Cheshire, North & Fawcett

Private International Law

Cheshire, North & Fawcett

Private International Law

Cheshire, North & Fawcett
Private International Law

FOURTEENTH EDITION

J J Fawcett LLB, PhD, Solicitor
Professor of Law, University of Nottingham

J M Carruthers LLB (Hons), Dip LP, PhD, Solicitor
Reader in Conflict of Laws, University of Glasgow

CONSULTANT EDITOR

Sir Peter North CBE, QC, MA, DCL, FBA
Former Principal of Jesus College, Oxford, and Vice-Chancellor of Oxford University

OXFORD
UNIVERSITY PRESS

OXFORD
UNIVERSITY PRESS

Great Clarendon Street, Oxford OX2 6DP

Oxford University Press is a department of the University of Oxford.
It furthers the University's objective of excellence in research, scholarship,
and education by publishing worldwide in

Oxford New York

Auckland Cape Town Dar es Salaam Hong Kong Karachi
Kuala Lumpur Madrid Melbourne Mexico City Nairobi
New Delhi Shanghai Taipei Toronto

With offices in

Argentina Austria Brazil Chile Czech Republic France Greece
Guatemala Hungary Italy Japan Poland Portugal Singapore
South Korea Switzerland Thailand Turkey Ukraine Vietnam

Oxford is a registered trade mark of Oxford University Press
in the UK and in certain other countries

Published in the United States
by Oxford University Press Inc., New York

British Library Cataloguing in Publication Data

Data available

Library of Congress Cataloging in Publication Data

Data available

Typeset by Cepha Imaging Private Ltd, Bangalore, India
Printed in Great Britain
on acid-free paper by
CPI Antony Rowe, Chippenham

ISBN 978–0–19–928425–2 (Hbk)
ISBN 978–0–19–928438–2 (Pbk)

10 9 8 7 6 5 4 3 2

Preface to the Fourteenth Edition

There have been more changes in private international law between the publication of the thirteenth edition of this book and this latest edition than has ever happened between editions in the past. This is partly due to the long interval between this edition and its predecessor, but is even more due to the increasing speed at which private international law changes. The Europeanisation of private international law has gathered pace following the establishment of Community competence in private international law by the Treaty of Amsterdam and the adoption of a programme of measures for the implementation of the principle of mutual recognition of decisions in civil and commercial matters. The Brussels Convention, though lingering in a few cases, has been largely replaced by the Brussels I Regulation. There is a new Lugano Convention and an EC/Danish Agreement. There are three new Regulations creating, respectively, a European Enforcement Order for Uncontested Claims, a European Small Claims Procedure and a European Order for Payment Procedure. The EC Service Convention has been replaced by a Regulation, itself superseded by a new Service Regulation. All of these developments have necessitated major changes to Chapters 10, 11 and 16. The rules on the applicable law in relation to obligations have not escaped this process of Europeanisation. The Rome II Regulation on the law applicable to non-contractual obligations has been introduced. The book has been written on the assumption that this Regulation is now in force, which soon will be the case. To reflect this development, Chapter 19 deals with all non-contractual obligations, replacing the old Chapters 19 and 20, which dealt separately with torts and restitution. The Rome I Regulation on the law applicable to contractual obligations is about to replace the Rome Convention, at least in most Member States. At the time of writing it is too early to say whether the United Kingdom will reverse its previous position and opt in to the Regulation (the Ministry of Justice has reached the provisional conclusion that it should do so). The book, in Chapter 18, therefore sets out the current law under the Rome Convention but contains detailed coverage of the changes to be effected by the Regulation. Family law too has been subject to major changes. In Chapters 21 and 24, full account is taken of the Brussels II *bis* Regulation concerning jurisdiction and the recognition and enforcement of judgments in matrimonial matters and matters of parental responsibility.

Areas where traditional English rules of private international law hold sway likewise have been subject to major changes. In particular, jurisdiction under the traditional rules now is dealt with by the numerous rules in Part 6 of the Civil Procedure Rules. The implications of the possible future adoption of the Hague Convention on Choice of Court Agreements 2005 are fully examined.

The case law on all the topics in the book is ever expanding. There are not only more reported cases than ever but the advent of electronic retrieval systems means that unreported cases are now accessible and have to be considered. Case law developments continue to be of enormous importance. Of particular note are the long awaited decisions of the European Court of Justice in *Turner*, *Owusu* and *Gasser*, which have dealt a hammer blow to cherished English practices in relation to international civil and commercial litigation. In Chapter 21 there is a consideration of what may be the implications of these decisions in the family law arena.

All of these developments have meant, perhaps inevitably, an increase in the length of the book. In the same way as previous editions, this edition of the book seeks to meet both practitioner and student requirements, a task that becomes increasingly difficult. The detail required to satisfy the practitioner means that the book is geared more towards the advanced student than the beginner.

On the theme of change, the reader will have noticed that the authorship of the book has altered. Sir Peter North has had a long association with the book, dating back to his co-authorship of the eighth edition in 1970, but decided that the time had come to hand over the responsibilities of co-authorship. It will be apparent that the new co-author is Dr Janeen Carruthers of the University of Glasgow. Sir Peter has remained as consultant editor and we are indebted to him for his advice and encouragement. Another notable change is that the book now is published by Oxford University Press. The first six editions were published by Oxford University Press, and so the book has returned to its original home.

As in the previous edition, we have adopted the post-Woolf reform terminology of "claimants" and "claim forms" in describing the law as it currently stands and in describing post-Woolf reform cases. But we have retained the old terminology in the description of the parties or proceedings in pre-Woolf reform cases. For convenience, references in the book are made to "England" but when statements are made as to the current law this should be taken to include Wales.

For help and guidance in the preparation of this edition, we should like particularly to thank Professors Elizabeth Crawford, Trevor Hartley, Jonathan Hill, Geoffrey Morse, Horton Rogers, Stephen Todd, Paul Torremans, and Dr Adeline Chong. Our thanks go to our families for their encouragement and support.

Our publishers have prepared all the various tables and the index and we thank them for this and for all their other help and co-operation.

We have endeavoured to state the law as on 1 November 2007, though it has been possible to include some more recent material, in particular the final version of the Rome I Regulation.

ADDENDUM ON THE ROME I REGULATION The United Kingdom Government is expected to announce its decision on whether to opt in to the Rome I Regulation by the end of July 2008. All the indications are that it is set to opt in.

Nottingham and Glasgow
April 2008
JJF and JMC

Preface to the First Edition

Convention demands that in the preface to a new book the author should excuse his temerity in adding to the literature on the subject and should also state the objects he hopes to attain. My excuse is the fascination, perhaps my readers will say the fatal fascination, of the subject. Of all the departments of English law, Private International Law offers the freest scope to the mere jurist. It is the perfect antithesis of such a topic as real property law. It is not overloaded with detailed rules; it has been only lightly touched by the paralysing hand of the Parliamentary draftsman; it is perhaps the one considerable department in which the formation of a coherent body of law is in course of process; it is, at the moment, fluid not static, elusive not obvious; it repels any tendency to dogmatism; and, above all, the possible permutations of the questions that it raises are so numerous that the diligent investigator can seldom rest content with the solution that he proposes. Despite its value as a subject of academic study it is curiously neglected in the legal education of this country, a fact which is remarkable if regard is had to the number of different legal systems that the British Empire comprises. On the Continent and in the United States of America, Private International Law is one of the major subjects of study at the Universities but in England it cannot claim a professorship of its own and it forms only an insignificant part of the chief law examinations.

The purpose of this book, however, is not merely to indulge my own fancy, but to provide students with a shorter account of the subject than most of those already published. Further, my object has been not to remain satisfied with mere exposition but to approach the more controversial topics in a spirit of constructive criticism. There are many instances in which I have found it impossible to agree with the views of such great masters as Dicey and Westlake, and in which I have ventured, perhaps rashly, to suggest that the relevant authorities indicate a somewhat different principle, but in all such cases I have been careful to present the reader with what may be called the generally accepted textbook view of each matter. Some of the mild strictures contained in this book may not be well founded, but even so they can do little harm, for there is no doubt that the subject in general sorely needs criticism. It may be doubted, indeed, whether all is well with the English system of Private International Law. Instances are numerous in the last thirty years in which the Courts have adopted some plausible principle, without serious investigation of its merits and without considering what the effect will be if it is applied to a case with slightly different facts. There are other cases in which it is difficult to extract the *ratio decidendi*, or indeed any clear principle, from the judgments. Private International Law, in fact, presents a golden opportunity, perhaps the last opportunity, for the judiciary to show that a homogeneous and scientifically constructed body of law, suitable to the changing needs of society, can be evolved without the aid of the legislature, and, though the task must necessarily be performed by the judges, there seems no reason why the jurist should stand aside in cloistered inactivity.

The book contains no account of the law relating to British nationality. This is a subject which should be dealt with solely in works on Constitutional Law, for it clearly has little, if any, connexion with Private International Law. Whether a person is a national of a particular country is relevant neither to the question of choice of law, nor, it is submitted, for purposes of jurisdiction.

Oxford
1 January 1935
G.C.C.

Summary Contents

PART IV THE LAW OF OBLIGATIONS

PART V FAMILY LAW

PART VI THE LAW OF PROPERTY

Contents

PART IV THE LAW OF OBLIGATIONS

PART V FAMILY LAW

Selected Bibliography

Anton *Private International Law; A treatise from the Standpoint of Scots law*, by A E Anton, 2nd edn (1990)

Anton: Jurisdiction *Anton & Beaumont's Civil Jurisdiction in Scotland*, by Paul Beaumont, 2nd edn (1995)

Audit *Droit International Privé*, by Bernard Audit (1991)

Barnett *Res Judicata, Estoppel, and Foreign Judgments*, by Peter R Barnett (2001)

Basedow and Kono *An Economic Analysis of Private International Law*, by J Basedow and T Kono (eds) (in co-operation with G Rühl) (2006)

Batiffol and Lagarde *Droit International Privé*, by Henri Batiffol and Paul Lagarde, 7th edn (1981–1983), 8th edn, Vol I (1993)

Baty *Polarized Law*, by T Baty (1914)

Beale *The Conflict of Laws*, by J H Beale (1935)

Beaumont and McEleavy *The Hague Convention on International Child Abduction*, by Paul Beaumont and Peter McEleavy (1999)

Bell *Forum Shopping and Venue in Transnational Litigation*, by Andrew S Bell (2003)

Benjamin *Interests in Securities: A Proprietary Law Analysis of the International Securities Markets*, by J Benjamin (2000)

Binchy *Irish Conflicts of Law*, by William Binchy (1988)

Boele-Woelki *Perspectives for the Unification and Harmonisation of Family Law in Europe*, by K Boele-Woelki (ed) (2003)

Briggs and Rees *Civil Jurisdiction and Judgments*, by Adrian Briggs and Peter Rees, 4th edn (2005)

Carruthers *The Transfer of Property in the Conflict of Laws*, by Janeen M Carruthers (2005)

Castel and Walker *Canadian Conflict of Laws*, by J Walker, 6th edn (2006)

Cavers *The Choice of Law Process*, by D F Cavers (1965)

Cavers: Essays *The Choice of Law: Selected Essays 1933–1983*, by D F Cavers (1985)

Clarkson and Hill *The Conflict of Laws*, by C M V Clarkson and J Hill, 3rd edn (2006)

Collier *Conflict of Laws*, by J G Collier, 3rd edn (2001)

Collins *The Civil Jurisdiction and Judgments Act 1982*, by Lawrence Collins (1983)

Collins: Essays *Essays in International Litigation and the Conflict of Laws*, by Lawrence Collins (1994)

Cook *Logical and Legal Bases of the Conflict of Laws*, by W W Cook (1942)

Currie *Selected Essays on the Conflict of Laws*, by Brainerd Currie (1963)

Crawford and Carruthers *International Private Law in Scotland*, by E B Crawford and J M Carruthers, 2nd edn (2006)

Dicey, Morris and Collins *The Conflict of Laws*, by Sir Lawrence Collins et al, 14th edn (2006)

Ehrenzweig *Private International Law* Vols I–III, by A A Ehrenzweig and E Jayme (1967–1977)

Ehrenzweig: Treatise *A Treatise on the Conflict of Laws*, by A A Ehrenzweig (1962)

Falconbridge *Essays on the Conflict of Laws*, by J D Falconbridge, 2nd edn (1954)

Fawcett *Declining Jurisdiction in Private International Law*, James J Fawcett (ed) (1995)

Fawcett *Reform and Development in Private International Law: Essays in Honour of Sir Peter North*, James Fawcett (ed) (2002)

Fawcett, Harris and Bridge *International Sale of Goods in the Conflict of Laws*, by James J Fawcett, Jonathan M Harris and Michael Bridge (2005)

Fawcett and Torremans *Intellectual Property and Private International Law*, by James J Fawcett and Paul Torremans (1998)

Fentiman *Foreign Law in English Courts*, by Richard Fentiman (1998)

Fletcher *Conflict of Laws and European Community Law*, by I F Fletcher (1982)

Fletcher *Insolvency and Private International Law*, by Ian F Fletcher, 2nd edn (2005)

Francescakis *La Théoirie du Renvoi*, by Ph Francescakis (1958)

Gaudemet-Tallon *Competence et Execution Des Jugements En Europe* by Hélène Gaudemet-Tallon, 3rd edn (2002)

Geeroms *Foreign Law in Civil Litigation*, by Sofie Geeroms (2004)

Graveson *Conflict of Laws: Private International Law*, by R H Graveson, 7th edn (1974)

Harris *The Hague Trusts Convention*, by J Harris (2002)

Hartley *Civil Jurisdiction and Judgments*, by T C Hartley (1984)

Hayton *European Succession Laws*, by D Hayton, 2nd edn (2002)

Hill *International Commercial Disputes*, by Jonathan Hill, 3rd edn (2005)

Hood *Conflict of Laws within the UK*, by Kirsty J Hood (2007)

Jackson (1975) *The "Conflicts" Process*, by David C Jackson (1975)

Jackson (2005) *The Enforcement of Maritime Claims*, by David C Jackson, 4th edn (2005)

Kaye *The New Private International Law of Contract of the European Community*, by Peter Kaye (1993)

Kaye *Law of the European Judgments Convention*, Vols one–five, by Peter Kaye (1999)

Kennett *The Enforcement of Judgments in Europe*, by Wendy Kennett (2000)

Kruger *Civil Jurisdiction Rules of the EU and their Impact on Third States*, by Thalia Kruger (2008)

Lalive *The Transfer of Chattels in the Conflict of Laws*, by Pierre A Lalive (1955)

Lasok and Stone *Conflict of Laws in the European Community*, by D Lasok and P A Stone (1987)

Layton and Mercer *European Civil Practice*, by Alexander Layton and Hugh Mercer et al (eds) 2nd edn (2004)

Leflar *American Conflicts Law*, by Robert A Leflar, 4th edn (1986)

Levontin *Choice of Law and Conflict of Laws*, by A V Levontin (1976)

Lorenzen *Selected Articles on the Conflict of Laws*, by Ernest G Lorenzen (1947)

McClean *Recognition of Family Judgments in the Commonwealth*, by J D McClean (1983)

McLachlan and Nygh *International Tort Litigation*, Campbell McLachlan and Peter Nygh (eds) (1996)

McLeod *The Conflict of Laws*, by James G McLeod (1983)

Magnus and Mankowski *Brussels I Regulation*, by U Magnus and P Mankowski (2007)

Mann *Foreign Affairs in English Courts*, by F A Mann (1986)

Mann: Money *The Legal Aspect of Money*, by F A Mann, 6th edn (2005)

Marsh *Marital Property in the Conflict of Laws*, by Harold Marsh (1952)

Meeusen, Pertegas, Straetmans and Swennen *International Family Law for the European Union*, J Meeusen, M Pertegas, G Straetmans and F Swennen (eds) (2007)

Miller *International Aspects of Succession*, by G Miller (2000)

Morris: Essays *Contemporary Problems in the Conflict of Laws*, essays in honour of J H C Morris (1978)

Morris *The Conflict of Laws*, by David McClean and Kisch Beevers, 6th edn (2005)

Morris and North *Cases and Materials on Private International Law*, by J H C Morris and P M North (1984)

Morse *Torts in Private International Law*, by C G J Morse (1978)

Nadelmann *Conflict of Laws: International and Interstate*, by K Nadelmann (1972)

North *The Private International Law of Matrimonial Causes in the British Isles and the Republic of Ireland*, by P M North (1977)

North: Contract *Contract Conflicts*, P M North (ed) (1984)

North *Private International Law Problems in Common Law Jurisdictions*, by Peter North (1993)

North: Essays *Essays in Private International Law*, by Peter North (1993)

Nygh *Autonomy in International Contracts*, by Peter Nygh (1999)

Nygh and Davies *Conflict of Laws in Australia*, by P E Nygh and M Davies, 6th edn (2002)

O'Hara *Economics of Conflict of Laws*, by E O'Hara (2007)

Ooi *Shares and Other Securities in the Conflict of Laws*, by Maisie Ooi (2003)

Palsson *Marriage and Divorce in Comparative Conflict of Laws*, by Lennart Palsson (1974)

Palsson: Marriage *Marriage in Comparative Conflict of Laws: Substantive Conditions*, by Lennart Palsson (1981)

Panagopoulos *Restitution in Private International Law*, by George Panagopoulos (2000)

Patchett *Recognition of Commercial Judgments and Awards in the Commonwealth*, by K W Patchett (1984)

Pertegas Sender *Cross-Border Enforcement of Patent Rights*, by Marta Pertegas Sender (2002)

Plender *The European Contracts Convention*, by Richard Plender and Richard Wilderspin, 2nd edn (2001)

Rabel *The Conflict of Laws: A Comparative Study*, by Ernst Rabel, 2nd edn (1958–1964)

Rammeloo *Corporations in Private International Law*, by Stephan Rammeloo (2001)

Read *Recognition and Enforcement of Foreign Judgments*, by H E Read (1938)

Restatement 2d *American Law Institute Restatement of the Law 2d: Conflict of Laws* (1971)

Robertson *Characterization in the Conflict of Laws*, by A H Robertson (1940)

Rose *Restitution and the Conflict of Laws*, Francis Rose (ed) (1995)

Savigny *A Treatise on the Conflict of Laws,* by Friedrich Carl Von Savigny, translated into English by W Guthrie (all references are to the first edition, published in 1869)

Scoles, Hay, Borchers and Symeonides *Conflict of Laws*, by E F Scoles, P Hay, P J Borchers and S C Symeonides 4th edn (2004)

Shapira *The Interest Approach to Choice of Law*, by Amos Shapira (1970)

Stark *International Family Law*, by B Stark (2005)

Story *Commentaries on the Conflict of Laws*, by Joseph Story, 8th edn, by G Melville Bigelow (1883)

Sykes and Pryles *Australian Private International Law*, by E I Sykes and M C Pryles, 3rd edn (1991)

Sykes and Pryles: Casebook *Conflict of Laws Commentary and Materials*, by E I Sykes and M C Pryles, 3rd edn (1988)

Symeonides *The American Choice-of-Law Revolution: Past, Present and Future*, by S C Symeonides (2006)

Takahashi *Claims for Contribution and Reimbursement in an International Context*, by Koji Takahashi (2000)

Weintraub *Commentary on the Conflict of Laws*, by Russell J Weintraub, 4th edn (2001)

Westlake *A Treatise on Private International Law*, by John Westlake, 7th edn by Norman Bentwich (1925)

Whincop and Keyes *Policy and Pragmatism in the Conflict of Laws*, by M J Whincop and M Keyes (2001)

Wolff *Private International Law*, by M Wolff, 2nd edn (1950)

Yeo *Choice of Law for Equitable Doctrines*, by T M Yeo (2004)

Zaphiriou *The Transfer of Chattels in Private International Law*, by G A Zaphiriou (1956)

Table of Statutes

INTRODUCTORY NOTE

This Table is set out in the following sections (in this order): UK (including Scotland and Northern Ireland) Statutes, followed by UK Statutory Instruments; EU Legislation (primary and secondary, excluding conventions); European Conventions; International Conventions; Bilateral Treaties; National Legislation of Other Countries (subdivided by country). Alphabetical order is followed within sections/subsections.

Table of Cases

The full alphabetical list of cases is followed by a list of European Court of Justice cases ordered by year and case number.

PART I

Introduction

Chapters

Introduction

Chapter 1

Definition, Nature and Scope of Private International Law

1. INTRODUCTION

Private international law is that part of English law which comes into operation whenever the court is faced with a claim that contains a foreign element. It is only when this element is present that private international law has a function to perform. It has three main objects.

First, to prescribe the conditions under which the court is competent to entertain such a claim.

Secondly, to determine for each class of case the particular municipal system of law by reference to which the rights of the parties must be ascertained.

Thirdly, to specify the circumstances in which (a) a foreign judgment can be recognised as decisive of the question in dispute; and (b) the right vested in the judgment creditor by a foreign judgment can be enforced by action in England.

The *raison d'être* of private international law is the existence in the world of a number of separate municipal systems of law—a number of separate legal units—that differ greatly from each other in the rules by which they regulate the various legal relations arising in daily life. Courts in one country must frequently take account of some rule of law that exists in another. A sovereign is supreme within his own territory and, according to the universal maxim of jurisprudence, he has exclusive jurisdiction over everybody and everything within that territory and over every transaction that is effected there. He can, if he chooses, refuse to consider any law but his own. Although the adoption of this policy of indifference might have been common enough in other ages, it is impracticable in the modern civilised world. Consequently, nations have long found that they cannot, by sheltering behind the principle of territorial sovereignty, afford to disregard foreign rules of law merely because they happen to be different from their own internal system of law. Moreover, as will be shown later, it is no derogation of sovereignty to take account of foreign law.

The recognition of a foreign law in a case containing a foreign element may be necessary for at least two reasons. In the first place, the invariable application of the law of the forum, ie the local law of the place where the court is situated, would often lead to gross injustice. Suppose that a person engaged in English litigation is required to prove that she is the lawful widow of a man who has just died, the marriage having taken place abroad many years ago. The marriage ceremony, though regular according to the law of the place where it was performed, did not perhaps satisfy the formal requirements of English law, but nevertheless to apply the English Marriage Act 1949 to such a union, and thereby to deny that the couple were man and wife, would be nothing but a travesty of justice.

Secondly, if the court is to carry out in a rational manner the policy to which it is now committed—that of entertaining actions in respect of foreign claims—it must, in the nature of things, take account of the relevant foreign law or laws. A claimant,[1] for instance, seeks damages for breach of a contract that was both made and to be performed in France. Under the existing practice the court is prepared to create and to enforce in his favour, if he substantiates his case, an English right corresponding as nearly as possible to that which he claims. However, neither the nature nor the extent of the relief to which he is rightly entitled nor, indeed, whether he is entitled to any relief can be determined if the law of France is disregarded. This is because to consider English law alone might reverse the legal obligations of the parties as fixed by the law to which their transaction, both in fact and by intention, was originally subjected. A promise, for instance, made by an Englishman in Italy and to be performed there, if valid and enforceable by Italian law, would not be held void by an English court merely because it was unsupported by consideration.[2]

---

[1] Following the reforms to civil procedure introduced in 1999, the term "claimant" is now used in place of "plaintiff". It needs to be borne in mind that the latter term was used in earlier English decisions and is still used in other common law jurisdictions.

[2] *Re Bonacina* [1912] 2 Ch 394; and see now the Contracts (Applicable Law) Act 1990.

In justifying this reference to a foreign law, English judges and textbook writers have frequently used[3] the term *comity of nations*, "a phrase which is grating to the ear, when it proceeds from a court of justice".[4] Although the term has been often used, analysis of it reveals that it has been employed in a meaningless or misleading way. The word itself is incompatible with the judicial function, for comity is a matter for sovereigns, not for judges required to decide a case according to the rights of the parties.[5] Again, if the word is given its normal meaning of courtesy it is scarcely consistent with the readiness of English courts to apply enemy law in time of war. Moreover, if courtesy formed the basis of private international law a judge might feel compelled to ignore the law of Utopia on proof that Utopian courts apply no law but their own, since comity implies a bilateral, not a unilateral, relationship. If, on the other hand, comity means that no foreign law is applicable in England except with the permission of the sovereign, it is nothing more than a truism. The fact is, of course, that the application of a foreign law implies no act of courtesy, no sacrifice of sovereignty. It merely derives from a desire to do justice.

Private international law, then, is that part of law which comes into play when the issue before the court affects some fact, event or transaction that is so closely connected with a foreign system of law as to necessitate recourse to that system. It has, accordingly, been described as meaning "the rules voluntarily chosen by a given State for the decision of cases which have a foreign complexion".[6] The legal systems of the world consist of a variety of territorial systems, each dealing with the same phenomena of life—birth, death, marriage, divorce, bankruptcy, contracts, wills and so on—but in most cases dealing with them differently. The moment that a case is seen to be affected by a foreign element, the court must look beyond its own internal law, lest the relevant rule of the internal system to which the case most appropriately belongs should happen to be in conflict with that of the forum. The forms in which this foreign element may appear are numerous. One of the parties may be foreign by nationality or domicile; a businessman may be declared bankrupt in England, having numerous creditors abroad; the action may concern property situated abroad or a disposition made abroad of property situated in England; if the action is on a bill of exchange, the foreign element may consist in the fact that the drawing or acceptance or endorsement was made abroad; a contract may have been made in one country to be performed in another; two persons may resort to the courts of a foreign country where the means of contracting or of dissolving a marriage are more convenient than in the country of their domicile. It is the existence of such foreign elements as these that has caused the courts to frame a number of different *rules for the choice of law* which demonstrate the most appropriate legal system to govern the issue that has arisen.

---

[3] Eg *Amin Rasheed Shipping Corpn v Kuwait Insurance Co* [1984] AC 50 at 65; *Spiliada Maritime Corpn v Cansulex Ltd* [1987] AC 460 at 477; *Société Nationale Industrielle Aérospatiale v Lee Kui Jak* [1987] AC 871 at 895; and *Arab Monetary Fund v Hashim (No 3)* [1991] 2 AC 114 at 136.

[4] De Nova (1964) 8 Am JLH 136, 141, citing the early American author, Livermore.

[5] Nadelmann, *Conflict of Laws: International and Interstate*, p 8; for further discussion see Wolff, pp 14–15; Yntema (1966) 65 Mich LR 1; Khan-Freund (1974) III Hague Recueil 147, 164.

[6] Baty, *Polarized Law*, p 148.

2. SPACE AND TIME

(a) Space

It is frequently stressed that the function of private international law is to indicate the area over which a rule of law extends—that it "deals primarily with the application of laws in space".[7] The essence of this is that a rule of substantive law, eg the English rule that every simple contract must be supported by consideration, is generally expressed in universal terms and seems to have no dimension in space, for according to its wording it applies to all contracts wherever made. But its dimension in space, ie its sphere of authority, is the very thing that is fixed by private international law, because a sovereign is free to provide, if he chooses, that the area over which a rule of substantive law, whether domestic or foreign, is to prevail shall be wider than the territorial jurisdiction in which it originated. If, for instance, an English court decides that the goods situated in England belonging to a man who died intestate and domiciled in France shall be distributed according to the provisions of the Code Napoléon, what it decides in effect is that the rule of the French internal law relating to intestacy is, in the case of persons domiciled in France, to be given effect outside the territorial limits of the French law-maker, provided of course that French law so permits. In the words of Savigny:

> It is this diversity of positive laws which makes it necessary to mark off for each, in sharp outline, the area of its authority, to fix the limits of different positive laws in respect to one another.[8]

This method of expressing the function of the subject does not mean that the sphere of application of each rule of law is, or can be, determined once and for all for every situation to which it may be relevant.[9] The area over which any given rule of law extends will vary with the particular circumstances in which its operation is under consideration. Consequently, the English rules governing contractual capacity will apply to certain transactions effected by domiciled Englishmen abroad, but not to others.

(b) Time

There are certain circumstances in which the factor of time as well as that of space may require consideration.[10] In the dimension of space, for instance, the rights of a husband and wife to each other's property are usually governed, in the absence of a marriage settlement, by the law of the domicile. But does this rule of selection refer to domicile at the time of the marriage or to domicile as it may change from time to time?[11] Again, whether a will has been effectively revoked by the execution of a later will or by its destruction is determinable by the law of the testator's domicile, but if his domicile does not remain

---

[7] Beale, p 1; see especially, Unger (1957) 43, Grotius Society 87, 94 et seq.

[8] *Private International Law*, Guthrie's translation, p 6.

[9] Cook, *Logical and Legal Bases of Conflict of Laws*, p 7.

[10] On this topic, see F A Mann (1954) 31 BYBIL 317; Grodecki (1959) 35 BYBIL 58; Spiro (1960) 9 ICLQ 357; Kahn-Freund (1974) III Hague Receuil 147, 441–446; Fassberg (1990) 38 ICLQ 956; Grodecki, 3 *International Encyclopedia of Comparative Law*, Chapter 8; Dicey, Morris and Collins, pp 60–72; Morris, paras 20-034–20-045.

[11] See infra, pp 1295 and 1297.

constant this selective rule will produce no decision until it has been decided whether the reference is to the law of the domicile at the time of the execution, or of the act of destruction, or at the time of the testator's death.[12]

Another type of case in which the factor of time is relevant arises where, subsequently to the transaction in issue, there has been a change in the foreign law selected to govern the rights of the parties. Here, it is essential to ascertain whether the English court must apply the foreign law as it stood at the time of the transaction or as it now exists after the change.[13] Generally, courts prefer the latter solution.[14]

A variety of situations in which the factor of time is pertinent will be considered at later stages in this book.

3. SCOPE OF PRIVATE INTERNATIONAL LAW

Private international law is not a separate branch of law in the same sense as, say, the law of contract or of tort. It is all-pervading.

> It starts up unexpectedly in any court and in the midst of any process. It may be sprung like a mine in a plain common law action, in an administrative proceeding in equity, or in a divorce case, or a bankruptcy case, in a shipping case or a matter of criminal procedure. . . . The most trivial action of debt, the most complex case of equitable claims, may be suddenly interrupted by the appearance of a knot to be untied only by Private International Law.[15]

Nevertheless, private international law is a separate and distinct unit in the English legal system just as much as the law of tort or of contract, but it possesses this unity, not because it deals with one particular topic, but because it is always concerned with one or more of three questions, namely:

(a) Jurisdiction of the English court.
(b) Recognition and enforcement of foreign judgments.
(c) The choice of law.

We must be prepared to consider almost every branch of private law, but only in connection with these three matters.

(a) Jurisdiction

The basic rule at common law is that the English court has no jurisdiction to entertain an action *in personam* unless the defendant has been personally served with a claim form in England or Wales. This rule, which cannot be satisfied while the defendant is abroad, applies, of course, whether the case has a foreign complexion or not, but there are three reasons which require the question of jurisdiction to be separately treated in a book on private international law. First, there are certain circumstances in which the court is

---

[12] See infra, pp 1275–1276.
[13] See for instance, infra, pp 880–881.
[14] *Re Chesterman's Trusts* [1923] 2 Ch 466 at 478.
[15] Frederic Harrison, *Jurisprudence and the Conflict of Laws*, pp 101–102.

empowered by statute to assume jurisdiction over absent defendants, a power which naturally is of greater significance in foreign than in domestic cases.[16] Secondly, there are certain types of action, such as a petition for divorce, where the mere presence of the defendant in the country does not render the court jurisdictionally competent.[17] Thirdly, there is a separate regime of jurisdictional rules in the case of a defendant domiciled (in a specially defined sense) in a Member State of the European Community.[18]

(b) Recognition

Where there has been litigation abroad, but the defendant has most of his assets in England, it will be important to ascertain whether English law will recognise or permit the enforcement of the foreign judgment. Provided that the foreign court had jurisdiction to adjudicate on the case, according to English private international law, the English court will generally recognise the foreign judgment as if one of its own and it can be enforced accordingly.[19] Again, our membership of the European Community has led to the introduction of important specific rules for the recognition of judgments from courts of the Member States.[20]

(c) Choice of law

If the English court decides that it possesses jurisdiction, then a further question, as to the choice of law, must be considered; ie which system of law, English or foreign, must govern the case?[21] The action before the English court, for instance, may concern a contract made or a tort committed abroad or the validity of a will made by a person who died domiciled abroad. In each case that part of English law which consists of private international law directs what legal system shall apply to the case, ie, to use a convenient expression, what system of internal law shall constitute the applicable law. English private international law, for instance, requires that the movable property of a British subject who dies intestate domiciled in Italy shall be distributed according to Italian law. These rules for the choice of law, then, indicate the particular legal system by reference to which a solution of the dispute must be reached. This does not necessarily mean that only one legal system is applicable, for different aspects of a case may be governed by different laws, as is the case with marriage where formal and essential validity are governed by different laws.[22]

The function of private international law is complete when it has chosen the appropriate system of law. Its rules do not furnish a direct solution of the dispute, and it has been said that this department of law resembles the inquiry office at a railway station where a passenger may learn the platform at which his train starts. If, for instance, the defence to an action for breach of contact made in France is that the formalities required by French law have not been observed, private international law ordains that the formal validity of the

---

[16] Infra, p 372.
[17] Infra, p 945 et seq.
[18] See infra, Chapter 11.
[19] Infra, p 513 et seq.
[20] Infra, p 595 et seq.
[21] For the view that this question is becoming less significant in comparison with jurisdictional issues, see Briggs (1989) 9 OJLS 251, 252–257; Fawcett [1991] Current Legal Problems 39.
[22] Infra, p 878 et seq.

contract shall be determined by French law. But it says no more. The relevant French law must then be proved by a witness expert in the subject.

It is generally said that the judge at the forum "applies" or "enforces" the chosen law, or alternatively that the case is "governed" by the foreign law. These expressions are convenient to describe loosely what happens, but they are not accurate. Neither is it strictly accurate to say that the judge enforces not the foreign law, but a right acquired under the foreign law.[23] The only law applied by the judge is the law of the forum, the only rights enforced by him are those created by the law of the forum. But owing to the foreign element in the case the foreign law is a fact that must be taken into consideration, and what the judge attempts to do is to create and to enforce a right as nearly as possible similar to that which would have been created by the foreign court had it been seised of a similar case which was purely domestic in character.[24]

4. MEANING OF "FOREIGN LAW"

For the purposes of private international law the expression "foreign system of law" means a distinctive legal system prevailing in a territory other than that in which the court functions. It therefore includes, not merely the law existing in a state under a foreign political sovereignty, but also the law prevailing in a sub-division of the political state of which the forum is part. Thus, for the purpose of private international law and so far as English courts are concerned, the law of Scotland, of the Channel Islands, of Northern Ireland, or of one of the member countries of the Commonwealth or European Community is just as much a foreign law as the law of Japan or Brazil.

5. INTERNATIONAL VARIETY OF PRIVATE INTERNATIONAL LAW RULES

Private international law is not the same in all countries. There is no one system that can claim universal recognition, though there has been a significant movement in recent years towards the harmonisation of private international law rules between groups of countries. This book is concerned solely with the English rules, ie with the rules that guide an English court whenever it is seised of a case that contains some foreign element. A writer on public international law may perhaps claim with some justification that the doctrines which he propounds are entitled to universal recognition. Thus, in theory at any rate, a German and a French jurist should agree as to what constitutes an effective blockade. But the writer on private international law can make no such claim. This branch of law as found, for instance, in Japan shows many striking contrasts with its English counterpart, and though the English and American rules show considerable similarity they are fundamentally different on a number of points. The many questions relating to the personal status of a party depend in England on the law of his domicile, but in France, Italy, Spain and most other Continental European countries on the law of

---

23 *Re Askew* [1930] 2 Ch 259 at 267.
24 Infra, pp 26–27, and see Lorenzen (1920) 20 Col LR 247, 259.

his nationality. Again, the principles applied by various legal systems to divorce jurisdiction may so conflict that the same two persons are deemed married in one jurisdiction but unmarried in another. On the other hand, though Scottish internal law differs substantially from that of England, the principles of private international law are so similar in both countries that an English decision is usually, though not invariably, followed in Scotland and vice versa.[25]

6. AVOIDING CONFLICTS

There are two possible ways in which this lack of unanimity among the various systems of private international law may be ameliorated.[26]

(a) Unification of internal laws

The first is to secure by international conventions the unification of the *internal* laws of the various countries on as many legal topics as possible. When attention is paid to the fundamental and basic differences in principle that distinguish one legal system from another, especially in the common law systems as contrasted with their civil law counterparts, it is obvious that this form of unification holds out no great prospect of success. Nevertheless, a certain amount of progress has been made in the few departments of law where this unity is imperative and possible.

An important example of unification is the Warsaw Convention of 1929 as amended at The Hague, 1955, and supplemented by the Guadalajara Convention, 1961,[27] which makes the international carriage of persons or goods by aircraft for reward subject to uniform rules as regards both jurisdiction and the law to be applied. It also provides that any agreement by the parties purporting to alter the rules on these matters shall be null and void. The Convention has been made binding in England by the Carriage by Air Act 1961. Further examples of the unification of internal laws are the Carriage of Goods by Sea Act 1924,[28] the Carriage of Goods by Road Act 1965, the Carriage of Passengers by Road Act 1974, the International Transport Conventions Act 1983 and the Merchant Shipping Act 1995, all of which give effect to conventions made at international conferences. Mention may also be made of the Berne Convention of 1886, since amended several times, by which an international union for the protection of the rights of authors over their literary and artistic works was formed. The Council of the League of Nations entrusted to the Institute for the Unification of Private Laws (UNIDROIT), established by the Italian Government in Rome, the task of indicating the lines along which further

---

[25] By virtue of the Scotland Act 1998, Scottish civil law (being a reference to the general principles of private law, including private international law—s 126(4)(a)) falls within the legislative competence of the Scottish Parliament. However, the private international law aspects of reserved matters (s 29(3)) are reserved to the Westminster Parliament. See Crawford and Carruthers, para 2-04.

[26] For an excellent account of the various methods of seeking unanimity, and an assessment of their success, see David, 2 *International Encyclopedia of Comparative Law*, Chapter 5.

[27] This was made part of the law of the United Kingdom by the Carriage by Air (Supplementary Provisions) Act 1962. The Warsaw Convention was modernised by the Montreal Convention for the Unification of Certain Rules relating to International Carriage by Air 1999.

[28] The Hague Rules which are contained in the Act were amended by a Brussels Protocol of 1968 which is embodied in the Carriage of Goods by Sea Act 1971, which came into force in 1977.

unification might be attained.[29] An important result of its labours, in conjunction with those of the Hague Conference,[30] was the conclusion at The Hague in 1964 of a convention which establishes a uniform set of rules on international sales of goods and also on the formation of contracts for such sales. These conventions were accepted by the United Kingdom and incorporated in the Uniform Laws on International Sales Act 1967[31] which, when its provisions apply, excludes the rules of private international law.[32] There is now a successor to the 1964 Convention, the United Nations Convention on Contracts for the International Sale of Goods of 1980,[33] prepared under the auspices of another body concerned with the unification of law, the United Nations Committee on International Trade Law (UNCITRAL). The United Kingdom is not a party to the 1980 Convention. On a smaller scale, the Scandinavian countries[34] and a number of Latin-American countries[35] have adopted conventions unifying various areas of their laws.

(b) Unification of private international law

The second method by which the inconvenience that results from conflicting national rules may be diminished is to unify the rules of private international law, so as to ensure that a case containing a foreign element results in the same decision irrespective of the country of its trial.[36] Several attempts have been made in the Hague Conference on Private International Law[37] to reduce the number of topics on which the rules for choice of law in different countries conflict, thus indicating the desirability of having a code of private international law common to the civilised world. Prior to the seventh session in 1951, the sessions were confined to the Continental states of Europe, for, owing to the fundamental differences between the common law and the civil law which forms the basis of most European systems, there seemed little prospect of agreement being reached between the two groups. The British delegates, however, attended the seventh and subsequent sessions, no longer as mere observers but as full members of the conference[38] and they have since been joined by delegations from other common law jurisdictions, including Australia, Canada and the USA.[39]

A step of great significance taken in 1951 was the drafting of a charter designed to place the Hague Conference on a lasting footing by the establishment of a permanent bureau. This charter has been accepted by many countries, including the United Kingdom, and the Bureau, consisting now of a Secretary-General, a Deputy Secretary-General, three First Secretaries and a small team of Legal Officers belonging to different countries, was

---

[29] See David, op cit, pp 133–141.

[30] Infra, pp 11–12.

[31] As amended by the Sale and Supply of Goods Act 1994, Sch 2.

[32] Graveson, Cohn and Graveson, *Uniform Laws on International Sales Act 1967*.

[33] See Honnold, *Uniform Law for International Sales Act under the 1980 United Nations Convention* (3rd edn, 1999).

[34] David, op cit, pp 181–188.

[35] Ibid, pp 148–150; and see Parra-Aranguren (1979) III Hague Recueil 55; Maekelt (1982) IV Hague Recueil 193; Juenger (1994) 42 AJCL 381.

[36] Vitta (1969) I Hague Recueil 111–232; van Loon, in *Forty Years On: The Evolution of Postwar Private International Law in Europe* (1990), pp 101–122; Pfund (1994) V Hague Recueil 9.

[37] See generally http://www.hcch.net.

[38] Van Hoogstraten (1963) 12 ICLQ 148.

[39] Nadelmann (1965) 30 Law & Contemporary Problems 291; Pfund (1985) 19 Int Lawyer 505; Reese (1985) 19 Int Lawyer 881; McClean in Borras (ed), *E Pluribus Unum* (1996), p 205.

established at The Hague. Its mission is to be a forum for the Member States for the development and implementation of common rules of private international law in order to co-ordinate the relationships between different private law systems in international situations and to promote international judicial and administrative co-operation in the fields of protection of the family and children, civil procedure and commercial law. Its chief functions are to examine and prepare proposals for the unification of private international law and to keep in touch with the Council of Europe and with governmental and non-governmental organisations, such as the Commonwealth Secretariat and the International Law Association.[40] The Bureau works under the general direction of the Standing Government Commission of the Netherlands, which was established by Royal Decree in 1897, with the object of promoting the codification of private international law. Fairly recent English statutes relating to private international law problems which owe their existence, at least in part, to acceptance by the United Kingdom of the Hague Conventions,[41] include the Wills Act 1963,[42] the Adoption Act 1968,[43] the Evidence (Proceedings in Other Jurisdictions) Act 1975,[44] the Child Abduction and Custody Act 1985,[45] Part II of the Family Law Act 1986[46] and the Recognition of Trusts Act 1987.[47]

In addition to the conventions mentioned above, many similar arrangements have been made between individual countries, as for example the bilateral conventions on civil procedure concluded by the United Kingdom with a large number of foreign states. An example of a limited multilateral convention is that concluded in 1969 between the Benelux states—Belgium, the Netherlands and Luxembourg—which unified the rules of private international law on the more important matters, such as capacity and status, succession to property on death and the essential validity of contracts.[48]

(i) Europeanisation of private international law[49]

A modern feature of private international law is the Europeanisation of the subject, by which is meant the assimilation of Member States' private international law rules, and the creation of a European "area of freedom, security and justice". The legal basis for this development is the Treaty of Amsterdam,[50] Articles 61 to 67, in terms of which the subject of judicial co-operation in civil matters became a matter of European Community

---

[40] On the work of the Hague Conference generally, see Nadelmann (1972) 20 AJCL 323; David, op cit, pp 141–148; Droz (1980) III Hague Recueil 123; Overbeck (1992) Hague Recueil 9; Boggiano, ibid, 99; McClean, ibid, 267; TMC Asser Institute, *The Influence of the Hague Conference on Private International Law* (1993); (1994) 57 Law & Contemporary Problems, No 3.

[41] See North, *Essays in Private International Law* (1993), pp 225–256.

[42] Infra, pp 1266–1277.

[43] See now Adoption and Children Act 2002, infra, p 1156 et seq.

[44] Infra, pp 86–87.

[45] Infra, p 1103 et seq.

[46] Infra, p 992 et seq.

[47] Infra, pp 1311–1312.

[48] For discussion of the activities of the six Inter-American Specialised Conferences on Private International Law, see http://www.oas.org/dil/privateintlaw_interamericanconferences.htm. Also Parra-Aranguren, in *Conflicts and Harmonisation* (1990) 155–175; and see Burman (1995) 28 Vand J of Transnational L 367; Parra-Aranguren in Borras (ed), *E Pluribus Unum* (1996), p 299.

[49] See generally Crawford and Carruthers (2005) 3 Jur Rev 251.

[50] Signed in 1997 and in force on 1 May 1999.

law rather than one merely of inter-governmental co-operation. By virtue of Article 65, measures in the field of judicial co-operation in civil matters having cross-border implications may be taken *in so far as necessary for the proper functioning of the internal market*, and shall include improving and simplifying the recognition and enforcement of decisions in civil and commercial cases; promoting the compatibility of the rules applicable in the Member States concerning the conflict of laws and of jurisdiction; and eliminating obstacles to the good functioning of civil proceedings, if necessary by promoting the compatibility of the rules on civil procedure applicable in the Member States. There followed, in 1998, the Vienna Action Plan[51] of the European Council and Commission on how best to implement the Amsterdam provisions, and subsequently, in 1999, there was convened in Tampere, Finland, an Extraordinary European Council Meeting, which produced a programme of work for the period 1999–2004, devoted to the development of the European judicial area. The results of the five-year Tampere programme were presented by the European Commission in June 2004, and in November that year, a new programme, termed the "Hague Programme",[52] was adopted by the European Council, with a view to strengthening and developing the EU Justice and Home Affairs legislative portfolio over the period 2005–09.

Title IV ("Area of Freedom, Security and Justice") of the Treaty of Lisbon, amending the Treaty on European Union and the Treaty establishing the European Community,[53] shall replace the pre-existing provision on visas, asylum, immigration and other policies related to free movement of persons. Article 65 in Chapter 3 of Title IV of the Lisbon Treaty concerns judicial co-operation in civil matters, and provides that:

1. The Union shall develop judicial cooperation in civil matters having cross-border implications, based on the principle of mutual recognition of judgments and of decisions in extrajudicial cases. Such cooperation may include the adoption of measures for the approximation of the laws and regulations of the Member States.

The wording of the new Article 65(2) is noteworthy:

2. For the purposes of paragraph 1, the European Parliament and the Council, acting in accordance with the ordinary legislative procedure, shall adopt measures, *particularly when necessary for the proper functioning of the internal market*,[54] aimed at ensuring:

   (a) the mutual recognition and enforcement between Member States of judgments and of decisions in extrajudicial cases;
   (b) the cross-border service of judicial and extrajudicial documents;

---

[51] OJ 1999 C 19.

[52] The Hague Programme: Strengthening Freedom, Security and Justice in the European Union (OJ 2003 C 53/1) and the Council and Commission Action Plan Implementing the Hague Programme on Strengthening Freedom, Security and Justice in the European Union (OJ 2005 C 198/1). See European Council 4/5 November 2004, Presidency Conclusions (Press Release, Brussels, 8 December 2004, 14292/1/04 REV1 CONCL3), and Communication from the Commission to the Council and the European Parliament: Report on the Implementation of the Hague Programme for 2006 (COM (2007) 373 final).

[53] Signed in Lisbon on 13 December 2007.

[54] Emphasis added. This requirement is less stringent than that which applies under Art 65 of the Treaty of Amsterdam.

(c) the compatibility of the rules applicable in the Member States concerning conflict of laws and of jurisdiction;

(d) cooperation in the taking of evidence;

(e) effective access to justice;

(f) the elimination of obstacles to the proper functioning of civil proceedings, if necessary by promoting the compatibility of the rules on civil procedure applicable in the Member States;

(g) the development of alternative methods of dispute settlement;

(h) support for the training of the judiciary and judicial staff.

Accordingly, the European Community has proved to be, and looks set to continue to be, a major force for the creation of uniform law within the Community and for the unification of private international law among EU Member States.[55] European harmonisation efforts have generated, for example and of note, in the area of civil and commercial jurisdiction, the 1968 Brussels Convention on jurisdiction and the enforcement of judgments in civil and commercial matters[56] (almost entirely replaced by Council Regulation (EC) No 44/2001 on jurisdiction and the recognition and enforcement of judgments in civil and commercial matters[57]), and in choice of law, the 1980 Rome Convention on contractual obligations,[58] implemented in the United Kingdom by means of the Contracts (Applicable Law) Act 1990. There now exist many EU directives, regulations and proposed regulations containing private international law measures, concerned not only with the allocation of jurisdiction and enforcement of judgments, but also with choice of law and matters of procedure. These will be identified and examined in context throughout the book.

For the European Union, there is an important, and sometimes difficult, balance to strike between securing regional harmonisation of laws, and participating in projects which seek to bring about global harmonisation of laws.[59] By virtue of membership of the European Union, Member States have lost the power to act autonomously in matters concerning judicial co-operation in civil matters which fall within European Union competence. In 2006, the European Community decided to accede to the Hague Conference on Private International Law, by means of declaration of acceptance of the Statute of the Hague Conference.[60] The Accession of the Community to the Hague Conference took place on

---

[55] *Harmonisation of Private International Law by the EEC* (ed Lipstein); Fletcher, *Conflict of Laws and European Community Law* (1982); Lasok and Stone, *Conflict of Laws in the European Community* (1987); North, in *Forty Years On: The Evolution of Postwar Private International Law in Europe* (1990), pp 29–48; Duintjer Tebbens, ibid, pp 49–69; Stone, *EU Private International Law Harmonisation of Laws* (2006).

[56] Implemented in the UK by means of the Civil Jurisdiction and Judgments Act 1982. See infra, Chapter 10 below.

[57] See, infra, Chapter 11.

[58] OJ 1980 L 266; North, *Contract Conflicts* (1982). See now also the Rome I Regulation, infra, Chapter 18.

[59] See H van Loon and A Schulz, 'The European Community and the Hague Conference on Private International Law' in B Martenczuk and S van Thiel (eds), *Justice, Liberty, Security: New Challenges for the External Relations of the European Union* (Institute for European Studies of the Free University of Brussels, 2007).

[60] Council Decision (EC) 2006/719 of 5 October 2006 on the accession of the Community to the Hague Conference on Private International Law OJ 2006 L 297/1. Membership of the Conference is open to Regional Economic Integration Organisations to which the member states thereof have transferred competence over matters of private international law (Art 3 of the amended version (1 January 2007) of the Statute of the Hague Conference).

3 April 2007.[61] The admission of the European Community to the Hague Conference is in addition to the individual membership of the Conference of the various European Union Member States.[62]

(ii) Impact of European Convention on Human Rights on private international law[63]

The Human Rights Act 1998 incorporates into the law of the United Kingdom the European Convention on Human Rights (ECHR). Human rights concerns were aired in private international law cases in the United Kingdom long before the passing of the 1998 Act,[64] but since its entry into force instances of this phenomenon have increased dramatically.

The rights incorporated are referred to under the Act as "Convention rights". In terms of section 6(1) of the 1998 Act, it is unlawful for a public authority, which includes a court or tribunal,[65] to act in a way which is incompatible with a Convention right. A court or tribunal determining a question which has arisen in connection with a Convention right must "take into account"[66] any judgment, decision, declaration or advisory opinion of the European Court of Human Rights (ECtHR), whenever made or given, so far as, in the opinion of the court or tribunal, it is relevant to the proceedings in which that question has arisen.[67] Moreover, in so far as it is possible to do so, primary legislation and subordinate legislation, whenever enacted,[68] must be read and given effect in a way which is compatible with the Convention rights.[69] If a court[70] is satisfied that a provision is incompatible with a Convention right, it may make a declaration of that incompatibility.[71]

In the context of private international law, discussion of the ECHR has most commonly focused upon the effect of Article 6, which provides the right to a fair trial.[72] Article 6 has been considered not only in the context of rules of jurisdiction,[73] but also in relation to

---

[61] See Schulz (2007) 56 ICLQ 939.

[62] On the distribution of competences between the Regional Economic Integration Organisation and its Member States, see Schulz (2007) 56 ICLQ 939, 945.

[63] See, generally, Fawcett (2007) 56 ICLQ 1; and Bell in Bottomley and Kinley (eds), *Commercial Law and Human Rights*, 115.

[64] Eg *J v C* [1970] AC 668, HL; *Oppenheimer v Cattermole* [1976] AC 249, 278 (per Lord CROSS), 283 (per Lord SALMON), HL; *Williams & Humbert Ltd v W & H Trade Marks (Jersey) Ltd* [1986] AC 368, 428 (per Lord TEMPLEMAN); *The Playa Larga* [1983] 2 Lloyd's Rep 171, 190, CA; *Settebello Ltd v Banco Toto and Acores* [1985] 1 WLR 1050, 1056, CA.

[65] S 6(3).

[66] Though not necessarily follow.

[67] S 2(1).

[68] S 3(2)(a).

[69] S 3(1).

[70] Meaning, for this purpose, the House of Lords; the Judicial Committee of the Privy Council; the Courts-Martial Appeal Court; in England and Wales or Northern Ireland, the High Court or the Court of Appeal; and in Scotland, the High Court of Justiciary sitting otherwise than as a trial court, or the Court of Session (s 4(5)).

[71] S 4(2).

[72] For full analysis of the impact of Art 6 on private international law rules, see Fawcett, op cit.

[73] In relation to jurisdiction in civil and commercial matters, see eg *OT Africa Line Ltd v Hijazy (The Kribi)* [2001] 1 Lloyd's Rep 76. The UK judicial response to arguments based on Art 6 sometimes has been fairly dismissive, eg *Lubbe v Cape plc* [2000] 1 WLR 1545; *Dow Jones & Co Inc v Yousef Abdul Latif Jameel* [2005] QB 946; and *AG of Zambia v Meer Care and Desai (A firm)* [2005] EWHC 2102 (Ch). See, in detail, infra, p 613. In relation to jurisdiction in matrimonial matters, see, eg *Mark v Mark* [2005] UKHL 42 (infra, Chapter 21).

recognition and enforcement of foreign judgments.[74] Decisions of the ECtHR have made clear the point that denial of access to national courts may amount to a breach of Article 6,[75] but it is equally clear that the right of access to a court is not absolute, and may be subject to restrictions, provided that these pursue a legitimate aim and are proportionate.[76]

With regard to other provisions of the Convention, United Kingdom courts have been required to consider, in a private international law context, the implications of Article 8 (right to respect for private and family life),[77] Article 10 (freedom of expression);[78] Article 12 (right to marry);[79] Article 14 (prohibition of discrimination);[80] and Article 1 of the First Protocol (protection of property).[81]

More detailed examination of particular Convention rights in their private international law context will be included in subsequent chapters, as appropriate.

7. THE NAME OF THE SUBJECT

The issue of the name or title of the subject may seem to be of little importance, but needs to be addressed, largely because there is no name which commands universal approval. The expression "Private International Law", coined by Story in 1834,[82] was adopted by the earlier English authors, such as Westlake and Foote, and is used in most

---

[74] Eg *Kuwait Airways Corpn v Iraqi Airways Co (Nos 4 and 5)* [2002] UKHL 19, [2002] 2 AC 883; *Maronier v Larmer* [2002] EWCA Civ 774, [2003] QB 620; *SA Marie Brizzard et Roger International v William Grant & Sons Ltd (No 2)* 2002 SLT 1365; *Al-Bassam v Al-Bassam* [2004] EWCA Civ 857; *Government of the United States of America v Montgomery (No 2)* [2004] UKHL 37, [2004] 3 WLR 2241; and *Orams v Apostolides* [2006] EWHC 2226 (QB). As regards the operation of public policy as a defence to recognition and enforcement, see *Krombach v Bamberski* [2001] QB 709; further, infra, pp 611–615. In relation to matrimonial matters, see, eg *Emin v Yeldag* [2002] 1 FLR 956 (concerning the grant of ancillary relief dependent upon recognition by the English court of a divorce obtained in the Turkish Republic of Northern Cyprus, a country not recognised by the British Government).

[75] Eg *Airey v Ireland*, Judgment of 9 October 1979, Series A, No 32; (1979) 2 EHRR 305; *Golder v UK*, Judgment of 21 February 1975, Series A, No 18; (1975) 1 EHRR 524; and *Osman v United Kingdom*, Judgment of 28 October 1998; (2000) 29 EHRR 245.

[76] *Ashingdane v United Kingdom*, Judgment of 28 May 1985, Series A, No 93, para 57; (1985) 7 EHRR 528; *Steel and Morris v United Kingdom*, Judgment of 15 Feb 2005, para 62.

[77] Eg *J v C* [1970] AC 668, HL; *Re I (Minors)* 23 April 1999 unreported, CA; *Re J (A Child) (Return to Foreign Jurisdiction: Convention Rights)* [2005] UKHL 40, [2005] 3 WLR 14; *S v B (Abduction: Human Rights)* [2005] 2 FLR 878; and *Re C (A Child) (Abduction: Residence and Contact)* [2006] 2 FLR 277.

[78] Eg *Skrine & Co v Euromoney Publications plc* [2002] EMLR 15; and *Prudential Assurance Co Ltd v Prudential Insurance Co of America (No 2)* [2003] EWCA Civ 1154, [2004] ETMR 29.

[79] Eg *Wilkinson v Kitzinger and Ors* [2006] EWHC 2022 (Fam), in which the petitioner, an English domiciliary, sought a declaration as to her marital status in terms of the Family Law Act 1986, s 55, failing which, a declaration of incompatibility, under s 4 of the 1998 Act, in relation to s 11(c) of the Matrimonial Causes Act 1973, which specifies that a marriage shall be void on the ground that parties are not respectively male and female. Dismissing the petition, the court concluded that neither Art 8, nor Art 12 of the ECHR guaranteed the petitioner the right to have her foreign same sex marriage recognised as having the status of a marriage in English law.

[80] Eg *Re J (A Child) (Return to Foreign Jurisdiction: Convention Rights)* [2005] UKHL 40, [2005] 3 WLR 14.

[81] Eg *Shanshal v Al-Kishtaini* [2001] EWCA Civ 264 at [50]–[62], [2001] 2 All ER (Comm) 601; *Kuwait Airways Corpn v Iraqi Airways Co* [2002] 2 AC 883; and *Orams v Apostolides* [2006] EWHC 2226 (QB), [36]. See Carruthers, paras 8.71–8.76.

[82] *Commentaries on the Conflict of Laws* (1st edn), S 9.

civil law countries. The chief criticism directed against its use is its tendency to confuse private international law with the law of nations or public international law, as it is usually called. There are obvious differences between the two. The latter primarily governs the relations between sovereign states and it may perhaps be regarded as the common law of mankind in an early state of development;[83] the former is designed to regulate disputes of a private nature, notwithstanding that one of the parties may be a sovereign state.[84] There is, at any rate in theory, one common system of public international law, consisting of the "customary and treaty rules which are considered legally binding by States in their intercourse with each other",[85] but, as we have seen, there are as many systems of private international law as there are systems of municipal law. Moreover, as often as not a question of private international law arises between two persons of the same nationality, as, for instance, where the issue is the validity of a divorce between two English persons in a foreign country.

It would, of course, be a fallacy to regard public and private international law as totally unrelated. Some principles of law, such as requirements of natural justice, are common to both; some rules of private international law, as for example the traditional common law doctrine of the "proper law" of a contract, have been adopted by a court in the settlement of a dispute between sovereign states; equally, some rules of public international law are applied by a municipal court when hearing a case containing a foreign element.[86]

An equally common title to describe the subject, and one generally used in the USA, is "The Conflict of Laws".[87] This is innocuous if it is taken as referring to a difference between the internal laws of two countries on the same matter. When, for instance, a question arises regarding whether the assignment in France of a debt due from a person resident in England ought to be governed by English or by French internal law, it may be said that these two legal systems are in conflict with each other in the sense that they can each put forward claims to govern the validity of the assignment. But the title is misleading if it is used to suggest that two systems of law are struggling to govern a case. If an English court decides that the assignment must be governed by French law, it does not do so because English law has been worsted in a conflict with the law of France, but because it is held by the law of England, albeit another part of the law of England, ie private international law, that in the particular circumstances it is expedient to refer to French law. In fact, the very purpose of private international law is to avoid conflicts of law. The one case where a genuine conflict arises is where two territorial systems, differing in themselves, both seek to regulate the same matter, as, for example, where the bequest of a Greek citizen dying domiciled in England is governed by the law of his domicile according to the English doctrine, but by the national law according to the Greek view.

---

83 Jenks, *The Common Law of Mankind*; Jessup, *Transnational Law*.

84 See, eg, *Re Maldonado's Estate* [1954] P 223; infra, pp 49–50.

85 Oppenheim, *International Law* (1967) 8th edn, Vol I, pp 4–5.

86 Eg the doctrine of sovereign immunity, infra, p 491 et seq. The interaction of public and private international law has been fully canvassed by Wortley (1954) I Hague Recueil 245; Hambro (1962) I Hague Recueil 1–68. See also Vallindas (1959) 8 ICLQ 620–624; Lipstein (1972) I Hague Recueil 104, 167–194; Kahn-Freund (1974) III Hague Recueil 147, 165–196; Lowenfeld (1979) II Hague Recueil 311; Mann, *Foreign Affairs in English Courts* (1986). See, for the interesting interface between private international law and public international law, *Kuwait Airways Corpn v Iraqi Airways Co* [2002] 2 AC 883, and comment thereon in Carruthers and Crawford (2003) 52 ICLQ 761.

87 For criticism of this title in the USA, see Maiea (1993) 56 Albany LR 753, 754.

The fact is that no title can be found that is accurate and comprehensive,[88] and the two titles "Private International Law" and "The Conflict of Laws" are so well known to, and understood by, lawyers that no possible harm can ensue from the adoption of either of them. It might be argued that the latter title is preferable, because it is a little unrealistic to speak in terms of international law if the facts of the case are concerned with England and some other part of the British Isles. However, the former is the title most widely used throughout the world and, significantly for this country, it is the description used in the European Community and most other international bodies of which the United Kingdom is a member.

---

[88] Other terms which have been used to describe the subject are "International Private Law", "Intermunicipal Law", "Comity", and the "Extra-territorial Recognition of Rights".

Chapter 2

Historical Development and Current Theories

Private international law as found in England is a substantive part of English law and was, until the last two or three decades, almost entirely the result of judicial decisions; though it is now the case that a considerable part of this field of law has been embodied in legislation. The writings of jurists in other countries, however, have influenced its growth to a considerable extent, especially through those doctrines that have found acceptance on the Continent. Twentieth century analyses of the basis of the subject, particularly those carried out in the USA, have been of more recent influence. It is difficult to study the subject without at any rate a slight acquaintance with the historical development of the earlier and current trends of thought. It is proposed, therefore, to start by giving a short sketch of the historical development of this branch of law[1] in England,[2] before moving on to look briefly at the varied approaches to the subject in the twentieth and early twenty-first centuries.

---

[1] For an account of the historical development of the subject more generally since Roman times and with particular emphasis on developments in Continental Europe, see the 12th edn of this book (1992), pp 15–23.

[2] The only separate work in English of an historical nature is Sack, *Conflicts of Laws in the History of the English Law*, in *Law: A Century of Progress 1835–1935*, Vol 3, pp 342–454. Beale gives a full and valuable outline of the general history of the subject in *Conflict of Laws*, pp 1881–1975. See also Wolff, pp 19–51; Westlake, pp 1–22; Yntema (1953) 2 AJCL 297; de Nova (1966) II Hague Recueil 441–477; Lipstein (1972) I Hague Recueil 104–166; and see Kegel (1964) II Hague Recueil 103–111; Juenger (1985) IV Hague Recueil 123, 136–169.

1. DEVELOPMENT OF ENGLISH PRIVATE INTERNATIONAL LAW

(a) Early history

Given that private international law issues had exercised the minds of civil lawyers for centuries, and given the growth of English activity as a trading nation, it seems at first sight surprising that English lawyers did not find it necessary to deal with choice of law problems until a couple of centuries ago. This, however, was the case and it was only in the eighteenth century that an awareness of the problems developed. Blackstone did not mention them and it was the middle of the nineteenth century before an English treatise on private international law was written, by Westlake. Sack has traced this tardiness of development to the special features of the common law and to the English system of administration of justice.[3] His explanation in brief is as follows.

The intra-national conflicts, that had long been inevitable on the Continent owing to the existence of different legal systems within the territory of a single nation, could not arise in England after the whole country had been brought under the sway of a single common law. International conflicts were precluded by the rule, established at an early date, that the common law courts were unable to entertain foreign causes. This rule was the necessary result of the practice by which the members of the jury were summoned from the place where the operative facts had occurred, since their function was to decide according to their knowledge of the facts. The sheriff could scarcely summon a jury from a foreign country in which the dispute between the parties had arisen. It is true that special courts were set up to deal with cases that might contain foreign elements. The King established courts to deal with complaints made by foreigners whom he had invited to England and who were, therefore, entitled to his protection. The staple courts and the pie-powder courts decided mercantile disputes. But in each of these cases the law administered was the law merchant which, at any rate in theory, was regarded as a universally binding system. There was no question of applying a foreign law at variance with the law of England.

When English traders began to extend their commercial activities beyond the seas, it was inevitable that they would occasionally suffer from this inability to obtain redress in respect of transactions effected abroad. A remedy ultimately became available to them in the Court of Admiralty, which extended its jurisdiction to foreign causes as early as the middle of the fourteenth century. By the middle of the sixteenth century it was competent to try disputes arising out of mercantile dealings abroad.[4] Again, however, there was no question of choice of law, for the court dispensed the general law maritime or, in cases of purely commercial matters, the general law merchant.[5]

By the end of the sixteenth century the common law courts had begun to compete for this jurisdiction. The technical difficulty that formerly stood in their way had disappeared, for the jury relied no longer on its own knowledge but on the testimony of witnesses.

---

[3] See Sack, *Conflicts of Laws in the History of English Law*, in *Law: A Century of Progress, 1835–1935* Vol III, pp 342–454; and see Anton (1956) 5 ICLQ 534; Nygh (1961) 1 U Tas LR 555; (1964) 2 U Tas LR 28.

[4] Sack, op cit, pp 353–355.

[5] Ibid, p 355.

The initial step was to deal with "mixed" cases, ie those in which some of the operative facts occurred in England, others abroad, as, for example, where the defendant failed to perform in Spain a charter-party that had been made in England.[6] The final step, that of trying cases connected solely with a foreign country, was facilitated by the new division of actions into local and transitory. In transitory actions, ie where the cause of action might have arisen anywhere, there was no necessity to summon the jury from one particular neighbourhood. The plaintiff could sue the defendant where he was to be found, and could lay the *venue* (ie the place from which the jury was summoned) where he liked. By Coke's time it was settled that the courts at Westminster could entertain all actions that were of a transitory nature, such as actions for breach of contract or on bills of exchange, notwithstanding that the relevant facts were connected with a foreign country.[7]

Thus the stage was reached at which it should have been necessary to deal with the familiar problem of choice of law. But in the case of mercantile disputes, which must have formed the bulk of those brought to court, the problem was avoided for many generations, since such disputes were decided according to the general law merchant common to European nations. By the nineteenth century, when the international nature of this law had ceased and it had been incorporated as one of the municipal branches of English law, the modern doctrines of private international law had already taken root in England.[8] Moreover, although the common law courts had expressed their willingness to take cognisance of foreign law, they were reluctant to entertain actions in which this would be necessary.[9] When the necessity became pressing, their first reaction was to require foreign cases to be tried by the appropriate court abroad, and to accompany this with a readiness to enforce the foreign judgment in England. This recognition of foreign judgments, which dates at least from 1607,[10] has never involved a reference to the foreign municipal law. All the English courts have ever done in this connection is to inquire whether the foreign court had jurisdiction in the international sense and whether its judgment was final.[11]

(b) Later development

The growth of the British Empire inevitably led to increased links between British subjects owing obedience to a variety of laws, and consequently to an increase in the number of disputes that required, if justice were to be done, a reference to something more than the common law of England. Yet the emergence of anything approaching a connected system of private international law proved to be a slow and laborious process.

The first hesitant steps are to be seen in *Robinson v Bland*[12] in 1760. This involved the question, which was discussed but not decided, whether a contract valid by the law of France where it was made, though void by English law, could be sued on in England.

---

[6] Ibid, pp 359–360.
[7] Ibid, pp 370–371.
[8] Ibid, pp 375–377.
[9] Ibid, p 381.
[10] *Wier's Case* (1607) 1 Roll Abr 530 K 12.
[11] The cases such as *Penn v Baltimore* (1750) 1 Ves Sen 444, in which equity exercises personal jurisdiction in respect of acts occurring abroad, do not involve the application of foreign law; infra, p 481 et seq.
[12] (1760) 1 Wm Bl 234, 2 Burr 1077.

The plaintiff had lent £300 to X in Paris, which X immediately lost to the plaintiff by gaming, together with an additional £372. X gave the plaintiff a bill of exchange payable in England for the whole amount. It was found that in France "money lost at play between gentlemen may be recovered as a debt of honour before the Marshals of France, who can enforce obedience to their sentences by imprisonment".[13] After the death of X the plaintiff brought assumpsit against his administrator on three counts: on the bill of exchange, for money lent, and for money had and received. It was held that the bill of exchange was void and that no action lay for the recovery of the money won at play. The plaintiff, however, was held entitled to recover on the loan.

The reason for the decision given by two of the three judges was that the laws of France and of England were the same on all these points, and that therefore it was unnecessary to consider which law would apply had there been a difference between them. The judges, however, expressed their opinions on the question. WILMOT J considered it "a great question", but inclined to the belief that a claim contrary to public policy could not be pursued in England. DENISON J felt that English law would govern since the plaintiff had chosen an English forum. It was left to Lord MANSFIELD to give a more modern flavour to the discussion.

> The general rule, established *ex comitate et jure gentium*, is that the place where the contract is made, and not where the action is brought, is to be considered in expounding and enforcing the contract. But this rule admits of an exception when the parties at the time of making the contract had a view to a different kingdom.[14]

He amplified his remark as to the exception in these words: "The law of the place can never be the rule, where the transaction is entered into with an express view to the law of another country, as the rule by which it is to be governed."[15] Although this was the first mention of the doctrine that the law to govern a contract is the law intended by the parties, what is more noteworthy about the decision is that as late as 1760 the rules on so important a matter were completely unsettled.

In 1775 in *Mostyn v Fabrigas*,[16] Lord MANSFIELD also adumbrated part of the rule that governed liability in tort until very recently,[17] though it was not finally settled until 1869.[18] He laid down that what was a justification by the law of the place of the tort could be pleaded as a defence to an action in England. Other principles suggested or established in the eighteenth century were that the law of the place of celebration governs the formal validity of a marriage,[19] that movables are subject to the law of the domicile of the owner for the purpose of succession[20] and bankruptcy distribution,[21] and that actions relating to foreign immovables are not sustainable in England.[22] It was not, however, until nearly

---

[13] WILMOT J described it as "this wild, illegal, fantastical Court of Honour"! 2 Burr at p 1083.
[14] 1 Wm Bl 234 at 258–259.
[15] 2 Burr 1077 at 1078.
[16] (1774) 1 Cowp 161.
[17] Infra, pp 766–767.
[18] *Phillips v Eyre* (1870) LR 6 QB 1, infra, p 766 et seq.
[19] *Scrimshire v Scrimshire* (1752) 2 Hag Con 395.
[20] *Pipon v Pipon* (1744) Amb 25.
[21] *Solomons v Ross* (1764) 1 Hy Bl 131 n.
[22] *Shelling v Farmer* (1725) 1 Stra 646.

the close of the century that a clear acknowledgment was made of the duty of English courts to give effect to foreign laws. It was made, once again, by Lord MANSFIELD.

> Every action here must be tried by the law of England, but the law of England says that in a variety of circumstances, with regard to contracts legally made abroad, the laws of the country where the cause of action arose shall govern.[23]

Thus the eighteenth century represents the embryonic period of private international law, a period which extended to at least the middle of the next century. As late as 1825, BEST CJ felt justified in remarking that "these questions of international law do not often occur",[24] and though the era of development was at hand, a considerable time had yet to pass before the main rules were determined. Thus, although rules to govern contracts, torts and legitimation were laid down in 1865, 1869 and 1881 respectively, it was not until 1895 that the dependence of divorce jurisdiction on domicile was established. Such matters as capacity to marry, choice of law in nullity and legitimacy are still unsettled. The formative period is not yet at an end.[25] There are still transactions and events common in daily life that are governed by comparatively ancient decisions, and there are others on which the decisions are so hesitating and vacillating that it is difficult to extract the governing principle with assurance. An important fact, and one that should never be overlooked either by the student or the practitioner, is that many of the older decisions are faulty and dangerous guides, and especially so when the point at issue has been the subject of more recent adjudication. Moreover, the number of decisions on choice of law issues is still relatively small[26] in comparison with the case law that surrounds such topics as contracts and torts. Indeed, this general state of the authorities, coupled with the movement in favour of unification by conventions,[27] the establishment of the Law Commissions,[28] and Europeanisation of the subject area[29] has led in recent years to increasing legislative intervention in the field of private international law.[30]

2. MODERN THEORIES AND DEVELOPMENTS[31]

The theoretical interest in, and development of, private international law did not end with the nineteenth century and more recent developments must now briefly be surveyed. Whilst the earlier theoretical development of the subject was very much a task

---

[23] *Holman v Johnson* (1775) 1 Cowp 341. Lord STOWELL spoke to the same effect in *Dalrymple v Dalrymple* (1811) 2 Hag Con 54.

[24] *Arnott v Redfern* (1825) 2 C & P 88 at 90.

[25] See Fentiman, in *Prescriptive Formality and Normative Relativity in Modern Legal Systems* (1994), pp 443 et seq.

[26] One area where there is a substantial number of reported decisions is that relating to jurisdictional disputes, infra, Chapters 11–14.

[27] Supra, pp 11–12; and see particularly the Civil Jurisdiction and Judgments Act 1982; Contracts (Applicable Law) Act 1990; Civil Jurisdiction and Judgments Act 1991.

[28] See, eg Domicile and Matrimonial Proceedings Act 1973; Matrimonial and Family Proceedings Act 1984, Part III; Foreign Limitation Periods Act 1984; Family Law Act 1986; Private International Law (Miscellaneous Provisions) Act 1995.

[29] Supra, pp 12–15.

[30] See North (1982) 46 RabelsZ 490, 500 et seq; Reese (1987) 35 AJCL 395.

[31] The diverse theories are conveniently summarised and analysed by Anton, pp 17–42; Nygh, Chapter 3; Morris, Chapter 21.

undertaken by civil lawyers,[32] more recently the mantle of theoretical analysis has passed to the common lawyers and, in particular, to theorists in the USA.

(a) Theory of acquired rights

The theory of vested or acquired rights[33] originated with the Dutch jurist Huber,[34] but it was elaborated earlier this century by common lawyers; by Dicey[35] in England and by Beale[36] in the USA. This theory is based on the principle of territoriality. A judge cannot directly recognise or sanction foreign laws nor can he directly enforce foreign judgments, for it is his own territorial law which must exclusively govern all cases that require his decision. The administration of private international law, however, raises no exception to the principle of territoriality, for what the judge does is to protect rights that have already been acquired by a claimant under a foreign law or a foreign judgment. Extra-territorial effect is thus given, not to the foreign law itself, but merely to the rights that it has created.[37]

Support for this theory is claimed from the judgment of Sir William SCOTT in *Dalrymple v Dalrymple*,[38] where the question at issue was whether Miss Gordon was the wife of Mr Dalrymple. Sir William SCOTT said:

> The cause being entertained in an English court it must be adjudicated according to the principles of English law applicable to such a case . . . the validity of Miss Gordon's marriage rights must be tried by reference to the law of the country where, if they exist at all, they had their origin.[39]

This theory of acquired rights receives scant support at the present day and it has, indeed, been devastatingly criticised.[40] It no doubt stresses one of the principal objects of private international law, for, as we have already seen, one of the elementary duties of a civilised court is impartially to protect existing rights even though they originated abroad. Nevertheless, it must be observed that to protect a right is to give effect to the legal system to which it owes its origin, for a right is not a self-evident fact, but a conclusion of law.[41]

---

[32] Civil lawyers' energies have been directed to the formulation of new or replacement codes; see Samuel (1988) 37 ICLQ 681; Symeonides (1989) 37 AJCL 187 (Switzerland); Palmer (1980) 28 AJCL 197 (Austria); Gabor (1980) 55 Tul LR 63 (Hungary); Dickson (1985) 34 ICLQ 231 (Federal Republic of Germany); Sarcevic (1985) 33 AJCL 283 (Yugoslavia); Lisbonne (1986) 75 Rev Crit dip 192 (Peru); Bruch (1987) 35 AJCL 255; Sucsuz (1991) 19 International Journal of Legal Information 97 (Turkey); Kim (1992) 40 AJCL 1 (Japan); Symeonides, ibid, 259, (1997) 48 Mercer LR 837 (Louisiana); Hay (1999) 47 AJCL 633 (Germany); Zvekov (1998–1999) 44 McGill LJ 525 (Russian Federation); Fiorini (2005) 54(2) ICLQ 499 (Belgium); and Parra-Aranguren in Einhorn and Siehr (eds), pp 264 et seq (Peru; Mexico; Quebec; and Venezuela). See generally on codification, Jayme (1982) IV Hague Recueil 9, and a symposium in (1990) 38 AJCL 423 et seq.

[33] See Morris, paras 21-008–21-010.

[34] For translations of the title *De Conflict Legum*, and for accounts of Huber's, influence, see Lorenzen, *Selected Articles on the Conflict of Laws*, Chapter 6; Llewelfryn Davies (1937) 18 BYBIL 49; and see Lipstein (1972) I Hague Recueil 97, 121–131.

[35] *Conflict of Laws* (5th edn), pp 17, 43; see Nadelmann, *Conflict of Laws: International and Interstate*, pp 14–18; Lipstein [1972B] CLJ 67–71.

[36] *Conflict of Laws*, pp 1967–1969.

[37] Holland, *Jurisprudence* (9th edn), pp 398–399; *Re Askew* [1930] 2 Ch 259 at 267.

[38] (1811) 2 Hag Con 54.

[39] Ibid, at p 58.

[40] Arminjon (1933) I Hague Recueil 1–105; Cook, *Logical and Legal Bases of the Conflict of Laws*, passim; Carswell (1959) 8 ICLQ 268; Kahn-Freund (1974) III Hague Recueil 147, 464–465.

[41] Carswell (1959) 8 ICLQ 268, 285.

The theory is open to several objections. First, it is advanced in explanation of the diffi-culty of reconciling the recognition of a foreign law with the general principle that the laws of a sovereign state have force only within its own territorial jurisdiction. But this difficulty is only an imagined one because it assumes too narrow a meaning of the expres-sion "territorial law", which is not confined to the positive rules that regulate acts and events occurring within the jurisdiction, but includes also rules for the choice of the applicable law.[42] English choice of law rules are part of the law of England and when a court, for instance, tests the substantial validity of a contract made by two foreigners in Paris by reference to French law, it applies a rule imposed by the English sovereign and it may accurately be described as putting into force part of the territorial law of England.

Secondly, the theory is futile if its supposed objective is to indicate what legal system governs each legal relation, for it begs the question and produces a vicious circle. A judge who is merely directed to protect a foreign acquired right is not far advanced on his jour-ney, for he still needs to identify the particular legal system, out of perhaps several possible choices, which is entitled to determine whether acquisition is complete. Such a search is not facilitated by the bald statement that a right once vested is inviolable. Once the appropriate law to govern a case has been determined, the rights that it has vested in the litigant ought certainly to be recognised as far as possible, but that fact can scarcely be called "the foundation of judicial decisions" on private international law.[43] As Cook has shown, there are no fundamental and logical principles which infallibly indicate in any given situation what court has jurisdiction and what law is applicable.[44]

Thirdly, the theory is untrue in fact, since the choice of law rules current in much of the common law world can require the enforcement of a right that is unrecognised, or even repudiated, by the chosen law.[45]

> A French widow, for instance, claims a share of her husband's English land. This claim raises a question either of succession or of the mutual property rights of hus-band and wife. If the English judge classifies the issue as one concerned with the mutual property rights of spouses, he must enforce whatever right is granted to a widow by that particular part of French law. But if French law would have classified the case as one of succession, it may well be that the English judge will enforce a right that would not have been admitted in France.

The theory as advocated by Beale is open to a difficulty of a different nature. He insisted that the municipal law of the country under which a right has been acquired must be followed *to the exclusion of its choice of law rules*. This no doubt is correct as a general prin-ciple;[46] but if so, the result will frequently be that the right enforced by the court of the forum will not correspond with that recognised by the relevant foreign law. The logic of the vested rights theory requires that the court of the forum shall apply, not merely the domestic rules, but also the choice of law rules, of the legal system under which the right is said to have been acquired. If, for instance, an American citizen were to die intestate

---

[42] Arminjon, op cit, p 27; see also Lord MANSFIELD in *Holman v Johnson* (1775) 1 Cowp 341 at 343.
[43] Dicey, *Conflict of Laws* (5th edn), p 18.
[44] *Logical and Legal Bases of the Conflict of Laws*, pp 18–19.
[45] Arminjon, op cit, pp 32–33, 47–48.
[46] Infra, pp 57 and 71.

domiciled in Italy, some American courts would apply the law of his domicile and would grant to the relatives such rights to the movable property of the deceased as would have been granted to them by the relevant provisions of the Italian Civil Code had the deceased been an Italian with no foreign connections. But Italian private international law, in its insistence that intestacy is governed by the law of the patriality, would deny that the relatives possess any such rights.

Again it was said by Dicey in his lifetime that, "the incidents of a right of a type recognised by English law acquired under the law of any civilised country must be determined in accordance with the law under which the right is acquired".[47] This is not completely true, for the incidents and consequences attached to a foreign right when enforced in England may differ from those recognised in its country of origin. An English court, for instance, may exact maintenance from a husband living in England, although he and his wife are domiciled in a country where no such obligation is recognised.

The theory of vested rights is analytically defective and is inadequate as an explanation of the pattern of rules of private international law. On the other hand, it may have performed a useful role in the development of the subject. As has already been pointed out, the theory stresses one of the primary objectives of private international law. It serves to emphasise the need to find solutions with an international flavour. The notion that a foreign right is vested and as such requires respect, although analytically a fiction, tends to induce the correct psychological background for the formulation of choice of law rules. The fiction of vested rights is a fiction inimical to insular prejudices.

(b) Local law theory

A second theory is that which has been called the *local law theory*.[48] This was expounded by Walter Wheeler Cook, who differed from earlier jurists with regard to the value of so-called fundamental principles. His method, congenial to English lawyers, was to derive the governing rules, not from the logical reasoning of philosophers and jurists, but by observing what the courts have actually done in dealing with cases involving private international law issues. He stressed that what lawyers investigate in practice is how judges have acted in the past, in order that it may be prophesied how they will probably act in the future. A statement of law is "true", not because it conforms to an alleged "inherent principle", but because it represents the past, and therefore the probable future, judicial attitude.

The gist of the local law theory as formulated by Cook is that the court of the forum recognises and enforces a local right, ie one created by its own law. This court applies its own rules to the total exclusion of all foreign rules. But, since it is confronted with a foreign-element case, it does not necessarily apply the rule of the forum that would govern an analogous case purely domestic in character. For reasons of social expedience and practical convenience, it takes into account the laws of the foreign country in question. It creates its own local right, but fashions it as nearly as possible on the law of the country in which the decisive facts have occurred.

---

[47] Dicey, *Conflict of Laws* (5th edn), p 43, General Principle No V.
[48] Cook, especially Chapter I; Lorenzen, *Selected Articles on the Conflict of Laws*, I; de Sloovère (1927) 41 Harv LR 421; Cheatham (1945) 58 Harv LR 561; Falconbridge (1937) 53 LQR 556; Falconbridge, *Conflict of Laws* (2nd edn), pp 30–37; Morris, para 21-011.

Since the court of the forum adopts the view that the chosen law would have taken not of the actual case, but of an equivalent domestic case, it does not necessarily recognise the right that would in fact have been vested in the claimant according to the chosen law. If the court of the chosen law had tried the actual case, it would not have regarded it as a domestic case. Owing to the presence of foreign elements, it would have been guided by its own choice of law rules, and therefore it might well have applied some law other than its own domestic system. Cook sums up the theory in these words:

> The forum, when confronted by a case involving foreign elements, always applies its own law to the case, but in doing so adopts and enforces as its own law a rule of decision identical, or at least highly similar though not identical, in scope with a rule of decision found in the system of law in force in another state or country with which some or all of the foreign elements are connected, the rule so selected being in many groups of cases, and subject to the exceptions to be noted later, the rule of decision which the given foreign state or country would apply, not to the very group of facts now before the court of the forum, but to *a similar but purely domestic group of facts involving for the foreign court no foreign element*. . . .
> The forum thus enforces, not a foreign right, but a right created by its own law.[49]

It is scarcely deniable, however, that this local law theory is little more than what one writer has stigmatised as a sterile truism—sterile because it affords no basis for the systematic development of private international law.[50] To remind an English judge, about to try a case containing a foreign element, that whatever decision he gives he must enforce only the law of the forum is a technical quibble that explains nothing and solves nothing. It provides no guidance whatever as to the limits within which he must have regard to the foreign law.

(c) The American revolution[51]

The major theoretical developments of private international law over the last few decades have taken place in the USA. Indeed they have been described as a new American revolution.[52] Whilst a variety of ways of tackling choice of law problems has been put forward in the USA, they tend to have a similar basic characteristic—an analysis of the issues arising in a particular case with a concern to devise the appropriate rule for this more narrowly formulated problem as compared with the far more broadly based conventional choice of law rules.[53] This analysis of issues in individual cases requires the court to examine the particular substantive rules of law in conflict in the case, to identify the policies at issue and to resolve any conflict so identified by choice of law rules appropriate to that narrowly defined conflict.

---

[49] Cook, pp 20–21.

[50] Yntema (1953) 2 AJCL 297, 317.

[51] See De Boer, *Beyond Lex Loci Delicti* (1987); Brilmayer, *Conflict of Laws: Foundations and Future Directions*, (1995) 2nd edn; (1995) 252 Hague Recueil 9; Symeonides (2003) 1 Hague Recueil 77; Symeonides, Perdue and von Mehren, *Cases and Materials on Conflict of Laws: American, Comparative and International* (2003) 2nd edn; and Scoles, Hay, Borcher and Symeonides, *Hornbook on Conflict of Laws* (2004) 4th edn. Also, from 1987 onwards, Annual Surveys of American Choice-of-Law Cases, cited in Symeonides (2005) 53 AJCL 559 at n 1.

[52] See Kegel (1964) II Hague Recueil 95.

[53] For a comparison of the two approaches, see Hay (1991) I Hague Recueil 281; Bliesener (1994) 42 AJCL 687.

In order to examine briefly these new developments, we shall have to look first at two general approaches common to most of the "revolutionaries" before looking at the main theoretical approaches put forward.

(i) Two general approaches

(a) Rule selection or jurisdiction selection?

English choice of law rules cover a wide variety of matters—such as the rule that the formal validity of a marriage is governed by the law of the place of celebration, that the essential validity of a contract is governed by the law chosen by the parties or (in the absence of choice) by the law of the country with which the contract is more closely connected, or that succession to movables is governed by the law of the testator's domicile. All these rules, however, have one thing in common. They are, in the terminology of the American writers, "jurisdiction-selecting" rules. They require the court to apply the law of the country chosen by the choice of law rule irrespective of the content of the particular rule of law thereby selected. This is to be compared with the technique of "rule-selection" favoured in the USA, which emphasises a choice between different substantive rules of law which in turn leads to a balancing of the respective "interests" involved in the application of a particular substantive rule of one legal system rather than a different substantive rule of another legal system.

The choice between a jurisdiction-selecting or a rule-selecting approach has been put thus:

> Should a court in dealing with a claim that a foreign law is applicable to the case before it or to an issue in that case choose between its own and the foreign legal system or, instead, choose between its own rule and the foreign rule?[54]

Rule-selection is preferred by the American writers and in some fields by the courts, but such an approach can take a variety of forms. Before attempting to outline some of these forms, it is necessary to examine a further general issue which may eradicate the need for any choice at all, namely the question whether there is a true or false conflict.

(b) True and false conflicts[55]

A jurisdiction-selecting approach to choice of law leads to the application of the rules of law of the chosen jurisdiction irrespective of which of the rules of substantive law of two or more apparently involved legal systems is to be applied. There is a basic assumption here that rules from two or more legal systems do have a claim to be applied. If they do not, and on analysis only one has such a claim, there is no choice to be made. This latter situation has been described as a "false conflict";[56] the former case where more than one set of rules has a legitimate claim to application, thereby necessitating the development

---

[54] Cavers (1970) III Hague Recueil 75, 122.

[55] Pryles (1987) 10 Sydney LR 284.

[56] This term covers the case where the laws of the two states are the same or would produce the same result, eg *Scheer v Rockne Motors Corpn* 68 F 2d 942 (1934) and where the laws are different but only one has an interest in being applied; eg *Babcock v Jackson* 12 NY 2d 473, 191 NE 2d 279 (1963); *Williams v Rawlings Truck Line Inc* 357 F 2d 581 (1965). See *Danziger v Ford Motor Co* 402 F Supp 2d 236 (DDC 2005).

of rules for choosing between them, is a "true conflict".[57] There is a third possibility,[58] which has been described as a "no-interest" case,[59] where a conflict of decision may result from the application of the laws of the different states, but where neither state has an interest in its law being applied.[60]

> The classic "no interest" case is one in which the plaintiff's state has a law favourable to the defendant and the defendant's state has a law favourable to the plaintiff. . . . The plaintiff's state has no interest in protecting the defendant who comes from another state and the defendant's state has no reason to give the plaintiff more compensation than he would get under the law of his own state.[61]

It will be apparent that in this whole area a two-stage analysis is involved. First, does the case concern a true or a false conflict? This question is to be answered by a proper interpretation of the rules in issue in the light of their respective purposes and the facts of the case.[62] Indeed, it is said that if, after such a test has been applied, a true conflict is seen to exist, the test should be applied more carefully again in the hope that on truer analysis the conflict will prove to be false and the need for choice of law rules that much the less.[63]

If, despite re-analysis, the choice of law problem still remains in the form of a "true" conflict, the next stage of analysis is reached, ie the selection between the various rules which have a legitimate claim to application. On this, American writers have put forward a variety of rule-selection techniques, which we must now examine.

(ii) Rule-selection techniques

(a) Governmental interest analysis

Currie, described as the father[64] of the governmental interest analysis approach, proposed[65] that the court should examine the policies expressed in the rules of substantive law in apparent conflict and assess the interests of the respective states in having the policies embodied in their rules applied in a fact situation not restricted to the one state. If, on careful assessment, the rules, policies and interests are found to be in conflict, a "true" conflict, then the law of the forum is to be applied. This is so notwithstanding the fact that the other state has an interest in the application of its own contrary policy.

The main role of interest analysis is to determine whether the conflict is true or false, but applying the law of the forum, without more, to a true conflict is, in truth, an abandonment of the internationalism of private international law.[66] Furthermore, the technique of interest analysis, particularly in a country like England where choice of law problems

---

[57] See Symeonides (2003) 51 AJCL 1, 13.

[58] For a range of seven possibilities, see Westen (1967) 55 Calif LR 74.

[59] Eg Currie, *Selected Essays on the Conflict of Laws* (1963), pp 152–156; and Symeonides (2003) 51 AJCL 1, 14.

[60] *Hurtado v Superior Court* 522 P 2d 666 (1974).

[61] Weintraub (1977) 41 Law and Contemporary Problems 146, 153.

[62] Cavers (1970) III Hague Recueil 75, 129.

[63] Currie (1963) 63 Col LR 1233, 1241–1242.

[64] *Bernhard v Harrah's Club* 546 P 2d 719 at 722 (1976).

[65] Currie, *Selected Essays on the Conflict of Laws* (1963), especially Chapters 4 and 12; (1963) 63 Col LR 1233.

[66] Eg *Erny v Estate of Merola* 792 A 2d 1208 (NJ 2002).

are more likely to be international than inter-state,[67] suffers from major defects.[68] The weighing of interests is limited to the identification of whether the conflict is true or false; it plays no part at the crucial stage of determining the applicable law. The latter is as important as the former. Furthermore, any weighing of interests is limited to state interests. This may be thought legitimate in the field of public international law; but in the context of private international law, the court should seek "conflicts justice"[69] and this requires due regard to be paid to the interests of the parties in the individual case.

Another disadvantage of governmental interest analysis is that it assumes a willingness and ability on the part of judges to identify and to evaluate the policies and interests expressed in the substantive laws under review. There are real difficulties here. How is the court to determine the policy underpinning a statutory rule;[70] and is the policy evident at the time the statute was passed still one that justifies its retention? There are similar problems caused by the passage of time in relation to judge-made law and the policies justifying the rule may never have been clearly articulated. The problems are compounded when the policy assessment has to be made in relation to the law of a foreign country whose legal system and law-making processes are very different from ours.[71] It is no answer to these difficulties to say that American courts have, mainly in the areas of tort and contract, applied interest analysis for more than three decades. Most of the relevant cases have involved inter-state rather than international conflicts[72] and, more often than not, no real attempt has been made to discover the policy basis of the rules in conflict. There tends to be merely a statement, without evidence, as to what the policies of the rules must be—very much a forum oriented assessment.

There are further difficulties with this approach. Not only is it inherently uncertain, but it also normally requires a judicial determination of where the balance of interests lies. This inhibits lawyers from giving advice and it suggests (as has proved to be the case) that the approach may best be used in areas such as the law of tort where "the function of the law is substantially pathological and the view of the court is essentially retrospective".[73] It has been little used in family law and in property matters where the law's function may more often be prospective, involving advice as to the future. A final disadvantage concerns what Currie described as "the disinterested third State".[74] This is the case where the interests of three states have to be assessed, where the forum has no interest in its law being applied but where there is a true conflict between the interests of the two other states. The Currie analysis breaks down; there is no merit in applying the law of the forum and no rule for deciding which other law to apply.

---

[67] See Shapira, *The Interest Approach to Choice of Law* (1970), pp 34–44.

[68] For criticism of Currie's views, see Kegel (1964) II Hague Recueil 95, 180–207; Reese (1965) 16 UTLJ 228; Shapira, op cit, pp 175–185; Cavers (1970) III Hague Recueil 75, 147–148; Kahn-Freund (1974) III Hague Recueil 147, 413–415; Reese (1976) II Hague Recueil 1, 44–62, 181–191; Hancock (1977) 26 ICLQ 799; North (1980) I Hague Recueil 9, 33–38; Juenger (1984) 32 AJCL 1, 25–50; cf Kay (1989) III Hague Recueil 9. For defence of Currie's views, see Posnak (1994) 40 Wayne LR 1121; Shaman (1997) 45 Buffalo LR 329.

[69] Kegel (1964) II Hague Recueil 95, 181–189.

[70] See Brilmayer (1980) 78 Mich LR 392.

[71] Fawcett (1982) 31 ICLQ 189.

[72] See Kegel (1979) 27 AJCL 615.

[73] North (1980) I Hague Recueil 9, 37. Eg *Gilbert v Seton Hall University* 332 F 3d 105 (2d Cir 2003).

[74] (1963) 28 Law and Contemporary Problems 754.

(b) Comparative impairment

There is a body of opinion in the USA which, though prepared to go much of the way with Currie's interest analysis and the identification, and thus elimination, of false conflicts, is not willing to accept that the law of the forum automatically be applied in cases of true conflicts. In contrast to Currie's views, such opinion believes that courts are able to and ought to weigh the conflicting interests. The criterion for such evaluation is suggested as that of "comparative impairment". This approach, first propounded in 1963 by Baxter[75] and since supported by the Supreme Court of California,[76] requires the court to determine which of the conflicting states' interests would be more impaired if its policy were subordinated to the policy of the other state. The essence of the comparative impairment approach has been summed up thus:

> the comparative impairment approach to the resolution of true conflicts attempts to determine the relative commitment of the respective states to the laws involved. The approach incorporates several factors for consideration: the history and current status of the states' laws: the function and purpose of those laws.[77]

Though this approach is open to all the objections that may be made against any rule-selection approach, with its underlying premise that the identification of governmental interests or state policies implicit in the conflicting rules is easy to accomplish, it does meet some of the criticisms of Currie's mechanistic forum-oriented approach and of his failure to solve the problem of the disinterested third state.

(c) Principles of preference

As long ago as 1933 Cavers advocated[78] the abandonment of a jurisdiction-selecting approach in favour of rule-selection. Later, he developed[79] his choice of law rules as "principles of preference". He and Currie have much in common. They were both supporters of rule-selection: both would utilise this analysis to identify cases of true and false conflict. Resolution of false conflicts is easy—there is no conflict. The parting of the ways comes with true conflicts. Cavers did not accept "Currie's stern rejection of all choice-of-law rules".[80] Instead, he sought to develop choice of law rules for the resolution of true conflicts. Accepting that the detailed development of rule-selection rules may be a long process, he suggested that the courts should develop broad principles of preference:

> The court is to seek a rule for choice of law or a principle of preference which would either reflect relevant multistate policies or provide the basis for a reasonable accommodation of the laws' conflicting purposes. A principle of preference would be applicable to all cases having the same general pattern of law and fact and would identify a preferred result on choice-of-law grounds. If the case could not thus be generalised, the court should state

---

[75] (1963) 16 Stan LR 1; and see Horowitz (1974) 21 UCLALR 719, 748–758.

[76] *Bernhard v Harrah's Club* 546 P 2d 719 (1976); *Offshore Rental Co Inc v Continental Oil Co* 583 P 2d 721 (1978); and see *Liew v Official Receiver* 685 F 2d 1192 (1982).

[77] *Offshore Rental Co Inc v Continental Oil Co*, supra, at 727. For criticisms of this approach, see Bradley (1976) 29 Stan LR 127, 146; Weintraub (1977) 41 Law and Contemporary Problems 146, 158; North (1980) I Hague Recueil 9, 38–40; Kay (1980) 68 Calif LR 577; and Juenger (1999) 73 Tul LR 1309.

[78] (1933) 47 Harv LR 173.

[79] *The Choice-of-Law Process* (1965); (1970) III Hague Recueil 75; (1977) 26 ICLQ 703; *The Choice of Law, Selected Essays* (1985).

[80] *The Choice-of-Law Process* (1965), p 94.

the reasons leading it to prefer one result to the other on choice-of-law grounds. In either case it should apply the law leading to the preferred result.[81]

This is the gradualist approach. It involves the introduction of broad principles of preference, worked out by Cavers in some fields, namely torts, contracts and conveyances, but not developed at all in others. The main objective is to do justice between the parties and, from these just principles, it is envisaged that more specific detailed rules will emerge as a result of judicial development.[82]

The main appeal of Cavers' approach is that it attempts a solution to the true conflict, but in the process it attracts all the criticisms of any rule selection approach.[83] It is still necessary to identify and evaluate state policies or interests. Uncertainty and unpredictability remain, even with principles of preference. This is because their evolution is seen in terms of judicial development, and choice of law rules based on principles of such detail as is necessary to accommodate so many varied policies will take a very long time to develop. This may be easier in a federal state, as Cavers himself admitted,[84] than with the type of international conflicts with which English courts tend to be faced.

(d) Interpretation of forum policy

Criticism of both the traditional jurisdiction-selecting approaches and more recent governmental interests analysis is found in the writings of Ehrenzweig.[85] In his view, a court, in searching for the appropriate choice of law rule, should give pre-eminence to the law of the forum—an approach described as "interpretation of forum policy".[86] He maintained that, in practice, the courts have applied the law of the forum as the general rule, and suggested that foreign law was not to be regarded as "applicable" to govern a case, merely that it should be "tolerated".[87] Reference to a foreign law is only to be made in exceptional circumstances where application of the law of the forum would be unfair to the parties or contrary to their intentions. Application of the law of the forum has the obvious advantages for all concerned in litigation that it is easy and cheap to apply; but it depends on knowing what the forum is going to be. Ehrenzweig's approach is a recipe for "forum-shopping", with the claimant seeking to sue in the country with the law most favourable to him. It is hardly satisfactory that the merits of his approach to choice of law issues depend on the availability of controls over jurisdictional rules. Furthermore, a forum-oriented approach cannot provide choice of law decisions in the absence of litigation.[88]

---

[81] *The Choice-of-Law Process* (1965), p 64.

[82] The courts have, in some cases, attempted to develop such detailed rules; see *Neumeier v Kuehner* 286 NE 2d 454 (1972); *First National Bank in Fort Collins v Rostek* 514 P 2d 314 (1973); *Bader v Purdom* 841 F 2d 38 (1988).

[83] For criticisms, see de Nova (1966) II Hague Recueil 597–603; Lipstein (1972) I Hague Recueil 157–161.

[84] (1933) 47 Harv LR 173, 203.

[85] *A Treatise on the Conflict of Laws* (1962); *Private International Law*, Vols I–III (1967–1977); (1960) 58 Mich LR 637; (1961) 49 Cal LR 240; (1968) II Hague Recueil 178.

[86] Cavers (1970) III Hague Recueil 75, 150.

[87] *A Treatise on the Conflict of Laws* (1962), p 311.

[88] For other criticisms, see Shapira, *The Interest Approach to Choice of Law* (1970), pp 205–208; Kegel (1964) II Hague Recueil 95, 224–236; Lipstein (1972) I Hague Recueil 144–147.

(e) Choice of law factors

There are two, fairly similar, American approaches to choice of law problems under which the applicable law is determined by reference to a variety of choice of law factors. The first of these is the American Law Institute's Restatement of the Conflict of Laws, Second, which adopts as its basic criterion for choice of law the application of the law of the state which has the most significant relationship to the particular issue under principles laid down in paragraph 6 of the Restatement. This requires the court to follow a statutory directive of its own state on choice of law but, in the absence of such a directive, the factors relevant to the choice of the applicable law include:

(a) the needs of the inter-state and international systems;
(b) the relevant policies of the forum;
(c) the relevant policies of other interested states and the relative interests of those states in the determination of the particular issue;
(d) the protection of justified expectations;
(e) the basic policies underlying the particular field of law;
(f) certainty, predictability and uniformity of result; and
(g) ease in the determination and application of the law to be applied.

The most significant relationship test, with these choice influencing factors, is applied to a whole variety of conflicts issues, ranging from contract and tort to marriage and property.

Reese, the Reporter of the Second Restatement and architect of this approach,[89] would describe the test provided in the Restatement as an "approach" to choice of law and not as providing in itself rules for the solution of specific choice of law problems.[90] Nevertheless, it is perceived as a means to the end of development of clear, precise rules:

> I believe that one ultimate goal, be it ever so distant, should be the development of hard-and-fast rules of choice of law. I believe that in many instances these rules should be directed, at least initially, at a particular issue. And I believe that in the development of these rules consideration should be given to the basic objectives of choice of law, to the relevant local law rules of the potentially interested states and, of course, to the contacts of the parties and of the occurrence with these states.[91]

The attraction of this approach is that, in reality, it attempts to have the best of all worlds. It provides specific choice of law rules, unlike the forum-oriented approach of Currie and Ehrenzweig. It does not require an analysis into true and false conflicts with its difficulties of determining in detail the interests of the states whose laws are competing, or the policies underlying the creation or retention of such rules; yet it provides some consolation, in the reference to "the relevant policies of other interested states and the relative interests of those states in the determination of the particular issue", to those who are supporters of interest analysis. It acknowledges the desirability of certainty and ease of application of the law, surely very necessary elements in the formulation of new rules of law. It requires a new look at the old choice of law rules, and encourages that new look to be

---

[89] Cheetham and Reese (1952) 52 Col LR 959. See Symeonides (1997) 56 Md LR 1246.
[90] Reese (1976) II Hague Recueil 1, 44–65.
[91] Ibid, p 180.

issue-oriented rather than aimed at whole areas of the law such as "contract", "tort" or "marriage". Indeed, it is both jurisdiction selecting and rule selecting at the same time.[92] The purpose of indicating that regard should be had to the policies of the interested states and their relative interests in the determination of the particular issue must be in order to aid the selection of the more appropriately applicable rule—a form of interest analysis or rule-selection. In giving consideration, as Reese does in the passage just quoted, to the contacts of the parties and of the occurrence with the interested states, Reese relies on a "grouping of contacts" approach which is predominantly jurisdiction-selecting.

Although the Restatement Second has had a significant impact on the decision of tort cases in the USA involving choice of law issues,[93] it does not escape criticisms,[94] which are of two main kinds. The first is that "the factors often point in different directions and carry in themselves no measure of their significance".[95] You cannot point in rule selection and jurisdiction selection directions at one and the same time. Secondly, it is hard to be certain as to the purpose of the Restatement's choice influencing factors. They read like an exhortation to a law reformer, as criteria to be weighed in formulating new rules. Their effectiveness depends both on litigation and on judicial creativity, on a willingness of judges to cast aside old rules in a search for better ones, despite any uncertainty that may bring. It is not surprising that their main impact has been in the field of choice of law in tort, where the role of the law is far more retrospective than prospective.

The second approach involving choice of law factors is that of Leflar who has advocated that courts resolve choice of law issues by reference to five "choice-influencing considerations". In no particular order of priority, he lists them[96] as:

(A) Predictability of result;
(B) Maintenance of interstate and international order;
(C) Simplification of the judicial task;
(D) Advancement of the forum's governmental interests;
(E) Application of the better rule of law.

All but the last of these essentially mirror factors to be found in the list in the Restatement Second. They have the same attractions and are subject to the same criticisms; but the fifth factor, that of "the better rule of law", calls for separate comment. It is a factor which has proved attractive to the judiciary, though one which is more likely to lead to a court concluding that its own, the forum's, rule of law is the better rule.[97] Nevertheless, it is a dangerous factor to use in the choice of law process because it confuses the issue of the reform of the substantive law of one country with that of choosing the most appropriate

---

[92] See Shapira, *The Interest Approach to Choice of Law* (1970), p 214.

[93] Eg *Babcock v Jackson* 191 NE 2d 279 (1963); *Pancotto v Sociedade de Safaris de Mocambique SARL* 422 F Supp 405 (1976).

[94] See the symposium in (1997) 56 Maryland LR 1193. Also *Dowis v Mud Slingers Inc* 621 SE 2d 413 (Ga 2005), 417–418.

[95] Cavers (1970) III Hague Recueil 75, 145.

[96] Leflar, *American Conflicts Law* (1986) 4th edn, pp 277–279. For an assessment of Leflar's work, see the symposium in (1980) 34 Ark LR 199. Also *Mikelson v United Services Auto Association* 111 P 3d 601 (Hawaii 2005).

[97] Eg *Clark v Clark* 222 A 2d 205 (1966); *Turcotte v Ford Motor Co* 494 F 2d 173 (1974); *Wille v Farm Bureau Mutual Insurance Co* 432 NW 2d 784 (1988); cf *Boucher v Boucher* 553 A 2d 313 (1988).

law to govern a dispute with links with two or more countries. It is certainly not the task of a judge in one country to try to reform the law in another.[98]

(iii) Impact of the revolution

Whilst the direct influence of these American developments of private international law theory is essentially limited to the USA,[99] writers from, for example, France,[100] Italy,[101] Germany[102] and Switzerland[103] have welcomed the developments as, at least, providing an impetus for reappraisal of the civil lawyer's[104] approach to choice of law problems. At the same time, however, the voices of American critics[105] of interest analysis and the like are growing ever stronger, concerned with many of the criticisms of the "revolution" which have been mentioned earlier. Few, however, are as robust as this:

> Conflicts of law has become a veritable playpen for judicial policymakers. . . . [The] courts are saddled with a cumbersome and unwieldy body of conflicts law that creates confusion, uncertainty and inconsistency, as well as complication of the judicial task. The approach has been like that of the misguided physician who treated a case of dandruff with nitric acid, only to discover that the malady would have been remedied with medicated shampoo. Neither the doctor nor the patient need have lost his head.[106]

In truth, the impact of the new ideas has been limited. Whilst its effects on choice of law have been substantial in the area of tort law,[107] and have been significant in the context of contract rules, interest analysis and its progeny have been little discussed in the context of family law[108] or property matters and have had little impact on judicial decisions in those fields.

---

[98] Cavers (1971) 49 Texas LR 211, 215; but contrast Juenger (1985) IV Hague Recueil 123, 253–318. See Symeonides (2001) 49 AJCL 1, 8 et seq; and *Jepson v General Cas Co of Wisconsin* 513 NW 2d 467, 473 (Minn 1994).

[99] Though some direct influence in England can be seen, on what were our choice of law rules in tort, in *Chaplin v Boys* [1971] AC 356, infra, pp 766–767. For a survey of the different approaches taken throughout the USA, see Symeonides (2001) 49 AJCL 13.

[100] Audit (1979) 27 AJCL 589.

[101] Vitta (1982) 30 AJCL 1.

[102] Kegel (1979) 27 AJCL 618.

[103] Siehr (1999–2000) 60 La LR 1354.

[104] See further the symposium papers collected in (1982) 30 AJCL 1–146; Jayme, in *Forty years On: The Evolution of Postwar Private International Law in Europe* (1990), pp 15–27.

[105] Eg Juenger (1984) 32 AJCL 1; (1985) 46 Ohio State LJ 509; (1985) IV Hague Recueil 123, 227–252; (1988) 21 UC Davis LR 515; Rosenberg (1981) 81 Col LR 946; Korn (1983) 83 Col LR 772; Brilmayer (1985) 46 Ohio State LJ 459; (1984) 35 Mercer LR 555; Dane (1987) 96 Yale LJ 1191; (1989) 98 Yale LJ 1277; and see Baxter (1987) 36 ICLQ 92; cf Weintraub (1984) 35 Mercer LR 629; Posnak (1988) 36 AJCL 681; Kay (1989) III Hague Recueil 9; Symeonides (2001) 37 Willamette LR 1; Whitten (2001) 37 Willamette LR 259; Maltz (2005) 36 Rutgers LJ 527; and Symeonides (2007) 32 Southern Illinois Law Journal. Also, Symposium (2000) 75 Ind LJ 399, including comment by Juenger (at 403), Symeonides (at 437), Simson (at 649) and Weintraub (at 679); Symeonides, *The American Choice-of-Law Revolution: Past, Present and Future* (2006); and Levin (2007) 60 Stan LR 247.

[106] *Paul v National Life* 352 NE 2d 550 at 551, 553 (1986).

[107] It is often the case that a court may be influenced by more than one approach, as in *Mitchell v Craft* 211 So 2d 509 (1968). For a striking example of a federal court applying a variety of approaches to different claims arising from one accident, see *Re Air Crash Disaster Near Chicago Illinois on May 25, 1979* 644 F 2d 594 (1981).

[108] North (1980) I Hague Recueil 9.

Economic analysis of the conflict of laws

In recent years, interesting developments in conflict of laws thinking, in the USA and elsewhere, have emerged from the "law and economics" movement.[109] To some extent, this has been the result of a growing awareness that the vigour of the American "revolution" has subsided, and that state-based methodological approaches to the subject, such as governmental interest analysis, are inadequate. A number of scholars have sought to analyse, from an economic perspective, the interplay of legal systems, particularly in the fields of choice of law in contract and tort.[110] The economic analysis, characteristically, is "transactional", focusing not exclusively, nor even primarily, on the interests of sovereign states, but rather on party interests,[111] the purpose of private international law being said to be the facilitation of private ordering.[112] Arguably, the emphasis on private, instead of state, interests fits more readily with the reality of globalisation,[113] internal market integration,[114] and the approximation of laws.[115]

(d) The English approach[116]

What, in the light of the theories and approaches discussed above, is the theoretical or doctrinal basis of English private international law? In considering its nature do we find ourselves perplexed by the enigma that apparently it subordinates the sovereignty of the law of the forum to that of a foreign power? To answer this last question first, the position surely is that for the forum of its own volition to give effect to a foreign law or to enforce a right that is the creature of that law involves no abdication of sovereignty. To describe a foreign right as vested may perhaps be misleading in so far as it implies that it *cannot* be disregarded. For this danger to be dispelled, however, it is only necessary to realise that the forum's recognition of the foreign right is not based on an admission that it has any force in itself, but on the forum's realisation that its own positive rules of law, though in its view best suited for matters solely connected with its own country, are not always the right and proper rules for the regulation of matters that contain some foreign element. It therefore provides its own special rules for dealing with such cases—rules which specify when its courts shall be competent to try a foreign-element case, and which indicate the particular legal system that shall guide the courts in their exercise of this jurisdiction.

---

[109] See, generally, Whincop and Keyes, *Policy and Pragmatism in the Conflict of Laws* (2001); Basedow and Kono (eds, in co-operation with Rühl), *An Economic Analysis of Private International Law* (2006); and O'Hara (ed), *Economics of Conflict of Laws* (2007).

[110] Eg Solimine (1989) 24 Georgia LR 49; Trachtman (2001) 42 Va J Int L 1; Berman (2002) 151 U Pa LR 311; Guzman (2002) 90 Geo LJ 333; Stephan (2002) 90 Geo LJ 957; Muir Watt (2003) Vol 7.3 EJCL; Berman (2005) 153 U Pa LR 1819; Berman (2005) 43 Colum J Transnat L 485; Berman (2005) 51 Wayne LR 1105; Michaels (2005) Duke Law School Legal Studies Paper No 74, (2005) 51 Wayne LR 1209, and (2006) 2 J Priv Int L 195; and Rühl (2006) 24 Berkeley J Int L 101.

[111] Whincop and Keyes, pp 6 and 186.

[112] Ibid, p 9.

[113] See Michaels (2005) Duke Law School Legal Studies Paper No 74; and Gottschalk, Michaels, Rühl and von Hein, *Conflict of Laws in a Globalized World* (2007).

[114] See Muir Watt (2003) Vol 7.3 EJCL, para 3.

[115] See, supra, p 11 et seq.

[116] The English approach is, through membership of the European Community, becoming an increasingly European approach (supra, p 12 et seq), seen, to date, most clearly in the context of the jurisdiction of the courts and recognition of foreign judgments (infra, Chapters 11 and 16) and choice of law in obligations (infra, Chapters 18 and 19).

These rules are as much part of its own territorial law as those that regulate the conveyance of land in its own country.

But on what principle are the rules constructed? Is there one overriding principle from which they can all be deduced? Must they conform to a single doctrine? Are there certain maxims or axioms by reference to which the correct solution of all the diverse cases that arise in practice can be discovered? Do our difficulties disappear if we are reminded that all laws are personal, or that they are all real, or that every right duly established under the law of a civilised country must in general be sanctioned by an English judge? Clearly, such theoretical analyses are unsupported in English private international law. They are alien to the common law tradition and if offered in argument would be a matter of surprise to an English judge. The instinct of the English lawyer is to test a proposed rule by its practical bearing on normal human activities and expectations. It is by this method that in his opinion the purpose of law, which at bottom is to promote justice and convenience, can best be furthered. He is nothing if not an empiricist and a pragmatist. This is the spirit in which our choice of law rules have been conceived until the stage has been reached at which it is possible to extract a general principle from the existing stream of authority. In so doing, regard will be had to the policy objectives of choice of law rules. This task is undertaken not, as in the USA,[117] to provide individual choice of law solutions for each case that arises, but in order to develop clear rules properly applicable to the generality of cases in a particular field.

There is no sacred principle that pervades all decisions, but when the circumstances indicate that the internal law of a foreign country will provide a solution more just, more convenient and more in accord with the expectations of the parties than the internal law of England, the English judge does not hesitate to give effect to the foreign rules. What particular foreign law shall be chosen depends on different considerations in each legal category. Neither justice nor convenience is promoted by rigid adherence to any one principle; it is preferable that the various principles should fit the needs of the different legal relations, and should harmonise with the social, legal and economic traditions of England. Thus, for instance, the law to govern capacity will vary according to whether the matter under consideration is a commercial contract, a contract of marriage or a disposition of property. Again, the law to govern the essential validity of a contract is, in the absence of choice, the law of the country with which the contract is most closely connected, but the ascertainment of this will necessitate the consideration of a variety of presumptions and other factors, such as the residence or place of central administration of the parties, the situs of any immovable property involved, the place of performance and the legal form of any contractual documents. The presumptions are rebuttable and weight is given to all the factors. None is exclusive. Private international law is no more an exact science than is any other part of the law of England; it is not scientifically founded on the reasoning of jurists, but it is beaten out on the anvil of experience.

---

[117] Supra, p 27 et seq.

PART II

Preliminary Topics

Chapters

PART II

Preliminary Topics

Chapter 3

Classification[1]

1. INTRODUCTION

In a case containing a foreign element, the English court will have to examine various matters in sequence. First, it will have to be determined that the English court has jurisdiction both over the parties and the cause of action. The detailed rules on jurisdiction are discussed later.[2] Then, having satisfied itself that it possesses jurisdiction, the court must next determine the juridical nature of the question that requires decision. Is it, for instance, a question of breach of contract or the commission of a tort? Until this is determined, it is obviously impossible to apply the appropriate rule for the choice of law and thus to ascertain the applicable law. This is the first issue of classification to be

---

[1] An alternative English word for classification is "characterization". In French it is called *qualification*. The problems that it raises, since their discovery by Kahn in 1891 and Bartin in 1897, have been widely discussed both in England and abroad. The following are the chief contributions in English: Beckett (1934) 15 BYBIL 46; Robertson, *Characterization in the Conflict of Laws* (1940); Falconbridge, pp 51–123; Cook, pp 211 et seq; Lorenzen (1920) 20 Col LR 247; Unger (1937) 19 Bellyard 3; Lederman (1951) 29 Can Bar Rev 3, 168; Inglis (1958) 74 LQR 493, 503 et seq; Lipstein, [1972B] CLJ 67, 77–83; Ehrenzweig, *XXth Century Comparative and Conflicts Law*, pp 395 et seq; Kahn-Freund (1974) III Hague Recueil 147, 367 et seq; Dine [1983] Jur Rev 73; Forsyth (1998) 114 LQR 141; Jackson, *The "Conflicts" Process*, Chapters 5 and 6; Levontin, *Choice of Law and Conflict of Laws*, Chapter 5; Anton, pp 65–75; Wolff, pp 146–167; Morris, paras 20-001–20-010; Dicey, Morris and Collins, paras 2-001–2-045.

[2] Infra, p 199 et seq.

discussed in this chapter—classification of the cause of action. The court, having done this, must next select the legal system that governs the matter. This selection will be conditioned by what has aptly been called a connecting factor,[3] ie some outstanding fact which establishes a natural connection between the factual situation before the court and a particular system of law. The connecting factor varies with the circumstances. If, for instance, a British subject dies intestate, domiciled in France, leaving movables in England and land in Scotland, his movables will be distributed according to the law of France because of his domicile in that country; but Scots law, as being the law of the situs, will determine the succession to the land. This raises the second issue of classification to be examined here—classification of a rule of law. This is the identification of the department of law under which a particular legal rule falls, in order to ascertain whether it falls within the department with regard to which the chosen law is paramount.

2. CLASSIFICATION OF THE CAUSE OF ACTION

(a) Meaning of classification

The "classification of the cause of action" means the allocation of the question raised by the factual situation before the court to its correct legal category. Its object is to reveal the relevant rule for the choice of law.[4] The rules of any given system of law are arranged under different categories, some being concerned with status, others with succession, procedure, contract, tort and so on, and until a judge, faced with a case involving a foreign element, has determined the particular category into which the question before him falls, he can make no progress, for he will not know what choice of law rule to apply. He must discover the true basis of the claim being made.[5] He must decide, for instance, whether the question relates to the administration of assets or to succession, for in the case of movables left by a deceased person, the former is governed by the law of the forum, the latter by the law of the domicile. Whether undertaken consciously or unconsciously, this process of classification must always be performed. It is usually done automatically and without difficulty. If, for instance, the defendant is sued for the negligent damaging in France of the claimant's goods, the factual situation before the court clearly raises a question of tort.

(b) Difficulties

Occasionally, however, the matter is far from simple. In the first place, it may be a case near the line in which it is difficult to determine whether the question falls naturally within this or that judicial category. Secondly, it may be a case where English law and the relevant foreign law hold diametrically opposed views on the correct classification. There may, in other words, be a conflict of classification, as, for instance, where the

---

[3] Falconbridge (1937) 53 LQR 235, 236, adopted by Robertson, *Characterization in the Conflict of Laws*, p 92.

[4] See *Tezcan v Tezcan* (1992) 87 DLR (4th) 503 at 509–511; and *Sweedman v Transport Accident Commission* [2006] HCA 8, per GLEESON CJ, GUMMOW, KIRBY and HAYNE JJ, at [25]–[32], and per CALLINAN J, at [110]–[116].

[5] *Re Musurus's Estate* [1936] 2 All ER 1666 at 1667; *Do Carmo v Ford Excavations Pty Ltd* (1984) 52 ALR 231, per WILSON J at 239–40; and *Air Link Pty Ltd v Paterson* (2005) 218 ALR 700, per CALLINAN J at 230.

question whether a will is revoked by marriage may be regarded by the forum as a question of matrimonial law, but by the foreign legal system as a testamentary matter.[6]

These two difficulties are well illustrated by the historic *Maltese Marriage* case,[7] decided by the Court of Appeal at Algiers in 1889, which made the problem of classification a fashionable subject of study.

> A husband and wife, who were domiciled in Malta at the time of their marriage, acquired a French domicile. The husband bought land in France. After his death his widow brought an action in France claiming a usufruct in one quarter of this land. There was uniformity in the rules for the choice of law of both countries: succession to land was governed by the law of the situs, but matrimonial rights were dependent on the law of the domicile at the time of the marriage.

The first essential, therefore, was to decide whether the facts raised a question of succession to land or of matrimonial rights. At this point, however, a conflict of classification emerged. In the French view the facts raised a question of succession; in the Maltese view a question of matrimonial rights. When a conflict of this nature arises it is apparent that, *if a court applies its own rule of classification*, the ultimate decision on the merits will vary with the country in which the action is brought. On this hypothesis, the widow would have failed in France but have succeeded in Malta.[8]

The crucial question, therefore, is—on what principles do English judges classify the cause of action? Or, to put it in another way—according to what system of law must the classification be made? Must it be made according to the internal law of England, on the ground that the internal rules and the rules of private international law in any country are based on the same legal conceptions?[9] It is arguable, for instance, that when English private international law submits intestate succession to movables to the law of the deceased's domicile, the expression "intestate succession" must be given the meaning that it bears in English internal law and not a more extensive meaning than may be attributed to it in the foreign domicile. In opposition to this view, which had wide support, it has been suggested that classification must be based on the "essential general principles of professedly universal application" of analytical jurisprudence and comparative law.[10] But, although it may be desirable to solve the problem in this scientific manner, it is scarcely practicable to do so whilst there are no commonly agreed general jurisprudential principles.

(c) Basis on which classification is made

There can be little doubt that, in practice, classification of the cause of action is effected on the basis of the law of the forum. Thus, by application of the principles of English law, an English judge makes an analysis of the question before him and, after determining its juridical nature in accordance with those principles, assigns it to a particular legal

---

[6] Cf *Re Martin, Loustalan v Loustalan* [1900] P 211.

[7] *Anton v Bartolo* (1891) *Clunet* 1171. For a fuller and more detailed account see Robertson, *Characterization in the Conflict of Laws*, pp 158–162; Beckett (1934), 15 BYBIL 46, 50, n 1; Wolff, p 149.

[8] In fact the French court applied the matrimonial law of Malta.

[9] Cf Jackson, *The "Conflicts" Process*, pp 72–82.

[10] Beckett (1934) 15 BYBIL 46, 59.

category.[11] Although English law principles are being applied here, the case is in fact one which contains a foreign element, and so the classification which is made will not necessarily be the same as that which would be made in a purely domestic case.[12] In this context, its object is to serve the purposes of private international law and, since one of the functions of this department of law is to formulate rules applicable to a case that impinges on foreign laws, it is obviously incumbent on the judge to take into account the accepted rules and institutions of foreign legal systems. It follows, therefore, that the judge must not rigidly confine himself to the concepts or categories of English internal law for, if he were to adopt this parochial attitude, he might be compelled to disregard some foreign concept merely because it was unknown to his own law. The concepts of private international law, such as "contract", "tort", "corporation", "bill of exchange",[13] must be given a wide meaning in order to embrace "analogous legal relations of foreign type".[14] In the words of one author:

> The various legal categories, into one of which the judge must decide that the question falls before he can select his conflicts rule, must be wider than the categories of the internal law, because otherwise the judge in a conflicts question will be unable to make provision for any rule or institution of foreign law which does not find its counterpart in his own internal law, and thus one of the reasons for the existence of the science of conflict of laws will be defeated.[15]

Two examples will show that English judges have been prepared to solve the problem of classification in this broad spirit. In *De Nicols v Curlier*[16] the facts were as follows:

> A couple, French by nationality and by domicile, were married in Paris without making an express contract as to their proprietary rights. Their property, both present and future, thus became subject by French law to the system of community of property. The husband died domiciled in England, leaving a will which disregarded his widow's rights under French law. The widow took proceedings in England to recover her community share.

The rule of English private international law is that the proprietary rights of a spouse to movables are governed primarily by any contract, express or implied, that the parties may have made before marriage. Failing a contract, the rights are determined by the law of the matrimonial domicile of the parties. Thus the problem of classification was whether the right claimed by the widow was to be treated as contractual or testamentary, for only after

---

[11] Statutory provision to this effect is made, in relation to tort claims, by the Private International Law (Miscellaneous Provisions) Act 1995, s 9(2), in respect of the interpretation of which, see *Trafigura Beheer BV v Kookmin Bank Co (Preliminary Issue)* [2006] EWHC 1450: "the words 'for the purposes of private international law' in s 9(2) indicate that Parliament intended that the court should examine relevant issues to decide whether they would be characterised as 'relating to tort' not only by reference to English legal concepts and classifications, but by taking a broad 'internationalist' view of legal concepts. It followed that the word 'tort' in s 9 was to be construed broadly, so as to embrace non-contractual civil wrongs that gave rise to a remedy." (AIKENS J, at [68]). See further, infra, pp 766–768 and 777–779.

[12] See *Macmillan Inc v Bishopsgate Trust (No 3)* [1996] 1 WLR 387; and see Forsyth (1998) 114 LQR 141; infra, pp 819–820—Characterisation as restitution and p 1245—Shares. Also *Raiffeisen Zentralbank Österreich AG v Five Star General Trading LLC and Ors* [2001] QB 825, per MANCE LJ at [26], and *Atlantic Telecom GmbH, Noter* 2004 SLT 1031, per Lord BRODIE at p [1044].

[13] *G & H Montage GmbH v Irvani* [1990] 1 WLR 667 at 678.

[14] Nussbaum (1940) 40 Col LR 1461, 1470.

[15] Robertson, op cit, p 33.

[16] [1900] AC 21.

that had been decided would it be possible to choose between the French law governing the contract and the English law governing testamentary questions. It was clear that in the eyes of English internal law no contract had been made, but the House of Lords held that according to French law a husband and wife are bound by an implied contract to adopt the system of community, despite the absence of an express agreement to that effect. Thus the court, by its readiness to recognise a foreign concept, widened the category of contracts as understood by English internal law.

A second illustration of the international spirit in which English judges fulfil the task of classification is that, when required to determine whether or not the property in dispute is to be regarded as land and thus subject to the law of the situs, they abandon the distinction between realty and personalty in favour of the more universal distinction between movables and immovables.[17] Thus land in England, subject to a trust for sale but not yet sold, is regarded under the domestic doctrine of conversion as already possessing the character of personalty. If, therefore, the owner dies intestate domiciled abroad, it is arguable that he has died entitled not to land, but to pure personalty, and that the relevant intestacy rules are those of the law of his domicile, not of the law of the situs. Despite this, it is held that his right must be classified as a right to an immovable to be governed by the law of the situs.[18]

There is, however, one type of case in which the English judge will probably not make the classification on the basis of English law as the law of the forum. This is where the only possible applicable law is either the law of country X or the law of country Y and both these laws classify the question in the same manner, though in a manner different from that usual in English law.[19]

3. CLASSIFICATION OF A RULE OF LAW

(a) The problem described

Once the main legal category has been determined the next step is to apply the correct choice of law rule in order that the governing law may be ascertained. As we have seen, the correct rule will depend on some connecting factor, such as domicile or the situation of immovables, which links the question to a definite legal system. X, for instance, dies intestate domiciled in France, leaving movables in England. Since he has been connected by domicile with France, the operative rule for the choice of law is, therefore, that the question of intestate succession must be governed by French law. However, at this stage the second process of classification has to be gone through. It may be necessary to identify the legal category into which some particular rule falls, in order to discover whether it falls within a category with regard to which the law selected by our choice of law rules is paramount. That law has a certain sphere of control, ie it governs some, but not all, aspects of the juridical question as classified by the English court in the sense already indicated. Thus, for instance, in an action brought in England for breach of a contract

---

[17] Discussed, infra, Chapter 27. See also Carruthers (2005), Chapter 1.
[18] *Re Berchtold* [1923] 1 Ch 192.
[19] Robertson, op cit, pp 76–78; Lorenzen (1920) 20 Col LR 247, 281; Beckett (1934) 15 BYBIL 46, 62.

made and performable in France, French law governs matters of formal and essential validity, but all questions of procedure are subject to English law. A French procedural rule is outside the sphere of control of the chosen French law relating to matters of substance. If, therefore, a particular French rule is pleaded and if it is doubtful whether it relates to procedure or to substance, its true nature must obviously be determined. It must be ignored if it is procedural in character, otherwise it must be applied. Likewise, an English domestic rule is excluded if it relates to form or substance, but is applicable if it is procedural in nature.

(b) Basis on which classification is made

The critical and controversial question is the basis on which the classification should be made, and illustrations from the authorities will now be given to show how English judges have dealt with the matter. It is, however, essential to appreciate that a rule either of the foreign chosen law or of English law itself may require to be classified and that the line of reasoning is not necessarily the same in each of these situations.

(i) Classification of an English rule

Leroux v Brown[20] illustrates the process applied to an English rule:

> By an oral agreement, made in France, the defendant, resident in England, undertook to employ the plaintiff in France for a period longer than a year. The substantive validity of the contract was governed by French law, by which the contract was valid as to substance. The defendant pleaded, however, that the plaintiff's claim to recover damages was unenforceable in England, since the Statute of Frauds provided that "no action shall lie upon a contract not to be performed within the space of one year from the making thereof" unless the agreement or some note thereof was in writing signed by the defendant.

This plea required the court to decide whether the statutory rule was of a procedural character.[21] If so it was fatal to the plaintiff, for being a rule of English procedure it was necessarily binding in an English action. Unfortunately, the members of the court took the line of least resistance and, ignoring the larger issues involved, confined their attention to the literal wording of the statute. The reasoning of MAULE J, for instance, lacked nothing in simplicity: the statute provides that no action shall be brought on an agreement not to be performed within a year, unless it is evidenced by a written memorandum; the present agreement is of this nature and there is no memorandum; "the case, therefore, plainly falls within the distinct words of the statute".[22]

The defect of this reasoning lay in basing classification on English internal law instead of on private international law. The court failed to appreciate that the classification of the statutory rule was required for an international case, not for a purely domestic one. The issues are different. The fact that a rule has been classified, or that it ought properly to be classified, in a particular way for a domestic transaction containing no foreign element,

---

[20] (1852) 12 CB 801; and see *Mahadervan v Mahadervan* [1964] P 233.
[21] For the present law, see infra, Chapter 6.
[22] (1852) 12 CB 801.

does not preclude an entirely different approach when a question of private international law is involved. In this latter type of case, a condition precedent to the classification of an English rule is to ascertain the policy that the rule is designed to serve. Was it, for instance, the policy of the Statute of Frauds that no oral contract of guarantee should be actionable in England, irrespective of the law by which it was governed or of the country in which it was performable? Unless this was clearly the policy of the Act, it was an unfortunate application of mechanical jurisprudence to read the words—*no action shall be brought*—in a rigid and literal sense and thus to deprive the plaintiff in that case of a right recognised as valid and enforceable by the law with which it was alone connected. To do this is to strike at the roots of private international law and to defeat one of its fundamental objects. At the present day, when the principles of this part of the law are more mature and its purpose better understood, it is believed that a court, if required to classify a rule of English law, would have regard to the foreign features of the case and would solve the problem more appropriately than the Court of Common Pleas did in *Leroux v Brown*.[23]

(ii) Classification of a foreign rule

(a) Parental consent to marry

The law reports contain several examples of the classification of a foreign rule. The best introduction to this issue, however, is provided by the controversial Court of Appeal decision in *Ogden v Ogden*:[24]

> This concerned a domiciled Frenchman, aged nineteen, who married a domiciled Englishwoman, in England, without first obtaining the consent of his parent, as required by Article 148 of the French Code. The husband obtained an annulment of this marriage in a French court on the ground of want of consent. The wife subsequently went through a ceremony of marriage in England with a domiciled Englishman, who, in the present action, petitioned for a decree of nullity on the ground that at the time of the ceremony the respondent was still married to the Frenchman.

The factual situation, therefore, raised the question of the validity of the French marriage. There were two connecting factors: the husband was domiciled in France; the marriage was solemnised in England. Guided by these factors, English private international law indicated two rules:

> First, the essential validity of the marriage, including the capacity of the husband, must be governed by French law.

> Secondly, the formal validity of the marriage ceremony must be tested by English law.

Only the essential validity of the marriage was controlled by French law. It followed, therefore, that if the purpose of Article 148 was to incapacitate the husband from

---

[23] Cf *Bernkrant v Fowler* 55 Cal 2d 558, 360 P 2d 906 (1961). Among other examples of the classification of an English rule, see *Anderson v Equitable Assurance Society of the United States* (1926) 134 LT 557, at 566; *Re Cohn* [1945] Ch 5 (the Law of Property Act 1925, s 184, dealing with *commorientes* classified as part of the substantive, not procedural, law, infra, pp 50 and 1271; *Re Priest* [1944] Ch 58 (rule that a gift to an attesting witness to a will renders the gift void goes to essential validity, not to form); *Re Maldonado's Estate* [1954] P 223, infra, pp 49–50, *Re Fuld's Estate (No 3)* [1968] P 675 at 697, 698 (rule as to knowledge and approval in the proof of wills is evidential and thus procedural).

[24] [1908] P 46.

matrimony unless he complied with its provisions, it affected the essential validity of any marriage that he might contract and should be granted extra-territorial recognition.

So far all is straightforward. Moreover, there is no difficulty if both English and French law agree on the juridical nature of the consent rule and therefore on its sphere of application. Complications arise, however, when the true nature of the rule is doubtful. The difficulty then is to discover the reasoning by which a solution must be reached. Is, for instance, the French classification to be followed blindly? Again, is the English view of an analogous rule in the internal law of England, presuming that one exists, to be adopted? Neither alternative is satisfactory. The rational method is for the English judge to examine the rule in its foreign setting, in order to ascertain its intended scope, the policy by which it has been dictated and the part that it is designed to play by the French legislature.

Only by this process can full and proper effect be given to the English choice of law rule. French law, having been chosen to govern essential validity, must be allowed within reason to determine which of its domestic rules are essential rather than formal. To take the opposite course and to uphold a marriage, which is essentially void under the personal law of the parties, by attributing a merely ceremonial character to a rule regarded as essential by that law would not only be the negation of so-called comity, but would incongruously debilitate the English choice of law rule. The only reservation is that a foreign classification must be repudiated, if to adopt it would contravene the English doctrine of public policy or be repugnant to some fundamental principle of English law.

In *Simonin v Mallac*,[25] decided forty-eight years before *Ogden v Ogden*, the court was confronted with a different French provision that was obviously not intended to affect capacity in the strict sense of the word.

> Two domiciled French persons came to England and went through a ceremony of marriage in the English form, returning to Paris two or three days later. The wife subsequently petitioned the English court for a decree of nullity on the ground of want of parental consent. By French law, the parties were capable of inter-marriage, but they were required to ask advice of their parents, a request which had to be repeated each month for three months if the parents were adverse to the marriage. At the end of the fourth month, the marriage might take place despite parental disapproval.

It was clear that absence of the consent required by this rule did not render the parties incapable of inter-marriage. The obtaining of consent was in essence an additional formality and, since the form of the ceremony is a matter solely for the law of the place of celebration, the marriage was rightly adjudged to be valid.[26]

In *Ogden v Ogden*, however, the relevant French rule was to this effect:

> The son who had not reached the age of twenty-five could not contract marriage without the consent of his father and mother.

Although it seems almost unarguable that the object of this provision was to impose a total incapacity on the parties unless they obtained parental consent, the Court of Appeal

---

[25] (1860) 2 Sw & Tr 67.
[26] Infra, Chapter 20.

held the marriage to be valid, since the ceremony had been performed in accordance with the requirements of English law, the law of the place of celebration. The latter marriage between the respondent and the Englishman was therefore bigamous. It is submitted that this case was not on the same footing as *Simonin v Mallac*, and that it is opposed to established principles. For the English court to classify the rule as formal was in effect to infringe the principle that the essential validity of a marriage falls to be determined by the law of the domicile.[27] The most unfortunate feature of *Ogden v Ogden* is its suggestion that every rule requiring parental consent to a marriage must be classified as formal.[28]

(b) Bona vacantia

Re Maldonado's Estate[29] provides an outstanding example of a foreign rule being construed in its context, with a view to deciding whether it fell within the sphere of control of the foreign governing law. The facts were these:

> A person died intestate domiciled in Spain leaving assets to the extent of some £26,000 in England. By Spanish law those assets passed to the Spanish state, since the deceased left no relatives entitled to take them by way of succession.

The English choice of law rule applicable to this factual situation is that intestate succession to movables must be determined according to Spanish law as being the law of the domicile. Therefore, the sphere of control of Spanish law in the instant case was confined to matters of succession, and the problem was whether the Spanish rule under which the assets passed to the state was to be classified as a rule of succession.

At this point it is pertinent to notice that, though the movables of a deceased owner who dies intestate without leaving recognised successors pass to the state in the great majority of countries, yet the capacity in which the state takes is not uniform throughout the world. In some countries, such as Italy and Germany, it has been regarded as an heir taking by way of succession; in others, such as Turkey, Austria and formerly England, the State has been held to act in its capacity as the paramount sovereign authority and confiscates the movables as being *bona vacantia*, ownerless goods.[30] If, for example, the deceased died domiciled in Turkey, the Turkish law, since it governs only questions of succession and since it does not regard the State as a successor, has been considered to have no say in the matter and movables found in England passed to the Crown.[31]

The provision of the Spanish code applicable to the facts of the *Maldonado* case was that "The State shall inherit" movables. Moreover, the expert evidence accepted by the court

---

[27] The Court of Appeal in *Ogden v Ogden* refused to recognise the French annulment of the marriage, with the result that the parties possessed the status of married persons in England, but of unmarried persons in France. Infra, Chapter 21.

[28] In *Lodge v Lodge* (1963) 107 Sol Jo 437, HEWSON J, after hearing expert evidence, held that a contravention of Art 148 of the French Code rendered the marriage voidable, and he followed *Ogden v Ogden*. The Law Commission has left any reform to judicial development: Law Com No 165 (1987). In contrast, see, for Scots law, Family Law (Scotland) Act 2006, s 38(5) (in respect of which, see Crawford and Carruthers, para 11-34).

[29] [1954] P 223; Lipstein [1954] CLJ 22.

[30] See Wolff, p 157. Under s 46(1)(vi) of the Administration of Estates Act 1925 it is arguable that the Crown takes by succession and not by virtue of a prerogative right to ownerless property: *Re Mitchell, Hatton v Jones* [1954] Ch 525; cf *Re Hanley's Estate* [1942] P 33; but see Ing, *Bona Vacantia*, pp 57–62. See also *Hanchett-Stamford v Attorney General and Anor (Barclays Bank Trust Co Ltd Intervening)* [2008] EWHC 330 (CH).

[31] *Re Musurus's Estate* [1936] 2 All ER 1666 (Turkey); *Re Barnett's Trust* [1902] 1 Ch 847 (Austria).

showed that in the Spanish view this was a true case of taking by way of succession, not a case of seizing ownerless goods. Thus the rule under which movables, failing relatives, pass to the state is classified as a rule of succession in Spain but as a confiscatory rule in England, and the short question was whether in an English action this foreign conception of the relationship between the State and the deceased was to prevail with regard to movables found in England. Could the law of the domicile dictate to the English court what meaning should be attributed to heirship?

It was argued for the Crown that the English rules of private international law are dominant so far as property in England is concerned, and that no one can be described as a "successor" in the eyes of English law unless he has a personal nexus with the deceased, a connection which certainly cannot be claimed by a sovereign state to which the property passes. This argument, however, did not prevail. It was held, both by BARNARD J and by the Court of Appeal, that the Spanish law of the domicile, which admittedly governed all questions of intestate succession, must be allowed to determine the sense and scope of the term "succession". Further, the alleged requirement of a personal nexus between the deceased and the heir was dismissed as a fallacy, for in the words of JENKINS LJ: "The heir or successor is surely the person, whether related to the deceased or not, who under the relevant law is entitled to inherit or to succeed."[32]

Finally, there was nothing contrary to public policy or repugnant to English law in allowing a sovereign state to take property in the capacity of an heir.

(c) Other examples

In an earlier case, of *commorientes*, the question was whether the relevant rule of the German law of the domicile was to be applied as affecting substance or to be rejected as being procedural in nature. UTHWATT J followed the same process of construing the rule in its foreign setting and, therefore, accepted the German classification.[33] In the later case of *Adams v National Bank of Greece and Athens*[34] DIPLOCK J found it necessary to decide whether a certain Greek decree related to status or to the discharge of contractual liabilities, and he was insistent that for this purpose he was bound "to look at the substance of the law, not merely at its form".[35] There is no need at this stage to discuss other cases in which English courts have classified foreign rules, since examples will appear from time to time in the course of the following pages.[36]

---

[32] [1954] P 223 at 249.

[33] *Re Cohn* [1945] Ch 5.

[34] [1958] 2 QB 59.

[35] [1958] 2 QB 59 at 75.

[36] *General Steam Navigation Co v Guillou* (1843) 11 M & W 877, infra, pp 91–92 (whether a French rule affected procedure or the substantive law of tort); *Re Doetsch* [1896] 2 Ch 836 and other similar cases, infra, p 91 (whether a rule regulating the order in which parties must be sued affected procedure or substance); *Huntington v Attrill* [1893] AC 150, infra, p 129 (whether a New York statutory rule was penal or remedial); *Re Martin, Loustalan v Loustalan* [1900] P 211, infra, pp 1276–1277 (whether revocation of a will by marriage was a testamentary or matrimonial question); *Re Wilks* [1935] Ch 645 (whether the time at which shares forming part of an estate must be sold was a question of succession or administration); *Re Korvine's Trusts, Levashoff v Block* [1921] 1 Ch 343 (whether a gift in the event of death is to be classed as a bequest or a gift *inter vivos*); *Metal Industries (Salvage) Ltd v S T Harle (Owners)* 1962 SLT 114; and *Raiffeisen Zentralbank Österreich AG v Five Star General Trading LLC and Ors* [2001] QB 825 (whether an assignee's claim under the assignment of a marine insurance policy, made with French insurers, but governed by English law, was to be treated as contractual or proprietary).

Chapter 4

The Incidental Question

1. WHAT IS AN INCIDENTAL QUESTION?

A case involving private international law may place a subsidiary issue, as well as a main question, before the court. Once the relevant choice of law rule has been applied and the law to govern the main issue thereby determined, a further choice of law rule may be required to answer the subsidiary question affecting the main issue.

This problem may be illustrated as follows.

> Suppose that W claims rights of intestate succession to H's immovables in Italy. According to English rules of private international law, this falls to be determined by Italian law as the law of the situs.[1] Assume further that, under English conflict rules, W is recognised as H's widow, but not under Italian rules, because, for instance, Italian law does not recognise H's divorce from his first wife. The main problem, whether W can succeed to H's estate, is clearly determinable by Italian law, but must the subsidiary problem of the validity of the marriage also be referred to that law?

A question of this nature has been aptly termed the "incidental question" by Wolff,[2] though the less satisfactory expression "the preliminary question" is also used.[3]

---

[1] Infra, pp 1277–1279.

[2] Op cit, p 206. The problem has been described by Ehrenzweig, p 340, as "another miscreant of a conceptualism gone rampant".

[3] For discussion of this problem, see Robertson, Chapter 6; Dicey, Morris and Collins, Chapter 2; Levontin, *Choice of Law and Conflict of Laws*, Chapter 4; Gotlieb (1955) 33 Can Bar Rev 523; de Nova (1966) II Hague Recueil 443, 557–569; Kahn-Freund (1974) III Hague Recueil 147, 437–440; Gotlieb (1977) 26 ICLQ 734;

2. THE ELEMENTS OF AN INCIDENTAL QUESTION

An incidental question properly so-called presumes the existence of three facts.[4] The main issue should, under the English rules of private international law, be governed by a foreign law. There should be a subsidiary question involving a foreign element which could have arisen separately and which has its own independent choice of law rule. This choice of law rule should lead to a conclusion different from that which would have been reached had the law governing the main question been applied. Without these prerequisites there is no "incidental question",[5] and in most of the cases where a true problem has arisen the court has not appreciated that a determination of the law to govern the incidental question is required. This is an issue on which the support of jurists may be found for a variety of solutions. Some support the law governing the main issue,[6] others the choice of law rules of the forum,[7] and others consider that the determination of the problem will depend on the nature of the individual case and the policy of the forum thereto.[8]

3. THE PROBLEM ILLUSTRATED

The way in which an incidental question arises may be illustrated by two decisions, one English, the other Canadian, on the inter-relation of the choice of law rules for divorce recognition and for capacity to marry.[9] The English case is *Lawrence v Lawrence*:[10]

> The first husband and his wife married in Brazil and lived there until 1970. In that year the wife obtained a divorce in Nevada, USA, which was not recognised in Brazil; but the next day she married the second husband in Nevada. Later, the second husband petitioned for a declaration as to the validity of this second marriage. An incidental question arose from the fact that, under Brazilian law, being that of the wife's domicile to which English choice of law rules referred capacity to marry, she lacked capacity to marry the second husband. On the other hand, the Nevada divorce was recognised in England under our divorce recognition rules.[11]

The Court of Appeal, by a variety of reasoning, upheld the validity of the second marriage.[12] The effect of this was to give primacy to the divorce recognition issue at the expense of that of capacity to marry.[13]

Juenger (1985) IV Hague Recueil, 123, 195–197; Wengler, Vol III *International Encyclopedia of Comparative Law*, Chapter 7; Schmidt (1992) II Hague Recueil 305.

[4] See Dicey, Morris and Collins, para 2-047.

[5] See the discussion of *Shaw v Gould* (1868) LR 3 HL 55, infra, pp 1143–1146, by Webb and Davis, *Casebook on the Conflict of Laws in New Zealand*, pp 86–87; cf Gotlieb (1955) 33 Can Bar Rev 523, 535–537. In the context of legitimacy, contrast *Motala v A-G* [1990] 2 FLR 261, [1990] Fam Law 340, infra, p 1148.

[6] Wolff, p 206; Robertson, p 141; Lipstein [1972B] CLJ 67, 90–96.

[7] Breslauer, pp 18–21; Nussbaum, pp 104–109; Falconbridge (1939) 17 Can Bar Rev 369, 377–378.

[8] Dicey, Morris and Collins, para 2-049; Crawford and Carruthers, para 4-06; and see Gotlieb (1955) 33 Can Bar Rev 523, 555.

[9] Infra, pp 913–915.

[10] [1985] Fam 106. Infra, p 914.

[11] Recognition of Divorces and Legal Separations Act 1971; see now Family Law Act 1986, Part II, infra, p 992 et seq.

[12] For a converse approach, see *R v Brentwood Superintendent Registrar of Marriages, ex p Arias* [1968] 2 QB 956.

[13] This result would now be reached by statute under the Family Law Act 1986, s 50.

The Canadian decision in *Schwebel v Ungar*[14] provides a converse example of the incidental question, where the capacity rule prevailed over that of divorce recognition. The facts were these:

> A Jewish husband and wife, domiciled in Hungary, decided to settle in Israel. When they were in Italy, en route to Israel, the husband divorced his wife by "gett". Under Hungarian law, the law of their domicile, and under Italian law this divorce was invalid, but it was effective according to Israeli law. They then acquired an Israeli domicile and whilst so domiciled the wife later visited Ontario and married a second husband who ultimately petitioned the Ontario court for a decree of nullity on the ground of his "wife's" bigamy.

The Canadian court had not only to consider the question of the wife's capacity to marry, governed under Ontario choice of law rules by Israeli law, but also the question of the validity of the wife's divorce by gett. Under the Ontario rules of private international law the divorce would not be recognised, but it would under the Israeli rules. The Supreme Court of Canada upheld the validity of the second marriage. It was valid by the law of Israel, the law governing capacity to marry, and this prevailed over the Ontario rule denying recognition to the divorce.[15] Here, capacity was regarded as the main question, to which divorce recognition was incidental.

The majority of the decisions in which an incidental question has arisen have applied the law applicable to the main issue, though often without an apparent realisation that an incidental question was involved.[16] So unthinking and mechanical an approach cannot be justified and the determination of this issue must vary according to the class of case under review. If it is one, such as succession to movables, in which the doctrine of total renvoi requires the whole law of the foreign country to be followed, then both the main and incidental questions should, probably, be referred to that law.[17] Where, on the other hand, it is one in which the court is referred to the internal law of the foreign country, as perhaps in the case of a question of torts,[18] then there should be a greater likelihood of the court's separating the incidental from the main question and applying the appropriate English choice of law rule to each. However, as *Schwebel v Ungar*[19] illustrates, even in this type of case the court may still apply the law governing the main question on the grounds that "to hold otherwise would be to determine the personal status of a person not domiciled in Ontario by the law of Ontario instead of by the law of that person's country of domicile".[20] However, if one turns the issue round and asks why, in a question of status,

---

[14] (1963) 42 DLR (2d) 622; affd 48 DLR (2d) 644; Lysyk (1965) 43 Can Bar Rev 363; Webb (1965) 14 ICLQ 659.

[15] This approach is approved in *Padolecchia v Padolecchia* [1968] P 314 at 338–340, though on the facts as found no true incidental question arose.

[16] Eg *Re Johnston* [1903] 1 Ch 821; *Baindail v Baindail* [1946] P 122 at 127; *Haque v Haque* (1962) 108 CLR 230; *Schwebel v Ungar*, supra; *R v Brentwood Superintendent Registrar of Marriages, ex p Arias*, supra; and see *Breen v Breen* [1964] P 144; Gotlieb (1977) 26 ICLQ 734 at 771 et seq.

[17] See, eg, *Re Johnson*, supra; *Baindail v Baindail*, supra; *Haque v Haque*, supra; Gotlieb (1955) Can Bar Rev 523, 545, 547; and see the interesting problem posed by Webb and Davis, *Casebook on the Conflict of Laws in New Zealand*, p 88.

[18] Cf *Re Degaramo's Estate* 33 NYS 502 (1895); and see *Meisenhelder v Chicago and North Western Rly Co* 170 Minn 317 (1927); Webb and Davis, op cit, pp 84–85; cf de Nova (1966) II Hague Recueil 443, 566–567.

[19] Supra, and see *Padolecchia v Padoleccha*, supra.

[20] (1963) 42 DLR (2d) 622 at 633.

should the law of the forum subordinate its own choice of law rules to those of some other jurisdiction, then any real justification for the decision in that case is harder to find.[21]

4. DÉPEÇAGE

A problem related to that of the incidental question is that of "picking and choosing"[22] or '*dépeçage*'. A case involving foreign elements may give rise to issues which involve different choice of law rules. To take the simplest example,[23] if a husband and wife, both domiciled in England, marry in France, then any dispute as to the validity of their marriage may have to be referred to English or French law. In fact, if the dispute is as to the formal validity of the marriage, reference will be made to French law as the law of the place of celebration, and if the issue is one of capacity, it will be determined according to English law as the ante-nuptial domiciliary law of the parties.[24] Here it is clear that the one general issue of the validity of the marriage has to be analysed into two separate sub-issues referable to different laws. The court will pick and choose between these two sub-issues. A similar example is provided in the law of contract where the parties are free to choose different laws to govern different parts of their contract.[25]

In other cases the question whether there are two issues referable to different laws or but one single issue is less easy to determine. Although a failure to distinguish separate issues may produce an unjust and distorted result, it might also be said that the decision to pick and choose may be motivated by a desire to avoid the application of a rule that is regarded as undesirable. The most commonly cited example relates to interspousal immunity in tort.[26] If a husband and wife, both domiciled in a foreign country, are involved in a motor accident in England in which the husband negligently injures the wife, this would be classified as a tort problem to which the appropriate choice of law rules would be applied, pointing as a general rule towards the application of English law,[27] though with the possibility of this being displaced in favour of the law of another country.[28] Let us assume, however, that although an action will lie between husband and wife under English law, it will not so lie under the law of their domicile. Are we to say that the question of interspousal immunity arising in a tort claim is a tort issue,[29] or should we adopt a more subtle categorisation and suggest that the interspousal immunity issue is a matter of status to be segregated from the tort context in which it arose and to be referred to the law of the domicile?[30] The latter is the better approach.

---

[21] Lysyk (1965) 43 Can Bar Rev 363 at 379; though cf *Breen v Breen* [1964] P 144.

[22] Cavers (1970) III Hague Recueil 137–140; Ehrenzweig, *Private International Law*, pp 119–121; Reese (1973) 73 Col LR 58.

[23] Lipstein (1972) I Hague Recueil 214.

[24] Infra, p 877.

[25] Contracts (Applicable Law) Act 1990, Sch 1, Art 3 (1), infra, pp 690–692; but see Mclachlan (1990) 61 BYBIL 311.

[26] Cavers (1970) III Hague Recueil 138.

[27] Infra, p 795 et seq.

[28] Which could be the law of the country of their common domicile.

[29] Eg *Schmidt v Government Insurance Office of New South Wales* [1973] 1 NSWLR 59; *Corcoran v Corcoran* [1974] VR 164, infra, p 790 et seq.

[30] Eg *Warren v Warren* [1972] Qd R 386.

The problem can become more complex, as where the law of the domicile would permit the spouses to sue, but its substantive tort rules would deny the wife recovery, for example, because she was guilty of contributory negligence, whilst under the law governing liability in tort a wife cannot sue her husband but, apart from that, she has a good claim in tort.[31] If one picks and chooses, then the law governing the tort issue may only be applied to the tort elements of the wife's claim, whilst the law of the domicile is applied to the question of interspousal immunity. The result is that the wife can recover by picking and choosing different laws to govern different issues, though had any one law been applied to all issues, she would have failed.

---

[31] Cavers (1970) III Hague Recueil 138.

Chapter 5

Renvoi[1]

1. THE PROBLEM STATED

Once it is decided that a court has jurisdiction, how the issue before it is to be character-ised in terms of private international law and what choice of law rules are applicable, it might be thought that the judge's task was reaching its conclusion. Nothing remains for him to do but apply the chosen law. If this is English law there is no doubt that what he is required to do is to give effect to English internal law. Thus, where a person dies intes-tate domiciled in England leaving movables here the rules of distribution contained in the Administration of Estates Act 1925 must be applied. There can be no question of paying any further regard to the private international law of England. The function of that department of the law is purely selective and its selection of English law as the

---

[1] The literature on the subject is immense; among the contributions in English see: Bate, *Notes on the Doctrine of Renvoi*; Mendelssohn-Bartholdy, *Renvoi in Modern English Law*; Rabel, i, 75 et seq; Lorenzen (1910) 10 Col LR 190, 327; Abbot (1908) 24 LQR 133; Falconbridge, pp 137–263; Lorenzen (1917) 27 Yale LJ 509; Schreiber (1917) 31 Harv LR 523; Griswold (1938) 51 Harv LR 1165; Morris (1937) 18 BYBIL 32; Cowan (1938) 87 U of Pa LR 34; Griswold, ibid 257; Falconbridge (1953) 6 Vanderbilt Law Review 708; Inglis (1958) 74 LQR 493; Von Mehren, *XXth Century Comparative and Conflicts Law*, 360; de Nova (1966) II Hague Recueil 443, 478–577; Kahn-Freund (1974) III Hague Recueil 147, 392–397, 431–437; Sauveplanne, *International Encyclopaedia of Comparative Law*, Vol III, Chapter 6 (1990); Briggs (1998) 47 ICLQ 877; Levontin, *Choice of Law and Conflict of Laws*, Chapter 3; Dicey, Morris and Collins, Chapter 4; Crawford and Carruthers, Chapter 5; and Morris, paras 20-016–20-033.

applicable law must perforce refer to English internal law, ie to the rules applicable to a purely domestic situation having no foreign complexion.

If, however, the applicable law is that of a foreign country the situation may be more complex. The difficulty is to determine what is meant by the applicable "law". If, for example, the English rule for the choice of law refers to the law of Italy, what meaning must be attributed to "the law of Italy"? The difficulty is not obvious at first sight, but it can be demonstrated by a simple illustration.

> X, a British subject, dies intestate, domiciled in Italy, and an English court is required to decide how his movables in England are to be distributed.

It is clearly desirable that the mode of distribution should be the same everywhere, in the sense that no matter what national court deals with the matter there ought to be universal agreement as to what particular legal system shall indicate the actual beneficiaries. The fact, however, that there are different systems of private international law militates against this ideal solution. Thus, according to the English rules for the choice of law, the question of intestate succession to movables is governed by Italian law as being the law of X's domicile at the time of death, but according to the Italian rules it must be referred to the law of England as being the law of his nationality. In the above example, for instance, an English court has no option but to refer the question of succession to Italian law; while an Italian judge if faced with this issue is under an equal necessity to apply the national law. The English judge, of course, is exclusively governed by his own system of private international law, and must therefore decide that X's goods shall be distributed according to Italian law. Despite this obvious conclusion, however, we are still confronted with the question—what is meant by Italian law? Does it mean Italian internal law, ie the rules enacted by the Italian Code analogous to section 46 of the Administration of Estates Act 1925 which regulate the distribution of an intestate's property? Or does it mean the whole of Italian law, including in particular the rules of private international law as recognised in Italy? If the latter is the correct meaning, a further difficulty is caused by the difference between the English and Italian rules of the choice of law; for on referring to Italian private international law we find ourselves referred back to English law. This being so, the question is whether we are to ignore the divergent Italian rule or to accept the reference back that it makes. If we accept the reference back, are we to stop finally at that point and to distribute X's goods according to the Administration of Estates Act?

2. POSSIBLE SOLUTIONS

When a case is complicated in this fashion, owing to a difference in the private international law of two countries, there are three possible solutions.[2] These are as follows:

The judge who is faced with this issue and who is referred by English private international law to, say, the law of Italy, may

(i) take "the law of Italy" to mean the internal law of Italy; *or*

---

[2] See *Tezcan v Tezcan* (1992) 87 DLR (4th) 503 at 519–521.

(ii) decide the case on the assumption that the doctrine of single renvoi is recognised by English law; *or*

(iii) take "the law of Italy" to mean the law which an Italian judge would administer if he were seised of the matter, ie the doctrine of double renvoi.

These possible courses will now be discussed to show that in some types of case the third solution, whether rightly or wrongly, has been frequently adopted by the judges.

(a) Apply internal law only

The first solution, and the one which is in general correct and desirable, is to read the expression "the law of the country" as meaning only the internal rules of that law. The following would seem to represent the sensible view:

> If England chooses the law of a person's domicile as the best one to apply to a certain relationship, does she mean the ordinary law for ordinary people, his friends and neighbours, in that domicile? Or does she include that country's rules for the choice of law? Common sense could answer that the last alternative is absurd and otiose: a rule for the choice of an appropriate law has already been applied, namely our own. To proceed to adopt a foreign rule is to decide the same question twice over.[3]

This would seem to be in accord with the intention of the propositus. If, for instance, a man voluntarily abandons England and acquires a domicile in Italy where he permanently resides until his death many years later, the natural inference is that he willingly submits himself to the internal law of that country. This seems also to be the obvious answer in those cases, such as contract,[4] where the parties are allowed expressly to choose the law to govern their relationship. Few businessmen would voluntarily choose the doctrine of renvoi. This approach has been definitely adopted in at least two early English decisions, one by a court of first instance,[5] the other by the Privy Council.[6] It is, and always has been, unconsciously adopted in a multitude of decisions.[7]

(b) Doctrine of single renvoi

The second solution is to apply the doctrine of renvoi, in the form of single renvoi. Such doctrine is to this effect: if a judge in country A is referred by his own rule of the choice of a law to the "law" of country B, but the rule of the choice of law in B refers such a case to the "law" of A, then the judge in A must apply the internal law of his own country. The operation of this famous but regrettable doctrine, which demands that a reference to the law of a country shall mean a reference to the whole of its law, including its private international law, is best explained by the example already given:

> X, a British subject, dies intestate, domiciled in Italy, and an English court is required to decide how his movables in England are to be distributed.

---

[3] Baty, *Polarised Law* (1914), p 116.

[4] Infra, p 689.

[5] *Hamilton v Dallas* (1875) 1 Ch D 257.

[6] *Bremer v Freeman* (1857) 10 Moo PCC 306; see also *Re Annesley* [1926] Ch 692 at 709; *Re Askew* [1930] 2 Ch 259 at 278; cf *Re Ross* [1930] 1 Ch 377 at 402.

[7] Infra, pp 72–73.

The English court is directed by its own private international law to refer this question of distribution to Italian law as being the law of the deceased's domicile. When, however, it examines the provision relating to the choice of the applicable law contained in the Italian Code, it finds that in the case of succession to movables the Code prefers the law of the deceased's nationality to that of his domicile, and that if an Italian court had been hearing this matter in the first instance it would have resorted to the law of England. Thus, the English court finds itself referred back to English law as being the law of X's nationality. There is a renvoi or remission to English law.

If the court accepts this remission and distributes the property according to the Administration of Estates Act 1925, it is true to say that the doctrine of renvoi is part of English law. Italian law has been allowed, not to give a direct solution to the problem under consideration, but to indicate what legal system shall furnish the final solution. Where the court that is hearing the matter accepts the remission and applies its own municipal law it recognises the doctrine in its simplest form. Renvoi, properly so called, is best exemplified by the well-known decision of the French Cour de Cassation in *Forgo's* case.[8]

> Forgo, a Bavarian national, died intestate in France, where he had lived since the age of five. The question before the French court was whether his movables in France should be distributed according to the internal law of France or of Bavaria. Collateral relatives were entitled to succeed by Bavarian law, but under French law the property passed to the French government to the exclusion of collaterals. French private international law referred the matter of succession to Bavarian law, but Bavarian private international law referred it to French law. The Cour de Cassation in France accepted the remission and applied the succession provisions of French law.

Where, as in *Forgo's* case, there are only two legal systems concerned—where the reference is merely from country A to country B and back from B to A—the doctrine of renvoi appears in its simplest form. It can best be described as *remission*. A case may occur, however, where the reference is from A to B, and from B to C. Suppose, for instance, that an Italian testator dies domiciled in France leaving movables in England, English law will refer the question of succession to movables to the law of his domicile, French law. If, however, France were to refer the same question to the law of his nationality, Italian law, this would be a case of reference from B to C, best described as *transmission*.

This particular doctrine of renvoi, whether in the form of remission or transmission, which is now generally called *partial* or *single* renvoi,[9] is not part of English law.[10] That is to say, if English law refers a matter to the law of the domicile and if the latter remits the question to English law, the judge does not automatically accept the remission and apply

---

[8] (1883) 10 Clunet 63; and see Juenger (1985) IV Hague Recueil 123, 197–199.
[9] Dicey, Morris and Collins, para 4-008.
[10] *Re Askew* [1930] 2 Ch 259 at 268: "An English court can never have anything to do with it [renvoi], except so far as foreign experts may expound the doctrine as being part of the *lex domicilii*", per MAUGHAM J.

English internal law. He does not act as the French court did in *Forgo's* case. It seems unnecessary, therefore, to elaborate the objections to which the doctrine is open.[11]

(c) Doctrine of total renvoi

(i) The doctrine stated

The third possible solution is to adopt what may be called the *foreign court theory* or the "doctrine of double renvoi" or total renvoi,[12] or "the English doctrine of renvoi". This demands that an English judge, who is referred by his own law to the legal system of a foreign country, must apply whatever law a court in that foreign country would apply if it were hearing the case. Let us assume, for example, a question arises concerning the testamentary dispositions of a British subject who dies domiciled in Belgium, leaving assets in England. A Belgian judge dealing with this matter would be referred by his rules of private international law to English law, but he would then find that the case was remitted to him by English law. Evidence must therefore be adduced in the English proceedings to show what the Belgian judge would in fact do. He might accept the remission and apply his own internal law, and this would be his course if renvoi in the *Forgo* sense (single renvoi) is recognised in Belgium, or he might reject the remission and apply English internal law. Whatever he would do inexorably determines the decision of the English judge.[13] If this third solution is adopted, it is vital to realise that the decision given by the English judge will depend on whether the doctrine of single renvoi is recognised by the particular foreign law to which he is referred. The doctrine, for instance, is repudiated in Italy but recognised in France. Therefore, if the issue in England is the intrinsic validity of a will made by a British subject domiciled in Italy, the judge, if he is to make an imaginary judicial journey to Italy, will reason as follows:

An Italian judge would refer the matter to English law, as being the national law of the propositus. English law remits the question to Italian law as being the law of his domicile.

> Italian law does not accept this remission, since it repudiates the single renvoi doctrine. Therefore an Italian judge would apply English internal law.[14]

A French domicile, however, would produce the opposite result, since a court sitting in France would accept the remission from England and would ultimately apply French internal law.[15]

(ii) Objections to the doctrine

This third solution does not lack support in England, North America and Australia.[16] Certain English decisions, which will be discussed later, may be cited in its favour;

---

[11] Rabel, i, 81.

[12] Dicey, Morris and Collins, para 4-009; Falconbridge, p 170.

[13] The doctrine is ambiguous in the sense that the grounds on which the English judge must arrive at the Belgian decision are far from clear. Must he reason on the basis of the actual circumstances of the case, especially the presence of the assets in England? Or, must he reason on a false assumption, namely, that the assets are in Belgium? There is judicial authority for both views. See Dobrin (1934) 15 BYBIL 36, 37–45.

[14] *Re Ross* [1930] 1 Ch 377, infra, p 68.

[15] *Re Annesley* [1926] Ch 692, infra, p 67.

[16] *Neilson v Overseas Projects Corpn of Victoria Ltd* (2005) 221 ALR 213; infra, pp 70–71.

throughout his life Dicey maintained its truth; the editor of his fifth edition was equally strong in advocating its merits;[17] and an American jurist sums up his conclusions in these words: "When a court is referred by its own conflicts rule to a foreign law, it should, as a matter of course, look to the entire foreign law as the foreign court would administer it."[18]

Before estimating the value of the English decisions, therefore, it is appropriate to consider a few of the objections that may be raised to this total renvoi doctrine. The burden of the following pages is that it is objectionable in principle, is based on unconvincing authority and cannot be said to represent the general rule of English law. It is submitted that, subject to certain well-defined exceptions, an English judge, when referred by a rule for the choice of law to the legal system of a foreign country, is not required to consider whether the renvoi doctrine is recognised by the private international law of either country, but must administer the internal law of the legal system to which he has been referred.

The following objections, among others, may be directed against the doctrine:[19]

(a) The total renvoi doctrine does not necessarily ensure uniform decisions

The laudable objective of those who favour the doctrine either of single or of total renvoi is to ensure that the same decision shall be given on the same disputed facts, irrespective of the country in which the case is heard. In truth, however, the doctrine of renvoi, in whatever form it is expressed, will produce this uniformity only if it is recognised in one of the countries concerned and rejected in the other—not if it is recognised in both. If, for example, the law of the domicile, to which the English judge is referred, ordains that the case is to be decided exactly as the national (English) court would decide it, what is the judge to do on finding that by English law his decision is to be exactly what it would be in the country of the domicile?[20] Where is a halt to be called to the process of passing the ball from one judge to another? There is no apparent way in which this inextricable circle can be broken—or in which this international game of tennis can be terminated.

Uniformity will, indeed, be attained if the law of the domicile repudiates the doctrine of total renvoi, ie if, instead of seeking guidance from a foreign judge, it categorically provides that the national (English) law shall govern the matter, for in this case English internal law will apply and harmony will prevail. It is true that the total renvoi doctrine is apparently unrecognised in countries outside the Commonwealth, but nonetheless it is difficult "to approve a doctrine which is workable only if the other country rejects it".[21] The fact is, of course, that uniformity of decisions is unattainable on any consistent principle with regard to matters that are determined in some countries by the law of the nationality, in others by the law of the domicile.

A second obstacle to uniformity of decisions is that the foreign court doctrine does not require, in fact does not allow, the English judge to don the mantle of his foreign colleague without any reservations. Matters that are classified as procedural in England

---

[17] Dicey, *Conflict of Laws* (5th edn), pp 863 et seq; Keith (1942) 24 JCL 69.
[18] Griswold (1938) 51 Harv LR 1165, 1183.
[19] See also Morris, paras 20-029–20-032.
[20] Morris (1937) 18 BYBIL 32, 37; and see Schreiber (1917) 31 Harv LR 523.
[21] Lorenzen (1941) 50 Yale LJ 743, 753.

must be submitted to English internal law, even though the foreign judge might have regarded them as substantive.[22] This may well lead to a discrepancy of result. Moreover, the application of a rule of foreign law will sometimes be excluded on grounds of public policy or because it is considered to be a penal, revenue or other public law matter.[23]

(b) The total renvoi doctrine signifies the virtual capitulation of the English rules for choice of law

Stripped of its verbiage, the doctrine involves nothing less than a substitution of the foreign for the English choice of law rules. In the case, for instance, of the British subject who dies intestate domiciled in Italy, the English rule selects the law of Italy as the governing law, but the equivalent Italian rule selects the law of England. When, therefore, the English judge defers to the decision that an Italian judge would have given, he applies the internal law of England and thus shows a preference for the Italian selective rule. The English rule is jettisoned, since it does not meet with the approval of the law-maker in Italy. This, indeed, is the apotheosis of comity.[24] Moreover, a rule for the choice of the applicable law is essentially selective in nature,[25] and that it should have no other effect than to select another and contradictory rule of selection savours of incompatibility and paradox. Furthermore, the application of the law selected by the foreign country's choice of law rules may be unacceptable in public policy terms.[26]

One acute critic, however, finds nothing strange in this surrender to a foreign rule for the choice of law.[27] He denies that there is any logical reason why an English rule of this nature should not be taken to indicate the private international law of a foreign country rather than its internal law. To regard a reference to the law of the domicile as a reference to the internal law is, he says, merely to beg the question. This argument, it is submitted, ignores both the nature and genesis of a rule for the choice of the applicable law. The truth is that such a rule is based on substantial grounds of national policy. It represents what appears to the enacting authority to be right and proper, having regard to the sociological and practical considerations involved. The English principle, for instance, that an intestate's movables shall be distributed according to the law of his last domicile is founded on the reasoning that rights of succession should depend on the law of the country where the deceased established his permanent home. Having voluntarily become an inhabitant of the country, it is the view of English law that in this matter he should be on the same footing as other inhabitants. Moreover, the natural inference is that he submits himself to the law which binds his friends and neighbours. This would seem to be his presumed intention. Thus, if the reference to the law of his domicile is regarded as a reference to whatever internal system the private international law of the domicile may choose, then not only is the deliberate policy of English law reversed, but the probable intention

---

[22] Infra, Chapter 6.

[23] Infra, Chapter 8.

[24] See the dissenting judgment of Taschereau J in the Canadian case of *Ross v Ross* (1894) 25 SCR 307; and see Schreiber (1917) 31 Harv LR 523, 561, 564.

[25] Ibid, 533.

[26] In such circumstances a Canadian court has applied the internal law of the country chosen by the forum's choice of law rules, ie ignored the doctrine of renvoi on public policy grounds: *Vladi v Vladi* (1987) 39 DLR (4th) 563.

[27] Griswold (1938) 51 Harv LR 1165, 1176, 1178.

of the propositus is ignored. Indeed, his expectations may be flouted. He may, for instance, have refrained from making a will, having been content with the local rules governing intestacy, the substance of which it will have been a simple matter for him to ascertain. A quite different set of rules, however, may operate if the private international law of his domicile is to have effect.

(c) The total renvoi doctrine is difficult to apply

The doctrine obliges the English judge to ascertain as a fact the precise decision that the foreign court would give. This confronts him with two difficulties. First, he must ascertain what view prevails in the foreign country with regard to the doctrine of single renvoi. Secondly, where the foreign rule for the choice of law selects the national law of the propositus, the judge must ascertain what is meant by national law.

As we have already seen, the chosen law that emerges from an application of the doctrine depends, inter alia, on whether the doctrine of single renvoi is recognised by the law of the domicile.[28] If the court of the domicile would accept the remission made to it by English law, it would determine the case according to its own internal law; otherwise it would apply the internal law of England. This dependence of the rights of the parties on the attitude of the law of the domicile to the renvoi doctrine is a cause of acute embarrassment. There are few matters on which it is more difficult to obtain reliable information, not least because of the undue influence of expert witnesses over the process. Alternatively, the English judge may be confronted with a somewhat arduous and invidious task, as witness the following remarks of WYNN-PARRY J:

> It would be difficult to imagine a harder task than that which faces me, namely, of expounding for the first time either to this country or to Spain the relevant law of Spain as it would be expounded by the Supreme Court of Spain, which up to the present time has made no pronouncement on the subject, and having to base that exposition on evidence which satisfies me that on this subject there exists a profound cleavage of legal opinion in Spain and two conflicting decisions of courts of inferior jurisdiction.[29]

The second difficulty that may arise is to ascribe a definite meaning to the expression "national law". When the private international law rules of the country in which the English judge is presumed to sit select the nationality of a person as the connecting factor, it becomes necessary to correlate the national law with some precise system of internal law by which the issue before the court may be determined. This is a simple matter when the person is a national of some country, such as Sweden, which has a unitary system of territorial law.[30] There is a single body of internal law applicable throughout the territory known as Sweden. The position is far different where the country of nationality comprises several systems of territorial law, as is true for example of the United Kingdom and the USA. What, for instance, is the national law of a British subject? For an English court, the question is really pointless, because the law that governs a British subject in personal

---

[28] Supra, pp 59–60.

[29] *Re Duke of Wellington* [1947] Ch 506 at 515; infra, pp 69–70.

[30] For a stimulating exposé of the present difficulty, see Falconbridge, pp 202–216. See also Morris (1940) 56 LQR 144. For judicial comment on the onerous nature of the doctrine, see *Barros Mattos Junior v MacDaniels Ltd* [2005] IL Pr 45, per Lawrence COLLINS J, at [108].

matters varies according to the territory of the foreign country in which he is domiciled. It is one system in England, another in Scotland, and so on. The case of *Re O'Keefe*[31] will serve to illustrate both the nature of the difficulty and the speciousness of the total renvoi doctrine. The facts were these:

> The question before the English court was the way in which the movables of X, a spinster who died intestate, were to be distributed. X's father was born in 1835 in Ireland, but at the age of 22 he went to India, and except for various stays in Europe lived there throughout his life and died in Calcutta in 1885. X was born in India in 1860; from 1867 to 1890 she lived in various places in England, France and Spain; but in 1890 she settled down in Naples and resided there until her death 47 years later in 1937. About the year 1878 she had made a short tour in Ireland with her father. She never lost her British nationality, but it was held that she had acquired a domicile in Italy.

The law selected by English private international law to govern the question of distribution was, therefore, the law of her domicile. Had an Italian judge been hearing the case, however, he would have been referred to her national law by the Italian Civil Code. He would have rejected any remission made to him by the national law, since the single renvoi doctrine had not been adopted in Italy. The Civil Code used the general expression "national law" and failed to define what this means when the country of nationality contains more than one legal system. Which system of internal law, then, out of those having some relation to X, would be regarded by an Italian court as applicable? The issue raised in the case was whether it was the law of England, Ireland or India. Which of these systems would be selected by a court in Italy? The expert witnesses agreed that it would be the law of the country to which X "belonged" at the time of her death. She certainly did not "belong", whatever that may mean, to England in the sense of attracting to herself English internal law, for she had spent no appreciable time in the country. She might perhaps, by reason of her birth in Calcutta, be regarded as belonging to India, though she had not been there for seventy years. The reasonable man might even be excused for thinking that she most properly belonged to Italy, the country where she had continuously spent the last forty-seven years of her life.[32] CROSSMAN J, however, would have none of these. He reverted to X's domicile of origin, and held that she belonged to Ireland because that was the country where her father was domiciled at the time of her birth. In the result, therefore, the succession to her property was governed by the law of the country which she had never entered except during one short visit some sixty years before her death; which was not even a separate political unit until sixty-two years after her birth; of whose succession laws she was no doubt profoundly and happily ignorant; and under the law of which it was impossible in the circumstances for her to claim citizenship. The convolutions by which such a remarkable result is reached are interesting. First, the judge is referred by the English rule to the law of the domicile, which in the instant case means the law of the domicile of choice; then he bows to the superior wisdom of a foreign legislator and allows the

---

[31] [1940] Ch 124. See Nadelmann (1969) 17 AJCL 418, 443–448.

[32] Morris points out ((1940) 56 LQR 144 at 46) that the originating summons did not suggest Italian law as a possible choice, and he assumes that the decision is no authority against the view that the internal law of the domicile should have been applied.

law of the domicile to be supplanted by the law of the nationality; then, upon discovering that the law of the nationality is meaningless, he throws himself back on the domicile of origin; and thus determines the rights of the parties by a legal system which is neither the national law nor the law of the domicile as envisaged by the English rule for choice of law.[33] Comment is surely superfluous.

(iii) Analysis of decisions supporting the doctrine

Although a number of cases are often cited in support of the total renvoi doctrine, they are far from satisfactory. The first of these is *Collier v Rivaz*,[34] where the facts were as follows:

> A British subject, who according to English law was domiciled in Belgium at the time of his death, had executed seven testamentary instruments, a will and six codicils. The will and two of the codicils had been executed in accordance with the formalities required by Belgian internal law. The remaining four codicils, though formally valid according to the Wills Act 1837, were not made in the form required by Belgian internal law. According to the law of Belgium the testator had never acquired a domicile in that country, since he had not obtained the necessary authorisation from the government. The question was whether the instruments could be admitted to probate in England.

Sir Herbert JENNER, after propounding the theory that he must sit as a Belgian judge, admitted the will and two codicils to probate because they satisfied the formalities of the internal law of the country in which the testator was domiciled in the English sense. He extended the same indulgence to the remaining codicils on the ground that, since the testator had not acquired a domicile in Belgium in the Belgian sense, a judge in Brussels would apply Belgian private international law, under which the formal validity of the instruments would be tested by English internal law.

This decision is open to many criticisms.[35] It is obvious that, when a choice of law rule selects a particular legal system as the one to govern a given question, it is necessary to decide whether this means the internal law or the private international law of the selected system. It cannot mean both, for the private international law rules may indicate some other legal system, the internal law of which differs from the internal law of the selected system. If the question in *Collier v Rivaz* had been, not the formal, but the essential, validity of the testamentary instruments, and if, for instance, some of them had been lawful by English internal law but unlawful by Belgian internal law, while others had been lawful in Belgium but unlawful in England, it would have been impossible to uphold them in their totality. Sir Herbert JENNER, however, had it both ways. He held that the formal validity of a will cannot be denied if it satisfies either the internal law or the private international law of the selected legal system. There is much to be said for this benevolent rule

---

[33] The difficulty of identifying the law to which a British national is subject was ignored in *Re Ross* [1930] 1 Ch 377, infra, p 68; *Re Askew* [1930] 2 Ch 259, infra, pp 68–69; and *Re Duke of Wellington* [1947] Ch 506, infra, pp 69–70. In these cases English law was chosen without argument.

[34] (1841) 2 Curt 855; see also *Frere v Frere* (1847) 5 Notes of Cases 593; cf *Bremer v Freeman* (1857) 10 Moo PCC 306, infra, p 1266.

[35] See especially: Abbot (1908) 24 LQR 133, 143; Falconbridge, pp 143–145, 151–152; Morris (1937) BYBIL 32, 43–44; Mendelssohn-Bartholdy, *Renvoi in English Law*, pp 58–64.

in the one case of formal validity, since it is obviously desirable that the intention of a testator, clearly expressed and not intrinsically objectionable, should be respected if reasonably possible.[36] What is impossible is that the rule should be allowed a wider general operation.[37]

In contrast to *Collier v Rivaz*, *Re Annesley*[38] was concerned with the essential validity of a will.

> An Englishwoman was domiciled at the time of her death in France according to the principles of English law, but was domiciled in England in the eyes of French law. This was because she had never obtained the authorisation of the French government which, before 1927, was necessary for the acquisition of domicile. Her testamentary dispositions were valid by English internal law, but invalid by French internal law, since she had failed to leave two-thirds of her property to her children.

RUSSELL J held that the validity of the dispositions must be determined by French law. His actual decision, therefore, was in accordance with the view that a reference to the law of a given country is a reference to its internal law,[39] but he did not reach his conclusion in this simple fashion. He preferred the total renvoi theory. Although the judge's reasoning is not altogether clear, it seems that he ultimately arrived at the application of French internal law by the following route:

> English private international law refers the matter to French law as being the law of the domicile.

> A French judge would be referred by his own rules to English law. He would, however, find himself referred back by English private international law to French law.

> Single renvoi is recognised in France.

> Therefore, a French court would accept the remission, and in the result would apply French internal law.

It is to be noted, however, that, had the judge not thought himself bound by previous authorities, he would have preferred to have based his decision on an alternative and simpler ground. This, the direct antithesis of the approach that we have just considered, was that the natural meaning of the expression "the law of a country" is the internal law of the country in question. "When we say that French law applies to the administration of the personal estate of an Englishman who dies domiciled in France, we mean that French municipal law which France applies in the case of Frenchmen."[40]

Another case concerned with the essential validity of a will is *Re Ross*.[41]

---

[36] Choice of law rules relating to wills are discussed infra, pp 1264 et seq and 1279 et seq.

[37] *Re Lacroix Goods* (1877) 2 PD 94 was another case where the English judge seems to have applied both the private international law rules and the internal law of the domicile; see Morris (1937) 18 BYBIL 32, 42. The operation of any renvoi doctrine in matters concerning the formal validity of wills has now been virtually excluded by the Wills Act 1963 which governs wills of testators dying after 1963, and under which there is a variety of systems of internal law by which the formal validity of a will may be tested; infra, pp 1266–1267.

[38] [1926] Ch 692.

[39] Supra, p 59.

[40] [1926] Ch 692 at 709. This view was rejected by LUXMOORE J in *Re Ross* [1930] 1 Ch 377 at 402; in a later case, *Re Askew* [1930] 2 Ch 259 at 278, MAUGHAM J considered that there was "much to be said for it".

[41] [1930] 1 Ch 377.

The testatrix, a British subject, who was domiciled in Italy, both in the English and the Italian sense, disposed of her property by a will which excluded her son from the list of beneficiaries. This exclusion was justifiable by English internal law, but contrary to Italian internal law which required that one-half of the property should go to the son as his *legitima portio*. She left land in Italy and movable property both in England and Italy.

Luxmoore J held with regard to the movables that in accordance with the English rule of the choice of law the claim of the son to his *legitima portio* must be determined by Italian law as being the law of the testatrix's domicile. He then put the question—What is meant by the law of the domicile? Does it refer merely to the municipal law of the domicile or does it include its rules of private international law?[42]

In the result the judge applied English internal law and disallowed the claim of the son. This was the conclusion which an Italian judge would have reached. He would have referred the matter to the law of the nationality and would have rejected the remission made to him by English law. As regards the land, the English rule for the choice of law referred the judge to Italian law as being the law of the situs. The expert evidence showed that an Italian court would again turn to the law of the nationality and would adopt the rule of English internal law applicable to land situated in England and belonging to an English testator. It was held once more, therefore, that the claim of the son failed. In this way Mrs Ross was allowed to evade one of the cardinal rules of the legal system, the protection of which she had enjoyed for the last fifty-one years of her life.

The next case, *Re Askew*,[43] raised an issue of legitimacy.

By an English marriage settlement made on the marriage of X, a British subject domiciled in England, to his first wife, Y, it was provided that X, if he married again, might revoke in part the settled trusts and make a new appointment to the children of *such subsequent marriage*. Some time before 1911, X, who had long been separated from Y, acquired a German domicile. In 1911, having obtained a divorce from a competent German court, he married Z, in Berlin. Some time *before the divorce* a daughter had been born to X and Z in Switzerland. In 1913 X exercised his power of revocation and made an appointment in favour of his daughter.

The question before the English court concerned the validity of this appointment. A short answer to this question, and one that would have involved no reference to private international law, was that the daughter of Z was in no sense a child of the "subsequent marriage", for the only marriage subsisting at the time of her birth was that between X and Y. She might be legitimate, but she could not possibly be the child of a non-existing marriage.[44] This fact, however, was not brought to the notice of Maugham J, who insisted that the validity of the appointment depended on whether the daughter was legitimate. She could not claim legitimacy under the Legitimacy Act 1926[45] since at the time of her

---

[42] [1930] 1 Ch 377, at 388, 389.

[43] [1930] 2 Ch 259, followed in *Collins v A-G* (1931) 145 LT 551.

[44] *Re Wicks' Marriage Settlement* [1940] Ch 475; cf *Colquitt v Colquitt* [1948] P 19 at 25 where it was suggested that no difference should be drawn between phrases such as a "legitimate child" and a "child of a subsisting marriage".

[45] Now replaced by the Legitimacy Act 1976.

birth her father was married to someone other than her mother.[46] By English private international law, however, her legitimacy depended on whether German law, being that of her father's domicile both at the time of her birth and also at the time of his marriage to Z, recognised legitimation by subsequent marriage. In such a case, German private international law referred the matter to the law of the father's nationality. Moreover, the doctrine of single renvoi was generally accepted in Germany. If, therefore, a German court were required to pronounce on the legitimacy of Z's daughter, it would first refer to English law, and then, on finding a remission made by English law to the law of the domicile, would accept this and apply German internal law. In other words, if the English reference to the law of the domicile was a reference to the private international law rules of the domicile, the daughter would be legitimate. MAUGHAM J felt that both on principle and on the authorities he was obliged to consider the private international law of Germany. He therefore decided in favour of the legitimacy of the daughter and the validity of the appointment.

The facts of *Re Duke of Wellington*,[47] another relevant case, were as follows:

> The Duke of Wellington, a British subject domiciled in England, left two wills, one dealing with his Spanish, the other with his English, property. By the former he left his land in Spain to the person who would succeed both to his English dukedom and to his Spanish dukedom of Ciudad Rodrigo.[48] He died a bachelor, with the result that by the internal law of England his English dukedom passed to his uncle, while by the internal law of Spain his sister succeeded to the Spanish dukedom. Therefore, the Spanish land remained undisposed of, since there was no one person qualified to take both dukedoms.

The problem, therefore, was to identify the person to whom the Spanish land passed, and this depended on whether the solution was to be found in the internal law of Spain or of England. By the former, the testator was entitled to devise only half of his land, the other half passing as on intestacy;[49] by English internal law, the land would pass to the next Duke of Wellington under the residuary gift contained in the English will.

WYNN-PARRY J decided in favour of English internal law for the following reasons: the English choice of law rule referred him in the first instance to Spanish law, which, having regard to such cases as *Re Ross*,[50] included the private international law of Spain; the Spanish code provided that testate and intestate succession was to be determined by the national law of the deceased, whatever be the country in which the property was situated; therefore, the question was whether a Spanish court, having thus been referred to the national (English) law, would accept the remission made by that law to the law of the situs. In short, was the doctrine of single renvoi recognised in Spain? After considering the conflicting evidence of the expert witnesses and the conflicting decisions of two Spanish courts of first instance, the judge reached the conclusion that a court in Spain

---

[46] Section 1(2) of the 1926 Act. This rule was abrogated by the Legitimacy Act 1959, s 1; see now the Legitimacy Act 1976, infra, pp 1152–1153.

[47] [1947] Ch 506.

[48] This will also disposed of his movables in Spain.

[49] This difference is not brought out in the report, see Morris (1948) 64 LQR 264, 266.

[50] Supra, p 68.

would not accept the remission made by the national law. Therefore, the Duke of Wellington was entitled to the land under the English will.

A further case to be considered is *Re Fuld's Estate (No 3)*[51] where the facts were as follows:

> The testator, a German by origin, had acquired Canadian nationality when resident in Ontario, but he died domiciled in Germany. His will and its second codicil were executed in England and were considered formally valid in England.[52] The three other codicils to his will were executed in Germany and, thus, according to English private international law, German law, as the law of his domicile, governed their formal validity. The last two of these codicils were invalid as to form under German domestic law, but valid under English and Ontario domestic law.

What had to be determined was whether reference to German law was to German internal law or the whole of German law, including its rules of private international law. This involved a difficult problem of the interpretation of the German Civil Code which allowed reference in such cases to either the law governing validity or that of the place of execution. SCARMAN J construed this latter reference as a reference to the internal law of Germany. However, the reference under German law to the law governing validity was to the law of Ontario as the law of the nationality. This was considered to be a reference to the whole of Ontario law, including its rules of private international law. These led to a reference back to German law, as the law of the domicile, and this reference back was accepted by German law under the Civil Code. German internal law was applied and, consequently, the codicils were invalid.

The nature and application of the renvoi doctrine was the focus of an important recent Western Australian case, *Neilson v Overseas Projects Corporation of Victoria Ltd*,[53] the facts of which were as follows:

> Mrs Neilson, an Australian citizen, domiciled in Western Australia, moved with her husband to China, he having accepted a position with the defendant Victoria corporation, which required him to work there. Subsequently, Mrs Neilson was injured at the couple's place of residence in China, and so sued her husband's employer, in contract and in tort, in Western Australia.

The point in issue was whether application of the Chinese *lex loci delicti* should include the Chinese choice of law rules, which, in the circumstances of the case, conferred a discretion on the forum to apply Australian substantive law, which had a more generous limitation period than domestic Chinese law. By majority,[54] the High Court of Australia held that where the *lex loci delicti* rule requires an Australian court to apply foreign law, the court must, ordinarily at least, apply foreign choice of law rules, and whichever law those rules yield. While three judges were of the view that, in resolving the appeal, it was "unnecessary to postulate a single theory of renvoi to govern all proceedings in Australian

---

[51] [1968] P 675; Graveson (1966) 15 ICLQ 937, 941–944.
[52] Under the Wills Act 1861, s 2.
[53] (2005) 221 ALR 213. For commentary, see Keyes (2005) 13 Torts Law Journal 1; Lu and Carroll (2005) 1 J Priv Int L 35; and Mortensen (2006) 2 J Priv Int L 1
[54] McHUGH J, dissenting.

courts requiring reference to foreign substantive law",[55] it is worthy of note that total renvoi was accepted by a majority of five judges.[56]

3. SCOPE OF THE APPLICATION OF RENVOI

(a) Renvoi inapplicable in many cases

This review of the principal decisions[57] discloses that the total renvoi doctrine is not of general application. Its scope appears to be limited to certain matters concerning either status or the disposition of property on death. In countless cases dealing with such matters as torts,[58] insurance, sale of movables, gifts *inter vivos* or *mortis causa*, mortgages, negotiable instruments, partnerships, dissolution of foreign companies and so on, the English courts, when referred to "the law" of a foreign country, have never had the slightest hesitation in applying the internal law of that country. One of the clearest rejections of any renvoi doctrine is to be found in the field of contract, it being thought that no sane businessman or his lawyers would choose the application of renvoi. Not only was the rejection made clear at common law,[59] but this position has been confirmed by Article 15 of the (1980) Rome Convention on the law applicable to contractual obligations to which effect is given by the Contracts (Applicable Law) Act 1990.[60] The clear terms of Article 15 are that the application of the law of any country specified by this Convention means the application of the rules of law in force in that country other than its rules of private international law.[61]

There are, however, as we have seen, decisions which do apply renvoi in certain limited areas. These cases perhaps show that the judges, in considering whether the reference may not be to the private international law of the chosen country, have taken the view that "the various categories of cases merit individual consideration in the light of expediency"[62] and that the entire problem is not to be decided on *a priori* reasoning. One writer, who has done much to illuminate the subject, suggests that the renvoi doctrine cannot be rejected in toto, since it has proved to be a useful and justifiable expedient for the solution of at least certain special questions.[63] The conclusion, in fact, is that generally a reference made by an English rule for choice of law to a foreign legal system is to the internal law,

---

[55] Per KIRBY J, at [175]; see also GUMMOW and HAYNE JJ, at [99].

[56] Per GUMMOW and HAYNE JJ, at [90]; GLEESON CJ, at para 13; KIRBY J, at [176] and [191]; HEYDON J, at [271]. See Mortensen, (2006) 2 J Priv Int L 1, 10. Nevertheless, Mortensen, at 12, remarks that *Neilson*, ". . . reinforces our understanding of the shortcomings of the doctrine of renvoi, and especially of double renvoi".

[57] It is thought that *Armitage v A-G* [1906] P 135 was not a case on renvoi, but rather a decision on the jurisdiction of the courts: Falconbridge, p 745; Lipstein [1972B] CLJ 66, 84–86.

[58] *M'Elroy v M'Allister* 1949 SC 110 at 126. See now the Private International Law (Miscellaneous Provisions) Act 1995, s 9(5), infra, pp 767–768. The Rome II Regulation contains an exclusion of renvoi clause (Art 24). See, in contrast, however, *Neilson v Overseas Projects Corpn of Victoria Ltd* [2005] HCA 54, supra, p 70; see, for a statement of principle, CALLINAN J, at [261]. Also Keyes (2005) 13 Torts Law Journal 1; Lu and Carroll (2005) 1 J Priv Int L 35; and Mortensen (2006) 2 J Priv Int L 1.

[59] *Re United Rlys of the Havana and Regla Warehouses Ltd* [1960] Ch 52 at 97; *The Evia Luck (No 2)* [1990] 1 Lloyd's Rep 319 at 327, affd sub nom *Dimskal Shipping Co SA v International Transport Workers Federation* [1992] 2 AC 152; *Amin Rasheed Shipping Corpn v Kuwait Insurance Co* [1984] AC 50 at 61–62; and *see Kutchera v Buckingham International Holdings Ltd* [1988] IR 61 at 68; cf Briggs (1989) 9 OJLS 251, 254–256.

[60] The general principle is reiterated in the Rome I Regulation, Art 20; infra, p 689.

[61] Cf Rome II Regulation, Art 24; infra, p 788.

[62] Rabel, i, 77.

[63] Falconbridge (1953) 6 Vanderbilt LR 708. For a more recent defence, see Briggs (1998) 47 ICLQ 877.

not to the private international law, of the chosen system, but that this general principle is subject to a number of exceptions.

As regards unjust enrichment, in *Barros Mattos Junior v MacDaniels Ltd*[64] counsel for the claimant argued that the applicable law should be construed as being that law, including its rules of private international law. Lawrence COLLINS J, while judging the argument to be premature, nevertheless opined that, although there is no authority directly in point, "the claim to the application of renvoi in restitution claims is weak".[65]

(b) Issues to which renvoi may apply

(i) Validity of bequests

Where the essential validity of a will[66] or intestate succession to movables[67] is determinable by the law of a foreign country, the view that would be taken of the matter by the foreign judge, if he were hearing the case, must be adopted. Also, in cases in which the testator died before 1964 and in cases in which, although he died after 1963, the formal validity of his will is considered under the old common law rule of reference to the law of the domicile, a grant of probate will not be denied on the ground of formal invalidity if the will is formally valid according to the private international law, though not according to the internal law, of the governing legal system.[68]

(ii) Claims to foreign immovables

Where a question arises of the right to foreign immovables, as in *Re Ross*,[69] the English court will apply the private international law rules of the country where the immovables are situated, if they would be applied by a court of the situs hearing the same question.[70] This may be justified on the ground that it promotes the security of title.[71]

(iii) Some cases of movables

If the English choice of law rule refers a disputed title to movables to the law of their situs at the time when the alleged title was said to have been acquired, it is probable that the court will apply the internal system of law that a court of the situs would apply in the particular circumstances of the case.[72]

---

[64] [2005] IL Pr 45.

[65] Para 121. See also Rome II Regulation, Art 24; infra, p 788.

[66] *Re Annesley* [1926] Ch 692, supra, p 67; *Re Ross* [1930] 1 Ch 377, supra, p 68; *Re Adams* [1967] IR 424. Proposed European harmonisation of choice of law rules concerning the essential validity of wills would "obviate the need for renvoi where all the connecting factors are situated in a Member State". See EU Green Paper, "Succession and Wills" COM (2005) 65 final, para 2.7; infra, Chapter 32.

[67] *Re O'Keefe* [1940] Ch 124, supra, p 65; cf *Re Thom* (1987) 40 DLR (4th) 184.

[68] *Collier v Rivaz* (1841) 2 Curt 855, supra, p 66; *Frere v Frere* (1847) 5 Notes of Cases 593; and see Wills Act 1963, infra, pp 1266–1267.

[69] [1930] 1 Ch 377, supra, p 68.

[70] *Re Ross*, supra, p 68; *Re Duke of Wellington* [1947] Ch 506, supra, p 69; *Re Bailey* [1985] 2 NZLR 656; *Re Schneider's Estate* 96 NYS 2d 652 (Surr Ct 1950), discussed by Morris (1951) 4 ILQ 268; Falconbridge (1953) 6 Vanderbilt LR 708, 725–731. See Carruthers, paras 1.43–1.45, and pp 276 and 293.

[71] Yntema (1957) 35 Can Bar Rev 721, 740.

[72] See *The Islamic Republic of Iran v Berend* [2007] EWHC 132 (QB), [2007] 2 All ER (Comm) 132, and note by Knight (2007) Conveyancer and Property Lawyer 564. In *Macmillan Inc v Bishopsgate Trust (No 3)* [1996] 1 WLR 387, STAUGHTON LJ said (at p 405) that renvoi did not apply to the choice of the law to determine

(iv) Family law issues

The one area of family law where there is clear authority for the application of renvoi is that of the recognition, at common law, of legitimation by subsequent marriage.[73] There is also some authority for the application of the doctrine of renvoi to matrimonial property issues[74] and to both formal[75] and essential[76] validity of marriage.[77] What is not wholly clear is whether renvoi allows the validity of a marriage to be upheld if it is valid either under the internal law of the country to which English choice of law rules refer or under that country's private international law rules—a rule of alternative reference.[78]

So too in relation to children, the Peréz-Vera Report on the 1980 Hague Convention on the Civil Aspects of International Child Abduction indicates that the applicable law in terms of the Convention includes its rules of private international law.[79]

---

who has title to shares in a company. But see *Winkworth v Christie, Manson and Woods Ltd* [1980] Ch 496 at 514; and infra, p 1213 et seq.

[73] *Re Askew* [1930] 2 Ch 259, supra, pp 68–69. It is doubtful whether the doctrine of renvoi applies to recognition of a foreign legitimation under the Legitimacy Act 1976, s 3, infra, pp 1153–1154.

[74] *Vladi v Vladi* (1987) 39 DLR (4th) 563.

[75] *Taczanowska v Taczanowski* [1957] P 301; see also *Hooper v Hooper* [1959] 2 All ER 575, infra, p 884.

[76] *R v Brentwood Superintendent Registrar of Marriages, ex p Arias* [1968] 2 QB 956, infra, pp 913–915. The actual decision in this case would now be different by reason of the Family Law Act 1986, s 50, infra, p 915.

[77] This view was provisionally supported in Law Commission Working Paper No 89 (1985), paras 2.39, 3.39; but not all commentators agreed, see Law Com No 165 (1987), paras 2.5–2.6. Similarly, use of renvoi is expressly permitted by the Civil Partnership Act 2004, s 54(10) in relation to testing the validity of civil partnerships registered outside England and Wales (cf s 124(10), for Scotland, and s 177(10) for Northern Ireland).

[78] Infra, pp 912–913.

[79] Explanatory Report (1981), paras 66 and 67. Infra, Chapter 24. See, eg, *Re JB (Child Abduction) (Rights of Custody: Spain)* [2003] EWHC 2130, [2004] 1 FLR 796, discussed by Beevers and Perez Milla (2007) 3 J Priv Int L 201.

Chapter 6

Substance and Procedure

1. DIFFERENCE BETWEEN SUBSTANCE AND PROCEDURE

(a) Procedure governed by the law of the forum

One of the eternal truths of every system of private international law is that a distinction must be made between substance and procedure, between right and remedy.[1] The substantive rights of the parties to an action may be governed by a foreign law, but all matters appertaining to procedure are governed exclusively by the law of the forum.[2]

---

[1] Cf Cook (1932–33) 42 Yale LJ 333; Szaszy (1966) 15 ICLQ 436, 455–456; and see Spiro (1969) 18 ICLQ 949. This distinction is, in principle, drawn by the Contracts (Applicable Law) Act 1990, infra, p 687, which excludes (in Sch 1, Art 1(2) (h)) from its rules for determining the law applicable to a contract matters of evidence and procedure, subject to a number of limited exceptions, discussed infra. Similar provision is made in the case of tort by the Private International Law (Miscellaneous Provisions) Act 1995, s 14(3)(b).

[2] *British Linen Co v Drummond* (1830) 10 B & C 903; *De la Vega v Vianna* (1830) 1 B & Ad 284; *Huber v Steiner* (1835) 2 Bing NC 202; *Don v Lippmann* (1837) 5 Cl & Fin 1 at 13; *Chaplin v Boys* [1971] AC 356 at

At first sight the principle seems almost self-evident. A person who resorts to an English court for the purpose of enforcing a foreign claim cannot expect to occupy a different procedural position from that of a domestic litigant. The field of procedure constitutes perhaps the most technical part of any legal system, and it comprises many rules that would be unintelligible to a foreign judge and certainly unworkable by a machinery designed on different lines. A party to litigation in England must take the law of procedure as he finds it. He cannot by virtue of some rule in his own country enjoy greater advantages than other parties here; neither must he be deprived of any advantages that English law may confer upon a litigant in the particular form of action.[3] To take an old example, an English creditor who sued his debtor in Scotland could not insist on trial by jury, nor, in the converse case, could a Scottish creditor suing in England refuse the intervention of a jury, on the ground that in Scotland, where the debt arose, the case would have been tried by a judge alone.[4]

(b) Importance of distinction between substance and procedure[5]

Although the principle is certain and universal, its application can give rise to considerable difficulty, especially when trying to establish a test by which a procedural rule can be distinguished from a substantive one. Unless the distinction is made with a clear regard to the underlying purpose of private international law, the inevitable result will be to defeat that purpose. So intimate is the connection between substance and procedure that to treat an English rule as procedural may defeat the policy which demands the application of a foreign substantive law. A glaring example of this is afforded by section 4 of the Statute of Frauds, which formerly provided that no action should be brought on certain contracts unless they were evidenced by a note or memorandum signed by the party to be charged or by his lawfully authorised agent. In *Leroux v Brown*:[6]

> An oral agreement was made in France by which the defendant, resident in England, agreed to employ the plaintiff, resident in France, for a period that was longer than a year. The contract was valid and enforceable by French law, which was the law by which it was to be governed, but had it been an English domestic contract it would, though valid, nevertheless have been unenforceable under the Statute of Frauds. An action brought in England for its breach failed on the ground that the statute imposed a rule of procedure which was binding on all litigants suing in England.

Although this decision might, possibly, be based on an intelligible principle of domestic law, it is repugnant to the principles on which English private international law is founded. That law exists to fulfil foreign rights, not to destroy them. The law governing the contract in *Leroux v Brown* undoubtedly entitled the plaintiff to recover damages for the

---

378–379, 381–382, 392–393, 394. Cf, in Canada, *Somers v Fournier* (2002) 214 DLR (4th) 611, CA (Ont); and *Volger v Szendroi* 2008 NSCA 18.

[3] *De la Vega v Vianna* (1830) 1 B & Ad 284 at 288; *Chaplin v Boys* [1971] AC 356 at 394.

[4] *Don v Lippmann* (1837) 5 Cl & Fin 1 at 14.

[5] See Fentiman, *Foreign Law in English Courts* (1998), pp 35–41, 92–94; and Carruthers (2004) 53 ICLQ 691.

[6] (1852) 12 CB 801; and see *Morris v Baron & Co* [1918] AC 1 at 15. The statute now just applies to a contract of guarantee: Law Reform (Enforcement of Contracts) Act 1954, s 1. In the case of contracts concerning land they need to be made by signed writing. If not, the contract is invalid: Law of Property (Miscellaneous Provisions) Act 1989, s 2.

breach of the undertaking and, had he obtained judgment in France in an action to which the defendant voluntarily appeared, nothing would have prevented him from succeeding in an action brought on the judgment in England. Moreover, he would have succeeded had he done something in furtherance of the contract that constituted an act of part performance in the eyes of English law.[7] To refuse him a right of action in England on the contract was tantamount to denying that the contract, admittedly governed as to substance by French law, conferred a right on him. It is a stultification of private international law to refuse recognition to a foreign right substantively valid under its governing law, unless its recognition will conflict with some rule of public policy so insistent as to override all other considerations. WILLES J attacked the decision in two later cases, and evidently thought that in the circumstances the statutory rule should not have been treated as procedural.[8]

The Court of Appeal took a somewhat different approach in *Monterosso Shipping Co Ltd v International Transport Workers' Federation*.[9]

> The plaintiff, a Maltese company, owned a ship which was managed by a Norwegian company with Norwegian officers and a Spanish crew. The defendants were an international federation of trade unions with whom the plaintiff had purported to enter into a collective agreement in 1980. However, the defendants "blacked" the ship when it started a regular run between Swedish ports, because the Swedish seamen's union objected to the use of a Spanish and not a Swedish crew. The plaintiff claimed damages for breach of the 1980 collective agreement, and the issue was raised of whether the law governing the agreement was English or Spanish. The Court of Appeal held that it was Spanish; but the court also had to consider whether to give effect to section 18 of the Trade Union and Labour Relations Act 1974, which declared that a collective agreement "shall be conclusively presumed not to have been intended by the parties to be a legally enforceable contract unless the agreement . . . states that the parties intend that the agreement shall be a legally enforceable contract". It was argued by the defendants that this section was procedural in effect so that an English court should apply the section irrespective of the law governing the contract.

The Court of Appeal held that section 18 was to be classed as substantive and not procedural. In so doing dissatisfaction was expressed[10] with the reasoning in *Leroux v Brown*[11] and, in holding section 18 of the 1974 Act to be substantive, Lord DENNING MR had this to say:

> It seems to me that the true distinction is between the existence of a contract (which is substantive law) and the remedies for breach of it (which is the procedural law). The right

---

[7] *Mahadervan v Mahadervan* [1964] P 233 at 242.

[8] *Williams v Wheeler* (1860) 8 CBNS 299 at 316; *Gibson v Holland* (1865) LR 1 CP 1 at 8. This view has been adopted in the USA; *Bernkrant v Fowler* 55 Cal 2d 588, 360 P 2d 906 (1961). However, in *G & H Montage GmbH v Irvani* [1990] 1 WLR 667 it was suggested that the reasoning in *Leroux v Brown* was "unassailable" and that only the House of Lords could overrule the decision: [1990] 1 WLR 667 at 684, and see at 690. On the other hand, in considering the Contracts (Applicable Law) Act 1990 and the Rome Convention on the Law Applicable to Contractual Obligations (infra, p 747) it should be borne in mind that it has been suggested that whether a contract has to be in writing may be regarded as a matter of the substantive formal validity of a contract: Giuliano and Lagarde Report OJ 1980 C 282/31.

[9] [1982] 3 All ER 841.

[10] Ibid, at 846.

[11] And with the leading cases on limitation of actions, see infra, p 80 et seq.

course is to analyse the statute and see whether it negatives the existence of a contract or not. If there is no contract, but the statute says it cannot be enforced (except in writing or within a stated period) that is procedural law. It is governed by the *lex fori*.

In this present case, as I construe s 18 of the 1974 Act, it negatives the existence of any contract at all.[12]

(c) How is the distinction to be made?

It remains to consider further how the line between substance and procedure is to be drawn for the purposes of private international law.[13] Only the most general definitions of "the law of procedure" have been given by the English judges. Perhaps the best known is that of LUSH LJ: "The mode of proceeding by which a legal right is enforced, as distinguished from the law which gives or defines the right, and which by means of the proceeding the court is to administer the machinery as distinguished from its product."[14] This substitution of "mode of proceeding" for "procedure" does not carry us far. Nor does the definition ensure a just and convenient solution. It implies that, since the owner has chosen to fashion his foreign-acquired right into a new form through the instrumentality of English machinery, he must rest content with the design and movement of that machine. This sounds sensible but if, as in *Leroux v Brown*, the machinery refuses to move, one part of private international law is nullified by another. Nor shall we arrive at a solution if we change the metaphor and concentrate on the contrast between right and remedy. They do not always admit of contrast in law. Historically they are inseparably connected. As GOULDING J has said:

> Within the municipal confines of a single legal system, right and remedy are indissolubly connected and correlated, each contributing in historical dialogue to the development of the other, and save in very special circumstances, it is as idle to ask whether the court vindicates the suitor's substantive right or gives the suitor a procedural remedy as to ask whether thought is a mental or cerebral process. In fact the court does both things by one and the same act.[15]

The truth is that substance and procedure cannot be relegated to clear-cut categories. There is no preordained dividing line between them which can be discovered by logic alone. Determining the nature of a rule as procedural or substantive cannot be done in the abstract. Although the two must be distinguished, the line between them should be drawn by having regard to the relativity of legal terms and the exact purpose for which the distinction is being made.

This problem was clearly faced by SCARMAN J in *Re Fuld's Estate (No 3)*[16] when he asked: "When is a question one of substantive law? When is a question merely one of evidence or procedure? I attempt no general answer to these questions; for answer can only be made after an analysis of the specific questions calling for decision, its legal background

---

[12] [1982] 3 All ER 841 at 846; and see at 848–849, per MAY LJ.

[13] Carruthers, op cit, 696.

[14] *Poyser v Minors* (1881) 7 QBD 329 at 333; adopted in *Re Shoesmith* [1938] 2 KB 637. See Carruthers, op cit, pp 694–696.

[15] *Chase Manhattan Bank NA v Israel-British Bank (London) Ltd* [1981] Ch 105 at 124.

[16] [1968] P 675 at 695.

and factual context." This shows that the line should not be drawn in the same place for all purposes.[17] It should be drawn in the light of the relevant circumstances, one of which is that the purposes of private international law as distinct from municipal law require fulfilment. Thus it is at least arguable that whether section 4 of the Statute of Frauds is of a procedural or substantive nature should be decided differently according to whether a foreign or purely English transaction is involved. The crux of the matter is—Why is the distinction between substance and procedure made in private international law? The answer presumably is—For the convenience of the court. The court, when faced with a conflict of laws problem, though bound to apply the law selected by the choice of law rules, cannot be expected to import all the relevant rules of the foreign law. To apply, for instance, the foreign rules concerned with such matters as service of process, evidence and methods of enforcing judgments would be not only inconvenient but impracticable. Nevertheless, the overriding policy is to apply the foreign substantive law, and if this will be defeated by a slavish adherence to the domestic distinction between substance and procedure, the court should consider whether in the circumstances such adherence is necessary. For: "It is not everything that appears in a treatise on the law of evidence that is to be classified internationally as adjective law, but only provisions of a technical or procedural character—for example rules as to the admissibility of hearsay evidence or what matters may be noticed judicially."[18]

"If we admit", says Cook, "that the 'substantive' shades off by imperceptible degrees into the 'procedural', and that the 'line' between them does not 'exist', to be discovered merely by logic and analysis, but is rather to be drawn so as best to carry out our purpose, we see that our problem resolves itself substantially into this: How far can the court of the forum go in applying the rules taken from the foreign system of law without unduly hindering or inconveniencing itself?"[19] One critic has replied, "Not much farther than we have already gone";[20] but at least it would be possible to go far enough to avoid such decisions as *Leroux v Brown*,[21] and a Canadian court has suggested that legislation should be categorised as procedural only if the question is beyond doubt.[22]

It should be borne in mind that the issue whether a rule is one of substance or procedure may arise in more than one context. The most common context, as illustrated by *Leroux v Brown*, is the determination of the nature of a rule of English law in circumstances where the governing law is foreign. If the English rule is procedural, it is applied notwithstanding the foreign governing law. If the English rule is substantive, it is ignored and the foreign law applied. The problem can, however, arise in circumstances where, although the applicable law is foreign, there is some doubt as to whether the rules of that country's

---

[17] Cook, op cit, at 344, 352 and 356.

[18] *Mahadervan v Mahadervan* [1964] P 233 at 243.

[19] Cook, *Logical and Legal Bases of the Conflict of Laws*, p 166. A more radical solution has been suggested by Cavers, *The Choice-of-Law Process*, p 289, that "Before trial each party could move . . . for the use of one or more specifically identified procedural rules, to be drawn from the law of the state supplying the substantive law of the case relevant to the issue or issues to which the procedural rules related and to be used for specified purposes in the trial or other proceedings in the case. If the motions were granted, the rules thereby allowed to be used would take the place of the rules of the forum that would otherwise be applied for the same purposes."

[20] Ailes (1941) 39 Mich LR 392, 418.

[21] Supra, p 76 et seq.

[22] *Block Bros Realty Ltd v Mollard* (1981) 122 DLR (3d) 323 at 328.

law are procedural (and to be ignored in England) or substantive (and to be applied in England).[23] In *Chase Manhattan Bank NA v Israel-British Bank (London) Ltd:*[24]

> The plaintiff, a New York bank, sought to trace and recover in equity £2 million paid by mistake to the account of the defendant bank. The issue was whether the plaintiff bank was entitled to trace the proceeds. Although the court held that there was no significant difference between the two relevant laws, English and New York law, on the right to trace, GOULDING J asked the question "whether the equitable right of a person who pays money by mistake to trace and claim such money under the law of New York is conferred by substantive law or is of a merely procedural character".[25] He concluded[26] that the view of an English court would be that the plaintiff New York bank had, under New York law, an equitable interest as a *cestui que* trust which was substantive in nature.

Why did the judge ask the question as to the nature of the equitable right to trace? Presumably, because if he had found the New York rule to be procedural, he would have been unwilling to apply it in England.

2. PARTICULAR ISSUES

Authority is scarcely needed for the proposition that all routine matters arising in the successive stages of litigation must be governed exclusively by English law as being the law of the forum. Such routine matters are generally said to include: service of process; the form that the action must take and whether any special procedure is permissible; the title of the action, eg by what persons and against what persons it should be brought; the competency of witnesses and questions as to the admissibility of evidence; the respective functions of judge and jury; the right of appeal, and, according to some writers, the burden of proof.[27]

It is necessary to consider separately certain issues whose classification as substantive or procedural raises difficulties.

(a) The time within which an action must be brought

Until 1984, English law was committed to the view that statutes of limitation, if they merely specified a certain time after which rights could not be enforced by action, affected procedure and not substance.[28] This meant that limitation was governed by English law, as the law of the forum, and any limitation provision of the applicable law was ignored.[29]

---

[23] Eg *Harding v Wealands* [2007] 2 AC 1.

[24] [1981] Ch 105.

[25] Ibid, at 122.

[26] Ibid, at 127.

[27] Lord REID has said in *Carl Zeiss Stiftung v Rayner and Keeler Ltd (No 2)* [1967] 1 AC 853 at 919 that "estoppel is a matter for the *lex fori* but the *lex fori* ought to be developed in a manner consistent with good sense," see infra, Chapter 15.

[28] *Black-Clawson International Ltd v Papierwerke Waldhof-Aschaffenburg AG* [1975] AC 591 at 630.

[29] *British Linen Co v Drummond* (1830) 10 B & C 903; *Huber v Steiner* (1835) 2 Bing NC 202; *Don v Lippmann* (1837) 5 Cl & Fin 1; *Harris v Quine* (1869) LR 4 QB 653. Contrast *Tolofson v Jensen* (1994) 120 DLR (4th) 289.

Where, however, it could be shown that the effect of a statute of limitation of the foreign applicable law was not just to bar the plaintiff's remedy, but also to extinguish his cause of action,[30] then the English courts would be prepared to regard the foreign rule as substantive and to be applied in England.[31]

The common law rule, which has been criticised in a number of common law jurisdictions,[32] tends to have no counterpart in civil law countries which usually treat statutes of limitation as substantive.[33] Furthermore, the Contracts (Applicable Law) Act 1990, implementing the European Community Convention on the Law Applicable to Contractual Obligations (1980),[34] provides that the law which governs the essential validity of a contract is to govern "the various ways of extinguishing obligations, and prescription and limitation of actions".[35] In 1982 the Law Commission concluded that "there is a clear case for the reform of the present English rule"[36] and their recommendations formed the basis of the Foreign Limitation Periods Act 1984.[37]

The general principle of the 1984 Act abandons the common law approach which favoured the application of the domestic law of limitation.[38] Instead, the English court is to apply the law which governs the substantive issue according to English choice of law rules, and this new approach is applied to both actions[39] and arbitrations[40] in England. In the case of those few tort claims, such as defamation, to which the common law choice of law rules still apply,[41] English law, as the law of the forum, will remain relevant[42] because of the choice of law rule which requires actionability both by the law of the forum and by the law of the place of the tort.[43] The corollary of the main rule is that English law is no longer automatically to be applied. There is, of course, a significant difference between a rule under which a claim is to be held to be statute barred in England if statute barred under the governing law, a reform which seems widely to be welcomed, and a further rule that, if the claim is not statute barred abroad, it must be allowed to proceed in England. This is more controversial and the question whether any, and if so what, restriction should be placed on the application of the foreign rule was examined at length by the Law

---

[30] Examples in English law are provided by acquisitive prescription under the Prescription Act 1832 or express extinction of the former owner's title under the Limitation Act 1980, ss 3 and 17.

[31] *Harris v Quine* (1869) LR 4 QB 653 at 656.

[32] Law Com No 114 (1982), paras 3.3–3.8.

[33] See Law Commission Working Paper No 75 (1980), paras 25–26. But see, in South Africa, *Society of Lloyd's v Price; Society of Lloyd's v Lee* 2006 5 SA 393 (SCA), discussed by Forsyth (2006) 2 J Priv Int L 169, and (2006) 2 J Priv Int L 425, and by Neels 2007 Journal of South African Law 178. See also *Society of Lloyd's v Romahn* 2006 4 SA 23 (C).

[34] Infra, p 667.

[35] Sch 1, Art 10(1)(d); and see North, *Contract Conflicts* (1982), p 16. Cf Rome I Regulation, Art 12 (1) (d) and Rome II Regulation, Art 15(h), examined infra, p 848.

[36] Law Com No 114 (1982), para 3.10.

[37] Carter (1985) 101 LQR 68; Stone [1985] LMCLQ 497. Cf, for Scotland, Prescription and Limitation (Scotland) Act 1984, s 4.

[38] S 1(5); but the doctrine of renvoi may be relevant in determining, under s 1(1), the relevant foreign substantive law; see Law Com No 114 (1983), para 4.33; Stone [1985] LMCLQ 497, 506–507.

[39] S 1(1)(a).

[40] Arbitration Act 1996, s 13(1)(4)(a).

[41] Under the Private International Law (Miscellaneous Provisions) Act 1995, s 13, infra, p 869.

[42] S 1(2), of the 1984 Act.

[43] *Metall und Rohstoff AG v Donaldson Lufkin & Jenrette Inc* [1990] 1 QB 391 at 438; *Arab Monetary Fund v Hashim* [1996] 1 Lloyd's Rep 589; and see, infra, p 767.

Commission.[44] At the end of the day, they decided not to adopt, for example, any "long-stop" provision such as that an action could not proceed after, say fifty years;[45] but concluded that the courts had adequate power under the doctrine of public policy to disapply either an extremely long or a very short foreign limitation period. Such a public policy exception to the general rule is to be found in section 2(1) of the 1984 Act; but it is worth noting that it is reinforced by a provision,[46] not found in the Law Commission's draft Bill, to the effect that the causing of undue hardship to a party by the application of the foreign period would be contrary to public policy. Such hardship has been held to arise where the defendants had agreed to an extension of time which proved to be ineffective under the governing law, the basis of the hardship being the parties' unawareness that that law would apply.[47]

There are some practical limits to the application of a foreign limitation rule. For example, it is for English law to determine the time at which the limitation period stops running against the claimant, eg when he commences litigation[48]—to do otherwise might involve the English court in detailed matters of foreign procedure. For similar reasons, the English court will ignore foreign rules as to the interruption of the running of the period because of the absence of a party from the jurisdiction.[49] On the other hand, if there is a discretion under the foreign law, eg to suspend the running of the period, the English court must attempt to exercise it in the same way as it would be exercised in the foreign courts.[50] The rule that equitable relief may be refused apart from a statute of limitation, if for example the claimant has been guilty of delay, has been preserved. Yet still, where there is a foreign applicable law, the English court must exercise its discretion by having regard to the relevant rules of any foreign applicable law.[51]

In 2006, the Legal Affairs Committee of the European Parliament[52] requested that the European Commission should submit a legislative proposal on limitation periods in relation to cross-border personal injury and fatal accident claims. The view of the Committee is that, given current divergencies among Member States as regards limitation periods, there may be sufficient justification for the setting of common minimum requirements throughout Europe, by means of legislation, at least in respect of cross-border litigation cases.[53]

(b) Evidence[54]

(i) Evidence a matter for the law of the forum

Every system of law has its own principles for deciding the way in which the truth of facts, acts and documents shall be ascertained, and it is obvious that those principles must

---

[44] Law Com No 114 (1982), paras 4.35–4.50.

[45] It might be noted that the Scottish Law Commission, having toyed with a similar idea, rejected it as inappropriate and undesirable; Scot Law Com No 74 (1983), para 7.8; cf Carter (1985) 101 LQR 68, 70.

[46] S 2(2); and see *Arab Monetary Fund v Hashim* [1996] 1 Lloyd's Rep 589 at 599–600.

[47] *The Komninos S* [1990] 1 Lloyd's Rep 541.

[48] S 1(3).

[49] S 2(3); and see Law Com No 114 (1982), paras 4.26–4.32.

[50] S 1(4).

[51] S 4(3). Section 3 of the 1984 Act which deals with foreign judgments on limitation points is discussed *infra*, Chapter 15. Cf, in Canada, *Vogler v Szendroi* 2008 NSCA 18.

[52] Having recourse to the special powers conferred on it by Art 192(2) of the EC Treaty.

[53] European Parliament, Legal Affairs Committee, Draft Report 2006/2014 (INI), PE 367.972v03-00 (May 2006).

[54] See generally Layton and Mercer, Chapter 7.

usually apply whether the question at issue is domestic or foreign in origin. If another system of evidence were admissible it would be equally reasonable to permit another mode of trial.[55]

> Whether a witness is competent or not [said Lord BROUGHAM], whether a certain matter requires to be proved by writing or not, whether certain evidence proves a certain fact or not, that is to be determined by the law of the country where the question arises.[56]

Leroux v Brown[57] is an outstanding example of the rule that the law of the forum determines whether written evidence is required.

There is, however, in the case of contracts an important statutory exception to the rule that proof of facts is for the law of the forum. Under the Contracts (Applicable Law) Act 1990,[58] a contract or an act intended to have legal effect may be proved in any way allowed by the law of the forum or by reference to any law governing the formal validity of the contract or act,[59] provided that the mode of proof under such law can be administered in the courts of the forum. This provision is echoed, in respect of non-contractual obligations, in Article 22(2) of the Rome II Regulation,[60] which provides that acts intended to have legal effect may be proved by any mode of proof recognised by the law of the forum or by any of the laws governing the formal validity of the act,[61] provided that such mode of proof can be administered by the forum.

(ii) Distinction between interpretation and proof of document

With regard to the evidence necessary to prove a certain fact, an important distinction exists where a document is in issue, in that the interpretation of the document must be distinguished from its proof. The foreign document must be interpreted according to the system of law by which it is governed, but it must be proved in accordance with the requirements of the law of the forum.[62] The English court that is hearing the matter must investigate the governing law as a fact and must take such expert evidence as shows what the construction would be in the foreign country, but at that point the reference to the foreign law must stop. What evidence that law admits or rejects is irrelevant.[63] For example, the meaning of technical expressions used in a charter-party must be ascertained by reference to the governing law, but the existence of the charter-party itself must be proved in the manner required by English law. Thus, in *Brown v Thornton*:[64]

> An action was brought in England to cover freight due under a charter-party that had been made in Batavia, by means of the instrument being written in the book of

---

[55] *Yates v Thomson* (1835) 3 Cl & Fin 544 at 587.

[56] *Bain v Whitehaven Rly Co* (1850) 3 HL Cas 1 at 19; and see *Mahadervan v Mahadervan* [1964] P 233 at 243; *Re Fuld's Estate (No 3)* [1968] P 675 at 697–698.

[57] (1852) 12 CB 801, supra, p 76. See now the Contracts (Applicable Law) Act 1990 and the Giuliano and Lagarde Report OJ 1980 C 282/31, infra, Chapter 18.

[58] Sch 1, Art 14(2). Cf Rome I Regulation, Art 18(2). For further statutory exceptions, see the Army Act 1955, the Medical Act 1983 and *McAllister v General Medical Council* [1993] AC 388.

[59] Art 9.

[60] Infra, Chapter 19.

[61] Art 21.

[62] Eg *Wicken v Wicken* [1999] Fam 224.

[63] *Yates v Thomson* (1835) 3 Cl & Fin 544 at 586.

[64] (1837) 6 Ad & El 185.

a notary, and signed by the parties. Each party received a copy, signed and sealed by the notary, and counter-signed by the principal governmental officer of Java. A charter-party was sufficiently proved in a Javanese court by production of the notary's book, but, since such books were not allowed to be removed from Java, courts in other parts of the Dutch dominions admitted the copies as evidence.

The plaintiff was nonsuited owing to his failure to prove the charter-party in the manner required by English law. The original contract contained in the notary's book was not produced. Secondary evidence would have been admissible had it been given in the form either of a copy made by the public officer of a court, or of a copy made by some person authorised by each party to give a binding copy, but neither of these ways was available.

The Crown, however, has power under the Evidence (Foreign Dominion and Colonial Documents) Act 1933[65] to issue Orders in Council providing that entries contained in the public registries of other countries, whether part of the Commonwealth or not, shall be admissible evidence in English proceedings, and that they shall be proved by means of duly authenticated official certificates.[66]

(iii) Taking of evidence within the EU:[67] Council Regulation (EC) No 1206/2001

This matter is regulated by Council Regulation (EC) No 1206/2001 on co-operation between the courts of the Member States in the taking of evidence in civil or commercial matters.[68] In order to facilitate the proper functioning of the internal market, it was thought necessary to improve co-operation between the courts of Member States in the taking of evidence; in particular to simplify and accelerate relevant procedures for the transmission and execution of requests for taking evidence,[69] and also to allow a court in one Member State (the requesting court), in accordance with its own law, to take evidence directly in another Member State (the requested court), if accepted by the latter State and subject to such conditions as the requested court may determine.[70] Each Member State is required to designate a "central body" to assist in the operation of the European scheme,[71] but it is expected that the transmission and execution of requests for the taking of evidence generally should be made directly and by the most rapid means possible between the courts of the Member States.

In terms of Article 21, the Regulation shall prevail over other provisions contained in bilateral or multilateral agreements concluded by Member States, including, in

---

[65] As amended by the Oaths and Evidence (Overseas Authorities and Countries) Act 1963, s 5; Fentiman, *Foreign Law in English Courts* (1998), p 225. Evidence of documents may also be admitted under s 7 of the Civil Evidence Act 1995 (see formerly, s 1 of the Evidence Act 1938: *Henaff v Henaff* [1966] 1 WLR 598). See Dicey, Morris and Collins, para 17-037 et seq.

[66] See *North v North* (1936) 52 TLR 380; *Motture v Motture* [1955] 3 All ER 242n, [1955] 1 WLR 1066.

[67] Except Denmark: Council Regulation (EC) No 1206/2001, recital (22).

[68] Entered into force on 1 July 2001, and having effect throughout the EU, with the exception of Denmark, as from 1 January 2004. See Report from the Commission to the Council, the European Parliament and the European Economic and Social Committee on the application of Regulation (EC) No 1206/2001 (COM (2007) 769 final), prepared in accordance with Art 23 of the Regulation. See also Practice Guide for the application of the Regulation, drawn up by the Commission Services, and available at: http://ec.europa.eu/civiljustice/evidence_ec_guide_en.pdf.

[69] Recitals (2) and (8).

[70] Recital (15).

[71] Art 3. The central body for England and Wales is the Senior Master, Queen's Bench Division, Royal Courts of Justice.

particular, the 1970 Hague Convention on the Taking of Evidence Abroad in Civil or Commercial Matters (to which the United Kingdom is a party), in relations between the Member States party thereto.

(a) Evidence by means of request

Chapter II of the Regulation deals with the transmission and execution of requests for the taking of evidence. Article 4 lays down strict rules regarding the form and content of requests, which must be presented in an official (or accepted) language of the requested state.[72]

The requested court is required to execute the request expeditiously[73] and in accordance with its own law.[74] If it is not possible for the request to be executed by the requested court within ninety days of the court's receipt thereof, the court should inform the requesting court, stating reasons for the delay in execution.[75] If the request cannot be executed because it does not contain all information required in terms of Article 4, the requested court shall inform the requesting court thereof without delay, and shall request that it send the missing information.[76]

If permitted by the law of the requesting court, parties and their representatives are entitled to be present at the taking of evidence,[77] and it is competent also for representatives of the requesting court to be present at the taking of evidence, if compatible with the law of the Member State of that court (and subject to such conditions as may be imposed by the requested court[78]), in order to enhance the evaluation of the evidence.[79] Alternatively, the requesting court may ask the requested court to utilise communications technology, such as video conferencing or teleconferencing.[80]

Where necessary in executing a request, the requested court shall apply the appropriate coercive measures in the instances and to the extent as are provided for by the law of the Member State of the requested court for the execution of a request made for the same purpose by its national authorities or one of the parties concerned.[81]

Possibilities for the requested court to refuse the request are confined to strictly limited, exceptional situations,[82] such as where a person claims the right to refuse to give evidence, or to be prohibited from giving evidence, under the law of the State of the requested court, or under the law of the State of the requesting court (subject to confirmation by the requesting court);[83] or where the request falls outside the scope of the Regulation, or where execution of the request falls outside the functions of the judiciary

---

[72] Art 5.
[73] Recital (10), and Art 6.
[74] Recital (12), and Art 10(2).
[75] Art 10(1).
[76] Art 8(1).
[77] Art 11.
[78] Art 12(4).
[79] Recital (14); and Art 12.
[80] Art 10(4).
[81] Art 13.
[82] Recital (11), and Art 14.
[83] Art 14(1).

of the requested court.[84] Significantly, Article 14.3 provides that execution of the request cannot be refused solely on the ground that under the law of the State of the requested court that court has exclusive jurisdiction over the subject matter of the action, or because the law of the State of the requested court would not admit the right of action on it.

As regards costs, Article 18 provides that the execution of a request for the taking of evidence shall not give rise to a claim for any reimbursement of taxes or costs. Nevertheless, the requested court may require the requesting court to ensure the prompt reimbursement of experts' and interpreters' fees, and costs occasioned by use of communications technology.[85]

(b) Direct taking of evidence by the requesting court

A request by the court of one Member State for the direct taking of evidence may be made in relation to judicial proceedings, commenced or contemplated.[86] Direct taking of evidence can take place only if it can be performed voluntarily, without need of coercive measures.[87] The taking of such evidence shall be performed by a member of the judicial personnel, or by a designated expert, in accordance with the law of the Member State of the requesting court.[88]

As with the taking of evidence by means of request, the requested court is required to act expeditiously and in accordance with its own law.[89] The central body of the requested Member State must inform the requesting court within thirty days of receipt if the request is accepted, and, if necessary, under what conditions the performance is to be carried out.[90] Similarly, the grounds for refusal to allow the direct taking of evidence are restricted to cases where the request does not fall within the scope of the Regulation; or where the request does not contain all the necessary information pursuant to Article 4; or where the direct taking of evidence requested is contrary to fundamental principles of law in its Member State.[91]

(iv) Taking of evidence outside the EU: Evidence (Proceedings in Other Jurisdictions) Act 1975; Protection of Trading Interests Act 1980

The Evidence (Proceedings in Other Jurisdictions) Act 1975[92] gives effect to the Hague Convention on the Taking of Evidence Abroad in Civil and Commercial Matters (1970).[93]

---

[84] Art 14(2)(a) and (b). Additionally, the request may be refused if the requesting court does not comply within 30 days with the request by the requested court to supply information pursuant to Art 8 (Art 14(2)(c)), or if a deposit or advance asked for in accordance with Art 18.3 has not been made within 60 days (Art 14(2)(d)).

[85] Art 18(2) and (3).

[86] Art 1(2).

[87] Art 17(2).

[88] Art 17(3).

[89] Art 17(6).

[90] Art 17(4). The central body may assign a court of its Member State to take part to ensure the proper application of Art 17.

[91] Art 17(5).

[92] See Sutherland (1982) 31 ICLQ 784; Collins (1986) 35 ICLQ 765.

[93] The English courts regard their jurisdiction hereunder as wholly statutory: *Boeing Co v PPG Industries Inc* [1988] 3 All ER 839. However, the US Supreme Court has held that the procedures of the Hague Convention are optional, not mandatory: *Société Nationale Industrielle Aérospatiale v United States District Court for the*

It empowers the High Court to order the taking of evidence (including its video record-ing)[94] in England when requested to do so by a foreign court, if the evidence is to be obtained for the purpose of actual or contemplated proceedings in any civil or commer-cial matter[95] or actual criminal proceedings.[96] In general, the court has a discretion whether or not to order such taking of evidence and it will refuse permission where the request amounts to a "fishing expedition";[97] but under the Protection of Trading Interests Act 1980 it must refuse to make an order if the request by the foreign court infringes the jurisdiction of the United Kingdom or is otherwise prejudicial to the United Kingdom.[98] The 1980 Act was passed because of concern over the effect of American anti-trust litiga-tion involving British companies[99] and it also permits[100] the Secretary of State to give directions prohibiting compliance with an order of a foreign court requiring a person in the United Kingdom to produce commercial documents, not within the territorial juris-diction of the foreign court, or to provide commercial information from such documents if it appears to the Secretary of State that the request infringes United Kingdom jurisdic-tion, or is otherwise prejudicial to the United Kingdom, or if compliance would be pre-judicial to the security of the United Kingdom or its relations with other governments.[101]

(v) Interpretation distinguished from evidence

Evidence must be distinguished from interpretation.[102] The rule of English law, for instance, that if a contract is written, "the writing is the grand criterion of what terms are intended to be contractual and what not"[103] and that therefore oral evidence is inadmis-sible to add to, vary or contradict the writing, is a rule of evidence properly so called that must be applied in every English action.[104] But, despite its deceptive similarity, the rule which admits oral evidence to show that the parties intended to incorporate a certain condition customarily included in a contract of a particular kind is a rule of

---

Southern District of Iowa 107 S Ct 2542 (1987); Slomanson (1988) 37 ICLQ 391; Minch (1988) 22 Int Lawyer 511; Prescott and Alley, ibid, 939; Born and Hoing (1990) 24 Int Lawyer 393; Griffin and Bravin (1991) 25 Int Lawyer 331; Black (1991) 40 ICLQ 901. For a comparative analysis, see Morse in Plender (ed), *Legal History and Comparative Law: Essays in Honour of Albert Kiralfy* (1990), p 159.

[94] *Barber & Sons v Lloyd's Underwriters* [1987] QB 103, [1986] 2 All ER 845; and *R v Forsyth* (1997) Times, 8 April, CA. For implications of the use of video and audio conferencing technology in transnational litigation, see Davies (2007) 55 AJCL 205.

[95] *Re State of Norway's Application (Nos 1 and 2)* [1990] 1 AC 723; Carter [1989] BYBIL 494; Lipstein (1990) 39 ICLQ 120. The House of Lords held that the proceedings had to be so classified under the law of both the requesting and requested states and, on this basis, included fiscal proceedings. A Special Commission (1989) of the Hague Conference on Private International Law has preferred an autonomous interpretation of the phrase; see Mann (1990) 106 LQR 354.

[96] *Re Westinghouse Electric Corpn Uranium Contract* [1978] AC 547; *Re Asbestos Insurance Coverage Cases* [1985] 1 WLR 331, HL; *R v Rathbone, ex p Dikko* [1985] QB 630; and see Sutherland (1982) 31 ICLQ 784.

[97] *Re State of Norway's Application (Nos 1 & 2)* [1990] 1 AC 723 at 766–767, 810; *First American Corpn v Zayed* [1999] 1 WLR 1154; cf *Lord Advocate, Petitioner* 1993 SC 638; and *Lord Advocate, Petitioner* 1998 SLT 835.

[98] S 4.

[99] Huntley (1981) 30 ICLQ 213; for rather different American perspectives, see Batista (1983) 17 Int Lawyer 61; Blythe (1983) 31 AJCL 99.

[100] S 2. For the effect of the 1980 Act on the recognition and enforcement of foreign judgments, see infra, Chapter 15.

[101] See *British Airways Board v Laker Airways Ltd* [1984] QB 142 at 195–198; affd on this issue [1985] AC 58 at 87–92.

[102] See *Re Barker* [1995] 2 VR 439.

[103] *Korner v Witkowitzer* [1950] 2 KB 128 at 162.

[104] [1950] 2 KB 128 at 162–163.

interpretation that is not necessarily applicable merely because the action is in England. It concerns interpretation, not proof.[105] Owing to the imperfect manner in which the contract has been drafted, the intention of the parties is not clear and the object of the particular rule is to explain what they meant.

A distinction must also be made between facts that are relevant and the evidence by which such facts are proved, for the former fall to be decided according to the law governing the transaction, while the latter is a matter of procedure for the law of the forum. This was considered in *The Gaetano and Maria*.[106]

> An action was brought in England on a bottomry bond given at the Azores by the master of a ship flying the Italian flag, without any communication with his owners. By Italian law the bond was valid; by English law its validity depended on proof that at the time it was given the ship was in distress and in need of repair and that the circumstances were such as to render it impossible for the master to communicate with the cargo-owners. It was argued that, since proof of the necessity of immediate repairs is a matter of evidence, the question of the validity of the bond must be determined by English law, being the law of the forum. The flaw in this argument was exposed by the Court of Appeal.

The sole fact in issue was one of substance, namely, whether the master had authority to give a valid bond. This was a question that fell to be determined by Italian law, the law of the flag. The equivalent English rule on this question no doubt differed from that under Italian law, but since it affected substance, not procedure, it was not to be invoked merely because the action was brought in England.

(vi) Presumptions and burden of proof

A controversial question is whether presumptions and burden of proof are matters that affect procedure or substance.[107] The classification of presumptions will depend on their nature and effect.[108] Presumptions of fact pose no problem for they raise no legal issue. Presumptions of law may be either irrebuttable or rebuttable. The former would appear to be substantive in effect,[109] but it is not clear how the latter should be classified. It has been suggested[110] that those which apply to a restricted class of case should be treated as substantive, but that it is uncertain how presumptions of general application, such as the presumptions of death or validity of marriage, should be classified. There is authority for treating the presumption as to the validity of a marriage as substantive so that a marriage may be upheld under the presumption of the foreign governing law.[111] But if the English law presumption favoured the validity of marriage whilst the foreign one did not, it is tempting to conclude that the public policy of the forum in favour of validity would prevail.

---

[105] [1950] 2 KB 128 at 163.

[106] (1882) 7 PD 137.

[107] See Wolff, pp 234–236.

[108] Dicey, Morris and Collins, paras 7-029–7-030.

[109] *Re Cohn* [1945] Ch 5; see *Monterosso Shipping Co v International Transport Workers Federation* [1982] 3 All ER 841.

[110] Dicey, Morris and Collins, paras 7-029–7-030; and see Morse, *Torts in Private International Law*, pp 178–179.

[111] *De Thoren v A-G* (1876) 1 App Cas 686; *Mahadervan v Mahadervan* [1964] P 233.

Whilst there may be much to be said for the view that the burden of proof is regulated by the law governing matters of substance,[112] the contrary view has been voiced.[113] Indeed, in *Re Fuld's Estate (No 3)*[114] SCARMAN J concluded that the English Probate Court "must in all matters of burden of proof follow scrupulously its own *lex fori*".[115]

The question whether a rule distributing the burden of proof affects substance or procedure has arisen in the USA on a plea of contributory negligence. There is authority for the view that the burden of proving contributory negligence is a question of substantive law, to be determined by the law governing such substantive issues.[116]

Again, in the case of contractual and non-contractual obligations, there are special legislative rules. The Contracts (Applicable Law) Act 1990 provides[117] that the rules of the law governing the substance of the contract which "raise presumptions of law or determine the burden of proof" shall be applied. It is only if these rules are to be classified as ones of substance that they are to be applied in place of the law of the forum. If they are merely procedural, they are inapplicable.[118] As regards non-contractual obligations, Article 22(1) of the Rome II Regulation[119] provides an equivalent rule, to the effect that the law governing a non-contractual obligation under the Regulation shall apply to the extent that, in matters of non-contractual obligations, it contains rules which raise presumptions of law or determine the burden of proof.

(c) Parties

Two questions need to be considered in connection with the identity of the parties to the action. The first is the determination of the appropriate person to sue,[120] and the second concerns the identity of the person to be sued.[121]

(i) The proper claimant

The first question is whether the name in which an action may be brought falls to be determined exclusively by the law of the forum on the ground that it is a mere matter of procedure. It is a question that arises principally where the claimant is not the original owner of the subject matter of the dispute, but has acquired it derivatively from the original owner, as, for instance, in the case of the assignment of a debt or other intangible movable. In those cases where English law requires the assignee to sue in the name of the assignor, it has been said,[122] and indeed on one occasion held,[123] that the requirement

---

[112] Dicey, Morris and Collins, para 7-027.

[113] *The Roberta* (1937) 58 Lloyd's Rep 159.

[114] [1968] P 675.

[115] Ibid, at 697; and see at 698–699.

[116] See *Fitzpatrick v International Rly* 252 NY 127 (1929); Hancock, *Torts in the Conflict of Laws*, 159 et seq; Webb and Brownlie (1962) 50 Can Bar Rev 79, 87–89; Morse, *Torts in Private International Law*, pp 174–178.

[117] Sch 1, Art 14(1). Cf Rome I Regulation, Art 18.

[118] Indeed they fall outside the legislation altogether: Art 1(2)(h), infra, Chapter 18.

[119] Infra, Chapter 19.

[120] See Crawford (2000) 6 Jur Rev 347; and *FMC Corpn v Russell* 1999 SLT 99.

[121] See Prott (1989) V Hague Recueil 215, 245–254; *International Association of Science and Technology for Development v Hamza* (1995) 122 DLR (4th) 92.

[122] *Wolff v Oxholm* (1817) 6 M & S 92 at 99.

[123] *Jeffery v M'Taggart* (1817) 6 M & S 126.

must be observed in an action in this country, even though it is not necessary by the law governing the transaction.

But on principle it is doubtful whether every rule that regulates the name in which an action must be brought is merely procedural in character. It would seem to be an unwarranted extension of the province of procedure, at any rate in cases falling within the sphere of private international law, to regard a rule as procedural if the effect is to deprive the claimant of a right which he has definitely acquired under the governing legal system.[124] If, for instance, English law still regarded a contractual right as so essentially personal as to be actionable only at the suit of the original contracting party, it would surely be the negation of principle, and indeed of justice, to enforce such a rule indiscriminately as being one of procedure, and thus to defeat a claimant who had acquired a contractual right derivatively under some legal system that regarded the transaction as valid. To adopt this attitude would be to mistake substance for procedure. There is little authority on the matter, but the early case of *O'Callaghan v Thomond*[125] at least shows that the English courts have not always adopted this attitude: the assignee of an Irish judgment brought an action of debt in his own name in England to recover the amount of the judgment. He was entitled so to sue by Irish law. The argument of counsel for the defendant was instructive. Though admitting the general principle that the law of one country would recognise and enforce obligations raised by the law of another country, he contended that the principle applied only to the substance of the contract, and could neither affect the form of enforcing an obligation in another country nor be allowed to contravene the general rule of English law that intangible movables were unassignable. He therefore argued that no action could be maintained in the present circumstances except in the name of the person who recovered the judgment. The court, however, was unanimous that the rule was a matter of substance, not procedure.

One problem which can arise in determining who is a proper claimant is whether a person will be permitted to sue in England in a representative capacity, relying on an appointment made under a foreign law. In *Kamouh v Associated Electrical Industries International Ltd*[126] the plaintiff was Lebanese and, because his brother had disappeared, he caused himself to be appointed by a court in Beirut as his brother's "judicial administrator" and, in that capacity, sought to bring an action in England on a contract made between his brother and the defendants. PARKER J refused to recognise his title to sue, observing[127] that, in such cases, there are two conflicting principles to be examined: first, that these courts should as a matter of comity give effect to the curator's or tuteur's right under foreign law to sue in his own name; secondly, that municipal procedure should be applied. The first principle prevails in the case of bankruptcy,[128]

---

[124] In *Bumper Development Corpn v Metropolitan Police Comr* [1991] 1 WLR 1362, the Court of Appeal, whilst accepting that the issue of whether a foreigner (here a ruined Indian Hindu temple recognised in India as a juristic person) could sue in England was a matter for English law as the law of the forum, took the broad view that it would not be contrary to public policy so to permit it.

[125] (1810) 3 Taunt 82. See also *Innes v Dunlop* (1800) 8 Term Rep 595; *Trimbey v Vignier* (1834) 1 Bing NC 151 at 160; cf *Regas Ltd v Plotkins* (1961) 29 DLR (2d) 282.

[126] [1980] QB 199.

[127] Ibid, at 206.

[128] *Macaulay v Guaranty Trust Co of New York* (1927) 44 TLR 99.

receivership[129] and the curatorship of the mentally ill;[130] whilst the second holds sway in respect of an administrator of the property of a deceased[131] or absent[132] person.

(ii) The appropriate defendant

The second question relates to the party sued. It has to be decided whether a foreign rule determining the identity of the party to be sued, or prescribing the order in which parties must be sued, is one of substance or of procedure. In order to do this, it is necessary to classify the exact nature and effect of the rule according to the legal system of which it forms a part.

The question is of special importance in partnership cases.[133] The doctrine, for instance, of English law that any one partner may be sued alone for the totality of the partnership debts is in sharp contrast with the rule, obtaining in many other jurisdictions, that a creditor cannot sue an individual partner until he has first sued the partners jointly and the assets of the firm have been exhausted. If a rule of this nature is pleaded as a bar to an English action, it has to be classified in its foreign context. It must not be dismissed as procedural, if the result will be to impose a liability that does not exist by the law governing the transaction; but if it merely requires the enforcement in a particular manner of an admitted liability, it must be dismissed as a rule affecting only the mode of process. The principle applied by the courts appears to be as follows:

> If the law governing matters of substance considers there to be no doubt as to the defendant's liability, even though the action is conditional on other parties being sued first, then this is a rule of procedure which, unless it obtains in England, is ignored in English proceedings. If, on the other hand, the governing law regards the defendant as being under no liability whatever unless other parties are sued first, it imposes a rule of substance that must be observed in English proceedings.[134]

Thus in an action brought against the executors of a deceased member of a Spanish firm, a claim that, according to Spanish law, creditors could not institute a suit against the separate estate of a deceased partner until they had had recourse to and had exhausted the property of the firm was not upheld because the rule in question merely determined the mode of procedure.[135]

---

[129] *Schemmer v Property Resources Ltd* [1975] Ch 273, where it is emphasised, at 287, that recognition will depend on there being sufficient connection between the defendant and the country in which the receiver was appointed; and see *Thorne, Ernst & Whinney Inc v Sulpetro Ltd* (1987) 47 DLR (4th) 315; *White v Verkouille* [1990] 2 Qd R 191.

[130] *Didisheim v London and Westminster Bank* [1900] 2 Ch 15, infra, pp 1186–1187.

[131] *New York Breweries Co v A-G* [1899] AC 62.

[132] *Kamouh v Associated Electrical Industries Ltd* [1980] QB 199.

[133] Eg *Oxnard Financing SA v Rahn (Legal Personality of Swiss Partnership)* [1998] 1 WLR 1465 (CA). It may also arise in cases where, under the foreign law, a creditor must sue the principal debtor before he can sue a surety. This rule has been held to be procedural: *Waung v Subbotovsky* [1968] 3 NSWR 499; affd on other grounds 121 CLR 337.

[134] *General Steam Navigation Co v Guillou* (1843) 11 M & W 877; *Bank of Australasia v Harding* (1850) 9 CB 661; *Bullock v Caird* (1875) LR 10 QB 276; *Re Doetsch* [1896] 2 Ch 836. The suggested principle is criticised by Wolff, p 240.

[135] *Re Doetsch*, supra.

The distinction was neatly raised in the leading case of *General Steam Navigation Co v Guillou*,[136] where the facts were as follows:

> The plaintiffs brought an action in England to recover damages for injury caused to one of their ships by the negligent navigation of a French ship which at the time of the accident was under the direction and management of the defendant's servants. The offending ship belonged to a French company of which the defendant was a shareholder and acting director.

The third plea to the action stated that:

> By the law of France the defendant . . . was not . . . responsible for or liable to be sued . . . individually, or in his own name or person, in any manner whatsoever, in respect of the said causes of action, . . . but by the law of France the said company alone . . . or the master in command for the time being of the said ship, was . . . responsible for, and liable to be sued . . . for, the said causes of action.

The one question, therefore, that fell to be decided here was whether the French law, as disclosed in the plea, absolved the defendant from all liability in any circumstances, or whether it imposed on him an undoubted, though a joint, liability. Although the court unanimously took this distinction,[137] the judges of the Court of Exchequer were equally divided on the question on the facts, although the plea clearly alleged a denial of liability by French law. Lord ABINGER and ALDERSON B held that French law merely required the defendant to be sued jointly with his co-owners in the name of the company; while Barons PARKE and GURNEY considered that according to the plea the defendant incurred no responsibility whatsoever, joint or several, for the acts of the master. This judicial difference of opinion on the question of fact is of no great moment, for the importance of the decision lies in the clearness with which the general principle is stated.

(d) Priorities

It has consistently been held that the order in which property in the possession of the court is distributable among creditors must be governed by English law. The priority of creditors in such a case is a procedural matter that is determinable by the law of the forum;[138] though it does not necessarily follow that the forum's rule as to priorities should be the same in an international claim as in a purely domestic case.[139] The law of the forum governs because the issue of priority forms no part of the transaction under which a creditor has acquired his right. It is extrinsic and comprises in effect a privilege dependent on the law of the country where the remedy is sought.[140] Thus priorities of creditors claiming in bankruptcy or in the administration of a deceased insolvent's estate are governed exclusively by the law of the forum.[141] It is the same in the case of liens. Where, for instance, two or more persons prosecute claims against a ship that has been arrested

---

[136] Supra.
[137] (1843) 11 M & W 877 at 895.
[138] *Pardo v Bingham* (1868) LR 6 Eq 485; *Re Melbourn* (1870) 6 Ch App 64; *The Colorado* [1923] P 102; *The Halcyon Isle* [1981] AC 221; distinguish priority of assignees of intangible movables, infra, Chapter 30.
[139] Carter (1983) 54 BYBIL 207, 211–212.
[140] *Harrison v Sterry* (1809) 5 Cranch 289 at 298; approved in *The Colorado* [1923] P 102 at 107.
[141] See Council Regulation (EC) No 1346/2000 on Insolvency Proceedings, Art 4(2)(i).

in England, the order in which they are entitled to be paid is governed exclusively by English law.[142]

In the case of a right *in rem* such as a lien, however, this principle must not be allowed to obscure the rule that the substantive right of the creditor depends on the governing law. The validity and nature of the right must be distinguished from the order in which it ranks in relation to other claims. Before it can determine the order of payment, the court should examine the law governing the transaction upon which the claimant relies in order to verify the validity of the right and to establish its precise nature. Once the nature of the right is ascertained in this way, then the principle of procedure should come into play and determine that the order of payment prescribed by English law for a right of that particular kind shall govern.

Whilst this is the basis on which courts ought to proceed, decisions in relation to maritime liens have not consistently followed this line.[143] A clear and, it is suggested, correct illustration of the approach to be adopted is provided by *The Colorado*.[144]

At least one earlier decision[145] had failed[146] to draw the crucial distinction between the substance of the right, an issue for the governing law, and the question of priorities, a remedial matter for the law of the forum. A similar failure is evident in the decision of the majority in the Privy Council in *The Halcyon Isle*.[147]

> An English bank had a mortgage on the *Halcyon Isle*, a British registered ship being repaired in the USA by American ship repairers. The repair bill was unpaid and the ship was arrested in Singapore and ordered by the court to be sold, but the proceeds were insufficient to satisfy the claims of both the bank and the repairers. So a question of priorities arose. Under Singapore law (which was the same as English law), the mortgagees had priority because the ship repairers were not regarded as having a maritime lien. Under US law, the repairers were regarded as having such a lien as would give them priority.

The Singapore Court of Appeal held in favour of the repairers,[148] but was reversed by a majority in the Privy Council who gave priority to the English bank. Whilst both the majority and the dissenting minority in the Privy Council agreed that matters of priority are procedural and to be governed by the law of the forum, they disagreed as to the

---

[142] *The Milford* (1858) Sw 362 at 366; *The Tagus* [1903] P 44; *American Surety Co of New York v Wrightson* (1910) 16 Com Cas 37; *The Colorado* [1923] P 102; *The Halcyon Isle* [1981] AC 221.

[143] Carter (1983) 54 BYBIL 207.

[144] [1923] P 102, in which the Court of Appeal held that while French law determined the substance of a mortgagee's right to a ship, English law determined whether the right ranked before or after an opposing claim. See also *The Acrux* [1965] P 391 at 404. In *The Zigurds* [1932] P 113, German necessaries men sought reimbursement from the proceeds of sale of a ship but failed to gain priority over the English mortgagee because, although they enjoyed such priority under German law, that was as a matter of German procedural (and not substantive) law; and it was for English procedural law to determine priorities. Also *The Ship Betty Ott v General Bills Ltd* [1992] 1 NZLR 655.

[145] *The Tagus* [1903] P 44.

[146] As is pointed out by the Supreme Court of Canada in *Todd Shipyards Corpn v Altema Compania Maritima SA* (1972) 32 DLR (3d) 571 at 575–576.

[147] [1981] AC 221.

[148] Following the decision of the Supreme Court of Canada in *Todd Shipyards Corpn v Altema Compania Maritima SA* (1972) 32 DLR (3d) 571.

analysis of the claims to be ranked in order of priority. Lord DIPLOCK, for the majority, concluded that the issue of priority depended "upon whether or not if the repairs to the ship had been done in Singapore, the repairers would have been entitled under the law of Singapore to a maritime lien on the *Halcyon Isle* for the price of them. The answer to that question is that they are not. The mortgagees are entitled to priority."[149]

This approach fails to give due consideration to the law of the USA. It is for that law, as the governing law, to consider both whether the claim by the repairers was valid and whether it would lead to the creation, *under US law*, of a maritime lien. The basis of the majority judgment seems to be that whether the repairs are entitled to a lien is solely a procedural matter, and Lord DIPLOCK claimed that such analysis is consistent with the decision in *The Colorado*.[150]

Much to be preferred is the analysis of the minority,[151] who found in favour of the ship repairers. The essence of their approach is succinctly expressed thus:

> The question is—does English law, in circumstances such as these, recognise the maritime lien created by the law of the United States of America, ie the *lex contractus* where no such lien exists by its own internal law? In our view the balance of authorities, the comity of nations, private international law and natural justice all answer this question in the affirmative. If this be correct then English law (the *lex fori*) gives the maritime lien created by the *lex loci contractus* precedence over the mortgagees' mortgage. If it were otherwise, injustice would prevail. The ship-repairers would be deprived of their maritime lien, valid as it appeared to be throughout the world, and without which they would obviously never have allowed the ship to sail away without paying a dollar for the important repairs.[152]

(e) The nature and extent of the remedy

It is obvious that a claimant who seeks to enforce a foreign claim in England can demand only those remedies recognised by English law. Even then, he cannot demand such remedies unless they harmonise with the right according to its nature and extent as fixed by the foreign law.[153] "Put in another way", to quote Lord PARKER CJ, in *Phrantzes v Argenti*,[154] "if the machinery by way of remedies here is so different from that in Greece as to make the right sought to be enforced a different right, that right would not, in my judgment, be enforced in this country". *Phrantzes* was concerned with the Greek law relating to the obligation of a man to provide a dowry for his son-in-law.[155] By that law, a father was obliged to establish a dowry for his daughter on her marriage, the amount of which depended, inter alia, on his finances, the number of his children and the social position of himself and his son-in-law. If a father failed to fulfil this obligation, his daughter, and she alone, had a cause of action to compel him to enter into a dowry contract not

---

[149] [1981] AC 221 at 241.

[150] Supra. See [1981] AC 221 at 238. He also, thereby, disapproved of the Supreme Court of Canada's decision in *Todd Shipyards Corpn v Altema Compania Maritima SA*, supra: [1981] AC 221 at 241–242.

[151] Lord SALMON and Lord SCARMAN.

[152] [1981] AC 221 at 246–247.

[153] *Chaplin v Boys* [1971] AC 356 at 381–382, 394; and see *Baschet v London Illustrated Standard* [1900] 1 Ch 73.

[154] [1960] 2 QB 19 at 35–36.

[155] For an American example, see *Slater v Mexican National Rly Co* 194 US 120 (1904).

with herself, but with her husband. If the father was abroad, he could be directed by the Greek court to conclude the contract, wherever he might happen to be, in the presence either of a public notary or the Greek consul. It was against this background that Mrs Phrantzes brought an action in England against her father, claiming a declaration that she was entitled to be provided with a dowry and petitioning that the amount properly due to her should be assessed. All parties were Greek nationals, and it was assumed that the father was domiciled in Greece.

Lord PARKER was satisfied that the obligation of a man to establish a dowry in favour of his son-in-law was one that on general principles was enforceable in England. It could not be excluded on the ground that the right of the beneficiary was unknown to English law.[156] Nevertheless, he held that for at least two reasons the action must fail.

> First, there was no remedy at common law appropriate to enforce the exact right vested in the plaintiff by Greek law, namely, "a right to obtain an order condemning someone to enter into a contract in a particular form with a person not even a party to the proceedings".[157]
>
> Secondly, the daughter did not come to the English court possessed of a right to a definite sum of money. What she was entitled to was such sum as, failing agreement, a court in its discretion might assess; and this assessment depended on a wide variety of factors such as the social position of the parties in a Greek environment.
>
> All these enquiries and decisions are essentially matters for the domestic courts, and matters largely for the discretion of those courts and not our courts.[158]

It is established that a claim to set-off affects procedure, not substance, since the issue that it raises is whether the relief claimed by the defendant shall be granted in the claimant's action or whether it is obtainable only by a counter-action.[159] If the court, in accordance with its own procedural code, refuses the privilege of set-off, it makes no attack on the substance of the defendant's claim, but, without adjudging the merits of the claim, merely rules that it must be put in suit in separate proceedings.[160]

(f) Damages[161]

The subject of damages raises a problem of some difficulty in private international law, not because the principles are obscure but because the English authorities are scanty.

Various questions must be segregated. In brief, remoteness of damage and heads of damage must be distinguished from measure of damages. The rules relating to remoteness indicate what kind of loss actually resulting from the commission of a tort or from a

---

[156] Distinguishing in this respect such decisions as *Re Macartney* [1921] 1 Ch 522, and *De Brimont v Penniman* (1873) 10 Blatch 436, where a New York court refused to enforce the duty, recognised by French law, of a father-in-law to support his son-in-law, infra, Chapter 15.

[157] [1960] 2 QB 19 at 35.

[158] Ibid, per Lord PARKER; cf *Khalij Commercial Bank Ltd v Woods* (1985) 17 DLR (4th) 358.

[159] *Meyer v Dresser* (1864) 16 CBNS 646; and see Wood, *English and International Set-off* (1989), Chapter 23. But see Dicey, Morris and Collins, para 7-032.

[160] But see Wolff, pp 233, 234, where it is shown that under Continental laws set-off is extra-judicial and is regarded as a matter of substance; and see Wood, op cit, Chapter 24.

[161] See, generally, Carruthers, op cit.

breach of contract is actionable; the rules for the measure of damages show the method by which compensation for an actionable loss is calculated. There is one principle of remoteness in tort, another in contract, with similar variations between the two causes of action as to the heads of damage or loss for which recovery may be made. However, the rule that regulates the measure of damages is the same for contracts as it is for torts. It requires *restitutio in integrum.*

(i) Remoteness of damage

There can be no doubt, at least in principle, that remoteness of damage must be governed by the law governing the obligation that rests on the defendant. Both the existence and the extent of an obligation, whether it springs from a breach of contract or the commission of a wrong, must be determined by the system of law from which it derives its source.[162] The governing law admittedly determines the nature and content of the right created by a contract, and it is clear that the kind of loss for which damages are recoverable on breach forms part of that content. Both the nature and the content of a contractual right depend in part on the question whether certain consequential loss that may ensue if the contract is unperformed will be too remote in the eye of the law. If the governing law determines what constitutes a breach, it also determines the consequences of a breach.[163]

> Suppose, for the sake of argument, that by French law a purchaser who sues a seller for non-delivery of goods is entitled to recover for the loss that he has suffered through failure to carry out any sub-contracts he may have made.

On this hypothesis, a purchaser under a French contract for the sale of goods acquires a right of perfectly definite extent. Furthermore, the principles of private international law as embodied in the Contracts (Applicable Law) Act 1990[164] require that his position in this respect shall be neither improved nor prejudiced by the fact that he happens to bring his action in England. If the court applies the rule of internal English law, that compensation cannot be recovered for sub-contract losses, the result is to diminish the content of the right as fixed by the governing law. Of course, an exception must be made when the type of loss for which recovery may be had in the foreign country is contrary to the distinctive policy of the law of the forum.[165]

In *D'Almeida Araujo Lda v Becker & Co Ltd*, a case of breach of contract, PILCHER J based his decision on the distinction between remoteness of damage and measure of damages.[166] The facts were these:

> By a contract, made on 20 March and governed by Portuguese law, the plaintiffs, merchants in Lisbon, agreed to sell 500 tons of palm oil to the defendants, a British company carrying on business in London. With a view to the fulfilment of their undertaking, the plaintiffs agreed to buy 500 tons of palm oil from one Mourao,

---

[162] *Slater v Mexican National Rly Co* 194 US 120 (1904).
[163] Contracts (Applicable Law) Act 1990, Sch 1, Art 10(1)(c) and cf Rome I Regulation, Art 12(1)(c), infra, Chapter 18; and see *Drew Brown v The Orient Trader* (1972) 34 DLR (3d) 339.
[164] Ibid.
[165] 1990 Act, Sch 1, Art 16. Cf Rome I Regulation, Art 21.
[166] [1953] 2 QB 329.

a Portuguese dealer. This contract provided that, in the event of its breach, the party in default should indemnify the other to the extent of 5 per cent of the total value of the contract, a sum that in fact amounted to the equivalent of £3,500. The plaintiffs were forced into the payment of this sum, since the defendants broke the contract of 20 March.

In the present action, the plaintiffs claimed to recover by way of damages the £3,500 which they had been obliged to pay under the indemnity. It was admitted that according to English law the loss suffered by reason of this payment would found no claim to damages, since it was not the kind of loss that ensued in the usual course of things from such a breach of contract. The judge, however, held that English law was irrelevant, concluding that the question whether the plaintiffs were entitled to claim from the defendants the £3,500 which they paid to Mourao, depended on whether such damage were too remote, a question which fell to be determined in accordance with Portuguese law.[167]

It should logically follow from the *D'Almeida* case that remoteness of damage in tort is also a matter of substance to be determined by the governing law,[168] for to rule otherwise would permit a claimant to exact compensation for what did not constitute a ground of liability under that law. This principle has been given legislative effect in Article 15(c) of the Rome II Regulation.[169]

(ii) Heads of damage

A further issue in which the distinction between substance and procedure has arisen is that of deciding whether a particular head of damage is recoverable, ie whether this is a matter of the quantification of the measure of damages and thus procedural, or whether it raises a substantive issue. Whilst there seems little doubt that, in the field of contract, this is a substantive issue for the law governing the contract, tort claims caused more difficulty because of the basic choice of law rule that the claim had to be actionable both by English law as the law of the forum and by the law of the place of the tort.[170] Although tort choice of law rules have now been placed on a statutory basis,[171] the determination of whether an issue is a matter of procedure or of substance is left to the common law.[172] It seems clear that, at common law, a claim for damages for pain and suffering or,[173] in a fatal accidents claim, for solatium,[174] is to be classed as substantive. Similarly, the question whether recovery may be had in a tort action for heads of economic loss is a matter of substance and not of procedure,[175] as is a claim for

---

[167] [1953] 2 QB 329 at 338, [1953] 2 All ER 288 at 293. The case would be decided the same way under the Contracts (Applicable Law) Act 1990.

[168] See Morse, *Torts in Private International Law*, pp 197–200; Morse (1996) 45 ICLQ 888 at 895–6; and *Edmunds v Simmonds* [2001] WLR 1003 at 1009.

[169] Infra, Chapter 19.

[170] Infra, p 767.

[171] Private International Law (Miscellaneous Provisions) Act 1995, Part III, infra, p 767.

[172] Ibid, s 14(3)(b), in respect of the interpretation of which, see *Harding v Wealands* [2007] 2 AC 1.

[173] See the majority in *Chaplin v Boys* [1971] AC 356, at 379 (per Lord HODSON), 393 (per Lord WILBERFORCE), 394–395 (per Lord PEARSON).

[174] Eg *Naftalin v London, Midland and Scottish Rly Co* 1933 SC 259; *McElroy v McAllister* 1949 SC 110; and see *Mackinnon v Iberia Shipping Co Ltd* 1955 SC 20; but cf Walker, *The Law of Delict in Scotland* (2nd edn), pp 67–68.

[175] *Mitchell v McCulloch* 1976 SC 1; *Breavington v Godleman* (1988) 169 CLR 41.

exemplary damages.[176] The position is less certain in relation to statutory caps on damages.[177]

(iii) Measure of damages

The next question is by what law is the measure of damages governed?[178] A rule as to the measure of damages in the narrow sense is a mere rule of calculation. Its function is to quantify in terms of money the sum payable by the defendant in respect of the injury, whether it be a tort or breach of contract, for which his liability has already been determined by the governing law. A claimant who seeks to recover compensation in England in respect of an obligation that is governed as to substance by a foreign law has already acquired a right the nature and extent of which have been fully determined. His object is that his right as established shall be converted by the English court into a right to receive a definite sum of money. He is entitled to be paid in full for the injury suffered and he takes advantage of the English process and machinery in order to exact this payment.

It would seem, therefore, that all questions that arise in the course of this quantification of the amount payable should be governed by English law as the law of the forum. This has been the approach, traditionally, of courts in the United Kingdom. Although PILCHER J has said that, "the quantification of damage, which according to the proper law is not too remote, should be governed by the *lex fori*",[179] some opposition has been expressed.[180] Indeed McNAIR J found, "the greatest possible difficulty in appreciating the distinction . . . between remoteness of damage and measure of damage".[181] Moreover, if the quantification of damages is considered to be a matter of procedure, to be governed by the *lex fori*, "difficulties will arise if the applicable law recognises a cause of action which is unknown to English domestic law [the *lex fori*], for the simple reason that there will be no English domestic rules on quantification and assessment for the English court to apply as the *lex fori*".[182] Nevertheless, the distinction has long been held both valid and valuable by the House of Lords.[183]

---

[176] *Waterhouse v Australian Broadcasting Corpn* (1989) 86 ACTR 1.

[177] See *Stevens v Head* (1993) 176 CLR 433 at 458; Morse (1996) 45 ICLQ 888 at pp 895–896; and *Harding v Wealands* [2007] 2 AC 1, per Lord HOFFMAN at [42]–[46]. Also, in *Harding*, per Lord RODGER at [72]: "Lord Hoffman has analysed the passage in *Dicey & Morris, The Conflict of Laws* [7th edn, 1958, p 1092], to the effect that 'statutory provisions limiting a defendant's liability are *prima facie* substantive; but the true construction of the statute may negative this view'. I respectfully agree with his analysis. In any event, as the passage recognises, in any given case the answer to the question must depend on the construction of the relevant provision in the context of the particular statute." See Dicey, Morris and Collins, paras 7-040–7-043.

[178] See *Edmunds v Simmonds* [2001] WLR 1003; *Roerig v Valiant Trawlers Ltd* [2002] 1 Lloyd's Rep 681; *Hulse v Chambers* [2001] 1 WLR 2386; and *Harding v Wealands* [2007] 2 AC 1. Also Carruthers, op cit; Panagopoulos (2005) 1 J Priv Int L 69; and Carruthers (2005) 1 J Priv Int L 323.

[179] The *D'Almeida Case* [1953] 2 QB 329 at 336.

[180] See the minority in *Stevens v Head* (1993) 176 CLR 433. Also *John Pfeiffer Pty Ltd v Rogerson* [2000] HCA 36; *Régie National des Usines Renault SA v Zhang* [2002] 187 ALR 1; and *Re T & N Ltd and Ors (No 2)* [2006] 1 WLR 1792 at [63].

[181] *N V Handel Maatschappij J Smits Import-Export v English Exporters Ltd* [1955] 2 Lloyd's Rep 69 at 72. This is a view with which Lord UPJOHN has sympathised, in *Boys v Chaplin* [1968] 2 QB 1 at 31; and see *Livesley v Horst* [1925] 1 DLR 159 at 164.

[182] Morse (1996) 45 ICLQ 888 at 895–896. See Carruthers (2004) 53 ICLQ 691, 699–700.

[183] *Chaplin v Boys* [1971] AC 356 at 378–379, 382–383, 392–393, 394. Cf, in Australia, the majority in *Stevens v Head* (1993) 176 CLR 433.

Opportunity for the House of Lords to revisit the distinction, and to review its merits, arose in *Harding v Wealands*,[184] the facts of which were as follows:

> The claimant, Giles Harding, an English national, domiciled in England, was rendered tetraplegic as a result of a motor accident in New South Wales in February 2003. The defendant was Mr Harding's partner, Tania Wealands, an Australian national who had lived in Australia until June 2001, at which time she moved to England to live with the claimant in a settled relationship. Ms Wealands conceded liability, but a preliminary issue arose before ELIAS J concerning the law applicable to the assessment of damages. ELIAS J held in favour of the claimant, concluding, inter alia, that the New South Wales statutory damages provisions were to be treated as procedural in nature, and subject, therefore, to the English *lex fori*.

Upon Ms Wealand's appeal, the Court of Appeal, by a majority,[185] reversed the decision of the judge at first instance,[186] and upheld Ms Wealand's contention that the claim for damages was to be determined in accordance with the law of New South Wales. The House of Lords, however, allowed Mr Harding's appeal, restoring the judgment of ELIAS J and affirming the "damages principle", holding that the question of the assessment of damages in tort, in terms of section 14(3) of the Private International Law (Miscellaneous Provisions) Act 1995, is to be regarded as a matter of procedure, governed by the *lex fori*. In the instant case, the provisions of the New South Wales Motor Accidents Compensation Act 1999[187] were characterised as procedural, meaning that the claimant's damages were to be quantified in accordance with English law.

Reference of the issue of measure of damages to the law of the forum will mean that if, for instance, the defendant pleads a tender of the amount due, he must prove that the tender is in accordance with English law. This is because if the task of the court is to fix the amount payable it must also be competent to decide whether in its view payment has in effect already been made.[188] Furthermore, the question whether the damages should be paid in a lump sum or by means of periodic payments is a procedural matter for the law of the forum.[189] The question whether collateral benefits accruing from the death of a deceased person ought to be deducted in calculating an award of damages for loss of dependency has been judged to be a matter of procedure, to be determined by the law of the forum.[190] Conversely, the question whether a claimant is contributorily negligent, leading to a reduction in the award of damages payable, has been held to be a factor relevant to the scope of the defendant's liability for the victim's injuries and the identification of actionable damage, and thus a substantive issue, rather than merely an aspect of the assessment of damages.[191]

---

[184] [2007] 2 AC 1. See Carruthers (2005) 1(2) J Priv Int L 323; Dougherty and Wyles (2007) 56 ICLQ 443; and Weintraub (2007) 43 Texas Int LJ 311.

[185] ARDEN LJ and Sir Wm ALDOUS; WALLER LJ, dissenting.

[186] See [2005] 1 WLR 1539, per ARDEN LJ at [52].

[187] In respect of which, see also *McNeilly v Imbree* [2007] NSWCA 156.

[188] *The Baarn* [1933] P 251.

[189] McGregor (1970) 33 MLR 1, 21 et seq.

[190] *Roerig v Valiant Trawlers Ltd* [2002] 1 WLR 2304 at [25]–[26]. The court indicated that the question of deductions is closely tied to policy considerations, and "with the way in which damages under the particular head are to be assessed overall" (at [26]).

[191] *Dawson v Broughton*, 31 July 2007 (unreported), considered at (2007) Journal of Personal Injury Law C186. See now Rome II Regulation, Art 15(b) ("division of liability"), examined, infra, Chapter 19.

The traditional approach of the English courts to the matter of quantification of damages will require to be abandoned when the Rome II Regulation comes into operation.[192] By virtue of Article 15(c) of Rome II, not only the existence and the nature of damage, but also the assessment of damage are matters to be determined by the law applicable to the non-contractual obligation.[193] This provision represents a major change in English private international law. Article 15(c) adopts the position taken in most Member States, which regard assessment of damages as a substantive matter to be determined by the applicable law, and it has the virtue of preventing forum shopping within the European Community for an assessment of damages advantage.[194] It broadly follows Article 10(1)(c) of the Rome Convention on the Law Applicable to Contractual Obligations. Under the Contracts (Applicable Law) Act 1990 the law governing the substance of the contract also governs "the consequences of breach, including the assessment of damages in so far as it is governed by rules of law", provided that the court of the forum has these powers according to its procedural law.[195] This is intended only to apply rules of law for the assessment of damages to be found in the governing law, since "questions of fact will always be for the court hearing the action".[196]

(iv) Payment of interest

The issue as to whether interest is payable necessitates consideration of whether interest is claimed by virtue of a term in a contract or as damages and whether what is in issue is the right to interest or the rate at which it is payable. It was well established at common law that whether interest was payable on a contractual debt, and if so at what rate, was a matter to be determined by the law governing the essential validity of the contract.[197] This would still appear to be the case under the Contracts (Applicable Law) Act 1990.[198] This rule has been applied in the case of dishonour of a bill of exchange. So, whether interest is recoverable on dishonour depends on the law governing the contract under which the defendant rendered himself liable.[199] Where damages for breach of contract are being claimed, rather than a debt, then the right to interest on the damages is governed by the law applicable to the contract.[200] There is some authority for the conclusion that the right to interest on damages in tort is governed by the law applicable to the substantive tort issue.[201]

Turning now to the rate at which interest is to be paid, or whether the interest is to be compound or simple, there seems little doubt again that, in the case of a contractual

---

[192] On 11 January 2009, per Rome II, Art 32.

[193] Infra, Chapter 19.

[194] For possible difficulties in application, see, infra, Chapter 19.

[195] Sch 1, Art 10(1)(c). Cf Rome I Regulation, Art 12(1)(c).

[196] Giuliano and Lagarde Report, OJ 1980 C 282/33.

[197] *Montreal Trust Co v Stanrock Uranium Mines Ltd* (1965) 53 DLR (2d) 594; and see *Shrichand & Co v Lacon* (1906) 22 TLR 245; *Mount Albert Borough Council v Australasian Temperance and General Mutual Life Assurance Society* [1938] AC 224; Law Com No 124 (1983), para 2.29.

[198] Sch 1, Art 10(1)(c).

[199] *Allen v Kemble* (1848) 6 Moo PCC 314; *Gibbs v Fremont* (1853) 9 Exch 25.

[200] See, at common law, *Miliangos v George Frank (Textiles) Ltd (No 2)* [1977] QB 489; cf *Midland International Trade Services Ltd v Sudairy* (1990) Financial Times, 2 May. Similarly, in a claim for restitutionary relief based on frustration, the law governing the frustrated contract has been applied to determine a claim to interest: *BP Exploration Co (Libya) Ltd v Hunt (No 2)* [1979] 1 WLR 783 at 845–850; affd [1983] 2 AC 352.

[201] *Ekins v East-India Co* (1717) 1 P Wms 395; Dicey, Morris & Collins, para 33-395. But see *Kuwait Oil Tanker Co SAK v Al Bader (No 3)* [2000] 2 All ER (Comm) 271, per MOORE-BICK J at 339–344.

claim for interest, these matters are governed by the law applicable to the contract.[202] There is less certainty as to the law to determine the rate of interest payable on damages. In an action for damages for breach of contract, it was decided in *Miliangos v George Frank (Textiles) Ltd (No 2)*[203] that the question of the rate of interest is a matter relating to measure of damages, and thus a matter of procedure governed by the law of the forum.[204] This has been dissented from by KERR J: "Both the right to interest and its amount should be determined by the proper law. The proper law results from the express or implied choice of both parties or from the nature of the transaction."[205]

There are no clear answers to be discerned from the Contracts (Applicable Law) Act 1990 which simply excludes matters of procedure from its scope, without defining them.[206] So we are thrown back on the common law decisions for guidance. There are difficulties with KERR J's approach in the case, for example, of contractual claims for damages in foreign currency. The currency of the law governing the contract may be different from the currency of account, the currency of the loss and the currency of the forum.[207] The rates of interest relevant to each may well reflect the strength and weaknesses of the various currencies. If the rate of interest is governed by the law of the forum,[208] this means that, in England, the court has a discretion as to the rate[209] and it has been made clear by the Court of Appeal that, prima facie, interest should be awarded at the rate applicable to the currency of the judgment.[210] This might not be possible if the governing law of the contract determined the rate. The Law Commission has considered this issue and concluded, though without proposing legislation on the matter, that the practical arguments in favour of the application of the law of the forum should prevail.[211]

(g) Judgments in foreign currency[212]

(i) Old rule: judgment must be in sterling

It was accepted in England for many years that an English court could not order payment of debts or damages except in English currency.[213] The amount due to the plaintiff in

---

[202] This was clearly the position at common law: *Fergusson v Fyffe* (1841) 8 Cl & Fin 121 at 140 (compound interest); *Mount Albert Borough Council v Australasian Temperance and General Mutual Life Assurance Society* [1938] AC 224 (rate of interest).

[203] [1977] QB 489; and see *The Funabashi* [1972] 1 WLR 666 at 671.

[204] See now Contracts (Applicable Law) Act 1990, Sch 1, Art 10(1)(c). Also Late Payment of Commercial Debts (Interest) Act 1998, s 12.

[205] *Helmsing Schiffahrts GmbH & Co KG v Malta Drydocks Corpn* [1977] 2 Lloyd's Rep 444 at 450.

[206] Sch 1, Art 1(2)(h).

[207] Infra, p 106.

[208] See *Lesotho Highlands Development Authority v Impregilo SpA* [2003] 2 Lloyd's Rep 497, per BROOKE LJ, at para 50; and *Rogers v Markel Corpn* [2004] EWHC 1375, per TREACY J, at [77]–[81], and [2004] EWHC 2046. See Dicey, Morris and Collins, at paras 33-397–33-400.

[209] Supreme Court Act 1981, s 35A (added by the Administration of Justice Act 1982, s 15 and Sch 1).

[210] *Shell Tankers (UK) Ltd v Astro Comino Armadora SA* [1981] 2 Lloyd's Rep 40 at 45–47; and see *Miliangos v George Frank (Textiles) Ltd (No 2)* [1977] QB 489; *Swiss Bank Corpn v State of New South Wales* (1993) 33 NSWLR 63. The prima facie rule was displaced in *Helmsing Schiffahrts GmbH & Co KG v Malta Drydocks Corpn*, supra.

[211] Working Paper No 80, *Foreign Money Liabilities* (1981), paras 4.23–4.27; Law Com No 124, *Foreign Money Liabilities* (1983), paras 3.55–3.56.

[212] Mann, *The Legal Aspect of Money*, (2005) 6th edn, Chapter 4; Goode, *Payment, Obligations and Financial Transactions* (1983), Chapter V; Bowles, *Law and the Economy* (1982), Chapter 9. The whole question of foreign money liabilities was considered by the Law Commission in Law Com No 124 (1983).

[213] *Manners v Pearson & Son* [1898] 1 Ch 581.

foreign currency had to be converted into sterling and the appropriate exchange rate was that at the date the cause of action arose, eg the date of the breach of a contract[214] or the commission of a tort.[215]

(ii) Miliangos v George Frank (Textiles) Ltd

The rule that judgment must be in sterling came under increasing attack, culminating in the decision of the House of Lords in *Miliangos v George Frank (Textiles) Ltd*.[216]

> By means of a contract governed by Swiss law, the plaintiff, a Swiss national, had agreed to sell a quantity of polyester yarn to the English defendants. The yarn was delivered in 1971. The money of account and of payment was Swiss francs. The defendant having failed to pay, the plaintiff sought payment of the sterling equivalent of the sum due in Swiss francs, at the date when payment should have been made. However, after a decision of the Court of Appeal allowing judgment to be given in a foreign currency,[217] the plaintiff in *Miliangos* was given leave to amend his claim so as to claim the amount due to him in Swiss francs.

The problem facing the House of Lords was a fairly simple one. Were they to act on the Practice Direction of 1966[218] and reverse an earlier but fairly recent decision of their own[219] and accept the line already taken by the Court of Appeal, or were they to confirm the well-established rule that judgment could only be given in sterling with a conversion date as of the date of breach? The significance of the decision to the plaintiff, in an era of rapidly fluctuating interest rates, was very considerable and especially given that the Swiss franc was strong and sterling weak. Judgment in Swiss francs, converted into sterling as at the date of judgment, would give him almost 50 per cent more in sterling than conversion as at the date of the breach. Their Lordships decided to abandon the old rule and allow judgment to be given in foreign currency, here Swiss francs.[220] This was a decision of major commercial and financial significance but it left a whole range of further issues undecided, many of which have since been resolved by judicial decision. The most important of them are: how far beyond judgments for debts expressed in foreign currency does the *Miliangos* decision go? And in what currency may a court give judgment?

(iii) Claims to which the Miliangos rule applies

The first issue to be considered is the scope of the *Miliangos* decision. Their Lordships were very careful to limit their new principle to the type of case before them, leaving it to

---

[214] Eg *Re United Rlys of the Havana and Regla Warehouses Ltd* [1961] AC 1007.

[215] Eg *SS Celia v SS Volturno* [1921] 2 AC 544.

[216] [1976] AC 443. It had already been decided that an arbitral award (*Jugoslavenska Oceanska Plovidba v Castle Investment Co Inc* [1974] QB 292) and a judgment for a debt (*Schorsch Meier GmbH v Hennin* [1975] QB 416) could be made in foreign currency. For Scots law on this issue, see Moran (1995) 44 ICLQ 72.

[217] *Schorsch Meier GmbH v Hennin* [1975] QB 416.

[218] [1966] 1 WLR 395. See now *Practice Direction (Judgments: Foreign Currency)* (1992) PD 11.

[219] *Re United Rlys of the Havana and Regla Warehouses Ltd* [1961] AC 1007, [1960] 2 All ER 332.

[220] Lord SIMON of Glaisdale dissented, believing that such a revolutionary change should only be made by Parliament; [1976] AC 443 at 470. However, the Law Commission subsequently examined the whole question of foreign money liabilities and concluded that "the principle underlying the decision in *Miliangos* and the consequences which flow from it are greatly to be preferred to the rules which that decision superseded": Law Com No 124 (1983), para 3.8; cf Bowles and Whelan (1982) 45 MLR 434.

future decisions to work out the further implications of it. Indeed, Lord WILBERFORCE said:

> I would confine my approval at the present time . . . to claims such as those with which we are here concerned, ie, to foreign money obligations, sc obligations of a money character to pay foreign currency arising under a contract whose proper law is that of a foreign country and where the money of account and payment is that of that country, or possibly of some other country, but not of the United Kingdom.[221]

Development came very rapidly. It started with cases of debt, then extended to liquidated damages for breach of contract and eventually to claims for unliquidated damages.[222] The result is that it is now established that the court can give judgment for a sum in foreign currency as damages for breach of contract[223] and as damages in tort.[224] Furthermore, the principle applies in contractual claims whether the law governing the contract is English law[225] or foreign law.[226] It also extends to restitutionary claims,[227] winding up orders[228] and voluntary liquidations,[229] and it also seems clear that it will apply to salvage claims.[230]

In all these cases it has normally been the claimant who sought payment in a currency other than sterling because of the depreciation of sterling. There is now much greater variation in exchange rates. "Sterling is no longer a stable currency, nor are US dollars, nor French francs. No currency is stable. They all swing about with every gust that blows."[231] So what happens when sterling appreciates? In the case of an action for a debt it seems clear that the claimant ought to be entitled to judgment in the currency of the debt, converted into sterling as at the date of payment, and not judgment in sterling converted from the currency of the debt as at the date of breach. As was said in *Miliangos*, "the creditor has no concern with pounds sterling: for him what matters is that a Swiss franc for good or ill should remain a Swiss franc".[232] A similar rule ought to apply to claims for damages in foreign currency. The claimant should be entitled to judgment in the currency of his loss[233] and not in sterling calculated as at the date the cause of

---

[221] [1976] AC 443 at 467–468; and see 497–498, 503; see *Owners of Eleftherotria v Despina R, The Despina R* [1979] AC 685 at 695. But see Mann (1976) 92 LQR 165, 166.

[222] For discharge of foreign currency obligations, especially debts, other than where there is a judgment, see Dicey, Morris and Collins, paras 36R-051–36-060.

[223] *Services Europe Atlantique Sud v Stockholms Rederiaktiebolag SVEA, The Folias* [1979] AC 685; and see *Kraut AG v Albany Fabrics Ltd* [1977] QB 182; *Federal Commerce and Navigation Co Ltd v Tradax Export SA* [1977] QB 324 at 341–342; revsd on other grounds [1978] AC 1; *The Texaco Melbourne* [1994] 1 Lloyd's Rep 473.

[224] *Owners of Elftherotria v Despina R, The Despina R* [1979] AC 685; *Hoffman v Sofaer* [1982] 1 WLR 1350.

[225] Eg *Services Europe Atlantique Sud v Stockholms Rederiaktiebolag SVEA, The Folias*, supra; *Barclays Bank International Ltd v Levin Bros (Bradford) Ltd* [1977] QB 270; *Federal Commerce and Navigation Co Ltd v Tradax Export SA*, supra, at 341–342.

[226] *Miliangos v George Frank (Textiles) Ltd (No 2)* [1977] QB 489.

[227] *BP Exploration Co (Libya) Ltd v Hunt (No 2)* [1979] 1 WLR 783, affd [1983] 2 AC 352.

[228] *Re Dynamics Corpn of America* [1976] 1 WLR 757.

[229] *Re Lines Bros Ltd* [1983] Ch 1; *Re Lines Bros Ltd (No 2)* [1984] Ch 438.

[230] *Services Europe Atlantique Sud v Stockholms Rederiaktiebolag SVEA, The Folias* [1979] QB 491 at 516; affd [1979] AC 685; and see *Miliangos v George Frank (Textiles) Ltd* [1976] AC 443 at 468.

[231] [1979] QB 491 at 513.

[232] [1976] AC 443 at 466.

[233] Discussed, infra, p 106 et seq.

action arose. In this way the claimant is protected against changes in the value of his currency as against sterling, but is not, and should not be, protected against changes in the internal value of his own currency.[234]

(iv) Interest

Interest may be allowed in an action for payment of a debt or damages in foreign currency at a rate which may be different from the English rate for sterling.[235] The rate of interest to be paid on a judgment given in a foreign currency is within the discretion of the court, and is not confined to the English statutory rate for judgment debts.[236]

(v) Procedural nature of the Miliangos rule

The rule propounded in the *Miliangos* decision is a rule of procedure and not of substance;[237] thus English law is applied as the law of the forum. This can be seen from the fact that the rule has been applied where the law governing the substance of the contract in question was foreign,[238] and without reference, at common law in tort, to the law of the place of the tort.[239]

(vi) Date for conversion of currency

Although judgment may be given in foreign currency, a question of conversion into sterling may still arise. The judgment may be satisfied by payment of the sum in foreign currency[240] but, failing such satisfaction, the claimant will seek to enforce the judgment and this will necessitate conversion of the judgment into sterling.[241] In fact in *Miliangos* itself, the House of Lords considered that the claim could be in the alternative, either for the foreign currency or the sterling equivalent at "the date of payment". It has been stated in the Court of Appeal that the conversion should be made "as close as practicable to the date of payment, having regard to the realities of enforcement procedures".[242] In normal cases, the "date of payment" at which conversion must be made will be the date at which the court authorises enforcement of the judgment in terms of sterling,[243] and this also

---

[234] *Owners of Eleftherotria v Despina R, The Despina R* [1979] AC 685 at 697.

[235] *Miliangos v George Frank (Textiles) Ltd (No 2)* [1977] QB 489; *Helmsing Schiffahrts GmbH & Co KG v Malta Drydocks Corpn* [1977] 2 Lloyd's Rep 444; *Shell Tankers (UK) Ltd v Astro Comino Armadora SA* [1981] 2 Lloyd's Rep 40; *Maschinenfabric v Altikar Pty Ltd* [1984] 3 NSWLR 152; *The Kefalonia Wind* [1986] 1 Lloyd's Rep 292 n; and see Bowles and Phillips (1976) 39 MLR 196.

[236] Private International Law (Miscellaneous Provisions) Act 1995, s 1(1), inserting a new s 44A to that effect into the Administration of Justice Act 1970. This provision implements a recommendation of the Law Commission, in Law Com No 124 (1983), para 4.15.

[237] *Owners of Eleftherotria v Despina R, The Despina R* [1979] AC 685 at 704.

[238] Eg *Miliangos v George Frank (Textiles) Ltd* [1976] AC 443.

[239] *Owners of Eleftherotria v Despina R, The Despina R* [1979] AC 685.

[240] See *Practice Direction* [1976] 1 WLR 83, as amended by *Practice Direction* [1977] 1 WLR 197; and *Practice Direction (Judgments: Foreign Currency)* (1992) PD 11.

[241] *Miliangos v George Frank (Textiles) Ltd* [1976] AC 443 at 497, 501.

[242] *Carnegie v Giessen and Ors* [2005] EWCA Civ 191; [2005] 1 WLR 2510, per CARNWORTH LJ, at [12].

[243] Ibid, at 468–469, 497–498, 501–502; and see *Practice Direction* [1976] 1 WLR 83, as amended by *Practice Direction* [1977] 1 WLR 197; *The Halcyon Skies (No 2)* [1977] 1 Lloyd's Rep 22; *George Veflings Rederi A/S v President of India* [1979] 1 WLR 59. The Law Commission re-examined this rule and supported its retention, but also made a number of detailed proposals for changes to the relevant procedural laws: Law Com No 124 (1983), Part V. On garnishee orders against foreign currency bank accounts, see *Choice Investments Ltd v Jeromnimon* [1981] QB 149, [1981] All ER 225; and now, Third Party Debt Orders *per* Civil Procedure Rules, Pt 72, in respect of which see Dicey, Morris and Collins, paras 24R-078–24-082. In the case of set-off, see

applies to the case of an arbitrator's award.[244] In the case of the winding up of a company (both compulsory and voluntary), the appropriate date will be the date of the winding-up order.[245]

There are various cases where it has been provided by statute that the conversion into sterling shall be made according to the rate of exchange prevailing at the time of judgment and, of course, these are unaffected by the *Miliangos* decision. The judgment-date rule applies to carriage by air[246] but not to carriage of goods by road.[247] In the case of foreign judgments expressed in foreign currency and registered in England under the Foreign Judgments (Reciprocal Enforcement) Act 1933[248] for the purposes of recognition and enforcement, they are to be registered in the foreign currency with conversion at the date of payment[249] just as if the claimant had sued on the original cause of action, or, it is assumed, as if there was an action on the judgment at common law.[250] There is no provision in the Civil Jurisdiction and Judgments Act 1982,[251] which governs the recognition and enforcement of judgments given in European Union States,[252] indicating the date for converting into sterling the currency in which the foreign judgment was given. It is assumed,[253] however, that the same principles will apply. The rules are different for the enforcement of foreign maintenance orders,[254] where the conversion date is not that, under the *Miliangos* rule, of actual payment or when enforcement is authorised, but rather the earlier date of the registration of the order.[255] This difference of approach can be justified on grounds of convenience.[256] It is quite impracticable for the sums due under a foreign maintenance order, often payable weekly, to vary from week to week in the light of currency fluctuations.[257] In the case of claims for damages falling within section 13 of the Merchant Shipping

---

The Transoceanica Francesca and Nicos V [1987] 2 Lloyd's Rep 155 (tort); *Smit Tak International Zeesleepen Berginsbedrijk BV v Selco Salvage Ltd* [1988] 2 Lloyd's Rep 398 (contract); and see *The Lu Schan* [1993] 1 Lloyd's Rep 259.

[244] Ibid, at 469; Law Com No 124 (1983), para 2.43; cf *Jugoslovenska Oceanska Plovidba v Castle Investment Co* [1974] QB 292.

[245] *Re Dynamics Corpn of America* [1976] 1 WLR 757; cf *Miliangos v George Frank (Textiles) Ltd* [1976] AC 443 at 469, 498 (compulsory); *Re Lines Bros Ltd* [1983] Ch 1; *Re Lines Bros (No 2)* [1984] Ch 438 (voluntary); and see *Re Gresham Corpn Pty Ltd* [1990] 1 Qd R 306.

[246] Carriage by Air Act 1961, Sch 1, Art 22(5), and see s 4(4).

[247] Carriage of Goods by Road Act 1965, Sch, Art 27(2).

[248] S 2(3), for the main provisions see infra, Chapter 15.

[249] Administration of Justice Act 1977, ss 4, 32(4), Sch 5, which also repeals the Bills of Exchange Act 1882, s 72(4).

[250] *East India Trading Co Inc v Carmel Exporters and Importers Ltd* [1952] 2 QB 439, [1952] 1 All ER 1053 would, it is suggested, be decided differently after *Miliangos*; see *Batavia Times Publishing Co v Davis* (1978) 88 DLR (3d) 144 especially at 151–154; and see Law Com No 124 (1983), para 2.38.

[251] Except in the case of maintenance orders, infra.

[252] Infra, Chapter 16.

[253] Collins, *The Civil Jurisdiction and Judgments Act 1982* (1983), p 116; Law Com No 124 (1983), paras 2.38–2.42, 3.45–3.46.

[254] Infra, Chapter 23.

[255] Maintenance Orders (Reciprocal Enforcement) Act 1972, s 16; Civil Jurisdiction and Judgments Act 1982, s 8; Civil Jurisdiction and Judgments Act 1991, Sch 2, para 2; cf *Re May's Marriage* (1987) 90 FLR 134.

[256] Law Com No 124 (1983), paras 2.48–2.51, 3.47–3.49.

[257] English maintenance orders may be made in foreign currency (eg *R v Cambridge County Court, ex p Ireland* [1985] Fam Law 23) but in such cases conversion is effected at the date the enforcement procedure is initiated: see Law Com No 124 (1983), para 2.52.

Act 1995[258] the rate of exchange is either that at the date of judgment or at the date agreed by the parties.[259]

(vii) In what currency should the court give judgment?

We have seen that the question whether damages can be given in a foreign currency is a procedural issue. This leads to a further issue of classification. Given that an English court can award damages in a foreign currency, is it for English law as the procedural law of the forum to provide the legal rules for deciding in which currency this is to be done, or is the question of the identification of the currency a matter of substantive law? For example, if the governing law of a contract is French, and the English court is prepared to give damages in a foreign currency, does the court use the English or the French rules for deciding which is the appropriate currency? This issue would appear to be a matter of substance. In the field of contract, the currency in which damages are to be calculated has been held to be a matter for the law governing substantive issues,[260] as in *Kraut AG v Albany Fabrics Ltd*,[261] in which the facts were as follows:

> The plaintiff, a Swiss company, sold cloth to the English defendants, by means of contract governed by Swiss law. The defendant failed to pay and the plaintiff sought payment of various sums owing to it and damages for breach of contract. The issue before the court was whether judgment could be given in Swiss francs.

This was the first case after *Miliangos v George Frank (Textiles) Ltd*[262] where the court had to consider whether the principle of that decision extended to a claim for damages for breach of contract, rather than a claim for the payment of a debt. In allowing the claim in Swiss francs, EVELEIGH J relied on Swiss law, the law governing the contract, under which law the defendant was treated as if it was a debtor. This justified the application of the *Miliangos* principle that judgment may be given in a foreign currency, but also indicated that the currency in which the loss is to be calculated should be determined by the governing law. The questions whether, in a contract action, judgment should be given in a foreign currency and, in a case where there is more than one possible currency, in which currency, have been held to depend on general principles of the law of contract and on rules of private international law:

> The former require application, as nearly as possible of the principle of *restitutio in integrum*, regard being had to what was in the reasonable contemplation of the parties. The latter involve ascertainment of the proper law of the contract, and application of that law. If the proper law is English, the first step must be to see whether, expressly or by implication, the contract provides an answer to the currency question.[263]

It ought logically to follow that, if the determination of the currency in which damages for breach of contract are to be calculated is a matter of substance for the law governing

---

[258] Giving effect to the Athens Convention on the Carriage of Passengers by Sea, contained in Sch 6, Part I of the 1995 Act.

[259] 1995 Act, Sch 6, Part I, Art 9.

[260] *Services Europe Atlantique Sud v Stockholms Rederiaktiebolag SVEA, The Folias* [1979] AC 685 at 700; and see *Miliangos v George Frank (Textiles) Ltd* [1976] AC 443 at 465.

[261] [1977] QB 182.

[262] [1976] AC 443.

[263] *Services Europe Atlantique Sud v Stockholms Rederiaktiebolag SVEA, The Folias* [1979] AC 685 at 700.

the contract, it should also be a matter of substance so far as claims in tort are concerned. The tort position is less clear because in the one relevant decision, *The Despina R*,[264] English law was applied without reference to the fact that the tort in question was committed in China. One can argue that, where foreign law is not pleaded, it is deemed to be the same as English law.[265]

Turning now to the English rules for determining the currency in which damages should be assessed, the House of Lords has taken the view[266] that, once the obligation to give judgment in sterling has been abandoned, any rule[267] that, where damages consisted of loss incurred directly in a foreign currency, the damages must be assessed in that currency, should also be abandoned. Instead the court must identify the currency of the claimant's loss for:

> a plaintiff, who normally conducts his business through a particular currency, and who, when other currencies are immediately involved, uses his own currency to obtain those currencies, can reasonably say that the loss he sustains is to be measured not by the immediate currencies in which the loss first emerges but by the amount of his own currency, which in the normal course of operation, he uses to obtain those currencies. This is the currency in which his loss is felt, and is the currency which it is reasonably foreseeable he will have to spend.[268]

Guidance in determining the currency of loss in claims for damages is provided by two decisions, which were consolidated on appeal to the House of Lords in 1979, one in contract, the other in tort. In *Services Europe Atlantique Sud v Stockholms Rederiaktiebolag SVEA, The Folias*[269] the facts were as follows:

> By contract governed by English law, the plaintiff, a French company, chartered a Swedish ship from the defendants. Owing to defective refrigeration, the cargo was damaged on arrival in Brazil. The plaintiff settled a claim by the receiver of the cargo, paying him in Brazilian currency. In arbitration proceedings, the defendants admitted liability, but maintained that they should reimburse the plaintiff in Brazilian currency, the currency the plaintiff had used to settle the claim, and not in French francs, the currency used by the plaintiff to buy the Brazilian cruzeiros.

Judgment was given in French francs as the currency most truly expressing the plaintiff's loss. Again, the significance of the decision lies in inflation, because the Brazilian currency had weakened greatly against the French franc between the date of settling the claim and the date of judgment. The decision, therefore, protected the plaintiff from the effects of this fluctuation.

Where a contract is governed by English law, the determination of the currency in which payment is to be made is ascertained in the first instance by reference to the terms of

---

[264] [1979] AC 685, infra, p 108. In *Hoffman v Sofaer* [1982] 1 WLR 1350, another tort case, both the law of the place where the tort was committed and the law of the forum were English.

[265] Infra, p 111 et seq.

[266] *Services Europe Atlantique Sud v Stockholms Rederiaktiebolag SVEA, The Folias* [1979] AC 685.

[267] Eg *Di Ferdinando v Simon, Smits & Co Ltd* [1920] 3 KB 409; *SS Celia v SS Volturno* [1921] 2 AC 544; *The Canadian Transport* (1932) 43 Lloyd's Rep 409.

[268] [1979] AC 685 at 697.

[269] [1979] AC 685; Bowles and Whelan (1979) 42 MLR 452; and see *Ozalid Group (Export) Ltd v African Continental Bank Ltd* [1979] 2 Lloyd's Rep 231; *Food Corpn of India v Carras (Hellas) Ltd* [1980] 2 Lloyd's Rep 577; *Société Francaise Bunge SA v Belcan NV* [1985] 3 All ER 378.

the contract. If it provides expressly or impliedly for the currency in which damages are to be calculated[270] then judgment should be given in that currency. In the absence of such provision in the contract, where the claimant incurs expenditure as a consequence of the defendant's breach of contract, judgment for damages should be in the currency most truly expressing the claimant's loss,[271] provided the parties can be taken reasonably to have this in contemplation.[272] This will not necessarily be the currency of the expenditure which may[273] or may not[274] be the currency of the contract.

The other 1979 House of Lords decision is in the tort field, *The Despina R*.[275]

> The plaintiff's ship and the defendants' ship, both Greek, were in collision in Shanghai harbour. The plaintiff's ship received temporary repairs in Shanghai and then went to Japan and eventually to the USA for further repairs. The plaintiff, having expended sums on repairs and other expenses in Chinese and Japanese currencies, in US dollars and in sterling, sought payment of these sums as damages for the harm negligently done to its ship, arguing that they should be expressed in US dollars, that being the currency in which it carried on its business.

Their Lordships held that damages in tort, as in contract, are payable in the currency of the plaintiff's loss, here US dollars, being the currency which the plaintiff is able to show is that in which he normally conducts trading operations.[276]

Reference to the currency of the claimant's loss must be qualified. This is because, if the claimant has exacerbated his loss by use of his own currency, he runs the risk that the use of his own currency may be too remote a consequence of the defendant's conduct as to justify quantifying his loss by reference to it.[277] The principle laid down in *The Despina R* is of general application, whatever the basis of the tort claim, even though that case only related to the torts of negligence and damage to property.[278] In *Hoffman v Sofaer*[279] the court was prepared to award the plaintiff, an American, damages in dollars for loss of earnings stemming from negligent medical treatment suffered in England. Damages for pain, suffering and loss of amenity were given in sterling, however, on the ground that it would be impossible to assess them in dollars.[280]

We have seen that judgments, other than for unliquidated damages, may be given in foreign currency. In the case of a debt or claim for liquidated damages, the contract may provide for the currency in which the debt is to be paid; and judgment should be given in that currency.[281] In other cases, where the money of account (the currency in which the

---

[270] Ibid, at p 700; and see *Jugoslavenska Oceanska Plovidba v Castle Investment Co Inc* [1974] QB 292 at 298;

[271] [1979] AC 685, 701–703, 705; and see *The Texaco Melbourne* [1994] 1 Lloyd's Rep 473.

[272] Ibid at p 701; see *Metaalhandel JA Magnus BV v Ardfields Transport Ltd* [1988] 1 Lloyd's Rep 197.

[273] *Federal Commerce and Navigation Co Ltd v Tradax Export SA* [1977] QB 324 at 341–342; revsd on other grounds [1978] AC 1.

[274] [1979] AC 685 at 702.

[275] [1979] AC 685; Knott (1980) 43 MLR 18; and see *The Lash Atlantico* [1987] 2 Lloyd's Rep 114.

[276] *Per* Lord WILBERFORCE at 698.

[277] See the Court of Appeal, [1978] QB 396 at 437; and see [1979] AC 685 at 697–699.

[278] Cf *North Scottish Helicopters Ltd v United Technologies Corpn Inc (No 2)* 1988 SLT 778.

[279] [1982] 1 WLR 1350; and see *Kraut AG v Albany Fabrics Ltd* [1977] QB 182 at 189.

[280] Ibid at 1357. Cf *Fullemann v McInnes's Executor* 1992 SLT 259.

[281] *Services Europe Atlantique Sud (SEAS) v Stockholms Rederiaktiebolag SVEA, The Folias* [1979] QB 491 at 514.

obligation is measured) is different from the money of payment (the currency in which the obligation is discharged), judgment should normally be given in the former.[282] If, however, the contract provides an agreed rate of exchange between the two, judgment should be given in the money of payment.[283] In the case of a restitutionary claim,[284] the award should be related not to the claimant's loss, but to the currency of the defendant's benefit. Where the benefit is money, the award should normally be for repayment by the defendant in the same currency as that in which he received payment. If the benefit is other than money, then the award should be in the currency in which the benefit can be "most fairly and appropriately valued".[285]

(h) Execution

Judgments and the execution of judgments, being integral parts of the process which the claimant has elected to adopt, are necessarily subject to the law of the forum. The particular mode of execution admitted by that law, whether more or less favourable to the claimant than that recognised by the law governing the transaction, has exclusive application. This principle covers such matters as whether the judgment may be satisfied out of land or goods;[286] whether debts in the hands of third parties can be attached by third party debt order; whether a receiver may be appointed; whether a writ *ne exeat regno* is procurable; or whether personal constraint is permissible. Thus, where a Portuguese, who had been arrested in the course of English proceedings for non-payment of a debt which was due to a Spaniard under a Portuguese contract, applied to be discharged from custody on the ground that he was not liable to arrest by the law governing the contract, the application was refused.[287]

---

[282] *George Veflings Rederi A/S v President of India* [1978] 1 WLR 92; affd [1979] 1 WLR 59; cf *BP Exploration Co (Libya) Ltd v Hunt (No 2)* [1979] 1 WLR 783 at 840–841.

[283] *President of India v Taygetos Shipping Co SA* [1985] 1 Lloyd's Rep 155.

[284] *BP Exploration Co (Libya) Ltd v Hunt (No 2)* [1979] 1 WLR 783 at 837–845 (affd [1983] 2 AC 352); see infra, Chapter 20.

[285] Ibid at 840.

[286] But where, in the case of a mortgage, the governing law provides that both the property mortgaged and other property of the debtor are liable for the debt, this amounts to a substantive rule, applicable even though the law of the forum restricts the claim to the property mortgaged; *Sigurdson v Farrow* (1981) 121 DLR (3d) 183; and see *243930 Alberta Ltd v Wickham* (1990) 73 DLR (4th) 474.

[287] *De la Vega v Vianna* (1830) 1 B & Ad 284.

Chapter 7

The Proof of Foreign Law[1]

1. FOREIGN LAW: A QUESTION OF FACT

The established rule is that knowledge of foreign law,[2] even of the law obtaining in some other part of the common law world, is not to be imputed to an English judge.[3] Even though the foreign law is notorious, it has been said that the court cannot take judicial notice of it.[4] Unless the foreign law with which a case may be connected is pleaded by the party relying thereon, it is assumed that it is the same as English law.[5] The onus of proving

---

[1] Fentiman, *Foreign Law in English Courts* (1998), (1992) 108 LQR 142; Geeroms, *Foreign Law in Civil Litigation* (2004)—for a comparative study; Hartley (1996) 45 ICLQ 271; Lando (1995) 2 Maastricht JECL 359, at 367–372; Hood (2006) 2 J Priv Int L 181. The EC Commission is required to produce a study (by 20 August 2011) on the way in which foreign law is treated in different jurisdictions and on the extent to which courts in Member States apply foreign law pursuant to the Rome II Regulation on non-contractual obligations, Art 30(1)(i); discussed, infra, pp 789–790.

[2] This can include Sharia law: *Shamil Bank of Bahrain EC v Bexico Pharmaceuticals Ltd* [2004] EWCA Civ 19, [2004] 1 WLR 1784; *Al-Bassam v Al-Bassam* [2004] EWCA Civ 857.

[3] *Nelson v Bridport* (1846) 8 Beav 547, though cf *Saxby v Fulton* [1909] 2 KB 208 at 211; *Harold Meyers Travel Service Ltd v Magid* (1975) 60 DLR (3d) 42 at 44; *El Ajou v Dollar Land Holdings plc* [1993] 3 All ER 717 at 736; revsd by the Court of Appeal [1994] 2 All ER 685 but not on this point; *Grupo Torras SA and Torras Hostench London Ltd v Sheikh Fahad Mohammed Al-Sabah* [1996] 1 Lloyd's Rep 7 at 18, CA. Judicial notice is taken of European Community law, which, of course, is not technically foreign law, see the European Communities Act 1972, s 3.

[4] *El Ajou v Dollar Land Holdings plc* [1993] 3 All ER 717 at 736; revsd by the Court of Appeal [1994] 2 All ER 685 but not on this point. For criticism of this see *Morgan Grenfell & Co Ltd v Istituto per I Servizi Assicurativi del Commercio* [2001] EWCA Civ 1932 at [53]. See generally Fentiman, *Foreign Law in English Courts* (1998), pp 248–251.

[5] *Macmillan Inc v Bishopsgate Investment Trust plc (No 4)* [1999] CLC 417, CA; *El Ajou v Dollar Land Holdings plc*, supra; *Kuwait Oil Tanker Co SAK v Al Bader* [2000] 2 All ER (Comm) 271 at 336, CA; *Al-Wazir v Islamic Press Agency Inc* [2001] EWCA Civ 1276 at [20], [42]–[43], [2002] 1 Lloyd's Rep 410; *Société Eram Shipping Co Ltd v Compagnie Internationale de Navigation* [2001] EWCA Civ 1317 at [45], [2001] 2 Lloyd's Rep

that it is different, and of proving what it is, lies on the party who pleads the difference.[6] If there is no such plea, or if the difference is not satisfactorily proved,[7] the court must give a decision according to English law, even though the case may be connected solely with some foreign country,[8] and the law of that foreign country is applicable according to English choice of law rules.[9] The difficulty that there can sometimes be in applying this presumption is illustrated by a decision of the High Court of Australia[10] where, although there was proof that there was a flexible exception to the general tort choice of law rule that exists under Chinese law, there was inadequate evidence as to how this was applied

---

627; revsd [2003] UKHL 30, [2004] 1 AC 260 without discussion of this point; *Concord Trust v The Law Debenture Trust Corpn plc* [2005] UKHL 27 at [44], [2005] 1 WLR 1591; *PT Pan Indonesia Bank Ltd TBK v Marconi Communications International Ltd* [2005] EWCA Civ 422 at [70]; *Balmoral Group Ltd v Borealis* [2006] EWHC 1900 (Comm) at [427]–[435]; [2006] 2 Lloyd's Rep 629; *Sharp v Ministry of Defence* [2007] EWHC 224 (QB). See also *McGowan v Summit at Lloyds* 2002 SLT 1258 at 1263; *Attorney-General for England and Wales v R* [2002] 2 NZLR 91 CA; *Backman v The Queen* (1999) 178 DLR (4th) 126, Fed CA; *Davison v Sweeney* (2005) 255 DLR (4th) 757. Foreign principles of public policy are presumed to be the same as English ones; *Royal Boskalis Westminster NV v Mountain* [1999] QB 675 at 725 (per PHILLIPS LJ), 689 (per STUART-SMITH LJ), CA. For criticism of the presumption in a case of defamation see *Schapira v Ahronson* [1998] IL Pr 587 at 599, CA and where the Court's process of execution was sought to be invoked see the *Société Eram Case* [2001] 2 Lloyd's Rep 394 at 398 (per TOULSON J) but cf the Court of Appeal, op cit, at [55]–[56]. See criticism where the foreign legal system is very different from the forum: *Neilson v Overseas Projects Corpn of Victoria Ltd* [2005] HCA 54 at [203] (per KIRBY J). See generally on exceptions to the presumption, Fentiman, *Foreign Law in English Courts* (1998), pp 146–148; *Damberg v Damberg* [2001] 52 NSWLR 492 at [119]–[162], NSWCA; *Shaker v El-Bedrawi* [2002] EWCA Civ 1452 at [64]–[72], [2003] Ch 350. This presumption may not be applied where the claimant asks for summary judgment: *National Shipping Corpn v Arab* [1971] 2 Lloyd's Rep 363. Nor in a case where an injunction is sought preventing acts of passing off abroad, *Dunhill v Sunoptic* [1979] FSR 337; or acts of infringement, *International Business Machines Corpn v Phoenix Intercontinental (Computers) Ltd* [1994] RPC 251. Nor has it been applied in a tax case involving German law, which is not a common law based system: *Damberg v Damberg*, supra, at [162], distinguished in *Tisand v Owners of the Ship MV Cape Moreton (Ex Freya)* [2005] FCAFC 68, (2005) 219 ALR 48. Nor has it been applied where the proper law of a contract was foreign and there was no proof of that law: *Global Multimedia v ARA Media Services* [2006] EWHC 3107 (Ch) at [37]–[40], [2007] 1 All ER (Comm) 1160. Nor has it been applied where there was only proof of part of the foreign law: *Tamil Nadu Electricity Board v St CMS Electricity Co* [2007] EWHC 1713 (Comm) at [97]–[98], [2007] 2 All ER (Comm) 701. It should be pointed out that there are a number of cases where an English court has not assumed the foreign law to be the same as English statute law: *R v Brixton Prison Governor, ex p Caldough* [1961] 1 All ER 606; *Osterreichische Länderbank v S'Elite Ltd* [1981] QB 565 at 569; and see *Purdom v Pavey & Co* (1896) 26 SCR 412; *BP Exploration Co (Libya) Ltd v Hunt* (1980) 47 FLR 317; *The Mercury Bell v Amosin* (1986) 27 DLR (4th) 641; *Shaker v El-Bedrawi*—possibly where an English statute cannot be applied without significant modification; cf *De Reneville v De Reneville* [1948] P 100; for Australia see *National Auto Glass Supplies v Nielsen & Moller Autoglass* [2007] FCA 1625 at [33]–[45]. See also Hartley (1996) 45 ICLQ 271, 285–289 who mentions exceptions in relation to criminal proceedings, international obligations not to enforce a contract and, without judicial authority to support this, status and illegality.

[6] *The King of Spain v Machado* (1827) 4 Russ 225 at 239; *Ascherberg Hopwood and Crew v Casa Musicale Sonzogno* [1971] 1 WLR 173, affd ibid at 1128; *Kutchera v Buckingham International Holdings Ltd* [1988] IR 61 at 68; *Kraus's Administrators v Sullivan* 1998 SLT 963; *Glencore International AG v Metro Trading International Inc (No 2)* [2001] 1 Lloyd's Rep 284 at [55]; the *PT Pan Indonesia Bank* Case, supra, at [70].

[7] In the latter situation, it is not necessary for the opposing party to adduce his own contradictory evidence: the *PT Pan Indonesia Bank* Case, supra, at [70].

[8] *Warner Bros v Nelson* [1937] 1 KB 209; *Cressington Court (Owners) v Marinero (Owners), The Marinero* [1955] 1 All ER 676; *Mount Cook (Northland) Ltd v Swedish Motors Ltd* [1986] 1 NZLR 720; cf *Guépratte v Young* (1851) 4 De G & Sm 217 at 224–225. As to the alternatives open to a court when a party fails to prove foreign law, see Kahn-Freund (1974) III Hague Recueil 139, 422–426. See generally North, *Essays*, pp 179–181.

[9] For torts see infra, pp 789–790; Fentiman, *Foreign Law in English Courts* (1998), p 106. For the position in relation to contract see, infra, p 696, n 257; Fentiman, op cit, pp 87 et seq. See also *Sharp v Ministry of Defence* [2007] EWHC 224 (QB) at [11]–[12].

[10] *Neilson v Overseas Projects Corpn of Victoria Ltd* [2005] HCA 54; Briggs [2006] LMCLQ 1.

and whether it would be applied in the circumstances of the present case. The majority applied the presumption and asked how an Australian court would construe an Australian statute, concluding, in the light of this, that this exception would be applied by a Chinese court.[11] There is much force in a critical dissenting judgment which pointed out that Australian law had no such flexible exception and argued that construction could not be divorced from what was being construed.[12]

Foreign law is, therefore, treated as a question of fact but it is "a question of fact of a peculiar kind".[13] To describe it as one of fact is no doubt apposite, in the sense that the applicable law must be ascertained according to the evidence of witnesses, yet there can be no doubt that what is involved is at bottom a question of law. This has been recognised by the courts.[14] The rule, for instance, in a purely domestic case is that an appellate court will disturb a finding of fact by the trial judge only with the greatest reluctance, but this is not so when the "fact" that has been found in the court below is the relevant rule of a foreign legal system.[15] In such a case the role of the appellate court has been described in terms of a "duty . . . to examine the evidence of foreign law which was before the justices and to decide for ourselves whether that evidence justifies the conclusion to which they came".[16] Nevertheless, the courts have concluded that a mistake as to foreign law is to be regarded as a mistake of fact.[17]

2. HOW FOREIGN LAW IS PROVED[18]

It is clear that the relevant foreign law on some particular matter must be proved, like other matters of which no knowledge is imputed to the judge, "by appropriate evidence, ie by properly qualified witnesses",[19] unless both parties agree to leave the investigation

---

[11] *Neilson v Overseas Projects Corpn of Victoria Ltd*, supra, at [125]–[127] (per GUMMOW and HAYNE JJ), [249] (per CALLINAN J), [267] (per HEYDON J).

[12] Ibid at [36] (McHUGH J). KIRBY J at [203] and GLEESON CJ at [16] also found the presumption of no assistance.

[13] *Parkasho v Singh* [1968] P 233 at 250; *Macmillan Inc v Bishopsgate Investment Trust plc (No 4)* [1999] CLC 417, CA; *Morgan Grenfell & Co Ltd v Istituto per I Servizi Assicurativi del Commercio* [2001] EWCA Civ 1932 at [45]; *King v Brandywine Reinsurance* Co [2005] EWCA Civ 655 at [66]–[67], [2005] 1 Lloyd's Rep 655, Briggs (2005) BYBIL 660; *Abu Dhabi Investment Co v H Clarkson & Co Ltd* [2006] EWHC 1252 (Comm) at [26], [2006] 2 Lloyd's Rep 381. Propositions of foreign law which a claimant advances in order to succeed against a person claiming contribution under the Civil Liability (Contribution) Act 1978, s 1, are not properly to be regarded as part of the factual basis of the claim against such person: *Arab Monetary Fund v Hashim (No 8)* (1993) Times, 17 June; see also *Arab Monetary Fund v Hashim (No 9)* (1994) Times, 11 October.

[14] See, eg, *Egmatra AG v Marco Trading Corpn* [1999] 1 Lloyd's Rep 862; *Reliance Industries Ltd v Enron Oil and Gas India Ltd* [2002] 1 Lloyd's Rep 645—Arbitration Act 1996, s 69 (appeals on a question of law) cases.

[15] *Grupo Torras SA and Torras Hostench London Ltd v Sheikh Fahad Mohammed Al-Sabah* [1996] 1 Lloyd's Rep 7 at 18, CA.

[16] *Parkasho v Singh*, supra; *Dalmia Dairy Industries Ltd v National Bank of Pakistan* [1978] 2 Lloyd's Rep 223 at 286; and see Webb (1967) 16 ICLQ 1152, 1155–1156; Fentiman, *Foreign Law in English Courts* (1998), pp 201–202. Proof of foreign law in an appellate court is discussed further, infra, pp 118–119.

[17] *The Amazonia* [1990] 1 Lloyd's Rep 236, CA; and see *Andre & Cie SA v Ets Michel Blanc & Fils* [1979] 2 Lloyd's Rep 427, CA.

[18] See generally Fentiman, *Foreign Law in English Courts* (1998), Chapter VI.

[19] *Nelson v Bridport* (1845) 8 Beav 527 at 536; *Beatty v Beatty* [1924] 1 KB 807 at 814; *Lazard Bros & Co v Midland Bank* [1933] AC 289; *El Ajou v Dollar Land Holdings plc* [1993] 3 All ER 717 at 736; revsd by the Court of Appeal [1994] 2 All ER 685 but not on this point; *Grupo Torras SA and Torras Hostench London Ltd v Sheikh Fahad Mohammed Al-Sabah* [1996] 1 Lloyd's Rep 7 at 17 et seq, CA; *R v Okolie* (2000) Times, 16 June, CA.

to the judge and to dispense with the aid of witnesses.[20] This method of proof by way of expert witnesses has been criticised on the basis that it can involve a vast amount of oral and written evidence, leading to inordinate delay and expense.[21] Efforts have been made under the civil procedure rules to remedy this by giving the courts power to control expert evidence;[22] even so, it remains the case that, subject to section 4(2) of the Civil Evidence Act 1972,[23] foreign law cannot be proved, for instance, by citing a previous decision of an English court in which the same foreign rule was in issue,[24] or by merely presenting the judge with the text of the foreign law and leaving him to draw his own conclusions,[25] or by referring to a decision in which a court of the foreign country has stated the meaning and effect of the law in question.[26] A fortiori, it cannot be proved by referring to a decision as to the law of the foreign country in question given in the courts of some other foreign country.[27] Nor can it be proved by the assertion of an opinion as to the effect of the foreign law without reference to the relevant authorities.[28] However, the parts of the United Kingdom form an exception to these rules in cases coming before the House of Lords as the ultimate appellate tribunal in civil matters. Thus Scottish law must be proved by evidence in the courts inferior to the House of Lords, but in the House of Lords itself, which is the common forum of both England and Scotland, it is a matter of which their Lordships have judicial knowledge.[29]

However, proof of foreign law, including Scots and Northern Irish law, is rendered easier by s 4(2) of the Civil Evidence Act 1972. It provides that, when any question of foreign law has been determined in civil or criminal proceedings in the High Court, the Crown Court, certain other courts or in appeals therefrom, or in proceedings before the Judicial Committee of the Privy Council on appeal from courts abroad,[30] any finding made or decision given in such proceedings shall, if reported in citable form,[31] be admissible in later civil proceedings as evidence of the foreign law.[32] Indeed, the foreign law shall be

---

Cf *Lear v Lear* (1973) 51 DLR (3d) 56. This is by no means a universal law. By German, Belgian and Netherlands law, for instance, foreign law is regarded as law, not fact and is commonly ascertained by personal research by the court itself, Geeroms, *Foreign Law in Civil Litigation* (2004), paras 2.132–2.175, Hartley, op cit, pp 275–276. In New Zealand, the court has power to decide a question of foreign law in the absence of other expert evidence: Evidence Act, 1908, s 40; *Dymocks Franchise Systems (NSW) Pty Ltd v Todd* [2002] UKPC 50, [2004] 1 NZLR 289.

[20] *Jabbour (F & K) v Custodian of Israeli Absentee Property* [1954] 1 WLR 139 at 147–148; *Dalmia Dairy Industries Ltd v National Bank of Pakistan* [1978] 2 Lloyd's Rep 223 at 236; *Islamic Republic of Iran v Berend* [2007] EWHC 132 (QB) at [35], [2007] 2 All ER 132.

[21] *Grupo Torras SA and Torras Hostench London Ltd v Sheikh Fahad Mohammed Al-Sabah*, supra, at 17.

[22] Discussed infra, p 117.

[23] Infra.

[24] *Lazard Bros & Co v Midland Bank Ltd*, supra; *McCormick v Garnett* (1854) 23 LJ Ch 777; *Re Marseilles Extension Rly and Land Co* (1885) 30 Ch D 598 at 602. But in *Re Sebba* [1959] Ch 166, DANCKWERTS J considered that in the circumstances he was justified in departing from this rule.

[25] *Buerger v New York Life Assurance Co* (1927) 96 LJKB 930 at 940.

[26] *Beatty v Beatty* [1924] 1 KB 807 at 814–815; *Guaranty Trust Co of New York v Hannay & Co* [1918] 2 KB 623 at 638, 667.

[27] *Callwood v Callwood* [1960] AC 659; Webb (1960) 23 MLR 556; Carter (1960) 36 BYBIL 408.

[28] *Mount Cook (Northland) Ltd v Swedish Motors Ltd* [1986] 1 NZLR 720. See also *Astra SA Insurance and Reinsurance Co v Sphere Drake Insurance Ltd* [2000] All ER (D) 672.

[29] *Elliot v Joicey* [1935] AC 209 at 236. This rule is unaffected by the Civil Evidence Act 1972, s 4(2), infra.

[30] S 4(4).

[31] S 4(5).

[32] See *Phoenix Marine Inc v China Ocean Shipping Co* [1999] CLC 478.

taken to be in accordance with such finding or decision unless the contrary is proved, provided it does not conflict with another finding of foreign law adduced in the same proceedings.[33]

The English courts have not adopted the practice in civil law systems according to which a government may be requested to give an official statement of the law on some particular matter. By the British Law Ascertainment Act 1859, however, a court within Her Majesty's Dominions, which is of the opinion that it is necessary or expedient for the disposal of a case to ascertain the law of some part of Her Majesty's Dominions, may remit to a superior court in the latter place the question of law on which a ruling is required.[34] The provisions of this Act may be extended by Order in Council to other British territories.[35]

Foreign law had formerly to be proved to the satisfaction of the jury, but the Supreme Court Act 1981[36] has now provided as follows:

Where . . . it is necessary to ascertain the law of any other country which is applicable to the facts of the case, any question as to the effect of the evidence given with respect to that law shall, instead of being submitted to the jury, be decided by the judge alone.

3. WITNESSES WHO CAN PROVE FOREIGN LAW[37]

It is obvious that no witness can speak to a question of law as a fact and that all he can do is to express his opinion. The rule is, therefore, that he must be an expert. The question as to who is a sufficient expert in this matter has not been satisfactorily resolved by the English decisions.[38] Though no doubt the court has a discretion in the matter, the general principle has been that no person is a competent witness unless he is a practising lawyer in the particular legal system in question, or unless he occupies a position or follows a calling in which he must necessarily acquire a practical working knowledge of the foreign law. In other words, practical experience is a sufficient qualification. Thus, in accordance with this principle:

A Roman Catholic bishop was allowed to testify to the matrimonial law of Rome, since a knowledge of its provisions was essential to the performance of his official duties.[39]

---

[33] Findings or decisions as to foreign law in earlier proceedings may only be adduced if notice is given to all other parties: s 4(3).

[34] S 1. The European Convention on Information on Foreign Law, sometimes referred to as the London Convention, Treaty Series No 117 (1969) (Cmnd 4229) sets out to achieve the same aims as the 1859 Act in respect of foreign countries generally. The Convention has been ratified by the United Kingdom, but has never been implemented. See Fentiman, *Foreign Law in English Courts* (1998), pp 239–244; Geeroms, *Foreign Law in Civil Litigation* (2004), paras 2.256–2.257; Dicey, Morris and Collins, para 9-024; Rodger and Van Doorn (1997) 46 ICLQ 151; Rodger 1998 SLT 80.

[35] Foreign Jurisdiction Act 1890, s 5, Sch 1.

[36] S 69(5), replacing Administration of Justice Act 1920, s 15 and Supreme Court of Judicature (Consolidation) Act 1925, s 102. The Act applies to criminal trials: *R v Hammer* [1923] 2 KB 786.

[37] See generally Fentiman, *Foreign Law in English Courts* (1998), pp 178–182.

[38] Falconbridge, op cit, pp 833–838.

[39] *The Sussex Peerage Case* (1844) 11 Cl & Fin 85; distinguish *R v Savage* (1876) 13 Cox CC 178; see also *R v Ilich* [1935] NZLR 90.

A hotel-keeper in London, a native of Belgium, who had formerly been a commissioner of stocks in Brussels, was admitted to prove the Belgian law of promissory notes, on the ground that his business had made him conversant with commercial law.[40]

An ex-Governor of Hong Kong was held competent to prove the marriage law of that colony.[41]

A secretary to the Persian Embassy was allowed to depose to the law of Persia, on it being shown that there were then no professional lawyers in that country, but that all diplomatic officials had to be thoroughly versed in the law.[42]

Where it was necessary to ascertain the meaning of a bill of exchange given in Chile, the evidence of a London bank director with long experience of banking in South America was preferred to that of a young man who had been at the Chilean Bar for four years.[43]

An experienced police officer from Quebec was able to prove the road traffic law of that Province before an Ontario court.[44]

The view taken by the courts was that a mere academic knowledge of foreign law scarcely qualified a person as an expert witness. Thus in *Bristow v Sequeville*[45] where it was necessary to prove the law in force at Cologne, a witness was called who stated that he was a jurist and legal adviser to the Prussian consul in England, and that having studied law at Leipzig University, but never practised in Prussia, he knew from his studies there that the Code Napoléon applied in Cologne. It was held that he was not a competent witness. But although it has been said that study alone is not sufficient qualification,[46] the courts did not consistently observe the requirement of practical experience. Thus the Reader in Roman-Dutch law to the Council of Legal Education, who had made a special study of that law for the purpose of his lectures, was admitted to testify to Rhodesian law;[47] an English barrister, who in the course of his profession had made researches into the marriage laws of Malta, was held competent to prove the validity of a marriage that had been solemnised at Valetta;[48] evidence as to the law of Chile was admitted from an English solicitor who, though never a practitioner in that country, stated that he had considerable experience of its laws;[49] and, in another case,[50] evidence as to Egyptian law was admitted from an English barrister who had practised before the mixed courts and British consular courts in Egypt until they ceased to function, thirteen years earlier. Since then he had had no right of audience in Egyptian courts, though he had done his best to keep his

---

[40] *Vander Donckt v Thellusson* (1849) 8 CB 812; distinguish *Perlak Petroleum Maatschappij v Deen* [1924] 1 KB 111.

[41] *Cooper-King v Cooper-King* [1900] P 65. The only lawyer who could be found to give such expert evidence had demanded "a prohibitive fee of fifteen guineas".

[42] *Re Dhost Aly Khan's Goods* (1880) 6 PD 6.

[43] *De Béche v South American Stores* [1935] AC 148. The evidence of a bank manager was also accepted in *Said Ajami v Customs Comptroller* [1954] 1 WLR 1405; distinguished in *Clyne v Federal Comr of Taxation (No 2)* (1981) 57 FLR 198.

[44] *Guerin v Proulx* (1982) 37 OR (2d) 558.

[45] (1850) 5 Exch 275; *Re Bonelli's Goods* (1875) 1 PD 69.

[46] *Re Turner* [1906] WN 27.

[47] *Brailey v Rhodesia Consolidated Ltd* [1910] 2 Ch 95; and see *Barford v Barford* [1918] P 140.

[48] *Wilson v Wilson* [1903] P 157.

[49] *Re Whitelegg's Goods* [1899] P 267.

[50] *Rossano v Manufacturers' Life Insurance Co Ltd* [1963] 2 QB 352.

knowledge of Egyptian law up to date. It has now been made clear, by section 4(1) of the Civil Evidence Act 1972, that evidence as to foreign law may be given by a person who is qualified to do so on account of his knowledge and experience "irrespective of whether he has acted or is entitled to act as a legal practitioner there".[51] Subsequently, a Dutch academic lawyer who had undertaken extensive research and had wide contact with Indonesian lawyers and practice was qualfied to give evidence as to the land law of Indonesia[52] and an academic lawyer has given evidence on UAE law.[53]

4. THE ROLE OF THE COURT[54]

Under the Civil Procedure Rules the courts have the power to control expert evidence for the purpose of reducing costs and delay. No party may call an expert or put in evidence an expert's report without the court's permission.[55] Expert evidence is to be given in a written report unless the court directs otherwise.[56] A party may put written questions to an expert instructed by another party about his report.[57] The court may, at any stage, direct a discussion between experts with a view to identifying issues and their reaching an agreed opinion on these issues.[58] Where two or more parties wish to submit expert evidence on a particular issue, the court may direct that the evidence on that issue is to be given by one expert only.[59] The court may give permission for oral evidence on a case management occasion. An expert has an overriding duty to help the court on the matters within his expertise.[60] This overrides any duty to the person from whom he has received instructions or by whom he is paid.[61]

Although he must state his opinion as based on his knowledge or practical experience of the foreign law, the expert may refer to codes, decisions or treatises for the purpose of refreshing his memory, but in such an event the court is at liberty to examine the law or passage in question in order to arrive at its correct meaning.[62] If the expert witnesses disagree the court must look at the sources of the foreign law.[63] Even if the expert witness is uncontradicted by other expert testimony, the court may examine the texts in order to reach its own conclusions on the foreign law, though where the expert evidence

---

[51] See in relation to evidence given by affidavit, *Practice Direction (Foreign Law Affidavit)* [1972] 1 WLR 1433.
[52] *PT Royal Bali Leisure v Hutchinson & Co Trust Co Ltd* [2004] EWHC 1014 (Ch) at [107].
[53] *Glencore International AG v Metro Trading International Inc (No 2)* [2001] 1 Lloyd's Rep 284 at [52]. See also *Evialis SA v SIAT* [2003] EWHC 863, [2003] 2 Lloyd's Rep 377 at [43]; *Shiblaq v Sadikoglu* [2004] EWHC 1890 (Comm) at [4]–[12], [2004] IL Pr 51; *Abu Dhabi Investment Co v H Clarkson & Co Ltd* [2006] EWHC 1252 (Comm), [2006] 2 Lloyd's Rep 381.
[54] Fentiman, *Foreign Law in English Courts* (1998), pp 188–202.
[55] CPR, r 35.4.
[56] CPR, r 35.5.
[57] CPR, r 35.6.
[58] CPR, r 35.12.
[59] CPR, r 35.7.
[60] CPR, r 35.3(1).
[61] CPR, r 35.3(2).
[62] *Concha v Murrietta* (1889) 40 Ch D 543; *Russian Commercial and Industrial Bank v Comptoir d'Escompte de Mulhouse* [1923] 2 KB 630 at 643; *Re Cohn* [1945] Ch 5; see 61 LQR 340; *De Beéche v South American Stores Ltd and Chilian Stores Ltd* [1935] AC 148 at 158–159; *Parkasho v Singh* [1968] P 233 at 250–252, 254.
[63] *Arros Invest Ltd v Rafik Nishanov* [2004] EWHC 576 (Ch) at [22], [2004] IL Pr 22.

is uncontradicted, the court should be reluctant to reject it,[64] unless it is absurd.[65] However, the power to reject the expert's opinion is not confined to instances of absurdity in at least one situation, namely where the English court interprets a foreign statute in accordance with English rules of construction, there being no evidence that different rules would govern the foreign court's interpretation.[66] Essentially the judge's finding is as to statutory interpretation and as such is one of law. The court should not examine texts which have not been relied on by the expert or by counsel.[67] Again, if there is a conflict of testimony between the expert witnesses on either side, the court must place its own interpretation on the foreign law in the light of all the evidence given,[68] having regard to the preponderance of legal opinion before it.[69] The evidence of one expert may be accepted as a whole over that of another but is, nevertheless, not accepted on a particular issue.[70] It may be necessary to find the proper construction of a particular foreign provision by inference from the evidence of one or both of the experts, applying the rules of construction under the foreign law.[71] The expert proves the foreign rules of construction and the court itself, in the light of these rules, determines the meaning of contractual documents.[72] In all cases, in fact, it is the right and duty of the court to examine and criticise the evidence.[73]

The question of proof of foreign law in an appellate court has been examined by Sir Jocelyn SIMON P who said:

> Foreign law is, it is true, regarded in English courts as a question of fact; and appellate courts are slow to interfere with trial courts on questions of fact; but that only applies with particular force as regards the assessment of relative veracity and the judgment of matters

---

[64] *Sharif v Azad* [1967] 1 QB 605 at 616; *Grupo Torras SA and Torras Hostench London Ltd v Sheikh Fahad Mohammed Al-Sabah* [1996] 1 Lloyd's Rep 7 at 18, CA; *James Hardie & Co v Hall* (1998) 43 NSWLR 554 at 573.

[65] The *Grupo Torras* case, supra. Contrast the view of expert evidence taken in *Re Russian Bank for Foreign Trade* [1933] Ch 745 with the view taken of the same expert's evidence in *Re Banque des Marchands de Moscou (Koupetschesky)* [1958] Ch 182 and see Civil Evidence Act 1972, s 4(2), supra, p 114.

[66] *Macmillan Inc v Bishopsgate Investment Trust plc (No 4)* [1999] CLC 417, CA; *Hunt v T & N plc* (1993) 109 DLR (4th) 16 at 29–30 (Sup Ct Can).

[67] *Bumper Development Corpn Ltd v Metropolitan Police Comr* [1991] 1 WLR 1362.

[68] *Trimbey v Vignier* (1834) 1 Bing NC 151; *Di Sora v Phillips* (1863) 10 HL Cas 624 at 636–642; *Lazard Bros & Co v Midland Bank Ltd* [1933] AC 289 at 298; *Sinfra Akt v Sinfra Ltd* [1939] 2 All ER 675; *Parkasho v Singh* [1968] P 233; *Grupo Torras SA and Torras Hostench London Ltd v Sheikh Fahad Mohammed Al-Sabah* [1996] 1 Lloyd's Rep 7 at 18, CA; *Macmillan Inc v Bishopsgate Investment Trust plc (No 4)* [1999] CLC 417, CA; *Gulf Consolidated v CSFB Ltd* [1992] 2 Lloyd's Rep 301 at 303; Fentiman, *Foreign Law in English Courts* (1998), pp 200–201.

[69] *Shiblaq v Sadikoglu* [2004] EWHC 1890 (Comm) at [10], [2004] IL Pr 51.

[70] *Gulf Consolidated v CSFB Ltd*, supra, at 303–304.

[71] Ibid.

[72] Dicey, Morris and Collins, para 9-019; *King v Brandywine Reinsurance Co* [2005] EWCA Civ 655 at [68], [2005] 1 Lloyd's Rep 655; *Evialis SA v SIAT* [2003] EWHC 863 (Comm) at [44], [2003] 2 Lloyd's Rep 377; *Toomey (Syndicate 2021) v Banco Vitalicio de España SA de Seguros y Reaseguros* [2003] EWHC 1102 (Comm) at [37], appeal dismissed without discussion of this point [2004] EWCA Civ 622 at [37], [2004] 1 CLC 965; *Svenska Petroleum Exploration v Government of the Republic of Lithuania (No 2)* [2005] EWHC 2437 (Comm) at [29], [2006] 1 Lloyd's Rep 181, appeal dismissed without discussion of this point [2006] EWCA Civ 1529.

[73] *Tallinna Laevaushisus (A/S) v Estonian State Steamship Line* (1947) 80 Lloyd's Rep 99 at 108; *Rouyer Guillet et Cie v Rouyer Guillet & Co Ltd* [1949] 1 All ER 244 n; *Re Fuld's Estate (No 3), Hartley v Fuld* [1968] P 675 at 700–703; as to the question of the court examining the constitutionality of foreign legislation, see Mann (1943) 59 LQR 155; Lipstein (1967) 42 BYBIL 265; Kahn-Freund (1974) III Hague Recueil 139, 449–452; Kahn-Freund, *Festschrift für F A Mann*, p 207.

of degree. Where the inference of fact depends on the consideration of written material, an appellate court is at no particular disadvantage compared to a trial court and will regard itself as freer to review the decision of the trial court.[74]

The Court of Appeal has interfered with the judge's finding of fact in the situation where this was contrary to the views of both side's experts.[75] The Court of Appeal is entitled and bound to form its own view, independently of the trial judge's view, on the issue of construction of a foreign statute, where its interpretation has been in accordance with English rules of construction, there being no evidence that different rules would govern the foreign court's interpretation.[76] Due regard must, however, be paid to the relevant circumstances as found by the judge.

---

[74] *Parkasho v Singh*, supra, at 254. See also *Grupo Torras SA and Torras Hostench London Ltd v Sheikh Fahad Mohammed Al-Sabah* [1996] 1 Lloyd's Rep 7 at 18, CA.

[75] *Grupo Torras SA and Torras Hostench London Ltd v Sheikh Fahad Mohammed Al-Sabah*, supra, at 23.

[76] *Macmillan Inc v Bishopsgate Investment Trust plc (No 4)* [1999] CLC 417, CA.

Chapter 8

Exclusion of Foreign Law

It is obvious that circumstances will occasionally arise in which the law of the forum must be preferred to the foreign law that would normally be applicable to the case. An outstanding example of this is the civil law doctrine of *ordre public* under which any domestic rule designed to protect the public welfare must prevail over an inconsistent foreign rule. The danger of a doctrine so vague as this is that it may be interpreted to embrace such a multitude of domestic rules as to provide a fatally easy excuse for the application of the law of the forum and thus to defeat the underlying purpose of private international law. The analogous English doctrine, though less unruly, is indeed not above suspicion in this respect. Summarily stated, it withholds all recognition from any foreign law or judgment which is repugnant to the distinctive policy of English law, and it refuses to enforce any foreign law which is of a penal, revenue or other public law nature.[1]

---

[1] Holder (1968) 17 ICLQ 926; Smart (1986) 35 ICLQ 704; Carter (1989) 48 CLJ 417; Lipstein in Banakas (ed), *United Kingdom Law in the 1980s*, p 38 and Forsyth, ibid, p 94.

Furthermore, foreign expropriatory laws will, in some circumstances, not be recognised, and, in other circumstances, although recognised, will not be enforced. Finally, the mandatory rules of the forum may be applied, with the result that, to that extent, a foreign law is excluded.

We will now deal separately with these four[2] cases.

1. FOREIGN REVENUE, PENAL AND OTHER PUBLIC LAWS

Dicey, Morris and Collins[3] employs a three-fold classification of foreign laws which will not be enforced by English courts, ie revenue laws, penal laws and other public laws. This classification, which was first adopted by Lord DENNING in *A-G of New Zealand v Ortiz*,[4] has been endorsed by the Court of Appeal on a number of occasions,[5] has been given the support of the House of Lords in *Re State of Norway's Applications (Nos 1 and 2)*,[6] and was enshrined in statutory form for the area of tort choice of law by the Private International Law (Miscellaneous Provisions) Act 1995.[7] The same classification has also been adopted by the High Court of Australia,[8] the Court of Appeal in New Zealand[9] and in the High Court in Ireland.[10] "Public laws" is, seemingly, the umbrella concept which encompasses both revenue and penal laws, but also allows for a category of "other public laws".[11] The common thread running through the exclusionary rule in relation to revenue, penal and other public laws is that laws will not be enforced if they involve an assertion of sovereign authority by one state within the territory of another.[12] If the exclusionary rule applies it has been said that, in conceptual terms, what the court is doing is declining to exercise its jurisdiction.[13] Whether the claim sought to be enforced in the English courts is one

---

[2] There is also the doctrine of foreign Act of State, which is beyond the scope of this book, see *Buttes Gas and Oil Co v Hammer (No 3)* [1982] AC 888; distinguished in *Kuwait Airways Corpn v Iraqi Airways Co (Nos 4 and 5)* [2002] UKHL 19, [2002] 2 AC 883; Dicey, Morris and Collins, paras 5-041–5-050.

[3] Dicey, Morris and Collins, para 5R-019.

[4] [1984] AC 1 at 20 et seq. Cf ACKNER LJ at 34 and O'CONNOR LJ at 35. The House of Lords decided the case on a narrow point of construction: infra, p 128, n 63.

[5] See *Williams & Humbert Ltd v W & H Trade Marks (Jersey) Ltd* [1986] AC 368 at 394, 401; see also in the House of Lords the judgment of Lord MACKAY at 437, cf Lord TEMPLEMAN at 428; *Re State of Norway's Application* [1987] QB 433 at 477–478; *United States of America v Inkley* [1989] QB 255 at 265–265; *Camdex International Ltd v Bank of Zambia (No 2)* (1997) CLC 714, CA; *Mbasogo v Logo Ltd* [2006] EWCA Civ 1370 at [51], [2007] QB 846; Briggs (2006) 77 BYBIL 554.

[6] [1990] 1 AC 723.

[7] S 14(3)(a)(ii); the 1995 Act is discussed infra, pp 767–768. Choice of law for non-contractual obligations is now largely governed by the Rome II Regulation; discussed infra, pp 770–858.

[8] *A-G (UK) v Heinemann Publishers Australia Pty Ltd (No 2)* (1988) 165 CLR 30.

[9] *A-G for the United Kingdom v Wellington Newspapers Ltd* [1988] 1 NZLR 129.

[10] *Bank of Ireland v Meeneghan* [1995] 1 ILRM 96 at 101.

[11] *USA v Inkley*, supra, at 264–265.

[12] *Re State of Norway's Applications (Nos 1 and 2)*, supra, at 807–808. See also *Mbasogo v Logo Ltd* [2006] EWCA Civ 1370 at [41], [50], [51], [2007] QB 846; Mills [2007] CLJ 3; Scott [2007] LMCLQ 296 and (2007) 2 J Priv Int L 309; *Tasarruff v Demirel* [2006] EWHC 3354 (Ch) at [63], [2007] IL Pr 8; affd without discussion of this point [2007] EWCA Civ 799, [2007] 1 WLR 2508. According to the *Mbasogo* case, the same principle underlies both the exclusion of foreign revenue, penal and other public laws and the act of state doctrine. See also *President of the State of Equatorial Guinea v Royal Bank of Scotland International* [2006] UKPC 7 at [23]–[28]; Briggs (2006) 77 BYBIL 554.

[13] *Re State of Norway's Applications (Nos 1 and 2)*, supra, at 807–808. The practical consequence is that the claim will be struck out as not justiciable. This means that the standard of proof in relation to the issue of

which involves a penal, revenue or other public law is an issue to be determined according to the criteria of English law.[14] It is irrelevant whether a foreign law so regards it.[15] The three related concepts of revenue, penal and other public laws will now be examined.

(a) Foreign revenue laws[16]

(i) The prohibition on enforcement

Although it has been generally accepted, at any rate since the time of Lord MANSFIELD,[17] that no action lies in England for the enforcement of a foreign revenue law, authority for the proposition long remained a little nebulous, with the issue only being raised clearly on just one or two occasions.[18] All doubts were, however, stilled in 1955 by the decision of the House of Lords in *Government of India v Taylor*,[19] where, after a company, registered in England but carrying on business in India, had gone into voluntary liquidation, a demand was made on it by the Indian Commissioner of Income Tax for the payment of a large sum of income tax in respect of the capital gain derived from the earlier sale of the business. The Commissioner claimed to prove for this debt in the liquidation, but his claim was rejected by the liquidator and by the lower courts. It was argued for the appellants in the House of Lords that the alleged rule excluding the recognition of foreign revenue laws did not extend to taxes similar to those imposed in England, but was confined to penal laws, and that in any event it demanded modification in the case of a foreign country belonging to the Commonwealth. Further, it was said that the rule, even if accepted in toto, did not apply to liquidation proceedings, for a liquidator is under a statutory duty to discharge all the "liabilities" of the company, which is a word of wide import not confined to debts directly enforceable by action.

These arguments were rejected. Their Lordships were unanimous in holding that the rule expressed by Lord MANSFIELD rested on a solid basis of authority and convenience.[20] They also held, with one dissentient,[21] that the duty of a liquidator in the winding up of a company is confined to the discharge of such liabilities as are legally enforceable.

---

exclusion is whether the claimant has a real prospect of succeeding (a serious issue to be tried) on the claim, rather than that of a good arguable case: *Tasarruff v Demirel* [2006] EWHC 3354 (Ch) at [62], [2007] IL Pr 8; affd without discussion of this point [2007] EWCA Civ 799, [2007] 1 WLR 2508, leave to appeal to the House of Lords dismissed [2007] 1 WLR 3066.

14 *USA v Inkley*, supra, at 265.

15 *Tasarruff v Demirel* [2006] EWHC 3354 (Ch) at [65], [2007] IL Pr 8; affd without discussion of this point [2007] EWCA Civ 799, [2007] 1 WLR 2508, leave to appeal to the House of Lords dismissed [2007] 1 WLR 3066.

16 See especially M Mann (1954) 3 ICLQ 465, and the judgment of KINGSMILL MOORE J in the Irish case of *Peter Buchanan Ltd and Macharg v McVey* [1955] AC 516 n, [1954] IR 89. See also Albrecht (1950) 30 BYBIL 454, 459–465; Castel (1964) 42 Can Bar Rev 277; Stoel (1967) 16 ICLQ 663, 671 et seq; F A Mann (1971) I Hague Recueil 115, 172–181; Carter (1984) 55 BYBIL 111.

17 *Holman v Johnson* (1775) 1 Cowp 341 at 343.

18 See eg *Sydney Municipal Council v Bull* [1909] 1 KB 7; *Re Visser* [1928] Ch 877. See also *The Eva* [1921] P 454; *King of the Hellenes v Brostrom* (1923) 16 Lloyd's Rep 167 and 190; *Metal Industries (Salvage) v Owners of the S T Harle* 1962 SLT 114; cf *The Acrux* [1965] P 391; Webb (1965) 28 MLR 591.

19 [1955] AC 491; see also *Williams and Humbert Ltd v W and H Trade Marks (Jersey) Ltd* [1986] AC 368 at 428, discussed infra, pp 135–137; *USA v Harden* (1963) 41 DLR (2d) 721; *Rothwells v Connell* (1993) 119 ALR 538 at 548–549.

20 But the rule will only operate if the English court classifies the claim as a tax or revenue claim, eg, *Weir v Lohr* (1967) 65 DLR (2d) 717; *Connor v Connor* [1974] 1 NZLR 632; the former case also indicates that the rule may well not operate between the states of a federal country; see also *Permanent Trustee Co (Canberra) Ltd v Finlayson* (1967) 9 FLR 424; revsd on another point (1968) 122 CLR 338.

21 Lord KEITH.

(ii) Indirect enforcement

The rule that no action lies to recover foreign taxes is not affected by the identity of the claimant or by the form in which the action is brought. "In every case the substance of the claim must be scrutinised, and if it then appears that it is really a suit brought for the purpose of collecting the debts of a foreign revenue it must be rejected."[22] That an indirect evasion of the rule will not be tolerated is well illustrated by *Rossano v Manufacturers' Life Insurance Co Ltd*:[23]

> The plaintiff was an Egyptian national resident in Alexandria, who brought an action to recover money due under three policies of life insurance issued by the defendant, an insurance company with a head office in Toronto and branches in many other countries. The first two policies required payment in London in pounds sterling; the third directed payment at New York in dollars.

One defence raised by the defendant was that two garnishee orders[24] had been served on three of its branches in Cairo which would render it responsible for the payment of certain taxes alleged to be due from the plaintiff to the Egyptian government if it paid him before he had satisfied this fiscal liability. The defence failed, for to allow the garnishee orders, which related solely to taxation debts, to defeat the plaintiff's cause of action would constitute an indirect enforcement of a foreign revenue law. The obvious result of dismissing the action would be the recovery of the taxes by the Egyptian government.[25]

However, the prohibition on indirect enforcement of foreign revenue laws does not prevent an English court from assisting a foreign state to obtain evidence against one of that state's taxpayers. Thus an English court will accede to a request by a foreign state that witnesses in England give oral evidence pursuant to the Evidence (Proceedings in Other Jurisdictions) Act 1975,[26] even though this is in connection with proceedings in the foreign state against one of its taxpayers.[27] Seemingly, this is the case regardless of whether the taxpayer supports the request.

It is questionable whether the general ban on indirect enforcement is not too rigid. If, for instance, in the *Rossano Case*, the defendants had in fact paid the taxes due to the government, would not an action based upon the unjust enrichment of the plaintiff have succeeded? It may even be questioned whether such a decision as that reached in *Municipal*

---

[22] *Peter Buchanan Ltd and Macharg v McVey* [1955] AC 516 n at 529, [1954] IR 89 at 107; approved by the House of Lords in *Government of India v Taylor*, supra; *QRS 1 ApS v Fransden* [1999] 1 WLR 2169, CA; *Air India Ltd v Caribjet Inc* [2002] 2 All ER (Comm) 76. But see on the first two of these cases *Williams and Humbert Ltd v W and H Trade Marks (Jersey) Ltd* [1986] AC 368 at 440; see also *Re Lord Cable* [1977] 1 WLR 7 at 13. It is suggested in this last case that proceedings in England by a foreign government for direct enforcement of that government's currency control regulations, even against a citizen of that country, would be contrary to the principle of non-enforcement of foreign revenue laws; but cf *Kahler v Midland Bank Ltd* [1950] AC 24 at 46–47, 57; see also *A-G of New Zealand v Ortiz* [1984] AC 1 at 24 (per Lord Denning MR in the Court of Appeal).

[23] [1963] 2 QB 352.

[24] As to garnishment (third party debt orders), see infra, pp 1238–1239.

[25] See, eg, *Peter Buchanan Ltd and Mackay v McVey* [1955] AC 516 n, [1954] IR 89; *Williams and Humbert Ltd v W and H Trade Marks (Jersey) Ltd* [1986] AC 368 at 437–441; cf *Ayres v Evans* (1981) 39 ALR 129.

[26] Supra, pp 86–87.

[27] *Re State of Norway's Applications (Nos 1 and 2)* [1990] 1 AC 723.

Council of Sydney v Bull,[28] where the plaintiff failed in its bid to recover a contribution imposed by a local statute in respect of certain street improvements effected in the area where the defendant owned property, accords with the practice of states and their subordinate bodies to furnish services in return for payment.

The narrow dividing line is illustrated by *Brokaw v Seatrain UK Ltd*:[29]

> In this case goods were shipped from the USA to England in an American ship. Whilst the ship was at sea, the US Treasury served a notice of levy, in respect of taxes unpaid by the owners of the goods, on the shipowners demanding that the goods should be surrendered. When the ship arrived at Southampton, the shipowners refused to deliver the goods to the consignee, who claimed delivery or their value.

By reason of interpleader proceedings, the court had to consider the claim of the US Treasury, which was rejected on the basis that to allow it amounted to indirect enforcement of a foreign revenue law by seizure of goods. However, had the notice of levy been effective to reduce the goods into the possession of the US Treasury, their claim would have been upheld, for the court would then have been enforcing a possessory title rather than a revenue law.

It is now necessary to consider the extent to which the rule against the indirect enforcement of foreign revenue laws has been affected by United Kingdom accession to the European Economic Community. It has not been affected by the United Kingdom becoming a Contracting State to the Convention on Jurisdiction and the Enforcement of Judgments in Civil and Commercial Matters of 1968 (the Brussels Convention), now replaced for virtually all purposes by the Brussels I Regulation.[30] The Court of Appeal in *QRS 1 ApS v Fransden*,[31] which involved a claim that undeniably fell foul of the English exclusionary rule, held that this was a revenue matter within the meaning of Article 1 of the Brussels Convention.[32] As such, it fell outside the scope of that Convention. Moreover, the English exclusionary rule was not incompatible with the EEC Treaty.[33] However, the exclusionary rule has been affected by the European Community Regulation on Insolvency Proceedings.[34] Art 39 of the Regulation gives tax authorities and social security authorities of Member States the right to lodge proof as creditors in insolvency proceedings conducted in other Member States, provided that the proceedings come within the scope of the Regulation.[35] More importantly, European Community Directives provide for mutual assistance and recovery as between Member States in relation to duties and taxes.[36]

---

[28] [1909] 1 KB 7.

[29] [1971] 2 QB 476; see *A-G of New Zealand v Ortiz* [1984] AC 1 at 31–32 (per ACKNER LJ in the Court of Appeal). See also *Re Van de Mark and Toronto-Dominion Bank* (1989) 68 OR (2d) 379.

[30] And by the EC/Danish Agreement, see infra, pp 204–342.

[31] [1999] 1 WLR 2169, CA; Briggs (1999) BYBIL 341; Smart (2000) 116 LQR 360.

[32] Discussed infra, p 215. If it had been a matter within the scope of the Convention, the English exclusionary rule could not be invoked because it would impair the effectiveness of the Convention, [1999] 1 WLR 2169 at 2177–2178, CA.

[33] In particular Art 59, [1999] 1 WLR 2169 at 2178–2180, CA.

[34] Council Regulation (EC) No 1346/2000 of 29 May 2000, OJ 2000 L 160/1.

[35] See Fletcher, *Insolvency in Private International Law* (2005) 2nd edn, para 2.94.

[36] Council Directive (EEC) No 76/308 (the Mutual Assistance Recovery Directive as amended by Council Directive (EEC) No 79/1071 and Council Directive (EC) No 2001/44 and as implemented by Commission Directive (EC) No 2002/94); implemented in the United Kingdom by SI 2004/674.

(iii) Recognition of a foreign revenue law

This rule that no action will lie at the instance of a foreign state to enforce a revenue law does not mean, despite what Lord MANSFIELD said in *Holman v Johnson*,[37] that such a law is to be totally ignored.[38] Refusal to enforce it implies no disclaimer of its lawful existence, and circumstances may require that its existence be recognised. Thus, on the ground that public policy demands the maintenance of harmonious relations with other nations, the courts will not countenance any transaction, such as a fraudulent tax-evasion scheme, which is knowingly designed to violate a revenue law of a foreign and friendly state.[39] If personal representatives have had personally to pay taxes on a foreign estate under foreign revenue laws, those foreign laws will be recognised here so as to enable the personal representatives to be indemnified from assets of the estate situated here.[40] Furthermore, in such cases the personal representatives should be given leave to remit the assets to the foreign country for payment of the taxes.[41]

(b) Foreign penal laws[42]

It is well settled that an English court will not lend its aid to the enforcement, either directly or indirectly, of a foreign penal law.[43] The imposition of a penalty normally reflects the exercise by a state of its sovereign power, and it is an obvious principle that an act of sovereignty can have no effect in the territory of another state.

(i) The meaning of a penalty

The word "penalty" is equivocal, and if understood without qualification it comprises penalties to the enforcement of which there can be no objection, as for example one incorporated in a commercial contract with the object of inducing the prompt performance of his contract by one of the parties.[44] What, therefore, is the meaning of the word in the present context? The answer given by the Privy Council in *Huntington v Attrill*,[45] the leading English authority on the subject, is that it is limited to a fine or other exaction imposed by the state for some violation of public order of a criminal complexion.[46]

---

[37] (1775) 1 Cowp 341 at 343: "No country takes notice of the revenue laws of another."

[38] *Regazzoni v KC Sethia (1944) Ltd* [1956] 2 QB 490 at 515; affd [1958] AC 301 at 319; *X, Y and Z v The Bank* [1983] 2 Lloyd's Rep 535 at 546–547; cf *Sharif v Azad* [1967] 1 QB 605 at 617; *Mackender v Feldia AG* [1967] 2 QB 590 at 601. See also *Bank of Ireland v Meeneghan* [1995] 1 ILRM 96.

[39] *Re Emery's Investment Trusts* [1959] Ch 410; *Pye Ltd v BG Transport Service Ltd* [1966] 2 Lloyd's Rep 300 at 308–309. See also *Euro-Diam Ltd v Bathurst* [1990] 1 QB 1 at 39–40.

[40] *Re Lord Cable* [1977] 1 WLR 7 at 25–26; and see *Re Reid* (1970) 17 DLR (3d) 199.

[41] *Re Lord Cable* [1977] 1 WLR 7 at 25–26; and see *Scottish National Orchestra Ltd v Thomson's Executor* 1969 SLT 325.

[42] See especially FA Mann (1954) 40 Grotius Society 25; M Mann (1956) 42 Grotius Society 133, and see Stoel (1967) 16 ICLQ 663.

[43] *Ogden v Folliott* (1790) 3 Term Rep 726; *Wolff v Oxholm* (1817) 6 M & S 92; *Huntington v Attrill* [1893] AC 150; *Frankfurther v WL Exner Ltd* [1947] Ch 629; *Empresa Exportadora de Azúcar v Industria Azucarera Nacional SA, The Playa Larga* [1983] 2 Lloyd's Rep 171; *X, Y and Z v The Bank* [1983] 2 Lloyd's Rep 535; *A-G of New Zealand v Ortiz* [1984] AC 1; *Williams and Humbert Ltd v W and H Trade Marks (Jersey) Ltd* [1986] AC 368. For Canada see *Pro Swing Inc v Elta Golf Inc* 2006 SCC 52.

[44] *Huntington v Attrill* [1893] AC 150 at 156.

[45] [1893] AC 150.

[46] See also *Lewis v Eliades* [2003] EWCA Civ 1758 at [50], [2004] 1 WLR 693 a penalty "normally means a sum payable to the state, and not to a private individual", leave to appeal to the House of Lords refused [2004] 1 WLR 1393; *Schemmer v Property Resources Ltd* [1975] Ch 273.

Applying this definition, an order made pursuant to a criminal statute confiscating a convicted person's assets will not be enforced, nor will a restraint order,[47] nor will an order committing a person to prison for contempt of court.[48] Nor will an order for contempt of court arising out of an action between private parties be enforceable.[49] Lord DENNING MR has indicated[50] that, in the context of recognition of foreign judgments, a judgment for exemplary damages is not to be denied recognition as being in respect of "a penalty".[51] A Canadian court has come to the same conclusion in relation to a judgment for punitive damages.[52] It may well be, therefore, that a foreign law as to exemplary or punitive damages will be applied here and will not be castigated as a penal law.[53] On the other hand, there is a statutory prohibition on the enforcement of foreign judgments for multiple damages,[54] such as treble damages under the USA anti-trust laws. These laws have been described as penal.[55] More recently, the Court of Appeal has accepted, obiter, that this is arguable but found it unnecessary to decide the point.[56]

(ii) Examples of the prohibition on indirect enforcement of a penal law

An example of an attempt to enforce a foreign penalty indirectly is *Banco de Vizcaya v Don Alfonso de Borbón y Austria*[57] where the facts were these:

> The former King of Spain had bought certain securities with his own money and had instructed that they should be held by a London bank to the order of his agents, the Banco de Vizcaya, a Spanish concern. The Spanish Republican Government later decreed that all his property, wherever situated, should be confiscated and that anything deposited with Spanish banks should be delivered to the Treasury. The plaintiffs claimed delivery of the securities from the London bank on the ground that they had a contractual right of recovery by virtue of the instructions given by King Alfonso at the time of the original deposit.

---

[47] *Bank of Ireland v Meeneghan* [1995] 1 ILRM 96.

[48] *Gersten v The Law Society of New South Wales* [2002] NSWCA 344.

[49] *Pro Swing Inc v Elta Golf Inc* 2006 SCC 52.

[50] *SA Consortium General Textiles v Sun and Sand Agencies Ltd* [1978] QB 279 at 299–300. See also *Old North State Brewing Co v Newlands Services Inc* [1999] 4 WWR 573, BC CA. But cf the decision of the German Federal Supreme Court in *Re the Enforcement of a United States Judgment for Damages* (Case IX ZR 149/91) [1994] IL Pr 602.

[51] Infra, p 557.

[52] *Old North State Brewing Co v Newlands Services Inc* [1999] 4 WWR 573, BC CA. See also *Benefit Strategies Group Inc v Prider* [2005] SASC 194, (2005) 91 SASR 544. cf *Schnabel v Yung Lui* [2002] NSWSC 115, 1 February 2002 (unreported)—punitive damages consituting a penal award because of a public element (failure to comply with a court order).

[53] Cf *Travelers Casualty and Surety Co of Europe Ltd v Sun Life Assurance Co of Canada (UK) Ltd* [2004] EWHC 1704 at [77], [2004] IL Pr 50.

[54] Protection of Trading Interests Act 1980, s 5; infra, pp 561–563. Under the 1980 Act the Secretary of State can make orders prohibiting persons in the United Kingdom from complying with foreign extra-territorial measures which are damaging to United Kingdom trading interests; see ss 1–3.

[55] *British Airways Board v Laker Airways Ltd* [1984] QB 142 at 163 per (PARKER J), and in the Court of Appeal at 201; Paterson [1995] UBCLR 241. But cf *Old North State Brewing Co v Newlands Services Inc* [1999] 4 WWR 573, BC CA (treble damages based on an unfair and deceptive trade practice statute not anti-trust).

[56] *Lewis v Eliades* [2003] EWCA Civ 1758 at [50], [2004] 1 WLR 693; discussed infra, pp 562–563.

[57] [1935] 1 KB 140. A similar case is *Frankfurther v W L Exner Ltd* [1947] Ch 629. For an early example, see *Ogden v Folliott* (1790) 3 Term Rep 726.

LAWRENCE J held that the plaintiffs were not in reality asserting their own contractual rights as they originally existed, but the rights of the Spanish Republic. Therefore their claim failed, since to countenance it would in effect be to enforce an admittedly penal law of the Republic.

A more recent case to discuss the question of enforcement of a foreign penal law is *A-G of New Zealand v Ortiz*:[58]

> A Maori carved door was removed from New Zealand without permission of the appropriate authorities and was eventually offered for sale by the first defendant by auction in London. The Attorney-General of New Zealand (the plaintiff) alleged that the state was the owner of the door and sought an injunction in the English courts restraining the sale and an order for delivery up of the door. The basis of this claim was a New Zealand statute which, in certain circumstances, provided for the forfeiture, without compensation, of historic articles.

STAUGHTON J, at first instance, gave judgment for the plaintiff. The Court of Appeal allowed an appeal on the basis of a point of construction of the New Zealand statute.[59] It was held that the statute only provided for the forfeiture of historic articles when the goods had been seized by the appropriate New Zealand authorities, and this had not happened in the present case. However, the Court of Appeal went on to discuss the wider point of the nature of the New Zealand statute. Lord Justices ACKNER and O'CONNER held, obiter, that the New Zealand statute was a penal law and, therefore, would not be enforced in England.[60] The claim was made by the Attorney-General on behalf of the state, the cause of action concerned a public right—the preservation of historic articles within New Zealand, and vindication of the right was sought through forfeiture of the property without compensation.[61] Lord DENNING expressed himself in different terms; he regarded the New Zealand statute as coming within the category of a public law[62] rather than a penal law.[63]

(iii) Characterisation of the foreign law/right of action

It is undeniable that the English court must itself characterise the alleged penal, revenue or other public law, but regard will be had to the attitude adopted in the courts in the

---

[58] [1984] AC 1; Nott (1984) 33 ICLQ 203. See generally on claims by foreign states for return of their property, Collins, *Essays*, pp 118–129.

[59] [1984] AC 1 at 17–18, 29, 35.

[60] At 31–34, 35.

[61] At 33–34 (per ACKNER LJ).

[62] At 20–24; see infra, pp 130–131.

[63] On appeal to the House of Lords, the decision of the Court of Appeal was upheld solely on the narrow point of construction of the New Zealand statute. The Law Lords, at 45–49 (per Lord BRIGHTMAN), having heard no argument on the point relating to the enforcement of a penal law, declined to express any opinion on the correctness of the obiter dicta on this matter in the Court of Appeal. The result of the case is to leave a problem over the return of unlawfully exported cultural heritage. But see now *Islamic Republic of Iran v Barakat* (2008) Times, 7 January—claim to allow recovery of Iranian cultural heritage allowed. For attempts to solve the problem by international arrangements, see the Commonwealth Scheme for the Protection of the Material Cultural Heritage, 1993; O'Keefe (1995) 44 ICLQ 147; the UNIDROIT Convention on the International Return of Stolen or Illegally Exported Cultural Objects (1995) 34 ILM 1322. For the position within the European Community see SI 1994/501, SI 1997/1719, SI 2001/3972, implementing Council Directive (EEC) No 93/7 of 15 March 1993 on the return of cultural objects unlawfully removed from the territory of a Member State.

foreign jurisdiction.[64] According to the Privy Council in *Huntington v Attrill*[65] nothing can be regarded as a penalty unless it is "recoverable at the instance of the State or of an official duly authorised to prosecute on its behalf, or of a public informer".[66] The facts of the case were as follows:

> A New York statute, designed, inter alia, to protect the public against company promoters, provided that the directors of a corporation should be personally liable for its debts on proof that false reports of its financial condition had been published. Sums recoverable under this provision were payable to creditors in satisfaction pro tanto of their claims. A creditor instituted a suit under the statute in a New York court and obtained judgment for a large sum. He later brought an action on the judgment in Ontario. The New York courts had decided that actions brought under the statute were of a penal character.

The Privy Council held, first, that it was for the Ontario court to put its own interpretation on the statutory provision; and, secondly, that the statute was remedial, not penal, since it permitted a subject to enforce a liability in his own interests and for the protection of his own private rights.[67]

In *United States of America v Inkley*,[68] the Court of Appeal was faced with a more complex case involving an action by a foreign state, but which was clothed in civil form.

> An action was brought by the US government for enforcement of a judgment for the amount of an appearance bond plus interest obtained in a federal court in Florida, sitting as a civil court, against the defendant who had been released on bail but had subsequently failed to appear to answer criminal charges.

The Court of Appeal refused to enforce the judgment on the basis that this was an action by a foreign state to enforce the execution of its own public/penal law. Dicey, Morris and Collins's three-fold classification of the exclusionary rule was adopted. "Public laws" was seen as the wide overall exclusionary category, and a foreign penal law will necessarily also be a foreign public law. Whether the right of action which it is sought to have enforced in England is public or private was said to depend on three considerations: the party in whose favour the right is created; the purpose of the law on which the right is based; the general context of the case as a whole. The Court of Appeal held[69] that the action was concerned with the right of the US government to ensure the due observance of its criminal law; the purpose of the action was part of a public law process aimed to ensure the attendance of persons accused of crime before the criminal courts; the general context was criminal or penal. The essentially public/penal law nature of the action was not affected by the fact that it was dressed up in civil form. Applying these considerations

---

[64] *United States of America v Inkley* [1989] QB 255 at 265.

[65] [1893] AC 150; and see *Metal Industries (Salvage) Ltd v Owners of S T Harle* 1962 SLT 114 at 116.

[66] At 157, 158. See *A-G of New Zealand v Ortiz* [1984] AC 1 at 32 (per ACKNER LJ). See also *Bank of Ireland v Meeneghan* [1995] 1 ILRM 96.

[67] The Supreme Court of the US reached the same conclusion: (1892) 146 US 657.

[68] [1989] QB 255; Carter (1988) BYBIL 347. Cf *United States Securities and Exchange Commission v Cosby* 2000 BCSC 338—judgment in civil action by SEC ordering disgorgement of ill-gotten gains not penal; see also *US (SEC v Shull)* (1999) BCSC.

[69] At 265–266.

to the facts of the case it was concluded that: "Notwithstanding its civil clothing, the purpose of the action initiated by the writ issued in this case was the due execution by the United States of America of a public law process aimed to ensure the attendance of persons accused of crime before the criminal courts."[70]

(iv) Recognition of foreign penal laws

The enforcement of a foreign penal law must be distinguished from its application or recognition.[71] Although enforcement will not be allowed, it is going too far to assert that "the penal laws of one country cannot be taken notice of in another".[72] This is scarcely true for, subject to the possible intervention of the doctrine of public policy,[73] such a law must be regarded as operative even in English proceedings if it is part of the foreign legal system which, according to the relevant rule for the choice of law, governs the transaction that is sub judice.[74] If, for example, a Ruritanian statute makes the export of certain raw materials a crime punishable by fine and confiscation of property, in no circumstances will the fine be recoverable by an action in England. Nevertheless, if a Ruritanian businessman, by a contract that falls to be governed by the law of that country, agrees to sell the prohibited materials to an Englishman, an action brought against him in England for non-delivery must necessarily fail. The illegality of the contract according to its governing law, though springing from a crime and from a penal law devoid of extra-territorial effect, cannot be ignored.[75]

(c) Other foreign public laws[76]

Judicial and statutory adoption[77] of Dicey, Morris and Collins's three-fold classification of foreign laws which will not be enforced means that this third category is now firmly established. What we are concerned with here are public laws which are not revenue or penal ones. It is not difficult to find examples of "other public laws". Dicey, Morris and Collins[78] give the following as illustrations: import and export regulations; trading with the enemy legislation; price control regulations; and anti-trust legislation.[79] However, it is much more difficult to give a precise definition to the concept of "public laws", since the common law does not as yet recognise any clear distinction between public and private laws.[80] In *A-G of New Zealand v Ortiz*[81] Lord DENNING admitted that the concept

---

[70] At 266.

[71] M Mann (1956) 42 Grotius Society 133, 135–136.

[72] *Ogden v Folliott* (1790) 3 Term Rep 726 at 733.

[73] Infra, pp 139–150.

[74] See *A-G of New Zealand v Ortiz* [1984] AC 1 at 31 (per ACKNER LJ in the Court of Appeal). See also *Bank of Ireland v Meeneghan* [1995] 1 ILRM 96.

[75] The same principle affects a foreign revenue law, supra, p 126.

[76] See generally Baade (1995) 30 Texas Int LJ 429. For an exception in Australia and the USA see the Australia-United States Free Trade Agreement, Art 14.7, Hogan-Doran (2006) 80 ALJ 361.

[77] Supra, p 122. But cf *United States of America v Ivey* (1996) 139 DLR (4th) 570, Ont CA; discussed infra, p 132.

[78] Dicey, Morris and Collins, para 5-033. See also *United States of America v Ivey* (1996) 139 DLR (4th) 570, Ont CA.

[79] Anti-trust laws may be penal, see supra, pp 126–127.

[80] *Re State of Norway's Application* [1987] QB 433 at 475, affd by the House of Lords without discussion of this specific point [1990] 1 AC 723, 458. The problem of identifying public laws also arises in the context of jurisdiction under the Brussels/ Lugano system, see infra, pp 215–217.

[81] [1984] AC 1.

of "other public laws" was very uncertain, but went on to explain that they are laws which are eiusdem generis with penal or revenue laws.[82] He found a common thread underlying these three categories in the principles applied in international law; in particular, in the principle that laws will not be enforced if they involve an exercise by a government of its sovereign authority over property beyond its territory.[83] He concluded that legislation providing for the automatic forfeiture to the state of works of art should they be exported would come within this principle, and, accordingly, within the category of other public laws. In *Camdex International Ltd v Bank of Zambia (No 2)*,[84] the Court of Appeal held that the English courts would not entertain proceedings to enforce a civil cause of action that, it was argued,[85] the Bank of Zambia had under Zambian law against a Zambian mining company to recover foreign exchange due under a direction issued by the bank, on the basis that this would constitute enforcement of Zambian public law. In giving the direction the bank was exercising its authority under a Zambian statute as the agent responsible for administering exchange control. That legislation was part of the public law of Zambia enforceable by right of the authority of the Zambian State rather than by way of a private right in the bank.

The exclusion of other public laws has been accepted by the High Court of Australia and the Court of Appeal in New Zealand in the *Spycatcher Cases*,[86] which involved the important issues of confidentiality and state security. The Attorney-General of the United Kingdom sought, inter alia, injunctions in Australia and New Zealand to prevent publication in those respective countries of the whole or parts of *Spycatcher*, the memoirs of Peter Wright—a former intelligence officer of the British Security Services. The Attorney-General's argument, that Wright was acting in breach of duties of confidence (fiduciary and contractual) owed to the United Kingdom government, was assumed to be correct. One of the defences in both cases was that the Australian and New Zealand courts will not enforce a foreign penal or other public law.

Both the Australian and New Zealand courts refused to grant the relief sought, albeit on different grounds. The High Court of Australia regarded the action as one whereby the United Kingdom government sought to protect the efficiency of its Security Services as part of the defence of the country; as such, it fell within the exclusion of "other public laws". The New Zealand Court of Appeal, however, took a different view. The duty of confidentiality was said to arise from the relationship between the parties as employer

---

[82] At 20.
[83] See also *Camdex International Ltd v Bank of Zambia (No 2)* (1997) CLC 714; *Gotha City v Sotheby's (No 2)* (1998) Times, 8 October; *Robb Evans v European Bank Ltd* (2004) 61 NSWLR 75, NSWCA 82 (proceedings to secure a governmental interest), Thomas (2005) 121 LQR 380. But cf *Islamic Republic of Iran v Barakat* (2008), Times 7 January, CA.
[84] (1997) Times, 28 January 1997, CA; Briggs (1997) 68 BYBIL 369. The issue of enforcement of a foreign public law arose in the context of garnishment (now called a third party debt order) of a debt, see infra, pp 1238–1239.
[85] This argument was rejected by the Court of Appeal.
[86] In Australia: *A-G (UK) v Heinemann Publishers Australia Pty Ltd (No 2)* (1988) 165 CLR 30; see also *Trade Practices Commission v Australia Meat Holdings Pty Ltd* (1988) 83 ALR 299 at 360–363; *Robb Evans v European Bank Ltd* (2004) 61 NSWLR 75, NSWCA. In New Zealand: *A-G for the United Kingdom v Wellington Newspapers Ltd* [1988] 1 NZLR 129. Criticised by Mann (1988) 104 LQR 497; Collier [1989] CLJ 33; see also Lord KEITH in *A-G v Guardian Newspapers Ltd (No 2)* [1990] 1 AC 109, 264–265. The exclusion of "other public laws" has also been accepted in Hong Kong in a different context: *Nonus Asia Ltd v Standard Chartered Bank* [1990] 1 HKLR 396.

and employee. An action for damages (an injunction having earlier been refused on the basis that the contents of the book were already in the public domain) was therefore not barred by the exclusionary rule in relation to foreign penal or other public laws. Nonetheless, this was not thought to be a proper case for protecting the United Kingdom's security secrets since there had been prior publication abroad of the information in *Spycatcher*; moreover, the New Zealand public interest justified publication.

In contrast, the Ontario Court of Appeal has regarded the public law exception as resting on a rather shaky foundation, without though closing the door on such an exception.[87] On the assumption that there was such an exception, a US law which allows the US government to bring an action for compensation under a US statute for the cost of cleaning up environmental damage was not regarded as being a public law.[88] There were two reasons for this. First, the claim was concerned with clearing up damage in the USA.[89] Secondly, although asserted by a public authority the action was said to be so close to a claim for nuisance that it was in substance of a commercial or private law character. Relevant to this was the fact that such an action could be brought between private parties or against the government.

There is some controversy[90] over whether an English court "will refuse to enforce all public laws . . . or whether the court should only refuse to enforce a foreign public law if enforcement is contrary to public policy".[91] The uncertainty over this is reflected in the wording of the Private International Law (Miscellaneous Provisions) Act 1995.[92] This does not simply provide an exception to the normal statutory tort choice of law rules for cases involving a foreign penal, revenue or other public law. It qualifies this by referring to a foreign penal, revenue or other public law "as would not otherwise be enforceable under the law of the forum". This deliberately does not answer the question when such a foreign law would not be enforceable at common law.

2. FOREIGN EXPROPRIATORY LEGISLATION

A somewhat troublesome question is the extent to which foreign expropriatory legislation is recognised in England when it is directed, not against a particular person, as in

---

[87] *United States of America v Ivey* (1996) 139 DLR (4th) 570, Ont CA.

[88] As a result, judgments granted in the USA were enforceable, see infra, p 561.

[89] The Ontario Court of Appeal approved the reasoning of SHARPE J (1995) 130 DLR (4th) 674, who stressed this point at 689. See also *Gotha City v Sotherby's (No 2)*, supra.

[90] See Dicey, Morris and Collins, para 5-040.

[91] Collins, Proceedings of the Special Public Bill Committee, Private International Law (Miscellaneous Provisions) Bill, Further Memorandum *HL Paper* 36 (1995), p 68; see also Beaumont, p 77. The former view is seemingly supported by Lord DENNING in the *Ortiz* case; the latter by STAUGHTON J in the same case, by Brennan J in the High Court of Australia in the *Spycatcher* case, supra at 50–52, and by the Court of Appeal in *Islamic Republic of Iran v Barakat* (2008) Times, 7 January. See generally Vischer (1992-I) 232 Hague Recueil 9 at 150–153.

[92] S 14 (3)(a)(ii); the 1995 Act is discussed infra, pp 767–768. Tort choice of law is now largely governed by the Rome II Regulation on non-contractual obligations, infra, pp 770–858.

Don Alfonso's Case,[93] or a particular item, as in the *Ortiz Case*,[94] but against national property generally. It would seem that legislation of this nature may take four forms.[95]

First, *requisition*, which term is generally confined to the seizure of property in the public interest for a limited period, usually until the end of some emergency, and in return for compensation.

Secondly, *nationalisation*, which is the permanent absorption of property into public ownership in furtherance of some political aim and in return for compensation.

Thirdly, *compulsory acquisition*, which is the permanent seizure of property in fulfilment of some economic or social aim, and in exchange for compensation.

Fourthly, *confiscation*, which is the permanent seizure of private property without payment of compensation.[96]

The main question of private international law in this connection is the extent to which, in the eyes of English law, a decree of a foreign state implementing one of these forms of expropriation affects property belonging either to nationals of that state or to aliens.

The general principles that have a bearing on the question defy simple harmonisation, for against the principles that neither foreign legislation nor foreign penal laws have extra-territorial effect, stands the equally fundamental doctrine that a foreign sovereign cannot normally be impleaded.[97] If, for instance, the Ruritanian government obtains possession of jewellery held by a London bank on the ground that it falls within the scope of a Ruritanian decree of confiscation and if the decree is not regarded by English law as applicable to property in England, how can this view be rendered effective against a sovereign power that is immune from the jurisdiction?

Another obstacle to a simple generalisation of the law is the doubt whether all forms of property stand on the same footing for the purpose of determining the effect of expropriation. The suggestion, for instance, by no means unsupported by authority, has been made that a merchant ship stands in a category of its own, since it has a permanent situs in the country to which it belongs.[98] If this is correct, a state which requisitions or confiscates its national ships exercises a quasi-territorial, not an extra-territorial, act of authority.

If an English judge is required to determine the effect of foreign expropriatory legislation, his decision will depend on three main factors, namely the interpretation of the foreign legislation; the situs of the property at the time of the legislative decree; and the question whether the foreign sovereign was in actual possession or control of the property outside his territory at the time when the facts giving rise to the litigation occurred. The present law appears to be as follows.

---

[93] Supra, pp 127–128.

[94] Supra, p 128.

[95] See *I Congreso del Partido* [1983] 1 All ER 1092 at 1103, CA, revsd on a different point [1983] 1 AC 244; *Williams and Humbert Ltd v W and H Trade Marks (Jersey) Ltd* [1986] AC 368; infra, pp 135–136.

[96] See in relation to discharge of a debt by governmental act, *Wight v Eckhardt Marine GmbH* [2003] UKPC 37, [2004] 1 AC 147.

[97] Infra, pp 491–501.

[98] McNair (1946) 31 Grotius Society 30.

(a) Property within the foreign jurisdiction at time of decree

The English courts recognise without hesitation that the ownership of property is conclusively and finally determined by the terms of the foreign decree of expropriation if the property is situated within the jurisdiction of the sovereign at the time of the decree, notwithstanding that it is later brought to England and is still there at the time of the action. For instance, in *Luther v Sagor*:[99]

> Timber, situated in Russia and belonging to the plaintiff, a private company incorporated according to the law of Russia, was seized by the Soviet authorities under a decree that had nationalised all profits belonging to industrial and commercial establishments. Part of the timber was later brought to England and there sold to the defendants by a Soviet agent. The plaintiff sued for damages in what is now called conversion (formerly trover) on the ground that the ownership of the timber was still vested in it.

The Court of Appeal, on grounds which were not identical, found for the defendant.

In the view of WARRINGTON LJ, no sovereign state must sit in judgment upon the acts of another foreign state affecting property within its own territory.[100] BANKES LJ found it impossible to ignore the law of Russia, the law of the situs at the time of the decree, under which the seller had acquired a good title to the goods.[101] SCRUTTON LJ, following perhaps a more doubtful line of reasoning, argued that, since the doctrine of immunity would have prevented any investigation of the Russian sovereign's title had the timber been found in England in the possession of a Russian official, it followed that no such investigation was possible where possession had been given to a private purchaser. "What the court cannot do directly, it cannot do indirectly."[102]

But surely the simple and decisive justification of the decision is the rule that a title to movables, valid according to the law of the situs at the time of its acquisition, is recognised by English law.[103] The law of the situs must prevail in such circumstances unless the rule of that law under which the title has been acquired is so immoral or so alien to the principles of justice as understood in England that it must be disregarded as being contrary to public policy. The Court of Appeal considered this objection, but found it impossible to regard the nationalisation decree as anything else but the expression of a policy designed, whether mistakenly or not, to promote the best interests of Russians. This can be contrasted with *Kuwait Airways Corpn v Iraqi Airways Co (Nos 4 and 5)*[104] where an

---

[99] [1921] 3 KB 532 at 548. Followed in *Princess Olga Paley v Weisz* [1929] 1 KB 718; and see *Oppenheimer v Cattermole* [1976] AC 249 at 282–283; *Buttes Gas and Oil Co v Hammer (No 3)* [1982] AC 888 at 931; *Williams and Humbert Ltd v W and H Trade Marks (Jersey) Ltd* [1986] AC 368; *Westland Ltd v AOI* [1995] QB 282. Cf *Carl Zeiss Stiftung v Rayner and Keeler Ltd (No 2)* [1967] 1 AC 853. Quaere whether the decision would be the same if the owner escaped with his property from the country after the decree but before he had been deprived of possession by the local authorities.

[100] [1921] 3 KB 532 at 548–549.

[101] Ibid, at 545.

[102] Ibid, at 555–556.

[103] See the remarks of DEVLIN J in *Bank voor Handel en Scheepvaart NV v Slatford* [1953] 1 QB 248 at 260. See also *Peer International Corpn v Termidor Music Publishers Ltd* [2003] EWCA Civ 1156, [2004] Ch 212.

[104] [2002] 2 AC 883, HL; Rogerson [2003] CLP 265; Carruthers and Crawford (2001) 52 ICLQ 761; discussed further infra, pp 145–146; distinguished in *Peer International Corpn v Termidor Music Publishers Ltd* [2003] EWCA Civ 1156, [2004] Ch 212.

Iraqi Resolution divesting the Kuwaiti owners of aircraft situated in Iraq of their title was not simply a governmental expropriation of property within its territory, but was part of an attempt to extinguish every vestige of Kuwait as a separate state. The House of Lords held that enforcement or recognition of the Resolution would be manifestly contrary to the public policy of English law.[105]

The principle of *Luther v Sagor* was followed by the House of Lords in *Williams and Humbert Ltd v W and H Trade Marks (Jersey) Ltd*.[106] One point that should be noted from the outset about this case is that at first instance and in the Court of Appeal the case was regarded as one of confiscation of property, ie expropriation *without* payment, whereas the House of Lords treated it as a case of compulsory acquisition, ie expropriation *with* payment. Nonetheless, the principle in *Luther v Sagor* was still applied in all three courts. The facts of the case, according to the House of Lords, were as follows:

> The Spanish government compulsorily acquired all the shares of a company incorporated in Spain, Rumasa, and of the subsidiary companies of Rumasa incorporated in Spain, including two banks—"Jerez" and "Norte". Rumasa also held all the shares in an English company, Williams and Humbert; this company was now, therefore, indirectly controlled by the Spanish government. The plaintiffs, the English company and the three above-named Spanish companies, at the instigation of the Spanish government, brought actions in England against the defendants, the original owners of the Spanish companies, the Mateos family, and a Jersey company, for the return of property (in the form of trade marks and money), which it was alleged had been improperly diverted from the English company and one of the Spanish companies, and for damages. The defendants argued that the proceedings were an attempt to enforce a foreign penal law and/or it would be contrary to public policy to grant the relief sought.

NOURSE J ordered that the defence be struck out, as disclosing no reasonable defence, and this was upheld by a majority of the Court of Appeal. There were appeals to the House of Lords.

The House of Lords unanimously dismissed the appeals. Lord TEMPLEMAN, with whom the other Law Lords concurred, examined the decision in *Luther v Sagor* and then stated the principle that "an English court will recognise the compulsory acquisition law of a foreign state and will recognise the change of title to property which has come under the control of a foreign state and will recognise the consequences of that change of title".[107] Here, the property was the shares in the Spanish companies and this property was situated in Spain, the companies being incorporated there. The change in ownership of the shares was, accordingly, recognised. The Spanish government would have no right to confiscate the English property, ie the shares in Williams and Humbert; but, according to Lord TEMPLEMAN, it did not purport to do so, since this property would remain in the

---

[105] Public policy operated as an exception to tort choice of law rules, but if there had been an action asserting title to the aircraft, public policy would have operated as an exception to the lex situs rule, at 192 (per Lord SCOTT).

[106] [1986] AC 368; F A Mann (1986) 102 LQR 191; (1987) 103 LQR 26; (1988) 104 LQR 346; (1985) 56 BYBIL 316; Carter (1986) 57 BYBIL 439.

[107] At 431.

ownership of Rumasa, one of the Spanish companies.[108] In reality though, the Spanish government would control Williams and Humbert. The Spanish government would, therefore, be able to achieve by indirect means (confiscation of Rumasa) what it could not achieve by direct confiscation.

When it came to the specific allegation that what was involved was enforcement of a foreign penal law, Lord TEMPLEMAN doubted if the Spanish law could be regarded as penal.[109] Even if it was accepted that it was a penal law there was no attempt directly to enforce this law in England,[110] since the objective of the law, to acquire and control various companies, had already been achieved in Spain. Nor was there an attempt indirectly to enforce the Spanish law, since the actions were brought by the companies, and under well-established principles of company law these were distinct entities from the Spanish government which owned the companies.[111] If the argument that it was a penal law were to be accepted, it would produce the anarchic result that none of the companies could pursue actions outside Spain and wrongdoers vis à vis the companies would be released from liability.[112]

The *Williams and Humbert* case is also interesting for its discussion at first instance[113] and in the Court of Appeal[114] of foreign confiscatory laws. The Court of Appeal[115] agreed with NOURSE J, at first instance, that confiscatory laws should be classified as follows:

Class 1 laws, which the English courts will not recognise:

A. Foreign confiscatory laws which, by reason of their being discriminatory on grounds of race, religion or the like, constitute so grave an infringement of human rights that they ought not to be recognised as laws at all.

B. Foreign laws which discriminate against nationals of this country in time of war by purporting to confiscate their moveable property situated in the foreign state.

Class 2 laws,[116] which will be recognised, but to which effect will not be given:

A. Foreign laws confiscating property situated in the foreign state, if they are penal.

B. Foreign laws which purport to confiscate property situated in this country.

Class 3 laws, to which effect will be given provided they do not fall within Class 1: Foreign laws which confiscate property in the foreign state and where title has been perfected there.[117]

It was argued, at first instance, by counsel for the defence that there was a further category within Class 1 of foreign confiscatory laws which are aimed at confiscating the property

---

[108] At 428, 433.

[109] At 428; see also 437 (per Lord MACKAY).

[110] At 428–429; see also 437–441 (per Lord MACKAY).

[111] At 429.

[112] At 429–430. Lord TEMPLEMAN rejected the suggestion that a receiver should be appointed to deal with English assets and to recover debts; cf F A Mann (1962) 11 ICLQ 471; (1986) 102 LQR 191.

[113] [1986] 1 AC 375 at 379.

[114] [1986] 1 AC 389; Forsyth [1985] CLJ 376.

[115] At 392, 414.

[116] On which see *Gotha City v Sotheby's (No 2)* (1998) Times, 8 October.

[117] This quotation is from *Settebello Ltd v Banco Totta* [1985] 1 WLR 1050 at 1056 where the Court of Appeal adopted the classification of NOURSE J in the *Williams and Humbert* case.

of particular individuals or classes of individuals,[118] but NOURSE J denied the existence of any such category. It was at this point that it was argued, unsuccessfully,[119] that on the facts of the case there was an attempt to enforce a foreign confiscatory law which was penal or a public law (Class 2A).

One final point to note about the *Williams and Humbert* case is that, seemingly, it introduces a principle that, for reasons of comity, a party cannot plead in a case of compulsory acquisition that the foreign government has acted in an oppressive way.[120] Neither will the English courts consider the merits of the compulsory acquisition or the motives of the foreign government.[121] What is new is the suggestion that such matters cannot even be pleaded by a party.

The last question which has to be asked is whether the principle of *Luther v Sagor* applies where the confiscated property, though situated within the jurisdiction of the confiscating state, belongs to aliens. This was the main issue raised in *Anglo-Iranian Oil Co v Jaffrate*, better known as *The Rose Mary*,[122] where the court took the view that *Luther v Sagor* does not condone the confiscation of movables belonging to an owner who is not a national of the confiscating state unless adequate compensation is paid to him in return. It has subsequently been held by UPJOHN J, however, that neither the nationality of the dispossessed owner nor the payment of compensation to him affects the general principle laid down in *Luther v Sagor* and other cases.[123] The principle is that English law recognises the extra-territorial effectiveness of confiscatory legislation passed by a foreign state in respect of movables situated within its territory or of contracts governed by its law, unless the object is to confiscate the property of individual persons or classes of persons.

(b) Property outside the foreign jurisdiction at time of decree

If the property was outside the territory of the confiscating or requisitioning sovereign at the time of the decree, whether in England, in a foreign country or on the high seas, the first task of the judge is to construe the decree in order to ascertain whether it is in terms confined to property within the jurisdiction or whether it purports to affect property outside the territory. It is for the judge to form his own opinion on this question after hearing the evidence of expert witnesses.

If he comes to the conclusion that the decree was neither expressly nor implicitly directed against property in other countries or on the high seas, then the question is no longer significant. This was the substantial basis of the House of Lords decision in *Lecouturier v Rey*.[124] Under a French statute, the Carthusian monks had been expelled from France and deprived of their property. They continued, but now in Spain, to

---

118 [1986] 1 AC 375 at 381.

119 See the judgment of NOURSE J at 382–386; the argument was also rejected in the Court of Appeal, LLOYD LJ dissenting; for the House of Lords see supra, pp 135–136.

120 [1986] AC 368 at 431, 434, 436.

121 See also *Settebello Ltd v Banco Totta* [1985] 1 WLR 1050—a case involving the issue of letters of request.

122 [1953] 1 WLR 246.

123 *Re Helbert Wagg & Co Ltd* [1956] Ch 323. However, see O'Connell (1955) 4 ICLQ 270; Wortley, *Expropriation in Public International Law*, pp 33–36, 95; F A Mann (1954) 70 LQR 181, 188–190.

124 [1910] AC 262; *The Jupiter (No 3)* [1927] P 122.

manufacture the liqueur known as Chartreuse, according to its original secret formula. Their Lordships held that the monks, rather than the French liquidator, were still free to exploit in England the reputation which Chartreuse had obtained there. The statute neither expressly nor by implication affected property outside France.

If, on the other hand, the judge comes to the conclusion that the foreign legislation is intended to have extra-territorial operation, the first general principle to be considered is that legislation has no extra-territorial effect. Broadly speaking, jurisdiction is coincident with power, and how can power be exerted within the territory of another sovereign?[125]

The clear implication of the territorial principle is that property situated, say, in England cannot be affected by a foreign decree of expropriation and that the rights of the owner remain unimpaired. Thus a Cuban law purporting to confiscate the copyright (situated in England) in certain Cuban musical works has been held to be ineffective.[126] The only doubt is whether the decree is effective against a national of the foreign state, since historical authority is not lacking for the view that the right to expropriate property may be based on the allegiance of its owner as well as upon its situs.[127] Whether this view is justifiable or not, it has found few adherents.[128] Thus in one case MAUGHAM J held that a Soviet confiscatory decree was ineffective with regard to property in England although the owner was a Soviet subject at the time of the decree.[129] The application of the principle, however, that the legislative power of a state is only territorial, may be frustrated by the impact of the equally well-established principle[130] that a foreign state or sovereign cannot normally be impleaded, for if the sovereign is in possession or control of the expropriated property, even though it may be in England, the owner is unable to enforce his rights.[131]

If property is not in the possession or control of the foreign state at the time of the proceedings and if it was outside the territorial jurisdiction of that state at the time of the expropriatory decree, it is now established that the rights of the owner are unaffected.[132] A contrary rule would conflict not only with the principle that legislative power is territorial, but also in the particular case of confiscation with the doctrine that the penal laws of another country will not be indirectly enforced in England.[133] Since the foreign state is not in possession at the time of the proceedings, the principle that the state is immune from the jurisdiction of the court has no application, for if the foreign state commences the proceedings this amounts to submission and there is no immunity.[134]

---

[125] *Jabbour (F & K) v Custodian of Israeli Absentee Property* [1954] 1 WLR 139 at 150, and authorities there cited; *Williams and Humbert Ltd v W and H Trade Marks (Jersey) Ltd* [1986] AC 368 at 427–428.

[126] *Peer International Corpn v Termidor Music Publishers Ltd* [2003] EWCA Civ 1156, [2004] Ch 212; Osborne [2004] CLJ 567. See also *Société Eram Shipping Co Ltd v Cie Internationale de Navigation* [2003] UKHL 30 at [54], [80], [2004] 1 AC 260.

[127] McNair (1946) 31 Grotius Society 30, 35 et seq.

[128] But see *Lorentzen v Lydden & Co* [1942] 2 KB 202, infra.

[129] *Re Russian Bank for Foreign Trade* [1933] Ch 745.

[130] Governed now by the State Immunity Act 1978, infra, pp 490–501.

[131] Eg *Compañia Naviera Vascongado v SS Cristina* [1938] AC 485, though there would now not appear to be immunity in such a case involving a ship used for commercial purposes, by reason of the State Immunity Act 1978, s 10(2).

[132] *Tallinna Laevauhisus (A/S) v Estonian State Steamship Line* (1947) 80 Lloyd's Rep 99; *Novello & Co Ltd v Hinrichsen Edition Ltd* [1951] Ch 595; *Bank voor Handel en Scheepvaart NV v Slatford* [1953] 1 QB 248.

[133] *Frankfurther v W L Exner Ltd* [1947] Ch 629 at 636–637.

[134] State Immunity Act 1978, s 2(3).

(c) Requisition of property

Owing to the decision of ATKINSON J in *Lorentzen v Lydden & Co*,[135] it was for some time doubtful whether an extra-territorial effect should not be attributed to the requisition, as distinct from the confiscation, of property by a foreign state. In that case the public policy exception was used in a positive way to give effect to a foreign government's act of requisition in relation to property situated in England. However, in *Bank voor Handel en Scheepvaart NV v Slatford*,[136] DEVLIN J followed an earlier Scots decision[137] in preference to that of ATKINSON J. DEVLIN J favoured "the simple rule that generally property in England is subject to English law and to none other".[138] The position is now finally settled by the Court of Appeal in *Peer International Corpn v Termidor Music Publishers Ltd*,[139] where this simple rule was applied and *Lorentzen v Lydden* was overruled. It was held that the public policy exception could not be used in a positive way to give effect to a foreign government's confiscatory act in relation to property situated in England, ie to give that act a validity that it would not otherwise have. The Court distinguished *Kuwait Airways Corpn v Iraqi Airways Co (Nos 4 and 5)*,[140] which was concerned with the very different situation where public policy was used in a negative way to deny recognition to a foreign government's confiscatory act in relation to property situated in that country, ie to deny that act a validity that it would otherwise have. The *Peer* Case involved confiscation but it supports the wider principle that English law will not enforce foreign laws that purport to have extra-territorial effect, a principle that applies equally to non-confiscatory cases as it does to confiscatory cases.

3. FOREIGN LAWS REPUGNANT TO ENGLISH PUBLIC POLICY[141]

(a) General principles

It is a well-established principle that any action brought in this country is subject to the English doctrine of public policy. Certain heads of the domestic doctrine of public policy command such respect, and certain foreign laws and institutions seem so repugnant to English notions and ideals, that the English view must prevail in proceedings in this country, for SCARMAN J has said that "an English court will refuse to apply a law which outrages its sense of justice and decency".[142] However, he also struck a note of caution in

---

[135] [1942] 2 KB 202.

[136] [1953] 1 QB 248.

[137] *The El Condado* (1939) 63 Lloyd's Rep 330, 1939 SC 413.

[138] [1953] 1 QB 248 at 260.

[139] [2003] EWCA Civ 1156, [2004] Ch 212.

[140] [2002] 2 AC 883, HL; discussed further supra, pp 134–135 and infra, pp 145–146.

[141] On this subject see Kahn-Freund (1953) 39 Grotius Society 39; Nygh (1964) 13 ICLQ 39; Kahn-Freund (1974) III Hague Recueil 139, 426–431; F A Mann, *Foreign Affairs in English Courts*, (1986), chapter 8; Sammartano and Morse, *Public Policy in Transnational Relationships* (1992); Lagarde, *International Encyclopaedia of Comparative Law*, Vol III, chapter II; Bucher (1993-II) 239 Hague Recueil 13; Carter (1993) 42 ICLQ 1; Enonchong (1996) 45 ICLQ 633; Leslie [1995] Jur Rev 477; Blom [2003] NILR 373.

[142] *Re Fuld's Estate (No 3)* [1968] P 675 at 698. See also *Kuwait Airways Corpn v Iraqi Airways Co (Nos 4 and 5)* [2002] UKHL 19 at [16] (per Lord NICHOLLS), [2002] 2 AC 883.

suggesting that "before it exercises such power it must consider the relevant foreign law as a whole".[143]

The occasional exclusion of a foreign law on the grounds of public policy is no doubt inevitable, but the English domestic doctrine of public policy covers a multitude of sins varying in their degree of turpitude, and it is essential to resist the suggestion that an action concerning a transaction governed by a foreign law must necessarily fail because it would have failed had the governing law been English. Judges in the past have now and then expressed somewhat extravagant views on the matter. Thus, for instance, in a restraint of trade case,[144] FRY J seemed to suggest that every limb of the domestic doctrine must apply in every action in England. This can scarcely be so. The conception of public policy is, and should be, narrower and more limited in private international law than in internal law.[145] A transaction that is valid by its foreign governing law should not be nullified on this ground unless its enforcement would offend some moral, social or economic principle so sacrosanct in English eyes as to require its maintenance at all costs and without exception. In the words of CARDOZO J in a New York case:

> We are not so provincial as to say that every solution of a problem is wrong because we deal with it otherwise at home . . . The courts are not free to refuse to enforce a foreign right at the pleasure of the judges, to suit the individual notion of expediency or fairness. They do not close their doors unless help would violate some fundamental principle of justice, some prevalent conception of good morals, some deep-rooted tradition of the common weal.[146]

English courts should not invoke public policy save in cases where foreign law is manifestly incompatible with public policy.[147]

The particular rule of public policy that the defendant invokes may be of this overriding nature and therefore enforceable in all actions. Or it may be local in the sense that it represents some feature of internal policy. If so it must be confined to cases where the governing law is English.[148] The mere fact that, for example, a contract, governed by a foreign law, infringes some rule of English domestic law such as the need for consideration to support a simple contract will not prevent its enforcement in England.[149]

To ascertain whether it is all-pervading or merely local, it must be examined "in the light of its history, the purpose of its adoption, the object to be accomplished by it, and the local conditions".[150] Perhaps the most important question to ask in each case is—what is the rule designed to prevent?[151] Presumably, for instance, the policy underlying the rule

---

[143] *Re Fuld's Estate (No 3)* [1968] P 675 at 698.

[144] *Rousillon v Rousillon* (1880) 14 Ch D 351 at 369. Actually the governing law in the circumstances of the case was English law. Therefore, of course, the domestic doctrine applied; cf *Timms v Nicol* 1968 (1) SA 299.

[145] *Vervaeke v Smith* [1983] 1 AC 145 at 164 (per Lord SIMON); *Kuwait Airways Corpn v Iraqi Airways Co (Nos 4 and 5)* [2002] UKHL 19 at [114] (per Lord STEYN), [2002] 2 AC 883.

[146] *Loucks v Standard Oil Co of New York* 224 NY 99 at 111 (1918); quoted in *Kuwait Airways Corpn v Iraqi Airways Co (Nos 4 and 5)*, supra, at [16] (per Lord NICHOLLS).

[147] *Gotha City v Sotheby's (No 2)* (1998) Times, 8 October.

[148] Cf *Mackender v Feldia AG* [1967] 2 QB 590 at 601; *Re Colt Telecom Group plc (No 2)* [2002] EWHC 2815 at [76]–[77] (Ch), [2003] BPIR 324.

[149] *Re Bonacina, Le Brasseur v Bonacina* [1912] 2 Ch 394. See now the Rome Convention, discussed infra, pp 741–743.

[150] Wharton, *Conflict of Laws* (3rd edn), i, 16.

[151] See, eg, *Block Bros Realty Ltd v Mollard* (1981) 122 DLR (3d) 323.

which invalidates a promise by an employee not to compete against his employer in the future is to further the economic well-being of the country by enabling every person freely to exploit in England the trade that he has learnt. If so, only a rigid doctrinaire would claim that this particular rule is of universal application, designed to control relations between employers and employees in other countries. The English prohibition of contracts in restraint of trade is only concerned with freedom of trade in *England*.[152]

If the court decides that, having regard to the particular circumstances, the distinctive policy of English law is in truth affected, then the incompatible foreign rule must, indeed, be totally excluded. Some of the older decisions, however, have perhaps tended to invoke the domestic doctrine of public policy in all its ramifications with remorseless determination.

Kaufman v Gerson[153] provides a striking example of insularity.

> The husband of the defendant had misappropriated money entrusted to him by the plaintiff. By a contract made and to be performed in France the defendant agreed to pay to the plaintiff by instalments out of her own money the full amount misappropriated, in consideration that the plaintiff would refrain from prosecuting the husband for what was a crime by French law. Both the plaintiff and defendant were French nationals domiciled in France; the misappropriation had occurred in France; the contract was valid by French law.

This contract could scarcely be regarded as offensive to some fundamental principle of justice, for there is nothing particularly reprehensible in allowing a person to escape criminal proceedings at the price of paying full compensation to the sufferer. Nevertheless, an action for the recovery of instalments still due was dismissed on the ground that "to enforce a contract so procured would be to contravene what by the law of this country is deemed an essential moral interest".[154]

In *Addison v Brown*,[155] however, a less insular interpretation was put on the reservation of public policy.

> A wife sued her husband to recover arrears of maintenance due under a contract that was governed by Californian law. It was expressly agreed that neither party would apply to any court for the variation of the contract and that if in fact it were varied by any court in subsequent divorce proceedings it would nevertheless remain in force as written. Ten years later the husband obtained a divorce in California, and the contract, far from being varied, was incorporated in the judgment.

The contract, since it contained an agreement by the parties to oust the jurisdiction of the court, was contrary to the doctrine of public policy as understood in England, and it was therefore pleaded that the action was not maintainable. STREATFIELD J, however, refused to treat this particular segment of the doctrine as being of universal application. He said

---

152 *Warner Bros v Nelson* [1937] 1 KB 209.
153 [1904] 1 KB 591, CA reversing WRIGHT J [1903] 2 KB 114. The decision was not followed in the Canadian case of *National Surety Co v Larsen* [1929] 4 DLR 918, but see *K(E) v K(D)* (2004) 257 DLR (4th) 549, BC CA.
154 [1904] 1 KB 591 at 599–600.
155 [1954] 1 WLR 779.

that there could be no objection in England to an agreement that purports to oust the jurisdiction of a foreign court.[156]

The principle that emerges in *Addison v Brown* is that, in order to apply the English domestic rules on public policy to an agreement, it must be shown that the agreement relates to England, in some important way. The same principle was applied, in a different context, in *Trendtex Trading Corpn v Crédit Suisse*.[157] There, the House of Lords held that, since an assignment of a cause of action savoured of champerty, it was contrary to public policy and therefore void. A crucial point in the case was that the assignment related to an *English* cause of action.

Before turning to a summary of cases where domestic policy is affected, one final general point has to be made, namely that most of these cases arise in the context of contract choice of law. This area has recently been put largely on a statutory footing.[158] However, the substance of the public policy exception would not appear to be affected.[159]

(b) Summary of cases where distinctive policy is affected

It is no easy matter to classify those cases in which the English court will refuse to enforce a foreign acquired right, on the ground that its enforcement would affront some moral principle the maintenance of which admits of no possible compromise. However, the following is suggested as the probable classification.

(i) Where the basic principles of English justice and fairness are affronted

Lord Nicholls in *Kuwait Airways Corpn v Iraqi Airways Co (Nos 4 and 5)*[160] has said that "the courts of this country must have a residual power, to be exercised exceptionally and with the greatest circumspection, to disregard a provision in the foreign law when to do otherwise would affront basic principles of justice and fairness which the courts seek to apply in the administration of justice in this country".[161] Two particular instances of this, namely a breach of human rights and a fundamental breach of international law, will be considered below. However, this principle cannot be confined to one particular category of unacceptable laws.[162] The established rule, which will be stated later,[163] that a foreign judgment cannot be recognised in England if it offends the principles of natural justice, as, for example, if the defendant was denied the opportunity of presenting his case to the foreign court, exemplifies this aspect of English public policy. Another example is the rule that a contract obtained by a class of duress so unconscionable that it will cause the English court, as a matter of public policy, to override the law governing the contract, is

---

[156] [1954] 1 WLR 779 at 784.

[157] [1982] AC 679; Thornley [1982] 41 CLJ 29. See also *Sigurdson v Farrow* (1981) 121 DLR (3d) 183; *Fraser v Buckle* [1996] 1 IR 1, SC. For the changing English domestic law attitude towards some instances of champerty see *Giles v Thompson* [1994] 1 AC 142, HL.

[158] See the Contracts (Applicable Law) Act 1990; infra, pp 741–743.

[159] But see the problems raised in relation to the comity of nations/public policy cases like *Foster v Driscoll* [1929] 1 KB 470; infra, pp 742–743.

[160] [2002] 2 AC 883, HL.

[161] Ibid, at [18]. (Lord HOFFMANN concurred with this judgment, as did Lord Scott on the public policy/recognition and enforcement point).

[162] Ibid.

[163] Infra, pp 563–565.

unenforceable in England.[164] Consistent with this, a foreign judgment granted in respect of a contract entered into under undue influence, duress or coercion may be refused enforcement in England on the ground of public policy.[165] As a final example, to permit a party which has not acted in good faith in relation to the purchase of stolen goods to benefit from a foreign limitation period as against a party who had no knowledge of the whereabouts of stolen goods and no possibility of recovering them, was against English public policy as expressed in the Limitation Act 1980.[166]

(ii) Where the English conceptions of morality are infringed

It cannot be doubted that a contract or other transaction which is objectionable in English eyes on the ground that it tends to promote sexual immorality,[167] such as a contract for prostitution, will receive no judicial recognition in England, though it may be innocuous according to its foreign governing law.[168] Similarly, an agreement to be performed abroad involving payment for the use of personal influence in securing a contract will not be enforced in England, at least not in the situation where the foreign place of performance applies the same public policy.[169] Neither, in this age of commercial fraud, will a contract drafted to deceive third parties be enforced.[170] On the other hand, Canadian courts have held that the enforcement of contracts relating to gambling debts would not violate Canadian concepts of essential judicial morality,[171] nor would enforcement of a foreign judgment for treble or punitive damages,[172] or for excessive damages.[173]

(iii) Where a transaction prejudices the interests of the United Kingdom or its good relations with foreign powers

An example of the first part of the above statement is the prohibition of business with an alien enemy.[174] In one case, for instance, an English company, owning mines in Spain,

---

[164] *Royal Boskalis Westminster NV v Mountain* [1999] QB 674 at 729 (per PHILLIPS LJ), CA. See, eg, *Kaufman v Gerson* [1904] 1 KB 591, supra, p 141. cf *Dimskal Shipping Co SA v International Transport Workers Federation* [1992] 2 AC 152, HL involving a different type of duress (ie economic). See also *Société des Hôtels Réunis SA v Hawker* (1913) 29 TLR 578; *Kahler v Midland Bank Ltd* [1950] AC 24 at 44–45; cf *A M Luther v James Sagor & Co* [1921] 3 KB 532 at 558–559.

[165] *Israel Discount Bank of New York v Hadjipateras* [1984] 1 WLR 137; infra, p 557. For public policy as a defence to recognition and enforcement of foreign judgments see *Vervaeke v Smith* [1983] 1 AC 145; generally infra, pp 556–558.

[166] *Gotha City v Sotheby's (No 2)* (1998) Times, 8 October.

[167] See, eg, *Pearce v Brooks* (1866) LR 1 Exch 213; *Ayerst v Jenkins* (1873) LR 16 Eq 275; *Taylor v Chester* (1869) LR 4 QB 309.

[168] *Robinson v Bland* (1760) 2 Burr 1077 at 1084.

[169] *Lemenda Trading Co Ltd v African Middle East Petroleum Co Ltd* [1988] QB 448; Carter (1988) BYBIL 356. See also *Westacre v Jugoimport* [2000] 1 QB 288, CA, discussed further, infra, pp 659–660; *Apple Corps Ltd v Apple Computer Inc* [1992] FSR 431; *Tekron Resources Ltd v Guinea Investment Co Ltd* [2003] EWHC 2577 (QB), [2004] 2 Lloyd's Rep 26.

[170] *Mitsubishi Corpn v Alafouzos* [1988] 1 Lloyd's Rep 191.

[171] *Boardwalk Regency Corpn v Maalouf* (1992) 88 DLR (4th) 612, Ont CA; *Auerbach v Resorts International Hotel Inc* (1991) 89 DLR (4th) 688, Quebec CA. These cases involved enforcement of foreign judgments, see infra, pp 556–558.

[172] *Old North State Brewing Co v Newlands Services Inc* [1999] 4 WWR 573, BC CA; discussed infra, p 558. See also *Benefit Strategies Group Inc v Prider* [2005] SASC 194, (2005) 91 SASR 544. Cf *Schnabel v Yung Lui* [2002] NSWSC 115.

[173] *Beals v Saldanha* 2003 SCC 72—damages in Florida were considerably larger than those that would be granted in a comparable case in Canada; discussed infra, p 558.

[174] *Robson v Premier Oil and Pipe Line Co* [1915] 2 Ch 124 at 136.

made a contract in 1910 for the delivery by instalments spread over a number of years of minerals to a German company.[175] The contract contained a suspensory clause which provided that in the event of war the obligations of the parties should be suspended during hostilities. The English company brought an action in 1916 claiming a declaration that the contract was not merely suspended but was abrogated by the existence of a state of war between Great Britain and Germany. The objection was taken that this was a German contract and that therefore it fell to be governed by German law. It was argued that illegality according to English law was irrelevant. What had to be shown was that the contract was illegal by German law. It was held, however, that the German character of the contract had no bearing on this question. "It is illegal for a British subject to become bound in a manner which sins against the public policy of the King's realm",[176] and it has long been established that the prohibition of trading with an alien enemy rests on public policy. It seems that payment in breach of United Nations sanctions as enacted in the relevant domestic law is akin to trading with the enemy for the purposes of public policy.[177]

Support for the second part of our statement may be derived from the rule that it is contrary to public policy as understood in all civilised nations for persons in England to enter into an engagement with the avowed object of causing injury to a friendly government,[178] as, for example, by raising a loan to further a revolt,[179] by an agreement to import liquor contrary to a prohibition law,[180] to defraud its revenue[181] or to export a prohibited commodity.[182] Such conduct is a breach of international comity and tends to injure the relations of the British government with friendly powers.[183] It is not, however, contrary to public policy to enforce a contract which is illegal and/or void by the law of a foreign and friendly state when the contract was made in England and involved the performance exclusively in England of acts entirely lawful under English law.[184] Nor is it against public policy to enforce a contract, judgment or arbitral award between nationals of two foreign countries, both friendly to the United Kingdom, even though the two foreign states are enemies of each other.[185] A court in this country cannot set itself up as a judge of the rights and wrongs of a controversy between two countries friendly to us.[186]

---

[175] *Dynamit Actien-Gesellschaft v Rio Tinto Co Ltd* [1918] AC 260.

[176] Ibid, at 294.

[177] *Royal Boskalis Westminster NV v Mountain* [1999] QB 674 at 693 (per Stuart-Smith LJ), CA.

[178] *British Nylon Spinners Ltd v ICI Ltd* [1955] Ch 37 at 52; *Bodley Head Ltd v Flegon* [1972] 1 WLR 680 at 687–688.

[179] *De Wutz v Hendricks* (1824) 2 Bing 314.

[180] *Foster v Driscoll* [1929] 1 KB 470; cf *Toprak v Finagrain* [1979] 2 Lloyd's Rep 98; *Tekron Resources Ltd v Guinea Investment Co Ltd* [2003] EWHC 2577 (QB), [2004] 2 Lloyd's Rep 26.

[181] *Re Emery's Investments Trusts* [1959] Ch 410; *Pye Ltd v BG Transport Service Ltd* [1966] 2 Lloyd's Rep 300 at 308–309.

[182] *Regazzoni v K C Sethia (1944) Ltd* [1958] AC 301. For a critical study of this decision, see F A Mann (1958) 21 MLR 130 et seq. Cf *Trinidad Shipping Co v Alston* [1920] AC 888; *Dalmia Dairy Industries Ltd v National Bank of Pakistan* [1978] 2 Lloyd's Rep 223 at 267–268; *Mahonia Ltd v JP Morgan Chase Bank* [2003] 2 Lloyd's Rep 911—extended to where the illegal purpose is known to just one party.

[183] This sort of case now will have to come within the statutory public policy exception introduced by the Contracts (Applicable Law) Act 1990, see infra, pp 742–743.

[184] *JSC Zestafoni v Ronly Holdings Ltd* [2004] EWHC 245 (Comm) at [75], [2004] 2 Lloyd's Rep 335. See also *Society of Lloyd's v Fraser* [1999] Lloyd's Rep IR 156, CA (Ch).

[185] *Dalmia Dairy Industries Ltd v National Bank of Pakistan*, infra, at pp 299–301.

[186] *Empresa Exportadora De Azúcar v Industria Azucarera Nacional SA, The Playa Larga* [1983] 2 Lloyd's Rep 171; Carter (1983) 54 BYBIL 297.

(iv) A gross infringement of human rights

Gross infringements of human rights are one instance, and an important instance, of a provision of a foreign law, which if recognised or enforced would affront basic principles of justice and fairness which the courts seek to apply in the administration of justice in this country.[187] A German decree during the Nazi era depriving Jewish émigrés of their German nationality and, consequentially, leading to the confiscation of their property is an example of a law which constitutes so grave an infringement of human rights that the English courts ought to refuse to recognise it as a law at all.[188] An English court will not apply a foreign law that involves such a grave infringement of human rights.[189] Nowadays, human rights are protected under the European Convention on Human Rights.[190] In recent years human rights law has been used to cast light on the public policy defence to recognition and enforcement of foreign judgments.[191]

(v) A fundamental breach of international law

As far back as 1973, the House of Lords accepted that it is part of English public policy that our courts should give effect to clearly established rules of international law.[192] The leading case developing this category of public policy is *Kuwait Airways Corpn v Iraqi Airways Co (Nos 4 and 5)*.[193]

> Following the Iraq invasion of Kuwait in 1990, aircraft belonging to the claimant, Kuwait Airways Corporation, were seized and flown by the defendant, Iraqi Airways Company, to Iraq. The Revolutionary Command Council of Iraq (RCC) passed Resolution 369 which purported to divest the claimant of its title to its aircraft and transfer this to the defendant. This was part and parcel of the Iraqi seizure

[187] *Kuwait Airways Corpn v Iraqi Airways Co (Nos 4 and 5)* [2002] 2 AC 883 at [18] (per Lord NICHOLLS, Lords HOFFMANN and SCOTT concurring), [114] (per Lord STEYN), [137] (per Lord HOPE).

[188] *Oppenheimer v Cattermole* [1976] AC 249 at 277–278, HL. This proposition was cited with approval in *Kuwait Airways Corpn v Iraqi Airways Co (Nos 4 and 5)*, supra, at [18] (per Lord NICHOLLS), [114] (per Lord STEYN), [137] (per Lord HOPE). For other cases arising out of the Nazi era contrast *Re Meyer* [1971] P 298 with *Igra v Igra* [1951] P 404. For early examples of foreign laws or status offending English conceptions of human liberty and freedom of action see in relation to slavery, see *Sommersett's Case* (1772) 20 State Tr 1; *Forbes v Cochrane* (1824) 2 B & C 448 at 467; *Regazzoni v K C Sethia (1944) Ltd* [1956] 2 QB 490 at 524; cf *Santos v Illidge* (1860) 8 CBNS 861. See also *Gotha City v Sotheby's (No 2)* (1998) Times, 8 October. US courts have refused to enforce English libel judgments on the basis that English libel law provides inadequate freedom of speech: *Bachchan v India Abroad Publications Inc* 588 NYS 2d 661 (Sup Ct 1992); *Matusevitch v Telnikoff* [1996] IL Pr 181, US District Ct for the District of Columbia; Maltby (1994) 94 Col LR 1978; Devgun (1994) 23 Anglo-Am LR 195. For the link between constitutional guarantees and public policy in Canada see *Pro Swing Inc v Elta Golf Inc* 2006 SCC 52 at [59]–[62].

[189] See the parallel situation where there was a fundamental breach of international law, discussed below. See also *Skrine & Co v Euromoney Publications plc* [2002] EMLR 15, CA—a contribution action following settlement of claims abroad.

[190] For enforcement of the Convention rights in the United Kingdom see the Human Rights Act 1998.

[191] Both under the Brussels system (see Case C-7/98 *Krombach v Bamberski* [2001] QB 709, [2000] ECR I-1935, discussed infra, pp 613–614, and the traditional English rules on enforcement (see *Al-Bassam v Al Bassam* [2004] EWCA Civ 857 at [45], discussed infra, pp 558–560). See also the use of human rights law when considering the public policy defence under the EU Insolvency Regulation (Reg 1346/2000) in C-341/04 *Eurofood IFSC Ltd* [2006] IL Pr 23 at para [67].

[192] *Oppenheimer v Cattermole* [1976] AC 249 at 277–278, HL.

[193] [2002] 2 AC 883, HL. Their Lordships, at [28] (per Lord NICHOLLS, with whose judgment Lord HOFFMANN concurred, as did Lord SCOTT on the public policy/recognition and enforcement point), at [114] (per Lord STEYN), [138] (per Lord HOPE) placed reliance on *Oppenheimer v Cattermole* [1976] AC 249. The *Kuwait Airways* Case also involved important points in relation to tort choice of law, which are discussed infra, pp 854–855.

of Kuwait and its assets and the assimilation of these assets into the structure of Iraq. The claimant brought proceedings in England for return of the aircraft or payment of their value, and damages.

MANCE J gave judgment for the claimant on liability. The Court of Appeal dismissed the defendant's appeal against this decision. The House of Lords, affirming this decision, held that in appropriate circumstances it is legitimate for an English court to have regard to the content of international law when deciding whether to recognise a foreign law.[194] The judiciary does not have to shut its eyes to a breach of international law when the breach is plain and, indeed, acknowledged.[195] The acceptability of a foreign law must be judged by contemporary standards.[196] This was not simply a governmental expropriation of property within its territory, it was part of an attempt to extinguish every vestige of Kuwait as a separate state. Expropriation in such circumstances was not acceptable in today's world. Iraq's invasion of Kuwait and seizure of its assets were gross violations of established rules of international law of fundamental importance. Enforcement or recognition of Resolution 369 therefore would be manifestly contrary to the public policy of English law.[197] In the case of a fundamental breach of international law, no connection with England is needed for the public policy exception to operate, since it is not based on a principle of English public policy which is domestic in character.[198] In this case public policy operated as an exception to the tort choice of law rules.[199] The House of Lords then applied the tort choice of law rules on the footing that the transfer of title purportedly made by Resolution 369 was to be disregarded.[200] This was because it was contrary to public policy to apply Iraqi law as the lex situs to exclude claims it would otherwise have under Iraqi law as the law of the place where the tort was committed.[201] In other words, the court applied the law of the place where the tort was committed minus that part of it which was against public policy to recognise. The upshot was that there was actionability under the law of Iraq.

(c) Cases involving a foreign status

Any attempt to classify the foreign laws that are offensive to the English concept of public policy is not easy to reconcile with decisions on the measure of recognition to be given to a foreign status. The short answer, no doubt, is that, though the court must recognise the existence of a person's status as fixed by the law of his foreign domicile, it need not

---

194 [2002] 2 AC 883 at [26] (per Lord NICHOLLS).

195 The non-justiciable principle under the Act of State doctrine does not require this, ibid at [26] (per Lord NICHOLLS), at [12]–[113] (per Lord STEYN), at [135]–[149] (per Lord HOPE).

196 Ibid, at [28] (per Lord NICHOLLS).

197 Ibid, at [29] (per Lord NICHOLLS); at [114] (per Lord STEYN), at [149] (per Lord HOPE). It would also be contrary to United Kingdom obligations under the UN Charter: Lord NICHOLLS at [29]; Lord STEYN at [114], at [141] (per Lord HOPE).

198 Ibid, at [166]–[167] (per Lord HOPE). There was a clear connection between Resolution 369, which was part of the law of the place where the tort was committed (which is what the court was concerned with in a tort choice of law case), and the breach of international law.

199 Ibid, at [33] (per Lord NICHOLLS), [114] (per Lord STEYN), [165]–[166] (per Lord HOPE). Public policy would have operated as an exception to the lex situs rule if there had been an action asserting title to the aircraft, at [192] (per Lord SCOTT).

200 Ibid, at [37] (per Lord NICHOLLS), at [117]–[118] (per Lord STEYN), [168]–[170]. Lord SCOTT dissenting at [172], [191]–[194].

201 Ibid, at [31]–[33] (per Lord NICHOLLS).

necessarily give effect to the results or incidents attributed to it by that law, including the capacities and incapacities of the person affected.[202] The problem, however, is to determine what incidents may be accepted, what must be repudiated. Obviously an incident must be repudiated if it is contrary to a positive rule of English internal law. Again, a remedy permitted by the foreign law of the status will not be granted if English law is not adapted to its enforcement. Thus, an English court was quite prepared to recognise that under Greek law a father should provide his daughter with a dowry, though the nature of the daughter's right was such that it should not be enforced here.[203] Finally, a foreign status or incident of status will be disregarded if it offends the English doctrine of public policy. So far as English internal law is concerned, it has long been settled that a judge is no longer free to invent new heads of public policy. He may expound, but must not expand, this branch of the law.[204] In the field of private international law, however, exposition has gradually blossomed into expansion to such an extent that apparently the judges now feel free to exclude the law of the domicile whenever[205] they feel it proper to do so in the circumstances.

The ancestry of this extreme view may be traced back to *Worms v De Valdor*[206] in 1880. That case was concerned with the French status of prodigality which arises when a court appoints an adviser, a *conseil judicaire*, to safeguard the interests of an adult person of extravagant habits. The court may prohibit him from compromising claims, borrowing or receiving money, alienating or mortgaging property and bringing or defending actions without the collaboration of his adviser. The question in *Worms v De Valdor* was whether an action for the cancellation of certain bills of exchange, brought by a prodigal in his own name and without the assistance of his *conseil judiciaire*, could succeed. FRY J, unaided by expert evidence, made his own researches into French law and concluded that the appointment of a *conseil judiciaire* neither changed the status of a prodigal nor subjected him to a personal disqualification. Had it done so, the judge intimated that he would have disregarded the disqualification as being penal in nature. He did in fact allow the action to proceed, but on the ground, it would seem, that whether the prodigal could sue in England in his own name was a procedural question determinable by English law as that of the forum.

In the case of *Re Selot's Trusts*,[207] the question was whether the status of prodigality, imposed on the plaintiff by the French law of his domicile, precluded his recovery of a legacy bequeathed to him by an English will. FARWELL J, affecting to follow *Worms v De Valdor*, held that the disability of the prodigal to bring an action without the assistance of his legal adviser was a penal restriction that had no effect in English proceedings. What the judge overlooked was that this was not the ratio decidendi of FRY J in the earlier case.[208]

---

202 Allen (1930) 46 LQR 277, 293 et seq; Inglis (1957) 6 ICLQ 202, 220–224; Falconbridge, p 751.

203 *Phrantzes v Argenti* [1960] 2 QB 19; supra, pp 94–95; Webb (1960) 23 MLR 446; Carter (1960) 36 BYBIL 412; and see *Shahnaz v Rizwan* [1965] 1 QB 390—recognition of deferred dower; cf *Re Macartney* [1921] 1 Ch 522; *Khalij Commercial Bank Ltd v Woods* (1985) 17 DLR (4th) 358.

204 *Fender v St John-Mildmay* [1938] AC 1 at 40; *Vervaeke v Smith* [1983] 1 AC 145 at 164—existing principles can be applied to new circumstances.

205 *Russ v Russ* [1964] P 315.

206 (1880) 49 LJ Ch 261.

207 [1902] 1 Ch 488.

208 The two decisions have sometimes been said to support the proposition that a foreign status unknown to English law will not be recognised in England. See, eg, *Republica de Guatemala v Nunez* [1927] 1 KB 669 at 701. The proposition is unfounded. For example, the married status of the parties to a polygamous marriage is

A later case concerned with a status of incompetence is *Re Langley's Settlement Trusts*.[209] The Court of Appeal held that the joint exercise of a power to withdraw part of settled funds by the settlor and his wife was effective, even though the settlor was disqualified as incompetent by the law of his residence and domicile, California. The exercise complied with English law which governed the settlement that created the power, since the document had been signed by a man who was not incompetent in the eyes of English internal law. It also complied with the law that governed the man's status, for the wife in signing the document had obeyed the express directions of the Californian court.

What, however, is more pertinent to the present discussion is that the Court of Appeal gave an alternative reason for the decision. The principle, it was said, is that it is a matter of judicial discretion whether a foreign status shall be recognised.[210] Had the only facet of the Californian law requiring investigation in the present case been the ban placed on the settlor's right to withdraw the settled funds, the court would have exercised its discretion against the recognition of his status of incompetence. But in order that the law may be reasonably certain and predictable it has long been established that judicial discretion must be exercised in accordance with settled rules, not in an arbitrary or capricious manner. It is not an unfettered discretion, but one, as Lord ELDON said in a specific performance case, that "must be regulated upon grounds that will make it judicial".[211] What, therefore, was the particular head of public policy that justified the rejection of the Californian status? The Court of Appeal, affirming BUCKLEY J in the court below, classified the status as penal since it deprived the settlor of his power to deal with a valuable interest. The word "penal", said BUCKLEY J, "means law of a kind which deprives the person affected of his rights or property in a way which adversely affects his interests".[212] But this is to attribute to the word a meaning that is warranted neither by the dictionary nor by the nature of the particular status. The object of the Californian order was not to penalise the invalid, but to protect him against the machinations of "artful or designing persons".[213] Similarly, the subjection of a spendthrift to the status of prodigality is designed to protect him against his own extravagance. It would seem, therefore, that to stigmatise as penal any law which deprives him of a valuable interest is to invent a new head of public policy that is supported by no authority except the doubtful decision of FARWELL J in *Re Selot's Trusts*. It is a proposition that scarcely accords with the views expressed in *Luther v Sagor*.[214]

Moreover, the proposition that a judge has a free discretion to exclude a foreign status or its incidents if he considers that in the particular circumstances it will adversely affect a person's right to deal with his property cannot be accepted with any degree of complacency. Its impact on the doctrine of public policy would, at first sight, be disastrous, for what has been laboriously shaped into a reasonably ordered form would become once

---

recognised and, indeed, English courts will grant matrimonial relief to the parties to such a marriage. So also was the status arising from a foreign adoption or a foreign legitimation *per subsequens matrimonium* recognised before those institutions were accepted by English internal law.

[209] [1961] 1 WLR 41; affd [1962] Ch 541; Grodecki (1962) 11 ICLQ 578.
[210] See *De Reneville v De Reneville* [1948] P 100 at 109.
[211] *White v Damon* (1802) 7 Ves 30 at 35.
[212] [1961] 1 WLR 41 at 46.
[213] Californian Probate Code, s 1466.
[214] [1921] 3 KB 532, supra, pp 133–134.

more amorphous and indeterminate. It is difficult to disagree with the criticism that it is "a revolutionary innovation in our private international law",[215] and that "the courts might just as well abandon any attempt to formulate and apply defined rules of law if these can be overridden by an undefinable discretion".[216]

However, this whole problem of a free discretion is perhaps, at the moment, more apparent than real. The most common situation where the recognition of a foreign status arises is in cases involving the effect of a foreign divorce, annulment or legal separation. But, as will be seen below, the whole area of recognition of foreign divorces, etc is now put on a legislative basis and it is clear that recognition cannot be refused on the ground of a lack of substantial justice. In the future though, the problem of a free discretion, and more generally of public policy, may re-emerge, when, as is likely, English courts are faced with having to decide whether they will recognise a same sex marriage or a same sex civil partnership, valid according to the law of the domicile of the parties, and whether they will give effect to the incidents of such a marriage or partnership.[217]

(d) Recognition of foreign divorces, etc[218]

At one time, the discretion to refuse to recognise a foreign status applied in the context of recognition of foreign divorces, annulments and legal separations. It was said that there was a power to refuse to recognise a foreign divorce "which offends against English ideas of substantial justice".[219] The inherent difficulty in defining this concept was a cause for concern, as was the width of the doctrine.[220] However, in the case of divorces, etc granted in a European Community Member State, recognition is now dealt with by a Community Regulation and, in the case of divorces granted outside a European Community Member State, is now put on a statutory basis. Under the relevant Regulation[221] and statute recognition has to be given to foreign divorces, etc unless one of a limited list of grounds of non-recognition applies. Similarly, under the relevant statute[222] recognition has to be given to foreign divorces, etc unless the the court exercises its discretion on a limited listed number of grounds to deny recognition. With both Regulation and statute these grounds do not contain any provision allowing the courts to refuse recognition on the basis of want of substantial justice. It is possible, though, to refuse recognition in cases where there has been, in effect, a denial of natural justice,[223] and in cases where recognition

---

[215] Nygh (1964) 13 ICLQ 39, 50.

[216] Nygh, op cit, at 51; and see *Chaplin v Boys* [1971] AC 356 at 378.

[217] See infra, pp 937–940.

[218] Public policy as a defence in cases of recognition of foreign divorces, etc is dealt with more fully, infra, pp 990–991 and 1018–1023.

[219] *Middleton v Middleton* [1967] P 62 at 69; see also *Gray (otherwise Formosa) v Formosa* [1963] P 259; *Lepre v Lepre* [1965] P 52. For the reintroduction of this concept, but now in the area of enforcement of foreign commercial judgments, see *Adams v Cape Industries plc* [1990] Ch 433 at 557 et seq; discussed infra, p 566.

[220] See Carter (1962) 38 BYBIL 497; Lewis (1963) 12 ICLQ 298; Blom-Cooper (1963) 26 MLR 94; Carter (1965–1966) 41 BYBIL 445; Unger (1966) 29 MLR 327. See also *Varanand v Varanand* (1964) 108 Sol Jo 693, cited in *Qureshi v Qureshi* [1972] Fam 173 at 201.

[221] Council Regulation (EC) No 2201/2003 of 27 November 2003 concerning jurisdiction and the recognition and enforcement of judgments in matrimonial matters and the matters of parental responsibility OJ 2003 L 338/1 (Brussels II *bis*), Art 22; discussed infra, pp 988–992.

[222] The Family Law Act 1986; see s 51.

[223] Brussels II *bis*, Art 22(b); Family Law Act 1986, s 51(3)(a).

would be "manifestly contrary to public policy".[224] It is not entirely clear whether the use of the common law concept of public policy as one of the statutory grounds of non-recognition and the exclusion of the concept of substantial justice represents a shift in substance or merely one of terminology.[225] However, it is clear that the courts have been willing to use public policy as a ground for non-recognition of foreign divorces in circumstances where one might have expected a reluctance to do so. Thus in *Joyce v Joyce*[226] public policy was used as a ground[227] for non-recognition of a Quebec divorce, even though this involved criticism of the laws and procedure of a foreign and friendly country as being unfair to the respondent. More recently, in *Vervaeke v Smith*[228] a foreign nullity decree was refused recognition in the House of Lords on the basis of public policy, where there was no unfairness to the respondent. No criticism was made of the foreign law.[229] Rather, their Lordships were concerned to uphold the English policy of maintaining the validity of sham marriages, which was to be preferred to the Belgian policy, and that this policy should not be avoided by petitioners going abroad to obtain a nullity decree,[230] especially when the petitioner had previously put forward a bogus case in England which had failed. A policy of upholding sham marriages is odd enough, but to give this policy overriding force in an international context is even stranger.

4. MANDATORY RULES

The concept of mandatory rules has only recently been introduced into English law. Mandatory rules of the forum have been described by the Law Commissions as domestic rules which "are regarded as so important that as a matter of construction or policy they must apply in any action before a court of the forum, even where the issues are in principle governed by a foreign law selected by a choice of law rule".[231] The statutory and EC rules on choice of law in respect of trusts,[232] contracts[233] and torts[234] all have rules providing for the application of the mandatory rules of the forum. An example of English mandatory

---

[224] Brussels II *bis*, Art 22(a); Family Law Act 1986, s 51(3)(c). There are a number of other circumstances in which public policy issues arise, in the context of family law. A foreign law of domicile governing capacity to marry may not be recognised if it is repugnant to English public policy: *Cheni v Cheni* [1965] P 85 at 98–99, infra, p 908. Restraint on remarriage after a foreign divorce may be regarded as penal, so that the restriction will be regarded as inoperative outside the jurisdiction in which it was imposed, see infra, p 916. See in relation to same sex marriages and civil partnerships, infra, p 939.

[225] See *Vervaeke v Smith* [1983] 1 AC 145 at 164 (per Lord SIMON, who seems to regard the two concepts as being, in substance, the same). The Law Commission regards the courts' treatment of the two concepts as involving the same approach, Law Com No 137 (1984), para 2.26.

[226] [1979] Fam 93; infra, pp 1018–1023; cf *Igra v Igra* [1951] P 404 at 412. The public policy defence did not succeed in *Sabbagh v Sabbagh* [1985] FLR 29; *Eroglu v Eroglu* [1994] 2 FLR 287; *Kellman v Kellman* [2000] 1 FLR 785.

[227] It was also decided that there had been a denial of the opportunity to take part in the proceedings under s 8(2)(a)(ii) of the Recognition of Divorces and Legal Separations Act 1971; now s 51(3)(a)(ii) of the Family Law Act 1986.

[228] [1983] 1 AC 145; Smart (1983) 99 LQR 24; Jaffey (1983) 32 ICLQ 500; infra, p 1019.

[229] See at 156 (per Lord HAILSHAM).

[230] At 156–157, 163–167.

[231] Law Com Working Paper No 87 (1984), Scot Law Com Consultative Memorandum No 62 (1984), para 4.5.

[232] Infra, pp 1322–1323.

[233] Infra, pp 731–738.

[234] Infra, pp 849–851.

rules is provided by the controls on exemption clauses contained in the Unfair Contract Terms Act 1977; the Act itself stipulates[235] that, in certain circumstances, these controls shall apply despite the parties' choice of a foreign law to govern the contract. The concept of mandatory rules is a positive one; the concern is to apply a particular domestic rule. This contrasts with the exclusionary rules previously examined in this chapter where the concern is that a foreign rule should not be applied, ie they are negative concepts.[236] However, the effect of the application of a mandatory rule of English law is that a foreign domestic law, which would otherwise govern under choice of law rules, is not applied. To that extent application of mandatory rules can be regarded as an exclusionary concept. At the same time, and this brings out the essentially different nature of mandatory rules, there can be circumstances where the concern is to apply the mandatory rules of a foreign country, rather than those of the forum. The statutory rules on choice of law for trusts and contracts[237] provide for the application of foreign mandatory rules. Naturally, under these particular provisions it is not a case of the exclusion of a foreign law, but of its application.

---

[235] S 27(2).

[236] See *Peer International Corpn v Termidor Music Publishers Ltd* [2003] EWCA Civ 1156, [2004] Ch 212; discussed supra, p 138. But see the argument that public policy in contract cases sometimes operates as a positive concept, the concern being to apply English law, infra, pp 736–737. See generally Blom [2003] NILR 373, 379–382.

[237] Infra, pp 1322–1323 and 738–741. Cf the position in relation to torts, see infra, p 851.

Chapter 9

Domicile, Nationality and Residence[1]

---

[1] Kahn, *South African Law of Domicile of Natural Persons* (1972); North (1990) I Hague Recueil 13, 26–48.

1. INTRODUCTION

It has been universally recognised that questions affecting the personal status of a human being should be governed constantly by one and the same law, irrespective of where he may happen to be or of where the facts giving rise to the question may have occurred.[2] But unanimity goes no further. There is disagreement on two matters. What is the scope of this "personal law", as it is called, and should its criterion be domicile or nationality?[3] In England, however, it has long been settled that questions affecting status are determined by the law of the domicile of the *propositus* and that, broadly speaking, such questions are those affecting family relations and family property.[4] To be more precise, the following are some of the matters that are to a greater or lesser extent governed by the personal law:[5] the essential validity of a marriage; the effect of marriage on the proprietary rights of husband and wife; jurisdiction in divorce and nullity of marriage, though only to a limited degree; legitimacy, legitimation and adoption; wills of movables, intestate succession to movables, and inheritance by a dependant.

When it comes to a definition of domicile, this is no easy matter. The concept of domicile is not uniform throughout the world. To a civil lawyer it means habitual residence, but at common law it is regarded as the equivalent of a person's permanent home.[6] Such a definition gives a misleading air of simplicity to the English concept of domicile. It fails to mention, for example, that there are two main classes of domicile; the *domicile of origin* that is communicated by operation of law to each person at birth, ie the domicile of his father or his mother, according as he is legitimate or illegitimate;[7] and the *domicile of choice* which every person of full age is free to acquire in substitution for that which he at present possesses. This distinction relates merely to the acquisition and loss of domicile, not to its effects. It also fails to point out that the acquisition of a domicile of choice requires not only residence in a territory subject to a distinctive legal system,[8] but also an intention by the *propositus* to remain there permanently. "There must be the act and there must be the intention."[9] But, as will be seen,[10] both the concept of permanency and the ascertainment of a person's intentions are fraught with difficulty.

The English concept of domicile is bedevilled by rules; these are complex, often impossible to justify in policy terms, and lead to uncertainty of outcome. Before looking at these rules in detail, one preliminary matter should be considered. This is the question of whether the same test for domicile applies, regardless of the context in which the matter is raised.

---

[2] Rabel, i, 109; and see Kahn-Freund (1974) III Hague Recueil 139, 334–335, 391–492.

[3] On the respective merits of nationality and domicile see infra, pp 179–181.

[4] It will be seen, infra, pp 210–213, that domicile is an important basis of jurisdiction in the very different context of jurisdiction in civil and commercial matters, where domicile is given a special meaning, see the Civil Jurisdiction and Judgments Order, SI 2001/3929, para 9 of Sch I and Art 60 of Council Regulation (EC) No 44/2001 of 22 December 2000 on jurisdiction and the recognition and enforcement of judgments in civil and commercial matters (the Brussels I Regulation), discussed infra, pp 204–341.

[5] See further *Mark v Mark* [2005] UKHL 42 at [38], [2006] 1 AC 98.

[6] *Whicker v Hume* (1858) 7 HL Cas 124 at 160.

[7] Infra, p 155.

[8] *Henderson v Henderson* [1967] P 77 at 79.

[9] *Munro v Munro* (1840) 7 Cl & Fin 842.

[10] Infra, p 159 et seq.

According to what W W Cook called the "single conception theory", English law takes the view that the test which determines the place of a person's domicile must remain constant no matter what the nature of the issue may be before the court. Cook,[11] however, denied that this was true in practice. He regarded "domicile" as a relative term which varies in meaning according to the different situations (eg taxation, divorce, intestate succession) to which it is applicable. A judge, he said, must inevitably focus his attention on the concrete problem before him, otherwise he will neglect the "social and economic" requirements of the situation. Although there appears to have been a tendency in the USA to adopt this view,[12] the conventional approach in England has been to reject it.[13] However, it should be noted that under the Inheritance Tax Act 1984[14] there is a special definition whereby, for certain purposes, persons are treated as domiciled in the United Kingdom. Also it is hard to believe that judges in this country have not been influenced by an awareness of the consequences of the finding as to domicile in the particular case before them.[15] There is evidence[16] that the courts wish to achieve a number of policy objectives: in particular, to validate wills. It is easy for courts to achieve the right result by manipulating the process for ascertaining the domicile, and this is a likely explanation of many cases which are otherwise hard to reconcile on their facts.

2. GENERAL RULES

There are five general rules that may be briefly discussed.

It is a settled principle that nobody shall be without a domicile,[17] and in order to make this effective the law assigns what is called a domicile of origin to every person at his birth, namely, to a legitimate child the domicile of the father, to an illegitimate child the domicile of the mother,[18] and to a foundling the place where he is found.[19] This domicile of origin prevails until a new domicile has been acquired,[20] so that if a person leaves the country of his origin with an undoubted intention of never returning to it again, nevertheless his domicile of origin adheres to him until he actually settles with the requisite intention in some other country.[21]

Secondly, a person cannot have two domiciles.[22] Since the object of the law in insisting that no person shall be without a domicile is to establish a definite legal system by which certain of his rights and obligations may be governed, and since the facts and events of his

---

[11] *Logical and Legal Bases of the Conflict of Laws*, pp 194 et seq; Kahn-Freund (1974) III Hague Recueil 139, 404–405.

[12] Reese (1955) 55 Col LR 589; Restatement 2d, section 11(2).

[13] Eg 7th Report of the Private International Law Committee, 1963 (Cmnd 1955), para 12.

[14] S 267; see the Income Tax (Earnings and Pensions) Act 2003, s 10; Income Tax (Trading and Other Income) Act 2005, s 636.

[15] See Fawcett (1985) 5 OJLS 378.

[16] Fawcett, ibid.

[17] *Mark v Mark* [2005] UKHL 42 at [37], [2006] 1 AC 98.

[18] *Udny v Udny* (1869) LR 1 Sc & Div 441 at 457.

[19] Westlake, s 248; Dicey, Morris and Collins, para 6R-025. See also *Re McKenzie* (1951) 51 SRNSW 293.

[20] *Munro v Munro* (1840) 7 Cl & Fin 842 at 876.

[21] Infra, pp 159–167.

[22] *Mark v Mark* [2005] UKHL 42 at [37], [2006] 1 AC 98. See also *IRC v Bullock* [1976] 1 WLR 1178 at 1184; *Lawrence v Lawrence* [1985] Fam 106 at 132.

life frequently impinge upon several countries, it is necessary on practical grounds to hold that he cannot possess more than one domicile at the same time, at least for the same purpose.[23]

Domicile signifies connection with what has conveniently been called a "law district",[24] ie a territory subject to a single system of law. In the case of a federation, where the legislative authority is distributed between the state and federal legislatures, this law district is generally represented by the particular state in which the *propositus* has established his home.[25] A resident in the USA for instance, is not normally domiciled in the USA as such, but in one of its states. Nevertheless, the doctrine of unity of domicile—one man, one domicile—may be modified by federal legislation. Thus the Family Law Act 1975, which has force throughout the Commonwealth of Australia, provides, inter alia, that proceedings for a decree of dissolution of marriage may be instituted if either party to the marriage is "domiciled in Australia".[26] Thus, the effect within a limited field is to create an Australian, as distinct from a state, domicile and, indeed, one that, because of statutory amendments in this limited context,[27] is different from domicile in a state for other purposes, eg succession.[28]

Thirdly, the fact that domicile signifies connection with a single system of territorial law does not necessarily connote a system that prescribes identical rules for all classes of persons. It may well be that in a unit such as India different legal rules apply to different classes of the population according to their religion, race or caste, but nonetheless it is the territorial law of India that governs each person domiciled there, notwithstanding that Hindu law may apply to one case, Moslem to another.

Fourthly, there is a presumption in favour of the continuance of an existing domicile. Therefore the burden of proving a change lies in all cases on those who allege that a change has occurred.[29] This presumption may have a decisive effect, for if the evidence is so conflicting or indeterminate that it is impossible to elicit with certainty what the resident's intention is, the court will decide in favour of the existing domicile.[30]

The standard of proof necessary to rebut the presumption is that adopted in civil actions, which requires the intention of the *propositus* to be proved on a balance of probabilities, not beyond reasonable doubt as is the case in criminal proceedings.[31] It has been said that

---

[23] Cf supra, pp 154–155, and see Restatement 2d, § 11(2).

[24] Dicey, Morris and Collins, para 6-016.

[25] Cf Nigeria: *Odiase v Odiase* [1965] NMLR 196.

[26] Family Law Act 1975, s 39(3)(b).

[27] Ibid, s 4(3); see Nygh (1976) 25 ICLQ 674.

[28] *Lloyd v Lloyd* [1961] 2 FLR 349; and see *Re Benko* [1968] SASR 243 (both decisions on the earlier Matrimonial Causes Act 1959); but now see the Domicile Act 1982, s 11 (adopted uniformly in Australia), and in New Zealand the Domicile Act 1976, s 10. The Canadian Divorce Act 1968 provided similarly that divorce jurisdiction could be exercised over a petitioner "domiciled in Canada": s 5(1); however, domicile is no longer used as a connecting factor in cases of divorce jurisdiction: Divorce and Corollary Relief Act 1985.

[29] *Winans v A-G* [1904] AC 287 at 289; *Re Lloyd Evans* [1947] Ch 695; *Messina v Smith* [1971] P 322 at 330; *Puttick v A-G* [1980] Fam 1 at 17; *Spence v Spence* 1995 SLT 335; *Bheekhun v Williams* [1999] 2 FLR 229, 234, CA; *Reddington v Riach's Executor* 2002 SLT 537 at [27], OH.

[30] See, eg, *Winans v A-G*, supra, Lord HALSBURY's speech.

[31] *Re Fuld's Estate (No 3)* [1968] P 675 at 685–686; *Re Flynn* [1968] 1 WLR 103 at 115; *Re Edwards, Edwards v Edwards* (1969) 113 Sol Jo 108; *Buswell v IRC* [1974] 1 WLR 1631 at 1637; but see *Lawrence v Lawrence* [1985] Fam 106 at 110, 111, where the matter was left open by LINCOLN J; affd by the Court of Appeal, ibid at 120, without discussion of this point.

there is a heavy burden of proof of loss of a domicile of origin[32] and Sir Jocelyn SIMON P has gone further and suggested that, when the displacement of a domicile of origin by a domicile of choice is alleged, "the standard of proof goes beyond a mere balance of probabilities".[33] This observation no doubt stems from such cases as *Winans v A-G*[34] which appear to regard the intention in favour of retaining the domicile of origin as an almost irrebuttable presumption. SCARMAN J, however, after observing that the language used in such cases emphasises as much the nature and quality of the intention to be proved as the standard of proof required, observed that: "Two things are clear—first that unless the judicial conscience is satisfied by evidence of change, the domicile of origin persists; and secondly, that the acquisition of a domicile of choice is a serious matter not to be lightly inferred from slight indications or casual words."[35] The Court of Appeal when endorsing this approach has actually disapproved of the use of the phrase "heavy burden".[36]

The fifth and final rule[37] is that, subject to certain statutory exceptions,[38] the domicile of a person is to be determined according to the English and not the foreign concept of domicile.[39]

3. THE ACQUISITION OF A DOMICILE OF CHOICE[40]

The two requisites for the acquisition of a fresh domicile are residence and intention. It must be proved that the person in question established his residence in a certain country with the intention of remaining there permanently. Such an intention, however unequivocal it may be, does not per se suffice.[41] These two elements of residence and intention must concur,[42] but this is not to say that there need be unity of time in their concurrence. The intention may either precede or succeed the establishment of the residence. The emigrant forms his intention before he leaves England for Australia; the émigré who flees from persecution may not form it until years later.

(a) Residence

Residence and intention are separate but inter-related concepts. "Residence in a country for the purposes of the law of domicile is physical presence in that country as an inhabitant of it."[43] In one case[44] a taxpayer who spent ten to twelve weeks each year in Quebec

---

[32] *Holden v Holden* [1968] NI 7.

[33] *Henderson v Henderson* [1967] P 77 at 80; *Steadman v Steadman* [1976] AC 536 at 563; *R v R (Divorce: Jurisdiction: Domicile)* [2006] 1 FLR 389 at [26].

[34] [1904] AC 287, infra, pp 161–162.

[35] *Re Fuld's Estate (No 3)* [1968] P 675 at 686; approved in *Cyganik v Agulian* [2006] EWCA Civ 129 at [7], [2006] 1 FCR 406. See also *Re Clare (No 2)* [1984] STC 609 at 614.

[36] *Brown v Brown* (1982) 3 FLR 212 at 218, 220.

[37] See infra, p 178.

[38] Family Law Act 1986 s 46(5), infra, p 994.

[39] See *Lawrence v Lawrence* [1985] Fam 106 at 132; *Rowan v Rowan* [1988] ILRM 65 at 67.

[40] The question of capacity to acquire a fresh domicile is discussed infra, p 178.

[41] *Harrison v Harrison* [1953] 1 WLR 865.

[42] *Mark v Mark* [2005] UKHL 42 at [39], [2006] 1 AC 98.

[43] *IRC v Duchess of Portland* [1982] Ch 314 at 318–319. See, eg, *Re S (Hospital Patient: Foreign Curator)* [1996] Fam 23 at 31.

[44] *IRC v Duchess of Portland*, supra.

for the purpose of maintaining her links with that Province with a view ultimately to returning to live was held not to be a resident of Quebec during her presence there since she was not there as an inhabitant. A Russian multi-millionaire who owned twenty houses round the world and used his two houses in England as mere stop-overs whilst on business trips was not resident in England.[45] Normally though, the requirement of residence is easy to establish. Residence is regarded as being a question of fact and one can be resident in a place where one has no right to be.[46]

Residence and intention are inter-related in that, strictly speaking, residence is a fact, though a necessary one, from which intention may be inferred.[47] Older cases adopted a presumption in favour of domicile which grew in strength with the length of the residence and was hard to rebut.[48] However, more recent cases,[49] including House of Lords authorities,[50] have attached less weight to the length of residence, and have taken the view that, although a material consideration, it is rarely decisive.

Whatever weight is given to the length of residence it is undeniable that time is not the sole criterion of domicile.[51] Long residence does not constitute, nor does brief residence negative, domicile. Everything depends on the attendant circumstances, for they alone disclose the nature of the person's presence in a country. In short, the residence must answer "a qualitative as well as a quantitative test".[52] Thus in *Jopp v Wood*[53] it was held that a residence of twenty-five years in India did not suffice to give a certain John Smith an Indian domicile because of his alleged intention ultimately to return to Scotland, the land of his birth. Again, in *IRC v Bullock*[54] a Canadian who had a domicile of origin in Nova Scotia was held not to have become domiciled in England, despite the fact that he had either served in the RAF or lived in England for over forty years. He retained his domicile in Nova Scotia because he intended to return there should his wife predecease him.

Conversely, brevity of residence is no obstacle to the acquisition of a domicile if the necessary intention exists. If a man clearly intends to live in another country permanently, as, for example, where an emigrant, having wound up his affairs in the country of his origin, flies off with his wife and family to Australia, his mere arrival there will satisfy the element of residence.[55]

---

[45] *High Tech International AG v Deripaska* [2006] EWHC 3276 (QB)—a case on domicile for the purposes of the Civil Jurisdiction and Judgments Order 2001, discussed infra, pp 210–211. See also *Cherney v Deripaska* [2007] EWHC 965 (Comm), [2007] IL Pr 49.

[46] *Mark v Mark* [2005] UKHL 42 at [47] (per Baroness HALE), [13] (per Lord HOPE), [2006] 1 AC 98.

[47] *Munro v Munro* (1840) 7 Cl & Fin 842 at 877.

[48] *Stanley v Bernes* (1830) 3 Hag Ecc 373; *Re Marret, Chalmers v Wingfield* (1887) 36 Ch D 400; *Hodgson v De Beauchesne* (1858) 12 Moo PCC 285 at 329; *Udny v Udny* (1869) LR 1 Sc & Div 441 at 455; *Re Liddell-Grainger's Will Trusts, Dormer v Liddell-Grainger* [1936] 3 All ER 173.

[49] Eg *Puttick v A-G* [1980] Fam 1 at 17.

[50] *Winans v A-G* [1904] AC 287 at 297–298; *Bowie (or Ramsay) v Liverpool Royal Infirmary* [1930] AC 588; both cases are discussed, infra, pp 161–163.

[51] *Hodgson v De Beauchesne* (1858) 12 Moo PCC 285 at 329, 330.

[52] *Bowie (or Ramsay) v Liverpool Royal Infirmary* [1930] AC 588 at 598. See *R v R (Divorce: Jurisdiction: Domicile)* [2006] 1 FLR 389 at [24], [26].

[53] (1865) 4 De GJ & Sm 616; and see *A-G v Yule* (1931) 145 LT 9.

[54] [1976] 1 WLR 1178.

[55] *Hodgson v de Beauchesne* (1858) 12 Moo PCC 285 at 330; *Bell v Kennedy* (1868) LR 1 Sc & Div 307 at 319; *PL v An tArd Chlaraitheoir* [1995] 2 ILRM 241; *In the Marriage of Ferrier-Watson & McElrath* [2000] FamCA 219 at [78]–[80]; *Blackett v Darcy* [2005] NSWSC at [13].

A striking example of this truth occurred in the United States.[56]

> A man abandoned his home in State X and took his family to a house in State Y, about half a mile from X, intending to live there permanently. Having deposited his belongings there, he and his family returned to X, in order to spend the night with a relative. He fell ill and died there. It was held that his domicile at death was in Y.

It is possible for a person to be resident in several countries at the same time. In such a case of dual or multiple residence a domicile of choice can only be acquired in a country if this can be shown to be the chief residence.[57] This was established in *Plummer v IRC*.[58] The taxpayer had an English domicile of origin. She spent the majority of each year in England, where she was being educated. However, she spent more than three months of each year in Guernsey, which had become her family home. HOFFMANN J held that, despite the taxpayer's retention of residence in England, her domicile of origin, she could acquire a domicile of choice in Guernsey if she could show that this was her chief residence. This she was unable to do. She had not yet settled in Guernsey. Accordingly she retained her English domicile. The case could, though, have been decided on the much simpler ground that she lacked the requisite intention for acquisition of a Guernsey domicile of choice.[59]

Problems in relation to residence would disappear if this concept were to be replaced by the simpler concept of presence.[60]

(b) The requisite intention

(i) The nature of the intention

(a) An intention to reside permanently

As has already been mentioned,[61] the acquisition of a domicile of choice requires an intention by the *propositus* to remain permanently in the territory in which he resides. This is not difficult to understand if the word permanent is used in its correct sense as signifying the opposite of "temporary". According to the *Shorter Oxford English Dictionary* it means "lasting or designed to last indefinitely without change", and this indeed is the definition that most of the judges have recognised when required to consider the nature of the intention necessary for a change of domicile. In *Udny v Udny*,[62] for instance, Lord WESTBURY described the intention as being one to reside "for an unlimited time".

---

[56] *White v Tennant* 31 W Va 790, 8 SE 596 (1888).

[57] For the meaning of main residence for the purpose of liability to council tax, see *Regina (Williams) v Horsham District Council* [2004] EWCA Civ 39, [2004] 1 WLR 1137.

[58] [1988] 1 WLR 292; Kunzlik [1988] CLJ 187; Carter [1988] 59 BYBIL 350; Smart (1990) 10 OJLS 572. However, dual residence can lead to a dual domicile for the purposes of the Civil Jurisdiction and Judgments Order 2001; cf *Daniel v Foster* 1989 SLT 90.

[59] But see Fentiman [1991] CLJ 445.

[60] This was one of the proposals of the Law Commissions, set out in Law Com No 168 (1987), Scot Law Com No 107 (1987), para 5.7; infra, pp 195–196. However, these proposals have been rejected, Law Com No 239 (1995) p 10, n 24. For Australia see *In the Marriage of Ferrier-Watson & McElrath* [2000] Fam, CA 219 at [80].

[61] Supra, p 157.

[62] (1869) LR 1 Sc & Div 441 at 458; followed in *Re Fuld's Estate (No 3)* [1968] P 675; *Bheekhun v Williams* [1999] 2 FLR 229, 232-233, CA; *Spence v Spence* 1995 SLT 335.

A more modern statement to the same effect is that of Baroness HALE who referred to an intention to reside "permanently or indefinitely".[63]

The essence, therefore, of these and many other similar statements is that the intended residence must not be for a limited period, whether the limitation is expressed in terms of time or made dependent on the occurrence of a contingency, such as the accomplishment of a definite task, that will occur if at all during the life of the *propositus*.

It is also clear that a conditional intention will not suffice. Thus in *Cramer v Cramer*[64] a woman with a French domicile of origin who came to England intending to remain here and marry an Englishman, who was already married, did not acquire an English domicile of choice. Her intention to remain was conditional on both herself and her proposed husband obtaining divorces and on their relationship continuing. It would, no doubt, have been different if she had intended to remain here come what may, but this was not her intention.

(b) Unlikely contingencies

In cases where the termination of residence is dependent on the occurrence of a contingency this will not prevent the acquisition of a domicile unless the contingency is itself unambiguous and realistic. In the words of SCARMAN J:

> If a man intends to return to the land of his birth upon a clearly foreseen and reasonably anticipated contingency, eg the end of his job, the intention required by law is lacking; but, if he has in mind only a vague possibility, such as making a fortune (a modern example might be winning a football pool) . . . such a state of mind is consistent with the intention required by law.[65]

Subsequently, a distinction has been drawn between the question whether a contingency itself is clear and the question whether a contingency which is clear will happen.[66]

If a contingency is not sufficiently clear to be identified then it cannot operate to prevent the acquisition of a domicile of choice. Thus in *Re Furse*[67] evidence that the *propositus*, who had a Rhode Island domicile of origin, would leave England, where he had lived for nearly forty years, if he was no longer able to live an active physical life on his farm was not fatal to a change of domicile, and it was held that the *propositus* had acquired an English domicile of choice. Similarly the vague possibility that in some undefined circumstances a person might decide to move to another country does not weigh against him.[68]

---

[63] *Mark v Mark* [2005] UKHL 42 at [39], [2006] 1 AC 98; *Cyganik v Agulian* [2006] EWCA Civ 129 at [45] (per MUMMERY LJ), [2006] 1 FCR 406. For use of "indefinitely" see also *Re Fuld's Estate (No 3)* [1968] P 675 at 684; and see *Re Edwards, Edwards v Edwards* (1969) 113 Sol Jo 108; *Cramer v Cramer* [1987] 1 FLR 116; *In re S (Hospital Patient: Foreign Curator)* [1996] Fam 23 at 31. For Australia see Domicile Acts 1982, s 10. For New Zealand see Domicile Act 1976, s 9.

[64] [1987] 1 FLR 116.

[65] *Re Fuld's Estate (No 3)*, supra, at 684–685; and see *Henderson v Henderson* [1967] P 77 at 80–81; *Buswell v IRC* [1974] 1 WLR 1631 at 1637; *IRC v Bullock* [1976] 1 WLR 1178 at 1186; *Re Furse* [1980] 3 All ER 838; *Cyganik v Agulian* [2006] EWCA Civ 129 at [6], [2006] 1 FCR 406; *Gould v Gould* 1968 SLT 98.

[66] *IRC v Bullock* [1976] 1 WLR 1178 at 1186.

[67] [1980] 3 All ER 838. See also *Doucet v Geoghegan* (1878) 9 Ch D 441; *Lawrence v Lawrence* [1985] Fam 106 at 110–111; affd by the Court of Appeal without discussion on this point. Distinguished in *Proes v Revenue Commissioners* [1998] 4 IR 176, where the contingency of "if no longer able to look after herself" was held to be clear.

[68] *North v Skipton Building Society* 2002 WL 1039545 at [21].

On the other hand, if the contingency can be identified, it has to be asked whether there is a substantial possibility of the contingency happening; if there is, this will prevent the acquisition of a domicile of choice. Thus in *IRC v Bullock*,[69] where a husband intended to return to Canada to live permanently if his wife predeceased him, it was held that the husband did not acquire an English domicile of choice, since there was a real possibility, in view of their ages, of this happening. Of course, if there is no substantial possibility of a contingency happening, the evidence evincing a desire to leave the residence will not prevent the acquisition of a domicile of choice.[70]

(c) The former attitude towards contingencies: *Winans v A-G, Ramsay v Liverpool Royal Infirmary*

That a contingency must be something more than a vague possibility if it is to prevent the acquisition of a domicile in the country of residence has not been invariably accepted by the courts. It has several times been affirmed, and more than once by the House of Lords, that the present residence of a man is not to be equated with domicile if he contemplates some remote or uncertain event, whose occurrence at some indeterminate time in the future might cause him to leave his country of residence. If this possibility is present to his mind, even an intention to reside indefinitely in the country is said to be ineffective.[71] This view appears to equate the word "permanent" with "perpetual", and to require for a change of domicile an irrevocable intention never to abandon the present place of domicile. Yet it is no part of the law that the intention to maintain the residence should be irrevocable,[72] for such a requirement would virtually exclude the acquisition of a domicile of choice.[73] Nevertheless, in *Winans v A-G*[74] and in *Bowie (or Ramsay) v Liverpool Royal Infirmary*,[75] the House of Lords came very near to regarding a vague possibility as if it were, to cite the words of SCARMAN J again, "a clearly foreseen and reasonably anticipated contingency".[76] The facts of the former case were these:

> Winans was born in 1823 in the USA, where he was continuously engaged in his father's business until 1850. From 1850 to 1859 he resided in Russia. He married a British subject and appears never to have set foot again in the USA. In 1859 he showed signs of consumption, and, being advised by the doctors to winter in Brighton in England, he reluctantly took rooms at a hotel there, and in 1860 leased two adjoining houses. He still held these houses at the time of his death. From 1860 to 1893 he spent time each year in England but also time in Scotland, Germany or Russia. From 1893 until he died in 1897 he lived entirely in England. The Crown

---

[69] [1976] 1 WLR 1178; Carter (1976–77) 48 BYBIL 362; *Cramer v Cramer* [1987] 1 FLR 116; see also *Qureshi v Qureshi* [1972] Fam 173.

[70] *Pletinka v Pletinka* (1964) 109 Sol Jo 72; see also *Osvath-Latkoczy v Osvath-Latkoczy* (1959) 19 DLR (2d) 495.

[71] *Moorhouse v Lord* (1863) 10 HL Cas 272 at 285–286; *Jopp v Wood* (1865) 4 De GJ & Sm 616; *Goulder v Goulder* [1892] P 240; *Winans v A-G* [1904] AC 287; *Bowie (or Ramsay) v Liverpool Royal Infirmary* [1930] AC 588; *A-G v Yule* (1931) 145 LT 9; *Wahl v A-G* (1932) 147 LT 382. The rigorous theory adopted in these decisions has been rejected in South Africa: *Eilon v Eilon* 1965 (1) SA 703 at 708–709.

[72] *Gulbenkian v Gulbenkian* [1937] 4 All ER 618 at 627; *IRC v Bullock* [1976] 1 WLR 1178 at 1184; *Lawrence v Lawrence* [1985] Fam 106 at 110–111; affd by the Court of Appeal, without discussion of this point.

[73] See *A-G v Pottinger* (1861) 30 LJ Ex 284 at 292.

[74] [1904] AC 287.

[75] [1930] AC 588.

[76] Supra, p 160.

claimed legacy duty on a comparatively small amount of property abroad. Such duty was payable only if he had acquired an English domicile at the time of his death.

The fact that he had resided principally in England for the last thirty-seven years of his life raised a very strong presumption in favour of an English domicile, but there was no direct evidence as to what his intention was. Lord MACNAGHTEN analysed with some particularity the hopes, projects and daily habits of Mr Winans. He found that, in addition to the care of his health, Mr Winans had two objects in life. The first was the construction in Baltimore of a large fleet of spindle-shaped vessels, which would give the USA superiority at sea over Britain. The second object was to develop a large property of about 200 acres in Baltimore. On this, wharves and docks were to be constructed for the spindle-shaped vessels, and a large house built in which Mr Winans intended to live in order that he might take personal command of the whole undertaking. He succeeded in getting control of the property only at the very end of his life, and at the time of his death he was working day and night on the scheme.

Lord MACNAGHTEN reached the conclusion that the domicile of origin in New Jersey had not been lost. He said that "up to the very last he had an expectation or hope of returning to America and seeing his grand scheme inaugurated".[77] Lord HALSBURY found it impossible to infer from the evidence what Mr Winans' intention was, and he held therefore that the Crown had not discharged its duty of proving a change of domicile. Lord LINDLEY vigorously dissented. In his view Winans had given up all serious idea of returning to America.[78]

Bowie (or Ramsay) v Liverpool Royal Infirmary[79] concerned one George Bowie, who had left a will that was formally valid if his domicile at death was Scottish but invalid if it was English. The story of his life was uneventful.

> He was born in Glasgow in 1845 with a Scottish domicile of origin. He gave up his employment as a commercial traveller at the age of thirty-seven and refused to do any more work during the remaining forty-five years of his life. But even the idle must be fed, and after residing with his mother and sisters in Glasgow, he moved his residence to Liverpool in 1892 in order to live on the bounty of his brother. At first he lived in lodgings, but moved to his brother's house when the latter died twenty-one years later, and resided there with his sole surviving sister until she died in 1920. He remained there until his own death in 1927.

Thus George lived in England for the last thirty-six years of his life. During that time he left the country only twice, once on a short visit to the USA, on the second occasion to take a holiday in the Isle of Man. Though he often said he was proud to be a Glasgow man, he resolutely refused on several occasions to return to Scotland, even for the purpose of attending his mother's funeral. On the contrary, he had expressed his determination never to set foot in Glasgow again and had arranged his own burial in Liverpool.

Thus evidence was completely lacking of any inclination, either by words or actions, to disturb a long and practically uninterrupted residence in England. Nevertheless the

---

[77] [1904] AC 287 at 298.

[78] [1904] AC 287 at 300. The decision against the acquisition of an English domicile was virtually that of Lord MACNAGHTEN alone. In the courts below, KENNEDY J, PHILLIMORE J (83 LT 634), COLLINS MR, STIRLING LJ and MATHEW LJ (85 LT 508), reached the opposite conclusion without any hesitation.

[79] [1930] AC 588.

House of Lords held unanimously that George died domiciled in Scotland. Their Lordships denied that his prolonged residence disclosed an intention to choose England as his permanent home. Rather, they inferred that had his English source of supply failed he would have retreated to Glasgow.

(d) Evaluation of judicial statements and decisions

It would, however, be a mistake to exaggerate the importance of judicial pronouncements or decisions which on the surface appear to distort the character of the intention that is necessary for the acquisition of a domicile. SCARMAN J has stressed that the difficulty of reconciling the numerous statements arises not from lack of clarity of judicial thought, but from the nature of the subject. The cases involve a detailed examination of the facts and it is not surprising that different judicial minds concerned with different factual situations have chosen different language to describe the law.[80] SCARMAN J would regard the difference between the statements of judges in earlier cases as showing a difference of emphasis and therefore as being of no great moment.[81]

It may well be, then, that to construct a formula which describes the precise intention required by English law for the acquisition of a domicile of choice is an impossibility, but perhaps the most satisfactory definition was that offered nearly a hundred and fifty years ago by KINDERSLEY V-C:

> That place is properly the domicile of a person in which he has voluntarily fixed the habitation of himself and his family, not for a mere special and temporary purpose, but with a present intention of making it his permanent home, unless and until something (which is unexpected or the happening of which is uncertain) shall occur to induce him to adopt some other permanent home.[82]

(e) Time at which intention is relevant

The traditional statement that there must be a *present* intention of permanent residence merely means that so far as the mind of the person at the relevant time was concerned he possessed the requisite intention. The relevant time varies with the nature of the inquiry. It may be past or present. If, for example, the inquiry relates to the domicile of a deceased person, it must be ascertained whether at some period in his life he had formed and retained a fixed and settled intention of residence in a given country. Once this is established, evidence of his subsequent fluctuations of opinion as to whether he would or would not move elsewhere will be ignored.[83] If, on the other hand, the essential validity of a proposed marriage depends on the law of X's domicile and if the identity of this law is in doubt, what must be examined is his immediate intention.

(f) A bona fide intention

The intention must be bona fide "in the sense of being genuine and not pretended for some other purpose, such as getting a divorce to which one would not be entitled by the law of the true domicile".[84]

---

[80] *Re Fuld's Estate (No 3)* [1968] P 675 at 682–683.
[81] Ibid, at 684.
[82] *Lord v Colvin* (1859) 4 Drew 366 at 376.
[83] *Re Marrett, Chalmers v Wingfield* (1887) 36 Ch D 400.
[84] *Mark v Mark* [2005] UKHL 42 at [47], [2006] 1 AC 98.

(ii) Evidence of intention

The question whether a person has formed the requisite intention is one of fact.[85] It is impossible to lay down any positive rule with respect to the evidence necessary to prove intention. All that can be said is that every conceivable event and incident in a man's life is a relevant and an admissible indication of his state of mind. Everything said and done during the whole of a person's life should be considered, taking account of things said and done after as well as before the time when it is alleged that the chosen domicile has been acquired.[86] It may be necessary to examine the history of his life with the most scrupulous care, and to resort even to hearsay evidence where the question concerns the domicile that a person, now deceased, possessed in his lifetime.[87] Nothing must be overlooked that might possibly show the place which he regarded as his permanent home at the relevant time.[88] No fact is too trifling to merit consideration.[89] Indeed, one of the defects of English law is that the evidence adduced in a disputed case of domicile is often both voluminous and difficult to assess. This is due to the over-scrupulous manner in which the courts attempt to discover a man's exact intention. The tendency is to investigate his actual state of mind, rather than to rest content with the natural inference of his long-continued residence in a given country. This, indeed, is to set sail on an uncharted sea. Nothing must be neglected that can possibly indicate the bent of the resident's mind. His aspirations, whims, *amours*, prejudices, health, religion, financial expectations—all are taken into account.[90]

Having regard, therefore, to the roving commission imposed on the courts, it is not surprising that their decisions exhibit a multiplicity of different factors that have been regarded as *indicia* of intention. Without attempting to give an exhaustive list, it may be useful to observe that at one time or another the following have been regarded as relevant criteria of intention: naturalisation,[91] retention of citizenship,[92] obtaining a passport,[93] purchase[94] or building of a house,[95] where income is earned,[96] purchase of a burial ground,[97] directions in a will as to burial in a particular country,[98] a long period of residence in a country,[99]

---

[85] *Mark v Mark* [2005] UKHL 42 at [47], [2006] 1 AC 98.

[86] *Bheekhun v Williams* [1999] 2 FLR 229, 237, CA.

[87] *Scappaticci v A-G* [1955] P 47.

[88] See, eg, the voluminous evidence considered by CHITTY J in *Re Craignish* [1892] 3 Ch 180.

[89] *Drevon v Drevon* (1864) 34 LJ Ch 129 at 133; and see *Re Flynn, Flynn v Flynn* [1968] 1 WLR 103 at 107; *Morgan v Cilento* [2004] EWHC 188 (Ch), [2004] All ER (D) 122.

[90] *Casdagli v Casdagli* [1919] AC 145 at 178.

[91] *D'Etchegoyen v D'Etchegoyen* (1888) 13 PD 132; *Qureshi v Qureshi* [1972] Fam 173 at 190–191.

[92] *IRC v Bullock* [1976] 1 WLR 1178; *Bheekhun v Williams* [1999] 2 FLR 229, 235, CA; *R v R (Divorce: Jurisdiction: Domicile)* [2006] 1 FLR 389 at [26]; *Dellar v Zivy* [2007] EWHC 2266 (Ch) at [35], [2007] IL Pr 60.

[93] *Bheekhun v Williams*, supra.

[94] *D'Etchegoyen v D'Etchegoyen*, supra; *Moorhouse v Lord* (1863) 10 HL Cas 272; for the history of this case see Thompson and Mackie [1979] Jur Rev 138; *Stevenson v Masson* (1873) LR 17 Eq 78; *Re Craignish* [1892] 3 Ch 180. See also *Henwood v Barlow Clowes International Ltd (in Liquidation)* [2007] EWHC 1579 (Ch), renting for 13 years.

[95] *Morgan v Cilento* [2004] EWHC 188 (Ch), [2004] All ER (D) 122.

[96] *R v R (Divorce: Jurisdiction: Domicile)* [2006] 1 FLR 389 at [24]; *Dellar v Zivy* [2007] EWHC 2266 (Ch) at [35], [2007] IL Pr 60.

[97] *Stevenson v Masson*, supra; *Haldane v Eckford* (1869) LR 8 Eq 631.

[98] *Reddington v Riach's Executor* 2002 SLT 537 at [29], OH.

[99] *Bheekhun v Williams* [1999] 2 FLR 229, 237, CA; *Reddington v Riach's Executor* 2002 SLT 537 at [29], OH; *R (On the Application of Haqq) v Knapman* [2003] EWHC 3366 at [51] (Admin); *Henwood v Barlow Clowes International*

the exercise of political rights,[100] such as voting,[101] not learning the language of the country in which you are living,[102] not acquiring a bank account or credit cards in that country,[103] the establishment of children in business,[104] the statutory declaration made by a candidate for naturalisation that he intends to reside permanently in the United Kingdom,[105] the place where a man's wife and family reside,[106] statements by an elderly person that the move would be his last,[107] departure from a country owing to compulsion of war,[108] the refusal of a foreign *fiancée* to leave her own country,[109] statements as to his domiciliary intentions made by a deceased person in his lifetime,[110] a statement by the *propositus* that the marriage should be dissolved in England because this was where he and his wife resided,[111] the effect of racial intolerance on domiciliary intention,[112] the fact that a family is split between England and abroad,[113] choosing on separation to come to a country rather than returning to one's homeland,[114] and remaining in a country after a spouse has died.[115]

Undue stress must not be laid on any single fact however impressive it may appear when viewed out of its context, for its importance as a determining factor may well be minimised when considered in the light of other qualifying events. Again, no one fact is of constant value, for every case varies in its circumstances, and what is of decisive importance in one may be of little weight in another.[116]

It is for this reason that it is impossible to formulate a rule specifying the weight to be given to particular evidence. All that can be gathered from the authorities in this respect is that more reliance is placed on conduct rather than declarations of intention, especially if they are oral.[117] Nevertheless, the common law rule, that expressions of intention by a living person cannot be received in evidence unless against his own interest, is not applicable to an issue of domicile,[118] and it is common enough for witnesses to testify

---

Ltd (in Liquidation) [2007] EWHC 1579 (Ch). See also *In the Marriage of Ferrier-Watson & McElrath* [2000] Fam, CA 219 at [83].

[100] *Drevon v Drevon* (1864) 34 LJ Ch 129 at 137.

[101] *Morgan v Cilento* [2004] EWHC 188 (Ch), [2004] All ER (D) 122; *R v R (Divorce: Jurisdiction: Domicile)* [2006] 1 FLR 389 at [24].

[102] *Irvin v Irvin* [2001] 1 FLR 178 at 194.

[103] *R v R (Divorce: Jurisdiction: Domicile)* [2006] 1 FLR 389 at [24].

[104] *Stevenson v Masson* (1873) LR 17 Eq 78.

[105] *Gulbenkian v Gulbenkian* [1937] 4 All ER 618; distinguish *Wahl v A-G* (1932) 147 LT 382 and see *Steiner v IRC* (1973) 49 TC 13.

[106] *Forbes v Forbes* (1854) Kay 341; *Aitchison v Dixon* (1870) LR 10 Eq 589; cf *IRC v Bullock* [1976] 1 WLR 1178 at 1185; *Cyganik v Agulian* [2006] EWCA Civ 129 at [46], [2006] 1 FCR 406.

[107] *Reddington v Riach's Executor* 2002 SLT 537 at [29], OH.

[108] *Re Lloyd Evans* [1947] Ch 695.

[109] *Donaldson v Donaldson* [1949] P 363.

[110] *Scappaticci v A-G* [1955] P 47.

[111] *Bheekhun v Williams* [1999] 2 FLR 229 at 238, CA.

[112] *Qureshi v Qureshi* [1972] Fam 173 at 193.

[113] *Begum v Entry Clearance Officer, Dacca* [1983] Imm AR 163.

[114] *Marsh v Marsh* 2002 SLT 87, Sh Principal.

[115] *Reddington v Riach's Executor* 2002 SLT 537 at [29], OH.

[116] *Hodgson v De Beauchesne* (1858) 12 Moo PCC 285 at 330; *Doucet v Geoghegan* (1878) 9 Ch D 441 at 445; *Wahl v A-G* (1932) 147 LT 382.

[117] *McMullen v Wadsworth* (1889) 14 App Cas 631 at 636, PC.

[118] *Bryce v Bryce* [1933] P 83; Civil Evidence Act 1968, s 2(1).

to parol declarations made during his life by the person whose domicile is in question. This kind of evidence, however, especially when given long after the conversation occurred, is suspect, for witnesses may lie or forget.[119] Little weight should be given to this kind of evidence.[120] Declarations should contain "a real expression of intention",[121] for it only too frequently happens that they cannot be taken at their face value. They may be interested statements designed to flatter or to deceive the hearer; they may represent nothing more than vain expectations unlikely to be fulfilled; and the very facility with which they can be made requires their sincerity to be manifested by some active step taken in furtherance of the expressed intention. The circumstances in which the statement is made need to be considered, and any declaration must be backed up by conduct consistent with the declared intention.[122]

Even lower in the scale of values is evidence given in the course of the trial by the person himself not of his past declarations, but of his past intention. This must be accepted with very considerable reserve, for on such a personal issue as his own place of domicile he is under a bias that is likely to influence his mind, perhaps even his veracity.[123] It is different, and some significance will be attached to the evidence, in the situation where the person whose domicile is in issue has nothing to be gained from the outcome of the present proceedings and his actions are consistent with this evidence.[124]

In at least two respects, motive, in the sense of the antecedent desire that determines the will to act, is one of the *indicia* of the intention requisite for the acquisition of a domicile of choice. First, it may throw light on the question whether the removal to another country was intended to be permanent. It will serve, for instance, to contrast the case of a man who flees to England to escape political persecution in his own country with that of a retired officer who goes to Jersey to avoid heavy taxation. Secondly, it may provide means of testing the sincerity of a declaration of intention. Thus, if a widower testifies that at the time of his wife's death he and she regarded Scotland as their permanent home, the fact that by Scots law he is entitled to one-half of his wife's property may make his testimony a little suspect.[125] Both of these points arose in *Spence v Spence*,[126] where the dominant reason for a couple's departure from Spain had been to avoid tax liability. It was held that the husband had not acquired a domicile of choice in Spain, where he had lived for nine years. The court was wary of his statement of an intention to remain in Spain in the future. It was also relevant that he had not registered as a Spanish resident, paid no taxes there, and his business ventures had links with a number of other countries.

---

[119] *Hodgson v De Beauchesne* (1858) 12 Moo PCC 285; *Re Liddell-Grainger's Will Trusts* [1936] 3 All ER 173; *Re Fuld's Estate (No 3)* [1968] P 675 at 691–692.

[120] *Cyganik v Agulian* [2006] EWCA Civ 129 at [13], [2006] 1 FCR 406.

[121] *Hodgson v De Beauchesne*, supra, at 325.

[122] *Ross v Ross* [1930] AC 1 at 6; and see *Qureshi v Qureshi* [1972] Fam 173 at 192–193; *Spence v Spence* 1995 SLT 335 at 340; *Marsh v Marsh* 2002 SLT 87; *Reddington v Riach's Executor* 2002 SLT 537 at [29], OH. In several cases even written declarations have been disregarded: *Re Martin* [1900] P 211—declaration in mortgage deed; *Re Liddell-Grainger's Will Trusts* [1936] 3 All ER 173—declaration in a will; *Wahl v A-G* (1932) 147 LT 382—declaration in naturalisation papers; *Buswell v IRC* [1974] 1 WLR 1631—declaration on an Inland Revenue form.

[123] *Bell v Kennedy* (1868) LR 1 Sc & Div 307 at 313; *Re Craignish* [1892] 3 Ch 180 at 190; *Chaudhary v Chaudhary* [1985] Fam 19 at 26, affd by CA, ibid at 33; *Spence v Spence* 1995 SLT 335 at 340.

[124] *PL v An tArd Chlaraitheoir* [1995] 2 ILRM 241. See also *Brown v Brown* (1982) 3 FLR 212 at 214–215 where the declaration was consistent with conduct.

[125] Cf *Re Craignish* [1892] 3 Ch 180.

[126] 1995 SLT 335.

It is important to realise that the only intention relevant to a change of domicile is an intention to settle permanently in a country. This will effect a change of domicile even if the *propositus* intended to retain his former personal law.[127] One of the legal consequences of an intention to settle in country X is that the person in question becomes subject to the law of X whether this is his wish or not. It is the inevitable effect of his residence in that country coupled with his intention to remain there without any limit of time.[128]

(c) Voluntary residence

It is a commonplace that to constitute domicile a residence must be voluntary—a matter of free choice,[129] not of constraint. In several cases, the circumstances may raise a doubt as to whether such freedom exists.

(i) Prisoners

A clear example of constraint preclusive of this freedom is imprisonment in a foreign country, and there is no doubt that a prisoner, except perhaps one transported or exiled for life, retains the domicile that he possessed before his confinement.[130]

(ii) Refugees/persons seeking asylum

It cannot be predicated that refugees necessarily retain their former domicile. The motive that induced the flight no doubt militates against the inference that there was an intention of permanent residence in the chosen asylum. There is a presumption against a change of domicile, but "what is dictated by necessity in the first instance may afterwards become a matter of choice",[131] and the presumption may well be reversed by subsequent circumstances, as, for example, by the continued retention of the residence after a return to the original country has become safe and practicable.[132]

(iii) Fugitives from justice

Another example of involuntary residence in a new country is that of the fugitive from justice. Nevertheless, if a man leaves his domicile in order to escape the consequences of crime, the natural inference is that he has left for ever and that a presumption arises in favour of the acquisition of a fresh domicile in the country of refuge. His departure, has indeed, been forced upon him, yet this does not necessarily mean that he intends it to be temporary. For example, in *Moynihan v Moynihan (Nos 1 and 2)*[133] it was held that the *propositus*, who had left the United Kingdom to avoid arrest on serious fraud charges, had, at his death, acquired a domicile of choice in the Philippines, where he had lived for

---

[127] *Douglas v Douglas* (1871) LR 12 Eq 617 at 644, 645; *Re Steer* (1858) 3 H & N 594. To the same effect, *Re Liddell-Grainger's Will Trusts* [1936] 3 All ER 173.

[128] *Re Craignish* [1892] 3 Ch 180 at 188, 189.

[129] It may perhaps be more accurate to say that in all cases physical presence in a country satisfies the requirement of residence, and that constraint is relevant only to the question of intention; see McClean (1962) 11 ICLQ 1156–1160.

[130] *Burton v Fisher* (1828) Milw 183; *Burton v Dolben* (1756) 2 Lee 312 at 318; *Re the late Emperor Napoleon Bonaparte* (1853) 2 Rob Eccl 606.

[131] *Winans v A-G* (1901) 85 LT 508 at 510.

[132] *De Bonneval v De Bonneval* (1838) 1 Curt 856; *May v May* [1943] 2 All ER 146; cf *Re Evans* [1947] Ch 695.

[133] [1997] 1 FLR 59.

twenty years, built up a thriving business, acquired properties, married and had children. In *Re Martin, Loustalan v Loustalan*,[134] however, LINDLEY LJ suggested that the "all-important" factor is whether there is a definite period after which a wrongdoer may return home in safety. In other words, if the crime ceases to be punishable or the sentence to be enforceable after a given number of years, residence in another country, unless fortified by other facts, does not effect a change of domicile; but if the fugitive remains perpetually liable to proceedings, then the new place of residence becomes the new domicile.[135] This view was not adopted by the other members of the court, RIGBY LJ remarking that to suggest that the fugitive in question intended at the time of his escape from France to return as soon as he could safely do so (twenty years in the particular case) was "so irrational that, in default of the strongest evidence, it ought not to be imputed to him".[136] It is, indeed, difficult to agree with LINDLEY LJ, except possibly where the offence is trifling and the term of prescription short. The judgment of LINDLEY LJ was not referred to in the judgment of Sir Stephen BROWN P in *Moynihan v Moynihan (Nos 1 and 2)*.

Re Martin was concerned with the possibility of a fugitive from justice being free to return to his domicile abroad; more recently, the entirely different problem has arisen of the possibility of a fugitive being forced to return to face justice abroad under an extradition treaty. If the fugitive never set up a home and has no affection for England, merely seeing it as a place of refuge, and is ready to move on if detection and arrest is imminent, a domicile of choice will not be acquired.[137]

(iv) Fugitive debtors

Freedom of choice is also affected when a man finds it desirable to flee the country to avoid his creditors. Whether this raises a presumption against an intention to return to his own country must obviously depend on a variety of circumstances, such as the amount of the debts, the possibility of meeting them, the imminence of legal proceedings, the activities of the debtor in his new residence and so on. It certainly cannot be said that the adoption of the new residence per se effects a change of domicile.[138]

(v) Invalids

The case of an invalid who settles in a foreign country for the sake of his health, not merely for the purpose of convalescence, should on principle cause no difficulty. The principle is that unless a man is a free agent his adoption of a new residence does not effect a change of domicile. He must have an alternative—either to stay or to go. But it would seem that an alternative is open to every invalid. To take even the extreme case, if a man, being assured by his doctors that he has only a few months to live, decides to spend the short remainder of his life in a country where the climate may alleviate his suffering, it would seem clear, if all sentiment of pity is dismissed, that of his own volition he has chosen a new and permanent home, since he intends to continue his new residence until death. The residence and intention essential for a change of domicile are present.

---

[134] [1900] P 211.
[135] Ibid, at 232.
[136] Ibid, at 235.
[137] *Puttick v A-G* [1980] Fam 1 at 18.
[138] Eg see *Pitt v Pitt* (1864) 4 Macq 627; *Udny v Udny* (1869) LR 1 Sc & Div 441; *Briggs v Briggs* (1880) 5 PD 163; *Re Robertson* (1885) 2 TLR 178; *Re Wright's Trusts* (1856) 25 LJ Ch 621 at 624.

Yet, this suggestion has been stigmatised by Lord KINGSDOWN as "revolting to common sense and the common feelings of humanity".[139] No doubt it is, and no doubt a court would in fact declare against a change of domicile in such circumstances, but nevertheless the decision would be difficult to reconcile with strict principle unless, perhaps, it could be buttressed by the argument that the invalid contemplated a return to his former home if the medical verdict should prove to be unfounded.

The case just put, however, is an extreme one. Where the necessity of selecting a different climate is of a less compelling nature, where there is no immediate danger,[140] the normal principle is consistently applied and the fact that the invalid's sole reason for departure is a desire to enjoy better health or to retard the progress of a disease cannot per se be regarded as excluding an intention to remain permanently in the chosen place. In such a case it has been said that the *propositus* "*was exercising a preference, and not acting upon a necessity*", and the judge refused to hold that the domicile cannot be changed.[141]

(vi) Miscellaneous cases

There are various other cases, somewhat analogous to those just discussed, in which the reason to which a change of residence is due has a rather more decisive effect on the question of intention. Thus, if a person resides abroad in pursuance of his duties as a public servant of his own government, as, for example, an ambassador, a military or naval officer or a consul, or if he is an employee under contract to go where sent, the inference to be drawn from the cause of the residence is that it is not intended to be permanent.[142]

In such cases the existing domicile is retained unless there are additional circumstances from which a contrary intention can be determined.[143] Thus, to take an extreme case, it has been held that even a member of the armed forces may acquire a domicile in a foreign country where he is compulsorily resident and whence he is liable to be removed at any moment by higher authority, if there is sufficient evidence of his intention to settle there permanently as soon as he once more becomes a free agent.[144] The fact that the area of his new home coincides with his area of service does not per se preclude him from acquiring a new domicile. It has also been held that, if the requisite residence and intention are satisfactorily proved, he may acquire a domicile in a country other than that in which he is compulsorily serving.[145] It would seem that a person who enters the armed forces of a foreign power, in such circumstances as to necessitate his indefinite residence in the foreign country, acquires a new domicile there.[146]

---

[139] *Moorhouse v Lord* (1863) 10 HL Cas 272; see also *Johnstone v Beattie* (1843) 10 Cl & Fin 42 at 139.

[140] *Hoskins v Matthews* (1856) 8 De GM & G 13 at 28.

[141] Ibid at 28–29 emphasis added. See also *Philippi v IRC* [1971] 1 WLR 684; cf *Re James* (1908) 98 LT 438.

[142] *Re Patten's Goods* (1860) 6 Jur NS 151 (naval); *A-G v Lady Rowe* (1862) 1 H & C 31 (Chief Justice of Ceylon); *Firebrace v Firebrace* (1878) 4 PD 63 (army officer); *Re Mitchell, ex p Cunningham* (1884) 13 QBD 418 (army officer); *Re Macreight, Paxton v Macreight* (1885) 30 Ch D 165 (Jerseyman serving in British Army); *A-G v Kent* (1862) 31 LJ Ex 391 at 397 (attaché to Portuguese Embassy); *Sharpe v Crispin* (1869) LR 1 P & D 611 (consul).

[143] *Re Smith's Goods* (1850) 2 Rob Eccl 332; and see *McEwan v McEwan* 1969 SLT 342.

[144] *Donaldson v Donaldson* [1949] P 363; *Cruikshanks v Cruikshanks* [1957] 1 WLR 564. So held also in Scotland: *Sellars v Sellars* 1942 SC 206.

[145] *Stone v Stone* [1958] 1 WLR 1287.

[146] *Re Mitchell, ex p Cunningham* (1884) 13 QBD 418 at 421, as qualified by the earlier remarks of PAGE WOOD V-C in *Forbes v Forbes* (1854) Kay 341 at 356.

(d) Precarious residence

A person can form an intention to remain in a place despite considerable uncertainty as to whether this will be possible.[147] The mere fact than an alien living in England under a certificate of registration is liable to deportation does not prevent him from acquiring an English domicile of choice,[148] or deprive him of a domicile already acquired.[149] Indeed, a domicile of choice may even continue after deportation if re-entry is lawful.[150] Neither the permissive nor the precarious character of his residence nullifies his intention to settle in England.[151] A domicile of choice in England can be acquired, even though that person's presence in the United Kingdom is unlawful. The House of Lords so decided in *Mark v Mark*[152] where the issue was whether a person can be habitually resident or domiciled in England for the purpose of jurisdiction to grant a divorce when that person's presence was a criminal offence under the Immigration Act 1971. Their Lordships held that there was no reason of public policy to deny acquisition of a domicile in England in such a case.[153] Indeed, if a person has chosen to make his home in a new country for an indefinite period of time, it is appropriate that he should be connected to that country's system of law for the kind of purposes for which domicile is relevant.[154] Neither is legality an essential element in either presence or in the formation of the requisite intention, both of which are issues of fact.[155] However, the legality of a person's presence is not completely irrelevant. As in the other cases of precarious residence, it may well be relevant as to whether that person had formed the requisite intention.[156]

(e) The burden of proof

The burden of proof that lies on those who allege a change of domicile varies with the circumstances. In this connection there are two observations that may be made. First, English judges have taken the view that it requires far stronger evidence to establish the abandonment of a domicile of origin in favour of a fresh domicile than to establish a change from one domicile of choice to another.[157] Secondly, and by way of contrast, there is authority for the view that a change of domicile from one country to another under the same sovereign, as from Jersey or Scotland to England, is more easily proved than

---

147 *Mark v Mark* [2005] UKHL 42 at [47], [2006] 1 AC 98.

148 *Boldrini v Boldrini* [1932] P 9; *May v May* (1943) 169 LT 42; *Zanelli v Zanelli* (1948) 64 TLR 556; *Szechter v Szechter* [1971] P 286; and see *Lim v Lim* [1973] VR 370. See also *Mark v Mark* [2005] UKHL 42 at [39], [2006] 1 AC 98.

149 *Cruh v Cruh* [1945] 2 All ER 545; *Mark v Mark* [2005] UKHL 42 at [39], [2006] 1 AC 98.

150 *Thiele v Thiele* (1920) 150 LT Jo 387; and see Dicey, Morris and Collins, para 6-060.

151 *Zanelli v Zanelli*, supra. See also *Mark v Mark* [2005] UKHL 42 at [49], [2006] 1 AC 98.

152 [2005] UKHL 42, [2006] 1 AC 98; Briggs (2005) 76 BYBIL 675. See to the same effect in Canada, *Jablonowski v Jablonowski* (1972) 28 DLR (3d) 440. Cf in Australia, *Solomon v Solomon* (1912) 29 WN NSW 68 and in South Africa, *Smith v Smith* 1962 (3) SA 930; discussed by Spiro (1963) 12 ICLQ 680; Kahn, op cit, pp 62–64.

153 *Mark v Mark*, supra, at [44]–[47] (Baroness HALE, Lords HOPE, NICHOLLS, HOFFMANN and PHILLIPS concurring).

154 Ibid, at [46].

155 Ibid at [47]–[49] (per Baroness HALE), [13] (per Lord HOPE).

156 Ibid, at [50] (per Baroness HALE), [13] (per Lord HOPE).

157 Infra, pp 171–173.

a change to a foreign country.[158] It is not lightly to be inferred that a man intends to settle permanently in a country where he will possess the status of an alien, with all the difficulties and conflict of duties that such a status involves.

(f) Change of domicile and change of nationality

It is important to emphasise that nationality and domicile are two different conceptions and that a man may change the latter without divesting himself of his nationality.[159] An Englishman may remain an Englishman in the sense that his allegiance renders him subject to certain duties to the Crown, and yet he may so change his residence that many of his legal rights and obligations will be determinable by a foreign system of law, as being the law of his domicile.[160]

4. DOMICILE OF ORIGIN AND DOMICILE OF CHOICE CONTRASTED

As compared with the views held in civil law countries, in the USA, in New Zealand and Australia,[161] the domicile of origin is regarded by English law[162] as fundamentally different from a domicile of choice. It differs in its character, in the conditions necessary for its abandonment and in its capacity for revival.

(a) Tenacity of the domicile of origin

There is the strongest possible presumption in favour of the continuance of a domicile of origin. As contrasted with the domicile of choice, it has been said by Lord MACNAGHTEN that "its character is more enduring, its hold stronger and less easily shaken off".[163] In fact, decisions such as *Winans v A-G*[164] and *Bowie (or Ramsay) v Liverpool Royal Infirmary*[165] warrant the conclusion that almost overwhelming evidence is required to shake it off. In the latter of these cases evidence was completely lacking of the slightest indication, either by words or actions, that George Bowie intended to live anywhere else than in England. Yet it was held that the tenacity of his Scottish domicile of origin had not yielded. Much more recently, in *Cramer v Cramer* Stephen Brown and Balcombe LJJ held that the burden of proving a change of domicile from one of origin to one of choice was a heavy one.[166]

---

158 *Lord v Colvin* (1859) 4 Drew 366 at 422–423; *Whicker v Hume* (1858) 7 HL Cas 124 at 159; *Moorhouse v Lord* (1863) 10 HL Cas 272 at 287.

159 *Boldrini v Boldrini* [1932] P 9 at 15; *Bradfield v Swanton* [1931] IR 446; *Re Adams* [1967] IR 424 at 447–448. For the converse case of a change of nationality without a change of domicile, see *Wahl v A-G* (1932) 147 LT 382. See the discussion by Westlake, *Private International Law* (7th edn), pp 348–354.

160 *Udny v Udny* (1869) LR 1 Sc & Div 441 at 452.

161 See the New Zealand Domicile Act 1976 and the Australian Domicile Acts 1982; Nygh and Davies, paras 13.10–13.11.

162 For proposals for reform, which have unfortunately been rejected, see infra, p 195.

163 *Winans v A-G* [1904] AC 287 at 290; and see *A-G v Yule and Mercantile Bank of India* (1931) 145 LT 9; *Wahl v A-G* (1932) 147 LT 382; *Hyland v Hyland* (1971) 18 FLR 461; *Cyganik v Agulian* [2006] EWCA Civ 129 at [56], [2006] 1 FCR 406.

164 Supra, pp 161–162.

165 [1930] AC 588, supra, pp 162–163.

166 [1987] 1 FLR 116; cf the attitude towards the domicile of origin shown in *Brown v Brown* (1982) 3 FLR 212, infra, p 173.

(b) Abandonment of an existing domicile

Since a domicile of choice is voluntarily acquired if there is the requisite intention and residence, so it is extinguishable in the same manner, ie merely by a removal from the country with an intention not to return and even without acquiring a fresh domicile of choice.[167] In cases of dual or multiple residence what is necessary is that the country ceases to be the chief residence[168] with, presumably, an intention not to reside there as the chief residence. The only distinction between acquisition and abandonment is that the latter requires less evidence than the former.[169] There cannot be abandonment by intention alone.[170]

But it has been objected by MEGARRY J, obiter, that to require proof of an intention not to return is too rigorous a test, since it denies effect to a departure from a country without an intention of returning. In his view, it is unnecessary to prove a positive intention not to return, since the "merely negative absence of any intention"[171] to resume the residence will suffice to effect an abandonment of the domicile. This negative test would cover the situation where a person departs from their domicile of choice and initially intends to return to live there. Gradually this resolve withers and eventually dies. At that point there would be the necessary intention for abandonment,[172] even though there might not yet be a definite resolve not to return. Literally, the negative test would also cover the situation where, at the time of departure, the person in question has not thought about whether to return or not. But it is questionable whether such an absence of thought would be enough for abandonment. A person who has thought about whether to return, but is in two minds, would not have the requisite intention for abandonment.[173] What is uncontroversial is that there will be no abandonment where there is a positive intention to return.[174]

But the domicile of origin, which in its inception is not a matter of free will but is communicated to a person by operation of law, is not extinguished by mere removal with an intention not to return. It cannot be lost by mere abandonment. It endures until supplanted by a fresh domicile of choice. *Bell v Kennedy*[175] is the leading authority for this rule.

> The domicile of origin of Bell was in Jamaica. In 1837, he left the island without any intention of returning, resided in Scotland, and occupied himself in looking

---

[167] *Udny v Udny* (1869) LR 1 Sc & Div 441 at 450; *Fielden v IRC* (1965) 42 TC 501 at 507; *Tee v Tee* [1974] 1 WLR 213 at 215.

[168] *Plummer v IRC* [1988] 1 WLR 292 at 295.

[169] *Re Evans* [1947] Ch 695.

[170] *Re Raffenel's Goods* (1863) 3 Sw & Tr 49; *Faye v IRC* (1961) 40 TC 103; *Re Adams* [1967] IR 424 at 452; *IRC v Duchess of Portland* [1982] Ch 314 discussed infra, p 179; *Rowan v Rowan* [1988] ILRM 65.

[171] *Re Flynn* [1968] 1 WLR 103 at 113; approved in *Qureshi v Qureshi* [1972] Fam 173 at 191; *Morgan v Cilento* [2004] EWHC 188 (Ch) at [15], [2004] All ER (D) 122; a negative test was used in *IRC v Duchess of Portland* [1982] Ch 314 at 318; *Proes v Revenue Commissioners* [1998] 4 IR 176. But cf *Irvin v Irvin* [2001] 1 FLR 178, 185; *Breuning v Breuning* [2002] EWHC 236 (Fam), [2002] 1 FLR 888, 904. See generally Crawford (2005) 54 ICLQ 829 at 851.

[172] See *Morgan v Cilento* [2004] EWHC 188 (Ch) at [15], [76], [2004] All ER (D) 122.

[173] Ibid, at [15].

[174] *Irvin v Irvin* [2001] 1 FLR 178.

[175] (1868) LR 1 Sc & Div 307.

for an estate in that country on which to settle down. He had not been successful in this when his wife died in 1838.

It was held that his domicile at that moment was in Jamaica. Although he had abandoned the island for good in 1837 and was resident in Scotland, he had not at that time decided to make his permanent residence there. The evidence showed that in 1838 his mind was vacillating with regard to his future home. Therefore, since he had not acquired a Scottish domicile of choice, he retained his domicile of origin.

A modern instance of removal from the domicile of origin with an intention not to return is *Brown v Brown*.[176] In this case there was evidence of a willingness by the court to infer the intention necessary for the acquisition of a domicile of choice, on the basis that the person in question, who worked for a multinational oil company, had severed his links with his domicile of origin in the USA, and the nature of his work meant that he had opportunities for the acquisition of a new domicile abroad.[177]

(c) Revival of the domicile of origin

If the domicile of origin is displaced as a result of the acquisition of a domicile of choice, the rule of English law is that it is merely placed in abeyance for the time being. It remains in the background ever ready to revive and to fasten upon the *propositus* immediately he abandons his domicile of choice.[178] The position may be illustrated by the following example.

> X, an adult with a Scots domicile of origin but who has lived all his life in England, has developed a strong dislike for the United Kingdom, leaves the country determined never to set foot here again. He acquires a domicile of choice in Peru. After residing there for forty years, in the course of which he has amassed a fortune, he leaves the country for good and takes up his temporary residence in New York, being undecided whether to settle permanently in Virginia or California.

The result is that immediately on his departure from Peru his Peruvian domicile ceases abruptly, but his Scots domicile of origin revives and remains attached to him until he has in fact acquired a domicile of choice in some other country. It is clear, of course, that during his period of indecision in New York there must be some personal law applicable to him. This might be either Peruvian or Scottish law. In the USA, where the doctrine of revival is not accepted,[179] it would be the law of Peru. According to Lord Chancellor HATHERLEY, however, to admit this is to be driven to the absurdity of asserting a person to be domiciled in a country which he has resolutely forsaken and cast off, simply because he may (perhaps for years) be deliberating before he settles himself elsewhere.[180]

Yet certain doubts suggest themselves. Is it so absurd to prefer the law under which the man has recently been living, perhaps for a prolonged period? Are the claims of the law

---

[176] (1982) 3 FLR 212. Cf *DT v FL* [2004] 1 ILRM 509, SC of Ireland—no immediate intention of returning. See also *Vien Estate v Vien Estate* (1988) 49 DLR (4th) 558.

[177] Op cit, at 215, 217.

[178] *Udny v Udny* (1869) LR 1 Sc & Div 441; *Tee v Tee* [1974] 1 WLR 213, at 215–216; see also Wade (1983) 32 ICLQ 1 at 12 et seq.

[179] *Re Jones' Estate* (1921) 192 Iowa 78, 182 NW 227.

[180] *Udny v Udny* (1869) LR 1 Sc & Div 441 at 450.

which is imposed on him at birth, independently of his volition, superior to that which he has voluntarily chosen and long retained? At any rate the advantages of preferring the domicile of origin in the case of our hypothetical X are not particularly conspicuous. The country that determines his personal law is one that he has never visited and for which he feels a repugnance. Nevertheless, if he wishes to marry, his capacity will be determined by reference to the law of Scotland. If he dies intestate leaving movables in England, they will be distributed according to Scots law and United Kingdom inheritance tax will be payable. These illustrations, which could be multiplied, provoke the thought that the virtues of the doctrine of revival are not so obvious as appeared to the mid-Victorian judges. The doctrine of revival has in fact been rejected in New Zealand[181] and in Australia,[182] and its rejection in the United Kingdom was proposed by the Law Commissions. However, the Law Commissions' proposals have themselves been rejected.[183]

5. DOMICILE OF DEPENDENT PERSONS

There are two classes of dependent persons—children[184] and mentally disordered persons.

(a) Children

(i) A child's domicile of origin

A child acquires at birth a domicile of origin by operation of law, namely, if legitimate and born in his father's lifetime, the domicile of his father,[185] if illegitimate[186] or born after his father's death,[187] the domicile of his mother.[188] A foundling is domiciled in the country where he is found.[189] If a child is born illegitimate, but is later legitimated, his father's domicile will be communicated to him from the date of legitimation, but it is probable that his domicile of origin remains that of his mother, presuming that at his birth his parents were domiciled in different countries.[190] It is important to note that a domicile of origin once acquired remains constant throughout life.[191]

---

[181] Domicile Act 1976, s 11; see Webb (1977) 26 ICLQ 194; but see generally for the position in Commonwealth countries, McClean, *Recognition of Family Judgments in the Commonwealth* (1983), Chapter 1.

[182] Domicile Acts 1982, s 7; Nygh and Davies, 13.11.

[183] Law Com No 239 (1995), p 10 n 24. See now, for Scots law, Family Law (Scotland) Act 2006, s 22; and Crawford and Carruthers, paras 6-05–6-06.

[184] Palmer (1974) 4 Fam Law 35; Binchy (1979) 11 Ottowa LR 279; Blaikie [1984] Jur Rev 1.

[185] *Forbes v Forbes* (1854) Kay 341 at 353; *Udny v Udny* (1869) LR 1 Sc & Div 441 at 457. Does an adopted child acquire a new domicile of origin on adoption based on the the domicile of his adoptive father (or mother, if not adopted by a couple or one of a couple) as at the date of adoption? See Adoption and Children Act 2002, s 67.

[186] *Udny v Udny*, supra; *Re Wright's Trusts* (1856) 2 K & J 595; *Urquhart v Butterfield* (1887) 37 Ch D 357; *Carmona v White* (1980) 25 SASR 525. See for proposals for reform, which have unfortunately been rejected, infra, pp 195–196; for New Zealand, see the Domicile Act 1976, s 6; for Australia the Domicile Acts 1982, s 9.

[187] There appears to be no English authority for this.

[188] Though see discussion of legitimacy, infra, pp 1142–1143. Although the Family Law Reform Act 1987 very largely assimilates the rights of children, regardless of whether they are legitimate or illegitimate, the concept of legitimacy is still relevant for domicile purposes. See, however, now in Scotland, Family Law (Scotland) Act 2006, s 22, which effects a change in the rules of Scots law concerning the domicile of persons under 16.

[189] Westlake, s 248; Dicey, Morris and Collins, para 6R-025.

[190] Wolff, pp 118–119.

[191] Except perhaps in the case of adoption, supra.

(ii) When an independent domicile can be acquired

Before reaching the age of 16, an unmarried child is incapable of acquiring by his own act an independent domicile of choice.[192] He is powerless to alter his civil status. Once that age is reached, then a child, whether male or female, is fully capable of having an independent domicile.[193] Furthermore, any child below that age who is validly married can acquire an independent domicile. Although this will not affect the status of English domiciled children, who are incapable of marriage until the age of 16, it does mean that any child below that age whose foreign marriage is recognised here[194] will be regarded as capable of having an independent domicile.

(iii) The effect of a change in the parent's domicile

Although an unmarried child under 16[195] is unable to acquire a domicile of choice by his own act there is nothing to prevent the acquisition of a domicile of choice *for* him by the act of one of his parents. This may be effected either by the father or by the mother. The primary rule is that the domicile of a legitimate child[196] automatically changes with any change that occurs in the domicile of the father.[197] This unity is not destructible at the will of the father. It is not terminated if he purports to create a separate domicile for his son, for instance, by setting him up in business abroad.[198] At one time, as between a living father and his legitimate child, there was a necessary unity of domicile, even though they may have resided in different countries, and even after a divorce and the mother had custody.[199] But this has been altered by the Domicile and Matrimonial Proceedings Act 1973[200] in the one case where both parents[201] are alive but are living apart. In such a case the child's domicile is that of the mother, if the child has his home with her and no home with his father,[202] or if he acquired his mother's domicile in this way and has not since then had a home with his father.[203] This latter provision means that a child who has his home with his mother keeps her domicile, though he ceases to live with her, provided he does not later have a home with his father. Furthermore, a child who has his mother's

---

[192] *Forbes v Forbes* (1854) Kay 341 at 353.

[193] Domicile and Matrimonial Proceedings Act 1973, s 3(1). A child who was over 16 or was married but was incapable of having an independent domicile before 1 January 1974 is regarded as capable from that date. Sections 3 and 4 of the 1973 Act are not retrospective, and, therefore, in considering the domicile of a child as at any time before 1 January 1974 (which it may be necessary to do when tracing that person's domicile up to the present day), the old law is still applicable. Under such rules a child is incapable of acquiring an independent domicile until reaching full age whether or not married: *Harrison v Harrison* [1953] 1 WLR 865. A female married child takes the domicile of her husband but if widowed reverts to that of her father until majority: *Shekleton v Shekleton* [1972] 2 NSWR 675.

[194] Eg *Alhaji Mohamed v Knott* [1969] 1 QB 1.

[195] Hereafter described as a "child".

[196] An adopted person is treated as the legitimate child of the adopters or adopter: Adoption and Children Act 2002, s 67.

[197] *D'Etchegoyen v D'Etchegoyen* (1888) 13 PD 132. As to whether a change in a guardian's domicile is communicated to his ward, see Spiro (1956) 5 ICLQ 196 et seq.

[198] Wolff, p 117.

[199] *Breuning v Breuning* [2002] EWHC 236 (Fam), [2002] 1 FLR 888, 902 (discussing the pre-1974 law).

[200] S 4(1); see *Williams, Petitioner* 1977 SLT (Notes) 2. The equivalent in Australia is the Domicile Acts 1982, s 9; in New Zealand the Domicile Act 1976, s 6.

[201] Including adoptive parents: Adoption and Children Act 2002, s 67.

[202] S 4(2)(a). On the meaning of "home", see *Re P (GE) (An Infant)* [1965] Ch 568 at 585–586; *Re Y (Minors) (Adoption: Jurisdiction)* [1985] Fam 136; and cf Family Law (Scotland) Act 2006, s 22.

[203] S 4(2)(b).

domicile by reason of these provisions continues to retain it after her death unless and until he has a home with his father.[204]

Two points should be stressed in relation to these statutory provisions. They apply only to the determination of a child's dependent domicile and do not appear to affect the determination of his domicile of origin. Thus, a child born of parents who are married but living apart at the time of his birth would appear to acquire his father's domicile as his domicile of origin[205] but, immediately thereafter, a domicile of dependence with his mother, where his home is. Secondly, these provisions apply only to the case where both parents are alive and are living apart, and provided the child is legitimate.[206] It is unfortunate that other cases giving rise to problems relating to a child's dependent domicile are left to be dealt with by the common law.[207] If a father, on the death of his wife, abandons his children and acquires a fresh domicile elsewhere, and the children are left to be cared for by grandparents, their domicile is still decided by obscure common law rules. However, it seems most unlikely that a court would affirm the inevitability of the application of the father's domicile. This was the view at common law, taken by Lord MACDERMOTT LCJ in the Northern Ireland case of *Hope v Hope*,[208] of the situation where the mother was alive, where he characterised the capacity of a father to change the domicile of his minor child as "a manifestation of parental authority and responsibility". Therefore he asked: "why should it apply to tie the domicile of the child to the will of a father who has abjured his responsibility by walking out of his child's life?"[209] It is suggested that this view is still valid in those cases unaffected by the Domicile and Matrimonial Proceedings Act 1973.

The domicile that a child acquires by reason of his father or mother moving to another country is a domicile of choice, or better perhaps of quasi-choice,[210] and his domicile of origin continues to be that imposed upon him at birth.[211] This rule may become important at a later stage in his life. For instance, a father, domiciled in England at the time of his son's birth, acquires a domicile of choice in France and retains it until after his son reaches the age of 16. At the age of 25, the son acquires a domicile of choice in Italy, but later abandons that country for good and dies without having acquired another permanent home. In these circumstances, the English domicile will revive on the loss of his Italian domicile and English law will govern testamentary or intestate succession to his movables.

A child acquires, on the death of his father, the domicile of his mother.[212] The question that has arisen here is whether such a child's domicile continues to follow that of

---

[204] S 4(3).

[205] See Palmer (1974) 4 Fam Law 35, 36; cf Dicey, Morris and Collins, para 6-028, where it is suggested that a child, born to parents who have been divorced, takes his mother's domicile at birth.

[206] S 4(4). This includes adopted: Adoption and Children Act 2002, s 67.

[207] See Palmer (1974) 4 Fam Law 35, 36–38.

[208] [1968] NI 1; not following the Scottish decision in *Shanks v Shanks* 1965 SLT 330; cf *Re B (S) (An Infant)* [1968] Ch 204 at 208.

[209] [1968] NI 1 at 5; and see Carter (1968–69) 43 BYBIL 239.

[210] *Harrison v Harrison* [1953] 1 WLR 865, suggested by counsel at 866.

[211] *Henderson v Henderson* [1967] P 77, [1965] 1 All ER 179.

[212] *Potinger v Wightman* (1817) 3 Mer 67. The domicile of a child whose father is dead, or of an illegitimate child, is unaffected by s 4 of the Domicile and Matrimonial Proceedings Act 1973: s 4(4). For Australia see the Domicile Acts 1982, s 9; for New Zealand the Domicile Act 1976, s 6.

the mother, or whether there are any circumstances in which it will remain unaffected by her acts. The general doctrine is that, if after the death of the father the child continues to live with the mother, then any new domicile acquired by the mother is prima facie to be regarded as communicated to the child.[213] But this is not necessarily so. It is recognised that the mother is empowered to change her children's domicile either by taking them to a new domicile acquired by her, or by leaving them where their father was domiciled at the time of his death[214] or even, it would seem, by placing them in another country under the care of a competent person. But this power must be exercised bona fide and with the sole object of promoting the welfare of the children. Thus, even the prima facie rule, that a new domicile acquired by the mother is communicated to her children, is displaced if this is disadvantageous to them or if the change of domicile is due to some fraudulent design on her part, as, for example, where her motive is to take advantage of a law of succession more beneficial to herself.[215]

(iv) Criticism of the existing law

It is hard to disagree with the criticism by the Law Commissions of the present rules, namely that they "discriminate between legitimate and illegitimate children and between their fathers and mothers. They also fail to deal adequately with the cases where a child is abandoned, his parents die, the child is fostered or is taken into the care of a local authority."[216] However, finding acceptable new rules to replace the present rules is not so easy.[217]

(b) Mental disorder or mental incapacity

Although there is no direct authority, it is generally agreed that the domicile of a mentally disordered or mentally incapacitated person cannot be changed either by himself, since he is incapable of forming an intention, or by the person to whose care he has been entrusted.[218] Of course, in accordance with the general principle applicable to children, the domicile of the father will be communicated to a child of unsound mind during the childhood of the latter, but a somewhat irrational distinction has been suggested as regards an adult who is mentally disordered or mentally incapacitated. If he has been continuously disordered or incapacitated both during childhood and after the age of 16, it is said that his domicile will continue to change with that of his father; but that if he first becomes disordered or incapacitated after reaching the age of 16, his then domicile becomes indelible, for if the power of changing it were vested in the father great danger might be done to "the interests of others".[219] There are two possible solutions, though

---

[213] *Johnstone v Beattie* (1843) 10 Cl & Fin 42 at 138.

[214] *Re Beaumont* [1893] 3 Ch 490; *Re G* [1966] NZLR 1028; Blaikie [1984] Jur Rev 1 at 4 et seq. This power would have gone if the Law Commissions' proposals had been accepted.

[215] *Potinger v Wightman* (1817) 3 Mer 67 at 79, 80.

[216] Law Com No 168 (1987), Scot Law Com No 107 (1987), para 3(2)(d).

[217] For the Law Commissions' proposals in relation to children, and their rejection, see infra, pp 195–196.

[218] *Urquhart v Butterfield* (1887) 37 Ch D 357 at 382; and see *Bempde v Johnstone* (1796) 3 Ves 198; *Sharpe v Crispin* (1869) LR 1 P & D 611; Westlake, p 251; cf *Re G* [1966] NZLR 1028. Nor probably can it be altered by the Court of Protection in exercise of its powers under the Mental Capacity Act 2005, see Dicey, Morris and Collins, paras 6R-105, 6-106, 6-107, 6-108.

[219] *Sharpe v Crispin* (1869) LR 1 P & D 611 at 618.

neither is supported by authority in England. First, as the paramount consideration is the interest of the mentally disordered or mentally incapacitated person, not of others, it might be advisable that the Court of Protection should be entitled to change his domicile if this appears to be for his benefit. Secondly, a rule could be adopted to the effect that an adult who is mentally disordered or mentally incapacitated should be domiciled in the country with which he is for the time being most closely connected.[220]

(c) Capacity to acquire a domicile

It has been suggested that the capacity of a dependent person to acquire a fresh domicile is not always governed by English law, the law of the forum. Such a possibility was adumbrated obiter in an English case in 1887,[221] and more recently it has been canvassed by Graveson.[222] It is submitted, however, that this thesis is based upon a fundamental misconception, since it overlooks the fact that domicile is no more than a connecting factor. Its acquisition is not *itself* a problem for the solution of which a rule for the choice of law is required. For the connecting factor in any English choice of law rule must logically always be interpreted according to English notions.[223]

6. DOMICILE OF MARRIED WOMEN[224]

(a) The abolition of dependency

Until 1974, the rule was that the domicile of a husband was communicated to his wife immediately on marriage and it was necessarily and inevitably retained by her for the duration of the marriage. This rule was much criticised as "the last barbarous relic of a wife's servitude"[225] and was abolished by section 1 of the Domicile and Matrimonial Proceedings Act 1973.[226] The domicile of a married woman as at any time on or after 1 January 1974 "shall, instead of being the same as her husband's by virtue only of marriage, be ascertained by reference to the same factors as in the case of any other individual capable of having an independent domicile".

This means that a married woman is to be treated as capable of acquiring a separate domicile; though in the vast majority of cases she and her husband will, independently, acquire the same domicile. It is, however, quite possible for happily married spouses to have separate domiciles as where, for example, a student at an English university who is domiciled in New York marries a fellow student domiciled in England, both intending at the end of their studies to go and live in New York.[227]

---

[220] See the rejected proposals of the Law Commissions: Law Com No 168 (1987), Scot Law Com No 107 (1987), Part IV.

[221] *Urquhart v Butterfield* (1887) 37 Ch D 357 at 384.

[222] (1950) 3 ILQ 149; and see Mendes de Costa, *Studies in Canadian Family Law* (1972), Vol II, pp 914–916; cf Nygh and Davies, 13.25; New Zealand Domicile Act 1976, s 5(2).

[223] *Re Martin* [1900] P 211 at 227; *Re Annesley* [1926] Ch 692 at 705. But see Family Law Act 1986, s 46(5).

[224] Palmer (1974) 124 NLJ 49, 73, 95.

[225] *Gray v Formosa* [1963] P 259 at 267; and see *Adams v Adams* [1971] P 188 at 216.

[226] S 1.

[227] See *Puttick v A-G* [1980] Fam 1 at 17; *IRC v Duchess of Portland* [1982] Ch 314 at 319–320.

(b) Transitional problems

The 1973 Act deals also with the transitional problem of the domicile of dependence of a wife acquired before 1974.[228] A woman, married before 1974, who, therefore, acquired her husband's domicile on marriage, is to be treated as retaining that domicile as a domicile of choice if it was not the wife's own domicile of origin, until it is changed by acquisition of a new domicile of choice or revival of the domicile of origin on or after 1st January 1974.[229] This means that, after that date, the wife's domicile is not to be treated as dependent on her husband but as her own domicile of origin, or of choice, until she acquires a new domicile of choice or until her domicile of origin revives.[230] The operation of these transitional provisions is shown in *IRC v Duchess of Portland*:[231]

> The taxpayer, who had a domicile of origin in Canada, married her husband, an English domiciliary, in 1948, thereby acquiring an English domicile of dependency. The couple set up home in England. However, the taxpayer, throughout her marriage, maintained close links with Canada, including retaining a bank account, owning a house and returning for visits for ten to twelve weeks each year. It was agreed that when her husband retired they would both live permanently in Canada.

Nourse J held that the taxpayer had not reacquired her domicile of origin in Canada and retained her domicile of choice in England during the period in question. He reasoned as follows: the 1973 Act turned the taxpayer's domicile of dependency into one of choice; she had not abandoned this English domicile of choice, notwithstanding her intention to return to Canada, since she had not ceased to reside in England.[232] The judge regarded the language of the transitional provisions as clear and said that the above construction "does not . . . lead to any result which is unjust and anomalous or absurd".[233]

7. DOMICILE AND NATIONALITY[234]

(a) Nationality and domicile contrasted

Nationality is a possible alternative to domicile as the criterion of the personal law. These are two different conceptions. Nationality represents a person's political status, by virtue

---

[228] In considering the domicile of a married woman as at any time before 1 January 1974, the old law will apply, so that she will be regarded as incapable of acquiring a domicile independent from that of her husband. Cf the position in Ireland where the Supreme Court has held the wife's dependent domicile rule to be unconstitutional, and a wife's domicile has to be worked out like that of any other independent person whether before or after 1986, when the domicile of dependency was abolished by the Domicile and Recognition of Foreign Divorces Act 1986, s 1: *W v W* [1993] 2 IR 476.

[229] Domicile and Matrimonial Proceedings Act 1973, s 1(2).

[230] For a different interpretation of s 1(2) of the 1973 Act, see Wade (1983) 32 ICLQ 1, particularly at 6 et seq.

[231] [1982] Ch 314; Wade, op cit, at 3 et seq; Thompson (1983) 32 ICLQ 237; Carter (1982) 53 BYBIL 295.

[232] The same approach was applied earlier in *Oundjian v Oundjian* (1979) 1 FLR 198 at 202.

[233] *Duchess of Portland*, supra, 320. However, the New Zealand Domicile Act 1976, ss 4 and 5 and the Australian Domicile Acts 1982, s 5(1) and (2) give a different solution. The English and Scottish Law Commissions in their rejected proposals set out in Law Com No 168 (1987) and Scot Law Com No 107 (1987) Part VIII, favoured the Australian and New Zealand solution, and the reversal of *IRC v Duchess of Portland*.

[234] de Winter (1969) III Hague Recueil 357–503; Nadelmann (1969) 17 AJCL 418; and see Palsson, *Marriage and Divorce in Comparative Conflict of Laws*, Chapter 3; North, *Private International Law of Matrimonial Causes*, pp 5–15.

of which he owes allegiance to some particular country; domicile indicates his civil status and it provides the law by which his personal rights and obligations are determined.[235] Nationality depends, apart from naturalisation, on the place of birth or on parentage; domicile, as we have seen, is constituted by residence in a particular country with the intention of residing there permanently. It follows that a person may be a national of one country but domiciled in another.

If one looks at the historical development, it will appear that, over the last two centuries, the ascertainment of the personal law, which ought to be governed by legal and practical considerations, has in fact been influenced by varying political and economic factors. The French revolution, the struggles of Italy to win independence, the wave of nationalism that swept Europe in the nineteenth century, the desire of the poorer countries to share in the prosperity of their emigrants—these and other similar circumstances have led to a widespread idolatry of the principle of nationality. At present many countries in Europe and South America adopt nationality as the criterion of personal law, whilst the common law jurisdictions of the Commonwealth and the USA, among others, still stand by the test of domicile. As immigration has increased in Western Europe since the Second World War, domicile has gained ground at the expense of nationality.[236]

It may be asked, what are the respective merits of domicile and nationality as a determinant of the law to govern status and personal rights generally? Each has its merits and demerits.[237]

(i) The merits and demerits of domicile

The English preference for domicile is based on two main grounds. First, domicile means the country in which a person has established his permanent home, and what can be more natural or more appropriate than to subject him to his home law? It is difficult to agree that he should be excommunicated from that law merely because technically he is a citizen of some state that he may have abandoned years ago.[238] Secondly, domicile furnishes the only practicable test in the case of such political units as the United Kingdom, Canada, Australia and the USA where the same nationality embraces a number of, sometimes diverse, legal systems. The expression "national law" when applied to a British subject is meaningless. It is one system for England, another in Scotland; similarly for a Canadian, there is one system in Ontario and a quite different one in Quebec.

In the course of its development in England, however, the law relating to domicile has acquired certain vices. A short mention of these will suffice here, as they have already been discussed in this chapter. First, it will not infrequently happen that the legal domicile of a person is out of touch with reality, for the exaggerated importance attributed to the domicile of origin, coupled with the technical doctrine of its revival, may well ascribe to a person a domicile in the country which by no stretch of the imagination can be called

---

[235] *Udny v Udny* (1869) LR 1 Sc & Div 441 at 457.

[236] Palsson (1986) IV Hague Recueil 316, 332 et seq.

[237] See de Winter, op cit, pp 400–418; Kahn-Freund (1974) III Hague Recueil 139, 314, 389–391, 467–468.

[238] Of course, if a country which adopts the principle of nationality also accepts the doctrine of renvoi, the practical result may be the substitution of the law of the domicile for the law of nationality, supra, pp 57–61.

his home.[239] Secondly, an equally irrational result may ensure from the view, sometimes accepted by the English courts, that long residence is not equivalent to domicile if accompanied by the contemplation of some uncertain event the occurrence of which will cause a termination of the residence.[240] Thirdly, the ascertainment of a person's domicile depends to such an extent on proof of his intention, the most elusive of all factors, that only too often it will be impossible to identify it with certainty without recourse to the courts.[241]

(ii) The merits and demerits of nationality

Nationality, as compared with domicile, enjoys the advantages that it is relatively easy to understand as a concept and normally it is easily ascertainable.[242] Nevertheless, it is objectionable as a criterion of the personal law on at least three grounds.[243]

First, it may point to a country with which the person in question has lost all connection, or with which perhaps he has never been connected. It is a strange notion, for instance, that a Neapolitan, who has emigrated to California in his youth without becoming naturalised in the USA, should throughout his life remain subject to Italian law with regard to such matters as marital and testamentary capacity. Secondly, nationality is sometimes a more fallible criterion than domicile. In the eyes of English law no person can be without a domicile, no person can have more than one domicile at the same time. On the other hand, the person may be stateless or may simultaneously be a citizen of two or more countries.[244] Thirdly, nationality cannot always determine the internal law to which a person is subject. This is the case, as we have seen, when one political unit such as the USA comprises a variety of legal systems. Similarly, nationality breaks down as a connecting factor in the case of the United Kingdom where, for many purposes, there is no such thing as United Kingdom law. The application of the concept of nationality in such circumstances will lead to eccentric decisions such as that given in *Re O'Keefe*.[245]

Perhaps a fair conclusion, speaking very generally, is to say that, as determinants of the personal law, nationality yields a predictable but frequently an inappropriate law; domicile yields an appropriate but frequently an unpredictable law.

This division of the world into those countries that adopt the principle of nationality and those that prefer the test of domicile is unfortunate, since it obstructs the movement for the unification of rules of private international law; the reconciliation of the opposing views is highly desirable. Moreover, whilst there has been a tendency on the Continent to substitute domicile for nationality as the test of personal law, there has been a natural

---

[239] Supra, p 171 et seq.

[240] Supra, p 159 et seq.

[241] Supra, p 164 et seq.

[242] See generally Law Com No 168 (1987), Scot Law Com No 107 (1987), para 3.9. It is ascertained by reference to the law of the state of the nationality concerned; eg *Oppenheimer v Cattermole* [1976] AC 249; see also *R v Secretary of State for the Home Department, ex p Bibi* [1985] Imm AR 134.

[243] North, *Private International Law of Matrimonial Causes*, pp 9–10. See also Law Com No 168 (1987), Scot Law Com No 107 (1987), paras 3.10–3.11.

[244] Eg *Torok v Torok* [1973] 1 WLR 1066.

[245] [1940] Ch 124, discussed supra, pp 65–66, and *Re Johnson* [1903] 1 Ch 821.

reluctance to absorb the English principles in toto.[246] This has led to international efforts to reach agreement on the meaning of both domicile and also residence as connecting factors.[247]

8. CONCEPTS OF RESIDENCE

Dissatisfaction with nationality as a connecting factor has led to a realisation of the defects of domicile also. This has had several consequences. One has been attempts in England to reform the concept of domicile,[248] but these have been successful only in relation to the dependent domicile of children and married women.[249] Problems in the basic definition of domicile remain. The failure, over many years, to reform domicile has led, in its turn, to a tendency to reject it as a connecting factor in favour of residence.[250] One of the main forces in this direction has been the fact that the Hague Conventions have relied on "habitual residence" as a connecting factor.[251] The Rome Convention on contract choice of law[252] also utilises this concept, but now in the commercial sphere. This has resulted in the concept being introduced into English law as legislation is passed to implement these conventions.[253] The wheel has been turned full circle as purely domestic legislation has also adopted "habitual residence" as a major connecting factor in matrimonial jurisdiction.[254] It is also used as a condition for eligibility for income support, housing benefit and council tax benefit.[255] Nonetheless, although habitual residence is increasingly being used as an alternative connecting factor, it would be wrong to introduce a general substitution of habitual residence for domicile.[256] For the connection between a person and a country provided by habitual residence is not sufficiently strong to justify that person's

---

[246] Folke Schmidt (1951) 4 ILQ 39–52; Cheshire, ibid, 52–59; de Winter (1969) III Hague Recueil 357, 419–423.

[247] Eg Council of Europe Resolution (72)1 on the Standardisation of the Legal Concepts of "Domicile" and of "Residence".

[248] Infra, pp 195–196.

[249] Domicile and Matrimonial Proceedings Act 1973, ss 1, 3, 4, supra, pp 174–179.

[250] North, *Private International Law of Matrimonial Causes*, pp 10–15.

[251] de Winter (1969) III Hague Recueil 357, 419–454; Cavers (1972) 21 Am ULR 475.

[252] See Arts 4(2) and 5, infra, pp 711–716.

[253] Eg Wills Act 1963, infra, p 1266 et seq; Adoption and Children Act 1976, infra, p 1160; Child Abduction and Custody Act 1985, infra, p 1103; Family Law Act 1986, Pt II, infra, p 994 et seq; Contracts (Applicable Law) Act 1990, infra, pp 711–716 and 726; The Hague Convention on Jurisdiction, Applicable Law, Recognition, Enforcement and Co-operation in respect of Parental Responsibility and Measures for the Protection of Children of 1996, also makes extensive use of habitual residence, see infra, pp 1136–1139; Clive [1998] Jur Rev 169.

[254] Domicile and Matrimonial Proceedings Act 1973, ss 5, 6, infra, pp 945–949; Family Law Act 1986, Parts I and III, infra, pp 1040–1045 and 1078–1088. See also the Child Support Act 1991, s 44(1). Council Regulation (EC) No 2201/2003 of 27 November 2003 concerning jurisdiction and the recognition and enforcement of judgments in matrimonial matters and the matters of parental responsibility OJ 2003 L 338/1 (Brussels II *bis*), discussed infra, pp 944–949 and 1080–1086, uses habitual residence as an alternative connecting factor for jurisdiction. See generally the comments of THORPE LJ in *Nessa v Chief Adjudication Officer* [1998] 2 All ER 728 at 737, CA; affd [1999] 1 WLR 1937, HL.

[255] See, eg, Income Support (General) Regulations, 1987 SI 1987/1967. See generally Hardy (1997) 19 JSW and FL 73.

[256] Law Com No 168 (1987), Scot Law Com No 107 (1987), paras 3.5–3.8. The proposals that the Law Commissions did put forward for reform have been rejected. Cf Irish Law Reform Commission's Report on Domicile and Habitual Residence as Connecting Factors in the Conflict of Laws of 1983; Binchy, *Irish Conflicts of Law*, pp 98–100. Cf *Cyganik v Agulian* [2006] EWCA Civ 129 at [58] (per LONGMORE LJ), [2006] 1 FCR 406 suggesting consideration of replacing domicile by habitual residence in the Inheritance (Provision for Family and Dependants) Act 1975.

affairs always being determined by the law of that country. Take the example of English expatriates working abroad, in countries such as Saudi Arabia, on long-term contracts. Their personal affairs, such as their capacity to enter a marriage, should be determined by the law of England, their domicile, not by the law of Saudi Arabia, their habitual residence.

(a) Ordinary residence[257]

"Ordinary residence" has been known as a connecting factor in English law for some time. It used to form a basis for service of a claim form out of the jurisdiction;[258] it used to be a basis of jurisdiction in matrimonial causes in the case of a petitioning wife;[259] it used to be a criterion for obtaining security for costs;[260] it is a significant connecting factor for the purposes of immigration[261] and social security law;[262] it is an important connecting factor in taxation statutes;[263] it has been the criterion used for determining eligibility for a mandatory student award from the local authority;[264] used as the basis for determining whether a student is a home or overseas student for the purpose of payment of university fees,[265] and for designating the local authority to be responsible in a care order.[266]

There is some authority on the meaning of "ordinary residence", though its precise meaning has caused difficulty.[267] One judge went so far as to say that the adjective adds nothing to the noun.[268] However, Lord SCARMAN in giving the judgment of the House of Lords in *Shah v Barnet London Borough*,[269] said that this adjective brings out two important features of ordinary residence, namely residence must be adopted voluntarily, ie not by virtue of kidnapping or imprisonment,[270] and for settled purposes, which can include for

---

[257] Smart (1989) 38 ICLQ 175. For the meaning of residence, simpliciter, see *K v M, M and L (Financial Relief: Foreign Orders)* [1998] 2 FLR 59 at 75. For residence as a component of domicile, see supra, pp 157–159.

[258] Ord 11, r 1(1)(c), of the old Rules of the Supreme Court, replaced by what is now r 6.20(1) of the CPR; see infra, pp 373–374. In Ireland, domicile for the purposes of jurisdiction in civil and commercial matters is defined in terms of ordinary residence, see *Deutsche Bank v Murtagh* [1995] 1 ILRM 381.

[259] Matrimonial Causes Act 1973, s 46(1)(b), repealed by the Domicile and Matrimonial Proceedings Act 1973, s 17(2), Sch 6.

[260] See *Leyvand v Barasch*, (2000) Times, 23 March. This has been replaced by residence: CPR, r 25.13(2)(a).

[261] *Man Chiu Yu v Secretary of State for the Home Department* [1981] Imm AR 1651; it must be questionable whether the case would now be decided the same way in the light of the decisions in *Shah v Barnet London Borough Council* [1983] 2 AC 309; *R v Secretary of State for the Home Department, ex p Margueritte* [1983] QB 180 (acquisition of UK citizenship); *Britto v Secretary of State for the Home Department* [1984] Imm AR 93.

[262] Eg National Insurance Decision No R (P) 1/72; Wikeley, Ogus and Barendt, *The Law of Social Security* (5th edn), pp 231–232.

[263] See *Levene v Inland Revenue Comrs* [1928] AC 217; *Inland Revenue Comrs v Lysaght* [1928] AC 234; *Reed v Clark* [1986] Ch 1.

[264] *Shah v Barnet London Borough Council* [1983] 2 AC 309; *R v Lancashire County Council, ex p Huddleston* [1986] 2 All ER 941.

[265] See *Orphanos v Queen Mary College* [1985] AC 761.

[266] The Children Act 1989, s 31(8); *C (A Child) v Plymouth County Council* [2000] 1 FLR 875, CA. See also s 105(6) of the 1989 Act; *North Yorkshire County Council v Wiltshire County Council* [1999] 2 FLR 560.

[267] McClean (1962) 11 ICLQ 1153, 1161–1166.

[268] *Hopkins v Hopkins* [1951] P 116 at 121–122.

[269] [1983] 2 AC 309 at 342. Lord SCARMAN was referring to the adverb "habitually" but he equated this with "ordinarily".

[270] Cf *Petrotrade Inc v Smith* [1998] 2 All ER 346 at 350–351—involuntary residence in situation where arrested and given bail on condition did not leave.

the purposes of "education, business or profession, employment, health, family or merely love of the place".[271] The words "ordinary residence" should be given their natural and ordinary meaning, and not an artificial legal construction,[272] which will be the same regardless of the context, unless it can be shown that the statutory framework requires a different meaning.[273] Ordinary residence does not connote continuous physical presence, but physical presence with some degree of continuity, notwithstanding occasional temporary absences.[274] There must, however, be some physical presence. Intention to reside is not, alone, sufficient.[275] It is a question of construction of a statute whether the word "lawful" should be implied so as to qualify the ordinary residence.[276] In *Shah* it was said obiter that a person cannot rely on his unlawful presence in breach of the immigration laws to constitute *ordinary* residence.[277] However, this is regarded as a rule of construction of the relevant statute which uses the ordinary residence criterion.[278] Thus for the purpose of United Kingdom tax laws there is no requirement that the ordinary residence must be lawful.[279] On the other hand, unlawful residence cannot be relied upon for the purposes of acquiring citizenship.[280] The difference between these two examples is that a person may benefit from being ordinarily resident in the United Kingdom for immigration purposes whereas a person will not so benefit for taxation purposes.[281] The state does have an interest in whether a person is ordinarily resident in the United Kingdom or not.[282] Moreover, it can be argued that, as a matter of general principle, a person should not benefit from his own unlawful conduct.

Each case must, of course, depend on its own peculiar facts, but the authorities show that even absence for a considerable time will not terminate a person's ordinary residence if it is due to some specific and unusual cause, as for instance when a wife accompanies her husband during his employment in a foreign country,[283] or a man is looking after his sick mother abroad.[284] Again, the significance of a comparatively prolonged absence will be weakened if, during the relevant period, the *propositus* has maintained a house or flat in

---

[271] The *Shah* case, supra, at 344; *Britto v Secretary of State for the Home Department* [1984] Imm AR 93. For Canada see *Trotter v Trotter* (1992) 90 DLR (4th) 554.

[272] *Gateshead Metropolitan Borough Council v L* [1996] 3 All ER 264 at 267.

[273] The *Shah* case, supra, at 341–343.

[274] *Levene v Inland Revenue Comrs* [1928] AC 217 at 232; *Shah v Barnet London Borough Council* [1983] 2 AC 309 at 341–342; *R v Immigration Appeal Tribunal, ex p Siggins* [1985] Imm AR 14; *Re Vassis* (1986) 64 ALR 407.

[275] National Insurance Decision No R(P) 1/72.

[276] *Mark v Mark* [2005] UKHL 42 at [31], [2006] 1 AC 98.

[277] *Shah v Barnet London Borough Council* [1983] 2 AC 309 at 343–344, 349; *Mark v Mark*, supra, at [32]. See also *R v Secretary of State for the Home Department, ex p Marguerrite* [1983] QB 180; British Nationality Act 1981, s 50(5) as amended by British Overseas Territories Act 2002, s 1(2); *Immigration Appeal Tribunal v Chelliah* [1985] Imm AR 192. On the lawfulness of a person's residence and the qualification to vote, see *Hipperson v Newbury District Electoral Registration Officer* [1985] QB 1060.

[278] *Mark v Mark* [2005] UKHL 42 at [31], [2006] 1 AC 98. See for Canada, *Blair v Chung* (2006) 271 DLR (4th) 311, illegal residence can in some circumstances constitute ordinary residence.

[279] *Mark v Mark*, supra, at [31].

[280] Ibid, at [32].

[281] Ibid, at [36].

[282] Ibid, at [45].

[283] *Stransky v Stransky* [1954] P 428; *Lewis v Lewis* [1956] 1 WLR 200; *Shah v Barnet London Borough Council*, supra, at 343.

[284] *R v Secretary of State for the Home Department, ex p Zahir Chugtai* [1995] Imm AR 559.

England ready for immediate occupation.[285] However, a person who, after living in England for seven years, returned to Pakistan and then sought unsuccessfully to re-enter England over a six-year period was not ordinarily resident in England during that period.[286] The ordinary residence of a new-born baby necessarily has to be dependent on the residence of its mother.[287] The ordinary residence of a small child or an adult who is too handicapped to form an intention is prima facie that of the parents.[288]

(b) Habitual residence[289]

The courts[290] have repeatedly followed the judgment of Lord SCARMAN in *R v Barnet London Borough Council, ex p Shah*,[291] holding that there is no difference in principle between the traditional concept of ordinary residence and the more fashionable concept of habitual residence[292] and that they both refer to a person's abode in a particular place or country which he has adopted voluntarily and for settled purposes as part of the regular order of his life for the time being, whether of short or of long duration. Whether a person is habitually resident in a particular country is said to be a question of fact, to be decided by reference to all the circumstances of any particular case.[293] Habitual residence is a concept without the various legal artificialities of domicile, such as the doctrine of revival, and analogies with that concept are not appropriate.[294] Nonetheless, determination of a person's habitual residence, particularly that of a child, has perhaps inevitably also become partly a question of law, and the law on habitual residence has become

---

[285] The *Stransky* case, supra, and see *Casey v Casey* 1968 SLT 56. But cf *Carmichael v Director-General of Social Welfare* [1994] 3 NZLR 477—keeping chattels in a room in a daughter's house.

[286] *R v Secretary of State for the Home Department, ex p Mohammed Butta* [1994] Imm AR 197.

[287] *C (A Child) v Plymouth County Council* [2000] 1 FLR 875, 879, CA.

[288] *R v Kent County Council, ex p S* [2000] 1 FLR 155.

[289] de Winter (1969) III Hague Recueil 357; Hall (1975) 24 ICLQ 1; Clive [1997] Jur Rev 137; Leslie 1996 SLT 145; Crawford [1992] Jur Rev 177 and [2000] Jur Rev 89; Rogerson (2000) 49 ICLQ 86; Stone (2000) 29 Anglo-Am LR 342 and see Council of Europe Resolution 72(1): Standardisation of the Legal Concepts of "Domicile" and "Residence".

[290] *Re M (Minors)(Residence Order: Jurisdiction)* [1993] 1 FLR 495 at 499, CA; on which see Cretney (1993) 109 LQR 538; *Re M (Abduction: Habitual Residence)* [1996] 1 FLR 887, CA; *M v M (Abduction: England and Scotland)* [1997] 2 FLR 263 at 267 (per BUTLER-SLOSS LJ), at 273 (per MILLETT LJ); *Ikimi v Ikimi* [2001] EWCA Civ 873, [2001] 3 WLR 672; *Mark v Mark* [2005] UKHL 42 at [27], [33], [2006] 1 AC 98, Rogerson [2006] CLJ 35. See also *Re B (Minors)(Abduction)(No 2)* [1993] 1 FLR 993; *Re V (Abduction: Habitual Residence)* [1995] 2 FLR 992 at 1001. For Scotland see *Dickson v Dickson* 1990 SCLR 692 at 703; *Findlay v Findlay* 1994 SLT 709 at 713. For Canada see *Chan v Chow* (2001) 199 DLR (4th) 478 (BCCA); *Korutowska-Wooff v Wooff* (2004) 242 DLR (4th) 385 (Ont CA). For New Zealand see *SK v KP* [2005] 3 NZLR 590, CA.

[291] See supra. For a definition from the French Cour de cassation see *Moore v Moore* [2006] IL Pr 628.

[292] Cf *Nessa v Chief Adjudication Officer* [1999] 1 WLR 1937 at 1941, HL, where it was said that there was a common core of meaning but there were shades of difference depending on the context and the object and purpose of legislation using the concepts. However, according to *Ikimi v Ikimi* [2001] EWCA Civ 873 at [31], [2001] 3 WLR 672, the two concepts mean the same thing in the field of family law.

[293] *Re J (A Minor)(Abduction: Custody Rights)* [1990] 2 AC 562 at 578 (per Lord BRANDON); *Re M (Abduction: Habitual Residence)*, supra, at 895, CA; *Re A (Minors)(Abduction: Habitual Residence)* [1996] 1 WLR 25; *Re M (Minors) (Residence Order: Jurisdiction)*, supra, at 499; *Re A (Abduction: Habitual Residence)* [1998] 1 FLR 497; *Re B (Abduction: Children's Objections)* [1998] 1 FLR 667; *Nessa v Chief Adjudication Officer* [1999] 1 WLR 1937 at 1942; *Al Habtoor v Fotheringham* [2001] EWCA Civ 186, [2001] 1 FLR 951; *Mark v Mark* [2005] UKHL 42 at [36], [2006] 1 AC 98. For Scotland see *Rellis v Hart* 1993 SLT 738; *Moran v Moran* 1997 SLT 541; *D v D* 2001 SLT 1104 at [19], First Division. For New Zealand see *SK v KP* [2005] 3 NZLR 590, CA.

[294] *Re S (A Minor)(Abduction)* [1991] 2 FLR 1 at 20, CA. See also *Re B (Minors)(Abduction)(No 2)* [1993] 1 FLR 993; *Al Habtoor v Fotheringham* [2001] EWCA Civ 186 at [42], [2001] 1 FLR 951; *W and B v H (Child Abduction: Surrogacy)* [2002] 1 FLR 1008.

increasingly complex. The burden of proof is upon the person seeking to show a change of habitual residence to establish this.[295]

(i) Acquisition of a new habitual residence

Re J (A Minor)(Abduction: Custody Rights)[296] held that residence for an appreciable period of time and a settled intention to reside on a long-term basis are needed for acquisition of a new habitual residence.[297]

(a) Residence

Before a child or adult can be habitually resident in a country he must be resident there.[298] This does not necessarily require physical presence at all times. Temporary absence, for example on holiday[299] or for educational purposes[300] or for an attempt to effect a reconciliation with an estranged spouse,[301] will not bring an end to habitual residence. Indeed it can continue despite considerable periods of absence.[302] In an extreme example, a petitioner was held to be habitually resident in England for the whole of the preceding year, despite spending 204 days of that year in a concurrent habitual residence in Nigeria.[303] An habitual residence in England has been held to continue despite a period of some two years nine months residing in Hong Kong.[304] Habitual residence for the purpose of divorce jurisdiction under section 5(2) of the Domicile and Matrimonial Proceeedings Act 1973[305] need not be lawful residence and can be acquired by a person who is in England illegally.[306] However, it is a question of statutory construction whether the word "lawfully" should be implied into a statutory provision which uses the concept of habitual residence.[307] There was no reason to imply this in the case of a statute dealing with divorce jurisdiction. Indeed, it is only right that persons with longstanding links with England should have their personal affairs dealt with in England and subject to English law.[308] This would not necessarily work to their benefit; it may be a disadvantage, so there is no question of benefiting from unlawful residence. But there are other statutory provisions, in particular those conferring entitlement to some benefit from the state where it

---

[295] *F v S (Wardship: Jurisdiction)* [1993] 2 FLR 686, CA. See also *Re E (Child: Abduction)* [1992] 1 FCR 541, CA (per PARKER LJ).

[296] [1990] 2 AC 562; distinguished in *Re S (A Minor)(Custody: Habitual Residence)* [1998] AC 750, HL.

[297] Supra, at 578–579.

[298] *Re M (Abduction: Habitual Residence)* [1996] 1 FLR 887 at 895 (per Sir John BALCOMBE), at 896 (per MILLETT LJ), CA.

[299] *Findlay v Findlay* 1994 SLT 709; *Rellis v Hart* 1993 SLT 738.

[300] *Re A (Wardship Jurisdiction)* [1995] 1 FLR 767.

[301] *Re B (Child Abduction: Habitual Residence)* [1994] 2 FLR 915; *H v H (Child Abduction: Stay of Proceedings)* [1994] 1 FLR 530.

[302] *Oundjian v Oundjian* (1979) 1 FLR 198, where over one-third of the period was spent abroad.

[303] *Ikimi v Ikimi* [2001] EWCA Civ 873, [2001] 3 WLR 672. Cf *Armstrong v Armstrong* [2003] EWHC 777 (Fam), [2003] 2 FLR 375.

[304] *C v FC (Brussels II: Free Standing Application For Parental Responsibility)* [2004] 1 FLR 317.

[305] Amended in the light of Council Regulation (EC) No 2201/2003 of 27 November 2003 concerning jurisdiction and the recognition and enforcement of judgments in matrimonial matters and the matters of parental responsibility OJ 2003 L 338/1 (Brussels II *bis*), discussed infra, pp 944–959, which gives pre-eminence to the jurisdiction rules contained therein.

[306] *Mark v Mark* [2005] UKHL 42 at [35], [2006] 1 AC 98.

[307] Ibid, at [31].

[308] Ibid, at [31]–[34]. Cf the reasoning of the Court of Appeal, [2004] EWCA Civ 168, [2005] Fam 267, which was based on a denial of access to the English courts contrary to Art 6(1) of the ECHR.

would be proper to imply a requirement that the residence be lawful.[309] Even where the word "lawfully" cannot be implied into a statute, the fact that the residence is unlawful might still be relevant to the factual question of whether that residence is "habitual".[310] Thus a person who went on the run after a deportation order might find it hard to establish that the residence was habitual.[311]

(b) A period of time

The formulation in *Re J (A Minor)(Abduction: Custody Rights)*,[312] requiring residence for an appreciable period of time, has been followed in numerous cases.[313] However, more recently the House of Lords in *Nessa v Chief Adjudication Officer*[314] has adopted rather different wording. Lord SLYNN said that, as a matter of ordinary language, a person is not habitually resident in any country unless that person has taken up residence and lived there for a period which shows that the residence has become "habitual" and will or is likely to continue to be habitual.[315] He went on to say though that this was what Lord Brandon in *Re J (A Minor)(Abduction: Custody Rights)* was referring to when he used the words an "appreciable period of time".[316] In *Nessa*, it was held that a woman who arrived in England from Bangladesh was not habitually resident for the purpose of entitlement to income support on the day that she arrived.[317] It follows that there may be a gap between habitual residence in one state and acquisition of habitual residence in another. A person may have no habitual residence at all.[318] However, it may be that for the purposes of making particular legislation effective, an example being the founding of jurisdiction, it may be necessary that a person is habitually resident in some state. In other words there would not be a gap. This would, exceptionally, be departing from the ordinary meaning of the words "habitual residence". The importance of the context when determining the meaning of habitual residence is shown in *Swaddling v Adjudication Officer*,[319] where the European Court of Justice held that a community Regulation concerned with income support for employed persons precluded the United Kingdom from adopting a definition of habitual residence (on which entitlement to the benefit was based) that looked to the length of residence, requiring an appreciable period of residence.[320]

---

[309] Supra, at [36]. See also the discussion in relation to ordinary residence, supra, p 184.

[310] Supra, at [36].

[311] Ibid.

[312] [1990] 2 AC 562; distinguished in *Re S (A Minor)(Custody: Habitual Residence)* [1998] AC 750, HL.

[313] *Re J (A Minor)(Abduction: Custody Rights)* [1990] 2 AC 562 at 578; cited without disapproval by Lord SLYNN in *Re S (A Minor)(Custody: Habitual Residence)* [1998] AC 750, HL; *Re F (A Minor)(Child Abduction)* [1992] 1 FLR 548, CA; *Re M (Minors)(Residence Order: Jurisdiction)* [1993] 1 FLR 495, CA; *M v M (Abduction: England and Scotland)* [1997] 2 FLR 263, CA; *Re B (Minors)(Abduction)(No 2)*, supra; *Re A (Abduction: Habitual Residence)* [1998] 1 FLR 497; *Ikimi v Ikimi* [2001] EWCA Civ 873, [2001] 3 WLR 672; *D v D* 2001 SLT 1104 at [19]. See also *Chan v Chow* (2001) 199 DLR (4th) 478 (BCCA).

[314] [1999] 1 WLR 1937, HL; Crawford [2000] Jur Rev 89.

[315] *Re J (A Minor)(Abduction: Custody Rights)* [1999] 1 WLR 1937 at 1942, HL; followed in *Re N (Abduction: Habitual Residence)* [2000] 2 FLR 899; *Al Habtoor v Fotheringham* [2001] EWCA Civ 186 at [25], [2001] 1 FLR 951. For continuing use of the appreciable period formula see *Ikimi v Ikimi*, supra, and *D v D*, supra.

[316] *Nessa v Chief Adjudication Officer*, supra, at 1942. See *M, Petitioner* 2005 SLT 2 equating the two.

[317] *Nessa v Chief Adjudication Officer*, supra.

[318] *Mark v Mark* [2005] UKHL 42 at [37], [2006] 1 AC 98. See also *SK v KP* [2005] 3 NZLR 590 at [48], CA; *WP V FP* [2007] EWHC 779 (Fam), [2007] 2 FLR 129.

[319] Case C-90/97 [1999] ECR I-1075.

[320] Ibid, at paras [30] and [34].

It is a question of fact whether and when the requisite habitual residence has been established. This depends very much on the circumstances of the particular case.[321] The requisite period is not a fixed one.[322] The period may in some circumstances be short.[323] Butler-Sloss LJ has said that a month can be an appreciable time for these purposes[324] and Lord Slynn has said that, if a person leaves one country to go to another with the established intention of settling there permanently, habitual residence may change very quickly.[325] In *V v B (A Minor)(Abduction)*[326] an habitual residence was acquired after less than three months' residence in Australia, the parties, according to the plaintiff, having decided to settle there. In contrast, in *Re A (Abduction: Habitual Residence)*[327] it was said, obiter, that three weeks in the circumstances of the case was not an appreciable time.[328] In *D v D* a few days was not enough.[329] In a difficult case, such as a local authority placing a child overseas without a final plan, even one or two years' residence may not be enough for losing an existing habitual residence and replacement by a new one abroad.[330] Temporary absence from a country will not prevent acquisition of an habitual residence there provided this is not inconsistent with an intention to settle.[331] The position where someone is resuming an habitual residence that they previously had is different from that where they are coming to England for the first time.[332] As with ordinary residence,[333] it is possible to be habitually resident in more than one place at the same time.[334] It follows that a person can be habitually resident in England for the whole of a one-year period despite also being habitually resident in another country.[335] However, in such a case the person must have spent an appreciable part of the year in England, 161 days being sufficient[336]

---

[321] *Nessa v Chief Adjudication Officer*, supra, at 1942.

[322] Ibid at 1943. See *Cameron v Cameron* 1996 SLT 306 at 313, no minimum period is required. Though see Brussels II *bis*, Art 3.1(a), indents 5 and 6, discussed infra, pp 945–946.

[323] *Nessa*, supra, at 1943.

[324] *Re F (A Minor)(Child Abduction)* [1992] 1 FLR 548 at 555, CA; *Re G (A Minor)(Enforcement of Access Abroad)* [1993] Fam 216, CA.

[325] *Re S (A Minor)(Custody: Habitual Residence)* [1998] AC 750, HL. See also *Re B (Minors)(Abduction)(No 2)*, supra, at 995.

[326] [1991] FCR 451, [1991] 1 FLR 266. See also *Re S (A Minor)(Abduction)* [1991] 2 FLR 1; *Cameron v Cameron* 1996 SLT 306. Cf *Adderson v Adderson* (1987) 36 DLR (4th) 631, Alberta CA—two short periods of a few months each not enough to establish an habitual residence in Hawaii.

[327] [1998] 1 FLR 497.

[328] Ibid at 505. See also *WP V FP* [2007] EWHC 779 (Fam), [2007] 2 FLR 129—7–8 days not enough; *Re M (Minors) (Residence Order: Jurisdiction)* [1993] 1 FLR 495.

[329] 2001 SLT 1104.

[330] *London Borough of Greenwich v Ms S, Mr A, B, C, D, E (by their Children's Guardian), Z* [2007] EWHC 820 (Fam), [2007] 2 FCR 141.

[331] *Re A (Abduction: Habitual Residence: Consent)* [2005] EWHC 2998 (Fam), [2006] 2 FLR 1.

[332] *Nessa v Chief Adjudication Officer*, op cit, at 1943, referring to Case C-90/97 *Swaddling v Adjudication Officer* [1999] ECR I-1075, ECJ.

[333] *IRC v Lysaght* [1928] AC 234; *Hopkins v Hopkins* [1951] P 116; *Shah v Barnet London Borough Council* [1983] 2 AC 309 at 342; *Leyvand v Barasch* (2000) Times, 23 March.

[334] *Mark v Mark* [2005] UKHL 42 at [37], [2006] 1 AC 98; *Ikimi v Ikimi* [2001] EWCA Civ 873, [2001] 3 WLR 672; *Breuning v Breuning* [2002] EWHC 236 (Fam), [2002] 1 FLR 888 at 900; *M v H* [2005] EWHC 1186 (Fam). But cf *Re V (Abduction: Habitual Residence)* [1995] 2 FLR 992, on which doubt is cast by *Ikimi*. Cf also the position in Scotland: *Dickson v Dickson* 1990 SCLR 692 at 703; *Findlay v Findlay* 1994 SLT 709; *Cameron v Cameron* 1996 SLT 306. Cf Blom (1973) 22 ICLQ 109, 136; Clive [1997] Jur Rev 137, at 144; Leslie 1996 SLT 145, 147–148.

[335] *Ikimi v Ikimi* [2001] EWCA Civ 873, [2001] 3 WLR 672. See also *C v FC (Brussels II: Free Standing Application For Parental Responsibility)* [2004] 1 FLR 317.

[336] *Ikimi v Ikimi*, supra.

and 71 days insufficient.[337] Less dramatically, it is possible, for example, to be habitually resident for part of the year in London and for the rest of the year in Corfu.[338]

(c) A settled intention

There must be a degree of settled intention or purpose.[339] This is not concerned with being settled in a country.[340] Instead it describes one's purpose in living where one does.[341] The element of "animus" required is less than that for domicile. There is no need to show a person intended to stay there permanently or indefinitely.[342] The settled intention can be for a limited period,[343] a period limited by the immediate purpose such as employment, even short-term employment of no more than six months.[344] Thus a person can be habitually resident in a country even though he intends at some future date to move to another country.[345] For example, a serviceman who is posted abroad, anticipating at least a three-year stay, can acquire an habitual residence there.[346] To take another example, in *Watson v Jamieson*[347] there was a settled purpose where children went to live with their father in Scotland for two years, the understanding between the separated parents from the outset being that the children would then go to live with their mother, who lived in New Zealand, for two years. The children were held to be habitually resident in Scotland. A move on a trial basis can constitute a settled purpose.[348] A person can have a settled intention despite disliking the environment in which he lives.[349]

According to Lord BRANDON in *Re J (A Minor)(Abduction: Custody Rights)*,[350] the settled intention refers to residing on a long-term basis. On the other hand, according to the Court of Appeal in *M v M (Abduction: England and Scotland)*[351] the settled purpose refers to "part of the regular order of his life for the time being, whether of short or of long duration". Under Scots law it is sufficient if there is an intention to reside for an appreciable period,[352] or for some time.[353] These differences in terminology should not be regarded as important since "A settled purpose is not something to be searched for

---

[337] *Armstrong v Armstrong* [2003] EWHC 777 (Fam).

[338] *Re V (Abduction: Habitual Residence)*, supra; *Re A (Abduction: Habitual Residence)* [1998] 1 FLR 497 at 505.

[339] The *Shah* case refers to a settled purpose, as do habitual residence cases expressly following it. The *Re J* case refers to a settled intention. There does not appear to be any difference between the two.

[340] *Moran v Moran* 1997 SLT 541; *Re R (Abduction: Habitual Residence)* [2003] EWHC 1968 (Fam), [2004] 1 FLR 216.

[341] *Moran* supra.

[342] *Re B (Minors)(Abduction)(No 2)* [1993] 1 FLR 993; *M v M (Abduction: England and Scotland)* [1997] 2 FLR 263 at 274 (per MILLETT LJ); *D v D* 2001 SLT 1104 at [19].

[343] *Moran v Moran* [1997] SLT 541; *Al Habtoor v Fotheringam* [2001] EWCA Civ 186 at [37], [2001] 1 FLR 951; *Re R (Abduction: Habitual Residence)* [2003] EWHC 1968 (Fam), [2004] 1 FLR 216.

[344] *Re R (Abduction: Habitual Residence)* supra.

[345] *M v M (Abduction: England and Scotland)* [1997] 2 FLR 263, CA.

[346] *Re A (Abduction: Habitual Residence)* [1996] 1 FLR 1.

[347] 1998 SLT 180. Cf *Punter v Secretary for Justice* [2003] NZCA 306 at [32].

[348] *Al Habtoor v Fotheringham* [2001] EWCA Civ 186, [2001] 1 FLR 951; *Cameron v Cameron* 1996 SC 17; *M, Petitioner* 2005 SLT 2. Cf *Re N (Abduction: Habitual Residence)* [2000] 2 FLR 899.

[349] *M, Petitioner* 2005 SLT 2 at [20].

[350] Supra, at 578. See also *Re V (Jurisdiction: Habitual Residence)* [2001] 1 FLR 253.

[351] [1997] 2 FLR 263.

[352] *Cameron v Cameron* 1996 SLT 306 at 313.

[353] *D v D (Parent and Child:Residence)* 2001 SLT 1104.

under a microscope. If it is there at all it will stand out clearly as a matter of general impression."[354]

How easy is it to show this settled intention? The longer the period of residence the easier it becomes.[355] Thus in *M v M (Abduction: England and Scotland)*,[356] it was clearly important in finding this settled purpose that the parties had actually been living in Scotland for as long a period as two years. Indeed, it has been suggested that where there is a long period of residence the objective facts will then point to this being the habitual residence.[357] The objective facts spoke for themselves where a child had been in a country for fifteen months.[358] Conversely, if the residence has been for a short period only, the intention becomes crucial. A few months, or even a month, can be enough for acquisition of an habitual residence,[359] but there would have to be evidence of the requisite settled intention.[360] Thus in *V v B (A Minor)(Abduction)*,[361] where an habitual residence was acquired after less than three months, it was crucial that the parties intended to settle in that country. In contrast, in *Re A (Abduction: Habitual Residence)*[362] it was held that there was no settled purpose in the situation where the intended period of stay was six weeks in order for a child to have holiday contact with its father and grandparents. Neither was there a settled purpose in *Re B (Child Abduction: Habitual Residence)*[363] where the wife visited her husband in Canada for a period of under three months for the purpose of attempting to effect a reconciliation. In these cases involving a period of short residence the residence was for a temporary purpose and this was fatal to the acquisition of an habitual residence.[364] When it comes to establishing an intention to settle, this was shown in one case by the fact, inter alia, that the family furniture was sent to that country.[365]

(d) Voluntarily

There is a further requirement in relation to adults that the residence must have been voluntary.[366] The equating of habitual residence with ordinary residence means that this requirement has the same meaning as that previously examined in the context of

---

[354] *Re B (Minors)(Abduction)(No 2)* [1993] 1 FLR 993 at 998; *Re A (Abduction: Habitual Residence)* [1998] 1 FLR 497.

[355] See Clive [1997] Jur Rev 137, 140 et seq.

[356] Supra.

[357] *Zenel v Haddow* 1993 SLT 975; 1993 SCLR 872. See also Leslie, op cit, 147. But see *M v M (Abduction: England v Scotland* [1997] 2 FLR 263 at 267 (per BUTLER-SLOSS LJ)—two years was not necessarily conclusive of habitual residence. See also *Breuning v Breuning* [2002] EWHC 236 (Fam), [2002] 1 FLR 888 at 899—evidence going back over a long period of time should be discouraged.

[358] *Zenel v Haddow*, supra.

[359] *M v M (Abduction: England and Scotland)* [1997] 2 FLR 263 at 267, CA. See also *Re B (Minors)(Abduction) (No 2)* [1993] 1 FLR 993.

[360] Acquisition of an habitual residence in such cases is criticised by Leslie 1996 SLT 145, 147.

[361] Supra.

[362] [1998] 1 FLR 497. See also *Re R (Wardship: Child Abduction)* [1992] 2 FLR 481, CA.

[363] [1994] 2 FLR 915. See also *H v H (Child Abduction: Stay of Domestic Proceedings)* [1994] 1 FLR 530.

[364] See also *Re S (Minors)(Abduction: Wrongful Retention)* [1994] Fam 70; *Re A (Minors)(Abduction: Habitual Residence)* [1996] 1 WLR 25 at 33; *Re A (Wardship: Jurisdiction)* [1995] 1 FLR 767; *Findlay v Findlay (No 2)* 1995 SLT 492.

[365] *A v A (Child Abduction)* [1993] 2 FLR 225.

[366] *Shah v Barnet London Borough Council* [1983] 2 AC 309 at 342; *Nessa v Chief Adjudication Officer* [1999] 1 WLR 1937 at 1943, HL; *M v M (Abduction: England and Scotland)*, supra; *Ikimi v Ikimi* [2001] EWCA Civ 873 at [34], [2001] 3 WLR 672. But cf *Cameron v Cameron* 1996 SLT 306 at 311; Clive [1997] Jur Rev 137 at 141; Leslie 1996 SLT 145 at 146; Crawford and Carruthers, para 6-40.

ordinary residence.[367] A serviceman who is stationed on a base abroad can be regarded as voluntarily resident in that country (he could have left the armed forces if he did not want to accept the posting) and, having made the family home there, he and his family will take this country as their habitual residence.[368]

(ii) Abandonment

A person can cease to be habitually resident in a country in a single day if he or she leaves it with a settled intention not to return to it but to take up long-term residence in another country instead.[369] For example in *Moran v Moran*[370] the parents, who were habitually resident in California, agreed that the mother and child should return to Scotland for a year, whilst the father remained in California to deal with business problems. It was held that the child's habitual residence ceased as from the date of departure from California. However, habitual residence in one jurisdiction does not necessarily come to an end merely because the person concerned leaves for a short period or for a temporary purpose,[371] such as formal education.[372] The abandonment of an habitual residence can take place without acquisition of another habitual residence elsewhere,[373] with the inevitable result that a person has no habitual residence.[374] Moreover, because an habitual residence can be abandoned in one day but not acquired until there has been residence for a period showing that residence has become habitual, this gap when there is no habitual residence will correspondingly last for that period. During this period, for example, a child will be without the protection of the legislation on child abduction[375] and an adult will not get income support.[376] It is in order to mitigate this that it has been accepted that in some circumstances the period may be short.[377] It has even been accepted that, exceptionally, for the purposes of making particular legislation effective, it may be necessary to ensure that there is no gap.[378] But to close the gap entirely in all cases it would be necessary to introduce an artificial rule, analogous to that in relation to a domicile of origin, that an habitual residence cannot be abandoned and it continues until replaced by another habitual residence elsewhere.[379]

(iii) Children[380]

The habitual residence of a child is not fixed but may change according to the circumstances of the parent or other principal carer with whom the child lives and who is

---

[367] Supra.

[368] *Re A (Minors)(Abduction: Habitual Residence)* [1996] 1 WLR 25 at 32–33.

[369] *Re J (A Minor)(Abduction: Custody Rights)* supra, at 578 (per Lord BRANDON). See also *Re M (Minors)(Residence Order: Jurisdiction)*, supra, at 501, CA; *F v F (Abduction: Habitual Residence)* [1993] Fam Law 199; *Re N (Abduction: Habitual Residence)* [2000] 2 FLR 899; *Al Habtoor v Fotheringham* [2001] EWCA Civ 186 at [25], [2001] 1 FLR 951.

[370] 1997 SLT 541.

[371] *Rellis v Hart* 1993 SLT 738 at 741.

[372] *P V P* [2006] EWHC 2410 (Fam), [2007] 2 FLR 439.

[373] *Re M (Abduction: Habitual Residence)* [1996] 1 FLR 887; *WP v FP* [2007] EWHC 779 (Fam), [2007] 2 FLR 129.

[374] *Mark v Mark* [2005] UKHL 42 at [37], [2006] 1 AC 98.

[375] *Re F (A Minor)(Child Abduction)* [1992] 1 FLR 548, CA.

[376] *Nessa v Chief Adjudication Officer* [1999] 1 WLR 1937, HL.

[377] Ibid.

[378] *Nessa v Chief Adjudication Officer*, supra.

[379] See Leslie 1996 SLT 145, 149.

[380] Crawford [1992] Jur Rev 177; Stone (1992) 4 JCL 170.

lawfully exercising rights of custody.[381] This has been criticised as detracting from the factual nature of the concept and as taking a parent-centred rather than child-centred approach.[382] If the parents are living together and the child is living with them it will take the parents' habitual residence.[383] There is authority to the effect that a new-born child takes this habitual residence immediately on birth, rather than having to reside for an appreciable period in that country before doing so.[384] There is a problem if the child is born abroad whilst on holiday to parents habitually resident in England. It has been said, obiter, that in these circumstances it is possible for the child to take an habitual residence in England from birth.[385] This would have to be on the basis of a rather surprising finding of fact[386] that the child is habitually resident in England.[387]

If both parents have joint parental responsibility, neither parent can unilaterally change the child's habitual residence by removing or retaining it wrongfully and in breach of the other party's rights.[388] Both parents must consent to the change of habitual residence.[389] A father can, for example, consent to the child being with the mother and therefore to a change of habitual residence.[390] Moreover, one parent may take no step to prevent the other parent from changing the child's home, which over a period, may amount to acquiescence.[391] In the unusual situation where a married couple lived with the children, and yet each parent had a different habitual residence, the habitual residence of the children could only change if the parents had a common intention to change their residence.[392]

---

[381] *Re M (Minors)(Residence Order: Jurisdiction)* [1993] 1 FLR 495 at 500, CA; *Re G (A Minor)(Enforcement of Access Abroad)* [1993] Fam 216, CA; *Re B (Minors)(Abduction)(No 2)* [1993] 1 FLR 993; *Re A (Abduction: Habitual Residence)* [1998] 1 FLR 497 at 503; *Re JS (Private International Adoption)* [2000] 2 FLR 638; *Re M (Abduction: Conflict of Jurisdiction)* [2000] 2 FLR 372. Cf *W and B v H (Child Abduction: Surrogacy)* [2002] 1 FLR 1008—habitual residence not taken from surrogate mother with whom no biological connection.

[382] Schuz (2001) 13 Child and Family Law Quarterly 1; *SK v KP* [2005] 3 NZLR 590 at [75], CA.

[383] *Re A (Minors)(Abduction: Habitual Residence)* [1996] 1 WLR 25.

[384] *B v H (Habitual Residence: Wardship)* [2002] 1 FLR 388 at 403; *PAS v AFS* [2005] 1 ILRM 306 at 317, SC of Ireland. See also Clive [1997] Jur Rev 137, 146.

[385] *B v H (Habitual Residence: Wardship)*, supra; *PAS v AFS*, supra.

[386] Cf *Re M (Abduction: Habitual Residence)* [1996] 1 FLR 887; discussed infra, p 193. See also MILLETT LJ in that case, at 895–896, "it is not possible for a person to acquire residence in one country while remaining throughout physically present in another".

[387] *W and B v H (Child Abduction: Surrogacy)* [2002] 1 FLR 1008 at [23].

[388] *Re M (Abduction: Habitual Residence)* [1996] 1 FLR 887 at 896, (per MILLETT LJ), CA. See also *H v H (Child Abduction: Stay of Domestic Proceedings)* [1994] 1 FLR 530; *Re S (Minors)(Abduction: Wrongful Retention)* [1994] Fam 70; *Re B (Minors)(Abduction)(No 2)*, supra; *Findlay v Findlay* 1994 SLT 709; *Findlay v Findlay (No 2)* 1995 SLT 492; *Moran v Moran* 1997 SLT 541; *Re B (Abduction: Children's Objections)* [1998] 1 FLR 667; *Re N (Abduction: Habitual Residence)* [2000] 2 FLR 899; *B v H (Habitual Residence: Wardship)* [2002] 1 FLR 388.

[389] *Re K (Abduction: Consent: Forum Conveniens)* [1995] 2 FLR 211, CA; *Findlay v Findlay (No 2)* 1995 SLT 492.

[390] *Re F (A Minor)(Child Abduction)* [1992] 1 FLR 548, CA; *Re H (Abduction: Habitual Residence: Consent)* [2000] 2 FLR 294; *D v D* 2001 SLT 1104 at [27]–[28] Lord CARLOWAY, overturned by the First Division without discussion of this point; *C v FC (Brussels II: Free Standing Applicaion For Parental Responsibility)* [2004] 1 FLR 317.

[391] *Re F (A Minor)(Child Abduction)* [1992] 1 FLR 548 at 556–557, CA. See also *Robertson v Robertson* 1998 SLT 468; *Singh v Singh* 1998 SLT 1084; *D v D (Parwent and Child: Residence)* 2001 SLT 1104. Cf *C v FC (Brussels II: Free Standing Application For Parental Responsibility)* [2004] 1 FLR 317.

[392] *Re N (Abduction: Habitual Residence)* [2000] 2 FLR 899. But see *Re A (A Child)* [2006] EWHC 3338 (Fam), [2007] 1 FLR 1589—habitual residence is a ultimately a question of fact and not always determinable by reference to the combined intention of the parents.

A court order determining rights of residence and custody can also change the child's habitual residence.[393] However, commonsense would suggest that if, for example, a child has been living with its mother for ten years it would take the same habitual residence as the mother, even though during this period the mother has been acting in defiance of a court order to return the child.[394] A child subject to a supervision requirement probably remains habitually resident at the home of his or her parent.[395]

The courts have rejected the idea of some sort of habitual residence of dependency on the parent, as being incompatible with the idea that habitual residence is a question of fact.[396] It follows that before a child can be habitually resident in a country it must be resident there.[397] Thus for a child's habitual residence to change to that of another country the child has to leave the country in which he is resident and reside in that other country.[398] The previous two sentences should not be regarded as statements of law but rather as assertions of fact.

If one parent has sole lawful custody of the child, his situation with regard to habitual residence will be the same as that of this parent.[399] According to the Court of Appeal in *Re M (Minors)(Residence Order: Jurisdiction)*,[400] lawful custody refers to the child being in the physical care of that parent. Thus a child who was in the care of grandparents in Scotland, with the agreement of the mother, had an habitual residence in Scotland.[401] This ended when the mother decided that this arrangement should end and the children came back to her in England. However, the children would not immediately take an English habitual residence. The result was that they were not habitually resident in either country.[402] If a child has been made a ward of court, a parent cannot then change its habitual residence without leave of the court.[403] If the mother is the sole carer, then dies, and relatives, with no parental rights over the child, have taken it out of the jurisdiction for a period of two days, this cannot result in the existing habitual residence being lost and a new one gained.[404] It is not clear at what age a person ceases to be a child for the purposes of habitual residence, but it is likely that this is at 16.[405] As with an adult, a child may have no habitual residence.[406]

---

[393] *Re F (A Minor)(Child Abduction)* supra; *Re S (Minors)(Abduction: Wrongful Retention)* [1994] Fam 70.

[394] *Re B (Abduction: Children's Objections)* [1998] 1 FLR 667 at 671. See also Clive [1997] Jur Rev 137, 145.

[395] *Glasgow City Council v M* 2001 SLT 396, 400.

[396] *Re M (Abduction: Habitual Residence)* [1996] 1 FLR 887 at 895 (per Sir John BALCOMBE), CA; *Al Habtoor v Fotheringham* [2001] EWCA Civ 186, [2001] 1 FLR 951.

[397] *Re M (Abduction: Habitual Residence)* [1996] 1 FLR 887 at 895 (per Sir John BALCOMBE), CA.

[398] Ibid (disapproving of *Re A (Wardship: Jurisdiction)* [1995] 1 FLR 767 at 773). See also *Re F (Abduction: Unborn Child)* [2006] EWHC 2199 (Fam), [2007] 1 FLR 627.

[399] *Re J (A Minor)(Abduction)* supra, at 578 (per Lord BRANDON); *Re M (Minor)(Residence Order: Jurisdiction)*, supra. See also *Re F (A Minor)(Child Abduction)* [1992] 1 FLR 548, CA; *Re O (A Minor)(Abduction: Habitual Residence)* [1993] 2 FLR 594. But cf *Rellis v Hart* 1993 SLT 738.

[400] [1993] 1 FLR 495, CA.

[401] See also *Re A (Wardship: Jurisdiction)* [1993] 1 FLR 767 at 772.

[402] See also *Al Habtoor v Fotheringham*, supra; *W and B v H (Child Abduction: Surrogacy)*, supra.

[403] *Re B-M (Wardship Jurisdiction)* [1993] 1 FLR 979; *Re W: Re B (Child Abduction: Unmarried Father)* [1998] 2 FLR 146 at 159.

[404] *Re S (A Minor)(Custody: Habitual Residence)* [1998] AC 750, HL. The longer the child remains in the new jurisdiction without opposition, the more likely it is that it will acquire the habitual residence of the new carer; see the Court of Appeal in the same case [1997] 1 FLR 958 at 962.

[405] Stone (1992) 4 JCL 170 at 173. See also Family Law Act 1986, s 41(1).

[406] See *W and W v H (Child Abduction: Surrogacy) (No 2)* [2002] 2 FLR 252.

(iv) Does habitual residence have different meanings in different contexts?

In general, it is true to say that habitual residence has the same meaning, regardless of the context. In *Shah*, it was said that the words "ordinary residence" should be given their natural and ordinary meaning, and not an artificial legal construction,[407] which will be the same regardless of the context, unless it can be shown that the statutory framework requires a different meaning.[408] The formula in *Shah* (that residence must be adopted voluntarily and for settled purposes) was derived from tax cases but was adopted in the instant case in the context of student awards from the local authority. It is evident too that the *Shah* formula has been subsequently applied in different contexts, for example it has been applied by Baroness HALE in *Mark v Mark* in the context of divorce jurisdiction under English traditional national rules.[409] These rules[410] provided that an English court had jurisdiction to entertain proceedings for divorce if either party to the marriage was either domiciled or habitually resident in England for a period of one year. *Shah* has even been followed in cases of divorce jurisdiction[411] where the question was whether the husband was habitually resident in England for the purpose of the EC divorce jurisdiction rules in the Brussels II Regulation.[412] The term "habitual residence" in that Regulation and its replacement, the Brussels II *bis* Regulation, must be given a Community meaning in accordance with the object and purpose of the Regulation.[413] It might therefore have been expected that the definition would be somewhat different in that context from that in other contexts, including other family law contexts.[414] However, the approach to be taken in the context of the Regulation has been regarded as being equivalent to that in other contexts, including in non-family cases.[415] It is also noticeable that in *Nessa*,[416] an income support case, the House of Lords was at pains to make the point that it was acting consistently with *Re J (A Minor)(Abduction:Custody Rights)* an abduction case.

However, the principle that habitual residence has the same meaning, regardless of the context, was acknowledged in *Shah*[417] as being subject to the proviso that this is so, unless it can be shown that the statutory framework requires a different meaning.[418] Recently, Baroness HALE in *Mark v Mark* has taken up this theme, stating that "habitual residence may have a different meaning in different statutes according to their context and purpose".[419] Although it has been said that it is essential that the word "habitually" should

---

[407] *Gateshead Metropolitan Borough Council v L* [1996] 3 All ER 264 at 267.

[408] *Shah* case, supra, at 341–343.

[409] *Mark v Mark*, supra, at [36].

[410] Domicile and Matrimonial Proceedings Act 1973, s 5(2).

[411] *Breuning v Breuning* [2002] EWHC 236 (Fam), [2002] 1 FLR 888; *Armstrong v Armstrong* [2003] EWHC 777 (Fam), [2003] 2 FLR 375. See also *C v FC (Brussels II: Free Standing Application For Parental Responsibility)* [2004] 1 FLR 317.

[412] Infra, pp 947–949.

[413] *M v H* [2005] EWHC 1186 (Fam) at [85]. See also *Moore v Moore* [2006] I L Pr 628, French Cour de Cassation.

[414] See generally Lamont (2007) 3 J Priv Int L 261.

[415] *M v H Nessa* case, supra.

[416] Supra, at 1942.

[417] *Shah*, case, supra at 341–343.

[418] Rogerson (2000) 49 ICLQ 86. See also McClean, op cit, at 1153; Smart, op cit, at 183. Also see *Gingi v Secretary of State for Work and Pensions* [2001] EWCA Civ 1685, [2002] 1 CMLR 20; Crawford (2003) 10 Journal of Social Security Law 52.

[419] [2005] UKHL 42 at [15], [37], [2006] 1 AC 98.

have the same meaning wherever it appears in a family law statute, it has been conceded that this would not necessarily be extended to international child abduction cases.[420] This difference in meaning in different contexts comes out in two different aspects of the concept of habitual residence. First, it comes out in relation to whether there is a requirement that the residence must be lawful. As has been seen,[421] this does indeed depend on the statute and its context and purpose. Secondly, it comes out in relation to the requisite period of residence. Normally, there can be a gap between habitual residence in one state and aquisition of habitual residence in another. However, it may be that for the purposes of making particular legislation effective, an example being the founding of jurisdiction, it may be necessary that a person is habitually resident in some state and so there will be no gap. This departs from defining habitual residence as a matter of ordinary language and gives habitual residence a different meaning, which depends on the context.

9. REFORM[422]

Attempts in the 1950s and 1960s at the wholesale reform of the law of domicile[423] were unsuccessful because they were thought to be too radical. More recently, the English and Scottish Law Commissions[424] put forward in a joint Report a set of proposals for reform of the major rules which, at least as regards the ease of change of a domicile, were more conservative. These proposals were strongly influenced by the reform of this area of law in New Zealand,[425] Australia[426] and Canada.[427]

The Law Commissions started off on the basis that it should be a little easier to acquire a new domicile. To achieve this it was proposed that the standard of proof in all acquisition cases should be the normal civil standard,[428] and that it should be sufficient to show that a person intended to settle in the country in question for an indefinite period.[429] In their view a person who makes his home in country A, and has no present intention to return to a country of an earlier domicile or to establish a home in another country, should be regarded as domiciled in country A. This would have overruled older cases like *Ramsay* but would not appear to involve a significantly different test from that adopted in more modern cases.[430] When it comes to domicile issues other than that of ease of change of domicile, a bolder line was taken which would have led to major improvements in the law.

---

[420] *Ikimi v Ikimi* [2001] EWCA Civ 873 at [31] (per Thorpe LJ), [2001] 3 WLR 672. See also *Armstrong v Armstrong* [2003] EWHC 777 (Fam) at [12], [2003] 2 FLR 375; *M v H* [2005] EWHC 1186 (Fam) at [91]–[92].

[421] Supra, pp 186–187.

[422] See Carter (1987) 36 ICLQ 713; North (1990) I Hague Recueil 13, 34, 48.

[423] See the Private International Law Committee's first report (Cmnd 9068 of 1954) and its seventh report (Cmnd 1955 of 1963); M Mann (1963) 12 ICLQ 1326.

[424] Law Com No 168 (1987); Scot Law Com No 107 (1987); Sheridan [1989] BTR 230. This followed Law Com Working Paper No 88 (1985), Scot Law Com Consultative Memorandum No 63, on which see Fawcett (1986) 49 MLR 225; Fentiman (1986) 6 OJLS 353. See also Hong Kong Consultation Paper on Rules for Determining Domicile [2004] HKLRCCP 1

[425] Domicile Act 1976.

[426] Domicile Acts 1982.

[427] The Domicile and Habitual Residence Act 1983 of Manitoba.

[428] Para 5.6.

[429] Paras 5.8–5.14.

[430] The Law Commissions' Working Paper had recommended a much more radical approach using a presumption as to the intention necessary to acquire a domicile, based on 7 year's habitual residence in a country:

The domiciles of origin, choice and dependency would have been abolished, to be replaced by a domicile for children and a domicile for adults.[431] This would have greatly simplified the law. No special tenacity would have been given to the domicile received at birth and the doctrine of revival would have been replaced by a rule that an adult's domicile would continue until another domicile was obtained. A child would be domiciled in the country with which he was for the time being most closely connected and there would be rebuttable presumptions for determining this. All in all, the Law Commissions' proposals represented "a further important step in the process of improving the structure, effectiveness and fairness of the rules of domicile",[432] and were supported by the judges of the Family Division.[433] It is greatly to be regretted then that these proposals have been rejected for England and Wales.[434] In contrast, in Scotland the law in relation to the domicile of persons under 16 has been reformed. Influenced, at least in part, by the Law Commissions' proposals, Scots law provides that where the parents are domiciled in the same country and the child has a home with a parent or with both of them, the child is domiciled in the same country as its parents.[435] Where this is not the case, the child is domiciled in the country with which it has for the time being the closest connection.[436] These rules make no reference to the terms "domicile of origin" and "domicile of choice". Regrettably, full consideration was not given to the implications of the new law for the domicile rules generally.[437]

Law Com Working Paper No 88 (1985), Scot Law Com Consultative Memorandum No 63 (1985), paras 5.11–5.16.

[431] See now in Scots law, Family Law (Scotland) Act 2006, s 22, discussed infra.

[432] North, op cit, p 45.

[433] See the Written Evidence of Sir Stephen Brown in the Proceedings of the Special Public Bill Committee 36 Official Report (1995), p 13.

[434] Law Com No 239 (1995), p 10, n 24.

[435] Family Law (Scotland) Act 2006, s 22(1) and (2); Maher 2006 SLT 149.

[436] S 22 (3).

[437] Crawford and Carruthers, para 6-05.

PART III

Jurisdiction, Foreign Judgments and Awards

Chapters

Jurisdiction, Foreign Judgments and Awards

Chapter 10

Jurisdiction of the English Courts
—An Introduction

"Jurisdiction" is a word susceptible of several different meanings, but in the present account it is used in its widest sense to refer to the question of whether an English court will hear and determine an issue upon which its decision is sought.[1] The position is complicated by the fact that there are numerous separate sets of rules determining the jurisdiction of English courts. First, there are the four different sets of rules under the Brussels/Lugano system, ie the rules contained in the Brussels I Regulation, the EC/Denmark Agreement, the Brussels Convention and the Lugano Convention. Secondly, there are the rules contained in a modified version of the Brussels I Regulation (the Modified Regulation). Thirdly, there are the traditional English rules on jurisdiction.

---

[1] *Tehrani v Secretary of State for the Home Department* [2006] UKHL 47 at [66] (per Lord SCOTT, [2007] 1 AC 521; *Fourie v Le Roux* [2007] UKHL 1 at [25] (per Lord SCOTT, [2007] 1 WLR 320.

1. JURISDICTION UNDER THE BRUSSELS/LUGANO SYSTEM

(a) The Brussels I Regulation

In broad terms, the rules on jurisdiction contained in the Brussels I Regulation apply where:

(a) the matter is within the scope of the Regulation (a civil and commercial matter); and

(b) the defendant is domiciled in a European Community Member State, apart from Denmark[2] (ie in Austria, Belgium, Bulgaria, Cyprus,[3] the Czech Republic, Estonia, Finland, France, Germany, Greece, Hungary, Ireland, Italy, Latvia, Lithuania, Luxembourg, Malta, the Netherlands, Poland, Portugal, Romania, Slovakia, Slovenia, Spain, Sweden and the United Kingdom). Even if the defendant is not so domiciled, certain provisions in the Regulation will still apply, eg where the case involves title to land in a Member State or where there is an agreement conferring jurisdiction on the courts of a Member State.

The Brussels I Regulation is discussed in Chapter 11.

(b) The EC/Denmark Agreement

In broad terms, the rules on jurisdiction contained in the EC/Denmark Agreement apply where:

(a) the matter is within the scope of the Brussels I Regulation (a civil and commercial matter); and

(b) the defendant is domiciled in Denmark. Even if the defendant is not so domiciled, certain provisions in the Regulation will still apply, eg where the case involves title to land in Denmark or where there is an agreement conferring jurisdiction on the courts of Denmark.

The EC/Denmark Agreement applies by international law the provisions of the Brussels I Regulation, with minor amendments. Accordingly, it is also discussed in detail in Chapter 11.

(c) The Brussels Convention

In broad terms, the rules on jurisdiction contained in the Brussels Convention are applied where:

(a) the matter is within the scope of the Convention (a civil and commercial matter); and

(b) the defendant is domiciled in one of the territories of the Contracting States[4] which fall within the territorial scope of the Brussels Convention and are excluded

---

[2] The Regulation is not directly applicable to Denmark. However, by virtue of the EC/Denmark Agreement, its provisions are applied by international agreement to the relations between the Community and Denmark.

[3] The Regulation does not apply in relation to the Turkish Republic of Northern Cyprus: *Orams v Apostolides* [2006] EWHC 2226 (QB), [2007] 1 WLR 241; Briggs (2006) 77 BYBIL 561. This matter has been referred by the Court of Appeal, 18 June 2007, to the Court of Justice: Case C-420/07.

[4] At the moment the Contracting States to the Brussels Convention are the original 15 Member States.

from the Regulation.[5] The territories in question are (in relation to France) the French overseas territories, such as New Caledonia and Mayotte, and (in relation to the Netherlands) Aruba.[6] Even if the defendant is not so domiciled, certain provisions in the Convention will still apply, eg where the case involves title to land in one of the French overseas territories or Aruba, or where there is an agreement conferring jurisdiction on the courts of one of the French overseas territories or Aruba.

The Brussels Convention is discussed in detail in Chapter 11.

(d) The Lugano Convention

In broad terms, the rules on jurisdiction contained in the Lugano Convention are applied in the United Kingdom and in other European Community Member States where:

(a) the matter is within the scope of the Convention (a civil and commercial matter); and

(b) the defendant is domiciled in an EFTA State (ie Iceland, Norway or Switzerland).[7] Even if the defendant is not so domiciled, certain provisions in the Convention will still apply, eg where the case involves title to land in an EFTA State or where there is an agreement conferring jurisdiction on the courts of an EFTA State.

The terms of the Lugano Convention have been aligned with those of the Brussels I Regulation and are accordingly also discussed in detail in Chapter 11.

2. JURISDICTION UNDER THE MODIFIED REGULATION

The Civil Jurisdiction and Judgments Act 1982 applies a modified version of the Brussels I Regulation in cases where:

(a) the matter is within the scope of the Brussels I Regulation (a civil and commercial matter); and

(b) the defendant is domiciled in the United Kingdom or the proceedings are of a kind where jurisdiction is allocated to the courts of a part of the United Kingdom regardless of domicile, eg the case involves title to land in part of the United Kingdom.

Because of its close links with the Brussels I Regulation, the Modified Regulation is also discussed in detail in Chapter 11.

3. JURISDICTION UNDER THE TRADITIONAL RULES

The traditional rules on jurisdiction are still applicable, in practical terms,[8] in cases falling outside the Brussels/Lugano system and the Modified Regulation. Before the advent

---

[5] Art 68(1). Territories are excluded from the Regulation pursuant to Art 299 of the EC Treaty.

[6] See Layton and Mercer, paras 11.061–11.071. See also Kruger, paras 1.026–1.037.

[7] It is possible for non-EFTA/European Community States to become parties to the Convention.

[8] In terms of theory the position is more difficult since Art 4 of the Brussels I Regulation provides that, if the defendant is not domiciled in a Member State, the jurisdiction of the courts of each Member state shall, subject to Arts 22 and 23, be determined by the national private international law rules of that Member State. This has

of the Brusssels/Lugano system and the Modified Regulation the traditional rules were applied in all cases, and their historical roots make it appropriate to refer to them as the traditional rules.

Jurisdiction under the traditional rules involves three major issues:

(a) Whether the English courts have power to hear the case

As will be seen in Chapter 12, the competence of the courts to hear a case is a procedural matter and is dependent on the service of a claim form on the defendant. A claim form can be served on the defendant if he is present within the jurisdiction, if he submits to the jurisdiction of the English courts, or if the courts authorise service of a claim form out of the jurisdiction under rule 6.20 of the Civil Procedure Rules.

(b) Whether the court will decline jurisdiction or stay the proceedings

Notwithstanding that it is competent to hear the case, the court can decline jurisdiction or stay the proceedings in cases where the doctrine of *forum non conveniens* applies or where a decision to proceed with the case would be contrary to an exclusive jurisdiction clause or an arbitration clause. The courts' discretionary powers to refuse to take jurisdiction will be discussed in Chapter 13.

(c) Whether there is a limitation upon the exercise of jurisdiction

Even though there has been service of process, the jurisdiction of the courts is subject to certain limitations, the effect of which is to render the court incompetent to determine the issue. These limitations relate to the subject matter of the issue (eg the case involves foreign land); the kind of relief sought (eg the case involves granting a divorce); and the persons between whom the issue is joined (eg the defendant is a foreign sovereign state). There are also certain statutory limitations on jurisdiction which derive from international conventions (eg the case involves international carriage by air). These limitations will be discussed in Chapter 14.

---

led to the idea that there is only one source of jurisdiction rules, namely the Regulation. See Opinion of the Court of Justice 1/03 Competence of the Community to conclude the new Lugano Convention [2006] ECR-I 1145 at para 148 and generally Kruger, paras 1.052–1.057.

Chapter 11

Jurisdiction Under the Brussels/ Lugano System

1. INTRODUCTION

In this chapter, jurisdiction under the Brussels/Lugano system (ie the Brussels I Regulation, the EC/Denmark Agreement, the Brussels Convention and the Lugano Convention) and under the Modified Regulation will be considered.

2. THE BRUSSELS I REGULATION

The Brussels I Regulation (Council Regulation (EC) No 44/2001 of 22 December 2000 on jurisdiction and the recognition and enforcement of judgments in civil and commercial matters)[1] came into force on 1 March 2002.[2] It directly applies in all the EC Member States,[3] with the exception of Denmark.[4] However, under the EC/Denmark Agreement[5] the provisions of the Regulation, with minor modifications, are applied by international law to the relations between the Community and Denmark. The aim of the Brussels I Regulation is to unify jurisdiction rules in civil and commercial matters and simplify formalities with a view to rapid and simple recognition and enforcement of judgments given in Member States.[6] The Treaty of Amsterdam established Community competence in private international law.[7] The Brussels I Regulation is one of a number of measures[8]

---

[1] OJ 2001 L 12/1 (amended by: Corrigendum, OJ 2001 L 307/28; Commission Regulation (EC) No 1496/2002, OJ 2002 L 225/13—amending Annex I and II; the Act concerning the conditions of accession of the Czech Republic, etc, OJ 2003 L 236/33; Commission Regulation (EC) No 2245/2004, OJ 2004 L 381/10—amending Annexes I, II, III and IV; Regulation (EC) No 1791/2006, OJ 2006 L 363/1). For commentaries see Briggs and Rees, *Civil Jurisdiction and Judgments* (2005), 4th edn, chapters 2, 3 and 7; Layton and Mercer, Vol 1, chapters 11–23; Dicey, Morris and Collins, paras 11-001R–11-095 and 11R-263–11-421; Magnus and Mankowski (eds), *Brussels I Regulation*; Ancel (2001) 3 Yearbook of Private International Law 101; Harris (2001) 20 CJQ 218; Kennett (2001) 50 ICLQ 725; Rodger [2001] Jur Rev 59 and 70; Stadler (2005) 42 CMLR 1637; Hartley (2006) 319 Hague Recueil ch VI. The Regulation is best referred to as "Brussels I", so as to avoid confusing it with "Brussels II", ie Council Regulation (EC) No 1347/2000 of 29 May 2000 on jurisdiction and the recognition and enforcement of judgments in matrimonial matters and in matters of parental responsibility for children of both spouses OJ 2000 L 160; replaced by Council Regulation (EC) No 2201/2003 of 27 November 2003 concerning jurisdiction and the recognition and enforcement of judgments in matrimonial matters and the matters of parental responsibility OJ 2003 L 338/1 (Brussels II *bis*); discussed infra, pp 945–952 and 988–992.

[2] Art 76. As far as jurisdiction is concerned, the Regulation applies only to legal proceedings instituted after the entry into force of the Regulation: Art 66. For the original 15 Member States (with the exception of Denmark) the Regulation came into force on 1 March 2002, for the 10 new entrants in 2004 the Regulation came into force on 1 May 2004, for the two 2007 new Member States on 1 January 2007.

[3] The United Kingdom and Ireland "opted in" to the Regulation, in accordance with Art 3 of the Protocol on the position of the United Kingdom and Ireland annexed to the Treaty on European Union and to the Treaty establishing the European Community.

[4] See the Protocol on the position of Denmark (the Danish opt-out) annexed to the Treaty on European Union and to the Treaty establishing the European Community.

[5] OJ 2005 L 299/61; discussed infra, p 341.

[6] See Recital (2) of the Regulation.

[7] See Beaumont (1999) 48 ICLQ 223; Basedow (2000) 37 CMLR 687; Israel (2000) 7 Maastricht JECL 81; Remien (2001) 38 CMLR 53.

[8] For other measures see: Council Regulation (EC) No1347/2000 of 29 May 2000 on jurisdiction and the recognition and enforcement of judgments in matrimonial matters and in matters of parental responsibility for children of both spouses OJ 2000 L 160/19; replaced by Council Regulation (EC) No 2201/2003 of 27 November 2003 concerning jurisdiction and the recognition and enforcement of judgments in matrimonial matters and the matters of parental responsibility OJ 2003 L 338/1; Council Regulation (EC) No 1348/2000 of 9 May 2000 on the service in the Member States of judicial and extra-judicial documents in civil or commercial

relating to judicial co-operation in civil matters having cross-border implications which are necessary for the sound operation of the internal market.[9] Such measures fall within the wider objective the Community has set itself[10] of establishing an area of freedom, security and justice, in which the the free movement of persons is ensured.[11] The Brussels I Regulation is based on, and updates, the earlier Brussels Convention,[12] which it replaces in virtually all cases.[13] That Convention came into force in 1973 and applied as between the original six members of the European Economic Community. The Brussels Convention was subsequently amended by four separate Accession Conventions.[14] Although the Brussels Convention has been replaced in virtually all cases by the Brussels I Regulation, unfortunately the Brussels Convention has not been consigned entirely to history. It still applies in relation to certain territories of Member States and will be examined later on in this chapter.[15] The legal basis for the Regulation is Title IV, in particular Article 61(c), of the Treaty on European Union which authorises the adoption of measures in the field of judicial co-operation in civil matters as provided for in Article 65, which specifically mentions the recognition and enforcement of decisions in civil and commercial matters. The great advantage of a Regulation is that it is directly applicable in the Member States. In contrast, a Convention has to be ratified by the Contracting States and, in the case of the United Kingdom, implementing legislation is also required. There have been delays in some Contracting States in the ratification of Accession Conventions to the Brussels Convention, which has led to the undesirable situation where at times different Member States have been applying different versions of the Convention. Before moving on to the substantive law relating to the jurisdiction of the courts under the Brussels I Regulation, a little needs to be said about impending reform of the Regulation. After that, three preliminary matters must be mentioned: the interpretation of the Brussels I Regulation;

---

matters, OJ 2000 L 160/37, replaced by Council Regulation (EC) No 1393/2007 OJ 2007 L 324/79 discussed infra, pp 300–301; Council Regulation (EC) No 1346/2000 of 29 May 2000 on insolvency proceedings OJ 2000 L 160/1 and Council Regulation (EC) No 1206/2001 of 28 May 2001 on co-operation between the courts of the Member States in the taking of evidence in civil or commercial matters OJ 2001 L 174/1, discussed supra, p 84; Regulation (EC) No 805/2004 of the European Parliament and of the Council of 21 April 2004 creating a European Enforcement Order for uncontested claims OJ 2004 L 143/15; Regulation (EC) No 1896/2006 of the European Parliament and of the Council of 12 December 2006 creating a European order for payment procedure; Regulation (EC) No 861/2007 of the European Council and of the Parliament of 11 July 2007 establishing a European Small Claims Procedure. See more generally Council Decision of 28 May 2001 establishing a European Judicial Network in civil and commercial matters OJ 2001 L 174/25. See generally Crawford and Carruthers [2005] Jur Rev 251.

  [9] See Recital (1) of the Regulation.

  [10] See Art 2 of the Treaty on European Union.

  [11] See Art 61(c) of the Treaty on European Union and the discussion in Chapter 1, supra, pp 12–15.

  [12] Convention on Jurisdiction and the Enforcement of Judgments in Civil and Commercial Matters of 1968. There was also a Protocol on Interpretation in 1971, which came into force in 1975. Both the original Convention and the Protocol are to be found in OJ 1978 L 304/77 and 97.

  [13] Art 68(1) of the Brussels I Regulation.

  [14] These are as follows: first, the United Kingdom, Danish and Irish Accession Convention of 1978 (OJ 1978 L 304/1); secondly, the Greek Accession Convention of 1982 (OJ 1982 L 388/1); thirdly, the Spanish and Portuguese Accession Convention of 1989—the San Sebastian Convention (OJ 1989 L 285/1); fourthly, the Austrian, Finnish and Swedish Accession Convention of 1996 (OJ 1997 C 15/1). A consolidated version of the 1968 Convention and 1971 Protocol, as amended by the four Accession Conventions, is set out in OJ 1998 C 27/1. All references to the "Brussels Convention" (or the "Convention") and the "1971 Protocol" are to the latest version amended by the four Accession Conventions.

  [15] See infra, p 342.

the allocation of jurisdiction within the United Kingdom; and the special definition of domicile.

(a) Reform of the Regulation

No later than five years after the entry into force of the Regulation, the Commission is required to present a Report on the application of the Regulation,[16] accompanied by proposals for such changes as are thought necessary. In pursuance of this obligation, albeit rather late, the Commission intends to produce a Green Paper in the near future. Two studies, funded by the Commission, have been produced, which will serve as the basis for the Green Paper. The first study is the *Report on the Application of Regulation Brussels I in the Member States* prepared by the Institue of Private International Law at the University of Heidelberg (the Hess, Pfeiffer and Schlosser Report).[17] This Report is an empirical study based on questionnaires sent out by the general reporters to national contributors, who, after addressing stakeholders, collecting statistical information, and conducting interviews with the profession and other interested parties, produced National Reports.[18] In the light of these National Reports, and the research of the general reporters themselves, the Hess, Pfeiffer and Schlosser Report identifies problems with the operation of the Regulation and indicates possible solutions. Reference will be made in this chapter to these problems and possible solutions. The second study is the *Study on Residual Jurisdiction* prepared by Nuyts (the Nuyts Report).[19] This is concerned with jurisdiction under traditional national rules of jurisdiction. The study is based on national reports from Member States.[20] It contains a comparative analysis of these national jurisdictional rules and options for their possible future harmonisation.

(b) Interpretation of the Regulation

(i) Referrals to the Court of Justice

Article 68 of the Treaty on European Union authorises the Court of Justice to give preliminary rulings, under Article 234 of the Treaty, on the interpretation of the Brussels I Regulation and of other acts of the institutions of the Community based on Title IV of the Treaty.[21] However, Article 68 contains two limitations on when a national court can request such a ruling. First, a court can only request a preliminary ruling "if it considers that a decision on the question is necessary to enable it to give judgment".[22] There is nothing to stop English courts from deciding that the meaning of the Regulation is clear

---

[16] Art 73. In preparing this Report special attention should be paid to the consumer provisions and their application in cases of electronic commerce, see the Joint Statement by the Council and the Commission relating to contracts concluded by consumers applicable to on-line transactions.

[17] Study JLS/C4/2005/03, Final Version September 2007, available at the European Commission-European Judicial Network—What's new website http://ec.europa.eu/civiljustice/news/whatsnew_en.htm.

[18] These are available at http://ec.europa.eu/civiljustice/news/whatsnew_en.htm.

[19] Study JLS/C4/2005/07-30, Final Version September 2007, available at http://ec.europa.eu/civiljustice/news/whatsnew_en.htm.

[20] The National Reports are available at http://ec.europa.eu/civiljustice/news/whatsnew_en.htm.

[21] In exceptional circumstances the Court can refuse to rule on a question referred to it, see Case C-111/01 *Gantner Electronic GmbH v Basch Exploitatie Maatschappij BV* [2003] ECR I-4207, at [33]–[41].

[22] The procedure for references from English courts is contained in CPR, Part 68 and Practice Direction 68. A national court when making a referral can rely on submissions of one party to the main proceedings of which it has not yet examined the merits: Case C-116/02 *Erich Gasser GmbH v Misat Srl* [2003] ECR I-4207.

and that a reference to the Court of Justice is not necessary. However, the English courts have made numerous references to the Court of Justice in relation to the interpretation of the Brussels Convention and are likely also to request rulings in relation to the interpretation of the Regulation. The second limitation is in respect of the courts which can request a ruling from the Court of Justice. The only court of a Member State which can do so is one against whose decisions there is no judicial remedy under national law.[23] In the case of the United Kingdom this normally means the House of Lords, which *must* request a ruling if it considers that a decision on the question is necessary to enable it to give judgment. This is more restrictive than the position under the Brussels Convention, where there is the Protocol on Interpretation of 1971, which allows references from the Court of Appeal.[24]

(ii) The principles and decisions laid down by the Court of Justice in respect of the Brussels Convention

The Brussels I Regulation should be interpreted in the light of the substantial body of case law decided under the Brussels Convention.[25] Many of the rules in the Regulation are the same as those in the Convention and their meaning has previously been explained by the Court of Justice after a reference from a Contracting State to the Convention. There may be no decision by the Court of Justice on the precise point at issue, but other decisions on the Brussels Convention by that Court are relevant in so far as they lay down principles of interpretation. These principles are important not only when interpreting rules in the Regulation which have been directly borrowed from the Brussels Convention but also when interpreting new rules introduced by the Regulation. The principles laid down by the Court of Justice when interpreting the Brussels Convention are as follows:

(i) The meaning of a provision should be ascertained in the light of its purpose rather than by taking its literal meaning, a principle which has been confirmed in relation to the Regulation.[26]

(ii) As a general principle, the terms of the Brussels Convention should be interpreted autonomously,[27] rather than by reference to national law. The reason for this is that many of the concepts in the Convention have different meanings under the separate national laws of the Contracting States and reference to national law inevitably leads to a lack of uniformity in interpretation. The objectives of the Convention therefore require that it should be given a uniform application throughout the Community. Applying this reasoning, the scope of the Convention and of particular provisions

---

[23] Art 68 of the Treaty on European Union; Case C-24/02 *Marseille Fret SA v Seatrano Shipping Co Ltd* [2002] ECR I-3383; Case C-555/03 *Magali Warbecq v Ryanair Ltd*. See also the opinion of AG Jacobs in Case C-18/02 *DFDS Torline v SEKO* [2004] ECR I-1417, [2004] IL Pr 10 at [26]. See Art 68(3) for referrals by Council, Commission or Member States.

[24] See infra, p 342. For an example of the Court of Appeal finding itself unable to make a reference under the Regulation see *Through Transport Mutual Insurance Association (Eurasia) Ltd v New India Assurance Association Co Ltd* [2004] EWCA (Civ) 1598 at [39], [2005] 1 Lloyd's Rep 67. But the Court of Appeal can still make a reference where the effect of the Regulation is to limit the number of appeals, as the Regulation does in relation to enforcement of judgments, see *Orams v Apostolides*, 18 June, 2007, referring to the Court of Justice Case C-420/07.

[25] See the opinion of AG Leger in Case C-281/02 *Owusu v Jackson* [2005] I-1383, [2005] QB 801 at [193]–[194].

[26] *Speed Investments Ltd v Formula One Holdings Ltd (No 2)* [2004] EWCA Civ 1512 at [22]–[28], [2005] 1 WLR 1936. See also *M v H* [2005] EWHC 1186 (Fam) at [85]—a Brussels II *bis* case.

[27] Case C-383/95 *Rutten v Cross Medical Ltd* [1997] ECR I-57 at 74; [1997] All ER (EC) 121 at 131; Case C-295/95 *Farrell v Long* [1997] QB 842, [1997] ECR I-1683 at 1704.

has consistently been given a Community meaning. Exactly the same reasoning applies in relation to the Regulation and its terms too should be given a Community meaning.[28] As regards other issues, reference to national law has only been made in exceptional cases where, because of the nature of the concept involved, it has been thought to be impossible to arrive at a definition without so doing.[29] These exceptional cases have to some extent, although not entirely, disappeared under the Regulation. A number of important changes have been introduced by the Regulation which share the theme of replacing rules which required, or had been interpreted as requiring, a reference to national law with autonomous definitions.[30]

(iii) There is another general principle which relates to the method of deciding upon what the Community meaning should be. The Court of Justice when defining concepts used in the Brussels Convention has considered two factors. First, it has looked at the objectives and scheme of the Convention.[31] The same should apply in relation to the Regulation. The objectives of the Regulation are the same as those of the Convention.[32] According to the Recitals, the Regulation has the objective of unifying the rules of jurisdiction in civil and commercial matters and simplifying formalities with a view to rapid and simple recognition and enforcement of judgments given in Member States.[33] The Court of Justice has also looked at the objectives of the provision in question[34] and has decided how it relates to other provisions in the Convention.[35]

(iv) In ascertaining the meaning of concepts used in the Regulation, regard should be had to the meaning of cognate concepts to be found in the EC Treaties or in secondary legislation.[36] The need for such an interpretation, which was warranted under the Brussels Convention,[37] is even more pertinent now that the Convention has been replaced by a Regulation and has therefore been integrated into the Community legal order in a more systematic and direct manner.[38]

(v) There are more specific principles where the Court of Justice has identified the purpose underlying a particular provision and has laid down policy considerations to be taken into account, in particular, whether a particular provision is to be narrowly or widely interpreted.[39]

---

[28] *M v H* [2005] EWHC 1186 (Fam) at [85]—a Brussels II *bis* case.

[29] See the opinion of the Advocate General in Case 150/77 *Bertrand v Ott* [1978] ECR 1431, and Case 12/76 *Industrie Tessili Italiana Como v Dunlop AG* [1976] ECR 1473. See also Case 129/83 *Zelger v Salinitri (No 2)* [1984] ECR 2397, on Art 21 of the Brussels Convention.

[30] See Art 5(1)(b) of the Regulation, discussed infra, pp 237–243, Art 30, discussed infra, pp 308–309, and Art 60, discussed infra, pp 211–213.

[31] Case 29/76 *Lufttransportunternehmen GmbH v Organisation Européenne pour la Securité de la Navigation Aérienne (Eurocontrol)* [1976] ECR 1541; Case C-172/91 *Sonntag v Waidmann* [1993] ECR I-1963.

[32] *Evialis SA v SIAT* [2003] EWHC 863 (Comm) at [93], [2003] 2 Lloyd's Rep 377.

[33] See Recital (2) of the Regulation.

[34] Reference to the Reports accompanying the Convention, discussed infra, p 209, have been helpful in this.

[35] Case 33/78 *Somafer v Saar-Ferngas* [1978] ECR 2183.

[36] Case C-271/00 *Gemeente Steenbergen v Baten* [2002] ECR I-10489, [2003] 1 WLR 1996 at [43].

[37] The Brussels Convention has been held to be "linked" to the EC Treaty, and the provisions of the latter apply to matters within the scope of the Convention: Case C-398/92 *Mund & Fester v Hatrex International Transport* [1994] ECR I-467; Briggs (1994) 14 YEL 557; Beaumont (1995) 44 ICLQ 220.

[38] See the opinion of AG TIZZANO in *Gemeente Steenbergen v Baten*, supra, at [44]. See also FORNER DELAYGUA JJ "Internet Jurisdiction in Business to Business On-Line Performed Contracts: Lessons From the Hague?" in JJ Barcelo III and KM Clermont (eds), *A Global Law of Jurisdiction and Judgments: Lessons from the Hague*.

[39] These apply equally to the Regulation: *Shahar v Tsitsekkos* [2004] EWHC 2659 (Ch) at [50].

(iii) Aids to interpretation

There is an Explanatory Memorandum from the Commission of the European Communities on the proposal for a Regulation to replace the Brussels Convention.[40] However, whilst useful, this is fairly brief and just sets out the view of the Commission.[41] There is no official report accompanying the Regulation itself. This contrasts with the position in relation to the Brussels Convention, the draft of which was accompanied by the Jenard Report.[42] This is a commentary prepared by the rapporteur of the committee of experts which drew up the draft Convention. Each of the first three Accession Conventions to the Brussels Convention is also accompanied by a Report.[43] The Court of Justice has not infrequently referred to the Jenard Report and to the subsequent Reports in order to ascertain the meaning of provisions in the Brussels Convention. Of course, these Reports are still relevant to interpreting the many provisions in the Regulation which have been taken unaltered from the Convention. What is lacking therefore is an authoritative Report explaining the changes introduced by the Regulation. However, recourse can be had to the 29 Recitals at the beginning of the Regulation. Another source of authority is the decisions of the courts of other Member States in relation to the Regulation and the Brussels Convention.[44] Whatever the normal attitude is towards the decisions of Continental judges, in this context their decisions ought to be of persuasive authority. Finally, English courts should always be prepared to consider the texts of the Regulation in other languages, which is what they have done with the Brussels Convention.[45]

(c) Allocating jurisdiction within the United Kingdom

The Regulation assigns jurisdiction to the courts of Member States.[46] The United Kingdom is the Member State under the Regulation; this raises the particular problem of whether the courts of England, Scotland or Northern Ireland are to have jurisdiction. With some of the provisions in the Regulation it is possible to identify a part or place in the United Kingdom which is to have jurisdiction.[47] It is not possible to do so where, for example, jurisdiction is allocated to the United Kingdom on the basis that the defendant is domiciled within the United Kingdom under Article 2 of the Regulation. Section 16 of the Civil Jurisdiction and Judgments Act 1982, as amended,[48] solves this problem by introducing a modified version of the Regulation,[49] which allocates jurisdiction within

---

[40] COM (1999) 348 final.

[41] For cases using the Explanatory Memorandum, see the Opinion of AG COLOMER in Case C-283/05 *ASML Netherlands BV v Semiconductor Industry Services GmbH (SEMIS)* at [50]–[51] of the opinion; *Tavoulareas v Tsavliris* [2006] EWCA Civ 1772 at [4]; *M v H* [2005] EWHC 1186 (Fam) at [77]–[115]—a Brussels II *bis* case where the Commission's Practice Gude was used by the court.

[42] OJ 1979 C 59.

[43] The Schlosser Report OJ 1979 C 59; the Evrigenis and Kerameus Report OJ 1986 C 298/1; the Almeida Cruz, Desantes Real, Jenard Report, OJ 1990 C 189/06. There is no report accompanying the Austrian, Finnish and Swedish Accession Convention of 1996.

[44] Case law on the Brussels Convention can be found in Digest of Case Law Relating to the European Communities, D Series and in Kaye, *European Case Law on the Judgments Conventions* (1998).

[45] See Art 68 of the Brussels Convention; Case 150/80 *Elefanten Schuh GmbH v Jacqmain* [1981] ECR 1671; *Newtherapeutics Ltd v Katz* [1991] Ch 226 at 243–245; *CFEM Façades SA v Bovis Construction Ltd* [1992] IL Pr 561.

[46] These are all the Member States of the European Community with the exception of Denmark.

[47] Eg under Art 5. See in relation to the Brussels Convention the Schlosser Report, p 98, and infra, pp 228–262.

[48] By SI 2001/3929, Art 4 and Sch 2, Part II, para 3.

[49] Set out in Sch 4 to the 1982 Act, as substituted by SI 2001/3929, Art 4 and Sch 2, Part II, para 4.

the United Kingdom. The Modified Regulation is examined in detail towards the end of this chapter.[50] Suffice it to say at this point that it goes further than was strictly necessary by dealing with internal United Kingdom cases (eg a Scotsman sues in England an English domiciled man in respect of land in England), and not merely with situations where the United Kingdom has been assigned jurisdiction under the Regulation (eg a Frenchman, having been injured in France, sues an English domiciled man in England).

(d) A special definition of domicile

Extensive use is made of the concept of domicile for the purpose of deciding when the Regulation applies, and, where it does, of allocating jurisdiction[51] to particular Member States. However, despite the importance of this concept, it is only partially defined in the Regulation. This raises a serious problem since the meaning of the concept differs from one Member State to another.

Article 59 of the Regulation deals with the question of which Member State's definition of domicile is to be used. The first paragraph states that the courts of the Member State seised of the matter shall apply their own definition of domicile to determine whether a party is domiciled in that Member State. According to the second paragraph, in order to determine whether a party is domiciled in another Member State, a court must apply the law of that State; eg if the United Kingdom courts, having decided (after using their own definition) that a person is not domiciled in the United Kingdom, want to know whether the defendant is domiciled in France, they must apply the French definition of domicile.[52]

The effect of these provisions is that the English courts are, initially at least, going to apply their own definition of domicile. What English law usually means by domicile is far removed from what civil law means.[53] The harmonisation of the law on jurisdiction would have been seriously undermined if the traditional English concept of domicile had been used in this context. The Civil Jurisdiction and Judgments Order 2001[54] therefore contains special provisions on the meaning of the domicile of an individual for the purposes of the Regulation. The simplest solution, which would have been to equate an individual's habitual residence with his domicile,[55] was not possible because of the separate reference in the Regulation to habitual residence.[56] Paragraph 9 of Schedule 1 of the Civil Jurisdiction and Judgments Order 2001 adopts a complicated solution, with different rules for each of the contexts under the Regulation in which an individual's domicile has to be ascertained. Thus, the rules[57] state when an individual is domiciled: (i) in the United Kingdom, (ii) in a particular part of the United Kingdom, (iii) in a particular

---

[50] Infra, pp 346–352.

[51] Infra, pp 222–228. The Modified Regulation does likewise, infra, pp 346–352.

[52] *Haji-Ioannou v Frangos* [1999] 2 Lloyd's Rep 337, 344, CA; *Bank of Credit and Commerce International SA (In Liquidation) v Wajih Sirri Al-Kaylani* [1999] IL Pr 278, CA—interrogatories can be administered to ascertain whether a person comes within the foreign definition. See also Layton and Mercer, Vol 2, chapters 47–64 at .051 in each of these chapters (for the definition of domicile in other European Community States).

[53] See the Schlosser Report, pp 95–97.

[54] SI 2001/3929.

[55] In Ireland domicile is, however, equated with ordinary residence: Sch 5, Part I of the Jurisdiction of Courts and Enforcement of Judgments (European Communities) Act 1988; *Deutsche Bank v Murtagh* [1995] 1 ILRM 380.

[56] See Art 5(2).

[57] See para 9(2) to (7), infra, pp 222–227 and 346–348.

place in the United Kingdom and (iv) in a state other than a Regulation State. For most of these purposes[58] domicile is equated with the state where (a) a person is resident[59] and (b) the nature and circumstances of his residence indicate that he has a substantial connection with it.[60] Showing a substantial connection is made easier by the use of a presumption (based on residence), which is available under some of these rules, but not others.[61] The onus is on the claimant to show a good arguable case that the defendant is domiciled in a particular State.[62]

The Hess, Pfeiffer and Schlosser Report points out that the determination of the domicile of natural persons is, in some cases, rather complex, and suggests that there should be discussion on whether an acceptable autonomous definition can be found.[63]

Under the Regulation the approach towards determining the domicile of companies has changed from that under the Brussels Convention.[64] In order "to make the common rules more transparent and to avoid conflicts of jurisdiction",[65] Article 60 of the Regulation[66] gives an autonomous definition to the concept of the domicile of a company, rather than leaving this to be determined by Member States applying their rules of private international law. It provides in paragraph (1) that, "for the purposes of this Regulation, a company or other legal person or association of natural or legal persons is domiciled at the place where it has its:

(a) statutory seat, or
(b) central administration, or
(c) principal place of business.

Because these are alternatives, a company can, in principle, be domiciled in more than one Member State. The concept of the statutory seat of a company is well known in civil law systems,[67] but has no equivalent under English or Irish law, which tend to refer to the place of incorporation[68] of a company. Article 60(2) caters for this difference by stating that:

For the purposes of the United Kingdom and Ireland "statutory seat" means the registered office or, where there is no such office anywhere, the place of incorporation or,

---

[58] But not when domicile in a particular place in the United Kingdom is being ascertained, see para 9(4).

[59] "Resident" is given its ordinary English meaning (discussed supra, pp 157–159: *Bank of Dubai Ltd v Abbas* [1997] IL Pr 308, CA. See also *Chellaram v Chellaram (No 2)* [2002] EWHC 632 (Ch) at [21], [2002] 3 All ER 17; *Foote Cone & Belding Reklin Hizmetleri v Theron* [2006] EWHC 1585; *High Tech International AG v Deripaska* [2006] EWHC 3276 (QB); *Cherney v Deripaska* [2007] EWHC 965 (Comm), [2007] IL Pr 49.

[60] A person may be resident in England but lack the substantial connection: *Petrotrade Inc v Smith* [1999] 1 WLR 457 at 461–462—one factor being that the defendant was unable to leave because of a bail condition.

[61] The presumption is contained in para 9(6). It can be used for the purposes of para 9(2) and (3), but not para 9(4) and (7). All of the rules of domicile will be examined more fully later on in the context in which they operate, see infra, pp 223–224, 227–228 and 346–348.

[62] *Chellaram v Chellaram (No 2)* [2002] EWHC 632 (Ch) at [23], [2002] 3 All ER 17.

[63] See para 873, Study JLS/C4/2005/03, Final Version September 2007, available at the European Commission—European Judicial Network—What's new website http://ec.europa.eu/civiljustice/news/whatsnew_en.htm.

[64] Cf Art 53, para 1 of the Brussels Convention, discussed infra, p 342.

[65] Recital (11) of the Regulation.

[66] See generally Benedettelli [2005] EBLR 55.

[67] See Weser (1961) 10 AJCL 323, 329–330; Rammeloo, *Corporations in Private International Law* (2000), p 323 et seq.

[68] Taking jurisdiction in England on this basis has given rise to the problem that the more appropriate forum may be abroad in a non-Member State, see infra, pp 321–329.

where there is no such place anywhere, the place under the law of which the formation took place.

This provision only applies "For the purposes of the United Kingdom and Ireland." Thus it will apply in the situation where an English court is determining whether it has jurisdiction on the basis of the company being domiciled in England but not where advice is being given as to whether a German court has jurisdiction on the basis of it being domiciled in Germany. Article 60 does not get rid of all the definitional problems that can arise in relation to the domicile of a company. What is the definition of the terms "statutory seat", "central administration" and "principal place of business"? Given that Article 60 is concerned to give an autonomous meaning to the concept of the domicile of a company, these terms should also be given an autonomous meaning. It is true that Article 59(1) says that the court seised of the matter shall apply its internal law to determine whether a "party" (and, in principle, this would include a company) is "domiciled" in a Member State. But this does not actually direct the court seised to apply its internal law to determine whether a "party" has its "statutory seat", "central administration" or "principal place of business" in a Member State. Article 59(1) is concerned with the "domicile" of a "party" and as far as companies are concerned this is dealt with by Article 60. In other words Article 59(1) is overidden by Article 60. The three alternative criteria used in Article 60(1) correspond to the three criteria (registered office, central administration or principal place of business) used in Article 48 (formerly 58) of the EC Treaty, which deals with the right of establishment of companies within the Community. Regard should be had to the case law on these Article 48 terms when ascertaining the meaning of the terms used in Article 60. As regards the meaning of "central administration", "administration" has been described as having something of the "back office" about it. [69] Administration "ensures that all runs smoothly: money is got in, debts are paid, leases and transport are arranged, personnel are looked after".[70] The "central" administration makes more sense in the case of a large organisation than a small one. The location of the company secretary's office in a major organisation might provide a good clue as to the "central" administration.[71] The central administration can be identified by looking at where important personnel, such as the chief executive officer and various departmental heads, are located.[72] Central administration is a different concept from central management and control. The latter is a concept used in the context of the Brussels Convention.[73] In ascertaining where a company has its central management and control it is relevant to look at where the directors are resident, hold meetings and decide major policy issues,[74] and whether the company has just started.[75] This emphasis on the board of directors is different from the back room emphasis of central administration.

---

[69] *King v Crown Energy Trading AG* [2003] EWHC 163 (Comm) at [12], [2003] IL Pr 28.
[70] Ibid.
[71] Ibid, at [13].
[72] Ibid.
[73] Infra, p 342.
[74] See *The Rewia* [1991] 1 Lloyd's Rep 69 at 74; this point was not disputed in the appeal which overruled the decision on other grounds [1991] 2 Lloyd's Rep 325, CA.
[75] *Royal & Sun Alliance Insurance plc v MK Digital FZE (Cyprus) Ltd* [2006] EWCA Civ 629 at [85]–[86], [2006] 2 Lloyd's Rep 110.

As regards the meaning of the "principal place of business", this is a concept with which the English courts are already familiar. LEGGATT LJ in *The Rewia* held, in the context of a choice of jurisdiction clause providing for trial in the principal place of business, that this referred to the "chief" or "most important" place of business, rather than the "main" place of business.[76] It is not necessarily the place where most of the business is carried out. This case has been described as "an essential tool" in deciding on the principal place of business for the purposes of Article 60 of the Regulation.[77] The principal place of business has been identified by looking at where important personnel, such as the chief executive officer and various departmental heads, are located. The place where day-to-day activities of the company are carried out may not be the principal place of business if those activities are subject to the control of senior management located elsewhere.[78] This evidence of where important personnel are located has also been used to identify the central administration of the same company.[79] It is not easy to see what the difference is between the "principal place of business" and the "central administration" of a company and there does appear to be a considerable overlap between the two concepts.[80] *The Rewia* was concerned with the meaning of a single concept. In contrast, Article 60 uses both the concept of "principal place of business" and that of "central administration". The former should be defined in a way that distinguishes it from the latter.

When it comes to the domicile of trusts, Article 60(3) reverts back to the approach adopted under the Brussels Convention and the courts seised of the matter are instructed to apply their rules of private international law.[81] The courts of a Member State must do likewise when ascertaining the seat of a company for the purposes of exclusive jurisdiction under Article 22(2) of the Regulation.[82]

(e) When does the Regulation apply?

(i) The matter must be within the scope of the Regulation

None of its provisions, whether on jurisdiction or on recognition and enforcement of judgments, will apply unless the matter is within the scope of the Regulation.

Article 1 is designed to deal with the scope of the Regulation. But before looking at this, various other limitations on the operation of the Regulation must be mentioned. First, the Regulation is doubtless only concerned with the *international jurisdiction* of Member States. This limitation was spelt out in the preamble to the Brussels

---

[76] [1991] 2 Lloyd's Rep 325, 334, CA.

[77] *King v Crown Energy Trading AG* [2003] EWHC 163 (Comm) at [14], [2003] IL Pr 28. See also *Ministry of Defence and Support of the Armed Forces for the Islamic Republic of Iran v FAZ Aviation Ltd* [2007] EWHC 1042 (Comm), [2007] IL Pr 42.

[78] *Ministry of Defence and Support of the Armed Forces for the Islamic Republic of Iran v FAZ Aviation Ltd* [2007] EWHC 1042 (Comm) at [29], [2007] IL Pr 42.

[79] *King v Crown Energy Trading AG*, supra, at [13], [31].

[80] Ibid, at [14].

[81] For the domicile of a trust for the purposes of the Regulation under English private international law see the Civil Jurisdiction and Judgments Order, SI 2001/3929, Art 3 and Sch 1, para 12. For domicile of the Crown see Civil Jurisdiction and Judgments Act 1982, s 46 and *Tehrani v Secretary of State for the Home Department* [2006] UKHL 47, [2006] 3 WLR 699.

[82] See infra, p 282, n 677.

Convention[83] but can be assumed to apply also in relation to the Regulation, even though it is not mentioned in the Recitals.[84] It follows that the Regulation should not apply where a dispute involves no foreign element or where the foreign element only involves another part of the United Kingdom.[85] However, the foreign element can be satisfied by connections with a non-Member State.[86] Thus the Regulation will apply where there are connections with two States, one of which is a Member State and the other a non-Member State, as, for example, where both parties are domiciled in a Member State and the events at issue occurred in a non-Member State.[87] The Regulation does not require connections with two Member States. Secondly, the Regulation does not affect certain other conventions on jurisdiction or recognition and enforcement which Member States have *in the past* entered into,[88] or statutes implementing them.[89] There is no provision, as there is under the Brussels Convention[90] for conventions entered into by Member States *in the future*. The Community does, however, have power to enter into international agreements.[91] In England, admiralty jurisdiction and carriage by road are examples of areas which are left largely untouched because of conventions entered into in the past.[92] Nonetheless, some of the provisions in the Brussels I Regulation will still apply. The application of the Regulation is precluded solely in relation to questions governed specifically by the specialised convention in question.[93] In so far as the latter is silent on a jurisdictional mat-

---

[83] See the Jenard Report, p 8; the Schlosser Report, p 123. See also Case C-281/02 *Owusu v Jackson* [2005] ECRI-1383, [2005] QB 801 at [25]; Opinion of the Court of Justice 1/03 Competence of the Community to conclude the new Lugano Convention [2006] ECR I-1145 at [143]–[145].

[84] Opinion of the Court of Justice 1/03 Competence of the Community to conclude the new Lugano Convention [2006] ECR I-1145 at [143]–[145].

[85] But see cases stating that certain Articles apply despite no international element: Art 23 (*Provimi v Aventis Animal Nutrition SA* [2003] EWHC 961 (Comm) at [74]–[75]—obiter, [2003] 2 All ER (Comm) 683; *Snookes v Jani-King (GB) Ltd* [2006] EWHC 289 (QB) at [39]–[45]—a provisional view, [2006] IL Pr 19; cf *British Sugar plc v Fratelli* [2004] EWHC 2560 at [34]—ratio, [2005] 1 Lloyd's Rep 332; Art 2 (the *British Sugar* Case—obiter).

[86] *Owusu v Jackson*, supra, at [26].

[87] Ibid.

[88] Art 71. Where the defendant does not enter an appearance the court must verify of its own motion whether it has jurisdiction under the specialised convention: Art 71(2)(a); Case C-148/03 *Nurnberger Allgemeine Versicherungs AG v Portbridge Transport International BV* [2004] ECR I-10327. The European Council can authorise Member States' accession to international conventions, see, eg, Council Decision (EC) No 2002/762 of 19 September 2002 in relation to the Bunkers Convention, OJ 2002 L 256/7.

[89] Arts 71 and 67: Case C-406/92 *Owners of cargo lately laden on board Tatry v Owners of Maciej Rataj, The Tatry* [1994] ECR I-5439, discussed infra, p 307; Art 69 lists bilateral conventions which are in fact superseded by this Regulation. For the effect of these provisions on recognition and enforcement of foreign judgments in England see infra, pp 600–601.

[90] Art 57 [1] of the Brussels Convention.

[91] See the Opinion of the Court of Justice 1/03 Competence of the Community to conclude the new Lugano Convention [2006] ECR I-1145 at [148]; the Joint Statement by the Council and the Commission on Arts 71 and 72 and on the negotiations within the framework of the Hague Conference on Private International Law, on which see Kruger (2006) 55 ICLQ 447. See for the difficulties that arise Takahashi (2003) 52 ICLQ 529. See more generally on external competence of the Community and private international law: Kotuby [2001] NILR 1; Beaumont in Fawcett (ed), *Reform and Development of Private International Law* at pp 25–29; Kruger, Chapter 7.

[92] See infra, pp 418–422, for the effect of the Brussels I Regulation on admiralty jurisdiction. The provisions in the Regulation affecting this are Arts 5(7) and 7; see in relation to the Brussels Convention the Schlosser Report, pp 108–111, 139–142. In cases where the Regulation does apply, Art 2 will operate in relation to an action in rem: *The Deichland* [1990] 1 QB 361. For the position in Scotland see *Ladgroup Ltd v Euroeast Lines SA* 1997 SLT 916. For carriage by road see the CMR Convention and *Royal & Sun Alliance Insurance plc v MK Digital FZE (Cyprus) Ltd* [2006] EWCA Civ 629, [2006] 2 Lloyd's Rep 110.

[93] *The Tatry*, supra.

ter, the Brussels I Regulation will still apply.[94] Thirdly, the rules on jurisdiction and recognition and enforcement make it clear that they do not apply to proceedings, or issues arising in proceedings, in Member States concerning the recognition and enforcement of judgments given in non-Member States.[95]

(a) Civil and commercial matters

Article 1 declares that "This Regulation shall apply in civil and commercial matters whatever the nature of the court or tribunal."

No definition is given of "civil and commercial matters",[96] although Article 1 goes on to say that it does not include "revenue,[97] customs[98] or administrative matters".[99] These words are there to make it clear that public law matters are excluded. The difficulty for English lawyers is that in domestic law the distinction between private and public law is not sharply drawn.[100] In civil law jurisdictions there is a clear distinction between the two, although the same criteria are not always applied when drawing the distinction. Some guidance on this definitional problem was given by the Court of Justice in the leading case of *LTU v Eurocontrol*[101] where it was held that a Community meaning had to be given to "civil and commercial matters", with the result that the Brussels Convention did not apply to the situation where a public authority was acting in the exercise of its powers. The public authority was an international organisation concerned with air safety; it was acting in the exercise of its powers when it sought to collect charges from an airline for the use of its services, the use of the services being obligatory and the rate of charge being fixed unilaterally.

The difficulty with requiring the public authority to be acting in the exercise of its powers, before the matter can be excluded from the Regulation, is that it is often hard to tell whether a public authority is acting in a private capacity or in the exercise of its powers.[102]

---

[94] Ibid. The Arrest Convention of 1952 is silent on *lis pendens* and therefore Arts 27 and 28, infra, pp 303–315, of the Brussels I Regulation (formerly Arts 21 and 22 of the Brussels Convention) will apply. See Briggs [1995] LMCLQ 161. The principle in *The Tatry* has been followed in relation to the CMR Convention on carriage by road: *Frans Maas Logistics (UK) Ltd v CDR Trucking BV* [1999] 2 Lloyd's Rep 179. But see the misapplication of this principle in *The Tatry* in *The "Bergen"* [1997] 1 Lloyd's Rep 380, discussed infra, p 419, in relation to what is now Art 23 of the Brussels I Regulation; *Deaville v Aeroflot* [1997] 2 Lloyd's Rep 67—a Warsaw Convention case.

[95] Case C-129/92 *Owens Bank Ltd v Bracco (No 2)* [1994] QB 509 at 544–546; Hartley (1994) 19 ELR 545.

[96] See the Jenard Report, p 9; the opinion of the Advocate General in Case 29/76 *LTU v Eurocontrol* [1976] ECR 1541; Betlem and Bernasconi (2006) 122 LQR 124.

[97] This excludes both direct and indirect attempts to enforce the revenue law of another State: *QRS 1 ApS v Frandsen* [1999] 1 WLR 2169, CA.

[98] This does not encompass where a guarantor has paid customs duties and seeks reimbursement from a third party, their relationship being governed by private law: Case C-265/02 *Frahuil SA v Assitalia SPA* [2004] ECR I-1543. Nor where a State seeks payment from the guarantor: Case C-266/01 *Preservatrice Fonciere TIARD SA v Staat der Nederlanden* [2003] ECR I-4867, at [44].

[99] See the Schlosser Report, p 82. See also *Re State of Norway's Application* [1987] QB 433 at 473–474, affd in *Re State of Norway's Application (Nos 1 and 2)* [1990] 1 AC 723, HL; *Short v British Nuclear Fuels plc* [1997] IL Pr 747, Irish Sup Ct.

[100] See the Advocate General's opinion in *LTU v Eurocontrol*, supra; the Schlosser Report, p 82; *Re State of Norway's Application*, supra. See also Philip (1978) II Hague Recueil 1, 63–72.

[101] Case 29/76 *Lufttransportunternehmen GmbH v Organisation Européene pour la Securité de la Navigation Aérienne (Eurocontrol)* [1976] ECR 1541; see Hartley (1977) 2 ELR 61. The decision is criticised by Giardina (1978) 27 ICLQ 263, 272–274; and by Fletcher, *Conflict of Laws and European Community Law* (1982), p 112.

[102] See the Schlosser Report, pp 83–84.

In *Netherlands State v Rüffer*[103] the Court of Justice held that a public authority, in this case the Dutch State, was acting in the exercise of its powers in respect of a public water-way when it sought to recover from a German shipowner the costs of removing a wreck, even though under Dutch law (the Dutch courts being seised of the matter) the action was classified as one in tort. The case was concerned with a Community concept and it would therefore be inappropriate to allow Dutch law to classify it according to domestic criteria. The action arose from international treaty obligations and would be regarded by many Member States as an administrative one, the common core of the national legal systems being an important consideration when giving a Community meaning to this concept. In contrast, a teacher, although the holder of a public office, was not acting in the exercise of public authority powers when supervising a pupil who was killed in an accident, even though this was covered under a social insurance scheme.[104] Nor was a public body acting in the exercise of public powers when it sought recovery under rules of civil law from a person of sums paid by it by way of social assistance to the divorced spouse and child of that person.[105] An action brought by a consumer protection organisation against a trader was held to be a civil matter.[106] The former was a private body. Moreover, it was not acting in the exercise of public powers since its action was concerned with making relationships governed by private law subject to review by the courts. Likewise an action brought by a state by which it sought to enforce against a person governed by private law a private law guarantee contract which was concluded to enable a third person to supply a guarantee required by that state was a civil and commercial matter.[107] Where an action was brought by a guarantor (A) against an importer (F) after A had paid customs duties owed by F it was necessary to examine the legal relationship between the parties to the dispute.[108] The relationship between A and F was governed by private law. The basis of the action had also to be examined. This was based on a civil law rule providing for subrogation. Accordingly the action fell within the concept of civil and commercial matters. An action by natural persons of a Contracting State against another Contracting State to obtain compensation for damage caused by the armed forces of the latter Contracting State when invading the territory of the first State does not constitute a civil and commercial matter.[109] Operations conducted by armed forces are one of the characteristic emanations of state sovereignty.[110] It follows that the acts complained of must be regarded as resulting from the

---

[103] Case 814/79 [1980] ECR 3807. For criticism see Hartley, pp 11–15 and (1981) 6 ELR 215. See also *LTU v Eurocontrol*, supra; *Re Senator Hanseatische* [1996] 2 BCLC 562; *Grovit v De Nederlandsche Bank* [2007] EWCA Civ 953, [2008] 1 WLR 51—a State bank was acting in the exercise of its public law powers when it sent out a letter which contained libellous material.

[104] Case C-172/91 *Sonntag v Waidmann* [1993] ECR I-1963; Briggs (1993) 13 YEL 517; Hartley (1994) 19 ELR 538; Plender (1993) 64 BYBIL 555.

[105] Case C-271/00 *Gemeente Steenbergen v Baten* [2003] 1 WLR 1996. See also Case C-433/01 *Freistaat Bayern v Jan Blijdenstein* [2004] ECR I-981 at [21], [2004] IL Pr 8. It is different if the public body is acting under a prerogative of its own, specifically conferred on it by the legislature (in this case to ignore an agreement between spouses limiting maintenance after divorce), see *Gemeente Steenbergen v Baten*, [36].

[106] Case C-167/00 *Verein Für Konsumenteninformation v K H Henkel* [2002] ECR I-8111 at [30].

[107] Case C-266/01 *Preservatrice Fonciere TIARD SA v Staat der Nederlanden* [2003] ECR I-4867 at [36].

[108] Case C-265/02 *Frahuil SA v Assitalia SPA* [2004] ECR I-1543 at [20], [2004] IL Pr 11.

[109] Case C-292/05 *Lekhoritou v Germany* [2007] IL Pr 14; Lyons (2007) ELR 563; Gartner (2007) 8 German LJ 417.

[110] Ibid, at [37].

exercise of public powers on the part of the state on the date when those acts were perpetrated.[111]

Article 1 states that the Regulation shall apply whatever the nature of the court or tribunal. It follows that a decision of a criminal court is within the Regulation provided that it relates to a civil or commercial matter.[112] An example is provided by the decision where a criminal court awarded damages to the family of a pupil negligently killed by a teacher.[113] Similarly, the Regulation would also apply to cases brought before tribunals provided that they do not relate to administrative matters.

Width is given to the scope of the Regulation by the inclusion of "civil" matters. This covers a number of areas which might otherwise be excluded, for example, certain torts, labour law matters including disputes over contracts of employment[114] and fines imposed by courts or tribunals provided they are for the benefit of a private claimant.[115] Likewise forfeiture proceedings for infringement of a trade mark brought by a Trading Standards Office in the Magistrates Court were a civil matter because they were for the benefit of a private individual.[116]

Article 1 also includes maintenance, which causes particular problems under the Regulation. There is a special basis of jurisdiction under Article 5(2) dealing with maintenance, from which it can be inferred that it comes within the scope of the Regulation. Maintenance is another one of the important concepts which is not defined in the Regulation.[117] It is clear that it can include lump sum as well as periodical payments.[118] It does not matter that the payments are ancillary to divorce proceedings, and are to be made after the divorce (even though divorce, as a matter of status, is outside the scope of the Regulation).[119] The subject of maintenance was discussed by the Court of Justice in the second *De Cavel* case,[120] where it was held that interim compensatory payments payable on a monthly basis by one spouse to another as part of a French judgment dissolving a marriage were in the nature of maintenance, a crucial point being that they were designed to support that spouse and were based on need. This meant that the case fell within the terms of the Brussels Convention. The application of these criteria to the financial orders that can be made by English courts is dealt with later on in the book, where maintenance is considered in detail.[121]

---

[111]   Ibid, at [38].

[112]   See, eg, Case 157/80 *Rinkau* [1981] ECR 1391, Hartley (1981) 6 ELR 483; Case C-7/98 *Krombach v Bamberski* [2001] QB 709 at [30]. See also Art 61 of the Regulation.

[113]   Case C-172/91 *Sonntag v Waidmann* [1993] ECR I-1963. See also *Haji-Ioannou v Frangos* [1999] 2 Lloyd's Rep 337 at 351, CA.

[114]   See the Jenard Report, pp 9, 24; the Schlosser Report, p 82; the opinion of the Advocate General in *Netherlands v Rüffer, supra;* Case 25/79 *Sanicentral GmbH v Collin* [1979] ECR 3423, (on which see Collins, p 8).

[115]   See the Schlosser Report, p 84.

[116]   *R v Harrow Crown Court, ex p UNIC Centre Sarl* [2000] 1 WLR 2122.

[117]   See generally the Schlosser Report, pp 101–105.

[118]   See ibid, p 102.

[119]   Jurisdiction and recognition of divorce judgments are dealt with infra, Chapter 21. However, a foreign maintenance order may be irreconcilable with an English divorce, see *Macaulay v Macaulay* [1991] 1 WLR 179, infra, pp 1071–1073.

[120]   Case 120/79 *De Cavel v De Cavel (No 2)* [1980] ECR 731. It does not matter whether it is an interim or final order, see the first *De Cavel* case, Case 143/78 [1979] ECR 1055; Hartley (1979) 4 ELR 222. The wording of Art 5(2) of the Brussels Convention was altered expressly to include payments ancillary to divorce proceedings, see the Schlosser Report, pp 84–87.

[121]   Infra, pp 1055–1061.

(b) Exclusions

Article 1 sets out a number of matters which are excluded from the scope of the Regulation, even though they are civil and commercial matters. It is intended that these matters should only be excluded where they are the principal object of the proceedings.[122]

(i) "The status or legal capacity of natural persons, rights in property arising out of a matrimonial relationship, wills and succession"

For English lawyers there are no real problems in understanding what is meant by status[123] or wills and succession.[124] The same cannot be said in respect of the concept of rights in property arising out of a matrimonial relationship.[125] No guidance is given in the Regulation as to the meaning of this term. According to the Schlosser Report it is designed to exclude the matrimonial regime used in civil law countries whereby special rules on separation or community of property are established in respect of family assets.[126] The Court of Justice in the first *De Cavel*[127] case held that rights in property arising out of a matrimonial relationship covered not only matrimonial regimes but also any proprietary relationship resulting directly from the marital relationship or its dissolution. It meant the exclusion of protective measures (freezing of assets) relating to the property of the spouses pending divorce proceedings before a French court. The Court of Justice has also held that an action in respect of the husband's management of his wife's property must be considered to be closely connected with the proprietary relationship of the parties flowing from the marriage and was therefore excluded.[128]

There are great difficulties in applying these principles in a common law context. There is no English equivalent of the Continental matrimonial regime. In English law, a dispute concerning matrimonial property may simply be concerned with general property law principles, and the Regulation will apply, for example, where there is a dispute between a wife and a mortgagee bank in respect of a matrimonial home mortgaged by the husband.[129] Where a spouse is ordered to make a lump sum payment as part of divorce proceedings the position is more complicated. According to the Court of Justice in *Van Den Boogaard v Laumen*,[130] if the purpose of the payment is to ensure the former spouse's maintenance, then it must be regarded as a matter relating to maintenance,[131] and therefore within the scope of what is now the Brussels I Regulation. On the other hand, if the purpose is the division of assets, rather than maintenance in any sense, it will concern "rights in property arising out of a matrimonial relationship", and hence be outside the

---

[122] See the Jenard Report, p 10.

[123] See the Schlosser Report, p 89. See also the discussion of Brussels II *bis*, infra, pp 944–952.

[124] See *Re Hayward* [1997] Ch 45 at 53–54. See generally infra, pp 1263–1292.

[125] See generally on matrimonial property, infra, pp 1293–1310.

[126] See the Schlosser Report, p 87. See also Collins, pp 25–26; Hartley, pp 17–19.

[127] Supra.

[128] Case 25/81 *CHW v GJH* [1982] ECR 1189. The case involved a provisional measure, see Art 31, discussed infra, pp 315–318.

[129] See *Williams and Glyn's Bank Ltd v Boland* [1981] AC 487.

[130] Case C-220/95 [1997] ECR I-1147. For the propositions to be derived from the case see *Moore v Moore* [2007] EWCA Civ 361 at [80], [2007] IL Pr 36. See also *DT v FL* [2006] IEHC 98, [2007] IL Pr 56.

[131] For maintenance under the Regulation, see supra, p 217, infra, pp 245–247.

scope of the Regulation.[132] It should be possible to deduce the aim of the payment from the reasoning of the court which made the order. "If this shows that a provision awarded is designed to enable one spouse to provide for himself or herself or if the needs and resources of each of the spouses are taken into consideration in the determination of its amount, the decision will be concerned with maintenance."[133] If no order has been made by a court but there is an application for an order, it is necessary to consider the terms of the application in so far as it sheds light on the aim of the application.[134] The same distinction and principle apply where there is a transfer of ownership of property, such as the matrimonial home, as part of divorce proceedings.[135]

(ii) "Bankruptcy, proceedings relating to the winding up of insolvent companies or other legal persons, judicial arrangements, compositions and analogous proceedings"[136]

It is intended that only proceedings arising directly from,[137] and closely connected with, the bankruptcy should be excluded from the Regulation.[138] In *Gourdain v Nadler*[139] the Court of Justice held that a French provision, under which a manager of a company in liquidation could be ordered to pay money to form part of the assets of the company, came within the bankruptcy exclusion, the legal foundation of this action being the French law of bankruptcy and it being very closely connected with the winding-up proceedings. It has been said, obiter, that claims in a compulsory liquidation by a liquidator under section 238 (transactions at an undervalue) or section 239 (preferences) of the Insolvency Act 1986 would be within the exception.[140]

In contrast, a claim by a trustee in bankruptcy to recover from a third party assets said to belong to the bankrupt's estate did not have bankruptcy as its principal subject matter, and thus fell outside the bankruptcy exclusion.[141] The issue was not as to bankruptcy law but as to the effect under the law of the situs of the fact that the third party was the sole registered proprietor of a villa. Likewise a claim by a trustee in bankruptcy for an order for the sale of the bankrupt's villa did not have bankruptcy as its principal subject matter.[142] It was a property claim that happened to be brought by a trustee in bankruptcy.

---

[132] See, eg, *Moore v Moore*, supra, at [81]–[95]. Where an order is designed in part to provide maintenance and in part to divide property it is possible to split up the enforceable under the Regulation and the unenforceable, *Van Den Boogard* case, supra, at 1184–1185.

[133] Ibid, at 1184–1185.

[134] *Moore v Moore*, supra, at [86].

[135] *Van Den Boogaard v Laumen*, supra.

[136] A question has been referred by the Bundesgerichtshof Germany to the Court of Justice in relation to this provision in Case C-339/07 *Rechtsanwalt Christopher Seagon v Deko Marty Belgium NV*.

[137] This does not encompass a dispute over rights under pre-liquidation transactions: *UBS AG v Omni Holding AG (In Liquidation)* [2000] 1 WLR 916.

[138] See the Jenard Report, pp 11–12; the Schlosser Report, pp 89–92. See generally Fletcher, *Conflict of Laws and European Community Law* (1982), Chapter 6.

[139] Case 133/78 [1979] ECR 733; Hartley (1979) 4 ELR 482.

[140] *UBS AG v Omni Holding AG (In Liquidation)* [2000] 1 WLR 916, at 922. See also *Oakley v Ultra Vehicle Design Ltd (In Liquidation)* [2005] EWHC 872 (Ch) at [42], [2005] IL Pr 55. In contrast, it has been suggested that an action under s 423 of the Insolvency Act 1986 (transactions prejudicial to creditors) falls outside the exception, Smart [1998] CJQ 149 at 153–160.

[141] *Re Hayward* [1997] Ch 45 at 53–55; Briggs (1996) 67 BYBIL 1577; Harris (1997) ELR 179; approved in *UBS AG v Omni Holding AG (In Liquidation)* [2000] 1 WLR 916, at 922. See also the *Oakley* case, supra, at [42].

[142] *Ashurst v Pollard* [2001] Ch 595, CA.

(iii) "Social Security"[143]

(iv) "Arbitration"[144]

Arbitration awards cannot be enforced under the Regulation.[145] More generally, the Court of Justice has said that the Brussels Convention does not apply to proceedings and decisions concerning applications for the revocation, amendment, recognition and enforcement of arbitration awards.[146] However, the exclusion goes wider than this. In *Marc Rich & Co v Società Italiana Impianti PA*[147] the Court of Justice held that arbitration is excluded in its entirety, including proceedings brought before the English courts for the appointment of an arbitrator. Whether a dispute is excluded from the scope of the Regulation is determined by reference solely to the subject matter of the dispute.[148] The fact that, during the course of the dispute, there has to be determined a preliminary issue, whatever that issue may be, cannot affect the exclusion. It followed that the litigation concerning the appointment of an arbitrator was excluded, even though the existence or validity of the arbitration agreement was raised as a preliminary issue in that litigation.

This still leaves the question of determining when the subject matter of the dispute falls within the arbitration exclusion. Clearly excluded, according to the Court of Justice, are proceedings which are ancillary to arbitration proceedings, such as the appointment or dismissal of arbitrators, the fixing of the place of arbitration or the extension of the time limit for making awards.[149] Provisional measures granted by a court using Article 31 of the Regulation[150] in support of arbitration proceedings are not ancillary to those proceedings but in parallel to them and are therefore not excluded.[151] They do not concern arbitration as such but the protection of a wide variety of rights. The English courts have referred to the exclusion of judicial proceedings which are integral to the arbitration process,[152] and of proceedings directed to the regulation and support of arbitration

---

[143] See the Schlosser Report, p 92; Case C-271/00 *Gemeente Steenbergen v Baten* [2003] 1 WLR 1996—action by the administration acting under rules of the ordinary civil law to recover from a person benefits paid by way of social assistance to the divorced spouse of that person not within this exclusion, [48]–[49].

[144] See the Schlosser Report, p 92.

[145] See *Allied Vision Ltd v VPS Film Entertainment GmbH* [1991] 1 Lloyd's Rep 392 at 399. They are covered by other conventions, infra, pp 654–661. If the award is turned into a judgment, this also falls within the exclusion: *Arab Business Consortium International Finance and Investment Co v Banque Franco Tunisienne* [1996] 1 Lloyd's Rep 485.

[146] Case C-391/95 *Van Uden Maritime BV (t/a Van Uden Africa Line) v Kommanditgesellschaft in Firma Deco-Line* [1999] QB 1225.

[147] Case C-190/89 [1991] ECR I-3855; Hartley (1991) 16 ELR 529; Briggs (1991) 11 YEL 527; Davidson 1992 SLT 267. The Court of Appeal's decision referring the matter to the Court of Justice is reported at [1989] 1 Lloyd's Rep 438. See also *Union Transport plc v Continental Lines SA* [1992] 1 WLR 15 at 17–18.

[148] For the problem of recognition and enforcement of foreign judgments where a court has taken jurisdiction despite an arbitration clause, see infra, pp 628–630.

[149] Case C-391/95 *Van Uden Maritime BV (t/a Van Uden Africa Line) v Kommanditgesellschaft in Firma Deco-Line* [1999] QB 1225.

[150] Infra, pp 315–318.

[151] The *Van Uden* case, supra.

[152] *Toepfer International GmbH v Molino Boschi srl* [1996] 1 Lloyd's Rep 510 at 513; *Union de Remorquage et de Sauvetage SA v Lake Avery Inc, The Lake Avery* [1997] 1 Lloyd's Rep 540 at 549. For an example of what is not encompassed, see: *Vale Do Rio Doce Navegacao SA v Shanghai Bao Steel Ocean Shipping Co Ltd (T/A Bao Steel Ocean Shipping Co)* [2000] 2 Lloyd's Rep 1.

proceedings and awards,[153] such as for security for the costs of an arbitration.[154] This looks to be entirely in line with the views of the Court of Justice. However, an English judge has said that the exclusion goes wider than this to cover matters falling within the ambit of application of international Conventions on arbitration.[155] The Court of Appeal has held that proceedings for enforcement of the arbitration agreement (by way of declarations that a party must refer a dispute to arbitration and that the bringing of proceedings abroad was in breach of the agreement to arbitrate and a claim for an injunction restraining the commencement or continuance of proceedings abroad) are also excluded,[156] on the basis that the principal focus of the proceedings is arbitration. The House of Lords has confidently given its opinion that proceedings for an injunction restraining a person from commencing or continuing proceedings abroad on the ground that such proceedings are in breach of an arbitration agreement are excluded since they "are entirely to protect the contractual right to have the dispute determined by arbitration".[157] Nonetheless, it is submitted that the law on this cannot be regarded as being *acte clair*[158] and a reference is needed to the Court of Justice to resolve the matter. This question of the scope of the arbitration exclusion arises incidentally when answering the question whether it is consistent with the Regulation for a court of a Member State to make an order to restrain a person from commencing or continuing proceedings *in another Member State* on the ground that such proceedings are in breach of an arbitration agreement.[159] The latter question has been referred by the House of Lords[160] to the Court of Justice and in answering that question it is possible that we may also get an answer to the incidental question in relation to arbitration.

The Court of Justice in the *Marc Rich* case did not decide whether, when the issue of the existence or validity of the arbitration agreement arises on its own (ie not as a preliminary issue), this comes within the arbitration exclusion.[161] In the situation where the issue of existence/validity arises as a preliminary one to an issue which is itself outside the scope of the Regulation, there is support for the view that this preliminary issue is also excluded.[162] Thus if proceedings for enforcement of the arbitration agreement are excluded so is the issue of the existence/validity of that agreement.[163] The Court of Justice, in a subsequent case, has said that the Brussels Convention does not apply to judgments

---

[153] *Lexmar v Nordisk* [1997] 1 Lloyd's Rep 289 at 292.

[154] *Lexmar v Nordisk* [1997] 1 Lloyd's Rep 289. At the other end of the spectrum, contrast *The Xing Su Hai* [1995] 2 Lloyd's Rep 15 at 21—no relief claimed in any way related to arbitration.

[155] See COLEMAN J in *Toepfer International GmbH v Société Cargill France* [1997] 2 Lloyd's Rep 98 at 103; and in *Lexmar v Nordisk* [1997] 1 Lloyd's Rep 289 at 292.

[156] *Through Transport Mutual Insurance Association (Eurasia) Ltd v New India Assurance Association Co Ltd* [2004] EWCA (Civ) 1598 at [38]–[51], [2005] 1 Lloyd's Rep 67. See also *Navigation Maritime Bulgare v Rustal Trading Ltd (The Ivan Zagubanski)* [2002] 1 Lloyd's Rep 106; *Toepfer v Cargill*, supra, at 102–105.

[157] *West Tankers Inc v RAS Riunione Adriatica di Sicurta SpA* [2007] UKHL 4 at [14], [2007] Lloyd's Rep 391.

[158] *Through Transport*, supra, at [39]. In *Toepfer International GmbH v Société Cargill France* [1998] 1 Lloyd's Rep 379, CA, Briggs (1997) 68 BYBIL 362, this question was referred to the Court of Justice for a decision, but the action was then settled.

[159] Discussed infra, pp 337–338.

[160] *West Tankers* case, supra.

[161] *Marc Rich & Co AG v Società Italiana Impianti PA (The "Atlantic Emperor") (No 2)* [1992] 1 Lloyd's Rep 624 at 628, 632, CA; Kaye [1993] CJQ 359. But see the opinion of AG DARMON in the *Marc Rich* case, supra at 3876, who thought it was excluded.

[162] See AG DARMON's opinion in the *Marc Rich* case, supra, at 3875–3876.

[163] *Toepfer v Cargill*, supra, at 105.

determining whether an arbitration agreement is valid or not or, because it is invalid, ordering the parties not to continue the arbitration proceedings.[164] Finally, an English court has held that claims designed to impugn the validity of an arbitration agreement fall outside the scope of the Lugano Convention.[165] The mere fact that the invalidity of the arbitration clause is dealt with as a preliminary issue does not bring the judgment as to the substance of the claim within the exclusion.[166]

The Hess, Pfeiffer and Schlosser Report advocates bringing ancillary proceedings in support of arbitration within the scope of the Regulation.[167]

(ii) Whether the defendant is domiciled in a Member State

It is necessary to distinguish between: (a) bases of jurisdiction (Chapter II, Sections 1–7); (b) other provisions on jurisdiction in Chapter II; (c) provisions on recognition and enforcement in Chapter III. It is only in the first of these, the bases of jurisdiction under the Regulation, that an initial basic distinction is drawn between the situation where the defendant is and is not domiciled in a Member State.[168] Section 1 of Chapter II gives two exceptions where this basic distinction does not operate. The position can be summarised as follows:

(a) Where the defendant is domiciled in a Member State the bases of jurisdiction under the Regulation will apply and not the traditional rules of jurisdiction of the forum.

(b) Where the defendant is not domiciled in a Member State, in general, the traditional rules of jurisdiction of the forum will apply.

(c) There are exceptions to (b), ie some of the bases of jurisdiction under the Regulation (Articles 22 and 23) will apply to defendants, even though they are not domiciled in a Member State.

Each of these will be looked at in more detail.

(a) Where the defendant is domiciled in a Member State

Article 2 in Section contains the most important basis of jurisdiction under the Regulation, that a defendant domiciled in a Member State is subject to the jurisdiction of the courts

---

[164] Case C-391/95 *Van Uden Maritime BV (t/a Van Uden Africa Line) v Kommanditgesellschaft in Firma Deco-Line* [1999] QB 1225; the opinion of AG Darmon in the *Marc Rich* case, supra, at 3876; the Schlosser Report, para 64; *The Lake Avery* [1997] 1 Lloyd's Rep 540 at 549; *The Ivan Zagubanski*, supra at [100]; *Philip Alexander Securities and Futures Ltd v Bamberger* [1997] IL Pr 73 at 100 (Waller J—regardless of whether invalidity was ruled on at a preliminary stage or together with a judgment on the substance of the dispute); but cf Leggat LJ in the Court of Appeal [1997] IL Pr 104 at 115, CA; Audit (1993) 9 Arbitration International 1. Cf *The Heidberg* [1994] 2 Lloyd's Rep 287; *Zellner v Phillip Alexander Securities and Futures Ltd* [1997] IL Pr 730 at 742; (1991) 7 Arbitration International, Schlosser Report, p 227 and Jenard Report, p 247. See generally Hascher (1997) 13 Arb Int 33.

[165] *A v B* [2006] EWHC 2006 (Comm), [2007] 1 Lloyd's Rep 237.

[166] *Zellner v Phillip Alexander Securities and Futures Ltd* [1997] IL Pr 730. See also *The Atlantic Emperor (No 2)*, supra, at 632–633; Waller J in *Philip Alexander Securities and Futures Ltd v Bamberger*, supra, at 94–102.

[167] Study JLS/C4/2005/03, Final Version September 2007, available at the European Commission—European Judicial Network—What's new website http://ec.europa.eu/civiljustice/news/whatsnew_en.htm. See paras 862–870. Exclusive jurisdiction over such proceedings would be granted to the courts of the Member State in which the arbitration takes place, see infra, p 283.

[168] For the position under the Regulation as regards other provisions on jurisdiction, see infra, p 301; for recognition and enforcement, see infra, pp 598–599.

of that State. If the defendant is to be sued in the courts of a Member State other than that of his domicile, Article 3(1) provides that this can only be done by virtue of the bases of jurisdiction set out in Sections 2 to 7. This prevents national courts from using their traditional rules on jurisdiction, including their exorbitant rules, against a defendant who is domiciled in a Member State. In the United Kingdom's case it is specifically provided in Article 3(2)[169] that, against such a defendant, jurisdiction can no longer be founded on presence of the defendant in the forum. It is also implicit from Article 3(2) that service out of the jurisdiction under rule 6.20 of the Civil Procedure Rules cannot be used.[170] Article 3(1) does not refer to the domicile of the *claimant*. It follows that, for example, a Japanese domiciliary, although not domiciled in a Member State, would have to use the bases of jurisdiction under the Regulation if he wished to sue in a Member State a defendant who was so domiciled.

Articles 2 and 3 require courts to decide whether a defendant is domiciled in a Member State. Paragraph 9 of Schedule 1 to the Civil Jurisdiction and Judgments Order 2001[171] contains a provision for determining, for the purposes of the Regulation, when an individual is domiciled in the United Kingdom.[172] He is so domiciled, if and only if (a) he is resident in the United Kingdom,[173] and (b) the nature and circumstances of his residence indicate that he has a substantial connection with the United Kingdom. The latter requirement shall be presumed to be fulfilled, unless the contrary is proved, if the individual has been resident in the United Kingdom, or part thereof, for the last three months or more.[174] If the individual is not domiciled in the United Kingdom it then has to be seen whether he is domiciled in another Member State. Paragraph 9 has no provisions for determining this. This is consistent with Article 59 of the Regulation, which, it will be recalled,[175] provides that, in order to determine whether a party is domiciled in another Member State, the courts shall apply the law of that state.

As regards the domicile of companies, recourse must be had to the autonomous definition contained in Article 60 of the Regulation. Accordingly, a company will be domiciled in the United Kingdom if it has its statutory seat, or central administration, or principal place of business there. In the situation where a court in the United Kingdom is deciding whether to apply the Regulation,[176] "statutory seat" means the registered office or, where there is no such office anywhere, the place of incorporation or, where there is no such place anywhere, the place under the law of which the formation took place. Article 60 will likewise apply in order to determine whether a company is domiciled in another Member State or in a non-Member State, as will the special provision equating the "statutory seat" with the registered office, etc. Under Article 60 a company may be domiciled

---

[169] And Annex I.

[170] See the Schlosser Report, p 100. CPR, r 6.20 is discussed infra, pp 372–397.

[171] SI 2001/3929, amended by SI 2007/1655.

[172] Para 9(2). The Modified Regulation will also apply if he is.

[173] See *Grupo Torras SA and Torras Hostench London Ltd v Sheikh Fahad Mohammed Al-Sabah* [1995] 1 Lloyd's Rep 374 at 444–446—the defendant may also be resident in another country. This was not part of the appeal to the Court of Appeal, [1996] 1 Lloyd's Rep 7, CA. See also *Canada Trust Co v Stolzenberg* [1997] 1 WLR 1582, CA; approved by the House of Lords [2002] 1 AC 1.

[174] Para 9(6).

[175] See supra, p 210.

[176] This is "for the purposes of the United Kingdom", as required by Art 60(2).

in more than one State. For example, it may have its statutory seat in Panama but its central administration in Germany. In such a case the company undoubtedly has a domicile in a Member State. The bases of jurisdiction contained in the Brussels I Regulation will apply and the company cannot be sued in a Member State under that State's traditional rules on jurisdiction.[177]

(b) The defendant is not domiciled in a Member State

Where the defendant is not domiciled in a Member State, Article 4 states that the jurisdiction of the courts of each Member State shall, subject to the provisions of Articles 22 and 23, be determined by the law of that Member State. If, to take an example, an Englishman wishes to sue a Californian domiciliary in England, he would have to do so under the traditional English rules on jurisdiction, which are, by and large, more generous to the claimant than their equivalent under the Regulation. Article 4 therefore recognises the use of exorbitant jurisdiction by Member States in certain circumstances. This has far-reaching consequences when it comes to enforcing judgments and declining jurisdiction in cases of *lis pendens*.[178]

Article 4 requires the courts of Member States to ascertain when a defendant is not domiciled in a Member State. Having decided that an individual defendant is not domiciled in the United Kingdom (under the United Kingdom definition), and is not domiciled in another Member State (under that state's definition), the defendant must be domiciled in a non-Member State. A person must have a domicile in one state or another for the purposes of the Regulation. In the rare situations where the particular non-Member state in which the defendant is domiciled has to be ascertained,[179] this is done by applying paragraph 9(7) of Schedule 1 to the Civil Jurisdiction and Judgments Order 2001, which provides that an individual is domiciled in a state other than a Regulation State if and only if (a) he is resident in that state, and (b) the nature and circumstances of his residence indicate that he has a substantial connection with that state.[180] In this particular context there is no presumption to aid in showing the required substantial connection, and it is possible, in rare cases, that an individual may not have a substantial connection with any one state at all. Where this happens one would have to be resigned to saying that the individual is domiciled in a non-Regulation State but it is not clear in which particular one.[181] As regards corporate defendants, Article 60 of the Brussels I Regulation will be applied to determine whether a company is domiciled in a non-Member State.

The Hess, Pfeiffer and Schlosser Report identified a problem with Article 4 in that it results in an unequal system of access to justice for European Community plaintiffs.[182]

---

[177] *The Deichland* [1990] 1 QB 361, CA; *The Rewia* [1991] 2 Lloyd's Rep 325, CA.

[178] See the Jenard Report, pp 20–21, and infra, pp 598–599 and 304.

[179] It may be necessary to ascertain the particular non-Regulation State because of Art 72, discussed infra, pp 626–627.

[180] Is "State" here referring to the political unit, eg the USA, or to a law district, eg New York? When para 9(7) refers to a Regulation State this means a political unit; it is arguable that "a state other than a Regulation State" likewise means a political unit. On the other hand, under para 9 England is applying its own jurisdictional rules and the normal meaning of a state in English private international law is that of a law district.

[181] See, supra, n 179.

[182] Study JLS/C4/2005/03, Final Version September 2007, available at the European Commission—European Judicial Network—What's new website http://ec.europa.eu/civiljustice/news/whatsnew_en.htm. See para 875 and paras 155–165.

This comes about because the national rules of jurisdiction in some Member States are open to plaintiffs, regardless of their domicile, whereas in other Member States they are only available to plaintiffs domiciled in that Member State. As a first step to solving this problem it is suggested that it might be advisable to extend Articles 5 and 6 to cases involving defendants who are domiciled outside the European Community and to only allow a reference to national rules of jurisdiction on the basis of a residual provision.

(c) The exceptions

Article 4 mentions just two exceptions to the rule that national bases of jurisdiction apply where the defendant is not domiciled in a Member State; these are contained in Articles 22 and 23.[183] The former Article gives exclusive jurisdiction in certain circumstances, regardless of the defendant's domicile. The latter Article is concerned with agreements on jurisdiction.[184] Other possible exceptions under Article 24 (submission), Article 13 (an agreement in a matter relating to insurance), Article 17 (an agreement in a consumer contract) and Article 21 (an agreement in an individual contract of employment) are discussed later.[185]

(d) Plaintiff's domicile

There is no requirement for the application of Chapter II of the Regulation that the plaintiff is domiciled in a Member State.[186] Thus the Regulation will apply in a dispute between a plaintiff domiciled in a non-Member State and a defendant domiciled in a Member State.[187] However, there are a small number of bases of jurisdiction which pre-suppose that the plaintiff is domiciled in a Member State.[188] If the plaintiff is not so domiciled these bases cannot be used. But it remains open to the plaintiff to use other bases of jurisdiction.

(f) Bases of jurisdiction

The first seven Sections of Chapter II set out the bases of jurisdiction under the Regulation, with each Section containing one or more bases of jurisdiction. The division into Sections emphasises that different types of jurisdiction are being dealt with. The Regulation provides for: (i) general jurisdiction (Section 1); (ii) special jurisdiction (Section 2); (iii) jurisdiction in matters relating to insurance (Section 3); (iv) jurisdiction over consumer contracts (Section 4); (v) jurisdiction over individual contracts of employment (Section 5); (vi) exclusive jurisdiction (Section 6); and (vii) prorogation of jurisdiction (Section 7).

---

[183] Infra, pp 275–296.

[184] See infra, pp 283–296.

[185] See infra, pp 266–275 and 297.

[186] Case C-412/98 *Universal General Insurance Co (UGIC) v Group Josi Reinsurance Co SA* [2001] QB 68; Peel, [2001] YEL 354.

[187] *Universal General Insurance* case, at [61]. See also Case C-190/89 *Marc Rich & Co v Società Italiana Impianti PA* [1991] ECR I-3855; Case C-406/92 *Owners of cargo lately laden on board the ship Tatry v Owners of the Ship Maciej Rataj* (Note) [1999] QB 515. See also Case C-281/02 *Owusu v Jackson* [2005] I-1383, [2005] QB 801 at [27].

[188] Arts 5(2), 9(1)(b) and 16(1). Art 23(1) requires one of the parties to be domiciled in a Member State. If not the defendant, it would have to be the plaintiff.

In some situations, the claimant will have to sue the defendant in the courts of the Member State which has been allocated exclusive jurisdiction under the Regulation. In other situations, the courts of more than one Member State will have jurisdiction and the claimant will be able to choose the Member State in which to sue the defendant. With the harmonisation of rules on jurisdiction in the different Member States, lawyers in the United Kingdom can now advise clients on whether they can sue or be sued not only in the United Kingdom but also in other Member States. This task is made easier by the absence from the Regulation of provisions giving a discretion to refuse to take jurisdiction.[189]

When the issue comes to trial in England, it is well established in cases where reliance is placed on special jurisdiction under Articles 5 and 6 that the claimant has to show a good arguable case that the terms of Article 5 or 6 are satisfied.[190] It is now settled that the same standard and burden of proof will apply where the claimant seeks trial in England relying on other bases of jurisdiction,[191] in particular on Article 2[192] or Article 23.[193] A good arguable case has a certain flexibility and suggests that one party has a much better argument on the evidence available.[194] The requirement of a good arguable case is intended to encapsulate the rule that the court must be as satisfied as it can be, having regard to the limitations of the interlocutory process, that factors exist which allow the court to take jurisdiction.[195] The application of the test may vary from case to case, both in order to take account of any relevant policy underlying the Regulation and in order to take account of the limitations imposed by the interlocutory process.[196] Moreover, there is a

---

[189] Art 27 deals with the specific problem of *lis pendens* but there is no discretion involved under this provision, see infra, p 305. On the question whether the English courts can use their traditional doctrine of *forum non conveniens*, see infra, pp 320–333.

[190] *Canada Trust Co v Stolzenberg (No 2)* [1998] 1 WLR 547 at 553–559, CA, approved by the House of Lords [2002] 1 AC 1 at 13 (per Lord STEYN, with whom the other Law Lords concurred); Briggs (2000) 71 BYBIL 446; Look Chan Ho, (2001) 50 ICLQ 632; *Masri v Consolidated Contractors International (UK) Ltd* [2005] EWCA Civ 1436 at [15], [2006] 1 WLR 830. See also in *Deutsche Ruckversicherung AG v La Fondiara Assicurazioni SpA* [2001] 2 Lloyd's Rep 621 at 622. This adopts the same test as applies for service out of the jurisdiction with the permission of the courts under the traditional rules, infra, p 373.

[191] *Bank of Tokyo-Mitsubishi Ltd v Baskan Gida Sanayi Ve Pazalarma AS* [2004] EWHC 945 (Ch) at [193], [2004] 2 Lloyd's Rep 394.

[192] *Haji-Ioannou v Frangos* [1999] 2 Lloyd's Rep 337, 348, CA; in *Royal & Sun Alliance Insurance plc v MK Digital FZE (Cyprus) Ltd* [2006] EWCA Civ 629 at [86]. See also *Latchin (t/a Dinkha Latchin Associates) v General Mediterranean Holdings SA)* [2002] CLC 330, 336–339; *Chellaram v Chellaram (No 2)* [2002] EWHC 632 (Ch) at [23], [2002] 3 All ER 17; *King v Crown Energy Trading AG* [2003] EWHC 163 (Comm) at [4], [2003] I L Pr 28. See also *Dubai Bank Ltd v Abbas* [1997] IL Pr 308.

[193] *Bols Distilleries v Superior Yacht Services Ltd* [2006] UKPC at [27]–[28], [2007] 1 WLR 12. See also *Carnoustie Universal v International Transport Workers Federation* [2002] EWHC 1624 (Comm) at [47], [2003] I L Pr 7; *Evialis SA v SIAT* [2003] EWHC 863 (Comm) 377 at [70]–[71], [2003] 2 Lloyd's Rep 377; the *Bank of Tokyo-Mitsubishi* case, supra, at [193]. For the position on the burden of proof where the defendant seeks to deny trial in England by relying on a clause providing for the exclusive jurisdiction of the courts of another Member State see infra, p 285.

[194] *Masri v Consolidated Contractors International (UK) Ltd* [2005] EWCA Civ 1436, [2006] 1 WLR 830; the *Bols Distilleries* case, supra, at [28]; the *Bank of Tokyo-Mitsubishi* case, supra, at [193]; *Konkola Copper Mines plc v Coromin Ltd* [2006] EWCA Civ 5 at [86], [2006] 1 Lloyd's Rep 410; *Benatti v WPP Holdings Italy srl* [2007] EWCA Civ 263 at [42]–[44] (per TOULSON LJ), [2007] 1 WLR 2316. But see also *Konkola* at [96] where RIX LJ suggests a different test where a jurisdictional issue goes to the heart of the merits. See also RIX LJ in *Royal & Sun Alliance Insurance PLC v MK Digital FZE (Cyprus) Ltd* [2006] EWCA Civ 629 at [62], [2006] 2 Lloyd's Rep 110.

[195] *Benatti v WPP Holdings*, supra, at [41]; the *Bols Distilleries* case, supra, at [28].

[196] Ibid.

threshold requirement, at least in cases of special jurisdiction, which the claimant has to satisfy before the defendant can be subjected to jurisdiction. The claimant's case must establish that there is a serious issue on the merits to be tried.[197] Common sense would suggest that the same requirement should apply in respect of the other bases of jurisdiction.[198]

(i) General jurisdiction

Article 2 provides that "persons domiciled in a Member State shall, whatever their nationality, be sued in the courts of that Member State".

The Regulation adopts the principle that, in general, persons should be sued[199] in the courts of the Regulation State where they are domiciled.[200] The words "shall . . . be sued" must not be taken literally. Other bases of jurisdiction make it clear that the defendant may, and, in some circumstances, must, be sued in the courts of a Member State other than that of his domicile.[201] Article 2 is concerned with the defendant's domicile at the moment of the issue of proceedings, rather than their subsequent service on the defendant.[202] Article 2 is applicable even where the claimant and the defendant are domiciled in the same Member State[203] and the dispute between them is connected with a non-Member State, rather than with another Member State.[204] In other words, what is involved is relationships between the courts of a single Member State and a non-Member State.[205]

In order to ascertain whether the defendant is domiciled in a Member State under Article 2, reference must be made (if an individual) to Article 59 of the Regulation and paragraph 9

---

[197] *ABKCO Music & Records Inc v Music Collection International Ltd* [1995] RPC 657, CA; *Mecklermedia Corpn v DC Congress GmbH* [1998] Ch 40 at 46; *Grupo Torras SA and Torras Hostench London Ltd v Sheikh Fahad Mohammed Al-Sabah* [1995] 1 Lloyd's Rep 374, the appeal to the Court of Appeal did not raise this point. Cf *Surzur Overseas Ltd v Koros* [1999] 2 Lloyd's Rep 611, at 613 CA, where the standard was wrongly described as being a good arguable case. The standard of proof as to the merits is a matter for national courts as part of determining their own jurisdiction: AG DARMON in Case C-68/93 *Shevill v Presse Alliance SA* [1995] 2 AC 18 at 49–50.

[198] See generally Briggs and Rees, para 2.208. The argument against is based on the analogy with the traditional rules, where there is no such requirement in relation to defendants within the jurisdiction; see in support of this argument the *Mecklermedia* case, supra.

[199] *National Justice Compañía Naviera SA v Prudential Assurance Co Ltd (The Ikarian Reefer (No 2)* [2000] 1 WLR 603, CA; Briggs (2000) 71 BYBIL 450—this does not include an application under s 51 of the Supreme Court Act 1981 to recover costs from a non-party.

[200] See the Jenard Report, pp 13 and 18–19. See also *SA Consortium General Textiles v Sun and Sand Agencies Ltd* [1978] QB 279 at 295, [1978] 2 All ER 339 at 351; *Citadel Insurance Co v Atlantic Union Insurance Co SA* [1982] 2 Lloyd's Rep 543 at 549; *Knauf UK GmbH v British Gypsum Ltd* [2001] EWCA Civ 1570 at [49], [2002] 1 Lloyd's Rep 199.

[201] Where Art 27 (lis pendens) applies it requires the courts of Member States, including that of the defendant's domicile, to decline jurisdiction.

[202] *Canada Trust Co v Stolzenberg (No 2)* [2002] 1 AC 1 at 8–12 (per Lord STEYN), 22–23 (per Lord HOFFMANN), 23 (per Lord COOKE), 23 (per Lord HOPE), 26 (per Lord HOBHOUSE), HL. See also *Ministry of Defence and Support of the Armed Forces for the Islamic Republic of Iran v FAZ Aviation Ltd* [2007] EWHC 1042 (Comm) at [5], [52], [53], [2007] IL Pr 42. For the position where proceedings are brought in Scotland see Lord HOPE at 23–26.

[203] There is no need for a connection with any other Member State according to *British Sugar plc v Fratelli* [2004] EWHC 2560 at [34] (obiter), [2005] 1 Lloyd's Rep 332 but such a case should fall outside the scope of the Regulation, supra, pp 213–214.

[204] Case C-281/02 *Owusu v Jackson* [2005] ECR I-1383, [2005] QB 801 at [24]–[37].

[205] Ibid, at [36].

of Schedule 1 to the Civil Jurisdiction and Judgments Order 2001 and (if a company) to Article 60 of the Regulation, which have already been discussed.[206] Where the Member State in which the defendant is domiciled is the United Kingdom, the Modified Regulation will apply to allocate jurisdiction between the courts of England, Scotland and Northern Ireland.[207]

(ii) Special jurisdiction

In some cases trial is permitted in the courts of a Member State other than the one in which the defendant is domiciled; this is known as special jurisdiction and the relevant provisions are found in Section 2 of Chapter II of the Regulation. This alternative form of jurisdiction is justified on the basis of a close link between the court and the action or in order to facilitate the sound administration of justice.[208] It is left to the claimant to decide whether he wishes to sue the defendant in the latter's domicile under Article 2, or whether he wishes to sue him in another Member State under Section 2. Where the Member State given special jurisdiction is the United Kingdom, the claimant will want to know whether he is to sue in England, Scotland or Northern Ireland or has the choice of suing in any of these. The amended version of the Regulation will not apply[209] to allocate jurisdiction within the United Kingdom. It has no need to. The provisions on special jurisdiction are designed to give local as well as international jurisdiction[210] and can be regarded as giving jurisdiction to the courts of a part of the United Kingdom and not merely to the courts of the United Kingdom as a whole. Many of the provisions give jurisdiction to the courts of a place in a Member State, and the place in the United Kingdom would be in England, Scotland or Northern Ireland, as indicated by the particular provisions. Other provisions give jurisdiction to the courts or a court of a Member State, but the context readily identifies which part of the United Kingdom is the appropriate one to have jurisdiction.

(a) Article 5

This is the most important of the three articles in Section 2. Article 5 provides that a person domiciled in a Member State may be sued in another Member State in seven specified situations. Before looking at these, it is important to realise that the use of the words "may be sued" is not intended to confer on courts a discretion to refuse to take jurisdiction.[211] Rather it emphasises that the claimant is allowed (but not required) to sue the defendant in a Member State other than where the defendant is domiciled. Nonetheless, the defendant's domicile is the normal place for trial. Article 5 is an exception to this general rule,[212] and its provisions must not be given an interpretation going

---

[206] Supra, pp 211–213.

[207] Infra, pp 346–352.

[208] Recital (12) of the Regulation. See also Case C-386/05 *Color Drack GmbH v LEXX International Vertriebs GmbH* at [22]. It may not be the state with the closest connection, Case C-288/92 *Custom Made Commercial Ltd v Stawa Metallbau GmbH* [1994] ECR I-2913.

[209] Infra, p 347.

[210] See the Schlosser Report, p 98; Hartley, p 40.

[211] *Tesam Distribution Ltd v Shuh Mode Team GmbH* [1990] IL Pr 149, CA; *Boss Group v Boss France SA* [1997] 1 WLR 351, CA.

[212] Case 56/79 *Zelger v Salinitri* [1980] ECR 89.

beyond the situations envisaged by the Regulation.[213] It is less clear whether this means that all its provisions should be given a restrictive interpretation.[214]

The seven situations where the defendant can be sued in a Member State other than that of his domicile are set out in Article 5(1) to (7) as follows:

Article 5(1)

(a)[215] in matters relating to a contract, in the courts for the place of performance of the
    obligation in question;
(b) for the purpose of this provision and unless otherwise agreed, the place of perform-
    ance of the obligation in question shall be:
      — in the case of the sale of goods, the place in a Member State where, under the con-
        tract, the goods were delivered or should have been delivered,
      — in the case of the provision of services, the place in a Member State where, under
        the contract, the services were provided or should have been provided,
(c) if subparagraph (b) does not apply then subparagraph (a) applies;

(i) What are matters relating to a contract?

In order for Article 5(1) to apply there must be a matter relating to a contract. The Court of Justice has given an independent community meaning to this concept, rather than applying the classification adopted under the national law of a Member State.[216]

A contractual relationship   There must be a contractual relationship between the parties.[217] In certain circumstances, this can present a problem, with no consensus under the substantive law of the Member States over whether there is such a relationship, and the Court of Justice has had to resolve the question. In the *Peters* case[218] the Court has had to consider the relationship between an association and its members. Not all Member States regard this as a contractual relationship. Nonetheless, the Court of Justice held that this came within Article 5(1) of the Brussels Convention. The Community definition of matters relating to a contract includes relationships which involve close links of the same kind as are created between parties to a contract. In *Jakob Handte & Co GmbH v Traitements Mecano-Chimiques des Surfaces SA (TMCS)*[219] the Court had to consider the relationship between a manufacturer and a sub-buyer who brings a claim in respect of

---

[213] C-26/91 *Jakob Handte & Co GmbH v Traitements Mecano-Chimiques des Surfaces SA (TMCS)* [1992] ECR I-3967, at [14]; Case C-433/01 *Freistaat Bayern v Jan Blijdenstein* [2004] ECR I-981, at [25]; [2004] IL Pr 8; Case C-168/02 *Kronhofer v Maier* [2004] IL Pr 27, at [14]; the opinion of AG JACOBS in Case C-167/00 *Verein Für Konsumenteninformation v K H Henkel* [2002] ECR I-8111, at [33].

[214] Cf the *Kronhofer* case, supra, with the denials by AG JACOBS in *Verein* and the Court of Justice in Case C–27/02 *Petra Engler v Janus Versand GmbH*, [2005] ECR I-481 at [48] (following AG JACOBS at [38] of his opinion) that Art 5(3) and the scope of 5(1) respectively should be restrictively interpreted. Art 5(2) should be so interpreted: the *Freistaat* case.

[215] For the use of Art 5(1) where the defendant is domiciled in Luxembourg, see Art 63 of the Regulation.

[216] Case 34/82 *Peters v Zuid Nederlandsee Aannemers Vereniging* [1983] ECR 987; Case C-26/91 *Jakob Handte & Co GmbH v Traitements Mecano-Chimiques des Surfaces SA (TMCS)* [1992] ECR I-3967.

[217] Case C-51/97 *Réunion Européenne SA v Spliethoff's Bevrachtingskantoor BV* [2000] QB 690.

[218] Case 34/82 [1983] ECR 987. See Hartley (1983) 8 ELR 262. See also *Bank of Scotland v Investment Management Regulatory Organisation Ltd* 1989 SLT 432; *Engdiv Ltd v G Percy Trentham Ltd* 1990 SLT 617. See also *Boss Group v Boss France SA* [1997] 1 WLR 351, CA; Crawford (2005) 54 ICLQ 829, 840.

[219] Case C-26/91 [1992] ECR I-3967; Briggs (1992) 12 YEL 667; Decker (1993) 42 ICLQ 366; Hartley (1993) 18 ELR 506; Fawcett (1993-I) 238 Hague Recueil 13, at 76–78.

damage to the product itself. Under French law there is liability in contract, whereas under English law, and that of many other Member States, usually there is no liability at all, either in contract or tort. The Court of Justice held that it was irrelevant how the relevant national court classified the matter or how it was classified under the applicable law; "matters relating to contract" had to be given an independent meaning. The action did not relate to a contractual matter since there was no contractual relationship between the parties[220] because the manufacturer had not undertaken any contractual obligation towards the sub-buyer,[221] and the nature of the manufacturer's liability was not regarded by the overwhelming majority of Contracting States to the Brussels Convention as being contractual. However, such liability (ie that imposed under French law) should be regarded as falling within the scope of Article 5(3) of the Regulation,[222] even though such liability is not regarded in Member States as being tortious in the strict sense.[223]

An identifiable obligation The Court of Justice in *Fonderie Officine Meccaniche Tacconi SpA v Heinrich Wagner Sinto Maschinenfabrik GmbH (HWS)*[224] has said that "while Article 5(1) of the Brussels Convention does not require a contract to have been concluded, it is nevertheless essential, for that provision to apply, to identify an obligation, since the jurisdiction of the national court is determined, in matters relating to a contract, by the place of performance of the obligation in question".[225] In that particular case there were negotiations that gave rise to expectations but the stage had not yet been reached when there were obligations.[226] The House of Lords in *Agnew v Lansforsakringsbolagens AB*[227] has held that the requirement of an identifiable obligation[228] is separate from the requirement that there be a matter relating to a contract.[229] The nature of this obligation has been examined by the House of Lords in both the *Agnew* case and in the earlier case of *Kleinwort Benson Ltd v Glasgow City Council*.[230] In *Kleinwort Benson* a majority of the House of Lords, influenced by the allocation of jurisdiction to the place of performance of the obligation in question, adopted a principle that a

---

[220] Cf *Atlas Shipping v Suisse Atlantique* [1995] 2 Lloyd's Rep 18—a contract between A and B to pay C held to be within Art 5(1) of the Brussels Convention, and to the same effect see *Benatti v WPP Holdings Italy SRL* [2007] EWCA Civ 263 at [52] (per Toulson LJ), [2007] 1 WLR 2316.

[221] The obligation must be freely assumed by one party towards the other, see infra, pp 232–233.

[222] AG Jacobs at 3989. In principle, this would not stop a national court from then classifying the action as contractual for choice of law purposes, AG Jacobs at 3984.

[223] The wide scope of Art 5(3) is discussed infra, pp 247–249.

[224] Case C-334/00 [2002] ECR I-7357.

[225] The *Fonderie* case, supra, at [22]. See also Case C–27/02 *Petra Engler v Janus Versand GmbH*, supra, at [50]; Case C-234/04 *Kapferer v Schlank & Schick GmbH* [2006] IL Pr 17 at [45] of the opinion of AG Tizzano (a contract does not need to have been formed).

[226] See the opinion of AG Geelhoed in the *Fonderie* case, supra, at [81]–[83].

[227] [2001] 1 AC 223.

[228] Ibid at 240 (per Lord Woolf), 246 (per Lord Cooke—an obligation so intimately connected with contract that it falls within Art 5(1), 250 (per Lord Hope), 262–266, (per Lord Millett), 233–234 (per Lord Nicholls).

[229] Ibid at 240 (per Lord Woolf), 246 (per Lord Cooke), 250 (per Lord Hope), 262–266. Lord Millett (262–266) accepted this requirement but regarded it as falling within the concept of matters relating to a contract, as, seemingly, did Lord Nicholls (233–234). The latter was the view in the earlier House of Lords case of *Kleinwort Benson Ltd v Glasgow City Council* [1999] 1 AC 153.

[230] [1999] 1 AC 153; Briggs (1997) 68 BYBIL 331; Dickinson [1998] RLR 104; Maher [1998] Jur Rev 131; McGrath [1999] CJQ 41; Virgo (1998) 114 LQR 386; Peel [1997] LMCLQ 22; Pitel [1998] CLJ 19. See also *Strathaird Farms Ltd v GA Chattaway & Co* 1993 SLT 36. See generally Peel, in Rose (ed) *Restitution and the Conflict of Laws*, (1995), Chapter 1.

claim can only come within Article 5(1) of the Modified Convention (now Modified Regulation),[231] allocating jurisdiction within the United Kingdom, if it is based on a particular contractual obligation, ie the obligation whose performance is sought in the judicial proceedings.[232] This makes clear that the obligation must be a contractual one and that it must also be a performance obligation. Support for both propositions can be found in terminology used by the Court of Justice in a number of cases.[233] The *Kleinwort Benson* case concerned a claim for restitution of money paid under a purported contract subsequently accepted by both parties as being *void ab initio*. This claim was based on the concept of unjust enrichment, not on a particular contractual obligation and, accordingly, fell outside the scope of Article 5(1).[234] Moreover, since it was accepted that the contract was *void ab initio*, there was no obligation and Article 5(1) could not apply.[235] This does not mean that all claims for restitution would fall outside Article 5(1). A restitutionary claim that is based on a contractual obligation will not do so.[236] A claim to recover money paid under a valid contract, on the ground of a failure of consideration following a breach of contract by the defendant, is capable of being classified under some systems as contractual and the concept of a contractual obligation may be broad enough to encompass this.[237]

The requirement that the claim has to be based on the performance of a particular contractual obligation raised concerns that Article 5(1) might not apply where the claim arises out of a pre-contractual obligation. However, these concerns were put to rest by the House of Lords in *Agnew v Lansforsakringsbolagens AB*,[238] which held by a majority[239] that a claim for a declaration that the plaintiffs were entitled to avoid (ie rescind) insurance contracts on the basis of misrepresentations and non-disclosure fell within Article 5(1) of the Lugano Convention. In other words, an "obligation", which in this case could variously be described as being to make a fair presentation of the risk, not to misrepresent the risk, or to disclose facts material to the risk,[240] included a pre-contractual obligation which if not fulfilled gave the plaintiffs the right to set aside the contract.[241] Doubts were expressed in the *Agnew* case as to whether it would be appropriate to refer to an

---

[231] It appears from their Lordships' judgments that these would have been exactly the same if it had been a case on the Brussels Convention. See also *Eddie v Alpa Srl* 2000 SLT 1062 at 1068. The Court of Justice in Case C-346/93 *Kleinwort Benson Ltd v Glasgow City Council* [1996] QB 57, infra, p 249, declined to give a ruling on the Art 5(1) point on the basis that it arose in the context of an intra-United Kingdom dispute under the Modified Convention, rather than in order to apply the Brussels Convention itself.

[232] At 167–171 (per Lord GOFF), 181 (per Lord CLYDE), 189 (per Lord HUTTON). See the powerful and convincing dissent of Lord NICHOLLS at 174–176, with whom Lord MUSTILL, at 174 et seq, concurred.

[233] Both the *De Bloos* case, supra 1508, at [11], [14] and the *Shenavai* case, supra, 256, at [18] refer to a contractual obligation. The latter also refers to "the contractual obligation . . . whose performance is sought in the judicial proceedings". See also the opinion of AG GEELHOED in the *Fonderie* case, supra, at [38]–[39].

[234] It also fell outside Art 5(3), see infra, p 249. See also *Eddie v Alpa Srl* 2000 SLT 1062—claim for restitution of overcharged payment outside Art 5(1) of the Brussels Convention.

[235] At 169 (per Lord GOFF), 181 and 183 (per Lord CLYDE), 195–196 (per Lord HUTTON). But cf the judgment of MILLET LJ in the Court of Appeal [1996] QB 678 at 698–699.

[236] Fawcett, Harris and Bridge paras 8.13–8.27.

[237] See Lord GOFF at 167 and 171.

[238] [2001] 1 AC 223; Briggs (2000) 71 BYBIL 451; Pester [2000] LMCLQ 289.

[239] Lords HOPE and MILLETT dissenting.

[240] Per Lord COOKE at 246. According to Lord WOOLF, at 239, the obligation was to disclose. Lord NICHOLLS, at 233–234, concurred with both Lords COOKE and WOOLF, which leaves the precise nature of the obligation uncertain.

[241] Cf the *Fonderie* case, supra, which concerned pre-contractual liability but no contract was ever concluded and the obligation was therefore based on a rule of law.

"obligation" not to be guilty of duress, or undue influence or inducing a contract by mistake in a case of a person seeking to rely on duress, etc.[242] Moreover, there could be no place of performance of such a negative obligation.[243] In contrast, where the negative obligation was not to commit yourself to other partners this was regarded by the Court of Justice as an obligation but the problem was that there was a multiplicity of places of performance in different Member States and therefore Article 5(1) could not be used.[244]

We must turn now to the statement in the *Fonderie* case that no contract need have been concluded.[245] This makes clear that Article 5(1) can apply where there is agreement on the main parts of the contract but not on all terms and conditions and there is no signed contract.[246] At this late stage, when there is almost a complete contract, it can be inferred from the circumstances that obligations have been assumed by the parties.

An obligation that is freely assumed   The Court of Justice has repeatedly held that, in order for there to be a matter relating to a contract, there must be an obligation freely assumed by one party towards another.[247] This requirement has come into play in two different situations.

The first is where there is no direct contractual relationship between the parties. This is illustrated by the *Jakob Handte* case[248] where, although there was no direct contractual relationship between a sub-buyer and the manufacturer, under French law the sub-buyer had a contractual claim against the manufacturer.[249] The Court of Justice said that the manufacturer "undertakes no contractual obligation to that [sub]buyer whose identity and domicile may legitimately be unknown to him".[250] Neither was this requirement met where a guarantor (A), who paid customs duties under a guarantee obtained by the forwarding agent (V), sought reimbursement from the owner of goods (F), who was not a party to the contract of guarantee.[251] It would, however, be met if F authorised the

---

[242] Supra, at 241 (per Lord WOOLF, with whom Lord NICHOLLS concurred), 265 (per Lord MILLETT, who, after examining the nature of the so-called obligation according to the applicable national law, thought there was no obligation in such cases).

[243] The requirement of an identifiable place of performance is discussed infra, p 233.

[244] Case C-256/00 *Besix SA v Wasserreinigungsbau Alfred Kretzschmar GmbH & Co KG (WABAG)* [2002] ECR I-1699; discussed infra, pp 240–241. See also in relation to a negative obligation *Crucial Music Corpn v Klondyke Management AG* [2007] EWHC 1782 (Ch), [2007] IL Pr 54, which held that the obligation can also be a warranty as to an existing state of affairs.

[245] The *Fonderie* case, supra, [22]. See also Case C–27/02 *Petra Engler v Janus Versand GmbH*, supra, at [45] and [50].

[246] See the opinion of AG Geelhoed in the *Fonderie* case, supra, at [83].

[247] The *Jakob Handte* case, supra, at 3994, at [15]; Case C-51/97 *Réunion Européenne SA v Spliethoff's Bevrachtingskantoor BV* [2000] QB 690, at [17] and [19], Hartley (2000) 25 ELR 89; Case C-334/00 *Fonderie Officine Meccaniche Tacconi SpA v Heinrich Wagner Sinto Maschinenfabrik GmbH (HWS)* [2002] ECR I-7357, [23]; Case C-265/02 *Frahuil SA v Assitalia SPA* [2004] ECR I-1543; the *Petra Engler* case, supra, at [50]; *Kapferer v Schlank & Schick GmbH* [2006] IL Pr 17 at [45] of the opinion of AG TIZZANO. For the problems raised by this requirement in the case of an action between a carrier and a third party holder of a bill of lading see Fawcett, Harris and Bridge, paras 5.21–5.26.

[248] Supra. For a different illustration see Case C-167/00 *Verein Für Konsumenteninformation v K H Henkel* [2002] ECR I-8111, at [39]–[40].

[249] The *Jakob Handte* case, supra. This is based on the theory that the intermediate supplier transmits to the sub-buyer his contractual rights against the manufacturer (or against a previous intermediary) as an accessory of the goods.

[250] Supra, at [20].

[251] Case C-265/02 *Frahuil SA v Assitalia SPA* [2004] ECR I-1543.

conclusion of the contract of guarantee.[252] There was also no contractual relationship freely entered into between the consignee of goods and a sub-carrier which was a third party to a transport contract between the consignee and another company which issued the bill of lading.[253]

The second situation where this requirement came into play arose in the *Fonderie* case.[254] There was no identifiable contractual obligation, the negotiations not having reached the stage where contractual obligations arose. The obligation in that case to make good the damage allegedly caused by the unjustified breaking off of negotiations could derive only from rules of law, in particular the rule which requires the parties to act in good faith in negotiations with a view to the formation of a contract.[255] Accordingly, there was no obligation freely assumed by one party towards another.[256]

But where there are contractual obligations, as there were in the *Agnew* case, these can arise both by virtue of the terms of the contract and under the general law (such as the obligations imposed on the seller by the Sale of Goods Act 1979). Contractual obligations arising by virtue of the terms of the contract are undeniably freely assumed by one party towards another. As regards obligations that arise by virtue of the general law, it can be said that by voluntarily entering into a contract the parties freely assume the legal incidents of the contract.[257] This means that the source of the obligation, whether it is the general law or the express terms of the contract, does not matter.[258] Neither is there any problem in meeting this requirement where there is a unilateral undertaking by a commercial body to award a prize.[259]

An identifiable place of performance Not only must there be an identifiable obligation, there must also be an identifiable place of performance.[260] This, like the requirement of an identifiable obligation, was regarded by the majority of Law Lords in the *Agnew* case as a separate requirement from there being a matter relating to a contract.[261] A single place of performance for the obligation in question must be identified.[262]

---

[252] Ibid.

[253] Case C-51/97 *Réunion Européenne SA v Spliethoff's Bevrachtingskantoor BV* [2000] QB 690; Peel [1998] YEL 7000; Briggs [1999] LMCLQ 333; Hartley (2000) 25 ELR 89; Takahashi [2001] LMCLQ 107. However, the action came within the scope of Art 5(3).

[254] Case C-334/00 [2002] ECR I-7357.

[255] Ibid, at [24]–[25].

[256] Ibid. However, this pre-contractual liability will come within Art 5(3), discussed infra, pp 247–258.

[257] *Agnew v Lansforsakringsbolagens AB* [2001] 1 AC 223, 264 (per Lord MILLETT).

[258] The *Agnew* case, supra, 240–244 (per Lord WOOLF), 233–234 (per Lord NICHOLLS), 253 (per Lord HOPE), 264 (per Lord MILLETT).

[259] Case C–27/02 *Petra Engler v Janus Versand GmbH*, supra, at [51]–[60]; *Kapferer v Schlank & Schick GmbH* [2006] IL Pr 17 at [45]–[50] of the opinion of AG TIZZANO.

[260] See the opinion of AG JACOBS in Case C–27/02 *Petra Engler v Janus Versand GmbH*, supra, at [33]; *Agnew v Lansforsakringsbolagens AB* [2001] 1 AC 223 at 240 (per Lord WOOLF), 246 (per Lord COOKE), 250 (per Lord HOPE), 233–234 (per Lord NICHOLLS).

[261] [2001] 1 AC 223 at 240 (per Lord WOOLF), 246 (per Lord COOKE), 250 (per Lord HOPE). Lord MILLETT (262–266) accepted this requirement but regarded it as falling within the concept of matters relating to a contract, as, seemingly, did Lord NICHOLLS (233–234). The latter was the view of the House of Lords in the earlier *Kleinwort* case, supra.

[262] Case C-256/00 *Besix SA v Wasserreinigungsbau Alfred Kretzschmar GmbH & Co KG (WABAG)* [2002] ECR I-1699; discussed infra, pp 240–241.

A claim for damages *SPRL Arcado v SA Haviland*[263] concerned two claims: one for the payment of commission under a commercial agency agreement; the other for damages for the wrongful premature repudiation of this agreement. The Court of Justice held that both claims came within the community concept of matters relating to a contract. The claim for commission was based on the agreement itself and thus undoubtedly was a matter relating to a contract. The claim for damages for wrongful repudiation raised more of a problem, the defendants arguing that this was based on quasi-delict. However, the Court of Justice held that this claim was also a matter relating to a contract, being based on the failure to fulfil a contractual obligation to give reasonable notice of termination. The Court found confirmation of this from the fact that the Rome Convention on contract choice of law undoubtedly regards such a claim as being contractual in nature.[264]

(ii) Disputes relating to the existence of the agreement

In *Effer v Kantner*[265] the Court of Justice held that jurisdiction under Article 5(1) of the Brussels Convention may be invoked by the claimant even where there is a dispute between the parties over the existence of the contract on which the claim is based. Courts would be too easily deprived of jurisdiction if an allegation by the defendant that no contract existed was sufficient to prevent the dispute falling within Article 5(1). The court seised of the matter may end up deciding that no contract exists but this is neither here nor there. All that matters is that this court is satisfied that the requirements of Article 5(1) are satisfied, including that it is a matter relating to a contract. When it comes to trial in England it has to be shown that there is a good arguable case that a contract exists, which may well involve going into the merits of the case.[266] Where a negative declaration is sought denying the existence of the contract the claimant can rely upon the fact that the defendant is seeking to enforce a contract against him.[267] The court whose jurisdiction is invoked under Article 5(1) may, of its own motion, examine its jurisdiction,[268] including the question of the existence of the contract, and decide that it does not have jurisdiction.

The *Effer* case involved an action for the enforcement of the performance of a contractual obligation, during the course of which the question of the existence of the contract arose as a preliminary issue.[269] Similarly, in *Boss Group Ltd v Boss France SA*[270] the Court

---

[263] Case 9/87 [1988] ECR 1539; Allwood (1988) 13 ELR 366; Briggs [1988] YEL 269; Stone [1988] LMCLQ 383.

[264] Infra, pp 755–756.

[265] Case 38/81 [1982] ECR 825; Hartley (1983) 8 ELR 235. See Art 22, Case 73/77 *Sanders v Van der Putte* [1977] ECR 2383; *Kapferer v Schlank & Schick GmbH* [2006] IL Pr 17 at [60] of the opinion of AG Tizzano.

[266] *Tesam Distribution Ltd v Shuh Mode Team GmbH* [1990] IL Pr 149; *Medway Packing Ltd v Meurer Maschinen GmbH & Co KG* [1990] 2 Lloyd's Rep 112, CA; *Rank Film Distributors Ltd v Lanterna Editrice SRL* [1992] IL Pr 58; *Deutsche Ruckversicherung AG v La Fondiara Assicurazioni SPA* [2001] 2 Lloyd's Rep 621.

[267] *Boss Group Ltd v Boss France SA*, supra at 356–357, CA.

[268] Where Art 26 of the Regulation applies the court will be under a duty to do so, see infra, p 302.

[269] This was used by Lords Clyde and Goff in the *Kleinwort Benson* case, supra, at 182 and 170, to reconcile the principle adopted by the majority of the House of Lords, that the claim must be based on a particular contractual obligation, with the decision in the *Effer* case allowing jurisdiction in relation to a dispute over the existence of the contract. But compare Lord Nicholls, Lord Mustill concurring, at 174. Lord Hutton, at 193–194, although in favour of the above principle did not attempt to reconcile it with the *Effer* case which he distinguished on the basis that it did not involve a contract accepted as being *void ab initio*.

[270] [1997] 1 WLR 351; Briggs (1996) 67 BYBIL 583; Forsyth [1996] LMCLQ 329; Peel (1996) 112 LQR 541. The decision was approved by Lord Clyde in the *Kleinwort Benson* case, supra, at 182.

of Appeal used Article 5(1) to take jurisdiction to grant the plaintiff a negative declaration that no contract existed in circumstances where the defendant was seeking to enforce a contractual obligation against the plaintiff. What would happen though if the question of the existence of the contract is the only matter in issue between the parties? Applying the principle adopted by the majority of the House of Lords in the *Kleinwort Benson* case, namely that the claim must be based on a particular contractual obligation, it cannot be said that the claim is so based and, accordingly, it would fall outside the scope of Article 5(1). Lord GOFF, obiter, expressed serious doubts regarding whether, as a general rule, a court can have jurisdiction to rule upon the validity of a contract.[271] Moreover, what would be the place of performance of the obligation in question in such a case?

(iii)   Which is the obligation in question?

A multiplicity of obligations (which may have different places of performance) can arise in complex contractual cases, yet the Regulation gives no indication in Article 5(1) as to which obligation is being referred to.

In *De Bloos v Bouyer*[272] the Court of Justice went some way towards a community definition for the obligation in question. It held that Article 5(1) of the Brussels Convention is referring not to any obligation under the contract but to the contractual obligation forming the basis of the legal proceedings, the one which the contract imposes on the defendant, the non-performance of which is relied upon by the claimant. Thus an English court had jurisdiction in a case where German defendants broke their obligation to give reasonable notice of termination of an exclusive distribution agreement to an English company in England.[273] There is a problem in identifying the obligation in question in cases where the claimant is seeking a negative declaration, ie a declaration that he is not liable to perform an obligation under the contract, on the basis that the other party has not performed a term of the contract. It has been suggested that the obligation in question is that term and not the claimant's obligation to perform the contract.[274] With certain contracts it is by no means easy to ascertain precisely what the obligations of the parties are.[275] It may also be necessary to ascertain whether an agreement has been superseded by a further

---

[271] At 170.

[272] Case 14/76 [1976] ECR 1497. See Giardina (1978) 35 ICLQ 263, 269–271; Hartley (1977) 2 ELR 60.

[273] *Medway Packaging Ltd v Meurer Maschinen GmbH & Co KG* [1990] 2 Lloyd's Rep 112, CA. See also *Waverley Asset Management Ltd v Saha* 1989 SLT (Sh Ct) 87; *Bitwise Ltd v CPS Broadcast Products BV* 2003 SLT 455.

[274] *AIG Europe (UK) Ltd v The Ethniki* [2000] 2 All ER 566, 574 at [27], CA. See also *Boss Group Ltd v Boss France SA* [1997] 1 WLR 351, CA; *Fisher v Unione Italiana de Riassicurazione SpA* [1998] CLC 682; *USF Ltd (t/a USF Memcor) v Aqua Technology Hanson NV/SA* [2001] 1 All ER (Comm) 856. The *Agnew* case, supra, would tend to support this.

[275] See generally on the parties' obligations where there is a distribution agreement: *Ferndale Films Ltd v Granada Television Ltd* [1994] IL Pr 180, Irish Supreme Court; *Boss Group Ltd v Boss France SA* [1997] 1 WLR 351, CA; *Carl Stuart Ltd v Biotrace Ltd* [1994] IL Pr 554, Irish High Court; *USF Ltd (t/a USF Memcor) v Aqua Technology Hanson NV/SA* [2001] 1 All ER (Comm) 856; *Bio-Medical Research Ltd v Delatex SA* [2001] 2 ILRM 51, Irish Supreme Court. For a concession agreement, see *Hacker Kuchen GmbH v Bosma Huygen Meubelimpex BV (Case 14.197)* [1992] IL Pr 379. For licences see *Rank Film Distributors v Lanterna Editrice Srl* [1992] IL Pr 58; *Olympia Productions Ltd v Mackintosh* [1992] ILRM 204. See generally on the above agreements, Fawcett and Torremans, pp 79–89. There can also be problems with a sale of goods contract: see *Viskase Ltd v Paul Kiefel GmbH* [1999] 1 WLR 1305, CA, Briggs (1999) 70 BYBIL 336; *MBM Fabri-Clad Ltd v Eisen-Und Huttenwerke Thale AG* [2000] IL Pr 505, CA, Fawcett, Harris and Bridge, paras 3.109–3.141; and with a settlement contract, see *Kenburn Waste Management Ltd v Bergmann* [2002] CLC 644, CA.

agreement imposing separate contractual obligations, one of which is being relied upon.[276] Moreover, if the claimant is seeking compensation a decision then has to be made as to whether this claim involves an independent contractual obligation (and therefore falls within Article 5(1)), or whether it involves a new obligation replacing the unperformed contractual obligation (which would be outside Article 5(1)). There is no consensus among the legal systems of the different Member States as to which of these two is the source of the right to claim compensation. The national court where trial is sought is therefore left to decide this in the light of the law applicable to the contract under its private international law rules. If English law applies, an obligation to pay unliquidated damages cannot form the basis of jurisdiction under Article 5(1) since this obligation is remedial in character, not an independent contractual obligation.[277]

A particular difficulty with the *De Bloos* approach is that the claimant may make several claims involving different obligations to be performed in different States. This problem was solved by the Court of Justice in *Shenavai v Kreischer*.[278] The judge dealing with the case is to identify the principal obligation on which the claimant's action is based and jurisdiction is to be determined in accordance with this. Thus, if the defendant shipowners are in breach of obligations under a charter-party to, first, nominate a vessel (this obligation to be performed in London) and, secondly, provide a vessel for the carriage of cargo (this obligation to be performed in Florida) the first obligation is the principal one, since it is the performance of this obligation that triggers other obligations.[279] The plaintiff is not allowed to camouflage the principal obligation by relegating it to a subordinate role by the way he chooses to express his claim.[280] If all the obligations are to be performed in the same country, there is no need to identify the principal obligation.[281] In the situation where the action is founded on two obligations of equal rank arising from the same contract, one obligation to be performed in one Member State and the other in another Member State, the same court does not have jurisdiction to hear the whole of an action.[282]

---

[276] *W H Martin Ltd v Felbinder Spezialfahrzeugwerke GmbH* [1998] IL Pr 794, CA.

[277] *Medway Packaging Ltd v Meurer Maschinen GmbH & Co KG* [1990] 1 Lloyd's Rep 383 at 389, HOBHOUSE J at first instance. The Court of Appeal did not discuss this point.

[278] Case 266/85 [1987] ECR 239; Allwood (1988) 13 ELR 60. See also *Campbell International Trading House Ltd v Peter Van Aart* [1992] 2 IR 305; *Ferndale Films Ltd v Granada Television Ltd* [1994] IL Pr 180, Irish Supreme Court; *Carl Stuart Ltd v Biotrace Ltd*, supra; *Gascoigne v Pyrah* [1994] IL Pr 82, CA; *Raiffeisen Zentral Bank Österreich Aktiengesellschaft v National Bank of Greece SA* [1999] 1 Lloyd's Rep 408; *Rank Film Distributors v Lanterna Editrice Srl* [1992] IL Pr 58; *AIG Europe v The Ethniki* [1998] 4 All ER 301, affd [2000] 2 All ER 566, CA; *Bitwise Ltd v CPS Broadcast Products BV* 2003 SLT 455.

[279] *Union Transport plc v Continental Lines SA* [1992] 1 WLR 15, HL; Briggs (1992) 108 LQR 186. For characterisation of the principal obligation in cases of: a bill of lading, see *RPS Prodotti Siderurgici srl v Owners and/or demise charterers of the Sea Maas, The Sea Maas* [2000] 1 All ER 536; carriage by road, see *Royal & Sun Alliance Insurance plc v MK Digital FZE (Cyprus) Ltd* [2006] EWCA Civ 629 at [87]–[105], [2006] 2 Lloyd's Rep 110; reinsurance, see *AIG Europe (UK) Ltd v The Ethniki* [2000] 2 All ER 566, CA; supply and delivery of goods, see *MBM Fabri-Clad Ltd v Eisen-Und Huttenwerke Thale AG* [2000] IL Pr 505, CA; a letter of credit, see *Crédit Agricole Indosuez v Chailease Finance Corpn* [2000] 1 Lloyd's Rep 348, CA; accountancy services, see *Barry v Bradshaw* [2000] IL Pr 706, CA.

[280] *The Ethniki*, supra, 573 at [25].

[281] *Boss Group Ltd v Boss France SA* [1997] 1 WLR 351, CA.

[282] Case C-420/97 *Leathertex Divisione Sinetici SpA v Bodetex BVBA* [1999] ECR I-6747, at [36]; Panagopoulos [2000] LMCLQ 150; Peel (2001) 20 YEL 331; distinguished in *The Ethniki*, op cit, 573 at [26], CA.

For the purposes of Article 5(1) the claims are split up and tried before the courts of different Member States. However, the claimant can avoid this by bringing the whole of the action in the Member State in which the defendant is domiciled.

(iv)   The place of performance of the obligation in question

One of the major innovations introduced by the Brussels I Regulation has been to introduce in Article 5(1)(b)[283] an autonomous definition of the place of performance of the obligation in question. The Brussels Convention contained no such definition[284] and the Court of Justice was not prepared to provide one. Instead, the place of performance of the obligation in question under Article 5(1) of the Brussels Convention was determined by the forum applying its rules of private international law. In *Tessili v Dunlop*[285] the Court of Justice held that the national court before which the matter is brought "must determine in accordance with its own rules of conflict of laws what is the law applicable to the legal relationship in question and define in accordance with that law the place of performance of the contractual obligation in question".[286] The autonomous definition was introduced to remedy the shortcomings in the *Tessili* approach,[287] which was criticised by academics[288] and by Advocates General.[289] Criticisms include the fact that it leads to a lack of harmonisation in the law of jurisdiction[290] and that the process that has to be gone through is undeniably complex and difficult to apply.[291] The Court of Justice has accepted that the *Tessili* approach can lead to jurisdiction being allocated to a forum which is not the one that has the closest connection with the dispute.[292] The autonomous definition is designed to reinforce the unification of the rules of jurisdiction whilst ensuring their predictability.[293] Article 5(1)(b) represents a compromise between the Member States, some of which wanted to retain the existing rule and others to abolish Article 5(1) altogether.[294] Article 5(1)(b) does not attempt to define the place of performance for every contractual obligation. Instead, it concentrates on the place of performance for two commonly encountered types of contract, namely ones for the sale of goods and the provision of services, rather than for particular obligations. When laying

---

[283]   See Fawcett, Harris and Bridge, paras 3.143–3.235, 3.298–3.301; Takahashi, (2002) 27 ELR 530.

[284]   Apart from for individual contracts of employment.

[285]   Case 12/76 [1976] ECR 1473. See Giardina (1978) 35 ICLQ 263, 271–272; Hartley (1977) 2 ELR 59. This decision was confirmed by the Court of Justice in: Case C-288/92 *Custom Made Commercial Ltd v Stawa Metallbau GmbH* [1994] ECR I-2913, Briggs (1994) 14 YEL 573; and in Case C-440/97 *GIE Groupe Concorde v The Master of the Vessel Suhadiwarno Panjan* [1999] ECR I-6307, at 6354 [33], Peel (2001) 20 YEL 331; the *Leathertex* case, supra, at 6791 [33].

[286]   [1976] ECR 1473 at 1485.

[287]   See the Explanatory Memorandum in the Proposal for a Council Regulation COM (1999) 348 final, p 14.

[288]   See Kennett *Yearbook of European Law* (1995), p 193; Anton and Beaumont, p 101; Hil (1995) ICLQ 591, 618; Reed [1997] NILQ 243. But for a defence of the rule see Briggs and Rees, para 2.129.

[289]   AG Leger in the *Leathertex* case, supra, AG Lenz In the *Custom Made* case, supra, and AG Ruiz-Jarabo Colomer in the *GIE* case, supra. See also AG Bot in Case C-386/05 *Color Drack GmbH v LEXX International Vertriebs GmbH* [2007] IL Pr 35 at [54]–[77].

[290]   AG Leger in the *Leathertex* case, supra, [128].

[291]   See AG Ruiz-Jarabo Colomer in the *GIE* case, supra, at 874–875. This has led to resistance from national courts, particularly in France, to applying the *Tessili* approach, see Droz [1997] Rec Dalloz 351, AG Ruiz-Jarabo Colomer in the *GIE* case, supra, at 878.

[292]   Case C-288/92 *Custom Made Commercial Ltd v Stawa Metallbau GmbH* [1994] ECR I-2913 at 2956–2957.

[293]   Case C-386/05 *Color Drack GmbH v LEXX International Vertriebs GmbH* [2007] IL Pr 35 at [24].

[294]   See Beaumont in Fawcett *Reform and Development of Private International Law*, p 15 et seq.

down the autonomous definition for each of these two types of contract Article 5(1)(b) applies the same definition, regardless of the obligation on which the claim is based.

The scope of Article 5(1)(b)   There are two clear limitations on the scope of Article 5(1)(b).[295] First, it is explicitly provided that the case must be one of the "sale of goods" or the "provision of services". Neither concept is defined in the Regulation. It is easier to say what each concept does not cover than what it does. We know from other provisions in the Regulation that "sale of goods" and "provision of services" do not cover insurance contracts, individual contracts of employment and consumer contracts. Neither, when working out the meaning of "sale of goods", does this cover the provision of services and vice versa. Turning to what "sale of goods" does cover, it is important to note that twenty-one of the twenty-six European Community Member States subject to the Brussels I Regulation are parties to the UN Convention on the International Sale of Goods (CISG) of 1980 (the Vienna Convention). The concept of sale of goods under that Convention represents the corpus of most of the legal systems of the Member States. It is submitted therefore that one should turn to the meaning of "sale of goods" under the Vienna Convention to answer the question of what is covered by the words "sale of goods" in Article 5(1)(b). This is helpful in determining whether a contract for the supply of goods to be manufactured is one for the "sale of goods". It also tells us that "goods" should be given a broad meaning to include minerals and crops and should also encompass the sale of software, whether contained on a disk or transferred over the internet.[296] On the other hand, "sale of goods" should not cover the sale of ships, since such sales are excluded from the Vienna Convention. The concept of the "provision of services" should be given an independent community meaning. A number of instruments refer to this concept and it is to these that one should turn for guidance—in particular, the European Community Directive on services in the internal market.[297] The concept covers not only professional services such as contracts for accountancy advice,[298] to design a website,[299] devising advertising material,[300] or contracts to act as commercial agent for someone,[301] but also the separate autonomous contracts under a letter of credit,[302] reinsurance contracts,[303] contracts of carriage, contracts for the inspection of goods, and franchise contracts.[304] However, the

---

[295] For these and other possible limitations, see Fawcett, Harris and Bridge, paras 3.146–3.170. A third possible limitation is that the contract contains no term as to the place of delivey of goods or place of provision of services: *Scottish & Newcastle International Ltd v Othon Ghalanos Ltd* [2008] UKHL 11 at [3] (per Lord BINGHAM obiter).

[296] For business to business e-commerce, see Fawcett, Harris and Bridge, paras 10.42–10.53. For licensing agreements, see infra, p 243.

[297] Directive (EC) No 2006/123 of 27 December 2006, Art 4 (any self-employed economic activity, normally provided for remuneration, as referred to in Art 50 of the Treaty) OJ 2006 L 376/36. A service provider can include a legal person as well as a natural person. Recitals (17)–(24) also refer to: transport services, financial services, postal services, electronic communications services, healthcare and pharmaceutical services, audiovisual services. See Fawcett, Harris and Bridge, para 3.300.

[298] See *Barry v Bradshaw* [2000] IL Pr 706, CA. But cf *Benatti v WPP Holdings Italy SRL* [2007] EWCA Civ 263 at [56]–[57] (per TOULSON LJ)—contract to act as a consultant not covered, [2007] 1 WLR 2316.

[299] *1st Mover APS v Direct Hedge SA* [2003] IL Pr 31, Eastern Court of Appeal, Denmark.

[300] *Société ND Conseil SA v Société Le Meridien Hotels* [2007] IL Pr 39, French Cour de Cassation.

[301] *Solinas v Société Fabrica Textil Riopele* [2007] IL Pr 7, French Cour de Cassation. See also a decision of the same court on 11 July 2006 concerning Wema Post Maschinen.

[302] But cf Beaumont in Fawcett (ed), *Reform and Development of Private International Law*, pp 22–23.

[303] These fall outside Section 3 and therefore within Art 5(1), see infra, pp 266–268.

[304] See Recital (17) of the Rome I Regulation.

"provision of services" should be interpreted as not covering contracts relating to a right in rem or a tenancy of immovable property.[305] Further guidance on the meaning of services can be found by looking at examples of contracts held to fall outside Article 5(1)(b) generally.[306] Distribution agreements involve elements of both sale and service and are therefore difficult to classify. This has led to the suggestion that they should fall outside the scope of Article 5(1)(b).[307] The typical arrangement is that the distribution agreement is the main contract (between A and B). This probably should be regarded as one for the provision of services.[308] But flowing from this will be a series of sale of goods contracts between A and B, with B re-selling the goods to C.[309]

The second clear limitation on the scope of Article 5(1)(b) is implicit from the part of Article 5(1)(b) that allocates jurisdiction. This is that the goods were delivered or should have been delivered/services were provided or should have been provided in *a place in a Member State*.

One final observation that should be made about the scope of Article 5(1)(b) relates to its width. It "applies regardless of the obligation in question, even where this obligation is the payment of the financial consideration for the contract. It also applies where the claim relates to several obligations."[310] This means that if goods are delivered in England the English courts will have jurisdiction under Article 5(1), even though the claim is for payment for the goods.[311] The width of the rule can be justified on the basis that delivery characterises the contract of sale,[312] and providing the service characterises the contract for the provision of services. At first sight this might suggest that it is no longer necessary to identify the obligation in question in cases of sale of goods[313] or the provision of services. However, this is still necessary because of the possibility of displacement of the place of delivery/provision of services rule that operates in such cases by an agreement on the place of performance of the obligation in question.

The place in a Member State where, under the contract, the goods were delivered or should have been delivered   Article 5(1)(b) allocates jurisdiction to the place where, "under the contract",

---

[305] See Art 4(1)(c) of the Rome I Regulation.

[306] Infra, p 243.

[307] See Briggs and Rees, para 2.128; Beaumont, op cit, p 20.

[308] See Recital (17) of the Rome I Regulation; the opinion of AG Leger in the *Leathertex* case, supra, at 6770 [130], n 55. But cf *Waeco International GmbH v Cardon*, French Cour de cassation [2007] IL Pr 38—neither sales nor service; *General Motors Ireland Ltd v SES-ASA Protection SpA* [2006] 1 ILRM 63 at 69–70—regarding the head contract as one for the sale of goods; *Nestorway Ltd v Ambaflex BV* [2006] IEHC 235, [2007] IL Pr 48—breach of exclusive distribution agreement involved neither sales nor service.

[309] See *General Motors Ireland*, supra, at 68.

[310] See the Explanatory Memorandum, in the Proposal for a Council Regulation COM (1999) 348 final, p 14; the opinion of AG Bot in Case C-386/05 *Color Drack GmbH v LEXX International Vertriebs GmbH* [2007] IL Pr 35 at [88] and the Court of Justice at [26].

[311] See the opinion of AG Bot in Case C-386/05 *Color Drack GmbH v LEXX International Vertriebs GmbH* [2007] IL Pr 35 at para 89; *Comet Group plc v Unika Computer SA* [2004] IL Pr 1. However, in such a case the displacement rule may apply, see infra, pp 242–243.

[312] *Color Drack*, supra, at [38], Court of Justice; AG Mayras in the *Tessili* case, supra; Takahashi, op cit, at 534. See also the importance attached to delivery by the Court of Appeal in the *MBM Fabri-Clad* and *Viskase* cases, supra, and by the Court of Session House in Scotland in *Ferguson Shipbuilders Ltd v Voith Hydro GmbH & Co KG* 2000 SLT 229 and in *Eddie v Alpa Srl* 2000 SLT 1062.

[313] Under the old law (ie the Brussels Convention) identification of the obligation in question dictated the place of performance in a sales case, see the *MBM Fabri-Clad* and *Viskase* cases, supra.

the goods were delivered or should have been delivered. This means that, when ascertaining this place, recourse must be had to the terms of the contract as agreed by the parties. The sales contract may, for example, expressly provide for delivery ex works or for delivery at frontier. In the situation where, according to English principles of sale of goods, delivery of goods as well as property and risk in respect of them has taken place upon shipment, that place must be treated as being the place of delivery for the purposes of Article 5(1)(b), not the place of ultimate destination of the goods.[314] The parties, by agreeing on the place of delivery, are effectively choosing the place to be allocated jurisdiction. Nonetheless there is no requirement that the formalities under Article 23 have to be met. In the absence of such an express agreement by the parties on the place of delivery, it may be possible to imply an agreement from the terms of the contract. It should also be possible to imply an agreement from the circumstances of the case, such as from the fact that the parties have contracted before and delivery has always been to one particular place. In the absence of an express or implied agreement as to the place of delivery, there is considerable uncertainty as to whether Article 5(1)(b) applies at all and, if it does, how the place where the goods were delivered or should have been delivered is to be identified. It is submitted that Article 5(1)(b) should still apply in this situation and that an autonomous community definition should be given to the concept of the place where the goods were delivered and the concept of the place where goods should have been delivered. This definition could be based on the substantive law rule on the place of delivery in the absence of agreement that applies under the Vienna Convention.[315]

Numerous problems arise with the place of delivery rule.[316] Two of the most obvious are as follows. First, what happens if goods are delivered to more than one place and these are in different Member States?[317]

> For example, asssume that there is a contract for the sale of 10,000 tons of grain, 3,000 tons to be delivered to England and 7,000 tons to Germany. All 10,000 tons are rendered defective by contact with a previous cargo. The claimant wishes to sue in one Member State in respect of the whole 10,000 tons. Article 5(1)(b) should not operate in this situation to give jurisdiction in respect of the whole 10,000 tons to both England and Germany, thereby giving the claimant a choice of fora.[318]

In *Besix SA v Wasserreinigungsbau Alfred Kretzschmar GmbH & Co KG (WABAG)*,[319] the Court of Justice held that Article 5(1) of the Brussels Convention had to be interpreted as meaning that, in the event that the relevant contractual obligation has been, or is to be,

---

[314] *Scottish & Newcastle International Ltd v Othon Ghalanos Ltd* [2008] UKHL 11. The contract was to all intents and purposes an FOB one, albeit described as a CFR contract in invoices. Lord MANCE, at [49]–[55], suggested, obiter, that the place of shipment should be regarded as the place of delivery for all types of FOB contract, even where the seller retains symbolic possession of the goods through the bills of lading until the goods are forwarded or received by the buyer. Lords BINGHAM, at [7], and RODGER, at [81]–[21], reserved their position on this. Lords BROWN and NEUBERGER made no comment on this.

[315] See Art 31 of the Vienna Convention.

[316] See Fawcett, Harris and Bridge, paras 3.204–3.226 and, for the place of delivery in cases of e-commerce, paras 10.55–10.75.

[317] Where the places of delivery are in the same Member State Art 5(1)(b) will apply and the court in the area of the principal place of delivery will have jurisdiction to hear all the claims based on the contract of sale: Case C-386/05 *Color Drack GmbH v LEXX International Vertriebs GmbH* [2007] IL Pr 35.

[318] Cf Art 6 of the preliminary draft Hague Judgments Convention.

[319] Case C-256/00 [2003] 1 WLR 327.

performed in a number of places, jurisdiction to hear and determine the case cannot be conferred on the court within whose jurisdiction any one of those places of performance happens to be located.[320] Instead, jurisdiction has to be based on Article 2. It was clear from the wording of the provision, which is in the singular (the place of performance), that a single place of performance for the obligation in question must be identified.[321] The Court was concerned to avoid a multiplicity of competent courts and the risk that the plaintiff is able to choose the place of performance which he judges to be most favourable to his interests. An alternative way of achieving a single court with jurisdiction over the whole of the goods would be to allocate jurisdiction to the court of the principal place of delivery, determined on the basis of economic criteria. This was the solution adopted by the Court of Justice in a case involving several places of delivery within the same Member State.[322] The position is more difficult in the situation where the claimant wishes to sue in England for merely the 3,000 tons delivered there. Again there is no single place of performance for the obligation to deliver but it is arguable that this does not fall foul of the spirit of the *Besix* case. There is not a multiplicity of competent fora in respect of the whole 10,000 tons. Neither does the claimant have a choice of bringing the action for the whole 10,000 tons in two different fora.

Secondly, what happens if there is a fictitious place of delivery, ie the contract provides for delivery in a place when this is designed not to determine where delivery will actually take place, but solely to establish that the courts of a particular place have jurisdiction? That this is the aim can be shown by the fact that a place of delivery has been designated which has no connection with the reality of the contract and the obligations under the contract, obligations which, because of their very nature or because of geographical fact, can only be performed in some other country.[323] Goods may then be delivered to this other country (Member State A), rather than to the fictitious place of delivery (Member State B). An attempt may be made to bring an action in the fictitious place of delivery (Member State B) on the basis that, under the contract, goods "should have been delivered" there within the wording of Article 5(1)(b). The Court of Justice has held that where there is a fictitious place of performance, this is governed not by Article 5(1) of the Brussels Convention but by Article 17 (Article 23 of the Brussels I Regulation) and the requirements of that provision must be met.[324] In other words, the fictitious place of performance is treated as an attempted jurisdiction clause. The same approach should be adopted towards a fictitious place of delivery, given that the place of delivery rule is being used to determine the place of performance of the obligation in question.

There are also problems: where there is delivery to alternative places; a deemed place of delivery; constructive delivery; a floating place of delivery; an agreement on the place of

---

[320] Ibid, at [28]. See also *Mora Shipping Inc v Axa Corporate Solutions Assurance SA* [2005] EWCA Civ 1069 at [21], [2005] 2 Lloyd's Rep 769.

[321] The *Besix* case, supra, at [29], [32]. See also Case C-386/05 *Color Drack GmbH v LEXX International Vertriebs GmbH* [2007] IL Pr 35 at [38].

[322] Case C-386/05 *Color Drack GmbH v LEXX International Vertriebs GmbH* [2007] IL Pr 35. This was without prejudice to the position where the places of delivery are in several Member States, see [16]. Where the principal place cannot be determined, the plaintiff may sue in the place of delivery of its choice (at [46]). This solution would not work in a case involving several Member States.

[323] Case C-106/95 *MSG v Gravières Rhénanes* [1997] ECR I-911.

[324] Case C-106/95 *MSG v Gravières Rhénanes* [1997] ECR I-911.

delivery entered into after the contract was made; a refusal to accept delivery; and identifying the place of delivery in cases of e-commerce.[325]

Jurisdiction is allocated to the place where the goods were delivered or *should have been delivered*. This deals with cases of non delivery and mis-delivery. Thus if goods are delivered to England when, under the contract, they should have been delivered to France, the place of performance of the obligation in question under Article 5(1)(b) will be France, rather than England.

The place in a Member State where, under the contract, the services were provided or should have been provided   Everything said in the previous section about the meaning of "under the contract" applies equally to this provision. Likewise the reference to the place where services should have been provided deals with cases of non-provision of services and mis-provision in the sense of a party providing services in the wrong place. When it comes to identification of the place in a Member State where, under the contract, the services were provided or should have been provided, the situation is analogous to that of identification of the place in a Member State where, under the contract, the goods were delivered or should have been delivered. Analogous problems can arise. For example, services may be provided in more than one place and these are in different Member States. For instance a distributor will commonly agree to distribute goods in a number of Member States. The solution to this is the same as for the delivery of goods in a number of different Member States. In practical terms it is unlikely to matter whether a contract is classified as one for the sale of goods or as one for the provision of services since both rules are likely to point to the same place. This though is not to deny that the operation of the services rule may throw up certain problems that may not arise or are less likely to arise under the sale of goods rule. A letter of credit, payment under which should be regarded as the provision of a service, may provide that "we shall pay you as per your instructions". This is a floating place of payment; there is no identifiable place of payment as at the time the contract is concluded but there is a mechanism for identifying this place and this place will crystallise later, when the beneficiary gives his instructions. Effect has been given by the Court of Appeal to a floating place of payment in a letter of credit for the purposes of identifying the place of performance of the obligation in question under Article 5(1) of the Brussels Convention.[326] However, this has now to be read in the light of the *Besix* case. If the payee nominating the place of payment is the claimant, he is effectively being given a choice of fora, which was a concern in the *Besix* case, and therefore jurisdiction cannot be conferred by Article 5(1) of the Brussels Convention and now Regulation. The same principle should apply where there is a floating place of delivery under a sale of goods contract.

Displacement where it is otherwise agreed   The special rule that operates in the case of the sale of goods and in the case of the provision of services is subject to the proviso that it applies "unless otherwise agreed". This proviso reduces the weakness in Article 5(1)(b) whereby it subjects all obligations, not just the obligation to deliver goods and the obligation to provide services, to the place of delivery of goods/provision of services.

---

[325] See Fawcett, Harris and Bridge, paras 3.142–3.301.
[326] *Crédit Agricole Indosuez v Chailease Finance Corpn* [2000] 1 Lloyd's Rep 348, CA.

Let us assume that goods have been delivered in Spain but it has been agreed that payment shall be made in England. The claimant wishes to sue in England for non-payment. The place of performance of the obligation to pay will be in England by virtue of the displacement rule. The displacement rule tells us that the place of delivery rule does not apply and then Article 5(1)(b) implicitly allocates jurisdiction to the place of performance of the obligation in question agreed by the parties.

For the displacement rule to apply there are three requirements. First, there must be an agreement. The European Community Commission seem to envisage that the agreement will be "explicit" but there is no reason in principle why an implicit agreement should not suffice. Nor is there any reason why the agreement should have to be in the sales/services contract. Secondly, the agreement must be on the place of performance of the obligation in question. Under the displacement rule it is vital to identify the obligation in question and hence its agreed place of performance. The agreed place of performance must not be a fictitious one, ie designed not to determine the place where the person liable is actually to perform the obligations incumbent on him, but solely to establish that the courts for a particular place have jurisdiction.[327] Thirdly, this agreed place must be somewhere other than where the goods were delivered or should have been delivered/services were provided or should have been provided.

Cases falling outside the scope of Article 5(1)(b)   Article 5(1)(c) is concerned with the situation where Article 5(1)(b) does not apply. Examples of contracts which are neither for the sale of goods nor the provision of services are a contract for the assignment of intellectual property rights,[328] a licensing agreement, an agreement to provide a joint tender for a construction project,[329] a contract for the payment of a prize,[330] a contract whereby a person received a percentage participation in an oil concession.[331] It has been assumed that Article 5(1)(c) will apply to an average guaranteee entered into between shipowners and cargo insurers,[332] and a loan agreement under a salvage agreement.[333] A further example is a contract relating to a right in rem or to a tenancy of immovable property.[334] Moreover, a contract for the sale of goods would fall outside the scope of Article 5(1)(b) in the situation where delivery is made or should have been made in a non-Member State.

Article 5(1)(c) provides that if 5(1)(b) does not apply then Article 5(1)(a) applies. Applying this last provision it is necesssary to identify the place of performance of the obligation in question. It is not entirely clear how this is to be done. The EC Commission

---

[327] *7E Communications Ltd v Vertex Antennentechnik GmbH* [2007] EWCA Civ 140 at [50], [2007] 1 WLR 2175; Case C-106/95 *Mainschiffahrts-Genossenschaft eG (MSG) v Les Gravières Rhénanes Sarl* [1997] QB 731; discussed infra, p 244.

[328] This falls outside the definition of services under Art 4 of the European Community Directive on services in the intenal market, supra, p 238.

[329] See the opinion of AG ALBER in Case C-256/00 *Besix SA v Wasserreinigungsbau Alfred Kretzschmar GmbH & Co KG (WABAG)* [2002] ECR I-1699, 1713–1714, [48].

[330] *Kapferer v Schlank & Schick GmbH* [2006] IL Pr 17 at [64] of the opinion of AG TIZZANO.

[331] *Masri v Consolidated Contractors International (UK) Ltd* [2005] EWHC 944 (Comm) at [74] and [99], affd without discussion of this point [2005] EWCA Civ 1436, [2006] 1 WLR 830.

[332] *Mora Shipping Inc v Axa Corporate Solutions Assurance SA* [2005] EWCA Civ 1069 at [21], [2005] 2 Lloyd's Rep 769.

[333] *Tavoulareas v Tsavliris* [2005] EWHC 2140 (Comm) at [48]–[55], [2006] 1 All ER (Comm), 109.

[334] Supra, pp 238–239.

envisages that this place will be identified using the traditional approach adopted by the Court of Justice in the *Tessili* case in relation to Article 5(1) of the Brussels Convention and the Court of Justice, and national courts have unthinkingly done this. [335] This is the natural solution, which has the advantage of familiarity. Reliance can be placed on the existing case law under Article 5(1) of the Brussels Convention. The alternative, and less desirable, solution would be for the Court of Justice to provide an autonomous definition for the place of performance of the obligation in question. This could be geared to the type of contract involved. This would involve considerable uncertainty until precedents have been built up.

The traditional approach in the *Tessili* case requires the national court: first, to determine in accordance with its own rules of conflict of laws[336] what is the law applicable to the legal relationship in question; and, secondly, to define in accordance with that law the place of performance of the contractual obligation in question.[337] Examination of the substantive domestic law of Member States shows that the same general approach towards determining the place of performance is applied throughout the European Community.[338] First, effect is given to an express stipulation as to the place of performance in the contract. It is common to find such an express stipulation. This can be done in an informal way without the formalities required for an agreement as to jurisdiction under Article 23,[339] even though the effect of such a contractual provision is to lead indirectly, by reason of Article 5(1), to a particular court having jurisdiction.[340] However, there is a qualification to this in the case of a fictitious place of performance.[341] If the agreement on the place of performance is designed not to determine the place where the person liable is actually to perform the obligations incumbent on him, but solely to establish that the courts for a particular place have jurisdiction, this is governed not by Article 5(1) but by Article 23, and the requirements of that provision must be met.[342] Moreover, a floating place of performance should not be permissible in the situation where the claimant is the person nominating the place of performance.[343] The only other proviso is that the clause specifying the place of performance must be valid under the law applicable to the contract.[344]

Secondly, in the absence of an express stipulation, it may be possible to imply a choice by the parties. This is a question of contractual interpretation. Thirdly, if this does not produce an answer each Member State has residual rules which determine the place of performance. It is at this stage that the question of the applicable law may become crucial,

---

[335] *Kapferer v Schlank & Schick GmbH* [2006] IL Pr 17, the opinion of AG Tizzano at [64]–[65]. See also *Masri v Consolidated Contractors International (UK) Ltd* [2005] EWHC 944 (Comm) at [99], affd without discussion of this point [2005] EWCA Civ 1436, [2006] 1 WLR 830; *Mora Shipping Inc v Axa Corporate Solutions Assurance SA* [2005] EWCA Civ 1069 at [21], [2005] 2 Lloyd's Rep 769; *Tavoulareas v Tsavliris* [2005] EWHC 2140 (Comm) at [48]–[55], [2006] 1 All ER (Comm), 109.

[336] See the Rome Convention, discussed infra, pp 667–764; Forsyth and Moser (1996) 45 ICLQ 190.

[337] [1976] ECR 1473 at 1485.

[338] See Kennett (1995) 15 YEL, p 193 et seq.

[339] Art 23 is discussed infra, pp 291–294.

[340] Case 56/79 *Zelger v Salinitri* [1980] ECR 89; noted by Hartley (1981) 3 ELR 61.

[341] Discussed supra, p 241.

[342] Case C-106/95 *Mainschiffahrts-Genossenschaft eG (MSG) v Les Gravières Rhénanes Sarl* [1997] QB 731; Hartley (1997) 22 ELR 360.

[343] Supra, p 241.

[344] The *Zelger* case, supra. See generally on the law applicable to the contract, infra, pp 667–764.

since these national rules sometimes provide different solutions.[345] For example, Member States differ on whether, in the absence of a stipulation on the due place of payment, the obligation to pay must be performed in the creditor's place of business or in the debtor's. [346]

An obligation performable in a number of places   As has been seen, the *Besix* case[347] establishes that, in the event that the relevant contractual obligation has been, or is to be, performed in a number of places, jurisdiction to hear and determine the case cannot be conferred by Article 5(1) of the Brussels Convention on the court within whose jurisdiction any one of those places of performance happens to be located.[348] Instead, jurisdiction has to be based on Article 2. A single place of performance for the obligation in question must be identified.[349] The *Besix* case concerned the situation where the place of performance of the obligation in question could not be determined because it consisted of an undertaking by the defendants not to do something (not to commit themselves to other partners) which was not subject to any geographical limit and was therefore characterised by a multiplicity of places of its performance.[350] The place of performance, in effect, was in any place in the world, including all the Contracting States to the Convention.

> **Article 5(2)** in matters relating to maintenance, in the courts for the place where the maintenance creditor is domiciled or habitually resident or, if the matter is ancillary to proceedings concerning the status of a person, in the court which, according to its own law, has jurisdiction to entertain those proceedings, unless that jurisdiction is based solely on the nationality of one of the parties.[351]

A maintenance creditor has the option to sue in his domicile or habitual residence under Article 5(2) or in the defendant's domicile (under Article 2). The Court of Justice[352] has given the concept of a "maintenance creditor" an autonomous Community meaning. This covers any person applying for maintenance, including a person bringing a maintenance action for the first time.[353] A "maintenance creditor" does not need to have obtained a maintenance order recognising her or his entitlement to maintenance. This provision is a rare case where the Regulation uses the concept of habitual residence. The domicile

---

[345] See *Definitely Maybe (Touring) Ltd v Marek Lieberberg Konzertagentur GmbH (No 2)* [2001] 1 WLR 1745; *Mercury Publicity Ltd v Wolfgang Loerke GmbH* [1993] IL Pr 142, CA; Forsyth and Moser (1996) 45 ICLQ 190 at 193.

[346] See the *Definitely Maybe* case, supra; *Bank of Scotland v Seitz* 1990 SLT 584; *Tavoulareas v Tsavliris* [2005] EWHC 2140 (Comm) at [52], [2006] 1 All ER (Comm), 109.

[347] Case C-256/00 *Besix SA v Wasserreinigungsbau Alfred Kretzschmar GmbH & Co KG (WABAG)* [2002] ECR I-1699, [2003] 1 WLR 327; discussed supra, pp 240–241.

[348] Ibid, 1727 at [28]. See also *Mora Shipping Inc v Axa Corporate Solutions Assurance SA* [2005] EWCA Civ 1069 at [21], [2005] 2 Lloyd's Rep 769.

[349] Ibid, 1727 at [29], [32].

[350] The earlier decision of the Court of Appeal in *Boss Group Ltd v Boss France SA* [1997] 1 WLR 351, where jurisdiction was taken under Art 5(1) of the Brussels Convention in a case involving a negative obligation performable "everywhere", including in England and France, can no longer be followed.

[351] Maintenance jurisdiction generally is discussed infra, p 1050 et seq. Under the Proposal for a Council Regulation on jurisdiction, applicable law, recognition and enforcement of decisions and co-operation in matters relating to maintenance obligations COM (2005) 649 final, new jurisdictional rules will replace those in Brussels I.

[352] Case C-295/95 *Farrell v Long* [1997] QB 842. See also *Moore v Moore* [2007] EWCA Civ 361 at [80], [86], [2007] IL Pr 36.

[353] The paternity of a child may still be in issue.

of an individual is defined under the Civil Jurisdiction and Judgments Order 2001[354] in a way that is so close to the English concept of habitual residence[355] that the use of habitual residence as an alternative to domicile under Article 5(2) is unlikely to widen the scope of that provision. Nonetheless, Article 5(2) is more obviously pro-claimant in its terms than any of the other forms of special jurisdiction in Article 5. It is designed to protect the weaker party, the maintenance creditor,[356] and is akin to the measures designed to protect the weaker party found under Sections 3, 4 and 5 of Chapter II of the Regulation.[357] At the same time, the claimant's domicile is an appropriate forum for trial, since a court there is best able to gauge the claimant's needs.[358]

Although Article 5(2) allows an action to be brought in the maintenance creditor's domicile or habitual residence, it does not say that this right is confined to the maintenance creditor. However, a public body which seeks reimbursement from the maintenance debtor of sums paid by way of an education grant to a maintenance creditor, to whose rights it is subrogated, cannot rely on Article 5(2).[359] This is because the public body is not in a weaker position with regard to the maintenance debtor.[360]

The major definitional problem that has arisen so far has been over the meaning of "matters relating to maintenance". This concept has already been discussed in relation to the scope of the Regulation.[361] One particular aspect of this which should be mentioned here is the problem posed by the practice of combining maintenance claims (which on their own are within the Regulation) with main proceedings for divorce (which on their own are outside the scope of the Regulation). The Court of Justice held that these ancillary claims for maintenance were within the scope of the Brussels Convention.[362] Article 5(2) of the Brussels Convention was, however, amended so as expressly to give jurisdiction in respect of the maintenance claim to the court which has jurisdiction, according to its own law, to entertain the proceedings as to status.[363] The language of Article 5(2) of the Regulation is identical to the amended Brussels Convention. To take an example of how this will affect the jurisdiction of the English courts to grant maintenance: there is jurisdiction to grant a divorce if, inter alia, the spouses are habitually resident or domiciled in England;[364] if one of these bases of jurisdiction is satisfied, the English courts will not only be able to grant a divorce but will also be able to grant maintenance where there are maintenance proceedings which are ancillary to the divorce proceedings. Where a maintenance

---

[354] See supra, pp 210–211.

[355] Discussed supra, pp 185–195.

[356] Case C-433/01 *Freistaat Bayern v Jan Blijdenstein* [2004] ECR I-981, at [29]; [2004] IL Pr 8.

[357] Infra, pp 266–275. For a criticism of the policy in relation to maintenance, see Hartley, pp 49–50.

[358] See the Jenard Report, p 25.

[359] Case C-433/01 *Freistaat Bayern v Jan Blijdenstein* [2004] ECR I-981, [2004] IL Pr 8.

[360] Ibid, at [30].

[361] Supra, pp 218–219.

[362] The second *De Cavel* case, Case 120/79 [1980] ECR 731. See also *Moore v Moore* [2007] EWCA Civ 361 at [68], [2007] IL Pr 36. See also *DT v FL* [2006] IEHC 98, [2007] IL Pr 56.

[363] See the Schlosser Report, p 80. See also *Moore v Moore*, supra, at [[68]–[76]. This does not apply if the jurisdiction as to status is one based solely on the nationality of one of the parties. English courts do not take jurisdiction on this basis, see infra, pp 945–949. Indeed neither does any other Member State. Brussels II *bis* does not allow divorce, etc jurisdiction on the basis of *one* party's jurisdiction. Art 3(1)(b) refers to nationality of *both* spouses.

[364] The rules on jurisdiction to grant a decree of divorce, legal separation or marriage annulment are discussed infra, pp 945–949.

obligation arises from an agreement rather than from a court order, this comes within Article 5(1) rather than Article 5(2).[365]

Article 5(3) in matters relating to tort, delict or quasi-delict, in the courts for the place where the harmful event occurred or may occur.

(i) What are matters relating to tort, delict or quasi-delict?

The Court of Justice in *Kalfelis v Schroder*[366] has held that the concept of "matters relating to tort, *delict* or *quasi-delict*" must be given a community definition. The question then arises of how widely or narrowly this concept is to be interpreted. In many cases this has not been regarded as problematic. So, for example, it has been held that actions for defamation,[367] negligent misstatement,[368] negligent and fraudulent misrepresentation;[369] negligence,[370] conversion,[371] infringement of intellectual property rights,[372] passing off,[373] unfair competition,[374] and actionable breaches of EC law giving rise to a claim for damages[375] come within Article 5(3). The crucial question is whether the concept of "tort, delict or quasi-delict" extends to cover an action in respect of a non-contractual obligation which is not characterised in the substantive domestic law of Member

---

[365] See the Schlosser Report, pp 101–102.

[366] Case 189/87 [1988] ECR 5565; Hartley (1989) 14 ELR 172; Briggs [1988] YEL 272.

[367] Case C-68/93 *Shevill v Presse Alliance SA* [1995] 2 AC 18.

[368] *Domicrest v Swiss Bank* [1999] QB 548; *Alfred Dunhill Ltd v Diffusion Internationale de Maroquinerie de Prestige* [2002] IL Pr 13. See also the obiter dicta in the Court of Appeal in *Viskase Ltd v Paul Kiefel GmbH* [1999] 1 WLR 1305 at 1320 (per CHADWICK LJ) and in *ABCI v Banque Franco-Tunisienne* [2003] EWCA Civ 205 at [41] (per MANCE LJ), [2003] 2 Lloyd's Rep 146. For Scotland see *William Grant & Sons International Ltd v Marie Brizard et Roger International SA* [1997] IL Pr 391.

[369] For negligent misrepresentation: see *RZB v NGB* [1999] 1 Lloyd's Rep 408—negligent misrepresentation under Greek law; the *Alfred Dunhill* case, supra,—negligent misrepresentation under s 2(1) of the Misrepresentation Act 1967. For fraudulent misrepresentation see: *Agnew v Lansforsakringsbolagens AB* [2001] 1 AC 223, 259, 252–253 (obiter dicta per Lord HOPE); *Raiffeisen Zentral Bank Österreich AG v Alexander Tranos* [2001] IL Pr 9—the claim was based on fraudulent or negligent misrepresentations); *The Bank of Tokyo-Mitsubishi Ltd v Baskan Gida Sanayi Ve Pazarlama AS* [2004] EWHC 945 (Ch) at [223], [2004] 2 Lloyd's Rep 395—a claim based on deceit and what was sometimes described as negligent misstatement and at other times as negligent misrepresentation.

[370] *Watson v First Choice Holidays* [2001] EWCA Civ 972 at [26], [2001] 2 Lloyd's Rep 339; *Messier Dowty Ltd v Sabena SA* [2000] 1 WLR 2040, at [48],CA—faulty design of a product.

[371] *Anton Durbeck GmbH v Den Norske Bank ASA* [2002] EWHC 1173 (Comm), varied [2003] QB 1160, CA, without an appeal on this point; *Bank of Tokyo-Mitsubishi Ltd v Baskan Gida Sanayi Ve Pazarlama AS*, supra, at [218]. See also *Re: Action for a Prohibitory Injunction* (II ZR 329/03) [2006] IL Pr 39, Bundesgerichtshof.

[372] *Molnlycke AB v Procter & Gamble Ltd (No 4)* [1992] 1 WLR 1112 at 1117; *Pearce v Ove Arup Partnership Ltd* [1997] Ch 293; revd by CA, [2000] Ch 403, Fentiman [1999] CLJ 286, Harris [1999] LMCLQ 360 without discussion of this point; *Fort Dodge Animal Health Ltd v Akzo Nobel NV* [1998] FSR 222; *Bonnier Media Ltd v Greg Lloyd Smith and Kestrel Trading Corpn* 2003 SC 36, [2002] ETMR 86. For the problem where invalidity is raised as a defence, see infra, pp 282–283, n 679. See generally, Fawcett and Torremans, p 150 et seq; Dutson (1998) 47 ICLQ 659; [1997] JBL 495; (1997) 46 ICLQ 918; Briggs (1997) 68 BYBIL 349; (1997) LQR 364; Fentiman [1997] CLJ 504; Tugendhat (1997) 113 LQR 360.

[373] *Modus Vivendi Ltd v British Products Sanmex Co Ltd* [1996] FSR 790; *Mecklermedia Corpn v DC Congress GmbH* [1998] Ch 40; the *Bonnier* case, supra.

[374] *Saba Molnlycke AS v Procter & Gamble Scandinavia Inc* [1997] IL Pr 704, Tonsberg Court of Appeal—a Lugano Convention case.

[375] *Schmidt v Home Secretary* [1995] 1 ILRM 301. See also *Provimi Ltd v Roche Products Ltd* [2003] EWHC 961 (Comm) at [126], [2003] 2 All ER (Comm) 683—damages for infringement of EU competition law. On the latter, see Withers [2002] JBL 250, 259–264. See also *SanDisk Corpn v Koninklijke Philips Electronics* [2007] EWHC 332 (Ch), [2007] IL Pr 22.

States as one in tort, such as one in unjust enrichment or non-contractual breach of confidence.[376]

The Court of Justice in *Kalfelis* also held that matters relating to tort, delict or quasi-delict "must be regarded as an independent concept covering all actions which seek to establish the liability of a defendant and which are not related to a 'contract' within the meaning of Article 5(1)".[377] This statement has been approved in numerous subsequent decisions of that Court[378] and has been followed in national courts.[379] The Court of Justice in these subsequent cases has interpreted this statement as setting out the scope of Article 5(3).[380] The technique adopted by the Court of Justice for determining whether Article 5(3) applies is as follows. The first question asked is whether there is a matter relating to a contract under Article 5(1).[381] If there is, that is the end of the matter and Article 5(3) cannot apply.[382] Once it has been decided that there is not, it must be held that it is a matter relating to tort, delict or quasi-delict.[383] This would suggest that Article 5(3) is a residual category literally covering all cases which seek to establish the liability of a defendant and which are not related to a "contract" within the meaning of Article 5(1).[384] This perhaps goes too far.[385] After all, there are Article 5 cases falling outside both Article 5(1) and 5(3), of which maintenance under Article 5(2) is an obvious example. There is also a requirement that there is a harmful event.[386] Nevertheless Article 5(3) is given a very wide scope. The Court of Justice has not inquired into whether under the law of the various Member States there was a tort in the substantive domestic law sense[387] and it has applied Article 5(3) in the situation where there is no such tort. This is shown most graphically in *Fonderie Officine Meccaniche Tacconi SpA v Heinrich Wagner Sinto Maschinenfabrik GmbH (HWS)*.[388] The Court of Justice held that a claim based on pre-contractual liability under Article 1337 of the Italian Civil Code, which provides that, in the context of the negotiation and formation of a contract, the parties must act in good faith, did not

---

[376] The classification of this cause of action is, as a matter of substantive law, unclear, see Fawcett and Torremans, pp 430–431.

[377] Supra, at 5585, [17].

[378] Case C-261/90 *Reichert v Dresdner Bank (No 2)* [1992] ECR I-2149; AG DARMON in Case C-89/91 *Shearson Lehman Hutton Inc v TVB* [1993] ECR I-139 at 178; AG JACOBS in Case C-26/91 *Jakob Handte & Co GmbH v Société Traitements Mécano-Chimiques des Surfaces SA (TCMS)* [1992] ECR I-3967 at 3984–3985; Case C-51/97 *Réunion Européenne SA v Spliethoff's Bevrachtingskantoor BV* [2000] QB 690; Case C-96/00 *Gabriel v Schlanck & Schick GmbH* [2002] ECR I-6367, 6398 at para 33; Case C-167/00 *Verein Fur Konsumenteninformation v K H Henkel* [2002] ECR I-8111, at [36]; Case C-334/00 *Fonderie Officine Meccaniche Tacconi SpA v Heinrich Wagner Sinto Maschinenfabrik GmbH (HWS)* [2002] ECR I-7357, at [21]; Case C-18/02 *DFDS Torline v SEKO* [2004] ECR I-1417, [2004] IL Pr 10, at [30] of the opinion of AG JACOBS; Case C-27/02 *Petra Engler v Janus Versand GmbH* [2005] ECR I-481 at [29].

[379] See, eg, *Re Mail Order Promise of Win in a Draw* [2003] IL Pr 46, Bundesgerichtshof.

[380] See the *Réunion Européenne*, *Verein*, *Gabriel* and *DFDS* cases, supra.

[381] The *Gabriel* case, supra, at [34].

[382] Case C-27/02 *Petra Engler v Janus Versand GmbH*, supra, at [60]; *Agnew v Lansforsakringsbolagens AB* [2001] 1 AC 223, 244–245 (per Lord WOOLF), 233–234 (per Lord NICHOLLS), 247 (per Lord COOKE), 259 (per Lord HOPE), 267 (per Lord MILLETT).

[383] See the *Réunion Européenne* case, supra, at [23]–[24]. See also the *Verein* case, supra, at [40]–[41]. See also the *Gabriel* case, supra, at 6398 [33]–[34], where the assumption was that if the action was not contractual in nature it would fall within Art 5(3).

[384] See the opinion of AG GEELHOED in the *Fonderie* case, supra, at [73].

[385] See the opinion of AG JACOBS in the *Engler* case, supra, at [57].

[386] See infra, pp 250–251.

[387] See the *Réunion Européenne*, *Verein* and *Gabriel* cases.

[388] Case C-334/00 [2002] ECR I-7357.

relate to a contract and in the light of this was a matter relating to tort, delict or quasi-delict within Article 5(3) of the Brussels Convention.[389] Article 1337 sets out a non-contractual obligation which is not regarded under Italian law as delictual.[390] There was no evidence that it was regarded as being delictual under the law of other Member States. This means that other non-contractual obligations which are not characterised as tortious, the most obvious ones being those of unjust enrichment and non-contractual breach of confidence, should be regarded as falling within the scope of Article 5(3),[391] provided, of course, that the other requirements (set out below) for coming within this provision are met.

Unfortunately for English lawyers, the House of Lords in *Kleinwort Benson Ltd v Glasgow City Council*[392] has given a narrow interpretation to Article 5(3), holding unanimously that a claim for restitution based on unjust enrichment did not fall within this provision.[393] Reliance was placed on another passage in the *Kalfelis* case[394] which states that "a court which has jurisdiction under Article 5(3) over an action in so far as it is based on tort or delict does not have jurisdiction over that action in so far as it is not so based". The House of Lords interpreted the first key passage, which has been relied upon so much by the Court of Justice, as merely being concerned with whether an independent meaning should be given to the term "tort", not with the question of scope, which in their Lordships' view was dealt with in the second passage.[395] This may have been a tenable interpretation at the time the *Kleinwort* case was decided but it cannot be reconciled with the recent decision in the *Fonderie* case, nor with other later decisions of that Court which have not asked whether there is a tort in the substantive domestic law sense. This leaves English judges, particularly when faced with cases of unjust enrichment,[396] in a quandary over conflicting authorities. Ultimately, the Court of Justice trumps the House of Lords on questions of interpretation of the Brussels Convention, and now Regulation, and the English courts must follow the former Court, in preference to the latter.[397]

---

[389] Ibid, at [27].

[390] Benatti, *La Responsabilita precontracttuale*, (1963), p 133 et seq.

[391] See the opinion of AG DARMON in Case C-89/91 *Shearson Lehman Hutton Inc v TVB* [1993] ECR I-139, at [102]. See also the decision of the Austrian Supreme Court in *Re Concurrent Claims (Royalties)* (Case 4 Ob 66/01), [2003] IL Pr 30—a non-contractual claim based on "any conceivable legal ground" held to fall within Art 5(3). In *Hewden Tower Cranes Ltd v Wolffkran GmbH* [2007] EWHC 857 (TCC), [2007] 2 Lloyd's Rep 138—a claim for contribution between tortfeasors, the classification of which is unclear under English domestic law, was held to come within Art 5(3).

[392] [1999] 1 AC 153.

[393] Ibid, at 172 (per Lord GOFF), 185 (per Lord CLYDE), 196 (per Lord HUTTON), 172 (per Lord MUSTILL), 177 (per Lord NICHOLLS). See also *Compagnie Commercial Andre SA v Artibell Shipping Co Ltd* 1999 SLT 1051. The Court of Justice in Case C-346/93 *Kleinwort Benson Ltd v Glasgow City Council* [1996] QB 57 declined to give a ruling on the question whether Article 5(3) has an extended meaning in relation to restitutionary claims on the basis that this question arose in the context of an intra-UK dispute under the Modified Convention (now the Modified Regulation), rather than in order to apply the Brussels Convention itself. It was left to the English courts to solve this difficult question of interpretation.

[394] Supra, at 5585, [19].

[395] Supra, at 196 (per Lord HUTTON). The more obvious explanation for the second passage is that it is dealing with concurrent actions in tort and contract (as well as unjust enrichment), ie the situation that actually arose in the *Kalfelis* case, see the *Réunion Européenne SA* case, supra, Peel [1998] LMCLQ 22 at 26. Concurrent actions are discussed infra, pp 251–252.

[396] But also in cases of non-contractual breach of confidence, see *Kitechnology BV v Unicor GmbH Plastmaschinen* [1994] IL Pr 568, CA.

[397] As far as a claim for restitution based on unjust enrichment is concerned there was another reason given for excluding this from the scope of Art 5(3), namely there was no harmful event, see infra, pp 250–251.

An action which seeks to establish the liability of a defendant   According to the Court of Justice in *Kalfelis*, to come within Article 5(3) the action must seek to establish the *liability* of a defendant.[398] In *Reichert v Dresdner Bank (No2)*,[399] the Court of Justice held that an action whereby a creditor sought to set aside a gift of property made by a debtor, which allegedly defrauded him of his rights (an action paulienne under French law) did not seek to establish the liability of a defendant in the sense understood in Article 5(3). There was no question of making good damage done to the creditor by the debtor's fraudulent act and the action was not just directed at the defendant debtor but also at the third party beneficiary of the disposition by the debtor.[400] "Liability" has been widely defined to encompass types of legal liability other than the obligation to make financial reparation, such as refraining from certain types of unlawful conduct.[401] Thus a plaintiff may seek to establish liability not just by claiming compensation. He could equally do so by seeking an injunction to prevent damage[402] or by seeking a declaration that certain conduct is unlawful as an essential precursor to an action for damages.[403] Each of these has been held to come within the scope of Article 5(3). It has also been held that an action for a declaration that that person is under no liability because no tort has been committed falls within Article 5(3).[404] The liability can be in respect of a non-contractual obligation, ie one that is not in a strict sense tortious or delictual.[405]

A harmful event   The House of Lords in *Kleinwort Benson* held that to come within Article 5(3) of the Modified Convention (now Modified Regulation) there must be a harmful event.[406] Other than in exceptional circumstances, a claim based on unjust enrichment does not presuppose such an event. This was the second line of reasoning used by the House of Lords to explain their decision in that case. In *Casio Computer Co Ltd v Sayo*,[407] the Court of Appeal held that a constructive trust claim based on dishonest assistance fell within Article 5(3), distinguishing *Kleinwort Benson* on the basis that, in the case in front of them, there was a harmful event. Whilst the result looks right, this ignores the narrow interpretation of the *Kalfelis* case adopted by the House of Lords. The separate issue of whether there was a matter relating to tort, delict or quasi-delict, and

---

[398] For the difficulties caused by this requirement see Briggs and Rees, para 2.138.

[399] Case C-261/90 [1992] ECR I-2149; Briggs (1992) 12 YEL 660.

[400] Cf *Cronos Containers NV v Palatin* [2002] EWHC 2819 (Comm) at [15], [2003] 2 Lloyd's Rep 489—a conversion case where proprietary restitution of money was sought. The claim was based on a wrongful act, ie the denial of title, and damages are payable for this.

[401] Case C-167/00 *Verein Für Konsumenteninformation v K H Henkel* [2002] ECR I-8111 at [35] of the opinion of AG Jacobs. See also AG Geelhoed in the *Fonderie* case, [2002] ECR I-7357 at [76] of his opinion who said that Art 5(3) covered a failure to comply with a legal rule regulating conduct.

[402] As in the *Verein* case, supra, p 248, n 378.

[403] Case C-18/02 *DFDS Torline v SEKO* [2004] ECR I-1417, [2004] IL Pr 10, at [19]–[28].

[404] *Equitas Ltd v Wave City Shipping Co Ltd* [2005] EWHC 923 (Comm), [2005] 2 All ER (Comm) 301, by analogy with the position under Art 5(1), supra, p 234.

[405] The *Fonderie* case, p 249, n 390.

[406] Supra, 172 (per Lord Goff), 185 (per Lord Clyde), 196 (per Lord Hutton), 172 (per Lord Mustill), 177 (per Lord Nicholls). See also the *Agnew* case, supra, at 267 (per Lord Millett); the opinion of AG Jacobs in the Engler case, supra, at para [61]—"generally, perhaps always, requires at least an allegation of harm or damage" and of AG Geelhoed in the Fonderie case, supra, at [42].

[407] [2001] IL Pr 164, CA; Briggs (2001) 72 BYBIL 470; Yeo (2001) 117 LQR 560. See also in relation to jurisdiction over constructive trustees *Dexter Ltd (In Administrative Receivership) v Harley* (2001) Times, 2 April; See also *Benatti v WPP Holdings Italy SRL* [2007] EWCA Civ 263 at [58] (per Toulson LJ), [2007] 1 WLR 2175—breach of fiduciary duty assumed to come within Art 5(3).

what that means, was not examined. The concept of a harmful event is a wide one and with regard to consumer protection it covers situations other than where an individual has personally suffered damage.[408]

(ii) Concurrent actions in tort and contract

We are concerned here with the situation where, for example, the claimant commences proceedings in one court involving parallel claims in contract and tort for failure to take care. Such actions raise particularly difficult problems in relation to the scope of Article 5(3) and to some extent Article 5(1). It is well established that an action cannot fall within both Article 5(1) and 5(3).[409] These two provisions are mutually exclusive.[410] The matter will have to be classified as either one relating to a tort or as one relating to a contract, but not both. And the claimant is unable to choose which it is. This follows from the principle in *Kalfelis* that Article 5(3) covers all actions which seek to establish the liability of a defendant and which are not related to a "contract" within the meaning of Article 5(1) and its corollary that if a case falls within Article 5(1) it does not fall within Article 5(3).[411] The *Kalfelis* case involved claims in tort and contract as well as for unjust enrichment and, in the second key passage in the case,[412] appears to be saying that in an action in tort and contract a court which has jurisdiction in respect of the former does not by that fact have jurisdiction in respect of the latter.[413] *Kalfelis* was followed by the Court of Appeal in *Source Ltd v TUV Rheinland Holding AG*,[414] where there were allegations of breach of contract and breach of a duty of care in failing to exercise reasonable skill and care in the preparation and supply of reports as to the quality of goods purchased by the plaintiffs. The Court of Appeal held that both causes of action were excluded from the scope of Article 5(3) because both related to a contract within Article 5(1).[415] Whilst the result looks to be right, the process of reasoning is hard to square now with the requirement stressed by the House of Lords in the subsequent *Kleinwort Benson* case that the claim is based on a particular contractual obligation. The tort claim cannot be so regarded. In the light of the *Kleinwort Benson* case, TUCKEY J has said, obiter, that he does not regard *Source* as still being good law.[416] But *Source* has also been approved, without discusssion of this point, in obiter dicta by MORISON J [417] and in another case by WARD LJ in the Court of Appeal.[418]

The decisions in the *Kalfelis* and *Source* cases raise three questions. First, in the *Source* case would Article 5(3) still not have applied if the action had been pleaded only in tort,

---

[408] The *Verein* case, supra, at [42]. In the instant case, the concept of a "harmful event" covered the undermining of legal stability by the use of unfair terms which it was the task of associations such as the Consumers' Association to prevent.

[409] AG GEELHOED in the *Fonderie* case, supra, at [71]; the *Agnew* case, supra, at 244–245 (per Lord WOOLF), 233-234 (per Lord NICHOLLS), 247 (per Lord COOKE), 267 (per Lord MILLETT).

[410] The *Agnew* case, supra, at 267 (per Lord MILLETT).

[411] AG GEELHOED in the *Fonderie* case, supra, at [41].

[412] Supra, p 249.

[413] See Peel [1998] LMCLQ 22 at 26; Briggs and Rees, para 2.138.

[414] [1998] QB 54.

[415] Ibid at 63 (per STAUGHTON LJ, WAITE and ALDOUS LJs concurring).

[416] *Raiffeisen Zentral Bank Österreich AG v National Bank of Greece* [1999] 1 Lloyd's Rep 408, 411.

[417] *Rayner v Davies* [2003] IL Pr 14 at [18]–[19], affd without discussion of this point [2002] EWCA Civ 1880; [2003] IL Pr 15.

[418] *Barry v Bradshaw* [2000] IL Pr 706, 713 at [10]. See also *Mazur Media Ltd v Mazur Media GMBH* [2004] EWHC 1566 (Ch) at [30], [2004] 1 WLR 2966.

with no mention of contract; and would the matter still be regarded as related to a contract simply because the parties have a contractual relationship and the claim could have been brought in contract? There are indications that the Court of Appeal would have answered this first question in the affirmative,[419] but this was before the decision of the House of Lords in the *Kleinwort Benson* case on the scope of Article 5(1). In the light of that decision, arguably Article 5(3) should apply. Secondly, if the tort claim is not a matter relating to contract can the court with jurisdiction under Article 5(1) over the contract claim also try the claim in so far as it is based on tort? The opinion of the Advocate General in the *Kalfelis* case, that the whole of the action should be channelled into the court with contract jurisdiction, appears to have been rejected by the Court of Justice in the second key passage in that case.[420] This means that the tort claim disappears altogether as far as Article 5(1) and 5(3) are concerned. The action is regarded for jurisdictional purposes as one solely in contract. The claimant is, of course, free to use some other basis of jurisdiction, such as Article 2, which is not concerned with whether the matter relates to tort or contract. Thirdly, if jurisdiction is based on Article 5(1) and the tort claim has disappeared for the purposes of that provision, does it follow that, as the proceedings unfold, the plaintiff is confined to a claim in contract? In particular, can the claimant rely on tort choice of law rules, rather than those in contract? In principle, this should be possible.[421]

In *Domicrest v Swiss Bank Corpn*,[422] Rix J distinguished the *Source* case on the basis that not only were the claims in contract and tort not parallel but they were also premised on opposite lines of argument.[423] The claim in contract was based on the argument that payment was due from the defendant bank under a payment order; the claim in tort on the basis that an employee of the bank was wrong to tell the plaintiff that a payment order was as good as cash. The two claims were entirely separate and accordingly had to be treated as such under Article 5. Article 5(1) would have to be satisfied in relation to the claim in contract and Article 5(3) in relation to the claim in tort.

(iii) Threatened wrongs

Article 5(3) provides that the defendant may be sued in the courts for the place where the harmful event occurred *or may occur*. This reference to where the harmful event may occur was added to the Regulation to make it clear that Article 5(3) covers an action to prevent a threatened wrong.[424] This is an important clarification since with certain torts, such as infringement of intellectual property rights, it is common to seek an injunction in the Member State in which the threat exists.[425]

---

[419] The *Source* case, supra, at 63–64. See also *Burke v Uvex Sports GmbH* [2005] IL Pr 26, Irish HC.

[420] The *Kaifelis* case, supra, at 5586 [19] (the second key passage) and [20]. See also Lords Goff and Clyde in the *Kleinwort Benson* case, supra, at 166–167, 183–184, who interpreted the judgment of the Court of Justice as rejecting the Advocate General's opinion.

[421] See the opinion of AG Jacobs in Case C-26/91 *Jacob Handte & Co GmbH v société Traitements Mécano-Chimiques des Surfaces SA (TMCS)* [1992] ECR I-3967 at 3984. It would be necessary to meet the criteria for the application of tort choice of law rules, see infra, pp 775–788.

[422] [1999] QB 548.

[423] Ibid, 561.

[424] For the position under the Brussels Convention, which lacks this additional wording see infra, p 342.

[425] It was possible even under the Brussels Convention to obtain an injunction in such cases by using Art 24 of the Convention (Art 31 of the Regulation), discussed infra, pp 315–318. See Fawcett and Torremans, pp 151–152, 217.

(iv) Where is the place where the harmful event occurred?

The Jenard Report deliberately left open the question of whether "the place where the harmful event occurred" referred to the place where the event giving rise to the damage occurred or the place where the damage occurred. The Court of Justice provided the answer in *Bier BV v Mines de Potasse D'Alsace SA*.[426] This provides a classic example of the situation in which the elements in a tort are split up among different states.

> It was alleged that the French defendants had polluted the waters of the Rhine in France. These waters flowed into the Netherlands, where damage was caused to a Dutch horticultural business. The Dutch plaintiffs wished to sue in the Netherlands; so it was necessary to decide on the place where the harmful event occurred.

The Court of Justice, on a reference from the Dutch courts, held that Article 5(3) of the Brussels Convention was intended to cover both the place where the damage occurred and the place of the event giving rise to it, where the two are not identical. The claimant therefore has the option of suing in either place. The Court of Justice justified this wide interpretation in three ways. First, Article 5(3) is concerned to give jurisdiction to an appropriate forum. Both the place of acting and of damage are appropriate places for trial. Secondly, it is designed to give the claimant the option of suing elsewhere than in the Contracting State where the defendant is domiciled. Applying a place of acting rule on its own would not normally allow this. Applying a place of damage rule on its own would ignore cases where the act took place somewhere other than in the State where the defendant is domiciled. Thirdly, there is artificiality in concentrating on one element in a tort or delict to the exclusion of the other elements.

The *Bier* rule was applied by the Court of Justice in the very different context of multi-state defamation in *Shevill v Presse Alliance SA*.[427]

> The first plaintiff was an English resident working at a bureau de change in Paris. She alleged that an article which appeared in "France Soir", published by a French incorporated company, suggested that she was involved in laundering drugs money. Proceedings were brought in England for libel. The House of Lords sought guidance, inter alia, on the interpretation of "the place where the harmful event occurred".

The Court of Justice held that the definition in the *Bier* case applied equally in the case of damage other than physical or pecuniary, and, in particular, applied to injury to reputation. Accordingly, the plaintiff had the option of suing either in the courts for the place where the damage occurred or in the courts for the place of the event which gave rise to and was at the origin of that damage. There is a question, which is examined below, of where these places are in a case of multi-state defamation. There is also a question that arises where, for example, the claimant bases jurisdiction on damage in England of

---

[426] Case 21/76 [1978] QB 708, [1976] ECR 1735; followed in *Shevill*, supra, at [20], *Verein*, supra, at [44], *DFDS*, supra, at [40].

[427] [1995] 2 AC 18; Briggs (1995) 15 YEL 487; Forsyth [1995] CLJ 515; Carter in McLachlan and Nygh, Chapter 7, at pp 118–121; Reed and Kennedy [1996] LMCLQ 108. See also *Ewins v Carlton* [1997] 2 ILRM 223; *Skogvik v Sveriges Television AB* [2003] IL Pr 417, Norwegian Supreme Court—libel on cable television. For the application of *Shevill* in cases of defamation over the internet see Bigos (2005) 54 ICLQ 585.

whether there has been such damage in England and of who is to decide this. The Court of Justice held that the criteria for assessing whether the event in question is harmful and the evidence required of the existence and extent of the harm alleged by the victim of the defamation are governed by the substantive law determined by the national private international law rules of the court seised, provided that the effectiveness of the Convention (now the Regulation) is not thereby impaired.[428] Moreover, the fact that damage is presumed under national law does not preclude the operation of Article 5(3). The case was referred back to the House of Lords which, applying the decision of the Court of Justice, held that where English law[429] presumed that the publication of a defamatory statement was harmful to the person defamed without specific proof thereof, that was sufficient for the application of Article 5(3).[430] Accordingly, the plaintiff was able to invoke the jurisdiction of the English courts under this Article.

The place of the event giving rise to the damage   In *Shevill*, the Court of Justice gave an autonomous meaning to the concept of the place of the event giving rise to the damage, rather than ascertaining this in the light of the elements of the tort under the substantive law of the forum or the applicable law. It held that, in the case of a libel distributed in several Contracting States, the place of the event giving rise to the damage "can only be the place where the publisher of the newspaper in question is established, since that is the place where the harmful event originated and from which the libel was issued and put into circulation".[431] The court of this place has jurisdiction to hear the action for damages for all the harm caused by the unlawful act. The same principles as in the *Shevill* case have been applied in the analogous situation of copyright infringement involving publications in several Member States.[432] In a case of allegedly unlawful industrial action by a trade union leading to the immobilising of a ship, the event giving rise to the damage was the notice of industrial action given by the union at its head office.[433]

The analogy of defamation has also been applied in a case of negligent misstatement.[434] In *Domicrest Ltd v Swiss Bank Corpn*,[435] Rɪx J held that in such a case the place where the harmful event giving rise to the damage occurs is where the misstatement originates, rather than where it is received and relied upon. In the case of a telephone conversation between persons in different countries, this is where the words constituting the misstatement are spoken (in the instant case, this was in Switzerland), rather than where they are

---

[428] The *Shevill* case, supra, at 63–64.

[429] English law was applied as the substantive law of the forum: [1996] AC 959 at 983. However, according to the Court of Justice in *Shevill* it should only be applied if it is the governing law according to national private international law rules.

[430] [1996] AC 959; Leslie 1997 SLT (News) 133; Briggs (1996) 67 BYBIL 586.

[431] *Shevill*, supra, at 62.

[432] *Wegmann v Elsevier Science Ltd* [1999] IL Pr 379, French Cour de Cassation.

[433] Case C-18/02 *DFDS Torline v SEKO* [2004] ECR I-1417, [2004] IL Pr 10 at [41].

[434] For conversion see *Cronos Containers NV v Palatin* [2002] EWHC 2819 (Comm) at [19], [2003] 2 Lloyd's Rep 489. For abuse of a dominant position, see *SanDisk Corpn v Koninklijke Philips Electronics* [2007] EWHC 332 (Ch), [2007] IL Pr 22. For the problem of identifying this in the situation where an indemnity is sought from a third party, see *Waterford Wedgwood plc v David Nagli Ltd* [1999] IL Pr 9. This is not the place where a decision to commit a tort is reached: *Anton Durbeck GmbH v Den Norske Bank ASA* [2002] EWHC 1173 (Comm), varied [2003] QB 1160, CA, without an appeal on this point.

[435] [1999] QB 548; Reed (1999) 18 CJQ 218.

heard (in the instant case, this was in England). Accordingly, the English court had no jurisdiction. There is no difference for these purposes between oral or other instantaneous communication and a written document. RIX J refused to follow the earlier negligent misstatement case of *Minster Investments Ltd v Hyundai Precision and Industry Co Ltd*.[436] In this case, which was decided before *Shevill*,[437] STEYN J decided to use a traditional English formula,[438] and ask "where in substance the cause of action in tort arises, or what place the tort is most closely connected with". The essence of the action for negligent misstatement was said to be the negligent advice and reliance on it. Certificates negligently produced in France and Korea were received and relied upon in England, and accordingly there was jurisdiction in England. However, as RIX J pointed out, the "substance" test "does not reflect either the wording or the philosophy of the Brussels Convention as laid down in the European Court's decisions".[439] Moreover, the plaintiff always has the option of suing in the place where the damage occurred, which is quite likely to be the place of receipt and reliance.[440] The *Domicrest* approach has been preferred to that in *Hyundai* by other judges at first instance,[441] including in a case involving certificates,[442] and by MANCE LJ in obiter dicta in the Court of Appeal. [443]

The Court of Justice in *Réunion Européenne v Spliethoff's Bevrachtingskantoor BV*[444] acknowledged that in certain cases it may be difficult or indeed impossible to determine the place where the event giving rise to the damage occurred. Such impossibility is illustrated by the facts of the case. Pears were shipped in refrigerated containers by the defendant maritime carrier from Australia to the Netherlands, then taken by road to France where the consignee discovered that the goods were damaged. There had been a breakdown in the cooling system in the containers. In such circumstances the claimant will have to rely on bringing the defendant maritime carrier before the courts for the place where the damage occurred.

In a case of threatened passing off and trade mark infringement where the threatened delict involved setting up a website outside Scotland which could be accessed in Scotland, it was held that the Scottish courts had jurisdiction under Article 5(3) of the Brussels Convention.[445]

---

[436] [1988] 2 Lloyd's Rep 621; Hartley (1988) 13 ELR 217. See also *Modus Vivendi Ltd v Sanmex Co Ltd* [1996] FSR 790.

[437] And before the decisions of the Court of Justice on the place where damage occurred, infra, pp 256–258.

[438] Taken from cases on the old tort head of Ord 11, RSC (now CPR, r 6.20), infra, p 385, n 305.

[439] The *Domicrest* case, supra, at 566–567.

[440] Ibid, at 567–568. But not in the *Domicrest* case, see infra, p 257.

[441] *Raiffeisen Zentral Bank Österreich AG v Alexander Tranos* [2001] IL Pr 9; *Alfred Dunhill Ltd v Diffusion Internationale de Maroquinerie de Prestige* [2002] IL Pr 13 at [31]; *Sunderland Marine Mutual Insurance Co Ltd v Wiseman* [2007] EWHC 1460 (Comm). But see *Raiffeisen Zentral Bank Österreich AG v National Bank of Greece* [1999] 1 Lloyd's Rep 408 where TUCKEY J refrained from expressing a view on which approach was correct and *Bank of Tokyo-Mitsubishi Ltd v Baskan Gida Sanayi Ve Pazarlama AS* [2004] EWHC 945 (Ch), [2004] 2 Lloyd's Rep 395, where Lawrence COLLINS J said at [223] that it was not necessary to decide whether *Domicrest* applied to fraudulent misrepresentation, or whether it was rightly decided.

[442] *London Helicopters Ltd v Heliportugal LDA-INAC* [2006] EWHC 108, [2006] IL Pr 28—where misstatement was put into circulation.

[443] *ABCI (Formerly Arab Business Consortium International Finance and Investment Co) v Banque Franco-Tunisienne* [2003] 2 Lloyd's Rep 146 at [41], CA.

[444] Case C-51/97 [2000] QB 690.

[445] *Bonnier Media Ltd v Greg Lloyd Smith and Kestrel Trading Corpn* 2003 SC 36, [2002] ETMR 86. See also *Re The Maritim Trademark* (Case 416 0294/00) [2003] IL Pr 297, the Landgericht, Hamburg; *Parkes v Cintec*

This applies a place of downloading rule.[446] The delict was potentially committed in every State in which the website could be seen but this was limited by saying that there would be no jurisdiction in a State where the impact of the website would be insignificant.

The place where the damage occurred   A number of problems arise in relation to this concept. First, it is not easy to ascertain what the damage is and hence where it occurs in cases where the damage is other than physical or pecuniary.[447] "In the case of an international libel through the press, the injury is to the honour, reputation and good name of a person, and this occurs in the places where the publication is distributed, when the victim is known in these places".[448] With passing off, damage occurs where the goodwill is damaged.[449] With unfair competition it is the place where direct economic loss to the claimant, in the form of loss of sales, was sustained.[450] It has been held in a case of non-contractual breach of confidence, that damage occurs where there is damage directly caused to the claimant's commercial interests in that State.[451] But what of a tort, such as infringement of intellectual property rights, where damage is not one of the elements of the tort? The concept of damage becomes highly artificial and difficult to ascertain in such a case.[452]

Secondly, is this referring just to the place where direct damage occurs or does it also allow jurisdiction where indirect damage occurs? This question has arisen in the context of financial harm. In *Dumez France and Tracoba v Hessische Landesbank*[453] the immediate victims of the alleged harmful act (of cancelling certain bank loans) committed in Germany were German subsidiary companies, which suffered financial harm in Germany, but as a consequence of this the parent companies also suffered financial loss in France where their head offices were situated. The Court of Justice held that Article 5(3) of the Brussels Convention could not be construed as allowing the parent companies to bring proceedings in France against German defendants. The *Bier* case, although allowing jurisdiction to be assumed in the State where the harm occurs, was concerned with cases where a direct consequence was felt in a Member State (this would be in Germany), not an indirect consequence, as occurred in France. This principle applies even more strongly to the situation where there is financial damage which has simultaneous and co-extensive consequences in a Member State (X), where the victim was domiciled and his assets were concentrated, other than that in which it arises and is suffered by the victim.[454] There is

---

International Ltd [2006] CSIH 30; Thunken (2002) 51 ICLQ 909; Fawcett and Torremans, pp 158–161, 167. For internet torts generally, see Bigos (2005) 54 ICLQ 585; Fawcett, Harris and Bridge, paras 10.137–10.161.

[446] See *Dow Jones & Co v Gutnick* (2002) 210 CLR 575, HC; discussed infra, pp 389–390.

[447] Locating the place where financial loss occurred is not always easy, see the *DFDS* case, supra, at [42]–[45]—damage caused by immobilising a ship located in flag state.

[448] The *Shevill* case, supra, at 62. See also *Hunter v Blom-Cooper* [2000] IL Pr 229, Irish High Court—a republication case.

[449] *Mecklermedia Corpn v DC Congress GmbH* [1998] Ch 40 at 51–52; *Modus Vivendi Ltd v British Products Sanmex Co Ltd* [1996] FSR 790 at 802–803.

[450] *Saba Molnlycke AS v Procter & Gamble Scandinavia Inc* [1997] IL Pr 704. See for abuse of dominant position *SanDisk Corpn v Koninklijke Philips Electronics* [2007] EWHC 332 (Ch), [2007] IL Pr 22.

[451] *Kitechnology BV v Unicor GmbH Plastmaschinen* [1994] IL Pr 568 at 581–582. This is assuming that such an action comes within the scope of Art 5(3).

[452] See Fawcett and Torremans, pp 164–167. But see *IBS Technologies (PVT) Ltd v APM Technologies SA* 7th April 2003 (unreported).

[453] Case 220/88 [1990] ECR 49; Hartley (1991) 16 ELR 71.

[454] Case C-168/02 *Kronhofer v Maier* [2004] ECR I-6009.

no jurisdiction in Member State X. The *Dumez* case was followed in *Marinari v Lloyds Bank plc (Zubaidi Trading Co Intervener)*,[455] which was a simpler case involving direct and indirect damage to the same person.

> The Italian domiciled plaintiff was arrested in England and promissory notes were sequestrated. The plaintiff subsequently brought an action in Italy, inter alia, for compensation for the damage he claimed to have suffered as a result of his arrest, the breach of several contracts and injury to his reputation.

The Court of Justice held that the place of damage was to be interpreted as not referring to the place where the victim claimed to have suffered financial loss consequential upon initial damage arising and suffered by him in another Member State. The Court of Justice was concerned to keep Article 5(3) within certain bounds so as to avoid multiplication of competent fora. It also wanted to avoid the situation where the plaintiff was able to sue in the place where he was domiciled. Consistently with the *Marinari* case, it was held in the *Domicrest* case that the damage occurred in Switzerland and Italy where, on the strength of the alleged negligent misstatement by the defendant bank, goods stored in those countries were released by the English plaintiff without prior payment.[456] It follows from this that, in a case of breach of confidence, there is no jurisdiction in the Member State where there is financial loss consequent on the damage to the claimant's commercial interests.[457] The reasoning in *Marinari* applies equally to cases of personal injury. In *Henderson v Jaouen*,[458] initial damage had been suffered by the claimant in a road traffic accident in France but his medical condition had deteriorated whilst living in England. The Court of Appeal held that there was no "harmful event" in England under Article 5(3) of the Brussels Convention. This concept is to be given an autonomous Community meaning. The decision was therefore unaffected by the fact that under French law deterioration constitutes a separate cause of action from the original injury.

Thirdly, in the situation where there is direct damage in more than one Member State, does Member State A which has jurisdiction on the basis of damage in that State also have jurisdiction in relation to the damage sustained in other Member States? This problem arose in the *Shevill* case. The Court of Justice held that each Member State in which the defamatory publication was distributed and in which the victim claims to have suffered injury to his reputation (in that state) only has jurisdiction to rule on the injury caused in

---

[455] Case C-364/93 [1996] QB 217; Briggs [1996] LMCLQ 27 and (1995) 15 YEL 511; Collier [1996] CLJ 216; Hartley (1996) 21 ELR 164. See also *Waterford Wedgwood plc v David Nagli Ltd* [1999] IL Pr 9 at 22–23; *Dexter Ltd (In Administrative Receivership) v Harley* (2001) Times, 2 April.

[456] The *Domicrest* case, supra, at 568. See also *Raiffeisen Zentral Bank Österreich AG v National Bank of Greece* [1999] 1 Lloyd's Rep 408, 414; *Bank of Tokyo-Mitsubishi Ltd v Baskan Gida Sanayi Ve Pazarlama AS* [2004] EWHC 945 at [223] (Ch); *Raiffeisen Zentral Bank Österreich AG v Alexander Tranos* [2001] IL Pr 9; *Alfred Dunhill Ltd v Diffusion Internationale De Maroquinerie De Prestige* [2002] IL Pr 13 at [53]–[55]; *London Helicopters Ltd v Heliportugal LDA-INAC* [2006] EWHC 108 at [21], [27], [2006] IL Pr 28; *Crucial Music Corpn v Klondyke Management AG* [2007] EWHC 1782 (Ch), [2007] IL Pr 54. See on these cases Fawcett, Harris and Bridge, paras 6.93–6.95.

[457] *Kitechnology BV v Unicor GmbH Plastmaschinen*, supra, at 581–582. See also in relation inability to exploit a copyright: *Mazur Media Ltd v Mazur Media GmbH* [2004] EWHC 1566 (Ch) at [44]–[52], [2004] 1 WLR 2966. And in relation to payment under a fraudulent insurance claim: *Sunderland Marine Mutual Insurance Co Ltd v Wiseman* [2007] EWHC 1460 (Comm).

[458] [2002] EWCA Civ 75, [2002] 1 WLR 2971; Briggs (2001) 72 BYBIL 458.

that state to the victim's reputation in that state.[459] It is obviously undesirable to have different aspects of the same dispute tried before different courts. However, the claimant can avoid this by bringing the entire claim in the Member State where the defendant is domiciled (using Article 2) or in the Member State where the publisher is established (using Article 5(3)), where this is different.

Fourthly, can the place where the damage is discovered be regarded as the place where the damage occurred? This question arose in *Réunion Européenne SA v Spliethoff's Bevrachtingskantoor*.[460] The Court of Justice held that the place (France) where the plaintiff consignee merely discovered the existence of the damage to the goods delivered to it could not constitute the place where the damage occurred.[461] This is consistent with their decisions in *Dumez* and *Marinari*; to decide otherwise would often mean attributing jurisdiction to the place of the plaintiff's domicile. In the case of an international transport operation of the kind in question, the place where the damage occurs can only be that where the actual maritime carrier was to deliver the goods, not the place of final delivery or where the consignee discovered the damage.

> **Article 5(4)** as regards a civil claim for damages or restitution which is based on an act giving rise to criminal proceedings, in the court seised of those proceedings, to the extent that the court has jurisdiction under its own law to entertain civil proceedings.[462]

> **Article 5(5)**[463] as regards a dispute arising out of the operations of a branch, agency or other establishment, in the courts for the place in which the branch, agency or other establishment is situated.

There are two requirements under Article 5(5): first, the defendant domiciled in a Member State must have a branch, agency or other establishment in another Member State. Secondly, the dispute must arise out of the operations of the branch, agency or other establishment.

(i) A branch, agency or other establishment

A literal interpretation would suggest that these three terms encompass different situations and are there to give width to Article 5(5). The Court of Justice has, instead, applied a teleological interpretation to this provision and has reached a different conclusion.[464] After looking at the purpose of the Brussels Convention and the place within it of Article 5(5) as an exception to Article 2, the Court of Justice has decided that this provision should be interpreted narrowly. The "branch", "agency" and "other establishment" are identified by characteristics which are said to be common to all three.[465] These are

---

[459] [1995] 2 AC 18 at 62. See also *Barclay v Sweeney* [1999] IL Pr 288 Cour d'Appel, Paris—invasion of privacy and the infringement by the press of the right to one's image.

[460] Case C-51/97 [2000] QB 690. See also the subsequent decision of the Cour de Cassation in [1999] IL Pr 613.

[461] The *Réunion* case, supra, at 6547 [37].

[462] See generally Case C-172/91 *Sonntag v Waidmann* [1993] ECR I-1963.

[463] See Fawcett (1984) 9 ELR 326.

[464] Case 14/76 *De Bloos v Bouyer* [1976] ECR 1497; Case 33/78 *Somafer v Saar-Ferngas* [1978] ECR 2183; Case 139/80, *Blanckaert and Willems v Trost* [1981] ECR 819; Case 218/86 *Sar Schotte GmbH v Parfums Rothschild Sarl* [1987] ECR 4905. See also Case C-439/93 *Lloyd's Register of Shipping v Société Campenon Bernard* [1995] ECR I-961.

[465] The approach in *Harada Ltd T/A Chequepoint UK Ltd v Turner* [2000] IL Pr 574 at [23], EAT, which simply looked at the fact that there was a registered branch in England must be regarded as being wrong.

as follows: the branch, agency or other establishment must (a) have a fixed permanent place of business, (b) be subject to the direction and control of the parent, (c) have a certain autonomy[466] and (d) act on behalf of and bind the parent. These are the characteristics of a typical branch office. Any other method of carrying on business is likely to fall outside the ambit of Article 5(5). The one characteristic that does separate the three terms is that of legal personality. A branch will not have a separate legal personality, whereas an establishment or agent can be a legally independent entity.

The Court of Justice has examined this matter in four cases. The *Somafer*[467] case concerned a sales representative.

> A French company (Somafer) carried on business in Germany by means of a sales representative who was one of their employees. There was no office or furniture in Germany and Somafer was not entered in a commercial register as a branch. A German company wished to sue Somafer in Germany and the question was whether Somafer had a branch, agency or other establishment in that country.

The Court of Justice stressed the need for a fixed permanent place of business in Germany and the sales representative having the power to act on behalf of and to bind his parent,[468] neither of which would appear to be satisfied on the above facts.

Blanckaert v Trost[469] involved a company carrying on business abroad by means of a commercial agent.

> A Belgian manufacturer of furniture appointed a German independent commercial agent to set up a sales network in Germany. The agent was free to arrange its own work, was not prevented from representing several other firms competing in the same sector, and transmitted orders to the parent without being involved in their terms or execution.

The Court of Justice, emphasising the need for the intermediary to be under the direction and control of the parent, held that such an agent did not have the character of a branch, agency or other establishment.[470]

The requirement of direction and control had first been introduced in *De Bloos v Bouyer*[471] which concerned an exclusive distributor rather than a commercial agent.

> The defendant French company granted exclusive distribution rights in Belgium for its products to the plaintiff Belgian company. The question arose of whether the plaintiff could sue the defendant in Belgium on the basis that the plaintiff was a Belgian branch, agency or other establishment of the defendant.

The Court of Justice held that it could not do so where the grantee of the concession was not subject to the direction and control of the parent. This would be the situation with a

---

[466] The Advocate General in *De Bloos*, supra, gave his opinion that the autonomy of an agency is less marked than that of a branch.

[467] Supra; see Hartley (1979) 4 ELR 127.

[468] Cf the *Harada* case, supra, at [23], which must be regarded as wrong.

[469] Supra; see Hartley (1981) 6 ELR 481.

[470] See also *New Hampshire Insurance Co v Strabag Bau AG* [1990] 2 Lloyd's Rep 61 at 68–69; appeal dismissed [1992] 1 Lloyd's Rep 361, CA.

[471] Supra; see Hartley (1977) 2 ELR 61.

typical grantee. The Court of Justice also made it clear that "an establishment" is based on the same essential characteristics as a branch or agency. Finally, it emerges from the case that Article 5(5) is designed for third parties who wish to sue the parent. It is doubtful whether an intermediary can ever rely on its own presence within a Member State to found jurisdiction in an action brought by it against the parent.[472] To allow this would, in effect, give the claimant the right to sue in his own residence whenever Article 5(5) is applicable. A third party claimant who wishes to found jurisdiction on Article 5(5) will not necessarily be suing in the State where he resides.

The Court of Justice was faced with a case involving a subsidiary company carrying on business through its parent in *Sar Schotte GmbH v Parfums Rothschild Sarl*.[473]

> The plaintiff German company provided atomisers to the defendant French company (French Rothschild). The defendant company was a wholly-owned subsidiary of a German company (German Rothschild). The plaintiff wished to sue the French defendant in Germany for the price of the atomisers supplied, and argued that German Rothschild was an "establishment" of French Rothschild.

The Court of Justice held that Article 5(5) would apply, even though under company law German Rothschild was an independent company with a separate legal personality.[474] German Rothschild and French Rothschild had the same name and identical management, and German Rothschild negotiated and conducted business in the name of French Rothschild, which used German Rothschild as an extension of itself and would appear as such to third parties.[475] The place of business of the branch, etc does not have to be owned by the defendant. The same principles will doubtless also apply in the more common situation where a parent carries on business through its subsidiary. This case shows that an "establishment" under Article 5(5) has a different meaning from a "branch" in so far as it covers a body with a separate legal personality. However, this is not much of an advance. German Rothschild only came within Article 5(5) because it acted, in effect, as if it were a branch of French Rothschild. The case is unusual in that a typical parent or subsidiary will act for itself and not on behalf of its subsidiary or parent, and will thus be outside the ambit of Article 5(5).

(ii) The dispute must arise out of the operations of the branch, agency or other establishment

This provision ensures that the Member State given jurisdiction under Article 5(5) is an appropriate one for trial. It presupposes that the branch, agency or other establishment has power to carry out activities itself (albeit on behalf of the parent); this ties in with the requirement, already mentioned, that the intermediary must have a certain autonomy. In the *Somafer* case the Court of Justice identified three sorts of actions comprised within the concept of a dispute arising out of the operations of a branch, agency or other establishment.[476] First, there are actions concerning the management of the intermediary

---

[472] See the Advocate General's opinion at 1519.

[473] Case 218/86 [1987] ECR 4905; Allwood (1988) 13 ELR 213. See *Zellner v Philip Alexander Securities and Futures Ltd* [1997] IL Pr 730, District Court Krefeld.

[474] There was previously considerable uncertainty over this situation: see the opinion of the Advocate General in *De Bloos, Somafer* and *Blanckaert*.

[475] See also Case C-89/91 *Shearson Lehman Hutton Inc v TVB Treuhandgesellschaft für Vermögensverwaltung und Beteiligungen mbH* [1993] ECR I-139 at 169–172 (per AG DARMON).

[476] But cf the *Harada* case, supra, at [22] which seems to have ignored this.

"such as those concerning the situation of the building . . . or the local engagement of staff to work there".[477] Secondly, there are actions relating to undertakings entered into in the name of the parent in the place where the intermediary is situated.[478] The Court of Justice subsequently, in *Lloyd's Register of Shipping v Société Campenon Bernard*,[479] held that the undertakings given by the intermediary might be performed outside the Contracting State where the intermediary was established, possibly by another ancillary establishment such as another branch office. The Court of Appeal in *Anton Durbeck GmbH v Den Norske Bank Asa* [480] regarded the *Lloyd's Register* case as demonstrating that there must be such nexus between the branch, etc and the dispute as to render it natural to describe the dispute as one that has arisen out of the activities of the branch.[481] Where the claim is in contract, that nexus can be derived from the negotiations between the claimant and the branch, etc which give rise to the contractual obligation, the alleged breach of which is the subject of the dispute.[482] This would include a case where the branch, etc conducts all the negotiations but the final contract is signed by the parent.[483] Thirdly, there are non-contractual actions arising from the activities of the intermediary. The Court of Appeal in *Anton Durbeck* has held, in the light of the *Lloyd's Register* case, that these activities do not have to be carried out at the place where the branch, etc is established.[484] Nor must the activities bring about the harmful event within the jurisdiction.[485] The same broad flexible criterion that applies in contract cases is equally applicable in tort cases, namely that there must be such nexus between the branch, etc and the dispute as to render it natural to describe the dispute as one that has arisen out of the activities of the branch.[486] It was not thought by the Court of Appeal to be desirable to formulate any more specific test to determine whether a tortious dispute has arisen out of the activities of a branch.[487] The answer must depend on the facts of the individual case. In the instant case there was a tortious claim for wrongful interference with a bill of lading following the arrest of a ship, as a consequence of which its cargo perished. The Court of Appeal held that the dispute arose out of the activities of the defendants' London branch.[488] The loan in respect of which security over a ship was given was negotiated by the London branch of the defendant Norwegian bank. The decision to enforce the security by arresting the ship was taken in London and the instructions and power of attorney to arrest the ship were given by the London branch.

---

[477] [1978] ECR 2183 at 2192–2193.

[478] See *Latchin (t/a Dinkha Latchin Associates) v General Mediterranean Holdings SA)* [2002] CLC 330 at [50]–[51].

[479] Case C-439/93 [1995] ECR I-961; Briggs (1995) 15 YEL 496; Hartley (1996) 21 ELR 163; Hill [1996] CJQ 94. See also the Advocate General in *Sar Schotte*, supra, at 4914–4915. Cf the Court of Justice in the *Somafer* case at 2192–2193.

[480] [2003] EWCA Civ 147, [2003] QB 1160—a case on Art 5(5) of the Lugano Convention. An appeal to the House of Lords on the question of a stay of the English proceedings was withdrawn, see infra, pp 345–346.

[481] Ibid, at [40].

[482] Ibid. The *Lloyd's Register* case, supra, at [20] supports this.

[483] But cf the opinion of AG SLYNN in Case 218/86 *SAR Schotte GmbH v Parfums Rothschild SARL* [1987] ECR 4905 at 4914. However, this was a case decided before the *Lloyd's Register* case with its wide view of the requirement that the dispute arises out of the operations of the branch, etc. Moreover, AG SLYNN would have preferred to interpret the requirement widely to encompass this situation.

[484] *Anton Durbeck*, supra, at [40].

[485] Ibid, at [38]–[40].

[486] Ibid, at [40].

[487] Ibid, at [41].

[488] Ibid, at [46].

Article 5(6) as settlor, trustee or beneficiary of a trust created by the operation of a statute, or by a written instrument, or created orally and evidenced in writing, in the courts of the Member State in which the trust is domiciled.[489]

Article 5(7) as regards a dispute concerning the payment of remuneration claimed in respect of the salvage of a cargo or freight, in the court under the authority of which the cargo or freight in question:

(a) has been arrested to secure such payment, or

(b) could have been so arrested, but bail or other security has been given; provided that this provision shall apply only if it is claimed that the defendant has an interest in the cargo or freight or had such an interest at the time of salvage.[490]

A proposed Art 5(8) The Hess, Pfeiffer and Schlosser Report recommends the introduction of a new head of Article 5 for cases where the object of the dispute is moveable property, which would allocate juridition to the courts of the Member State in which the property is situated.[491]

(b) Special jurisdiction under Article 6

The four situations where the defendant may be sued in a Member State other than that of his domicile are as follows:

Article 6(1) where he is one of a number of defendants, in the courts for the place where any one of them is domiciled, provided the claims are so closely connected that it is expedient to hear and determine them together to avoid the risk of irreconcilable judgments resulting from separate proceedings;[492]

A person domiciled in a Member State cannot be sued before the courts of another Member State in which an action has been brought against a co-defendant who is not domiciled in any of the Member States.[493] The proceedings must be brought before the courts of a Member State where one of the parties is domiciled.[494] If trial[495] is sought in England, the claimant has to establish a good arguable case that the first defendant was domiciled in England. The relevant time for establishing domicile is that of process being issued, rather than at the time of its service on the first defendant[496] or at the time at which

---

[489] It does not apply to constructive or implied trusts. In order to determine where the trust is domiciled for the purposes of the Regulation, see Art 60(3) and SI 2001/3929, Art 3, Sch 1, para 12. Domicile is tested as at the date of the proceedings: *Chellaram v Chellaram (No 2)* [2002] EWHC 632 (Ch), [2002] 3 All ER 17. For allocation within the United Kingdom, see para 7 of Sch 1 to SI 2001/3929.

[490] See the Schlosser Report, pp 108–109. Salvage of a ship is dealt with under the Brussels Convention of 1952 on the Arrest of Seagoing Ships and the Brussels I Regulation does not apply.

[491] See para 876 of Study JLS/C4/2005/03, Final Version September 2007, available at the European Commission—European Judicial Network—What's new website http://ec.europa.eu/civiljustice/news/whatsnew_en.htm.

[492] See generally Fawcett (1995) 44 ICLQ 744, at 749–754. The interraction of this provision with the special rules for contracts of employment (Section 5) has been referred to the Court of Justice in C-462/06 *Glaxosmithkline v Rouard*.

[493] Case C-51/97 *La Réunion Européenne v Spliethoff's Bevrachtingskantoor* [2000] QB 690.

[494] Ibid, at [44]. The Hess, Pfeiffer and Schlosser Report, para 878, recommends that consideration should be given to extending Art 6(1) so that other bases of jurisdiction are sufficient.

[495] There is no restriction in Art 6 on the type of action. It can include a claim for an anti-suit injunction: *The Eras EIL Actions* [1995] 1 Lloyd's Rep 64.

[496] *Canada Trust Co v Stolzenberg (No 2)* [2002] 1 AC 1 at 8–12 (per Lord STEYN), 22–23 (per Lord HOFFMANN), 23 (per Lord COOKE), 23 (per Lord HOPE), 26 (per Lord HOBHOUSE), HL. For the position where proceedings are brought in Scotland see Lord HOPE at 23–26.

it was sought to join the additional defendants or the time at which they were actually joined.[497] Article 6(1) does not require service on the first defendant prior to the issue or service of proceedings on other defendants.[498] Neither does it require that the defendants are defendants in the same set of proceedings, there can be separate actions in the same Member State.[499]

However, there is a danger of misuse of this provision with proceedings being brought against a number of defendants solely with the object of ousting the jurisdiction of the courts of the Member State in which one of the defendants is domiciled. Accordingly, the Regulation contains a proviso that "the claims are so closely connected that it is expedient to hear and determine them together to avoid the risk of irreconcilable judgments resulting from separate proceedings".[500] There is though no further need to establish separately that the claims were not brought with the sole object of ousting the jurisdiction of the courts of the Member State where one of the defendants was domiciled.[501] The Court of Justice in *Roche Nederland BV v Primus* has left open the question whether "irreconcilable" should be widely construed as being equivalent to "contradictory".[502] However, the Court of Justice went on to hold that in order that decisions may be regarded as contradictory, it is not sufficient that there be a divergence in the outcome of the dispute, but that divergence must also arise in the context of the same situation of fact and law.[503] Thus, even under this broad definition, Article 6(1) will not apply where infringement proceedings are brought in a number of courts in different Member States in respect of a European patent granted in each of those States, against defendants domiciled in those States in respect of acts allegedly committed in their territory, since any divergences between the decisions given by the courts concerned would not arise in the context of the same factual and legal situation.[504] In this scenario, Article 6(1) will not apply even though

---

[497] *Petrotrade Inc v Smith* [1999] 1 WLR 457.

[498] The *Canada Trust* case, supra, at 12–13 (per Lord Steyn), 23 (per Lord Hoffmann), 23 (per Lord Cooke), 23 (per Lord Hope), 26 (per Lord Hobhouse).

[499] *Masri v Consolidated Contractors International (UK) Ltd* [2005] EWCA Civ 1436, [2006] 1 WLR 830 (appeal to the House of Lords pending).

[500] Under the Brussels Convention this requirement was laid down by the Court of Justice in Case 189/87 *Kalfelis v Schröder* [1988] ECR 5565, rather than being contained in the Convention. For examples of where there was the requisite connection see *Carnoustie Universal SA v International Transport Workers' Federation* [2002] EWHC 1624 (Comm) at [120]–[134], [2002] 2 All ER (Comm) 657); *The Bank of Tokyo-Mitsubishi Ltd v Baskan Gida Sanayi Ve Pazarlama AS* [2004] EWHC 945 (Ch) at [216], [2004] 2 Lloyd's Rep 395; *King v Crown Energy Trading AG* [2003] EWHC 163 (Comm), [2003] IL Pr 28; *Oakley v Ultra Vehicle Design Ltd (In Liquidation)* [2005] EWHC 872 (Ch) at [55], [2005] IL Pr 55; *Et Plus SA v Welter* [2005] EWHC 2115 (Comm), [2006] 1 Lloyd's Rep 251; *Dadourian Group International Inc v Simms* [2006] EWCA Civ 399 at [34], [2006] 1 All ER (Comm) 709. The concern is whether the claims are related as at the time of institution of the proceedings: the *Kalfelis* case at [12]; *Messier Dowty Ltd v Sabena SA* [2000] 1 WLR 2040 at [50], CA, noted by Briggs (2000) 71 BYBIL 455; *FKI Engineering Ltd v Dewind Holdings Ltd* [2007] EWHC 72 (Comm), [2007] IL Pr 17.

[501] Case C-98/06 *Freeport plc v Olle Arnoldsson* [2007] IL Pr 58 at [59].

[502] Case C-539/03 [2007] IL Pr 9 at [23]–[25]; Briggs [2006] LMCLQ 447. "Irreconcilable" for the purposes of Art 22 of the Brussels Convention (Art 28 of the Regulation) is defined in terms of "contradictory", see infra, p 313. AG Leger at [79]–[106] gave his opinion that a narrower definition should be given to "irreconcilable" in the context of Art 6(1).

[503] However, there is no requirement that the legal basis of the claims against the two defendants is the same, see Case C-98/06 *Freeport plc v Olle Arnoldsson* [2007] IL Pr 58, infra, p 264.

[504] Case C-539/03 *Roche Nederland BV v Primus* [2007] IL Pr 9—factually, the defendants were different and the infringements, committed in different Member States, and legally each patent is governed by different

the defendant companies belong to the same group and may have acted in an identical or similar manner in accordance with a common policy elaborated by one of them.[505]

According to earlier English case law, judgments may be irreconcilable because they involve contradictory findings of fact, or contradictory legal conclusions drawn from those facts.[506] This appears to fit in with what was later said in the *Roche* case. However, English case law providing that judgments may be irreconcilable because they involve contradictory remedies[507] falls foul of the statement in *Roche* that a mere divergence in the outcome of the dispute is not enough. If the claims against the various defendants are substantially the same in law and fact, such as where the defendants are joint debtors or joint tortfeasors,[508] there is an obvious risk of irreconcilable judgments. Even where the claims are largely based on different facts, there can be a risk of an inconsistent finding of fact in relation to a particular central matter.[509] In contrast, there is no such risk where there are proceedings for the infringement of parallel intellectual property rights (eg an English defendant infringes the claimant's United Kingdom copyright and a German defendant the claimant's German copyright) since these are regarded as being different rights.[510] Nor is there any such risk if the case just concerns England and Scotland and is going to go on appeal to the House of Lords, whose judgment would be binding on both law districts.[511] The Court of Justice has held that the fact that claims brought against a number of defendants have different legal bases does not preclude the application of Article 6(1).[512] An example of this would be where the claim against one defendant is based on contractual liability and the claim against the other defendant is based on liability in tort or delict.[513] It is for the national court to assess whether there is a risk of irreconcilable judgments if the claims are tried separately and to take into account all the factors in the case.[514] This may lead it to take into consideration the legal bases of the actions. In some circumstances, a claim against one defendant in contract and the other in tort, can, if the claims are tried separately, lead to the risk of irreconcilable judgments.[515] In such a case, Article 6(1) will apply.

---

national laws ([27]–[32]). See also *Fort Dodge Animal Health Ltd v Akzo Nobel NV* [1998] FSR 222, CA. See generally Fawcett and Torremans, pp 172–174.

[505] Ibid.

[506] *Gascoigne v Pyrah* [1994] IL Pr 82, CA; *Casio Computer Co Ltd v Sayo* [2001] EWCA Civ 661, [2001] IL Pr 43—applying the analogy of Art 22 of the Brussels Convention (Art 28 of the Regulation), discussed infra, p 313; *Latchin (t/a Dinkha Latchin Associates) v General Mediterranean Holdings SA* [2002] CLC 330. See also *MacDonald v FIFA* [1999] SLT 1129; *Compagnie Commercial Andre SA v Artibell Shipping Co Ltd* 1999 SLT 1051. But see *Watson v First Choice Holidays* [2001] EWCA Civ 972, [2001] 2 Lloyd's Rep 339, which referred to the Court of Justice the question whether judgments can be irreconcilable when this is based on irreconcilable findings of fact but the case was subsequently removed from the register.

[507] *Société Commerciale de Réassurance v Eras* [1995] 1 Lloyd's Rep 64 at 78–79—an English court would grant an anti-suit injunction against a defendant when a foreign court, faced with essentially the same facts, would not.

[508] See, eg, *Pearce v Ove Arup Partnership Ltd* [2000] Ch 403, CA. See also *Chiron Corpn v Evans Medical Ltd* [1996] FSR 863, involving a licensee under a patent.

[509] The *Gascoigne* case, supra.

[510] *Coin Controls Ltd v Suzo International (UK) Ltd* [1999] Ch 33 at 52.

[511] *Barclays Bank plc v Glasgow City Council* [1994] QB 404, CA.

[512] Case C-98/06 *Freeport plc v Olle Arnoldsson* [2007] IL Pr 58 at [47].

[513] Case C-98/06 *Freeport plc v Olle Arnoldsson* [2007] IL Pr 58. Earlier obiter dicta in *Réunion Européenne SA v Spliethoff's Bevrachtingskantoor BV*, supra, at [50], that have been interpreted as laying down a requirement that the legal bases was the same, were regarded in *Freeport* at [42]–[46] (and see AG MENGOZZI at [32]–[46], as being confined to the facts of that case and interpreted (somewhat unconvincingly) as just reinforcing the point that Art 6(1) only applies where proceedings are brought in a Member State where one of the defendants is domiciled.

[514] The *Freeport* case, supra, at [41].

[515] See *Watson v First Choice Holidays* [2001] EWCA Civ 972 at [31], [2001] 2 Lloyd's Rep 339. Cf *Messier Dowty Ltd v Sabena SA* [2000] 1 WLR 2040, at [50], CA. If the claims against both defendants are in both

Again to prevent abuse, there are additional requirements to be satisfied before this provision can be used.[516] First, English courts have held that there must be a valid claim[517] against the defendant domiciled in the forum.[518] The Court of Justice has effectively confirmed this requirement by saying that Article 6(1) cannot be interpreted in such a way as to allow a plaintiff to make a claim against a number of defendants for the sole purpose of removing one of them from the jurisdiction of the courts of the Member State in which that defendant is domiciled.[519] Secondly, the second defendant must be a necessary or proper party to the action against the first defendant.[520] This was not satisfied where a German domiciled defendant was added merely in order to obtain discovery of documents.[521]

Article 6(2) as a third party in an action on a warranty or guarantee or in any other third party proceedings, in the court seised of the original proceedings, unless these were instituted solely with the object of removing him from the jurisdiction of the court which would be competent in his case.[522]

Article 6(3) on a counterclaim[523] arising from the same contract or facts on which the original claim was based,[524] in the court in which the original claim is pending.

---

contract and tort it may be possible to show the requisite connection, see *Clodagh Daly v Irish Group Travel Limited Trading as "Crystal Holidays"* [2003] IL Pr 38, Irish High Court.

[516] Requirements to be found under the multi-defendant provision under the traditional rules, CPR, r 6.20(3), discussed infra, pp 374–377.

[517] As at the date of the issue of the claim form: *Zair v Eastern Health and Social Services Board* [1999] IL Pr 823, CA.

[518] *The Rewia* [1991] 2 Lloyd's Rep 325 at 335–336, CA; *Gascoigne v Pyrah*, supra; *Gannon v B & I Steam Packet Co Ltd* [1994] IL Pr 405; *Kelly v McCarthy* [1994] IL Pr 29; *The Xing Su Hai* [1995] 2 Lloyd's Rep 15; the *Andrew Weir Shipping* case, supra; according to the *Et Plus SA* case, supra, at [59] and *FKI Engineering Ltd v Dewind Holdings Ltd* [2007] EWHC 72 (Comm) at [32], [2007] IL Pr 17—a real or serious issue to be tried.

[519] Case C-103/05 *Reisch Montage AG v Kiesel Baumaschinen Handels GmbH* [2006] ECR I-6827 at [32]; Briggs [2006] LMCLQ 447. However, Art 6(1) can still apply even though an action is regarded under a national provision as inadmissible (because of bankruptcy acting as a procedural bar) from the time it is brought in relation to the first defendant.

[520] *Mölnlycke AB v Procter & Gamble Ltd (No 4)* [1992] 1 WLR 1112, CA; *Oakley v Ultra Vehicle Design Ltd (In Liquidation)* [2005] EWHC 872 (Ch) at [56], [2005] IL Pr 55.

[521] *Mölnlycke*, supra, at 1116–1117. Cf *Messier Dowty Ltd v Sabena SA* [2000] 1 WLR 2040, at [49].

[522] See Case C-365/88 *Kongress Agentur Hagen GmbH v Zeehaghe BV* [1990] ECR I-1845; Hartley (1991) 16 ELR 73; North in Nouveaux itinéraires en droit: Hommage à Rigaux, p 373. See also *Kinnear v Falconfilms NV* [1996] 1 WLR 920; *Waterford Wedgwood plc v David Nagli Ltd* [1999] IL Pr 9; *Caltex Trading Pte Ltd v Metro Trading International Inc* [1999] 2 Lloyd's Rep 724; *National Justice Compania Naviera SA v Prudential Assurance Co Ltd (No 2)* [2000] 1 WLR 603, CA; *Knauf UK GmbH v British Gypsum Ltd (No 2)* [2002] 2 Lloyd's Rep 416; *British Sugar plc v Babbini* [2004] EWHC 2560 (TCC), [2005] 1 Lloyd's Rep 332; *Barton v Golden Sun Holidays Ltd* [2007] 151 SJLB 1128, [207] IL Pr 57. On the proviso under Art 6(2), see *Hough v P & O Containers* [1999] QB 834. Art 23 takes priority over Art 6(2): the *Hough* case ibid. Art 6(2) is applicable to third party proceedings between insurers based on multiple insurance, in so far as there is a sufficient connection between the original proceedings and the third party proceedings to support the conclusion that the choice of forum does not amount to an abuse: Case C-77/04 *GIE Réunion Européenne v Zurich España* [2005] IL Pr 456.

[523] This does not cover set-off as a defence: Case C-341/93 *Danvaern Production A/S v Schuhfabriken Otterbeck GmbH & Co* [1995] ECR I-2053; Briggs (1995) 15 YEL 498; Hartley (1996) 21 ELR 166. See also *Dollfus Mieg & Cie v CDW International Ltd* [2004] IL Pr 12—counterclaim does not include a cross-claim by by a person not an original defendant, on which see also *Jordan Grand Prix v Baltic Insurance Group* [1999] 2 AC 127, HL. For criticism of a restrictive German interpretation, see Sturner 2007 I P Rax 41.

[524] This is not to be construed in the same way as "related actions" under Art 28(3) of the Regulation (infra, pp 313–314): the Opinion of AG Léger in the *Danvaern* case, supra, at 2068–2070. The question whether it is a more restrictive concept was referred to the Court of Justice by the District Court in Luxembourg in *Reichling v Wampach* [2002] IL Pr 42 but the Court of Justice in Case C-69/02 [2002] IL Pr 43 held that that court was not authorised to request a reference.

Article 6(4) in matters relating to a contract, if the action may be combined with an action against the same defendant in matters relating to rights *in rem* in immovable property, in the court of the Member State in which the property is situated.[525]

(c) Special jurisdiction under Article 7

Article 7 provides that:

Where by virtue of this Regulation a court of a Member State has jurisdiction in actions relating to liability arising from the use or operation of a ship, that court, or any other court substituted for this purpose by the internal law of that Member State, shall also have jurisdiction over claims for limitation of such liability.[526]

(iii) Jurisdiction in matters relating to insurance

Section 3 of Chapter II of the Regulation (namely Articles 8 to 14)[527] deals with matters relating to insurance,[528] although it does not define the term. Section 3 does not apply to disputes between a reinsurer and a reinsured in connection with a reinsurance contract because neither party is in a weaker position vis à vis the other.[529] Generally, it only applies in the situation where the defendant is domiciled in a Member State,[530] although there is the possible exception of the situation where there is an agreement as to jurisdiction under Article 13. An extended meaning is given to domicile in this context.[531] Where an insurer not domiciled in a Member State has a branch, agency or other establishment in a Member State, and the dispute arises out of the latter's operations,[532] the insurer is deemed to be domiciled in that State.[533] The provisions contained in Section 3 are exclusive.[534] Where they apply it is not possible to rely on other bases of jurisdiction under the Regulation.[535] It differs from exclusive jurisdiction under Section 6 in two important respects. First, jurisdiction is not assigned to a single Member State under Section 3; instead the claimant, where he is the weaker party, is allowed a limited choice

---

[525] See the Almeida Cruz, Desantes Real and Jenard Report, para 24.

[526] See the Schlosser Report, pp 109–110. For service out of the jurisdiction see *ICL Shipping Ltd v Chin Tai Steel Enterprise Co Ltd* [2004] 1 All ER (Comm) 246.

[527] Arts 7–12A of the Brussels Convention (on which see the Schlosser Report, pp 112–117).

[528] This does not include third party proceedings between insurers, based on alleged multiple insurance: Case C-77/04 *GIE Réunion Européenne v Zurich España* [2005] IL Pr 456. "Insurance" does not cover an application by insurers for costs against a non-party under the Supreme Court Act 1981, s 51 even though there were main proceedings relating to insurance: *National Justice Compañía Naviera SA v Prudential Assurance Co Ltd (No 2)* [2000] 1 WLR 603 at 616, CA.

[529] Case C-412/98 *Société Group Josi Reinsurance Co SA v Compagnie d'Assurances Universal General Insurance Co Ugic* [2001] QB 68. See also *Agnew v Lansförsäkringsbolagens AB* [2001] 1 AC 223, at 238–239 (per Lord WOOLF), 233–234 (per Lord NICHOLLS), 245–246 (per Lord COOKE), 249 (per Lord HOPE), 262 (per Lord MILLETT).

[530] See Art 8, which says that Section 3 is without prejudice to Art 4; see also Arts 9 and 12.

[531] Art 9(2). For application of this provision within the United Kingdom (the Modified Regulation does not have such a provision), see SI 2001/3929, Art 3, Sch 1, para 11.

[532] For interpretation of this phrase see the opinion of AG ELMER in Case C-439/93 *Lloyd's Register of Shipping v Société Campenon Bernard* [1995] ECR I-961 at 971.

[533] See the opinion of AG LEGER in Case C-281/02 *Owusu v Jackson* [2005] QB 801 at [132]–[134]. See, eg, *S & W Berisford plc v New Hampshire Insurance Co* [1990] 2 QB 631.

[534] Art 8, which is without prejudice to Arts 4 and 5(5).

[535] Art 24 of the Regulation (Art 18 of the Brussels Convention) may be an exception to this, see the Jenard Report, p 29.

of forum. Secondly, the parties may in certain limited circumstances depart from the provisions of Section 3. These two aspects of Section 3 will be examined in more detail.

Section 3 contains protective provisions, designed to protect the party in a weaker position.[536] In a dispute between the policyholder (ie the other party to the contract of insurance)[537] and the insurer, this will be the policyholder in those cases where he is faced with a standard form non-negotiable contract. The claimant is given a choice of forum when suing the defendant insurer. According to Article 9(1), where the insurer is the defendant he can be sued: (a) in the Member State where he is domiciled; or (b) in another Member State, in the case of actions brought by the policyholder, the insured or a beneficiary, in the courts for the place where the plaintiff is domiciled; or (c) if he is a co-insurer, in the courts of a Member State in which proceedings are brought against the leading insurer.[538] Article 9 of the Regulation extends the right (granted under the Brussels Convention) of the policyholder as plaintiff to sue in his domicile to the insured[539] and to a beneficiary. Where the insurer is the claimant, he is given no choice of forum. According to Article 12 he may bring proceedings only in the courts of the Member State in which the defendant is domiciled,[540] whether he is the policyholder, the insured or a beneficiary.[541] Article 12 can be used by a claimant insurer who is not domiciled in any Member State.[542]

The policy of favouring the insured party has been strongly criticised by English lawyers; it gives an unwarranted opportunity for the insured to forum-shop, and is based on the erroneous assumption that the insured is always the weaker party, whereas, in reality, the insured may be a wealthy enterprise which is every bit as strong as the insurer.[543] Nonetheless, Section 3 will still operate.[544]

The validity of this criticism is lessened to some extent by the fact that Section 3 can be departed from by an agreement on jurisdiction. Article 13 requires the agreement to satisfy one of five alternatives set out in that Article.[545] These are as follows: (i) the agreement is entered into after the dispute has arisen; (ii) the agreement allows the policyholder, the insured or a beneficiary to bring proceedings in courts other than those indicated in Section 3; (iii) the agreement is concluded between a policyholder and an insured, both of whom are at the time of conclusion of the contract domiciled or

---

[536] Recital (13) of the Regulation.

[537] See the Jenard Report, p 31; the Schlosser Report, p 117.

[538] The options are extended in cases of liability insurance, or insurance of immovable property, see Arts 10 and 11. Art 11(2) allows the injured party to bring an action directly against the insurer before the courts for the place in a Member State where that injured party is domiciled, provided that such a direct action is permitted and the insurer is domiciled in a Member State: Case C-463/06 *FBTO Schadeverzekeringen NV v Jack Odenbreit*.

[539] Normally this will also be the policyholder. For an example of where this would not be the case, see the Schlosser Report, p 117.

[540] Or, in the case of a counterclaim (which means a counterclaim against the original claimant, ie not one involving new parties) in the Member State in which the original claim is pending, see *Jordan Grand Prix Ltd v Baltic Insurance Group* [1999] 2 AC 127, HL.

[541] This is not an exhaustive list, and Art 12 can apply to other defendants provided that the claim relates to insurance: *Jordan Grand Prix Ltd v Baltic Insurance Group* [1998] 1 WLR 1049, affd by HL [1999] 2 AC 127, HL, which found it unnecessary to discuss this point; Briggs (1998) 69 BYBIL 346.

[542] *Jordan Grand Prix Ltd v Baltic Insurance Group* [1999] 2 AC 127, HL.

[543] Collins, at p 68, and in Lipstein (ed), *Harmonisation of Private International Law by the EEC* (1978), pp 99–100; Kerr (1978) 75 LS Gaz 1190, 1191.

[544] See *New Hampshire Insurance Co v Strabag Bau AG* [1992] 1 Lloyd's Rep 361, CA.

[545] See also Art 14.

habitually resident in the same Member State, and confers jurisdiction on that State even if the harmful event were to occur abroad, provided that such an agreement is not contrary to the law of that State;[546] (iv) the agreement is concluded with a policyholder who is not domiciled in a Contracting State except in so far as the insurance is compulsory or relates to immovable property in a Contracting State; (v) the agreement relates to a contract of insurance in so far as it covers one or more of the risks set out in Article 14.[547] The agreement would also have to satisfy the requirements relating to agreements as to jurisdiction under Article 23 of the Regulation.[548] Under Article 23, the defendant does not have to be domiciled in a Member State. Article 13 allows all the other provisions in Section 3 (including any requirement as to the defendant being domiciled in a Member State) to be departed from. It therefore appears that an agreement conferring jurisdiction in a matter relating to insurance does not require that the defendant be domiciled in a Member State.[549] There is a suggestion in the Jenard Report[550] that Section 3 can also be departed from by the defendant submitting to the courts of a Member State by entering an appearance under what is now Article 24 of the Regulation.

(iv) Jurisdiction over consumer contracts

Section 4 (Articles 15 to 17[551]) applies in matters relating to a contract[552] concluded[553] by a consumer (ie a person who concludes a contract for a purpose outside his present or future[554] trade or profession[555]) and the contract is one of the three alternative types listed

---

[546] The jurisdiction agreement cannot be relied upon against a beneficiary under the insurance contract who has not expressly subscribed to that clause and is domiciled in a Contracting State other than that of the policyholder and the insurer: Case C-112/03 *Société financière et industrielle du Peloux v Axa Belgium* [2006] QB 251.

[547] See generally *Charman v WOC* [1993] 2 Lloyd's Rep 551, CA; *Charterers Mutual Assurance Association Ltd v British and Foreign* [1998] IL Pr 838 at 850; *Tradigrain SA v SIAT SpA* [2002] EWHC 106 (Comm) at [39]–[43], [2002] 2 Lloyd's Rep 553; *Minister for Agriculture, Food and Forestry v Alte Leipziger Versicherüng Aktiengesellschaft* [2002] 1 ILRM 306, Irish Supreme Court; *Standard Steamship Owners' Protection and Indemnity Association (Bermuda) Ltd v GIE Vision Bail* [2004] EWHC 2919 (Comm) at [58]–[64], [2005] 1 All ER (Comm) 618. The Regulation in Art 14(5) extends the risks to cover "large risks" as defined in Council Directive (EEC) No 73/239, as amended by Council Directives (EEC) Nos 88/357 and 90/618, as they may be amended.

[548] *Gerling v Italian Treasury*, supra. For the need for an "agreement" under Art 23, see *Evialis SA v SIAT* [2003] EWHC 863 (Comm) at [59]–[69], [2003] 2 Lloyd's Rep 377. See also *Tradigrain SA v SIAT SpA* [2002] EWHC 106 (Comm) at [44]–[62], [2002] 2 Lloyd's Rep 553.

[549] See Collins, p 51.

[550] Jenard Report, p 30.

[551] Arts 13–15 of the Brussels Convention (on which see the Schlosser Report, pp 117–120).

[552] The claim must be contractual in nature but extends to claims which are so closely linked to the consumer contract as to be indivisible: Case C-96/00 *Gabriel v Schlanck & Schick GmbH* [2002] ECR I-6367 at 6402–6404 at [53]–[57]—a claim for a prize to be awarded on condition that the consumer ordered goods, which he did. Cf Case C–27/02 *Petra Engler v Janus Versand GmbH*, supra, at [36]–[38]; *Re Jurisdiction in a claim based on a prize draw notification* [2007] IL Pr 15, Bundesgerichtshof. A reference has been made to the Court of Justice in relation to this in Case C-180/06 *Renate Ilsinger v Martin Dreschers (Administrator in the Insolvency of Schlank & Schick GmbH)*.

[553] Where a contract has not been concluded it may be possible to use Art 5(1): the *Petra Engler* case, supra, at [36]; *Kapferer v Schlank & Schick GmbH* [2006] IL Pr 17 at [43]–[44] of the opinion of AG Tizzano.

[554] Case C-269/95 *Benincasa v Dentalkit Srl* [1997] ECR I-3767.

[555] Art 15. For purposes partly within and partly outside a trade or profession, see Case C-464/01 *Gruber v Bay Wa AG* [2006] QB 204—business purpose must have been negligible; the court cannot take account of facts of which the other party may have been aware when the contract was concluded unless the person wishing to rely on s 4 behaved in such a way to give the other party the legitimate impression that he was acting for the purposes of his business. See also *Standard Bank London Ltd v Apostolakis (No 1)* [2002] CLC 933 at 936–937—consumer includes private investor entering into foreign exchange contract; cf the decision to the contrary of a Greek

in Article 15. The first type (Article 15(1)(a)) is a contract for the sale of goods[556] on instalment credit, a term which has been given a community meaning by the Court of Justice.[557] The second type (Article 15(1)(b)) is a contract for a loan payable by instalments. The third type (Article 15(1)(c)) applies in all other cases and encompasses two alternatives. The first is where "the contract has been concluded with a person who pursues commercial or professional activities in the Member State of the consumer's domicile". The second alternative is where the contract has been concluded with a person who "by any means, directs such activities to that Member State or to several States including that Member State". In both cases the contract must fall within the scope of such activities.

Article 15(1)(c) is worded differently from its predecessor under the Brussels Convention[558] because of concerns over electronic commerce.[559] The new wording involves three major changes when compared with its predecessor. First, Article 15(1)(c) just refers to "in all other cases" whereas its predecessor referred to "any other contract for the supply of goods or a contract for the supply of services".

The second change is to introduce the new concept of activities pursued in (under the first alternative) or directed towards (under the second alternative) a Member State. This replaces a requirement that in the state of the consumer's domicile the conclusion of the contract was preceded by a specific invitation addressed to him or by advertising. The old provision was very specific in naming the activities of the defendant in the consumer's domicile that would subject him to trial there. The new provision is much more general, merely referring to "activities" (without specifying what these are) pursued in or directed towards a Member State. However, the requirement, under the old provision, of positive conduct by the seller or provider of services, normally preceding the involvement of the consumer,[560] will doubtless still apply in relation to the new provision under the Regulation. The idea presumably also remains that the trader must have taken steps to market his goods or services in the country where the consumer resides.[561] "Directing activities"

---

court when faced with the same facts in *Standard Bank London v Apostolakis* (Decision 8032/2001) [2003] IL Pr 29, Multi-Member First Instance Court Athens; *Prostar Management Ltd v Twaddle* 2003 SLT (Sh Ct) 11. Where a consumer assigns his contractual rights to a non-consumer, the latter cannot rely on the protective rules of Arts 15–17 which the consumer could have relied on: Case C-89/91 *Shearson Lehman Hutton Inc v TVB Treuhandgesellschaft für Vermogensverwaltung und Beteiligungen mbH* [1993] ECR I-139; Briggs (1993) 13 YEL 511; Hartley (1994) 19 ELR 537; Plender (1993) 64 BYBIL 557. This was followed in Case C-167/00 *Verein Für Konsumenteninformation v K H Henkel* [2002] ECR I-8111 at [33], which held that a consumer protection organisation which brings an action on behalf of consumers is not a consumer.

[556] This does not include unit trusts: *Waverley Asset Management Ltd v Saha* 1989 SLT (Sh Ct) 87, a case on the Modified Convention (now Modified Regulation).

[557] Case 150/77 *Bertrand v Ott* [1978] ECR 1431; see Hartley (1979) 4 ELR 47. This does not encompass a contract involving manufacture and payment in full (by instalments) before possession is transferred. Case C-99/96 *Mietz v Intership Yachting Sneek BV* [1999] ECR I-2277; Peel [2001] YEL 359.

[558] Art 13(3) of the Brussels Convention. But see in the context of contract choice of law, Art 5(2) of the Rome Convention, discussed infra, p 726, where the same terminology as under Art 13(3) of the Brussels Convention is used.

[559] See generally on Art 15(1)(c) of the Brussels I Regulation and e-commerce: Oren (2003) 52 ICLQ 665.

[560] See *Rayner v Davies* [2002] EWCA 1880 at [24] (per MUMMERY LJ), [2003] IL Pr 15—a case on Art 13(3) of the Brussels Convention of a consumer going to Italy where a surveyor was domiciled and negotiations carried on there but fax sent by surveyor to England with a formal offer, held no invitation by surveyor to consumer in England. Art 15(1)(c) of the Brussels I Regulation would doubtless not be met either.

[561] See Case C-96/00 *Gabriel v Schlanck & Schick GmbH* [2002] ECR I-6367 at 6400-6401, [42]–[44]—a case on Art 13(3) of the Brussels Convention.

towards a Member State can be "by any means". This new concept is designed to make clear that Article 15(1)(c) applies to consumer contracts concluded via an interactive website accessible in the state of the consumer's domicile.[562] Such a contract is treated in the same way as a contract concluded by telephone, fax and the like, and activates the grounds of jurisdiction provided for in Section 4. In determining whether activities have been directed towards a Member State, a relevant factor is that this internet site solicits the conclusion of distance contracts and that a contract has been concluded at a distance.[563] The language or currency that a website uses is not relevant. In contrast to an interactive website, the intention is that the fact that a consumer simply had knowledge of a service or possibility of buying goods via a passive website accessible in his country of domicile will not trigger the protective jurisdiction.[564]

The third major change is to get rid of the condition in the predecessor provision[565] that the consumer must have taken necessary steps for the conclusion of the contract in his home state. This change too was prompted by a consideration of the position where contracts are concluded via an interactive website.[566] For such contracts the place where the consumer takes these steps was seen as being difficult or impossible to determine, and they might in any event be irrelevant to creating a link between the contract and the consumer's state.[567] The philosophy of the new Article 15 is that the co-contractor creates the necessary link when directing his activities towards the consumer's state.[568]

Article 15(1)(c) has been the most contentious of all the changes introduced by the Brussels I Regulation, with the European Parliament suggesting amendments and even that the introduction of the Regulation should be delayed.[569] The Commission refused to accept these suggestions[570] but said that it was planning to pursue current initiatives on alternative consumer dispute-settlement schemes. This is to be welcomed. For all the attention paid to Article 15 of the Brussels I Regulation, international litigation is not the best way of solving cross-border consumer disputes.[571] Also welcome is the introduction of a European Small Claims Procedure.[572]

---

[562] See the Explanatory Memorandum in the Proposal for a Council Regulation COM (1999) 348 final, p 16 (herein after "the Explanatory Memorandum"). There is no protection for professionals who do not know where the consumer is domiciled.

[563] See the Joint Statement by the Council and Commission on Arts 15 and 73.

[564] The Explanatory Memorandum, p 16. See also the Joint Statement by the Council and Commission on Articles 15 and 73.

[565] Art 13(3)(b) of the Brussels Convention.

[566] See the Explanatory Memorandum, p 16.

[567] Ibid.

[568] Ibid.

[569] See the European Parliament's Committee on Citizen's Freedoms and Rights, Justice and Home Affairs; the European Parliament's Committee on Legal Affairs Report on the proposed Brussels I Regulation Final A5-0253/2000. Similar views were expressed by the European and Social Committee in their Opinion OJ 2000 C 117/6. See also Amendment 37 in the Proposal from the Parliament.

[570] COM (2000) 0689 final—CNS 99/0154, 2.2.2.

[571] For the importance of alternative methods of dispute settlement, see the Joint Statement by the Council and Commission on Arts 15 and 73, and the Proposal for a European Parliament and Council Directive on certain aspects of mediation in civil and commercial matters COM (2004) 718.

[572] European Parliament and Council Regulation (EC) No 861/2007 establishing a European Small Claims Procedure OJ 2007 L 199/1; discussed infra, pp 646–648. This introduces a cheaper and simplified procedure. It is optional and covers claims of up to 2,000 Euros. Jurisdiction is still needed in accordance with the Brussels

It is expressly provided that Section 4 on consumer protection shall not apply to contracts of transport other than a contract which, for an inclusive price, provides for a combination of travel and accomodation (package holidays).[573] It also only applies (arguably apart from agreements as to jurisdiction under Article 17 of the Regulation) where the defendant is domiciled in a Member State,[574] and this is extended to cover a defendant with a branch, agency or other establishment in one of the Member States, provided that the dispute arises out of the latter's operations.[575] Section 4 adopts the same approach towards allocating jurisdiction as does Section 3: the normal rules on jurisdiction do not apply (Section 4 should therefore be interpreted so as to be strictly limited to its objectives);[576] the claimant, where he is the weaker party, is given a choice of forum; and the provisions of Section 4 can be departed from by agreement in certain limited circumstances.

Section 4 is, like Section 3, a protective provision; in this case it is the consumer who is in the weaker position.[577] Under Article 16 the consumer is given the choice of suing the other party to a contract either in the defendant's domicile or in his own domicile.[578] Where the roles are reversed, the other party can only sue the defendant consumer in the latter's domicile. Section 4 can be departed from by an agreement which complies with one of the three alternatives under Article 17 (an agreement which is entered into after the dispute has arisen, or an agreement which allows the consumer to bring proceedings in courts other than those indicated in the Section, or an agreement which confers jurisdiction on the courts of the common domicile or habitual residence of the parties) and, presumably, also complies with Article 23. One further limitation on the use of jurisdiction agreements in consumer cases is that the agreement must not infringe the Unfair Terms in Consumer Contracts Regulations 1999.[579] A jurisdiction clause which has not been individually negotiated and which confers exclusive jurisdiction on the seller's or supplier's principal place of business must be regarded as being unfair,[580] as must a clause which involves an imbalance of convenience (alternative jurisidictions available to the claimant but not to the defendant consumer), which took the consumer by surprise (no translation and no careful explanation).[581] Under Article 23, the defendant does not have to be domiciled in a Member State.[582] The position is arguably the same in

---

I Regulation. See also European Parliament and Council Regulation (EC) No 1896/2006 creating a European Order for payment procedure OJ 2006 L 399/1, discussed infra, pp 644–646.

[573] Art 15(3).

[574] Art 15 is without prejudice to Arts 4 and 5(5); Case C-318/93 *Brenner and Noller v Dean Witter Reynolds Inc* [1994] ECR I-4275; Briggs (1994) 14 YEL 578.

[575] Art 15(2); see the opinion of AG LEGER in Case C-281/02 *Owusu v Jackson* [2005] QB 801 at [132]–[134]. For the application of this provision within the United Kingdom (the Modified Regulation does not contain such a provision), see SI 2001/3929, Art 3, Sch 1, para 11. If, as a result of using the deemed domicile provision under Art 15(2), both parties are now domiciled in the same Member State, AG DARMON has given his opinion that the Brussels Convention will not apply since there is no issue of international jurisdiction, the *Bremner* case, supra, at 4282. For interpretation of the phrase "branch . . . operations", see the opinion of AG ELMER in the *Lloyd's Register of Shipping* case, supra, at 971.

[576] *Bertrand v Ott*, supra.

[577] See Recital (13) of the Regulation.

[578] For allocation within the United Kingdom, see the Civil Jurisdiction and Judgments Order, SI 2000/3929, Art 3 and Sch 1, para 7.

[579] SI 1999/3159.

[580] Case C-240/98 *Oceano Grupo Editorial SA v Rocio Murciano Quintero* [2000] ECR I-4941.

[581] *Standard Bank London Ltd v Apostolakis (No 2)* [2002] CLC 939.

[582] Art 4(1) of the Regulation.

Section 4 cases.[583] It is likely that Section 4 can also be departed from under Article 24, ie where the defendant submits to the courts of a Member State by entering an appearance.[584]

(v) Jurisdiction over individual contracts of employment

Section 5 (Articles 18–21) is concerned with matters relating to individual contracts of employment. The Brussels Convention contained certain provisions designed to protect the employee,[585] as the weaker party to the contract. The Brussels I Regulation takes things a stage further by introducing a Section devoted entirely to individual contracts of employment, putting such contracts on the same footing as insurance and consumer contracts. "Matters relating to individual contracts of employment" refers to the situation where claims are made under (ie based on) individual contracts of employment.[586] Thus it is limited to claims in contract and does not cover tortious claims. Section 5 does not define "individual contracts of employment".[587] However, it is clear that "individual" contracts of employment are to be contrasted with collective agreements between employers and workers' representatives.[588] Moreover, guidance can be found in *Shenavai v Kreischer*,[589] where the Court of Justice had to decide in the context of Article 5(1) of the Brussels Convention whether the case involved a contract of employment. *Shenavai* involved a claim by an architect for fees in connection with the drawing up of plans for the building of houses. The Court of Justice held that this was not a contract of employment. It was said[590] that contracts of employment had certain peculiarities, distinguishing them from other types of contract: they created a lasting bond bringing the worker to some extent within the organisational framework of the business of the employer; "they are linked to the place where the activities are pursued, which determines the application of mandatory rules and collective agreements". The relationship of the parties in a contract of employment has also been described as one of subordination of the employee to the employer.[591] The Court of Appeal has emphasised the personal nature of the relationship between employer and employee and the inequality of bargaining power inherent in this. It has held that a contract appointing an advertising agency as a sole commercial agent was not one of employment.[592] Nor was a contract one of employment where a person had his hours expressed in maximum, not minimum, terms, was paid a low

---

[583] See Collins, p 60; Layton and Mercer, para 16.003; see the argument on this point in relation to insurance, supra, p 268. But cf the opinion of AG Darmon in the *Brenner* case, supra, 4281—the *only exception* to Art 4 is contained in Art 13.

[584] *Re Jurisdiction in a Consumer Contract* (Case 2U 1788/99) [2002] IL Pr 14, Regional Court of Appeal, Koblenz.

[585] See Arts 5(1) and 17(5).

[586] *Swithenbank Foods Ltd v Bowers* [2002] EWHC 2257 (QB), [2002] 2 All ER (Comm) 974; *Samengo-Turner v J & H Marsh & McLennan (Services) Ltd* [2007] EWCA Civ 723, [2007] IL Pr 52.

[587] See generally on this concept Allwood (1987) YEL 131 at 137 et seq.

[588] See the Jenard and Möller Report, which accompanied the 1988 Lugano Convention (replaced by the 2007 Lugano Convention), p 73.

[589] Case 266/85 [1987] ECR 239. See also *Benatti v WPP Holdings Italy Srl* [2007] EWCA Civ 263 at [45]–[51] (per Toulson LJ), [75]–[82] (Buxton LJ), [98]–[100] (per Clarke MR), [2007] 1 WLR 2316.

[590] Supra, at 255–256. See also Case 32/88 *Six Constructions Ltd v Humbert* [1989] ECR 341; Hartley (1989) 14 ELR 236.

[591] The Jenard and Möller Report, p 73; *WPP Holdings v Benatti* EWHC 1641 (Comm) at [69], [2006] 2 Lloyd's Rep 610; affd in *Benatti v WPP Holdings Italy Srl* [2007] EWCA Civ 263, [2007] 1 WLR 2316.

[592] *Mercury Publicity Ltd v Wolfgang Loerke GmbH* [1993] IL Pr 142, CA.

retainer plus commission, was allowed to spend a substantial amount of time on other business interests and, if he used a financial adviser in the performance of his duties, had to pay for this himself.[593]

Section 5 also only applies (apart from, arguably, agreements as to jurisdiction under Article 21) where the defendant is domiciled in a Member State,[594] and this is extended to cover a defendant employer with a branch, agency or other establishment in one of the Member States, provided that the dispute arises out of the latter's operations.[595] Where the provisions in Section 5 apply it is not possible to rely on other bases of jurisdiction under the Regulation.[596]

Section 5 is, like Sections 3 and 4, a protective provision: in this case it is the employee who is the weaker party.[597] Under Article 19 the employee is given the choice of suing the employer either in the Member State where the employer is domiciled or in another Member State in the place[598] where the employee habitually carries out his work or in the courts for the last place where he did so. Allocation of jurisdiction to the place where the employee habitually carries out his work has been justified[599] on the basis that this points to the Member State whose law may well be applicable,[600] and on the basis that this best protects the employee as the weaker party.[601] However, a rule based on this place is not without its problems. In the situation where an employee works in several Member States, where is the place where he habitually carries out his work? In *Rutten v Cross Medical,*[602] the Court of Justice held that this is the place where he has established the effective centre of his working activities.[603] The identification of this place is a matter for the national court. However, it is necessary to take into account whether the employee spent most of his working time[604] in one of the Member States and whether the employee has an office where he organises his business activities and to which he returns after each business trip abroad. In the instant case, the employee spent approximately two-thirds of his working hours in the Netherlands and the remaining one-third in four other countries. Moreover, he carried out his work from an office in his home in the Netherlands to which he returned after each business trip. It cannot be open to doubt that he habitually carried out his work in the Netherlands. However, the employee may not have an office that constitutes

---

[593] The *Benatti* case, supra.

[594] Art 18(1) is without prejudice to Arts 4 and 5(5).

[595] Art 18(2). For the application of this provision within the United Kingdom (the Modified Regulation does not contain such a provision), see SI 2001/3929, Art 3, Sch 1, para 11.

[596] Art 18(1), which is without prejudice to Arts 4 and 5(5). Art 24 may be a possible exception to this.

[597] See Recital (13) of the Regulation.

[598] Work on the Continental shelf adjacent to a Member State is regarded as work in that State: C-37/00 *Weber v Universal Ogden Services Ltd* [2002] QB 1189.

[599] See Case 133/81 *Ivenel v Schwab* [1982] ECR 1891; Hartley (1983) 8 ELR 328. The decision is criticised by McClellan and Kremlis (1983) 20 CMLR 529, 542. It was distinguished in *Mercury Publicity Ltd v Wolfgang Loerke GmbH* [1993] IL Pr 142, CA.

[600] The Rome Convention on the Law Applicable to Contractural Obligations (1980), Art 6, discussed, infra, pp 726–727.

[601] Case C-437/00 *Pugliese v Finmeccanica SpA* [2003] ECR I-10829.

[602] Case C-385/95 [1997] ECR I-57.

[603] This takes into account their earlier decision in Case C-125/92 *Mulox IBC Ltd v Geels* [1993] ECR I-4075; Hartley (1994) 19 ELR 540; Plender (1993) 64 BYBIL 558.

[604] Rather than looking just at where he works at the point of dismissal: *Harada Ltd t/a Chequepoint UK Ltd v Turner* [2000] IL Pr 574 at [26], EAT.

the effective centre of his working activities. In such a case, the place where he "habitually" works is that where, taking account of all the circumstances of the case, he actually performs the essential part of his duties.[605] If the employee performs the same activities in several countries, failing other criteria, he will habitually work where he has worked the longest. Applying these criteria it may still be impossible to identify the "habitual" place of work either because there are two places of work of equal importance or because there is no place with a sufficiently strong connection to be regarded as the main link. Article 19(2)(b) provides that "if the employee does not or did not habitually carry out his work in any one country, the employer can be sued in the place where the business which engaged the employee is or was situated". This rule has the virtue of ensuring that jurisdiction is not given to a multiplicity of different Member States.[606] Furthermore, the law of the country in which is situated the place of business through which the employee was engaged will normally be applied, at least in the absence of a choice of the applicable law by the parties.[607] There is no requirement that the countries in which the employee habitually carries out work are Member States. Obviously, though, the place where the business, which engaged the employee, was or is now situated, must be in a Member State. A place of business, in this context, is intended to be understood in a broad sense: "in particular, it covers any entity such as a branch or agency with no legal personality".[608] If the place of business which engaged the employee changes between the time of engagement of the employee and the time when proceedings are brought, the employee can bring proceedings in either place. Under the Brussels Convention the employee was also given the same choice of places in which to sue the employer.[609] What is different under the Regulation is that the position where the employer[610] sues the employee is spelt out. He can only do so in the Member State where the employee is domiciled.[611] He does not have the option, which he had under the Brussels Convention, of suing in the place where the employee habitually carries out his work.[612]

The question can arise of who the employee is working for. A contract of employment may be suspended whilst the employee works for another employer in a different place. The place where the employee habitually carries out his work can be the latter place, provided that at the time of the conclusion of the second contract the first employer has an interest in the employee's performance for the second employer.[613] In determining whether the requisite interest exists it is relevant to consider such factors as whether the

---

[605] Case C-37/00 *Weber v Universal Ogden Services Ltd* [2002] QB 1189, 1211 at [58]. See also Case C-555/03 *Magali Warbecq v Ryanair Ltd* [2004] IL Pr 17, Tribunal De Travail De Charleroi, Belgium, which referred to the Court of Justice (Case 555/03) the problem of identifying the place where a member of air crew habitually works but that Court had no jurisdiction to decide the matter. The Provincial Labour Court of Appeal, Mecklenberg-Vorpommern, Germany, has referred several questions to the Court of Justice in relation to employees working on a ship: Case C-413/07 *Haase v Superfast Ferries SA.*

[606] The Jenard and Möller Report, p 73.

[607] Art 6(2)(b) of the Rome Convention, infra, pp 726–727.

[608] The Jenard and Möller Report, p 73.

[609] See Art 5(1) of the Brussels Convention.

[610] For the meaning of employer, see *Samengo-Turner v J & H Marsh & McLennan (Services) Ltd* [2007] EWCA Civ 723 at [32]–[35], [2007] IL Pr 52.

[611] Art 20(1). However, the employer has the right to bring a counterclaim in the court in which the original claim is pending: Art 20(2).

[612] But if the employee did not habitually carry out his work in any one country the employer had to sue him in his domicile and could not sue in the place of business which engaged him.

[613] The *Pugliese* case, supra, n 601.

second contract was envisaged when the first contract was concluded; the first contract was amended on account of the second; there were organisational or economic links between the two employers.[614]

Section 5 may be departed from by an agreement which complies with one of the two alternatives under Article 21 (an agreement which is entered into after the dispute has arisen, or one which allows the employee to bring proceedings in courts other than those indicated in Section 5). The latter alternative means that a claimant employee can rely on an agreement conferring jurisdiction entered into before the dispute has arisen. In this situation the agreement does not confer exclusive jurisdiction since the claimant employee, instead of suing in the Member State agreed upon, could opt to sue under Article 19 in the Member State of the employer defendant's domicile or in another Member State in the place where the employee habitually carries out his work, etc. On the other hand, an employee in the position of defendant cannot rely on an agreement entered into before the dispute has arisen. An employer, whether acting as claimant or defendant, can only rely on an agreement conferring jurisdiction entered into after the dispute has arisen.[615] The same two alternatives were to be found in the Brussels Convention.[616] The agreement must presumably also comply with Article 23. Under Article 23, the defendant does not have to be domiciled in a Member State.[617] The position is arguably the same in Section 5 cases.[618] It is likely that Section 5 can also be departed from under Article 24, ie where the defendant submits to the courts of a Member State by entering an appearance.

(vi) Exclusive jurisdiction

Article 22[619] allocates jurisdiction to the courts of the Member State which is thought to be uniquely well placed to deal with the subject matter listed in that Article. So strong is this desire to allocate jurisdiction that Article 22 expressly provides that it applies regardless of domicile. It is therefore an exception to the normal rule that the bases of jurisdiction under the Regulation only apply where the defendant is domiciled in a Member State.[620] Where jurisdiction is assigned to the United Kingdom under Article 22, the Modified Regulation will apply to allocate jurisdiction to a part of the United Kingdom. For example, where the proceedings concern the ownership of land in England, the English courts will have exclusive jurisdiction. The jurisdiction under Article 22 is exclusive in the sense that a Member State other than the one which has been allocated jurisdiction under it is deprived of jurisdiction, even though it would otherwise have had it under one of the other bases of jurisdiction such as the domicile of the defendant. Article 22 therefore trumps other bases of jurisdiction, even jurisdiction based on the agreement of the parties.[621] The courts of Member States are required by Article 25 to

---

[614] Ibid at [24], where other factors are listed.

[615] *Samengo-Turner v J & H Marsh & McLennan (Services) Ltd* [2007] EWCA Civ 723 at [37], [2007] IL Pr 52.

[616] Art 17(5) of the Brussels Convention.

[617] Art 4(1) of the Regulation.

[618] See argument on this point in relation to insurance, supra, p 268.

[619] Art 16 of the Brussels Convention.

[620] Case C-343/04 *Land Oberosterreich v CEZ AS* [2006] IL Pr 25 at [21]. See generally supra, pp 224–225. Both the claimant and defendant could be domiciled in a non-Member State, see Case C-281/02 *Owusu v Jackson* [2005] ECR I-1383, [2005] QB 801 at [28].

[621] See Recital (14) of the Regulation. For the relationship between Arts 22 and 27 (*lis pendens*) see infra, pp 310–312.

275

declare of their own motion that they do not have jurisdiction where they are seised of a claim which is principally concerned[622] with a matter over which the courts of another Member State have exclusive jurisdiction by virtue of Article 22. This requirement applies to Member States regardless of their own rules on procedure, which may require the jurisdictional point to be raised by one of the parties, and regardless of what steps have been taken by the defendant.[623] It has meant a fundamental change of procedure for United Kingdom courts, which had, in the past, only acted after submissions from the parties.[624]

Article 22 applies to proceedings involving: (i) immovable property; (ii) certain company law matters; (iii) validity of entries in public registers; (iv) certain matters involving intellectual property; (v) enforcement of judgments. Article 25 suggests that Article 22 only applies where the claim is principally concerned with one of these matters.[625] Where more than one Member State is allocated jurisdiction under Article 22 (eg the claim concerns land in two Member States), Article 29 provides that any court other than the one first seised shall decline jurisdiction.[626]

There are five heads under Article 22, one for each of the above matters. The reported cases on the corresponding provision in the Brussels Convention (Article 16), have given a Community meaning to its terms and have interpreted the heads in the light of their purpose and their place within the scheme of the Convention. This provision must not be given a wider interpretation than is required by its objective.[627] Sometimes this has led to Article 16 of the Brussels Convention (Article 22 of the Regulation) being given a narrow interpretation, on other occasions to a wide interpretation.[628] The head which has the most startling repercussions is the first one and this will be examined in detail; the remaining four heads will merely be stated.

Article 22 provides that the following courts shall have exclusive jurisdiction, regardless of domicile:

> **Article 22(1)** in proceedings which have as their object rights *in rem* in immovable property or tenancies of immovable property, the courts of the Member State in which the property is situated.[629]

---

[622] In *Coin Controls Ltd v Suzo International (UK) Ltd* [1999] Ch 33, Laddie J at 50–51 gave a wide interpretation to the phrase "principally concerned" so that "something which is a major feature of the litigation is not incidental" and therefore comes within this. The result was to preclude jurisdiction for infringement of a patent registered in another Member State in the situation where its validity (see Art 22(4) infra) was going to be raised during the infringement proceedings. The decision was affirmed in *Fort Dodge Animal Health Ltd v Akzo Nobel NV* [1998] FSR 222, CA; Dutson [1998] LMCLQ 505 and in *Prudential Assurance Co Ltd v Prudential Insurance Co of America* [2003] EWCA Civ 327, [2004] FSR 25. See generally Fawcett and Torremans, pp 202–208. Cf *Re Polly Peck International plc (No 2)* [1998] 3 All ER 812 at 828, CA—"principally" means "chiefly", "for the most part".

[623] Case 288/82 *Duijnstee v Goderbauer* [1983] ECR 3663; Hartley (1984) 10 ELR 64.

[624] See the Schlosser Report, p 81.

[625] See the opinion of the Advocate General in the *Duijnstee* case, supra.

[626] See *Prudential Assurance Co Ltd v Prudential Insurance Co of America* [2003] EWCA Civ 327 at [25], [2003] 1 WLR 2295.

[627] Case 73/77 *Sanders v van der Putte* [1977] ECR 2383 at [17]–[18]; *Klein v Rhodos Management Ltd* [2005] ECR I-8667 at [15], [2006] IL Pr 2; Case C-343/04 *Land Oberosterreich v CEZ AS* [2006] IL Pr 25 at [26]–[27].

[628] Cf *Duijnstee v Goderbauer*, supra (on what is now Art 22(4)), and Case 73/77 *Sanders v van der Putte* [1977] ECR 2383, with Case 241/83 *Rösler v Rottwinkel* [1986] QB 33 and *Speed Investments Ltd v Formula One Holdings Ltd (No 2)* [2004] EWCA Civ 1512, [2005] 1 WLR 1936.

[629] Art 16(1)(a) of the Brussels Convention, prior to that Art 16(1).

The immovable property must be situated in a Member State or States.[630] If the dispute relates to property situated in two Member States (eg it concerns the existence of a lease over such property) the Court of Justice in *Scherrens v Maenhout*[631] has held that normally each Member State has exclusive jurisdiction over the property situated in the territory of the state. Nonetheless, in certain exceptional circumstances one State may be given exclusive jurisdiction over the entire property. An example given of where this might happen would be where property is subject to a single lease, the land in one Member State is adjacent to the land in the other Member State and the property is situated almost entirely in one of those two Member States. In cases where the property is situated in the United Kingdom, the Modified Regulation will apply to allocate jurisdiction to a part of the United Kingdom. If the immovable property is situated outside a Member State, Article 22(1) will not apply, but, depending on the circumstances, other bases of jurisdiction under the Regulation may still be applicable, eg the domicile of the defendant in a Member State. Article 22(1) covers two sorts of proceedings: ones which have as their object (ie are based upon) rights in rem in immovable property and ones which have as their object tenancies of immovable property.

(a) Rights in rem

The proceedings must have as their object a right which is enforceable against the whole world (a right in rem), not a right which is merely enforceable against a particular person (a right in personam). Thus proceedings involving a claim to legal ownership of one-half of a villa in Minorca, together with an order that steps be taken to rectify the Minorcan property register and an order for the sale of the villa and division of proceeds, have as their object a right in rem.[632] The essence of the proceedings was an attempt by the trustee to establish, protect and perfect his title.[633] In contrast, the following have as their object a right in personam, and are accordingly outside the scope of Article 22(1): proceedings for rescission of a contract of sale of land and for consequential damages;[634] proceedings to decide whether a contract for the transfer of land had been entered into;[635] proceedings for a declaration that the defendant holds property on trust for the claimant and for an order requiring him to execute documents vesting legal title in the claimant;[636] proceedings for a declaration that a person is an equal owner in equity of property;[637] proceedings brought by a trustee in bankruptcy for an order for the sale of a villa with vacant possession (which did not involve establishing, protecting or perfecting his title to the land);[638] proceedings for compensation for the use of a flat, otherwise than under a tenancy and the ownership of which was not in dispute;[639] proceedings to determine the existence

---

[630] The effect where the property is in a non-Member State is discussed later on in this chapter, infra, pp 327–328.

[631] Case 158/87 [1988] ECR 3791; Hartley (1989) 11 ELR 57.

[632] *Re Hayward* [1997] Ch 45 at 56–57; *Webb v Webb* [1991] 1 WLR 1410.

[633] *Re Hayward*, supra, at 48; distinguished in *Ashurst v Pollard* [2001] Ch 595, 608, CA, on which see Carruthers, paras 2.39–2.50.

[634] Case C-518/99 *Gaillard v Chekili* [2001] ECR I-2771.

[635] *Sorensen v Pedersen* [2006] IL Pr 26, Eastern Court of Appeal, Denmark.

[636] Case C-294/92 *Webb v Webb* [1994] QB 696; Briggs (1994) 110 LQR 526; (1994) 14 YEL 563; Hartley (1994) 19 ELR 547; Rogerson [1994] CLJ 462; Birks (1994) 8 Trust Law Int 99; MacMillan [1996] Conv 125.

[637] *Prazic v Prazic* [2006] EWCA Civ 497, [2006] 2 FLR 1125.

[638] *Ashurst v Pollard* [2001] Ch 595, CA; Briggs (2000) 71 BYBIL 443; Harris [2001] LMCLQ 205.

[639] Case C-292/93 *Lieber v Göbel* [1994] ECR I-2535; Briggs (1994) 14 YEL 572.

or scope of an easement;[640] proceedings for the restoration of property to its original condition;[641] and proceedings for infringement of an intellectual property right.[642] An action to terminate the appointment of a manager of a timeshare development in Spain and eject him from the property did not have as its object rights in rem in immovable property.[643] According to the Court of Justice in *Reichert v Dresdner Bank*[644] Article 16(1) of the Brussels Convention (Article 22(1) of the Regulation) is only concerned with actions which determine "the extent, content, ownership or possession of immovable property or the existence of other rights *in rem* therein and to provide the holders of those rights with the protection of the powers which attach to their interest". Applying this narrow Community definition the Court held that an action whereby a creditor sought to have set aside a gift of the legal ownership of immovable property which he alleged was made by the debtor to defraud his creditors (an action paulienne) did not come within the scope of Article 16 (1) of the Brussels Convention (Art 22(1) of the Regulation). This action did not concern the rules and customs of the situs and accordingly there was no reason why it should come within the exclusive jurisdiction of the courts of the situs. Likewise, applying this narrow Community definition, the Court of Justice has held that Article 16(1) of the Brussels Convention does not apply to an action, possibly preventative, for cessation of a nuisance.[645] Although the basis of such an action was the interference with a right in rem in immovable property, the real and immovable nature of that right was, in that context, of only marginal significance.[646] Moreover, considerations of the sound administration of justice which underlie exclusive jurisdiction under Article 16(1) did not apply to this particular case of nuisance, which involved a claimant and defendant with land in different states, requiring an assessment of facts relating to both States.[647] Finally, this narrow definition would exclude actions for damages based on infringement of rights in rem or on damage to property in which rights in rem exist, since the existence and content of such rights in rem, usually rights of ownership, are of only marginal significance.[648]

(b) Tenancies

Article 22(1) also applies to proceedings which have as their object tenancies of immovable property. Leases involve complex social legislation and the courts of the Member State where this is in force are best able to apply their own law and are accordingly given exclusive jurisdiction.[649] There is little authority on what is meant by a tenancy for the purposes of this provision. It does not include the situation where one party transfers ownership to another, compensation being sought for the use of the property following the annulment of the transfer of ownership.[650] The difficulty with including tenancies

---

[640] Case C-343/04 *Land Oberosterreich v CEZ AS* [2006] IL Pr 25, opinion of AG Maduro at [82].
[641] *Fondation Solomon v Guggenheim v D Helion* [1997] I L Pr 457 (French Sup Ct).
[642] *Pearce v Ove Arup Partnership* [1997] Ch 293 at 302; revsd by CA on a different point [2000] Ch 403.
[643] *Barratt International Resorts Ltd v Martin* 1994 SLT 434.
[644] Case 15/88 [1990] ECR I-27; Hartley (1991) 16 ELR 69. See also the earlier Scots case of *Ferguson's Trustee v Ferguson* 1990 SLT (Sh Ct) 73.
[645] Case C-343/04 *Land Oberosterreich v CEZ AS* [2006] IL Pr 25.
[646] Ibid, at [34].
[647] Ibid, at [37]–[38].
[648] Ibid, at [33].
[649] See the Jenard Report, pp 34–35.
[650] *Lieber v Göbel*, supra, n 639.

under Article 22(1) is that in some cases a dispute between a landlord and a tenant may relate essentially to the land itself (this is within Article 22(1)); whereas, in other cases, the issue may relate more obviously to the contractual rights and obligations between the parties (which are less obviously within the ambit of Article 22(1)).

In *Sanders v Van der Putte*[651] the Court of Justice held that, where the dispute relates to the existence or interpretation of the lease, compensation for damage caused by the tenant[652] or for giving up possession of the premises, it was within Article 16(1) of the Brussels Convention (the corresponding provision to Article 22(1) of the Regulation). The effect of including disputes relating to the existence of the lease is that a court's jurisdiction under Article 16(1) of the Brussels Convention (Article 22(1) of the Regulation) cannot be defeated by an allegation that the lease is void.[653] The Court of Justice, which was not prepared to give Article 16(1) of the Brussels Convention a wider ambit than was required by its objectives, went on to hold that Article 16(1) of the Brussels Convention did not apply to a dispute between an original tenant and a sub-lessee as to the existence of an agreement under which the sub-lessee agreed to rent and run the original tenant's retail business, the emphasis in the agreement being on this latter aspect. The main object of the agreement was the operation of a business undertaking. By analogy with this decision, the Court of Justice in *Hacker v Euro-Relais*[654] held that there was no tenancy agreement within Article 16(1) of the Brussels Convention (Article 22(1) of the Regulation) where a travel agent and a client entered into a contract for a travel package involving the provision of a number of different services, including making reservations for the journey, for an inclusive price, even where one of these services was the use of holiday accommodation. *Hacker* involved a complex contract comprising a range of services. Likewise there was no tenancy agreement where there was a type of timeshare involving a membership contract enabling the member to acquire, for a user fee, the right to use an apartment (within a complex but not individually designated) but also with the service of enabling the member to exchange their holiday accommodation (plus the right to further services at the complex). There was a separate membership fee and user fee, the former costing nearly five times the latter.[655] It is different, and Article 22(1) of the Regulation will apply, where there are services, such as insurance in the event of cancellation or a guarantee of reimbursement in the event of the tour operator's insolvency, which are merely ancillary to a contract's principal status as a tenancy agreement. [656] Such services cannot alter the status of the tenancy agreement, especially when these are not in issue before the court.[657] Moreover Article 22(1) is not rendered inapplicable because the dispute is between a professional tour operator who is subrogated to the rights of the owner and the tenant who had rented the accommodation from the tour operator.[658]

Sanders only dealt with a limited range of the issues that can arise in disputes between a landlord and a tenant. For example, the Court of Justice gave no answer as to whether

---

[651] [1977] ECR 2383; see Hartley (1978) 3 ELR 164.
[652] See also Case C-8/98 *Dansommer A/S v Gotz* [2000] ECR I-393.
[653] See also Case 38/81 *Effer v Kantner* [1982] ECR 825.
[654] [1992] ECR I-1111; Briggs (1992) 12 YEL 657; Plender (1992) 63 BYBIL 607; Hartley (1992) ELR 17.
[655] Case C-73/04 *Klein v Rhodos Management Ltd* [2005] ECR I-8667, [2006] IL Pr 2.
[656] Case C-8/98 *Dansommer A/S v Gotz* [2000] ECR I-393; Peel (2001) YEL 357.
[657] Ibid, 414 at [34].
[658] Ibid, 415 at [38].

claims for the payment of rent and other outgoings were within Article 16(1) of the Brussels Convention. Subsequently, the Court of Justice in *Rösler v Rottwinkel*[659] departed from the spirit of narrow interpretation in *Sanders* by holding that Article 16(1) of the Brussels Convention (Article 22(1) of the Regulation) applies to disputes concerning the respective obligations of the landlord and tenant under the agreement.[660] This would cover, for instance, a simple action for unpaid rent or other outgoings, an action in respect of repairs and decoration of property, and an action in respect of damage to movable property caused by the tenant.[661]

Such disputes are accordingly subject to the exclusive jurisdiction of the Member State in which the immovable property is situated. In favour of this, it can be said that one Member State will be allocated jurisdiction in respect of most of the disputes that can arise between a landlord and a tenant. This is preferable to having an action which involves, for example, a claim for possession and for unpaid rent split up between different Member States. Also the rationale of Article 22(1) of the Regulation leads to a wide interpretation, since many Member States have social legislation in respect of rents and therefore ought to be able to hear a case which involves a claim for rent in respect of property situated in their territory.

The *Rösler* case also establishes, by way of contrast, that proceedings which only indirectly concern the use of the property, such as a claim by a landlord for damages for lost enjoyment of a holiday in the property let (and for travel expenses) following the alleged breach by a tenant of a user clause in the lease, do not have as their object the tenancy of immovable property and accordingly fall outside the scope of Article 22(1).

The Court of Appeal in *Jarrett v Barclays Bank plc*[662] held that timeshare agreements in respect of properties in Spain and Portugal were to be regarded as tenancies within the meaning of Article 16(1) of the Brussels Convention since they involved the right to the exclusive occupation of immovable property owned by the vendors for a specified period in return for a sum of money. However, proceedings brought by purchasers of timeshares against banks which financed the purchase did not have as their object tenancies of immovable property, being based on the debtor-creditor-supplier agreements rather than the timeshare agreements. Accordingly, Article 16(1) of the Brussels Convention did not apply and the English courts could try the actions. In contrast, an action for the payment of the price agreed for a timeshare has been held to come within this provision.[663]

The Hess, Pfeiffer and Schlosser Report voices concern over the necessity for exclusive jurisdiction in contracts relating to the rental of office space and recommends narrowing the scope of Article 22(1) in favour of a more flexible approach.[664]

---

[659] [1986] QB 33. Criticised by F A Mann (1985) 101 LQR 329 and Hartley (1985) 10 ELR 361.

[660] See also the opinion of the Advocate General in *Sanders v Van der Putte*, supra; Anton and Beaumont's *Civil Jurisdiction in Scotland*, para 7.10. Cf the Jenard Report, p 35.

[661] It is not clear whether the damage to property mentioned in *Sanders* was only referring to the immovable property.

[662] [1999] QB 1; Briggs (1996) 67 BYBIL 577.

[663] *Re a Claim for Payment for a Timeshare* [1997] IL Pr 524, Darmstadt District Court.

[664] Para 879 of Study JLS/C4/2005/03, Final Version September 2007, available at the European Commission—European Judicial Network—What's new website http://ec.europa.eu/civiljustice/news/whatsnew_en.htm.

(c) Short-term holiday lets

The *Rösler* case involved a short-term holiday let. Such lets (ie ones for a maximum period of six months) are now subject to the second paragraph of Article 22(1),[665] which provides as follows:

> However, in proceedings which have as their object tenancies of immovable property concluded for temporary private use for a maximum period of six consecutive months, the courts of the Member State in which the defendant is domiciled shall also have jurisdiction, provided that the tenant is a natural person and that the landlord and the tenant are domiciled in the same Member State;

This provision[666] is designed to deal with criticisms levelled at *Rösler v Rottwinkel*. In this case the Court of Justice held, inter alia, that a claim by a plaintiff landlord against a defendant tenant in respect of outgoings, such as water and gas, in relation to the short-term holiday let of a villa in Italy, had to be tried in Italy where the property was situated. This was despite the fact that both parties were resident in Germany and that therefore trial in Italy would be very inconvenient to them. Moreover, the drafters of the Brussels Convention did not intend to give exclusive jurisdiction to the Contracting State in which the property was situated in cases involving short-term holiday lets.[667]

The second paragraph of Article 22(1) meets these criticisms by providing that in a case like this the Member State in which the defendant is domiciled shall also have jurisdiction. The plaintiff in the *Rösler* case could now therefore, if he wanted to, sue in Germany. On the other hand, if he preferred, he could still sue in Italy under the first paragraph of Article 22(1). Both the Member State in which the defendant is domiciled and the Member State in which the property is situated have exclusive jurisdiction under Article 22(1). This could result in concurrent proceedings in two different Member States; eg one party may sue in Italy and the other party in Germany. In such a situation Article 29 will operate so that the court other than the one first seised must decline jurisdiction.[668]

The first requirement that has to be satisfied before jurisdiction is given to the Member State in which the defendant is domiciled is that the proceedings have as their object tenancies of immovable property. The meaning of this has already been examined in relation to the first paragraph of Article 22(1),[669] where the same phrase is used, and the *Rösler* case is still no doubt good authority on this point. The other requirements are largely, but not exclusively, geared to the facts of the *Rösler* case. The second requirement is that it must be a short-term let (for a maximum period of six consecutive months). The third requirement is that the tenant must be a natural person. Legal persons, such as companies, are excluded on the basis that they are generally engaged in commercial transactions. This involves a relaxation from the predecessor wording under the Brussels Convention,[670] which required

---

[665] Art 16(1)(b) of the Brussels Convention.

[666] See the Almeida Cruz, Desantes Real and Jenard Report, para 25. The introduction of this provision into the Brussels Convention followed the 1988 Lugano Convention (on which see the Jenard and Möller Report OJ 1990 C 189/57) with some modifications. The 1988 Convention has been replaced by the 2007 Lugano Convention.

[667] See the Jenard and Möller Report, p 75; the Schlosser Report, para 164.

[668] Infra, p 310.

[669] Supra, pp 277–278.

[670] Art 16(1)(b) of the Brussels Convention. But followed Art 16(1)(b) of the 1988 Lugano Convention (replaced by Art 22(1) of the 2007 Lugano Convention), infra, pp 342–346.

that the landlord must also be a natural person, [671] a requirement based on the facts of the *Rösler* case. Fourthly, both parties must be domiciled in the same Member State.[672]

At the same time, the second paragraph of Article 22(1) is wide enough to cover a dispute between the landlord and tenant that relates (unlike in the *Rösler* case) to the land itself, so that inspection of the land may be necessary. The most appropriate place for trial in such a case is the Member State in which the land is situated; nonetheless, the Member State in which the defendant is domiciled also has jurisdiction, provided that the above requirements are met.

The Hess, Pfeiffer and Schlosser Report has suggested that further consideration needs to be given to the problems of an exclusive jurisdiction in cases concerning the rent of holiday homes and that a more flexible approach seems to be advisable.[673]

Article 22(2) in proceedings which have as their object the validity of the constitution, the nullity or the dissolution of companies[674] or other legal persons or associations of natural or legal persons,[675] or of the validity of the decisions of their organs,[676] the courts of the Member State in which the company, legal person or association has its seat.[677] In order to determine that seat, the court shall apply its rules of private international law;

Article 22(3) in proceedings which have as their object the validity of entries in public registers, the courts of the Member State in which the register is kept.[678]

Article 22(4) in proceedings concerned with the registration or validity of patents, trade marks, designs, or other similar rights required to be deposited or registered, the courts of the Member State in which the deposit or registration has been applied for, has taken place or is under the terms of a Community instrument or an international convention deemed to have taken place.[679]

---

[671] The Almeida Cruz, Desantes Real and Jenard Report, para 25; see also *Jarrett v Barclays Bank plc* [1999] QB 1 at 13–14.

[672] See the *Dansommer* case, supra, where this requirement was not met but the first para of Art 22(1) applied.

[673] Para 880 of Para 879 of Study JLS/C4/2005/03, Final Version September 2007, available at the European Commission—European Judicial Network—What's new website http://ec.europa.eu/civiljustice/news/whatsnew_en.htm.

[674] See *Re Senator Hanseatische* [1996] 2 BCLC 562 at 577; affd by CA at 597 without discussion of this point. This is concerned with the dissolution of solvent companies: *Re Drax Holdings Ltd* [2003] EWHC 2743 (Ch) at [28], [2004] 1 WLR 1049.

[675] This covers an English partnership: *Phillips v Symes* [2002] 1 WLR 853.

[676] *Speed Investments Ltd v Formula One Holdings Ltd (No 2)* [2004] EWCA Civ 1512 at [22]–[34], [2005] 1 WLR 1936—dispute about the composition of the Board; Briggs (2004) 75 BYBIL 543; *Shahar v Tsitsekkos* [2004] EWHC 2659 (Ch) at [47]–[50].

[677] The Regulation differs from the Brussels Convention in making it clear that it is only concerned with the *validity* of the decisions of organs, etc. It covers proceedings *principally concerned with* the validity of directors' exercise of their powers: *Newtherapeutics Ltd v Katz* [1991] Ch 226; Kaye (1991) 10 CJQ 220; Carter (1990) 61 BYBIL 397. See also the *Phillips* case, supra, at [44]–[50]. But not an action concerning misappropriation of the company's money by the directors, *Grupo Torras SA v Sheikh Fahad Mohammed Al-Sabah* [1996] 1 Lloyd's Rep 7, CA, or contractual claims, *FKI Engineering Ltd v Dewind Holdings Ltd* [2007] EWHC 72 (Comm). An "organ" can include a court appointed officer: *Papanicolaou v Thielen* [1997] IL Pr 37 (Irish HC). See also *Bank of Scotland v Investment Management Regulatory Organisation Ltd* 1989 SLT 432. Partnerships are also included, see the Schlosser Report, p 120. See also SI 2001/3929, Art 3, Sch 1, para 10 for a special definition of the seat of a corporation for the purpose of Art 22(2).

[678] *Re Fagin's Bookshop plc* [1992] BCLC 118; *Re Hayward* [1997] Ch 45 at 55–57; *Caledonian Contracting Partnership Ltd v Thomas Rodger* [2004] EWHC 851 (Ch).

[679] See generally the Schlosser Report, p 124; the Jenard Report, p 36; *Duijnstee v Goderbauer* [1984] ECR 3363; Fawcett and Torremans, pp 15–27, 61–62; Wadlow (1985) 10 ELR 305. It covers a petition for revocation

Article 22(5) in proceedings concerned with the enforcement of judgments,[680] the courts of the Member State in which the judgment has been or is to be enforced.[681]

A proposed Article 22(6) The Hess, Pfeiffer and Schlosser Report[682] advocates the introduction of an Article 22(6), according to which exclusive jurisdiction over ancillary proceedings concerned with the support of arbitration proceedings would be granted to the courts of the Member State in which the arbitration takes place.[683]

(vii) Prorogation of jurisdiction

This is referring to jurisdiction selected by the parties. It takes the form of either an agreement on jurisdiction (Article 23), or the defendant's submission to the forum by appearing before its courts (Article 24). In both cases the Regulation respects the wishes of the parties, subject to exclusive jurisdiction under Article 22 which trumps the jurisdiction under Articles 23 and 24.[684]

(a) An agreement on jurisdiction

(i) The effect of the agreement

Article 23[685] is concerned with one type of agreement, ie one which satisfies the requirements in relation to the agreement set out in that article, but it gives the agreement one of two possible effects, depending on where the parties to the agreement are domiciled. The agreement will either give the courts of a Member State jurisdiction (which will be

---

of a patent alleging invalidity: *Napp Laboratories v Pfizer Inc* [1993] FSR 150; *Chiron Corpn v Evans Medical Ltd* [1996] FSR 863 at 866; but not disputes concerning the right to a patent involving an invention of an employee, *Duijnstee v Goderbauer*, supra. Actions for infringement are governed by the general rules in the Convention, including Art 5(3), not by Art 22(4), Case C-4/03 *Gesellschaft für Antriebstechnik mbH & Co KG (GAT) v Luk Lamellen und Kupplungsbau Beteiligungs KG* [2006] ECR I-6509 at [16]; Briggs [2006] LMCLQ 447; see generally supra, p 247, n 372; as are actions for a declaration of non-infringement, the *Chiron* case, supra, at 866–867. In the situations where invalidity is raised as a defence to infringement or a declaration is sought of non-infringement on the basis of invalidity the Court of Justice in *GAT* has ruled that Art 16(4) of the Brussels Convention (Art 22(4) of the Regulation) will apply. See Torremans (2007) (29) EIPR 195–203. Where invalidity is raised as a defence, English courts had come to the same conclusion: *Coin Controls Ltd v Suzo International (UK) Ltd* [1999] Ch 33; *Fort Dodge Animal Health Ltd v Akzo Nobel NV* [1998] FSR 222, CA. See generally on the issue of invalidity as raised in different ways during infringement proceedings, Fawcett and Torremans, pp 201–214 and Fawcett in Fawcett (ed), *Reform and Development of Private International Law*, Chapter 6. The second para of Art 22(4) provides that: "Without prejudice to the jurisdiction of the European Patent Office the courts of each Member State shall have exclusive jurisdiction, regardless of domicile, in proceedings concerned with the registration or validity of any European patent granted for that State." For suggestions for reform of Art 22(4) and more generally for intellectual property cases, see the Hess, Pfeiffer and Schlosser Report, paras 917–925.

[680] See Art 38, infra, pp 605–610: Case C-129/92 *Owens Bank Ltd v Bracco* [1994] QB 509 at 545.

[681] The provision does not cover a set-off between the right whose enforcement is being sought and a claim over which the courts of the Member State would have no jurisdiction if it were raised independently—see Case 220/84 *AS Autoteile Service GmbH v Malhé* [1985] ECR 2267; Hartley (1986) 11 ELR 98. Nor does it cover an action paulienne under French law: Case C-261/90 *Reichert v Dresdner Bank (No 2)* [1992] ECR I-2149. It applies to a third party debt (garnishee) order: *Kuwait Oil Tanker Co SAK v Qabazard* [2003] UKHL 31, [2004] 1 AC 300; Briggs [2003] LMCLQ 418; Rogerson [2003] CLJ 576. It does not prevent a court from granting a world-wide freezing injunction pending enforcement of the English judgment in a Member State: *Babanaft International Co SA v Bassatne* [1990] Ch 13 at 35, 46, CA. See also *Interpool Ltd v Galani* [1988] QB 738, CA.

[682] Study JLS/C4/2005/03, Final Version September 2007, available at the European Commission—European Judicial Network—What's new website http://ec.europa.eu/civiljustice/news/whatsnew_en.htm. See paras 863–865.

[683] The place of arbitration would be defined by a new Recital, see the Hess, Pfeiffer and Schlosser Report, para 870.

[684] See Recital (14) of the Regulation.

[685] Art 17 of the Brussels Convention.

exclusive unless the parties have agreed otherwise) or merely preclude the courts of other Member States from having jurisdiction.

(a) An agreement giving jurisdiction

Where there is an agreement giving jurisdiction under Article 23, the courts of the Member State selected by the parties have jurisdiction (without any discretionary power to refuse to take jurisdiction[686]). Such jurisdiction shall be exclusive unless the parties have agreed otherwise.[687] The consequence of the courts of a Member State being allocated exclusive jurisdiction is that the courts of other Member States[688] are deprived of jurisdiction.[689] In the situation where the parties have agreed otherwise, non-exclusive jurisdiction is allocated. The consequence of this is that the courts of other Member States are not deprived of jurisdiction.

An agreement can only give jurisdiction if one or more of the parties is domiciled in a Member State.[690] It is not specified whether the party domiciled in a Member State should be the defendant or the claimant.[691] However, it is clear, if one looks at Article 4, that it can be either. Article 4 acccepts that Article 23 can operate in the situation where the defendant is not domiciled in a Member State. Article 4 declares that where the defendant is not domiciled in a Member State each Member State shall apply its own law on jurisdiction and not the bases of jurisdiction under the Regulation. But this is expressly made subject to Articles 22 and 23.

(b) An agreement precluding the courts of other Member States from having jurisdiction

Article 23(3) provides that where neither party[692] is domiciled in a Member State "the courts of other Member States shall have no jurisdiction over their disputes unless the court or courts chosen have declined jurisdiction".

Under this provision the Regulation does not give jurisdiction to the court or courts of the Member State selected by the parties. Instead, this court will apply its national rules on jurisdiction, the defendant being domiciled in a non-Member State,[693] and will have

---

[686] See infra, pp 321–327.

[687] Non-exclusive jurisdiction is discussed infra, pp 289–290.

[688] The jurisdiction of non-Member States is not precluded by Art 23: *Ultisol v Bouygues* [1996] 2 Lloyd's Rep 140; appeal allowed on a different point in *Bouygues Offshore SA v Caspian Shipping (Nos 1, 3, 4 and 5)* [1998] 2 Lloyd's Rep 461, CA.

[689] According to the Schlosser Report (p 81), the courts of other Member States must of their own motion consider if what is now Art 23 applies.

[690] Case C-387/98 *Coreck Maritime GmbH v Handelsveem BV* [2000] ECR I-9337—in a case involving third parties one of the parties to the original contract must be so domiciled.

[691] Where both are domiciled in the same Member State, and particularly where the parties also agree on jurisdiction in that State, there is a basic problem of whether the dispute is international in character: see the Schlosser Report, p 123 and the Jenard Report, pp 37–38; the opinion of AG Darmon in Case C-318/93 *Brenner and Noller v Dean Witter Reynolds Inc* [1994] ECR I-4275 at 4282; the opinion of AG Leger in Case C-281/02 *Owusu v Jackson* [2005] ECR I-1383, [2005] QB 801 at [102]. If the dispute is not international in character it should be regarded as being outside the scope of the Regulation; see supra, pp 213–214. But see English cases stating that Art 23 applies despite no international element: *Provimi v Aventis Animal Nutrition SA* [2003] EWHC 961 (Comm) at [74]–[75]—obiter, [2003] 2 All ER (Comm) 683; *Snookes v Jani-King (GB) Ltd* [2006] EWHC 289 (QB) at [39]–[45]—a provisional view, [2006] IL Pr 19; cf *British Sugar plc v Fratelli* [2004] EWHC 2560 at [34]—ratio, [2005] 1 Lloyd's Rep 332.

[692] This is referring to the original contracting parties.

[693] Art 4.

to decide whether it has jurisdiction under those rules. However, an agreement on jurisdiction does preclude courts in other Member States from having jurisdiction; it is only
when the court agreed upon has decided that it has no jurisdiction (or, presumably, has
decided, even though it has jurisdiction, that it is going to use a discretion to decline to
take jurisdiction) that the courts of other Member States can decide whether they have
jurisdiction under their national rules.[694]

This means that parties to an international contract who are domiciled in non-Member
States can oust the jurisdiction of the courts of other Member States by including an
English jurisdiction clause in the contract. Moreover, the subsequent English judgment
will have to be recognised and enforced in other Member States under the Brussels I
Regulation.[695]

(ii) The requirements in relation to the agreement

For an agreement to come within Article 23 two requirements must be satisfied: (i) the
parties must have agreed that a court or the courts of a Member State are to have jurisdiction to settle any disputes which have arisen or which may arise in connection with a
particular legal relationship; (ii) the agreement must satisfy certain requirements as to
form. A claimant who seeks to establish the jurisdiction of the English courts under
Article 23 must show a good arguable case that its terms have been met.[696] However, if
the defendant claims that an English court, which would otherwise have jurisdiction, has
no jurisdiction because of a clause providing for the exclusive jurisdiction of the courts of
another Member State, it has been suggested that the burden lies on the defendant.[697] If
the defendant challenges the jurisdiction under Article 23 by arguing that there was a
contract of employment under Section 5 of the Regulation, it is not up to the claimants
to show they had a much better argument that this was not the case.[698] Before looking in
more detail at these requirements it must be stressed that they apply equally to agreements

---

[694] See the Schlosser Report, p 124.

[695] See infra, pp 598–599.

[696] *Bols Distilleries v Superior Yacht Services Ltd* [2006] UKPC 45 at [28] (per Lord RODGER), [2007] 1 WLR
12. See also *Glencore International AG v Metro Trading International Inc (No 1)* [1999] 2 Lloyd's Rep 632 at 642;
Carnoustie Universal v International Transport Workers Federation [2002] EWHC 1624 (Comm) at [47], [2003]
IL Pr 7; *SSQ Europe SA v Johann & Backes OHG* [2002] 1 Lloyd's Rep 465 at 476; *Evialis SA v SIAT* [2003]
EWHC 863 (Comm) 377 at [70]–[71], [2003] 2 Lloyd's Rep 377; the *Bank of Tokyo-Mitsubishi* case, supra, at
[193]. But see *Standard Steamship Owners' Protection and Indemnity Association (Bermuda) Ltd v GIE Vision Bail*
[2004] EWHC 2919 (Comm) at [27], [2005] 1 All ER (Comm) 618—standard of proof is on a balance of
probabilities where facts have to be decided at the jurisdictional stage and will not be decided later.

[697] *Konkola Copper Mines plc v Coromin Ltd* [2006] EWCA Civ 5 at [95], [101], [2006] 1 Lloyd's Rep
410—not finally deciding the issue; *Hewden Tower Cranes Ltd v Wolffkran GmbH* [2007] EWHC 857 at [46]
(TCC), [2007] 2 Lloyd's Rep 138. See the judgment of David STEEL J in *Knauf UK GmbH v British Gypsum Ltd*
[2001] EWCA Civ 1570 at [41], [2002] 1 Lloyd's Rep 199—the Court of Appeal did not comment on whether
this was correct; *Bank of Tokyo-Mitsubishi Ltd v Baskan Gida Sanayi Ve Pazarlama AS*, supra, at [193]. But cf the
Carnoustie case, supra, at [46]; *Provimi Ltd v Roche Products Ltd* [2003] EWHC 961 (Comm) at [55], [2003] 2
All ER (Comm) 683. The standard of proof is not settled but there has been a tendency to apply a flexible good
arguable case test (consistent with the idea of one side having a much better argument on the material available),
Konkola, at [75]–[96]; *Hewden*, at [46]; *Bols Distilleries*, supra, at [28]; *Benatti v WPP Holdings Italy SRL* [2007]
EWCA Civ 263 at [42]–[44], [2007] 1 WLR 2316. But see the suggestion of RIX LJ in *Konkola* at [96] for a
different test, at least where a jurisdictional issue goes to the heart of the merits. See also RIX LJ in *Royal & Sun
Alliance Insurance plc v MK Digital FZE (Cyprus) Ltd* [2006] EWCA Civ 629 at [62]; [2006] 2 Lloyd's Rep 110.

[698] *Benatti v WPP Holdings Italy Srl* [2007] EWCA Civ 263 at [37]–[44] (per TOULSON LJ), [2007] 1 WLR
2316.

which give jurisdiction and to agreements which merely preclude the courts of other Member States from having jurisdiction.

(a) The parties[699] *must have agreed that a court or the courts of a Member State*[700] *are to have jurisdiction to settle any disputes which have arisen or which may arise in connection with a particular legal relationship*[701]

An agreement Normally, the parties will agree on the court which is to have jurisdiction; however, it can also be conferred by a trust instrument.[702] A choice of jurisdiction clause contained in the statutes of a company can constitute an agreement for the purposes of Article 23, which is binding on all the shareholders.[703] It is not necessary for the jurisdiction clause to be phrased in such a way that the competent court can be identified on its wording alone.[704] It is sufficient that the clause states the objective factors on the basis of which the parties have agreed to choose a court to which they wish to submit disputes. The concept of an "agreement" is to be given an autonomous meaning.[705] In accordance with this, the relationship between shareholders and companies is to be regarded as contractual, irrespective of how national law characterises it. It does not matter that the shareholder has not agreed to the clause. By becoming and remaining a shareholder he agrees to be bound by the contents of the statutes of the company.[706] This takes a relaxed view of the concept of an "agreement". Article 23 stipulates the form which the agreement must take, and the Court of Justice has held that requirements as to form under national law are no longer applicable.[707] To require parties to comply with two sets of formal requirements would impose such a burden on the parties that this would interfere with normal commercial practices.

A question may arise as to the material validity of the "agreement" (ie the jurisdiction clause).[708] Material validity encompasses issues of formation and consent to the agreement.[709] For example, there may be a jurisdiction clause in writing but it is alleged that this is not incorporated into the contract between the parties or that the "contract" containing the jurisdiction clause was never concluded.[710] It might be alleged that, as a result of mistake, misrepresentation, duress or undue influence, there was no consent to

---

[699] An agent can agree: see *Standard Steamship Owners' Protection and Indemnity Association (Bermuda) Ltd v GIE Vision Bail* [2004] EWHC 2919 (Comm) at [52]–[55], [2005] 1 All ER (Comm) 618.

[700] Art 23 will not apply where the clause confers jurisdiction on a state which at the time the action is begun is not a Member State: *Re Exchange Control and a Greek Guarantor* [1993] IL Pr 298, German Federal Supreme Court.

[701] Case C-214/89 *Powell Duffryn plc v Petereit* [1992] ECR I-1745 at 1777–1778.

[702] Art 23(4).

[703] Case C-214/89 *Powell Duffryn plc v Petereit*, supra, at 1772–1775; Briggs (1992) 12 YEL 664; Hartley (1993) 18 ELR 225; Polak (1993) 30 CMLR 406. See also *Re Jurisdiction in Internal Company Matters* [1995] IL Pr 425, German Federal Supreme Court. For satisfying the requirement as to form of the agreement see infra, pp 291–294.

[704] Case C-387/98 *Coreck Maritime GmbHv Handelsveem BV* [2000] ECR I-9337 at [15]—jurisdiction was allocated to the country where the carrier had its principal place of business; noted by Peel (2001) YEL 340.

[705] *Powell Duffryn plc v Petereit*, supra.

[706] Ibid.

[707] Case 150/80 *Elefanten Schuh GmbH v Jacqmain* [1981] ECR 1671; Hartley (1983) 8 ELR 237. The Court of Justice classified the Belgian requirement as to the language of the contract as one of form.

[708] The Schlosser Report, p 125. See generally: Briggs and Rees, para 2.97; Dannemann in Rose (ed), *Lex Mercatoria-Essays on International Commercial Law in Honour of Francis Reynolds* (2000) Chapter 11.

[709] See Art 8 of the Rome Convention, discussed infra, pp 744–745.

[710] *Bols Distilleries v Superior Yacht Services Ltd* [2006] UKPC 45 at [14], [2007] 1 WLR 12.

the clause. The authorities are split on whether the material validity of the "agreement" is to be determined by reference to national substantive law as identified by the relevant private international law rules for determining the applicable law,[711] or by giving the concept of an "agreement" an autonomous Community meaning.[712] The weight of authority favours the latter view. Nevertheless, the former view is the better one in terms of principle. It would seem wrong not to test the validity of this term (ie the jurisdiction agreement) by the law governing the contract, just as one would test the material validity of other terms of the contract by that law. The Hess, Pfeiffer and Schlosser Report sees a solution to the existing problems in relation to material validity in the prospect of some degree of Community harmonisation of the substantive law on formation of contracts.[713]

Where national laws go beyond matters of form and consensus and, as a matter of public policy, have a rule prohibiting agreements conferring jurisdiction in certain cases, for example, in contracts of employment, this national law is overridden by the Regulation and the agreement will have full effect provided, of course, that it complies with all the other requirements under Article 23.[714] It may be alleged that under national law the contract containing the jurisdiction clause is void. Any such dispute is governed by the applicable law determined by the private international law of the Member State of the court having jurisdiction.[715] The courts of the Member State with exclusive jurisdiction under Article 23 also have exclusive jurisdiction in relation to such a dispute,[716] provided that, according to the national court, the jurisdiction clause covers this dispute.[717]

---

[711] Case C-214/89 *Powell Duffryn v Petereit* [1992] ECR I-1745 at [32]–[33]—the questions whether the dispute arose out of the legal relationship in connection with which the jurisdiction agreement was made and whether the scope of the clause applied to the dispute are both a matter for the national court applying national laws. However, the Court at [14] also said that the concept of an agreement conferring jurisdiction must be regarded as an independent one, and see *Provimi Ltd v Roche Products Ltd* [2003] EWHC 961 (Comm) at [83], [2003] 2 All ER (Comm) 683. For national support for this solution see: *Lafi Office and International Business SL v Meriden Animal Health Ltd* [2001] 1 All ER (Comm) 54; *Les Verreries De Saint-Gobain SA v Martinswerk GmbH* [1999] IL Pr 296, Cour de Cassation; *Re a Wood-Cutting Machine* [1995] IL Pr 191, Oberlandesgericht, Dusseldorf.

[712] Case C-288/92 *Custom Made Commercial Ltd v Stawa Metallbau GmbH* [1994] ECR I-2913 at 2946–2948 (AG Lenz, who expressly discusses the matter); Case C-269/95 *Benincasa v Dentalkit Srl* [1997] ECR I-3767, 3797 at [25], criticised by Harris (1998) 23 ELR 279; Case C-159/97 *Transporti Castelletti Spedizioni Internazionali SpA v Hugo Trumpy SpA* [1999] ECR I-1597 at [49] and [51], Hartley (2000) 25 ELR 178, Peel (2001) YEL 340; Case C-116/02 *Erich Gasser v Misat Srl* [2003] ECR I-4207 at [51] and more explicitly by AG Leger at [78] and [81]. For national support see: *Knauf UK GmbH v British Gypsum Ltd* [2001] 2 All ER (Comm) 332, the Court of Appeal left this point open [2001] EWCA Civ 1570 at [61], [2002] 1 Lloyd's Rep 199; *Provimi Ltd v Roche Products Ltd* [2003] EWHC 961 (Comm) at [82], [2003] 2 All ER (Comm) 683. See also Case 25/76 *Galeries Segoura Sprl v Bonakdarian* [1976] ECR 1851 at 1860. Even if the requirements of Art 23 cannot be supplemented by substantive requirements of national law, they are always subject to the requirements of European law. So a jurisdiction clause must not, for example, infringe the Unfair Terms in Consumer Contract Regulations 1999, SI 1999/3159; Case C-240/98 *Oceano Grupo Editorial SA v Rocio Murciano Quintero* [2000] ECR I-4941; Staudenmayer, (2000) 8 ERPL 547; *Standard Bank London Ltd v Apostolakis (No 2)* [2002] CLC 939.

[713] Study JLS/C4/2005/03, Final Version September 2007, available at the European Commission—European Judicial Network—what's new website http://ec.europa.eu/civiljustice/news/whatsnew_en.htm. See para 881.

[714] Case 25/79 *Sanicentral GmbH v Collin* [1979] ECR 3423; Hartley, pp 72–73, and in (1980) 5 ELR 73. See also Case C-269/95 *Benincasa v Dentalkit Srl* [1997] ECR I-3767 at 3797; *Bankers Trust International plc v RCS Editori SpA* [1996] CLC 899. *Snookes v Jani-King (GB) Ltd* [2006] EWHC 289 (QB) at [13]-[32], [2006] IL Pr 19, accepting, obiter, that a jurisdiction clause in breach of the Unfair Contract Terms Act 1977 is unenforceable appears to be wrong.

[715] Case C-269/95 *Benincasa v Dentalkit Srl* [1997] ECR I-3767 at 3797 [25].

[716] Ibid, at 3798–3799.

[717] Ibid; Case C-214/89 *Powell Duffryn plc v Petereit* [1992] ECR I-1745, discussed infra, p 292.

This solution is consistent with that adopted in relation to Articles 5(1) and 22(1).[718] According to the Court of Justice, any other solution would mean that a party could frustrate the operation of what is now Article 23 simply by claiming that the whole of the contract was void.

It is possible to have an incorporation of a jurisdiction clause by reference to another document or contract.[719] For example, a contract may refer to general conditions of trading, a reinsurance contract may incorporate the terms of an insurance contract and a bill of lading may incorporate the terms of a charter-party.[720] The body of terms to be incorporated must be clearly identified. However, in the absence of specific language the court may not be able to conclude that the parties have demonstrated clearly and precisely the existence of a consensus to incorporate clauses, such as a jurisdiction clause, which are ancillary to the subject matter of the contract.

Conferring jurisidiction The agreement must confer jurisdiction on the courts of a Member State. According to the Court of Appeal, the question whether a choice of jurisdiction should be implied in a contract governed by English law, is a matter of English law, which only recognises an express choice of a forum by the parties, eg "all disputes are to be tried before the French courts"; there cannot be an implied choice.[721] In general, Article 23 does not apply where the parties merely specify the Member State which is the place of performance of a contractual obligation, even though the effect of this is to give a Member State jurisdiction under Article 5(1).[722] However, the requirements of Article 23 cannot be evaded by an agreement on a fictitious place of performance. If the agreement on the place of performance is designed solely to establish jurisdiction, not to determine the place where the person liable is actually to perform the obligations incumbent on him, then the requirements of Article 23 must be met.[723]

On the courts of a Member State Article 23 only refers to an agreement that the courts of a "Member State", in the singular, are to have jurisdiction. However, the Court of Justice in *Meeth v Glacetal Sarl*[724] held that an agreement giving jurisdiction to the courts of two Member States was within what is now Article 23. The agreement provided that the parties, who were domiciled in different Member States, could only be sued in the courts of their respective States. This could result in two Member States having exclusive jurisdiction under Article 23 if each party decided to sue the other. Article 29 would then apply

---

[718] *Effer v Kantner*, discussed supra, p 234; *Sanders v Van der Putte*, discussed supra, p 279.

[719] Case 24/76 *Colzani v RUWA* [1976] ECR 1831; *Crédit Suisse Financial Products v Société Générale d'Enterprises* [1997] CLC 168, CA; *AIG v Ethniki* [1998] 4 All ER 301, [2000] 2 All ER 566, CA; *AIG v QBE International Insurance Ltd* [2001] 2 Lloyd's Rep 268; Briggs (2001) 71 BYBIL 452; *Evialis SA v SIAT* [2003] EWHC 863 (Comm) 377 at [25]–[36] and [74]–[80], [2003] 2 Lloyd's Rep 377; *Tradigrain SA v SIAT SpA* [2002] EWHC 106 (Comm), [2002] 2 Lloyd's Rep 553; *Siboti K/S v BP France SA* [2003] 2 Lloyd's Rep 364; *Prifti on behalf of Lloyds Syndicates v Musini Sociedad Anonima de Segouras y Reaseguros* [2003] EWHC 2796 (Comm).

[720] For incorporation by reference to another document see *Evialis SA v SIAT* [2003] EWHC 863 (Comm) 377 at [25]–[36] and [74]–[80], [2003] 2 Lloyd's Rep 377.

[721] *New Hampshire Insurance Co v Strabag Bau AG* [1992] 1 Lloyd's Rep 361 at 371–372. But cf the Schlosser Report, pp 123–124; *British Sugar plc v Babbini* [2004] EWHC 2560 (TCC), [2005] 1 Lloyd's Rep 332.

[722] Case 56/79 *Zelger v Salinitri* [1980] ECR 89, discussed supra, p 244.

[723] Case C-106/95 *Mainschiffahrts-Genossenschaft eG (MSG) v Les Gravières Rhénanes Sarl* [1997] ECR I-911. For discussion of how the purpose of the agreement on the place of performance is to be established, see supra, p 244.

[724] Case 23/78 [1978] ECR 2133; Hartley (1979) 4 ELR 125.

and the court seised of the matter second would defer to the court first seised. The contractual clause in *Meeth* did not give the parties a choice of forum in which to sue. Nonetheless, it is clear that a clause providing, for example, that "the courts of England and Germany are to have exclusive jurisdiction in any proceedings brought by either party" comes within Article 23.[725] Such a clause is exclusive in the sense that it precludes the jurisdiction of the courts of other Member States. Moreover, an agreement which only gives one party a choice of Member States in which to sue will also come within Article 23.[726]

Non-exclusive jurisdiction agreements The parties may agree to confer either exclusive or non-exclusive jurisdiction on the courts of a Member State. It is a matter for national law to determine which it is. As far as English law is concerned, it should be for the law governing the jurisdiction agreement,[727] rather than the agreement as a whole,[728] to determine, as a matter of construction,[729] whether the clause is "exclusive"[730] or not.[731] The burden of proving that the clause is exclusive is said to rest on the party who relies on it.[732] The Brussels I Regulation has clarified the position where the parties have agreed on non-exclusive jurisdiction (ie the agreement purports to give jurisdiction but does not purport to oust the jurisdiction of other states) by adding a sentence to Article 23, which provides that the jurisdiction allocated under Article 23 "shall be exclusive unless the parties have agreed otherwise".[733] This addition makes two things clear. First, an agreement on non-exclusive jurisdiction gives jurisdiction under Article 23 to the courts of the Member State agreed upon. Secondly, such an agreement gives non-exclusive jurisdiction to these

[725] *Kurz v Stella Musical Veranstaltungs GmbH* [1992] Ch 196. See also Case 22/85 *Anterist v Crédit Lyonnais* [1986] ECR 1951 at 1962–1963.

[726] *Anterist v Crédit Lyonnais*, supra. See also *Banque Cantonale v Waterlily* [1997] 2 Lloyd's Rep 347; *Gamlestaden plc v CDS* [1994] 1 Lloyd's Rep 433.

[727] For Scots authority in favour of this solution see *McGowan v Summit at Lloyds* 2002 SLT 1258 at [15]. This will be determined under traditional common law rules; the Rome Convention excludes agreements on jurisdiction from its scope, infra, pp 684–685.

[728] But see *Continental Bank NA v Aeakos Compañía Naviera SA* [1994] 1 WLR 588 at 592, CA, where both pointed to English law.

[729] *Sohio Supply Co v Gatoil (USA) Inc* [1989] 1 Lloyd's Rep 588 at 591, CA; *S&W Berisford plc v New Hampshire Insurance Co* [1990] 2 All ER 321 at 326; *Continental Bank NA v Aeakos Compania Naviera SA*, supra, at 592–594; *Svendborg v Wansa* [1997] 2 Lloyd's Rep 183 at 186, CA; *Insured Financial Structures Ltd v Elektrocieplownia Tychy SA* [2003] EWCA Civ 110 at [8], [2003] QB 1280; *Standard Bank London Ltd v Apostolakis (No 1)* [2002] CLC 933; *Konkola Copper Mines PLC v Coromin Ltd* [2005] EWHC 898 (Comm) at[69]-[73], [2005] 2 Lloyd's Rep 555; affd without discussion of this point [2006] EWCA Civ 5, [2006] 1 Lloyd's Rep 410; *Konkola Copper Mines plc v Coromin Ltd (No 2)* [2006] EWHC 1093 (Comm) at [22]–[24], [2006] 2 Lloyd's Rep 446. See also *FAI General Insurance v Ocean Marine Mutual* (1996–1997) 41 NSWLR 117.

[730] *Evans Marshall v Bertola SA* [1973] 1 WLR 349.

[731] For the relevant principles of construction where English law governs, see: *Pathe Screen Entertainment v Handmade Films* 1989 attached to *Tonicstar Ltd v American Home* [2004] EWHC 1234 (Comm), [2005] Lloyd's Rep IR 32; the *Continental Bank* case, supra, at 593–594; *Sohio Supply Co v Gatoil (USA) Inc*, supra. For the effect of there also being an English choice of law clause cf *British Aerospace plc v Dee Howard Co* [1993] 1 Lloyd's Rep 368, *Sinochem International Oil (London) Co Ltd v Mobil Sales and Supply Corp (No 2)* [2000] 1 Lloyd's Rep 670 at 676 with *Axa v Ace* [2006] EWHC 216 at [29]–[30], [2006] Lloyd's Rep IR 683; *Sea Trade Maritime Corpn v Hellenic Mutual War Risks Association (Bermuda) Ltd (The Athena) (No 2)* [2006] EWHC 2530 (Comm), [2007] 1 Lloyd's Rep 280. See generally Peel [1998] LMCLQ 182 at 182–185. The clause does not have to provide in express terms that the chosen court is to be the exclusive forum. Nor does a non-exclusive agreement have to be express: *Evialis SA v SIAT* [2003] EWHC 863 (Comm) 377 at [68], [2003] 2 Lloyd's Rep 377. For the similar if not identical principles of construction under Scots law see *McGowan v Summit at Lloyds* 2002 SLT 1258.

[732] *Evans Marshall v Bertola SA*, supra, at 361.

[733] Compare the position under the Brussels Convention, infra, p 342.

courts (ie it does not oust the jurisdiction of the courts of other Member States). Article 23 gives full effect to the wishes of the parties. If the parties have agreed on non-exclusive jurisdiction then this is what is conferred under Article 23.

Allocating jurisdiction within the United Kingdom   Where the Member State whose courts are given jurisdiction under Article 23 is the United Kingdom, there is the usual problem of allocating jurisdiction within the United Kingdom. Where the Modified Regulation applies[734]—ie (a) the subject matter of the proceedings is within the scope of the Regulation and (b) the defendant is domiciled in the United Kingdom or the proceedings are of a kind mentioned in Article 22 (exclusive jurisdiction regardless of domicile)—this will provide the answer.[735] Where the Modified Regulation does not apply, the position is less straightforward. It will be necessary to interpret Article 23 as giving jurisdiction not merely to the courts of the United Kingdom, but to the courts of a part of the United Kingdom. This is easy enough where the parties have specifically agreed on trial in England, Scotland, or Northern Ireland. It is not so easy in the unlikely event of the parties merely agreeing on trial in "the United Kingdom", without any further specification.[736]

Conferring jurisdiction on the courts of a non-Member State   Where the parties confer jurisdiction on the courts of a non-Member State, Article 23 will not apply.[737] Other bases of jurisdiction under the Regulation may, however, still be applicable, eg Article 2. A court in a Member State must assess the validity of such a jurisdiction clause according to its own rules for determining the applicable law.[738] The effect to be given to such a clause, if it is valid, is less clear. In particular, can such a clause be used as a ground for declining jurisdiction under the Regulation? This raises the whole question of whether there is a discretion to stay actions under the Regulation, which is considered later in this chapter.[739]

To settle any disputes which have arisen   The agreement must be to settle any disputes "which have arisen or which may arise".[740] It follows that an agreement as to jurisdiction may be made after the dispute has arisen, as well as beforehand. It is for the national court to interpret the clause conferring jurisdiction invoked before it in order to determine whether the dispute in question comes within its scope.[741] The Court of Appeal has held that this raises a question of construction of the clause, and that that is a question of law to be determined by the governing law.[742] This should be the law applicable to the clause

---

[734] See infra, pp 346–348.

[735] See infra, pp 346–352.

[736] See Briggs and Rees, para 2.93.

[737] The *Coreck* case, supra, para 19.

[738] Ibid.

[739] Infra, pp 320–333.

[740] See *British Steel Corpn v Allivane International Ltd* 1989 SLT (Sh Ct) 57.

[741] Case C-214/89 *Powell Duffryn plc v Petereit* [1992] ECR I-1745; Case C-269/95 *Benincasa v Dentalkit Srl* [1997] ECR I-3767 at 3798. See *Hewden Tower Cranes Ltd v Wolffkran Gmbh* [2007] EWHC 857 at [34]–[39] (TCC), [2007] 2 Lloyd's Rep 138.

[742] *Continental Bank NA v Aeakos Compañía Naviera SA* [1994] 1 WLR 588 at 592, CA. See also *Re Leyland Daf Ltd* [1994] 1 BCLC 264; affd [1994] 2 BCLC 106, CA, without discussion of this point; *Ocarina Marine Ltd v Marcard Stein & Co* [1994] 2 Lloyd's Rep 524; *Maimann v Maimann* [2001] IL Pr 27; *Carnoustie Universal v International Transport Workers Federation* [2002] EWHC 1624 (Comm) at [92]–[106], [2003] IL Pr 7; *Provimi Ltd v Roche Products Ltd* [2003] EWHC 961 (Comm) at [57], [2003] 2 All ER (Comm) 683; *Evialis SA v SIAT* [2003] EWHC 863 (Comm) 377 at [60]–[61], [2003] 2 Lloyd's Rep 377; *Snookes v Jani-King (GB) Ltd*

rather than the law applicable to the agreement as a whole.[743] Accordingly, where English law governs, the relevant English principles of construction[744] will apply. The same court has been prepared to determine whether disputes arising in Greek proceedings come within a clause governed by English law.[745] The disputes which the agreement is dealing with must be "in connection with a particular legal relationship". This has been interpreted to mean that, if the courts of a Member State have exclusive jurisdiction under what is now Article 23, the same courts are not precluded from considering a set-off by the defendant against the plaintiff, thereby cutting out superfluous procedure.[746]

(b) The form of the agreement

A choice of jurisdiction clause may be included within the varied terms of a standard form contract and there is a danger of it going unnoticed by one of the parties. Article 23 contains specific requirements[747] as to the form of the agreement in order to prove the genuine consensus of the parties. The agreement must be (a) in writing[748] or evidenced in writing, or (b) in a form which accords with practices which the parties have established between themselves, or (c) in international trade or commerce, in a form which accords with a usage of which the parties are or ought to have been aware and which in such trade or commerce is widely known to, and regularly observed by, parties to contracts of the type involved in the particular trade or commerce concerned. Before looking at these requirements a few words are necessary on the attitude of the Court of Justice towards their interpretation. The Court of Justice has considered, on the one hand, the purpose of the requirements as to form and the place of Article 17 within the Brussels Convention, which corresponds to Article 23 in the Regulation, both of which lead to a strict interpretation, and, on the other hand, the need to uphold normal commercial practices, which necessitates that the formal requirements be not unduly onerous.

In writing or evidenced in writing The *in writing* requirement is clearly satisfied where there is a written contract which contains a choice of jurisdiction clause in the text and the contract is signed by both parties. Any variant of this causes problems. Where the choice of jurisdiction clause is contained in general conditions on the back of a written and signed contract there is a danger that, although it is in writing, it will still go unnoticed. Accordingly, the Court of Justice has held that the text of the contract must contain

---

[2006] EWHC 289 (QB) at [52], [2006] IL Pr 19; *Clare Taverns v Charles Gill* [2000] ILRM 98 at 109–111; *Bio-Medical Research Ltd v Delatex SA* [2001] 2 ILRM 51, SC of Ireland; *Leo Laboratories v Crompton BV* [2005] 2 ILRM, SC of Ireland. For Scotland see *Mackays Stores Ltd v Topward Ltd* 2006 SLT 716.

[743] The two were the same in the *Continental Bank* case.

[744] Set out in the *Continental Bank* case, supra, at 592–593; see also *Kitechnology BV v Unicor GmbH Plastmaschinen* [1994] I L Pr 568 at 574–577, CA. Under English law the scope of a jurisdiction agreement in an interntional commercial contract should be construed liberally: *Fiona Trust & Holding Corpn v Privalov* [2007] EWCA Civ 20 at [18] (per Longmore LJ), [2007] 2 Lloyd's Rep 267; appeal dismissed sub nom *Premium Nafta Products Ltd v Fili Shipping Co Ltd* [2007] UKHL 40, [2007] 2 All ER (Comm) 1053; discussed infra, p 452. For explicit support in the House of Lords for the views of Longmore LJ see at [26] (per Lord Hope), [38] (per Lord Brown).

[745] Criticised infra, pp 310–311.

[746] Case 23/78 *Meeth v Glacetal* [1978] ECR 2133. For counterclaims see the Advocate General's opinion in that case and Art 6(3).

[747] See also the requirement of form where a person is domiciled in Luxembourg, see Art 63(2).

[748] For the procedural classification of a requirement as to writing under English private international law, see *Leroux v Brown* (1852) 12 CB 801, supra, pp 76–77.

an express reference to these general conditions.[749] The text of the contract[750] does not have to contain an express reference to the jurisdiction clause, it is enough that it refers to the general conditions containing this clause.[751] The fact that the other party does not have a copy of these general conditions is irrelevant.[752] Similarly, where the contract refers to earlier offers which had general conditions on the back, the text of the contract must refer expressly to the earlier offers.[753] Where the written contract contains the choice of jurisdiction clause in the text but has only been signed by one party, there is, again, a danger of it going unnoticed by the other party. The Court of Justice has held that the consent of the other party has also to be in writing, either in the document itself or in a separate document.[754] The effect of these cases is that not only must the choice of jurisdiction clause be in writing but also the consensus on its application must be in writing. Although this strict approach remains good law,[755] subsequent cases raising different issues have taken a more liberal line. The mere fact that a written agreement containing a choice of jurisdiction clause has expired is not fatal if it can be shown that under the relevant applicable law the parties can validly extend the initial contract without observing the requirements of writing.[756] In the case of a shareholder, the requirement of form is complied with if the statutes containing the jurisdiction clause are lodged in a place to which the shareholder may have access or in a public register.[757]

Article 23(2) provides that: "Any communication by electronic means which provides a durable record of the agreement shall be equivalent to 'writing'." This is a new provision which is concerned with contracts concluded by electronic means. It ensures that the need for the agreement to be in writing or evidenced in writing does not invalidate a jurisdiction agreement concluded in a form that is not written on paper but is accessible on screen.[758]

The *evidenced in writing* alternative is designed to deal with the situation where there is an oral contract which is confirmed in writing.[759] In *Galeries Segoura Sprl v Firma Rahim Bonakdarian*[760] the Court of Justice held that, where an oral agreement is made subject

---

[749] Case 24/76 *Colzani v Rüwa* [1976] ECR 1831. See also *Marine Contractors Inc v Shell Petroleum Development Co of Nigeria* [1984] 2 Lloyd's Rep 77; *Richard SA v Pavan* [1998] I L Pr 193, French Sup Ct (illegible choice of jurisdiction clause—Art 17 of the Brussels Convention not satisfied); *Lafarge Plasterboard Ltd v Fritz Peters & Co KG* [2000] 2 Lloyd's Rep 689 at 697; *Lafi Office and International Business SL v Meriden Animal Health Ltd* [2001] 1 All ER (Comm) 54—party sending terms and conditions cannot argue it did not consent; *7E Communications Ltd v Vertex Antennentechnik GmbH* [2007] EWCA Civ 140, [2007] 1 WLR 2175; *Stryker Corpn v Sulzer Metco AG* [2006] IEHC 60, [2007] IL Pr 47.

[750] The contract may be contained in two documents, see *7E Communications Ltd v Vertex Antennentechnik GmbH* [2007] EWCA Civ 140 at [33]–[37], [2007] 1 WLR 2175.

[751] *7E Communications*, supra, at [30]–[32].

[752] *Crédit Suisse Financial Products v Société Générale d'Entreprises* [1997] IL Pr 165, CA.

[753] The *Colzani* case, supra, at [12]. The conditions must have been expressly referred to in the offer and must have been communicated to the other party.

[754] Case 71/83, *Partenreederei MS Tilly Russ v Haven and Vervaebedriff Nova NV* [1985] QB 931, [1984] ECR 2417; see the notes by Wilderspin (1984) 9 ELR 456, and North [1985] LMCLQ 177.

[755] *Siboti K/S v BP France SA* [2003] EWHC 1278 (Comm) at [39], [2003] 2 Lloyd's Rep 364.

[756] Case 313/85 *Iveco Fiat SpA v Van Hool NV* [1986] ECR 3337; Allwood (1987) 12 ELR 461.

[757] Case C-214/89 *Powell Duffryn plc v Petereit* [1992] ECR I-1745.

[758] See the Explanatory Memorandum in the Proposal for a Council Regulation COM (1999) 348 final, p 18.

[759] But see *Middle East Tankers & Freighters Bunker Services SA v Abu Dhabi Container Lines PJSC* [2002] EWHC 957 (Comm), [2002] 2 Lloyd's Rep 643 at 651–652.

[760] Case 25/76 [1976] ECR 1851.

to general conditions of sale, the confirmation in writing (accompanied in that case by notification of the general conditions of sale which contained a clause conferring jurisdiction) must be accepted in writing by the other party. It was reasoned that in such a case there is no initial oral agreement as to a clause conferring jurisdiction which is capable of being evidenced by the confirmation in writing. Subsequently, the Court of Justice has shown a concern that the requirements as to form should not be so onerous as to impede normal commercial practices, and has adopted a rather more liberal line. In *Partenreederi MS "Tilly Russ" v Nova NV*[761] it held that where the choice of jurisdiction clause is in writing (in the instant case, in printed conditions in a bill of lading[762]) this can be regarded as written confirmation of an earlier communicated oral agreement between the parties expressly referring to that clause.

The same willingness to recognise that there has been confirmation in writing is evident in the decision of the Court of Justice in *F Berghoefer GmbH and Co Kg v ASA SA*.[763] Here it was held that, in the situation where there is an oral agreement expressly dealing with jurisdiction,[764] the formal requirements of Article 17 of the Brussels Convention (the corresponding provision to Article 23 of the Regulation) were satisfied if written confirmation of the agreement by one of the parties was received by the other and the latter raised no objection. It was not required that the confirmation comes from the party who stands to lose from the clause. Thus in the instant case it was a German plaintiff who confirmed the oral agreement that the German courts should have exclusive jurisdiction.

In a form which accords with practices which the parties have established between themselves   This provision gives effect to the idea developed by the Court of Justice that the consensus of the parties may be shown by a continuous business relationship between them which was subject to the general conditions containing the jurisdiction clause.[765]

In international trade or commerce, in a form which accords with a usage of which the parties are or ought to have been aware and which in such trade or commerce is widely known to, and regularly observed by, parties to contracts of the type involved in the particular trade or

---

[761] Supra.

[762] The bill of lading may come into existence after the creation of the contract of carriage to which the jurisdiction clause relates; however, Art 23 does not require the agreement on jurisdiction to be contemporaneous with the original contract. See on this aspect of the case, North [1985] LMCLQ 177.

[763] Case 221/84 [1985] ECR 2699; Hartley (1986) 11 ELR 470. For an English case taking this liberal line, see *Middle East Tankers & Freighters Bunker Services SA v Abu Dhabi Container Lines PJSC* [2002] EWHC 957 (Comm), [2002] 2 Lloyd's Rep 643. See also Case 313/85 *Iveco Fiat SpA v Van Hool NV* [1986] ECR 3337.

[764] See *Bols Distilleries v Superior Yacht Services Ltd* [2006] UKPC at [38], [2007] 1 WLR 12—not evidenced in writing where no evidence jurisdiction agreement ever discussed and agreed.

[765] *Partenreederei M S Tilley Russ v Haven and Vervaebedriff Nova NV*, supra; *Segoura v Bonakdarian*, supra. See also *O T Africa Line Ltd v Hijazy (The Kribi)* [2001] 1 Lloyd's Rep 76 at 89; *SSQ Europe SA v Johann & Backes OHG* [2002] 1 Lloyd's Rep 465—a good arguable case established that the defendant had traded for a long period (with 672 invoices) in the knowledge that the claimant was only willing to deliver on its standard terms and the defendant knew the content of these terms and never once objected to them; *Middle East Tankers & Freighters Bunker Services SA v Abu Dhabi Container Lines PJSC* [2002] EWHC 957 (Comm), [2002] 2 Lloyd's Rep 643, 652; *Lafarge Plasterboard Ltd v Fritz Peters & Co KG* [2000] 2 Lloyd's Rep 689 at 698; *Standard Steamship Owners' Protection and Indemnity Association (Bermuda) Ltd v GIE Vision Bail* [2004] EWHC 2919 (Comm) at [45], [2005] 1 All ER (Comm) 618; *Oakley v Ultra Vehicle Design Limited (In Liquidation)* [2005] EWHC 872 (Ch) at [54], [2005] IL Pr 55.

commerce concerned[766]   This provision on trade usage was introduced[767] because of fears that the Court of Justice had interpreted the original requirements on writing or evidenced in writing so restrictively that businessmen would find it hard to meet them.[768] This relaxation of the formal requirements has repercussions on the issue of the reality of the consensus of the parties to the jurisdiction clause. This consensus is presumed to exist where commercial usages in the relevant branch of international trade or commerce exist in this regard of which the parties are or ought to have been aware.[769] A usage in international trade or commerce must exist.[770] The form must accord with established usages. This is assessed solely in the light of commercial usages, not by national requirements. [771] No independent requirements are laid down for this, such as that the jurisdiction clause is contained in a written document. The parties must have been or ought to have been aware of the usage.[772] There is an additional requirement[773] that this usage must, on the one hand, be widely known to, and, on the other hand, regularly observed by, parties to contracts of the type involved in the particular trade or commerce concerned.[774] The Hess, Pfeiffer and Schlosser Report sees a solution to the existing problems in relation to determining usages in the prospect of some degree of Community harmonisation of the substantive law on formation of contracts.[775]

Which party can allege that the requirements relating to form have not been met? Clearly the party who did not have notice of the choice of jurisdiction clause can do so. This was the position in the *Colzani* and *Segoura* cases. But if this party wishes to rely on the clause, can the other party, who knew about it from the outset, challenge the clause on the basis of lack of compliance with the requirements as to form? Since the purpose of these requirements is to prevent choice of jurisdiction clauses going unnoticed by one of the parties, it is arguable that only the party who did not have notice of the clause should be able to challenge it.[776] On the other hand, if, as the Schlosser Report suggested in relation to the Brussels Convention,[777] the courts of Member States must of their own motion determine whether Article 17 (Article 23 of the Regulation) operates to prevent them from having jurisdiction, these are requirements which apply regardless of the arguments of the parties, and it should be irrelevant which party raises the issue.

---

[766] Case C-106/95 *Mainschiffahrts-Genossenschaft eG (MSG) v Les Gravières Rhénanes Sarl* [1997] ECR I-911; Seatzu (1998) 49 NILQ 327; AG Lenz's opinion in Case C-288/92 *Custom Made Commercial Ltd v Stawa Metallbau GmbH* [1994] ECR I-2913 at 2934–2948; Case C-159/97 *Transporti Castelletti Spedizione Internatzionali SpA v Hugo Trumpy SpA* [1999] ECR I-1597.

[767] See the 1978 Accession Convention to the Brussels Convention.

[768] See the Schlosser Report, p 125. It may be that both the *Colzani* and *Segoura* cases would now come within this, as would *The Tilly Russ* (see *SSQ Europe SA v Johann & Backes OHG* [2002] 1 Lloyd's Rep 465 at 481).

[769] Case C-106/95 *Mainschiffahrts-Genossenschaft eG (MSG) v Les Gravières Rhénanes Sarl*, supra, at 201–202; Case C-159/97 *Trasporti Castelletti Spedizioni Internazionali SpA v Hugo Trumpy SpA* [1999] ECR I-1597.

[770] The *Trasporti Castelletti* case, supra, 1651, at [30]; *Standard Steamship Owners' Protection and Indemnity Association (Bermuda) Ltd v GIE Vision Bail* [2004] EWHC 2919 (Comm) at [44], [46], [2005] 1 All ER (Comm) 618. See also *Clare Taverns v Charles Gill* [2000] ILRM 98, 109.

[771] See the *Trasporti Castelletti* case, supra, at [39].

[772] Ibid at para 45. See also *The Kribi*, supra, at 90; *Clare Taverns v Charles Gill* [2000] ILRM 98, 109.

[773] Originally added to the Brussels Convention by the 1989 Accession Convention, Art 7.

[774] See *The Kribi*, supra, at 90.

[775] Study JLS/C4/2005/03, Final Version September 2007, available at the European Commission—European Judicial Network—what's new website http://ec.europa.eu/civiljustice/news/whatsnew_en.htm. See para 882.

[776] For the position in respect of a third party in relation to a contract of insurance, see Case 201/82 *Gerling v Italian Treasury* [1983] ECR 2503.

[777] Schlosser Report, p 21; see also the *Colzani* case.

(iii)   Third parties and jurisdiction agreements

Do the requirements as to form apply in relation to third parties? In *Gerling v Italian Treasury*[778] the Court of Justice held that a third party beneficiary would be entitled to rely on a choice of jurisdiction clause inserted for his benefit in a contract (which satisfied Article 17 of the Brussels Convention requirements) between an insurer and a policy-holder, even though the third party had satisfied the requirements as to form. The Court pointed out that the provisions on insurance in the Convention were designed to protect the policyholder. It would be pointless to require a third party to go through these formalities; and in those cases where the beneficiary was not told of the jurisdiction clause, impossible for him to do so. Consistent with this, in the later *Tilly Russ*[779] case it was held that a third party who, under the applicable national law, stood in the shoes of an original shipper, succeeding to his rights and obligations under a bill of lading (which did comply with Article 17 of the Brussels Convention, corresponding to Article 23 of the Regulation), could not avoid the obligations in respect of jurisdiction under this by arguing that he did not consent to the jurisdiction clause.[780] But, according to the Court of Justice in *Coreck Maritime GmbH v Handelsveem BV*,[781] a jurisdiction clause is only valid as against a third party who succceeded by virtue of the applicable national law to the shipper's rights and obligations. If the third party bearer of the bill of lading, succeeded by virtue of the applicable law to the shipper's rights and obligations when he acquired the bill of lading there is no need to ascertain whether he accepted the jurisdiction clause in the original contract.[782] However, if, under the applicable national law, the party not privy to the original contract did not succeed to the rights and obligations of one of the original parties, the court seised must ascertain, having regard to the requirements laid down in the first paragraph of Article 17 of the Brussels Convention, whether he actually accepted the jurisdiction clause relied on against him.[783] The crucial question whether a party not privy to the original contract has succeeded to the rights and obligations of one of the original parties must be determined according to the applicable national law.[784] The principle in *Tilly Russ* applies equally to the situation where neither

---

[778] Case 201/82 [1983] ECR 2503; Hartley (1983) 8 ELR 264 Applied in: *Re Leyland Daf Ltd* [1994] 2 BCLC 106, CA—involving a receiver of a company; *Glencore International AG v Metro Trading International Inc (No 1)* [1999] 2 Lloyd's Rep 632—involving an assignee of a debt. See also Case C-112/03 *Société Financière & Industrielle du Peloux v Société AXA Belgium* [2006] QB 251, discussed supra, p 268.

[779] Case 71/83 [1985] QB 931, [1984] ECR 2417.

[780] Under English law a third party holder of a bill of lading will so succeed: *The Kribi*, supra, at 90. A receiver of a company is bound by an agreement on jurisdiction entered into by the company: *Re Leyland Daf Ltd* [1994] 2 BCLC 106, CA; *Glencore International AG v Metro Trading International Inc (No 1)*, supra. See also *WPP Holdings Italy Srl v Benatti* [2006] EWHC 1641 (Comm) at [102]–[108], [2006] 2 Lloyd's Rep 610; it was not necessary to discuss this point on appeal in *Benatti v WPP Holdings Italy SRL* [2007] EWCA Civ 263, [2007] 1 WLR 2316—appeal allowed in relation to one claimant and dismissed in relation to other claimants.

[781] Case C-387/98 [2000] ECR I-9337. See also *Siboti K/S v BP France SA* [2003] 2 Lloyd's Rep 364; *Hapag Lloyd Container Line GmbH v La Réunion Européenne* [2003] IL Pr 51, French Cour de Cassation.

[782] The *Coreck* case, supra, at [25]. Cf the attitude of the Court of Justice towards the use of Art 5(1) of the Brussels Convention, see supra, pp 229–230.

[783] Ibid, at [26]. See *Astilleros Zamakona SA v MacKinnons* 2002 SLT 1206; *Andromeda Marine SA v OW Bunker & Trading A/S (The Mana)* [2006] EWHC 777 (Comm), [2006] 2 Lloyd's Rep 319; *Hewden Tower Cranes Ltd v Wolffkran Gmbh* [2007] EWHC 857 at [52]–[60] (TCC), [2007] 2 Lloyd's Rep 138. Regard must be had to the formalities under Art 23(1) of the Brussels I Regulation.

[784] The *Coreck* case, supra, at [24]. The national court must apply its rules of private international law to determine this law: ibid, [30].

party is privy to the original contract of carriage. [785] The original contracting parties must have consented to the jurisdiction clause (which means satisfying the formal requirement) and each new party must have succeeded to the rights and obligations of an original party.

(iv) Limitations on the effectiveness of the agreement

First, Article 23(5) provides that the courts which have exclusive jurisdiction under Article 22 cannot be deprived of it by an agreement under Article 23, and any agreement which purports to do so shall have no legal force. It also provides that agreements conferring jurisdiction are also of no legal force if they are contrary to Article 13, 17 or 21. [786] This means that in matters relating to insurance, in consumer contracts and in individual contracts of employment, any agreement conferring jurisdiction must comply with both the requirements of Article 23 and Article 13, 17 or 21.

Secondly, there is another limitation on the effectiveness of the agreement, which is not mentioned in Article 23. The Court of Justice has held that the defendant's submission to the courts of a Member State under Article 18 of the Brussels Convention (Article 24 of the Regulation) overrides an agreement conferring jurisdiction under Article 17 of the Convention (Article 23 of the Regulation). [787]

Thirdly, [788] Article 27 of the Regulation (*lis pendens*) operates as a limitation on the effectiveness of an agreement on jurisdiction. A party who does not wish to be bound by an agreement providing, for example, for the exclusive jurisdiction of the English courts can bring pre-emptive proceedings before the courts of another Member State. The court seised first may decide that it has no jurisdiction because of the jurisdiction agreement. But there will inevitably be a delay before it reaches its decision on this matter and, depending on the Member State in question, this may be an excessive delay. In the meantime, the court seised second has to stay its proceedings until the court seised first has declared that it has no jurisdiction. [789] Alternatively, the court seised first may declare that the agreement does not apply and takes jurisdiction. The English court being seised second cannot examine the jurisdiction of the court first seised. [790] It must stay its proceedings until the jurisdiction of the court seised first is established and, once it is, must then decline jurisdiction.

(b) Submission to the forum

Article 24 (Article 18 of the Brussels Convention) provides that "a court of a Member State before which a defendant enters an appearance shall have jurisdiction". This means that where the defendant submits to the courts of a Member State he will give that State jurisdiction even though it would not otherwise have had it under the Regulation. Once the defendant has submitted, this covers the whole of the proceedings, including any

---

[785] Case C-159/97 *Trasporti Castelletti Spedizioni Internazionali SpA v Hugo Trumpy SpA* [1999] ECR I-1597. See the opinion of AG Leger at 1617 [79].

[786] For the burden of proof see *Benatti v WPP Holdings Italy Srl* [2007] EWCA Civ 263 at [37]–[44] (per Toulson LJ), [2007] 1 WLR 2316; discussed supra, p 226.

[787] Case 150/80 *Elefanten Schuh GmbH v Jacqmain* [1981] ECR 1671.

[788] There is a fourth limitation that applies under Art 17 of the Brussels Convention, see infra, p 342.

[789] C-116/02 *Erich Gasser v Misat Srl* Case [2003] ECR I-4207; discussed infra, pp 310–312.

[790] Ibid.

earlier orders or decisions in the proceedings.[791] Where the appearance is before the United Kingdom courts the familiar problem of allocating jurisdiction within the United Kingdom arises.[792] Where the Modified Regulation applies, this will allocate jurisdiction to a part of the United Kingdom. Where it does not, the Regulation itself can be regarded as allocating jurisdiction to the courts of England, Scotland or Northern Ireland, depending on which court the defendant actually appears before.

For Article 24 to apply there are two conditions. First, it is arguable that in principle the defendant must be domiciled in a Member State.[793] The argument for this is as follows. Article 24 must be read in the light of Articles 3 and 4. Unless there is something in the wording of Article 24 to indicate that it applies regardless of the defendant's domicile, those articles would confine it to the situation where the defendant is domiciled in a Member State. There is nothing in the wording of Article 24 to indicate that it is intended to apply regardless of domicile. The wording of this provision can be contrasted with that of Article 23 which does indicate that it is intended to apply regardless of the defendant's domicile.[794] There is an argument against this, albeit of less weight. Article 23 applies regardless of the defendant's domicile, and so should Article 24 since both articles are dealing with prorogation of jurisdiction;[795] indeed Article 24 can override Article 23.[796] A counter-argument to this is that with Article 23 it has recently been spelt out in Article 4 of the Regulation that it applies, regardless of the defendant's domicile. Article 4 does not treat Articles 23 and 24 the same. The failure to also mention Article 24 would suggest that it is not intended to so apply. As regards authority on this vexed question, there seems to be a comment from Advocate General DARMON[797] that Article 18 of the Brussels Convention (Article 24 of the Regulation) is an exception to Article 4 and applies regardless of the defendant's domicile. More importantly, the Court of Justice has said in a case that did not involve this provision that under Article 18 of the Convention the defendant's domicile is not relevant.[798] But these were comments made in relation to the earlier Brussels Convention. What we are now concerned with is the Regulation, with its alteration of Article 4 to include Article 23 but with no mention of Article 24.

Secondly, the defendant must enter an appearance before a court of a Member State. The Regulation does not define the meaning of entering an appearance. According to the Jenard Report, referring to the Brussels Convention, it will be for the court seised of the proceedings to determine this in accordance with its own rules of procedure.[799]

---

[791] *Marc Rich & Co AG v Società Italiana Impianti PA, The Atlantic Emperor (No 2)* [1992] 1 Lloyd's Rep 624 at 633, CA—a case involving enforcement under the traditional English rules, discussed infra, p 520 et seq.

[792] Supra, pp 209–210.

[793] See supra, p 225. See also the Jenard Report, p 38; Gaudemet-Tallon, point 79; Hartley, p 76. Cf Collins, p 51; Briggs and Rees, para 2.67; Layton and Mercer, para 20.120.

[794] Art 4 makes the point crystal clear.

[795] See *Transocean Towage Co Ltd v Hyundai Construction Co Ltd* [1987] ECC 282, Netherlands Sup Ct.

[796] *Elefanten Schuh v Jacqmain*, supra; Case 48/84 *Spitzley v Sommer Exploitation SA* [1985] ECR 787.

[797] Case C-318/93 *Brenner and Noller v Dean Witter Reynolds Inc* [1994] ECR I-4275 at 4280.

[798] Case C-412/98 *Universal General Insurance Co (UGIC) v Group Josi Reinsurance Co SA* [2001] QB 68 at [44].

[799] At p 38. See also the opinion of the Advocate General in *Elefanten Schuh v Jacqmain*, supra. See in relation to English procedure for defending a claim: *Ace Insurance SA-NV (Formerly Cigna Insurance Co of Europe SA NV) v Zurich Insurance Co* [2001] EWCA Civ 173 at [14]; [2001] 1 Lloyd's Rep 618, CA; *IBS Technologies (PVT) Ltd v APM Technologies SA*, 7 April 2003 (unreported) at [16]–[29]. See also *Caltex Trading Pte Ltd v Metro Trading*

Article 24 does, though, make it clear that not all the situations where the defendant enters an appearance come within its scope.[800] Article 24 also only refers to the *defendant* entering an appearance; it would not appear to cover the case where a claimant enters an appearance to contest a set-off sought by the defendant in response to the claimant's original claim. However, the Court of Justice in *Spitzley v Sommer Exploitation SA*[801] held that a court of a Member State, which would not otherwise have had jurisdiction in respect of the set-off, had it under Article 18 of the Brussels Convention (corresponding to Article 24 of the Regulation) because of the plaintiff's appearance before the court. Whilst this interpretation flies in the face of the wording of Article 18 (Article 24), it is not unfair to the parties who have both (one by seeking the original claim, the other by seeking a set-off) elected for trial in that Member State. There is also economy of procedure if both the claim and set-off are dealt with in the same Member State.

There are two limits on the application of Article 24.

First, Article 24 does not apply where the appearance was entered to contest jurisdiction. The defendant must be extremely careful as to how he conducts his defence where proceedings are commenced against him in a Member State. Where the defendant enters an appearance and fights the action on its merits (eg denies he is in breach of contract), the court of the Member State before which he appears will have jurisdiction. Where the defendant merely denies that the court of a Member State has jurisdiction over him (eg he points out that it is using a traditional exorbitant basis of jurisdiction against him and that this is prohibited by the Regulation), the court of the Member State before which he appears will not have jurisdiction. A defendant does not submit to the jurisdiction of the English courts merely by acknowledging service and applying to stay the action.[802] The distinction between fighting on the merits and contesting jurisdiction is well known to English lawyers,[803] and is easy to apply where the defendant acts in only one of these ways. What if the defendant appears before the courts of a Member State and argues in the alternative, that there is no jurisdiction over him and that, even if there is, he did not, for instance, break the contract? It is helpful at this point to look at the history of Article 24. The corresponding provision predecessor to this under the Brussels Convention (Article 18) is differently worded in that it refers in the English language version to the submission rule not applying where appearance was entered *solely* to contest jurisdiction. A literal interpretation of Article 18 of the Brussels Convention would suggest that the court before which the defendant has appeared is given jurisdiction in this situation, because the defendant has not appeared *solely* to contest jurisdiction. Article 24 of the Regulation, by omitting the word "solely", avoids any such suggestion. It clarifies the point that the defendant does not submit if he argues in the alternative. This rewording also gets rid of an inconsistency between different language versions of the submisssion provision.

International Inc and Ors and Glencore International AG and Ors (Third Parties) and Sea Victory Shipping Corp Procopiou and Baker Services Inc (Fourth Parties) [1999] 2 Lloyd's Rep 724, 730–732—issuing a summons for discovery of documents.

[800] See, infra, the limitations on the application of Art 24.

[801] Case 48/84 [1985] ECR 787; Hartley (1986) 11 ELR 98.

[802] CPR, Part 11; *The Sydney Express* [1988] 2 Lloyd's Rep 257. See also *Kurz v Stella Musical Veranstaltungs GmbH* [1992] Ch 196 at 201–202; *British Steel Corpn v Allivane International Ltd* 1989 SLT (Sh Ct) 57.

[803] Infra, pp 521–526; Collins, pp 92–93.

The French text of Article 18 of the Brussels Convention does not even contain an equivalent of the word "solely". It is also important to look at the decision of the Court of Justice in *Elefanten Schuh v Jacqmain*,[804] which involved Article 18 of the Brussels Convention. The Court held that one of the objectives of the Convention is to give the defendant the right to defend himself, and he should not be handicapped from going into matters of substance by this having the effect of destroying his arguments as to jurisdiction. It may actually be necessary for him to go into matters of substance in order to protect his property from seizure. The defendant, therefore, does not submit if he argues in the alternative. There can be no objections to this principle when it is applied, as it has been by the Court of Appeal, in the situation where the primary purpose of the defence is to challenge the jurisdiction.[805] But the principle would also appear to cover the situation where the primary purpose of the defence is to fight the action on its merits. Spurious arguments as to a lack of jurisdiction may be added on to what is, in essence, a defence based on substance, in order to avoid the application of Article 24 of the Regulation. The Court of Justice has stopped the defendant from tacking on arguments as to jurisdiction at a late stage, holding that it must be clear to the claimant and the court from the time of the defendant's first defence on the merits that it is intended to contest the court's jurisdiction; if not, Article 24 will give jurisdiction to the courts of the Member State before which the defendant has appeared.[806] In other words, the challenge to jurisdiction must be made before or at the same time as (but not after) the argument on the merits.[807] This does nothing to stop the well advised defendant who, at an early stage of the proceedings, includes a specious defence which contests jurisdiction. A defendant who contests jurisdiction at the right stage can participate in a full trial on the merits and still maintain his objection to jurisdiction.[808]

Secondly, Article 24 also does not apply where another court has exclusive jurisdiction by virtue of Article 22. Article 24 does not say whether it is subject to Article 23. By only mentioning Article 22 it can be inferred that it is not. The Court of Justice has confirmed this by holding that an appearance under Article 18 of the Brussels Convention (Article 24 of the Regulation) overrides an agreement conferring jurisdiction under Article 17 of the Convention (Article 23 of the Regulation).[809] This is only right and proper; both Articles 23 and 24 are dealing with selection of jurisdiction by the parties and a later selection by appearance should take precedence over an earlier selection by agreement.

---

[804] Supra. Followed in Case 25/81 *CHW v GJH* [1982] ECR 1189; Case 27/81 *Röhr v Ossberger* [1981] ECR 2431; Case 201/82 *Gerling v Italian Treasury* [1983] ECR 2503. See also *Luis Marburg & Söhne GmbH v Società Ori Martin SpA* [1987] ECC 424, Italian Supreme Court; *Campbell International Trading House Ltd v Peter Van Aart* [1992] 2 IR 305, Supreme Court of Ireland.

[805] See *Marc Rich & Co AG v Società Italiana Impianti PA, The Atlantic Emperor (No 2)* [1992] 1 Lloyd's Rep 624 at 633, CA; *Toepfer v Molino Boschi* [1996] 1 Lloyd's Rep 510 at 514–515.

[806] *Elefanten Schuh v Jacqmain*, supra. Where the challenge to jurisdiction is not a preliminary matter see the Advocate General's opinion in *CHW v GJH*, supra. See also *Devrajan v District Judge Ballagh* [1993] 3 IR 381, Supreme Court of Ireland; *Strathaird Farms Ltd v GA Chattaway & Co* 1993 SLT (Sh Ct) 36; *SSQ Europe SA v Johann & Backes OHG* [2002] 1 Lloyd's Rep 465—intention to contest jurisdiction clear despite a counterclaim as well as a defence on merits.

[807] *Harada Ltd (t/a Chequepoint) v Turner* [2003] EWCA Civ 1695 at [29] (per Simon Brown LJ).

[808] Ibid at [38] (per Simon Brown LJ), [50] (per Mance LJ).

[809] *Elefanten Schuh v Jacqmain*, supra. See also *The Sydney Express* [1988] 2 Lloyd's Rep 257.

(g) Procedure—service of the claim form

Under the traditional English rules on jurisdiction, service of a claim form performs the dual functions of providing the basis of jurisdiction and giving the defendant notice of the proceedings. The Regulation has bases of jurisdiction which do not depend on service of a claim form. Procedure is largely left as a matter for national law, rather than being dealt with by the Regulation. The procedure under English law where the Regulation applies is as follows. A claim form can be served out of the jurisdiction[810] without the permission of the court, provided that each claim[811] included in the claim form is one which the court has power to determine under the Judgments Regulation[812] and:

(a) no proceedings between the parties concerning the same claim are pending in the courts of any other part of the United Kingdom or any other Regulation State; and

   (i) the defendant is domiciled in the United Kingdom or in any Regulation State;

   (ii) Article 22 of the Judgments Regulation refers to the proceedings; or

   (iii) the defendant is a party to an agreement conferring jurisdiction to which Article 23 of the Judgments Regulation refers.

As regards the practicalities of service, where service is to be effected in another Member State, Regulation (EC) No 1393/2007 of the European Parliament and Council on the service in the Member States of judicial and extrajudicial documents in civil or commercial matters[813] applies.[814] This is concerned to improve and expedite the transmission of documents for service between the Member States[815] and, in relation to matters to which it applies, replaces the Hague Convention of 1965 on the Service Abroad of Judicial and Extrajudicial Documents in Civil or Commercial Matters and any bilateral or regional instruments between Member States.[816] The Court of Justice has power to give a ruling

---

[810] CPR, r 6.19(1A). For the accompanying statement required by r 6.19(3) see Practice Direction—Service out of the Jurisdiction, 6BPD.2, 1.3A; *Trustor AB v Barclays Bank plc* (2000) Times, 22 November 2000.

[811] See *Shahar v Tsitsekkos* [2004] EWHC 2659 (Comm) at [96].

[812] *Swithenbank Foods Ltd v Bowers* [2002] EWHC 2257, [2002] 2 All ER (Comm) 974; *Mercury Communications Ltd v Communication Telesystems International* [1999] 2 All ER (Comm) 33—a Brussels Convention case.

[813] OJ 2007 L 324/79. This replaces Council Regulation (EC) No 1348/2000, OJ 2000 L 160/37 (the 2000 Service Regulation). The Regulation is not directly applicable to Denmark. However, by virtue of an Agreement between the European Community and Denmark, as from 1 July 2007 the provisions in the original Service Regulation are applied by international agreement to the relations between the Community and Denmark (this is a separate Agreement from the EC/Denmark Agreement extending the Brussels I Regulation to Denmark). The 2000 Service Regulation was based on the 1997 Convention on the service in the Member States of the European Union of judicial and extrajudicial documents in civil and commercial matters OJ 1997 C 261/1. The Explanatory Report acccompanying the Service Convention is set out at OJ 1997 C 261/26. See generally on the Service Convention, Kennett [1998] CJQ 284. For English procedural rules, see CPR r 6.26A and Practice Direction—Service out of the Jurisdiction, 6BPD.1.

[814] As from from 13 November 2008. The Regulation cannot be subverted by using an alternative method of service (as authorised by CPR, r 6.8) such as by serving the defendant's English lawyers within the jurisdiction: *Knauf UK GmbH v British Gypsum Ltd* [2001] EWCA Civ 1570 at [47] and [58], [2002] 1 Lloyd's Rep 199; *Bentinck v Bentinck* [2007] EWCA Civ 175 at [49] (per Lawrence COLLINS LJ), [2007] IL Pr 391 or by dispensing with service (CPR, r 6.9). *Phillips v Nussberger* [2008] UKHL 1 at [39], [2008] 1 WLR 181. Dispencing with service may be allowed in a Brussels/Lugano case in exceptional circumstances where there is no such subverting: *Olafsson v Gissurarson* [2008] EWCA 152.

[815] Recital (2).

[816] Art 20(1). However, Member States are not precluded from concluding between themselves arrangements to expedite further or simplify the transmission of documents, provided that they are compatible with the Regulation: Art 20(2). The United Kingdom is a party to the 1965 Hague Convention and has also entered into

on the interpretation of the European Community Service Regulation, on the matter being referred to it by a national court. The Regulation applies in civil and commercial matters where a judicial or extra-judicial document has to be transmitted from one Member State to another for service there.[817] However, it does not apply where the address of the person to be served with the document is not known.[818] The United Kingdom and Ireland have "opted in" to the Regulation, but it does not apply in Denmark. The Regulation provides for the establishment of a transmitting agency and a receiving agency in each Member State[819] and for the direct transmission of documents between agencies in different Member States.[820] This is designed to avoid the delays which, in the past, have built up due to transmission being effected through a chain of intermediaries. The receiving agency is under a duty to serve a document or have it served on the defendant as soon as possible, and in any event within one month of receipt.[821] The addressee can refuse to accept a document if it is not written in, or accompanied by a translation into, a language which the addressee understands or the official language of the state addressed.[822] Member States are free to use certain other specified means of transmission and service of documents,[823] including service by post directly to persons residing in another Member State.[824] The Regulation sets up a Committee which assists the Commission in implementing the Regulation.[825] The Service Regulation is also concerned with the notice of the proceedings that is given to the defendant and, as will be seen later in this chapter,[826] has provisions designed to safeguard his interests.

(h) Other provisions relating to jurisdiction

There are provisions on jurisdiction in Chapter II of the Brussels I Regulation dealing with matters other than bases of jurisdiction, eg dealing with minimum standards in relation to notice of the proceedings and declining jurisdiction in cases of *lis pendens*. These provisions can, as a matter of principle, apply regardless of where the defendant is domiciled.[827] This is subject to the wording of the provision in question which, in some instances, makes it clear that it only relates to the situation where a defendant is domiciled in a Member State.

---

various bilateral Civil Procedure Conventions. See generally CPR, rr 6.24, 6.25 and 6.26. It will continue to use these arrangements in cases where the Regulation does not apply.

[817] Art 1(1). The Regulation does not extend to revenue, customs or administrative matters or to liability of the State for actions or omissions in the exercise of state authority (*acta iure imperii*).

[818] Art 1(2).

[819] Art 2.

[820] Art 4.

[821] Art 7. After one month the receiving agency must continue to take all necessary steps to serve: Art 7(2)(b).

[822] Art 8. See in relation to sending the translation required: Case C-433/03 *Leffler v Berlin Chemie AG* [2006] IL Pr 6; Mankowski (2006) 43 CMLR 1689. See also *Benatti v WPP Holdings Italy SRL* [2007] EWCA Civ 263 at [68]–[69] (per Toulson LJ), [86]–[90] (per Buxton LJ), [97] (per Clarke MR), [2007] 1 WLR 2316. A reference on the interpretation of Art 8 of the 2000 Service Regulation has been made by the Bundesgerichtshof to the Court of Justice in Case C-14/07 *Ingenieurburo Michael Weiss und Partner GbR v Industrie und Handelskammer Berlin*. AG Trstenjak has delivered her opinion.

[823] Arts 12–15.

[824] Art 14; *Benatti v WPP Holdings Italy SRL*, supra, at [88] (per Buxton LJ). These are alternatives to service under Arts 4 to 11 and both may be used, see Case C-473/04 *Plumex v Young Sports NV*.

[825] Art 18.

[826] Infra.

[827] See Arts 3 and 4, and supra, pp 222–225.

(i) Safeguarding the rights of the defendant

The Brussels I Regulation safeguards the rights of the defendant in two ways.

(a) The duty to examine jurisdiction where the defendant does not enter an appearance

A court of a Member State before which a defendant (domiciled in another Member State) is sued, but in circumstances where he does not enter an appearance,[828] is required to examine its own jurisdiction and declare of its own motion that it has no jurisdiction unless this is derived from the provisions of the Regulation.[829] Hitherto, an English court acted on the basis of the submissions of the parties.[830]

(b) Minimum standards in relation to notice

A court of a Member State "shall stay the proceedings so long as it is not shown that the defendant has been able to receive the document instituting the proceedings or an equivalent document in sufficient time to enable him to arrange for his defence, or that all necessary steps have been taken to this end".[831] It is intended that this will only apply where the defendant is domiciled in one Member State, is sued in another, and does not enter an appearance.[832] This provision was introduced with civil law systems in mind, under some of which there is a danger of a defendant having a judgment entered against him in default of appearance without having any knowledge of the action. Where the defendant does not enter an appearance, the court of a Member State before which an action is brought is required to consider its own procedure, to see that it conforms with these minimum standards, before entering a default judgment.

This is not likely to lead to stays of proceedings in Member States for three reasons. First, the minimum standards in relation to notice set out in the Brussels I Regulation are replaced by those in Article 19 of the 2000 European Union Service Regulation (to be replaced by Article 19 of the 2007 Service Regulation, which is virtually identical in wording[833]) if the document instituting the proceedings has to be transmitted from one Member State to another pursuant to this Regulation.[834] Article 19 of the 2000 Service Regulation provides that, if the defendant did not appear, judgment shall not be given unless it is established that either the document was served in compliance with the law of the State addressed, or the document was actually delivered to the defendant or to his residence by another method provided for by the 2000 Service Regulation. In either case, it must also be shown that service or delivery was effected in sufficient time to enable the defendant to defend. The Hess, Pfeiffer and Schlosser Report points out that the

---

[828] Contesting jurisdiction is not entering an appearance, see Case C-148/03 *Nurnberger Allgemeine Versicherungs AG v Portbridge Transport International BV* [2004] ECR I-10327.

[829] Art 26(1). For application of this requirement where jurisdiction is based on a special convention under Art 71 see the *Nurnberger* case, supra.

[830] See the Schlosser Report, pp 81–82. See also Art 25 and Case 288/82 *Duijnstee v Goderbauer* [1983] ECR 3663. See generally Kohler (1985) 34 ICLQ 563, 573–574.

[831] Art 26(2).

[832] See the Jenard Report, pp 39–40. Also Case 228/81 *Pendy Plastic Products BV v Pluspunkt Handelsgesellschaft mbH* [1982] ECR 2723; Anton and Beaumont's, *Civil Jurisdiction in Scotland*, para 7.33.

[833] The Brussels I Regulation will need to be amended to refer to the 2007 Service Regulation, which replaces the 2000 Service Regulation.

[834] Art 26(3) of the Brussels I Regulation.

interaction of the Brussels I Regulation and Article 19 of the 2000 Service Regulation is very difficult for practitioners to understand and that it may be advisable to find a more simple solution.[835] Secondly, where the provisions of the 2000 Service Regulation are not applicable,[836] eg the document is not to be transmitted to another Member State, Article 15 of the Hague Convention of 1965 on the Service Abroad of Judicial and Extrajudicial Documents in Civil or Commercial Matters applies if the document instituting the proceedings or an equivalent document had to be transmitted abroad pursuant to that Convention.[837] The minimum standards for notice contained in Article 15 are the same as those contained in Article 19 of the 2000 Service Regulation. The latter effectively incorporated the terms of the former. Article 15 of the Hague Service Convention, like Article 19 of the 2000 Service Regulation, does not apply where the address of the person to be served is not known. Thirdly, in cases falling outside both the 2000 Service Regulation and the Hague Service Convention, eg where the address of the person to be served is not known, Member States will use their own rules for service abroad. English courts are likely to assume that their procedure for service abroad[838] will comply with the minimum standards for notice set out in the Brussels I Regulation since the procedure for service abroad was introduced after the Civil Jurisdiction and Judgments Act 1982 (implementing the Brussels Convention with the same minimum standards) was passed.[839]

The English procedure will come in for scrutiny from the courts of other Member States which are asked to recognise or enforce a judgment of an English court. Conversely, English courts will have to consider foreign procedure when asked to recognise the judgments of courts in other Member States.[840]

(ii) Lis pendens—related actions

(a) Lis pendens[841]

Article 27[842] provides that:

1. Where proceedings involving the same cause of action and between the same parties are brought in the courts of different Member States, any court other than the court first seised shall of its own motion stay its proceedings until such time as the jurisdiction of the court first seised is established.
2. Where the jurisdiction of the court first seised is established, any court other than the court first seised shall decline jurisdiction in favour of that court.

The Regulation will often give jurisdiction to the courts of more than one Member State in respect of a single dispute, eg an Italian claimant, who is injured in Italy by the

---

[835] Para 872 of Study JLS/C4/2005/03, Final Version September 2007, available at the European Commission—European Judicial Network—What's new website http://ec.europa.eu/civiljustice/news/whatsnew_en.htm.

[836] See Art 1 of the 2000 European Community Service Regulation.

[837] Art 26(4) of the Brussels I Regulation; see also *Pendy Plastic Products v Pluspunkt*, supra.

[838] See supra, p 300.

[839] See Collins, p 96.

[840] See Art 34(2); Case 166/80 *Klomps v Michel* [1981] ECR 1593; Hunnings [1985] JBL 303; infra, pp 615–622.

[841] See generally Fawcett *Declining Jurisdiction*, pp 27–46; Herzog (1995) 43 AJCL 379; Hartley (2006) 139 Hague Recueil 166–169.

[842] Art 21 of the Brussels Convention.

negligent driving of a defendant domiciled in France, can sue either in Italy under Article 5(3) or in France under Article 2. There is an obvious need for a provision to deal with the problems of forum shopping, concurrent proceedings and conflicting judgments in the courts of different Member States.[843] Whilst Article 27 is limited to concurrent[844] proceedings[845] in Member States, it should be noted that it is not limited to proceedings under the bases of jurisdiction set out in the Regulation.[846] Article 27 will apply where proceedings involving the same cause of action and parties have been commenced in two Member States under their traditional rules on jurisdiction (the bases of jurisdiction under the Regulation being inapplicable).[847] The Court of Justice, following a reference from the Court of Appeal, held in *Overseas Union Insurance Ltd v New Hampshire Insurance Co* that there is no requirement that either party be domiciled in a Member State.[848] This is clear from the wording and purpose of Article 27. Of course, for Article 27 to apply, the proceedings have to be within the scope of the Regulation.[849] It should also be noted that Article 27 is a purely mechanical rule. The court of the Member State first seised of the matter takes priority, and any court of another Member State must of its own motion decline jurisdiction, once the jurisdiction of the court first seised is established in that State.[850] The court seised second normally cannot examine the jurisdiction of the court first seised.[851] This is so even when the court "seised second"

---

[843] See Case 42/76 *De Wolf v Cox BV* [1976] ECR 1759; Hartley (1977) 2 ELR 146; the case is discussed infra, pp 634–635.

[844] The proceedings must be pending, not concluded (*Berkeley Administration Inc v McClelland* [1995] IL Pr 201, CA; *Prudential Assurance Co Ltd v Prudential Insurance Co of America* [2003] EWCA Civ 327 at [26], [2003] 1 WLR 2295) or discontinued (*International Nederlanden v CAA* [1997] 1 Lloyd's Rep 80 at 93–94) or struck out on the basis that they are bound to fail (*QRS I Aps v Frandsen* [1999] IL Pr 432). See also *Gamlestaden plc v Casa de Suecia SA* [1994] 1 Lloyd's Rep 433; *Tavoulareas v Tsavliris (No 2)* [2005] EWHC 2643 (Comm), [2006] 1 All ER (Comm) 130, Art 27 does not apply where judgment is given in the court first seised at the time the court second seised makes its determination as to whether to decline. Art 27 will apply where the court first seised has declared that it is without jurisdiction but an appeal is pending (*Moore v Moore* [2007] EWCA Civ 361 at [102]–[103], [2007] IL Pr). It will also apply where the decision of the court first seised that it has jurisdiction is itself under appeal (*William Grant & Sons International Ltd v Marie Brizard et Roger International* SA 1998 SC 536).

[845] This does not include provisional proceedings: *Miles Platts Ltd v Townroe Ltd* [2003] EWCA Civ 145 at [21]–[22], [2003] 1 All ER (Comm) 561; *Boss Group Ltd v Boss France SA* [1997] 1 WLR 351, CA (but cf *The Winter* [2000] 2 Lloyd's Rep 298, 302—provisional measure raising substantive matters); nor those concerning the recognition and enforcement of judgments given in non-Contracting States, Case C-129/92 *Owens Bank Ltd v Bracco* [1994] QB 509; *Bank of Dubai Ltd v Abbas* [1998] IL Pr 391. Nor does it mean issues raised in proceedings: *The Happy Fellow* [1998] 1 Lloyd's Rep 13, CA. Amended proceedings are treated as separate from original proceedings: *Grupo Torras SA and Torras Hostench London Ltd v Sheikh Fahad Mohammed Al-Sabah* [1995] 1 Lloyd's Rep 374 at 431, this was not part of the appeal; affd [1996] 1 Lloyd's Rep 7, CA. Proceedings encompasses an application to a court to establish a liability limitation fund: Case C-39/02 *Maersk Olie & Gas AS v M De Haan en W De Boer* [2004] I-9657 at [33].

[846] See *The Nordglimt* [1988] QB 183.

[847] See Arts 3 and 4, supra, pp 222–225; the Jenard Report, pp 20–21.

[848] Case C-351/89 [1992] 1 QB 434; Briggs (1991) 11 YEL 521; Hartley (1992) 17 ELR 75.

[849] *Toepfer v Société Cargill* [1998] 1 Lloyd's Rep 379, CA.

[850] See the Schlosser Report, p 125. See also *Carnoustie Universal SA v International Transport Workers' Federation* [2002] EWHC 1624 (Comm) 657 at [45]–[46], [2002] 2 All ER (Comm) 657—onus is on the claimant to show a good arguable case that the English court should take jurisdiction, ie that Art 27 does not apply. The court must be satisfied of this whether or not the defendant mounts a challenge. See also *Kolden Holdings Ltd v Rodette Commerce Ltd* [2007] EWHC 1597 (Comm), [2007] IL Pr 50.

[851] *Overseas Union Insurance Ltd v New Hampshire Insurance Co*, supra; *Haji-Ioannou v Frangos* [1999] 2 Lloyd's Rep 337 at 351, CA—a Brussels Convention case which summarises the principles to be applied.

has Article 23 exclusive jurisdiction.[852] There is no discretion given to the courts of either Member State as to whether they should take jurisdiction. A mechanical rule tends to produce certainty; this does not mean that there are no problems with Article 27.

(i) The two sets of proceedings must involve the same cause of action. According to the Court of Justice in *Gubisch Maschinenfabrik KG v Giulio Palumbo*[853] this, like the other terms in Article 21 of the Brussels Convention (Article 27 of the Regulation) concerned with whether a situation of *lis pendens* exists, must be given an independent Community meaning. The cause of action refers to the "facts and the rule of law relied on as the basis of the action".[854] There is, though, a separate (albeit closely related) requirement, which does not appear in the English language version of Article 27: the *subject matter* or *object* of the proceedings, ie "the end the action has in view",[855] must be the same.[856] We are concerned with the subject matter (and other substantive requirements, namely the same cause of action and same parties) as at the time when the *lis pendens* comes into existence (ie from the moment when two courts of two Member States are seised of an action).[857] This happens at an early stage before the defendants have been able to put forward their arguments. It follows that in determining the subject matter (and other substantive requirements), account should be taken only of the claims of the respective applicants, not of the defence that may be raised by a defendant.[858] The Court of Justice in the *Gubisch* case held that the same subject matter requirement was satisfied in circumstances where one party brought an action in Italy for the recission or discharge of an international sales contract whilst an action by the other party to enforce the same contract was pending before a court in Germany. The same question whether the contract was binding lay at the heart of both actions and it was not required that the two claims be entirely identical. Whilst this broad interpretation is understandable, it does tend to break down the distinction between this provision and Article 28, which deals with related actions.

---

[852] Infra, pp 310–312. But there is an exception in transitional cases: Case C-163/95 *Von Horn v Cinnamond* [1998] QB 214; distinguished in: *Davy International v Voest Alpine* [1999] 1 All ER 103, CA; *Advent Capital plc v Ellinas Imports-Exports Ltd* [2005] EWHC 1242 (Comm), [2005] 2 Lloyd's Rep 607; Briggs (2005) 76 BYBIL 654, 658. See also *M v H* [2005] EWHC 1186 (Fam)—a Brussels II *bis* case. See also Layton and Mercer, paras 31.008–31.009.

[853] Case 144/86 [1987] ECR 4861; Hartley (1988) 13 ELR 216.

[854] Case C-406/92 *The Owners of the Cargo Lately Laden on Board the Ship Tatry v The Owners of the Ship Maciej Rataj* [1994] ECR I-5439 at 5475; [1999] QB 515; Case C-39/02 *Maersk Olie & Gas AS v M De Haan en W De Boer* [2004] ECR I-9657 at [38]; *Haji-Ioannou v Frangos* [1999] 2 Lloyd's Rep 337 at 351, CA; *JP Morgan Europe Ltd v Primacom AG* [2005] EWHC 508 (Comm) at [39]–[49], [2005] 2 Lloyd's Rep 665. For examples where the cause of action was the same, see the *Carnoustie* case, supra, at [86]–[91]; *Glencore International AG v Metro Trading International Inc (No 1)* [1999] 2 Lloyd's Rep 632, 638; *The Winter* [2000] 2 Lloyd's Rep 298, 305; *Bank of Tokyo-Mitsubishi Ltd v Baskan Gida Sanayi Ve Pazarlama AS* [2004] EWHC 945 (Ch) at [207], [2004] 2 Lloyd's Rep 395; *JP Morgan Europe*, supra, at [39]–[49]; *Jacobs & Turner Ltd v Celsius sarl* [2007] CSOH 76 at [68]. See also *Kloeckner & Co AG v Gatoil Overseas Inc* [1990] 1 Lloyd's Rep 177, where each purchase and sale agreement stemming from a basic contract was treated as a separate cause of action.

[855] *The Tatry*, supra, at 5475; Case C-111/01 *Gantner Electronic GmbH v Basch Exploitatie Maatschappij BV* [2003] ECR I-4207 at [25]; *Haji-Ioannou v Frangos* [1999] 2 Lloyd's Rep 337 at 351, CA.

[856] For examples of where this requirement was satisfied, see the *Carnoustie* case, supra, at [88]; *The Winter*, supra, 305; *Bank of Tokyo-Mitsubishi*, supra, at [208]; *JP Morgan Europe*, supra, at [39]–[49]; *Jacobs & Turner Ltd*, supra, at [68]–[75]; *Kolden Holdings Ltd v Rodette Commerce Ltd* [2007] EWHC 1597 (Comm) at [60], [2007] IL Pr 50.

[857] The *Gantner* case, supra, at [27]; following Case 129/83 *Zelger v Salinitri (No 2)* [1984] ECR 2397; Hartley (1985) 10 ELR 56.

[858] The *Gantner* case, supra, at [32]; *Jacobs & Turner Ltd*, supra, at [70]; *Kolden Holdings Ltd v Rodette Commerce Ltd* [2007] EWHC 1597 (Comm) at [66], [2007] IL Pr 50.

This broad interpretation was followed in *The Tatry*,[859] where the Court of Justice held that an action seeking to have the defendant held liable for causing loss and to pay damages constituted the same cause of action and subject matter as earlier proceedings by that defendant for a negative declaration that he was not liable for that loss. Allowing negative declarations to come within Article 27[860] gives the green light to pre-emptive forum shopping by a party who fears that proceedings are going to be commenced against him.[861] The cause of action in one set of proceedings may be broader than that in the other. If the cause of action is broader in the court second seised, Article 27 will operate in respect of the element common to both sets of proceedings.[862] This is consistent with the approach adopted by the Court of Justice in relation to multi-party cases.[863] A simple example of where the cause of action is not the same in the two sets of proceedings is where one cause of action is for infringement of a trade mark and the other is for passing off.[864] The object is not the same where one claim is for the recovery of money and the other is in large part the tracing of that money into the assets acquired with it and a claim to a beneficial interest.[865] Neither the cause of action nor the object were the same where a shipowner sought to limit liability by establishing a liability limitation fund and a victim sought damages from the shipowner.[866] As regards the cause of action, the legal rule which formed the basis of each of these applications was different, one action being based on an international Convention and national law giving effect to it, the other being based on the law of non-contractual liability.[867] As regards the object, one action sought to have the defendant declared liable, whereas the other sought to limit liablity in the event that that person was held liable.[868]

---

[859] Case C-406/92 *The Owners of the Cargo Lately Laden on Board the Ship Tatry v The Owners of the Ship Maciej Rataj* [1994] ECR I-5439; [1999] QB 515; Briggs [1995] LMCLQ 161; and (1994) 14 YEL 579; Davenport (1995) 111 LQR 366; Fentiman [1995] CLJ 261.

[860] See also Case C-351/96 *Drouot Assurances SA v Consolidated Metallurgical Industries* 485 [1999] QB 497; Case C-116/02 *Erich Gasser v Misat Srl* [2003] ECR I-4207; *Messier Dowty Ltd v Sabena SA* [2000] 1 WLR 2040, at 2049, CA; *Kinnear v Falconfilms NV* [1996] 1 WLR 920.

[861] See generally the criticism by Collins (1992) 108 LQR 545; *Mélanges En L'Honneur De Jacques-Michel Grossen*, p 386 and *Essays*, p 274 and 283 et seq; more specifically in respect of the decision of the Court of Justice: Fentiman, op cit; Davenport, op cit. See also Lawrence COLLINS J in *Bank of Tokyo-Mitsubishi Ltd*, supra, at [198].

[862] See the opinion of AG TESAURO in *The Tatry*, supra; *William Grant & Sons International Ltd v Marie Brizard et Roger International* SA 1998 SC 536; *Glencore International AG v Metro Trading International Inc (No 1)* [1999] 2 Lloyd's Rep 632, 638–639; *Jacobs & Turner Ltd*, supra, at [46].

[863] See the discussion, infra, of *The Tatry*, supra.

[864] *Mecklermedia Corpn v DC Congress GmbH* [1998] Ch 40. For other examples, see: *Sarrio SA v Kuwait Investment Authority* [1997] 1 Lloyd's Rep 113, CA, revsd by the House of Lords [1999] 1 AC 32 without discussion of this point; *Berkeley Administration Inc v McClelland* [1996] IL Pr 72 at 786, CA; *Toepfer v Molino Boshci* [1996] 1 Lloyd's Rep 510 at 513; *Charterers Mutual Assurance Association Ltd v British and Foreign* [1998] IL Pr 838 at 855; *Glencore International AG v Shell Trading and Shipping Co Ltd* [1999] 2 All ER (Comm) 922; *Lafi Office and International Business SL v Meriden Animal Health Ltd* [2001] 1 All ER (Comm) 54 at 70–71; *JP Morgan Europe Ltd v Primacom AG* [2005] EWHC 508 (Comm) at [54]–[56], [2005] 2 Lloyd's Rep 665; *Prazic v Prazic* [2006] EWCA Civ 497 at [16], [2006] 2 FLR 1128. It is unclear whether the cause of action is the same in the situation where there are actions in two Member States under Art 5(1) of the Regulation, there being two obligations of equal weight each to be performed in the two different Member States (See Case C-420/97 *Leathertex Divisione Sinetici SpA v Bodetex BVBA* [1999] ECR I-6747 at [36]; Panagopoulos [2000] LMCLQ 150. The European Commission asssumed in their arguments that it would be).

[865] *Haji-Ioannou v Frangos* [1999] 2 Lloyd's Rep 337 at 351, CA. For other examples see *Glencore International AG v Shell Trading and Shipping Co Ltd*, op cit; *JP Morgan Europe Ltd v Primacom AG* [2005] EWHC 508 (Comm) at [51]-[53], [2005] 2 Lloyd's Rep 665.

[866] Case C-39/02 *Maersk Olie & Gas AS v M De Haan en W De Boer* [2004] ECR I-9657 at [42].

[867] Ibid, at [38].

[868] Ibid, at [35].

(ii) The two sets of proceedings must be between the same parties.[869] This requirement has raised problems in maritime actions. The Court of Justice in *The Tatry*[870] held that if one action is brought in personam (against a person) in one Contracting State and the other is brought in rem (against a ship) in another Contracting State, and has subsequently continued both in rem and in personam, or solely in personam, according to the distinctions drawn by the national law of that other Member State, the parties are the same. It was said that the distinction drawn under national law between an action in personam and one in rem is not material for the interpretation of Article 21 of the Brussels Convention (Article 27 of the Regulation). It follows that the result in the case would have been exactly the same if the action in rem had continued as such according to national law.[871] Multi-party cases have also raised problems. In *The Tatry*, the Court of Justice adopted a party-by-party approach, holding that "the second court seised is required to decline jurisdiction only to the extent to which the parties to the proceedings before it are also parties to the action previously commenced; it does not prevent the proceedings from continuing between the other parties".[872]

> Thus, if in the court first seised A, B and C sue X, and in the court second seised X sues A and B, the latter court must decline jurisdiction in relation to all the parties in the proceedings before it. Whereas in the converse situation, ie if in the court first seised A and B sue X, and in the court second seised X sues A, B and C, Article 27 will not operate in respect of the action brought against C.[873]

In ascertaining whether the parties are the same, it is possible to look beyond their strict formal identities. An insurer and an insured can be considered to be the same party for the purposes of Article 27 in the situation where their interests are the same, such as where an insurer, by virtue of its right of subrogation, brings or defends an action in the name of its insured, but not where their interests diverge.[874] It is for the national court to decide whether it is such a situation.[875] On a reference back to the French courts it was held on the facts that an insurer of a hull who does not cover fault on a shipowner's part is not the same party as the insured (ie the owner).[876] It may also be unreal to regard a wholly-owned subsidiary as being a different party from its parent.[877] The deployment of a related company in a group of companies as claimant in proceedings may be a sham to

---

[869] For examples where the requirement was not met, see *Bank of Scotland v SA Banque Nationale De Paris* 1996 SLT 103; the *Lafi* case, supra, 70. Cf in the area of maintenance *J v P* [2007] EWHC 704 (Fam) at 48.

[870] Case C-406/92 *The Owners of the Cargo Lately Laden on Board the Ship Tatry v The Owners of the Ship Maciej Rataj* [1999] QB 515, [1994] ECR I-5439.

[871] See the judgment of Lord Steyn, with whom the other Law Lords concurred, in *Republic of India v India Steamship Co Ltd (No 2)* [1998] AC 878 at 910, 913.

[872] *The Tatry*, supra, at 5474. See also *Haji-Ioannou v Frangos* [1999] 2 Lloyd's Rep 337 at 351, CA; *Glencore International AG v Shell Trading and Shipping Co Ltd*, supra, 925; *Glencore International AG v Metro Trading International Inc (No 1)*, supra, 637.

[873] The court second seised is able, though, to use Art 28, discussed infra, pp 312–315, to stay the proceedings against C on the ground that they are related, see *The Tatry*, supra, at 5477–5480.

[874] Case C-351/96 *Drouot Assurances SA v Consolidated Metallurgical Industries* [1999] QB 497; Handley (2000) 116 LQR 191; Peel (1998) 18 YEL 689; Seatzu (1999) 24 ELR 540.

[875] See, eg, *Kolden Holdings Ltd v Rodette Commerce Ltd* [2007] EWHC 1597 (Comm), [2007] IL Pr 50— assignee held to be same party as assignor.

[876] *Drouot Assurances SA v Consolidated Metallurgical Industries* [2000] IL Pr 421, French Cour de Cassation.

[877] See *Berkeley Administration Inc v McClelland* [1995] IL Pr 201 at 211 (per Dillon LJ), CA.

avoid the application of Article 27, in which case the court will look at the reality of the situation and the parties will be regarded as being the same.[878]

(iii) Article 27 could lead to a race between the parties,[879] the winner being the one who can show that the court where he brought the action is first seised of jurisdiction. The Brussels I Regulation has filled what has been seen as a gap in the law[880] by defining in Article 30 the precise moment at which a court is first seised for the purposes of Articles 27, 28 and 29. Arriving at a uniform definition which would apply in all Member States was not easy because of the different procedural systems adopted by different Member States. The solution adopted in Article 30 has been to provide two alternative definitions. One is for Member States where the claim is lodged with the court before service of the document instituting the proceedings. This is what happens in England. The other is for Member States, such as France, where service precedes lodging with the court. In Member States where the claim is lodged with the court before service, a court is deemed to be seised "at the time when the document instituting the proceedings or an equivalent document is lodged with the court, provided that the plaintiff has not subsequently failed to take the steps he was required to take to have service effected on the defendant . . . ".[881] In the case of England, the courts will be seised on the date of the issue of the claim form.[882] The steps the plaintiff is required to take to effect service will depend on the legal system in question. They may include transmission to the court of all material facts enabling it to serve notice, or the handing over of the document already registered with the court to the competent authority for service.[883] In Member States where the document has to be served before being lodged with the court, a court is deemed to be seised "at the time when it is received by the authority responsible[884] for service, provided that the plaintiff has not subsequently failed to take the steps he was required to take to have the document lodged with the court".[885] It is to be noted that in this scenario the moment when a court is deemed to be seised is not the time of actual service,[886] it will be prior to that when the document is received by the authority responsible for service.[887] Being seised is different from having been served service and so it does not

---

[878] *Turner v Grovit* [2000] QB 345, CA. This point was not discussed by the House of Lords [2001] UKHL 651, [2002] 1 WLR 107.

[879] This is the opposite of the culture which the English CPR seek to promote, see *Messier Dowty v Sabena SA* [2000] 1 WLR 2040, 2047, CA.

[880] See the views of the European Commission in the Explanatory Memorandum in the Proposal for a Council Regulation COM (1999) 348 final, p 20.

[881] Art 30(1). See *Tavoulareas v Tsavliris* [2005] EWHC 2140 (Comm), [2006] 1 All ER (Comm) 109.

[882] See Dicey, Morris and Collins, para 12-060; *WPP Holdings Italy SRL v Benatti* [2006] EWHC 1641 (Comm) at [28], [2006] 2 Lloyd's Rep 610; Lesage (2006) EU Lp 157—this point was not mentioned on appeal in *Benatti v WPP Holdings Italy SRL* [2007] EWCA Civ 263, [2007] 1 WLR 2316 (appeal allowed in relation to one claimant and dismissed in relation to other claimants). This date is entered on the form by the court: CPR r 7.2.

[883] See the views of the European Commission in the Explanatory Memorandum in the Proposal for a Council Regulation COM (1999) 348 final, p 20.

[884] There is uncertainty in Member States about the definition of responsible authority, see the Hesss, Pfeiffer and Schlosser Report, at para 897, which recommends clarification of its meaning.

[885] Art 30(2).

[886] *Benatti v WPP Holdings Italy SRL* [2007] EWCA Civ 263 at [96] (per CLARKE MR), [2007] 1 WLR 2316.

[887] It is unclear whether this is referring to the transmitting agency or the receiving agency under the EC Service Regulation. BUXTON LJ in *Benatti v WPP Holdings Italy Srl*, supra, at [85] assumes it is the former.

matter that the service was invalid under the European Community Service Regulation.[888] All that Article 30(2) requires is that the claimant, after lodging the document with the authority responsible for service, must not have failed to take the steps he was required to take to have the document lodged with the court (which no doubt might include steps to facilitate service as a pre-requisite to lodgement with the court).[889] The fact that Member States will not all be applying the same definition runs the risk, in theory at least, that the race to become first seised is still going to be run on unequal terms. However, this risk is more apparent than real since both definitions take as the moment of being first seised the earliest practicable moment in the sequence of events under that procedural system. There is also a practical problem for an English court in determining when a foreign court is seised. Whether a document is effective to institute proceeedings in another Member State should be for the national law of that foreign Member State to determine, rather than for the English court. [890]

(iv) Article 27 is limited to concurrent proceedings in different Member States.[891] To take an example, it would not apply to concurrent actions in Japan and the United Kingdom. In many such cases (eg a Japanese domiciliary sues a United Kingdom domiciliary in Japan, and there are concurrent proceedings in the United Kingdom where the United Kingdom domiciliary sues the Japanese domiciliary) the Regulation would not apply to the action brought in the United Kingdom and the courts would use traditional bases of jurisdiction and can also use the accompanying rules on stays of action on the ground of *forum non conveniens*, which are used to deal with cases of *lis pendens*.[892] In other cases (eg a Japanese domiciliary sues a United Kingdom domiciliary in the United Kingdom, and there are concurrent proceedings in Japan where the United Kingdom domiciliary sues the Japanese domiciliary), the Regulation would apply to the action brought in the United Kingdom. Nonetheless, Article 27 does not apply and there would appear to be no power to decline jurisdiction under any other provision in the Regulation,[893] even though it may be inappropriate to take jurisdiction in the light of the other proceedings in the non-Member State. Moreover, the English courts should not use the traditional English doctrine of *forum non conveniens* to stay the English proceedings.[894]

(v) It may be perfectly clear which court of a Member State is first seised of the proceedings, but jurisdiction may be challenged in that court. The court seised second must of its own motion[895] stay its proceedings[896] until such time as the jurisdiction of the court first seised is established.[897] Once it has been, the court seised second must then

---

[888] *Benatti*, supra, at [66]–[67] (per Toulson LJ), [92]–[97] (per Clarke MR). Cf Buxton LJ in *Benatti* at [84]–[85] and *Tavoulareas v Tsavliris* [2004] EWCA Civ 48 at [31], [2004] 1 Lloyd's Rep 445.

[889] *Benatti*, supra, at [66] (per Toulson LJ), [92]–[97] (per Clarke MR).

[890] *Benatti*, supra, at [84] (per Buxton LJ). But cf *Tavoulareas v Tsavliris* [2005] EWHC 2140 (Comm) at [60], [61], [2006] 1 All ER (Comm), 109; Briggs (2005) 76 BYBIL 654, 656.

[891] The effect where the *lis pendens* involves a non-Member State is discusssed later in this chapter, infra, p 327.

[892] See infra, in this chapter pp 329–331, and infra, pp 440–443 for the relevant English rules.

[893] However, Art 27 may have "reflexive" effect, see infra, p 327.

[894] See infra, pp 320–329.

[895] For the effect on the burden of proof on the parties see *Benatti v WPP Holdings Italy Srl* [2007] EWCA Civ 263 at [62] (per Toulson LJ), [2007] 1 WLR 2316.

[896] But can still make a provisional order: *JP Morgan Europe Ltd v Primacom AG* [2005] EWHC 508 (Comm) at [70]–[72], [2005] 2 Lloyd's Rep 665.

[897] The court first seised decides upon its jurisdiction: *Advent Capital plc v Ellinas Imports-Exports Ltd* [2005] EWHC 1242 (Comm) at [105], [2005] 2 Lloyd's Rep 607. The jurisdiction of an English court is not "established"

decline jurisdiction. This two-stage process avoids the danger of the court seised of the action second declining jurisdiction in favour of the court first seised; but, then the latter court decides subsequently that it has no jurisdiction. Both actions would have been dismissed and starting an action afresh might run into time-bar problems.

(vi) Article 27 is wide enough to cover cases where two Member States have exclusive jurisdiction. Nonetheless, the point is expressly covered by Article 29[898] which, like Article 27, requires a court, other than the one first seised, to decline jurisdiction in favour of that court. Article 29 does not stipulate whether it is referring to exclusive jurisdiction under Article 22 or Article 23,[899] and must be assumed to cover both.

(vii) The question may arise in the court second seised of whether the proceedings before it are within the scope of the Regulation. That court can decide this question and does not have to stay its proceedings so that there can be a decision on this matter by the court first seised.[900]

(viii) More problematical is the situation where a court in one Member State regards itself as having exclusive jurisdiction under Article 22 or 23, but a court in another Member State, nonetheless, has previously allowed the commencement of proceedings in that State. This situation arose before the Court of Justice in *Erich Gasser v Misat Srl,* [901] which was the first of three important decisions[902] of that Court to hold that English practices in relation to international litigation were inconsistent with the Brussels Convention. In *Gasser* the Court of Justice held that a court seised second whose jurisdiction has been claimed under an agreement conferring jurisdiction has nevertheless to stay proceedings until the court first seised has declared that it has no jurisdiction. It is for the court first seised to pronounce as to its jurisdiction in the light of the jurisdiction clause.[903] In the past the English courts took a different view. The Court of Appeal in *Continental Bank NA v Aeakos Compañia Naviera SA*[904] held that a dispute brought first before the Greek courts came within an English exclusive jurisdiction clause, and that since the English court "second seised" had jurisdiction in relation to any such dispute conferred on it by the agreement of the parties under Article 17 of the Brussels Convention (Article 23 of

---

if it has stayed its proceedings: *The Xin Yang* [1996] 2 Lloyd's Rep 217 at 222. But it would be still seised: *Viking Line ABP v The International Transport Workers' Federation* [2005] EWHC 1222, [2006] IL Pr 4 at [73].

[898] Art 23 of the Brussels Convention, on which see the Jenard Report, p 42.

[899] On the provision under the Brussels Convention (Art 17) corresponding to Art 23 of the Regulation, see Case 23/78 *Meeth v Glacetal Sarl* [1978] ECR 2133.

[900] *Through Transport Mutual Insurance Association (Eurasia) Ltd v New India Assurance Association Co Ltd* [2004] EWCA (Civ) 1598 at [23]–[37], [2005] 1 Lloyd's Rep 67.

[901] Case C-116/02 [2003] ECR I-4207; Baatz [2004] LMCLQ 25; Fentiman [2004] CLJ 312. and (2005) 42 CMLR 241; Hartley in (2005) 54 ICLQ 813 and *Le droit international privé: esprit et methodes (Melanges en l'honneur de Paul Lagarde)* (Dalloz, Paris, 2005), p 383; Mance (2004) 120 LQR 357. In Case C-351/89 *Overseas Union Insurance Ltd v New Hampshire Insurance Co,* supra, the position in this situation was left open by the Court of Justice. See also *JP Morgan Europe Ltd v Primacom AG* [2005] EWHC 508 (Comm) at [36], [2005] 2 Lloyd's Rep 665; Briggs (2005) 76 BYBIL 641, 648–650.

[902] The other two cases were Case C-281/02 *Owusu v Jackson* [2005] ECR I-1383, [2005] QB 801, discussed infra, pp 323–329, and Case C-159/02 *Turner v Grovit* [2004] ECR I-3565, [2005] 1 AC 101, discussed infra, pp 334–337. See generally on all three cases, Hartley in (2005) 54 ICLQ 813 and in (2006) 319 Hague Recueil des cours, 169–184.

[903] Distinguished in the *Through Transport* case, supra, at [36] on the basis that in the latter case there was a question whether the claim in England was within the Regulation, see infra, pp 337–338.

[904] [1994] 1 WLR 588; Bell (1994) 10 LQR 204; Briggs [1994] LMCLQ 158; Hartley (1994) 19 ELR 549; Rogerson [1994] CLJ 241. *Continental Bank* was followed in many cases. The same approach was adopted in Scotland: *Bank of Scotland v SA Banque Nationale De Paris* 1996 SLT 103.

the Regulation), this took precedence over Article 21 of the Convention (Article 27 of the Regulation).[905] This was on the basis that Article 17 deprives the courts of other Contracting States of jurisdiction in relation to disputes coming within the scope of the clause and therefore these courts cannot be "first seised". Likewise, Advocate General LEGER in his opinion in the *Gasser* case was concerned to uphold the effectiveness of choice of jurisdiction agreements and proposed that Article 17 of the Convention (Article 23 of the Regulation) should constitute an exception to Article 21 of the Convention (Article 27 of the Regulation). But the Court of Justice decided that Article 21 of the Convention trumps Article 17. In terms of the structure and objectives of the Regulation this must be right. *Continental Bank* is open to the criticism that the English court was making a decision on whether the Greek court had jurisdiction. As the Court of Justice in *Gasser* pointed out, "the court second seised is never in a better position than the court first seised to determine whether the latter has jurisdiction".[906] This consideration should outweigh the commercial importance of giving effect to jurisdiction agreements.[907] Moreover, there is an alternative way of giving effect to such agreements, namely by awarding damages for breach of the jurisdiction agreement.[908]

There is, though, the very real practical problem of a party adopting delaying tactics, commencing pre-emptive proceedings before a court which he knows lacks jurisdiction because of an exclusive jurisdiction clause, thereby preventing trial in the Member State agreed on until the court first seised has declared that it has no jurisdiction.[909] To make things worse, there are Member States, one of which is Italy, in which in general the duration of proceedings (from commencement to obtaining a decision on jurisdiction) is excessively long.[910] This will involve a breach of Article 6 of the European Convention for the safeguard of Human Rights and Fundamental Freedoms (ECHR). Nevertheless, the Court of Justice in *Gasser* held that Article 21 of the Brussels Convention (Article 27 of the Regulation) will still give priority to the court first seised, even where the duration of proceedings before the courts of the Contracting State in which the court first seised is established is excessively long.[911] The mutual trust which the Contracting States accord to each other's legal systems and judicial institutions, on which the Brussels Convention is based, was said to dictate this.[912] An alternative approach, which was advocated by the United Kingdom government, would have been to have an exception to the *Gasser* principle which would allow the court second seised to examine the jurisdiction of the court first seised where the claimant has brought an action before that court in bad faith (in order to block proceedings in another Contracting State) and that court has not decided the question of jurisdiction within a reasonable time.[913] The difficulty with this approach is that this exception would normally apply in every case where the court first seised is one where excessive delay is routine. The exception

---

[905] The Court of Appeal went on to grant an injunction restraining proceedings in Greece. Such an injunction has since been held to be incompatible with the Brussels Convention, see infra, pp 333–337.

[906] Gasser, supra, at [48].

[907] But cf the opinion of AG LEGER ibid, at [67] and [83].

[908] See Merrett (2006) 55 ICLQ 315.

[909] See Hartley in Nafziger and Symeonides (eds), *Law and Justice in a Multistate World* (2002), p 73.

[910] The *Gasser* case, supra, at [57].

[911] Ibid, at [73].

[912] Ibid, at [72]. See generally on mutual trust under the Brussels Convention, Blobel and Spath (2005) 30 ELR 528.

[913] The *Gasser* case, supra at [63].

effectively becomes country specific, rather than case specific, hence the concern with mutual trust among Contracting States. Nonetheless, it cannot be right that a concern with mutual trust should outweigh both the commercial importance of giving effect to jurisdiction agreements and the human rights of the party seeking to uphold the jurisdiction agreement. What is more, the Member State whose courts are seised second may find itself in breach of Article 6 of the ECHR for failing to try the case with reasonable dispatch.[914] The Hess, Pfeiffer and Schlosser Report [915] advocates a different approach from that of the United Kingdom government, ie to allow parallel proceedings if the risk of conflicting decisions on jurisdiction can be minimised.[916] This gives hope that *Gasser* will be overturned in an amended Brussels I Regulation.

Gasser was concerned with the relationship between the provisions on choice of jurisdiction agreements and *lis pendens*. The position is different in a case involving Article 22 of the Regulation. In this situation the court seised second with exclusive jurisdiction under Article 22 is not required to stay its proceedings in favour of the court seised first.[917] Article 22 cases can be distinguished from Article 23 cases on two grounds. First, in Article 22 cases, but not in Article 23 cases, the court seised first is required to declare of its own motion that it has no jurisdiction if the courts of another Member State have exclusive jurisdiction under Article 22.[918] The jurisdiction of the court first seised is not capable of being established.[919] Secondly, a court in another Member State will not recognise a judgment if it conflicts with Article 22, but it will if it conflicts with Article 23.[920]

Reform: Article 27A

The Hess, Pfeiffer and Schlosser Report advocates the introduction of a new Article 27A to deal with concurrent litigation on the validity of an arbitration agreement in different Member States, giving priority to the court of the Member State which is the place of arbitration.[921]

(b) Related actions

Article 28 of the Regulation is concerned with related actions. Article 28(1) provides that: "Where related actions are pending[922] in the courts of different Member States,

---

[914] See Hartley, op cit.

[915] Study JLS/C4/2005/03, Final Version September 2007, available at the European Commission—European Judicial Network—What's new website http://ec.europa.eu/civiljustice/news/whatsnew_en.htm.

[916] At paras 888–891. One possibility they raise for achieving this is by introducing an additional mode for concluding an exclusive choice of forum agreeement by way of a short and clear-cut standard form.

[917] See the opinion of AG LEGER in the *Gasser* case, supra, at [52]; the *Overseas Union Insurance* case, supra, at [26]; *Prudential Assurance Co Ltd v Prudential Insurance Co of America* [2003] EWCA Civ 327 at [22], [2003] 1 WLR 2295; *Speed Investments Ltd v Formula One Holdings Ltd* [2004] EWCA Civ 1512 at [35]–[38], [2005] 1 WLR 1936.

[918] Art 25. This distinction was used by the Court of Justice to justify their decision in the *Gasser* case, supra, at [52]. See also the *Prudential Assurance* case, supra, at [22].

[919] The *Prudential Assurance* case, supra, at [22].

[920] Art 35(1) of the Regulation. This point was made by the Commission in the *Gasser* case, which treated Art 16 of the Brussels Convention (Art 22 of the Regulation) cases differently from Art 17 of the Convention (Art 23 of the Regulation) cases, see [35]–[36]. See also the opinion of AG LEGER in that case at [75].

[921] See paras 866–868 of Study JLS/C4/2005/03, Final Version September 2007, available at the European Commission—European Judicial Network—What's new website http://ec.europa.eu/civiljustice/news/whatsnew_en.htm.

[922] Cf Art 22(1) of the Brussels Convention, which requires both actions to be pending *at the first instance stage*. The Regulation is worded so as to avoid this requirement.

any court other than the court first seised may stay its proceedings." There is also power under Article 28(2) for the court seised second to decline jurisdiction if the court first seised has jurisdiction over the related actions in question and its law permits the consolidation thereof.[923]

Related actions are defined as ones which are so closely connected that it is expedient to hear them together to avoid irreconcilable judgments from separate proceedings[924] in courts of different Member States.

The Court of Justice has held that this definition must be broadly interpreted[925] and covers all cases where there is a risk of conflicting decisions, even if, because the parties are different, the judgments can be separately enforced and their legal consequences are not mutually exclusive.[926] The concern is to prevent conflicting judgments, albeit only as regards their reasoning, and the court second seised should be able to use Article 28 whenever it considers that the reasoning of the court first seised may concern issues likely to be relevant to its own decision.[927] The House of Lords applied these principles in *Sarrio SA v Kuwait Investment Authority*[928] and, reversing the decision of the Court of Appeal,[929] held that no distinction is to be drawn between the primary or essential issues necessary to establish a cause of action and other matters not essential to the court's conclusion. Adopting this broad common sense approach, their Lordships affirmed the decision of MANCE J, at first instance,[930] that the actions were related[931] where there were allegations common to both sets of proceedings in relation to whether negotiations leading to a sale were conducted by or on behalf of the defendant.

---

[923] Both actions must be pending at first instance, on which see *William Grant & Sons International Ltd v Marie Brizard et Roger International SA* [1997] IL Pr 391 at 401, Court of Session; *Bank of Scotland v SA Banque Nationale de Paris* 1996 SLT 103 at 131–132.

[924] Art 28(3).

[925] *The Tatry*, supra. See also *Sarrio SA v Kuwait Investment Authority* [1999] AC 32, HL; Briggs (1997) 68 BYBIL 331; Harris [1998] LMCLQ 145; *Prazic v Prazic* [2006] EWCA Civ 497 at [17].

[926] *The Tatry*, supra. It follows that "irreconcilable" under Art 28(3) has a different and wider meaning from that in the context of Art 34(3), infra, pp 622–624. On which see Case C-539/03 *Roche Nederland BV v Primus* [2007] IL Pr 9 at [23].

[927] See the opinion of AG TESAURO in *The Tatry*, supra.

[928] Supra.

[929] [1997] 1 Lloyd's Rep 113.

[930] [1996] 1 Lloyd's Rep 650.

[931] See also as examples of related actions: *The Happy Fellow* [1998] 1 Lloyd's Rep 13, CA—collision and limitation actions related; *Toepfer v Molino Boschi* [1996] 1 Lloyd's Rep 510 at 513–514; *Glencore International AG v Metro Trading International Inc (No 1)*, supra, 646–647; *Cronos Containers NV v Palatin* [2002] EWHC 2819, [2003] 2 Lloyd's Rep 489; *Evialis v SIAT* [2003] EWHC 863 (Comm) at [123] and [125], [2003] 2 Lloyd's Rep 377; *Bank of Tokyo-Mitsubishi Ltd v Baskan Gida Sanayi Ve Pazarlama AS* [2004] EWHC 945 (Ch) at [226], [2004] 2 Lloyd's Rep 395; *In the Matter of Intercare Ltd* [2004] 1 ILRM 351; *Prazic v Prazic* [2006] EWCA Civ 497 at [18], [2006] 2 FLR 1128. Cf *Mecklermedia Corpn v DC Congress GmbH* [1998] Ch 40 at 54; *Charterers Mutual Assurance Association Ltd v British and Foreign* [1998] IL Pr 838 at 855; the *Lafi* case, supra, 71; *Miles Platts Ltd v Townroe Ltd* [2003] EWCA Civ 145 at [28]–[34], [2003] 1 All ER (Comm) 561; *Bank of Tokyo-Mitsubishi*, supra, at [241]; *Leo Laboratories v Crompton BV* [2005] 2 IRLM 423—one action in tort, the other in contract following the delivery of contaminated defective product; *Jacobs & Turner Ltd*, supra, at [77]; *Sony Computer Entertainment Ltd v RH Freight Services Ltd* [2007] EWHC 302 (Comm) at [27]–[34], [2007] IL Pr 21; *J v P* [2007] EWHC 704 (Comm) at [49]–[52]; *Landis & Gyr Ltd v Scaleo Chip ET* [2007] EWHC 1880 (QB) at [46]–[50], [2007] IL Pr 53.

Article 28 is concerned with situations that fall outside Article 27, ie the cause of action and subject matter, or the parties,[932] or even both[933] will not be the same.[934] There is no risk of irreconcilable judgments if there is no intention of pursuing the proceedings, commenced in two different Member States, anywhere other than in one Member State,[935] or if one set of proceedings has been definitively terminated,[936] or if one action is for provisional measures and the other is as to the merits.[937] It is not permissible to examine whether the courts of another Member State have exercised properly their jurisdiction under the Regulation when determining whether actions are related.[938] It seems to be implicit from the part of the definition of related actions that refers to it being expedient to hear the two actions together[939] that the court first seised is able to try both actions together, not just in relation to Article 28(2), which makes this an express requirement, but also in relation to Article 28(1); where this is not the case the actions cannot come within Article 28.[940] At the same time it is important to note that Article 28 itself does not confer jurisdiction.[941] In particular, it does not accord jurisdiction to a court of a Member State to try an action which is related to another action in respect of which it has jurisdiction under the Regulation. One final observation on the definition of related actions is that the same wording is to be found in Article 6(1) of the Regulation.[942] Cases decided in the latter context have been relied on for guidance in the present context, and vice versa.[943] However, the Court of Justice has left open the question whether the same definition of "irreconcilable" should be used in these two different contexts,[944] or whether a narrower interpretation should be given in the context of Article 6(1).[945]

---

[932] *The Tatry*, supra; *The Nordglimt* [1988] 1 QB 183 at 201—if the facts were to occur now the parties would be regarded as being the same and Art 27 would apply.

[933] See *Sarrio SA v Kuwait Investment Authority*, supra.

[934] See the opinion of AG Tesauro in *The Tatry*, supra.

[935] *Fox v Taher* [1997] IL Pr 441, CA.

[936] Case C-39/02 *Maersk Olie & Gas AS v M De Haan en W De Boer* [2004] ECR I-9657 at [40].

[937] *Rank Film Distributors v Lanterna Editrice Srl* [1992] IL Pr 58. It might be different if the provisional measure raises issues as to the merits as it did in the *Miles Platt* case, although on the facts of that case there was little duplication of issues and therefore the actions were held not to be related.

[938] *AGF v Chiyoda* [1992] 1 Lloyd's Rep 325; following *Overseas Union Insurance Co v New Hampshire Insurance Co*, supra. For the exceptions to the principle prohibiting an examination of the jurisdiction of the court first seised, see supra, pp 312 and 305.

[939] The actions may be connected but not capable of being heard together in a real sense because their basis is very different: *JP Morgan Europe Ltd v Primacom AG* [2005] EWHC 508 (Comm) at [57], [2005] 2 Lloyd's Rep 665.

[940] *Haji-Ioannou v Frangos* [1999] 2 Lloyd's Rep 337 at 352, CA; *L A Gear Inc v Gerald Whelan & Sons Ltd* [1991] FSR 670; *De Pina v MS Birka ICG* [1994] IL Pr 694. But cf *Centro Internationale Handelsbank AG v Morgan Grenfell Trade Finance Ltd* [1997] CLC 870.

[941] Case C-420/97 *Leathertex Divisione Sinetici SpA v Bodetex BVBA* [1999] ECR I-6747, 6792 at [30].

[942] Supra, pp 263–264.

[943] In considering Art 6(1), it has been said that it is necessary to have in mind the related actions provision: *Messier-Dowty v Sabena SA* [2000] 1 WLR 2040, 2053, CA; *Coin Controls v Suzo (UK) Ltd* [1999] Ch 33 at 46 and vice versa (*King v Crown Energy Trading AG* [2003] EWHC 163 (Comm) at [36], [2003] IL Pr 28).

[944] Case C-539/03 *Roche Nederland BV v Primus* [2007] IL Pr 9 at [23]–[25]—an Art 6(1) case.

[945] AG Leger was in favour of a narrower definition for Art 6(1), see [79]–[105] of his opinion.

Any court other than the court first seised may (rather than must) stay its proceedings[946] or decline jurisdiction.[947] This gives a discretion,[948] in exercising which "regard may be had to the question of which court is in the best position to decide a given question".[949] The court may consider matters "such as the extent of the relatedness, the stage reached in each set of proceedings and the proximity of each Court to the subject matter of the case".[950] This involves considerations of *forum conveniens*,[951] but there is one crucial additional consideration that is unique to this area, namely that there is a risk of irreconcilable judgments if a stay is not granted. There is a strong presumption in favour of granting a stay so as to avoid this.[952] However, it has been said, obiter, that this presumption would be rebutted where the action in the court first seised was brought in breach of an agreement providing for the exclusive jurisdiction of the English courts.[953]

The Hesss, Pfeiffer and Schlosser Report has highlighted the problem that exists under the current law where the court first seised declines jurisdiction but the court second seised may consider also that it has no jurisdiction. To avoid this danger it recommends that the court second seised should be under an an obligation to try the case. [954]

(iii) Provisional measures [955]

(a) Jurisdiction as to the substance

A court which has jurisdiction[956] as to the substance of a case in accordance with Articles 2 and 5 to 24 also has jurisdiction to order any provisional or protective measures which

---

[946] Under Art 28(1). See *Kloeckner & Co AG v Gatoil Overseas Inc* [1990] 1 Lloyd's Rep 177 at 206; Case 150/80 *Elefanten Schuh GmbH v Jacqmain* [1981] ECR 1671.

[947] Under Art 28(2). See *Owens Bank Ltd v Bracco* [1992] 2 AC 443, [1992] 2 WLR 127, CA; *Sarrio SA v Kuwait Investment Authority*, supra; *Haji-Ioannou v Frangos* [1999] 2 Lloyd's Rep 337 at 352, CA.

[948] See *IP Metal Ltd v Ruote OZ SpA* [1993] 2 Lloyd's Rep 60; *The MV Turquoise Bleu* [1996] 1 ILRM 406. The discretion can be exercised on the application of just one claimant, even though there are several claimants in the court first seised: *The Happy Fellow* [1998] 1 Lloyd's Rep 13, CA.

[949] See the opinion of AG LENZ in Case C-129/92 *Owens Bank Ltd v Bracco (No 2)* [1994] QB 509 at 542.

[950] *Grupo Torras SA and Torras Hostench London Ltd v Sheikh Fahad Mohammed Al-Sabah* [1995] 1 Lloyd's Rep 374 at 418, 437; the Court of Appeal in [1996] 1 Lloyd's Rep 7 found it unnecessary to discuss this point following the opinion of AG LENZ in *Owens Bank Ltd v Bracco*, supra, at 541.

[951] The *Grupo Torras* case, supra. See also *Mecklermedia Corpn v DC Congress GmbH* [1998] Ch 40 at 55–56; *Tradigrain v SIAT SpA* [2002] EWHC 106 (Comm) at [66], [2002] 2 Lloyd's Rep 553; *Miles Platts Ltd v Townroe Ltd* [2003] EWCA Civ 145 at [34], [2003] 1 All ER (Comm) 561; *Bank of Tokyo-Mitsubishi*, supra, at [228]. But cf *J v P* [2007] EWHC 704 (Comm) at [50], [71]–[73]. *Forum conveniens* is discussed infra, pp 399–411.

[952] *Virgin Aviation v CAD Aviation* [1991] IL Pr 79 at 88; the opinion of AG LENZ in *Owens Bank Ltd v Bracco*, supra, at 541. See also *The Linda* [1988] 1 Lloyd's Rep 175 at 179; MANCE J in the *Grupo Torras* case, supra—caution must be exercised before refusing a stay, and in *Sarrio Sa v Kuwait Investment Authority* [1996] 1 Lloyd's Rep 650 at 661—neither the Court of Appeal nor the House of Lords discussed this point; *Jacobs & Turner Ltd*, supra, at [78]. This has led to statements that the discretion is not one based on *forum non conveniens*: *The Linda*, supra; *Virgin Aviation v CAD Aviation*, supra; the *Miles Platts* case, supra, at [34]. Cf on the burden of proof *Centro Internationale Handelsbank AG v Morgan Grenfell Trade Finance Ltd* [1997] CLC 870.

[953] *JP Morgan Europe Ltd v Primacom AG* [2005] EWHC 508 (Comm) at [65]–[66], [2005] 2 Lloyd's Rep 665.

[954] Op cit, para 896.

[955] Collins, *Essays*, Chapter 1; (1981) 1 YEL 249; Matthews [1995] CJQ 190; Kennett (1993) 56 MLR 342; Hill, Chapter 10; Maher and Rodger (1999) 48 ICLQ 302; Hartley (1999) 24 ELR 674; Petrochilos [2000] LMCLQ 99; Aird (2002) 21 CJQ 271.

[956] A court will still have jurisdiction, even though it has stayed its proceedings under Art 27(1): *JP Morgan Europe Ltd v Primacom AG* [2005] EWHC 508 (Comm) at [70]–[73], [2005] 2 Lloyd's Rep 665.

may prove necessary.[957] This is not subject to any further conditions, such as that the measure sought must be capable of enforcement in the state of that court. Thus it would allow a Dutch court, using its Kort-geding (summary) procedure, to grant an interim injunction prohibiting the infringement of a patent outside the Netherlands[958] or an English court to grant a world-wide freezing injunction. However, a court of a Member State has no power to order a provisional or protective measure on the above basis if the parties have referred the settlement of their dispute to arbitration, since the effect of this is to deprive the court of jurisdiction under the Regulation as to the substance of the case.[959]

(b) Article 31

In addition there is Article 31,[960] which allows a court to order provisional or protective measures even if it does not have jurisdiction as to the substance of the case.[961] This provides that: "Application may be made to the courts of a Member State for such provisional, including protective, measures as may be available under the law of that State, even if, under this Regulation, the courts of another Member State have jurisdiction as to the substance of the matter."

According to the Court of Justice, "provisional or protective measures" under Article 24 of the Brussels Convention, which corresponds to Article 31 of the Regulation, are ones which are intended to maintain a legal or factual situation in order to safeguard rights.[962] This encompasses the English freezing (Mareva) injunction[963] and search (Anton Piller) order, the Continental *saisie conservatoire*, an ordinary interlocutory injunction under English law[964] and a French process of appointing a judicial expert, who investigated and protected evidence of facts but could not impose any final solution of the dispute on the parties, regarded by French law as interim proceedings.[965] Provisional payments of money owed under a contract can fall within Article 31 subject to certain conditions. The interim payment of a sum of money claimed to be due under a contract under the Dutch Kort-geding procedure does not constitute a provisional measure within the meaning of Article 31 unless, first, repayment to the defendant of the sum awarded is guaranteed if the claimant is unsuccessful as regards the substance of his claim and, secondly, the measure

---

[957] Case C-391/95 *Van Uden Maritime BV (t/a Van Uden Africa Line) v Kommanditgesellschaft in Firma Deco-Line* [1999] QB 1225; Peel (1998) YEL 693; Rodger (1999) 18 CJQ 199.

[958] See the criticism of this in *Chiron Corpn v Organon Teknika Ltd (No 10)* [1995] FSR 325 at 338. For the circumstances where an injunction was granted by an English court restraining the Dutch proceedings, see *Fort Dodge Animal Health Ltd v Akzo Nobel NV* [1998] FSR 222, CA; this is no longer possible, see infra, pp 334–338. See also the more general criticism of the Kort-geding procedure in *Mietz v Intership Yachting Sneek BV* [1996] IL Pr 661, German Federal Supreme Court. However, the Court of Justice has held that this procedure is of a type envisaged by Art 24 of the Brussels Convention (Art 31 of the Regulation): Case C-99/96 *Mietz v Intership Yachting Sneek BV* [1999] ECR I-2277, at [43].

[959] The *Van Uden* case, supra. Recourse can, however, be had to Art 31 of the Regulation, discussed infra. The arbitration exclusion is discussed supra, pp 220–222.

[960] Art 24 of the Brussels Convention.

[961] The *Van Uden* case, supra.

[962] *Reichert v Dresdner Bank (No 2)* Case C-261/90 [1992] ECR-I 2149; the *Van Uden* case, supra.

[963] For recognition and enforcement of freezing injunctions, see infra, pp 602–603.

[964] See *Kitechnology BV v Unicor GmbH Plastmaschinen* [1994] IL Pr 568, CA; infra, p 319 but not an injunction restraining foreign proceedings; but cf Briggs [1994] LMCLQ 158 at 162.

[965] *Miles Platts Ltd v Townroe Ltd* [2003] EWCA Civ 145, [2003] 1 All ER (Comm) 561.

sought relates only to specific assets of the defendant located or to be located within the confines of the territorial jurisdiction of the court to which application is made.[966] An order for maintenance pending trial has been held not to be a provisional measure because, on the facts, of the lack of a realistic prospect of repayment.[967] "Provisional or protective measures" do not encompass an *action paulienne* under French law, which, rather than maintaining the status quo, allows a disposition of property to be set aside.[968] Moreover, it finally determines the position. Neither does the phrase cover a measure ordering the hearing of a witness for the purpose of enabling the applicant to decide whether to bring the case.[969]

The granting of provisional or protective measures on the basis of Article 31 is conditional on, inter alia, the existence of a real connecting link between the subject matter of the measures sought and the territorial jurisdiction of the Member State of the court before which those measures are sought.[970] This requirement will be met if the assets subject to the measures sought are located in the Member State in which those measures are sought. It may not be met if a world-wide freezing injunction[971] is sought or if a Dutch court grants an injunction prohibiting the infringement of a patent outside the Netherlands.

Article 31 has been interpreted by the Court of Justice as only applying to provisional measures which relate to matters within the scope of the Regulation.[972] It has to be asked what rights a provisional measure seeks to protect and, if these rights are outside the scope of the Regulation, a provisional measure cannot be granted under Article 31. Provisional measures may be granted under Article 31 even though the proceedings as to the substance of the case are to be conducted before arbitrators, despite the fact that arbitration is excluded from the scope of the Regulation.[973] There is no requirement that the main proceedings in the other Member State must have actually started when the interim relief is sought, or that they will start in the future. All that is required is that the possibility of substantive proceedings exists under national law.[974] Article 31 obviously allows a provisional measure to be granted in support of proceedings as to the substance of

---

966 The *Van Uden* case, supra. See also Case C-99/96 *Mietz v Intership Yachting Sneek BV* [1999] ECR I-2277, at [43]. On the second requirement see *Bachy SA v Belbetoes Fundacoes E Betoes Especiais LDA* [1999] IL Pr 743, French Cour de cassation.

967 *Wermuth v Wermuth* [2003] EWCA Civ 50 at [31] (per HENRY LJ) and [43] (per Lawrence COLLINS J), [2003] 1 WLR 942—neither was it a protective measure. See also *Comet Group plc v Unika Computer SA* [2004] IL Pr 1 at [23].

968 The *Reichert* case, supra.

969 Case C-104/03 *St Paul Dairy Industries NV v Unibel Exser BVBA* [2005] ECR I-3481, [2005] IL Pr 31.

970 The *Van Uden* case, supra. See *Banco Nacional De Comercio Exterior SNC v Empresa De Telecommunicaciones De Cuba SA* [2007] EWCA Civ 662, [2007] IL Pr 51, [2007] CLJ 495; *SanDisk Corpn v Koninklijke Philips Electronics* [2007] EWHC 332 (Ch), [2007] IL Pr 22.

971 It is unclear whether it is enough if there are assets in England as well as abroad, and the freezing injunction relates to the former as well as the latter. But cf Briggs [2003] LMCLQ 418 at 424–425 who argues that such orders are still permissible.

972 Case 143/78 *De Cavel v De Cavel* [1979] ECR 1055; Case 25/81 *CHW v GJH* [1982] ECR 1189; the *Reichert* case, supra; the *Van Uden* case, supra. For the special problem with matrimonial property of not knowing at the time of the interim order what substantive rights are going to be enforced later, see Hartley, pp 17–18.

973 The *Van Uden* case, supra. See also *Toepfer v Cargill* [1997] 2 Lloyd's Rep 98 at 107–108. For the reasons for this, see supra, pp 220–222.

974 The *Van Uden* case, supra: it was enough that proceedings "may be commenced"; see also the opinion of AG LEGER in the *same case*. But cf *Fort Dodge Animal Health Ltd v Akzo Nobel NV* [1998] FSR 222 at 245, CA.

the case in another Member State. However, it does not appear to preclude a provisional measure being granted in support of proceedings as to the substance of the case in the same Member State in which the provisional measure is sought.[975] The court granting the provisional measure can base its jurisdiction to do so on traditional national rules of jurisdiction, including exorbitant rules prohibited under Article 3 of the Regulation.[976]

The Hess, Pfeiffer and Schlosser Report reserves its strongest criticism of the Regulation for Article 31.[977] It it is highly critical of the lack of any provision which would allow a court having jurisdiction over the substance of the dispute to set aside or modify in pursuance with their own law a provisional or protective order granted by a court of another Member State. It recommends that such a provision should be introduced.

(c) Section 25 of the 1982 Act

Article 31 does not allow provisional measures to be granted where none were available beforehand. It requires the courts of the Member State before which an application is made to grant the provisional measures which are available under the law of that State.[978] If none are available in the particular circumstances,[979] Article 31 would not help. There was a danger of this happening under English law. A freezing injunction was regarded as being an ancillary order which was only available where the English courts had jurisdiction over the main action.[980] If this rule had remained, Article 24 of the Brussels Convention (Article 31 of the Regulation) would have been of no practical effect in England. Section 25[981] of the 1982 Act altered the rule to prevent this happening.[982] It provides that English courts can grant interim relief[983] where proceedings[984] have been or

---

[975] No objection was made by the Court of Justice in the *Van Uden* case, which involved provisional measures sought before the Dutch courts, to the fact that proceedings as to substance took place in the Netherlands where arbitration proceedings were instituted.

[976] Ibid.

[977] Study JLS/C4/2005/03, Final Version September 2007, available at the European Commission—European Judicial Network—What's new website http://ec.europa.eu/civiljustice/news/whatsnew_en.htm. See paras 907–916.

[978] *Republic of Haiti v Duvalier* [1990] 1 QB 202 at 212, CA.

[979] Eg it may not be available under the law of X, if the parties confer jurisdiction on Member State Y and intended provisional measures to be sought there, see Collins, p 90.

[980] *The Siskina* [1979] AC 210; *Mercedes-Benz AG v Leiduck* [1996] AC 284, PC. See McLachlan (1987) 36 ICLQ 669.

[981] As extended by SI 1997/302 and amended by SI 2001/3929, Art 4, Sch 2, Part IV, para 10.

[982] *Babanaft International Co SA v Bassatne* [1990] Ch 13 at 30; *Republic of Haiti v Duvalier*, supra, at 210; *X v Y* [1990] 1 QB 220 at 227–228. See generally Hogan (1989) 14 ELR 191. S 25 is discussed infra. See also s 24, as amended by SI 2001/3929, Art 4, Sch 2, Part IV, para 9 (interim relief in cases of doubtful jurisdiction) and s 26 (security in Admiralty proceedings), as amended by s 11 of the Arbitration Act 1996. S 25 also applies in relation to the Brussels and Lugano Conventions.

[983] See s 25(7). A claim form for an interim remedy under s 25(1) may be served out of the jurisdiction with the permission of the court: CPR, r 6.20(4). But where the defendant is domiciled in a Member State it would appear that the claim form can be served out of the jurisdiction without the permission of the court by virtue of CPR, r 6.19(1A) (quoted supra, p 300). But cf Dicey, Morris and Collins, paras 8.025, 11.265 n 53. An English court granting interim relief can consider a counterclaim: *Balkanbank v Taher (No 2)* [1995] 1 WLR 1067, CA.

[984] This does not cover arbitration proceedings. However, s 2 of the Arbitration Act 1996 provides that the power to grant interim relief in support of arbitration applies even if the seat of the arbitration is outside England and Wales or Northern Ireland and even if no seat has been determined or designated.

are to be commenced[985] in another state. This could be in a Regulation State, a Brussels Convention or Lugano Convention Contracting State or in a non-Member/non-Contracting State.[986] It could be in another part of the United Kingdom. Although this is a wide provision, it does require that the provisional measure is used in support of *foreign* proceedings, which will resolve the merits of the dispute.[987] Thus an English court could grant a world-wide freezing injunction over assets in England and abroad, pending trial in France, the object being to preserve the English assets for when the French judgment is enforced in England under the Brussels I Regulation.[988] The usefulness of section 25 and Article 31 goes beyond this. They allow an interlocutory injunction to be granted stopping a wrong in England or abroad, such as the infringement of an intellectual property right or a breach of confidence, or a threatened wrong, even though the English courts are unable to try the substantive dispute because they lack jurisdiction under the Regulation.[989] There is no requirement under section 25 that the subject matter of the proceedings is within the scope of the Brussels I Regulation[990] or that the defendant be domiciled in an European Community Member State.[991] It follows that interim relief could be granted, for example, in support of foreign insolvency proceedings.[992]

The court may refuse to grant interim relief if the fact that it is exercising an ancillary jurisdiction in support of substantive proceedings elsewhere makes it inexpedient to grant it.[993] Five considerations should be born in mind when determining whether it is inexpedient to grant relief: (i) whether the order would interfere with the management of the case in the primary court; (ii) whether it was the policy in the primary jurisdiction not itself to make world-wide freezing/disclosure orders; (iii) whether there was a danger that the orders made would give rise to disharmony and/or risk of inconsistent orders in other jurisdictions; (iv) whether there was likely to be a potential conflict as to jurisdiction; (v) whether the court would be making an order it could not enforce.[994] Account should

---

[985] See *Alltrans Inc v Interdom* [1991] 2 Lloyd's Rep 571.

[986] See SI 1997/302. See also Capper [1998] CJQ 35; IRS [1997] CJQ 185. For Scotland see Maher 1998 SLT 225; Crawford and Carruthers, paras 7.57–7.58.

[987] *Channel Tunnel Group Ltd v Balfour Beatty Construction Ltd* [1993] AC 334 at 365; *Balkanbank v Taher (No 2)* [1995] 1 WLR 1067 at 1073; *Neste Chemicals SA v DK Line SA The Sargasso* [1994] 3 All ER 180 at 187–188; *Crédit Suisse Fides Trust SA v Cuoghi* [1998] QB 818 at 825, CA.

[988] See *Republic of Haiti v Duvalier* [1990] 1 QB 202, CA. The object may be, as in this case, to discover where the assets are. The foreign equivalent of an English freezing injunction cannot be enforced in England under the Regulation, see infra, pp 602–603. All of this has to be read now in the light of the *Van Uden* case, discussed supra, p 316.

[989] *Kitechnology BV v Unicor GmbH Plastmaschinen* [1994] IL Pr 568, CA; *Coin Controls Ltd v Suzo International (UK) Ltd* [1999] Ch 33 at 53. See also Fawcett and Torremans, pp 214–218. Recourse can be had to traditional exorbitant national bases of jurisdiction according to the Court of Justice in the *Van Uden* case, supra.

[990] See s 25(3)(b) (as amended by Art 4, Sch 2, Part IV, para 10), and SI 1997/302.

[991] *X v Y*, supra, at 229.

[992] See Smart [1998] CJQ 149 at 150–153.

[993] S 25(2); *Motorola Credit Corpn v Uzan (No 2)* [2003] EWCA Civ 752, [2004] 1 WLR 113; *Crédit Suisse Fides Trust SA v Cuoghi* [1998] QB 818; petition for leave to appeal to the House of Lords dismissed: [1998] 1 WLR 474; *Refco Inc v ETC* [1999] 1 Lloyd's Rep 159, CA; *Ryan v Friction Dynamics Ltd* (2000) Times, 14 June; *State of Brunei Darussalam v Bolkiah* (2000) Times 5 September; *Bas Capital Funding Corpn v Medfinco Ltd* [2003] EWHC (Ch), [2004] 1 Lloyd's Rep 652 at [201]; *Banco Nacional de Comercio Exterior SNC v Empresa de Telecommunicaciones De Cuba SA* [2007] EWCA Civ 662, [2007] IL Pr 51.

[994] The *Motorola* case, supra. See in relation to (b) and (c), *Banco Nacional De Comercio Exterior SNC*, supra.

also be taken of the need[995] for the existence of a real connecting link between the subject matter of the measures sought and the territorial jurisdiction of the Member State of the court before which those measures are sought.[996] Where there was reason to suppose that the order made against a foreign defendant would be disobeyed and that, in this eventuality, no sanction would exist, then the court should refrain from making the order.[997] Relief is not limited to remedies which could be granted by the court trying the substantive dispute.[998] Thus the Court of Appeal has approved the grant of a world-wide freezing injunction in support of proceedings in Switzerland, even though the Swiss courts had no power to make such an order.[999]

(i) Is there a discretion to stay proceedings?

(i) In the Regulation itself?

A distinctive feature of the law relating to jurisdiction in common law systems is the presence of a discretionary power to refuse to take jurisdiction on the basis of *forum non conveniens*; ie the appropriate forum for trial is abroad.[1000] There is no such power in civil law systems.[1001] Given that the Regulation is based on the Brussels Convention which had civil law origins, it is not surprising to find that it contains no general discretion to stay actions on the basis of *forum non conveniens*.[1002] Moreover, whilst there is a provision on *lis pendens* in Article 27 this clearly does not involve a discretion.[1003]

(ii) Can the traditional English doctrine of forum non conveniens be used?

An English court must not act in a manner which is inconsistent with the Regulation.[1004] In answering the question whether, by using the doctrine of *forum non conveniens*, it is so acting, it is important to distinguish four different situations.

(a) The Regulation is inapplicable

In the situation where the Regulation is inapplicable (ie the matter is not within the scope of the Regulation)[1005] the courts in the United Kingdom will be able to apply their rules on stays of action (whether these are based on *forum non conveniens*, or on a foreign choice of jurisdiction clause)[1006] as well as their traditional bases of jurisdiction.

---

[995] The *Van Uden* case, supra, p 316.

[996] *Banco Nacional De Comercio Exterior SNC v Empresa de Telecommunicaciones de Cuba SA* [2007] EWCA Civ 662 at [29], [2007] IL Pr 51.

[997] The *Motorola* case, supra.

[998] The *Crédit Suisse* case, supra, at 829.

[999] Ibid.

[1000] See generally Fawcett, *Declining Jurisdiction*, pp 10–27; *Forum non conveniens* is discussed infra, pp 426–443.

[1001] See ibid, pp 10, 21–27; Kennett (1995) 54 CLJ 552.

[1002] See the opinion of the Advocate General in Case 12/76 *Tessili v Dunlop* [1976] ECR 1473; Case 42/76 *De Wolf v Cox* [1976] ECR 1759. See also the hostile attitude of the Court of Justice towards the use of the idea of an appropriate forum in connection with the basis of jurisdiction in Case C-288/92 *Custom Made Commercial Ltd v Stawa Metallbau* [1994] ECR I-2913.

[1003] There is a discretion to stay under Art 28 (related actions) but this is not one exercised on the basis of *forum non conveniens*, supra, p 315.

[1004] *Mazur Media Ltd v Mazur Media GMBH* [2004] EWHC 1566 (Ch) at [69], [2004] 1 WLR 2966.

[1005] Supra, pp 213–222.

[1006] See *A v B* [2006] EWHC 2006 (Comm), [2007] 1 Lloyd's Rep 237—claims designed to impugn the validity of an arbitration agreement fell outside the scope of the Lugano Convention.

(b) The Regulation is applicable and the bases of jurisdiction set out therein come into play

We are concerned here with the situation where the matter is within the scope of the Regulation and the bases of jurisdiction set out in the Regulation apply (these apply where the defendant is domiciled in a Member State or Article 22 or 23 applies). In this situation, it has to be decided whether the court of the Member State which has been assigned jurisdiction by the Regulation has to take it. If so, to grant a stay would be inconsistent with the Regulation. Continental lawyers[1007] have taken the view that any court of a Contracting State allocated jurisdiction under the Brussels Convention (replaced in virtually all cases by the Regulation) must try the case and that courts in the United Kingdom cannot use their *forum non conveniens* discretion in such circumstances. However, English lawyers, when discussing the Brussels Convention, have not been prepared to give up their doctrine of *forum non conveniens* so easily, and have distinguished between cases where the alternative forum is a Contracting State and those where it is a non-Contracting State. After examining the English authorities attention will turn to the decision of the Court of Justice in *Owusu v Jackson*,[1008] which overturns the English law in this area.

(i) The English authorities

In *S & W Berisford plc v New Hampshire Insurance Co*[1009] and *Arkwright Mutual Insurance Co v Bryanston Insurance Co Ltd*[1010] it was held that there was no general discretionary power to stay the proceedings when jurisdiction had been allocated to England under Article 2 of the Brussels Convention, even if the alternative forum was a non-Contracting State.

However, the Court of Appeal in *Re Harrods (Buenos Aires) Ltd*[1011] disagreed. Proceedings were brought in England for, inter alia, the winding up of an English incorporated company. It was argued that the most appropriate forum for trial was Argentina, where the company exclusively carried on its business, and a stay was sought of the English proceedings. The Brussels Convention applied by virtue of the company's English domicile. Nonetheless, it was held that there was power to stay the English proceedings on the ground of *forum non conveniens* and a stay was granted. A fundamental distinction was drawn between cases where the alternative forum was, as here, in a non-Contracting State and cases where it was in a Contracting State. The *forum non conveniens* discretion could still be exercised in the former case, but not in the latter.[1012] The Court of Appeal

---

[1007] See the Schlosser Report, pp 97–99; Kohler (1985) 31 ICLQ 563, 571–574; Droz, *Compétence judiciaire et effets des judgments dans le marché commun*, p 128; Tebbens in Sumampouw (ed), *Law and Reality: Essays on National and International Procedural Law in Honour of Voskuil*, p 47; Gaudemet-Tallon (1991) Rev crit dr int privé 491.

[1008] Case C-281/02 [2005] ECR I-1383; [2005] QB 801.

[1009] [1990] 2 QB 631.

[1010] [1990] 2 QB 649; Collins (1990) 106 LQR 535; Briggs [1991] LMCLQ 10.

[1011] [1992] Ch 72; Briggs (1991) 107 LQR 180; Kaye [1992] JBL 47; Hartley (1992) 17 ELR 553. For critical Continental reaction see Gaudemet-Tallon op cit; Tebbens, op cit.

[1012] The unavailability of the discretionary power to stay in cases where the alternative forum was a Contracting State was confirmed in *Messier Dowty Ltd v Sabena SA* [2000] 1 WLR 2040, 2047, CA; *Aiglon v Gau Shan* [1993] 1 Lloyd's Rep 164; *Lafi Office and International Business SL v Meriden Animal Health Ltd* [2001] 1 All ER (Comm) 54; *Carnoustie Universal SA v The International Transport Workers Federation* [2003] EWHC 1108 (Comm) at [27], [2004] IL Pr 2; *Mahme Trust v Lloyds TSB Bank plc* [2004] EWHC 1931, [2004] IL Pr 43; *Mazur Media Ltd v Mazur Media Gmbh* [2004] EWHC 1566 (Ch) at [71], [2004] 1 WLR

accepted the argument[1013] that the Convention was intended to regulate jurisdiction as between Contracting States and not as between a Contracting and a non-Contracting State. Exercise of the discretion to stay in a case involving a non-Contracting State would therefore not be inconsistent with the Convention. Although a controversial decision,[1014] *Re Harrods* was followed by differently constituted Courts of Appeal on a number of occasions.[1015] These subsequent decisions showed that the principle in *Re Harrods* was not limited to cases where no other Member State was involved and it was applied in the situation where the defendant was domiciled not in England but in another Member State and the alternative forum abroad was a non-Member State.[1016] The principle also looked to be applicable regardless of the basis of jurisdiction.[1017] It was applied in cases where jurisdiction was based not on domicile but on special jurisdiction under Article 6(1),[1018] on the insurance provisions under Section 3,[1019] on submission,[1020] and on exclusive jurisdiction under Article 17 of the Convention (Article 23 of the Regulation).[1021] The Court of Appeal[1022] also applied the principle in the situation where the English courts were being asked to stay the proceedings not on the basis of *forum non conveniens* but on the closely related basis that the action had been brought in breach of an agreement conferring exclusive jurisdiction on the courts of a non-Member State,[1023] the alternative forum being the courts of that state.

2966. But cf *White Sea & Onega Shipping Co Ltd v International Transport Workers Federation* [2001] 1 Lloyd's Rep 421, disapproved by CA. For post-Case C-281/02 *Owusu v Jackson* [2005] ECR I-1383, [2005] QB 801 confirmation, see *Viking Line ABP v The International Transport Workers' Federation* [2005] EWHC 1222, [2006] IL Pr 4 at [73]–[75]; Briggs (2005) 76 BYBIL 641, 646–647.

[1013] Put forward by Collins (1990) 106 LQR 535.

[1014] Cf the criticism in the 13th edn of this book, pp (1999), 264–265; Briggs and Rees, (2000) 3rd edn, para 2.216 and (2005) 4th edn, para 2.223; and Layton and Mercer, paras 13.023–13.026 with Dicey and Morris (2000) 13th edn, paras 12-017–12-018. See generally Fentiman [2000] Cambridge Yearbook of European Legal Studies 107.

[1015] *The Po* [1991] 2 Lloyd's Rep 206, CA; *The Nile Rhapsody* [1994] 1 Lloyd's Rep 382, CA; *Haji-Ioannou v Frangos* [1999] 2 Lloyd's Rep 337 et 346, CA (which regarded itself as being bound as a matter of precedent), Briggs (1999) 70 BYBIL 474; *Ace Insurance SA-NV (Formerly Cigna Insurance Co of Europe SA NV) v Zurich Insurance Co* [2001] EWCA Civ 173 at [39] (which also regarded itself as being bound as a matter of precedent), [2001] 1 Lloyd's Rep 618, CA, Briggs (2001) 72 BYBIL 474. For Ireland see *In the Matter of Intercare Ltd* [2004] 1 ILRM 351, 358.

[1016] *Eli-Lilly and Co v Novo Nordisk A/S* [2000] IL Pr 73, CA; *Ace Insurance*, supra, at [31]; *The Po* [1991] 2 Lloyd's Rep 206, where England had jurisdiction by virtue of the Collision Convention, preserved by Art 57 of the Brussels Convention (Art 71 of the Regulation), and not by virtue of the defendant's domicile in England. See also the restatement of the *Re Harrods* principle by Lord Bingham in The *Haji-Ioannou* case, supra, at 346. Cf the judgment of DILLON LJ in *Re Harrods*.

[1017] See the restatement of the *Re Harrods* principle by Lord BINGHAM in The *Haji-Ioannou* case, supra, at 346.

[1018] *Aiglon v Gau Shan*, supra.

[1019] *American Motorists Insurance Co (Amico) v Cellstar Corpn* [2003] EWCA Civ 206 at [49], [2003] I L Pr 22—it was accepted that *Re Harrods* would apply, if it was a correct decision.

[1020] The *Ace Insurance* case, supra.

[1021] The *Eli-Lilly* case, supra—it appears to have been a case of an exclusive jurisdiction clause; *Sinochem International Oil (London) Ltd v Mobil Sales and Supply Corp Ltd (No 2)* [2000] 1 Lloyd's Rep 670—an exclusive jurisdiction clause; *Mercury Communications Ltd v Communication Telesystems International* [1999] 2 All ER (Comm) 33—non-exclusive jurisdiction agreement.

[1022] *The Nile Rhapsody* [1994] 1 Lloyd's Rep 382, CA. However, the Court of Appeal, at 392, was prepared to assume that a reference to the Court of Justice was needed to clarify the law on this point but that a reference should not be made in this particular case because of the expense and delay to the parties this would involve.

[1023] See infra, pp 328–329.

(ii) The decision of the Court of Justice in Owusu v Jackson

When the Court of Appeal decision in *Re Harrods (Buenos Aires) Ltd* was appealed to the House of Lords, the issue of the correctness of the principle adopted in that case was referred to the Court of Justice;[1024] but before the Court could consider the matter, the action was settled. In *Lubbe v Cape plc*, Lord BINGHAM, with whom the other Law Lords concurred, agreed that the law in this area was not clear and said obiter that this matter should be referred to the Court of Justice.[1025] This has now happened in *Owusu v Jackson*,[1026] where the claimant, domiciled in England, brought proceeedings in England against the first defendant, who was also domiciled in England, after being injured in Jamaica whilst staying at a villa he had rented from the first defendant. The latter sought a stay of the procededings on the basis of *forum non conveniens*. The Court of Appeal[1027] referred to the Court of Justice[1028] the correctness of the principle in *Re Harrods*.

The Court of Justice held that Article 2 of the Brussels Convention applied even though the claimant and one of the defendants were domiciled in the same Contracting State and even though the dispute had links with a non-Contracting State and not with another Contracting State.[1029] It then went on to hold that the Brussels Convention precludes a court of a Contracting State from declining the jurisdiction conferred on it by Article 2 of that Convention on the ground that a court of a non-Contracting State would be a more appropriate forum for the trial of the action even if the jurisdiction of no other Contracting State is in issue or the proceedings have no connecting factors to any other Contracting State.[1030]

The decision in *Owusu* on the declining jurisdiction point was based on three considerations[1031] and the reasoning is entirely convincing. First, Article 2 is "mandatory in nature and that, according to its terms, there can be no derogation from the principle it lays down except in the cases expressly provided for by the Convention".[1032] The Court followed a theme that ran through their earlier decisions in *Gasser*[1033] and *Turner v Grovit*,[1034]

[1024] Case C-314/92 *Ladenimor SA v Intercomfinanz SA*.

[1025] [2000] 1 WLR 1545, 1562, HL. The House of Lords avoided the contentious matter of the correctness of the decision in *Re Harrods (Buenos Aires) Ltd* by finding that under *forum non conveniens* principles no stay would be granted. See also *Intermetal Group Ltd & Trans-World (Steel) Ltd v Worslade Trading Ltd* [1998] IL Pr 765, Irish Sup Ct.

[1026] Case C-281/02 [2005] ECR I-1383, [2005] QB 801; Briggs (2005) 121 LQR 535 and [2005] LMCLQ 378; Fentiman [2005] CLJ 303 and [2006] CMLR 705; Rodger (2006) 2 J Priv Int L 71; Cuniberti (2005) 54 ICLQ 973; Hare [2006] JBL 157; Harris (2005) 54 ICLQ 933; Hartley (2005) 54 ICLQ 813; Ibili [2006] NILR 127; Peel [2005] LMCLQ 363; Knight [2007] CLJ 288.

[1027] [2002] EWCA Civ 877, [2002] IL Pr 45, CA; Briggs (2002) 73 BYBIL 453. See also *American Motorists Insurance Co (Amico) v Cellstar Corpn* [2003] EWCA Civ 206, [2003] IL Pr 22, where the Court of Appeal referred the same question to the Court of Justice in *Owusu* with a view to it being combined with the reference in that case.

[1028] Case C-281/02.

[1029] Ibid, at [23]–[36].

[1030] Ibid, at [54]. This follows criticism of the use of *forum non conveniens* in the European Community context by AG RUIZ-JARABO COLOMER in Case C-159/02 *Turner v Grovit* [2004] ECR I-3565 at [35]; discussed infra, pp 334–337.

[1031] The *Owusu* case, supra, at [38]–[47]. AG LEGER, at [235]–[259] of his opinion mentioned a fourth consideration, that the scheme of the Convention supported this conclusion.

[1032] Ibid, at [37].

[1033] [2003] ECR I-14693, [2005] QB 1 at [72]; discussed supra, pp 310–312.

[1034] Supra, at [24].

which also held that English practices in relation to international litigation were incompatible with the Convention, and that the Convention lays down a compulsory system of jurisdiction which the courts in Contracting States are required to respect.[1035]

Secondly, the authors of the Convention did not provide for an exception on the basis of *forum non conveniens*, although the question of so providing was discussed.

Thirdly, application of the doctrine of *forum non conveniens* would undermine certain objectives of the Convention,[1036] namely: respect for the principle of legal certainty;[1037] the strengthening in the Community of the legal protection of persons established therein; and the laying down of common rules of jurisdiction to the exclusion of derogating national rules. When it comes to the first of these objectives, the discretionary nature of the doctrine of *forum non conveniens* is liable to undermine the predictability of the rules of jurisdiction, in particular of Article 2, and consequently the principle of legal certainty. As regards the second objective, the legal protection of persons established in the Community would also be undermined in that a defendant, who is generally better placed to conduct his defence before the courts of his domicile, would not be able reasonably to foresee before which other court he may be sued. The legal protection of the claimant is also undermined in that, under this doctrine, it is for the claimant to establish that he would not obtain justice before the foreign court.[1038] Finally, turning to the third objective, allowing *forum non conveniens* in the context of the Brussels Convention when this doctrine has developed only in the United Kingdom and Ireland, and not in the other Contracting States, would be likely to affect the uniform application of the rules contained in the Convention, thereby defeating the objective of laying down common rules of jurisdiction to the exclusion of derogating national rules. Concern that the objectives of the Convention may be undermined not only provides a positive reason for rejecting the doctrine of *forum non conveniens*, it also destroys what might be argued is a justification for the use of *forum non conveniens*. The Court of Justice in an earlier case has drawn a difficult distinction between jurisdiction (dealt with by the Convention) and procedure (which is for national law).[1039] But application of procedural rules must not, according to the Court, impair the effectiveness of the Convention.[1040] According to Advocate General LEGER in *Owusu*, if it is asssumed for the sake of argument that *forum non conveniens* is a procedural rule it is one that impairs the effectiveness of the Convention.[1041]

[1035] The *Owusu* case, supra, at [38].

[1036] This would in turn undermine the effectiveness of the Convention: AG LEGER at [271].

[1037] This principle has been described as the basis of the Convention, see Case C-539/03 *Roche Nederland BV v Primus*, supra, at [37]. See also Case C-256/00 *Besix*, supra, at [24]–[26] and Case C-4/03 *GAT*, supra, at [28].

[1038] The *Owusu* case, supra, at [43]. This would be at the second stage of the *forum non conveniens* process, discussed infra, pp 434–439. AG LEGER, at [268] of his opinion, pointed out that this plea may be raised by a defendant as a delaying tactic and, at [272], that a claimant by being denied trial in a Contracting State is also denied the benefit of the recognition and enforcement rules under the Convention.

[1039] Case 365/88 *Kongress Agentur Hagen GmbH v Zeehaghe BV* [1990] ECR I-1845.

[1040] Ibid.

[1041] The *Owusu* case, at [260]–[261]. The same point has been made by the Court of Justice in Case C-159/02 *Turner v Grovit* [2004] ECR I-3565, [2005] 1 AC 101 at [29], discussed infra, pp 334–337, in relation to injunctions restraining foreign proceedings.

Owusu was a Brussels Convention case but the reasoning of the Court of Justice is equally applicable to the Brussels I Regulation. Indeed, Advocate General Leger said[1042] that the eleventh Recital in the Preamble to the Regulation, which states that "the rules of jurisdiction must be highly predictable", confirmed his view that a court of a Contracting State is precluded from declining jurisdiction on the ground that a court of a non-Contracting State would be more appropriate for the trial of the action.[1043]

(iii) Altering the facts

The Court of Appeal referred a further question to the Court of Justice, namely, if the Court holds that the use of *forum non conveniens* is inconsistent with the Convention in the circumstances of the *Owusu* case itself, is the use of that doctrine ruled out in all circumstances or just in certain circumstances? The Court of Justice refused to answer this hypothetical question, pointing out that its function was confined to answering questions necesssary for the effective resolution of a dispute.[1044] This inevitably raises a number of questions relating to whether the result would be any different if the material facts were altered. First, would the result be any different if the parties were not domiciled in the same Member State but instead one was domiciled in a Member State and the other in a non-Member State (and the events in issue occurred within that non-Member State or some other non-Member State)? This is materially no different from *Owusu*. This new situation involves the relationships betweeen the court of a single Member State and those of a non-Member State(s) and, according to the Court of Justice, Article 2 would apply.[1045] This new situation would then fall squarely within the ruling of the Court of Justice that, in Article 2 cases, the use of *forum non conveniens* is precluded "even if the jurisdiction of no other Contracting State is in issue or the proceeedings have no connecting factors to any other Contracting State".[1046] But what would happen if the jurisdiction of another Member State is in issue or there is a connecting factor with another Member State? For example, let us assume that the parties were domiciled in different Member States (and the event at issue occurred in one of those Member States or in some other Member State) or the parties were domiciled in the same Member State (and the event at issue occurred in another Member State). This involves the relationships between the courts of different Member States and there is no question but that Article 2 will apply.[1047] The objections raised by the Court of Justice to declining jurisdiction in favour of a court of a non-Member State apply equally to declining jurisdiction in favour of a court of a Member State and the English courts should not decline jurisdiction in the latter situation.[1048] However, this situation is unlikely to come before the Court of Justice since it is accepted in England that there is no power to decline jurisdiction in favour of another Member State.[1049]

[1042] The *Owusu* case, supra, at [278].

[1043] See also Layton and Mercer, para 13.027.

[1044] The *Owusu* case, supra, at [48]–[53]. The Advocate General's Opinion, at [64]–[81] and [217], deliberately keeps strictly to the facts of the *Owusu* case.

[1045] Ibid, at [36].

[1046] Ibid, at para [54].

[1047] Ibid, at [36].

[1048] *Viking Line ABP v The International Transport Workers' Federation* [2005] EWHC 1222, [2006] IL Pr 4 at [73]–[75].

[1049] Supra, p 321.

Secondly, would the result be any different if the jurisdiction of a Member State was based not on Article 2 but on some other basis set out in the Brussels I Regulation? *Owusu* obviously applies where jurisdiction is based on Article 12 (insurer suing in the defendant's domicile).[1050] In *Owusu* Advocate General LEGER said that where jurisdiction is based on Articles 5 and 6 and Sections 3 and 4 of the Convention the case will necessarily involve relations between two Contracting States and not relations between a Contracting State and a non-Contracting State[1051] (with the unsaid but implicit result that the doctrine of *forum non conveniens* cannot be used). This oversimplifies the position. The case may involve two Member States and a non-Member State. For example, the English court's jurisdiction over a defendant domiciled in another Member State may be based on special jurisdiction under Article 6(1) but the alternative forum for trial is in a non-Member State, with which the dispute has strong connections. Prior to *Owusu* an English court has applied *Re Harrods* in this precise situation.[1052] It is submitted that it should no longer do so. The objections to the use of the doctrine of *forum non conveniens* raised by the Court of Justice in terms of the authors of the Convention not providing for such an exception and its use undermining certain objectives of the Convention (the second and third considerations set out above) are equally applicable, regardless of which of the bases of jurisdiction set out in the Regulation is used by the English court. The only possible difference that the basis used can make is over the question whether that particular basis is, like Article 2, mandatory (the first consideration). Admittedly the wording of special jurisdiction under Articles 5, 6 and 7 and jurisdiction under Sections 3, 4 and 5 of the Regulation is less obviously mandatory than the wording of Article 2. Nonetheless, there is no hint in the wording of Articles 5, 6 and 7 and Sections 3, 4 and 5 that the principles laid down in these provisions can be derogated from. *Owusu* has been applied by GLOSTER J where jurisdiction was based on Article 6(1).[1053] In her view it would equally apply whenever there is jurisdiction under the Regulation.[1054] Where jurisdiction is based on Articles 22 or 23 of the Regulation[1055] (Articles 16 and 17 of the Convention), this can involve, as in *Owusu*, the relationships between the courts of a Member State and a non-Member State.[1056] Nonetheless these provisions will still apply.[1057] Again, the wording of Articles 22 and 23 of the Regulation is less obviously mandatory than the wording of Article 2. But there is no hint in the wording of Articles 22 and 23 that the principles laid down in these provisions can be derogated from. Indeed, the case for regarding Articles 22 and 23 as being mandatory in nature is particularly compelling and the Court of Justice has described jurisdiction under Article 22 as being mandatory in nature.[1058] It has to be remembered that under these provisions the case for

---

[1050] *CNA Insurance Co Ltd v Office Depot International (UK) Ltd* [2005] EWHC 456 (Comm) at [26].

[1051] The *Owusu* case, supra, at [24] of his opinion.

[1052] *Aiglon v Gau Shan*, supra.

[1053] *Viking Line ABP v The International Transport Workers' Federation* [2005] EWHC 1222, [2006] IL Pr 4 at [70]–[72].

[1054] Ibid, at [71].

[1055] The position would be same in Art 24 of the Regulation cases. See generally on Art 23 and *Owusu*, Baatz [2006] LMCLQ 143 at 149.

[1056] The *Owusu* case, supra, at [28].

[1057] Ibid.

[1058] Case C-4/03 *Gesellschaft für Antriebstechnik mbH & Co KG (GAT) v Luk Lamellen und Kupplungsbau Beteiligungs KG* [2006] ECR I-6509 at [24].

the courts of a particular Member State having jurisdiction is so strong that it is given exclusive jurisdiction. It would be extraordinary if a Member State could then decline jurisdiction when it cannot do so when jurisdiction is based on Article 2 (which does not give exclusive jurisdiction). Here too it is submittted that to decline jurisdiction in favour of the courts of a non-Member State would be inconsistent with the Regulation. In the situation where Article 23 gives non-exclusive jurisdiction (ie there is a non-exclusive jurisdiction clause), the position is essentially the same as where jurisdiction is based on Articles 5, 6 and 7 or Sections 3, 4 and 5 of the Regulation. As in those cases, declining jurisdiction in favour of the courts of a non-Member State would be inconsistent with the Regulation.[1059]

Thirdly, can the principle in *Re Harrods* (and hence the doctrine of *forum non conveniens*) still be used in the situation where the jurisdiction of a Member State is based on Article 2 (or some other basis set out in the Regulation) but a court of a non-Member State has previously been seised of a claim liable to give rise to *lis pendens* or related actions. *Re Harrods* has been used in the past in this situation.[1060] The Court of Justice regarded the hypothetical question referred to them as to whether the use of *forum non conveniens* is precluded in all circumstances, which it refused to answer, as being asked in connection with, inter alia, this situation.[1061] Advocate General LEGER was at pains to make clear that he was not dealing with this situation.[1062] Nonetheless, it is wrong to think that *Owusu* tells us nothing about how this situation would be dealt with if it came before the Court of Justice.[1063] On the contrary, it is easy to predict what the answer would be. The reasoning of the Court of Justice that precluded the declining of jurisdiction on the ground that a court of a non-Contracting State would be more appropriate is equally applicable in this situation. However, what is left open for a future decision is the possibility, in this situation, of the Brussels Regulation having "reflexive" effects, which is a very different concept from that of *forum non conveniens* and one which has its advocates among Continental lawyers. This theory will be discussed later on in this chapter.[1064]

Fourthly, can the principle in *Re Harrods* (and hence the doctrine of *forum non conveniens*) still be used in the situation where the jurisdiction of a Member State is based on Article 2 (or some other basis set out in the Regulation) but the links connecting the dispute with a non-Member State are of a kind referred to in Article 22 of the Regulation (Article 16 of the Brussels Convention)? Even before *Re Harrods*, English courts were suggesting that there was a discretion to stay the English proceedings in this situation.[1065] The Court of Justice regarded the hypothetical question referred to them as to whether

---

[1059] But see the doubts expresssed, without deciding the point, in *Antec International Ltd v Biosafety USA Inc* [2006] EWHC 47 (Comm) at [17]–[26]. See also where it was unnecessary to decide the point because the criteria for a stay were not met, *HIT Entertainment Ltd v Gaffney International Licensing Pty* [2007] EWHC 1282 (Ch).

[1060] The *Ace Insurance* case, supra.

[1061] The *Owusu* case, supra, at [48]. The Court of Justice also said that the question was asked in connection with the situation where a "Convention" granted jurisdiction to the court of a non-Contracting State.

[1062] Ibid, at [69], [217] and [281]. AG LEGER at [71]–[72], gave his opinion that the wide reference by the Court of Appeal, which would have involved discussion of, inter alia, this situation, was inadmissible.

[1063] But cf Briggs and Rees, para 2.226. See also Peel [2005] LMCLQ 363, 374–376; Briggs [2005] LMCLQ 378.

[1064] Infra, p 333.

[1065] *Arkwright Mutual Insurance Co v Bryanston Insurance Co Ltd*, supra, at 663.

the use of *forum non conveniens* is precluded in all circumstances, which it refused to answer, as also being asked in connection with this situation.[1066] Advocate General LEGER was also at pains to make clear that he was not dealing with this situation.[1067] However, the reasoning of the Court of Justice that precluded the declining of jurisdiction on the ground that a court of a non-Contracting State would be more appropriate is equally applicable in this situation. Accordingly, the *forum non conveniens* discretion should not operate in this situation.[1068] But what is left open for a future decision is the possibility, in this situation, of the Brussels I Regulation having "reflexive" effects.[1069]

There is a separate question that arises in the situation where the links connecting the dispute with a non-Member State are of a kind referred to in Article 22 of the Regulation (Article 16 of the Brussels Convention). Will the traditional subject matter limitations on jurisdiction, which preclude an English court from trying a case, apply? This question is best answered below[1070] when examining these limitations on juridiction.

Fifthly, what is the effect of *Owusu* in the situation where the jurisdiction of a Member State is based on Article 2 (or some other basis set out in the Regulation) but a court of a non-Member State has been designated by an agreement conferring jurisdiction? Even before *Re Harrods*, English courts were suggesting that there was a discretion to stay the English proceedings in this situation.[1071] Under the English traditional rules on stays of actions the ground for obtaining a stay in this situation would not be *forum non conveniens* but the related ground that there has been a breach of an agreement providing for trial abroad.[1072] This raises a question of principle of whether the result would be any different if a stay was granted on what is a discretionary basis other than *forum non conveniens*?[1073] The Court of Justice was concerned with cases of *forum non conveniens* and never seems to have thought about this situation. Advocate General LEGER was at pains to make clear that he was not dealing with this situation.[1074] Nonetheless, the reasoning of the Court of Justice is equally applicable to it. The wording of Article 2 is still mandatory, Member States which concluded the Regulation had no intention of including a discretionary power to stay on the basis of a breach of a jurisdiction agreement, and when it comes to achieving the objectives of the Regulation the same objections can be made to this discretionary power to stay as were made to the *forum non conveniens* discretionary power. Accordingly, the grant of a stay on this basis should also be precluded in this situation.[1075] But, as with the *lis pendens* and Article 22 situations, what is left open for a

---

[1066] The *Owusu* case, supra, at [48].

[1067] Ibid, at [70], [217] and [281].

[1068] But see *Konkola Copper Mines plc v Coromin Ltd* [2005] EWHC 898 (Comm), [2005] Lloyd's Rep 555; affd without discussion of this point [2006] EWCA Civ 5, [2006] 1 Lloyd's Rep 410; discussed infra, p 329. See also Peel [2005] LMCLQ 363, 374–376; Briggs [2005] LMCLQ 378.

[1069] Discussed infra, p 333.

[1070] Infra, pp 487–489.

[1071] See *S & W Berisford plc v New Hampshire Insurance Co* [1990] 2 QB 631 at 643; *Arkwright Mutual Insurance Co v Bryanston Insurance Co Ltd*, [1990] 2 QB 649 at 663.

[1072] Infra, pp 443–448.

[1073] The question whether there is a residual discretion to stay is discussed infra, pp 332–333.

[1074] The *Owusu* case, supra, at [69], [217] and [281].

[1075] But cf Briggs and Rees, para 2.224; Peel [2005] LMCLQ 363, 374–376; Briggs [2005] LMCLQ 378. See generally Harris (2005) 54 ICLQ 933, 943-945. It is unclear whether the *Re Harrods* principle will operate in cases involving an agreement to go to arbitration in a non-Member State. There is the added complication in such cases that it is not clear whether they come within the scope of the Regulation in the first place. If they do, there is then

future decision is the possibility, in this situation, of the Regulation having "reflexive" effects.[1076]

Unfortunately, COLMAN J in *Konkola Copper Mines Plc v Coromin Ltd* [1077] has said obiter that the discretion to stay proceedings brought in breach of a choice of jurisdiction clause providing for trial abroad in a non-Contracting State can still be used in the situation where the English court's jurisdiction is based on Article 2 of the Brussels Convention. *Owusu* was distinguished on the totally unconvincing basis that that case involved use of the *forum non conveniens* discretion, whereas *Konkola* involved the discretion that applies where there is a breach of a foreign jurisdiction clause.[1078] This entirely misses the point that the Court of Justice clearly regarded the use of discretionary powers as being incompatible with the objectives of the Convention. Reliance was placed on pre-*Owusu* case law,[1079] rather than on the reasoning in that case. COLMAN J appeared to regard the position where the links connecting the dispute with a non-Contracting State are of a kind referred to in Article 16 of the Brussels Convention (Article 22 of the Regulation) as being in principle the same as that where there was a clause conferring jurisdiction on the courts of a non-Contracting State.[1080] Accordingly, he might have been prepared to allow a discretion in that situation as well. But he regarded the *lis pendens* in a non-Contracting State situation as being different.[1081]

(c) The Regulation is applicable but none of the bases of jurisdiction set out therein come into play

We are concerned here with the situation where the matter is within the scope of the Regulation but none of the bases of jurisdiction set out therein come into play (the defendant is domiciled in a non-Member State and neither Article 22 nor 23 applies). According to Article 4 of the Regulation, in this situation jurisdiction is determined by the law of each Member State. The English law of jurisdiction includes not only bases of jurisdiction but also the discretion to stay on the ground of *forum non conveniens*.[1082] But what if the alternative forum is a Member State? Can the doctrine of *forum non conveniens* still be used?

---

the complication that s 9 of the Arbitration Act 1996, infra, pp 450–454, directs the English court to stay the proceedings. For a case granting a s 9 stay because of arbitration in Paris, see *Et Plus SA v Welter* [2005] EWHC 2115 (Comm) at [50], [2006] 1 Lloyd's Rep 251. A claim in relation to arbitration may fall outside the scope of the Regulation altogether and therefore a stay can be granted even in favour of another Member State, see *A v B* [2006] EWHC 2006 (Comm), [2007] 1 Lloyd's Rep 237.

[1076] Discussed infra, p 333.

[1077] [2005] EWHC 898 (Comm), [2005] Lloyd's Rep 555; affd [2006] EWCA Civ 5, [2006] 1 Lloyd's Rep 410 but without an appeal on this particular point; Briggs (2005) 76 BYBIL 641.

[1078] Contrast *Konkola* with *CNA Insurance Co Ltd v Office Depot International (UK) Ltd* [2005] EWHC 456 (Comm) at [26], holding that *Owusu* precludes a stay on case management grounds.

[1079] The *Arkwright* case, supra. Reliance was also placed on the Schlosser Report, para 176, which says that there is nothing in the Convention to support the conclusion that agreements conferring jurisdiction on courts of non-Contracting States must be inadmisssible in principle. But as COLMAN J had to admit, there was nothing to suggest that the Report was thinking of the English discretion. Indeed what it may have been referring to was the reflexive effect of the Convention. COLMAN J, at [94]–[95], said that the decision of the ECJ in Case C-387/98 *Coreck Maritime GmbH v Handelsveem BV* [2000] ECR I-9337 (a case discussing the question of the law that applies to determine the validity of a jurisdiction agreement) did not solve the problem in the existing case. Cf the signifance attached to the case in Briggs and Rees, para 2.224. *Coreck* is a pre-*Owusu* case saying nothing directly on stays of action.

[1080] The *Konkola* case, supra, at [98].

[1081] Ibid.

[1082] *The Xin Yang* [1996] 2 Lloyd's Rep 217 at 220; *Sarrio SA v Kuwait Investment Authority* [1996] 1 Lloyd's Rep 650 at 654, affd by the Court of Appeal [1997] 1 Lloyd's Rep 113, revsd by the House of Lords without discussion of this point [1999] 1 AC 32.

(i) Alternative forum is a Member State

The Court of Appeal in *Sarrio SA v Kuwait Investment Authority*,[1083] adopting the analysis of MANCE J at first instance,[1084] decided that, in the light of what Article 4 provides,[1085] the doctrine of *forum non conveniens* can operate in cases where Article 4 applies, even where the alternative forum is another Contracting State. Moreover, to separate out the inextricably linked concepts of bases of jurisdiction and the courts' discretion to decline jurisdiction on the ground of *forum non conveniens*, so that once a basis of jurisdiction was satisfied the English courts would have to try the case, would lead to an anomaly given that one of the bases of jurisdiction under the traditional rules, service of a claim form out of the jurisdiction, under what is now rule 6.20 of the Civil Procedure Rules,[1086] is itself a discretionary form of jurisdiction.[1087] A discretion would operate in rule 6.20 cases but not where the basis of jurisdiction is service of a claim form within the jurisdiction.

How is this affected by *Owusu*? Advocate General LEGER in that case said that where jurisdiction of a court of a Contracting State is established pursuant to Article 4 of the Convention this does not prevent the court in question from declining to exercise its jurisdiction, in accordance with the doctrine of *forum non conveniens* on the ground that a court of a *non-Contracting State* would be more appropriate to deal with the substance of the case.[1088] This is not dealing with the situation that arose in the *Sarrio* case, which concerned an alternative forum in a Contracting State. However, Advocate General LEGER did accept that Article 4 cases are to be treated differently from Article 2 cases, and to that extent can be said to support the *Sarrio* case. Nonetheless, the position in the *Sarrio* situation is unclear and a reference is needed to the Court of Justice to resolve it.[1089] Until there is such a decision, or one from the House of Lords, overruling the principle in *Sarrio*, that decision remains as a binding authority.

A practical problem arises if the English court exercises its discretion and stays the English proceedings in circumstances where the "alternative forum" is another Member State. The danger is that no Member State will end up trying the case. If the jurisdiction is "established", the court in the other Member State, which is second seised, will have to decline jurisdiction because of Article 27 of the Regulation, assuming, of course, that the requirements of that provision have been met. However, this danger can be avoided in various ways: by the English court dismissing the action rather than merely staying it (which is the best solution),[1090] by the foreign court regarding the jurisdiction of the

---

[1083] [1997] 1 Lloyd's Rep 113; Briggs (1996) 67 BYBIL 592; revsd by the House of Lords without discussion of this point [1999] 1 AC 32, H. See also *The Xin Yang* [1996] 2 Lloyd's Rep 217; Harris (1997) 113 LQR 557; Newton [1997] LMCLQ 337.

[1084] [1996] 1 Lloyd's Rep 650 at 654–656. See also MANCE J in *Grupo Torras SA v Al Sabah* [1995] 1 Lloyd's Rep 374 at 441; the Court of Appeal [1996] 1 Lloyd's Rep 7 did not discuss this point.

[1085] The *Sarrio* case, supra, (MANCE J). See also *The Xin Yang*, supra, at 220.

[1086] At that time Order 11, r 1(1) of the Rules of the Supreme Court. CPR, 620 is discussed infra, pp 372–413.

[1087] [1997] 1 Lloyd's Rep 113 at 123, CA.

[1088] The *Owusu* case, supra, at [235].

[1089] This was recognised (prior to *Owusu*) in *Haji-Ioannou v Frangos* [1999] 2 Lloyd's Rep 337, 348, CA, and since *Owusu* in *Luiz Vicente Barros Mattos v Macdaniels Ltd* [2005] EWHC 1323 (Ch) at [137], [2005] IL Pr 630. See also Briggs and Rees, para 2.228.

[1090] See *Haji-Ioannou v Frangos* [1999] 2 Lloyd's Rep 337, 347–348, CA.

English court as not being "established" in the situation where it has stayed its proceedings,[1091] or by the English court refusing to stay its proceedings.[1092]

(ii) Alternative forum is a non-Member State

The *Sarrio* case involved the situation where the alternative forum was a Member State.[1093] Where the alternative forum is a non-Member State it can be said with some confidence that the *forum non conveniens* discretion can still be used.[1094] There is support for this in the Opinion of Advocate General LEGER in the *Owusu* case[1095] and in earlier obiter dicta in an English case, *The Xin Yang*. [1096] What is less clear is the basis for the availability of *forum non conveniens*. Advocate General LEGER took the view that the principle in *Re Harrods* can still be used in this situation. However, the better view is that Article 4 cases are different from Article 2 cases for the reasons explained in *Sarrio* and, under this view, whether the alternative forum is a Member State or a non-Member State is irrelevant. In *The Xin Yang*, it is not entirely clear which of these two views underlay the support for the use of the *forum non conveniens* discretion.[1097]

Once it has been decided that the English court should stay or decline jurisdiction under Articles 27 or 28 of the Regulation,[1098] it becomes immaterial to consider whether England is the appropriate or inappropriate forum for trial.[1099] To grant a stay on the grounds of *forum non conveniens* in this situation would be inconsistent with the Regulation.[1100]

(d) The knock on effect of *Owusu* in multi-defendant cases

In the situation where there are two defendants, one domiciled in England and the other in a non-Member State, it is necessary to look separately at each defendant. There is no power to stay on the ground of *forum non conveniens* the proceedings against the English defendant. But there is power to stay the proceedings against the second defendant. However, the English court when exercising the *forum non conveniens* discretion may be reluctant to grant a stay because this will involve splitting up the multi-defendant action, leading to concurrent proceedings in two different countries. Indeed in the English first instance decision in *Owusu* a stay was refused against Jamaican co-defendants for this very reason.[1101]

(e) Article 71 of the Regulation applies

We are concerned here with the situation where the English court's jurisdiction is derived from an international Convention, and is accordingly preserved by Article 71 of the

---

[1091] *The Xin Yang*, supra; the *Sarrio* case in the Court of Appeal, supra, at 123.

[1092] The *Sarrio* case in the Court of Appeal, supra, at 123.

[1093] As did *The Xin Yang*, supra.

[1094] Cf Briggs and Rees, para 2.227.

[1095] The *Owusu* case, supra, at [235].

[1096] [1996] 2 Lloyd's Rep 217 at 222.

[1097] Ibid.

[1098] Supra, pp 303–315.

[1099] *Sarrio SA v Kuwait Investment Authority* [1996] 1 Lloyd's Rep 650 at 656, MANCE J, whose analysis was adopted by the Court of Appeal [1997] 1 Lloyd's Rep 113; reversed by the House of Lords without discussion of this point. See *Haji-Ioannou v Frangos* [1999] 2 Lloyd's Rep 337, 347, CA.

[1100] See in relation to the Brussels Convention the judgment of KERR LJ in *The Sennar (No 2)* [1984] 2 Lloyd's Rep 142 at 154, CA.

[1101] Judge BENTLEY QC had earlier decided that he had no power to stay the proceeedings against the English defendant.

Regulation. The principle in *Re Harrods* has been applied in this situation.[1102] However, the Article 71 situation is essentially the same as that in relation to Article 4 and everything said in the previous section is equally applicable here.

(iii) Is there a residual discretion?

The English courts in the past have held that they have a residual discretion to decline jurisdiction in Brussels Convention cases so as to prevent an abuse of process,[1103] as where the claimant's claim is purely speculative and is bound to fail.[1104] Abuse of process has been explained in terms of preventing frivolous or vexatious actions.[1105] The justification that has been given for this residual discretion is as follows. The Brussels Convention is not concerned with questions of procedure except in so far as they impair the effectiveness of the Convention.[1106] It has been argued that the doctrine of abuse of process is a procedural rule and one that does not impair the effectiveness of the Convention.[1107] However, it is very doubtful whether such an argument would be accepted by the Court of Justice. In *Turner v Grovit*,[1108] the Court of Justice has held that the Brussels Convention precludes the grant of an injunction whereby a court of a Contracting State prohibits a party to proceedings pending before it from commencing or continuing legal proceedings before a court of another Contracting State, even where that party is acting in bad faith with a view to frustrating the existing proceedings.[1109] The procedural rule argument was raised in the *Turner* case but rejected on the basis that, even if an injunction was a procedural rule, it was one that impaired the effectiveness of the Convention.[1110] The procedural argument was also rejected by Advocate General LEGER in the *Owusu* case in the context of the English courts staying their own proceedings on the basis of *forum non conveniens*. He gave his Opinion that if it is assumed for the sake of argument that *forum non conveniens* is a procedural rule, it is one that impairs the effectiveness of the Convention.[1111] The discretionary nature of *forum non conveniens* that goes to undermine the objective under the Convention/Regulation of achieving legal certainty[1112] is equally a feature of a residual discretion to stay to prevent abuse of process. However, until there is a decision of the Court of Justice or the House of Lords providing to the contrary, the

---

[1102] *The Po* [1991] 2 Lloyd's Rep 206. See in relation to in rem jurisdiction infra, pp 419–422.

[1103] *Boss Group Ltd v Boss France SA* [1997] 1 WLR 351 at 358, CA; *Pearce v Ove Arup Partnership Ltd* [1997] Ch 293 at 309; revsd by the Court of Appeal on the basis that the judge had been wrong to hold that the claim was bound to fail, [1997] 1 All ER 769, CA; *Bank of Scotland v SA Banque Nationale de Paris* 1996 SLT 103 at 133–134. It is doubtful whether there is a discretion to stay as part of the CPR case management powers and, if there is, it should not be exercised: the *Lafi* case, supra, 74; but cf *Et Plus SA v Welter* [2005] EWHC 2115 (Comm) at [91], [2006] 1 Lloyd's Rep 251.

[1104] The *Pearce* case, supra.

[1105] The *Boss* case, supra. This does not include seeking a negative declaration where it serves no useful purpose: *USF Ltd (t/a USF Memcor) v Aqua Technology Hanson NV/SA* [2001] 1 All ER (Comm) 856 at [24]–[26].

[1106] Case 365/88 *Kongress Agentur Hagen GmbH v Zeehaghe BV* [1990] ECR I-1845—a decision in relation to the Brussels Convention.

[1107] See *Berkeley Administration Inc v McClelland* [1996] IL Pr 772, CA.

[1108] Case C-159/02 [2004] ECR I-3565, [2005] 1 AC 101, discussed infra.

[1109] Ibid, at [32].

[1110] Ibid, at [29].

[1111] The *Owusu* case, supra, at [260]–[261].

[1112] See ibid, at [42]. AG LEGER at [266], [272] mentioned that the objectives of the Convention were also undermined by the procedural consequences of a stay and the denial to the claimant of simplified recognition and enforcement.

English courts may feel bound by earlier precedents providing for a residual discretion in the circumstances outlined above.

(iv) Does the Regulation have "reflexive" effects?

Continental lawyers have argued that there is power to decline jurisdiction in certain limited situations on the basis that the Brussels Convention (Regulation) should have "reflexive" effects.[1113] The first is where jurisdiction has been taken under what is now the Regulation, but the parties have agreed on trial in a non-Member State. The second situation is where there are links connecting the dispute with a non-Member State of a kind referred to in Article 22 of the Regulation. The third is where a court in a non-Member State has previously been seised of a claim liable to give rise to *lis pendens* or related actions. Under this theory, Articles 23, 22 and 27 of the Regulation would give an implied authority to decline jurisdiction in these three specific situations. This is a solution that is best regarded as coming from within the Regulation itself[1114] and is very different from a national court granting a stay on the basis of a traditional ground of its own, as happened in *Re Harrods*. Moreover, since these Articles involve a duty to dismiss, what would appear to be involved if they are given "reflexive" effects is likewise a duty to dismiss the proceedings, rather than a discretion to stay, as there is under *forum non conveniens*.[1115] The Court of Justice in the *Owusu* case refused to discuss the second and third situations[1116] and Advocate General LEGER was at pains to make clear that he was not dealing with these three situations.[1117] This appears to leave it open for a national court to decline jurisdiction in these three situations on the basis of the "reflexive" effects theory.[1118] A decision of the Court of Justice is needed on whether the Regulation precludes the grant of a stay on this basis. It is to be noted, though, that the objection that the Court of Justice had to *forum non conveniens* in terms of its discretionary nature[1119] and the objection that Advocate General LEGER also had in terms of the procedural consequences of a stay,[1120] do not apply to a duty to dismiss proceedings.

(j) Is there a discretion to restrain foreign proceedings?[1121]

(i) In the Regulation itself?

As well as the doctrine of *forum non conveniens*, there is another distinctive feature of the law relating to jurisdiction in common law jurisdictions, namely the discretionary power,

---

[1113] See Gaudemet-Tallon (1991) Rev crit dr int privé 491; Droz, *Compétence judiciaire et effets des judgments dans le marché commun*, p 108; Gothot and Holleaux, *La Convention de Bruxelles du 27 Septembre 1968*, pp 83–84; and generally Kennett (1995) 54 CLJ 552, 563–566. For English support, see Layton and Mercer, para 13.022. See also Case C-163/95 *Von Horn v Cinnamond* [1998] QB 214, where the Commission raised the reflexive effect but the Court of Justice found it unnecessary to discuss this.

[1114] See Kruger, paras 3.10–3.19.

[1115] See Briggs and Rees, para 2.224.

[1116] The *Owusu* case, [48]–[52] and the discussion supra, pp 327–328.

[1117] Ibid, at [217].

[1118] The Court of Appeal in *Ace Insurance SA-NV (formerly Cigna Insurance Co of Europe SA NV) v Zurich Insurance Co* [2001] EWCA Civ 173 at [42]; [2001] 1 Lloyd's Rep 618, had found it unecessary to decide whether Art 17 of the Brussels Convention had "reflexive" effect. See also the comments of LONGMORE J at first instance, [2000] 2 Lloyd's Rep 423 at [21].

[1119] The *Owusu* case, supra, at [42].

[1120] Ibid, at [266].

[1121] Briggs in Andenas and Jacobs (eds), *European Community Law in the English Courts*, pp 287–292.

in certain circumstances, to grant an injunction restraining a party from commencing or continuing as claimant in foreign proceeedings.[1122] This is described as restraining or enjoining foreign proceedings. Although the injunction operates in personam, it is recognised that this constitutes an interference with the jurisdiction of the foreign court. The fact that the court has the power does not necessarily mean that it will grant an anti-suit injunction. The traditional English criteria for the grant of such an injunction[1123] have to be satisfied. In contrast, civil law jurisdictions, when faced with the same problem of forum shopping abroad, deal with it in an indirect way at the stage of recognition and enforcement of the foreign judgment obtained in an inappropriate forum for trial.[1124] It is not surprising, therefore, to find that the Regulation, with its civil law origins, contains no such power to restrain foreign proceedings.

(ii) Can the traditional English power to restrain foreign proceedings be used?

There is an obligation on the courts of Member States not to act in a way that is incompatible with the Regulation. So the real question is whether the Regulation precludes the use of the traditional English power to restrain foreign proceedings. In cases falling outside the scope of the Regulation there can be no question of the Regulation precluding the use of this power,[1125] and the traditional English power to restrain foreign proceedings, including proceedings in another Member State, can be used. In cases falling within the scope of the Regulation the position is more complex. In such cases it is important to distinguish instances where proceedings in a Member State are being restrained from those where proceedings in a non-Member State are being restrained.

(a) Restraining proceedings in a Member State

(i) The English case law

In the past, the Court of Appeal has held that it had power to restrain proceedings in another Contracting State to the Brussels Convention in situations where there had been a breach of a clause providing for the exclusive jurisdiction of the English courts,[1126] and a breach of an arbitration clause.[1127] This power was then extended by the Court of Appeal in *Turner v Grovit*[1128] to the situation where, in the view of the English court, that court was first seised of the proceedings and, accordingly, Article 21 of the Convention (Article 27 of the Regulation) would apply. The *Turner* case also went on to extend the power to the situation where proceedings are launched in another Contracting State for no purpose other than to harass and oppress a party who was already a litigant in England.

[1122] Fawcett, *Declining Jurisdiction*, pp 62–65.

[1123] Infra, pp 455–475.

[1124] Fawcett, *Declining Jurisdiction*, pp 66–67. But see now *Banque Worms v Brachot* 11 November 2002, 2003 Rev Crit 816.

[1125] *Deaville v Aeroflot* [1997] 2 Lloyd's Rep 67; *Through Transport Mutual Insurance Association (Eurasia) Ltd v New India Assurance Association Co Ltd* [2004] EWCA (Civ) 1598, [2005] 1 Lloyd's Rep 67. But which European Community State is to decide whether the Regulation is inapplicable?

[1126] *Continental Bank NA v Aeakos Compañía Naviera SA* [1994] 1 WLR 588, CA; followed in *Fort Dodge Animal Health Ltd v Akzo Nobel NV* 1998] FSR 222, CA— a case involving exclusive jurisdiction under Art 16 of the Brussels Convention (Art 22 of the Regulation).

[1127] *The Angelic Grace* [1995] 1 Lloyd's Rep 87, CA.

[1128] [2000] QB 345, CA; Briggs (1999) 70 BYBIL 332; Fentiman [2000] CLJ 45; Harris (1999) 115 LQR 576; Hartley (2000) 49 ICLQ 166. The decision of the House of Lords and Court of Justice are discussed infra.

(ii) The effect of Erich Gasser GmbH v Misat Srl

The power to restrain foreign proceedings in another Member State in the situation where there had been a breach of a clause providing for the exclusive jurisdiction of the English courts was severely limited as a result of the decision of the Court of Justice in *Erich Gasser GmbH v Misat Srl*. [1129] It will be recalled that the Court held that a court seised second whose jurisdiction has been claimed under an agreement conferring jurisdiction has nevertheless no power to stay proceedings until the court first seised has declared that it has no jurisdiction. It is for the court first seised to pronounce as to its jurisdiction in the light of the jurisdiction clause.[1130] In such circumstances, an English court second seised cannot claim that there has been a breach of an exclusive jurisdiction clause providing for trial in England and is therefore unable to restrain on this basis the foreign proceedings in the Member State first seised.[1131] Of course, this did not affect the power to restrain proceedings in another Member State in the situation where the English court was first seised. Nor did it affect situations where the power has been exercised in situations other than where there had been a breach of a jurisdiction clause. The fatal blow to the power to restrain proceedings in other Member States came from the decision of the Court of Justice in *Turner v Grovit*,[1132] which was the second (in time) of the three recent decisions of the Court of Justice to hold that English practices in relation to international litigation were inconsistent with the Brussels Convention.[1133]

(iii) Turner v Grovit

The facts of the case were simple.

> Turner brought an action in England against his employer (an English company) for unfair dismissal. A Spanish company (in the same group of companies) for which Turner had previously worked brought an action in Spain for damages. The Court of Appeal granted an injunction ordering the defendants, which included the English and Spanish companies, not to continue the Spanish action, having concluded that this action had been brought in bad faith to harass Turner. The defendants appealed to the House of Lords on the basis that there was no power to grant an injunction in such circumstances.

The House of Lords [1134] referred to the Court of Justice the narrow question whether it is inconsistent with the Brussels Convention "to grant restraining orders against defendants who are threatening to commence or continue legal proceedings in another Convention country when those defendants are acting in bad faith with the intent and purpose of frustrating or obstructing proceedings properly brought before the English courts?". The Court of Justice[1135] held that the Brussels Convention precludes the grant

---

[1129] Case C-116/02 [2003] ECR I-4207; discussed supra, pp 310–312.

[1130] Ibid.

[1131] *Through Transport Mutual Insurance Association (Eurasia) Ltd v New India Assurance Association Co Ltd* [2004] EWCA (Civ) 1598 at [89], [2005] 1 Lloyd's Rep 67.

[1132] Case C-159/02 [2005] 1 AC 101.

[1133] The first decision was the *Gasser* case, supra; discussed supra, pp 310–312. The third was *Owusu*, supra; discussed supra, pp 323–329.

[1134] [2001] UKHL 65, [2002] 1 WLR 107; Briggs (2001) 72 BYBIL 436; Ambrose (2003) 52 ICLQ 401.

[1135] Case C-159/02 [2005] 1 AC 101; Briggs (2004) 120 LQR 529; Hare [2004] CLJ 570; Hartley (2005) 54 ICLQ 813; Kruger (2004) 53 ICLQ 1030.

of an injunction whereby a court of a Contracting State prohibits a party to proceedings pending before it from commencing or continuing legal proceedings before a court of another Contracting State, even where that party is acting in bad faith with a view to frustrating the existing proceedings.[1136] The Court said that any injunction restraining a party from commencing or continuing proceedings before a foreign court constituted an interference with the jurisdiction of the foreign court which, as such, was incompatible with the system of the Convention.[1137] Arguments put forward by the House of Lords and by the United Kingdom government in support of the use of such injunctions were rejected. This interference could not be justified on the basis that it was only an indirect interference and was intended to prevent an abuse of process by the defendant in the proceedings in the forum state. The defendant was criticised for having recourse to the jurisdiction of another Contracting State. A decision by an English court as to the abusive nature of the defendant's conduct involved an assessment of the appropriateness of bringing proceeeedings in another Contracting State which ran counter to the principle of mutual trust underpinning the Convention.[1138] Even if one was prepared to accept for the sake of argument that the grant of an injunction was a procedural measure, it was one which impaired the effectiveness of the Convention.[1139] The grant of injunctions did not contribute to minimising the risk of conflicting decisions and avoiding a multiplicity of proceeeedings. Injunctions restraining foreign proceedings rendered ineffective the specific mechanisms provided by the Brussels Convention for cases of *lis pendens* and related actions.[1140] Moreover, such injunctions could give rise to conflicts for which the Convention contained no rules.[1141] An injunction could be issued in one Contracting State but a decision given in another. There could be two Contracting States issuing contradictory injunctions.

(iv) Going beyond cases of bad faith

On its facts, the *Turner* case involved the situation where proceedings were launched in another Contracting State for no purpose other than to harass and oppress a party who was already a litigant in England and the reference from the House of Lords was a narrrow one which referred specifically to this situation. However, the language and reasoning of the Court of Justice is not so confined. The Court of Justice regarded it as being axiomatic that any injunction restraining a party from bringing proceedings before a foreign court constituted an interference with the jurisdiction of that court. The grant of an injunction in the situation where, for example, there has been a breach of an exclusive jurisdiction clause would equally constitute an interference with the jurisdiction of the foreign court.[1142] The English courts exercise the power to grant injunctions restraining foreign proceedings in a wide variety of different situations and, as will be seen,[1143] it is by no

---

[1136] Case C-159/02 [2005] 1 AC 101 at [32].
[1137] Ibid, at [27].
[1138] Ibid, at [28]. For application of this principle in the context of setting aside a judgment subject to payment into court, see *Tavoulareas v Tsavliris* [2005] EWHC 2140 (Comm) at [44], [2006] 1 All ER (Comm) 109.
[1139] Para 29; referring to Case C-365/88 *Kongress Agentur Hagen GmbH v Zeehaghe BV* [1990] ECR I-1845.
[1140] *Turner v Grovit*, supra, at [30].
[1141] Ibid.
[1142] Many cases will be dealt with by the principles in the *Gasser* case, supra, pp 310–312. It may be possible to obtain damages for breach of the jurisdiction agreement, see Merrett (2006) 55 ICLQ 315.
[1143] Infra, pp 455–475.

means easy to categorise the cases where such an injunction has been granted. The prohibition on the grant of an injunction restraining proceedings before a court of another Member State should apply regardless of the category of case involved.[1144] The only qualification to this relates to the situation where an injunction is granted to restrain a party from commencing or continuing proceedings brought in a breach of an arbitration agreement. This raises a question of the scope of the Regulation.

(v) Breach of an arbitration agreement[1145]

The Court of Appeal in *Through Transport Mutual Insurance Association (Eurasia) Ltd v New India Assurance Association Co Ltd*[1146] has held that the English courts have power to grant an anti-suit injunction in a case where a party to an arbitration agreement begins proceeedings in the courts of a Member State in breach of an arbitration clause in a contract. According to the Court of Appeal the crucial distinction between this situation and the ones that arose in the *Gasser*[1147] and *Turner* cases is that a claim in England for such an injunction falls outside the scope of the Regulation,[1148] whereas those cases involved proceedings in two Member States both sets of which fell within the scope of what is now the Regulation.[1149] But the more compelling point is surely that the proceedings in the Member State abroad did fall within the Regulation.[1150] It follows that the injunction undermines the jurisdiction granted to the courts of that state by the Regulation. This is contrary to the *Turner* case.[1151] Although the Court of Appeal decided that it had the power to grant an anti-suit injunction, on the facts of the case it decided not to do so because there was no breach of contract in bringing the proceedings in the Member State abroad.[1152] The House of Lords in *West Tankers Inc v RAS Riunione Adriatica di Sicurta SpA*[1153] has referred to the Court of Justice the question whether it is consistent with the Regulation for a court of a Member State to make an order to restrain a person from commencing or continuing proceedings in another Member State on the ground that such proceedings are in breach of an arbitration agreement. In case it might be of assistance to

---

[1144] But see the *Through Transport* case, supra, at [91] and [95], which seems to confine *Turner* to cases of vexation and oppression. Cf *Advent Capital plc v Ellinas Imports-Exports Ltd* [2005] EWHC 1242 (Comm) at [98], [2005] 2 Lloyd's Rep 607.

[1145] See generally Gross [2000] LMCLQ 11.

[1146] [2004] EWCA (Civ) 1598 at [66]–[92], [2005] 1 Lloyd's Rep 67; Briggs (2004) 75 BYBIL 549; Merrett [2005] CLJ 308; Pengelley (2006) 2 J Priv Int L 397; *Through Transport Mutual Insurance Association (Eurasia) Ltd v New India Assurance Association Co Ltd* [2005] EWHC 455 (Comm), [2005] 2 Lloyd's Rep 378 (for the follow-up on the facts). The decision of the Court of Appeal was followed in *West Tankers Inc v Ras Riunione Adriatica di Sicurta SpA* [2005] EWHC 454 (Comm); Briggs (2005) 76 BYBIL 641, at 648; but see the reference from the House of Lords [2007] UKHL 4 to the Court of Justice (discussed infra). See also Ambrose (2003) 52 ICLQ 401, 419–421.

[1147] The Court of Appeal had earlier held that the court second seised can decide whether the proceedings before it are within the scope of the Regulation, see supra, p 310. The Court, at [83], accepted that if that were wrong the *Gasser* case would apply.

[1148] Ibid, at [47]; supra, p 221. This meant that Arts 27 and 28 would not apply. For an analogous argument in relation to stays of action, see *A v B* [2006] EWHC 2006 (Comm), [2007] 1 Lloyd's Rep 237—claims designed to impugn the validity of an arbitration agreement fell outside the scope of the Lugano Convention and therefore a stay of the claims could be granted under the English courts' inherent jurisdiction.

[1149] Ibid, at [83].

[1150] The Court of Appeal appears to have accepted this. The court of the Member State abroad held that the arbitration clause did not apply to a third party.

[1151] See the *Turner* case, supra, at [27].

[1152] The *Through Transport* case, supra, at [95].

[1153] [2007] UKHL 4, [2007] 1 Lloyd's Rep 391; Fentiman [2007] CLJ 493; Steinbruck [2007] CJQ 358.

that Court, the House of Lords has given its opinion that such proceedings fall within the arbitration exclusion, are thus outside the scope of the Regulation,[1154] and therefore the proceedings for an injunction cannot be inconsistent with the Regulation. Their Lordships accepted that there was an argument that any proceedings (whether within the scope of the Regulation or not), which restrain a party from invoking a jurisdiction available under the Regulation (the situation in the present case), conflict with the Regulation because they amount to an indirect interference with that jurisdiction.[1155] But their Lordships regarded this argument as going far beyond the reasoning in *Gasser* and *Turner* and as being being outweighed by the need to support arbitration as a means of resolving commercial disputes.[1156] The Court of Justice may decide the case on the simple ground that the proceedings in question are not excluded from the scope of the Regulation. But regardless of what, if anything, is decided on that point, the Court of Justice will be concerned, as it was in *Turner*, to prevent an interference by the English courts with the jurisdiction under the Regulation of the courts of another Member State. That interference will still be there, regardless of whether the proceedings in England for an injunction are within the scope of the Regulation or not. Pleas to uphold the integrity of arbitration are likely to have as little effect as the need to uphold the integrity of choice of jurisdiction agreements had in *Gasser*. The Court of Justice is likely to be much more concerned to uphold the integrity of the Regulation than the integrity of arbitration, and to hold that the grant of a restraining order is inconsistent with the Regulation.

(vi) What if jurisdiction is not founded on a Regulation ground?

The Court of Justice was concerned to prevent interference with the jurisdiction of the foreign court. In the *Turner* case, the jurisdiction of the Spanish court was founded on one of the bases of jurisdiction under the Brussels Convention since the defendant in the Spanish proceedings was domiciled in the United Kingdom. Would the position be any different in the situation where the Regulation applies (ie the matter is within the scope of the Regulation) but none of the bases of jurisdiction set out in the Regulation apply to the proceedings which are being restrained (ie the defendant in the proceedings being restrained is domiciled in a non-Member State and Articles 22 and 23 do not apply)? Article 4 of the Regulation applies, according to which the jurisdiction of each Member State is determined by the law of that state. To take an example, a German court has taken jurisdiction under some traditional German basis of jurisdiction in an action brought against a New York defendant, and there is no question of Article 22 or 23 either giving the German courts jurisdiction or ousting their jurisdiction. The jurisdiction of the German court is directly derived from German national rules on jurisdiction, even if the authority for the German courts to use their national rules is derived from Article 4 of the Regulation. The Court of Justice in the *Turner* case referred to an injunction of the kind at issue limiting the application of the rules on jurisdiction "laid down by the Convention"[1157] and this is referring to the bases of jurisdiction set out in the Convention.[1158]

[1154] The *West Tankers* case, supra, at [12]–[14]; discussed supra, p 221.
[1155] Ibid, at [15].
[1156] Ibid, at [15]–[21].
[1157] The *Turner* case, supra, at [30].
[1158] Ibid, at [25].

Nonetheless, it is submitted that the Court of Justice should be concerned to prevent interference with the jurisdiction of the German courts in the above situation. One of the objections to injunctions restraining foreign proceedings made by the Court of Justice in the *Turner* case was that they rendered ineffective the specific mechanisms provided by the Brussels Convention for cases of *lis pendens* and related actions. Those mechanisms apply even where the jurisdiction of Member States is based on national rules on jurisdiction. So this criticism is equally valid in the present situation.

(vii) An injunction preventing the commencement or continuation of proceedings

The injunction sought in the *Turner* case was to prevent the continuance of proceedings previously commenced. An injunction sought at an earlier stage which seeks to prevent the commencement of proceedings in another Member State would equally be prohibited by the decision in that case.

(b) Restraining proceedings in a non-Member State

We are concerned here with the situation where an English court has jurisdiction under one of the bases of jurisdiction set out in the Regulation and the claimant in English proceedings seeks to restrain a party from commencing or continuing proceedings in a non-Member State. The injunction, if granted, constitutes an interference with the jurisdiction of the foreign court. But in this situation it is submitted that this would not be incompatible with the system of the Regulation. In the *Turner* case it was the fact that the injunction prohibited a party to proceedings pending before it from commencing or continuing legal proceedings *before a court of another Contracting State* that made the injunction incompatible with the Convention system. In the present situation, if anything, the injunction is being used to uphold the jurisdiction allocated under the Regulation and its grant should not be regarded as being incompatible with the Regulation. Accordingly, there is power to grant the injunction. Thus an injunction may be granted restraining proceedings brought in a non-Member State in breach of a clause which gives the English courts exclusive jurisdiction under Article 23 of the Regulation.[1159] In *Samengo-Turner v J & H Marsh & McLennan (Services) Ltd*, an injunction was granted in relation to proceedings in New York in the situation where the defendant English domiciled employees who worked in London had the right to be sued only in England by virtue of Section 5 of the Brussels I Regulation.[1160] The acceptance that there was power to grant an injunction in this situation must be right,[1161] there was no incompatibility with the Regulation. What is more questionable, though, is the fact that, because there was the right under that section to be sued exclusively in England, this right provided the ground for granting the injunction.[1162] The same reasoning would apply to cases where the English courts are allocated exclusive jurisdiction under Article 22 of the Regulation.

[1159] *Advent Capital plc v Ellinas Imports-Exports Ltd* [2005] EWHC 1242 (Comm) at [100], [2005] 2 Lloyd's Rep 607. See also *Ultisol v Bouygues* [1996] 2 Lloyd's Rep 140—a Brussels Convention case. An appeal was allowed against the decision on the basis of changes in the position since the first instance judgment was given: *Bouygues Offshore SA v Caspian Shipping Co (Nos 1, 3, 4 and 5)* [1998] 2 Lloyd's Rep 461, CA. There was, however, no denial of the power to grant an injunction.

[1160] [2007] EWCA Civ 723, [2007] IL Pr 52.

[1161] This was common ground by counsel.

[1162] See infra, p 476.

The grant of an anti-suit injunction is not restricted by Article 6 of the Human Rights Act, which provides a right to have civil rights determined "by an independent and impartial tribunal established by law".[1163] This does not deal with *where* the right to such a hearing is to be exercised. What is required is that rights are determined *somewhere* by a hearing and before a tribunal in accordance with Article 6. Of course, the traditional English criteria for the grant of an injunction restraining foreign proceedings have to be met.[1164] In the above example, they will be because what is involved in an Article 23 case is the invasion of a legal right not to be sued abroad. In the past, an injunction restraining proceedings in a non-Contracting State has not been granted merely because the action was brought outside the Contracting State in which the defendant was domiciled.[1165] The reasoning behind this was that there was no "right" to be sued in the Contracting State in which the defendant was domiciled, at least in cases where the alternative forum was a non-Contracting State.[1166] But now the *Owusu* case effectively establishes such a "right".[1167] It follows that an injunction should be granted for breach of this. When an anti-suit injunction has been granted there is always the practical problem of whether it will be effective in cases where the defendant is neither living in England nor has substantial assets there.[1168]

(k) Future impact of the Hague Convention on Choice of Court Agreements

In 2005, a Convention on Choice of Court Agreements was adopted by the Hague Conference on Private International Law.[1169] This is concerned to ensure the effectiveness of exclusive choice of court agreements. The European Community in 2007 became a member of the Hague Conference[1170] and any ratification of the Convention would be by the European Community alone,[1171] rather than by the Community plus the Member States.[1172] Delays in ratification have been caused by delays in finalisation of the accompanying Explanatory Report by Hartley and Dogauchi.[1173] The terms of the Convention are considered in detail in Chapter 12.[1174]

When it comes to the issue of the impact that ratification would have on the Brussels I Regulation, as far as jurisdiction is concerned the Convention will prevail over the

---

[1163] *OT Africa Line Ltd v Hijazy (The Kribi)* [2001] 1 Lloyd's Rep 76, 86–87.

[1164] See *First National Bank Association v Compagnie Nationale Air Gabon* [1999] IL Pr 617 at [26]–[27].

[1165] *Société Commerciale de Réassurance v Eras International Ltd (No 2)* [1995] 2 All ER 278 at 298–299.

[1166] Reliance was placed on *Re Harrods*, supra.

[1167] Supra, pp 323–325.

[1168] Infra, p 456.

[1169] See http://www_hcch.net. See the Explanatory Report (2007) by Hartley and Dogauchi, available on this website; Hartley (2006) 31 ELR 414; Hartley (2006) 319 Hague Recueil 137–141; Kruger (2006) 55 ICLQ 447; Teitz (2005) 53 AJCL 543; Tu (2007) 55 AJCL 347. Attempts at a much wider Hague jurisdiction and judgments convention failed, see McClean in Fawcett (ed), *Reform and Development of Private International Law*, Chapter 11; O'Brian (2003) 66 MLR 491. See also Schulz (2006) 2 J Priv Int L 243.

[1170] See Schulz (2007) 56 ICLQ 915.

[1171] In the light of Opinion 1/03 of the Court of Justice holding that the Community had exclusive competence to conclude the new Lugano Convention; on which see Lavranos (2006) 43 CMLR 1087.

[1172] Negotiations at the Hague were carried out on the pragmatic basis of a shared competence with Member States; see the Joint Statement by the Council and the Commission on Articles 71 and 72 [of the Brussels I Regulation] and on the negotiations within the framework of the Hague Conference on Private International Law.

[1173] Ratifications are now starting, see the Hague Conference website.

[1174] Infra, pp 422–424.

Regulation where one of the parties is resident in a Contracting State to the Convention that is not a European Community Member State. [1175] Apart from this, the Regulation is largely unaffected. [1176]

3. THE EC/DENMARK AGREEMENT

Under an Agreement between the European Community and Denmark, the provisions of the Brussels I Regulation, with minor modifications, are applied by international law to the relations between the Community and Denmark (hereinafter referred to as the EC/Denmark Agreement). [1177] The Agreement does not affect the application of the Brussels I Regulation by the Members of the Community other than Denmark. [1178] In matters of jurisdiction, the Agreement applies where the defendant is domiciled[1179] in Denmark, or where Article 22 or 23 of the Regulation confers jurisdiction on the courts of Denmark. [1180] The Agreement also applies in relation to a *lis pendens* or to related actions, provided for in Articles 27 and 28 of the Regulation, when proceedings are instituted in a Member State (other than Denmark) and in Denmark. Prior to the entry into force of this Agreement, the Brussels Convention applied in relation to Denmark. For the purposes of the Agreement the application of the provisions of the Regulation is modified. However, there are no modifications in relation to Chapter II (Jurisdiction) of the Regulation. [1181] Denmark is not bound by amendments to the Brussels I Regulation but it can decide to implement the contents of such amendments. [1182] International agreements entered into by the Community which affect the Regulation are also not binding upon Denmark. [1183] Finally, when it comes to interpretation of the Agreement, the Danish courts are required to request a ruling from the European Court of Justice in the same circumstances as the courts of another Member State are required to do so in relation to the Regulation. [1184]

[1175] Art 26(6)(a).

[1176] Art 23 of the Regulation would need to be co-ordinated with the rules in the Convention, see the Hess, Pfeiffer and Schlosser Report Study JLS/C4/2005/03, Final Version September 2007, available at the European Commission—European Judicial Network—What's whats new website http://ec.europa.eu/civiljustice/news/whatsnew_en.htm. See para 884.

[1177] OJ 2006 L 120/22. For consequential amendments in the UK see SI 2007/1655. The Agreement applies to legal proceedings instituted after its entry into force (on 1 July 2007): Art 9(1) of the Agreement. There is a separate EC/Denmark Agreement extending the terms of the EC Service Regulation to Denmark.

[1178] Art 10(1) of the Agreement.

[1179] The Civil Jurisdiction and Judgments Order, SI 2001/3929, with its definition of domicile of an individual, applies equally to the Agreement as to the Brussels I Regulation, see SI 2007/1655.

[1180] Art 10(2)(a) of the Agreement. It will also have to be a civil and commercial matter under Art 1 of the Regulation.

[1181] Art 2(2). The modifications relate to: Ch III (Recognition and Enforcement), Art 50 (legal aid and decisions given by an administrative authority in Denmark in respect of maintenance); Ch V (General Provisions), Art 62 (in matters relating to maintenance, court to include Danish administrative authorities), Art 64 (notification of consular officer in certain disputes involving ships registered in Denmark); Ch VI (Transitional Provisions), Art 66; Relations with Other Instruments (Ch VII), Arts 70(2), 72; (Ch VIII) Final Provisions, Art 76; and Annexes I,II, III and IV.

[1182] Art 3.

[1183] Art 5.

[1184] Art 6.

4. THE BRUSSELS CONVENTION

The Brussels Convention on Jurisdiction and the Enforcement of Judgments in Civil and Commercial Matters of 1968,[1185] as amended by four Accession Conventions,[1186] has been replaced in virtually all cases by the Brussels I Regulation. However, one has to say "virtually" because the Convention continues to apply in relation to the territories of the Contracting States[1187] which fall within the territorial scope of that Convention and are excluded from the Regulation.[1188] The territories in question are (in relation to France) the French overseas territories, such as New Caledonia and Mayotte, and (in relation to the Netherlands) Aruba.[1189] The rules on jurisdiction contained in the Brussels Convention are therefore applied in the United Kingdom and in the other Contracting States in the situation where the matter is within the scope of the Convention (a civil and commercial matter) and the defendant is domiciled in one of these territories, or Article 16 (exclusive jurisdiction) or 17 (an agreement on jurisdiction) of the Convention allocates jurisdiction to the courts of one of these territories. The rules on jurisdiction under the Brussels Convention are significantly different from those of the Brussels I Regulation. The former are described fully in the previous edition of this book[1190] and the reader is referred to what is said there for futher details. It is possible that the Community will decide to extend the application of the Brussels I Regulation to territories currently governed by the Brussels Convention.

5. THE LUGANO CONVENTION

The European Free Trade Association (EFTA) bloc was at one time the single most important trading partner of the European Community, and the need for legal and economic co-operation between the two blocs was recognised. A convention on jurisdiction and the recognition and enforcement of judgments was seen as part of this process of co-operation. There were difficulties in the EFTA countries acceding to the Brussels Convention, in particular over the role of the Court of Justice in interpreting that Convention. Instead, a parallel Convention was agreed at Lugano in 1988.[1191] As the European Community has expanded to take in Austria, Finland and Sweden, which were formerly part of the EFTA bloc, and the EFTA bloc has correspondingly contracted, being confined for the purposes of Lugano to just Iceland, Norway and Switzerland,[1192]

[1185] There is also a Protocol on Interpretation in 1971, which came into force in 1975.

[1186] Both the original Convention and the Protocol are to be found in OJ 1978 L 304/77 and 97. The four Accesssion Conventions are listed supra, p 205, n 14. All references to the "Brussels Convention" (or the "Convention") and the "1971 Protocol" are to the latest version amended by the four Accession Conventions. For implementation of the Convention in the United Kingdom, see s 2(1) of the Civil Jurisdiction and Judgments Act 1982, as amended. The latest version of the Convention is to be found in OJ 1998 C 27/1 and also in the latest United Kingdom implementing legislation, SI 2000/1824, which implements the fourth Accession Convention.

[1187] At the moment the Contracting States to the Brussels Convention are the original 15 Member States.

[1188] Art 68(1). Territories are excluded from the Regulation pursuant to Art 299 of the EC Treaty.

[1189] See Layton and Mercer, paras 11.061–11.071. See also Kruger, paras 1.026–1.037.

[1190] See the 13th edn of this book (1999), pp 182–262.

[1191] OJ 1988 L 391/9. This is set out in Sch 3C to the Civil Jurisdiction and Judgments Act 1982, added by s 1(1) of the Civil Jurisdiction and Judgments Act 1991. See generally the 13th edn of this book (1999), pp 278–283.

[1192] Liechtenstein is an EFTA State but not a Contracting State to Lugano.

the practical significance of the Lugano Convention, at least for European Community Member States, has diminished. The 1988 Lugano Convention mirrored the Brussels Convention by adopting the same fundamental principles but there were some crucial differences in the terms of the two Conventions. With the replacement of the Brussels Convention in virtually all cases by the Brussels I Regulation it was desirable for the terms of the Lugano Convention to be amended to bring them into line so far as possible with the Regulation.[1193] A new Lugano Convention was concluded in 2007, which replaces the 1988 Convention.[1194] The Community had exclusive competence to conclude this new Convention, rather than there being a shared competence between the Community and Member States.[1195] The Contracting parties were the European Community, Denmark, Iceland, Norway and Switzerland. The European Community Member States are bound by the Convention because the European Community concluded it.[1196] The states bound by the Convention are accordingly the twenty-seven European Community Member States and the three EFTA States. The Convention allows for the accession of future EFTA Member States,[1197] European Community Member States acting on behalf of non-European territories that are part of their territory[1198] and even for third states to accede to the Convention.[1199] The Convention comes into force on the first day of the sixth month following the date on which the European Community and a Member of EFTA deposit their instruments of ratification.[1200] In the case of the United Kingdom, no implementing legislation is required to implement the Convention.[1201]

(a) When does the Lugano Convention apply?

A matter of concern to the European Community Member States, including the United Kingdom, is the relationship of the Lugano Convention to the Brussels I Regulation, the Brussels Convention[1202] and the EC/Denmark Agreement. The Lugano Convention provides that these instruments continue to apply in the circumstances previously outlined in this chapter, unaffected by the Lugano Convention.[1203] The Lugano Convention

---

[1193] The EFTA States were consulted on the substantive changes to be made to the Brussels Convention with a view to a future new Lugano Convention which would be in the same terms as the Convention. However, as a result of the Brussels Convention being replaced, not with another Convention but with a Regulation, the EFTA States had to wait until the Regulation had come into force and new negotiations were then necessary.

[1194] Art 69(6) of the 2007 Lugano Convention OJ 2007 L 339/3. However, the old system of exchange of information is preserved until a new system is set up: Protocol 2, Art 3(3).

[1195] Opinion of the ECJ 1/03. Signature will be by a person on behalf of the Community: Council Decision (EC) No 2007/712.

[1196] Art 300(7) of the EC Treaty.

[1197] Arts 70(1)(a) and 71 of the Lugano Convention (all references to "the Lugano Convention" refer to the 2007 Convention).

[1198] Arts 70(1)(b) and 71 of the Lugano Convention.

[1199] Arts 70(1)(c) and 72 of the Lugano Convention. Poland, prior to becoming a European Community Member State, acceded to the 1988 Lugano Convention.

[1200] Art 69 of the Lugano Convention. Ratification is likely to happen during 2008. This part of the chapter, dealing with the Lugano Convention, has been written on the assumption that the new convention is in force. (The convention has been approved by the Council, assent by the European Parliament is pending.) The Convention applies only to legal proceedings instituted after its entry into force in the State of origin: Art 63(1).

[1201] Cf the position under the 1988 Lugano Convention, implemented by the Civil Jurisdiction and Judgments Act 1991. However, an Order in Council will be needed parallel to the Civil Jurisdiction and Judgments Order, SI 2001/3929 for such matters as the definition of the domicile of an individual.

[1202] And the Protocol on interpretation of that Convention.

[1203] Art 64(1) of the Lugano Convention.

is applied by courts in the Member States, including the United Kingdom, in relation to jurisdiction in the situation where the matter is within the scope of the Convention and the defendant is domiciled[1204] in Iceland, Norway or Switzerland, or Article 22 (exclusive jurisdiction) or 23 (agreement as to jurisdiction) of the Convention gives jurisdiction to the courts of Iceland, Norway or Switzerland.[1205] As far as the Member States are concerned, the provisions in the Lugano Convention on *lis pendens* and related actions[1206] will apply if there are concurrent proceedings in an Community Member State and in Iceland, Norway or Switzerland.[1207] The Convention does not affect any conventions by which the contracting parties and/or the states bound by the Convention are bound and which in relation to particular matters govern jurisdiction or the recognition or enforcement of judgments.[1208] This covers conventions entered into in the past. The position is the same under the Regulation.[1209] The Convention goes on to provide that it does not prevent contracting parties from entering into such conventions in the future.[1210]

(b) Interpretation of the Lugano Convention

It is desirable that the Convention should have as uniform an interpretation as posssible in the states in which it is applied[1211] and, with this in mind, Protocol 2 (uniform interpretation) is attached to the Convention. The Convention is part of Community rules and, accordingly, the Court of Justice has jurisdiction to give rulings on the interpretation of its provisions.[1212] However, a reference for such a ruling can only be made from a court or tribunal of a European Community Member State, not from the courts of one of the three EFTA contracting parties. Where a reference to the Court of Justice is made for such a ruling, the EFTA States are entitled to submit statements of case or written observations.[1213] Any court applying and interpreting the Convention is required to pay due account to the principles laid down in any relevant decision of the Court of Justice.[1214] This obligation covers not only the courts in the Member States but also the courts in the three EFTA States.[1215] Independently of this, the courts of Member States have obligations

---

[1204] See Arts 59 and 60 of the Convention. The special defintion of domicile adopted for the purposes of the 1988 Lugano Convention (ss 41–46 of the Civil Jurisdiction and Judgments Act 1982, as amended by the Civil Jurisdiction and Judgments Act 1991, Sch 2, paras 16–21) will need to be amended by an Order in Council for the purposes of the 2007 Lugano Convention.

[1205] Art 64(2)(a) of the Lugano Convention. As far as the three EFTA States are concerned, their courts will apply Lugano where the matter is within the scope of the Convention and the defendant is domiciled in the territory of a state where the Convention applies (ie a Member State or EFTA State) or Arts 22 or 23 of the Convention confer jurisdiction on the courts of such a state.

[1206] Arts 27 and 28.

[1207] Art 64(2)(b) of the Lugano Convention. As far as the three EFTA States are concerned, Arts 27 and 28 of the Convention will apply if there are concurrent proceedings in an EFTA State and a Member State/EFTA State.

[1208] Art 67(1) of the Lugano Convention. Provisions on jurisdiction or recognition or enforcement in acts of the institutions of the European Community are treated in the same way as conventions: Protocol 3(1).

[1209] Art 71 of the Brussels I Regulation.

[1210] Art 67(1) of the Lugano Convention.

[1211] See the Preamble to Protocol 2 attached to the Convention.

[1212] See the Preamble to Protocol 2 attached to the Convention. The authority for the Court of Justice giving preliminary rulings is Art 68 of the Treaty on European Union. The limitations on when a national court can make such a ruling are discussed supra, pp 206–207.

[1213] Protocol 2, Art 2.

[1214] Art 1(1), Protocol 2.

[1215] Ibid.

in relation to the Court of Justice resulting from the Treaty of European Union.[1216] The courts in Member States are bound by the jurisprudence of that Court.[1217]

Due account must also be paid by the courts of both Member States and the three EFTA States to the principles laid down by any relevant decision rendered by the national courts of the states bound by the Convention.[1218] A relevant decision, whether of the Court of Justice or a national court, may concern not just a provision of the Lugano Convention (2007) but also any similar provision of the Brussels I Regulation, the Brussels Convention or the EC/Denmark Agreement.[1219] A relevant decision of a national court may concern the 1988 Lugano Convention.[1220]

(c) The terms of the Lugano Convention

The Lugano Convention has been aligned with the Brussels I Regulation and the terms of the two are very similar. Indeed, these are much closer than the 1988 Lugano Convention was to the parallel Brussels Convention. There are obvious differences in terminology between the Lugano Convention and the Regulation. Thus all references in the latter to "a Member State" are replaced by a reference to "a State bound by this Convention".[1221] But as far as jurisdiction is concerned,[1222] there are only two differences of substance.[1223] First, Article 5(2) of the Lugano Convention (special jurisdiction in matters relating to maintenance) sets out an additional alternative State (bound by the Convention) in which a person domiciled in a State bound by the Convention may be sued, namely:

> (c) in the court which, according to its own law, has jurisdiction to entertain proceedings concerning parental responsibility, if the matter relating to maintenance is ancillary to those proceedings, unless that jurisdiction is based solely on the nationality of one of the parties.

Secondly, Article 22(4) (exclusive jurisdiction in proceedings concerned with the registration or validity of patents etc) expressly provides that this provision applies "irrespective of whether the issue is raised by way of an action or as a defence". Article 22(4) of the Brussels I Regulation does not say this but that provision has been interpreted by the Court of Justice to so provide.[1224] The Lugano Convention therefore merely incorporates the effect of existing case law, which would have been applied to the Convention.

(d) Stays of action

An English court must not act in a way which is inconsistent with the Convention.[1225] The question of when a stay of English proceedings is inconsistent with the Brussels

---

[1216] Art 1(2), Protocol 2.

[1217] Art 10 of the Treaty on European Union.

[1218] Art 1(1), Protocol 2.

[1219] Ibid.

[1220] Ibid. No reference could be made to the ECJ in relation to interpretation of the 1988 Lugano Convention.

[1221] As defined in Art 1(3). The 1988 Lugano Convention referred to "a Contracting State".

[1222] Title 2, Arts 2–31 of the Lugano Convention. For service of documents see Protocol 1, Art I.

[1223] Art 26 has been altered but not seemingly in substance.

[1224] Case C-4/03 *Gesellschaft für Antriebstechnik mbH & Co KG (GAT) v Luk Lamellen und Kupplungsbau Beteiligungs KG* (a Brussels Convention case); supra, p 282, n 679.

[1225] S 49 of the Civil Jurisdiction and Judgments Act 1982, as amended by Sch 2, para 24 of the Civil Jurisdiction and Judgments Act 1991 so provided in relation to the 1988 Lugano Convention.

Convention (and the Brussels I Regulation) has been discussed previously when examining *Owusu v Jackson*[1226] and what has been said there need not be repeated here. It is likely that the English courts will apply the same principles in relation to the Lugano Convention as are applied in relation to the Brussels Convention/Regulation. This would mean, for example, that if, in a case involving a Swiss defendant, an English court has been allocated jurisdiction under Article 5 of the Lugano Convention, that court is precluded from declining jurisdiction on the ground that a court of a state bound by the Convention or even a state which is not bound would be more appropriate for the trial of the action.[1227]

6. THE MODIFIED REGULATION[1228]

(a) When does the Modified Regulation apply?

Section 16 of the Civil Jurisdiction and Judgments Act 1982[1229] is headed "allocation within UK of jurisdiction in certain civil proceedings". Section 16(1) states that the Modified version of Chapter II of the Regulation set out in Schedule 4 of the 1982 Act:[1230]

> shall have effect for determining, for each part of the United Kingdom,[1231] whether the courts of law of that part . . . have . . . jurisdiction in proceedings where:
>
> (a) the subject-matter of the proceedings is within the scope of the Regulation as determined by Article 1 of the Regulation (whether or not the Regulation has effect in relation to the proceedings); and
>
> (b) the defendant . . . is domiciled in the United Kingdom or the proceedings are of a kind mentioned in Article 22 of the Regulation (exclusive jurisdiction regardless of domicile).

It follows from section 16 that for the Modified Regulation to apply three conditions must be satisfied.

(i) The situation must concern allocation of jurisdiction within the United Kingdom

This presupposes that courts in the United Kingdom have jurisdiction. There are two situations where this will be so: first, in cases where the Brussels I Regulation, the Brussels Convention or the Lugano Convention has allocated jurisdiction to courts in the United Kingdom;[1232] secondly, in internal United Kingdom cases, where for example a Scotsman sues an Englishman in respect of land in England. Rules are needed to determine which part of the United Kingdom should have jurisdiction, although it would have been quite

---

[1226] Supra, pp 320–333.

[1227] The correctness of the *Re Harrods* principle was due to be considered by the House of Lords in the context of the Lugano Convention in *Anton Durbeck GmbH v Den Norske Bank Asa* but the appeal was withdrawn. The decision of the Court of Appeal is reported at [2003] EWCA Civ 147, [2003] 2 WLR 1296.

[1228] Sch 4 to the Civil Jurisdiction and Judgments Act 1982; as substituted by SI 2001/3929, art 4 and Sch 2, Part II, para 4. See generally Hood, *Conflict of Laws Within the UK* (2007), paras 5.12–5.33.

[1229] As amended by SI 2001/3929, Art 4 and Sch 2, Part II, para 3.

[1230] For the limited exclusions from Sch 4, see s 17 and Sch 5 (as amended). For special provisions with respect to trusts and consumer contracts, see s 10, as substituted by SI 2001/3929, Art 3 and Sch 1, para 7.

[1231] S 50 defines this as England and Wales, Scotland or Northern Ireland.

[1232] See the Schlosser Report, p 98; supra, pp 209–210 and infra.

possible to leave the traditional English rules on jurisdiction to do this. The Brussels I Regulation and the Brussels and Lugano Conventions themselves are inapplicable in internal United Kingdom cases.[1233]

(ii) The subject matter of the proceedings must be within the scope of the Regulation as determined by Article 1

The scope of the Brussels I Regulation has already been dealt with.[1234] Section 16(1)(a) provides that the Modified Regulation will apply "whether or not the Regulation has effect in relation to the proceedings". In an internal United Kingdom case the proceedings may be within the provisions on the scope of the Regulation set out in Article 1 (ie a civil and commercial matter), yet the Regulation would not be applied. It will be recalled that the Regulation is only concerned with the international jurisdiction of Member States.[1235] This additional wording in section 16(1)(a) gets over this particular problem.

(iii) The defendant must be domiciled in the United Kingdom or the proceedings must be of a kind mentioned in Article 22 of the Regulation

The Modified Regulation is only concerned with proceedings where the defendant is domiciled in the United Kingdom or the proceedings are of a kind mentioned in Article 22 of the Regulation (exclusive jurisdiction regardless of domicile). Where jurisdiction is allocated under Article 2 (the defendant is domiciled in a Member State) or under Article 22 (exclusive jurisdiction regardless of domicile), this refers to international jurisdiction (ie jurisdiction is conferred on the United Kingdom) and not local jurisdiction (ie jurisdiction conferred on a part of the United Kingdom).[1236] Where jurisdiction is assigned to the courts in the United Kingdom under other articles, it is necessary to regard jurisdiction as being allocated to the courts in a part of the United Kingdom. In general, there is no problem where Article 5 applies, as this is designed to give local jurisdiction.[1237] Most of the heads of Article 5 are phrased in terms of the courts for a "place" in a Member State having jurisdiction.[1238] For example, Article 5(3) refers to the courts for the place where the harmful event occurred; ascertaining the "place" where the harmful event occurred inevitably pinpoints a part of the United Kingdom whose courts are to have jurisdiction. Where Articles 23 and 24 of the Regulation apply, as has already been seen,[1239] there may be more difficulty in allocating jurisdiction to a part of the United Kingdom.

The requirement under section 16(1)(b) of the 1982 Act that the defendant be domiciled in the United Kingdom causes the usual definitional problems. In principle, a person is domiciled in England, Scotland, or Northern Ireland, not in the United Kingdom. Section 41(2) of the 1982 Act solves this difficulty by defining, for the purposes of the Act, whether an individual is domiciled in the United Kingdom. This is only so if (a) he

---

[1233] Supra, pp 209–210.
[1234] Supra, pp 213–222.
[1235] See supra, pp 213–214.
[1236] See the Schlosser Report, p 98.
[1237] Ibid.
[1238] There is, however, a problem with Art 5(6) which gives jurisdiction to the courts of the Member State in which a trust is domiciled and does not refer to "the place".
[1239] Supra, pp 275 and 296–297.

is resident in the United Kingdom, and (b) the nature and circumstances of his residence indicate that he has a substantial connection with the United Kingdom. Showing this substantial connection is made easier by the introduction of a presumption under section 41(6), according to which, where an individual (a) is resident in the United Kingdom, or in a particular part; and (b) has been so resident for the last three months or more, the requirement as to a substantial connection is presumed to have been fulfilled, unless the contrary is shown. With corporations, section 42(3) basically provides that for the purposes of the 1982 Act a corporation has its seat in the United Kingdom if (a) it was incorporated and has its registered office in the United Kingdom, or (b) its central management and control is exercised in the United Kingdom.

(b) Interpretation of the Modified Regulation

The wording of the Modified Regulation closely follows that of the Brussels I Regulation. Prior to the Modified Regulation there was a Modified Convention based closely on the Brussels Convention. Section 16(3)(a) of the 1982 Act requires the English courts to pay regard to the decisions of the Court of Justice and to the relevant principles followed by it in relation to the jurisdictional provisions in Title II of the Brussels Convention or Chapter II of the Brussels I Regulation. Thus the House of Lords, when interpreting Article 5(1) of the earlier Modified Convention, took the decisions of the Court of Justice in relation to the identically worded (where relevant) provision of the Brussels Convention fully into account.[1240] However, the Modified Convention did not apply the Brussels Convention as such (and the Modified Regulation does not apply the Brussels I Regulation as such); it merely takes it as a model. Accordingly, the Court of Justice held that it did not have jurisdiction to give a preliminary ruling on a question of interpretation of the Brussels Convention, not in order to apply that Convention but in order to apply the identically worded (where relevant) provision in the Modified Convention.[1241] Each Report[1242] accompanying the Brussels Convention and the three Accession Conventions of 1978, 1982 and 1989 may be considered.[1243] If the Court of Justice interprets the Brussels Convention in a way of which the United Kingdom disapproves, the United Kingdom can alter the Modified Regulation to nullify such decisions in relation to allocating jurisdiction within the United Kingdom.[1244]

(c) The terms of the Modified Regulation

Although there was no necessity for the allocation of jurisdiction within the United Kingdom to be based on the Brussels Convention, and now the Brussels I Regulation,

---

[1240] *Kleinwort Benson Ltd v Glasgow City Council* [1999] 1 AC 153 at 163–164 (per Lord GOFF—although at one point he questions whether it would always be appropriate to apply the same interpretation to the Modified Convention as to the identically worded provision in the Brussels Convention), 178–179 (per Lord CLYDE), 186–187 (per Lord HUTTON); discussed supra, pp 230–231. See also *Strathaird Farms Ltd v G A Chattaway & Co* 1993 SLT (Sh Ct) 36.

[1241] Case C-346/93 *Kleinwort Benson Ltd v Glasgow City Council* [1996] QB 57; Briggs (1995) 15 YEL 492; Turkki (1996) 21 ELR 419; Peel [1996] LMCLQ 9; Collins (1995) 111 LQR 541; Bishop (1995) 20 ELR 495; Betlem (1996) 33 CMLR 137. It would be different if there was a direct and unconditional renvoi to provisions of community law.

[1242] Supra, p 209.

[1243] S 16(3)(b) of the 1982 Act. There is no report accompanying the 1996 Accession Convention.

[1244] S 47(1)(b) of the 1982 Act.

this is the form it was decided it should take.[1245] The effect of this can be seen in two examples. In the first example, the defendant is domiciled in the United Kingdom; the claimant will be able to sue him in England (if he is domiciled there),[1246] or in Scotland (if special jurisdiction under rule 3 of the Modified Regulation[1247] gives jurisdiction to Scotland), or in Northern Ireland (if there is an agreement on jurisdiction under rule 12 of the Modified Regulation giving jurisdiction to Northern Ireland—under this provision the jurisdiction given is not exclusive[1248]). In the second example, the dispute concerns the ownership of land in England; the claimant will have to sue in England (under rule 11(a)(i) of the Modified Regulation).

The Modified Regulation is different from the Brussels I Regulation. The modifications that make it different will now be examined.

(i) The modifications

Some of these modifications are necessary to allocate jurisdiction within the United Kingdom. Where the Regulation refers to a *Member State*, the Modified Regulation instead refers to a *part of the United Kingdom*. Thus, under rule 1 "persons domiciled in a part of the United Kingdom shall be sued in the courts of that part". According to rule 3 they "may be sued in the courts of another part of the United Kingdom only by virtue of rules 3 to 13 of this Schedule [which correspond to Articles 5–7 and 15–24 of the Regulation]".

In order to determine whether an individual is domiciled in a particular part of the United Kingdom one must refer to section 41(3) of the 1982 Act. This uses the same criteria as are used under section 41(2) when ascertaining whether an individual is domiciled in the United Kingdom, ie it looks for residence and a substantial connection with that part. The presumption under section 41(6) based on three months' residence is also applicable. Even if the presumption can be rebutted, this is not the end of the matter. Section 41(5) declares that, where the substantial connection cannot be shown in relation to any particular part of the United Kingdom, an individual shall be treated as domiciled in the part of the United Kingdom in which he is resident. Applying these rules, a person could be domiciled in two parts of the United Kingdom at the same time (eg a person has a home in England where he lives all winter but he has spent the previous three months of the summer at his home in Scotland), and both parts would have jurisdiction.[1249] As far as companies are concerned, section 42(4) provides in broad terms that a company has a seat in a particular part of the United Kingdom only if it has its registered office in that part, or its central management and control is exercised in that part, or it has a place of business in that part. It may also be necessary in the case of some bases of jurisdiction to ascertain the place in the United Kingdom where an individual is domiciled. Section 41(4) provides a definition for determining this.[1250]

[1245] See Anton and Beaumont's *Civil Jurisdiction in Scotland*, paras 1.33, 9.01–9.04. Originally when it was decided to base the Modified Convention on the Brussels Convention this was, in part, because Scotland wished to replace its traditional rules on jurisdiction with rules based on the Brussels Convention. See also Crawford and Carruthers, paras 7.53–7.54.

[1246] Under s 41 of the 1982 Act a person may have a dual domicile in different parts of the United Kingdom, so the claimant can sue in either part: *Daniel v Foster* 1989 SLT 90.

[1247] This is the equivalent to Art 5 of the Brussels I Regulation.

[1248] *Snookes v Jani-King (GB) Ltd* [2006] EWHC 289 (QB) at [56]–[62], [2006] IL Pr 19,

[1249] For stays of action, see infra, pp 351–352.

[1250] S 41(4) has to be used where Art 5(2) or Art 6 is applicable. For companies, see s 42(5).

There are also modifications of substance, the most important of which are as follows. Rule 3(a) of the Modified Regulation starts off like Article 5(1)(a) of the Brussels I Regulation by providing special jurisdiction "in matters relating to a contract, in the courts for the place of performance of the obligation in question". However, it does not go on to define the place of performance of the obligation in question for contracts for the sale of goods or the provision of services.

The Modified Regulation contains two additional bases of special jurisdiction. Rule 3(h) deals, inter alia, with proceedings concerning debts secured on immovable property and gives jurisdiction to the courts of the part of the United Kingdom in which the property is situated. Rule 4 of the Modified Regulation deals with proceedings which have as their object a decision of an organ of a company and gives jurisdiction to the courts of the part of the United Kingdom in which the company has its seat. This rule is treated as one of special jurisdiction. In contrast, the Regulation deals with such proceedings by allocating exclusive jurisdiction to the courts of the seat of the company.[1251]

Rule 12 of the Modified Regulation, which deals with jurisdiction agreements, differs from Article 23 of the Regulation in a number of respects. First, the effect of an agreement on jurisdiction is different. Rule 12 of the Modified Regulation provides that, if the parties have chosen the courts of a part of the United Kingdom (eg the English courts) as the forum for trial, those courts will have jurisdiction. However, in contrast to Article 23 of the Brussels I Regulation, such an agreement on jurisdiction does not give exclusive jurisdiction,[1252] and a claimant will be able to use the other bases of jurisdiction set out in the Modified Regulation to sue in another part of the United Kingdom.[1253] Nor is there any equivalent in rule 12 of Article 23(3), which does not give jurisdiction but merely precludes other courts from having jurisdiction. Secondly, for jurisdiction to be conferred by Rule 12 of the Modified Regulation there is a requirement that the defendant is domiciled in the United Kingdom.[1254] For jurisdiction to be conferred by Article 23 of the Brussels I Regulation it is sufficient if the plaintiff is domiciled in a Member State. Thirdly, if the parties have not specified which part of the United Kingdom has jurisdiction conferred on it (ie the agreement just says that trial is to take place in the United Kingdom), Rule 12 of the Modified Regulation will not apply, and the other bases of jurisdiction under the Modified Regulation will have to be used to allocate jurisdiction within the United Kingdom. Fourthly, there is no requirement in respect of the form of agreement, though there must still be a real agreement between the parties.[1255] Fifthly, the agreement, however, must be effective to confer jurisdiction under the law of that part of the United Kingdom whose courts the parties have agreed are to have jurisdiction.

[1251] Art 22(2) of the Brussels I Regulation.

[1252] Under Art 23 of the Brussels I Regulation jurisdiction is exclusive unless the parties have agreed otherwise.

[1253] See *British Steel Corpn v Allivane International Ltd* 1989 SLT (Sh Ct) 57. Cf *Jenic Properties Ltd v Andy Thornton Architectural Antiques* 1992 SLT (Sh Ct) 5, and *McCarthy v Abowall (Trading) Ltd* 1992 SLT (Sh Ct) 65—if it is an exclusive jurisdiction clause, effect will be given to this and jurisdiction is precluded in another part of the United Kingdom.

[1254] See s 16(1)(b) of the Civil Jurisdiction and Judgments Act 1982, as amended by SI 2001/3929 Art 4, Sch 2, Part II, para 3.

[1255] *British Steel Corpn v Allivane International Ltd*, supra.

Finally, the provisions on jurisdiction in matters relating to insurance and exclusive juris-diction in relation to patents,[1256] which are contained in the Regulation, are omitted from the Modified Regulation. This means that other bases of jurisdiction under the Modified Regulation will have to be used in these cases. There is also no provision on *lis pendens* in the Modified Regulation.

(d) Stays of action

(i) Lis pendens

The absence of a provision on *lis pendens* from the Modified Regulation does not cause any problems. Where the Brussels I Regulation is applicable, Article 27 is worded in such a way as to require all courts in the United Kingdom, whether in England, Scotland or Northern Ireland, to decline jurisdiction where the courts of another Member State are first seised of the action. In internal United Kingdom cases, the Brussels I Regulation is inapplicable and the traditional English rules on the discretion to stay,[1257] including those on *lis pendens*, can be used.

(ii) A general discretion to stay

The wording of the Modified Regulation, being based on the Brussels I Regulation, con-tains no suggestion that there is a discretion to stay proceedings on the basis of *forum non conveniens*. Section 49 of the 1982 Act merely provides that a stay of action must not be inconsistent with the Brussels Convention or the Lugano Convention. A stay of action must also not be inconsistent with the Brussels I Regulation. It would, therefore, appear that a discretion to stay actions on the basis of *forum non conveniens* exists under the Modified Regulation, where its use is not inconsistent with the Brussels I Regulation, the Brussels Convention or the Lugano Convention. In deciding whether its use is inconsist-ent it is important to distinguish between, on the one hand, situations where the Brussels I Regulation, the Brussels Convention or the Lugano Convention applies (as well as the Modified Regulation) and, on the other hand, situations where the Modified Regulation applies on its own (internal United Kingdom cases).

Where the Brussels I Regulation, the Brussels Convention or the Lugano Convention applies, there is no discretion to stay proceedings on the basis of *forum non conveniens*, even where the alternative forum is a non-European Community/EFTA State.[1258] Thus, an English court cannot stay proceedings on the basis that the alternative forum is, for example, France or New York. However, where the Modified Regulation then applies to allocate juris-diction within the United Kingdom, it is likely that there is a discretion to stay on this basis. It can be argued that the allocation of jurisdiction within the United Kingdom is a purely internal matter, and other Member or Contracting States can have no objection to a discre-tion to stay being used to transfer actions from one part of the United Kingdom to another.[1259]

[1256] For the more general exclusion of patent proceedings from the Modified Regulation see Sch 5, para (2) of the 1982 Act, on which see generally (in relation to the earlier Modified Convention) Anton and Beaumont's *Civil Jurisdiction in Scotland*, para 9.12.

[1257] Infra, pp 425–455.

[1258] See supra, pp 320–333.

[1259] See the Schlosser Report, p 98; Briggs and Rees 2.231; Hartley, p 80; Collins, pp 45–46; Stone (1983) 29 ICLQ 477, 496–499.

A stay will only be granted if there is an alternative forum with jurisdiction elsewhere in the United Kingdom. This avoids the danger of all the parts of the United Kingdom staying the proceedings, thereby denying the claimant his right, under the Brussels I Regulation, the Brussels Convention or the Lugano Convention to sue the defendant domiciled in the United Kingdom in that Member State.

In internal United Kingdom cases the Brussels I Regulation, Brussels Convention and Lugano Convention are inapplicable and therefore courts in the United Kingdom can use a discretion to stay on the basis of *forum non conveniens* without having to concern themselves with whether this is inconsistent with any of these instruments.[1260]

[1260] *Cumming v Scottish Daily Record and Sunday Mail Ltd* [1995] EMLR 538; *Lennon v Scottish Daily Record* [2004] EWHC 359 (QB); Collins (1995) 111 LQR 541; *Ivax Pharmaceuticals UK Ltd v Akzo Nobel BV* [2005] EWHC 2658 (Ch), [2006] FSR 43; *Sunderland Marine Mutual Insurance Company Ltd v Wiseman* [2007] EWHC 1460 (Comm) at [38], [2007] 2 All ER (Comm) 937. Drake J in *Cumming* departed from his earlier decision in *Foxen v Scotsman Publications Ltd* [1995] 3 EMLR 145; criticised by Collins and Davenport (1994) 110 LQR 325. See also *Kelly Banks v CGU Insurance plc*, Outer House Court of Session, 5 November 2004 (unreported), per Lady Smith. See generally Briggs and Rees, para 2.209; Hartley, op cit; Collins, op cit. But for a contrary view, see Hood, *Conflict of Laws Within the UK* (2007), paras 5.16–5.17.

Chapter 12

The Competence of the English Courts Under the Traditional Rules[1]

1. ACTIONS IN PERSONAM

An action in personam is designed to settle the rights of the parties as between themselves,[2] eg an action for damages for breach of contract, an action for an injunction in a tort case, or an action for possession of tangible property. The most striking feature of the English common law rules relating to competence in actions in personam is their purely procedural character. Anyone may invoke or become amenable to the jurisdiction, provided only that the defendant has been served with a claim form.[3]

---

[1] See generally Hartley (2006) 319 Hague Recueil, Ch IV. For Scots residual national rules see Sch 8 to the Civil Jurisdiction and Judgments Act 1982, as substituted by Civil Jurisdiction and Judgments Order, SI 2001/3929, Sch 2(III), para 7.

[2] *Tyler v Judges of the Court of Registration* (1900) 175 Mass 71.

[3] For the procedure for disputing the English court's jurisdiction see CPR, Part 11. Prior to April 1999, the defendant had to be served with a writ of summons, or its equivalent, eg an originating summons.

This procedural approach has meant that, apart from cases where matrimonial relief is sought,[4] the courts have not been concerned with the connection that the parties to the dispute have with England. Two important consequences stem from this. First, the mere service of a claim form will give the English courts power to try actions which may be inappropriate for trial in England; eg the defendant may be a foreigner who is only transiently in England and the cause of action may have no factual connection with England. The development of a wide, flexible discretion to stay actions on the basis of *forum non conveniens* is an effective solution to this problem. This allows courts, although competent to try the case, to refuse to do so where there is a clearly more appropriate forum for trial abroad.[5]

The second consequence of this procedural approach is the converse of the first. If the defendant is not present within the jurisdiction, the English courts are denied power to try actions in many cases in which it would be appropriate for trial to be held here, such as when a tort has been committed in England or when the defendant is domiciled, but not physically present, in England. This defect was recognised many years ago and was remedied by statute so as to give a discretionary power to the courts (now contained in the Civil Procedure Rules[6]) to authorise service of a claim form on a defendant abroad in certain cases. Another exception to the normal principle that the courts have no power to entertain an action against a defendant who is outside the jurisdiction was found to be necessary to deal with cases where the defendant submitted to the English court's jurisdiction.

The result of these developments is that the English courts are now competent to try an action in personam in three situations:

(a) where there has been service of a claim form on a defendant present within the jurisdiction;
(b) where the defendant has submitted to the English court's jurisdiction;
(c) where there has been service of a claim form out of the jurisdiction under rule 6.20 of the Civil Procedure Rules.

(a) Service of a claim form on a defendant present within the jurisdiction

(i) Individuals

As has already been seen, at common law "whoever is served with the King's writ [now called a claim form] and can be compelled consequently to submit to the decree made is a person over whom the courts have jurisdiction".[7] Jurisdiction accordingly depends on the presence of the defendant in England. Once the court has asserted its power by service of process on the defendant it is not rendered incompetent by his subsequent departure from the country.[8] The corollary to this is that if a defendant escapes service, by reason of his absence abroad, no proceedings can be brought against him.[9]

---

⁴ Infra, p 944 et seq.
⁵ Infra, pp 426–443.
⁶ CPR, r 6.20.
⁷ *John Russell & Co Ltd v Cayzer, Irvine & Co Ltd* [1916] 2 AC 298 at 302, HL.
⁸ *Razelos v Razelos (No 2)* [1970] 1 WLR 392; cf the American case of *Michigan Trust Co v Ferry* 228 US 346 (1913).
⁹ *Laurie v Carroll* (1958) 98 CLR 310; *Myerson v Martin* [1979] 1 WLR 1390, CA; *Mondial Trading Pty Ltd v Interocean Marine Transport Inc* (1985) 65 ALR 155; cf *Porter v Freudenberg* [1915] 1 KB 857 at 887–888.

Even the mere transient presence of a person in England suffices to render him amenable to the jurisdiction of the courts. If a claim form is served, eg on a Japanese person during a visit of a few hours to London, an action may then be brought against him in his absence concerning a matter totally unrelated to anything that has occurred in England.[10] Not only is the justice of this exercise of power suspect, but in many cases it will be ineffective, for, in this example a judgment given in the action will be of no use to the claimant unless followed by proceedings in Japan for its enforcement, and a Japanese court can scarcely be expected to recognise a jurisdiction based on such flimsy grounds. This English doctrine is inevitable in domestic law because of the procedural significance of the claim form, but it is unfortunate from the point of view of private international law that no jurisdictional distinction is drawn between presence and residence.[11] Nevertheless, it has been twice confirmed by the Court of Appeal, holding that the court had jurisdiction over a defendant who was served whilst visiting England for a few days unconnected with the litigation,[12] or even whilst visiting England for Ascot races.[13] Similarly service on a defendant who has been brought within the jurisdiction in police custody or who has come in answer to a witness summons has been held to be good and to confer jurisdiction on the court.[14] If, however, a defendant is enticed within the jurisdiction fraudulently or improperly, then service of the claim form may be set aside.[15]

Part 6 of the Civil Procedure Rules sets out rules on the method of service of documents[16] (including a claim form) within the jurisdiction. In principle, Part 6 should not alter the fundamental rule that a defendant may only be served with originating process within the jurisdiction if he is present within the jurisdiction at the time of service or deemed service.[17] It is only concerned with the *method* of service. However, the Court of Appeal has recently disagreed, holding that service can be effected using a method authorised by Part 6 (leaving a claim form at the defendant's place of business[18]) to serve a defendant who was temporarily abroad at the time of service, and that there is no longer any such

---

[10] Cf *Carrick v Hancock* (1895) 12 TLR 59, infra, p 518.

[11] The Foreign Judgments (Reciprocal Enforcement) Act 1933, whose object it is to facilitate the enforcement in England of judgments obtained abroad, specifies the residence, not the mere presence, of the defendant in the country as one of the circumstances sufficient to found the jurisdiction of a court of that country, infra, p 581.

[12] *Colt Industries Inc v Sarlie* [1966] 1 WLR 440, following *Carrick v Hancock* (1895) 12 TLR 59 at 60.

[13] *HRH Maharanee Seethaderi Gaekwar of Baroda v Wildenstein* [1972] 2 QB 283, CA. The presence rule has been accepted by the US Supreme Court in *Burnham v Superior Court of California* 109 L Ed 2d (1990); Collins (1991) 107 LQR 10. See for Australia: *John Pfeiffer Pty Ltd v Rogerson* (2000) 203 CLR 503 at [13], HC of Australia; *BHP Billiton Ltd v Schultz* (2004) 221 CLR 400 at [17], HC of Australia.

[14] *Doyle v Doyle* (1974) 52 DLR (3d) 143; *John Sanderson & Co (NSW) Pty Ltd v Giddings* [1976] VR 421; *Baldry v Jackson* [1976] 1 NSWLR 19; affd without discussion of this issue [1976] 2 NSWLR 415.

[15] *Watkins v North American Land and Timber Co Ltd* (1904) 20 TLR 534, HL; *Colt Industries Inc v Sarlie*, supra, at 443–444.

[16] See *Godwin v Swindon BC* [2001] EWCA Civ 1478, [2002] 1 WLR 997.

[17] *Bank of Swaziland v Hahn* [1986] 1 WLR 506, HL; *Chellaram v Chellaram (No 2)* [2002] EWHC 632 (Ch) at [47], [2002] 3 All ER 17; *Fairmays v Palmer* [2006] EWHC 96 (Ch). But see the criticism by Zuckerman (2006) 25 CJQ 127. Service by an alternative method (formerly called substituted service), discussed infra, cannot be used to get round this: *Cadogan Properties Ltd v Mount Eden Land Ltd* [2000] IL Pr 722, CA.

[18] See CPR, r 6.5(6); discussed infra, p 356. Service other than personal service, eg by post, was available prior to the CPR.

fundamental rule.[19] Part 6 provides[20] that a document may be served by any of the following methods: (a) personal service (ie leaving it with that individual[21]); (b) first class post; (c) leaving the document at a place specified in rule 6.5; (d) through a document exchange; (e) by fax or other means of electronic communication.[22] The court may make an order permitting service by an alternative method[23] and can dispense with service.[24] The court will serve a document which it has issued or prepared, subject to a number of exceptions,[25] one of which is where the party on whose behalf the document is to be served notifies the court that he wishes to serve it himself.[26] Where the court is to serve a document, it is for the court to decide which of the methods of service specified above is to be used.[27]

As regards the method of service by leaving the document at a place specified in rule 6.5, this provides that, except for cases of service out of the jurisdiction, a document must be served within the jurisdiction.[28] A party must give an address for service within the jurisdiction.[29] Where a party does not give the business address of his solicitor as his address for service, and resides or carries on business within the jurisdiction, he must give his residence or place of business as his address for service.[30] Where no solicitor is acting[31] for the party to be served and the party has not given an address for service, the document must be sent or transmitted to, or left at, the place shown in a table.[32] In the case of an individual, this is the usual or last known residence.[33] In the case of the proprietor of a business, it is the usual or last known residence, or place of business or last known place

---

[19] *City & County Properties v Kamali* [2006] EWCA Civ 1879, [20007] 1 WLR 1219. The decision of the House of Lords in *Bank of Swaziland* was distinguished as one simply of construction of the then procedural rule.

[20] CPR, r 6.2(1).

[21] CPR, rule 6.4(3). There is an exception where a solicitor is authorised to accept service, r 6.4(2), on which see *Nanglegan v Royal Free Hampstead NHS Trust* [2002] 1 WLR 1043.

[22] On (e) see: CPR, 6PD.3; *Molins plc v GD SpA* [2000] 1 WLR 1741, CA; *BAS Capital Funding Corpn v Medfinco Ltd* [2003] EWHC 1798 (Ch) at [167], [2004] 1 Lloyd's Rep 652.

[23] CPR, r 6.8. This cannot be made retrospectively (*Anderton v Clwyd CC (No2)* [2002] EWCA Civ 933, [2002] 1 WLR 3174 at 3185) or used to avoid conventions providing the mechanism for service out of the jurisdiction (*Knauf UK GmbH v British Gypsum Ltd* [2002] 1 WLR 907, CA; distinguished in *Phillips v Nussberger* [2008] UKHL 1 at [39], [2008] 1 WLR 180). For examples of "good reason" for alternative service: see *Marconi v PT Pan Indonesia Bank Ltd TBK* [2004] EWHC 129 (Comm) at [39]–[45], [2004] 1 Lloyd's Rep 594—very extensive delay under Indonesian procedure; appeal on a different point dismissed [2005] EWCA Civ 422; *Phillips v Symes* [2003] EWHC 1172 (Ch) (Peter SMITH J)—speed was essential.

[24] CPR, r 6.9. See *Phillips v Nussberger* [2008] UKHL 1 at [34]–[35], [2008] 1 WLR 180; *Olafsson v Gissurarson* [2008] EWCA Civ 152. This power should not be used to circumvent the requirements of a service convention: *Shiblaq v Sadikoglu* [2004] EWHC 1890 (Comm) at [57], [2004] IL Pr 51. See also *Lakah Group v Al Jazeera Satellite Channel* [2003] EWCA (Civ) 1781 at [10]–[13].

[25] CPR, r 6.3(1).

[26] CPR, r 6.3(1)(b).

[27] CPR, 6.3(2).

[28] CPR, r 6.5(1). Does this mean that in a case where service within the jurisdiction is problematic, a claimant who goes straight for service out of the jurisdiction may fall foul of this provision?

[29] CPR, r 6.5(2).

[30] CPR, r 6.5(3).

[31] *Marshall Rankine v Maggs* [2006] EWCA Civ 20.

[32] CPR, r 6.5(6). In the case of a natural person, the table sets out alternative methods of service, more than one of which may be used: *Phillips v Symes* [2002] 1 WLR 863 at [26] (HART J).

[33] Even if the defendant did not receive it: *Akram v Adam* [2004] EWCA 1601; *Smith v Hughes* [2003] EWCA Civ 656, [2003] 1 WLR 2441. The latter case also establishes that it does not matter that the claimant knows or believes that the defendant was no longer living at that address. *Smith v Hughes* was distinguished

of business. In the case of an individual who is suing or being sued in the name of a firm, it is the usual or last known residence, or the principal or last known place of business of the firm.

(ii) Partnerships

In the case of a partnership,[34] the claimant may serve the claim form on an individual partner who is present in England, or on the partnership firm under the Civil Procedure Rules.[35] Where the claim is against the partnership, these Rules provide that co-partners carrying on business in England must be sued in the name of the firm, unless it is inappropriate to do so.[36] The Civil Procedure Rules deal with the method of service and state that, where partners are being sued in the name of their firm, a document is served personally on a partnership by leaving it with a partner, or a person who, at the time of service, has the control or management of the partnership at its principal place of business.[37] It is also possible to serve a document by post, leaving it at a place specified in rule 6.5,[38] through a document exchange or by fax or other means of electronic communication.[39] Therefore, service which is effected on the person who has the control or management of the English business operates as a valid service on all the partners, even in the case of a foreign firm all the members of which are resident abroad.[40] Again, service on one partner present in England is effective against the co-partners out of the jurisdiction,[41] and service effected with the permission of the court under rule 6.20[42] on one partner out of the jurisdiction is a good service on all the other partners out of the jurisdiction.[43] Service on the partnership in England will allow the claimant to seek permission to serve a partner abroad, under rule 6.20(3) as a "necessary or proper party to that claim".[44] In the situation where there is a foreign partnership which does not carry on business

---

in *Marshall Rankine v Maggs*, supra. See also *Burns-Anderson v Wheeler* [2005] EWHC 575, [2005] 1 Lloyd's Rep 580.

[34] The nature and status of an entity is a matter for the law under which it is created: *Oxnard Financing SA v Rahm* [1998] 1 WLR 1465, CA.

[35] CPR, r 7.2A and CPR, PD 7.

[36] CPR, PD 7, 5A. Where an individual foreigner carries on a business here in a name other than his own name, a claim may be brought against the business name: CPR, PD 7, 5C. Valid service can be effected on a person acting on a partner's instructions to accept service: *Kenneth Allison Ltd v A E Limehouse & Co* [1992] 2 AC 105, HL.

[37] CPR, r 6.4(5). See also PD 6, para 4.2 (accompanying notice). This provision will not apply to a limited liability partnership. The partnership is a separate entity and the *partners* are not being sued in the name of the firm. Such a partnership is a body corporate according to s 1(2) of the Limited Liability Partnerships Act 2000 (partnership law is also disapplied by s 1(5)). It is therefore a "Corporation incorporated in England and Wales other than a company" and by virtue of CPR, r 6.6 can be sued at the principal office of the corporation or any place within the jurisdiction where the corporation carries on its its activities and which has a real connection with the claim. The Companies Act 1985 provisions in relation to service (discussed infra, pp 358–363) could be extended to cover limited liability partnerships (see s 15 of the Limited Liability Partnerships Act 2000) allowing service at its registered office.

[38] See, eg, *Lexi Holdings plc v Shaid Luqman*, 22 October 2007 (unreported), service on one of the partners (sued in the name of the partnership) by leaving document at his usual or last known address.

[39] CPR, r 6.2(1).

[40] *Worcester City and County Banking Co v Firbank, Pauling & Co* [1894] 1 QB 784, CA.

[41] *Lysaght Ltd v Clark & Co* [1891] 1 QB 552.

[42] Discussed, infra, p 372 et seq.

[43] *Hobbs v Australian Press Association* [1933] 1 KB 1, CA.

[44] *West of England Steamship Owners Protection and Indemnity Association Ltd v John Holman & Sons* [1957] 1 WLR 1164; infra, pp 374–377.

within the jurisdiction, it is permissible to sue the partnership in England by naming as defendants the individual partners being sued in their capacity as partners.[45] Service of the claim form on these individuals will have to be effected within the jurisdiction or out of the jurisdiction using rule 6.20.

(iii) Companies[46]

The same principle applies for corporate defendants as for individual defendants: the defendant is subject to the jurisdiction of the English court if he is present in England. Of course, a company cannot literally be present in England. It is therefore necessary to give an artificial presence to a corporate defendant, according to which a foreign company can be present in England by virtue of the transaction of business. Originally, jurisdiction was determined by the application of common law rules,[47] but now recourse must be had to the rules contained in the Companies Act 1985[48] and to Part 6 of the Civil Procedure Rules, which contains alternative methods of service on foreign companies. The law on service on a foreign company using the Companies Act 1985 is well settled, whereas, in contrast, it is as yet not entirely clear what Part 6 does and does not allow. It follows that, where a case falls clearly within the Companies Act 1985, this is the set of rules that should be used. However, in cases falling outside this Act, recourse should be had to Part 6, which may allow service on the foreign company.

(a) The Companies Act 1985

(i) A company registered in England

A company registered in England under the Companies Act 1985 is regarded as present in England and a document may be served on a company by leaving it at, or sending it by post to, the company's registered office.[49] A company registered in Scotland which carries on business in England can be served with a document by sending it to the principal place of business in England with a copy to its registered office.[50]

(ii) A foreign company

The position of a foreign company is less straightforward. Prior to 1992, the 1985 Act allowed for service within the jurisdiction in respect of a foreign company if it established a place of business in Great Britain. However, following an amendment to the Act in 1992,[51] it now distinguishes between foreign companies which have a branch in Great

---

[45] *Oxnard Financing SA v Rahn* [1998] 1 WLR 1465, CA.

[46] See generally Enonchong (1999) 48 ICLQ 921.

[47] *Okura & Co Ltd v Forsbacka Jernverks Aktiebolag* [1914] 1 KB 715 at 718, CA; *The Theodohos* [1977] 2 Lloyd's Rep 428.

[48] *The Theodohos* [1977] 2 Lloyd's Rep 428; *The Vrontados* [1982] 2 Lloyd's Rep 241 at 244 (Lord DENNING), CA; *South India Shipping Corpn Ltd v Export-Import Bank of Korea* [1985] 1 WLR 585 at 588, CA; *Boocock v Hilton International Co* [1993] 1 WLR 1065, CA. Cf *Bethlehem Steel Corpn v Universal Gas and Oil Co Inc* (1978) Times, 3 August, per Lord SCARMAN.

[49] Companies Act 1985, s 725 (1). This is unaffected by the fact that the CPR have introduced various methods of service. Service under s 725 or under one of the methods introduced by the CPR are alternatives: see CPR, r 6.2(2); *Murphy v Staples UK Ltd* [2003] EWCA Civ 656; [2003] 1 WLR 2441.

[50] Companies Act 1985, s 725 (2), (3).

[51] SI 1992/3179.

Britain and those that have established a place of business, which is not a branch, in Great Britain. Separate regimes apply to these two different situations.

A foreign company which has a branch in Great Britain   A limited company which is incorporated outside the United Kingdom and Gibraltar and has a branch in Great Britain is required to register with the registrar of companies the names and addresses of all persons resident in Great Britain authorised to accept on the company's behalf service of process in respect of the business of the branch.[52] Process in respect of the carrying on of the business of a branch is sufficiently served if addressed to any such person and is left at or sent by post to that address.[53] Where a company fails to comply with its statutory obligations to so register, or if all the persons named are dead or have ceased to reside in Great Britain, or refuse to accept service on the company's behalf, or for any other reason cannot be served, a document may be served on the company in respect of the carrying on of the business of the branch by leaving it at, or sending it by post to, any place of business established by the company in Great Britain.[54] This means that service can be effected at somewhere other than the branch, provided that the company has established a place of business there.[55]

For these provisions to come into play the claimant must establish a good arguable case that: first, the foreign company has a *branch* in Great Britain; and secondly, the document which is served on the company must be *in respect of the carrying on of the business of the branch*.[56] These two requirements will now be examined.

A branch   The branch provisions were introduced into English law by way of implementation of the Eleventh Company Law Directive,[57] and a "branch" means a branch within the meaning of this Directive.[58] Unfortunately, the Directive does not actually give a definition of a "branch". However, it is clear from its preamble that it is different from a subsidiary company; the obvious difference being that a branch lacks legal personality whereas a subsidiary is a separate legal entity. Applying this distinction, a branch should also be regarded as being different from an independent commercial agent. We have some idea therefore of what it is not. When it comes to what it is, in *Saab v Saudi American Bank*[59] it was common ground that a branch is a more permanent establishment than a mere place of business.[60] The fact that a "branch" means a branch within the meaning of the Directive indicates that a European definition should be given to this term. This can be done by applying the definition given by the Court of Justice to a "branch, agency or other establishment" under Article 5(5) of the Brussels Convention.

---

[52] 1985 Act, s 690A and Sch 21A, para 3(e).
[53] S 694A(2).
[54] S 694A(3).
[55] For the definition of establishment of a place of business see infra, pp 361–363.
[56] *Saab v Saudi American Bank* [1999] 1 WLR 1861 at 1873 (per CLARKE LJ). He was referring to the standard of proof in relation to the second requirement but would doubtless apply the same standard to the first requirement.
[57] Council Directive (EEC) No 89/666.
[58] S 698(2)(b); inserted by SI 1992/3179, Sch 2, para 13. Where a branch comprises places of business in more than one part of the United Kingdom the branch is treated as being situated in the part of the United Kingdom where its principal place of business is situated, s 698(2)(a).
[59] [1999] 1 WLR 1861, CA.
[60] Ibid, at 1868.

This would be to define a branch in terms of certain characteristics, as previously described.[61] Admittedly, the Court of Justice was concerned in that context with whether there was a branch, agency or other establishment and not with whether there was a branch as such. This means that if an entity lacks the characteristics of a branch, agency or other establishment it clearly cannot be a branch for the present purposes. But even if it has these characteristics it can be argued that it is an agency or other establishment rather than a branch. This will clearly be so if there is a separate legal entity, ie a subsidiary or independent commercial agent. But if there is no such separate legal entity it is a hard argument to make, since the Court of Justice has regarded the branch, agency and other establishment, aside from the separate legal entity point, as being essentially the same.[62] A further point in favour of adopting the Court of Justice's definition of a branch, etc in relation to Article 5(5) is the fact that the requirement that the document that is served on the company is "in respect of the carrying on of the business of the branch", mirrors that to be found in Article 5(5), namely that the dispute arises out of the operations of the branch, etc. However, the Court of Appeal in the Saab case, which was concerned with the requirement that the document served on the company must be "in respect of the carrying on of the business of a branch", has held that these words must be construed as they stand without reference to Article 5(5) and the decisions of the Court of Justice.[63] Whatever the rights and wrongs of this approach in relation to this second requirement, it is submitted that it should not be applied in relation to defining a branch, where recourse should be had to the decisions of the Court of Justice.

In respect of the carrying on of the business of the branch   The requirement that the document served on the company must be in respect of the carrying on of the business of the branch was introduced by the amendment to the 1985 Act. It was not there under the pre-1992 law on establishing a place of business, nor is it required under the post-1992 law under the separate provisions that apply where the foreign company has established a place of business which is not a branch. The meaning of this requirement was explained by the Court of Appeal in *Saab v Saudi American Bank*.[64]

> The defendant Saudi bank had represented that it had the ability and resources to market shares on a global basis and that its London branch would be actively involved in the marketing. The plaintiffs alleged that these were misrepresentations. Part of the complaint was that the London branch did not play its part in the marketing project. The complaint was also in part in respect of the defendant's business elsewhere.

The Court of Appeal held that process would be "in respect of the carrying on of the business" of the branch if it is in part in respect of the carrying on of the business, unless the connection between the process and the carrying on of the business is *de minimis*, ie of so little significance that it should be disregarded.[65] It affirmed the decision of TUCKEY J at

---

[61] Supra, pp 258–260.
[62] Case 14/76 *Ets A de Bloos SPRL v Bouyer* [1976] ECR 1497 at 1510. See also the Advocate General at 1519, who has said that the autonomy of an agency is less marked than that of a branch.
[63] *Saab v Saudi American Bank* [1999] 1 WLR 1861, 1871, CA.
[64] Ibid.
[65] Ibid, at 1872.

first instance that the process in this particular case was in respect of the carrying on of the business of the bank's London branch, since it was partly in respect of that business. This adopts a very different, and much easier to satisfy, test than that adopted by the Court of Justice in relation to the virtually identical requirement under Article 5(5) that the dispute arises out of the operations of the branch, etc.[66] But, as has been mentioned, the Court held that, as far as the requirement under the Companies Act is concerned, the words must be construed as they stand without reference to Article 5(5) and the decisions of the Court of Justice. In interpreting the requirement under the Act, the Court was trying to keep the gap between the two separate sets of provisions in the Act (dealing with branches and the establishment of a place of business other than a branch) as narrow as possible.[67] This approach is not compatible with the European origins of the branch provisions or the European definition that should be given to a "branch".

A foreign company which has established a place of business, which is not a branch, in Great Britain A company incorporated elsewhere than in Great Britain which establishes a place of business in Great Britain (this does not include a limited company which is incorporated outside the United Kingdom and Gibraltar, and has a branch in the United Kingdom[68]) is required to file with the registrar of companies the names and addresses of some one or more persons resident in Great Britain authorised to accept service of process on its behalf.[69] If a person is so named service must be effected on this person.[70] So long as the name of such a person remains on the file, service of a document on him renders the company subject to the jurisdiction of the court even though the company no longer carries on business in England.[71] It can be said in favour of this approach that it prevents foreign companies from running up debts in England and then shutting up shop. However, it can sometimes involve unfairness to the defendant company. In such circumstances it is always possible for the defendant to seek a stay of proceedings on the basis of *forum non conveniens*.[72] A more radical solution, advocated in the Court of Appeal in *Rome v Punjab National Bank (No 2)*,[73] would be to amend the Companies Act so that a company which had ceased to carry on business and had removed itself would only be subject to jurisdiction in relation to matters which arose during the period in which the company carried on business in England. If a company fails to comply with its statutory obligations, or if the persons on the register are dead or no longer resident here, or refuse to accept service on the company's behalf, or for any reason cannot be served, the document may be served on the company by leaving it at, or sending it by post to, "any place of business established by the company in Great Britain".[74] These last words have been interpreted to mean a place of business that is still established at the time

---

[66] Supra, pp 260–261.
[67] The *Saab* case, supra, 1872.
[68] S 690B.
[69] S 691.
[70] *Boocock v Hilton International Co* [1993] 1 WLR 1065, CA. However, the courts have a discretionary power, under CPR, r 3.10, to remedy any procedural error, on which see the *Boocock* case, supra.
[71] *Rome v Punjab National Bank (No 2)*, [1989] 1 WLR 1211; *Sabatier v Trading Co* [1927] 1 Ch 495.
[72] *Rome v Punjab National Bank (No 2)* [1989] 1 WLR 1211 at 1220 (per Sir John May).
[73] Ibid, at 1221 (per Parker LJ and Sir Roualeyn Cumming-Bruce).
[74] Companies Act 1985, s 695.

of service.[75] Service is not adequate if effected at a former place of business that has ceased to function.

For these provisions to come into play the claimant must show a good arguable case that the foreign company has *established a place of business, other than a branch*, in Great Britain. We know that this is referring to a less permanent establishment than a branch.[76] Establishment of a place of business is deliberately different from merely carrying on business.[77] Ultimately it is a question of fact whether a place of business has been established in Great Britain.[78] Prior to 1992, the Companies Act did not contain a separate provision for branches and the only question was whether a place of business had been established. There are pre-1992 cases determining this question[79] which can still be used as guidance now,[80] with the proviso that some of them may in fact have involved a branch. There are also cases decided after 1992, endorsing the earlier approach.[81] The combined case law indicates that it is relevant to see whether the business is carried on from a fixed and definite place and whether the company uses an agent that can bind it contractually.[82] Indeed, the latter factor should be regarded as being a powerful one, albeit not determinative.[83] The business premises do not have to be owned or leased by the company.[84] If the foreign company carries on business in England by means of an independent commercial "agent", the latter will doubtless own or lease the business premises. Nonetheless, the foreign company may have established a place of business in England.[85] On the other hand, it is not enough for the company to have an office if it does not carry on any business at that place.[86] Nor is it enough merely to own land in England; it has to be shown that the business of the foreign company is habitually carried on from that land.[87] However, a private residence of one of the directors of the company can constitute a place of business if the company transacts business from there.[88] The lack of some external manifestation of the defendant company, such as a nameplate or its modern equivalent (a website setting out

---

[75] *Deverall v Grant Advertising Inc* [1955] Ch 111, CA; and see *Bethlehem Steel Corpn v Universal Gas and Oil Co Inc* (1978) Times, 3 August, HL.

[76] The *Saab* case, supra, at 1868.

[77] *Rakusens Ltd (A Company) v Baser Ambalaj Plastik Sanayi Ticaret AS* [2001] EWCA Civ 1820 at [33] (per ARDEN LJ), [2002] 1 BCLC 104.

[78] The *Rakusens* case, ibid. See also *Reuben v Time Inc* [2003] EWHC 1430 QB at [33].

[79] See *South India Shipping Corpn Ltd v Import-Export Bank of Korea* [1985] 1 WLR 585, CA; *Re Oriel Ltd* [1985] 1 WLR 180, CA; *Adams v Cape Industries plc* Ch 433 at 530–531; *Cleveland Museum of Art v Capricorn Art International SA* [1990] 2 Lloyd's Rep 166.

[80] See the *Rakusens* case, supra; *Domansa v Derin Shipping And Trading Co Inc* [2001] 1 Lloyd's Rep 362, 365–366; *Matchnet plc v William Blair & Co LLC* [2002] EWHC 2128 (Ch) at [7], [2003] 2 BCLC 195; *Harrods Ltd v Dow Jones & Co Inc* [2003] EWHC 1162 (QB).

[81] Ibid.

[82] The *Rakusens* case, supra, at [17] (per BUXTON LJ), [39] (per ARDEN LJ); *Harrods Ltd v Dow Jones & Co Inc* [2003] EWHC 1162 (QB) at [21].

[83] The *Adams* case, supra, at 531; followed by ARDEN LJ in the *Rakusens* case, supra, at [40], [41] and in *Reuben v Time Inc* [2003] EWHC 1430 QB at [40], [41].

[84] *Re Oriel Ltd* [1986] 1 WLR 180, CA, a case under s 106 of the Companies Act 1948, which discusses ss 407 and 412 of that Act (now ss 691 and 695 of the Companies Act 1985).

[85] *Cleveland Museum of Art v Capricorn Art Internationals A* [1990] 2 Lloyd's Rep 166. The English proceedings were, however, stayed, see infra, p 442.

[86] The *Matchnet* case, supra.

[87] *Re Oriel Ltd*, supra, at 223.

[88] Ibid, at 222.

its business address[89]) at the premises, although a relevant factor, is not a decisive one. Statements on the company's website have to be treated with caution because they are not designed to be legal statements.[90] It is not necessary to show that the activities in England constitute a substantial part of the foreign company's business; and no objection has been made to the fact that activities in London were merely incidental to the defendant's main objects.[91] In cases where a foreign company carries on business in England by means of a wholly-owned subsidiary company, [92] the question will arise of whether the English subsidiary is carrying on its own business or that of its parent. The ability of the former to bind the latter contractually will be an important factor in determining this. In most cases, the English subsidiary will carry on its own business and not that of the parent, [93] with the result that the foreign parent company will not be present/resident in England. This places undue reliance on traditional notions of agency. It would be better, as US courts have done, to look at the economic realities of the situation; if the parent and subsidiary form one economic unit it should be possible to found jurisdiction against the foreign parent on the basis of the presence of its subsidiary in England, or indeed against a foreign subsidiary on the basis of the presence of the parent in England.[94] More generally, the whole of the law on jurisdiction against corporate defendants would make more sense if instead of applying a misleading analogy with individuals it was recognised that corporate defendants are very different and that jurisdiction should be based on the notion of their economic presence within the jurisdiction rather than on the establishment of a place of business.[95]

There is no requirement that the dispute has to relate to the activities of the business carried on at the place of business which has been established in Great Britain. This stands in marked contrast to the position in respect of branches where, as has been seen, the provisions on service are dealing with service *in respect of the carrying on of the business of the branch*. It is hard to see in policy terms why there should be such a distinction.

(b) The Companies Act 2006

The Companies Act 1985 is in the process of being replaced by the Companies Act 2006, which makes fundamental changes in relation to overseas companies.

(i) A company registered in England and Wales

Part 37 of the Companies Act 2006,[96] which will be brought into force on 1 October 2008, deals with service on companies. A document may be served on a company

---

[89] *Commonwealth Bank of Australia v White* [1999] 2 VR 681, 692.

[90] The *Matchnet* case, supra; *Lakah Group v Al Jazeera Satellite Channel* [2003] EWHC 1297 at [46]–[47]; affd [2003] EWCA (Civ) 1781 without discussion of this point.

[91] The *South India Shipping* case, supra, per ACKNER LJ who followed a case decided under the common law: *Hercules Aktieselskabet Dampskib v Grand Trunk Pacific Rly Co* [1912] 1 KB 222, CA.

[92] See *Adams v Cape Industries plc* [1990] Ch 433, a case on enforcement of a foreign judgment, discussed infra, pp 518–520.

[93] See, eg, the *Matchnet* case, supra. Under principles of company law the foreign parent and English subsidiary are separate legal entities. But for an example where the parent acted on behalf of the subsidiary, see Case 218/86 *Sar Schotte GmbH v Parfums Rothschild* [1987] ECR 4905, a case concerned with jurisdiction under Art 5(5) of the Brussels Convention, discussed supra, p 260; *Amalgamated Wireless (Australasia) Ltd v McDonnell Douglas Corpn* (1988) 77 ALR 537 at 540.

[94] See *Bulova Watch Co Inc v Hattori and Co Ltd* 508 F Supp 1322 at 1342 (1981); Fawcett (1988) 37 ICLQ 645 at 663 et seq. Such an approach was rejected in *Adams v Cape Industries plc* [1990] Ch 433 at 532 et seq, CA.

[95] Fawcett, op cit. Cf *Ets Soules et Cie v Handgate Co Ltd SA, The Handgate* [1987] 1 Lloyd's Rep 142.

[96] This Part will be implemented "with relevant provisions".

registered under the Act by leaving it at, or sending it by post to, the company's registered office.[97] There is a special rule for the situation where a company registered in Scotland or Northern Ireland carries on business in England and Wales. The process of any court in England and Wales may be served on the company by leaving it at, or sending it by post to, the company's principal place of business in England and Wales, addressed to the manager or other head officer in England and Wales of the company.[98] Provision is also made for service of documents on a director or secretary of a company.[99] There is no suggestion that this can be used to bring an action against the company.

(ii) An overseas company

The new regime   Part 34 of the Companies Act 2006, which will be brought into force on 1 October 2008, empowers the Secretary of State to make provision by regulations in relation to overseas companies. An overseas company is defined as a company incorporated outside the United Kingdom.[100] This is a wider definition than that under section 744 of the Companies Act 1985, which refers to companies incorporated outside Great Britain that establish a place of business in Great Britain. The regulations will be able to specify the connection with the United Kingdom that gives rise to the various disclosure obligations under Part 34.[101] At the time of writing, these regulations have not been produced. However, we know at least in part what the content of the Regulations will be. This is because Part 34 in places specifies what the Regulations must require. Thus the Regulations must require a company to register particulars if the company opens a branch[102] in the United Kingdom.[103] We also know what the Company Law Review Steering Group proposed in relation to overseas companies,[104] but until the regulations appear we do not know whether their recommendations will be adopted in full. The intention of the Steering Group is that the two separate regimes under the 1985 Act, one for foreign companies that have a branch in Great Britain and the other for foreign companies that have established a place of business, which is not a branch, in Great Britain, will be replaced by a single regime. This is very much to be welcomed. First, it simplifies the law. Secondly, it avoids having to determine whether an established place of business in the United Kingdom is a branch or not. The new single regime would align the two present separate regimes in the following way. First, it would apply to foreign companies that have established a place of business in the United Kingdom.[105] Using the existing concept of establishment of a place of business[106] has the advantage of familiarity. It also means that there would be no lessening of the protection available to third parties who enter into legal transactions with overseas companies. The concept of establishing a place of business would include a branch but will go wider than that.[107] Secondly,

---

[97] Companies Act 2006, s 1139(1).

[98] S 1139(4).

[99] S 1140.

[100] S 1044.

[101] See the Explanatory Notes to the Companies Act 2006.

[102] This means a branch within the meaning of the Eleventh Company Law Directive (EEC) No 89/666.

[103] Companies Act 2006, s 1046(2)(a).

[104] See Company Law Review Steering Group (CLRSG) *Modern Company Law: Reforming the Law Concerning Oversea Companies* Consultation Document October 1999; CLRSG *Final Report*, paras 11.21–11.33.

[105] *Reforming the Law Concerning Oversea Companies,* paras 19–22.

[106] On which, see supra, pp 361–363.

[107] *Reforming the Law Concerning Oversea Companies,* para 24.

the registration requirements imposed on the overseas company would be based on those imposed under the Companies Act 1985 where there is a branch, rather than the less onerous requirements imposed where there is the establishment of a place of business, which is not a branch.[108] This would ensure that the United Kingdom implements the Eleventh Company Law Directive, which lays down registration and other requirements in relation to branches.[109]

The Regulations must require an overseas company to register: (a) particulars identifying every person resident in the United Kingdom authorised to accept service of documents on behalf of the company, or (b) a statement that there is no such person.[110] Provision may be made by the regulations requiring an overseas company to give notice of ceasing to have a registrable presence.[111]

Service on an overseas company   A document may be served on an overseas company whose particulars are registered: (a) by leaving it at, or sending it by post to, the registered address of any person resident in the United Kingdom who is authorised to accept service of documents on the company's behalf, or (b) if there is no such person, or if any such person refuses service or service cannot for any other reason be effected, by leaving it at or sending it by post to any place of business of the company in the United Kingdom.[112] As previously mentioned,[113] the Act makes provision for service on directors and secretaries of companies.[114] When it comes to an overseas company whose particulars have been registered under Part 34, regulations[115] will specify the position, the holder of which can be served.[116] The 2006 Act says nothing about the situation where an overseas company fails to register any particulars under Part 34. The concern that there should be no lessening of the protection available to third parties who enter into legal transactions with overseas companies means that the regulations will have to deal with this situation. Presumably regulations will provide that, where an overseas company does not register any particulars, service can be effected, by leaving it at or sending it by post to any place of business of the company in the United Kingdom. In such a case, the introduction of a single regime of rules coupled with the need to comply with the Eleventh Company Law Directive means that one of the requirements that will now be imposed in relation to any overseas company that has established a place of business in the United Kingdom, whether a branch or not, is that the document served on the foreign company must be in respect of the carrying on of the business of the established place of business. This will cure the jurisdictional anomaly that arises under the Companies Act 1985 where the document served on the foreign company is not in respect of the carrying on of the business of the

---

[108] Ibid, para 21.

[109] Ibid, para 24.

[110] Companies Act 2006, s 1056. Provision is made for regulations in respect of overseas companies that are required to register, or have registered, in more than one part of the United Kingdom.

[111] Companies Act 2006, s 1058.

[112] S 1139(2). See also the company communications provisions (ss 1144–1148 and Schs 4 and 5). Provisions on service are contained in Part 37 of the Act (supplementary provisions), which will come into force on 1 October 2008.

[113] Supra, pp 363–364.

[114] S 1140.

[115] Under s 1046 in Part 34.

[116] S 1140 (2)(b). See s 1140(6) for where an appointment is terminated and for where an overseas company ceases to have a registrable presence.

outlet in England, whereby a foreign company which establishes a place of business, which is not a branch, is subject to jurisdiction (because there is no requirement that the document served is in respect of the carrying on of the business of the established place of business) whereas a foreign company which opens a branch is not (because there is such a requirement). Under the Companies Act 2006 neither will be subject to jurisdiction in this situation, at least not under the jurisdiction rules contained in that Act. [117]

(c) Part 6 of the Civil Procedure Rules

As has been seen, the Companies Act 1985 sets out methods of service in relation to overseas companies. However, as an alternative to these methods of service a company may be served by any method permitted under Part 6 of the Civil Procedure Rules.[118] The argument that Part 6 is ultra vires in providing these alternative methods of service has been rejected by LONGMORE J in *Sea Assets Ltd v PT Garuda Indonesia*.[119] After looking at these alternative methods of service, three related questions have to be addressed in relation to service under Part 6. What is the relationship between Part 6 and the Companies Act 1985? Which foreign companies can be served using these alternative methods of service under Part 6? What are the advantages in using these alternative methods?

(i) The alternative methods of service

One of these is leaving the document at a specified place. The obligation of a party to give an address for service applies equally to companies as it does to individuals. Where a company does not give the business address of its solicitor as its address for service and carries on business within the jurisdiction it must give its place of business as its address for service.[120] Where no solicitor is acting for the party to be served and the party has not given an address for service the document must be sent or transmitted to, or left at, the place shown in the table set out in rule 6.5(6). For a company registered in England and Wales,[121] the specified place of service is the principal office of the company, or any place of business of the company within the jurisdiction which has a real connection with the claim. For any other company it is any place of business of the company within the jurisdiction.

Another method is that of personal service. A document is served personally on a company or other corporation by leaving it with a person holding a senior position within the company or corporation,[122] such as a director. There is some uncertainty over whether this provision can be used in relation to a foreign company. The accompanying Practice

---

[117] See infra, pp 368–369 for how CPR, Part 6 can be used to get over this jurisdictional problem.

[118] CPR, r 6.2(2). See *Murphy v Staples UK Ltd* [2003] EWCA Civ 656, [2003] 1 WLR 2441.

[119] [2000] 4 All ER 371.

[120] CPR, r 6.5(3). This rule does not distinguish between individuals and companies. Thus it refers to a party and then to his residing or carrying on business within the jurisdiction. The former term seems designed just to cover individuals, since a company cannot literally be resident anywhere and can only have an artificial residence. If a company is given an artificial residence, at common law this was where it carried on business, see generally Fawcett (1988) 37 ICLQ 645. It follows that in the case of a company the term reside appears to adds nothing to that of carrying on business.

[121] This does not include an oversea company which has obtained a branch registration certificate, see the *Sea Assets* case, supra; discussed infra, pp 368–369.

[122] CPR, r 6.4. See 6PD.6.2 for the definition of "a person holding a senior position".

Direction[123] is phrased in narrower terms than the rule itself. It states that personal service on a "registered company or corporation" (ie one registered in England) is effected by leaving a document with a person holding a senior position. When it defines what is meant by a person holding a senior position it again refers to a "registered company or corporation".[124] The intention is seemingly that this method of service cannot be used with a foreign company. It would be absurd if service on a director of a foreign company (which may have no branch or other established place of business or even carry on business in England) who happens to be transiently present in England were to be regarded as being effective service on that company. This has never been the position under English law. However, GRAY J was, seemingly, prepared to use personal service in respect of a foreign company, not one registered in England.[125] This is a weak authority because this point was not raised by counsel. Moreover, on the facts of the case personal service was not effective because it was not made on a senior officer of the defendant company. The Court of Appeal affirmed the decision of GRAY J.[126] This specific point was not discussed but it was said more generally that GRAY J had applied the correct tests.[127]

(ii) What is the relationship between Part 6 and the Companies Act 1985?

The relationship between the Companies Act 1985 and the methods of service under Part 6 of the Civil Procedure Rules is by no means clear. Two cases discussing Part 6 have assumed that this is an alternative basis of jurisdiction to the Companies Act 1985.[128] More significantly, one of the few cases specifically discussing the point has adopted this view.[129] Under this wide view of the role of Part 6, compliance with the methods of service under Part 6 provides the basis of jurisdiction. However, it could be argued that the methods of service in Part 6 are precisely that, just methods of service, and are not as such bases of jurisdiction against foreign companies. Under this narrow view of the role of Part 6, the question of which foreign companies can be served is dealt with under the Companies Act 1985 and this requires the foreign company to have a branch or an established place of business other than a branch in England. Only if this requirement is met are you entitled to go on to the next stage, which is the method of service. This appears to be the view adopted in the two other cases specifically to address the point.[130] In one of these cases, it was said that "the wording of the CPR does not enable one to by-pass the need to demonstrate that a place of business has been established within this jurisdiction".[131] The argument in favour of this narrow view and against the wide view is that the

---

[123] 6PD.6.1.

[124] It does, though, have a definition of such a person in respect of a "corporation which is not a registered company": 6PD.6.2(2).

[125] *Lakah Group v Al Jazeera Satellite Channel* [2003] EWHC 1297 (QB) at [27]–[33]; affd [2003] EWCA (Civ) 1781.

[126] [2003] EWCA (Civ) 1781.

[127] Ibid, at [8].

[128] *Sea Assets Ltd v PT Garuda Indonesia* [2000] 4 All ER 371; the *Saab* case, supra, at 324–325 (per CLARKE LJ).

[129] *Lakah Group v Al Jazeera Satellite Channel*, [2003] EWHC 1297 at [39]–[41]; affd [2003] EWCA (Civ) 1781. However, *Harrods Ltd v Dow Jones & Co Inc* [2003] EWHC 1162 (QB) and *Reuben v Time Inc* [2003] EWHC 1430 (QB) took a different view, discussed below.

[130] The *Harrods* case, supra, and the *Reuben* case, supra.

[131] The *Harrods* case, supra, at [33]. This view has been expressly adopted and applied by another High Court judge in the first instance decision in the *Reuben* case, supra, at [30], [31].

latter would widen the jurisdiction of English courts considerably and the provisions in the Companies Act 1985 dealing with jurisdiction against foreign companies would become largely redundant. It is hard to believe that either of these consequences was intended when Part 6 was introduced. This narrow interpretation of Part 6 is further supported by a decision in relation to service on an individual using Part 6[132] where it was held that, although this contained general rules about service, it had not swept away the general principle that a defendant could only be served within the jurisdiction if he were present in the jurisdiction at the time of service.[133] The same could be said to be true of companies and whether a company is present is determined by the Companies Act 1985.

(iii) Which foreign companies can be served using these alternative methods?

Companies that have registered as an overseas company or should have registered under the 1985 Companies Act   According to *Sea Assets Ltd v PT Garuda Indonesia*,[134] if a company has obtained a branch registration certificate under the Companies Act, service can be effected under the method set out in that Act or by any of the methods set out in Part 6 of the Civil Procedure Rules. But what of a foreign company that has not so registered either in respect of a branch or an established place of business other than a branch? If the company has a branch or an established place of business other than a branch in England within the meaning of the Companies Act, again service can be effected under the methods set out in that Act or, as an alternative, by any of the methods set out in Part 6. This is uncontroversial. Even under the narrow view of the role of Part 6, it is clear that the alternative methods of service in Part 6 can be used in this situation.

Foreign companies that have a place of business within the jurisdiction   Under rule 6.5(6) of the Civil Procedure Rules service has to be effected at any place of business[135] within the jurisdiction. This presupposes that the foreign company has a place of business within the jurisdiction. Whether service on such a company using the methods set out in Part 6 forms a basis of jurisdiction depends on whether the wide view of the role of Part 6 is adopted, or the narrow.

(iv) What are the advantages in using these alternative methods?

There are two advantages in using Part 6 of the Civil Procedure Rules (as widely interpreted), rather than the Companies Act 1985. First, there is no requirement that service is in respect of the carrying on of the business of the branch. Secondly, service can be effected on a foreign company which merely has a place of business within the jurisdiction.

No requirement that service is in respect of the carrying on of the business of the branch   In *Saab v Saudi American Bank*,[136] CLARKE LJ discussed obiter the position where the method of service is that of leaving the document at a place specified under rule 6.5(6) of the Civil Procedure Rules. He said that "it appears . . . that process can be served on a foreign company with a place of business in, say, London without the necessity for

---

[132] The case concerned service by first class post at the usual or last known residence under CPR, r 6.5(6).

[133] *Chellaram v Chellaram (No 2)* [2002] EWHC 632 (Ch) at [47], [2002] 2 All ER 17.

[134] The *Sea Assets* case, supra.

[135] The meaning of this is examined infra, pp 369–370.

[136] [1999] 1 WLR 1861.

establishing any link between the process and the business being conducted in London".[137] This dictum was applied by LONGMORE J in *Sea Assets Ltd v PT Garuda Indonesia*.[138] In this case, the claim form was served at the branch office of a company incorporated in Indonesia, which had obtained a branch registration certificate under the Companies Act. The dispute did not relate to the carrying on of the business of the defendant's London branch. Accordingly, it was not possible to rely on service under section 694A of the Companies Act 1985. Instead the claimant sought to rely on service under Part 6 of the Civil Procedure Rules, arguing that service was effected at "any place of business of the company within the jurisdiction" under rule 6.5(6). LONGMORE J held that the claim form had been validly served under this provision. The argument that Part 6 was ultra vires in providing alternative methods of service to those contained in the Companies Act 1985 was rejected. Also rejected was the argument that for the purposes of rule 6.5(6) the defendant was a company registered in England and Wales by virtue of its obtaining a branch registration certificate under the Companies Act. It was a company whose essence was overseas. If this argument had succeeded then the service would not have been valid. It will be recalled that with a company registered in England and Wales the place of service is the principal office of the company or any place of business of the company within the jurisdiction which has a real connection with the claim. The branch office at which the process was served did not fall within either of these two categories.

If the narrow view of the role of Part 6 is adopted, this raises a question over the correctness of the decision in the *Sea Assets* case. The requirement in the Companies Act 1985 that, in the case of a branch, the document served must be in respect of the carrying on of the business of the branch, whilst admittedly appearing in the sections of the Act dealing with service, does not appear to be concerned with the method of service. It is not concerned with how and where the process is served. It looks to be a substantive requirement. If one looks at Article 5(5) of the Brussels I Regulation this contains two substantive requirements, namely that there is a branch, etc and that the dispute arises out of the operations of the branch, etc. The position is arguably the same under the Companies Act 1985. If one accepts that this is a substantive requirement, it should then apply regardless of the method of service. Accordingly, it would apply even where the method employed is one set out in Part 6 of the Civil Procedure Rules.

Service on a foreign company which has a place of business within the jurisdiction
There is an obvious difference between the wording of the Companies Act 1985, which requires that the foreign company has "established" a place of business and rule 6.5(6) of the Civil Procedure Rules, which merely requires that a foreign company has a place of business within the jurisdiction. "Establishing" a place of business within the meaning of the Companies Act 1985 "connotes a degree of formality and permanence of location which is not required by Part 6.5(6)".[139] However, the requirement of a "place of business" remains under the Civil Procedure Rules.[140] That means that service on an address

---

[137] Ibid, at 324–325.
[138] [2000] 4 All ER 371.
[139] *Lakah Group v Al Jazeera Satellite Channel* [2003] EWHC 1297 at [41]; the Court of Appeal, in affirming the decision at first instance, said it was unnecessary to discuss this point [2003] EWCA (Civ) 1781 at [8].
[140] Ibid, at [41]; affd [2003] EWCA (Civ) 1781. CPR, r 6.5(6) refers also to service where a corporation "carries on its activities". According to the Court of Appeal at [8], the test for this is the same as for "any place of

with which the company has no more than a transient or irregular connection will not be valid.[141] It must be the defendant's place of business; what is needed is evidence of actual business activity on the part of the defendant. Business activity on the part of an associated company is not enough.[142] Nevertheless, if the wide view of the role of Part 6 is adopted, it is going to be easier to use rule 6.5(6) as the basis of jurisdiction than the Companies Act 1985. Some situations will come within the former but fall outside the latter. It follows that, if a foreign company has not registered as an 'oversea company' under the 1985 Act, recourse should be had to Part 6, rather than trying to show that it should have registered under the 1985 Act (ie that it has a branch or has established a place of business other than a branch). In contrast, if the narrow view of the role of Part 6 is adopted, it would be necessary to show that the foreign company not only has a place of business within the jurisdiction (to satisfy rule 6.5(6)) but also has a branch or has established a place of business other than a branch within the meaning of the 1985 Act.

(b) Submission to the jurisdiction

Despite the fundamental principle that the court cannot entertain an action against a defendant who is absent from England, it has long been recognised that an absent defendant may confer jurisdiction on the court by submitting to it. This may be done in a variety of ways, such as by the defendant acknowledging service but without applying to the court for an order declaring that it has no jurisdiction,[143] or instructing a solicitor to accept service on his behalf.[144] Commencing an action as a claimant will give the court jurisdiction over a counterclaim.[145] A foreign claimant who commences an action in England submits willingly to the jurisdiction and does so without reservation and is subject to all the incidents of litigation in England, including his amenability to a counterclaim.[146] In contrast, a foreign defendant who is brought to jurisdiction by answering a claim within rule 6.20 of the Civil Procedure Rules is brought to England unwillingly and can limit his submission to the jurisdiction; prima facie he is regarded as submitting only on a claim-by-claim basis.[147] Although a defendant who acknowledges service and contests the case on its merits will be held to have submitted to the jurisdiction,[148] an acknowledgment of service

---

business". It therefore does not matter whether the defendant is a corporation or a company and in the *Lakah* case there was no attempt to say which it was.

[141] *Lakah Group v Al Jazeera Satellite Channel* [2003] EWCA (Civ) 1781 at [8].

[142] *Lakah Group v Al Jazeera Satellite Channel* [2003] EWHC 1297 at [48]; affd without discussion of this point [2003] EWCA (Civ) 1781.

[143] CPR, r 11(5). There is no submission by acknowledging service but failing to tick the box indicating an intention to contest jurisdiction and the defendant has 14 days to make his application: *IBS Technologies (PVT) Ltd v APM Technologies SA* 2003 (unreported).

[144] CPR, r 6.4(2). See also *Manta Line Inc v Sofianites and Midland Bank plc* [1984] 1 Lloyd's Rep 14, CA; *Sphere Drake Insurance plc v Gunes Sigorta Anonim Sirketi* [1987] 1 Lloyd's Rep 139; *Jordan v Schatz* (2000) 189 DLR (4th) 62, BC Court of Appeal.

[145] CPR, r 20(4). See also *Balkanbank v Taher (No 2)* [1995] 1 WLR 1067, CA.

[146] *Glencore International AG v Exter Shipping Ltd* [2002] EWCA Civ 528 at [45]–[56], [2002] All ER (Comm) 1.

[147] Ibid.

[148] *Boyle v Sacker* (1888) 39 Ch D 249, CA; cf *Redhead v Redhead and Crothers* [1926] NZLR 131; *Brealey v Board of Management of Royal Perth Hospital* (1999) 21 WAR 79. See also *Obikoya v Silvernorth Ltd* (1983) Times, 6 July. As will a counterclaim, see *CAN Insurance Co Ltd v Office Depot International (UK) Ltd* [2005] EWHC 456 (Comm) at [26].

merely to protest that the court does not have jurisdiction will not constitute submission,[149] even if the defendant also seeks a stay of proceedings pending the outcome of proceedings abroad.[150] Nor will the retention of the claim form and acknowledgment of service, by themselves, amount to a waiver of any irregularity.[151] Where a defendant has complied with Part 11 of the Civil Procedure Rules with a view to challenging the jurisdiction, and the time for making his application has not expired, any conduct on his part must be wholly unequivocal to amount to a submisssion to the jurisdiction and a waiver of that right of challenge.[152] Any submission must not have been induced by misrepresentation.[153]

Furthermore, any person may contract, either expressly or impliedly, to submit to the jurisdiction of a court to which he would not otherwise be subject.[154] Thus, in the case of an international contract it is common practice for the parties, one or even both of whom are resident abroad, to agree that any dispute arising between them shall be settled by the English court or by an arbitrator in England.[155] A party to such a contract, having consented to the jurisdiction, cannot afterwards contest the binding effect of the judgment.[156] Such an agreement is recognised and made procedurally effective by a rule of procedure which permits the parties to a contract to prescribe, in the event of an action, the method by which the claim form shall be served on the defendant, whether in England or elsewhere.[157] For example, the parties may agree in a contract that service is to be effected on an agent of the defendant in England. The defendant out of the jurisdiction will be deemed to have been served by service on his agent within the jurisdiction.[158] However, if the parties agree on a method of service which involves service out of the jurisdiction, the claim form shall not be deemed to have been duly served abroad unless permission has been granted under rule 6.20 or service of the claim form is allowed without permission under rule 6.19.[159]

---

[149] CPR, r 11; for the time for making such a protest see r 11(4), *Monrose Investments v Orion Nominees* [2002] IL Pr 21 and *Midland Resources Ltd v Gonvarri Industrial SA* [2002] IL Pr 8. For extension of time, see *CAN Insurance Co Ltd v Office Depot International (UK) Ltd* [2005] EWHC 456 (Comm) at [26]. See generally *Re Dulles' Settlement (No 2), Dulles v Vidler* [1951] Ch 842, CA; and see *Tallack v Tallack and Broekema* [1927] P 211; *Razelos v Razelos (No 2)* [1970] 1 WLR 392 at 403; see also *Air Nauru v Nive Airlines Ltd* [1993] 2 NZLR 632; cf *Solvalub Ltd v Match Investments Ltd* [1998] IL Pr 419 (going beyond a protest as to jurisdiction and into the merits constituted submission), Jersey CA; *Trans-Continental Textile Recycling v Partenreederei MS Erato* [1998] IL Pr 129, Federal Court of Canada. The principle is the same when it comes to enforcement of foreign judgments: Civil Jurisdiction and Judgments Act 1982, s 33, as amended, discussed infra, pp 522–526.

[150] *Williams and Glyns Bank plc v Astro Dinamico Cia Naviera SA* [1984] 1 WLR 438, HL; cf *The Messiniaki Tolmi* [1984] 1 Lloyd's Rep 266, CA; *Finnish Marine Insurance Co Ltd v Protective National Insurance Co* [1990] 1 QB 1078; *Prudential Assurance Co Ltd v Prudential Insurance Co of America* [2003] FSR 97 at 101–105.

[151] *Caribbean Gold Ltd v Alga Shipping Co Ltd* [1993] 1 WLR 1100. See also on waiver *The Xing Su Hai* [1995] 2 Lloyd's Rep 15.

[152] *SMAY Investments Ltd v Sachdev (Practice Note)* [2003] EWHC 474 (Ch), [2003] 1 WLR 1973.

[153] *Beecham Group plc v Norton Healthcare Ltd* [1997] FSR 81 at 88.

[154] *Feyerick v Hubbard* (1902) 71 LJKB 509; *Copin v Adamson* (1875) 1 Ex D 17, CA, infra, p 520; Pryles (1976) 25 ICLQ 543; Kahn-Freund (1977) 26 ICLQ 825; Anton and Beaumont's, *Civil Jurisdiction in Scotland*, paras 10.72–10.77.

[155] Infra, p 701. It is most unlikely that English courts would accept an implied agreement to submit; cf *Adams v Cape Industries plc* [1990] Ch 433, infra, pp 520–521.

[156] A choice of the law to govern a contract does not, of itself, amount to agreement to submit to that jurisdiction: *Dunbee Ltd v Gilman & Co (Australia) Pty Ltd* [1968] 2 Lloyd's Rep 394; cf *Acrow (Automation) Ltd v Rex Chainbelt Inc* [1971] 1 WLR 1676 at 1683, CA.

[157] CPR, r 6.15. See *Society of Lloyd's v Tropp* [2004] EWHC 33 (Comm).

[158] This follows the common law rule in *Tharsis Sulphur and Copper Co Ltd v Société Industrielle et Commerciale des Métaux* (1889) 58 LJQB 435.

[159] CPR, r 6.15(2); *McCulloch v Bank of Nova Scotia* [EWHC] 790 (Ch) at [33], [2006] 2 All ER (Comm) 714.

If no method of service is prescribed by the parties, rule 6.19 or 6.20 will have to be resorted to in respect of a foreign defendant.[160]

It must be noted that the parties cannot by submission confer jurisdiction on the court to entertain proceedings beyond its authority.[161] Submission will not, for example, confer jurisdiction in divorce or nullity proceedings,[162] or over proceedings principally concerned with a question of title to foreign land.[163]

(c) Service of a claim form on a defendant out of the jurisdiction[164]

The rule at common law, that no action in personam will lie against a defendant unless he has been served with a claim form while present in England, often precludes a claimant from enforcing a claim in the most appropriate forum. Because of this an entirely different kind of jurisdiction, generally called "assumed" jurisdiction, was introduced many years ago,[165] which gave the courts a discretionary power to summon absent defendants, whether English or foreign. The exercise of this jurisdiction is now governed by rule 6.20 of the Civil Procedure Rules.[166] The overriding objective of the latter is to enable the court to deal with cases justly.[167]

Rules 6.19 and 6.20 permit service of a claim form on a defendant who is out of the jurisdiction (ie not to be found in England or Wales) in the circumstances that will be considered below. In some cases service is allowed without the permission of the court. However, in many cases service is only allowed with the permission of the court. This contrasts with the position in a number of common law jurisdictions in which this requirement has been dispensed with altogether.[168] There is much to be said for the latter approach.[169] An amendment to the English rules on service out of the jurisdiction to reflect this has been considered but has not been introduced.

(i) Service of a claim form out of the jurisdiction with the permission of the court

Rule 6.20 empowers the court, upon an application being made to it,[170] to permit service[171] of a claim form[172] on a defendant who is abroad. However, permission will only be given

---

[160] Where the court's permission is required r 6.20(5)(d) allows the court to grant this, infra, p 382.

[161] *Re Paramount Airways Ltd (In Administration)* [1992] Ch 160 at 171.

[162] Infra, pp 944–952.

[163] Civil Jurisdiction and Judgments Act 1982, s 30, as amended by the Civil Jurisdiction and Judgments Act 1991, Sch 2, para 13 and the Civil Jurisdiction and Judgments Order 2001/3929 Sch 2(IV), para 13; infra, pp 486–487.

[164] Collins (1972) 21 ICLQ 656; reprinted in *Essays*, p 226.

[165] By the Common Law Procedure Act 1852.

[166] Previously by Ord 11, r 1(1) RSC.

[167] CPR, r 1.1.

[168] For Canada, see Castel and Walker, *Canadian Conflict of Laws* (6th edn), para 11.5; Blom in Fawcett (ed), *Declining Jurisdiction*, pp 121–124. For New Zealand, see NZ High Court Rule 219; *Kuwait Asia Bank EC v National Mutual Life Nominees Ltd* [1991] 1 AC 187, [1990] 3 All ER 404 (service can nonetheless be set aside on the application of the defendant); Barnard in Fawcett, *Declining Jurisdiction*, pp 343–345.

[169] Infra, p 410.

[170] For the requirement of supporting written evidence see r 6.21(1); *ANCAP v Ridgley* [1996] 1 Lloyd's Rep 570; *The Kurnia Dewi* [1997] 1 Lloyd's Rep 552 at 562–563.

[171] For retrospective permission see *Nesheim v Kosa* [2007] EWHC 2710 (Ch).

[172] A counterclaim should be treated as a claim form: *Shahar v Tsitsekkos* [2004] EWHC 2659 (Ch) at [92]. For service out of the jurisdiction of documents other than claim forms see CPR, r 6.30; *C Inc plc v L* [2001] 2 All ER (Comm) 446.

if England and Wales is the proper place in which to bring the claim.[173] The court has to be satisfied: first, that there is a good arguable case that one of the grounds (paragraphs) of rule 6.20 is satisfied; secondly, that there is a reasonable prospect of success (a serious issue to be tried on the merits); thirdly, that the discretion should be exercised to permit service out of the jurisdiction. The onus is on the claimant to satisfy these three points.[174]

(a) The grounds of rule 6.20

The Civil Procedure Rules made a number of drafting changes in order to produce a list of grounds for service out of the jurisdiction which is clearer and simpler than the list under the predecessor rules.[175] Although there has been a change of wording, principles expounded in former authorities relating to the old grounds remain applicable.[176] The claimant must show a good arguable case that one of the grounds of rule 6.20 is satisfied.[177] The standard for a good arguable case is less stringent than a balance of probabilities but more than that of a real prospect of success.[178] A good arguable case is a concept with a certain flexibility and suggests that one party has a much better argument on the evidence available.[179] The court must not appear to pre-try the central issue in the case but at the same time must carefully scrutinise the factor which gives jurisdiction.[180] However, where jurisdiction depends on a question of law or construction, the court will decide it rather than apply the good arguable case test.[181] The following are the cases where the service of a claim form out of the jurisdiction is allowed with the permission of the court.

(i) General grounds

(1) Where "a claim is made for a remedy against a person domiciled within the jurisdiction".[182] This ground is an extensive departure from common law principles. It renders jurisdiction possible over practically any kind of claim[183] against an absent person (including a corporation), provided that he is domiciled in England. In this context, domicile is

---

[173] CPR, r 6.21(2A).

[174] On the first two points see *Seaconsar Far East Ltd v Bank Markazi Jomhouri Islami Iran* [1994] 1 AC 438 at 454 et seq, HL; on the third see *Spiliada Maritime Corpn v Cansulex Ltd* [1987] AC 460 at 481 and *Berezovsky v Michaels* [2000] 1 WLR 1004, HL.

[175] See the Lord Chancellor's Department Consultation Paper on the Civil Procedure Rules—Service of Court Process Abroad, para 23.

[176] *Petroleo Brasiliero SA v Mellitus Shipping Inc (The Baltic Flame)* [2001] EWCA Civ 418 at [31], [2001] 2 Lloyd's Rep 203. Cf *Crédit Agricole Indosuez v Unicof Ltd* [2003] EWHC 2676 (Comm) at [16], [2004] 1 Lloyd's Rep 196.

[177] *Seaconsar Far East Ltd v Bank Markazi Jomhouri Islami Iran* [1994] 1 AC 438 at 453–454, 456–457, HL. See also *Bank of Baroda v Vysya Bank Ltd* [1994] 2 Lloyd's Rep 87 at 90.

[178] *Carvill America Inc v Camperdown UK Ltd* [2005] EWCA Civ 645 at [45], [2005] 2 Lloyd's Rep 457.

[179] *Canada Trust Co v Stolzenberg (No 2)* [1998] 1 WLR 547 at 555–556 (per WALLER LJ), approved by HL [2002] 1 AC 1 at 13 (per Lord STEYN with whom the other Law Lords agreed). See *Tasarruff v Demirel* [2006] EWHC 3354 (Ch) at [40], [2007] IL Pr 8, affirmed without discussion of this point [2007] EWCA Civ 799, [2007] 1 WLR 2508, leave to appeal to the House of Lords dismissed [2007] 1 WLR 3066; also supra, p 226. See the application of this principle in relation to r 6.20(6) infra, pp 382–383. See generally Crawford (2005) 54 ICLQ 829, 840–841.

[180] *Canada Trust Co v Stolzenberg (No 2)*, supra, 555–556 (per WALLER LJ).

[181] *Chellaram v Chellaram (No 2)* [2002] EWHC 632 (Ch) at [136], [2002] 2 All ER 17.

[182] CPR, r 6.20(1); formerly Ord 11, r (1)(1)(a) RSC.

[183] *Re Liddell's Settlement Trusts* [1936] Ch 365, CA.

now determined in accordance with the definition contained in the Brussels I Regulation and the Civil Jurisdiction and Judgments Order 2001.[184] This definition is used in cases arising within the Brussels I Regulation, and as has been seen,[185] is a very complex one. Of course, the jurisdiction rules contained in the Brussels I Regulation and/or the Modified Regulation will apply in a case where the defendant is domiciled in England provided that the dispute concerns international jurisdiction and it is a civil and commercial matter. This ground is therefore concerned with cases which do not involve this.[186]

(2) Where "a claim is made for an injunction ordering the defendant to do or refrain from doing an act within the jurisdiction".[187] The courts refuse to grant permission under this ground unless the substantial and genuine dispute between the parties is whether an injunction against some act in England[188] ought to be granted. It follows that this ground cannot be used in the case of an anti-suit injunction restraining a defendant from pursuing proceedings abroad.[189] The claimant cannot found the jurisdiction of the English court by claiming an injunction that is only incidental to the remedy that he in fact desires.[190] This ground is wide enough to cover a permanent injunction restraining threatened breaches of contract and torts within the jurisdiction.[191] However, it does not cover the issue of a freezing injunction (previously known as a "Mareva"[192] injunction), ie an *interlocutory* injunction[193] to restrain a defendant from removing his assets from the jurisdiction or from dissipating them pending the trial of an action against him. There is no power to order the issue of a claim form out of the jurisdiction under this ground merely because a freezing injunction is sought.[194] There is, however, a separate ground under rule 6.20 which permits this.[195]

(3) Where "a claim is made against someone on whom the claim form has been or will be served (otherwise than in reliance on this paragraph) and: (a) there is between the claimant and that person a real issue which it is reasonable for the court to try; and (b) the claimant wishes to serve the claim form on another person who is a necessary or proper

---

[184] CPR, r 6.18(g) referring to the Judgments Regulation and paras 9–12 of Sch 1 of the 2001 Order.
[185] Supra, pp 210–211.
[186] See, eg, *Bank of Dubai v Abbas* [1997] IL Pr 308, CA.
[187] CPR, r 6.20(2); formerly Ord 11, r 1(1)(1)(b). See *Re Baltic Real Estate Ltd* [1992] BCC 629 at 635.
[188] See *King v Lewis* [2004] EWCA (Civ) 1329 at [2], [2005] IL Pr 16—no act in England where an injunction was sought against publication on a website controlled abroad. Cf the differently worded Scots interdict provision and *Bonnier Media Ltd v Greg Lloyd Smith and Kestrel Trading Corpn* [2002] ETMR 86.
[189] *Amoco (UK) Exploration Co v British American Offshore Ltd* [1999] 2 Lloyd's Rep 772 at 778. But r 6.20(5) can be used, see infra, pp 378–382.
[190] *Rosler v Hilbery* [1925] Ch 250, CA.
[191] *James North & Sons Ltd v North Cape Textiles Ltd* [1984] 1 WLR 1428, CA.
[192] *Mareva Cia Naviera SA v International Bulk Carriers SA* [1980] 1 All ER 213 n, CA.
[193] Under s 37 of the Supreme Court Act 1981.
[194] *Siskina (Cargo Owners) v Distos Cia Naviera SA, The Siskina* [1979] AC 210, HL; applied by the Privy Council in *Mercedes Benz AG v Leiduck* [1996] AC 284; Collins (1996) 112 LQR 8; Andrew [1996] CLJ 12; Smart (1996) 112 LQR 397; and see *Perry v Zissis* [1977] 1 Lloyd's Rep 607 at 616–617, CA; *Serge Caudron v Air Zaire* [1986] ILRM 10, Supreme Court of Ireland, distinguised in *McKenna v EH* [2002] 2 ILRM 117. But cf the dissent of Lord NICHOLLS in the *Mercedes-Benz* case, supra, at 312–314; followed in *Krohn GmbH v Varna Shipyard* [1998] IL Pr 614, Royal Court Jersey. Cf also an injunction under s 30 of the Merchant Shipping Act 1894, re-enacted in Merchant Shipping Act 1995, Sch 1, para 6: *The Mikado* [1992] 1 Lloyd's Rep 163.
[195] See CPR, r 6.20(4); discussed infra, p 378.

party to that claim".[196] Permission to serve a person abroad may be obtained under this ground in circumstances that are not covered by any of the other heads—for instance, when a tort has been committed in a foreign country by two persons jointly, only one of whom is subject to the court's jurisdiction.[197] Moreover, unlike Article 6(1) of the Brussels I Regulation,[198] it can be used where there are claims against different defendants based on different causes of action.[199] This provision is concerned with the situation where there are two defendants:[200] a first (or anchor) defendant, who has actually been served or will be served; and a second defendant whom the claimant now wishes to serve out of the jurisdiction. There are separate requirements in respect of each defendant.

It is a condition of the grant of permission in respect of the second defendant that the first defendant has already been validly served[201] or will be served.[202] The service can be within the jurisdiction or out of the jurisdiction under rule 6.20, provided this is not in reliance on rule 6.20(3). It must also be shown that the claim is made against the defendant who has been served or will be served. However, it need no longer be shown, as was the case with its predecessor, that the first defendant was "duly served".[203] There is, though, a separate requirement under rule 6.20(3)(a) that there is between the claimant and the first defendant a real issue which it is reasonable for the court to try.[204] The claimant's application for service out of the jurisdiction under rule 6.20(3) must be supported by written evidence stating the grounds for the witness's belief that there is a real issue between the claimant and the first defendant.[205] This merits threshold test[206] protects the first defendant, who can be served with a claim form, from spurious claims being brought against him solely in order to obtain jurisdiction over the second defendant who is outside the jurisdiction. It also, of course, protects the second defendant. There will not be "a real issue which it is reasonable for the court to try" if the claimant has no real prospect

---

[196] CPR, r 6.20(3); formerly Ord 11, r 1(1)(c) RSC. See generally Fawcett (1995) 44 ICLQ 744, 746–749.

[197] *Croft v King* [1893] 1 QB 419.

[198] See supra, pp 262–265.

[199] See, eg, *Owusu v Jackson* [2002] EWCA Civ 877, [2002] IL Pr 45.

[200] They do not need to be joint or even alternative defendants: *Bank of New South Wales v Commonwealth Steel Co Ltd* [1983] 1 NSWLR 69; *Westpac Banking Corpn v Commonwealth Steel Co Ltd* [1983] 1 NSWLR 735.

[201] *Kuwait Oil Tanker Co SAK v Al Bader* [1997] 1 WLR 1410, CA; *The Xing Su Hai* [1995] 2 Lloyd's Rep 15; *The Cienvik* [1996] 2 Lloyd's Rep 395; *Amoco (UK) Exploration Co v British American Offshore Ltd* [1999] 2 Lloyd's Rep 772, 779; *Chellaram v Chellaram (No 2)* [2002] EWHC 632 (Ch), [2002] 3 All ER 17. It was possible to validate the purported leave with retrospective effect under RSC, Ord 2, r 1 (see now CPR, para 3.10); this aspect is criticised by Briggs (1997) 68 BYBIL 360.

[202] This ground cannot be used if the action against the first defendant has been stayed: *Haji-Ioannou v Frangos* [1999] 2 Lloyd's Rep 337, 361, CA.

[203] On which see *Derby and Co Ltd v Larsson* [1976] 1 WLR 202, HL.

[204] *Morin v Bonhams & Brooks Ltd* [2003] EWHC 467 (Comm), [2003] IL Pr 25, the Court of Appeal affirmed the decision at first instance that Monegasque law governed the tort claim [2003] EWCA Civ 1802, [2004] 1 Lloyd's Rep 702; *Chase v Ram Technical Services Ltd* [2000] 2 Lloyd's Rep 418 at [11]–[13]; *C Inc plc v L* [2001] 2 All ER (Comm) 446 at [94]; *Crédit Agricole Indosuez v Unicof Ltd* [2003] EWHC 2676 (Comm) at [16], [2004] 1 Lloyd's Rep 196; *Booth v Phillips* [2004] EWHC 1437 at [11]–[23], [2004] 2 Lloyd's Rep 457. For cases on the requirement under Ord 11, r 1(1)(c) RSC that there was a serious issue on the merits in respect of the first defendant: see *The Ines* [1993] 2 Lloyd's Rep 492 at 493; *Grupo Torras SA and Torras Hostench London Ltd v Sheikh Fahad Mohammed Al Sabah* [1995] 1 Lloyd's Rep 374 at 380; appeals to the CA dismissed without discussion of this point, [1996] 1 Lloyd's Rep 7; *New Hampshire Insurance Co v Aerospace Finance Ltd* [1998] 2 Lloyd's Rep 539 at 542; *The Ikarian Reefer (No 2)* [1999] 2 Lloyd's Rep 621 at 627.

[205] See CPR, r 6.21(2); *ISC v Guerin* [1992] 2 Lloyd's Rep 430 at 432.

[206] *De Molestina v Ponton* [2002] 1 Lloyd's Rep 271 at [37].

of succeeding on that issue.[207] "Real" is to be contrasted with "fanciful".[208] This requirement will not be met if the claim against the first defendant is bound to fail. It will also not be met if the claim against the first defendant is not a bona fide one, ie the first defendant is joined with the sole object of subjecting the second defendant to the jurisdiction of the English courts.[209]

The claimant must establish a good arguable case[210] that the second defendant, whom the claimant wishes to serve out of the jurisdiction, is "a necessary or proper party"[211] to the claim against the first defendant. In determining whether a person is a proper party the courts have been very much influenced by English procedural rules on joinders of parties.[212] Generally a person who may be joined in proceedings in accordance with the English rules as to joinder of parties is a "proper party".[213] There is nothing to suggest that the power of the court to give permission for service out under rule 6.20(3) is narrower than under its predecessor or that the circumstances in which a person may properly be joined as a defendant are narrower under the Civil Procedure Rules than under their predecessor.[214] The second defendant will not be a necessary or proper party if he has a good defence in law to the claim and therefore it is bound to fail;[215] nor will it be the

---

207 *Owusu v Jackson* [2002] EWCA Civ 877 at [32], [2002] IL Pr 45.

208 Ibid. The Court said that CPR, r 6.20(3) introduces the language of r 24.2(a)(i) and in that context "real" contrasts with "fanciful", citing *Swain v Hillman* [2001] 1 All ER 91 at [10].

209 *Konamaneni v Rolls-Royce Industrial Power (India) Ltd* [2002] 1 WLR 1269 at [44].

210 *Carvill America Incorporated v Camperdown UK Ltd* [2005] EWCA Civ 645 at [45], [2005] 2 Lloyd's Rep 457.

211 CPR, r 6.20(3)(b). See generally *Massey v Heynes and Co* (1888) 21 QBD 330; *Qatar Petroleum v Shell International Petroleum* [1983] 2 Lloyd's Rep 35; *International Commercial Bank plc v Insurance Corpn of Ireland plc* [1989] IR 453; *ISC v Guerin* [1992] 2 Lloyd's Rep 430; *Tromso Sparebank v Byrne* [1992] IL Pr 73, Irish Supreme Court; *O'Toole v Ireland* [1992] ILRM 218; *Short v British Nuclear Fuels plc* [1997] IL Pr 747, Irish Supreme Court; *International Credit v Adham* [1994] 1 BCLC 66; *Barings plc v Coopers & Lybrand* [1997] IL Pr 12 at 23–24; affd by CA [1997] IL Pr 576 at 585; *Krohn GmbH v Varna Shipyard* [1998] IL Pr 607, Royal Court Jersey; *Bouygues Offshore SA v Caspian Shipping Co (No 3)* [1997] 2 Lloyd's Rep 493; *C Inc plc v L* [2001] 2 All ER (Comm) 446 at [94]; *McCarthy v Pillay* [2003] 2 ILRM 284; *Crédit Agricole Indosuez v Unicof Ltd* [2003] EWHC 2676 (Comm), [2004] 1 Lloyd's Rep 196; *Caltex Trading Pte Ltd v Metro Trading International Inc* [1999] 2 Lloyd's Rep 724, 737; *OT Africa Line Ltd v Magic Sportswear Corpn* [2005] EWCA Civ 710 at [14], [2005] 2 Lloyd's Rep 170; *Marciano v Puterman* (2005) 258 DLR (4th) 356, Sask CA.

212 *Massey v Heynes & Co* (1888) 21 QBD 330 at 338 (per Lord ESHER MR), quoted by MAY LJ in *Multinational Gas and Petrochemical Co v Multinational Gas and Petrochemical Services Ltd* [1983] Ch 258 at 274, CA; *The Eras Eil Actions* [1992] 1 Lloyd's Rep 570, CA; *Arab Monetary Fund v Hashim (No 4)* [1992] 1 WLR 1176, CA; *Barings plc v Coopers & Lybrand* [1997] IL Pr 12 at 18; affd by CA [1997] IL Pr 576 at 585; *Fremont Insurance Ltd v Fremont Indemnity Co* [1997] CLC 1428. See also *Analog Devices BV v Zurich Insurance Co* [2002] 2 ILRM 366, SC of Ireland. See also *Konamaneni v Rolls-Royce Industrial Power (India) Ltd* [2002] 1 WLR 1269 at [44].

213 *Petroleo Brasiliero SA v Mellitus Shipping Inc (The Baltic Flame)* [2001] EWCA Civ 418 at [33], [2001] 2 Lloyd's Rep 203; Takahashi (2002) 51 ICLQ 127. See also *United Film Distribution Ltd v Chhabria* [2001] EWCA Civ 416 at [32]–[38], [2001] 2 All (Comm) 865; the *Owusu* case, supra, at [9]; *Trumann Investment Group Ltd v Société Générale SA* [2004] EWHC 1769 (Ch); *Carvill America Inc v Camperdown UK Ltd* [2005] EWCA Civ 645 at [48]–[49], [2005] 2 Lloyd's Rep 457. The English rules on joinder are contained in CPR, r 19. CPR, r 7.3 provides that a claimant may use a single claim form to start all claims which can be conveniently disposed of in the same proceedings.

214 *United Film Distribution Ltd v Chhabria*, supra, at [38].

215 *Multinational Gas and Petrochemical Co v Multinational Gas and Petrochemical Services Ltd* [1983] Ch 258 at 273, 287, CA. See also *The Ines* [1993] 2 Lloyd's Rep 492 at 494; *The Kurnia Dewi* [1997] 1 Lloyd's Rep 552 at 564; *Borealis AB v Stargas Ltd* [1999] QB 863, CA, affd by the House of Lords on different grounds [2002] 2 AC 205.

case if the claimant's rights are predominantly against the first defendant.[216] More surprisingly, it has been held that this requirement is not met if the claim should have been principally brought against the *second defendant*.[217] It is, therefore, possible for the courts to protect the first defendant in cases where the action brought against the first defendant was not a bona fide one, by holding that the second defendant is not a necessary or proper party to that action.[218]

When it comes to the exercise of the discretion to serve out of the jurisdiction, special care is needed with this ground, "in the sense that the court will give careful examination to the cause of action relied on, both as to its substance and its prospects (is it bound or very likely to fail?), whether it is brought in good faith or with some improper motive or ulterior purpose, and whether or not full and fair disclosure has been made".[219] Establishing that England is the clearly appropriate forum for trial will not be easy because the rule applies to cases where there is no territorial connection between the claim which is the subject of the relevant action and the jurisdiction of the English courts.[220] Nevertheless, this is a good provision in terms of litigational convenience, allowing for the consolidation of litigation in one state. This is a factor which may properly encourage a judge to lean in favour of allowing service out of the jurisdiction in the absence of positive counter-indications.[221] In cases where the action against the first defendant is not a bona fide one, or where it is bound to fail, this has been regarded as a relevant factor to be taken into account against exercising the discretion to allow service out of the jurisdiction.[222] Permission has also not been granted where there are substantial defendants who are subject to the jurisdiction and there is no real advantage to the claimant in joining further defendants who are abroad.[223]

(3A) Where "a claim is a Part 20 claim and the person to be served is a necessary or proper party to the claim against the Part 20 claimant".[224] This is a new ground which is concerned with Part 20 claims.[225] These include counterclaims by a defendant and claims by a defendant for contribution or indemnity.[226] In determining whether to permit service out of the jurisidiction under this ground the court should, as with other grounds, be influenced by the interests of the parties and practical justice.[227]

---

[216] *Re Schintz* [1926] Ch 710.

[217] *Rosler v Hilbery* [1925] Ch 250, CA.

[218] See *Multinational Gas and Petrochemical Co v Multinational Gas and Petrochemical Services Ltd*, supra, at 279.

[219] *Petroleo Brasiliero SA v Mellitus Shipping Inc (The Baltic Flame)* [2001] EWCA Civ 418 at [21], [2001] 2 Lloyd's Rep 203.

[220] *Multinational Gas and Petrochemical Co v Multinational Gas and Petrochemical Services Ltd* [1983] Ch 258 at 271 (per MAY LJ), CA.

[221] The *Petroleo Brasiliero* case, supra, at [22].

[222] *Rosler v Hilbery*, supra; *Tyne Improvement Comrs v Armement Anversois, The Brabo*, supra, at 349–350; *The Manchester Courage* [1973] 1 Lloyd's Rep 386 at 391; *Multinational Gas and Petroleum Co v Multinational Gas and Petroleum Services Ltd*, supra, at 279.

[223] *Chaney v Murphy* [1948] WN 130, 64 TLR 489. See also *International Marine Services Inc v National Bank of Fujairah* [1997] IL Pr 468, CA.

[224] CPR, r 6.20(3A).

[225] See, eg, *Petroleo Brasiliero SA v Mellitus Shipping Inc (The Baltic Flame)* [2001] EWCA Civ 418, [2001] 2 Lloyd's Rep 203 (a contribution case).

[226] CPR, r 20.2. For counterclaims against a non-party see *Shahar v Tsitsekkos* [2004] EWHC 2659 (Ch) at [85]–[92].

[227] The *Petroleo Brasiliero* case, supra, at [38].

(ii) Claims for interim remedies

(4) Where "a claim is made for an interim remedy under section 25(1) of the 1982 [Civil Jurisdiction and Judgments] Act".[228] At one time a freezing injunction could not be granted in support of foreign proceedings.[229] However, this restriction on the issue of freezing injunctions was subsequently doubted[230] and was eventually swept aside by section 25[231] of the Civil Jurisdiction and Judgments Act 1982 as extended.[232] This allows an English court to grant "interim relief",[233] such as a freezing injunction, in respect of proceedings which have been or are to be commenced[234] in another state (regardless of whether this is a Brussels I Regulation State, Brussels/Lugano Convention Contracting State or a non-Regulation/Convention State) or in another part of the United Kingdom. The court may refuse to grant an interim remedy if the fact that it is exercising an ancillary jurisdiction in support of substantive proceedings elsewhere makes it inexpedient to grant it.[235] The approach towards the exercise of this power is the same in non-Regulation/Convention cases as it is in Regulation/Convention cases.[236] Rule 6.20(4) provides that a claim form for an interim remedy under section 25(1)[237] may be served out of the jurisdiction with the permission of the court. Section 24 of the 1982 Act provides that the English courts can grant a freezing injunction pending trial in England where the issue to be tried is whether the court has jurisdiction to entertain the proceedings.

(iii) Claims in relation to contracts

(5) Where "a claim is made in respect of a contract" in four alternative specified cases.[238] The predecessor of this ground was much more detailed, requiring that "the claim is

---

[228] CPR, r 6.20(4); formerly Ord 11, r 8A. For the need for such a provision see *Mercedes Benz AG v Leiduck* [1996] 1 AC 284 at 304–305 (per Lord Mustill), PC.

[229] *The Siskina*, supra, at 255; *Channel Tunnel Group Ltd v Balfour Beatty Construction Ltd* [1993] AC 334, at 362, HL. For the position in respect of a search order, see *Altertext Inc v Advanced Data Communications Ltd* [1985] 1 WLR 457 at 463. The general question of jurisdiction over movables is discussed infra, pp 391–393 and 413–414. *The Siskina* is still relevant where a freezing injunction is used in support of domestic proceedings. For a separate aspect of the legacy of *The Siskina*, see *The Veracruz I* [1992] 1 Lloyd's Rep 353, CA; criticised by Collins (1992) 108 LQR 175; Marshall [1992] LMCLQ 161; Wilde [1993] LMCLQ 309.

[230] *Channel Tunnel Group Ltd v Balfour Beatty Construction Ltd* [1993] AC 334 at 340–342 (per Lords Browne–Wilkinson, Keith and Goff), HL; Collins (1993) 19 LQR 342; Hill [1993] LMCLQ 465. See also the majority of the Privy Council in *Mercedes Benz AG v Leiduck*, supra, at 304 which expressed no conclusion on whether there was this power; cf the dissent of Lord Nicholls at 305–310. There is power to grant interim relief in support of foreign arbitration proceedings: *Channel Tunnel Group Ltd v Balfour Beatty Construction Ltd* [1993] AC 334, HL; see also Arbitration Act 1996, s 2. See generally Capper [1996] CJQ 211. See also *C Inc plc v L* [2001] 2 All ER (Comm) 446 at [75]—claim for substantive relief made abroad. The restriction has been rejected in Jersey, *Solvalub Ltd v Match Investments Ltd* [1998] IL Pr 419, CA Jersey, following the dissent of Lord Nicholls in the *Mercedes Benz* case, supra, at 305–310.

[231] As amended to reflect the introduction of the Lugano Convention and the Brussels I Regulation.

[232] SI 1997/302. S 25(3) authorises this extension.

[233] It has been doubted whether this includes security for costs, see *Bank Mellat v Helliniki Techniki SA* [1984] QB 291.

[234] See *Fourie v Le Roux* [2007] UKHL 1, [2007] 1 WLR 320; Devonshire (2007) 123 LQR 361.

[235] S 25(2) of the Civil Jurisdiction and Judgments Act 1982.

[236] *Refco Inc v ETC* [1999] 1 Lloyd's Rep 159 at 172, 174, CA. See supra, pp 318–320.

[237] This is a requirement for the operation of para (4) *Tasarruff v Demirel* [2006] EWHC 3354 (Ch) at [84]–[87], [2007] IL Pr 8; affirmed without discussion of this point [2007] EWCA Civ 799, [2007] 1 WLR 2508, leave to appeal to the House of Lords dismissed [2007] 1 WLR 3066.

[238] CPR, r 6.20(5); formerly Ord 11, r 1(1)(d) RSC.

brought to enforce, rescind, dissolve, annul or otherwise affect a contract, or to recover damages or obtain any other remedy in respect of the breach of a contract". It is unlikely that this drafting change was intended to have any substantive effect on the court's powers. [239] Cases that fell within the predecessor ground will doubtless fall within the new ground. Thus, for example, a claim for an anti-suit injunction to uphold an exclusive jurisdiction agreement in favour of the English court came within the predecessor provision because it was one to "enforce" the contract [240] and should now be regarded as a claim made in respect of a contract. More significantly, whatever the intention underlying the rewording, the new simpler wording can be interpreted as bringing within the new ground cases that were not within its predecessor. Thus the Court of Appeal held in relation to a predecessor of rule 6.20(5) of the Civil Procedure Rules[241] that it was necessary to assert that there was a contract and that the cause of action was based upon this contract.[242] The new wording, which merely requires that a claim is made *in respect of* a contract (ie it relates to or is connected with the contract),[243] given its natural meaning, leads to the result that the cause of action does not have to be based on the contract.[244] Thus a restitutionary claim for the return of an overpayment of money by one contracting party to another, which is based on unjust enrichment, has been held to fall within the new provision.[245] This was despite the fact that there is now a restitution ground which would encompass cases that are so based.[246] The claimant in the above circumstances therefore has overlapping alternatives under rule 6.20. A claim for damages for fraudulent misrepresentation inducing the claimant to enter a contract[247] and a claim for tortious interference with a contract[248] did not fall within the predecessor provision. The question now is whether such a claim is made in respect of a contract. [249] A claim in respect of a contract should not encompass a claim for a declaration that no contract exists since a new ground for service out of the jurisdiction has been added to the list of grounds to cover such a claim.[250] Neither does it encompass a claim for interpleader relief

---

[239] This particular drafting change probably stems from the objective of producing a list of grounds for service out of the jurisdiction which is clearer and simpler: see the Lord Chancellor's Department Consultation Paper on the Civil Procedure Rules—Service of Court Process Abroad, para 23.

[240] *Youell v Kara Mara Shipping Co* [2000] 2 Lloyd's Rep 102.

[241] Ord 11, r 1(1)(d) RSC.

[242] *DVA v Voest Alpine* [1997] 2 Lloyd's Rep 279 at 287 (per HOBHOUSE LJ), 291 (per MORRITT LJ), CA.

[243] *Albon v Naza Motor trading* [2007] EWHC 9 (Ch), [2007] 1 Lloyd's Rep 297.

[244] Compare this with the tort ground, discussed infra, p 384 which requires that the claim is "made" in tort, ie based on a tort.

[245] *Albon v Naza Motor trading* [2007] EWHC 9 (Ch), [2007] 1 Lloyd's Rep 297. The predecessors of r 6.20(5) encompassed restitutionary claims arising out of what was then regarded as an implied contract. That was before the development of unjust enrichment, which did not satisfy the former requirement that the claim was based on a contract. In so far as restitutionary claims are still in some instances based on contract, it is uncontroversial that they would come within r 6.20(5). See in relation to claims that a contract is frustrated and for consequent relief: *BP Exploration Co (Libya) Ltd v Hunt* [1976] 1 WLR 788. See generally Fawcett, Harris and Bridge, paras 8.64–8.81.

[246] CPR, r 6.20(15).

[247] *Arab Business Consortium International Finance and Investment Co v Banque Franco-Tunisienne* [1996] 1 Lloyd's Rep 485 at 492.

[248] *Amoco (UK) Exploration Co v British American Offshore Ltd* [1999] 2 Lloyd's Rep 772 at 779.

[249] The term "contract" refers to the English concept of a contract: *Youell v Kara Mara Shipping Co* [2000] 2 Lloyd's Rep 102.

[250] CPR, r 6.20(7); discussed infra, p 384.

since this involves a claim to be released from proceedings, not a claim for a substantive right.[251]

The four alternative cases specified in rule 6.20(5) are as follows:

(a) Where the contract[252] "was made within the jurisdiction".[253] In principle, the English rules on formation of a contract should be used to ascertain whether the contract was made within the jurisdiction since the place where a contract is made is a connecting factor and, as such, should be defined by English law.[254] However, there is authority which assumes that if a foreign law was applicable to the contract this will determine when and where the contract is made.[255] It is sufficient for this provision if the contract was substantially made within the jurisdiction.[256] In principle, it is possible to have a contract made in more than one country, such as where the parties' deliberately signed separate copies in different countries so as to avoid giving the other party an advantage in terms of where the contract was finalised.[257] If one of these countries is England, the terms of rule 6.20(5)(a) will be met. English law provides that in the case of a contract of employment the employer may be sued either in tort or for breach of contract if he neglects his implied duty to take reasonable care for the safety of the employee. If, therefore, the contract is made in England for employment abroad, or, indeed, if the contract is governed by English law,[258] the employee may invoke this part of the rule without being driven to rely on rule (8) given below which is confined to a tort where the damage was sustained, or resulted from an act committed, in England.[259]

(b) Where the contract "was made by or through an agent trading or residing within the jurisdiction".[260] This ground is applicable even though the agent has no authority to

---

[251] *Cool Carriers AB v HSBC Bank USA* [2001] 2 Lloyd's Rep 22.

[252] It is not enough that an earlier contract was so made if the latter contract does not give effect to the earlier one: *ABCI (Formerly Arab Business Consortium International Finance and Investment Co) v Banque Franco-Tunisienne* [2003] EWCA Civ 205 at [17], [2003] 2 Lloyd's Rep 146.

[253] CPR, r 6.20(5)(a); formerly Ord 11, r 1(1)(d)(i) RSC. Eg *Mackender v Feldia AG* [1967] 2 QB 590; *Aaronson Bros Ltd v Maderera del Tropico SA* [1967] 2 Lloyd's Rep 159; *Howard Houlder and Partners Ltd v Marine General Transporters Corpn, The Panaghia P* [1983] 2 Lloyd's Rep 653; *Bank of Baroda v Vysya Bank Ltd* [1994] 2 Lloyd's Rep 87 at 94; *Minories v Afribank* [1995] 1 Lloyd's Rep 134; *Kelly v Cruise Catering Ltd* [1994] 2 ILRM 394; *Bastone & Firminger Ltd v Nasima Enterprises (Nigeria) Ltd* [1996] CLC 1902; *Williams v Society of Lloyd's* [1994] 1 VR 274; *Saab v Saudi American Bank* [1999] 1 WLR 1861 at [6], CA; *Eastern Power Ltd v Azienda Comunale Energia e Ambiente* [2001] IL Pr 6, Ont CA; *Burrows v Jamaica Private Power Co Ltd* [2002] CLC 255; *ABCI (Formerly Arab Business Consortium International Finance and Investment Co) v Banque Franco-Tunisienne* [2003] EWCA Civ 205 at [23]–[27], [2003] 2 Lloyd's Rep 146. For criticism of this ground in the light of e-commerce see Fawcett, Harris and Bridge, paras 10.99–10.100; Hogan-Doran (2003) 77 ALJ 377.

[254] English law was applied in *Brinkibon Ltd v Stahag Stahl und Stahlwarenhandelsgesellschaft GmbH* [1983] 2 AC 34 but the question of which state's rules on formation should be applied was not in issue. See also *Eastern Power Ltd v Azienda Comunale Energia e Ambiente* [2001] IL Pr 6, Ont CA.

[255] *Marconi v PT Pan Indonesia Bank Ltd TBK* [2004] EWHC 129 (Comm), [2004] 1 Lloyd's Rep 594; affd [2005] EWCA Civ 422 at [70]–[71].

[256] *BP Exploration Co (Libya) Ltd v Hunt* [1976] 1 WLR 788 at 797–798.

[257] *Apple Corps Ltd v Apple Computer Inc* [2004] EWHC 768 (Ch), [2004] IL Pr 34.

[258] See (c) infra, p 381.

[259] *Matthews v Kuwait Bechtel Corpn* [1959] 2 QB 57.

[260] CPR, r 6.20 (5)(b); formerly Ord 11, r 1(1)(d)(ii) RSC; on which see, eg, *Gibbon v Commerz und Creditbank Aktiengesellschaft* [1958] 2 Lloyd's Rep 113; *Burrows v Jamaica Private Power Co Ltd* [2002] CLC 255; *Munchener Ruckversicherungs Gesellschaft v Commonwealth Insurance Co* [2004] EWHC 914 (Comm) at [21]

effect a completed contract. Thus in *National Mortgage and Agency Co of New Zealand Ltd v Gosselin*[261] the London agent of a Belgian firm, who was employed merely for the purpose of obtaining orders, sent the firm's price list to the plaintiff. The plaintiff gave an order which was forwarded by the agent and accepted through the post by the Belgian firm. It was held that the contract had been made "through" the agent, for, though the final acceptance did not lie with him, he had negotiated its terms. It is implicit that the agent is acting on behalf of the foreign defendant who is the principal.[262] The agent must not be acting as a broker on behalf of the claimant.[263]

(c) Where the contract[264] "is governed by English law".[265] Ascertainment of the governing law is a matter for the rules contained in the Rome Convention of 1980.[266] Rule 6.20(5)(c) presupposes that one law governs the whole of the contract.[267] Yet under the Rome Convention it is possible for different laws to govern different parts of the contract.[268] If the dispute only relates to part of the contract it should be enough that this part of the contract is governed by English law.

The court normally has only to reach a tentative or provisional conclusion that English law governs,[269] but this presupposes that there is room for further investigation of facts or law later on.[270] If the facts are before the court and not in dispute, a definite conclusion as to the applicable law should be reached at this jurisdictional stage of the action.[271]

---

and [24]; *Marconi v PT Pan Indonesia Bank Ltd TBK* [2004] EWHC 129 (Comm), [2004] 1 Lloyd's Rep 594; affd [2005] EWCA Civ 422 at [72]. Cf *Bank of Baroda v Vysya Bank Ltd* [1994] 2 Lloyd's Rep 87 at 96. See also *Commonwealth Bank of Australia v White* [1999] 2 VR 681 at 694–696. For service on the principal by means of serving the agent see CPR, r 6.16.

[261] (1922) 38 TLR 832, CA. See also *Citadel Insurance Co v Atlantic Union Insurance Co SA* [1982] 2 Lloyd's Rep 543, CA; *Lincoln National Life Insurance Co v Employers Reinsurance Corpn* [2002] EWHC 28, [2002] Lloyd's Rep IR 853.

[262] This was explicit in Ord 11, r 1(1)(d)(ii) RSC.

[263] *Gill and Duffus Landauer Ltd v London Export Corpn GmbH* [1982] 2 Lloyd's Rep 627. See also *Union International Insurance Co Ltd v Jubilee Insurance Co Ltd* [1991] 1 WLR 415.

[264] There must be a contract between the claimant and defendant: *The Flecha* [1999] 1 Lloyd's Rep 612—a bill of lading case.

[265] CPR, r 6.20(5)(c); formerly Ord 11, r 1(1)(d)(iii) RSC.

[266] Discussed infra, pp 667–764. See, eg, *PT Pan Indonesia Bank Ltd TBK v Marconi Communications International Ltd* [2005] EWCA Civ 422 at [39] where this was common ground; *Egon Oldendorff v Liberia Corpn* [1995] 2 Lloyd's Rep 64 at 68; *Marubeni Hong Kong and South China Ltd v Mongolian Government* [2002] 2 All ER (Comm) 873; appeal on a different issue dismissed [2005] EWCA Civ 395, [2005] 1 WLR 2497. See also *Samcrete Egypt Engineers and Contractors SAE v Land Rover Exports Ltd* [2001] EWCA Civ 2019, [2002] CLC 533 (*forum non conveniens*). For an argument that the traditional English rules on the proper law of the contract should apply see Morse [1994] LMCLQ 560 at 561–563, for a counter-argument see the 13th edn of this book, p 304. On the question whether the Court of Justice would accept a reference from the English courts in relation to the interpretation of the Rome Convention when it arises in the jurisdictional context, see infra, p 673.

[267] See *Armar Shipping Co Ltd v Caisse Algérienne d'Assurance et de Réassurance, The Armar* [1980] 2 Lloyd's Rep 450 at 456.

[268] Infra, pp 690–692.

[269] *Compañia Naviera Micro SA v Shipley International Inc, The Parouth* [1982] 2 Lloyd's Rep 351 at 354; *Mitsubishi Corpn v Aristidis Alafouzos* [1988] 1 Lloyd's Rep 191 at 193; *Attock Cement Co Ltd v Romanian Bank for Foreign Trade* [1989] 1 WLR 1147 at 1152–1156, CA; Collier [1990] CLJ 39; *Finnish Marine Insurance Co Ltd v Protective National Insurance Co* [1990] 1 QB 1078 at 1084.

[270] *E F Hutton & Co (London) Ltd v Mofarrij* [1989] 1 WLR 488 at 485, CA; *Islamic Arab Insurance Co v Saudi Egyptian American Reinsurance Co* [1987] 1 Lloyd's Rep 315 at 317, CA.

[271] *Ilyssia Cia Naviera SA v Ahmed Abdul Qawi Bamaodah, The Elli 2* [1985] 1 Lloyd's Rep 107 at 114, CA; *Enichem Anic Spa v Ampelos Shipping Co Ltd, The Delfini* [1988] 2 Lloyd's Rep 599 at 602–603; appeal on other

Whilst at one time the courts showed a considerable reluctance to exercise their discretion under this particular head,[272] this has been replaced by a neutral attitude.[273] The exercise of the discretion depends on the individual circumstances of the case.[274]

(d) Or where the contract[275] "contains a term to the effect that the court shall have jurisdiction to determine any claim in respect of the contract".[276] Where there is a jurisdiction clause providing for trial in England, this will often meet the requirements of Article 23 of the Brussels I Regulation[277] and jurisdiction will be allocated to the English courts by virtue of that provision.[278] Rule 6.20(5)(d) is concerned with the situation where Article 23 does not apply, for example because neither party to the jurisdiction agreement is domiciled in a European Community Member State. Under rule 6.20(5)(d) the idea is that the parties should be bound by the jurisdiction clause[279] to which they have agreed unless there is some strong reason to the contrary.[280] This provision encompasses not only clauses providing for the exclusive jurisdiction of the English courts but also clauses providing for the non-exclusive jurisdiction of the English courts (ie the parties are not precluded from commencing proceedings abroad). [281]

(6) Where "a claim is made in respect of [282] a breach of contract committed within the jurisdiction".[283] The claimant must establish a good arguable case as to the elements of

---

grounds dismissed [1990] 1 Lloyd's Rep 252; *Ophthalmic Innovations International (United Kingdom) Ltd v Ophthalmic Innovations International Inc* [2004] EWHC 2948 (Ch), [2005] IL Pr 10; *Chellaram v Chellaram (No 2)* [2002] EWHC 632 (Ch) at [136], [2002] 2 All ER 17; *Marubeni Hong Kong and South China Ltd v Mongolian Government* [2002] 2 All ER (Comm) 873 at [29]–[30]; appeal on a different issue dismissed [2005] EWCA Civ 395, [2005] 1 WLR 2497.

[272] *Amin Rasheed Shipping Corpn v Kuwait Insurance Co*, supra, at 68 (per Lord DIPLOCK).

[273] *Spiliada Maritime Corpn v Cansulex Ltd* [1987] AC 460; following Lord WILBERFORCE in the *Amin Rasheed* case at 72.

[274] *Spiliada Maritime*, supra, at 481–482; see infra, pp 401–402.

[275] There must be a contract between the claimant and defendant: *The Flecha* [1999] 1 Lloyd's Rep 612—a bill of lading case. See also *ABCI (Formerly Arab Business Consortium International Finance and Investment Co) v Banque Franco-Tunisienne* [2003] EWCA Civ 205 at [17], [2003] 2 Lloyd's Rep 146—no jurisdiction over settlement agreement merely because a share subscription agreement contained a jurisdiction clause.

[276] CPR, r 6.20(5)(d); formerly Ord 11, r 1(1)(d)(iv) RSC. On the question of the law to be applied in order to determine whether the contract contains such a term see Art 8 of the Rome Convention, discussed infra, pp 744–746.

[277] Discussed supra, pp 283–296.

[278] For a case that appears to have ignored this point see *OT Africa Line Ltd v Magic Sportwear Corpn* [2006] EWCA Civ 710, [2005] 2 Lloyd's Rep 170.

[279] This can take an indirect form, see *Bhatia Shipping v Alcobex Metals* [2004] EWHC 2323 (Comm) at [17], [2005] 2 Lloyd's Rep 336—agreement on jurisdiction in the place of delivery of goods.

[280] *Unterweser Reederei GmbH v Zapata Off-Shore Co, The Chaparral* [1968] 2 Lloyd's Rep 158; *Citi-March v Ltd v Neptune Orient Lines Ltd* [1997] 1 Lloyd's Rep 72. See also the discussion of *forum conveniens* infra, pp 402–404, and of *forum non conveniens*, infra, pp 431–432. When proceedings were brought before the US courts an injunction was, originally, granted enjoining the parties from proceeding in England, but the US Supreme Court ruled that the English jurisdiction clause should be enforced unless such enforcement would be unreasonable or unjust: *The Chaparral* [1972] 2 Lloyd's Rep 315.

[281] *Gulf Bank KSC v Mitsubishi Heavy Industries Ltd* [1994] 1 Lloyd's Rep 323; *Standard Steamship Owners' Protection and Indemnity v Gann* [1992] 2 Lloyd's Rep 528; Fawcett [2001] LMCLQ 234, 244–245.

[282] See *GAF Corpn v Amchem Products Inc* [1975] 1 Lloyd's Rep 601 at 605–606. Restitutionary claims based on unjust enrichment arising in the context of a contract should fall outside this ground: see Fawcett, Harris and Bridge, para 8.83 but cf the case on the outmoded concept of quasi-contract of *McFee Engineering Pty Ltd v CBS Construction Pty Ltd* (1980) 44 FLR 340.

[283] CPR, r 6.20(6); formerly Ord 11, r 1(1)(e) RSC. *Citadel Insurance Co v Atlantic Union Insurance Co SA* [1982] 2 Lloyd's Rep 543; *Cantieri Navali Riuniti SpA v NV Omne Justitia. The Stolt Marmaro* [1985] 2 Lloyd's

contract, breach and place of breach. But if the central issue to be tried is as to whether there was a contract at all, the court must be careful not to give the appearance of pre-try-ing this issue, whilst at the same time carefully scrutinising whether there was a breach committed within the jurisdiction.[284] This provision can apply in the situation where there are distinguishable and independent obligations, some of which have a place of performance within the jurisdiction and others of which have a place of performance outside the jurisdiction.[285] But what of the position where the obligations are not inde-pendent of each other? *Johnson v Taylor Bros & Co Ltd*[286] was such a case.

> Swedish sellers failed to ship goods that they had sold to English buyers under a contract cif Leeds. The shippers failed both to deliver the shipping documents and to ship the goods. The obligations are linked for if the goods have not been shipped, the shipping documents will never have come into existence. The former breach occurred in England but the latter occurred in Stockholm.

The English courts should be regarded as having jurisdiction under rule 6.20(6) for breach of the obligation to deliver the shipping documents on the basis that the shippers failed to deliver these in England. The wording of the predecessor of this provision was amended[287] to specify that it applied irrespective of whether some other breach was com-mitted out of the jurisdiction,[288] thereby ensuring that this situation came within the breach ground. It was considered unnecessary to retain this additional wording in rule 6.20. It has been argued that this turns the clock back so that the breach ground does not apply where, although there was a breach committed within the jurisdiction, the sub-stantial breach was committed out of the jurisdiction.[289] But this change was one of the minor drafting changes introduced by the Civil Procedure Rules, designed to produce a list of grounds for service out of the jurisdiction which was clearer and simpler than its predecessor and was not intended to have any substantive effect on the court's powers.[290] Permission cannot be granted under this ground unless three conditions are fulfilled: the alleged contract must in fact have been made; it must have been broken; and the breach

---

Rep 428; *Banque Paribas v Cargill International SA* [1992] 2 Lloyd's Rep 19 at 23, CA; *Agrafax Public Relations Ltd v United Scottish Society Inc* [1995] IL Pr 753, CA; *Marconi v PT Pan Indonesia Bank Ltd TBK* [2004] EWHC 129 (Comm), [2004] 1 Lloyd's Rep 594; affd [2005] EWCA Civ 422 at [73]. See also *Analog Devices BV v Zurich Insurance Co* [2002] 2 ILRM 366, SC of Ireland. For the application of this ground in cases of international sale of goods see Fawcett, Harris and Bridge, para 4.51–4.89.

[284] *Canada Trust Co v Stolzenberg (No 2)* [1998] 1 WLR 547 at 555–556 (per WALLER LJ), approved by HL [2002] 1 AC 1 at 13 (per Lord STEYN with whom the other Law Lords agreed).

[285] *Rein v Stein* [1892] 1 QB 753 at 757 (per LINDLEY LJ), CA. See also *Robey v Snaefell Mining Co* (1887) 20 QBD 152; *The Eider* [1893] P 119 at 126 (per the President, Sir Francis H JEUNE), at 126.

[286] [1920] AC 144.

[287] This was because the House of Lords in the *Johnson* case, which was faced with a differently worded breach provision, refused permission for service of process out of the jurisdiction on the basis that, although the failure to deliver the shipping documents represented a breach in England, the substantial breach was the non-shipment of the goods at Stockholm.

[288] Ord 11, r 1(1)(e) RSC said "and irrespective of the fact, if such be the case, that the breach was preceded or accompanied by a breach committed out of the jurisdiction that rendered impossible the performance of so much of the contract as ought to have been performed within the jurisdiction".

[289] See the argument of counsel in *Network Telecom (Europe) Ltd v Telephone Systems International Inc* [2003] EWHC 2890 (QB), [2004] 1 All ER (Comm) 418 at [101]–[103]—the court did not decide the point.

[290] See the Lord Chancellor's Department Consultation Paper on the Civil Procedure Rules—Service of Court Process Abroad, para 23.

must have occurred in England. If the breach involves a failure to perform, it is necessary to look at where the performance was to take place.[291] It has been held that the court in its discretion may grant permission where the claimant seeks an account against a person abroad, despite the fact that usually the foreign forum is the most convenient place for the production of the relevant books and documents.[292]

(7) Where "a claim is made for a declaration that no contract exists where, if the contract was found to exist, it would comply with the conditions set out in paragraph (5)".[293] This is a new ground of jurisdiction, added by the Civil Procedure Rules, which makes it clear that rule 20.6(5) applies where there is a claim for a negative declaration that no contract exists.[294] This ensures that the position under the traditional rules on jurisdiction[295] is the same as that under the Brussels I Regulation.[296] Rule 6.20(7) does not cover a claim made for a declaration of non-liability.

(iv) Claims in tort

(8) Where "a claim is made in tort where (a) damage was sustained within the jurisdiction; or (b) the damage sustained resulted from an act committed within the jurisdiction".[297] A claim is "made" in tort when it is founded (ie based) on a tort,[298] ie there must be liability under English or foreign law which is to be classified as being tortious.[299] If the claim is founded on what is, in English law, a tort then clearly it should be classified as tortious for jurisdictional purposes.[300] This encompasses the situation where the claimant relies on the English law of tort or on a foreign cause of action that is known to English law, such as negligence under New York law. However, the introduction of statutory tort choice of law rules, and now European Community choice of law rules for non-contractual obligations, means that the English courts will now be faced with actions for invasion of privacy under French law and the like.[301] With a cause of action like this,

---

[291] See *Brinkibon Ltd v Stahag Stahl und Stahlwarenhandelsgesellschaft GmbH* [1983] 2 AC 34, 49–50, HL; *Gill and Duffus Landauer Ltd v London Export Corpn GmbH* [1982] 2 Lloyd's Rep 627, 630.

[292] *International Corpn Ltd v Besser Manufacturing Co* [1950] 1 KB 488.

[293] CPR, r 6.20(7).

[294] See the Lord Chancellor's Department Consultation Paper on the Civil Procedure Rules—Service of Court Process Abroad, para 21.

[295] The position previously was unclear. Cf *Finnish Marine Insurance Co Ltd v Protective National Insurance Co* [1990] 1 QB 1078—not within the contract head, with *DR Insurance Co v Central National Insurance Co* [1996] 1 Lloyd's Rep 74—within the head if agreement entered into with intent to create legal relations.

[296] For the use of Art 5(1) of the Brussels Convention to take jurisdiction to grant a negative declaration that no contract existed, see *Boss Group Ltd v Boss France SA* [1997] 1 WLR 351, CA.

[297] CPR, r 6.20(8); formerly Ord 11, r 1(1)(f) RSC.

[298] Ord 11, r 1(1)(f) RSC so provided. The change in wording in r 6.20(8) doubtless simply reflects the desire for simpler and clearer grounds. Claims founded on a constructive trust do not come within this ground: *Metall und Rohstoff AG v Donaldson Lufkin and Jenrette Inc* [1990] 1 QB 391 at 474; overruled on a different point in *Lonrho plc v Fayed* [1992] 1 AC 448, HL; *Nycal (UK) Ltd v Lacey* [1994] CLC 12. See also *ISC v Guerin* [1992] 2 Lloyd's Rep 430—equitable restitutionary remedies for breach of trust or fiduciary duty held to be not founded on a tort. It would include a claim for restitution for tortious wrongdoing but not if it is based on unjust enrichment, see Fawcett, Harris and Bridge, para 8.87–88, 8.93; Briggs in Rose (ed), *Restitution and the Conflict of Laws*, pp 57–60. It also includes a claim by a tortfeasor for contribution under a statute: *FFSB Ltd v Seward & Kissel LLP* [2007] UKPC 16.

[299] *OT Africa Line Ltd v Magic Sportswear Corpn* [2004] EWHC 2441 (Comm) at [24], [2005] 1 Lloyd's Rep 252; appeal dismissed without discussion of this point [2005] EWCA Civ 710, [2005] 2 Lloyd's Rep 170.

[300] See *Metall und Rohstoff AG v Donaldson Lufkin and Jenrette Inc* [1990] 1 QB 391 at 449, CA; overruled on a different point in *Lonrho plc v Fayed* [1992] 1 AC 448.

[301] Infra, p 766 et seq.

unknown to English law, how are the courts to determine whether the claim is founded on a tort?[302] The fact that the foreign state whose law is relied upon regards the cause of action as tortious (or delictual) should be regarded as persuasive evidence of this; the case for this becomes even stronger if it can be shown generally that other countries that have this cause of action also adopt this characterisation.[303]

Rule 6.20(8) makes it clear that jurisdiction can be taken in England if *either* the damage was sustained[304] *or* the damage resulted from an act committed in England.[305] The result is to make the tort head a very wide one,[306] and to bring tort cases under rule 6.20 into line with tort cases under the jurisdiction rules to be found under the Brussels/Lugano system.[307] By using the tort provision under that system as the model for rule 6.20(8), not only are the virtues of the former (its width and clarity) incorporated into rule 6.20, but also its weaknesses. Thus it is not appropriately worded to deal with cases of libel, since these do not require proof of *damage* to be actionable; nor does it solve all the definitional problems that can arise. Before turning to examine these definitional problems, it should be pointed out that rule 6.20(8) does not on its wording appear to cover injunctions to restrain threatened wrongs.[308] This reflects the fact that rule 6.20(8) is based on the Brussels Convention,[309] rather than on the more recent Brussels I Regulation, which has additional wording to make it clear that the tort provision applies to threatened wrongs.[310]

Damage was sustained within the jurisdiction   There can be problems over whether the damage is sustained in England. If the act and injury take place in State A, but the claimant is hospitalised in State B, is damage sustained there?[311] This raises the question

---

[302] See generally Harris (1998) 61 MLR 33.

[303] Cf the position under the Rome II Regulation, infra, p 790 et seq.

[304] See, eg, *Short v Ireland* [1997] 1 ILRM 161.

[305] This avoids the definitional problem encountered under a predecessor provision, which referred to "a tort committed within the jurisdiction"; see *Distillers Co (Biochemicals) Ltd v Thompson* [1971] AC 458. The problem of where a tort is committed can still arise in the context of jurisdiction (infra, pp 387–389), as well as that of choice of law (infra, pp 869–872). Cf Kaye in McLean (ed), *Compensation for Damage: An International Perspective*, Chapter 8 1993. This old test is still used in the Bahamas, see *FFSB Ltd v Seward & Kissel LLP* [2007] UKPC 16.

[306] But for examples which do not come within either, see *ABCI v BFT* [1997] 1 Lloyd's Rep 531, CA; *Shahar v Tsitsekkos* [2004] EWHC 2659 (Ch) at [35]–[40].

[307] See Art 5(3) of the Brussels I Regulation, Brussels and Lugano Conventions; Case 21/76 *Bier v Mines de Potasse* [1978] QB 708, supra, pp 253–258.

[308] But see to the contrary *Beecham Group plc v Norton Healthcare Ltd* [1997] FSR 81 at 97. CPR, r 6.20(2) may, however, be applicable; see *James North and Sons Ltd v North Cape Textiles Ltd* [1984] 1 WLR 1428 at 1431, supra, p 374. It is also possible to use s 25 of the Civil Jurisdiction and Judgments Acts 1982, supra, p 378, to grant an interim injunction to prevent a threatened wrong in England.

[309] But Art 5(3) of the Brussels Convention has been interpreted to cover threatened wrongs, see Case C–167/00 *Verein v Henkel* [2002] ECR I–8111; Case C–18/02 *DFDS Torline v SEKO* [2004] ECR I–1417.

[310] Supra, p 252.

[311] In favour of an affirmative answer see *Booth v Phillips* [2004] EWHC 1437 at [33]–[47], [2004] 1 WLR 3293. For Canadian support see: *Vile v Von Wendt Zurich Insurance Co* (1979) 103 DLR (3d) 356. See also in Canada (a significant connection under the real and substantial connection test): *Duncan v Neptunia Corpn* (2001) 199 DLR (4th) 354; *Muscutt v Courcelles* (2002) 213 DLR (4th) 577, Ont CA; *Doiron v Bugge* (2005) 258 DLR (4th) 716, Ont CA. But for a denial of jurisdiction in international cases (where it is more difficult to justify jurisdiction) as not satisfying the real and substantial connection test: see *Leufkens v Alba Tours International Inc* (2002) 213 DLR (4th) 614, Ont CA; *Lemmex v Bernard* (2002) 213 DLR (4th) 627, Ont CA; *Sinclair v Cracker Barrel Old Country Store Inc* (2002) 213 DLR (4th) 643, Ont CA; *Gajraj v DeBernardo* (2002) 213 DLR (4th) 651, Ont CA; distinguished in *Doiron*. Cf for inter-provincial cases (satisfying this test) the *Muscutt* case;

whether the damage caused must be direct or whether it can include indirect damage. The better view is that damage refers to the direct damage sounding in monetary terms which the wrongful act produced upon the claimant.[312] This is the same definition of damage as that applied by the European Court for the purposes of Article 5(3) of the Brussels I Regulation. The adoption of this European Community definition for the purposes of service out of the jurisdiction[313] acknowledges the fact that the tort ground for service out of the jurisdiction was reworded to align with Article 5(3).[314] If a widow sues in her own right for loss of dependency the damage will be direct and located where she lives, rather than where her husband was killed abroad.[315] If a libel is published in England and the claimant has a reputation in England it is accepted that rule 6.20 (8) will apply.[316] This is on the basis that significant damage to reputation was sustained within the jurisdiction.[317] As regards libel over the internet, where the libel is contained in text which is uploaded[318] abroad and downloaded[319] in England, publication takes place in England.[320]

Damage to the claimant might have been suffered in more than one country, particularly in a case involving an economic tort. The Court of Appeal in *Metall und Rohstoff AG v Donaldson Lufkin and Jenrette Inc*[321] held that it is not necessary that all the damage has been sustained within the jurisdiction; it is "enough if some significant damage has been

---

Touchburn v O'Brien (2002) 210 DLR (4th) 668, Novia Scotia CA. For Australian support see *Thomas v Penna* [1985] 2 NSWLR 171, but now see *Flaherty v Girgis* (1987) 71 ALR 1, High Court of Australia.

[312] *ABCI (Formerly Arab Business Consortium International Finance and Investment Co) v Banque Franco-Tunisienne* [2003] EWCA Civ 205 at [44], [2003] 2 Lloyd's Rep 146; *Beecham Group plc v Norton Healthcare Ltd* [1997] FSR 81 at 97–98; *Bastone & Firminger Ltd v Nasima Enterprises (Nigeria) Ltd* [1996] CLC 1902; *Newsat Holdings Ltd v Zani* [2006] EWHC 342 (Comm) at [46]–[49], [2006] 1 Lloyd's Rep 707. There is also Canadian authority in favour of a direct damage rule in *National Bank of Canada v Clifford Chance* (1996) 30 OR (3d) 746. But cf *Barings plc v Coopers & Lybrand (A Firm)* [1997] IL Pr 12 at 24–25, affd by CA, [1997] IL Pr 576 at 585; *Booth v Phillips*, supra; *Baxter v RMC Group plc* [2003] 1 NZLR 304, 316.

[313] *ABCI (Formerly Arab Business Consortium International Finance and Investment Co) v Banque Franco-Tunisienne* [2003] EWCA Civ 205 at [44], [2003] 2 Lloyd's Rep 146 at [44]. See also Rix J in the *Bastone* case, supra, at 1912, who quoted in support of the direct damage principle a decision of the Court of Justice on the meaning of damage for the purposes of Art 5(3) of the Brussels Convention; and to the same effect *Newsat Holdings Ltd v Zani* [2006] EWHC 342 (Comm) at [46]–[49], [2006] 1 Lloyd's Rep 707.

[314] *ABCI (Formerly Arab Business Consortium International Finance and Investment Co) v Banque Franco-Tunisienne* [2003] EWCA Civ 205 at [43], [2003] 2 Lloyd's Rep 146.

[315] *Booth v Phillips*, supra, at [45], which is correct on this point.

[316] *King v Lewis* [2004] EWCA (Civ) 1329, [2005] IL Pr 16; *Dow Jones & Co Inc v Jameel* [2005] EWCA (Civ) 75 at [49], [2005] QB 946.

[317] In *Berezovsky v Michaels* [2000] 1 WLR 1004, HL, it was accepted by counsel that the tort ground of service out (at that time Ord 11, r 1(1)(f) RSC) was satisfied because significant damage (to the claimants' reputations in England) was sustained in England. See also *Dow Jones & Co Inc v Gutnick* (2002) 210 CLR 575 at [46], HC of Australia; discussed infra, p 389.

[318] Ie the information is made available over the internet by placing it in a storage area managed by a web-server.

[319] On to the computer of a person who has used a web-browser to pull the material from the web-server.

[320] *Godfrey v Demon Internet Ltd* [2001] QB 201 at 208–209; *Loutchansky v Times Newspapers Ltd* [2001] EWCA Civ 1805 at [58], [2002] QB 783; *King v Lewis*, supra, where this was common ground; *Dow Jones & Co Inc v Jameel* [2005] EWCA (Civ) 75 at [48]–[49], [2005] QB 946; *Dow Jones & Co Inc v Gutnick* (2002) 210 CLR 575, HC of Australia; discussed infra, p 389. For Canada see *Bangoura v Washington Post* (2004) 258 DLR (4th) 341; and for New Zealand *Nationwide News Pty v University of Newlands* CA, 9 December 2005. See also *Ashton Investments Ltd v OJSC Russian Aluminium RUSAL* [2006] EWHC 2545 (Comm) at [62], [2007] 1 Lloyd's Rep 311, damage in England by hacking (from Russia) into a server in England.

[321] [1990] 1 QB 391; overruled on a different point in *Lonrho plc v Fayed* [1992] 1 AC 448.

sustained in England".[322] "Damage" can include the situation where the acts of the defendant expose the claimant to claims by others which are pursued in England, and if successful will result in judgment against the claimant.[323] But in a case of financial loss it is not enough to show that a company has its seat in England.[324]

An act committed within the jurisdiction[325]   The tortious act from which the damage resulted may have been committed partly within the jurisdiction and partly without. According to the Court of Appeal in the *Metall und Rohstoff* case,[326] it is not necessary that all of the acts have been committed within the jurisdiction. It is enough if "substantial and efficacious acts" have been committed within the jurisdiction, even if substantial and efficacious acts have also been committed outside the jurisdiction. In determining where a tortious act was committed, regard should be had to the case law identifying the place of the event giving rise to the damage for the purpose of Article 5(3) of the Brussels I Regulation or the earlier Brussels Convention.[327] It follows that, in a case of negligent or fraudulent misrepresentation, the damage sustained resulted from an act committed within the jurisdiction if the misstatement was made in England, rather than being received in England.[328]

Exercise of the discretion   The courts showed a distinct willingness to exercise their discretion to allow service out of the jurisdiction under the predecessor to rule 6.20(8). The House of Lords in *Berezovsky v Michaels*[329] followed earlier Court of Appeal cases[330] in holding that, when exercising the *forum conveniens* discretion, regard is to be had to the principle that the jurisdiction in which a tort was committed is prima facie the natural

---

[322] Ibid, at 437. See also *Morin v Bonhams & Brooks Ltd* [2003] EWHC 467 (Comm) at [61], [2003] I L Pr 25. The Court of Appeal affirmed the decision at first instance that Monegasque law governed the tort claim [2003] EWCA Civ 1802, [2004] 1 Lloyd's Rep 702. See also *Jones v Ministry of the Interior of the Kingdom of Saudi Arabia* [2005] QB 699 at [29], CA—psychological damage in England after torture abroad; reversed without discussion of this point, [2006] UKHL 26, [2007] 1 AC 270.

[323] *The Eras Eil Actions* [1992] 1 Lloyd's Rep 570. For another example of damage, see *Crédit Agricole Indosuez v Unicof Ltd* [2003] EWHC 2676 (Comm) at [20], [2004] 1 Lloyd's Rep 196.

[324] The *Eras Eil Actions*, supra. See also *Deuruneft v Bullen* [2004] 1 WWR 535 at [51]–[60].

[325] See, eg, *Saab v Saudi American Bank* [1999] 1 WLR 1861 at [6], CA.

[326] Supra. See also *Grupo Torras SA and Torras Hostench London Ltd v Sheikh Fahad Mohammed Al-Sabah* [1995] 1 Lloyd's Rep 374 at 450, appeals to CA dismissed without discussion of this point [1996] 1 Lloyd's Rep 7, CA; *Morin v Bonhams & Brooks Ltd* [2003] EWHC 467 (Comm) at [61], [2003] IL Pr 25, the Court of Appeal affirmed the decision at first instance that Monegasque law governed the tort claim [2003] EWCA Civ 1802, [2004] 1 Lloyd's Rep 702; *Ashton Investments Ltd v OJSC Russian Aluminium RUSAL* [2006] EWHC 2545 (Comm) at [63], [2007] 1 Lloyd's Rep 311.

[327] See *ABCI (Formerly Arab Business Consortium International Finance and Investment Co) v Banque Franco-Tunisienne* [2003] EWCA Civ 205 at [41], [2003] 2 Lloyd's Rep 146. This case law is discussed supra, pp 254–256.

[328] *Newsat Holdings Ltd v Zani* [2006] EWHC 342 (Comm), [2006] 1 Lloyd's Rep 707.

[329] [2000] 1 WLR 1004, HL; Briggs (2000) 71 BYBIL 440; Hare [2000] CLJ 461; Harris (2000) 116 LQR 562. For other *forum conveniens* cases involving libel, see *Kroch v Rossell* [1937] 1 All ER 725, CA; *Schapira v Ahronson* [1998] IL Pr 587, CA; *Chadha v Dow Jones & Co Inc* [1999] IL Pr 829, CA; *Reuben v Time Inc* [2003] EWHC 1430 QB and, earlier, *Reuben v Time Inc* [2003] EWCA Civ 06 at [14]; *Harrods Ltd v Dow Jones & Co Inc* [2003] EWHC 1162 (QB). See more generally *Markel International Insurance Co Ltd v La República Compañía Argentina de Seguros Generales SA* [2004] EWHC 1826 (Comm) at [29]; [2005] Lloyd's Rep IR 90 QBD (Comm).

[330] *Cordoba Shipping Co Ltd v National State Bank, Elizabeth, New Jersey, The Albaforth* [1984] 2 Lloyd's Rep 91; Fawcett [1985] LMCLQ 6; Carter (1984) 55 BYBIL 347; *AG v Donaldson Lufkin and Jenrette Inc* [1990] 1 QB 391 at 484. See also *ISC v Guerin* [1992] 2 Lloyd's Rep 430 at 435; *The Xin Yang* [1996] 2 Lloyd's Rep 217 at 223, CA; *International Marine Services Inc v National Bank of Fujairah* [1997] IL Pr 468 at 470, CA.

forum for the determination of the dispute.[331] Two Russian businessmen alleged that they were libelled by the editor and publishers of an American business magazine and claimed damages in England restricted to the injury to their reputations in England. There was publication of the libel in England because of the distribution of copies of the magazine there. This publication constituted a separate tort which was committed in England.[332] This meant that England was prima facie the natural forum for trial. The number of copies distributed in England (some 1,900 compared to over 785,000 in the USA and Canada) was said to be significant.[333] This was important because the tort committed within the jurisdiction must be substantial.[334] Moreover, on conventional *Spiliada* principles the claimants had significant connections with England and reputations to protect in England.[335] It was also highly relevant that the claimants were only seeking damages for the loss of their reputation *in England*.[336] Trial in Russsia would not redress damage to the plaintiffs' reputation in England.[337] In contrast, if the plaintiffs had had a reputation in the USA and were suing for damage to that reputation, this would point to trial in the USA. The majority[338] concluded that England was the appropriate forum for trial. In contrast, if publication takes place abroad there will be considerable difficulty in persuading the court to permit service out of the jurisdiction.[339]

The House of Lords in *Berezovsky* examined the relationship between the natural forum principle and the *forum conveniens* test laid down in the *Spiliada* case. All the Law Lords agreed that the two were consistent with each other.[340] Lord STEYN went on to explain that the former went to the weight of evidence.[341] The latter was concerned with a high level of generality and the former with a much lower level of generality. Lord HOPE added that the natural forum principle was no more than a starting point for identification of the most appropriate forum.[342] This idea has been repeated by the Court of Appeal in *King v Lewis*.[343] This subtle shift in emphasis has the potential for the presumption becoming a weak one. Lord Hope dissented from the majority on the question whether England was the clearly appropriate forum (ie in his view the presumption was rebutted).

---

[331] But cf for Australia *BHP Billiton Ltd v Schultz* (2004) 221 CLR 400 at [18] (per GLEESON CJ, McHUGH and HEYDON JJ, HC of Australia). CALLINAN J at [259] adopts the same principle as in *Berezovsky*.

[332] In the House of Lords, it was accepted by counsel that the tort ground of service out (at that time Ord 11, r 1(1)(f) RSC) was satisfied because significant damage (to their reputations in England) was sustained in England.

[333] The *Berezovsky* case, supra, at 1013 (per Lord STEYN), 1033 (per Lord HOBHOUSE).

[334] Ibid, at 1014 (per Lord STEYN), 1033 (per Lord HOBHOUSE), following *Kroch v Rossell* [1937] 1 All ER 725, CA. See also *Reuben v Time Inc* [2003] EWHC 1430 QB at [53]—over 13,000 copies. Cf *Dow Jones & Co Inc v Jameel* [2005] EWCA (Civ) 75 at [70], [2005] QB 946; Briggs (2005) 76 BYBIL 668, service set aside where only 5 subscribers in England accessed the offending text. See also *Al Amoudi v Brisard* [2006] EWHC 1062 (QB).

[335] The *Berezovsky* case, supra, at 1014 (per Lord STEYN), 1033 (per Lord HOBHOUSE), 1016 (per Lord NOLAN).

[336] Ibid, at 1017 (per Lord NOLAN), 1014–1015 (per Lord STEYN), 1033 (per Lord HOBHOUSE).

[337] Ibid, at 1014–1015 (per Lord STEYN), 1033 (per Lord HOBHOUSE).

[338] Lords STEYN, NOLAN, and HOBHOUSE. Lords HOFFMANN and HOPE dissenting.

[339] *Reuben v Time Inc* [2003] EWCA Civ 06 at [14].

[340] The *Berezovsky* case, supra, at 1014 (per Lord STEYN), 1033 (per Lord HOBHOUSE), 1017 (per Lord NOLAN), 1019–1021 (per Lord HOFFMANN), 1030–1032 (per Lord HOPE).

[341] Ibid, at 1014; at 1033 (per Lord HOBHOUSE).

[342] Ibid, at 1032.

[343] [2004] EWCA (Civ) 1329 at [26], [2005] IL Pr 16; Briggs (2004) 75 BYBIL 565. See also *Richardson v Schwarzenegger* [2004] EWHC 2422 (QB); Briggs (2004) 75 BYBIL 565 at 570.

However, this appears to be because he disagreed with the majority finding that the claimants had significant connections with England.[344] Lord HOPE's judgment, and other case law on international libel,[345] has led the Court of Appeal in *King v Lewis* to state the following general proposition for such cases. The more tenuous the claimant's connection with England (and the more substantial any publication abroad) the weaker the consideration that England is the natural forum becomes.[346] With transnational libels (ie publication in many different States), including internet torts, the global picture has to be considered.[347] With such libels the place where the tort is committed ceases to be very meaningful.[348]

This natural forum principle requires the court to ascertain where a tort is committed. Whilst it is easy enough to state and apply the rule as to where the tort of defamation is committed, namely where the defamation is published,[349] it is by no means always easy to state or apply the rule as to where many other torts are committed.[350] The identification of the place where a tort is committed when this has occurred over the internet is particularly problematic,[351] even for defamation. In *Dow Jones & Co Inc v Gutnick* [352] the High Court of Australia held that ordinarily the place where the tort of defamation is committed is where the material alleged to be defamatory is downloaded on to the computer of a person who has used a web-browser to pull the material from the web-server. This was preferred to the place of uploading (ie the place where information is made available over the internet by placing it in a storage area managed by a web-server).[353] In England, it is well established that a libel is committed where publication takes place and that a text on the internet is published at the place where it is downloaded.[354] The Court of Appeal in

---

[344] [2000] 1 WLR 1004, 1032-1033. See also the dissent of Lord HOFFMANN at 1023–1024.

[345] In particular *Chadha v Dow Jones & Co Inc* [1999] IL Pr 829, CA.

[346] *King v Lewis*, supra, at [27]. See also *Richardson v Schwarzenegger* [2004] EWHC 2422 (QB) at [23].

[347] *King v Lewis*, supra, at [28], following Lord Steyn in the *Berezovsky* case, supra, at 1012.

[348] The *King* case, supra. Two other propositions (in relation to internet torts and juridical advantages) are discussed infra, pp 389–390.

[349] On the facts of the *Berezovsky* case, all the constituent elements of the tort were said to have occurred in England, per Lord STEYN at 1013, and so there was no difficulty over where the tort was committed. See also *Reuben v Time Inc* [2003] EWCA Civ 06 at [14]; *King v Lewis*, supra, at [27]. For Canada see *Direct Energy Marketing Ltd v Hillson* [2000] IL Pr 102, 114–115.

[350] See generally the cases decided under the old tort head of Ord 11, r 1(1) which required that a tort was committed within the jurisdiction: *Distillers v Thompson* [1971] AC 458; *Diamond v Bank of London and Montreal* [1979] QB 333; *Castree v Squibb* [1980] 1 WLR 1248; the *Cordoba* case, supra. See also the identification of the place of the tort under the common law tort choice of law rules discussed infra, pp 767 and 871–872. See for an example of the difficulty, the position in relation to negligent misstatements and negligent and fraudulent misrepresentations discussed in Fawcett, Harris and Bridge, paras 6.110–6.113. For fraudulent conspiracy see *ABCI (Formerly Arab Business Consortium International Finance and Investment Co) v Banque Franco-Tunisienne* [2003] EWCA Civ 205 at [41], [2003] 2 Lloyd's Rep 146.

[351] See, eg, *Bonnier Media Ltd v Greg Lloyd Smith and Kestrel Trading Corpn* [2002] ETMR 86 (trade mark infringement and passing off) and more generally Fawcett, Harris and Bridge, paras 10.169 (defamation); 10.185 (negligent misstatement); 10.198 (conversion); 10.212 (inducement of breach of contract); 10.220 (negligence).

[352] (2002) 210 CLR 575, HC of Australia; Briggs (2003) 119 LQR 210; Kohl (2003) 52 ICLQ 1049; Rolph (2002) 24 Sydney LR 263; Fitzgerald (2003) 27 Melbourne ULR 590.

[353] Ibid.

[354] *Godfrey v Demon Internet Ltd* [2001] QB 201, 208–209; *Loutchansky v Times Newspapers Ltd* [2002] QB 783 at [58], CA; *Harrods Ltd v Dow Jones & Co Inc* [2003] EWHC 1162 (QB) at [36]; *King v Lewis*, supra (this was accepted by the parties); *Richardson v Schwarzenegger* [2004] EWHC 2422 (QB) at [19]; *Dow Jones & Co Inc v Jameel* [2005] EWCA (Civ) 75 at [48]–[49], [2005] QB 946. See also Lord HOFFMANN in the *Berezovsky* case, supra, at 1024.

King v Lewis[355] said that a publisher who chooses the internet, which is a global medium, cannot be too fastidious about the part of the world where he is made a libel defendant.[356] The Court rejected the notion that the court should be more ready to stay proceedings where the defendants did not target their publications towards the jurisdiction in which they have been sued.[357] It was pointed out that a defendant targets every jurisdiction in which his text may be downloaded. But this is too simplistic an approach. It is questionable whether the same attitude should be adopted where it is not a commercial on-line publisher (who could equally well publish in conventional form abroad, and would then be subject to jurisdiction there, as on-line) but instead a private individual who is not out to make a profit and has no subscribers. Moreover, there are situations where the defendant commercial on-line publisher may not reasonably foresee the text being downloaded in England, such as where a defendant on-line publisher makes it clear that he will not contract with subscribers in England but an English resident lies or uses an anonymising technique to take out a subscription.[358] In such a case, the English courts should be willing to stay the action.

The natural forum principle was introduced at the time when service out of the jurisdiction in tort cases was based on the commission of a tort within the jurisdiction[359] and when the tort choice of law rules also required this place to be ascertained.[360] However, it makes less sense now that the tort ground does not seek to find a single place which is where the tort was committed but, instead, looks at both the place of damage and the place where the act from which the damage resulted was committed. Neither do the tort choice of law rules require this place to be ascertained,[361] apart from in cases of defamation,[362] where the old common law rules still operate. We would be better served not having presumptions when exercising a discretion and not having a principle that the jurisdiction in which a tort was committed is prima facie the natural forum for the dispute. Instead, what we should look at in tort cases is the law applicable to the tort,[363] which is the idea underlying the presumption.[364] If the law applicable to the tort is English law, this should be recognised as strong evidence in favour of England clearly being the appropriate forum for trial.[365] Let us take the example of a case where jurisdiction is based on damage sustained in England. Normally, the English court will then go on to apply English law. In a defamation case, if the tort is committed in England, English law will be applicable. In these situations there is a strong case for exercising the discretion in favour of allowing service out of the jurisdiction.

---

[355] Supra.

[356] Ibid, at [31].

[357] Ibid, at [34]–[35].

[358] See Fawcett, Harris and Bridge, para 10.15–10.16.

[359] *Cordoba Shipping Co Ltd v National State Bank, Elizabeth, New Jersey (The Albaforth)* [1984] 2 Lloyd's Rep 91, CA.

[360] The common law tort choice of law rules are discussed infra, pp 766–767.

[361] The statutory and EC tort choice of law rules are discussed infra, pp 766–869.

[362] See infra, pp 871–872.

[363] See *Ark v True North Capital* [2005] EWHC 1585 (Comm) at [68], [2006] 1 All ER (Comm) 138. It may be necesssary to ascertain this at the jurisdictional stage to show that there is a reasonable prospect of success, see the *Metall und Rohstoff* case, supra, and infra, p 399.

[364] See *Voth v Manildra Flour Mills Pty Ltd* (1990) 171 CLR 538 at 566 et seq, High Court of Australia.

[365] Ibid.

(v) Enforcement

(9) Where "a claim is made to enforce any judgment or arbitral award".[366] The identically worded predecessor of this ground was introduced in the light of the Civil Jurisdiction and Judgments Act 1982. The background to it is the rule that any action in England to enforce a foreign judgment at common law requires the English rules as to jurisdiction and service of claim forms to be satisfied.[367] If the claimant was unable to satisfy this requirement, he was always left with the option of bringing a new action on the original cause of action, with the possibility of using service out as the basis of jurisdiction. Section 34 of the Civil Jurisdiction and Judgments Act 1982 prevents the claimant from doing this,[368] hence the need for some basis for serving a claim form on a defendant in order to enforce the foreign judgment. Rule 6.20(9) provides the means for satisfying this requirement. The claimant must show a good arguable case that a judgment would be given in England based on the foreign judgment and ordinarily that he can reasonably expect a benefit from the English judgment.[369] However, there is no requirement under paragraph (9) that the defendant has assets in England.[370] Paragraph (9) also applies in respect of arbitral awards.[371] An action for a pre-judgment freezing injunction in support of foreign proceedings does not come within this provision.[372] A freezing injunction does not "enforce" anything and there is no "judgment" to be enforced.

(vi) Claims about property within the jurisdiction

(10) Where "the whole subject matter of a claim relates to property located within the jurisdiction".[373] This is a wholly new formulation, the purpose of which is to lay down a single rule in place of three earlier rules.[374] It embraces and extends beyond the contents of those rules.[375] In considering the application of this provision it is necessary to examine how the case was put, and what in substance it involved. [376]The elements of this ground for service out of the jurisdiction are as follows.

A claim This provision extends to any claim for relief, whether for damages or otherwise, so long as it is related to property located within the jurisdiction.[377] It cannot be

---

[366] CPR, r 6.20(9); formerly Ord 11, r 1(1)(m) RSC.

[367] *Perry v Zissis* [1977] 1 Lloyd's Rep 607, see infra, p 516.

[368] Infra, p 544.

[369] *Demirel v Tasarruff* [2007] EWCA Civ 799 at [29], [2007] 1 WLR 2508; leave to appeal to the House of Lords dismissed [2007] 1 WLR 3066.

[370] *Demirel v Tasarruff* [2007] EWCA Civ 799 at [10]–[25].

[371] However, it has been doubted whether committal proceedings to enforce a freezing injunction come within this head: *Mansour v Mansour* [1990] FCR 17, [1989] 1 FLR 418.

[372] *Mercedes-Benz AG v Leiduck* [1996] AC 284 at 298–299 (per Lord MUSTILL), PC.

[373] CPR, r 6.20(10).

[374] *Re Banco Nacional de Cuba* [2001] 1 WLR 2039, 1254, 1255.The case is also reported as *Banca Carige v BNC* [2001] 2 Lloyd's Rep 147. The three earlier rules are RSC, Ord 11, r 1(1)(g), (h), (i). These provided as follows: (g) the whole subject matter of the action is land situate within the jurisdiction (with or without rents or profits) or the perpetuation of testimony relating to land so situate; (h) the claim is brought to construe, rectify, set aside or enforce an act, deed, will, contract, obligation or liability affecting land situate within the jurisdiction; (i) the claim is made for a debt secured on immovable property or is made to assert, declare or determine proprietary or possessory rights, or rights of security, in or over *movable* property, or to obtain authority to dispose of *movable* property, situate within the jurisdiction.

[375] *Re Banco Nacional de Cuba*, supra, 2055.

[376] *Sahar v Tsitsekkos* [2004] EWHC 2659 (Ch) at [41]–[42]; *The Republic of Pakistan v Zardari* [2006] EWHC 2411 (Comm) at [157], [2006] 2 CLC 667.

[377] *Re Banco Nacional de Cuba*, supra, 2055.

construed as being confined to claims relating to the ownership or possession of property,[378] such as one for the recovery of land,[379] although these will commonly be the sort of claims where this ground will be invoked. Thus this provision applied where a declaration was sought that a transfer of shares constituted a transaction at an undervalue within the meaning of the Insolvency Act 1986.[380] It is enough that the claim relates to a transaction affecting the property, rather than as to the property or some interest therein. In principle therefore, it can extend to, for example, a claim for damages arising from a breach of contract or a tort relating to property located within the jurisdiction.

The whole subject matter of a claim If the subject matter of the claim relates to property in England and also to property abroad it cannot be said that "the whole subject matter" of the claim relates to property within the jurisdiction. On the other hand, if the claim is made solely in relation to that part of the property located in England then the ground will be satisfied.

Relates to A declaration sought about the disposition of shares "relates to" this property.[381] This phrase has been widely construed so that the claim does not have to have a direct effect on the property itself, its possession or title. If, for example, a buyer sues the seller for damages for breach of contract alleging that the goods situated in England are defective, the claim "relates to" property located within the jurisdiction.[382] This is because compensation is sought in respect of the diminished value of that property arising out of its defective state. A predecessor, and more restrictively worded, property ground[383] encompassed an action against the assignee of a lease for breach of covenant to repair,[384] a claim by a tenant of a farm to recover compensation for improvements,[385] and an action to enforce obligations under a declaration of trust in respect of land which had been sold at the time of the action.[386] These actions would all come within rule 6.20(10). An action for the recovery of rent[387] and one concerning royalties in respect of the production of oil[388] were not covered in the past[389] but would be now since they "relate to" property in the wide sense which has been given to this phrase.

Property This provision is not limited to land, but extends to personal property.[390] In conflict of laws terminology, this is not limited to immovable property but extends to movable property. This could be tangible movable property, such as physical goods, or intangible movable property, such as shares.[391] Property includes confidential

---

378 Ibid.
379 *Agnew v Usher* (1884) 14 QBD 78; affd 51 LT 752. This came within a predecessor of Ord 11, r 1(1)(g) RSC.
380 *Re Banco Nacional de Cuba*, supra.
381 *Re Banco Nacional de Cuba*, supra, 2056.
382 Ibid.
383 Ord 11, r 1(1)(h) and its predecessors.
384 *Tassell v Hallen* [1892] 1 QB 321.
385 *Kaye v Sutherland* (1887) 20 QBD 147.
386 *Official Solicitor v Stype Investments (Jersey) Ltd* [1983] 1 All ER 629.
387 *Agnew v Usher* (1884) 14 QBD 78.
388 *BHP Petroleum Pty Ltd v Oil Basins Ltd* [1985] VR 725.
389 Under Ord 11, r 1(1)(h). The action had to directly affect the land itself: *Casey v Arnott* (1876) 2 CPD 24.
390 *Re Banco Nacional de Cuba*, supra, 2055.
391 Ibid. See also *Walanpatrias Stiftung v Lehman Brothers International (Europe)* [2006] EWHC 3034 (Comm) at [25].

information[392] and money,[393] including money representing the proceeds of sale of land.[394] So disputed funds paid into a bank account in England would come within paragraph (10) but no doubt permission for service out of the jurisdiction would be refused where the connection with England was so tenuous.[395] An action in relation to a life policy assigned to a lender as security for a loan was covered by a previous property ground[396] and would now come within rule 6.20(10).

Located within the jurisdiction[397]   Immovable property is easily located. However, movable property obviously may be moved from one country to another. We should be concerned with location at the time of the commencement of the proceedings, which should be regarded as being the moment when permission is sought for service out of the jurisdiction.[398] Whilst there is normally no difficulty in fixing the location of tangible movable property, this can be problematic with intangible movable property, such as shares.[399]

Exercise of the discretion   Where there is a dispute about title to real property in England, depending on English law, it is almost impossible to envisage where England would not be the clearly appropriate forum for trial.[400] Where the dispute more broadly relates to the ownership of property (and the proceeds of sale) in England, England may still be the clearly appropriate forum.[401]

(vii) Claims about trusts, etc

(11) Where "a claim is made for any remedy which might be obtained in proceedings to execute the trusts of a written instrument where (a) the trusts ought to be executed according to English law;[402] and (b) the person on whom the claim form is to be served is a trustee of the trusts".[403] This ground is in terms concerned with express trusts and accordingly does not apply to constructive trusts.[404] There is a separate ground dealing with such trusts.[405] There is no need for the property subject to the trusts to be situated in England. So, for example, this ground will apply where a defendant trustee has sold the entire trust funds and has departed abroad with the proceeds.[406]

---

[392] *Ashton Investments Ltd v OJSC Russian Aluminium RUSAL* [2006] EWHC 2545 (Comm) at [67], [2007] 1 Lloyd's Rep 311.

[393] The *Walanpatrias* case, supra, at [25].

[394] *The Republic of Pakistan v Zardari* [2006] EWHC 2411 (Comm) at [157]–[159], [2006] 2 CLC 667.

[395] Ibid.

[396] See *Deutsche National Bank v Paul* [1898] 1 Ch 283, which held that such a claim did not fall within one of the contract heads. This led to the introduction of a new head of Ord 11 (eventually Ord 11, r 1(1)(i)) to deal with this.

[397] See *Shahar v Tsitsekkos* [2004] EWHC 2659 (Ch) at [42].

[398] We are concerned with domicile as at the moment of the issue of proceedings, rather than the subsequent service on the defendant, *Canada Trust Co v Stolzenberg (No 2)* [2002] 1 AC 1, HL.

[399] See infra, pp 1244–1245.

[400] *The Republic of Pakistan v Zardari* [2006] EWHC 2411 (Comm) at [171], [2006] 2 CLC 667. See also *Khyentse Hope* [2005] 3 NZLR 501.

[401] The *Republic of Pakistan* case, supra, at [171]–[181].

[402] The question whether English law applied to the trusts is tested as at the time when permission to serve out was sought: *Chellaram v Chellaram (No 2)* [2002] EWHC 632 (Ch) at [148]–[153], [2002] 3 All ER 17.

[403] CPR, r 6.20(11); formerly Ord 11, r 1(1)(j) RSC.

[404] *Chellaram v Chellaram (No 2)* [2002] EWHC 632 (Ch) at [137], [138], [2002] 3 All ER 17.

[405] CPR, r 6.20(14); set out infra, p 394.

[406] At one time, under a differently worded ground, the property subject to the trusts had to be situated in England (see *Winter v Winter* [1894] 1 Ch 421 and *Official Solicitor v Stype Investments (Jersey) Ltd* [1983] 1 All

(12) Where "a claim is made for any remedy which might be obtained in proceedings for the administration of the estate of a person who died domiciled[407] within the jurisdiction".[408]

(13) Where "a claim is made in probate proceedings which includes a claim for the rectification of a will".[409] This ground applies to an action for the grant of probate, or letters of administration of an estate, or for the revocation of such a grant, or for a decree pronouncing against the validity of a will, provided the action is not non-contentious or common form probate business. Rule 6.20(13) has added wording to make it clear that this ground includes a claim for the rectification of a will.

(14) Where "a claim is made for a remedy against the defendant as constructive trustee where the defendant's alleged liability arises out of acts committed within the jurisdiction".[410] This replaces an earlier provision which was explicit in specifying the remedy sought in such cases and also answered the question of who can commit the act in question. It allowed for service out of the jurisdiction where "the claim is brought for money had and received or for an account or other remedy against the defendant as constructive trustee, and the defendant's alleged liability arises out of acts committed, whether by him or otherwise, within the jurisdiction". It was doubtless not intended that these changes should have any substantive effect on the court's powers.[411] It follows that recourse probably can be had to the old wording and to the authorities under that provision. These authorities establish that the constructive trust ground will cover knowing participation in acts[412] in England in a fraudulent breach of trust committed in England.[413] Probably, it also covers knowing receipt abroad of the proceeds of such frauds, the knowledge having been acquired abroad.[414] The concept of a constructive trust is wide enough to cover a proprietary equitable claim.[415] Bribes and the property from time to time representing the bribe are held on a constructive trust for the person injured.[416] It is not necessary that all the acts have been committed within the jurisdiction.[417] It is enough

---

ER 629), but this limitation was removed.

[407] Domicile is now determined in accordance with the definition contained in the Brussels I Regulation and the Civil Jurisdiction and Judgments Order 2001 (discussed supra, pp 210–213): CPR, r 6.18(g).

[408] CPR, r 6.20(12); formerly Ord 11, r 1(1)(k) RSC. See *Dellar v Zivy* [2007] EWHC 2266 (Ch), [2007] IL Pr 60. It is very debatable whether the discretion would be exercised in the case of foreign immovables; see Davis (1966) 2 NZULR 243 at 244–245.

[409] CPR, r 6.20(13); formerly Ord 11, r 1(1)(l) RSC.

[410] CPR, r 6.20(14); formerly Ord 11, r 1(1)(t) RSC, on which see *Insurance Co "Ingosstrakh" Ltd v Latvian Shipping Co* [2000] IL Pr 164, CA.

[411] See the Lord Chancellor's Department Consultation Paper on the Civil Procedure Rules—Service of Court Process Abroad, para 22, which notes that a number of minor drafting changes were proposed which did not affect the substance. This appears to be another of these changes.

[412] But probably not an omission: *Battalion Investment & Trust Co Ltd v Clifford*, 2002 (unreported).

[413] *ISC v Guerin* [1992] 2 Lloyd's Rep 430 at 433, HOFFMAN J; *ISC v Radcliff*, 7 December 1990 (unreported) (MILLETT J).

[414] *ISC v Guerin*, supra; *Polly Peck International plc v Nadir* (1992) The Independent, 2 September. Cf *ISC v Radcliff*, supra.

[415] *NABB Brothers Ltd v Lloyds Bank International (Guernsey) Ltd* [2005] EWHC 405 (Ch) at [68]–[73], [2005] IL Pr 37.

[416] *The Republic of Pakistan v Zardari* [2006] EWHC 2411 (Comm) at [164], [2006] 2 CLC 667.

[417] See in relation to constructive trusts *ISC v Guerin*, [1992] 2 Lloyd's Rep 430, 433, HOFFMANN J; *Polly Peck International v Nadir* (1992) The Independent, 2 September, revsd by the Court of Appeal (1993). The Times, 22 March, but HOFFMANN LJ said obiter that he adhered to his view in the *ISC* case. See also *The Republic of*

that "substantial and efficacious acts" have been committed within the jurisdiction, even if substantial and efficacious acts have also been committed outside the jurisdiction.[418] There must be some link between the acts committed within the jurisdiction and the defendant but those acts do not have to be those of the defendant.[419] If the principal fraudster gives instructions for money in England to be paid abroad to a knowing recipient, it is not necessary for the recipient to have done anything in England for rule 6.20(14) to apply to allow service out of the jurisdiction against the recipient.[420]

(15) Where "a claim is made for restitution where the defendant's alleged liability arises out of acts committed within the jurisdiction".[421] This is a new ground for service out of the jurisdiction introduced by rule 6.20 of the Civil Procedure Rules. A claim for a restitutionary remedy that is based on unjust enrichment is undeniably a claim "made for restitution". However, this phrase would appear to go much wider than this and would cover all cases where a restitutionary remedy is sought, regardless of what the claim is based on.[422] It could be based on contract or on wrongdoing. It would cover an equitable proprietary claim.[423] Seemingly, it can also cover an action for equitable relief for breach of confidence.[424] Acts may have been committed partly within the jurisdiction and partly outside the jurisdiction. The same problem has arisen with both the tort ground[425] and the constructive trust ground.[426] The position adopted in relation to those grounds should also be adopted in relation to this ground. Thus it should not be necessary that all the acts have been committed within the jurisdiction. It should be enough that "substantial and efficacious acts" have been committed within the jurisdiction, even if substantial and efficacious acts have also been committed outside the jurisdiction. There is no difficulty in coming within paragraph (10) where there are separate breaches of the equitable duty of confidentiality and one of these takes place in England by virtue of publication of photos (taken in New York in circumstances of breach of confidence).[427]

Pakistan v Zardari [2006] EWHC 2411 (Comm) at [166]–[168], [2006] 2 CLC 667. Cf *ISC v Radcliff*, 7 December 1990 (unreported) (MILLETT J).

[418] *Nycal (UK) Ltd v Lacey* [1994] CLC 12, a case decided under Ord 11, r 1(1)(t) RSC. Substantial and efficacious acts committed within the jurisdiction between breach of duty and receipt of relevant property were acts out of which liability arose even where committed by persons other than the defendant. See also in relation to the tort ground *Metall und Rohstoff AG v Donaldson Lufkin and Jenrette Inc* [1990] 1 QB 391, CA; overruled on a different point in *Lonrho plc v Fayed* [1992] 1 AC 448.

[419] *NABB Brothers Ltd v Lloyds Bank International (Guernsey) Ltd* [2005] EWHC 405 (Ch) at [86], [2005] IL Pr 37; *The Republic of Pakistan v Zardari* [2006] EWHC 2411 (Comm) at [169], [2006] 2 CLC 667.

[419] *NABB Brothers*, supra, at [86].

[420] Ibid, at [87].

[421] CPR, r 6.20(15).

[422] See Fawcett, Harris and Bridge, paras 8.37–8.38. Contrast the wording of the tort ground, a claim "made *in* tort". Observe also the grouping of the restitution ground with four other grounds all concerned with the remedy sought.

[423] *NABB Brothers Ltd v Lloyds Bank International (Guernsey) Ltd* [2005] EWHC 405 (Ch) at [77], [2005] IL Pr 37.

[424] *Douglas v Hello! Ltd (No 2)* [2003] EWCA Civ 139 at [23]–[26], [2003] EMLR 28, where this was common ground for counsel. But not every such claim, see *Ashton Investments Ltd v OJSC Russian Aluminium RUSAL* [2006] EWHC 2545 (Comm) at [69], [2007] 1 Lloyd's Rep 311.

[425] Supra, p 387.

[426] Supra, pp 394–395.

[427] *Douglas v Hello! Ltd (No 2)*, supra, at [36].

(viii) Claims by HM Revenue and Customs

(16) Where "a claim is made by the Commissioners for HM Revenue and Customs relating to duties or taxes against a defendant not domiciled[428] in Scotland or Northern Ireland".[429]

(ix) Claim for costs order in favour of or against third parties

(17) Where "a claim is made by a party to proceedings for an order that the court exercise its power under section 51 of the Supreme Court Act 1981 to make a costs order in favour of or against a person who is not a party to those proceedings; (Rule 48.2 sets out the procedure where the court is considering whether to exercise its discretion to make a costs order in favour of or against a non-party)".[430]

(x) Admiralty claims

(17A) Where "a claim is—(a) in the nature of salvage and any part of the services took place within the jurisdiction; or (b) to enforce a claim under section 153, 154 or 175 of the Merchant Shipping Act 1995".[431] Admiralty "other claims" (ie formerly called in personam claims)[432] are in general subject to the same rules for service out of the jurisdiction as any other claim.[433] However, rule 6.20(17A) is a special rule providing for service out of the jurisdiction where the claim is in the nature of salvage or where the claim arises from oil pollution. The Civil Procedure Rules also provide that a claim form in a collision claim may not be served out of the jurisdiction unless there is a specified connection with England or the defendant has submitted to or agreed to submit to the jurisdiction of the court.[434]

(xi) Claims under various enactments

(18) Where "a claim is made under an enactment specified in the relevant practice direction".[435]

---

[428] Domicile is determined in accordance with the definition contained in the Brussels I Regulation and the Civil Jurisdiction and Judgments Order 2001: CPR, r 6.18(g); discussed supra, pp 210–213.

[429] CPR, r 6.20(16); formerly Ord 11, r 1(1)(n) RSC.

[430] CPR, r 6.20(17). For the need for this provision see *National Justice Compañía Naviera SA v Prudential Assurance Co Ltd (The Ikarian Reefer (No 2)* [2000] 1 Lloyd's Rep 129 at 137. See *OT Africa Line Ltd v Magic Sportswear Corpn* [2004] EWHC 2441 (Comm) at [26]–[28], [2005] 1 Lloyd's Rep 252; appeal dismissed without discussion of this point [2005] EWCA Civ 710 at [15], [2005] 2 Lloyd's Rep 170.

[431] CPR, r 6.20 (17A).

[432] See Part 61PD 12.1.

[433] Subject to CPR, Part 61 and PD, provisions on limitation and collision claims, "other claims" proceed in accordance with Part 58 (Commercial Court).

[434] CPR, r 61.4(7). See also in relation to limitation claims CPR, r 61.11(5), *ICL Shipping Ltd & Steamship Mutual Underwriting Association (Bermuda) Ltd v ChinTai Steel Enterprise Co Ltd* [2003] EWHC 2320 (Comm).

[435] CPR, r 6.20(18); replacing Ord 11, r 1(1)(o), (q), (r), (s), (u). The relevant enactments are set out in the CPR 6BPD.6, 5.2 and are as follows: the Nuclear Installations Act 1965; Schedule 2 to the Immigration Act 1971; the Inheritance (Provision for Family and Dependents) Act 1975; Council Directive (EEC) No 76/308 dated 15 March 1976, where service is to be effected in a Member State of the European Union (this Directive deals with claims for an agricultural levy or other sum); Part VI of the Criminal Justice Act 1988; the Social Security Contributions and Benefits Act 1992; the Drug Trafficking Offences Act 1994; Part II of the Immigration and Asylum Act 1999; the Financial Services and Markets Act 2000.

(xii) The interaction of the different grounds of rule 6.20

It should be pointed out that an overlap between the various paragraphs of rule 6.20 is possible, and one case may come within several grounds. At the same time, the grounds under rule 6.20 are to be read disjunctively and each paragraph is complete in itself and independent of the others.[436] This means, for example, that an employee, who has suffered personal injury abroad (following a negligent act there) during the course of his employment and who can sue his employer for damages either for breach of contract or in tort, can elect to frame his action in contract rather than in tort, thereby bringing his case within one of the grounds of rule 6.20 (previously Order 11, rule 1(1)).[437] However, if service abroad has been allowed under one of the grounds, the claimant is not allowed later to add to his particulars of claim a claim for another cause of action for which permission to serve a claim form out of the jurisdiction would not have been given.[438]

(b) A reasonable prospect of success

An application for permission to serve a claim form out of the jurisdiction under rule 6.20 must be supported by written evidence stating that the claimant believes that his claim has a reasonable prospect of success.[439] This is synonymous with "a real prospect of success".[440] "Real is to be contrasted with fanciful or imaginary".[441] The test is the same or substantially the same as that previously laid down by the House of Lords in *Seaconsar Far East Ltd v Bank Markazi Jomhouri Islami Iran*[442] in relation to service out of the jurisdiction under Order 11, rule 1(1) of the Rules of the Supreme Court, the predecessor of rule 6.20.[443] In that case, the House of Lords held that the claimant has to establish that there is a serious issue to be tried in that there is "a substantial question of fact or law or both, arising on the facts disclosed by the affidavits, which the [claimant] . . . bona fide

---

[436] *Matthews v Kuwait Bechtel Corpn* [1959] 2 QB 57 at 62 (an Ord 11 RSC case); and see *Tassell v Hallen* [1892] 1 QB 321.

[437] *Matthews v Kuwait Bechtel Corpn*, supra, a case dealing with Ord 11, r 1(1) RSC.

[438] *Waterhouse v Reid* [1938] 1 KB 743; *The Siskina* [1979] AC 210 at 254–255; *Donohue v Armco Inc* [2001] UKHL 64 at [21], [2002] 1 All ER 749. Cf *FFSB Ltd v Seward & Kissel LLP* [2007] UKPC 16.

[439] CPR, r 6.21(1)(b).

[440] *Swiss Reinsurance Company Ltd v United India Insurance Co* [2002] EWHC 741 (Comm) at [27], [2004] IL Pr 4 at 62; *Carvill America Inc v Camperdown UK Ltd* [2005] EWCA Civ 645 at [24], [2005] 2 Lloyd's Rep 457; *The Republic of Pakistan v Zardari* [2006] EWHC 2411 (Comm) at [136], [2006] 2 CLC 667; *Tasarruff v Demirel* [2006] EWHC 3354 (Ch) at [39], [2007] IL Pr 8, affd without discussion of this point [2007] EWCA Civ 799. The wording "real prospect of success" is to be found in CPR, Parts 3 and 24.

[441] The *Swiss Reinsurance Co* case, supra; the *Carvill America* case, supra, at [24].

[442] [1994] 1 AC 438; Briggs [1994] LMCLQ 1; Carter (1993) BYBIL 464; Perkins [1994] CLJ 244.

[443] The *Swiss Reinsurance Company* case, supra (the same or substantially the same); *Navigators Insurance Co v Atlantic Methanol Production Co* [2003] EWHC 1706 (Comm) at [33] (treated as the same); *BAS Capital Funding Corpn v Medfinco Ltd* [2003] EWHC 1798 at [153] (no reason to believe differs in any material way), [2004] IL Pr 16; *MRG (Japan) Ltd v Engelhard Metals Japan Ltd* [2003] EWHC 3418 (Comm) at [7]–[10] (the same), [2004] 1 Lloyd's Rep 731; *Ophthalmic Innovations International (United Kingdom) Ltd v Ophthalmic Innovations International Inc* [2004] EWHC 2948 (Ch) at [39], [2005] IL Pr 109; *NABB Brothers Ltd v Lloyds Bank International (Guernsey) Ltd* [2005] EWHC 405 (Ch) at [53], [2005] IL Pr 37; *Pearson Education Ltd v Prentice Hall of India Private Ltd* [2005] EWHC 655 (QB); *Ashton Investments Ltd v OJSC Russian Aluminium (RUSAL)* [2006] EWHC 2545 (Comm), [2007] 1 Lloyd's Rep 311; *The Republic of Pakistan v Zardari* [2006] EWHC 2411 (Comm) at [136], [2006] 2 CLC 667. The merits threshold under CPR, r 6.20 should not differ in substance from that of summary judgment under r 24.2 (in other words, the court should not subject a foreign defendant to proceedings which the defendant would be entitled to have summarily dismissed): *De Molestina v Ponton* [2002] 1 Lloyd's Rep 271, 281; the *Carvill America* case, supra, at [24]; *Chris Sawyer v Atari Interactive Inc* [2005] EWHC 2351 (Ch) at [49]–[50], [2006] IL Pr 8.

desires to try . . .".[444] An issue that is imaginary or fanciful is not a serious issue to be tried.[445] Conversely, a claimant has a real prospect of success if his chances of success are not fanciful.[446]

The threshold test of a reasonable prospect of success (serious issue on the merits) is a low one.[447] It is a lower standard of proof than that of a good arguable case, the standard that previously applied to the merits. This inquiry is an element in the exercise of the court's discretion[448] but is separate and distinct from the *forum conveniens* element.[449] With many grounds of rule 6.20, eg paragraphs (1) and (18), once the ground is established there will have to be a separate inquiry into the merits.[450] It seems that this will also be necessary in respect of paragraph (2).[451] In contrast, with paragraph (6) this will not be necessary.[452] In order to have invoked this ground the claimant will have had to establish the elements of contract, breach and place of breach; in effect, the claimant will have already established a good arguable case on the merits and no separate issue as to the merits to which a lower standard of proof is applicable will arise. The position in relation to paragraph (5) is more complex.[453] Sub-paragraphs (a), (b), (c) and (d) all require the relevant contract to be proved.[454] Once that is done, there arises a separate issue as to the merits of the claim relative to that contract.[455] The position under paragraph (3) is equally complex.[456] The claimant has to show that there is a serious issue which it is reasonable for the court to try in respect of the defendant who has been or will be served.[457] In deciding whether a person is a proper party it is necessary to identify the common questions of law or fact which arise in the claim against the person served (or to be served) and the other person sought to be served. This goes to establishing the ground, and the standard is that of a good arguable case. It is then necessary to be satisfied that these questions of law or fact raise a serious issue to be tried on the merits.[458] With paragraph (8), a separate inquiry is necessary, it being accepted in the *Seaconsar* case that the standard of proof for establishing negligence was a lesser one than

---

[444] *Seaconsar Far East Ltd v Bank Markazi Jomhouri Islami Iran* [1994] 1 AC 438 at 452 (per Lord GOFF), HL.

[445] The *Swiss Reinsurance Co* case, supra.

[446] The *Carvill America* case, supra, at [24].

[447] *Morin v Bonhams & Brooks Ltd* [2003] EWHC 467 (Comm) at [46], [2003] IL Pr 25; affd [2003] EWCA 1802, [2004] IL Pr 24; the *Carvill America* case, supra, at [24].

[448] See CPR, r 6.21(2A), infra, p 399.

[449] The *Seaconsar* case, supra, at 455–456.

[450] The *Seaconsar* case, ibid, at 454, referring to Ord 11, r 1(1) (a), (q),(r) and (s).

[451] See *Chemische Fabrik Vormals Sandoz v Badische Anilin und Soda Fabriks* (1904) 90 LT 733 at 735; approved in the *Seaconsar* case.

[452] The *Seaconsar* case, supra, at 453–454. See also *Agrafax Public Relations Ltd v United Scottish Sociey Inc* [1995] IL Pr 753.

[453] The *Seaconsar* case, supra, at 454–455.

[454] With sub-para (a) a good arguable case will also have to be shown that the contract was made within the jurisdiction, the *Seaconsar* case, supra. See also *Apple Corps Ltd v Apple Computer Inc* [2004] EWHC 768 (Ch) at [34]–[35], [2004] IL Pr 34; *Bank of Baroda v Vysya Ltd* [1994] 2 Lloyd's Rep 87 at 95.

[455] The *Seaconsar* case, supra, at 454–455. See also *DR Insurance Co v Central National Insurance Co* [1996] 1 Lloyd's Rep 74 at 80.

[456] The *Seaconsar* case, supra, at 455.

[457] *Grupo Torras SA and Torras Hostench London Ltd v Sheikh Fahad Mohammed Al-Sabah* [1995] 1 Lloyd's Rep 374 at 380; appeals to the CA dismissed without discussion of this point, [1996] 1 Lloyd's Rep 7.

[458] *Barings plc v Coopers & Lybrand (A Firm)* [1997] IL Pr 12 at 23–24; affd by CA [1997] IL Pr 576 at 585.

that for establishing that the negligence occurred within the jurisdiction (which goes to establishing the terms of the ground).[459]

If the law is in issue but there is no serious issue to be tried in relation to the facts, the court may determine the point of law at the application to serve out stage and refuse permission for such service.[460] Establishing a reasonable prospect of success (a serious issue on the merits) can raise choice of law questions at the jurisdictional stage of the action. Thus in *Metall und Rohstoff AG v Donaldson Lufkin and Jenrette Inc*[461] the Court of Appeal applied the English common law tort choice of law rules to determine whether the claimant had established the case on the merits.[462] At that time,[463] for the claimant to succeed, actionability by English law had to be shown, which there was in respect of the claim for inducement of a breach of contract, but not in respect of the claim, as pleaded, for conspiracy.

(c) The exercise of the discretion under rule 6.20

The courts *may*, rather than *must*, allow service of a claim form out of the jurisdiction. Where the case falls within one of the grounds of rule 6.20, the exercise of assumed jurisdiction in any given case lies within the discretion of the court[464] and the court will not give permission for service out of the jurisdiction unless satisfied that England and Wales is the proper place in which to bring the claim.[465] The onus is on the claimant to show good reason why service out should be permitted.[466] The criterion for exercise of the rule 6.20 discretion is that of *forum conveniens*,[467] ie service out of the jurisdiction will only be

---

[459] The *Seaconsar* case, supra, at 455; approving the judgment of Lord TUCKER in *Vitkovice Horni a Hutni Tezirstvro v Korner* [1951] AC 869 at 889, HL. See also *Barings plc v Coopers & Lybrand (A Firm)* [1997] IL Pr 12 at 25–26; affd by CA, [1997] IL Pr 576 at 585.

[460] The *De Molestina* case, supra, at 281; *Nima Sarl v Deves Insurance Public Co Ltd (The Prestrioka)* [2002] EWCA Civ 1132 at [18], [2003] 2 Lloyd's Rep 327; the *Carvill America* case, supra, at [25].

[461] [1990] 1 QB 391; overruled on a different point in *Lonhro plc v Fayed* [1992] 1 AC 448, HL; Fentiman [1989] CLJ 191; Fawcett [1991] Current Legal Problems 39, 42–43. See also *Morin v Bonhams & Brooks Ltd* [2003] EWHC 467 (Comm), [2003] IL Pr 25; aff'd [2003] EWCA 1802, [2004] IL Pr 24.

[462] At that time the standard was that of a good arguable case.

[463] See now the choice of law rules under the Rome II Regulation on non-contractual obligations, infra, Chapter 19.

[464] For an appeal court's powers to review the discretion vested in a judge see *Hadmor Productions Ltd v Hamilton* [1983] 1 AC 191; *Spiliada Maritime Corpn v Cansulex Ltd* [1987] AC 460, HL; *Berezovsky v Michaels* [2000] 1 WLR 1004 at 1021 (per Lord HOFFMANN); *Owusu v Jackson* [2002] EWCA Civ 877 at [30], [2002] IL Pr 45; *King v Lewis* [2004] EWCA (Civ) 1329 at [35], [2005] IL Pr 16; *Limit (No 3) Ltd v PDV Insurance Co* [2005] EWCA Civ 383 at [69], [2005] 2 All ER (Comm) 347; *Galaxy Special Maritime Enterprise v Prima Ceylon Ltd (The Olympic Galaxy)* [2006] EWCA Civ 528 at [30], [2006] 2 Lloyd's Rep 27.

[465] CPR, r 6.21(2A). This is differently worded from its predecessor (Ord 11, r 4) but the principles expounded in former authorities relating to Ord 11 remain applicable: *Petroleo Brasiliero SA v Mellitus Shipping Inc (The Baltic Flame)* [2001] EWCA Civ 418 at [31], [2001] 2 Lloyd's Rep 203. Where the application is for permission to serve a claim form in Scotland or Northern Ireland and it appears that the claimant may also be entitled to a remedy there, the courts in deciding whether to grant permission shall compare the cost and convenience of proceeding there or in England: r 6.21(3).

[466] *Ophthalmic Innovations International (United Kingdom) Ltd v Ophthalmic Innovations International Inc* [2004] EWHC 2948 (Ch) at [41], [2005] IL Pr 10.

[467] This presupposes that there is an obvious alternative forum abroad available to the claimant in the sense that there is no barrier to taking proceedings there, even if the remedy sought is not available there, see *Petroleo Brasiliero* case, supra, at [35]. If there is not it is proper to allow service out of the jurisdiction: *Ets Soules et Cie v Handgate Co Ltd SA, The Handgate* [1987] 1 Lloyd's Rep 142. See also *New Hampshire Insurance Co v Strabag Bau AG* [1992] 1 Lloyd's Rep 361 at 369–370, CA.

allowed where England is clearly the most appropriate forum in the interests of the parties and the ends of justice. The law in this area has been exhaustively re-examined and restated by the House of Lords in *Spiliada Maritime Corpn v Cansulex Ltd*[468] where Lord GOFF, with whom the other Law Lords concurred, set out the relevant principles for the exercise of the discretion.

(i) The basic principle

Lord GOFF said that the underlying fundamental principle was "to identify the forum in which the case can be suitably tried for the interests of all the parties and for the ends of justice".[469] The same principle underlies the discretion to stay actions on the basis of *forum non conveniens* after the service of a claim form.[470] Lord GOFF then went on to state a number of other principles which help to explain the basic principle. These principles relate to the following: the appropriate forum; other considerations; the exorbitant nature of rule 6.20 jurisdiction; and the particular ground of rule 6.20 being employed.

(ii) The appropriate forum

The burden of proof is on the claimant to show that England is the appropriate forum for trial,[471] and that this is clearly so.[472] Appropriateness comprises a wide range of considerations. "The court must take into account the nature of the dispute, the legal and practical issues involved, such questions as local knowledge, availability of witnesses and their evidence[473] and expense."[474] It also involves looking at the expense and inconvenience to a foreign defendant in having trial in England.[475] As well as these matters of litigational convenience, the courts have considered the connections that the parties and the cause of action have with the alternative fora.[476] Beyond this, the circumstances of an individual case may raise other considerations. For example, the fact that England is the only forum in which all of the claims against the defendants can be heard is a powerful

---

[468] [1987] 1 AC 460. Confirmed in *Berezovsky v Michaels* [2000] 1 WLR 1004, HL.

[469] The *Spiliada* case, supra, at 480.

[470] Infra, p 428. This is entirely consistent with the overriding objective of the CPR to deal with cases justly. See also *Voth v Manildra Flour Mills Pty Ltd* (1990) 171 CLR 538 at 563–564, High Court of Australia. The Australian test for service out of the jurisdiction is, however, easier for the claimant to satisfy than the English one, only being concerned with whether the forum is clearly inappropriate, see Collins (1991) 107 LQR 182; Epstein in Fawcett (ed), *Declining Jurisdiction*, p 82 et seq.

[471] On an application by the defendant to set aside permission previously granted the onus is on the claimant to establish this is so as at the date on which the order granting permission was made: *ISC v Guerin* [1992] 2 Lloyd's Rep 430 at 434–435; *Mohammed v Bank of Kuwait and the Middle East KSC* [1996] 1 WLR 1483 at 1493, CA. But cf *BMG Trading Ltd v A S McKay* [1998] IL Pr 691 at 694, CA.

[472] *Spiliada Maritime Corpn v Cansulex Ltd* [1987] AC 460 at 481; the *Berezovsky* case, supra. Nonetheless, the defendant must identify clearly the issues where he alleges that it is appropriate that some of these should be tried abroad: *Limit (No 3) Ltd v PDV Insurance Co* [2005] EWCA Civ 383 at [72] (per CLARKE LJ), [2005] All ER (Comm) 347; *Chris Sawyer v Atari Interactive Inc* [2005] EWHC 2351 (Ch) at [54], [2006] IL Pr 8.

[473] *Abbassi v Abbassi* [2006] EWCA Civ 355. Use of video-links reduces the inconvenience of travelling to England but this is a relatively minor factor: *Nima Sarl v Deves Insurance Public Co Ltd (The Prestrioka)* [2002] EWCA Civ 1132 at [76], [2003] 2 Lloyd's Rep 327.

[474] Per Lord WILBERFORCE in *Amin Rasheed Corpn v Kuwait Insurance Co* [1984] AC 50 at 72.

[475] *Société Générale de Paris v Dreyfus Bros* (1885) 29 Ch D 239 at 242; *George Monro Ltd v American Cyanamid and Chemical Corpn* [1944] KB 432; *Cordova Land Co Ltd v Victor Bros Inc* [1966] 1 WLR 793 at 801–802.

[476] *Kroch v Rossell et Cie* [1937] 1 All ER 725; *Amanuel v Alexandros Shipping Co, The Alexandros P* [1986] 1 QB 464; *Spiliada Maritime Corpn v Cansulex Ltd* [1987] AC 460; *International Marine Services Inc v National Bank of Fujarah* [1997] IL Pr 468, CA.

factor in favour of trial in England.[477] Conversely, the interests of justice may be best served by submission of a whole suit to a single tribunal abroad which can adjudicate on all the matters in issue, rather than having trial continuing partly in England and partly abroad.[478] It is not particularly significant whether a contract was made within the jurisdiction or not.[479] The fact that English[480] law is applicable to the dispute in question may point towards England as being the appropriate forum for trial.[481]

Lord GOFF in the *Spiliada* case[482] said that the fact that English law is the law governing the contract would in some cases be of very great importance, and, in others, of little importance,[483] depending on the circumstances. On the facts of the case this was said to be a relevant factor in the exercise of the discretion.[484] Indeed, this was said to be by no means an insignificant factor[485] since the dispute was, inter alia, as to the nature of the obligation under the contract. This is a significant factor where there is evidence that the foreign court may not apply English law despite an express choice of this as the governing law.[486] The fact that English law governs a contract is of very great importance in cases raising an issue of English public policy.[487] It is highly desirable that such an issue should be determined by an English court. In contrast, where no difference between the competing laws is shown, this factor is given little weight.[488] Nor is it given any significant weight when a reinsurance contract governed by English law relates to liability under the law

---

[477] *Booth v Phillips* [2004] EWHC 1437 (Comm) at [51], [2004] 2 Lloyd's Rep 457. See also *Sinochem International Oil (London) Ltd v Mobil Sales and Supply Corpn Ltd (Sinochem International Oil Co Ltd, third party) (No 2)* [2000] 1 All ER (Comm) 758, 773; *Attorney General of Zambia v Meer Care & Desai (A Firm)* [2005] EWHC 2120 (Ch); appeal on other grounds dismissed [2006] EWCA Civ 390, [2006] 1 CLC 436. See also *Pei v Bank Bumiputra Malaysia Berhad* (1998) 41 OR (3d) 39.

[478] See *Donohue v Armco Inc* [2001] UKHL 64, [2002] 1 All ER 749—a case involving breach of an English exclusive jurisdiction agreement; discussed infra, pp 470–473. See also *American Motorists Insurance Co v Cellstar Corpn* [2002] EWHC 421, [2002] 2 Lloyd's Rep 216; affd [2003] EWCA Civ 206, [2003] IL Pr 370.

[479] *Bank of Baroda v Vysya Bank Ltd* [1994] 2 Lloyd's Rep 87 at 96.

[480] See *Downing v Al Tameer Establishment* [2002] EWCA 721, [2002] 2 All ER (Comm) 545—reference to "UK" interpreted as referring to English.

[481] *Cordoba Shipping Co Ltd v National State Bank, Elizabeth, New Jersey, The Albaforth* [1984] 2 Lloyd's Rep 91 at 93–94, CA (involving tort); *Spiliada Maritime Corpn v Cansulex Ltd* [1987] AC 460, HL (contract), discussed infra, pp 411–412; *Banque Paribas v Cargill International SA* [1992] 2 Lloyd's Rep 19, CA; *Overseas Union Insurance Ltd v Incorporated General Insurance Ltd* [1992] 1 Lloyd's Rep 439, CA; *CGU International Insurance plc v Szabo* [2002] 1 All ER (Comm) 83; *Apple Corps Ltd v Apple Computer Inc* [2004] EWHC 768 (Ch) at [68], [2004] IL Pr 34; *Dellar v Zivy* [2007] EWHC 2266 (Ch) at [46], [2007] IL Pr 60. But cf *Trade Indemnity v Försäkrings AB Njord* [1995] 1 All ER 796—English law applicable outweighed by fact that focus of dispute was business practices of Swedish insurance co; see also *Voth v Manildra Flour Mills Pty Ltd* (1990) 171 CLR 538 at 566 et seq, High Court of Australia.

[482] *Spiliada Maritime Corpn v Cansulex Ltd* [1987] AC 460, 481, HL.

[483] See, eg, *Egon Oldendorff v Liberia Corpn* [1995] 2 Lloyd's Rep 64 at 76.

[484] At 486.

[485] See also *CGU International Insurance plc v Szabo* [2002] 1 All ER (Comm) 83; *Apple Corps Ltd v Apple Computer Inc* [2004] EWHC 768 (Ch) at [68], [2004] IL Pr 34.

[486] *Chris Sawyer v Atari Interactive Inc* [2005] EWHC 2351 (Ch) at [62], [2006] IL Pr 8.

[487] *Mitsubishi Corpn v Aristidis I Alafouzos* [1988] 1 Lloyd's Rep 191 at 196; *E I Du Pont de Nemours and Co v I C Agnew* [1987] 2 Lloyd's Rep 585 at 594–595.

[488] *Macsteel Commercial Holdings (Pty) Ltd v Thermasteel V (Canada) Inc* [1996] CLC 1403, CA; *Chase v Ram Technical Services Ltd* [2000] 2 Lloyd's Rep 418 at 421; *Konamaneni v Rolls-Royce Industrial Power (India) Ltd* [2002] 1 WLR 1269 at [170]; *Chellaram v Chellaram (No 2)* [2002] EWHC 632 (Ch) at [170], [2002] 3 All ER 17; *Navigators Insurance Co v Atlantic Methanol Production Co LLC* [2003] EWHC 1706 (Comm) at [48], [2004] Lloyd's Rep IR 418. See also *Galaxy Special Maritime Enterprise v Prima Ceylon Ltd (The Olympic Galaxy)* [2006] EWCA Civ 528 at [23], [2006] 2 Lloyd's Rep 27.

of Texas.[489] The issues arising in the case may not raise significant points of law[490] and in so far as English law is applied it may be easy for a foreign court to state and apply this.[491] The fact that the dispute involves complex questions of foreign law may be a strong pointer towards trial abroad in the country whose law governs.[492] But the governing law may be of little weight where it is not so complex that it cannot be dealt with easily by the English courts.[493] Where the defendant seeks trial abroad so as to take advantage of foreign choice of law rules this has been regarded as a factor in favour of trial in England.[494] On the other hand, if trial in England would lead to a multiplicity of proceedings, with concurrent overlapping actions taking place in England and abroad, this would be a ground for exercising the discretion against allowing service out of the jurisdiction.[495] This consideration can outweigh the fact that English law governs the contract.[496] However, the weight to be attached to the concurrent proceedings factor depends on how far the proceedings have advanced abroad.[497] The parties and issues do not have to be identical.[498] It is enough that there is a risk of inconsistent findings.[499]

In cases involving an exclusive jurisdiction clause providing for trial in England,[500] the discretion, in the absence of strong reason to the contrary, will be exercised in favour of

---

[489] *Ace Insurance SA-NV (Formerly Cigna Insurance Co of Europe SA NV) v Zurich Insurance Co* [2001] EWCA Civ 173 at [47]; [2001] 1 Lloyd's Rep 618, CA—a *forum non conveniens* case.

[490] *Limit (No 3) Ltd v PDV Insurance Co* [2005] EWCA Civ 383 at [46]–[49], [2005] 2 All ER (Comm) 347; *Royal & Sun Alliance Insurance plc v Retail Brand Alliance Inc* [2004] EWHC 2139 (Comm) at [25], [2005] Lloyd's Rep IR 110, QBD (Comm).

[491] *Nima SARL v Deves Insurance Public Co Ltd (The Prestrioka)* [2002] EWCA Civ 1132 at [73], [2003] 2 Lloyd's Rep 327; *Galaxy Special Maritime Enterprise v Prima Ceylon Ltd (The Olympic Galaxy)* [2006] EWCA Civ 528 at [23], [2006] 2 Lloyd's Rep 27.

[492] *American Motorists Insurance Co v Cellstar Corpn* [2002] EWHC 421, [2002] 2 Lloyd's Rep 216; affd [2003] EWCA Civ 206 at [48], [2003] IL Pr 370; *Tryg Baltica International (UK) Ltd v Boston Compañía de Seguros SA* [2004] EWHC 1186 (Comm) at [42], [2005] Lloyd's Rep IR 40, QBD. See also *Burrows v Jamaica Private Power Co Ltd* [2002] CLC 255—foreign law and jurisdiction. The parties may accept the importance of the applicable law: *Samcrete Egypt Engineers and Contractors SAE v Land Rover Exports Ltd* [2001] EWCA Civ 2019, [2002] CLC 533.

[493] *Music Sales Ltd v Shapiro Bornstein & Co Inc* [2005] EWHC 759 (Ch) at [25], [2006] 1 BCLC 371.

[494] *Tiernan v The Magen Insurance Co Ltd* [2000] IL Pr 517 at [18].

[495] *The Hagen* [1908] P 189; *El du Pont de Nemours & Co v I C Agnew and K W Kerr* [1987] 2 Lloyd's Rep 585; *DR Insurance Co v Central National Insurance Co* [1996] 1 Lloyd's Rep 74; cf *The Bank of Baroda v The Vysya Bank Ltd* [1994] 2 Lloyd's Rep 87 at 97–98; *Chase v Ram Technical Services Ltd* [2000] 2 Lloyd's Rep 418; *American Motorists Insurance Co v Cellstar Corpn* [2003] EWCA Civ 206 at [48], [2003] IL Pr 370; *Galaxy Special Maritime Enterprise v Prima Ceylon Ltd (The Olympic Galaxy)* [2006] EWCA Civ 528, [2006] 2 Lloyd's Rep 27. Cf *Amoco (UK) Exploration Co v British American Offshore Ltd* [1999] 2 Lloyd's Rep 772, 780—no risk of inconsistent decisions; *Markel International Insurance Co Ltd v La República Compañía Argentina de Seguros Generales SA* [2004] EWHC 1826 (Comm) at [38], [2005] Lloyd's Rep IR 40, QBD. See also *Spiliada Maritime Corpn v Cansulex Ltd*, supra—a case involving third party proceedings.

[496] *New Hampshire Insurance Co v Strabag Bau AG* [1992] 1 Lloyd's Rep 361, CA. See also *Galaxy Special Maritime Enterprise v Prima Ceylon Ltd (The Olympic Galaxy)* [2006] EWCA Civ 528, [2006] 2 Lloyd's Rep 27. But cf *CGU v Szabo* [2002] 1 All ER (Comm) 83.

[497] *Ark v True North Capital* [2005] EWHC 1585 (Comm) at [70], [2006] 1 All ER (Comm) 138. See further infra, pp 442–443.

[498] *BAS Capital Funding Corpn v Medfinco Ltd* [2003] EWHC 1798 at [107], [2004] IL Pr 16; *Konamaneni v Rolls-Royce Industrial Power (India) Ltd* [2002] 1 WLR 1269 at [172]–[173].

[499] The *BAS* and *Konamaneni* cases, supra.

[500] In such cases, often Art 23 of the Brussels I Regulation, discussed supra, pp 283–296, will apply. We are concerned here with the situation where that provision does not apply. Normally, where there is an English jurisdiction

holding parties to their bargain.[501] The normal principle established in *Spiliada*, that the burden of proof is on the claimant to satisfy the court that England is clearly and distinctly the appropriate forum for trial, is replaced in cases where there is an agreement as to jurisdiction.[502] This means that the court will give effect to the submission to jurisdiction, although still retaining a discretion to grant a stay if the defendant can show strong reasons against holding the parties to their bargain. A good reason for not granting permission may be some factor that could not have been foreseen at the time that the contract was made.[503] Instances where good reason can be shown are likely to be rare.[504] An example would be where the interests of parties other than the parties bound by the exclusive jurisdiction clause are involved or grounds of claim not the subject of the clause are part of the relevant dispute so that if the agreement is upheld there is a risk of parallel proceedings and inconsistent decisions.[505] However, if this risk was foreseeable, the contractual bargain will be upheld and service out refused.[506] The position is less certain in cases where the parties have agreed on the non-exclusive jurisdiction of the English courts.[507] There are cases where the same principle has been applied as in cases involving an exclusive jurisdiction clause.[508] However, other cases have rightly regarded a non-exclusive jurisdiction clause differently from an exclusive one[509] and the Court of Appeal has applied the normal principle in the *Spiliada* case to a non-exclusive

---

clause English law will govern the contract as well, see infra, pp 701–704. For the significance to be attached to arbitration in England, see *Egon Oldendorff v Liberia Corpn* [1995] 2 Lloyd's Rep 64 at 76.

[501] *Unterweser Reederei GmbH v Zapata Off-Shore Co (The Chaparral)* [1968] 2 Lloyd's Rep 158 at 163 (per WILLMER LJ).

[502] *The Standard Steamship Owners Protection and Indemnity Association (Bermuda) Ltd v Gann* [1992] 2 Lloyd's Rep 528. See also *Insurance Co "Ingosstrakh" Ltd v Latvian Shipping Co* [2000] IL Pr 164, CA; *Citi-March Ltd v Neptune Orient Lines Ltd* [1997] 1 Lloyd's Rep 72; *BAS Capital Funding Corpn v Medfinco Ltd* [2003] EWHC 1798 at [192], [2004] IL Pr 16; *OT Africa Line Ltd v Magic Sportswear Corporation* [2005] EWCA Civ 710 at [19], [2005] 2 Lloyd's Rep 170.

[503] *Marubeni Hong Kong and South China Ltd v Mongolian Government* [2002] 2 All ER (Comm) 873 at [43]; appeal on a different issue dismissed [2005] EWCA Civ 395. See also *Mercury Communications Ltd v Communication Telesystems International* [1999] 2 All ER (Comm) 33 at 41; *JP Morgan Securities Asia Private Ltd v Malaysian Newsprint Industries SDN BHD* [2001] 2 Lloyd's Rep 41 at [51]; *Import-Export Metro Ltd v Compañía Sud Americana de Vapores SA* [2003] EWHC 11 (Comm), [2003] 1 Lloyd's Rep 405; *Antec International Ltd v Biosafety USA Ltd* [2006] EWHC 47 (Comm) at [7]. Cf *British Aerospace plc v Dee Howard Co* [1993] 1 Lloyd's Rep 368 at 376—this is the only factor providing good reason; the *BAS Capital Funding Corpn* case, supra, at [191]; *Konkola Copper Mines plc v Coromin Ltd (No 2)* [2006] EWHC 1093 (Comm) at [32], [2006] 2 Lloyd's Rep 446—a case concerning a foreign jurisdiction clause.

[504] The *Mercury Communications* case, supra, at 41.

[505] *Donohue v Armco Inc* [2001] UKHL 64, [2002] 1 All ER 749—an example of strong reasons for not upholding the agreement in the context of not granting an anti-suit injunction in relation to foreign proceedings and also in the context of stays of action on the basis of a foreign jurisdiction clause; infra, pp 444 and 470–473.

[506] *Konkola Copper Mines plc v Coromin Ltd (No 2)* [2006] EWHC 1093 (Comm), [2006] 2 Lloyd's Rep 446. See also on the significance of unforeseeability in the context of permitting service out of the jurisdiction, supra.

[507] See generally Fawcett [2001] LMCLQ 234, 245–248. For the identification of a clause as being non-exclusive, see supra, p 289 and Fawcett, ibid, at 235–241. For discussion of such clauses in the context of *forum non conveniens* see infra, p 432.

[508] The *Standard Steamship Owners* case, supra; *Gulf Bank KSC v Mitsubishi Heavy Industries Ltd* [1994] 1 Lloyd's Rep 323; the *Mercury Communications* case, supra, at 41; the *Marubeni* case, supra, at [63]–[64]; the *JP Morgan* case, supra, at [43]; *Breams Trustees Ltd v Upstream Downstream Simulation Services Inc* [2004] EWHC 211 (Ch); *Antec International Ltd v Biosafety USA Ltd* [2006] EWHC 47 (Comm) at [7]; *HIT Entertainment Ltd v Gaffney International Licensing Pty Ltd* [2007] EWHC 1282 (Ch).

[509] *Evans Marshall & Co v Bertola SA* [1973] 1 WLR 349 at 361 (KERR J); the *Sinochem* case, supra. See also the *BAS Capital Funding Corpn* case, supra, at [192].

jurisdiction clause.[510] When applying this principle it is relevant to take into account the fact that the parties have implicitly agreed that England is *an* appropriate forum for trial.[511] However, they are not agreeing that it is *the* appropriate forum. A feature which may justify not taking jurisdiction in England would be where there are overlapping proceedings abroad.[512]

Where the parties have agreed to trial abroad, they should be kept to their agreement and it takes a strong cause to permit the court to ignore a foreign exclusive jurisdiction clause.[513] When the question is whether to give leave for service out of the jurisdiction, rather than to stay otherwise well founded proceedings, there is an even heavier burden to discharge upon the applicant who asks the court not to enforce a foreign jurisdiction clause.[514] Where the issue arises of whether there is a foreign jurisdiction clause in a contract, the claimant has to establish a good arguable case that there was not.[515] The considerations material to the exercise of the discretion in such a case (ie a service out case where there is a foreign jurisdiction clause) are the same as in cases involving a stay of English proceedings where there is a foreign jurisdiction clause.[516] If the foreign jurisdiction clause is non-exclusive, there is no breach of agreement in commencing proceeedings in England and the normal principle in the *Spiliada* case should apply.[517] As with a non-exclusive jurisdiction clause providing for trial in England, the parties have implicitly agreed that the foreign court is *an* appropriate forum for trial, but not *the* appropriate forum.[518] In determining whether England is the clearly appropriate forum, a relevant consideration is whether proceedings are pending in the forum abroad designated by the non-exclusive jurisidiction clause.[519] Where they are so pending, the continuance of the English proceedings has been regarded as involving a breach of the non-exclusive jurisdiction clause (by not agreeing to submit to that foreign court).[520] That clause has

---

[510] *Colonia Versicherung AG v Amoco Oil, The "Wind Star"*, 1993 (unreported).

[511] *S & W Berisford plc and NGI Precious Metals Inc v New Hampshire Insurance Co* [1990] 1 Lloyd's Rep 454 at 463.

[512] The *BAS Capital Funding* case, supra, at [193]—especially if started abroad by the claimant in England.

[513] *Mackender v Feldia AG* [1967] 2 QB 590 at 604; *Unterweser Reederei GmbH v Zapata Off-Shore Co, The Chaparral* [1968] 2 Lloyd's Rep 158 at 163–164; *Evans Marshall & Co Ltd v Bertola SA* [1973] 1 WLR 349; *Citi-March Ltd v Neptune Orient Lines Ltd* [1997] 1 Lloyd's Rep 72; the *Sinochem* case, supra, at 766; *Insurance Co "Ingosstrakh" Ltd v Latvian Shipping Co* [2000] IL Pr 164, 169, CA; *Burrows v Jamaica Private Power Co Ltd* [2002] 1 All ER (Comm) 374 at [9]; *Dornoch Ltd v Mauritius Union Assurance Co Ltd* [2006] EWCA Civ 389 at [12], [2006] 2 Lloyd's Rep 475; *Advanced Cardiovascular Systems Inc v Universal Specialties Ltd* [1997] 1 NZLR 186. For the position where the contract provides for arbitration abroad, see *A and B v C and D* [1982] 1 Lloyd's Rep 166, affd sub nom *Qatar Petroleum v Shell International Petroleum* [1983] 2 Lloyd's Rep 35, CA. Foreign choice of jurisdiction clauses are also important when it comes to stays of action, discussed infra, pp 443–450.

[514] The *Insurance Co "Ingosstrakh"* case, supra, at 169; The *Sinochem* case, supra, at 767.

[515] *Dornoch Ltd v Mauritius Union Assurance Co Ltd* [2006] EWCA Civ 389 at [18], [2006] 2 Lloyd's Rep 475. The fact that the defendant can also establish a good arguable case does not matter. So far this principle has been applied in reinsurance cases where the question of the governing law has arisen.

[516] *Citi-March Ltd v Neptune Orient Lines Ltd*, supra; the *Insurance Co "Ingosstrakh"* case, supra, 169–170. See infra, pp 443–448.

[517] *E D & F Man Ship Ltd v Kvaerner Gibraltar Ltd, The Rothnie* [1996] 2 Lloyd's Rep 206 at 211—a stay case; *BP plc v Aon Ltd* [2005] EWHC 2554 (Comm) at [21]–[22], [2006] 1 Lloyd's Rep 549; *Catlin Syndicate Ltd v Adams Land & Cattle Co* [2006] EWHC 2065 (Comm) at [19]. But cf *Excess Insurance Co Ltd v Allendale Mutual Insurance Co*, CA, 8 March 1995 (unreported)—involving a service of suit clause which is akin to a non-exclusive jurisdiction clause; *Burrows v Jamaica Private Power Co Ltd* [2002] CLC 255 at 258–259.

[518] *BP plc v Aon Ltd*, supra, at [23].

[519] Ibid at [31]; *Catlin Syndicate*, supra, at [47].

[520] *BP plc v Aon Ltd*, supra, at [23].

therefore been regarded as being akin to an exclusive jurisdiction clause and the claimant has had to show strong reasons justifying trial in England in preference to trial abroad in the designated forum.[521] Whereas one forum may be appropriate for determining points of construction, another may be appropriate for the trial of the facts. If, as is normally desirable, facts and law are to be tried in the same proceedings, the appropriate forum for determining the facts should take priority.[522]

(iii) Other considerations

Identification of "the forum in which the case can be suitably tried for the interests of all the parties and for the ends of justice" involves looking not only at factors of appropriateness but at other considerations as well.[523] Guidance on the range of considerations to be taken into account when exercising the rule 6.20 discretion can be found in cases on the discretion to stay actions on the basis of *forum non conveniens* after the service of a claim form within the jurisdiction.[524] This follows from the fact that the same basic principle underlies the exercise of the discretion in both areas, although there are differences between the burdens of proof and in respect of the fact that rule 6.20 is regarded as an exorbitant form of jurisdiction.[525] Two particular considerations, which have not been mentioned so far, need to be examined.

First, there is the question, which was asked even before the *Spiliada* case, of whether justice will be obtained in the foreign court.[526] If it appears probable that the claimant, owing to political or other reasons, will not receive a fair trial abroad, the court may well exercise its discretion in favour of the application for service out of the jurisdiction, even though both parties to the suit are foreigners and even though their rights fall to be governed by foreign law.[527] Such an allegation, though, has to be made out to a high standard of cogency.[528] The Court of Appeal has been prepared to take this idea of not receiving a fair trial abroad further and has held[529] that, where the foreign jurisdiction is "compelled to apply a law which is contrary to the general understanding of

---

[521] Ibid; relying on *Ace Insurance SA-NV (Formerly Cigna Insurance Co of Europe SA-NV) v Zurich Insurance Co* [2001] EWCA Civ 173 at [62], [2001] 1 Lloyd's Rep 618, CA—a *forum non conveniens* case, infra, p 432.

[522] *New Hampshire Insurance Co v Phillips Electronics North America Corpn* [1998] IL Pr 256, CA.

[523] *Metall Und Rohstoff AG v Donaldson and Jenrette Inc* [1990] 1 QB 391; overruled on a different point in *Lonrho plc v Fayed* [1992] 1 AC 448, HL.

[524] Infra, pp 430–443.

[525] *Spiliada Maritime Corpn v Cansulex Ltd* [1987] AC 460 at 481. See generally Edinger (1986) 64 Can Bar Rev 283. If a case involves some defendants outside the jurisdiction, and others within the jurisdiction, the case is looked at in the round: *EI Du Pont de Nemours & Co v I C Agnew and K W Kerr* [1987] 2 Lloyd's Rep 585 at 593; *Travelers Casualty and Surety Co of Europe Ltd v Sun Life Assurance Co of Canada (UK) Ltd* [2004] EWHC 1704, [2004] IL Pr 50.

[526] *Aaronson Bros Ltd v Maderera del Tropico SA* [1967] 2 Lloyd's Rep 159 at 162; and *Unterweser Reederei GmbH v Zapata Off-Shore Co, The Chaparral* [1968] 2 Lloyd's Rep 158.

[527] *Oppenheimer v Louis Rosenthal and Co AG* [1937] 1 All ER 23. Cf in a modern context *Cortese v Nowsco Well Service Ltd* [2001] IL Pr 16, CA of Alberta. See generally on the modern attitude towards allegations of injustice abroad, infra, pp 434–439.

[528] *International Marine Services Inc v National Bank of Fujairah* [1997] IL Pr 468 at 470, CA; *Limit (No 3) Ltd v PDV Insurance Co* [2005] EWCA Civ 383 at [63]–[66], [2005] 2 All ER (Comm) 347. Cf the rather more relaxed attitude in Ontario: *Pei v Bank Bumiputra Malaysia Berhad* (1998) 41 OR (3d) 39.

[529] *Coast Lines v Hudig and Veder Chartering NV* [1972] 2 QB 34. See also *Seashell Shipping Corpn v Mutualidad de Seguros Del Instituto Nacional De Industria, The Magnum ex Tarraco Augusta* [1989] 1 Lloyd's Rep 47 at 53 (the foreign court might not apply the law agreed by the parties); Carter (1989) 60 BYBIL 482; *Kloeckner & Co AG v Gatoil Overseas Inc* [1990] 1 Lloyd's Rep 177 at 207.

commercial men",[530] this is a good reason for the exercise of the discretion to allow service abroad, notwithstanding the inconvenience to the defendant. The House of Lords has held that substantial justice would not be done abroad in a country where no financial assistance was available, the nature and complexity of the case being such that it could not be tried at all without the benefit of financial assistance.[531] This has led to the suggestion that the level of injustice abroad must be such as to deprive the claimant of any remedy at all.[532] Thus evidence of delay in trial in India of between four and five years, or possibly up to ten years, was not enough to constitute substantial injustice.[533] But evidence that delay in trial in Indonesia of more than ten years was usual was enough.[534] The English courts are also concerned with whether the defendant would receive a fair trial in England.[535] If for some reason he would not, then trial should take place abroad.

Secondly, there is the question whether the claimant will obtain a legitimate personal or juridical advantage from trial in England. This has traditionally been one of the factors to be considered when exercising the discretion to stay on the basis of *forum non conveniens*. The effect of the *Spiliada* case is to introduce this factor as a consideration when exercising the discretion to allow service out of the jurisdiction in rule 6.20 cases.[536] Lord GOFF said[537] that the court should not be deterred from refusing permission in what are now rule 6.20 cases simply because the claimant will be deprived of an advantage, such as higher damages or a more generous limitation period,[538] provided that the court is satisfied that substantial justice will be done in the available appropriate forum abroad. It is envisaged that the sort of advantage mentioned above, which is to the benefit of the claimant and to the detriment of the defendant, will not be decisive.[539] However, the position may be different in the situation where the advantage to the claimant is not to

---

[530] *Coast Lines v Hudig and Veder Chartering NV*, supra, at 45; see also *Britannia Steamship Insurance Association Ltd v Ausonia Assicurazioni SpA* [1984] 2 Lloyd's Rep 98 at 102, *Cadre SA v Astra Asigurari* [2004] EWHC 2504 (QB) at [16]; cf *Catlin Syndicate Ltd v Adams Land & Cattle Co* [2006] EWHC 2065 (Comm) at [42]–[46].

[531] *Connelly v RTZ Corpn plc* [1998] AC 854, HL—a stay of proceedings case, discussed infra, pp 434–435. See also *Lubbe v Cape* [2000] 1 WLR 1545, HL, infra, p 435. Cf *Hewitson v Hewitson* [1999] 2 FLR 74.

[532] *Konamaneni v Rolls-Royce Industrial Power (India) Ltd* [2002] 1 WLR 1269 at [175]–[177]. This constituted "no alternative forum" abroad but compare the meaning of this phrase in cases of *forum non conveniens*, infra, pp 428–430.

[533] Ibid. See also *Chellaram v Chellaram (No 2)* [2002] EWHC 632 (Ch) at [177], [2002] 3 All ER 17. For similar cases in relation to *forum non conveniens*, see infra, p 435.

[534] *Marconi v PT Pan Indonesia Bank Ltd TBK* [2004] EWHC 129 (Comm) at [38], [2004] 1 Lloyd's Rep 594; affd [2005] EWCA Civ 422 at [77].

[535] See *Attorney General for Zambia v Meer Care & Desai* [2006] EWCA Civ 390, [2006] 1 CLC 436, the fact that the defendants could not get to England to defend in person did not mean that trial would be unfair when alternative arrangements were made to hear their evidence.

[536] Not to be taken into account in the initial search for the appropriate forum, see the *Metall und Rohstoff* case, supra, 488. But see the criticism of the Court of Appeal in *King v Lewis* [2004] EWCA (Civ) 1329, [2005] IL Pr 16.

[537] [1987] AC 460 at 482–484. See also the *Connelly* case, supra, at 872.

[538] If the English proceedings are set aside, this may be on condition that the defendant should waive its right to rely on the time bar in the foreign proceedings, per Lord GOFF at 487–488; *Nima Sarl v Deves Insurance Public Co Ltd, The Prestrioka* [2002] EWCA Civ 1132 at [80], [2003] 2 Lloyd's Rep 327—only exceptionally will this not be required. See on time-bars, *Metall und Rohstoff AG v Donaldson Lufkin and Jenrette Inc* [1990] 1 QB 391 at 488; overruled on a different point in *Lonrho plc v Fayed* [1992] 1 AC 448, HL. Problems with time-bars have arisen in the context of foreign choice of jurisdiction agreements, see infra, p 445.

[539] See also *King v Lewis*, supra, at [20]—fact that action could not be brought sucessfully abroad but could in England not to be taken into account.

the disadvantage of the defendant. Thus, on the facts of the *Spiliada* case one crucial point was that the claimants obtained an advantage from trial in England in that similar proceedings involving the same defendant company, lawyers, expert witnesses and insurers had been commenced and eventually settled in England.[540] The advantage that this gave to the claimants in terms of "efficiency, expedition and economy" did not involve a countervailing disadvantage to the defendants. Indeed, it was in the objective interests of justice that trial should take place in England. The result was that the House of Lords allowed service out of the jurisdiction. The advantage that the claimant obtains from the award of costs in English proceedings has been taken into account on the basis that substantial justice would not be done in the foreign proceedings if the claimant would have to pay costs there,[541] as has the advantage of trial before an English court which would uphold an arbitration agreement, whereas the alternative forum abroad might not,[542] and the advantage of the availability of urgent interlocutory relief.[543]

There is no fixed list of the considerations that can be taken into account. Thus it has been held in a case involving connections with three states that it is not in the interests of the parties or of justice to refuse trial in England in the situation where there was another appropriate court in State X to which neither party wished to resort, producing the result that the case should be tried in State Y, which was clearly less appropriate for trial than England.[544] The fact that a claimant gets no legitimate benefit from trial in England is a relevant consideration. It will ordinarily not be just to permit service out of the jurisdiction unless there is a real prospect of a legitimate benefit to the claimant from the English proceedings.[545]

On the other hand, it seems that certain considerations cannot be taken into account when exercising the discretion. The courts are not "to embark upon a comparison of the procedures, or methods, or reputation or standing of the courts of one country as compared with those of another".[546] Nonetheless,[547] the Court of Appeal has held that the ease with which an English judgment can be enforced in other European countries by virtue of what is now the Brussels I Regulation constitutes a legitimate advantage to the claimant.[548]

---

[540] The *Spiliada* case, supra, at 484–486. See also *Crédit Agricole Indosuez v Unicof Ltd* [2003] EWHC 2676 (Comm) at [19], [2004] 1 Lloyd's Rep 196.

[541] *Roneleigh Ltd v MII Exports Inc* [1989] 1 WLR 619 at 623; cf *Pride Shipping Corpn v Chung Hwa Pulp Corpn* [1991] 1 Lloyd's Rep 126 at 135.

[542] *Union de Remorquage et de Sauvetage SA v Lake Avery Inc, The "Lake Avery"* [1997] 1 Lloyd's Rep 540.

[543] *Intermetal Group Ltd & Trans-World (Steel) Ltd v Worslade Trading Ltd* [1998] IL Pr 765, Irish Supreme Court.

[544] *Banque Paribas v Cargill International SA* [1992] 2 Lloyd's Rep 19 at 25, CA.

[545] *Demirel v Tasarruff* [2007] EWCA Civ 799 at [27], [2007] 1 WLR 2508, leave to appeal to the House of Lords dismissed [2007] 1 WLR 3066.

[546] *Amin Rasheed Corpn v Kuwait Insurance Co* [1984] AC 50 at 72 (per Lord WILBERFORCE), at 67 (per Lord DIPLOCK) See also *Jayaretnam v Mahmood* (1992) Times, 21 May; *New Hampshire Insurance Co v Strabag Bau AG* [1992] 1 Lloyd's Rep 361 at 371; *Bank of Baroda v Vysya Bank Ltd* [1994] 2 Lloyd's Rep 87 at 98; *Trade Indemnity v Försäkrings AB Njord* [1995] 1 All ER 796 at 809. See further infra, pp 436–437.

[547] *Coast Lines v Hudig and Veder Chartering NV* [1972] 2 QB 34 at 45, CA; Bissett-Johnson (1972) 21 ICLQ 53; cf Collins (1972) 21 ICLQ 656; Graupner (1963) 12 ICLQ 357. See also *Kutchera v Buckingham International Holdings Ltd* (1988) 9 ILRM 501 at 505–506, Supreme Court of Ireland.

[548] *International Credit and Investment Co (Overseas) Ltd v Shaikh Kamal Adham* [1999] IL Pr 302, CA. Cf *Coast Lines v Hudig and Veder Chartering NV* [1972] 2 QB 34 at 45, CA; Bissett-Johnson (1972) 21 ICLQ 53; cf Collins (1972) 21 ICLQ 656; Graupner (1963) 12 ICLQ 357. See also *Kutchera v Buckingham International Holdings Ltd* (1988) 9 ILRM 501 at 505–506, Sup Ct of Ireland.

(iv) Negative declarations[549]

One important factor that is taken into account in deciding whether the case is a proper one for service out of the jurisdiction, not mentioned by Lord GOFF in the *Spiliada* case, is that the claimant seeks a negative declaration from the English courts. The modern approach towards the grant of negative declarations is set out in *Messier-Dowty v Sabena SA (No 2)*,[550] where Lord WOOLF MR said that:

> The deployment of negative declarations should be scrutinised and their use rejected where it would serve no useful purpose. However, where a negative declaration would help to ensure that the aims of justice are achieved the courts should not be reluctant to grant such declarations. They can and do assist in achieving justice.[551]

No valid reason could be seen for taking an adverse view of negative declaratory relief.[552] The crucial question therefore is whether such a declaration would serve a useful purpose. An example of where it would do so is where the person against whom it is sought is "temporising" (ie was not prepared to come forward and make his claim).[553] Where the negative declaration would serve a useful purpose the normal *forum conveniens* principles (or *forum non conveniens*) will then apply.[554] Where the negative declaration would serve no useful purpose, permission for service out of the jurisdiction should be refused or, in a case of *forum non conveniens*, a stay granted.[555] Careful scrutiny must be exercised not just to test utility but also to ensure that inappropriate forum shopping is not allowed.[556] If the possibility exists that the claimant in the English proceedings will be sued by the defendant in an alternative forum abroad, the English court must be particularly careful to ensure that the negative declaration is sought for a valid and valuable purpose and not in an illegitimate attempt to pre-empt the jurisdiction in which the dispute between the parties is to be resolved.[557] Likewise, where there are existing proceedings abroad, if the

---

[549] Collins, *Essays*, Chapter 5; Dicey, Morris and Collins, paras 12-039–12-041; Bell (1995) 111 LQR 674; Bell, *Forum Shopping and Venue in Transnational Litigation*, paras 3.106, 4.250–4.293.

[550] [2000] 1 WLR 2040, CA—a Brussels Convention case discussing the principles to be applied under the traditional English rules of jurisdiction; Briggs (2000) 71 BYBIL 455. See also *New Hampshire Insurance Co v Phillips Electronics North America Corpn* [1998] IL Pr 256, CA.

[551] The *Messier-Dowty* case, supra, at 2050.

[552] Ibid, at 2049.

[553] *Bristow Helicopters Ltd v Sikorsky Aircraft Corpn* [2004] EWHC 401 (Comm) at [25], [2004] 2 Lloyd's Rep 150—a *forum non conveniens* case. See also *Bhatia Shipping v Alcobex Metals* [2004] EWHC 2323 (Comm) at [24]–[26], [2005] 2 Lloyd's Rep 336.

[554] See *Swiss Reinsurance Co Ltd v United India Insurance Co* [2002] EWHC 741 (Comm) at [27], [2004] IL Pr 4—a case on service out of the jurisdiction; *Travelers Casualty and Surety Co of Europe Ltd v Sun Life Assurance Co of Canada (UK) Ltd* [2004] EWHC 1704 (Comm), [2004] IL Pr 50—a case involving both *forum conveniens* and *forum non conveniens*; *CGU International Insurance plc v Szabo* [2002] 1 All ER (Comm) 83; *Tryg Baltica International (UK) Ltd v Boston Compañía de Seguros SA* [2004] EWHC 1186 (Comm) at [10]–[40], [2005] Lloyd's Rep IR 40, QBD; *Ark v True North Capital* [2005] EWHC 1585 (Comm) at [72], [2006] 1 All ER (Comm) 138. In the *Messier-Dowty* case, supra, a negative declaration was refused because the joinder of the party against whom it was sought was improper.

[555] See *American Motorists Insurance Co v Cellstar Corpn* [2002] EWHC 421, [2002] 2 Lloyd's Rep 216; affd [2003] EWCA Civ 206, [2003] IL Pr 370—without discussion of this point; *Chase v Ram Technical Services Ltd* [2000] 2 Lloyd's Rep 418 at 420–421.

[556] *Travelers Casualty and Surety Co of Europe Ltd v Sun Life Assurance Co of Canada (UK) Ltd* [2004] EWHC 1704 (Comm) at [90]–[92], [2004] IL Pr 50.

[557] *New Hampshire Insurance Co v Phillips Electronics North America Corpn* [1998] IL Pr 256, CA. See also *Burrows v Jamaica Private Power Co Ltd* [2002] 1 All ER (Comm) 374 at [7]; *Ark v True North Capital*, supra, at [73]–[78].

negative declaration does serve a useful purpose, the court must consider whether it is proper to grant permission for service out of the jurisdiction notwithstanding the undesirability of concurrent proceedings.[558]

(v) An exorbitant basis of jurisdiction

The predecessor of what is now rule 6.20 was regarded as being an "exorbitant" or "extraordinary" basis of jurisdiction.[559] It is a wider jurisdiction than we recognise in others, in that if a foreign court took jurisdiction in similar circumstances English courts would not be prepared to recognise that court's judgment.[560] Assumed jurisdiction has been seen as conflicting with the general principles of comity between civilised nations, and, because of this, at one time it was said that the power to allow service out of the jurisdiction should be exercised with extreme caution.[561]

Such views now seem rather old fashioned. Nonetheless, this traditional reluctance to allow service out of the jurisdiction continues to exert an influence in the form of a number of general principles, all of which operate against the exercise of assumed jurisdiction. The power conferred by what is now rule 6.20 is only exercisable by the court in cases "which seem to it to fall within the spirit as well as the letter of the various classes of case provided for".[562] As has been seen,[563] the claimant must show that there is a reasonable prospect of success. If, in the circumstances, the construction of the ground is at all doubtful it should be resolved in favour of the defendant.[564] The claimant must also show that England is *clearly* the appropriate forum.[565] Moreover, since the application for permission is made without notice being served on any other party, full and fair disclosure of all the material facts,[566] such as that proceedings have been commenced abroad,[567] is necessary.[568] Any unreasonable delay by the claimant in seeking leave militates against

---

[558] *Ark v True North Capital*, supra, at [76].

[559] *Spiliada Maritime Corpn v Cansulex Ltd* [1987] AC 460 at 481. See generally De Winter (1968) 17 ICLQ 706; Collins (1991) 107 LQR 10.

[560] See infra, pp 529–530. For the position under the Brussels I Regulation, see supra, p 223.

[561] *Cordova Land Co Ltd v Victor Bros Inc* [1966] 1 WLR 793 at 796; *Mackender v Feldia AG* [1967] 2 QB 590 at 599; *Amin Rasheed Corpn v Kuwait Insurance*, supra, at 65. Cf *Hyde v Agar* (1998) 45 NSWLR 487.

[562] *Johnson v Taylor Bros* [1920] AC 144 at 153.

[563] Supra, pp 397–399.

[564] *The Hagen* [1908] P 189 at 201; *The Siskina* [1979] AC 210 at 254–255; cf *Buttes Gas and Oil Co v Hammer* [1971] 3 All ER 1025 (for later proceedings, see [1975] QB 557); *Chellaram v Chellaram (No 2)* [2002] EWHC 632 (Ch) at [153], [2002] 3 All ER 17; *Network Telecom (Europe) Ltd v Telephone Systems International Inc* [2003] EWHC 2890 (QB), [2004] 1 All ER (Comm) 418 at [53]–[55].

[565] *Spiliada Maritime Corpn v Cansulex Ltd* [1987] AC 460 at 481; *Islamic Arab Insurance Co v Saudi Egyptian American Reinsurance Co* [1987] 1 Lloyd's Rep 315 at 318–319.

[566] Ie material to showing that the claimant has a reasonable prospect of success and all the other matters the judge has to consider: *MRG (Japan) Ltd v Engelhard Metals Japan Ltd* [2003] EWHC 3418 (Comm) at [26]–[31], [2004] 1 Lloyd's Rep 731.

[567] *Tiernan v The Magen Insurance Co Ltd* [2000] IL Pr 517 at [21]; *Network Telecom (Europe) Ltd v Telephone Systems International Inc*, supra; *Ophthalmic Innovations International (United Kingdom) Ltd v Ophthalmic Innovations International Inc* [2004] EWHC 2948 (Ch) at [45], [2005] IL Pr 10.

[568] *Kuwait Oil Co (KSC) v Idemitsu Tankers KK, The Hida Maru* [1981] 2 Lloyd's Rep 510; *Trafalgar Tours Ltd v Alan James Henry* [1990] 2 Lloyd's Rep 298; *Newtherapeutics Ltd v Katz* [1991] Ch 226, [1991] 2 All ER 151; *Grupo Torras SA and Torras Hostench London Ltd v Sheikh Fahad Mohammed Al-Sabah* [1995] 1 Lloyd's Rep 374 at 449, appeals to the Court of Appeal dismissed without discussion of this point, [1996] 1 Lloyd's Rep 7; *ANCAP v Ridgley* [1996] 1 Lloyd's Rep 570; *Konamaneni v Rolls-Royce Industrial Power (India) Ltd* [2002] 1 WLR 1269 at [179]–[187]; *Chellaram v Chellaram (No 2)* [2002] EWHC 632 (Ch) at [189]–[193], [2002] 3 All ER 17; the *Network Telecom* case, supra; *JP Morgan Securities Asia Private Ltd v Malaysian Newsprint Industries*

leave being given.[569] Strict compliance with the procedural requirements under what is now rule 6.20 is usually required and irregularities cannot normally be cured at a later stage of the action.[570]

Whilst a reluctance to exercise jurisdiction under what is now rule 6.20 is understandable, it should perhaps be tempered by a realisation that other countries have exorbitant bases of jurisdiction.[571] Moreover, we should not be over critical of the grounds used under rule 6.20 (and over reluctant to exercise jurisdiction on these grounds). Under the Brussels/Lugano system jurisdiction is required to be taken in England, without any discretionary rule in the Regulation/Conventions to decline to do so,[572] in cases where, if the traditional rules on jurisdiction had to be used, one of the grounds of rule 6.20 would be applicable.[573] Now that we have a *forum non conveniens* discretion to stay actions once a claim form has been served, it would rationalise the English law on jurisdiction if service out of the jurisdiction was automatically available without the leave of the court. The *forum non conveniens* discretion could then come into play once the claim form had been served. After all, this discretion is based on the same fundamental principle as the rule 6.20 discretion. However, it is the notion that rule 6.20 is an exorbitant form of jurisdiction with the consequential placing of the burden of proof on the claimant, coupled with a fear of defendants being forced to respond to unmeritorious actions which would have been filtered out by a permission requirement, that stands in the way of this rationalisation.

(vi) The significance of the particular ground of rule 6.20

Whilst accepting that what is now rule 6.20 is an exorbitant form of jurisdiction, Lord GOFF has pointed out that the circumstances specified under the different grounds vary greatly, and that this affects the court's willingness to exercise the discretion in favour of allowing service out of the jurisdiction.[574] In cases coming under rule 6.20(3) special care is needed[575] because of the lack of connection, under this ground, between the claim and an English forum.[576] In contrast to this, if the parties have agreed on trial in England by

---

SDN BHD [2001] 2 Lloyd's Rep 41 at [58]–[65]; the *BAS Capital Funding Corpn* case, supra, at [196]–[199]; *Pearson Education Ltd v Prentice Hall India PTE Ltd* [2005] EWHC 636 (QB), [2006] FSR 8; *Albon v Naza Motor Trading* [2007] EWHC 9 (Ch) at [34]–[38], [2007] 1 Lloyd's Rep 297.

[569] *The Nimrod* [1973] 2 Lloyd's Rep 91.

[570] *Ophthalmic Innovations International (United Kingdom) Ltd v Ophthalmic Innovations International Inc* [2004] EWHC 2948 (Ch) at [43], [2005] IL Pr 10 following *Camera Care Ltd v Victor Hasselblad AB* (1986) Times, 6 January, [1986] ECC 373—a case under Ord 11, RSC; *Leal v Dunlop Bio-Processes Ltd* [1984] 2 All ER 207. Cf *Midland International Trade Services Ltd v Sudairy* (1990) Financial Times, 2 May. Cf *Spargos Mining NL v Atlantic Capital Corpn* (1995) Times, 11 December. A fresh application for permission may be made: *Albon v Naza Motor trading* [2007] EWHC 9 (Ch) at [16], [2007] 1 Lloyd's Rep 297.

[571] See De Winter (1968) 17 ICLQ 706; Art 3 of the Brussels I Regulation and Brussels and Lugano Conventions, discussed supra, pp 222–223.

[572] On the question whether an English court can use the traditional English doctrine of *forum non conveniens*, see supra, pp 320–333.

[573] See *James North and Sons Ltd v North Cape Textiles Ltd* [1984] 1 WLR 1428 at 1433–1434, on the importance of harmonising English law with that in other European Community countries as a factor in favour of exercising the discretion to allow service abroad.

[574] *Spiliada Maritime Corpn v Cansulex Ltd* [1987] AC 460 at 481.

[575] *Petroleo Brasiliero SA v Mellitus Shipping Inc (The Baltic Flame)* [2001] EWCA Civ 418 at [21], [2001] 2 Lloyd's Rep 203; see supra, pp 374–377.

[576] *Multinational Gas and Petrochemical Co v Multinational Gas and Petrochemical Services* [1983] Ch 258 at 271–272, CA.

putting an English jurisdiction clause in their contract, the courts have been very willing to allow service out of the jurisdiction under rule 6.20(5)(d),[577] unless there was a strong reason to the contrary, since the parties should abide by their agreement and there is a strong prima facie case that the jurisdiction chosen is an appropriate one.[578] In tort cases the starting point for the operation of the discretion has been a willingness to allow service out of the jurisdiction. As has already been mentioned,[579] the House of Lords in *Berezovsky v Michaels*[580] has confirmed the principle that the jurisdiction in which a tort was committed is prima facie the natural forum for the determination of the dispute.

However, the real question is always whether it is appropriate *in the circumstances of the particular case* for a claim form to be served out of the jurisdiction. It is certainly important to look at the relevant ground of rule 6.20 invoked by the claimant, to ask whether there is a close connection with England on the facts of the case, whether English law will apply and whether the parties have agreed on trial in England, but generalisations or presumptions about particular grounds of rule 6.20 do not help. Lord GOFF in the *Spiliada* case said that the importance to be attached to any particular ground of what is now rule 6.20 may vary from case to case.[581] Thus, as has already been seen,[582] the fact that English law is the law governing the contract would, in some cases, be of very great importance, and, in others, of little importance, depending on the circumstances. In the *Spiliada* case itself it was by no means an insignificant factor.[583]

(vii) The operation of the principles

This can be best illustrated by examining the *Spiliada* case[584] itself.

> The plaintiff shipowners, a Liberian company, alleged that the *Spiliada* had been damaged by wet sulphur being loaded on it by order of the defendant shippers, a British Columbia company, and sought damages for breach of contract. A similar action had previously been started by different plaintiffs against, inter alia, the defendants, following damage to the ship *Cambridgeshire*. In the *Spiliada* action it was held at first instance that there was a contract governed by English law.

Although one of the grounds of what is now rule 6.20 was satisfied, the Court of Appeal held that it was not a proper case for exercising the discretion to allow service out of the jurisdiction and set aside the writ.

The House of Lords allowed the appeal. Lord GOFF stated the principles to be applied in relation to the exercise of what is now the rule 6.20 discretion, as set out above.[585] The availability of witnesses and the risk of a multiplicity of proceedings were examined. However, the crucial point was the *Cambridgeshire* factor. If the *Spiliada* action also took place in England there would be teams of lawyers and experts available who had prepared

---

[577] Infra, p 582.
[578] Supra, pp 402–403.
[579] Supra, pp 387–389.
[580] [2000] 1 WLR 1004.
[581] [1987] AC 460 at 481.
[582] Supra, pp 401–402.
[583] Supra, p 401.
[584] *Spiliada Maritime Corpn v Cansulex Ltd* [1987] AC 460.
[585] Supra, p 399 et seq.

for the *Cambridgeshire* action. This would contribute to the efficient administration of justice.[586] The court would be assisted in reaching a just decision, and the possibility of a settlement of the proceedings (as happened in the *Cambridgeshire* action) would be enhanced. Trial in England was not merely a matter of financial advantage to the plaintiff (without being to the disadvantage of the defendant) but was "in the objective interests of justice". Moreover, it was a relevant factor that the litigation was being fought under a contract governed by English law, and on the facts this was by no means an insignificant factor.[587]

(ii) Service of a claim form out of the jurisdiction without the permission of the court

Rule 6.19 allows service of a claim form out of the jurisdiction *without* the permission of the court in two situations. The first[588] is where the court has jurisdiction by virtue of the Brussels I Regulation[589] or the Civil Jurisdiction and Judgments Act 1982.[590] This statute, as amended by the Civil Jurisdiction and Judgments Act 1991, is concerned with cases coming within the Brussels and Lugano Conventions and the Modified Regulation; the question of service of the claim form in such cases has already been discussed.[591] At one time a question was raised over whether the predecessor of this rule[592] was wide enough to cover the situation where an interim remedy, such as a freezing injunction, was sought in England in support of proceedings in another state or in another part of the United Kingdom by virtue of section 25 of the Civil Jurisdiction and Judgments Act 1982.[593] However, a special ground providing for service of the claim form out of the jurisdiction with the permission of the court has been introduced to deal with this situation.[594] Rule 6.19 requires that the defendant is domiciled in a Brussels I Regulation State[595] or in a Contracting State to the Brussels Convention or a State bound by the Lugano Convention.[596] The second[597] is where the court has power to hear and determine the claim by virtue of any other enactment, even though the defendant is not within the jurisdiction or the facts giving rise to the claim did not occur within the jurisdiction. An example of such an enactment is the Protection of Trading Interests Act 1980.[598] Rule 6.19 will also apply to actions brought under certain statutes passed as the result of international conventions which give a party the right to sue in England, such as the Carriage by Air Act 1961, the Carriage by Air (Supplementary Provisions) Act 1962, the Carriage

---

[586] [1987] AC 460 at 485–486. See also *Reeves v Sprecher* [2007] EWHC 117 (Ch).

[587] Supra.

[588] A statement is required by CPR, r 6.19(3) of the grounds on which the claimant is entitled to serve the claim form out of the jurisdiction; for the form this takes see 6BPD.2.

[589] CPR, r 6.19(1A).

[590] CPR, r 6.19(1).

[591] Supra, pp 300–301.

[592] Ord 11, rule 1(2) RSC.

[593] Cf *Mercedes-Benz AG v Leiduck* [1996] AC 284 at 302, PC with *Republic of Haiti v Duvalier* [1990] 1 QB 202. S 25 is discussed supra, pp 318–320.

[594] CPR, r 6.20(4); discussed supra, p 378.

[595] Ie a European Community Member State, apart from Denmark. However, by virtue of the EC/Denmark agreement the provisions of Brussels I are applied by international agreement to the relations between the Community and Denmark.

[596] Or that the case comes within Arts 22 or 23 of the Regulation, Arts 16 or 17 of the Brussels Convention or Arts 22 or 23 of the Lugano Convention.

[597] CPR, r 6.19(2). See *Re Harrods (Buenos Aires) Ltd* [1992] Ch 72 at 115–116.

[598] See infra, pp 561–563.

of Goods by Road Act 1965, the Civil Aviation Act 1982 and the Merchant Shipping Act 1995.[599] In a multi-defendant case, each defendant is looked at separately so that service out of the jurisdiction may be effected on one defendant without permission, provided that the normal requirements for this are met, irrespective of whether the claims against the other defendants satisfy these requirements.[600] Where a claim form can be served under rule 6.19 it must be so served and the claimant does not have the option of seeking permission to serve under rule 6.20,[601] under which the period for responding to a claim form is calculated differently.[602]

(iii) Service of the claim form

Where service of a claim form out of the jurisdiction is allowed, there is the practical problem of how this is to be effected on a defendant who is abroad. Service within the European Union is dealt with by the Union's Service Regulation.[603] What we are concerned with now is service outside the European Union.[604] Actions that contain a foreign element must frequently require the assistance of judicial and administrative officers in other countries, and the United Kingdom has therefore concluded conventions with a number of states in order to facilitate the conduct of legal proceedings in civil and commercial matters, and is a party to the Hague Convention[605] on the service abroad of judicial and extra-judicial documents in civil or commercial matters, which came into effect in 1969.[606]

(d) Are there other bases of competence?

A doctrine of arrestment *ad fundandam jurisdictionem* operates in Scotland[607] and in certain civil law countries[608] under which an action may be brought against a person

---

[599] See generally Dicey, Morris and Collins, Chapter 15.

[600] See SI 1996/2892, reg 2.

[601] *The Reefer Creole* [1994] 1 Lloyd's Rep 584 at 586.

[602] See CPR, 6PD.8.

[603] Supra, pp 300–301.

[604] See generally CPR, rr 6.24–6.31.

[605] (1964) Cmnd 1613; see (1965) 14 ICLQ 564–572. For alternative methods of service allowed under the Convention see: *Molins plc v GD SpA* [2000] 1 WLR 1741, CA; *Arros Invest Ltd v Rafik Nishanov* [2004] IL Pr 22. The parties can agree on a method of service: *McCulloch v Bank of Novia Scotia* [2006] EWHC 790 (Ch), [2006] 2 All ER (Comm) 714.

[606] CPR, r 6.8 (service by a method not permitted by the CPR rules, on which see *Addax BV Geneva Branch v Coral Suki SA* [2004] EWHC 2882 (Comm), [2005] 2 All ER (Comm) 137) cannot be used to avoid application of the Hague Service Convention or a bilateral convention: *Knauf UK GmbH v British Gypsum Ltd* [2002] 1 WLR 907; distinguished in *Phillips v Nussberger* [2008] UKHL 1, [2008] 1 WLR 180; *Marconi v PT Pan Indonesia Bank Ltd TBK* [2004] EWHC 129 (Comm) at [39]–[45], [2004] 1 Lloyd's Rep 594; appeal on a different point dismissed [2005] EWCA Civ 422. The principles in *Knauf* have been applied to CPR, r 6.9 (power to dispense with service) in *Shiblaq v Sadikoglu* [2004] EWHC 1890 (Comm) at [56]–[58], [2004] IL Pr 51. For service where the country abroad is not a party to the Hague Service Convention and with which there is no bilateral convention, see CPR, rr 6.24 and 6.25, *BAS Capital Funding Corpn v Medfinco Ltd* [2003] EWHC 1798 at [156]–[168], [2004] IL Pr 16; *Habib Bank Ltd v Central Bank of Sudan.* [2006] EWHC 1767 (Comm), [2006] 2 Lloyd's Rep 412. For the use of CPR, rr 6.9 and 6.24 in a Lugano Convention case, see *Olafsson v Gissurarson* [2008] EWCA 152.

[607] This doctrine does not apply where the defendant is domiciled in the United Kingdom: Civil Jurisdiction and Judgments Act 1982, Sch 8, r 2(h). Nor does it apply where the case is within the scope of the Brussels I Regulation or Brussels or Lugano Convention and the defendant is domiciled in a Regulation State, Contracting State to the Brussels Convention or a State bound by the Lugano Convention, Art 3 of the Regulation and Conventions: discussed supra, pp 222–224.

[608] For Germany see s 23 ZPO; BGH 2.7.1991, NJW 1991, 3092 (a sufficient connection with Germany is required); Dannemann (1992) 41 ICLQ 632. A Regulation State or Contracting State to the Brussels Convention

absent from the forum if movables[609] situated there and belonging to him have been taken into the custody of the law at the instance of the claimant.[610] The court can deal with a claim unconnected with the movables and deliver a personal judgment against the owner that will be wholly or partially satisfied by their sale. Another instance is the jurisdiction *quasi in rem* that is recognised in the USA, which enables a personal claim against a defendant living abroad to be satisfied out of chattels owned by him but situated in the forum. Attachment of the chattels confers jurisdiction on the court of the situs, but any judgment that may be given is limited in its effect to the value of the property attached.[611]

English law stands aloof from this doctrine,[612] at least in cases where the claim is unrelated to the movables. An attempt in *The Siskina*[613] to introduce indirectly a ground based on the presence of assets in the forum was unsuccessful. However, where the claim is related to the movables the position is very different. Rule 6.20(10) of the Civil Procedure Rules allows a claim form to be served out of the jurisdiction with the permission of the court where the whole subject matter of a claim relates to property (and this includes movable property) located within the jurisdiction.[614]

It is not open to the courts to introduce new additional bases of competence.[615] Any extension of the jurisdiction of the courts over foreign defendants requires subordinate legislation by the rules committee if not primary legislation by Parliament itself.[616]

2. ACTIONS IN REM[617]

(a) An action against a ship as defendant

In Roman law an action in rem was one brought in order to vindicate a jus in rem, ie a right such as ownership available against all persons, but the only action in rem known to English law is that which lies in an Admiralty court against a particular res, namely a ship or some other res, such as cargo, associated with the ship.[618] The Supreme Court Act

---

or State bound by the Lugano Convention cannot use this form of jurisdiction in the situation where the case is within the scope of the Regulation or either Convention and the defendant is domiciled in a Regulation State, Contracting State to the Brussels Convention or a State bound by the Lugano Convention: Art 3 of the Regulation and Conventions, discussed supra, pp 222–224.

[609] Jurisdiction over immovables is discussed infra, pp 478–489.

[610] For Scots law see Civil Jurisdiction and Judgments Act 1982, Sch 8, r 2(h); Anton and Beaumont's *Civil Jurisdiction in Scotland*, paras 10.36–10.38; Anton, *Private International Law*, pp 188–193; Crawford and Carruthers, para 7-04.

[611] Restatement 2d, Conflict of Laws, § 66; Hay (1986) 35 ICLQ 32; *Shaffer v Heitner* 433 US 186 at 210 (1977); *Rush v Savchuck* 444 US 320 (1980).

[612] See also in relation to Canada *Marren v Echo Bay Mines Ltd* (2003) 226 DLR (4th) 622, BC CA.

[613] *Siskina (owners of cargo lately laden on board) v Distos Cia Naviera SA, The Siskina* [1979] AC 210.

[614] Discussed supra, pp 391–393. It may be posssible to use r 6.20(3); discussed supra, pp 374–377.

[615] *Siskina (owners of cargo lately laden on board) v Distos Cia Naviera SA, The Siskina* [1979] AC 210. See also *Serge Caudron v Air Zaire* [1986] ILRM 10, Supreme Court of Ireland.

[616] At 260 (Lord DIPLOCK); see also at 262–263 (Lord HAILSHAM).

[617] Jackson, *Enforcement of Maritime Claims* (2005) 4th edn, paras 2.31–2.239. For an examination of this whole subject in Australia, see (1986) ALRC 33; the Admiralty Act 1988 (Cth); Davenport [1987] LMCLQ 317; Crawford [1997] LMCLQ 519.

[618] "Ship" can include a dredger, *The Von Rocks* [1998] 2 Lloyd's Rep 198, Supreme Court of Ireland. For cargo, see *Sembawang Salvage Pte Ltd v Shell Todd Oil Services Ltd* [1993] 2 NZLR 97. The owner and other

1981 lists the claims that lie within the Admiralty Court[619] and goes on to make detailed provision as to when an action in rem may be brought.[620] To take one instance, the rule has long been that a maritime lien attaches to and remains enforceable against a ship that collides with and damages another.[621] Such a lien "is a privileged claim upon a vessel in respect of service done to it or injury caused by it, to be carried into effect by legal process. It is a right acquired by one over a thing belonging to another—a *jus in re aliena*".[622]

That the ship is the defendant in an action brought to enforce the lien is underlined by the legal process available to the claimant. After the issue of an in rem claim form, service may be made by fixing a copy of the claim form on the outside of the ship.[623] The claimant is entitled to have the ship arrested, in which case the Admiralty Marshal will effect service.

The person is the ship, and therefore it is essential that it should be "so situated as to be within the lawful control of the State under the authority of which the court sits".[624] In short, the court is competent to entertain the action if the ship lies within the territorial waters of England. It has been held that the issue of a warrant for the arrest of property in an Admiralty action in rem is no longer[625] a discretionary remedy.[626] So long as a claimant's case is not bound to fail, which means that he has an arguable case, he is entitled to proceed with it.[627] Accordingly, there is no duty of full and frank disclosure.[628] However, it is possible that the court might have a general discretion to set aside a warrant of arrest on the basis that its effects are unjust.[629] The court has power to release a ship under arrest,[630]

---

persons interested are also made defendants. The action also lies against an aircraft, Supreme Court Act 1981, s 21(3), or hovercraft, Hovercraft Act 1968, s 2(1).

[619] See Supreme Court Act 1981, s 20, amended by Merchant Shipping (Salvage and Pollution) Act 1994, s 1(6), Sch 2, para 6, and Merchant Shipping Act 1995, s 314(2), Sch 13, para 59(2)(a), (b), (c) and (d) and the Merchant Shipping and Maritime Security Act 1997, s 29(1) and Sch 6, para 2. This includes, eg, a claim "arising out of any agreement relating to the carriage of goods in a ship or to the use or hire of a ship": s 20(2)(h), on which see *The Antonis P Lemos* [1985] AC 711; *Petrofina SA v AOT Ltd* [1992] QB 571; *The Lloyd Pacifico* [1995] 1 Lloyd's Rep 54; *The Bumbesti* [2000] QB 559; see also *Gatoil International Inc v Arkwright-Boston Manufacturers Mutual Insurance Co* [1985] AC 255, HL. It also includes a claim "in respect of goods . . . supplied to a ship for her operation": s 20(2)(m), on which see *The River Rima* [1988] 1 WLR 758, HL; Jackson [1988] LMCLQ 423; *The Edinburgh Castle* [1999] 2 Lloyd's Rep 362; *The Nore Challenger* [2001] 2 Lloyd's Rep 103.

[620] S 21. For procedural rules see CPR, Part 61 and Practice Direction (Admiralty Claims); Tsimplis and Gaskell [2002] LMCLQ 520.

[621] S 21 (3).

[622] *The Ripon City* [1897] P 226 at 242.

[623] CPR, Part 61, PD 3.6. There are other alternative ways in which service can be made.

[624] *Castrique v Imrie* (1870) LR 4 HL 414 at 429; *General Motors-Holdens Ltd v The Ship Northern Highway* (1982) 29 SASR 138.

[625] See *The Vasso (formerly Andria)* [1984] 1 Lloyd's Rep 235.

[626] *The Varna* [1993] 2 Lloyd's Rep 253, CA; Dockray (1994) 110 LQR 382. This decision reflected changes to the procedural rules. Since *The Varna* these have been altered yet again (see now CPR, r 61.5) but this probably does not alter the position, see Tsimplis and Gaskell, op cit, at pp 522–526.

[627] *The Yula Bondarovskaya* [1998] 2 Lloyd's Rep 357 at 361.

[628] *The Varna*, supra. CPR, Part 61, PD 5.3 sets out the particulars required in the declaration by the party making an application for arrest.

[629] *The Varna*, supra, at 258.

[630] See, eg, *The Bumbesti*, supra, 572–575 (adequate other security). Release can be made subject to conditions, see eg *The Vanessa Ann* [1985] 1 Lloyd's Rep 549. For subsequent arrest and subsequent provision of security, see Art 3(3) of the Arrest Convention; *The Tjaskemolen No 2* [1997] 2 Lloyd's Rep 476.

and the shipowner can protect itself by giving security. The usual practice is that the ship will only be released on the provision of sufficient security to cover the amount of the claim plus costs.[631]

The granting of security aspect of the action in rem is underlined by the fact that the ship or other chattel can be sold under the authority of the court and the proceeds adjudged to the claimant in satisfaction of his claim.[632] If a sale is ordered, the judgment operates in rem in the sense that it divests the property in the ship from the owners and confers an absolute title on the purchaser, good against all persons.[633]

The formal position is that the ship is the defendant. However, the House of Lords in *Republic of India v India Steamship Co (No 2)*[634] held that the reality is that an action in rem is an action against the owner of the ship. This means that the latter is a party to the action in rem. This is important, inter alia, when it comes to the operation of section 34 of the Civil Jurisdiction and Judgments Act 1982, which is concerned with the estoppel effect of a foreign judgment.[635]

(b) An action against a ship other than the primary ship

Normally the action lies only against the primary ship (eg the offending ship in a collision case[636]) but in the case of certain claims that arise in connection with a ship for which "the relevant person" (ie the owner, charterer, person in possession or control of the ship) would be liable in an action in personam,[637] section 21(4) of the Supreme Court Act 1981 allows an action in rem to be brought against either (i) that ship (the primary ship) or (ii) another ship owned by "the relevant person,"[638] but not both.[639] However, it does not allow an action to be brought against a ship owned by a sister company of the owners of the primary ship.[640]

In cases where the action is brought against the primary ship "the relevant person" must be, at the time when the action is brought, either the beneficial owner of that ship[641] or

---

[631] *The Bazias 3* [1993] QB 673, CA—the usual practice applies even though the claim is subject to an arbitration clause. For retention of the ship for satisfaction of any arbitration award, see the Arbitration Act 1996, s 11, infra, p 417.

[632] *The Henrich Björn* (1886) 11 App Cas 270 at 276–277. For priority amongst creditors, see *The Turiddu* [1998] 2 Lloyd's Rep 278.

[633] *Minna Craig Steamship Co v Chartered Mercantile Bank of India, London and China* [1897] 1 QB 460.

[634] [1998] AC 878, HL; Briggs (1997) 68 BYBIL 355; Rose [1998] LMCLQ 27; Teare [1998] LMCLQ 33; Davenport (1998) 114 LQR 169.

[635] Infra, p 544.

[636] Eg *The Beldis* [1936] P 51; *The Atlantic Star* [1974] AC 436.

[637] See *The Gulf Venture* [1984] 2 Lloyd's Rep 445.

[638] Eg *The Soya Margareta* [1961] 1 WLR 709; *The Span Terza* [1982] 1 Lloyd's Rep 225; *The Mawan* [1988] 2 Lloyd's Rep 459. For ships flying the flag of a non-Contracting State, see *In the matter of MV Kapitan Labunets* [1995] 1 ILRM 430, Sup Ct of Ireland.

[639] *The Banco* [1971] P 137; *The Stephan J* [1985] 2 Lloyd's Rep 344; *The Afala* [1995] 2 Lloyd's Rep 286. It is, however, possible to have claim forms issued against several ships and then to serve one of these claim forms on the ship which comes conveniently within the jurisdiction, see *The Berny* [1979] QB 80; Supreme Court Act 1981, s 21(8); see also *The Helene Roth* [1980] QB 273; *The Freccia Del Nord* [1989] 1 Lloyd's Rep 388.

[640] *The Evpo Agnic* [1988] 1 WLR 1090. See also *The Tiang Shen No 8* [2000] 2 Lloyd's Rep 430, HK CA.

[641] Cf for Australia *The Cape Moreton* [2005] 219 ALR 48; Hetherington [2005] LMCLQ 428.

the charterer of it under a charter by demise,[642] under which he would have full possession and control but not ownership.

In cases where the action is brought against another ship it must be shown that "the relevant person" is the beneficial owner of that ship. It is clear from the wording of section 21(4)[643] that it is not enough to show that "the relevant person" is a charterer under a charter by demise. However, if "the relevant person" does own another ship the ambit of section 21(4) is very wide. Since "the relevant person" can include a mere charterer, whether under a charter by demise or under some other type of charter,[644] of the primary ship, it follows that an action can be brought against another ship owned by a charterer of the primary ship[645] although this is not a sister ship.

(c) A stay of proceedings which is subject to conditions

A problem may arise, once an action in rem against a ship has been brought and the ship arrested or security for it given, if the defendant seeks to have the proceedings stayed. The court has a discretion to order the stay of the proceedings if the parties have agreed to submit their dispute to a foreign court[646] or if a foreign court would be a more appropriate forum.[647] If the case falls under section 9 of the Arbitration Act 1996,[648] a stay is mandatory. If the action in rem is stayed the arrested ship or other security can be retained as a security for the satisfaction of any arbitration award or judgment;[649] alternatively, the court can make the staying of the action conditional on the defendant giving some other security.[650] It is irrelevant whether or not the other proceedings have actually started.[651] However, it seems that these provisions in respect of security where Admiralty proceedings are stayed cannot apply if the proceedings are outside the jurisdiction of the Admiralty Court.[652]

---

[642] S 21(4). See *The Nazym Khikmet* [1996] 2 Lloyd's Rep 362, CA; *The Guiseppe di Vittorio* [1998] 1 Lloyd's Rep 136, CA; *The Looiersgracht* [1995] 2 Lloyd's Rep 411, Canada Federal Court Trial Division; *The Tjaskemolen* [1997] 2 Lloyd's Rep 465 (sham transfer ignored). Cf *Ocean Industries v Steven C* (1991) 104 ALR 353.

[643] Cf s 21(4)(i) with s 21(4)(ii).

[644] *The Span Terza* [1982] 1 Lloyd's Rep 225, CA (involving a time charterer); *The Tychy* [1999] 2 Lloyd's Rep 11, CA (slot charterers—the issue of their replacement was considered in *The Tychy (No 2)* [2001] 2 Lloyd's Rep 403, CA), Baughen [2006] LMCLQ 129; *The Faial* [2000] 1 Lloyd's Rep 473; *The Sextum* [1982] 2 Lloyd's Rep 532 (HK Supreme Court).

[645] *The Span Terza* [1982] 1 Lloyd's Rep 225, CA; *The Sextum* [1982] 2 Lloyd's Rep 532 (HK Supreme Court); *Laemthong International Lines Co Ltd v BPS Shipping Ltd* (1997) 190 CLR 181 High Court of Australia. Cf the obiter dicta by Lord DIPLOCK in *The Jade*, sub nom *The Exchersheim* [1976] 1 All ER 920 at 925; and see *The Maritime Trader* [1981] 2 Lloyd's Rep 153.

[646] Infra, pp 443–448; see *The Athenee* (1922) 11 Lloyd's Rep 6; *The Fehmarn* [1957] 1 WLR 815; *The Eleftheria* [1970] P 94.

[647] Infra, pp 426–443; see *The Cap Bon* [1967] 1 Lloyd's Rep 543; *The Atlantic Star* [1974] AC 436.

[648] Infra, pp 450–454; see *The Golden Trader* [1975] QB 348; *Marazura Navegación SA v Oceanus Mutual Underwriting Association (Bermuda) Ltd* [1977] 1 Lloyd's Rep 283 at 287–288; *The Rena K* [1979] QB 377.

[649] Civil Jurisdiction and Judgments Act 1982, s 26; Arbitration Act 1996, s 11. See *The Vasso* [1984] 1 Lloyd's Rep 235 at 243; *Spiliada Maritime Corpn v Cansulex Ltd* [1987] AC 460, HL; *The World Star* [1986] 2 Lloyd's Rep 274; *The Silver Athens (No 2)* [1986] 2 Lloyd's Rep 583; *The Emre II* [1989] 2 Lloyd's Rep 182.

[650] Conditions other than this can be imposed under the 1982 Act, s 26 (see *The Havhelt* [1993] 1 Lloyd's Rep 523) but not under the 1996 Act, s 11.

[651] *The Jalamatsya* [1987] 2 Lloyd's Rep 164; *The Nordglimt* [1988] 1 QB 183 at 204.

[652] *The Nordglimt*, ibid.

(d) The effect of the Brussels/Lugano system[653]

(i) The basis of jurisdiction

The Brussels I Regulation normally applies in cases where the defendant is domiciled in a European Community Member State[654] and the matter in question is a civil and commercial matter.[655] The Brussels Convention normally applies in cases where the defendant is domiciled in one of the French overseas territories, such as New Caledonia and Mayotte, or (as regards the Netherlands) Aruba and the matter in question is a civil and commercial matter. The Lugano Convention normally applies in cases where the defendant is domiciled in an EFTA State and it is a civil and commercial matter. However, Article 71 of the Regulation, Article 57 of the Brussels Convention and Article 67 of the Lugano Convention preserve other conventions relating to jurisdiction previously entered into by the United Kingdom, eg the Convention Relating to the Arrest of Sea-Going Ships of 1952 (the Arrest Convention[656]). The Court of Appeal in *The Anna H*[657] rejected the argument that Admiralty jurisdiction in cases of arrest had been altered or that the jurisdiction to entertain the claim and rule upon its merits had been taken away. It follows that English courts are still able to take jurisdiction under the provisions of the Supreme Court Act 1981, in so far as these provisions are derived from the Arrest Convention,[658] even if the defendant is domiciled in a Regulation State or a Contracting State to the Brussels Convention or a State bound by the Lugano Convention, and even if that State is not a party to the Arrest Convention.[659] To take an example, it is still possible to bring an action in rem against a ship, owned by a Frenchman, which is arrested in English waters following a collision at sea. On the other hand, in cases coming within the Regulation or the Brussels or Lugano Convention, jurisdiction has to be taken under the Regulation or that Convention, and cannot be taken under any provision in the Supreme Court Act 1981, if that provision is not derived from the Arrest Convention.

The Arrest Convention requires a ship actually to be arrested. In *The Deichland*[660] a writ in rem was served on a ship in England, but then, as is commonly the case, the demise charterers (Deich) gave undertakings as to security in consideration of the ship not being arrested. There was jurisdiction under the 1981 Act (ignoring for the moment the

---

[653] See in relation to the Brussels/Lugano system: Jackson, *Civil Jurisdiction and Judgments—Maritime Claims* (1987); *The Enforcement of Maritime Claims* (2005) 4th edn, paras 6.1–6.63; Dicey, Morris and Collins, paras 13-022–13-035; Brice [1987] LMCLQ 281; Blackburn [1988] LMCLQ 91.

[654] With the exception of Denmark. However, by virtue of the EC/Denmark Agreement the provisions of Brussels I are applied by international agreement to the relations between the Community and Denmark.

[655] Discussed supra, pp 213–225.

[656] Also, rather confusingly, often referred to as the Brussels Convention. The 1999 Arrest Convention is an up-dated version, which will enter into force when 10 states ratify it. This has not yet happened. The United Kingdom is unwilling to ratify.

[657] [1995] 1 Lloyd's Rep 11, CA; Hartley [1995] LMCLQ 31. For the position in Scotland see *Ladgroup Ltd v Euroeast Lines SA* 1997 SLT 916.

[658] *The Deichland* [1990] 1 QB 361; *The Sea Maas* [1999] 2 Lloyd's Rep 281 at 282. On the complex question of the extent to which the 1981 Act is based on the Arrest Convention, see *Gatoil International Inc v Arkwright-Boston Manufacturers Mutual Insurance Co* [1985] AC 255, HL; *The Deichland*, supra.

[659] Art 71 of the Brussels I Regulation, Art 57 of the Brussels Convention and Art 67 Lugano Convention, supra, pp 214–215. However, the Arrest Convention must, of course, apply in respect of that particular defendant, see Jackson, *The Enforcement of Maritime Claims* (4th edn 2005), paras 6.12–6.21.

[660] [1990] 1 QB 361; Carter (1989) 60 BYBIL 489. Cf *The Po* [1991] 2 Lloyd's Rep 206. Cf *The Anna H*, supra, where it was unsuccessfully argued that the arrest did not come within the Arrest Convention.

Brussels/Lugano system) but this was not based on the Arrest Convention, since the ship had not been arrested. Deich was domiciled in Germany and under Article 2 of the Brussels Convention (corresponding to Article 2 of the Brussels I Regulation, which would now apply on the facts) had to be sued there. The Court of Appeal granted a declaration that the English courts lacked jurisdiction. Although this was an action in rem, Deich was treated as the defendant for the purposes of Article 2 of the Brussels Convention. However, a ship can be arrested under the Arrest Convention, which requires that the arrest is to secure a maritime claim, even though bail or other security has already been given.[661]

Moreover, in cases coming within the Brussels/Lugano system, it is not possible to take jurisdiction in rem against aircraft, hovercraft or against property connected with a ship, ie the cargo or freight, since the Arrest Convention only provides for jurisdiction against a ship. Instead, jurisdiction has to be taken under the Brussels/Lugano system.[662]

Article 71 of the Regulation, Article 57 of the Brussels Convention and Article 67 of the Lugano Convention also preserve the 1952 International Convention on Certain Rules Concerning Civil Jurisdiction in Matters of Collision (the Collision Convention).[663] What matters is that the United Kingdom legislation, which was designed to implement the Collision Convention, is in accordance with that Convention. It does not matter that that Convention has not been directly implemented in the United Kingdom.[664]

In the situation where jurisdiction is derived from the Arrest Convention it has been held in *The Bergen*[665] that an English court is not deprived of jurisdiction by a foreign choice of jurisdiction clause coming within Article 17 of the Brussels Convention (corresponding to Article 23 of the Brussels I Regulation, which would now apply on the facts). However, this decision appears to be wrong. The Brussels/Lugano system will continue to apply in so far as the Arrest Convention is silent on a jurisdictional matter,[666] and the latter says nothing about the effect of agreements on jurisdiction. Accordingly, Article 23 of the Brussels I Regulation will still apply to deprive an English court of jurisdiction.

(ii) Stays of action

The power to stay an action in rem, unlike the action in rem itself, does not derive from an international convention. It is part of the English courts' inherent jurisdiction and cannot be used in circumstances where to grant a stay would be inconsistent with the Brussels I Regulation or the Brussels or Lugano Conventions.[667] In determining whether the grant of a stay would be inconsistent, three different situations need to be examined. The first is where the alternative forum is a non-European Community Member State

---

[661] *The Anna H*, supra. See also *The Prinsengracht* [1993] 1 Lloyd's Rep 41.

[662] See, in particular, Art 5(7) of the Brussels I Regulation and Brussels and Lugano Conventions, discussed supra, p 262.

[663] See *The Po* [1991] 2 Lloyd's Rep 206; Hartley [1991] LMCLQ 446. Cf *Doran v Power* [1997] IL Pr 52, Irish Supreme Court.

[664] *The Po*, supra, at 211.

[665] [1997] 1 Lloyd's Rep 380; Siig [1997] LMCLQ 362.

[666] Case C-406/92 *Owners of cargo lately laden on board Tatry v Owners of Maciej Rataj, The Tatry* [1994] ECR I-5439, [1999] QB 515n; discussed supra, p 307.

[667] See supra, pp 320–333.

(and a non-Contracting State to the Brussels Convention and not a State bound by the Lugano Convention). In *The Po*[668] the Court of Appeal applied the doctrine of *forum non conveniens* to a case involving jurisdiction under the Collision Convention, despite the fact that the defendants were domiciled in Italy, which, at that time, brought the case within the Brussels Convention (now the Brussels I Regulation would apply on the facts). It is important to note that the case was argued on the basis that the alternative forum for trial was Brazil.[669] This was a case decided before the landmark decision of the Court of Justice in *Owusu v Jackson*,[670] which held that where the jurisdiction of a court of a Contracting State is based on Article 2, the Brussels Convention precludes that court from declining jurisdiction on the ground that a court of a non-Contracting State would be a more appropriate forum for the trial of the action. However, in a case of jurisdiction in rem under, for example, the Arrest Convention or Collision Convention (as preserved by Article 71 of the Brussels I Regulation, Article 57 of the Brussels Convention and Article 67 of the Lugano Convention) this is not based on Article 2 or, indeed, on any other of the bases of jurisdiction set out in the Regulation or Brussels or Lugano Conventions. This means that the doctrine of *forum non conveniens* should still operate in this situation. There is support for this view in the Opinion of Advocate General LEGER in *Owusu*, who discussed the analogous situation where Article 4 of the Brussels Convention applies (ie where the defendant is domiciled outside a Contracting State and therefore national rules of jurisdiction apply).[671] Advocate General LEGER said that where the jurisdiction of a court of a Contracting State is established pursuant to Article 4 of the Brussels Convention this does not prevent the court in question from declining to exercise its jurisdiction, in accordance with the doctrine of *forum non conveniens* on the ground that a court of a non-Member State would be more appropriate to deal with the substance of the case.[672]

The second situation that must be considered is where, again, there is jurisdiction in rem under the Arrest or Collision Convention but this time the alternative forum is a Regulation State (or a Contracting State to the Brussels or Lugano Conventions). Applying the analogy of Article 4 cases, there is authority in *Sarrio SA v Kuwait Insurance Authority*[673] that in such cases the doctrine of *forum non conveniens* can operate, even where the alternative forum is another Member State. It is as yet unclear how this is affected by the decision of the Court of Justice in *Owusu v Jackson* and another decision of that court is needed to clarify the matter.

The third situation is where there is jurisdiction in rem under the Arrest or Collision Conventions but the defendant is domiciled outside a Brussels I Regulation State[674] and Articles 22 and 23 of the Regulation[675] do not apply. According to CLARKE J in *The Xin*

---

[668] [1991] 2 Lloyd's Rep 206. See also *The Nordglimt* [1988] 1 QB 183 at 205.

[669] However, on the particular facts the first instance decision refusing a stay was upheld, the defendants having failed to show that Brazil was a clearly more appropriate forum.

[670] Case C-281/02 [2005] QB 801; discussed supra, pp 323–333.

[671] Supra, p 330.

[672] At [235].

[673] [1997] 1 Lloyd's Rep 113, CA; reversed by the House of Lords without discussion of this point.

[674] Or Brussels Convention Contracting State or state bound by the Lugano Convention.

[675] Arts 16 and 17 of the Brussels Convention, Arts 22 and 23 of the Lugano Convention.

Yang,[676] Article 4 of the Brussels Convention (on these facts this would now be Article 4 of the Brussels I Regulation) would apply. Jurisdiction is therefore to be determined by the law of each Member State and in the case of England this encompasses not only bases of jurisdiction (including the provisions in the Supreme Court Act 1981 dealing with actions in rem[677]) but also the discretion to stay on the ground of *forum non conveniens*.[678] As has been seen,[679] according to *Sarrio*, in Article 4 cases the doctrine of *forum non conveniens* can operate even where the alternative forum is another Member State.[680] CLARKE J, following this line of authority, held that the Netherlands was the appropriate forum for trial and stayed the English proceedings in rem. This, though, is now subject to the decision of the Court of Justice in *Owusu v Jackson* and it is unclear whether *Sarrio* can still stand in the light of that decision. However, in an Article 4 case where the alternative forum is a non-Member State there are comments from Advocate General LEGER in *Owusu* to the effect that the *forum non conveniens* discretion can still operate. [681] There is another way of analysing this third situation. It is arguable that Article 4 should not apply to cases, of which *The Xin Yang* appears to be one, coming within Article 71 of the Regulation.[682] The latter preserves bases of jurisdiction set out in specialised conventions and thereby creates a regime which falls outside those provisions in the Regulation[683] concerned with bases of jurisdiction, such as Article 4. However, if the case is treated as an Article 71 case, rather than as an Article 4 case, this should not make any difference since the two cases are analogous and the analysis in relation to the grant of a stay on the ground of *forum non conveniens* is the same in each case.

Whatever the position may be in relation to *forum non conveniens*, it is clear that Articles 27 (lis pendens) and 28 (related actions) of the Brussels I Regulation[684] can apply in cases where jurisdiction has been brought under the Arrest Convention. The application of the Regulation is precluded solely in relation to questions specifically governed by the specialised convention in question; in so far as the latter is silent on a jurisdictional matter, the Regulation will continue to apply.[685] Whilst Article 71 of the Regulation[686] preserves the Arrest Convention, the latter says nothing about proceedings brought in two different jurisdictions and nothing about the question of which court is to decline jurisdiction.[687] It will be recalled that Article 27 requires that the two

---

[676] [1996] 2 Lloyd's Rep 217; Newton [1997] LMCLQ 337.

[677] *The Xin Yang*, supra, at 220.

[678] *The Xin Yang*, ibid; *Sarrio SA v Kuwait Insurance Authority* [1996] 1 Lloyd's Rep 650 at 654; affd by the Court of Appeal [1997] 1 Lloyd's Rep 113; revsd by the House of Lords without discussion of this point [1999] 1 AC 32.

[679] Supra, pp 329–331.

[680] *Sarrio SA v Kuwait Insurance Authority* [1997] 1 Lloyd's Rep 113, CA; revsd by the House of Lords without discussion of this point.

[681] At [235].

[682] Or Art 57 of the Brussels Convention or Art 67 of the Lugano Convention.

[683] Or Brussels or Lugano Convention.

[684] Supra, pp 303–315. Arts 21 and 22 of the Brussels Convention and Arts 27 and 28 of the Lugano Convention.

[685] Case C-406/92 *Owners of Cargo lately laden on board Tatry v Owners of Maciej Rataj, The Tatry* [1994] ECR I-5439, [1999] QB 515 n; a case on the Brussels Convention discussed supra, p 307.

[686] Art 57 of the Brussels Convention and Art 67 of the Lugano Convention.

[687] *The Tatry*, supra. See also *The Linda* [1988] 1 Lloyd's Rep 175 at 178. The position is the same in relation to the Geneva Convention on the Contract for the International Carriage of Goods by Road of 1956 (the CMR Convention), *Sony Computer Entertainment Ltd v RH Freight Services Ltd* [2007] EWHC 302 (Comm) at [27].

sets of proceedings involve the same parties. It will also be recalled that, according to the Court of Justice in *The Tatry*,[688] if one action is in personam and the other in rem, and the latter has subsequently continued both in rem and in personam, or solely in personam, according to the distinctions drawn by the national law of that other Member State, the parties are the same. Moreover, the answer would be the same, even if the action in rem had continued as such according to national law,[689] since the distinction drawn by the law of a Member State between an action in personam and an action in rem is not material for the interpretation of Article 27. The court first seised of the action takes priority and any other court must decline jurisdiction once the jurisdiction of the court first seised has been established. With an action in rem an English court is seised of the proceedings from the moment when the document instituting the proceedings is lodged with the court[690] (ie on the date of the issue of the claim form) and not from the time of service of a claim form or arrest of a ship.[691] In the situation where an English court has declined jurisdiction under Article 27, the arrested ship can be retained as security and made available to meet a judgment in the foreign action in the court first seised of the proceedings.[692]

3. FUTURE DEVELOPMENTS: THE HAGUE CONVENTION ON CHOICE OF COURT AGREEMENTS 2005

In 2005, a Convention on Choice of Court Agreements was adopted by the Hague Conference on Private International Law.[693] The process of ratification of the Convention and the involvement of the European Community in this has already been discussed,[694] as has the lack of impact the Convention would have on the Brussels I Regulation. However, if the United Kingdom were to be bound by the Convention, its impact on the traditional English rules of jurisdiction would be considerable.

The Convention applies in international cases[695] to exclusive choice of court agreements concluded in civil or commercial matters.[696] There are, though, various exclusions from its

---

[688] *The Tatry,* supra. See also *The Winter* [2000] 2 Lloyd's Rep 298 (on whether cause of action was the same).

[689] *Republic of India v India Steamship Co Ltd (No 2)* [1998] AC 878 at 913, HL (per Lord STEYN with whom the other Law Lords concurred).

[690] Art 30(1) of the Brussels I Regulation.

[691] The position under the Lugano Convention is the same as under the Brussels I Regulation. Under the Brussels Convention it is unclear whether an English court is seised from the moment of service (see *Neste Chemicals SA v DK Line SA, The Sargasso* [1994] 3 All ER 180, CA) or whether, as an alternative, it can be from the time of arrest when this is earlier (see *The Freccia del Nord* [1989] 1 Lloyd's Rep 388 and *The Sargasso,* supra, footnote d).

[692] Civil Jurisdiction and Judgments Act 1982, s 26; *The Nordglimt* [1988] 1 QB 183 at 203–204. The position is more problematical if security has been given to prevent arrest; Hartley (1989) 105 LQR 640 argued that Art 22 of the Brussels Convention (corresponding to Art 28 of the Regulation) has to be used in such a case.

[693] See http://www.hcch.net. See the Explanatory Report by Hartley and Dogauchi, which is available on this website; Hartley (2006) ELR 414 and (2006) 319 Hague Recueil 137–141; Kruger (2006) 55 ICLQ 447; Teitz (2005) 53 AJCL 543; Tu (2007) 55 AJCL 347.

[694] Supra, pp 340–341.

[695] As defined in Art 1(2) and (3).

[696] Art 1(1).

scope.[697] It does not apply to exclusive choice of court agreements to which a natural person acting primarily for personal, family or household purposes (a consumer) is a party.[698] Nor does it apply to exclusive choice of court agreements where they relate to contracts of employment, including collective agreements.[699] There is also a long list of matters excluded from the scope of the Convention.[700] Many are familiar to us, being matters that are either also excluded from the scope of the Brussels I Regulation[701] or matters in repect of which exclusive jurisdiction is allocated under Article 22 of the Regulation.[702] But the Convention goes beyond this and, for instance, also excludes claims for personal injury brought by or on behalf of natural persons[703] and tort or delict claims for damage to tangible property that do not arise from a contractual relationship.[704]

The Convention is, in general, confined to "exclusive" choice of court agreements.[705] If it had included non-exclusive agreements, there would have been the risk of parallel proceedings in different states, which would have necessitated a *lis pendens* provision. An exclusive choice of court agreement is defined by Article 3, which requires the agreement to be concluded or documented in writing, or by any other means of communication which renders information accessible so as to be usable for subsequent reference.[706] A choice of court agreement which designates the courts of one Contracting State or one or more specific courts of one Contracting State shall be deemed to be exclusive unless the parties have expressly provided otherwise.[707] The courts of a Contracting State designated by such an agreement have jurisdiction to decide a dispute to which the agreement applies, unless the agreement is null and void under the law of that state (including its choice of law rules which may refer to the substantive law of some other state),[708] and are forbidden to decline to exercise jurisdiction on the ground that the dispute should be tried in a court of another state.[709]

A court in a Contracting State other than that of the chosen court is required to suspend or dismiss proceedings to which the agreement applies unless one of five alternative limitations operates.[710] These are that: (a) the agreement is null and void under the law of the state of the chosen court (including its choice of law rules); (b) a party lacked the capacity to conclude the agreement under the law of the state of the court seised; (c) giving effect

---

[697] Art 2.

[698] Art 2(1)(a).

[699] Art 2(1)(b).

[700] Art 2 (2)(a)–(p). See also Art 2(4).

[701] See Art 2(2): (a) status and legal capacity of natural persons; (c) family law matters, including matrimonial property regimes; (d) wills and succession; (e) insolvency; and Art 2(4) arbitration. The scope of the Regulation is discussed supra, pp 213–222.

[702] See Art 2(2): (l) rights in rem in immovable property and tenancies; (m) validity, nullity or dissolution of legal persons; (n) validity of intellectual property rights; (p) validity of entries in public registers. Art 22 of the Regulation is discussed supra, pp 275–283.

[703] Art 2(2)(j).

[704] Art 2(2)(k).

[705] Recognition and enforcement can be extended to non-exclusive agreements by reciprocal declarations made by Contracting States, see Art 22.

[706] Art 3(c).

[707] Art 3(b).

[708] Art 5(1). See the Hartley and Dogauchi Report, para 125.

[709] Art 5(2).

[710] Art 6.

to the agreement would lead to a manifest injustice or would be manifestly contrary to the public policy of the state of the court seised; (d) for exceptional reasons beyond the control of the parties, the agreement cannot reasonably be performed; or (e) the chosen court has decided not to hear the case. Unlike under the Brussels I Regulation,[711] there is no *lis pendens* rule in the Convention which could be used to trump the agreement.

A judgment given by a court of a Contracting State designated in the agreement will be recognised and enforced in other Contracting States,[712] subject to limited grounds of refusal.[713] Recognition of judgments under the Convention is discussed further in Chapter 15.[714]

---

[711] See the *Gasser* case, discussed supra, pp 310–312.
[712] Art 8.
[713] Art 9.
[714] Infra, pp 593–594.

Chapter 13

Stays of English Proceedings and Restraining Foreign Proceedings

1. STAYS OF ENGLISH PROCEEDINGS

Even though an English court has power to try a case, ie a claim form has been served on the defendant in accordance with the rules set out in the previous chapter,[1] it can, nonetheless, refuse to take jurisdiction and stay the English proceedings.[2] Although the English court is technically only regulating its own jurisdiction, the effect of a stay is to force a claimant to go abroad to sue or, in some cases, to go to arbitration.[3] The court is therefore, in reality, choosing between alternative fora for trial, or between trial and arbitration.[4]

---

[1] England must also be available as a forum in the sense that the defendant would obtain a fair trial in England, see *Attorney General for Zambia v Meer Care & Desai* [2006] EWCA Civ 390, [2006] 1 CLC 436.

[2] The procedure for disputing the court's jurisdiction or arguing that the court should not exercise its jurisdiction is set out in Part 11 of the CPR. The stay should be sought at the time when the proceedings are commenced; any delay may be used as a reason for not exercising the discretion to stay, see *Coupland v Arabian Gulf Oil Co* [1983] 1 WLR 1136; *Lee v Mindel* [1994] IL Pr 217, CA.

[3] The arbitration may be in England or abroad, see infra, pp 450–451.

[4] In cases where there is an arbitration agreement, a stay of proceedings will be mandatory; infra, pp 450–454.

The power to stay English proceedings is derived from the court's inherent jurisdiction,[5] which is preserved by statute,[6] and from statutory provision on arbitration.[7] The power is exercised in three situations:

(a) where the doctrine of *forum non conveniens* applies;
(b) where there is a foreign choice of jurisdiction clause;
(c) where there is an agreement on arbitration.

Each of these three situations will be examined in turn. After which, a different sort of stay, namely one granted pending the determination of proceedings abroad, will be considered.

(a) Forum non conveniens[8]

It has already been seen that the discretionary power to allow service of a claim form out of the jurisdiction is exercised on the basis of *forum conveniens*.[9] There is also a general discretionary power to stay actions on the basis of *forum non conveniens* (ie where the clearly appropriate forum for trial is abroad).[10] Whilst there has been such a power in Scotland[11] and the USA[12] for a considerable length of time, it is only relatively recently that a general doctrine of *forum non conveniens* has been accepted in England.[13] The English discretion to stay is now indistinguishable from the Scottish doctrine of *forum non conveniens*.[14] That this is the case has been endorsed by the House of Lords in the leading authority on stays of action, *Spiliada Maritime Corpn v Cansulex Ltd*.[15] It is clear

---

[5] There is a separate power to stay proceedings using domestic general powers of case management under CPR, r 3.1(f). It may be difficult to persuade the court to exercise this power in an international case, see *Affymetrix Inc v Multilyte Ltd* [2004] EWHC 291 (Ch), [2005] IL Pr 34.

[6] See s 49(3) of the Supreme Court Act 1981. A court has power to stay an action in which its own jurisdiction is in issue: *Williams and Glyn's Bank plc v Astro Dinamico Compañía Naviera SA* [1984] 1 WLR 438.

[7] The Arbitration Act 1996, s 9; discussed infra, pp 450–454.

[8] Bell, *Forum Shopping and Venue in International Litigation* (2003); Briggs and Rees, paras 4.10–4.21; Dicey, Morris and Collins, paras 12R-001–12-041; Fawcett, *Declining Jurisdiction*, especially pp 10–27 (for a comparative survey); Brand (2002) 37 Texas Int LR 467; International Law Association, Third Interim Report: Declining and Referring Jurisdiction in International Litigation; Briggs (1983) 3 LS 74; [1984] LMCLQ 227; [1985] LMCLQ 360; Barma and Elvin (1985) 101 LQR 48; Schuz (1986) 35 ICLQ 374; (for a comparison with Dutch law) Verheul (1986) 35 ICLQ 413; Robertson (1987) 103 LQR 398; Slater (1988) 104 LQR 554; Fawcett (1989) 9 OJLS 205; Beaumont, in Fawcett (ed), *Declining Jurisdiction*, pp 207–223.

[9] Supra, pp 399–412.

[10] For the application of this doctrine in the area of family law see infra, pp 960–964.

[11] Anton, *Private International Law* (1990), 2nd edn, pp 212–218; Crawford and Carruthers, paras 7-45–7-46. *Crédit Chimique v James Scott Engineering Group Ltd* 1979 SC 406, 1982 SLT 131.

[12] Scoles, Hay, Borchers and Symeonides, paras 11.8–11.13; Leflar, *American Conflicts Law*, (1986) 4th edn, pp 152–156; *Gulf Oil Corpn v Gilbert* 330 US 501 (1946); *Piper Aircraft Co v Reno* 454 US 235 (1981).

[13] By Lord DIPLOCK in *The Abidin Daver* [1984] AC 398 at 411. Lords EDMUND-DAVIES, KEITH and TEMPLEMAN concurred with Lord DIPLOCK. For earlier relaxation in the law see *The Atlantic Star* [1974] AC 436, at 454, 468; *MacShannon v Rockware Glass Ltd* [1978] AC 795. For much earlier cases confining the grant of a stay to cases of vexation and oppression, see *Logan v Bank of Scotland (No 2)* [1906] 1 KB 141; *Egbert v Short* [1907] 2 Ch 205; *Re Norton's Settlement* [1908] 1 Ch 471.

[14] *The Abidin Daver*, supra, at 411 (per Lord DIPLOCK).

[15] [1987] AC 460; Briggs [1987] LMCLQ 1; Collier [1987] CLJ 33; Carter (1986) 57 BYBIL 429. See also *Connelly v RTZ Corpn plc* [1998] AC 854, HL; *Lubbe v Cape plc* [2000] 1 WLR 1545, HL; *Tehrani v Secretary of State for the Home Department* [2006] UKHL 47, [2007] 1 AC 521.

from this case that the same basic criterion applies in cases involving stays of action as in cases involving the exercise of the discretion to serve a claim form out of the jurisdiction.[16] The *Spiliada* case set off a chain reaction in a number of common law jurisdictions, and has been followed[17] in New Zealand,[18] Canada,[19] Hong Kong,[20] Brunei,[21] Singapore,[22] Gibraltar,[23] the Caribbean[24] and Ireland,[25] but not in Australia,[26] where a majority of the High Court, in a very unclear and much criticised decision, required there to be vexation or oppression for the grant of a stay, but could not agree on what this meant. However, it has been established subsequently that this can be shown by the fact that the forum is a clearly inappropriate one for trial[27] (a formula loaded in favour of trial in the forum[28]).

(i) The principles on which the discretion to stay is exercised

The law was exhaustively considered and restated by the House of Lords in *Spiliada Maritime Corpn v Cansulex Ltd*,[29] where Lord GOFF, giving the unanimous judgment of

---

[16] Supra, pp 399–407 and 411–412.

[17] For Scots reaction see *Sokha v Secretary of State for the Home Department* 1992 SLT 1049; *Morrison v Panic Link Ltd* 1993 SLT 602; reclaiming motion refused 1994 SLT 232; *PTKF Kontinent v VMPTO* 1994 SLT 235.

[18] *McConnell Dowell Constructors Ltd v Lloyd's Syndicate 396* [1988] 2 NZLR 257, CA; *Club Mediterranee NZ v Wendell* [1989] 1 NZLR 216, CA; *Crane Accessories Ltd v Lim Swee Hee* [1989] 1 NZLR 221; Paterson (1989) 13 NZULR 337; *Society of Lloyd's v Hyslop* [1993] 3 NZLR 135, CA; see generally Barnard in Fawcett (ed), *Declining Jurisdiction*, pp 348–358.

[19] *Amchem Products Inc v Workers' Compensation Board* (1993) 102 DLR (4th) 96 at 107–112 (per SOPINKA J); Edinger [1993] Can BR 366; *Holt Cargo Systems Inc v ABC Containerline NV (Trustees of)* (2001) 207 DLR (4th) 577, SC of Canada; *Spar Aerospace Ltd v American Mobile Satellite Corpn* (2002) 220 DLR (4th) 54 at 80–85, SC of Canada; Walker (2003) 118 LQR 567; *Bourdon v Stelco Inc* (2006) 259 DLR (4th) 34, SC of Canada. For the differences between the Canadian and English doctrines, see Blom in Fawcett (ed), *Declining Jurisdiction*, p 127 et seq.

[20] *The Adhiguna Meranti* [1988] 1 Lloyd's Rep 384, HK CA; *The Kapitan Shvetsov* [1998] 1 Lloyd's Rep 199, HK CA; Svantesson (2005) 35 HKLJ 395.

[21] *Syarikat Bumiputra Kimonis v Tan Kok Voon* [1988] 3 MLJ 315.

[22] *Brinkerhoff Maritime Drilling Corpn v PT Airfast Services Indonesia* [1992] 2 SLR 776; *Eng Liat Kiang v Eng Bak Hern* [1995] 3 SLR 97; *Oriental Insurance Co Ltd v Bhavani Stores Pte Ltd* [1998] SLR 253; *PT Hutan Domas Raya v Yue Xiu Enterprises* [2001] 2 SLR 49; *Yuninshing v Edward Mondong* [2002] 2 SLR 506.

[23] *Aldington Shipping Ltd v Bradstock Shipping Corpn and Mabanaft GmbH, The Waylink and Brady Maria* [1988] 1 Lloyd's Rep 475, Gibraltar CA.

[24] *Barclays Bank plc v Kenton Capital Ltd et al* (1994–95) Cayman Islands Law Reports 489; McDowell (2000) 49 ICLQ 108.

[25] *Intermetal Group Ltd & Trans-World (Steel) Ltd v Worslade Trading Ltd* [1998] IL Pr 765, Irish Sup Ct; *McCarthy v Pillay* [2003] 2 ILRM 284, Irish Sup Ct.

[26] *Oceanic Sun-Line Special Shipping Co Inc v Fay* (1988) 165 CLR 197, High Court of Australia. See Pryles (1988) 62 ALJ 774; Reynolds (1989) 105 LQR 4; Briggs (1989) 105 LQR 200; Briggs [1989] LMCLQ 216; Collins (1989) 105 LQR 364; Garner (1989) 38 ICLQ 361; Mclachlan [1990] CLJ 37.

[27] *Voth v Manildra Flour Mills Pty Ltd* (1990) 171 CLR 538, HC of Australia: following DEANE J in the *Oceanic Case*, supra, at 247–248. See Collins (1991) 107 LQR 182; Pryles (1991) 65 ALJ 442; Brereton (1991) 40 ICLQ 895; Epstein in Fawcett (ed), *Declining Jurisdiction*, p 82 et seq; Marasinghe (1993) 23 UWA LR 264; Prince (1998) 47 ICLQ 573; Garnett (1999) 23 Melbourne ULR 30. See also *Dow Jones & Company Inc v Gutnick* (2002) 210 CLR 575, HC of Australia. Where a person has been served outside Australia there is a power under Part 10, r 6A (2)(b) of the Supreme Court Rules 1970 (NSW) to set service aside on the ground that the court is an inappropriate forum (a less emphatic test). This still requires the defendants to establish vexation or oppression: *Régie Nationale Des Usines Renault SA v Zhang* (2001) 210 CLR 491, HC of Australia.

[28] For the reasons for this formulation see *BHP Billiton Ltd v Schultz* (2004) 221 CLR 400 at [9]–[11], HC of Australia.

[29] [1987] AC 460. The facts of the case are discussed supra, pp 411–412.

the Law Lords, set out a number of principles on which the discretion should be exercised. These principles have been affirmed and further explained by Lord GOFF[30] in the House of Lords in *Connelly v RTZ Corpn plc*[31]and by Lord BINGHAM[32] in the House of Lords in *Lubbe v Cape plc*.[33] Before turning to examine these principles, one general point needs to be made. The decision on the exercise of the discretion is essentially one for the judge at first instance, and an appellate court should not interfere merely because it would give different weight to the factors involved.[34]

(a) The basic principle

> The basic principle is that a stay will only be granted on the ground of forum non conveniens where the court is satisfied that there is some other available forum, having jurisdiction, which is the appropriate forum for trial of the action, ie in which the case may be tried more suitably for the interests of all the parties and the ends of justice.[35]

This is the most important of the principles and sums up the whole basis of the *forum non conveniens* discretion. Lord GOFF, however, did lay down a number of other subordinate principles which have been frequently followed. He referred to a two-stage inquiry. The first stage is concerned with whether there is another available forum which is clearly more appropriate than the English forum; the second stage with the requirements of justice.[36]

(b) The two-stage inquiry

(i) The first stage: another available forum which is clearly more appropriate.

The burden of proof is on the defendant to show that there is another available forum which is clearly or distinctly more appropriate than the English forum.[37] The defendant will find it all the easier to discharge this burden where it has only a tenuous connection with the forum.[38] The same has been said to apply where service was effected out of the jurisdiction, at least where the defendant did not earlier seek to set aside service out on the basis that the claimant had not shown that England was the clearly appropriate forum.[39]

Another available forum   The defendant must show that there is another "available" forum abroad.[40] In the *Spiliada* case availability refers to another court abroad having

---

[30] With whom the other Law Lords concurred.

[31] [1998] AC 854, HL. Lord HOFFMANN dissented on the application of those principles to the facts of the case.

[32] With whom the other Law Lords concurred.

[33] [2000] 1 WLR 1545, HL.

[34] The *Spiliada* case, supra.

[35] Ibid, at 476. See also *Connelly v RTZ Corpn plc* [1998] AC 854 at 868–869, HL; the *Lubbe* case, supra, at 1554.

[36] Cf the Canadian doctrine which considers the juridical advantage when determining the appropriate forum: *Amchem Products Inc v Workers' Compensation Board* (1993) 102 DLR (4th) 96 at 110, SC of Canada.

[37] The *Spiliada* case, supra, at 474; the *Lubbe Case*, supra, at 1554.

[38] The *Spiliada* case, supra, at 477.

[39] *Hindocha v Gheewala* [2003] UKPC 77 at [26]. But the claimant will have had to show that England was the clearly appropriate forum in order to obtain permission for service out of the jurisdiction.

[40] It has also been held that there must be real issues to be tried between the parties. If there is no arguable defence, a stay will be refused: *Adria Services YU v Grey Shipping Co Ltd* 30 July 1993, (unreported), CLARKE J.

"competent jurisdiction" to try the case.[41] Lord WALKER, delivering the judgment of the Privy Council in *Hindocha v Gheewala*,[42] has said that an alternative forum is not available (in the relevant sense) unless it is open to the claimant to institute proceedings as of right in that forum.[43] Taken literally this might suggest that the defendant must be present in the forum abroad.[44] But this is not the case. The crucial point is that the foreign court has jurisdiction and the basis on which this is taken should not matter. This is born out by the fact that a forum can be available abroad solely by virtue of the defendant's undertaking before the judge in England, when he was considering *forum non conveniens*, to submit to the jurisdiction of the foreign court.[45] It seems that, in principle, it is possible to have an implied undertaking to submit.[46] In carrying out this inquiry into availability the court is concerned with evidence as at the date of the defendant's application for a stay.[47] However, in exceptional and extreme cases a stay could be granted on the basis of a change of circumstances between that date and the date of the hearing.[48] The same principles in relation to the time element no doubt apply to all aspects of the *forum non conveniens* inquiry.[49]

Evans LJ, with whom SAVILLE and MORRITT LJJ concurred, in *Mohammed v Bank of Kuwait and the Middle East KSC*[50] gave "availability" a more complex and more questionable meaning. They said that this meant "available in practice to this plaintiff to have his dispute resolved", and that the question whether substantial justice is likely to be achieved is relevant to this issue.

> There was evidence in the case showing that the Iraqi plaintiff, who had worked in Kuwait for a Kuwait bank against which he commenced proceedings in England, was unable to visit Kuwait personally and there were perhaps diplomatic and legal restrictions which could affect his ability to have a legal representative of his choice whom he could fully and properly instruct for the purpose of proceedings there.

In the light of this evidence, it was held that Kuwait was not shown by the defendant to be available to the plaintiff in a practical sense as an alternative forum for trial, and the decision of the judge at first instance granting a stay was reversed.

The difficulty with this definition of "availability" is that it requires the court to distinguish between different types of injustice. One type goes to availability of the alternative forum and is considered at the first stage of the *Spiliada* inquiry; consequently the onus

---

[41] See the approval by Lord GOFF of the classic statement of Lord KINNEAR in *Sim v Robinow* (1892) 19 R 665. See also *Lubbe v Cape plc* [2000] 1 WLR 1545 at 1565-1566 (per Lord HOPE, the other Law Lords concurring); *Tehrani v Secretary of State for the Home Department* [2006] UKHL 47, [2007] 1 AC 521. Cf *Petroleo Brasiliero SA v Mellitus Shipping Inc* [2001] EWCA Civ 418 at [35] (per POTTER LJ), [2001] 2 Lloyd's Rep 203. For Australia see *Reinsurance Australia Corporation Ltd v HIH Casualty and General Insurance (in Liquidation)* [2003] FCA 56.

[42] [2003] UKPC 77; Merrett [2004] CLJ 309 and (2005) 54 ICLQ 211.

[43] *Hindocha v Gheewala*, supra, at [22].

[44] Or has assets in the forum: *Lubbe v Cape plc* [2000] 1 WLR 1545 at 1565–1566 (per Lord HOPE, who was presumably thinking of when a Scots court has jurisdiction as of right).

[45] The *Lubbe* case, supra, *Hindocha v Gheewala*, supra, at [22].

[46] *Hindocha v Gheewala*, supra, at [24]–[25].

[47] *Lubbe v Cape plc* [2000] 1 WLR 1545 at 1565–1566 (per Lord HOPE), 1556 (per Lord BINGHAM with whom the other Law Lords concurred); *Hindocha v Gheewala* supra, at [22]; *Mohammed v Bank of Kuwait and the Middle East KSC* [1996] 1 WLR 1483, CA. Cf *ISC v Guerin* [1992] 2 Lloyd's Rep 430 at 434.

[48] The *Mohammed* case, supra.

[49] *BMG Trading Ltd v AS McKay* [1998] IL Pr 691 at 694, CA.

[50] [1996] 1 WLR 1483, CA; Briggs (1996) 67 BYBIL 587.

is on the defendant to show that there is no such injustice. The other type does not go to availability and is raised at the second stage of the inquiry; consequently the onus is on the claimant to show circumstances by reason of which justice demands that a stay should not be granted. This is not a distinction that it is easy to draw, and merely serves to complicate the law on *forum non conveniens*. In the *Mohammed* case, Evans LJ clearly regarded the evidence mentioned above as going to availability, whereas allegations that the plaintiff would not get a fair trial in Kuwait because of hostility to Iraqis following the Iraqi invasion of Kuwait were not so regarded and were said to be a matter to be raised at the second stage of the inquiry.[51] It would have been best if "availability" had been confined to the issue of whether the alternative forum abroad had jurisdiction to try the case on the merits[52] and that substantial justice had been regarded as irrelevant at this stage of the inquiry. Given, though, that this distinction has been drawn, it would be best to confine the idea of injustice that goes to "availability" to the facts of the *Mohammed* case.

It is encouraging to note that a differently constituted Court of Appeal has accepted that there is substance in the criticisms of the *Mohammed* case, and that in a future case in which the onus of proof is vital it might be necessary to consider whether that decision can stand against the *Spiliada* case.[53] Moreover, the House of Lords in a subsequent case[54] regarded injustice that took the form of not being able to try the case at all abroad because financial assistance was not available there, and the nature and complexity of the case required such assistance, as arising at the second stage of the inquiry. There was no suggestion that this went to "availability", although the case would have been a stronger authority if this argument had been raised and rejected. This has been followed by another House of Lords case to the same effect.[55]

Clearly more appropriate   The other available forum must be clearly or distinctly more appropriate than the English forum.[56] Another way of putting it is to say the other available forum must be the "natural forum".[57] The terms "natural forum" and "appropriate forum" have been used synonymously.[58] It is not enough just to show that England is not the natural or appropriate forum for trial. Neither is it enough to establish a mere balance of convenience in favour of the foreign forum.[59] This principle is designed to reflect the fact that, in cases where a stay is sought on the basis of *forum non conveniens*, jurisdiction will have been founded as of right, ie a claim form will have been served within the jurisdiction.[60]

---

[51] The *Mohammed* case, supra, at 1495.

[52] Likewise, if the foreign court refuses to exercise its jurisdiction and stays the action the alternative forum abroad is not available.

[53] *Askin v Absa Bank Ltd* [1999] IL Pr 471 at [29]–[30], CA; Briggs (1999) 70 BYBIL 319.

[54] *Connelly v RTZ Corpn plc* [1998] AC 854, HL; infra, pp 434–435.

[55] The *Lubbe* case, supra.

[56] For examples of where the natural forum was abroad, see *Rockware Glass Ltd v MacShannon* [1978] AC 795; *The Al Battani* [1993] 2 Lloyd's Rep 219; *The Xin Yang* [1996] 2 Lloyd's Rep 217.

[57] Ie the country with which the action has the most real and substantial connection: the *MacShannon* case, supra, at 829. See also *The Abidin Daver* [1984] AC 398 at 415 (Lord KEITH); *The Forum Craftsman* [1984] 2 Lloyd's Rep 102 at 108 (SHEEN J); affd by the Court of Appeal [1985] 1 Lloyd's Rep 291.

[58] See *Spiliada Maritime Corpn v Cansulex Ltd Rockware Glass Ltd v MacShannon* [1978] AC 795 at 812 (per Lord DIPLOCK); see also *Trendtex Trading Corpn v Crédit Suisse* [1980] 3 All ER 721 at 734; *European Asian Bank AG v Punjab and Sind Bank* [1982] 2 Lloyd's Rep 356 at 364.

[59] The *Spiliada* case, supra, at 474; *Banco Atlantico SA v British Bank of the Middle East*, supra, at 508.

[60] See the *Lubbe* case, supra, at 1554.

In ascertaining whether there is a clearly more appropriate forum abroad, the search is for the country with which the action has the most real and substantial connection.[61] The court will look for connecting factors "and these will include not only factors affecting convenience or expense (such as availability of witnesses),[62] but also other factors such as the law governing the relevant transaction[63] . . . , and the place where the parties respectively reside or carry on business".[64]

These are the same factors considered when determining the *forum conveniens* for the purposes of service out of the jurisdiction. The weight to be attached to the fact that English law governs the contract or that a foreign law governs has been considered in that context[65] and what is said there need not be repeated here. Likewise, the significance of the fact that a tort was committed in England or was committed abroad has been considered previously.[66] The presumption that the natural forum for trial is where the tort was committed applies equally to cases of *forum non conveniens* as to cases of *forum conveniens*.[67] When it comes to a stay of English proceedings on *forum non conveniens* grounds in a case where the parties have agreed on the exclusive jurisdiction of the English courts,[68] there has been a lack of consistency of approach by the courts. In most cases, it has been accepted that the courts retain their discretion to stay the English proceedings but there is no agreement on whether the normal principles of *forum non conveniens* apply (with the agreement operating as an important factor against the grant of a stay[69]) or whether a special rule should be adopted by analogy with the special rule that operates in the situation where there is an exclusive jurisdiction clause providing for trial abroad (the court will uphold the agreement unless strong reasons can be shown.[70]) As an example of the

---

[61] *Spiliada Maritime Corpn v Cansulex Ltd* [1987] AC 460 at 477–478.

[62] For location of documents see *Arab Banking Corpn v First Union National Bank*, 2001 (unreported).

[63] See, eg, *The Xin Yang* [1996] 2 Lloyd's Rep 217; *Luiz Vicente Barros Mattos Junior v Macdaniels Ltd* [2005] EWHC 1323 (Ch) at [138]. If there is a dispute as to the applicable law and this cannot be tried as a preliminary issue, this is a neutral factor: *Lubbe v Cape plc* [1999] IL Pr 113 at 126, CA (the first CA case); Briggs (1998) 67 BYBIL 336; affd without discussion of this point [2000] 1 WLR 1545, HL. Cf the treatment of choice of law on the facts of the case in the second Court of Appeal case, [2000] IL Pr 439, Briggs (1999) 68 BYBIL 319, revsd by the House of Lords on the injustice abroad point.

[64] The *Spiliada* case, supra, at 478. For Canada see *Spar Aerospace Ltd v American Mobile Satellite Corpn* (2002) 220 DLR (4th) 54, 80–85, SC of Canada; *Eastern Power Ltd v Azienda Communale Energía and Ambiente* (1999) 178 DLR (4th) 409, Ontario CA; *Markandu v Benaroch* (2004) 242 DLR (4th) 101, Ont CA.

[65] Supra, pp 401–402.

[66] Supra, pp 387–389. For Australia see: *Dow Jones & Co Inc v Gutnick* (2002) 210 CLR 575 (tort committed in Victoria, no stay because Victoria not a clearly inappropriate forum); *Régie National des Usines Renault SA v Zhang* (2002) 210 CLR 491 at 521. For Ontario see *Mutual Life Assurance Co of Canada v Peat Marwick* (1998) 172 DLR (4th) 379, Ont CA.

[67] *Lennon Scottish Daily Record* [2004] EWHC 359 (QB) at [36]–[38]. See also *Reuben v Time Inc* [2003] EWCA Civ 06 at [14].

[68] We are concerned with the situation where Article 23 of the Brussels I Regulation (discussed supra, pp 283–296) does not apply. Where it does, which will often be the case, the English courts have no power to stay the English proceedings on *forum non conveniens* grounds (see supra, pp 326–327). For a case which did not discuss whether Art 23 applied in relation to an English jurisdiction clause see *OT Africa Line Ltd v Magic Sportswear Corpn* [2005] EWCA Civ 710, [2005] 2 Lloyd's Rep 170. For Canadian reaction to an English jurisdiction agreement see *OT Africa Line Ltd v Magic Sportswear Ltd* 2006 FCA 284, [2007] 1 Lloyd's Rep 85.

[69] *The Volvox Hollandia* [1987] 2 Lloyd's Rep 520 at 529, appeal on a separate point allowed [1988] 2 Lloyd's Rep 61, CA; *The Hida Maru* [1981] 2 Lloyd's Rep 510, CA; *Eli Lilly and Co v Novo Nordisk A/S* [2000] IL Pr 73 at 80, CA. See also *Bouygues v Caspian* [1997] IL Pr 472, CA.

[70] *Akai Pty Ltd v People's Insurance Co Ltd* [1998] 1 Lloyd's Rep 90 at 104–105; *UBS AG v Omni Holding AG (In Liquidation)* [2000] 1 WLR 916 at 925; *Import-Export Metro Ltd v Compania Sud Americana De Vapores SA*

latter approach it has been said that, when it comes to showing the strong cause needed for a stay, this must go beyond matters of mere convenience and must enter into the interests of justice itself[71] or refer to some matter that was unforeseeable at the time of entering into the contract.[72] The disregarding of foreseeable matters assumes that the parties acted freely in adopting the clause.[73] An even more radical suggestion is that, where there is a clause providing for the exclusive jurisdiction of the English courts, the courts have no discretion to stay the English proceedings on the ground of *forum non conveniens*.[74] Where there is a non-exclusive jurisdiction agreement providing for trial in England there is still a discretion to stay the English proceedings but there is again no consistency as to how the agreement is to be factored into the exercise of the discretion. One approach has been to adopt a modified version of the *Spiliada* principles, whereby the parties are precluded from raising factors of appropriateness;[75] unless the factor could not have been foreseen by the defendant when the contract was entered into;[76] the other has been to apply the *Spiliada* principles in the normal way but to treat a non-exclusive jurisdiction clause as a very important factor.[77] Where there is a clause providing for the exclusive jurisdiction of a foreign court, a stay of the English proceeedings will ordinarily be granted, not on the ground of *forum non conveniens*,[78] but on the separate ground that the court should uphold the agreement of the parties.[79] Where there is a clause providing for the non-exclusive jurisdiction of a foreign court similar principles have been adopted as in cases where there is a clause providing for the non-exclusive jurisdiction of an English court. Thus one approach has been to apply a modified version of the *Spiliada* principles precluding the consideration of any factors of appropriateness, even seemingly those the parties could not have foreseen at the time the contract was entered into;[80] another approach has been to apply the *Spiliada* principles in the normal way, treating the clause as a very important factor in ascertaining the appropriate forum. Turning to other factors of appropriateness, what has been said earlier about the significance of the fact that a negative declaration is sought[81] and the importance of the fact that all the litigation

---

[2003] EWHC 11 (Comm), [2003] 1 Lloyd's Rep 405. The special rule for foreign jurisdiction clauses is discussed infra, pp 443–448.

[71] *Sinochem International Oil (London) Ltd v Mobil Sales and Supply Corpn Ltd (No 2)* [2000] 1 All ER (Comm) 758, 772. For the significance of this factor in cases of forum conveniens see supra, pp 402–403.

[72] See the *Import-Export Metro Ltd Case*, supra. See the same approach applied in relation to a foreign service of suit clause in *Ace Insurance SA-NV (Formerly Cigna Insurance Co of Europe SA-NV) v Zurich Insurance Co* [2001] EWCA Civ 173 at [62], [2001] 1 Lloyd's Rep 618, CA, infra, p 447.

[73] *Import-Export Metro Ltd Case*, supra. See also *Mercury v Communication Telesystems* [1999] 2 All ER (Comm) 33.

[74] *Berisford v New Hampshire* [1990] 1 Lloyd's Rep 454, 458 (Hobhouse J—obiter). But cf the approach of Hobhouse LJ in *Bouygues v Caspian*, supra.

[75] *British Aerospace plc v Dee Howard Co* [1993] 1 Lloyd's Rep 368.

[76] Ibid; *Mercury v Communication Telesystems* [1999] 2 All ER (Comm) 33; the *Import-Export Metro Ltd* case, supra, at [14]. See also *Sinochem (No 2)* [2000] 1 All ER (Comm) 758 (a case involving an exclusive English jurisdiction clause applying the foreseeability approach).

[77] *Berisford v New Hampshire* [1990] 1 Lloyd's Rep 454 at 463.

[78] Under that doctrine this is a strong indication that the appropriate forum is abroad: *Trendtex Trading Corpn v Crédit Suisse* [1980] 3 All ER 721 at 737 and in the Court of Appeal, at 758, affd by the House of Lords, [1982] AC 679.

[79] Infra, pp 443–448.

[80] *The Rothnie* [1996] 2 Lloyd's Rep 206.

[81] Supra, pp 408–409.

can be heard together in one state, rather than having to be split between states,[82] is equally applicable in the present context. Where the subject matter of a dispute concerns the internal management of a company, the location of the company is particularly important.[83]

Cases where there is no clearly more appropriate forum abroad　In cases where there is no clearly more appropriate forum abroad, ie where either there is no country which is the natural forum or England is the natural forum, the courts will ordinarily refuse a stay of proceedings.[84] Examples of cases where there was no natural forum for trial and a stay was therefore refused are: where banks were in dispute over payment under a letter of credit;[85]and where there was a collision on the high seas.[86] A stay will likewise be refused in cases where it is possible to identify the natural forum and this is England.[87] In cases where the court has exercised its discretion to allow service out of the jurisdiction under rule 6.20 of the Civil Procedure Rules, the court has already decided that England is the most appropriate forum for trial.[88] It follows that a stay of proceedings will not be granted subsequently on the basis of *forum non conveniens*. In practice, therefore, stays are normally sought in cases where a claim form has been served within the jurisdiction, rather than in cases where a claim form has been served out of the jurisdiction under rule 6.20.[89]

Since the *Spiliada* case, numerous cases have been decided on the basis that there was no clearly more appropriate forum abroad. But what is noticeable about these cases is that in virtually all of them the courts have considered all the circumstances of the case, including considerations going beyond those of appropriateness. This has often been on the basis that the ultimate question is what justice demands and all the factors for and against a stay have to be considered together.[90] As will be seen, in cases where there is a clearly

---

[82] Supra, pp 400–401.

[83] *Incorporated Broadcasters Ltd v Canwest Global Communications Corp*n (2003) 223 DLR (4th) 627, Ont CA.

[84] *Spiliada Maritime Corpn v Cansulex Ltd* [1987] AC 460 at 478; *Lubbe v Cape plc* [2000] 1 WLR 1545 at 1554. See also *Metal Scrap Trade Corpn v Kate Shipping Co Ltd* [1990] 1 WLR 115 at 133 (per Lord GOFF) HL; *The Maciej Rataj* [1991] 2 Lloyd's Rep 458 at 467; *BCCHK v Sonali* [1995] 1 Lloyd's Rep 227; *Dubai Bank Ltd v Abbas* [1998] IL Pr 391; *PTKF Kontinent v VMPTO Progress* 1994 SLT 235; *Bristow Helicopters Ltd v Sikorsky Aircraft Corpn* [2004] EWHC 401 (Comm) at [27], [2004] 2 Lloyd's Rep 150.

[85] *European Asian Bank AG v Punjab and Sind Bank* [1982] 2 Lloyd's Rep 356. This was a pre-*Spiliada* case but one which was used by Lord GOFF to illustrate his third principle. See also *Luis Vincente Barros Mattos v Macdaniels Ltd* [2003] EWHC 1173 (Ch).

[86] *Spiliada Maritime Corpn v Cansulex Ltd*, supra, at 477; *The Vishva Abha* [1990] 2 Lloyd's Rep 312 at 314. The position may be the same after a collision in territorial waters, see *The Po* [1990] 1 Lloyd's Rep 418; affd by the Court of Appeal [1991] 2 Lloyd's Rep 206. But cf *The Wellamo* [1980] 2 Lloyd's Rep 229; *The Abidin Daver* [1984] AC 398.

[87] *OTM Ltd v Hydronautics* [1981] 2 Lloyd's Rep 211; *The Hamburg Star* [1994] 1 Lloyd's Rep 399; *Meridien Biao Bank GmbH* [1997] 1 Lloyd's Rep 437, CA; *Zivlin v Baal Taxa* [1998] IL Pr 106; *Schapira v Ahronson* [1998] IL Pr 587, CA. Cf *Pillai v Sarkar* (1994) The Times, 21 July.

[88] Supra, pp 399–400.

[89] A defendant who fails to ask for service out of the jurisdiction to be set aside on the basis that England is not the *forum conveniens* can still seek a stay on grounds of *forum non conveniens*: *Hindocha v Gheewala* [2003] UKPC 77 at [26].

[90] See, eg, *Charm Maritime Inc v Minas Xenophon Kyriakou and David John Mathias* [1987] 1 Lloyd's Rep 433 at 447. See also *The Po* [1990] 1 Lloyd's Rep 418 at 424; affd by the Court of Appeal [1991] 2 Lloyd's Rep 206; *Arkwright Mutual Insurance Co v Bryanston Insurance Co Ltd* [1990] 2 Lloyd's Rep 70 at 83; cf *Meadows Indemnity*

more appropriate forum abroad the courts will necessarily go on to consider the other relevant circumstances in the case.

(ii) The second stage: the requirements of justice

Lord GOFF has said that:

> if there is some other available forum which prima facie is clearly more appropriate for the trial of the action, it [the court] will ordinarily grant a stay unless there are circumstances by reason of which justice requires that a stay should nevertheless not be granted.[91]

Once it has been shown that there is a clearly more appropriate forum for trial abroad the burden of proof shifts to the claimant to justify coming to England.[92] The court is concerned with the question whether justice requires that a stay should not be granted.[93] This second stage of the inquiry has been considered and further explained by Lord GOFF in the House of Lords in *Connelly v RTZ Corpn plc*.[94]

> The plaintiff, who was domiciled in Scotland, worked in Namibia at a uranium mine operated by a Namibian subsidiary of the first defendant, an English company. After being found to be suffering from cancer, the plaintiff commenced proceedings in England against the first defendant and one of its English subsidiaries for negligence. No financial assistance was available to the plaintiff in Namibia, whereas it was available to the plaintiff in England, in the form either of legal aid or a conditional fee agreement. The defendants sought a stay of the English proceedings, which was granted by the judge at first instance. The Court of Appeal lifted the stay.[95] The defendants appealed to the House of Lords.

The House of Lords dismissed the defendants' appeal.[96] It was accepted by the plaintiff that Namibia was the jurisdiction with which the action had the closest connection, with the result that prima facie a stay should be granted.[97] The point at issue in the case was therefore whether a stay should nevertheless be refused because justice so required. Lord GOFF, by way of further explanation of his classic statements in the *Spiliada* case, enunciated a principle that "if a clearly more appropriate forum overseas has been identified, generally speaking the plaintiff will have to take that forum as he finds it, even if it is in certain respects less advantageous to him than the English forum".[98] Applying this

---

Co Ltd v Insurance Corpn of Ireland Ltd and International Commercial Bank plc [1989] 1 Lloyd's Rep 181 at 190; affd [1989] 2 Lloyd's Rep 298; *Saab v Saudi Arabian Bank* [1999] 1 WLR 1861, 1882, CA.

[91] *Spiliada Maritime Corpn v Cansulex Ltd*, supra, at 478; the *Lubbe* case, supra, at 1554.

[92] [1987] AC 460 at 476. This has been described as an evidential burden: *Charm Maritime Inc v Minas Xenophon Kyriakou and David John Mathias* [1987] 1 Lloyd's Rep 433 at 448.

[93] *Spiliada Maritime Corpn v Cansulex Ltd* [1987] AC 460 at 478, HL.

[94] [1998] AC 854, HL; Briggs (1997) 68 BYBIL 357. See also *Carlson v Rio Tinto plc* [1999] CLC 551.

[95] [1997] IL Pr 643, CA.

[96] The plaintiff also appealed to the House of Lords from a decision of a differently constituted Court of Appeal: [1996] QB 361; English [1996] CLJ 214, dismissing the plaintiff's appeal against the stay. This appeal to the House of Lords was upheld. For comment on both Court of Appeal decisions, see Briggs (1996) 67 BYBIL 587; Peel (1997) 113 LQR 43. The plaintiff's appeal was concerned with the availability of legal aid; the defendant's appeal was concerned with the impact of a conditional fee agreement. The House of Lords held that s 31(1)(b) of the Legal Aid Act 1988 did not preclude the court from taking the availability of legal aid into account in considering a stay.

[97] The *Connelly* case, supra, at 872.

[98] Ibid, at 872; *Lubbe v Cape plc*, supra, at 1554.

principle, it was said that as a general rule the court will not refuse to grant a stay simply because the plaintiff has shown that no financial assistance, eg in the form of legal aid, will be available to him in the appropriate forum, whereas such financial assistance will be available to him in England.[99] However, this was an exceptional case since it was clear that the nature and complexity of the case was such that it could not be tried at all without the benefit of financial assistance.[100] Accordingly, substantial justice would not be done in the particular circumstances of the case if the plaintiff had to proceed in the appropriate forum where no financial assistance was available.[101] Likewise, the circumstances in *Lubbe v Cape plc*[102] were special and unusual. If the English proceedings were stayed in favour of the more appropriate forum in South Africa the probability was that the plaintiffs would have no means of obtaining the professional representation and the expert evidence which would be essential if their claims were to be justly decided.[103] This would amount to a denial of justice.

In determining whether justice requires that a stay should not be granted, all the circumstances of the case will be taken into account. The court will consider the fact that a claimant may not obtain justice abroad because, for example, the judiciary is not independent.[104] It has also been held that it is not conducive to justice to require a claimant, who had an arguable claim under what we would regard as the governing law, to litigate abroad in a country which would summarily reject the claimant's action.[105] Inordinate delay of the order of magnitude of ten years before an action comes to trial abroad has also been held to be a denial of justice;[106] as has a derisory low limit on damages imposed by the foreign court.[107] In another case, doubts were expressed as to whether any foreign judge "could conscientiously resolve with any confidence that he was reaching a correct answer" to a question as to the effect of a contract as a matter of English public policy.[108] Neither is it just to stay proceedings in England when the claimant would be liable to imprisonment if he were to return to the alternative forum abroad.[109] Much more commonly,

---

[99] The *Connelly* case, supra, at 873; *Lubbe v Cape plc*, supra, at 1554.

[100] The *Connelly* case, supra, at 873–874. It might have been different if it had been possible to put on a rudimentary presentation abroad and the plaintiff sought to put on a Rolls-Royce presentation in England, supra, at 874.

[101] Lord Hoffmann dissented on this point.

[102] [2000] 1 WLR 1545, HL; Briggs (2000) 71 BYBIL 435; Muchlinski (2001) 50 ICLQ 1; Peel (2001) 117 LQR 187; Sinclair [2001] LMCLQ 197.

[103] The *Lubbe* case, supra, at 1559.

[104] *The Abidin Daver* [1984] AC 398 at 411. See cases cited infra, p 437, n 122. See also *Middle East Banking Co SA v Al-Haddad* (1990) 70 OR (2d) 97 (complete breakdown of the administration of justice because of civil war).

[105] *Banco Atlantico SA v British Bank of the Middle East* [1990] 2 Lloyd's Rep 504 at 509.

[106] *The Vishva Ajay* [1989] 2 Lloyd's Rep 558 at 560 (delay in India). Cf *Ceskoslovenska Obchodni Banka AS v Nomura International plc* [2003] IL Pr 20—4 or even up to 6 years, delay in Czech Republic; *Crédit Agricole Indosuez v Unicof Ltd* [2004] 1 Lloyd's Rep 196 at 205 (delay in Kenya). The delays in India are now less, so as not to amount to a substantial injustice; see *RHSP v EIH* [1999] 2 Lloyd's Rep 249 at 253–254 and the following *forum conveniens* cases: *Konamaneni v Rolls-Royce Industrial Power (India) Ltd* [2002] 1 WLR 1269 at [175]–[177] (evidence of 4 to 5 years' or might be up to 10); *Chellaram v Chellaram (No 2)* [2002] EWHC 632 (Ch) at [177], [2002] 3 All ER 17 (evidence of 4 to 5 years). For a *forum conveniens* case similar to *The Vishva Ajay* see *Marconi v PT Pan Indonesia Bank Ltd TBK* [2004] EWHC 129 (Comm) at [38], [2004] 1 Lloyd's Rep 594—more than 10 years' delay usual in Indonesia; affd [2005] EWCA Civ 422 at [77].

[107] *BMG Trading Ltd v A S McKay* [1998] IL Pr 691, CA; *The Adhiguna Meranti* [1988] 1 Lloyd's Rep 384 at 395–396, Hong Kong Court of Appeal; see also *The Falstria* [1988] 1 Lloyd's Rep 495.

[108] *E I Du Pont de Nemours & Co v Agnew and Kerr* [1987] 2 Lloyd's Rep 585 at 595; see also *Mitsubishi Corpn v Aristidis I Alafouzos* [1988] 1 Lloyd's Rep 191 at 196.

[109] *Purcell v Khayat* (1987) The Times, 23 November.

though, what is considered is whether, by staying the proceedings, the claimant will be deprived of some advantage that he would have obtained from trial in England.

Treatment of the advantage to the claimant   The mere fact that the claimant obtains a legitimate[110] personal[111] or juridical (ie substantive law[112] or procedural) advantage cannot be decisive.[113] The claimant will not ordinarily discharge the burden lying upon him by showing that he will enjoy procedural advantages, or a higher scale of damages or more generous rules of limitation if he sues in England.[114] As has been mentioned, generally speaking the claimant will have to take the clearly more appropriate forum overseas as he finds it, even if it is in certain respects less advantageous to him than the English forum.[115]

Comparing the quality of justice   The House of Lords has held that the courts should not engage in the invidious task of comparing the quality of justice obtained under the English common law system of procedure with that obtained under a civil law system.[116] A differently constituted House of Lords has held that the English courts should be careful to reject a procedural comparison between England and South Africa in relation to the handling of group actions.[117] The fact that trial in England would take place before the Commercial Court or the Admiralty Court, with their great experience and international standing, should no longer be taken into account as an advantage to the claimaint.[118] When it comes to other forms of procedural advantage, the effect of this prohibition on making comparisons between different legal systems is less clear. The House of Lords in *Spiliada Maritime Corpn v Cansulex Ltd* was prepared to regard a more complete procedure for discovery (disclosure) as an advantage to the plaintiff,[119] along with other juridical advantages, but was not prepared to give decisive weight to such advantages when operating the discretion.[120] Certainly, when faced with *undisputed evidence* of a specific substantial procedural advantage to the claimant of trial in England,

---

[110] *Rockware Glass Ltd v MacShannon* [1978] AC 795 at 812. Lord SCARMAN in *Castanho v Brown and Root (UK) Ltd* [1981] AC 557 at 575 said that time should not be spent in speculating about the meaning of "legitimate advantage".

[111] Ie the claimant is an English resident: *Rockware Glass Ltd v MacShannon* [1978] AC 795 at 819.

[112] *The Atlantic Star* [1974] AC 436 at 468 (per Lord WILBERFORCE); *Power Curber International Ltd v National Bank of Kuwait SAK* [1981] 1 WLR 1233.

[113] *Spiliada Maritime Corpn v Cansulex Ltd* [1987] AC 460 at 482. See also *De Dampierre v De Dampierre* [1988] AC 92 at 109–110.

[114] *Lubbe v Cape plc* [2000] 1 WLR 1545, at 1554 (per Lord BINGHAM with whom the other Law lords concurred), HL.

[115] *Connelly v RTZ Corpn plc* [1998] AC 854, at 872, HL; *Lubbe v Cape plc* [2000] 1 WLR 1545, at 1554, HL.

[116] *Amin Rasheed Shipping Corpn v Kuwait Insurance Co* [1984] AC 50 at 67; *The Abidin Daver* [1984] AC 398 at 410. See also *Aratra Potato Co Ltd v Egyptian Navigation Co, The El Amria* [1981] 2 Lloyd's Rep 119 at 127, CA. See *BCCHK v Sonali* [1995] 1 Lloyd's Rep 227; *RHSP v EIH* [1999] 2 Lloyd's Rep 249 at 254.

[117] *Lubbe v Cape plc* [2000] 1 WLR 1545 at 1559 (per Lord BINGHAM with whom the other Law Lords concurred).

[118] *The Abidin Daver* [1984] AC 398 at 424–425; *Hawke Bay Shipping Co Ltd v The First National Bank of Chicago, The Efthimis* [1986] 1 Lloyd's Rep 244 at 260; *Ceskoslovenska Obchodni Banka AS v Nomura International plc* [2003] IL Pr 20. But see *Islamic Arab Insurance Co v Saudi Egyptian American Reinsurance Co* [1987] 1 Lloyd's Rep 315 at 319, 320; Slater (1988) 104 LQR 554.

[119] *Bank of Tokyo Ltd v Karoon* [1987] AC 45 n at 62–63 (per GOFF LJ), CA. See also *Trendtex Trading Corpn v Crédit Suisse* [1980] 3 All ER 721 at 737—decided before the House of Lords cases forbidding the making of comparisons; *Metall Und Rohstoff AG v ACLI Metals (London) Ltd* [1984] 1 Lloyd's Rep 598—a case on restraining foreign proceedings. Cf *The Traugutt* [1985] 1 Lloyd's Rep 76 at 79.

[120] [1987] AC 460 at 482–483. See also *Ceskoslovenska Obchodni Banka AS v Nomura International plc* [2003] IL Pr 20 at [17].

the courts have been willing to take this into account.[121] Similarly if there is positive and cogent evidence that the claimant, if forced to litigate abroad, would not obtain justice, eg because the judiciary is not independent, then this should be considered.[122] Inevitably whenever there is held to be injustice abroad the English court is making a comparison between the quality of justice there and in England, where there is no such injustice. English courts are concerned that a minimum standard of justice is available in the alternative forum and the Court of Appeal has warned that "the court must not be too unworldly in its approach" and that "there are other parts of the world where things are badly wrong".[123] The courts are, however, not going to be easily convinced of the existence of such injustice. Thus the courts could not find any justification for holding that Kuwaiti judges would not have acted fairly if an Iraqi citizen appeared as plaintiff before them, despite the earlier Iraqi invasion and Gulf War.[124] This difficulty in convincing the court is particularly marked when it is alleged that injustice arises in a country which is one with which the United Kingdom has close ties, such as a fellow European Community State.[125] So far the discussion has been about a comparison of procedural matters; but neither will the English courts decide whether the substantive law of England is better than that of a foreign country.[126]

The weight to be attached to the advantage to the claimant At one time great weight was attached to this factor, and if the claimant obtained a substantial advantage from trial in England the courts were unlikely to grant a stay of the English proceedings. The House of Lords in the *Spiliada* case sought to reduce the weight given to the advantage to the claimant when exercising the discretion to stay. Hence the principle that the mere fact that the claimant has a legitimate personal or juridical advantage in proceedings in England cannot be decisive.[127] Lord GOFF gave an example:[128] an English court would not, in ordinary circumstances, hesitate to stay English proceedings even though the plaintiff would be deprived of a higher award of damages available here. The same example was given by Lord GOFF in the *Connelly* case[129] when he enunciated the general

---

[121] *The El Amria* [1981] 2 Lloyd's Rep 119 at 127; *The Jalakrishna* [1983] 2 Lloyd's Rep 628 at 630–631; *The Po* [1991] 2 Lloyd's Rep 206 at 213.

[122] *The Abidin Daver* [1984] AC 398 at 411. See also *Ziraat Muduroglu Ltd v TC Bankasi* [1986] QB 1225; *Aldington Shipping Ltd v Bradstock Shipping Corpn and Mabanaft GmbH, The Waylink and Brady Maira* [1988] 1 Lloyd's Rep 475 at 482, Gibraltar Court of Appeal; *Crédit Agricole Indosuez v Unicof Ltd* [2004] 1 Lloyd's Rep 196 at 205—replacement of judges in Kenya; *Limit (No 3) Ltd v PDV Insurance Co* [2005] EWCA Civ 383 at [63]–[66]; *Al-Koronky v Time Life Entertainment Group Ltd* [2006] EWCA Civ 1123. But cf *Jayaretnam v Mahmood* (1992) Times, 21 May; *Skrine and Co (A Firm) v Euromoney Publications plc* (2000) Times, November 10. For Australia and Canada see *JLM v Director General, NSW Dept of Community Services* (2001) 180 ALR 402—acceptance that judges corrupt in Mexico seemingly without evidence, and *Pei v Bank Bumiputra Malaysia Bd* (1998) 41 OR (3d) 39, Ont Court (Gen Div). But compare *Westec Aerospace Inc v Raytheon Aircraft Co* (1999) 173 DLR (4th) 498, British Columbia Court of Appeal—cogent evidence needed.

[123] *Muduroglu Ltd v TC Ziraat Bankasi* [1986] QB 1225 at 1248.

[124] *Mohammed v Bank of Kuwait and the Middle East KSC* [1996] 1 WLR 1483 at 1496, CA. See also *Cortese v Nowsco Well Service Ltd* [2001] IL Pr 196, CA of Alberta—attitude of Alberta court towards prosecution in Italy.

[125] *Dubai Electricity Co v Islamic Republic of Iran Shipping Lines, The Iran Vojdan* [1984] 2 Lloyd's Rep 380 at 388.

[126] *Herceg Novi v Ming Galaxy* [1998] 4 All ER 238 at 247, CA.

[127] Cf in Canada *Van Dooselaere v Holt Cargo Systems Inc* [1999] IL Pr 634, Canadian Fed CA.

[128] The *Spiliada* case, supra, at 482. See *RHSP v EIH* [1999] 2 Lloyd's Rep 249 at 254.

[129] [1998] AC 854 at 872, HL; the *Lubbe* case, supra, at 1554.

principle that, normally speaking, the claimant will have to take the clearly more appropriate forum overseas as he finds it, even if it is in certain respects less advantageous to him than the English forum. The claimant may also have to do without the more generous English system of discovery (disclosure) of documents,[130] and accept the foreign forum's system of court procedure,[131] including rules of evidence. Trial abroad does not amount to an injustice.[132] The claimant will also normally have to accept the fact that financial assistance, eg in the form of legal aid, is not available abroad.[133] Neither can the claimant justify trial in England on the basis that there is a higher limit of liability here than abroad.[134] There was no injustice in trial abroad in such a case. Likewise there has been held to be no injustice in denying the claimant the advantage sought, if the action against the defendant was not stayed, of being able to join further defendants (the case against whom was very weak) who were out of the jurisdiction using the multi-defendant ground under what is now rule 6.20 of the Civil Procedure Rules.[135] Neither, standing on its own, was there any injustice in trial in South Africa from the lack of established procedures for handling group actions.[136] Instead this involved the kind of procedural comparison which the courts should be careful to avoid. There are suggestions from Lord GOFF that the attitude towards the advantage to the claimant may be different where jurisdiction has been founded on an exorbitant basis of jurisdiction such as the transient presence of the defendant in the forum.[137] In such a case, the court may be prepared to help the claimant by refusing a stay to enable him to keep the benefit of an advantage available to him in this country.

Nonetheless, Lord GOFF was concerned to pay regard to the interests of all the parties and of the ends of justice. All the circumstances of the case have to be considered. Circumstances can arise which lead to a different conclusion and to the refusal of the grant of a stay. This is graphically illustrated by the *Connelly* case, where it will be recalled that substantial justice would not be done in the particular circumstances of the case if the plaintiff had to proceed in the appropriate forum abroad where no financial assistance was available, the nature and complexity of the case being such that it could not be tried at all without the benefit of financial assistance. Lord GOFF also said in the *Spiliada* case that, in the situation where the claimant is time-barred from proceeding abroad but comes within the English limitation period, it would not be just to deprive him of the benefit of trial in England if he acted reasonably in commencing proceedings here and did not act

---

[130] The *Connelly* case, supra, at 872; *The Xin Yang* [1996] 2 Lloyd's Rep 217 at 224, CA; *Ceskoslovenska Obchodni Banka AS v Nomura International Plc* [2003] IL Pr 20 at [17]. See also *Lubbe* case, supra, at 1554. For Ontario see *Ash v Corpn of Lloyd's* [1993] IL Pr 330, Ont CA.

[131] See *Westec Aerospace Inc v Raytheon Aircraft Co* (1999) 173 DLR (4th) 498 at 514, British Columbia CA.

[132] The *Ceskoslovenska Obchodni Banka AS* case, supra.

[133] The *Connelly* case, supra, at 873.

[134] *Herceg Novi v Ming Galaxy* [1998] 4 All ER 238, CA; Briggs (1998) 69 BYBIL 340; disapproving of *Caltex v BP* [1996] 1 Lloyd's Rep 286, *Caspian Basin v Bouygous (No 4)* [1997] 2 Lloyd's Rep 507 at 530, appeal dismissed [1998] 2 Lloyd's Rep 461, CA. Cf *The Kapitan Shvetsov* [1998] 1 Lloyd's Rep 199, HK CA.

[135] *Haji-Ioannou v Frangos* [1999] 2 Lloyd's Rep 337 at 360–361, CA. Even if there was jurisdiction against the first defendant, service out against the further defendants would not have been permitted. Cf *Charm Maritime Inc v Minas Xenophon Kyriakou and David John Mathias* [1987] 1 Lloyd's Rep 433.

[136] The *Lubbe* case, supra, at 1559.

[137] The *Connelly* case, supra, at 873.

unreasonably in failing to commence proceedings in the foreign jurisdiction.[138] Seemingly, if the claimant obtains an advantage from trial in England, which does not involve a corresponding disadvantage to the defendant (eg there is a similar action before the English courts involving the same defendant, expert witnesses, lawyers and insurers), there may be injustice to the claimant in depriving him of this advantage by staying the English action.[139] The fact that an English court can award costs to a successful litigant can be an important advantage and one that operates for the benefit of both parties.[140] An advantage to the claimant can include matters relevant to the aftermath of the trial such as the ease of enforcement of an English judgment elsewhere in Europe.[141]

The concern to reduce the weight to be attached to the advantage to the claimant is a development to be welcomed. Although there has been considerable judicial condemnation of the practice of forum shopping,[142] it appears in the past that the more the claimant had to gain from this practice the more likely he was to be allowed to continue his action in England.[143] The emphasis in the House of Lords is now very much on chauvinism being replaced by judicial comity.[144] However, the extent to which this new spirit has filtered down to lower courts is questionable. In many cases the courts have concluded that the interests of justice demand that a stay be refused, even though the clearly most appropriate forum is abroad. As has been seen, there are numerous recent examples of cases where English courts have held that there would be positive injustice in trial abroad or an important advantage to the claimant in trial in England.

(c) Public interest factors[145]

In *Lubbe v Cape plc*, the Court of Appeal held that public interest considerations[146] supported trial in South Africa.[147] This referred to South Africa's interest in trying cases of personal injury following mining operations in South Africa which affected persons employed and resident there. The public interest was not directly spelt out but seemingly

---

[138] The *Spiliada* case, at 483–484; the *Lubbe* case, supra, at 1554. See also *Metall Und Rohstoff AG v Donaldson Lufkin & Jenrette Inc* [1990] 1 QB 391 at 486–488; overruled on a different point in *Lonrho plc v Fayad* [1992] 1 AC 448, HL; *BMG Trading Ltd v A S McKay* [1998] IL Pr 691 at 700; *Baghlaf v PNSC* [1998] 2 Lloyd's Rep 229, CA; *Baghlaf v PNSC (No 2)* [2000] 1 Lloyd's Rep 1, CA; *Goliath Portland Cement Co Ltd v Bengtell* (1994) 33 NSWLR 414, CA. See also, infra, p 445.

[139] The *Spiliada* case, supra, at 485–486; see also supra, pp 411–412.

[140] *The Vishva Ajay* [1989] 2 Lloyd's Rep 558; *The Al Battani* [1993] 2 Lloyd's Rep 219; *Roneleigh Ltd v MII Exports Inc* [1989] 1 WLR 619; see also *International Group Ltd and Trans-World (Steel) Ltd v Worstade Trading Ltd* [1998] IL Pr 765, Irish Supreme Court—availablity of urgent interlocutory relief; cf *The Varna (No 2)* [1994] 2 Lloyd's Rep 41 at 48; *The Polessk* [1996] 2 Lloyd's Rep 40; *RHSP v EIH* [1999] 2 Lloyd's Rep 249 at 254.

[141] *International Credit and Investment Co (Oveseas) Ltd v Shaikh Kamal Adham* [1999] IL Pr 302, CA. See also *Dubai Bank Ltd v Abbas* [1998] IL Pr 391 at 404; *Inter-Tel Inc v Ocis Plc* [2004] EWHC 2269 (QB).

[142] *Chaplin v Boys* [1971] AC 356 at 406, 380, 383; *The Atlantic Star* [1974] AC 436 at 454; see Fawcett (1984) 35 NILQ 141; Schuz (1986) 35 ICLQ 374; Bell (1995) 69 ALJ 124. For robust defence of forum shopping, see Slater (1988) 104 LQR 554; Juenger (1994) 16 Sydney LR 5, the reply by Opeskin at 14 and the rejoinder by Juenger at 28.

[143] Cf GOFF LJ in *Bank of Tokyo Ltd v Karoon* [1987] AC 45 at 62–63, CA.

[144] See *The Abidin Daver* [1984] AC 398 at 411 (per Lord DIPLOCK). See also *Owens Bank Ltd v Bracco* [1991] 4 All ER 833 at 858, CA in relation to litigation within the European Community in cases outside the Brussels Convention.

[145] See Morse (2002) 37 Texas Int LJ 541.

[146] See *Gulf Oil Corpn v Gilbert* (1947) 330 US 501.

[147] [2000] 1 Lloyd's Rep 139, 161–162, (per PILL LJ, ALDOUS and TUCKEY LJJ concurring), CA. This was the second Court of Appeal case. The first is reported at [1999] IL Pr 113, CA.

could lie in the fact that, for example, questions could be raised as to whether local regulations were ignored and whether these were stringent enough.[148] It was an opportunity for a developing country to pass judgment on behalf of its own people.[149] Although this was not mentioned, England could have been said to have a public interest in not trying the case in that there were at least three thousand foreign plaintiffs who would be legally aided, which could have had implications for the legal aid fund. However, this approach was disapproved by the House of Lords.[150] Lord Hope said that the basic principle on which the doctrine of *forum non conveniens* is exercised, which looks to the interests of the parties and the ends of justice, left no room for consideration of public interest or public policy which cannot be related to the private interests of the parties or the ends of justice.[151] This means that where the plea of *forum non conveniens* has failed (ie it cannot be shown that there is some other available forum in which the case may be tried more suitably for the interests of all the parties and the ends of justice) trial must take place in England however desirable on grounds of public interest or public policy that the litigation should be tried abroad. Conversely, there is a public interest in favour of trial in England in that when foreigners litigate in England, this forms a valuable invisible export[152] and confirms judicial pride in the English legal system. Nonetheless, where the plea of *forum non conveniens* is successful a stay ought to be granted however desirable it may be on grounds of public interest or public policy that the action should be tried here.[153] Lord HOPE explained that not only does the basic principle not allow for consideration of public interest factors but also the English courts are not equipped to conduct the sort of enquiry that would be needed if such factors were to be considered.[154]

(ii) Multiplicity of proceedings

If litigation involving the same parties and the same issues is continuing simultaneously in two different countries, this is referred to as a case of *lis alibi pendens*.[155] In such cases the issue facing the English court is not simply that of deciding to which of the alternative fora the claimant should have to go to bring his action. Instead, the choice is between, on the one hand, trial in England *plus* trial abroad (if a stay is refused) and, on the other hand, trial abroad (if a stay is granted). It is highly undesirable to have concurrent actions in England and abroad: this involves more expense and inconvenience to the parties than if the trial were held in merely one country; it can also lead to two conflicting judgments, with an unseemly race by the parties to be the first to obtain a judgment and to subsequent problems of estoppel.[156] The objection to concurrent proceedings has been said to be

---

[148] This point was made in *Re Union Carbide Corpn Gas Plant Disaster at Bhopal, India* 634 F Supp 842 (SDNY 1986), which was quoted with approval at 161–162.

[149] *Re Union Carbide Corpn, supra.*

[150] [2000] 1 WLR 1545.

[151] Ibid at 1566, at 1561 (per Lord BINGHAM with whom the other Law Lords concurred). But see CPR, r 1.1 (overriding objective), particularly r 1.1(2)(e).

[152] Kerr (1978) 41 MLR 1; Lord Devlin, *Samples of Lawmaking* (1962), pp 29–30. See also *Camilla Cotton Oil Co v Granadex SA* [1976] 2 Lloyd's Rep 10 at 14.

[153] The *Lubbe* case, op cit, at 1567 (per Lord HOPE), 1561 (per Lord BINGHAM with whom the other Law Lords concurred).

[154] Ibid, at 1567.

[155] On the significance of a multiplicity of proceedings in CPR, r 6.20 cases see supra, pp 400–401.

[156] *The Abidin Daver* [1984] AC 398 at 412 (per Lord DIPLOCK), 423–424 (per Lord BRANDON). See also *The Messiniaki Tolmi* [1983] 1 Lloyd's Rep 666 at 672. On estoppel see infra, pp 544–550.

even stronger if this involves in one of the two states proceedings for a negative declaration (a declaration that a person is not liable in an existing action).[157] But this was before the adoption by the courts of a more relaxed attitude towards the granting of such declarations.[158] If it is in the interest of justice, such a declaration may still be granted.[159] If there is a multiplicity of proceedings in England and abroad, but the parties or the issues are different in each of the actions, this is technically not a case of *lis alibi pendens*; nonetheless, it is undesirable to have this multiplicity of proceedings and some, if not all, of the objections inherent in cases of *lis alibi pendens* will still be applicable.[160]

In cases where the concurrent proceedings are in the United Kingdom and in another European Community State or in an EFTA State, the *lis alibi pendens* provision contained in Article 27[161] of the Brussels I Regulation (or Article 21 of the Brussels Convention or Article 27 of the Lugano Convention) may be applicable. However, what we are concerned with in this chapter are cases which do not fall within these Articles, eg where there are concurrent proceedings in England and New York.

The common law has no separate *lis alibi pendens* rule.[162] Instead, the fact that the refusal of a stay of English proceedings will lead to a multiplicity of proceedings in England and abroad is an important additional element to be taken into account under the doctrine of *forum non conveniens*. Lord GOFF in the *Spiliada* case did not explain how the new restated principles in relation to *forum non conveniens* would operate in cases involving a multiplicity of proceedings. However, in *De Dampierre v De Dampierre*[163] he said that the "same principle is applicable whether or not there are other relevant proceedings already pending in the alternative forum".[164] The defendant[165] has to show that there is a

---

[157] *First National Bank of Boston v Union Bank of Switzerland* [1990] 1 Lloyd's Rep 32 at 38–39. See also *Saipem Spa v Dredging V02 BV and Geosite Surveys Ltd, The Volvox Hollandia* [1988] 2 Lloyd's Rep 361 at 371, CA; *Sohio Supply Co v Gatoil (USA) Inc* [1989] 1 Lloyd's Rep 588 at 593.

[158] See supra, pp 408–409.

[159] *Smyth v Behbehani* [1999] IL Pr 584, CA—in the interest of justice that proceedings in relation to comparable transactions should all be tried at one and the same time.

[160] See *Metall Und Rohstoff AG v ACLI Metals (London) Ltd* [1984] 1 Lloyd's Rep 598, CA; *Hawke Bay Shipping Co Ltd v The First National Bank of Chicago, The Efthimis* [1986] 1 Lloyd's Rep 244, CA; *New Hampshire Insurance Co v Aerospace Finance Ltd* [1998] 2 Lloyd's Rep 539. But cf *Eli Lilly and Co v Novo Nordisk A/S* [2000] IL Pr 73, 80, CA.

[161] Supra, pp 303–312. Cf the position in Australia, on which see *Rocklea Spinning Mills Pty Ltd v Consolidated Trading Corpn* [1995] 2 VR 181.

[162] *Canada Trust Co v Stolzenberg (No 2)* [2002] 1 AC 1 at [20] (per Lord HOFFMANN).

[163] [1988] AC 92. For Canada see: *472900 BC Ltd v Thrifty Canada Ltd* (1999) 168 DLR (4th) 602, British Columbia CA; *Westec Aerospace Inc v Raytheon Aircraft Co* (1999) 173 DLR (4th) 498, British Columbia CA; appeal dismissed (2001) 197 DLR (4th) 211, SC of Canada; *Western Union Insurance Co v Re-Con Building Products Inc* (2001) 205 DLR (4th) 184, British Columbia CA; *Blinds To Go Inc v Harvard Private Capital Holdings Inc* (2003) 232 DLR (4th) 340, New Brunswick CA.

[164] *De Dampierre v De Dampierre*, supra, at 108. See also *The Varna (No 2)* [1994] 2 Lloyd's Rep 41. Cf the earlier position set out in *The Abidin Daver* [1984] AC 398. See *Galaxy Special Maritime Enterprise v Prima Ceylon Ltd (The Olympic Galaxy)* [2006] EWCA Civ 528 at [25]–[26], [2006] 2 Lloyd's Rep 27, which regards *The Abidin Daver* as being largely untouched. This must be regarded as being wrong.

[165] For cases involving the claimant seeking a stay of English proceedings, see *A-G v Arthur Andersen & Co (United Kingdom)* [1989] ECC 224; *Australian Commercial Research and Development Ltd v ANZ McCaughan Merchant Bank Ltd* [1989] 3 All ER 65; and see *Doe v Armour Pharmaceutical Co Inc* [1995] IL Pr 148, Irish SC.

clearly more appropriate forum abroad, ie *the* natural forum must be abroad.[166] This will be determined in the light of the fact that the case involves a multiplicity of proceedings.

The modern approach towards a multiplicity of proceedings can be illustrated by looking at *Cleveland Museum of Art v Capricorn Art International SA*,[167] where there were concurrent proceedings in Ohio and England between the same parties involving the same issues. HIRST J applied the basic principle used in the *Spiliada* case. He examined the factors in favour of trial in Ohio and England, took into account the fact that the action was now ready for trial in Ohio and the undesirable consequences of concurrent litigation, both in terms of expense and inconvenience to the parties and in terms of the possibility of conflicting judgments, and concluded that the Ohio court was clearly the more appropriate forum for trial of the action, in the sense of being the one in which the case may be tried more suitably for the interests of all the parties and the ends of justice. A stay of the English proceedings was accordingly granted.

In contrast to this, the operation of the same approach by the Court of Appeal led to the refusal of a stay, despite the undesirability of having concurrent proceedings, in a case where the contract was governed by English law.[168] Questions of English public policy would arise and doubts were expressed as to whether any foreign court could fairly resolve them. Similarly, an English choice of jurisdiction clause may outweigh the multiplicity of proceedings factor, with the result that a stay will be refused.[169] A stay will also be refused if there is no country which is a natural forum for trial, even if this will mean a multiplicity of proceedings. Thus a stay was refused in a case where a collision occurred in international waters between two ships of different nationalities. [170]

The weight to be attached to the factor of multiplicity of proceedings will depend on the circumstances of the case. It is not a decisive factor in the sense of automatically making a foreign forum clearly more appropriate and shifting the burden of proof to the claimant to justify trial in England.[171] It does not matter, in principle, whether the action was commenced first in England or abroad; this is merely an accident of timing.[172] But the date when trial would be held in each country has been taken into account.[173] It is also seemingly relevant whether it is a case of the same claimant starting proceedings in two

---

[166] Cf Lord DIPLOCK's formulation in the earlier case of *The Abidin Daver* [1984] AC 398. It is inappropriate now to use Lord DIPLOCK's formulation, see *Arkwright Mutual Insurance Co v Bryanston Insurance Co Ltd* [1990] 2 QB 649 at 665.

[167] [1990] 2 Lloyd's Rep 166.

[168] *E I Du Pont de Nemours & Co v Agnew and Kerr* [1987] 2 Lloyd's Rep 585. See also *Hawke Bay Shipping Co Ltd v The First National Bank of Chicago, The Efthimis* [1986] 1 Lloyd's Rep 244; *Dellar v Zivy* [2007] EWHC 2266 (Ch) at [45]–[48], [2007] IL Pr 60, concerning a will to be interpreted according to English law.

[169] *Akai Pty Ltd v People's Insurance Co Ltd* [1998] 1 Lloyd's Rep 90 at 107.

[170] *The Coral Isis* [1986] 1 Lloyd's Rep 413.

[171] *Meadows Indemnity Co Ltd v Insurance Corpn of Ireland Ltd and International Commercial Bank plc* [1989] 1 Lloyd's Rep 181 at 189; affd [1989] 2 Lloyd's Rep 298, CA.

[172] *The Coral Isis* [1986] 1 Lloyd's Rep 413; *E I Du Pont de Nemours & Co v Agnew and Kerr* [1987] 2 Lloyd's Rep 585 at 593; *Mitchell v Mitchell* 1993 SLT 123. Cf Art 27 of the Brussels I Regulation, supra, pp 303–312. See also *McConnell Dowell Constructors Ltd v Lloyd's Syndicate 396* [1988] 2 NZLR 257 at 273; *Western Union Insurance Co v Re-Con Building Products Inc* (2001) 205 DLR (4th) 184, British Columbia Court of Appeal; appeal dismissed (2001) 197 DLR (4th) 211, Sup Ct of Canada; *Ingenium Technologies Corp v McGraw-Hill Companies, Inc* (2005) 255 DLR (4th) 499, British Columbia CA.

[173] *Eli Lilly and Co v Novo Nordisk A/S* [2000] IL Pr 73, 80, CA; *XN Corpn Ltd v Point of Sale Ltd* [2001] IL Pr 35 (expedited trial in England).

different jurisdictions or a case where the claimant in one jurisdiction is the defendant in another jurisdiction and vice versa. In the former case the claimant will generally be forced to elect the country in which he wants trial.[174] If he elects for trial abroad the court will then dismiss the English proceedings. It is also relevant to look at the motivation behind the commencement of the foreign proceedings and the progress made in them. If an action is commenced abroad not because of a genuine desire for trial in that country but merely to avoid being time-barred and to demonstrate the possibility of trial in that country, the factor of multiplicity of proceedings will be given no weight.[175] Likewise, if no substantial progress has been made in the foreign proceedings, eg there has been no discovery,[176] or the foreign proceedings are unlikely to survive a jurisdictional challenge in that country,[177] the multiplicity of proceedings will be given little weight. On the other hand, if genuine proceedings have developed abroad to the stage where they have some impact upon the dispute, especially if this is likely to be of continuing effect, then this may be relevant.[178] In one case,[179] the fact that the dispute might come to trial abroad during the year made the multiplicity of proceedings a relevant factor. In *The Abidin Daver* one of the factors pointing towards Turkey as the natural forum for trial was the fact that proceedings were promptly started there soon after a collision in Turkish waters between a Cuban-owned vessel and a Turkish-owned vessel, and were proceeding with dispatch; indeed, the Turkish court had appointed a surveyor who had already interviewed relevant witnesses and prepared a report for the court.[180]

(b) Foreign jurisdiction clauses[181]

If parties have agreed on trial in a European Community or EFTA State, Article 23 of the Brussels I Regulation, Article 17 of the Brussels Convention or Article 23 of the Lugano Convention may be applicable,[182] according to which the European Community or EFTA State on which jurisdiction has been conferred by the parties is given exclusive jurisdiction. What we are concerned with here, however, are cases where Article 23 (or Article 17) is not applicable, eg where the parties have agreed on trial in New York.

---

[174] See *Australian Commercial Research and Development Ltd v ANZ McCaughan Merchant Bank Ltd* [1989] 3 All ER 65 at 70; *Ledra Fisheries Ltd v Turner* [2003] EWHC 1049 (Ch); *Khaled Salam Racy v Salah Jacques Hawila* [2004] EWCA Civ 209; *A-G v Arthur Andersen & Co* [1989] ECC 224. See also *Manufacturers Life Insurance Co v Guarantee Co of North America* (1988) 62 OR (2d) 147. Cf *Merrill Lynch v RAFFA* [2001] IL Pr 31. See also Smart [1990] LMCLQ 326.

[175] *De Dampierre v De Dampierre*, supra, at 108. See also *Irish Shipping Ltd v Commercial Union Assurance Co plc* [1991] 2 QB 206 at 232, 245.

[176] *Arkwright Mutual Insurance Co v Bryanston Insurance Co Ltd* [1990] 2 Lloyd's Rep 70 at 80.

[177] *Meridien Biao GmbH v Bank of New York* [1997] 1 Lloyd's Rep 437 at 445, where MILLETT LJ did not dissent from the view of the trial judge on this point, CA.

[178] *De Dampierre v De Dampierre*, supra. See also *The Coral Isis*, supra; *Henry v Henry* (1995) 185 CLR 571, High Court of Australia; *Mackay Refined Sugars (NZ) Ltd v New Zealand Sugar Co Ltd* [1997] 3 NZLR 476.

[179] *Meadows Indemnity Co Ltd v Insurance Corpn of Ireland Ltd and International Commercial Bank plc* [1989] 1 Lloyd's Rep 181 at 189; affd [1989] 2 Lloyd's Rep 298, CA.

[180] [1984] AC 398 at 410, 421.

[181] Pryles (1976) 25 ICLQ 543; Kahn-Freund (1977) 26 ICLQ 825; Robertson (1982) 20 Alberta LR 296; Briggs [1984] LMCLQ 227 at 241–248; Barma and Elvin (1985) 101 LQR 48 at 65–67; Peel [1998] LMCLQ 182; Fawcett [2001] LMCLQ 234.

[182] Supra, pp 283–296.

(i) The exercise of the discretion to stay[183]

As has been seen,[184] an English court will be most reluctant to permit service out of the jurisdiction in the face of an agreement by the parties to submit their disputes to the exclusive jurisdiction of a foreign court. In the situation where the English court has undoubted jurisdiction over actions properly instituted in England, there is an inherent discretion in the court to stay English proceedings brought in breach of an express foreign jurisdiction clause. This differs from the previous situation in so far as there is a heavier burden in the service out of the jurisdiction cases on the claimant to persuade the court not to give effect to the express clause.[185] The question may arise whether the dispute that has arisen falls within the scope of an exclusive jurisdiction clause. English courts give such clauses, as between the parties to them, a generous interpretation.[186] Lord BINGHAM in the House of Lords in *Donohue v Armco Inc*[187] summarised the principles that apply when exercising the discretion to stay English proceedings brought in breach of a foreign exclusive jurisdiction clause.[188] The case concerned an injunction sought to restrain proceedings brought abroad in breach of an English exclusive jurisdiction clause. But Lord BINGHAM widened the discussion to refer more generally to the principles that apply where there has been a breach of an exclusive jurisdiction clause, which includes the situation where proceedings are brought in England in breach of a foreign jurisdiction clause:

> If contracting parties agree to give a particular court exclusive jurisdiction to rule on claims between those parties, and a claim falling within the scope of the agreement is made in proceedings in a forum other than that which the parties have agreed, the English court will ordinarily[189] exercise its discretion (whether by granting a stay of proceedings in England, or by restraining the prosecution of proceedings in the non-contractual forum abroad, or by such other procedural order as is appropriate in the circumstances) to secure compliance with the contractual bargain, unless the party suing in the non-contractual forum (the burden being on him) can show strong reasons for suing in that forum.[190]

Whether a party can show strong reasons, sufficient to displace the other party's prima facie entitlement to enforce the contractual bargain, will depend on all the facts and

---

[183] Cf Civil Code of Quebec, Art 3148, para 2, under which a Quebec court has no jurisdiction to decide a case if the parties have agreed to submit all disputes to a foreign court or arbitrator, unless the defendant submits to the Quebec court; *GreCon Dimter Inc v JR Normand Inc* (2005) 255 DLR (4th) 257, Sup Ct of Canada.

[184] Supra, p 404.

[185] *Evans Marshall & Co Ltd v Bertola SA* [1973] 1 WLR 349 at 362; *Insurance Co "Ingosstrakh" Ltd v Latvian Shipping Co* [2000] IL Pr 164, 169; *Sinochem International Oil (London) Ltd v Mobil Sales and Supply Corpn Ltd (No 2)* [2000] 1 All ER (Comm) 758, 767.

[186] *Donohue v Armco Inc* [2001] UKHL 64 at [14] (per Lord BINGHAM, Lords MACKAY and NICHOLLS concurring), [60]–[61] and [68] (per Lord SCOTT), [2002] 1 All ER 749. See also *Fiona Trust & Holding Corpn v Privalov* [2007] EWCA Civ 20 at [18] (per Lord LONGMORE LJ), [2007] 2 Lloyd's Rep 267; appeal dismissed sub nom *Premium Nafta Products Ltd v Fili Shipping Co Ltd* [2007] UKHL 40, [2007] 2 All ER (Comm) 1053 without discussing choice of jurisdiction agreements.

[187] [2001] UKHL 64, [2002] 1 All ER 749.

[188] Lords MACKAY at [40] and NICHOLLS at [41] concurred with the judgment of Lord BINGHAM. Lords HOBHOUSE and SCOTT delivered judgments coming to the same conclusion as Lord BINGHAM and agreed that these were the principles to be applied.

[189] This recognises that it is a discretion. Also a party may lose his claim to equitable relief by dilatoriness or other unconscionable conduct, supra, at [24].

[190] Ibid, at [24].

circumstances of the particular case.[191] The House of Lords approved[192] the judgment of BRANDON J in *The Eleftheria*,[193] a case on the stay of English proceedings brought in breach of a foreign exclusive jurisdiction clause which has been repeatedly cited and approved over the years.[194] BRANDON J listed some of the matters which might properly be regarded by the court when exercising its discretion.[195]

(a) In what country the evidence on the issues of fact is situated, or more readily available, and the effect of that on the relative convenience and expense of trial as between the English and foreign courts.[196] (b) Whether the law of the foreign court applies and, if so, whether it differs from English law in any material respects.[197] (c) With what country either party is connected, and how closely.[198] (d) Whether the defendants genuinely desire trial in the foreign country, or are only seeking procedural advantages.[199] (e) Whether the plaintiffs would be prejudiced by having to sue in the foreign court because they would: (i) be deprived of security for their claim;[200] (ii) be unable to enforce any judgment obtained; (iii) be faced with a time bar not applicable in England;[201] or (iv) for political, racial, religious or other reasons be unlikely to get a fair trial.[202]

This list is not intended to be exhaustive.[203] After examining many of the authorities, Lord BINGHAM concluded that, where the dispute is between two contracting parties,

---

[191] Ibid.

[192] Ibid.

[193] [1970] P 94.

[194] Most importantly, *The Eleftheria* was affirmed by the Court of Appeal in the *El Amria* [1981] 2 Lloyd's Rep 119, by the House of Lords in *The Sennar (No 2)* [1985] 1 WLR 490 at 500; see also *Trendtex Trading Corpn v Crédit Suisse* [1980] 3 All ER 721; affd by the House of Lords [1982] AC 679. They were also seemingly accepted by Lord GOFF in *The Pioneer Container* [1994] 2 AC 324, PC; Toh [1995] LMCLQ 183. See also *Kutchera v Buckingham International Holdings Ltd* (1988) 9 ILRM 501, Supreme Court of Ireland; *Apple Computer Inc v Apple Corps SA* [1990] 2 NZLR 598; *Air Nauru v Niue Airlines Ltd* [1993] 2 NZLR 632; *Society of Lloyd's & Oxford Members Agency Ltd v Hyslop* [1993] 3 NZLR 135; *Kidd v van Heeren* [1998] 1 NZLR 324 and [2006] 1 NZLR 393. For New Brunswick see *A/S Nyborg Plast v Lameque Quality Group Ltd* (2001) 213 DLR (4th) 301, New Brunswick CA.

[195] [1970] P 94, at 99–100.

[196] *The Panseptos* [1981] 1 Lloyd's Rep 152.

[197] *Trendtex Trading Corpn v Crédit Suisse* [1980] 3 All ER 721 at 735; affd by the House of Lords, [1982] AC 679; *The Panseptos* [1981] 1 Lloyd's Rep 152.

[198] The courts have also looked more generally at the connections that the facts of the case have with the alternative fora. If there is no connection with England it has been said that only a perverse exercise of the discretion would lead to refusal of a stay: *The Sennar (No 2)* [1985] 1 WLR 490 at 501, HL (per Lord BRANDON); see also *The Star of Luxor* [1981] 1 Lloyd's Rep 139.

[199] *The Vishva Prabha* [1979] 2 Lloyd's Rep 286; *The Atlantic Song* [1983] 2 Lloyd's Rep 394; *The Pia Vesta* [1984] 1 Lloyd's Rep 169; *The Iran Vojdan* [1984] 2 Lloyd's Rep 380; *The Frank Pais* [1986] 1 Lloyd's Rep 529.

[200] This factor appears to be no longer of importance because of s 26 of the Civil Jurisdiction and Judgments Act 1982 (stay subject to retention of security, etc), supra, p 417; *The Havhelt* [1993] 1 Lloyd's Rep 523 at 524. See also *The Bergen (No 2)* [1997] 2 Lloyd's Rep 710 at 721.

[201] See *The Adolf Warski* [1976] 2 Lloyd's Rep 241; *The El Amria and El Minia* [1981] 2 Lloyd's Rep 539; *The Blue Wave* [1982] 1 Lloyd's Rep 151; *The Sennar (No 2)* [1984] 2 Lloyd's Rep 142, CA; affd [1985] 1 WLR 490, HL; *The Indian Fortune* [1985] 1 Lloyd's Rep 344; *The Pioneer Container*, supra; *Citi-March Ltd v Neptune Orient Lines Ltd* [1997] 1 Lloyd's Rep 72; *The MC Pearl* [1997] 1 Lloyd's Rep 566; *The Bergen (No 2)* [1997] 2 Lloyd's Rep 710; *Baghlaf Al Zafer v PNSC* [1998] 2 Lloyd's Rep 229 at 237, CA; *Insurance Co "Ingosstrakh" Ltd v Latvian Shipping Co* [2000] IL Pr 164, CA. See also *Spiliada Maritime Corpn v Cansulex Ltd* [1987] AC 460, HL; *Nima Sarl v Deves Insurance Public Co Ltd (The Prestrioka)* [2002] EWCA Civ 1132 at [76], [2003] 2 Lloyd's Rep 327 (a *forum conveniens* case); *Snookes v Jani-King (GB) Ltd* [2006] EWHC 289 (QB) at [67]–[75], [2006] IL Pr 19.

[202] See *Carvalho v Hull, Blyth (Angola) Ltd* [1979] 1 WLR 1228. This can include delays in coming to trial: *Baghlaf Al Zafer v PNSC* [1998] 2 Lloyd's Rep 229 at 235–236, CA.

[203] The *Donohue* case, supra, at [24].

and the interests of other parties are not involved, effect will in all probability be given to the exclusive jurisdiction clause.[204] In contrast, the English court may well decline to grant a stay (or grant an anti-suit injunction as the case may be) where the interests of parties other than the parties bound by the exclusive jurisdiction clause are involved or grounds of claim not the subject of the clause are part of the relevant dispute so that there is a risk of parallel proceedings and inconsistent decisions.[205] However, if this risk was foreseeable, a stay will be granted.[206] The above factors have been decisive in refusing a stay, although not fitting easily within any of the considerations set out in the *The El Amria*, which shows the non-exclusive nature of the list of considerations. In *The El Amria*[207] BRANDON LJ added that judges should not be drawn into making comparisons between the two different systems of administering justice used by English courts on the one hand and foreign courts on the other.[208] It has been said in other cases that it ill be-hoves a party who has agreed to trial in a particular foreign country subsequently to argue that he would suffer some procedural disadvantage from trial there,[209] or to argue that the substantive law which would be applied by the foreign court would be disadvantageous to him.[210] Even if one assumes that such disadvantages can be taken into account in the present context, they will be of considerably less weight than under the second stage of the *Spiliada* test.[211] There has been a tentative suggestion that the necessary strong cause to rebut the prima facie case for a stay is easier to find where the jurisdiction clause is a standard one incorporated into a contract (without any previous course of dealing between the parties) than where it has been specifically negotiated.[212] Another, and

---

[204] Ibid, at [25]. An early exception is *The Fehmarn* [1958] 1 WLR 159. A more recent one is *Domansa v Derin Shipping and Trading Co Inc* [2001] 1 Lloyd's Rep 362.

[205] The *Donohue* case, supra, at [27] referring to the following stay cases: *The El Amria*, supra, *Citi-March Ltd v Neptune Orient Lines Ltd* [1997] 1 Lloyd's Rep 72 at 78; *The MC Pearl* [1997] 1 Lloyd's Rep 566. For similar refusal of stay cases not mentioned see *The Rewia* [1991] 1 Lloyd's Rep 69 at 75; overruled on a different point [1991] 2 Lloyd's Rep 325, CA; *SCB v PNSC* [1995] 2 Lloyd's Rep 365; *Sinochem International Oil (London) Ltd v Mobil Sales and Supply Corpn Ltd (No 2)* [2000] 1 All ER (Comm) 758, 772. Lord BINGHAM also referred to anti-suit injunction cases: *Bouygues Offshore SA v Caspian Shipping Co (Nos 1, 3, 4 and 5)* [1998] 2 Lloyd's Rep 461; Briggs (1998) 69 BYBIL 342; *Crédit Suisse First Boston (Europe) v MLC (Bermuda) Ltd* [1999] 1 All ER (Comm) 237 and to *Evans Marshal & Co Ltd v Bertola SA* [1973] 1 WLR 349 (a service out case). For post-*Donohue* cases see *Konkola Copper Mines plc v Coromin Ltd* [2006] EWCA Civ 5, [2006] 1 Lloyd's Rep 410—also taking into account that there was only a provisionally found foreign jurisdiction clause; *Konkola Copper Mines plc v Coromin Ltd (No 2)* [2006] EWHC 1093 (Comm), [2006] 2 Lloyd's Rep 446.

[206] *Konkola Copper Mines plc v Coromin Ltd (No 2)* [2006] EWHC 1093 (Comm), [2006] 2 Lloyd's Rep 446. See also on the significance of unforeseeability in the context of permitting service out of the discretion, supra, p 403.

[207] [1981] 2 Lloyd's Rep 119.

[208] Ibid, at 127. See also *The Abidin Daver* [1984] AC 398, discussed supra, pp 436–437; *The Bergen (No 2)* [1997] 2 Lloyd's Rep 710 at 715. But see in relation to delays in coming to trial: *Baghalf Al Zafer v PNSC* [1998] 2 Lloyd's Rep 229 at 235–236, CA.

[209] *Trendtex Trading Corpn v Crédit Suisse* [1980] 3 All ER 721 at 736–737; affd by the House of Lords, [1982] AC 679; *The Kislovodsk* [1980] 1 Lloyd's Rep 183 at 186; *Konkola Copper Mines plc v Coromin Ltd (No 2)* [2006] EWHC 1093 (Comm) at [31], [2006] 2 Lloyd's Rep 446.

[210] *The Benarty* [1984] 2 Lloyd's Rep 244 at 251, CA.

[211] *The Nile Rhapsody* [1992] 2 Lloyd's Rep 399 at 414; Briggs (1993) 109 LQR 382; appeal dismissed, [1994] 1 Lloyd's Rep 382, CA; *Banco de Honduras SA v East West Insurance Co* [1996] 1 LRLR 74 at 80.

[212] *The Bergen (No 2)* [1997] 2 Lloyd's Rep 710 at 715. See also *Akai Pty Ltd v People's Insurance Co Ltd* [1998] 1 Lloyd's Rep 90 at 105–106. In the USA, jurisdiction clauses are subject to judicial scrutiny for fairness: *Carnival Cruise Lines Inc v Shute* 111 S Ct 1614 (1991); Richman (1992) 40 AJCL 977; Purcell (1992) 40 UCLA LR 423. See also *Trepanier v Kloster Cruise Ltd* (1995) 23 OR (3d) 398.

probably better, distinction that could be drawn is whether the parties acted freely in adopting the clause.[213]

The criteria listed in *The El Amria* encompass the same factors which are considered under the doctrine of *forum non conveniens*,[214] and the attitude towards individual factors is the same in both contexts.[215] Thus a stay should not be granted where a claimant has acted reasonably in commencing proceedings in England and not unreasonably in allowing time to expire in the agreed foreign jurisdiction.[216] Nonetheless, the law has not yet reached the stage where the two forms of discretion can be assimilated.[217] The principle that the parties should abide by their agreement is of great importance in cases involving an exclusive jurisdiction clause. The starting point is that the English proceedings should be stayed if there is such a clause providing for the exclusive jurisdiction of a foreign court, whereas under the *forum non conveniens* discretion the starting point is that an action properly commenced in England should be allowed to continue. This means that the burden of proof is different under each discretion.[218] In cases involving foreign exclusive jurisdiction clauses the burden is on the claimant to show why a stay should not be granted.[219] In cases of *forum non conveniens* the burden is on the defendant, at least as regards showing that the natural forum is abroad.[220] Moreover, a claimant cannot complain of the procedure of the foreign court if that court has been chosen by the parties.[221]

So far we have been discussing foreign exclusive jurisdiction clauses. If the foreign jurisdiction clause is non-exclusive the position is very different.[222] There is no breach of agreement in commencing proceedings in England and in principle it looks to be wrong to apply the same principles in the case of a non-exclusive jurisdiction clause as are applied in the case of an exclusive one. The right approach in the case of a non-exclusive jurisdiction clause is to apply the principles of *forum non conveniens* and to grant a stay on

---

[213] *Import-Export Metro Ltd v Compañia Sud Americana de Vapores SA* [2003] EWHC 11 (Comm), [2003] 1 Lloyd's Rep 405; *Mercury v Communication Telesystems* [1999] 2 All ER (Comm) 33—cases concerned with the exclusive jurisdiction of the English courts, supra, p 432.

[214] See *The Frank Pais* [1986] 1 Lloyd's Rep 529 at 535; *Citi-March Ltd v Neptune Orient Lines Ltd* [1997] 1 Lloyd's Rep 72 at 74. These are also the same factors as in *forum conveniens*, supra, pp 399–407.

[215] See *The Pioneer Container*, supra, at 348, where Lord GOFF quoted his comments in the *Spiliada* case on time bars. See also *The Bergen (No 2)* [1997] 2 Lloyd's Rep 710 at 715, citing the *Spiliada* case; *Baghlaf Al Zafer v PNSC* [1998] 2 Lloyd's 229 at 237. But cf *Citi-March Ltd v Neptune Orient Lines Ltd* [1997] 1 Lloyd's Rep 72 at 76–77.

[216] *The Pioneer Container*, supra; *The Bergen (No 2)*, supra; *Baghlaf Al Zafer v PNSC*, supra—a stay can be granted on terms that the defendant waives the time bar; *Nima Sarl v Deves Insurance Public Co Ltd, The Prestrioka* [2002] EWCA Civ 1132 at [80], [2003] 2 Lloyd's Rep 327 (a *forum conveniens* case).

[217] *Baghlaf Al Zafer v PNSC*, supra; *Citi-March Ltd v Neptune Orient Lines Ltd*, supra; *The Polessk* [1996] 2 Lloyd's Rep 40 at 42; see also *The Rothnie* [1996] 2 Lloyd's Rep 206; *The Nile Rhapsody* [1992] 2 Lloyd's Rep 399, appeal dismissed [1994] 1 Lloyd's Rep 382, CA, where there were attempts to use the two tests in conjunction with each other. Cf Briggs [1984] LMCLQ 227 at 241–248; Barma and Elvin (1985) 101 LQR 48 at 65–67.

[218] *Trendtex Trading Corpn v Crédit Suisse* [1980] 3 All ER 721 at 734–735; affd by the House of Lords [1982] AC 679.

[219] If the plaintiff discharges this burden, a stay will not be granted to the defendant on the basis of *forum non conveniens*, see *The Frank Pais* [1986] 1 Lloyd's Rep 529 at 535.

[220] Supra, p 428.

[221] *Trendtex Trading Corpn v Crédit Suisse* [1980] 3 All ER 721 at 734–735; affd by the House of Lords [1982] AC 679. See also *The Nile Rhapsody* [1992] 2 Lloyd's Rep 399 at 414; appeal dismissed [1994] 1 Lloyd's Rep 382, CA.

[222] The rules for determining whether a clause is exclusive or non-exclusive are discussed supra, pp 289–290.

that basis.[223] However, the Court of Appeal has applied the principles to be applied to a foreign exclusive jurisdiction clause to a foreign service of suit clause, which is akin to a non-exclusive jurisdiction clause.[224]

(ii) Reliance on, escape from, exclusive jurisdiction clauses

The impact of a foreign exclusive jurisdiction clause on service out of the jurisdiction under rule 6.20 of the Civil Procedure Rules and on stays of action is such that a defendant who does not wish to face trial in England will seek to rely on such a clause wherever possible, whereas a claimant who wishes to bring his action in England will seek to escape from such a clause.

(a) When can a defendant rely on an exclusive jurisdiction clause?

A defendant who is not a party to a contract containing an exclusive jurisdiction clause will not be able to rely on it, unless he can show that under the governing law he has an enforceable right to invoke the clause.[225]

(b) When can a claimant escape from an exclusive jurisdiction clause?

A claimant cannot avoid a foreign exclusive jurisdiction clause by simply framing his action in tort, since it is for the law governing (presumably) the agreement on jurisdiction, and not for English law as the law of the forum, to determine whether the claim lies in contract or in tort.[226] Furthermore, if a foreign court has given a judgment deciding that the exclusive jurisdiction clause applies to the claim, this may create an issue estoppel preventing the claimant from denying this.[227]

However, a claimant can escape from a foreign exclusive jurisdiction clause by showing that it is void[228] and therefore of no effect.[229] It will only be in rare cases that the claimant will succeed in establishing this. It is not enough to show that part of the agreement between the parties is void, if the foreign choice of jurisdiction clause is still left intact.[230] Neither it appears will it necessarily be enough for the claimant to show

---

[223] *The Rothnie* [1996] 2 Lloyd's Rep 206; Fawcett [2001] LMCLQ 234, at 253–255. See also *Morrison v Panic Link Ltd* 1994 SLT 232.

[224] *Ace Insurance SA-NV (Formerly Cigna Insurance Co of Europe SA-NV) v Zurich Insurance Co* [2001] EWCA Civ 173 at [62], [2001] 1 Lloyd's Rep 618, CA. See also the obiter dicta in *Import-Export Metro Ltd v Compañía Sud Americana de Vapores SA* [2003] EWHC 11 (Comm) at [14], [2003] 1 Lloyd's Rep 405—applying the same principles as where there is an English non-exclusive jurisdiction agreement (for the latter see supra, p 432 for *forum non conveniens* and supra, pp 403–404 for *forum conveniens*).

[225] *The Forum Craftsman* [1985] 1 Lloyd's Rep 291. Quaere whether this is the law governing the agreement on jurisdiction or of the contract as a whole. For the question under English law of whether shipowners can rely on an exclusive jurisdiction clause, see *The Mahkutai* [1996] AC 650, PC; *Bouygues Offshore SA v Caspian Shipping Co* [1997] IL Pr 472, CA.

[226] *The Sindh* [1975] 1 Lloyd's Rep 372, CA; cf *The Makefjell* [1976] 2 Lloyd's Rep 29; Knight (1977) 26 ICLQ 664. See also *The Sennar (No 2)* [1984] 2 Lloyd's Rep 142 at 148–149, CA; although this decision was affd by the House of Lords [1985] 1 WLR 490, it was thought unnecessary to express any view on this particular matter, per Lord BRANDON at 500.

[227] *The Sennar (No 2)* [1985] 1 WLR 490, discussed infra, pp 549–550.

[228] A final judgment is needed to this effect even where it is alleged the contract is *void ab initio*: *Morrison v The Society of Lloyd's* [2000] IL Pr 92, New Brunswick QB.

[229] It is not clear on which party the burden of proof lies in respect of the validity of the exclusive jurisdiction clause.

[230] *Trendtex Trading Corpn v Crédit Suisse* [1982] AC 679.

that the *whole* agreement of which the jurisdiction agreement is a part is void. There is support for the idea that a jurisdiction agreement (whether foreign or English) should be regarded as severable from the main contract in which the jurisdiction agreement is contained (in a clause).[231] This is on the basis that the parties, when nominating a court to settle their disputes, may well have expected this court to try the issue of the validity of the main contract.[232] This draws an analogy with the position in relation to arbitration agreements, which can be void or voidable only on grounds which relate directly to the arbitration agreement.[233] Applying this analogy, where it is argued that there never was a main contract at all (eg because of forgery), that will also be an attack on the validity of the jurisdiction agreement contained within the main contract.[234] In contrast, an argument that the main contract can be rescinded because it was procured by bribery may affect the main contract but does not undermine the jurisdiction agreement.[235]

As regards the validity of the whole agreement, the existence and validity of a contract is governed by the rules on the applicable law set out in the Rome Convention.[236] A fundamental breach of contract may result in termination of the contract and the non-application of the clause therein, including a jurisdiction clause.[237] When it comes to the question of the validity of just the exclusive jurisdiction clause it has been held that this is to be decided by applying the governing law, and the clause will be struck down if it is void according to this law.[238] In principle, this should be the law governing the agreement on jurisdiction, not the contract as a whole.[239]

---

[231] See Dicey, Morris and Collins, para 12-099; approved obiter in *Fiona Trust & Holding Corpn v Privalov* [2007] EWCA Civ 20 at [27] (per LONGMORE LJ), [2007] 2 Lloyd's Rep 267; appeal dismissed sub nom *Premium Nafta Products Ltd v Fili Shipping Co Ltd* [2007] UKHL 40, [2007] 2 All ER (Comm) 1053. The House of Lords only discussed severability in relation to arbitration agreements. See generally on recent cases involving incorporation of jurisdiction and arbitration agreements into contracts, Briggs (2006) 77 BYBIL 581.

[232] Dicey, Morris and Collins, para 12-099.

[233] See infra, p 452.

[234] See infra, p 452. See also *Mackender v Feldia AG* [1967] 2 QB 590 at 598 (per Lord DENNING), 602-603 (per DIPLOCK LJ); *Crédit Suisse First Boston (Europe) Ltd v Seagate Trading Co Ltd* [1999] 1 Lloyd's Rep 784— where the attack on the main contract also involved a direct attack on an English exclusive jurisdiction agreement.

[235] Infra, p 452.

[236] Art 8(1), infra, pp 744–745. The issue of incorporation of a clause has been held to be one of material validity of the *contract* and hence to be determined by the application of Art 8(1): *Egon Oldendorff v Liberia Corpn* [1995] 2 Lloyd's Rep 64. For the treatment of this issue in Australia see *Oceanic Sun-Line Special Shipping Co Inc v Fay* (1988) 165 CLR 197, High Court of Australia.

[237] *ZI Pompey Industrie v Ecu-Line NV* [2000] IL Pr 600, Fed Ct (Canada) and [2000] IL Pr 608, Fed Ct of Canada.

[238] *The Iran Vojdan* [1984] 2 Lloyd's Rep 380; *The Frank Pais* [1986] 1 Lloyd's Rep 529 at 530; *OT Africa Line Ltd v Magic Sportswear Corpn* [2005] EWCA Civ 710 at [58]–[61], [83], [2005] 2 Lloyd's Rep 170; Baatz [2006] LMCLQ 143; Briggs (2005) 76 BYBIL 650; *Horn Linie GmbH & Co v Panamericana Formas E Impresos SA* [2006] EWHC 373 (Comm) at [10], [2006] 2 Lloyd's Rep 44.

[239] To be determined under traditional common law rules (the Rome Convention excludes agreements on jurisdiction from its scope, infra, pp 684–685): *OT Africa Line Ltd v Magic Sportswear Corpn* [2005] EWCA Civ 710 at [60] (per RIX LJ), [2005] 2 Lloyd's Rep 170. However, LONGMORE LJ, at [1]–[2] and [20]–[23], favoured the law governing the *contract as a whole*. Unhelpfully, LAWS LJ agreed with both RIX LJ and LONGMORE LJ. LONGMORE LJ was followed in the *Horn Linie* case, supra, at [20].

An exclusive jurisdiction clause may also be void because of the terms of a statute.[240] In *The Hollandia*,[241] the House of Lords held that an exclusive jurisdiction clause providing for trial in the Netherlands was rendered null and void and of no effect by virtue of the Hague-Visby Rules, which are part of English law.[242] The Rules provide, inter alia, that any clause lessening the liability of the carrier otherwise than as provided for under the Rules shall be null and void.[243] The Dutch exclusive jurisdiction clause had the effect, albeit indirectly, of lessening the carrier's liability, since, if trial was held in the Netherlands, the Dutch courts would apply Dutch law which set a lower maximum limit on the carrier's liability than that provided for under the Rules.[244] In the absence of an exclusive jurisdiction clause and of any other basis for the granting of a stay, the shipper's action was allowed to proceed.[245]

In *The Hollandia* the continuance of the plaintiff's action depended ultimately on the wording of the Hague-Visby Rules. The same is true of the later case of *The Benarty*.[246] In that case the Court of Appeal held that an exclusive jurisdiction clause providing that actions should be brought in the Indonesian courts was not rendered void under the Hague-Visby Rules, since the case concerned a tonnage limitation (ie one calculated on the tonnage of the ship carrying the goods), and not a package limitation[247] as in the *The Hollandia* (ie one calculated on the number of packages or on their weight). In consequence, the principle that the parties should abide by their agreement was applied and a stay of the English[248] proceedings was granted.

(c) Arbitration agreements[249]

Section 9 of the Arbitration Act 1996[250] substantially gives effect to Article II of the New York Convention on the Recognition and Enforcement of Arbitral Awards (1958).[251] It applies to all written arbitration[252] agreements.[253] Section 9 applies even if the seat of the

---

[240] *The Hollandia* [1983] 1 AC 565; *Akai Pty Ltd v People's Insurance Co Ltd* (1996) 71 ALJR 156 High Court of Australia.

[241] [1983] 1 AC 565, [1982] 3 All ER 1141; sub nom *The Morviken* [1983] 1 Lloyd's Rep 1; Mann (1983) 99 LQR 376, 400–406. *The Hollandia* is unaffected by the Rome Convention, see infra, p 763.

[242] See the Carriage of Goods by Sea Act 1971.

[243] See the Schedule to the Carriage of Goods by Sea Act 1971, Art III, para 8.

[244] [1983] 1 AC 565 at 574–575. Defendants can undertake not to take advantage of the lower limit, in which case the jurisdiction clause is no longer disregarded: *Baghlaf Al Zafer v PNSC* [1998] 2 Lloyd's Rep 229 at 238, CA.

[245] *The Hollandia*, supra, at 576–577.

[246] [1984] 2 Lloyd's Rep 244; Reynolds [1984] LMCLQ 545.

[247] Ibid, at 250–251, 253–254.

[248] Ibid, at 251, 255.

[249] Hill, paras 20.2.1–20.2.37.

[250] For interpretation of the 1996 Act, see Departmental Advisory Committee (DAC) Report on Arbitration Law, February 1996, on the relevance of which see *Halki Shipping Corpn v Sopex Oils Ltd* [1998] 1 WLR 726 at 732, CA.

[251] And replaces s 2 of the Arbitration Act 1975 and s 4 of the Arbitration Act 1950.

[252] *Walkinshaw v Diniz* [2000] 2 All ER (Comm) 237. For agreements on alternative dispute resolution see *Cable & Wireless plc v IBM United Kingdom Ltd* [2002] EWHC 2059 (Comm), [2002] 2 All ER (Comm) 1041.

[253] 1996 Act, s 5 (agreement to be in writing); s 6 (definition of arbitration agreement, which can include incorporation of arbitration clause from another document—on which see *Trygg Hansa v Equitas* [1998] 2 Lloyd's Rep 439; *The Delos* [2001] 1 Lloyd's Rep 703); replacing 1975 Act, s 7(1); *Excomm Ltd v Ahmed Abdul-Qawi Bamordah, The St Raphael* [1985] 1 Lloyd's Rep 403; *Zambia Steel v Clark and Eaton* [1986] 2 Lloyd's Rep 225.

arbitration is outside England and Wales or Northern Ireland or no seat has been desig-nated or determined.[254] Section 9 will doubtless also apply regardless of whether the arbitration agreement is governed by English or foreign law.[255]

A party[256] to an arbitration agreement against whom legal proceedings[257] are brought (whether by way of claim or counterclaim) in respect of a matter which under the agree-ment is to be referred to arbitration[258] may (upon notice to the other parties to the pro-ceedings) apply to the courts in which the proceedings have been brought to stay the proceedings so far as they concern that matter.[259] Most arbitration clauses refer any "dis-pute" to arbitration. The question whether there is a "dispute" between the parties that they have agreed to refer to arbitration therefore arises. There is a "dispute" whenever there is a claim which the other party refused to admit or did not satisfy.[260] It does not matter whether there is an answer to the claim in fact or law.[261] The fact that an applica-tion may be made to stay a counterclaim, as well as a claim, represents a change to the previous statutory position. Another statutory provision provides that an application may be made notwithstanding that the matter is to be referred to arbitration only after the exhaustion of other dispute resolution procedures.[262] An application may not be made by a person before taking the appropriate procedural step (if any) to acknowledge the legal proceedings against him or after he has taken any step in those proceedings to answer the substantive claim.[263] The court must be satisfied that there was an arbitration clause and that the subject of the action was within that clause.[264] Under English law,

---

[254] 1996 Act, s 2(2)(a). For the determination of the seat see *Dubai Paymentech* [2001] 1 Lloyd's Rep 65.

[255] See *Nova (Jersey) Knit Ltd v Kammgarn Spinnerei GmbH* [1977] 1 WLR 713.

[256] This includes any person claiming under or through a party to the agreement: 1996 Act, s 82(2). See in relation to the same phrase under the 1975 Act, *Grupo Torras SA and Torras Hostench London Ltd v Sheikh Fahad Mohammed Al-Sabah* [1995] 1 Lloyd's Rep 374 at 450–451; appeals dismissed [1996] 1 Lloyd's Rep 7, CA. See in relation to an assignee, *The Leage* [1984] 2 Lloyd's Rep 259. For a stay using s 49(3) of the Supreme Court Act 1981 pending arbitration abroad between a party to the litigation and a third party (not involved in the litigation), see *Reichhold Norway ASA v Goldman Sachs International* [2000] 1 WLR 173, CA; discussed infra, pp 454–455.

[257] This includes where one party seeks declaratory relief from the court, including where the applicant seeks in the alternative an extension of time to come to arbitration: *Grimaldi Compagnia di Navigazione SpA v Sekihyo Line Ltd* [1998] 3 All ER 943.

[258] See *NB Three Shipping Ltd v Harebell Shipping Ltd* [2004] EWHC 2001 (Comm), [2005] 1 Lloyd's Rep 509. The matter must be capable of settlement by arbitration: 1996 Act, s 81(1)(a); Hill, paras 20.2.9–20.2.11.

[259] Arbitration Act 1996, s 9(1). The Court of Appeal will entertain an appeal against a decision as to wheth-er to stay under s 9: *Inco Europe v First Choice Distribution* [2000] 1 WLR 586, HL. For the relationship between ss 9 and 12 (extension of time to come to arbitration), see *Grimaldi Compagnia di Navigazione SpA v Sekihyo Line Ltd* [1998] 3 All ER 943.

[260] *Halki Shipping Corpn v Sopex Oils Ltd* [1998] 1 WLR 726, CA; Whiteley [1998] LMCLQ 164; *Wealands v CLC Contractors* [1999] 2 Lloyd's Rep 739, CA; *Exfin Shipping Ltd v Tolani Shipping Co Ltd* [2006] EWHC 1090 (Comm), [2006] 2 Lloyd's Rep 389. See also *Loon Energy Inc v Integra Mining* [2007] EWHC 1876 (Comm) at [85]–[87].

[261] The *Halki* case, supra.

[262] Arbitration Act 1996, s 9(2). This deals with a point made by Lord Mustill in *Channel Tunnel Group Ltd v Balfour Beatty Construction Ltd* [1993] AC 334 at 354.

[263] Arbitration Act 1996, s 9(3). See *Patel v Patel* [2000] QB 551, CA—application for a default judgment to be set aside and for leave to defend and counterclaim was not such a step.

[264] *Al-Naimi v Islamic Press Agency Inc* [2000] 1 Lloyd's Rep 522, CA; *Albon v Naza Motor Trading Sdn Bhd (No 3)* [2007] EWHC 327 (Ch), [2007] 2 Lloyd's Rep 1. See on the scope of the clause: *Wealands v CLC Contractors* [1999] 2 Lloyd's Rep 739, CA; *Capital Trust Investments Ltd v Radio Design TJ AB* [2002] CLC 787; *Sonatrach Petroleum Corpn v Ferrell International Ltd* [2002] 1 All ER (Comm) 627 at 639–640; *Anglia Oils Ltd v Owners of the Vessel "Marine Champion"* [2002] EWHC 2407 (Admiralty); *El Nasharty v J Sainsbury* [2003]

arbitration clauses in international commercial contracts are to be liberally construed.[265] Construction of the arbitration clause starts from the asssumption that the parties, as rational businesssmen, are likely to have intended any dispute arising out of the relationship into which they have entered or purported to enter to be decided by the same tribunal, unless the the language makes it clear that certain questions were intended to be excluded from the arbitrator's jurisdiction.[266] Thus an arbitration clause was construed to cover a dispute as to whether the contract of which it formed part was procured by bribery.[267] The staying of the proceedings is mandatory[268] unless the court is satisfied that the arbitration agreement is null and void,[269] inoperative[270] or incapable of being performed.[271] Under English arbitration law an arbitration agreeement is separable from the main contract of which it forms part.[272] It follows that the invalidity or rescission of the main contract does not necessarily entail the invalidity or rescission of the arbitration agreement.[273] The arbitration agreement is a distinct agreement and can be void or voidable only on grounds which relate directly to the arbitration agreement.[274] An argument that the main contract can be rescinded because it was procured by bribery may affect the main contract but does not undermine the arbitration ageement as a distinct agreement.[275] On the other hand, where it is argued that there never was a main contract at all (eg because of forgery), that will be an attack on the validity of the arbitration agreement contained within the main contract.[276] The relevant time for ascertaining validity and whether it is capable of being performed is as at the date of commencement of the proceedings to be stayed, rather than as at the date of the application for a stay.[277] The burden

---

EWHC 2195 (Comm) at [29], [2004] 1 Lloyd's Rep 309; *Law Debenture Trust v Elektrim Finance* [2005] EWHC 1412 (Ch), [2005] 2 All ER (Comm) 476 at [32]–[37]. For the use of the court's inherent jurisdiction where the court is not sure of this see infra, pp 453–454.

[265] *Fiona Trust & Holding Corpn v Privalov* [2007] EWCA Civ 20 at [18] (per LONGMORE LJ), [2007] 2 Lloyd's Rep 267; appeal dismissed sub nom *Premium Nafta Products Ltd v Fili Shipping Co Ltd* [2007] UKHL 40, [2007] 2 All ER (Comm) 1053. For explicit support in the House of Lords for the views of LONGMORE LJ see at [26] (per Lord Hope), [38] (per Lord BROWN).See also *Mabey and Johnson Ltd v Danos* [2007] EWHC 1094 (Ch) at [12]–[15].

[266] *Fiona Trust & Holding Corpn v Privalov* sub nom *Premium Nafta Products Ltd v Fili Shipping Co Ltd* [2007] UKHL 40 (per Lord HOFFMANN), [22] (per Lord HOPE), [36] (per Lord SCOTT), [37] (per Lord WALKER), [38] (per Lord BROWN), [2007] 2 All ER (Comm) 1053.

[267] Ibid. With the result that a stay of the court proceedings for a declaration that the contracts had been rescinded was granted.

[268] And must be unconditional: *The Rena K* [1979] QB 377 at 400, supra, p 417. *The Vasso, formerly Andria* [1984] 1 Lloyd's Rep 235 at 242. However, security available in an action in rem can be retained: 1996 Act, s 11.

[269] See *Inco Europe v First Choice Distribution* [1999] 1 WLR 270, CA; affd on the question of the jurisdiction of the Court of Appeal to hear the appeal: [2000] 1 WLR 586, HL.

[270] See *The Merak* [1965] P 223 at 239, decided under s 4(2) of the Arbitration Act 1950; *Astro Valiente Compañía Naviera SA v Pakistan Ministry of Food and Agriculture (No 2)* [1982] 1 WLR 1096; *Kaverit Steel and Crane Ltd v Kone Corpn* (1992) 87 DLR (4th) 129.

[271] Arbitration Act 1996, s 9(4).

[272] Ibid, s 7.

[273] *Fiona Trust & Holding Corpn v Privalov* sub nom *Premium Nafta Products Ltd v Fili Shipping Co Ltd* [2007] UKHL 40 at [17] (per Lord HOFFMANN), [22] (per Lord HOPE), [36] (per Lord SCOTT), [37] (per Lord WALKER), [38] (per Lord BROWN), [2007] 2 All ER (Comm) 1053.

[274] Ibid.

[275] Ibid at [35] (per Lord HOPE), [17]–[21] (per Lord HOFFMANN), [36] (per Lord SCOTT), [37] (per Lord WALKER), [38] (per Lord BROWN)

[276] Ibid, at [17] (per Lord HOFFMANN), [22] (per Lord HOPE), [36] (per Lord SCOTT), [37] (per Lord WALKER), [38] (per Lord BROWN), [2007] 2 All ER (Comm) 1053.

[277] *Traube v Perelman*, 2001 (unreported).

of proof is on the party alleging this.[278] No choice of law rule is provided for these issues.

The question whether an arbitration agreement is null and void is a matter for the law governing the arbitration agreement.[279] The same law governs the question whether a contract contains an arbitration clause.[280] The determination of the scope of an arbitration clause and whether it covers the matter in dispute between the parties is likewise an issue for the law governing the arbitration agreement.[281] "Inoperative" encompasses the situation where the arbitration agreement has come to an end.[282] The question whether the arbitration agreement is incapable of being performed relates not to whether one of the parties can satisfy any award that may be made but rather to whether the agreement can be performed up to the stage of an award being made.[283]

Under the previous statutory provision there was a further ground for not granting a stay, namely that there was not in fact any dispute between the parties with regard to the matter agreed to be referred to arbitration.[284] If the claimant could show that there was no defence to the claim, the court could at the same time refuse a stay and give a summary judgment[285] in favour of the claimant.[286] The Arbitration Act 1996 omits this ground for not granting a stay on the basis that it is confusing and unnecessary.[287] The intention of the 1996 Act was to exclude this summary judgment jurisdiction based on an investigation of what was in fact disputable.[288] A stay will be granted and the claimant's application for summary judgment will be dismissed, even though the claimant claims that the defendant has no arguable defence.[289]

One final matter concerns the extent to which the courts can use their inherent jurisdiction to stay proceedings in cases involving arbitration. One of the general principles set out in the Arbitration Act 1996, in the light of which all the provisions in the Act must be read, is that "in matters governed by this Part [Part I, ie sections 1 to 84] the court

---

[278] *Overseas Union Insurance Ltd v AA Mutual International Insurance Co Ltd* [1988] 2 Lloyd's Rep 63 at 70.

[279] See *Astro Venturoso Compañia Naviera v Hellenic Shipyards SA, The Mariannina* [1983] 1 Lloyd's Rep 12; *Weissfisch v Julius* [2006] EWCA Civ 218, [2006] 1 Lloyd's Rep 716. This will be determined according to traditional common law rules; the Rome Convention excludes arbitration agreements from its scope, infra, pp 684–685.

[280] *Marc Rich & Co AG v Societa Italiana Impianti PA, The Atlantic Emperor* [1989] 1 Lloyd's Rep 548; the case was referred to the European Court of Justice on a different point, see supra, p 220. See also *O T M Ltd v Hydronautics* [1981] 2 Lloyd's Rep 211. Cf *The Rena K* [1979] QB 377. However, the issue of incorporation of an arbitration clause has been held to be one of material validity of the *contract* and hence to be determined by the application of Art 8(1) of the Rome Convention: *Egon Oldendorff v Liberia Corpn* [1995] 2 Lloyd's Rep 64. But where a foreign court gives a judgment on the question of incorporation this may create an estoppel, see *Tracomin SA v Sudan Oil Seeds Co Ltd (Nos 1 and 2)* [1983] 1 WLR 1026, discussed infra, pp 570–571.

[281] *Nova (Jersey) Knit Ltd v Kammgarn Spinnerei GmbH* [1977] 1 WLR 713 at 718–719, 730; *Abu Dhabi Investment Co v H Clarkson & Co Ltd* [2006] EWHC 1252 (Comm), [2006] 2 Lloyd's Rep 381.

[282] *Downing v Al Tameer* [2002] EWCA Civ 721, [2002] CLC 1291.

[283] *The Rena K* [1979] 1 QB 377 at 393. See also *Grupo Torras SA and Torras Hostench London Ltd v Sheikh Fahad Mohammed Al-Sabah* [1995] 1 Lloyd's Rep 374 at 451–452; appeals dismissed [1996] 1 Lloyd's Rep 7, CA.

[284] 1975 Act, s 1(1).

[285] See now CPR, Part 24; previously RSC, Ord 14.

[286] *Channel Tunnel Group Ltd v Balfour Beatty Construction Ltd* [1993] AC 334 at 356, HL.

[287] DAC Report (1996), para 55. See also *Hayter v Nelson* [1990] 2 Lloyd's Rep 265.

[288] *Halki Shipping Corpn v Sopex Oils Ltd* [1998] 1 WLR 726 at 750 (per HENRY LJ), CA.

[289] Ibid. There must, of course, be a dispute between the parties that they have agreed to refer to arbitration, supra, p 451.

should not intervene except as provided by this Part".[290] It follows that a court cannot use its inherent jurisdiction to stay proceedings where the matter is governed by Part I. Thus it cannot do so where the conditions for the application of Article 9 are satisfied but a stay is refused because the arbitration agreement is incapable of being performed. On the other hand, there is nothing in the 1996 Act to prevent a court from using its inherent jurisdiction where the matter is not governed by Part I. Moreover, to use its inherent jurisdiction in this situation is supported by House of Lords authority in relation to the statutory predecessor of section 9 of the 1996 Act, where it was held that, whether or not the procedure for resolving disputes agreed between the parties amounted to an arbitration agreement falling within section 1 of the Arbitration Act 1975, the court had an inherent jurisdiction to stay the proceedings.[291] This leaves the question: which matters are not governed by Part I of the 1996 Act? Two examples have been suggested.[292] The first is an oral arbitration agreement;[293] the second, an agreement to refer a dispute to an alternative dispute resolution mechanism other than arbitration.[294] Going beyond this, it has been suggested in the Court of Appeal that a stay under the inherent jurisdiction might be sensible in the situation where the court could not be sure that there was an arbitration agreement or that the subject of the action was within that agreement.[295] Thus recourse has been had to the inherent jurisdiction and a stay granted in relation to claims designed to impugn the validity of an arbitration agreement.[296] However, the case would be an exceptional one before the court would grant a stay, leaving these matters to an arbitrator, in circumstances where the court was uncertain as to whether there was an arbitration agreement.[297]

(d) Stays pending the determination of proceedings abroad

So far, stays of English proceedings where the effect of the stay has been to force the claimant to go abroad to sue or to go to arbitration abroad have been considered. However, the English courts also have power[298] to stay English proceedings pending the final determination of arbitration or trial abroad,[299] in other words, to suspend temporarily the English proceedings. This involves less of an interference with the claimant's right to bring his action in England. Nevertheless, this power will only be exercised in rare and

---

[290] Arbitration Act 1996, s 1(c).

[291] *Channel Tunnel Group Ltd v Balfour Beatty Construction Ltd* [1993] AC 334; Reymond (1993) 109 LQR 337. This involves a discretionary power which is based on the idea that the parties should abide by their agreement and is analogous to upholding foreign choice of jurisdiction agreements, discussed supra, pp 443–448.

[292] Hill, para 20.2.39.

[293] See the Arbitration Act 1996, ss 5 (agreement to be in writing) and 81 (saving any rule of law, consistent with the provisions of Part I, as to the effect of an oral arbitration agreement).

[294] See *Channel Tunnel Group Ltd v Balfour Beatty Construction Ltd* [1993] AC 334, HL— a case decided in relation to the Arbitration Act 1975, s 1.

[295] *Al-Naimi v Islamic Press Agency Inc* [2000] 1 Lloyd's Rep 522 at 525 (per WALLER LJ) and 528 (per CHADWICK LJ), CA. See also *Fiona Trust & Holding Corpn v Privalov* [2007] EWCA Civ 20 at [37]-[38] (per LONGMORE LJ), [2007] 2 Lloyd's Rep 267; appeal dismissed sub nom *Premium Nafta Products Ltd v Fili Shipping Co Ltd* [2007] UKHL 40, [2007] 2 All ER (Comm) 1053; *Albon v Naza Motor Trading Sdn Bhd (No 3)* [2007] EWHC 327 (Ch) at [16], [2007] 2 Lloyd's Rep 1.

[296] *A v B* [2006] EWHC 2006 (Comm), [2007] 1 Lloyd's Rep 237.

[297] *El Nasharty v J Sainsbury* [2003] EWHC 2195 (Comm) at [29], [2004] 1 All ER (Comm) 728; *Albon v Naza Motor Trading Sdn Bhd (No 3)* [2007] EWHC 327 (Ch) at [24]–[25], [2007] 2 Lloyd's Rep 1.

[298] Under its inherent jurisdiction expressly preserved by s 49(3) of the Supreme Court Act 1981.

[299] *Reichhold Norway ASA v Goldman Sachs International* [2000] 1 WLR 173, CA.

compelling circumstances.[300] It was correctly exercised in *Reichhold Norway ASA v Goldman Sachs International*.[301]

> X began an action against Y before the English courts. X then commenced arbitration proceedings against Z in Norway. The two sets of concurrent proceedings overlapped to a significant degree. Y obtained a stay of the English proceedings pending the determination of the arbitration in Norway.

2. RESTRAINING FOREIGN PROCEEDINGS

An English court cannot prohibit a foreign court from trying an action. However, it does have a discretionary power, in certain circumstances, to grant an injunction restraining a party from commencing or continuing as claimant in foreign proceedings.[302] This power is not restricted by the Human Rights Act,[303] Article 6 of which is not concerned with *where* the right to a fair and public hearing is to be exercised by a litigant but rather with the fact that civil rights must be exercised *somewhere* by a hearing and before a tribunal in accordance with the provisions of that Article.

(a) Underlying principles

First, the restraining order is directed not against the foreign court but against the party proceeding or threatening to proceed in the foreign court.[304] It binds only that party, in personam.[305] If the order is disobeyed, the person against whom it is directed can be punished for contempt of court. However, the reality is that, if the defendant neither lives in England nor has substantial assets there, the injunction is unlikely to be enforceable except by the foreign court recognising and giving effect to the injunction, or, if it refuses to do so, as may well be the case, by the English court refusing to recognise or enforce the judgment of the foreign court.[306]

---

[300] Ibid at 186 (per Lord BINGHAM delivering the judgment of the Court of Appeal). For refusal to grant a stay: see *Konkola Copper Mines plc v Coromin Ltd* [2006] EWCA Civ 5, [2006] 1 Lloyd's Rep 410; *Mabey and Johnson Ltd v Danos* [2007] EWHC 1094 (Ch).

[301] [2000] 1 WLR 173, CA. Cf *National Westminster Bank v Utrecht-America Finance Co* [2001] EWCA Civ 658 at [24]–[25], [2001] 3 All ER 733.

[302] See generally Briggs and Rees, paras 5.34–53; Dicey, Morris and Collins, paras 12-067–12-081; Briggs in Rose (ed), *Lex Mercatoria: Essays in International Commercial Law in Honour of Francis Reynolds*, p 219; Fentiman in Cheong *et al* (eds), in *Current Issues in International Commercial Litigation*, pp 44–71; Collins in, Cheong *et al* (eds), *Current Issues in International Commercial Litigation*, pp 5–10; Wilson [1997] JBL 424; Bell and Gleeson (1997) 71 ALJ 955; Males [1998] LMCLQ 543; Hartley (1987) 35 AJCL 48; Ho (2003) 52 ICLQ 697. This power to restrain foreign proceedings is also referred to as enjoining foreign proceedings. The injunction is often referred to as an anti-suit injunction. For the powers of the High Court in respect of injunctions, see the Supreme Court Act 1981, s 37. For the powers of an appeal court to interfere with the exercise of the discretion by a lower court see *Donohue v Armco Inc* [2001] UKHL 64, [2002] 1 All ER 749 at [37]–[38]. The terms of the injunction may take the form of not contesting certain matters in the foreign court, see *Banque Cantonale v Waterlily Maritime Inc* [1997] 2 Lloyd's Rep 347 at 357. For an injunction restraining arbitration in England see *Elektrim SA v Vivendi Universal SA (No 2)* [2007] EWHC 571 (Comm), [2007] 2 Lloyd's Rep 8.

[303] *OT Africa Line Ltd v Hijazy (The Kribi)* [2001] 1 Lloyd's Rep 76 at [41]–[44].

[304] *Donohue v Armco Inc* [2001] UKHL 64, [2002] 1 All ER 749, 757; *Turner v Grovit* [2001] UKHL 65 at [23], [2002] 1 WLR 107; *Société Nationale Industrielle Aérospatiale v Lee Kui Jak* [1987] AC 871, 892.

[305] *Turner v Grovit*, supra, at [23].

[306] *Phillip Alexander Securities and Futures Ltd v Bamberger* [1997] IL Pr 73 at 117, CA. The German court in this case refused to permit the injunctions to be served in Germany, regarding them as an infringement of their sovereignty. For the refusal to enforce the foreign judgment, see infra, p 614.

Secondly, an injunction will only be issued restraining a party who is amenable to the jurisdiction of the court, against whom an injunction will be an effective remedy.[307] This is a consequence of the fact that, unlike the situation in which a court grants a stay of English proceedings, a court when restraining foreign proceedings is not regulating its own jurisdiction. There is no difficulty in a case where the person against whom the injunction is directed is an English resident. The position is more complicated in a case where he is a foreign resident. There is jurisdiction to grant the injunction if the person against whom it is directed has submitted to the English court's jurisdiction,[308] or if he has sufficient connection with England to justify this,[309] eg where he has brought an action abroad in breach of an agreement providing for arbitration in England.[310] Furthermore, if a claim form has been or could be served out of the jurisdiction on the defendant under rule 6.20 of the Civil Procedure Rules, the courts will thereby have power to grant an injunction, restraining foreign proceedings.[311] If there is jurisdiction to grant the injunction, the courts, when deciding whether to exercise their discretion to grant this, will not consider the possibility that a foreign defendant will not obey this order.[312] The grant of an injunction does not require the English court to make any finding as to the jurisdiction of the foreign court.[313]

Thirdly, although the claim form is directed at a person there is, nonetheless, an implicit interference with the jurisdiction of a foreign court whenever an English court grants an injunction restraining foreign proceedings. There are obvious comity problems inherent in the exercise of the power to restrain foreign proceedings; for this reason it has often been said that the power must be exercised with caution.[314] "Considerations of comity grow in importance the longer the foreign suit continues and the more the parties and the Judge have engaged in its conduct and management."[315]

---

[307] *Castanho v Brown and Root (UK) Ltd* [1981] AC 557, HL; *Midland Bank plc v Laker Airways Ltd* [1986] QB 689; *Bank of Tokyo Ltd v Karoon* [1987] AC 45 n at 59, CA; *Société Industrielle Aérospatiale v Lee Kui Jak* [1987] AC 871 at 892; *Donohue v Armco Inc*, supra, at 757; *Turner v Grovit*, supra, at [23]; Thomas [1983] LMCLQ 692.

[308] *Glencore International AG v Exter Shipping Ltd* [2002] EWCA Civ 528 at [52], [2002] 2 All ER (Comm) 1. See also *Royal Exchange Assurance Co Ltd v Compañía Naviera Santi SA, The Tropaioforos* [1962] 1 Lloyd's Rep 410; *Castanho v Brown and Root (UK) Ltd*, supra.

[309] *The Tropaioforos*, supra; *Castanho v Brown and Root (UK) Ltd*, supra.

[310] *Tracomin SA v Sudan Oil Seeds Co Ltd (Nos 1 and 2)* [1983] 1 WLR 1026, an agreement to arbitrate in England can alternatively be regarded as a submission to jurisdiction for these purposes.

[311] *Donohue v Armco Inc*, supra, at 758. See also *Royal Exchange Assurance v Compañía Naviera Santi SA, The Tropaioforos*, supra. The injunction ground under CPR, r 6.20(2) cannot be used: *Amoco (UK) Exploration Co v British American Offshore Ltd* [1999] 2 Lloyd's Rep 772.

[312] *Castanho v Brown and Root (UK) Ltd*, supra.

[313] *Turner v Grovit*, supra, at [26]

[314] See, eg, *Castanho v Brown and Root (UK) Ltd*, supra; *British Airways Board v Laker Airways Ltd* [1985] AC 58 at 95 (per Lord SCARMAN), HL; *South Carolina Insurance Co v Assurantie NV* [1987] AC 24 at 40, HL (per Lord BRANDON); *Société Nationale Industrielle Aérospatiale v Lee Kui Jak*, supra, at 892; *Airbus Industrie GIE v Patel* [1999] 1 AC 119 at 133, HL; *Donohue v Armco Inc*, supra, at 757; *Sabah Shipyard (Pakistan) Ltd v Islamic Republic of Pakistan* [2002] EWCA Civ 1643 at [40]; [2003] 2 Lloyd's Rep 571, CA. On comity see also *Amoco (UK) Exploration Co v British American Offshore Ltd* [1999] 2 Lloyd's Rep 772 at 780.

[315] *Royal Bank of Canada v Cooperative Centrale Raiffeisen-Boerenleenbank BA* [2004] EWCA Civ 7 at [50], [2004] 1 Lloyd's Rep 471.

Fourthly, and more specifically, an anti-suit injunction will not be granted in circumstances which amount to a breach of comity. In *Airbus Industrie GIE v Patel* Lord GOFF, giving the unanimous judgment of the House of Lords, said that:

> As a general rule, before an anti-suit injunction can properly be granted by an English court to restrain a person from pursuing proceedings in a foreign jurisdiction in cases of the kind under consideration in the present case, comity requires that the English forum should have a sufficient interest in, or connection with, the matter in question to justify the indirect interference with the foreign court which an anti-suit injunction entails.[316]

This was stated "as a general rule", which inevitably begs the question of what the exception is to this. Lord GOFF contemplated that there may be extreme cases, "for example where the conduct of the foreign state exercising jurisdiction is such as to deprive it of the respect normally required by comity", where no such limit is required to the exercise of the jurisdiction to grant an anti-suit injunction.[317]

Fifthly, different principles apply to cases where an injunction is sought to restrain a party from proceeding in a foreign court in breach of an arbitration agreement or a clause providing for exclusive jurisdiction in England.[318] In particular, there is not the same concern with comity. This affects the operation of the third and fourth principles.

Sixthly, the broad principle underlying the jurisdiction is that it is to be exercised when the ends of justice require it.[319]

Finally, judicial decisions limit when it may be considered just to grant an injunction.[320] The power to make the order is dependent upon there being wrongful conduct of the party to be restrained of which the applicant is entitled to complain and has a legitimate interest in seeking to prevent.[321] The conduct in question should fit within the description of being unconscionable in the eye of English law.[322] The use of the word unconscionable makes the point that the remedy is a personal one for the wrongful conduct of an individual. It is essentially a fault-based remedial concept.[323] It is unconscionable conduct that founds the right, legal or equitable, for the protection of which an injunction can be granted.[324]

(b) Categorisation of the cases

It is possible to divide up the cases where an injunction has been granted into various categories, and each category contains more specific criteria for the grant of an injunction.

---

[316] *Airbus Industrie GIE v Patel, supra,* at 138.

[317] Ibid, at 140.

[318] *Aggeliki Charis Compañía Marítima SA v Pagnan SpA, The Angelic Grace* [1995] 1 Lloyd's Rep 87, CA; infra, pp 474–475.

[319] *Airbus Industrie GIE v Patel,* supra, at 133 (per Lord GOFF), HL; *Société Aérospatiale v Lee Kui Jak,* supra, at 892, PC; *Donohue v Armco Inc,* supra, at 757; *Turner v Grovit,* supra, at [24].

[320] *Turner v Grovit,* supra, at [22].

[321] Ibid, at [24]. For criticism of the legitmate interest of the applicant requirement see infra, p 464.

[322] Ibid; following *British Airways Board v Laker Airways Ltd* [1985] AC 58 at 81 (per Lord DIPLOCK).

[323] *Turner v Grovit,* supra, at [24].

[324] *Glencore International AG v Exter Shipping Ltd* [2002] EWCA Civ 528 at [42], [2002] 2 All ER (Comm) 1; *OT Africa Line Ltd v Magic Sportswear Corpn* [2005] EWCA Civ 710 at [63] and [83], [2005] 2 Lloyd's Rep 170.

However, neither the judges in the leading cases[325] nor writers[326] are able to agree on what these categories are. This is partly because different attempts at categorisation emphasize different things: some focus on the conduct of the party to be restrained; others on the right of the applicant to complain. Lord HOBHOUSE giving the judgment in the most recent House of Lords case on the topic, *Turner v Grovit*,[327] was more concerned with identifying and explaining what he saw as being the requirement that runs through the case law than with identifying different categories of case. This is the requirement that there is wrongful conduct of the party to be restrained of which the applicant is entitled to complain and has a legitimate interest in seeking to prevent.[328] *Turner* has been interpreted by the Court of Appeal as laying down two categories[329] and this is the categorisation that will be applied here, namely:

(i)   where the conduct of the party to be restrained is unconscionable;
(ii) where the bringing of the proceedings abroad is in breach of an agreement.

It is upon these two categories that the present discussion will focus. But before doing so, it is important to stress that the power to grant injunctions is not restricted, and should not be restricted, to certain limited categories.[330] New categories should be capable of introduction where the ends of justice require it.[331] However, according to Lord HOBHOUSE the grant of an injunction is subject to the requirement that there is wrongful

---

[325] Cf *South Carolina Co v Assurantie NV* [1987] AC 24 at 40, HL (three categories: invasion of a legal or equitable right not to be sued abroad; bringing of the proceedings abroad would be unconscionable; there is another forum which is more appropriate in the interests of justice) with *Airbus Industrie GIE v Patel* [1999] 1 AC 119, HL (vexation or oppression, breach of an agreement, unconscionability) and then *Turner v Grovit*, supra, at [24] (unconscionable conduct). Cf these English cases with *Amchem Products Inc v Workers' Compensation Board* (1993) 102 DLR (4th) 96, Supreme Court of Canada; *CSR Ltd v Cigna Insurance Australia Ltd* (1997) 189 CLR 345, High Court of Australia; *Australian Broadcasting Corpn v Lenah Game Meats Pty Ltd* (2001) 185 ALR 1.

[326] Dicey, Morris and Collins, paras 12R-001 and 12-067–12-077 (where the injunction is necessary in the interests of justice but with a separate section on single forum cases); Briggs and Rees, paras 5.39–5.43 (breach of a legal or equitable right not to be sued abroad; the latter means where this would be unconscionable conduct and the most important instance would be where it is vexatious or oppressive); Hill, paras 11.2.2–11.2.22 (unconscionable behaviour, including vexation or oppression, or infringement of a legal or equitable right not to be sued abroad); Harris (1997) 17 OJLS 477, 485–488 (vexation or oppression, or possibly breach of contract). See also Ho (2003) 52 ICLQ 697.

[327] [2001] UKHL 65, [2002] 1 WLR 107; followed in *Glencore International AG v Exter Shipping Ltd* [2002] EWCA Civ 528 at [42], [2002] 2 All ER (Comm) 1.

[328] *Turner v Grovit*, supra, at [24].

[329] *Sabah Shipyard (Pakistan) Ltd v Islamic Republic of Pakistan* [2002] EWCA Civ 1643 at [39]; [2003] 2 Lloyd's Rep 571, CA; *Royal Bank of Canada v Cooperative Centrale Raiffeisen-Boerenleenbank BA* [2004] EWCA Civ 7 at [8], [2004] 1 Lloyd's Rep 471; *Seismic Shipping Inc v Total E&P UK plc (The Western Regent)* [2005] EWCA Civ 985 at [44]–[46], [2005] 2 Lloyd's Rep 359; *OT Africa Line Ltd v Magic Sportwear Corpn* [2006] EWCA Civ 710 at [63], [83], [2005] 2 Lloyd's Rep 170. The restatement in *Seismic* of the principles to be applied was followed in *Cadre SA v Astra Asigurari SA* [2005] EWHC 2626 (Comm), [2006] 1 Lloyd's Rep 560.

[330] *Castanho v Brown and Root (UK) Ltd* [1981] AC 557 at 573 (per Lord SCARMAN, with whom the other Law Lords concurred), HL; *British Airways Board v Laker Airways Ltd* [1985] AC 58 at 81, HL; *Société Nationale Industrielle Aérospatiale v Lee Kui Jak* [1987] AC 871 at 892; *Barclays Bank plc v Homan* [1993] BCLC 680 at 685–687 (HOFFMANN J), [1993] BCLC 680 at 705, CA. Cf *South Carolina Insurance Co v Assurantie NV* [1987] AC 24 at 39–41 (per Lord BRANDON—Lords BRIDGE and BRIGHTMAN concurring, Lords GOFF and MACKAY dissented on this point), HL; Carter (1986) 57 BYBIL 434; note (1987) 103 LQR 157; Forsyth [1988] CLJ 177.

[331] *Castanho v Brown and Root (UK) Ltd*, supra, at 573; *British Airways Board v Laker Airways Ltd*, supra, at 81; *Société Natonale Industrielle Aérospatiale v Lee Kui Jak*, supra, at 892; *Bank of Tokyo Ltd v Karoon* [1987] AC 45 n at 59, CA. This is also implicit in *Airbus Industrie GIE v Patel*, supra, with its statement of the underlying principle being the ends of justice.

conduct of the party to be restrained of which the applicant is entitled to complain and has a legitimate interest in seeking to prevent.[332]

(i) Where the conduct of the party to be restrained is unconscionable

In *British Airways Board v Laker Airways Ltd*[333] the House of Lords held that:

> The power of the English court to grant the injunction exists, if the bringing of the suit in the foreign court is in the circumstances so unconscionable that in accordance with our principles of a "wide and flexible" equity it can be seen to be an infringement of an equitable right of the applicant.[334]

This is a very broad category and for the purposes of analysis it is important to divide it up into two very different sub-categories, which deal with very different situations and involve very different considerations. The first of these sub-categories is where the pursuit of proceedings abroad is vexatious or oppresssive. This is the most important instance of unconscionable conduct. In this sub-category the right not to be sued derives from the inappropriateness of the forum abroad.[335] The second sub-category is what can be called other instances of unconscionable conduct. Here the right not to be sued derives from the conduct itself and not from the inappropriateness of the forum abroad.[336] These two categories are so different that it is legitimate to refer to the grant of an injunction on the ground of vexation or oppression.

(a) Where the pursuit of proceedings abroad is vexatious or oppressive

The House of Lords in *South Carolina Insurance Co v Assurantie NV*[337] held that unconscionable conduct included "conduct which is oppressive or vexatious". Lord GOFF in the House of Lords in *Airbus Industrie GIE v Patel* described the grant of an injunction on this ground as a particular application of the broad principle underlying the jurisdiction to grant an injunction restraining foreign proceedings, namely that this is to be exercised when the ends of justice require it.[338] According to Lord HOBHOUSE in *Turner v Grovit*, the terms "vexatious" and "oppressive" are other phrases used to criticise unconscionable conduct.[339] But these are not to be taken as limiting definitions.[340] He too emphasised "the basic principle of justice".[341] What we are concerned with are English ideas of justice.[342] There is not and should not be any choice of law issue in relation to the

---

[332] But for the introduction of what is in effect a new category which ignores this requirement see *Samengo-Turner v J & H Marsh & McLennan (Services) Ltd* [2007] EWCA Civ 723 at [38]–[44], [2007] IL Pr 52.

[333] [1985] AC 58, [1984] 3 All ER 39, HL; Collier [1984] CLJ 253; Carter (1984) 55 BYBIL 358.

[334] *British Airways Board v Laker Airways*, supra, at 95 (per Lord SCARMAN); see also 81 (per Lord DIPLOCK); *Airbus Industrie GIE v Patel* [1999] 1 AC 119 at 134 (per Lord GOFF), HL; *Midland Bank plc v Laker Airways Ltd* [1986] QB 689 at 701, 711–712.

[335] *Turner v Grovit*, supra, at [25].

[336] Ibid.

[337] [1987] AC 24.

[338] [1999] 1 AC 119 at 133, HL.

[339] *Turner v Grovit*, supra, at [24]. See also *DVA v Voest Alpine* [1997] 2 Lloyd's Rep 279 at 286, CA; *Toepfer v Société Cargill* [1998] 1 Lloyd's Rep 379 at 384, CA; Harris (1997) 17 OJLS 477 at 487; *Seismic Shipping Inc v Total E & P UK plc (The Western Regent)* [2005] EWCA Civ 985 at [44]–[46], [2005] 2 Lloyd's Rep 359.

[340] *Turner v Grovit*, supra, at [24].

[341] Ibid; following Lord GOFF in *Société Nationale Industrielle Aérospatiale v Lee Kui Jak* [1987] AC 871 at 893.

[342] *Barclays Bank plc v Homan* [1993] BCLC 680 at 687 (HOFFMANN J), [1993] BCLC 680 at 705, CA.

right not to be sued abroad.[343] When discussing the grant of an injunction on this ground it is important to distinguish two different situations. The first is where there are two or more available fora for trial, one of which is England. The second is where trial is available in alternative fora abroad, but not in England. In the former situation an injunction will be granted where the pursuit of the proceedings abroad is vexatious or oppressive. In the latter situation, as a general rule an injunction will not be granted even though the pursuit of the proceedings abroad is vexatious or oppressive.

(i) There are two or more available fora for trial (one of which is England)

In this situation the courts are deciding whether trial should take place in England or abroad, for the effect of granting an injunction restraining foreign proceedings is to force the claimant to sue in England. For many years the courts exercised the power to restrain foreign proceedings on the basis of vexation or oppression.[344] The widening of the principles to be applied in respect of the stay of English proceedings soon filtered through to cases on restraining foreign proceedings. At one time it was said that the principle was the same, regardless of whether the remedy sought was a stay of English proceedings or a restraint of foreign proceedings.[345] Lord GOFF in the *Spiliada* case[346] was careful to state the principles on *forum non conveniens* without reference to injunctions restraining foreign proceedings. Nonetheless, the danger, after *Spiliada*, was that, in practice, injunctions restraining foreign proceedings would simply be granted on the basis that England was the natural forum for trial. This was recognised by the Privy Council in *Société Nationale Industrielle Aérospatiale v Lee Kui Jak*,[347] which held that it was no longer right, in the light of the *Spiliada* case, to apply the same criteria to restraining foreign proceedings as those applied when granting a stay of English proceedings. To do so would be against comity and would disregard the fundamental requirement that an injunction will only be granted where the ends of justice so require.

When it comes to the criteria to be applied for determining whether to grant an injunction, Lord GOFF resurrected the old language of vexation and oppression:

> in a case such as the present where a remedy for a particular wrong is available both in the English . . . court and in a foreign court, the English . . . court will, generally speaking, only restrain the plaintiff from pursuing proceedings in the foreign court if such pursuit would be vexatious or oppressive.[348]

This old terminology was then combined with the modern terminology of the natural forum. According to Lord GOFF, the vexation or oppression test that is now being adopted generally presupposes that the English court has first concluded that it provides the natural forum for trial.[349] If the only issue is whether an English or a foreign court is the more appropriate forum for trial of the action, that question should normally be decided

---

[343] Cf Briggs [1997] LMCLQ 90. For a rebuttal see Harris [1997] LMCLQ 413. See in relation to foreign causes of action and the scope of a jurisdiction clause, infra, pp 470–471, n 450.

[344] See *Cohen v Rothfield* [1919] 1 KB 410.

[345] *Castanho v Brown and Root (UK) Ltd* [1981] AC 557 at 574 (per Lord SCARMAN).

[346] [1987] AC 460 at 480. See also *Société Nationale Industrielle Aérospatiale v Lee Kui Jak* [1987] AC 871 at 896.

[347] [1987] AC 871; Kunzlik [1987] CLJ 406; Briggs [1987] LMCLQ 391; Carter (1988) 59 BYBIL 342.

[348] The *Société Aérospatiale* case, at 896.

[349] Ibid; *Airbus Industrie GIE v Patel* [1999] 1 AC 119 at 134 (per Lord GOFF); *Donohue v Armco Inc* [2001] UKHL 64, [2002] 1 All ER 749 at [20]. See also *Amchem Products Inc v Workers' Compensation Board* (1993) 102

by the foreign court applying the principle of *forum non conveniens*.[350] The English court preferably should not pre-empt the foreign court's decision as to its jurisdiction by granting an injunction before the decision is made.[351] But vexation or oppression requires more than that England is the natural forum (and hence is a more stringent test than that used prior to the *Société Aérospatiale* case).[352] It has to be shown that there would be injustice to the defendant if the claimant was allowed to pursue the foreign proceedings. Since the court is ultimately concerned with the ends of justice, account must also be taken of the claimant's position: "the court will not grant an injunction if, by doing so, it will deprive the plaintiff of advantages in the foreign forum of which it would be unjust to deprive him".[353] These principles have been applied by the House of Lords in *Donohue v Armco Inc*,[354] by the Court of Appeal in numerous cases[355] and have been accepted, obiter, by the House of Lords in *Airbus Industrie GIE v Patel*,[356] in which Lord Goff delivered the judgment of the House of Lords, and in *Turner v Grovit*.[357] They have also found broad acceptance in the Supreme Court of Canada,[358] have influenced the High Court of Australia[359] and been applied in Scotland.[360]

The application of these principles to particular facts can be seen by looking at the *Société Aérospatiale* case:

> The plaintiffs were the widow and administrators of the estate of a businessman, resident in Brunei, who was killed when the helicopter on which he was a passenger crashed in Brunei. The helicopter was manufactured by the defendant S, a French company, and operated by the defendant BM, a Malaysian company. The plaintiffs instituted proceedings against S and BM both in Brunei and Texas (where S carried on business). S sought an injunction in Brunei restraining the plaintiffs from continuing with the Texas action. This was refused by the Court of Appeal of Brunei.

DLR (4th) 96 at 118 (per Sopinka J). For examples of where an injunction was refused because England was not the natural forum, see the *Donohue* case, supra, *Bouygues v Caspian Shipping Co (No 2)* [1997] 2 Lloyd's Rep 485.

[350] *Barclays Bank plc v Homan* [1993] BCLC 680 at 701, CA; *Arab Monetary Fund v Hashim (No 6)* (1992) Times, 24 July

[351] *Amchem Products Inc v Workers' Compensation Board* (1993) 102 DLR (4th) 96 at 118 (per Sopinka J), Sup Ct of Canada; *Deaville v Aeroflot* [1997] 2 Lloyd's Rep at 67; *Pan American World Airways Inc v Andrews* 1992 SLT 268.

[352] *Lee Kui* Jak, supra, *Cadre SA v Astra Asigurari SA* [2005] EWHC 2626 (Comm) at [13], [2006] 1 Lloyd's Rep 560.

[353] The *Société Aérospatiale* case, supra, at 896.

[354] [2001] UKHL 64, [2002] 1 All ER 749 at 757–758 (per Lord Bingham, Lords Mackay and Nicholls concurring), at 768 (per Lord Hobhouse).

[355] *El du Pont de Nemours & Co and Endo Laboratories Inc v Agnew (No 2)* [1988] 2 Lloyd's Rep 240; *Hemain v Hemain* [1988] 2 FLR 388; *Barclays Bank plc v Homan* [1993] BCLC 680, CA; *Hughes v Hannover* [1997] 1 BCLC 497, CA; *Royal Bank of Canada v Cooperative Centrale Raiffeisen-Boerenleenbank BA* [2004] EWCA Civ 7 at [37], [2004] 1 Lloyd's Rep 471; *Seismic Shipping Inc v Total E & P UK plc (The Western Regent)* [2005] EWCA Civ 985 at [44]–[46], [2005] 2 Lloyd's Rep 359.

[356] [1999] 1 AC 119 at 133, HL.

[357] Supra, at [23]–[29].

[358] *Amchem Products Inc v Workers' Compensation Board* (1993) 102 DLR (4th) 96; Glenn (1994) 28 UBCLR 193.

[359] *CSR Ltd v Cigna Insurance Australia Ltd* (1997) 189 CLR 345; Briggs (1998) 114 LQR 27; *Australian Broadcasting Corpn v Lenah Game Meats Pty Ltd* (2001) 185 ALR 1.

[360] *Pan American World Airways Inc v Andrews* 1992 SLT 268; *Shell UK Exploration and Production Ltd v Innes* 1995 SLT 807; *FMC Corpn v Russell* 1999 SLT 99; and Brown 1995 SLT (News) 253.

On appeal to the Privy Council it was held that an injunction should be granted. The natural forum for trial of the plaintiffs' action against S was held to be Brunei. This was on the basis of the strong connections with Brunei, including the fact that the accident happened there, Brunei law was applicable, the deceased was resident there and carried on his principal business there. However, this in itself was not enough to justify the grant of an injunction restraining the foreign proceedings. Generally speaking, what has to be shown is vexation or oppression. Trial in Texas would involve serious injustice to S amounting to oppression in that the company might be unable to claim a contribution from BM in the Texas proceedings. Instead, S might have to bring a separate action in Brunei against BM with attendant difficulties. At the same time, there was no injustice in depriving the plaintiffs of trial in Texas. Any advantages that the plaintiffs obtained from trial in Texas (such as superior means of gathering evidence to mount a case against S, availability of expert counsel, the contingency fee system, prospects of an early trial) were effectively neutralised by undertakings given by S that, for example, evidence already obtained in the Texas proceedings would be available in Brunei proceedings.

A number of problems arise out of this decision.

First, what is meant by vexation or oppression?[361] We know that these terms are another way of criticising unconscionable conduct.[362] Despite what was said in the Privy Council,[363] older cases can be of little value in ascertaining this. The problem faced by the courts nowadays is that of claimants forum shopping in countries, such as the USA, where a very wide jurisdiction is taken, a very different sort of problem from that faced by courts in the nineteenth century.[364] The use of language from the nineteenth century only serves to obscure the basic considerations that should be taken into account in this area: the interests of the parties; the connections with the alternative fora; the dictates of comity and the need for caution before restraining foreign proceedings.[365] A modern example of oppression is provided by *Airbus Industrie GIE v Patel*.[366] There were two appropriate fora for an action, but the plaintiffs sought to sue in a third forum, Texas, which was clearly inappropriate (none of the parties had any connection with Texas, none of the causes of action arose there, nor had any loss been suffered there, and the law of Texas was irrelevant to the settlement of the dispute). The conduct of the plaintiffs was prima facie oppressive. To take another example, requiring the defendant to fight in two different jurisdictions can amount to substantial injustice.[367] Other examples of the sort of material injustice amounting to oppression include such situations as where a party is prevented from properly preparing his case, or the foreign court is being misled, or a party is forced to incur expense not apparently connected with

---

[361] For a very narrow Australian view of this concept, see *CSR Ltd v Cigna Insurance Australia Ltd* (1997) 189 CLR 345 at 393–394, High Court of Australia.

[362] *Turner v Grovit*, supra, at [24].

[363] The *Société Aérospatiale* case, supra, at 896.

[364] Ibid at 894.

[365] See *Metall und Rohstoff AG v ACLI Metals (London) Ltd* [1984] 1 Lloyd's Rep 598.

[366] [1997] 2 Lloyd's Rep 8, CA; reversed by the House of Lords [1999] 1 AC 119 but not on the oppression point. It was accepted, at 140, that the conduct in the case may properly be regarded as oppressive.

[367] *SCOR v Eras EIL (No 2)* [1995] 2 All ER 278; *Advanced Portfolio Technologies Inc v Ainsworth* [1996] FSR 217; Harris [1997] CJQ 279; *FMC Corpn v Russell* 1999 SLT 99 at 102; *General Star v Stirling Cooke* [2003] EWHC 3 (Comm), [2003] IL Pr 19; *Albon v Naza Motor Trading Sdn Bhd (No 4)* [2007] EWHC 1879 (Ch), [2007] 2 Lloyd's Rep 420.

the case;[368] where the defendant would not have a fair trial abroad[369] or when the claim abroad is brought in bad faith, or is doomed to fail;[370] or where there was no good reason for seeking to have the dispute tried abroad (the action being started abroad as a defensive step to prevent other courts from taking jurisdiction).[371] Continuance of foreign proceedings brought in breach of a contractual clause providing for the exclusive jurisdiction of the English courts may well in itself be vexatious and oppressive.[372] On the other hand, the fact that there are concurrent proceedings does not in itself mean that there is oppression,[373] although the court recognises the undesirable consequences that may follow, namely conflicting judgments or a rush to obtain a judgment creating a situation of *res-judicata*.[374] There is no oppression in suing a defendant abroad in a state with which the proceedings have very real connections, such as US plaintiffs, mostly US or non-English defendants, and a fraudulent scheme that allegedly arose in New York.[375]

Secondly, what is meant in the present context by an advantage to the claimant? As an example, it has been held that the fact that a ship has been arrested abroad to obtain security for a claim is an advantage for these purposes.[376] On the other hand, it is doubtful whether this would encompass the higher damages, eg punitive damages, available in the USA. Indeed, it seems to be suggested[377] that the fact that the plaintiffs sought this advantage in Texas might have had some relevance as evidence of oppression if this point had not been neutralised by undertakings given by the plaintiffs. Similarly, availability of contingency fees and pre-trial discovery proceedings abroad have been held not to be legitimate advantage unless the forum abroad is the single or natural forum.[378]

Thirdly, *Société Aérospatiale* was a case where the plaintiffs had started proceedings in two different fora. Nonetheless, the principles set out by the Privy Council are seemingly equally applicable in cases where the roles of the parties are reversed, ie the claimant in the foreign proceedings is the defendant in the English proceedings and vice versa.[379] It has been suggested that the courts should be even more cautious about granting an injunction in reversed role cases than in cases where a claimant has instituted proceedings in two different jurisdictions, on the ground that in the former case the claimant in the

---

[368] *FMC Corpn v Russell* 1999 SLT 99 at 102.

[369] *Al-Bassam v Al-Bassam* (2004) EWCA Civ 857.

[370] *SCOR v Eras EIL (No 2)* [1995] 2 All ER 278; *Shell International Petroleum Co Ltd v Coral Oil Co Ltd (No 2)* [1999] 2 Lloyd's Rep 606. See also *Trafigura Beheer BV v Kookmin Bank Co (No 2)* [2006] EWHC 1921 (Comm) at [51], [52], [2007] 1 Lloyd's Rep 669; Briggs (2007) 123 LQR 18.

[371] *Cadre SA v Astra Asigurari SA* [2005] EWHC 2626 (Comm) at [18], [2006] 1 Lloyd's Rep 560.

[372] *Sohio Supply Co v Gatoil (USA) Inc* [1989] 1 Lloyd's Rep 588. See infra, pp 469–474.

[373] *Lee Kui Jak*, supra, at 894; *Seismic Shipping*, supra, at [44].

[374] *Seismic Shipping*, supra, at [44].

[375] *Donohue v Armco Inc* [2001] UKHL 64, [2002] 1 All ER 749 at [20] (per Lord BINGHAM, Lords MACKAY and NICHOLLS concurring), [45] (per Lord HOBHOUSE). For other examples see also *Kornberg v Kornberg* (1991) 76 DLR (4th) 379; *Pan American World Airways Inc v Andrews* 1992 SLT 268; *Through Transport Mutual Insurance Association (Eurasia) Ltd v New India Assurance Co Ltd* [2004] EWCA (Civ) 1598 at [96].

[376] *The Irini A* [1999] 1 Lloyd's Rep 196.

[377] [1987] 1 AC 871 at 899. But cf *FMC Corpn v Russell* 1999 SLT 99 at 105.

[378] *Simon Engineering plc v Butte Mining plc* [1996] 1 Lloyd's Rep 104 n at 110–111; *Simon Engineering plc v Butte Mining plc (No 2)* [1996] 1 Lloyd's Rep 91 at 98–100; following *Smith Kline & French Laboratories Ltd v Bloch* [1983] 1 WLR 730, CA. See also *Shell UK Exploration and Production Ltd v Innes* 1995 SLT 807 at 824; *Amchem Products Inc v Workers' Compensation Board* (1993) 102 DLR (4th) 96 at 110–111 (SOPINKA J) Sup Ct of Canada.

[379] *E I Du Pont & Co v I C Agnew* [1988] 2 Lloyd's Rep 240. Cf the position in relation to stays of English proceedings in cases involving a multiplicity of proceedings.

foreign proceedings has been compelled to appear in the English proceedings.[380] Moreover, it is probably the case that an English court can grant an injunction enjoining foreign proceedings, even if proceedings in respect of the main cause of action have not yet been commenced here. The only concern is that England is available as a forum.

Fourthly, what are the comity considerations in a case like the *Société Aérospatiale* case? The House of Lords has subsequently held that there is no infringement of comity where England is the natural forum for the resolution of the dispute.[381] This provides England with a sufficient interest in, or connection with, the matter in question to justify the interference with the foreign court that an anti-suit injunction entails.

(ii) Trial is available in alternative fora abroad (but not in England)

This is the situation that arose in *Airbus Industrie GIE v Patel*.[382]

> Following an aircraft crash in India, the defendants, English residents, brought proceedings in Texas against the plaintiffs, manufacturers of the aircraft. The plaintiffs sought from the English courts an injunction restraining the defendants from continuing with the Texas proceedings.

The House of Lords, reversing the decision of the Court of Appeal,[383] held that the grant of an injunction in the circumstances was inconsistent with comity. The English courts had no interest in, or connection with, the matter in question to justify such interference. This was despite the fact that the natural forum for trial was India; but the courts there were unable to grant effective injunctive relief in respect of the English defendants,[384] whereas the English courts could grant effective relief to prevent the pursuit of proceedings in Texas which may properly be regarded as oppressive. Nor was the fact that Texas, at that time, did not recognise and apply the doctrine of *forum non conveniens* so extreme as to deprive that state of the respect required by comity. Accordingly, there could be no exception to the general rule requiring a sufficient interest in, or connection with, the matter in question. Lord HOBHOUSE in *Turner v Grovit*[385] has caused some confusion by referring to the need for the *applicant* to have a legitimate interest in making his application[386] and interpreting *Airbus Industrie GIE v Patel* as being a case where the applicant had no such interest. According to Lord HOBHOUSE, what this case shows is that the necessary legitimate interest of the applicant must be the existence of proceedings in England which need to be protected by the grant of a restraining order.[387] This misunderstands the reasoning in the case where the concern was with *England's* interest Moreover, whilst the two different tests in relation to the relevant interest lead to the same result in a case like

---

[380] *Hemain v Hemain* [1988] 2 FLR 388, 390, quoting from *Cohen v Rothfield* [1919] 1 KB 410 at 414. The latter case was cited with approval in the *Société Aérospatiale* case at 892. For the significance of the *Hemain* case in relation to matrimonial causes see infra, p 964.

[381] *Airbus Industrie GIE v Patel* [1999] 1 AC 119 at 134, 138–139 (per Lord GOFF), HL.

[382] [1999] 1 AC 119, HL; Briggs (1998) 69 BYBIL 332; Peel (1998) 114 LQR 543; approved in *Turner v Grovit*, supra, at [27].

[383] [1997] 2 Lloyd's Rep 8; Briggs (1996) 67 BYBIL 601; Fentiman [1997] CLJ 46.

[384] COLEMAN J refused to enforce at common law a judgment of the Indian court purporting to restrain the defendants from claiming damages other than in India, [1996] IL Pr 465.

[385] *Turner v Grovit*, supra, at [27].

[386] See Ambrose (2003) 52 ICLQ 401, 406.

[387] *Turner v Grovit*, supra, at [27].

Airbus Industrie GIE v Patel, the legitimate interest of the applicant test causes real problems in single forum cases.[388]

(b) Other instances of unconscionable conduct

Lord HOBHOUSE in *Turner v Grovit* said that there were instances of unconscionable conduct where the right not to be sued abroad derives from the conduct itself and not from the inappropriateness of the forum abroad (eg as in the *Société Aérospatiale* case) or the breach of an agreement.[389] There is a judicial reluctance to define what is meant by "unconscionable" conduct.[390] In principle it simply means contrary to the rules of English equity.[391] What is unconscionable cannot and should not be defined exhaustively.[392] Guidance on the meaning of unconscionable conduct can also be found in *British Airways Board v Laker Airways Ltd*[393] where Lord DIPLOCK said that unconscionable conduct encompasses the bringing of an action against a person who has a right not to be sued because a defence, such as estoppel in pais, promissory estoppel, election, waiver, standing by and laches, is available to him under English law.[394] In contrast, it is not unconscionable to continue with an action in Texas for damages following a collision at sea after an English court has granted a decree limiting the shipowner's liability.[395] The purpose of an injunction is not to ensure that a foreign court recognises an English judgment but to prevent unconscionable conduct.[396] There does not appear to be a case where an injunction has been granted solely in aid of an English judgment[397] and it is unclear whether an injunction can ever be granted in support of an English judgment.[398] The House of Lords in *South Carolina Insurance Co v Assurantie NV*[399] held that unconscionable conduct included not only conduct which is oppressive or vexatious but also conduct "which interferes with the due process of the court". The meaning of vexatious and oppressive has previously been examined. Attention will now turn to the concept of conduct which interferes with the due process of the court or, as it is sometimes called, abuse of process.

(i) Interference with the due process of the court

Turner v Grovit on its facts concerned abuse of process, which is another way of expressing the same general ideas as "unconscionable" conduct but with particular reference to the effect of the unconscionable conduct upon pending English proceedings.[400] The facts of the case have been examined previously.[401] The House of Lords held that it was proper

---

[388] Infra, pp 466–469.

[389] Supra, at [25].

[390] See *South Carolina Insurance Co v Assurantie NV* [1987] AC 24 at 41, HL.

[391] *Barclays Bank plc v Homan* [1993] BCLC 680 at 687 (HOFFMANN J); [1993] BCLC 680 at 705, CA.

[392] *Glencore International AG v Exter Shipping Ltd* [2002] EWCA Civ 528 at [42], [2002] 2 All ER (Comm) 1.

[393] [1985] AC 58.

[394] Ibid, at 81.

[395] *Seismic Shipping Inc v Total E & P UK plc (The Western Regent)* [2005] EWCA Civ 985, [2005] 2 Lloyd's Rep 359, Briggs (2005) 76 BYBIL 663. There was no reason to think that the Texan court would not give full consideration to the English decree, at [49].

[396] The *Seismic Shipping* case, supra, at [48] (per CLARKE LJ, NOURSE LJ concurring).

[397] Ibid, at [66] (per RIX LJ, NOURSE LJ concurring).

[398] Cf RIX LJ at [67] (who contemplates that it can) with CLARKE LJ at [48] (who appears to suggest that it cannot).

[399] [1987] AC 24, HL.

[400] *Turner v Grovit* [2001] UKHL 65 at [24], [2002] 1 WLR 107.

[401] Supra, p 335.

for the Court of Appeal to grant an injunction on these facts because: (a) the applicant was a party to existing legal proceedings in England; (b) the defendants had in bad faith commenced and proposed to prosecute proceedings in another jurisdiction for the purpose of frustrating or obstructing the proceedings in England; (c) the court considered that it was necessary in order to protect the legitimate interest of the applicant in the English proceedings to grant the applicant a restraining order against the defendants.[402] However, the proceedings abroad were in another European Community Member State, Spain, and this raised the question, referred to the Court of Justice, whether it was inconsistent with the Brussels Convention to grant an injunction in such circumstances. The Court of Justice held that it was, even where the party commencing proceedings before the court of another Member State was acting in bad faith with a view to frustrating the existing proceedings.[403]

Lord HOBHOUSE in *Turner v Grovit* highlighted the need for there not only to be wrongful conduct of the party to be restrained but also for the applicant to be entitled to complain about this conduct and to have a legitimate interest in seeking to prevent it.[404] Lord HOBHOUSE went on to say that where there has been clearly unconscionable conduct on the part of the party sought to be restrained, as there was in the instant case, this is a sufficiently strong element to support the affected party's application for an order to restrain such conduct.[405] This is not based upon the complaint that the action has been brought in an inapppropriate forum.[406] But where there was unconscionable conduct for some non-contractual reason, the necessary legitimate interest must be the existence of proceedings in England which need to be protected by the grant of a restraining order.[407] This latter requirement was met on the facts of the case.

Another and very obvious example of unconscionable conduct can be seen in *Glencore International AG v Exter Shipping Ltd*,[408] where the plaintiffs in an action in Georgia had no legitimate interest in pursuing claims in Georgia. This was part of a deliberate strategy of harassment and vexation, designed to wear down the applicant (a defendant in the Georgia action) by subjecting it to the burden of litigating on several fronts, and designed to put off the day when a conclusion was reached on the issues dividing the parties.[409] There was a clear need to protect existing English proceedings[410] and the appeal against the grant of an injunction was dismissed.

(ii) Single forum cases

Lord HOBHOUSE in *Turner v Grovit* did not discuss "single" forum cases. This phrase covers not only cases where an injunction is sought restraining proceedings in the only

---

[402] *Turner v Grovit*, supra, at [29].

[403] Case C-159/02 *Turner v Grovit* [2004] All ER (EC) 485; supra, pp 335–336.

[404] *Turner v Grovit* [2001] UKHL 65 at [24], [2002] 1 WLR 107.

[405] Ibid, at [25].

[406] Ibid.

[407] Ibid, at [27].

[408] [2002] EWCA Civ 528 at [65]–[70], [2002] 2 All ER (Comm) 1; Briggs (2002) 73 BYBIL 463. See also *Noble Assurance Co v Gerling-Konzern General Insurance Co* [2007] EWHC 253 (Comm); *Benfield Holdings Ltd v Elliot Richardson* [2007] EWHC 171 (QB).

[409] The *Glencore* case, supra, at [69].

[410] Ibid at [62]–[64].

state which has jurisdiction[411] but also cases where there was only one state in which the claimant could bring a successful action.[412] The contrast has been made with alternative forum cases, ie the English court is choosing between two or more alternative fora for trial, such as in the *Société Aérospatiale* case. In the past, the language of unconscionability has been used in "single" forum cases,[413] whereas the language of vexation and oppression has been used in alternative forum cases. *Turner v Grovit* on its facts does not fall easily within either category. It is not a single forum case (both England and Spain had jurisdiction) but neither is it like the *Société Aérospatiale* case where the only unconscionable conduct complained of is the fact that the proceedings abroad have been commenced in an inappropriate forum. "Single" forum cases should be examined as a separate group of cases because of the need for extra caution before granting an injunction in such cases.

In the *South Carolina* case a party to an English action sought to obtain in the USA discovery of documents from a third party. US pre-trial procedure allows this evidence to be obtained, whereas English procedure does not. The House of Lords held that there was no unconscionable conduct. There was no interference with the due process of the English courts. The English courts still controlled their own procedure, since it is up to the parties to obtain, either in England or abroad, the relevant evidence.[414] Moreover, mere extra cost and inconvenience to the parties cannot be characterised as interference with the court's control of its own process.[415] In contrast, an injunction was granted preventing the obtaining of witness statements in the USA when it was intended to call those witnesses in England and they might be discouraged from attending if witness statements had been obtained in the USA.[416]

In *British Airways Board v Laker Airways Ltd*[417] the House of Lords unanimously allowed an appeal against the grant of an injunction restraining an action in the USA by Laker Airways Ltd (Laker), a Jersey company with its principal office in London, against British Airways and another British airline. The action was for multiple damages for breach of US anti-trust laws by conspiring to eliminate Laker as a competitor by fixing "predatory" air fare tariffs. There was no cause of action under English law, and the only country in which Laker could obtain a remedy was the USA. For this reason the case was distinguishable from cases where a choice is being made between alternative fora; those cases were of no assistance here.[418] Caution was said to be a "very necessary" in these single forum cases.[419] It was not unconscionable to allow the proceedings in the USA to continue, seemingly, because no complaint could be made about Laker's conduct. It had been argued that, since Laker was admitted to the scheduled airlines' club and submitted to the regulations required by the club, it could not complain about the conduct of fellow

---

[411] *Airbus Industrie GIE v Patel*, supra, at 134.

[412] See *Barclays Bank plc v Homan* [1993] BCLC 680 at 698, CA.

[413] *Airbus Industrie GIE v Patel*, supra, at 134. For criticism of this distinction between alternative forum and single forum cases see Peel (1998) 114 LQR 543 at 544.

[414] Supra, at 41–44.

[415] Ibid, at 42–43.

[416] *Omega Group Holdings Ltd v Kozeny* [2002] CLC 132.

[417] [1985] AC 58, HL.

[418] [1985] AC 58, at 80, 85.

[419] Ibid, at 95.

members of the club that was permitted by the club's rules in relation to fares. This argument was rejected on the basis that Laker's action was founded not on the actual fares charged but on the fact that the other airlines were allegedly in breach of US law.[420] It is to be noted that in exercising their discretion their Lordships did not give weight to the fact that it would be impossible to enforce in England an American judgment for multiple damages in an anti-trust case.[421]

On the other hand, in *Midland Bank plc v Laker Airways Ltd*[422] the Court of Appeal held it to be unconscionable conduct for Laker to bring an anti-trust suit in the USA against the Midland Bank and an injunction was allowed restraining those threatened proceedings. The alleged liability of the bank arose out of banking acts done in England and intended to be governed by English law; the bank had never submitted to US anti-trust law or US jurisdiction; and there was no claim against it in England.[423] It was also relevant that the evidence of conspiracy under US law was weak, although the court was reluctant to examine the question of the weight of the evidence too closely. However, in rare cases where it is clear that the action abroad is bound to fail, this will make the claimant's foreign action frivolous and vexatious and therefore unconscionable.[424] But the fact that a party will be exposed to pre-trial discovery in the US proceedings is not a source per se of injustice.[425]

The requirement that, as a general rule, the English forum should have a sufficient interest in, or connection with, the matter in question to justify the interference with the foreign court that an anti-suit injunction entails, applies as much to single forum as to alternative forum cases.[426] The decision in the *Midland Bank* case has been described by Lord GOFF as being consistent with this requirement in that the relevant transaction was overwhelmingly English in character.[427] In contrast, the grant of an injunction in the *British Airways Board* case could not be justified in this way.[428] Lord HOBHOUSE in *Turner v Grovit* has muddied the waters by introducing the requirement that the *applicant* has a legitimate interest in seeking to prevent the wrongful conduct and that where there was unconscionable conduct for some non-contractual reason, the necessary legitimate interest of the *applicant* must be the existence of proceedings in England which need to be protected by the grant of a restraining order.[429] There were no such English proceedings in the *Midland Bank* case. However, Lord HOBHOUSE was not referring to single forum cases and his words should not be taken as limiting the right to grant an injunction in such cases. He was thinking of *Airbus Industrie GIE v Patel* and seems not to have understood the concern in that case that *England* should have an interest. Looking at that requirement, what Lord GOFF's comments (in *Airbus Industrie GIE v Patel*) in relation to

---

[420] [1985] AC 58, at 84–85.

[421] See the Protection of Trading Interests Act 1980, s 5, discussed infra, pp 561–563. See also the judgment of PARKER J at first instance [1984] 1 QB 142 at 162–163.

[422] [1986] QB 689, CA. Distinguished in *Barclays Bank plc v Homan* [1993] BCLC 680 at 688, 692; [1993] BCLC 680 at 705, CA.

[423] [1986] QB 689 at 699–700, 704–705, 712–713.

[424] Ibid, at 700, 702, 710, 712–713. See also *British Airways Board v Laker Airways Ltd* [1985] AC 58 at 86.

[425] [1986] QB 689 at 714.

[426] *Airbus Industrie GIE v Patel* [1999] 1 AC 119 at 134, 138 (per Lord GOFF), HL.

[427] Ibid at 138.

[428] Ibid.

[429] *Turner v Grovit*, supra, at [27].

the *Midland Bank* case show is that the requisite interest of the English forum can still be shown even where there are no proceedings in England which need to be protected.

In principle, there is even more need for caution in restraining foreign proceedings in cases where the claimant has only a single forum in which he is able to bring an action (ie which has jurisdiction) than there is in cases when there are alternative fora for trial, since the effect of granting the stay is to deny the claimant trial in any country at all. On the other hand, it is questionable whether the need for extra caution exists in those cases (such as the *Laker* cases) where the claimant is being denied the opportunity to bring a successful action, but does in fact have a choice of fora (ie two states have jurisdiction).[430]

The need for caution is even stronger if a judgment has actually been obtained in the forum abroad and a world-wide injunction is sought to restrain a party from relying on this judgment. Even if that party is acting unconscionably the court may exercise its discretion and refuse to grant the injunction.[431]

(ii) The bringing of the proceedings abroad would be in breach of an agreement

Where proceedings abroad would be in breach of a valid[432] exclusive jurisdiction clause[433] providing for trial in England,[434] the English courts have an inherent power to restrain a party from bringing or continuing the proceedings abroad, for that would constitute a breach of contract.[435] The same principles apply where proceedings abroad would be in breach of a valid arbitration clause.[436] Less commonly, the breach of an agreement is in *bringing the proceedings* abroad rather than being in breach of an exclusive jurisdiction clause or arbitration clause, which relates to where the proceeedings must be brought or what type of proceedings must be brought. Nonetheless the same principles will apply.[437] In cases where there would be a breach of an agreement, different principles in relation to the grant of an injunction apply from cases where there is no such agreement.

---

[430] The courts still refer to these as single forum cases, but are using the term in a different sense from that where only one state has jurisdiction.

[431] *E D & F Man (Sugar) Ltd v Yani Haryanto (No 2)* [1991] 1 Lloyd's Rep 161 at 167–168.

[432] See supra, pp 448–450 on the validity of an exclusive jurisdiction clause. See specifically in the present context *Crédit Suisse First Boston (Europe) Ltd v Seagate Trading Co Ltd* [1999] 1 Lloyd's Rep 784; *OT Africa Line Ltd v Magic Sportwear Corpn* [2006] EWCA Civ 710, [2005] 2 Lloyd's Rep 170.

[433] An agreement on jurisdiction can take the form of a consent order in foreign proceedings whereby the parties agree not to challenge the jurisdiction of the English courts: *General Motors Corpn v Royal & Sun Alliance Insurance Group* [2007] EWHC 2206 (Comm).

[434] Such a clause will often fall within Art 23 of the Brussels I Regulation, supra, pp 283–296. It is submitted that this does not preclude the English courts from granting an injunction in relation to proceedings in a non-Member State, see supra, pp 339–340.

[435] This power has been recognised for many years see *Ellerman Lines Ltd v Read* [1928] 2 KB 144; *Mike Trading and Transport Ltd v R Pagnan and Fratelli, The Lisboa* [1980] 2 Lloyd's Rep 546, CA; *British Airways Board v Laker Airways Ltd* [1985] AC 58 at 81; *Continental Bank NA v Aeakos Compañia Naviera SA* [1994] 1 WLR 588, CA. It must be not merely arguable that there is a breach: *National Westminster Bank v Utrecht-America Finance Co* [2001] EWCA Civ 658, [2001] 3 All ER 733; *American International Specialty Lines Insurance Co v Abbott Laboratories* [2002] EWHC 2714 (Comm) at 275. It must be shown to a high degree of probability that the case is right: the *American International Specialty Lines Insurance* case.

[436] *Aggeliki Charis Compañia Marítima SA v Pagnan SpA, The Angelic Grace* [1995] 1 Lloyd's Rep 87, CA. For earlier cases see *Pena Copper Mines Ltd v Rio Tinto Co Ltd* (1911) 105 LT 846; *Tracomin SA v Sudan Oil Seeds Co Ltd (Nos 1 and 2)* [1983] 1 WLR 1026.

[437] *National Westminster Bank v Utrecht-America Finance Co* [2001] EWCA Civ 658, [2001] 3 All ER 733.

First, the requirement that there is wrongful conduct of the party to be restrained of which the applicant is entitled to complain and has a legitimate interest in seeking to prevent[438] is easily met in such cases. The conduct of the party acting in breach of the agreement is unconscionable.[439] A contractual jurisdiction or arbitration clause will provide a right not to be sued in another forum.[440] The applicant does not have to show that the contractual forum is more appropriate than any other; the contractual agreement does that for him. Where the applicant is relying upon a contractual right not to be sued in the foreign country then, in the absence of some special circumstance, he has by reason of his contract a legitimate interest in enforcing that right against the other party to the contract.[441] Secondly, a party to an exclusive English jurisdiction clause has a right to have the contract enforced and this can only be displaced by strong reasons being shown by the opposite party why an injunction should *not* be granted.[442] The same principle applies in relation to breach of an arbitration clause.[443] Where there is no such clause a party has to show that justice requires that he should be granted an injunction.[444] Thirdly, the principle that the power to grant an injunction restraining foreign proceedings must be exercised with caution does not apply in breach cases.[445] Fourthly, there is not the same concern with comity in such cases.[446] This underlies the first and third of the above points. A separate point to note in relation to the breach of an agreement is that a claimant is able to recover as damages its reasonable expenses in litigating abroad (as defendant) where this was in breach of an exclusive jurisdiction clause.[447] This includes the costs of defending such part of the action abroad as fell within the clause.[448]

(a) Breach of an exclusive jurisdiction agreement

It will be recalled that Lord BINGHAM in the House of Lords in *Donohue v Armco Inc*[449] summarised the principles to be applied where there has been a breach of an exclusive jurisdiction agreement as follows. Where contracting parties agree to give a particular court exclusive jurisdiction to rule on claims between those parties, and a claim falling

---

[438] *Turner v Grovit*, supra, at [24].

[439] Ibid, at [27]. See also *OT Africa Line Ltd v Magic Sportswear Corpn* [2005] EWCA Civ 710 at [63] and [83], [2005] 2 Lloyd's Rep 170.

[440] *Turner v Grovit*, supra, at [25]. See also *British Airways Board v Laker Airways Ltd* [1985] AC 58 at 81.

[441] *Turner v Grovit*, supra, at [27]. See also *Airbus Industrie GIE v Patel* [1999] 1 AC 119, 138, HL.

[442] The *Donohue* case, supra, at [45] (per Lord HOBHOUSE).

[443] See infra, pp 474–475.

[444] The *Donohue* case, supra, at [45] (per Lord HOBHOUSE).

[445] *Aggeliki Charis Compañía Maritima SA v Pagnan SpA, The Angelic Grace* [1995] 1 Lloyd's Rep 87, 96, CA; *Glencore International AG v Exter Shipping Ltd* [2002] EWCA Civ 528 at [43], [2002] 2 All ER (Comm) 1. See also the *Donohue* case, supra, at 757, which only referred to this principle when discussing vexation or oppression.

[446] Infra, pp 472–473.

[447] *Union Discount Co Ltd v Zoller* [2001] EWCA Civ 1755, [2002] 1 WLR 1517; Briggs (2001) 72 BYBIL 446; *Donohue v Armco Inc* [2001] UKHL 64 at [75] (per Lord SCOTT), [48] (per Lord HOBHOUSE), [2002] 1 All ER 749; *A/S Svendborg v Ali Hussein Akar* [2003] EWHC 797 (Comm); *National Westminster Bank v Rabobank Nederland* [2007] EWHC 1742 (Comm), [2008] 1 All ER (Comm) 266; Tan and Yeo [2003] LMCLQ 435; Tham [2004] LMCLQ 46; Ho (2003) 52 ICLQ 697, 707–710. See in relation to damages for breach of an arbitration clause: *DVA v Voest Alpine* [1997] 2 Lloyd's Rep 279, 285; *A v B (No 2)* [2007] EWHC 54 (Comm), [2007] 1 Lloyd's Rep 358.

[448] *Donohue v Armco Inc* [2001] UKHL 64 at [75] (per Lord SCOTT), [48] (per Lord HOBHOUSE), [2002] 1 All ER 749. See also *A v B (No 2)* [2007] EWHC 54 (Comm), [2007] 1 Lloyd's Rep 358 (indemnity costs for breach of an arbitration agreement).

[449] [2001] UKHL 64, [2002] 1 All ER 749.

within the scope of the agreement[450] is made in proceedings in a forum other than that on which the parties have agreed, the English court will ordinarily[451] exercise its discretion by restraining the prosecution of proceedings in the non-contractual forum abroad (or by granting a stay of proceedings in England, or by such other procedural order as is appropriate in the cicumstances) to secure compliance with the contractual bargain, unless the party suing in the non-contractual forum (the burden being on him) can show strong reasons for suing in that forum.[452] These principles apply in both the contexts of an injunction restraining foreign proceedings brought in breach of an exclusive jurisdiction clause providing for trial in England and of a stay of English proceedings brought in breach of an exclusive jurisdiction clause providing for trial abroad.[453] The matters that might properly be regarded by the court when exercising its discretion in the latter context are equally relevant in the former context. It follows that the matters listed by BRANDON J in *The Eleftheria*, set out earlier in this chapter when discussing stays of action,[454] should be considered when exercising the discretion to grant an injunction.[455] This is not intended to be an exhaustive list.[456] After examining many of the authorities from both areas, Lord BINGHAM concluded that, where the dispute is between two contracting parties, and the interests of other parties are not involved, effect will in all probability be given to the exclusive jurisdiction clause.[457] In contrast, the English court may well decline to grant an anti-suit injunction (or a stay as the case may be) where the interests of parties other than the parties bound by the exclusive jurisdiction clause are involved or grounds of claim not the subject of the clause are part of the relevant dispute so that there is a risk of parallel proceedings and inconsistent decisions.[458] The principle that applies in cases of *forum non conveniens* that, where there is a clause providing for the exclusive jurisdiction of the English courts, the courts should refuse to pay regard to matters of convenience that were foreseeable at the time the contract was concluded,[459] has been applied in the present context.[460]

The *Donohue* case concerned an injunction sought to restrain proceedings brought in New York in breach of English exclusive jurisdiction clauses contained in agreements relating to the sale of shares. The defendants in the English proceedings were able to show

---

[450] An English court will decide whether claims brought abroad under a foreign cause of action fall within the scope of the exclusive jurisdiction clauses, see *Donohue v Armco Inc* [2000] 1 Lloyd's Rep 579 at 586–589; revd by the House of Lords [2001] UKHL 64, [2002] 1 All ER 749, where the scope of the clauses was not in issue. See also *National Westminster Bank v Utrecht-America Finance Co* [2001] EWCA Civ 658, [2001] 3 All ER 733; *AWB (Geneva) SA v North America Steamships Ltd* [2007] EWCA Civ 739, [2007] 2 Lloyd's Rep 315.

[451] This recognises that it is a discretion.

[452] The *Donohue* case, supra, at [24].

[453] On the latter see supra, pp 444–448.

[454] Supra, p 445.

[455] *Beazley v Horizon Offshore Contractors Inc* [2004] EWHC 2555 (Comm) at [24]; [2005] IL Pr 11.

[456] The *Donohue* case, supra, at [24].

[457] Ibid, at [25]. See *Horn Linie GmbH & Co v Panamericana Formas e Impresos SA (The Hornbay)* [2006] EWHC 373 (Comm), [2006] 2 Lloyd's Rep 44, a cargo insurer seeking to avoid the parties' bargain.

[458] The *Donohue* case, supra, at [27] referring to the following anti-suit injunction cases: *Bouygues Offshore SA v Caspian Shipping Co (Nos 1, 3, 4 and 5)* [1998] 2 Lloyd's Rep 461; *Crédit Suisse First Boston (Europe) v MLC (Bermuda) Ltd* [1999] 1 All ER (Comm) 237. The stay cases referred to are cited supra, p 446, n 205. See more generally on refusal to grant an injunction: *Akai Pty Ltd v People's Insurance Co Ltd* [1998] 1 Lloyd's Rep 90 at 104 et seq; *Shell v Coral Oil* [1999] 1 Lloyd's Rep 72 at 79.

[459] Supra, pp 431–432.

[460] The *Beazley case*, supra, at [29].

the requisite strong reasons, sufficient to displace the claimant's prima facie entitlement to enforce the contractual bargain, and an injunction restraining the proceedings in New York was refused. There were other defendants in the New York proceedings who were potential co-claimants in the English proceedings,[461] some of whom were not parties to the exclusive jurisdiction clauses. The strong reasons lay in the prospect, if the injunction were to be granted, of litigation between the defendants on the one side and the claimant and the potential co-claimants on the other continuing partly in England and partly in New York.[462] The interests of justice were best served by the submission of the whole suit to a single tribunal which could adjudicate on all the matters in issue, namely the New York courts.[463]

In contrast, the parties were held to their bargain and an injunction granted in relation to proceedings brought in Canada in breach of an agreement providing for the exclusive jurisdiction of the English courts, even though there were real connections with that country and there was also a Canadian statute which rendered a jurisdiction clause in a bill of lading, which provided for trial outside Canada, as being of no effect and which was equivalent to the internationally agreed Hamburg Rules.[464]

Lord BINGHAM in *Donohue* has said that a party may lose his claim to equitable relief by dilatoriness or other unconscionable conduct.[465] This is consistent with earlier statements that the longer the delay before the application was made the more likely it was that there would be good reason to refuse it, and that equally voluntary submission to the jurisdiction of the foreign court would very often amount to such good reason, especially where the proceedings have progressed for any period of time, a fortiori where an application for a stay of the foreign proceedings had been made and failed.[466]

The principles governing the grant of injunctions and stays are not entirely the same, a point acknowledged by Lord BINGHAM in the *Donohue* case,[467] in that considerations of comity arise in the former case but not in the latter. However, a concern with comity has not been evident in cases where the ground for an injunction is that of a breach of an agreement.[468] Indeed, Lord BINGHAM did not think that this difference in the principles governing the grant of injunctions and stays needed to be explored in the instant case

---

[461] They could not be joined to the English action as claimants because they had no cause of action entitling them to an anti-suit injunction on the ground of vexation or oppression, supra, at [17]–[22] (per Lord BINGHAM) and [45] (per Lord HOBHOUSE).

[462] The *Donohue* case, supra, at [33] (per Lord BINGHAM) and [75] (per Lord SCOTT).

[463] Ibid, at [34].

[464] *OT Africa Line Ltd v Magic Sportswear Corpn* [2005] EWCA Civ 710, [2005] 2 Lloyd's Rep 170. See also *Horn Linie GmbH & Co v Panamericana Formas e Impresos SA (The Hornbay)* [2006] EWHC 373 (Comm), [2006] 2 Lloyd's Rep 44.

[465] The *Donohue* case, supra, at [24].

[466] *Svendborg v Wansa* [1997] 2 Lloyd's Rep 183, CLARKE J; the Court of Appeal said that there could be no criticism of the way that the judge had exercised the discretion, ibid. See generally on delay *Toepfer International GmbH v Molino Boschi Srl* [1996] 1 Lloyd's Rep 510 at 518; *Philip Alexander Securities and Futures Ltd v Bamberger*, supra, at 92–93 (WALLER J), appeal to the Court of Appeal dismissed without discussion of this point; *Society of Lloyd's v White (No 1)* [2002] IL Pr 10; *Advent Capital plc v GN Ellinas Importers-Exporters Ltd* [2003] EWHC 3330 at [26]–[27], [42]–[44], [2004] IL Pr 23; cf *Akai Pty Ltd v People's Insurance Co Ltd* [1998] 1 Lloyd's Rep 90 at 107–108; *DVA v Voest Alpine* [1997] 2 Lloyd's Rep 279 at 288, CA.

[467] Supra, at [24].

[468] Lord GOFF in *Airbus Industrie GIE v Patel* when discussing comity stressed that he was not discussing cases where the choice of forum was the subject of an agreement between the parties, ibid, at 138.

(one where there was a breach of an exclusive jurisdiction agreement).[469] The Court of Appeal has said that there is no reason in principle why comity should stand in the way of granting an injunction where proceedings are brought in breach of an English exclusive jurisdiction clause.[470] In *The Angelic Grace* it was thought that no court would be offended by the grant of an injunction to restrain a party from invoking a jurisdiction which he had promised not to invoke and which it was its own duty to decline.[471] This has proved to be unduly optimistic and the German courts have regarded the issue of anti-suit injunctions, in a case involving a consumer contract which provided for arbitration in London but where the German court did not regard itself as obliged to stay its proceedings in such circumstances, as an infringement of its sovereignty and refused to permit the injunctions to be served.[472] WALLER J in *Philip Alexander Securities and Futures Ltd v Bamberger*, aware of the fact that the German courts were offended by the grant of an anti-suit injunction by the English courts, distinguished *The Angelic Grace*, inter alia, on this ground, and held that it was not a case where it was appropriate to grant an injunction.[473] The Court of Appeal in the *Bamberger* case, recognising the comity problem where effect needs to be given to the injunction by a foreign court, thought that the English practice in relation to the grant of anti-suit injunctions may need reconsideration in the light of the facts of this case.[474] However, many subsequent cases have followed the principles in *The Angelic Grace*, ignoring the reaction of foreign courts to the grant of an injunction.[475] Nonetheless, it is submitted that where there is clear evidence that a foreign court would be offended[476] a degree of caution is desirable even in cases involving breach of an agreement. When it comes to whether a foreign court will be offended by the grant of an injunction it may be necessary to distinguish common law jurisdictions which are used to granting such an injunction themselves and are therefore not likely to be offended[477] and civil law jurisdictions which are not and are therefore likely to be offended.

Many of the cases of restraining by injunction a breach of a jurisdiction agreement have involved an injunction restraining proceedings in another European Community State.

---

[469] The *Donohue* case, supra, at [24].

[470] *National Westminster Bank v Utrecht-America Finance Co* [2001] EWCA Civ 658, [2001] 3 All ER 733. See also *OT Africa Line Ltd v Magic Sportwear Corpn* [2006] EWCA Civ 710 at [32], [83], [2005] 2 Lloyd's Rep 170.

[471] *Aggeliki Charis Compañía Marítima SA v Pagnan SpA, The Angelic Grace* [1995] 1 Lloyd's Rep 87, CA. See also *Through Transport Mutual Insurance Association (Eurasia) Ltd v New India Assurance Co Ltd* [2004] EWCA (Civ) 1598; *West Tankers Inc v Ras Riunione Adriatica di Sicurta SpA (The Front Comor)* [2005] EWHC 454 (Comm), [2005] 2 Lloyd's Rep 257, Hill [2006] LMCLQ 166, the House of Lords referred a question of European law to the Court of Justice, supra, pp 337–338.

[472] *Re the Enforcement of an English Anti-Suit Injunction* [1997] IL Pr 320; Harris [1997] CJQ 283.

[473] [1997] IL Pr 73 at 93–94.

[474] [1997] IL Pr 73 at 117, CA. See generally Males [1998] LMCLQ 543 at 547 et seq.

[475] *Through Transport Mutual Insurance Association (Eurasia) Ltd v New India Assurance Co Ltd* [2004] EWCA (Civ) 1598, [2005] 1 Lloyd's Rep 67; the *West Tankers Case*, supra, at [43]–[52]. See also *Navigation Maritime Bulgare v Rustal Trading Ltd (The Ivan Zagubanski)* [2002] 1 Lloyd's Rep 106 at [115]–[119]; *XL Insurance Ltd v Owens* [2000] 2 Lloyd's Rep 500. Cf *OT Africa Line ltd v Hijazy (The Kribi)* [2001] 1 Lloyd's Rep 76 at [83]; *Evialis SA v SIAT* [2003] 2 Lloyd's Rep 377 at 388–389.

[476] See *The Kribi*, supra, at [83].

[477] *Beazley v Horizon Offshore Contractors Inc* [2004] EWHC 2555 (Comm) at [40], [2005] IL Pr 11; *Society of Lloyd's v White (No 2)* [2002] IL Pr 11 at [54]–[56]. But see *Commonwealth Bank of Australia v White (No 4)* [2001] VSC 511, Moshinsky (2005) 79 ALJ 82, court refused to stay its proceedings, despite an English anti-suit injunction granted on the basis of breach of a jurisdiction agreement.

However, since the decision of the Court of Justice in *Turner v Grovit*[478] this is no longer possible.

Where the agreement provides for the non-exclusive jurisdiction of the English courts there is no breach of agreement in bringing proceedings abroad and therefore an injunction will not be granted on the basis of breach of an agreement.[479] However, if one party (A) by way of a pre-emptive strike seeks an injunction abroad whereby the other party (B) will be permanently restrained from making any demand under a contract (containing a non-exclusive English jurisdiction clause) in the hope of preventing B from starting proceedings in England, this is a breach of contract and vexatious.[480] An injunction restraining A from continuing the proceedings abroad will then be granted on the basis of vexation or oppression.[481] Moreover, the nature of the jurisdiction clause may be such that, although not exclusive, it does not contemplate parallel proceedings and pursuing proceedings abroad would be vexatious or oppressive.[482] Normally, though, a non-exclusive jurisdiction agreement will contemplate the possibility of simultaneous trials in England and abroad and, if trial is pursued abroad, there will not only be no breach of agreement but also no vexatious or oppressive conduct.[483]

(b) Breach of an arbitration agreement

According to the Court of Appeal in the *The Angelic Grace*, where there is an agreement valid under its governing law to arbitrate and foreign court proceedings are pending, the English courts have an inherent power to restrain the parties from bringing or continuing the foreign proceedings, for that would constitute a breach of contract.[484] In such cases, the court need feel no diffidence in granting the injunction, provided that it is sought promptly and before the foreign proceedings are too far advanced.[485] The often expressed principle that the power to issue an anti-suit injunction must be exercised with caution was said to have no application in such a case. There has often been said to be no difference in principle between an injunction to restrain proceedings in breach of an arbitration clause and one to restrain proceedings in breach of an exclusive jurisdiction clause.[486]

---

[478] Case C-159/02 [2004] All ER (EC) 485; discussed supra, pp 335–336.

[479] *Royal Bank of Canada v Cooperative Centrale Raiffeisen-Boerenleenbank BA* [2004] EWCA Civ 7, [2004] 1 Lloyd's Rep 471, Briggs (2004) 75 BYBIL 558; *Continental Bank v Aeakos* [1994] 1 WLR 588, CA; *A/S Svendborg v Wansa* [1997] 2 Lloyd's Rep 183, CA; Fawcett [2001] LMCLQ 234 at 255–257.

[480] *Sabah Shipyard (Pakistan) Ltd v Islamic Republic of Pakistan* [2002] EWCA Civ 1643; [2003] 2 Lloyd's Rep 571, CA, Briggs (2003) 74 BYBIL 528.

[481] The *Sabah* case, supra.

[482] Ibid, [36]–[37], [52] (per PILL LJ).

[483] *Royal Bank of Canada v Cooperative Centrale Raiffeisen-Boerenleenbank BA* [2004] EWCA Civ 7, [2004] 1 Lloyd's Rep 471.

[484] See *Aggeliki Charis Compañía Marítima SA v Pagnan SpA, The Angelic Grace* [1995] 1 Lloyd's Rep 87, CA; followed in, eg, *Bankers Trust Co v PT Jakarta International Hotels and Development* [1999] 1 Lloyd's Rep 910; approved most recently in *Through Transport Mutual Insurance Association (Eurasia) Ltd v New India Assurance Co Ltd* [2004] EWCA (Civ) 1598; the *West Tankers* case, supra. For where the sole purpose of proceeding abroad is to obtain arrest of a ship, see *Petromin SA v Secnav Marine Ltd* [1995] 1 Lloyd's Rep 603. See also *The Kallang* [2006] EWHC 2825 (Comm), [2007] 1 Lloyd's Rep 160—arrest abroad used to undermine arbitration clause.

[485] *The Angelic Grace*, supra, at 96 (per MILLETT LJ); the *Through Transport* case, supra, at [90].

[486] *The Angelic Grace*, supra, at 96 and the *Through Transport* case, supra, at [90]. See also the *Natwest Bank* case, supra, at [32]; the *American International Specialty Lines Insurance Co* case, supra, at 275; *Goshawk Dedicated Ltd v ROP Inc* [2006] EWHC 1730 (Comm), [2006] Lloyd's Rep IR 711. In arbitration cases, the

The justification for the grant of an injunction in either case is that, without it, the claimant will be deprived of his contractual rights in a situation in which damages are manifestly an inadequate remedy.[487] The ground for granting the injunction to restrain the foreign proceedings is the clear and simple one that the defendant has promised not to bring them.[488] Moreover, the principles in the *Donohue* case[489] (a case concerned with exclusive jurisdiction clauses) have been applied where an injunction was sought to restrain proceedings brought in breach of a clause providing for arbitration in England.[490] There are numerous examples of restraining by injunction a breach of an arbitration agreement where the injunction was used to restrain proceedings in another European Community State. The English courts have continued to grant such injunctions, even after the decision of the Court of Justice in *Turner v Grovit*, although whether they are justified in so doing is by no means clear and needs to be resolved by the Court of Justice.[491] Where a person, who is not a party to the arbitration agreement and is therefore not in breach of this, but is, nonetheless, bound to arbitrate in England because of the nature of its foreign statutory claim as classified under English conflict of laws, the principles in *The Angelic Grace* will not be applied by way of parity of reasoning.[492]

3. STAYS OF ENGLISH PROCEEDINGS AND RESTRAINING FOREIGN PROCEEDINGS IN CASES WHERE THE BRUSSELS/LUGANO SYSTEM APPLIES

The discussion in this chapter has been conducted so far on the assumption that jurisdiction has been taken under the traditional rules.[493] In cases coming within the Brussels/Lugano system,[494] there is the added complication of whether the English courts can exercise their powers to stay English proceedings or restrain foreign proceedings.[495]

New York Convention does not provide a ground for refusal of an anti-suit injunction: *West Tankers Inc v Ras Riunione Adriatica Di Sicurta SpA (The Front Comor)* [2005] EWHC 454 (Comm) at [57], [2005] 2 Lloyd's Rep 257; affd on this point [2007] UKHL 4.

[487] *Aggeliki Charis Compañía Marítima SA v Pagnan SpA, The Angelic Grace* [1995] 1 Lloyd's Rep 87, CA.

[488] *Toepfer International GmbH v Société Cargill France* [1998] 1 Lloyd's Rep 379 at 384, CA; the *Through Transport* case, supra, at [90].

[489] Supra, pp 470–471.

[490] *Welex AG v Rosa Maritime Ltd* [2003] EWCA Civ 938 at [47]–[52], [2003] 2 Lloyd's Rep 509; followed in *Through Transport Mutual Insurance Association (Eurasia) Ltd v New India Assurance Co Ltd* [2003] EWHC 3158 (Comm), [2004] 1 Lloyd's Rep 509; overruled in part but without disapproval of this point —[2004] EWCA (Civ) 1598; *Cv D* [2007] EWHC 1541 (Comm), [2007] 2 Lloyd's Rep 367, appeal dismissed [2007] EWCA Civ 1282. Cf *Toepfer International GmbH v Société Cargill France* [1997] 2 Lloyd's Rep 98 at 110. The Court of Appeal at [1998] 1 Lloyd's Rep 379 at 386 held that COLMAN J did not err in principle in the exercise of his discretion. Effect will also be given to the arbitration agreement by appointing an arbitrator in England, despite proceedings abroad: *Atlanska Plovidba v Consignaciones Asturianas SA (The Lapad)* [2004] EWHC 1273 (Comm), [2004] 2 Lloyd's Rep 109.

[491] See the discussion supra, pp 332–338.

[492] *Through Transport Mutual Insurance Association (Eurasia) Ltd v New India Assurance Co Ltd* [2004] EWCA (Civ) 1598 at [95]–[97] (involving a statutory transfer of rights of action).

[493] Supra, pp 353–422.

[494] For when the Brussels I Regulation, Brussels and Lugano Conventions apply see supra, pp 213–225.

[495] A stay may be inconsistent with the Warsaw Convention 1929, see *Milor SRL v British Airways plc* [1996] QB 702, CA, and with the CMR Convention *Royal & Sun Alliance plc v MK Digital FZE (Cyprus) Ltd* [2005]

This question has already been examined in detail[496] and the reader should refer to the earlier discussion of this important matter.

In the situation where the English courts have power to grant an injunction, the question will then arise of whether an injunction should be granted. In so far as the English courts still have power to restrain proceedings in another Member State, they should not refuse to exercise the discretion to grant an anti-suit injunction on the basis that the injunction is restraining proceedings in another Member State.[497]

Turning now to the situation where the question is whether an injunction should be granted restraining proceedings in a non-Member State;[498] in *Samengo-Turner v J & H Marsh & McLennan (Services) Ltd*[499] an injunction was granted in relation to proceedings in New York as the only means of giving effect to the defendants' right under the Brussels I Regulation to be sued only in England.[500] This extends the grant of anti-suit injunctions by effectively creating a new category. Two criticisms can be levelled at this decision. First, it does not satisfy Lord HOBHOUSE's requirement in *Turner v Grovit* that there is wrongful conduct of the party to be restrained.[501] On the contrary, that party had commenced procedings in New York acting in reliance on an agreement between the parties providing for the exclusive jurisdiction of the New York courts. Secondly, in terms of comity, New York courts cannot be expected to be sympathetic to an English assertion of exclusive jurisdiction under a Regulation to which New York is not a party or to the English courts striking out of the exclusive jurisdiction agreement by virtue of that Regulation. The situation is very different from one where there has been a breach of an exclusive jurisdiction agreement. TUCKEY LJ accepted that the case for granting an injunction was not as strong as one where there had been a breach of an exclusive jurisdiction agreement.[502] But nonetheless, an injunction was granted.

EWHC 1408 (Comm), [2005] IL Pr 51, appeal allowed without discussion of this point [2006] EWCA Civ 629, [2006] 2 Lloyd's Rep 110.

[496] Supra, pp 320–340.

[497] *West Tankers Inc v Ras Riunione Adriatica di Sicurta SpA* [2007] UKHL 4 at [6].

[498] There is power to grant an injunction in this situation, even though the basis of jurisdiction is one set out in the Regulation, see supra, pp 339–340.

[499] [2007] EWCA Civ 723 at [38]–[44], [2007] IL Pr 52; Briggs [2007] LMCLQ 433.

[500] See supra, p 339.

[501] Supra, p 458.

[502] The *Samengo-Turner* case, supra, at [41].

Chapter 14

Limitations on Jurisdiction

1. INTRODUCTION

Jurisdiction under the traditional rules is subject to certain limitations, the effect of which is to render the court incompetent to determine the issue notwithstanding that the defendant has been properly served with a claim form. These limitations have been judicially classified into the following three types.[1]

(i) Limitations that affect the subject matter of the issue Broadly stated, these limitations preclude a right of action if the issue relates to foreign immovables,[2] foreign intellectual property rights,[3] foreign taxes,[4] the rights and liabilities arising under a foreign penal or other public law,[5] or discovery of documents outside the jurisdiction.[6]

(ii) Limitations that affect the kind of relief sought These restrict the power of the court to grant relief affecting the matrimonial status of the parties. In this type of case it is not

---

[1] *Garthwaite v Garthwaite* [1964] P 356 at 387.
[2] Infra, p 478 et seq.
[3] Infra, pp 489–490.
[4] Supra, p 123 et seq.
[5] Supra, p 126 et seq.
[6] *MacKinnon v Donaldson Lufkin and Jenrette Securities Corpn* [1986] Ch 482.

enough that the respondent has been served with process. As will be seen in Chapter 21 on matrimonial and related causes, the competence of the court to proceed with the trial is conditioned by such factors as the habitual residence or domicile of the parties.[7]

(iii) Limitations relating to persons between whom the issue is joined   There are certain persons against whom the jurisdiction cannot be enforced, and others by whom it cannot be invoked.[8]

There is one further limitation which should be added to this list.

(iv) Limitations on jurisdiction imposed by certain statutes[9]   It is intended in this chapter to deal with limitations in respect of foreign immovables and foreign intellectual property rights, limitations relating to the parties and limitations imposed by certain statutes. The other limitations mentioned above are more appropriately dealt with elsewhere in the book.

2. JURISDICTION IN RESPECT OF FOREIGN PROPERTY

(a) Foreign immovables[10]

The limitations on jurisdiction in relation to foreign immovables are derived from two sources: first, certain common law rules; secondly, the Brussels/Lugano system. Each of these limitations will be examined in turn.

(i) The common law limitation

(a) The exclusionary rule

An English court has no jurisdiction to adjudicate upon the right of property in, or the right to possession of, foreign immovables, even though the parties may be resident or domiciled in England.[11] This general rule is based on the practical consideration that only the court of the situs can make an effective decree with regard to land.

It was at one time thought, however, that as regards England the rule was not based on substantial grounds, but was due to the technicalities of the English law of procedure. A distinction was made between local and transitory actions. If a cause of action was one that might have arisen anywhere, it was *transitory*; if it was one that could have arisen only in one place, it was *local*. In local matters, such as claims to the ownership of land,[12] the *venue* had to be laid with accuracy, but in transitory matters the plaintiff was allowed to lay the *venue* where he pleased. However, local venues were abolished by the Judicature Act 1873. This removed the technical objection to the possibility of bringing an action

---

[7] Infra, pp 944–965.

[8] Infra, pp 490–510.

[9] Infra, pp 510–511.

[10] On the distinction between movables and immovables, see infra, pp 1193–1197.

[11] *British South Africa Co v Companhia de Moçambique* [1893] AC 602; *Deschamps v Miller* [1908] 1 Ch 856; *Hesperides Hotels Ltd v Muftizade* [1979] AC 508; Merrills (1979) 28 ICLQ 523; Carter (1978) 49 BYBIL 286. For a Canadian and an Australian authority on this point, see *Jeske v Jeske* (1982) 29 RFL (2d) 348; *Dagi v BHP (No 2)* [1997] 1 VR 428. Cf *Rowe v Silverstein* [1996] 1 VR 509.

[12] The place from which the jury was summoned.

in respect of foreign immovables before an English court, and it was not long before it was suggested, and indeed decided, that such actions could now be entertained. This argument was strongly pressed in *British South Africa Co v Companhia de Moçambique*.[13]

> This was an action of trespass brought against the defendants for having broken into and taken possession of large tracts of lands and mines in South Africa.

The Court of Appeal held that, local *venues* having been abolished, such an action could properly be brought here.[14] The House of Lords, however, reversed this decision and held that an English court has no jurisdiction to entertain a suit with respect to foreign immovables and, moreover, it finally dispelled the idea that this principle ever rested on a technical rule of procedure.[15] Stated more explicitly, what this decision now signifies is that the jurisdiction of the court is barred where the action raises the issue of the title to, or right to possession of, land abroad.

This exclusion of jurisdiction is justified on the basis that any judgment in rem that might be given would be totally ineffective unless it were accepted and implemented by the authorities in the situs.[16] However, this issue must be raised directly, for "it is the action *founded on* a disputed claim of title to foreign lands over which an English court has no jurisdiction, and . . . where no question of title arises, or only arises as a collateral incident of the trial of other issues, there is nothing to exclude the jurisdiction".[17] Examples of a refusal of jurisdiction on this ground are: proceedings for the partition of land in Ireland;[18] an action to test the validity of a devise of land situated in Pennsylvania;[19] an action[20] or a petition of right[21] to recover possession of Colonial land; a claim to obtain inspection of documents, possessed by the defendant in England, in aid of an action for the recovery of land that was pending in India;[22] an action for a declaration of title to fishery rights.[23]

A question that has arisen is whether an action to recover arrears of rent charged on land abroad is maintainable in England. In *Whitaker v Forbes*:[24]

> An English testator devised land in Australia to the defendant, but charged it with the payment of an annuity of £500 to the plaintiff.

---

[13] [1893] AC 602.

[14] [1892] 2 QB 358.

[15] [1893] AC 602 at 629.

[16] It is unlikely that foreign judgments relating to title to English land will be recognised in this country, see infra, p 534.

[17] *St Pierre v South American Stores (Gath and Chaves) Ltd* [1936] 1 KB 382 at 397, interpreting the speech of Lord HERSCHELL in the *Moçambique* case [1893] AC 602 at 626; and see *Tito v Waddell (No 2)* [1977] Ch 106 at 262–264, 310. See also *Dagi v BHP (No 2)* [1997] 1 VR 428 at 441—the claim must essentially concern rights to or over foreign land. The rule in the *Moçambique* case will not apply where what is involved is more than a mere dispute between private individuals, see *Buttes Gas and Oil Co v Hammer (No 3)* [1982] AC 888.

[18] *Cartwright v Pettus* (1676) 2 Cas in Ch 214.

[19] *Pike v Hoare* (1763) Amb 428.

[20] *Roberdeau v Rous* (1738) 1 Atk 543.

[21] *Re Holmes* (1861) 2 John & H 527.

[22] *Reiner v Marquis of Salisbury* (1876) 2 Ch D 378.

[23] *Toome Eel Fishery (Northern Ireland) v Jangaard and Butler* [1960] CLY 1297.

[24] (1875) 1 CPD 51.

An action to recover arrears of this rentcharge inevitably failed, for it had been commenced before the abolition of the rules of *venue* by the Judicature Act, and thus the court had no option but to enforce the technical rule that the action was local and therefore not maintainable. Lord CAIRNS, however, remarked that it might possibly be maintainable in the future.[25] In this particular case, of course, the defendant, having assumed no contractual obligation, was liable solely on the ground of privity of estate arising from his possession of the land, and there can be no doubt that a liability which rests on privity of contract, as where a borrower charges his land with the repayment of the loan, will be enforceable in English proceedings.

(b) Exceptions to the exclusionary rule

There are two exceptions to the exclusion of jurisdiction under the rule in the *Moçambique* case.

(i) *Action founded on a personal obligation*[26]

If the conscience of the defendant is affected in the sense that he has become bound by a personal obligation to the claimant, the court, in the exercise of its jurisdiction in personam, will not shrink from ordering him to convey or otherwise deal with foreign land. For the argument that a court cannot, by its judgments or decrees, directly bind or affect land that lies within the confines of another state has no force where the issue before the court is not a right in rem relating to foreign immovables, but an obligation enforceable in personam against the defendant.[27]

The primary essential is that the defendant should be subject to the general jurisdiction of the court.[28] This jurisdiction, as we have seen, is founded on his presence in England, but as regards the power to pronounce a decree in personam against him it is equally well founded by service of a claim form under rule 6.20 of the Civil Procedure Rules.[29] Once the court is thus empowered to take cognizance of the matter, the doctrine that equity acts in personam may be freely and effectively applied. A decree may be issued which, though personal in form, will indirectly affect land abroad. The operation of this rule may readily be illustrated by recent decisions on the making of search orders, ie orders without notice for the inspection of property, in relation to property abroad. If the defendant has been properly served in England, the court has power to, and may well make, the order. It is, however, a discretionary order and though an order has been granted for the inspection of premises in one foreign state,[30] an order has been refused in relation to premises in another foreign state.[31] Furthermore, if the jurisdiction of the court is based on service of the claim form out of the jurisdiction following an application without notice under rule 6.20, execution of the search order abroad may be suspended

---

[25] Ibid, at 52.

[26] See generally Yeo, *Choice of Law for Equitable Doctrines*, paras 1.03–1.26.

[27] *Ewing v Orr Ewing* (1883) 9 App Cas 34 at 40. For the position under the Brussels Convention (Brussels I Regulation), which reaches the same conclusion, see Case C-294/92 *Webb v Webb* [1994] QB 696, supra, p 277.

[28] *Razelos v Razelos (No 2)* [1970] 1 WLR 392 at 403. See also *Bheekhun v Williams* [1999] 2 FLR 229 at 242, CA.

[29] *Re Liddell's Settlement Trusts* [1936] Ch 365 at 374. For CPR, r 6.20, see supra, pp 372–413.

[30] *Cook Industries Inc v Galliher* [1979] Ch 439.

[31] *Protector Alarms Ltd v Maxim Alarms Ltd* [1978] FSR 442.

until the defendant has had an opportunity to seek to set aside the service of the claim form.[32]

If, for instance, a mortgagee of land in New York refuses to reconvey on receipt of principal, interest and costs, there is no way by which a direct transfer of the property to the mortgagor can be effected at the instance of the English court. But the court can indirectly produce the desired result by saying to the recalcitrant mortgagee, "You are subject to our jurisdiction by reason of your presence in England, and if you refuse to take the steps required by the law of the situs for a reconveyance of the property to the mortgagor, we shall imprison you or sequestrate your English property until you comply." The distinction is that the court cannot act upon the land directly, but acts on the conscience of the defendant.[33]

This right to affect foreign land was finally established by the decision in *Penn v Baltimore*[34] in 1750. In that case:

> A contract had been made in England between the plaintiff and the defendant, by which a scheme was arranged for fixing the boundaries of Pennsylvania and Maryland. To a claim for specific performance brought in this country the defendant objected that the court had no jurisdiction, since it could neither make an effectual decree nor execute its own judgment.

Lord Hardwicke, while admitting that he could not make a decree in rem, granted specific performance, on the ground that the strict primary decree in a court of equity was in personam.

The exercise of this jurisdiction, of course, is not confined to questions concerning foreign land. It extends to any case where the defendant has been guilty of conduct that in the eyes of the court is contrary to equity and good conscience. An important example of the general jurisdiction occurs where a person who is amenable to the jurisdiction commences legal proceedings abroad, the institution of which is inequitable. In such circumstances the court has a power to issue an injunction restraining the foreign proceedings, for a decree of this nature is not directed against the authority of the foreign court but merely commands a person within the English jurisdiction what he is to do.

Even where a person has actually obtained judgment abroad, an injunction may be issued restraining him from reaping its fruits, if he has obtained it in breach of some contractual or fiduciary duty or in a manner contrary to the principles of equity and conscience.[35]

We must now, however, confine the discussion to the manner in which the exercise of this personal jurisdiction may affect foreign land. The fundamental requirement is that the defendant should be subject to some personal obligation arising from his own act, for it is only when his conscience is affected that the court is entitled to interfere. This personal obligation can arise "out of contract or implied contract, fiduciary relationship, or fraud, or other conduct which, in the view of the Court of Equity in this country, would

---

[32] *Altertext Inc v Advanced Data Communications Ltd* [1985] 1 WLR 457.
[33] *Cranstown v Johnston* (1796) 3 Ves 170 at 182; *Companhia de Moçambique v British South Africa Co* [1892] 2 QB 358 at 364.
[34] (1750) 1 Ves Sen 444.
[35] *Ellerman Lines Ltd v Read* [1928] 2 KB 144.

be unconscionable, and [does] not depend for [its] existence on the law of the *locus* of the immovable property".[36] It will lead, perhaps, to a better appreciation of the subject if we attempt to tabulate the various circumstances that have been considered sufficient to raise the necessary personal equity. It should, however, be stressed that the courts may decide that a personal equity exists without going on to categorise the situation before them. Thus the Court of Appeal has held[37] that there is jurisdiction to grant a wife an order restraining her husband from disposing of a villa in Spain, since the right to financial relief arising from divorce proceedings is concerned with a personal equity and this is enough to give jurisdiction.

Contracts relating to foreign land   It is clear that a party to a contract concerning foreign land is subject to a personal obligation which affects his conscience and which can be enforced by the personal process of a court of equity,[38] even if his contractual right can only be pursued by an uncontested assertion of his title to foreign land.[39] The existence of a contractual obligation was the ground of the decision in *Penn v Baltimore*.[40] In a very early case,[41] the defendant, who refused to perform a contract for the sale of land in Ireland, was successfully sued for specific performance while on a casual visit to England. Again, a decree for specific performance was made against the English executors of a testator who had agreed for valuable consideration to execute a legal mortgage of land in the island of Dominica;[42] and an action has lain in England for recovery of rent due under a lease of land in Chile.[43] More recently, specific performance of a contract for the sale of land in Scotland has been decreed against an English purchaser, notwithstanding the argument that there was considerable difference between Scots and English land law.[44] In Canada, specific performance has been granted by a New Brunswick court against a vendor who attempted to repudiate a contract for the sale of land in Quebec.[45] It has been said *per curiam* that the fact that land is situated abroad should affect the choice of law, not jurisdiction, if the case is one in which it is sought to enforce an equitable claim in personam.[46] Thus a claim to have foreign land conveyed to the claimant, based on an English contract and made against a purchaser of the land with prior notice of that contract (who would be considered to be acting unconscionably), could in principle succeed, provided the foreign law would not overreach the English doctrine of notice.[47]

---

[36] *Deschamps v Miller* [1908] 1 Ch 856 at 863. See also Westlake, s 173; Foote, p 224; Dicey, Morris and Collins, paras 23-041–23-050; *Companhia de Moçambique v British South Africa Co* [1892] 2 QB 358 at 364.

[37] *Hamlin v Hamlin* [1986] Fam 11. See also *Hlynski v Hlynski* (1999) 176 DLR (4th) 132, Sask CA.

[38] *Cood v Cood* (1863) 33 LJ Ch 273; *British South Africa Co v De Beers Consolidated Mines Ltd* [1910] 2 Ch 502 at 523, 524; *St Pierre v South American Stores (Gath and Chaves) Ltd* [1936] 1 KB 382.

[39] *Tito v Waddell (No 2)* [1977] Ch 106 at 264, 310; infra, p 483.

[40] (1750) 1 Ves Sen 444.

[41] *Archer v Preston*, undated, but cited in *Arglasse v Muschamp* (1682) 1 Vern 76 at 77.

[42] *Re Smith, Lawrence v Kitson* [1916] 2 Ch 206.

[43] *St Pierre v South American Stores (Gath and Chaves) Ltd* [1936] 1 KB 382.

[44] *Richard West & Partners (Inverness) Ltd v Dick* [1969] 2 Ch 424; affd, ibid, at 435. In view of the general requirement of jurisdiction over the defendant, discussed supra, p 353 et seq, it is hard to see why HARMAN LJ [1969] 2 Ch 424 at 436 was unwilling to commit himself if the defendant was not domiciled in England.

[45] *Ward v Coffin* (1972) 27 DLR (3d) 58.

[46] *R Griggs Group Ltd v Evans* [2004] EWHC 1088 (Ch) at [110], [2005] Ch 153. See also *Macmillan Inc v Bishopsgate Investment Trust plc (No 3)* [1995] 1 WLR 978 at 989, affd on other grounds [1996] 1 WLR 387, CA.

[47] *R Griggs Group Ltd v Evans*, supra, at [111].

Fraud and other unconscionable conduct   Fraud is an extrinsic, collateral act, violating all proceedings, even those of courts of justice,[48] and it always creates a right in the injured party to sue the defendant in personam wherever he can find him, no matter where the cause of action has arisen or where the subject matter of the action is situated. The leading case is *Cranstown v Johnston*.[49]

> The plaintiff was liable to pay to the defendant in London over £2,500 but was unable to make the payment at the required time. He was entitled to a plantation of great value in the island of St Christopher. The law of that island allowed a creditor to proceed against an absent debtor. After judgment had been obtained without any actual notice to the plaintiff, the plantation was seized and the plaintiff's interest therein sold to the defendant for £2,000, which was far less than its true value. The plaintiff filed a bill for relief in the English Court of Equity.

The Master of the Rolls decreed that on receipt of what was due for principal, interest and costs the defendant should reconvey the plantation to the plaintiff. He did not deny that what had been done was in accordance with the law of the situs, but he pointed out that the defendant had used the local law not to satisfy the debt, but to obtain an estate at an inadequate price. This was a "gross injustice" sufficient to justify the court in acting on the conscience of the defendant.

Fiduciary relationship   A trust attached to foreign land may be enforced by the English court, provided that the trustee is present in this country.[50] This is so, even though the author of the trust is not subject to the English jurisdiction.[51] However, two different types of problem may arise in relation to a trust or other equitable obligation concerning foreign land. The first is where the dispute before the court concerns the enforcement of the trust. It may be that a beneficiary can only establish his right to benefit under the trust by asserting evidence of his title to foreign land. In that event, the question of title to the land, though relevant to the claimant's claim, is only incidental to the dispute before the court, namely the enforcement of the trust, such as a trust of royalties from the mining of land.[52] If, on the other hand, there are rival claimants to the land, then the claimant's assertion of title is part of the subject matter of the dispute and would come within the *Moçambique* rule, whether the claim related to a trust[53] or to a contractual obligation[54] concerning the foreign land. A claim that is based on legal ownership of immovable property abroad will come within the *Moçambique* rule, even though the remedy sought is that of a constructive trust.[55]

Mortgage and foreclosure   Again, a personal equity arising from a mortgage of foreign land may justify an action in this country. Thus, where the mortgagor of land in Jamaica had obtained a decree from the English court which directed certain accounts to be taken

---

[48] *Duchess of Kingston's Case* (1776) 20 State Tr 355 at 544; *White v Hall* (1806) 12 Ves 321.

[49] (1796) 3 Ves 170. See also *Arglasse v Muschamp* (1682) 1 Vern 76; *Cook Industries Inc v Galliher* [1979] Ch 439.

[50] *Kildare v Eustace* (1686) 1 Vern 437; see also *Razelos v Razelos (No 2)* [1970] 1 WLR 392. It is not clear, in the latter case, whether jurisdiction was assumed on the basis of fraud or of a fiduciary relationship: Chesterman (1970) 33 MLR 209, 212–213.

[51] *Ewing v Orr Ewing* (1883) 9 App Cas 34; and see *Chellaram v Chellaram* [1985] Ch 409 at 426–427.

[52] *Tito v Waddell (No 2)* [1977] Ch 106 at 262–264, 272, 310.

[53] Ibid, at 263, 310.

[54] Supra, p 482.

[55] *Re Polly Peck International plc (In Administration) (No 2)* [1998] 3 All ER 812 at 828, CA.

with a view to redemption, the court granted an injunction restraining the mortgagees, who were present in England, from instituting foreclosure proceedings in Jamaica.[56] The mortgagor had a clear equity to be protected from a double account. The same principle applies to foreclosure proceedings. In English proceedings a decree in a foreclosure action is merely a decree in personam since it destroys the right of redemption given by equity to the mortgagor, and it can therefore be made by an English court against a mortgagor who is within the jurisdiction, although the subject of the mortgage may be immovables situated abroad.[57] Whether a personal obligation is such as to affect the defendant's conscience is a matter to be determined solely by English law. According to *Re Courtney*,[58] the court does not refuse to exercise its equitable jurisdiction merely because the right, recognised by English law as springing from the personal relationship between the parties, is one that is not recognised by the law of the situs.

Limitations on the doctrine   The doctrine of *Penn v Baltimore*, however, is subject to two limitations. First, it must be possible for the decree issued by the English court to be carried into effect in the country where the land is situated.[59] This restriction requires no elaboration, for the futility of ordering the defendant to perform some act which would be forbidden by the law of the situs is obvious.[60]

Secondly, the personal obligation which is the basis of the English court's jurisdiction must, to use an expression of Beale, "have run from the defendant to the plaintiff",[61] ie there must be privity of obligation between the parties to the action.

It is firmly established that the court acts only against the actual person who, as a result of his *own* conduct, is under a personal obligation to the claimant, and it stops short of exercising the jurisdiction against a third party, even though he may have acquired the land from one who is contractually, or otherwise personally, liable to the claimant.[62] There must be privity of obligation between claimant and defendant, and that privity must arise from some transaction effected by the claimant with the defendant.

> If A agrees to sell foreign land to B, there is no doubt that A incurs a personal liability that is justiciable in England. But if, in breach of his contract, A sells the land to X, there is no personal equity which B can enforce against X. There is no contract by X with B, no unconscionable conduct by X towards B personally.

What is involved in such a case is a claim of title to foreign land advanced by two contesting parties who are strangers to each other so far as mutual dealings are concerned.

---

[56] *Beckford v Kemble* (1822) 1 Sim & St 7; cf *Inglis v Commonwealth Trading Bank of Australia* (1972) 20 FLR 30; Pryles (1973) 22 ICLQ 756.

[57] *Toller v Carteret* (1705) 2 Vern 494; *Paget v Ede* (1874) LR 18 Eq 118.

[58] (1840) Mont 8 Ch 239 at 251; *Re Anchor Line (Henderson Bros) Ltd* [1937] Ch 483 at 488.

[59] *Waterhouse v Stansfield* (1851) 9 Hare 234; cf *Richard West & Partners (Inverness) Ltd v Dick* [1969] 2 Ch 424 at 429–430, 436; *Razelos v Razelos (No 2)* [1970] 1 WLR 392 at 403–405.

[60] *Re Courtney* (1840) Mont & Ch 239 at 250–251.

[61] (1906) 20 HLR 382, 390.

[62] *Martin v Martin* (1831) 2 Russ & M 507; *Waterhouse v Stansfield* (1851) 9 Hare 234; *Norris v Chambers* (1861) 29 Beav 246; affd 3 De G F & J 583; *Hicks v Powell* (1869) 4 Ch App 741; *Norton v Florence Land Co* (1877) 7 Ch D 332; *Catania v Giannattasio* (1999) 174 DLR (4th) 170, Ont CA.

Such a question of title is, of course, determinable exclusively by the law of the situs and is subject exclusively to the jurisdiction of the courts at the situs. [63]

There may, of course, be exceptional circumstances in which an equity that has arisen between A and B can be enforced against C under the doctrine of *Penn v Baltimore*. It is always a question of personal obligation. Is the defendant, though not a party to the original transaction which gave rise to the dispute, contractually or otherwise personally bound? Thus where the defendants had agreed to take land in Mexico subject to an express obligation in favour of existing debenture-holders, it was clearly unconscionable that they should rely exclusively on the law of the situs.[64]

Concluding remarks on the doctrine Such, then, is the doctrine that the English court invokes to justify an order which, though personal in form, may affect the title to foreign land. It is a doctrine that in some cases has undoubtedly been carried to an extent scarcely warranted by the principles of international law,[65] as, for instance, where an Englishman resident in Chile was ordered to carry out a contract concerning land, binding according to English law, which the Chilean courts had held not to be binding.[66] In fact, Lord ESHER MR once went so far as to say that the decision in *Penn v Baltimore*, "seems to me to be open to the strong objection, that the Court is doing indirectly what it dare not do directly".[67]

An interesting question that has never arisen in England is whether a foreign judgment based on the same principle as that adopted in *Penn v Baltimore*, but affecting *English* land, will be granted extra-territorial effect.[68]

> If, for instance, a Californian court decrees that X, resident in California, shall reconvey English land to Y, from whom he had obtained it by fraud, will the English court, in proceedings brought by Y, compel X to carry the decree into effect?

Comity, if it means anything, would dictate an affirmative answer. However, any attempt by a foreign court to regulate the disposition of land outside its jurisdiction not unnaturally provokes a certain animosity in the state where the property is situated and it is doubtful whether in this particular context the English judges would be imbued with any spirit of reciprocity. The Supreme Court of Canada, indeed, has satisfied itself that English courts do not regard their own decrees in personam affecting land abroad as having any extra-territorial effect, and that therefore no recognition will be granted to similar decrees of foreign courts.[69]

---

[63] *Norris v Chambres* (1861) 29 Beav 246; affd (1861) 3 De G F & J 583. Followed in *Deschamps v Miller* [1908] 1 Ch 856; and see *Re Hawthorne, Graham v Massey* (1883) 23 Ch D 743; *Cook Industries Inc v Galliher* [1979] Ch 439.

[64] *Mercantile Investment and General Trust Co v River Plate Trust, Loan and Agency Co* [1892] 2 Ch 303.

[65] Story, p 758.

[66] *Cood v Cood* (1863) 33 LJ Ch 273.

[67] *Companhia de Moçambique v British South Africa Co* [1892] 2 QB 358 at 404–405.

[68] Dicey, Morris and Collins, paras 14R-099–14-108.

[69] *Duke v Andler* [1932] SCR 734; see Gordon (1933) 49 LQR 547; Anderson (1999) 48 ICLQ 167; cf *Chapman Estate v O'Hara* [1988] 2 WWR 275. In the USA, although the Supreme Court in *Fall v Eastin* 215 US 1 (1909) held that recognition need not be given to judgments in personam concerning land, most states are prepared to recognise such judgments: Scoles, Hay, Borchers, Symeonides, para 24.10; Restatement 2d § 102, comment d.

(ii) Questions affecting foreign land arising incidentally in an English action

The second exception, which lacks direct authority but which undoubtedly exists in practice, is apparent from such well-known cases as *Re Duke of Wellington*[70] and *Nelson v Bridport*,[71] to take only two examples.[72] In each of these cases jurisdiction was assumed although quite clearly the title to foreign land was the matter in dispute. Since parties cannot consent to the exercise of a jurisdiction which the court admittedly does not possess,[73] how is this divergence from the general principle to be explained? The usual explanation is that if an estate or a trust, which includes English property and foreign immovables, is being administered in English proceedings,[74] the court is prepared to determine a disputed title to the foreign immovables.[75] Perhaps Lord HERSCHELL had this practice in mind when he accepted that the courts could take jurisdiction to determine incidental matters involving title to foreign land.[76] Although a stern critic might question whether the title to the Spanish land in *Re Duke of Wellington* was a mere incident in the proceedings, there is no doubt that in the course of dealing with such a matter as a trust or a will subject to English law the courts have in fact not hesitated to determine the title to foreign land. The jurisdictional difficulty that arises appears to have been canvassed only once,[77] and all that can be said is that the practice comes perilously near to destroying the supposedly universal principle that jurisdiction concerning the title to, or possession of, immovables resides only in the state in which the property is situated.

(c) Damages for trespass to foreign land

Until fairly recently the limitations at common law extended to prevent jurisdiction in cases where the action raised the issue of the recovery of damages for trespass to foreign land, even though no question of title to the land arose.[78] This rule came in for much criticism and was abolished by section 30(1) of the Civil Jurisdiction and Judgments Act 1982,[79] which provides that:

> the jurisdiction . . . to entertain proceedings for trespass to, or any other tort affecting, immovable property shall extend to cases in which the property in question is situated

---

[70] [1948] Ch 118, supra, p 69.

[71] (1846) 8 Beav 547, infra, pp 1199–1200.

[72] See also *Re Piercy* [1895] 1 Ch 83; *Re Hoyles* [1911] 1 Ch 179; *Re Ross* [1930] 1 Ch 377, supra, pp 67–68. Cf *Buttes Gas and Oil Co v Hammer (No 3)* [1982] AC 888.

[73] Duncan and Dykes, *Principles of Civil Jurisdiction*, 258; see also the doubt expressed by SOMERVELL LJ in *The Tolten* [1946] P 135 at 166.

[74] The jurisdiction of the English court to administer an *inter vivos* trust of land in a European Community or EFTA State is subject to Arts 1(1) and 22(1) of the Brussels I Regulation (Arts 1(1) and 16(1)(a) of the Brussels Convention and Arts 1(1) and 22(1) of the Lugano Convention), supra, pp 276–278 and 342.

[75] *Jubert v Church Comrs for England* 1952 SC 160; *Re Bailey* [1985] 2 NZLR 656; Morris (1946) 64 LQR 264, 268. Morris suggests that the English and foreign property must be subject to similar limitations, but is this right?

[76] *British South Africa Co v Companhia de Moçambique* [1893] AC 602, at 626. See also Westlake, op cit, s 173.

[77] *Re Duke of Wellington* [1948] Ch 118 at 120, gives the misleading impression that if the parties consent the court can arrogate a jurisdiction that it does not possess. It must be admitted, however, that this was done in *The Mary Moxham* (1876) 1 PD 107. See also *Couzens v Negri* [1981] VR 824.

[78] *St Pierre v South American Stores (Gath and Chaves) Ltd* [1936] 1 KB 382 at 396; *Hesperides Hotels Ltd v Aegean Turkish Holidays Ltd* [1979] AC 508. See also *Dagi v BHP (No 2)* [1997] 1 VR 428, 443 (negligence).

[79] Applied in *Trawnik v Lennox* [1985] 1 WLR 532.

outside [England] unless the proceedings are principally concerned with a question of the title to, or right to possession of, that property.

According to the Court of Appeal in *Re Polly Peck International plc (In Administration) (No 2)*,[80] "principally" is used in the ordinary sense of "for the most part" or "chiefly",[81] so that section 30(1) preserves the *Moçambique* rule only in cases where the real issue in the proceedings is the question of title to, or the right to possession of, foreign land, and all other questions are merely incidental thereto.[82] The applicants claimed to own and be entitled to immediate possession of land, buildings and other immovable property in the Northern part of Cyprus, properties which were expropriated after the 1974 Turkish invasion. The applicants' claim was undeniably concerned with a question of title to, and the right to possession of, that property. However, it was seriously arguable[83] that the proceedings were not principally so concerned because they raised substantial questions, such as whether Polly Peck International itself committed any acts of trespass and whether Polly Peck International could be liable for acts of trespass by its subsidiaries, which were not principally concerned with a question of title to, or the right to possession of, the property in Cyprus. It followed that the court could entertain the proceedings.

(ii) The limitation under the Brussels/Lugano system

The limitation on jurisdiction in respect of foreign immovables under the Brussels/Lugano system stems from Article 22(1) of the Brussels I Regulation,[84] Article 22(1) of the Lugano Convention and Article 16(1)(a) of the Brussels Convention,[85] the effect of which is to prevent a court in the United Kingdom from taking jurisdiction in proceedings which have as their object rights in rem in, or tenancies of, immovable property situated in another European Community State or in an EFTA State,[86] since the courts of the European Community/EFTA State in which the property is situated are given exclusive jurisdiction over such proceedings.

If Article 22(1) of the Regulation or Lugano Convention, or Article 16(1)(a) of the Brussels Convention, is applicable, the common law rules on jurisdiction in relation to foreign immovables are overridden by this Article.[87] It is important to note that the limitation under Article 22(1) (Article 16(1)(a)) is wider in two respects than that under the common law rules. First, Article 22(1) (Article 16(1)(a)) is not confined to proceedings

---

[80] [1998] 3 All ER 812; Briggs (1998) 69 BYBIL 356; Dickinson [1998] LMCLQ 519.

[81] *Re Polly Peck (No 2)*, supra, at 828.

[82] Ibid, at 829. It was said, at 828, that this approach was consistent with the interpretation of Art 19 of the Brussels Convention (Art 25 of the Brussels I Regulation), supra, pp 275–276, in *Fort Dodge Animal Health Ltd v Akzo Nobel* [1998] FSR 222 and *Coin Controls Ltd v Suzo International (UK) Ltd* [1999] Ch 33 at 50–51. But there, "principally" has been equated with "not arising incidentally" which is a much laxer test than "chiefly".

[83] It was not necessary to determine this matter definitively before the trial on the merits, ibid, at 827.

[84] Under the EC/Denmark Agreement the provisions of the Regulation, with minor modifications, are applied by international law to the relations between the Community and Denmark.

[85] See supra, pp 276–282.

[86] For the position where the immovable property is situated in Scotland or Northern Ireland, see para 11(a) of the Modified Regulation in the Civil Jurisdiction and Judgments Act 1982, Sch 4, discussed generally supra, pp 348–349.

[87] *Pearce v Ove Arup Partnership Ltd* [1999] 1 All ER 769 at 793, CA. The Civil Jurisdiction and Judgments Act 1982, s 30 is also subject to the Brussels I Regulation, the Lugano and Brussels Conventions and the Modified Regulation; see s 30(2) and the Civil Jurisdiction and Judgments Order, SI 2001/3929 Sch 2(IV), para 13.

raising the issue of the title to, or the right to possession of, foreign immovables. The provision has been widely interpreted to encompass, for example, a simple action for unpaid rent in respect of a villa in Italy.[88] Secondly, apart from the case of short-term lets,[89] there are no exceptions to the limitation contained in Article 22(1) (Article 16(1)(a)). It follows that English courts will not be able to take jurisdiction, for example, in a case involving fraud or unconscionable conduct,[90] if Article 22(1) (Article 16(1)(a)) is applicable. However, if the matter affecting the foreign land only arises incidentally, the proceedings will not come within Article 22(1) (Article 16(1)(a)) since they will not have rights in rem "as their object";[91] English courts will, accordingly, be able to take jurisdiction in such a case, as they can do at common law.[92]

What if Article 22(1) (Article 16(1)(a)) is not applicable as, for example, in a case where there is a dispute over the title to land in a non-European Community/EFTA State, such as New York? Can the exclusion in the *Moçambique* case be used to deny jurisdiction to English courts? In cases where the traditional bases of jurisdiction apply, clearly it can. But if jurisdiction has been allocated to the United Kingdom under the Brussels/Lugano system[93] (eg the defendant is domiciled in the United Kingdom), this probably should not be denied on the basis of the exclusion contained in the *Moçambique* case.[94] The wording of Article 2 of the Brussels Convention (Brussels I Regulation) is mandatory and not optional.[95] In addition, the application by the English courts of the exclusion contained in the *Moçambique* case would undermine one of the objectives of the Convention, namely the uniform application of the rules contained in the Convention,[96] unless it can be shown that all the other Member States operate the same rule.[97] Moreover, an English court should not use its discretionary powers to stay the proceedings on the basis that New York is the appropriate forum for trial.[98] However, there are worrying indications that English courts are prepared to continue to use discretionary powers when they should not do so. COLMAN J has said, obiter, that discretionary powers to stay the English proceedings can still be used in a case involving an agreement providing for jurisdiction in a non-European Community State[99] and his reasoning indicates that in his view a discretionary power to stay would also still operate in a case where there is a dispute

---

[88] See Case 241/83 *Rösler v Rottwinkel* [1986] QB 33, [1985] ECR 99, discussed supra, pp 280–282.

[89] Art 22(1) of the Brussels I Regulation and Lugano Convention (Art 16(1)(b) of the Brussels Convention). This provision is, in substance, worded in the same way in the first two instruments but differently in the third instrument, supra, pp 281–282 and 342.

[90] See supra, p 483 for the common law position.

[91] Case 115/88 *Reichert v Dresdner Bank* [1990] ECR I-27, particularly at 35 (per the Advocate General).

[92] See supra, p 483.

[93] Supra, pp 225–299.

[94] See, however, for suggestions to the contrary: Droz, paras 165–169; Dicey, Morris and Collins, para 23-027; note by AM 1987 SLT 52; Briggs and Rees, para 2.225.

[95] Case 281/02 *Owusu v Jackson* [2005] QB 801, discussed supra, pp 323–325. This was concerned with the discretionary doctrine of *forum non conveniens* but much of the reasoning of the ECJ would apply equally to the subject matter limitation on jurisdiction in the *Moçambique* case.

[96] See the reasoning in the *Owusu* case, supra, pp 323–325.

[97] France has no such rule.

[98] Supra, pp 327–328. All the reasoning in *Owusu* applies in this situation.

[99] See *Konkola Copper Mines plc v Coromin* [2005] EWHC 898 (Comm), [2005] 2 Lloyd's Rep 555, criticised supra, pp 328–329; affd [2006] EWCA Civ 5, [2006] 1 Lloyd's Rep 410 but with no appeal on this point.

over land in a non-Member State.[100] This could spill over into continued use of the non-discretionary exclusionary rule contained in the *Moçambique* case. Rather than use this rule or *forum non conveniens*, a safer way for refusing to try the case would be to argue that jurisdiction can be declined by giving "reflexive" effect to Article 22(1) (Article 16(1)(a)).[101]

(b) Foreign intellectual property rights[102]

In England it has been assumed until recently that the exception in the *Moçambique* case was confined to cases involving foreign *immovable* property. However, in *Tyburn Productions Ltd v Conan Doyle*[103] VINELOTT J applied the *Moçambique* case to exclude actions relating to foreign intellectual property rights.[104] The historical distinction between *local* and *transitory* actions was resurrected. Any question of validity of title to, or infringement of, a foreign copyright, patent or trade mark was a local one for the courts of the country by whose law the copyright, patent or trade mark was created, such rights being territorially limited to that country. It followed that the question raised in the case, namely whether the defendant was entitled to copyright under the law of the USA, was not justiciable in the English courts. This misunderstands the *Moçambique* case, which was decided on a point of substance as to whether an English court could give an effective judgment and not on the basis of a procedural distinction between *local* and *transitory* actions.[105]

Moreover, policy considerations for and against having such a limitation on jurisdiction were ignored.[106] The Court of Appeal in *Pearce v Ove Arup Partnership Ltd*[107] has said, in effect, that the views of VINELOTT J should be confined to the facts of the case before him, ie a case where a declaration was sought and the issue was as to the existence and validity of the right, and that the *Tyburn* decision is of little or no assistance in the different situation where there is an action for infringement abroad of a foreign intellectual property right, the existence and validity of which are not in issue. However, the Court of Appeal found it unnecessary to decide whether such an action was justiciable in the English courts. Nor was *Tyburn* thought to be helpful in a case where it was held that the court in the exercise of its equitable in personam jurisdiction could order a person, who had acquired intellectual property situated abroad with sufficient notice of an earlier obligation to transfer the property to another, to assign that property to its equitable owner,

---

[100] See COLEMAN J's reliance on *Arkwright Mutual Insurance Co v Bryanston Insurance Co Ltd* [1990] 2 QB 649 at 663, a pre-*Owusu* case, which should now be regarded as wrong.

[101] Supra, p 333.

[102] Trooboff in McLachlan and Nygh, Chapter 8; Austin (1997) 113 LQR 321; Fentiman [1997] CLJ 503; Fawcett and Torremans, pp 283–295; Lipstein [2002] CLJ 295.

[103] [1991] Ch 75; Carter (1990) 61 BYBIL 400; following the High Court of Australia's decisions in *Potter v Broken Hill Pty Co Ltd* (1906) 3 CLR 479; *Steinhardt & Son Ltd v Meth* (1961) 105 CLR 440. See also *Atkinson Footwear Ltd v Hodgskin* (1995) 31 IPR 186.

[104] Such rights are not classified as immovable property, accordingly s 30 of the 1982 Act does not apply: *Coin Controls Ltd v Suzo International (UK) Ltd* [1999] Ch 33; *Pearce v Ove Arup Partnership Ltd* [1997] Ch 293, (LLOYD J), appeal allowed on a different point [2000] Ch 403, CA; *R Griggs Group Ltd v Evans* [2004] EWHC 1088 (Ch) at [119], [2005] Ch 153; Fawcett and Torremans, pp 281–283, 287.

[105] Supra, pp 478–479.

[106] Fawcett and Torremans, pp 290–293.

[107] [2000] Ch 403, CA; Briggs (1999) 70 BYBIL 337; Harris [1999] LMCLQ 360.

provided that the English equity was not extinguished by foreign law. This was especially so where the original contract was governed by English law and the rights existed in manifold jurisdictions.[108]

What is clear is that in cases where jurisdiction is based on the Brussels/Lugano system there is no limitation in relation to the infringement of foreign intellectual property rights,[109] at least where invalidity is not raised as a defence and these rights are created in a European Community/EFTA State and probably also even where they are created outside such a State.[110] In cases where jurisdiction is based on the traditional English rules, it is submitted that there should be no limitation on jurisdiction in respect of actions involving either the infringement or the validity of foreign intellectual property rights. It is understandable that judges should be reluctant to decide whether a person has infringed a foreign intellectual property right or whether that right is a valid one,[111] but it is always possible for a stay of the proceedings to be granted using the doctrine of *forum non conveniens*. An inflexible blanket limitation on jurisdiction is both unnecessary and undesirable.

3. JURISDICTION OVER THE PARTIES

(a) Persons who cannot invoke the jurisdiction

The one person precluded from suing in an English court is an alien enemy. Before a person can bear this character there must, of course, be a state of war between the United Kingdom and an enemy country at the time of the attempted proceedings, and whether the countries are still at war despite the cessation of hostilities is conclusively settled by a certificate from the Secretary of State for Foreign and Commonwealth Affairs.[112] Given a state of war, however, the question whether a person is an alien enemy does not depend on his nationality but on where he resides or carries on business. A British subject or a neutral who is voluntarily resident, or who is carrying on business, in enemy territory or in territory under the effective control of the enemy is treated as an alien enemy and is in the same position as a subject of hostile nationality resident in hostile territory.[113] A person of hostile nationality who is within the Queen's peace, as, for example, when he is resident in England under a cartel[114] or by permission of the Crown,[115] is temporarily free from his enemy character and may invoke the jurisdiction.[116]

---

[108] *R Griggs Group Ltd v Evans* [2004] EWHC 1088 (Ch) at [139]–[140], [2005] Ch 153.

[109] *Fort Dodge Animal Health Ltd v Akzo Nobel NV* [1998] FSR 222, CA; Dutson [1998] LMCLQ 505; *Coin Controls Ltd v Suzo International (UK) Ltd* [1999] Ch 33; *Pearce v Ove Arup Partnership Ltd* [2000] Ch 403, CA; Fawcett and Torremans, pp 190–193; supra, pp 282–283.

[110] Fawcett and Torremans, pp 193–195; Briggs (1997) 113 LQR 364 at 366; Dutson (1997) 46 ICLQ 918 at 921.

[111] See *Plastus Kreativ AB v Minnesota Mining and Manufacturing Co* [1995] RPC 438.

[112] *R v Bottrill* [1947] KB 41, CA; *Amin v Brown* [2005] EWHC 1670 (Ch), [2006] IL Pr 5.

[113] *Porter v Freudenberg* [1915] 1 KB 857 at 869; *Sovracht (vo) v Van Udens Scheepvart en Agentuur Maatschappij (NV Gebr)* [1943] AC 203. See McNair (1942) 58 LQR 191. For the purposes of the Trading with the Enemy Act 1939, which penalises persons trading with the enemy, *de facto* residence, though not voluntary, is sufficient: *Vamvakas v Custodian of Enemy Property* [1952] 2 QB 183.

[114] *The Hoop* (1799) 1 Ch Rob 196 at 201.

[115] Eg when he was registered under the Aliens Restriction Act 1914: *Princess Thurn and Taxis v Moffit* [1915] 1 Ch 58; *Schaffenius v Goldberg* [1916] 1 KB 284.

[116] *Johnstone v Pedlar* [1921] 2 AC 262.

An alien enemy can neither initiate an action nor continue one that was commenced before hostilities.[117] The disability of suing is based on public policy, but there are no considerations of public policy that make it desirable to suspend actions *against* alien enemies, and it is now well established that they may be sued.[118] Moreover, when sued they can plead a set-off in diminution of the claim of the claimant; they can take all the usual procedural steps, and they are at liberty to challenge an adverse judgment by appealing to a higher tribunal.[119]

(b) Persons who may claim exemption from the jurisdiction[120]

(i) Sovereigns and sovereign states[121]

The basic rule at common law was that a foreign sovereign or sovereign foreign state was immune from the jurisdiction of the English courts, though the court would take jurisdiction if the sovereign submitted thereto. This immunity extended both to direct actions against the sovereign and to indirect actions involving his property. However, this whole question was the subject of the European Convention on State Immunity (1972)[122] which led to the law being placed on a statutory basis by the State Immunity Act 1978.[123] Legislative authority for immunity is essential. An argument that the European Community should have an independent claim to sovereign immunity by analogy to a foreign state has been rejected because of the lack of legislative authority for this.[124] When a question of immunity arises under the 1978 Act this must be tried as a preliminary issue before the substantive action can proceed.[125] Before turning to the provisions of the 1978 Act, it must be mentioned that there is now a United Nations Convention on State Immunity.[126]

---

117 *Porter v Freudenberg*, supra. An alien enemy, respondent to a petition for the revocation of a patent, has been allowed, however, to amend his specification by way of disclaimer, since this constitutes a defence to the petition: *Re Stahlwerk Becker Aktiengesellschaft's Patent* [1917] 2 Ch 272. His right of action is generally abrogated, but sometimes merely suspended; see *Ertel Bieber & Co v Rio Tinto Co* [1918] AC 260; *Schering Ltd v Stockholms Enskilda Bank Aktiebolag* [1946] AC 219.

118 *Robinson & Co v Continental Insurance Co of Mannheim* [1915] 1 KB 155; *Porter v Freudenberg*, supra.

119 *Porter v Freudenberg* [1915] 1 KB 857.

120 See Fox, *The Law of State Immunity*; Lewis, *State and Diplomatic Immunity* (1989) 3rd edn; Sinclair (1980) II Hague Recueil 114; Watts (1994-III) 247 Hague Recueil 13; Marasinghe (1991) 54 MLR 664.

121 We are concerned here with recognised states. On the question whether an unrecognised state can sue or be sued in an English court, see *Gur Corpn v Trust Bank of Africa Ltd* [1987] QB 599; Warbrick (1987) 50 MLR 84; Beck (1987) 36 ICLQ 348. On the recognition of a foreign regime as the government of a state, see *Republic of Somalia v Woodhouse Drake & Carey (Suisse) SA* [1993] QB 54, Kingsbury (1993) 109 LQR 377; Leslie [1997] Jur Rev 110; Crawford [1993] CLJ 4; *Sierra Leone Telecommunications Co Ltd v Barclays Bank plc* [1998] 2 All ER 821.

122 Cmnd 5081; Sinclair (1973) 22 ICLQ 254; Mann (1973) 36 MLR 18.

123 See Bowett [1978] CLJ 193; White (1979) 42 MLR 72; Mann (1979) 50 BYBIL 43; Delaume (1979) 73 AJIL 185; Lewis [1980] LMCLQ 1. For similar legislation abroad see Foreign States Immunities Act 1981 (South Africa); Foreign Sovereign Immunities Act 1976 (USA); and State Immunity Act 1982 (Canada). See, though, for New Zealand and Australia, where the common law still applies: *Governor of Pitcairn v Sutton* [1995] 1 NZLR 426; *Controller and Auditor-General v Davison* [1996] 2 NZLR 278, CA; and *Reid v Republic of Nauru* [1993] 1 VR 251. The 1978 Act also implements the provisions of the 1926 Brussels Convention on Immunity of State-owned Ships, together with the Protocol thereto of 1934.

124 *J H Rayner (Mincing Lane) Ltd v Department of Trade and Industry* [1989] Ch 72 at 198–203, 223, 252–253, CA; affd [1990] 2 AC 418, 516, HL without deciding this point.

125 Ibid, at 194, 252; affd by HL, supra, without deciding this point.

126 United Nations Convention on Jurisdictional Immunities of States and Their Property of 2004; Denza (2006) 55 ICLQ 395; Fox (2006) 55 ICLQ 399; Gardiner (2006) 55 ICLQ 407. Criticised by Hall (2006) 55

Consultations are taking place on whether the United Kingdom should sign and eventually ratify this Convention. Related to this, is the question whether ratification would require amendment to the 1978 Act. In the meantime, the Convention is regarded by the English courts as powerfully demonstrating international thinking on state immunity.[127]

(a) Scope of the State Immunity Act 1978

The immunity conferred by the 1978 Act is not limited to those states which are parties to the 1972 Convention but is world-wide in effect.[128] It applies to any foreign or Commonwealth state, other than the United Kingdom, to the sovereign or other head of that state[129] in his public capacity,[130] to the government of that state and to any department thereof.[131] An official or agent of a foreign state enjoys state immunity *ratione materiae* in respect of his acts of a sovereign or governmental nature.[132] Applying this principle, there is an absolute right to claim immunity, even in respect of civil claims against state officials for systematic torture committed outside the country of suit.[133] Provision is made for the application of the Act by Order in Council to the constituent territories of a federal state.[134] This is because such constituent territories do not automatically enjoy immunity under the 1972 Convention but only if the federal state so declares.[135] A difficult question before the passing of the 1978 Act was to determine whether a state corporation such as a state bank, or the US Shipping Board, could properly claim to be an emanation of the foreign state and thus entitled to immunity.[136] This problem is

---

ICLQ 411; McGregor (2006) 55 ICLQ 411. The International Law Commission has produced in 2001 draft articles on the Responsibility of States for Internationally Wrongful Acts.

[127] *Jones v The Kingdom of Saudi Arabia* [2006] UKHL 26 at [8], [2007] 1 AC 270, following *AIG Capital Partners Inc v Republic of Kazakhstan* [2005] EWHC 2239 at [80] (Comm), [2006] 1 All ER 284.

[128] For the provisions as to recognition of foreign judgments see, infra, pp 587–588.

[129] For proposals for reform, see the Resolution of the Institute of International Law of 2001 on "The Immunities from Jurisdiction and Execution of Heads of State and Heads of Government in International Law", on which see Fox (2002) 51 ICLQ 119.

[130] A sovereign, or head of state, when acting outside his public capacity, is entitled to immunity under the Diplomatic Privileges Act 1964 (infra, p 502); 1978 Act, s 20(1)(a); *BCCI v Price Waterhouse* [1997] 4 All ER 108; Hopkins [1998] CLJ 4; *Harb v Aziz* [2005] EWCA Civ 632; *Aziz v Aziz* [2007] EWCA Civ 712 at [57].

[131] 1978 Act, s 14(1). For the immunity of a department see *Jones v Ministry of the Interior of the Kingdom of Saudi Arabia* [2006] UKHL 26, [2007] 1 AC 270.

[132] *Propend Finance Pty Ltd v Sing* (1997) 111 ILR 611, CA; *Jones v Ministry of the Interior of the Kingdom of Saudi Arabia* [2006] UKHL 26, [2007] 1 AC 270, discussed infra, pp 495–496; *Grovit v De Nederlandsche Bank* [2005] EWHC 2944 (QB), [2006] 1 Lloyd's Rep 636, affd by the Court of Appeal without any discussion of the state immunity point [2007] EWCA Civ 953, [2008] 1 WLR 51; *Re P (Diplomatic Immunity: Jurisdiction)* [1998] 1 FLR 1026. See also *Walker (Litigation Guardian of) v Bank of New York* (1994) 111 DLR (4th) 186, Ont CA; *Jaffe v Miller* (1993) 103 DLR (4th) 315, Ont CA. See also Art 2(1)(b)(iv) of the UN Convention of 2004. For the immunity of an official at common law see *Holland v Lampen-Wolfe* [2000] 1 WLR 1573, HL.

[133] The *Jones* case, supra. See also obiter dicta in *R v Bow Street Magistrate, ex p Pinochet (No 3)* [2000] 1 AC 147, 264 (per Lord HUTTON), 278 (per Lord MILLETT), 280–281 (per Lord PHILLIPS). The human rights concerns involved are discussed infra, pp 494–496. See generally Fox [2006] EHRLR 142. For the position where extradition of a former head of state is sought for criminal offences of torture, see *R v Bow Street Magistrate, ex p Pinochet (No 1)* [2000] 1 AC 61, HL; *R v Bow Street Magistrate, ex p Pinochet (No 3)* [2000] 1 AC 147, HL.

[134] 1978 Act, s 14(5); SI 1993/2809. For the situation where an order has not been made, see s 14(6); *BCCI v Price Waterhouse*, supra.

[135] Art 28, see Sinclair (1973) 22 ICLQ 254, 279–280.

[136] *Trendtex Trading Corpn v Central Bank of Nigeria* [1977] QB 529; *C Czarnikow Ltd v Rolimpex* [1979] AC 351; *I Congreso del Partido* [1983] 1 AC 244 at 258.

dealt with in the 1978 Act through the use of the concept of "a separate entity".[137] Such an entity, being distinct from the executive organs of the government of the foreign state and being capable of suing or being sued, is not entitled to immunity unless the proceedings relate to something done by the "separate entity" in the exercise of sovereign authority and the circumstances were such that the state would have been immune.[138] The question of when a "separate entity" is exercising sovereign authority came before the House of Lords[139] where it was held that this term refers to the common law concept of *acta jure imperii*,[140] and that Iraqi Airways was so acting when it removed aircraft from Kuwait following the Iraqi invasion. The airline was closely involved with the State of Iraq in the last stage of an enterprise which entailed both the seizure and removal of the aircraft.[141] However, the subsequent retention and use of the aircraft did not amount to so acting, even though this was done in consequence of a legislative decree vesting the aircraft in the airline.[142] Indeed, once this decree was passed the situation changed, and the acts of Iraqi Airways were no longer in the exercise of sovereign authority but were commercial acts. In subsequent proceedings, it was held that perjured evidence had been given to the House of Lords and that Iraqi Airways had even earlier than this done acts which were no longer in the exercise of sovereign authority, namely engaging in the process of the absorption of the Kuwaiti aircraft into the Iraqi Airways fleet by registration, repainting and insurance of some of the aircraft with a view to their subsequent commercial use.[143]

Part I of the 1978 Act (proceedings in the United Kingdom by or against other states) does not apply to proceedings relating to anything done by or in relation to the armed forces of another state whilst present in the United Kingdom.[144] In such cases immunity depends upon common law principles, including the one referred to above, namely that a foreign sovereign is only entitled to immunity in respect of acts within the sphere of sovereign activity, ie *acta jure imperii*.[145] There is no single test for determining this. It requires consideration of the whole of the context in which the claimant's claim was made.[146] Relevant factors can include where the act happened, whom it involved and what kind of act it was (ie whether it was wholly military or primarily private

---

[137] This probably refers to a "separate entity" of a state: *Kuwait Airways Corpn v Iraqi Airways Co* [1995] 1 WLR 1147 at 1158, HL.

[138] 1978 Act, ss 14(1), (2). Employees of the separate entity are also entitled to immunity, subject to the same provisos: *Grovit v De Nederlandsche Bank* [2005] EWHC 2944 (QB), [2006] 1 Lloyd's Rep 636; affd by the Court of Appeal without any discussion of the state immunity point [2007] EWCA Civ 953, [2008] 1 WLR 51.

[139] *Kuwait Airways Corpn v Iraqi Airways Co* [1995] 1 WLR 1147; Fox (1996) 112 LQR 186; reversing in part [1995] 1 Lloyd's Rep 25, CA, Staker (1994) 66 BYBIL 496, Fox (1994) 110 LQR 199; Marks [1994] CLJ 213; Talmon (1995) 15 OJLS 295; for criticism of the first instance decision of EVANS J denying immunity, see Fox (1994) 43 ICLQ 193 at 196.

[140] The *Kuwait Airways* case, supra, at 1156.

[141] Ibid, at 1163.

[142] Lords MUSTILL and SLYNN dissenting. For the subsequent conversion action see *Kuwait Airways Corpn v Iraqi Airways Co (Nos 4 and 5)* [2002] UKHL 19, [2002] 2 AC 883.

[143] *Kuwait Airways Corpn v Iraqi Airways Co (No 11)* [2003] EWHC 31, [2003] 1 Lloyd's Rep 448. This separate fraud action follows *Kuwait Airways Corpn v Iraqi Airways Co (No 8) (Petition for Variation of Order)* [2001] 1 WLR 429, HL.

[144] The 1978 Act, s 16(2).

[145] *Littrell v United States of America (No 2)* [1995] 1 WLR 82, CA; Staker (1994) BYBIL 491; Collier [1995] CLJ 7; applied in *Holland v Lampen-Wolfe* [2000] 1 WLR 1573, HL.

[146] *Littrell v United States of America (No 2)*, supra, at 95 (per HOFFMANN LJ).

or commercial).[147] After considering these factors it was held that the US Government was immune from suit in an action for personal injury brought by a US serviceman who was treated at a US military hospital in England, the operation of which was required for the maintenance of the US armed forces in the United Kingdom.[148] Similarly there was immunity from suit in an action for defamation brought by a US citizen, a civilian instructor at a US military base in England, against another US citizen, who was a civilian education services officer at the base, the provision within a military base of education for military personnel being part of a state's sovereign function of maintaining its armed forces.[149]

The basic principle of the 1978 Act is that a foreign state is immune from the jurisdiction[150] of the English courts and effect is to be given to that immunity whether or not the state appears in the proceedings.[151]

(b) State immunity and human rights[152]

The European Court of Human Rights (ECtHR) in *Al-Adsani v United Kingdom* has accepted that, in cases of sovereign immunity, the right of access to a court under Article 6(1) of the European Convention on Human Rights is engaged.[153] It follows that, to be compatible with Article 6(1), the limitation on jurisdiction under the doctrine of sovereign immunity has to pursue a legitimate aim and be proportionate.[154] The ECtHR considered the application of these criteria in the context of a civil claim against the State of Kuwait alleging torture in that state. A majority of the ECtHR said that "the grant of sovereign immunity to a State in civil proceedings pursues the legitimate aim of complying with international law to promote comity and good relations between States through the respect of another State's sovereignty".[155] Moreover, the restriction is proportionate to the aim pursued since state immunity reflects "a generally accepted rule of international law".[156] The majority of the ECtHR concluded that the use of state immunity, even in these circumstances, does not constitute an unjustified restriction on the claimant's right of access to the courts as laid down by Article 6(1).[157] This confirms the correctness of an

---

[147] *Littrell v United States of America (No 2)*, supra at 95 (per HOFFMANN LJ).

[148] Ibid.

[149] *Holland v Lampen-Wolfe* [2000] 1 WLR 1573, HL; Tomonori (2001) 64 MLR 472; Yang [2001] CLJ 17. The immunity was claimed by the USA on behalf of the defendant.

[150] This includes English proceedings for recognition of a foreign judgment against a foreign state granted in that state: *AIC Ltd v Federal Government of Nigeria* [2003] EWHC 1357 (QB).

[151] 1978 Act, s 1.

[152] Lloyd Jones (2003) 52 ICLQ 463.

[153] Judgment of 21 November 2001 at [52]; (2001) 34 EHRR 273, ECtHR. See also *McElhinney v Ireland*, Judgment of 21 November 2001 at [26]; [2002] 34 EHRR 13, ECtHR; *Fogarty v United Kingdom*, Judgment of 21 November 2001 at [28]; [2002] 34 EHRR 12, ECtHR; App No 50021/00, *Kalogeropoulou v Greece and Germany*, 12 December 2002; Garnett (2002) 118 LQR 367; Voyiakis (2003) 52 ICLQ 293.

[154] *Al-Adsani v United Kingdom*, supra, at [53]; following *Waite and Kennedy v Germany*, Judgment of 18 February 1999; (1999) 30 EHRR 261—immunity granted to an international organisation (the European Space Agency). See also *NCF and AG v Italy* (1995) 111 ILR 153, European Commission on Human Rights.

[155] *Al-Adsani v United Kingdom*, supra, at [54]. See also the *McElhinney Case*, supra, at [35]; the *Fogarty Case*, supra, at [34].

[156] *Al-Adsani v United Kingdom*, supra at [56]–[57]. See also the *McElhinney Case*, supra at [35]–[40]; the *Fogarty Case*, supra at [38]; and *Holland v Lampen-Wolfe* [2000] 1 WLR 1573 at 1578–1579 (per Lord HOPE), 1581 (per Lord CLYDE).

[157] *Al-Adsani v United Kingdom*, supra; the *Jones* case, supra.

earlier decision of the Court of Appeal that state immunity applies even where the sovereign acts outside the law of nations by violating fundamental human rights by torturing prisoners.[158] According to the ECtHR in *McElhinney v Ireland*, neither was there a breach of Article 6(1) where state immunity was used to deny access to the Irish courts in a case involving a civil claim in tort brought against the British government following acts by its agent (a soldier) within the sphere of *de jure imperii*.[159] The same Court in *Fogarty v United Kingdom* decided that there was no breach of Article 6(1) where state immunity was used to deny access to the English courts in a case involving a civil claim for discrimination brought against the US government by an applicant for re-employment at the US embassy.[160]

The English courts in *Jones v Ministry of the Interior of the Kingdom of Saudi Arabia*[161] were faced with a more complex case than *Al-Adsani*. Following alleged torture abroad, civil claims for damages were brought against both a foreign state, the Kingdom of Saudi Arabia, and individual defendants who were officials of that state.[162] The House of Lords agreed with the Court of Appeal[163] that the Kingdom was entitled to immunity.[164] But, unlike the Court of Appeal,[165] it regarded the position of individual defendants as being the same as that of the Kingdom[166] with the result that immunity also applied in relation to the claims against the individual defendants. On a straightforward application of the State Immunity Act 1978, immunity would apply in relation both to the Kingdom and to the individual defendants.[167] The claimants argued that to apply the 1978 Act would be incompatible with the right of access to the English courts provided by Article 6. Their Lordships expressed doubts[168] as to the correctness of the unanimous decision of the ECtHR in *Al-Adsani* that Article 6 was engaged in a case of state immunity but were prepared to assume that it was.[169] The claimants sought to show that the restriction imposed by the law of State immunity was disproportionate by arguing that the proscription of torture by international law, having the authority of a peremptory norm,[170] precludes the grant of immunity to states or individuals sued for committing acts of torture since such acts cannot be governmental acts or exercises of state authority entitled to

---

[158] *Al-Adsani v Government of Kuwait (No 2)* (1996) 107 ILR 536, CA; Fox (1994) 138 SJ 854.

[159] Judgment of 21 November 2001; [2002] 34 EHRR 13, ECtHR.

[160] Ibid, at 12, ECtHR.

[161] [2006] UKHL 26, [2007] 1 AC 270. See also *Grovit v De Nederlandsche Bank* [2005] EWHC 2944 (QB), [2006] 1 Lloyd's Rep 636; affd without discussion of the state immunity point [2007] EWCA Civ 953, [2008] 1 WLR 51; *Republic of Ecuador v Occidental Exploration and Production Co* [2005] EWCA Civ 1116 at [49], [2006] QB 432.

[162] Under the UN Convention on State Immunity it is unclear whether such a claim would attract immunity, see Art 6(2)(b).

[163] [2004] EWCA Civ 1394, [2005] QB 669; Fox (2005) 121 LQR 353 and (2006) EHRLR 142; Yang (2005) 64 CLJ 1. Distinguished in *Republic of Ecuador v Occidental Exploration and Production Co* [2005] EWCA Civ 1116 at [49], [2006] QB 432.

[164] [2006] UKHL 26 at [29] (per Lord BINGHAM), at [36] (per Lord HOFFMANN), [2007] 1 AC 270. Lords RODGER at [103], WALKER at [104] and CARSWELL at [105] concurred with these two speeches.

[165] [2004] EWCA Civ 1394, [2005] QB 669 at [92].

[166] [2006] UKHL 26 at [10]–[13] (per Lord BINGHAM), at [66] (per Lord HOFFMANN).

[167] Ibid, at [13] (per Lord BINGHAM). See also Lord HOFFMANN at [66].

[168] Approving the obiter dicta of Lord MILLETT in *Holland v Lampen-Wolfe* [2000] 1 WLR 1573 at 1588. Cf MANCE LJ in the Court of Appeal in the *Jones* case, supra, at [82].

[169] [2006] UKHL 26 at [14] (per Lord BINGHAM), [64] (per Lord HOFFMANN), [2007] 1 AC 270.

[170] It was common ground that this was so, ibid, at [13] (per Lord BINGHAM).

protection of state immunity *ratione materiae*.[171] The House of Lords was unable to accept that torture cannot be a governmental or official act.[172] Immunity under the 1978 Act was not disproportionate as inconsistent with a peremptory norm of international law and, accordingly, there was no infringement of the claimants' rights under Article 6.[173] In a much easier case, immunity granted to employees of the Dutch Central Bank, who were sued, along with the Bank, for defamation, was not disproportionate where there was an effective remedy in the Netherlands and the gravity of the allegations against the defendants was much less than in the *Jones* case.[174]

(c) Exceptions from immunity

The State Immunity Act 1978 provides a substantial list of exceptions from state immunity. Section 3 provides an exception of major significance. A foreign state is not immune as respects any proceedings relating to a commercial transaction entered into by that state,[175] bearing in mind the wide definition of state already discussed. Until fairly recently, the position at common law was that a foreign state was immune even with regard to its purely commercial activities.[176] However, this wide immunity was rejected in a series of cases, culminating in two decisions of the House of Lords.[177] Instead, the "restrictive"[178] doctrine of immunity was applied, both to actions in rem and in personam, under which a foreign state was entitled to immunity in respect of its governmental acts but not in respect of its commercial transactions.

These common law developments are now, in substance, embodied in the 1978 Act.[179] "Commercial transaction" is defined[180] to include not only contracts for the supply of goods or services but also the provision of finance through loans and the like, and any guarantee or indemnity in respect of such transactions. Even more widely it extends to "any other transaction or activity (whether of a commercial, industrial, financial, professional or other similar character) into which a state enters or in which it engages

---

171 Ibid, at [17] (per Lord Bɪɴɢʜᴀᴍ).

172 [2006] UKHL 26 at [19], [27] (per Lord Bɪɴɢʜᴀᴍ), at [85] (per Lord Hᴏғғᴍᴀɴɴ), [2007] 1 AC 270.

173 Ibid at [28] (per Lord Bɪɴɢʜᴀᴍ).

174 *Grovit v De Nederlandsche Bank* [2005] EWHC 2944 (QB), [2006] 1 Lloyd's Rep 636; affd without discussion of the state immunity point [2007] EWCA Civ 953, [2008] 1 WLR 51. See also the *Holland* case, supra, at 1578–1579 (per Lord Hᴏᴘᴇ), 1581 (per Lord Cʟʏᴅᴇ).

175 S 3(1)(a).

176 Eg *Kahan v Pakistan Federation* [1951] 2 KB 1003; *Baccus SRL v Servicio Nacional del Trigo* [1957] 1 QB 438.

177 *The Philippine Admiral* [1977] AC 373; *Trendtex Trading Corpn v Central Bank of Nigeria* [1977] QB 529; Lewis [1979] LMCLQ 460; *Hispano Americana Mercantil SA v Central Bank of Nigeria* [1979] 2 Lloyd's Rep 277; *Planmount Ltd v Republic of Zaire* [1981] 1 All ER 1110; *I Congreso del Partido* [1983] 1 AC 244; Fox (1982) 98 LQR 94; Mann (1982) 31 ICLQ 573; *Alcom Ltd v Republic of Colombia* [1984] AC 580; Ghandi (1984) 47 MLR 597; Lloyd Jones [1984] CLJ 222; Crawford (1984) 55 BYBIL 340; Fox (1985) 34 ICLQ 115. See also *Empresa Exportadora de Azúcar v Industria Azucarera Nacional SA, The Playa Larga* [1983] 2 Lloyd's Rep 171.

178 See generally, Sornarajah (1982) 31 ICLQ 661; Crawford (1983) 54 BYBIL 75.

179 See *Planmount Ltd v Republic of Zaire* [1981] 1 All ER 1110; *I Congreso Del Partido* [1983] 1 AC 244 at 260; *Alcom Ltd v Republic of Colombia* [1984] AC 580.

180 S 3(3). See *Alcom Ltd v Republic of Colombia* [1984] AC 580 at 601–603; *Arab Republic of Egypt v Gamal-Eldin* [1996] 2 All ER 237 at 247; *Svenska Petroleum Exploration AB v Government of the Republic of Lithuania (No 2)* [2006] EWCA Civ 1529 at [129]–[131], [2007] QB 886; Kawharu [2007] LMCLQ 136. Cf the definition under Art 2(2) of the UN Convention on State Immunity. On the relevance of the common law cases, see Fox (1982) 98 LQR 94. For the position in the USA, see *Saudi Arabia v Nelson* [1993] IL Pr 555, SC.

otherwise than in the exercise of sovereign authority".[181] Indeed, this commercial exception from immunity extends further to include any obligation of the foreign state which by virtue of a contract, whether or not a commercial transaction, falls to be performed in whole or in part in the United Kingdom.[182] This would include contracts made in the exercise of sovereign authority to be performed here, such as contracts for the building of warships. There must also be "proceedings relating to" a commercial transaction. This refers to claims arising out of the transaction.[183] These will usually be contractual claims. It does not cover tortious claims arising independently of the transaction but in the course of its performance.[184]

There is a variety of other exceptions to immunity. In the case of contracts of employment, there is no immunity in respect of proceedings between the state and an individual where the contract was made in the United Kingdom or the work is to be wholly or partly performed here.[185] There is no immunity as regards proceedings for death or personal injury or damage to or loss of tangible property caused by an act or omission in the United Kingdom;[186] nor is there immunity in the case of proceedings relating to United Kingdom patents, trade marks, and similar rights belonging to the state, or to the alleged infringement in the United Kingdom by the foreign state of such rights, including copyright.[187]

Immunity is excluded in the case of proceedings relating to the state's interest in immovables in England or to an obligation arising from such an interest.[188] Thus the French government, who were tenants of a house in London which was not being used for the purpose of a diplomatic mission,[189] did not have immunity in respect of an action by the landlords for damages for loss sustained as a result of an alleged refusal by the tenants to

---

[181] S 3(3)(c). See *Svenska Petroleum Exploration AB v Government of the Republic of Lithuania (No 2)* [2006] EWCA Civ 1529 at [132]–[133], [2007] QB 886. Special provision is made in s 10 for ships that are used for commercial purposes.

[182] S 3(1)(b). See *J H Rayner (Mincing Lane) Ltd v Department of Trade and Industry* [1989] Ch 72 at 194–195, 222, 252; affd by HL [1990] 2 AC 418 without discussion of this point. The exception from immunity provided by s 3 is inapplicable if the parties to the dispute are states or have otherwise agreed in writing or if the contract (not being a commercial transaction) was made in the territory of the foreign state and the obligation is governed by its administrative law: s 3(2).

[183] *Holland v Lampen-Wolfe* [2000] 1 WLR 1573 at 1587 (per Lord MILLETT); *Svenska Petroleum Exploration AB v Government of the Republic of Lithuania (No 2)* [2006] EWCA Civ 1529 at [134]–[137], [2007] QB 886. See also *Bouzari v Iran (Islamic Republic)* (2004) 243 DLR (4th) 406, Ont CA.

[184] *Holland v Lampen-Wolfe*, supra. Proceedings for registration of a foreign judgment relate to the judgment and not to a commercial transaction, even if the transaction underlying the judgment was commercial: *AIC Ltd v Federal Government of Nigeria* [2003] EWHC 1357 (QB).

[185] S 4(1); see generally Fox (1995) 66 BYBIL 97; Garnett (2005) 54 ICLQ 705. This is subject to exception in the case of contrary agreement in writing or where the employee is a national of the foreign state or is neither a United Kingdom national nor resident in England: s 4(2), (3) and (5), as amended by Zimbabwe Act 1979, s 6(3) and Sch 3, and by British Nationality Act 1981, s 52(6) and Sch 7 and see the transitional provision in s 23(3)(b). See *Sengupta v Republic of India* [1983] ICR 221. See also *Arab Republic of Egypt v Gamal-Eldin* [1996] 2 All ER 237. S 4(1) is also subject to s 16 (diplomatic immunity).

[186] S 5. See *United States of America v Friedland* (1999) 182 DLR (4th) 614, Ont CA; *Schreiber v Canada (Attorney General)* (2002) 216 DLR (4th) 513, Sup ct of Canada; *Bouzari v Iran (Islamic Republic)* (2004) 243 DLR (4th) 406, Ont CA. For the position in Ireland see *McElhinney v Williams* [1994] 2 ILRM 115.

[187] S 7. See *A Ltd v B Bank and Bank of X* [1997] FSR 165.

[188] S 6(1); and see *The Charkieh* (1873) LR 4 A & E 59 at 97; *Alcom Ltd v Republic of Colombia* [1984] AC 580 at 603.

[189] See s 16(1)(b); discussed infra, p 504.

permit entry to carry out repairs.[190] Furthermore, the state has no immunity in the case of proceedings relating to its interest in other immovable or movable property by way of succession, gift or *bona vacantia*.[191] There is no requirement that the property be situated in England but the circumstances in which a judgment based on this exception must be recognised elsewhere are limited.[192] In the case of the administration of estates or trusts, or insolvency, the court's jurisdiction is unaffected by the fact that a foreign state may claim an interest in the property.[193] There is also an exception to immunity in the case of a state which is a member of a corporate or unincorporated body, or a partnership, which has members other than states and which is incorporated or constituted under United Kingdom law or is controlled from or has its principal place of business in the United Kingdom.[194] There is no immunity as regards proceedings for VAT, customs or excise duties, or rates on commercial premises.[195]

An important practical exception from immunity is that relating to ships in use, or intended for use, for commercial purposes. In the case of such ships, there is no immunity in Admiralty proceedings (or proceedings on a claim which could be made the subject of Admiralty proceedings) relating to an action in rem against a ship belonging to the foreign state or to an action in personam for enforcing a claim in connection with such a ship.[196]

Finally, there is no immunity if the state has submitted to the jurisdiction of the courts;[197] and there is a related exception in the case where a state has agreed in writing to submit a dispute to arbitration,[198] for there is then no immunity with regard to court proceedings

---

[190] *Intpro Properties (UK) Ltd v Sauvel* [1983] QB 1019.

[191] S 6(2).

[192] See 1978 Act, s 19(3) for the limitations on the recognition here of foreign judgments involving this exemption; and see Art 20(3) of the European Convention on State Immunity (1972) and s 31 of the Civil Jurisdiction and Judgments Act 1982, discussed infra, pp 588–589.

[193] S 6(3); *Re Rafidain Bank* [1992] BCLC 301; cf *United States of America and Republic of France v Dollfus Mieg et Cie SA and Bank of England* [1952] AC 582 at 617–618.

[194] S 8. See *Maclaine Watson & Co Ltd v International Tin Council* [1989] Ch 253 at 282–283.

[195] S 11.

[196] S 10(1), (2). Cf *The Guiseppe Di Vitorio* [1998] 1 Lloyd's Rep 136, CA. Special provision is made for actions in rem against one ship in connection with another ship, actions concerning cargo, or proceedings where the foreign state is a party to the Brussels Convention covering the Immunity of State-owned Ships (1926): ss 10(3)–(6), 17(1).

[197] S 2(1); *Svenska Petroleum Exploration AB v Government of the Republic of Lithuania (No 2)* [2006] EWCA Civ 1529 at [124]–[128], [2007] QB 886; *Donegal International Ltd v Zambia* [2007] EWHC 197 (Comm), [2007] 1 Lloyd's Rep 397. A state is deemed to have submitted if it has instituted the proceedings (s 2(3)(a), *Schreiber v Canada (Attorney General)* (2002) 216 DLR (4th) 513, Sup ct of Canada) or has taken any step in the proceedings (s 2(3)(b)) and this would include where it seeks a stay on the grounds of *forum non conveniens*: *A Co Ltd v B Co Ltd and Republic of Z*, 1993 (unreported); *Kuwait Airways Corpn v Iraqi Airways Co* [1995] 1 Lloyd's Rep 25, CA; revsd, but not on this point, by the House of Lords [1995] 1 WLR 1147; cf *Jaffe v Miller* (1993) 103 DLR (4th) 315. For the purposes of s 2(3)(b) action taken by a member of the mission or its solicitors must be authorised by the head of mission: *Aziz v Republic of Yemen* [2005] EWCA Civ 745. For counterclaims see s 2(6); *United States of America v Friedland* (1999) 182 DLR (4th) 614, Ont CA; *Schreiber v Federal Republic of Germany* (2001) 196 DLR (4th) 281, Ont CA; affd by SC of Canada in *Schreiber v Canada (Attorney General)* (2002) 216 DLR (4th) 513. Submission does not imply submission to the enforcement jurisdiction of the courts; see s 13(3), and *Alcom Ltd v Republic of Colombia* [1984] AC 580 at 600.

[198] *Svenska Petroleum Exploration AB v Government of the Republic of Lithuania (No 2)* [2006] EWCA Civ 1529 at [114]–[116], [2007] QB 886.

which relate to the arbitration.[199] This includes proceedings for enforcement of a foreign arbitration award.[200] There are detailed rules as to what constitutes submission by the foreign state. Submission may be by prior written agreement[201] or after the dispute has arisen;[202] but a provision in an agreement that the law of a part of the United Kingdom is to govern does not constitute submission.[203] In fact, the only way it could have been regarded as submission would have been if the choice of English law was regarded as an implied choice of English jurisdiction and if that was then regarded as implied submission. Any intervention by a foreign state for the purpose only of claiming immunity or asserting an interest in property in circumstances such that the state would have been entitled to immunity had the proceedings been brought against that state does not amount to submission.[204] A state is, however, deemed to submit if it has instituted the proceedings or, subject to what has just been said, if it intervenes in the proceedings,[205] unless it does so in reasonable ignorance of facts entitling it to immunity, and immunity is claimed as soon as is reasonably practicable.[206]

(d) Indirect impleading

It has been assumed so far that the question of the immunity to which a sovereign state is entitled arises in the course of proceedings in which the state is named as defendant, ie direct impleading. In practice, however, what is far more common is "indirect impleading". In this type of case the issue of state immunity arises either because of interpleader proceedings by the state or because one party to the proceedings claims, for example, that the goods in issue[207] are subject to the power of a foreign state and that to proceed with the claim would indirectly implead that state. Before the State Immunity Act 1978 a variety of issues had been held to implead a foreign sovereign, such as an action which put his title to goods in issue or which related to property in the possession of the foreign state[208] or which the state had the right to possess,[209] or even property "in the control" of the foreign sovereign.[210] Most cases of indirect impleading involved chattels but the

---

[199] S 9(1). This is subject to contrary provision in the arbitration agreement. See also in relation to the Commonwealth Secretariat Act 1966, *Mohsin v The Commonwealth Secretariat* [2002] EWHC 377 (Comm). Nor does it apply to an arbitration agreement between states: s 9(2).

[200] *Svenska Petroleum Exploration AB v Government of the Republic of Lithuania (No 2)* [2006] EWCA Civ 1529 at [117]–[122], [2007] QB 886.

[201] See, eg, *A Company Ltd v Republic of X* [1990] 2 Lloyd's Rep 520; *Sabah Shipyard (Pakistan) Ltd v Islamic Republic of Pakistan* [2002] EWCA Civ 1643 at [18]–[27] (per WALLER LJ), [48]–[51] (per PILL LJ), [2003] 2 Lloyd's Rep 571. See also s 17(2).

[202] S 2(2); and see the transitional provision in s 23(3)(a); cf *Duff Development Co Ltd v Kelantan Government* [1924] AC 797; *Kahan v Pakistan Federation* [1951] 2 KB 1003. The head of the state's diplomatic mission in the United Kingdom is deemed to have authority to submit, as is any person who entered into a contract on behalf of the state in matters relating to that contract: s 2(7); cf *Baccus SLR v Servicio Nacional del Trigo* [1957] 1 QB 438 at 473.

[203] Ibid.

[204] S 2(4); see generally, *London Branch of the Nigerian Universities Commission v Bastians* [1995] ICR 358.

[205] S 2(3). See *Fusco v O'Dea* [1994] 2 ILRM 389.

[206] S 2(5). Any submission extends to an appeal, but not to a counterclaim unless it arises out of the same legal relationship or facts as the original claim: s 2(6). See also *Kubacz v Shah* [1984] WAR 156.

[207] Eg *The Parlement Belge* (1880) 5 PD 197.

[208] Eg *Compañia Naviera Vascongada v SS Cristina* [1938] AC 485.

[209] Eg *United States of America and Republic of France v Dollfus Mieg et Cie SA and Bank of England* [1952] AC 582.

[210] Eg *The Broadmayne* [1916] P 64.

doctrine of immunity was extended to cases where the subject matter of the action was a chose in action to which title was claimed by a foreign state.[211] Finally, the foreign state did not have to prove its title to the property in issue. It was sufficient for evidence to be adduced that the claim of the foreign state was not illusory or founded on a manifestly defective title.[212] It had to be an arguable issue.[213] Another example of indirect impleading is the situation where a civil claim for damages is brought against individual state officials, following alleged official torture abroad.[214] The foreign state is indirectly impleaded since the acts of the officials are attributable to it. If these claims against individual defendants were to proceed and be upheld, the interests of the foreign state would obviously be affected, even though it is not a named party.

The question of "indirect impleading" is not dealt with, as such, in the State Immunity Act 1978 even though it is the most likely circumstance in which the issue of sovereign immunity will arise. Nevertheless, this aspect of sovereign immunity is very substantially regulated. First, it is clear that the immunity, and the exceptions thereto, provided by the 1978 Act are intended to apply whether the foreign state is a party to the action or intervenes by means of interpleader proceedings. This is apparent from section 2(4) which provides that a state does not submit to the jurisdiction merely by intervening in proceedings to assert an interest in property in circumstances such that the state would have been immune if directly impleaded. Secondly, the problems of indirect impleading surface in section 6(4) which provides that a court may entertain proceedings against a person other than a state notwithstanding that the proceedings relate to property in the possession or control of a state or in which a state claims an interest. This is the indirect impleading situation where the state does not necessarily intervene; but the court's power to entertain such proceedings depends on the state not being immune if the proceedings were brought directly against it and, in the case where the proceedings relate to property in which the state claims an interest, the state's claim must be neither admitted nor supported by prima facie evidence.

The result is that in a case of indirect impleading, the law is much as before. There will be immunity unless the case falls within an exception under the 1978 Act, and it is unlikely that the exceptions in the 1978 Act would have altered the decisions in favour of immunity in many of the cases, other than those relating to ships,[215] decided at common law,[216] for there is no statutory exception to immunity in most cases involving movables. The requirement of property being in the possession or control of the foreign state indicates little change; though the need to adduce prima facie evidence in support of a claim to an interest in the goods perhaps imposes a heavier burden than at common law. Finally, the reference in section 6(4) of the 1978 Act to "property", without qualification, suggests that the provision covers both corporeal and incorporeal property, ie choses in action.

---

[211] *Rahimtoola v Nizam of Hyderabad* [1958] AC 379.

[212] *Juan Ysmael & Co Inc v Indonesian Government* [1955] AC 72 at 88–90. Cf *Shearson Lehman Bros Inc v Maclaine Watson & Co Ltd (International Tin Council intervening) (No 2)* [1988] 1 WLR 16, 29–31, HL—a sovereign asserting a right of property in a document in the possession of a third party.

[213] *Rahimtoola v Nizam of Hyderabad* [1958] AC 379 at 410.

[214] *Jones v Ministry of the Interior of the Kingdom of Saudi Arabia* [2006] UKHL 26 at [31], [2007] 1 AC 270.

[215] See the exceptions to immunity in the 1978 Act, s 10.

[216] Mann (1973) 36 MLR 18, 23–24.

In the situation where the indirect impleading arises out of a claim against individual officials following alleged torture abroad, the 1978 Act has been applied to provide immunity for these individuals.[217]

(e) Procedural and other miscellaneous matters in the 1978 Act

There are a number of other miscellaneous, but significant, matters dealt with by the State Immunity Act 1978. Provision is made for the service of process on a foreign state and for a number of other procedural matters.[218] These include immunity from injunctive relief[219] and from the processes of execution except with the state's written consent or in respect of property in use or intended for use for commercial purposes.[220] It has been held that a credit balance in a bank account kept for the purpose of meeting the day-to-day expenditure of a foreign embassy was not used for commercial purposes and was therefore immune from the processes of execution.[221] Some of the expenditure would no doubt come within the concept of commercial purposes under the Act, but other expenditure clearly did not, and the bank balance was one and indivisible; it was not susceptible of dissection to reflect the different expenditure. Power is given to provide by Order in Council for the restriction or extension of the Act's immunities and privileges. They may be restricted where they exceed those accorded by the foreign state in relation to the United Kingdom; and they may be extended where they are less than those required by any international agreement between the United Kingdom and the foreign state.[222] Nothing in the list of exceptions to the general principle of immunity is to affect the immunities and privileges conferred by the Diplomatic Privileges Act 1964 or the Consular Relations Act 1968;[223] but the 1964 Act is extended to apply to a head of state, his family and his private servants.[224]

One final issue which may arise is whether the party in question is a foreign state for the purposes of the 1978 Act. This is an issue which arose in relation to sovereign immunity before this Act and the position is, in effect, unchanged. The status of a foreign sovereign is a matter of which the court takes judicial notice, that is to say it is a matter that the

---

[217] *Jones v Ministry of the Interior of the Kingdom of Saudi Arabia* [2006] UKHL 26, [2007] 1 AC 270; discussed supra, pp 495–496.

[218] 1978 Act, ss 12, 13, 14(3)–(5); see *Kuwait Airways Corpn v Iraqi Airways Co* [1995] 1 WLR 1147, HL—service has to be transmitted through the Foreign and Commonwealth Office to the Ministry of Foreign Affairs in the state in question; *ABCI (Formerly Arab Business Consortium International Finance and Investment Co) v Banque Franco-Tunisienne* [2002] 1 Lloyd's Rep 511, appeals dismissed [2003] 2 Lloyd's Rep 146, CA—service in an agreed way; *Westminster City Council v Government of the Islamic Republic of Iran* [1986] 1 WLR 979; *Crescent Oil and Shipping Services Ltd v Importang UEE* [1998] 1 WLR 919.

[219] See *Soleh Boneh International Ltd v Government of the Republic of Uganda* [1993] 2 Lloyd's Rep 208 at 213.

[220] 1978 Act, s 13; *Sabah Shipyard (Pakistan) Ltd v Islamic Republic of Pakistan* [2002] EWCA Civ 1643 at [18]–[27] (per WALLER LJ), [48]–[51] (per PILL LJ), [2003] 2 Lloyd's Rep 571; Wilkes (2004) 53 ICLQ 512. See also *Coreck Maritime GmbH v Sevrybokholodflot* 1994 SLT 893. See in relation to the property of a state's Central Bank: s 14(4), *AIC Ltd v Federal Government of Nigeria* [2003] EWHC 1357 at [44]–[59] (QB); *AIG Capital Partners Inc v Republic of Kazakhstan* [2005] EWHC 2239 (Comm), [2006] 1 All ER 284.

[221] *Alcom Ltd v Republic of Colombia* [1984] AC 580, HL; Ghandi (1984) 47 MLR 597; Lloyd Jones [1984] CLJ 222. The onus is on the judgment creditor to show the commercial purpose.

[222] 1978 Act, s 15. See in relation to the USSR/Russian Federation, SI 1978/1524, SI 1997/2591; *Coreck Maritime GmbH v Sevrybokholodflot* 1994 SLT 893; *The Guiseppe Di Vittorio* [1998] 1 Lloyd's Rep 136, CA.

[223] Infra, p 502 et seq.

[224] 1978 Act s 20, discussed infra, p 508 et seq.

court is either assumed to know or to have the means of discovering without embarking upon a contentious inquiry.[225] Where it was doubtful whether a person enjoyed sufficient independence to entitle him to immunity, as, for instance, in the case of a ruler in Malaya[226] or in a case after the Indian Independence Act 1947 of a former ruler of an independent state in India,[227] the court applied to the Secretary of State for Foreign and Commonwealth Affairs whose answer was final and conclusive, and this rule is embodied in the 1978 Act.[228]

(ii) Ambassadors and other diplomatic officers[229]

It has long been recognised that the representatives in the United Kingdom of a foreign state are sent on the understanding that they shall have an immunity from the civil and criminal jurisdiction of the local courts which reflects that enjoyed by the sovereign whom they represent.[230] The Diplomatic Privileges Act 1708,[231] which was declaratory though not exhaustive of the common law,[232] provided in accordance with this principle that "all writs and processes" against a foreign ambassador or other public minister should be "utterly null and void".[233] At common law the immunity is shared by the members of the foreign envoy's family, if living with him; by his diplomatic family, as it is sometimes called, such as his counsellors, secretaries and clerks; and by his domestic staff, such as chauffeurs.

This principle of immunity is a feature of all systems of law, but since its application has been far from uniform, especially as regards the position of domestic servants, the law on the subject was ultimately codified in 1961 by the Vienna Convention on Diplomatic Intercourse and Immunities.[234] Effect has been given to this Convention by the Diplomatic Privileges Act 1964,[235] which, in respect of the matters dealt with therein, replaces any previous enactment or rule of law. It applies not only to diplomatic representatives of foreign countries but also to the diplomatic representatives of Commonwealth countries and the Republic of Ireland and their staffs.[236] Furthermore the Act is retrospective in operation and applies to actions begun before the date on which it came into force.[237]

---

[225] *Mighell v Sultan of Johore* [1894] 1 QB 149 at 161. See also *Federal Republic of Yugoslavia v Croatia* [2000] IL Pr 591, French Cour de Cassation.

[226] *Mighell v Sultan of Johore*, supra.

[227] *Sayce v Ameer Ruler Sadig Mohammad Abbasi Bahawalpur State* [1952] 2 QB 390.

[228] S 21(a). See *Trawnik v Lennox* [1985] 1 WLR 532.

[229] For a discussion of the historical development, see Young (1964) 40 BYBIL 141.

[230] *The Parlement Belge* (1880) 5 PD 197 at 207.

[231] See Blackstone's Commentaries, i, 255.

[232] *The Amazone* [1940] P 40.

[233] S 3.

[234] See generally Denza, *Diplomatic Law* (1998) 2nd edn.

[235] S 1. See Samuels (1964) 27 MLR 689; Buckley (1965–1966) 41 BYBIL 321; and see Hardy, *Modern Diplomatic Law*, pp 52–68; Brown (1988) 37 ICLQ 53. The Act has been amended in minor respects by the Diplomatic and Other Privileges Act 1971, and the Diplomatic and Consular Premises Act 1987; and see the State Immunity Act 1978, ss 16(1), 20.

[236] Diplomatic Privileges Act 1964, s 8(4), Sch 2, repealing the Diplomatic Immunities (Commonwealth Countries and Republic of Ireland) Act 1952, s 1(1), and thereby limiting the immunity in the case of the staff of Commonwealth High Commissions, eg *Empson v Smith* [1966] 1 QB 426.

[237] *Empson v Smith*, supra.

(a) The persons entitled to privileges

The persons entitled to immunity are allocated to three categories, and the particular privileges allowed them vary according to the category to which they belong. Any doubt as to whether a person is entitled to a privilege is conclusively settled by a certificate given by the Secretary of State.[238] No immunity is conferred until the representative of the foreign state has been accepted or received in this country.[239] The three categories are as follows:

(i) Diplomatic agents

These comprise the head of the mission and the members of his diplomatic staff,[240] as for instance, the secretaries, counsellors and attachés. Arms control inspectors and observers are now included in the definition.[241]

Such a person is exempt from the civil[242] and criminal jurisdiction of the English courts[243] in respect both of his official and private acts, and, though he himself may institute proceedings,[244] no remedy is enforceable against him in the United Kingdom at the instance of either a private citizen or the state. Thus no action will lie against a High Commissioner for unfair dismissal.[245] But this immunity does not import immunity from legal liability.[246] Thus, if a diplomatic agent commits a tort against which he has insured himself he can claim to be indemnified by the insurer. If a diplomatic agent is a citizen of the United Kingdom and Colonies or if he is permanently resident in the United Kingdom, his immunity from the civil jurisdiction is limited to official acts performed in the exercise of his functions.[247] The diplomatic agent must be treated with due respect and all appropriate steps must be taken to prevent any attack on his person, freeedom or dignity.[248]

---

[238] Diplomatic Privileges Act 1964, s 4. See, eg, *R v Governor of Pentonville Prison, ex p Teja* [1971] 2 QB 274; *R v Governor of Pentonville Prison, ex p Osman (No 2)* [1989] COD 446. However, such a certificate whilst conclusively settling that a child is a dependant will not settle that the child is a member of the household of the diplomat, which is what is required, see infra: *Re P (Children Act: Diplomatic Immunity)* [1998] 1 FLR 624 at 626.

[239] *R v Governor of Pentonville Prison, ex p Teja*, supra; *R v Lambeth Justices, ex p Yusufu* [1985] Crim LR 510; *R v Governor of Pentonville Prison, ex p Osman (No 2)*, supra. However, the position appears to be different in immigration cases: *R v Secretary of State for the Home Department, ex p Bagga* [1991] 1 QB 485 at 496–497, 508–509.

[240] Diplomatic Privileges Act 1964, Sch1, Art 1(a)–(e).

[241] Arms Control and Disarmament (Privileges and Immunities) Act 1988. See also the Vienna Document 1992 (Privileges and Immunities) Order 1992, SI 1992/1727. For the position of foreign personnel assisting after a nuclear accident see the Atomic Energy Act 1989, Sch.

[242] Including a divorce petition: *Shaw v Shaw* [1979] Fam 62.

[243] 1964 Act, Sch 1, Art 31(1). Furthermore, the private residence of a diplomatic agent is inviolable, as are the premises of the mission. But see *Re B (A Child) (Care Proceedings: Diplomatic Immunity)* [2002] EWHC 1751 (Fam), [2003] 1 WLR 168. On diplomatic and consular premises, see generally the Diplomatic and Consular Premises Act 1987.

[244] *Baron Penedo v Johnson* (1873) 29 LT 452.

[245] *Omerri v Uganda High Commission* (1973) 8 ITR 14.

[246] *Dickinson v Del Solar* [1930] 1 KB 376 at 380; *Re P (Diplomatic Immunity: Jurisdiction)* [1998] 1 FLR 1026.

[247] Diplomatic Privileges Act 1964, s 2(6); Sch 1, Art 38(1). This limited immunity may, however, be extended by Order in Council.

[248] Art 29 of the Vienna Convention. On which see *Harb v Aziz* [2005] EWCA Civ 632; *Aziz v Aziz* [2007] EWCA Civ 712.

By way of exception to the exemption from civil jurisdiction there are three types of action that lie against a diplomatic agent, namely:

(a) a real action relating to private immovable property in England, unless it is held on behalf of the sending state for the purposes of the mission[249]—it has been decided that a diplomatic agent's private residence was not held for the purposes of the mission;[250]

(b) an action relating to succession in which the diplomatic agent is involved as executor, administrator, heir or legatee in his capacity as a private person;

(c) an action relating to any professional or commercial activity pursued by him in the United Kingdom[251] outside his official functions.[252]

This last exception reverses the previous law, under which a person of diplomatic rank was not liable to be sued in respect of his commercial or private transactions.[253]

No writ of execution may be issued against a diplomatic agent, except where judgment has been given against him in an action relating to immovable property, to succession or to any private commercial transaction, and even then no measure may be taken that will infringe the inviolability of his person or residence.[254]

The general rule is that a diplomatic agent is exempt from all dues and taxes, personal or real, national, regional or municipal.[255]

The above privileges granted to a diplomatic agent are also possessed by the members of his family forming part of his household,[256] provided that they are of alien nationality.[257]

(ii) Members of the administrative and technical staff[258]

This category includes such persons as clerks, typists, archivists and radio or telephone operators. Such members of the staff, together with the members of their families, provided that they are neither citizens of the United Kingdom and Colonies nor permanently resident in the United Kingdom, are immune from the civil jurisdiction, but only in respect of acts done within the scope of their duties.[259] They are also on the same footing as diplomatic agents with regard to the exemption from taxes and other dues.[260]

---

[249] See State Immunity Act 1978, s 16(1)(b).

[250] *Intpro Properties (UK) Ltd v Sauvel* [1983] QB 1019. Even if the premises are held for professional purposes, for the immunity to apply there must be proceedings concerning a state's title to or its possession of property.

[251] But not outside, see *BCCI v Price Waterhouse* [1997] 4 All ER 108 at 111–112.

[252] Diplomatic Privileges Act 1964, Sch 1, Art 31(1).

[253] *Taylor v Best* (1854) 14 CB 487.

[254] Diplomatic Privileges Act 1964, Sch 1, Art 31(3).

[255] Ibid, Sch 1, Arts 33, 34, 36.

[256] A dependent child, although a member of the diplomat's family, may not form part of his household: *Re P (Children Act: Diplomatic Immunity)* [1998] 1 FLR 624 at 626.

[257] The 1964 Act, Sch 1, Art 37(1); see also *Re C (An Infant)* [1959] Ch 363; Wilson (1965) 14 ICLQ 1265; O'Keefe (1976) 25 ICLQ 329.

[258] Diplomatic Privileges Act 1964, Sch 1, Art 1; eg *Empson v Smith* [1966] 1 QB 426. See also Arms Control and Disarmament (Privileges and Immunities) Act 1988.

[259] *Re B (A Child) (Care Proceedings: Diplomatic Immunity)* [2002] EWHC 1751 (Fam), [2003] 1 WLR 168.

[260] Diplomatic Privileges Act 1964, Sch 1, Art 37(2).

(iii) Members of the service staff

Members of the service staff, who are defined by the Convention as "members of the staff of the mission in the domestic staff of the mission",[261] include such persons as butlers, cooks, maids and chauffeurs. These enjoy no privileges if they are either citizens of the United Kingdom and Colonies or if they are permanently resident in the United Kingdom. Otherwise, they enjoy immunity from the civil jurisdiction of the courts, but only in respect of acts performed in the course of their duties; and they are exempt from income tax on the emoluments paid to them by the sending state and from liability to pay contributions under social security legislation.[262]

(b) Cessation of immunities and privileges

The immunities and privileges enjoyed by any person normally cease at the moment when he leaves the United Kingdom[263] or on the expiry of a reasonable time within which to do so, provided that his functions have come to an end. Nevertheless, his immunity continues to endure in respect of acts already done by him in the exercise of his official duties.[264] On the other hand his immunity in respect of acts already done in his private capacity no longer avails him.[265] However, diplomatic immunity which comes into existence after an action has been started will necessitate a stay of those proceedings until such time as the immunity may cease to be enjoyed.[266]

(c) Waiver of privileges

It was recognised at common law that a diplomatic agent or other member of the diplomatic staff might waive his immunity from the civil and criminal jurisdiction of the local courts, either by expressly consenting through his solicitor to the proceedings, or by entering an appearance to the writ or by commencing proceedings as plaintiff. Since, however, the privilege is the privilege of the sending state, not of the individual diplomat, it was essential that consent to its waiver should have been given by the sending state in the case of proceedings against the head of the mission, and by the head of the mission where the proceedings were against a subordinate member of the state. It followed that, even if a subordinate member had waived the privilege, he might later obtain a stay of proceedings by showing that he had not acted with the consent of his superior.[267]

These rules have been little affected by the Act of 1964. In the first place, the authority of the sending state to waive the privilege is retained;[268] and it is enacted that a waiver by the head of the mission shall be deemed to be a waiver by that state.[269] The words of this last provision are wide enough to embrace the case where the head of the mission waives his

---

[261] Ibid, Sch 1, Art 1(g).

[262] Ibid, s 2(4); Sch 1, Arts 33, 37.

[263] *Shaw v Shaw* [1979] Fam 62; see also *Re Regina and Palacios* (1984) 45 OR (2d) 269.

[264] Diplomatic Privileges Act 1964, Sch 1, Art 39(2).

[265] *Zoernsch v Waldock* [1964] 1 WLR 675 at 692; *Re P (Diplomatic Immunity: Jurisdiction)* [1998] 1 FLR 1026—taking children from the jurisdiction at the end of a posting.

[266] *Ghosh v D'Rozario* [1963] 1 QB 106.

[267] *R v Madan* [1961] 2 QB 1, and authorities there cited.

[268] Diplomatic Privileges Act 1964, Sch 1, Art 32(1). See *Propend Finance v Sing* (1997) 111 ILR 611, CA; *Re P (Children Act: Diplomatic Immunity)* [1998] 1 FLR 624.

[269] Diplomatic Privileges Act 1964, s 2(3).

own privilege, not merely that of a subordinate member of the staff.[270] It is enacted that a waiver must always be express.[271] It is possible to waive personal immunity, but at the same time to maintain immunity in respect of a diplomatic document.[272]

Where, under the former law, a person entitled to immunity waived his privilege and commenced an action as claimant, it was doubtful whether it was permissible for the defendant to plead a counterclaim. The Act now settles this doubt by providing that:

> the initiation of proceedings by . . . a person enjoying immunity from jurisdiction . . . shall preclude him from invoking immunity from jurisdiction in respect of any counterclaim directly connected with the principal claim.[273]

The rule at common law that a judgment given against a foreign diplomat cannot be executed, notwithstanding that he has waived his immunity from the jurisdiction,[274] has been confirmed. There can be no enforcement of a judgment unless there has been a separate waiver of the immunity from execution.[275] Failing a separate waiver, the judgment remains unenforceable until the defendant has ceased to be a member of the foreign mission.

(d) Restriction of privileges and immunities

It sometimes happens that the privileges granted to a British mission in a particular foreign state are less than those enjoyed by the mission of that state in the United Kingdom. In that event, an Order in Council may be made withdrawing the statutory immunities and privileges to such extent or in respect of such persons as appears to Her Majesty to be proper.[276] Furthermore, reciprocal arrangements for wider immunities than those contained in the 1964 Act may be continued.[277]

(e) International organisations[278]

It is clear, then, that immunity from jurisdiction is enjoyed by the diplomatic representatives of foreign states who reside in the United Kingdom during the performance of their duties. The International Organisations Act 1968[279] provides that certain privileges may be conferred on persons who are present for a limited time in the United Kingdom as the representatives of some organisation of which the United Kingdom and one or more Sovereign Powers are members.[280] What organisations are eligible and what particular

---

270 For the difficulties involved in such a waiver, see *Fayed v Al-Tajir* [1988] QB 712 at 733, 737. KERR LJ appears to doubt whether the head of the mission can waive his own privilege (at 737), whereas MUSTILL LJ appears to accept this (at 733).

271 Diplomatic Privileges Act 1964, Sch 1, Art 32(2). See *A Company Ltd v Republic of X* [1990] 2 Lloyd's Rep 520, which held that the waiver must be given to the court itself; Mann (1991) 17 LQR 362.

272 *Fayed v Al-Tajir*, supra.

273 Diplomatic Privileges Act 1964, Sch 1, Art 32(3).

274 *Re Suarez, Suarez v Suarez* [1918] 1 Ch 176.

275 Diplomatic Privileges Act 1964, Sch 1, Art 32(4).

276 Diplomatic Privileges Act 1964, s 3(1); re-enacting the Diplomatic Immunities Restriction Act 1955.

277 Ibid, s 7(1).

278 See generally Gaillard and Pingel-Lenuzza (2002) 51 ICLQ 1. In certain cicumstances, an international organisation may sue in England, see *Arab Monetary Fund v Hashim (No 3)* [1991] 2 AC 114, CA; Mann (1991) 107 LQR 357; Carter (1991) 62 BYBIL 447; Hill (1992) 12 OJLS 135.

279 As amended by the Diplomatic and Other Privileges Act 1971; the European Communities Act 1972, s 4(1), Sch 3, Part IV; the International Organisations Act 1981, and the International Organisations Act 2005.

280 Replacing the International Organisations (Immunities and Privileges) Act 1950, as amended by the Diplomatic Privileges Act 1964. The 1968 Act has been extended to Commonwealth organisations; see International

immunities they are to enjoy must be specified by Order in Council.[281] Examples of organisations that have been specified are the United Nations, the Commission of the European Communities, the European Bank for Reconstruction and Development,[282] the Council of Europe,[283] the International Labour Organisation, the World Health Organisation, the International Court of Justice, the International Criminal Court, the European Court of Human Rights and the International Tribunal for the Law of the Sea.

The maximum immunities that may be granted to an organisation or to a representative thereof vary with each case. Thus, high officers and members of committees and missions may be put on the same footing as heads of diplomatic missions with regard to immunity from suit and legal process, inviolability of residence and exemption from taxes and privileges as to the importation of certain articles, and there is the like inviolability of official premises as is accorded in respect of the premises of a diplomatic agent;[284] but the maximum privileges of other officers and representatives are limited to immunity from suit and legal process in respect of things done in the course of their employment, to exemption from income tax on their official salaries, to exemption from certain other customs duties and taxes and to privileges as to the importation of certain articles.[285] Although an officer of an international organisation has immunity, this is granted for the benefit of the organisation and may be waived by it. Accordingly, there is no limitation on jurisdiction in an action by the organisation against the officer.[286] The immunity of an officer only extends to official acts and cannot include the situation where the officer is accepting a bribe for his own benefit.[287]

Special provision is made in the International Organisations Act 1968 for conferring diplomatic exemptions and privileges on officers of specialised agencies of the United Nations,[288] and also on other organisations, including international commodity organisations, of which the United Kingdom is not a member,[289] on bodies established under the Treaty on European Union,[290] on persons involved in international judicial proceedings[291] and on representatives at international conferences in the United Kingdom.[292]

Organisations Act 1981, s 1. See also the Commonwealth Secretariat Act 1966, as amended by the International Organisations Act 2005, ss 1–3; *Mohsin v The Commonwealth Secretariat* [2002] EWHC 377 (Comm).

[281] International Organisations Act 1968, s 1. Orders in Council made under the 1950 Act are to continue to have effect: s 12(5), (6).

[282] *Mukoro v European Bank for Reconstruction and Development* [1994] ICR 897.

[283] Of which the European Commission of Human Rights is an organ: *Zoernsch v Waldock* [1964] 2 All ER 256. For immunities for United Kingdom representatives to the Consultative Assembly of the Council of Europe, see s 4 of the International Organisations Act 1981.

[284] International Organisations Act 1968, Sch I, Pt II; as amended by s 5 of the International Organisations Act 1981.

[285] The 1968 Act, Sch I, Pt III; as amended by the International Organisations Act 1981, s 5.

[286] *Arab Monetary Fund v Hashim* [1996] 1 Lloyd's Rep 589, CA.

[287] Ibid.

[288] The 1968 Act, s 2. See also *Re Immunity of Special Rapporteur* (1999) Times, 19 May, ICJ.

[289] International Organisations Act 1968, s 4; and s 4A, added by s 2 of the International Organisations Act 1981.

[290] International Organisations Act 1968, s 4B, added by s 5 of the International Organisations Act 2005.

[291] The 1968 Act, s 5; extended by ss 7 and 8 of the International Organisations Act 2005. See in relation to the International Tribunal for the Law of the Sea, SI 2005/2047. See also the International Criminal Court Act 2001, Sch 1, para 1, extended by the International Organisations Act 2005, s 6.

[292] International Organisations Act 1968, s 6; see also s 5A added by the International Organisations Act 1981, s 3.

(f) Immunity of foreign sovereigns

In placing the whole question of sovereign immunity on a statutory basis, the State Immunity Act 1978[293] has limited the immunity formerly enjoyed by a foreign sovereign or head of state. In so far as the immunities conferred by the Diplomatic Privileges Act 1964 are wider than those under the 1978 Act, it has been thought desirable to apply the appropriate immunities of the 1964 Act to a sovereign or other head of state, the members of his family forming part of his household and his private servants;[294] though without the qualifications in the 1964 Act relating to residence or nationality.[295]

(g) Consular immunities

The regulation of consular immunity, so far as foreign consuls and their staffs are concerned,[296] is governed by the Consular Relations Act 1968,[297] giving effect to the Vienna Convention on Consular Relations 1963. Consular officers[298] are not liable to arrest, save in the case of a grave crime,[299] and are only subject to restrictions on personal freedom in execution of judicial decisions of final effect.[300] In the case of civil proceedings, consular officers and employees are not amenable to the jurisdiction of the courts of this country in respect of acts performed in the exercise of consular functions except, in the case of a contractual action, where such officer or employee does not contract expressly or impliedly as an agent of his sending state, and in the case of an action by a third party for damage arising from an accident in the United Kingdom caused by a vessel, vehicle or aircraft.[301] There is power for these various exemptions to be waived by the sending state.[302]

There are provisions dealing also with exemption from social security provisions, taxation, customs and estate duties.[303] Special provision is made for the fact that the varied privileges and immunities shall not be accorded to consular employees and the families of members of a consular post who carry on private gainful occupations in the United Kingdom.[304] Again, as with the Diplomatic Privileges Act 1964, there is provision for

---

[293] Supra, p 491 et seq.

[294] State Immunity Act 1978, s 20. See *Harb v Aziz* [2005] EWCA Civ 632; *Aziz v Aziz* [2007] EWCA Civ 712. A former head of state has immunity from criminal jurisdiction for acts done in his official capacity as head of state: *R v Bow Street Magistrate, ex p Pinochet (No 3)* [1999] 2 All ER 97, HL. However, this does not extend to official acts of torture committed after ratification of the International Convention against Torture and Other Cruel, Inhuman or Degrading Treatment or Punishment 1984.

[295] State Immunity Act 1978, s 20(2).

[296] For the position of consular officers from the Commonwealth and the Republic of Ireland see the Consular Relations Act 1968, s 12, as amended by the Diplomatic and Other Privileges Act 1971 and the Commonwealth Countries and Republic of Ireland (Immunities and Privileges) Order 1985, SI 1985/1983, as amended by the Commonwealth Countries and Republic of Ireland (Immunities and Privileges) Order 2005, SI 2005/246.

[297] See Woodliffe (1969) 32 MLR 59; and see the State Immunity Act 1978, s 16(1).

[298] Defined in Sch I, Art 1.

[299] Defined in s 1(2).

[300] Sch I, Art 41. A consular official is within the United Kingdom for the purposes of the hearsay rule and s 23 of the Criminal Justice Act 1988; see *R v Carmenza Jiminez-Paez* (1993) 98 Cr App Rep 239, CA.

[301] Sch I, Art 43. See Lee, *Vienna Convention on Consular Relations*, pp 143–146.

[302] Sch I, Art 45.

[303] Sch I, Arts 48–51.

[304] Sch I, Art 57.

those cases where there is already agreement for additional or reduced privileges[305] and for the withdrawal of privileges.[306]

(iii) The Brussels/Lugano system

To what extent are these rules on sovereign and diplomatic immunity affected by the Brussels/Lugano system? It will be recalled that this system only applies in relation to civil and commercial matters. If the action concerns the commercial transactions of a foreign state or diplomat this would appear to relate to a civil and commercial matter. However, there is authority to the effect that where an action involves the governmental acts of a foreign state or the official acts of a diplomat (ie the situation where immunity is granted) it will fall outside this concept. This is because, as has been seen, actions involving a public authority acting in the exercise of its powers have been held to fall outside the scope of the Brussels Convention (Brussels I Regulation) and Lugano Convention.[307]

The first of these authorities, and the leading case on the relationship between state immunity and the scope of the Brussels Convention, is *Lechouritou v Germany*.[308] The Court of Justice held that an action by natural persons of a Contracting State against another Contracting State to obtain compensation for damage caused by the armed forces of the latter Contracting State when invading the territory of the first State did not constitute a civil and commercial matter.[309] The reasoning of the Court is highly instructive in the present context. It was said that operations conducted by armed forces are one of the characteristic emanations of state sovereignty.[310] It followed that the acts complained of must be regarded as resulting from the exercise of public powers on the part of the state on the date when those acts were perpetrated.[311] The question whether the acts carried out in the exercise of these public powers were lawful made no difference to this.[312] In the light of this finding the Court held that there was no need to discuss the second question referred to the Court, namely whether a plea of state immunity is compatible with the Brussels Convention.[313] Likewise in *Grovit v De Nederlandsche Bank*,[314] the Court of Appeal held that a claim for defamation brought against the Dutch Central Bank and two of its employees, all of whom were entitled to immunity,[315] was not a civil one within the meaning of the Regulation. The first defendant was a public authority and the defamation was contained in a letter written during the exercise of public powers.

If the Brussels/Lugano system were to apply in cases involving the governmental acts of a foreign state or official acts of a diplomat, the question would arise of whether the

---

[305] S 3.
[306] S 2.
[307] Supra, pp 215–216.
[308] Case C-292/05 [2007] IL Pr 14.
[309] Case C-292/05 *Lekhoritou v Germany* [2007] IL Pr 14.
[310] Ibid, at [37].
[311] Ibid, at [38].
[312] Ibid, at [43].
[313] Ibid, at [47].
[314] [2007] EWCA Civ 953, [2008] 1 WLR 51, affirming [2005] EWHC 2944 (QB), [2006] 1 Lloyd's Rep 636.
[315] See s 14(2) of the 1978 Act.

limitations on jurisdiction outlined above would also apply. The problem is an acute one. Much of the law on sovereign and diplomatic immunity stems from international conventions. There could be a clash between obligations arising under these conventions and the obligations that arise under the Brussels I Regulation, EC/Denmark Agreement and Brussels/Lugano Conventions. In *Grovit v De Nederlandsche Bank*, Tugendhat J, at first instance, held that the Regulation is to be read subject to the law of state immunity.[316] This is on the basis that the Regulation must be read subject to international law and that state immunity is part of international law. There is, though, an alternative basis for so reading the Regulation. This is that Article 71 of the Regulation[317] preserves the Basle Convention, which the 1978 Act implements. It is also to be noticed that Parliament appears to have drafted the Civil Jurisdiction and Judgments Act 1982 on the basis that the limitations in respect of sovereign and diplomatic immunity will still apply.[318]

4. STATUTORY LIMITATIONS ON JURISDICTION

There are a number of statutes, all of which implement international conventions, which preclude the jurisdiction of the English courts over actions in rem and in personam in particular situations.[319] The situations may be defined either by reference to ministerial decision or by the statutes and conventions themselves. The first case may be illustrated by the Supreme Court Act 1981, section 23 of which provides that no court in England shall have jurisdiction to entertain any claim certified by the Secretary of State to be such as falls to be determined under the Rhine Navigation Convention.[320] Similarly, the jurisdiction of any court in the United Kingdom is excluded under the Nuclear Installations Act 1965 in the case of any claim certified by the Minister to be one which, under any relevant international agreement, falls to be determined by some other United Kingdom or foreign court.[321]

Other statutes, mainly those implementing international transport conventions, stipulate that actions may be brought only under the jurisdictional rules stated in the conventions. For example, the Carriage by Air Act 1961 requires that in the case of international carriage[322] any action for damages must be brought in the territory of one

---

[316] [2005] EWHC 2944 (QB) at [47], [2006] 1 Lloyd's Rep 636; Briggs (2005) 76 BYBIL 641, 645; affd by the Court of Appeal without any discussion of the state immunity point [2007] EWCA Civ 953, [2008] 1 WLR 51. See also *Gimenez-Exposito v Federal Republic of Germany* [2005] IL Pr 7, French Cour de Cassation.

[317] Discussed supra, p 214.

[318] See s 31 of the 1982 Act which deals with judgments against states other than the United Kingdom. This section applies to judgments given in, inter alia, EC/EFTA states yet its wording presupposes the continued existence of rules on state immunity. See Anton and Beaumont's, *Civil Jurisdiction in Scotland*, para 3.04.

[319] These conventions are not affected by the Brussels I Regulation, Danish Agreement and the Brussels/Lugano Conventions; see Art 71(1) of the Brussels I Regulation (which preserves existing agreements, which in relation to particular matters govern jurisdiction, but does not allow for the United Kingdom entering into such agreements after the Regulation came into force), Art 57 of the Brussels Convention and Art 67(1) of the Lugano Convention, supra, pp 214 and 342.

[320] See Jackson, *Enforcement of Maritime Claims* (2005) 4th edn, para 12.153.

[321] S 17(1).

[322] Sch 1, Art 1(2).

of the High Contracting Parties to the convention,[323] either before the court at the place of destination or before the court having jurisdiction where the carrier ordinarily resides or has his principal place of business or has an establishment by which the contract has been made.[324] Similar jurisdictional rules are prescribed under the Carriage by Air (Supplementary Provisions) Act 1962,[325] the Carriage of Goods by Road Act 1965,[326] the Carriage of Passengers by Road Act 1974,[327] and the International Transport Conventions Act 1983.[328]

---

[323] The Warsaw Convention 1929, as amended at The Hague in 1955, supplemented by the Guadalajara Convention 1961, and modernised by the Montreal Convention for the Unification of Certain Rules relating to International Carriage by Air 1999.

[324] Carriage by Air Act 1961, Sch 1, Art 28(1).

[325] Sch, Art VIII.

[326] Sch, Art 31(1).

[327] Sch, Art 21(1). Other statutes containing specific jurisdictional rules based upon or by reference to international conventions are the Supreme Court Act 1981, ss 20–22, amended by the Merchant Shipping (Salvage and Pollution) Act 1994, s 1(6), Sch 2, para 6, and Merchant Shipping Act 1995, s 314(2), Sch 13, para 59(2)(a), (b), (c) and (d); and the Merchant Shipping Act 1995, Part VI, Chapter III (ss 152–171, as amended by SI 2006/1244), s 183(1).

[328] S 1 and Appendix A of the Convention concerning International Carriage by Rail, Cmnd 8535 (1982) which is given the force of law by the 1983 Act. Most of the 1983 Act is repealed and replaced by the Railways (Convention on International Carriage by Rail) Regulations, SI 2005/2092, which comes into effect on a day to be appointed.

Chapter 15

Recognition and Enforcement of Foreign Judgments: the Traditional Rules

1. INTRODUCTION

(a) The effect given to foreign judgments

Unsatisfied foreign judgments give rise to complicated questions of private international law. If a claimant fails to obtain satisfaction of a judgment in the country where it has been granted, the question arises as to whether it is enforceable in another country where the defendant is found. It is clear at the outset that owing to the principle of territorial sovereignty a judgment delivered in one country cannot, in the absence of international agreement, have a direct operation of its own force in another. Levy of execution, for instance, cannot issue in England in respect of a judgment delivered in New York. Nevertheless, the common law systems have long permitted the enforcement of a foreign judgment within certain defined limits, since otherwise one of the essential objects of private international law, the protection of rights acquired under a foreign system of law, would not be fully attained.[1]

(b) The theory underlying recognition and enforcement[2]

The attitude adopted by English law from the earliest days has been to permit the successful suitor to bring an action in England on the foreign judgment. But over the years the courts have changed their view as to the ground upon which this privilege is based. The older cases put it solely on the ground of comity.[3] It is unnecessary, however, to consider this historical theory further, for it has been supplanted by a far more defensible principle that has been called "the doctrine of obligation".[4] This doctrine, which was laid down in 1842, is that, where a foreign court of competent jurisdiction has adjudicated a certain sum to be due from one person to another, the liability to pay that sum becomes a legal obligation that may be enforced in this country by an action of debt.[5] Once the judgment is proved the burden lies on the defendant to show why he should not perform the obligation.

> The judgment of a court of competent jurisdiction over the defendant imposes a duty or obligation on him to pay the sum for which judgment is given, which the courts in this country are bound to enforce.[6]

In other words, a new right[7] has been vested in the creditor and a new obligation imposed on the debtor at the instance of the foreign court. Lord ESHER once said that "the liability of the defendant arises upon an implied contract to pay the amount of the

---

[1] Bar, p 895

[2] Briggs and Rees, para 7.44; Briggs (1987) 36 ICLQ 240 and (2004) 8 BYBIL 1; Ho (1997) 46 ICLQ 443; Harris (1997) 17 OJLS 477.

[3] See *Geyer v Aguilar* (1798) 7 Term Rep 681 at 97; Piggott, *Foreign Judgments*, Part i, p 10 et seq.

[4] Piggott, *Foreign Judgments*, p 10 et seq.

[5] *Russell v Smyth* (1842) 9 M & W 810. See also *Adams v Cape Industries plc* [1990] Ch 433 at 552–553; *Owens Bank Ltd v Bracco* [1992] 2 AC 443 at 484, HL; *Murthy v Sivajothi* [1999] 1 WLR 467, CA; *Lewis v Eliades* [2003] EWCA Civ 1758 at [48] (per POTTER LJ), [2004] 1 WLR 692; *Gordon Pacific Developments Pty Ltd v Conlon* [1993] 3 NZLR 760.

[6] *Schibsby v Westenholz* (1870) LR 6 QB 155 at 159.

[7] See *Cambridge Gas Transportation Corpn v Official Committee of Unsecured Creditors of Navigator Holdings plc* [2006] UKPC 26 at [13], [2007] 1 AC 508.

foreign judgment".[8] This does not mean that the justification for the enforcement of the obligation is an implied contract, but that for procedural purposes the debtor is regarded as having implicitly promised to pay.[9] This may be illustrated by the fact that the creditor's action is barred under the Limitation Act 1980 after six years, not after twelve years as in the case of an English judgment.[10]

The doctrine of obligation has in turn come in for criticism in that it fails to reveal the policy considerations underlying the rules on recognition and enforcement.[11] It is more concerned with explaining in theoretical terms why we recognise and enforce foreign judgments than with explaining in theoretical terms which foreign judgements should be recognised and enforced. The Supreme Court of Canada has considered the latter. It has referred to a modern and more clearly defined concept of comity which is concerned with "justice, necessity and convenience".[12]

> Comity in the legal sense is neither a matter of absolute obligation, on the one hand, nor of mere courtesy and good will, upon the other. But it is the recognition which one nation allows within its territory to the legislative, executive or judicial acts of another nation, having due regard both to international duty and convenience, and to the rights of its own citizens or of other persons who are under the protection of its laws.[13]

This allows for the adoption of rules in the light of modern conditions. Old common law rules that were based on an outmoded view of the world that emphasised sovereignty and independence often at the cost of fairness have been rejected.[14] "Greater comity is required in our modern era when international transactions involve a constant flow of products, wealth and people across the globe".[15] The end result is a new Canadian rule which provides for recognition and enforcement when the judgment granting state has properly or appropriately exercised jurisdiction,[16] a test which is near to one of jurisdictional reciprocity.

(c) The Brussels/Lugano system

One very important recent development is the introduction of the Brussels I Regulation on jurisdiction and the recognition and enforcement of judgments in civil and commercial matters. This follows the United Kingdom's accession to the Brussels Convention, which in virtually all cases is replaced by the Regulation,[17] and to the parallel 1988 Lugano Convention (replaced now by the 2007 Lugano Convention). In cases where the rules on recognition and enforcement of foreign judgments under the Brussels/Lugano system

---

[8] *Grant v Easton* (1883) 13 QBD 302 at 303.

[9] Read, *Recognition and Enforcement of Foreign Judgments*, pp 112–113.

[10] *Re Flynn (No 2)* (1968) 112 Sol Jo 804; and see *Re Flynn (No 3)* [1969] 2 Ch 403; *Berliner Industriebank AG v Jost* [1971] 2 QB 463; *Lax v Lax* (2004) 239 DLR (4th) 683, Ont CA.

[11] Ho, op cit.

[12] *Morguard Investments Ltd v De Savoye* (1991) 76 DLR (4th) 256; discussed infra, pp 530–531. See also *Beals v Saldanha* 2003 SCC 72, Sup Ct of Canada; discussed infra, p 531.

[13] The *Marguard* case, supra, at 269. This adopts the definition in *Hilton v Guyot* 159 US 113 (1895) at 163–164.

[14] *Hunt v T & N plc* (1993) 109 DLR (4th) 16, Supreme Court of Canada.

[15] Ibid.

[16] For identifying this see infra, p 531.

[17] Under the EC/Denmark Agreement the provisions of the Regulation, with minor amendments, are applied by international law to the relations between the Community and Denmark.

apply, these rules supersede all other rules on recognition and enforcement. The place of the Brussels/Lugano system within the existing framework of rules on recognition and enforcement of foreign judgments is considered briefly later on in this chapter and the relevant rules under the Brusssels/Lugano system are considered in detail in the next chapter.

(d) Family law

It should be stressed that there are special rules dealing with the recognition of foreign divorces, annulments and legal separations, foreign maintenance orders, and foreign orders relating to children. These rules are examined later in Part V of this book, on family law.

2. RECOGNITION AND ENFORCEMENT AT COMMON LAW

We must now consider the principles on which the successful litigant may take advantage of a foreign judgment at common law.[18] A foreign judgment creditor has an alternative. He may either sue on the obligation created by the judgment, or he may plead the judgment as *res judicata* in any proceedings which raise the same issue. The common law doctrine is that a foreign judgment, though creating an obligation that is actionable in England, cannot be enforced in England without the institution of fresh legal proceedings. Nevertheless, if a fresh action is brought in England on the foreign judgment that action is subject to the Civil Procedure Rules and, for example, the claimant may apply for summary judgment under Part 24 on the basis that the defendant has no defence to the claim.[19] A foreign judgment cannot be enforced by, for example, the appointment of a receiver without such a fresh action in England. Furthermore, any action in England will require the English rules as to jurisdiction and service of claim forms to be satisfied.[20]

(a) Jurisdiction of the foreign court:[21] judgments in personam

A judgment in personam determines the existence of rights against a person.[22] The first and overriding essential for the effectiveness of a foreign judgment in personam in England is that the adjudicating court should have had jurisdiction in the international sense over the defendant. A foreign court may give a judgment which, according to the system of law under which it sits, is conclusively binding on the defendant, but unless the circumstances are such as in the eyes of English law to justify the court in having assumed jurisdiction, the judgment does not create a cause of action that is actionable in England.[23]

---

[18] The foreign decision must, of course, always be one that is regarded as a judgment: *Berliner Industriebank AG v Jost* [1971] 2 All ER 1513—entry of a debt in the record as a judgment in bankruptcy proceedings; *Midland International Trade Services Ltd v Sudairy* (1990) Financial Times, 2 May—a decision of an administrative tribunal.

[19] *Grant v Easton* (1883) 13 QBD 302.

[20] *Perry v Zissis* [1977] 1 Lloyd's Rep 607. Amendments to the rules on service out of the jurisdiction have made this easier: see now CPR, r 6.20(9), supra, p 391.

[21] Clarence Smith (1953) 2 ICLQ 510; Pryles (1972) 21 ICLQ 61; Von Mehren (1980) II Hague Recueil 9 at 55 et seq; Briggs (1987) 36 ICLQ 240.

[22] *Cambridge Gas Transportation Corpn v Official Committee of Unsecured Creditors of Navigator Holdings plc* [2006] UKPC 26 at [13], [2007] 1 AC 508. Judgments in rem will be considered infra, p 532.

[23] See eg *Sirdar Gurdyal Singh v The Rajah of Faridkote* [1894] AC 670.

In other words, in the view of English law, the foreign court must have been entitled to summon the defendant and subject him to judgment.[24]

Since a foreign judgment is actionable only because it imposes an obligation on the defendant, it follows that any fact which negatives the existence of that obligation is a bar to the action. One of the negative facts must necessarily be that the defendant owes no duty to obey the command of the tribunal which has purported to create the obligation. There must be a correlation between the legal obligation of the defendant and the right of the tribunal to issue its command. The tests that determine whether obedience is due to an English court should, on grounds of reciprocity, also be adopted when the inquiry relates to the competence of a foreign court. Personal jurisdiction in this country under the traditional rules depends on the right of a court to summon the defendant. Apart from special powers conferred by statute,[25] it is obvious that, since the right to summon depends on the power to summon, jurisdiction is in general exercisable only against those persons who are present in England.[26] If the defendant is absent from a country and has no place of business there, then, whether he be a citizen or an alien, he would appear to be immune from the jurisdiction, unless he has voluntarily submitted to the decision of the court.[27] The burden of proof is on the person seeking to enforce the judgment of a foreign court to establish that the court had jurisdiction in the international sense over the defendant.[28]

Let us now consider, in more detail, what are the criteria of jurisdiction in the international sense.

(i) Residence and, possibly, presence of defendant in the foreign country at the time of the suit

(a) An individual defendant

There is no doubt that the residence of the defendant within the foreign country is sufficient for jurisdiction.[29] What is more debatable is whether the mere presence of the defendant in the foreign country for a short time will suffice.[30] The argument in favour of jurisdiction on such a basis is that persons who happen to be within a territorial dominion owe obedience to its sovereign power—obedience, that is to say, to the jurisdiction of its courts and in certain respects to its laws. "By making himself present he contracts-in to a network of obligations, created by the local law and by the local courts."[31] This duty of obedience results from mere presence in the territory, and therefore the length of time for which the presence continues is immaterial.[32]

---

[24] *Pemberton v Hughes* [1899] 1 Ch 781 at 790 et seq; *Salvesen v Austrian Property Administrator* [1927] AC 641 at 659.

[25] Supra, pp 372–413.

[26] *Employers' Liability Assurance Corpn v Sedgwick, Collins & Co* [1927] AC 95 at 114.

[27] *Harris v Taylor* [1915] 2 KB 580 at 589.

[28] *Adams v Cape Industries plc* [1990] Ch 433 at 550; *Owens Bank Ltd v Bracco* [1992] 2 AC 443 at 489, HL; *Akande v Balfour Beatty Construction Ltd* [1998] IL Pr 110 at 113.

[29] *Emanuel v Symon* [1908] 1 KB 302 at 309; *Schibsby v Westenholz* (1870) LR 6 QB 155 at 161. Residence without presence at the date of commencement of proceedings is seemingly enough: *State Bank of India v Murjani Marketing Group Ltd*, 27 March 1991(unreported), CA. Cf, however, *Adams v Cape Industries plc* [1990] Ch 433 at 518.

[30] See generally Oppong (2007) 3 J Priv Int L 321.

[31] *Adams v Cape Industries plc*, supra, at 553.

[32] *Carrick v Hancock* (1895) 12 TLR 59; *Adams v Cape Industries plc*, supra, at 517–518.

Furthermore, the jurisdiction of the English court may be based on the mere presence of the defendant within the jurisdiction.[33]

This view is supported by *Carrick v Hancock*:[34]

> A domiciled Englishman appeared after a writ was served on him in Sweden while he was on a short visit to that country. It was held that despite his fleeting stay in Sweden an action on the judgment lay against him in this country.

It has been endorsed, obiter, by the Court of Appeal in *Adams v Cape Industries plc*.[35] The temporary presence must be voluntary, ie not induced by compulsion, fraud or duress.[36] The date of service of process in the foreign country is probably the relevant one for examining whether the defendant is present abroad, rather than the date of issue of proceedings.[37] It is not the date of the cause of action arising.[38]

There is, however, much to be said for the view that casual presence, as distinct from residence, is not a desirable basis of jurisdiction. Where, for instance, both parties are foreigners and the cause of action is based entirely on facts occurring abroad and subject to foreign law, it is strange that the defendant should be bound by the decision of a court in whose jurisdiction he may by chance have been temporarily present. "The court is not a convenient one for either of the parties, nor is it in a favourable position to deal intelligently either with the facts or with the law."[39] Furthermore, any analogy based on the jurisdiction of the English courts is not particularly convincing, since the rules on jurisdiction are operated in conjunction with a discretion to stay the proceedings, and the exercise of the discretion is likely to be an issue when jurisdiction is founded on mere presence.

(b) A corporate defendant

A company cannot literally be resident or present in a foreign country. It may, though, carry on business abroad. The circumstances in which this can amount to an artificial residence or presence in a foreign country were set out by the Court of Appeal in *Adams v Cape Industries plc*.[40] It has to be shown that: (i) the corporation has its own fixed place of business (a branch office) there, from which it has carried on its own business for more than a minimal time, or a representative has carried on the corporation's business for more than a minimal time from a fixed place of business;[41] and (ii) the corporation's business is transacted from that fixed place of business. This second requirement is

---

[33] Supra, pp 354–370. See also *Wendel v Moran* 1993 SLT 44.

[34] (1895) 12 TLR 59.

[35] Supra, at 517–518. See also *Richman v Ben-Tovim* 2007 (2) SALR 283, South African Supreme Court. Cf *Re Carrick Estates Ltd and Young* (1988) 43 DLR (4th) 161.

[36] *Adams v Cape Industries plc*, supra, at 517–518.

[37] Ibid. But cf *Akande v Balfour Beatty Construction Ltd* [1998] IL Pr 110 at 117.

[38] *Emanuel v Symon*, supra; see also *Wendel v Moran* 1993 SLT 44; *Re McTavish & Hampton Securities and Investments Ltd* (1983) 150 DLR (3d) 27; *Rafferty's Restaurant Ltd v Sawchuk* [1983] 3 WWR 261; *Re Kelowna and District Credit Union and Perl* (1984) 13 DLR (4th) 756; *Hull v Wilson* (1995) 128 DLR (4th) 403.

[39] Dodd (1929) 23 Ill LR 427, 437–438.

[40] [1990] Ch 433 at 530–531; Collier [1990] CLJ 416; Carter (1990) 61 BYBIL 402. Cases on the jurisdiction of English courts over claims against foreign companies are relevant in this context: see supra, pp 358–370.

[41] Following *Littauer Glove Corpn v F W Millington (1920) Ltd* (1928) 44 TLR 746. See also *TDI Hospitality Management Consultants Inc v Browne* (1995) 117 DLR (4th) 289, Manitoba CA; *Hull v Wilson* (1996) 128 DLR (4th) 403, Alberta, CA. See also *Long Beach Ltd v Global Witness Ltd* [2007] EWHC 1980 (QB), website

unlikely to cause any difficulties if a branch office is established.[42] However, if business is carried on abroad by a representative the question will arise of whether this person is carrying on the corporation's business or no more than his own. It will then be necessary to look into the functions which this representative has been performing and his relationship with the overseas corporation. This will involve looking at such things as acquisition of business premises, payment of the representative, reimbursement of expenses, the degree of control by the corporation, and display of the corporation's name. The representative's power to bind the corporation contractually is of particular importance. If the representative lacks this power this is a powerful factor counting against the presence or residence of the overseas corporation.

In the *Adams* case these principles were applied to the situation where the corporation carried on business abroad by means of a subsidiary company.

> The defendants, an English company concerned with mining asbestos, and its world-wide marketing subsidiary, another English company, carried on business in the USA through its US marketing subsidiary, NAAC and its successor CPC, companies incorporated in Illinois. Asbestos mined by the defendants was sold for use in an asbestos factory in Texas. The 206 plaintiffs, who were mainly employees injured whilst working at this factory, commenced proceedings for damages in the US Federal District Court at Tyler, Texas. The defendants took no part in these proceedings (the Tyler 2 actions), although they had taken part in earlier asbestos-related proceedings involving different plaintiffs (the Tyler 1 actions),[43] and a default judgment was awarded against them by the US Court.

SCOTT J dismissed the action to enforce the default judgment in England, and this was affirmed by the Court of Appeal. It was held that the defendants were not present in Illinois, since NAAC and CPC, the representatives of the defendants, were carrying on exclusively their own business and not that of the defendants.[44] Relevant to this was the fact that, inter alia, NAAC leased premises itself, bought and stored asbestos, paid taxes on its profits and had its own creditors/debtors. The position of CPC was even weaker since it was an independently owned company and not even a subsidiary of either of the defendants. Moreover, whilst NAAC and CPC performed valuable services for the defendants as intermediaries, neither had power to, and never did, bind the defendants contractually.

A subsidiary will normally act just for itself and not for the overseas parent.[45] Counsel for the plaintiffs tried to get round this difficulty by arguing that the defendants and NAAC were all part of a single economic unit.[46] This radical idea, which is based on the economic reality of the situation and has found favour in the USA,[47] was rejected by the

---

accessible from judgment granting state not enough; cf the position in Canada, *Disney Enterprises Inc v Click Enterprises Inc* (2006) 267 DLR (4th) 291.

[42] There is no requirement, as under the Brussels/Lugano system, that the branch has a certain autonomy, see the discussion of Art 5(5) of the Brussels I Regulation supra, pp 258–260.

[43] This raises arguments in relation to submission, discussed infra, p 527.

[44] [1990] Ch 433 at 545 et seq.

[45] But see Case 218/86 *Sar Schotte Gmbh v Parfums Rothschild* [1987] ECR 4905, which is concerned with jurisdiction under Art 5(5) of the Brussels Convention, discussed supra, pp 258–261.

[46] [1990] Ch 433 at 532 et seq; Fawcett (1988) 37 ICLQ 645.

[47] See *Bulova Watch Co Inc v K Hattori and Co Ltd* 508 F Supp 1322 at 1342 (1981).

Court of Appeal, who emphasised the traditional company law notion that parent and subsidiary are separate legal entities. This means that an English company can set up its business abroad in such a way that it is not present/resident there. Provided that the company does not submit to the jurisdiction of the foreign court, judgments against it in that country will not be enforced in England. The principles in the *Adams* case apply equally to the situation where a defendant company carries on business abroad by means of companies in the same group, which are not subsidiaries, and by means of companies in which it has a shareholding.[48] Normally, these associated companies will act for themselves and not for the defendant company.

What if the defendant had been present/resident in Illinois? Without expressing a final decision on this issue, there are some surprising suggestions, albeit rather hesitant ones, from the Court of Appeal that this would have been sufficient, even though the trial took place in Texas.[49] This was on the basis that the trial took place in a federal district court (ie a US court) rather than a state of Texas court. This was despite the fact that a federal court judge sitting in Texas has to apply that state's rules on both jurisdiction in personam and choice of law, and a federal judgment is itself a foreign judgment when it comes to its enforcement within the USA.

(ii) Submission to the foreign court

(a) Submission by virtue of being the claimant in the foreign action

It is perfectly clear that, if a person voluntarily and unsuccessfully submits his case as claimant to the decision of a foreign tribunal, he cannot afterwards, if sued upon the judgment in England, aver that he was not subject to the jurisdiction of that tribunal.[50]

(b) Agreements to submit

What may be regarded as a particular example of submission arises where the defendant has previously contracted to submit himself to the foreign jurisdiction,[51] as, for instance, in *Feyerick v Hubbard*,[52] where a domiciled British subject resident in London agreed to sell his patent rights to a Belgian, the contract of sale containing a provision that all disputes should be submitted to the jurisdiction of the Belgian courts. A less explicit agreement was held to be sufficient in *Copin v Adamson*,[53] where it was held that the articles of association of a company, which provided that all disputes that might arise during liquidation should be submitted to the jurisdiction of a French court, constituted a contract on the part of every shareholder that he should be bound by a judgment so obtained. "It appears to me", said Lord CAIRNS, "that, to all intents and purposes, it is as if there had been an actual and absolute agreement by the defendant [shareholder]".[54]

---

[48] *Akande v Balfour Beatty Construction Ltd* [1998] IL Pr 110.

[49] [1990] Ch 433 at 550 et seq. Cf *Akande v Balfour Beatty Construction Ltd* [1998] IL Pr 110 at 122.

[50] *Schibsby v Westenholz* (1870) LR 6 QB 155 at 161; *Novelli v Rossi* (1831) 2 B & Ad 757.

[51] *Emanuel v Symon* [1908] 1 KB 302; *Copin v Adamson* (1874) LR 9 Exch 345 at 354.

[52] (1902) 71 LJKB 509. Distinguish an agreement which merely selects the law of a foreign country as the governing law of a contract: *Dunbee Ltd v Gilman & Co (Australia) Pty Ltd* [1968] 2 Lloyds Rep 394, NSW CA; infra, p 700.

[53] (1874) LR 9 Ex Ch 345; affd (1875) 1 Ex D 17; *Vallée v Dumerque* (1849) 4 Exch 290.

[54] (1875) 1 Ex D 17 at 19.

If the agreement was entered into under undue influence it will not constitute submission, but the defendant cannot raise in England the issue of undue influence if this defence was available to him in the foreign proceedings and he failed to raise it there.[55]

In *Copin v Adamson* and other cases[56] the agreement to accept the foreign jurisdiction was express and the weight of authority was in favour of the view that an agreement to submit cannot be implied.[57] Despite this body of opinion, DIPLOCK J held in *Blohn v Desser*[58] that a partner in an Austrian firm who was resident in England and took no part in the conduct of the business would be held impliedly to have agreed to submit to the jurisdiction of the Austrian courts.[59] This conclusion has been strongly criticised, extra-judicially,[60] and was rejected by ASHWORTH J in *Vogel v R and A Kohnstamm Ltd*,[61] who refused to countenance an implied agreement to submit. The Court of Appeal in *New Hampshire v Strabag Bau*[62] expressed a preference for this view rather than that of DIPLOCK J in *Blohn v Desser*.

In *Adams v Cape Industries plc*[63] it was argued that the defendants, by their conduct in participating in the earlier asbestos-related actions (the Tyler 1 actions) in the same court, had represented that they would similarly participate in future claims (ie the Tyler 2 actions) brought in that court, and in that sense had impliedly agreed to submit to the jurisdiction. SCOTT J, speaking obiter, seemed to accept that an implied agreement to submit might suffice. However, a clear indication of consent to the exercise of the foreign court's jurisdiction was needed. Furthermore, in the case of a representation, as opposed to a contractual agreement, this would have to be acted upon by the claimants in some way.

(c) Submission by voluntary appearance[64]

(i) An appearance to fight on the merits

The defendant submits to the jurisdiction of the foreign court by voluntary appearance if he has fought the action on its merits, and so taken his chance of obtaining a judgment in his own favour.[65] A person's submission in respect of a claim against him can also be taken as a submission, first, in respect of claims concerning the same subject matter,

---

[55] *Israel Discount Bank of New York v Hadjipateras* [1984] 1 WLR 137, CA; discussed infra, p 557.

[56] *Bank of Australasia v Harding* (1850) 9 CB 661; *Bank of Australasia v Nias* (1851) 16 QB 717.

[57] *Sirdar Gurdyal Singh v The Rajah of Faridkote* [1894] AC 670 at 685–686; *Emanuel v Symon* [1908] 1 KB 302 at 305, 313–314.

[58] [1962] 2 QB 116; and see *Sfeir & Co v National Insurance Co of New Zealand Ltd* [1964] 1 Lloyd's Rep 330 at 339–340.

[59] In the event, however, the defendant was held not to be liable, since the judgment was not final and conclusive; infra, pp 536–538.

[60] Lewis (1961) 10 ICLQ 910; Cohn (1962) 11 ICLQ 583; ibid, Abel, 587; Carter (1962) 38 BYBIL 493; and see the 8th edn of this book (1970), pp 627–628. But cf Briggs and Rees, para 7.42.

[61] [1973] QB 133; Cohn (1972) 21 ICLQ 157.

[62] [1992] 1 Lloyd's Rep 361 at 372.

[63] [1990] Ch 433 at 463–467. The first instance decision in relation to submission was not challenged on appeal.

[64] For the position where there has been undue influence, see *Israel Discount Bank of New York v Hadjipateras* [1984] 1 WLR 137, CA; discussed supra and infra, at p 557.

[65] *Molony v Gibbons* (1810) 2 Camp 502; *Guiard v De Clermont and Donner* [1914] 3 KB 145; *The Atlantic Emperor (No 2)* [1992] 1 Lloyd's Rep 624 at 633, CA; *Pattni v Ali and Dinky International SA* [2006] UKPC 51 at [39]. On what amounts to an appearance, see *Re Overseas Food Importers & Distributors Ltd and Brandt* (1981) 126 DLR (3d) 422; *Mid-Ohio Imported Car Co v Tri-K Investments Ltd* (1995) 129 DLR (4th) 181, British Columbia CA.

and, secondly, in respect of related claims which might properly be brought against him under the foreign court's rules of procedure, either by the original claimant or by others who were parties to the proceedings (eg co-defendants who subsequently brought a cross-claim) at the time he submitted.[66] It is suggested that if the defendant is represented by a lawyer who has no authority to act for him this should not be regarded as a submission.[67] The finding of a foreign court that the defendant had authorised a lawyer to act on his behalf, and had accordingly submitted to the jurisdiction, may create an issue estoppel preventing this issue of authority being relitigated in England.[68]

(ii) An appearance to protest against jurisdiction

The case that for many years caused difficulty was where a defendant entered an appearance with the sole object of protesting against the jurisdiction of the foreign court.

At common law an illogical distinction was drawn between a protest as to the existence of jurisdiction and as to the exercise of a discretion in relation to jurisdiction. In *Henry v Geoprosco International Ltd*:[69]

> The defendant, a company registered in Jersey, appeared before a court in Alberta and argued, unsuccessfully, that service out of the jurisdiction should be set aside, on the ground, inter alia, that the court was not the *forum conveniens*.

When it came to enforcement of the Alberta judgment in England, the Court of Appeal held that an appearance, such as this, to ask the court to use its discretion not to exercise its jurisdiction constituted submission. However, the court left open the question of whether an appearance solely to protest against the existence of the jurisdiction of a foreign court constituted submission. Not only was the above distinction unjustifiable, but also its application led to the absurd result that, in certain circumstances, a defendant who appeared before a foreign court to protest that it had no jurisdiction over him would be deemed to have submitted to that court's jurisdiction.

The old law has been replaced by section 33 of the Civil Jurisdiction and Judgments Act 1982,[70] which is designed to get rid of this absurdity; but, as will be seen, there are still some problems which are caused by the wording of this section.

Section 33(1) provides that:

> For the purposes of determining whether a judgment given by a court of an overseas country should be recognised or enforced in England and Wales or Northern Ireland, the person against whom the judgment was given shall not be regarded as having submitted to the

---

[66] *Murthy v Sivajothi* [1999] 1 WLR 467, CA, Briggs (1998) 69 BYBIL 349; *Whyte v Whyte* [2005] EWCA Civ 858.

[67] This point was left open in *First National Bank of Houston v Houston E & C Inc* [1990] 5 WWR 719 at 725. But see under the Brussels Convention, Case C–78/95 *Hendrikman v Magenta Druck & Verlag GmbH* [1997] QB 426.

[68] *Desert Sun Loan Corpn v Hill* [1996] 2 All ER 847, CA.

[69] [1976] QB 726, CA; Carter (1974–1975) 47 BYBIL 379; Collier [1975] CLJ 219; Collins (1976) 92 LQR 268–287; Solomons (1976) 25 ICLQ 665. *Henry v Geoprosco* has not been followed in Canada, see *Clinton v Ford* (1982) 137 DLR (3d) 281; Lange (1983) 61 Can Bar Rev 637.

[70] For Australia see s 7(5) of the Foreign Judgments Act 1991 (Cth); *de Santis v Russo* [2002] 2 Qd R 230, CA.

jurisdiction of the court by reason only of the fact that he appeared (conditionally or otherwise) in the proceedings for all or any one or more of the following purposes, namely:

(a) to contest the jurisdiction of the court;
(b) to ask the court to dismiss or stay the proceedings on the ground that the dispute in question should be submitted to arbitration or to the determination of the courts of another country;
(c) to protect, or obtain the release of, property seized or threatened with seizure in the proceedings.

Section 33 only applies to a judgment given by a court of an "overseas country", ie "any country or territory outside the United Kingdom".[71] It does not distinguish between recognition and enforcement at common law and by statute[72] and can, therefore, apply to both, except in so far as section 33(2) applies.

Section 33(2)[73] provides that:

> Nothing in this section shall affect the recognition or enforcement in England and Wales or Northern Ireland of a judgment which is required to be recognised or enforced there under the 1968 Convention or the Lugano Convention or the [Brussels I] Regulation.

This means that, although, in principle, section 33 applies to judgments covered by the Brussels/Lugano system, it remains subject to this system.[74]

Section 33(1) is a negative provision; it does not define what amounts to submission to the jurisdiction of a foreign court, but merely states that an appearance for one or more specified purposes does not amount to submission. *Henry v Geoprosco*[75] shows that a defendant may, in fact, put in an appearance to argue:

(1) that the foreign court has no jurisdiction because no basis of jurisdiction is applicable;
(2) that the foreign court should use its discretionary powers to set aside service out of the jurisdiction on the basis that it is not the *forum conveniens*;
(3) that the foreign court should use its discretionary powers to stay the proceedings on the basis of *forum non conveniens*;
(4) that the foreign court should use its discretionary powers to stay the proceedings because of an agreement on jurisdiction;
(5) that the foreign court should/must stay the proceedings because of an arbitration agreement;
(6) that the foreign court should dismiss or stay the proceedings because of a *Scott v Avery*[76] arbitration clause, ie one which provides not merely for arbitration but that

---

[71] S 50 of the 1982 Act. For judgments given within the United Kingdom, see infra, pp 574–576.

[72] As far as enforcement under the Foreign Judgments (Reciprocal Enforcement) Act 1933 is concerned, s 33 of the 1982 Act merely replaces a similarly worded provision under the 1933 Act (s 4(2)(a)(i)), discussed infra, p 581.

[73] As amended by the Civil Jurisdiction and Judgments Act 1991, Sch 2, para 15 and the Civil Jurisdiction and Judgments Order, SI 2001/3929, Sch 2(IV), para 15.

[74] In cases coming within the Brussels/Lugano system, recognition and enforcement are not dependent on whether the defendant has submitted to the foreign court (see infra, pp 596–597) and therefore s 33 is irrelevant, see Collins, *The Civil Jurisdiction and Judgments Act 1982*, p 144.

[75] [1976] QB 726, CA; discussed supra, p 522.

[76] *Scott v Avery* (1856) 5 HL Cas 811.

an action cannot be maintained until the matter in dispute has first been referred to and decided by arbitrators.

If a defendant puts in an appearance for any one of these purposes, how is this treated under section 33? The answer is to be found by looking at the six categories above and considering them in relation to the three sub-sections under section 33(1).

The three purposes of appearance, specified under section 33(1), which do not amount to submission are as follows:

Section 33(1)(a) *an appearance "to contest the jurisdiction of the court"*
Section 33(1)(a) is of the same effect as, and virtually identical in wording to, the end part of section 4(2)(a)(i) of the Foreign Judgments (Reciprocal Enforcement) Act 1933, which it replaces.[77] It follows that, although section 33(1)(a) will be significant in relation to both recognition at common law and under the 1933 Act, it only introduces a major change in the law in respect of recognition at common law.

Section 33(1)(a) follows the 1933 Act in not defining what is meant by contesting the jurisdiction. Given the history of this area of law it is to be regretted that this concept was not clearly spelled out in the 1982 Act. Category (1), of the six categories set out above, clearly comes within section 33(1)(a).[78] There is more difficulty with category (2). A narrow interpretation of section 33(1)(a) would be that only arguments as to the bases of jurisdiction (category (1)) come within it. The distinction drawn in *Henry v Geoprosco* between the existence of jurisdiction and the exercise of a discretion, with category (2) coming within the latter, could still be followed under section 33(1)(a), due to the imprecise wording of this provision. However, it would be better to give a wide interpretation to section 33(1)(a) so that it encompasses any argument in relation to jurisdiction, whether as to the existence of jurisdiction or as to the exercise of a discretion. The wording of the provision allows this interpretation. Moreover, the distinction drawn in *Henry v Geoprosco* was strongly criticised at the time[79] and section 33(1) was intended to overrule that decision.[80] If this wide interpretation of section 33(1)(a) is accepted, it would also encompass category (3).

Section 33(1)(b) *"an appearance to ask the court to dismiss or stay the proceedings on the ground that the dispute in question should be submitted to arbitration or to the determination of the courts of another country"*
It was necessary to have a separate provision in section 33(1) to deal with the situation set out in section 33(1)(b) because of a line of reasoning adopted by the Court of Appeal in *Henry v Geoprosco*.[81] There, the defendant appeared and sought a stay of proceedings abroad on the basis, inter alia, that there was a *Scott v Avery* type of arbitration clause in the contract between the parties. According to the Court of Appeal,[82] this defence involved an assertion that the plaintiff had no accrued cause of action, and this meant that the

---

[77] See s 54 and Sch 14 of the 1982 Act, and infra, p 581.
[78] See *Desert Sun Loan Corpn v Hill* [1996] 2 All ER 847 at 861, CA (per Roch LJ). But cf Evans LJ and Stuart-Smith LJ who ignored this provision.
[79] See the 10th edn of this book (1979), p 640; Collins (1976) 92 LQR 268, 287; cf Carter (1974–1975) 47 BYBIL 379, 381.
[80] This becomes even more apparent when one looks at s 33(1)(b), discussed infra.
[81] [1976] QB 726; discussed supra, p 522.
[82] [1976] QB 726 at 732–735, 750.

defendants were voluntarily asking the court to adjudicate on the merits of that part of the defence. The defendants had, therefore, submitted to the jurisdiction of the court. Section 33(1)(b) makes it clear that there is no submission in this situation (ie category 6).[83]

Section 33(1)(b) can also, with some confidence, be said to cover category (5).[84] In the first reported decision on section 33, *Tracomin SA v Sudan Oil Seeds Co Ltd*,[85] Staughton J held that Sudanese sellers who appeared before the Swiss courts to ask for a stay of proceedings because of an arbitration clause, which provided that disputes should be submitted to arbitration in London, had not submitted to the jurisdiction of the Swiss courts. The judge did not say whether this situation came within section 33(1)(a) or (1)(b). It is submitted that the more natural place for it is under section 33(1)(b). Section 33(1)(b) does not just deal with agreements on arbitration; it also appears from the context to be designed to deal with agreements on the choice of court (category 4).

Section 33(1)(c) *An appearance "to protect, or obtain the release of, property seized or threatened with seizure in the proceedings"*
Under the common law rules, a defendant who possessed property abroad was placed in a particularly awkward situation. If he ignored the foreign proceedings, he stood to lose his property in the event of a default judgment being granted. On the other hand, if he put in an appearance in order to safeguard his foreign property he stood to lose not only his foreign property but also his English property as well, because his appearance would, in some circumstances, amount to a submission to the foreign court and that court's judgment would accordingly be enforceable in England. Section 33(1)(c) enables the defendant to appear abroad to safeguard his property without running this risk.

Like section 33(1)(a), this provision is closely modelled on the end part of section 4(2)(a)(i) of the Foreign Judgments (Reciprocal Enforcement) Act 1933 which it replaces.[86] Although section 33(1)(c) applies to both recognition at common law and under the 1933 Act, it will only effect a major change in the law in respect of recognition at common law, and is a development to be welcomed as bringing uniformity to these two different types of enforcement.

Section 33(1)(c) follows section 4(2)(a)(i) of the 1933 Act in applying regardless of whether the defendant is seeking to protect property that has already been seized in the proceedings, or whether he is acting with foresight to protect property that is merely threatened with seizure.[87] It thus gets rid of the distinction under the common law between the situation where property had already been seized (an appearance to protect this property would not amount to submission)[88] and where the property was merely

---

[83] The Court of Appeal, ibid at 750, said that this defence could be raised as a plea in bar and not merely where a stay is sought; hence s 33(1)(b) refers to an appearance to ask the court to "dismiss" the proceedings, as well as referring to an appearance to ask the court to stay the proceedings.

[84] In *Henry v Geoprosco*, supra, a stay was sought in Alberta on the basis of both categories (5) and (6).

[85] [1983] 1 WLR 662, 670–672, affd by the Court of Appeal [1983] 1 WLR 1026; the only point raised on appeal was whether s 33, which came into force during the course of the first instance hearing, could apply to an action commenced and a judgment given before the 1982 Act came into force or had been passed.

[86] See s 54 of and Sch 14 to the 1982 Act and infra, p 581.

[87] See *The Eastern Trader* [1996] 2 Lloyd's Rep 585 at 600—a counterclaim to obtain the release of property threatened with seizure did not amount to a submission.

[88] *Henry v Geoprosco International Ltd* [1976] QB 726 at 746–747. See also *Clinton v Ford* (1982) 137 DLR (3d) 281; *Amopharm Inc v Harris Computer Corpn* (1992) 93 DLR (4th) 524.

threatened with seizure (an appearance to protect this property would amount to submission).[89] Now, in neither case is there submission to the foreign court.

(iii) Arguing in the alternative

Where the defendant's plea that the foreign court lacked jurisdiction fails and he then goes on to fight the action on its merits, he has clearly submitted to the foreign court's jurisdiction.[90] However, it is different and there is no submission if the defendant merely raises an initial plea on the merits at the same time as his defence as to lack of jurisdiction, but does not go on actually to fight on the merits.[91] A defendant may do this because he is required under some legal systems to plead a defence on the merits at the outset if he is to raise this defence later on, and he may wish to keep alive this possibility.[92] After the defence as to lack of jurisdiction fails, the defendant may then decide to take no further part in the proceedings. The defendant should not be regarded as having submitted in this situation. According to the Court of Appeal in *The Atlantic Emperor (No 2)*,[93] section 33 should not be construed too narrowly. Even if the defendant is not required to plead a defence on the merits at the outset, where he does so he will not be regarded as having submitted in the situation where he makes it abundantly clear that his primary purpose is to challenge the foreign court's jurisdiction, provided he takes no further part in the proceedings after the defence of lack of jurisdiction fails.

(iv) Appeals against judgments in default

A foreign judgment that is given against an absent defendant in default of his appearance is clearly not actionable in England, but is this so if he later moves to have the default judgment set aside and is unsuccessful? The answer would seem to depend on the grounds for the appeal. If the appeal is as to the merits of the claim, then this will constitute submission,[94] and will normally amount to submission to the judgment of the court of first instance.[95] However, an appeal, or application for leave to appeal, merely as to a jurisdictional issue would not constitute submission.[96]

---

[89] *De Cosse Brissac v Rathbone* (1861) 6 H & N 301; *Voinet v Barrett* (1885) 55 LJQB 39; *Guiard v De Clermont* [1914] 3 KB 145.

[90] *Boissière and Co v Brockner & Co* (1889) 6 TLR 85; *The Atlantic Emperor (No 2)* [1992] 1 Lloyd's Rep 624 at 633, CA.

[91] *The Atlantic Emperor (No 2)* [1992] 1 Lloyd's Rep 624 at 633, CA; *The Eastern Trader* [1996] 2 Lloyd's Rep 585 at 601; Collins, *The Civil Jurisdiction and Judgments Act 1982*, p 144. But cf *Gourmet Resources International Inc v Paramount Capital Corpn* [1993] IL Pr 583, Ont; *Mid-Ohio Imported Car Co v Tri-K Investments Ltd* (1995) 129 DLR (4th) 181, British Columbia CA.

[92] See eg Case 150/80 *Elefanten Schuh GmbH v Jacqmain* [1981] ECR 1671; discussed supra, pp 298–299. See also *The Eastern Trader* [1996] 2 Lloyd's Rep 585 at 600.

[93] Supra, at 633. See also *Starlight International Inc v AJ Bruce* [2002] EWHC 374 at [14], [2002] IL Pr 35.

[94] *SA Consortium General Textiles v Sun and Sand Agencies Ltd* [1978] QB 279 at 299, 304, 308–309; and see *Guiard v De Clermont* [1914] 3 KB 145.

[95] The *SA Consortium General Textiles Case*, supra, at 299, 304; cf *Guiard v De Clermont*, supra, at 155. In so far as these cases discuss appeals on jurisdictional issues they must now be read in the light of s 33 of the 1982 Act, discussed supra, pp 522–525.

[96] The *SA Consortium General Textiles Case*, supra, at 305, 308–309; s 33 of the 1982 Act. It seems that, in two of the Canadian cases where recognition was denied to a default judgment even though the defendant had moved to set it aside, namely *McLean v Shields* (1885) 9 OR 699 and *Esdale v Bank of Ottawa* (1920) 51 DLR 485, the ground on which the defendant moved to set aside the original judgment was want of jurisdiction; see Read, op cit, pp 168–170. In the third it was not clear what the basis for seeking to set aside the original judgment was: *Re Carrick Estates Ltd and Young* (1988) 43 DLR (4th) 161.

(v) Taking procedural steps in the foreign country[97]

In *Adams v Cape Industries plc*[98] SCOTT J held that the defendants' participation in a consent order given by the Federal District judge extinguishing the cause of action against them as part of a settlement of the litigation in the Tyler 1 actions amounted to submission to the jurisdiction of the Federal District Court in Texas, in relation to those proceedings. The defendants had thereby waived the jurisdictional objections that they had raised earlier. However, for such a waiver the defendants must have "taken some step which is only necessary or only useful if the objection has been actually waived, or if the objection has never been entertained at all".[99] There was no such step where a defendant entered a conditional appearance and sought to set aside leave to serve out of the jurisdiction.[100] In the *Adams* case, the argument that submission to the Tyler 1 actions was also submission to the Tyler 2 actions (in respect of which the enforcement proceedings were brought), on the ground that there was just one unit of litigation, was rejected. The basis of submission is consent and participation in the order in relation to the Tyler 1 actions was no evidence of consent to the trial of future actions not yet started (the Tyler 2 actions). More generally, it was said[101] that:

> If the [procedural] steps would not have been regarded by the domestic law of the foreign court as a submission to the jurisdiction, they ought not, in my view, to be so regarded here.

(iii) Nothing else founds jurisdiction

The results so far of our inquiry into the international competence of foreign courts is that jurisdiction sufficient to render a judgment actionable in England exists in two cases, namely, where the defendant was resident or, possibly, present in the country of the forum at the time of the action, or where he submitted to the jurisdiction. The question now is whether there are any other grounds of competency.[102]

(a) Political nationality

Is the fact that the defendant is a national of the foreign country where the judgment has been obtained sufficient to render him amenable to the jurisdiction of the local courts? There is no English authority that contains an actual decision to this effect, but the suggestion that this is enough has been affirmed obiter in several cases.[103]

---

[97] See generally Briggs and Rees, para 7.41.

[98] [1990] Ch 433, supra, pp 518–520. See also *The Eastern Trader* [1996] 2 Lloyd's Rep 585 at 600; *Starlight International Inc v AJ Bruce* [2002] EWHC 374 at [41], [2002] IL Pr 35; *Von Wyl v Engeler* [1998] 3 NZLR 416, CA.

[99] The *Adams* case, supra, at 458. Cf *Starlight International Inc v AJ Bruce* [2002] EWHC 374 at [41], [2002] IL Pr 35—waiver according to US Federal Law.

[100] *Akande v Balfour Beatty Construction Ltd* [1998] IL Pr 110 at 114–116.

[101] The *Adams* case, supra, at 461. See also *Starlight International Inc v A J Bruce* [2002] EWHC 374 at [15]–[16], [2002] IL Pr 35.

[102] See generally *Adams v Cape Industries plc* [1990] Ch 433 at 515; and also *Emanuel v Symon* [1908] 1 KB 302 at 309; *Schibsby v Westenholz* (1870) LR 6 QB 155 at 161; *Rousillon v Rousillon* (1880) 14 Ch D 351 at 371. See also *State of New York v Fitzgerald* (1983) 148 DLR (3d) 176.

[103] *Douglas v Forrest* (1828) 4 Bing 686; *Schibsby v Westenholz* (1870) LR 6 QB 155 at 161; *Rousillon v Rousillon* (1880) 14 Ch D 351 at 371; *Emanuel v Symon* (1908) 1 KB 302 at 309; *Harris v Taylor* [1915] 2 KB 580 at 591; *Forsyth v Forsyth* [1948] P 125 at 132. See also *Gavin Gibson & Co v Gibson* [1913] 3 KB 379 at 388.

It is also adopted by certain textbook writers.[104] It has been rejected by the Irish High Court.[105]

It is submitted with some confidence that nationality per se is not, and has been rejected as, a reason which, on any principle of private international law, can justify the exercise of jurisdiction.[106] The argument advanced in its favour, namely that "a subject is bound to obey the commands of his Sovereign, and, therefore, the judgments of his sovereign courts",[107] is no doubt true, but, as WOLFF pointed out, it is not the duty of another sovereign to aid the enforcement of the obligation.[108] Indeed the undesirability of such a rule becomes abundantly clear when it is remembered that it is essentially within the competence of a state to decide who are and who are not its nationals. The granting or withholding of nationality is sometimes an instrument of political policy. Even if this is not the case, the legal tie of nationality may have an extremely slender factual basis. If a Japanese court were to give judgment in personam against a person who, though born in Japan, had left that country in his infancy and acquired a domicile in England without taking out letters of naturalisation, it is difficult to appreciate the justification for holding the judgment actionable in England. Again, to make nationality the basis of jurisdiction is scarcely practicable in the case of states, such as the United Kingdom,[109] the USA,[110] Canada or Australia, which contain several separate law districts. Finally, there is no question of reciprocal recognition, for the British nationality of a defendant does not suffice to found the jurisdiction of the English court.

(b) Domicile

If mere allegiance suffices to give jurisdiction, so also, it might be presumed, does domicile. The connection between a person and the country in which he is domiciled is generally a very real one, but the tie of allegiance may be of the loosest description. An ineffective exercise of jurisdiction ought not to be tolerated, and it is undeniable that a judgment based on domicile is superior on the score of effectiveness to one based merely on allegiance. Yet the curious thing is that those writers who are content to make political allegiance a ground of jurisdiction deny without hesitation the sufficiency of domicile. It is suggested that on this point at least they must be right and that domicile alone will not suffice as a ground of jurisdiction.[111]

---

104 Westlake, p 399; Foote, p 398; Schmitthoff, *Conflict of Laws* (3rd edn), p 465. It is rejected by Wolff, p 126; Graveson, pp 621–622 (though he suggests exceptions). But see Read, op cit, pp 151–155; Dicey, Morris and Collins, para 14-078.

105 *Rainford v Newell Roberts* [1962] IR 95; Jackson (1963) 26 MLR 563.

106 *Blohn v Desser* [1962] 2 QB 116 at 123; and see *Rossano v Manufacturers' Life Insurance Co Ltd* [1963] 2 QB 352 at 382–383; *Vogel v R and A Kohnstamm Ltd* [1973] QB 133 at 141; the *Adams* case, supra, at 515.

107 Dicey (6th edn), p 357.

108 Wolff, p 126. He further points out that allegiance is not sufficient even in those civil law countries where nationality is the criterion of the personal law.

109 See *Patterson v D'Agostino* (1975) 58 DLR (3d) 63.

110 See *Dakota Lumber Co v Rinderknecht* (1905) 6 Terr LR 210 at 221–224.

111 Read, op cit, p 160.

(c) Locality of cause of action

According to the decisions that have dealt with the matter up to the present, it is undoubted that the various circumstances considered above exhaust the possible cases in which a foreign court possesses international competence. Thus it is not sufficient that the cause of action, as, for instance, a breach of contract or the commission of a tort,[112] occurred in a foreign country.[113]

(d) Choice of governing law

It has been held by the Supreme Court of New South Wales that an agreement to submit to the jurisdiction of the English courts is not to be inferred from an agreement to make English law the governing law of a contract.[114]

(e) Possession of property

It was once thought, on the authority of *Becquet v MacCarthy*,[115] that the possession of immovable property within the foreign country was sufficient to found jurisdiction. It is safe to conclude that this decision would not be followed now for it has since been decided by the Court of Appeal in *Emanuel v Symon*[116] that neither the fact of possessing property in a foreign country nor the fact of making a partnership contract there relating to the property is sufficient to render the possessor amenable to the local jurisdiction.

(f) Foreign judgment based on service out of the jurisdiction

The practice, illustrated by rule 6.20 of the Civil Procedure Rules,[117] under which the courts of a country assume jurisdiction over absentees, raises the question whether a foreign judgment given in these circumstances will be recognised in England.[118] The authorities, so far as they go, are against recognition. The question arose in *Buchanan v Rucker*[119] where it was disclosed that, by the law of Tobago, service of process might be effected on an absent defendant by nailing a copy of the summons on the door of the court house. It was held that a judgment given against an absentee after service in this manner was an international nullity having no extra-territorial effect. Indeed, the suggestion that it should be actionable in England prompted Lord ELLENBOROUGH to ask with some disdain: "Can the island of Tobago pass a law to bind the rights of the whole world? Would the world submit to such an assumed jurisdiction?"[120]

---

[112] Eg *Gyonyor v Sanjenko* [1971] 5 WWR 381.

[113] *Sirdar Gurdyal Singh v Faridkote* [1894] AC 670 at 684; *Phillips v Batho* [1913] 3 KB 25 at 30; *Wendel v Moran* 1993 SLT 44; cf *Schibsby v Westenholz* (1870) LR 6 QB 155 at 161.

[114] *Dunbee Ltd v Gilman & Co (Australia) Pty Ltd* [1968] 2 Lloyd's Rep 394; and see *Mattar and Saba v Public Trustee* [1952] 3 DLR 399.

[115] (1831) 2 B & Ad 951.

[116] [1908] 1 KB 302; and see *Sirdar Gurdyal Singh v Faridkote* [1894] AC 670 at 685.

[117] Supra, pp 372–413.

[118] See Clarence Smith (1953) 2 ICLQ 524–526.

[119] (1808) 9 East 192.

[120] Ibid, at 194.

A less fanciful process again raised the question in *Schibsby v Westenholz*,[121] where a judgment had been given by a French court against Danish subjects resident in England. The defendants were notified of the proceedings in the customary manner, which involved forwarding the summons to the consulate of the country where the defendant resided, with instructions to deliver it to him if practicable. The defendants failed to appear and judgment was given against them. It was held that no action lay on the judgment. Had the principle on which judgments are enforceable been comity, the Court of Queen's Bench intimated that having regard to the English practice of service out of the jurisdiction it would have reached a different conclusion. Since, however, the basis of enforcement is that a judgment imposes an obligation on the defendant, it followed that there must be a connection between him and the forum sufficiently close to make it his duty to perform that obligation. No such duty could be spelt out of the inactivity of the defendants, who were aliens resident in a foreign country. WRIGHT J reached the same conclusion in a later case where a New Zealand judgment had been given against an absentee under an assumed jurisdiction substantially similar to that countenanced by the English rules on service out of the jurisdiction.[122]

It is not without significance, however, that in this general context the Court of Appeal in *Travers v Holley*[123] acted on the basis of reciprocity and held that what entitles an English court to assume divorce jurisdiction is equally effective in the case of a foreign court. In a later case, however, HODSON LJ observed that *Travers v Holley* was: "a decision limited to a judgment *in rem* in a matter affecting matrimonial status, and it has not been followed, so far as I am aware, in any case except a matrimonial case".[124] Thus, any suggestion that the advance towards "internationalism"[125] made by that decision should be extended to jurisdiction assumed under provisions substantially similar to those contained in the English rules on service out of the jurisdiction has so far not been accepted, and the present position is that the rules set out above remain intact.[126]

(iv) The real and substantial connection test

The Supreme Court of Canada in *Morguard Investments Ltd v De Savoye*[127] has adopted a radically different approach towards the recognition and enforcement of foreign judgments at common law in inter-provincial cases. The concern is to produce a greater

---

[121] (1870) LR 6 QB 155.

[122] *Turnbull v Walker* (1892) 67 LT 767.

[123] [1953] P 246; see also *Re Dulles' Settlement (No 2)* [1951] Ch 842 at 851. For the current law on recognition of foreign divorces, etc see infra, p 986 et seq.

[124] *Re Trepca Mines Ltd* [1960] 1 WLR 1273 at 1281–1282; and see *Schemmer v Property Resources Ltd* [1975] Ch 273 at 287; *Henry v Geoprosco International Ltd* [1976] QB 726 at 745; *Felixstowe Dock and Rly Co v United States Lines Inc* [1989] QB 360; *Murthy v Sivajothi* [1999] 1 All ER 721 at 730, CA; *Gordon Pacific Developments Pty Ltd v Conlon* [1993] 3 NZLR 760. See also *Morguard Investments Ltd v De Savoye* (1991) 76 DLR (4th) 256, Sup Ct of Canada.

[125] Kahn-Freund, *The Growth of Internationalism in English Private International Law*, p 30 et seq.

[126] *Société Cooperative Sidmetal v Titan International Ltd* [1966] 1 QB 828 at 841; and see *Crick v Hennessy* [1973] WAR 74.

[127] (1991) 76 DLR (4th) 256; Castel and Walker, *Canadian Conflict of Laws* (6th edn), para 14.5d; Blom (1991) 70 Can Bar Rev 733; Glenn (1992) 37 McGill LJ 537; confirmed in *Hunt v T & N plc* (1993) 109 DLR (4th) 16 (Supreme Court of Canada); Walsh (1994) 73 Can Bar Rev 304.

degree of recognition and enforcement within the Canadian federation than has hitherto been the case under the English-based common law rules. A judgment granted in another province is entitled to recognition and enforcement provided that the judgment granting court "properly, or appropriately, exercised jurisdiction in the action". This requirement is satisfied where the forum that had assumed jurisdiction and given judgment has "a real and substantial connection with the action".[128] This is a more flexible test than that under the English common law and may be satisfied in the situation where the defendant was neither resident in the judgment granting state nor submitted to its courts.[129] This approach is not concerned solely with Canadian federalism but also more widely with "the need in modern times to facilitate the flow of wealth, skills and people across state lines in a fair and orderly manner".[130] It is not surprising therefore that the Supreme Court of Canada in *Beals v Saldanha* has extended this approach to the recognition and enforcement at common law of judgments granted outside Canada.[131] It is for the enforcing court to decide whether there is the requisite real and substantial connection. However, it would be "odd indeed if a Canadian court would refuse to recognise and enforce a judgment of a foreign court in a situation where the foreign court assumed jurisdiction on the same basis on which Canadian courts assume jurisdiction".[132] There is much to be said for adopting the real and substantial connection test, or something similar, in England.[133] Indeed, its origin is to be found in a decision of the House of Lords on the recognition of foreign divorces at common law.[134] However, the introduction of any such wider test for the international jurisdiction of a foreign court for enforcement purposes would need to be accompanied by a re-examination of the natural justice and public policy defences so as to protect defendants who have been subject to injustice abroad.[135]

---

[128] For some of the factors relevant to determining this, see *Bank of Credit and Commerce International (Overseas) Ltd v Gokal* [1995] IL Pr 316 at 319 (Warren J SC of British Columbia); *Moses v Shore Boat Builders Ltd* (1993) 106 DLR (4th) 654 at 667, British Columbia CA. This requirement is also satisfied if the defendant was in the jurisdiction at the time of the action or submitted to the jurisdiction. The new rule can therefore be regarded as adding to the existing common law rules.

[129] As in the *Morguard* case itself.

[130] La Forest J in *Morguard*, supra, at 269.

[131] 2003 SCC 72; criticised by Atrill [2004] CLJ 574, Walker (2004) 120 LQR 365. The parties remain free to submit or agree to the jurisdiction in which the dispute is to be resolved, at [34] and [37]. The real and substantial connection test is subject to a different statutory approach, see at [28]–[29]; *Hull v Wilson* [1996] IL Pr 307, CA of Alberta.

[132] *Moses v Shore Boat Builders Ltd* (1993) 106 DLR (4th) 654 at 667, British Columbia CA. See also the *Beals* case, supra, at [29]. For enforcement of a judgment of a foreign state where jurisdiction was based on service out of the jurisdiction see *Frymer v Brettschneider* [1996] IL Pr 138, Ont CA—the subject matter of the litigation must have a real connection with that state.

[133] See Briggs (1992) 109 LQR 549 at seq and (1987) 36 ICLQ 240, who favours recognition and enforcement where the foreign court is the natural forum. See also Rogerson [1998] CJQ 91 at 102. Cf Harris (1997) 17 OJLS 477, who would base recognition and enforcement on whether or not the English courts are willing to restrain the foreign proceedings by anti-suit injunction.

[134] *Indyka v Indyka* [1969] 1 AC 33. For the present rules, which are statutory, see infra, p 986 et seq.

[135] See Walker, op cit; the dissenting judgments of Binnie, Iacobucci and LeBel JJ in the *Beals* case.

(b) Judgments in rem

(i) The definition of a judgment in rem

The jurisdictional elements that must exist before a foreign judgment in rem can claim recognition in England are not difficult to specify, but it is first necessary to appreciate the correct meaning of this species of judgment. It has been defined as:

> a judgment of a court of competent jurisdiction determining the status of a person or thing (as distinct from the particular interest in it of a party to the litigation); and such a judgment is conclusive evidence for and against all persons whether parties, privies or strangers of the matters actually decided.[136]

More recently, a judgment in rem has been defined as the judicial determination of the existence of rights over property.[137] In contrast, a judgment in personam determines the existence of rights against a person.[138] There is no reason why a judgment should be characterised as either wholly in rem or wholly in personam.[139] This is not a mattter of severance, rather it is a matter of analysis of the extent to which a judgment operates in part in rem and in part in personam. An order of a bankruptcy court in the USA during bankruptcy proceedings there has been held to be neither a judgment in rem nor one in personam since such proceedings are not concerned with the determination of the existence of rights.[140] The two parts of the above-quoted definition will now be considered.

(a) The subject matter of a judgment in rem

The *res* which may form the subject matter of a judgment in rem is not confined to physical things. If the essence of such a judgment is that it constitutes an adjudication on status, it follows that certain decrees declaring the status of persons must also be classed as operating in rem.[141] Thus, the word *res* as used in this context includes those human relationships, such as marriage, which do not originate merely in contract, but which constitute what may be called institutions recognised by the state.[142] A foreign court which issues, for instance, a decree of divorce or nullity of marriage will, if competent in respect of jurisdiction, be deemed to have pronounced a judgment in rem that is conclusive in England and binding on all persons.[143]

---

[136] *Lazarus-Barlow v Regent Estates Co Ltd* [1949] 2 KB 465 at 475. And see *Fracis Times & Co v Carr* (1900) 82 LT 698 at 701; *Pattni v Ali and Dinky International SA* [2006] UKPC 51 at [19]–[23], [2007] 2 AC 85; Spencer Bower, Turner and Handley, *The Doctrine of Res Judicata* (3rd edn), para 234-5.

[137] *Cambridge Gas Transportation Corpn v Official Committee of Unsecured Creditors of Navigator Holdings plc* [2006] UKPC 26 at [13], [2007] 1 AC 508; Briggs [2007] LMCLQ 129 and (2006) 77 BYBIL 575.

[138] *Cambridge Gas Transportation*, supra, at [13].

[139] *Pattni v Ali and Dinky International SA* [2006] UKPC 51 at [37], [2007] 2 AC 85; Briggs [2007] LMCLQ 129 and (2006) 77 BYBIL 575; Tham [2007] LMCLQ 129.

[140] *Cambridge Gas Transportation Corpn v Official Committee of Unsecured Creditors of Navigator Holdings plc* [2006] UKPC 26, [2007] 1 AC 508. According to Lord HOFFMANN, at [14], "Bankruptcy proceedings provide a mechanism for collective execution against the property of the debtor by creditors whose rights are admitted or established."

[141] *Salvesen v Administrator of Austrian Property* [1927] AC 641 at 662 (per Lord DUNEDIN), and see per Lord HALDANE, ibid, at 652–653.

[142] Cf Lord HALDANE in *Salvesen's Case* [1927] AC 641 at 652–653.

[143] For the estoppel effect of foreign nullity decrees, see *Vervaeke v Smith* [1983] 1 AC 145; discussed infra, pp 567–568.

There is some authority for the view that judgments in personam that are ancillary to such judgments in rem are equally binding in England. An illustration of this is afforded by *Phillips v Batho*[144] where the facts were as follows:

> The plaintiff, domiciled in India, obtained a divorce from his wife in an Indian court, and was awarded damages against the defendant, as co-respondent. The defendant was not present in India at the time of the suit, nor did he submit to the jurisdiction. The plaintiff then sued him in England to recover the damages awarded by the Indian judgment.

This judgment, if treated as one in personam, was not actionable in England, since the Indian court had no jurisdiction in personam over the defendant. Neither, in the opinion of the judge, could the plaintiff sue in England on the original cause of action, for the English court had divorce jurisdiction, at that time, only where the parties were domiciled in England. Scrutton J avoided the difficulties by holding that the judgment awarding damages was ancillary to the judgment in rem dissolving the marriage and, as such, was probably conclusive everywhere, and at any rate was conclusive in another part of the Commonwealth.[145] This decision has been subjected to devastating criticism;[146] it has been disapproved in New Zealand,[147] ignored in Canada[148] and is probably wrong. The judgment should be treated as one in personam whose recognition should be denied on the ground of lack of jurisdiction.

(b) The effect of a judgment in rem

The effect, for instance, of a condemnation in the Admiralty court in prize proceedings is to vest the ship in the captors and thus to alter its status. Such a judgment differs fundamentally from one in personam. A judgment in rem settles the destiny of the res itself "and binds all persons claiming an interest in the property inconsistent with the judgment even though pronounced in their absence";[149] a judgment in personam, although it may concern a res, merely determines the rights of the litigants *inter se* to the res. The former looks beyond the individual rights of the parties, the latter is directed solely to those rights.[150] Thus a judgment of a Kenyan court that two defendants "do transfer all the 100% shares in the 3rd defendant [World Duty] to the plaintiff as per the said sale and purchase agreement . . ." was held to be a judgment in personam, rather than one in rem.[151] It did not constitute or involve any form of adjudication or purported adjudication in rem relating to the shares in World Duty. Nor did it even purport actually to transfer or deal with the shares. Rather, what it did was to determine the parties' rights and duties relating to them.

---

[144] [1913] 3 KB 25.
[145] "A holding which created a new type of judgment—a hybrid obtained by crossing an action *in rem* with an action *in personam*, with the dominant jurisdictional characteristics being possessed by the former." Read, op cit, p 264.
[146] Ibid, pp 264–267.
[147] *Redhead v Redhead and Crothers* [1926] NZLR 131; see Webb & Davis, pp 182–183.
[148] *Patterson v D'Agostino* (1975) 58 DLR (3d) 63.
[149] *Dollfus Mieg et Compagnie SA v Bank of England* [1949] Ch 369 at 383.
[150] *Castrique v Imrie* (1870) LR 4 HL 414 at 427.
[151] *Pattni v Ali and Dinky International SA* [2006] UKPC 51 at [39], [2007] 2 AC 85.

(ii) Recognition of judgments in rem: the jurisdictional requirements

A foreign judgment which purports to operate in rem will not attract extra-territorial recognition unless it has been given by a court internationally competent in this respect. In the eyes of English law, the adjudicating court must have jurisdiction to give a judgment binding all persons generally.

(a) Judgments relating to immovables

If the judgment relates to immovables, it is clear that only the court of the situs is competent.[152] So English courts will not recognise foreign judgments concerning title under a will to land in England,[153] even though our courts might take jurisdiction to determine the validity of wills as to foreign land.[154] Similarly, though jurisdiction is taken here over actions in personam concerning foreign land,[155] foreign judgments in personam concerning English land are unlikely to be recognised here.[156]

(b) Judgments relating to movables

In the case of movables, however, the question of competence is not so simple, since there would appear to be at least three classes of judgments in rem.[157]

(i) Judgments that immediately vest the property in a certain person as against the whole world

These occur, for instance, where a foreign court of Admiralty condemns a vessel in prize proceedings. The Privy Council has said, obiter, that a judgment in rem of a Kenyan court transferring Isle of Man shares (as required by a sale and purchase agreement) cannot be recognised as having in rem effect.[158] However, it will not be ignored for all purposes. It could arguably operate to create an issue estoppel abroad preventing the defendants from arguing they were not in breach of the sale and purchase agreement.[159]

(ii) Judgments that decree the sale of a thing in satisfaction of a claim against the thing itself

A judgment which orders a chattel to be sold is a judgment in rem if the object of the sale is to afford a remedy, not by execution against the general estate of the defendant, but by appropriating the chattel in satisfaction of the claimant's claim. Such a judgment is not the same as the sentence of an Admiralty court in a prize case which immediately vests the property in the claimant, but it is analogous thereto if the money demand of the claimant in respect of which it is given is a demand against the chattel and not against the owner personally.[160] In all cases, therefore, the nature of a foreign judgment that has ordered the sale of some chattel must be determined by ascertaining whether, according to the foreign

---

[152] *Re Trepca Mines Ltd* [1960] 1 WLR 1273 at 1277.
[153] *Boyse v Colclough* (1854) 1 K & J 124; and see *Re Hoyles* [1911] 1 Ch 179 at 185–186.
[154] Supra, p 486.
[155] Supra, pp 480–486.
[156] See *Duke v Andler* [1932] SCR 734, supra, p 485; see also White (1982) 9 Sydney LR 630. Cf *Chapman Estate v O'Hara* [1988] 2 WWR 275.
[157] Westlake, s 149.
[158] *Pattni v Ali and Dinky International SA* [2006] UKPC 51 at [38], [2007] 2 AC 85.
[159] Ibid.
[160] *Imrie v Castrique* (1860) 8 CBNS 405 at 411, 412.

law, the original action was a suit against the chattel. The subject was elaborately considered by fourteen judges in the leading case of *Castrique v Imrie*:[161]

> The owner of a British ship mortgaged her to X while she was on a voyage. During the voyage the master drew a bill of exchange on the owner for the cost of certain repairs and indorsed it to a Frenchman at Le Havre. The indorsee brought an action on the bill against the master at Le Havre, and obtained a judgment which declared as follows: "The Tribunal condemns Benson in his quality (capacity) of captain of the vessel *Ann Martin*, and *by privilege on that vessel* to pay to the plaintiff" the amount of the bill. The court declared the master to be free from arrest to which otherwise he would have been liable. A higher court, though having an opinion from the Attorney-General that by English law the mortgagee had a better right than the indorsee, affirmed the decision and ordered the ship to be sold. The ship, having been sold, ultimately arrived in England, and the mortgagee brought an action in the Court of Common Pleas to recover her, on the ground that the sale in France was illegal and void.

The decision necessarily depended on the nature of the French judgment. If it was in rem, then the plaintiff must fail, since the ship was in France at the time of the proceedings. If the judgment was in personam, it was not binding on the mortgagee, since he had been absent from the French proceedings. The Court of Common Pleas held the judgment to be in personam, but the Exchequer Chamber and the House of Lords reversed this decision.

The "privilege" which the judgment created on the ship was, according to French law, a species of lien, and although the proceedings were started against the master as well as against the ship, the sale was ordered not in execution of the judgment debt, but in enforcement of the lien. A more striking example of the manner in which English courts pay recognition to foreign judgments in rem is afforded by *Minna Craig Steamship Co v Chartered Bank of India*,[162] for there the lien that had been declared by a German court was one which conflicted with the principles of English internal law. In this type of case, the only court competent to give a judgment affecting the status of a res that will command general recognition is the court of the country where the res was situated at the time of the action.

(iii) Judgments that order movables to be sold by way of administration[163]

If, in the course of administering an estate in bankruptcy or on death, a foreign court orders the sale of chattels, the sale will be regarded as conferring a title on the purchaser valid in England. In the case of succession on death, jurisdiction to make such an order resides in the court of the country where the deceased died domiciled.[164] Subject to the European Community Insolvency Regulation,[165] the English courts will recognise the bankruptcy jurisdiction of a foreign court if the debtor was domiciled in the foreign country or submitted to the jurisidiction of the foreign court.[166]

---

[161] (1860) 8 CBNS 405; revsd, ibid, p 405; reversal affd (1870) LR 4 HL 414.
[162] [1897] 1 QB 55; affd, ibid, 460.
[163] Westlake, s 149.
[164] See *Re Trufort, Trafford v Blanc* (1887) 36 Ch D 600.
[165] Council Regulation (EC) 1346/2000 on insolvency proceedings.
[166] Dicey, Morris and Collins, para 31R-059.

(iii) Enforcement of judgments in rem

Whilst recognition of a foreign judgment in rem may be fairly common and relatively straightforward, enforcement of such judgments in England raises different issues. No foreign judgment relating to immovables abroad can be enforced in England. If the judgment relates to movables, the real issue is whether it was sufficient to pass title to the property, ie a question of recognition rather than enforcement.[167] A rare example of enforcement of a foreign judgment by an action in rem in England is provided by *The City of Mecca*.[168] Sir Robert PHILLIMORE held that a Portuguese judgment for damages for the loss caused by a collision on the high seas between a Spanish ship and a British ship was a judgment in rem which could be enforced in England by an action in rem against the ship. Although on appeal this decision was set aside on the ground that the Portuguese judgment was, in fact, a judgment in personam,[169] the first instance decision is still of good authority and has been applied by SHEEN J in *The Despina GK*.[170]

(c) Finality of the judgment

A foreign judgment does not create a valid cause of action in England unless it is *res judicata* by the law of the country where it was given. It must be final and conclusive in the sense that it must have determined all controversies between the parties. If it may be altered in later proceedings between the same parties *in the same court*, it is not enforceable by action in England.[171] These principles will now be examined.

A provisional judgment is not *res judicata* if it contemplates that a fuller investigation leading to a final decision may later be held. This aspect of the meaning of finality and conclusiveness is illustrated by the leading case of *Nouvion v Freeman*.[172]

> X, who had sold certain land in Seville to Y, brought an "executive" action in Spain against Y and obtained a "remate" judgment for a large sum of money. There were two kinds of proceedings under Spanish law; executive or summary proceedings, and "plenary" or ordinary proceedings. In an executive action, on proof of a prima facie case, the judge without notice to the defendant made an order for the attachment of his property. Notice of the attachment was given to the defendant and he was at liberty to appear and defend the action. But the defences open to him were limited in number, and in particular he could not set up any defence that denied the validity of the transaction upon which he was sued. Either party who failed in executive proceedings could institute plenary proceedings before the same judge, and in these could set up every defence that was known to the law.

---

[167] *Castrique v Imrie* (1870) LR 4 HL 414 at 429.

[168] (1879) 5 PD 28.

[169] (1881) 6 PD 106.

[170] [1983] 1 QB 214; see also *SS Pacific Star v Bank of America National Trust and Savings Association* [1965] WAR 159.

[171] *Nouvion v Freeman* (1889) 15 App Cas 1; *Re Riddell* (1888) 20 QBD 512 at 516; *Blohn v Desser* [1962] 2 QB 116. Interim payments are now enforceable under the Foreign Judgments (Reciprocal Enforcement) Act 1933, see infra, p 580.

[172] (1889) 15 App Cas 1; applied in *Colt Industries Inc v Sarlie (No 2)*, [1966] 1 WLR 1287; *Berliner Industriebank AG v Jost* [1971] 2 All ER 1513; distinguished in *Audrain v Aero Photo Inc* (1983) 138 DLR (3d) 177.

It was held by the House of Lords, affirming the Court of Appeal, that no action lay on the remate judgment. Since it was liable to be abrogated by the adjudicating court, it was not *res judicata* with regard to either party, neither did it extinguish the original cause of action.

A more modern illustration is afforded by *Blohn v Desser*.[173] In that case, an action was brought against the defendant personally on an Austrian judgment that had been given not against her individually, but against a firm of which she was a member. To have rendered her personally liable under Austrian law would have necessitated a separate action against her individually, but in this event certain defences would have been available to her that could not have been raised in the proceedings against the firm. Therefore, even if the judgment could be regarded as given against her personally, it was not final and conclusive. Again, to take another important example, a judgment in default of appearance, whilst it can be final and conclusive,[174] does not satisfy the condition of finality if it is given in a country where the defendant is allowed to apply within a limited time for its rescission by the adjudicating court.[175]

The necessity for finality and conclusiveness appears in a slightly different aspect in the cases dealing with foreign maintenance orders. As is the case in England, foreign courts usually have power to vary the amount of maintenance orders. Thus in *Harrop v Harrop*[176] the issue was the recognition of an order for maintenance made in Perak. A magistrate could order a person to pay a monthly allowance for maintenance of his wife, and, if such order was disregarded, could direct the amount due to be levied in the manner in which fines were levied. On application by the husband or wife and on proof of a change in the circumstances of the parties, the magistrate could vary the amount to be paid. In the present case a magistrate had ordered the payment of a monthly sum, and later, when this fell into arrears, had ordered that payment of the arrears should be enforced by the appropriate method. The wife failed in the action which she brought in England on these orders. SANKEY J, in the course of his judgment, put the gist of the matter in these words: "In my view a judgment or order cannot be said to be final and conclusive if (1) an order has to be obtained for its enforcement, and (2) on application for such an order the original judgment is liable to be abrogated or varied."[177]

If a court is empowered to vary the amount of future payments of maintenance but cannot alter its order as to accrued instalments, then instalments that are already due under the foreign judgment may be recovered by action in England.[178] *Harrop v Harrop* is not inconsistent with this rule, for in that case no evidence was given to show that the amount of accrued instalments was unalterable.

---

[173] [1962] 2 QB 116. Austrian judgments are now enforced under the Brussels I Regulation.

[174] *Starlight International Inc v A J Bruce* [2002] EWHC 374 at [17], [2002] IL Pr 35—it must be *res judicata* in the foreign legal system; *Schnabel v Yung Lui* [2002] NSWSC 15.

[175] Wolff, op cit, pp 264, 265. Cf *Barclays Bank Ltd v Piacun* [1984] 2 Qd R 476; *Re Dooney* [1993] 2 Qd R 362.

[176] [1920] 3 KB 386; and see *Re Macartney* [1921] 1 Ch 522. But cf *McC v McC* [1994] 1 IR 293.

[177] [1920] 3 KB 386 at 399. Provision for reciprocal enforcement of foreign maintenance orders is now made by statute, infra, pp 1069–1073.

[178] *Beatty v Beatty* [1924] 1 KB 807; and see *Patton v Reed* (1972) 30 DLR (3d) 494; *Lear v Lear* (1974) 51 DLR (3d) 56; *Stark v Stark* (1979) 94 DLR (3d) 556; *McLean v McLean* [1979] 1 NSWLR 620.

A decision that is final and conclusive is not provisional. As regards an interlocutory decision or order, decisions that are interlocutory in the sense of being made pending final determination of the case, such as an interlocutory injunction pending trial, are not final and conclusive.[179] But where a case is *res judicata*, has been decided on a full consideration of the merits, and the matter cannot be challenged or reheard by the same court it will be final and conclusive, even though it remains possible that an adjustment may be made to the damages by the same court on the application of either party (but which does not challenge the existence of the debt).[180]

The requirement of finality means that the judgment must be final in the particular court in which it was pronounced.[181] It does not mean that there must be no right of appeal. Neither the fact that the judgment may be reversed on appeal, nor even the stronger fact that an actual appeal is pending in the foreign country, is a bar to an action brought in England;[182] though where an appeal is pending the English court has an equitable jurisdiction to stay execution, which it will generally exercise.[183] If, however, the effect under the foreign law of a pending appeal is to stay execution of the judgment, it would seem that, in the interim, the judgment is not actionable in England.[184]

(d) The judgment, if in personam, must be for a fixed sum

As we have seen, the ground on which a foreign judgment is enforceable in England is that the defendant has implicitly promised to pay the amount due under the judgment.[185] It follows that there can be no question of enforcing a foreign decree for specific performance or for the specific delivery or restitution of chattels. Moreover, the law implies a promise to pay a definite, not an indefinite, sum.[186] Unless in an action in personam the foreign court has definitely and finally determined the amount to be paid, no action is maintainable in England.[187] In *Sadler v Robins*[188] a court in Jamaica had decreed that the defendant should pay to the plaintiff £3,670 9s 1/4d, first deducting therefrom the full costs expended by the defendant, such costs to be taxed by a master of the court. It was held that until taxation the plaintiff had no cause of action in England, since the sum due

---

179 *Desert Sun Loan Corpn v Hill* [1996] 2 All ER 847 at 863 (per STUART-SMITH LJ), at 856 (per EVANS LJ), CA.

180 *Lewis v Eliades* [2003] EWHC 368 (QB) at [54]–[56], [2003] 1 All ER (Comm) 850; appeal allowed in part without discussion of this point [2003] EWCA Civ 1758, [2004] 1 WLR 692. The adjustment to the damages arose out of the fact that there was an application for a separate judgment from the same court trebling the damages because of racketeering contrary to the US RICO Act. See also *Schnabel v Yung Lui* [2002] NRWSC 15.

181 *Beatty v Beatty*, supra, at 815, 816.

182 *Scott v Pilkington* (1862) 2 B & S 11; *Colt Industries Inc v Sarlie (No 2)* [1966] 1 WLR 1287; *Lewis v Eliades* [2003] EWCA Civ 1758 at [18], [2004] 1 WLR 692. See also *Four Embarcadero Center Venture v Mr Greenjeans Corpn* (1988) 64 OR (2d) 746; affd 65 OR (2d) 160. A judgment enforcing a foreign judgment, which is then overturned, will be set aside: *Benefit Strategies Group Inc v Prider* [2007] SASC 250.

183 *Scott v Pilkington*, supra; *Nouvion v Freeman* (1889) 15 App Cas 1 at 13; *Four Embarcadero Center Venture v Mr Greenjeans*, supra; *Arrowmaster Inc v Unique Forming Ltd* [1995] IL Pr 505, Ontario Ct of Justice; *Old North State Brewing Co v Newlands Service Inc* (1998) 155 DLR (4th) 250; *cf Colt Industries Inc v Sarlie (No 2)*, supra.

184 *Patrick v Shedden* (1853) 2 E & B 14; cf *Berliner Industriebank AG v Jost* [1971] 2 QB 463 at 470–471.

185 *Grant v Easton* (1883) 13 QBD 302.

186 *Sadler v Robins* (1808) 1 Camp 253 at 256. But see White (1982) 9 Sydney LR 630.

187 *Sadler v Robins*, supra; *Henderson v Henderson* (1844) 6 QB 288. For enforcement of judgments expressed in a foreign currency and charging ordrers see *Carnegie v Giessen* [2005] EWCA Civ 191.

188 Supra.

on the Jamaican decree was indefinite. A sum, however, satisfies the requirement of certainty if it can be ascertained by a simple arithmetical process.[189]

This is the position in England. In contrast, the Supreme Court of Canada in *Pro Swing Inc v Elta Golf Inc*[190] has held that the traditional common law rule that limits recognition and enforcement to fixed sum judgments should be revised so as to open the door to equitable orders, such as injunctions, which are key to an effective modern-day remedy. However, this change must be accompanied by a judicial discretion enabling the Canadian court to consider relevant factors, including the criteria that guide Canadian courts when crafting domestic equitable orders, such as the territorial scope of an injunction being specific and clear.[191]

(e) Conclusiveness of foreign judgments

(i) A foreign judgment is not impeachable on its merits

It is well established that in an action on a foreign judgment the English court is not entitled to investigate the propriety of the proceedings in the foreign court.[192] Erroneous judgments delivered by a foreign court are not void in England.[193] The merits of the case have been argued and determined, and if one of the parties is discontented with the decision his proper course is to take appellate proceedings in the forum of the judgment. The English tribunal, in other words, cannot sit as a Court of Appeal against a judgment pronounced by a court which was competent to exercise jurisdiction over the parties.[194]

(a) Mistakes by the foreign court

(i) Mistakes as to facts or as to law

The defendant in England may show that the foreign court had no jurisdiction to try the case, or he may plead a limited number of defences, such as fraud, which will be considered later,[195] but he is not at liberty to show that the court mistook either the facts or the law on which its judgment was founded.[196]

A more difficult question is whether a foreign judgment can be impeached on the ground that the court made an obvious mistake with regard to English law when purporting to give a decision according to that law. It has been decided that such a mistake does not excuse the defendant from performing the obligation that has been laid upon him by the

---

[189] *Beatty v Beatty* [1924] 1 KB 807.

[190] 2006 SCC 52, (2007) 273 DLR (4th) 663; Pitel (2007) 3 J Priv Int L 241; Oppong (2007) 70 MLR 670.

[191] Ibid at [15], [30]–[31]. The uncertain territorial scope of the injunction in question led to it not being enforced in Canada.

[192] *Henderson v Henderson* (1844) 6 QB 288; *Bank of Australasia v Nias* (1851) 16 QB 717; *Vanquelin v Bouard* (1863) 15 CBNS 341; *Goddard v Gray* (1870) LR 6 QB 139; *Messina v Petrocochino* (1872) LR 4 PC 144; *Vadala v Lawes* (1890) 25 QBD 310 at 316; *Pemberton v Hughes* [1899] 1 Ch 781 at 790; *Merker v Merker* [1963] P 283. For earlier doubts, see *Smith v Nicolls* (1839) 5 Bing NC 208 at 221.

[193] *Imrie v Castrique* (1860) 8 CBNS 405 at 428.

[194] *Dent v Smith* (1869) LR 4 QB 414 at 446; *Imrie v Castrique*, supra; *Ferdinand Wagner v Laubscher Bros & Co* [1970] 2 QB 313 at 318.

[195] Infra, pp 551–556.

[196] *Bank of Australasia v Nias*, supra, at 735; *Goddard v Gray*, supra, at 150.

judgment.[197] The doctrine that a foreign judgment cannot be impeached as to merits has been carried to its logical conclusion. Thus in *Goddard v Gray*:[198]

> The plaintiffs, who were Frenchmen, sued the defendants (Englishmen) in France on a charter-party, the proper law of which was English law. The charter-party contained the clause: "Penalty for non-performance of this agreement estimated amount of freight." The effect of such a clause under English law was not to quantify the damages exactly, but to leave them to be assessed according to the actual loss suffered; but the French court, believing that the language of the charter-party was to be understood in its natural sense, fixed the damages payable by the defendant at the exact amount of freight.

When sued on the judgment in England, the defendants pleaded this mistaken view of English law in defence. The plea failed. The court held that there could be no difference between a mistake as to English law and any other mistake.

(ii) A mistake as to its own jurisdiction

What, for many years, has been less certain is whether the foreign court must have had internal competence, ie jurisdiction under its own law. LINDLEY LJ once said that the jurisdiction which alone is important in connection with a foreign judgment is the competence of the foreign court in the international sense. "Its competence or jurisdiction in any other sense is not regarded as material by the courts of this country."[199] According to this view, action will lie in England on a foreign judgment although delivered by a court that, according to its own internal law, had no jurisdiction whatsoever over the cause of action. If, for instance, the foreign court has adjudicated on a claim in excess of the legally permitted amount, is it to be no answer to an action on the judgment in England that the court lacked internal jurisdiction? To admit this would be inconsistent with principle. According at any rate to the English rule, a judgment delivered by a court with no jurisdiction is a complete nullity, and it seems curious that what was null and void in the foreign country can be regarded as valid for the purposes of an English action. Such a foreign judgment creates no rights whatsoever in favour of the claimant, yet it is because a right has been vested in him that, according to the doctrine of obligation, he may sue on the judgment in England. The dictum of LINDLEY LJ, for it was nothing more, was not applied in *Papadopoulos v Papadopoulos*,[200] where one of the grounds on which the Cypriot decree of nullity was held to be ineffective was that the court had no power by the law of Cyprus to declare the marriage null and void. Similarly, in *Adams v Adams*[201] recognition was refused to a Rhodesian divorce decree because, under Rhodesian law as

---

[197] *Castrique v Imrie* (1870) LR 4 HL 414; *Goddard v Gray* (1870) LR 6 QB 139; *Good Challenger Navegante SA v Metalexportimport SA (The Good Challenger)* [2003] EWCA Civ 1668 at [56], [2004] 1 Lloyd's Rep 67.

[198] (1870) LR 6 QB 139. Approved by Lord SIMON in *Vervaeke v Smith* [1983] 1 AC 145 at 162, HL. See also *Tracomin SA v Sudan Oil Seeds Co Ltd* [1983] 1 WLR 662 at 674 (STAUGHTON J); *Tracomin SA v Sudan Oil Seeds Co Ltd* [1983] 1 Lloyd's Rep 560 at 577 (LEGGATT J); *Benefit Strategies Group Inc v Prider* [2005] SASC 194 at [76]–[80], (2005) 91 SASR 544.

[199] *Pemberton v Hughes* [1899] 1 Ch 781. See also *Adams v Cape Industries plc* [1990] Ch 433 at 549–550, CA; cf the judgment at first instance, at 492.

[200] [1930] P 55.

[201] [1971] P 188.

interpreted in England, the decree was invalid as it had been pronounced by a judge who was not a judge *de jure* of the High Court of Rhodesia.[202]

(iii) A procedural mistake

It is essential to observe that if the foreign court is internally competent the fact that it has erred in its own rules of procedure is no answer to an action in England. This is the explanation of *Pemberton v Hughes*,[203] the case in which LINDLEY LJ delivered his dictum. In that case:

> A decree for divorce had been pronounced by the competent court in Florida in an undefended suit brought by a husband against his wife, both parties being domiciled and resident in Florida. It appeared that she had received only nine days' notice of the proceedings instead of ten days as required by the law of Florida.

It was held by the Court of Appeal that the decree was final and was binding in England. LINDLEY LJ in the course of his judgment said:

> All that the English courts look to are the finality of the judgment and the jurisdiction of the court, in this sense and to this extent—namely its competence to deal with the sort of case that it did deal with, and its competence to require the defendant to appear before it.[204]

In other words, the Florida court was not only internally competent to deal with a case of divorce, but also internationally competent, since the defendant was domiciled in Florida. The judge then concluded as follows:

> If the court had jurisdiction in this sense, and to this extent, the courts of this country never inquire whether the jurisdiction has been properly or improperly exercised, provided that no substantial injustice, according to English notions has been committed.[205]

At first sight the decision of the Court of Common Pleas in *Vanquelin v Bouard*[206] may seem difficult to reconcile with this statement of the law.

> This was an action in England on a judgment obtained in France on a bill of exchange. The defendant pleaded that by French law the French court had no jurisdiction, since the defendant was not a trader and was not resident at Orleans where the bills were drawn. The plea was disallowed.

If the plea meant that the French action had been brought in the wrong court[207] and if this were so, it is arguable that the judgment was a nullity. ERLE CJ denied, however, that the court lacked internal jurisdiction. Thus, to repeat the words of LINDLEY LJ, the French tribunal was competent "to deal with the sort of case that it did deal with", though perhaps the defendant might have pleaded in defence that he personally was not within that

---

[202] Cf *Re James (An Insolvent)* [1977] Ch 41 at 65–66, 77–78; see now the requirement of effectiveness for the recognition of foreign divorces, etc, infra, pp 995–996.

[203] [1899] 1 Ch 781.

[204] Ibid, at 790.

[205] Ibid, at 790–791.

[206] (1863) 15 CBNS 341.

[207] See *Pemberton v Hughes* [1899] 1 Ch 781 at 791.

competence. In explanation of both *Pemberton v Hughes* and *Vanquelin v Bouard* it has been said that:

> The court had competence in the sort of case involved, but there was a mistake or irregularity of procedure in the exercise of that competence which rendered the right created by the judgment merely voidable, capable of being made void by subsequent proceedings.[208]

A significant feature of *Vanquelin v Bouard* is that the defendant let the French proceedings go by default. Further, he did not plead in the English action that the French judgment was a complete nullity.

A more recent example of these rules in operation is provided by *Merker v Merker*.[209] A German court had annulled a marriage, declaring it to be "null and void" in circumstances where, under German law, it should have been declared to be "a non-existent marriage". Although the German court had jurisdiction, its decree would be regarded as a complete nullity by other German courts. Nevertheless, the decree was recognised in England. As the German court had jurisdiction, the English court "must accept the actual decision and exclude any evidence impugning it which falls short of showing that it was obtained by fraud or is contrary to natural justice".[210]

(b) Raising defences available abroad

A closely related rule is that defences that were available before the foreign court cannot be raised in England. In such a case the defendant should have raised the defence in the foreign proceedings. Thus in *Ellis v M'Henry*:[211]

> Judgment had been given in Canada in an action that would have failed had the defendant pleaded a certain composition deed. The plaintiff sued on this judgment in England, and the question was whether the defendant was entitled at that stage to set up the deed as a defence.

Bovill CJ dismissed the contention on the basis that this "would go to impeach the propriety and correctness of the judgment, and is a matter which cannot be gone into after the judgment has been obtained".[212]

This doctrine was applied more recently by the Court of Appeal in *Israel Discount Bank of New York v Hadjipateras*:[213]

> A judgment was granted in New York against two defendants in respect of guarantees given by them to the plaintiff bank. The guarantees provided that the defendants submitted to the jurisdiction of the New York courts. The second defendant, who was aged 21 when he entered into his guarantee, alleged that he only did so under the undue influence of his father, the first defendant. He raised this issue for

---

[208] Read, *Recognition and Enforcement of Foreign Judgments*, p 100.

[209] [1963] P 283, infra, p 995.

[210] Ibid, at 298–299.

[211] (1871) LR 6 CP 228. See also *Henderson v Henderson* (1844) 6 QB 288; *Martelli v Martelli* (1983) 148 DLR (3d) 746; *Dallal v Bank Mellat* [1986] QB 441.

[212] *Ellis v M'Henry*, supra, at 238–239.

[213] [1984] 1 WLR 137; Collier [1984] CLJ 47. See also *Tracomin SA v Sudan Oil Seeds Co Ltd* [1983] 1 Lloyd's Rep 560 (Leggatt J), reversed on another point, [1983] 1 WLR 1026; *E D & F Mann (Sugar) Ltd v Yani Haryanto (No 2)* [1991] 1 Lloyd's Rep 429, CA.

the first time when enforcement of the New York judgment was sought in England, although he could have raised it during the New York proceedings.

The Court of Appeal accepted that, in principle, undue influence could come within the ambit of the defence that enforcement of the judgment would be against public policy, as could duress and coercion.[214] However, since the defence of undue influence was "available" to him in New York (New York law on this defence being the same as English law), he could not now raise it in England. STEPHENSON LJ, relying on *Ellis v M'Henry*, said that "a defendant must take all available defences in a foreign country"[215] and is at fault if he does not do so. Underlying this principle were considerations of "comity and the duty of the courts to put an end to litigation".

Whilst the principle is undeniably a sound one, the question that arises in the instant case is whether an exception should be made to it in cases involving the defence of public policy. Public policy is treated as an exception to normal private international law rules in other areas[216] and could be treated in the same way in this context. It has to be seriously questioned whether it is right to enforce a judgment when an allegation of a matter as serious as undue influence has not been considered in either the foreign or the English proceedings.[217] Moreover, as will shortly be seen, where the defendant is relying on the analogous defence of fraud, he is allowed to raise this defence in England even though it was available to him abroad, and was not raised there.[218] There are therefore weighty arguments against the decision; nonetheless, it is submitted that the Court of Appeal's decision was the right one. The proper place for defences to be raised is before the foreign court, and it is not unfair to the defendant to prevent him from raising a defence in England, provided that the defence was available to him abroad and he therefore had the opportunity of raising it there.[219]

This inevitably raises the question of what is meant by a defence being "available" to a defendant abroad. In the instant case it was shown that New York law had a defence of undue influence and it was accepted that this was the same as the English defence.[220] Presumably, if New York law had been different from English law and did not have a defence of undue influence, or had a narrower concept of undue influence which did not allow the defence to operate in a situation where the English defence would operate, the defence would not be "available" abroad and the second defendant would have been able to raise the issue in England. What is not clear is whether the concept of availability of a defence abroad is referring solely to the existence of a rule which allows a particular defence, or whether it is also referring to the existence of evidence which goes to establish the defence. If new factual existence of undue influence had only come to light after the New York proceedings had ended, it cannot be said, except in the most limited sense, that the defence was "available" to the defendant abroad. Neither can it be said that the

---

[214] Per STEPHENSON LJ at 143; GOFF LJ at 147 concurring.

[215] At 144, see also O'CONNOR LJ at 146.

[216] Supra, pp 139–150.

[217] See *Syal v Heyward* [1948] 2 KB 443, concerning the analogous defence of fraud, infra, p 556. Cf the fraud/public policy defence under the Brussels/Lugano system, infra, pp 611–615.

[218] Infra, p 556.

[219] This principle should also apply in relation to fraud, see infra, p 556.

[220] Because of the presumption that foreign law is the same as English law unless the contrary is proved, see [1984] 1 WLR 137 at 140, 146 and generally on the presumption, supra, pp 111–112.

defendant was at fault in failing to raise the defence. In this situation the defendant should be allowed to raise the defence in England.

What if the defendant has raised the issue of undue influence during the foreign proceedings and this plea has failed; can he re-raise the issue in England? The conclusiveness principle in *Ellis v M'Henry*,[221] which was quoted with approval in the instant case,[222] prevents the defendant from doing so.

(ii) Estoppel per rem judicatam[223]

A cause of action, once it has been adjudicated by a court of competent jurisdiction, becomes *res judicata*, and as such it raises an estoppel against the unsuccessful party.

> The rule of estoppel by *res judicata*, which is a rule of evidence, is that where a final decision has been pronounced by a judicial tribunal of competent jurisdiction over the parties to and the subject-matter of the litigation, any party or privy to such litigation as against any other party or privy is estopped in any subsequent litigation from disputing or questioning such decision on the merits.[224]

(a) Estoppel as a defence[225]

According to this doctrine, at common law, a foreign judgment was conclusive in two respects in favour of the defendant in England.

First, in the situation where the claimant lost abroad, the judgment provided the successful defendant in the foreign proceedings with an effective defence if he was sued by the other party in England on the original cause of action. The claimant was estopped from denying the conclusiveness of the judgment.[226]

Secondly, in the situation where the claimant won abroad, but had not been awarded full compensation, the common law rule was that the satisfied judgment of the foreign court provided a good defence to an action brought by the claimant in England for the residue of his claim.[227]

This common law rule has now been superseded by the much wider statutory rule in section 34 of the Civil Jurisdiction and Judgments Act 1982.[228] This provides that:

> No proceedings may be brought by a person in England and Wales . . . on a cause of action in respect of which a judgment has been given in his favour in proceedings between the same parties or their privies, in a court in another part of the United Kingdom or in a court of an overseas country, unless that judgment is not enforceable or entitled to recognition in England and Wales . . .

---

[221] (1871) LR 6 CP 228, 238; supra, p 542.

[222] [1984] 1 WLR 137 at 144 (STEPHENSON LJ).

[223] See generally Barnett, *Res Judicata, Estoppel, and Foreign Judgments* (2001).

[224] *Carl Zeiss Stiftung v Rayner and Keeler Ltd (No 2)* [1967] 1 AC 853 at 933, citing Spencer Bower, *The Doctrine of Res Judicata*, p 3.

[225] See, however, for an example of a claimant who wished to enforce a foreign judgment (using issue estoppel to prevent the defendant from denying that he had authorised a lawyer to act on his behalf, and had accordingly submitted to the foreign court's jurisdiction) *Desert Sun Loan Corpn v Hill* [1996] 2 All ER 847, CA. See also *The Varna (No 2)* [1994] 2 Lloyd's Rep 41 at 48.

[226] *Ricardo v Garcias* (1845) 12 Cl & Fin 368 at 406.

[227] *Taylor v Hollard* [1902] 1 KB 676; *Barber v Lamb* (1860) 8 CBNS 95 at 100.

[228] The section applies also in Northern Ireland, but not in Scotland.

The effect of this provision is that, if the judgment is enforceable or entitled to recognition in England and Wales, the claimant has to sue on the judgment obtained[229] and cannot bring fresh proceedings based on the original cause of action.[230] To allow the claimant to bring fresh proceedings in England would be unjust.[231] There is no requirement that the foreign judgment has been satisfied; it must merely have been "given". The operation of this provision has been examined by the House of Lords in *Republic of India v India Steamship Co Ltd*[232] and in *Republic of India v India Steamship Co Ltd (No 2).*[233]

> Following a fire on board the defendant's ship, a small number of the cargo of artil-
> lery shells were jettisoned and the remainder were damaged. In 1988, the plaintiff,
> a cargo owner, commenced proceedings in personam against the shipowner in
> India for short delivery and obtained a judgment in its favour in December 1989.
> Previously, in August 1989, the plaintiff had launched proceedings in rem in
> England in respect of damage to the whole of the cargo.

The House of Lords in *Republic of India v India Steamship Co Ltd (No 2)* held that the plaintiffs' action in England was barred by section 34. A number of important points emerge from this litigation. First, it did not matter that the English proceedings were launched before the Indian judgment was obtained. Section 34 prohibits proceedings being "brought" in England and this is wide enough to prevent proceedings being continued.[234] Secondly, according to the House of Lords in *Republic of India v India Steamship Co Ltd* the cause of action in the Indian proceedings (for short delivery) and the English proceedings (for damage to the whole of the cargo) was the same. This was despite the fact that the Indian judgment was for only the rupee equivalent of £7,200, whereas the English claim was for the equivalent of £2.6 million. In both sets of proceedings the cause of action came under the same contract of carriage and depended on the same breach of that contract. Moreover, both actions were concerned with a single incident, ie the fire. There may have been a breach of more than one term of the contract but it was not necessary to distinguish these breaches because the factual basis giving rise to the breaches was the same. Thirdly, according to *(No 2)* the parties were the same even though one action was in personam and the other in rem. For the purposes of section 34 an action in rem is an action against the shipowners from the moment that the Admiralty Court is seized with jurisdiction.[235] Fourthly, section 34 does not use the idea that a cause of action is lost by its merger in the judgment. It creates a bar against proceedings by the claimant, rather

---

[229] In this situation the claimant will be able to ask for service of a claim form out of the jurisdiction under CPR, r 6.20(9), discussed supra, p 391.

[230] The section applies regardless of whether the judgment is enforceable or entitled to recognition at common law, by statute, or under the Brussels/Lugano system; in the case of the latter, s 34 merely confirms the existing rule under that system, see Case 42/76 *De Wolf v Harry Cox BV* [1976] ECR 1759, discussed infra, pp 634–635.

[231] *Republic of India v India Steamship Co Ltd* [1993] AC 410 at 422, HL; *Republic of India v India Steamship Co Ltd (No 2)* [1998] AC 878 at 910, HL.

[232] [1993] AC 410; Beckwith (1994) 43 ICLQ 185; Briggs [1993] LMCLQ 451; Carter (1993) 64 BYBIL 470; Davenport (1994) 110 LQR 25. This reversed the decision of the Court of Appeal [1992] 1 Lloyd's Rep 124; Collins (1992) 108 LQR 393.

[233] [1998] AC 878; Briggs (1997) 68 BYBIL 355.

[234] The *Republic of India (No 2)* case, supra, at 912. But what if the English proceedings had been commenced before those in India?

[235] Ibid, at 913. This moment is when the claim form is served or deemed to have been served.

than excluding the jurisdiction of the court.[236] Accordingly, this defence can be defeated by waiver, estoppel or contrary agreement.[237]

It is not required that the claimant should have been the original party in the overseas proceedings or that such proceedings be exclusively civil in character, provided that the judgment is enforceable or entitled to recognition in England.[238] However, the stronger domestic policy of protecting the interests of minors has meant that this provision may not operate to prevent them from bringing fresh proceedings, when the foreign proceedings were not in their interests and there are questions over their consent to the foreign proceedings.[239]

It must still be the case, though, that if the claimant has two causes of action founded on the same damage against separate defendants, as where the drivers of two vehicles have collided and caused him injury, a judgment of a foreign court against one of them does not bar him from suing the other in England.[240] He cannot, however, sustain such an action if the amount awarded him by the foreign judgment is sufficient to compensate him fully for the damage suffered, for English law does not tolerate double satisfaction.[241]

(b) Cause of action and issue estoppel

So far as English judgments are concerned, estoppel *per rem judicatam* is a generic term which comprises two species.

The first, called *cause of action estoppel*, "is that which prevents a party to an action from asserting or denying, as against the other party, the existence of a particular cause of action, the non-existence or the existence of which has been determined by a court of competent jurisdiction in previous litigation between the same parties".[242] In such a case, a further action for the same cause can never succeed.

The second species, called *issue estoppel*, becomes relevant where the determination of a cause of action has necessitated the determination of a number of different issues.[243] In the case of an English judgment, the rule then is that the parties to an action are estopped from contesting a particular issue which has already been determined in previous proceedings to which they were also parties.[244] It is immaterial that the cause of action is not the same in both proceedings.[245]

---

[236] See Collins, op cit. See *Messer Griersheim GmbH v Goyal MG Gases PVT Ltd* [2006] EWHC 79 (Comm), [2006] 1 CLC 283, setting aside default judgment and granting summary judgment on the merits.

[237] *Republic of India v India Steamship Co Ltd*, supra, at 424. On the facts there was no estoppel by convention or acquiescence: *Republic of India v India Steamship Co Ltd (No 2)*, supra, at 914–916. The House of Lords in *(No 2)* found it unnecessary to decide whether the wider principle in *Henderson v Henderson* (1844) 6 QB 288, which prevents points being raised in subsequent proceedings and which could and should have been raised in earlier proceedings (see supra, p 542), applied in cases where s 34 did not do so. CLARKE J, at first instance, thought that in principle it could apply: [1994] 2 Lloyd's Rep 331 at 356–357, as did the Court of Appeal [1998] AC 878 at 897–898.

[238] *Black v Yates* [1992] QB 526; Carter (1991) 62 BYBIL 458.

[239] *Black v Yates*, supra.

[240] See *Kohnke v Karger* [1951] 2 KB 670.

[241] Ibid.

[242] *Thoday v Thoday* [1964] P 181 at 197.

[243] The expression "issue estoppel" was coined by HIGGINS J in the Australian case of *Hoystead v Taxation Comr* (1921) 29 CLR 537, 561; on appeal, [1926] AC 155.

[244] *Fidelitas Shipping Co Ltd v V/O Exporteklab* [1966] 1 QB 630 at 640, 642; *Carl Zeiss Stiftung v Rayner and Keeler Ltd (No 2)* [1967] 1 AC 853 at 913–917, 933–935, 964–965.

[245] *Marginson v Blackburn Borough Council* [1939] 2 KB 426.

There is abundant authority that cause of action estoppel applies to foreign judgments,[246] and it is now clear that issue estoppel also applies to foreign judgments.[247] In *Carl Zeiss Stiftung v Rayner and Keeler Ltd*[248] a majority of the Law Lords[249] were of the opinion that there can be an issue estoppel in respect of a foreign judgment. However, the doctrine was not applied in that particular case since the essentials for the application of the doctrine[250] were not satisfied. Since then a number of cases have accepted that issue estoppel applies in respect of foreign judgments,[251] and the matter was put beyond any doubt by the House of Lords' decision in *The Sennar (No 2)*,[252] in which issue estoppel was applied to a Dutch judgment. Lord DIPLOCK said that "it is far too late, at this stage of the development of the doctrine, to question that issue estoppel can be created by the judgment of a foreign court".[253]

(c) Prerequisites of estoppel

The same prerequisites apply for a cause of action and an issue estoppel. In both cases an estoppel will not apply unless three conditions are satisfied.[254]

First, the previous decision must have been final and conclusive[255] on the merits,[256] and must have been given by a court of competent jurisdiction.[257] The requirement that the decision is on the merits has been relaxed by the Court of Appeal, which has accepted that, in principle, an issue estoppel can arise from a judgment of a foreign court on a

---

[246] Supra, pp 544–546.

[247] See generally Campbell (1994) 16 Sydney LR 311; Rogerson [1998] CJQ 91.

[248] [1967] 1 AC 853.

[249] Contra Lord GUEST.

[250] Discussed infra.

[251] *Westfal-Larsen and Co A/S v Ikerigi Compañia Naviera SA* [1983] 1 All ER 382; *Tracomin SA v Sudan Oil Seeds Co Ltd* [1983] 1 WLR 662 (STAUGHTON J), affd by the Court of Appeal [1983] 1 WLR 1026, CA; *The Jocelyne* [1984] 2 Lloyd's Rep 569 (LLOYD J); *Vervaeke v Smith* [1983] 1 AC 145 at 156, 160, 162 discussed infra, pp 567–568, a case of an English judgment creating an issue estoppel; *The European Gateway* [1987] QB 206.

[252] [1985] 1 WLR 490.

[253] At 493; the other Law Lords agreed; the case is discussed infra, pp 549–550.

[254] *Carl Zeiss Stiftung v Rayner and Keeler Ltd (No 2)* [1967] 1 AC 853 at 909–910, 935, 942, 967–971; *The Sennar (No 2)* [1985] 1 WLR 490 at 493–494, 499. On the application of these prerequisites to US judgments approving the settlement of class actions, see Dixon (1997) 46 ICLQ 134.

[255] See *Desert Sun Loan Corpn v Hill* [1996] 2 All ER 847 at 855 et seq, 863 (per STUART-SMITH LJ); *Buehler AG v Chronos Richardson Ltd* [1998] 2 All ER 960, CA; *Boss Group Ltd v Boss France SA* [1997] 1 WLR 351 at 359, CA; *Kirin-Amgen Inc v Boehringer Mannheim GmbH* [1997] FSR 289, CA; *The Irini A (No 2)* [1999] 1 Lloyd's Rep 189; *Svenska Petroleum Exploration AB v Government of the Republic of Lithuania* [2005] EWHC 9 (Comm) at [35]–[38], [2005] 1 Lloyd's Rep 515; *Leibinger v Stryker Trauma GmbH* [2005] EWHC 690 (Comm); *Svenska Petroleum Exploration AB v Government of the Republic of Lithuania (No 2)* [2006] EWCA Civ 1529 at [91]–[104]; *Barrett v Universal-Island Records Ltd* [2006] EWHC 1009 (Ch) at [176]–[190]. A judgment for enforcement of a foreign judgment is not conclusive: *Cortes v Yorkton Securities Inc* (2007) 278 DLR (4th) 740; cf *Morgan Stanley & Co International Ltd v Pilot Lead Investments Ltd* [2006] 4 HKC 93, criticised by Smart (2007) 81 ALJ 349.

[256] *Carl Zeiss Stiftung v Rayner and Keeler Ltd (No 2)*, supra, at 918–919, 926, 936, 949, 969–970; *Charm Maritime Inc v Kyriakou and Mathias* [1987] 1 Lloyd's Rep 433; *Tracomin SA v Sudan Oil Seeds Co Ltd* [1983] 1 WLR 662 (STAUGHTON J); *The Sennar (No 2)*, supra, at 494, 499, discussed infra. An issue estoppel may arise out of a judgment which is subject to appeal, see *Hawke Bay Shipping Co Ltd v The First National Bank of Chicago, The Efthimis* [1986] 1 Lloyd's Rep 244 at 247; *Good Challenger Navegante SA v Metalexportimport SA (The Good Challenger)* [2003] EWCA Civ 1668, [2004] 1 Lloyd's Rep 67. The judgment on the merits can be implicit: *The Republic of Kazakhstan v Istil Group Inc* [2006] EWHC 448 (Comm), [2006] 2 Lloyd's Rep 370.

[257] *Carl Zeiss Stiftung v Rayner and Keeler Ltd (No 2)*, supra, at 942; *Tracomin SA v Sudan Oil Seeds Co Ltd* (STAUGHTON J), supra; *The Sennar (No 2)*, supra, at 499; *Good Challenger Navegante SA v Metalexportimport SA (The Good Challenger)* [2003] EWCA Civ 1668, [2004] 1 Lloyd's Rep 67.

procedural, ie non-substantive, issue.[258] Seemingly, this would include a finding by the foreign court that the defendant had authorised a lawyer to act on his behalf and had accordingly submitted to the jurisdiction.[259]

Secondly, there must be identity of parties,[260] that is to say, the parties to the previous decision or their privies must be the same persons as the parties to the later action or their privies.

Thirdly, the cause of action or issue before the court must be identical with that previously determined.[261]

Nonetheless, when it comes to applying these common rules there is an important difference between cases involving a cause of action estoppel and those involving issue estoppel. When applying the doctrine of issue estoppel the need for caution has been stressed.[262] There are good reasons for adopting this attitude. Confronted with an unfamiliar procedure, it may be difficult for an English judge to ascertain, for instance, the exact issues that have been determined by the foreign court and whether each of them has been determined beyond the possibility of further litigation. Issues may not be fully argued abroad because, in cases of a trivial nature, the defendant may have regarded it as impracticable, in terms of time and expense, to defend fully. It may then be unjust to estop the defendant from raising these issues in England. The application of the principles of issue estoppel is subject to the overriding consideration that it must work justice and not injustice.[263] Issue estoppel is a rule of evidence and, as such, is no doubt governed by the law of the forum, but this is a case where the law of the forum ought to be applied "in a manner consistent with good sense".[264] Two further points to note are that determination of the issue said to give rise to the issue estoppel must have been necessary for the decision of the

---

[258] *Desert Sun Loan Corpn v Hill* [1996] 2 All ER 847, CA; Briggs (1996) 67 BYBIL 596.

[259] The foreign court made no such specific finding in the *Desert Sun Loan Corpn* case, supra, at 860 (per EVANS LJ) and 863 (per STUART-SMITH LJ).

[260] *Carl Zeiss Stiftung v Rayner and Keeler Ltd (No 2)*, supra, at 910–913, 928–936, 937, 943–946, 968 et seq; *The Sennar (No 2)*, supra, at 499; *House of Spring Gardens Ltd v Waite* [1991] 1 QB 241 at 252–254; *Republic of India v India Steamship Co Ltd (No 2)* [1998] AC 878, HL; discussed supra, p 545; *Kivin-Amgen Inc v Boehringer Mannheim GmbH* [1997] FSR 289, CA; *Baker v Ian McCall International Ltd* [2000] CLC 189; *Good Challenger Navegante SA v Metalexportimport SA (The Good Challenger)* [2003] EWCA Civ 1668, [2004] 1 Lloyd's Rep 67. See generally Handley (2000) 116 LQR 191.

[261] *Carl Zeiss Stiftung v Rayner and Keeler Ltd (No 2)*, supra, at 913, 935, 942–944, 967–968; *The Sennar (No 2)*, supra, at 494–495, 498–500; *Hawke Bay Shipping Co Ltd v The First National Bank of Chicago, The Efthimis* [1986] 1 Lloyd's Rep 244 at 247; *Siporex Trade SA v Comdel Commodities Ltd* [1986] 2 Lloyd's Rep 428; *Republic of India v India Steamship Co Ltd* [1993] AC 410, discussed supra, pp 545–546; *Desert Sun Loan Corpn v Hill* [1996] 2 All ER 847, CA; *Buehler AG v Chronos Richardson Ltd* [1998] 2 All ER 960, CA; *Kirin-Amgen Inc v Boehringer Mannheim GmbH* [1997] FSR 289, CA; *Baker v Ian McCall International Ltd* [2000] CLC 189; *Air Foyle Ltd v Center Capital Ltd* [2002] EWHC 2535 (Comm), [2003] 2 Lloyd's Rep 753; *Masters v Leaver* [2000] IL Pr 387; *Good Challenger Navegante SA v Metalexportimport SA (The Good Challenger)* [2003] EWCA Civ 1668, [2004] 1 Lloyd's Rep 67.

[262] *Carl Zeiss Stiftung v Rayner and Keeler Ltd (No 2)* [1967] 1 AC 853 at 917, 918 (Lord REID), 925–926 (Lord HODSON), 947 (Lord UPJOHN), 967 (Lord WILBERFORCE); *Westfal-Larsen & Co A/S v Ikerigi Compañía Naviera SA* [1983] 1 All ER 382, 388–389. See also *The Sennar (No 2)* [1985] 1 WLR 490 at 500; *Owens Bank Ltd v Bracco* [1991] 4 All ER 833 at 856, CA; affd [1992] 2 AC 443, HL; *Desert Sun Loan Corpn v Hill* [1996] 2 All ER 847, CA; *Good Challenger Navegante SA v Metalexportimport SA (The Good Challenger)* [2003] EWCA Civ 1668, [2004] 1 Lloyd's Rep 67.

[263] Ibid, [2003] EWCA Civ 1668 at [54], [75]–[78], [75]–[78], [2004] 1 Lloyd's Rep 67.

[264] [1967] 1 AC 853 at 919.

foreign court[265] and it is irrelevant that the English court may form the view that the decision of the foreign court was wrong either on the facts or as a matter of English law.[266]

The requirements for an estoppel were discussed by the House of Lords in *The Sennar (No 2)*.[267]

A bill of lading presented by the original sellers of groundnuts to the original buyers contained an exclusive jurisdiction clause, providing that all actions under the contract of carriage should be brought only before the court of Khartoum or Port Sudan and that the law of the Sudan should apply. Nonetheless, GfG, a German company which was the subsequent buyer, brought an action in the Netherlands against the defendant shipowners for damages for the equivalent of a tort, claiming that a false date had been put on the bill of lading by the master of the defendant's ship, *The Sennar*, as a result of which it had incurred liabilities. The Dutch court declined jurisdiction, reasoning that GfG could only found a claim on the contract contained in the bill of lading and the contract had in it the Sudanese exclusive jurisdiction clause. The plaintiff, another German company, which was successor in title to GfG, brought an action in England against the defendant for damages in tort for deceit/negligence in respect of the same cause of action. One of the issues that had to be decided was whether the plaintiff was estopped by the Dutch decision from asserting that its claim did not fall within the exclusive jurisdiction clause, which only dealt with claims under the contract.

The House of Lords unanimously held that the plaintiff was estopped from asserting this; the Sudanese exclusive jurisdiction clause applied with the result that the English proceedings were stayed.[268] Since the substance of the claim had not been decided by the Dutch court, this was not a case of cause of action estoppel but one of issue estoppel. There were, however, problems in the instant case in satisfying two of the prerequisites for an estoppel.

First, was the Dutch decision, which only concerned a preliminary matter of jurisdiction and did not raise the substance of the dispute, decided "on the merits"? Lord BRANDON gave a wide definition to this concept thus:

Looking at the matter negatively a decision on procedure alone is not a decision on the merits. Looking at the matter positively a decision on the merits is a decision which establishes certain facts as proved or not in dispute; states what are the relevant principles of law applicable to such facts; and expresses a conclusion with regard to the effect of applying those principles to the factual situation concerned.[269]

Lord BRANDON concluded that the Dutch decision was not a procedural one[270] and therefore came with the above definition.[271] Lord DIPLOCK agreed that the Dutch deci-

---

[265] *Good Challenger Navegante SA v Metalexportimport SA (The Good Challenger)* [2003] EWCA Civ 1668 at [58]–[74], [2004] 1 Lloyd's Rep 67.

[266] Ibid, at [55]–[57].

[267] [1985] 1 WLR 490. Only Lords DIPLOCK and BRANDON gave detailed judgments. Lords FRASER, ROSKILL and BRIDGE concurred with these two Law Lords.

[268] The discretionary power to stay proceedings in this type of case is discussed supra, pp 443–448.

[269] [1985] 1 WLR 490 at 499; see also 494 (per Lord DIPLOCK).

[270] Ibid, at 499. Cf *Harris v Quine* (1869) LR 4 QB 653. That case is now affected by s 3 of the Foreign Limitation Periods Act 1984, discussed infra, p 586.

[271] See also *Tracomin SA v Sudan Oil Seeds Co Ltd* [1983] 1 WLR 662 (STAUGHTON J).

sion was as to the merits. He held that the Dutch court did not simply decide that it did not have jurisdiction; it decided, first, that the only claim against the shipowners was for breach of contract, and, second, that as a result of the Sudanese exclusive jurisdiction clause that claim was enforceable only in the courts of the Sudan. There was, therefore, a judgment on the merits in respect of these two issues.[272]

Secondly, was the issue the same in the Dutch and English courts? In the Dutch court, although the action was framed in tort, the issue was whether it could be founded in tort or only on the contract (in the latter eventuality, the issue was whether the exclusive jurisdiction clause applied). However, in the English court, the action was framed in tort and undeniably could be founded in tort and the isssue was whether the action would come within the exclusive jurisdiction clause. Nevertheless, the basic issue was held to be the same, ie whether, even though the claim was framed in tort rather than in contract, the exclusive jurisdiction clause applied to such a claim.[273]

There was no need for the exercise of caution in the use of issue estoppel in the instant case[274] since all the issues decided in the Netherlands had been fully litigated. Also the reason why caution is needed is so that issue estoppel does not unjustly prevent *defendants* from raising issues in England. In the instant case, it was being used to prevent claimants from relitigating the same claim on another basis in a different jurisdiction.[275] Indeed, there are strong policy reasons why a court should be very willing to use issue estoppel in a case like *The Sennar (No 2)*:[276] shipowners are vulnerable to having their ships arrested and to forum shopping by claimants; exclusive jurisdiction clauses are designed to fix the place of trial and therefore claimants should not be able to avoid such clauses by going from one country to another seeking a classification of the cause of action which achieves this objective; having tried this once abroad, a claimant should not be able to have another bite of the cherry in England.

(iii) Abuse of process

Quite apart from issue estoppel, the courts have an inherent power to prevent any abuse of process which may be involved in an attempt to litigate matters for a second time.[277] This doctrine has been used recently by the Privy Council to strike out a defence of fraud (in respect of which there was no prima facie evidence), thereby avoiding re-opening this issue when it had been determined abroad.[278] According to Lord Templeman:[279]

> No strict rule can be laid down; in every case the court must decide whether justice requires the further investigation of alleged fraud or requires that the plaintiff

---

[272] [1985] 1 WLR 490, at 494–495.

[273] Ibid, at 499–500 (per Lord Brandon).

[274] Ibid, at 500 (per Lord Brandon).

[275] See Kerr LJ in the Court of Appeal [1984] 2 Lloyd's Rep 142 at 152–153.

[276] See generally, Lord Diplock at 493, Lord Brandon at 501; Kerr LJ in the Court of Appeal, supra, at 149–154.

[277] *Desert Sun Corpn v Hill* [1996] 2 All ER 847 at 859 (per Evans LJ), 864 (per Stuart-Smith LJ), CA. See on abuse by not bringing forward the full case in earlier proceedings, *Baker v Ian McCall International Ltd* [2000] CLC 189; *Air Foyle Ltd v Center Capital Ltd* [2002] EWHC 2535 (Comm), [2003] 2 Lloyd's Rep 753; *Good Challenger Navegante SA v Metalexportimport SA (The Good Challenger)* [2003] EWCA Civ 1668 at [100]–[101], [2004] 1 Lloyd's Rep 67.

[278] *Owens Bank Ltd v Etoile Commerciale SA* [1995] 1 WLR 44; discussed infra, pp 555–556. See also *House of Spring Gardens Ltd v Waite* [1991] 1 QB 241 at 254–255.

[279] The *Owens Bank* case, supra, at 51.

having obtained a foreign judgment, shall no longer be frustrated in enforcing that judgment.

Recourse to what justice requires makes it difficult to predict when this doctrine will operate.[280] What is clear, though, is that it is not confined to cases where the issue is that of fraud,[281] and it avoids having to determine whether the prerequisites of issue estoppel have been met.[282] It is an alternative to issue estoppel but also involves some overlap with that doctrine in that an attempt to litigate a matter for a second time may fall foul of both doctrines.[283]

(iv) Judgments in personam and in rem

The principle of *res judicata* applies both to actions in personam and actions in rem, for as regards their degree of conclusiveness these actions differ from each other only in the number of persons who are bound by the judgment. A judgment in personam binds the parties and their privies if they litigate the same issue in England. A judgment in rem has a wider operation, since it is conclusive against all the world.[284] Both judgments in rem and judgments in personam are conclusive upon the point decided, but in the former "the point", since it is the determination of status, is conclusive against the whole world, while in the latter, since it is unconcerned with status, is conclusive only between parties and privies.[285]

(f) Defences available to the defendant[286]

Despite the fact that the foreign judgment on which the defendant is sued is final and conclusive, it is still open to him to escape liability not only by pleading that the foreign court had no jurisdiction, but also by pleading any one of nine further defences set out below.

(i) Foreign judgment obtained by fraud

If we omit all reference to private international law for the moment, we find a well-established rule that a domestic judgment may be impeached on the ground that it was obtained by fraud.[287] The unsuccessful party, instead of appealing or applying for a new trial, may bring an independent action to set aside the judgment.[288] It is not a method that is encouraged,[289] or one which, owing to the strict burden of proof imposed on the claimant,

---

[280] See generally Rogerson [1998] CJQ 91 at 100–102.

[281] See the *Desert Sun Loan Corpn* case, supra. See also *J H Rayner (Mincing Lane) Ltd v Bank für Gemainwirtschaft AG* [1983] 1 Lloyd's Rep 462, CA; *Dallal v Bank Mellat* [1986] QB 441; *Kirin-Amgen Inc v Boehringer Mannheim GmbH* [1997] FSR 289, CA.

[282] See the *Owens Bank* case, supra.

[283] See the *House of Spring Gardens* case; the *Desert Sun Loan Corpn* case, supra, at 864 (per STUART-SMITH LJ).

[284] Supra, p 532. Estoppel in divorce, etc cases is discussed, infra, pp 1013–1015.

[285] *Ballantyne v Mackinnon* [1896] 2 QB 455 at 462.

[286] These defences may be pleaded not only by a defendant resisting an action in England on a foreign judgment in favour of the claimant, but also by a claimant suing in England on the original cause of action who is met by the defence of a foreign judgment in favour of the defendant; *Jacobson v Frachon* (1927) 138 LT 386 (natural justice); *Manolopoulos v Pnaiffe* [1930] 2 DLR 169 (fraud).

[287] *Duchess of Kingston's* case (1776) Smith LC (13th edn), ii, 641 at p 717; *R v Humphrys* [1977] AC 1 at 21, 30; Gordon (1961) 77 LQR 358–381; 533–559; Garnett (2002) 1 JICL 161.

[288] *Flower v Lloyd* (1877) 6 Ch D 297; *Jonesco v Beard* [1930] AC 298.

[289] *Flower v Lloyd (No 2)* (1879) 10 Ch D 327 at 333–334, per JAMES LJ, though BAGALLAY LJ dissented.

easily succeeds. It will not succeed unless he alleges and proves that new facts, evidential of fraud, have been discovered since the judgment and that they were not reasonably discoverable at the time of the trial. He must further prove that this new evidence, had it been adduced in the original action, would in all probability have had a material effect on the decision.[290]

Turning now to private international law, it is firmly established that a foreign judgment is impeachable for fraud in the sense that upon proof of fraud to a high degree of probability by the person alleging it[291] the judgment cannot be enforced by action in England.[292]

(a) Types of fraud

It is clear that, as in domestic law,[293] a judgment will be denied recognition if the court had been imposed upon by a trick not apparent at the time of the trial, but discovered later. Thus in *Ochsenbein v Papelier*:[294]

> A French seller, in the course of a dispute in Paris with an English buyer, produced a writ showing that he had begun an action to recover the price of the goods. When remonstrated with, however, he burnt the writ then and there and agreed to refer the dispute to arbitration in London. He nevertheless proceeded with the action behind the buyer's back and obtained judgment by default. The seller brought an action in the Court of Queen's Bench on this judgment, and the Court of Chancery, when asked by the buyer to restrain the action, refused an injunction as being unnecessary. It was unnecessary because the above facts, if proved, would afford a good defence to the common law action. The fraud may consist of perjury by the successful party or witnesses.[295]

The rule that a judgment is impeachable for fraud applies in those rare cases where the foreign court itself has acted in a fraudulent manner. This occurred in *Price v Dewhurst*[296] where, acting under Danish law, certain persons formed themselves into a court for the purpose of administering the property of a deceased testator. On proof that they, or some of them, were interested parties, their decision was treated by SHADWELL V-C as fraudulent and void in so far as it favoured the judges themselves.[297]

(b) Fraud and going into the merits of the foreign judgment

When fraud is alleged English courts have gone into the merits of the foreign judgment. This has happened both in the situation where the allegation of fraud has been raised and dismissed abroad, and in the situation where the defendant failed to raise this defence abroad, although it was available to him.

---

[290] *Boswell v Coaks (No 2)* (1894) 86 LT 365 n; *Falcke v Scottish Imperial Insurance Co* (1887) 57 LT 39; *Birch v Birch* [1902] P 130.

[291] *Bater v Bater* [1951] P 35; *Ahmed v Habib Bank Ltd* [2001] EWCA Civ 1270 at [32], [2002] 1 Lloyd's Rep 444. See also *Benefit Strategies Group Inc v Prider* [2005] SASC 194, (2005) 91 SASR 544.

[292] *Vadala v Lawes* (1890) 25 QBD 310 at 316; *Ellerman Lines Ltd v Read* [1928] 2 KB 144.

[293] *Duchess of Kingston's Case* (1776) Smith LC (13th edn), ii, 641 at 651.

[294] (1873) 8 Ch App 695.

[295] *Benefit Strategies Group Inc v Prider* [2005] SASC 194, (2005) 91 SASR 544—allegation of perjury by process servers abroad.

[296] (1837) 8 Sim 279.

[297] See also the effect of fraud on the recognition of foreign divorces and annulments, discussed infra, pp 1018–1023.

(i) Fraud has been raised abroad

The authorities   In the case of foreign as distinct from domestic judgments, the English appeal courts have, on no fewer than four occasions, proceeded on the same evidence that was given at the original trial and have sustained a charge of fraud that had been investigated and dismissed by the foreign court. The first of these cases is *Abouloff v Oppenheimer.*[298]

> This was an action brought on a Russian judgment which ordered the return of certain goods unlawfully detained by the defendant, or, alternatively, the payment of their value. One defence was that the judgment had been obtained by fraud in that the plaintiff had falsely represented to the Russian court that the defendant was in possession of the goods, the truth being that the plaintiff himself continued in possession of them throughout. It was demurred that this was an insufficient answer in point of law, since the plea was one which the Russian court could, and as a matter of fact did, consider, and that to examine it again would mean a new trial on the merits. The demurrer was overruled.[299]

Lord ESHER, at any rate, had no inhibitions. He said:

> I will assume that in the suit in the Russian courts the plaintiff's fraud was alleged by the defendants and that they gave evidence in support of the charge: I will assume even that the defendants gave the very same evidence which they propose to adduce in this action; nevertheless the defendants will not be debarred at the trial of this action from making the same charge of fraud and from adducing the same evidence in support of it.[300]

The next case is *Vadala v Lawes,*[301] which raised the simple point whether an allegation of fraud which has already been fully investigated by a foreign court can once more be investigated in England. The Court of Appeal unanimously answered the question in the affirmative, and ordered a new trial with a view to discovering whether there had been fraud in relation to certain bills of exchange.

These two cases were followed in the third case, *Jet Holdings Inc v Patel.*[302]

> The plaintiffs brought an action in California to recover money allegedly misappropriated by the defendant. The defendant appeared and claimed that he had suffered and been threatened with violence by or on behalf of the president of the plaintiff companies. A default judgment was awarded against the defendant after he failed to attend for a medical examination in California. An action was brought in England to enforce the judgment. This action failed.

The Court of Appeal held that the plaintiffs had implicitly, and even to some extent expressly, asserted to the Californian court that the defendant's account of violence and threats was untrue. If it was true, this, together with the actual incidents of violence relied upon, was capable of amounting to fraud. On the other hand, fraud cannot be a defence

---

[298] (1882) 10 QBD 295. See also *Baden v Société Générale SA* [1993] 1 WLR 509 n.

[299] It should be noticed, of course, that by demurring to the plea the plaintiff admitted the truth of the facts it alleged.

[300] The *Abouloff* case, supra, at 306.

[301] (1890) 25 QBD 310. See also *Norman v Norman (No 2)* (1968) 12 FLR 39.

[302] [1990] 1 QB 335; Carter (1988) 59 BYBIL 360.

if the foreign court has not been deceived,[303] or if what the defendant alleges is plainly untrue.[304] The fraud alleged did not relate, as in the previous two cases, to the cause of action (here, the issue of whether the defendant had misappropriated the money); it was instead an example of what was described as being "collateral" fraud. However, this made no difference to the principles to be applied. In either case, "the foreign courts' views on fraud are neither conclusive nor relevant".[305] The issue of fraud had to go on trial in England, where the facts would be considered afresh to see whether the defendant was entitled to resist enforcement on this basis.

Finally, in *Owens Bank Ltd v Bracco*[306] the House of Lords has affirmed the common law rule as set out in *Abouloff* and *Vadala*. The case involved statutory enforcement under the Administration of Justice Act 1920. It was held that the defence of fraud under that Act uses the term "fraud" in the common law (ie *Abouloff* and *Vadala*) sense. Accordingly, the defendants were entitled to show that a St Vincent judgment had been obtained by fraud irrespective of whether they could produce fresh evidence not available to them, or reasonably discoverable by them, before the judgment was delivered. The statutory concept of fraud was settled and could not be altered except by further legislation. Lord BRIDGE, giving the unanimous decision of the Law Lords, went on to say,[307] obiter, that, whilst there might be strong policy arguments for giving a foreign judgment the same finality as an English judgment, it was out of the question to alter the common law rule so that it was different from the statutory rule; to do so would lead to absurdity.

The effect of these decisions is that the doctrine as to the conclusiveness of foreign judgments is materially and most illogically prejudiced. The Privy Council, in a subsequent case, has said that it does not regard the decision in the *Abouloff* case with enthusiasm, especially in its application to countries whose judgments the United Kingdom has agreed to register and enforce.[308] The Supreme Court of Canada in *Beals v Saldanha* has adopted a very different rule whereby the merits of a foreign judgment can be challenged for fraud only where the allegations are new and not the subject of prior adjudication.[309] If the House of Lords were to be faced with a case of fraud arising in the context of

---

[303] If a foreign court still gives judgment for a claimant, despite being aware of attempts to mislead that court and of violence against the defendant, enforcement in England would no doubt be against public policy, discussed infra, pp 556–560.

[304] [1990] 1 QB 335 at 346.

[305] At 345.

[306] [1992] 2 AC 443; Briggs (1992) 109 LQR 549; Carter (1992) 63 BYBIL 522; Collier [1992] CLJ 441. The issue of fraud was also raised in Italian proceedings for enforcement of the St Vincent judgment. This raised questions under the Brussels Convention, which the House of Lords referred to the Court of Justice, see Case C-129/92 *Owens Bank Ltd v Bracco (No 2)* [1994] ECR I-117; discussed supra, p 215, which held that the Convention was inapplicable.

[307] *Owens Bank v Bracco*, supra, at 489.

[308] *Owens Bank Ltd v Etoile Commerciale SA* [1995] 1 WLR 44 at 50, PC. *Abouloff* has not been followed in Australia, see *Keele v Findley* (1990) 21 NSWLR 444; doubted in *Yoon v Song* [2000] NSWC 1147; but see now *Toubia v Schwenke* [2002] NSWCA 34—fresh evidence needed but no requirement that it could not have been discovered by the exercise of due diligence. Also compare the attitude towards fraud in Brussels I Regulation cases, see *Interdesco SA v Nullifire Ltd* [1992] 1 Lloyd's Rep 180; discussed infra, pp 612–613. *Abouloff* has not been extended to enforcement of foreign arbitration awards, see *Westacre v Jugoimport* [2000] 1 QB 288 at 309–310, 316–317, CA; petition for leave to appeal to House of Lords dismissed [1999] 1 WLR 1999.

[309] 2003 SCC 72 at [51]. The defendant has to show the facts raised could not have been discovered by due diligence prior to the judgment, at [52].

enforcement at common law, it could overrule the common law rule as set out in *Abouloff*, although this would lead to the absurdity mentioned in *Owens Bank Ltd v Bracco*.[310] In the meantime, it is necessary to find ways of avoiding the *Abouloff* rule.

Ways of avoiding the *Abouloff* rule   There are two ways[311] of so doing: the first is to distinguish this rule; the second is to use the court's inherent power to prevent misuse of its process.

The first way was adopted by the Court of Appeal in *House of Spring Gardens Ltd v Waite*,[312] where the fact that the issue of fraud had already been litigated in Ireland estopped defendants from alleging, at the enforcement stage, that the prior Irish judgment had been obtained by fraud. What differentiated this case from the first three decisions[313] mentioned above was said to be that the issue of fraud had been examined in Ireland in a second action (in 1987) separate from the original one (in 1983) in respect of which enforcement was sought.[314] It was the judgment in this second action which created the estoppel. The result would have been different and the question of whether there had been fraud re-examined if it had been possible either to impeach the 1987 judgment on the basis that this judgment had itself been obtained by fraud or to produce new evidence of fraud in relation to the 1983 judgment.[315]

The crucial distinction that has to be drawn is between those foreign judgments which create an estoppel in relation to the issue of fraud and those that do not.[316] It is doubtless easier to satisfy the requirements for an estoppel[317] if there has been a separate action abroad dealing solely with the issue of fraud, but it may be possible to satisfy these requirements without this. Furthermore the foreign judgment creating the estoppel does not have to have been obtained in the country which granted the original judgment for which enforcement is now sought.[318] The English courts have a discretion to stay the English trial determining whether a foreign judgment was obtained by fraud, pending trial of the same issue in another country.[319]

The second way was adopted by the Privy Council in *Owens Bank Ltd v Etoile Commerciale SA*.[320] Lord TEMPLEMAN, giving the decision of the Privy Council, pointed out that every

---

[310] See *Clarke v Fennoscandia Ltd* (No 2) 2001 SLT 1311 at [28]—inconceivable that *Owens Bank* would not be followed at common law.

[311] There is in addition a possible exception to the rule in cases where it is unconscionable for the claimant to assert that the judgment was fraudulent having regard to his subsequent conduct, as where the claimant had previously relied on a fraudulent judgment, knowing of the fraud: *Baden v Société Générale SA* [1993] 1 WLR 509 at 596–597.

[312] [1991] 1 QB 241; Carter (1990) 61 BYBIL 405.

[313] *Owens Bank Ltd v Bracco*, supra, had not yet been decided.

[314] [1991] 1 QB 241 at 251.

[315] Ibid.

[316] *Owens Bank Ltd v Bracco* [1991] 4 All ER 833 at 855-857, CA; affd without discussing this point [1992] 2 AC 443, HL. See also *Owens Bank Ltd v Etoile Commerciale SA* [1995] 1 WLR 44 at 50, PC.

[317] Supra, pp 547–550.

[318] *Owens Bank Ltd v Bracco*, supra, at 857, CA; affd without discussing this point [1992] 2 AC 443, HL.

[319] Ibid.

[320] [1995] 1 WLR 44. This was the alternative ground used by the Court of Appeal in *House of Spring Gardens Ltd v Waite*, supra. See generally Briggs and Rees, para 7.50.

court has an inherent power to prevent misuse of its process,[321] whether by a claimant or a defendant, and that:

> Where allegations of fraud have been made and determined abroad, summary judgment or striking out in subsequent proceedings are appropriate remedies in the absence of plausible evidence disclosing at least a prima facie case of fraud.[322] No strict rule can be laid down; in every case the court must decide whether justice requires the further investigation of alleged fraud or requires that the plaintiff, having obtained a foreign judgment, shall no longer be frustrated in enforcing that judgment.[323]

(ii) Fraud has not been raised abroad

The decision of the Court of Appeal in *Syal v Heyward*[324] takes matters even further, for it allows retrial in England notwithstanding that the claimant deliberately refrained from raising in the original trial the facts upon which the allegation of fraud is based. The strange result appears to follow that an English defendant to a foreign action may reserve a defence of fraud available to him with the intention of raising it if he is sued on the judgment in England.[325] This is an indulgence that has nothing to commend it. Moreover, it contrasts with the decision of the Court of Appeal in *Israel Discount Bank of New York v Hadjipateras*,[326] which was concerned with a failure to raise a defence available abroad in the analogous area of undue influence. There can also be a retrial in England even though there had been an attempt to raise the defence of fraud abroad at a late stage and this had not been allowed.[327]

(ii) Foreign judgment contrary to public policy of English law

No action is sustainable on a foreign judgment which is contrary to the English principles of public policy.[328] There is no need to add anything here to what has already been said about the subject of general public policy,[329] except to give some examples of the application of the doctrine to the particular case of a foreign judgment.[330]

---

[321] Supra, pp 550–551.

[322] See also *Commercial Innovation Bank Alfa Bank v Kozeny* [2002] UKPC 66—(a triable issue of fraud).

[323] *Owens Bank Ltd v Etoile Commerciale SA*, supra, at 51.

[324] [1948] 2 KB 443; approved obiter in *Owens Bank Ltd v Bracco* [1992] 2 AC 443 at 487, HL. See also *Adams v Cape Industries plc* [1990] Ch 433 at 568–569; *Svendborg v Wansa* [1997] 2 Lloyd's Rep 183 at 189, CA.

[325] Cowen (1949) 65 LQR 82, 84; though see *Svirskis v Gibson* [1977] 2 NZLR 4 at 10.

[326] [1984] 1 WLR 137, CA; discussed supra, pp 542–543. For the position in relation to natural justice, see infra, pp 563–565.

[327] *Owens Bank Ltd v Bracco*, supra.

[328] *Re Macartney* [1921] 1 Ch 522 at 527; and see *Dalmia Dairy Industries v National Bank of Pakistan* [1978] 2 Lloyd's Rep 223 at 299–301. The same principle applies in Canada, see eg *Bank of Montreal v Snoxell* (1982) 143 DLR (3d) 349.

[329] Supra, pp 139–150.

[330] An early example is *Re Macartney* [1921] 1 Ch 522; distinguished *Stark v Stark* (1979) 94 DLR (3d) 556. There were two other grounds on which *Re Macartney* was based. The first was that the judgment was not final and conclusive, supra, pp 536–538. The second was that the cause of action was unknown in England, a ground which is supported by *De Brimont v Penniman* (1873) 10 Blatch 437; *Mayo-Perrott v Mayo-Perrott* [1958] IR 336; but Read, op cit, pp 293–295, suggests that such a ground is of dubious merit, on the authority of *Burchell v Burchell* (1928) 58 QLR 527. See also *Phrantzes v Argenti* [1960] 2 QB 19, supra, p 147; *Cablevision Systems Development Co v Shoupe* (1986) 39 WIR 1, Anderson (1993) 42 ICLQ 697. Cf *Telnikoff v Matusevitch* 702 A2d 230 (Md CA)—refusal to enforce English libel judgment; Kyu Ho Youm (2000) 49 ICLQ 131.

(a) Application of general principles of public policy to enforcement of foreign judgments

Israel Discount Bank of New York v Hadjipateras[331] shows that undue influence, duress and coercion can come within the ambit of the public policy defence. However, as has already been seen,[332] even though the defence was one of public policy it could not be raised in the instant case because, although it had been available in New York proceedings, it had not been put forward there. The public policy defence also guards against the enforcement of a judgment given by a court that is biased or corrupt.[333]

In *Vervaeke v Smith*[334] the House of Lords held that recognition of a Belgian judgment invalidating a sham marriage (ie where the parties had no intention of living together as husband and wife) would be against public policy.[335]

In *Soleimany v Soleimany*, there are obiter dicta in the Court of Appeal to the effect that it would be against public policy to recognise a foreign judgment enforcing a contract in the situation where the foreign court has found as a fact that it was the common intention of the parties to commit an illegal act in a state which England regards as a foreign and friendly state.[336]

As an example going the other way, courts in Canada have enforced foreign judgments for gambling debts even though such debts are not recoverable under the law of the province where enforcement was sought and the activity giving rise to the debt would be criminal.[337] One particularly difficult question that arises is whether the enforcement of a foreign judgment for exemplary or punitive damages would be against public policy.[338] It has been said in the Court of Appeal that there is:

> nothing contrary to English public policy in enforcing a claim for exemplary damages, which is still considered to be in accord with the public policy in the United States and many of the great countries of the Commonwealth.[339]

---

[331] [1984] 1 WLR 137, CA.

[332] Supra, pp 546–543.

[333] *Beals v Saldanha* 2003 SCC 72 at [72].

[334] [1983] 1 AC 145, HL. The case involved recognition of a foreign nullity decree and is, therefore, discussed more fully infra, pp 1018–1020.

[335] Both at common law and under the Foreign Judgments (Reciprocal Enforcement) Act 1933, on which see infra, p 584. See also *E D & F Mann (Sugar) Ltd v Yani Haryanto (No 2)* [1991] 1 Lloyd's Rep 161 at 167; affd by the Court of Appeal but on the basis that there had been a prior English judgment [1991] 1 Lloyd's Rep 429, infra, pp 567–568. The *Vervaeke* case was also decided on an estoppel point, discussed infra, pp 567–568.

[336] [1998] 3 WLR 811 at 821, CA. See also *Society of Lloyd's v Saunders* (2001) 210 DLR (4th) 519, Ont CA. Cf *Westacre v Jugoimport* [2000] 1 QB 288, CA; petition for leave to appeal to House of Lords dismissed [1999] 1 WLR 1999; discusssed infra, p 659.

[337] *Boardwalk Regency Corpn v Maalouf* (1992) 88 DLR (4th) 612, Ont CA; *Auerbach v Resorts International Hotel Inc* (1991) 89 DLR (4th) 688, Quebec CA. For other examples: see *Bolton v Marine Services Ltd* [1996] 2 NZLR 15, CA—irregularly obtained foreign judgment enforced against a defendant in contempt of the foreign court; *Reeves v One World Challenge LLC* [2006] 2 NZLR 184, CA, enforcement of judgment upholding a contract which would not be enforced by a New Zealand court not against public policy.

[338] See Merkin (1994) 1 IJIL 19. See generally Brand (1996) 43 NILR 143.

[339] *SA Consortium General Textiles v Sun and Sand Agencies Ltd* [1978] QB 279 at 300, infra, p 582.

The British Columbia Court of Appeal[340] and the Supreme Court of South Australia (Full Court)[341] have held that the enforcement of a judgment for punitive damages was not against public policy. The former court held that the enforcement of a judgment for treble damages was akin to one for exemplary damages and was not against public policy.[342] Damages awarded, even though not punitive damages, may appear to be excessive. Nonetheless, the Supreme Court of Canada has held that, although the sums awarded by a jury in Florida were considerably larger than those that would be granted as damages in a comparable case in Canada (and indeed appeared disproportionate to the original value of the land in question), this in itself would not bar enforcement under the public policy defence.[343] It did not violate Canadian principles of morality.

In contrast, the German Federal Supreme Court has refused on public policy grounds to enforce that part of a Californian judgment which was in respect of exemplary and punitive damages.[344] However, no objection was made to the fact that under the judgment 40 per cent of the money received was to be handed over to the plaintiff's lawyer under a contingency fee agreement. Nor was any objection made to the fact that the damages for pain and suffering were more than twenty times what a German court would award.

(b) Using human rights law to cast light on the public policy defence

The public policy defence is informed by the requirements under Article 6 of the European Convention on Human Rights (ECHR). It sheds light on when there would be a denial of a fair trial abroad. This is the position under the Brussels/Lugano system[345]and it applies equally to enforcement under the traditional rules. The Court of Appeal in *Al-Bassam v Al-Bassam*[346] said that LEWISON J, at first instance, was correct to voice his concern that the judgment of a foreign court given in proceedings which, in the eyes of English law, had failed to meet the requirements of a fair trial, would not be recognised in England.[347] This was because an English court when applying its rules on recognition of foreign judgments "will have regard to its own obligation to act in a manner which is not inconsistent with the Convention right to a fair trial".[348] The English rule on the recognition of foreign judgments that would have to be applied to prevent recognition would be the public policy defence.

---

[340] *Old North State Brewing Co v Newlands Services Inc* [1999] 4 WWR 573, BC Court of Appeal. See also *Beals v Saldanha* 2003 SCC 72—no public policy objection made to damages which included punitive damages.

[341] *Benefit Strategies Group Inc v Prider* [2005] SASC 194 at [60]–[75], (2005) 91 SASR 544. Cf *Schnabel v Yung Lui* [2002] NSWSC 15, 1 February 2002 (unreported)—punitive damages with a public element for failing to comply with an order of a US court.

[342] *Old North State Brewing Co v Newlands Services Inc* [1999] 4 WWR 573, BC Court of Appeal. The Court also held that the judgment for treble damages was not penal. Cf on this latter point *Lewis v Eliades* [2003] EWCA Civ 1758, [2004] 1 WLR 692, where this point was said not to be clear. A foreign judgment for treble damages cannot be enforced in England, see the Protection of Trading Interests Act 1980; discussed infra, pp 561–563.

[343] *Beals v Saldanha* 2003 SCC 72.

[344] *Re the Enforcement of a United States Judgment for Damages* (Case IX ZR 149/91) [1994] IL Pr 602; Bungert [1993] Int Lawyer 1075; Hay (1992) 40 AJCL 729; Zekoll (1992) 30 Col J Trans L 641. See also *Schnabel v Yung Lui* [2002] NSWSC 15—same result but achieved by regarding punitive/exemplary damages as penal. See Art 33 of the preliminary draft Hague Judgments Convention, Interim Text of 20 June 2001, which was eventually abandoned. This allowed non-compensatory damages (including punitive or exemplary damages), which are grossly excessive, to be enforced to a lesser amount.

[345] *Maronier v Larmer* [2002] EWCA Civ 774, [2003] QB 620; discussed infra, p 613.

[346] [2004] EWCA Civ 857.

[347] Ibid at [45].

[348] Ibid.

(iii) A breach of Article 6 of the ECHR[349]

There is a separate defence, the source of which is Article 6 of the ECHR[350] and the jurisprudence of the European Court of Human Rights (ECtHR), rather than the English rules on recognition and enforcement of foreign judgments. Judge MATSCHER in the ECtHR in *Drozd and Janousek v France and Spain*[351] said that an ECHR Contracting State may incur responsibility by reason of assisting in the enforcement of a foreign judgment, originating from a Contracting State or a non-Contracting State, which has been obtained in conditions which constitute a flagrant breach of Article 6, whether it is a civil or criminal judgment.[352] This is an example of how the ECHR has indirect effect. It means that an English court which enforces a foreign judgment which has been obtained in such circumstances will itself be in breach of Article 6. The ECtHR in *Pellegrini v Italy*[353] adopted a wider principle than this by not requiring the breach to be "flagrant". It held that the Italian courts, before authorising the enforcement of a decision of the Vatican courts, should have satisfied themselves that the Vatican court proceedings fulfilled the guarantees of Article 6 and that "A review of that kind is required where a decision in respect of which enforcement is requested emanates from the courts of a country which does not apply the Convention."[354]

The Court of Appeal in *Al-Bassam v Al-Bassam*[355] refused to accept that the ECHR has this indirect effect, even though the decision of the ECtHR in *Pellegrini v Italy* was cited to it. It accepted that a foreign judgment, granted in circumstances where a fair trial had been denied abroad, would not be recognised. But the reason for this was because the English rules on recognition say it should not be, not because human rights law says it should not.[356] Nonetheless, as has been seen,[357] the human rights position was not irrelevant. When operating the private international law rules on recognition of foreign judgments, account would be taken of the human rights position. In other words human rights law is used to cast light upon private international law concepts.

However, in a case decided a few weeks after *Al-Bassam*, the House of Lords in *Government of the United States of America v Montgomery (No 2)*[358] accepted that Article 6 can have indirect effect in cases of enforcement of foreign judgments. The case concerned the registration in England under section 97 of the Criminal Justice Act 1988 of a confiscation order made in the USA in circumstances where the fugitive disentitlement doctrine, under which a court does not have to hear or decide the appeal of a fugitive, was applied. Registration requires the High Court to be "of the opinion that enforcing the order in

---

[349] See Fawcett (2007) 56 ICLQ 1.

[350] Supra, p 15.

[351] Judgment of 26 June 1992, Series A No 240; (1992) 14 EHRR 745, 749.

[352] There is no breach of the Canadian Charter of Rights and Freedoms in such a case, see *Beals v Saldanha* 2003 SCC 72 at [78], Sup Ct of Canada.

[353] Judgment of 20 July 2001; (2001) 35 EHRR 44.

[354] At [40]. It is unclear whether *Pellegrini* applies where the judgment was granted in an ECHR Contracting State.

[355] [2004] EWCA Civ 857.

[356] Ibid at [35], [45].

[357] Supra, p 558.

[358] [2004] UKHL 37, [2004] 3 WLR 2241; Briggs (2004) 75 BYBIL 537.

England and Wales would not be contrary to the interests of justice".[359] BURNTON J, at first instance, had decided that it would not be contrary to the interests of justice to do so, even though the order would have been made in breach of the requirements of Article 6 of the ECHR if that Article had applied to the making of that order (which it did not because it was made in the USA). On appeal to the Court of Appeal,[360] it was argued that: (i) if the ECHR had applied in the USA, the confiscation order would have been made in contravention of Article 6 and of Article 1 of Protocol 1 in the ECHR; (ii) this being the case, if the courts registered the order, they would be contravening section 6 of the Human Rights Act 1998. The Court of Appeal did not accept that there had been a breach by the US courts of the standards required by Article 6. But even if there had been such a breach, it could not be said that the decision to register gave rise to any breach of Article 6 of the Convention by the English court. The House of Lords affirmed the decision of the Court of Appeal. However, Lord CARSWELL, who delivered the unanimous judgment of the House of Lords, followed the dictum of Judge MATSCHER in the *Drozd* case and accepted that enforcement of a foreign judgment might in principle give rise to responsibility on the part of a Convention State.[361] Under this principle there must be a flagrant breach of Article 6 and on the facts of the instant case there was no such breach. The fugitive disentitlement doctrine applied in the USA, although it failed to secure all of the protection required by Article 6, was said to be a rational approach which had commended itself to the federal jurisdiction in the USA. As such, it could not be described as a flagrant breach. The House of Lords refused to accept that *Pellegrini v Italy* gave rise to a wider principle under which it was not necessary to show that there had been a flagrant breach abroad. *Pellegrini* was distinguished on the basis that it turned on the relationship between the Italian civil courts and the Vatican court. This confines the *Pellegrini* case to its facts, ie the enforcement of Vatican court judgments in Italy. According to this view, it is therefore not an authority in the private international law situation where the courts in one state are being asked to recognise and enforce the judgment granted in another state. This is an example of the English courts getting human rights law wrong.[362]

(iv) Foreign revenue, penal or other public laws

English courts will not enforce foreign revenue, penal or other public laws either directly[363] or through the recognition of a foreign judgment.[364] Thus in *USA v Inkley*[365] the Court of Appeal refused to enforce a judgment granted in Florida relating to a bail appearance bond, where the purpose of the enforcement action was the execution of a foreign public law/penal process. However, the foreign judgment will be denied recognition only if it falls directly within the area of revenue, penal or other public laws, strictly construed. So, a foreign judgment for costs may be recognised even though the costs would be payable

---

[359] S 97(1)(c) of the Criminal Justice Act 1988.

[360] [2003] EWCA Civ 392, [2003] 1 WLR 1916; criticised by Hartley (2004) 120 LQR 211, Briggs (2003) 74 BYBIL 553.

[361] At [27]; criticised by Briggs, (2004) 75 BYBIL 537.

[362] Fawcett (2007) 56 ICLQ 1, 35–36.

[363] Supra, pp 121–132.

[364] *USA v Harden* (1963) 41 DLR (2d) 721. See, however, as exceptions the Criminal Justice Act 1988, s 97 (foreign confiscation orders); *Government of the USA v Montgomery (No 2)* [2004] UKHL 37, [2004] 3 WLR 2241; discussed supra, p 559, and Art 39 EC Regulation on Insolvency Proceedings; discussed supra, p 125.

[365] [1989] QB 255.

into a foreign legal aid fund.[366] A foreign judgment in respect of an action brought by the USA for compensation under a US statute for the cost of clearing up environmental damage in the USA has been held to be enforceable, the action being regarded as close to one for nuisance.[367]

A civil judgment, though combined with a penal judgment, may be actionable in England as creating a separate and independent cause of action, despite the general principle[368] that penalties imposed abroad are disregarded. Thus in *Raulin v Fischer*:[369]

> The defendant, a young American lady, while recklessly galloping her horse in the Bois de Boulogne, ran into the plaintiff, a French officer, and seriously injured him. She was prosecuted by the French State for her act of criminal negligence. By French law a person who is injured by a crime may intervene in the prosecution and make a claim for damages, whereupon his civil action is tried together with the prosecution and one judgment is pronounced on both matters. The plaintiff did so intervene. The defendant was convicted of the crime and ordered to pay a fine of 100 francs to the State and 15,917 francs by way of damages and costs to the plaintiff.

It was held on these facts, in an action brought by the plaintiff in England to recover the sterling equivalent of 15,917 francs, that the French judgment was severable. That part of it which awarded the plaintiff damages was not tainted with the penal character of the rest of the proceedings, and therefore might be recovered in England without involving recognition of a penal judgment.

(v) The Protection of Trading Interests Act 1980[370]

The background to this Act is the United Kingdom resentment[371] at the extra-territorial application of anti-trust laws by the USA. Diplomatic attempts at solving what is a political as well as an economic and legal problem failed and led to legal warfare. Under the Act, the Secretary of State is given wide powers to counter foreign measures for regulating international trade which affect the trading interests of persons in the United Kingdom.[372]

---

[366] *Connor v Connor* [1974] 1 NZLR 632.

[367] *United States of America v Ivey* (1996) 139 DLR (4th) 570, Ont CA.

[368] Supra, pp 126–130.

[369] [1911] 2 KB 93; and see *SA Consortium General Textiles v Sun and Sand Agencies Ltd* [1978] QB 279, infra, p 582; *A-G of New Zealand v Ortiz* [1984] AC 1, at 31–35, CA, discussed supra, p 128; *Lewis v Eliades* [2003] EWCA Civ 1758, [2004] 1 WLR 692, discussed infra, pp 562–563. See also *Benefit Strategies Group Inc v Prider* [2005] SASC 194 at [74]–[75], (2005) 91 SASR 544; *Schnabel v Yung Lui* [2002] NSWSC 15.

[370] See Huntley (1981) 30 ICLQ 213 at 229–233; Jones [1981] CLJ 41; AV Lowe (1981) 75 AJIL 257; Blythe (1983) 31 AJCL 99; Bridge (1984) 4 Legal Studies 2. For analogous statutes in Australia and Canada, see the Foreign Anti-Trust Judgments (Restriction of Enforcement) Act 1979 (Cth) and the Foreign Extraterritorial Measures Act 1985; see generally Patchett, *Recognition of Commercial Judgments and Awards in the Commonwealth* (1984), para 3.24; Castel and Walker, *Canadian Conflicts of Laws* (6th edn), para 14.29b; Castel (1983) 1 Hague Recueil 9, 79–92; Collins [1986] JBL 372 and 452.

[371] See *British Nylon Spinners Ltd v ICI Ltd* [1953] Ch 19; *Re Westinghouse Electric Corpn Uranium Contract Litigation NDL Docket No 235* [1978] AC 547. The resentment is also shared by Australia and Canada, see supra, n 370.

[372] See ss 1–4. See also the Protection of Trading Interests (US Antitrust Measures) Order 1983, SI 1983/900; the Protection of Trading Interests (Australian Trade Practices) Order, SI 1988/569, on which see *Trade Practices Commission v Australian Meat Holdings Pty Ltd* (1988) 83 ALR 299; Protection of Trading Interests (Hong Kong) Order, SI 1990/2291; US Reexport Control Order, SI 1982/885; and Protection of Trading Interests (US Cuban Assets Control Regulations) Order, SI 1992/2449.

Alongside this, there are restrictions on the enforcement of certain overseas judgments. Section 5(2) provides that a court in the United Kingdom cannot enforce:[373]

(a) a judgment for multiple damages, ie one "for an amount arrived at by doubling, trebling or otherwise multiplying a sum assessed as compensation for the loss or damage sustained by the person in whose favour the judgment is given";[374]

(b) a judgment based on a competition law which is specified in an order made by the Secretary of State;[375]

(c) where a judgment coming within (a) or (b) has been given against a third party, a judgment on a claim for contribution.

Three points should be noted about section 5. First, although the Act does not mention any specific foreign country, the reference to multiple damages shows beyond any doubt that the target at which the Act is aimed is US anti-trust laws,[376] although it operates against multiple damages in other contexts as well.[377] Secondly, the prohibition on the enforcement of a judgment for multiple damages applies to all of the multiplied award and not merely to the non-compensatory part.[378] However, where a foreign court gives a composite judgment comprising both a multiplied award and ordinary compensatory damages for separate private causes of action similar to those available under English law, it is possible to separate the different parts and enforce the latter but not the former. This is what happened in *Lewis v Eliades*.[379]

> A court in the USA gave a composite judgment for over $8 million, which included over $1.1 million damages for racketeering contrary to the RICO Act ($396,000 basic damages trebled up[380]) plus over $6.8 million damages in respect of separate causes of action for breach of fiduciary duty and fraud. Counsel for the claimant conceded that the whole of the $1.1 million racketeering damages (ie including the basic damages of $396,000) was irrecoverable but sought enforcement of $6.8 million damages for breach of fiduciary duty and fraud.

The Court of Appeal enforced that latter part of the judgment. Thirdly, the prohibition on enforcement does not depend on whether the overseas court applied its anti-trust laws extra-territorially. It has been pointed out[381] that section 5 can apply to the enforcement

---

[373] Either at common law, or by statute under the Administration of Justice Act 1920, discussed infra, p 576 et seq, or Part 1 of the Foreign Judgments (Reciprocal Enforcement) Act 1933, discussed infra, p 578 et seq, see s 5(1). S 5 will not, however, apply to cases coming within the Brussels/Lugano system, discussed infra, pp 595–636, but see especially p 610. For the significance of s 5 in relation to restraining foreign proceedings, see *Simon Engineering plc v Butte Mining plc* [1996] 1 Lloyd's Rep 104 n; *SCOR v Eras EIL (No 2)* [1995] 2 All ER 278 at 308–312.

[374] S 5(3).

[375] S 5(2)(b) and (4).

[376] See *British Airways Board v Laker Airways Ltd* [1985] AC 58 at 89 (per Lord DIPLOCK).

[377] See *Lewis v Eliades* [2003] EWCA Civ 1758, [2004] 1 WLR 692; discussed infra. Cf the position in Canada, on which see *Old North State Brewing Co v Newlands Services Inc* [1999] 4 WWR 573, British Columbia CA.

[378] *Lewis v Eliades* [2003] EWCA Civ 1758 at [41] (per POTTER LJ), [55] (per CARNWATH LJ) but cf at [62] (JACOB LJ), [2004] 1 WLR 692.

[379] [2003] EWCA Civ 1758, [2004] 1 WLR 692; leave to appeal to the House of Lords refused [2004] 1 WLR 1393; Kellman (2004) 53 ICLQ 1025.

[380] Prior to the order abroad to treble the damages there is no judgment for multiple damages and the basic damages can be enforced, see *Lewis v Eliades* [2003] EWHC 368 (QB), [2003] 1 All ER (Comm) 850. By the time the appeal was heard the damages had been trebled and so this situation was not discussed.

[381] See *British Airways Board v Laker Airways Ltd* [1984] QB 142 at 161–162 (PARKER J).

of a judgment in an anti-trust suit brought by one US corporation against another US corporation, which has assets in the United Kingdom, following anti-trust infringements which took place wholly within the USA. The rationale of this section is not, therefore, that there has been an invasion of United Kingdom sovereignty; instead, it is more akin to that underlying the prohibition of enforcement in cases of foreign penal laws or in cases where enforcement would be against public policy.[382]

Section 5 is a negative provision. More controversial is the accompanying positive provision contained in section 6. This gives a "qualifying"[383] defendant, who has actually paid some or all of the multiple damages, the right to recover in the United Kingdom the non-compensatory part of the payment. This claw-back provision is no doubt designed to discourage private litigants from instigating civil proceedings for multiple damages and to persuade the USA to alter its anti-trust stance in respect of United Kingdom defendants.[384] Section 6 provides a unique cause of action; for this to be of any assistance to a claimant in England jurisdictional and enforcement problems have also to be overcome. The 1980 Act helps with both problems. Section 6(5) provides that "a court in the United Kingdom may entertain proceedings on a claim under this section notwithstanding that the person against whom the proceedings are brought is not within the jurisdiction of the court". A claim form will still have to be served on the defendant, but the leave of the court is not required for service out of the jurisdiction.[385] Section 7[386] allows for Orders in Council to be made providing for the enforcement in the United Kingdom of foreign judgments clawing-back sums paid pursuant to an award of multiple damages. This is done on a reciprocal basis[387] so that an overseas country must provide for the enforcement in that country of judgments given in the United Kingdom under section 6. Section 7 applies regardless of whether or not the foreign claw-back provision corresponds to section 6.[388] It follows that an Order in Council could specify that the whole of a foreign judgment, including the claw-back of the compensatory part of an award of multiple damages, is to be enforced in the United Kingdom, even though section 6 does not allow the claw-back of this compensatory part in proceedings in the United Kingdom.[389]

(vi) Foreign judgment contrary to natural justice

(a) The meaning of contrary to natural justice

Although the judges have frequently asserted that a foreign judgment obtained in proceedings which contravene the principles of natural justice cannot be enforced in England, it is extremely difficult to fix with precision the exact cases in which the contravention is sufficiently serious to justify a refusal of enforcement. SHADWELL V-C once said that

---

[382] Ibid, at 162–163; Blythe (1983) 31 AJCL 99, 123.

[383] Ie a citizen of the United Kingdom, or a body incorporated in the United Kingdom, or a person carrying on business in the United Kingdom, s 6(1). See also s 6(3) and (4).

[384] Blythe, op cit, at 126–127.

[385] CPR, r 6.19(2), see supra, pp 412–413. S 6(5) will not apply in the unlikely event of the jurisdiction rules under the Brussels/Lugano system, discussed supra, p 204 et seq, applying (European Community and EFTA States are not likely to give judgments for multiple damages).

[386] As amended by s 38 of the Civil Jurisdiction and Judgments Act 1982.

[387] See, eg, the United Kingdom-Australia Agreement (1991) Cmnd 1394, Art 2(2).

[388] This is the effect of the amendment introduced by s 38 of the 1982 Act.

[389] See Anton & Beaumont's *Civil Jurisdiction in Scotland* (1984), paras 11–15.

"whenever it is manifest that justice has been disregarded, the court is bound to treat the decision as a matter of no value and no substance".[390] But this goes too far. As we have already seen, a foreign judgment is enforceable notwithstanding that it patently proceeded upon a wrong view of the evidence or of the foreign law, or even of English law, but it would not be extravagant to suggest that this is a questionable application of natural justice. Such a judgment is in a wide sense unjust, but it is difficult to trace delicate gradations of injustice so as to reach a definite point at which it deserves to be called the negation of natural justice. It is therefore not enough to allege that the decision is very wrong or works injustice in the particular case.[391]

The expression "contrary to natural justice" has, however, figured so prominently in judicial statements that it is essential to fix, if possible, its exact scope. When applied to foreign judgments it relates merely to alleged irregularities in the procedure adopted by the adjudicating court, and has nothing to do with the merits of the case. For many years the courts have been vigilant to ensure that the defendant has been given due notice and a proper opportunity to be heard,[392] and natural justice was regarded as being confined to these two requirements. However, there is recent authority to the effect that these are merely instances of a wider principle of natural justice, according to which the court has to consider whether there has been a procedural defect such as to constitute a breach of an English court's views of substantial justice.[393]

(b) Due notice and proper opportunity to be heard

Concern over due notice has arisen in the situation where jurisdiction has been exercised over absent defendants.[394] The English courts are reluctant to criticise the procedural rules of foreign countries on this matter and will not measure their fairness by reference to the English equivalents but, if the mode of citation has been manifestly insufficient as judged by any civilised standard, they will not hesitate to stigmatise the judgment as repugnant to natural justice and for that reason to treat it as a nullity. The relevant cases in modern times have been confined largely to foreign divorces and annulments, and want of notice or of an opportunity to be heard are now dealt with specifically in the Family Law Act 1986.[395] If the foreign court, in proceedings in personam, is prepared to dispense with notice of the proceedings, or to allow notice to be served in a manner inadequate to satisfy an English court, it is not for the English court to dispute the foreign judgment,[396] even where the foreign court's jurisdiction is based solely on an agreement by the defendant to submit thereto.[397] Due notice is concerned with notice of the proceedings[398] and not of the steps

---

[390] *Price v Dewhurst* (1837) 8 Sim 279 at 302.

[391] *Robinson v Fenner* [1913] 3 KB 835 at 842.

[392] *Jacobson v Frachon* (1927) 138 LT 386 at 390 (Lord HANWORTH), 392, (ATKIN LJ); *Buchanan v Rucker* (1808) 9 East 192; *Rudd v Rudd* [1924] P 72.

[393] *Adams v Cape Industries plc* [1990] Ch 433.

[394] See, eg, *Angba v Marie* (2006) 263 DLR (4th) 562.

[395] Infra, pp 1015–1018.

[396] *Jeannot v Fuerst* (1909) 100 LT 816; and see *Vallée v Dumergue* (1849) 4 Exch 290 at 303.

[397] *Feyerick v Hubbard* (1902) 71 LJKB 509; *Jeannot v Fuerst*, supra.

[398] See, eg, *Cortes v Yorkton Securities Inc* (2007) 278 DLR (4th) 740. The proceedings could refer to appellate proceedings: *Boele v Norsemeter Holding AS* [2002] NSWCA 363 (notice to former foreign lawyer not enough).

necessary to defend those proceedings.[399] If the defendant had knowledge of the foreign proceedings the lack of due notice defence cannot be used.[400]

As regards the requirement of a proper opportunity to be heard, it is a violation of natural justice if a litigant, though present at the proceedings, was unfairly prejudiced in the presentation of his case to the court. A clear example of this would be if he were totally denied a right to plead, but the defence of unfair prejudice is not one that is lightly admitted. It is not sufficient, for instance, that his personal evidence was excluded, if the procedural rule of the forum is that parties may not give evidence on their own behalf.[401] On the other hand, granting judgment against an unrepresented litigant, who had attended with documents, without hearing the litigant or adjourning to allow the material to be put into proper form, was effectively a denial of a hearing on the merits and thus against natural justice.[402] It is a breach of the ECHR to deny the defendant's lawyers permission to put forward the defence case in relation to a civil claim as a penalty for non-appearance by the defendant at a criminal trial[403] and when it comes to enforcement of a foreign judgment given in such circumstances the natural justice defence should apply. The question whether the defendant had a proper opportunity to present his side of the case arose in *Jacobson v Frachon*.[404]

> A French court, before giving judgment in an action brought by an English buyer of goods, alleged to be of inferior quality, against a French seller, appointed an expert to examine the goods in London. The expert, who was a relative of the defendant, made no proper examination, and, though deputed by the court to take evidence, refused to hear the evidence of the plaintiffs and their witnesses. He ultimately made a report adverse to the plaintiffs which was found by ROCHE J to be the uncandid production of a biased and prejudiced mind. Judgment for the defendant was given by the French court. The plaintiffs then sued the defendant in England for breach of the original contract. The defendant pleaded the French judgment in bar of action, but the plaintiffs replied that this judgment was contrary to natural justice.

The Court of Appeal held that the judgment was not void as contravening the requirements of natural justice, since the plaintiffs had not been prevented from presenting their case to the court. It appeared that by French law the court was not bound by the expert's report, but could reject it if satisfied of its inaccuracy. The plaintiffs therefore were at liberty to produce witnesses to the court and to attack the report. It further appeared that the plaintiffs had taken this course, although without success. It could not, therefore, be said that the court had refused to hear the evidence of the litigant.

---

[399] *Beals v Saldanha* 2003 SCC 72 at [68], Sup Ct of Canada.

[400] *Commercial Innovation Bank Alfa Bank v Kozeny* [2002] UKPC 66. See also *Re Cavell Insurance Co Ltd* (2006) 269 DLR (4th) 679, Ont CA.

[401] *Scarpetta v Lowenfeld* (1911) 27 TLR 509; *Robinson v Fenner* [1913] 3 KB 835.

[402] *Leaton Leather & Trading Co v Ngai Tak Kong* (1997) 147 DLR (4th) 377. See also *Kidron v Green* (2000) 48 OR 3rd 775—breach of natural justice where jury awarded damages for emotional distress without substantial evidence of condition of plaintiff.

[403] *Krombach v France* Application no 29731/96 (ECtHR) at paras [90]–[91]. See also *Motorola Credit Corpn v Uzan* [2003] EWCA Civ 752 at [54]–[58], [2004] 1 WLR 113, CA.

[404] (1928) 138 LT 386. See also *Society of Lloyd's v Saunders* (2001) 210 DLR (4th) 519, Ont CA.

(c) Substantial justice

Normally, an allegation that there has been a lack of natural justice will involve either or both of the requirements of due notice and a proper opportunity to be heard. However, the Court of Appeal in *Adams v Cape Industries plc*[405] did not regard the defence as being restricted to these two instances.[406] The ultimate question was whether there was a procedural defect which constituted "a breach of an English court's views of substantial justice".[407] The defendants in the present case had proper notice of the proceedings but chose not to contest them. Nevertheless, it was said, obiter, that there was a breach of natural justice in the way that the Federal District Court judge in Texas had assessed damages in favour of the 206 plaintiffs; this was fixed between the plaintiffs and judge on an average basis per plaintiff rather than on the basis of their individual entitlement according to the evidence.[408] The conclusion of the Court of Appeal that, in such circumstances, a judgment should not be enforced in England is no doubt correct. But it is questionable whether the use of a wide definition of the concept of natural justice was the best way of achieving this result. It opens up a gap between, on the one hand, commercial cases and, on the other hand, cases of recognition of foreign divorces and annulments, where the natural justice defence is expressly confined to instances of want of due notice and opportunity to be heard.[409] Want of substantial justice was a much criticised concept, and is no longer a basis for the refusal of recognition of foreign divorces, etc.[410] The use of the concept of substantial injustice in relation to the recognition and enforcement of foreign judgments creates new uncertainty over the ambit of the defence of natural justice. Cases of procedural unfairness which do not involve a lack of due notice or opportunity to be heard would be better dealt with under the defence of public policy.[411]

(d) The availability of a remedy in the judgment-granting country

The question was raised in the *Adams* case of whether the defendants should have sought a remedy in Texas in respect of the lack of natural justice. The Court of Appeal said,[412] using the analogy of fraud,[413] that in cases involving lack of due process and opportunity to be heard it may well be that the defendant does not have to show that he has sought to take advantage of any available remedy in the foreign courts before he can raise the defence of lack of natural justice in England at the enforcement stage. However, in cases involving a lack of substantial justice other than the two primary kinds the position is different; here it is relevant to consider the fact that there is the possibility of the correction of error in the country where the judgment was obtained. Nonetheless, this was not fatal to the use of the natural justice defence on the facts of the case, since there was no

---

[405] [1990] Ch 433 at 557 et seq. For the facts of the case see supra, pp 518–520. Followed in *Masters v Leaver* [2000] IL Pr 387.

[406] See also the position in Canada: *Beals v Saldanha* 2003 SCC 72 at [59]–[70], defendant must have been given a fair process abroad, which includes judicial independence.

[407] [1990] Ch 433 at 564.

[408] See also the *Masters* case, supra, at [39]—failure abroad to use the procedure required by the original decision on liability by which quantum is to be assessed.

[409] Infra, pp 1015–1018.

[410] Supra, pp 149–150.

[411] Supra, pp 556–558.

[412] At 568 et seq.

[413] Supra, pp 551–556.

evidence that the defendants had any knowledge of the method used for the assessment of the damages in the USA until the stage when enforcement of the judgment was sought in England. Likewise the exhaustion of appeal procedures in the judgment-granting state cannot be a prerequisite in the situation where the possible ground of appeal is not apparent to the defendant in adequate time to pursue this course.[414]

What happens if the defendant actually raised the issue of natural justice in the foreign judgment-granting court, and the issue was determined by that court? The *Jacobson* case suggests that in such a case the defence of lack of natural justice (at least when referring to a lack of due notice and opportunity to be heard) is no longer available. However, this proposition was doubted in *Jet Holdings Inc v Patel*,[415] a case decided on the basis of fraud which also raised the issue of a lack of natural justice. In fraud cases the normal rule is that an English court at the enforcement stage can go into this issue, even though it has previously been litigated in the judgment-granting country.[416] The Court of Appeal expected that the same rule would apply in cases involving a lack of natural justice, although it did not finally decide this point.

(vii) A foreign judgment on a matter previously determined by an English court[417]

A foreign judgment will not be recognised if there has been a prior English judgment in respect of the same matter. The House of Lords so held in *Vervaeke v Smith*:[418]

> In 1954, the appellant, a Belgian domiciled woman, entered into a sham marriage (ie the parties did not intend to live as husband and wife thereafter) with an Englishman (Smith) in order to avoid deportation. In 1970 the appellant married in Italy, Messina, who died on the day of the ceremony. The appellant wished to inherit Messina's property as his "wife". An obvious obstacle to this was her earlier marriage to Smith. She, therefore, sought a decree of nullity in England in respect of her first marriage on the ground of lack of consent. This petition was dismissed;[419] the marriage was not invalidated, even though it was a sham marriage. Later, the appellant went to Belgium and obtained a nullity decree on the ground that the marriage was a sham. Armed with this decree, the appellant returned to England and sought a declaration that the Belgian decree was entitled to recognition here (the first petition), and a declaration that, this being so, the marriage between the appellant and Messina was valid (the second petition).

WATERHOUSE J dismissed both petitions and an appeal to the Court of Appeal was dismissed. The appellant then appealed to the House of Lords.

The House of Lords unanimously dismissed both petitions, thereby refusing recognition of the Belgian judgment.[420] The earlier English judgment, which determined the validity

---

[414] *Masters v Leaver* [2000] IL Pr 387.

[415] [1990] 1 QB 335 at 345.

[416] Supra, pp 553–556.

[417] There is substantially the same defence in cases of recognition under the Brussels/Lugano system see infra, pp 622–624 and 638.

[418] [1983] 1 AC 145, HL; Lipstein [1981] CLJ 20 (on the Court of Appeal's decision); Carter (1982) 53 BYBIL 302; Jaffey (1983) 32 ICLQ 500; Smart (1983) 99 LQR 24; Jaffey (1986) CJQ 35.

[419] *Messina v Smith* [1971] P 322.

[420] The case was also decided on the basis of public policy, discussed supra, p 557. It raised problems of recognition under the Foreign Judgments (Reciprocal Enforcement) Act 1933, discussed infra, p 584.

of the marriage, meant that the matter was *res judicata*.[421] As far as the appellant's first petition was concerned, the English judgment operated as a cause of action estoppel preventing the same matter from being raised before the English courts. It would prevent the appellant from directly seeking a nullity decree in England, and it was said that she should be in no better position by virtue of proceeding indirectly by obtaining a judgment abroad and then seeking recognition of this judgment.[422] The Belgian judgment was in respect of the very matter, ie the validity of the marriage, which had previously been determined in the English judgment. As regards the second petition, the English judgment operated as an issue estoppel preventing the granting of the declaration which the appellant sought.[423] Although the English judgment did not actually determine the validity of the appellant's second marriage, it did decide the issue upon which this was dependent, the validity of the appellant's first marriage.

Vervaeke leaves open two questions.[424] First, what would happen if the English judgment in respect of the same matter is given *after* the foreign judgment for which recognition is sought.[425] The reasoning of the House of Lords could apply equally well to prevent recognition of the foreign judgment in this situation. Secondly, what would happen where there are two inconsistent foreign judgments given in different states in respect of the same matter, both of which are required to be recognised at common law? This presents more of a problem since the principles in *Vervaeke* do not provide an answer. However, the Privy Council in *Showlag v Mansour*[426] has now provided an answer to the question, which is examined below.[427]

One final observation should be made in connection with *Vervaeke*. The specific question raised in that case of recognition of a foreign nullity decree following an earlier English decision in the same matter is now dealt with by Brussels II *bis*[428] and the Family Law Act 1986.[429] However, *Vervaeke* still remains a good authority on the general principles to be applied in cases involving recognition of foreign judgments (other than divorces, annulments or judicial separations)[430] on matters previously determined by an English court, and has been applied subsequently in a commercial context.[431]

---

[421] At 156–157 (per Lord Hailsham), 158–160 (per Lord Diplock).

[422] Per Lord Diplock, at 160. There is, however, a question as to whether the issue was the same in the earlier English judgment and in the present proceedings for recognition of the Belgian judgment, see Jaffey (1983) 32 ICLQ 500.

[423] At 156 (per Lord Hailsham), at 160 (per Lord Diplock).

[424] See generally Stone [1983] LMCLQ 1, 22–23. For the solution to these questions where recognition and enforcement comes within the Brussels/Lugano system, see infra, pp 622–624.

[425] This situation is unlikely to arise because the foreign judgment would normally operate to prevent the English action, see supra, pp 544–546.

[426] [1995] 1 AC 431.

[427] Infra, p 569.

[428] Art 22.

[429] S 51(1); Law Com No 137, para 6.65; see the criticisms of Jaffey (1986) CJQ 35; infra, p 1014.

[430] These are dealt with by Art 22 of Brussels II *bis*; s 51(1) of the Family Law Act 1986.

[431] *E D & F Mann (Sugar) Ltd v Yani Haryanto (No 2)* [1991] 1 Lloyd's Rep 429, CA; Carter (1991) 62 BYBIL 461.

(viii) A foreign judgment on a matter previously determined by a court in another foreign state

We are concerned here with the situation where there are two irreconcilable foreign judgments, each pronounced by a court of competent jurisdiction and both being final and not open to impeachment on any ground. This situation arose in *Showlag v Mansour*.[432]

> The legal representatives of a deceased businessman, believing that money deposited in London banks had been stolen by the defendant employee of the deceased, instituted proceedings against him in various jurisdictions. In 1990 an English court held that this money had been stolen by the defendant. In 1991 an Egyptian appeal court dismissed the legal representatives' civil claim on the ground that the money had been a gift to the defendant. Some of the money was held in Jersey and actions were brought there for its return. It was argued before the Jersey courts that the question of whether the money was a gift was *res judicata* following the English judgment. The Court of Appeal of Jersey held that the legal representatives could not insist on the English judgment being applied in their favour and suggested to the parties that they might prefer to relitigate in Jersey the issue of whether there had been a gift. The legal representatives appealed to the Privy Council.

The Privy Council held that it was necessary to determine which of the two conflicting judgments should be given priority and that the earlier of the two judgments (ie the English judgment) must be recognised and given effect to the exclusion of the other.[433] In coming to this conclusion the Privy Council was influenced by the fact that the same solution was adopted by the Brussels Convention in the situation where there are two irreconcilable judgments; one granted in a Contracting State, the other in a non-Contracting State.[434]

(ix) An overseas judgment given in proceedings brought in breach of agreement for settlement of disputes

Section 32 of the Civil Jurisdiction and Judgments Act 1982 provides an important defence which is that:

> a judgment given by a court of an overseas country in any proceedings shall not be recognised or enforced in the United Kingdom if—
> (a) the bringing of those proceedings in that court was contrary to an agreement under which the dispute in question was to be settled otherwise than by proceedings in the courts of that country; and
> (b) those proceedings were not brought in that court by, or with the agreement of, the person against whom the judgment was given; and

---

[432] [1995] 1 AC 431; Morgan (1995) 33 Can YBIL 3; followed in *The Joanna V* [2003] EWHC 1655 (Comm), [2003] 2 Lloyd's Rep 617.

[433] This is subject to a proviso, which is part of the law of *res judicata*, see supra, p 544 et seq, that there may be circumstances under which the person holding the earlier judgment may be estopped from relying on it (following *Republic of India v India Steamship Co Ltd* [1993] AC 410—a case of estoppel by representation), ibid, at 440–441.

[434] See Art 27(5) of the Brussels Convention (Art 34(4) of the Brussels I Regulation) discussed infra, pp 624–625. See also Art 22 of Brussels II *bis* and s 51(1) of the Family Law Act 1986, discussed infra, pp 990 and 1014–1015.

(c) that person did not counterclaim in the proceedings or otherwise submit to the jurisdiction of that court.

The background to section 32[435] is that some legal systems are much stricter than others
in their requirements as to when an arbitration or choice of court agreement is incorporated into a contract. A party who wants to avoid such an agreement may be able to do so
by seeking trial in a country which does not accept the agreement as being effective. He
may then obtain a judgment as to substance in his favour. If the English courts recognise
the agreement, section 32 provides that they shall not recognise and enforce this foreign
judgment.

Within a short time of section 32 coming into force, the English courts had to consider
the operation of this section in *Tracomin SA v Sudan Oil Seeds Co Ltd (Nos 1 and 2)*.[436] A
dispute arose between the Sudanese sellers of peanuts and the Swiss buyers. The contracts
between the parties contained a clause providing for the settlement of disputes by arbitration in London. Despite this, the buyers brought an action for damages before the Swiss
courts. The sellers unsuccessfully sought a stay of those proceedings, relying on the arbitration clause. The Swiss courts decided that the arbitration clause was invalid, because it
had not been properly incorporated into the contracts under Swiss law—no evidence of
English law, which governed the contracts, having been given. Under English law the
arbitration clause had been incorporated into the contracts.

In *Tracomin (No 1)* the buyers sought an injunction in England restraining the arbitration in London, on the basis that the Swiss judgment created an estoppel in relation to
the issue of the validity of the arbitration clause. The Court of Appeal applied section 32
and refused to recognise the Swiss judgment.[437] Sir John DONALDSON MR (ACKNER and
FOX LJJ concurring) confined his comments to the precise point of the appeal, whether
sections 32 and 33 applied to a foreign judgment granted before those provisions had
come into force.[438] Having decided that in the circumstances of the case[439] they did, it
was accepted without argument that the requirements for non-recognition under section
32 were satisfied. This is clearly right. The reasons were explained by STAUGHTON J at first
instance. There was an agreement under which the dispute was to be settled otherwise
than by proceedings in Switzerland, since the arbitration clause had been validly incorporated into the contracts according to the governing law. The decision of the Swiss court
that there was no valid arbitration agreement was immaterial because of section 32(3),[440]
which provides[441] that a court in the United Kingdom is not bound by any decision
of the overseas court relating to any of the matters in, inter alia, section 32(1). The first
requirement under section 32(1)(a) was, therefore, satisfied. These Swiss proceedings
were not brought with the agreement of the sellers; the second requirement under

---

[435] See Collins, *The Civil Jurisdiction and Judgments Act 1982*; pp 141–143.

[436] [1983] 1 WLR 1026, CA.

[437] Affirming the decision of STAUGHTON J [1983] 1 WLR 662. Swiss judgments are now recognised and
enforced under the Lugano Convention, infra, pp 589–590.

[438] See Sch 13, Part 1, para 2, and Pt II, paras 8(1) and 9(1).

[439] The reasoning of the Court of Appeal (at 1029–1030) was that Sch 13, Part II, para 8 lists the judgments
on which s 32 is not to have retrospective effect; since this judgment did not come within the categories specified
therein, s 32 could apply retrospectively to it.

[440] See the decision of STAUGHTON J, *Tracomin (No 1)*, supra, at 670.

[441] Infra, p 573.

section 32(1)(b) was, therefore, also satisfied. The sellers, although they appeared, did not, according to section 33(1)(b) of the 1982 Act, submit to the jurisdiction of the Swiss courts since they only appeared in order to ask the court to stay the proceedings on the ground that the dispute should be submitted to arbitration. The third requirement under section 32(1)(c) was, therefore, also satisfied.

In *Tracomin (No 2)*, which was decided on the next day, the Court of Appeal used their discretionary powers to grant the sellers an injunction restraining the buyers from litigating in Switzerland.[442] The jurisdictional basis for granting this was the existence of the agreement to submit disputes to English arbitration.[443]

(a) The scope of the section

Section 32 only applies to a judgment given by a court of an "overseas country", ie any country or territory outside the United Kingdom.[444] This means that it does not apply to the judgments of Scottish or Northern Ireland courts.[445]

Section 32(1) does not distinguish between recognition and enforcement at common law and by statute and, as will be seen, the defence can operate in respect of at least some of the forms of statutory recognition and enforcement.[446] However, its impact will be felt most at common law because there was already a similarly worded provision to section 32 under the Foreign Judgments (Reciprocal Enforcement) Act 1933,[447] which it replaces.[448]

(b) The three requirements for the operation of section 32

(i) There must be an agreement under which the dispute was to be settled otherwise than by proceedings in the courts of the country where the proceedings were brought, and the bringing of the proceedings in that country must be contrary to that agreement (section 32(1)(a)).[449] This requirement would be satisfied in the following examples: proceedings were brought in Japan when an agreement provided that all disputes were to be settled by trial in England; proceedings were brought in New York when an agreement provided that all disputes were to be settled by arbitration in Switzerland;[450] proceedings were

---

[442] Reversing the decision of Leggatt J [1983] 1 Lloyd's Rep 571 on the exercise of this discretion. See generally on injunctions restraining a party from litigating abroad, supra, pp 455–475.

[443] See Leggatt J [1983] 1 Lloyd's Rep 571, at 576 and the Court of Appeal [1983] 1 WLR 1026 at 1035. See also *The Angelic Grace* [1995] 1 Lloyd's Rep 87, CA.

[444] See s 50 of the 1982 Act.

[445] For recognition of these, see infra, pp 574–576.

[446] It applies to judgments recognised and enforced under the Administration of Justice Act 1920, and to most judgments coming under the Foreign Judgments (Reciprocal Enforcement) Act 1933. However, it does not affect judgments given in proceedings which arise under a number of international conventions and which are recognised or enforced under Part I of the 1933 Act (see s 32(4)(b) of the 1982 Act, as amended by the Statute Law (Repeals) Act 2004, Sch 1(14), para 1), see infra, p 578. It does not affect judgments required to be recognised or enforced under the Brussels/Lugano system (s 32(4), as amended by the Civil Jurisdiction and Judgments Act 1991, Sch 2, para 14 and the Civil Jurisdiction and Judgments Order, 2001/3929 Sch 2 (IV)), para 14); *The Atlantic Emperor (No 2)* [1992] 1 Lloyd's Rep 624 at 632, CA; *The Heidberg* [1994] 2 Lloyd's Rep 287 at 297; see infra, pp 628–629.

[447] S 4(3)(b) of the 1933 Act, see infra, pp 583–584.

[448] S 54 of the 1982 Act and Sch 14.

[449] For an agreement by the parties that a judgment is to only have local effect, see *Black Gold Potato Sales Inc v Joseph Garibaldi* [1996] IL Pr 171, Ontario Court of Justice.

[450] See *Deutsche Schachtbau-und Tiefbohrgesellschaft mbH v Shell International Petroleum Co Ltd* [1990] 1 AC 295 at 311; the case went to the House of Lords on a garnishment (third party debt order) point, ibid, at 323.

brought in Brazil when an agreement provided that all disputes were to be settled by arbitration in Brazil. The agreement for settlement of disputes will normally take the form of a choice of jurisdiction clause or an arbitration clause contained in a written contract between the parties. It could, however, take the form of an agreement made after the dispute had arisen and could, whenever it was made, be an oral agreement.

The party seeking recognition or enforcement of the overseas judgment can, however, challenge the agreement. Section 32(2) provides that the defence under section 32(1) does not apply where the agreement was "illegal, void or unenforceable or was incapable of being performed for reasons not attributable to the fault of the party bringing the proceedings in which the judgment was given". In the absence of a foreign decision creating an issue estoppel,[451] an English court will have to determine these matters itself. A decision on whether an agreement is illegal, void or unenforceable raises a problem of the applicable law. This will be solved by applying the law governing the agreement as identified using traditional English choice of law principles.[452] In *Tracomin SA v Sudan Oil Seeds Co Ltd*,[453] it will be recalled that the question arose of whether an arbitration clause had been validly incorporated into the contracts. By English law the arbitration clause had been incorporated into the contracts but by Swiss law it had not. STAUGHTON J accepted that English law, as the governing law, should be applied on this question, and that the arbitration clause was validly incorporated into the contracts.[454]

(ii) It must be shown that the person against whom the judgment was given neither brought the proceedings in the first place nor agreed to the proceedings being brought in that court by the other party (section 32(1)(b)). This is a negative requirement and is concerned to ensure that the agreement for settlement of disputes has not been overridden by either of the above two types of conduct.

(iii) It must be shown that the person against whom the judgment was given did not counterclaim or otherwise submit to the jurisdiction of that court (section 32(1)(c)). This shows a similar concern to that shown under section 32(1)(b), but is dealing with the conduct of the party against whom the judgment was given *after* the proceedings have been brought. The losing party abroad must not have submitted to the jurisdiction by putting in a counterclaim or in any other way (eg by fighting the action on its merits). Only such counterclaims as amount to a submission count for these purposes.[455] It is important to note that, in deciding whether there has been submission, section 33 of the 1982 Act will apply.[456] Thus a counterclaim to obtain the release of property threatened with seizure does not amount to a submission and, accordingly, section 32 will operate.[457]

---

[451] Supra, pp 544–550 and infra.

[452] See Art 1(2)(d) of the Rome Convention, infra, pp 684–685.

[453] [1983] 1 WLR 662. Affd by the Court of Appeal [1983] 1 WLR 1026; discussed supra, p 525.

[454] [1983] 1 WLR 662, 668; the point was not argued before him. The Court of Appeal also implicitly accepted this point [1983] 1 WLR 1026. This has now to be read in the light of the introduction of the Rome Convention and *Egon Oldendorff v Liberia Corpn* [1995] 2 Lloyd's Rep 64, where MANCE J held that the issue of incorporation of an arbitration agreement into a contract was one for the law governing the contract (as identified using Art 8 of the Rome Convention) rather than one for the law governing the arbitration agreement (to be identified using traditional English choice of law rules), see infra, pp 744–745.

[455] *The Eastern Trader* [1996] 2 Lloyd's Rep 585 at 600.

[456] See *Tracomin SA v Sudan Oil Seeds Co Ltd* [1983] 1 WLR 1026, CA; *The Atlantic Emperor (No 2)* [1992] 1 Lloyd's Rep 624 at 633, CA.

[457] *The Eastern Trader*, supra, at 600.

Nor does an alternative defence on the merits amount to a submission where the defendant makes it abundantly clear that his primary purpose is to challenge the jurisdiction of the foreign court.[458]

(c) Decisions of foreign courts in respect of the above matters

Section 32(3) provides that "a court in the United Kingdom shall not be bound by any decision of the overseas court relating to any of the matters mentioned in subsection (1) and (2)". Thus, as has already been mentioned, in *Tracomin SA v Sudan Oil Seeds Co Ltd*[459] a Swiss court, applying Swiss law, had held that the English arbitration clause was not validly incorporated into the contracts. When the question of recognition of the judgment arose in England, section 32 was raised as a defence. In deciding that there was a valid agreement on arbitration, STAUGHTON J held that the decision of the Swiss court was immaterial, according to section 32(3).

Section 32(3) does not apply to the decision of a court other than the overseas court which gave the judgment. Instead, the normal principles of issue estoppel[460] will apply, and, according to these principles, issues relating to an agreement on jurisdiction may have to be regarded as being settled by the decision of a foreign court.[461] To take an example:

> Section 32 is raised as a defence to a judgment given in State A and an English court has to decide whether an agreement providing for jurisdiction in State B is valid. The overseas court in State A decided that it was not. The English court is not bound by this decision because section 32(3) applies. However, a court in State C had decided that the agreement was valid. If this judgment is recognised it may create an estoppel in England which prevents any denial that the agreement is valid.

3. DIRECT ENFORCEMENT OF FOREIGN JUDGMENTS BY STATUTE

The common law doctrine that a foreign judgment, though creating an obligation that is actionable in England, cannot be enforced in England except by the institution of fresh legal proceedings is subject to important exceptions introduced by a number of statutes, the most important of which are the Civil Jurisdiction and Judgments Act 1982, as amended by the Civil Jurisdiction and Judgments Act 1991 (which deals with both recognition and enforcement within the United Kingdom and under the Brussels Convention (now replaced in virtually all cases by the Brussels I Regulation) and the Lugano Convention); the Administration of Justice Act 1920, Part II; the Foreign Judgments (Reciprocal Enforcement) Act 1933; the European Communities Act 1982 and the State Immunity Act 1978. We will deal with these statutes separately. As far as the Civil

---

[458] *The Atlantic Emperor (No 2)*, supra, at 633.
[459] [1983] 1 WLR 662 at 670. Affirmed by the Court of Appeal in this case without argument on the point.
[460] Supra, pp 544–550.
[461] See *The Sennar (No 2)* [1985] 1 WLR 490, HL, discussed supra, pp 549–550.

Jurisdiction and Judgments Act 1982, as amended, is concerned, the provisions therein on recognition and enforcement within the United Kingdom and under the Brussels and Lugano Conventions will also be dealt with separately. Recognition and enforcement under the Brussels I Regulation also constitutes an exception to the common law doctrine but is not a statutory exception and will therefore be considered in another part of this chapter.

(a) The Civil Jurisdiction and Judgments Act 1982: recognition and enforcement within the United Kingdom[462]

(i) Enforcement of United Kingdom judgments in other parts of the United Kingdom

Where a judgment is given in one part of the United Kingdom (ie England and Wales, Scotland and Northern Ireland), section 18 of the 1982 Act provides for its enforcement in another part of the United Kingdom by way of registration under Schedules 6 (money provisions) or 7 (non-money provisions). A judgment to which section 18 applies can be enforced in another part of the United Kingdom only in this way,[463] ie the common law rules on enforcement cannot be used. Schedules 6 and 7 will only apply where there is a "judgment" as defined under section 18.

Section 18 initially gives a wide definition to the concept of a judgment.[464] It means, inter alia, "any judgment or order . . . given or made by a court of law in the United Kingdom". A judgment of an inferior court is therefore covered, as is a judgment in rem. It also includes "any award or order made by a tribunal" and "an arbitration award".[465] The section then gives a detailed list of judgments which it does not cover.[466] To take some examples, it does not apply to: (i) a judgment given in a magistrates' court; (ii) any judgment or order given in the exercise of jurisdiction in relation to insolvency law, within the meaning of section 426 of the Insolvency Act 1986;[467] (iii) so much of a judgment as concerns the status of an individual;[468] (iv) so much of a judgment as is a provisional measure other than an interim payment; (v) a maintenance order which is enforceable under the separate statutory provisions dealing with enforcement of maintenance orders in another part of the United Kingdom.[469] Finally, to further complicate matters,

---

[462] See generally Hartley, *Civil Jurisdiction and Judgments*, pp 100–101; Collins, *The Civil Jurisdiction and Judgments Act 1982*, pp 131–135; Anton and Beaumont's, *Civil Jurisdiction in Scotland*, paras 9.33–9.43; Dicey, Morris and Collins, para 14R-239.

[463] S 18(8). There is an exception in respect of arbitration awards within s 18(2)(e).

[464] S 18(2). The Proceeds of Crime Act 2002 (Investigations in different parts of the United Kingdom) Order, SI 2003/425 Part 6, art 34 adds to this definition.

[465] Cf the position under the Brussels/Lugano system, infra, pp 599–600.

[466] See s 18(3), (5), (6), (7).

[467] S 18(3)(6a). Under s 426 "insolvency law" means a provision under the Insolvency Act 1986 and accordingly does not include the power to grant an extra-territorial injunction; see *Hughes v Hannover* [1997] 1 BCLC 497; Smart [1998] CJQ 149 at 160–163; (1998) 114 LQR 46. S 426(1) deals with enforcement within the United Kingdom of a judgment or order in the exercise of jurisdiction in relation to insolvency. For general discussion of s 426, see Woloniecki (1986) 35 ICLQ 644.

[468] S 18(5)(b) and (6), as amended by the Courts and Legal Services Act 1990, Sch 16, para 41.

[469] S 18 (5)(a); see also s 18(7). The statute in question is the Maintenance Orders Act 1950 (see s 16 of that Act), as amended by the Courts and Legal Services Act 1990, Sch 20.

section 18 contains a few limited specific inclusions within its scope,[470] eg fines for contempt of court.

(a) Enforcement of money provisions

In cases where there is a judgment as defined under section 18, the procedure under Schedule 6 for enforcement of money judgments is as follows.[471]

A certificate in respect of the judgment is obtained in the original court, whether it is a judgment of a superior or inferior court. This is then registered in the prescribed manner in the superior court of the other part of the United Kingdom in which enforcement is sought—in England and Wales or Northern Ireland the High Court, in Scotland the Court of Session. A registered certificate is of the same force and effect as a judgment of the registering court, which has the same powers in relation to enforcement as if it had given the original judgment.[472]

There are few defences to enforcement under Schedule 6. A defendant cannot impeach the judgment on its merits and, unlike at common law, cannot plead that the court in the other part of the United Kingdom lacked jurisdiction. Moreover, the defences available at common law cannot be used,[473] and section 32 of the 1982 Act cannot apply because the judgment is not given by a court of an "overseas" country.

The only defences to enforcement under Schedule 6 that a defendant is allowed under the 1982 Act are to be raised after registration and are as follows: first, the registering court *must* set aside the registration if the procedure in the Schedule has not been complied with; secondly, it *may* set aside the registration if satisfied that there was an earlier judgment dealing with the matter in dispute given by another court having jurisdiction in the matter.[474] The limited nature of the defences means that the party who objects to the judgment given in the original court has to go there and appeal against it, rather than raise his objections when enforcement of the judgment is sought in another part of the United Kingdom.

This, however, raises the problem of an appeal against the original judgment overturning or amending that judgment. This is met in Schedule 6 by providing that a certificate shall not be issued unless, under the law of the part of the United Kingdom in which the judgment was given: "(a) either the time for an appeal has expired or the appeal has finally been disposed of; and (b) enforcement is not stayed and the time available for its enforcement has not expired".[475]

Even after registration there is a power given to the registering court to stay proceedings for enforcement pending the outcome of an application, under the law of the part of the United Kingdom in which the judgment was given, to set aside or quash the judgment.[476]

There are special provisions on costs and interest.[477]

---

[470] S 18(4).

[471] Sch 6, paras 2–6; see also CPR, Part 74, paras 74.14–74.18.

[472] Sch 6, para 6.

[473] See *Clarke v Fennoscandia Ltd* 1998 SLT 1014—interim interdict against the enforcement of an English order for costs on the ground that it had been obtained by fraud refused.

[474] Sch 6, para 10.

[475] Sch 6, para 3; criticised by Stone (1983) 32 ICLQ 477, 487–488.

[476] Sch 6, para 9.

[477] Sch 6, paras 7 and 8.

(b) Enforcement of non-money provisions

The 1982 Act extends the previous statutory law by providing in Schedule 7 for the enforcement of non-money provisions. A non-money provision is defined as "any relief or remedy not requiring payment of a sum of money";[478] this would include an injunction, a decree of specific performance and a declaration as to title. The provisions in this Schedule are very similar to those in Schedule 6. There are, however, some minor procedural differences,[479] and, more importantly, there is a major difference of substance. It is stated that "a judgment shall not be registered . . . if compliance with the non-money provisions contained in the judgment would involve a breach of the law of that part of the United Kingdom".[480]

(ii) Recognition of United Kingdom judgments in other parts of the United Kingdom

Section 19(1) simply states that:

> a judgment to which this section applies given in one part of the United Kingdom shall not be refused recognition in another part of the United Kingdom solely on the ground that, in relation to that judgment, the court which gave it was not a court of competent jurisdiction according to the rules of private international law in force in that other part.

With a few exceptions, section 19 applies to the same judgments as section 18.[481] It is a curiously worded provision in that it is phrased in negative terms and does not impose a positive duty to recognise judgments.[482] It could be read literally so as to infer that there are defences available to prevent recognition[483] and that included in these is a defence of lack of jurisdictional competence, provided that this allegation is combined with another defence.

(iii) The effect of a judgment given in another part of the United Kingdom

This is dealt with by section 34 of the 1982 Act, which, it will be recalled,[484] abolishes the non-merger rule in respect of foreign judgments. Once a judgment has been given in another part of the United Kingdom, the claimant may not bring proceedings in England and Wales on the same cause of action unless that judgment is not enforceable or entitled to recognition in England and Wales.

(b) Administration of Justice Act 1920[485]

This Act makes provision for the enforcement within the United Kingdom of judgments obtained in a superior court of any part of the Commonwealth.[486]

---

[478] Sch 7, para 1.

[479] See Sch 7, paras 2–5; CPR, Part 74, para 74.16.

[480] Sch 7, para 5(5). See *G v Caledonian Newspapers Ltd* 1995 SLT 559. Obviously there is no provision on interest as such, but costs carry interest, Sch 7, para 7(2).

[481] S 19(2); for exclusions from s 19 that are included within s 18, see s 19(3).

[482] See generally, Anton and Beaumont's *Civil Jurisdiction in Scotland*, para 9.34.

[483] Ie the defences at common law, see Stone [1983] LMCLQ 1; Lane (1986) 35 ICLQ 629; Layton and Mercer, 39.041. Cf Anton and Beaumont's *Civil Jurisdiction in Scotland*, para 9.34.

[484] Supra, p 544.

[485] Some minor amendments have been made to this Act by the Civil Jurisdiction and Judgments Act 1982, s 35; ss 10 and 14 of the 1920 Act are amended.

[486] S 13. See generally, Patchett, *Recognition of Commercial Judgments and Awards in the Commonwealth*, Chapters 1–4.

(i) When registration of Commonwealth judgments is allowed

A person who has obtained a judgment in a territory forming part of the Commonwealth may within twelve months apply to the High Court in England or Northern Ireland or to the Court of Session in Scotland for its registration, whereupon the court may, if in all the circumstances of the case they think it is just and convenient that the judgment should be enforced in the United Kingdom, order the judgment to be registered.[487] Thus, registration is not a right, as it is in cases of recognition and enforcement within the United Kingdom, but lies wholly within the discretion of the court. A judgment cannot be registered, however, unless it is one under which a sum of money is made payable.[488] Neither can a judgment for multiple damages be registered.[489]

(ii) When registration is not allowed

Under section 9(2) of the 1920 Act registration is not allowed if the original court acted without jurisdiction or if the judgment debtor did not voluntarily submit to the jurisdiction of the adjudicating court, unless he was carrying on business[490] or was ordinarily resident within that jurisdiction.[491] It is assumed that questions of jurisdiction are to be determined by reference to the common law rules as to the jurisdiction of the foreign court.[492] The other defences available under section 9(2) are also similar to those available at common law,[493] namely that the judgment debtor was not served and did not appear in the original proceedings, that the judgment was obtained by fraud,[494] and that the original cause of action was one which, for reasons of public policy or for some other similar reason, could not have been entertained in England. A judgment may not be registered if the judgment debtor satisfies the English court either that an appeal is pending or that he is entitled to appeal against the judgment.[495] The defences mentioned so far are ones laid down by the 1920 Act itself. In addition, the defence laid down by section 32 of the Civil Jurisdiction and Judgments Act 1982, in respect of an overseas judgment given in proceedings brought in breach of an agreement for settlement of disputes,[496] will apply to cases coming within the 1920 Act. A judgment given in a foreign state against that state cannot be registered under the 1920 Act.[497]

---

[487] S 9(1); *Akande v Balfour Beatty Construction Ltd* [1998] IL Pr 110 at 123. The registration of a judgment against a state can attract state immunity: *AIC Ltd v Federal Government of Nigeria* [2003] EWHC 1357 (QB), [2003] All ER (D) 190.

[488] S 12. The *Akande* case, supra.

[489] Protection of Trading Interests Act 1980, s 5; discussed supra, pp 561–563.

[490] See *Sfeir & Co v National Insurance Co of New Zealand* [1964] 1 Lloyd's Rep 330; *Akande v Balfour Beatty Construction Ltd* [1998] IL Pr 110. The meaning of this is the same as at common law—the *Akande* case at 119.

[491] See *Brower v Sunview Solariums Ltd* (1998) 156 DLR (4th) 752.

[492] Supra, pp 516–527.

[493] Supra, p 551 et seq. The common law cases must be referred to for the meaning of these defences: *Owens Bank Ltd v Bracco* [1992] 2 AC 443.

[494] This term is used in the common law sense, *Owens Bank Ltd v Bracco*, supra, p 554.

[495] S 9(2)(e). There is no such common law defence, see supra, p 538.

[496] Supra, pp 569–573. It is suggested that if there are irreconcilable judgments it would not be regarded as just and convenient to enforce the judgment, see Hill, para 12.6.6.

[497] *AIC Ltd v Federal Government of Nigeria* [2003] EWHC 1357 (QB), [2003] All ER (D) 190 (s 1 of the State Immunity Act 1978 applies).

(iii) The effect of registration

A judgment registered under the Act is of the same force and effect, and it may be followed by the same proceedings, as if it had originally been obtained in the registering court.[498] A claimant is in no way deprived of his right to sue at common law upon the obligation created by a foreign judgment,[499] but if he sues on a judgment that is registrable under the Act he is not entitled to the costs of the action unless registration has been refused or unless the court otherwise orders.[500]

(iv) Reciprocity

The Act, however, does not render a judgment registrable within the United Kingdom unless its provisions have been extended by Order in Council to the country in which the judgment has been obtained. Reciprocity is essential. When reciprocal provisions have been made by a Commonwealth country for the enforcement of English, Scottish and Northern Ireland judgments, an Order in Council may be made extending the Act to the country in question.[501] The Act has been extended to a substantial number of Commonwealth countries.[502]

(c) Foreign Judgments (Reciprocal Enforcement) Act 1933[503]

(i) The object of the Act

The policy of facilitating the direct enforcement of foreign judgments in England, and of ensuring that English judgments are enforced abroad,[504] received a further impulse from the Foreign Judgments (Reciprocal Enforcement) Act 1933, which applies the principle of registration, not only to the Commonwealth, but also to foreign countries.

(ii) The countries to which the provisions of the Act are extended

The provisions made by the Act for the registration of foreign judgments in England may be extended by Order in Council to any country which is prepared to afford substantial reciprocity of treatment to judgments obtained in the United Kingdom.[505] It is undesirable that there should be two systems of registration, one for the Commonwealth, the

---

[498] S 9(3)(a), (b); as amended by the Administration of Justice Act 1956, s 40(b).

[499] *Yukon Consolidated Gold Corpn v Clark* [1938] 2 KB 241 at 252.

[500] S 9(5).

[501] S 14; as amended by the Civil Jurisdiction and Judgments Act 1982, s 35(3). The reciprocity is no longer exact in the case of some Commonwealth jurisdictions which now make United Kingdom judgments registrable under their counterparts, not of the 1920 Act, but of the Foreign Judgments (Reciprocal Enforcement) Act 1933.

[502] See SI 1985/1994. But see now in relation to Australia SI 1994/1901, infra, p 590, and Gibraltar SI 1997/2601 and SI 1997/2602, infra, pp 589–590. The 1920 Act no longer applies in relation to Hong Kong.

[503] The 1933 Act is amended by the Civil Jurisdiction and Judgments Act 1982, s 35(1) and Sch 10. Parts of the 1933 Act are repealed by s 54 and Sch 14. The 1933 Act must also now be read in the light of ss 32 and 33 of the 1982 Act, discussed, generally, supra, pp 569–573 and 521–526 and, more particularly in this context, infra, pp 581 and 584. See generally on the 1933 Act, Vallat, *International Law and the Practitioner*, Chapter V; Patchett, *Recognition of Commercial Judgments and Awards in the Commonwealth*, Chapters 1–4.

[504] *Yukon Consolidated Gold Corpn v Clark* [1938] 2 KB 241 at 253; and see *Ferdinand Wagner v Laubscher Bros & Co* [1970] 2 QB 313 at 319–320.

[505] S 1; as amended by s 35 (1) and Sch 10 of the 1982 Act. Enforcement of a judgment abroad may affect whether security for costs is given in England: *Compagnie Française v Thorn Electrics* [1981] FSR 306; *Porzelack KG v Porzelack (UK) Ltd* [1987] 1 WLR 420.

other for countries outside the Commonwealth, and therefore a policy of the gradual supersession of the 1920 Act has been adopted. With this object in view power is given to render the 1933 Act applicable by Order in Council to countries forming part of the Commonwealth, and it is provided that the Administration of Justice Act 1920 shall cease to apply to any such country except those to which it extended at the date of the Order in Council,[506] which was introduced in 1933.[507] However, in order for the 1933 Act to be applied to any particular Commonwealth country, a further specific Order in Council is required, both in the case of a jurisdiction to which the 1920 Act had never been applicable[508] and of one to which it had.[509] Orders to this effect have been made for Pakistan,[510] Bangladesh,[511] India, Australia and the Australian states,[512] Jersey, Guernsey, the Isle of Man, and Tonga. The Act has also been extended to Canada.[513]

As regards countries outside the Commonwealth, orders have been made extending the provisions of the Act to Austria,[514] Belgium, France, Israel, Italy, the Netherlands, Norway, the Federal Republic of Germany and Suriname.[515] These orders provide that judgments in civil and commercial matters shall be mutually recognised and enforced, notwithstanding that the adjudicating court followed rules for the choice of law different from those that would have been followed in the country where enforcement is sought. The provisions of the Act apply also to foreign judgments given in proceedings which arise under a number of international conventions.[516]

(iii) Prerequisites of registration

The successful party to proceedings in a foreign country to which the Act has been extended may apply to the High Court at any time within six years[517] for registration of the

---

[506] S 7.

[507] SR & O 1933 No 1073.

[508] *Yukon Consolidated Gold Corpn v Clark*, supra, (Ontario).

[509] *Jamieson v Northern Electricity Supply Corpn (Private) Ltd* 1970 SLT 113 (Zambia). If an order is made under the 1933 Act applicable to a country to which there is already an Order in force made under the 1920 Act, then the latter ceases to apply: 1933 Act, s 7(2).

[510] See Pakistan Act 1990, Sch, para 8.

[511] Bangladesh Act 1973, s 1(1).

[512] SI 1994/1901, infra, pp 589–590.

[513] SI 1987/468, infra, pp 589–590.

[514] Judgments given in Austria, Belgium, France, Italy, the Netherlands, Norway and Germany will usually come within the Brussels/Lugano system and will be recognised and enforced under one of these rather than under the 1933 Act, see infra, p 596 et seq.

[515] The 1933 Act does not extend to the USA and this has been the source of judicial comment, eg *Perry v Zissis* [1977] 1 Lloyd's Rep 607 at 614, 617. A draft bilateral UK/US recognition convention, quite independent of the 1933 Act, was prepared: (1976) Cmnd 6771; but it was never agreed, see infra, p 590.

[516] Eg Carriage of Goods by Road Act 1965, s 4, Sch, Art 31(1). See generally, Dicey, Morris and Collins, paras 15-024–15-027. The provisions of the 1933 Act may also apply to foreign judgments clawing back sums paid pursuant to an award of multiple damages: Protection of Trading Interests Act 1980, s 7, discussed supra, pp 561–563.

[517] S 2.

judgment[518] in England.[519] A "judgment" now includes arbitration awards which have been turned into judgments.[520] It does not, however, include a judgment on a judgment,[521] eg a judgment given in State A providing for the enforcement of a judgment given in State B. The judgment no longer has to be delivered by a superior court.[522] It is, however, required that the judgment was delivered by a recognised court[523] (which refers to the identity of the court and not the capacity in which it is acting)[524] or tribunal;[525] the judgment is final and conclusive or requires an interim payment to be made;[526] a sum of money is adjudged to be payable to the applicant, other than a sum in respect of taxes or in respect of a fine or other penalty.[527] This latter phrase does not include an award of exemplary damages or damages for "resistance abusive" under French law.[528] A judgment is not to be registered if it is one for multiple damages.[529] A judgment is also not to be registered if it has been wholly satisfied or if it cannot be enforced by execution in the foreign country.[530] A judgment, however, is to be deemed final and conclusive, notwithstanding that an appeal may be pending against it or that it may still be subject to appeal in the foreign courts.[531] The Act differs from the earlier Act of 1920 in that no discretion is left to the High Court. It is expressly provided that: "On any such application the court shall, subject to proof of the prescribed matters and to the other provisions of this Act, order the judgment to be registered."[532]

(iv) Setting aside of registration

There are, however, certain circumstances in which, on the application of the party against whom the registered judgment is enforceable, the registration *must* be set aside and other circumstances in which it *may* be set aside.

---

[518] Or part of the judgment, see s 2(5); *Ahmed v Habib Bank Ltd* [2001] EWCA Civ 1270 at [55]–[58], [2002] 1 Lloyd's Rep 444.

[519] The judgment can be registered in foreign currency: Administration of Justice Act 1977, s 4(2)(b), supra, p 105; and see *Batavia Times Publishing Co v Davis* (1978) 88 DLR (3d) 144; *Principality of Monaco v Project Planning* (1980) 32 OR (2d) 438; *Clinton v Ford* (1982) 137 DLR (3d) 281.

[520] S 10A; added by s 35(1) and Sch 10, para 4 of the 1982 Act. See *ABCI v BFT* [1996] 1 Lloyd's Rep 485 at 489.

[521] S 1(2A); added by s 35(1) and Sch 10, para 1 of the 1982 Act. For the position under the Brussels I Regulation, see infra, p 600.

[522] Cf the original s 1(1) with the amended version introduced by s 35(1) and Sch 10, paras 1 and 2 of the 1982 Act. See also s 54 and Sch 14 of the 1982 Act.

[523] S 1; as amended by s 35(1) and Sch 10, para 1 of the 1982 Act. For the problems in relation to County Court judgments, see Matthews (1996) 112 LQR 221.

[524] *Ahmed v Habib Bank Ltd* [2001] EWCA Civ 1270, [2002] 1 Lloyd's Rep 444.

[525] S11(1); as amended by s 35(1) and Sch 10, para 5 of the 1982 Act.

[526] S11(2); as amended by s 35(1) and Sch 10, para 1 of the 1982 Act.

[527] S 1(2); as amended by s 35(1) and Sch 10, para 1 of the 1982 Act. See *Patterson v Vacation Brokers Inc* [1998] IL Pr 482, Ont CA—an order for costs on an indemnity basis not a penalty.

[528] *SA Consortium General Textiles v Sun and Sand Agencies Ltd* [1978] QB 279 at 299–300, 305–306.

[529] S 5 of the Protection of Trading Interests Act 1980; discussed supra, at pp 561–563. It is unclear whether such a judgment is one for a penalty, see *Lewis v Eliades* [2003] EWCA Civ 1758 at [50] (per POTTER LJ), [2004] 1 WLR 692. Cf *Old North State Brewing Co v Newlands Services Inc* [1999] 4 WWR 573, BC Court of Appeal (not penal).

[530] S 2(1); and see *SA Consortium General Textiles v Sun and Sand Agencies Ltd*, supra, at 297, 300–302.

[531] S 1(3). But it is provided by s 5(1) that on an application to set aside registration the court may do so or may adjourn the application if satisfied that an appeal is pending or that the defendant is entitled and intends to appeal; see, for examples where such an application was refused: *Re A Debtor (No 11 of 1939)* [1939] 2 All ER 400; *SA Consortium General Textiles v Sun and Sand Agencies Ltd* [1978] QB 279 at 297, 298, 306, 307. See also *Hunt v BP Exploration Co (Libya) Ltd* [1980] 1 NZLR 104. Under the Act of 1920 the fact that an appeal is pending is a bar to registration, supra, p 577.

[532] S 2.

(a) When registration *must* be set aside

(i) Lack of jurisdiction

The first case in which the registration must be set aside is if the foreign court acted without jurisdiction.[533] The rules by which the 1933 Act specifies the circumstances in which a foreign court shall be deemed to have had jurisdiction are very similar to the common law rules[534] and vary according to whether the original action was in personam or in rem.

Bases of jurisdiction in personam In the case of a judgment given in an action in personam the original court is deemed to have had jurisdiction on three main bases: residence, submission and having an office or place of business within the foreign jurisdiction.

(1) Residence In the case of residence, the 1933 Act provides that there is jurisdiction "if the judgment debtor, being a defendant in the original court, was at the time when the proceedings were instituted resident in, or being a body corporate had its principal place of business in, the country of that court".[535] As residence is required, temporary presence would appear to be excluded.[536] In the case of corporations, the requirement is not just the one at common law or under the 1920 Act of carrying on business,[537] but rather that the principal place of business be in the foreign country.

(2) Submission The second basis of jurisdiction is submission and three instances of this are provided in section 4(2)(a) of the 1933 Act:[538]

(i) if the judgment debtor, being a defendant in the original court, submitted to the jurisdiction of that court by voluntarily appearing in the proceedings;[539] or

(ii) if the judgment debtor was plaintiff in, or counter-claimed in, the proceedings of the original court; or

(iii) if the judgment debtor, being a defendant in the original court, had before the commencement of the proceedings agreed, in respect of the subject matter of the proceedings, to submit to the jurisdiction of that court or of the courts of the country of that court.

What in general constitutes submission through a voluntary appearance to contest the jurisdiction of the court is likely to be determined in the same way as at common law.[540] The likelihood of this being the case is strengthened by the fact that section 33 of the Civil Jurisdiction and Judgments Act 1982, which provides that in three situations there is no submission by voluntary appearance, applies to recognition or enforcement under the 1933 Act as well as to recognition or enforcement at common law.[541] It will be recalled that under section 33 there is no submission where the appearance is to contest

---

[533] Cf the Australian position, on which see *Hunt v BP Exploration Co (Libya) Ltd* (1979) 144 CLR 565, and in New Zealand, *Hunt v BP Exploration Co (Libya) Ltd* [1980] I NZLR 104.
[534] Supra, p 516 et seq.
[535] S 4(2)(a)(iv).
[536] Cf the common law position, supra, pp 517–518.
[537] Supra, pp 518–520 and 577.
[538] As amended by s 54 and Sch 14 of the Civil Jurisdiction and Judgments Act 1982.
[539] Including an appeal, see *SA Consortium General Textiles v Sun and Sand Agencies Ltd* [1978] QB 279 at 309.
[540] *Henry v Geoprosco International Ltd* [1976] QB 726, supra, p 522 et seq.
[541] Supra, p 523. S 33 of the 1982 Act replaces a similarly worded provision contained in the end part of s 4(2)(a)(i), see s 54 and Sch 14 of the 1982 Act.

the jurisdiction of the court, to seek a stay of proceedings on the ground that there should be an arbitration or trial in another country, or to protect property.

Whilst there is no doubt that an express agreement to submit would fall within section 4(2)(a)(iii), there remains the problem of an implied agreement to submit. Despite some faint Scottish indication to the contrary,[542] it is suggested that, as at common law,[543] an implied agreement will never suffice.[544]

The operation of some of these provisions on submission was considered in *SA Consortium General Textiles v Sun and Sand Agencies Ltd*:[545]

> The plaintiff, a French textile company, sold clothing to the defendant, an English company. The goods came from the plaintiff's branches in Lille and Paris and the invoice from Lille provided that all disputes were to be referred to the commercial court there, whilst the other invoice gave exclusive jurisdiction to the Seine commercial court. The plaintiff claimed the sums due under both invoices and damages for "resistance abusive" in proceedings before the Lille commercial court. Judgment was given for the plaintiff in default of appearance, though the defendant had been served with notice of the proceedings. The defendant failed to appeal within the three-month period allowed under French law. The plaintiff then sought enforcement of the Lille judgment in England, whereupon the defendant applied to the President of the Court of Appeal in Douai for leave to appeal, and then in fact appealed to the full Court of Appeal. The defendant sought, unsuccessfully, to resist the enforcement of the default judgment of the Lille court on a variety of grounds, such as that it could not be enforced by execution in France,[546] or that damages for "resistance abusive" were penal.[547] The main issue, however, was whether the defendant could be taken to have submitted to the jurisdiction of the French courts in respect of both claims.

Section 4(2)(a)(iii) of the 1933 Act was interpreted by a majority in the Court of Appeal as not covering an agreement to submit to all the courts of the foreign country by agreeing to submit to one, so that agreement to submit the issues arising under one invoice to the Seine court did not amount to agreement to submit that issue to any other of the courts of France, including the Lille court.[548] However, the appeal to the Court of Appeal in Douai on the merits of the claim did amount to submission as to both claims,[549] as did a statement by the defendant's English solicitors, when proceedings against the defendant were contemplated in England, that *all* disputes must be brought before the Lille court.[550]

(3) Jurisdiction based on having a place of business The third basis of jurisdiction and one not to be found at common law is provided by section 4(2)(a)(v) of the 1933 Act, namely "if the judgment debtor, being a defendant in the original court, had an office or

---

542 *Jamieson v Northern Electricity Supply Corpn (Private) Ltd* 1970 SLT 113 at 116.
543 Supra, pp 520–521.
544 Thus the decision in *Vogel v R and A Kohnstamm Ltd* [1973] QB 133, supra, p 521 would be the same today even though the 1933 Act has now been extended to Israel.
545 [1978] QB 279; Carter (1979) 50 BYBIL 252. The points raised in the case in respect of the 1933 Act are not affected by the alterations made to that Act by s 35(1) of the 1982 Act.
546 1933 Act, s 2(1)(b), supra, p 580.
547 Ibid, s 1(2)(b), supra, p 580.
548 [1978] QB 279 at 302–304, 309; cf Lord DENNING MR at 298–299.
549 Ibid at 299, 308–309; see supra, p 526.
550 Ibid at 299, 307–308; cf GOFF LJ at 303–304.

place of business in the country of that court and the proceedings in that court were in respect of the transaction effected through or at that office or place".

Limitations on jurisdiction   The three bases of jurisdiction are subject to qualification in that, notwithstanding them, the foreign court shall not be deemed to have had jurisdiction if the case concerned immovables outside the country of the foreign court or if the defendant was under the rules of public international law entitled to immunity from the jurisdiction of the foreign court and did not submit thereto.[551]

Special statutory grounds of jurisdiction   Where a foreign judgment is registered under the 1933 Act pursuant to one of the various statutory provisions[552] embodying international conventions, the different statutes provide that the jurisdictional grounds in the 1933 Act shall all be replaced by special jurisdictional grounds relevant to the particular convention in question.[553]

Meaning of action in personam   It is expressly enacted that the expression "action in personam" shall not include any matrimonial cause,[554] or any proceedings connected with matrimonial matters, the administration of the estates of deceased persons, bankruptcy, winding up of companies, lunacy or the guardianship of minors.[555]

Statutory grounds of jurisdiction are exclusive   In the case of an action in personam, no other ground of jurisdiction will render a foreign judgment registrable under the Act. The fact, for instance, that the claimant has obtained leave from the foreign court to serve process on the defendant in England does not per se generate jurisdiction for the purposes of registration.[556]

Jurisdiction over action in rem   The original court is deemed to have had jurisdiction over an action in rem if the subject matter of the action, whether movable or immovable, was situated in the foreign country at the time of the proceedings.[557]

(ii) Other circumstances where registration must be set aside

There are a number of circumstances in addition to want of jurisdiction[558] where, according to the 1933 Act, [559] registration must be set aside, most of which are very similar to the common law defences:[560]

(i)   if the judgment is not one to which the Act applies;

---

[551] S 4(3); as amended by s 54 and Sch 14 of the Act. S 4(3)(b) of the 1933 Act has been repealed and has been replaced, in effect, by s 32 of the 1982 Act, see supra, p 569 et seq.

[552] Supra, p 579.

[553] Eg Carriage of Goods by Road Act 1965, s 4, Sch, Art 31(1). The defence under s 32 of the 1982 Act will not apply: s 32(4)(b).

[554] But see *Vervaeke v Smith* [1983] 1 AC 145, HL, discussed infra, p 585.

[555] S 11(2).

[556] *Société Cooperative Sidmetal v Titan International Ltd* [1966] 1 QB 828, infra, p 591; *Coast Lines Ltd v Hudig and Veder Chartering NV* [1972] 2 QB 34 at 45.

[557] Section 4(2)(b), subject to the qualifications provided by s 4(3) as amended by s 54 and Sch 14 of the 1982 Act, discussed, supra.

[558] S 4(1)(a)(ii).

[559] S 4(1)(a).

[560] Supra, pp 551–573. It is arguable that, as a foreign judgment once registered under the 1933 Act shall be of the same force and effect as if it had been a judgment of the English court (s 2(2)), it is open to all defences available under English domestic law.

(ii) if the judgment debtor, being the defendant in the original proceedings, did not (despite service of process in accordance with the foreign law) receive notice of the proceedings in sufficient time to enable him to defend them and did not appear;[561]

(iii) if the judgment was obtained by fraud;[562]

(iv) if the enforcement of the judgment would be contrary to public policy in England;[563]

(v) if the rights under the judgment are not vested in the applicant.

One further instance of where registration *must* be set aside is provided by section 32 of the Civil Jurisdiction and Judgments Act 1982:[564]

(vi) if the judgment was given in proceedings brought in breach of an agreement for the settlement of disputes.

(b) When registration *may* be set aside

Registration *may* be set aside if the registering court is satisfied that the matter adjudicated upon had already been the subject of a final and conclusive judgment by a court having jurisdiction in that matter.[565]

(v) The effect of a foreign judgment

(a) A judgment which has been registered

A judgment registered under the Act is, for the purposes of execution, of the same force and effect and subject to the same control as if it had originally been given in the registering court.[566] One significance of this provision would appear to be that the grounds on which registration may or must be set aside may be different from those on which enforcement will be refused. Once the foreign judgment is registered, then it would appear that not only may the registration be set aside for failure to satisfy section 4 of the 1933 Act, but also the registered judgment may be set aside and enforcement refused for any one of the various reasons for setting aside English judgments[567] which may be appropriate to a foreign judgment.

---

[561] This is similar to, but narrower than, the common law defence that the foreign proceedings were contrary to natural justice, supra, pp 563–565; and see *Brockley Cabinet Co Ltd v Pears* (1972) 20 FLR 333; *Barclays Bank Ltd v Piacun* [1984] 2 Qd R 476. Instances of a lack of natural justice falling outside this narrow provision could be treated as coming within the public policy provision, *Society of Lloyd's v Saunders* (2001) 210 DLR (4th) 519, Ont CA.

[562] When an application is made on this ground, the same rules apply as where the defence of fraud is raised to an action at common law on a foreign judgment, supra, pp 551–556; *Syal v Heyward* [1948] 2 KB 443; *Owens Bank Ltd v Bracco* [1992] 2 AC 443 at 489, HL. See also *Ahmed v Habib Bank Ltd* [2001] EWCA Civ 1270, [2002] 1 Lloyd's Rep 444.

[563] For a recognition case where this applied, see *Vervaeke v Smith* [1983] 1 AC 145, HL, at 156 (per Lord HAILSHAM) and 159 (per Lord DIPLOCK); discussed infra, at pp 1018–1020. This provision does not preclude the recognition of a judgment for exemplary damages or damages for "resistance abusive" under French law: *SA Consortium General Textiles v Sun and Sand Agencies Ltd* [1978] QB 279 at 299, 300, 305, 306.

[564] Discussed, supra, pp 569–573.

[565] S 4(1)(b); *Vervaeke v Smith* [1983] 1 AC 145, HL at 156 (per Lord HAILSHAM) and 159 (per Lord DIPLOCK); discussed infra, pp 1013–1014.

[566] S 2(2). So a foreign judgment, registered in England, will, for the purposes of the exercise of the discretion whether to grant a stay of execution, be treated as if it were an English judgment: *Ferdinand Wagner v Laubscher Bros & Co* [1970] 2 QB 313. See also *Susin v Delazzer* (1998) 155 DLR (4th) 170.

[567] See, eg, Gordon (1961) 77 LQR 358, 533.

(b) A judgment which is capable of registration

Section 6 of the 1933 Act provides that: "No proceedings for the payment of a sum payable under a foreign judgment to which this Part of this Act applies, other than proceedings by way of registration of the judgment, shall be entertained by any court in the United Kingdom." This clearly means that no action for enforcement at common law can be brought on a judgment that is registrable, but, seemingly, *this provision* did not prevent the claimant from suing on the original cause of action. However, the claimant is now prevented from doing so by section 34 of the Civil Jurisdiction and Judgments Act 1982 which, as has been seen,[568] abolishes the non-merger rule.

(vi) Conclusiveness of foreign judgments

Section 8[569] of the 1933 Act preserves the common law[570] rules as to the conclusiveness of foreign judgments, but it also provides[571] that a judgment to which the registration provisions of the Act apply, or would apply had a sum of money been payable thereunder, whether or not it can be or is registered, is to be recognised in England as conclusive between the parties in all proceedings founded on the same cause of action.

(a) An exception to the conclusiveness rule

However, a foreign judgment is not recognised as conclusive under the Act if the registration has been set aside or, where the judgment has not been registered, it would have been set aside if it had been registered.[572] The grounds on which registered judgments are set aside are contained in section 4 of the Act.[573] The operation of this proviso was considered in *Vervaeke v Smith*,[574] where it was held that a Belgian judgment in respect of the validity of a marriage[575] would not be entitled to recognition under section 8 of the 1933 Act because the matter in dispute had previously been the subject of a final and conclusive judgment in England[576] and also because recognition would be against public policy.[577]

(b) A prerequisite for recognition: the judgment must have been given on the merits

The rule in section 8, unlike the general registration provisions, applies to a judgment in favour of a defendant; ie a foreign judgment to which the Act applies in which the claimant's claim is dismissed will be recognised in England as conclusive between the parties. However, as with the common law rule on conclusiveness,[578] the judgment must have

---

[568] Supra, p 544.

[569] S 8(3).

[570] Supra, pp 539–551.

[571] S 8(1).

[572] S 8(2). See *Barclays Bank Ltd v Piacun* [1984] 2 Qd R 476.

[573] Discussed supra, pp 539–551.

[574] [1983] 1 AC 145, HL.

[575] On the question of whether the judgment (a nullity decree) came within the 1933 Act, see infra, pp 586–587. See also *Maples v Maples* [1988] Fam 14.

[576] Per Lord DIPLOCK at 159–160, Lord HAILSHAM at 156, Lords BRANDON and KEITH concurring at 167. Registration *may* be set aside in such a case according to s 4(1)(b).

[577] Per Lord HAILSHAM at 156; Lord BRANDON concurring at 167; Lord DIPLOCK at 159 and 161. Registration *must* be set aside in such a case according to s 4(1)(a)(v).

[578] *The Sennar (No 2)* [1985] 1 WLR 490, supra, pp 549–550.

been given on the merits. Thus in *Black-Clawson International Ltd v Papierwerke Waldhof-Aschaffenburg AG*:[579]

> Just within the six-year limitation period under English law, the English plaintiff began proceedings, on bills of exchange which had been dishonoured, in England and in Germany. The limitation period under German law was three years and had expired, and the German trial court dismissed the action on that ground.[580] In the English proceedings, the German defendant argued that the German judgment should be recognised in England under the 1933 Act and, relying on section 8(1), that it was conclusive between the parties as the English and German proceedings were both founded on the same cause of action.

A majority of the House of Lords held that section 8(1), unlike the main provisions of the 1933 Act, applied to judgments in favour of a defendant as well as of a plaintiff. However, the German judgment, dismissing the action because it was time-barred under the German law as to limitation which merely barred the remedy and did not extinguish the right, was not a decision on the merits even though regarded, in Germany, as a decision on substance. The German judgment was not therefore conclusive, though the English proceedings were stayed until the outcome of a final German appeal was known.

Black-Clawson remains good authority on the general point that a foreign judgment must be given on the merits in order to come within section 8 of the Act. It is, however, no longer good authority on the specific point of the effect of a foreign judgment involving a limitation period. This is because of section 3 of the Foreign Limitation Periods Act 1984,[581] which treats a foreign judgment on a limitation matter as being conclusive "on its merits". Section 3 applies regardless of whether the foreign court has applied its own law on limitation periods or that of any other country, including England and Wales. It also applies regardless of whether recognition is sought under statutory rules or at common law, and therefore, overturns the common law decision in *Harris v Quine*.[582]

(c) The scope of section 8: matrimonial causes

The provisions on recognition (section 8), unlike those on enforcement, are not confined to cases where there is a money judgment. This raises the major question of whether section 8 can apply to matrimonial causes, for example foreign decrees of divorce or nullity. For many years this question remained unanswered. However, it is now clear that an overseas divorce, etc cannot be recognised under the 1933 Act.[583] The 1933 Act is concerned with "actions",[584] whether in personam or in rem.[585] In matrimonial causes,

---

[579] [1975] AC 591; Jaffey (1975) 38 MLR 585; Carter (1974–1975) 47 BYBIL 381.

[580] The analysis of the trial court was that the issue of limitation was one of substance, to be referred to English law as the law governing the contract. English law would classify the issue as procedural to be referred to German law as the law of the forum and German law would accept the renvoi and apply its own law. The effect of German law (though regarded as substantive) was to bar the remedy but not extinguish the right. A German appellate court then decided that the English 6-year period applied. A final appeal to the Federal Supreme Court was pending at the time of the English proceedings.

[581] See Law Com No 114 (1982), paras 4.58–4.71; Stone [1985] LMCLQ 497; Carter (1985) 101 LQR 68; supra, pp 80–82.

[582] (1869) LR 4 QB 653, supra, p 549.

[583] *Maples v Maples* [1988] Fam 14. For recognition of overseas divorces, etc, see infra, p 986 et seq.

[584] See s 4(2); s 4(1)(a)(ii); s 8(2)(b).

[585] These terms are defined supra, pp 353 and 414.

"proceedings" are brought before the English courts rather than "actions". Moreover, section 8(1) is concerned with judgments which affect "the parties thereto". A judgment of marital status has a wider significance and can affect others, such as the state and children of the marriage.

(d) European Community judgments

As a result of the European Communities (Enforcement of Community Judgments) Order 1972[586] any Community judgment[587]to which the Secretary of State has appended an order for enforcement shall be registered by the High Court if application is made by the person entitled to enforce it. The judgments to which the Order applies are not those of the national courts of the Member States of the European Community[588] but rather judgments of the courts and institutions of the Community itself, ie judgments of the European Court of Justice, and decisions of the Arbitration Committee of the European Atomic Energy Community, of the High Authority of the European Coal and Steel Community which impose a pecuniary obligation, and of the Council and of the Commission of the European Community which impose a pecuniary obligation on persons other than states.

The effect of registration is that such Community judgments and decisions shall, for all purposes of execution, have the same force and effect as if they were judgments of the High Court. The High Court would appear to have no discretion as to whether to register such judgments;[589] but the European Court of Justice may order that enforcement of such a registered judgment shall be suspended. Such order then must be registered by the High Court and when registered shall have effect as if it were an order of the High Court staying the execution of the judgment and no steps to enforce the judgment may be taken while the order remains in force.

The judgments which may be registered are not restricted to those under which a sum of money is payable.[590] If, in the case of a Community money judgment,[591] it has been partly satisfied at the date of registration, then it is to be registered only in respect of the sum outstanding; and if the judgment is satisfied in whole or in part after registration, then the registration shall be appropriately cancelled or varied.

(e) Judgments against states

(i) Judgments against the United Kingdom: the State Immunity Act 1978

It will be recalled that the State Immunity Act 1978 implements the European Convention on State Immunity (1972). The major significance of the Convention and of the 1978

---

[586] SI 1982/1590, made under s 2(2) of the European Communities Act 1972; amended by SI 1998/1259 (to make provision for Council Regulation (EC) 40/94 on the Community trade mark) and SI 2003/3204 (to make provision for Council Regulation (EC) 6/2002 on Community designs).

[587] There are similar rules for the registration and enforcement of Euratom inspection orders.

[588] As to recognition of which, see infra, p 596 et seq.

[589] Also the defence under s 32 of the Civil Jurisdiction and Judgments Act 1982 will not apply because there is no judgment of a court "of an overseas country" (as defined under s 50).

[590] SI 1972/1590, para 2(1): and see *Re Westinghouse Electric Corpn Uranium Contract* [1978] AC 547 at 636.

[591] A judgment can be registered in a foreign currency: Administration of Justice Act 1977, s 4(2)(b).

Act is to provide for the circumstances when a sovereign state is to be immune from the jurisdiction of our courts.[592] However, provision is also made for the recognition here of judgments given against the United Kingdom by a court in another state which is a party to the 1972 Convention.[593] Recognition must be given to such a judgment if it was a final judgment and if the United Kingdom was not entitled to immunity under the Convention.[594] Such a judgment, and any settlement before a court in a Convention State which is treated under the law of that state as equivalent to a judgment,[595] shall be regarded here as conclusive between the parties.[596] Recognition may, however, be denied on a number of grounds:[597] that recognition would be manifestly contrary to public policy; that a party to the proceedings had no adequate opportunity to present his case; that the procedural requirements of the Convention had not been complied with; if prior similar proceedings between the same parties are pending before a court in the United Kingdom, or before a court in a Convention State whose judgment would be required to be recognised; if there are prior inconsistent judgments of a United Kingdom court or a court in a Convention State; in the case of a judgment concerning the interest of the United Kingdom in movable or immovable property by way of succession, gift or *bona vacantia*, if the foreign court would not have had jurisdiction under rules equivalent to the English rules appropriate to such a claim, or if the foreign court applied a law other than that which would have been applied by an English court and would have reached a different conclusion had it applied that latter law.

(ii) Judgments against other states: the Civil Jurisdiction and Judgments Act 1982

The 1978 Act did not deal with the recognition of foreign judgments against states other than the United Kingdom. These are now dealt with by the Civil Jurisdiction and Judgments Act 1982, section 31(1) of which provides that:

A judgment given by a court of an overseas country against a State other than the United Kingdom or the State to which that court belongs[598] shall be recognised and enforced in the United Kingdom, if and only if—

(a) it would be so recognised and enforced if it had not been given against a State; and

(b) that court would have had jurisdiction in the matter if it had applied rules corresponding to those applicable to such matters in the United Kingdom in accordance with sections 2 to 11 of the State Immunity Act 1978.

---

[592] Supra, p 491 et seq.

[593] 1978 Act, ss 18, 19; and see Sinclair (1973) 22 ICLQ 254, 266–267, 273–276.

[594] S 18(1).

[595] S 18(3).

[596] S 18(2).

[597] S 19. S 32 of the Civil Jurisdiction and Judgments Act 1982 will not apply, since it only concerns judgments against persons.

[598] A foreign judgment against a state given in that state cannot be registered under the 1920 Act or seemingly the 1933 Act because it attracts immunity under Art 1 of the 1978 Act: *AIC Ltd v Federal Government of Nigeria* [2003] EWHC 1357 (QB), [2003] All ER (D) 190. For a rule preventing enforcement under the 1933 Act of judgments against persons, such as diplomats, entitled to immunity from jurisdiction, see s 4(3)(c) of the 1933 Act.

The concept of "a judgment given against a State" is defined under the 1982 Act,[599]as is the concept of a "State" (ie to include the constituent territories in a federal state).[600] Section 31(1) will not affect judgments given in proceedings which arise under a number of international conventions, and which are recognised and enforced under the 1933 Act.[601]

(f) The Brussels and Lugano Conventions

The Brussels Convention, which is implemented by the Civil Jurisdiction and Judgments Act 1982, has been replaced in virtually all cases by the Brussels I Regulation. One has to say "virtually" because the Brussels Convention continues to apply to judgments given in relation to the territories of the Contracting States[602] which fall within the territorial scope of the Brussels Convention and are excluded from the Regulation.[603] The territories in question are (in relation to France) the French overseas territories, such as New Caledonia and Mayotte, and (in relation to the Netherlands) Aruba.[604] The free circulation of judgments within the European Community, which was provided by the Brussels Convention, was extended to what was left of the EFTA bloc[605] by the 1988 Lugano Convention.[606] This Convention, which was implemented by the Civil Jurisdiction and Judgments Act 1991 (amending the 1982 Act), was a parallel one to the Brussels Convention, closely based on the latter, but not identical to it. The 1988 Convention has been replaced by the 2007 Lugano Convention, which aligns the Convention with the Brussels I Regulation. Recognition and enforcement under the Brussels and Lugano Conventions is considered in Chapter 16, as is the Brussels I Regulation.

The Brussels Convention provided a new impetus for other countries to enter into bilateral recognition and enforcement conventions with the United Kingdom.[607] The requirement that English courts must recognise all judgments of the courts of other Contracting States, even where jurisdiction was taken against a defendant domiciled in a non-Contracting State under an exorbitant basis of jurisdiction, caused considerable anxiety in, for example, the USA[608] and Australia.[609] However, Article 59 of the Brussels Convention[610] allowed[611] a Contracting State to conclude conventions with other countries under which judgments of the courts of other Contracting States[612] against persons described as habitually resident in such other countries shall not be recognised in the first

---

[599] S 31(2).

[600] S 31(5).

[601] S 31(3); as amended by the Statute Law (Repeals) Act 2004, Sch 1(14), para 1.

[602] At the moment the Contracting States to the Brussels Convention are the original 15 Member States.

[603] Art 68(1). Territories are excluded from the Regulation pursuant to Art 299 of the EC Treaty.

[604] See Layton and Mercer, paras 11.061–11.071. See also Kruger, paras 1.026–1.037.

[605] Ie Iceland, Norway, and Switzerland.

[606] Infra, p 638 et seq.

[607] It has also led in part to the reconsideration of common law rules and the adoption of a principle of full faith and credit for cases of enforcement within Canada: *Morguard Investments Ltd v De Savoye* (1991) 76 DLR (4th) 256 at 272; discussed supra, pp 530–531.

[608] Nadelmann (1977) 41 Law and Contemporary Problems 54, 58–62, and see infra, pp 635–636.

[609] Pryles and Trindade (1974) 42 ALJ 185, 192–195.

[610] Art 59, discussed infra, pp 635–636.

[611] And still allows in the few cases where the Brussels Convention still applies.

[612] And those granted in Gibraltar: SI 1997/2602 para 5.

Contracting State. This was the genesis of a draft UK/US Judgments Convention.[613] However, this Convention was never implemented because of United Kingdom alarm at the prospect of having to enforce American judgments for large awards of damages. Negotiations with Canada and Australia were more successful, with agreement being reached on a UK/Canada Convention[614] and a UK/Australia Convention.[615] As previously mentioned, the Brussels Convention has been replaced in virtually all cases by the Brussels I Regulation and this contains no equivalent of Article 59.[616] However, bilateral agreements containing the Article 59 let-out entered into prior to the entry into force of the Regulation are still honoured. The 2007 Lugano Convention, like the earlier 1988 Convention, contains an equivalent of Article 59 so that bilateral agreements containing the Article 59 let-out entered into prior to the entry into force of the 2007 Convention are honoured, as are conventions entered into in the future.[617]

4. INTER-RELATION OF THE COMMON LAW AND STATUTES

One problem which has been touched on already[618] and might usefully be examined a little more fully is that of the inter-relation of the common law rules of recognition and those provided by statute (other than the Civil Jurisdiction and Judgments Act 1982[619]), especially in the fields of jurisdiction and defences. It will be recalled[620] that at common law the grounds of jurisdiction of the foreign court which will be recognised in England are based on residence and submission. Under section 4(2)(a) of the Foreign Judgments (Reciprocal Enforcement) Act 1933,[621] there are listed five grounds of jurisdiction in actions in personam,[622] the underlying bases of which are residence, submission and having an office or place of business within the country. The problems to be examined are whether the statutory regime is to be regarded merely as a codification of the common law principles and, if not, whether in a case which falls outside the statute, the basis of statutory recognition should affect common law recognition.

---

[613] (1976) Cmnd 6771; see Hay and Walker (1976) 11 Texas Int LJ 421; Smit (1977) 17 VA J Int L 443; Mathers (1977) 127 NLJ 777; North (1978) 128 NLJ 315; Alford (1979) 18 Colum J Transnat L 119; North, *Essays*, Chapter 8; Kerr (1980) Europarecht 353, 356–357.

[614] See the Schedule to SI 1987/468. See also Patchett, *Recognition of Commercial Judgments and Awards in the Commonwealth* (1984), pp 32–35; Castel and Walker, *Canadian Conflict of Laws* (6th edn), para 14.27; SI 1987/468, amended by SI 1987/2211, SI 1988/1304 and 1853, SI 1989/987, SI 1991/1724, SI 1992/1731 and SI 1995/2708 extends the Foreign Judgments (Reciprocal Enforcement) Act 1933 to designated Provinces of Canada (Alberta, British Columbia, Manitoba, New Brunswick, Newfoundland, Nova Scotia, Ontario, Prince Edward Island, the Yukon Territory, Saskatchewan, Northwest Territories): supra, pp 578–579.

[615] See the Schedule to SI 1994/1901. This Order extends the 1933 Act, supra, pp 578–587, to the judgments of designated courts of Australia. Before this, the 1920 Act was extended to Australian states.

[616] See infra, pp 626–627.

[617] Infra, pp 638–639.

[618] Supra, pp 579–584.

[619] For the very different rules for recognition and enforcement under the Brussels/Lugano system, see infra, pp 596–640.

[620] Supra, p 516 et seq.

[621] As amended by s 54 of and Sch 14 to the Civil Jurisdiction and Judgments Act 1982.

[622] Supra, pp 581–582.

Just such issues arose in *Société Coopérative Sidmetal v Tital International Ltd*.[623]

> The defendant, an English company, had agreed to sell steel to the plaintiff, a Belgian company, and to ship the steel direct to an Italian company which had bought the steel from the plaintiff. Dissatisfied with the steel, the Italian company sued the plaintiff in Belgium and the plaintiff sought to join the defendant as a third party and a Belgian writ was served on it in England. The defendant took no part in the Belgian proceedings, but judgment was given against the defendant and in favour of the plaintiff. The plaintiff had the Belgian judgment registered in England under the Foreign Judgments (Reciprocal Enforcement) Act 1933 and the defendant sought to have the registration set aside.

The real issue was whether the Belgian court had jurisdiction such as to permit an English court to recognise and enforce the Belgian judgment. None of the jurisdictional requirements listed in section 4(2) of the 1933 Act was satisfied, nor were any of the heads of jurisdiction laid down at common law in *Emanuel v Symon*.[624] Nevertheless, it was argued for the plaintiff that the effect of the 1933 Act was fundamentally to change the basis on which foreign judgments are recognised in England, namely that the 1933 Act approaches the question of recognition "on the principle that, if there is reciprocity between the courts of this country and the courts of the country in which the judgment was obtained, then comity of nations requires that the jurisdiction of the courts of that country should be recognised for the purposes of the Act".[625] On such a basis, a Belgian judgment should be recognised either if an English court would have had jurisdiction in similar circumstances, ie service of the claim form out of the jurisdiction,[626] or if a Belgian court would have recognised the jurisdiction of the English court in a similar case, mutatis mutandis.

Whilst WIDGERY J accepted that the 1933 Act did not constitute a codification of the common law principles,[627] he was not prepared to accept that this Act had reintroduced comity or reciprocity as the underlying basis for the recognition of foreign judgments either at common law, or under the 1933 Act.[628] The bases of jurisdiction laid down in section 4(2)(a) of the 1933 Act are exclusive.[629]

A different question is whether, in so far as the provisions of the 1933 Act are broader than those of the common law, the 1933 Act could influence the development of the common law recognition rules. It is suggested that it could, and should, as in the case of jurisdiction based on having an office or place of business in the foreign country.[630]

---

[623] [1966] 1 QB 828; Webb (1966) 15 ICLQ 269; followed in *Gordon Pacific Developments Pty Ltd v Conlon* [1993] 3 NZLR 760; *Re Word Publishing Co Ltd* [1992] 2 Qd R 336. Recognition and enforcement of Belgian judgments will usually come now within the Brussels I Regulation discussed infra, pp 596–637.

[624] [1908] 1 KB 302 at 309.

[625] [1966] 1 QB 828 at 845.

[626] Cf supra, pp 529–530.

[627] [1966] 1 QB 828 at 841, 846. See for the Australian position, *Hunt v BP Exploration Co (Libya) Ltd* (1979) 144 CLR 565 and for New Zealand, *Hunt v BP Exploration (Libya) Ltd* [1980] 1 NZLR 104. Cf *Re Trepca Mines Ltd* [1960] 1 WLR 1273 at 1281–1282; *Rossano v Manufacturers' Life Insurance Co* [1963] 2 QB 352 at 383.

[628] [1966] 1 QB 828 at 841, 847; and see *Blohn v Desser* [1962] 2 QB 116 at 123; *Vogel v R and A Kohnstamm Ltd* [1973] QB 133 at 134; *Henry v Geoprosco International Ltd* [1976] QB 726 at 751.

[629] And see *Sharps Commercials Ltd v Gas Turbines Ltd* [1956] NZLR 819.

[630] 1933 Act, s 4(2)(a)(v), supra, pp 582–583.

Certainly it is true in the case of the defence of fraud, illustrated by *Syal v Heyward*,[631] that decisions on recognition at common law may be relied upon for the purposes of the application of the 1933 Act. What one cannot do is to determine the present common law rules by reference to the 1933 Act, for one "cannot ascertain what the common law is by arguing backwards from the provisions of the statute".[632]

5. THE BRUSSELS I REGULATION

The jurisdictional provisions of the Brussels I Regulation have already been considered,[633] but the Regulation provides also for the recognition and enforcement in this country of judgments given in civil and commercial matters in European Community Member States, with the exception of Denmark. Under the EC/Denmark Agreement the provisions of the Regulation, with minor modifications, are applied by international law to the relations between the European Community and Denmark. This means that judgments given in another European Community State[634] that are within the scope of the Regulation must now be recognised and enforced under this scheme rather than under the 1920 Act,[635] the 1933 Act[636] or the common law rules.[637] There is no implementing legislation in the United Kingdom for the Brussels I Regulation. It is directly applicable in Member States, with the exception of Denmark, and cannot therefore be regarded as a United Kingdom statutory scheme of enforcement.[638] The provisions on recognition and enforcement under the Regulation are complex, despite the Regulation's aim of simplifying this area of law. Moreover, these provisions are markedly different from the rules on recognition and enforcement at common law or under the 1933 Act.[639] For these reasons, it has been thought best to deal with recognition and enforcement under the Brussels I Regulation in a separate chapter.[640] That chapter will also consider three related Regulations: the European Enforcement Order Regulation, which applies where there is a judgment on an uncontested claim; the European Order for Payment Procedure Regulation; and the European Small Claims Procedure Regulation.

---

[631] [1948] 2 KB 443, supra, p 556. See also *Owens Bank Ltd v Bracco* [1992] 2 AC 443 at 489, HL; supra, p 554. This is also true in relation to the 1920 Act.

[632] *Henry v Geoprosco International Ltd* [1976] QB 726 at 751.

[633] Supra, p 204 et seq.

[634] Ie in Austria, Belgium, Bulgaria, Cyprus, the Czech Republic, Estonia, Finland, France, Germany, Greece, Hungary, Ireland, Italy, Latvia, Lithuania, Luxembourg, Malta, Netherlands, Poland, Portugal, Romania, Slovakia, Slovenia, Spain and Sweden. For the territories covered see Layton and Mercer, paras 11.061–11.071. See the statement by the United Kingdom in relation to Gibraltar attached to the Regulation, whereby other Member States are to enforce Gibraltar judgments as if they are United Kingdom judgments.

[635] Orders were made extending the 1920 Act to Cyprus and Malta.

[636] Orders were made extending the 1933 Act to Austria, Belgium, France, Italy, the Netherlands and Germany. See supra, pp 578–579. For the relationship between the 1933 Act and the Regulation see infra, pp 598–599.

[637] The common law rules were used for Bulgaria, the Czech Republic, Luxembourg, Denmark, Estonia, Finland, Ireland, Greece, Hungary, Latvia, Lithuania, Poland, Romania, Slovakia, Slovenia, Spain, Portugal, and Sweden; supra, p 516 et seq. For the relationship between the common law rules and the Regulation see infra, pp 598–599.

[638] There are, however, United Kingdom provisions in support of the Regulation contained in the Civil Jurisdiction and Judgments Order, SI 2001/3929.

[639] This is a relevant consideration when deciding whether to award security for costs: *Porzelack KG v Porzelack (UK) Ltd* [1987] 1 WLR 420.

[640] Infra, p 696 et seq.

6. THE HAGUE CONVENTION ON CHOICE OF COURT AGREEMENTS 2005

Work carried out at the Hague Conference on private international law on a multilateral convention on jurisdiction, recognition, and enforcement of foreign judgments in civil and commercial matters ended in failure.[641] However, in 2005, a Convention on Choice of Court Agreements was adopted.[642] This is concerned to ensure the effectiveness of exclusive choice of court agreements.[643] The provisions on jurisdiction have already been discussed.[644] A judgment given by a court of a Contracting State designated in the agreement will be recognised in other Contracting States,[645] subject to a number of grounds of refusal.[646] Where one of these grounds is established, recognition or enforcement *may* be refused, rather than must be. The court addressed is not precluded from recognition or enforcement and Contracting States will be able to lay down criteria for recognition of judgments where one of these grounds applies.[647] The grounds include where: the agreement was null and void under the law of the state of the chosen court (including its choice of law rules), unless the chosen court has determined that the agreement is valid;[648] a party lacked the capacity to conclude the agreement under the law of the requested state;[649] the document which instituted the proceedings was not notified to the defendant in sufficient time and in such a way as to enable him to arrange for his defence, unless the defendant entered an appearance and presented his case without contesting notification in the court of origin;[650] the judgment was obtained by fraud in connection with a matter of procedure; [651] recognition or enforcement would be manifestly incompatible with the public policy of the requested state;[652] the judgment is inconsistent with a judgment given in the requested state in a dispute between the same parties; the judgment is inconsistent with an earlier judgment given in another state between the same parties on the same cause of action, provided that the earlier judgment fulfils the conditions necessary for its recognition in the requested state.[653] These last five grounds are very similar to, and at times identical with, those found in the defences to recognition of judgments within the European Community under the Brussels I Regulation.[654] The Convention also provides that recognition or enforcement of a judgment may be refused if, and to the extent that, the judgment awards damages, including exemplary or punitive damages, that do not compensate a party for actual loss or harm suffered.[655] Overall, the Convention

---

[641] See supra, p 340.
[642] See http://www.hcch.net and supra, pp 422–424.
[643] As defined in Art 3.
[644] Supra, pp 422–424.
[645] Art 8.
[646] Art 9.
[647] The Hartley and Dogauchi Report, http://www.hcch.net, paras 125 and 183.
[648] Art 9(a).
[649] Art 9(b).
[650] Art 9(c).
[651] Art 9(d).
[652] Art 9(e).
[653] Art 9(g).
[654] See Art 34 of the Regulation, discussed infra, pp 610–627.
[655] Art 11(1).

would have a dramatic effect on cases where there is a jurisdiction agreement providing for trial abroad, which are at present dealt with under the common law rules or under the 1920 or 1933 Acts. Thus, for example, if the United Kingdom[656] and the USA applied this Hague Convention, recognition and enforcement of judgments granted in the USA, consequent on a jurisdiction agreement, would be dealt with, not under the common law rules, but under the very different rules under the Convention.[657]

---

[656] The Convention would be ratified by the EC alone. Member States would then be bound by this.

[657] The impact of the Hague Convention on Choice of Court Agreements on enforcement under the Brussels I Regulation is considered infra, pp 636–637.

Chapter 16

Recognition and Enforcement of Judgments Under the Brussels/Lugano System

1. THE BRUSSELS I REGULATION[1]

(a) Introduction

The Brussels I Regulation[2] is concerned to simplify formalities with a view to rapid and simple recognition and enforcement of judgments given[3] in Member States.[4] This is seen as being essential for the sound operation of the internal market.[5] The objective is to have free movement of judgments within the Member States in civil and commercial matters.[6] In order to achieve this the Regulation provides that: first, the recognition of judgments is automatic, in the sense that none of the usual conditions found in cases of recognition

---

[1] For commentaries on recognition and enforcement under the Regulation see Briggs and Rees, paras 7.03–7.24; Layton and Mercer, Vol 1, Chapters 24–29; Dicey, Morris and Collins, paras 14R-185–14-238; Hartley (2006) 319 Hague Recueil, Ch XX.; Magnus and Manikowski (eds), *Brussels I Regulation*.

[2] Council Regulation (EC) No 44/2001 of 22 December 2000 on jurisdiction and the recognition and enforcement of judgments in civil and commercial matters OJ 2001 L 12/1 (amended by: Corrigendum, OJ 2001 L 307/28; Commission Regulation (EC) No 1496/2002, OJ 2002 L 225/13—amending Annex I and II; the Act concerning the conditions of accession of the Czech Republic, etc, OJ 2003 L 236/33; Commission Regulation (EC) No 2245/2004, OJ 2004 L 381/10—amending Annexes I, II, III and IV; Regulation (EC) No 1791/2006, OJ 2006 L 363/1). The background to the Regulation and its provisions on jurisdiction are discussed supra, pp 203–340. The Regulation entered into force on 1 March 2002.

[3] As regards the original 15 Member States (but not Denmark), it applies to judgments given following proceedings instituted in the Member State of origin after the entry into force of the Regulation on 1 March 2002 (Art 66(1)). Proceedings in the Member State of origin instituted before this date resulting in a judgment after that date can be recognised under the transitional provision in Art 66(2). As regards the 10 new 2004 Member States, the position is the same but the relevant date is 1 May 2004 (the date of their accession to the European Community). As regards the 2 new 2007 Member States, the relevant date is 1 January 2007. For the position in relation to Denmark see infra, p 637.

[4] Recital (2) of the Regulation. This is the same purpose as that of the Brussels Convention (which it replaces in virtually all cases, infra, p 637), on which see Case C-7/98 *Krombach v Bamberski* [2001] QB 709 at [19]. The Member States in respect of which the Regulation is directly applicable are the 27 European Community Member States, with the exception of Denmark (ie Austria, Belgium, Bulgaria, Cyprus, the Czech Republic, Estonia, Finland, France, Germany, Greece, Hungary, Ireland, Italy, Latvia, Lithuania, Luxembourg, Malta, the Netherlands, Poland, Portugal, Romania, Slovakia, Slovenia, Spain, Sweden and the United Kingdom). Under the EC/Denmark Agreement, discussed infra, p 637, the provisions of the Regulation, with minor modifications, are applied by international law to the relations between the Community and Denmark.

[5] Recital (1) of the Regulation. For the legal basis for the Regulation see Arts 61(c) and 65 of the Treaty on European Union. The latter specifically mentions the recognition and enforcement of decisions in civil and commercial matters.

[6] Recital (6) of the Regulation.

and enforcement at common law or under the Foreign Judgments (Reciprocal Enforcement) Act 1933[7] have to be satisfied before recognition can take place; secondly, enforcement follows on from recognition and is largely a procedural matter; and thirdly, the defences available under the Regulation against recognition and enforcement are limited—in particular, a court in another Member State is under a duty to recognise and enforce a judgment even though the court which granted it misapplied the rules on jurisdiction under the Regulation.

Such liberal provisions on recognition and enforcement can only work where there is mutual trust among the Member States. This requires safeguards to be built into the system.[8] The first, and most obvious, one is that the Regulation is a double instrument; ie it contains direct rules both on jurisdiction and on recognition and enforcement.[9] The two sets of rules on jurisdiction and on recognition and enforcement are each part of a single scheme. In order to achieve the objective of the free movement of judgments it is necessary that the rules on jurisdiction are unified.[10] The fact that the Member States share the same rules on jurisdiction means that, when it comes to recognition and enforcement, the Regulation does not need to impose a requirement that the court in the second Member State, in which enforcement is sought, should have to check the basis on which the court in the first Member State, which gave judgment, took jurisdiction. Moreover, the bases of jurisdiction under the Regulation are narrow; exorbitant bases are prohibited and there are special provisions on natural justice designed to protect the defendant where he has not entered an appearance at the trial.[11] The second safeguard is that there are still defences which can be considered by the court in the Member State in which recognition and enforcement of the judgment is sought.[12]

The emphasis under the Regulation is away from litigation at the stage of recognition and enforcement (and in the country where this is sought); instead, any disputes as to jurisdiction should be dealt with in the Member State in which the trial of the substantive issue takes place. A defendant can no longer ignore the original action and decide instead to defend by challenging the recognition and enforcement of the judgment when this is sought in another Member State. A defendant is virtually forced to defend the original action; once the judgment is given, there will often be nothing he can do to stop its recognition and enforcement in other Member States. This is not unfair to a defendant who is domiciled in a Member State: the Regulation's rules on jurisdiction will frequently mean that the trial takes place in the Member State of his domicile anyway. Even when he has to go to another Member State to defend the action, this will still be within the Community. It is more questionable, however, whether the Regulation is fair in its treatment of defendants domiciled in non-Member States. As will shortly be shown, any judgment given against them in a Member State is to be recognised and enforced under

---

[7] Supra.
[8] See the Jenard Report, OJ 1979 C 59/1, 42; Case 125/79 *Denilauler SNC v Couchet Frères* [1980] ECR 1553.
[9] For the rules on jurisdiction, see supra, pp 203–340.
[10] Recital (6) of the Regulation.
[11] See Arts 3, 25 and 26, discussed supra, pp 223, 276 and 302–303; the Jenard Report, OJ 1979 C595/1, 47.
[12] Discussed infra, pp 610–627.

the Regulation.[13] This is despite the fact that defendants domiciled in non-Member States are denied the jurisdictional safeguards available to defendants domiciled in Member States; in particular, they are subject to the exorbitant bases of jurisdiction used in Member States. These defendants will have to defend away from home and may have to travel long distances in order to do so.

The Brussels I Regulation is based on, and updates, the earlier Brussels Convention, which it replaces in virtually all cases. The exception being that the Brussels Convention still applies in relation to certain overseas territories of some Member States.[14] The Regulation applies to legal proceedings instituted and to documents formally drawn up or registered as authentic after its entry into force on 1 March 2002.[15] However, there is a transitional provision stating that, if proceedings in the judgment-granting Member State were instituted before this date but the judgment was given after it, this will be recognised and enforced in accordance with the Regulation, provided that certain conditions are met.[16]

The Commission is due shortly to produce a Green Paper dealing with reform of the Regulation.[17] The Hess, Pfeiffer and Schlosser Report,[18] which will serve as the basis for the Green Paper, identifies a number of problems with the operation of Chapter III of the Regulation and indicates possible solutions. These will be considered at various points in this chapter and there will also be further discussion of future developments at the end of the chapter.

(b) When do the rules on recognition and enforcement under the Brussels I Regulation apply?

Chapter III (Articles 32 to 56) of the Regulation deals with the recognition and enforcement of judgments. In cases coming within this title traditional national rules cannot be used.[19] Chapter III applies, regardless of which rules on jurisdiction have been applied in the court which gave the judgment, to the situation where recognition and enforcement is sought in one Member State of a judgment given in another Member State in respect of a matter coming within the scope of the Regulation. As will be seen, it does not cover orders without notice.

(i) Regardless of which rules on jurisdiction have been applied

Chapter III of the Regulation applies equally to judgments given by the courts of Member States granted after jurisdiction was taken under the Regulation's rules (contained in Chapter II) and to judgments granted after jurisdiction was taken under

---

[13] See infra. See also the Jenard Report, p 42. For non-EU reaction to the Brussels Convention (now in virtually all cases replaced by the Regulation) see infra, pp 635–636.

[14] Infra, p 637.

[15] Art 66(1).

[16] Art 66(2).

[17] Supra, p 206.

[18] Available at the European Commission—European Judicial Network—What's new website http://ec. europa.eu/civiljustice/news/whatsnew_en.htm.

[19] The English rules are set out supra, p 514 et seq.

traditional national rules (the defendant being domiciled in a non-Member State).[20] It would even apply to the situation where a court has relied upon an exorbitant basis of jurisdiction, eg a French court takes jurisdiction over an American on the basis of the claimant's French nationality.[21] It also applies to judgments granted after jurisdiction was taken under other conventions, eg in cases of admiralty jurisdiction.[22] The basic distinction drawn for jurisdictional purposes between situations where the defendant is and is not domiciled in a Member State does not apply when it comes to recognition and enforcement of judgments. At this stage, any judgment is entitled to recognition irrespective of the domicile of the defendant.

(ii) There must be a judgment given in a Member State[23]

"Judgment" is widely defined under Article 32 of the Regulation as "any judgment given by a court or tribunal of a Member State". There is no limitation on the type of court and, therefore, the judgments of inferior as well as of superior courts are covered. The awards of tribunals are also included, provided that the tribunal is of a Member State. In other words, the tribunal must be a state rather than a private body. The fact that this requirement would exclude most arbitration awards from Article 32 is of no practical importance since Article 1 excludes arbitration from the scope of the Regulation anyway.[24] Neither does it matter what the judgment is called; it includes "a decree, order, decision or writ of execution, as well as the determination of costs or expenses".[25] This is a very wide definition, and it follows, for example, that maintenance orders come within Article 32.[26] It can also include judgments on preliminary issues.[27] A "judgment" must be distinguished, though, from a court settlement. The former is a decision which emanates from a judicial body deciding on its own authority on the issues between the parties,[28] whereas the latter is essentially contractual, its terms depending first and foremost on the parties' intentions.[29]

---

[20] For an example, see Case 178/83 *Firma P v Firma K* [1984] ECR 3033. For the rules as to when traditional bases of jurisdiction apply, see supra, pp 224–225.

[21] Art 14 of the French Civil Code. The effect of the Regulation on exorbitant bases of jurisdiction is discussed supra, pp 222–223.

[22] See Collins, pp 34–35. Of course, if the particular convention also has rules on recognition and enforcement, these will apply rather than the recognition and enforcement rules under the Brussels I Regulation, see infra, p 600.

[23] See Arts 33 and 38. See also Case C-129/92 *Owens Bank Ltd v Bracco (No 2)* [1994] QB 509 at 544; Briggs (1994) 14 YEL 557; Fentiman [1994] CLJ 239; Hartley (1994) 19 ELR 545; Peel (1994) 110 LQR 386.

[24] See supra, pp 220–222.

[25] Art 32. Orders of a procedural nature are not, however, included, see the Schlosser Report, OJ 1979, C 59/1, paras 184–187; Anton and Beaumont's *Civil Jurisdiction in Scotland*, para 8.05.

[26] See the Schlosser Report, pp 132 and 134; Civil Jurisdiction and Judgments Order, SI 2001/3929, Art 3 and Sch 1, para 3; and infra, pp 1071–1073. Not all maintenance orders come within the Regulation, see Art 71, discussed infra, p 600.

[27] *The Heidberg* [1994] 2 Lloyd's Rep 287 at 297; *CFEM Facades SA v Bovis Construction Ltd* [1992] IL Pr 561.

[28] Case C-414/92 *Solo Kleinmotoren GmbH v Boch* [1994] ECR I-2237; Briggs (1994) 14 YEL 568.

[29] The *Solo Kleinmotoren* case, supra. For the special rules on recognition and enforcement of authentic instruments (on which see Case C-260/97 *Unibank A/S v Christensen* [1999] ECR I-3715, Peel [2001] YEL 363) and court settlements see Chapter IV of the Regulation (Art 57 (ex Art 50), on which see *S & T Bautrading v Nordling* [1997] 3 All ER 718, CA and Art 58), and CPR, r 74.11. A "consent judgment", which can be obtained from the English courts, is within what is now Art 32: the opinion of AG GULMANN in the *Solo* case, supra, at 2245; *Landhurst Leasing plc v Marcq* [1998] IL Pr 822, CA.

There is no requirement that the judgment must be a final one and it is intended that, in principle, provisional orders will be covered.[30] In contrast to the position in respect of recognition and enforcement in England, at common law or under existing bilateral treaties, the Regulation is not limited to money judgments, and can, therefore, include an order for specific performance or an injunction.[31] The Schlosser Report, when discussing the Brussels Convention, envisaged that, on enforcement of a foreign judgment for specific performance, the same penalties for contempt of court should be imposed as if it were an English judgment.[32] It also envisaged that a foreign judgment imposing a penalty for disregarding a court order can come within what is now the Regulation,[33] although it is not clear whether it will do so when it is a fine which accrues to the state rather than to a judgment creditor.[34] A court order in one Member State for the enforcement of a judgment given in another state, whether a Member or a non-Member State, falls outside Chapter III of the Regulation.[35] To decide otherwise would mean, in effect, that a court in Member State A would have to recognise a judgment given in a non-Member State (X) simply because a court in Member State B had recognised the judgment given in State X and had granted an enforcement order in respect of it.[36] This would be contrary to one of the basic principles of the Regulation; the Regulation is only concerned with recognition of judgments *given in Member States* and is not intended to affect the recognition of judgments given in non-Member States.

(iii) In respect of a matter coming within the scope of the Regulation

Two preliminary points must be made before looking at the scope of the Regulation as defined by Article 1. First, Chapter III is only concerned with the *international* recognition and enforcement of judgments;[37] it will not apply to an internal United Kingdom case as, for example, where an English court is asked to recognise a Scottish judgment.[38] Secondly, Article 71 provides that the Regulation "shall not affect any conventions to which the Member States are parties and which in relation to particular matters, govern jurisdiction or the recognition or enforcement of judgments". The effect of this is to preserve a number of conventions dealing with jurisdiction or recognition and enforcement in respect of certain specific matters, such as maintenance obligations towards children.[39] It follows that, if another convention is applicable and has rules on recognition and enforcement, these rules will apply and not those contained in Chapter III of the

---

[30] See the Schlosser Report, p 126; Case 143/78 *De Cavel v De Cavel* [1979] ECR 1055. This contrasts with the requirement that the judgment be "final and conclusive" under the traditional English rules, see supra, pp 536–538. However, provisional orders without notice are not included under Chapter III, see infra, pp 602–603. Moreover, under Art 38 the judgment must be enforceable in the state in which it was given before it can be enforced, see infra, p 607. There may, therefore, be problems even with provisional orders, which are not made without notice.

[31] See *Barratt International Resorts Ltd v Martin* 1994 SLT 434; *Berkeley Administration Inc v McClelland* [1995] IL Pr 201 at 220 (per HOBHOUSE LJ), CA.

[32] The Schlosser Report, p 132. See Collins, p 116.

[33] The Schlosser Report, p 132. It is implicit from Art 49 that penalties are included in some circumstances; see also Anton and Beaumont's *Civil Jurisdiction in Scotland*, para 8.36.

[34] See the Schlosser Report, p 132.

[35] See the opinion of AG LENZ in Case C-129/92 *Owens Bank Ltd v Bracco*, supra, at 522–524.

[36] See Hartley, pp 84–85; Collins, p 106; Anton and Beaumont's *Civil Jurisdiction in Scotland*, para 8.05; Layton and Mercer, paras 24.037–24.042. But cf McEvoy (1994) 68 ALJ 576, 580.

[37] See Arts 33 and 38, and more generally on the international scope of the Regulation, supra, pp 213–214.

[38] For rules on this see ss 18 and 19 of the 1982 Act, discussed supra, pp 574–576.

[39] Infra, p 1070.

Brussels I Regulation. This can be justified on the ground that these other conventions usually involve obligations towards non-Member States and should not therefore be altered by a European Community Regulation which is confined to Member States of the Community.[40] Article 71 is only concerned with conventions which Member States have entered into *in the past* (ie prior to the Regulation coming into force on 1 March 2002). There is no provision, as there is under the Brussels Convention,[41] for conventions entered into by Member States in the future.

What has already been said in the context of jurisdiction[42] about the meaning of civil and commercial matters under Article 1 need not be repeated. It is, however, important to realise that the interpretation of Article 1 can arise at two stages in the litigation process and in the courts of two Member States.[43] Where a court of a Member State has taken jurisdiction under the rules set out in the Regulation, the question of the scope of the Regulation will arise both at that stage and at the recognition and enforcement stage in the Member State in which recognition or enforcement is sought. Even where the court which gave the judgment decided after full argument that the matter came within the scope of the Regulation, the recognising and enforcing court will have to decide the matter afresh, if necessary by referring any question of interpretation to the Court of Justice of the European Communities. If the recognising court considers that the matter does not come within the scope of the Regulation, the Regulation is being interpreted differently in the Member States and a reference to the Court of Justice is desirable. Indeed, many of the cases on the interpretation of Article 1 discussed earlier in Chapter 11 are ones where the reference to the Court of Justice came from the court in which recognition and enforcement was sought.[44]

In contrast to this, where jurisdiction has been taken under national rules, the first time that the scope of the Regulation is considered may well be at the recognition and enforcement stage.

Where the matter is not within the scope of the Regulation, judgments given in other Member States will be recognised and enforced in the United Kingdom at common law or under existing bilateral treaties.[45] The Regulation supersedes the bilateral treaties previously entered into by the United Kingdom with many European Community States.[46] These earlier arrangements will, however, still operate where the United Kingdom is asked to recognise and enforce a judgment given in one of these states which is in respect of a matter to which the Regulation does not apply.[47] It is for national courts to interpret

---

[40] See the Jenard Report, pp 59–61.

[41] Art 57 of the Brussels Convention.

[42] Supra, pp 215–222.

[43] See Giardina (1978) 27 ICLQ 263, 275.

[44] See eg Case 143/78 *De Cavel v De Cavel* [1979] ECR 1055; Case 29/76 *LTU v Eurocontrol* [1976] ECR 1541; Case 120/79 *De Cavel v De Cavel (No 2)* [1980] ECR 731; Case C-172/91 *Sonntag v Waidmann* [1993] ECR I-1963.

[45] See Art 56. See Cases 9 and 10/77 *Bavaria Fluggesellschaft Schwabe v Eurocontrol* [1977] ECR 1517; Anton and Beaumont's *Civil Jurisdiction in Scotland*, para 3.02; Hartley, pp 11 and 13. For the English rules on enforcement at common law and by statute, see supra, pp 516–590.

[46] The United Kingdom has bilateral treaties with Austria, France, Belgium, the Federal Republic of Germany, Italy and the Netherlands.

[47] Art 70. See also Cases 9 and 10/77 *Bavaria Fluggesellschaft Schwabe v Eurocontrol* [1977] ECR 1517; Hartley (1977) 2 ELR 461. The bilateral treaties also apply to judgments given before the entry into force of the Regulation: Art 70, para 2. For transitional provisions generally, see Art 66.

the scope of these bilateral agreements and where these courts use the concept of civil and commercial matters they may interpret it differently from the community concept under the Regulation.

Where a judgment is in respect of several matters, some of which are enforceable under the Regulation and others are not, the judgment is split and recognition and enforcement is only authorised for those matters within the scope of the Regulation.[48]

(iv) Orders without notice are not included

In *Denilauler v SNC Couchet Frères*:[49]

> The question arose of whether an order from a French court, during the course of proceedings for payment under a contract (the main action), for a *saisie conservatoire* freezing certain of the German defendant's assets in Germany, thereby preventing the defendant from thwarting enforcement of the judgment in the main action, was enforceable in Germany under the Brussels Convention.

With a provisional and protective measure without notice,[50] such as the English freezing injunction (formerly Mareva injunction) or the Continental *saisie conservatoire*, the defendant is not summoned to appear and it is intended that there should be enforcement without prior service. The Court of Justice held that what is now Chapter III does not cover decisions resulting from proceedings which by their very nature neither allow the defendant to state his case nor give him an opportunity to do so. However, there is English authority[51] to the effect that, if an English freezing injunction is made after notice has been served on the defendant or after the defendant had an opportunity to resist the claimant's application for the order, it is entitled to recognition and enforcement under the Brussels Convention (now replaced in virtually all cases by the Regulation), provided at least that the injunction is in aid of substantive proceedings in England.[52] This will be so even if the order relates to assets in another Member State.

In deciding to exclude decisions which were not based on adversary proceedings the Court of Justice was influenced by two considerations. First, there are a number of important provisions in what is now Chapter III which are concerned with whether there has been service of process and compliance with basic requirements of natural justice in the court which granted the judgment.[53] These presuppose that, in principle, both parties can participate in the proceedings, although it may be the case that the defendant, having been summoned, does not actually appear. They are not designed, and by inference neither is what is now Chapter III, to deal with the situation where the defendant has not even been summoned to appear. Secondly, the defendant is denied a fundamental right

---

[48] Art 48. If the excluded matter is only incidentally raised, the recognition rules under the Regulation will still apply. There is no defence under the Regulation. Cf Art 27(4) of the Brussels Convention.

[49] Case 125/79 [1980] ECR 1553; Hartley (1981) 6 ELR 59.

[50] See generally on protective measures and what is now the Regulation: Collins (1981) 1 European Year Book of International Law 249; Lipstein (1987) 36 ICLQ 873; Hogan (1989) 14 ELR 191.

[51] *Babanaft International Co SA v Bassatne* [1990] Ch 13 at 31–32. (per KERR LJ, who was referring obiter to a pre-judgment freezing injunction), followed in *Normaco v Lundman* [1999] IL Pr 381.

[52] Collins doubted whether an English freezing injunction in aid of foreign substantive proceedings by virtue of s 25 of the Civil Jurisdiction and Judgments Act 1982 were enforceable under the Brussels Convention: (1989) 105 LQR 262 at 293–294.

[53] See Art 34(2); Art 54 and Annex V. These provisions are discussed infra, pp 615–622.

by not being able to put his side of the case in the original proceedings;[54] yet, this is one of the safeguards which is used to justify the liberal provisions on recognition and enforcement under what is now Chapter III.

The principle in the *Denilauler* case equally excludes a permanent injunction without notice if the defendant has not been served with process in the judgment-granting state and has not been given an opportunity to be heard before the order was made.[55]

Given that protective measures without notice cannot be recognised and enforced in other Member States, what the claimant has to do is either to wait until the adversarial stage is reached and then seek enforcement of the measure under the Regulation[56] or to apply under Article 31[57] for a protective measure in the courts of each of the Member States in which the defendant has assets. Where the defendant has assets in several Member States this involves considerable inconvenience to the claimant. On the other hand, it leaves the decision on the granting of the protective measure to the court in the state where the assets are situated, which is the court best able to decide the issue. It also means that there will be a full examination of all the relevant considerations before an order is granted. In certain circumstances an English court may grant a world-wide freezing injunction (ie over assets abroad).[58] In theory this avoids problems of enforcement of the measure abroad or the need for an application for a protective measure in another Member State. In practice it will normally be followed up with one of these steps.

(c) Problems of interpretation

The points made in the context of jurisdiction in relation to interpretation of the Regulation and in relation to referrals to the Court of Justice[59] are equally applicable here. When it comes to the question of which courts can make a referral to the Court of Justice, the position in recognition and enforcement cases under the Regulation is very much more restrictive than that under the Brussels Convention.[60]

(d) Recognition[61]

The issue of recognition can arise in three different ways: (i) in order for a judgment to be enforced under the Regulation, it must first be recognised;[62] (ii) recognition will apply on

---

[54] The party against whom the order is directed would know nothing about this in the original state, or in the state where enforcement was sought, until after the enforcement order (now a declaration of enforceability) had been granted. The Advocate General in *Denilauler* gave his opinion that courts in some Member States might use the public policy defence to avoid enforcing *ex parte* (ie without notice) protective measures if these were within what is now Chapter III.

[55] *EMI Records Ltd v Modern Music Karl-Ulrich Waltebach GmbH* [1992] QB 115.

[56] See Case C-99/96 *Mietz v Intership Yachting Sneek BV* [1999] ECR I-2277; discussed infra, p 627.

[57] Discussed supra, pp 316–318. Under Art 31 a court in a Member State can grant a provisional measure even if it does not have jurisdiction under the Regulation in respect of the substance of the matter. For doubts on whether the English procedure for providing security for costs comes within Art 24 of the Brussels Convention (Art 31 of the Regulation), see *Bank Mellat v Helliniki Techniki SA* [1983] 3 All ER 428 at 434.

[58] See *Babanaft International Co SA v Bassatne* [1990] Ch 13, CA; Collins (1989) 105 LQR 262; supra, pp 318–320.

[59] Supra, pp 206–209.

[60] Infra, p 637.

[61] See Section 1 of Chapter III (Articles 33–37).

[62] See generally Droz, *Compétence Judiciaire et Effets des Jugements dans le Marché Commun*, p 273; the opinion of the Advocate General in Case 42/76 *De Wolf v Cox* [1976] ECR 1759; Hartley (1977) 2 ELR 146 and also Hartley, p 82.

its own, without any question of enforcement, where a judgment is used as a defence to a new action;[63] and (iii) recognition can operate on its own in a more positive way, eg in order to establish a title to property or by way of a set-off.[64]

Article 33, paragraph 1 provides that "a judgment given in a Member State shall be recognised in the other Member States without any special procedure being required".[65] The Regulation makes recognition of judgments mandatory between Member States and does so without any conditions having to be satisfied. In contrast to the rules on recognition at common law and under the Foreign Judgments (Reciprocal Enforcement) Act 1933, it does not have to be shown that the judgment is final and conclusive,[66] or that the foreign court had jurisdiction in an international sense;[67] nor is it required that the foreign judgment was on the merits.[68] The Jenard Report, when discussing the Brussels Convention, emphasised the point by describing recognition as being automatic under the Convention.[69] This must be qualified by pointing out that there are defences;[70] and a better way of putting it is to say that there is a rebuttable presumption that judgments are to be recognised.[71] A foreign judgment recognised by virtue of Article 33 in principle has the same effects in the state in which enforcement is sought as it does in the state in which it was given.[72] Article 33 will not apply to a decision of a court of a Member State on an issue arising in proceedings to enforce a judgment given in a non-Member State, such as the question whether the judgment in question was obtained by fraud.[73] This is dictated by the principle that if a dispute falls outside the scope of the Regulation the existence of a preliminary issue which the court must resolve in order to determine the dispute cannot justify application of the Regulation.[74]

Section 1 of Chapter III (Articles 33 to 37) contains no procedural provisions in respect of recognition. In the situation where recognition is merely a first step towards enforcement, the enforcement procedure under Section 2 (Articles 38 to 52)[75] will obviously be used. If recognition is used merely as a defence to an action, no procedure is necessary;

---

[63] See, eg, *De Wolf v Cox*, supra, discussed infra, pp 634–635; *Berkeley Administration Inc v McClelland* [1995] IL Pr 201 at 221 (per Hobhouse LJ), CA.

[64] See Anton and Beaumont's *Civil Jurisdiction in Scotland*, para 8.09. For the position in respect of counterclaims, see Hartley, p 83.

[65] English law has never required any special procedure for recognition. This aspect of para 2, therefore, represents no change in the law of England.

[66] For the traditional English rules requiring this see supra, pp 536–538. However, the Regulation does have rules dealing with the case where there is an appeal in the state in which the judgment was granted, see infra, pp 630–634.

[67] Cf the traditional English rules, supra, pp 516–527. For the problem of whether the court has internal jurisdiction, see Art 35, para 3, discussed infra, pp 625–626.

[68] Cf the traditional English rules, supra, pp 516–527 and 547–548. For the position under the Brussels Convention (now replaced in virtually all cases by the Regulation), see Collins, pp 86–87; Anton and Beaumont's *Civil Jurisdiction in Scotland*, para 8.11.

[69] At p 74.

[70] See infra, pp 610–627.

[71] See the opinion of the Advocate General in Case 42/76 *De Wolf v Cox* [1976] ECR 1759; also the Jenard Report, p 43. Certain documents must, nonetheless, be produced by the party seeking recognition, see Art 53, para 1.

[72] Case 145/86 *Hoffmann v Krieg* [1988] ECR 645.

[73] Case C-129/92 *Owens Bank Ltd v Bracco (No 2)* [1994] QB 509 at 545.

[74] Ibid at 546. Following Case C-190/89 *Marc Rich and Co AG v Società Italiana Impianti PA* [1991] ECR I-3855.

[75] Infra, pp 605–610.

but this still leaves a minority of cases where there is a need for some procedural rules. Article 33, para 2 provides that, if recognition of a judgment is the principal issue in the dispute, an interested party[76] may apply for the judgment to be recognised in accordance with the enforcement procedure under Section 2.[77] The example given in the Jenard Report[78] is of a negotiable instrument declared to be invalid in Italy and presented to a bank in Belgium. The bank can apply for the judgment in Italy to be recognised using the simplified enforcement procedure in Section 2. If a party opposes recognition, however, the normal rules of procedure of the recognising state will have to be used, and if the outcome of the proceedings in a court of a Member State depends on the determination of an incidental question of recognition, that court shall have jurisdiction over that question.[79]

(e) Enforcement[80]

The Court of Justice decided in *De Wolf v Cox*[81] that, in situations where what is now Chapter III applies, the enforcement procedure in those sections *must* be used. National rules cannot be used as an alternative. The procedure for enforcement involves making a without notice application in the Member State in which enforcement is sought. The judgment is declared enforceable on completion of certain formalities. The other party is informed of this and has rights of appeal and, if that party does appeal, the proceedings then become contentious. Before considering the details of this procedure the policy considerations underlying these rules should be examined.

(i) Policy matters

The Regulation seeks to ensure that the procedure for making enforceable in one Member State a judgment given in another is efficient and rapid.[82] At the same time, it seeks to provide safeguards for both parties.[83]

(a) An efficient and rapid procedure

The application for a declaration of enforceability is made without notice, ie the other party will have no warning and is not entitled to make any submissions on the application.[84] This simplifies the procedure, which is in the interests of both parties. The Regulation has simplified the procedural formalities incumbent on the applicant. The only documents that he has to provide when applying for a declaration of enforceability

---

[76] A party seeking recognition—*Re An Application By National Organisation Systems SA* (Decision 3265/2003) [2005] IL Pr 52, the One Member First Instance Court of Athens.

[77] The provisions under Section 3 (Arts 53–56) must also be complied with. See, generally, the opinion of the Advocate General in *De Wolf v Cox*, supra; the Schlosser Report, p 27. If recognition is refused and the applicant wishes to appeal, the enforcement procedure under the Regulation (infra, pp 605–610) will be used. In England, Article 33, para 2 must be read in conjunction with CPR, Part 74.10.

[78] At pp 74–75.

[79] Art 33, para 3.

[80] See Section 2 of Chapter III (Arts 38–52). See also CPR, Part 74.2–74.13.

[81] Case 42/76 [1976] ECR 1759; Hartley (1977) 2 ELR 146. For further discussion of the case, see infra, pp 634–635.

[82] See Recital (17) of the Regulation.

[83] See Recital (18).

[84] Art 41. For the documents which have to be produced with the application, see Arts 53 and 55 and CPR, Part 74.9, 74.12, 74.13. See also the Civil Jurisdiction and Judgments Order, SI 2001/3929, Art 3 and Sch 1, para 11. For the consequences of non-disclosure, see *Landhurst Leasing plc v Marcq* [1998] IL Pr 822, CA.

are a copy of the judgment and a certificate from the court in the judgment-granting state containing all the information that the court deciding on the application requires.[85] More significantly, the Regulation has modified the enforcement procedure to reduce the time taken for the declaration of enforceability.[86] To ensure a rapid procedure, the declaration of enforceability is issued virtually automatically after purely formal checks of the documents supplied, without there being any possibility for the court to raise of its own motion any of the grounds for non-recognition (and hence non-enforcement) provided by the Regulation under Articles 34 and 35.[87] These grounds may be reviewed only in the course of an appeal from the party against whom enforcement has been authorised.

(b) Safeguarding the applicant's interests

The applicant's interests are protected in six ways:

(i)   By the adoption of a unilateral procedure in respect of the declaration of enforceability, the party against whom enforcement is sought is prevented from removing assets out of the jurisdiction in order to thwart the applicant.[88]

(ii) Simplifying the procedural requirements incumbent on the applicant when applying for a declaration of enforceability.

(iii) Making the issue of a declaration of enforceability virtually automatic.

(iv) Protective measures can be obtained without a declaration of enforceability being required. When a judgment must be recognised in accordance with the Regulation, "nothing shall prevent the applicant from availing himself of provisional, including protective, measures in accordance with the law of the Member State requested".[89] Once there has been a declaration of enforceability, the applicant is entitled as of right to protective measures, such as a freezing injunction preventing the other party from removing assets.[90] The applicant cannot be denied the right to a protective measure by being required, for example, to obtain a court order authorising this, even though this is required by national law.[91] To require this would go against the basic policy of the Regulation that a party who has a declaration of enforceability or has registered a judgment may proceed with protective measures. But there is nothing incompatible with the Regulation in requiring an applicant for an English freezing injunction to provide the usual undertaking to protect third parties, this being a feature of the English measure.[92] Even before this stage is reached, an English court which has given the original judgment may safeguard the applicant's interests

---

[85] Art 53 of the Regulation. Cf Arts 46 and 47 of the Brussels Convention, which involve more documents.

[86] See the Explanatory Memorandum in the Proposal for a Council Regulation COM (1999) 348 final, p 7 (hereinafter "the Explanatory Memorandum").

[87] Recital (17) of the Regulation. See also Art 41 and the Explanatory Memorandum, p 21.

[88] The Schlosser Report, p 134; *Denilauler v SNC Couchet Frères* [1980] ECR 1553; Hartley (1981) 6 ELR 59; Case 178/83 *Firma P v Firma K* [1984] ECR 3033; Hartley (1985) 10 ELR 233.

[89] Art 47(1). This provision does not provide an English court with jurisdiction to grant a world-wide freezing order: *Banco Nacional de Comercio Exterior SNC v Empresa de Telecommunicaciones de Cuba SA* [2007] EWCA Civ 662 at [24]–[26], [2007] IL Pr 51. See Kennett (2001) 50 ICLQ 725 at 735 for difficulties in interpretation of this provision.

[90] Art 47, para 2. See also *Rayner v Republic of Brazil* [1999] 2 Lloyd's Rep 750—a Brussels Convention case.

[91] Case 119/84 *Capelloni v Pelkmans* [1985] ECR 3147; Hartley (1986) 11 ELR 96; *Elwyn (Cottons) Ltd v Pearle Designs Ltd* [1989] IR 9.

[92] *Banco Nacional de Comercio Exterior SNC v Empresa de Telecommunicaciones de Cuba SA* [2007] EWCA Civ 662 at [44]–[46], [2007] IL Pr 51.

by granting a world-wide freezing injunction over assets in another Member State, pending proceedings for the enforcement of the judgment under the Regulation.[93]

(v) If a declaration of enforceability is refused, the applicant can appeal against this.[94]

(vi) If the application for a declaration of enforceability is successful, the defendant is not given an excessive number of avenues for appeal, which could be used as delaying tactics.[95]

(c) Safeguarding the interests of the party against whom enforcement is sought

This party is protected in three ways:

(i) A declaration of enforceability can be granted only if the judgment is "enforceable" in the Member State in which it was granted.[96] The Court of Justice has held that the term "enforceable" is referring solely to the enforceability, in formal terms, of foreign decisions and not to the circumstances in which such decisions may be executed in the state of origin.[97] Moreover, "the question whether a decision is, in formal terms, enforceable in character must be distinguished from the question whether that decision can any longer be enforced by reason of payment of the debt or some other cause". This is a very narrow view of the term "enforceable", and it casts doubt on whether the enforceability requirement will now operate in two situations in which it was previously thought that it would do so. The first is where an appeal is pending in the Member State in which the judgment was given, and the effect of this is to suspend enforcement in that state.[98] The second is where the judgment has already been enforced in the state in which it was given. The enforceability requirement would, it was thought,[99] prevent the claimant from recovering twice.

(ii) If the application for a declaration of enforceability is successful (and it usually will be, given that the issue of a declaration of enforceability is virtually automatic), the defendant is notified and can appeal against the declaration of enforceability[100] but only on the basis that one of the defences under Articles 34 and 35 applies.[101]

---

[93] *Babanaft International Co SA v Bassatne* [1990] Ch 13, CA; criticised by Hogan (1989) 14 ELR 191 at 197 et seq. See supra, p 319.

[94] See infra, p 608.

[95] See Case C-432/93 *Société d'Informatique Service Réalisation Organisation (SISRO) v Ampersand Software BV* [1996] QB 127 at 160; discussed infra, p 610.

[96] Arts 53(2), 54 and Annex V. A certificate obtained in accordance with these provisions is evidence that the judgment is enforceable in the Regulation state of origin, see the Civil Jurisdiction and Judgments Order SI 2001/3929, Art 3 and Sch 1, para 8(1)(b).

[97] Case C–267/97 *Coursier v Fortis Bank* [1999] ECR I-2543; Peel [2001] YEL 352. Execution is governed by the domestic law of the court in which execution is sought, Case 145/86 *Hoffmann v Krieg* [1988] ECR 645. It may be clear that a judgment is enforceable but not clear what is enforceable (a judgment fixing the amount payable by reference to insolvency law or one ordering payment). Registration in England can be adjourned so that further evidence can be obtained from the foreign court: *La Caisse Régional du Crédit Agricole Nord de France v Ashdown* [2007] EWCA Civ 574.

[98] See the Schlosser Report, at p 130. Where the appeal does not have this effect Art 46 will come into play, see infra, pp 631–633.

[99] Ibid, at p 134.

[100] Art 43. Normally the defendant must appeal at this stage and cannot raise arguments at the stage of execution of the judgment: Case 145/86 *Hoffmann v Krieg*, supra.

[101] Art 45(1). Arts 34 and 35 are discussed infra, pp 610–627. A foreign judgment may not be reviewed as to its substance: Art 36.

(iii) If a declaration of enforceability is refused, the applicant may appeal against this;[102] but the other party must be summoned to appear before the appellate court. If he fails to do so, the natural justice provisions in Article 26 of the Regulation will apply,[103] even though this party is not domiciled in a Member State and Article 26 would therefore not normally apply. The requirement to summon the other party is a very strict one; it applies even though the application for a declaration of enforceability has been dismissed in the lower court on the purely formal ground that the correct documents as required under Article 53 have not been produced, and even where the enforcement order is applied for in a state which is not the state of residence of the party against whom enforcement is sought.[104] By summoning a party to appear there is an obvious danger (at least where the declaration of enforceability is sought against him in a state other than that of his residence) that he will remove assets from that state before the declaration of enforceability is granted; nonetheless he must still be summoned.[105] An English freezing injunction or its Continental equivalent should be sought to prevent him removing assets.

(ii) Procedural rules

These are derived from the Regulation, the Civil Jurisdiction and Judgments Order 2001 and the Civil Procedure Rules.[106] There are separate rules for maintenance orders.[107] The enforcement procedure under the Regulation has two stages: the application for and grant of a declaration of enforceability, and subsequent appeals.

(a) The application for and grant of a declaration of enforceability

The basic provision is Article 38 which provides that: "A judgment given in a Member State and enforceable in that State shall be enforced in another Member State when, on the application of any interested party, it has been declared enforceable there."

Where the Member State in which enforcement is sought is the United Kingdom, the judgment is enforced in that part (ie England and Wales, Scotland, or Northern Ireland) in which it has been registered for enforcement.[108] If enforcement is required in more than one part of the United Kingdom, the judgment must be registered in each part where enforcement is sought. The application is submitted in England to the High Court;[109] the procedure for the registration is left to English law,[110] and is similar to that

---

[102] The procedure is discussed infra, p 609.

[103] Art 43, para 4. Art 26 is discussed supra, pp 302–303.

[104] See Case 178/83 *Firma P v Firma K* [1984] ECR 3033 where documents were not produced at the correct time.

[105] Ibid.

[106] See Sections 2 and 3 of Chapter III of the Regulation, the Civil Jurisdiction and Judgments Order, SI 2001/3929, Art 3 and sch 1, paras 2–6 and CPR, Part 74.

[107] See the Civil Jurisdiction and Judgments Order, SI 2001/3929, Art 3 and Sch 1, para 3.

[108] Art 38, para 2. See the Schlosser Report, p 132.

[109] Art 39, para 1. In the case of a maintenance judgment the application is submitted to a magistrates' court on transmission by the Secretary of State. For other Member States see the list of courts in Annex II. The jurisdiction of the court is determined "by reference to the place of domicile of the party against whom enforcement is sought, or to the place of enforcement": Art 39, para 2. Cf Art 32 of the Brussels Convention.

[110] Art 44. For the procedure, see the Civil Jurisdiction and Judgments Order, SI 2001/3929, Art 3 and Sch 1, para 2 and CPR, Part 74.2–74.7. For maintenance orders, see para 3 of Sch 1 to the Civil Jurisdiction and Judgments Order 2001. Proving the authenticity of judgments is dealt with by para 8 of Sch 1 to the 2001 Order.

used where there is registration under the traditional rules. The Regulation merely lays down requirements as to the documents to be attached to the application[111] and as to furnishing an address for service.[112] A judgment, the enforcement of which is authorised and registered under the Regulation, is of the same force and effect, and the registering court has the same powers in relation to enforcement, as if the judgment had been given by the registering court in England.[113] Interest for the period after the judgment is given can be recovered on a registered judgment provided that, in accordance with the law of the Regulation State in which judgment was given, this is recoverable under the judgment.[114]

(b) Appeals

If, as will usually be the case, the declaration of enforceability is granted, this must be served on the party against whom enforcement is sought, accompanied by the judgment, if not already served on that party.[115] Article 43(5) provides that this party has a month from the service of the declaration of enforceability, or two months where notice was served on a party not domiciled within the jurisdiction, in which to appeal.[116] During this period, and until the appeal has been determined, no measures of enforcement may be taken other than protective ones[117] (such as a freezing injunction). Service of the declaration of enforceablity must be made in accordance with the procedural rules of the Member State in which enforcement is sought.[118] In cases of defective service the mere fact that the party against whom enforcement is sought has notice of that decision is not sufficient to cause time to run for the purposes of the time limit in which to appeal.[119] The Court of Justice has held that the right of appeal under what is now Article 43(5) is only given to the party against whom enforcement is sought and any redress for interested third parties is excluded, even where the national law of the Member State in which the enforcement order (now declaration of enforceability) is granted gives such parties a right of action.[120] In England, the appeal must be made to the High Court in accordance with

---

[111] Art 40, para 3. For the documents in question, see Art 53. See also Case 178/83 *Firma P v Firma K* [1984] ECR 3033. The Regulation does not require proof of service of the judgment at this stage. Cf Art 47(1) of the Brussels Convention, on which see Case C-275/94 *Van der Linden v Berufsgenossenschaft der Feinmechanik und Elektrotechnik* [1996] ECR I-1393.

[112] Art 40, para 2; Case 198/85 *Carron v Germany* [1986] ECR 2437; Hartley (1987) 12 ELR 64. See *Rhatigan v Textiles Confecciones Europeas SA* [1992] IL Pr 40, Irish Sup Ct.

[113] See the Civil Jurisdiction and Judgments Order, SI 2001/3929, Art 3 and Sch 1, para 2(2). See *Noirhomme v Walklate* [1992] 1 Lloyd's Rep 427 at 431—on the equivalent provision in relation to the Brussels Convention (s 4(3) of the Civil Jurisdiction and Judgments Act 1982) and which suggests that there is a discretionary power to order a stay. For maintenance orders, see para 3(3) of the 2001 Order.

[114] See the Civil Jurisdiction and Judgments Order, SI 2001/3929, Art 3 and Sch 1, para 5. For the position in respect of legal aid, see Art 50 of the Regulation.

[115] Art 42(2) of the Regulation.

[116] See also CPR, Part 74.8. See on extension of time for an appeal, *Citibank NA v Rafidian Bank* [2003] EWHC 1950, [2003] IL Pr 49.

[117] Art 47(3); CPR, Part 74.9. See Case 119/84 *Capelloni v Pelkmans* [1985] ECR 3147; Hartley (1986) 11 ELR 96; Stone (1983) 32 ICLQ 477, 480. See also *Rayner v Republic of Brazil* [1999] 2 Lloyd's Rep 751, 764, CA.

[118] Case C-3/05 *Verdoliva v JM Van der Hoeven BV* [2006] IL Pr 31—a Brussels Convention case.

[119] Ibid.

[120] Case 148/84 *Deutsche Genossenschaftsbank v Brasserie du Pecheur SA* [1985] ECR 1981—the third party may be able to contest execution though. This was a case on Art 36 of the Brussels Convention which is worded differently from Art 43(5) of the Regulation but the latter clearly refers to the party against whom enforcement is sought and so the result would be the same under the Regulation.

its rules of procedure.[121] The judgment[122] given on appeal[123] is subject to a single further appeal on a point of law to the Court of Appeal or to the House of Lords (if there is an appeal direct from the High Court to the House of Lords under the leap-frog procedure in the Administration of Justice Act 1969).[124] This further appeal cannot be brought by interested third parties, even where the domestic law of the state in which enforcement is sought confers a right of appeal on such parties.[125]

A similar procedure for bringing appeals in England is followed where the application is against a *refusal* to grant a declaration of enforceability.[126]

(f) Defences

It is part of the claimant's case when seeking recognition or enforcement to show that the Regulation applies, and, in a case of enforcement, that the judgment is enforceable in the Member State in which it was given. The court in the Member State in which an application for a declaration of enforceability is sought will check that the documents supplied by the claimant are correct and these documents include evidence that the judgment is indeed enforceable in the Member State in which it was given.[127] The enforcement procedure does not appear to give an opportunity for the defendant to raise any of these matters by way of a defence. At the application stage the party against whom enforcement is sought is not entitled to make any submissions.[128] At the subsequent appeal stage the only grounds for revoking a declaration of enforceability are those specified in Articles 34 and 35.[129] Nonetheless, it would be extraordinary if the defendant cannot raise at the appeal stage the question of whether the Regulation applies,[130] and whether

---

[121] Art 43, para 2. In the case of a maintenance order the appeal is lodged with a magistrates' court.

[122] This does not include a preliminary or interlocutory order, see Case 258/83 *Brennero v Wendel GmbH* [1984] ECR 3971.

[123] This does not include a decision under Art 46, para 1, infra, pp 631–633, refusing a stay of proceedings and ordering the party to whom the enforcement order was granted to provide security (Case C-183/90 *BJ Van Dalfsen v B Van Loon* [1991] ECR I-4743; Briggs (1991) 11 YEL 530) or lifting a stay previously ordered (Case C-432/93 *Société d'Informatique Service Réalisation Organisation (SISRO) v Ampersand Software BV* [1996] QB 127; Briggs (1995) 15 YEL 506; Collier [1996] CLJ 8; Hartley (1996) ELR 169). The court seised of a further appeal on a point of law has no jurisdiction to impose or reimpose such a stay.

[124] Art 44, para 2 of the Regulation, and the Civil Jurisdiction and Judgments Order, SI 2001/3929, Art 3 and Sch 1, para 4. If the action relates to the recognition or enforcement of a maintenance order the single further appeal is to the High Court.

[125] Case C-172/91 *Sonntag v Waidmann* [1993] ECR I-1963 at 1998–1999.

[126] See Art 43 of the Regulation, and CPR, Part 74.8(4)(b), under which the appellant has only 1 month to appeal even if the notice was served on a party not domiciled within the jurisdiction. The other party must be summoned to appear before the appellate court; this requirement is discussed supra, at pp 607–608. On the single further appeal on a point of law, see Art 44 of the Regulation and the Civil Jurisdiction and Judgments Order, SI 2001/3929, Art 3 and Sch 1, para 4.

[127] Arts 53(2), 54 and and Annex V of the Regulation. A certificate obtained in accordance with these provisions is evidence that the judgment is enforceable in the Regulation State of origin, see the Civil Jurisdiction and Judgments Order, SI 2001/3929, Art 3 and Sch 1, para 8(1)(b).

[128] Art 41.

[129] Art 45.

[130] See Dicey, Morris and Collins, para 14-223, which regards this as being a drafting error. The defendant can do so under the Brussels Convention, which has a different enforcement procedure, see the Schlosser Report, p 134. The defendant can also raise under the Convention the issue whether the proper formalities for presenting an application were observed (see *Artic Fish Sales Co Ltd v Adam (No 2)* 1996 SLT 970). This appears to be not possible under the Regulation.

the judgment is indeed enforceable in the Member State of origin. Articles 34 and 35 set out exhaustively the defences to recognition,[131] but since there can be no enforcement without recognition, they are also implicitly defences to enforcement. Paragraph 1 of Article 45 spells this out by providing expressly that the defences specified in Articles 34 and 35 operate as reasons for refusing or revoking a declaration of enforceability.

Where a defence under Articles 34 and 35 is established, the judgment will not be recognised or enforced in other Member States. Likewise, if a judgment is not enforceable in the Member State in which it was given, it cannot be enforced in other Member States. In contrast to this, where the Regulation does not apply, it may still be possible for a judgment to be recognised and enforced in another Member State under an existing bilateral treaty or at common law.[132]

Articles 34 and 35 are an obstacle to the free movement of judgments and should, accordingly, be interpreted strictly.[133]

Finally, in this part of the chapter, the position where enforcement is sought of a provisional or protective measure will be examined.

(i) Defences under Article 34

Article 34 sets out four defences: (i) public policy; (ii) natural justice; (iii) a conflict with a judgment given in the Member State in which recognition is sought; (iv) a conflict with a judgment given in another Member State or in a non-Member State. The Regulation has sought to narrow the defences[134] and there is one fewer than under the Brussels Convention.[135] Likewise the Regulation has reworded individual defences in a restrictive manner so as to improve the free movement of judgments.[136]

(a) Public policy

Article 34(1) (Article 27(1) of the Brussels Convention) provides that a judgment shall not be recognised "if such recognition is manifestly contrary to public policy in the Member State in which recognition is sought".

(i) Whose definition of the concept of public policy is to be applied?

The wording of Article 34(1) strongly suggests that the recognising court is to apply its own concept of public policy when considering this defence.[137] However, because of the differences in the meaning of public policy in the separate Member States,[138] it would be most undesirable for national courts to apply their own concept of public policy automatically. National courts are undoubtedly left with some latitude in deciding on the

---

[131] Case C-414/92 *Solo Kleinmotoren GmbH v Boch* [1994] ECR I-2237 at 2253—a Brussels Convention case.

[132] Supra, pp 516–587.

[133] The *Solo* case, supra, at 2256, discussed infra, p 623.

[134] See the Explanatory Memorandum, p 21.

[135] Infra, p 637.

[136] The Explanatory Memorandum, p 22.

[137] See also the opinion of AG Lenz in Case C-129/92 *Owens Bank Ltd v Bracco (No 2)* [1994] QB 509 at 523, [21]; *CFEM Façades SA v Bovis Construction Ltd* [1992] IL Pr 561 at 571.

[138] See generally Lloyd, *Public Policy: A Comparative Study in English and French Law* (1953).

meaning of the concept, but they must give it a meaning which is appropriate in the context of the Regulation, and the Court of Justice may intervene if they fail to do so.[139] Thus we are left with the position whereby the recognising court of a Member State determines, according to its own conceptions, what public policy requires, but there are limits to that concept which are subject to review by the Court of Justice.[140] These limits are a matter for interpretation of the Regulation.[141]

(ii) What public policy includes

The public policy defence should only be used in exceptional cases.[142] The word "manifestly" has been added by the Regulation to underscore the exceptional nature of this defence.[143] The Jenard Report states that public policy should not be used to criticise the *decision* of the court which gave the judgment. It is the *recognition* of the judgment rather than the judgment itself which must be contrary to public policy.[144] This negative approach is not particularly helpful in understanding what is included within the concept.[145]

The Schlosser Report envisages that fraud in the proceedings in the Member State in which the judgment was given can, in some circumstances, come within the public policy exception.[146] However, it also accepts that there are some situations involving allegations of fraud where it would not be appropriate to use public policy as a defence. Two situations come to mind. First, where the allegation of fraud has been raised and dismissed in the court which gave the judgment, to reopen the matter at the recognition and enforcement stage, in the absence of new evidence, involves both an implicit criticism of the original judgment and going into the substance of the matter. This is prohibited by Article 36.[147] Secondly, where the issue of fraud *could* have been raised in the state in which the judgment was given, or can still be raised there, it is questionable

---

[139] See Anton and Beaumont's *Civil Jurisdiction in Scotland*, para 8.14; Collins, p 108; Dicey, Morris and Collins, paras 14-208–14-210; Layton and Mercer, paras 26.013–26.024; Rasmussen (1978) 15 CMLR 249, 264–266; d'Oliveira in *The Common Law of Europe and the Future of Legal Education*, p 276 et seq.

[140] Case C-7/98 *Krombach v Bamberski* [2001] QB 709 at [22]; Case C-38/98 *Régie Nationale des Usines Renault SA v Maxicar SpA* [2000] ECR I-2973 at [27].

[141] Ibid.

[142] Case 145/86 *Hoffmann v Krieg* [1988] ECR 645; Case C-78/95 *Hendrikman v Magenta Druck & Verlag GmbH* [1997] QB 426 at 442; the *Krombach* case, supra, at [21]; the *Renault* case, supra, at [26].

[143] The Explanatory Memorandum, p 23. The same word was introduced in the earlier Brussels II Convention and then Regulation (Art 15(1)(a) of Council Regulation (EC) No 1347/2000 of 29 May 2000 on jurisdiction and the recognition and enforcement of judgments in matrimonial matters and in matters of parental responsibility for children of both spouses, OJ 2000 L 160, replaced by Council Regulation (EC) No 2201/2003 of 27 November 2003 concerning jurisdiction and the recognition and enforcement of judgments in matrimonial matters and the matters of parental responsibility, OJ 2003 L 338/1 (Brussels II *bis*)).

[144] See the Jenard Report, at p 44. The recognising court is said to be under a *duty* to verify whether recognition would be contrary to public policy, see the Jenard Report, at p 44. In Case 27/81 *Röhr v Ossberger* [1981] ECR 2431, public policy was raised as a defence but the Court of Justice interpreted Art 18 of the Brussels Convention (Art 24 of the Regulation) in such a way that the defence collapsed.

[145] It is, however, useful in ascertaining what is not included within the defence, see infra, pp 614–615.

[146] See the Schlosser Report, at p 128. There is no provision in the Regulation dealing expressly with fraud; it would, therefore, have to come within Art 34(1) if it is to provide a defence; cf the English common law rules, supra, pp 551–556. For fraud and public policy in the area of recognition of foreign divorces, see infra, pp 990 and 1018–1022. An example coming within the public policy exception suggested by English lawyers is multiple damages under the Protection of Trading Interests Act 1980, discussed supra, pp 561–563; see Anton and Beaumont's *Civil Jurisdiction in Scotland*, para 8.16; Hartley, p 89; Stone (1983) 32 ICLQ 477, 480–481.

[147] *Interdesco SA v Nullifire Ltd* [1992] 1 Lloyd's Rep 180 at 187. Cf the English common law decisions on fraud discussed supra, pp 551–556. On Art 36 see infra, p 628.

whether fraud should be available as a defence under Article 34(1). Indeed, PHILLIPS J in *Interdesco SA v Nullifire Ltd*[148] refused to allow the defence of fraud in this situation. To deny a party a defence in these circumstances encourages persons who want to raise the question of fraud to do so in the Member State in which the judgment was given,[149] which is the best place for deciding the issue. It is best to confine the public policy defence in cases of fraud to the situation in which (i) there is evidence of fraud which was unavailable and unexamined earlier on in the proceedings, and (ii) the evidence arises at such a late stage that it cannot be raised on appeal in the state which granted the judgment, and the only court in which the fraud can be considered is the recognising court.

Moving beyond the issue of fraud, in *Krombach v Bamberski*[150] the Court of Justice held that recourse to public policy can be envisaged only where recognition or enforcement would infringe a rule of law regarded as essential in the legal order of the state in which enforcement is sought or a right recognised as being fundamental within that legal order.[151] In determining whether rights are fundamental the Court of Justice took into account the case law of the European Court of Human Rights. It followed that a German recognising court was entitled to hold that a refusal by a French judgment-granting court to hear the defence by counsel of an accused person, who was not present at the hearing of a civil claim based on a criminal offence, constituted a manifest breach of a fundamental right.[152] Turning to the decisions of national courts, the Court of Appeal has held that a defendant, who was unaware that Dutch proceedings that had been stayed for twelve years had been reactivated until after the time for an appeal had passed, had manifestly not received the fair trial that Article 6 of the European Convention on Human Rights required. Accordingly, recognition of the Dutch judgment would be contrary to the public policy of England.[153] However, this was an exceptional case. The English courts apply a strong but not irrebuttable presumption that the procedures of other signatories to the Convention are compliant with Article 6.[154] The constitution, procedures and conduct of a court of another Member State may involve the infringement of the defendant's rights under Article 6 but it is necessary to look at the foreign proceedings as a whole, including any appeals by way of a rehearing before courts which are compliant with

---

[148] [1992] 1 Lloyd's Rep 180; approved by the Court of Appeal in *Société d'Informatique Service Réalisation Organisation v Ampersand Software BV* [1994] IL Pr 55 at 60, CA; *Artic Fish Sales Co Ltd v Adam (No 2)* 1996 SLT 970; *Banco Nacional de Comercio Exterior SNC v Empresa de Telecomunicaciones de Cuba SA* [2007] EWHC 2322 (Comm) at [19], [2007] IL Pr 59. See also *Turczynski v Wilde and Partners* [2003] IL Pr 64, French Cour de Cassation.

[149] See the Schlosser Report, at p 128; Hartley, pp 85–86; Collins, pp 101–108; Layton and Mercer, para 26.024.

[150] Case C-7/98 [2001] QB 709; Peel [2001] YEL 347; followed in Case C-341/04 *Eurofood IFSC Ltd* [2006] IL Pr 23.

[151] The *Krombach* case, supra, at [37].

[152] Ibid, at [40]. The District Court of Appeal, Milan, Italy, has referred several questions to the Court of Justice in relation to the public policy defence after the failure to allow a defendant to present any form of defence following the grant of a debarring order for failure to comply with an injunction.

[153] *Maronier v Larmer* [2002] EWCA Civ 774 at [37]–[38], [2003] QB 620 at 632; Briggs (2002) 73 BYBIL 468. Cf *Citibank NA v Rafidian Bank* [2003] EWHC 1950, [2003] IL Pr 49. For France see *Stolzenberg v Daimler Chrysler Canada Inc* [2005] IL Pr 24, French Cour de Cassation.

[154] The *Maronier* case, supra, at [25].

Article 6.[155] This would mean that the earlier infringement has been rectified or that it could be said that no infringement has ever occurred.[156]

The Court of Appeal has also held that if a defendant, after receiving notice of an anti-suit injunction granted by an English court restraining proceedings in another Member State, nevertheless continues with those proceedings and obtains a judgment on the merits in his favour, this will be refused recognition in England on the ground of public policy.[157] However, it is strongly arguable that this is raising the question of the jurisdiction of the judgment-granting court and the public policy defence cannot be used in this situation.[158] Perhaps more importantly, the practical significance of this use of the public policy defence has been much reduced by the fact that it is now clear that the grant of such an injunction will in most, but seemingly not all,[159] cases be incompatible with the Regulation.[160] It has also been suggested that the public policy defence may operate in England in the situation where the action has been brought in a foreign Member State in breach of a valid arbitration agreement.[161] French courts have held that it is contrary to the French concept of public policy to recognise a foreign judgment which does not state the reasoning on which it is based[162] or an English judgment for costs set at a disproportionately high level.[163]

(iii) What public policy does not include

It is easier to say what public policy does not encompass than what it does. As has already been mentioned, the Jenard Report states that the defence should not be used to criticise the decision of the court which gave the judgment.[164] Neither can it be applied to review the jurisdiction of the court of the Member State in which the judgment was given.[165] This prevents it being used to criticise exorbitant jurisdiction taken against defendants domiciled in non-Member States,[166] or even in Member States.[167] The recognising court

---

[155] *SA Marie Brizzard et Roger International v William Grant & Sons Ltd (No 2)* 2002 SLT 1365, 1379 at [67].

[156] Ibid.

[157] *Philip Alexander Securities and Futures Ltd v Bamberger* [1997] IL Pr 73 at 115, CA; *Through Transport Mutual Insurance Association (Eurasia) Ltd v New India Assurance Co Ltd (The "Hari Bhum")* [20003] EWHC 3158 (Comm) 206 at [42], [2004] 1 Lloyd's Rep 206 at 215; appeal allowed in part but without discussion of the recognition and enforcement point [2004] EWCA (Civ) 1598.

[158] See the opinion of AG RUIZ-JARABO COLOMER in Case C-159/02 *Turner v Grovit* [2004] All ER (EC) 485 at [36], who was clearly of the view that the public policy defence could not be used.

[159] See the *Through Transport* case [2004] EWCA (Civ) 1598, discussed supra, pp 337–338 (anti-suit injunction granted where there had been breach of an arbitration agreement).

[160] Supra, pp 333–340.

[161] *Philip Alexander Securities and Futures Ltd v Bamberger* [1997] IL Pr 77 at 101–102 (WALLER J), see infra, pp 629–630.

[162] *Sàrl Polypetrol v Société Générale Routière* [1993] IL Pr 107 (it is necessary for the claimant to produce documents which are equivalent to the missing reasoning), French Cour de Cassation; *Pordea v Times Newspapers Ltd* [2000] IL Pr 763, French Cour de Cassation. But cf *Materiel Auxiliaire d'Informatique v Printed Forms Equipment Ltd* [2006] IL Pr 803, French Cour de Cassation and see the criticism in Dicey, Morris and Collins, para 14-208.

[163] The *Pordea* case, supra.

[164] At p 76. This prevents an examination of the law and procedure of the court which granted the judgment; it surely does not prevent the recognising court from considering new evidence as to, for example, an allegation that the trial judge was bribed.

[165] Art 35, para 3; see the opinion of the Advocate General in *Röhr v Ossberger*, supra.

[166] The Jenard Report, p 44.

[167] The *Krombach* case, supra, at [34].

cannot refuse recognition solely on the ground that there is a discrepancy between the legal rule applied in the judgment-granting state and that which would have been applied by the recognising court if it had been seised of the matter.[168] This is because Article 36 prohibits a foreign judgment being reviewed as to its substance. It would be different if recognition would involve the infringement of a fundamental principle as explained in the *Krombach* case. But this will only happen in the most exceptional cases of error.[169] There was no such infringement in *Régie Nationale des Usines Renault SA v Maxicar SpA*.[170] It was alleged that the judgment-granting court made an error of Community law by recognising the existence of certain intellectual property rights, rights which would not be recognised in the judgment-recognising state. The question then arose as to whether recognition of the judgment would be against public policy. The Court of Justice held that, in this situation, there was no breach of a rule of law regarded as essential in the legal order of the state in which recognition was sought.[171] Public policy cannot be used in situations covered elsewhere in Article 34.[172] Accordingly, this defence will not protect a defendant whose rights have been infringed by a lack of natural justice as dealt with under Article 34(2) (and therefore that defence applies).[173] But this defence may be used where the requirements of natural justice as laid down in Article 34(2) have been met (and therefore that defence does not apply) in circumstances where there has been inter-ference with the defendant's ability to arrange his defence.[174] Nor can the defence be used when the issue is whether a foreign judgment is compatible with a judgment given in the state in which recognition is sought.[175]

In some of the above situations the concept of public policy used in civil law systems would apply,[176] as would the concept of public policy used in common law systems.[177] The fact that Article 34(1) is not intended to apply in these same situations shows the limited nature of the public policy defence under the Regulation.

(b) Natural justice

Article 34(2) (Article 27(2) of the Brussels Convention) provides that a judgment shall not be recognised:

Where it [the judgment] was given in default of appearance, if the defendant was not served with the document which instituted the proceedings or with an equivalent docu-ment in sufficient time and in such a way as to enable him to arrange for his defence,

---

[168] Ibid, at [36].

[169] See the opinion of AG ALBER in Case C-38/98 *Régie Nationale des Usines Renault SA v Maxicar SpA* [2000] ECR I-2973 at [67].

[170] Case C-38/98 [2000] ECR I-2973; Peel [2001] YEL 347. See *Viking Line ABP v The International Transport Workers' Federation* [2005] EWHC 1222, [2006] IL Pr 4 at [78]–[81].

[171] The *Renault* case, supra, [31].

[172] Case C-78/95 *Hendrikman v Magenta Druck & Verlag GmbH* [1997] QB 426. See also *Artic Fish Sales Co Ltd v Adam (No 2)* 1996 SLT 970 at 973.

[173] The *Hendrikman* case, supra. See also the opinion of the Advocate General in *Röhr v Ossberger*, supra.

[174] *Re Enforcement of a Judgment (Date Error in Translated Summons)* (Case IX ZB 14/00) [2003] IL Pr 32, German Federal Supreme Court.

[175] Case 145/86 *Hoffmann v Krieg* [1988] ECR 645. Art 34(3) deals with this, infra, pp 622–624.

[176] See Forde (1980) 29 ICLQ 259, 272–273.

[177] See supra, pp 139–150 and 556–558.

unless the defendant failed to commence proceedings to challenge the judgment when it was possible for him to do so.[178]

There is concern that the rights of the defendant should be fully protected by the Regulation. When a judgment has been given in default of appearance there is a particular concern as to whether the service on the defendant was such as to give him the opportunity to defend himself properly.[179] Article 34(2) is intended to ensure that a judgment is not recognised or enforced under the Regulation if the defendant has not been given such an opportunity.[180]

(i) The interaction with jurisdictional provisions on natural justice

Where the natural justice safeguards at the jurisdictional stage of proceedings apply under Article 26,[181] Article 34(2) operates as a double check on natural justice, with the recognising court examining the same issue that has been examined and decided upon by the court which gave the judgement.[182] In this situation, the defence under Article 34(2) is only likely to be used in exceptional cases.[183]

Where Article 26 does not apply, eg because the defendant is domiciled in a non-Member State, or is not sued in the Member State in which he is domiciled, Article 34(2) provides a check on whether basic requirements of natural justice have been satisfied in the Member State in which the judgment was given. It is more important to have a check in this situation than in the situation where Article 26 applies, and the defence is correspondingly more likely to be used. The court which gave the judgment may not have even examined the issue of natural justice, and, if it has done so, may only have inadequate procedural safeguards.

(ii) Establishing the defence

Article 34(2) has not infrequently been used as a defence. It comprises the following elements:

(a) The judgment was given in default of appearance

Non-recognition under Article 34(2) is possible only where the defendant was in default of appearance in the original proceedings. Consequently it may not be relied upon where the defendant appeared.[184] Article 34(2) does not look at the reasons why a defendant did

---

[178] See generally, the Jenard Report, pp 44–45; Hunnings [1985] JBL 303; Kennett [1992] CJQ 115.

[179] See Art 26(2), discussed supra, pp 302–303. For the position where there is a default judgment, see Art 53(2) and Annex V at 4.4.

[180] Case 166/80 *Klomps v Michel* [1981] ECR 1593; Case C-123/91 *Minalmet v Brandeis* [1992] ECR 1-5661; Case C-172/91 *Sonntag v Waidmann* [1993] ECR I-1963 at 2000; Case C-474/93 *Hengt Import BV v Campese* [1995] ECR I-2113 at 2127; Case C-78/95 *Hendrikman v Magenta Druck v Verlag GmbH* [1997] QB 426 at 441–442.

[181] Supra, pp 302–303.

[182] Case 228/81 *Pendy Plastic Products v Pluspunkt* [1982] ECR 2723; Case 166/80 *Klomps v Michel* [1981] ECR 1593; Hartley (1982) 7 ELR 419; Case C-522/03 *Scania Finance SA v Rockinger Spezialfabrik Fur Anhangerkupplungen GmbH & Co* [2006] IL Pr 1. See also Hartley, pp 90–92. The Advocate General in the *Plendy Plastic* case referred to the duty of the court to ascertain whether the requirements of Art 27(2) of the Brussels Convention had been complied with. However, the French Cour de Cassation has held that a court is not required to consider this provision of its own motion: *Wagner v Tettweiler* [1985] ECC 258.

[183] See infra.

[184] Case C-172/91 *Sonntag v Waidmann* [1993] ECR I-1963 at 2000.

appear. Whether he appeared merely to contest the jurisdiction of the court, or actually to fight the action on its merits, does not matter; in both cases the judgment would not be considered as being given in default of appearance.[185] Appearance should be given an autonomous meaning.[186] But, whatever the definition, if a defendant has neither lodged any formal document with the foreign court (once the proceedings were begun) nor was present when the proceedings came to trial, he cannot be regarded as having appeared.[187] Appearances after the judgment has been given raise particularly difficult problems.

> In *Klomps v Michel*[188] a judgment which was treated as being in default of appearance was given in Germany.[189] Subsequently, the defendant raised an objection (based on the service of documents) to this judgment before the same German court which had given the judgment in default. This was held to be inadmissible because the time for lodging objections had expired. A Dutch court which was asked to enforce the German judgment referred a number of issues of interpretation of Article 27(2) of the Brussels Convention to the Court of Justice, including whether, in these circumstances, a judgment is to be regarded as given in default.

The Court of Justice held, inter alia, that the judgment was given in default of appearance, despite the fact that the defendant had appeared to have it set aside. The reasoning of the Court was that the defendant had not submitted a defence as to substance, and since the objection he did raise was held to be inadmissible, this left the original decision in default intact.

There can also be problems where a claim for compensation is joined to criminal proceedings. In *Sonntag v Waidmann*[190] the Court of Justice, adopting an autonomous interpretation of the concept of appearance, held that a defendant is deemed to have appeared if he answered at the trial, through counsel of his own choice, to the criminal charges but did not express a view on the civil claim, on which oral argument was also submitted in the presence of his counsel. It is possible, though, for the defendant to decline to appear in the civil action when answering the criminal charges. Technically there may be an appearance by the defendant in that lawyers purporting to represent the defendant appeared before the court. Nonetheless, Article 34(2) still applies if the proceedings were instituted without the defendant's knowledge and lawyers appeared without his authority (having been appointed by business associates of the defendant), since, in such circumstances, the defendant is powerless to defend himself.[191]

(b) The defendant was not served

This is a vital question and one that cannot pass unnoticed at the time when recognition and enforcement is sought. Article 53(2)[192] requires the party seeking recognition or

---

[185] *Tavoulareas v Tsavliris (No 2)* [2006] EWCA Civ 1772 at [12], [2007] 1 WLR 1573; Briggs (2006) 77 BYBIL 593.

[186] Case C-78/95 *Hendrikman v Magenta Druck & Verlag GmbH* [1997] QB 426; Hartley (1997) 22 ELR 364.

[187] *Tavoulareas v Tsavliris (No 2)* [2006] EWCA Civ 1772 at [11]–[16], [2007] 1 WLR 1573.

[188] Case 166/80 [1981] ECR 1593.

[189] The case involved a German order said to be equivalent to one given in default.

[190] Case C-172/91 [1993] ECR 1-1963; Briggs (1993) 13 YEL 517; Plender (1993) BYBIL 555.

[191] Case C-78/95 *Hendrikman v Magenta Druck & Verlag GmbH* [1997] QB 426.

[192] See also Annex V, 4.4.

enforcement to produce certain evidence which establishes that the party in default was served with the document instituting the proceedings. The Regulation has altered the natural justice defence so as to no longer require that the defendant was "duly" served.[193] This required reference to the legislation of the state in which the judgment was given and to its conventions on service.[194] The requirements of due service and service in sufficient time constituted two separate and concurrent safeguards for a defendant who failed to appear. If a document was not duly served this in itself triggered the operation of the natural justice defence, even if the defendant had sufficient time to arrange for his defence.[195] The intention under the Regulation is that this should no longer be so. It is enough for the defendant in the judgment-granting state to have been served with notice in sufficient time and in such a way as to enable him to arrange for his defence.[196] This means, for example, that a mere formal irregularity in the service procedure, as where it is not accompanied by a required translation, will not debar recognition or enforcement under the Regulation,[197] provided the service was in sufficient time and in such a way as to enable the defendant to arrange his defence. A formal irregularity, which does not affect the capacity of the defendant to understand the elements of the claim and his capacity to defend his rights, can be ignored.[198] This is another example of the way in which defences have been reworded so as to narrow them down, thereby improving the free movement of judgments. But at the same time the rights of the defendant must have been effectively protected.[199]

Article 34(2) requires that the defendant was "served" and it is not enough that he was merely notified of the proceedings.[200] This raises the difficult question of what constitutes "service" in the present context. This could be referring to service according to the procedures of the judgment-granting state. However, certain irregularities in these procedures will not be fatal.[201] An alternative view, which has found favour with the Court of Appeal, is that this refers to service according to the European Community Service Regulation.[202] But given the purpose of the rewording of Article 34(2), a mere formal irregularity in compliance with that Regulation should not be enough to deny that there has been service. "Service" should be widely construed and the really important question is whether

---

[193] This is still required under Art 27(2) of the Brussels Convention, see infra, p 637.

[194] See the Jenard Report, p 44; *Klomps v Michel*, supra; Case C-305/88 *Lancray v Peters* [1990] I-2725 at 2750; Case C-39/02 *Maersk Olie & Gas v Firma Mm de Haan en W de Boer* [2004] ECR I-9657 at [60]; Case C-522/03 *Scania Finance SA v Rockinger Spezialfabrik Fur Anhangerkupplungen GmbH & Co* [2006] IL Pr 1—where there is a service convention between the granting and enforcing state due service is determined solely in the light of this.

[195] See Case C-305/88 *Lancray v Peters* [1990] I-2725.

[196] See the Explanatory Memorandum, p 23.

[197] See Ibid, p 23; Case C-283/05 *ASML Netherlands BV v Semiconductor Industry Services GmbH (SEMIS)* [2007] IL Pr 4 at [41]–[47]. But it will do so under the Brussels Convention, see Case C-305/88 *Lancray v Peters* [1990] ECR I-2725.

[198] AG Ruiz-Jarabo Colomer in *ASML Netherlands BV v Semiconductor Industry Services GmbH (SEMIS)*, supra, at [69].

[199] Ibid, at [20].

[200] Ibid, at [41]–[47], the opinion of AG Ruiz-Jarabo Colomer at [65]; *Tavoulareas v Tsavliris (No 2)* [2006] EWCA Civ 1772, [2007] 1 WLR 1573. See Briggs and Rees, para 7.14; Dicey, Morris and Collins, para 14-214; Layton and Mercer, para 26.026. See also *Re The Enforcement of An Austrian Judgment* (Case 3 W 91/03) [2005] IL Pr 29, Oberlandesgericht (Appeal Court), Dusseldorf.

[201] Layton and Mercer, para 26.052.

[202] *Tavoulareas v Tsavliris (No 2)* [2006] EWCA Civ 1772 at [8], [2007] 1 WLR 1573.

this was in sufficient time and in such a way as to enable the defendant to arrange his defence.

In *Klomps v Michel*[203] the Court of Justice held that Article 27(2) of the Brussels Convention does not require proof that the document instituting the proceedings was actually brought to the knowledge of the defendant. No objection was made to the method of notice employed in that case, although it did not involve personal service on the defendant. The same must be true under the Regulation.

(c) With the document which instituted the proceedings or with an equivalent document

In *Klomps v Michel*, which was a case decided under the Brussels Convention, it was held that this was referring to "any document ... service of which enables the plaintiff, under the law of the State of the court in which the judgment was given to obtain, in default of appropriate action taken by the defendant, a decision capable of being recognised and enforced under the Convention".[204] This included an order for payment under German law, but not a subsequent German enforcement order; the latter was the judgment that was enforceable under the Convention and therefore could not be the document which instituted the proceedings. A different and rather better definition, in that it relates to the purpose of what is now Article 34(2), was adopted by the Court of Justice in the subsequent case of *Hengst Import BV v Campese*,[205] which referred to "the document or documents which must be duly and timeously served on the defendant in order to enable him to assert his rights before an enforceable judgment is given in the State of origin".[206] The document in this case encompassed a summary order for the payment of money under Italian law, which together with the application instituting the proceedings was served on the defendant.[207] This started time running for the defendant to oppose the order, which was not enforceable before the expiry of the time limit. The question of how much detail the document must contain, eg whether it must mention the amount of a claim, has been raised before the Court of Justice but left unanswered.[208] The reference to "an equivalent document" encompasses the situation where an order provisionally determining the maximum amount of liability has at first been provisionally adopted by the court at the conclusion of a unilateral procedure, which was then followed by reasoned submissions by both parties.[209]

(d) In sufficient time and in such a way as to enable him to arrange for his defence

It is for the court where enforcement is sought to determine whether service was effected in sufficient time and in such a way as to enable the defendant to arrange for his defence, account being taken of all the facts of the case.[210] The concepts of sufficiency of time and the "way" in which service is effected are dealing with different situations and problems.

---

[203] Case 166/80 [1981] ECR 1593; Case C-305/88.

[204] Supra, at 1606.

[205] Case C-474/93 [1995] ECR I-2113; Briggs (1995) 15 YEL 502.

[206] The *Hengst Import* case, supra, at 2128.

[207] The Court of Justice would not go into the question of whether the Italian court had made an error of law in granting the order, see infra, p 628.

[208] Case C-172/91 *Sonntag v Waidmann* [1993] ECR I-1963 at 2000–2002.

[209] Case C-39/02 *Maersk Olie & Gas v Firma Mm de Haan en W de Boer* [2004] ECR I-9657 at [59].

[210] See the *Klomps* case, supra, at [20]; the *Debaecker* case, supra at [31]; the *Maersk* case, supra, at [61].

In sufficient time   We are concerned here with the situation where there has been service and the defendant has notice which enables him from that point onwards to defend. Where there has been service, it can usually be assumed that the defendant is able to defend from that moment onwards; this can be assumed even though there was no personal service on the defendant (Article 34(2) does not require actual knowledge of the document instituting the proceedings). The question then arises of whether the defendant has *sufficient time* in which to defend himself. The *time* in question is that available to the defendant for the purposes of preventing the issue of a judgment in default enforceable under the Regulation.[211] This involves looking at the procedural law in the judgment-granting state. Under German procedural law a valid notice of appearance entered at any time prior to the issue of a default judgment will prevent its issue.[212] The period in question therefore goes right up to the date of issue of the default judgment. In *Klomps v Michel* the judgment in question was the German enforcement order; this meant that the period after it was granted, during which objections could be made, was disregarded. Time will begin to run from the date on which service is effected.

A more difficult question is whether the time available is *sufficient* to prevent the judgment in default being issued. The recognising court will have to look at all the circumstances of the case. In *Klomps v Michel* the Court of Justice seemed to regard sufficiency of time as being solely a question of fact. But it is hard to see how a court could answer the question without having some yardstick to which the facts could be related. The criterion for sufficiency of time could be left to the law of the state in which the judgment was given, or to the law of the state in which recognition is sought, or by having regard to both of these,[213] or it could be left to be determined by an independent Community meaning to be given to the concept. It would be wrong to leave the matter to the law of the state in which the judgment was given, since this would not provide the check on abuse of natural justice which Article 34(2) was designed to achieve. The most effective way of achieving this objective would be to give a Community definition to the concept of sufficiency of time, although, in the absence of this, national courts may well fall back on their own idea of what is sufficient time.

And in such a way   This wording was introduced by the Regulation and is not to be found in the Brussels Convention. It appears to be concerned with the manner of service and the effect that this has on the defendant's ability to arrange for his defence. It would deal with the problem of inadequate service. That is the situation where, although there was service, there may have been inadequate notice to enable the defendant to defend himself from that point onwards. This will only occur in exceptional cases. Under the Brussels Convention this problem had to be dealt with within the context of sufficiency of time by the rather unsatisfactory device of holding that time has not yet begun to run, with the result that the defence applies.[214] Now it can be dealt with by holding that the defendant was not served "in such a way" as to enable him to arrange for his defence.

---

[211] *TSN Kunststoffrecycling GmbH v Jurgens* [2002] EWCA Civ 11 at [49], [2002] 1 WLR 2459 at 2472; Briggs (2002) 73 BYBIL 468.

[212] The *TSN Kunststoffrecycling* case, supra.

[213] See *Re Recognition of a Default Judgment* (Case 16 W 12/02) [2005] IL Pr 23 at [5], Oberlandesgericht (Court of Appeal), Cologne.

[214] *Klomps v Michel*, supra; Case 49/84 *Debaecker v Bouwman* [1985] ECR 1779; Hartley (1987) 2 ELR 220; applied in *Artic Fish Sales Co Ltd v Adam (No 2)* 1996 SLT 970.

In determining whether service has been adequate to enable the defendant to prepare his defence, all the circumstances have to be considered, "including the means employed for effecting service, the relations between the plaintiff and the defendant or the nature of the steps which had to be taken in order to prevent judgment being given in default".[215] It means that, sometimes, personal service will be required and merely serving process at the defendant's address, although in accordance with the law of the state in which the judgment was given, would not be enough. The Advocate General in the *Klomps* case gave as an example the situation where the defendant was in hospital.

The court of the Member State in which enforcement is sought may take into account exceptional circumstances which have arisen after service has been effected. The Court of Justice so decided in *Debaecker v Bouwman*,[216] where it was said that, in deciding whether there had been a breach of the natural justice defence under Article 27(2) of the Brussels Convention, it was relevant to consider the fact that after fictitious service had been made on the defendant—at a police station in Antwerp—the plaintiff had become apprised of the defendant's post office box address in Essen, but had made no effort to contact him there. However, it was also relevant to consider the fact that the defendant was responsible for the earlier failure of the served document to reach him by leaving premises without giving notice and without leaving a forwarding address.

The question of adequacy of service was regarded by the Court of Justice in *Klomps v Michel* and *Debaecker v Bouwman* as being solely one of fact. As with the question of sufficiency of time, it would be better to fix some yardstick to which the facts can be related. If this is to be done, it would be desirable to have a Community standard rather than leaving the standard to be that of the law of the state in which recognition is sought.

Giving the recognising court the power to consider the adequacy of service is an important measure. Without it there would be no substantial check by the recognising court on whether the defendant was able to prepare his defence in the Member State in which the judgment was given. It is a necessary measure in view of the fact that the concept of "service" does not itself provide a proper check on natural justice by the recognising court.

Unless the defendant failed to commence proceedings to challenge the judgment when it was possible for him to do so This proviso was introduced by the Regulation. If the defendant was in a position to appeal on grounds of procedural irregularity in the judgment-granting state and has not done so,[217] he is not entitled to invoke that procedural irregularity as a ground for refusing or revoking a declaration of enforceability in the enforcing state.[218] This is yet another example of the Regulation narrowing down defences so as to improve the free movement of judgments. It is unclear whether this requirement comes into play in cases where service has not been effected in the first place and whether it can be satisfied by an appeal in the judgment-granting state after the application for enforcement has been made.[219] It is only "possible" for the defendant to

---

[215] *Klomps v Michel*, supra, at 1609.
[216] [1985] ECR 1779.
[217] See, eg, Case C-123/91 *Minalmet GmbH v Brandeis Ltd* [1992] ECR I-5661.
[218] The Explanatory Memorandum, p 23. See also *Re The Enforcement Of A Portuguese Judgment* (Case IX ZB 2/03) [2005] IL Pr 28, Bundesgerichtshof (German Federal Supreme Court).
[219] *Tavoulareas v Tsavliris (No 2)* [2006] EWCA Civ 1772 at [17], [2007] 1 WLR 1573.

challenge the default judgment in the judgment-granting state if he has knowledge of its contents.[220] Due service (ie compliance with all the formal rules applicable to service) of the default judgment is not required. A parallel is drawn with service of the document instituting the proceedings so that the default judgment must have been served on the defendant in sufficient time to enable him to arrange for his defence before the courts of the state in which the judgment was given.[221] Where this is not the case, the proviso will not apply.

(iii) Interaction with the public policy defence

There are circumstances where there has been an interference with the defendant's ability to arrange his defence but the defence in Article 34(2) does not operate. To take some examples: the judgment was not given in default of appearance but the judge was biased; the service on the defendant was unobjectionable but the court refused to hear counsel for the defendant;[222] the original service was unobjectionable but the defendant was unaware that proceedings were reactivated after a long period during which they had been stayed, without any re-service.[223] In such circumstances the public policy defence can operate.[224]

(c) A conflict with a judgment given in the Member State in which recognition is sought

Article 34(3) provides that a judgment shall not be recognised "if it [the judgment] is irreconcilable with a judgment given in a dispute between the same parties in the Member State in which recognition is sought". Where there are contemporaneous proceedings between the same parties in two Member States, in respect of the same or a related cause of action, the Regulation requires one court to decline jurisdiction in favour of the other.[225] The position is more difficult where the cause of action in the two Member States is neither the same nor related. There is no provision requiring one of the courts to decline jurisdiction in favour of the other, and there can be conflicting judgments in two Member States. Article 34(3) solves this problem, in so far as the conflict is between a judgment given in the Member State in which recognition is sought and a judgment given in another Member State, by providing that the judgment given in the recognising Member State takes priority.[226] The court of the Member State in which recognition is sought must refuse recognition; it has no discretionary power to authorise recognition on the basis that the foreign judgment does not sufficiently disturb the rule of law.[227]

---

[220] Case C-283/05 *ASML Netherlands BV v Semiconductor Industry Services GmbH (SEMIS)* [2007] IL Pr 4 at [49].

[221] Ibid, at [41]–[47].

[222] See the *Krombach* case, supra, p 613.

[223] See the *Maronier* case, supra, p 613.

[224] See supra, p 611.

[225] See Section 9, Chapter II (Arts 27–30) of the Regulation, discussed supra, pp 303–315. Nonetheless, even in cases where the cause of action is the same there can still be conflicting judgments, see Hartley, pp 92–93.

[226] See the Jenard Report, p 45.

[227] Case C-80/00 *Italian Leather SpA v WECO Polstermobel GmbH & Co* [2002] ECR I-4995 at 5026–5027, [50]–[52]; Kramer (2003) 40 CMLR 953.

All that is required for a defence to operate is that: (i) a judgment[228] has been given in the recognising Member State—this can be before or after the judgment is given in the other Member State;[229] (ii) it is given in a dispute between the same parties; (iii) this judgment is irreconcilable with the judgment given in the other Member State. In order to ascertain this, the Court of Justice in *Hoffman v Krieg*[230] has said that the two judgments should be examined to see whether they entail legal consequences that are mutually exclusive. Applying this test, it was held that a German judgment ordering a husband to pay maintenance to his wife as part of his conjugal obligations was irreconcilable with a subsequent Dutch judgment pronouncing a divorce. "Judgment" has the same meaning as under Article 32 and therefore includes proceedings for interim measures.[231] A foreign decision on interim measures ordering an obligor not to carry out certain acts is irreconcilable with a decision on interim measures refusing to grant such an order.[232] The fact that the irreconcilability arose from different procedural requirements in the two states, rather than from legal reasons, is irrelevant.[233] Irreconcilability lies in the *effects* of judgments, it does not concern the procedural requirements that determine whether judgment can be given which differ from Member State to Member State.[234] It is left to the recognising court to decide whether a judgment has been *given* in their Member State.[235] Where only an interim judgment (as to substance) has been given or where the judgment is subject to an appeal, this may be a difficult decision. Moreover, because the defence does not apply in the situation where proceedings are merely pending in the recognising Member State, the effect of Article 34(3) will be to induce applicants to race to seek recognition before a conflicting judgment is actually given.

When recognition is sought in England, as far as Article 34(3) is concerned the Member State in which recognition is sought must be the United Kingdom (ie the Member State of the European Community) rather than the individual countries within the United Kingdom. This means that a French judgment will not be recognised in England if it is irreconcilable with a Scottish or Northern Ireland judgment.

It has been suggested[236] that a judgment *given* in the Member State in which recognition is sought (State A) can include the situation where the judgment has in fact been delivered in another state (State B) but is entitled to recognition in Member State A.

---

[228] An enforceable settlement reached before a court does not constitute a "judgment" under Art 32, supra, p 599, and hence under this provision: Case C-414/92 *Solo Kleinmotoren GmbH v Boch* [1994] ECR I-2237. The mere fact that there are *proceedings* in the recognising Member State is not a ground for refusing to register the judgment: *Landhurst Leasing plc v Marcq* [1998] IL Pr 822, CA.

[229] See the opinion of AG GULMANN in the *Solo* case, supra, at 2244.

[230] Case 145/86 [1988] ECR 645; Hartley (1991) 16 ELR 64; Briggs [1988] 265; Stone [1988] LMCLQ 393. Followed in *Macaulay v Macaulay* [1991] 1 WLR 179, infra, pp 1071–1073. See also *DT v FL* [2006] IEHC 98 at [75]–[76], [2007] IL Pr 56; *Commune De Macot La Plagne v SA Sebluxl* [2007] IL Pr 12, French cour de Cassation; *Materiel Auxiliaire D'Informatique v Printed Forms Equipment Ltd* [2006] IL Pr 44, French cour de Cassation.

[231] Case C-80/00 *Italian Leather SpA v WECO Polstermobel GmbH & Co* [20002] ECR I-4995 at 5025, [41]. See also *AGF Kosmos Assurances Générales v Surgil Trans Express* [2007] IL Pr 24, French cour de Cassation.

[232] *Italian Leather*, supra, at 5026, [47].

[233] Ibid, at 5008, [61] (opinion of AG LEGER).

[234] Ibid, at [44].

[235] See the Jenard Report, p 45.

[236] The Jenard Report, p 45; Collins, p 110. Cf Anton and Beaumont's *Civil Jurisdiction in Scotland*, para 8.19.

The wording of Article 34(3) does not support this wide interpretation. However, in its favour it has to be pointed out that in certain cases it would be a way of resolving the problem of giving priority to one of the conflicting judgments. The first such case would be where the conflicting judgments are both granted in Member States other than the one in which recognition is sought.[237] Article 34(4) has been extended by the Regulation to deal with this situation but it may not apply (eg because of the sequence in which the judgments were given).[238]Article 34(3) will not apply unless this wide interpretation of the word *given* is adopted. The second case is where one of the conflicting judgments is granted in a non-Member State. Article 34(4), which is designed to deal with this situation, may not apply (eg because of the sequence in which the judgments were given).[239] Again, Article 34(3) will only apply if the wide interpretation of the word *given* is adopted. An alternative way of dealing with these two cases would be by invoking the public policy defence and then giving priority to the earlier judgment.[240]

The Hess, Pfeiffer and Schloser Report criticises the fact that Article 34(3) gives priority to a judgment granted in the recognising state even though that judgment may not have respected the *lis pendens* rule under the Regulation. It therefore suggests adding an extra requirement for Article 34(3) to operate, namely that the pendency of the parallel proceedings or the irreconcilability could not have been sought in the court proceedings in the Member State of origin.[241]

(d) A conflicting judgment given in another Member State or in a third State

Article 34(4) provides that a judgment shall not be recognised "if it [the judgment] is irreconcilable with an earlier judgment given in another Member State or in a third State involving the same cause of action and between the same parties, provided that the earlier judgment fulfils the conditions necessary for its recognition in the Member State addressed".

This provision, like Article 34(3), is concerned with the situation where there are two irreconcilable judgments and with ensuring that priority is given to one of them.[242] The *lis pendens* provisions in the Regulation, requiring one court to decline jurisdiction in favour of another, can only operate where the proceedings are in two different Member States.[243] Where the proceedings are in a third state (ie a non-Member State) and a Member State, there is a real possibility of two judgments being given, both of which have to be recognised. This is a serious situation which could give rise to diplomatic

---

[237] See generally, Hartley, p 93; Anton and Beaumont's *Civil Jurisdiction in Scotland*, para 8.20; Layton and Mercer, para 26.081. Art 27 of the Regulation (*lis pendens*) will often prevent this situation from arising, see supra, pp 303–312, but will not do so where the cause of action is not the same in the actions in the two Member States.

[238] See infra.

[239] See infra.

[240] Hill, para 13.3.37.

[241] Study JLS/C4/2005/03, Final Version September 2007, available at the European Commission—European Judicial Network—what's new website http://ec.europa.eu/civiljustice/news/whatsnew_en.htm. See paras 564–565. This would be a partial alignment of the position with Art 21 of the European Order for uncontested claims, discussed infra, pp 643–644.

[242] See the Schlosser Report, pp 131–131; cf the Jenard Report, p 45.

[243] See Art 27, discussed supra, pp 303–312.

problems with non-Member States. To avoid this,[244]Article 34(4) gives priority to the judgment given in the non-Member State, and the judgment given in the Member State is not recognised.

There was a gap in the Brussels Convention in that it did not deal with the situation where the earlier judgment was in another Member State.[245] The *lis pendens* provisions in the Regulation will normally prevent a judgment being given in the court second seised but it will not do so if that court does not accept that the parties or the cause of action are the same. The Regulation has closed this gap by extending Article 34(4) to cover this situation.

For Article 34(4) to operate it must be shown that: (i) the judgment given in the non-Member State is the earlier one; (ii) it is entitled to recognition;[246] (iii) it is irreconcilable with the later judgment given in the Member State; (iv) it involves the same cause of action and the same parties.[247]

There is still a problem where one of these requirements is not satisfied, with the result that Article 34(4) does not apply. If faced with conflicting judgments given in a Member State (A) and in another Member State (B) or a third state (C), it is possible to solve the conflict by applying the wide interpretation of Article 34(3) set out above[248] to give priority to the judgment of the other Member State (B) or the third state (C), as the case may be. An alternative is that, in the absence of a defence, the judgment given first could be given priority.[249]

The Hess, Pfeiffer and Schloser Report advocates the introduction of the additional requirement, suggested for Article 34(3),[250] for Article 34(4) as well.

(ii) Defences under Article 35

This provides a defence to recognition in two situations; both involve an examination of the jurisdiction taken by the court which delivered the judgment.

(a) The judgment conflicts with Sections 3, 4 or 6 of Chapter II of the Regulation[251]

A judgment will not be recognised if it conflicts with the jurisdictional provisions in Section 3 (insurance matters, Articles 8 to 14), Section 4 (consumer contracts, Articles 15 to 17),[252] or Section 6 (exclusive jurisdiction, Article 22) of Chapter II of the Regulation. Normally, the recognising court cannot review the jurisdiction taken by the court in the Member State in which the judgment was granted.[253] Article 35 provides an exception to

---

[244] The problem could also be avoided by dismissing proceedings. This would have to be on the basis that the Regulation has "reflexive" effect, see supra, p 333.

[245] See the Explanatory Memorandum, p 23.

[246] See the Schlosser Report, at p 131. In England this would be at common law or by statute; see *Owens Bank Ltd v Bracco* [1991] 4 All ER 833 at 841, CA, affd by the House of Lords [1992] 2 AC 443, and generally supra, pp 516–587.

[247] This is assessed by the recognising court and not by the court seised second of the original proceedings.

[248] Supra, pp 622–624.

[249] See Layton and Mercer, para 26.082.

[250] Supra, p 624.

[251] See *Berkeley Administration Inc v McClelland* [1995] IL Pr 201 at 213 (per Dillon LJ), CA.

[252] See Case C-99/96 *Mietz v Intership Yachting Sneek BV* [1999] ECR I-2277.

[253] Art 35, para 3.

this which can be justified because Sections 3, 4 and 6 depart from the normal rules of jurisdiction. As indeed does Section 5 (individual contracts of employment, Articles 18 to 21). Yet curiously this is not included in the list that allows a defence. The explanation for this is that any review of jurisdiction would only affect the applicant, who will generally be the employee.[254] In examining jurisdiction, the recognising court is bound by the findings of fact on which the court which gave the judgment based its jurisdiction;[255] this avoids unnecessary duplication of effort. The recognising court will, however, examine whether these special rules on jurisdiction were correctly applied by the court which gave the judgment. It appears to be irrelevant whether jurisdiction has been challenged in the court which gave the judgment. Sections 3, 4 and 6 are complex provisions; there is every likelihood of the recognising court interpreting these provisions differently from the way in which they have been interpreted by the court which gave the judgment and holding that the latter court did not have jurisdiction. In order to avoid conflicting interpretations, wherever possible, there should be a referral to the Court of Justice for a definitive interpretation.

The Hess, Pfeiffer and Schlosser Report recommends the deletion of this defence since it is not in line with the principle of mutual trust.[256]

(b) The case is provided for under Article 72

A judgment will not be recognised in a case provided for under Article 72.[257] This is concerned with agreements entered into by Member States, prior to the Regulation entering into force, pursuant to Article 59 of the Brussels Convention,[258] whereby a Contracting State has agreed with a non-Contracting State that, in certain circumstances, it will not recognise judgments given in other Contracting States against defendants from that non-Contracting State. The United Kingdom had entered into conventions with Canada and Australia incorporating the obligation under Article 59. This means that, to take an example, a French judgment will not be recognised in England if jurisdiction could only have been taken in France against a person domiciled or habitually resident in Canada or Australia on one of the exorbitant bases of jurisdiction referred to in Article 3(2)[259] of Title II of the Brussels Convention. This means that the English court would have to examine the jurisdiction of the French court to see whether it could *only* have been founded on one of the specified exorbitant bases. When examining jurisdiction, it is not clear from the wording of Article 35 whether the recognising court is bound by the findings of fact of the court in which the judgment was given.[260] There is no equivalent of Article 59 in the Regulation. Once the Regulation came into force no new agreements of that kind could be entered into by virtue of the Regulation. The defence in relation to

---

[254] See the Explanatory Memorandum, p 23.
[255] Art 35, para 2; the Jenard Report, p 46.
[256] Study JLS/C4/2005/03, Final Version September 2007, available at the European Commission—European Judicial Network—what's new website http://ec.europa.eu/civiljustice/news/whatsnew_en.htm. See para 901.
[257] Art 35, para 1.
[258] Discussed infra, pp 635–636.
[259] See supra, pp 222–223.
[260] Hartley thinks that it is bound, p 87.

Article 59 agreements is therefore confined to agreements entered into prior to the entry into force of the Regulation.

(iii) Enforcement of a provisional or protective measure

The jurisdiction recognised by Article 31 of the Regulation constitutes a special regime. If a court, after adversarial proceedings,[261] grants a provisional or protective measure, basing its jurisdiction on national law in conjunction with Article 31,[262] the court to which the application for enforcement of this judgment was made may examine whether the measure ordered was indeed a provisional or protective measure within the meaning of this Article.[263] If it concludes that it was not, the order is not capable of being the subject of an enforcement order under Chapter III of the Regulation.[264] The judgment may be silent as to the basis of its jurisdiction, in which case, in order to ensure that the Regulation rules are not circumvented, the judgment will be construed as meaning that the court founded its jurisdiction on Article 31. If, on the other hand, the court granting a provisional or protective measure has jurisdiction as to the substance of the case under Articles 2 or 5 to 24, the normal prohibition on the review of the jurisdiction of the judgment-granting court will apply.

(g) Non-defences

(i) Other defences are not available

The duty to recognise and enforce a judgment under the Regulation applies unless one of the defences under Articles 34 and 35 is available; it follows that all other defences are implicitly rejected. The Regulation reinforces this point by expressly providing that two very important matters may not be raised as defences.

(a) A review of jurisdiction

Article 35, para 3 provides that "the jurisdiction of the court of the Member State of origin may not be reviewed". This provision is wide enough to exclude two arguments in respect of jurisdiction.[265] First, it prevents any suggestion that the court which gave the judgment must have had jurisdiction in the international sense.[266] Strictly speaking, it was not necessary to exclude this expressly since the Regulation implicitly does so by providing for recognition and enforcement without any reference to the international jurisdiction of the court which delivered the judgment.[267] Secondly, it stops any enquiry into the internal jurisdiction of the court which gave the judgment. It cannot be argued that this court misapplied the jurisdictional rules under the Regulation.[268] Neither can it

---

[261] The judgment will then be within the scope of Chapter III of the Regulation, supra, pp 602–603.

[262] In contrast to having jurisdiction as to the substance of the case, supra, p 315.

[263] Case C-99/96 *Mietz v Intership Yachting Sneek BV* [1999] ECR I-2277.

[264] Ibid, at [56]. See also *Comet Group plc v Unika Computer SA* [2004] IL Pr 1 at [24]–[31].

[265] For the position where a national court acts in breach of Art 35, para 3, see Kohler (1985) 34 ICLQ 563 at 578–580.

[266] The concept of international jurisdiction and how it differs from internal jurisdiction is discussed supra, pp 516–517.

[267] See supra, pp 603–604 and 608–609.

[268] See Case 7/98 *Krombach v Bamberski* [2001] QB 709 at [31]–[32]. This is subject to the defences under Art 35, discussed supra, pp 625–626.

be argued that the court which granted the judgment misapplied its traditional national rules on jurisdiction. The prohibition against examining jurisdiction cannot be evaded by using the public policy defence,[269] even where an exorbitant basis of jurisdiction has been used against a defendant domiciled in another Member State.[270]

It is questionable whether it was right to exclude a defence of lack of internal jurisdiction. It would have been possible under the Regulation to lay down a double check on jurisdiction, the court granting the judgment making sure that it has jurisdiction under the Regulation, and the recognising and enforcing court checking this. The Regulation sets up a system of double checks in respect of natural justice but not in respect of jurisdiction, presumably because it is satisfied that a court will only take jurisdiction under the Regulation's rules when it ought to. Despite the safeguards built into the rules on jurisdiction in the Regulation, this may be unduly optimistic. It also makes no allowance for the fact that jurisdiction may be taken in a Member State under traditional national rules, and those rules may be misapplied.

(b) A review of substance

Article 36[271] provides that "under no circumstances may a foreign judgment be reviewed as to its substance". The courts of the Member State in which recognition is sought cannot refuse recognition solely on the ground that there is a discrepancy between the legal rule applied by the judgment granting court from that which would have been applied by the recognising court if it had been seised of the dispute.[272] It cannot be alleged that the foreign court made a mistake of fact or a mistake of law.[273] Even though a defence based on an allegation that there has been a mistake of law is not expressly excluded by Article 36, it is implicitly excluded by the terms of Articles 34 and 35, which provide the *only* defences to recognition.[274] Thus, in *Hengst Import BV v Campese*[275] the Court of Justice refused to go into an allegation that the Italian court had made an error of law in granting the order in question. The "substance" of a judgment applies to a legal rule allowing judgment without hearing defence counsel, which is a procedural rule.[276] Procedural irregularities in the judgment-granting state can be examined in order to establish one of the defences under Articles 34 and 35.[277]

(ii) The special problem where there is a breach of an agreement for the settlement of disputes

From an English lawyer's viewpoint the most noticeable omission from the defences under Articles 34 and 35 is that of a provision equivalent to section 32 of the Civil

---

[269] Art 35, para 3.

[270] See the *Krombach* case, supra, at [34], discussed supra, p 613.

[271] See also Art 45, para 2.

[272] See the *Krombach* case, supra, at [36]; the *Renault* case, supra, at 29. The question of when the public policy defence can be used in cases of discrepancy is discussed supra, pp 614–615.

[273] See the *Krombach* case, supra, at [36]; the *Renault* case, supra, at [29].

[274] It does not appear to be a matter of public policy, see supra, p 614.

[275] Case C-474/93 [1995] ECR I-2113 at 2129; discussed supra, p 619. See also *Westpac Banking Corpn v Dempsey* [1993] 3 IR 331 at 340.

[276] See the *Krombach* case, supra, at [36]–[37]. Cf the opinion of AG JACOBS in Case C-78/95 *Hendrikman v Magenta Druck & Verlag GmbH* [1997] QB 426 at 437.

[277] Ibid at 436–437.

Jurisdiction and Judgments Act 1982, which, it will be recalled,[278] provides that an overseas judgment shall not be recognised or enforced in the United Kingdom if it was given in proceedings brought in breach of an agreement for settlement of disputes otherwise than by proceedings in the courts of that country.

(a) A breach of an agreement providing for trial in a particular state

Under the Regulation there is a duty to recognise and enforce a judgment obtained in another Member State, despite the fact that there was an agreement between the parties providing for the trial of disputes in a state (whether a Member or non-Member State) other than the one in which trial took place. Following on from this, because the judgment is required to be recognised or enforced under the Regulation, section 32 of the 1982 Act will not apply.[279]

The reason for the absence of a defence under the Regulation to deal with this situation is not clear. Admittedly, Article 23[280] will operate in many cases and thereby prevent a court in another Member State from taking jurisdiction in defiance of the agreement. But this is not a complete answer. Article 23 will not always apply; eg it will not do so where the agreement on jurisdiction provides for trial in a non-Member State. Even where Article 23 ought to have been applied, there is always the possibility that a court in a Member State might misconstrue its provisions and fail to apply them.

(b) A breach of an agreement to go to arbitration

There is no defence where recognition or enforcement is sought of a judgment granted by a court in a Member State which has taken jurisdiction despite an agreement by the parties to go to arbitration in that or some other state. However, the more basic question arises as to whether there is a duty to recognise or enforce a judgment in the first place in these circumstances. This question has to be asked because Article 1 excludes arbitration from the scope of the Regulation.[281] There is little authority directly on the issue of whether this provision excludes not only arbitration proceedings themselves (including arbitration awards[282]) but also, and this is crucial in the present context, judgments of courts where there has been a breach of an agreement to go to arbitration.[283] If such judgments are excluded from the scope of the Regulation, the result is that the non-Regulation rules on recognition and enforcement will apply, including, in England, section 32 of the 1982 Act and, subject to the terms of that provision, the judgment will not be recognised or enforced. On the other hand, if such judgments are within the scope of the Regulation

---

[278] See supra, pp 569–573.

[279] Supra, p 571. See *The Atlantic Emperor (No 2)* [1992] 1 Lloyd's Rep 624 at 632, CA; *The Heidberg* [1994] 2 Lloyd's Rep 287 at 297.

[280] See supra, pp 283–296.

[281] Supra, pp 220–222.

[282] See Case C-391/95 *Van Uden Maritime BV (t/a Van Uden Africa Line) v Kommanditgesellschaft in Firma Deco-Line* [1999] QB 1225; *Allied Vision Ltd v VPS Film Entertainment GmbH* [1991] 1 Lloyd's Rep 392 at 399. An arbitration award that has been made enforceable as a judgment in the state in which it was granted also falls outside the scope of the Regulation: *ABCI v BFT* [1996] 1 Lloyd's Rep 485—a case on the Brussels Convention.

[283] See supra, pp 220–222; Collins, pp 29 and 112; Anton and Beaumont's *Civil Jurisdiction in Scotland*, paras 3.23–3.26, 8.26; Davidson 1992 SLT 267, at 268–270; Briggs in Andenas and Jacobs (eds), *European Community Law in the English Courts*, pp 293–295; Van Houtte (1997) 13 Arb Int 85.

the normal duty to recognise and enforce the foreign judgment under the Regulation will apply, and section 32 of the 1982 Act will not affect this.

It has been suggested that the Regulation should be narrowly interpreted so as to exclude from its scope judgments based on proceedings brought in breach of an arbitration agreement.[284] However, against this the Regulation is not concerned with arbitration and we now have a decision from the Court of Justice in the *Marc Rich* case[285] on the scope of the arbitration exclusion, albeit in the context of a different issue in relation to arbitration, which suggests that judgments in cases where there has been a breach of an agreement to go to arbitration are, nonetheless, within the scope of the Regulation.[286] The Court of Justice held that, in determining whether a dispute falls within the scope of the Brussels Convention, reference must be made solely to the subject matter of the dispute, rather than to any preliminary issue that has to be resolved in order to determine the dispute. The subject matter of the dispute in the present context is presumably the enforcement of a foreign judgment. This is clearly not part of the process of arbitration, and is accordingly not excluded by the arbitration exclusion.

What little direct authority there is on the matter supports this view of the scope of the arbitration exclusion. In *The Heidberg*, Judge DIAMOND said that it was "beyond doubt" that the judgment of a foreign Contracting State on the substance of a dispute, even if given in breach of a valid arbitration agreement, must be recognised under the Brussels Convention.[287] However, WALLER J has said that, although such a judgment comes within the Brussels Convention, the public policy defence may operate with the result that it is not recognised.[288] A decision of the Court of Justice is needed on this question.[289] Of course, if the arbitration agreement is invalid there is no breach of an agreement to go to arbitration. The judgment-granting court may well have given a decision, as a preliminary issue, that the arbitration agreement is indeed invalid. This mere fact does not bring the judgment as to the substance of the claim within the arbitration exclusion.[290] As regards the decision on validity, the Court of Justice has said that the Brussels Convention does not apply to judgments determining whether an arbitration agreement is valid or not or, because it is invalid, ordering the parties not to continue the arbitration proceedings.[291]

(h) Appeals in the State in which the judgment was given

It is unfair to the judgment debtor for a judgment to be recognised or enforced where there is a possibility of it being altered subsequently on appeal in the Member State in

---

[284] See Briggs and Rees, para 7.08. See in relation to the Brussels Convention: Hartley, pp 96–97. See generally Layton and Mercer, paras 12.045–12.053.

[285] Case C-190/89 *Marc Rich and Co AG v Società Italiana Impianti PA* [1991] ECR I-3855, supra, p 220.

[286] But cf Briggs (1991) 11 YEL 527, 529.

[287] [1994] 2 Lloyd's Rep 287 at 301.

[288] *Phillip Alexander Securities and Futures Ltd v Bamberger* [1997] I L Pr 72 at 101–102.

[289] *Marc Rich & Co AG v Società Italiana Impianti PA, The Atlantic Emperor (No 2)* [1992] 1 Lloyd's Rep 624 at 632–633, CA.

[290] *Zellner v Phillip Alexander Securities and Futures Ltd* [1997] IL Pr 730. See also *The Atlantic Emperor (No 2)*, supra, at 632–633; *Phillip Alexander Securities and Futures Ltd v Bamberger*, supra, at 102.

[291] The *Van Uden* case, supra; discussed supra, pp 315–317.

which it was granted.[292] Articles 38, 37 and 46 of the Regulation may prevent recognition or enforcement in this situation.

(i) Article 38

Article 38 contains a requirement that before enforcement can take place it must be shown that the judgment is enforceable in the Member State in which it was given.[293] This requirement is not specifically designed to deal with appeals. However, the effect of an appeal in the judgment-granting Member State may be to prevent the judgment from being enforceable there, with the result that the judgment is not enforceable in other Member States. This still leaves a problem in other cases where the appeal does not have this effect or where recognition alone, and not enforcement, is sought.

(ii) Articles 37 and 46

Articles 37 and 46 of the Regulation are specifically designed to deal with the difficulties raised by appeals in the Member State in which the judgment was given.

Article 37(1) gives the recognising court a power to stay its proceedings if an "ordinary appeal" against the judgment was granted. The idea is that there should be a stay of proceedings until the appeal is finally disposed of.

Article 46(1) gives the court with which an appeal against the decision granting a declaration of enforceability is lodged under Article 43 (in England this is the High Court) or Article 44 (in England this is concerned with a single further appeal on a point of law) power, in certain circumstances, to stay the proceedings. If a stay is refused,[294] or a stay previously ordered is lifted,[295] this is not subject to a further appeal. Article 46(1) is a similar provision to that contained in Article 37, but with the following important differences.[296] First, the party appealing against the decision granting a declaration of enforceability must apply for a stay of the proceedings; the court cannot act on its own motion. Secondly, the power to stay applies not only to cases where an ordinary appeal has been lodged, but also to cases where an ordinary appeal has not been lodged, if the time for such an appeal has not yet expired.[297] In this case, the court may specify the time within which such an appeal is to be lodged. Thirdly, the court with which an appeal has been lodged against a decision granting a declaration of enforceability has power to make enforcement conditional on the provision of security,[298] but only when it gives judgment

---

[292] See the Jenard Report, p 52; the opinion of the Advocate General in Case 43/77 *Industrial Diamond Supplies v Riva* [1977] ECR 2175. It is equally unfair to the judgment creditor, who has lost his action, for the judgment to be recognised in other Member States when this judgment is subject to an appeal.

[293] Supra, p 607.

[294] Case 183/90 *Van Dalfsen v Van Loon* [1991] ECR I-4743.

[295] Case C-432/93 *Société d'Informatique Service Réalisation Organisation (SISRO) v Ampersand Software BV* [1996] QB 127. The court seised of a further appeal on a point of law (in England the Court of Appeal or the House of Lords under the leapfrog procedure) has no jurisdiction to impose or reimpose such a stay and it is irrelevant that it has this power under its domestic procedural law.

[296] The Jennard Report, p 52.

[297] See *Noirhomme v Walklate* [1992] 1 Lloyd's Rep 427 at 431.

[298] Art 46, para 3. The Court of Session in *Re Petition of Marie Brizard et Roger International SA* referred to the Court of Justice (Case C-126/96) a number of questions in relation to the interpretation of this provision but the action was settled.

on the appeal, since it is only at this time that the original judgment can be enforced, and the judgment debtor needs this form of protection in case a further appeal succeeds.[299]

Two aspects of Articles 37 and 46 cause particular problems: (i) these provisions are only concerned with "ordinary" appeals; and (ii) the power to stay proceedings is a discretionary one.

(a) An ordinary appeal

An "ordinary" appeal must have been lodged against the judgment in the state in which it was given, or, under Article 46 (but not Article 37), the time for an "ordinary" appeal must not yet have expired. In civil law systems, an "ordinary" appeal is often contrasted with an "extra-ordinary" appeal. The English legal system has no such distinction and this may cause difficulty for both foreign and English courts.

It would be particularly hard for a foreign court, which has been asked to recognise or enforce under the Regulation an English judgment subject to an appeal, to determine whether this was an "ordinary" appeal when there is no such concept under English law.[300] Article 37(2) therefore provides that, where enforcement is suspended in the United Kingdom by reason of an appeal, a court in another Member State in which recognition is sought may stay the proceedings for recognition.[301] Article 46(2) provides that, where the judgment was given in the United Kingdom, "any form of appeal available in the Member State of origin shall be treated as an ordinary appeal".

This still leaves a problem for English courts; they will have to grapple with an unfamiliar concept when determining whether an "ordinary" appeal has been lodged in the foreign Member State in which the judgment was given. An "ordinary" appeal is, however, a concept that has now been defined by the Court of Justice.

In *Industrial Diamond Supplies v Riva*,[302] a case decided under the Brussels Convention, the Court of Justice gave a Community meaning to the concept of an ordinary appeal. This was necessary because some Contracting States do not have the concept, and those that do have it do not always define it in the same way. In deciding what this Community definition should be, the Court of Justice was concerned to ensure that the recognising and enforcing court was able to stay the proceedings "whenever reasonable doubt arises with regard to the fate of the decision in the State in which it was given".[303] The court held that an ordinary appeal under Articles 30 and 38 of the Brussels Convention (Articles 37 and 46 of the Regulation) is any appeal which: (a) may result in the annulment or amendment of the original judgment, and (b) for which there is a specific time for appealing

---

[299] Case 258/83 *Brennero v Wendel GmbH* [1984] ECR 3971; Hartley (1986) 11 ELR 95.

[300] Since a Community meaning is given to the concept, see infra, this would not be an impossible task.

[301] It is not clear whether Art 37(1) is replaced by Art 37(2) in cases coming within that paragraph. The wording of Art 37 suggests that, as an alternative, a stay can be granted in the situation where an "ordinary" appeal has been lodged in England, see Hartley, p 95. However, according to the Schlosser Report (p 130), the intention was to replace the concept of an "ordinary" appeal by Art 30(2) of the Brusssels Convention (Art 37, para 2 of the Regulation) in the situation where recognition is sought of a judgment from a court in the United Kingdom.

[302] Case 43/77 [1977] ECR 2175; Hartley (1978) 3 ELR 160, and generally Hartley, p 94. See also the Schlosser Report, p 130. Cf *Interdesco SA v Nullifire Ltd* [1992] 1 Lloyd's Rep 180.

[303] At 2189.

which starts to run by virtue of the judgment. It is not an ordinary appeal if it is one which is either dependent on events unforeseeable at the time of the original trial or on action taken by persons extraneous to the case who are not bound by the period for making an appeal.

The first of these two criteria is suitable for an appeal which has actually been lodged, and is relevant to Articles 37 and 46 of the Regulation; the second is suitable for the situation where an appeal has not been lodged, but the time for this has not expired, and is therefore only relevant to Article 46 of the Regulation. Since the Court of Justice wanted the same criteria to apply to both what are now Articles 37 and 46 of the Regulation, it put the two elements together for a common definition of an ordinary appeal. However, adopting this two-part definition produces curious results. Where an appeal has been lodged the first part of the definition would be satisfied, since the danger of the original judgment being altered exists. But, if this lodged appeal is of a type for which there is no time limit on when it can be brought, the second part of the definition would not be satisfied. It does not seem right to exclude an appeal which has actually been lodged because it was of a type for which there was no time limit as to when it could have been lodged.[304]

(b) A discretionary power

The recognising or enforcing court has a discretion to stay the proceedings; it is under no duty to grant a stay and one can be refused even though an ordinary appeal has been lodged, or, under Article 46, the time for such an appeal has not yet expired. The criteria on which this discretion is to be exercised have not as yet been fully developed by the Court of Justice. The Court of Justice has, however, held that a court, when deciding whether to grant a stay of proceedings, may take into account only such submissions as the party lodging the appeal against the decision authorising the enforcement of a judgment was unable[305] to make before the court of the state in which the judgment was given.[306] According to Advocate General LEGER, the refusal in the judgment-granting state to stay the enforcement of the judgment may be a relevant factor when making an assessment of the appeal's chances of success, but is never decisive.[307] Advocate General LEGER is clearly of the view that the recognising or enforcing court can consider the likelihood of the appeal's chances of success.[308] However, the Court of Justice in an earlier case has said that this is not something that can be considered.[309] There is English authority on the exercise of the discretion in *Petereit v Babcock International Holdings Ltd*.[310] The court laid down a general principle that prima facie a foreign judgment should be enforced.

---

[304] Hartley interprets the decision in *Industrial Diamond Suppliers v Riva*, supra, in such a way as to avoid this, p 94.

[305] The Court of Session in *Re Petition of Marie Brizard et Roger International SA* [1997] IL Pr 373 referred a number of questions to the Court of Justice to clarify the meaning of this idea (Case C-126/96) but the case was settled.

[306] Case C-183/90 *BJ Van Dalfsen v B Van Loon* [1991] ECR I-4743.

[307] See the opinion of AG LEGER in Case C-432/93 *Société d'Informatique Service Réalisation Organisation (SISRO) v Ampersand Software BV* [1996] QB 127 at 154–155.

[308] Ibid. See also *Petereit v Babcock International Holdings Ltd* [1990] 1 WLR 350 at 355.

[309] *Van Dalfsen*, supra, at 4775. Applied in *Banco Nacional de Comercio Exterior SNC v Empresa de Telecomunicaciones de Cuba SA* [2007] EWHC 2322 (Comm) at [10]–[11], [2007] IL Pr 59.

[310] [1990] 1 WLR 350; Kaye [1991] JBL 261. See also *Banco Nacional de Comercio Exterior SNC v Empresa de Telecomunicaciones de Cuba SA* [2007] EWHC 2322 (Comm) at [12]–[13], [2007] IL Pr 59.

In deciding whether to grant a stay pending the result of the appeal abroad the court considered the economic consequences to the parties of, on the one hand, granting a stay and, on the other hand, enforcing the judgment; for what is being decided is which party is to have the use of the judgment money during the period up to the result of the appeal being known. In deciding to grant a stay[311] the judge was influenced by the prospect of the defendant suffering potential losses, in terms of cash flow problems and currency exchange losses, which could not be adequately dealt with by the provision of security by the plaintiff. The most likely situation for the exercise of the discretion against a stay is going to arise before courts in other Member States which are asked to recognise or enforce judgments given in the United Kingdom and which are subject to an appeal. The extreme width of Articles 37(2) and 46(2), which are not limited to "ordinary" appeals,[312] needs to be countered by the use of the discretion to refuse a stay.[313]

(i) The estoppel effect of a judgment obtained in a Member State

In *De Wolf v Cox*,[314] a case decided under the Brussels Convention, the Court of Justice held that, once a judgment which is enforceable under the Convention has been obtained in one Contracting State, the party who has obtained the judgment in his favour is prevented from bringing a new action before a court in another Contracting State for a judgment in the same terms. The Court came to this conclusion because it foresaw a number of problems that could arise if bringing a new action was allowed. First, it could involve the courts of another Contracting State going into the substance of the dispute when this is a matter for the courts of the Contracting State in which the original judgment was given.[315] Secondly, if a judgment is given in the second Contracting State which conflicts with that given in the first, it means that the court in the second has failed in its duty to recognise the first judgment.[316] Thirdly, the *lis pendens* provisions under the Convention show the general desire to avoid having two sets of proceedings and two judgments in respect of the same cause of action.[317] Fourthly, allowing a new action could result in a creditor possessing two orders for enforcement in respect of the same debt.

On the facts of the case, whilst there were two sets of proceedings there were not two inconsistent judgments, since the Dutch court, before which a new action was brought, recognised the judgment granted earlier in Belgium. The Court of Justice was therefore reacting more against potential problems than actual ones and, by forcing the parties to use the enforcement procedure under the Convention, imposed greater expense upon the parties than would have been the case if the plaintiff had been allowed to bring fresh proceedings in the Netherlands.

The effect of the decision in *De Wolf* is that a judgment given in a Member State which is enforceable under the Regulation creates what in English law is regarded as an estoppel

---

[311] Conditional on the defendant providing adequate security to protect the plaintiff's position.
[312] Discussed supra, pp 632–633.
[313] See the Schlosser Report, p 130.
[314] Case 42/76 [1976] ECR 1759; Hartley (1977) 2 ELR 146.
[315] See Art 36 and Art 45(2) of the Regulation.
[316] See Art 33 of the Regulation, discussed supra, pp 603–604.
[317] See Art 27 of the Regulation, discussed supra, pp 303–312.

from the moment that it has been given.[318] The facts of *De Wolf* only concerned the situation where the estoppel principle prevents the claimant, having obtained a judgment in his favour, from obtaining another judgment against the same defendant in new proceedings involving the same cause of action and subject matter in a different Member State. However, this principle applies equally to prevent a claimant who has lost his action from obtaining a judgment against the same defendant in new proceedings in a different Member State.[319] Where, for the purposes of Article 27 of the Regulation, the parties, cause of action and subject matter are the same, a foreign judgment will be recognised as binding between all those parties.[320]

(j) Foreign reaction

(i) *The automatic recognition of judgments without jurisdictional safeguards*

American lawyers have been outspoken in their criticism of the Brussels Convention[321] and their criticism is equally applicable to the Regulation. The basis of their objection is that what is now the Regulation provides for the automatic recognition and enforcement of judgments against defendants domiciled in non-Member States,[322] despite the absence of the jurisdictional safeguards provided for defendants domiciled in Member States. Minimum standards in relation to natural justice[323] do not have to be complied with. The Regulation also recognises the use of exorbitant bases of jurisdiction against defendants domiciled in non-Member States (but not those domiciled in Member States[324]), and under Article 4(2) even extends their use. This provision, to take an example, allows a French domiciliary to use Article 14 of the French Civil Code, under which jurisdiction is based on the claimant's French nationality, to found jurisdiction against a defendant from a non-Member State and to have that judgment recognised and enforced throughout the European Community.

From a Community point of view there is as great a need for the free circulation of judgments where defendants are domiciled in non-Member States as there is where they are domiciled in Member States,[325] since there is the same risk of a defendant thwarting the claimant by moving his assets from one Member State to another. It is also understandable that the jurisdictional rules in the Regulation, since they are only concerned with allocating jurisdiction to Member States, should involve a basic distinction between the situation where the defendant is and is not domiciled in a Member State. But, when you add these two elements together, the result is that defendants domiciled in non-Member

---

[318] See supra, p 544.

[319] *Berkeley Administration Inc v McClelland* [1995] IL Pr 201, CA.

[320] Ibid at 211 (per Dillon LJ). A foreign judgment which is recognised under Art 33 may also lead to an issue estoppel, provided that the normal requirements at common law for this (supra, pp 544–550) are satisfied: *Berkeley Administration Inc v McClelland* [1996] IL Pr 772 at 787 (per Sir Richard Scott V-C), CA; see also *Boss Group Ltd v Boss France SA* [1997] 1 WLR 351 at 359.

[321] Von Mehren (1981) 81 Col LR 1044; Von Mehren (1980) II Hague Recueil 9, 95 et seq; Nadelmann (1967) 67 Col LR 995, reprinted in *Conflict of Laws: International and Interstate*, p 238; Nadelmann (1967) 5 CMLR 409. For Australian reaction see Pryles and Trindale (1974) 42 ALJ 185; McEvoy (1994) 68 ALJ 576, 582.

[322] Supra, pp 598–599.

[323] See Art 26, discussed supra, pp 302–303. The safeguards at the recognition and enforcement stage will, however, apply, see supra, pp 615–622.

[324] Supra, pp 222–224.

[325] See the Jenard Report, p 20.

States are treated unfairly.[326] This whole problem was, seemingly, only recognised at a late stage by the drafters of the Brussels Convention who, almost as an afterthought, introduced Article 59 to deal with it.[327]

(ii) Article 59 of the Brussels Convention

Article 59 allowed a Contracting State to the Brussels Convention to enter into a convention with a third state (ie a non-Contracting State), under which the former agrees not to recognise judgments given against defendants domiciled or habitually resident in the latter where the judgment could only be founded on an exorbitant basis of jurisdiction specified in Article 3(2) of the Brussels Convention. It was never a satisfactory solution to the problem of unfairness to defendants domiciled in non-Contracting States.[328] But it did at least have the great merit for European Community States of putting them in a very strong bargaining position when it came to negotiating bilateral treaties with third states. The free circulation of judgments founded on exorbitant bases of jurisdiction acted as the stick and the let-out allowed by Article 59 as the carrot to bring third states to the negotiating table.[329] That is all now in the past. There is no equivalent of Article 59 in the Regulation.[330] The European Commission explain this by saying that it would be out of place to have such a provision in a Community Regulation.[331] The Commission would like to have exclusive external competence in matters covered by the Regulation.[332] The notion of Member States negotiating and entering into bilateral agreements, which affect the Community rules on recognition, with non-Member States is seen as being inappropriate. However, the Council and Commission can negotiate international agreements that would mitigate the consequences of Chapter III of the Regulation for persons domiciled in third states.[333] Moreover, bilateral agreements containing the Article 59 let-out entered into prior to the entry into force of the Regulation are still honoured.[334]

(k) Future impact of the Hague Convention on Choice of Court Agreements

In 2005, the Hague Conference on Private International Law adopted a Convention on Choice of Court Agreements.[335] Under this Convention a judgment given by a court of a Contracting State designated in the agreement will be recognised in other Contracting

---

[326] For an attempt to justify the Brussels Convention's treatment of defendants domiciled in non-Contracting States, see Hauschild, in Goode and Simmonds (eds), *Commercial Operations in Europe* (1978), pp 57–58; see also Kohler (1985) 35 ICLQ 563, 580–581. Cf Nadelmann, *Conflict of Laws: International and Interstate*, pp 246–248; (1967) 5 CMLR 409, 414–419.

[327] For the origins of Art 59, see Nadelmann (1967) 5 CMLR 409.

[328] See the 13th edn of this book (1999), p 516.

[329] Nadelmann advocated US retaliation against this: *Conflict of Laws: International and Interstate*, pp 267–268.

[330] Art 59 still exists under the Brussels Convention, see infra, p 637.

[331] The Explanatory Memorandum, supra, pp 7–8.

[332] See Beaumont in Fawcett (ed), *Reform and Development of Private International Law* (2002), Chapter 1, p 25. See also Opinion 1/03 of the ECJ holding that conclusion of a new Lugano Convention falls within the exclusive competence of the Community.

[333] See the Joint Statement by the Council and the Commission on Arts 71 and 72.

[334] Art 72 of the Regulation; discussed supra, pp 626–627.

[335] Discussed supra, pp 422–424.

States,[336] subject to limited grounds of refusal.[337] Ratification would be by the European Community. If this were to happen, the Brussels I Regulation would continue to apply in relation to the recognition or enforcement of judgments as between European Community Member States.[338]

2. THE EC/DENMARK AGREEMENT

Under an Agreement between the EC and Denmark the provisions of the Brussels I Regulation, with minor modifications,[339] are applied by international law to the relations between the Community and Denmark.[340] In matters of recognition and enforcement, the Agreement applies where Denmark is either the state of origin or the state addressed.[341] As far as recognition and enforcement is concerned, the application of the provisions in Chapter III of the Regulation is subject to just one very minor amendment.[342] Prior to the entry into force of this Ageement, the Brussels Convention applied in relation to Denmark.[343]

3. THE BRUSSELS CONVENTION

The Brussels Convention has been replaced in virtually all cases by the Brussels I Regulation. However, one has to say "virtually" because the Brussels Convention still applies in relation to the territories of the Contracting States[344] which fall within the territorial scope of the Brussels Convention and are excluded from the Regulation.[345] The territories in question are (in relation to France) the French overseas territories, such as New Caledonia and Mayotte, and (in relation to the Netherlands) Aruba.[346] It follows that the rules on recognition and enforcement under the Brussels Convention are still applied in the United Kingdom and in the other Contracting States[347] where, for example, a judgment was given in New Caledonia in respect of a matter within the scope of the Convention. The rules on recognition and enforcement under the Brussels Convention are significantly different from those of the Brussels I Regulation. The former are described fully in the previous edition of this book[348] and the reader is referred to what is said there for further details.

---

[336] Art 8.

[337] Art 9.

[338] Art 26(6)(b).

[339] As regards recognition and enforcement, there are amendments to Arts 50 (legal aid and decisions given by an administrative authority in Denmark in respect of maintenance), 62 (in matters relating to maintenance, court to include Danish administrative authorities), and 64 (notification of consular officer in certain disputes involving ships registered in Denmark), see Art 2(2) of the Agreement.

[340] See generally the discussion in the context of jurisdiction, supra, p 341.

[341] Art 10(2)(c) of the Agreement.

[342] This is to Art 50 (legal aid and decisions given by an administrative authority in Denmark in respect of maintenance), see Art 2(2)(b) of the Agreement. The other modifications are listed supra, p 341, n 1181.

[343] For transitional provisions concerning procedings instituted in the state of origin before the entry into force of of the Agreement see Art 9 of the Agreement.

[344] At the moment the Contracting States to the Brussels Convention are the original 15 Member States.

[345] Art 68(1). Territories are excluded from the Regulation pursuant to Art 299 of the EC Treaty.

[346] See Layton and Mercer, paras 11.061–11.071. See also Kruger, paras 1.026–1.037.

[347] At the moment the Contracting States are the original 15 European Community, Member States.

[348] See the 13th edn of this book (1999), pp 480–516. See also Briggs and Rees, paras 7.29–7.35; Dicey and Morris, (13th edn), paras 14R-183–14-229.

4. THE LUGANO CONVENTION

The 1988 Lugano Convention extended the free circulation of judgments beyond the European Community to what is left of the EFTA bloc (Iceland, Norway and Switzerland). It did this by means of a parallel Convention to the Brussels Convention, based closely on that Convention, albeit not identical to it. The 1988 Lugano Convention has been replaced by the 2007 Lugano Convention,[349] the terms of which have been aligned with the Brussels I Regulation. The states bound by the Convention are the twenty-seven European Community Member States and the three EFTA States (Iceland, Norway and Switzerland). The Lugano Convention has been examined earlier in the context of jurisdiction.[350] Some of the same issues that were discussed there need to be addressed now in relation to the recognition and enforcement of foreign judgments: when do the rules on recognition and enforcement under the Lugano Convention apply? What are the differences between the Lugano Convention and the Brussels I Regulation?

(a) When do the rules on recognition and enforcement under the Lugano Convention apply?[351]

The Lugano Convention applies in matters of recognition and enforcement, where either the state of origin or the state addressed is not applying the Brussels I Regulation, the Brussels Convention or the EC/Denmark Agreement,[352] but is, of course, bound by the Lugano Convention. Thus if a United Kingdom court is asked to recognise a Swiss, Norwegian or Icelandic judgment, or vice versa, the Lugano Convention will apply. If both states are members of EFTA, the Lugano Convention will also apply. The Lugano Convention provides that the Brussels I Regulation, the Brussels Convention and the EC/Denmark Agreement continue to apply, unaffected by the Convention.[353] Thus if a United Kingdom court is asked to recognise a French judgment, the Brussels I Regulation will apply.

(b) Differences between the Lugano Convention and Brussels I Regulation

The alignment of the Lugano Convention with the Brussels I Regulation has resulted in a close similarity between the two. Nonetheless, there are a number of differences in substance, most of which can be traced back to provisions in the 1988 Lugano Convention.

First, the Lugano Convention provides that Contracting Parties can enter into Conventions with third states incorporating Article 59 of the Brussels Convention type obligation.[354] There is no such provision in the Regulation.[355] The power to enter into the let-out in the

---

[349] OJ 2007 L 339/3, Art 69(6).

[350] Supra, pp 342–346.

[351] Where recognition or enforcement is sought, the Convention applies only to proceedings instituted after its entry into force in the state of origin and in the state addressed: Art 63(1). However, if proceedings in the state of origin were instituted before this date, judgments given after that date will still be recognised under the Convention if certain conditions are met: Art 63(2).

[352] Art 64(2)(c) of the Lugano Convention.

[353] Art 64(1) of the Lugano Convention.

[354] Art 68(1) of the Lugano Convention. Art 59 of the Brussels Convention is discussed supra, p 636.

[355] Art 72 of the Regulation; discussed supra, pp 626–627.

future was present in the 1988 Lugano Convention,[356] which was based on the Brussels Convention, and is retained in the 2007 Lugano Convention. This is not as big a difference from the Regulation as it might appear. The Contracting Parties to the Convention are the three EFTA States, Denmark and the European Community, not the individual European Community Member States. Moreover, the European Council and Commission can negotiate international agreements that would mitigate the consequences of Chapter III (Recognition and Enforcement) of the Brussels I Regulation in third states.[357] The let-out allowed in the Lugano Convention is a narrow one. It only applies to the exorbitant bases of jurisdiction listed in the Convention. This does not include jurisdiction under rule 6.20 of the Civil Procedure Rules. Moreover, there is an additional limitation on its use. In broad terms, it cannot apply where jurisdiction is based on the presence of the defendant's property in the forum and the action relates to this property.[358]

Secondly, there is an additional defence in Article 64(3) of the Lugano Convention.[359] This was introduced in the 1988 Convention[360] and arose because of a concern raised by EFTA States. It has then been repeated in the 2007 Convention. Article 64(3), contains a discretionary power[361] to refuse to recognise or enforce a judgment "if the ground of jurisdiction on which the judgment has been made differs from that resulting from this Convention". This is designed to deal with the situation where a European Community State takes jurisdiction under a differently worded provision of the Brussels I Regulation, Brussels Convention or Danish Agreement, when it should have taken jurisdiction under the Lugano Convention.[362] With the alignment of the Lugano Convention with the Brussels I Regulation this will very seldom happen but could do so in a case involving maintenance.[363] The defence only applies where recognition or enforcement is sought against a party domiciled in a state where the Lugano Convention applies but not the Brussels I Regulation, Brussels Convention or Danish Agreement; ie an Icelandic, Norwegian or Swiss domiciliary. The defence will not apply if the judgment "may otherwise be recognised or enforced under any rule of law in the State addressed", ie under its common law rules.

Thirdly, there is a further additional defence under Article 67(4),[364] which is concerned with the situation where jurisdiction has been taken under a convention on a particular matter, eg the Warsaw Convention on international carriage by air of 1929. When negotiating the 1988 Lugano Convention, the EFTA States would not agree to the open system that then operated under Article 57 of the Brussels Convention[365] (the predecessor of Article 71 of the Brussels I Regulation[366]). A safeguard was accordingly introduced and this has been

---

356 Art 59 of the 1988 Lugano Convention.

357 See the Joint Statement by the Council and the Commission on Arts 71 and 72 of the Brussels I Regulation; supra, p 636.

358 Art 68(2) of the Lugano Convention.

359 See generally Art 35(1) of the Lugano Convention.

360 Art 54(B)(3) of the 1988 Lugano Convention. It was not in the Brussels Convention.

361 See Case C-80/00 *Italian Leather SpA v WECO Polstermobel GmbH & Co* [2002] ECR I-4995 at 5027, [51].

362 See the Jenard and Moller Report, p 68, for the purpose of the predecessor provision in the 1988 Lugano Convention (Art 54B(3) of that Convention).

363 Supra, p 345.

364 See generally Art 35(1) of the Lugano Convention.

365 See the Jenard and Moller Report, p 92.

366 Discussed supra, p 600.

repeated in the 2007 Lugano Convention. Article 67(4) of the 2007 Convention provides a discretionary power to refuse to recognise or enforce a judgment if the state addressed is not bound by the convention under which jurisdiction is asserted and the person against whom recognition or enforcement is sought is domiciled in that state. This defence does not operate solely for the benefit of domiciliaries of the EFTA States; a judgment granted in an EFTA State could be denied recognition in a European Community State on this ground. The 2007 Lugano Convention has introduced additional wording, not to be found in the 1988 Convention, to deal with the situation where the convention on a particular matter is one which would have to be concluded by the European Community.[367] In this situation, the defence applies where the state addressed is a Member State of the European Community, is not bound by the convention which would have to be concluded by the European Community, and the defendant is domiciled in any European Community Member State. Again, the defence will not apply if the judgment may otherwise be recognised or enforced under any rule of law in the state addressed.

Fourthly,[368] Switzerland reserves the right to declare upon ratification that it will not apply the proviso in the natural justice defence in Article 34(2) of the Convention, which says "unless the defendant failed to commence proceedings to challenge the judgment when it was posssible for him to do so".[369] If Switzerland makes such a declaration, the other Contracting Parties must apply the same reservation in respect of judgments granted in Switzerland.[370]

5. THE EUROPEAN ENFORCEMENT ORDER REGULATION

Where there is a judgment, court settlement or authentic instrument on an uncontested claim,[371] the creditor, as an alternative to seeking recognition and enforcement under the Brussels I Regulation,[372] can seek this under the European Enforcement Order Regulation (Regulation (EC) No 805/2004 creating a European Enforcement Order for uncontested claims),[373] which applies[374] in all the European Community Member States

---

[367] The individual European Community Member States no longer have power to conclude conventions which in particular matters govern jurisdiction or the recognition or enforcement of judgments, see supra, pp 600–601.

[368] There is a fifth difference which concerns decisions in Denmark, Iceland or Norway in respect of maintenance and legal aid: Art 50(2) of the Lugano Convention. There was a similar provision in the 1988 Lugano Convention.

[369] Protocol 1, Art III(1) attached to the Lugano Convention. Art 34(2) of Lugano follows Art 34(2) of the Brussels I Regulation discussed supra, pp 615–622. This proviso was not in the 1988 Lugano Convention (Art 27(2)). Other Contracting Parties can make the same reservation in respect of judgments granted in non-European Community/EFTA States which have acceded to the Lugano Convention: Protocol 1, Art III(2).

[370] Protocol 1, Art III(1).

[371] For obtaining such a judgment see, in relation to claims in relation to uncontested debts, the Proposal for a Regulation creating a European order for payment procedure COM (2004) 173 final, p 3.

[372] Art 27 of the European Enforcement Order Regulation.

[373] OJ 2004 L 143/15. See also the Commission's Proposal for the Council Regulation: Brussels, 18 April 2002 COM (2002) 159 final. For commentaries see Briggs and Rees, paras 7.25–7.28; Dicey, Morris and Collins, paras 14-229–14-234. For English procedural rules see CPR, Part 74, Section V and CPR, PD 74B.

[374] The Regulation entered into force on 21 January 2004 and applies from 21 October 2005: Art 33. For a transitional provision see Art 26.

with the exception of Denmark.[375] The Regulation, like the Brussels I Regulation, is one of the measures[376] relating to judicial co-operation in civil matters that are regarded as being necessary for the proper functioning of the internal market.[377] The advantage in using the former as compared with the exequatur procedure under the latter is that it permits the free circulation of judgments, etc throughout the Member States without any intermediate proceedings needing to be brought in the Member State of enforcement prior to recognition and enforcement.[378] The creation of a European Enforcement Order for uncontested claims is the first stage in a programme[379] of measures for implementation of the principle of mutual recognition of decisions in civil and commercial matters.[380]

(a) Subject matter, scope and definitions

The purpose of the Regulation is to create a European Enforcement Order for uncontested claims[381] to permit, by laying down minimum standards, the free circulation of judgments,[382] court settlements and authentic instruments[383] throughout all Member States without any intermediate proceedings needing to be brought in the Member State of enforcement[384] prior to recognition and enforcement.[385] The scope of the Regulation is virtually the same as that of the Brussels I Regulation.[386] A claim is regarded as uncontested in four alternative situations:[387] the debtor has expressly agreed to it by admission or by means of a settlement;[388] or the debtor has never objected to the claim in the course of the court proceedings;[389] or the debtor has not appeared or been represented at a court hearing regarding that claim after having initially objected to the claim in the course of the court proceedings;[390] or the debtor has expressly agreed to the claim in an authentic instrument.[391]

(b) European enforcement order

The Regulation is concerned that a judgment that has been certified as a European Enforcement Order by the court of origin[392] should, for enforcement purposes, be treated as if it had been delivered in the Member State in which enforcement is sought.[393] Article

---

[375] Art 2(3).

[376] See for these measures supra, p 204.

[377] Recital (1) of the Regulation. See also Art 61(c) of the Treaty establishing the European Community.

[378] Recital (9) and Art 1.

[379] Adopted by the European Council on 30th November 2000, OJ 2001 C 12/1; discussed infra, p 649.

[380] Recital (4).

[381] "Claim" is defined in Art 4(2).

[382] As defined in Art 4(1).

[383] As defined in Art 4(3).

[384] As defined in Art 4(5).

[385] Art 1.

[386] Art 2. There is one additional exclusion, namely "the liability of the State for acts and omissions in the exercise of State authority ('acta iure imperii')". For the scope of the Brussels I Regulation see supra, pp 213–222.

[387] Art 3(1).

[388] Art 3(1)(a).

[389] Art 3(1)(b).

[390] Art 3(1)(c).

[391] Art 3(1)(d).

[392] As defined in Art 4(6).

[393] Recital (8).

5 is headed "Abolition of exequatur" and provides that "A judgment which has been certified as a European Enforcement Order in the Member State of origin[394] shall be recognised and enforced without the need for a declaration of enforceability and without any possibility of opposing its recognition."

Article 6 then sets out the requirements for certification as a European Enforcement Order.[395] It states that a judgment on an uncontested claim delivered in a Member State shall, upon application at any time to the court of origin, be certified as a European Enforcement Order provided that certain conditions are met.[396] First, the judgment is enforceable in the Member State of origin. Secondly, the judgment does not conflict with the rules on jurisdiction in Sections 3 (matters relating to insurance)[397] and 6 (exclusive jurisdiction under Article 22)[398] of Chapter II of the Brussels I Regulation. Thirdly, the court proceedings in the Member State of origin met the minimum standards for uncontested claims procedures as set out in Chapter III of the Regulation.[399] Fourthly, in cases where the claim relates to a consumer contract[400] and the debtor is the consumer, the judgment was given in the Member State of the debtor's domicile.[401]

(c) Minimum standards for uncontested claims procedures

Where a court in a Member State has given judgment on an uncontested claim in the absence of participation of the debtor in the proceedings, there is an obvious concern that the debtor was not informed of the proceedings, or provided with due information about the claim or the procedural steps necessary to contest the claim.[402] Chapter III therefore lays down minimum standards in relation to these matters. These procedural requirements apply[403] where there is a judgment on a claim that is uncontested in the sense that the debtor has never objected to the claim in the course of the court proceedings[404] or has not appeared or been represented at a court hearing regarding that claim after having initially objected to the claim in the course of the court proceedings.[405] A judgment on a claim that is uncontested within either of the above two meanings can be certified as a European Enforcement Order only if the court proceedings in the Member State of origin met the procedural requirements as set out in Chapter III.[406] The court in the Member State of enforcement has no power to check that the procedural requirements in Chapter III

---

[394] As defined in Art 4(4).

[395] For issue of the European Enforcement Order Certificate see Art 9. For its rectification or withdrawal see Art 10.

[396] Art 6(1).

[397] Discussed supra, pp 266–268.

[398] Discussed supra, pp 275–283.

[399] This requirement only applies where the claim is uncontested within the meaning of Art 3(1)(b) (debtor has never objected to the claim) or (c) (debtor has not appeared or been represented).

[400] Ie it relates to a contract concluded by a person, the consumer, for a purpose which can be regarded as being outside his trade or profession: Art 6(1)(d).

[401] It is also required that the claim is uncontested within the meaning of Art 3(1)(b) or (c). Domicile is defined according to Art 59 of the Brussels I Regulation, discussed supra, p 210.

[402] Recitals (10)–(13).

[403] Art 12(1).

[404] Art 3(1)(b).

[405] Art 3(1)(c).

[406] Art 12(1).

have been met.[407] The check is carried out by the court of origin before certifying the judgment as a European Enforcement Order. There are differences between the Member States as regards the service of documents, Chapter III therefore sets out detailed provisions for the minimum standard for this.[408] The document instituting the proceedings may be served on the debtor by various methods where there is proof of receipt by the debtor.[409] This includes personal service attested by an acknowledgment of receipt, including the date of receipt, which is signed by the debtor.[410] Postal service[411] and service by electronic means such as fax or e-mail[412] is also permissible provided that, in both cases, it is attested by an acknowledgment of receipt. Service without proof of receipt by the debtor is also permissible in certain circumstances,[413] such as by personal service at the debtor's personal address on persons who are living in the same household[414] or by deposit of the document in the debtor's mailbox[415] or at a post office (with notification in the debtor's mailbox).[416] Service may also have been effected on a debtor's representative.[417] In order to ensure that the debtor was provided with due information about the claim, the document instituting the proceedings must have contained: the names and addresses of the parties; the amount of the claim; if interest is sought, the interest rate and period for which it is sought; a statement of the reason for the claim.[418] Certain specified information must also have been provided about the procedural steps necessary to contest the claim.[419] Non-compliance with all the minimum standards mentioned above can be cured and the judgment certified as a European Enforcement Order if certain requirements are met.[420] The judgment can only be certified as a European Enforcement Order if the law of the Member State of origin has minimum standards for review of the judgment in specified exceptional cases.[421]

(d) Enforcement

Enforcement procedures are governed by the law of the Member State of enforcement.[422] A judgment certified as a European Enforcement Order is enforced under the same conditions as a judgment handed down in the Member State of enforcement.[423] However, enforcement will, upon application by the debtor, be refused if the judgment certified as a European Enforcement Order is irreconcilable with an earlier judgment given in any Member State or in a third country.[424] This is subject to a number of provisos. First, the

---

[407] Recital (10).
[408] Recital (13).
[409] Art 13.
[410] Art 13(1)(a).
[411] Art 13(1)(c).
[412] Art 13(1)(d).
[413] Art 14.
[414] Art 14(1)(a).
[415] Art 14(1)(c).
[416] Art 14(1)(d).
[417] Art 15.
[418] Art 16.
[419] Art 17.
[420] Art 18.
[421] Art 19.
[422] Art 20(1).
[423] Ibid.
[424] Art 21(1).

earlier judgment involved the same cause of action and was between the same parties. Secondly, the earlier judgment was given in the Member State of enforcement or fulfils the conditions necessary for its recognition in that state. Thirdly, the irreconcilability was not and could not have been raised as an objection in the court proceedings in the Member State of origin. The Regulation does not affect agreements entered into pursuant to Article 59 of the Brussels Convention.[425] Under no circumstances may the judgment or its certification as a European Enforcement Order be reviewed as to their substance in the Member State of enforcement.[426] There are powers in certain limited circumstances to stay the enforcement proceedings or limit them to protective measures.[427]

6. THE EUROPEAN ORDER FOR PAYMENT PROCEDURE REGULATION

Regulation (EC) No 1896/2006[428] creates a European order for payment procedure, which is intended to ensure the swift and efficient recovery of outstanding debts over which no legal controversy exists. The Regulation applies[429] in all the European Community Member States with the exception of Denmark.[430] The Regulation, like the Brussels I Regulation, the European Enforcement Order Regulation and the European Small Claims Procedure Regulation, is one of the measures[431] relating to judicial co-operation in civil matters that are regarded as being necessary for the proper functioning of the internal market.[432] The European order for payment procedure is available to a claimant as an alternative to the procedure existing under the law of a Member State or under Community law.[433]

(a) Scope and definitions

The Regulation applies to civil and commercial matters[434] in cross-border cases.[435] A cross-border claim is defined as one in which at least one of the parties is domiciled[436] or habitually resident in a Member State other than the Member State of the court seised.[437] A number of matters are excluded from the scope of the Regulation. These include some

---

[425] Art 22. Such agreements are discussed supra, p 636.

[426] Art 21(2).

[427] Art 23.

[428] OJ 2006 L 399/1. See also the Commission Green Paper on Improving the Efficiency of the Enforcement of Judgments in the European Union: The Attachment of Bank Accounts, COM (2006) 618 final, 24 October 2006.

[429] The Regulation entered into force on 31 December 2006 and applies from 12 December 2008, with the exception of Arts 28–31 (Member States communicating information to the Commission), which apply from 12 June 2008.

[430] Art 2(3).

[431] See for these measures supra, p 204.

[432] Recital (1) of the Regulation. See also Art 61(c) of the Treaty establishing the European Community.

[433] Art 1(2).

[434] For the meaning of this concept see supra, pp 315–322. Art 2(1) of the European Order for Payment Procedure Regulation spells out that the Regulation does not apply to revenue, customs or administrative matters or to the liability of the state for acts and omissions in the exercise of state authority.

[435] Art 2(1).

[436] To be determined in accordance with Arts 59 and 60 of the Brussels I Regulation, supra, pp 210–213: Art 3(2) of the European Order for Payment Procedure Regulation.

[437] Art 3(1).

of the matters excluded from the scope of the Brussels I Regulation, namely rights of property arising out of a matrimonial relationship,[438] wills and succession,[439] bankruptcy, etc[440] and social security.[441] In addition, there is the exclusion of one matter that is not excluded from the scope of the Brussels I Regulation, that is claims arising from non-contractual obligations.[442]

(b) The European order for payment procedure

The European order for payment procedure has been "established for the collection of pecuniary claims for a specific amount that has fallen due at the time when the the application for a European order for payment is submitted".[443] For the purpose of applying the Regulation, jurisdiction is to be determined in accordance with the relevant rules of Community law, in particular the Brussels I Regulation.[444] In the situation where a claim for payment is brought against a consumer, only the courts of the Member State where the defendant is domiciled have jurisdiction.[445]

An application for a European order for payment is made using standard form A, which is set out in Annex I of the Regulation. The court seised of the application must examine, as soon as posssible and on the basis of the application form whether the requirements set out in the Regulation have been met and whether the claim appears to be founded.[446] If the answer is in the negative, the application will be rejected.[447] If, on the other hand, these requirements are met, the court will issue as soon as possible, and normally within thirty days of the lodging of an application, a European order for payment using standard form E as set out in Annex IV. The order will inform the defendant of his options, namely to pay or to oppose the order.[448] The court will ensure that the order is served on the defendant in accordance with national law by a method that meets the minimum standards laid down in the Regulation.[449] The defendant may lodge a statement of opposition to the European order for payment with the court of origin.[450] This must be sent within thirty days of service of the order on the defendant.[451] After the expiry of that time limit, the defendant is entitled, in exceptional cases, to apply for a review of the order

---

[438] Art 2(2)(a), for the meaning of this exclusion see Art 1(2) (a) of the Brussels I Regulation, discussed supra, pp 218–219.

[439] Art 2(2)(a), for the meaning of this exclusion see Art 1(2) (a) of the Brussels I Regulation, discussed supra, pp 218–219.

[440] Art 2(2)(b), for the meaning of this exclusion see Art 1(2) (b) of the Brussels I Regulation, discussed supra, p 219.

[441] Art 2(2)(c), for the meaning of this exclusion see Art 1(2) (c) of the Brussels I Regulation, discussed supra, p 220.

[442] Art 2(2) (d). The exclusion applies unless: (i) the claims have been the subject of an agreement between the parties or there has been an admission of debt, or (ii) they relate to liquidated debts arising from joint ownership of property.

[443] Art 4.

[444] Art 6(1).

[445] Art 6(2). This repeats Art 16(2) of the Brussels I Regulation. Under the latter Regulation, Art 16(2) can be departed from by an agreement on jurisdiction. This would not appear to be possible under Art 6.

[446] Art 8.

[447] Art 11.

[448] Art 12(3).

[449] Art 12(5). These minimum standards are laid down in Arts 13, 14 and 15 of the Regulation.

[450] Using standard form F as set out in Annex VI.

[451] Art 16(2).

before the competent court in the Member State of origin.[452] The defendant is so entitled where, inter alia, he was prevented from objecting to the claim by reason of force majeure or due to extraordinary circumstances without any fault on his part.[453]

(c) Recognition and enforcement in other Member States

A European order for payment which has become enforceable in the Member State of origin will be recognised and enforced in the other Member States without the need for a declaration of enforceability and without any possibility of opposing its recognition.[454] In other words, exequatur is abolished. There is, though, a defence to enforcement.[455] This is substantially the same as the irreconcilable judgments defence that is to be found in the European Enfocement Order Regulation.[456] The enforcement procedure is partly governed by the law of the Member State of enforcement and partly laid down by the Regulation.[457] Where the defendant has applied for a review,[458] the competent court in the Member State of enforcement may limit the enforcement proceedings to protective measures or, under exceptional circumstances, stay the enforcement proceedings.[459]

7. THE EUROPEAN SMALL CLAIMS PROCEDURE REGULATION

The European Small Claims Procedure Regulation (Regulation (EC) No 861/2007)[460] establishes a European procedure for small claims, which is intended to simplify and speed up litigation in cross-border cases and to reduce costs. The Regulation applies[461] in all the European Community Member States with the exception of Denmark.[462] The Regulation, like the Brussels I Regulation, the European Enforcement Order Regulation and the European Order for Payment Procedure Regulation, is one of the measures[463] relating to judicial co-operation in civil matters that are regarded as being necessary for the proper functioning of the internal market.[464] The European small claims procedure is available to litigants as an alternative to the procedures existing under the laws of Member States.[465]

---

[452] Art 20.
[453] Art 20(1)(b).
[454] Art 19.
[455] Art 22(1).
[456] See Art 21(1) of the European Enforcement Order Regulation; discussed supra, pp 643–644.
[457] Art 21.
[458] Under Art 20, supra.
[459] Art 23.
[460] OJ 2007 L 199/1.
[461] The Regulation entered into force on 1 August 2007 and applies from 1 January 2009, with the exception of Art 25 (Member States communicating information to the Commission), which applies from 1 January 2008.
[462] Art 2(3).
[463] See for these measures supra, p 204.
[464] Recital (1) of the Regulation. See also Art 61(c) of the Treaty establishing the European Community.
[465] Art 1.

(a) Scope and definitions

The Regulation applies in cross-border cases, to civil and commercial matters.[466] A cross-border claim is defined as one in which at least one of the parties is domiciled[467] or habitually resident in a Member State other than the Member State of the court or tribunal seised.[468] The Regulation is limited to where the value of the claim does not exceed 2,000 Euros.[469] However, it is not confined to consumer claims and can include commercial claims.[470] A number of matters are excluded from the scope of the Regulation. These are the same matters as are excluded from the scope of the Brussels I Regulation[471] plus four additional mattters which are not excluded from the latter. These are as follows: maintenance obligations;[472] employment law;[473] tenancies of immovable property, with the exception of actions on monetary claims;[474] violations of privacy and of rights relating to personality, including defamation.[475]

(b) The European small claims procedure

A claimant commences the European Small Claims Procedure by filling in a standard form (form A), which is set out in Annex I to the Regulation, and lodging it with the court or tribunal with jurisdiction[476] directly, by post or by any other means of communication, such as fax or e-mail, acceptable to the Member State in which the procedure is commenced.[477] The court or tribunal with jurisdiction must have jurisdiction "in accordance with the rules" in the Brussels I Regulation.[478] It is contemplated that, normally, this will be one of the bases of jurisdiction set out in that Regulation[479] but it could presumably also include a case where jurisdiction is taken under traditional national rules of jurisdiction, which Article 4 of the Brussels I Regulation instructs the courts of Member States to apply in the situation where the defendant is not domiciled in a Member State (and Articles 22 and 23 of that Regulation do not apply).[480] The European small claims procedure is a written one.[481] But the court or tribunal will hold an oral hearing if it considers this to be necessary or if a party so requests.[482] A copy of the claim form is served on

---

[466] Art 2. For the meaning of this concept see supra, pp 315–322. Art 2(1) spells out that the Regulation does not apply to revenue, customs or administrative matters or to the liability of the state for acts and omissions in the exercise of state authority.

[467] To be determined in accordance with Arts 59 and 60 of the Brussels I Regulation, supra, pp 210–213, Art 3(2) of the European Small Claims Procedure Regulation.

[468] Art 3(1).

[469] Art 2(1).

[470] See Recital (4).

[471] See Art 2(2)(a)–(e) of the European Small Claims Procedure Regulation, for the meaning of these exclusions see Art 1(2) of the Brussels I Regulation, discussed supra, pp 218–222.

[472] Art 2(2)(b) of the European Small Claims Procedure Regulation.

[473] Art 2(2) (f).

[474] Art 2(2)(g).

[475] Art 2(h). The meaning of this phrase is examined infra, pp 784–785.

[476] Member States must inform the Commission which courts or tribunals have jurisdiction to give a judgment in the European Small Claims Procedure: Art 25(1).

[477] Art 4(1). Member States must inform the Commission which means are acceptable to them: Art 4(2).

[478] See Annex I, form A, guideline 4.

[479] See box 4 in form A, which, in effect, sets out the bases of jurisdiction under the Brussels I Regulation.

[480] The list of bases of jurisdiction in box 4 includes "Other" bases (than those under the Regulation).

[481] Art 5(1).

[482] Ibid.

the defendant who must respond within thirty days by filling in standard answer form C, as set out in Annex III.[483] Within fourteen days a copy of this response is dispatched to the claimant.[484] The claimant has thirty days to respond to any counterclaim.[485] Within thirty days of the receipt of the response from the defendant or the claimant, the court or tribunal will give a judgment.[486] Member States must inform the Commission whether an appeal is available under their procedural law against a judgment given in the European small claims procedure.[487] A judgment is enforceable in the state in which it was given notwithstanding any possible appeal.[488] However, where a party has challenged a judgment given in the the European small claims procedure or where such a challenge is still possible, the court or tribunal with jurisdiction can limit the enforcement proceedings to protective measures or make enforcement conditional on the provision of such security as it shall determine or, under exceptional circumstances, stay the enforcement proceedings.[489] There are minimum standards for the review of a judgment in situations where the defendant was not able to contest the claim.[490]

(c) Recognition and enforcement in other Member States

A judgment given in a Member State in the European small claims procedure will be recognised and enforced in other Member States without the need for a declaration of enforceability and without any possibility of opposing its recognition.[491] Thus exequatur is abolished. There is, though, a defence to enforcement,[492] which is in substance the irreconcilable judgments defence that is to be found in the European Enforcement Order Regulation.[493] The enforcement procedure is partly governed by the law of the Member State of enforcement and partly laid down by the Regulation.[494] Where a party has challenged a judgment given in the European small claims procedure or where such a challenge is still possible, the competent authority in the Member State of enforcement may limit the enforcement proceedings to protective measures or, under exceptional circumstances, stay the enforcement proceedings.[495]

8. FUTURE DEVELOPMENTS

The European Council, meeting in Tampere in 1999, confirmed that mutual recognition of judicial decisions throughout the European Union is the cornerstone of judicial

---

[483] Art 5 (2) and (3).

[484] Art 5(4).

[485] Art 5(6).

[486] Art 7(1). Alternatively the court or tribunal can (a) demand further details or (b) take evidence or (c) summon the parties to an oral hearing.

[487] Art 17.

[488] Art 15(1).

[489] Arts 15(2) and 23.

[490] See Art 18.

[491] Art 20(1).

[492] Art 22(1).

[493] Se Art 21(1) of the European Enforcement Order Regulation; discussed supra, pp 643–644.

[494] Art 21. The court or tribunal giving the judgment issues a certificate using standard form D, as set out in Annex IV: Art 20(2). The party seeking enforcement produces a copy of this to the enforcing court: Art 21.

[495] Art 23.

co-operation. The present system under the Brussels I Regulation requires the court in the Member State in which enforcement is sought to make a declaration of enforceability. This leads to delays and there can even be a refusal to recognise and enforce the judgment granted in another Member State. A Programme on Mutual Recognition has been adopted[496] with the ultimate aim of getting rid of this system of "exequatur" so that judgments will not be treated differently or be subject to additional procedures because they were granted in another Member State. Priority was given to creating a European Enforcement Order for uncontested claims.[497] This was followed by the European Order for Payment Procedure Regulation and the European Small Claims Procedure Regulation, both of which have also abolished exequatur.

The European Enforcement Order for uncontested claims is a pilot project, and the first stage in a process leading to the eventual abolition of exequatur for all contested claims. The second stage will be the revision of the Brussels I Regulation. The Hess, Pfeiffer and Schlosser Report mentions a number of changes that could be made to improve the existing system.[498] These include reducing the grounds of non-recognition by abolishing Article 35 (examination of grounds of jurisdiction); amending the irreconcilable judgments defences under Article 34,[499] improving remedies; further simplification of the exequatur proceedings; giving binding effect to the certificate issued by the judgment-granting state.

The third stage envisaged in the Programme on Mutual Recognition will be the final abolition of exequatur under the Brussels I Regulation. The Hess, Pfeiffer and Schlosser Report discusses this possibility but sees it as an alternative to improving the present situation, rather than as a third stage.[500] The Report notes that, in the three Regulations where exequatur has been abolished, this has been replaced by a complementary procedural safeguard in the form of review proceedings being made available in the judgment-granting state.[501] The Report goes on, in the light of this, to discuss a posssible way in which the abolition of exequatur could operate under the Brussels I Regulation. This would involve the introduction of co-ordinated review procedures in the Member State of origin and in the Member State of enforcement. Redress against fraud and procedural irregularity would be mainly centred in the judgment-granting Member State. However, if such means of redress do not exist or are not sufficiently efficient, the debtor may request the refusal of enforcement in the Member State of enforcement. In addition there would be a limited recourse to a public policy defence in extreme cases. There would also be a need for the partial harmonisation of the procedural law in Member States.

---

[496] See OJ 2001 C 12/1; for the background to this, see Kennett, *Enforcement of Judgments in Europe* (2000 OUP) Chapters 1 and 2. See also the Hague Programme: Strengthening Freedom, Security and Justice in the European Union (OJ 2005 C 53/1 at 3.4.2), adopted by the European Council in November 2004, and the Council and Commission Action Plan Implementing the Hague Programme (OJ 2005 C198/1 at 4.3).

[497] Discussed supra, pp 640–644.

[498] Study JLS/C4/2005/03, Final Version September 2007, available at the European Commission— European Judicial Network—what's new website http://ec.europa.eu/civiljustice/news/whatsnew_en.htm. See paras 901–902.

[499] Supra, pp 622–625.

[500] At para 900.

[501] At paras 903–905.

Chapter 17

Foreign Arbitral Awards[1]

A foreign arbitral award is on a similar footing to a foreign judgment in that it may be enforced in England in a variety of ways. An action may be brought at common law to recover the sum awarded. Statutory provision is also made for the enforcement of foreign arbitral awards. Before looking at the various methods of enforcement in detail one general point should be made. The Limitation Act 1980 provides that an action to enforce an award "shall not be brought after the expiration of six years from the date on which the cause of action accrued".[2] This provision applies regardless of the method of enforcement.[3] It has been held that an action to enforce an arbitration award is an independent cause of action.[4] Accordingly, time runs, not from the date of the original breach of contract which had been the subject of the arbitration, but from the date of the failure to honour the arbitration award.[5]

---

[1] Mustill and Boyd, *Commercial Arbitration* (1989) 2nd edn, pp 421–427 and Companion Volume 2001; Redfern and Hunter, *International Commercial Arbitration* (2004) 4th edn, Chapter 2; Hill, Chapter 25; Dicey, Morris and Collins, paras 16-095–16-183.

[2] S 7. This section does not apply where the submission is by an instrument under seal.

[3] *Minister of Public Works of the Government of the State of Kuwait v Sir Frederick Snow & Partners* [1983] 1 WLR 818 at 823–824, CA, see the obiter dicta by KERR LJ; the House of Lords affirmed this decision, without discussing this point [1984] 1 AC 426.

[4] *Agromet Motoimport v Maulden Engineering Co (Beds) Ltd* [1985] 1 WLR 762.

[5] Ibid. See also *Good Challenger Navegante SA v Metalexportimport SA (The Good Challenger)* [2003] EWCA Civ 1668, [2004] 1 Lloyd's Rep 67.

Also, if a foreign award has been entered as a judgment abroad, it seems that this not only can[6] but must be enforced under the rules on enforcement of judgments (provided it is capable of being so enforced) and not as an award.[7]

1. ENFORCEMENT AT COMMON LAW

The basic elements for the successful enforcement of a foreign arbitration award in England are that the parties submitted to arbitration, that the arbitration was conducted in accordance with the submission and that the award is both final and valid by the law of the country in which it was made.[8]

There must be a valid submission to arbitration; the validity of such agreement is determined by the proper law of the arbitration agreement.[9] This law will also determine whether the arbitration agreement has been rendered void by subsequent illegality.[10] The proper law of the arbitration agreement is usually the same as the law governing the contract as a whole.[11] The parties can choose the law governing the contract (or indeed the arbitration itself); in the absence of an express choice there is a strong inference that the contract (and thus the arbitration agreement) is governed by the law of the place where the arbitration is to take place.[12] The actual arbitration proceedings, in the absence of an express choice of the law to govern the arbitration proceedings,[13] will be governed by the law of the place of arbitration.[14] That law will determine whether the award is valid;[15] though whether the arbitrator has jurisdiction is a matter for the arbitration agreement and its proper law.[16] The award, to be enforceable in England, must, like a foreign judgment, be final and conclusive.[17] However, the fact that the foreign award is not enforceable in the place where it was made until it has been confirmed by a court probably does not prevent its enforcement in England, provided the law of the place of arbitration regarded the award as final.[18] One justification for this conclusion is that the action in

---

[6] See, eg, *East India Trading Co Inc v Carmel Exporters and Importers Ltd* [1952] 2 QB 439; *International Alltex Corp v Lawler Creations Ltd* [1965] IR 264.

[7] S 34 of the Civil Jurisdiction and Judgments Act 1982; supra, p 544. Cf Dicey, Morris and Collins, paras 16-105, 16-106. In Australia the common law non-merger rule still applies: *Brali v Hyundai Corpn* (1988) 15 NSWLR 734. For the situation where the award has not been entered as a judgment see *Trade Fortune Inc v Amalgamated Mill Supplies Ltd* [1995] IL Pr 370, SC of BC; Hill, paras 23.6.12–23.6.13; Dicey, Morris and Collins, para 16-104.

[8] *Norske Atlas Insurance Co Ltd v London General Insurance Co Ltd* (1927) 43 TLR 541.

[9] *Dalmia Dairy Industries Ltd v National Bank of Pakistan* [1978] 2 Lloyd's Rep 223. This is not affected by the Rome Convention, see Art 1(2)(d), infra, pp 684–685.

[10] *Dalmia Dairy Industries Ltd v National Bank of Pakistan* [1978] 2 Lloyd's Rep 223.

[11] *Black-Clawson International Ltd v Papierwerke Waldhof-Aschaffenburg AG* [1981] 1 Lloyd's Rep 446 at 455. For the law governing the contract as a whole reference now has to be made to the Rome Convention, infra, pp 667–764.

[12] Infra, pp 701–703.

[13] *International Tank and Pipe SAK v Kuwait Aviation Fuelling Co KSC* [1975] QB 224 at 232–233. See also *Naviera Amazonica Peruvia Sa v Cia International de Seguros del Peru* [1988] 1 Lloyd's Rep 116 at 119.

[14] *James Miller & Partners Ltd v Whitworth Street Estates (Manchester) Ltd* [1970] AC 583; *Dalmia Dairy Industries Ltd v National Bank of Pakistan* [1978] 2 Lloyd's Rep 223.

[15] *Norske Atlas Insurance Co Ltd v London General Insurance Co Ltd* (1927) 43 TLR 541.

[16] *Dalmia Dairy Industries Ltd v National Bank of Pakistan* [1978] 2 Lloyd's Rep 223.

[17] Ibid, at 246–250.

[18] Cf *Union Nationale des Cooperatives Agricoles de Céréales v R Catterall & Co Ltd* [1959] 2 QB 44; *Dalmia Dairy Industries Ltd v National Bank of Pakistan*, supra, at 249–250.

England to enforce the award is an action on the award and not on either the contract to which the award gives effect,[19] or on a foreign judgment. If the foreign arbitral award includes an award of interest, the English court in an action on the award will not make a further award of interest at a higher rate.[20]

It is suggested,[21] though there are few reported decisions, that the recognition or enforcement of a foreign arbitral award may be subject to the obvious defences that the arbitrator lacked jurisdiction,[22] that the award was obtained by fraud,[23] that its recognition or enforcement would be contrary to English public policy[24] or that it was obtained in proceedings which contravene the rules of natural justice.[25]

A foreign arbitral award which does not fall within the various statutory provisions for recognition and enforcement based on international conventions[26] may be enforced either by an action on the award at common law,[27] or by recourse to section 66 of the Arbitration Act 1996, which provides that, with leave of the court, an award may be enforced in the same manner as a judgment or order of the court to the same effect. This discretionary procedure is not restricted to domestic English awards but is available for the enforcement of foreign awards,[28] though the award will have to satisfy the other requirements for enforcement in the 1996 Act.[29] Leave to enforce an award will not be given where the tribunal lacked substantive jurisdiction to make the award.[30] It will also have to be enforceable here in the same manner as a judgment and, whilst it is possible for an award in foreign currency to be enforced in England,[31] it is not possible for an award for a sum to be paid in a foreign country to be enforced here under section 66 of the 1996 Act, though such an award will still be enforceable by action at common law.[32] In the case of a purely domestic award it has been suggested that the discretion under section 66 should be exercised to allow enforcement in nearly all cases, ie unless there is real ground for doubting the validity of the award.[33]

---

[19] *Norske Atlas Insurance Co Ltd v London General Insurance Co Ltd*, supra.

[20] *Dalmia Dairy Industries Ltd v National Bank of Pakistan* supra, at 272–275, 301–303.

[21] See Dicey, Morris and Collins, 16R-118–16-123.

[22] *Dalmia Dairy Industries Ltd v National Bank of Pakistan*, supra; and see *Kianta Osakeyhtio v Britain and Overseas Trading Co Ltd* [1954] 1 Lloyd's Rep 247.

[23] *Oppenheim & Co v Mahomed Haneef* [1922] 1 AC 482 at 487.

[24] *Hamlyn & Co v Talisker Distillery* [1894] AC 202 at 209, 214; *Dalmia Dairy Industries Ltd v National Bank of Pakistan*, supra, at 267–269, 299–301.

[25] Cf *Dalmia Dairy Industries Ltd v National Bank of Pakistan*, supra, at 269–270.

[26] Infra, pp 654–661.

[27] CPR, r 6.20(9) (formerly Ord 11, r1(1)(m) RSC) was introduced, inter alia, to provide jurisdiction in such cases, see supra, p 391.

[28] *Dalmia Cement Ltd v National Bank of Pakistan* [1975] QB 9.

[29] Such as the arbitration agreement being in writing; 1996 Act, s 5; on which see infra, p 655, n 49.

[30] 1996 Act, s 66(3). The defences of public policy and that the matter is not capable of settlement by arbitrators apply to s 81(a) and (c).

[31] *Jugoslovenska Oceanska Plovidba v Castle Investment Co Inc* [1974] QB 292; *Dalmia Cement Ltd v National Bank of Pakistan*, supra, at 23–26; and see *Miliangos v George Frank (Textiles) Ltd* [1976] AC 443, supra, pp 102–104; Law Com No 124 (1983), paras 2.44–2.47 which makes no recommendations for change in the law on this point.

[32] See *Dalmia Cement Ltd v National Bank of Pakistan* [1975] QB 9 at 23–27.

[33] *Middlemiss and Gould v Hartlepool Corpn* [1972] 1 WLR 1643 at 1647; cf *Re Boks & Co and Peters, Rushton & Co Ltd* [1919] 1 KB 491 at 497. A freezing injunction and disclosures order can be granted in aid of enforcement of a domestic award: *Gidrxslme Shipping Co Ltd v Tantomar-Transportes Maritimos Ltd* [1995] 1 WLR 299.

Where enforcement of a foreign arbitral award is in issue, the discretion is likely to be exercised with considerably more caution.[34]

2. ENFORCEMENT UNDER THE CIVIL JURISDICTION AND JUDGMENTS ACT 1982

Foreign arbitral awards and judgments of courts incorporating such awards are not enforceable under the Brussels/Lugano system.[35] Thus, to take an example, an arbitral award granted in France cannot be enforced in the United Kingdom under the Brussels I Regulation. However, an arbitration award granted in one part of the United Kingdom can be enforced in another part under the Civil Jurisdiction and Judgments Act 1982. As has already been seen,[36] enforcement in one part of the United Kingdom of a judgment[37] obtained in another part of the United Kingdom is dealt with by section 18 of the Civil Jurisdiction and Judgments Act 1982, which provides for a system of registration of United Kingdom judgments and allows very few defences to enforcement. Section 18 defines a "judgment" very widely and includes "an arbitration award which has become enforceable in the part of the United Kingdom in which it was given in the same manner as a judgment given by a court of law in that part".[38] It should, however, be noted that, unlike other forms of judgment, an arbitration award obtained in the United Kingdom does not have to be enforced under section 18.[39] It is still possible for a claimant, if he so chooses, to seek enforcement of the arbitration award at common law or by recourse to section 66 of the Arbitration Act 1996.[40] It should also be noted that section 19 of the 1982 Act, which deals with recognition of United Kingdom judgments, does not apply to arbitration awards.[41]

3. ENFORCEMENT UNDER THE ARBITRATION ACT 1950

Provision is made for the enforcement of certain foreign arbitral awards by Part II of the Arbitration Act 1950, which Act consolidates the Arbitration Acts 1889 to 1934. The background to this provision is afforded by a Protocol of 1923 and a Convention of 1927, both of which were signed by the United Kingdom at Geneva. The former deals with the international validity of arbitration agreements, the latter with the enforcement in one country of arbitral awards made in another. Part II of the Arbitration Act 1950

---

[34] *Dalmia Cement Ltd v National Bank of Pakistan* [1975] QB 9 at 14–15, 23; and see *Union Nationale des Cooperatives Agricoles de Céréales v Catterall* [1959] 2 QB 44 at 52 (an award enforceable under Part II of the 1950 Act, infra).

[35] Supra, p 220. See generally Hascher (1996) 12 Arb Int 233. As regards judgments incorporating awards (as under s 66 of the 1996 Act) see *ABCI v BFT* [1996] 1 Lloyd's Rep 485; affd [1997] 1 Lloyd's Rep 531, CA; the Schlosser Report, para 65; cf Schmitthoff (1987) 24 CMLR 143 at 154–155.

[36] Supra, pp 574–576.

[37] The judgment may concern money provisions (Sch 6 of the 1982 Act) or non-money provisions (Sch 7 to the 1982 Act).

[38] S 18(2)(e).

[39] See s 18(8).

[40] Supra, pp 653–654.

[41] S 19(3)(b).

applies to foreign arbitral awards[42] made in pursuance of an arbitration agreement to which the 1923 Protocol applies[43] and made between persons who are subject to the jurisdiction of different countries, both of which, by reason of their reciprocal provisions, have been declared by Order in Council to be parties to the 1927 Convention. The award must also have been made in such a country.[44] Part II of the 1950 Act will seldom operate. Most states which were parties to the Geneva Convention subsequently became parties to the New York Convention,[45] and enforcement is then dealt with under the latter.

4. ENFORCEMENT UNDER THE ARBITRATION ACT 1996

The Arbitration Act 1975[46] enabled the United Kingdom to accede to the New York Convention on the Recognition and Enforcement of Foreign Arbitral Awards 1958. The 1975 Act has been repealed and replaced by Part III of the Arbitration Act 1996 which, by and large, is to the same effect.[47] The 1996 Act provides for the recognition and enforcement in the United Kingdom of "New York Convention awards", ie awards[48] made, in pursuance of a written[49] arbitration agreement,[50] in a foreign country which is a party to the New York Convention.[51] If it is declared by Order in Council[52] that a state is a party to the New York Convention, or is a party in respect of any territory so specified, this is to be conclusive evidence of that fact.[53] The relevant date for ascertaining whether a foreign country is a party to the Convention is the date when proceedings to enforce an award are begun.[54] If a state is a party to the New York Convention at that date,

---

[42] But not to awards made under an arbitration agreement governed by English law: s 40(b), or New York Convention awards, infra, pp 655–661; see the Arbitration Act 1996, s 99.

[43] Arbitration Act 1950, Sch 1, para 1.

[44] Arbitration Act 1950, ss 35(1).

[45] For the few states which are parties to the Geneva Convention but not to the New York Convention see Dicey, Morris and Collins, para 16-096. The New York Convention is discussed infra, pp 655–661.

[46] See Lew (1975) 24 ICLQ 870; Thomas [1992] CJQ 352. The 1975 Act applied to awards made before the Act came into force: *Minister of Public Works of the Government of the State of Kuwait v Sir Frederick Snow & Partners* [1984] AC 426.

[47] See the Departmental Advisory Committee (DAC) Report on the Arbitration Bill (1996).

[48] This does not include an interlocutory order: *Resort Condominiums International Inc v Bolwell* (1994) 118 ALR 655; nor a judgment of the Sharia Council of Great Britain: *Al-Midani v Al-Midani* [1999] 1 Lloyd's Rep 923. An award can be enforced in part: *ACN 006 397 413 Pty Ltd v International Movie Group (Canada) Inc* [1997] 2 VR 31. If the award includes an order for costs, this is also enforceable under the Convention, see *Bank Mellat v Helliniki Techniki SA* [1984] QB 291 at 308.

[49] The requirement of writing is satisfied if the agreement is made in writing, by exchange of communications in writing, or evidenced in writing, or the parties agree by reference to terms which are in writing: s 5 of the 1996 Act.

[50] 1996 Act, s 100(2). See *Dardana Ltd v Yukos Oil Co* [2002] EWCA Civ 543, [2002] 2 Lloyd's Rep 326, CA.

[51] S 100(1).

[52] See SI 1984/168; SI 1989/1348; SI 1993/1256.

[53] 1996 Act, s 100(3); other evidence may be given to show that a state is a party to the Convention, see *Government of the State of Kuwait v Sir Frederick Snow & Partners* [1981] 1 Lloyd's Rep 656 at 666; overruled by the Court of Appeal and House of Lords on another point [1984] AC 426. Cf the 1950 Act which only applies if persons are "subject to the jurisdiction" of different states, supra.

[54] *Minister of Public Works of the Government of the State of Kuwait v Sir Frederick Snow & Partners* [1984] AC 426. Cf the position under the Arbitration Act 1950, s 35; the Foreign Judgments (Reciprocal Enforcement) Act 1933, s 1(2)(c) (as amended by the Civil Jurisdiction and Judgments Act 1982, Sch 10, para 1(2)).

an arbitration award made in that state will be a New York Convention award (provided, of course, that the award was made in pursuance of a written arbitration agreement), even though the state was not a party at the date when the arbitration award was made.[55] An award is treated as "made" at the seat of the arbitration, regardless of where it was signed, despatched or delivered to any of the parties.[56] Moreover, unless otherwise agreed by the parties, where the seat of the arbitration is in England and Wales or Northern Ireland, any award in the proceedings shall be treated as made there, regardless of where it was signed, despatched or delivered to any of the parties.[57] The "seat of the arbitration" means the juridical seat of the arbitration.[58] This can be designated by the parties to the arbitration agreement, any institution or person authorised by the parties, or the arbitral tribunal if authorised by the parties.[59] In the absence of any such designations, it is determined having regard to the parties' agreement and all the relevant circumstances.[60] This ensures that, as far as English law is concerned, every arbitration has a seat.

A New York Convention award may, by leave of the court, be enforced in the same manner as a judgment or order of the court[61] to the same effect.[62] Where leave is so given,[63] judgment may be entered in terms of the award.[64] The granting of leave is subject to the discretion of the court, which may be exercised with caution in the case of foreign awards.[65]

A New York Convention award is recognised as binding on the persons as between whom it was made, and may accordingly be relied on by these persons by way of defence, set off or otherwise in any legal proceedings in the United Kingdom.[66] In order for an award to be recognised or enforced the person wishing to do so merely has to produce the award and the original arbitration agreement, or certified copies, and a certified translation if either is in a foreign language.[67]

---

[55] *Minister of Public Works of the Government of the State of Kuwait v Sir Frederick Snow & Partners*, supra.

[56] 1996 Act, s 100(2)(b); overturning the principle in *Hiscox v Outhwaite* [1992] 1 AC 562, HL; Davidson (1992) 41 ICLQ 637; Reymond (1992) 108 LQR 1; Mann (1992) 108 LQR 6.

[57] 1996 Act, s 53, dealing specifically with the situation that arose in the *Hiscox* case. The result would now be different if the facts of that case arose.

[58] 1996 Act, s 3.

[59] Ibid.

[60] Ibid.

[61] S 105.

[62] S 101(2). For security for costs in enforecement proceedings, see *Gater Assets Ltd v Nak Naftogaz Ukrainiy* [2007] EWCA Civ 988, [2007] 2 Lloyd's Rep 588; *Dardana Ltd v Yukos Oil Co* [2002] 2 Lloyd's Rep 261.

[63] For the principles on extension of time to challenge the granting of leave, see *Soinco SACI v Novokuznetsk Aluminium Plant* [1998] 2 Lloyd's Rep 337, CA.

[64] 1996 Act, s 101(3). The judgment is treated like any other judgment; in principle the court can grant a stay of execution but in practice will rarely if ever do so: *Far Eastern Shipping Co v AKP Sovcomflot* [1995] 1 Lloyd's Rep 520.

[65] See *Dalmia Cement Ltd v National Bank of Pakistan* [1975] QB 9 at 23, supra, pp 653–654.

[66] 1996 Act, s 101(1).

[67] S 102.

There are, however, a number of grounds on which the defendant may resist recognition or enforcement.[68] The court has a discretion[69] to refuse enforcement if the defendant proves any of the following:[70]

(a) that a party to the arbitration agreement was under some incapacity.[71] The question of capacity is to be governed by the law applicable to that party under English contract choice of law rules. Furthermore, enforcement of the award can be refused whichever party to the arbitration agreement lacked capacity;

(b) that the arbitration agreement was invalid[72] under the law to which the parties subjected it, ie the law chosen by the parties.[73] Failing any indication of such law, validity is to be determined by the law of the country where the award was made;[74]

(c) that the defendant was not given proper notice of the appointment of the arbitrator or of the arbitration proceedings or was otherwise unable to present his case;[75]

(d) that the award deals with a difference not contemplated by or not falling within the terms of the submission to arbitration or contains matters beyond the scope of the submission to arbitration;[76]

(e) that the composition of the arbitral tribunal or the arbitral procedure was not in accordance with the agreement of the parties[77] or, failing such agreement, with the law of the country where the arbitration took place. It can be assumed from this defence that the parties are free to choose the procedural law to govern the arbitration and that, in the absence of choice, the curial law will be that of the country where the arbitration took place;

(f) that the award has not yet become binding on the parties, or has been set aside or suspended by a competent authority of the country in which, or under the law of

---

[68] The grounds listed in the 1996 Act, s 102 are the only ones available: s 103(1).

[69] See *China Agribusiness Development Corpn v Balli Trading* [1998] 2 Lloyd's Rep 76; *Dardana Ltd v Yukos Oil Co* [2002] EWCA Civ 543 at [8] and [18], [2002] 2 Lloyd's Rep 326, CA; *Svenska AB v Republic of Lithuania* [2005] EWHC 9 (Comm) at [27], [2005] 1 Lloyd's Rep 515.

[70] 1996 Act, s 103(2); the reasons for an award can be referred to in order to ascertain whether any of the circumstances under this section apply, see *Mutual Shipping Corpn of New York v Bayshore Shipping Co of Monrovia, The Montan* [1985] 1 WLR 625 at 631. As to the burden of proof, see *Dalmia Dairy Industries Ltd v National Bank of Pakistan* [1978] 2 Lloyd's Rep 223 at 238.

[71] *Irvani v Irvani* [2000] 1 Lloyd's Rep 412 at 423–425, CA.

[72] See *Dallal v Bank Mellat* [1986] QB 441 at 455–456; Kunzlik [1986] CLJ 377; *Irvani v Irvani* [2000] 1 Lloyd's Rep 412 at 425, CA. Proof that a person against whom recognition is invoked was not a party to the arbitration agreement falls within this provision: *Dardana Ltd v Yukos Oil Co* [2002] EWCA Civ 543 at [8], [2002] 2 Lloyd's Rep 326, CA; *Svenska AB v Republic of Lithuania* [2005] EWHC 9 (Comm) at [7], [2005] 1 Lloyd's Rep 515. This may include continuing, as well as initial, validity: *Dalmia Dairy Industries Ltd v National Bank of Pakistan*, supra, at 238.

[73] This would appear to include an inferred choice of the proper law, infra, p 666.

[74] See *Dallal v Bank Mellat* [1986] QB 441 at 455–456.

[75] *Minmetals Germany GmbH v Ferco Steel Ltd* [1999] CLC 647; *Irvani v Irvani* [2000] 1 Lloyd's Rep 412 at 426–427, CA; *Kanoria v Guiness* [2006] EWCA Civ 222, [2006] 1 Lloyd's Rep 701. See also *Re Schreter and Gasmac Inc* (1992) 89 DLR (4th) 365; *Iran Aircraft Industries v Avco Corpn* 980 F 2d 141 (2nd Cir, 1992).

[76] Subject to the proviso in s 103(4) of the 1996 Act that an award containing decisions on matters not submitted to arbitration may be recognised or enforced to the extent that it contains decisions on separate matters which were so submitted. See, on s 103(2)(d), *Agromet Motoimport v Maulden Engineering Co (Beds) Ltd* [1985] 1 WLR 762 at 775–776—a case on the same provision under the 1975 Act.

[77] *China Agribusiness Development Corpn v Balli Trading* [1998] 2 Lloyd's Rep 76.

which, it was made.[78] Under the 1950 Act an award is unenforceable, as at common law, if it is not "final",[79] rather than if it is "not yet binding".

There is a further discretion to refuse recognition or enforcement of the award which may be exercised by the court either of its own motion or on the application of a party to the arbitration agreement. Recognition or enforcement may be refused if the award is in respect of a matter which is not capable of settlement by arbitration, or if it would be contrary to public policy to recognise or enforce the award.[80] Whether a matter is capable of settlement by arbitration would appear to be determined by English law as the law of the country where recognition or enforcement is sought.[81] Denial of recognition or enforcement of an award as being contrary to English public policy is less extensive than the equivalent provision under the 1950 Act[82] in that recognition or enforcement cannot be denied under the 1996 Act on the ground that it would be contrary to the law of England. What has to be shown is that "there is some element of illegality or that the enforcement of the award would be clearly injurious to the public good or, possibly, that enforcement would be wholly offensive to the ordinary reasonable and fully informed member of the public".[83] Applying this definition, the enforcement of an award arrived at after arbitrators had applied "internationally accepted principles of law governing contractual relations" (the *lex mercatoria)* has been held not to be against public policy.[84]

It is consistent with this definition that, in the decision of the Court of Appeal in *Soleimany v Soleimany,*[85] an award was refused enforcement on public policy grounds where it referred on its face to an illegal enterprise under which it was the joint intention that carpets would be exported illegally out of Iran. This was a case of illegality from the outset (present when the underlying contract was made),[86] but WALLER LJ in obiter dicta went further. An award will not be enforced where the underlying contract is governed by the law of a foreign and friendly country, or which requires performance in such a country,

---

[78] See *Rosseel NV v Oriental Commercial and Shipping (UK) Ltd* [1990] 1 WLR 1387. See generally Petrochilos [1999] 48 ICLQ 856. If an application has been made to a competent authority to set aside or suspend a New York Convention award, the English court has a discretion to adjourn the decision on the recognition or enforcement of the award and to order security to be given: 1996 Act, s 103(5). On the latter, see *Soleh Boneh International Ltd v Government of the Republic of Uganda and National Housing Corpn* [1993] 2 Lloyd's Rep 208, CA; *Apis AS v Fantazia Kereskedelmi* [2001] 1 All ER (Comm) 348; *Dardana Ltd v Yukos Oil Co* [2002] EWCA Civ 543, [2002] 2 Lloyd's Rep 326, CA and *Dardana Ltd v Yukos Oil Co* [2002] 2 Lloyd's Rep 261; *IPCO (Nigeria) Ltd v Nigerian National Petroleum Corpn* [2005] EWHC 726 (Comm), [2005] 2 Lloyd's Rep 326.

[79] Supra, pp 536–538.

[80] 1996 Act, s 103(3).

[81] See Lew (1975) 24 ICLQ 870 at 876.

[82] S 37(1).

[83] *Deutsche Schachtbau-Und Tiefborhgesellschaft MBH v Shell International Petroleum Co Ltd (t/a Shell International Trading Co)* [1990] 1 AC 295 at 316, 322, CA. The case went to the House of Lords (ibid, at 323) on a separate Third Party Debt Order (garnishment) point, discussed infra, pp 1239–1240. See also *IPCO (Nigeria) Ltd v Nigerian National Petroleum Corpn* [2005] EWHC 726 (Comm) at [22]–[24], [2005] 2 Lloyd's Rep 326; *Amaltal Corpn Ltd v Maruha (NZ) Corpn Ltd* [2004] 2 NZLR 614, CA. Cf *Resort Condominiums International Inc v Bolwell* (1994) 118 ALR 655.

[84] The *Deutsche Schachtbau-Und Tiefborhgesellschaft mbH Case,* supra. See Rivkin (1993) 9 Arb Int 67. However, it appears that the parties cannot choose the *lex mercatoria* as the governing law under the Rome Convention on the law applicable to contractual obligations, see infra, pp 698–699.

[85] [1999] QB 785, CA; Harris and Meisel [1998] LMCLQ 568; Enonchong [1999] LMCLQ 495.

[86] *Soleimany v Soleimany,* supra, at 803 (per WALLER LJ).

if performance is illegal by the law of that country.[87] This was distinguished by the Court of Appeal in *Westacre Investments Inc v Jugoimport-SDPR Holding Co Ltd*, a case concerning a contract for the purchase of personal influence (lobbying rather than corruption), which, looking at the award and the reasons stated, was not illegal (or against public policy) by the law of the place of performance or under the governing law and curial law.[88] Whilst the award is not isolated from the underlying contract, it is relevant that the English court is considering the enforcement of an award, and not the underlying contract.[89] The underlying contract, on the facts as they appeared from the award, did not infringe one of those rules of public policy where the English court would not enforce it whatever its governing law or place of performance.[90] There is nothing which offends English public policy if a foreign arbitral tribunal enforces a contract for the purchase of personal influence which does not offend the domestic public policy under either the governing law of the contract or its curial law, even if English domestic public policy might have taken a different view.[91] What if there is illegality by the foreign place of performance? In the case of a contract for the purchase of personal influence that in itself is not enough to lead to non-enforcement of the contract or the subsequent award.[92] This represents a retreat by WALLER LJ from his earlier wide obiter dicta in *Soleimany*.[93] Subsequently in *OTV v Hilmarton*,[94] a case of a contract to lobby public servants, an award has been enforced even though there was a finding by the arbitrator of illegality under the law of the place of performance. *Soleimany* was distinguished on the basis that, unlike in that case, the illegality fell short of corruption or illicit practice.[95]

It is more difficult where the arbitrator has considered an allegation of illegality or of bribery and corruption and has rejected it. Where the allegation was a central one, was made, entertained and rejected at the arbitration and, on appeal, before a federal tribunal in that state, authority apart and in the absence of new evidence, there can be no justification for refusing to enforce the award.[96] Obiter dicta supporting the idea of some kind of a preliminary inquiry[97] have been doubted.[98] Moreover, according to these obiter dicta, in determining whether this is an appropriate case for making such a preliminary inquiry,

---

[87] Ibid. *Soleimany* has been subsequently reinterpreted by WALLER LJ as being decided on the basis that it was plain on the face of the award that the enterprise was unlawful under the law of the place of performance: *Westacre Investments Inc v Jugoimport-SDPR Holding Co Ltd* [2000] 1 QB 288 at 302, CA. Moreover, an award will not be enforced if the underlying contract, which is governed by English law or is to be performed in England, is illegal by English domestic law, *Soleimany* at 803.

[88] [2000] 1 QB 288 at 302–305, CA. *Soleimany* was distinguished by WALLER LJ, at 302, on the basis that, in that case, it was plain on the face of the award that the enterprise was unlawful under the law of the place of performance. *Westacre* was followed in *OTV v Hilmarton* [1999] 2 Lloyd's Rep 222.

[89] The *Westacre* case, supra, at 305.

[90] Following *Lemenda Trading Co Ltd v African Middle East Petroleum Co Ltd* [1988] QB 448—a case on enforcement of the contract rather than an award. The former point is discussed infra, p 741.

[91] Ibid.

[92] The *Westacre* case, supra, at 304–305 (per WALLER LJ); following the *Lemenda* case, supra.

[93] *Soleimany v Soleimany*, supra, at 803.

[94] [1999] 2 Lloyd's Rep 222; criticised by Hill [2000] LMCLQ 311.

[95] *OTV v Hilmarton*, supra, at 225.

[96] *Westacre Investments Inc v Jugoimport-SDPR Holding Co Ltd* [2000] 1 QB 288 at 316–317 (per MANTELL and HIRST LJJ); cf the dissent of WALLER LJ at 310–316, CA.

[97] *Soleimany v Soleimany*, supra, at 800–803. See also *Soinco SACI v Novokuznetsk Aluminium Plant* [1998] 2 Lloyd's Rep 337, CA.

[98] *Westacre Investments Inc v Jugoimport-SDPR Holding Co Ltd* [2000] 1 QB 288 at 316–317 (per MANTELL and HIRST LJ); cf the dissent of WALLER LJ at 310–316, CA.

the court will consider whether: there was evidence before the tribunal that this was a straightforward, commercial contract; the arbitrator made a specific finding that the underlying contract was not illegal; there was anything to suggest incompetence on the part of the arbitrators; there was any reason to suggest collusion or bad faith in the obtaining of the award.[99] The application of these criteria may well lead to the rejection of reopening the facts.[100]

Enforcement will be refused on public policy grounds if the award was obtained by fraud, such as perjured evidence.[101] However, the principle that enforcement of a foreign judgment can be attacked on the ground of fraud without any requirement that the evidence must not have been available at the trial[102] has not been extended to foreign arbitration awards, which, because the tribunal has been chosen by the parties, should be put into the same category as domestic arbitration awards and not into the same category as foreign judgments.[103] With foreign arbitration awards, normally the conditions to be fulfilled for re-opening the issue of fraud will be (a) that the evidence to establish the fraud was not available to the party alleging the fraud at the time of the hearing before the arbitrators; and (b) where perjury is the fraud alleged, ie where the very issue before the arbitrators was whether the witnesses were lying, the evidence must be so strong that it would reasonably be expected to be decisive at a hearing.[104] Normally, an English court will not reinvestigate allegations of procedural defects, which have already been considered by the supervisory court abroad.[105] It must be noted that recognition or enforcement cannot be refused on the basis that the arbitrator made an error of fact or law.[106] Nor can recognition or enforcement be refused on the basis that there was a subsequent inconsistent decision from a court in another country.[107] Where there are conflicting final decisions each pronounced by a body of competent jurisdiction, the earlier in time is to be recognised and given effect.[108]

The 1996 Act contains two provisions which interrelate with other bases for enforcement. If a New York Convention award would also be a foreign award within the meaning of the 1950 Act, that Act is not to apply to it but the award's recognition or enforcement shall be governed by the 1996 Act.[109] Secondly, nothing in the 1996 Act prejudices the right to enforce or rely on a New York Convention award at common law,[110] ie by an

---

[99] *Westacre Investments Inc v Jugoimport-SDPR Holding Co Ltd* [2000] 1 QB 288 at 316–317; *Soleimany v Soleimany*, supra, at 800.

[100] See the *Westacre* case, supra.

[101] *Westacre Investments Inc v Jugoimport-SDPR Holding Co Ltd* [2000] 1 QB 288.

[102] Supra, pp 551–555.

[103] The *Westacre* case, supra, at 309. See also *Re Schreter and Gasmac Inc* (1992) 89 DLR (4th) 365 at 379. See generally Harris and Meisel, [1998] LMCLQ 568, on the question of whether public policy in the context of enforcement of arbitration awards raises the same issues as in cases of enforcement of foreign judgments.

[104] The *Westacre* case, supra, at 309.

[105] *Minmetals Germany GmbH v Ferco Steel Ltd* [1999] CLC 647 at 659–662.

[106] *Mutual Shipping Corpn of New York v Bayshore Shipping Co of Monrovia, The Montan* [1985] 1 WLR 625 at 631.

[107] *The Joanna V* [2003] EWHC 1655 (Comm), [2003] 2 Lloyd's Rep 617.

[108] Ibid, at 628. Following *Showlag v Mansour* [1995] 1 AC 431, PC.

[109] 1996 Act, s 99.

[110] Ibid, s 104; in *Minister of Public Works of the Government of the State of Kuwait v Sir Frederick Snow & Partners* [1984] AC 426, the defences under the 1975 Act were said to cover the whole field of the defences which would be available in a common law action, see, supra, p 653.

action on the award, or under section 66 of the 1996 Act[111] (by leave of the court, enforcement in the same manner as a judgment or order of the court to the same effect).

5. ENFORCEMENT UNDER THE ADMINISTRATION OF JUSTICE ACT 1920 AND THE FOREIGN JUDGMENTS (RECIPROCAL ENFORCEMENT) ACT 1933

The provisions of the Administration of Justice Act 1920 whereby judgments given in Commonwealth countries may be registered and enforced in England[112] apply equally to arbitral awards.[113] The Foreign Judgments (Reciprocal Enforcement) Act 1933[114] now also extends to foreign arbitral awards.[115] However, a foreign arbitral award, which is registrable under the Act, unlike other judgments, does not have to be enforced under the Act.[116] The claimant, if he so chooses, can, instead, seek enforcement of the arbitration award at common law or by recourse to section 66 of the Arbitration Act 1996.[117]

6. ENFORCEMENT UNDER THE ARBITRATION (INTERNATIONAL INVESTMENT DISPUTES) ACT 1966

The Arbitration (International Investment Disputes) Act 1966 implements a convention made at Washington, DC in 1965 which established the International Centre for the Settlement of Investment Disputes between Contracting States and the nationals of other Contracting States.[118] Subject to the written consent of the parties, the Centre's arbitration tribunal has jurisdiction to settle any legal dispute arising out of such an investment.[119] An arbitral award made by the Centre's tribunal, if registered in the High Court, has, as respects the pecuniary obligations which it imposes, the same force and effect as if it had been a judgment of the High Court.[120] There is a discretion to stay English proceedings in breach of an agreement to submit to the Centre's arbitration.[121]

---

[111] 1996 Act, s 104.
[112] Supra, pp 576–578.
[113] Administration of Justice Act 1920, s 12(1).
[114] Supra, pp 578–587.
[115] S 10A of the 1933 Act, added by Sch 10, para 4 of the Civil Jurisdiction and Judgments Act 1982.
[116] See ss 10A and 6 of the 1933 Act.
[117] Supra, p 653.
[118] 1966 Act, Sch, Art 1.
[119] Ibid, Sch, Art 25. Choice of law rules are provided in Art 42.
[120] Ibid, ss 1, 2. The award may be registered in foreign currency: Administration of Justice Act 1977, s 4(2)(a), (b); see also Law Com No 124 (1983), paras 2.44–2.47.
[121] The 1996 Act, s 3(2), applying the Arbitration Act 1996, s 9, supra, pp 450–454.

PART IV

The Law of Obligations

Chapters

The Law of Obligations

Chapter 18

Contracts

1. INTRODUCTION

(a) The nature of the problem

The problem of ascertaining the applicable law is more perplexing in the case of contracts than in almost any other area. There are three reasons for this. First, there is the diversity of connecting factors that can be raised by the facts of the case: the place where the contract is made; the place of performance; the domicile, nationality or place of business of the parties; the situation of the subject matter and so on. In most areas of private international law the decisive connecting factor on which ascertainment of the applicable law depends is reasonably clear. There is general agreement, for instance, that it is the place of celebration which indicates the law to govern the formal validity of a marriage. But with contracts the sheer multiplicity of connecting factors makes it hard to identify one single connecting factor as the determinant of the applicable law. Secondly, contracts are planned transactions and the parties may well have considered the question of what law should govern the contract in the event of a dispute arising between them. They may have made provision in the contract, choosing the applicable law. Thirdly, a wide variety of different contractual issues can arise. For example, there can be a problem over whether a contract has been validly created, concerning how it should be interpreted, about whether it has been discharged. This raises the question whether the same law should govern all of these issues. Moreover, there are many different types of contract. A sale of goods contract has different features from an insurance contract or a contract for carriage of goods by sea. Should the same law govern regardless of the type of contract involved, or do the special features of particular contracts necessitate special choice of law rules?

(b) Various solutions to the problem[1]

As one would expect from the complex nature of the problem, a wide variety of different solutions have been tried in different countries over the years. In the USA a preference was formerly shown for a rigid and inflexible test, represented by the place of contracting in some of the states but by the place of performance in others. However, the choice of law revolution in that country[2] has affected not only tort cases but also contract cases, and a wide range of modern approaches is now used in this area.[3] Most of the countries of the European Continent rejected a rigid test and, instead, adopted the doctrine of autonomy under which the parties were free to choose the governing law, though divergent views obtained on the question whether their freedom was absolute or was restricted to the choice of a law with which the contract was factually connnected.[4] In the absence of choice by the parties, most of these countries adopted a flexible approach, leaving the judge to select the decisive connecting factors from the various elements of the contract and the circumstances of the case.[5]

English law, until fairly recently, applied the "proper law of the contract",[6] which was a succinct expression to describe the law governing many of the matters affecting a contract. The doctrine of the proper law was of common law origin and a vast case law developed to take account of the difficulties outlined above. It was both sophisticated and flexible in its approach. The key features of the doctrine were as follows. The parties could choose the proper law, with very little restriction on this right. If the parties did not express a choice, and one could not be inferred by the courts, an objective test was applied. This sought to localise the contract by looking for the system of law with which the transaction was most closely connected. The twin theories which underlay the proper law were therefore the subjective theory, which looked to the intentions of the parties, and the objective theory, which sought to localise the contract. Special rules were adopted for particular issues. The proper law was usually relevant, but the court was required to go

---

[1] See generally Lando, *3 International Encyclopedia of Comparative Law*, Chapter 24; North, *Private International Law Problems in Common Law Jurisdictions* (1993), Chapter V.

[2] Supra, pp 27–35.

[3] *Auten v Auten* 308 NY 155, 124 NE 2d 99 (1954)—grouping of contacts; Restatement, 2d, §§ 187, 188; *Lilienthal v Kaufman* 395 P 2d 543 (1964)—governmental interest analysis; *Haines v Mid-Century Insurance Co* 177 NW 2d 328 (1970)—choice influencing considerations. See generally Weintraub (1984) IV Hague Recueil 239; Penn and Cashel [1986] JBL 333, 497; Nygh (1995) 251 Hague Recueil 281–292; Scoles, Hay, Borchers and Symeonides, Chapter 18, especially at para 18.21.

[4] For a detailed account, see Rabel, ii 370 et seq.

[5] See Lando (1987) 24 CMLR 159, 188–199.

[6] For a detailed analysis see the 11th edn (1987) of this book, Chapter 18; Dicey and Morris, (1987) 11th edn, Chapters 32 and 33; Anton, Chapter 10.

beyond the proper law when considering certain issues. Thus, for example, with the issue of illegality the courts were concerned not only with illegality by the proper law but also with illegality by the law of the place of performance. There were also special rules for particular contracts, such as insurance contracts. These rules either made special provision for ascertaining the proper law or departed from the proper law altogether.

Choice of law in contract is now put on a statutory footing. The Contracts (Applicable Law) Act 1990 has largely replaced the common law rules and the doctrine of the proper law of the contract. The Act implements the EEC Convention on the law applicable to contractual obligations of 1980 (the Rome Convention), and it is with this Convention that this chapter is mainly concerned.

The Rome Convention is to be replaced in the near future by the Rome I Regulation and its provisions modernised.[7] The terms of this Regulation will also be examined.

2. THE ROME CONVENTION[8]

(a) Preliminary remarks

(i) The history and purpose of the Convention, the Rome I Regulation

(a) History of the Convention

As early as 1967 there was a proposal from the governments of the Benelux countries to the Commission of the European Communities for the unification of private international law rules, particularly in the field of contract law. Experts from the then six Member States of the Community prepared a preliminary draft Convention before the United Kingdom, Ireland and Denmark joined the European Community. At that time, this draft also covered non-contractual obligations. In negotiations between experts from the then nine Member States of the European Community there was extensive revision of the draft Convention, culminating in a final Convention (the Rome Convention) in 1980.[9] This was only concerned with contractual obligations. By the end of 1981 the Convention had been signed by all of the then Member States. In 1984, the Greek Accession Convention (the Luxembourg Convention) was concluded. This did not alter the substance of the Rome Convention. However, ratification of the Rome Convention was delayed whilst problems in relation to what powers, if any, the European Court of Justice should have as regards interpretation of the Convention were resolved. In 1988,

---

[7] See infra, pp 669–670.

[8] Dicey, Morris and Collins, Chapter 32; Kaye, *The New Private International Law of Contract of the European Community* (1993); Hill, *International Commercial Disputes* (2005) 3rd edn, Chapter 14; Plender, *The European Contracts Convention* (2001) 2nd edn; North (ed), *Contract Conflicts—The EEC Convention on the Law Applicable to Contractual Obligations: A Comparative Study* (1982); Fletcher, *Conflict of Laws and European Community Law* (1982) Chapter 5; Lasok and Stone, *Conflict of Laws in the European Community* (1987), pp 340–387; Anton, Chapter 11; North [1980] JBL 382; Bennett (1980) 17 CMLR 269; Williams [1981] LMCLQ 250; note (1981) 2 VA J IntL 91; Morse (1982) 2 YEL 107; Weintraub (1984) IV Hague Recueil 239, at 278–290; Williams (1986) 35 ICLQ 1; Lando (1987) 24 CMLR 159; RMM [1991] JBL 205; Young [1991] LMCLQ 314. The Rome Convention served as the model for the Inter-American Convention on the Law Applicable to International Contracts (the Mexico Convention): see (1994) 33 ILM 733; Juenger (1994) 42 AJCL 381. It has also influenced law reform proposals in Australia; see ALRC Rep No 58 (1992); Kincaid (1995) 8 Jo Contract Law 231.

[9] OJ 1980 L 266.

two protocols on interpretation of the Convention were signed. The Convention eventually received the requisite number of ratifications and came into force on 1 April 1991. At first, it only applied to the then ten Member States of the European Community (Belgium, Denmark, France, Germany, Greece, Ireland, Italy, Luxembourg, the Netherlands and the United Kingdom). However, subsequently there has been the 1992 Spanish and Portuguese Accession Convention[10] and the 1996 Austrian, Finnish and Swedish Accession Convention.[11] These two Accession Conventions only make minor alterations to the original version of the Rome Convention.[12] The ten 2004 new European Community Member States[13] have all signed[14] an Accession Convention[15] which will enter into force in a Contracting State after ratification. The United Kingdom and a number of other Member States have not yet ratified this Accession Convention. It is contemplated that any country which in the future joins the European Community should accede to the Convention.[16] There is as yet no Accession Convention for the two latest (2007) Member States (Bulgaria and Romania). The Convention is not open to signature by non-Members of the European Community.[17] However, there is nothing to stop other countries incorporating the rules contained in the Rome Convention into their private international law. Indeed, Belgium, Luxembourg, Denmark, the Netherlands and Germany all did this prior to the Convention itself coming into force in 1991.[18]

(b) The purpose of the Convention

According to its preamble, the purpose of the Convention is to establish uniform choice of law rules for contractual obligations throughout the Community.[19] In general terms, the Convention has been seen as a continuation of the work on unification begun by the Brussels Convention on jurisdiction and the enforcement of judgments in civil and commercial matters (replaced in virtually all cases by the Brussels I Regulation),[20] and like that Convention is concerned with creating the right conditions for an internal market with the free movement of persons, goods, services and capital among the Member States. More particularly, since the law will be the same wherever trial takes place in the Community, it inhibits the forum shopping that the Brussels Convention (Brussels I

---

[10] OJ 1992 L 333/1. See Gaudemet-Tallon [1993] RTD eur 61; Beaumont (1993) 42 ICLQ 728.

[11] OJ 1997 C 15/10. See the Explanatory Report in OJ 1997 C 191/11. This has been in force in the United Kingdom from 2001, see SI 2000/1825.

[12] From henceforth, in this chapter, all references to "the Rome Convention" or "the Convention" are to this version, ie as amended by these two Accession Conventions. This is set out in OJ 1998 C 27/34. The Austrian, Finnish and Swedish Accession Convention also makes minor amendments to the Protocol annexed to the Rome Convention and to the First Protocol on interpretation of 1988 (the latest version of which is set out at OJ 1998 C 27/47).

[13] Ie the Czech Republic, Cyprus, Estonia, Hungary, Latvia, Lithuania, Malta, Poland, Slovakia, Slovenia.

[14] On 14 April 2005.

[15] OJ 2005 C 169/01. This has also been signed by the 15 existing Member States.

[16] See the Joint Declaration attached to the Convention, at III. However, when the Rome Convention becomes the Rome I Regulation, see infra, p 669, this will be directly applicable in all the EC Member States, with the exception of Denmark. The Ministry of Justice has provisionally concluded that the United Kingdom should opt in. The Republic of Ireland has elected to opt in.

[17] Art 28(1).

[18] See generally Lando (1987) 24 CMLR 159; Triebel (1988) 37 ICLQ 935; De Boer (1990) 54 Rabels Z 24, 40 et seq.

[19] Para 3 of the Preamble.

[20] Para 2 of the Preamble. However, there is nothing in Art 220 of the Treaty of Rome about contract choice of law; cf the origins of the Brussels Convention and Brussels I Regulation, supra, pp 204–205.

Regulation) allows.[21] It was also said that such a Convention would increase legal certainty and make it easier to anticipate more easily the law to be applied.[22]

(c) The Rome I Regulation

In 2005, the European Commission put forward a proposal that the Rome Convention should be converted to the Rome I Regulation and its provisions modernised.[23] Harmonisation of choice of law rules is regarded as helping to facilitate the mutual recognition of judgments.[24] The proper functioning of the internal market is said to create a need for such harmonisation.[25] For the same reason there is said to be a need to achieve harmony between between three key instruments: the Brusssels I Regulation; Rome I and Rome II (on non-contractual obligations).[26] The legal basis for the proposed Regulation is Title IV, in particular Article 61(c), of the Treaty on European Union, which authorises the adoption of measures[27] in the field of judicial co-operation in civil matters as provided for in Article 65, which specifically mentions promoting the compatibility of the rules applicable in Member States concerning the conflict of laws (ie the applicable law).

The final version of the Regulation is based on a proposal contained in a European Parliament legislative resolution of 29 November 2007.[28] Prior to this there were informal contacts between the Council, the European Parliament and the Commission with a view to avoiding the need for a second reading and conciliation. The Council formally adopted the Regulation on 6 June 2008.[29] The Regulation will then not apply until eighteen months after the date of its adoption and then only to contracts concluded after the date from which it applies.

The United Kingdom, after stakeholder consultations, elected in 2006 not to opt in to the proposed Rome I Regulation.[30] Among the critics of the proposed Regulation[31] was the Financial Markets Law Committee,[32] which took the view that it would cause significant

---

[21] See the Giuliano and Lagarde Report OJ 1980 C 282 of 31 October, at pp 4–5 which quotes from the address by Vogelaar at the meeting of government experts in 1969.

[22] Ibid.

[23] Proposal for a Regulation of the European Parliament and the Council on the law applicable to contractual obligations (Rome I) COM (2005) 650 final. See Dutson (2006) 122 LQR 374 and (2006) IFL 36; Lando and Nielson (2007) 3 J Priv Int L 29; Dickinson (2007) 3 J Priv Int L 53; Gillies (2007) 3 J Priv Int L 89; Crawford and Carruthers, para15–49. For the earlier Green Paper of 14 January 2003 see COM (2002) 654 final; on which see Carruthers and Crawford 2003 SLT 137.

[24] Recital (3) of the Proposal, Recitals (4) and (6) of the final version of Rome I.

[25] Recital (4) of the Proposal, Recital (6) of the final version of Rome I.

[26] Recital (4) of the proposal. This is not mentioned in the Recitals in the final version of the Regulation.

[27] In accordance with Art 67(5).

[28] COM (2005) 0650-C6-0441/2005-2005/0261(COD), (hereinafter refered to as "proposal for a Rome I Regulation EP (first reading)").

[29] The Rome Convention will remain in force for certain territories of Member States, Art 24 of the Regulation. This is the same as the position in relation to the Brussels Convention, supra, p 342.

[30] The Republic of Ireland has elected to opt in. The Regulation would not be applied by Denmark. However, a parallel agreement between the EC and Denmark may be possible, see Lando and Nielson (2007) 3 J Priv Int L 29.

[31] See Dutson (2006) 122 LQR 374, [2006] JBL 608 and (2006) IFLR 36; Dickinson (2007) 3 J Priv Int L 53; Gillies (2007) 3 J Priv Int L 89.

[32] See http://www.fmlc.org.

uncertainty in the financial markets.[33] The prospect of having to consider giving effect to the overriding mandatory provisions of foreign countries generated the greatest concern in this regard, although other provisions also caused concern. Nonetheless, the United Kingdom government saw clear benefits in a coherent European Union choice of law regime and attended the subsequent negotiations, without voting rights. The United Kingdom can still opt in to the Regulation at the end of the negotiation process,[34] subject to the permission of the Commission. Now that negotiations on Rome I are complete, the United Kingdom is conducting a full public consultation before deciding whether to opt in or not. In its Consultation Paper (CP 05/08), the Ministry of Justice has taken the view that the Articles that were of greatest concern to the United Kingdom stakeholders during negotiations have either been removed, substantially revised or returned to their Convention form subject to later review. The Ministry of Justice has also argued that the Regulation improves upon the Convention in a number of respects, in particular in terms of improved drafting. All of this has led to its provisional conclusion that the United Kingdom should opt in to the Rome I Regulation. The views of stakeholders are sought on this conclusion. It remains to be seen whether the limited nature of the provision on overriding mandatory rules of foreign countries in the Regulation[35] will satisfy stakeholders. If the United Kingdom does not opt in, it will continue to apply the Rome Convention, leading to a lack of Europe-wide uniformity.

(ii) The Contracts (Applicable Law) Act 1990

The introduction of the Rome Convention into English law was a matter of considerable controversy with enthusiasts[36] and critics[37] taking polarised positions. The controversy ranged over both the need for harmonisation of contract choice of law rules and the nature and form of the new law. Nonetheless, when the 1990 Act was presented to Parliament it was said[38] that the Convention would produce benefits in terms both of harmonisation and, more questionably, improved certainty in the law. The Convention uses ill-defined Continental concepts (eg mandatory rules and characteristic performance), and when it does use a familiar concept (eg the parties' freedom to choose the applicable law) this is put in unfamiliar language and in the unfamiliar form of a Code. Moreover, unlike when the Brussels Convention came into force in the United Kingdom, the Rome Convention was not accompanied by decisions of the Court of Justice interpreting it. On the other hand, it is uncontroversial in that the substance of the law is largely unaltered.

---

[33] See para 17.1 of the Committee's Legal assessment of the conversion of the Rome Convention to a Community instrument and the provisions of the proposed Rome I Regulation, available at http://www.fmlc.org.

[34] The United Kingdom would not have to apply the Regulation in intra-United Kingdom cases, Art 22 of the Regulation, but the Ministry of Justice, in Consultation Paper CP 05/08, is proposing to apply similar rules in such cases.

[35] See infra, pp 740–741.

[36] North, *Contract Conflicts*, p 23; Jaffey (1984) 33 ICLQ 531 and *Topics in Choice of Law* (1996), Chapter 2.

[37] See Mann (1983) 32 ICLQ 265; (1989) 38 ICLQ 715; Briggs [1990] LMCLQ 192.

[38] See the Lord-Advocate, Hansard, (HL) 12 December 1989 vol 513, cols 1258–1260; Lord Chancellor, (HL) 24 April 1990, vol 518, col 439; Solicitor-General, (HC) Second Reading Committee 20 June 1990, cols 3–6.

The Contracts (Applicable Law) Act 1990[39] is closely modelled on the Civil Jurisdiction and Judgments Act 1982, which implemented the Brussels Convention.[40] The 1990 Act is very short. It provides that the Rome Convention, Luxembourg Convention (the Greek Accession Convention to the Rome Convention), Funchal Convention (the Spanish and Portuguese Accession Convention to the Rome Convention, as adjusted by the Luxembourg Convention), 1996 Accession Convention (of Austria, Finland and Sweden) and Brussels Protocol (the first Protocol on interpretation of the Rome Convention) shall have the force of law in the United Kingdom,[41] and sets out the four Conventions and the first Protocol in Schedules to the Act. There is a provision dealing with interpretation of the Conventions and Protocol,[42] which will be examined shortly.[43] Two other important matters are dealt with in the Act. The first is concerned with reservations under the Rome Convention. On ratifying the Convention the United Kingdom, as it was entitled to,[44] reserved the right not to apply Articles 7(1) (mandatory rules of foreign countries) and 10(1)(e) (the consequences of nullity of a contract). Section 2(2) therefore states that these two provisions shall not have the force of law in the United Kingdom. The second is concerned with intra-United Kingdom disputes,[45] as where, for example, there is a trial in England of a dispute involving a Scotsman who contracted in Scotland with an Englishman to deliver goods to England. According to the Convention,[46] the United Kingdom was not bound to apply the rules in the Convention to such a case. However, section 2(3) provides that "the Convention shall apply in the case of conflicts between the laws of different parts of the United Kingdom". This is to be welcomed. To have to apply separate rules for intra-United Kingdom cases would have been an unnecessary complication.

The effect of implementation of the Rome Convention is that, for contracts made after the Convention came into force, the traditional common law rules on contract choice of law are largely replaced by the rules contained in the Convention.[47] It is not possible for the parties to contract out of the Convention, for this would defeat its purpose.[48] Nor do the terms of the Convention support this possibility. Nevertheless, as will shortly be seen, the traditional common law rules continue to be applied even to contracts made after the Convention came into force in a number of situations. English courts therefore still have to operate two different regimes for contract choice of law: for Convention cases (ie cases coming within the scope of the Convention) there are the Convention rules; for non-Convention cases (ie cases outside the scope of the Convention) there are the traditional

---

[39] As amended by SI 1994/1900, in the light of the Spanish/Portuguese Accession Convention to the Rome Convention and by SI 2000/1825 in the light of the Austrian, Finnish and Swedish Accession Convention. From henceforth in this chapter all references to the Contracts (Applicable Law) Act 1990 or to "the 1990 Act" are to this amended version.

[40] Supra, p 205.

[41] S 2(1).

[42] S 3.

[43] Infra, pp 672–673.

[44] Art 22.

[45] Discussed infra, pp 680–681.

[46] Art 19(2).

[47] As regards statutes, eg the Unfair Contract Terms Act 1977, see infra, pp 731–736.

[48] North, *Essays*, pp 185–187; Kaye, p 120; Dicey, Morris and Collins, para 32-044; Fentiman, *Foreign Law in English Courts* (1998), p 83; Hogan (1992) 108 LQR 12; Rinze [1994] JBL 412 at 417. Cf Mann (1991) 107 LQR 353.

common law rules.[49] This undoubted complication in the law could have been avoided if the 1990 Act had provided that the rules in the Rome Convention were to be applied to all contracts made after the Convention came into force, even in non-Convention cases, thereby assimilating the two sets of rules.[50]

(iii) Interpretation[51]

(a) Referrals to the Court of Justice

Two Protocols on interpretation of the Rome Convention by the Court of Justice were signed in Brussels in 1988.[52] The first Protocol, which is set out in a Schedule to the 1990 Act, defines the scope of the jurisdiction of the Court of Justice and the conditions under which that jurisdiction is to be exercised. States accept the jurisdiction of the Court of Justice under this Protocol. The second Protocol confers powers on the Court of Justice to interpret the Rome Convention. The two-Protocol system allows some Member States to proceed with allowing referrals to the Court of Justice ahead of other Member States, such as Ireland, which have internal problems relating to allowing such a reference. The commencement of the first Protocol became possible following the ratification of the second Protocol by all fifteen Contracting States and it came into force for the United Kingdom on 1 March 2005.[53] References to the Court of Justice from United Kingdom courts are now therefore possible.

There was considerable controversy over the whole question of referrals of interpretation to the Court of Justice, but there is no doubt that without this there would be a danger that the courts in each Contracting State would interpret the Convention differently, with the consequent risk that harmonisation of contract choice of law rules within the Community would not be achieved.[54] Two limitations on when a national court can request a preliminary ruling on interpretation are contained in the first Protocol. First, a court can only make such a request "if that court considers that a decision on the question is necessary to enable it to give judgment".[55] There is nothing to stop English courts from deciding that the meaning of the Convention is clear and a reference to the Court of Justice is not necessary. This is the same wording as that adopted in respect of referrals to the Court of Justice in cases of interpretation of the Brussels Convention on jurisdiction and the enforcement of judgments. The second limitation is in respect of the courts which can request a ruling from the Court of Justice. The House of Lords and any other courts from which no further appeal is possible, and any court when acting as an appeal court, *may* request a preliminary ruling.[56] Judges at first instance can never so request.

---

[49] See the 11th edn (1987), of this book, Chapter 18. The common law rules were subject to a small number of statutory provisions, ibid.

[50] See North in *Contract Conflicts*, p 12; Fletcher, *Conflict of Laws and European Community Law* (1982), p 155.

[51] See Plender, paras 2.01–2.32.

[52] OJ 1989 L 48. There is a Report by Professor Tizzano on the Protocols: OJ 1990 C 219. See Kaye, pp 415–430.

[53] The Contracts (Applicable Law) Act 1990 (Commencement No 2) Order, SI 2004/3448. The first Protocol came into force internationally on 1 August 2004.

[54] See Kohler (1982) 7 ELR 103, 113; the opinion of the Commission of the European Community OJ 1980 L 94/39.

[55] Art 2.

[56] Ibid.

It is noticeable that, in contrast to the Protocol on interpretation of the Brussels Convention,[57] this Protocol states that the specified courts *may* (rather than must) request a ruling if they consider that a decision is necessary to enable them to give judgment. The lack of compulsion on courts to make referrals to the Court of Justice is deliberate. Some Member States, including the United Kingdom, argued that provision for the Court of Justice to have jurisdiction in relation to interpretation of the Convention was undesirable.[58] Many international contracts which have nothing to do with England nevertheless provide for trial in England and for English law to govern the contract. It was feared that foreign businessmen would, in future, opt for trial outside England and, indeed, outside the Community rather than face the prospect of a compulsory referral to the Court of Justice, which would delay the settlement of their dispute. The power to refer a question of interpretation was therefore made a discretionary one. In exercising this discretion national courts can take into account any appropriate factor including the wishes of the parties, who may want a speedy outcome to the litigation.[59] The result is that there are likely to be fewer referrals to the Court of Justice under the Rome Convention than there have been under the Brussels Convention.[60]

There is also, no doubt, a third limitation on referrals to the Court of Justice, which is not spelt out in the first Protocol. The Court of Justice is concerned with interpretation of the Convention as harmonised European law,[61] and not with interpretation of purely national rules of private international law. Many of the cases on interpretation of the Rome Convention coming before the English courts will arise in the context of whether the court has jurisdiction under rule 6.20 of the Civil Procedure Rules.[62] The Court of Justice may well refuse to accept a reference on interpretation of the Convention from the English courts in such a case.[63] The same is doubtless the case in relation to a reference on interpretation arising out of an intra-United Kingdom dispute.[64]

(b) The principles and decisions laid down by the Court of Justice

Section 3(1) of the 1990 Act provides that, where the meaning of the Convention[65] is not referred to the Court of Justice, it must be determined "in accordance with the principles laid down by, and any relevant decision of, [that Court]". This section adopts the same wording employed in the Civil Jurisdiction and Judgments Act 1982 in relation to interpretation of the Brussels Convention. The effect of section 3(1) is that the English courts have to act in accordance with two different types of authority: first, any relevant decisions of the Court of Justice; secondly, the principles laid down by the Court of Justice.

---

[57] Supra, p 207.

[58] The Tizzano Report, sections 23 et seq.

[59] Ibid, section 34.

[60] See generally Hansard (HL) 24 April 1990, vol 518, col 440. But see now the more restrictive rules on referrals in relation to the Brussels I Regulation, supra, pp 206–207.

[61] See Art 18, discussed infra, p 674.

[62] See CPR, r 6.20(5)(c), discussed supra, pp 381–382.

[63] But see Morse [1994] LMCLQ 560, 562. It presumably would accept a reference on the issue of whether CPR, r 6.20 is a procedural rule and thus excluded from the scope of the Convention.

[64] See Case C-346/93 *Kleinwort Benson Ltd v Glasgow City Council* [1996] QB 57; discussed supra, p 348. But see Plender, paras 2.28–2.32.

[65] And the Luxembourg and Funchal Conventions, the 1996 Accession Convention and the Brussels Protocol.

If the Court of Justice has previously given a decision on the provision in issue, this must be followed. A relevant decision for these purposes could include one of the decisions of the Court of Justice discussing the Rome Convention[66] in a jurisdiction case on a reference under the Protocol on interpretation of the Brussels Convention or on a reference under Article 234 of the Treaty on European Union on interpretation of the Brussels I Regulation. Judicial notice must be taken of any relevant decisions of, or expression of opinion by, the Court of Justice.[67] However, the provision which is in issue may not have been previously discussed by the Court of Justice. In this situation, the English courts must act in accordance with the principles of interpretation previously laid down by the Court of Justice. As yet there have been no referrals under the 1988 Protocol on interpretation of the Rome Convention. This raises two questions. What principles is the Court of Justice likely to apply in relation to interpretation of the Rome Convention? What are the English courts to do in the meantime?

The Court of Justice is likely to apply the same general principles of interpretation to the Rome Convention as it applies to other areas of law. For example, the meaning of a provision is ascertained in the light of its purpose rather than by looking at its literal meaning. The Rome Convention too should be given a purposive interpretation. More importantly, the Court of Justice has laid down certain general principles of interpretation in relation to the Brussels Convention (Brussels I Regulation); such as normally giving concepts an autonomous Community definition.[68] The same principles are likely to be applied by the Court of Justice in relation to another Community Convention which is also concerned with the unification of rules of private international law. The English courts should apply the principles that the Court of Justice is likely to apply. Indeed, the wording of section 3(1) is wide enough to compel the English courts to act in accordance with general principles of interpretation laid down by the Court of Justice in other contexts. It is encouraging to note that English judges when construing the Rome Convention have adopted a purposive approach[69] and have given the scope of the Convention an autonomous meaning.[70]

(c) The principle of uniform interpretation

One principle that the Court of Justice and national courts are bound to follow is the principle of uniform interpretation, which is set out in the Convention itself. Article 18[71] provides that "In the interpretation and application of the preceding uniform rules, regard shall be had to their international character and to the desirability of achieving uniformity in their interpretation and application". This means that courts should not define concepts by reference to national systems, but instead give independent

---

[66] See, eg, Case 133/81 *Ivenel v Schwab* [1982] ECR 1891, discussed supra, p 273; Case 9/87 *SPRL Arcado v SA Haviland* [1988] ECR 1539, discussed supra, p 234. Case C-89/91 *Shearson Lehman Hutton v TVB Treuhandgesellschaft für Vermogensverwaltung und Beteiligungen mbH* [1993] ECR I-139, discussed supra, p 269.

[67] S 3(2) of the Contracts (Applicable Law) Act 1990.

[68] Supra, pp 207–208.

[69] *Ennstone Building Products Ltd v Stanger Ltd* [2002] EWCA Civ 916 at [26], [2002] 1 WLR 3059; *Egon Oldendorff v Liberia Corpn* [1996] 1 Lloyd's Rep 380 at 387 (CLARKE J).

[70] *Raiffeisen Zentralbank Osterreich AG v Five Star Trading LLC* [2001] EWCA Civ 68 at [33], [2001] QB 825.

[71] The same provision is to be found in Art 7 of the United Nations Convention on Contracts for the International Sale of Goods of 1980.

Community meanings to the terms used in the Convention. This provision also has important consequences when it comes to aids to interpretation, which will now be considered.

(d) Aids to interpretation[72]

(i) The Giuliano and Lagarde Report[73]

The Rome Convention is accompanied by the Giuliano and Lagarde Report, which is a commentary by members of the Working Group responsible for drafting the Convention. Section 3(3) of the Contracts (Applicable Law) Act 1990 allows this Report, and the Tizzano Report on the 1988 Protocols on interpretation,[74] to be considered by the English courts in ascertaining the meaning or effect of any provisions in the Rome Convention or first Protocol on interpretation. This follows the pattern of the Civil Jurisdiction and Judgments Act 1982, which allowed the Jenard and Schlosser Reports to be considered by English courts when interpreting the European Community law on jurisdiction and enforcement of judgments.[75] The latter Reports have been constantly referred to by the Court of Justice and national courts when interpreting the Brussels Convention. The Giuliano and Lagarde Report has been treated by the English courts as being of the same high authority when it comes to interpretation of the Rome Convention.

(ii) Other matters which under English law can be used in interpretation of a Convention

Section 3(3) of the 1990 Act states that allowing the courts to refer to the Giuliano and Lagarde Report is without prejudice to any practice as to other matters which may be considered. This is the result of an amendment to the Act during its passage through the Lords, when concern was expressed that it should be made clear that textbook commentaries on the Act could be considered by the courts.[76]

(iii) The decisions of Continental courts

Whatever the normal attitude of English judges towards the decisions of Continental courts, in this context foreign decisions on interpretation of the Rome Convention are of persuasive authority. Article 18 (uniformity of interpretation) enables parties to rely on foreign decisions.[77] This will include the decisions of Continental courts in Member States which have applied the Convention in anticipation of to its coming into effect,[78] as well as decisions subsequent to this.

---

[72] See generally Kaye, pp 78–81.

[73] OJ 1980 C 282.

[74] OJ 1990 C 219.

[75] Supra, p 209.

[76] Hansard (HL) 5 April 1990, vol 517, cols 1541–1542.

[77] The Giuliano and Lagarde Report, p 38. See, eg, *Raiffeisen Zentralbank Osterreich AG v Five Star Trading LLC* [2001] EWCA Civ 68 at [49]–[52], [2001] QB 825.

[78] See, eg, the decisions of courts in the Netherlands: *Compagnie Européene des Petroles SA v Sensor Nederland BV* (1983) 22 ILM 66; *Machinale Glasfabriek de Maas BV v Emaillerie* [1985] 2 CMLR 281; *Buenaventura v Ocean Trade Co* [1984] ECC 183; *Société Nouvelle de Papeteries de l'Aa v Machinefabriek BOA*, 25 September 1992, NJ (1992) No 750, RvdW (1992) No 207. For German cases, see Horlacher (1994) 27 Cornell Int LJ 173. See also the Academy of European Law in Trier database at http://www.rome-convention.org.

(iv) Texts in other languages

The 1990 Act appears to give the force of law[79] to the Convention in its different languages texts, all of which are equally authentic,[80] rather than just to the English text, which is merely set out in the Act for ease of reference. Moreover, there is Court of Justice authority to the effect that courts of Member States should always be prepared to consider the texts of the Brussels Convention in other languages.[81] The same principle applies in relation to the Rome Convention.[82]

(v) The Brussels Convention and Brussels I Regulation

It has already been mentioned[83] that the effect of section 3(1) is to oblige English courts to follow decisions on interpretation of the Brussels Convention and the subsequent Brussels I Regulation which are relevant to interpretation of the Rome Convention. The most obvious example is the decision in *Ivenel v Schwab*,[84] which discusses the Rome Convention. Going beyond this, some of the provisions in the Rome Convention use the same concepts as,[85] or are even lifted word for word from,[86] the Brussels Convention. In such a situation, it is only right and proper that the earlier interpretation of this concept or term under the Brussels Convention should be looked at, and, unless there is a good reason to the contrary, followed.[87]

(vi) The traditional common law rules

Much of the Convention appears familiar to English lawyers and there may be a temptation to resort to the old common law rules when interpreting the Convention.[88] However, this is not usually justified and would be a dangerous habit to get into.[89] The provisions in the Convention are not normally based on English law or on that of any other country's national law but on a common core of ideas used in Community countries.[90] A rule which may appear at first sight to be the same as the common law rule it has replaced may turn out, on closer examination, to be different in some respect.[91] The aim of uniformity of interpretation throughout the Community will not be achieved if English courts interpret the

---

[79] S 2.

[80] See Art 33.

[81] Case 150/80 *Elefanten Schuh GmbH v Jacqmain* [1981] ECR 1671. See also *Newtherapeutics Ltd v Katz* [1991] Ch 226 at 243–245.

[82] *Ennstone Building Products Ltd v Stanger Ltd* [2002] EWCA Civ 916 at [28]–[29], [2002] 1 WLR 3059—looking at the French version of the Convention.

[83] Supra, p 673.

[84] Case 133/81 [1982] ECR 1891; discussed supra, p 273.

[85] See, eg, the concept of a contractual obligation used in Art 1(1) of the Rome Convention and Art 5(1) of the Brussels Convention and Brussels I Regulation; discussed supra, pp 229–235.

[86] See, eg, Art 5 (certain consumer contracts) of the Rome Convention which borrowed from Art 13 of the Brussels Convention (the wording of the Brussels I Regulation has been altered), discussed supra, pp 268–271. See Case C-89/91 *Shearson Lehman Hutton v TVB Treuhandgesellschaft für Vermogensverwaltung und Beteiligungen mbH* [1993] ECR I-139 at 174 (Opinion of AG DARMON).

[87] See, eg, *Base Metal Trading Ltd v Shamurin* [2004] EWCA Civ 1316, [2005] 1 WLR 1157.

[88] This was advocated by the Lord Chancellor, Hansard (HL) 15 February 1990, vol 515, col 1489.

[89] See in relation to Art 4, *Iran Continental Shelf Oil Co v IRI International Corp* [2002] EWCA 1024 at [16], [2004] 2 CLC 696. But cf *Marconi Communications International Ltd v PT Pan Indonesia Bank Ltd TBK* [2005] EWCA Civ 422, [2007] 2 Lloyd's Rep 72; discussed infra, pp 718–721.

[90] See *Raiffeisen Zentralbank Osterreich AG v Five Star Trading LLC* [2001] EWCA Civ 68 at [33]–[34], [2001] QB 825.

[91] See, eg, inferred choice of the applicable law, discussed infra, pp 701–706.

Convention as a codification of the proper law of the contract. Article 18 (uniform interpretation) serves as a reminder that national courts should not act in this way.[92]

(b) When does the Convention apply?

The Convention applies to matters coming within its scope, and it has universal application, ie it applies equally to contracts having no connection with a European Community State and to contracts with such a connection. Before turning to examine in detail these two aspects of the application of the Convention, four general points need to be made. First, the Convention does not have retrospective effect.[93] It only applies in a Contracting State to contracts made after the Convention has entered into force in that state (1 April 1991 in the case of the United Kingdom); the traditional common law rules will continue to apply to contracts made before the Convention has entered into force. Secondly, the Convention does not prejudice the application of other international conventions to which a Contracting State is a party, or becomes a party.[94] This means, for example, that, as far as the United Kingdom is concerned, carriage of goods by sea will still be dealt with by the Hague-Visby Rules, implemented by the Carriage of Goods by Sea Act 1971, and not by the Rome Convention. Thirdly, acts of the institutions of the European Communities, eg Community Regulations and Directives, and national laws implementing such acts,[95] laying down choice of law rules relating to contractual obligations, take precedence over the Convention.[96] Fourthly, Contracting States are allowed unilaterally to introduce choice of law rules inconsistent with those contained in the Convention.[97] However, they can only do so in regard to a particular category of contract, eg contracts made by travel agents. Furthermore, a process of informing and consulting with other Contracting States must be gone through first.

(i) The scope of the Convention

(a) Contractual obligations in any situation involving a choice between the laws of different countries

Article 1(1) states that "The rules of this Convention shall apply to contractual obligations in any situation involving a choice between the laws of different countries". There are two separate requirements under this provision. First, the obligation must be contractual. Secondly, there must be a choice of law problem.

(i) A contractual obligation

This concept should be given an autonomous meaning that is not blinkered by national conceptions such as consideration or even privity.[98] The issue in the case must be characterised, according to English principles of characterisation,[99] to see whether it is contractual

---

[92] See the Giuliano and Lagarde Report, p 38.

[93] Art 17.

[94] Art 21, discussed infra, p 763.

[95] See, eg, Reg 9 of the Unfair Terms in Consumer Contracts Regulations 1999; discussed infra, p 734.

[96] Art 20, discussed infra, p 762.

[97] Art 23. See also Art 24.

[98] *Raiffeisen Zentralbank Osterreich AG v Five Star Trading LLC* [2001] EWCA Civ 68 at [33], [2001] QB 825. See also *Atlantic Telecom GmbH, Noter* 2004 SLT 1031.

[99] The *Raiffeisen* case, supra; the *Atlantic Telecom* case, supra. The principles are discussed supra, pp 41–50.

or, for example, proprietary or tortious. The process of characterisation can be guided by the subject matter and wording of the Convention itself. A provision in the Convention may show a clear intention to embrace a particular issue.[100] Applying these principles it has been held[101] that the issue of whether, following an assignment (of the benefit of an insurance policy), the obligor (the insurer) had to pay (the proceeds of the insurance policy) to the asssignee (a bank) rather than the assignor (a vessel owner) fell within the contractual rather than the proprietary umbrella.[102] Also falling within this contractual umbrella are such issues as whether a contract has been novated, and whether a third party may enforce a right conferred on him from the outset under a contract.[103] Novation and making new contracts with third parties are instances of the parties' freedom to contract and it is this party autonomy that is the dominant theme influencing the modern international view of contract.[104] A contractual obligation "is by its very nature one which is voluntarily assumed by agreement".[105] Where a tortious or equitable duty of care is imposed, this arises from a voluntary assumption of responsibility[106] and not from agreement and therefore the Convention will not apply.[107] Not only do tortious obligations and property rights fall outside the scope of the Convention but so also do intellectual property rights[108] and claims that arise as a matter of company law and company regulation.[109] The position in relation to quasi-contract is more complicated. At first sight the Convention appears to encompass this matter. The Convention contains a provision dealing with "the consequences of nullity of the contract",[110] which under English law is regarded as being a quasi-contractual issue. However, its presence in the Convention is due to the fact that this issue is regarded by other Member States as being contractual. More importantly, a preliminary draft of the Convention,[111] which dealt with both contractual and non-contractual obligations, included in its provisions on non-contractual obligations a provision dealing with restitution. The Rome II Regulation on the law applicable to non-contractual obligations elaborates on this by having separate provisions for two different types of restitutionary claim.[112] One provision deals with non-contractual obligations arising out of unjust enrichment, the other with non-contractual obligations arising out of an act performed without due authority (*negotiorum gestio*). Moreover, in the context of jurisdiction, a claim in restitution has not been regarded

---

[100] The *Raiffeisen* case, supra, at [43].

[101] The *Raiffeisen* case, supra.

[102] The *Raiffeisen* case, supra. Accordingly Art 12, discussed infra, pp 1235–1237, applied.

[103] The *Raiffeisen* case, supra, at [43].

[104] Ibid.

[105] *Base Metal Trading Ltd v Shamurin* [2004] EWCA Civ 1316 at [28], [2005] 1 WLR 1157; Briggs (2004) BYBIL 572. This definition raises a difficulty where a contractual obligation is imposed by law as under s 2 of the Carriage of Goods by Sea Act 1992, see generally Fawcett, Harris and Bridge, paras 14.02–14.06.

[106] Or involuntary, eg strict liability.

[107] The *Base Metal* case, supra, at [28].

[108] See the Giuliano and Lagarde Report, p 10. However, a *contractual obligation* in respect of an intellectual property right, eg a licensing agreement, would come within the scope of the Convention. There was an unsuccessful attempt in the House of Lords to amend the 1990 Act to exclude this: Hansard (HL) 5 April 1990, vol 517, cols 1544–1547. See generally Fawcett and Torremans, p 551; Wadlow [1997] 1 EIPR 11, at 11–12.

[109] *Atlantic Telecom GmbH, Noter* 2004 SLT 1031.

[110] Art 10(1)(e); discussed infra, pp 757–758, and supra, p 671.

[111] Art 13 of the preliminary draft; see generally, Collier in Lipstein (ed), *Harmonisation of Private International Law by the EEC*, 81 et seq.

[112] Infra, pp 818–819.

as a matter relating to a contract.[113] Issues in restitution should therefore be regarded as being outside the scope of the Convention.

In cases where there is concurrent liability in contract and tort, the position prior to the introduction of the Rome II Regulation was very favourable to the claimant. The claimant was, for choice of law purposes, free to frame the action in tort rather than contract.[114] Indeed, the position was the same as under English domestic law and the claimant had the option of framing his claim in contract, or tort, or both.[115] The introduction of the Rome II Regulation means that this needs rethinking. The analogy should be drawn with jurisdiction under Article 5(1) and (3) of the Brussels I Regulation[116] and the obligation should be classsified as contractual or non-contractual but not both, so that there would be no question of the claimant being able to choose.[117]

(ii) A choice between the laws of different countries[118]

A preliminary draft of the Convention stated that it only applied "in situations of an international character".[119] This requirement was criticised[120] for the definitional problems it created, and it was replaced by the more straightforward requirement that there be a situation involving a choice between the laws of different countries. As far as the United Kingdom is concerned this merely makes explicit what was implicit under the traditional common law rules on contract choice of law. However, the fact that this is now spelt out in statutory form means that some attention needs to be given to this point. Under English private international law a choice of law problem exists whenever the court is faced with a dispute that contains a foreign element.[121] With a contractual dispute, typical examples of a foreign element are as follows: one of the parties to the contract is a foreign national or is habitually resident abroad; the contract is concluded abroad; the contract is to be performed by one of the parties abroad. In such cases the foreign country has a claim to have its law applied, and the uniform rules in the Convention are intended to apply.

The position is more difficult if the court is faced with a dispute involving a foreign element, but in respect of what is an essentially domestic contract. This can arise in two different types of case. The first is where, for example, there is a purely German contract, which is the subject of trial in England, subsequent to the defendant having moved his

---

[113] See *Kleinwort Benson Ltd v Glasgow City Council* [1999] 1 AC 153, HL; discussed supra, pp 230–231.

[114] *Base Metal Trading Ltd v Shamurin* [2004] EWCA Civ 1316 at [31]–[35], [2005] 1 WLR 1157. See also Dicey, Morris and Collins, paras 32-025–32-026.

[115] The *Base Metal Case*, supra, at [35]. See also Dicey, Morris and Collins, para 33-083. Cf Briggs [2003] LMCLQ 12 and the position in respect of jurisdiction under the Brussels I Regulation, supra, pp 251–252. See generally on choice law and concurrent claims arising out of the international sale of goods, Fawcett, Harris and Bridge, Chapter 20.

[116] Supra, p 251.

[117] This was advocated by Briggs [2003] LMCLQ 12 even before the introduction of Rome II. For discussion on which classification should be adopted see Chapter 19, infra, pp 779–780.

[118] See generally Lando in Lipstein (ed), *Harmonisation of Private International Law by the EEC*, p 15; (1987) 24 CMLR 159 at 163–164; Diamond (1986) IV Hague Recueil 236 at 248–251; Plender, paras 3.01–3.04, 3.15–3.17; Kaye, pp 107–111.

[119] Art 1 of the preliminary draft Convention.

[120] See, eg, Collins (1976) 25 ICLQ 35, 41. But see the definition of "international" in Art 1 of the Inter-American Convention on the Law Applicable to International Contracts of 1994.

[121] Supra, p 4 et seq.

business to England after concluding the contract. The situation involves a foreign element in that one of the parties now carries on his business in England. However, what is lacking is any relevant connection with a country other than Germany of the sort which would give that other country's law a claim to be applied.[122] Nonetheless, it is desirable that such cases come within the Convention.[123] The object of the Convention of achieving harmonisation of choice of law rules in contract is most likely to be attained if the scope of the Convention is given as wide an interpretation as possible. The above example should therefore be regarded as one involving a choice between the laws of different countries. The second type of case is where there is, for example, a purely English contract, but the parties have agreed that French law shall govern the contract. It is implicit from the terms of Article 3(3)[124] that the Convention will apply in this situation.[125] However, the Convention will not apply if there is a purely English contract which merely incorporates French law by, for example, setting out verbatim a provision of French law as a term of the contract.[126]

There is another problem in relation to the requirement that there is "a choice between the laws of different countries" which is less easily solved. Under English law, if foreign law is not pleaded or proved, the court gives a decision according to English law.[127] The courts are free to apply this rule in relation to the Rome Convention because matters of evidence and procedure are excluded from the scope of the Convention.[128] If the English court is going automatically to apply English law it is arguable that this is not a situation involving a choice between the laws of different countries. However, the purpose of the Convention is not going to be met if the English courts allow the parties to side-step the uniform rules contained therein by a simple omission to plead and prove foreign law. It would therefore be better if this sort of case was regarded as coming within the Convention.[129]

The choice must be between the laws of different *countries*. A country is defined under the Convention in the normal private international law sense as a territorial unit with its own rules of law, in this case relating to contractual obligations.[130] A French court, for example, will have to apply English law, or Scottish, or Northern Irish law under the Convention, even though the United Kingdom is the Contracting State to the Convention. Similarly, an English court may have to apply, for example, Ontario or New South Wales law under the Convention. Indeed, the Convention can apply to an inter-state dispute involving connections with the "countries" of California and New York, provided that trial takes place in a Contracting State to the Convention. However, the Convention makes it clear that it is for the United Kingdom to decide whether it wants to apply the rules in the Convention to intra-United Kingdom disputes. It is certainly not

---

122 See the Giuliano and Lagarde Report, p 10, which presupposes the existence of such a claim.
123 See Lando, op cit, pp 15–17. Diamond has no doubts that such cases come within it: ibid, pp 250–251.
124 Discussed infra, pp 695–697.
125 See generally Nygh, *Autonomy in International Contracts* (1999), pp 52–55.
126 Incorporation of foreign law is discussed infra, p 701.
127 Supra, p 111 et seq.
128 Art 1(2)(h), see infra, p 687.
129 There are problems then of whether the parties have made a choice of the applicable law, infra, p 694.
130 Art 19(1).

bound to do so,[131] but the obvious inconvenience of having a different regime for intra-United Kingdom contractual disputes from all other cases has led to a provision in the Contracts (Applicable Law) Act 1990 applying the Convention to such disputes.[132] The upshot is that England, Scotland and Northern Ireland are separate countries for the purposes of the Convention, even in intra-United Kingdom disputes.

(iii) The Rome I Regulation

Article 1 of the Regulation is headed "Material Scope" and provides that: "This Regulation shall apply, in situations involving a conflict of laws, to contractual obligations in civil and commercial matters. It shall not apply, in particular, to revenue, customs or administrative matters."[133] This adopts the wording on the scope of the Rome II Regulation on non-contractual obligations.[134] This new terminology and how it differs from that in the Rome Convention is analysed below.[135]

(b) Exclusions[136]

Article 1(2) to (4) excludes a wide variety of matters from the scope of the Convention. These matters can be put into three main categories. First and foremost, it excludes certain commercial contracts such as arbitration agreements and certain contracts of insurance. Secondly, it excludes non-commercial contracts, such as agreements to make wills and agreements to pay maintenance. Thirdly, it excludes certain matters which do not involve contract choice of law, such as evidence and procedure, or which under the laws of some Member States do not involve contract choice of law, such as negotiable instruments and the issue of capacity to contract. The matters excluded from the scope of the Convention, and the reasons for their exclusion, will now be examined, in the order in which they are set out in the Convention. These are as follows:

(i) Questions involving the status or legal capacity of natural persons, without prejudice to Article 11[137]

This phrase is a familiar one, and is to be found in the list of exclusions from the Brussels Convention and Brussels I Regulation.[138] Questions of status are clearly outside the scope of a Convention concerned with contract choice of law, and do not need expressly to be excluded. The exclusion of legal capacity is more controversial. To common lawyers capacity to contract is a matter falling squarely within the ambit of rules on contract choice of law. But to civil lawyers this is regarded as a matter relating to status, hence its exclusion from the Convention.[139] This particular exclusion only relates to natural persons. The exclusion of the legal capacity of corporations is dealt with under a separate provision.[140]

---

[131] Art 19(2).

[132] S 2(3).

[133] Art 1(1) of the Rome I Regulation.

[134] Art 1(1) of Rome II. This also expressly excludes "the liability of the State for acts and omissions in the exercise of State authority (acta iure imperii)".

[135] Infra, pp 775–780.

[136] See Plender, paras 4.01–4.54; Kaye, pp 111–142.

[137] Art 1(2)(a) of the Rome Convention.

[138] Supra, pp 218–219.

[139] See North in *Contract Conflicts*, p 10.

[140] Art 1(2)(e), discussed infra, p 685.

The result of the exclusion is that national courts are left to apply their traditional rules of private international law to the issue of capacity to contract; in England's case this will be the traditional common law rules. However, there is one exception to this. The exclusion of capacity to contract is subject to Article 11 of the Convention, which is a fairly narrow rule designed to protect a party who contracts with a natural person under an incapacity from being caught unawares by this. The English common law rules on capacity to contract, and Article 11, will be examined later on in this chapter in the section on particular issues.[141]

The same exclusion of questions involving status, etc applies under the Rome I Regulation.

(ii) Contractual obligations relating to:

(a) wills and succession,

(b) rights in property arising out of a matrimonial relationship,

(c) rights and duties arising out of a family relationship, parentage, marriage or affinity, including maintenance obligations in respect of children who are not legitimate.[142]

This provision is concerned with non-commercial contracts. Indeed, most disputes relating to the matters listed above will not even involve contractual obligations. For example, disputes in relation to wills are not normally contractual, but are concerned with issues such as the validity of the will. This provision makes it clear that, in the rare cases which raise contractual obligations, for example an agreement to make a will, the Convention will not apply.

The phrases "wills and succession" and "rights in property arising out of a matrimonial relationship" are to be found among the list of exclusions from the scope of the Brussels Convention and Brussels I Regulation,[143] and their meaning has been fully discussed in that context. There is no need under the Rome Convention to distinguish between rights in property arising out of a matrimonial relationship and maintenance since, as we will see next, the latter is also normally excluded from the scope of the Convention.

The Rome I Regulation adopts the wording of the Rome II Regulation on non-contractual obligations and excludes "obligations arising out of matrimonial property regimes, property regimes of relationships deemed by the law applicable to such relationships to have comparable effects to marriage, and wills and succession".[144] This provision and how it differs from the Rome Convention are discussed in the context of Rome II.[145]

Turning back to the Rome Convention, the third exclusion listed above, "rights and duties arising out of a family relationship", etc, does not feature in the Brussels Convention and was intended to ensure that contractual obligations relating to any family law matter were excluded from the Rome Convention.[146] In particular, it normally excludes maintenance obligations, which are included within the Brussels Convention and

---

[141] Infra, pp 750–753.
[142] Art 1(2)(b) of the Rome Convention.
[143] Art 1(1) of the Brussels I Regulation; discussed supra, pp 218–219.
[144] Art 1(2)(c) of the Regulation. Art 1(2)(b) of Rome II.
[145] Infra, pp 782–783.
[146] The Giuliano and Lagarde Report, p 10.

Brussels I Regulation.[147] However, the exclusion of maintenance is not all-embracing. The Giuliano and Lagarde Report[148]appears to distinguish between, on the one hand, obligations to pay maintenance which are imposed by law in respect of which there is also an agreement to pay (these are excluded from the scope of the Convention) and, on the other hand, purely contractual obligations to do so (these are within the scope of the Convention). Thus the case of a father who is under a legal obligation to maintain his children after a divorce, but who also agrees to maintain them, although involving a contractual obligation, is excluded from the scope of the Convention. In contrast to this, if a person who is not under a legal obligation to provide maintenance for a member of the family, nonetheless agrees to do so, as where a child agrees to maintain a parent, this would fall within the scope of the Convention.

The Rome I Regulation contains a separate provision to deal with this third exclusion. It provides that the Regulation will not apply to "obligations arising out of family relationships[149] and relationships deemed by the law applicable to such relationships to have comparable effects,[150] including maintenance obligations".[151] This adopts the wording of the exclusion in the Rome II Regulation on non-contractual obligations.[152] The difference in wording from that in the Rome Convention is discussed later on in the context of Rome II.[153]

(iii) Obligations arising under bills of exchange, cheques and promissory notes and other negotiable instruments to the extent that the obligations under such other negotiable instruments arise out of their negotiable character[154]

Under English law, negotiable instruments involve contractual obligations, but have long been subject to special rules, including those contained in the Bills of Exchange Act 1882, rather than being governed by the proper law of the contract.[155] The effect of the exclusion of negotiable instruments from the Convention is to preserve these special rules. The exclusion applies to bills of exchange, cheques and promissory notes, each of which category is well known to English lawyers. It also applies to "other negotiable instruments to the extent that the obligations under such other negotiable instruments arise out of their negotiable character". "Other negotiable instruments" is not defined under the Convention, and Contracting States may have different ideas on whether an instrument is negotiable. However, the Giuliano and Lagarde Report[156]states that it is for the private international law of the forum to determine whether a document is to be characterised as being negotiable. If the transfer takes place in England, the instrument is negotiable if English mercantile custom or a statute so provides. Examples of instruments

---

[147] See Art 5(2) of the Brussels I Regulation, discussed supra, pp 245–247.
[148] At p 10.
[149] This "should cover parentage, marriage, affinity and collateral relatives": Recital (8) of the Regulation.
[150] The reference "to relationships having comparable effects to marriage and other family relationships should be interpreted in accordance with the law of the Member State in which the court is seised": Recital (8) of the Regulation.
[151] Art 1(2)(b) of the Regulation.
[152] Art 1(2)(a) of Rome II.
[153] Infra, pp 781–782.
[154] Art 1(2)(c) of the Rome Convention. See the Giuliano and Lagarde Report, p 11; Kaye, pp 116–118.
[155] Dicey, Morris and Collins, 33R-322–33-378.
[156] At p 11.

which are negotiable in England include bonds issued by foreign governments and debentures issued to bearer by English companies. On the other hand, a bill of lading which is transferred in England is not negotiable, and is therefore within the scope of the Convention.

Even if it can be shown that what is involved is a negotiable instrument other than a bill of exchange, cheque or promissory note, the exclusion is limited to cases in which the obligation arises out of the negotiable character of the instrument. This would cover a dispute where, for example, an acceptor of the instrument wants payment but the other party refuses, alleging that the acceptor is not a holder in due course of the instrument. Such a dispute would be outside the scope of the Convention. On the other hand, contracts for the issue of, for example, Government bonds or for purchase/sale of such bonds are not concerned with the negotiable character of the instrument, and are thus within the scope of the Convention.[157]

The Rome I Regulation contains an identically worded exclusion.[158] It also contains a Recital which confirms the existing position by providing that the exclusion covers "bills of lading to the extent that the obligations under the bill of lading arise out of its negotiable character".[159]

(iv) Arbitration agreements and agreements on the choice of court[160]

The exclusion of arbitration agreements and agreements on the choice of court was probably the most controversial of the exclusions from the Convention, with the United Kingdom delegation arguing unsuccessfully that such agreements should be subject to the rules contained in the Convention.[161] The exclusion applies not only to arbitration or choice of jurisdiction agreements, ie agreements whose sole or main purpose is to provide for arbitration or a place of trial for a particular dispute, but also to arbitration or choice of jurisdiction clauses contained within a contract, which under English law are themselves regarded as separate agreements. However, when an arbitration or choice of jurisdiction clause is excluded,[162] this only affects the clause itself; the remaining clauses in the contract will be within the scope of the Convention and judges and arbitrators will have to apply the rules under the Convention to them. This exclusion obviously relates to any choice of law issues that arise with regard to arbitration agreements and agreements on the choice of court: such as the formation, validity[163] and effects of such agreements. It is also said to relate to any procedural questions that arise in relation to the arbitration.[164]

---

[157] Ibid.
[158] Art 1(2)(d) of the Regulation.
[159] Recital (9) of the Regulation.
[160] Art 1(2)(d) of the Rome Convention.
[161] For the reasons for this see infra, p 685.
[162] Nonetheless, according to the Giuliano and Lagarde Report, p 12, the clause remains relevant to the ascertainment of the applicable law under Art 3(1), see infra, pp 701–703.
[163] *Akai Pty Ltd v People's Insurance Co Ltd* [1998] 1 Lloyd's Rep 90 at 98. Some issues which may appear to be ones of validity of the jurisdiction agreement end up being regarded as ones of validity of the contract as a whole see: *Egon Oldendorff v Liberia Corpn* [1995] 2 Lloyd's Rep 64 (MANCE J), discussed infra, p 745. For cases where it appears to have been accepted that the issue was as to validity of the jurisdiction clause but that the law governing this issue was the law governing the contract as a whole (ie the Rome Convention) see: *OT Africa Line Ltd v Magic Sportswear Corpn* [2005] EWCA Civ 710 at [1]–[2], [22] (per LONGMORE LJ), [2005] 2 Lloyd's Rep 170 (but cf RIX LJ at [60]); *Horn Linie GmbH & Co v Panamericana Formas E Impresos SA (The Hornbay)* [2006] EWHC 373 (Comm) at [20], [2006] 2 Lloyd's Rep 44.
[164] The Giuliano and Lagarde Report, p 12.

The result of the exclusion is that national courts will continue to apply their own rules of private international law to arbitration agreements and agreements on the choice of court. In England's case this means the traditional common law rules.[165]Contracts will have to be split up so that a question, for example, of interpretation of a choice of jurisdiction clause will have to be determined under the traditional common law rules, whereas the rest of the contract will be governed by the rules applicable under the Convention. This can lead to different laws governing the agreement on arbitration/choice of court and the rest of the contract.[166]One could end up with a contract which is void according to the rules on the applicable law contained in the Convention, but which contains an arbitration agreement which is valid according to its proper law. It was in order to avoid such splitting of the contract that the United Kingdom argued that arbitration and choice of jurisdiction agreements should not be excluded from the scope of the Convention.

The Rome I Regulation contains an identically worded exclusion.[167]

(v) *Questions governed by the law of companies and other bodies corporate or unincorporate such as the creation, by registration or otherwise, legal capacity, internal organisation or winding up of companies and other bodies corporate or unincorporate and the personal liability of officers and members as such for the obligations of the company or body*[168]

This provision clarifies the point that, if contractual matters are raised in a company law context, they fall outside the scope of the Convention. Examples of matters excluded by this provision are the contract which, under English law, is contained in the memorandum and articles of association of a company, and a shareholders' agreement to wind up a company. The legal capacity of a company to contract is also excluded from the scope of the Convention.[169] On the other hand, an agreement by promoters to form a company is apparently not excluded from the scope of the Convention.[170] This is presumably on the basis that this is a purely contractual matter and is not governed by company law.

The Rome I Regulation contains an almost identically worded exclusion.[171]

(vi) *The question whether an agent is able to bind a principal, or an organ to bind a company or body corporate or unincorporate, to a third party*[172]

The exclusion is only concerned with the relationship between a principal and a third party, and is confined to the specific question of whether the principal is bound vis à vis

---

[165] The *Akai* case, supra.

[166] See Lipstein in Lipstein (ed), *Harmonisation of Private International Law by the EEC*, p 3.

[167] Art 1(2)(e) of the Regulation.

[168] Art 1(2)(e) of the Rome Convention; the Giuliano and Lagarde Report, p 12.

[169] *Continental Enterprises Ltd v Shandong Zhucheng Foreign Trade Group Co* [2005] EWHC 92 (Comm). This is a total exclusion. For an example of a case raising this issue, see *Janred Properties Ltd v Ente Nazionale Italiano per il Turismo* [1989] 2 All ER 444. Cf the position of natural persons under an incapacity—Art 11 may apply, on which see infra, pp 752–753.

[170] The Giuliano and Lagarde Report, p 12. See also *Base Metal Trading Ltd v Shamurin* [2003] EWHC 2419 (Comm) at [42], [2004] IL Pr 5; respondent's notice rejected without discussing this point [2004] EWCA Civ 1316, [2005] 1 WLR 1157.

[171] Art 1(2)(f) of the Regulation.

[172] Art 1(2)(f) of the Rome Convention. For criticism see Lasok and Stone, *Conflict of Laws in the European Community* (1987), p 354.

third parties by the acts of the agent.[173] It follows that, for example, a contractual dispute between the principal and agent arising out of the contract of agency is not excluded. The exclusion is therefore a narrow one. However, it does encompass the question whether an organ of a company can bind the company. This raises the question of ultra vires, which under English law is a question of company law. The exclusion has been explained[174] on the basis that the principle of freedom of contract, which is deeply enshrined in the Convention's rules on the applicable law,[175] is difficult to accept in relation to the matter excluded. As far as English law is concerned, the effect of the exclusion is the retention of the common law rule under which the proper law of the contract concluded between the agent and third party governs the question of whether the principal is bound vis à vis third parties by the acts of the agent.[176]

The question whether an agent is able to bind a principal is also excluded from the scope of the Rome I Regulation.[177] The original proposal for a Regulation did not exclude this question and contained a proposed new choice of law rule dealing with this issue and other issues arising where a contract is concluded by an agent.[178] However, this special rule was subsequently deleted and the original exclusion in the Rome Convention was restored, albeit with slightly modified wording.

(vii) The constitution of trusts and the relationship between settlors, trustees and beneficiaries[179]

The English concept of a trust is said to define the subject matter of this exception.[180] This raises the question of why this exclusion of the common law trust was introduced. It is presumably because, under English law, the constitution of trusts and the relationship between trustee/beneficiary and settlor/trustee are not based on contract. The exclusion is for the sake of clarity. There are Continental equivalents of a trust which are contractual in origin and thus appear to come within the Convention. However, these will also be excluded if they exhibit the same characteristics as a common law trust.[181] It is noticeable that the exclusion does not extend to trust property, although this can in fact raise contractual problems. For example, a trustee could invest in property abroad and could then be sued in contract by the vendor of the property. This situation appears to come within the scope of the Convention.

The Rome I Regulation contains an identically worded exclusion.[182]

---

[173] The Giuliano and Lagarde Report, p 13.
[174] Ibid.
[175] Infra, p 690.
[176] See *Marubeni Hong Kong and South China Ltd v Government of Mongolia* [2004] EWHC 472 (Comm) at [105]–[110], [2004] 2 Lloyd's Rep 198.
[177] Art 1(2)(g) of the Regulation.
[178] Art 7 of the Proposal for a Regulation of the European Parliament and the Council on the law applicable to contractual obligations (Rome I) COM (2005) 650 final.
[179] Art 1(2)(g) of the Rome Convention. See Morse [1993] JBL 168, 180. For trusts generally in private international law see infra, Chapter 34.
[180] The Giuliano and Lagarde Report, p 13.
[181] Ibid.
[182] Art 1(2)(h) of the Regulation.

(viii) Evidence and procedure, without prejudice to Article 14[183]

This provision excludes two matters, procedure and evidence. The exclusion of evidence is not total, but is subject to Article 14,[184] which subjects two specific evidential matters, the burden of proof (in so far as this raises rules of substance) and proving a contract, to the rules of the Convention. The exclusion of evidence and procedure was said by the Giuliano and Lagarde Report to require no comment.[185] Nonetheless, two obvious questions need to be asked. First, why were these matters expressly excluded from the scope of the Convention? Presumably, this is just for the sake of clarity. Procedural and evidential matters would not appear to come within the scope of a Convention which is concerned with contract choice of law (a matter of substance) and therefore do not need expressly to be excluded. Secondly, there is the vital question of when a matter is to be classified as being one of procedure. Procedure is a very different matter from the other matters excluded in that it involves a potential escape device, ie if you classify a matter as being purely procedural you escape from the choice of law rules under the Convention. National courts are likely to resort to their own traditional ideas of what is a procedural matter. However, English courts cannot automatically assume that the classifications which they have adopted in the past will continue to be appropriate under the Convention. For example, the question of whether a contract has to be in writing was classified at common law as being one of procedure. Under the Convention, seemingly, it is to be regarded as a matter of substance raising an issue of formal validity of the contract.[186] The danger of different states classifying the same matter differently can be avoided by adherence to the principle of uniform interpretation. Once it has been decided that the issue is one of evidence or procedure, the effect of the exclusion is that this issue is left to be governed by the forum's rules on private international law. Under English private international law all procedural matters (including evidence) are automatically a matter for the law of the forum.[187]

The Rome I Regulation contains a substantially identical exclusion.[188]

(ix) Insurance[189]

Certain contracts of insurance are excluded from the scope of the Convention. This is an important exclusion, involving a common type of commercial contract. However, the exclusion is only in respect of contracts of insurance which cover risks situated in the territories of the Member States of the European Community.[190] In order to determine whether a risk is situated in the European Community the court applies its internal law, which means its internal domestic law and not its private international law.[191] The exclusion

---

[183] Art 1(2)(h) of the Rome Convention.

[184] Discussed supra, pp 83 and 89.

[185] At p 38.

[186] Ibid, p 31; infra, p 747.

[187] Supra, pp 75–76.

[188] Art 1(3) of the Regulation.

[189] Art 1(3) of the Rome Convention.

[190] For risks situated in both Member and non-Member States see: *American Motorists Insurance Co (Amico) v Cellstar Corpn* [2003] EWCA Civ 206 at [13]–[40], [2003] IL Pr 22; *Travelers Casualty and Surety Co Ltd v Sun Life Assurance Co of Canada (UK) Ltd* [2004] EWHC 1704, [2004] IL Pr 50.

[191] Art 1(3); the Giuliano and Lagarde Report, p 13. The Contracts (Applicable Law) Act 1990, s 2(1A) provides that the internal law as far as the United Kingdom is concerned is contained in the provisions of the regulations for the time being in force under the Financial Services and Markets Act 2000, s 424(3).

does not apply to contracts of reinsurance.[192] In so far as insurance comes within the Convention, there are special rules in relation to consumer contracts,[193] which include contracts for the provision of services such as insurance. The exclusion is explained by the fact that it was intended that there should be Community Directives containing special choice of law rules for the insurance of risks situated within the European Community. These Directives have since been issued.[194] Contracts of insurance, in so far as they are excluded from the scope of the Convention and were entered into before these other European Community rules came into effect, will be subject to the traditional common law rules,[195] according to which the proper law of the contract is applied, but subject to special rules for ascertaining the objective proper law.

The Rome I Regulation introduces a major change by extending the scope of the Regulation to cover most insurance contracts. The only exclusion is of insurance contracts arising out of operations carried out by organisations other than undertakings referred to in Article 2 of the consolidated life assurance Directive[196] "the object of which is to provide benefits for employed or self-employed persons belonging to an undertaking or group of undertakings, or a trade or group of trades, in the event of death or survival or of discontinuance or curtailment of activity, or of sicknessss related to work or accidents at work".[197] The Regulation goes on to provide specific choice of law rules for such contracts.[198]

(x) Obligations arising out of dealings prior to the conclusion of a contract

The Rome I Regulation differs from the Convention by expressly excluding obligations arising out of dealings prior to the conclusion of a contract[199] on the basis that these fall within the scope of the Rome II Regulation, [200] which has a separate free-standing provision dealing with non-contractual obligations arising out of dealings prior to the conclusion of a contract.[201] There is no such express exclusion in the Convention but the

---

[192] Art 1(4). See *AIG Group (UK) Ltd v The Ethniki* [1998] 4 All ER 301 at 310. See generally Lasok and Stone, *Conflict of Laws in the European Community* (1987), pp 385–386 who argue that there should be special rules for reinsurance.

[193] See Art 5; discussed infra, p 726.

[194] See Directive (EC) No 88/357, OJ 1988 L 172 (amended by Directive (EC) No 1992/49 and (EC) No 2002/13), the Second Council Directive on Non-Life Insurance, on which see *Crédit Lyonnais v New Hampshire Insurance Co* [1997] 2 Lloyd's Rep 1, CA; Directive (EC) No 92/49, OJ 1992 L 228/1, the Third Council Directive on Non-Life Insurance; Directive (EC) No 2002/83, OJ 2002 L 345/1, the consolidated life assurance Directive. The choice of law rules are discussed in: Dicey, Morris and Collins, paras 33R-136–33-208; Kaye, pp 138–140; Plender, paras 4.49–4.54; Seatzu, *Insurance in Private International Law* (2003); Merrett (2006) 2 J Priv Int L 409; MacNeil (1995) 44 ICLQ 19; Smulders and Glazener (1992) 29 CMLR 775; Reich (1992) 29 CMLR 861, 870 et seq; Reichert-Facilides and d'Oliveira (eds), *International Insurance Contract Law*. See also the Law Com and Scottish Law Com Report on the Choice of Law Rules in the Draft Non-Life Insurance Services Directive, 11 April 1979. For criticism of the insurance exclusion see North in *Contract Conflicts*, p 11.

[195] See Dicey, Morris and Collins, 33-121–33-123.

[196] Directive (EC) No 2002/83 of 5 November 2002, OJ 2002 L 345/1. The Directive is amended by Directive (EC) No 2007/44.

[197] Art 1(2)(j) of the Regulation.

[198] Art 7 of the Regulation, discussed infra, pp 727–728.

[199] Art 1(2)(i) of the Regulation.

[200] See Recital (10) of the Rome I Regulation. See for the classification of such obligations in the context of the Brussels I Regulation, supra, pp 230–233.

[201] Art 12 of Rome II; discussed infra, pp 832–837.

Convention should not apply because obligations arising out of a pre-contractual relationship should be regarded as non-contractual.

(ii) The universal application of the Convention

The Rome Convention is intended to be of universal or world-wide application, ie it applies in any Contracting State forum, regardless of whether the contract has any connection with a European Community Contracting State.[202] In particular, there is no need for either party to the contract to be domiciled or resident in a Contracting State. The only thing that matters is that the dispute is tried in a Contracting State to the Convention. Thus a contractual dispute between a New York resident and an Ontario resident which is tried before the Commercial Court in England will be subject to the Convention. This avoids the need to distinguish for choice of law purposes between Contracting States and non-Contracting States, a distinction which would be particularly difficult to apply to contracts which involve connections with both a Contracting and a non-Contracting State.[203]

Article 2[204] provides that: "Any law specified by this Convention shall be applied whether or not it is the law of a Contracting State." This provision makes it clear that if the uniform rules under the Convention point, for example, to Japanese law as the law governing the contract, the courts of Contracting States will apply that country's law, even though Japan is not a Contracting State to the Convention. However, Article 2 only deals with one aspect of the universal application of the rules in the Convention. It says nothing about whether the situation or the parties must have a connection with a Contracting State. It is the Giuliano and Lagarde Report[205] which makes it clear that the Convention is intended to have universal application and, in particular, will apply to nationals of third states and to persons domiciled or resident therein.[206]

Article 2 is repeated almost verbatim in the Rome I Regulation.

(c) The applicable law

The provisions on the applicable law are at the heart of the Convention. A basic distinction is drawn between the situation where the law is chosen by the parties and the situation where the applicable law is ascertained in the absence of choice. Choice is concerned with the actual intentions of the parties (either expressed by the parties or inferred by the court) and absence of choice requires reference to objective connections localising the contract. The applicable law under the Convention, whether chosen or not, refers to the domestic law of the country in question, and there is no place for the doctrine of renvoi.[207] It is presupposed that there has to be an applicable law at the time when the

---

[202] See the Solicitor-General in Hansard (HC) Second Reading Committee 20 June 1990, col 4.

[203] Lagarde (1981) 22 VA J Int L 91, 93.

[204] See the Giuliano and Lagarde Report, p 13.

[205] Ibid, pp 8, 13.

[206] See the unsuccessful attempt to amend the 1990 Act so as to limit it to parties habitually resident in a Contracting State: Hansard (HL), 15 February 1990, vol 515, cols 1474–1490.

[207] Art 15; Kaye, pp 343–344. Obiter dicta in *Caterpillar Financial Services Corpn v SNC Passion* [2004] EWHC 569 (Comm) at [31]–[44], [2004] 2 Lloyd's Rep 99, which take into account French rules of private international law must be regarded as wrong.

contract is concluded.[208] It follows that the choice of a "floating" proper law, ie a proper law which was non-existent at the time when the contract was made but which was crystallised later on by the unilateral act of one of the parties. will be ineffective at the time when the contract is made. However, the Convention does allow the parties to vary the applicable law during the subsequent life of the contract.[209]

(i) The law is chosen by the parties

Any reference to choice of the applicable law raises a number of points which will be examined under the following headings: freedom of choice; limitations on choice; express choice; inferred choice; consent to choice. Before doing so, it must be pointed out that there are no formalities to be satisfied in relation to the parties' choice.[210]

(a) Freedom of choice

(i) The basic principle

Article 3 is entitled "Freedom of choice", and paragraph (1) sets out the basic principle that "a contract shall be governed by the law chosen by the parties". The parties' freedom to choose the governing law had been accepted in all the Member States of the European Community for many years.[211] In the United Kingdom the philosophical origin of this freedom is to be found in the fidelity of the Victorian judges to the Benthamite dogma of laissez-faire,[212] although authority for allowing the parties expressly to select the governing law pre-dates this.[213] In more modern policy terms, party autonomy provides the certainty and predictability which are essential in commercial matters. The philosophy of freedom of choice underlies not only the basic principle of allowing the parties to choose the law governing the contract but also some of the more detailed provisions relating to choice. Parties are given the freedom to pick and choose the applicable law so that it governs the whole or merely part of the contract. The parties are free to exercise their choice at any time and to vary their choice. These freedoms will now be examined.

Article 3(1) of the Regulation restates the basic principle on freedom of choice set out in the Convention.

(ii) Dépeçage[214]

The last sentence of Article 3(1) provides that: "By their choice the parties can select the law applicable to the whole or a part only of the contract." The parties are given the freedom to pick and choose (dépeçage) the applicable law and thereby sever the contract.[215]

---

[208] See Arts 3(2) and 4(2).

[209] Art 3(2); discussed infra, pp 692–694. See also the discussion of a "floating" applicable law, infra, p 700.

[210] *Oakley v Ultra Vehicle Design Ltd (In Liquidation)* [2005] EWHC (Ch) at [61], [2005] IL Pr 55. Cf Art 23 of the Brussels I Regulation, supra, pp 291–295.

[211] See the Giuliano and Lagarde Report, pp 15–16; Lando (1987) 24 CMLR 159, 171–179. It has also been accepted outside the Community, see Nygh (1995) 251 Hague Recueil Ch II and *Autonomy in International Contracts* (1999), Chapters 1 and 2. See more generally Harris (2000) 20 OJLS 247; Hartley (2006) 319 Hague Recueil Ch XII.

[212] Graveson, *Lectures on the Conflict of Laws and International Contracts* (1951), pp 6–8.

[213] See *Gienar v Meyer* (1796) 2 Hy Bl 603.

[214] See generally supra, pp 54–55. See in relation to the Rome Convention: Morse (1982) 2 YEL 107, 117–119.

[215] The same freedom is to be found in relation to trusts under Art 9 of the Hague Convention on the law applicable to trusts and on their recognition, implemented by the Recognition of Trusts Act 1987; see infra, pp 1315–1316.

The parties can choose different laws for different parts of the contract. Thus there could be an express choice of French law to govern one part, but an express choice of German law to govern the rest of the contract. The choice can be expressed by the parties or inferred by the court. If the parties choose different laws for different parts of the contract the choices must be logically consistent, ie they "must relate to elements in the contract which can be governed by different laws without giving rise to contradiction".[216] The Giuliano and Lagarde Report gives two contrasting examples.[217] An index linking clause may be made subject to a law different from the rest of the contract. On the other hand, it was thought unlikely that repudiation of the contract for non-performance could be subjected to two different laws, one for the vendor and the other for the purchaser. If the chosen laws cannot be reconciled, both choices fail and the rules on the applicable law in the absence of choice[218] have to be used. The "general obligation" under a contract (ie the contractual obligations governing the core of the parties' relationship, such issues as whether the contract is discharged by frustration or the innocent party can terminate the contract on account of the other party's breach) can only be governed by one law.[219] But it is possible for the general obligation under an agreement to be governed by New York law whilst payment instruments (ie cheques) and their validity, etc are governed by the drawee's law (with drawees from many different jurisdictions).[220] A breach of an insurance policy condition precluding the insured from making recovery from the insurer under a particular part of the policy can be severed from the insured's rights under other parts of the policy.[221] But the words of the policy defining the insured cannot be severed so as to be interpreted by different laws and given possibly different meanings, depending on the part of the globe in which events may occur giving rise to the claim.[222] The parties can choose a law to govern part of the contract but exercise no choice in respect of the remainder of the contract. In this situation the applicable law for the remainder of the contract must be ascertained, again, by the rules on the applicable law in the absence of choice. The Working Group rejected the notion of a presumption that the law chosen for one part of the contract should govern the entirety.[223]

What is meant by *part* of the contract? Obviously this covers the separate clauses in a contract. Thus the parties can choose one law to govern a particular clause,[224] and a different law to govern other clauses. From the example given above relating to repudiation of the contract, it also appears that *part* can include a particular issue[225] relating to the contract. Accordingly, the parties can choose one law to govern the interpretation of the contract and a different law to govern its discharge. On the other hand, it seems from the same example that the parties are not free to take a single issue, such as repudiation of

---

[216] The Giuliano and Lagarde Report, p 17.

[217] Ibid.

[218] See Art 4, discussed infra, pp 707–725.

[219] *Centrax v Citibank NA* [1999] 1 All ER (Comm) 557 at 562 (per WARD LJ), 569 (WALLER LJ), CA—citing Dicey and Morris, (1993)12th edn, p 1207.

[220] The *Centrax* case, supra.

[221] *CGU International Insurance plc v Szabo* [2002] 1 All ER (Comm) 83 at [39].

[222] Ibid.

[223] The Giuliano and Lagarde Report, p 17.

[224] Ibid.

[225] This is the type of severing of the contract that "dépeçage" usually refers to: see supra, pp 54–55. However, see Plender, para 5.17.

the contract, and to split this so that one law governs one party's rights and a different law governs the other party's rights. This is regarded as involving two choices which are logically inconsistent. Some contracts are, by their very nature, severable, for example a contract which turns out to consist of several independent contracts. Different laws can clearly be applied to these different contracts, without having to resort to the dépeçage provision.[226]

The Regulation repeats virtually verbatim the sentence on dépeçage used in the Convention.

(iii) Timing of choice

The first sentence of Article 3(2) provides that: "The parties may at any time agree to subject the contract to a law other than that which previously governed it, whether as a result of an earlier choice under this Article or of other provisions of this Convention." The policy underlying this provision[227] is that of providing maximum freedom as to when the parties can make their choice.[228] It can be made before the contract is concluded, at the time of or even after the conclusion of the contract. If the parties' choice is made for the first time after the conclusion of the contract, then the applicable law at the time of the conclusion of the contract will have to be determined by reference to the rules determining the applicable law in the absence of choice (Article 4). This law will apply until the parties subsequently exercise their choice, which may involve a variation in the applicable law.

This provision on timing of choice is adopted almost verbatim in the Regulation.

(iv) Variation of choice[229]

The parties' freedom to vary the applicable law follows on logically from their right to choose the applicable law at any time. For example, the parties may have agreed at the time of contracting that Californian law shall govern the contract. They have the freedom under Article 3(2) to agree subsequently[230] that, instead, Japanese law shall govern the contract.[231] It is irrelevant that Californian or Japanese law might not allow variation.[232] Equally, at the time the contract is made Luxembourg law may be applicable by virtue of the rules on the applicable law in the absence of choice (Article 4). The parties may subsequently agree that New York law shall govern. This subsequent agreement involves an exercise of the parties' freedom of choice under Article 3(1) and so can be

---

[226] See, however, Art 4(1) which has a provision on dépeçage in relation to contracts which are by their nature severable; infra, pp 709–710.

[227] See the Giuliano and Lagarde Report, p 17.

[228] This is referring to the parties' choice under Art 3(1), discussed infra, pp 700–705.

[229] See North, *Essays*, Chapter 3; Dicey, Morris and Collins, paras 32-084–32-085; Plender, paras 5.19–5.24.

[230] For the situation where there is an agreement at the time the contract is made to vary the applicable law in the future, see infra, p 700.

[231] See generally Diamond (1986) IV Hague Recueil 236, 262–264.

[232] For criticism of this aspect of Art 3(2), see Diamond [1979] Current Legal Problems 155, 162–165, who argues that variation should be a matter for the original governing law; Fletcher in *Conflict of Laws and European Community Law* (1982), at p 160, argues it should be for both the original and the substitute governing laws. This is supported by Kaye, p 156. Nygh argues it should be for the new law chosen, *Autonomy in International Contracts* (1999), p 101.

expressed or inferred.[233] In *The Aeolian*[234] the Court of Appeal held that a supply contract, which was governed by Japanese law, had not been varied by a subsequent undertaking (governed by English law) in relation to a claim for payment under a separate spares contract, even though both parties must be taken to have had in mind that the defence would rely, as a set-off to the claim for payment, on a cross-claim for breach of the supply contract. The agreement in the undertaking was confined to the claim for payment and did not extend to the cross-claim arising out of the supply contract.[235] The undertaking made no reference to the supply contract and no inference could be drawn from the circumstances of the case that English law should govern the cross-claim.[236] If the variation is made during the course of legal proceedings, it is for the forum's law of procedure to decide the extent to which this is effective.[237]

The Working Group on the Rome Convention recognised that there were certain dangers in allowing a variation of the applicable law by the parties. The second sentence of Article 3(2) provides a safeguard in the following terms: "Any variation by the parties of the law to be applied made after the conclusion of the contract shall not prejudice its formal validity under Article 9 or adversely affect the rights of third parties."

As regards formal validity, the concern was that the new law chosen by the parties might contain formal requirements which were not known under the law originally applicable. This could create doubts as to the validity of the contract during the period preceding the new agreement between the parties;[238] hence the rule that any variation by the parties is not to prejudice the formal validity of the contract under Article 9. The other danger recognised by the Working Group is in relation to third parties, who may have already acquired rights at the time of the conclusion of the contract between the original contracting parties. These rights cannot be affected by a subsequent change in the choice of the applicable law.

There are two other potential dangers that can arise from the parties' variation of the applicable law. First, the parties might thereby evade the mandatory rules (eg controls on exemption clauses) of the country whose law was originally applicable.[239] However, the normal limitations on the right to choose the applicable law will doubtless apply to a subsequent choice of the governing law in the same way that they apply to an initial choice. As will shortly be seen,[240] there are limitations on choice which deal to some extent with this problem of evasion. Secondly, the parties might choose a new law which invalidates the contract. Logically, the contract appears to be rendered invalid. This presupposes, however, that the new choice of the applicable law is itself valid. This is a matter

---

[233] See *ISS Machinery Services Ltd v Aeolian Shipping SA (the Aeolian)* [2001] EWCA Civ 1162 at [15] (per POTTER LJ), [27] (per MANCE LJ), [2001] 2 Lloyd's Rep 641; the Giuliano and Lagarde Report, p 18; cf Morse, op cit, p 120.

[234] *ISS Machinery Services Ltd v Aeolian Shipping SA (the Aeolian)* [2001] EWCA Civ 1162, [2001] 2 Lloyd's Rep 641.

[235] Ibid at [31] (per MANCE LJ).

[236] Ibid at [15]–[16] (per POTTER LJ).

[237] The Giuliano and Lagarde Report, p 18.

[238] The Giuliano and Lagarde Report, p 18.

[239] See Collins (1976) 25 ICLQ 35, 44; cf North, *Essays*, pp 60–61.

[240] Infra, pp 694–700.

for the new law that has been chosen.[241] Thus the validity of a New York choice of law clause (which operates as a subsequent choice) is a matter for New York law.

The position in relation to variation of choice under the Regulation is the same as under the Convention.

(v) Choice and the English rules on pleading and proof of foreign law [242]

What happens if the parties choose Utopian law to apply but subsequently neither party pleads Utopian law? The Convention does not provide an answer to this. On the one hand, the English procedural rule preserved by the Convention[243] indicates that English law must be applied automatically.[244] This would suggest that you can have a procedural variation of the applicable law.[245] On the other hand, Article 3(1) is phrased in strong terms: the "contract *shall* be governed by the law chosen by the parties".[246] But if foreign law has to be applied, this leads on to a practical problem of what an English judge is to do if the parties fail to plead and prove foreign law.[247] In view of this difficulty, English courts are likely to take a pragmatic line and simply apply English law under the English procedural rule. There would be no problem if it could be said that the failure to plead foreign law operates as a new agreement as to the applicable law by the parties replacing the original choice.[248] However, the parties' choice of the applicable law (whether an original or a later choice) must be expressed by the parties or demonstrated with reasonable certainty by the terms of the contract or the circumstances of the case.[249] A mere omission to plead and prove foreign law would not appear to satisfy this requirement.[250]

The position in relation to choice and the English rules on pleading and proof of foreign law is the same under the Regulation as under the Convention.

(b) Limitations on choice

Any discussion of freedom of choice inevitably leads on to the question of whether there is any restriction on the parties' freedom to choose the governing law.[251] The Convention also lays down restrictions on the parties' right to choose the governing law,[252] which will now be examined.

---

[241] See Art 8(1), infra, pp 744–745.

[242] See generally Fentiman, *Foreign Law in English Courts* (1998), pp 87 et seq.

[243] Art 1(2)(h), supra, p 687.

[244] But see Fentiman, *Foreign Law in English Courts* (1998), p 93 who suggests that how foreign law is pleaded is for English law but whether it should be pleaded is for the Rome Convention.

[245] See North, op cit, p 61; Diamond, op cit, p 262. See also Hartley (1996) 45 ICLQ 271 at 290–291; Dicey, Morris and Collins, para 9-011.

[246] The emphasis is the authors'. See also Fentiman (1992) 108 LQR 142, 144; Kaye, p 98.

[247] See Kaye, p 98.

[248] Fentiman, *Foreign Law in English Courts* (1998); Dicey, Morris and Collins, para 9-011 n 45.

[249] Art 3(1).

[250] Cf Hartley, op cit, p 291 n 101. See Lando (1987) 24 CMLR 159, 186–188 who suggests that the parties, in cases where the expense of proving foreign law is justified, are to be asked whether they intend to submit their contract to the law of the forum.

[251] See generally Nygh, *Autonomy in International Contracts* (1999), Chapter 3.

[252] Rinze [1994] JBL 412.

(i) Article 3(3)[253]

The only limitation mentioned in Article 3 itself is contained in Article 3(3) which provides that:

> The fact that the parties have chosen a foreign law, whether or not accompanied by the choice of a foreign tribunal, shall not, where all the other elements relevant to the situation at the time of the choice are connected with one country only, prejudice the application of rules of the law of that country which cannot be derogated from by contract, hereinafter called "mandatory rules".

This provision is concerned with the situation where there is an essentially domestic contract which is turned into a conflict of laws case by virtue simply of the parties' choice of a foreign applicable law. Article 3(3) provides a limitation on the right to choose in this situation, but only to the extent of preserving the *mandatory rules* of the country where all the other relevant connections are situated. According to Article 3(3) mandatory rules are ones that "cannot be derogated from by contract".[254] As an example of English mandatory rules, there are the rules providing controls on exemption clauses contained in the Unfair Contract Terms Act 1977. This Act makes it clear that these controls will, in certain circumstances, apply despite the parties' choice of a foreign law to govern the contract.[255] The effect of Article 3(3) is that if the parties to an entirely German contract, which contains an exemption clause, choose, for example, French law to govern, the court of any Contracting State which tries the case will have to apply any controls on exemption clauses contained in a German equivalent of the 1977 Act. The parties' choice of French law would appear to have been made with a view to evading the German controls on exemption clauses (assuming there are such controls). Article 3(3) will stop many cases of evasion of the law,[256] although it goes wider than this and it will ensure that any German controls on exemption clauses apply even if the parties have chosen French law for some perfectly legitimate reason, such as the fact that this is the applicable law under some related contract between the parties.

There are a number of points that can be made in relation to Article 3(3). First, it requires the parties to have chosen a "foreign" law. This raises a problem in the following type of case:

> Two Californian residents enter into an essentially Californian contract but choose English law to govern the contract. Trial of a subsequent dispute takes place in England. English law is "foreign" to the parties and the contract, but not "foreign" to the forum. Article 3(3) is concerned with the choice of a foreign law and with the situation at the time of the choice. At that time, English law was a foreign law, ie was foreign to the parties and the contract.

---

[253] Hartley (1997) 266 Hague Recueil 341, 366–368; Kaye, pp 159–168.

[254] This means that in a domestic context the rule cannot be contracted out of, see infra, pp 729–731. But see the obiter dicta on Art 3(3) in *Caterpillar Financial Services Corpn v SNC Passion* [2004] EWHC 569 (Comm) at [31]–[44], [2004] 2 Lloyd's Rep 99, which should be regarded as wrong.

[255] S 27(2); discussed infra, pp 732–734.

[256] But not necessarily all cases, see the discussion, infra, p 696, in relation to *Golden Acres Ltd v Queensland Estates Pty Ltd* [1969] Qd R 378; affd sub nom *Freehold Land Investments v Queensland Estates Ltd* 123 CLR 418. See Lando (1987) 24 CMLR 159, 182–183; Fawcett [1990] CLJ 44.

The result is that Article 3(3) operates and Californian mandatory rules are applicable.[257]

Secondly, Article 3(3) requires "all the other elements relevant to the situation"[258] to be connected with a country in order that its mandatory rules are to be applied. But when is an element *relevant* to the situation? Take the facts of the well-known case of *Golden Acres Ltd v Queensland Estates Pty Ltd*.[259]

> The case concerned the rate of commission to be paid to an estate agent. Many of the connections were with Queensland, but the plaintiff company was incorporated in Hong Kong. Was the place of incorporation a relevant element, or was the only relevant thing about the company the fact that it acted as an estate agent in Queensland?

Under the common law this case was decided on the basis that the choice of Hong Kong law to govern the contract was not made in good faith. Under the Convention the parties' motives are immaterial, but whilst one problem (ascertaining motives) has now disappeared, another problem (ascertaining whether all the relevant elements are with one country) has sprung up in its place.[260] In *Caterpillar Financial Services Corp v SNC Passion*:[261]

> A loan transaction had a number of connections with France: the borrower was a French company; the loan transaction was originally set up by French companies; it was argued that the loan agreement was made in France; the loan was for building a ship which would fly the French flag with a charter-party subject to French law. But the loan agreement was expressly governed by English law.

It was held that Article 3(3) had no application[262] because significant elements of the loan transaction involved a connection with a jurisdiction other than France. The most important of these was that the lender bank was a Delaware bank which acted through its office in Tennessee. Moreover, the loan agreement was intimately connected with a shipbuilding contract with advances being made directly to the shipbuilder in Singapore. This was a clear-cut case and it would have been astonishing if the opposite conclusion had been reached.

Thirdly, the structure of the Convention suggests that the country whose mandatory rules have to be applied will be a foreign country and not the forum. However, there is nothing to say that mandatory rules of the forum are excluded under Article 3(3). Indeed, it is important that Article 3(3) should encompass the mandatory rules of the forum,

---

[257] Where neither party pleads and proves Californian law, English law is likely to be applied either because of Art 1(2)(h) or for pragmatic reasons (see supra, p 694). But see Hartley, op cit, p 291; Fentiman, *Foreign Law in English Courts* (1998), pp 93–95. What is clear is that the failure to plead cannot operate in the context of mandatory rules as a new agreement.

[258] As opposed to relevant to the *contract*.

[259] Supra.

[260] However, there is no such problem in relation to connections if Art 7(2) is used. This is concerned with the mandatory rules of the forum; infra, pp 731–738. See also Fawcett [1990] CLJ 44, 58–60.

[261] [2004] EWHC 569 (Comm) at [21]–[30], [2004] 2 Lloyd's Rep 99.

[262] For another example, see *Bankers Trust International plc v RCS Editori SpA* [1996] CLC 899 at 905. See also *Shell International Petroleum Co Ltd v Coral Oil Co Ltd* [1999] 1 Lloyd's Rep 72 at 78–79.

since Article 7(2), although specifically designed to cover the mandatory rules of the forum, is concerned with a different and narrower type of mandatory rule.[263]

Fourthly, you have to look to the law of the country with which there are all the other relevant connections to see whether under *that country's law* the domestic rule is one which cannot be derogated from by contract.

Fifthly, the effect of applying a mandatory rule is to override the parties' choice of law, rather than to destroy it. Reverting to the earlier example, the German controls on exemption clauses will apply despite a French choice of law clause. Nonetheless, the choice of French law will still operate to govern other issues, such as interpretation of the contract, provided that this is an area where German law does not have mandatory rules.

The sixth and final point about Article 3(3) is that it tells us something, by implication, about freedom of choice. Article 3(3) is only concerned with mandatory rules. It follows that, even if all the other relevant connections are with Country X, the choice of law of Country Y will still apply as far as non-mandatory rules are concerned. This means that the parties can choose, as the applicable law, the law of a country with which there is no relevant connection.

The Rome I Regulation retains Article 3(3) in substance, but adopts a slightly different wording so as to align the provision as far as possible with the Rome II Regulation on non-contractual obligations.[264] The new Article 3(3) provides that:

> Where all other elements relevant to the situation at the time of the choice are located in a country other than the country whose law has been chosen, the choice of the parties shall not prejudice the application of provisions of the law of that other country which cannot be derogated from by agreement.[265]

The most obvious change in wording is that the confusing term "mandatory rules" is no longer used.[266]

(ii) The Rome I Regulation: Mandatory rules of Community law

Article 3(4) of the Rome I Regulation introduces an additional limitation on the parties' freedom to choose the applicable law. This provides that:

> Where all other elements relevant to the situation at the time of the choice are located in one or more Member States, the parties' choice of applicable law other than that of a Member State shall not prejudice the application of provisions of Community law, where appropriate as implemented in the Member State of the forum, which cannot be derogated from by agreement.[267]

---

[263] Infra, pp 730–731.

[264] See Recital (15) of the Regulation. This Recital follows the Rome Convention by providing that the rule applies, whether or not the choice of law rule was accompanied by a choice of court or tribunal. For the equivalent limitation under Rome II, see Art 14(2), discussed infra, p 840.

[265] Art 3(3) of the Regulation.

[266] See the discussion of Art 9 of the Regulation (overriding mandatory provisions), infra, pp 738–741.

[267] Art 3(4) of the Regulation.

This follows an almost identically worded limitation in the Rome II Regulation on non-contractual obligations.[268] It spells out a limitation that doubtless already exists in relation to the Rome Convention.[269]

(iii) Other provisions on mandatory rules,[270] public policy[271]

These limitations are more appropriately dealt with later on, where they will be looked at in some detail.

We have dealt with the limitations on choice specifically set out in the Convention itself. Nonetheless, there are a number of other possible limitations which have to be considered.

(iv) Logically consistent choices

As has already been seen,[272] if the parties are choosing two different laws for different parts of the contract, these choices must be logically consistent.

(v) A meaningless choice of law

In keeping with the above limitation, a meaningless choice of law will be ignored. This was established by the Court of Appeal in *Shamil Bank of Bahrain v Beximco Pharmaceuticals Ltd*:[273]

> A choice of law clause provided that the contract was governed by English law "subject to the principles of the Glorious Sharia'a". It was common ground that only the law of a country[274] can be chosen and therefore it was argued that incorporated into English law were specific principles of Sharia law. But there was no reference to or identification of those aspects of Sharia law which were intended to be incorporated into the contract. The principles of Sharia law were therefore repugnant to the choice of English law and rendered the clause self-contradictory and meaningless.

The construction adopted of the clause by the Court was that English law governed and the additional wording merely reflected the Islamic religous principles according to which the bank held itself out as doing business rather than a system of law intended to trump the application of English law. In contrast, at common law mere difficulty in ascertaining the governing law did not render the choice ineffective.[275] The position would doubtless be the same under the Convention and under the Regulation.

(vi) Choice of the law of a country

Under Article 3(1) the parties have the right to choose the applicable *law*, and this refers to the law of a country.[276] The Convention does not sanction the choice of a non-national

---

[268] Art 14(3) of Rome II is discussed infra, p 840.

[269] Mandatory rules under Art 7(2) of the Convention include community mandatory rules, infra, p 737.

[270] Arts 5(2) and 6(1), infra, p 726; Art 7, infra, pp 728–738; Art 9(6), infra, p 749.

[271] Art 16, infra, pp 741–743.

[272] Supra, pp 690–692.

[273] [2004] EWCA Civ 19, [2004] 1 WLR 1784.

[274] As defined in Art 19(1).

[275] See *The Blue Wave* [1982] 1 Lloyd's Rep 151.

[276] *Shamil Bank of Bahrain v Beximco Pharmaceuticals Ltd* [2004] EWCA Civ 19 at [48], [2004] 1 WLR 1784. But cf *Samcrete Egypt Engineers and Contractors SAE v Land Rover Exports Ltd* [2001] EWCA Civ 2019 at [39] (per POTTER LJ), [2002] CLC 533. See Art 1(1) on the scope of the Convention, which refers to a choice

system of law such as the *lex mercatoria*.[277] Such a choice refers not to the national law of any country but rather to a kind of transnational law consisting of internationally accepted principles of trade law, to be ascertained by arbitrators. Other examples of the choice of a non-national system of law are "general principles of law," the rules of law in the UN Convention on the International Sale of Goods 1980,[278] the law of Sharia[279] and Jewish law.[280] Such a reference is outside the parties' freedom to choose the applicable law.[281] However, it is possible to incorporate, by reference, provisions of the Sharia or other international code, such as the UN Convention on the International Sale of Goods 1980, provided that the parties in their contract have sufficiently identified specific provisions.[282] It is also possible to incorporate "Jewish law", without any such proviso, at least where the dispute is between Orthodox Jews who are agreed there is such a distinct body of law.[283]

The original proposal for a Rome I Regulation gave a boost to the principle of freedom of choice by allowing the parties to choose as the applicable law the law of a non-state.[284] Under this provision the parties were able to choose "the principles and rules of the substantive law of contract recognised internationally or in the Community".[285] This would include UNIDROIT principles, the UN Convention on the International Sale of Goods (the Vienna Convention) and the *Principles of European Contract Law*.[286] It was not intended to cover the *lex mercatoria*, which was regarded as not being precise enough, or private codifications not adequately recognised by the international community.[287] It has been questioned whether such a change in the law would do more than assist in interpretation of the contract since remedies, if they are to be effective, would have to flow from the law of a country.[288] The provision allowing a choice of non-state law was subsequently deleted.[289] However, under the Regulation the parties are free to incorporate by reference into their contract a non-state body of law or an international Convention.[290] Moreover, should the Community adopt in an appropriate legal instrument rules of substantive

---

between the laws of different "countries" and Art 3(3) which specifically refers to the law of a "country". For the meaning of country see Art 19(1) and supra, pp 680–681.

[277] See generally Lando (1985) 34 ICLQ 747; Lord Justice MUSTILL in Bos and Brownlie (eds), *Liber Amicorum for Lord Wilberforce* (1987), p 149; the symposium in (1989) 63 Tul L R, articles by Delaume at 575, Highet at 613; Smit at 631, Park at 647; North, *Private International Law Problems in Common Law Jurisdictions* (1993), pp 109–111; Chukwumerije [1994] Anglo-Am LR 265, 269 et seq; Nygh (1995) 251 Hague Recueil 269, 308–309; *Autonomy in International Contracts* (1999), Chapter 8.

[278] See Fawcett, Harris and Bridge, paras 13.86–13.94.

[279] The *Shamil Bank of Bahrain* case, supra, at [48].

[280] *Halpern v Halpern* [2007] EWCA Civ 291 at [19]–[29], [2007] 2 Lloyd's Rep 56.

[281] If the parties agree on the application of the *lex mercatoria*, or of "other considerations" an arbitral tribunal will apply this, see s 46(1)(b) of the Arbitration Act 1996. It is implicit in the Inter-American Convention on the Law Applicable to International Contracts of 1994 that a choice of the *lex mercatoria* is permissible: see Arts 3, 9 and 10.

[282] The *Shamil Bank of Bahrain* case, supra, at [49]–[52]. See infra, p 701.

[283] *Halpern v Halpern* [2007] EWCA Civ 291 at [33], [2007] 2 Lloyd's Rep 56.

[284] See the Explanatory Memorandum, COM (2005) 650 final, p 6.

[285] Art 3(2) of the original Proposal for a Regulation, COM (2005) 650 final.

[286] See the Explanatory Memorandum, p 6.

[287] The Explanatory Memorandum, p 6. For criticism of this see Lando and Nielson (2007) 3 J Priv Int L 29, 30–34.

[288] *Halpern v Halpern* [2007] EWCA Civ 291 at [39], [2007] 2 Lloyd's Rep 56.

[289] Art 3 of the Regulation. It was deleted in the April 2007 compromise package from the Presidency, agreed by the Council, 8022/07 JUSTCIV 73 CODEC 306 of 13 April 2007.

[290] Recital (13) of the Regulation.

contract law, including standard terms and conditions, that instrument may provide that the parties may choose to apply those rules.[291]

(vii) A "floating" applicable law

The parties cannot choose a "floating" applicable law to govern the contract. The applicable law must exist and be identifiable at the time when the contract is made.[292] It follows that a clause which, for example, gives one party the option to determine the applicable law in the future by selecting the law to govern from a list of possible alternatives, will be ineffective under the Convention, as it was at common law.[293] At least it will be ineffective at the time when the contract is made, and at this stage the applicable law will be determined objectively under Article 4 of the Convention. But what happens if one party makes the selection at some future date?[294] This subsequent choice may have been ineffective under the common law rules,[295] but the choice at this future date will be given retrospective effect under the Convention,[296] since variation of the applicable law is permissible.[297] The form of the variation is just rather unusual in this situation, in that the agreement is from the outset for a change of the applicable law in the future.

The position is the same under the Regulation.

(c) An express choice

The parties can express a choice simply by including a choice of law clause in the contract stating that, for example, all disputes shall be governed by English law.[298] Any question as to the validity or existence of this choice is governed by the rules on consent to choice, which will be examined later.[299] Parties may choose a particular law for a variety

---

[291] Recital (14) of the Regulation.

[292] *CGU International Insurance plc v Szabo* [2002] 1 All ER (Comm) 83 at [37].

[293] For the position at common law, see *Dubai Electricity Co v Islamic Republic of Iran Shipping Lines, The Iran Vojdan* [1984] 2 Lloyd's Rep 380 at 385; *Cantieri Navali Riuniti SpA v NV Omne Justitia, The Stolt Marmaro* [1985] 2 Lloyd's Rep 428 at 435; cf *Astro Venturoso Compañía Naviera v Hellenic Shipyards SA, The Mariannina* [1983] 1 Lloyd's Rep 12 at 15. But see *King v Brandywine Reinsurance Co (UK) Ltd* [2004] EWHC 1033 (Comm) at [45], [2004] 2 Lloyd's Rep 670; appeal dismissed without discussion of this point [2005] EWCA Civ 235, [2005] 1 Lloyd's 655. See in relation to an implied floating applicable law, *The Star Texas* [1993] 2 Lloyd's Rep 445, CA (no implied choice). These common law cases are still relevant to the law governing a jurisdiction or arbitration agreement, see *Sonatrach Petroleum Corpn v Ferrell International Ltd* [2002] 1 All ER (Comm) 627.

[294] It is very doubtful whether a selection can be made many years after a contract has expired: *Heath Lambert Ltd v Sociedad de Corretaje de Seguros* [2003] EWHC 2269 (Comm) at [18]–[19].

[295] See *Armar Shipping Co Ltd v Caisse Algérienne* [1981] 1 WLR 207 at 216; cf *Black Clawson International Ltd v Papierwerke Waldhof-Aschaffenburg AG* [1981] 2 Lloyd's Rep 446 at 456; *E I Du Pont de Nemours & Co v Agnew and Kerr* [1987] 2 Lloyd's Rep 585 at 592. See generally Beck [1987] LMCLQ 523.

[296] *CGU International Insurance plc v Szabo*, supra, at [37]—rejecting the idea of a "harlequin" proper law so that an insurance policy means different things according to the country of the person claiming under it. See also *Bhatia Shipping v Alcobex Metals* [2004] EWHC 2323 (Comm) at [16], [2005] 2 Lloyd's Rep 336.

[297] Art 3(2), discussed supra, pp 692–694; *King v Brandywine Reinsurance Co (UK) Ltd* [2004] EWHC 1033 (Comm) at [45], [2004] 2 Lloyd's Rep 670; appeal dismissed without discussion of this point [2005] EWCA Civ 235, [2005] 1 Lloyd's 655; Nygh (1995) 251 Hague Recueil 269, 320–321; *Autonomy in International Contracts* (1999), p 99; Dicey, Morris and Collins, 32-086–32-087; Kaye, p 148. But cf Howard [1995] LMCLQ 1 at 7. STEYN LJ in *The Star Texas*, supra, at 450, left this point open.

[298] See Briggs [2003] LMCLQ 389. See on the battle of the forms, Dannemann in Rose (ed), *Lex Mercatoria: Essays in Honour of Francis Reynolds* (2000), Chapter 11; Fawcett, Harris and Bridge, paras 13.57–13.61.

[299] Art 3(4) discussed infra, p 707.

of reasons.[300] It is usually convenient for a party to have the familiar law of their home state apply. One country's law may be more developed than another's in technical commercial areas such as banking and insurance, when English law is commonly chosen by the parties. It may have become standard practice for a particular country's law to apply to certain transactions. The content of one country's law may be more favourable to one of the parties than that of another. Whatever the law chosen, it is important that the parties should make an express choice, for without this there is considerable uncertainty as to the applicable law.

The express selection of the proper law must be distinguished from the quite different process of the incorporation in the contract of certain domestic provisions of a foreign law, which thereupon became terms of the contract.[301] Article 3 is only concerned with selection of the applicable law. Incorporation may be effected either by a verbatim transcription of the relevant provisions or by a general statement that the rights and liabilities shall in certain respects be subject to these provisions. The latter is only a shorthand method of expressing the agreed terms. Thus the parties to an English contract may expressly provide that their duties with regard to performance shall be regulated by certain specific rules contained in the French Civil Code. English law is then applied as the governing law to a contract into which the foreign rules have been incorporated.[302] It is possible to incorporate by reference the terms of the Sharia or of an international code. However, the doctrine of incorporation can only sensibly operate where the parties have, by the terms of their contract, sufficiently identified specific "black letter" provisions of the foreign law or international code.[303] It is common in cases involving carriage of goods by sea to incorporate the Hague Rules. It is posssible to incorporate all of the Hague Rules or merely specific provisions. Whether a particular term incorporated in this manner is valid and effective is a matter for determination by the applicable law under the Convention.[304] At common law, once a foreign law was incorporated into the contract as a term it remained constant in the sense that it was unaffected by any change in the relevant foreign law occurring after the date of the contract. The position appears to be the same under the Convention.

The position on express choice is the same under the Regulation as it is under the Convention.

(d) An inferred choice

Article 3(1) provides, as an alternative to an express choice, that there can be a choice "demonstrated with reasonable certainty by the terms of the contract or the circumstances of the case". This provision is concerned with a real choice by the parties, the court inferring what the parties' actual intentions[305] were from the terms of the contract or the circumstances of the case. This concept of an inferred or implied choice is well

---

[300] See Collins in *Contract Conflicts*, p 215.

[301] *Shamil Bank of Bahrain v Beximco Pharmaceuticals Ltd* [2004] EWCA Civ 19 at [48]–[52], [2004] 1 WLR 1784.

[302] Ibid, at [51].

[303] Ibid.

[304] Art 8(1); discussed infra, p 744.

[305] See *Hellenic Steel Co v Svolamar Shipping Co Ltd; The Komninos S* [1991] 1 Lloyd's Rep 370 at 374, CA; Reynolds (1992) 108 LQR 395.

known in English law, and is to be found in civil law countries as well.[306] Inferred choice under the Convention appears at first sight to be very close to the English law in this area. Nonetheless, there are differences, and cases decided at common law should be treated with caution. It is to be regretted therefore that the Court of Appeal has, when examining the idea of a real choice under the Convention, drawn an analogy with the common law concept of an implied term, namely one that must have been intended or was so obvious that it went without saying and was one to which the parties would have said "of course" if anyone had suggested it.[307]

(i) Drawing the inference

An inference as to the parties' intentions can be drawn from either the terms of the contract or the circumstances of the case.

The terms of the contract   The Giuliano and Lagarde Report[308] provides a number of examples of situations where a court may draw an inference as to the parties' intentions. In most of these examples the inference is being drawn from the terms of the contract. Thus an inference can be drawn in cases where: the contract is in a standard form known to be governed by a particular system of law, such as a Lloyd's policy of Marine Insurance; the contract contains a choice of forum clause or an arbitration clause naming the place of arbitration (at least in circumstances indicating that the arbitrator should apply the law of that place); or there is a reference to specific articles of the French Civil Code.[309] The reasoning in such cases is that if, for example, the parties intended that trial should take place in England they must also have intended that English law should apply, it being inconvenient and expensive for a foreign law to be applied.

The interesting thing about these examples, from an English point of view, is that the first three are the standard examples of an inferred choice under the common law rules. Thus in *Amin Rasheed Shipping Corpn v Kuwait Insurance Co*[310] Lord DIPLOCK[311] said that the terms of a standard Lloyd's SG form of policy showed by necessary implication that the parties (a Liberian company and a Kuwaiti insurance company) intended that the English law of marine insurance should apply. Kuwait had no law of marine insurance at that time, and the parties could not have intended Kuwaiti law to apply. The House of Lords unanimously held that the proper law of the contract was English law. This sort of case will be decided in exactly the same way under the Convention.[312] Similarly, where a reinsurance contract was placed in London on the London market, it was held that the terms of the slip (referring to standard form clauses used in England where they were

---

[306] The Giuliano and Lagarde Report, pp 15–17; Lando (1987) 24 CMLR 171–179. For inferred choice under German law, see Von Hoffmann in *Contract Conflicts*, pp 221, 224–225. See generally Nygh, *Autonomy in International Contracts* (1999), Chapter 5.

[307] *American Motorists Insurance Co (Amico) v Cellstar Corpn* [2003] EWCA Civ 206 at [44], [2003] IL Pr 22.

[308] At p 17.

[309] Instead of a choice of French law this may involve an incorporation by reference, supra, p 701.

[310] [1984] AC 50. The case involved service out of the jurisdiction under what is now CPR, r 6.20(5)(c).

[311] At 64–67; Lords ROSKILL, BRIGHTMAN and BRANDON concurred. Lord WILBERFORCE reached the same result by applying the objective proper law of the contract.

[312] *Gan Insurance Co Ltd v Tai Ping Insurance Co Ltd* [1999] IL Pr 729 at [31] and [36], CA.

developed) pointed to an implied choice of English law under the Convention.[313] Similarly, as at common law, a choice can be inferred from an arbitration clause or a choice of jurisdiction clause.[314] Thus in *Egon Oldendorff v Liberia Corpn*,[315] a clause providing for arbitration in London[316] was treated as an inferred choice of English law to govern the contract by virtue of Article 3(1). It was also relevant in this case when inferring intention that the parties used a well-known English language form of charter-party containing standard clauses with well-known meanings in English law. The case for an inferred choice is even stronger if the arbitration clause not only provides for arbitration in England but also expressly refers to the English Arbitration Acts.[317] Likewise a jurisdiction clause providing for trial in England has been treated as an inferrred choice of English law under the Convention.[318]

These are only examples of situations where it is possible to infer a choice from the terms of the contract, albeit particularly good ones. Could such an inference be drawn, for example, from the fact that the currency in which payment is to be made is that of a particular country? At common law the English courts drew inferences as to parties' intentions from a wide variety of factors relating to the terms of the contract, including this very factor. However, a note of caution should be struck when it comes to inferring a choice under the Convention. First, the inferred choice must be demonstrated "with reasonable certainty". If it is not, you move on to the provisions on the applicable law in the absence of choice (Article 4) to decide the case. Secondly, you are looking for the actual or real intentions of the parties.[319] It is just about credible to say in a case like *Amin Rasheed* (or in cases involving arbitration or choice of jurisdiction clauses) that the parties had real intentions, but the same cannot be said in a case where all that can be shown is that, for example, there is a clause in the contract relating to the currency in which payment is to be made. In the common law cases, although the language of inferred intent was often used it was by no means clear that the courts were looking for a real or actual

---

[313] Ibid. See also *Tiernan v The Magen Insurance Co Ltd* [2000] IL Pr 517 at 522–523; *Tryg Baltica International (UK)) Ltd v Boston Compañía de Seguros SA* [2004] EWHC 1186 (Comm) at [8], [2005] Lloyd's Rep IR 40; *Markel International Insurance Co Ltd v La República Compañía Argentina de Seguros Generales SA* [2004] EWHC 1826 (Comm) at [37], [2005] Lloyd's Rep IR 90; *Cadre SA v Astra Asigurari* [2004] EWHC 2504 (QB); *Dornach Ltd v Mauritius Union Assurance Co Ltd* [2006] EWCA Civ 389 at [43], [2006] 2 Lloyd's Rep 475. Cf *Evialis SA v SIAT* [2003] EWHC 863, [2003] 2 Lloyd's Rep 377.

[314] Courts in some other Contracting States have been more reluctant to draw the inference, see the Green Paper of 14 January 2003 on the conversion of the Rome Convention, COM (2002) 654 final, pp 23–25, and inferred choice under the Rome I Regulation, infra, pp 706–707.

[315] [1996] 1 Lloyd's Rep 380 (CLARKE J)—determining whether English law governed; [1995] 2 Lloyd's Rep 64 (MANCE J)—earlier on determining for the purposes of service out of the jurisdiction whether English law governed. See also *JSC Zestafoni v Ronly Holdings Ltd* [2004] EWHC 245 (Comm) at [75], [2004] 2 Lloyd's Rep 335.

[316] At common law, a clause providing for arbitration in Beijing or London at the defendant's option did not give rise to an implied choice: *The Star Texas* [1993] 2 Lloyd's Rep 445 at 448, 452, CA. The position would doubtless be the same under the Rome Convention.

[317] *American International Specialty Lines Insurance Co v Abbott Laboratories* [2002] EWHC 2714 (Comm), [2003] 1 Lloyd's Rep 267 at 272.

[318] *Marubeni Hong Kong and South China Ltd v Mongolian Government* [2002] 2 All ER (Comm) 873.

[319] *Egon Oldendorff v Liberia Corpn* (CLARKE J), supra, at 387–388.

intention on the parties' part.[320] The upshot is that it may be harder to draw an inference of intention under the Convention than it was under the common law rules.[321]

The circumstances of the case [322]   The inference can be drawn not only from the terms of the contract, but also from the circumstances of the case.[323] The Giuliano and Lagarde Report[324] gives two examples of inferred choice which would seem to fit within this category. The first is the situation where there is an express choice in a related transaction. However, whether the inference can be drawn will depend very much on the facts of the case. It will be recalled that in *The Aeolian*[325] the Court of Appeal held that an inference as to the law governing a supply contract, out of which a counterclaim arose, could not be drawn from the fact that the parties agreed that English law governed an undertaking in relation to a claim for payment under a separate spares contract. On the other hand, an inference could be drawn from the fact that an excess insurance policy followed the choice of law in the primary reinsurance policy.[326] The second is the situation where there is a previous course of dealing under contracts containing an express choice of the applicable law and this choice of law clause has been omitted in circumstances which do not indicate a deliberate change of policy by the parties. The English courts, under the common law rules, used the language of inferred intent in similar circumstances. They also inferred an intent from purely objective factors, such as the residence of the parties[327] or the nature and location of the subject of the contract.[328] This approach has continued to be used in relation to the Rome Convention. In *American Motorists Insurance Co (Amico) v Cellstar Corp* [329] the Court of Appeal inferred a choice of Texas law from the fact that a company from its base in Texas chose on behalf of its whole group of companies to negotiate world-wide cover in Texas with insurers also based in Texas. Whatever the position was at common law, it is submitted that it is inappropriate to infer an actual intention as required under the Convention from objective factors. The circumstances of the case can also be taken into account to show that no inference can be drawn as to the governing law. This was the situation in *Samcrete Egypt Engineers and Contractors SAE v Land Rover Exports Ltd*[330] where the fact that one party put forward a choice of law clause and the

---

[320] In *Coast Lines Ltd v Hudig and Veder Chartering NV* [1972] 2 QB 34 at 50 it was clear that STEPHENSON LJ in the Court of Appeal was not. There was much confusion at common law over the meaning of intention, and between the intentions of the parties and objective factors, infra, pp 708–709.

[321] See Morse, (1982) 2 YEL 107, 116–117. The same will be true in Germany, see Triebel (1988) 37 ICLQ 935 at 942. Cf Plender, para 5.07.

[322] Cf Art 2 of the (1955) Hague Convention on the law applicable to international sales of goods. It is unclear whether the "circumstances of the case" can include subsequent conduct which shows the parties' earlier intentions at the time of conclusion of the contract, see Plender, paras 5.13–5.15. Cf Dicey, Morris and Collins, 32-057–32-059.

[323] It is a moot point whether this means that the test for an inferred choice is wider than the test for an implied choice at common law. Cf POTTER LJ in *ISS Machinery Services Ltd v Aeolian Shipping SA (the Aeolian)* [2001] EWCA Civ 1162 at [16], [2001] 2 Lloyd's Rep 641 and *Samcrete Egypt Engineers and Contractors SAE v Land Rover Exports Ltd* [2001] EWCA Civ 2019 at [28], [2002] CLC 533 with MANCE LJ in *American Motorists Insurance Co (Amico) v Cellstar Corpn* [2003] EWCA Civ 206 at [44], [2003] IL Pr 22.

[324] At p 17.

[325] *ISS Machinery Services Ltd v Aeolian Shipping SA (the Aeolian)* [2001] EWCA Civ 1162, [2001] 2 Lloyd's Rep 641; discussed supra, p 693.

[326] *Dornach Ltd v Mauritius Union Assurance Co Ltd* [2006] EWCA Civ 389 at [41], [2006] 2 Lloyd's Rep 475.

[327] *Jacobs v Crédit Lyonnais* (1884) 12 QBD 589.

[328] *Lloyd v Guibert* (1865) LR 1 QB 115 at 122–123.

[329] [2003] EWCA Civ 206, [2003] IL Pr 22.

[330] [2001] EWCA Civ 2019, [2002] CLC 533.

other party deleted it from the draft contract was a positive indication that the parties made no choice as to the applicable law under Article 3(1).[331] The result was that no choice of English law could be inferred from the fact that this was a guarantee contract which was dependant on a principal contract which was governed by English law. Without taking into account the circumstances of the case, there would have been a strong argument for drawing such an inference.[332]

(ii) Conflicting inferences

The Giuliano and Lagarde Report states[333] that any inference which arises from a choice of jurisdiction clause "must always be subject to the other terms of the contract and all the circumstances of the case" (ie the very matters from which an inference can be drawn). For example, a choice of jurisdiction clause may point to an intention that the law of Country A shall apply, whereas a previous course of dealing may point to an intention that the law of Country B shall apply. However, no conflicting inference could be drawn from the fact that an earlier draft of the contract contained an express choice of law clause (providing that English law governed) and this clause was deleted.[334] A jurisdiction clause (providing for trial in England) still gave rise to a good arguable case that there was an inferred choice that English law was applicable. This notion of conflicting inferences is not confined to the situation where an inferred choice is being drawn from the presence of a choice of jurisdiction clause in the contract. Thus with an excess reinsurance contract, the inference to be drawn from the fact that the primary reinsurance was governed by Mauritian law conflicted with the inference to be drawn from the fact that the excess reinsurance was written on a Lloyd's slip in the London market on London market terms.[335] There was a stalemate.[336] If there are conflicting inferences it cannot be said that the choice has been demonstrated with reasonable certainty, and Article 3(1) does not permit the court to infer a choice of law that the parties might have made if they had no clear intention of making a choice.[337] The result is that you have to turn to the rules on the applicable law in the absence of choice[338] to determine the governing law.[339]

What is less clear is how the inference to be drawn from the terms of the contract and the circumstances of the case stands in relation to the objective connections that the contract has with different countries. For example, a previous course of dealing may raise the inference that English law governs, but many of the objective connections, such as the residence of the parties and the place of performance, could be with France. Under the Convention there is, quite properly, a rigid separation of intention (dealt with under

---

[331] Ibid, at [28].

[332] Ibid, at [23].

[333] At p 17. See also *Marubeni Hong Kong and South China Ltd v Mongolian Government* [2002] 2 All ER (Comm) 873 at [35].

[334] *Marubeni Hong Kong and South China Ltd v Mongolian Government* [2002] 2 All ER (Comm) 873 at [42]–[43]; distinguishing *Samcrete Egypt Engineers and Contractors SAE v Land Rover Exports Ltd* [2001] EWCA Civ 2019, [2002] CLC 533. There were subsequent proceedings dealing with other issues.

[335] *Dornach Ltd v Mauritius Union Assurance Co Ltd* [2006] EWCA Civ 389 at [43], [2006] 2 Lloyd's Rep 475.

[336] Ibid.

[337] The Giuliano and Lagarde Report, p 17; the *Dornach* case, supra, at [43].

[338] Art 4.

[339] The *Dornach* case, supra, at [43].

Article 3) from objective connecting factors (dealt with under Article 4). The inference that the parties intended English law to govern can seemingly only be challenged by a conflicting inference, ie by evidence showing a real intention that French law should govern. It is possible, though, to take a robust view that such an inference can be drawn from the factual connections with France. These could be considered on the basis that they constitute the surrounding circumstances.[340]

This robust view was adopted by MANCE J in *Egon Oldendorff v Liberia Corpn*.[341]

> In this case the plaintiff company was German, the defendant Japanese, and the contract provided for arbitration in London. It was argued that the arbitration clause was a minor factor and that other factors pointed objectively to Japanese law. Not only was the defendant corporation Japanese but also a Japanese shipbroker acted as intermediary between the parties, and the ships chartered were to be delivered and redelivered in Japan.

MANCE J rejected this argument, saying that these matters were inadequate to lead him to conclude that the parties intended London arbitration under Japanese law,[342] and held that there was a good arguable case for the purposes of service out of the jurisdiction that English law governed. Thus, although it is possible to draw a conflicting inference from objective factors, it seems that the circumstances where it will be right to do so may be relatively rare. Once it had been decided that there was jurisdiction, the issue arose of whether English law did in fact govern. CLARKE J held that it did.[343] Having agreed a "neutral forum", the reasonable inference is that the parties intended that forum to apply a "neutral" law, namely English law. In the circumstances, the arbitration clause was a strong indication of the parties' intention to choose English law. CLARKE J thought that the approach towards arbitration clauses under Article 3 was little or any different from that at common law,[344] and at common law inferences were drawn from factual connections.

(iii) Inferred choice under the Rome I Regulation

The Regulation contains two changes in relation to the inferred choice of the applicable law. First, such a choice has to be "clearly demonstrated".[345] This is a change of wording from Article 3(1) of the Rome Convention, which requires such a choice to be demonstrated with "reasonable certainty". It is unclear whether this represents a change in substance, requiring a higher standard to be demonstrated. Secondly, the Regulation also spells out the impact of a choice of jurisdiction agreement. Recital (12) states that: "An agreement between the parties to confer on one or more courts or tribunals of a Member State exclusive jurisdiction to determine disputes under the contract should be one of the factors to be taken into account in determining whether a choice of law has

---

[340] See the *Marubeni* case, supra, at [35].

[341] [1995] 2 Lloyd's Rep 64.

[342] Ibid, at 69.

[343] *Egon Oldendorff v Liberia Corpn* [1996] 1 Lloyd's Rep 380 (CLARKE J).

[344] The result would have been the same under the proper law of the contract in a three-country case like this. See *Compañía Naviera Micro SA v Shipley International Inc, The Parouth* [1982] 2 Lloyd's Rep 351, CA. Cf *Compagnie d'Armement Maritime SA v Cie Tunisienne de Navigation SA* [1971] AC 572, HL, treated as a two-country case.

[345] Art 3(3) of the Regulation.

been clearly demonstrated." [346] The background to this Recital is that a choice of jurisdiction agreement is an example of an inferred choice under the Rome Convention, but courts in some Contracting States have been more reluctant than the English courts have been to draw the inference in such a case.[347] The original proposal for a Regulation therefore provided that if the parties have agreed to confer jurisdiction on one or more courts or tribunals of a Member State to hear and determine disputes that have arisen or may arise out of the contract, they shall be presumed to have chosen the law of that Member State.[348] But this provision, which would have represented a change of substance in the law, was subsequently deleted. The Recital does not go as far as the presumption would have done in terms of the impact of a choice of jurisdiction agreement. As far as England is concerned, it will make no difference to drawing an inference. But it is possible that it might prompt the courts in other Member States to draw the inference when they would not have done so otherwise.

(e) Consent to choice

There can be a dispute as to whether one of the parties has consented to the choice. Article 3(4) provides that issues in relation to the validity and existence of consent are determined in accordance with the special rules in the Convention relating to material validity (Article 8), formal validity (Article 9) and incapacity (Article 11). These provisions will be discussed later in this chapter. Article 3(4) has been criticised.[349] The effect of it appears to be that one party can choose the law to govern the issue of consent to choice. If there is no valid consent to the choice, presumably the applicable law must be determined under the rules on the applicable law in the absence of choice.[350]

Article 3(4) is replicated in the Regulation.[351]

(ii) The applicable law in the absence of choice

In a surprising number of cases the parties fail to choose the applicable law. This may be because they have contracted without first consulting lawyers, or they cannot agree on the applicable law. The determination of the applicable law in the absence of choice is dealt with under Article 4, which consists of three main parts. First, there is the basic rule that the contract shall be governed by the law of the country with which it is most closely connected.[352] Secondly, there is a general presumption, based on the concept of characteristic performance, designed to identify the country with which the contract is most closely connected,[353] together with special presumptions[354] for two particular types of contract. Thirdly, there is a provision which, inter alia, states that the presumptions shall

---

[346] Recital (12) of the Regulation.

[347] See the Green Paper of 14 January 2003 on the conversion of the Rome Convention, COM (2002) 654 final, pp 23–25.

[348] Art 3(1) of the original Proposal for a Regulation, COM (2005) 650 final.

[349] See Cavers (1975) 48 So Cal L R 603 at 609; Nadelmann (1976) 24 AJCL 1, 8–9; Kaye, pp 168–170; cf Morse, op cit, at 119.

[350] Art 4. Cf the 1985 Hague Convention on the law applicable to contracts for the international sale of goods, Art 10(1) which spells this out.

[351] Art 3(5) of the Regulation.

[352] Art 4(1).

[353] Art 4(2).

[354] Art 4(3) and (4).

be disregarded if it appears that the contract is more closely connected with another country.[355] These provisions seek to combine certainty, provided by the presumptions, with flexibility, provided by the more closely connected test and the power to rebut the presumptions. Nonetheless, the scheme of Article 4 raises an initial dilemma, which is as yet unresolved. It is not clear whether what is intended is a three-, two- or even one-stage process.[356] The sequence in which the provisions are set out in Article 4 points to a three-stage process.[357] However, the Giuliano and Lagarde Report[358] envisages, at least in many cases, a one-stage process which starts and finishes with the presumptions. This view is supported by Continental case law.[359] Against this, it is hard to see how a court can decide whether it is appropriate to rebut a presumption unless it has first applied the more closely connected test. This would suggest a two-stage process, which starts with a presumption, but then moves on[360] to consider the more closely connected test in order to see whether this presumption can be rebutted. This view is supported by English case law.[361] The question of whether it is normally a one-stage or two-stage process becomes particularly important when it comes to the question of how easy it is to displace the general presumption. The three parts of Article 4 will now be examined.

(a) The most closely connected test

(i) The objective test

Article 4(1) provides that: "To the extent that the law applicable to the contract has not been chosen in accordance with Article 3, the contract shall be governed by the law of the country with which it is most closely connected."

Article 4(1) applies in the situation where the law has not been chosen by the parties or their choice has been ineffective.[362] The applicable law is determined by looking objectively at the connections, unlimited by any categorisation of the relevant factors,[363] linking the contract to a particular country. This rule is based on the common core of the law in Member States, where the same sort of flexible approach has been commonly used.[364] Under the proper law of the contract approach, in the absence of an express or inferred choice, the court looked for the system of law with which the transaction was most closely connected. This took into account such factors as the place of residence[365] or business[366] of the parties, the place where the relationship between the parties was centred,[367]

---

[355] Art 4(5).

[356] Going into this question has been described as being unhelpful, *Definitely Maybe (Touring) Ltd v Marek Lieberberg Konzertagentur GmbH* [2001] 1 WLR 1745 at [15].

[357] See generally Collins (1976) 25 ICLQ 35, 48.

[358] At p 21.

[359] See infra, pp 718–721; and generally Nygh (1995) 251 Hague Recueil 269, at 332–334. See also Dicey, Morris and Collins, para 32-125.

[360] At least where a party seeks to rely on Art 4(5), see infra, pp 718–721.

[361] See *Samcrete Egypt Engineers and Contractors SAE v Land Rover Exports Ltd* [2001] EWCA Civ 2019 at [37], [2002] CLC 533; and the discussion infra, pp 719–720.

[362] Eg, there are two inconsistent choices, see supra, p 698; see the Giuliano and Lagarde Report, p 20.

[363] *Apple Corps Ltd v Apple Computer Inc* [2004] EWHC 768 (Ch) at [57]–[60], [2004] IL Pr 34.

[364] See the Giuliano and Lagarde Report, pp 19–20. This approach is found in the USA under the American Restatement, Second, see Lando (1982) 30 AJCL 19, 31.

[365] *Jacobs v Crédit Lyonnais* (1884) 12 QBD 589 at 600, 602.

[366] *Re Anglo-Austrian Bank* [1920] 1 Ch 69.

[367] *XAG v A Bank* [1983] 2 Lloyd's Rep 535 at 543—banker and customer.

the place where the contract was made[368] or was to be performed,[369] or the nature and subject matter[370] of the contract. These factors are still relevant under the Convention.[371] However, in contrast to the proper law of the contract approach, it is now possible to take account of factors which have supervened after the conclusion of the contract.[372] Article 4 applies a purely objective test,[373] so it is therefore inappropriate to talk about the intentions of the parties.[374] It follows that the fact that the contract would be valid under one country's law but not under another's cannot be considered under Article 4, since this factor is only relevant to the determination of the parties' intentions (ie the parties would expect the contract to be valid[375]). Furthermore, although terms of the contract, such as a choice of jurisdiction or arbitration clause, should presumably be considered in the context of Article 4 in the situation where no clear inference can be drawn from them as to the intentions of the parties under Article 3(1),[376] their relevance when operating the objective test is limited to showing an objective connection with a country, and not as evidence of the parties' intentions. There can be little doubt that when the English courts set out to ascertain the objective proper law of the contract they sought to achieve certain underlying policy objectives, such as giving business efficacy to the contract.[377] English courts are going to find it harder to achieve such objectives under the Convention. The presence of the presumptions and the fact that the law is codified reduces the flexibility, and thus the room for manoeuvre, for a court that wants to achieve a particular result.[378]

(ii) Severing the contract[379]

The last sentence of Article 4(1) states that: "A severable part of the contract which has a closer connection with another country may by way of exception be governed by the law of that other country."

As has been seen,[380] the parties have the freedom to sever the contract when exercising their choice as to the applicable law. The courts have the same power when determining the applicable law in the absence of choice, and may decide, for example, that one part of

---

[368] *Lloyd v Guibert* (1865) LR 1 QB 115 at 122; *Cantieri Navali Riuniti SpA v N V Omne Justitia, The Stolt Marmaro* [1985] 2 Lloyd's Rep 428 at 433–435.

[369] *The Assunzione* [1954] P 150.

[370] *British South Africa Co v De Beers Consolidated Mines Ltd* [1910] 1 Ch 354 at 383, revsd on another point, [1912] AC 52.

[371] See *CGU International Insurance plc v Szabo* [2002] 1 All ER (Comm) 83 at [22].

[372] The Giuliano and Lagarde Report, p 20; *Caledonia Subsea Ltd v Micoperi SRL* 2002 SLT 1022, where Lord Cameron said that supervening factors refers to ones not existing at the time of conclusion of the contract and which could not have been reasonably contemplated. For criticism, see Lasok and Stone, *Conflict of Laws in the European Community*, p 363; Plender, para 6.04; cf Nygh (1995) 251 Hague Recueil 269, 346–347.

[373] This is clear from the title of Art 4 and the opening words of para (1).

[374] See *Crédit Lyonnais v New Hampshire Insurance Co* [1997] 2 Lloyd's Rep 1 at 5, CA. Under the objective proper law approach the courts have often referred to the parties' intentions, in the sense of the intentions that they would have had if they had considered the matter, or ought to have had as reasonable persons, see the 11th edn of this book (1987), pp 461–462.

[375] However, a policy of validation underlies Art 9(1) of the Convention, infra, pp 746–749.

[376] Supra, pp 690–707.

[377] Wyatt (1974) 37 MLR 399; Jaffey, *Topics in Choice of Law* (1996), p 32.

[378] However, Jaffey argues that the presumption of characteristic performance will often achieve the desired business efficacy, op cit, 32 et seq. See on achieving the latter, Atrill (2004) 53 ICLQ 549.

[379] See generally, Diamond (1986) IV Hague Recueil 236, 285–287; Pryles in *Contract Conflicts*, pp 323, 334 et seq; Plender, paras 6.05–6.08; Nygh (1995) 251 Hague Recueil 269, 347–348; Kaye, pp 475–477.

[380] Supra, pp 690–692.

the contract has its closest connection with France but another part with Italy.[381] However, severance is an exception to normal principles and the power of severance should be exercised by the courts "as seldom as possible".[382] This provision requires there to be a *severable* part of the contract. In other words, the nature of the contract must be such that part of the contract is independent from the rest and can be severed from it. The Giuliano and Lagarde Report gives, as examples, joint ventures and complex contracts.[383] An English example of severance is provided by *Libyan Arab Foreign Bank v Bankers Trust Co*,[384] a case decided before the Convention came into force. STAUGHTON J held that a single banking contract relating to bank accounts in New York and London was governed in part by New York law and in part by English law (as regards the plaintiff's London account). The judge referred to the power to sever a contract under Article 4 of the Convention, and the result would no doubt be the same now that the Convention is in force. Severability under Article 4(1) does not relate to the dispute; a court presumably cannot apply different laws to particular contractual issues, such as interpretation and discharge of the contract.[385] Finally, Article 4(1) is phrased in terms that a severable part of the contract *may* be governed by a different law from the rest of the contract. It is not clear whether this is intended to confer a discretion on the court, which would enable it to refuse to sever the contract, even though part of that contract was independent and severable.

(iii) The law of the country rather than the system of law

Under Article 4(1) the court has to ascertain the law of the country,[386] rather than the system of law, with which the contract is most closely connected, the former being more appropriate than the latter, given that Article 4(1) is not concerned with the intentions of the parties.[387] In many cases the difference between these two formulations may not be significant. However, an example of where it might be important can be seen from the facts of the common law decision in *James Miller & Partners Ltd v Whitworth Street Estates (Manchester) Ltd*.[388]

> In this case a Scottish company agreed to carry out alterations to an English company's premises in Scotland. The contract was in the standard form provided by the Royal Institute of British Architects. The form, style and legal language of the contract pointed towards English law. If the formulation of the test referred to the system of law you would expect English law to be the applicable law. However, the other factors in the case (such as the place of performance for both parties) pointed strongly towards Scotland. This would appear to be the *country* with which the contract had the closest connections.

---

[381] Pryles, op cit, at 339, suggests that the presumption under Art 4(2) should not be used for ascertaining the law applicable to a severable part of the contract; cf Plender, para 6.08.

[382] The Giuliano and Lagarde Report, at p 23.

[383] Ibid.

[384] [1989] QB 728; Carter (1989) 60 BYBIL 502.

[385] Cf the position under Art 3(1), supra, pp 690–692; cf Fletcher, *Conflict of Laws and European Community Law*, p 161.

[386] For the definition of country see Art 19, discussed supra, pp 680–681.

[387] *Crédit Lyonnais v New Hampshire Insurance Co* [1997] 2 Lloyd's Rep 1 at 5, CA.

[388] [1970] AC 583. Under the proper law of the contract approach, connection with the system of law was more commonly required, although two Law Lords in the *James Miller* case combined the two tests.

Under Article 4(1), Scots law would, accordingly, seem to be applicable.[389]

(iv) The contract

The connection is between the *contract* and the country whose law is to be applied, not between the dispute or transaction and that country. The fact that the connection must be with the *contract* rather than the issue, acts to discourage dépeçage[390] which, as has been mentioned, is only intended to operate in exceptional circumstances.

(b) The presumptions

The difficulty with any objective test that seeks to localise the contract is that of uncertainty. The Convention tries to resolve this uncertainty by the use of presumptions.[391] The Giuliano and Lagarde Report contemplates that the applicable law can be determined solely by applying the presumptions, without searching for the country with the closest connection.[392] The introduction of presumptions turns the clock back as far as English law is concerned. Although popular at one time, presumptions went out of fashion and were rejected,[393] one criticism being the very point that they diverted attention from the necessity to consider every single factor under the objective test. Nonetheless, the common law rule was not as open ended and flexible as might at first appear. In order to promote certainty in the law the courts identified specific factors as having great weight in identifying the closest connection in relation to certain contracts. For example, for insurance contracts the objective proper law would normally be the law of the state where the insurer carried on business.[394]

(i) The general presumption relating to characteristic performance

Article 4(2) provides that:

> Subject to the provisions of paragraph 5 [non-application of presumptions] of this Article, it shall be presumed that the contract is most closely connected with the country where the party who is to effect the performance which is characteristic of the contract has, at the time of conclusion of the contract, his habitual residence, or, in the case of a body corporate or unincorporate, its central administration . . .

Article 4(2) falls into two parts. First, the characteristic performance under the contract has to be identified. Secondly, this is given a geographical location by referring to the habitual residence of the party who is to effect the characteristic performance.

---

[389] See North, *Private International Law Problems in Common Law Jurisdictions* (1993), p 127. Compare Dicey, Morris and Collins,para 32-110.

[390] Vischer in Lipstein (ed), *Harmonisation of Private International Law by the EEC*, p 25. See also generally Lando (1987) 24 CMLR 167–169.

[391] See also the Australian proposals for reform of contract choice of law set out in ALRC Rep No 58 (1992). Cf Art 8, the 1985 Hague Convention on the law applicable to contracts for the international sale of goods and Art 9 of the Inter-American Convention on the Law Applicable to International Contracts of 1994.

[392] At p 21. The use of presumptions, it is said, "greatly simplifies the problem of determining the law applicable in the absence of choice . . . There is no longer any need to determine where the contract was concluded . . . Seeking the place of performance becomes superfluous". Cf the Advocate General in Case 266/85 *Shenavai v Kreischer* [1987] ECR 239 at 249.

[393] *Coast Lines Ltd v Hudig and Veder Chartering NV* [1972] 2 QB 34 at 47, 50.

[394] See Dicey, Morris and Collins, paras 33-141–33-143.

Characteristic performance[395]   Apart from the concept of mandatory rules, this is the most difficult concept used in the Convention. It does not help that the concept is not defined under the Convention nor that its origin is to be found in Swiss private international law.[396] As far as English law is concerned, the place of performance is well known as a connecting factor, but it suffers from the obvious defect that in a typical contract both parties have to perform and may have to do so in different states. The concept of characteristic performance seeks to avoid this difficulty by concentrating on just one performance, the one which is characteristic of the contract as a whole—ie the one which constitutes the essence of the contract. It is this feature of characteristic performance which was used by the Working Group to justify its elevation, above all other connections, to the position of becoming a presumption.[397] More grandiosely, and harder to understand, it was said that "the concept of characteristic performance essentially links the contract to the social and economic environment of which it will form a part".[398]

This still leaves the problem of identifying the characteristic performance. Under Swiss law this depends on the type of contract involved. Again there is no difficulty if only one party has to perform as, for example, in the case of a contract of gift, or a unilateral contract involving payment of a termination fee on discontinuance of a project.[399] But more typically, one party will perform services or provide goods, and the other will pay money for these. It is not immediately obvious which of these performances constitutes the essence of the contract. As far as each party is concerned what is important to them is the counter-performance by the other party. However, the Giuliano and Lagarde Report states[400] that the characteristic performance is usually the performance for which the payment is due; eg the delivery of goods, the granting of a right to make use of property, the provision of a service. Applying this principle, the English and Scots courts have had no difficulty in identifying the characteristic performance of contracts for the sale of goods (the characteristic performance is that of the seller delivering the goods)[401] and contracts for the provision of different types of service[402] and even contracts where one

---

[395] For criticism of the concept, see generally: Collins (1976) 25 ICLQ 35, 44 et seq; D'Oliveira (1977) 25 AJCL 303; Kaye, pp 187–191; Dicey, Morris and Collins, paras 32-113–32-123; Hill, paras14.2.41–14.2.48; Juenger in *Contract Conflicts*, pp 300–302; Schultz ibid, pp 186–187; Morse, op cit, pp 126–132; Fletcher, op cit, pp 161–165; Lasok and Stone, op cit, pp 362–363. Cf Lipstein (1981) 3 Northwestern J of Int L and Bus 402; Blaikie 1983 SLT 241; Jaffey, *Topics in Choice of Law* (1996), pp 32 et seq; Plender, paras 6.09–6.21. Cf ALRC Rep No 58 (1992), Draft Bill, s 9(6), recommending adoption of this concept in Australia.

[396] For the position in Switzerland, see the Swiss Federal Statute on Private International Law of 18 December 1987, Art 117. The statute is set out in (1989) 37 AJCL 193.

[397] The Giuliano and Lagarde Report, p 20.

[398] Ibid.

[399] *Ark Therapeutics plc v True North Capital Ltd* [2005] EWHC 1585 (Comm) at [55], [2006] 1 All ER (Comm) 138. See also *Armstrong International Ltd v Deutsche Bank Securities Inc* QBD 11 July 2003—payment of a fee allegedly due to a recruitment agency which had no contractual obligation to make an introduction.

[400] At p 20. See also Forsyth and Moser (1996) 45 ICLQ 190, at 193–194.

[401] *Iran Continental Shelf Oil Co v IRI International Corpn* [2002] EWCA Civ 1024 at [19], [2004] 2 CLC 696; *Ferguson Shipbuilders Ltd v Voith Hydro GmbH & Co KG* 2000 SLT 229 at 232, (OH); *William Grant & Sons International Ltd v Marie Brizard España SA* 1998 SC 536. See also *Machinale Glasfabriek De Maas BV v Emaillerie Alsacienne SA* [1985] 2 CMLR 281, [1984] ECC 123—a Dutch Supreme Court case applying the Convention as part of its private international law prior to the Convention coming into force. See generally Fawcett, Harris and Bridge, para 13.114.

[402] Eg an insurer providing insurance, on which see *Crédit Lyonnais v New Hampshire Insurance Co* [1997] 2 Lloyd's Rep 1 at 6, CA; *American Motorists Insurance Co (Amico) v Cellstar Corpn* [2003] EWCA Civ 206 at [47], [2003] IL PR 22; reinsurers providing reinsurance: *AIG Group (UK) Ltd v The Ethniki* [1998] 4 All ER 301 at

party provides both goods and services.[403] *Print Concept GmbH v GEW (EC) Ltd*[404] involved an oral distributorship agreement, which has proved to be more problematic.

> Print Concept (the distributor) was under an implied obligation to maximise sales in the German-speaking marketplace and GEW was under an implied obligation to supply its products to Print Concept which the latter would purchase.

The Court of Appeal held that it was the supply of the products that was characteristic of the distribution agreement, for the penetration of the German market could not take place without the supply and purchase of the products.[405] With a contract of guarantee, the characteristic performance is that of payment of money by the guarantor.[406] In *Bank of Baroda v Vysya Bank*[407] MANCE J regarded the position of a bank confirming a letter of credit as being analogous to that of a guarantor. The characteristic performance of the contract between the confirming bank and the issuing bank was the honouring by the confirming bank of its confirmation of credit in favour of the beneficiary.[408] The characteristic performance of the contract between the issuing bank and the beneficiary was the issue of the letter of credit[409] and that between the confirming bank and the beneficiary was that of the bank providing the banking service of payment under the letter of credit.[410] In ascertaining the characteristic performance, one is not confined to the terms of the contract.[411] The global picture must be assessed[412] and the background to the contract may be of particular importance.[413]

A number of criticisms can be levelled at the concept of characteristic performance and at the way it has been defined in the Giuliano and Lagarde Report. First, there are some

---

310; *Tiernan v The Magen Insurance Co Ltd* [2000] IL Pr 517; *Tryg Baltica International (UK) Ltd v Boston Compania De Seguros SA* [2004] EWHC 1186 (Comm), [2005] Lloyd's Rep IR 40; but cf *Dornach Ltd v Mauritius Union Assurance Co Ltd* [2006] EWCA Civ 389 at [41], [2006] 2 Lloyd's Rep 475—payment in the event of a claim as characteristic performance; providing the services of a pop group: *Definitely Maybe (Touring) Ltd v Marek Lieberberg Konzertagentur GmbH* [2001] 1 WLR 1745 at [5]; provision of testing and consultancy services: *Ennstone Building Products Ltd v Stanger Ltd* [2002] EWCA Civ 916 at [13], [2002] 1 WLR 3059; architectural services: *Latchin (t/a Dinkha Latchin Associates) v General Mediterranean Holdings SA* [2002] CLC 330 at [65]; provision of diving services: *Caledonia Subsea Ltd v Micoperi SRL* 2002 SLT 1022 at [21]; commercial agency agreement: *Albon v Naza Motor Trading* [2007] EWHC 9 (Ch), [2007] 1 Lloyd's Rep 297. For development of a website, see *1st Mover APS v Direct Hedge SA* [2003] IL Pr 31 at [11]–[12], Eastern Court of Appeal, Denmark. For the characteristic performance of a broking contract, see *HIB v Guardian Insurance Co* [1997] 1 Lloyd's Rep 412; and provision of an indemnity, see *Opthalmic Innovations International (United Kingdom) Ltd v Opthalmic Innovations International Inc* [2004] EWHC 2948 Ch at [53], [2005] IL Pr 109.

[403] See *Iran Continental Shelf Oil Co v IRI International Corpn* [2002] EWCA Civ 1024 at [19], [2004] 2 CLC 696.

[404] [2001] EWCA Civ 352, [2002] CLC 352.

[405] Ibid, at [34]. See also *Optelec v Midtronics* [2003] IL Pr 4, French Cour De Cassation.

[406] *Samcrete Egypt Engineers and Contractors SAE v Land Rover Exports Ltd* [2001] EWCA Civ 2019 at [38], [2002] CLC 533. See also the Giuliano and Lagarde Report, p 20; *Bloch v Soc Lima* (Versailles 14e ch, Feb 6 1991) [1992] JCP 21972. See also *RZB v NBG* [1999] 1 Lloyd's Rep 408 at 413—breach of a warranty.

[407] [1994] 2 Lloyd's Rep 87.

[408] Ibid, at 92. For the characteristic performance in relation to a bank account, see *Sierra Leone Telecommunications Co Ltd v Barclays Bank plc* [1998] 2 All ER 821; discussed infra, p 715.

[409] Supra, at 93.

[410] *Marconi Communications International Ltd v PT Pan Indonesia Bank Ltd TBK* [2005] EWCA Civ 422 at [54] and [59], [2007] 2 Lloyd's Rep 72.

[411] *Apple Corps Ltd v Apple Computer Inc* [2004] EWHC 768 (Ch) at [50]–[51], [2004] IL Pr 34.

[412] *Print Concept GmbH v GEW (EC) Ltd* [2001] EWCA Civ 352 at [34], [2002] CLC 352.

[413] *Iran Continental Shelf Oil Co v IRI International Corpn* [2002] EWCA Civ 1024 at [24], [2004] 2 CLC 696.

contracts which cannot be fitted easily within the concept, as the *Print Concept* case illustrates. Letters of credit are another example. Article 4(2) assumes the ability to identify a single party charged with the single performance characteristic of the contract.[414] But with a letter of credit there are a number of autonomous bilateral contracts and it is desirable that each contractual relationship arising in the course of the transaction has the same governing law.[415] With a contract of loan the characteristic performer could equally be regarded as being the borrower or the lender.[416] Even worse, there are some contracts that cannot be fitted at all within the concept. With a contract of barter it is difficult, if not impossible, to say that one party's performance is more characteristic of the contract than the other's.[417] The same is true with complex contracts for the commercial exploitation of intellectual property rights.[418] It was not possible to identify the characteristic performance of a trade mark agreement under which each party had to do (or refrain from doing) the same acts vis à vis the other (ie using their marks in their respective defined fields of use).[419] However, the Convention allows for this by providing in Article 4(5) that, if the characteristic performance cannot be determined, the presumption does not apply.

Secondly, the definition of characteristic performance in terms of the performance for which payment is due does not stand up well to close scrutiny. The payment of money was presumably rejected as the characteristic performance because this is a common feature of many contracts and therefore fails to distinguish between different types of contract. Nonetheless, there are some contracts where the payment of money is arguably the essence of the obligation, for example contracts of pledge or hire-purchase, or repayment of a loan.[420] The Working Group qualified their statement about the payment of money by saying that this is not *usually*[421] the essence of the obligation. The payment of money can, in unusual cases, constitute the characteristic performance. For example, the characteristic performance of a reinsurance contract has been described as being the making of payment in the event of a claim.[422]

Thirdly, the effect of generally denying that the payment of money constitutes the essence of the contract is to favour the seller of goods over the buyer. This has been justified on the basis that the seller's performance is generally more complicated and to a greater

---

[414] The *Marconi* case, supra, at [61].

[415] Ibid.

[416] *Atlantic Telecom GmbH, Noter* 2004 SLT 1031 at 1051–1052, where a preference was shown for the lender.

[417] *Caledonia Subsea Ltd v Micoperi SRL* 2002 SLT 1022 at [21]. See the representations of the German Government in Case 266/85 *Shenavai v Kreischer* [1987] ECR 239 at 255.

[418] Fawcett and Torremans, pp 559–561; Wadlow [1997] 1 EIPR 11 at 14.

[419] *Apple Corps Ltd v Apple Computer Inc* [2004] EWHC 768 (Ch) at [52]–[55], [2004] IL Pr 34.

[420] Collins (1976) 25 ICLQ 35 at 48; see also Diamond, op cit, p 274. But see the Giuliano and Lagarde Report, p 21. But with a loan see the *Atlantic Telecom* case, supra, in favour of service of providing the loan as characteristic performance. Cf *Tavoulareas v Tsavliris* [2005] EWHC 2140 (Comm) at [51], [2006] 1 All ER (Comm), 109, repayment of loan as characteristic performance. See also *Halpern v Halpern* [2007] EWCA Civ 291 at [28], [2007] 2 Lloyd's Rep 56—action to enforce compromise agreement allegedly entered into by executors.

[421] At p 20.

[422] *Dornach Ltd v Mauritius Union Assurance Co Ltd* [2006] EWCA Civ 389 at [41], [2006] 2 Lloyd's Rep 475. For another example see *Ark Therapeutics plc v True North Capital Ltd* [2005] EWHC 1585 (Comm) at [55], [2006] 1 All ER (Comm) 138, supra, p 399.

extent regulated by rules of law than that of the buyer.[423] However, it is questionable whether this is sufficient to justify completely ignoring the buyer's performance in most cases.

Fourthly, in terms of economic strength, the large enterprise, the manufacturer of goods, the provider of services (such as banks and insurance companies) and the professional is favoured against the other party who may well be in a weaker economic position.[424] It is curious to find a pro-manufacturer stance being taken in a Convention which is sufficiently concerned about protecting weaker parties to have special rules for consumers and employees.

Habitual residence, etc   Despite the emphasis placed on characteristic performance, Article 4(2) does not apply the law of the place of such performance. Instead, reference is made to the country where the party who is to effect the characteristic performance has his habitual residence, or, in the case of a company, its central administration. If the contract is entered into in the course of the trade or profession[425] of the party who is to effect the characteristic performance, reference is made to the principal place of business of that party or to another place of business (if, under the terms of the contract, performance is to be effected through that place).[426] Thus in a contract in relation to a bank account, performance by way of repayment of the sum deposited is effected through the branch where the account is kept. If the account is kept in England, English law will govern.[427] In a contract between a bank issuing a letter of credit and another bank confirming this, if the performance characteristic of the contract (honouring the confirmation) is effected through the confirming bank's London office, English law will govern the contract.[428] In determining whether the principal place of business is to to be displaced by some other place of business, it is necesssary to ascertain whether "under the terms of the contract" the characteristic performance is to be effected through that other place of business. An express or implied term must require performance in this other place so that that there would be a breach of contract if it were performed through another place.[429] It is not enough that the parties anticipated that performance would be effected through a place of business other than the principal place of business.[430] The question whether the characteristic performance is "effected through" that other place of business involves looking at the type of contract involved and if the obligation of the characteristic performer is,

---

[423] See Fletcher, op cit, p 163.

[424] For attempts to justify this, see Lagarde (1981) 22 VAJ Int L 91 at 97 n 32. See also Vischer in Lipstein (ed), *Harmonisation of Private International Law by the EEC* p 28; Lando (1987) 24 CMLR 159, at 202 et seq.

[425] There is no guidance in the Convention or Report as to when a contract is entered into in the course of the trade or profession of that party. The same difficulty arises under the Unfair Contract Terms Act 1977 and the Unfair Terms in Consumer Contracts Regulations 1999, see infra, pp 733–735. See also Art 15 of the Brussels I Regulation, supra, p 268, for the phrase "outside his trade or profession".

[426] Art 4(2).

[427] *Sierra Leone Telecommunications Co Ltd v Barclays Bank plc* [1998] 2 All ER 821. See also the Giuliano and Lagarde Report, p 21.

[428] *Bank of Baroda v Vysya Bank* [1994] 2 Lloyd's Rep 87 at 92. But where an Indian bank issued a letter of credit in London through an English bank, the law of India, as the place of central administration of the Indian bank, was applied under Art 4(2): ibid at 93.

[429] *Ennstone Building Products Ltd v Stanger Ltd* [2002] EWCA Civ 916 at [24]–[36], [2002] 1 WLR 3059. But cf the obiter dicta of CLARKE LJ in *Iran Continental Shelf Oil Co v IRI International Corpn* [2002] EWCA Civ 1024 at [65], [2004] 2 CLC 696.

[430] The *Ennstone* case, supra, at [24]–[36].

for example, to ship the goods then the question will be whether this is arranged by that place of business.[431]

Whatever the merits of the concept of characteristic performance, these become less important when the concept is diluted by the addition of another connecting factor in this way.[432] Moreover, it is questionable whether reference to a personal connecting factor such as a habitual residence is appropriate in the context of commercial contracts.[433] Article 4(2) also makes it clear that reference is to be made to the habitual residence or central administration as at the time of the conclusion of the contract, because of the possibility of changes in this connecting factor. It is noticeable that, whilst provision is made for the situation where characteristic performance cannot be ascertained, there is no corresponding provision dealing with the situation where the habitual residence, etc cannot be ascertained.[434] Presumably the forum will have to use its own national definitions of these concepts.[435]

Unless a presumption is easy to apply it will not produce the certainty in determining the objective applicable law that is its raison d'être.[436] Unfortunately, the presumption in Article 4(2) is a complex one, involving considerable definitional problems. Moreover, with a presumption, one connection is elevated to a position of importance above all others. It is doubtful whether the combination of habitual residence and characteristic performance merits this.

(ii) Special presumptions

Although, in principle, the concept of characteristic performance is applicable regardless of the type of contract involved, it has been thought necessary to have special presumptions relating to immovable property (Article 4(3)) and carriage of goods (Article 4(4)).

With immovable property the presumption is that the contract is most closely connected with the country where the immovable property is situated. However, this provision only applies to the extent that the subject matter of the contract is a right in immovable property or a right to use immovable property.[437] A contract for the sale of property or for the rental of a holiday home would come within this, but a contract for construction or repair would not because the main subject matter of the contract is not the immovable property itself.[438] This presumption, like the general one of characteristic performance, can be rebutted if the contract is more closely connected with another country. The Giuliano and Lagarde Report gives as an example a contract between two Belgians for the rental of an Italian holiday home.[439] It is said that Belgian law would govern this contract.

---

[431] *Iran Continental Shelf Oil Co v IRI International Corpn* [2002] EWCA Civ 1024 at [64]–[76], [2004] 2 CLC 696.

[432] Cf the Giuliano and Lagarde Report, at pp 20–21. Supported by Jaffey, *Topics in Choice of Law* (1996), p 35.

[433] Collins (1976) 25 ICLQ 35, 45–46; cf Jaffey, op cit.

[434] The preliminary draft Convention contained such a provision in Art 4.

[435] "Habitual residence" is discussed supra, pp 185–195. "Central administration" can doubtless be equated with "central management and control", discussed supra, p 212. "Place of business" is discussed supra, pp 369–370.

[436] Cf Jaffey, op cit, pp 36 et seq. See also generally Lando, op cit, p 203.

[437] See generally Fletcher, p 164; Plender, paras 6.22–6.27.

[438] The Giuliano and Lagarde Report, p 21.

[439] Ibid.

Contracts for the carriage of goods[440] were regarded by the Working Group as having peculiarities which merited a separate special rebuttable presumption, which refers to the principal place of business of the carrier at the time the contract was concluded. One of a number of alternative connections with that country must also be satisfied, eg that it is also the place of loading or discharge. If not, no presumption operates and the applicable law must be ascertained using Article 4(1).[441] Contracts for the carriage of passengers are subject to the general characteristic performance presumption under Article 4(2).[442] A mixed contract for the carriage of goods and passengers will be subject to two different presumptions with possibly two different applicable laws. With contracts of carriage other international conventions may apply, and these take precedence over the Rome Convention.[443]

(c) Non-application of the presumptions

Article 4(5) provides that: "Paragraph 2 [the basic presumption] shall not apply if the characteristic performance cannot be determined, and the presumptions in paragraphs 2, 3 and 4 [the basic and special presumptions] shall be disregarded if it appears from the circumstances as a whole that the contract is more closely connected with another country." This deals with two very different situations. The first is where the characteristic performance cannot be determined. In this case it is impossible to apply the basic presumption. The second is where the contract is more closely connected with another country. In this case the presumptions are disregarded.

(i) Impossibility in applying the basic presumption

If the characteristic performance cannot be determined,[444] Article 4(2) (the basic presumption) does not apply and the applicable law has to be determined by using the closest connection approach under Article 4(1). In such cases there will be the usual problems that arise under an objective approach which seeks to localise the contract. The court will have to ascertain all the connections with the different countries, give weight to these, and, if they are evenly balanced between two countries, find one especially important connection which tips the balance in favour of one country. [445]

(ii) Disregarding the presumptions

All the presumptions under Article 4 are to be disregarded if it appears from the circumstances as a whole that the contract is more closely connected with another country. The onus is on the party relying on Article 4(5) to establish that it is a proper case for

---

[440] According to Art 4(4), "carriage of goods" encompasses "single voyage charter-parties and other contracts the main purpose of which is the carriage of goods". See generally Schultz in *Contract Conflicts*, pp 185 et seq; Fletcher, op cit, pp 164–165; Plender, paras 6.28–6.32; Kaye, pp 197–202.

[441] Case C-440/97 *GIE Groupe Concorde v The Master of the vessel Suhadiwarno Panjan* [1999] ECR I-6307 at [41] (Opinion of AG Ruiz-Jarabo Colomer).

[442] The Giuliano and Lagarde Report, p 22.

[443] Art 21, discussed infra, p 763.

[444] For examples see supra, p 714.

[445] See *Apple Corps Ltd v Apple Computer Inc* [2004] EWHC 768 (Ch) at [61]–[64], [2004] IL Pr 34. See generally in relation to contracts for the commercial exploitation of intellectual property rights, Fawcett and Torremans, pp 561–570.

disregarding Article 4(2).[446] There are examples of where the English courts have simply ascertained the applicable law according to the presumption under Article 4(2) and have not gone on even to discuss Article 4(5), presumably because it was not raised by either party.[447] This may be because it is obvious that application of Article 4(5) does not produce a different result.[448] The power to disregard the presumptions provides flexibility[449] and was thought to be necessary because of the wide variety of different types of contract that have to be dealt with under the Convention, which has few special rules for particular contracts.[450] However, the price for this flexibility is the risk of uncertainty and lack of predictability[451] inherent in the weakening of the presumptions.[452]

When it comes to the inter-relationship of Article 4(2) and 4(5)[453] there are worrying differences between the approach adopted by the English courts and that adopted by the Dutch and Scots courts.[454] These differences relate to the weight to be given to the presumption and when it comes to evidence in favour of displacement the significance to be given to the place of performance by the characteristic performer.

The English approach At one time the English atttitude was that Article 4(5) "formally makes the presumption very weak"[455] and the presumption is displaced if the court considers that it is not appropriate to apply it in the circumstances of the case. This supports the two-stage process under Article 4.[456] The courts followed the proposition in Dicey and Morris[457] that the presumption may most easily be displaced in those cases where the place of performance differs from the place of business of the party whose performance is characteristic of the contract. In this situation, displacement in practice means applying the law of the place of performance by the characteristic performer, rather than the law of the place of business of the characteristic performer. This strikes at the heart of Article 4(2) because it favours the place of performance over the place of business. This is what

---

[446] *Definitely Maybe (Touring) Ltd v Marek Lieberberg Konzertagentur GmbH* [2001] 1 WLR 1745 at [15]; *Caledonia Subsea Ltd v Micoperi SRL* 2002 SLT 1022 (per Lord CAMERON).

[447] See cases where insurance or reinsurance services are provided, eg *Tiernan v The Magen Insurance Co Ltd* [2000] IL Pr 517; *Tryg Baltica International (UK) Ltd v Boston Compañía de Seguros SA* [2004] EWHC 1186 (Comm), [2005] Lloyd's Rep IR 40. For a case decided seemingly just on the basis of Art 4(1) see MORISON J in *ISS Machinery Services Ltd v Aeolian Shipping SA (the Aeolian)* this was not appealed against in [2001] EWCA Civ 1162, [2001] 2 Lloyd's Rep 641.

[448] *Print Concept GmbH v GEW (EC) Ltd* [2001] EWCA Civ 352 at [35], [2002] CLC 352.

[449] This has been welcomed by an American writer, see Juenger in *Contract Conflicts*, p 307. See also Kay (1989) III Hague Recueil 194. Flexibility can be used to achieve a particular result in a case: Diamond, op cit, pp 284–285.

[450] The Giuliano and Lagarde Report, p 22.

[451] Reese (1987) 35 AJCL 395 at 400; Schultz in *Contract Conflicts*, p 187.

[452] See *Crédit Lyonnais v New Hampshire Insurance Co* [1997] 2 Lloyd's Rep 1 at 5, CA; *Kenburn Waste Management Ltd v H Bergmann* [2002] EWCA Civ 98 at [32], [2002] IL Pr 33.

[453] See Hill (2004) 53 ICLQ 325, 339–350 and in Hill, paras 14.2.69–14.2.80; Atrill (2004) 53 ICLQ 549; the case notes by Briggs in (2001) 72 BYBIL 465 and (2002) 73 BYBIL 473.

[454] See generally *Definitely Maybe (Touring) Ltd v Marek Lieberberg Konzertagentur GmbH* [2001] 1 WLR 1745 at [9]–[15]; *Caledonia Subsea Ltd v Micoperi SRL* 2002 SLT 1022. See also Crawford and Carruthers, paras 15–16.

[455] *Crédit Lyonnais v New Hampshire Insurance Co* [1997] 2 Lloyd's Rep 1 at 5, CA. See also the *Bank of Baroda* case. For the argument that the presumption should be used as a tie-breaker, see Hill, 14.2.69.

[456] Supra, pp 707–708.

[457] Dicey and Morris (1993) 12th edn, pp 1137–1138, now Dicey, Morris and Collins, (2006) 14th edn, para 32-127.

happened in *Bank of Baroda v Vysya Bank*,[458] a decision of MANCE J applying Article 4(5). The case concerned a letter of credit.[459] This involved several separate contracts and MANCE J was concerned that these should not be governed by different laws.[460] Otherwise, this could lead to the situation where the applicable law varied according to the bank against which the beneficiary decided to enforce the credit. According to Article 4(2), English law governed the contract between the beneficiary and the plaintiff confirming bank, whereas Indian law governed the contract between the beneficiary and the defendant issuing bank. The result of applying Article 4(5) in relation to the latter contract was that it too was governed by English law. The other important factor in relation to this latter contract was that the place of performance differed from the place of business of the party whose performance was characteristic of the contract.[461] Similarly, in *Definitely Maybe (Touring) Ltd v Marek Lieberberg Konzertagentur GmbH*,[462] Article 4(5) was applied where the claimant characteristic performer, which provided the services of the pop group Oasis, was located in England whereas the place of characteristic performance was in Germany (where Oasis were to perform).[463] The defendant also had to perform contractual obligations in Germany. The presumption in favour of English law was displaced in favour of German law.

The stated attitude of the English courts towards Article 4(2) has subsequently shifted so as to give more weight to the presumption. The leading case is *Samcrete Egypt Engineers and Contractors SAE v Land Rover Exports Ltd*,[464] where POTTER LJ said that "unless art 4(2) is regarded as a rule of thumb which requires a preponderance of contrary connecting factors to be established before that presumption can be disregarded, the intention of the convention is likely to be subverted"[465] and that the Article 4(2) presumption "should . . . only be disregarded in circumstances which clearly demonstrate the existence of connecting factors justifying [this]".[466] This is a flexible approach compared with that adopted in the Netherlands.[467] The process involves looking at all the relevant connecting factors, one of which is the place of performance of the person who is to effect the

---

[458] [1994] 2 Lloyd's Rep 87; Morse [1994] LMCLQ 560; Struycken [1996] LMCLQ 18, at 22–23; Moloney [1997] LMCLQ 344, 348 et seq. See more generally Radicati Di Brozolo (2000) 48 AJCL 307, 318–322.

[459] See also on letters of credit *Trafigura Beheer BV v Kookmin Bank Co* [2005] EWHC 2350 (Comm); *Trafigura Beheer BV v Kookmin Bank Co* [2006] EWHC 1921 (Comm) at [48]; *Marconi Communications International Ltd v PT Pan Indonesia Bank Ltd TBK* [2005] EWCA Civ 422 at [44], [2005] 2 All ER (Comm) 325. For a common law case following *Bank of Baroda* see *Habib Bank Ltd v Central Bank of Sudan* [2006] EWHC 1767 (Comm), [2006] 2 Lloyd's Rep 412.

[460] *Bank of Baroda*, supra, at 93. See also Lagarde (1981) 22 VA J Int L 91, at 97–98: "A subcontract, for example, might be governed by the same law governing the principal contract between the contractor and the employer, rather than by the law of the country in which the subcontractor has his place of business."

[461] The *Bank of Baroda* case.

[462] [2001] 1 WLR 1745; Fentiman [2002] CLJ 50.

[463] See at [15] for approval of the Dicey and Morris (now Dicey, Morris and Collins) proposition.

[464] [2001] EWCA Civ 2019, [2002] CLC 533.

[465] Ibid, at [41]. Followed in *Marconi Communications International Ltd v PT Pan Indonesia Bank Ltd TBK* [2005] EWCA Civ 422 at [44], [2005] 2 All ER (Comm) 325; *Caledonia Subsea Ltd v Micoperi SRL* 2002 SLT 1022 (per Lord President CULLEN), but cf the support for the Dutch approach by Lords CAMERON and MARNOCH (infra, p 722).

[466] The *Samcrete* case, supra, at [45]. Followed in *Ennstone Building Products Ltd v Stanger Ltd* [2002] EWCA Civ 916 at [41], [2002] 1 WLR 3059; *Iran Continental Shelf Oil Co v IRI International Corpn* [2002] EWCA Civ 1024 at [81]–[82], [2004] 2 CLC 696; *Opthalmic Innovations International (United Kingdom) Ltd v Opthalmic Innovations International Inc* [2004] EWHC 2948 (Ch) at [49], [2005] IL Pr 109.

[467] The *Samcrete* case, supra, at [42]; the *Marconi* case, supra, at [48].

performance which is characteristic of the contract. Each case depends on its merits [468] and the weight to be attached to the place of performance will depend on the circumstances of the case.

This sounds a very balanced approach. But in practice the English courts can be accused of still giving too much significance to the place of performance and not enough to the place of business of the characteristic performer. There is continuing support for the proposition in Dicey and Morris (now Dicey, Morris and Collins) that the presumption may most easily be rebutted in those cases where the place of performance differs from the place of business of the party whose performance is characteristic of the contract. This proposition was cited[469] and applied in the *Samcrete case*.[470] According to the presumption in Article 4(2), Egyptian law governed a contract of guarantee. The fact that the guarantee was written in English was of little weight. Of greater significance was the fact that the obligation characteristic of the guarantee (payment under it by the guarantor), which was to be performed by the Egyptian defendant, was to be performed in England. In addition, the claimant's obligation to supply the product, the express consideration for the guarantee, was also to be performed in England. It was held that there was sufficient material before the court to justify disregarding the presumption in Article 4(2).[471] This has echoes of the common law, under which, where both parties performed in the same state this was a particularly important connecting factor which could tip the balance in favour of the application of the law of that country.[472] Article 4(5) was also applied in *Marconi Communications International Ltd v PT Pan Indonesia Bank Ltd TBK*.[473] Like the *Vysya Bank case*, this concerned a letter of credit, in this case the contract between the beneficiary and the confirming bank. As was said in that case, it was desirable that each of the contractual relationships arising in the course of the transaction should be governed by the same law.[474] Under the presumption, Indonesian law governed (the Indonesian bank effected the performance characteristic of the contract, namely, payment under the letter of credit). However, POTTER LJ said[475] that in the context of the overall purpose of a letter of credit, the factors which have the most significance when considering the closest connection are not the location of the central administration or the place of business of the issuing or confirming bank but the place where documents necessary to procure payment to the beneficiary are to be presented and checked and the place where payment is to be made against those documents. On the facts, not only was the contemplated place of payment England but also, for the purposes of negotiation, the documents would be submitted and checked in England before payment was made.[476] The problem with the line of argument in this case is that it can

---

[468] *Iran Continental Shelf Oil Co v IRI International Corpn* [2002] EWCA Civ 1024 at [90], [2004] 2 CLC 696.

[469] The *Samcrete* case, supra, at [43].

[470] See also *Kenburn Waste Management Ltd v H Bergmann* [2002] EWCA Civ 98, [2002] IL Pr 33—an obligation by characteristic performer habitually resident in Germany to abstain from issuing threats of patent infringement proceedings against parties in England (Art 4(5) applied).

[471] For an example of displacement which was regarded as obvious, see *American Motorists Insurance Co (Amico) v Cellstar Corpn* [2003] EWCA Civ 206 at [47], [2003] IL Pr 22.

[472] [1954] P 150.

[473] [2005] EWCA Civ 422, [2005] 2 All ER (Comm) 325; Hare [2005] LMCLQ 417.

[474] The *Marconi Communications* case, supra, at [61].

[475] Ibid, at [63].

[476] Ibid, at [66].

equally be said with other types of contract that the central administration or place of business is not an important connection whereas the place of performance is.[477] The presumption regards the central administration or place of business as an important connection and the Court of Appeal can be criticised for paying insufficient regard to this.

It is instructive to now look at the cases where the presumption under Article 4(2) has not been displaced. In *Ennstone Building Products Ltd v Stanger Ltd*[478] there was insufficient connection with Scotland for the presumption that English law governed by virtue of Article 4(2) to be disregarded.[479] The characteristic performance of the contract was the supply of advice to the claimant by the defendant, which had its principal place of business in England. The investigatory work would be performed in Scotland but the written advice, which was the vital part of the services to be provided, was to be received in England. This was therefore not a case where the characteristic performance was wholly in a country other than that where the characteristic performer had its principal place of business. The building causing the problem was in Scotland but the stone, which became stained, supplied by the claimant was quarried in England. Both companies were English, though it was the defendant's Scottish office that was involved in doing the work. In *Iran Continental Shelf Oil Co v IRI International Corp*,[480] there were connections with three countries, which is a scenario where it is unlikely that there is one country with which the contract is more closely connected.

> The case concerned the refurbishment of an oil rig in Iran (provision of goods and services) with performance to be effected by the defendant, which had its principal place of business in Texas, through its English office (hence English law applied under the presumption). There was physical shipment of goods from Texas but the technical requirements for refurbishment were identified by an expert from the defendant's English office after visiting Iran. The English office also had a formal role under the contract as shipper and supplier to avoid the appearance of buying goods direct from America.

English law governed by virtue of the presumption and it did not clearly appear from the circumstances that the contract was more closely connected with Texas than with England.

The Dutch and Scots approach   The attitude of the Dutch Supreme Court in *Société Nouvelle des Papeteries de l'Aa v Machinefabriek BOA*[481] is that the presumption is of great weight and should only be rebutted in exceptional cases, that Article 4(2) is the main rule not Article 4(1), and that the law identified by the presumption prevails unless it has no real significance as a connecting factor. This supports the one-stage view of the process under Article 4. The Dutch Supreme Court refused to apply Article 4(5) to rebut the

---

[477] See, eg, *Definitely Maybe (Touring) Ltd v Marek Lieberberg Konzertagentur GmbH* [2001] 1 WLR 1745 at [12].

[478] [2002] EWCA Civ 916, [2002] 1 WLR 3059—a decision of KEENE and POTTER LJJ. See also *Opthalmic Innovations International (United Kingdom) Ltd v Opthalmic Innovations International Inc* [2004] EWHC 2948 Ch at [53], [2005] IL Pr 109; *Armstrong International Ltd v Deutsche Bank Securities Inc* QBD, 11 July 2003 (unreported) at [20].

[479] The *Ennstone* case, supra, at [42].

[480] [2002] EWCA Civ 1024, [2004] 2 CLC 696.

[481] 25 September, NJ (1992) No 750, RvdW (1992) No 207; Struycken [1996] LMCLQ 18. For French discussion of Art 4(5) see *Bloch v Soc Lima SpA* (Versailles 14e ch, 6 February 1991) [1992] JCP 21972.

presumption that Dutch law applied, even though the only connection with the Netherlands was that it was the place of business of the person whose performance was characteristic of the contract, whereas many elements of the case linked the contract to France, including the fact that performance of the contract by this person took place there.[482] This case adopts a very different approach towards the situation where the place of performance differs from the place of business of the party whose performance is characteristic of the contract from that adopted by the English courts.

The Dutch approach has been rejected by the Court of Appeal in England as being too rigid.[483] However, it has been approved by a majority (Lords CAMERON and MARNOCH) in the First Division of the Court of Session in Scotland in *Caledonia Subsea Ltd v Micoperi SRL*.[484] The presumption in Article 4(2) was said to be a strong one,[485] which could only be displaced in *exceptional* cases.[486] Lord President CULLEN disagreed with the Dicey and Morris proposition that the presumption may most easily be rebutted in those cases where the place of performance differs from the place of business of the party whose performance is characteristic of the contract and made the point that, whilst relevant, the place of performance may be only one of a number of factors to be assessed in the exercise of Article 4(5).[487] The place of performance was regarded as playing a subordinate role as a circumstance in fixing the applicable law.[488]Although the contract was performed in Egypt by a characteristic performer with its principal place of business in Scotland, there were distinct connections with Scotland both prior to the conclusion of the contract and during its currency. This was not considered to be an exceptional case and the presumption in favour of Scotland could not be displaced.

(d) The applicable law in the absence of choice under the Rome I Regulation

(i) Article 4

Article 4 of the Rome I Regulation sets out one of the most radical departures from the position under the Convention.

Article 4(1) In order to achieve certainty, it is provided in Article 4(1) that, where the law applicable to the contract has not been chosen by the parties, there should be a list of fixed rules dealing with many of the most commonly encountered contracts.[489] Thus, a

---

[482] The *Société Nouvelle* case, supra.

[483] The *Samcrete* case, supra, at [42]; the *Marconi* case, supra, at [48].

[484] 2002 SLT 1022 (per Lords CAMERON and MARNOCH). Lord President CULLEN approved the approach in the *Sancrete* case, supra, at [41]. But see the analysis of Lord CAMERON's judgment by the Court of Appeal in *Marconi Communications International Ltd v PT Pan Indonesia Bank Limited TBK* [2005] EWCA Civ 422 at [48], [2005] 2 All ER (Comm) 325. See also *William Grant v Marie Brizard et Roger International SA* 1998 SC 536; *Krupp Uhde GmbH v Weir Westgarth Ltd*, 31 May 2002 (unreported) (Lord EASSIE).

[485] The *Caledonia Subsea* case, supra, (per Lord MARNOCH). See also Lord CAMERON.

[486] Ibid (per Lord CAMERON). See also Lord MARNOCH—"very special circumstances".

[487] Ibid.

[488] Ibid (per Lord CAMERON).Cf *Ferguson Shipbuilders Ltd v Voith Hydro GmbH & Co AG* 2000 SLT 229 at 232.

[489] See Art 4(1) of the Regulation. See the Explanatory Memorandum accompanying the Proposal for a Regulation of the European Parliament and the Council on the law applicable to contractual obligations (Rome I) COM (2005) 650 final, at pp 6–7. The European Parliament in its draft Report (PE 374.427v01-00 of 22 August 2006 and 7 December 2006) originally proposed a closest connection rule with a series of presumptions for particular types of contract.

contract for the sale of goods [490] shall be governed by the law of the country where the seller has his habitual residence.[491] A contract for the provision of services[492] shall be governed by the law of the country where the service provider has his habitual residence.[493] A contract relating to a right in rem in immovable property or to a tenancy of immovable property shall be governed by the law of the country where the property is situated.[494] A tenancy of immovable property concluded for temporary private use for a period of no more than six consecutive months shall be governed by the law of the country where the landlord has his habitual residence, provided that the tenant is a natural person and has his habitual residence in the same country.[495] A franchise contract shall be governed by the law of the country where the franchisee has his habitual residence.[496] A distribution contract shall be governed by the law of the country where the distributor has his habitual residence.[497] A contract for the sale of goods by auction shall be governed by the law of the country where the auction takes place, if such a place can be determined.[498] There is finally a special rule for contracts concluded at a financial market, which provides that a contract concluded within a multilateral system which brings together or facilitates the bringing together of multiple third party buying and selling interests in financial instruments,[499] in accordance with non-discretionary rules and governed by a single law, shall be governed by that law.[500] The original proposal for a Regulation contained a rule for contracts relating to intellectual or industrial property rights, but the compromise package of the Presidency of April 2007, agreed by the Council, deleted this rule and it is not present in the final version of the Regulation. The original proposal for a Regulation also contained a rule under Article 4(1) for contracts of carriage[501] but this rule did not form part of the compromise package of the Presidency of April 2007 agreed by the Council and there is no such rule under Article 4 of the final version of the Regulation. However, there is a separate Article 5 setting out a separate regime of rules for contracts of carriage.

Under most of these fixed rules[502] the result is the same as that obtained applying the characteristic performance presumptions under Article 4(2) and (3) of the Rome Convention. But under Article 4(1) of the Regulation the route to the result is more direct in that it would be no longer necessary to identify what the characteristic performance of a particular contract is. It is noticeable, though, that there is no attempt to

---

[490] "Sale of goods" should be defined in the same way as when applying Art 5(1)(b) of the Brussels I Regulation (discussed supra, p 238): Recital (17) of the Regulation.

[491] Art 4(1)(a) of the Regulation.

[492] "Provision of services" should be defined in the same way as when applying Art 5(1)(b) of the Brussels I Regulation (discussed supra, pp 238–239): Recital (17) of the Regulation.

[493] Art 4(1)(b) of the Regulation.

[494] Art 4(1)(c) of the Regulation.

[495] Art 4(1)(d) of the Regulation.

[496] Art 4(1)(e) of the Regulation.

[497] Art 4(1)(f) of the Regulation.

[498] Art 4(1)(g) of the Regulation.

[499] As defined by Art 4(1), point (17) of Directive (EC) No 204/39. See also Recital (18) of the Regulation.

[500] Art 4(1)(h) of the Regulation.

[501] See Art 4(1)(c) of the Regulation.

[502] But not for distribution contracts (on which see *Print Concept GmbH v GEW (EC) Ltd* [2001] EWCA Civ 352 at [35], [2002] CLC 352; discussed supra, pp 712–713), auctions and, arguably, franchise contracts (the characteristic performance could be regarded as that of the person granting the franchise for which the franchised person pays, see generally supra).

co-ordinate choice of law and jurisdiction.[503] This is understandable. With a contract for the sale of goods, jurisdiction in some cases will be allocated to the buyer's home state (as the place of delivery),[504] the courts of which will apply the law of the seller's home state. But in other cases it will be allocated to the seller's home state (as the place of delivery). In other words, the jurisdiction is not geared to the buyer's or seller's home state but to the more complex concept of place of delivery, which in some cases will be the seller's home state and in others the buyer's.

Article 4(2)   Article 4(2) deals with two situations: first, where the contract is not covered by Article 4(1); and, secondly, where the elements of the contract would be covered by more than one of the fixed rules in Article 4(1). In both situations, Article 4(2) provides that the contract shall be governed by the law of the country where the party required to effect the characteristic performance of the contract has his habitual residence. In the case of a contract consisting of a bundle of rights and obligations capable of being characterised as falling within more than one of the specified types of contract, the characteristic performance of the contract should be determined having regard to its centre of gravity.[505] So the criterion of characteristic performance is retained but what is a presumption under Article 4(2) of the Convention becomes a rule under the Regulation.

Article 4(4)   This leaves a problem where the law applicable cannot be determined pursuant to Article 4(1) or (2). This would arise where the contract is one of those for which there is a fixed rule under Article 4(1) but the applicable law cannot be determined under that rule or the performance of the contract which is characteristic of the contract cannot be identified under Article 4(2). The same problem arose under Article 4 of the Convention and the solution adopted under the Regulation[506] is the same one, namely that the contract shall be governed by the law of the country with which it is most closely connected. In order to determine that country, account should be taken, inter alia, of whether the contract in question has a very close relationship with another contract or contracts.[507]

Article 4(3)   Under the original proposal for a Regulation the rules in Article 4(1) and (2) were fixed ones with no exception, as under Article 4(5) of the Convention, which would allow the rule to be disregarded if it appears from the circumstances as a whole that the contract was more closely connected with another country. The desirability of achieving certainty in the law was given overriding importance. The price of this would have been total inflexibility. This was subject to scathing criticism.[508] It is very welcome then to see that Article 4(3) of the Regulation contains a flexible let-out.[509] This states that "Where it is clear from all the circumstances of the case that the contract is manifestly more closely connected with a country other than that indicated in paragraphs 1 or 2, the law of that other country shall apply." When applying this let-out, account should be taken, inter alia, of whether the contract in question has a very close relationship with another

---

[503] Except in respect of the definition of "sale of goods" and "provision of services".
[504] See Art 5(1)(b) of the Brussels I Regulation, discussed supra, pp 239–240.
[505] Recital (19) of the Regulation.
[506] Art 4(4) of the Regulation.
[507] Recital (21) of the Regulation.
[508] See Dutson (2006) 122 LQR 374 and (2006) IFLR 36.
[509] Originally introduced in the compromise package of the Presidency of 13 April 2007, agreed by the Council, 8022/07 JUSTCIV 73 CODEC 306.

contract or contracts.[510] It is not enough to show that the contract is more closely connected, it has to be "manifestly" more closely connected. The addition of the word "manifestly" is doubtless designed to underscore the exceptional nature of this let-out,[511] which appears to be intended to be a narrower one than that under Article 4(5) of the Rome Convention. This could be regarded as being an acceptable compromise which reconciles the needs of certainty and flexibility.[512] Whether the English courts would, in practice, interpret this new let-out more narrowly than the old let-out would remain to be seen.[513] With any flexible let-out, a lack of uniform interpretation in different Member States is likely in the absence of a decision of the Court of Justice.

(ii) Habitual residence

Article 4(1) makes much use of the concept of habitual residence. Article 19(1) of the Regulation introduces a definition of habitual residence for a company. This provides that, for the purposes of the Regulation, "the habitual residence of companies and other bodies, corporate or unincorporated, shall be the place of central administration". Provision is then made for the situations where the contract is concluded in the course of the operations of a branch, agency or any other establishment, or if, under the contract, performance is the responsibility of such a branch, agency or establishment. In these situations, the place where the branch, agency or any other establishment is located shall be treated as the place of habitual residence.[514] There is no definition of the habitual residence of a natural person, except for the situation where such a person is acting in the course of his business activity. Article 19(1) provides that, in this situation, the habitual residence of a natural person shall be his principal place of business. The idea of giving an autonomous definition to the concept of the habitual residence of a company, echoes the defining of the domicile of a company under the Brussels I Regulation. The intention is to produce certainty in the law. It was not possible to adopt the same definition for contract choice of law as has been adopted for jurisdiction. It will be recalled that the latter definition is in terms of three alternatives.[515] Whilst it is fine for jurisdictional purposes for a company to be located in three different states, for choice of law purposes the company must be located in just one state; there cannot be three different laws applying.[516] The definition of the habitual residence of a company in terms of its place of central administration follows that contained in the Rome II Regulation on non-contractual obligations.[517] When determining habitual residence, the relevant point in time is that of the conclusion of the contract.[518]

---

[510] Recital (20) of the Regulation.

[511] See the addition of the word "manifestly" to the public policy defence under the Brussels I Regulation, supra, p 612.

[512] See Lando and Nielsen (2007) 3 J Priv Int L 29 at 38.

[513] The Ministry of Justice, in Consultation Paper CP 05/08, has reached the provisional conclusion that the United Kingdom should opt in to the Regulation.

[514] Art 19(2) of the Regulation.

[515] See Art 60(1) of the Brussels I Regulation, discussed supra, pp 211–213.

[516] Recital (39) of the Regulation.

[517] Art 23 of Rome II; discussed infra, pp 788–789.

[518] Art 19(3) of the Regulation.

(d) Special contracts

In general, the Convention applies the same rules regardless of the type of contract involved. Nonetheless, the Convention acknowledges that particular contracts can produce special problems. The introduction of flexibility into Article 4 by allowing the presumption of characteristic performance to be rebutted was explained on this basis.[519] More particularly, there are special rules in the Convention in relation to contracts for immovable property,[520] carriage of goods,[521] consumer contracts[522] and individual employment contracts.[523] These exceptions have been justified on the basis that application of the normal rules under the Convention may produce inequitable or unrealistic results.[524] As has been seen,[525] the special rules for immovable property and carriage of goods are only concerned with the presumptions used for ascertaining the applicable law in the absence of choice. However, when it comes to consumer contracts[526] and individual employment contracts,[527] the Convention goes further and, in Articles 5 and 6, introduces special choice of law rules which are concerned with both choice and the applicable law in the absence of choice. In both situations the aim of these rules is to provide protection for the consumer and the employee.[528] The way this is done is by, first, ensuring that the protection given to the consumer or employee by mandatory rules is not thwarted by the parties' choice of the applicable law.[529] Secondly, in the absence of choice pre-eminence is given to the law of the consumer's habitual residence and the employee's habitual place for carrying on work.[530] Finally, the rules in the Convention dealing with the issue of formal validity make special provision for consumer contracts[531] and contracts for immovable property.[532]

(i) The Rome I Regulation

The Rome I Regulation retains the existing means for providing protection for consumers and employees.[533] There are some differences in detail. Reference is no longer made to "mandatory rules"; but instead to "provisions that cannot be derogated from by contract".[534] This avoids any confusion with the concept of overriding mandatory provisions

---

[519] The Giuliano and Lagarde Report, p 22.

[520] Art 4(3); see also Art 9(6).

[521] Art 4(4).

[522] Art 5; see also Art 9(5). The definition of a consumer contract is similar to that in Art 13 of the Brussels Convention (discussed supra, pp 268–270), see the Opinion of AG LEGER in Case C-99/96 *Mietz v Intership Yachting Sneek NV* [1999] ECR I-2277; *Rayner v Davies* [2002] EWCA Civ 1880, [2003] IL Pr 15.

[523] Art 6.

[524] Lagarde (1981) 22 VA J Int L 91, 98.

[525] Supra, pp 716–717.

[526] See Hartley in *Contract Conflicts*, pp 111 et seq; (1997) 266 Hague Recueil 341, 370–373; Morse (1992) 41 ICLQ 1, 2–11; Plender, paras 7.01–7.33; Kaye, pp 203–220. See generally on choice of law, consumers and e-commerce: Tang (2007) 3 J Priv Int L 113; Gillies (2007) 3 J Priv Int L 89.

[527] See Morse in *Contract Conflicts*, at pp 143 et seq; (1992) 41 ICLQ 1, 11–21; Plender, paras 8.01–8.36; Hartley (1997) 266 Hague Recueil 341, 373–378; Kaye, pp 221–238; Smith and Cromack (1993) 22 Industrial LJ 1; Smith and Villiers [1996] Jur Rev 167.

[528] See generally on weaker parties, Nygh, *Autonomy in International Contracts* (1999), Chapter 7.

[529] Arts 5(2), 6(1).

[530] Arts 5(3), 6(2).

[531] Art 9(5).

[532] Art 9(6).

[533] See Arts 6 (consumer contracts) and 8 (individual employment contracts) of the Rome I Regulation.

[534] Arts 6(2) and 8(1) of the Rome I Regulation.

under Article 9 of the Regulation. Some of the terminology in relation to consumer contracts[535] has been altered to bring this into line with the consumer agreement jurisdiction rules under the Brussels I Regulation, the idea being that this is better suited to e-commerce.[536] The Regulation also excludes a number of additional contracts from the consumer protection provisions.[537] As regards individual employment contracts, the law has been amplified to deal with personnel working on-board aircraft[538] and to provide guidance as to whether an employee posted abroad is temporarily employed there.[539]

More radically, Article 5 of the Rome I Regulation introduces special rules for contracts of carriage.[540] This has separate rules for carriage of goods and for carriage of passengers. The choice of law rule for contracts for the carriage of goods (Article 5(1)) is in substance very similar to that contained in Article 4(4) of the Rome Convention.[541] What is new is the introduction of a special choice of law rule for carriage of passengers (Article 5(2)). This restricts the parties' freedom to choose the applicable law to five designated countries, one of which is the country where the passenger has his habitual residence. In the absence of choice, the applicable law will normally be the law of the country where the passenger has his habitual residence. Where it is clear from all the circumstances of the case that the contract, in the absence of a choice of law, is manifestly more closely connected with a country other than that indicated in paragraphs 1 or 2, the law of that other country will apply.[542]

The most radical feature of the Regulation,[543] at least as regards special rules, is the introduction in Article 7[544] of special rules for insurance contracts. These special rules are intended to replace those in various insurance directives[545] and essentially reflect the position under those directives. This has the advantage of the relevant choice of law rules being contained in one instrument. Article 7 applies to insurance contracts covering large risks, whether or not the risk covered is situated in a Member State, and to all other insurance contracts covering risks situated inside the territory of the Member States.[546] Insurance contracts falling outside the special rules but which are not excluded from the scope of the Regulation[547] will be governed by the general choice of law rules under Articles 3 and 4 of the Regulation. The general choice of law rules will also apply

---

[535] In particular, in relation to the additional connection with the consumer's habitual residence required under Art 6.

[536] Art 6(1) of the Regulation. See Recitals (24) and (25) of the Regulation. But for a denial of this, see Gillies (2007) 3 J Priv Int L 89.

[537] Art 6(4)(d) and (e). Difficult definitional problems are raised in relation to exclusions for which guidance is provided by Recitals (26)–(31).

[538] Art 8(2) of the Rome I Regulation.

[539] Recital (36) of the Regulation. The Explanatory Memorandum, p 8. Further clarification of Art 8 is provided in Recitals (34) and (35).

[540] S 5 of the Rome I Regulation.

[541] The definition of "contracts of carriage of goods" is the same as that under Art 4(4) of the Convention, see Recital (22) of the Rome I Regulation.

[542] Art 5(3) of the Rome I Regulation.

[543] A revised Rome I text, presented by the Finnish and German Presidencies on 12 December 2006, proposed bringing insurance generally within Rome I. This was not part of the original proposal for a Regulation of 2005.

[544] For further detail see Recital (33) of the Regulation.

[545] See supra, p 687.

[546] Art 7(1) of the Rome I Regulation. For the definition of large risks, see Art 7(2). See also Recital (33).

[547] Art 1(2)(i) of the Rome I Regulation, discussed supra, p 688.

to reinsurance. The choice of law rules in Article 7 are complex and fall outside the scope of this book, which has previously left insurance to more specialised works.

(e) Limitations on the dominance of the applicable law

(i) Mandatory rules [548]

(a) General comments

The concept of mandatory rules is one of the key concepts under the Convention, with no fewer than six different provisions using it. It is a particularly difficult concept for English lawyers to apply because it is not known under English law, at least not under that name. Before turning to look at the definition of the concept under the Convention and at the provisions in which the concept is used, it is important to look at the background to its introduction into the Convention.

(i) The background to the concept

In domestic contract law there are now two very different sorts of rules.[549] There are the traditional rules which are concerned with settling disputes between parties, such as the rules on consideration. There are then the more modern rules which are concerned with protecting a group of persons or the national economic system—rules that arise as the result of state interference with contracts. The concept of mandatory rules only deals with this second class of rules. Consumers and employees provide good examples of groups of persons who are given special protection under the law. There are rules controlling exemption clauses and laying down requirements in relation to hire purchase and consumer credit transactions which are designed to protect consumers. There are also rules on industrial safety and hygiene and in relation to periods of notice for dismissal which are designed to protect employees. When it comes to protecting the national economic system, rules on monopolies, anti-trust, import and export prohibitions, price controls, exchange control legislation,[550] and the regulation of estate agents[551] are all designed to serve this purpose.

A state's interest in upholding protectionist laws may be so strong that it prohibits the parties from contracting out of such rules in a domestic situation. Going beyond this and into the realms of private international law, the state's interest in upholding certain laws may dictate that those laws must apply even though the issue is, in principle, governed by a different law selected by contract choice of law rules. An exception to the normal choice of law rules is thereby created. This sort of exception is well known in a number of Member States. The Giuliano and Lagarde Report[552] refers to the Dutch decision in the

---

[548] See generally Hartley (1997) 266 Hague Recueil 341; (1979) 4 ELR 236; (2006) 319 Hague Recueil Ch XIII; Diamond (1986) IV Hague Recueil Ch IV; Nygh (1995) 251 Hague Recueil, Ch V; *Autonomy in International Contracts* (1999), Chapter 9; Guedj (1991) 39 AJCL 661; Kaye, Chapter 12; Knofel [1999] JBL 239; Tillman [2002] JBL 45; Wojewoda (2000) 7 Maastricht Journal of European and Comparative Law 183; Plender, paras 9.01–9.13. See in relation to international commercial arbitration: Zhilsov [1995] NILR 91; Hochistrassen [1994] J Int Arb 57. See also ALRC Rep No 58 (1992), Draft Bill, s 9(9).

[549] Vischer (1974) II Hague Recueil Ch 2; Jaffey (1984) 33 ICLQ 531 at 538 et seq.

[550] See the Giuliano and Lagarde Report, p 28; Art 7(2) infra, pp 731–738.

[551] Hartley (1997) 266 Hague Recueil 341, 404–410.

[552] At 26.

Alnati case[553] which is a predecessor of Article 7(1) of the Convention (the general provision dealing with mandatory rules of a foreign country). The Dutch Supreme Court said that there could be cases when the interest of a foreign state in having its law applied outside its territory was so great that the Dutch courts should take this into account and give priority to the application of such provisions in preference to the law of another state chosen by the parties. In England, there is the Unfair Contract Terms Act 1977 with its provisions restricting the parties' freedom to choose the applicable law.[554] This is an example of what in English law is called an overriding statute,[555] ie the statute overrides normal choice of law rules so as to apply the rules in the statute. Thus the parties may have chosen French law to govern the contract, but in certain circumstances the controls on exemption clauses contained in the 1977 Act will still apply. The Working Group was concerned to retain this sort of exception.

(ii) The definition of mandatory rules

Mandatory rules are defined in Article 3(3) as rules "which cannot be derogated from by contract". This definition applies universally to all of the provisions on mandatory rules. In order to determine whether rules of a particular country are mandatory, reference must be made to the law of that country. For example, if an English court is concerned to ascertain whether a French domestic rule is a mandatory one, it has to ask whether under French law that particular rule cannot be derogated from by contract. The essence of mandatory rules is that a rule is applied because *that country's* law requires it to be so applied.[556] This definition of mandatory rules is an unfortunate one in that it can be construed as asking simply whether the parties can agree to depart from the rule in *domestic* cases, rather than the private international question of whether the rule is intended, according to the law of its country of origin, to apply regardless of the governing law.[557] Yet the effect given to mandatory rules under the Convention is to override the normal rules on the applicable law contained in the Convention. If one accepts the above construction of the definition, it follows that mandatory rules may be given a wider effect under the Convention than they have under the law of the country from which they originate. It would have been much better to have had a definition of mandatory rules that clearly reflects the principle that a domestic rule will only be given the effect under the Convention that it has under the law of its country of origin.[558] At the same time, this problem may not be as great as might at first sight appear. As will shortly be seen, it does not arise in relation to what are likely to be the most commonly used provisions in the Convention on mandatory rules. Furthermore, if English law is anything to go by, mandatory rules are likely to be ones which not only cannot be departed from by agreement in a purely domestic context but which also, according to their country of origin, override

---

[553] Nederlandse Jurisprudentie 1967, p 3; Rev Crit 1967, p 522; though later Dutch decisions seem to have resiled from this approach. See generally Schultsz (1983) 47 Rabels Z 267; Hartley, op cit, at 356–359.

[554] S 27(2); infra, pp 733–734.

[555] See the 11th edn of this book (1987), pp 466–471. See also *DR Insurance Co v Central National Insurance Co* [1996] 1 Lloyd's Rep 74 at 82—Insurance Companies Acts regarded as overriding statutes.

[556] This is particularly clear under Arts 7(1), 7(2) and 9(6).

[557] See Jackson in *Contract Conflicts*, pp 59, at 65–66; Plender, para 5.26; Dicey, Morris and Collins, para 32-073.

[558] See generally Morse, op cit, 123–124.

normal choice of law principles.[559] As will be seen, there are different types of mandatory rule under the Convention.

(iii) The provisions on mandatory rules

The concept of mandatory rules is used in no fewer than six different provisions in the Convention. Reference has already been made to three of these provisions: Articles 3(3) (the limitation on freedom of choice);[560] 5(2) (consumer contracts);[561] 6(1) (individual employment contracts).[562] In each of these provisions mandatory rules operate as a limitation on the freedom to choose the applicable law. These three provisions only apply in very limited circumstances. There is a fourth provision on mandatory rules contained in Article 9(6)[563] which is also very limited, in this case to matters of formal validity in respect of contracts for the use of immovable property. However, there are two general provisions on mandatory rules contained in Article 7(1) and (2) of the Convention, which are of much wider scope. Article 7(1)[564] is concerned with the mandatory rules of a foreign country and Article 7(2)[565] with the mandatory rules of the forum. As far as the United Kingdom is concerned, only the latter provision is of direct significance. Section 2(2) of the Contracts (Applicable Law) Act 1990 provides that Article 7(1) shall not have the force of law in the United Kingdom.[566]

(iv) Differences between the separate provisions on mandatory rules

The six provisions on mandatory rules, whilst sharing the same definition of a mandatory rule, are different from each other in three major respects. First, they differ on the question of which country's[567] mandatory rules are being referred to. For example, it may be the forum or that of a foreign country, and if the latter the extent of the connection required with that country may differ. This is a spatial difference which one would expect to find.

Secondly, and this is much more surprising, the provisions differ as to the type of mandatory rules with which they are dealing. There appear to be two different types of mandatory rules relevant under the Convention.[568] First, there is the basic wide type of mandatory rule, where all that has to be shown is that the definition of a mandatory rule is satisfied, ie under the law of the country with whose rule one is concerned, the rule cannot be derogated from by contract. Articles 3(3),[569] 5(2),[570] and 6(1) are all concerned with this basic wide type of mandatory rule. Secondly, there are the narrower overriding

---

[559] See, eg, the Unfair Contract Terms Act 1977, infra, pp 732–734; the Employment Rights Act 1996, infra, p 732.

[560] Supra, pp 695–697.

[561] Supra, p 726.

[562] Supra, p 726.

[563] Infra, p 749.

[564] Infra, p 738.

[565] Infra, pp 731–738.

[566] This is by virtue of the exercise of the power of reservation under Art 22(1)(a) of the Convention.

[567] Mandatory rules contained in European Community Regulations and Directives also come within the Convention, see infra, p 737.

[568] The French version of the Convention refers to "dispositions impératives" (see Art 3(3)) and also to "Lois de police" (see the heading to Art 7). See generally Plender, paras 5.25–5.27, 9.07; Kaye, pp 72 et seq.

[569] But see the obiter dicta in *Caterpillar Financial Services Corpn v SNC Passion* [2004] EWHC 569 (Comm) at [31]–[44], [2004] 2 Lloyd's Rep 99, which should be regarded as wrong.

[570] But see Plender, paras 9-14–9-17.

mandatory rules. With these, it must not only be shown that the rule is a mandatory one, within the above definition, but also that under the law of the country with whose rules you are concerned, the mandatory rule overrides the applicable law. Articles 7(1), 7(2) and 9(6) all require this additional element. Thus under Article 7(2) mandatory rules are applied in "a situation where they are mandatory irrespective of the law otherwise applicable to the contract". Under Article 7(1) it must be shown that "those [mandatory] rules must be applied whatever the law applicable to the contract". Under Article 9(6) the mandatory requirements must be "imposed irrespective of the country where the contract is concluded and irrespective of the law governing the contract". Naturally, a rule falling within this narrower type of mandatory rule will automatically come within the wider type as well. If the parties' right expressly to choose the governing law is taken away, it follows that the domestic rule is one that cannot be contracted out of. Using the same expression for two very different concepts causes confusion and the Rome I Regulation addresses this by using the term "overriding" mandatory rules when this term is being used in the Article 7 sense and by not using the term "mandatory" at all when referring to provisions that cannot be derogated from by agreement.[571]

Thirdly, the effect given to a mandatory rule under the Convention differs depending on the provision in question. With Articles 3(3), 5(2) and 6(1), the effect given to the mandatory rule under the Convention is merely to override the parties' freedom to choose the applicable law. With mandatory rules under Articles 7(1), 7(2) and 9(6) the effect given to the rule under the Convention is much greater. The mandatory rule is able to override all of the rules on the applicable law under the Convention (including the rules on the applicable law in the absence of choice).[572]

(b) The mandatory rules of the forum

Article 7(2) states that: "Nothing in this Convention shall restrict the application of the rules of the law of the forum in a situation where they are mandatory irrespective of the law otherwise applicable to the contract." The opening words of Article 7(2) make it clear that this provision was inserted so that the forum could continue to apply its own mandatory rules to override contract choice of law rules even after the new regime under the Rome Convention entered into force.[573] The existing law is therefore preserved. The Giuliano and Lagarde Report[574] gives some examples of the sort of protectionist domestic rules which Contracting States were anxious to preserve as overriding rules: rules on cartels, competition and restrictive practices, consumer protection and certain rules concerning carriage. Article 7(2), unlike the other provisions on mandatory rules, leads to no difficulty in identifying the country whose mandatory rules are in issue: they are solely the mandatory rules of the forum. However, it is not enough merely to show that the forum has a mandatory rule[575] (ie a rule which cannot be derogated from by contract).

---

[571] Infra, pp 738–739.

[572] There are problems, however, with statutes of limited overriding effect, discussed infra, pp 732–735.

[573] See the Giuliano and Lagarde Report, p 28. See also the Lord Advocate, Hansard (HL) 12 December 1989, vol 513, col 1260. An analogous provision is to be found in the Hague Convention on the Law applicable to Trusts and on their Recognition: Art 16, infra, p 1316.

[574] At p 28.

[575] Art 7(2) does not actually use the phrase "mandatory rules" but it does refer to rules "in a situation where they are mandatory".

It has to be shown that what is involved is "a situation where [the rules] are mandatory irrespective of the law otherwise applicable to the contract". According to the law of the forum the rule must, in the situation in question, be given an overriding effect. This still leaves the problem for the forum of identifying such rules and of identifying a situation when such rules are given overriding effect.

(i) Mandatory statutory rules

Assuming that England is the forum, English rules expressing a strong socio-economic policy are more likely to be contained in statutes than in common law rules. Moreover, when it comes to identifying such rules this may be much easier with statutory rules than with common law rules. Unlike a common law rule, a statute may state whether it is intended to have overriding effect.[576] The statute could expressly provide that in certain situations: it is to have complete overriding effect; it is to have limited overriding effect; it is to have no overriding effect. Alternatively, the statute may say nothing about its overriding effect, in which case it is a matter of statutory construction as to whether, in particular situations, it is intended to have overriding effect. These different possibilities will now be examined.

The statute expressly provides that it is to have complete overriding effect A statute of complete overriding effect is one that, under the law of its country of origin, overrides not only the parties' choice of the applicable law but also the applicable law in the absence of choice, so that forum law is intended to apply even though the objective applicable law is foreign. An example of an English statute which, according to its own terms, is intended completely to override normal contract choice of law rules, is provided in the Employment Rights Act 1996. Section 204(1) states that, for the purposes of the Act, it is immaterial whether the law governing the contract is the law of part of the United Kingdom or not. Article 7(2) will only apply in a *situation* where rules are mandatory irrespective of the law applicable to the contract. Section 94(1) of the 1996 Act, which gives employees the right not to be unfairly dismissed, has been interpreted as being impliedly territorially limited. The paradigm case for its application is where an employee works in Great Britain.[577] Let us assume that the case falls within the territorial limitation. This is the situation where the rules are mandatory irrespective of the law otherwise applicable to the contract.[578]

The statute expressly provides that it is to have limited overriding effect A statute of limited overriding effect is one that, under the law of its country of origin, overrides the parties' freedom to choose the applicable law, but does not override the applicable law in the absence of choice. The Unfair Contract Terms Act 1977 provides an example of an English statute which by its own terms makes it clear that it is of only limited

---

[576] See generally on the problems of the interaction between English statutes and the Convention, Morse in *Contract Conflicts*, pp 143, 163 et seq; Collins (1976) 25 ICLQ 35, 37–38. See also Jaffey, *Topics in Choice of Law* (1996), pp 57 et seq; Dutson (1997) 60 MLR 668, 686 et seq; Reynolds [1997] LMCLQ 177; ALRC Rep No 58 (1992), pp 32–39.

[577] *Lawson v Serco Ltd, Botham v Ministry of Defence, Crofts v Veta Ltd* [2006] UKHL 3, [2006] ICR 250; Briggs (2006) 77 BYBIL 572; overruling *Lawson* [2004] EWCA Civ 12, [2004] ICR 204, on which see Briggs (2004) 75 BYBIL 580; overruling *Botham* [2005] EWCA Civ 400; affirming *Crofts v Cathay Pacific* [2005] 599, [2005] ICR 1436. However, peripatetic and expatriate employees may come within the territorial limitation.

[578] An employee who wants the protection of the 1996 Act is best advised to rely on Art 7(2) rather than Art 6 (individual employment contracts) under which it is necessary to show that English law is applicable in the absence of choice.

overriding effect.[579] With such a statute, the question of whether there is a *situation* where the rules are mandatory irrespective of the law otherwise applicable to the contract becomes particularly important.

The 1977 Act provides a wide-ranging set of controls over exemption clauses in many kinds of contract. Some are rendered void; others are subjected to a reasonableness test. What is significant for our purposes is that the 1977 Act also provides for the operation of these controls in the international context. The important provision, which lays down the overriding nature of the rules on exemption clauses under the Act, is section 27(2),[580] which states:

> This Act has effect notwithstanding any contract term which applies or purports to apply the law of any country outside the United Kingdom, where (either or both)—
> (a) the term appears to the court, or arbitrator or arbiter to have been imposed wholly or mainly for the purpose of enabling the party imposing it to evade the operation of this Act; or
> (b) in the making of the contract one of the parties dealt as consumer, and he was then habitually resident in the United Kingdom, and the essential steps necessary for the making of the contract were taken there, whether by him or by others on his behalf.

The essential purpose of this sub-section is easy to state. It is intended to prevent parties to a contract, which is most closely connected with this country, from contracting out of the controls of the 1977 Act by a choice[581] of the law of a country outside the United Kingdom. The 1977 Act does not, as such, strike down the choice of a foreign law. It leaves it to take effect, and the foreign law is to be applied to the contract, subject to effect being given to the controls of the 1977 Act.[582] However, there is an important limitation on the effectiveness of section 27(2) in that the controls in the 1977 Act do not apply to "international supply contracts".[583] In such contracts the parties will remain free to rely on exemption clauses.

Section 27(2) overrides the parties' freedom to choose a foreign law to govern the contract. Article 7(2) will apply therefore to cases coming within this section.[584] However, section 27(2) is only concerned with the situation where there has been a choice by the parties.[585]

---

[579] For an example of an Australian statute, see s 8 of the Insurance Contracts Act 1984; *Akai Pty Ltd v People's Insurance Co Ltd* (1996) 71 ALJR 156, HC of Australia; Reynolds [1997] LMCLQ 177.

[580] The Law Commissions have made proposals for changes to this provision, see Law Com (2005) No 292 and Scot Law Com (2005) No 199, paras 8.82–8.85 (for consumer contracts), paras 7.30–7.34 (for business contracts).

[581] S 27(2) refers to "any contract term" which applies or purports to apply the law of some other country. This will include an express choice of law clause but it is unlikely to include an inferred choice through an arbitration or choice of court clause in the contract.

[582] For the difficulties thereby created, see Mann (1974) 90 LQR 42, 51–54; (1977) 26 ICLQ 903, 910.

[583] S 26; *Ocean Chemical Transport Inc v Exnor Craggs Ltd* [2000] 1 Lloyd's Rep 446; *Amiri Flight Authority v BAE Systems plc* [2003] EWCA 1447, [2003] 2 Lloyd's Rep 767; *Balmoral Group Ltd v Borealis (UK) Ltd* [2006] EWHC 1900 (Comm) at [436]–[449], [2006] 2 Lloyd's Rep 629. This provision appears to be inconsistent with the Rome Convention which contains no such limitation. See Hartley (1997) 266 Hague Recueil 341, 381–384. The Law Commissions have proposed that s 26 should not be replicated for consumer contracts, Law Com (2005) No 292 and Scot Law Com (2005) No 199, para 8.80. S 26 would be replaced with an exemption for business contracts under which goods are exported overseas, para 7.58.

[584] See the Giuliano and Lagarde Report, p 26; Hansard (HL) 12 December 1989, vol 513, col 1260.

[585] See the marginal note to s 27. Cf Hartley (1997) 266 Hague Recueil 341, 382 n 85.

In cases where there has been no such choice and the objective applicable law is foreign it seems that the Act's controls on exemption clauses will not apply; it cannot be said that the controls on exemption clauses in the Act apply irrespective of the law that otherwise applies to the contract. Article 7(2) will accordingly not operate in this situation. However, the controls on exemption clauses contained in the Act would, of course, be applicable if the governing law under the Convention was English law.[586] Moreover, in the absence of proof of the content of foreign law, the Act, including section 27 and the limitation on the use of that provision where there is an international supply contract, will apply.[587]

The Unfair Terms[588] in Consumer[589] Contracts Regulations 1999,[590] which implement the EEC Council Directive on unfair terms in consumer contracts,[591] contain a similar provision to section 27(2), albeit much simpler and more flexible than that section. Regulation 9 states that:

> These Regulations shall apply notwithstanding any contract term which applies or purports to apply the law of a non-Member State, if the contract has a close connection with the territory of the Member States.

The English courts should apply Regulation 9, not by virtue of Article 7(2) of the Rome Convention, but because it is a choice of law rule in a Community law instrument and accordingly takes precedence over that Convention.[592] Regulation 9 can be seen to be similar in impact to section 27(2) in that overriding effect is given to the substantive law and the choice of the foreign law is not struck out. Moreover, it is only concerned with the situation where there has been a choice by the parties. It is, however, a wider provision than section 27(2) in that there is no limitation in relation to "international supply contracts" and the close connection required is not limited to a specified set of circumstances as happens under section 27(2)(b).[593] What is more, the requisite close connection can be with the territory of the Member States of the European Community and not just with the United Kingdom.[594] There is, though, uncertainty over the meaning of "a close connection", which is not defined.[595] There is also uncertainty in the situation where the parties choose the law of another Member State to govern. The Law Commissions have proposed that the laws of other Member States should be applied if they would be

---

[586] See, however, s 27(1) of the 1977 Act which imposes a limitation on a right to choose English law as the governing law. This appears to be inconsistent with the Rome Convention, which contains no such limitation. See generally, Hartley, op cit. The Law Commissions have proposed that this provision should not be replicated for consumer contracts but should be for business contracts, Law Com (2005) No 292 and Scot Law Com (2005) No 199, paras 7.29, 8.81.

[587] *Balmoral Group Ltd v Borealis (UK) Ltd* [2006] EWHC 1900 (Comm) at [436]–[449], [2006] 2 Lloyd's Rep 629.

[588] A choice of jurisdiction clause may be an unfair term, see *Standard Bank London Ltd v Apostolakis (No 2)* [2002] CLC 939.

[589] Defined in Reg 3; *Standard Bank London Ltd v Apostolakis (No 1)* [2002] CLC 933 at 936–938.

[590] SI 1999/2083, amended by SI 2001/1186, replacing SI 1994/3159.

[591] Council Directive (EEC) No 93/13 OJ 1993 L 95/29.

[592] Art 20 of the Rome Convention; discussed supra, p 677 and infra, p 762.

[593] For overlaps and differences between the Unfair Contract Terms Act 1977 and the Unfair Terms in Consumer Contracts Regulations 1999 and proposals for a unified regime, see Law Com (2005) No 292 and Scot Law Com (2005) No 199.

[594] There is, though, no alternative to the close connection criterion specifically dealing with cases of evasion; cf s 27(2)(a) of the Unfair Contract Terms Act 1977.

[595] Cf the German implementing legislation which sets out an example: s 12 of the Standard Contract Terms Act; Knofel (1998) 47 ICLQ 439, 440–442.

applicable by virtue of existing rules of private international law as long as the consumer is afforded the protections contemplated by the Directive.[596]

There are a number of other United Kingdom Regulations implementing European Community Directives in relation to consumers,[597] provisions of which should be regarded as being mandatory rules of the forum.

The statute expressly provides that it is to have no overriding effect Article 7(2) will not be applicable in this case. There does not appear to be an example of such a statute under English law.

The statute has no express provision on its overriding effect but has a provision on its territorial scope In cases where a statute says nothing about its overriding effect it is a matter of construction of the statute to ascertain whether it is intended to have overriding effect in a particular situation.[598] Drawing this inference is much easier if the statute has a provision dealing with its territorial scope, albeit whilst not spelling out explicitly whether it is intended to have overriding effect. This can be illustrated by *Boissevain v Weil*.[599] The case concerned a Defence Regulation, made under the powers conferred by the Emergency Powers (Defence) Act 1939. This regulation made it an offence, subject to severe penalties, for a *British subject*[600] to carry out certain currency transactions. In the House of Lords, Lord RADCLIFFE declared that whether such an offence was committed could not depend on whether the law governing a loan contract was English or foreign. In other words, it was a regulation which, in the situation in the case, was construed as being of complete overriding effect. Article 7(2) would now apply, and the result would be the same under the Convention. Similarly, in *Chiron Corpn v Organon Teknika (No 2)*,[601] the Court of Appeal held that section 44 of the Patents Act 1977, sub-section (1) of which strikes down certain provisions (constituting an abuse of patent rights) in contracts relating to patents, applies regardless of whether English law governs the contract.[602] Section 44 is territorially limited to United Kingdom patents. The court was not prepared, in the light of this important restriction, to add on a further requirement that the contract had to be governed by English law.[603] Again, the result would be the same under the Convention by virtue of Article 7(2).

The statute has no express provision as to its overriding effect and no provision on its territorial scope Many statutes say nothing about their extra-territorial scope or their overriding effect. The construction of such a statute to ascertain whether it is intended to

---

[596] Law Com (2005) No 292 and Scot Law Com (2005) No 199, paras 7.20–7.26.

[597] See, eg, the Consumer Protection (Distance Selling) Regulations 2000, implementing Directive (EEC) No 97/7 of 20 May 1997 on the protection of consumers in respect of distance contracts; the Sale and Supply of Goods to Consumers Regulations 2002, implementing the Directive on certain aspects of the the sale of consumer goods and associated guarantees 1999/44 of 25 May 1999; Directive (EC) No 99/44.

[598] See Pryles in *Contract Conflicts*, pp 331 et seq.

[599] [1949] 1 KB 482, CA; affd [1950] AC 327. See also *The Hollandia* [1983] 1 AC 565—a case on the Carriage of Goods by Sea Act 1971; cf *Mediterranean Shipping Co SA v Trafigura Beheer BV* [2007] EWCA Civ 794. The position is different in respect of the Carriage of Goods by Sea Act 1992, on which see Sing [1994] LMCLQ 280.

[600] Defence (Finance) Regulations 1939, reg 2, as amended; Emergency Powers (Defence) Act 1939, s 3(1).

[601] [1993] FSR 567, CA.

[602] The case concerned a contractual defence to a tort action, see infra, pp 865–868. The defence applies where contractual provisions are void under this section.

[603] The *Chiron Corpn* case, supra, at 572.

have an overriding effect in a particular situation is especially difficult. In *English v Donnelly* [604] a Scottish court gave at least limited overriding effect to Scottish mandatory hire purchase requirements, with the result that the parties were not allowed to contract out of the statute in question by an express choice of law clause. In *Irish Shipping Ltd v Commercial Union Assurance Co plc* [605] STAUGHTON LJ showed some concern that "The intention of Parliament could be frustrated if it were open to the parties to a contract of insurance to exclude the operation of section 1 [of the Third Parties (Rights against Insurers) Act 1930] by choosing a foreign proper law". On the other hand, in *Sayers v International Drilling Co NV* [606] the Court of Appeal did not give overriding effect to the Law Reform (Personal Injuries) Act 1948, which is concerned to protect injured employees from clauses exempting the employer from liability. [607] A majority of the Court of Appeal held that the objectively determined proper law of the contract—Dutch law—applied, according to which the exemption clause was valid.

(ii) Mandatory common law rules

Whilst in principle it is possible to have mandatory common law rules, examples are likely to be very rare because of the difficulty in identifying such rules. [608] It has been suggested [609] that in some of the cases decided at common law where the English courts have refused to apply a foreign law on grounds of public policy and have instead applied English law, eg in those where the fundamental concepts of English justice were disregarded, [610] public policy operates in a positive way, the concern being to apply English law, and, accordingly such cases should be regarded as involving a mandatory rule of the forum. In other cases, it is admitted that public policy operates in a negative way, the concern being not to apply an objectionable foreign law (the effect is then that English law will apply), and it is rightly said that in such cases Article 16 of the Convention [611] will apply rather than Article 7(2). However, it is submitted that public policy primarily operates in a negative way [612] and it is extremely difficult to identify with any precision cases where public policy operates in a positive way, [613] given that the consequence is that the foreign proper law was not applied. In truth, each case of public policy has a positive and negative aspect but the latter dominates. The better approach is to treat all of these cases of public policy at common law, where the foreign proper law has not been applied and

---

[604] 1958 SC 494; see also the High Court of Australia's decision in *Kay's Leasing Corpn Pty Ltd v Fletcher* (1964) 116 CLR 124.

[605] [1991] 2 QB 206.

[606] [1971] 1 WLR 1176, infra, pp 863–865. Cf *Brodin v A R Seljan* 1973 SC 213.

[607] However, the case was argued by counsel on the narrow point as to what the proper law of the contract was.

[608] See the discussion in relation to tort, infra, pp 850–851.

[609] Hartley (1997) 266 Hague Recueil 341, 351–353; Kaye, pp 245–247; Jaffey, *Topics in Choice of Law* (1996), pp 54–56.

[610] See *Kaufman v Gerson* [1904] 1 KB 591; discussed supra, p 141. For a Canadian example, see *Society of Lloyd's v Saunders* (2002) 210 DLR (4th) 519, CA (Ont).

[611] Discussed infra, pp 741–743.

[612] See Nygh (1995) 251 Hague Recueil 269, 379–380; Vischer (1992) I Hague Recueil 9, 165.

[613] Note the lack of agreement between Hartley, op cit, Kaye, op cit, and Jaffey, op cit, over examples where public policy operates in this way.

instead English law has been applied, as operating in a negative way and therefore coming not within Article 7(2) but within Article 16.[614]

(iii) Mandatory rules in Community legislation

It is not only national rules that can be mandatory. So can provisions of Community legislation.[615] This was established in *Ingmar GB Ltd v Eaton Leonard Technologies Inc*, [616] where the Court of Justice held that Articles 17 and 18 of the self-employed commercial agents Directive, which guarantee certain rights to commercial agents after termination of agency contracts, [617]were mandatory provisions[618] in the sense used in Article 7(2).[619] These Articles applied even though the expressly chosen applicable law was that of California. The Court reached this conclusion in the light of the purpose of the Directive and of these Articles and in the light of Article 19, which provides that the parties may not derogate from Articles 17 and 18 to the detriment of the commercial agent. There was no express provision in the Directive on the territorial scope of these two provisions. However, looking at their purpose the Court held that Articles 17 and 18 applied where the situation was closely connected with the Community, in particular where the commercial agent carries on his activity in the territory of a Member State. These Articles would therefore apply even though the principal was established in a non-Member State country, California. On the facts, the Rome Convention did not come into play because the contract was concluded in 1989. However, it seems that the result would have been the same if the contract had been made after the Convention came into force and the Convention had come into play. The mandatory rules in the Directive[620] would then presumably have applied by virtue of Article 7(2).[621]

(iv) The effect given to mandatory rules under Article 7(2)[622]

Article 7(2) operates as an exception to the normal choice of law rules under the Convention by giving overriding effect to mandatory rules. Obviously it overrides the rules on the applicable law under Article 3 (choice) and Article 4 (the applicable law in the absence of choice). But Article 7(2) probably has an even wider effect than this. The opening wording of Article 7(2) is that: "Nothing in this Convention shall restrict the application of the rules of the law of the forum." This suggests that Article 7(2) should be regarded as a general exception to *all* the choice of law rules contained in the Convention, in the same way that public policy, which is more clearly worded in this respect, provides

---

[614] See Dicey, Morris and Collins, para 32-230–32-237.

[615] This is recognised in Art 3(4) of the Rome I Regulation, supra, p 707. If the Community legislation contains a choice of law rule, Art 20 of the Rome Convention will apply, see infra, p 762 for examples.

[616] Case C-381/98 [2000] ECR I-9305; Verhagen (2002) 51 ICLQ 135.

[617] Council Directive (EEC) No 86/653 of 18 December 1986 on the coordination of the laws of the Member States relating to self-employed commercial agents, OJ 1986 L 382/17; implemented in the United Kingdom by the Commercial Agents (Council Directive) Regulations 1993.

[618] Cf the position in relation to rules such as Arts 6(1) and 13 of the Directive which can be derogated from by a Member State, see the Opinion of AG LEGER at [81]–[85]. It is suggested that the E-Commerce Directive also contains mandatory rules, see Fawcett, Harris and Bridge, para 21.110.

[619] See the Opinion of AG LEGER at [87]–[89].

[620] Strictly speaking the United Kingdom implementing legislation would have applied, rather than the Directive itself.

[621] See the Opinion of AG LEGER at [87]–[89]. This will be subject to the point that if a Directive contains choice of law rules then Art 20 will then take it outside the Rome Convention.

[622] The same problem arises in relation to Art 7(1), see infra, p 738.

such an exception.[623] This means that the special rules for particular issues, such as formal validity, and for special contracts will also be overriden.[624] However, there is a particular problem in relation to consumer contracts and individual employment contracts, in that there are provisions on mandatory rules contained in the special regimes set out in Articles 5 and 6. Nevertheless, Article 7(2) should be regarded as overriding the other provisions in the Convention on mandatory rules. The result is that English mandatory rules would take priority over foreign mandatory rules. This has wide implications. For example, in a case where the applicable law under Article 4 of the Convention may be French and English law has mandatory rules, then, in principle, Article 7(2) should operate so that the English mandatory rules override the French ones. However, it must be for English law to decide whether its own mandatory rules are of such importance that they should apply in such a case.

(c) The mandatory rules of other countries[625]

Article 7(1) provides that:

> When applying under this Convention the law of a country, effect may be given to the mandatory rules of the law of another country with which the situation has a close connection, if and in so far as, under the law of the latter country, those rules must be applied whatever the law applicable to the contract. In considering whether to give effect to these mandatory rules, regard shall be had to their nature and purpose and to the consequences of their application or non-application.

Article 7(1) is the widest of the provisions on mandatory rules and is also the least clear. First, which country's mandatory rules are being referred to? The answer is a vague one: any country with which the situation has a close connection. Secondly, the forum does not have to give effect to the mandatory rules of a country with which there is a close connection. Instead, it is given a discretion as to whether to do so. These two features inevitably lead to uncertainty in the law, and several Contracting States, at the negotiating stage, objected to Article 7(1) on this ground. Because of this the Convention provides that any Contracting State can reserve the right not to apply Article 7(1).[626] The United Kingdom has entered such a reservation, and, in accordance with this, section 2(2) of the Contracts (Applicable Law) Act 1990 provides that Article 7(1) shall not have the force of law in the United Kingdom.[627]

(d) Overriding mandatory provisions under the Rome I Regulation

Article 9 is headed "Overriding mandatory provisions". This adopts the heading used in Rome II on non-contractual obligations.[628] The drafters of both Regulations have

---

[623] See the Giuliano and Lagarde Report, p 31; infra, pp 741–743.

[624] Cf Lasok and Stone, pp 378, 383–384. See also Williams (1986) 35 ICLQ 1, 24.

[625] See generally, Kaye, pp 248–261; note (2001) 114 Harv LR 2462; Chong (2006) 2 J Priv Int L 27; Dickinson (2007) 3 J Priv Int L 53.

[626] Art 22(1)(a).

[627] See the Solicitor-General, HC Second Reading Committee, 20 June 1990, col 4; Lord-Advocate, HL 12 December 1989, vol 513, cols 1258, 1271. See earlier Collins (1976) 25 ICLQ 35, 49–51; for a more extreme criticism in terms of disapproval of statutory regulation of contracts, see Mann in Lipstein (ed), *Harmonisation of Private International Law by the EEC*, p 31. Germany also has not included Art 7(1) in its legislation incorporating the Convention into its private international law. Reservations have also been entered by Ireland, Latvia, Luxembourg, Portugal and Slovenia. Cf ALRC Rep No 58 (1992), Draft Bill, s 9(9).

[628] See Art 16 of the Rome II Regulation.

been keen to avoid the confusion caused under the Rome Convention by using the term "mandatory rules" in two different senses.[629] This concern is apparent not only from the introduction of the term "overriding" mandatory provisions in Article 9 but also from the fact that Article 3(3) of the Regulation[630] avoids using the term mandatory rules altogether, instead referring to provisions which cannot be derogated from by agreement.[631] The former concept should be construed more restrictively than the latter.[632] The key features of Article 9 are as follows.

(i) A definition of overriding mandatory provisions[633]

Article 9 of the Regulation departs from the Convention by introducing a definition of overriding mandatory provisions.[634] Paragraph 1 defines these as "provisions the respect for which is regarded as crucial by a country for safeguarding its public interests, such as its political, social or economic organisation, to such an extent that they are applicable to any situation falling within their scope, irrespective of the law otherwise applicable to the contract under this Regulation". This definition is inspired by the decision of the Court of Justice in *Ardblade*,[635] which was concerned with the relationship between national mandatory provisions of Member States and the EC Treaty. This definition brings out the protectionist nature of mandatory provisions. The danger of defining what overriding mandatory provisions are protecting is that this may restrict the use of the concept. In particular, the definition will exclude provisions which aim to protect purely private interests. The other feature that is brought out in Article 9(1) is the overriding nature of such provisions. They are applicable "irrespective of the law otherwise applicable to the contract under this Regulation". This idea is familiar to us from the wording of Article 7(1) and (2) of the Convention. Under the Regulation, the equivalent provisions, namely Article 9(2) and (3) omit reference to this idea, it being mentioned in Article 9(1) instead.

The advantage of introducing a definition of overriding mandatory provisions under Article 9(1) is that it helps to separate out the two different senses in which the concept of mandatory provisions is used in Articles 3(3) and 9 of the Regulation (Articles 3(3) and 7 of the Convention).

(ii) The overriding mandatory provisions of the forum

Article 9(2) of the Regulation provides that "Nothing in this Regulation shall restrict the application of the overriding mandatory provisions of the law of forum." This is in substance the same as Article 7(2) of the Convention, subject to the point above that one must turn to look at the definition of mandatory provisions in Article 9(1), rather than looking for guidance in Article 9(2).

---

[629] See Recital (37) of the Rome I Regulation.

[630] Supra, pp 695–697.

[631] As do Arts 6(2), 8(1), 11(5) of the Rome I Regulation. Art 11(5) of the Regulation also refers to "requirements imposed irrespective of the country where the contract is concluded and irrespective of the law governing the contract". Art 11(5) is discussed infra, p 750.

[632] Recital (37) of the Rome I Regulation.

[633] Criticised by Dickinson (2007) 3 J Priv Int L 53, 66–68.

[634] Art 9(1) of the Regulation.

[635] Cases C-369/96 [1999] ECR I-8453 and C-374/96 [1998] ECR I-8385 at [31].

(iii) The overriding mandatory provisions of other countries [636]

Article 9(3) of the Regulation[637] provides that:

> Effect may be given to the overriding mandatory provisions of the law of the country where the obligations arising out of the contract have to be or have been performed, in so far as those overriding mandatory provisions render the performance of the contract unlawful. In considering whether to give effect to those provisions, regard shall be had to their nature and purpose and to the consequences of their application or non-application.

The background to this rule is that reservations by Member States in relation to particular Articles are in principle incompatible with a Regulation.[638] This means that if the United Kingdom were to opt in to the Regulation, its courts would for the first time have to consider giving effect to the mandatory provisions of other countries in an Article 9(3) situation. This was the most important single objection that the United Kingdom had to opting in to the Regulation. It was objected that the introduction in the United Kingdom of an Article 7(1) of the Rome Convention type of rule would create uncertainty,[639] in particular in the financial markets.[640] There has been an attempt to meet such concern by limiting the new rule in the final version of the Regulation in two major respects. First, Article 9(3) of the Regulation is only concerned with the overriding mandatory provisions of the law of "the country where the obligations arising out of the contract have to be or have been performed". This is much more certain than the wording of Article 7(1) of the Rome Convention, with its reference to the mandatory rules of law of another country with which the situation has a close connection. Secondly, Article 9(3) is only concerned with that country's overriding mandatory provisions in so far as they render the performance of the contract unlawful. Article 9(3) would enable the English courts to deal with cases of illegality by the foreign place of performance. Such cases were a concern at common law and, because of the absence in the United Kingdom of a provision on foreign mandatory rules, are not effectively dealt with by the Rome Convention.[641] In the absence of such a provision, they would not be effectively dealt with under the Regulation either.

There appears to be a further difference between Article 9(3) of the Regulation and Article 7(1) of the Convention, which is less welcome. Under Article 7(1) of the Convention it is expressly stated that what we are concerned with is whether, *under the law of that other country* whose mandatory rules are being considered, the rule must be applied whatever the law applicable to the contract. Article 9(1) unfortunately omits this wording. This would suggest that, when considering the mandatory provisions of a foreign country, now the test is whether that foreign country regards the provision as so important that the Regulation requires other countries to give it overriding effect under the Regulation.

---

[636] See Dickinson (2007) 3 J Priv Int L 53.

[637] The original proposal for a Rome I Regulation contained the same provision as Art 7(1) of the Rome Convention.

[638] It might have been possible for the United Kingdom to negotiate a reservation to Art 9(3) but this might only have been for a limited period.

[639] See Dickinson (2007) 3 J Priv Int L 53; Dutson (2006) 122 LQR 374.

[640] See para 17.1 of the Financial Markets Law Committee's Legal assessment of the conversion of the Rome Convention to a Community instrument and the provisions of the proposed Rome I Regulation, available at http://www.fmlc.org.

[641] See Chong (2006) 2 J Priv Int L 27 and more generally infra, pp 760–761.

This would be a more uncertain test to apply than being guided by what the law of the foreign country whose provision is being considered says about the overriding effect of that provision.

(ii) Public policy[642]

Article 16 of the Convention is entitled "Ordre public" and provides that the "application of a rule of the law of any country specified by this Convention may be refused only if such application is manifestly incompatible with the public policy ('ordre public') of the forum". In civil law countries ordre public operates as a well-established exception to normal choice of law rules, as does public policy in common law jurisdictions. Any clash between the civil and common law concepts of public policy is resolved by the reference to the application of a rule of law being "manifestly" incompatible with the public policy of the forum. This word has been regularly used in Hague Conventions on private international law in an attempt to restrain the use of the doctrine. This adds nothing as far as English law is concerned since there has long been a reluctance to invoke the public policy doctrine in this country.[643] However, for civil lawyers it makes clear that what is in issue is the narrow concept of international ordre public as opposed to the wide concept of domestic ordre public. It has to be shown that the *application* of a foreign rule of law is against the forum's public policy. The circumstances of the case have to be considered. If, for example, a contract governed by French law restrains a party from competing in *England* then the application of a French rule allowing restraint of trade would appear to be contrary to the well-known English public policy against restraint of trade because of the involvement of England. This limitation is entirely consistent with common law decisions on public policy, which normally have required some relevant connection with England which justifies English courts in invoking the public policy exception.[644] The intention then is that Article 16 will only be used in exceptional circumstances.[645]

When Article 16 does apply, it provides an exception to all of the preceding choice of law rules contained in the Convention, and is clearer in its wording in this respect than is the mandatory rules exception. Presumably, it can even operate to override the provisions on mandatory rules which are themselves an exception to normal choice of law principles.[646] Thus, an English court could refuse to apply the mandatory rules of a foreign country on the basis that the application of that mandatory rule would be against English public policy. It is possible to envisage this happening in cases where a foreign mandatory rule is in conflict with an English mandatory rule.

---

[642] See Philip (1978) II Hague Recueil 1, 55 et seq; Diamond, op cit, at 292 et seq; Moscani (1989) V Hague Recueil 9; Plender, paras 9.23–9.26; Kaye, pp 345–350; Dicey, Morris and Collins, paras 32R-229–32-243. See more generally, Enonchong (1996) 45 ICLQ 633, 634–636. Public policy includes Community public policy: the Giuliano and Lagarde Report, p 38.

[643] See the discussion of the public policy defence in relation to the recognition of foreign divorces, etc, infra, pp 1018–1023.

[644] Supra, pp 141–142. The fact that an agreement also offended the public policy of the foreign place of performance could provide justification: *Lemenda Trading Co Ltd v African Middle East Petroleum Co Ltd* [1988] QB 448; Carter (1988) 59 BYBIL 356; Collier [1988] CLJ 169; *Apple Corps Ltd v Apple Computer Inc* [1992] FSR 431; *Westacre Investments Inc v Jugoimport-SPDR Holding Co Ltd* [2000] 1 QB 288, CA.

[645] The Giuliano and Lagarde Report, p 38; see also the United Kingdom submission in Case 150/80 *Elefanten Schuh GmbH v Jacqmain* [1981] ECR 1671, [1982] 3 CMLR 1.

[646] See Fletcher, *Conflict of Laws and European Community Law*, p 172.

Common law cases[647] which involved the consideration of an objectionable foreign law which was held to be contrary to our distinctive English public policy will doubtless be decided in the same way under the Convention, using Article 16.[648] Thus the English court will continue not to enforce such contracts as those in restraint of trade, assigning a cause of action, involving a certain type of duress, or contracts for prostitution, provided normally[649] that the circumstances involve a sufficient connection with England to justify this.[650] However, there was a very different category of public policy cases at common law based on the notion of the comity of nations. Thus, in one case[651] the Court of Appeal held that it would be against the comity of nations to enforce a contract, the whole object of which was to import whisky into the USA contrary to the prohibition laws of that country.[652] Such cases do not appear to fit within Article 16.[653] This is a negative provision, being concerned with a refusal to apply some objectionable foreign rule.[654] If the English forum's concern, as appears to be the case in the above example, is to uphold a foreign law[655] on a matter of great importance to that foreign country, this does not look to come within either the wording or purpose of Article 16. The appropriate provision to refer to under the Convention is Article 7(1).[656] However, Article 7(1) is not available in the United Kingdom.

Is it possible to use Article 7(2)? It has been suggested that such cases involve a domestic rule of English law which can be regarded as a mandatory rule of English law within this provision.[657] However, to regard a common law rule of public policy based on the

---

[647] Supra, pp 142–144.

[648] But see the argument, discussed supra, pp 150–151, that some common law cases of public policy involve mandatory rules of the forum.

[649] See Dicey, Morris and Collins, para 32-233.

[650] Cf *Re Colt Telecom Group plc (No 2)* [2002] EWHC 2815 (Ch), [2003] BPIR 324—no-action clause enforced.

[651] *Foster v Driscoll* [1929] 1 KB 470. English law governed the contract. However, the result doubtless would have been the same if the contract had been governed by a foreign law, according to which the contract had been enforceable. See also *Regazzoni v K C Sethia (1944) Ltd* [1956] 2 QB 490; affd [1958] AC 301; *Euro-Diam Ltd v Bathurst* [1990] 1 QB 1 at 40; *Royal Boskalis Westminster NV v Mountain* [1998] 2 WLR 538 at 555, 565; Briggs (1997) 68 BYBIL 364; *Ispahani v Bank Melli Iran* [1998] Lloyd's Rep Bank 133, (1997) Times, 29 December, CA; *Westacre Investments Inc v Jugoimport-SDPR Holding Co Ltd* [2000] 1 QB 288, CA; *Tekron Resources Ltd v Guinea Investment Co Ltd* [2003] EWHC 2577 (QB), [2004] 2 Lloyd's Rep 26; Enonchong (1996) 45 ICLQ 633 at 649–650. For continuing use of the common law comity principle: in arbitration cases, *JSC Zestafoni v Ronty Holdings Ltd* [2004] EWHC 245 (Comm), [2004] 2 Lloyd's Rep 335; where English law was applied, *Society of Lloyd's v Fraser* [1999] Lloyd's IR 156, CA; *Tekron Resources* supra, *Mahonia Ltd v JP Morgan Chase Bank* [2003] EWHC 1927 (Comm), [2003] 2 Lloyd's Rep 911; and in the context of restitution, *Barros Mattos Junior v General Securities and Finance Ltd* [2004] EWHC 1188 (Ch), [2004] 2 Lloyd's Rep 475.

[652] Distinguished in the *JSC Zestafoni* case, supra—illegality in a foreign court but performance in England where there was no illegality.

[653] Hartley, op cit, 353; (1996) 45 ICLQ 271, 289 n 87; Kaye, p 69. Cf Lasok and Stone, op cit, pp 372–374.

[654] The Giuliano and Lagarde Report, at p 38; Philip, op cit, 57.

[655] But see Kaye, p 347 and Hill, para 14.3.20. English courts are not always so concerned. Cf *Akai Pty Ltd v People's Insurance Co Ltd* [1998] 1 Lloyd's Rep 90; Reynolds [1998] LMCLQ 1; where Thomas J, applying the traditional contract choice of law rules, which include the doctrine of public policy, gave effect to the agreement of the parties, rather than to an Australian mandatory rule rendering void a clause choosing English as the applicable law and conferring jurisdiction on the English courts; approved in *OT Africa Line Ltd v Magic Sportswear Corpn* [2005] EWCA Civ 710, [2005] 2 Lloyd's 170.

[656] Supra, p 738.

[657] Hartley (1997) 266 Hague Recueil 341, 403, 388–391. Admittedly, *Foster v Driscoll* appears as an example of contracts illegal at common law on grounds of public policy in Cheshire, Fifoot and Furmston's *Law of Contract* (13th edn), p 380.

comity of nations, and which therefore only applies in international cases, as a domestic law rule would appear to be a fiction. It looks more like a private international law rule, and, as such, is implicitly abolished by the Rome Convention in all cases where the latter applies.

(a) Public policy under the Rome I Regulation

Article 21 of the Rome I Regulation[658] is in substance the same as Article 16 of the Convention. The position in relation to objectionable foreign laws will therefore be the same. However, when it comes to the category of public policy cases at common law based on the notion of the comity of nations, the position may be affected by the introduction of Article 9(3) of the proposal for a Regulation.[659] Effect may be given to the overriding mandatory provisions of the place of performance in the situation where performance is rendered unlawful in that country.[660]

(f) Particular issues

The scheme of the Convention is that, having set out the rules on the applicable law, there are then special rules dealing with the particular issues of material validity,[661] formal validity,[662] incapacity[663] and a number of other matters.[664] By implication, all other issues must be governed by the rules on the applicable law set out earlier in the Convention. The point is spelt out by a provision on the scope of the applicable law[665] which gives particular instances of issues governed by the rules on the applicable law. With special rules for particular issues, a problem of classification inevitably arises. Under the common law rules, the English courts adopted the system of classification employed in the domestic law of contract. However, under the Convention it is important that the classification of issues is made in the light of the intentions of the drafters of the Convention and of the principle of uniform interpretation.[666] For example, the issue of whether a contract has to be in writing is intended to come within the category of formal validity[667] under the Convention, whereas this was classified as a procedural issue under the common law rules. The provisions in the Convention relating to particular issues will now be examined,[668] after which one issue that causes a special problem for the United Kingdom, that of illegality, will be considered.

---

[658] Art 21 substitutes provision of law for rule of law.

[659] Discussed supra, p 740.

[660] In *Foster v Driscoll* [1929] 1 KB 470 there was no illegality in the foreign place of performance (which was not in the USA). However, the objective of the scheme was that the whisky would end up eventually in the USA, hence the concern with the comity of nations.

[661] Art 8.

[662] Art 9.

[663] Art 11.

[664] Arts 12, 13, 14.

[665] Art 10.

[666] The Giuliano and Lagarde Report, p 38.

[667] Art 9, infra, p 747; see the Giuliano and Lagarde Report, p 31.

[668] Ie apart from Art 12 (voluntary assignment), Art 13 (subrogation) and Art 14 (burden of proof, proving the contract). These matters are more appropriately dealt with elsewhere in the book, see supra, pp 83 and 88, infra, pp 1232–1238.

(i) Material validity

Article 8 is entitled "Material Validity" and contains two provisions.[669] Before examining these provisions it is necessary to see what is encompassed within the concept of material validity.

(a) What is meant by material validity?

Material validity under the Convention covers a wide variety of different issues. This is apparent from both Article 8(1), which is concerned with "the existence and validity of a contract", and Article 8(2), which deals with the existence of consent. The intention is that not only are issues of material validity in the English sense covered (eg the issue of illegality), but also issues relating to formation of the contract[670] (eg offer and acceptance, and consideration). The validity of consent to the contract, (eg issues of mistake, misrepresentation and duress) is doubtless also covered under Article 8(1). Issues relating to the existence and validity of the contract itself are obviously covered, but so also are such issues in relation to the terms of the contract.[671] As has already been mentioned,[672] the existence and validity of consent to a choice of the applicable law are to be referred to Article 8.[673] Nonetheless, not all issues of validity are dealt with under Article 8; formal validity has a special rule to itself under Article 9.[674]

(b) The putative applicable law [675]

Article 8(1) states that: "The existence and validity of a contract, or of any term of a contract, shall be determined by the law which would govern it under this Convention if the contract or term were valid." This means that the normal rules on the applicable law under the Convention are applied to the issue of material validity. The only gloss on this is that with material validity one has to assume that the contract or term is valid in the first place before ascertaining the applicable law. In the terminology of the common law rules, the "putative" governing law is applied. As the Giuliano and Lagarde Report explains: "This is to avoid the circular argument that where there is a choice of the applicable law no law can be said to be applicable until the contract is found to be valid."[676] The important point of substance is that the parties are free to choose the governing law under Article 3 of the Convention, eg by putting a choice of law clause in the contract, even though the issue in the case is whether a valid contract exists between them. When it comes to validity of terms of the contract it means that the validity of a New York choice of law clause is governed by New York law. Similarly, the question whether a clause

---

[669] Art 8(1) and (2).

[670] The Giuliano and Lagarde Report, p 28. See *Continental Enterprises Ltd v Shandong Zhucheng Foreign Trade Group Co* [2005] EWHC 92 (Comm) in relation to illegality. Art 8(1) has been applied to determine *where* a contract was made for the purposes of service out of the jurisdiction: *Marconi Communications International Ltd v PT Indonesia Bank Ltd TBK* [2004] EWHC 129 (Comm) at [32]–[33], [2004] 1 Lloyd's Rep 594; appeal dismissed [2005] EWCA Civ 422, [2005] 2 All ER (Comm) 325.

[671] *Thierry Morin v Bonhams & Brooks Ltd* [2003] EWHC 467 (Comm), [2003] IL Pr 25; affd [2003] EWCA Civ 1802 at [21]–[23], [2004] IL Pr 24—upholding the decision at first instance as to the law governing the tort.

[672] See the discussion on Art 3(4), supra, p 707.

[673] The Giuliano and Lagarde Report, p 28. See generally Hill, para 14.4.5.

[674] Capacity is dealt with under Art 11.

[675] See Crawford (2005) 54 ICLQ 829; Harris (2004) 57 CLP 305, 316–321.

[676] At p 30.

providing for arbitration in England is validly incorporated into a contract is governed by English law (the arbitration clause being an inferred choice of the governing law).[677] In other words, the parties are able to pull themselves up by their own bootstraps. The principle has much to commend it. Businessmen use choice of law clauses in order to avoid the problems of ascertaining the objective governing law and their wishes should be respected whatever the issue.[678] However, this can lead to unfairness to one of the parties. The Working Group acknowledged this particular problem and included a safeguard in relation to consent to the contract.

(c) The safeguard in relation to consent[679]

This is contained in Article 8(2) which provides that: "Nevertheless a party may rely upon the law of the country in which he has his habitual residence to establish that he did not consent if it appears from the circumstances that it would not be reasonable to determine the effect of his conduct in accordance with the law specified in the preceding paragraph." This is designed[680] to cater for the following sort of example:

A makes an offer to B, and inserts a choice of law clause in the contract stating that the law of Utopia will govern all disputes between the parties. B remains silent, neither expressly accepting nor rejecting the offer. Under the law of Utopia silence can constitute an acceptance. It would be manifestly unfair for B to be contractually bound. The effect of Article 8(2) is that B can assert that he did not consent to the contract according to the law of his habitual residence.

The major proviso is that it would have to appear from the circumstances that it would not be reasonable to determine the effect of his conduct under Utopian law. On the above facts, doubtless it would not be. The circumstances to be taken into account include the parties' previous practices inter se and their business relationship[681] and whether the transaction is a conventional one.[682]

---

[677] *Egon Oldendorff v Liberia Corpn* [1995] 2 Lloyd's Rep 64 (MANCE J)—the issue was one for the law governing the *contract* rather than one of material validity of the arbitration agreement. Where the issue is one of material validity of an arbitration or choice of jurisdiction agreement this is a matter for the law governing the arbitration or choice of jurisdiction agreement. But see cases treating it as a matter for the law governing the contract: *OT Africa Line Ltd v Magic Sportswear Corpn* [2005] EWCA Civ 710 at [1]–[2], [22] (per LONGMORE LJ), [2005] 2 Lloyd's Rep 170 (but cf Rix LJ at [60]); *Horn Linie GmbH & Co v Panamericana Formas e Impresos SA (The Hornbay)* [2006] EWHC 373 (Comm) at [20], [2006] 2 Lloyd's Rep 44. The law governing the arbitration or choice of jurisdiction agreement is identified using traditional English choice of law rules (see Art 1(2)(d) supra, pp 684–685). See also *Egon Oldendorff v Liberia Corpn* [1996] 1 Lloyd's Rep 380 at 385 (CLARKE J); *Welex AG v Rosa Maritime Ltd (The Epsilon Rosa) (No 1)* [2002] EWHC 762 (Comm), [2002] 2 Lloyd's Rep 81; an appeal on the issues of incorporation in and grant of an anti-suit injunction was dismissed [2003] EWCA Civ 938, [2003] 2 Lloyd's Rep 509. This did not challenge the Art 8(1) point.
[678] See Dicey, Morris and Collins, paras 32R-154–32-168 and the common law cases of *Compañía Naviera Micro SA v Shipley International Inc, The Parouth* [1982] 2 Lloyd's Rep 351; *The Heidberg* [1994] 2 Lloyd's Rep 287 at 303 et seq. Cf Briggs [1990] LMCLQ 192; Jaffey, *Topics in Choice of Law*, pp 62 et seq; Kaye, pp 270–274. For Australian authority applying the law of the forum to the issue of formation of the contract, see *Oceanic Sun Line Special Shipping Co Inc v Fay* (1988) 165 CLR 197, HC of Australia.
[679] Criticised by Carter (1986) 57 BYBIL 1, 26, n 108. See generally Jaffey, op cit, pp 70–71.
[680] See the Giuliano and Lagarde Report, p 28.
[681] Ibid.
[682] *Welex AG v Rosa Maritime Ltd (The Epsilon Rosa) (No 2)* [2002] EWHC 2035 (Comm) at [11]–[12], [2002] 2 Lloyd's Rep 701; an appeal on the issues of incorporation in and the grant of an anti-suit injunction was dismissed [2003] EWCA Civ 938, [2003] 2 Lloyd's Rep 509. This did not challenge the Art 8(2) point.

The burden is on the party who wishes to displace Article 8(1) to show that the terms of Article 8(2) have been met.[683] Article 8(2) allows a party to rely on the law of his habitual residence to deny the existence of a contract. It cannot be used in a positive way to create a contract which did not exist under the applicable law. It was specifically devised with the question of silence constituting acceptance of an offer in mind. Nonetheless, it is wide enough to cover any issue of offer and acceptance. It is, though, only concerned with the *existence* of consent, not with the *validity* of consent (eg with duress, mistake, misrepresentation). In cases raising these issues Article 8(1) will no doubt apply; but, on its own, without the safeguard contained in Article 8(2). As far as the issue of consent is concerned, the combined effect of Article 8(1) and (2) is that the contract can be invalidated either by reference to the applicable law or by reference to the law of the habitual residence of the party denying that he consented.

There was an unsuccessful attempt in *Egon Oldendorff v Liberia Corpn*[684] to use Article 8(2) in a very different situation from that for which it was designed. The Japanese defendants sought to rely on Japanese law, which allegedly requires (in an agreement "subject to details") recapitulation and confirmation of contractual details by both parties, to establish that they did not consent to the incorporation of an arbitration clause into the contract. MANCE J held that the onus was on the party who sought to invoke Article 8(2) to negative consent, and that reliance could only be placed on Japanese law if it was not reasonable to determine the effect of the defendants' conduct in accordance with English law. It was unreasonable to determine consent in accordance with Japanese law because this would mean ignoring the English arbitration clause and to do this would appear to be contrary to ordinary commercial expectations when everything suggested that the defendants must already have considered and accepted the clause. The issue of consent raised by Japanese law looks to have more to do with the validity of consent than with its existence.[685] Accordingly, the case could have been decided on the basis that this issue fell outside the scope of Article 8(2), without going on to apply the "reasonableness" test.

(d) The Rome I Regulation

Article 10 of the Regulation[686] is virtually identical in wording to Article 8 of the Convention.

(ii) Formal validity[687]

Article 9 of the Convention deals with this issue. It contains general rules relating to the formal validity of contracts, a rule for unilateral acts intended to have legal effect (such as notice of termination of a contract), and special rules for consumer contracts and contracts in respect of immovable property.

---

[683] *(The Epsilon Rosa) (No 2)*, supra, at [11].

[684] [1995] 2 Lloyd's Rep 64 (MANCE J) who had to determine for the purposes of service out of the jurisdiction whether English law governed. Once it had been decided that there was jurisdiction CLARKE J had to decide whether English law did in fact govern: [1996] 1 Lloyd's Rep 380. See also *(The Epsilon Rosa) (No 2)*, supra, at [11]–[12]; the *Thierry Morin* case, supra, at [24]. The approach of MANCE J was followed in *Horn Linie GmbH & Co v Panamericana Formas e Impresos SA (The Hornbay)* [2006] EWHC 373 (Comm) at [19]–[21], [2006] 2 Lloyd's Rep 44—involving validity of a choice of law clause in a contract of carriage.

[685] See likewise the *Horn Linie* case, supra.

[686] This provision remains in substance unaltered from the original 2005 proposal for a Rome I Regulation.

[687] See Kaye, pp 281–295.

(a) What is meant by formal validity?

It is not always easy to decide whether a matter is one of form or substance. English lawyers have particular difficulty with the classification of issues as ones of form because of the relative dearth of formal requirements under English law. This has meant that issues have sometimes been given a surprising classification. For example, the issue of whether a contract has to be in writing looks to be one of form, yet traditionally this has been classified under English law as one of procedure, and thus to be determined by the law of the forum.[688] However, it now appears that under the Convention this issue should be classified as one of form. The Giuliano and Lagarde Report gives welcome guidance as to what formal validity encompasses. It includes "every external manifestation required on the part of a person expressing the will to be legally bound, and in the absence of which such expression of will would not be regarded as fully effective".[689] The following were given as examples of formal requirements:[690] the requirement that there must be two signatures to the contract; that the contract must be made in duplicate; and, of most interest to English lawyers, that a non-competition clause in a contract of employment must be in writing. On the other hand, it was said[691] that it did not include the special requirements which have to be fulfilled where an act is to be valid against third parties, eg the need in English law for a notice of a statutory assignment of a chose in action. It would be best if the concept of formal validity were to be given an independent Community meaning. If it is left to national laws to determine whether the issue is one of formal validity, the English courts will need to take a broader view of the concept than they have in the past.

(b) The general rules

(i) The contract is concluded between persons who are in the same country

The first of the general rules on formal validity is contained in Article 9(1) which provides that: "A contract concluded between persons who are in the same country is formally valid if it satisfies the formal requirements of the law which governs it under this Convention or of the law of the country where it is concluded." The policy underlying this provision is clear: to avoid the invalidation of contracts on the basis of formal defects. It does this by a validating rule of alternative reference. The normal rules on the applicable law under the Convention are applied, but if the contract is formally invalid under those rules, as an alternative, recourse can be had to the law of the country where the contract was concluded in order to validate it.

The Working Group[692] justified the reference to the law of the place where the contract was concluded on the basis of the historical importance of this law. A modern policy justification would be that disputes as to form arise at the time when and in the country where the contract is concluded. It is therefore convenient that that country's law should be applied to resolve the dispute. There is no problem in determining where a contract

---

[688] *Leroux v Brown* (1852) 12 CB 801; supra, pp 76–78. See also *G & H Montage GmbH v Irvani* [1990] 1 WLR 667 at 684, 690; *Rothwells v Connell* (1993) 119 ALR 538—a requirement that a deed be stamped for it to be admissible in evidence held to be procedural.

[689] At p 29.

[690] At p 31.

[691] At p 29.

[692] At p 30.

was concluded because of the limitation of Article 9(1) to contracts concluded between parties who are in the same country.[693]

When it comes to applying, as an alternative, the law that governs the contract, there are a number of difficulties. The first is that this law can be varied by the parties after the contract has been concluded. However, Article 3(2)[694] provides that a subsequent variation will not prejudice the formal validity of the contract. A subsequent variation of the governing law will not be allowed to invalidate the contract. On the other hand, a subsequent variation of the governing law which has the effect of formally validating a contract, invalid at its inception, will presumably be allowed,[695] validating the contract from that date. The second difficulty stems from the fact that different laws may govern different parts of the contract. Which of these governing laws is to determine its formal validity? According to the Giuliano and Lagarde Report "it would seem reasonable to apply the law applicable to the part of the contract most closely connected with the disputed condition on which its formal validity depends".[696] Thirdly, when Article 9 refers to the law that governs the contract, apparently this means the *putative* governing law, ie the law which would govern the contract if it were formally valid.[697]

(ii) The contract is concluded between persons who are not in the same country

If the parties are not in the same country at the time of the conclusion of the contract, the second general rule, which is contained in Article 9(2), applies. According to this: "A contract concluded between persons who are in different countries is formally valid if it satisfies the formal requirements of the law which governs it under this Convention or of the law of one of those countries." This means that recourse may be had to the law of up to three different countries in order to validate the contract. In the situation where offer and acceptance has been made by an exchange of e-mails, it is not easy to determine when the contract is concluded, and hence the place where each party is at that time.[698] The rules in Article 9(1) and (2) set out alternatives for validating the contract, rightly without giving a priority to any one alternative.

(iii) Acts intended to have legal effect

The third and last part of the general rules[699] is concerned with formal requirements in respect of acts[700] intended to have legal effect, such as an offer or notice of termination, and is analogous to Article 9(1) in that it refers, as alternatives, to the law applicable under the Convention or the law of the country where the act was done.

---

[693] Where the contract is concluded by an agent, reference has to be made to the country in which the agent acts: Art 9(3).

[694] Supra, pp 692–694.

[695] The Giuliano and Lagarde Report, p 30.

[696] Ibid.

[697] Ibid.

[698] Green Paper of 14 January 2003 on the conversion of the Rome Convention, COM (2002) 654 final, pp 38–39.

[699] Art 9(4).

[700] The act must relate to an existing or contemplated contract: the Giuliano and Lagarde Report, p 29.

(c) The special rules for particular contracts

(i) Consumer contracts

The first of the special rules is concerned with consumer contracts. The formal validity of a consumer contract is governed by the law of the country in which the consumer has his habitual residence.[701] This means that, for consumer contracts,[702] formal validity is governed by the law that governs the substance of the contract, and the consumer is protected by having the law of his habitual residence applied.[703]

(ii) Immovable property

The second special rule is concerned with contracts relating to immovable property. Article 9(6) states that:

> Notwithstanding paragraphs 1 to 4 of this Article, a contract the subject matter of which is a right in immovable property or a right to use immovable property shall be subject to the mandatory requirements of form of the law of the country where the property is situated if by that law those requirements are imposed irrespective of the country where the contract is concluded and irrespective of the law governing the contract.

This provision shows a concern to give effect to the mandatory rules of form of the law of the situs in cases involving immovable property.[704] It is not enough to show simply that these rules are mandatory (cannot be derogated from by contract). It must also be shown that the mandatory requirement of form is imposed "irrespective of the country where the contract is concluded and irrespective of the law governing the contract". In other words, according to the law of the situs the mandatory rule has to have overriding effect.[705]

(d) Formal validity under the Rome I Regulation

Article 11 (formal validity) of the proposal for a Regulation is by and large the same in substance as Article 9 of the Convention.[706] There is, though, one significant difference. The rules in the Convention on formal validity are now regarded as being too restrictive in the light of the growing frequency of contracts made at a distance.[707] In order to facilitate the formal validation of contracts, a third alternative connecting factor has been introduced. Thus, under Article 11(2)[708] (a contract is concluded between persons who, or whose agents, are in different countries at the time of conclusion), a contract is formally valid if it satisfies the formal requirements of: (i) the law which governs it in substance under the Regulation or (ii) the law of either of the countries where either of the parties or their agent is present at the time of conclusion or (iii) the law of the country where either of the parties had his habitual residence at that time. This third alternative is also introduced in relation to a unilateral act intended to have legal effect.[709]

---

[701] Art 9(5); see the Giuliano and Lagarde Report, pp 31–32.
[702] Ie ones to which Art 5 applies. The contract must be concluded in the circumstances mentioned in Art 5 (2).
[703] Morse in *Contract Conflicts*, pp 143, 151 criticises this for erring in favour of the consumer.
[704] See the Giuliano and Lagarde Report, p 31.
[705] See ibid, p 32, which makes this clear.
[706] More radical changes under the original proposal were dropped.
[707] Explanatory Memorandum, p 9.
[708] Rome I Regulation.
[709] Art 11(3) of the Rome I Regulation, replacing Art 9(4) of the Convention.

One further difference, albeit not one of substance, between the Regulation and the Convention relates to Article 11(5) of the former, which replaces Article 9(6) of the latter.[710] Article 11(5) does not use the confusing term "mandatory" requirements. Instead it spells out that in the present context we are concerned with requirements which (a) are imposed irrespective of the country where the contract is concluded and irrespective of the law governing the contracts [711] and (b) cannot be derogated from by agreement.

(iii) Capacity

As has already been seen, questions involving the capacity of corporations are excluded altogether from the scope of the Rome Convention.[712] When it comes to natural persons the position is more complex. The status or legal capacity of natural persons is, in general, excluded from the scope of the Convention.[713] Contracting States are therefore left to apply their traditional private international law rules to the issue of capacity to contract. However, this is subject to Article 11 of the Convention. This is a narrow rule concerned with protecting parties who have contracted with a natural person under an incapacity from being caught unawares by this. The traditional English common law rules on capacity will now be examined, and then Article 11 of the Convention.

(a) The traditional common law rules

What law governs capacity to make a commercial contract is a matter of speculation so far as the English common law authorities are concerned. There is no clear decision and the dicta are not very helpful. It is clear, though, that the choice lies between the law of the domicile,[714] the law of the place where the contract was made[715] and the proper law in the objective sense.

It may be conceded that in modern conditions of trade domicile is not a satisfactory test. It is incompatible with justice and with the trust that lies at the basis of commercial dealing that, for instance, a person over eighteen years of age should be able to escape liability for the price of goods sold or delivered to him in a London shop on the ground that he is still a minor by the law of his domicile abroad.[716] Indeed, under civil law systems the rule that capacity is governed by the personal law cannot be relied on by a person who, though lacking capacity by his personal law, has capacity according to the law of the place where the contract was made.[717] Under English law, in many cases, contracts by persons under

---

[710] Discussed supra, p 749.

[711] See Art 9 of the Regulation, discussed supra, pp 738–741.

[712] Art 1(2)(e) of the Rome Convention, supra, p 685.

[713] Art 1(2)(a), supra, p 681.

[714] *Sottomayor v De Barros* (1877) 3 PD 1 at 5. Although this was a marriage case, COTTON LJ applied his statement in support of the law of the domicile to any contract. He was severely criticised in *Sottomayor v De Barros (No 2)* (1879) 5 PD 94 at 100; but see *Re Cooke's Trusts* (1887) 56 LJ Ch 637 at 639; *Cooper v Cooper* (1888) 13 App Cas 88 at 99, 100, 108.

[715] *Baindail v Baindail* [1946] P 122 at 128; and see *Simonin v Mallac* (1860) 2 Sw & Tr 67; *Republica de Guatemala v Nunez* [1927] 1 KB 669 at 689.

[716] See Morris, paras 13.035–13.037.

[717] Wolff, pp 281–282.

18 years of age are not enforceable against them,[718] but the court might well restrict this rule (and it would be reasonable for it to do so) to contracts in respect of which the objective proper law is English law.[719] It is also argued that, in the converse case, capacity conferred by the law of the domicile should not be invalidated by the proper law, ie a person should be regarded as capable if capable by the law of his domicile.[720] So far, however, English courts have not been pressed to adopt such attitudes.

Not only has it been advocated frequently that the law of the place where the contract was made governs the question of capacity,[721] but there is also one old English decision to this effect.[722] This view, if it implies that the law of that place exclusively governs the matter, is clearly untenable, for it would enable a party to evade an incapacity imposed upon him by the law that governs the contract in other respects by the simple device of concluding the contract in a country where the law is more favourable. Moreover, the law of the place of contracting is ill adapted to govern the matter if, as may well happen, the parties conclude the contract in a place where they are only transiently present.

Such modern authority as there is would indicate that capacity to conclude a commercial contract is regulated by the proper law of the contract objectively ascertained. This is supported by the Canadian decision in *Charron v Montreal Trust Co*.[723] It was held there that capacity to enter a separation agreement is to be determined by the law of the country with which the contract is most substantially connected,[724] ie the proper law; though in the actual case this was also the law of the place where the contract was made.

More recently, the issue of capacity arose in *Bodley Head Ltd v Flegon*:[725]

> The defendant argued, inter alia, that an agreement between the Russian author, Alexander Solzhenitsyn, and H, a Swiss lawyer, was invalid as Solzhenitsyn had no capacity under Russian law, which was both the law of the domicile and the law of the place where the contract was made, to enter a contract to appoint an agent to contract abroad on his behalf.

Whilst doubting the correctness of the allegation that Solzhenitsyn was incapable under Russian law, BRIGHTMAN J had no doubt that the question of his capacity was to be decided by Swiss law as the proper law of the contract. Although the point was not discussed, the facts of this case did raise the issue that, in stating that capacity is governed by the proper law of the contract, this expression must be taken to mean the law of the country with which the contract is most substantially connected. Intention cannot here be allowed free play.[726] A person cannot confer capacity upon himself by deliberately submitting himself to a law to which factually the contract is unrelated.

---

[718] See Law Com No 134; the Minors' Contracts Act 1987.
[719] See Morris, paras 13.035–13.037.
[720] Dicey, Morris and Collins, para 32-225; Restatement, 2d § 198.
[721] *Baindail v Baindail* [1946] P 122 at 128; Anton, pp 276–278.
[722] *Male v Roberts* (1790) 3 Esp 163; and see *Bondholders Securities Corpn v Manville* [1933] 4 DLR 699.
[723] (1958) 15 DLR (2d) 240.
[724] Ibid, at 244–245.
[725] [1972] 1 WLR 680.
[726] *Cooper v Cooper* (1888) 13 App Cas 88 at 108. This was accepted by counsel in *Marubeni Hong Kong and South China Ltd v Mongolian Government* [2002] 2 All ER (Comm) 873 at [19].

(b) Article 11

Article 11 of the Rome Convention is entitled "Incapacity"[727] and states that:

> In a contract concluded between persons who are in the same country, a natural person who would have capacity under the law of that country may invoke his incapacity resulting from another law only if the other party to the contract was aware of this incapacity at the time of the conclusion of the contract or was not aware thereof as a result of negligence.

This is an unusual article in that it grafts a specific rule dealing with one aspect of capacity onto national rules of private international law on this topic. The aspect it is concerned with is the position of a party who contracts with a natural person who is under an incapacity but where the first party is unaware of this incapacity. In certain circumstances it protects such a party by imposing a limitation on the right of the natural person under the incapacity to invoke his own incapacity. This idea has its origin in the law of certain civil law countries. In order for this limitation to apply, certain stringent conditions have to be satisfied.[728]

First, there must be a contract concluded between persons who are in the same country. The Working Group did not want to prejudice the protection of, for example, minors when a contract was made at a distance. The person under an incapacity must be a natural person. However, there is no such requirement as regards the other party, and this could presumably be a corporation. In cases where the incapacity of a corporation is at issue the traditional common law rules will apply, and in such cases this is not subject to Article 11. Secondly, it must be a situation where, according to the traditional private international law rules applicable in the forum, a natural person has capacity under the law of the country where the contract was concluded, but lacks capacity under another law. For example, a Contracting State under its traditional private international law rules may apply the proper law (as in the case of England) or the law of the domicile or nationality (as in the case of some civil law countries) to the issue of capacity, and under that law a person lacks capacity. Under Article 11 it is then necessary to turn to the law of the place where the contract was concluded in order to see if there is capacity by that law. There is no difficulty in identifying the country where the contract was concluded in cases where (as will always be the case under Article 11) both parties are in the same country at the time of the conclusion of the contract. On the other hand, if a Contracting State to the Convention applies the law of the place of contracting to the issue of capacity under its traditional private international law rules, Article 11 will not operate.

If these requirements are met, the limitation on the right of an incapacitated person to invoke his own incapacity applies. The person under the incapacity can only invoke his own incapacity if the other party was aware of this incapacity or was not aware thereof as a result of negligence. The burden of proof as to this lies on the incapacitated party.[729] If satisfied, the incapacitated party lacks capacity to contract. On the other hand, if the incapacitated party does not satisfy the burden of proof he will have capacity to contract. The limitation is a narrow one. It only affects the rights of the person acting under the incapacity. The other party can raise an incapacity that exists according to the law applied

---

[727] This includes incapacity in relation to consent to choice: Art 3(4), supra, p 707.
[728] The Giuliano and Lagarde Report, p 34. See generally Kaye, pp 312–319.
[729] The Giuliano and Lagarde Report, p 34. See generally Kaye, pp 312–319.

by the traditional private international law rules of the forum even though he or she knew of the incapacity at the time of contracting. Furthermore, it only affects the rights of the person acting under the incapacity when that person is seeking to invoke his own incapacity. It does not prevent, for example, a minor from seeking to uphold a contract, and the other party cannot escape from a contract (valid by the applicable law) by saying that he was unaware that he was contracting with a minor.

Under the Rome I Regulation the position in relation to incapacity is in substance the same as that under the Convention.[730]

(iv) Scope of the applicable law[731]

Article 10 of the Rome Convention is entitled "Scope of the Applicable Law" and in paragraph (1) gives a number of examples of issues coming within the scope of the law applicable to the contract by virtue of Articles 3 to 6 and 12.[732] This is not intended to be an exhaustive list,[733] and it is implicit that all other issues are governed by the rules on the applicable law. The only exceptions are issues classified as ones of formal validity or incapacity. Material validity is, of course, governed by the rules on the applicable law because of Article 8(1). The examples provided by Article 10 are as follows:

(a) Interpretation

Under the common law rules the province of interpretation was to discover the true intent and meaning of the parties as expressed by the language of the contract. This was a question of fact. Nevertheless, a question of choice of law could arise for, if an expression was ambiguous and if it bore different meanings in different legal systems, its interpretation had to be determined by reference to one only of those systems. This distinction between fact and law is still valid under the Convention, since the Convention is only concerned with choice of law. When a choice of law problem arises, the Convention adopts the simple solution that the law applicable to the contract will govern the issue of interpretation.[734] A problem which arises from this approach can be illustrated by the situation where the contract is governed by Utopian law, but the parties have expressly provided that the contract is to be interpreted according to the law of Ruritania. At common law it seems that Ruritanian law would govern the interpretation of the contract. Under the Convention it appears, at first glance, that Utopian law has to be applied, since this is the law applicable to *the contract*. However, Article 10(1) refers to the law applicable to the contract "by virtue of Articles 3–6". Under Article 3 the parties are able to choose a law for *part* of the contract which may include a specific issue such as interpretation. The law applicable to the issue of interpretation in the above example would accordingly be Ruritanian law, which has been expressly chosen to govern that part of the contract.

---

[730] See the general exclusion in relation to natural persons: (Art 1(2)(a) of the Regulation. This is subject to Art 13, which replicates, with the addition of a comma, Art 11 of the Convention.

[731] See Plender, paras 11.01–11.18; Kaye, pp 297–310; Lagarde in *Contract Conflicts*, pp 49 et seq.

[732] In cases of dépeçage the law applicable will be that governing the relevant part of the contract; cf Anton, pp 339–340.

[733] "The law applicable to a contract . . . shall govern in particular": Art 10(1). See Plender, para 11.02, where it is suggested that "effects of a contract" are omitted from the list.

[734] Art 10(1)(a).

(b) Performance

(i) What is encompassed within the concept of performance?

Whilst interpretation of a contract is a fairly self-explanatory category, some explanation is needed of what is encompassed within the concept of performance under Article 10(1)(b). The Giuliano and Lagarde Report gives helpful examples of issues coming within Article 10:

> The diligence with which the obligation must be performed; conditions relating to the place and time of performance; the extent to which the obligation can be performed by a person other than the party liable; the conditions as to performance of the obligation both in general and in relation to certain categories of obligation (joint and several obligations, alternative obligations, divisible and indivisible obligations, pecuniary obligations); where performance consists of the payment of a sum of money, the conditions relating to the discharge of the debtor who has made the payment, the appropriation of the payment, the receipt, etc.[735]

It is not clear whether all of these examples come within Article 10(1)(b) or whether some of them are intended to come within Article 10(1)(c) (failure to perform) or (d) (the various ways of extinguishing obligations). However, it is not necessary to decide this since the position is the same under each of the sub-paragraphs of Article 10(1): the applicable law by virtue of Articles 3 to 6 and 12 governs. Nonetheless, it is important to distinguish all of these cases relating to the substance of performance from "the manner of performance and the steps to be taken in the event of defective performance" because of the special provision in Article 10(2), which deals with the latter.

(ii) The manner of performance: a special rule

Article 10(2) provides that: "In relation to the manner of performance and the steps to be taken in the event of defective performance regard shall be had to the law of the country in which performance takes place." This provision deals with the situation where the law of the country of the place of performance is different from the law of the country whose law is applicable under Articles 3 to 6 and 12 of the Convention.[736] Two questions arise in relation to Article 10(2). The first is a question of definition: what matters fall within the concept of manner of performance? The second is a question of substance: what is a court supposed to do if it is faced with a matter of the manner of performance?

The definitional question   The Working Group[737] said that they did not want to give a strict definition to the concept of manner of performance. However, they have provided examples of matters normally falling within this category: rules governing public holidays, the manner in which goods are to be examined, and the steps to be taken if they are refused. Ultimately, it is for the law of the forum to decide if the issue is one relating to the manner of performance. An example of this concept from the English courts is the rule under Chilean law that goods must be delivered to a customs warehouse.[738] The following have been held to be matters relating to the manner of performance under the old

---

[735] At pp 32–33.

[736] If the two are the same the court would have to apply that country's law as the applicable law.

[737] The Giuliano and Lagarde Report, at p 33.

[738] *East West Corpn v DKBS 1912* [2002] EWHC 83 (Comm) at [131], [2002] 2 Lloyd's Rep 182; appeals on other issues dismissed [2003] EWCA Civ 83, [2003] 1 Lloyd's Rep 239. The issue was whether this discharged

common law rules; questions over the money of payment, ie the currency in which a debt is dischargeable,[739] the date at which lay days begin to run,[740] the hours during which delivery may be tendered,[741] and the meaning to be attributed to the word "alongside" in a stipulation providing that the cargo is "to be taken from alongside the steamer".[742] In all of these examples what is really being talked about are the minor details of performance. These examples would doubtless be classified in the same way under the Convention, for they are entirely compatible with the examples of manner of performance given in the Giuliano and Lagarde Report.[743] The big difference between the Convention and the common law rules is in respect of the rule to be applied to the issue of manner of performance.

The question of substance This brings us on to the second question in relation to Article 10(2). What is a court supposed to do if it is faced with a matter of the manner of performance? The court does not have to apply the law of the country in which performance takes place. It is merely required to have regard to that law. The court is thus given a discretion as to whether to apply that law or not, as it so chooses.[744] If it does apply that law it can do so in whole or in part. At common law there was no such discretion; if the issue was one relating to the mode and manner of performance, the law of the place of performance was applied.[745] It may well be that the English courts will do as they used to do and simply apply the law of the place of performance.[746] The adoption of a discretion under the Convention introduces new and unwelcome uncertainty into this area. Obvious questions are raised. How much regard is to be given to this law? What are to be the criteria for the exercise of the discretion? The only guidance given on this by the Working Group is a reference to the court doing justice between the parties. It is surprising to find a discretion, particularly one to be exercised on such a vague criterion, in a Convention which places such emphasis on achieving uniformity and certainty in the law. And unlike Article 7(1), which is the other provision in the Convention involving the exercise of a discretion, Contracting States are not given a power of reservation in relation to Article 10(2).

(c) **Within the limits of the powers conferred on the court by its procedural law, the consequences of breach, including the assessment of damages in so far as it is governed by rules of law[747]**

(i) What is encompassed within the concept of consequences of breach?

According to the Giuliano and Lagarde Report,[748] "the consequences of breach" encompasses such matters as the liability of the party to whom the breach is attributable, claims

---

the carrier's delivery obligations. See also *Import Export Metro Ltd v Compañía Sud Americana de Vapores SA* [2003] EWHC 11 (Comm) at [20], [2003] 1 All ER (Comm) 703.

[739] *Temperance and General Mount Albert Borough Council v Australasian Mutual Life Assurance Society* [1938] AC 224 at 241.

[740] *Norden Steamship Co v Dempsey* (1876) 1 CPD 654.

[741] Dicey, Morris and Collins, paras 32.194–32.200; and see *Robertson v Jackson* (1845) 2 CB 412.

[742] Mann (1937) 18 BYBIL 97, 108, citing *Pulgrave, Brown & Son Ltd v SS Turid* [1922] 1 AC 397.

[743] Cf Kaye, pp 301–303. For a not very convincing suggestion that manner of performance can include exchange control regulations which make payment illegal, see Diamond, op cit, at 296; discussed infra, p 760.

[744] The Giuliano and Lagarde Report, p 33.

[745] The 11th edn of this book (1987), pp 492–495.

[746] See, eg, *East West Corpn v DKBS 1912*, supra.

[747] Art 10(1)(c).

[748] At p 33.

to terminate the contract for breach, and any "requirement of service of notice on the party to assume his liability". There is also guidance to be found in the European Court of Justice's decision in *SPRL Arcado v SA Haviland*.[749] This case involved, inter alia, an action for damages for wrongful repudiation of an independent commercial agency agreement. A jurisdictional question arose, namely whether the proceedings related to a contract under Article 5(1) of the Brussels Convention. In deciding that they did, the Court of Justice was influenced by the fact that any choice of law problem in relation to this claim was regarded as being contractual according to Article 10 of the Rome Convention. It was said that this Article "governs the consequence of total or partial failure to comply with obligations arising under it and consequently the contractual liability of the party responsible for such breach".[750] Finally, a Dutch court,[751] discussing the Convention before it came into effect, has said that "the consequences of breach" must be construed widely and can therefore include strikes. The court ordered striking crew members of a Saudi Arabian ship lying at Rotterdam to return to work on the basis that the strike was unlawful under Philippines law, which was the expressly chosen applicable law. The issues raised by the case were held to fall within Article 10(1)(c). Arguably, the "consequences of breach" could also encompass the issue of whether specific performance is available as a remedy.[752]

(ii) Assessment of damages

Article 10(1)(c) provides that the consequences of breach include the issue of assessment of damages, but this is only in so far as the assessment is "governed by rules of law". This draws a distinction between circumstances when assessment of damages raises questions of fact and those when it raises questions of law. If the question in relation to assessment is only one of fact (eg a jury is to calculate the amount of damages), this is a matter purely for the court hearing the action and the applicable law under the Convention will not govern the issue. On the other hand, if the question raised is one of law (the Giuliano and Lagarde Report[753] gives as examples cases where the contract prescribes the amount of damages in cases of non-performance or there is an international convention fixing a limit to the right to compensation), then Article 10(1)(c) will apply. Under the English common law the assessment or quantification of damages is a procedural matter for the law of the forum,[754] whereas the questions of heads of damage available and of remoteness of damage are ones of substance for the applicable law. The effect of Article 10(1)(c) is therefore that English courts will now have to apply the law applicable to the contract to the issue of assessment of damages in so far as this raises questions of law.

(iii) The procedural limitation

The scope of Article 10(1)(c) is limited by its opening words: "within the limits of the powers conferred on the court by its procedural law". It has been suggested[755] that this

---

[749] Case 9/87 [1988] ECR 1539.

[750] At p 1555.

[751] *Buenaventura v Ocean Trade Co* [1984] ECC 183 at 186.

[752] But see the procedural limitation in relation to Art 10(1)(c), infra, pp 756–757; Lasok and Stone, p 370.

[753] At p 33.

[754] Supra, pp 98–100.

[755] See Morse's comments on Art 10(1)(c) in his annotations to the 1990 Act in Current Law Statutes; Plender, para 11.13.

would, for example, allow an English court to refuse to award damages in the form of periodical payments (as required by the foreign applicable law) on the basis that there is no procedural mechanism under English law for the award of damages in this form. It may also allow a let-out to an English court which is reluctant to grant specific performance, as required by a foreign applicable law.[756]

(d) The various ways of extinguishing obligations, and prescription and limitation of actions

This provision[757] brings together what are, to English eyes, two very different sorts of issue. The first of these is the various ways of extinguishing obligations, of which there is a wide variety: eg by performance; by bankruptcy; by legislation;[758] by a moratorium; by subsequent impossibility; by novation, ie by a new contract which substitutes an existing obligation for another obligation, as, for example, by changing debtors. Any choice of law problems that arise in relation to these situations are a matter for the applicable law under the Convention, including the provisions on severing the contract.

The second issue covered is prescription and limitation of actions, which is likewise subject to the applicable law as determined by the Convention. This provision was, in part, responsible for the changes in the English law on limitation of actions. At one time the matter of limitation was regarded under English law as being a procedural one for the law of the forum. However, as has been seen,[759] the Foreign Limitation Periods Act 1984 changed this rule by adopting the principle that the English court is to apply to the issue of limitation the law which governs the substantive issue according to the English choice of law rules. Thus, even before the Rome Convention came into force, the English law on limitation produced the same effect in contract cases as that now produced by Article 10(1)(d). However, it was an awareness of the latter provision which helped to lead to the 1984 Act.[760]

(e) The consequences of nullity of the contract

This provision,[761] which was added at a very late stage of the negotiation of the Rome Convention, was designed to make it clear that the issue of whether money paid under a void contract is recoverable is to be subject to the rules on the applicable law under the Convention.[762] In some Member States the consequences of nullity are regarded as being non-contractual in nature. Indeed, under English and Scots law the right to recover money paid under a void contract forms part of the law of restitution, not of contract.[763] Because of this, Contracting States were allowed to enter a reservation, reserving the right not to apply Article 10(1)(e). Accordingly, the United Kingdom has entered a reservation

---

[756] Lasok and Stone, p 370.
[757] Art 10(1)(d).
[758] See *Wight v Eckhardt Marine GmbH* [2003] UKPC 37, [2004] 1 AC 147—discussing the borderline between discharge by government act and expropriation.
[759] Supra, pp 80–82.
[760] See Law Com No 114 (1982), para 3.9.
[761] Art 10(1)(e).
[762] The Giuliano and Lagarde Report, p 33; North in *Contract Conflicts*, pp 16–17.
[763] For choice of law in relation to restitution, see infra, Chapter 19.

and section 2(2) of the 1990 Act provides that Article 10(1)(e) is not part of United Kingdom law.[764]

(f) Scope of the applicable law and the Rome I Regulation

The Regulation leaves the terms of Article 10 of the Convention largely unaltered.[765] Nonetheless, for the United Kingdom and other Member States that have entered a reservation in relation to Article 10(1)(e) the fact that this provision will be contained in a Regulation will alter things, since reservations are incompatible with a Regulation.

(v) The special problem in relation to illegality

Article 8[766] subjects illegality[767] to the normal rules under the Convention. Thus, a court will not enforce a contract which is illegal by the law applicable to the contract. This was equally true under the traditional common law rules.[768] One of the few ways open to United Kingdom courts for dealing with illegality by the law of a particular country[769] is to hold, in cases where there has been no choice by the parties, that the law of that country is the objectively applicable law under Article 4, and there is sufficient flexibility within this Article for the courts to reach this conclusion if they are so minded.

This still leaves the problem of the effect of illegality under a law which is not the law applicable to the contract. There are no special rules under the Convention to deal with this problem. This contrasts with the position under the traditional common law rules, under which there were special rules to deal with issues of illegality.[770] However, Article 7(1) (the discretion to apply the mandatory rules of a foreign country) is a general rule which is effective to deal with the issue of illegality by a foreign law and can be used for this purpose by those other Contracting States which have not excluded its application. In the absence of this provision in United Kingdom law, the only way to deal with the problem of the effect of illegality under a law which is not the applicable law is for English courts to use other rules in the Convention, in particular those contained in Article 10(2) (manner of performance), Article 7(2) (mandatory rules of the forum) and Article 16 (public policy). Four situations involving illegality, which have been much discussed under the common law rules, will now be examined to ascertain what the position is under the Convention.

(a) An agreement to break a foreign law

At common law such an agreement, even though subject to a foreign law, was probably against the English doctrine of public policy and the comity of nations, and was

---

[764] See the Lord Advocate, Hansard (HL) 12 December 1989, col 1271.

[765] See Art 12 of the Regulation. Art 12(1)(c) refers to the consequences of the "total or partial" breach "of obligations", rather than to the consequences of breach.

[766] Supra, pp 744–746.

[767] On what constitutes illegality see *Continental Enterprises Ltd v Shandong Zhucheng Foreign Trade Group Co* [2005] EWHC 92 (Comm) at [48]–[49].

[768] See *Kahler v Midland Bank Ltd* [1950] AC 24. See generally on illegality at common law, Hartley (2006) 319 Hague Recueil Ch XIV.

[769] For proof of foreign law in relation to illegality, see Fentiman, *Foreign Law in English Courts*, pp 137, 255–256.

[770] See the 11th edn of this book (1987) pp 482–489. See also Hartley (1997) 266 Hague Recueil 341 at 385–395, 401–403.

not enforceable. As has already been seen,[771] cases decided on this basis appear to fall more appropriately within Article 7(1) than within the public policy provision in Article 16. Nonetheless, because of the absence of the former provision in the United Kingdom, this type of case will have to be considered under Article 16.

(b) Illegality by the law of the foreign place of performance in cases where the applicable law is English law

This situation arose in the well-known case under the common law of *Ralli Bros v Cia Naviera Sota y Aznar*.[772] This case was concerned not with illegality from the outset of the contract but with the rather different situation of supervening illegality, ie the illegality in the place of performance only arose after the contract had been made. A simple example would be a contract, made in January, the performance of which is rendered illegal by a statute passed in June. The facts of the *Ralli* case were as follows:

> An English firm chartered a Spanish ship from a Spanish firm to carry jute from Calcutta to Barcelona at a freight of £50 per ton. At the time when payment had fallen due the Spanish government had issued a decree ordaining that freight on jute must not exceed a figure considerably lower than the contractual freight. Freight was tendered at the rate allowed by Spanish law but the receivers of the cargo refused to pay the excess amount.

An action was brought in England to recover freight at the contractual rate. The action failed. The vital point in the case was that the proper law of the contract was English law. The court, therefore, was bound to apply and did in fact apply the internal law, not the private international law, of England. The familiar English cases dealing with impossibility of performance were cited and SCRUTTON LJ summed up their effect on the instant facts in the following words: "Where a contract requires an act to be done in a foreign country, it is, in the absence of very special circumstances, an implied term of the continuing validity of such a provision that the act to be done in the foreign country shall not be illegal by the law of that State."[773]

The position under the Convention with regard to such a case would appear to be as follows. The normal rules for the determination of the applicable law would apply to the issue of illegality by virtue of Article 8. The applicable law was English. Under the English domestic law of contract's doctrine of frustration, an agreement to perform that which it later becomes illegal to perform is unenforceable.[774] The result in the case would therefore

---

[771] Supra, pp 742–743.

[772] [1920] 2 KB 287. For continuing use of the common law illegality principle in the context of restitution, see *Barros Mattos Junior v General Securities and Finance Ltd* [2004] EWHC 1188 (Ch), [2004] 2 Lloyd's Rep 475 and in the context of arbitration, see *Tamil Nadu Electricity Board v ST-CMS Electric Co Private Ltd* [2007] EWHC 1713 (Comm), [2007] 2 All ER (Comm) 701.

[773] The *Ralli* case, supra, at 304.

[774] See Cheshire, Fifoot and Furmston's *Law of Contract* (13th edn), p 583. If the performance takes place abroad, the domestic rule on frustration is then phrased in terms of illegality by the law of the foreign place of performance: *Bangladesh Export Import Co Ltd v Sucden Kerry SA* [1995] 2 Lloyd's Rep 1 at 5–6, CA. The Law Commission has declined to express a view on whether *Ralli Bros* was truly a case of frustration, Consultation Paper No 154 (1999): Illegal Transactions, para 1.15.

be the same under the Convention as under the common law rules it replaces, and the action to recover the freight would fail.[775]

(c) Illegality by the law of the foreign place of performance in cases where the applicable law is foreign

No case arose at common law which required the court to consider the effect of illegality at the foreign place of performance on a contract the proper law of which was the law of yet another foreign country; in other words, a case like the *Ralli* case, but now involving a foreign proper law under which there was no illegality. There have been frequent dicta attributing decisive effect to illegality by the law of the place of performance,[776] although it has been consistently argued in this book[777] that such an approach is contrary to principle, and not dictated by the authorities.

Turning to the Convention, there is no special rule dealing with illegality by the law of the place of performance and, on the above facts, there is no illegality under the foreign applicable law. When a foreign country makes conduct illegal this may well involve a foreign mandatory rule, within Article 7(1), which deals with the mandatory rules of a foreign country with which there is a close connection.[778] However, the exclusion of Article 7(1) from United Kingdom law means that the English courts have no discretion to apply such foreign rules.

If the issue is classified as one relating to the manner of performance under Article 10(2), then it may be appropriate to apply the law, including any rules on illegality, of the country in which performance takes place. The "manner of performance" is, however, a fairly narrow category[779] and it would not be possible to regard the *Ralli* case as one relating to this issue. It has, nevertheless, been suggested[780] that the concept of manner of performance could include the question of whether payment is illegal because of exchange control regulations; and if these regulations are contained in the law of the place of performance it would then be appropriate to apply that country's law under Article 10(2).

Consideration needs also to be given, in the context of illegality by the foreign law of the place of performance, to the public policy provision of Article 16. The first problem with its application in this context is that the suspect English common law rule whereby a contract will not be enforced if it is to be performed in a foreign country where its performance is illegal by the law of that country, seeks to uphold a foreign law and thus appears to fall outside the negative concept of public policy used in Article 16.[781] The second problem is whether a case involving illegality by the law of a foreign place of

---

[775] Hartley (1997) 266 Hague Recueil 341, 392.

[776] *Toprak v Finagrain* [1979] 2 Lloyd's Rep 98 at 114; *United City Merchants (Investments) Ltd v Royal Bank of Canada* [1982] QB 208 at 228; revsd by the House of Lords on other points [1983] 1 AC 168; *XAG v A Bank* [1983] 2 Lloyd's Rep 535 at 543; *Euro-Diam Ltd v Bathurst* [1990] 1 QB 1 at 15, affd by CA at 30; *Libyan Arab Foreign Bank v Bankers Trust Co* [1989] QB 728; *Apple Corps Ltd v Apple Computers Ltd* [1992] FSR 431 at 442. For an attempt to codify this rule see ALRC Rep No 58 (1998), Draft Bill, s 9(10).

[777] See the 11th edn of this book (1987), pp 486–488. See also Reynolds (1992) 109 LQR 553; Hill, para 14.4.42.

[778] The place of performance constitutes such a connection: the Giuliano and Lagarde Report, p 27.

[779] Supra, pp 754–755.

[780] Diamond, op cit, at 296.

[781] Supra, pp 741–743.

performance can be regarded as raising public policy considerations for the forum. There was a tendency in the more recent common law decisions discussing the principle of illegality by the law of the place of performance, to describe this principle as being rooted in the notion of not acting against the comity of nations.[782] It is, however, submitted that the comity of nations aspect is very much more important in cases where the parties, from the outset, set out to break a foreign law than it is in cases where the parties act in good faith, but find subsequently that performance becomes impossible because of a change in the law of the place of performance. The upshot is that it is very doubtful whether cases of illegality by the foreign law of the place of performance can be regarded as falling within Article 16.[783]

Can Article 7(2) be used? It cannot be seriously suggested that the suspect common law rule in relation to illegality by the law of the foreign place of performance is a domestic rule of English law.[784] It is a rule of private international law, and, as such, is implicitly abolished by the Rome Convention in all cases where the latter applies.

The Rome I Regulation

The position would be very different if the provisional conclusion of the Ministry of Justice is followed and the United Kingdom opts in to the Rome I Regulation. Under the Rome I Regulation, Article 9(3) allows a court of a Member State to give effect to the overriding mandatory provisions of the place of performance in so far as those provisions render performance of the contract unlawful.[785]

(d) Illegality by the law of the English place of performance in cases where the applicable law is foreign

At common law such a contract would not be enforced, and this situation provided an exception to the normal rules on the application of the proper law of the contract.[786] Under the Convention this situation will arguably involve a mandatory rule of the forum; if so, Article 7(2) will lead to the application of English law and the contract will be unenforceable. Even if not, Article 16 would lead to the same conclusion.

(vi) Set-off under the Rome I Regulation

The Rome I Regulation introduces a rule for set-off, which aims to make set-off easier whilst respecting the legitimate concerns of the person who did not take the initiative.[787]

---

[782] *Toprak v Finagrain* [1979] 2 Lloyd's Rep 98 at 107; affd by the Court of Appeal at 112, without mentioning this specific point; *United City Merchants (Investments) Ltd v Royal Bank of Canada* [1982] QB 208 at 228, 242, revsd by the House of Lords on other points [1983] AC 168; *Euro-Diam Ltd v Bathurst* [1987] 1 Lloyd's Rep 178 at 187. See also *Lemenda Trading Co Ltd v African Middle East Petroleum Co Ltd* [1988] QB 448 discussed supra, p 741, n 644. See generally Kincaid (1995) 8 Jo Contract Law 231, 239–240. For the application of Art 16 in cases involving the comity of nations, see supra, pp 741–742.

[783] Dicey, Morris and Collins, para 32-150; Kaye, p 260; Hill, para 14.4.42. Cf Leslie [1995] Jur Rev 477, 483.

[784] But see Kaye, pp 260–261. Cf the suggestion in respect of the common law public policy/comity of nations rule, supra, pp 742–743.

[785] See the discussion, supra, pp 740 and 743.

[786] Dicey and Morris, (11th edn), pp 1218–1219. At common law if there was no illegality by the law of the English place of performance, it mattered not that there was a breach of some other country's law: *Fox v Henderson Investment Fund Ltd* [1999] 2 Lloyd's Rep 303.

[787] The Explanatory Memorandum, p 9.

Article 17 provides that: "Where the right to set-off is not agreed by the parties, set-off shall be governed by the law applicable to the claim against which the right to set-off is asserted."[788] This will cover cases of statutory offsetting. Where the right to set-off is agreed by the parties (contractual set-off), the set-off is subject to the general rules in Articles 3 and 4.[789]

(g) Relationship with other provisions of Community law

Under the Rome Convention acts of the institutions of the European Communities, eg Community Regulations and Directives, and national laws implementing such acts,[790] laying down choice of law rules relating to contractual obligations, take precedence over the Convention.[791]

The Rome I Regulation is to the same effect. Article 23 provides that: "With the exception of Article 7, this Regulation shall not prejudice the application of provisions of Community law which, in relation to particular matters, lay down conflict-of-law rules relating to contractual obligations." This Article is closely modelled on a parallel provision under the Rome II Regulation on non-contractual obligations.[792] The opening words make it clear that the special choice of law rules for insurance contracts in Rome I take precedence over the existing choice of law rules contained in various European Community directives. Recital (40) of the Rome I Regulation follows the Rome II Regulation in explaining that the Rome I Regulation should not restrict the free movement of goods and services as regulated by the E-Commerce Directive.[793] The difficult relationship between that Directive and Rome II is examined below.[794] What is said there is equally true with regard to the relationship between the Directive and Rome I.

---

[788] Art 17 of the Regulation.

[789] The Explanatory Memorandum, p 9.

[790] See, eg, Reg 9 of the Unfair Terms in Consumer Contracts Regulations 1999; discussed supra, p 734.

[791] Art 20. See, eg, (EC) No Directive 1993/7 of 15 March 1993 on the return of cultural objects; Directive (EC) No 96/71 of the European Parliament and the Council of 16 December 1996 concerning the posting of workers in the framework of the provision of services OJ 1997 L 18/1. The original proposal for a Rome I Regulation explicitly acknowledged these as examples, see Art 22(a) and Annex I (the final version of the Regulation omits to do so). A number of Directives provide that, if the contract has a direct link to the territory of one or more Member States, Community law will apply, even if the parties have chosen the law of a third country. These should not be regarded as choice of law rules and therefore Art 20 will not apply. Examples are: the unfair terms in consumer contracts Directive (EC) No 1993/13 of 5 April 1993; Timeshare Directive (EC) No 1994/47 of 26 October 1994; Directive (EC) No 97/7 of 20 May 1997 on the protection of consumers in respect of distance contracts; Directive (EC) No 1999/44 of 25 May 1999 on the sale and guarantees of consumption goods; Directive No 2002/65 of 23 September 2002 on distance sales of financial services. However, Art 7 (mandatory rules), discussed supra, pp 728–738 and particularly at p 737 (mandatory rules in community legislation) will operate. See generally Knöfel (1998) 47 ICLQ 439; Jayme and Kohler (1995) 84 RCDIP 1. The Green Paper of 14 January 2003 on the conversion of the Rome Convention of 1980 into a community instrument and its modernisation Brussels, COM (2002) 654 final, pp 17–18 discusses the issue of the proliferation of Directives having an impact on the applicable law.

[792] Art 27 of Rome II, discussed infra, pp 856–857.

[793] Directive (Ec)No 2000/31 of 8 June 2000, OJ 2000 L178/1.

[794] Infra, p 857.

(h) Relationship with other conventions

Article 21 states that: "This Convention shall not prejudice the application of international conventions to which a Contracting State is, or becomes, a party." This provision has two effects. First, it makes it clear that existing conventions covering some of the same ground as the Rome Convention are preserved. The United Kingdom has entered into a number of such Conventions in relation to carriage.[795] Cases which fell within one of these Conventions were governed by the rules in the particular carriage Convention (once implemented by legislation) and not by the proper law of the contract.[796] The rules in these carriage Conventions will continue to apply, unaffected by the Rome Convention. Secondly, it allows Contracting States to enter into new conventions covering some of the same ground as the Rome Convention.[797]

The Rome I Regulation

Under the Rome I Regulation the position will be largely the same with regard to *existing* conventions. Article 25[798] adopts the wording in Rome II on non-contractual obligations[799] and provides that the Regulation will: "not prejudice the application of international conventions to which one or more Member States are parties at the time when this Regulation is adopted and which lay down conflict-of-laws rules relating to contractual obligations".[800] The original proposal for a Regulation went on to suggest an exception to this principle so that the Regulation would take precedence over two multilateral conventions that have been entered into by a number of Member States, namely the Hague Convention of 15 June 1955 on the law applicable to international sales of goods and the Hague Convention of 14 March 1978 on the law applicable to agency.[801] But this proposal was dropped. The final version of the Regulation therefore has no exception for these multilateral conventions. However, the Regulation does have an exception in respect of conventions concluded exclusively between two or more Member States. The Regulation takes precedence over such conventions in so far as they concern matters governed by the Regulation.[802]

However, the position with regard to *future* conventions will be very different under the Rome I Regulation from that under the Convention. Member States will no longer be able to enter into any multilateral conventions as from the date that the Regulation enters into force.[803] The Community, though, does have power to enter

---

[795] See the Law Commission Consultative Document (August 1974) on the preliminary draft Convention, pp 93–95; Dicey, Morris and Collins, paras 33R-249–33-262.

[796] *The Hollandia* [1983] 1 AC 565. See also *Kenya Railways v Antares Co Pte Ltd, The Antares (Nos 1 and 2)* [1987] 1 Lloyd's Rep 424.

[797] If a Contracting State wishes to do so, it must follow the consultation procedure set out in Arts 23 and 24.

[798] Rome I Regulation.

[799] Art 28 of Rome II; discusssed infra, pp 857–858. The only difference between the two provisions is that Rome I refers to contractual obligations and Rome II to non-contractual obligations.

[800] Art 25(1) of the Rome I Regulation. Art 26(1) of the Rome I Regulation imposes an obligation on Member States to notify the Commission of the list of such multilateral conventions to which they are a party.

[801] Art 23(2) of the original proposal for a Regulation.

[802] Art 25(2) of the Regulation.

[803] See the analogous position under the Brussels I Regulation, supra, p 214.

into international agreements.[804] Moreover, the EC Council can authorise Member States' accession to international conventions.[805] It is envisaged that Member States will be able to negotiate and conclude on their own behalf agreements with third countries "in individual and exceptional cases, concerning sectoral matters", containing provisions on the law applicable to contractual obligations.[806]

ADDENDUM ON THE ROME I REGULATION

In July 2008 the United Kingdom government expressed the wish to opt in to the Rome I Regulation, and sought the consent of the Council of the European Union and of the European Commission to the United Kingdom's participation. The Rome I Regulation has been published in the Official Journal, OJ 2008 L 177/6. The Regulation will apply from 17 December 2009, to contracts concluded after that date. The regulation is entitled Regulation (EC) No 593/2008 of the European Parliament and of the Council of 17 June 2008 on the law applicable to contractual obligations (Rome I).

---

[804] See the Opinion of the Court of Justice 1/03 Competence of the Community to conclude the new Lugano Convention [2006] ECR-I 1145 at [148].

[805] See, eg, Council Decision (EC) No 2002/762 of 19 September 2002 in relation to the Bunkers Convention, OJ 2002 L 256/7.

[806] Recital (42) of the Rome I Regulation, which also provides that the Commission will make a proposal to the European Parliament and the Council concerning the procedures and conditions for this, ibid.

Chapter 19

Non-Contractual Obligations

1. INTRODUCTION

English law has traditionally had separate choice of law rules for torts, restitution and equitable obligations. These rules have been largely replaced by Regulation ((EC) No 864/2007) on the law applicable to non-contractual obligations (Rome II). This chapter is primarily concerned with the Regulation but, before turning to examine this in detail, it is useful to say something about the problems involved in ascertaining the applicable law for non-contractual obligations and how English law solved these problems prior to the introduction of the Regulation.

(a) Torts

The problem of ascertaining the applicable law in the case of torts is scarcely less perplexing than that in the case of contract. The reasons for this are as follows. First, there is a variety of different connecting factors that can be raised by the facts of the case: the place where the tort was committed; the residence, habitual residence, domicile, or nationality of the parties; the place where the parties' relationship was centred. Secondly, in the situation where, for example, a wrongful act takes place in one country and the consequent injury in another, there is a serious definitional problem in determining the place where the tort was committed. Thirdly, a wide variety of tortious issues may arise. For example, there can be issues of capacity, vicarious liability, defences and immunities, damages, limitations on recovery, wrongful death, or intra-family immunities. Should the same law govern all of these issues? Furthermore, there are many different types of tort or delict, ranging from negligent driving, nuisance, defamation, and fraudulent misrepresentation, to infringement of intellectual property rights and torts involving ships or aircraft. Should the same rule apply, regardless of the type of tort involved? Fourthly, if a foreign tort law is to be applied, this could lead to liability being imposed for torts unknown to English law, such as invasion of privacy or unfair competition, torts which may reflect radically different views and protect radically different interests from those recognised under English law.[1] Fifthly, the question arises of whether the parties should be allowed to choose the law applicable to a tort, and if so, what safeguards are needed.

Since 1996 the English tort choice of law rules[2] have been a combination of common law and statutory rules.[3] These rules will continue to apply in relation to those torts (including invasion of privacy and defamation) falling outside the scope of Rome II.[4] The common law rules in respect of foreign torts are derived from *Phillips v Eyre*,[5] as modified by the House of Lords in *Chaplin v Boys*[6] and the Privy Council in *Red Sea Insurance Co Ltd*

---

[1] Briggs (1989) 105 LQR 359, 362.

[2] For the very different common law tort choice of law rules in Australia, Canada and the USA: see (for Australia) *John Pfeiffer Pty Ltd v Rogerson* (2002) 203 CLR 503; *Régie Nationale des Usines Renault SA v Zhang* [2002] HCA 10, (2003) 210 CLR 491; *Neilson v Overseas Projects Corpn of Victoria Ltd* [2005] HCA 54, (2005) 221 ALR; (for Canada) *Tolofson v Jensen* (1994) 120 DLR (4th) 289; (for the USA) the conflicts revolution, discussed supra, pp 27–35.

[3] See further the 13th edn of this book (1999), Chapter19; Dicey, Morris and Collins, Chapter 35.

[4] Infra, pp 868–872.

[5] (1870) LR 6 QB 1 at 18–19 (per WILLES J).

[6] [1971] AC 356.

v Bouygues SA.[7] There is a general rule of double actionability (ie there must be actionability by the law of the forum and the law of the place of the tort), with a flexible exception to this introduced by *Chaplin v Boys*, seemingly based on the concept of the most significant relationship. The exception has been applied in the situation where the parties are from the same country, this also being the forum,[8] and has been extended to enable a claimant to rely exclusively on the foreign law of the place where the tort was committed, even if his claim would not be actionable under the law of the forum. [9] Where a tort is alleged to have been committed in England, the English courts have always applied English law to such a claim.[10] It is doubtful whether the "flexibility" introduced by *Boys v Chaplin* would permit English law to be displaced in favour of the application of some more appropriate law.[11] The place where a tort is committed is to be determined by asking the following question: "where in substance did this cause of action arise?" [12] There is a considerable body of case law applying this test to particular torts.

Part III of the Private International Law (Miscellaneous Provisions) Act 1995 put tort choice of law rules largely on a statutory basis by abolishing these common law rules and by introducing new statutory rules. There is a general rule, which applies the law of the country in which the events constituting the tort or delict in question occur.[13] Where the elements of these events occur in different countries, there is a series of rules to identify the applicable law.[14] Thus, for example, for a cause of action in respect of personal injury the applicable law is that of the country where an individual sustained the injury.[15] There is also a displacement rule, which applies a flexible exception. [16] This provides that where it is substantially more appropriate for the applicable law for determining the issues arising in the case to be the law of some other country (than that provided for under the general rule), the general rule will be displaced and the law of that other country will apply.[17] There are no special rules for particular torts, with the exception of defamation,

---

[7] [1995] 1 AC 190.

[8] *Chaplin v Boys* [1971] AC 356 at 378 (per Lord HODSON), 389–393 (per Lord WILBERFORCE); *Church of Scientology of California v Metropolitan Police Comr* (1976) 120 Sol Jo 690; *Johnson v Coventry Churchill International Ltd* [1992] 3 All ER 14.

[9] The *Red Sea* case, supra, distinguished in *Ennstone Building Products Ltd v Stanger Ltd* [2002] EWCA Civ 916, [2002] 1 WLR 3059.

[10] See, eg, *Szalatnay-Stacho v Fink* [1947] KB 1.

[11] *Metall und Rohstoff AG v Donaldson Lufkin & Jenrette Inc* [1990] 1 QB 391, CA; overruled on a different point in *Lonrho plc v Fayed* [1992] 1 AC 448, HL. See also *Connelly v RTZ Corpn plc* [1999] CLC 533 at 545. However, the *Red Sea* case, supra, accepted that (with a tort committed abroad) English law could be displaced by a foreign law. Numerous cases proceed on the basis that there is no exception, without the point being raised by counsel. But on their facts, if there was an exception, it would not have applied anyway. See, eg, *Ennstone Building Products Ltd v Stanger Ltd* [2002] EWCA Civ 916 at [48], [2002] 1 WLR 3059; *King v Lewis* [2004] EWCA (Civ) 1329, [2005] IL Pr 16.

[12] *Metall und Rohstoff AG v Donaldson Lufkin & Jenrette Inc* [1990] 1 QB 391; overruled on a different point in *Lonrho plc v Fayed* [1992] 1 AC 448, HL.

[13] S 11(1).

[14] S 11(2).

[15] S 11(2)(a).

[16] S 12.

[17] For cases applying the displacement rule, see: *Edmunds v Simmonds* [2001] 1 WLR 1003 (both parties normally resident in England); *Dawson v Broughton*, 31 July 2007 (unreported), Manchester County Court (both parties English but settled in France, English law applied under displacement rule). For cases rejecting the application of the displacement rule see: *Roerig v Valiant Trawlers Ltd* [2002] EWCA Civ 21, [2002] 1 WLR 2304 (one party Dutch, the other English); *Harding v Wealands* [2004] EWCA Civ 1735, [2005] 1 WLR 1539; overruled by the House of Lords without discussion of this point, [2006] UKHL 32, [2007] 2 AC 1 (one party

which is excluded from the scope of Part III of the 1995 Act.[18] The common law rules therefore continue to apply in defamation cases. There are also no special rules for particular issues.[19] The choice of law rules in Part III apply equally to events occurring in England as they apply to events occurring abroad.[20] Overall the 1995 Act has the effect of getting rid of the idiosyncrasies of the common law and bringing English rules closer to those in other European countries.

(b) Restitution

The problem of ascertaining the applicable law in cases of restitution is arguably more difficult than in respect of other obligations. First, there is a problem of terminology. At the heart of restitution lies the principle of unjust enrichment, which is concerned with reversing a defendant's enrichment at the claimant's expense. There is a view among common lawyers that restitution and unjust enrichment cover the same area of law, restitution being the response to unjust enrichment.[21] Continental lawyers, though, whilst accepting a principle of unjustifiable enrichment, would also include within the ambit of restitution or quasi-contract the principle of *negotiorum gestio*.[22] Secondly, the English substantive law of restitution, although rapidly developing, is not as well developed as that of contract or tort. Moreover, it is an area where there is much, perhaps over-much, theoretical discussion of what comes within the ambit of restitution and, within this topic, what the different categories of restitution are. All of this raises particularly acute problems of characterisation in private international law. Thirdly, restitutionary claims can arise in an exceptionally wide variety of different situations: for example, where money has been paid under a void contract; or by way of a bribe; or where a person has voluntarily intervened to pay a debt. This raises an important question: should the same choice of law rule apply to all of these different situations? Fourthly, as in tort cases, the English courts may be faced with a restitutionary claim in respect of a cause of action that is unknown to English law, eg for *negotiorum gestio* (the voluntary bestowal of a benefit).[23] This raises the question whether the English courts should allow recovery in respect of such a cause of action.

It can be stated with some confidence that in English cases of unjust enrichment decided under the pre-Rome II Regulation law, the obligation to make restoration is governed by the proper law of the obligation.[24] Dicey, Morris and Collins identifies the proper law by means of three sub-rules, each one dealing with a different type of claim to restitution.[25]

---

a national of the state whose law applied under the general rule); *Regina (Al-Jedda) v Secretary of State for Defence* [2006] EWCA Civ 327, [2007] QB 621, affd [2007] UKHL 58 (a claim by a British citizen against the British government but the issue was the legality of detention in Iraq, whose law applied under the general rule).

[18] S 13, which defines defamation widely to include malicious falsehood.

[19] Though the displacement rule in s 12 of the 1995 Act is concerned with the issues arising in the case, on which see *Regina (Al-Jedda) v Secretary of State for Defence* [2006] EWCA Civ 327, [2007] QB 621, affd [2007] UKHL 58.

[20] S 9(6).

[21] Birks, *Introduction to the Law of Restitution*, pp 16–22; Burrows, *The Law of Restitution* (2nd edn), Chapter 1. See also the Restatement 2d, Conflict of Laws, para 221 comment a.

[22] Zweigert and Müller-Gindullis in Lipstein (ed), *International Encyclopedia of Comparative Law*, Vol III, Chapter 30.

[23] Infra, pp 831–832.

[24] Dicey, Morris and Collins, Chapter 34; the 13th edn of this book (1999), Chapter 20.

[25] Rule 230(2).

Thus it seems that, if the obligation arises in connection with a contract, its proper law is the law applicable to the contract. If it arises in connection with a transaction concerning an immovable (land), its proper law is the law of the country where the immovable is situated. If it arises in any other circumstances, its proper law is the law of the country where the enrichment occurs. Although there has been a tendency for the courts to apply these sub-rules,[26] some cases have preferred to adopt a flexible solution, according to which the closest and most real connection is identified in the light of the whole facts and circumstances, without the use of sub-rules.[27]

(c) Equitable obligations[28]

The forms of liability which may arise from a breach of an equitable obligation are very varied. Such breaches may give rise to liability not only under the law of trusts but also in contract or tort, under the law of restitution, under the law of property or in the context of succession. There is a basic problem regarding whether separate choice of law rules for equitable obligations are needed, at least for some equitable obligations, or whether such obligations should always be fitted within the existing well-recognised choice of law categories. The problem is particularly acute where there is an equitable obligation whose domestic classification is uncertain, an obvious example being breach of confidence. There is a further problem in that any attempt to use existing choice of law categories raises the obvious question: which of the existing categories should be used in a particular case?

Authority on these questions is sparse.[29] Academic opinion is divided on whether separate choice of law rules should be adopted for at least some equitable obligations.[30] The most appropriate separate choice of law rule would be the application of the proper law of the equitable obligation, this being "the legal system governing the relationship in terms of which general access was gained to the beneficiary's assets".[31] When it comes to deciding which of the existing categories of choice of law a case should fall within, it appears that, if an equitable claim is to disgorge an unjust enrichment, this will fall within the unjust enrichment choice of law rules.[32] As far as breach of confidence is concerned, there is authority for this falling within the unjust enrichment choice of law rules, even where there was no element of disgorgement.[33]

---

[26] See Dicey, Morris and Collins, paras 34-020–34-031.

[27] *Arab Monetary Fund v Hashim* [1996] 1 Lloyd's Rep 589 at 597, CA, following Evans J [1993] Lloyd's Rep 543 at 566; *Baring Bros & Co Ltd v Cunninghame District Council* [1997] CLC 108, (1996) The Times, 30 September.

[28] See, generally, Yeo (2004); Dicey, Morris and Collins, paras 34-033–34-041; the 13th edn of this book (1999), p 1044.

[29] There is some authority which tends to support the application of the law of the forum, *United States Surgical Co v Hospital Products International Pty Ltd* [1982] 2 NSWLR 766 at 796–799; *A-G (UK) v Heinemann Publishers Australia Pty Ltd* (1987) 75 ALR 353 at 414–415.

[30] Cf (in favour of separate equitable choice of law rules) Barnard [1992] CLJ 474; the 13th edn of this book (1999), p 1044 with (against separate rules) Clarkson and Hill, pp 228, and 246–247; Dicey, Morris and Collins, paras 34-033–34-041; Yeo (2004).

[31] Barnard, p 507. See also *Grupo Torras SA v Al-Sabah (No 5)* [2001] Lloyd's Rep Bank 36.

[32] See Dicey, Morris and Collins, paras 34-033–34-041.

[33] *Douglas v Hello! Ltd (No 3)* [2005] EWCA Civ 595 at 97, [2006] QB 125; discussed infra, p 792.

2. THE ROME II REGULATION[34]

(a) Preliminary remarks

As from 11 January 2009,[35] the Rome II Regulation (Regulation (EC) No 864/2007) on the law applicable to non-contractual obligations directly applies in all the European Community Member States,[36] with the exception of Denmark.[37] However, it may be that the European Community and Denmark will enter into an Agreement,[38] under which the provisions of the Regulation, with minor modifications, are applied by international law to the relations between the Community and Denmark.

(i) The history, legal basis and justification of the Regulation

(a) History of the Regulation

In 1972 the original six Member States of the European Community prepared a preliminary draft Convention on the Law Applicable to Contractual and Non-Contractual Obligations.[39] However, in 1978 attention focused on contractual obligations, culminating in the Rome Convention in 1980. After years, without any progress being made on the harmonisation of choice of law rules in relation to non-contractual obligations, this project was back on the agenda in 1996[40] and a working party was set up by the Council of the European Union.[41] A Green Paper was produced in 2002 with a preliminary draft proposal[42] and, after consultation on this,[43] there was a proposal for a Regulation in 2003 (the Proposal).[44] The European Parliament sought fifty-four amendments, some

---

[34] Regulation (EC) No 864/2007, OJ 2007 L 199/40. This chapter has been written on the assumption that the Regulation already applies.

[35] Art 32. Except for Art 29 (notification of international conventions entered into by Member States), which applies from 11 July 2008.

[36] The United Kingdom and Ireland "opted in" to the Regulation, in accordance with Art 3 of the Protocol on the position of the United Kingdom and Ireland annexed to the Treaty on European Union and to the Treaty establishing the European Community, see Recital (39). The United Kingdom Government's decision to opt in was criticised by the House of Lords EU Committee, HL Paper 66 (2004), paras 80–82. Cf the United Kingdom original position in relation to Rome I, supra, p 669.

[37] See Recital (40) of the Regulation and the Protocol on the position of Denmark (the Danish opt-out) annexed to the Treaty on European Union and to the Treaty establishing the European Community.

[38] Along the lines of the EC/Denmark Agreement in relation to the Brussels I Regulation, discussed supra, p 341.

[39] See the Law Commissions' Consultative Document of 1974. The provisions on non-contractual obligations are set out in Law Commission Working Paper No 87 (1984), Appendix.

[40] See the Council Resolution of 14 Oct 1996, OJ 1996 C 319/1.

[41] The European Group for Private International Law, a private body but whose project was financed by the Commission, adopted a Proposal for a European Convention on the law applicable to non-contractual obligations, which was sent to the Council's General Secretariat to assist the working party, see [1998] NILR 465.

[42] Criticised by Dickinson [2002] EBLR 369; Roebuck and Mason (2003) 9 CTLR 1.

[43] For a summary of the responses by the Directorate Justice and Home Affairs and the contributions themselves see http://europa.eu.int/comm/justice-home/unit/civil/consultation/contributions-en.htm. For the response of the United Kingdom government of October 2002, see http://www.lcd.gov.uk/consult/general/eurocom.htm.

[44] COM (2003) 427 final of 22 July 2003, OJ 2004 C 96/8. For United Kingdom reaction, see House of Lords, European Union Committee, 8th Report of Session 2003–4, HL Paper 66, published 7 April 2004; Carruthers and Crawford 2004 SLT 19, (2005) Edin LR 65 and 239; Fawcett, Harris and Bridge, paras 17.165–17.182, 19.98–19.100; Stone (2006), Chapters 14 and 15. For international reaction (Borchers, Glenn, Symeonides, Watt, Weintraub) see http://www.dianawallismep.org.uk/pages/rome2.html.The Hague Programme, adopted by the Council on 5 November 2004, OJ 2004 C 53/1, called for work to be pursued actively on Rome II.

of major importance.[45] This led to an amended proposal from the Commission in 2006 (the Amended Proposal).[46] This accepted in whole or part some of the European Parliament's amendments but rejected others.[47] The Council adopted its common position in September 2006 (the Common Position).[48] The European Parliament proposed nineteen amendments to the Common Position.[49] The main issues at stake related to: violation of personality rights (including defamation); road traffic accidents; unfair competition; the definition of "environmental damage"; the relationship with other Community instruments; the treatment of foreign law; the review clause. The Council could not accept all of these amendments and recourse had to be had to the conciliation procedure, which produced the present Regulation. This was regarded as a satisfactory compromise by the relevant parties.[50] Three of the most contentious issues (namely: the choice of law rules that should apply to non-contractual obligations arising out of violations of privacy and rights relating to personality, including defamation; the position of cross-border victims of road traffic accidents; the way in which foreign law is treated in different Member States) were resolved by the Commission undertaking to produce reports on these issues as part of the process of review of the Regulation.[51] The Regulation was adopted in July 2007.

(b) The legal basis and justification of the Regulation

The legal basis for the Regulation is Title IV, in particular Article 61(c), of the Treaty on European Union, which authorises the adoption of measures[52] in the field of judicial co-operation in civil matters having cross-border implications as provided for in Article 65, which specifically mentions promoting the compatibility of the rules applicable in Member States concerning the conflict of laws[53] (ie the applicable law). Such measures are authorised "in so far as necessary for the proper functioning of the internal market".[54] Such measures fall within the wider objective the Community has set itself[55] of establishing an area of freedom, security and justice, in which the free movement of persons is ensured.[56] Rome II is one of a number of measures[57] relating to judicial co-operation in civil matters. The Brussels I Regulation is another such measure.

Harmonisation of choice of law rules ensures that the same substantive national law applies, irrespective of the Member State in which the action is brought. Recital (6) of the

---

[45] See the European Parliament Report on the proposal A66-0211/2005 final of 27 June 2005 (the Wallis Report). This was at the first reading stage before the European Parliament.

[46] COM (2006) 83 final of 21 February 2006. See Crawford and Carruthers, paras 16.29–16.35.

[47] See the Explanatory Memorandum accompanying the Amended Proposal.

[48] Council's Common Position of 25 September, OJ 2006 C 289/68.

[49] This was at the second reading stage before the European Parliament, concluded on 18 January 2007.

[50] See the Report to the European Parliament of its delegation to the Conciliation Committee A6-0257/2007 of 28 June 2007, Explanatory Statement, at pp 6–9, recommending approval by the European Parliament at the third reading.

[51] See Art 30; discussed infra, p 858.

[52] In accordance with Art 67(5).

[53] Art 65(b).

[54] The EU Committee of the House of Lords concluded that the Commission had not shown a convincing case of necessity, HL Paper 66 (2004), para 184. See also Dickinson [2002] EBLR 369. It is possible that in future there will be challenges to Rome II on the basis of *vires* (lack of competence of the Community).

[55] See Art 2 of the Treaty on European Union.

[56] See Art 61(c) of the Treaty on European Union and the discussion in Chapter 1 supra, pp 12–15.

[57] For other measures see supra, pp 204–205.

Regulation states that the proper functioning of the internal market creates a need for this. It goes on to say that this is in order "to improve the predictability of the outcome of litigation, certainty as to the law applicable and the free movement of judgments". The first two of these advantages were used to justify the Rome Convention. As regards the third advantage, harmonisation of choice of law rules has been regarded for some time as facilitating the mutual recognition of judgments.[58] However, this line of argument is hard to understand since there is semi-automatic recognition and enforcement of judgments within the Community, regardless of the law applied in the judgment-granting Member State.[59] The justification for the Regulation given in terms of preventing distortions of competition between community litigants[60] is equally unconvincing.[61] No mention is made of the advantage to be gained from harmonisation of inhibiting the forum shopping that the Brussels I Regulation allows. This is surprising, given that this was used to justify the introduction of the Rome Convention.[62] The most convincing justification for Rome II is that it is an extension of the Brussels I Regulation (which deals with jurisdiction in relation to both contractual and non-contractual obligations) and the Rome Convention (which deals with the law applicable to contractual obligations).[63]

(ii) Interpretation

(a) Referrals to the Court of Justice

Article 68 of the Treaty on European Union authorises the Court of Justice to give preliminary rulings, under Article 234 of the Treaty, on the interpretation of acts of the institutions of the Community based on Title IV of the Treaty. This includes Rome II. It also includes the Brussels I Regulation. The two limitations under Article 68 on when a national court can request such a ruling have previously been examined in the context of jurisdiction under the Brussels I Regulation[64] and need not be repeated here.

(b) The principles and decisions laid down by the Court of Justice

Where the meaning of the Regulation is not referred to the Court of Justice, it should be determined in accordance with the principles laid down by, and any relevant decision of, that Court.[65] This means that the English courts should act in accordance with two different types of authority: first, any relevant decisions of the Court of Justice; secondly, the principles laid down by the Court of Justice.

If the Court of Justice has previously given a decision on the provision in issue, this must be followed. However, the provision which is in issue may not have been previously

---

[58] See the joint Commission and Council programme of measures for implementation of the principle of mutual recognition of decisions in civil and commercial matters adopted by the Council on 30 November 2000, OJ 2001 C 12/1.

[59] See the Brussels I Regulation, supra, Chapter 16. See HL Paper 66 (2004), paras 55–56, referring to the evidence of North and Fentiman.

[60] Recital (13).

[61] See HL Paper 66 (2004), paras 57–59, referring to the evidence of Collins.

[62] See the Giuliano and Lagarde Report (1980) OJ 1980 C 282/4–5.

[63] See the Explanatory Memorandum from the Commission, accompanying the Proposal for Rome II (hereinafter "the Explanatory Memorandum"), p 3. But cf Fentiman, Written Evidence, HL Report 66 (2004), 110.

[64] Supra, pp 206–207.

[65] This is the position in relation to the Brussels system, supra, pp 207–208, and Rome Convention, supra, pp 673–674.

discussed by the Court of Justice. In this situation, the English courts should act in accordance with the principles of interpretation previously laid down by the Court of Justice.

The Court of Justice is likely to apply the same general principles of interpretation to Rome II as it applies in relation to the Brussels I Regulation.[66] These are as follows.

(i) The meaning of a provision should be ascertained in the light of its purpose rather than by taking its literal meaning.

(ii) The terms used in the Convention/Regulation should be given an autonomous meaning, rather than by reference to national law. This is confirmed in relation to Rome II by its Recitals. These state that a number of concepts should be given an autonomous meaning[67] and also provide definitions for terms used to set out the scope of a number of choice of law rules.[68]

(iii) When deciding upon what the Community meaning should be, two factors should be considered: first, the objectives and scheme of the Convention/Regulation; secondly, the objectives of the provision in question and how they relate to other provisions in the Convention/Regulation. The same should apply in relation to the Rome II Regulation.

(iv) In ascertaining the meaning of concepts used in the Regulation, regard should be had to the meaning of cognate concepts to be found in the European Community Treaties or in secondary legislation.[69]

In the absence of decisions of the Court of Justice in relation to interpretation of Rome II, the English courts should apply the principles that the Court of Justice is likely to apply. This is what has happened, in the absence of decisions of the Court of Justice, in relation to interpretation of the Rome Convention.[70] However, unlike the Rome Convention, the Regulation does not set out a principle of uniform interpretation.[71]

(c) Aids to interpretation

(i) Recitals

Recourse can be had to the forty Recitals at the beginning of the Regulation. Although Rome II has fewer Articles than the Brussels I Regulation, it has considerably more Recitals than the latter. There has been a recent tendency to put in the Recitals, not just explanations but also a number of amplifications[72] and definitions[73] that could, and perhaps should, have gone in the text.

(ii) The Explanatory Memorandum

There is an Explanatory Memorandum from the Commission of the European Communities on the Proposal for a Rome II Regulation.[74] Both the Court of Justice and

---

[66] Supra, pp 207–208.
[67] Recital (11) (non-contractual obligations), Recital (30) (*culpa in contrahendo*).
[68] See Recitals (23), (24), (26).
[69] Case C-271/00 *Gemeente Steenbergen v Baten* [2002] ECR I-10489, [2003] 1 WLR 1996, at [43].
[70] Supra, p 674.
[71] Discussed supra, pp 674–675.
[72] See Recital (8).
[73] See Recitals (9), (10).
[74] COM (2003) 427 final of 22 July 2003, OJ 2004 C 96/8.

English courts have used the Explanatory Memorandum accompanying the Brussels I Regulation to interpret it.[75] The Explanatory Memorandum on the Proposal for Rome II is reasonably detailed and, although it just sets out the view of the Commission, this view sometimes merely repeats the comments in earlier expert reports, what can be described as earlier influences.

(iii) Earlier influences

The Regulation adopts a substantial number of the provisions in the preliminary draft Convention on the Law Applicable to Contractual and Non-Contractual Obligations of 1972.[76] This was accompanied by the Giuliano, Lagarde and Van Sasse Van Ysselt Report.[77] This acknowledged that the 1972 draft was in turn influenced by the Hague Convention on the law applicable to Traffic Accidents of 1971 and the Hague Convention on the law applicable to Products Liability of 1973. The former is accompanied by the Essen Report and the latter by the Von Mehren Report. In so far as provisions in Rome II can be traced back to these Hague Conventions and Reports,[78] the latter are relevant to the interpretation of the former. The 1972 draft was the subject of a Law Commission Consultative Document which contains interesting comment and criticism but does not set out the views of the two Law Commissions.

(iv) The Brussels I Regulation and the instruments dealing with the law applicable to contractual obligations

Recital (7) of Rome II says that the substantive scope and the provisions of the Regulation "should be consistent with the Brussels I Regulation and the instruments dealing with the law applicable to contractual obligations". The instruments referred to are the Rome Convention and, in due course, the Rome I Regulation.[79] At first sight, this could be read as simply an explanation that concepts and terminology used in Rome II have in some case been lifted from the Brussels I Regulation and the Rome Convention.[80] Some concepts have been lifted from the Brussels I Regulation, as interpreted by the Court of Justice.[81] However, Recital (7) has important implications for the interpretation of Rome II. The need for consistency means that borrowed concepts and terminology should be interpreted in the light of the meaning given to them, in the past and in the future, in these other instruments. Indeed, the need for consistency could in principle come into play even where there is no borrowed concept or terminology.

(v) The views of the European Parliament

The Regulation is significantly different in places from the Proposal because of amendments sought by the European Parliament. The history of the Regulation as it progressed through the European Parliament provides an invaluable insight into the thinking underlying these changes.

---

[75] For cases using the Explanatory Memorandum on the proposal for the Brussels I Regulation see supra, p 209.

[76] See Arts 15 and 17 of Rome II.

[77] Commission Doc XIV/408/72-E.

[78] See Arts 15 and 17 of Rome II.

[79] Supra, pp 669–670.

[80] See, eg, Art 14(2) of Rome II, which is virtually the same as Art 3(3) of the Rome Convention.

[81] See Art 4(1) of Rome II and its reference to direct damage and the discussion of Art 5(3) of the Brussels I Regulation, supra, pp 256–257.

(b) When does the Regulation apply?

The Regulation applies to matters coming within its scope, and it has universal application, ie it applies equally to cases having no connection with a European Community
State and to cases with such a connection. Before turning to examine in detail these two
aspects of the application of the Regulation, three general points need to be made. First,
the Regulation does not have retrospective effect. It only applies in a Member State to
events giving rise to damage which occur after its entry into force.[82] But when does the
Regulation enter into force? The obvious answer would be on the date of its application
(from 11 January 2009).[83] However, earlier versions of the Regulation show an intention
that the Regulation should be regarded as entering into force on the date of its adoption
(11 July 2007) and this should be taken as being the relevant date. The traditional English
statutory and common law rules[84] will continue to apply to events giving rise to damage
which occur before that date. Secondly, the Regulation does not prejudice the application of international conventions to which a Member State was a party at the date when
the Regulation was adopted.[85] Thirdly, the Regulation does not prejudice the application
of provisions of Community law which, in relation to particular matters, lay down
conflict of law (ie choice of law) rules relating to non-contractual obligations.[86]

(i) The scope of the Regulation

(a) Application, in situations involving a conflict of laws, to non-contractual obligations in civil and commercial matters

Article 1(1) states that "This Regulation shall apply, in situations involving a conflict of
laws, to non-contractual obligations in civil and commercial matters." There are three
separate requirements under this provision. First, the situation must involve a conflict of
laws. Secondly, there must be a non-contractual obligation. Thirdly, there must be a civil
and commercial matter.

(i) A conflict of laws

The situation must involve a "conflict of laws". The Regulation frequently uses this term.
Conflict of laws is a confusing term for common lawyers since it is used to cover not just
choice of law but also jurisdiction and the enforcement of foreign judgments. Moreover,
the Regulation does not use the same terminology as the Rome Convention, which refers
to a choice between the laws of different countries.[87] Nevertheless, the Regulation is
undoubtedly concerned only with the question of the applicable law, as its full title and
its contents makes clear. In other words it is concerned with situations involving a choice of
law, ie a choice between the laws of different countries. This is clear from the Explanatory
Memorandum, which explains that a conflict of laws situation was one where "there are

---

[82] Art 31
[83] Art 32.
[84] Supra, pp 766–769.
[85] Art 28, discussed infra, pp 857–858.
[86] Art 27, discussed infra, pp 856–857.
[87] See supra, pp 679–681. However, the Rome I Regulation replacing the Rome Convention follows Rome
II by referring to situations involving a conflict of laws, Art 1(1).

one or more elements that are alien to the domestic social life of a country that entail applying several systems of law".[88]

This brings out the point that there must be a foreign element, not a purely domestic situation. This idea is familiar to English lawyers. Under English private international law a choice of law problem exists whenever the court is faced with a dispute that contains a foreign element.[89] With a non-contractual dispute, typical examples of a foreign element are as follows: one of the parties to the tort is a foreign national or is habitually resident abroad; the harmful event or the damage occurred abroad. In such cases the foreign country has a claim to have its law applied, and the uniform rules in the Regulation are intended to apply.

The position is more difficult if the court is faced with a dispute involving a foreign element, but in respect of what is an essentially domestic non-contractual obligation. This can arise in two different types of case. The first is where, for example, there is a purely German tort, which is the subject of trial in England, subsequent to the defendant having moved his business to England after the tort was committed. The situation involves a foreign element in that one of the parties now carries on his business here. However, what is lacking is any relevant connection with a country other than Germany of the sort which would give that other country's law a claim to be applied. Nonetheless, it is desirable that such cases come within the Regulation.[90] The object of the Regulation of achieving harmonisation of choice of law rules for non-contractual obligations is most likely to be attained if the scope of the Regulation is given as wide an interpretation as possible. The above example should therefore be regarded as one involving a choice between the laws of different countries. The second type of case is where there is, for example, a purely English tort or unjust enrichment, but the parties have agreed that French law shall govern this non-contractual obligation. It is implicit from the terms of Article 14(2)[91] that the Regulation will apply in this situation.[92]

There is another problem which is less easily solved. This relates to the requirement that the foreign element must entail applying several different systems of law, in other words there must be a choice between different laws. Under English law, if foreign law is not pleaded or proved the court gives a decision according to English law.[93] The courts are free to apply this rule in relation to the Regulation because matters of evidence and procedure are excluded from its scope.[94] If the English court is going automatically to apply English law, it is arguable that there is no element of choice between different laws. However, the purpose of the Regulation is not going to be met if the English courts allow the parties to side-step the uniform rules contained therein by a simple omission to plead and prove foreign law. It would therefore be better if this sort of case was regarded as coming within the Regulation.[95]

---

[88] At p 8.
[89] Supra, p 4 et seq.
[90] See the parallel problem in contract cases, supra, pp 679–680.
[91] Discussed infra, p 840.
[92] See the parallel problem in contract cases, supra, pp 679–680.
[93] Supra, p 111 et seq.
[94] Art 1(3), see infra, p 786.
[95] There are problems then of whether the parties have made a choice of the applicable law, infra, p 839.

The Explanatory Memorandum refers to applying several *systems of law*. Nonetheless, the choice of law rules in the Regulation consistently refer to the application of the law of a *country*. It is clear therefore that, for the purposes of the scope of the Regulation, the choice must be between the laws of different *countries*. A country is defined under the Regulation in the normal private international law sense as a territorial unit with its own rules of law, in this case relating to non-contractual obligations.[96] A German court, for example, will have to apply English law, or Scottish, or Northern Ireland law under the Regulation, even though the United Kingdom is the Member State under the Regulation. Similarly, an English court will have to apply, for example, Ontario or New South Wales law under the Regulation. Indeed, the Regulation will apply to an inter-state dispute involving connections with the "countries" of California and New York, provided that trial takes place in a European Community Member State.

However, the Regulation makes it clear that it is for the United Kingdom to decide whether it wants to apply the rules in the Regulation to intra-United Kingdom disputes.[97] It is certainly not bound to do so,[98] but the obvious inconvenience of having a different regime for intra-United Kingdom non-contractual disputes from all other cases is likely to lead to legislation applying the Regulation to such disputes. This is what happened in relation to contract choice of law.[99] This will then mean that England, Scotland and Northern Ireland will be treated as separate countries for the purposes of the Regulation, even in intra-United Kingdom disputes.

(ii) Non-contractual obligations

The Regulation applies to "non-contractual obligations". This concept varies in meaning from one Member State to another and therefore for the purposes of the Regulation it should be given an autonomous definition.[100] However, the Regulation gives only very limited guidance on what this definition should be. Thus we are told that the choice of law rules in the Regulation should also cover non-contractual obligations arising out of strict liability[101] and that the Regulation also applies to non-contractual obligations that are likely to arise.[102]

Non-contractual The word "non-contractual" does not tell us expressly what obligations are covered. Rather, we are told what is not covered, namely "contractual obligations". Contractual obligations in any situation involving a choice between the laws of different countries fall within the scope of the Rome Convention. The meaning of "contractual obligations" has been examined in Chapter 18 and the reader is referred to the discussion there[103] for more detail on this.

The word "non-contractual" obligations literally covers *all obligations* which are not contractual. This encompasses not only tortious/delictual and restitutionary obligations but also equitable obligations. The Explanatory Memorandum confirms that the inclusion

---

[96] Art 25(1).
[97] See generally Carruthers and Crawford (2005) Edin LR 65, 70–76.
[98] Art 25(2). At the time of writing, no decision has been made on this.
[99] See s 2(3) of the Contracts (Applicable Law) Act 1990.
[100] Recital (11).
[101] Ibid.
[102] Art 2(2).
[103] Supra, pp 677–679.

of all obligations, except those expressly excluded under Article 1(2), is what is intended.[104] The text of the Regulation also supports this interpretation. The fact that it was thought necessary expressly to exclude from the scope of the Regulation non-contractual obligations arising out of wills and succession[105] suggests that, without this, they would have come within the Regulation.

Obligations There must be an "obligation". In private international law there is a fundamental distinction between property, which has its own choice of law rules, and obligations, to which separate choice of law rules apply.[106] The Regulation is only concerned with obligations and leaves choice of law for property untouched.[107] As will be seen, difficult questions arise as to whether a tort (within the meaning of Chapter II of the Regulation) or property classification should be adopted. Equally, the question can arise as to whether an unjust enrichment or property classification should be adopted.

Non-contractual obligations and the scope of the choice of law rules We must now examine the relationship between the scope of the Regulation (non-contractual obligations) and the scope of the separate choice of law rules contained in Chapters II and III of the Regulation. Chapter II is headed "Torts/Delicts". Its scope is limited to where there is "a non-contractual obligation arising out of a tort/delict". Chapter III is headed "Unjust enrichment, *negotiorum gestio* and *culpa in contrahendo*". Its scope is limited to where there is "a non-contractual obligation arising out of unjust enrichment, *negotiorum gestio* and *culpa in contrahendo*". At first sight it might be thought that these provisions on the scope of Chapters II and III cut back the width of the concept of "non-contractual obligations" so as to exclude equitable obligations. There is no mention of equitable obligations in Chapters II and III and no separate Chapter IV headed "equitable obligations". However, no separate mention of equitable obligations is necessary. "Torts/Delicts" should be regarded as a residual category that covers all non-contractual obligations other than those expressly excluded under Article 1(2) and those covered in Chapter III.[108] The scope of the Regulation should be consistent with Brussels I.[109] This interpretation is consistent with the residual nature of jurisdiction under Article 5(3) of the Brussels I Regulation. This examination of the scope of Chapters II and III enables us to define "non-contractual obligations" in a positive way. These are obligations arising out of tort/delict, unjust enrichment, *negotiorum gestio* or *culpa in contrahendo*. This link between non-contractual obligations and these four concepts is shown by the fact that Article 2, which "defines" non-contractual obligations, in fact defines damage which is a requirement in relation to the scope of torts/delicts under Chapter II, rather than non-contractual

---

[104] See the Explanatory Memorandum, p 8. See also HL Paper 66 (2004), para 9.

[105] Art 1(2)(b); discussed infra, p 782.

[106] See generally Yeo, *Choice of Law for Equitable Doctrines*, Chapter 5.

[107] The Regulation does, though, contain choice of law rules for subrogation (Art 19) and multiple liability (Art 20), which are best discussed infra, Chapter 30.

[108] The Proposal for a Regulation was worded differently, having one section for non-contractual obligations arising out of a tort or delict and another section for non-contractual obligations arising out of an act other than a tort or delict. This made it more obvious that an equitable obligation would be covered. However, the change in wording should not be regarded as being significant. Indeed, the original wording was adopted simply to avoid technical language, see the Explanatory Memorandum, pp 8 and 21.

[109] Recital (7).

obligations as such.[110] Moreover, once it has been decided that there is, for example, unjust enrichment it cannot be anything other than a non-contractual obligation. There is no such thing as, for example, a contract arising from unjust enrichment.

It will be necessary later on to examine the meaning of the four concepts of tort/delict, unjust enrichment, *negotiorum gestio* and *culpa in contrahendo*.[111] This is because there can be questions as to whether, for example, an obligation arises out of tort or contract, out of contract or unjust enrichment, out of tort or unjust enrichment.

Concurrent liability   In cases where there is concurrent liability in contract and tort, the position prior to the introduction of the Rome II Regulation was very favourable to the claimant. The claimant was, for choice of law purposes, free to frame the action in tort rather than contract.[112] Indeed, the position was the same as under English domestic law and the claimant had the option of framing his claim in contract, or tort, or both.[113] The introduction of the Rome II Regulation means that this needs rethinking. The analogy should be drawn with jurisdiction under Article 5(1) and (3) of the Brussels I Regulation[114] and the obligation should be classified as contractual or non-contractual but not both, so that there would be no question of the claimant being able to choose.[115] This leaves the question of how concurrent liability should be classified for the purposes of the Regulation. The first alternative is to say that where there is concurrent liability in contract and tort, the latter should also be regarded as being contractual and therefore cannot be tortious. An English court has adopted this contractual classification of concurrent liability for the purposes of jurisdiction.[116] However, this classification of concurrent liability for jurisdictional purposes is by no means certain[117] and this uncertainty will extend into the area of choice of law. The second, and better, alternative is to say that, whatever the position in relation to jurisdiction, a tortious classification should be adopted for the purposes of the Regulation. There is a strong argument in favour of this solution, namely that the terms of the Regulation fit in much better with a tortious classification of concurrent liability than a contractual one. The Regulation envisages that there can be a tortious obligation in the situation where the parties have a pre-existing contractual relationship[118] and that there can be a tortious obligation to which there is a contractual defence.[119] These situations, although not confined to instances of concurrent liability,[120] will commonly occur in that context. Whatever solution the English courts adopt obviously does

---

[110] Indeed, damage is defined as covering "any consequence arising out of tort/delict, unjust enrichment, *negotiorum gestio* or *culpa in contrahendo*".

[111] Infra, pp 790–794, pp 819–825, pp 831–832, pp 832–834.

[112] *Base Metal Trading Ltd v Shamurin*, supra, at [31]–[35]. See also Dicey, Morris and Collins, paras 32-025–32-026.

[113] The *Base Metal* case, supra, at [35]. See also Dicey, Morris and Collins, para 33-083. Cf Briggs [2003] LMCLQ 12 and the position in respect of jurisdiction under the Brussels I Regulation, supra, p 251. See generally on choice law and concurrent claims arising out of the international sale of goods, Fawcett, Harris and Bridge, Chapter 20.

[114] Supra, pp 251–252.

[115] This was advocated by Briggs even before the introduction of Rome II.

[116] See *Source Ltd v TUV Rheinland Holding AG* [1998] QB 54; discussed supra, p 251. According to *Source*, this would be unaffected by the fact that the claim was only brought in tort or only brought in contract.

[117] Supra, pp 251–252.

[118] Art 4(3), discussed infra, pp 799–802.

[119] Art 15(b), discussed infra, pp 842–843.

[120] See the discussion, infra, of claims in tort and contract which are not parallel ones.

not mean that other courts will follow suit. Until the Court of Justice provides an autonomous solution to the problem of concurrent liability under the Regulation there is every possibility of different classifications being adopted in different Member States.[121] There may be claims in tort and contract which do not involve concurrent liability because the claims are not parallel ones, being based on separate lines of argument.[122] In this situation, Rome II will apply in relation to the claim in tort. There may be claims in tort, contract and unjust enrichment;[123] in so far as these involve concurrent claims, the same principles will apply as in cases of the more common concurrent claims in tort and contract.

(iii) A civil and commercial matter

Rome II applies in civil and commercial matters,[124] irrespective of the nature of the court or tribunal seised.[125] The concept of civil and commercial matters has also been used to limit the scope of the Brussels I Regulation (and previously the Brussels Convention). It has been borrowed from Brussels I so as to achieve consistency between these two instruments.[126] The meaning of "civil and commercial matters" has been extensively explored by the Court of Justice and by national courts in the context of the Brussels system, and the reader is referred to that discussion for its meaning in the present context.[127] Article 1(1) also goes on to provide that the Regulation shall not apply, in particular, to revenue, customs or administrative matters or to the liability of the state for acts or omissions in the exercise of state authority ("*acta iure imperii*"). The first three of these specifically excluded matters are also specifically excluded from the scope of the Brussels I Regulation and have also been borrowed from that Regulation.[128] The meaning of these three concepts is familiar to us from that context. The fourth specifically excluded matter is "*acta iure imperii*". Recital (9) clarifies the meaning of *acta iure imperii* by stating that this phrase "should include claims against officials who act on behalf of the State and liability for acts of public authorities, including liability of publicly appointed office-holders". These are just examples of *acta iure imperii* and are not intended as a complete definition. *Acta iure imperii* is not specifically excluded from the scope of the Brussels I Regulation. However, there is Court of Justice authority suggesting that that such claims fall outside the scope of Brussels I.[129]

(b) Exclusions

Article 1(2) and (3) expressly excludes a wide variety of matters from the scope of the Regulation. These matters can be put into two categories. First and foremost, Article 1 excludes certain non-contractual obligations. Secondly, it excludes certain matters which

---

[121] See the Explanatory Memorandum, pp 12–13. The doctrine of secondary connection under Art 4 of the Regulation mitigates this problem, see infra, pp 799–803.

[122] See *Domicrest v Swiss Bank Corpn* [1999] QB 548; discussed supra, p 252.

[123] See Case 189/87 *Kalfelis v Schroder* [1988] ECR 5565; discussed supra, p 251.

[124] Art 1(1).

[125] Recital (8). Cf the Brussels I Regulation, where Art 1(1) makes this point, rather than a Recital.

[126] See Recital (7).

[127] Supra, pp 215–217.

[128] For the meaning of "revenue, customs or administrative matters", see the discussion of the scope of the Brussels I Regulation, supra, p 215.

[129] *Lechouritou v Germany* Case C-292/05 [2007] IL Pr 14; discussed supra, pp 216–217 and 509.

do not involve the law applicable to non-contractual obligations, namely evidence and procedure. Most of these exclusions are also exclusions from the scope of the Rome Convention. The Commission has asserted that, as exceptions, these exclusions should be interpreted strictly.[130]

(i) The exclusion of certain non-contractual obligations

The matters excluded from the scope of the Regulation, and the reasons for their exclusion, will now be examined. These are as follows:

(a) non-contractual obligations arising out of family relationships and relationships deemed by the law applicable to such relationships to have comparable effects including maintenance obligations[131]

Family relationships are defined as covering "parentage, marriage, affinity and collateral relatives".[132] There is a similar exclusion of family relationships under the Rome Convention.[133] The availability of a pre-existing relationship provision under which the law governing the pre-existing relationship may also govern the non-contractual obligation led some to argue that the family relationship exclusion should be removed from the Regulation. However, this would have meant application of the law governing the pre-existing relationship. There are no harmonised choice of law rules for determining the governing law for family relationships. This would mean that the non-contractual obligation would be governed by a different substantive domestic law depending on the forum and its choice of law rules for family relationships. In such circumstances it was thought better to keep the family relationship exclusion.[134]

The exclusion in Rome II goes further than that in the Rome Convention and extends to "relationships deemed by the law applicable to such relationships to have comparable effects". It is not clear how the law applicable to such relationships is to be identified. One would expect this to be done by the forum applying its choice of law rules. But Recital (10) states that the reference to relationships having comparable effects to family relationships "should be interpreted in accordance with the law of the Member State in which the court is seised". This suggests that the forum automatically applies its own substantive domestic law to determine this.[135] Non-contractual obligations arising out of family relationships, etc are said to include "maintenance obligations".[136] There is a Proposal for a European Community Regulation on, inter alia, the applicable law relating to maintenance obligations.[137]

Non-contractual obligations are seldom going *to arise out of* a family relationship. However, an example would be where there is an action for compensation for damage

---

[130] The Explanatory Memorandum, p 9; criticised by Briggs, Written Evidence, HL Report 66 (2004), 95.
[131] Art 1(2)(a).
[132] Recital (10) of the Regulation.
[133] Art 1(2)(b) of the Rome Convention, discussed supra, p 682.
[134] See the Explanatory Memorandum, p 8.
[135] It might be argued that "law" of the Member State seised refers not to its substantive domestic law but to its private international law. But see the exclusion of renvoi by Art 24, discussed infra, p 788.
[136] The exclusion of maintenance under the Rome Convention is not all-embracing, see supra, p 683.
[137] Proposal for a Council Regulation on jurisdiction, applicable law, recognition and enforcement of decisions and cooperation in matters relating to maintenance obligations COM (2005) 649 final; see infra, p 1074.

caused by the late payment of maintenance.[138] In contrast, an action by a wife, who has suffered personal injury, against her husband following his negligent driving does not *arise out of* their family relationship but out of his negligent driving. Accordingly, it is not excluded from the scope of the Regulation.

(b) non-contractual obligations arising out of matrimonial property regimes, property regimes of relationships deemed by the law applicable to such relationships to have comparable effects to marriage, and wills and succession[139]

This exclusion covers two rather different things: first, non-contractual obligations arising out of matrimonial property regimes (and comparable regimes); and secondly, non-contractual obligations arising out of wills and succession. The phrase "matrimonial property regimes" is not defined in Rome II. However, there is a Commission Green Paper on conflict of laws in matters concerning matrimonial property regimes,[140] which defines such regimes as "Matrimonial property rights of the spouses" and as "the sets of legal rules relating to the spouses' financial relationships resulting from their marriage, both with each other and with third parties, in particular their creditors".[141] The Brussels system and the Rome Convention, all of which pre-date Rome II, exclude "rights in property arising out of a matrimonial relationship".[142] It is not obvious what difference, if any, there is between "rights in property arising out of a matrimonial relationship" and "matrimonial property regimes". There is no need under Rome II to distinguish between non-contractual obligations arising out of matrimonial property regimes and those arising out of maintenance since, as has been seen, the latter are also excluded from the scope of the Regulation.

The exclusion covers not just matrimonial property regimes but also "property regimes of relationships deemed by the law applicable to such relationships to have comparable effects to marriage". The same problem of how the law applicable to such relationships is to be determined arises as with the exclusion under *(a)* above. The wording of Article 1(2)(b) suggests that this should be done by the forum applying its choice of law rules. Recital (10) provides that relationships having comparable effects to marriage "should be interpreted in accordance with the law of the Member State in which the court is seised". This suggests that the forum automatically applies its own substantive domestic law to determine this.[143]

The phrase "wills and succession" is to be found among the list of exclusions from the scope of the Brussels Convention and Brussels I Regulation;[144] and its meaning has been fully discussed in that context. "Wills and succession" are also excluded from the scope of the Rome Convention.[145] Most disputes in relation to wills and succession will not involve non-contractual obligations but are concerned with issues such as the validity of

---

[138] The Explanatory Memorandum, p 8.

[139] Art 1(2)(b).

[140] COM (2006) 400 final.

[141] Ibid, at p 2.

[142] Art 1(1) of the Brussels I Regulation, discussed supra, pp 218–219; Art 1(2)(b) of the Rome Convention, discussed supra, pp 682–683.

[143] It might be argued that "law" of the Member State seised refers not to its substantive domestic law but to its private international law. But see the exclusion of renvoi by Art 24, discussed infra, p 788.

[144] Art 1(1) of the Brussels I Regulation, discussed supra, pp 218–219.

[145] Art 1(2)(b) of the Rome Convention, discussed supra, pp 682–683.

the will. This provision makes it clear that, in the rare cases which involve non-contractual obligations, the Regulation will not apply.

(c) non-contractual obligations arising under bills of exchange, cheques and promissory notes and other negotiable instruments to the extent that the obligations under such other negotiable instruments arise out of their negotiable character[146]

The identical exclusion but in respect of contractual obligations is to be found in the Rome Convention.[147] The reason for the incorporation of the same exclusion in Rome II is the same as the reason for its incorporation in the Rome Convention, namely that "the Regulation is not the proper instrument for such obligations, that the Geneva Conventions of 7 June 1930 and 19 March 1931 regulate much of this matter and that these obligations are not dealt with uniformly in the Member States".[148] The exclusion applies to bills of exchange, cheques and promissory notes, each of which category is well known to English lawyers. It also applies to "other negotiable instruments to the extent that the obligations under such other negotiable instruments arise out of their negotiable character". The meaning of this phrase has already been examined in the context of the Rome Convention[149] and the reader is referred to what is said there on this.

(d) non-contractual obligations arising out of the law of companies and other bodies corporate or unincorporated regarding matters such as the creation, by registration or otherwise, legal capacity, internal organisation or winding up of companies and other bodies corporate or unincorporated, the personal liability of officers and members as such for the obligations of the company or body and the personal liability of auditors to a company or its members in the statutory audits of accounting documents[150]

This provision clarifies the point that, if non-contractual obligations arise in a company law context, they fall outside the scope of the Regulation. A very similarly worded exclusion is to be found in the Rome Convention.[151] But the Rome II exclusion gives an additional example of the matters with regard to the law of companies that the exclusion is concerned with, namely "the personal liability of auditors to a company or its members in the statutory audits of accounting documents". The latter would encompass an action for negligence brought by a company or a member[152] against the auditor of a company. The Proposal for a Rome II Regulation contained a much narrower and very specific exclusion which was confined to the personal liability of officers and members as such for the debts of a company and the personal liability of auditors, etc. It was explained in relation to the former that the question of the personal liability of officers could not be separated from the law governing companies (applicable to the company in connection with whose management the question of liability arose).[153] An example of where the exclusion would operate can be seen in a pre-Regulation case, where a claim was brought by a company against one of its directors based on a breach by the latter of his equitable

---

[146] Art 1(2)(c).
[147] Art 1(2)(c) of the Rome Convention, discussed supra, pp 683–684.
[148] The Explanatory Memorandum, p 9.
[149] Supra, pp 683–684.
[150] Art 1(2)(d).
[151] Supra, p 685.
[152] But an action by a buyer of a company against its auditors would not be excluded.
[153] The Explanatory Memorandum, p 9.

duty of care to the former.[154] That duty was held to have arisen only from the director's relationship with the company.[155] If it did not relate to the constitution of the company, it related to its internal management.[156] It was held that the equitable duty was governed by the law of the company's place of incorporation. Under the Regulation the non-contractual obligation (ie the equitable duty) should be regarded, as it is under English law, as arising out of the law of companies (being concerned with the internal organisation of the company) and, accordingly, outside the scope of the Regulation. The English court would apply its national private international law rules according to which the director's equitable duty to his company is governed by the law of the company's place of incorporation.

(e) non-contractual obligations arising out of the relations between the settlors, trustees and beneficiaries of a trust created voluntarily[157]

This exclusion is explained on the simple basis that "trusts are a sui generis institution" and that they are also excluded from the Rome Convention.[158] The latter contains a wider exclusion: first, it also excludes the constitution of trusts; secondly, the Rome Convention exclusion is not confined to trusts created voluntarily.[159] Thus non-contractual obligations arising out of the relations between trustees and beneficiaries of a constructive trust are not excluded from Rome II.

(f) non-contractual obligations arising out of nuclear damage[160]

This exclusion, which is not to be found in the Rome Convention, has been explained[161] by "the importance of the economic and State interests at stake and the Member States' contribution to measures to compensate for nuclear damage in the international scheme of liability" established by various international Conventions.[162]

(g) non-contractual obligations arising out of violations of privacy and rights relating to personality, including defamation[163]

This excludes two matters: violations of privacy and rights relating to personality. The latter includes defamation. As regards violations of privacy, many civil law countries have laws on invasion of privacy. There is no such cause of action under English law. However, English law has expanded the wrong of breach of confidence to cover cases involving misuse (by publication) of private information.[164] This protects one aspect of privacy.[165] These cases of misuse of private information borne out of non-contractual breach of

---

[154] *Base Metal Trading Ltd v Shamurin* [2004] EWCA Civ 1316, [2005] 1 WLR 1157.

[155] Ibid, at [56].

[156] Ibid.

[157] Art 1(2)(e).

[158] The Explanatory Memorandum, p 9.

[159] The Proposal for Rome II followed the Rome Convention in not confining the exclusion to trusts created voluntarily.

[160] Art 1(2)(f).

[161] The Explanatory Memorandum, p 9.

[162] Namely, the Paris Convention of 29 July 1960 and the Additional Convention of Brussels of 31 January 1963, the Vienna Convention of 21 May 1963, the Convention on Supplementary Compensation of 12 September 1997 and the Protocol of 21 September 1988.

[163] Art 1(2)(g).

[164] *Campbell v MGN Ltd* [2004] UKHL Ltd, [2002] 2 AC 457; *Douglas v Hello!* [2007] UKHL 21, [2008] 1 AC. Breach of confidence traditionally covers secret (ie confidential) information.

[165] *Campbell v MGN Ltd*, supra, at [15] (per Lord Nicholls); *Douglas v Hello!*, supra, at [255].

confidence would undoubtedly be regarded in civil law jurisdictions as instances of invasion of privacy or injury to rights of personality. Accordingly they should fall within this
exclusion.

Rights relating to personality goes much wider than defamation. Under Swiss law the
tort of injury to rights of personality encompasses the right to live, the right to physical
integrity, the right to move, to sexual freedom, to protection of one's body after death, the
right to marry, to have a family, rights related to the name, to one's image and voice, the
right to privacy, the right to one's honour.

A question arises of whether the exclusion of defamation can be avoided by re-labelling
the tort as unfair competition, which is within the scope of the Regulation. Under English
law, if a business rival disparages the business reputation of a competitor, recourse can be
had to the law of defamation. In some other countries the same act of disparagement
would allow recourse to the law of unfair competition. The terms "defamation" and
"unfair competition" should be defined for the purposes of the Regulation in the light of
their meaning in Member States generally. This would suggest that this act should be
regarded as one of unfair competition and hence within the Regulation. In some countries, there is a cause of action for loss of self-esteem, for bringing a president or the government into disrepute by undermining public confidence in its capacity to govern, and
for insult. With these three causes of action there may be liability under the foreign law
even though the statement is true. This appears to be so far removed from the idea
of defamation that these causes of action should not be classified as defamation for the
purposes of the defamation exclusion.[166]

The Proposal for a Regulation did not exclude violations of privacy and rights relating to
personality. However, it was recognised that there were constitutional concerns over violation of freedom of the press and that the normal tort choice of law rules set out in the
Regulation could not apply on their own.[167] A special choice of law rule was therefore
proposed which made it explicit that the law designated under the normal tort choice of
law rules must be disapplied in favour of the law of the forum if it was incompatible with
the public policy of the forum in relation to freedom of the press.[168] The European
Parliament wanted a different rule[169] and sought amendments, which were unacceptable
to the Commission as being too favourable to editors. The European Parliament withdrew its amendments on the inclusion of these rules as part of the overall compromise on
the Regulation. These matters were regarded as being left over to be dealt with in the
future. The Commission is required by 31 December 2008 to produce a study on the

---

[166] It was suggested that these causes of action did not constitute defamation for the purposes of the defamation exclusion under the English statutory tort choice of law rules, see the 13th edn of this book (1999),
pp 654–656, but cf Dicey, Morris and Collins, pp 35–128. Under the Regulation, recourse should be had to
the public policy exception to prevent the claimant recovering under such foreign causes of action, see infra,
pp 851–855.

[167] See the Explanatory Memorandum, p 18. This rule was dropped in the amended Proposal.

[168] See Art 6(1) of the Proposal for a Regulation; the Explanatory Memorandum, pp 17–18. A special provision was also needed on the law governing the right of reply, see Art 6(2) of the Proposal for a Regulation.

[169] As did the House of Lords EU Committee, see HL Paper 66 (2004), para 130, which wanted a country of
origin rule.

situation where a non-contractual obligation arises out of violations of privacy and rights relating to personality, including defamation.[170]

(ii) Evidence and procedure, without prejudice to Articles 21 and 22[171]

Article 1(3) provides that the Regulation "shall not apply to evidence and procedure, without prejudice to Articles 21 and 22". The same exclusion is to be found in the Rome Convention.[172] Strictly speaking it was not necessary to expressly exclude evidence and procedure,[173] since these matters would not appear to come within the scope of a Regulation which is concerned with the law applicable to non-contractual obligations (a matter of substance). Presumably, this express exclusion is just for the sake of clarity. Article 1(3) excludes two matters, evidence and procedure.

Evidence   The exclusion of evidence is not total, but is subject to Article 21,[174] which contains a rule on the formal validity of a unilateral act intended to have legal effect and relating to a non-contractual obligation, and Article 22,[175] which subjects two specific evidential matters, rules which raise presumptions of law or determine the burden of proof and proving acts intended to have legal effect, to the rules of the Regulation.

Procedure   When it comes to procedure there is the vital question of when a matter is to be classified as being one of procedure, rather than one of substance. Procedure is a very different matter from the other matters excluded in that it involves a potential escape device, ie if you classify a matter as being purely procedural you escape from the choice of law rules under the Regulation. In the absence of guidance from the Court of Justice, national courts are likely to resort to their own traditional ideas of what is a procedural matter. However, English courts cannot automatically assume that the classifications which they have adopted in the past will continue to be appropriate under the Regulation. The concept of procedure should be given a community definition. The English courts should pay regard to the classification commonly adopted in other Member States, thereby avoiding the danger of adopting a different classification from that used in other Member States.

The terms of the Regulation sometimes make it clear that a different classification should be adopted from that under English law. Two examples can be given to illustrate this. The first example is concerned with damages. The issue of assessment or quantification of damages was classified at common law as being one of procedure, whereas the issue of heads of liability for which damages could be recovered was one of substance.[176] The position was

---

[170] The study must take into account rules relating to freedom of the press and freedom of expression in the media, and conflict of laws issues relating to Directive (EC) No 95/46 of the European Parliament and of the Council of 24 October 1995 on the protection of individuals with regard to the processing of personal data and on the free movement of such data.

[171] Art 1(3).

[172] Art 1(2)(h) of the Rome Convention; discussed supra, p 687.

[173] And the Proposal for a Regulation did not do so, see the Explanatory Memorandum accompanying the Proposal, p 9.

[174] Discussed infra, p 856.

[175] Discussed supra, p 89. This is lifted from Art 14 of the Rome Convention.

[176] Supra, pp 97–100. Contributory negligence, which may reduce damages under the law of some countries, was regarded as being substantive: *Dawson v Broughton*, 31 July 2007 (unreported), Manchester County Court. Contributory negligence falls clearly within the scope of the choice of law rules under the Rome II Regulation, see Art 15(b), discussed infra, pp 842–843.

the same under the statutory tort choice of law rules. In that context, it was held that the issue of whether accrued benefits (state benefits, employment pension, personal pension) had to be deducted when assessing damages was a procedural one.[177] Similarly, a statutory ceiling on damages was held to be a matter of assessment of damages and therefore procedural.[178] However, under the Regulation it is expressly stated that the issue of assessment of damage falls within the scope of the law applicable under the Regulation.[179] This follows the classification adopted in most civil law jurisdictions. It is suggested below[180] that this issue only falls within the scope of the rules on the applicable law in so far as assessment is prescribed by a rule of law. Rules on the deduction of accrued benefits and a statutory ceiling on damages are undeniably rules of law, and so for the purposes of the Regulation, the application of these rules is a matter for the rules on the applicable law and not a procedural matter.

The second example is that of the issue of limitation of liability. In the past, this been classified as procedural.[181] Again, under the Regulation it is expressly stated that this issue falls within the scope of the law applicable under the Regulation.[182]

Once it has been decided that the issue is one of evidence or procedure, the effect of the exclusion is that this issue is left to be governed by the forum's rules on private international law. Under English private international law all procedural matters (including evidence) are automatically a matter for the law of the forum.[183]

(ii) The universal application of the Regulation

The Rome II Regulation is intended to be of universal or world-wide application, ie it applies, regardless of whether the situation giving rise to the non-contractual obligation and the obligation itself has any connection with a European Community Member State. In particular, there is no need for either party to the dispute to be domiciled or resident in a Member State. The only thing that matters is that the dispute is tried in a Member State. Thus a tortious dispute between a New York resident and an Ontario resident which is tried before the High Court in England will be subject to the Regulation.

Article 3 provides that: "Any law specified by this Regulation shall be applied whether or not it is the law of a Member State." This provision makes it clear that, if the uniform rules under the Regulation point, for example, to Russian law as the law governing the non-contractual obligation, the courts of Member States will apply that country's law, even though Russia is not a European Community Member State. However, Article 3

---

[177] *Roerig v Valiant Trawlers* [2002] EWCA Civ 21, [2002] 1 WLR 2304. See also *Edmunds v Simmonds* [2001] 1 WLR 1003.

[178] *Harding v Wealands* [2006] UKHL 32, [2007] 2 AC 1; following *Stevens v Head* (1993) 176 CLR 433, HC of Australia. Cf *McNeilly v Imbree* [2007] NSWCA 156.

[179] Art 15(c); discussed infra, pp 843–846.

[180] Infra, pp 844–846.

[181] *Caltex Singapore Pte Ltd and Ors v BP Shipping Ltd* [1996] 1 Lloyd's Rep 86, concerned with limitation of liability in maritime cases under the Merchant Shipping Act 1995; approved in *Harding v Wealands*, supra, at [47] (per Lord HOFFMANN, [2] (per Lord WOOLF), [78] (per Lord RODGER), [79] (per Lord CARSWELL). See also *Seismic Shipping Inc v Total E & P UK plc (The Western Regent)* [2005] EWCA Civ 985 at [52], [2005] 2 Lloyd's Rep 359.

[182] Art 15(b), discussed infra, pp 842–843.

[183] Supra, pp 75–76.

only deals with one aspect of the universal application of the rules in the Convention. It says nothing about whether the situation giving rise to the non-contractual obligation, including the residence of the parties, must have a connection with a Member State. It is the Explanatory Memorandum[184] which makes it clear that the Regulation is intended to have universal application and will apply to situations giving rise to a non-contractual obligation which have no connection with a Member State. This principle of universal application is well established and is also to be found in the Rome Convention[185] and in the Brussels I Regulation (in the sense that that Regulation governs both purely "intra-Community" situations and situations involving a non-Member State).[186] It avoids the need to distinguish for choice of law purposes between intra-Community cases and extra-Community cases, a distinction which is both highly artificial and difficult to draw.[187] It also avoids the complexity of Member States having two sets of choice of law rules and the distortions in competition that would result if Member States applied their own national choice of law rules to extra-Community cases.[188]

(c) The applicable law: preliminary remarks

At the heart of the Regulation lie the rules on the applicable law. There are separate sets of rules for torts/delicts (in Chapter II) and unjust enrichment, *negotiorum gestio* and *culpa in contrahendo* (collectively referred to as unjust enrichment, etc) (in Chapter III). There is then a series of rules (in Chapter IV) allowing the parties to submit non-contractual obligations to the law of their choice.

(i) Exclusion of renvoi

The applicable law under the Regulation, whether chosen or not, refers to the domestic law of the country in question, and there is no place for application of that country's rules of private international law under the doctrine of renvoi.[189]

(ii) Definition of habitual residence

A number of the rules on the applicable law, in the absence of choice, provide for the application of the law of the country of the parties' habitual residence. The Regulation defines the habitual residence of companies but, apart from in one specific situation, not that of natural persons (ie individuals). This approach is broadly consistent with the defining of domicile for the purposes of the Brussels I Regulation. Article 23(1) of Rome II simply provides that "For the purposes of this Regulation, the habitual residence of companies and other bodies, corporate or unincorporated, shall be the place of central administration." The term "central administration" is used to define the domicile of companies under the Brussels I Regulation.[190] The same autonomous Community

---

184 At pp 9–10.
185 Supra, p 689.
186 Supra, p 214.
187 The Explanatory Memorandum, p 10.
188 Ibid.
189 Art 24. The position is the same for contract choice of law under the Rome Convention, supra, p 689.
190 Under Art 60 of the Brussels I Regulation domicile is defined in terms of three alternatives and so a company can be domiciled in three different states; this would not work for choice of law purposes hence the use of habitual residence as the connecting factor, rather than domicile.

meaning should be given to the concept in both contexts.[191] The place of central administration rule is qualified by a special rule in Article 23(1) to deal with the situation where the event giving rise to the damage occurs, or the damage arises, in the course of operation of a branch, agency or other establishment. In this situation, the place where the branch, etc is located is treated as the place of habitual residence of the company. The same meaning should be given to "branch, agency or other establishment" in the present context as has been given to it by the Court of Justice for the purposes of Article 5(5) of the Brussels Convention (Brussels I Regulation). The Court of Justice has also defined the concept of "a dispute arising out of the operations of a branch", etc for the purposes of Article 5(5). The requirement under Article 23(1) that the event or damage arises "in the course of operation of a branch", etc looks to be in substance the same, so that recourse can again be had to the case law under Article 5(5).

The one situation where Article 23 defines the meaning of the habitual residence of a natural person is where such a person is "acting in the course of his or business activity". In this situation, the habitual residence of the natural person is his or her principal place of business. The term "principal place of business" is used to define the domicile of companies under the Brussels I Regulation. The same autonomous Community meaning should be given to the concept in both contexts.[192] In all other situations, the English courts will have to have recourse to the meaning of habitual residence attributed to it under English law. In due course, it is to be hoped that there will be guidance from the Court of Justice on the meaning of the habitual residence of a natural person in the present context, as there has been in the context of income support for employed persons.[193] In the meantime, any guidance on the meaning of the concept from that Court in other contexts[194] should be borne in mind.

(iii) Definition of damage

Many of the choice of law rules use the concept of damage. Damage covers any consequence arising out of tort/delict, unjust enrichment, *negotiorum gestio* or *culpa in contrahendo*[195] and also damage that is likely to occur.[196]

(iv) Proof of foreign law

The normal English rules on proof of foreign law apply in relation to the Regulation. However, it is an open question how long this will remain the case. Different practices are followed in different Member States in relation to the treatment of foreign law.[197] The European Parliament unsuccessfully sought an amendment to the Regulation that would have required the court seised to establish the content of the foreign law of its own

---

[191] For the meaning given to the concept in the context of the Brussels I Regulation, see supra, p 212.

[192] For the meaning given to the concept in the context of the Brussels I Regulation, see supra, p 212.

[193] Case C-90/97 *Swaddling v Adjudication Officer* [1999] ECR I-1075; discussed supra, p 187.

[194] Guidance may also arise in the context of Council Regulation (EC) No 2201/2003 of 27 November 2003 concerning jurisdiction and the recognition and enforcement of judgments in matrimonial matters and the matters of parental responsibility, known as Brussels II *bis*; discussed infra, pp 945–949.

[195] Art 2(1).

[196] Art 2(3)(b).

[197] See supra, pp 111–115.

motion[198] so as to ensure a more uniform approach to the application of foreign law by courts throughout the European Union. The European Parliament dropped this amendment as part of the overall compromise on the Regulation. The matter was settled by the Commission undertaking to produce a study on the effects of the way in which foreign law is treated in the different jurisdictions and on the extent to which courts in the Member States apply foreign law in practice pursuant to the Rome II Regulation.[199] The Commission has made a statement which suggests that the study will not be confined to just the application of foreign law in Rome II cases but more generally in civil and commercial matters.[200] This study will be included in a more general report on the application of the Regulation, accompanied, if necessary, by proposals to adapt the Regulation.[201] This report must be submitted by 20 August 2011.

(d) The applicable law for torts/delicts

(i) The scope of Chapter II

Chapter II is headed "Torts/Delicts". A process of characterisation has to be gone through to determine whether an obligation arises out of: tort/delict; unjust enrichment, *negotiorum gestio* or *culpa in contrahendo*; or contract. If the obligation arises out of tort/delict it is a non-contractual obligation that falls within Chapter II. If the obligation arises out of unjust enrichment, *negotiorum gestio* or *culpa in contrahendo* tort/delict it is a non-contractual obligation that falls within Chapter III. If the obligation arises out of contract it is a contractual obligation and falls outside the scope of the Regulation altogether.

How is this process of characterisation to be carried out? If English judges apply the same approach as they have applied in relation to the Rome Convention, this would be according to English principles of characterisation.[202] However, the process of characterisation should be guided by the subject matter and wording of the Regulation itself. Moreover, this is subject to the implicit instruction in Recital (7) of the Regulation that "torts/delicts", being concerned with scope, should be interpreted in a way that is consistent with the meaning attached to this concept under Article 5(3) of the Brussels I Regulation (matters relating to tort, delict or quasi-delict). Article 5(3) goes wider than tort/delict in that it also covers quasi-delict. But quasi-delict is what is referred to in some Member States as quasi-contract (or restitution). Under Rome II quasi-delict or restitution law is dealt with in Chapter III. This means that there is a true analogy between the tort/delict part of Article 5(3) and torts/delicts under Chapter II of Rome II. Applying these principles we can examine what is covered by "torts/delicts" and what is not covered.

(a) What is covered

It will be recalled that "matters relating to tort, delict or quasi-delict" under Article 5(3) has been widely interpreted by the Court of Justice to cover all actions which seek to

---

[198] See EP Report A6-0211/2005 of 27 June 2005 (the Wallis Report), Amendment 43, Art 11 b (new), para 1. According to para 2 of this proposal, if it is impossible to establish the content of the foreign law and the parties agree, the law of the court seised shall be applied. But what if they do not agree?

[199] Art 30(1)(i).

[200] See, attached to the Regulation, the Commission statement on the treatment of foreign law.

[201] Art 30(1).

[202] Supra, p 677.

establish the liability of a defendant and which are not related to a contract within Article 5(1) of that Regulation.[203] This definition covers matters which are tortious according to the domestic substantive law of Member States. Thus it has been held to cover negligence, conversion, negligent misstatement, negligent and fraudulent misrepresentation.[204] But Article 5(3) goes beyond this. It is a residual category which covers matters which are not in a strict sense tortious, ie they are not classified as tortious under domestic substantive law. For example, Article 5(3) has been held by an English court to cover a constructive trust claim based on dishonestly assisting a breach of fiduciary duty[205] and has been assumed to cover a claim for breach of fiduciary duty.[206] In both cases, under English substantive law what is involved is a breach of an equitable obligation.

Torts/delicts for the purposes of Chapter II should also cover negligence and negligent misstatement, unless the misstatement is made during dealings prior to the conclusion of a contract.[207] We know from the terms of the Regulation that the concept of torts/delicts encompasses product liability; unfair competition; acts restricting free competition; environmental damage; infringement of intellectual property rights; industrial action. This is because there are separate specific rules for all of these in Articles 5 to 9 of Chapter II.

Torts/delicts for the purposes of Chapter II should be regarded as a residual category, as it is in jurisdictional cases. In principle therefore it should be capable of covering equitable obligations, including breach of a fiduciary duty and dishonestly procuring or assisting a breach of fiduciary duty.[208] On this basis, non-contractual breach of confidence, when it is concerned with protecting secret information,[209] should also come within Chapter II.[210] However, the position with equitable obligations is complicated by the fact that it can be argued that such obligations should fall within the category of unjust enrichment and, accordingly, within Chapter III.[211] Where a breach of an equitable obligation gives rise to liability under the law of trusts this will often come within the Hague Convention on the Law Applicable to Trusts and on their Recognition 1986, and recourse must then be had to the choice of law rules in that Convention,[212] rather than those in the Regulation.[213]

Tort/delict for the purpose of Chapter II is a narrower residual category than Article 5(3) of the Brussels I Regulation in that Chapter II does not include unjust enrichment,

---

[203] Supra, pp 247–248.

[204] Supra, p 247.

[205] *Casio Computer Co Ltd v Sayo* [2001] IL PR 164, CA; discussed supra, p 250.

[206] *Benatti v WPP Holdings Italy SRL* [2007] EWCA Civ 263 at [58] (per TOULSON LJ), [2007] 1 WLR 2316.

[207] This would constitute *culpa in contrahendo*, discussed infra, pp 832–834.

[208] See Yeo, para 8.58.

[209] When it is concerned with protecting privacy it is submitted that it is excluded from the scope of the Regulation, supra, pp 784–786.

[210] Usually this will be within Art 4 but for the purposes of the Regulation targeting a competitor by the disclosure of business secrets, which would be regarded under English law as a breach of confidence, should be regarded as an act of unfair competition within Art 6, see infra, p 809. In *Kitechnology BV and Ors v Unicor GMBH Plastmaschinen and Ors* [1994] IL Pr 568, the Court of Appeal found it impossible to express a concluded view on whether such a claim came within Art 5(3) of the Brussels Convention. See Fawcett and Torremans, pp 433–439.

[211] Discussed infra, pp 823–824.

[212] Discussed infra, pp 1315–1320.

[213] Art 28 of the Regulation; discussed infra, pp 857–858.

negotiorum gestio and *culpa in contrahendo* (because they fall within Chapter III), whereas an instance of *culpa in contrahendo* has been held to come within Article 5(3).[214] Moreover, Article 5(3) encompasses property matters,[215] whereas the law of property is not part of the law of obligations and therefore falls outside the scope of the Regulation altogether.[216]

The Regulation applies to non-contractual obligations that are likely to arise[217] so would cover the threat of a tort. This is consistent with the Brussels I Regulation which specifically applies to threatened wrongs.[218]

(b) What is not covered

Chapter II does not apply to non-contractual obligations arising out of unjust enrichment, *negotiorum gestio* and *culpa in contrahendo*. These are subject to the choice of law rules in Chapter III.

(i) Tort or unjust enrichment

Equitable obligations   Equitable obligations will fall within the tort choice of law rules in Chapter II, unless they are classified as unjust enrichment (within the meaning of Article 10 of the Regulation). Under the pre-Regulation classification for choice of law purposes the Court of Appeal found persuasive the argument that a claim for breach of confidence[219] fell to be categorised as a restitutionary claim for unjust enrichment.[220] The case in question involved a claim for damages,[221] rather than for an account for profits, and so made no sense as a matter of domestic classification. Under domestic English law this would not constitute unjust enrichment or restitution for wrongdoing. It would be very odd to adopt, for the purposes of the Regulation, a classification that is not followed as a matter of English substantive law or doubtless under the law of any other Member State. It is submitted therefore that such a case should be classified as tortious (within the wide meaning to be given to that phrase under Chapter II). However, if the disgorgement of profits was sought from the defendant (an account of profits) this would be regarded under English law as an example of restitution for equitable wrongdoing. It is argued below[222] that such cases fall within the meaning of unjust enrichment under the Regulation, and, accordingly, the choice of law rules in Chapter III (Article 10)

---

[214] Case C-334/00 *Fonderie Officine Meccaniche Tacconi SpA v Heinrich Wagner Sinto Maschinenfabrik GmbH (HWS)* [2002] ECR I-7357; discussed supra, p 248. The difficulties over whether unjust enrichment falls within Art 5(3) are discussed supra, p 249.

[215] This is provided that the action seeks to establish the liability of the defendant, see supra, p 250.

[216] See the discussion of conversion, infra, p 794.

[217] Art 2(2).

[218] Art 2(2).

[219] It was in fact a case of breach of confidence involving invasion of privacy and so would be outside the scope of the Regulation, supra, p 784. But what was said in the case is relevant for the discussion of the other type of breach of confidence involving confidential information.

[220] See *Douglas v Hello! Ltd (No 3)* [2005] EWCA Civ 595 at 97, [2006] QB 125.

[221] For distress and for having to deal hurriedly with the selection of photos.

[222] Infra, pp 824–825.

would have to be applied. The same principles should apply to other instances of breach of equitable obligations,[223] such as breach of a fiduciary duty.[224]

Contribution and indemnity   The difficult question of classification that arises as to whether a non-contractual obligation should be regarded as arising out of a tort/delict or unjust enrichment can be illustrated by examining the situation where a tortfeasor seeks a contribution or indemnity from another tortfeasor. The right to a contribution or indemnity can arise from a contract. Where this happens, the obligation will be contractual rather than non-contractual and will fall outside the scope of the Rome II Regulation altogether, but within the Rome Convention. Where the contribution or indemnity does not arise out of a contract, the Regulation tells us that the rules on the applicable law under the Regulation apply.[225] But which choice of law rules? Is this the tort/delict choice of law rules in Chapter II or the unjust enrichment choice of law rules in Chapter III? A contribution is probably best not regarded as a tort in the strict sense.[226] The better alternative would be to classify it as being based on unjust enrichment. [227] This has been the classification favoured by the Law Commissions, [228] again in a pre-Regulation context. If this classification is adopted under the Regulation, the unjust enrichment choice of law rules in Chapter III will apply, rather than the tort/delict choice of law rules in Chapter II. Similarly, an indemnity that does not arise from a contract is probably best not regarded as a tort in the strict sense.[229] The right to an indemnity has been regarded by an Australian court as being *sui generis* and not to be classified as either tortious or contractual.[230] This would fall within the wide definition of a tort/delict for the purposes of Chapter II. The probably better alternative would be to classify an action for an indemnity as being based on unjust enrichment. Chapter III will then apply.

(ii) *Tort or* culpa in contrahendo

A negligent misstatement that is made during dealings prior to the conclusion of a contract will fall within the concept of *culpa in contrahendo* and, accordingly, the choice of

---

[223] See generally Dicey, Morris and Collins, paras 34-033–34-037 for pre-Regulation cases where compensation was sought for breach of an equitable obligation and the unjust enrichment choice of law rules were not applied.

[224] This accords with the pre-Regulation classification of accounting for breach of fiduciary duty for choice of law purposes, see *Kuwait Oil Tanker Co SAK v Al-Bader* [2000] 2 All ER (Comm) 271, CA. The case also concerned a constructive trust, see generally infra, p 823.

[225] Art 15(a), discussed infra, p 842.

[226] Law Com No 193 (1990), para 3.48.

[227] See Dicey, Morris and Collins, paras 34-011, 34-051; and generally Takahashi, *Claims for Contribution and Reimbursement in an International Context*; Yeo, paras 9.34–9.41. The English statutory rules on contribution have been regarded as being what we now call under the Regulation an overriding mandatory rule of the forum: *Arab Monetary Fund v Hashim (No 9)* (1994) Times, 11 October, see infra, pp 849–850.

[228] Law Com No 193 (1990), paras 3.47–3.48. A claim between joint tortfeasors has been classified by the Australian courts as quasi-contractual and thus governed by the law governing the obligation: *Plozza v South Australian Insurance Co Ltd*, supra, at 127; *Stewart v Honey*, supra, at 592; and see *Nominal Defendant v Bagot's Executor and Trustee Co Ltd* [1971] SASR 347 at 365–367; revsd on other grounds (1971) 124 CLR 179; but see *Baldry v Jackson* [1977] 1 NSWLR 494. Contribution has, however, been held to fall within Art 5(3) (tort, delict or quasi-delict) of the Brussels I Regulation: *Hewden Tower Cranes Ltd v Wolffkran GmbH* [2007] EWHC 857 (TCC), [2007] 2 Lloyd's Rep 138; supra, p 249. A claim for contribution has been regarded as being founded upon a tort for the purpose of service out of the jurisdiction but not as a cause of action in tort: *FFSB Ltd v Seward & Kissel LLP* [2007] UKPC 16 at [22].

[229] Law Com No 193 (1990), para 3.48.

[230] *Borg-Warner (Australia) Ltd v Zupan* [1982] VR 437; Law Com No 193 (1990), para 3.48.

law rules in Chapter III will apply.[231] If it is not so made, it will fall within the concept of tort/delict. The English law of fraudulent and negligent misrepresentation is a form of pre-contractual liability and will fall within *culpa in contrahendo*.[232]

(iii) Tort or property

The common law is unusual in treating claims for interference with property rights as part of the law of tort. With the common law tort of conversion, the claimant seeks damages. In contrast, civil law countries treat interference with property as part of the law of property. The claimant seeks revendication, rather than damages.[233] Such a claim should be regarded as falling outside the scope of the Regulation, altogether. But what of a claim for damages for conversion under English law or that of some other common law country? The English courts have held that conversion falls within Article 5(3) of the Brussels Convention (Regulation)[234] but that provision encompasses property matters, whereas such matters fall outside the scope of the Regulation, not being part of the law of obligations. When it comes to choice of law, the Court of Justice, looking at how civil law jurisdictions classify the matter, is likely to decide that any claim for interference with property, including for conversion, is to be classified as part of the law of property and thus falls outside the scope of the Regulation. Such a classification presents the English courts with a major problem: what choice of law rules are they then to apply? There are no English property choice of law rules that would deal with a case of conversion. Such a case would fall naturally within the statutory tort choice of law rules[235] that applied prior to the introduction of the Rome II Regulation and still apply to torts falling outside the scope of the Regulation. It is to these statutory tort choice of law rules that the English courts should have recourse.

(iv) Tort or property or unjust enrichment

An action claiming ownership of a painting and for conversion has been classified by an English court in a pre-Regulation case as a restitutionary proprietary claim and not as one in tort in the strict sense.[236] Neither should it come within a tort in the wide sense for the purposes of choice of law. Such a claim is based on unjust enrichment (and thus within Chapter III) or is based on the law of property (and is thus outside the scope of the Regulation altogether).[237]

Questions of scope also arise in relation to the separate choice of law rules in Chapter II. These questions of scope will be considered below.[238]

(ii) The structure of Chapter II

Chapter II creates a flexible framework of choice of law rules, which seek to reconcile the requirement of legal certainty with the need to do justice in the individual case.[239]

---

[231] See infra, p 833.

[232] See infra, pp 833–834.

[233] See Fawcett, Harris and Bridge, paras 6.33–6.41.

[234] Supra, p 247.

[235] Discussed supra, pp 767–768.

[236] *Gotha City v Sotheby's (No 2)* (1998) Times, 8 October.

[237] This difficult question of classification is discussed infra, p 821.

[238] Infra, pp 795–818.

[239] Recital (14).

Article 4 is entitled the "General rule". Articles 5 to 9 then set out a number of specific rules for special torts "where the general rule does not allow a reasonable balance to be struck between the interests at stake".[240] The "general rule" applies for all other torts/delicts and the term must be understood as contrasting with the specific rules for special torts. For certain provisions there is a let-out which allows for a departure from fixed rules where it is clear from all the circumstances of the case that the tort/delict is manifestly more closely connected with another country.[241]

(iii) Article 4: General rule[242]

The so-called general rule comprises three separate rules: first, a general principle; secondly, an exception to this; thirdly, an escape clause, which operates as a let-out in relation to both the general principle and its exception.[243] It is noticeable that the general principle and the exception to it are rules and not presumptions. The escape clause is designed to be truly exceptional. These three rules are by and large not dissimilar from the English statutory tort choice of law rules.

(a) The scope of Article 4

Article 4 applies to "a non-contractual obligation arising out of a tort/delict". Despite the all-embracing language, Article 4 does not encompass the following torts/delicts: product liability; unfair competition; acts restricting free competition; environmental damage; infringement of intellectual property rights; industrial action. There are separate rules for these in Articles 5 to 9 of the Regulation. The scope of each of these special rules for specific torts will be examined later. Suffice it to say at this stage that difficult problems can arise as to whether the general rule under Article 4 should apply or one of the specific rules for special torts. For example, non-contractual breach of confidence should normally come within Article 4. However, for the purposes of the Regulation, targeting a competitor by the disclosure of business secrets, which would be regarded under English law as a breach of confidence, should be regarded as an act of unfair competition within Article 6.[244] Once it has been decided that there is a tort/delict within the meaning of Article 4 it follows that the obligation that arises out of this tort must be regarded as non-contractual.[245] Article 4 presupposes that damage occurs. It cannot therefore apply to a tort which does not require damage. As has been seen, damage includes any consequence arising out of tort/delict[246] and damage that is likely to occur.[247]

---

[240] Recital (19).

[241] Recital (14).

[242] For the application of the general rule to internet torts, see Fawcett, Harris and Bridge, paras 21. 203–21.210.

[243] See Recital (18).

[244] Supra, p 792.

[245] Supra, pp 777–779.

[246] Art 2(1).

[247] Art 2(3)(b).

(b) Article 4(1): a place of damage general principle

Article 4(1) provides that:

> Unless otherwise provided for in this Regulation, the law applicable to a non-contractual
> obligation arising out of a tort/delict shall be the law of the country in which the damage
> occurs irrespective of the country in which the event giving rise to the damage occurred
> and irrespective of the country or countries in which the indirect consequences of that
> event occur.

(i) Unless otherwise provided for

The opening words, "Unless otherwise provided for in this Regulation", make it clear
that this provision is subject to other provisions in the Regulation. Article 4(1) is subject
to the exception in Article 4(2) and the escape clause in Article 4(3), to the specific rules
for special torts (Articles 5 to 9), to the right of the parties to choose the applicable law
(Article 14), and to the limitations on the applicable law, namely overriding mandatory
provisions of the forum (Article 16) and public policy (Article 26).

(ii) The definitional problem and adoption of a place of damage rule

Virtually all the Member States are agreed on the application of the law of the place where
the tort was committed (*lex loci delicti commissi*) as the basic rule for tort/delict choice of
law. However, a definitional problem arises where the component factors of the case are
spread over several countries. There is no agreement among the Member States on the
definition of this place.[248] The basic choice is between the law of the country in which
the damage occurs (*lex damni*) and that of the country in which the event giving rise to
the damage occurred. In the Regulation, the former was preferred to the latter for two
reasons. First it is said that a connection with the country where the direct damage occurred
"strikes a fair balance between the interests of the person claimed to be liable and the
person sustaining the damage".[249] Secondly, it is said to "reflect the modern approach to
civil liability and the development of systems of strict liability".[250] In some cases, there
will be very little connection with the country in which the damage occurred. The classic
example is that of a car journey from Country A to Country E via Countries B, C and D.
The driver drives negligently in Country D and injures his passenger. Both parties are
from Country A. The fact that the damage occurred in Country D is fortuitous. Hence
the need for the exception in Article 4(2) and the escape clause in Article 4(3).

Article 4(1) not only makes it clear that the law of the country in which the damage
occurs is applicable but also spells out, in true belt and braces fashion, that one must not
apply the law of the country in which the event giving rise to the damage occurred[251] or
is likely to occur.[252] This seems to be entirely unnecessary. Perhaps it has been inserted
because of the position under the Brussels I Regulation in relation to jurisdiction in cases

---

[248] Some apply a place of acting rule (Austria), others a place of damage rule (the Netherlands, France,
Switzerland), yet others an alternative reference rule (Germany, Poland), in some it is not clear (Spain). The
Explanatory Memorandum, at p 11, says that recent codifications in Member States have adopted a place of
damage rule.

[249] Recital (16).

[250] Ibid.

[251] Art 4(1).

[252] Art 2(3)(a).

of tort/delict. It will be recalled that Article 5(3) has been interpreted by the Court of Justice to allocate jurisdiction to both the place of the event giving rise to damage and to the place of damage. But for choice of law purposes it cannot cover both because this would lead to two laws being applicable in cases where the two occurred in different countries.

(iii) Identification of the country in which damage occurs

Article 4(1) presupposes that it is always possible to identify the country where damage occurs. Identification of this country is normally easy enough in cases of personal injury or damage to property. In a case of personal injury the country in which the damage occurs should be the country where the injury was sustained.[253] In a case of damage to property the country in which the damage occurs should be the country where the property was damaged.[254] The place where property was damaged is usually easy to identify but what of the situation where perishable goods are carried across Europe in a refrigerated truck. At some unknown point the refrigeration breaks down and the goods gradually rot. For jurisdictional purposes the place where the damage is discovered cannot constitute the place of damage, [255] but for choice of law purposes it is hard to see any other solution than that of where the damage was discovered. The position is more straightforward in cases where the damage occurred in several countries and it is possible to identify these countries.[256] In this situation the laws of all of these countries will have to be applied on a distributive basis,[257] with a different law governing each instance of damage. With an economic tort such as negligent misstatement,[258] there can be very real problems in ascertaining the place of damage.[259] In cases where the country has had to be artificially fixed or is particularly difficult to identify, it should be that much easier to show that the tort is manifestly more closely connected with another country under the escape clause in Article 4(3).

(iv) Direct damage

Article 2(1) provides that damage covers "any consequence arising out of tort/delict . . .". This is potentially very wide and could cover indirect consequences as well as direct consequences. However, Article 4(1) then limits the meaning of damage by confining it to direct damage and excluding indirect damage. It does this by adding, after the instruction to apply the law of the country in which the damage occurs, the words "irrespective of the country or countries in which the indirect consequences of that event occur". If damage had included both direct and indirect damage this could have led to two or more

---

[253] See Recital (17).

[254] Ibid.

[255] Case C-51/97 *Réunion Européenne v Spliethoff's Bevrachtingskantoor BV* [2000] QB 690; discussed supra, p 258.

[256] See, eg, the pre-Regulation case of *Protea Leasing Ltd v Royal Air Cambodge* [2002] 2 All ER 224, damage was failure to pay for aircraft under leases (in a bank account outside Cambodia) and failure to maintain aircraft (in Cambodia). See also the pre-Regulation case of *Morin v Bonhams & Brooks Ltd* [2003] EWCA Civ 1802, [2004] 1 Lloyd's Rep 702, discussed infra, p 837 as an example of *culpa in contrahendo*.

[257] See Explanatory Memorandum, p 11. This is known as "Mosaikbetrachtung" (mosaic principle) in German law.

[258] If the misstatement arises out of dealings prior to the conclusion of a contract, Art 12 (*culpa in contrahendo*) will apply; see infra, p 833.

[259] See the jurisdiction case of *Raiffeisen Zentral Bank Osterreich AG v Alexander Tranos* [2001] IL Pr 85, which would now have to be dealt with as *culpa in contrahendo*; Fawcett, Harris and Bridge, paras 6.93–6.95.

countries' laws being applicable, which would be unworkable. Moreover, limiting damage to direct damage is consistent with Article 5(3) of the Brussels I Regulation, as interpreted by the Court of Justice. We can now look at some examples—drawn from the context of jurisdiction under Article 5(3)—of how the direct damage rule will operate. Where an Italian domiciled plaintiff is arrested in England (and promissory notes are sequestrated) and the plaintiff subsequently brings an action in Italy, inter alia, for compensation for the damage he claims to have suffered as a result of his arrest, the breach of several contracts and injury to his reputation, the damage occurs in England, not in Italy.[260] Likewise where initial damage has been suffered by the claimant in a road traffic accident in France but his medical condition has deteriorated whilst living in England, the damage occurs in France.[261] This is unaffected by the fact that under French law deterioration constitutes a separate cause of action from the original injury. Article 4(1) does not explain what happens where direct harm is suffered by an indirect victim,[262] as where, for example, A is injured in State X but B as a consequence suffers nervous shock witnessing this (say on the television) in State Y. As regards the claim by B, does the damage occur in X or Y? Article 4(1) does not specify that the damage is referring to the damage to the claimant. Nonetheless, in this situation it makes more sense for this to be read into Article 4(1) and for the law of Y to apply, rather than that of X.

(v) Threatened damage

Damage includes damage that is likely to occur.[263]

(c) Article 4(2): the common habitual residence exception

Article 4(2) sets out an exception to Article 4(1). This provides that "however, where the person claimed to be liable and the person sustaining damage both have their habitual residence in the same country at the time when the damage occurs, the law of that country shall apply". Article 4(2) is an inflexible rule. The only room for argument is over where the parties are habitually resident, which means that in cases where there is any room for argument over the habitual residence that will become a live issue. Many Member States apply the law of the parties' common residence or habitual residence in a tort choice of law case.[264] Under the English common law and statutory tort choice of law rules there is a flexible exception and the personal connecting factor is one of the factors to be taken into account. Indeed, it is an important factor and English law has been applied under both the common law and statutory rules exception in circumstances where the parties were normally resident in England[265] or resident in England.[266]

---

[260] See Case C-364/93 *Marinari v Lloyds Bank plc (Zubaidi Trading Co Intervener)*, [1996] QB 217. See also Case 220/88 *Dumez France and Tracoba v Hessische Landesbank* [1990] ECR 49; discussed supra, pp 256–257.

[261] See *Henderson v Jaouen* [2002] EWCA Civ 75, [2002] 1 WLR 2971; discussed supra, p 257.

[262] HL Paper 66 (2004), para 98, referring to the Written Evidence by Briggs at 95.

[263] Art 2(3)(b).

[264] See, eg, Switzerland and Germany (common habitual residence), the Netherlands (common residence) and Italy (common residence and nationality). See the Explanatory Memorandum, p 12.

[265] *Chaplin v Boys* [1971] AC 356 at 378 (per Lord HODSON), 389–393 (per Lord WILBERFORCE). The parties were servicemen temporarily stationed in Malta. See in relation to the statutory rules, *Edmunds v Simmonds* [2001] 1 WLR 1003.

[266] *Church of Scientology of California v Metropolitan Police Comr* (1976) 120 Sol Jo 690; *Johnson v Coventry Churchill International Ltd* [1992] 3 All ER 14.

The same result will apply under the Regulation, but now by virtue of a rigid rule[267] that only looks at the common habitual residence, rather than as the result of a wider flexible exception. However, the rigidity of the former rule and the flexibility of the latter can lead to a difference in result. Under the pre-Regulation law there is an instance of the English courts not applying the flexible exception, even though both of the parties appeared to be habitually resident in England.[268] In contrast, under the Regulation the habitual residence exception would operate in such a case.[269] Habitual residence is at least partially defined under Article 23.[270] The habitual residence of one or both parties can change during the course of events. Article 4(2) is concerned with habitual residence at the time when the damage occurs.

(d) Article 4(3): the manifestly more closely connected escape clause

(i) The escape clause

Article 4(3) is an escape clause. It provides that: "Where it is clear from all the circumstances of the case that the tort/delict is manifestly more closely connected with a country other than that indicated in paragraphs 1 or 2, the law of that other country shall apply." Like Article 4(5) of the Rome Convention, this is designed to produce flexibility so that individual circumstances can be taken into account in order as to apply the law that reflects the centre of gravity of the situation.[271] German private international law has virtually the same escape clause and Switzerland a similar one.[272] It is not enough to show that the tort/delict is more closely connected with a country other than that indicated in paragraphs 1 or 2, it has to be "manifestly" more closely connected. The addition of the word "manifestly" is designed to underscore the exceptional nature of this escape clause.[273] The use of rules in Article 4(1) and (2), rather than presumptions, is also designed to make clear that the exception really is exceptional.[274] Experience with the Rome Convention shows that a presumption can lead to States starting off with the exception, rather than the presumption. The requisite connection under Article 4(3) is shown from all the circumstances of the case. A particular example is given, namely where there is a pre-existing relationship between the parties, and this will be examined below. But this is only an example and, in principle, there may be other situations where it is clear from all the circumstances of the case that the tort/delict may be shown to be manifestly more closely connected with another country. How easy it will be to demonstrate this in practice remains to be seen. But the intention appears to be to set a high threshold. An example suggested of where Article 4(3) should operate is that of a single defendant being sued

---

[267] However, this can be escaped from by recourse to Art 4(3), infra.

[268] *Regina (Al-Jedda) v Secretary of State for Defence* [2006] EWCA Civ 327, [2007] QB 621—a claim by a British citizen, who appears to have been habitually resident in England, against the British government where the issue was the legality of detention in Iraq, whose law applied under the general rule.

[269] An English court may then be tempted to apply the escape clause in Art 4(3) in such a case. But the issue in the case does not appear to have any relevance under Art 4(3), see infra.

[270] Discussed supra, pp 788–789.

[271] See the Explanatory Memorandum, p 12.

[272] See the German Introductory Law to the Civil Code, the 1999 Codification, Art 41; the Swiss Federal Statute on Private International Law Statute 1987, Art 15.

[273] The Explanatory Memorandum, p 12. See also the addition of the word "manifestly" to the public policy defence under the Brussels I Regulation, supra, p 612.

[274] See the Explanatory Memorandum, p 12.

by numerous claimants, who have been injured in different countries.[275] It is the *tort* that must be manifestly more closely connected.[276] The issue that arises in the particular case does not appear to have any relevance.[277] The escape clause uses the criterion of connections.[278] The connection must be with a country, rather than the law of a country.[279]

(ii) A pre-existing relationship

Article 4(3) provides an example of a manifestly closer connection: "A manifestly closer connection with another country might be based in particular on a pre-existing relationship between the parties, such as a contract, that is closely connected with the tort/delict in question."

A very similar example is given under German private international law.[280] The pre-existing relationship is referred to as a secondary connection.[281] The idea is that the law of the country governing the secondary connection will also govern the non-contractual obligation.[282] This rule has been justified on the basis that by "having the same law apply to all their relationships, this solution respects the parties' legitimate expectations and meets the need for the sound administration of justice".[283] Under the English statutory tort choice of law rules it was possible to take into account a pre-existing relationship and the law governing that relationship when operating the displacement rule.[284] However, the governing law would just be one factor amongst a number of factors. The Regulation gives more significance to this factor by providing that the manifestly closer connection with another country might be *based on* a pre-existing relationship between the parties. In other words, this on its own might be enough for Article 4(3) to operate. It is unclear what significance should be attached to a choice of jurisdiction clause in the parties' contract. In so far as it determines the governing law, the same significance should be attached to it as to a choice of law clause. But if the governing law is different, the choice of jurisdiction clause should just be treated as one factual connection amongst many other factual connections.[285]

The example given in Article 4(3) of a pre-existing relationship is that of a contract. It is not uncommon for the parties to a claim in tort to have a contractual relationship. In cases of concurrent liability (provided this is classified as being tortious), this will be the case.[286] It would also arise where there are claims in tort and contract which are not

---

[275] Briggs, Written Evidence, HL Report 66 (2004), 95.

[276] This parallels Art 4(5) of the Rome Convention.

[277] Criticised by Morse, Written Evidence, HL Paper 66 (2004), 126. Contrast s 12(1) of the Private International Law (Miscellaneous Provisions) Act 1995.

[278] This parallels Art 4(5) of the Rome Convention. Contrast s 12(1) of the Private International Law (Miscellaneous Provisions) Act 1995, which, after comparing the significance of connecting factors, refers to it being substantially more "appropriate" that the law of some other country should apply.

[279] See Briggs, Written Evidence, HL Report 66 (2004), 95, who would have preferred these as alternatives.

[280] Art 41(2) of the German Introductory Law to the Civil Code, the 1999 Codification.

[281] See the Explanatory Memorandum, pp 8 and 12–13.

[282] Ibid.

[283] The Explanatory Memorandum, p 13.

[284] *Trafigura Beheer BV v Kookmin Bank Co* [2006] EWHC 1450 (Comm) at [103]–[104], [2006] 2 Lloyd's Rep 455. Cf MANCE LJ in *Morin v Bonham & Brooks Ltd* [2003] EWCA Civ 1802 at [23], [2004] 1 Lloyd's Rep 702, who left the matter open.

[285] This was the position under the statutory tort choice of law rules, see *Trafigura*, supra, at [104].

[286] See the discussion supra, pp 779–780.

parallel ones. It could also arise where there is a claim based on a non-contractual obligation and where, although there is a contract between the parties, there is no contractual
liability.[287] This pre-existing contractual relationship could presumably cover a contract
that has been annulled,[288] certainly after the tort was committed. The position is more
uncertain in relation to a contract annulled before the tort was committed. In such a case,
there may be little connection between the non-contractual obligation and the law governing the tort and the exception would not operate.[289] Where the contract that constitutes the pre-existing relationship is a consumer contract or an employment contract the
consumer and the employee are protected in relation to contractual obligations by special
contract choice of law rules under the Rome Convention. Thus if an employee habitually carries out his work in State A but the contract of employment has a choice of law
clause providing for the application of the law of State B, the employee can still rely on
the mandatory (protectionist) rules of State A. But as far as non-contractual obligations
are concerned it would appear that the law applicable would be that of State B. No mandatory rules of contract come into play.

The Commission has foreseen this problem and has said that the secondary connection
mechanism cannot have the effect of depriving the weaker party of the protection of the
law otherwise applicable (State A in our example).[290] But what is there in the Regulation
to stop this? There is no express provision to deal with this situation. The Commission
has said this is implicit in the protective rules in the Rome Convention but this looks to
be an inadequate response and it would have been better to incorporate into the Regulation
a restriction of the secondary connection rule.

In principle, a pre-existing relationship could include a pre-contractual relationship
where a contract has not been entered into.[291] But in practice this question will presumably not arise because there is a separate rule in the Regulation for cases of pre-contractual
liability.[292] The relationship between a guest passenger and a host driver who subsequently injures the passenger by his negligent driving is another example of a pre-existing
relationship.[293] In this example the pre-existing relationship is undeniably closely connected with the tort/delict in question. The pre-existing relationship could in principle
be a family relationship.[294] In practice this scenario is not normally going to face the
courts. This is because the Regulation excludes from its scope non-contractual obligations arising out of family relationships.[295] However, it is possible to have a family relationship in respect of which the exclusion does not operate because the non-contractual
obligation does not arise out of this, as where, for example, a husband negligently injures
his wife in a car crash. In this situation the question is whether the relationship of husband

---

[287] See the facts of the pre-Regulation case of *Trafigura Beheer BV v Kookmin Bank Co* [2006] EWHC 1450
(Comm), [2006] 2 Lloyd's Rep 455.
[288] The Explanatory Memorandum, p 13.
[289] See infra, p 802.
[290] The Explanatory Memorandum, p 13.
[291] The Explanatory Memorandum, p 13.
[292] Art 12, discussed infra, pp 832–835.
[293] See, eg, *Babcock v Jackson* [1963] 2 Lloyd's Rep 286, 12 NY 2d 473, 240 NYS 2d 743, New York Court of
Appeals.
[294] The Explanatory Memorandum, pp 8 and 13.
[295] Art 1(2)(a), discussed supra, p 781.

and wife is closely connected with the tort of negligent driving. A family relationship can include an annulled relationship.[296]

Closely connected with the tort/delict in question   The pre-existing relationship must be closely connected with the tort/delict in question.

Application of the law governing the pre-existing relationship   Let us assume that there is a pre-existing relationship between the parties that is closely connected with the tort/delict in question. A manifestly closer connection with another country might be based on this relationship. But which country does this point to? Take the example of where there is a contractual relationship. The Explanatory Memorandum envisages that the law of the country governing the contract will also govern the non-contractual obligation.[297] Likewise the law of the country governing the family relationship would govern the non-contractual obligation.[298] But what law governs the relationship of husband and wife? There are no harmonised rules of choice of law for marriage in the European Community so this would be a matter to be determined by the national choice of law rules of the forum. At common law the law of the domicile would govern the relationship of husband and wife. Indeed, it is possible at common law to classify the question whether one spouse is liable to the other in tort as a matter of status to be referred to the law of the domicile.[299] Similarly, whether a child can sue his parents may be similarly so classified.[300] The Rome II Regulation would produce the same result albeit by a different route. Rather than classifying the claim as family law it is classified as tort but to be governed by the law governing the family relationship.

The lack of harmonisation of choice of law rules for marriage means that different substantive domestic laws would apply to the family relationship depending on which Member State the trial was held in.[301] But what law governs a guest host relationship? Ultimately the search is for a manifestly closer connection with another country. This could be based on where the guest host relationship is centred. Thus if this relationship starts and is to end in New York, New York law should apply, rather than the law of Ontario where the car crash occurred and the guest was injured by the host.[302]

A discretion?   The wording of the pre-existing relationship example in Article 4(3) makes clear that even if there is a pre-existing relationship between the parties, such as a contract, which is closely connected with the tort/delict in question, there will not automatically

---

[296] The Explanatory Memorandum, p 13. But the same question arises as with an annulled contract (discussed supra) as to whether this would include a relationship annulled after the tort.

[297] At p 8.

[298] Ibid.

[299] This is the general view in the USA: *Haumschild v Continental Casualty Co* 7 Wis 2d 130, 95 NW 2d 814 (1959); cf *Schwartz v Schwartz* 103 Ariz 562, 447 P 2d 254 (1968) where the same conclusion was reached applying the choice of law rule of the Restatement 2d § 145. Australian courts have taken different views on this matter. Cf *Warren v Warren* [1972] Qd R 386 at 390–391 (application of the law of the domicile) with *Schmidt v Government Insurance Office of New South Wales* [1973] 1 NSWLR 59 and *Corcoran v Corcoran* [1974] VR 164 (application of tort choice of law rules). The Law Commissions reached no conclusion on the characterisation of intra-family immunities: Law Com No 193 (1990), paras 3.45–3.46.

[300] *Balts v Balts* 273 Minn 419, 142 NW 2d 6 (1966); and see *Emery v Emery* 45 Cal 2d 421, 289 P 2d 218 (1955); cf *Pierce v Helz* 314 NYS 2d 453 (1970).

[301] See the Explanatory Memorandum, p 8. This unfortunate result helped prompt the desire by some to exclude family relationships from the scope of the Regulation.

[302] These are the facts of *Babcock v Jackson*, supra.

be a manifestly closer connection with another country. There "might be". The court is said to have a degree of discretion to decide whether there is a significant connection between the non-contractual obligation and the law applicable to the relationship.[303] This is not a discretion in the sense that the term is used under English private international law in, for example, *forum conveniens* cases, instead it is just making the point that a fine judgment may have to be made as to whether the secondary connection will apply. The question ultimately is whether there is a manifestly closer connection with another country.

(iii) The effect of the secondary connection rule: mitigating problems of classification

The secondary connection rule has the effect of mitigating problems of classification. There are two particular areas where this is particularly noticeable. The first area is that of concurrent liability. The secondary connection rule has considerable implications for such cases.[304] Until the Court of Justice has determined the classification of such liability there is a danger of different national courts adopting different classifications. However, the undesirable lack of uniformity that this would entail is said to be mitigated by the secondary connection rule.[305] This needs a few words of explanation. Let us assume that a French court has adopted a contractual classification and applies French law as the law governing the contract. If an English court adopted a tortious classification it could also apply French law to govern the non-contractual obligation on the basis that the tortious relationship between the parties is governed by French law.

The second area where problems of classification arise is that of the consequences of nullity of a contract. This issue comes within the scope of the Rome Convention.[306] However, some Member States regard this issue as non-contractual and have been allowed to enter a reservation against the application of the Rome Convention to this issue. The effect of the secondary connection rule is that the same result will be achieved in states which have adopted a reservation and apply the Rome II Regulation as in states which apply the Rome Convention.[307]

(iv) An escape from Article 4(1) and (2)

Article 4(3) operates as an escape from both Article 4(1) and Article 4(2).

An exception to Article 4(1)   The scenario of both parties having a common habitual residence that is dealt with in Article 4(2) will be very much the exception and so Article 4(3) is likely to operate more commonly as an exception to Article 4(1), rather than Article 4(2). Apart from cases where there is a pre-existing relationship between the parties, situations where Article 4(3) would operate as an exception to Article 4(1) are likely to be relatively rare. At common law the flexible exception operated where the parties had

---

[303] The Explanatory Memorandum, p 12.

[304] See the Explanatory Memorandum, pp 12–13. The secondary connection rule applies to any cases of concurrent liability but in particular to those cases where a contractual defence is raised to a claim, see infra, pp 865–868.

[305] Ibid.

[306] See supra, pp 757–758.

[307] The Explanatory Memorandum, p 13. This assumes that, in states which have entered a reservation, the issue in classified as tortious/delictual and therefore Chapter II of the Rome II Regulation will apply. But in the United Kingdom it is regarded a restitutionary, see generally infra, p 822.

the same normal residence. This situation would now probably involve Article 4(2) (common habitual residence), rather than Article 4(1). So the question that would arise is whether Article 4(3) would operate as an escape from Article 4(2). Another situation where the common law flexible exception operated was where there were strong connections with the country where the tort was committed (eg Saudi Arabia) with the result that Saudi Arabian law governed. In contrast, Article 4(3) operates to displace the law of the country where damage occurred and so could not operate in such a case. One situation where it is suggested that Article 4(3) might operate (in the absence of a pre-existing relationship) is where the parties have a common nationality, particularly if this is accompanied by a common residence.

An exception to Article 4(2)   The scenario we are concerned with here is as follows:

> The law of country A is applicable under Article 4(1), the exception under Article 4(2) then leads to the application of the law of Country B. The question then is whether there is a manifestly closer connection with Country C with the result that under Article 4(3) the law of that country will apply to displace that of Country B.

In the absence of a pre-existing relationship between the parties, it is hard to envisage Article 4(3) operating in a three-country case. The parties' common habitual residence constitutes a strong connection with Country B, as does the occurrence of damage with Country A. If there are strong connections with two countries, it is unlikely that there is a manifestly closer connection with a third country, Country C. So displacement of Article 4(2) by Article 4(3) is likely to be even harder than displacement of Article 4(1) by Article 4(3), at least in a three-country case.

However, there is another possibility that needs to be considered. This involves a two country scenario.

> Let us assume that there are strong connections with the country of damage (Country A), quite apart from the fact that damage occurred there. The parties have a common habitual residence in Country B so that the exception under Article 4(2) will apply. But can the law of Country A be applied by virtue of Article 4(3)?

This raises a question of principle. Can Article 4(3) be used to displace the law applicable under Article 4(2) by the law applicable under Article 4(1)? The wording of Article 4(3) suggests that it can. Article 4(3) refers to the tort being manifestly more closely connected with a country other than that indicated in paragraph 1 *or* 2. The applicable law under Article 4(3) does not have to displace that indicated in both paragraph 1 and 2. So Article 4(3) could operate in a two-country situation. In terms of the balance of connections, the fact that damage occurred in Country A is a strong connection and if there are other weighty connections this could outweigh the common habitual residence connection. This would appeal to the English courts which, in a case decided under the common law tort choice of law rules, have used the flexible exception to apply the law of the country where the tort was committed.[308] More significantly, the English courts have, under the statutory tort choice of law rules, applied Iraqi law under the general rule and refused to apply the displacement rule, despite the fact that both parties appeared to be

---

[308] *Red Sea Insurance Co Ltd v Bouygues SA* [1995] 1 AC 190.

habitually resident in England.[309] The same result could be reached under the Regulation by applying Iraqi law by virtue of Article 4(3).[310]

(e) Article 4 and road traffic accidents

The choice of law rules in Article 4 apply to the issue of the assessment of damages.[311] So damages are assessed according to the law of the place of damage. This can be unsatisfactory in road traffic accident cases. The victim may be injured in a country other than the one in which he habitually resides. After the accident he will return to his home country and will have to live with the consequences of his injury in that state. It would be better for assessment to be determined by the law of the country in which the victim habitually resides. The European Parliament suggested an amendment to the Regulation to what is now Article 4 to produce this effect. This was not accepted but the European Parliament was able to secure the introduction in the recitals of a statement which ensures that the victim's actual circumstances will be taken into account when damages are quantified.[312] This is seen as a short-term solution. As regards a long-term solution, the European Parliament has managed to secure a commitment by the Commission to examine the problems arising where European Union residents are involved in a road traffic accident in a Member State other than the Member State of their habitual residence and to produce a study on this before the end of 2008.[313] This study will look at all options, including insurance aspects, for improving the position of cross-border victims from the European Union, which would pave the way for a Green Paper. There is a further problem in relation to road traffic accidents, namely that many Member States (but not the United Kingdom) have entered into the Hague Convention on the Law Applicable to Traffic Accidents of 1971. These states will continue to apply the choice of law rules in the Convention, rather than those in Article 4.[314] The Commission is required to produce, by 20 August 2011, a report on the application of the Regulation, which will include a study on the effects of the 1971 Hague Convention.[315]

(iv) Specific rules for special torts

Articles 5 to 9 set out what are described as specific rules for special torts:[316] namely, for product liability, unfair competition, acts restricting competition, environmental damage, infringement of intellectual property rights and industrial action. Some of these (product liability, acts restricting competition and infringement of intellectual property rights) are recognisable to common lawyers as torts. Others (unfair competition, environmental damage and industrial action) are broad concepts which are more familiar to civil lawyers than common lawyers but encompass what common lawyers would regard as a number of different torts. According to Recital (19) specific rules should be laid down "where the general rule does not allow a reasonable balance to be struck between

---

[309] *Regina (Al-Jedda) v Secretary of State for Defence* [2006] EWCA Civ 327, [2007] QB 621.

[310] But the decision in *Regina (Al-Jedda)* was influenced by the issue in the case, namely whether the detention in Iraq was lawful. Under Art 4(3) the issue in the case does not appear to be relevant.

[311] Art 15(c), discussed infra, pp 843–846.

[312] Recital (33), discussed further when Art 15 (c) is discussed infra, p 846.

[313] See the Commission Statement on road accidents attached to the Regulation.

[314] Art 28(1), discussed infra, pp 857–858.

[315] Art 30(1)(ii).

[316] See Recital (19).

the interests at stake". The introduction of specific rules for special torts follows the model adopted in a number of European civil law jurisdictions[317] and in relation to contract choice of law under the Rome Convention but rejected in England under its choice of law rules in tort [318] on the ground that any special rule might be difficult to put into statutory language and would make the position more complex.[319] In the United Kingdom, the case for having in the Regulation some of these specific rules was not thought to have been made out.[320] The European Parliament was also unconvinced and unsuccessfully sought the deletion of some of these rules.[321]

(a) Product liability[322]

Within the European Community, much of the substantive law of product liability has been harmonised by the EC Product Liability Directive.[323] Nonetheless, choice of law problems still arise.[324] Article 5 sets out a special choice of law rule to solve these problems. Product liability has long been regarded as a special tort that requires specific choice of law rules. This was recognised at the Hague Conference on Private International Law, which in 1973 concluded the Hague Convention on the law applicable to products liability. This has entered into force in six European Community Member States.[325] These Member States will continue to apply the 1973 Hague Convention, rather than Article 5 of Rome II.[326]

(i) The scope of Article 5

The heading of Article 5 is "product liability", which is not defined.[327] Article 5 applies where there is "a non-contractual obligation arising out of damage caused by a product". Both "damage" and "product" are defined under the European Community Product Liability Directive[328] and the intention is that recourse should be had to these definitions when deciding whether Article 5 applies.[329] However, Article 5 does not appear to be confined to claims brought under the strict liability regime of the Directive (or to be more accurate, under national laws implementing the Directive). In England, claims which could have been brought under the Directive are sometimes brought in negligence, which is more familiar. Such a claim literally falls within the scope of Article 5. Moreover, it would be most undesirable for the claimant to be allowed to avoid the application of

---

[317] And in the USA under the Restatement of the Conflict of Laws 2d.

[318] Apart from for defamation, discussed infra, p 868.

[319] Law Commission Working Paper No 87 (1984), paras 5.1–5.70.

[320] HL Paper 66 (2004), paras 106 (referring to product liability), 109 (unfair competition), 134 (violation of the environment).

[321] Ie the specific rules for unfair competition and acts restricting free competition.

[322] For a comparative study of different choice of law solutions in Europe and a discussion of the Proposal and the European Parliament's response see Graziano (2005) 54 ICLQ 475.

[323] Council Directive (EEC) No 85/374 of 25 July 1985, OJ 1985 L 210.

[324] The harmonisation within Europe has only been partial and there is no world-wide harmonisation; see generally Fawcett (1993-I) 238 Hague Recueil des cours, Chapter II.

[325] Finland, France, Luxembourg, the Netherlands, Slovenia, France. It was signed but not ratified in Belgium, Italy and Portugal.

[326] Art 28, discussed infra, pp 857–858.

[327] Nor is it defined in the Product Liability Directive.

[328] See Arts 9 and 2. The Proposal for the Rome II Regulation in Art 4 referred to a "defective" product. But this requirement was dropped.

[329] See the Explanatory Memorandum, p 13.

Article 5 (with the aim of getting a different law to apply under Article 4) by suing in negligence. Once it has been decided that there is damage caused by a product within the meaning of Article 5, it follows that there is a tort and the obligation that arises out of this tort must be regarded as non-contractual. Article 5 presupposes that damage[330] occurs. This will necessarily be the case because damage is one of the elements of the tort of product liability.

(ii) The law applicable to product liability

Article 5 has two paragraphs. The first paragraph is undeniably complicated, reflecting the wide range of possible connecting factors.[331] It sets out a "cascading" series of rules to which there is a lack of foreseeability exception. All of this is subject to Article 4(2) (the common habitual residence exception). The second paragraph of Article 5 provides an escape from paragraph 1, based on a manifestly closer connection with another country.

A "cascading" series of rules[332] The first of these is Article 5(1)(a), which provides that the law applicable is "the law of the country in which the person sustaining the damage[333] had his or her habitual residence[334] when the damage occurred, if the product was marketed in that country". The victim will normally have acquired the product and been injured in the state of his habitual residence (and would expect the law of that state to apply) but even if he acquires it abroad (perhaps whilst travelling) and is injured in a state other than his habitual residence, the law of his habitual residence will still apply. The requirement that the product was marketed in that country is designed to protect the interests of the producer. The latter normally controls its sales network and if the product is marketed in a state would expect the law of that state to be applied. The reference to "the product" being marketed in the country of habitual residence does not make clear whether it is referring to the actual product that caused the injury or to the line of product from which the injuring product came, which seems to be what was intended.[335] If the product is not marketed in the country in which the person sustaining the damage had his or her habitual residence, paragraph (a) does not apply and one moves on to paragraph (b). This provides that the law applicable is "the law of the country in which the product was acquired, if the product was marketed in that country". It does not say who the product must have been acquired by. It does not say that this must have been the victim. Failing paragraph (b), one moves on to paragraph (c). This provides that the law applicable is "the law of the country in which the damage occurred, if the product was marketed in that country".

There is no fall back rule for cases that do not fall within paragraph (a), (b) or (c). Yet this is possible.[336] Rules (a), (b) and (c) all require the product to have been marketed in the country whose law is applicable. But this may not have happened. If the case does not fall

---

[330] As defined in Art 2(1) and 2(3)(b).

[331] Cf Art 4 of the Proposal for a Regulation.

[332] See Recital (20).

[333] So if the right to sue is assigned, the habitual residence of the person sustaining the damage will apply not that of the assignee.

[334] The meaning of habitual residence is discussed supra, pp 788–789.

[335] See the Explanatory Memorandum, p 14. This would be important in a case of travelling abroad and acquiring a product. If the line was marketed in the habitual residence it would be foreseeable to the producer that that country's law would apply.

[336] Art 4(2) will in some, but not all, cases provide an answer, see infra.

within (a), (b) or (c), the specific rules for product liability in Article 5 are inapplicable and one would have to go back to the "general rule" in Article 4. It is perfectly possible to apply those rules to the special tort of product liability.[337] Indeed, the English courts have traditionally applied rules of general application to product liability cases. Article 5(1)(a) requires the moment when the damage occurred to be identified (at least when a person is in the process of changing their habitual residence) and Article 5(1)(c) requires the country in which the damage occurred to be ascertained. This country will normally be easy to ascertain but not always. What of the situation where pills are taken as a person moves across Europe and these have a cumulative effect? The country in which the individual sustained damage will have to be artificially fixed, the best solution probably being to fix it where the first impact was felt.[338]

A lack of foreseeability exception   Article 5(1) provides an exception to (a), (b) and (c) in the situation where the person claimed to be liable "could not reasonably foresee the marketing of the product, or a product of the same type, in the country the law of which is applicable under (a), (b) or (c)". This could happen where a product is marketed in a country without the consent of the person claimed to be liable. In this situation, the law applicable is that of the country in which the person claimed to be liable[339] is habitually resident. This provision appears to have been influenced by the 1973 Hague Convention, which contains a non-foreseeability rule.[340]

A common habitual residence exception   Article 5(1) is without prejudice to Article 4(2), which provides that "where the person claimed to be liable and the person sustaining the damage both have their habitual residence in the same country at the time when the damage occurs, the law of that country shall apply". Starting Article 5(1) with the words "Without prejudice to Article 4(2)" makes it clear that this common habitual residence exception operates not only as an exception to the law applicable under paragraph 1(a), (b) and (c) but also to the law applicable under the lack of foreseeability exception set out in the last sentence of Article 5(1).

The manifestly more closely connected escape clause   Paragraph (2) provides an escape from the law "indicated in paragraph 1", based on a manifestly closer connection with another country. This provision is identical in wording to Article 4(3). The structure and wording of Article 5 would suggest that the Article 5(2) escape clause will not only override the law applicable under the cascading rules and the lack of foreseeability exception but also the law applicable under Article 4(2). Application of the law of the country of common habitual residence under Article 4(2) is "indicated in paragraph 1". Moreover, this interpretation is consistent with Article 4 where the manifestly more closely connected escape clause operates as an escape from the common habitual residence exception.

---

[337] The Commission regarded the "country in which the damage occurs" rule as unsatisfactory in that it could be unrelated to the situation, unforeseeable to the producer and no source of protection to the victim, see the Explanatory Memorandum, pp 13–14.

[338] When applying the place of damage rule under Art 4(1), where damage is sustained in different countries the laws of all the countries will apply on a distributive basis. This solution will not work in the present context.

[339] Under the Product Liability Directive liability is imposed on the producer proper (as widely defined to extend beyond the manufacturer of the finished product) but also on the importer into the Community and in some circumstances the supplier, see Art 3.

[340] Art 7.

(b) Unfair competition[341]

Article 6 is concerned with two different torts, unfair competition (paragraphs 1 and 2) and acts restricting free competition (paragraph 3). The former will be considered in this section and the latter under the heading (Restricting free competition) in (c) below.

(i) The scope of the unfair competition choice of law rules

Article 6 is headed, inter alia, "Unfair competition" and paragraph 1 goes on to provide that the rules on the applicable law apply to "a non-contractual obligation arising out of an act of unfair competition". The purpose of rules against unfair competition is to protect competition by obliging all participants to play the game by the same rules.[342]The definition of "unfair competition" is particularly problematic.[343] Although most civil law systems have a substantive law of unfair competition there are huge differences over what is covered by these laws. The intention is that unfair competition should cover, among other things, "acts calculated to influence demand (misleading advertising, forced sales, etc), acts that impede competing supplies (disruption of deliveries by competitors, enticing away a competitor's staff, boycotts), and acts that exploit a competitor's value (passing off and the like)."[344] It is also intended to encompass industrial espionage, disclosure of business secrets and inducing breach of contract.[345] There is no tort of unfair competition under English law but there are specific torts of passing off, malicious falsehood and defamation (which can be used in a business context). Passing off is clearly an act of unfair competition. Where malicious falsehood and defamation are used in a business context and involve a competitor's goods or business, they should be regarded as coming within the ambit of unfair competition under Article 6.[346] Under English law, disclosure of business secrets would be regarded as coming within breach of confidence. But for the purposes of Article 6 this should be regarded as an act of unfair competition. The specific tort of inducing breach of contract should likewise be so regarded. Once it has been decided that there is an act of unfair competition within the meaning of Article 6(1) it follows that this is a tort and the obligation that arises out of this tort must be regarded as non-contractual. Where an act of unfair competition affects exclusively the interests of a specific competitor, the choice of law rule in Article 6(2)[347] applies Article 4 and therefore presupposes that damage[348] occurs. Most national laws on unfair competition require damage or the threat of damage so in practice there will be damage.

---

[341] At one time the Hague Conference on private international law had on its agenda for future work the law applicable to unfair competition (see the note drawn up by the permanent Bureau, Prel Doc No 5 of April 2000) but this was dropped in 2006, Prel Doc No 11 of June 2006. Swiss law has special tort choice of law rules for unfair competition and restraints of competition.

[342] The Explanatory Memorandum, p 15.

[343] See Fawcett and Torremans, pp 409–410.

[344] The Explanatory Memorandum, p 15.

[345] Ibid, at p 16.

[346] For why defamation in the business context should be regarded as unfair competition (within the scope of the Regulation) and not defamation (excluded from the scope of the Regulation), see supra, p 785.

[347] Art 6(1), discussed below, does not presuppose that there is damage.

[348] As defined in Art 2(1) and (3)(b).

(ii) The law applicable to unfair competition

There are two different choice of law rules in relation to unfair competition. The two separate rules reflect the fact that unfair competition law seeks to protect not only the market, competitors interests overall, consumers and the public in general but also specific competitors.[349]

Article 6(1)   The first choice of law rule is concerned with "where competitive relations or the collective interests of consumers are, or are likely to be, affected" (Article 6(1)). This is concerned with the effect on the market in general, on competitors' interests in general and the effect on the interests of consumers generally.[350] This would cover an action for an injunction based on unfair competition brought by a consumer association against the defendant.[351] It is, however, not confined to actions brought by consumer associations.

Under Article 6(1), the law applicable is that of the country where competitive relations or the collective interests of consumers are, or are likely to be, affected. This is the market where competitors are seeking to gain the customers' favour.[352] In determining which markets are likely to be affected only the direct substantial effects of an act of unfair competition should be taken into account.[353] This rule has been justified on the basis that it generally satisfies the objectives of protecting competitors, consumers and the general public and ensuring that the market economy functions properly.[354] The rule has been described as not being an exception to the general rule in Article 4(1) (the country of damage rule) but rather as a clarification of that rule.[355] Often the place of damage under the latter rule will coincide with the place where competitive relations are affected.[356] However, Article 6(1), unlike Article 4(1), has no common habitual residence exception or manifestly more closely connected escape clause.[357] It is a totally inflexible rule.

Article 6(2)   The second choice of law rule is concerned with where "an act of unfair competition affects exclusively the interests of a specific competitor" (Article 6(2)). In other words, a specific competitor is targeted. This would, for example, encompass enticing away a competitor's staff, corruption, industrial espionage, disclosure of business secrets or inducing breach of contract.[358] It would also cover passing off and those instances of malicious falsehood and defamation that come within the concept of unfair competition.

Under Article 6(2) it is provided that Article 4 will apply. In other words, unfair competition is not treated as a special tort and there is no special rule for it. It is to be noted that the whole of Article 4 will apply, not just the country of damage rule but also the common

---

[349] The Explanatory Memorandum, p 15.

[350] On the concept of consumers' interests, see Directive (EC) No 98/27 of 19 May 1998 on injunctions for the protection of consumers' interests, OJ 1998 L 166/51.

[351] The Explanatory Memorandum, p 15. This is consistent with the jurisdictional position, see Case C-167/2000 *Verein Für Konsumenteninformation v K H Henkel* [2002] ECR I-8111.

[352] The Explanatory Memorandum, p 16.

[353] Ibid.

[354] Recital (21).

[355] Ibid.

[356] For an example where they do not coincide, see the Explanatory Memorandum, p 16.

[357] These rules are said to be "not adapted to this matter in general": the Explanatory Memorandum, p 16.

[358] The Explanatory Memorandum, p 16.

habitual residence exception and the manifestly more closely connected escape clause. The underlying philosophy is that where a specific competitor has been targeted, that person should enjoy the benefit of the flexibility in Article 4(2) and (3).[359]

Article 6(4)   This provides that the law applicable under Article 6 cannot be derogated from by an agreement of the parties as to the governing law pursuant to Article 14. This limitation rule was not in the Proposal for a Regulation and so there is no explanation for it in the Explanatory Memorandum. It is perhaps rather surprising to find this limitation on the parties' normal freedom to choose the law applicable to a non-contractual obligation in Article 6(2) cases. After all, the choice of law rule is the flexible one set out in Article 4. So why not allow flexibility in the form of a choice of the applicable law by the parties? A possible justification for this could be that a denial of the freedom to choose also applies to infringements of intellectual property rights. Not uncommonly a claim for infringement is accompanied by one for passing off, a tort which would fall within Article 6(2). It would be undesirable for one part of the claim to be governed by the parties' choice and the other part not so governed.

(c) Restricting free competition

Article 6(3) sets out a choice of law rule for acts restricting free competition.[360] The substantive law background to this rule is Articles 81 and 82 of the Treaty on European Union, which deal with competition law within the European Union. In addition, individual Member States have their own competition laws. Any actionable breach of community law which gives rise to a claim in damages should be categorised as a tort/delict, being a breach of statutory duty.[361] A breach of competition rules has been held to come within the scope of Article 5(3) of the Brussels Convention.[362]

(i) The scope of Article 6(3)

Article 6 is headed, inter alia, "acts restricting free competition" and Article 6(3) applies to "a non-contractual obligation arising out of a restriction of competition". Recital (23) explains that the concept of restrictions of competition should cover four things: first, prohibitions on agreements between undertakings which have as their object or effect the prevention, restriction or distortion of competition within a Member State or within the internal market; secondly, prohibitions on decisions by associations of undertakings which have as their object or effect, etc; thirdly, prohibitions on concerted practices which have as their object or effect, etc; fourthly, prohibitions on the abuse of a dominant position within a Member State or within the internal market. This definition is taken almost verbatim from Articles 81 and 82 of the Treaty and those Articles can be consulted for particular instances of such agreements, decisions, concerted practices and abuses. To reinforce the link with those Articles, Recital (23) goes on to provide that such agreements, decisions, concerted practices or abuses must be prohibited by Articles 81

---

[359] The Explanatory Memorandum, p 16. See also s 4(2) Dutch Private International Law Act 2001, s 4(2) and Swiss Federal Private International Law Act 1987, s 136(2).

[360] There was no such rule in the Proposal for a Regulation.

[361] *Garden Cottage Foods v Milk Marketing Board* [1984] AC 130.

[362] *Norburt Schmidt v Home Secretary of the Government of the United Kingdom* [1995] 1 ILRM 301; Fawcett and Torremans, pp 423–425.

and 82 of the Treaty or by the law of a Member State.[363] So non-contractual obligations arising out of restrictions of competition cover infringements of both Community and national competition law.[364] Once it has been decided that there is an act restricting free competition within the meaning of Article 6(3), it follows that this is a tort and the obligation that arises out of this tort must be regarded as non-contractual.

Most actions for breach of competition law are brought by the Commission. Such an action would presumably fall outside the scope of the Regulation on the basis that this is not a civil and commercial matter. In contrast, an action by an individual (or company) who has suffered damage would clearly satisfy this requirement. The basic choice of law rule for a restriction of competition set out in Article 6(3)(a) does not presuppose that damage occurs [365] and so this cannot be regarded as an implied limitation on the scope of this Article. In practice, though, there is going to be damage when an individual brings the action.

(ii) The law applicable to acts restricting free competition

Article 6(3) sets out two choice of law rules. Article 6(3)(a) applies where the market is, or is likely to be, affected in just one country. Under this rule the law applicable is that of the country where the market is, or is likely to be, affected.[366] Article 6(3)(b) applies where the market is, or is likely to be, affected in more than one country. In this situation, the claimant[367] is able in certain circumstances[368] to choose to base his claim on the law of the court seised.[369] The law applicable under Article 6(3) may not be derogated from by an agreement pursuant to Article 14.[370]

(d) Environmental damage

Although there has been a gradual harmonisation within the European Community of the substantive law in relation to environmental damage, choice of law problems remain in the world-wide context and even within the European Community.[371] The Hague Conference on private international law has on its agenda future work leading to a possible Convention, "the conflict of jurisdictions, applicable law and international judicial and administrative co-operation in respect of civil liability for environmental damage".[372] So it is not surprising to find a specific rule in the Regulation for this situation. This is contained in Article 7.[373]

---

[363] Recital (23).

[364] Recital (22).

[365] However, Art 3(b) (where the market is affected in more than one country) does so.

[366] For where the market is affected in relation to unfair competition see supra, p 810.

[367] Who sues in the defendant's domicile.

[368] "provided that the market in that Member State is amongst those directly and substantially affected by the restriction of competition out of which the non-contractual obligation on which the claim is based arises". There is a variant of this proviso for the situation where the claimant sues more than one defendant.

[369] See Recital (23).

[370] Art 6(4).

[371] The Explanatory Memorandum, p 19.

[372] Council on General Affairs and Policy of the Conference (2–4 April 2007), Conclusion 2(b), Prel Doc No 24 of July 2007. See also the note drawn up by Bernasconi from the Permanent Bureau, Prel Doc No 8 of May 2000.

[373] See in relation to the Proposal, Betlem and Bernasconi (2006) 122 LQR 124, 137–151.

(i) The scope of Article 7

Article 7 is headed "environmental damage". Recital (24) explains that "environmental damage" means "adverse change in a natural resource, such as water, land or air, impairment of a function performed by that resource for the benefit of another natural resource or the public, or impairment of the variability among living organisms".[374] Article 7 applies to "a non-contractual obligation arising out of environmental damage or damage sustained by persons or property as a result of such damage". It is designed to cover two sorts of damage.[375] First, it covers damage to the environment itself. Many civil law states have introduced special rules dealing with the protection of the environment. Thus, under Italian law, he who nonchalantly violates environmental law must compensate the state for the damage caused. Secondly, it covers damage to persons or property which is as a result of environmental damage. This would cover cases brought under the English law of nuisance, trespass and negligence as well as the rule in *Rylands v Fletcher*.[376] With both types of damage, the damage must be the result of human activity.[377] Once it has been decided that there is environmental damage within the meaning of Article 7, it follows that this is a tort for the purposes of the Regulation and the obligation that arises out of this tort must be regarded as non-contractual.

(ii) The law applicable to environmental damage

In cases coming within the scope of Article 7 the law applicable "shall be the law determined pursuant to Article 4(1), unless the person seeking compensation for damage chooses to base his claim on the law of the country in which the event giving rise to the damage occurred". This provides for the application of the law of the country in which the damage occurs but with the claimant having the option of choosing the application of the law of the country in which the event giving rise to the damage occurred.

The place of damage rule　The starting point under Article 7 is the application of the law determined under Article 4(1), which provides for the application of the law of the country in which the damage occurs. This rule has been justified on the basis that it conforms to "recent objectives of environmental protection policy, which tends to support strict liability".[378] Moreover, it obliges operators established in low protection countries to abide by the greater protection afforded in neighbouring countries, removing the incentive to establish in low protection countries. This is said to be "conducive to a policy of prevention".[379] No recourse can be had to the Article 4(2) common habitual residence exception or the Article 4(3) manifestly more closely connected escape clause. This is doubtless because the place of damage rule is thought to work so well in the context of environmental damage that the use of an exception and a let-out is regarded as being unnecessary or inappropriate. The place of damage rule is the default rule that operates unless the claimant exercises the option to base his or her claim on the law of the country in which the event giving rise to the damage occurred.

---

[374] This definition is in line with other European Union instruments, such as the Directive on Environmental Liability.

[375] See also the general definition of damage in Art 2(1) and (3)(b).

[376] (1868) LR 3 HL 330.

[377] See the Explanatory Memorandum, p 19.

[378] Ibid.

[379] Ibid.

The option This allows the person seeking compensation for damage to base his or her claim on the law of the country in which the event giving rise to the damage occurs, rather than on the law of the country in which the damage occurs. If the claimant exercises this option, the applicable law is that of the country in which the event giving rise to the damage occurred.[380] The claimant can therefore choose the applicable law from two alternatives. This is a one-sided rule, with no such option given to the defendant. Article 7 can therefore be seen to be a pro-claimant rule.[381] The claimant victim is given this option so as to provide him or her with greater protection than is afforded by a place of damage rule. The victim should get the same protection as victims in neighbouring countries.[382] This can be illustrated by taking the following example:

> A polluter establishes its facilities in Country A by a river which flows into the neighbouring Country B, a low protection country. The victim should get the same protection as victims in Country A.[383]

If the victim could only rely on the law of the place of damage this would encourage businesses to establish their facilities on the border of low protection countries. So overall the option should raise the level of environmental protection. The stage at which the victim must exercise this option, ie the last moment at which it is possible to file a new claim, is for the procedural law of the forum to determine.[384] Giving the person seeking compensation the option of choosing to base his claim on the law of the country where damage was sustained or the law of the country in which the event giving rise to the damage occurred ties in with the jurisdictional choice of the same two countries given to the claimant under Article 5(3) of the Brussels I Regulation.

Rules of safety and conduct Article 17 contains a general limitation on the law applicable under the Regulation, which is concerned with rules of safety and conduct in force at the place of the event giving rise to liability. Environmental damage is an area where this rule may come into play. Operators are required to comply with public law rules as to safety and conduct.

> Let us assume that an operator complies with the rules, eg in relation to the level of toxic emissions, in the country in which it operates (Country A). Nonetheless, it causes damage in the adjacent Country B. The level of emissions exceeds those allowed under the rules of that country. Under the place of damage rule, the law of Country B will apply and the operator will be liable to the victim.

The effect of Article 17 is that the forum, in assessing the conduct of the operator, must take account "as a matter of fact and in so far as is appropriate, of the rules of safety and conduct" which were in force in Country A. This does not mean applying the law of Country A, rather it is a matter of taking account of its rules of conduct and safety to determine questions of fact.[385]

---

[380] This is not expressly stated in Art 7 but is implicit. It is also clearly the intention of the provision, see the Explanatory Memorandum, pp 19–20.

[381] See Recital (25) for the justification for this.

[382] The Explanatory Memorandum, pp 19–20.

[383] Ibid.

[384] The Explanatory Memorandum, p 20; Recital (25).

[385] See further infra, p 855.

(e) Infringement of intellectual property rights

Article 8 provides specific rules for infringement of intellectual property rights. Infringement was regarded as a special tort because of the significance given under intellectual property conventions[386] to the territoriality principle which attaches great importance to the law of the country in which protection is claimed.[387] However, it is only right to point out that there are no specific and clear-cut choice of law rules in these conventions.[388]

(i) The scope of Article 8

Article 8 is headed infringement of intellectual property rights and this provision applies to "a non-contractual obligation arising from an infringement of an intellectual property right . . .".[389] For the purposes of the Regulation the term "intellectual property rights" is to "be interpreted as meaning, for instance, copyright, related rights, the *sui generis* right for the protection of databases and industrial property rights".[390] "Industrial property rights" is a term used in the Berne Convention and in civil law jurisdictions to encompass patents, trade marks and registered designs. These are only instances of intellectual property rights. There can be other instances such as plant rights. Once it has been decided that there is an infringement of an intellectual property right within the meaning of Article 8, it follows that this is a tort and the obligation that arises out of this tort must be regarded as non-contractual. The choice of law rules in Article 8 do not presuppose that there is damage and so this cannot be regarded as an implied limitation on the scope of this Article. Under English law, the statutory provisions do not require any presence, let alone evidence, of damage.[391]

(ii) The law applicable to intellectual property rights

Article 8 sets out two separate choice of law rules. The first rule is set out in Article 8(1), the second in Article 8(2).

Article 8(1) This is concerned with infringements of intellectual property rights conferred under national legislation or international conventions, such as a United Kingdom patent or a European patent. Article 8(1) provides that: "The law applicable to a non-contractual obligation arising from an infringement of an intellectual property right shall be the law of the country for which protection is claimed." The country for which protection is claimed is, for a registered right, the country where it is registered. For copyright it is where the infringement was committed. To take an example of the operation of this rule, let us assume that a patent has been registered in England. It is claimed that this English patent has been infringed. If, as is usually the case, validity is raised as a defence

---

[386] See the Berne Convention for the Protection of Literary and Artistic Works of 1886 and the Paris Convention for the Protection of Industrial Property of 1883.

[387] The Explanatory Memorandum, p 20.

[388] See Fawcett and Torremans, Chapter 9. Rules referring to the law of the country in which protection is claimed could be regarded as unilateral rules explaining when substantive law applies.

[389] Art 8(1).

[390] Recital (26).

[391] It is assumed that any infringing act constitutes a wrong which will give rise to damage, see Fawcett and Torremans, p 132.

to the infringement, the English courts will have exclusive jurisdiction[392] and, by virtue of Article 8(1), will apply English law to determine whether the defendant is liable for infringement. English law also governs the validity point. English substantive law only provides protection for patents that have not only been registered in England but have also been infringed in England. Let us now assume that the patent has been registered in ten different European Community countries. If validity is raised as a defence, each of the ten European Community countries will have exclusive jurisdiction in relation to the patent that is registered in its country.[393] The claimant would have to bring ten actions in ten different Member States. Under Article 8(1) each Member State would then apply its own law to determine whether there has been infringement. Article 8(1) adopts the territorial principle that is found in intellectual property conventions, and has been used to justify special rules for infringement cases in the first place, but turns it into a choice of law rule.[394] This principle is regarded as being so important that there is no common habitual residence exception or "manifestly more closely connected" escape clause from the "country for which protection is claimed" rule.

Article 8(2) The second choice of law rule is concerned with infringements of unitary Community rights, ie a Community trade mark or a Community design. A Community right provides protection in every Member State. Article 8(1) does not work in this situation. The country for which protection is claimed is every European Community Member State. A different choice of law rule was therefore needed. Article 8(2) provides that: "In the case of a non-contractual obligation arising from an infringement of a unitary Community intellectual property right, the law applicable shall, for any question that is not governed by the relevant Community instrument, be the law of the country in which the act of infringement was committed." Article 8(2) only applies to questions that are not governed by the relevant Community instrument. The Community Trade Mark Regulation harmonises the basic rules on infringement so the question of infringement itself is governed by the Community instrument. However, the Community Trade Mark Regulation only has very limited rules on sanctions. Many issues in relation to sanctions (what are available, in what circumstances, etc) are left to be dealt with by national substantive law and these national rules can vary from one Member State to another. This resulting choice of law question will be determined by the application of the law of the country in which the act of infringement was committed. There is no common habitual residence exception or manifestly more closely connected escape clause from this rule.

Article 8(3) Provides that the law applicable under Article 8 cannot be derogated from by an agreement of the parties as to the governing law pursuant to Article 14. This is the same as with unfair competition, which can operate as a complementary tort to infringement. The only "explanation" given for this limitation in the case of infringement of intellectual property rights is that freedom of choice in this area would not be "appropriate",

---

[392] Case C-4/03 *Gesellschaft für Antriebstechnik mbH & Co KG (GAT) v Luk Lamellen und Kupplungsbau Beteiligungs KG* [2006] ECR I-6509; discussed supra, p 282.

[393] If validity is not raised as a defence, the defendant can be sued in its domicile or in another Member State under Art 5(3) of the Brussels I Regulation. However, validity can be raised at any stage, in which eventuality the exclusive jurisdiction provision will kick in.

[394] See the Explanatory Memorandum, p 20.

which is no real explanation at all.[395] The actual reason is presumably that the territorial principle that underlies the special choice of law rules for infringements is regarded as being so important that the parties should not be allowed to choose the law of a country other than the one arrived at by the application of that principle.

(f) Industrial action

Article 9 provides that:

> Without prejudice to Article 4(2), the law applicable to a non-contractual obligation in respect of the liability of a person in the capacity of a worker or an employer or the organisations representing their professional interests for damages caused by an industrial action, pending or carried out, shall be the law of the country where the action is to be, or has been, taken.[396]

(i) The scope of Article 9

Article 9 is entitled "Industrial action" and the choice of law rule is concerned with the law applicable to "a non-contractual obligation in respect of the liability of a person in the capacity of a worker or an employer or the organisations representing their professional interests for damages caused by an industrial action, pending or carried out". No definition of industrial action is provided. However, Recital (27) gives two examples of such action, namely strike action and lock-outs. More cryptically, Recital (27) points out that the exact concept of industrial action varies from one Member State to another "and is governed by each Member State's internal rules". Is this stating the position immediately prior to the Regulation coming into force or is it saying that there should be no community definition of the concept? If the latter, which Member State's internal rules should then provide the definition? The obvious answer would be the forum. But Recital (27) goes on to say: "Therefore, this regulation assumes as a general principle that the law of the country where the industrial action was taken should apply . . ." This might suggest that the law of the country where the action was taken should determine whether it is industrial action. In English and other common law jurisdictions, there is no tort of industrial action as such. However, a number of torts can arise out of strikes and lock-outs: namely, inducement of breach of contract;[397] causing loss by unlawful means; intimidation and unlawful conspiracy. Once it has been decided that there is an obligation in respect of the liability of a person in the capacity of a worker or an employer or the organisations representing their professional interests for damages caused by an industrial action, pending or carried out within the meaning of Article 9, this obligation must be regarded as non-contractual.

(ii) The law applicable to industrial action

In cases coming within the scope of Article 9, the law applicable is "the law of the country where the [industrial] action is to be, or has been, taken". This rule is designed to protect

---

[395] The Explanatory Memorandum, p 22.

[396] There was no such rule in the Proposal for a Regulation. The Explanatory Memorandum is therefore no guidance as to its meaning.

[397] Where the inducement of breach of contract does not arise from a strike or lock-out, it will constitute unfair competition, supra, p 809.

the rights of workers and employers.[398] It has been justified on the basis of the difficulty in defining "industrial action".[399] Some Member States were not happy with this rule because it means that vessels would be exposed to substantive law rules which varied according to the laws of the states of their ports of call, irrespective of whether those vessels were in full conformity with the laws of the flag state.[400] This rule is without prejudice to Article 4(2), the common habitual residence exception. However, the manifestly more closely connected escape clause in Article 4(3) does not apply. The specific rule on industrial action is "without prejudice to the conditions relating to the exercise of such action in accordance with national law and without prejudice to the legal status of trade unions or of the representative organisations of workers as provided for in the law of the Member States".[401]

(e) The applicable law for unjust enrichment, negotiorum gestio and culpa in contrahendo

Chapter III is concerned with obligations that arise neither out of a contract nor out of a tort/delict within the meaning of Chapter II.[402] More specifically it is concerned with obligations that arise out of unjust enrichment, *negotiorum gestio* and *culpa in contrahendo*. Obligations arising out of these three concepts are necessarily non-contractual obligations.[403] The first two concepts are concerned with the law of restitution. The third is concerned with the very different matter of pre-contractual obligations. The Commission, in the Proposal for a Regulation, acknowledged the difficulty in devising choice of law for these areas. They accepted that the substantive law and the choice of law rules were still evolving rapidly in most of the Member States, which meant that the law was far from certain.[404] The answer in the Proposal was to avoid technical terms and to provide a mixture of specific rules, whilst leaving sufficient flexibility to Member States to adapt the rules to their national system.[405] The final version of the Regulation is markedly different from the Proposal. It is much clearer in that it adopts separate regimes of specific rules for each of the three concepts dealt with in Chapter III, rather than a confusing combination of general rules and specific rules for particular concepts.[406] But this development has necessitated the use of technical terms with attendant definitional problems.

Before turning to examine these special rules, it should be noted that there is one exception to the principle that non-contractual obligations that arise out of unjust enrichment,

---

[398] Recital (27).

[399] Ibid.

[400] See the Statement by the Cypriot and Greek Delegations on Art 9, CODEC 838 JUSTCIV 181 of 14 September 2006. See also, at the same reference, the Joint Declaration of Latvia and Estonia, that Art 9 should only apply to cases which arise directly from exercise of the essential right to industrial action.

[401] Recital (28).

[402] The Explanatory Memorandum, p 21. See also Recital (29): "Provision should be made for special rules where damage is caused by an act other than a tort/delict, such as unjust enrichment, *negotiorum gestio* and *culpa in contrahendo*."

[403] See supra, pp 777–780.

[404] See the Explanatory Memorandum, p 21.

[405] Ibid. The UK government and the House of Lords EU Committee preferred confining the Regulation solely to torts/delicts, see United Kingdom Response (2002), para 20; HL Paper No 66 (2004), para 144, and the Written Evidence of Crawford, 100, Fentiman, 112, and Morse, 126.

[406] See Art 9 of the Proposal for a Regulation.

negotiorum gestio and *culpa in contrahendo* are dealt with by the special choice of law rules in Chapter III. The exception is concerned with non-contractual obligations that arise from the infringement of intellectual property rights. For example, a non-contractual obligation may be based on unjust enrichment arising from an infringement of intellectual property rights. In theory two sets of special choice of law rules under the Regulation could come into play in respect of the same dispute, namely the infringement of intellectual property rules in Article 8 of Chapter II and the unjust enrichment rules in Article 10 of Chapter III. To avoid this, Article 13 provides that Article 8 shall apply to non-contractual obligations arising from an infringement of an intellectual property right.[407] This means that the non-contractual obligation based on unjust enrichment is governed by the same law as the infringement itself.[408]

(i) Unjust enrichment

Article 10 sets out the special choice of law rules for unjust enrichment.

(a) The scope of Article 10

Article 10 is headed "Unjust enrichment" and applies where there is "a non-contractual obligation arising out of unjust enrichment".[409] Unjust enrichment includes "payment of amounts wrongly received".[410] This would cover a claim for restitution of an overpayment of money. This gives an example of unjust enrichment but there is no attempt to go further and to define "unjust enrichment".

(i) Characterisation as unjust enrichment

The nature of the problem Difficult problems of classification arise in relation to unjust enrichment. It is not always clear whether an obligation arises out of unjust enrichment, contract, tort, or equity. If the obligation arises out of unjust enrichment it will fall within Article 10. If the obligation arises out of contract it will fall outside the scope of the Regulation altogether, but within the Rome Convention. If the obligation arises out of tort or equity it will fall within Chapter II of the Regulation. If the matter is essentially proprietary it will fall outside the Regulation and instead come within the property choice of law rules.

Does it make any practical difference which set of choice of law rules is applied? In many cases it will make no practical difference whether the contract or unjust enrichment choice of law rules are applied. The result will be the same. This is because under Article 10 of the Regulation, normally, the law governing the contractual relationship will also govern the non-contractual obligation arising out of unjust enrichment.[411] Nonetheless, in a minority of cases the effect of Article 10 is that the law of some country other than that whose law is applicable to the contract will apply.[412] It is therefore crucial to decide whether the contract choice of law rules or the unjust enrichment choice of law

---

[407] See the Explanatory Memorandum, p 22.
[408] Ibid.
[409] Art 10(1).
[410] Ibid.
[411] Art 10(1), discussed infra.
[412] Art 10(2), (3) and (4), discussed infra.

rules should be applied. The same is true in relation to whether the tort choice of law rules[413] or the unjust enrichment choice of law rules are applied. The difference between the unjust enrichment choice of law rule under Article 10 and the English choice of law rules for property is much more marked and makes the question of characterisation on this borderline particularly important.

The approach to be adopted towards characterisation　At common law the English courts characterised the cause of action and the issue. The leading pre-Regulation case on characterisation in the context of restitution is *Macmillan Inc v Bishopsgate Investment Trust plc (No 3)*,[414] which concerned the developing notion of a receipt-based restitutionary claim. In this case, the Court of Appeal accepted that the claim was one in restitution, but characterised the issue as being proprietary with the result that the property choice of law rules applied. AULD LJ referred to the danger of looking at characterisation through domestic eyes, and said that "the 'receipt-based restitutionary claim' is a notion of English domestic law that may not have a counterpart in many other legal systems and is one that it may not be appropriate to translate into the English law of conflict".[415] In the absence of an issue whose characterisation is so clear-cut, it will be the characterisation of the cause of action that matters. This is what will happen in many cases.

Under the Regulation, it has to be decided whether there is a non-contractual obligation and, if there is, whether this arises out of unjust enrichment. This does not tell us precisely what is being characterised. If the facts of *Macmillan* were to arise under the Regulation, is one supposed to characterise the issue or the cause of action?

In the context of the Regulation the process of characterisation should not be carried out through English eyes. The approach adopted in *Macmillan* is designed to ensure that this does not happen. Ultimately the question is which set of choice of law rules in the Regulation should you apply and the flexible approach adopted in *Macmillan* is particularly well suited to answering this.

(ii) Specific problems

Property or unjust enrichment?[416]　Under English substantive law it is unclear to what extent proprietary claims should be characterised as restitutionary.[417] At first sight, this produces a considerable dilemma for the private international lawyer. However, under the pre-Regulation law it appears that, regardless of the characterisation of the cause of action, where the issue in the case is essentially a proprietary one, recourse must be had to the choice of law rules in relation to property issues.[418] The leading pre-Regulation case is *Macmillan Inc v Bishopsgate Investment Trust plc (No 3)*.[419]

---

[413] These will govern not just obligations characterised as tortious but also those characterised as equitable.

[414] [1996] 1 WLR 387; Forsyth (1998) 114 LQR 141.

[415] At 604. See also Briggs [1995] Rest LR 94, at 97.

[416] See Bird in Rose (ed), *Restitution*, pp 79–83; Pitel in Neyers, MacInnes and Pitel (eds), *Understanding Unjust Enrichment in the Conflict of Laws* (Hart 2004).

[417] See R Stevens in Rose (ed), *Restitution*, pp 182–183.

[418] See generally on the extent to which proprietary claims should be regarded as being restitutionary, R Stevens, op cit, pp 182–184.

[419] [1996] 1 WLR 387; Bird [1996] LMCLQ 57; Briggs (1996) 67 BYBIL 604; Swadling [1996] LMCLQ 63; R Stevens (1996) 112 LQR 198; J Stevens (1996) 59 MLR 741; Grantham and Rickett [1996] LMCLQ 463.

The plaintiff, a Delaware corporation, brought an action against a number of banks claiming that it was beneficially entitled to shares in a New York corporation, that these were held on constructive trust by the defendants for the benefit of the plaintiff, and seeking their return or compensation for their loss. The question arose of the applicable law. This in turn raised a question of characterisation: was the issue in the case restitutionary, in which case the restitution choice of law rules would apply, or proprietary, in which case the property choice of law rules would apply?

The Court of Appeal held that the issue in the case, namely whether the defendants could defeat the plaintiff's interest by establishing that they were bona fide transferees for value without notice, was essentially a proprietary one. Turning therefore to the choice of law rules in relation to property issues, it was held that the law applicable to questions of title to shares in a company was that of the place where the shares were situated, which in the ordinary way was that where the company was incorporated. Accordingly, New York law applied.

It has earlier been submitted that the *Macmillan* approach towards characterisation should be adopted in Regulation cases. This means that, if the facts of *Macmillan* were to arise now, the result should be the same, namely the property choice of law rules should apply, rather than the Regulation.

The question of characterisation as unjust enrichment or property also arises in relation to proprietary restitution.[420] A claim for proprietary restitution would arise where, for example, a seller delivers goods to the buyer and the latter fails to pay. The seller wants the goods themselves back. If title has passed to the buyer the seller would ask that the goods revest in him. The question is whether such a claim is based on unjust enrichment (and thus falls within Article 10 in Chapter III) or is based on the law of property (and thus falls outside the scope of the Regulation altogether). Under English substantive law there is considerable controversy over the classification of such claims.[421] In such circumstances, it was suggested under the pre-Regulation law that a bold line should be adopted and, rather than relying on a domestic English law classification, claims for proprietary restitution should be regarded as being based on property, since property rights are ultimately at stake.[422] This approach is even more attractive under the Regulation because other Member States do not recognise proprietary restitution[423] and so it is not possible to obtain any guidance from their domestic classification.

---

[420] *Macmillan* was not a case of proprietary restitution; it was one of a restitutionary claim to which there was a proprietary defence (Panagopoulos, 44–45) or better analysed as a direct assertion of a proprietary right (Panagopoulos, Burrows, op cit, 616). We are concerned here with proprietary restitution without a trust. For the situation where there is a trust, see Chong (2005) 54 ICLQ 855 and, in the context of international sale of goods, Fawcett, Harris and Bridge, paras 19.74–19.87.

[421] Cf Burrows, *The Law of Restitution* (2002) 2nd edn, pp 60–75 (proprietary or unjust enrichment depending on the circumstances) with Virgo, *The Principles of the Law of Restitution* (2006) 2nd edn, Chapter 20 (a proprietary claim).

[422] See Fawcett, Harris and Bridge, paras 19.69–19.73.

[423] See Dickson (1987) 36 ICLQ 751, 783 (referring to equitable interests); Bell, Boyron and Whittaker, *Principles of French Law* (1998), pp 402–403; Beatson and Schrage (eds), *Cases, Materials and Texts on Unjustified Enrichment* (2003), p 33 (referring to equitable interests); Gretton in Johnston and Zimmermann, *Unjustified Enrichment: Key Issues in Comparative Perspective* (2002), p 571; Panagopoulos, *Restitution in Private International Law* (2002), pp 11, 61.

Contract or unjust enrichment?[424] A claim by a buyer of goods for restitution of an overpayment of money to the seller arises out of unjust enrichment, rather than contract. This can be said with confidence because Article 10(1) provides that unjust enrichment includes "payment of amounts wrongly received".[425] A contract may be void *ab initio* and one of the parties seeks return of money paid in advance. Article 10(1)(e) of the Rome Convention[426] makes it clear that "the consequences of nullity" is to be characterised as contractual for the purposes of the European Community private international law of obligations. For most Member States what will then happen is that they will apply the contract choice of law rules set out in that Convention. However, there is a dilemma for those Contracting States (of which the United Kingdom is one) that entered a reservation in respect of this provision. The courts in the United Kingdom will have to decide what choice of law rules to apply in relation to this issue. The Commission contemplates that a tortious classification will be adopted in Member States that have entered a reservation to Article 10(1)(e) of the Rome Convention but that, applying Chapter II of the Rome II Regulation, the secondary connection rule under Article 4(3) of the Regulation will mitigate the effect of this.[427] However, under English law this issue has been regarded as restitutionary rather than contractual.[428] Indeed, this was why the United Kingdom entered a reservation against Article 10(1)(e) of the Rome Convention. If England adopted a restitutionary classification then, again, the secondary connection nature of Article 10(1) would also mitigate differences in classification between Member States. In other words, the English courts would end up applying the law governing the putative contractual relationship between the parties to the issue of unjust enrichment. This would produce the same result as adopting a contractual classification in the first place.

There is, though, a very different approach that could be applied. There is a strong argument that the English courts should not apply the rules in Article 10 of the Rome II Regulation because as a matter of European Community choice of law this issue is intended to come within the Rome Convention. It is wrong in principle for some Member States to be applying the Rome Convention to the issue and others applying the Rome II Regulation. This would leave a restitutionary issue which falls outside Article 10. The result is that the English courts would continue to apply the common law choice of law rules for unjust enrichment to the issue of the consequences of nullity.[429] However, under these rules if the restitutionary obligation arises in connection with a contract (including a void contract), the obligation is governed by the law applicable to the contract.[430] Looking to the near future, the Rome I Regulation provides that this issue falls within the scope of the contract choice of law rules and Member States would not be able to enter a reservation. If the United Kingdom opts in to the Rome I Regulation,[431] the current

---

[424] See generally Brereton in Rose (ed), *Restitution*, Chapter 4; Fawcett, Harris and Bridge, paras 8.12–8.26, for characterisation as contract or unjust enrichment for the purposes of jurisdiction under the Brussels I Regulation.

[425] Art 10(1).

[426] Discussed supra, pp 757–758.

[427] Supra, p 803.

[428] Criticised by Brereton, op cit, pp 172–174.

[429] See the 13th edn of this book (1999), pp 676–692; Dicey, Morris and Collins, Chapter 34. See in particular, *Baring Bros & Co Ltd v Cunninghame District Council* [1997] CLC 108, (1998) Times, 30 September.

[430] Dicey, Morris and Collins, paras 34R-001, 34-021.

[431] The Ministry of Justice has provisionally concluded that it should do so.

dilemma would be solved and courts in the United Kingdom would apply the contract choice of law rules under that Regulation.

A restitutionary obligation may arise out of discharge of a contract. This does not relate to "the consequences of nullity".[432] Under English law this would probably be regarded as restitutionary rather than contractual[433] and, if this classification is adopted for the purposes of the Rome II Regulation, recourse has to be had to Article 10. However, in some civil law countries, eg Germany, the right to have a contract unwound, and obtain restitution, following a serious breach of contract is regarded as contractual.[434] This is likely to be the classification adopted by the Court of Justice for the purposes of the Rome II Regulation. Such a case would then fall within the Rome Convention.[435]

Tort or unjust enrichment?   The borderline between unjust enrichment and tort has previously been examined when discussing the scope of Chapter II,[436] where it was seen that contribution and indemnity are probably best classified as arising out of unjust enrichment.

Equity and unjust enrichment   Prior to the Rome II Regulation it was suggested that the equitable parts of the law of restitution, such as the restitutionary remedy of rescission for common mistake in equity, should be characterised as restitutionary (unjust enrichment) rather than as equitable.[437] The question now is whether this should be regarded as falling within the meaning of unjust enrichment under the Regulation. If it is so regarded, Article 10 will apply. It was also suggested that the question whether a person holds on constructive trust is best regarded as coming within the restitution choice of law rules.[438] It is no doubt true that constructive trusts are restitutionary in cases where the constructive trust is imposed where there is unjust enrichment by subtraction or restitution for wrongdoing.[439] With the introduction of the Regulation, such cases would fall within Article 10. But there are other cases where a constructive trust is held to exist where there is no unjust enrichment by subtraction or restitution for wrongdoing.[440] A claim may assert that property is held on constructive trust because the transferee has equitable title to the property. The basis of such a claim is proprietary.[441] The appropriate choice of law rule to be applied will depend on whether the constructive trust falls within the Recognition of Trusts Act 1987,[442] which gives effect to the Hague Convention on the Law Applicable to Trusts and on their Recognition. If it does, then the choice of law rules

---

[432] Brereton, op cit, pp 166–167.

[433] Ibid.

[434] Ibid.

[435] See Art 10(1)(c) (consequences of breach) of the Rome Convention.

[436] Supra, pp 792–793.

[437] Bird in Rose (ed), *Restitution*, pp 77–79.

[438] Dicey, Morris and Collins, para 34.047; Bird, op cit, pp 82–83. See also the pre-Regulation case of *Kuwait Oil Tanker Co SAK v Al Bader* [2000] 2 All ER (Comm) 271 (this involved a claim for breach of fiduciary duty and thus liability to account as constructive trustees). Cf Barnard (1992) 51 CLJ 474, 479–480.

[439] These terms are explained infra, pp 824–825. This situation is more accurately known as constructive trusteeship, see *Paragon Finance v DB Thakerar and Co* [1999] 1 All ER 400 at 409.

[440] R Stevens, op cit, pp 215–218.

[441] See Chong (2005) 54 ICLQ 855. For the jurisdictional position, see *NABB Brothers Ltd v Lloyds Bank International* [2005] EWHC 405 (Ch), [2005] IL Pr 37.

[442] R Stevens ibid. There are different views on the applicability of the Act to constructive trusts: cf Fawcett, Harris and Bridge, para 19.76–19.80 (most constructive trusts will be covered) with Dicey, Morris and Collins, para 34-050, which confines the operation of the Act to the situation once a constructive trust has

in the Act will apply. This is unaffected by the advent of the Regulation, which does not prejudice the application of this Hague Convention.[443] If the constructive trust does not fall within the 1987 Act, the property choice of law rules should apply.[444] The position is equally unsettled when it comes to resulting trusts. Although it has been argued that, in principle, there are restitutionary resulting trusts and that these should be characterised as restitutionary,[445] the better view is that, as a matter of substantive law, resulting trusts should be regarded as proprietary.[446] This would suggest a proprietary characterisation for the purposes of choice of law. The property choice of law rules would then apply[447] (rather than those in the Regulation), except to the extent, and this is unclear,[448] that resulting trusts fall to be dealt with by the choice of law rules contained in the Recognition of Trusts Act 1987.[449] In which case the choice of law rules in the Act would apply, unaffected by the Regulation. Finally, it was suggested that, in the situation where the cause of action is in unjust enrichment, the right to trace should be determined by the unjust enrichment choice of law rules.[450] This is on the basis that tracing is a process of identification. With the introduction of the Regulation this would mean that Article 10 would apply.

Restitution for wrongdoing and unjust enrichment   Under English substantive law there is a concept of restitution for wrongdoing. The wrongdoing which must be established may be contractual or tortious or an equitable wrong. An example of restitution for contractual wrongdoing would be where a seller breaks his contract with the buyer and sells goods for £1,000 more to a third party. The original buyer seeks restitutionary damages of £1,000. An example of restitution for tortious wrongdoing would be where A wrongfully sells goods belonging to B (the tort of conversion) and B claims for the value of the sale, rather than the loss caused to him. An example of restitution for equitable wrongdoing would be where a person in a fiduciary position (such as a company director) makes an unauthorised profit and a claim is made for him to disgorge it by way of an account of profits. Under English substantive law the classification of restitution for wrongdoing is particularly difficult. A number of different views have

---

arisen. Chong, op cit, argues that the Act does not apply to constructive trusts governed by a foreign law. The Act is discussed infra, pp 1312 and 1315–1320.

[443] Art 28(1).

[444] See Stevens, op cit; Chong (2005) 54 ICLQ 855. Stevens argues that the choice of law rules for equitable wrongs (restitution for equitable wrongdoing is now encompassed within Art 10 of the Regulation) should apply where the trust arises by virtue of such a wrong.

[445] Bird, op cit, p 83; R Stevens, op cit, p 218. See also Millett (1998) 114 LQR 399, 415.

[446] *Westdeutsche Landesbank Girozentrade v Islington Borough Council* [1996] AC 669, HL.

[447] See Chong, op cit.

[448] See Dicey, Morris and Collins, para 29-007; Hayton (1987) 36 ICLQ 260, 263–264; infra, p 1314. Cf Fawcett, Harris and Bridge, para 19.77 for an assertion that most resulting trusts will fall within the Act. See also Chong, op cit, who argues that the Act does not apply to constructive trusts governed by a foreign law.

[449] Bird, op cit, p 83. See also Stevens, op cit. See also Fawcett, Harris and Bridge, para 19.77.

[450] Dicey, Morris and Collins, para 34-047; Panagopoulos (1998) 6 Rest LR 73; Fawcett, Harris and Bridge, para 19.96. There is a question whether a procedural classification should be adopted. MILLETT J in *El Ajou v Dollar Land Holdings plc* [1993] 3 All ER 717 at 736 found it unnecessary to decide this point since on the facts English law applied in either eventuality. However, the same judge has said in a conference paper that he inclines to the view that the matter is one of substance to be governed by the law of the restitutionary obligation, 8th Singapore Conference on International Business Law 30 October–1 November 1996. For tracing of trust property generally, see Harris (2002) 73 BYBIL 65; Fawcett, Harris and Bridge, paras 19.90–19.95.

been expressed on this.[451] Some leading common law commentators regard this category as coming within the category of unjust enrichment, but consider that unjust enrichment by wrongdoing (or dependent unjust enrichment) is different from the more usual unjust enrichment by subtraction (or autonomous unjust enrichment).[452] With unjust enrichment by wrongdoing, the defendant's gain has been acquired by committing a wrong against the claimant. So the enrichment results from the wrongful act of the person enriched. However, the better view, which enjoys the greatest academic support, is that the cause of action is in tort, contract or equity, and this triggers a restitutionary remedy.[453] Under English law, then, restitution for wrongdoing exists and it is almost universally agreed that it is very different from unjust enrichment by subtraction.[454]

In civil law jurisdictions the position is entirely different. The concept of restitution for wrongdoing is not known as such.[455] Civil law jurisdictions such as Germany, Greece[456] and France[457] classify such actions under unjust enrichment by subtraction. In the light of this, it is not surprising to find that the Regulation does not contain a special choice of law rule for restitution for wrongdoing or explain which of the choice of law rules it falls within. However, the failure to provide an explanation under the Regulation leaves uncertainty in relation to claims based on restitution for wrongdoing.

One possibility would be to adopt the English substantive law classification. Lack of agreement on this classification, makes this a rather unattractive proposition. But if one adopts, for the purposes of the Regulation,[458] the most commonly held view, namely that the cause of action is in tort, contract or equity, and this triggers a restitutionary remedy,[459] the result is as follows. Where the obligation is tortious or equitable, Chapter II (Article 4) will apply. But where the obligation is contractual, this will be excluded from the scope of the Regulation altogether.

A better alternative would be to adopt the civil law classification, namely that situations falling within the common law concept of restitution for wrongdoing simply come under unjust enrichment by subtraction. Article 10 would then apply. It is likely that the Court of Justice would adopt this classification for the purposes of the Regulation. This is supported by the wording of Article 10, which envisages that there can be unjust enrichment where the parties do not have just a contractual relationship but also have a tortious or other relationship that is closely connected with the unjust enrichment. The most obvious example of this situation is where there is what common lawyers would call restitution for tortious or equitable wrongdoing.

---

[451] See generally Bird, op cit, pp 72–76; Fawcett, Harris and Bridge, para 8.89; Rotherham (2007) 66 CLJ 172.

[452] Burrows, *The Law of Restitution*, pp 5–6, 44 and Chapter 14; Birks, *An Introduction to the Law of Restitution*, Chapters I and X. Birks later changed his mind, see in Cornish, Nolan, O'Sullivan and Virgo (eds) *Restitution: Past, Present and Future*, pp 14–15 and in *Unjust Enrichment* (2005) 2nd edn.

[453] Virgo, op cit, 445–448; Panagopoulos, op cit, 16–17, 81–84, 228; Bird, op cit, 74.

[454] But see Beatson, *The Use and Abuse of Unjust Enrichment* (1991), pp 25–28, who regards restitution for wrongdoing as falling within unjust enrichment by subtraction.

[455] See Beatson and Schrage (eds), *Cases, Materials and Texts on Unjustified Enrichment*, p 523.

[456] Panagopoulos, op cit, 228.

[457] See Beatson and Schrage (eds), *Cases, Materials and Texts on Unjustified Enrichment*, p 543.

[458] See Virgo, Written Evidence, HL Paper 66 (2004), 134.

[459] Virgo, op cit, 425–428; Panagopoulos, op cit, 16–17, 81–84, 228; Bird, op cit, 74.

(iii) Other aspects of scope

Once it has been decided that there is unjust enrichment within the meaning of Article 10 it follows that the obligation that arises out of this unjust enrichment must be regarded as non-contractual.[460] Article 10 does not presuppose that there is damage. This is not surprising given that damage is not one of the essential elements of unjust enrichment.

(b) The law applicable to unjust enrichment

Article 10 contains four rules, with a separate paragraph for each rule. The first paragraph is concerned with the specific situation where there is a relationship existing between the parties. The second paragraph is a fall-back provision which deals with the situation where the applicable law cannot be determined on the basis of the first paragraph. The third paragraph is a further fall-back provision now dealing with the situation where the applicable law cannot be determined on the basis of the first and second paragraphs. The fourth paragraph contains a manifestly more closely connected escape clause, which allows an escape from the first three paragraphs. Article 10 is very similar to the position under German law.[461]

(i) Where there is a relationship existing between the parties

Article 10(1) provides that:

> If a non-contractual obligation arising out of unjust enrichment, including payment of amounts wrongly received, concerns a relationship existing between the parties, such as one arising out of a contract or a tort/delict, that is closely connected with that unjust enrichment, it shall be governed by the law that governs that relationship.

This rule adopts the philosophy of secondary connection that is also to be found in Article 4(3).[462] The justification for the rule is that the non-contractual obligation arising out of unjust enrichment is so closely connected with the pre-existing relationship between the parties that it is preferable for the entire legal situation to be governed by the same law.[463] The same approach had its advocates in England.[464]

When does Article 10(1) apply?   In order for Article 10(1) to apply, the following must be shown:

First, there must be a non-contractual obligation arising out of unjust enrichment. In other words, the obligation must come within the scope of Article 10, examined above.

Secondly, the non-contractual obligation must concern a relationship existing between the parties. Article 10(1) goes on to give two examples of such a relationship, namely "one arising out of a contract or a tort/delict". Unjust enrichment most commonly arises out of the situation where the parties have a contractual relationship.[465] But the relationship

---

[460] Supra, pp 777–780.

[461] Introductory Law to the Civil Code, the 1999 Codification, Arts 38 and 41. See also Swiss law, the Swiss PIL Statute 1987, Arts 128 and 15.

[462] The Explanatory Memorandum, p 21. Art 4(3) is discussed supra, pp 799–805.

[463] Ibid.

[464] See Dicey, Morris and Collins, Rule 230(2)(a) and supra, p 800.

[465] The Rome Convention will apply to determine whether there is a contract between the parties. If there is no contract the parties could still have a relationship but this would have to have choice of law rules governing that relationship.

between the parties can also arise out of a tort/delict.[466] Where there is such a relation-ship, it may be that the obligation arises out of tort, rather than unjust enrichment and therefore Chapter II will apply, rather than Chapter III. So what is envisaged here is that there is a relationship existing between the parties arising out of a tort but that, neverthe-less, the obligation arises out of unjust enrichment. The most obvious example of this situation is where there is what common lawyers would call restitution for tortious wrongdoing (assuming that this falls within Article 10 in the first place).[467] The wording of Article 10(1) makes it clear that the relationship between the parties can arise out of something other than a contract or tort. This would include a relationship based on equity, such as a fiduciary relationship. The relationship must be implicitly limited by the need to fall within a category that has choice of law rules governing that relationship. Article 10(1) refers to a relationship "existing" between the parties. The use of the present tense raises the question whether a past relationship that has subsequently ceased, such as where a contract has been avoided, would come within this provision.[468] However, where, for example, a party seeks the return of money paid in advance under a contract that is void *ab initio*, this will fall outside the scope of Article 10 altogether. A relationship "aris-ing out of" a contact would obviously encompass the relationship between the two par-ties to that contract. But would it cover a pre-contractual relationship, which can give rise to pre-contractual obligations and where there may be no contract entered into by the parties? Article 12[469] deals with these cases and so Article 10 should be interpreted as not covering them.

Thirdly, the relationship existing between the parties must be closely connected with that unjust enrichment.

Application of the law that governs the relationship between the parties Where the parties have a contractual relationship, the law governing that contract will also govern the non-contractual obligation arising out of unjust enrichment. An example of the operation of this rule where there is a tortious relationship between the parties is as follows. A wrongfully sells goods belonging to B (the tort of conversion) and B claims for the value of the sale, rather than the loss caused to him. This is an example of tortious wrongdoing. Under Article 10(1) the law governing the tort of conversion will also govern the obligation to pay the value of the goods. In a case of restitution for equitable wrongdoing the law governing the fiduciary relationship would also govern the obliga-tion to restore the benefit obtained by the defendant by his wrongdoing.

(ii) Where the law applicable cannot be determined on the basis of paragraph (1)

Article 10(2) provides that: "Where the law applicable cannot be determined on the basis of paragraph 1 and the parties have their habitual residence in the same country when the event giving rise to unjust enrichment occurs, the law of that country shall apply."

---

[466] The Rome II Regulation will apply to determine whether the parties have a tortious relationship.

[467] Supra, pp 824–825.

[468] Art 9(1) of the Proposal for a Regulation referred to a pre-existing relationship so as to cover void contracts and pre-contractual relationships (see the Explanatory Memorandum, p 21) but Art 9 was replaced by Arts 10, 11 and 12 of the final version of the Regulation, which are markedly different.

[469] Supra, p 818.

When does Article 10(2) apply? There are two requirements for this provision to apply. First, the law applicable cannot be determined on the basis of paragraph 1. So this is a fall-back provision. We are familiar with the idea of a choice of law rule based on the parties' habitual residence from Article 4 but that operates as an exception to the general principle in Article 4(1), rather than a fall-back where the law applicable cannot be determined on the basis of that provision. The law applicable cannot be determined on the basis of Article 10(1) where the non-contractual obligation arising out of unjust enrichment does not concern a relationship existing between the parties that is closely connected with that unjust enrichment. This could be because there is no relationship existing between the parties, eg a seller delivers goods to the wrong person with whom it has no contractual or other relationship and seeks restitutionary damages equivalent to the value of the goods,[470] or there may be such a relationship but it is not closely connected with that unjust enrichment. If the law can be determined on the basis of paragraph 1, then that provision will apply, not Article 10(2). This will be the case even though the parties have a common habitual residence in some other country. This is different from Article 4(2) where the common habitual residence rule operates as an exception to Article 4(1), applying it to trump that provision. However, it is important to bear in mind that Article 10(4) operates as an escape from paragraph 1 (as well as paragraphs 2 and 3) and where the parties have a common habitual residence it can plausibly be argued that the non-contractual obligation is more closely connected with a country, ie the common habitual residence, other than that indicated in paragraph 1.

The second requirement for Article 10(2) to apply is that the parties must have their habitual residence in the same country. The meaning of habitual residence has previously been examined. The habitual residence of a party can change as events unfold. Article 10(2) is concerned with habitual residence at the time when the event giving rise to unjust enrichment occurs. For example, in a case of payment of amounts wrongly received it would be when the money is received.

Application of the law of the country of common habitual residence This common habitual residence rule is familiar to us from Article 4(2). However, as has been seen, the place of the rule within the scheme of the Article as a whole is much reduced in Article 10 from that in Article 4. The common habitual residence rule has been justified on the basis that it reflects the legitimate expectations of the parties where they are habitually resident in the same country.[471]

(iii) Where the law applicable cannot be determined on the basis of paragraph 1 or 2

"Where the law applicable cannot be determined on the basis of paragraphs 1 or 2, it shall be the law of the country in which the unjust enrichment took place."

When does Article 10(3) apply? Paragraph 3 requires that the law applicable cannot be determined on the basis of paragraph 1 or 2. So this is a further fall-back provision to that in Article 10(2). We are therefore dealing with a situation where there is no relationship

---

[470] Neither would there appear to be a tortious relationship. Under English law the mere unauthorized retention of another's goods is not conversion of them: *Kuwait Airways Corpn v Iraqi Airways Co (Nos 4 and 5)* [2002] 2 AC 883 at 1084 (per Lord NICHOLLS).
[471] The Explanatory Memorandum, p 21.

between the parties that is closely connected with that unjust enrichment (and thus paragraph 1 does not apply) and, where that is the case, there is no common habitual residence (and thus paragraph 2 does not apply).

Application of the law of the country in which the unjust enrichment took place   Where paragraph 3 applies, the applicable law is that of the country in which the unjust enrichment took place. The only explanation of the adoption of this fall-back rule[472] is that it is found in Swiss law[473] and in the European Group for Private International Law's Proposal for a European Convention on the law applicable to non-contractual obligations.[474] The major problem with this rule is the definitional one. Which is the country in which the unjust enrichment took place? [475] This could be referring to: the place where the legal event giving rise to the claim occurred (the *lex loci condictionis*); the place in which the act was committed responsible for conferring the benefit or enrichment (the *lex loci actus*); the place where the impoverishment occurs;[476] the place where the enrichment occurs. Deciding on the place does not end the definitional problem. Whichever solution is adopted, there is an attendant definitional problem under that solution.[477]

The Swiss choice of law rule for unjust enrichment refers directly to the law of the State in which the enrichment occurred, [478] rather than the more ambiguous law of the country in which the unjust enrichment took place. The position is the same under German law[479] and under the Proposal of the European Group for Private International Law.[480] Common lawyers have also directly applied the law of a country in which the enrichment occurred rule.[481] Dicey, Morris and Collins sets out a sub-rule using this point of contact.[482] Given the popularity in the European Community of reference to a country in which the enrichment occurred rule, particularly in Germany whose law appears to have been influential in the development of Article 10, it is submitted that the country in which the unjust enrichment took place should be defined in terms of the country in which the enrichment occurred.

However, the concept of the country in which the enrichment occurs itself involves a definitional problem: is this the place where the benefit accrues to the person who is enriched; or where the loss to the person who is impoverished occurs; or does it vary, depending on the particular situation? The best solution looks to be where the benefit

---

[472] Ibid, at 22.

[473] See Art 128(2) of the Swiss Federal Statute on Private International Law of 1987. And in German law, see Introductory Law to the Civil Code, the 1999 Codification, Art 38(3).

[474] Art 7(3).

[475] See Gutteridge and Lipstein (1939) 7 CLJ 80, 89–90; Collier in Lipstein (ed), *Harmonisation of Private International Law by the EC* pp 81, 85–86; Blaikie [1984] Jur Rev 112, 118–122; Bennett (1990) 39 ICLQ 136, 146–150.

[476] See Cohen (1956) 31 LA Bar Bull 71; Bird, op cit, pp 112–113.

[477] Bird, op cit, pp 110–116.

[478] See Art 128(2) of the Swiss Federal Statute on Private International Law of 1987.

[479] Introductory Law to the Civil Code, the 1999 Codification, Art 38(3).

[480] See Art 7(3) of the EGPIL Proposal for a European Convention on the law applicable to non-contractual obligations.

[481] See the American Restatement, First, para 453. For academic support in favour of a place where the enrichment occurred rule see, eg, Gutteridge and Lipstein, op cit, 89–90; Leslie (1998) Edin LR 233 (with a closest connection exception).

[482] Rule 230(2)(c) at paras 34R-001 and 34-052–34-053. This rule is merely the starting point for the identification of the proper law of the obligation to make restitution.

occurs,[483] but is this where it first occurs or, if goods or money are moved to another country, where the person continues to benefit?[484] If money is paid into a branch in Country A to be transferred to an account in a branch of the same bank in Country B does the benefit accrue where the immediate benefit occurred (A) or in the country of ultimate enrichment (B)?[485] What if money is paid mistakenly into bank accounts in a number of different countries?[486] Rather than applying a series of different laws it would be better to apply the escape clause under Article 10(4). The place where the benefit occurs will be difficult to ascertain where this consists in saving the defendant from expenditure; presumably it is where the expenditure would have been incurred. [487]

The other problem with a country in which the enrichment occurred rule is that this may be in a country with which the facts have little real connection, for example money may have merely been paid into a bank account there.[488] However, in such a case recourse can be had to the manifestly more closely connected escape clause in Article 10(4).

(iv) The manifestly more closely connected escape clause

Article 10(4) contains an escape clause, which provides that: "Where it is clear from all the circumstances of the case that the non-contractual obligation arising out of unjust enrichment is manifestly more closely connected with a country other than that indicated in paragraphs 1, 2 and 3, the law of that other country shall apply." This adopts the manifestly more closely connected escape clause that is used in Article 4(3) of the Regulation, subject to one difference. Article 4(3) goes on to give an example of a manifestly closer connection, explaining that this might be based in particular on a pre-existing relationship between the parties, such as a contract. Article 10(4) omits this example. This is because a scenario whereby basing Article 10(4) on a pre-existing relationship would produce a different result from that produced by Article 10, paragraph (1) (which is itself based on the parties' pre-existing relationship), (2) or (3) is not going to arise. The absence of any example as to what might constitute a manifestly closer connection under Article 10(4) means that it is going to be more uncertain as to when the escape clause operates here than under Article 4(3). It may also mean that it is going to be that much more difficult to establish the manifestly more closely connected criterion than is the case under Article 4(3).

Article 10(4) operates as an escape from paragraphs (1), (2) and (3). In determining whether the escape clause should operate as an escape from paragraph (1), it needs to be remembered that that paragraph adopts the secondary connection principle, which is one that is strongly held under the Regulation. The position here is therefore very different from that of Article 4(3) where it is a strongly held principle that forms the basis of the escape clause. Nevertheless, we have already seen a situation where it can at least plausibly be argued that Article 10(4) should operate as an escape from paragraph (1),

---

[483] Virgo, Written Evidence, HL Paper 66 (2004), p 135.

[484] Blaikie, op cit, pp 121–122.

[485] The example is given by Dicey, Morris and Collins, para 34-052.

[486] See Virgo, Written Evidence, HL Paper 66 (2004), p 135.

[487] Virgo, Written Evidence, HL Paper 66 (2004), p 135.

[488] See under the pre-Regulation law, *Baring Bros & Co Ltd v Cunninghame District Council* [1997] CLC 108, (1996) Times, 30 September; *Barros Mattos Junior v Macdaniels* [2005] EWHC 1323 at [118], [2005] IL Pr 630.

namely where there is a relationship existing between the parties who have a common habitual residence.

Escaping from paragraph (2) is harder to envisage. Where the applicable law is that of the common habitual residence under paragraph (2) it may be difficult to show that the non-contractual obligation is manifestly more closely connected with some other country. If Article 10(2) applies, this necessarily means that paragraph (1) does not apply so there is no relationship between the parties that is closely connected with that unjust enrichment. So the classic case for the application of the escape clause in Article 4(3), namely where there is a pre-existing relationship between the parties, is not going to arise.

When it comes to escaping from paragraph (3), one is dealing with a situation where there is no relationship between the parties that is closely connected with that unjust enrichment (and thus paragraph (1) does not apply) and there is no common habitual residence (and thus paragraph (2) does not apply). As has been seen, the place in which the unjust enrichment took place may have little connection with the facts, eg money is simply paid into a bank account in that country. In such a case, it may be possible to show that the non-contractual obligation is manifestly more closely connected with some other country.

Until there is guidance from the Court of Justice on the interaction of paragraphs (1) and (4) there is a risk that courts in Member States will be influenced by their traditional national choice of law rules for unjust enrichment. Thus in England, where there has been strong support for the secondary connection principle without any escape clause, there may well be an unwillingness to use the paragraph (4) escape clause. On the other hand, in Scotland, where there has been support for a flexible solution,[489] the courts may be much more willing to be persuaded that paragraph (4) should apply.

(ii) Negotiorum gestio

There is a special provision in Article 11 dealing with *negotiorum gestio*, which has been referred to as agency without authority.[490] The technical definition of this concept is, according to Article 11, "an act performed without due authority in connection with the affairs of another person". *Negotiorum gestio* is concerned with the situation where services are rendered by a person that enable another person to avoid personal injury or loss of assets.[491] The idea is that there has been the voluntary bestowal of a benefit entitling the intervenor (gestor) to a measure of recovery. Civil law jurisdictions recognise this concept, whereas there is no like concept or cause of action in common law systems.[492] Trans-border cases involving *negotiorum gestio* have been rare in the past.[493] The classic case where this has arisen has been that of salvage, ie one ship rendering help to another ship.[494] Continental writers regard *negotiorum gestio* as coming within the broad ambit of restitution or quasi-contract, albeit distinct from unjustifiable enrichment. The Regulation

---

[489] The *Cunninghame* case, supra, p 769, n 27.

[490] See the Explanatory Memorandum, p 21.

[491] Ibid.

[492] But see Sheehan (2006) 55 ICLQ 253.

[493] See the Hamburg Group for Private International Law's Comments on the Proposal for a Rome II Regulation, 34.

[494] The fact that salvage involves a *maritime* non-contractual obligation raises a particular difficulty, see infra, p 863.

follows this classification by placing *negotiorum gestio* in Chapter III, which is concerned with obligations that arise neither out of a contract nor out of a tort/delict within the meaning of Chapter II. Having a separate provision for *negotiorum gestio* recognises that it is different from unjust enrichment.

(a) The scope of Article 11

Article 11 applies where there is a non-contractual obligation arising out of an act performed without due authority in connection with the affairs of another person. Some cases involve acts of assistance, meaning one-off initiatives taken on an exceptional basis by the "agent", who acted in order to preserve the interests of the "principal". Some cases instead involve measures of interference in the assets of another person, as in the case of payment of a third-party debt. The choice of law rules do not distinguish between these two situations.[495] Article 11(2) (the common habitual residence rule) presupposes that damage occurs.

(b) The rules on the applicable law

These are in substance the same as those in Article 10.[496] There are obviously, though, some differences in language to reflect the fact that concern is now with "an act performed without due authority in connection with the affairs of another person", rather than with unjust enrichment. The use of the same choice of law rules in each article is not surprising when one bears in mind that both articles are concerned with the law of restitution.

(iii) Culpa in contrahendo

Article 12 is headed "*Culpa in contrahendo*" and sets out special choice of law rules for a non-contractual obligation arising out of dealings prior to the conclusion of a contract.[497] Such liability[498] raises difficult problems of classification both under substantive domestic law and under private international law. Some Member States may regard the obligation that arises out of pre-contractual dealings as contractual, others as tortious, yet others as *sui generis*.[499] The Rome II Regulation introduces a special rule for such cases in order to avoid the danger of different classifications being adopted in different Member States. It is thereby adopting a *sui generis* classification. The fact that obligations arising out of dealings prior to the conclusion of a contract are placed within the Rome II Regulation has in turn led to its express exclusion from the Rome I Regulation.[500] According to the Commission, *culpa in contrahendo* does not arise out of tort/delict as

---

[495] Cf Art 9(4) of the Proposal for a Regulation, on which see the Explanatory Memorandum, p 22.
[496] Supra, pp 826–831.
[497] German lawyers use the term *culpa in contrahendo* when referring to pre-contractual liability (see the German national Report by Lorenz in Hondius, *Pre-Contractual Liability: Reports to the XIIIth Congress International Academy of Comparative Law Montreal Canada 18–24 August 1990* (1991)). The two terms can be used synonomously.
[498] For a valuable comparative study of the substantive law see Hondius, *Pre-Contractual Liability: Reports to the XIIIth Congress International Academy of Comparative Law Montreal Canada 18–24 August 1990* (1991).
[499] See the Explanatory Memorandum, p 8.
[500] Art 1(2)(i) of the Rome I Regulation, discussed supra, pp 688–689. See the Explanatory Memorandum from the Commission accompanying the Proposal for the Rome I Regulation, para 4.2.

understood in Chapter II,[501] so it cannot fall within that Chapter. It is therefore placed in Chapter III, even though it is very different from unjust enrichment and *negotiorum gestio*.

Under English substantive domestic law there are no general principles of *culpa in contrahendo*.[502] However, a wide range of claims can arise "as a result of negotiations failing or an argument that a concluded contract is the result of untruths made in the course of the negotiations that preceded it".[503] Not surprisingly, prior to the Rome II Regulation, under English law there were no special choice of law rules for *culpa in contrahendo*. A difficult question of classification would arise as to whether the pre-contractual obligation on which the cause of action was based was contractual, tortious, restitutionary or equitable. Different causes of action could well involve a different classification and different choice of law rules.

(a) The scope of Article 12

(i) Culpa in contrahendo

Article 12 applies to "a non-contractual obligation arising out of dealings prior to the conclusion of a contract".[504] According to Recital (30), *culpa in contrahendo* for the purposes of the Regulation "is an autonomous concept and should not necessarily be interpreted within the meaning of national law". Recital (30) goes on to give two examples of what this concept includes, namely the violation of the duty of disclosure and the breakdown of contractual negotiations. These two situations reflect the two different types of pre-contractual liability under the substantive law. First, there is pre-contractual liability where no contract ensues. This includes duties in negotiation of a contract. For example, under Italian law[505] there is a requirement to act in good faith during the negotiation of a contract.[506] There is no such requirement or cause of action under English law but there may be liability in tort[507] under *Hedley Byrne v Heller*[508] for negligent misstatements made during the course of negotiations or liability in tort for fraudulent misrepresentation. Secondly, there is pre-contractual liability where a contract ensues. In most countries, once a contract ensues there is no need for pre-contractual liability. Nonetheless, most countries have duties of disclosure. Under English law there can be an action to avoid (ie rescind) an insurance contract on the basis of non-disclosure prior to entering the contract.[509] The English law of misrepresentation also constitutes a form of

---

[501] But see the Explanatory Memorandum from the Commission accompanying the Proposal for the Rome I Regulation, para 4.2, which says that pre-contractual obligations should be treated for the purposes of private international law as a matter of tort/delict.

[502] See Allen, "The English National Report" in Hondius, op cit, p 143, and more generally for a discussion of pre-contractual liability under English law.

[503] Ibid.

[504] Art 12(1).

[505] Article 1337 of the Italian Civil Code. For the position under French law see Giliker (2003) 52 ICLQ 970, 979–985.

[506] Case C-334/00 *Fonderie Officine Meccaniche Tacconi SpA v Heinrich Wagner Sinto Maschinenfabrik GmbH (HWS)* [2002] ECR I-7357; discussed supra, where such a claim was held to fall within Art 5(3) of the Brussels Convention.

[507] See Giliker, op cit, 974–978.

[508] [1964] AC 465.

[509] See *Agnew v Lansforsakringsbolagens AB* [2001] 1 AC 223; discussed supra, p 231, where the House of Lords held that such a claim fell within Art 5(1) of the Lugano Convention.

pre-contractual liability. This would cover liability for fraudulent misrepresentation (such as a claim under the tort of deceit[510]), negligent misrepresentation (such as a claim for damages under the Misrepresentation Act 1967[511] or, more rarely, in tort for negligent misstatement) and innocent misrepresentation (such as a claim for damages in lieu of rescission under the Misrepresentation Act 1967[512]).

The problem of characterisation   The introduction of the special category of *culpa in contrahendo* does not avoid the question of characterisation altogether. This question of characterisation will still arise as to whether the non-contractual obligation arises out of dealings prior to the conclusion of a contract or out of contract or unjust enrichment. An example is the situation where a restitutionary claim (for return of money paid in advance) is made consequent on rescission of a contract for misrepresentation.[513] It was suggested earlier that such a claim should be regarded as being based on contract, rather than unjust enrichment. But a further possibility is that it should be regarded as arising out of dealings prior to the conclusion of the contract. The result, though, would be the same, regardless of whether a contractual or *culpa in contrahendo* characterisation is adopted. In both cases, the law applicable to the contract would govern the non-contractual obligation.[514]

(ii) A non-contractual obligation

Article 12 is concerned with "a non-contractual obligation" arising out of dealings, etc. Once it has been decided that there is *culpa in contrahendo* within the meaning of Article 12 it follows that the obligation that arises out of this must be regarded as non-contractual.[515] If one were to say that there was a contractual obligation arising out of *culpa in contrahendo* this would open up a gap in the law since such an obligation would fall not only outside the Rome II Regulation but also outside the Rome I Regulation.

(iii) Arising out of dealings

The non-contractual obligation must *arise out of* dealings prior to the conclusion of the contract. There must be a direct link between the non-contractual obligation and the dealings.[516] This means that if, while a contract is being negotiated, a party suffers personal injury, Article 4 or another relevant provision of the Regulation will apply, rather than Article 12.[517]

(iv) Prior to the conclusion of the contract

The non-contractual obligation must arise out of dealings *prior to* the conclusion of a contract. It follows that a negligent misrepresentation/negligent misstatement made at the pre-contractual stage will come within Article 12 and Chapter III, whereas a

---

[510] Or a claim for rescission of a contract. This could be on the basis not only of a fraudulent misrepresentation but also a negligent or innocent one.

[511] S 2(1).

[512] S 2(2).

[513] Another example would be where a restitutionary claim is made consequent on rescission of a contract induced by mistake.

[514] See the Rome Convention, and Art 12(1) of the Rome II Regulation.

[515] Supra, pp 777–780.

[516] Recital (30) of the Regulation.

[517] Ibid.

negligent misstatement made after a contract has been entered into will come within Chapter II.

(v) Regardless of whether the contract was actually concluded or not

Article 12(1) provides that Article 12 applies "regardless of whether the contract was actually concluded or not". This reflects the two types of pre-contractual liability under the substantive law, namely pre-contractual liability where no contract ensues and pre-contractual liability where a contract ensues.

(vi) Damage

Article 12 presupposes that there is damage.[518]

(b) The rules on the applicable law

Culpa in contrahendo is a very different concept and cause of action from unjust enrichment and *negotiorum gestio*. It is not surprising to find that the rules on the applicable law are also different. Article 12(1) sets out a primary rule. There is then in Article 12(2) a fall-back position to deal with the situation where the law applicable cannot be determined on the basis of paragraph 1.

(i) The primary rule

Article 12(1) provides that: "The law applicable to a non-contractual obligation arising out of dealings prior to the conclusion of a contract, regardless of whether the contract was actually concluded or not, shall be the law that applies to the contract or that would have been applicable to it had it been entered into."

It will be recalled that Article 12 applies regardless of whether the contract was actually concluded or not. If it was concluded the law applicable to the non-contractual obligation will be the law that applies to the contract. Identification of this law presents no particular difficulty, or at least no more difficulty than any other case where the law applicable to a contract has to be determined. If a contract was not actually concluded, the law applicable to the non-contractual obligation will be the law that would have been applicable to the contract had it been entered into. This presents particular difficulties. First, there is a difficulty over choice of the applicable law. Let us assume that the parties were negotiating over the terms of the contract, with each party trying to impose its preferred choice of law or choice of jurisdiction clause on the other. However, the parties had not agreed on these terms. In determining which law would have been applicable had the contract been entered into, is the court supposed to speculate on which party was likely to win in this battle of the terms? This would be absurd and an agreement on the applicable law could only operate if the parties have actually agreed those terms, even if they have not entered into a contract. In other words, the parties may have agreed on a choice of law clause providing for the application of English law but have never agreed, for example, on the contract price. Secondly, what happens where the contractual negotiations are broken off at a very early stage? It may be impossible to ascertain the applicable law in any meaningful way.[519] Where it is impossible to determine the law applicable to

---

[518] As defined in Art 2(1) and (3)(b).

[519] It may be easier to come to a finding under the Rome I Regulation, with its emphasis on types of contract, than under the Rome Convention, with its use of connections.

the contract, as opposed to being merely difficult to do so, the fall-back position under Article 12(2) will come into play and provide an answer as to the law applicable to the non-contractual obligation.

Article 12(1) is a rigid rule that has no exception, for example for cases where the parties have a common habitual residence, and no escape clause for cases where the non-contractual obligation is manifestly more closely connected with another country. It is only when one moves on to the fall-back position in Article 12(2) where the law applicable cannot be determined on the basis of paragraph 1 that familiar rules based on the common habitual residence of the parties and a manifestly more closely connected escape clause come into play. The lack of an exception or escape from Article 12(1) means that it is very different therefore from Article 4(1). Perhaps more interestingly it is also different from Articles 10 and 11. We are familiar with a fall-back position under those Articles where the law applicable cannot be determined under the primary rule in the first paragraph of those Articles but they at least have a manifestly more closely connected escape clause that allows escape from the primary rule. Article 12 does not.

(ii) The fall-back position

Article 12(2) sets out the fall-back position. This only comes into play in the situation where the law applicable cannot be determined on the basis of paragraph 1. That would be the case where it is impossible to identify the law applicable to the contract. It is hard to see this operating in the situation where a contract has been concluded, but it is possible to envisage this operating in the situation where the contract was not actually concluded. The contractual negotiations may have been at such an early stage that it is impossible to identify the law that would have been applicable to the contract. At the same time, though, for Article 12 to apply in the first place there must have been sufficient dealings between the parties to give rise to an obligation. This scenario is likely to be rare.

The rules on the applicable law in Article 12(2) are very similar to those in Article 4. So, where contract choice of law does not provide an answer, tort choice of law has to do so. Recourse to tort choice of law rules may appear at first sight to be rather unprincipled but can be forgiven when one bears in mind that there is a case for classifying *culpa in contrahendo* as tortious.[520] Familiar rules are used in Article 12(2), ie country of damage rule, a common habitual residence rule and a manifestly more closely connected rule but all within a limited fall-back framework. Article 12 (2), like Article 4, contains three provisions: a general rule; an exception; and a manifestly more closely connected escape clause.

The general rule   Article 12(2)(a) provides that the applicable law is "the law of the country in which the damage occurs, irrespective of the country in which the event giving rise to the damage occurred and irrespective of the country or countries in which the indirect consequences of that event occurred". This is virtually identical to Article 4(1).[521] In a case of negligent misstatement, or negligent or fraudulent misrepresentation, identification

---

[520] Supra, p 832.
[521] Discussed supra, pp 796–798. The only difference is a change of tense from the present (occurs) under Art 4 to the past (occurred) under Art 12(2)(a).

of the country in which the damage occurs can be problematic.[522] There can also be losses incurred in more than one country. For example, as a result of a negligent misstatement concerning the mileage of a classic car in an auction catalogue in England, a claimant may incur loss in England in the form of the cost of an airline ticket to go to an auction in Monaco, where there is further loss in the form of entering into an adverse contractual commitment to pay an excessive amount for the car.[523] Under the mosaic principle,[524] English law will apply to the damage occurring in England and the law of Monaco to that occurring in Monaco.

The exception   Article 12(2)(b) provides that "where the parties have their habitual residence in the same country at the time when the event giving rise to the damage occurs, the law of that country" shall apply. This is the same as Article 4(2) except that under Article 12(2)(b) one is concerned with the habitual residence at the time when the event giving rise to the damage occurs, whereas with Article 4(2) one is concerned with habitual residence at the later time when the damage occurs.

The manifestly more closely connected escape clause   Article 12(2)(c) provides that "where it is clear from all the circumstances of the case that the non-contractual obligation arising out of dealings prior to the conclusion of a contract is manifestly more closely connected with a country other than that indicated in points (a) and (b), the law of that other country" shall apply. This is identical to Article 4(3). However, that provision goes on to provide that a manifestly closer connection with another country might be based in particular on a pre-existing relationship between the parties. Article 12(2)(c) has no such provision.[525] This is because a scenario whereby basing paragraph 12(2)(c) on a pre-existing relationship would produce a different result from that produced by paragraph (1), (2)(a) or (b) is not going to arise.[526]

(f) Choice of the applicable law

(i) Freedom of choice

Chapter IV is entitled "Freedom of choice" and contains just one Article, ie Article 14. This is also headed "Freedom of choice" and sets out the basic principle that "The parties may agree to submit non-contractual obligations to the law of their choice." Recital (31) gives two justifications for allowing the parties to choose the law applicable to a non-contractual obligation: first, the principle of party autonomy; secondly, the enhancement of legal certainty. This freedom of choice applies to all non-contractual obligations, except for those arising from an act of unfair competition,[527] a restriction of competition[528]

---

[522] See, eg, *Raiffeisen Zentral Bank Osterreich AG v Alexander Tranos* [2001] IL Pr 85—a jurisdiction case involving misrepresentations made during pre-contractual dealings.

[523] These are the facts of the pre-Regulation case of *Morin v Bonhams & Brooks Ltd* [2003] EWCA Civ 1802, [2004] 1 Lloyd's Rep 702.

[524] Supra, p 797, n 256.

[525] This is the same as the manifestly more closely connected escape clause in Arts 10 and 11.

[526] This is explained by the fact that Art 12(1) is based on the parties' existing relationship and by the interaction of the different paragraphs in Art 12.

[527] Art 6(4).

[528] Ibid.

or an infringement of an intellectual property right.[529] The extension of freedom of choice to non-contractual obligations follows the national private international law rules in a number of European states[530] and makes clear what was previously unclear under English law.[531] It is not clear whether the freedom to choose extends to allowing the parties to vary the governing law.[532]

(ii) Conditions imposed on the choice

In order to protect the weaker party, certain conditions are imposed on the choice.[533] The agreement must satisfy one of two alternatives. It must have been entered into after the event giving rise to the damage occurred[534] or, where all the parties are pursuing a commercial activity, also by an agreement "freely negotiated" before the event giving rise to the damage.[535]

An agreement entered into after the event giving rise to the damage occurred is less problematic than one entered into before that event. Once a dispute has arisen, it is assumed that the weaker party is not going to agree to the application of a foreign law that adversely affects him. The situation where there is an obvious need for protection of the weaker party is that where the agreement was entered into before the event giving rise to the damage.[536] The requirement that this agreement was "freely negotiated" is designed to provide this protection.[537] There is no explanation of what precisely is meant by these words. Let us assume, though, that the agreement was not freely negotiated. In this situation, the parties' choice of the law to govern non-contractual obligations will not take effect under Article 14. Curiously, though, the parties' agreement on the law applicable to their contractual obligations, which may not have ben freely negotiated, could operate indirectly to fix the law applicable to non-contractual obligations by virtue of Article 4(3). There is a further problem with a pre-dispute agreement. This is likely to be a clause in a contract between the parties. This can raise the thorny issue of concurrent liability in tort and contract, and whether there is a non-contractual obligation or a contractual one.[538] Of course, the issue of concurrent liability will not always be raised where there is a contract between the parties and a claim is brought in respect of non-contractual liability. There can be claims in contract and tort which are not parallel claims based on the same facts. There can also be a claim based on a non-contractual obligation and where, although there is a contract between the parties, there is no contractual liability.

---

[529] Art 8(3).

[530] See the Swiss Private International Law statute, Art 132; the German Introductory Law to the Civil Code, the 1999 Codification, Art 42. This is also allowed by the law of Austria, Liechtenstein and the Netherlands.

[531] See Law Commission Working Paper No 87 (1984), p 265 and para 4.21, which recommended that this should be allowed, but the Law Commissions' Report was silent on this. See generally at common law, North, *Essays*, pp 85–86, 187–191. See also *Morin v Bonhams & Brooks Ltd* [2003] IL Pr 25 at [33], no right to choose; affd without discussion of this point [2003] EWCA Civ 1802, [2004] 1 Lloyd's Rep 702.

[532] Cf Art 3(2) of the Rome Convention; discussed supra, pp 692–694.

[533] Recital (31).

[534] Art 14(1)(a).

[535] Art 14(1)(b).

[536] The Proposal for the Regulation did not allow for such an agreement, see Art 10(1) and the Explanatory Memorandum, p 22.

[537] Cf the technique for protecting weaker parties under the Brussels I Regulation, Arts 13, 17 and 21 (agreement must be entered into after dispute has arisen).

[538] There is a strong argument in favour of a tortious, rather than contractual, classification.

(iii) An express or inferred choice

The choice must be "expressed or demonstrated with reasonable certainty by the circum-stances of the case".[539] This phrase has been taken from the Rome Convention.[540] Its meaning has already been examined in the context of the discussion of that Convention. Suffice it to say in the present context that an express choice refers to a choice of law clause. A choice demonstrated with reasonable certainty by the circumstances of the case refers to an inferred choice, two examples of which are a choice of jurisdiction clause and an arbitration clause. One issue that will arise in the context of the Rome II Regulation is whether a choice of law clause or a jurisdiction clause in a contract between the parties is wide enough in its scope to cover a dispute in relation, not to contract, but to a non-contractual obligation. This issue has arisen before the English courts in relation to choice of jurisdiction clauses (in the context of jurisdiction)[541] but not choice of law clauses because of the lack of freedom to choose the governing law under the English traditional tort and restitution choice of law rules.

(iv) Choice and the English rules on pleading and proof of foreign law[542]

The same problem arises under the Rome II Regulation as arises under the Rome Convention, namely what happens if the parties choose Utopian law to apply but subse-quently neither party pleads Utopian law? The Regulation does not provide an answer to this. It is suggested[543] that the English courts should take a pragmatic line and simply apply English law under the English procedural rule that is preserved by Article 1(3) of the Regulation, which provides that the Regulation shall not apply to evidence and procedure.

(v) Choice and third parties

The parties' choice will not prejudice the rights of third parties.[544] The typical example of this is said to be the insurer's obligation to reimburse damages payable by the insured.[545]

(vi) Limitations on choice

The Regulation lays down restrictions on the parties' right to choose the governing law which will now be examined. Article 14 itself sets out two such limitations. The first of these (Article 14(2)) is concerned with provisions of law that cannot be derogated from by agreement; the second (Article 14(3)) with provisions of Community law that cannot be derogated from by agreement. More generally, the Regulation imposes limitations on the dominance of the applicable law.

---

[539] Art 14(1).

[540] Art 3(1), discussed supra, pp 700–701.

[541] Supra, pp 290–291.

[542] See generally Fentiman, *Foreign Law in English Courts* (1998), p 87 et seq.

[543] See the discussion in relation to the Rome Convention, supra, p 694.

[544] Art 14(1). Art 3(2) of the Rome Convention, discussed supra, p 693, provides that variation of choice shall not prejudice the rights of third parties.

[545] The Explanatory Memorandum, 22.

(a) Article 14(2): Provisions that cannot be derogated from by agreement

Article 14(2) provides that:

> Where all the elements relevant to the situation at the time when the event giving rise to the damage occurs are located in a country other than the country whose law has been chosen, the choice of the parties shall not prejudice the application of provisions of the law of that other country which cannot be derogated from by agreement.

This provision is in substance the same as Article 3(3) of the Rome Convention and is concerned with rules which cannot be departed from in a domestic context (dispositions imperatives). The most noticeable difference between Article 3(3) of the Rome Convention and Article 14(2) of the Rome II Regulation is that the latter wisely does not use the term mandatory rules to describe provisions which cannot be derogated from by agreement.[546] In accordance with the principle of consistency between these two instruments,[547] Article 14(2) of the Rome II Regulation should be interpreted in the light of the interpretation of Article 3(3) of the Convention.

(b) Article 14(3): Provisions of Community law that cannot be derogated from by agreement

Article 14(3) provides that:

> Where all the elements relevant to the situation at the time when the event giving rise to the damage occurs are located in one or more of the Member States, the parties' choice of the law applicable other than that of a Member State shall not prejudice the application of provisions of Community law, where appropriate as implemented in the Member State of the forum, which cannot be derogated from by agreement.

This provision treats the European Community as effectively one country and highlights the importance of Community mandatory rules. However, given that national law includes Community law, it is open to question whether it will in fact add anything to what is already provided for by Article 14(2).

(c) Overriding mandatory provisions[548] and public policy[549]

These limitations are more appropriately dealt with later on, where they will be looked at in detail.

(d) Certain special torts

The law applicable to a non-contractual obligation arising out of an act of unfair competition or a restriction of competition cannot be derogated from by an agreement under Article 14.[550] Likewise, the law applicable to a non-contractual obligation arising from an infringement of an intellectual property right cannot be derogated from by an agreement

---

[546] The use of the term mandatory rules in Art 3(3) of the Rome Convention causes confusion with the very different type of mandatory rule, overriding mandatory rules, under Art 7 of the Rome Convention (Art 16 of the Rome II Regulation).

[547] Recital (7), discussed supra, p 724.

[548] Discussed infra, pp 849–851.

[549] Discussed infra, pp 851–855.

[550] Art 6(4).

under Article 14.[551] No other torts are singled out for their own special limitation on the right to choose the applicable law.

(e) Other limitations

We have dealt with the limitations on choice specifically set out in the Regulation itself. Nonetheless, there are a number of other limitations which doubtless apply by analogy with limitations on the right to choose the law governing a contract.[552] Thus the parties cannot choose a meaningless applicable law or a floating applicable law.

(g) Scope of the law applicable

Chapter V is entitled "Common rules", ie rules common to Chapters II, III and IV. The first of these is Article 15, which is entitled "Scope of the law applicable" and in paragraphs (a) to (h) gives a number of examples of issues coming within the scope of the law applicable to non-contractual obligations by virtue of Chapters II, III and IV. What it does not do is say with regard to any particular issue is whether Chapter III applies or Chapter II or indeed both. Nonetheless, giving examples helps to clarify the position in relation to certain issues, such as limitation periods and assessment of damage, in respect of which different Member States have traditionally adopted a different classification, some regarding the issue as one of substance to be determined by the applicable law, others as procedural to be determined by the law of the forum.[553] The applicable law is given a wide function so as to provide certainty in the law.[554] Paragraphs (a) to (h) are not intended to be an exhaustive list,[555] and it is implicit that there are other issues that are governed by the rules on the applicable law. At the same time it is important to bear in mind that the Regulation in Articles 18 to 22[556] contains some special rules for particular issues and for those issues it is to these special rules that one most turn, rather than to the rules on the applicable law in Chapters II, III and IV. For example, Article 15 does not cover the issue of the burden of proof,[557] which is dealt with in Article 22.

The examples provided by Article 15 are in some cases drawn from the Rome Convention but even more influential have been the Hague Convention on the Law Applicable to Traffic Accidents of 1971 and the Hague Convention on the Law Applicable to Products Liability of 1973. The striking similarity between the provisions on the scope of the law applicable in these two Conventions[558] and the provisions on scope of the law applicable in Article 15 of the Rome II Regulation means that the Reports accompanying the two Conventions[559] are a valuable source on the meaning of the terms used in Article 15. The examples listed in Article 15 are as follows.

---

[551] Art 8(3).
[552] Discussed supra, pp 698–700.
[553] The Explanatory Memorandum, p 23.
[554] Ibid.
[555] "The law applicable to non-contractual obligations . . . shall govern in particular": Art 15.
[556] Discussed infra, pp 855–856.
[557] Cf Art 8(8) on the scope of the Hague Convention on the Law Applicable to Products Liability of 1973.
[558] See Art 8 of the1971 Convention and Art 8 of the 1973 Convention.
[559] See the Essen Report on the Road Traffic Convention and the Von Mehren Report on the Product Liability Convention.

(i) The basis and extent of liability, including the determination of persons who may be held liable for acts performed by them[560]

The basis of liability is concerned with intrinsic factors of liability[561] and encompasses such matters as: "the nature of liability (strict or fault based); the definition of fault, including the question whether an omission can constitute fault; the causal link between the event giving rise to the damage and the damage; the persons potentially liable . . .".[562]

The extent of liability encompasses the maximum extent of liability laid down by law,[563] such as a ceiling on liability, and the contribution to be made by each of the persons liable for the damage which is to be compensated.[564] It also includes "the determination of persons who may be held liable for acts performed by them". This is designed to cover the division of liability between joint perpetrators.[565] Extent of liability is also intended to cover actions for contribution or indemnity between joint-tortfeasors.[566] This is subject to the proviso that, where the contribution or indemnity is based on a contract, it will fall outside the scope of the Regulation.

(ii) The grounds for exemption from liability, any limitation of liability and any division of liability[567]

This provision is concerned with three issues relating to liability. All three can be regarded as extrinsic factors of liability,[568] ie conditions for exoneration from liability.[569] First, there is the issue of grounds for exemption from liability. This would cover acts of God and supervening acts of a third party,[570] as well as such well-known (at least in common law jurisdictions) phenomena as: guest statutes (preventing a guest passenger suing a host driver), interspousal immunity laws (preventing a wife from suing her husband and vice versa);[571] intra-family immunity laws (preventing children suing their parents and vice versa). It would also cover "force majeure, necessity, third-party fault and fault by the victim".[572] Under English law the fault of a victim is known as contributory negligence and operates to reduce damages rather than as an exemption of liability. What is contemplated therefore is the situation where the injury is entirely the fault of the victim.[573] Grounds for exemption from liability would also cover laws which exclude the

---

[560] Art 15(a).

[561] The Explanatory Memorandum, p 23. Extrinsic factors of liability are dealt with under Art 15(b); discussed infra.

[562] The Explanatory Memorandum, p 23.

[563] Ibid.

[564] Ibid.

[565] Ibid.

[566] See the Von Mehren Report on the Hague Convention on the Law Applicable to Products Liability 1973 (Art 8(1) of which also refers to "the basis and extent of liability"), 21.Cf the Essen Report on the Hague Traffic Accidents Convention 1971 at p 28, para 4.3, which makes clear that extent of liability does not cover recourse actions between tortfeasors. But this is explained by the fact that this Convention expressly excludes such actions: Art 2(5). The question whether the tort or unjust enrichment rules should apply is discussed supra, p 793.

[567] Art 15(b).

[568] Explanatory Memorandum, p 23.

[569] See the Giuliano, Lagarde and Van Sasse Van Ysselt Report, p 58.

[570] See the Von Mehren Report, p 21.

[571] Ibid.

[572] Explanatory Memorandum, p 23.

[573] See the Essen Report, p 29, para 5.1. Contributory negligence reducing damages comes within division of liability under Art 15(b).

perpetrator's liability in relation to certain categories of persons.[574] Any limitation of liability would cover provisions on limitation of liability for maritime claims as provided for by international convention.[575] It seems that grounds for exemption from liability and any limitation of liability is intended to cover an exemption or limitation clause in a contract, which is used as a defence to a claim in respect of a non-contractual obligation. Admittedly, although the Explanatory Memorandum mentions a significant number of examples of exemption from liability,[576] it does not mention exemption or limitation clauses in contracts. But the Essen Report on the Hague Convention on the Law Applicable to Traffic Accidents of 1971, which was the template for Article 15 of the Regulation, explains that grounds for exemption and limitation of liability (in Article 8(2) of that Convention) seemingly encompass contractual exemption or limitation clauses.[577] Under the Hague Convention the validity of such clauses falls within the scope of the law applicable to liability in that Convention.[578] The significance of this will be examined below[579] when the topic of contractual defences to an action in tort is considered more fully.

As regards division of liability, this would cover contributory negligence on the part of the victim.[580]

This provision does not effect any change in English private international law since the issues coming within it would all be regarded as ones of substance and accordingly governed by the applicable law.

(iii) The existence, the nature and the assessment of damage or the remedy claimed[581]

(a) The existence and the nature of damage

This is concerned with determining the damage for which compensation may be due; eg whether this includes for personal injury, damage to property, moral damage, environmental damage, financial loss or loss of an opportunity[582] and whether loss of profits can be recovered.[583] Existence of damage would no doubt cover the issue of remoteness of damage. Article 15(c) should also include the question whether compensation can be

---

[574] Explanatory Memorandum, p 23.

[575] The English rules contained in the Merchant Shipping Act 1995, s 185 and Sch 7, have in the past been given a procedural classification: *Caltex Singapore Pte Ltd and Ors v BP Shipping Ltd* [1996] 1 Lloyd's Rep 286; approved in *Harding v Wealands* [2006] UKHL 32, [2007] 2 AC 1; *Seismic Shipping Inc v Total E & P UK plc (The Western Regent)* [2005] EWCA Civ 985 at [52], [2005] 2 Lloyd's Rep 359. Under the Regulation, this looks to be wrong. It is arguable, though, that these English provisions are mandatory rules of the forum, discussed infra, p 850.

[576] At p 23. As does the Giuliano, Lagarde and Van Sasse Van Ysselt Report, p 53.

[577] At p 29, para 5.1. See also the Law Commissions' Consultative Document 1974, para 11.2.2. The Von Mehren Report, at p 21, suggests it covers non-contractual as well as contractual limitations in adverts and in documents accompanying a product.

[578] The Essen Report, p 29, para 5.1.

[579] Infra, pp 865–868.

[580] The Essen Report, p 29, para 5.2.

[581] Art 15(c).

[582] The Explanatory Memorandum, p 23. This refers to the Proposal for a Rome II Regulation which was more clearly worded. Art 11(c) referred to "the existence and kinds of injury or damage for which compensation may be due".

[583] See the Von Mehren Report, p 21.

recovered for pain and suffering or loss of amenity, ie the question of recovery of heads of damage. Under the English common law the issues of heads of damage available and of remoteness of damage are ones of substance for the applicable law, so the Rome II Regulation does not effect a change in English private international law on this point. The issue may arise of recovery of punitive and exemplary damages. This too should be determined by the law applicable to the non-contractual obligation.[584] This would be on the basis that it falls within the concept of the existence and nature of damage. If it falls outside that concept it should still be a matter to be determined by the law applicable to the non-contractual obligation. It should be recalled that Article 15 only provides examples of matters falling within the scope of the applicable law. There can be other examples which do not fall within Article 15(a) to (h) but which, nonetheless, are within the scope of the applicable law, and this would be one such example. In the case of punitive or exemplary damages, the question arises of whether the application of a law providing for such damages is manifestly incompatible with the public policy of the forum. This question will be examined below when discussing more generally the public policy limitation on the applicable law.[585]

(b) Assessment of damage

Article 15(c) provides that the assessment of damage is a matter to be determined by the law applicable to the non-contractual obligation. This adopts the position taken in most Member States, which regard assessment of damages as a substantive matter to be determined by the applicable law. It also broadly follows Article 10(1)(c) of the Rome Convention,[586] although there are some noticeable differences in the wording of the two provisions which will be examined below. In contrast, English private international law has traditionally regarded the assessment or quantification of damages as a procedural matter for the law of the forum.[587] Article 15(c) therefore represents a major change in English private international law. Subjecting this issue to the law governing the non-contractual obligation has the virtue of preventing forum shopping within the European Community for an assessment of damages advantage.

In so far as the foreign applicable law has legal rules in relation to assessment of damage, the effect of Article 15(c) is clear enough. The English court must apply these rules. However, the assessment of damage can involve questions of fact.[588] The amount of damages awarded in any state is going to be influenced by the social and economic conditions in that country. This is to do with fact rather than a rule of law. Questions of fact should be determined by the forum. This is acknowledged in Article 10(1)(c) of the Rome Convention, which draws a distinction between circumstances when assessment of damages raises questions of fact and those when it raises questions of law. If the question in relation to assessment is only one of fact, this is a matter purely for the court hearing the action and the applicable law under the Convention will not govern the issue. On the

---

[584] But this is subject to the public policy limitation on the dominance of the applicable law; discussed infra, pp 851–855.

[585] Infra, pp 851–852.

[586] Discussed supra, p 755.

[587] Supra, pp 98–100.

[588] See generally the Giuliano and Lagarde Report, p 33, discussing Art 10(1)(c) of the Rome Convention.

other hand, if the question raised is one of law then Article 10(1)(c) will apply. The Proposal for a Rome II Regulation followed Article 10(1)(c) of the Rome Convention and drew the same distinction. It stated that the scope of the applicable law covered the measure of damages "in so far as prescribed by law".[589] So it is only where the applicable law has rules of law on the measure of damages that the forum is required to apply that rule.[590] Regrettably, in the final version of the Rome II Regulation, Article 15(c) contains no such wording. However, there is nothing to suggest from the history of the amendments to the Regulation as it went through the legislative process to suggest that this was a deliberate omission designed to ensure that even factual matters would be subject to the applicable law.[591] The court seised would have great difficulty in operating such a rule. It would be sensible therefore to interpret Article 15(c) as being implicitly limited to the assessment of damages "in so far as prescribed by law".[592]

This leaves the difficulty of determining whether there is a rule of law in relation to assessment or whether it is a question of fact. A ceiling on damages in a statute or an international convention clearly involves a rule of law[593] and is subject to the applicable law.[594] With a ceiling on damages it could be argued that this is concerned with limiting liability (in which case it would fall within Article 15(b)), rather than with assessment of damages. In either event, the law governing the non-contractual obligation would apply to determine this issue. Similarly, a rule which requires accrued benefits (state benefits, employment pension, personal pension) to be deducted when assessing damages is a rule of law and is subject to the applicable law.[595] The more difficult thing to identify is a question of fact. In so far as the calculation takes into account the social and economic conditions in that country, this must be regarded as a question of fact. But is a particular method of calculation a rule of law or a matter of fact?[596] In the past it has not been necessary to make this distinction. Now, under the Regulation, where the evidence is simply

---

[589] Art 11(e) of the Proposal for a Regulation.

[590] The Explanatory Memorandum, p 24.

[591] "in so far as prescribed by law" was dropped when assessment of damage was added to Art 15(c), rather than being a separate rule (as was the case under the proposal for a Regulation), see the Council's Common Position of 11 August 2006 (JUSTCIV 137). The European Parliament had earlier proposed this shift (see the Wallis Report A6-0211/2005 of 27 June 2005, Amendment 40). The Commission (see the Explanatory Memorandum, pp 6–7, accompanying the Amended Proposal for a Rome II Regulation of 21 February 2006 2003/0168 (COD)) rejected an amendment proposed by the European Parliament (Amendment 41 in the Wallis Report), providing that the court seised would normally apply its national rules relating to the quantification of damages.

[592] The Hague Convention on the Law Applicable to Products Liability does not appear to be so limited, see the Von Mehren Report, pp 21–22. But cf the Essen Report in relation to the Hague Convention on the Law Applicable to Road Traffic Accidents, para 7.2, the judge is not prevented from fixing the amount of damages according to his own personal convictions. Under the pre-Regulation English tort choice of law rules the distinction for assessment of damages purposes between rules of law and questions of fact was rejected: *Re T & N Ltd (No 2)* [2005] EWHC 2990 (Ch), [2006] 1 WLR 1792.

[593] See the Giuliano and Lagarde Report, p 33.

[594] Cf the procedural classification under the English statutory tort choice of law rules, discussed supra, p 99.

[595] See ibid. However, a foreign applicable law may be overridden by English law, which it has been said operates as a mandatory rule of the forum: see the interpretation of *Roerig v Valiant Trawlers Ltd* [2002] EWCA Civ 21, [2002] 1 WLR 2304 by ARDEN LJ in *Harding v Wealands* [2004] EWCA Civ 1735 at [48], [2005] 1 WLR 1539 (revsd by the House of Lords without discussion of this example [2006] UKHL 32, [2007] 2 AC 1).

[596] The Giuliano and Lagarde Report, p 33, seems to regard it as a matter of fact.

that a foreign court applies a different method of assessment,[597] or would make a lower award of general damages in tort than an English court,[598] further evidence would be needed as to whether this difference is the result of a rule of law or a matter of fact.

One particular problem that is likely to arise is where in the state whose law is applicable a jury fixes the amount of damages in tort cases.[599] This does not normally happen under English law, so there is no mechanism for adopting this procedure. Is the English court now required to introduce such a mechanism? In the case of contractual obligations the answer is no. It could be argued that this involves a matter of fact rather than a rule of law.[600] More importantly, there is an explicit procedural limitation on the scope of Article 10(1)(c) of the Rome Convention from the opening words of that Article. These provide that "within the limits of the powers conferred on the court by its procedural law" the assessment of damages is a matter for the applicable law. If the forum has no mechanism for jury trials to assess damages it cannot be expected to use this method of assessment, even though the applicable law is that of a state which uses this method. However, Article 15(c) of the Rome II Regulation contains no such procedural limitation. Nonetheless, common sense requires that Article 15(c) should be interpreted as being implicitly procedurally limited in the same way as Article 10(1)(c) of the Rome Convention is explicitly so limited.

Finally, in relation to assessment of damages the European Parliament raised concerns in relation to road traffic accidents where the victim is injured in a country other than the one in which he habitually resides. Under Article 4(1) the amount of compensation will have to be calculated according to the law and standards of the country in which the damage occurs, and not those of the country where the victim habitually resides. The European Parliament regarded this as unsatisfactory and secured the introduction of Recital (33), which ensures that the court seised of the dispute will "take into account all the relevant actual circumstances of the specific victim, including in particular the actual losses and costs of after-care and medical attention".[601]

(c) The remedy

This would cover, for example, whether in a case of conversion recovery should take the form of money damages or return of goods.

(iv) Within the limits of powers conferred on the court by its procedural law, the measures which a court may take to prevent or terminate injury or damage or to ensure the provision of compensation[602]

This provision is concerned with two sorts of measures. First, it is concerned with measures which a court may take to prevent or terminate injury or damage. A claimant may seek an injunction to prevent damage occurring or to stop further damage where this has

---

[597] See the facts of the pre-Regulation case *Edmunds v Simmonds* [2001] 1 WLR 1003.

[598] See the facts of the pre-Regulation case *Hulse v Chambers* [2001] 1 WLR 2386.

[599] This was classified as a procedural matter under the pre-Regulation law: *Harding v Wealands* [2004] EWCA Civ 1735 at [57], [2005] 1 WLR 1539; revsd by the House of Lords without discussion of this example [2006] UKHL 32, [2007] 2 AC 1.

[600] See the Giuliano and Lagarde Report, p 33.

[601] The long-term solution to this problem is discussed supra, p 805.

[602] Art 15(d).

already occurred. This will commonly happen in cases, for example, of infringement of intellectual property rights and nuisance. The applicable law will determine whether a court may take this measure, in other words whether the criteria for the grant of an injunction have been met. Secondly, it is concerned with measures which a court may take to ensure the provision of compensation. This would cover the issue of whether lump sum compensation is adequate or whether periodic payments of compensation are required. Where an English court awards a lump sum for special damages whereas a foreign court would only award instalments,[603] the applicable law should determine which of the two is to be used.[604]

However, the scope of Article 15(d) is limited by its opening words: "within the limits of the powers conferred on the court by its procedural law". In other words, the forum is not required to order measures that are unknown in the procedural law of the forum.[605] English law allows for the grant of injunctions in the case of non-contractual obligations and has a mechanism for the grant of periodical payments of compensation.

(v) The question whether a right to claim damages or a remedy may be transferred, including by inheritance[606]

This provision is largely self-explanatory.[607] A right to claim damages may be transferred in various ways, most obviously by assignment or by inheritance. The applicable law will govern the question whether the right to claim damages that the deceased victim would have had if he had survived is capable of being transferred on death to his estate.[608] The question of who will benefit from the survival of the cause of action is a matter governed by the law governing the succession.[609] As far as English private international law is concerned, this provision represents no change in the law.[610] Assignment could be by contract or it could be by a method which is non-contractual, for example by way of gift. The law applicable to the non-contractual obligation will determine whether a claim in respect of this obligation is assignable and the relationship between the assignor and debtor.[611]

(vi) Persons entitled to compensation for damage sustained personally[612]

This is concerned with the issue of whether a person can recover for damage he himself has suffered by reason of injury to another person (the direct victim).[613] For example, this would cover whether a widow and children can recover for financial loss to *them* following the death of the husband/father[614] and whether a person can recover for emotional

---

[603] See the facts of *Hulse v Chambers*, supra.

[604] This is the position under the Hague Convention on the Law Applicable to Products Liability, see the Von Mehren Report, p 21.

[605] The Explanatory Memorandum, p 24.

[606] Art 15(e).

[607] See the Explanatory Memorandum, p 24.

[608] For English law, see the Law Reform (Miscellaneous Provisions) Act 1934, s 1(1).

[609] The Explanatory Memorandum, p 24. So the law governing succession will determine who the heir is.

[610] See Law Com Working Paper No 87 Private International Law Tort and Delict, para 2.62.

[611] The Explanatory Memorandum, p 24. Assignment of non-contractual obligations is discussed further, infra, p 1232.

[612] Art 15(f).

[613] See the Explanatory Memorandum, p 24; the Von Mehren Report, p 22.

[614] Under English law dependants can recover for this loss under the Fatal Accidents Act 1976.

distress suffered by having witnessed physical injury being done to another. It would also encompass the issue of whether a person can recover solatium (damages for injury to feelings) in respect of the death of a relative under Scots law. The applicable law will determine the answer to these questions, as was the position at common law.[615]

(vii) Liability for the acts of another person[616]

This is concerned with the issue of vicarious liability.[617] This could be liability of parents for their children, of principals for their agents or of employers for their employees. This represents no change in English private international law, which has traditionally regarded vicarious liability as a matter of substance to be determined by the law applicable to the tort.[618]

(viii) The manner in which an obligation may be extinguished and rules of prescription and limitation, including rules relating to the commencement, interruption and suspension of a period of prescription or limitation[619]

This provision is virtually identical with a provision in the Rome Convention.[620] It brings together what are, to English eyes, two very different sorts of issue. The first of these is the manner in which a non-contractual obligation may be extinguished: eg by payment of compensation or repayment of money in a case of unjust enrichment; by a judgment; by accord and satisfaction; by waiver; by bankrupcy. Any choice of law problems that arise in relation to these situations are matters for the applicable law under the Regulation.

The second issue covered is prescription and limitation of actions, which is likewise subject to the applicable law as determined by the Regulation. Prescription and limitation includes rules relating to the commencement, interruption and suspension of a period of prescription or limitation. Prescription and limitation involves loss of a right by failure to exercise it and accordingly can be seen to have some similarity to the manner in which an obligation may be extinguished. At one time the matter of limitation was regarded under English law as being a procedural one for the law of the forum. However, as has been seen,[621] the Foreign Limitation Periods Act 1984 changed this rule by adopting the principle that the English court is to apply to the issue of limitation the law which governs the substantive issue according to the English choice of law rules. Thus, even before the Rome II Regulation came into force, the English law on limitation produced the same effect in non-contractual obligation cases as that now produced by Article 15(h).

(ix) Capacity

Article 15 does not mention the issue of capacity to incur liability. This would include the issue of the age at which a person can incur capacity. It would also include the question of whether a company can incur liability on some basis other than vicarious liability, which is already covered under Article 15(g). However, Recital (12) makes it clear that

---

[615] See Law Com Working Paper No 87 Private International Law Tort and Delict, paras 2.67–2.76.
[616] Art 15(g).
[617] See the Explanatory Memorandum, p 24.
[618] See *Church of Scientology of California v Metropolitan Police Comr* (1976) 120 SJ 690, CA.
[619] Art 15(h).
[620] Art 10(1)(d) of the Rome Convention.
[621] Supra, pp 80–82.

the law applicable should also govern the question of the capacity to incur liability in tort/delict.[622]

(h) Limitations on the dominance of the law applicable

Considerations of public policy are said to justify giving the courts of Member States the possibility of applying exceptions based on the overriding mandatory provisions of the forum and public policy.[623] It is envisaged that these two exceptions will only apply in exceptional circumstances.[624]

(i) Overriding mandatory provisions of the forum

(a) Article 16

Article 16 is headed "overriding mandatory provisions" and goes on to provide that "Nothing in this Regulation shall restrict the application of the provisions of the law of the forum in a situation where they are mandatory irrespective of the law otherwise applicable to the non-contractual obligation". It makes clear that the forum can continue to apply its own mandatory rules to override the rules on the applicable law under the Regulation, including the rules allowing a choice of the applicable law. Article 16 is in substance worded identically to Article 7(2) of the Rome Convention. Much has already been said in the context of contract about the concept of mandatory rules and about how such rules are to be identified.[625] What is said there is equally relevant in the present context. Article 16 is concerned with *overriding* mandatory rules, as contrasted with provisions of the law of a country that cannot be derogated from by agreement, as in Article 14(2) of the Regulation. The addition of the word "Overriding" in the heading to Article 16 is to be welcomed. It is noticeable that under the Rome II Regulation the drafters have been concerned to avoid the confusion caused under the Rome Convention by using the same term "mandatory rules" in two different senses.[626] Under the Regulation not only is Article 16 headed "Overriding mandatory rules" but also Article 14(2) avoids using the term mandatory rules altogether.

(b) English overriding mandatory rules

English law is familiar with the concept of overriding mandatory rules of the forum in tort cases. The statutory tort choice of law rule expressly preserved the mandatory rules of the forum exception that existed at common law.[627]

(i) Examples of statutory mandatory rules of the forum

There is a distinct lack of authority in relation to the application of the mandatory rules of the forum exception in tort cases. This is because, under the common law tort choice

---

[622] See Briggs, Written Evidence, HL Report 66 (2004), p 96, who suggests Art 15(a) will apply.
[623] Recital (32).
[624] Ibid.
[625] Supra, pp 731–738.
[626] Supra, pp 730–731.
[627] Private International Law (Miscellaneous Provisions) Act 1995, s 14(4) states that: "This Part has effect without prejudice to the operation of any rule of law which either has effect notwithstanding the rules of private international law applicable in the particular circumstances or modifies the rules of private international law that would otherwise be so applicable."

of law rules, there was an automatic reference to English law anyway. Nonetheless, in a pre-Regulation case, the right to contribution, which can arise between joint tortfeasors under the Civil Liability (Contribution) Act 1978, has been held to be a matter solely of construction of the language of the Act.[628] The argument that the Act was only applicable where the law governing the right to contribution was English law was rejected. The Act is applicable once liability against joint tortfeasors has been established, applying tort choice of law rules. It is suggested that English statutory rules limiting the effect of certain exclusion clauses in contracts of employment,[629] might operate as mandatory rules in a negligence action brought by an injured employee against the employer.[630] It could also be argued that the provisions on limitation of liability for maritime claims contained in the Merchant Shipping Act 1995,[631] giving the force of law to an international Convention, should be regarded as mandatory rules.[632] In the past, these provisions have been given a procedural characterisation,[633] and so the question of whether they were mandatory rules did not arise. But the Regulation provides that limitation of liability comes within the scope of the rules on the applicable law.[634] Finally there is judicial authority stating that section 4 of the Fatal Accidents Act 1976[635] is a mandatory rule of English law.[636]

(ii) Common law rules of substantive law

The examples given so far all involve statutory provisions. But much of the English law of tort is of common law origin. In principle, it is possible to have a common law mandatory rule of the forum. But this leaves the practical problem of how such rules are to be identified. With a statutory provision, it may be possible to ascertain that it was Parliament's intention that this provision should apply, regardless of the law applicable to the tort. This can be done by looking at other provisions in the statute expressly stating that the whole or part of it is to have overriding effect or imposing a territorial limit on the scope of the statute. But with a common law rule, how is this intention to be ascertained? Indeed, whose intention are we concerned with? Presumably that of the judges, but which particular judge or judges? The upshot is that it is likely that examples of common law mandatory rules of the forum will be very rare. One possible example, though, has been suggested.[637] This is concerned with passing off. Let us assume that the act of passing off occurred in England and the claimant has goodwill in England. In so far as goodwill is territorially limited, an analogy can be drawn with the statutory tort of

---

[628] *Arab Monetary Fund v Hashim (No 9)* (1994) Times, 11 October; Briggs [1995] LMCLQ 437. In this situation, the mandatory rules of the forum rule is probably best regarded as an exception to unjust enrichment choice of law rules.

[629] See the Law Reform (Personal Injuries) Act 1948, s 1(3); infra, pp 863–864.

[630] Infra, pp 866–867.

[631] S 185 and Sch 7.

[632] See, for carriage of goods by sea, *The Hollandia* [1983] 1 AC 565; discussed supra, p 735.

[633] *Caltex Singapore Pte Ltd and Ors v BP Shipping Ltd* [1996] 1 Lloyd's Rep 286; approved in *Harding v Wealands* [2006] UKHL 32, [2007] 2 AC 1; *Seismic Shipping Inc v Total E & P UK plc (The Western Regent)* [2005] EWCA Civ 985 at [52], [2005] 2 Lloyd's Rep 359.

[634] Art 15(b); discussed supra, pp 842–843.

[635] This provides that in assessing damages in respect of a person's death, accrued benefits are to be ignored.

[636] See under the pre-Regulation law the interpretation of *Roerig v Valiant Trawlers Ltd* [2002] EWCA Civ 21, [2002] 1 WLR 2304 by Arden LJ in *Harding v Wealands* [2004] EWCA Civ 1735 at [48], [2005] 1 WLR 1539 (revsd by the House of Lords without discussion of this example [2006] UKHL 32, [2007] 2 AC 1).

[637] See Fawcett and Torremans, p 668.

infringement, which is also territorially limited. Prior to the Regulation, the statutory English tort of infringement, because it was territorially limited, was regarded as a mandatory rule of the forum in the situation where a United Kingdom right had been infringed in England.[638] After the introduction of the Regulation, the specific choice of law rule for the special tort of infringement of an intellectual property right ensures that English law will apply in this situation[639] and so there is no need to have recourse to the mandatory rules of the forum exception. But this need still exists in relation to passing off and can be justified on the basis that goodwill is territorially limited. This means that English law would apply to an act of passing off that occurred in England and the claimant has goodwill in England, even though the law applicable to the tort is that of a foreign country.

(c) No provision on the overriding mandatory rules of foreign countries

It is noticeable that there is no equivalent in the Rome II Regulation of Article 7(1) of the Rome Convention,[640] which provides for the application of the mandatory rules of a foreign country with which the situation has a close connection.[641] Such a provision is highly controversial.[642] Under the Rome Convention, Contracting States were allowed to reserve the right not to apply Article 7(1) and the United Kingdom and six other Contracting States to the Convention have done so. Allowing a Member State to enter a reservation would be incompatible under a Regulation. The upshot is that Member States which do not want to apply the mandatory rules of foreign countries would have been forced to consider giving effect to such rules. This could have jeopardised the willingness of these countries to vote for the Rome II Regulation.[643]

(ii) Public policy of the forum

(a) Article 26: General discussion

Article 26 of the Regulation is entitled "Public policy of the forum" and provides that the "application of a provision of the law of any country specified by this Regulation may be refused only if such application is manifestly incompatible with the public policy ('ordre public') of the forum". Recital (32) helpfully gives an example of a situation which may, depending on the circumstances of the case and the legal order of the Member State of the court seised, be regarded as being contrary to the public policy of the forum, namely where "the application of a provision of the law designated by the Regulation has the effect of causing non-compensatory exemplary or punitive damages of an excessive nature to be awarded".[644] Such a law may, "depending on the circumstances of the case and the legal order of the Member State of the court seised", be regarded as contrary to public policy.

---

[638] Ibid at 600. See also the 13th edn of this book (1999), p 651.

[639] Art 8(1); discussed supra, pp 815–816.

[640] Supra, p 738.

[641] There was such a provision in the Proposal and Amended Proposal but it was dropped and did not appear in the Common Position.

[642] The United Kingdom Government Response (2002), para 23, and HL Rep 66 (2004), para 146, proposed deleting this provision.

[643] But see Art 9(3) of the Rome I Regulation, supra, pp 740–741.

[644] Recital (32).

The addition of the words "of an excessive nature"[645] appears to be making the point that exemplary or punitive damages are not *ipso facto* excessive. [646] The forum may decide that the exemplary or punitive damages to be awarded will not be excessive, with the result that the public policy exception will not apply.[647] It will then award exemplary or punitive damages, the assessment of which will be a matter for the applicable law.[648] This means that, in a case where the Regulation applies and Ruritanian law is applicable, an English court could apply the Ruritanian law on exemplary or punitive damages. Technically, exemplary and punitive damages do not cover multiple damages for breach of US anti-trust law but nonetheless such damages should be regarded as against English public policy.[649] Recital (32) is only concerned with exemplary and punitive damages and does not include other types of non-compensatory damages, such as restitutionary damages.[650]

Article 26 is virtually identical to Article 16 of the Rome Convention. We know from the discussion of the latter,[651] and from the discussion of public policy in the context of the Brussels I Regulation,[652] the following. First, in civil law countries *ordre public* operates as a well-established exception to normal choice of law rules, as does public policy in common law jurisdictions. Any clash between the civil and common law concepts of public policy is resolved by the reference to the application of a rule of law being "manifestly" incompatible with the public policy of the forum. This adds nothing as far as English law is concerned since there has long been a reluctance to invoke the public policy doctrine in this country. However, for civil lawyers it makes clear that what is in issue is the narrow concept of international *ordre public* as opposed to the wide concept of domestic *ordre public*. The intention then is that Article 26 will only be used in exceptional circumstances. Secondly, it has to be shown that the *application* of a foreign rule of law is against the forum's public policy. The circumstances of the case have to be considered. This is entirely consistent with common law decisions on public policy, which normally have required some relevant connection with England which justifies English courts in invoking the public policy exception.[653] Thirdly, public policy under the Regulation is a negative concept, involving the *refusal* to apply a foreign law. Article 26 is concerned with an objectionable foreign law that is contrary to the public policy of the forum. Fourthly, when Article 26 does apply, it provides an exception to all of the preceding choice of law rules contained in the Regulation. Presumably, it can even operate to override provisions that cannot be derogated from by agreement under Article 14(2) which are themselves an exception to normal choice of law principles. Thus, an English

---

[645] Art 24 of the Proposal for a Rome II Regulation did not contain these additional words. Art 24 was a categorical rule with no discretion in the court seised. The European Parliament wanted a more discretionary rule (which again did not contain these additional words), see the Wallis Report, p 33. The Amended Proposal accepted this amendment in part, subject to redrafting.

[646] See the Explanatory Memorandum to the Amended Proposal, p 5.

[647] At common law a foreign law awarding exemplary or punitive damages may well be applied and not regarded as penal, supra, p 127.

[648] Art 15(c); discussed supra, pp 843–846.

[649] See Law Com Working Paper No 87 (1984), para 5.63. See also the discussion of foreign penal laws, supra, pp 126–130.

[650] Cf Art 24 of the Proposal, criticised by Virgo, Written Evidence, HL Paper 66 (2004), p 135–136.

[651] Supra, pp 741–743.

[652] Supra, pp 611–615.

[653] Supra, pp 141–142.

court could refuse to apply a rule which cannot be derogated from by agreement on the basis that the application of that rule would be against English public policy. It is possible to envisage this happening in cases where a foreign rule that cannot be derogated from by agreement is in conflict with an English rule which cannot be derogated from by agreement. Fifthly, Article 26 operates when the application of a provision of the law of any country specified by the Regulation is manifestly incompatible with the public policy ("*ordre public*") of *the forum*. National courts are undoubtedly left with some latitude in deciding on the meaning of the concept, but they must give it a meaning which is appropriate in the context of the Regulation, and the Court of Justice may intervene if they fail to do so. The courts of a Member State determine, according to its own conceptions, what public policy requires, but there are limits to that concept which are subject to review by the Court of Justice.[654] These limits are a matter for interpretation of the Regulation.[655] Sixthly, public policy is concerned with the situation where application of the foreign law would involve a manifest breach of a fundamental right in the Member State seised of the matter.[656] When using the public policy exception a court can be guided by the case law of the European Court of Human Rights.[657] It is submitted that it would be against public policy to apply a foreign law in circumstances where that law operates to deny rights guaranteed by the European Convention on Human Rights. In some countries, there is a cause of action for loss of self-esteem, bringing a president or the government into disrepute by undermining public confidence in its capacity to govern, and for insult.[658] If liability is imposed even where the statement is true, this may involve a breach of the right to freedom of expression. If so, the foreign law should not be applied, regardless of the law governing the tort. It has been suggested that a foreign law that provides that torture is lawful would be against public policy, and even a foreign law which provides inadequate redress by domestic standards might be contrary to public policy.[659]

Public policy may also come into play where there has been some divergence from European Community law. One area where this could arise is that of product liability. It is suggested that a court in a Member State should not apply the product liability law of another Member State in so far as this has diverged from the terms of the European Community Product Liability Directive and is thereby incompatible with European Community law.[660] Another suggested, but more doubtful, example is where a foreign law is applied under the Regulation which denies the protection given to internet service providers by the E-Commerce Directive.[661]

---

[654] Case C-7/98 *Krombach v Bamberski* [2001] QB 709 at [22]; Case C-38/98 *Régie Nationale des Usines Renault SA v Maxicar SpA* [2000] ECR I-2973 at [27]. Both cases are discussed supra, pp 613–615.

[655] See the *Krombach* and *Reneault* cases, supra.

[656] This applies the analogy of recognition of judgments granted in another Member State, on which see Case C-7/98 *Krombach v Bamberski* [2001] QB 709.

[657] Ibid.

[658] It is argued supra, p 785, that such laws should not fall within the defamation exclusion under Art 1(2)(g).

[659] See HL Paper 66 (2004), para 153 referring to the evidence of Sir Lawrence COLLINS. See also the Written Evidence of the AIRE centre, JUSTICE and REDRESS, p 89. An alternative way of dealing with such cases would be by applying English law as a mandatory rule of the forum under Art 16, discussed supra, p 849. But because the content of the foreign law is being considered, such cases are best regarded as coming within public policy.

[660] See Fawcett (1993-I) 238 Hague Recueil 13, 215–216.

[661] HL Paper 66 (2004), para 159, referring to the written evidence by Reed.

We must now consider when Article 26 would operate in cases where the forum is England. In other words, when is the application of a provision of the law of a foreign country specified by this Regulation manifestly incompatible with the public policy of England?

(b) Against the public policy of England

It is a well-established principle of English private international law that the English courts will not apply a foreign law when to do so would be inconsistent with the fundamental public policy of English law.[662] There are numerous examples of the operation of this doctrine in choice of law cases in contract,[663] but there was a distinct shortage of authority in England in relation to torts under the common law choice of law rules. The reason for this is easily explained. The requirement under the first limb of the double actionability rule of actionability according to English law meant that the English courts seldom got as far as applying a foreign law. The English courts would not be faced with the situation where an objectionable foreign law imposed liability in circumstances where English law would not do so. With the introduction of the statutory tort choice of law rules, abolishing the first limb of the double actionability rule and setting out an explicit public policy exception to the statutory rules,[664] this was due to change and it is likely that a body of case law would have developed on the operation of the doctrine of public policy in the context of statutory tort choice of law.

Under the Regulation, English courts will not infrequently be faced with causes of action that are unknown to English law. If these were to be routinely struck down as being manifestly incompatible with English public policy it could seem as if the common law rules had never been abolished. This would defeat the purpose of the Regulation. To take a practical example, it would be inappropriate for an English court, when faced with a claim for unfair competition based on Swiss law, to say that the application of such a law is against England's distinctive public policy. The Regulation envisages that Member States will apply the unfair competition law of other states, indeed the Regulation has special choice of law rules for unfair competition. Whilst no such cause of action exists under English law, there is nothing so extreme or objectionable about this Swiss law as to justify not applying it. Moreover, there is authority, in the different context of an action in relation to a dowry, to the effect that public policy cannot be invoked simply on the basis that the foreign cause of action is unknown in England.[665]

The situation at common law where public policy did operate was where there was actionability under English law but no actionability under the second limb of the double actionability rule because of an objectionable law. Thus, in a tort choice of law case at common law, the House of Lords refused to apply an Iraqi law providing for the expropriation of Kuwaiti assets following the invasion of that country on the basis that this law involved a breach of international law.[666] Enforcement or recognition of that law would

---

[662] Supra, pp 139–150.
[663] Supra, pp 142–144.
[664] Private International Law (Miscellaneous Provisions) Act 1995, s 14(3)(a)(i) sets out a public policy exception to the statutory tort choice of law rules.
[665] See *Phrantzes v Argenti* [1960] 2 QB 19.
[666] *Kuwait Airways Corpn v Iraqi Airways Co (Nos 4 and 5)* [2002] 2 AC 883, HL; discussed supra, pp 145–146.

be manifestly contrary to the public policy of English law.[667] The position would doubtless be the same under the Regulation.

(i) Rules of safety and conduct

Article 17 provides that: "In assessing the conduct of the person claimed to be liable, account shall be taken, as a matter of fact and insofar as is appropriate, of the rules of safety and conduct which were in force at the place and time of the event giving rise to the liability." This provision is derived from the Hague Convention on the Law Applicable to Traffic Accidents of 1971, the Hague Convention on the Law Applicable to Products Liability of 1973[668] and the national choice of law rules of Member States.[669] The effect of Article 17 is that, although the law governing the non-contractual obligation is that of Country A, account must be taken of the rules of safety and conduct in operation in the country in which the harmful act was committed (Country B).[670] The rule is said to strike a reasonable balance between the parties.[671] The perpetrator will have to comply with the rules of safety and conduct in the country in which it operates. The phrase "rules of safety and conduct" should be interpreted as referring to "all regulations having any relation to safety and conduct, including, for example, road safety rules in the case of an accident".[672]

But "account" is only required to be taken of rules of safety and conduct. "Taking account of" is not the same as applying the law of the place of the event giving rise to liability.[673] The law applicable under the rules in the Regulation will still govern. Moreover, account is only to be taken of such rules "as a matter of fact and insofar as is appropriate". The rules of safety and conduct of the place of the event giving rise to liability will only be taken account of *as a point of fact*, eg "when assessing the seriousness of the fault or the author's good or bad faith for the purposes of the measure of damages".[674] It is not clear what, if anything, taking account of rules *insofar as is appropriate* adds to what comes before.

To take an example of the operation of Article 17, the parties may have their common habitual residence in Country A but one injures the other in a road traffic accident in Country B. The issue is whether the defendant was, as a question of fact, driving negligently. In order to determine this, account must be taken of the road safety rules in Country B. A further example was given in the context of environmental damage.[675]

(j) Special rules for particular issues

Rome II contains a number of special rules for particular issues. Most of these are more appropriately discussed elsewhere in this book.[676] The two remaining issues: namely,

---

[667] No connection with England is needed in such a case because public policy is not based on a principle of English public policy, which is domestic in character.

[668] Art 7 of the former and Art 9 of the latter.

[669] The Explanatory Memorandum, p 25.

[670] Recital (34).

[671] Ibid.

[672] Ibid.

[673] The Explanatory Memorandum, p 25.

[674] Ibid.

[675] Supra, p 814.

[676] For Arts 19 (subrogation) and 20 (multiple liability), see infra, p 1238; Art 22 (burden of proof), supra, p 89.

direct action against the insurer of the person liable and formal validity, will be discussed here.

(i) Direct action against the insurer of the person liable

In common law jurisdictions the classification of a claim by a victim of a road accident under legislation permitting a direct action against the wrongdoer's insurance company has proved to be particularly difficult. The claim has been classified as tortious, as a *sui generis* statutory extension of contractual liability or as quasi-contractual, to be governed by the law governing the insurance contract.[677]

Article 18 of the Regulation adopts a different approach by providing that the person having suffered damage may bring his or her claim directly against the insurer of the person liable to provide compensation if the law applicable to the non-contractual obligation or the law applicable to the insurance contract so provides. This rule is designed to strike a balance between the interests of the victim and the insurance company.[678] It gives the victim two bites of the cherry when it comes to proceeding directly against the insurer. At the same time it limits the laws applicable to the two that the insurer can legitimately expect to be applied, namely the law applicable to the non-contractual obligation and the law applicable to the insurance contract.

(ii) Formal validity

The issue of formal validity will seldom arise in the creation of non-contractual obligations but could do so in the context of a unilateral act by one or other of the parties.[679] The Regulation adopts a rule modelled on Article 9(1) of the Rome Convention.[680] Article 21 of the Regulation provides that: "A unilateral act intended to have legal effect and relating to a non-contractual obligation shall be formally valid if it satisfies the formal requirements of the law governing the non-contractual obligation in question or the law of the country in which the act is performed."

(k) Relationship with Community law and existing international conventions

(i) Relationship with Community law

When discussing the law applicable to contractual obligations it was seen that there has been a growing problem of the insertion in community instruments of provisions which have an impact on private international law.[681] In some cases the instrument undeniably contains a choice of law rule, but in other cases it can be a moot point whether the provision is in truth a choice of law rule. It may merely explain when an instrument applies, but not explain what law governs in the event that the instrument does not apply (which a choice of law rule would do). The possibility cannot be excluded that there may be choice of law rules relating to non-contractual obligations in Community instruments dealing with particular matters and that these are inconsistent with the rules in the

---

[677] See 13th edn of this book (1999), p 665.
[678] See the Explanatory Memorandum, pp 25–26.
[679] Ibid, p 26.
[680] Supra, pp 746–749.
[681] Supra, p 762.

Rome II Regulation.[682] There is a particular concern that the provisions on the applicable law in the Rome II Regulation should not restrict the free movement of goods and services as regulated by Community instruments.[683] Article 27 therefore provides that the Regulation "shall not prejudice the application of provisions of Community law which, in relation to particular matters, lay down conflict of law [ie choice of law] rules relating to non-contractual obligations". Unlike with contracts, though, it is difficult to find clear examples of choice of law rules relating to non-contractual obligations in Community instruments. It seems to be suggested that the E-Commerce Directive[684] is one such instrument.[685] This contains a country of origin rule,[686] which appears to have an impact on the law applicable, but it is questionable whether this is a choice of law rule as such.[687] If it is accepted that it is,[688] the problems really start; for the impact of the Directive and of its country of origin rule on internet torts is very uncertain.[689]

(ii) Relationship with existing international conventions

Article 28 states: "This Regulation shall not prejudice the application of international conventions to which one or more Member States are parties at the time when this Regulation is adopted and which lay down conflict-of-law rules relating to non-contractual obligations." This provision makes it clear that existing conventions covering some of the same ground as the Rome II Regulation are preserved. Many Member States have entered into the Hague Convention on the Law Applicable to Traffic Accidents of 1971, which determines the law applicable to civil non-contractual liability arising from traffic accidents, and the Hague Convention on the Law Applicable to Products Liability of 1973, which determines the law applicable, in international cases, to products liability. For these Member States the rules in these Conventions will continue to apply, unaffected by the Rome II Regulation. However, the United Kingdom has entered into neither Convention and will accordingly apply the provisions in the Regulation in road traffic and products liability cases. The upshot is a lack of harmonised tort choice of law rules in the European Community in these two areas.[690] The United Kingdom, like only a small number of other Member States,[691] has entered into the Hague Convention on the Law Applicable to Trusts and on their Recognition of 1986 which lays down choice of law rules relating to non-contractual obligations (equitable obligations). So, again, there will

---

[682] Recital (35), para 1.

[683] Recital (35), para 2.

[684] Directive (EC) No 2000/31 of 8 June 2000, OJ 2000 L 178/1; implemented in the United Kingdom by the Electronic Commerce (EC Directive) Regulations 2002, SI 2002/2013.

[685] Recital (35), para 2.

[686] Art 3(1).

[687] See Fawcett, Harris and Bridge, paras 21.01–21.19. It has been argued that the provisions in the Directive should apply as mandatory rules of the forum, see ibid, paras 21.15–21.20, 21.110.

[688] Or if it applies as a mandatory rule of the forum. There is a further possibility, Recital (35), para 2 could be interpreted as giving priority to the country of origin rule, even if it does not lay down a choice of law rule.

[689] See HL Paper 66 (2004), paras 158–162; Fawcett, Harris and Bridge, paras 21.01–21.19, 21.120–21.210. See also Law Commission, *Defamation and the Internet: a Preliminary Investigation*, Scoping Study No 2, December 2002; Dicey, Morris and Collins, paras 35-158–35-162.

[690] For the concern that this has given rise to in road traffic accident cases, see supra, p 805.

[691] Italy, Luxembourg and the Netherlands, see http:// www.hcch.net.

be a lack of harmonisation in this area also. Member States are required to notify[692] the Commission of the conventions referred to in Article 28(1).[693]

Article 28 preserves the application of *existing* international conventions, ie conventions to which a Member State is a party at the time when the Regulation is adopted. However, it has no provision allowing Member States to enter into conventions *in the future* covering some of the same ground as the Regulation. This contrasts with the position under the Rome Convention, which allows for this. It would be out of place to have in a Regulation a provision which allows Member States to negotiate and enter into bilateral agreements which affect the Community rules.[694] However, the Community does have power to enter into international agreements.[695] Moreover, the European Community Council can authorise Member States' accession to international conventions.[696] It is envisaged that Member States will be able to negotiate and conclude on their own behalf agreements with third countries "in individual and exceptional cases, concerning sectoral matters", containing provisions on the law applicable to non-contractual obligations.[697]

Article 28(2) qualifies the preservation of existing international conventions by providing that the Rome II Regulation "shall, as between Member States, take precedence over conventions concluded exclusively between two or more of them insofar as such conventions concern matters governed by this Regulation".

(I) Review of the Regulation

The Commission is required, by 20 August 2011, to submit a report on the application of the Regulation, accompanied, if necessary, by proposals for its adaptation.[698] The review will include studies on two specific matters which were of particular concern to the European Parliament: namely, proof of foreign law;[699] and the law applicable to traffic accidents.[700] Another matter of great concern to the European Parliament was that of violations of privacy and rights relating to personality, including defamation. As part of the overall compromise on the Regulation, the European Parliament had to withdraw its amendments on the inclusion of special choice of law rules for violations of privacy and rights relating to personality. However, the Commission is required, by 31 December 2008, to produce a study on the situation where a non-contractual obligation arises out of violations of privacy and rights relating to personality, including defamation.[701]

---

[692] By 11 July 2008.

[693] Art 29(1). After 11 July 2008, the Member States are required to notify the Commission of denunciations. The Commission will publish in the Official Journal lists of notifications and denunciations: Art 28(2).

[694] Likewise both the Brussels I Regulation, on which see supra, p 214, and the Rome I Regulation (Art 25(1)) only allow for the preservation of existing international conventions.

[695] See the Opinion of the Court of Justice 1/03 Competence of the Community to conclude the new Lugano Convention [2006] ECR I-1145 at para 148.

[696] See, eg, Council Decision (EC) No 2002/762 of 19 September 2002 in relation to the Bunkers Convention, OJ 2002 L 256/7.

[697] Recital (37), which also provides that the Commission will make a proposal to the European Parliament and the Council concerning the procedures and conditions for this, ibid.

[698] Art 30(1).

[699] Art 30(1)(i); see the discussion supra, pp 789–790.

[700] Art 30(1)(ii); see the discussion supra, p 805.

[701] See supra, pp 784–786.

3. MARITIME NON-CONTRACTUAL OBLIGATIONS

(a) Maritime torts

The effect of the introduction of the Regulation in cases involving maritime torts is a matter of considerable difficulty. The Regulation has no specific choice of law rules for maritime torts. So the only rules that can possibly apply are those in Chapter II (normally Article 4 but Article 9 (industrial action) could apply[702]). However, Chapter II provides for the application of the law of a "country". The scope of that chapter is thus implicitly limited by the need for the identification of a "country", for it cannot operate without this. As has been seen, country is defined under the Regulation in the normal private international law sense as a territorial unit with its own rules of law. Article 4(1) applies the law of the country in which damage occurs. How should the country in which damage occurs be defined in relation to maritime torts? If one looks literally at where damage occurs, ie identifying the waters in which it occurs, it follows that if damage occurs within territorial waters, Chapter II will operate as usual.[703] In contrast, if damage occurs on the high seas, Chapter II would appear not to apply.

An alternative and much more radical approach would be to say that damage occurs in the country of the flag of the ship.[704] A law of the flag rule has the advantage that Chapter II would apply, regardless of the waters in which the damage occurs. There was a provision in the Proposal for a Regulation that in effect adopted a law of the flag rule[705] but this was deleted in the Amended Proposal.[706] It has been accepted in the past that, in the absence of a special provision dealing with torts committed on the high seas, the Community tort choice of law rules cannot operate.[707] The deletion of the special provision indicates that when interpreting the Regulation, a country should not be identified by looking at the law of the flag. Even if it were still legitimate to adopt a law of the flag rule, such a rule has substantial drawbacks. First, a law of the flag rule does not work if there is a collision between two ships flying different flags, so it does not provide the certainty needed under the Regulation.[708] Secondly, ships frequently fly a flag of convenience so that the applicable law could be that of Panama, even though the parties and events have no connection with that country. To be sure, there is under Article 4(2) the common habitual residence exception and under Article 4(3) the manifestly more closely connected escape clause but the spread of connections in maritime cases will often mean that these provisions are inapplicable. Thirdly, the English courts traditionally have applied a literal approach to where damage occurs in cases where it occurs within territorial waters.[709] Even where it occurs on the high seas, the law of the flag has not been

---

[702] See the Statement by the Cypriot and Greek Delegations on Art 9, supra, p 818.

[703] The Cypriot and Greek Delegations in their Statement on Art 9, supra, p 818, assume that it will apply to industrial action in territorial waters.

[704] See generally George (2007) 3 J Priv Int L 137, 168–171.

[705] Art 18 of the Proposal. This showed an intention to bring torts committed on the high seas within the tort choice of law rules.

[706] It is not clear why this provision was deleted.

[707] See the Giuliano, Lagarde and Van Sasse Van Ysselt Report, p 50, referring to the 1972 preliminary draft convention which contained no such special provision.

[708] Law Commission Working Paper 87 (1984), paras 5.79–5.81.

[709] *The Arum* [1921] P 12; and see *The Mary Moxham* (1876) 1 PD 107; *The Waziristan* [1953] 1 WLR 1446. But see Law Commission Working Paper No 87 (1984), para 5.77 which supported application of the law of the

applied where acts did not all occur on board a single vessel.[710] Indeed, the distinction between torts committed in territorial waters and torts committed on the high seas is a basic one as far as English lawyers have been concerned.[711] In conclusion, it is submitted that the country in which damage occurs should be defined in a literal sense in terms of the waters in which damage occurs. It is important, therefore, to distinguish between two different situations: first where damage occurs in territorial waters, secondly where it occurs on the high seas.

(i) Damage occurs within territorial waters

In this situation, Article 4 will apply. The place where damage occurs points to a country, namely the country in whose territorial waters the damage occurs. The idea of applying the normal tort choice of law rules to torts committed within territorial waters is a familiar one to English private international lawyers.[712] Applying Article 4(1), it may be entirely fortuitous that damage occurs in the country in question. For example, a ship may just be passing through or at anchor in a particular country's territorial waters when the damage occurs. It is possible that the common habitual residence exception (Article 4(2)) will apply or the manifestly more closely connected escape clause (Article 4(3)) but the spread of connections in maritime cases will often mean that these provisions are inapplicable.

(ii) Damage occurs on the high seas

The English High Court has jurisdiction to entertain an action in respect of injurious acts done on the high seas,[713] even though both the litigants are foreigners.[714] When it comes to determining the applicable law, Article 4(1) of the Regulation will not apply because damage does not occur in a "country". Article 4(2) cannot then apply because that is an exception to Article 4(1). Neither can Article 4(3) apply because that displaces the law applicable under Article 4(1) and (2). Member States must therefore apply their national choice of law rules to identify the applicable law.

In the case of England, identification of the choice of law rules to be applied for damage that occurs on the high seas is no easy matter. It has previously been seen that the English national rules are a combination of common law rules and statutory rules, which have largely replaced the common law rules. The effect of the introduction of the statutory tort choice of law rules in cases involving maritime torts is a matter of some difficulty. Section 10 of the Law Reform (Miscellaneous Provisions) Act 1995 abolishes the "ordinary" common law tort choice of law rules, ie the double actionability rule and flexible exception. But special tort choice of law rules (ie common law rules not abolished by section 10) are preserved by section 14(2). It follows that, to the extent that at common law special tort choice of law rules were to be applied to torts committed on the high seas,

---

flag in this situation; *Sayers v International Drilling Co NV* [1971] 1 WLR 1176.

[710] Infra, pp 861–863.

[711] See the 13th edn of this book (1999), pp 661–664; Dicey, Morris and Collins, 35-068–35-076.

[712] See at common law *The Arum* [1921] P 12; and see *The Mary Moxham* (1876) 1 PD 107; *The Waziristan* [1953] 1 WLR 1446; *Mackinnon v Iberia Shipping Co Ltd* [1954] 2 Lloyd's Rep 372, 1955 SLT 49; Carter (1957) 33 BYBIL 342–343. But cf *Sayers v International Drilling Co NV* [1971] 1 WLR 1176.

[713] *The Tubantia* [1924] P 78.

[714] *Chartered Mercantile Bank of India v Netherlands India Steam Navigation Co* (1883) 10 QBD 521 at 536–537.

these special rules will continue to apply rather than the statutory rules.[715] However, what is not entirely clear is precisely when, on the one hand, such special rules were to be applied at common law and when, on the other hand, ordinary tort choice of law rules (ie ones abolished by section 10) were to be applied. In the latter situation, of course, the statutory tort choice of law rules will now apply. In answering this question a distinction must be drawn between cases where the acts complained of have all occurred on board a single vessel and those where the acts are external to the ship in the sense that they have affected persons or property not on board, as, for example, where there is negligent navigation leading to a collision or to the destruction of a submarine cable.

(a) Acts occurring on board a single vessel

At common law the law of the flag was the decisive factor whenever the acts complained of had all occurred on board a single vessel, for a ship was regarded for certain purposes as a floating island over which the national law prevailed.[716] If, therefore, the tort was committed on board an English vessel, English law would alone apply; but if it was committed wholly on a foreign ship and an action was brought in England, the claimant, if the analogy of wrongs done in a foreign country was followed, would have to prove that the act was actionable both by the law of the flag and by English law.

This double actionability rule is abolished by section 10 of the 1995 Act. To be sure, the second limb of this rule, by referring to the law of the flag, takes an unusual form; nonetheless, the wording of section 10 is wide enough to encompass this rule. What it abolishes, inter alia, are "The rules of the common law, in so far as they . . . require actionability under both the law of the forum and the law of another country for the purpose of determining whether a tort or delict is actionable". The law of the flag rule refers to the "law of another country". Recourse must now be had to the general rule under section 11 and the displacement rule under section 12 of the 1995 Act. When operating the general rule, the law of the country in which the events constituting the tort or delict in question occurred should be regarded as being the law of the flag.[717] This is the country to which the ship belongs.[718] Where a flag is common to a political unit containing several different systems of law, as in the case of Canada or the USA, the law of the flag means the law of the port at which the ship is registered.[719]

(b) External acts

(i) Collisions

There is no doubt that, prior to the introduction of the statutory tort choice of law rules, the commonest kind of external act, namely, one that causes a collision, was governed solely by the general maritime law as administered in England, and not by that combination

---

[715] S 14(2) of the 1995 Act; Law Com No 193 (1990), para 3.27.

[716] *R v Anderson* (1868) LR 1 CCR 161 at 168; *R v Keyn* (1876) 2 Ex D 63 at 94. But not for the purpose of jurisdiction, *Chung Chi Cheung v R* [1939] AC 160; *O'Daly v Gulf Oil Terminals (Ireland) Ltd* [1983] ILRM 163.

[717] *Roerig v Valiant Trawlers Ltd* [2002] EWCA Civ 21 at [7], [2002] 1 WLR 2304. See Law Com No 193 (1990), para 3.27 74. See also Law Commission Working Paper No 87 (1984), para 2.110.

[718] Law Commission Working Paper No 87 (1984), para 5.84.

[719] *Canadian National Steamship Co v Watson* [1939] 1 DLR 273; *Gronlund v Hansen* (1969) 4 DLR (3d) 435. See also Law Commission Working Paper No 87 (1984), paras 2.110 and 5.85.

of English and foreign law which is required by the double actionability rule as laid down in *Phillips v Eyre*, as amended by *Boys v Chaplin* and the *Red Sea* case.[720] It was said that: "All questions of collision are questions *communis iuris*"[721] and must be decided by the law maritime.[722]

This special tort choice of law rule is preserved, and the statutory tort choice of law rules will not apply to collisions on the high seas. This raises the question of what is meant by "general maritime law". The natural inference to draw from this expression is that there exists a body of law which is universally recognised as binding on all nations in respect of acts occurring at sea. There is, however, no such body of law.[723] The expression, in truth, means nothing more than that part of English law which, either by statute or by reiterated decisions, has been evolved for the determination of maritime disputes.[724] It is the law which, despite the views of Westlake,[725] must be applied to all questions of collision unless international regulations have been laid down by a convention between states.[726]

(ii) Other external acts

The question that now arises is whether this maritime law applied to all external acts, ie to all cases where the alleged wrong consists of some act, other than a collision, done by a foreign ship to the property of another, as, for example, where a submarine cable is fouled[727] or where possession is seized of a wreck that is being salvaged by a third party.[728] Prior to the introduction of the statutory tort choice of law rules, it was strongly argued that the law maritime should apply to all external acts.[729] Moreover, the sphere of authority possessed by the general maritime law has been described in such comprehensive terms by the judges that it would appear to cover all torts committed on the high seas,[730] including an action under the Fatal Accidents Acts arising from a collision between a Latvian trawler and a Panamanian tanker off the coast of the USA.[731] It can be confidently stated, therefore, that the law maritime applied to all external acts. This was also

---

[720] However, in *Gronlund v Hansen* (1969) 4 DLR (3d) 435, a Canadian court seemed prepared to apply the original *Phillips v Eyre* rule to a claim arising from a death resulting from a collision on the high seas.

[721] *The Johann Friedrich* (1839) 1 Wm Rob 36 at 37.

[722] *The Wild Ranger* (1862) Lush 553; *The Zollverein* (1856) Sw 96; *The Leon* (1881) 6 PD 148; *Chartered Mercantile Bank of India, London and China v Netherlands Steam Navigation Co Ltd* (1883) 10 QBD 521; Dicey, Morris and Collins, paras 35-073–35-074; Foote, pp 524–525. Cf the position in Australia, see *Blunden v Commonwealth* (2004) 218 CLR 330, HC of Australia.

[723] *Lloyd v Guibert* (1865) LR 1 QB 115 at 123–125.

[724] *The Gaetano and Maria* (1882) 7 PD 137 at 143.

[725] Westlake, pp 290–291.

[726] The collision regulations at present in force are those which are laid down by various international conventions and given effect by the Merchant Shipping Act 1995. Damage to structures erected for the exploitation of the sea-bed of the Continental Shelf over which the United Kingdom exercises rights falls under the Continental Shelf Act 1964, as amended by the Oil and Gas (Enterprise) Act 1982, see Dicey, Morris and Collins, para 35-072 and the Informal Briefing by the draftsman HL Paper 36 (1995), pp 65–68.

[727] *Submarine Telegraph Co v Dickson* (1864) 15 CBNS 759.

[728] *The Tubantia* [1924] P 78.

[729] See the 12th edn of this book (1992), pp 559–560.

[730] *Chartered Mercantile Bank of India v Netherlands India Steam Navigation Co* (1883) 10 QBD 521 at 536–537; and see *Lloyd v Guibert* (1865) LR 1 QB 115 at 125; *The Gaetano and Maria* (1882) 7 PD 37; ibid, p 137 at 143; *Davidsson v Hill* [1901] 2 KB 606; *The Esso Malaysia* [1975] QB 198.

[731] *The Esso Malaysia*, supra.

the view of the Law Commissions.[732] The law maritime will continue to apply to all such acts, and the statutory tort choice of law rules will not apply.

(b) Maritime non-contractual obligations (other than torts)

Other non-contractual obligations can arise in the maritime context. For example, it has been seen earlier that a common example of *negotiorum gestio* is salvage, ie one vessel renders service to another. Looking at the choice of law rules on *negotiorum gestio*, Article 11(1) and (2) do not refer to the place of damage or the place where the act performed without authority occurred, and can therefore be applied to a case of maritime *negotiorum gestio*. However, Article 11(3) applies the law of the country in which the act was performed and the search for the manifestly more closely connected country under Article 11(4) should include the connection with this country. It is easy enough to identify the country where the act occurred if this is in territorial waters but this is problematic if the act occurs on the high seas.

The pragmatic approach would be to start by trying to apply Article 11(1) and (2) and if the circumstances are such that they provide an answer then that is the law that is applied. It would still be possible to go on to apply Article 11(3) and (4) in cases where the act took place in territorial waters. A more principled approach would be to say that Article 11 cannot be split up into its separate components in this way and therefore none of it can apply to maritime *negotiorum gestio*. In other words, one should treat maritime *negotiorum gestio* like maritime torts. This would leave Member States to apply their national choice of law rules on *negotiorum gestio*, as modified where necessary to take into account the maritime element, to solve the problem. This looks, as a matter of principle, to be the better approach. However, there is a practical problem in that English law has never articulated such choice of law rules.

4. MIXED ISSUES RELATING TO NON-CONTRACTUAL OBLIGATIONS AND CONTRACT

The problem of contractual defences to tort claims is one of the most intractable in private international law. This was the case under the English pre-Regulation choice of law rules[733] and remains the case under the Regulation.

(a) The nature of the problem

The leading English case at common law is the pre-Regulation case of *Sayers v International Drilling Co NV*.[734] The facts neatly illustrate the nature of the problem that faces the courts when mixed questions of tort and contract arise.

> The plaintiff was an Englishman who entered a contract of employment with a Dutch company, the defendants, to work on their oil rigs. The plaintiff was sent to work on a rig in Nigerian territorial waters and was injured by the alleged negligence

---

[732] Law Com No 193 (1990), para 3.27 74.
[733] See the 13th edn of this book (1999), pp 666–669.
[734] [1971] 1 WLR 1176; see Collins (1972) 21 ICLQ 320; Carter (1971) 45 BYBIL 404.

of his fellow employees. He brought an action for damages in England. It was not clear whether this was in tort or contract or both.[735] The contract contained a clause excluding all remedies for such injuries, other than those expressly provided by the contract. Such a clause was valid under Dutch law in the case of international contracts, but void under English domestic law by reason of the Law Reform (Personal Injuries) Act 1948.[736]

Which law governs the issue of validity of the clause? This in turn raises the question of whether this is to be determined by the application of the contract choice of law rules under the Rome Convention, or the tort choice of law rules under the Rome II Regulation, or some *sui generis* approach, or by some combination of both tort and contract rules.

(b) The nature of the obligation

The starting point under the Regulation is to determine the nature of the obligation on which the claim is based. Is this a contractual obligation or a non-contractual obligation? Where an employee is suing the employer this will raise the problem of concurrent liability in tort and contract.[737] It has been seen that in such a case, in the absence of a ruling from the Court of Justice, different Member States may well adopt different classifications, some opting for a contractual classification of the obligation, whilst others adopt a tortious classification. It has also been seen that there is a strong argument for adopting a tortious classification.

After determining the classification of the obligation, the next question is how this obligation interacts with the contractual defence provided by the exemption clause. To answer this, it is necessary to look separately at, on the one hand, the situation where the obligation is contractual and, on the other hand, where it is non-contractual.

(c) A contractual obligation to which there is a contractual defence

In this situation, there is no problem of a clash between tort choice of law rules and contract choice of law rules. The law governing the contract will determine the validity of the exemption clause.

To see how a contractual defence to an obligation which has been classified as contractual operates, we can look at the judgment of the majority of the Court of Appeal in *Sayers*, bearing in mind that it was a pre-Regulation case and so is not an authority on whether a contractual classification should be adopted for the purposes of the Regulation. The Court of Appeal held unanimously that the plaintiff's claim for damages for his personal injuries should fail. A majority,[738] applying common law contract choice of law rules,[739] without considering the tortious aspect of the case,[740] decided that the proper

---

[735] The plaintiff sought damages for the negligence of his fellow employees.

[736] S 1(3). See also the Unfair Contract Terms Act 1977, s 2(1).

[737] Discussed supra, p 779.

[738] SALMON and STAMP LJJ.

[739] The case went on appeal to the Court of Appeal on the question of what the proper law of the contract was.

[740] A similar approach to that of the majority in *Sayers* would appear to have been adopted by the High Court of Australia in *Oceanic Sun Line Special Shipping Co Inc v Fay* (1988) 165 CLR 197; North [1990] I Hague Recueil 9, 228–229. Though see GAUDRON J, (1988) 165 CLR 197 at 266.

law of the contract was Dutch law. Applying that law, the majority held that the exemption clause was valid and any claim in tort was defeated thereby. [741]

If the case arose now and a contractual characterisation were to be adopted, the Unfair Contract Terms Act 1977 would have to be considered, as would the Rome Convention.[742] However, the result may well be the same.[743] It is likely that Dutch law would be applicable under the Rome Convention.[744] The Court of Appeal, unfortunately, did not address the issue of whether the English domestic rules in the 1948 Act should be regarded as mandatory ones. There is thus no authority to suggest that such rules are within Article 7(2) of the Convention. [745]

(d) A non-contractual obligation to which there is a contractual defence

This situation would arise where: there is only liability in tort; where there are claims in tort and contract but these are not parallel claims (hence there is no concurrent liability) and it is the tort claim that is in issue; or where, although there is concurrent liability, the courts regard the obligation as being non-contractual.[746] There is, then, a contractual defence to this claim.[747] This is conceptually the most difficult situation to deal with because it involves an interaction of tortious and contractual elements. In determining the validity of the exemption clause there are in theory four different approaches that could be applied:[748] the exclusive application of contract choice of law rules; the exclusive application of tort choice of law rules; a *sui generis* approach; or an approach where choice of law rules in both contract and tort have roles to play, but different roles. The Regulation seemingly provides an answer in Article 15(b), which adopts the exclusive application of tort choice of law rules approach.

Article 15(b): Application of tort choice of law rules

Article 15(b) provides that the law applicable to non-contractual obligations under the Regulation governs in particular "the grounds for exemption from liability, [and] any limitation of liability". It seems that this phrase is intended to cover an exemption or limitation clause in a contract, which is used as a defence to a claim in respect of a non-contractual obligation.[749] In particular, the issue of the validity of such clauses falls

---

[741] Lord DENNING also applied Dutch law but on a different basis. He regarded the claim as one in tort to which there was a contractual defence. He adopted a proper law of the issue approach, combining elements of the common law proper law of the tort and proper law of the contract approaches.

[742] See generally, Morse in Contract Conflicts, p 158 et seq; Morse (1982) 2 YEL 107, 141–142; Lasok and Stone, Conflict of Laws in the European Community, pp 375–376; Hartley (1997) 266 Hague Recueil 341, at 413–416.

[743] But cf Law Com No 193 (1990), para 3.50; Dicey, Morris and Collins, para 35-049.

[744] See Art 6(2) of the Rome Convention; discussed supra, p 726.

[745] Supra, p 736. The rules in the Unfair Contract Terms Act 1977 are of only limited overriding effect, supra, pp 732–734, with the result that the Act itself does not indicate that its rules are mandatory ones in a case like Sayers.

[746] The strong argument for doing so is put supra, p 779.

[747] If the contract between the parties does not contain any clause which provides a defence, the contract choice of law rules have no role to play and recourse must be had solely to the tort choice of law rules in the Regulation. This is the explanation of the pre-Regulation common law case of *Coupland v Arabian Gulf Oil Co* [1983] 1 WLR 1136..

[748] See Law Com No 193 (1990), para 3.50.

[749] Supra, pp 842–843; criticised by Briggs, Written Evidence, HL Report 66 (2004), 96.

within the scope of the law applicable to liability under the Regulation.[750] This particular issue will be examined first and then other issues that can arise where an exemption clause or other contractual defence is used as a defence to tortious liability.

(a) Validity of the exemption clause

(i) Application of Article 4

If the facts of *Sayers* arose now (and the obligation on which the claim was based was classified as tortious) the tort choice of law rules under Article 4 of the Regulation would have to be applied to determine the validity of the exemption clause. On the facts of the *Sayers* case there is some difficulty in identifying the country in which the damage occurred for the purposes of Article 4(1). The accident took place on a Dutch rig in Nigerian territorial waters and it is arguable that, in the case of matters purely internal to the rig, Dutch, rather than Nigerian, law should be regarded as the law of the country in which the damage occurred.[751] However, the better view is that, for the purposes of the Regulation, the country in which damage occurs should be defined in a literal sense in terms of the waters in which damage occurs,[752] ie Nigeria. Under Article 4(1) therefore, it is for Nigerian law as the law of the country in which the damage occurs to decide whether the exemption clause is valid and can therefore provide a defence. However, there is a pre-existing contractual relationship between the parties. This means that it is likely that Article 4(3) will apply, with the result that the law of the country that governs the contract (Dutch law) will also govern the obligation in tort. This illustrates how the secondary connection rule in Article 4(3) can take the sting out of different classifications being adopted for the obligation in a case like *Sayers*. The result will be the same regardless of whether a contractual or tortious classification is adopted.

(ii) Overriding mandatory rules of the forum

The discussion of the *Sayers* case has proceeded so far on the basis that Dutch law will apply by virtue of Article 4 of the Regulation. However, there is an important further possibility to be considered. This is that English law[753] will apply by virtue of Article 16,[754] ie as an overriding mandatory rule of the forum, to deny effect to the exemption clause as a defence to an action in tort. There is much to be said for taking this view and there is a precedent for doing so under the pre-Regulation law.

The Court of Session in a very similar pre-Regulation case to *Sayers*, *Brodin v A/R Seljan*,[755] insisted on the application of the statutory prohibition against exemption clauses.

> The deceased, a Norwegian, domiciled in Scotland, was injured on board an oil tanker as it was docking in Scotland. He later died. The law of the forum and the law of the place of the tort were, therefore, Scottish. The proper law of the deceased's contract of employment was Norwegian and it contained an express choice of law clause which also excluded liability for personal injuries. Such an exemption is void

---

[750] Supra, p 843.
[751] Supra, p 859.
[752] Supra, pp 859–860.
[753] Law Reform (Personal Injuries) Act 1948, s 1(3).
[754] Discussed supra, pp 849–850.
[755] 1973 SC 213.

under Scots domestic law by reason of the Law Reform (Personal Injuries) Act 1948.[756]

The Court of Session held that Scots law alone was applicable to a claim for damages by the deceased's widow and that no defence based on such an exemption clause was available, irrespective of its effects under Norwegian law. The court was applying what we would now describe as a mandatory rule of the forum.[757]

(b) Whether a valid exemption clause can provide an effective defence

"Exemption from liability" would cover not just the issue of validity of the exemption clause. It would also cover the issue that arose in the pre-Regulation case of *Canadian Pacific Railway v Parent*.[758]

A widow sued her late husband's employers after he was killed in the course of his employment. The employer sought to rely on an exemption clause in the husband's contract of employment. There was no question raised as to the validity of the exemption clause. However, if the widow was suing in her own right as a dependent,[759] the exemption clause would not be effective to provide a defence. In contrast, if she could only sue for rights her husband would have had if he had lived,[760] the exemption clause would have been effective to provide a defence.

The different countries involved took different views of the basis of the widow's right to sue. Under the Regulation, the law governing the tort would determine the basis of the widow's right to sue and hence whether the exemption clause was an effective defence. The application of tort choice of law rules looks to be particularly appropriate.[761]

(c) The scope of the exemption clause

The issue can arise as to whether the exemption clause is worded adequately to exclude liability in tort. According to Article 15(b), the tort choice of law rules must be applied to determine this question. In principle, this does not make much sense. It would surely be better if the law governing the contract were to be applied to determine the scope of a contractual clause. However, in practice, the secondary connection rule under Article 4(3) will ensure that the law of the country that governs the contract will also determine the scope of the contractual clause.

(d) Other contractual defences

There are contractual defences to actions in tort, other than an exemption clause. "Grounds for exemption from liability, [and] any limitation of liability" under Article 15(b) will cover any such other contractual defence. An example of such a defence can be seen

---

[756] S 1(3).

[757] Law Com No 193 (1990), para 3.50.

[758] [1917] AC 195.

[759] In England, see the Fatal Accidents Act 1976.

[760] For survival of causes of action under English law, see the Law Reform (Miscellaneous Provisions) Act 1934.

[761] In *CPR v Parent*, the common law tort choice of law rules were applied to determine whether the exemption clause provided a defence. There is no contractual relationship between the parties (the widow and employer) and so Art 4(3) of the Regulation would not apply.

in the pre-Regulation case of *Chiron Corpn v Organon Teknika Ltd (No 2)*.[762] The defendants pleaded section 44(3) of the Patents Act 1977 as a defence to an infringement action. This provides a defence where there is a contract relating to the patent containing a term or condition which has been rendered void under section 44(1) of the 1977 Act on the basis that the patentee has abused his monopoly of power. It was held that section 44(1) applied, regardless of whether English law governed the contract. For the present purpose, what is important is that at common law the question of the applicable law in respect of this contractual defence to an infringement action was treated as a contractual matter, to which English rules on the law governing the contract applied. There was, though, no discussion of the problem raised by the fact that this was an action in tort. Under the Regulation the section 44(3) defence is an example of a ground for exemption from liability. The law applicable to this contractual defence would therefore be the law governing the tort of infringement of the intellectual property right.[763]

5. NON-CONTRACTUAL OBLIGATIONS OUTSIDE THE SCOPE OF THE ROME II REGULATION

The Regulation expressly excludes from its scope "non-contractual obligations arising out of violations of privacy and rights relating to personality, including defamation".[764] Member States must apply their traditional national choice of law rules for these matters. In the case of England, the statutory tort choice of law rules in Part III of the Private International Law (Miscellaneous Provisions) Act 1995 have largely replaced the common law tort choice of law rules. However, section 13 of the 1995 Act excludes defamation claims from Part III.[765] "Defamation" is widely defined in section 13(2)(a) to cover any claim under the law of any part of the United Kingdom for libel or slander and any claim under the law of Scotland for verbal injury. Section 13(2)(b) goes further and covers "any claim under the law of any other country corresponding to or otherwise in the nature of a claim mentioned in paragraph (a) above". This would encompass, for example, a claim for libel under Ontario law. Section 13 went even further and included malicious falsehood. However, it is submitted that this tort does not fall within the defamation exclusion under the Regulation and therefore the choice of law rules in the Regulation will apply.[766] As was seen earlier, under English law there are separate common law choice of law rules for restitution and breach of equitable obligations.

We must now examine the matters expressly excluded from the scope of the Regulation and determine whether the statutory tort choice of law rules or the common law tort choice of law rules apply, or indeed the choice of law rules for restitution or equitable obligations, and then comment on the application of these rules.

---

[762] [1993] FSR 567.

[763] See Art 8 of the Regulation, discussed supra, pp 815–817.

[764] Art 1(2)(g); discussed supra, pp 784–786. See in particular the meaning of defamation for the purposes of this exclusion. It is argued above that defamation arising in the business context should be regarded as coming within the unfair competition choice of law rules set out in Art 6 of the Regulation.

[765] For the reasons for this see the 13th edn of this book (1999), pp 656–657.

[766] See Art 6, discussed supra, p 809.

(a) Violations of privacy and rights relating to personality (excluding defamation)

The statutory tort choice of law[767] rules will apply to violations of privacy which are tortious, such as an action brought in England for invasion of privacy under Swiss law. In cases of misuse of private information borne out of non-contractual breach of confidence, the position is more difficult. It has been argued above that such cases fall within the exclusion from the Regulation of violations of privacy and rights relating to personality. But it is unclear how such an action should then be classified for the purposes of application of English national choice of law rules. As a matter of substantive law classification, there is support for the view that the expanded wrong of breach of confidence involving publication of private information is a tort.[768] This would mean that the statutory tort choice of law rules would apply. It could, though, be argued that, because of the use of the concept of breach of confidence, recourse should be had to the common law choice of law rules for equitable obligations. The counter-argument is that the misuse of private information is to be regarded as a cause of action separate from misuse of confidential information (even though both fall within the category of breach of confidence),[769] which might suggest a different classification for misuse of private information from that for misuse of confidential information. Finally, in the choice of law context the Court of Appeal has found persuasive the tentative suggestion[770] that a claim for expanded breach of confidence should be classified as a restitutionary claim for unjust enrichment.[771] This would mean that the common law choice of law rules for unjust enrichment would apply.

The statutory tort choice of law rules will also apply to rights relating to personality (excluding defamation), such as the right to the use of a name. The application of these rules to invasion of privacy and the right to the use of a name is particularly problematic because these are causes of action that are unknown to English law.[772]

(b) Defamation

The consequence of the exclusion of defamation claims—as widely defined by section 13(2)—from the scope of Part III is that the common law tort choice of law rules[773] will continue to be applied to such claims. They are rules which, as regards torts committed abroad, are anomalous, unjust and uncertain, and will discourage claimants in an international defamation case from bringing the action in England.

---

[767] Discussed in outline, supra, pp 767–768, and more fully in the 13th edn of this book (1999), pp 614–654.

[768] *Campbell v MGN Ltd* [2004] UKHL 22 at [14]–[15], [2004] 2 AC 457; *McKennitt v Ash* [2006] EWCA Civ 1714 at [8], [2007] 3 WLR 194.

[769] *Douglas v Hello! Ltd* [2007] UKHL 21 at [255], [2007] 2 WLR 920.

[770] In Dicey and Morris, 13th edn, para 34-029. See now Dicey, Morris and Collins, para 34-040.

[771] *Douglas v Hello! Ltd (No 3)* [2005] EWCA Civ 595 at [97]; [2006] QB 125.

[772] See the 13th edn of this book (1999) pp 619 (misguided attempts to exclude such causes of action from the scope of Part III), pp 646–647 (misguided attempts to use the public policy defence).

[773] See in relation to defamation: Prosser (1953) 51 Mich LR 959; Handford (1983) 32 ICLQ 452; Castel (1990) 28 Osgoode Hall LJ 153; Reed (1996) 15 CJQ 305, 306–309.

(i) Defamation committed abroad

The general rule of double actionability (ie there must be actionability by the law of the forum and the law of the place of the tort[774]) will apply to claims in respect of defamation committed abroad. This means that the claimant will be subject to injustice in having a double hurdle to surmount. There is, then, the possibility of the flexible exception (seemingly based on the concept of the most significant relationship) being applied,[775] with all the uncertainty involved in the operation of this exception. The application of these rules in cases of libel and slander will now be considered.

Application of the general rule of double actionability means that a defendant will be able to rely on defences available under English law, such as absolute and qualified privilege, even though the publication was abroad and such a defence is not available under the law of the foreign country where the tort was committed. Even if there is actionability under English law, the claim may fail because there is no actionability under the law of the foreign country where the tort was committed. In many foreign countries, particularly those that have a tort of invasion of privacy, it is much harder to establish defamation than it is under English law. Nonetheless, it may be possible to satisfy both limbs of the rule. An example of where this happened is *Church of Scientology of California v Metropolitan Police Comr.*[776] The claim concerned an alleged libel committed in Germany. There was actionability under both English and German law and the claim succeeded. When it comes to the application of the flexible exception to this general rule, there is one obvious situation where this may come into play. This is where both parties are resident in the same country and this is a country other than the one in which the tort was committed.[777]

(ii) Defamation committed in England

The leading authority on the rule that, if a tort is committed in England, the English courts will apply English law, is a defamation case, *Szalatnay-Stacho v Fink.*[778]

> The defendant, an official of the Czech government, then in exile in England during the Second World War, sent to the President of the Czech Republic, also in England, documents alleging misconduct by the plaintiff, the Czech Acting Minister in Egypt. These documents which were published in England were clearly defamatory of the plaintiff. Under Czech law the documents were absolutely privileged, but under English law only the defence of qualified privilege was available.

The Court of Appeal decided that English law was applicable to this tort committed in England, but that the conduct of the defendant fell within the defence of qualified privilege. Indeed, it was suggested that foreign law could only be applied in a case such as this if it was expressly provided for by legislation.[779]

---

[774] Supra, pp 766–767.

[775] Supra, p 767.

[776] (1976) 120 Sol Jo 690.

[777] See the defamation example discussed by the Law Commissions in Working Paper No 87 (1984), para 5.91.

[778] [1947] KB 1.

[779] Ibid, at 13.

This case was decided before the introduction of the flexible exception to the general rule of double actionability in the case of foreign torts. It is doubtful whether there is likewise a flexible exception in the case of torts committed in England.[780] But if, for the sake of argument, it is assumed that there is such an exception, when will this come into play? The Law Commissions gave the facts of *Fink's* case as an example of circumstances which might justify the application of a foreign law, ie Czech law.[781] This was because of the strong personal connection of the parties with Czechoslovakia.

(iii) Where is defamation committed?

It is well established that the tort of libel is committed where the libel is published. In *Bata v Bata*,[782] where defamatory letters had been written by the defendant in Zurich and posted to certain addresses in London, it was argued on the basis of the private international law rule, which at that time applied to cases of negligence, that the tort had been committed in Switzerland where the letters had been written and that, therefore, leave to serve the defendant out of the jurisdiction should not be granted. The Court of Appeal, however, held that, since publication is the material element that completes the tort of libel, the cause of action had arisen in England.[783] This was a case decided in the context of jurisdiction. However, the same reasoning was seemingly applied by the Court of Appeal in the choice of law context in *Church of Scientology v Metropolitan Police Comr*.[784] English police officers published an allegedly libellous report to a German Police Authority. The court acted on the basis that the tort was committed in Germany.

Furthermore, in *Jenner v Sun Oil Co*[785] an action was brought against the owners of a radio station who were alleged to have defamed the plaintiff by remarks broadcast in the USA and heard in Ontario. The Ontario High Court granted leave for service out of the jurisdiction, holding that the alleged tort had been committed in Ontario.[786]

The identification of the place where the tort of defamation is committed when this has occurred over the internet is particularly problematic.[787] In *Dow Jones & Co Inc v Gutnick*[788] the High Court of Australia had to determine the place where the tort of defamation was committed[789] in the situation where the alleged defamatory material was contained in an on-line journal. It held that, in this situation, ordinarily the place where the tort of defamation is committed is where the material alleged to be defamatory is downloaded on to the computer of a person who has used a web-browser to pull the material from

---

[780] See supra, p 767.

[781] Law Commission Working Paper No 87 (1984), para 5.91.

[782] [1948] WN 366; 92 Sol Jo 574.

[783] See too, *Kroch v Rossell et Cie* [1937] 1 All ER 725, where it was enough for publication that a few copies of a foreign newspaper had been sold in England.

[784] Supra.

[785] [1952] 2 DLR 526; see also *Pindling v National Broadcasting Corpn* (1984) 14 DLR (4th) 391.

[786] See also *Gordon v Australian Broadcasting Commission* (1973) 22 FLR 181.

[787] There is a further problem with internet defamation, namely the uncertain impact of the E-Commerce Directive (Directive (EC) No 2000/31 of 8 June 2000, OJ 2000 L 178/1 (implemented in the United Kingdom by the Electronic Commerce (EC Directive) Regulations 2002, SI 2002/2013), on the law applicable to this tort. See Law Commission, *Defamation and the Internet: a Preliminary Investigation*, Scoping Study No 2, December 2002; Dicey, Morris and Collins, paras 35-158–35-162; Fawcett, Harris and Bridge, paras 21.01–21.19 and 21.120–21.134.

[788] (2002) 210 CLR 575, HC of Australia; discussed supra, p 389.

[789] This was in the context of *forum non conveniens*. If forum law is applicable this is likely to be decisive.

the web-server. This was preferred to the place of uploading (ie the place where informa-tion is made available over the internet by placing it in a storage area managed by a web-server). In England, it is well established that a libel is committed where publication takes place and that a text on the internet is published at the place where it is downloaded.[790] The authorities on this have arisen largely in the jurisdictional context of *forum conven-iens* where, in order to determine whether England is the natural forum for trial, it has to be decided whether English law is applicable.[791]

(iv) Multi-state defamation

One edition of a newspaper may be read in numerous countries around the world. A radio broadcast may also be heard in numerous countries. Defamation over the inter-net inevitably involves multi-state defamation. Under English law, each publication is regarded as a separate publication and gives rise to a separate cause of action If a text is downloaded in a hundred countries, there are a hundred publications and the tort is committed in a hundred countries. If the claimant were to bring a claim based on a hun-dred separate publications this would not only give rise to choice of law problems (the obvious inconvenience of having to apply a hundred different laws[792]) but also to juris-dictional problems. However, a claimant can base a claim solely on publication in England.[793] If this is established, the English courts will have jurisdiction[794] and will apply the English law of defamation.[795]

---

[790] *Godfrey v Demon Internet Ltd* [2001] QB 201, 208–209; *Loutchansky v Times Newspapers Ltd* [2002] QB 783 at [58], CA; *Harrods Ltd v Dow Jones & Co Inc* [2003] EWHC 1162 (QB) at [36]; *King v Lewis* [2004] EWCA (Civ) 1329 at [26], [2005] IL Pr 16 (this was accepted by the parties); *Richardson v Schwarzenegger* [2004] EWHC 2422 (QB) at [19]; *Dow Jones & Co Inc v Jameel* [2005] EWCA (Civ) 75 at [48]–[49], [2005] QB 946; *Al Amoudi v Brisard* [2006] EWHC 1062 (QB) (the claimant must prove that the information was accessed and downloaded, there is no presumption of law that availability means substantial publication). See also Lord HOFFMANN in *Berezovsky v Michaels* [2001] 1 WLR 1004 at 1024.

[791] See *Harrods Ltd v Dow Jones & Co Inc*, supra; *King v Lewis*, supra.

[792] This has led to various suggestions for a separate choice of law rule for multi-state defamation not based on the place of publication. See Castel (1990) 28 Osgoode Hall LJ 153; the Restatement 2d, Conflict of Laws, § 150(2); *Australian Broadcasting Corpn v Waterhouse* (1991) 25 NSWLR 519 at 539; ALRC No 58 1992, Draft Choice of Law Bill, cl 6(5) applying a claimant's residence rule for all cases of defamation. Application of the flexible exception could result in just one law being applicable, thereby avoiding this difficulty, see *Woodger v Federal Capital Press of Australia Pty Ltd* (1996) 107 ACTR 1 at 36.

[793] This is what happened in *Berezovsky*, supra, and in the internet cases of *Harrods Ltd v Dow Jones & Co Inc*, supra; *King v Lewis*, supra; *Dow Jones & Co Inc v Jameel*, supra; *Richardson v Schwarzenegger*, supra. For jurisdic-tional purposes it is important that the claimant does so, see supra, p 388.

[794] Under both the Brussels I Regulation, supra, pp 253–256, and the traditional English rules (there must be *substantial* publication in England), supra, pp 385–388.

[795] See the discussion, supra, of defamation committed in England.

PART V

Family Law

Chapters

Family Law

Chapter 20

Marriage and Other Adult Relationships[1]

---

[1] Maddaugh (1973) 23 U Tor LJ 117; Swan (1974) 24 U Tor LJ 17, 18–41; Jaffey (1978) 41 MLR 38; North (1980) I Hague Recueil 9; Jaffey (1982) 2 OJLS 368, 369–373; North (1990) I Hague Recueil 9, 49–96 and see Audit, *La Fraude à la Loi*, pp 308–323.

1. THE MEANING OF "MARRIAGE"

A contract to marry differs fundamentally from a commercial contract,[2] since it creates a status that affects both the parties themselves and the society to which they belong. It is *sui generis*. It is fulfilled on the solemnisation of the marriage ceremony, and thereafter there is a change in the law that governs the relationship between the parties.

There are many different situations in which the existence of a marriage must be established as a preliminary to legal proceedings. The matter may concern many different parts of the law. Thus the institution of a matrimonial cause, such as a petition for divorce or judicial separation, implies that the parties are related to each other as husband and wife. If a person claims an inheritance or money due under an insurance policy as the widow or widower of the deceased; if a beneficiary under a will claims to be free from liability to inheritance tax as being the surviving spouse of the testator; in each case a preliminary to success is proof that a regularly constituted marriage exists. The existence of a marriage tie is equally essential in several departments of criminal law, as, for instance, where a person is prosecuted for bigamy. Again, social security benefits and the operation of the immigration laws may depend on the existence of a valid marriage. All these matters, and indeed many others, may raise a problem of private international law, since the parties in question may, for instance, have gone through a marriage ceremony abroad which, though valid by the law of the place of celebration or by the law of the domicile, does not create the status of marriage according to English law.

Each legal system must determine the attributes of the consensual union between man and woman,[3] the common factor, in the eyes of English law, of every marriage, which are necessary to create the relationship of husband and wife. In 1866 Lord PENZANCE defined marriage "as the voluntary union for life of one man and one woman to the exclusion of all others".[4] Although, as we shall see,[5] in the intervening years English law has come to accept as valid for many purposes marriages which are polygamous in nature or in fact, the requirement of a life long union (despite the prevalence of divorce) is still a necessary characteristic of marriage in the eyes of English law.

This requirement does not mean that a marriage must be indissoluble, but that in the eyes of the law of the place of celebration it must be potentially indefinite in duration. The facility with which, according to that law, it may be dissolved is irrelevant to its nature at the time of its creation. The one essential in this respect is that the parties have married in a form which envisages that, in the ordinary course of things, they will cohabit as husband and wife for the rest of their lives. This was affirmed in *Nachimson v Nachimson*,[6]

---

[2] Under the Law Reform (Miscellaneous Provisions) Act 1970, s 1, an agreement to marry does not have effect as a contract.

[3] *Corbett v Corbett (otherwise Ashley)* [1971] P 83; *Bellinger v Bellinger* [2003] UKHL 21; *J v C (Void Marriage: Status of Children)* [2006] EWCA Civ 551, [2006] 2 FLR 1098; *Wilkinson v Kitzinger and Ors* [2006] EWHC 2022 (Fam); Matrimonial Causes Act 1973, s 11(c); Norrie (1994) 43 I CLQ 757, 766–775; and see *Re North and Matheson* (1974) 52 DLR (3d) 280.

[4] *Hyde v Hyde* (1866) LR 1 P & D 130 at 133.

[5] Infra, p 918 et seq.

[6] [1930] P 217.

where a marriage had been celebrated in Moscow in 1924 between parties domiciled in Russia. At that date unilateral divorce was permissible by Russian law. In a suit for judicial separation brought in England, it was argued that the marriage was "of such a flimsy nature" that it could not be regarded as a union for life.[7] This argument was dismissed by the Court of Appeal as untenable. It was demonstrated that the dissolubility of a marriage can have no effect on its original character, for the valid creation of any contract, whether matrimonial, commercial or otherwise, stands apart from the conditions of its avoidance.[8] The remedy of divorce is an incident not of the marriage contract, but of the resulting status and, as such, is not necessarily the concern of the law of the country of the domicile at the time of marriage.

The ease of international travel has given, in the field of family law and elsewhere, added impetus in recent decades to the development of private international law rules.[9] Of particular importance in relation to marriage and matrimonial causes has been the incidence of immigration into the United Kingdom of many people from differing social, cultural and religious backgrounds. Until the middle of the nineteenth century, English choice of law rules relating to marriage were undeveloped and simple. All matters were to be referred to the law of the country where the marriage was celebrated. However, in 1861, the House of Lords in *Brook v Brook*[10] drew a distinction between the rules governing formalities and those governing capacity to marry. The facts were these:

> A marriage was celebrated in Denmark between a domiciled Englishman and his deceased wife's sister, also domiciled in England. The marriage was legal by Danish law, but illegal at that date (1850) by English law.

Although the marriage was valid by Danish law, the place where it was celebrated, the House of Lords was unwilling to allow the man to evade the prohibitions of English law, the law of his domicile. In applying English law and holding that the marriage was void, Lord CAMPBELL LC drew the following distinction:

> But while the forms of entering into the contract of marriage are to be regulated by the *lex loci contractus*, the law of the country in which it is celebrated, the essentials of the marriage depend upon the *lex domicilii*, the law of the country in which the parties are domiciled at the time of the marriage, and in which the matrimonial residence is contemplated.[11]

In the light of this decision, two major choice of law issues have to be examined: the choice of law rules governing the formal validity of a marriage and those rules governing its essential validity or capacity to marry, and it is necessary in addition to consider the special problems posed by polygamous marriages, and same sex unions.

---

[7] Ibid, at 220, per counsel.

[8] *Warrender v Warrender* (1835) 2 Cl & Fin 488 at 533.

[9] See, eg, EC Commission Press Release IP/07/42 (15 January 2007) regarding the European Community's role in "facilitating family law between Member States".

[10] (1861) 9 HL Cas 193.

[11] Ibid, at 207.

2. FORMALITIES OF MARRIAGE[12]

(a) The general rule

(i) The rule

There is no rule more firmly established in private international law than that which applies the maxim *locus regit actum* to the formalities of a marriage, ie that an act is governed by the law of the place where it is done. Whether any particular ceremony constitutes a formally valid marriage depends solely on the law of the country where the ceremony takes place.[13] Courts have frequently stressed the absolute nature of both the positive and negative aspects of this principle. "Every marriage must be tried according to the law of the country in which it took place",[14] and if it is good by that law, then, so far as its formal validity alone is concerned "it is good all the world over, no matter whether the proceedings or ceremony which constituted marriage according to the law of the place would or would not constitute marriage in the country of the domicile of one or other of the spouses".[15] The reverse is equally true. "If the so-called marriage is no marriage in the place where it is celebrated, there is no marriage anywhere, although the ceremony or proceedings if conducted in the place of the parties' domicile would be considered a good marriage."[16]

It is also important to note that the application of the law of the place of celebration to the formalities of a marriage is not disturbed even though the sole object of the parties in celebrating their marriage abroad is to evade some irksome requirement of the law of their domicile.[17] Thus in *Simonin v Mallac*:[18]

> Two persons, French by domicile, contracted a marriage in London which, though formally valid according to English law, would have been void if tested by French law since the parental consent required by the Code Napoleon had not been obtained. The wife later petitioned for a decree of nullity.

---

[12] See Sykes (1952) 2 ICLQ 78; Mendes da Costa (1958) 7 ICLQ 217; Parry, 8 *British Digest of International Law*, pp 513 et seq; Palsson, *Marriage and Divorce in Comparative Conflict of Laws*, Chapter 6; North (1980) I Hague Recueil 9, 69–77.

[13] *Scrimshire v Scrimshire* (1752) 2 Hag Con 395; *Dalrymple v Dalrymple* (1811) 2 Hag Con 54; *Warrender v Warrender* (1835) 2 Cl & Fin 488 at 530; *Harvey v Farnie* (1882) 8 App Cas 43 at 50; *Berthiaume v Dastous* [1930] AC 79, PC; *Kenward v Kenward* [1951] P 124; and see *R v Bham* [1966] 1 QB 159; *Re X's Marriage* (1983) 65 FLR 132; *Burke v Burke* 1983 SLT 331; *McCabe v McCabe* [1994] 1 FCR 257; *Wicken v Wicken* [1999] 1 FLR 293; *Vuong v Hoang* [1999] CLY 3734; *Chief Adjudication Officer v Bath* [2000] 1 FLR 8; *M v M (Divorce: Jurisdiction: Validity of Marriage)* [2001] 2 FLR 6; *Gandhi v Patel* [2002] 1 FLR 603; *Alfonso-Brown v Milwood* [2006] EWHC 642; and *AH v Secretary of State for the Home Department* [2006] UKIAT 38, [2006] INLR 517. See now, in Scots law, Family Law (Scotland) Act 2006, s 38(1). As to the method of proving a foreign marriage in English proceedings, see Dicey, Morris and Collins, paras 17-037 et seq; and *Wicken v Wicken* [1999] 1 FLR 293, per HOLMAN J, at 228. If there is no ceremony and the courts of the country where the parties are domiciled and resident recognise a marriage by repute, then so will the English courts: *Re Green* (1909) 25 TLR 222. Cf in Scotland *Walker v Roberts* 1998 SLT 1133; and *Ackerman v Logan's Executor (No 1)* 2002 SLT 37.

[14] *Herbert (Lady) v Herbert (Lord)* (1819) 3 Phillim 58 at 63.

[15] *Berthiaume v Dastous* [1930] AC 79 at 83. Cf, in USA, Symeonides (2003) 51 AJCL 82, citing *Xiong v Xiong* 648 NW 2d 900; *Donlam v Maggurn* 55 P 3d 74; and *Hudson Trail Outfitters v District of Columbia Department of Employment Services* 801 A 2d 987.

[16] Ibid. This general rule is subject to certain exceptions, discussed, infra, p 884 et seq.

[17] Eg *Scrimshire v Scrimshire* (1752) 2 Hag Con 395; *Ogden v Ogden* [1908] P 46.

[18] (1860) 2 Sw & Tr 67.

The court dismissed the petition, for, since the necessary consent, as we have seen,[19] was nothing more than a formality, its absence could not affect a marriage celebrated in England.[20] If, however, a marriage, valid as to form under the law of the place of celebration, but formally void according to the personal law of the parties is later annulled in the courts of their domicile, the decree of nullity will be recognised as effective by an English court even if the marriage was celebrated in England.[21]

One conclusion to be drawn from the rule that the law of the place of celebration governs the formal validity of a marriage is that no marriage in England is formally valid unless it complies with the requirements of English law as laid down, primarily,[22] in the Marriage Act 1949.[23] Therefore a marriage according to Romany custom,[24] a marriage in polygamous form,[25] a marriage in an unregistered building,[26] or a marriage by an unauthorised celebrant[27] are, in the absence of any further civil ceremony, void. Indeed such a marriage is regarded not so much as a void marriage but as no marriage at all.[28] If there is a civil ceremony as well, it is this alone which the law recognises.[29] Where, however, parties marry in England without acting "knowingly and wilfully" in breach of the provisions of the Marriage Act 1949,[30] the marriage is not necessarily denied effect. This point arose in *Chief Adjudication Officer v Bath*:[31]

---

[19] Supra, pp 48–49. As regards third party consent to a marriage, see also *M v M (Divorce: Jurisdiction: Validity of Marriage)* [2001] 2 FLR 6, per HUGHES J, at para 14 (permission of the government of Saudi Arabia required where the intended wife was a national of that country and the intended husband was not).

[20] And see *Ramos v Ramos* (1911) 27 TLR 515 where failure to register a marriage as required by the law of the domicile did not affect the validity of the marriage.

[21] Infra, p 992 et seq; see *Salvesen v Administrator of Austrian Property* [1927] AC 641; *De Massa v De Massa* [1939] 2 All ER 150 n; *Galene v Galene* [1939] P 237; *Merker v Merker* [1963] P 283.

[22] Occasionally, additional special rules must be complied with, eg, s 19 of the Asylum and Immigration (Treatment of Claimants, etc) Act 2004, and Immigration (Procedure for Marriage) Regulations, SI 2005/15. Eg *R (on the application of Baiai) v Secretary of State for the Home Department* [2006] EWHC 823, [2006] 2 FLR 645; and *R (on the application of Baiai) v Secretary of State for the Home Department* [2006] EWHC 1454, [2007] 1 WLR 735.

[23] See, eg, *Gandhi v Patel* [2002] 1 FLR 603. The parties, in marrying at an Indian restaurant in London in a Hindu ceremony presided over by a Brahmin priest acted in knowing and wilful disregard of English law ([16], [40] and [45]). Per PARK J, at [45]: "In the present case the Hindu ceremony . . . purported to be a marriage according to a foreign religion, and it made no attempt to be an English marriage within the Marriage Acts." See also *Gereis v Yagoub* [1997] 1 FLR 854 (Coptic Orthodox Christians married in England according to the rites of their church without any civil formalities required under the 1949 Act); despite the religious ceremony being followed by consummation and a period of cohabitation, AGLIONBY J granted a nullity decree on the basis that the parties had knowingly and wilfully intermarried in England in disregard of the requirements of English law.

[24] National Insurance Decision No R (S) 4/59.

[25] Cf *R v Ali Mohamed* [1964] 2 QB 350 n; *R v Bham* [1966] 1 QB 159.

[26] Marriage Act 1949, s 41; *Gereis v Yagoub* [1997] 1 FLR 854; and *M v M (Divorce: Jurisdiction: Validity of Marriage)* [2001] 2 FLR 6, per HUGHES J, at [39]. There is special provision for the marriage of Quakers and Jews and for the marriage by Registrar General's licence and by Archbishop's licence.

[27] *Gereis v Yagoub* [1997] 1 FLR 854.

[28] On the distinction between a void marriage and a "non-marriage", see *Gereis v Yagoub* [1997] 1 FLR 854, per AGLIONBY J, at 857 (a void marriage case); *M v M (Divorce: Jurisdiction: Validity of Marriage)* [2001] 2 FLR 6, per HUGHES J, at [23]; and *Gandhi v Patel* [2002] 1 FLR 603, per PARK J, at paras [31], [37], [45]–[47] (a non-marriage case).

[29] *Qureshi v Qureshi* [1972] Fam 173 at 186.

[30] Pt III, s 49.

[31] [2000] 1 FLR 8. Regrettably the court did not hear any submissions on *Gereis v Yagoub* [1997] 1 FLR 854; see Robert WALKER LJ in *Chief Adjudication Officer v Bath*, at [8].

A couple went through a Sikh marriage ceremony conducted by a Sikh priest in accordance with Sikh custom and religion at a Sikh temple in London which, at the material time, was not registered.[32] The marriage was not registered in a register office. The result was that there had not been a valid ceremony in accordance with the Marriage Act 1949. However, it could not be inferred that the couple had "knowingly and wilfully" failed to comply with the relevant statutory provisions.

The court relied on the common law presumption that when there is evidence of a ceremony of marriage having been gone through, followed by the cohabitation of the parties, everything necessary for the validity of the marriage will be presumed in the absence of evidence to the contrary. Having established that the couple was unaware of the fact of the temple's non-registered status, Evans LJ stated:

> There is no statutory provision that a marriage otherwise carried out in proper form, by an authorised celebrant and at a place of worship eligible to be registered under the [1949] Act, is invalid merely on the ground that the building was not registered for whatever reason.[33]

The marriage was not rendered void by section 49 of the 1949 Act. Robert Walker LJ reached the same decision by reference to the presumption of marriage arising from long cohabitation,[34] and the absence of compelling evidence to rebut that presumption:[35] "Apart from the presumption, the law as to validity of marriages solemnized (or said to have been solemnized) in England is not wholly statutory".[36]

(ii) Retrospectivity

It seems almost axiomatic that the question whether the status of husband and wife has been acquired must be determined once and for all by reference to the law of the place of celebration as it stood at the time when the parties went through the ceremony of marriage. According to this view, the verdict of that law at that time, whether in favour of, or adverse to, the acquisition of a married status, will be unaffected by a later change in its provisions. Otherwise the relationship between the parties will remain insecure. In *Starkowski v A-G*,[37] however, this conclusion was not fully accepted by the House of Lords, which held that a marriage void at the time of its celebration may be validated by a subsequent and retroactive change in the law of the place of celebration.[38]

---

[32] Subsequently it became registered.

[33] At [33].

[34] A presumption of formal validity operates also when the marriage ceremony took place abroad: *Mahadervan v Mahadervan* [1964] P 233 (marriage in Ceylon); *Vuong v Hoang* [1999] CLY 3734 (marriage before ancestral stones in China and not registered under Chinese law), in which Curl J held that the strong presumption of a valid marriage arising when a marriage ceremony is followed by cohabitation had not been diminished by increasingly liberal social attitudes; *Wicken v Wicken* [1999] 1 FLR 293 (civil marriage ceremony in England followed by Muslim marriage ceremony in the Gambia); and *Pazpena de Vire v Pazpena de Vire* [2001] 1 FLR 460 (parties lived together as husband and wife for 35 years following proxy marriage ceremony in Uruguay; Mark Harrison QC held that where there had been a lengthy cohabitation, the presumption of marriage could be rebutted only by clear evidence that there had been no marriage ceremony or that formalities had not been complied with. There was no such evidence in the instant case, and therefore the presumption was not rebutted).

[35] *M v M (Divorce: Jurisdiction: Validity of Marriage)* [2001] 2 FLR 6, per Hughes J, at [34] et seq.

[36] At p [41].

[37] [1954] AC 155; and see *Re Howe Louis* (1970) 14 DLR (3d) 49.

[38] If an act such as registration is required for the retrospective validation of a marriage, then the marriage remains invalid until that act is done: *Pilinski v Pilinska* [1955] 1 All ER 631; see Thomas (1954) 3 ICLQ 353;

H and W, Polish both by nationality and domicile, were married in Austria on 19 May 1945. The marriage was void by Austrian law since the ceremony was religious. On 12 June, a daughter, Barbara, was born to them. As from 30 June, Austrian legislation retrospectively validated such religious marriages, subject to their registration in a public register. In 1949, by which time H and W had both acquired a domicile in England, their marriage was registered in Austria, so that, by Austrian law, the parties were then regarded as having been lawfully married since 19 May 1945. In 1950 W and X went through a ceremony of marriage at Croydon. They had a son, Christopher, born before this marriage.

As indicated earlier, the existence of a marriage may be called into question in many different situations, and here the House of Lords was concerned with the question of Christopher's legitimacy.[39] If the marriage between H and W was still valid in 1950, W and X were bigamously married, Barbara was legitimate, and Christopher illegitimate. On the other hand, if it was void, Barbara was illegitimate, but Christopher had been legitimated by the ceremony of 1950. Thus the crucial question was whether the validity of the marriage between H and W was determinable according to the state of Austrian law on 19 May or on 30 June, when the retrospective legislation came into force. It was held that the latter was the appropriate date.

The answers to the two main arguments against this solution were not altogether convincing. The objection that the status of parties domiciled in England can scarcely be altered by the law of the country with which they are no longer connected was ruled out on the ground that the Austrian legislation dealt with formalities rather than with status. The further objection, that the parties to a void marriage will be unable to rely on their unmarried status if the ceremony remains liable to validation, was met by the reflection that validation will normally not be long delayed.

If the marriage between W and X had preceded the retrospective validation of the marriage between W and H, then it is suggested that the validation would not be recognised so as to nullify the second marriage which was wholly valid when entered into.[40] Similarly, if an English court had granted a decree of nullity in relation to the first marriage, the validity of that decree ought not to be affected by any later act of registration.[41] If the marriage between W and X came after the retrospective validation of the earlier marriage, but W was domiciled at the time of her second marriage in a country which did not recognise the effect of the validation, then the second marriage ought to be regarded in England as valid.[42]

Mendes da Costa (1958) 7 ICLQ 217, 251–260; Sinclair (1952) 29 BYBIL 479, (1953) 30 BYBIL 523.

[39] Cf *Azad v Entry Clearance Officer (Dhaka)* [2001] Imm AR 318, [2001] INLR 109; and *R (Shamsun Nahar) v The Social Security Commissioners* [2002] 1 FLR 670.

[40] This point is left open by the House of Lords in *Starkowski v A-G* [1954] AC 155 at 168, 171–172, 176, 182; but support for this conclusion is provided by *Ambrose v Ambrose* (1961) 25 DLR (2d) 1.

[41] *Salvesen v Administrator of Austrian Property* [1927] AC 641 at 651.

[42] See Law Commission Working Paper No 89 (1985), para 2.11. The Commission recommended, at paras 4.1–4.13, that there should be no legislative reform of the rules on retrospectivity, a view adopted in Law Com No 165 (1987), para 2.13. The rule now contained in the Family Law (Scotland) Act 2006, s 38(1) does not specify the time at which the formal validity of a marriage should be determined.

(iii) What are matters of form?

The statement that a marriage good by the law of the place of celebration is good all the world over is accurate only if confined to the question of formal validity. Essential validity is, as we shall see,[43] a matter for the personal law of the parties. This distinction may raise the question whether a particular rule obtaining in the place of the ceremony affects form or essence. Some matters seem clearly to be formal in character,[44] such as whether a religious or civil ceremony is required, the time and place of the ceremony, the persons by whom marriage ceremonies may be conducted, the need for witnesses, registration of the marriage, prior notification of the ceremony or a requirement of premarital blood tests. It has been established, for instance, that a rule which permits a marriage by proxy must be classified as formal since it is concerned with the manner in which the marriage ceremony may be performed.[45] Thus, if a woman, domiciled and resident in England, executes a power of attorney appointing X to act as her representative in the celebration of a marriage between her and Y in a country where marriage by proxy is recognised,[46] and the ceremony is in fact performed, the formal validity of the marriage cannot be impugned. A marriage ceremony solemnised in such a manner, though not possible in England, is not regarded as contrary to English public policy.[47] Indeed, the Court of Appeal has upheld the formal validity of a foreign marriage under customary law where neither spouse was present, both being in England at the time of the foreign ceremony.[48] The other important area where the issue of the classification of a particular rule as one of capacity or form has arisen is that of parental consent to marry. It has been seen[49] that English law classifies this as a question of form in relation to consent both under English and under foreign law.[50]

(iv) Marriages in foreign consulates and embassies

It is not wholly clear what the present law is as to celebration of marriages in consulates and embassies. The question of the formal validity of a marriage celebrated in a foreign consulate abroad was considered in *Radwan v Radwan (No 2)*:[51]

> In 1951, the husband, domiciled in Egypt, married Ikbal in Egypt in polygamous form. In 1952, he married the petitioner, Mary, a domiciled Englishwoman, in the Egyptian Consulate General in Paris, in polygamous form, and their matrimonial home was established in Egypt. In 1953, the husband divorced Ikbal by *talak*. In 1956, the husband and Mary came to live in England, where they acquired a domicile. In 1970, the husband obtained a *talak* divorce from Mary in the Egyptian Consulate General in London and then Mary petitioned the English courts for divorce.

---

[43] Infra, p 895 et seq.

[44] See, eg, *Gandhi v Patel* [2002] 1 FLR 603, per PARK J, at [34].

[45] *Apt v Apt* [1948] P 83; *Ponticelli v Ponticelli* [1958] P 204; *Birang v Birang* (1977) 7 Fam Law 172; and *Pazpena de Vire v Pazpena de Vire* [2001] 1 FLR 460.

[46] Cf National Insurance Decision No R (G) 3/74.

[47] *Apt v Apt*, supra; *Ponticelli v Ponticelli*, supra; *Pazpena de Vire v Pazpena de Vire*, supra.

[48] *McCabe v McCabe* [1994] 1 FCR 257. Cf *Alfonso-Brown v Milwood* [2006] EWHC 642.

[49] Supra, pp 47–49.

[50] *Simonin v Mallac* (1860) 2 Sw & Tr 67; *Ogden v Ogden* [1908] P 46; *Lodge v Lodge* (1963) 107 Sol Jo 437; see also *Bliersbach v McEwen* 1959 SC 43; Anton and Francescakis [1958] Jur Rev 253.

[51] [1973] Fam 35.

This matrimonial saga raises a number of separate issues, not all of which were considered in a logical sequence in the proceedings and some of which must be dealt with at greater length elsewhere. First, it was held that the *talak* divorce in the Egyptian Consulate General could not be recognised in England because the diplomatic premises were to be regarded as English and not Egyptian territory.[52] There was, however, the logically anterior question of the validity of the marriage in the Egyptian Consulate General in Paris and this was considered in the later proceedings in the case.[53] Two questions had to be examined—whether the parties had capacity and whether the marriage was formally valid. CUMMING-BRUCE J decided that, although Mary was incapable by English law of entering a polygamous marriage, she was capable by Egyptian law, the law of the intended matrimonial home.[54] As to formal validity, the court held that the Egyptian Consulate General in Paris was to be regarded as French, and not Egyptian, territory.[55] French law, as the law of the place of celebration, had to be applied to questions of formal validity. The court presumed the marriage to be formally valid in the absence of decisive evidence of French law to rebut this presumption.

Whilst this case provides clear authority for the view that a marriage abroad in a foreign embassy or consulate[56] must comply with the formalities of the receiving state, there remains the problem of marriages in England in foreign diplomatic premises.[57] There is some authority for the view that such marriages are formally valid if both parties are nationals and, perhaps, domiciliaries of the foreign state.[58] The opinion has been expressed at the diplomatic, rather than judicial, level that marriages in a foreign embassy between nationals of the sending state will be regarded as valid, but that, apart from diplomatic convention, consular marriages must comply with the formalities of English law.[59] The rejection of the idea of extra-territoriality is certainly consistent with the reasoning in *Radwan v Radwan (No 2)*[60] where the decision that the marriage in Paris must comply with French law was supported by reference to the earlier conclusion[61] that the divorce in London must be regarded as an English and not an Egyptian divorce.

(v) Renvoi

It has been assumed up to this point that formalities are to be governed by the internal law of the place of celebration; but there is some authority that the doctrine of renvoi[62] applies in this area with the result that a marriage will be formally valid if it complies with

---

[52] *Radwan v Radwan* [1973] Fam 24; Polonsky (1973) 22 ICLQ 343. The divorce recognition aspect of the case is considered infra, pp 1004–1005.

[53] [1973] Fam 35.

[54] This aspect of the case is discussed infra, p 901.

[55] See also *R v Turnbull, ex p Petroff* (1971) 17 FLR 438.

[56] Marriages abroad in British consulates are discussed infra, pp 885–886.

[57] And see *Khan v Khan* (1959) 21 DLR (2d) 171 at 176.

[58] *Bailet v Bailet* (1901) 17 TLR 317; and see *Pertreis v Tondear* (1790) 1 Hag Con 136; *Ruding v Smith* (1821) 2 Hag Con 371 at 386.

[59] Parry, 8 *British Digest of International Law*, pp 631–645.

[60] [1973] Fam 35.

[61] *Radwan v Radwan* [1973] Fam 24.

[62] Supra, p 73.

the formal requirements of whatever law is selected by the choice of law rules of the place of celebration.[63] In *Taczanowska v Taczanowski*:[64]

> Two Polish nationals, domiciled in Poland, were married in Italy in 1946 in a military camp, the husband being a member of the Allied occupation forces in Italy. The ceremony did not comply with the formal requirements of Italian law, but the court considered[65] the rule of Italian law that the marriage would be regarded as valid by the Italian courts if it complied with the formal requirements of Polish law, the law of the parties' common nationality.

In fact the marriage was not formally valid under Polish law, though it was held valid in England as an exception to the general rule of reference to the law of the place of celebration.[66] Nevertheless, it seems to have been assumed that the English courts would have regarded the marriage as formally valid had Polish law so regarded it, applying the renvoi doctrine of transmission from Italian law.

What is the position if a marriage satisfies the formal requirements of the domestic law of the place of celebration, but not those of the country referred to by its choice of law rules? Although there is no direct authority on this issue,[67] it has been suggested that, in the interests of upholding the validity of marriage, the English courts should regard the marriage as valid if it complies either with the domestic law of the place of celebration or with the system of law which would be applied by that country's choice of law rules. The Law Commission,[68] whilst supporting generally the application of the doctrine of renvoi in the case of formal validity of marriage in the interests of upholding the validity of marriages and promoting uniformity of status,[69] rejected such an alternative reference rule, despite its convenience, on the ground that it would lead to the marriage being regarded in England as formally valid, though not so regarded in the place of celebration.

(b) Exceptions to the general rule

There are two statutory exceptions and one common law exception to the rule that the law of the place of celebration governs formalities.

---

[63] The Family Law (Scotland) Act 2006 is silent on the subject of renvoi. Since the Act does not expressly exclude the operation of renvoi, a Scottish court may be open to applying the *lex loci celebrationis* in its entirety; see Crawford and Carruthers, para 11-24.

[64] [1957] P 301, and see *Hooper v Hooper* [1959] 1 WLR 1021.

[65] Ibid, at 305, 318.

[66] Infra, p 890 et seq.

[67] In *Hooper v Hooper* [1959] 1 WLR 1021 a marriage in Baghdad was held formally invalid for failure to comply with the requirements of English law, which law was to be applied under Iraqi choice of law rules; but it does not appear from the brief report whether the domestic law of Iraq had been satisfied.

[68] Law Commission Working Paper No 89 (1985), paras 2.39–2.42; and see the views of the Irish Law Reform Commission: LRC 19–1985, p 152.

[69] A view not broadly supported on consultation: Law Com No 165 (1987), para 2.5.

(i) The two statutory exceptions

(a) Consular marriages[70]

What is generally called a "consular marriage" is the first exception.[71] The Foreign Marriage Act 1892, as amended by the Foreign Marriage Act 1947 and the Foreign Marriage (Amendment) Act 1988, provides that any marriage between parties, one of whom at least is a United Kingdom national,[72] solemnised before a "marriage officer" in a foreign country[73] in the manner prescribed by the Act, shall be as valid as if it had been solemnised in the United Kingdom with a due observance of all forms required by law.[74] The persons who may be appointed marriage officers include British ambassadors, High Commissioners and consular officers, but they must hold a marriage warrant from the Secretary of State.[75]

The 1892 Act lays down various requirements as to such matters as parental consent,[76] the giving of notice of the marriage[77] and the registration of the marriage.[78] Section 8 is the most important section and it provides that every marriage must be solemnised at the official house[79] of the marriage officer, with open doors, in the presence of two or more witnesses and according to such form and ceremony as the parties see fit to adopt. Where a statement that the parties know of no impediment to their marriage would not otherwise be included in the ceremony adopted, they must each declare:

> I solemnly declare that I know not of any lawful impediment why I *AB* [*or CD*] may not be joined in matrimony to *CD* [*or AB*]

Similarly, if not otherwise stated in the ceremony adopted, each party must make the following declaration:

> I call upon these persons here present to witness that I *AB* [*or CD*] take thee *CD* [*or AB*] to be my lawful wedded wife [*or husband*].[80]

It has been held[81] that section 8 is the crucial section of this Act and is mandatory in nature, whilst other sections, namely 2, 3, 4, 7 and 9, are administrative or procedural and are only directory in nature. Failure to comply with these latter sections does not render the marriage invalid.

---

[70] See Civil Partnership Act 2004, s 210 and Civil Partnership (Registration Abroad and Certificates) Order, SI 2005/2761 for corresponding provisions regarding the registration of civil partnerships by a British Consular Officer.

[71] This exception to the *lex loci celebrationis* rule has been expressly retained in Scots law in the statutory formulation of the rule now contained in the Family Law (Scotland) Act 2006, s 38(1). It is not clear whether that rule affords any other exception: see Crawford and Carruthers, paras 11-28–11-30.

[72] Defined in s 1(2) of the 1892 Act, added by s 1(2) of the 1988 Act, and amended by the British Overseas Territories Act 2002, s 2(3).

[73] This means any country outside the Commonwealth.

[74] S1; eg *Ramsay-Fairfax v Ramsay-Fairfax* [1956] P 115.

[75] S 11; and see Law Commission Working Paper No 89 (1985), para 2.5.

[76] S 4, as substituted by s 2(1) of the 1988 Act.

[77] Ss 2, 3.

[78] S 9, as amended by s 5(1) of the 1988 Act.

[79] Defined in SI 1970/1539, para 5.

[80] Ibid, s 8(2)–(4), as substituted by s 4 of the 1988 Act.

[81] *Collett v Collett* [1968] P 482.

A marriage contracted under these statutory provisions is necessarily formally valid in England, even though it might be void under the law of the country where it took place.[82] However, any real danger that a marriage solemnised under the Act may be regarded as void under the law of the place of celebration has been virtually eliminated by the Foreign Marriage Order 1970.[83] This provides that a marriage officer must not solemnise a marriage in a foreign country unless he is satisfied:[84]

(a) that at least one of the parties is a United Kingdom national; and
(b) that the authorities of that country will not object to the solemnisation of the marriage; and
(c) that insufficient facilities exist for the marriage of the parties under the law of that country; and
(d) that the parties will be regarded as validly married by the law of the country in which each party is domiciled.

Furthermore, the 1892 Act provides that a marriage officer is not required to solemnise a marriage if to do so "would be inconsistent with international law or the comity of nations".[85] It is far from clear what this means and, indeed, whether it is of any force in the light of the conditions just listed above. However, nothing in the 1892 Act is to confirm, impair or affect the validity of a marriage celebrated abroad other than as the Act provides.[86] This means that a marriage valid under some other exception to the general rule is still to be regarded as valid.

(b) Marriages[87] of members of British forces serving abroad

Section 22 of the Foreign Marriage Act 1892,[88] as substituted by the Acts of 1947 and 1988,[89] provides as follows:

(1) A marriage solemnised in any foreign territory[90] by a chaplain serving with any part of the naval, military, or air forces of His Majesty[91] serving in that territory or by a person authorised . . . by the commanding officer of any part of those forces serving in that territory shall, subject as hereinafter provided, be as valid in law as if the marriage had been solemnised in the United Kingdom with a due observance of all forms required by law.

(1A) Subsection (1) above shall not apply to a marriage unless—
(a) at least one of the parties to the marriage is a person who—

---

[82] *Hay v Northcote* [1900] 2 Ch 262. In this case the marriage was held to be valid despite its annulment in the common domicile of the parties, but such an annulment would now be recognised in England, infra, p 986 et seq.

[83] SI 1970/1539.

[84] Ibid, para 3(1), as amended by SI 1990/598.

[85] Foreign Marriage Act 1892, s 19.

[86] Ibid, s 23.

[87] See Civil Partnership Act 2004, s 211 and The Civil Partnership (Armed Forces) Order, SI 2005/3188 for corresponding provisions regarding the registration of a civil partnership in respect of a member of Her Majesty's armed forces serving abroad.

[88] For Orders in Council made under the Act, see SI 1964/1000; SI 1965/137; SI 1990/2592.

[89] And as amended by SI 2005/3129.

[90] This is defined, in s 22(2), as any territory other than the Commonwealth, colonies, British protectorates and other territories under the protection or jurisdiction of the Crown. The original s 22 was limited to "British lines".

[91] The original s 22 was limited to the army.

    (i) is a member of the said forces serving in the foreign territory concerned or
        is employed in that territory in such other capacity as may be prescribed by
        Order in Council; or
    (ii) is a child of a person falling within sub-paragraph (i) above and has his
        home with that person in that territory; and
  (b) such other conditions as may be so prescribed are complied with.
(1B) In determining for the purposes of subsection (1A) above whether one person is
     the child of another, a person who is or was treated by another as a child of the fam-
     ily in relation to—
    (a) a marriage to which the other is or was a party; or
    (b) a civil partnership in which the other is or was a civil partner, shall be
        regarded as the other's child.[92]

"Foreign territory" includes, inter alia, ships which are for the time being in the waters of
any foreign territory.[93] A marriage celebrated under the Act is valid whether the armed
forces are on active service, or in the occupation of foreign territory after the successful
conclusion of hostilities, or merely stationed there. There is no necessity for one of the
parties to be a British subject,[94] but Commonwealth forces are excluded.[95]

(ii) The common law exception

There are certain exceptional circumstances in which a marriage may be recognised even
though it has not been solemnised according to the law of the place of celebration,
provided it satisfies the form required by the common law of England. Before discussing
the nature of these exceptional circumstances, the meaning of a "common law marriage"
must be clarified.

(a) Meaning of "common law marriage"[96]

It has long been admitted that there may be peculiar circumstances which allow a marriage
not solemnised according to the law of the place of celebration to be recognised as valid
if it satisfies the forms required by the common law of England. Before discussing the
nature of these circumstances, it must be made clear what is meant by a "common law
marriage", or, as it is better called, a "canon law marriage", since it emerged at a time when
the canon law governed the matrimonial affairs of Christians throughout Western
Europe.[97]

The only essential to the formal validity of a marriage required by the original common
law was that the parties should take each other as husband and wife. In 1843, however,
the further common law condition was added that an episcopally ordained priest or dea-
con, whether of the English or Roman Catholic Church, should perform the ceremony.

---

[92] Substituted by SI 2005/3129, Sch 4, para 1.
[93] S 22(3).
[94] *Taczanowska v Taczanowski* [1957] P 301.
[95] Foreign Marriage Act 1947, s 3.
[96] Hall [1987] CLJ 106.
[97] There is Irish authority that a potentially polygamous marriage is excluded: *Conlon v Mohamed* [1989]
ILRM 523.

This was decided by the House of Lords in *R v Millis*,[98] where it was held, though in a rather unsatisfactory manner,[99] that a marriage celebrated in Ireland by a Presbyterian minister according to the rites of the Presbyterian Church[100] was invalid. Lord HARDWICKE's Marriage Act[101] did not extend to Ireland, and therefore marriages in that country were governed by the common law. This rule, that no common law marriage is valid without the intervention of an episcopally ordained priest, is one that almost certainly lacks historical justification;[102] but its applicability to English common law marriages seems clear, although it may well be thought undesirable.[103]

There are several situations in which a marriage may be celebrated out of England and we shall have to consider them in turn to determine whether the marriage is formally valid if it satisfies the requirements of the common law.

(b) Where the common law is in force in the foreign country

The first situation is where the common law of England continues to govern the parties even in the foreign country where they take each other as husband and wife. This can be illustrated by the early days of colonialism. It was consistently recognised as a matter of constitutional law that the British settlers in such countries as Australia took English common law with them, but only so much of it as was suitable to the local conditions.[104] Tested by this principle, it seems clear that the rule of the common law requiring the intervention of an episcopally ordained priest could scarcely be extended to a marriage contracted in a colony during the early days of the colonisation when there was no Church establishment and no division of the country into parishes.[105] The weight of judicial opinion was for many years in favour of treating the rule in *R v Millis* as being confined to marriages in England and Ireland;[106] and in *Catterall v Catterall*[107] Dr LUSHINGTON held that a marriage which had been celebrated in Sydney in 1835 by a Presbyterian minister was valid at common law.

The position may be illustrated by two cases from a rather more modern setting. In *Wolfenden v Wolfenden*:[108]

---

[98] (1844) 10 Cl & Fin 534.

[99] The four judges of the Irish Court of Queen's Bench were equally divided, and PERRIN J, who had held the marriage valid, formally withdrew his judgment in order that an appeal might be taken to the House of Lords. The case was there argued before 6 Law Lords and 10 judges. A unanimous opinion of all the judges in favour of the invalidity of the marriage was read by TINDAL CJ, who explained, however, that lack of time had prevented a proper investigation of the case. The Law Lords, were, however, equally divided.

[100] Whose ministers are not episcopally ordained.

[101] Of 1753.

[102] The majority of canonists and historians consider the decision in *R v Millis* to be wrong; see Pollock and Maitland, *History of English Law*, Vol II, pp 370–372; *Merker v Merker* [1963] P 283 at 293–294; and see Lucas [1990] CLJ 117.

[103] Hall [1987] CLJ 106, 120.

[104] Blackstone, *Commentaries on the Laws of England*, i, 108.

[105] *Maclean v Cristall* (1849) Perry's Oriental Cases 75.

[106] *Beamish v Beamish* (1861) 9 HL Cas 274 at 348, 352; *Lightbody v West* (1903) 18 TLR 526.

[107] (1847) 1 Rob Eccl 580. There was in fact a local marriage statute which had not been observed, but Dr LUSHINGTON had already held in *Catterall v Sweetman* (1845) 1 Rob Eccl 304 that the statute did not avoid all marriages failing to satisfy its requirements.

[108] [1946] P 61. A similar case was *Phillips v Phillips* (1921) 38 TLR 150.

A Canadian, whose domicile of choice appears to have been English, went through a ceremony of marriage with a Canadian woman in China. The ceremony was performed, not by an episcopally ordained priest, but by the local minister of the Church of Scotland Mission. A Chinese Order in Council was in force which, after reciting that a treaty had given His Majesty the King jurisdiction in the Republic of China, proceeded to establish a system of judicature there and provided that the civil jurisdiction of every court acting under the Order should "as far as circumstances permit be exercised on the principle of and in conformity with English law for the time being in force".

Lord MERRIMAN P held that the marriage was valid at common law. The parties had freely consented to it and the circumstances precluded the presence of an episcopally ordained priest.

A similar decision was reached in *Penhas v Tan Soo Eng*.[109] Certain charters of justice issued in the first half of the nineteenth century introduced English law into Singapore, but provided that it should be administered in such manner as the religions, manners and customs of the inhabitants would admit. Therefore, a marriage ceremony in 1937 between a Jew and a Chinese woman, both British subjects domiciled in Singapore, at which the man observed the Jewish custom but the woman followed the Chinese rites, was held to be valid at common law. The parties intended the composite ceremony to record that they took each other as man and wife. The rule in *R v Millis* was inapplicable.

It has never been doubted that a marriage in a foreign country, where local formalities are non-existent or where those that exist are inapplicable to an English marriage, is valid if it is contracted in the presence of an episcopally ordained priest.[110] What is not clear is whether the requirement of celebration by an episcopally ordained priest can be ignored even if there is no difficulty in obtaining such services. In such a case, the weight of authority favours compliance with the requirement.[111] Strictly speaking, a marriage held to be valid in the types of case just considered is not a true exception to the doctrine *locus regit actum* for, so far as the parties are concerned, the law of the place of celebration is none other than the common law.[112]

(c) Insuperable difficulty

The second exceptional situation is where the parties, though not subject to the common law in the foreign place of celebration have, nevertheless, without regard to the local formalities, taken each other as husband and wife at a ceremony performed, usually, by an episcopally ordained priest. In such a case the marriage will be regarded as valid if compliance with the local formalities had been prevented by some insuperable difficulty.[113] What is meant by insuperable difficulty has been expressed in various ways. Lord STOWELL considered that "legal or religious difficulties" might justify a relaxation of the principle

---

[109] [1953] AC 304.
[110] *Limerick v Limerick* (1863) 32 LJPM & A 92; *Phillips v Phillips* (1921) 38 TLR 150.
[111] *Taczanowska v Taczanowski* [1957] P 301 at 326; *Collett v Collett* [1968] P 482 at 487; *Kuklycz v Kuklycz* [1972] VR 50; cf *Preston v Preston* [1963] P 411 at 436.
[112] *Taczanowska v Taczanowski* [1957] P 301 at 327, 328.
[113] *Kent v Burgess* (1840) 11 Sim 361.

locus regit actum.[114] Lord ELDON was clear that the parties might invoke the common law if they could not avail themselves of the law of the place of celebration or if there was no local law. He accordingly held that a marriage between Protestants at Rome solemnised by a Protestant priest was valid, since no Catholic priest would be allowed to perform the ceremony.[115] The parties have to have found it impossible, or virtually impossible,[116] to comply with the local law. It is not enough that they found it inconvenient, embarrassing or distasteful so to comply, as in *Kent v Burgess*[117]where a marriage in Belgium was held void for non-compliance with Belgian residence requirements there being no insuperable difficulty in the parties waiting the prescribed six-month period.

Australian courts have considered that "insuperable difficulty" existed in Germany in 1945 at a time when no register offices were open and the registrars had left their posts,[118] and in the Ukraine in 1942 as the German army advanced,[119] but not in Saigon in 1978.[120] The marriages in the first two cases were upheld as valid according to the common law.[121]

Although it has usually been the case that, when a marriage has been upheld under this exceptional head of insuperable difficulty, it has been celebrated by an episcopally ordained priest,[122] it is suggested that this is not a necessary requirement and that celebration by some other minister or even by none at all will suffice.[123]

(d) Marriages of military forces in belligerent occupation[124]

Circumstances can be envisaged where, although compliance with the local law is not impossible, it might be thought unreasonable. Such a problem arose in Europe at the end and in the aftermath of the Second World War, when many people married without recourse to the civilian, often Nazi, authorities. The problem is illustrated by the leading decision in *Taczanowska v Taczanowski*:[125]

> Two Polish nationals, domiciled in Poland, were married in Italy in 1946 by a Polish Army Chaplain, an episcopally ordained priest of the Roman Catholic Church, and therefore their marriage was valid according to the English common law. The husband was serving in the Polish 2nd Corps, an independent command in belligerent occupation in Italy. The ceremony did not comply with the local forms and was therefore void by Italian domestic law, but it would be recognised as valid by that country's private international law if it was valid by the national law of

---

[114] *Ruding v Smith* (1821) 2 Hag Con 371.

[115] *Lord Cloncurry's Case* (1811), cited by Cruise, *Dignities and Titles of Honour*, 276; and see the *Sussex Peerage Case* (1844) 11 Cl & Fin 85 at 92, 102.

[116] *Preston v Preston* [1963] P 411 at 432; or perhaps where conformity with the local law would be contrary to conscience: *Kochanski v Kochanska* [1958] P 147 at 151–152.

[117] (1840) 11 Sim 361.

[118] *Savenis v Savenis* [1950] SASR 309.

[119] *Kuklycz v Kuklycz* [1972] VR 50; cf *Persian v Persian* [1970] 2 NSWR 538.

[120] *Re X's Marriage* (1983) 65 FLR 132.

[121] It is an interesting question whether laws prohibiting inter-racial marriages could be regarded as creating insuperable difficulty: cf *Conlon v Mohamed* [1989] ILRM 523.

[122] Eg *Savenis v Savenis* [1950] SASR 309 (Roman Catholic priest); *Kuklycz v Kuklycz* [1972] VR 50 (Greek Orthodox priest).

[123] As in the first common law marriage exception, discussed supra, p 887.

[124] See Mendes da Costa (1958) 7 ICLQ 217; Andrews (1959) 22 MLR 396; Brownlie and Webb (1963) 39 BYBIL 457.

[125] [1957] P 301.

the parties. It was, however, not valid by Polish law. The parties came to England in 1947 and, in 1955, the wife petitioned for a decree of nullity on the ground that the marriage was void for non-compliance with the local forms.

The Court of Appeal felt that, since the parties were presumed not to have submitted themselves to the Italian law of the place of celebration, that law did not have to be applied. It was considered that there will often be no submission by a member of the military forces in occupation of a country, and such was held to be the case here. As Italian law was not applicable and the law of the parties' domicile was considered irrelevant,[126] English common law was applied and the validity of the marriage upheld.[127] The result was that the Court of Appeal, animated perhaps by a desire to save other similar marriages, said to number between three and four thousand, recognised as valid at common law a marriage void both by the law of the place of celebration and by the personal law of the parties.

A further step was taken in *Kochanski v Kochanska*.[128]

Here, two Polish nationals, occupants of a displaced persons' camp in Germany, to whom everything German was anathema, were married by a Catholic priest without compliance with the local forms.

Although this case was distinguishable from previous decisions in that neither party to the marriage could be described as a member of the armed forces of occupation, SACHS J upheld the validity of the marriage. He concluded that there was no submission to the local law; and having thus eliminated German law, the judge held the marriage to be valid on the ground that the ceremony satisfied the common law; though he would have preferred to fall back on the Polish law of the domicile had authority justified that course.

In moving beyond the narrow category of members of the armed forces of occupation, SACHS J gave support to the general idea that the requirement of compliance with the law of the place of celebration is based on submission thereto by the parties. In the case before him there was no submission and so the common law was applied. Such a general principle of submission underlies the decision in *Lazarewicz v Lazarewicz*,[129] where a Polish corporal, serving with the Polish army in Italy, was married in 1946 at Barletta in Italy to an Italian national. The ceremony, performed at a Polish refugee camp by a Catholic priest, did not comply with Italian law. PHILLIMORE J distinguished the case before him from the two earlier cases on the ground that there was evidence of the parties' intention to submit to Italian law: the husband had married not as a member or within the lines of the army of occupation, but as an ordinary sojourner in and subject to the laws of the foreign state.[130] Reliance on the common law was, therefore, precluded and the marriage was void.

---

[126] As the court was not concerned with a question of capacity; see also *Kochanski v Kochanska* [1958] P 147 at 154–155; *Kuklycz v Kuklycz* [1972] VR 50 at 52; cf *Maksymec v Maksymec* (1955) 72 WNNSW 522.

[127] The argument of the husband that the marriage was valid by virtue of the Foreign Marriage Act 1892, s 22 failed, since the Polish army chaplain was not officiating under the orders of a commanding officer of the British army serving abroad.

[128] [1958] P 147; followed in *Jaroszonek v Jaroszonek* [1962] SASR 157; cf *Fokas v Fokas* [1952] SASR 152; *Grzybowicz v Grzybowicz* [1963] SASR 62.

[129] [1962] P 171; and see *Dukov v Dukov* (1968) 13 FLR 149.

[130] *Merker v Merker* [1963] P 283 at 295.

This decision adds further support to a general theory that the basis of the rule *locus regit actum* is the presumed intention of the parties to submit themselves to the law of the place of celebration. It is suggested, however, that this theory of submission, if it purports to represent a general principle applicable to marriages other than those in an occupied country or in a country where it is insuperably difficult to comply with the local law, is neither supported by previous authority nor free from other objections. Clear authority against such a general rule is provided by the statement of the Privy Council in 1930 that: "If the so-called marriage is no marriage in the place where it is celebrated it is no marriage anywhere, although the ceremony or proceeding if conducted in the place of the parties' domicile would be considered a good marriage."[131]

If this rule stated in such categorical terms by the Privy Council is to give way to the presumed intention of the parties, certainty will be displaced by uncertainty, unless it is made clear what evidence suffices to establish an intention not to submit to the law of the place of celebration.[132] It will be seen[133] that evidence that the parties did not wish to observe the local law obviously cannot suffice.[134] In the result, the suggestion that the control of the law of the place of celebration depends on the intention of the parties, whatever its future fate may be, confused what was formerly reasonably clear.

Later decisions have not relied on the dangerous concept of submission. In *Merker v Merker*,[135] Sir Jocelyn SIMON P was faced with another marriage in occupied enemy territory:

> The parties were Polish domiciliaries who were serving in the Polish Armoured Division, part of the allied forces occupying Germany. They were married in a local German church by a Roman Catholic priest, a Polish army chaplain. German local law was not complied with. Later a German court granted a decree declaring the marriage to be null and void. After the wife had become resident in England, she petitioned for a declaration as to her status.

The first issue before the court was that of the validity of her marriage.[136] One of the arguments put to the court was that a person marrying in a foreign country could elect whether or not to submit to the local law, and, if he did not submit, then English common law, as the law of the forum, should determine the validity of his marriage. Such a general principle was emphatically rejected, for its effect "would be to leave the rule in *Berthiaume v Dastous*[137] in tatters and to introduce anarchy in a field where order and comity are particularly required".[138] Sir Jocelyn SIMON P confined the principle of *Taczanowska's* case to cases of: "Marriages within the lines of a foreign army of occupation (which constitute, so to speak, an enclave within which it is reasonable to hold that the local law has no application), or of persons in a strictly analogous situation to the members of such an army, such as members of an organised body of escaped prisoners

---

[131] *Berthiaume v Dastous* [1930] AC 79 at 83. Cf *Gandhi v Patel* [2002] 1 FLR 603, per PARK J, at [34].
[132] Carter (1957) 33 BYBIL 335.
[133] *Merker v Merker* [1963] P 283 at 295; *Preston v Preston* [1963] P 411 at 427.
[134] See, eg, *Gandhi v Patel* [2002] 1 FLR 603, per PARK J, at [16] and [45].
[135] [1963] P 283.
[136] The problems stemming from recognition of the German decree are considered infra, p 995.
[137] Supra, p 878.
[138] [1963] P 283 at 295; see also *Milder v Milder* [1959] VR 95.

of war."[139] Applying such a narrow principle, the marriage before him was, nevertheless, valid according to English common law.

This more restrictive decision was followed by that of the Court of Appeal in *Preston v Preston*[140] where the court had to consider the validity at common law of a marriage, in the same camp as that of *Kochanski v Kochanska*,[141] which had failed to comply with the law of the place of celebration. On the evidence before it, the court considered that the camp in question was part of the organisation of the allied forces in occupation. ORMEROD LJ interpreted *Taczanowska's* case as deciding that persons who marry in a foreign country are assumed to have submitted to the local law except in the case of the members of forces in belligerent occupation.[142] The general rule that persons are deemed to submit to the marriage laws of the place of celebration cannot be evaded merely because the parties claim that they did not intend to submit to that law. The circumstances where this general rule is inapplicable were narrowly, though not explicitly, defined.[143]

The conclusion to be drawn is that the principle of submission canvassed in the *Taczanowska* case and other decisions is very limited. It is relevant only to marriages contracted by a member of a conquering force in the conquered country.[144] This is the one type of case in which it is not unreasonable to offer the parties an alternative to the law of the place of celebration, for the incongruity of compelling a conqueror to submit to the conquered is obvious.[145]

(e) Marriages on the high seas

There is little authority as to what constitutes a valid marriage solemnised in a merchant ship while on the high seas.[146] The general principle is that the law of the flag governs transactions on board a vessel, for, as BYLES J once said, a British ship is regarded as a floating island on which British law prevails.[147] This raises two difficulties in the case of British ships.

First, since there is no one system of law common to all the countries that employ the British flag, it is difficult to decide which particular legal system constitutes the law of the flag. The alternative seems to lie between English law and the municipal law of the country in which the ship is registered. The latter is the more reasonable rule and the one that is generally advocated.[148]

Presuming this view to be correct, the second difficulty is to discover from the authorities what part of English law governs a marriage on a ship that is registered in England. Is it

---

[139] [1963] P 283 at 295.

[140] [1963] P 411.

[141] Supra, p 891.

[142] This casts doubt on the decision in *Kochanski v Kochanska*, supra, and also on *Oleszko v Pietrucha* (1963) Times, 22 March, where the parties were members of what was considered to be a displaced persons' camp.

[143] [1963] P 411 at 427–428.

[144] Eg *Rosenthal v Rosenthal* (1967) 111 Sol Jo 475; cf *Dukov v Dukov* (1968) 13 FLR 149.

[145] As, perhaps, also with members of an organised body of escaped prisoners of war: *Merker v Merker* [1963] P 283 at 295.

[146] White (1901) 17 LQR 283; Charteris [1907] Jur Rev 178.

[147] *R v Anderson* (1868) LR 1 CCR 161 at 168; but see *R v Carr* (1882) 10 QBD 76 at 85.

[148] Dicey, Morris and Collins, para 17-025; and see *Bolmer v Edsell* 90 NJ Eq 299 (1919); cf *Fisher v Fisher* 250 NY 313 (1929). Cf the rule relating to torts committed on board a ship, supra, p 859.

the common law or the common law as regulated by statute? The latter alternative appears clearly to be excluded. There is no statute that deals particularly with marriages at sea[149] and the "floating island" theory can scarcely be pressed so far as to suggest that the Marriage Acts are applicable.[150] Thus, the common law is in force on a ship, as in the analogous case of a colony, except where the common law has been modified by statute. To make the analogy complete it must also be conceded that only so much of the law is imported into the ship as is suitable to the local conditions. That raises the further question whether it suffices that the parties have freely taken each other as husband and wife, or whether, in accordance with *R v Millis*,[151] it is necessary that the ceremony should have been performed by an episcopally ordained priest. That the presence of an episcopally ordained priest is sufficient for validity seems generally to be admitted,[152] but that it is essential appears unwarranted.[153] The impossibility of procuring a priest on the high seas is even more apparent than in the case of a remote part of China, and it is difficult to resist the conclusion that the rule laid down in *Wolfenden v Wolfenden*[154] applies equally to a ship. The argument sometimes advanced, that a ship must sooner or later put into a port where advantage may be taken of the facilities offered by the local law or by the Foreign Marriage Acts, is of little weight. It can be countered by the reflection that the same facilities were open to parties in a remote part of China if they were prepared to make the necessary journey.

It has been sometimes suggested that the absence of a priest is fatal to the validity of a marriage at sea, unless it is a *marriage of necessity*. What this ambiguous expression means is not clear but there is little doubt that it is taken from the Irish case of *Du Moulin v Druitt*[155] in 1860, which is no longer a safe guide. In that case:

A woman stowaway was discovered on a troopship during a voyage to Australia. The commanding officer ordered that she and one of the soldiers on board should immediately be married, and the marriage was celebrated in his presence. In fact, as soon as the ship arrived in Sydney, the woman left her "husband" and went to live with the officer who had acted as clerk in the marriage ceremony. Later they married, in the lifetime of the soldier, and the issue arose as to the validity of her ship-board marriage.

The court held that the rule in *R v Millis*[156] applied and that the ship-board marriage was void on the ground that the marriage was not one "of necessity", since the vessel would touch at places where a priest would be obtainable.[157] Having regard to *Wolfenden v*

---

[149] The provisions of the Merchant Shipping Act 1894, ss 240(6) and 253(1)(viii), requiring particulars of marriages celebrated at sea to be entered in the ship's log were repealed without replacement by the Merchant Shipping Act 1970, ss 100(3), 101(4), Sch 5.

[150] Indeed the theory itself is now hard to sustain: *R v Gordon-Finlayson, ex p an Officer* [1941] 1 KB 171 at 178–179; *Oteri v R* [1976] 1 WLR 1272 at 1276.

[151] (1844) 10 Cl & Fin 534; supra, p 888.

[152] Elphinstone (1889) 5 LQR 44, 53.

[153] *Merker v Merker* [1963] P 283 at 294.

[154] [1946] P 61; supra, pp 888–889.

[155] (1860) 13 ICLR 212.

[156] (1844) 10 Cl & Fin 534.

[157] Cf *Maclean v Cristall* (1849) Perry's Ori Cas 75; and also *Culling v Culling* [1896] P 116—where the validity of a marriage before the ship's captain on board a warship was upheld; see now the Foreign Marriage Act 1892, s 22, supra, p 885.

Wolfenden,[158] it would seem that this peculiar reasoning need no longer be considered seriously.

It is submitted, then, that if parties, whatever their domicile or nationality, voluntarily take each other as husband and wife while at sea in a vessel registered at an English port, the marriage is formally valid in the eyes of English law provided, probably, that there is some element of urgency about their marriage.[159]

3. CAPACITY TO MARRY[160]

(a) Introduction

We turn now to consider the second major issue relating to choice of law in the context of marriage, namely, the law to govern capacity or, as it is sometimes described, essential validity. There is general agreement that this terminology includes matters of legal capacity[161] such as consanguinity and affinity, bigamy and lack of age. Consideration is given later to the law to govern matters of consent[162] and physical incapacity.[163] The fact that capacity as a term encompasses a wide range of matters does not necessitate the conclusion that all matters of capacity should be subject to the same choice of law rule—a matter to which we shall return.[164] A further preliminary point which ought to be borne in mind is that, provided that a person has capacity under the relevant law,[165] the fact that he is, for example, under age according to English law will not invalidate the marriage in the eyes of English law as the law of the forum—at least if the marriage does not take place in England.[166]

There are two main views as to the law which should govern capacity to marry—the dual domicile doctrine, and the intended matrimonial home doctrine.[167] These must now be examined more closely.

---

[158] [1946] P 61, supra, pp 888–889.

[159] Dicey, Morris and Collins, para 17-025.

[160] See Jaffey (1978) 41 MLR 38; (1982) 2 OJLS 368; North (1980) I Hague Recueil 9, 53–69; Fentiman [1985] CLJ 256.

[161] With regard to mental capacity, see *Sheffield City Council v E* [2004] EWHC 2808, [2005] 1 FLR 965, per MUNBY J at [141], to the effect that the test in relation to mental capacity is whether an individual has capacity to understand the nature of the marriage contract, and the duties and responsibilities that normally attach to marriage. See also *M v B* [2005] EWHC 1681, [2006] 1 FLR 117—23-year-old woman with severe learning disability at risk of parents arranging her marriage overseas, in particular SUMNER J, at [36]; *Re SA (Vulnerable Adult with Capacity: Marriage)* [2005] EWHC 2942 (Fam), [2006] 1 FLR 867—18-year-old woman, vulnerable adult, deaf and mute, at risk of unsuitable arranged marriage overseas; *X City Council v MB* [2006] EWHC 168—23-year-old man with severe autistic spectrum disorder at risk of parents arranging his marriage overseas; and *Westminster City Council v IC (A Protected Party by His Litigation Friend) and Ors* [2008] EWCA Civ 198, [2008] WCR (D) 92.

[162] Infra, p 972 et seq.

[163] Infra, p 979 et seq.

[164] See *Radwan v Radwan (No 2)* [1973] Fam 35 at 51, infra, pp 910–911.

[165] In relation to capacity to marry, the standard of proof required to rebut the presumption of a valid matrimonial union is the normal civil standard of a balance of probabilities: *Wicken v Wicken* [1999] Fam 224, per HOLMAN J, at 229.

[166] Eg *Mohamed v Knott* [1969] 1 QB 1, infra, p 936.

[167] Some more recently developed alternative approaches are examined, infra, pp 911–913.

(b) The two main theories

(i) The theories stated

The traditional and still prevalent view is that capacity to marry is governed by what may conveniently be called the *dual domicile doctrine*.[168] This prescribes that a marriage is invalid unless, according to the law of the domicile of both contracting parties at the time of the marriage, they each have capacity to contract that particular marriage.[169] This is said to be true whether the incapacity is "absolute", ie one which forbids a person, such as a child below a particular age, to marry anyone; or "relative", ie one which forbids two individual persons, such as an uncle and niece, to marry each other.[170] Under this doctrine, a marriage, for instance, between a man of the Jewish faith domiciled in Egypt and a woman of the same faith domiciled in England, the latter being his niece, is invalid, since a marriage between persons so related, though permissible in Egypt,[171] is prohibited by English law.

The alternative doctrine, and the one which has been supported strongly in earlier editions of the book,[172] is that which submits the question of capacity to what may briefly be termed the law of the *intended matrimonial home*. More fully stated, the doctrine is this:

> The basic presumption is that capacity to marry is governed by the law of the husband's domicile at the time of the marriage, for normally it is in the country of that domicile that the parties intend to establish their permanent home. This presumption, however, is rebutted if it can be inferred that the parties at the time of the marriage intended to establish their home in a certain country and that they did in fact establish it there within a reasonable time.

(ii) Evaluation of the two theories

Postponing for the moment a consideration of the actual decisions, the question must now be asked—what are the respective merits and demerits of the two rival doctrines?

(a) The intended matrimonial home doctrine

On social grounds it can be argued that the doctrine of the dual domicile is inferior to that of the intended matrimonial home. Marriage is an institution that closely concerns the public policy and the social morality of the state. The general laws which dictate its incidents, however, vary considerably between different countries, and where a woman domiciled in one country marries a man domiciled in another the question naturally arises—what state is to control the incident of capacity? Which state is in the nature of things entitled to demand pre-eminent consideration for its code of social morality? One clear answer might be—the state in which the parties set up their home.

A choice of law rule commands little respect if it is framed without regard to its impact on the social life of the community that will be most intimately affected by its operation.

---

[168] See, in Scots law, a statutory version of the rule: Family Law (Scotland) Act 2006, s 38(2)(a). See Crawford and Carruthers, para 11-16.

[169] Dicey, Morris and Collins, paras 17R-054 et seq; Wolff, pp 332–337.

[170] Westlake, s 21, p 57.

[171] Cf *Cheni v Cheni* [1965] P 85.

[172] Eg 7th edn of this book (1965), pp 276 et seq.

It seems reasonably clear that whether the inter-marriage of two persons should be prohibited for social, religious, eugenic or other like reason is a question that affects the community in which the parties live together as man and wife.[173]

In support of the argument that it is the law which is in force there which should be allowed to assess the propriety or impropriety of the marriage one might take the example of the extreme case of an absolute incapacity. If an English girl, aged fifteen and a half, contrary to the law of England, marries a foreigner domiciled in a country whose law permits marriage at this early age, it might be doubted whether it is justifiable to regard the marriage as void, for the social life of England is unaffected if the girl goes to live with him in his country, as the girl proposes to sever her connection with England. As against that, however, it is arguable that rules as to the age of marriage are designed to protect minors whether they intend to live abroad or not. It is also arguable that a matter so important as capacity to marry should not be determined by the intentions of the parties.[174]

Apart from social considerations, principle might seem to support the view that, where the parties are domiciled in different countries before their marriage, questions of the essential validity of the marriage, including their personal capacity, should be governed by the law of the place where they establish their joint home.[175] This is at least compatible with the rule that capacity to enter into a commercial contract is governed by the law of the country with which the contract has the closest connection.[176] Broadly speaking, domicile signifies the country with which the *propositus* is most closely connected since it is there that he has established his home.[177]

But owing to the peculiar reverence that English law still pays to the domicile of origin, it may well happen that the country in which a party is technically domiciled immediately prior to marriage in no sense represents his or her home, whether actual or contemplated. Could it be said, for instance, that George Bowie, the work-shy Scotsman in *Bowie (Ramsay) v Liverpool Royal Infirmary*,[178] had his home in, or any substantial connection with, Scotland? Finally, not only is just one law to be applied under the intended matrimonial home theory, but it may be more effective than the dual domicile test in supporting a policy of upholding the validity of marriages and of giving effect to the legitimate expectations of the parties.[179]

When one turns to the disadvantages of the intended matrimonial home theory, then several objections of a practical matter may be advanced against it.[180] It may be objected that any rule is undesirable which renders it impossible to decide whether a marriage is valid or void at the time of its celebration.[181] Such may be the case if it is doubtful whether

---

[173] Report of the Royal Commission on Marriage and Divorce (1956) Cmnd 9678, para 889; and see *Bliersbach v McEwan* 1959 SLT 81 at 89.

[174] Anton, p 429; and see *Cooper v Cooper* (1888) 13 App Cas 88 at 108; *Muhammad v Suna* 1956 SC 366 at 370.

[175] *Lawrence v Lawrence* [1985] Fam 106 at 127.

[176] Supra, pp 750–753.

[177] *Warrender v Warrender* (1835) 2 Cl & Fin 488 at 536.

[178] [1930] AC 588, supra, p 162.

[179] Law Commission Working Paper No 89 (1985), para 3.34; and see Jaffey (1978) 41 MLR 38; (1982) 2 OJLS 368.

[180] Law Commission Working Paper No 89 (1985), para 3.35; and see Glenn (1977) 4 Dalh LR 157.

[181] Dicey, Morris and Collins, para 17-061; and see *Lawrence v Lawrence* [1985] Fam 106 at 127–128.

the parties genuinely intend to establish their home in the alleged country. Again, it may be asked what is the position if they delay unreasonably in going to the chosen country or never go there at all, or intend never to set up a matrimonial home?[182] Answers to these criticisms have been propounded. First, the question whether a marriage is void for incapacity, unless it arises incidentally in the course of some other proceedings, will require the institution of a nullity suit for its answer, by which time it will be known whether the alleged intention of the parties was in fact fulfilled. The difficulty with such an answer is that it ignores the fact that a marriage which is *void ab initio* does not require a decision of a court to determine the parties' status. If it is void, it is void. If the parties have to wait and see what law is to govern their capacity, then their marital status remains in doubt. The second suggested answer is that it is not true that the status of the parties will remain indeterminate, for if the place of their future home is doubtful it is presumed to be in the domicile of the husband at the date of their marriage. However, in that case it is not easy to find merit in a discriminatory solution which refers the issue of a wife's capacity to marry to the law of the husband's ante-nuptial domicile.

It is also the case that arguments of principle have been advanced against the intended matrimonial home theory, it being suggested that post-nuptial intentions should be irrelevant when determining ante-nuptial capacity, and that it enables rules which are the legitimate concern of the domiciliary law to be evaded by an intention to set up home elsewhere.

(b) The dual domicile theory

The greatest merit of the dual domicile theory is that it refers capacity to marry to that law which, up to that time, has governed the status of each party.[183] The law of the domicile is the law of the country to which a person "belongs".[184] Furthermore, it preserves equality of the sexes by looking to the law of each party's domicile.[185] This is of added weight since a wife no longer automatically takes her husband's domicile on marriage.[186]

Varied criticisms have been made of the dual domicile theory, eg it tends towards the invalidity of marriages.[187] This is because, where the domiciliary laws differ as to the validity of the marriage, the marriage will be regarded as invalid. It is also said to be inefficacious as a practical working rule, in that it is a rule which admits of its own evasion. Suppose, for instance, that a woman domiciled in England wishes to marry her uncle who lives and is domiciled in Egypt. English internal law would prohibit the marriage. Being properly advised, however, she travels to Cairo for the marriage ceremony with the intention of remaining there for the rest of her married life, and thus acquires a domicile of choice, the law of which permits a marriage between an uncle and a niece. She is now of full capacity in the eyes of English private international law. Thus, it is said that the protection

---

[182] Eg *Vervaeke v Smith* [1983] 1 AC 145.
[183] *Lawrence v Lawrence* [1985] Fam 106 at 127.
[184] Hartley (1972) 35 MLR 571, 576.
[185] Morris, p 199.
[186] Domicile and Matrimonial Proceedings Act 1973, s 1.
[187] Hartley (1972) 35 MLR 571, 578.

supposedly afforded to an Englishwoman by the dual domicile rule is somewhat illusory. The evasion involved here amounts to as substantial a step as deciding to establish a matrimonial home in Egypt.

Another criticism which might be voiced is that, because of the inflexibility of many of the rules relating to acquisition and loss of a domicile, a person's capacity to marry may be determined by the law of a country he has never visited. Such criticism, however, may provide a reason for changing the rules relating to domicile,[188] rather than those concerning capacity to marry.

(iii) The rule as deducible from the English decisions[189]

We must turn now from theory and attempt to ascertain whether judicial authority in England supports the view that capacity to marry is governed by the law of the ante-nuptial domicile of each party, or by the law of the intended matrimonial home. It is submitted that many of the relevant decisions[190] are rather inconclusive. It will be seen that in such cases the decision would have been the same whether it had been based on the application of the law of the matrimonial home or on the dual domicile theory.

(a) Inconclusive decisions

For example, in *Brook v Brook*,[191] where, it will be recalled,[192] a Danish marriage was held void because both spouses lacked capacity under English law, the law of their domicile and of the intended matrimonial home, Lord CAMPBELL LC had this to say:

> But I am by no means prepared to say, that the marriage now in question ought to be or would be held valid in the Danish courts, proof being given that the parties were British subjects domiciled in England, that England was to be their matrimonial residence, and that by the law of England such a marriage is prohibited. The doctrine being established that the incidents of the contract of marriage celebrated in a foreign country are to be determined according to the law of the country in which the parties are domiciled and mean to reside, the consequence seems to follow that by this law must its validity or invalidity be determined.[193]

It is not possible to conclude in favour of one theory or the other on the basis of this case.[194]

---

[188] Supra, p 195.

[189] And see North, *Private International Law of Matrimonial Causes*, pp 119 et seq.

[190] *Mette v Mette* (1859) 1 Sw & Tr 416; *Brook v Brook* (1861) 9 HL Cas 193; *Re De Wilton* [1900] 2 Ch 481; *Re Paine* [1940] Ch 46; *Pugh v Pugh* [1951] P 482; and see *In the Will of Swan* (1871) 2 VR (IE & M) 47. In *Ali v Ali* [1968] P 564 infra, p 926, CUMMING-BRUCE J at 576–577, suggested that both views were tenable and neither concluded by authority. On the facts of the case, the law of the domicile and the law of the intended matrimonial home were both English law.

[191] (1861) 9 HL Cas 193.

[192] Supra, p 877.

[193] (1861) 9 HL Cas 193 at 213; see also at 224, 230–231, 239.

[194] Though see, at 212, Lord CAMPBELL's explanation of *Warrender v Warrender* (1835) 2 Cl & Fin 488. See also *Sottomayor v de Barros* (1877) 3 PD 1, infra, p 904.

Mette v Mette[195] is the earliest decision on this matter in which the parties were domiciled in different countries prior to their marriage:

> A domiciled Englishman contracted a marriage in Frankfurt with his deceased wife's half-sister, a domiciled German woman. This marriage, then prohibited by English law but valid by German law, was held to be void.

This decision does not conclude the controversy, since it is again compatible both with the dual domicile doctrine and the doctrine of the intended matrimonial home. The man was domiciled in England until his death; both parties contemplated a matrimonial residence in England; and therefore English law, as being the law of the matrimonial home, was the appropriate legal system to determine the matter. In the words of the judge, the husband "remained domiciled in this country".[196] The ratio decidendi is in fact rather doubtful. After remarking that "there could be no valid contract unless each was competent to contract with the other", words which suggest a preference for the dual domicile doctrine, Sir Cresswell CRESSWELL finally concluded that, since the husband had remained domiciled in England, and the marriage was with a view to subsequent residence here, the English prohibition was necessarily operative.[197]

(b) Support for the intended matrimonial home theory

Having considered and discarded such rather inconclusive decisions, one must turn to those which provide more specific support for one theory or the other, starting with those in favour of the intended matrimonial home view. The most persuasive early decision is that in the Australian case of *In the Will of Swan*,[198] where the issue was whether a marriage, which was celebrated on a temporary visit to Scotland between parties domiciled in the State of Victoria, could be held to revoke a will made by the husband before marriage. The wife was the niece of the husband's deceased wife and it was assumed that the marriage, though voidable by Victorian law, was void by Scots law. In upholding the validity of the marriage and thus of the revocation of the will, MOLESWORTH J said:

> The validity of marriages as to ceremonial and so forth depends upon the law of the place of the marriage, but . . . the policy of the occurrence of such marriages and their results, should depend, I think, upon the laws of the country of the parties in which they are afterwards probably to live.[199] No doubt, however, a similar result would have been achieved through the dual domicile test.

There are, moreover, judicial pronouncements which refer the question of the legality of a marriage to the law of the matrimonial domicile, though in all these cases the remarks are made obiter as no issue of capacity to marry was directly involved. In the first of these, *De Reneville v De Reneville*,[200] Lord GREENE MR had this to say:

> The validity of a marriage so far as regards the observance of formalities is a matter for the *lex loci celebrationis*. But this[201] is not a case of forms. It is a case of essential validity.

---

[195] (1859) 1 Sw & Tr 416.

[196] Ibid, at 424.

[197] Ibid, at 423–424.

[198] (1871) 2 VR (IE & M) 47; Fleming (1951) 4 ILQ 389, 392–393.

[199] *In the Will of Swan*, supra, at 50. This latter law was presumed to be Victorian.

[200] [1948] P 100. See also a similar statement by BUCKNILL LJ in *Casey v Casey* [1949] P 420 at 429, 430.

[201] Ie the effect on the marriage of the impotence and wilful refusal of one of the parties, see infra, p 970 et seq.

By what law is that to be decided? In my opinion by the law of France, either because that is the law of the husband's domicile at the date of the marriage or (preferably, in my view) because at that date it was the law of the matrimonial domicile in reference to which the parties may have been supposed to enter into the bonds of marriage.[202]

A further judgment which shows a similar trend is that of DENNING LJ in *Kenward v Kenward*,[203] where he affirmed, with no ambiguity, that the "substantial validity" of a marriage contracted between persons domiciled in different countries is governed by the law of the country where they intend to live and on the basis of which they agreed to marry.

In *Radwan v Radwan (No 2)*[204] CUMMING-BRUCE J, after a careful review of the authorities, held that capacity to contract a polygamous marriage is governed by the law of the intended matrimonial home,[205] a conclusion of some significance, for the wife was domiciled in England whilst the husband's domicile and the law of the intended matrimonial home was Egyptian. However, he did not maintain that the matrimonial home view provides the universal test, for he said that "Nothing in this judgment bears upon the capacity of minors, the law of affinity, or the effect of bigamy upon capacity to enter into a monogamous marriage."[206]

Support for an approach at least similar to the intended matrimonial home test has been voiced more recently in two decisions where the major issue was the recognition of foreign decrees. In *Vervaeke v Smith*,[207] where the main issue was the recognition of a foreign nullity decree relating to a sham marriage, Lord Simon GLAISDALE gave support to a choice of law rule which amounted to applying the law of the country with which the marriage has the most real and substantial connection.[208] Similar support is found for such an approach in the judgment of LINCOLN J, at first instance, in *Lawrence v Lawrence*,[209] a decision on the effect of the recognition of a foreign divorce on capacity to remarry,[210] but which also provides a rare example of a case where the dual domicile test would mean that the marriage was void, whilst the application of the intended matrimonial home/real and substantial connection test had the result that the marriage was valid.[211] Although both judges formulated their real and substantial connection test as an application of the "intended matrimonial domicile" doctrine, it is more convenient to consider a real and substantial connection test separately and more fully below.[212]

---

[202] [1948] P 100 at 114, and see BUCKNILL LJ, at 121–122. In *Ponticelli v Ponticelli* [1958] P 204 at 214, SACHS J assumed that the personal capacity of a spouse is governed by "the *lex domicilii* which normally coincides with the law pertaining to the country of the husband's domicil at the time of the marriage".

[203] [1951] P 124 at 144, 146; see also *Bliersbach v McEwan* 1959 SC 43 at 55.

[204] [1973] Fam 35, supra, pp 882–883.

[205] The whole question of capacity to enter a polygamous marriage is considered in more detail, infra, p 927 et seq.

[206] [1973] Fam 35 at 54. For discussion of whether different rules should apply to different forms of incapacity, see infra, pp 910–911.

[207] [1983] 1 AC 145, infra, p 1024.

[208] Ibid, at 166.

[209] [1985] Fam 106 at 112, 115. The Court of Appeal did not think that the case raised general issues relating to the law governing capacity to marry.

[210] Infra, pp 913–915.

[211] [1985] Fam 106 at 112.

[212] Infra, pp 911–912.

(c) Support for the dual domicile theory

We must now turn to those decisions which can be said to support the dual domicile theory, and which, it is submitted, are of greater weight than those cited in favour of the opposite theory.[213] There was clear reliance on the dual domicile theory in *Re Paine*:[214]

> An English testatrix left a sum of money on trust for her daughter, W, for life, and, if she died leaving any child or children surviving, then on trust for her absolutely. W was a British subject domiciled in England. In 1875 she travelled to Germany and married H, her deceased sister's husband, a German subject. H had lived in England for some time shortly before the marriage,[215] and he and his wife continued to live there until their respective deaths. H died in 1919, W died some twenty years later. One daughter of the marriage survived W.

In these circumstances the legacy to W would not become absolute unless the surviving daughter was her legitimate child, for the law then was that a reference in a will to a "child" meant a legitimate child only, unless a different intention could be determined from the context.[216] Whether the daughter was legitimate depended on whether the marriage in 1875 was valid. At that time a marriage between a woman and her deceased sister's husband was prohibited in English law, but allowed by German law. BENNETT J adopted the dual domicile doctrine and held the marriage to be void because of the incapacity attaching to W under the law of her ante-nuptial domicile. However, the result was exactly what it would have been had he applied the doctrine of the intended matrimonial home.[217] Since England was the country where the woman was domiciled, where the man was resident before the marriage, where they intended to reside together and where in fact they resided throughout their married lives, the decision that English law must prevail could scarcely have been different.

A later case, which raised a question of capacity in the narrow sense of the term, is *Pugh v Pugh*,[218] where the facts were these:

> A British officer, domiciled in England but stationed in Austria, married a Hungarian girl in Austria in 1946. The girl, whose domicile of origin was Hungarian, had gone to Austria with her parents to escape from the Russian advance. She was only 15 years of age and therefore, if her capacity had been governed by English domestic law, the marriage would undoubtedly have been rendered void by the Age of Marriage Act 1929 which prohibited a marriage "between persons either of whom is under the age of sixteen".[219] By Austrian law the marriage was valid, and by Hungarian law it had become valid in that it had not been avoided before she had attained the age of 17.

---

[213] See *Lawrence v Lawrence* [1985] Fam 106 at 122.

[214] [1940] Ch 46. This decision is at first sight difficult to reconcile with that of ROMER J in *Re Bischoffsheim* [1948] Ch 79, infra, p 1147, where, however, the question of the legitimacy of the children was held not to depend on the validity of their parents' marriage.

[215] See the facts as reported in (1940) 161 LT 266 at 267.

[216] See now the Family Law Reform Act 1987, s 19, as amended by the Adoption and Children Act 2002, Sch 3, para 52. See *Upton v National Westminster Bank plc* [2004] EWHC 1962, [2004] WTLR 1339.

[217] *Radwan v Radwan (No 2)* [1973] Fam 35 at 50.

[218] [1951] P 482; cf *Vida v Vida* (1961) 105 Sol Jo 913; and see North, *Private International Law of Matrimonial Causes*, p 120; (1980) I Hague Recueil 9, 57–69.

[219] See now the Marriage Act 1949, s 2.

The wife submitted that the marriage was void for want of capacity, first because the husband was a British subject with an English domicile and therefore bound by the 1929 Act; secondly, and alternatively, because the essential validity of the marriage was determinable by English law as being either the law of the husband's domicile or the law of the country of the proposed matrimonial home. PEARCE J granted a decree of nullity, holding that the wife was entitled to succeed on both submissions. The 1929 Act, he said, was intended to affect "all persons domiciled in the United Kingdom wherever the marriage might be celebrated".[220] He also agreed with the second submission, "since by the law of the husband's domicil it was a marriage into which he could not lawfully enter".[221] This passage, coupled with the citation of *Re Paine*,[222] undoubtedly suggests that the judge applied English law as being the law of the husband's domicile before marriage, though the fact remains that the decision is compatible with the doctrine of the intended matrimonial domicile.

There has been further express approval of the dual domicile theory, though again in circumstances where a similar result would have been achieved by the intended matrimonial home test.[223] However, a more significant decision is that of Sir Jocelyn SIMON P in *Padolecchia v Padolecchia*.[224] The facts were as follows:

> The husband, at all times domiciled in Italy, married there in 1953. He was later granted a divorce decree, by proxy, by a Mexican court, which decree would not be recognised in Italy. He went to live in Denmark and, on a one-day visit to England in 1964, he "married" the respondent who was resident and domiciled in Denmark. They both returned to Denmark to live and then the husband petitioned the English court for a decree of nullity on the ground that he was already married when he "married" the respondent.

Having decided that the court had jurisdiction,[225] Sir Jocelyn SIMON P had to determine by what law to test the petitioner's capacity to marry the respondent.[226] There was no doubt that, by Italian law, the law of the domicile, the divorce would not be recognised and hence that he had no capacity to marry. The position was probably the same under Danish law, though the evidence of Danish law was not wholly satisfactory. Had the case turned on Danish law, which would seem certain to be classed as the law of the intended matrimonial home, then further investigation of that law would have been necessary. However, the judge had no doubts that the capacity of the petitioner had to be referred to Italian law, the law of the domicile. His examination of the position under other possibly relevant laws seems to have been on the hypothesis that one of them might have been considered to be the law of the domicile.[227]

---

[220] [1951] P 482 at 493.

[221] Ibid, at 494.

[222] Supra, p 902.

[223] Eg *R v Brentwood Superintendent Registrar of Marriages, ex p Arias* [1968] 2 QB 956; *Crickmay v Crickmay* (1967) 60 DLR (2d) 734.

[224] [1968] P 314; and see *Szechter v Szechter* [1971] P 286 at 295.

[225] This aspect of the case is considered, infra, Chapter 21.

[226] Had the issue been classified as one concerned with the recognition of foreign divorces the outcome would have been the same, as the petitioner was domiciled at all material times in Italy, by whose law the Mexican decree was not recognised: [1968] P 314 at 338. It also seems most unlikely that the Mexican decree would be recognised under the Family Law Act 1986, infra, p 992 et seq.

[227] Further support for the approach in this case may be drawn from *Shaw v Gould* (1868) LR 3 HL 55; *Schwebel v Ungar* (1963) 42 DLR (2d) 622; affd (1964) 48 DLR (2d) 644, supra, p 53; Lysyk (1965) 43 Can BR

This decision would seem to provide a clear and explicit authority for the dual domicile theory.[228] Further support for this view may be drawn from two statutory provisions.[229] The first is the Marriage (Enabling) Act 1960, which modified the former rules of affinity. It has long been the rule that, after the death of his wife, a man may marry her sister, aunt or niece; and may also marry the wife of his brother, uncle or nephew after her husband is dead. The Act of 1960 eliminated the condition that the wife, brother, uncle or nephew must be dead at the time of the proposed marriage.[230] Thus, for example, it is now permissible for a man to marry the sister of his divorced wife while the latter is still alive. Having made this change in English internal law, the Act lays down a rule for the choice of law by providing that no such marriage shall be valid "if either party to it is at the time of the marriage domiciled in a country outside Great Britain, and under the law of that country there cannot be a valid marriage between the parties".[231] Despite the argument that this choice of law provision was not discussed in Parliament,[232] it does provide a clear statutory reference to the dual domicile theory, though in admittedly limited circumstances.[233]

The second statutory provision is section 11(d) of the Matrimonial Causes Act 1973[234] which stipulates that an actually polygamous marriage celebrated abroad is void if either party was domiciled in England at the time of the marriage.[235]

In Scots law, the statutory crystallisation of the dual domicile theory in section 38(2) of the Family Law (Scotland) Act 2006 is thought to have foreclosed any possibility of seeking to persuade a Scots court to apply the intended matrimonial home doctrine.[236]

(c) Further issues

It is now necessary to consider a number of further issues related to the operation of either the dual domicile or the intended matrimonial home approaches.

(i) The rule in Sottomayor v De Barros (No 2)[237]

The rule in *Sottomayor v De Barros (No 2)*[238] provides what may appear to be an exception to the two choice of law theories which have just been examined. Two related decisions need to be considered together here:

> The husband and wife were first cousins. They were presumed to be domiciled in Portugal by whose law marriage between first cousins was prohibited in the absence of a Papal dispensation. They married in England and lived together in the same house, though without consummating the marriage, for six years.

363, 368–370; and see *Ungar v Ungar* [1967] 2 NSWR 618.

[228] See also National Insurance Decision No R (G) 3/75.

[229] The Marriage (Scotland) Act 1977, ss 1(1), 2(1), specifically refer to persons domiciled in Scotland in relation to the questions of lack of age and consanguinity and affinity; and see also ss 3(5), 5(4).

[230] Marriage (Enabling) Act 1960, s 1(1).

[231] Ibid, s 1(3); see *Crickmay v Crickmay* (1967) 60 DLR (2d) 734.

[232] See 7th edn of this book (1965), p 288.

[233] See *Radwan v Radwan (No 2)* [1973] Fam 35 at 51.

[234] As amended by the Private International Law (Miscellaneous Provisions) Act 1995, Sch, para 2.

[235] The provision is discussed more fully, infra, p 928 et seq.

[236] See Crawford and Carruthers, para 11-16.

[237] See Clarkson (1990) 10 Legal Studies 80, 84 et seq.

[238] (1879) 5 PD 94; see also *Ogden v Ogden* [1908] P 46.

The Court of Appeal held[239] that the question of capacity must depend on the law of the domicile. If they were both domiciled in Portugal, the marriage would be void. This decision provides some further support for the dual domicile theory, though it is not conclusive for it appears that the parties never intended to live together as husband and wife, never really had a matrimonial home, and so reference to the law of Portugal as the law of the husband's domicile is compatible with the statement of the intended matrimonial home doctrine.[240]

The actual determination of the parties' domicile fell to be considered in later proceedings,[241] where it was decided that the husband was domiciled in England but the wife in Portugal. What effect, then, did this conclusion have on the validity of the marriage? If it is true to say that a marriage is invalid where either party is incapacitated by his or her personal law, the decision in this case should have been adverse to the legality of the marriage, but Sir James HANNEN P held that it constituted a valid marriage. It must be admitted that he did not base his decision on the matrimonial residence of the parties in England, but on the fact that the law of the place of celebration was English. Impressed by the "injustice which might be caused to our own subjects if a marriage were declared invalid on the ground that it was forbidden by the law of the domicile of one of the parties",[242] he refused to give effect to the prohibition imposed on the wife by Portuguese law. The decision has never been overruled. How, then, is it to be rendered compatible with the dual domicile doctrine? The difficulty is usually surmounted by framing an exception to that doctrine. It has been formulated as follows:

> The validity of a marriage celebrated in England between persons of whom the one has an English, and the other a foreign, domicile is not affected by an incapacity which, though existing under the law of such foreign domicile, does not exist under the law of England.[243]

In other words, capacity must be tested by the law of the domicile of each party, but, when one of them has an English domicile, a foreign incapacity affecting the other and unknown to English law must be utterly disregarded if the marriage takes place in England. This suggested rule has been stigmatised as "anomalous"[244] and as "unworthy of a place in a respectable system of the conflict of laws",[245] as well as being criticised by the Law Commission.[246] It is xenophobic in that it gives preference to the law of the place of celebration of the marriage if that is English, but not if it is foreign. It is likely to lead

---

[239] *Sottomayor v De Barros* (1877) 3 PD 1.

[240] Supra, p 896. It should be mentioned, however, that in the lower court the Queen's Proctor had argued, unsuccessfully, for the application of English law as that of the intended matrimonial home: (1877) 2 PD 81 at 82.

[241] *Sottomayor v De Barros (No 2)* (1879) 5 PD 94.

[242] (1879) 5 PD 94 at 104.

[243] Dicey, Morris and Collins, para 17E-106. In addition to *Sottomayor v De Barros (No 2)* (1879) 5 PD 94, the exception is supported by dicta: *Ogden v Ogden* [1908] P 46 at 74–77; *Chetti v Chetti* [1909] P 67 at 81–88; *Vervaeke v Smith* [1981] Fam 77 at 122 (the point was not referred to in the House of Lords: [1981] 1 AC 145); and see *R v Brentwood Superintendent Registrar of Marriages, ex p Arias* [1968] 2 QB 956 at 968–969; see also *MacDougall v Chitnavis* 1937 SC 390; cf Anton, pp 431–432. The exception can also be relied on to justify the decision in *Perrini v Perrini* [1979] Fam 84.

[244] *Radwan v Radwan (No 2)* [1973] Fam 35 at 50.

[245] Falconbridge, *Conflict of Laws*, p 711.

[246] Law Commission Working Paper No 89 (1985), para 3.17; and see paras 3.45–3.48. See also Law Com No 165 (1987), paras 2.7–2.8, 2.15.

to "limping" marriages, valid in England but not in the country of the domicile of one spouse. Thus, the case for the abandonment of the rule seems clear.

The *Sottomayor* decision could, on the facts, though not on the reasoning, be regarded as supporting the intended matrimonial home theory. A better view would be to regard this decision as an inelegant exception to the dual domicile theory and, if it is to remain, one to be interpreted as restrictively as possible by confining it, for example, "to a condition imposed by the law of the domicile that a specified consent or consents should be given".[247] Even if such restrictive interpretation is not accepted, there has been a narrowing of the scope of the rule by reason of the Marriage (Enabling) Act 1960,[248] for a marriage covered by that Act is not validated if either party is domiciled in a country under whose law there cannot be a valid marriage between the parties. Furthermore, to apply *Sottomayor v De Barros (No 2)* other than to cases of invalidity caused through want of consents would mean that its application would depend on the particular degree of affinity in question.

(ii) The role of the law of the place of celebration[249]

How far is the law of the place of celebration relevant to capacity to marry? This issue has arisen in two contexts. The first is whether there are issues as to essential validity which should be referred exclusively to the law of the place of celebration. Some support for such an approach is to be found in the speech of Lord SIMON of Glaisdale in *Vervaeke v Smith*[250] where he suggested that matters of "quintessential validity", such as whether, as in the case before him, a sham marriage could constitute a marriage at all, might be referred to the law of the place of celebration. It seems hard to justify such an approach in the case of matters going to the fundamental nature of marriage, especially as the parties may have had only a limited connection with the place of celebration.[251] Furthermore, the authorities on which the judge relied either ante-date the distinction which has been maintained since the mid-nineteenth century between form and essential validity[252] or were primarily concerned with formal validity.[253]

The second context in which the application of the law of the place of celebration has arisen is in deciding whether the rules of that law relating to essential validity must be satisfied *in addition* to those of the parties' personal law.[254] Clear authority for the rejection of any reference to the law of the place of celebration is found in *In the Will of Swan*.[255] However, in more recent years, there have been dicta[256] and the decision in

---

[247] As can be implied from *Miller v Teale* (1954) 92 CLR 406 at 414.

[248] Supra, p 904.

[249] Clarkson (1990) 10 Legal Studies 80, 81–84. See, in relation to Scots law, Family Law (Scotland) Act 2006, s 38(3). See also Crawford and Carruthers, para 11-18; the Family Law (Scotland) Act 2006 is silent on the question of the requirement of capacity by the *lex loci celebrationis* where that law is other than Scottish.

[250] [1983] 1 AC 145 at 165–166.

[251] For a detailed rejection of the law of the place of celebration as the law generally to be applied to issues of essential validity, see Law Commission Working Paper No 89 (1985), paras 3.21–3.23. Contrast the approach in South Africa: *Phelan v Phelan* 2007 (1) SA 483 (C).

[252] *Warrender v Warrender* (1835) 2 Cl & Fin 488 at 530.

[253] *Berthiaume v Dastous* [1930] AC 79 at 83.

[254] Bradshaw (1986) 15 Anglo-Am LR 112; and see Law Com No 165 (1987), para 2.6.

[255] (1871) 2 VR (IE & M) 47, supra, pp 725–726.

[256] Eg *Lendrum v Chakravarti* 1929 SLT 96 at 103. It is not clear why reference was made in *Schwebel v Ungar* (1963) 42 DLR (2d) 622 at 633–634 to the proposition that the law of the place of celebration might be relevant

Breen v Breen[257] which have indicated that the law of the place of celebration is relevant and should be considered in addition to the personal law, so that a marriage will be regarded as invalid if the parties lack capacity by the law of the place of celebration, even though they are capable under their personal law.

In *Breen v Breen*[258] the parties were at all relevant times domiciled in England. They married in Ireland during the lifetime of the husband's former wife, that first marriage having been dissolved by an English court. The second wife petitioned for a decree of nullity on the grounds that the divorce decree would not be recognised in Ireland and that, therefore, her "husband" lacked capacity to marry by Irish law. KARMINSKI J concluded, after examination of the Constitution of Ireland, that since the English divorce decree would be recognised in Ireland the second marriage was valid. However the only connection with Ireland that this marriage had was that it was celebrated there, yet reference was made to Irish law on an issue of capacity. One can conclude that as an authority for referring issues of capacity to the law of the place of celebration, this case is "a sorry and inarticulate precedent [which] should be considered insufficient to establish a rule of very doubtful merit".[259]

While it is true that the law of the place of celebration cannot always be disregarded,[260] a distinction should be drawn between cases where the law of the place of celebration is that of the forum and other cases. An English registrar, for instance, cannot be required to sanction a marriage if it would be void for incapacity under an English statute and an English court is unlikely, for policy reasons, to uphold such a marriage.[261] It is probably true to say that all marriages celebrated in England must comply with English law, not only as to formal validity but also as to matters of essential validity.[262]

On the other hand, incapacity by the law of a foreign place of celebration should be ignored,[263] as is illustrated by the Canadian decision in *Reed v Reed*:[264]

> The husband and wife were first cousins domiciled in British Columbia. The wife was aged 18 and could not marry in British Columbia without parental consent, which was refused. As a consequence, the parties were married in the State of Washington where all the necessary formal requirements were satisfied, but under whose law first cousins lacked capacity to marry. The wife petitioned, unsuccessfully, in British Columbia for a nullity decree.

---

to capacity to marry but without applying it. In that case an incapacity did exist by the law of the place of celebration, which was also the law of the forum, but the marriage in question was upheld; see Lysyk (1965) 43 Can Bar Rev 363, 369–370.

[257] [1964] P 144; Unger (1961) 24 MLR 784.

[258] [1964] P 144.

[259] Unger (1961) 24 MLR 784, 787.

[260] And see the Marriage (Scotland) Act 1977, s 2(3)(a), and Family Law (Scotland) Act 2006, s 38(3).

[261] Support might be inferred from *Padolecchia v Padolecchia* [1968] P 314 at 335; *Vervaeke v Smith* [1983] 1 AC 145 at 152; and also from *Pugh v Pugh* [1951] P 482 at 491–492.

[262] The Marriage (Scotland) Act 1977, ss 1(2) and 2(1)(a) provide expressly that a marriage celebrated in Scotland is void if the requirements as to age or consanguinity and affinity are not satisfied. See also s 38(3) of the Family Law (Scotland) Act 2006 (to which s 38(2)—the dual domicile rule—is expressly subject), which states that: "If a marriage entered into in Scotland is void under a rule of Scots internal law, then, notwithstanding subsection (2), that rule shall prevail over any law under which the marriage would be valid."

[263] This seems to be the inference in Scots law, in the Family Law (Scotland) Act 2006, s 28(3).

[264] (1969) 6 DLR (3d) 617.

Lack of parental consent was characterised as an issue of form to be referred to the law of the place of celebration, Washington, by which law the marriage was formally valid. Consanguinity was a matter of capacity to be referred to the law of the domicile, British Columbia, by which law the parties were capable. The court declined to apply the law of the place of celebration to the issue of capacity.

(iii) Public policy

Where a foreign domiciliary law governs the capacity of the parties to a marriage, it will not be recognised if it is repugnant to public policy.[265] The court has a discretionary power to repudiate a capacity or an incapacity on the ground that to give effect to it would be unconscionable.[266] This discretion, however, is to be exercised sparingly.[267] Thus, so far as repudiation of capacity is concerned, in *Cheni v Cheni*,[268] a case which is considered later in another context,[269] it was argued that a marriage celebrated in Cairo between an uncle and a niece, both domiciled in Egypt, was incestuous by the general consent of Christendom or at least by the general consent of civilised nations. Sir Jocelyn SIMON P disagreed. He insisted that a reasonable tolerance must be shown in applying the doctrine of public policy.[270] Marriages between uncle and niece were accepted by general Jewish law and by many Lutheran churches, and were not totally condemned even by the Catholic Church. It would, therefore, be unjustifiable to stigmatise as unconscionable a capacity acceptable "to many people of deep religious convictions, lofty ethical standards and high civilisation".[271]

It does seem clear, however, that the courts would be prepared, albeit with caution, to deny recognition to a wide variety of incapacities imposed by the law of the domicile such as incapacity to marry at all,[272] or inability to marry other than according to the tenets of a particular faith,[273] or incapacity to marry outside one's caste[274] or race.[275]

A subject which has given rise to some controversy in recent years is whether, and if so what, recognition should be afforded in England to same sex or transsexual relationships.[276]

---

[265] Cf, in Scots law, the Family Law (Scotland) Act 2006, s 38(4). See Crawford and Carruthers, para 11-21. There is also a minor statutory restriction, namely that imposed on descendants of George II by the Royal Marriages Act 1772; see Dicey, Morris and Collins, paras 17E-092–17-097; MacNeill (1922) 38 LQR 74; Parry (1956) 5 ICLQ 61.

[266] *Cheni v Cheni* [1965] P 85 at 98.

[267] *Vervaeke v Smith* [1983] 1 AC 145 at 164.

[268] Supra.

[269] Infra, p 924.

[270] And in *Mohamed v Knott* [1969] 1 QB 1, infra, p 936, the validity of the foreign marriage of a 13-year-old Nigerian girl was upheld.

[271] [1965] P 85 at 99.

[272] Eg because the person is a monk or a nun: *Sottomayor v De Barros (No 2)* (1879) 5 PD 94 at 104.

[273] Cf *Gray (otherwise Formosa) v Formosa* [1963] P 259; *Lepre v Lepre* [1965] P 52; and see *Papadopoulas v Papadopoulas* [1930] P 55 at 64; cf *Corbett v Corbett* [1957] 1 All ER 621, where incapacity to marry outside the Jewish faith was recognised.

[274] *Chetti v Chetti* [1909] P 67.

[275] *Sottomayor v De Barros (No 2)*, supra, at 104; cf *Conlon v Mohamed* [1989] ILRM 523.

[276] Similar controversies have arisen elsewhere, including in the USA and Canada. See Symeonides (2003) 51 AJCL 80; Symeonides (2004) 52 AJCL 66; Symeonides (2004) 52 AJCL 984, citing *In re Kandu* 315 BR 123, *Goodridge v Department of Public Health* 798 NE 2d 941; and Symeonides (2005) 53 AJCL 642, citing *Wilson v Ake* 354 F Supp 2d 1298, *Smelt v County of Orange* 374 F Supp 2d 861, and *Langan v St Vincent's Hospital of New York* 802 NYS 2d 476.

Section 11(c) of the Matrimonial Causes Act 1973 provides that a marriage shall be void on the ground that the parties are not respectively male and female.[277] The Civil Partnership Act 2004, however, allows same sex partners to register their relationship, in England and Wales, Scotland, and Northern Ireland, as a civil partnership.[278] The subject of civil partnership is examined more fully below.[279]

As regards transsexual persons, account must be taken in the United Kingdom of the Gender Recognition Act 2004,[280] the purpose of which is to provide transsexual persons with legal recognition in their acquired gender. By virtue of section 1 of the 2004 Act, a person of either gender, who is at least 18 years of age, may make an application in the United Kingdom to a Gender Recognition Panel, for the issue of a gender recognition certificate, on the basis of living in the other gender, or having changed gender under the law of a country or territory outside the United Kingdom.[281] The Act does not specify a requirement that the applicant have a personal or other connection with the United Kingdom, by way of, for example, nationality, domicile or residence.

Section 21 of the Act concerns foreign gender change and marriage. A person's gender is not to be regarded as having changed by reason only that it has changed under the law of a country or territory outside the United Kingdom.[282] A person who has changed gender in a country or territory outside the United Kingdom must make an application for a gender recognition certificate in the United Kingdom under section 1 of the Act. The Gender Recognition Panel must grant the application if the applicant satisfies the conditions listed in section 2 of the Act, including, in the case of an application under section 1(1)(b),[283] the condition that the country or territory under the law of which the applicant changed gender is "approved".[284]

---

[277] See also *Bellinger v Bellinger* [2003] UKHL 21, [2003] 2 AC 467; *KB v NHS Pensions Agency* [2004] ECR I-541; *J v C (Void Marriage: Status of Children)* [2006] EWCA Civ 551, [2006] 2 FLR 1098; and *Wilkinson v Kitzinger* [2007] EWHC 2022 (Fam), [2007] 1 FLR 295.

[278] See also Civil Partnership Act 2004 (Overseas Relationships) Order, SI 2005/3135; and Civil Partnership (Jurisdiction and Recognition of Judgments) Regulations, SI 2005/3334.

[279] Infra, p 937 et seq.

[280] See also SI 2005/54. The 2004 Act was introduced subsequent to the decision in *Bellinger v Bellinger* [2003] UKHL 21, in which the House of Lords concluded that s 11(c) of the Matrimonial Causes Act 1973 referred to a person's biological gender as determined at birth, so that, for the purposes of marriage, a person born with one sex could not subsequently become a person of the opposite sex. The effect of this interpretation was that English law, in not recognising a marriage between two individuals who were of the same gender at birth, but one of whom later underwent (prior to the marriage) gender reassignment treatment, was held to be incompatible with the applicant's right to respect for her private life under Art 8 of the ECHR and with her right to marry under Art 12 thereof. See also *Goodwin v UK* (2002) 35 EHRR 18.

[281] The application must be supported by appropriate medical evidence: s 3.

[282] S 21(1). Accordingly, a person is not to be regarded as being married by reason of having entered into a foreign post-recognition marriage: s 21(2). However, if a full gender recognition certificate is issued in the United Kingdom to a person who has entered into a foreign post-recognition marriage, after the issue of the certificate the marriage is no longer to be regarded as being void on the ground that, at the time it was entered into, the parties to it were not respectively male and female: s 21(3). In other words, the foreign post-recognition marriage will have no standing in the United Kingdom until such time as the party who changed gender abroad has also gained recognition in the acquired gender in the United Kingdom.

[283] Where the applicant has changed gender under the law of a country of territory outside the United Kingdom.

[284] S 2(2) and (4); see SI 2005/874.

If a gender recognition certificate is applied for and granted in the United Kingdom, the applicant shall, for all purposes, be treated as belonging to the gender recognised by the certificate.[285] In particular, the applicant will be able to marry someone of the opposite gender to his/her acquired gender.[286]

(iv) Renvoi

There is some authority that a reference to the personal law as governing issues of capacity should include a reference to its rules of private international law, ie that the doctrine of renvoi applies in this context. In *R v Brentwood Superintendent Registrar of Marriages, ex p Arias*[287] the facts were these:

> The husband, an Italian national domiciled in Switzerland, was married to a Swiss wife. He obtained a divorce in Switzerland. His wife remarried. He wished to remarry in England, but his Swiss divorce was not recognised in Italy.

The court upheld the Registrar's objections to the marriage. The husband's capacity to marry was referred to the law of Switzerland, his ante-nuptial domicile and the intended matrimonial home. It was agreed on the facts that Swiss law would refer the issue of his capacity to Italian law. This seems clearly to be an application of the doctrine of renvoi, though the matter is not discussed by the court; and it had the consequence that the husband was incapable of remarrying even in the country of his domicile and notwithstanding the remarriage in the same country of his first wife.[288]

(v) Should the same rule apply to all issues of capacity?

The discussion of the law governing capacity to marry has, so far, proceeded on the assumption that all incapacitating factors give rise to the same problems and are susceptible of the same solution in choice of law terms. Whilst it is true that, on the balance of the authorities, the ante-nuptial domiciliary law determines issues of capacity[289] such as consanguinity and affinity,[290] lack of age[291] and, indeed, bigamy,[292] it has been suggested that:

> It is an over-simplification of the common law to assume that the same test for purposes of choice of law applies to every kind of incapacity—non age, affinity, prohibition of

---

[285] Ss 9–21 and Schs 3–6 set out the consequences of the issue of a gender recognition certificate.

[286] S 11 and Sch 4. The Matrimonial Causes Act 1973, s 12 has been amended to the effect that a marriage celebrated after 31 July 1971 shall be voidable on the ground that (g) an interim gender recognition certificate has, after the time of the marriage, been issued to either party to the marriage, or (h) the respondent is a person whose gender at the time of the marriage had become the acquired gender under the Gender Recognition Act 2004.

[287] [1968] 2 QB 956; and see the Marriage (Scotland) Act 1977, s 3(5).

[288] The Law Commission has supported the application of renvoi to capacity to marry; see Working Paper No 89 (1985), para 3.39, Law Com No 165 (1987), para 2.6; and so has the Irish Law Reform Commission: LRC 19-1985, p 153. The decision in the *Brentwood* case would now be different by reason of the Family Law Act 1986, s 50, infra, pp 913–915.

[289] The questions whether consent and physical incapacities, such as impotence or wilful refusal to consummate, are to be regarded as matters of essential validity governed by the law of the domicile are considered, infra, p 970 et seq, as these issues will tend normally to arise in the context of nullity petitions.

[290] Eg *Mette v Mette* (1859) 1 Sw & Tr 416; *Brook v Brook* (1861) 9 HL Cas 193; *Sottomayor v De Barros* (1877) 3 PD 1; *Re Paine* [1940] Ch 46. The effect of the Marriage (Enabling) Act 1960, s 1(3) has already been considered supra, p 904.

[291] *Pugh v Pugh* [1951] P 482.

[292] *Padolecchia v Padolecchia* [1968] P 314.

monogamous contract by virtue of an existing spouse, and capacity for polygamy. Different public and social factors are relevant to each of these types of incapacity.[293]

There is no doubt that there are issues relating to capacity which are governed by special rules. For example, the rules governing capacity to marry following a divorce are now governed by specific statutory provisions,[294] and, as the passage just quoted illustrates, there is some authority for saying that, even though the dual domicile test applies to many forms of incapacity, the intended matrimonial home test ought to apply to capacity to enter a polygamous marriage.[295] It has also been suggested that different rules should apply to matters of "quintessential validity" as compared with other issues of essential validity.[296]

The virtue of a situation in which different choice of law rules may be applied to different issues of essential validity is that it enables the courts to retain the flexibility necessary to reach just results in difficult cases. It is hard to argue against a desire for justice but, in fact, that way lies uncertainty, anarchy and ultimately injustice. Whilst a limited number of exceptions from a general choice of law rule may be justifiable, it is not acceptable to permit the judge to decide which rule to apply essentially by reference to the factual circumstances of a particular case. It is suggested, for example, that there is no justification for applying the intended matrimonial home test to determine whether a man may marry polygamously[297] but the dual domicile test to determine whether he may marry his niece[298]—especially if she is to be his second wife! There would appear to be no social or policy factors justifying a different approach to the two types of case.

(d) Alternative approaches

It has been assumed so far that, in determining the general choice of law rule to select the law to govern the essential validity of marriage, the choice lies between the dual domicile or the intended matrimonial home approaches. Whilst it is true that the case law overwhelmingly supports one or other of these approaches, consideration has been given in more recent years to other ways of determining the applicable law, some of which will be examined here.

(i) Real and substantial connection[299]

In *Vervaeke v Smith*,[300] Lord SIMON of Glaisdale suggested that the "quintessential validity" of a marriage, this being in the case before him the validity of a "sham" marriage, should be governed by the law of the country "with which the marriage has the most real and substantial connection". A similar test was applied by LINCOLN J in *Lawrence v*

---

[293] *Radwan v Radwan (No 2)* [1973] Fam 35 at 51; and see Jaffey (1978) 41 MLR 38; Downes (1986) 35 ICLQ 170.

[294] Family Law Act 1986, s 50, infra, pp 913–915. The courts have also been prepared to accept the need for a special rule as to capacity in this context, see *Lawrence v Lawrence* [1985] Fam 106 at 114–115, 134.

[295] Discussed more fully, infra, p 927 et seq.

[296] *Vervaeke v Smith* [1983] 1 AC 145 at 165–166.

[297] *Radwan v Radwan (No 2)* [1973] Fam 35.

[298] Eg *Cheni v Cheni* [1965] P 85.

[299] See, supra, p 901.

[300] [1983] 1 AC 145 at 165–166.

Lawrence[301] to the issue of capacity to marry after a foreign divorce.[302] This approach had received some academic support in the past[303] and these two decisions have prompted further support.[304] It has, however, been vigorously rejected by the Law Commission:

> It is an inherently vague and unpredictable test which would introduce an unacceptable degree of uncertainty into the law. It is a test which is difficult to apply other than through the courtroom process and it is therefore unsuitable in an area where the law's function is essentially prospective, ie a yardstick for future planning.[305]

It does seem to be a retrograde step to introduce into the field of validity of marriage a test which, because of its inherent uncertainty, was abandoned in the field of divorce recognition in 1971.[306] It also seems unworkable where there is a real and substantial connection with more than one country.[307]

(ii) Alternative reference

A criticism that can be advanced against the dual domicile approach is that it favours invalidity, because the marriage will be invalid if either party lacks capacity by their ante-nuptial domiciliary law. To counter this disadvantage, and in order to differentiate between rules designed to protect the public interest and those designed to protect the parties, it has been suggested[308] that, in cases other than those such as non-age, impotence or wilful refusal, where the purpose of the rule is to protect the parties, the marriage should be regarded as valid if either the dual domicile or the intended matrimonial home test is satisfied. This embodies a clear policy in favour of upholding the validity of marriages, and this is a policy which has, in the present context, attracted some judicial support.[309] There are, however, major disadvantages with such an alternative reference approach which led to its rejection by the Law Commission.[310] Not only does it suffer from many of the disadvantages of the intended matrimonial home test, it may also require the substantive marriage laws of three different legal systems to be investigated. Furthermore, it does seem to depend on a distinction being made between grounds of invalidity on the basis of some form of assessment of the purpose of individual invalidating rules, thus introducing into the field of family law many of the problems of American "interest analysis".[311] Finally, it seems unwarranted to give such prominence to a policy

---

[301] [1985] Fam 106 at 112–115; though no specific support for this approach is to be found in the judgments in the Court of Appeal. See also *Entry Clearance Officer, Dhaka v Ranu Begum* [1986] Imm AR 461 at 464–465, 466–467; *R v Immigration Appeal Tribunal, ex p Rafika Bibi* [1989] Imm AR 1.

[302] Infra, p 913 et seq.

[303] Sykes suggested that essential validity should be governed by the proper law of the contract to marry, ie the law of that country with which the contract has the most real connection: (1955) 4 ICLQ 159, 168; and see supra, p 750 et seq, for the application of such a test to general contractual capacity.

[304] Fentiman [1985] CLJ 256; Smart (1985) 14 Anglo-Am LR 225; Fentiman (1986) 6 OJLS 353, 354–360.

[305] Working Paper No 89 (1985), para 3.20. This approach (and the next two examined here) were not discussed further in Law Com No 165 (1987).

[306] By the Recognition of Divorces and Legal Separations Act 1971, abrogating the decision in *Indyka v Indyka* [1969] 1 AC 33; see now the Family Law Act 1986, Part II, infra, p 986 et seq.

[307] *R v Immigration Appeal Tribunal, ex p Rafika Bibi* [1989] Imm AR 1 at 4–5.

[308] Primarily by Jaffey (1978) 41 MLR 38; (1982) 2 OJLS 368; and see Royal Commission on Marriage and Divorce (1956) Cmd 9678, para 891.

[309] *Lawrence v Lawrence* [1985] Fam 106 at 115, 134; and see *Minister of Employment and Immigration v Narwal* (1990) 26 RFL (3d) 95.

[310] Working Paper No 89 (1985), para 3.27.

[311] See North (1980) I Hague Recueil 9.

in favour of the upholding of marriages that it becomes the fundamental basis of the choice of law rule.

(iii) Elective dual domicile test

Concern for upholding the validity of a marriage has led to the suggestion[312] that, instead of declaring a marriage invalid if either party lacks capacity under his or her ante-nuptial domiciliary law, the marriage should be valid if it is so regarded under either law. Where, however, the issue arises prior to the celebration of the marriage, as where a registrar refuses a licence, it is suggested that the orthodox dual domicile test be applied.[313] This approach also was provisionally rejected by the Law Commission[314] for much the same reasons as the alternative reference test was rejected. It does not appear justified to prefer the rules of one party's domiciliary law to those of the other—to do so could lead to evasion and limping marriages. This approach would, again, give undue prominence to a domestic policy in favour of upholding the validity of marriages.

(e) Capacity and recognition of foreign divorces or annulments

(i) Effect of valid divorce or annulment on capacity to remarry[315]

An allegation of incapacity to marry on the grounds of bigamy involves most frequently in private international law a question of the recognition of a foreign divorce or annulment. In such a case the marriage will be bigamous only if the English courts decline to recognise the foreign divorce or annulment. Whilst the whole general question of the rules for the recognition of foreign divorces or annulments is considered later,[316] it is necessary at this point to examine the effect of such recognition on capacity to remarry.

The first problem to consider, taking the case of a foreign divorce, is that which arises where the divorced spouse is domiciled in one foreign country and is divorced in another, and the divorce is recognised in England but not in the country of the domicile. Here there is a conflict of private international law rules—a problem of the "incidental question".[317] If we ask whether the spouse has capacity to remarry, reference to the law of the domicile will reveal he is already married. If we ask whether he is single because validly divorced, English divorce recognition rules will reveal that he is single, with the corollary that he ought to be free to remarry.

Until fairly recently the resolution of this conflict necessitated separate examination of the effects of recognising foreign divorces and annulments and of whether the remarriage was in the United Kingdom or abroad. If the foreign divorce was recognised and the marriage was in the United Kingdom, any incapacity under the law of the domicile was, by statute, to be ignored.[318] If the remarriage was abroad the statute was silent and it was a

---

[312] Hartley (1972) 35 MLR 571, 576–578.

[313] Ibid, at p 578.

[314] Working Paper No 89 (1985), para 3.38.

[315] See Law Com No 137; Scot Law Com No 88 (1984), paras 2.35, 6.49–6.60.

[316] Infra, p 986 et seq.

[317] Supra, Chapter 4.

[318] Recognition of Divorces and Legal Separations Act 1971, s 7; reversing *R v Brentwood Superintendent Registrar of Marriages, ex p Arias* [1968] 2 QB 956.

matter of doubt as to whether recognition of the divorce carried with it capacity to remarry.[319] However, in 1985 in *Lawrence v Lawrence*[320] the Court of Appeal upheld the validity of a marriage abroad, following a divorce in Nevada which was recognised in this country but not in Brazil, the country of the remarrying wife's domicile.[321] The judge at first instance and the members of the Court of Appeal unanimously decided in favour of the validity of the second marriage, but they reached that decision by different routes. One was to apply the law of the country with which the marriage had the most real and substantial connection, which was held to be England as the intended matrimonial home (LINCOLN J[322] and Sir David CAIRNS[323]). Another was that a recognition of the divorce carried with it the right to remarry, even abroad, ie a judicial extension of the statutory rule for United Kingdom marriages to foreign marriages (ACKNER LJ[324] and Sir David CAIRNS[325]). The third was that, if a foreign divorce is recognised on the basis that it was obtained in the country of the domicile, determined in the foreign rather than the English sense,[326] then this domiciliary law (here Nevada) and not that of the domicile determined by English law (Brazil) governed the issue of capacity to remarry (PURCHAS LJ[327]).

In the case of a foreign annulment followed by the remarriage of one of the former spouses, there is authority that, if the foreign annulment is recognised in England, a remarriage in England will be regarded as valid even though the annulment is not recognised in the country of that spouse's domicile.[328] This conclusion mirrored for nullity the then current statutory rule in divorce; and there is no direct authority on the validity of a remarriage abroad. Finally, there are the cases of a divorce or nullity decree granted in England and followed by a marriage in England or elsewhere. Would a party to such a decree be regarded as incapable of marrying if the decree was not recognised in the country of his domicile? Despite some English authority to the contrary,[329] it seems only right that an English court should regard an English divorce, for example, as permitting a divorced spouse to remarry and not to be in a less advantageous position than that of a person whose foreign divorce is recognised in England.

This confused state of affairs was examined by the Law Commission in 1984[330] with the conclusion that the same rule should apply to divorces and annulments, whether granted

---

[319] See Law Com No 137; Scot Law Com No 88 (1984), para 6.52.

[320] [1985] Fam 106. The decision attracted much comment, see: Carter (1985) 101 LQR 496, (1986) 57 BYBIL 441; Collier [1985] CLJ 378; Jaffey (1985) 48 MLR 465; Downes (1986) 35 ICLQ 170; Lipstein (1986) 35 ICLQ 178.

[321] It is not easy to reconcile this conclusion with the decision of the House of Lords in *Shaw v Gould* (1868) LR 3 HL 55, infra, p 1143 et seq.

[322] [1985] Fam 106 at 114–115.

[323] Ibid, at 134.

[324] Ibid, at 124–125.

[325] Ibid, at 134–135.

[326] See Family Law Act 1986, s 46(1), (5), infra, p 992 et seq.

[327] [1985] Fam 106 at 131–134. This approach is strongly, and rightly, criticised by Carter (1985) 101 LQR 496, 500–501; Jaffey (1985) 48 MLR 465, 468–469.

[328] *Perrini v Perrini* [1979] Fam 84.

[329] *Breen v Breen* [1964] P 144, where, following a divorce in England, reference was nevertheless made to Irish law as that of the place of celebration to determine capacity to remarry.

[330] Law Com No 137; Scot Law Com No 88 (1984), paras 6.49–6.60.

in England or obtained elsewhere and recognised in England, and whether followed by a marriage in the United Kingdom or abroad. In all cases the fact that the divorce or annulment was not recognised in the country of the domicile or anywhere else should not affect the validity of a later marriage. This proposal is now embodied in section 50 of the Family Law Act 1986:[331]

Where, in any part of the United Kingdom—

(a) a divorce or annulment has been granted by a court of civil jurisdiction, or

(b) the validity of a divorce or annulment is recognised by virtue of this Part,[332] the fact that the divorce or annulment would not be recognised elsewhere shall not preclude either party to the marriage from forming a subsequent marriage or civil partnership in that part of the United Kingdom or cause the subsequent remarriage or civil partnership of either party (wherever it takes place) to be treated as invalid in that part.

The effect of this provision is to provide one clear straightforward rule embodying a principle which may well already have been the law.[333]

(ii) Effect on capacity to marry of non-recognition of a divorce or annulment

Section 50 of the 1986 Act only applies where a foreign divorce or annulment is recognised in England. There can be a similarly difficult, but converse, case where a foreign divorce or annulment is recognised by the law of the domicile, or of the country of the intended matrimonial home at the time of the remarriage, but not in England. There is Canadian authority in *Schwebel v Ungar*[334] for resolving this incidental question in a converse way to that to be found in section 50, ie by regarding the main question as that of capacity to marry, holding the spouse capable notwithstanding the non-recognition of the divorce under the forum's divorce recognition rules. The Law Commission examined this problem but concluded that no legislative provision should be made for it.[335] The Commission's reasons were essentially practical ones—there is no point in introducing legislation to resolve a problem unlikely to arise in real life. In the case of remarriage in England, conflict between the recognition and capacity rules is not likely to arise given that capacity by English law will be required.[336] In the case of remarriage abroad, there is the further factor that English recognition rules are so broad that conflict with the law governing capacity is unlikely, except where recognition is denied in England on grounds of public policy. In such a case recognition of the later re-marriage might well be justified.

---

[331] As amended by the Civil Partnership Act 2004, Sch 27, para 125. There is no provision equivalent to s 50 in the Brussels II *bis* Regulation, presumably because in the light of virtually automatic recognition of European divorces, etc among Member States, such a provision would be largely unnecessary. But see Crawford and Carruthers, para 12–26.

[332] Infra, p 992 et seq.

[333] See, eg Lipstein (1986) 35 ICLQ 178; cf *Lawrence v Lawrence* [1985] Fam 106 at 131–132 per PURCHAS LJ; Carter (1986) 57 BYBIL 441, 444.

[334] (1963) 42 DLR (2d) 622; affd 48 DLR (2d) 644, supra, p 53.

[335] Law Com No 137; Scot Law Com No 88 (1984), para 6.60; cf Jaffey (1985) 48 MLR 465, 469; Briggs (1989) 9 OJLS 251, 258.

[336] Supra, pp 906–908.

(iii) Prohibitions against remarriage

There is one final problem which relates to foreign divorces and capacity to marry. Some foreign divorce decrees, though purporting to dissolve the marriage, provide restrictions or prohibitions on remarriage by one or both of the parties. Restrictions of this kind appear to fall roughly into two classes, namely, those that are directed against the "guilty" party and those that postpone the date at which either party may contract a further marriage.[337]

To take the latter class first, it may be said that a foreign decree which forbids the parties to remarry before a certain period has elapsed has not finally and conclusively restored the parties to the unmarried status. This view was adopted for English law in *Warter v Warter*,[338] where the parties, who had been divorced in Calcutta, were prohibited by the Indian law of their domicile from marrying again before six months. It was held that a marriage in England contracted by the wife within six months with a domiciled Englishman was invalid.[339]

On the other hand, a decree which finally dissolves the marriage, but which by way, presumably, of punishment, imposes a restriction on the "guilty" party, is regarded by English law as imposing a penalty. We have already seen that the penal laws of foreign countries may be disregarded in England.[340] Thus in *Scott v A-G*:[341]

> Two persons domiciled in South Africa were divorced in that country, and thereupon became subject to a rule of South African law which provided that the guilty party could not remarry as long as the other party remained unmarried. The wife, who was the guilty party, remarried in England, her former husband being still unmarried.

This second marriage was upheld by the English court on the ground that the restriction on remarriage was a penalty, and therefore inoperative out of the jurisdiction under which it was inflicted.[342] The correctness of this decision would seem, indeed, to rest on an even simpler reason. Since the divorce decree had effected a complete dissolution of the marriage according to South African law, the woman, being no longer a wife, was free to acquire her own separate domicile.[343] She had in fact acquired a new domicile in England at the time of her remarriage, and therefore there was no possible ground on which her capacity to marry could be referred to South African law.[344]

---

[337] On this subject, see M Mann (1952) 42 Transactions of the Grotius Society 133, 138–141; Hartley (1967) 16 ICLQ 680, 694–699.

[338] (1890) 15 PD 152; but see now *Boettcher v Boettcher* [1949] WN 83; *Buckle v Buckle* [1956] P 181. See the Australian case, *Miller v Teale* (1954) 92 CLR 406; Webb (1956) 5 ICLQ 137.

[339] But why was it not held valid under the exceptional rule in *Sottomayor v De Barros (No 2)* (1879) 5 PD 94, supra, pp 904–906.

[340] Supra, p 126 et seq.

[341] (1886) 11 PD 128.

[342] As explained in *Warter v Warter* (1890) 15 PD 152 at 155.

[343] She would now, of course, always be free to acquire a separate domicile, supra, p 178 et seq.

[344] (1886) 11 PD 128 at 131; and see Wolff, p 379.

4. REFORM OF GENERAL RULES

There have been various initiatives for reform of the choice of law rules relating to marriage. None has borne significant fruit.[345] On the broader international scene, the Hague Conference on Private International Law in 1978 agreed a Convention on Celebration and Recognition of the Validity of Marriage, but few states have ratified it.[346] The United Kingdom has rejected it,[347] rightly so because the Convention rules are both unacceptable and incomplete.[348]

Closer to home, the Irish Law Reform Commission[349] had no doubt that, in the absence of effective international agreement, reform of the Irish choice of law rules was needed to eradicate uncertainty and complexity and to ensure that practical difficulties for the non-lawyers who have to apply them are avoided. In the Commission's view, this was a task requiring legislative reform and restatement. In making a wide range of recommendations, heavy reliance was placed on Working Paper (No 89) produced in 1985 by the English and Scottish Law Commissions on the same topic.[350] This examined both the desirability of reform of particular rules and, where appropriate, what specific changes might be made. The Commissions' provisional proposals were primarily concerned to produce clarity and certainty and few, if any, proposed radical change. Confirmation that the law of the place of celebration should govern formal validity amounted to nothing new, nor did the idea that there should be some exception founded on the lines of the present common law marriage exception.[351] Again, the provisional proposals that essential validity should be governed by the dual domicile test, that renvoi should apply to the law governing both formal and essential validity and that there should be a public policy safeguard to enable a foreign law not to be applied, either confirmed existing law or did little more than resolve matters of current debate.[352] More substantial were the suggestions that the rule in *Sottomayor v De Barros (No 2)*[353] be abolished and that, in determining essential validity, reference should be made in all cases to the law of the place of celebration as well as to that of the domicile.[354] There were also detailed proposals for minor reforms of the Foreign Marriage Act 1892 and its related delegated legislation.

The Irish recommendations have not been implemented and the provisional proposals in England and Wales have, with the exception of the reform of the Foreign Marriage

---

[345] Except in Scotland, where the rules now rest on a statutory footing: s 38 of the Family Law (Scotland) Act 2006.

[346] Though it has been accepted in Australia and implemented in the Marriage Amendment Act 1985, see Neave (1990) 4 Aus J Fam Law 190; Nygh in Borras (ed), *E Pluribus Unum* (1996), pp 253–267.

[347] Law Com No 165 (1987), para 1.2.

[348] For a range of criticisms of the Convention, see Batiffol (1977) 66 Rev crit dr int pr 451; Glenn (1977) 55 Can Bar Rev 586; Reese (1977) 25 AJCL 393; (1979) 20 Va J Int L 25; Lalive (1978) 34 *Annuaire suisse de droit international* 31; North (1981) 6 Dalh LJ 417, 430–433; (1990) I Hague Recueil 9, 74–81.

[349] LRC 19–1985.

[350] For criticisms, see Fentiman (1986) 6 OJLS 353, 354–360.

[351] Supra, p 887 et seq.

[352] Supra, p 895.

[353] (1879) 5 PD 94, supra, p 904.

[354] This view was, rightly, abandoned in the Law Commissions' Report: Law Com No 165 (1987), para 2.6.

Act 1892,[355] been abandoned.[356] The Law Commissions decided against recommending comprehensive legislation primarily because, in their view, there were no major areas "where, in practice, the law seems to go wrong, ie to lead to an undesirable result",[357] because satisfactory resolution of uncertainties in the law would require complex legislation, and because statutory intervention was thought undesirable whilst the law is still in a state of development. These reasons for doing nothing are not convincing. The solution of complex problems does not necessarily lead to complex legislation.[358] Aspects of the current law are undoubtedly undesirable; nor can there be doubt that other elements of the marriage choice of law rules are uncertain or unclear. It is perverse then to rely, as in effect the Commissions did, on that uncertainty as a reason for doing nothing, in the hope that the courts will in due course provide the appropriate new, clear rules.[359] The experience of the last hundred years is unlikely to convince those varied officials who have to advise on and apply marriage choice of law rules that the much needed clarification will in fact be forthcoming through judicial decisions.

5. POLYGAMOUS MARRIAGES[360]

(a) Introduction

Since the middle of the nineteenth century, it has been the case that a marriage which was both formally and essentially valid under the laws to be applied under English rules of private international law could still be regarded as invalid—or as a marriage to which no effect will be given—if it was actually or potentially polygamous. There was a steady erosion, during the twentieth century, of the circumstances in which a different attitude was taken by the law to polygamous marriages from that taken to monogamous marriages. Although differences still remain, they are now for all practical purposes limited to marriages which are actually, rather than potentially, polygamous.[361]

The high water mark of the antipathy to polygamy is to be seen in the judgment of Lord PENZANCE in *Hyde v Hyde*:[362] an Englishman, who had embraced the Mormon faith, married a Mormon lady in Utah according to the Mormon rites. After cohabiting with her for three years and having children by her, he renounced his faith and soon afterwards became the minister of a dissenting chapel in England. He petitioned for a decree of divorce after his wife had contracted another marriage in Utah according to the Mormon faith. Lord PENZANCE assumed that a Mormon marriage was potentially polygamous,

---

[355] See the Foreign Marriage (Amendment) Act 1988, supra, p 885.

[356] Law Com No 165 (1987), paras 2.13–2.14.

[357] Ibid, para 2.13.

[358] The statutory solution adopted in Scotland (s 38 of the Family Law (Scotland) Act 2006) can be accused of being simplistic, or at least silent on certain important topics, such as renvoi.

[359] Law Com No 165 (1987), para 2.14.

[360] Beckett (1932) 48 LQR 341; Morris (1953) 66 Harv LR 961; Hartley (1969) 32 MLR 155; Poulter (1976) 25 ICLQ 475; Jaffey (1978) 41 MLR 38; James (1979) 42 MLR 533; Shah (2003) 52 ICLQ 369; Rehman (2007) 21 International Journal of Law, Policy and the Family 108; and Beilfuss, "Islamic Family Law in the EU", Chapter 13 in Meeusen, Pertegas, Straetmans and Swennen (eds), *International Family Law for the European Union* (2007).

[361] Infra, p 932 et seq.

[362] (1866) LR 1 P & D 130.

and he refused to dissolve the marriage. He defined "marriage, as understood in Christendom . . . as the voluntary union for life of one man and one woman to the exclusion of all others".[363] The matrimonial laws of England are adapted to the Christian marriage, he thought, and are wholly inapplicable to polygamy. Parties to a polygamous marriage, therefore, "are not entitled to the remedies, the adjudication, or the relief of the matrimonial law of England".[364] Although the determination of the nature of the marriage is no longer of importance in deciding whether the parties are entitled to matrimonial relief from the English courts,[365] it is still, as will be seen,[366] of some importance in other areas of the law, such as its effect on succession, a later re-marriage, or social security entitlement.

(b) Nature of a polygamous marriage

Some further consideration must be given to Lord PENZANCE's definition. Although the form of marriage recognised by English law is generally described as a "Christian marriage",[367] this reference to religion is misleading. Whatever may be the religion of the parties or of the country in which they marry, their union is a marriage in the English sense provided that, in the eyes of the relevant law, it possesses the two attributes of indefinite duration and the exclusion of all other persons. Monogamy, for instance, is not and never has been the monopoly of Christianity. Given these two attributes, the union constitutes an English marriage notwithstanding that it may have been contracted in what mid-Victorian judges called an "infidel country", or contracted between non-Christians.[368]

The exclusion of polygamy from the English concept of marriage has been held to extend to a marriage that, although actually monogamous, is potentially polygamous.[369] If a husband has been entitled by the law that determined the nature of his marriage to take a plurality of wives, his marriage was considered to be polygamous notwithstanding that at the time when the question was raised he had not exercised that right nor ever intended to.[370] If the marriage was potentially polygamous at its inception then, though it might be possible to change it into a monogamous marriage, it retained its polygamous nature until such change was actually made.

---

[363] Ibid, at 133. For a more recent assessment, see Poulter (1979) 42 MLR 409.

[364] Ibid, at 138.

[365] Matrimonial Causes Act 1973, s 47, replacing with minor amendments, s 1 of the Matrimonial Proceedings (Polygamous Marriages) Act 1972, and amended by the Private International Law (Miscellaneous Provisions) Act 1995, s 8(2), Sch, para 2, discussed infra, p 942 et seq. See also *M v M (Divorce: Jurisdiction: Validity of Marriage)* [2001] 2 FLR 6 at paras 48 et seq.

[366] Infra, p 932 et seq.

[367] Eg *Warrender v Warrender* (1835) 2 Cl & Fin 488 at 532.

[368] *Brinkley v A-G* (1890) 15 PD 76—marriage in Japan between an Englishman domiciled in Ireland and a Japanese woman; *Spivack v Spivack* (1930) 99 LJP 52—Jewish marriage; *Penhas v Tan Soo Eng* [1953] AC 304—marriage between a Jew and a non-Christian solemnised according to mixed Chinese and Jewish rites; and see *Ali v Ali* [1968] P 564 at 576.

[369] This is now only of practical importance once the marriage becomes actually polygamous, infra, p 932 et seq.

[370] *Hyde v Hyde* (1866) LR 1 P & D 130; *Sowa v Sowa* [1961] P 70; *Cheni v Cheni* [1965] P 85 at 88–89. What law determines the nature of his marriage is discussed infra, p 920 et seq.

Thus in *Sowa v Sowa*:[371]

> A polygamous marriage was celebrated in Ghana where the parties were domiciled. Prior to the ceremony the husband promised the wife that he would go through a later ceremony which, according to the law of Ghana, would convert the union into a monogamous marriage. He failed to carry out his promise.

It was held that, despite his promise and despite the fact that the husband had not taken an additional wife, the marriage continued to be regarded as polygamous. In conformity with this reasoning, *Mehta v Mehta*[372] indicates that a marriage that is monogamous at its inception is not to be regarded as potentially polygamous merely because the husband is free later to change his religion and join a polygamous sect.[373] It should also be noted that the suggestion in this case that the inception of the marriage is the only time for determining its nature has been disapproved.[374] Such a marriage will remain monogamous until there has been the requisite change.

The border-line between polygamy and concubinage presents a problem in determining the nature of a marriage. In *Lee v Lau*,[375] a marriage in Hong Kong in which the husband, under Chinese customary law, though not permitted to remarry during the lifetime of his first wife, could take "*tsipsis*", ie concubines or secondary wives, was held to be potentially polygamous. In the words of the judge:

> Under a Chinese customary marriage, even if the title of "wife" is given only to the woman who was joined to the man at the marriage ceremony, that ceremony cannot be said to bring about a union to the exclusion of all others, since the husband can take fresh partners to whose status some legal recognition is given.[376]

(c) What law determines the nature of a marriage?

In effect, the inquiry here is to identify the law that determines whether the union conforms to the English concept of marriage. As we have seen, two requirements must be satisfied, the first of which is that the union is potentially for an indefinite period. The relevant law to govern this question is clear beyond all doubt, namely that of the place of celebration.[377]

On the other hand, the law that determines whether the marriage is monogamous or polygamous has not yet been settled beyond all doubt.

> If, for instance, a woman domiciled in England marries a Muslim in London and then cohabits with him in Pakistan where he is domiciled, what law determines whether her marriage is monogamous or polygamous in nature?[378]

---

[371] [1961] P 70.
[372] [1945] 2 All ER 690.
[373] But contrast *M v M (Divorce: Jurisdiction: Validity of Marriage)* [2001] 2 FLR 6, per HUGHES J, at [54].
[374] Infra, p 923 et seq.
[375] [1967] P 14; cf *Ng Ping On v Ng Choy Fund Kam* [1963] SRNSW 782; and see *Re Ah Chong* (1913) 33 NZLR 384; *Yuen Tse v Minister of Employment* (1983) 32 RFL (2d) 274; *Tang Lai Sau-kiu v Tang Loi* [1987] HKLR 85 at 90.
[376] *Lee v Lau* [1967] P 14 at 20.
[377] *Nachimson v Nachimson* [1930] P 217.
[378] The question whether it is a *valid* marriage, of whatever nature, is discussed, infra, p 923 et seq.

The choice lies between English law as the law of the place of celebration and the law of her ante-nuptial domicile, and Pakistani law as the law of his ante-nuptial domicile and, presumably, of both their post-nuptial domiciles. There is, unfortunately, no case in which this issue has been squarely raised and fully discussed. Whichever be the law, there is much to be said for the view that its function is to determine the nature and incidents of the marriage according to its own view, but not necessarily to impose that classification on the court of the forum. This approach may be seen from *Lee v Lau*[379] where Chinese customary law, being the law to which it was considered that reference should be made to determine the nature of the marriage, regarded the marriage as monogamous. Nevertheless CAIRNS J considered that, although reference should be made to the law of the place of celebration to determine the nature and incidents of the union by that law, the ultimate decision on the classification of the nature of the marriage, as with issues of classification generally, must be made by the law of the forum.

There is much to be said in favour of the view that the appropriate law by which to test the monogamous or polygamous character of a marriage is the law of the domicile. To apply the law of the place of celebration runs against the fundamental principle that matters of status, especially the status of husband and wife, are regulated by the law of the domicile. The proposition that the nature of a marriage should be determined by the law of the domicile, not by the law of the place of celebration, is certainly not devoid of judicial support.[380]

Determination of the nature of a marriage by reference to the law of the domicile does, however, create a number of real difficulties. Given that a married woman may have a domicile separate from her husband,[381] the problem would arise of deciding whether the domicile of the husband or of the wife, if different, should determine the nature of the marriage. If such a difficulty is to be avoided, and surely it should be, then the nature of a marriage ought to be determined by the law of the place of celebration. Furthermore, to do otherwise would mean acceptance of the fact that a marriage in an English register office could be a polygamous marriage. Such a conclusion should be reached only on the clearest authority. There is a further argument against reference to the law of the domicile. In some jurisdictions, both monogamous and polygamous marriages are recognised and therefore the nature of a particular marriage in such a country depends on the form of the ceremony by which it is celebrated. This, as has been seen,[382] indicates a matter to be considered by the law of the place of celebration.[383]

When one turns to consider what authority there is for reference to the law of the place of celebration, it is true that one will find that a number of the cases often cited in favour

---

[379] Supra; and see *Hassan v Hassan* [1978] 1 NZLR 385 at 390.

[380] *Warrender v Warrender* (1835) 2 Cl & Fin 488 at 535; *Kenward v Kenward* [1951] P 124 at 145; *Russ v Russ* [1964] P 315 at 326; *Ali v Ali* [1968] P 564 at 576–577; *Hussain v Hussain* [1983] Fam 26, infra, p 930, Carter (1982) 53 BYBIL 298; and see Briggs (1983) 31 ICLQ 737, 738. It seems also to have been assumed in *Radwan v Radwan (No 2)* [1973] Fam 35 that the law of the domicile or of the intended matrimonial home determined that the marriage in question was polygamous, because the place of celebration was held (at pp 42–43) to be France.

[381] Domicile and Matrimonial Proceedings Act 1973, s 1.

[382] Supra, p 878.

[383] Eg *Sowa v Sowa* [1961] P 70; *Kassim v Kassim* [1962] P 224; and see *Mohamed v Knott* [1969] 1 QB 1; Mendes da Costa (1966) 44 Can Bar Rev 293, 302.

of this view[384] have, as the result of careful analysis, been properly described as "either irrelevant or ambiguous".[385] *Hyde v Hyde*[386] itself is not clear on this matter for it is not certain whether the husband was domiciled in Utah where the marriage was celebrated, and so there may have been no conflict between the law of the domicile and of the place of celebration.

It is clear that the crucial case for the determination of this issue is one where the law of the place of celebration is different from that of the domicile.[387] Such a case was *Re Bethell*:[388]

> The deceased had "married" a native girl in Bechuanaland (now Botswana) at a ceremony in accordance with the custom of her tribe, the Barolong tribe, by whose custom marriage was considered to be potentially polygamous. Just after his death, a child was born and a question arose as to whether the child was legitimate for the purposes of an English will.

Having accepted the uncontroverted evidence that the deceased was domiciled in England at the time of his marriage, STIRLING J nevertheless concluded that the marriage was a Barolong marriage and thus polygamous. It is clear that the deceased's domiciliary law did not determine the nature of the marriage; though whether, in considering Barolong custom, STIRLING J can be said to be referring to the law of the place of celebration is a little doubtful without evidence of the law prevailing in Bechuanaland at that time.[389]

Reference to the law of the place of celebration was assumed to be beyond doubt in *Qureshi v Qureshi*:[390]

> The parties were both Moslems. The husband was domiciled at all material times in Pakistan. The wife was apparently domiciled before her marriage in India and, after her marriage, she assumed her husband's domicile in Pakistan. By both personal laws the marriage was potentially polygamous. They married in an English register office, followed by a religious ceremony. The question arose of recognition in England of an extra-judicial divorce by *talak*.[391]

Although not essential to his decision, Sir Jocelyn SIMON P had no doubt that this was a monogamous marriage, for the marriage "having taken place in England, where monogamy is the rule, must be regarded as monogamous for the purpose of invoking the jurisdiction of the court".[392]

---

[384] *Hyde v Hyde* (1866) LR 1 P & D 130; *Chetti v Chetti* [1909] P 67; *R v Hammersmith Marriage Registrar* [1917] 1 KB 634, CA; *R v Naguib* [1917] 1 KB 359; *Maher v Maher* [1951] P 342 (this last case was overruled as regards another point by *Russ v Russ* [1964] P 315, CA); *Risk v Risk* [1951] P 50. The Scottish decision in *Lendrum v Chakravati* 1929 SLT 96 favours the law of the place of celebration (overruled on another point by *MacDougall v Chitnavis* 1937 SC 390).

[385] Bartholomew (1964) 13 ICLQ 1022, 1058.

[386] (1866) LR 1 P & D 130.

[387] In *Iman Din v National Assistance Board* [1967] 2 QB 213 at 218–219, SALMON LJ went so far as to infer that whether a marriage is polygamous is determined by reference to both the personal law of the parties and the law of the country in which it was celebrated, but this seems to be a doubtful proposition.

[388] (1888) 38 Ch D 220.

[389] Bartholomew (1964) 13 ICLQ 1022, 1052–1053.

[390] [1972] Fam 173; and see *Chetti v Chetti* [1909] P 67; *Ohochuku v Ohochuku* [1960] 1 All ER 253.

[391] Discussed, infra, p 999 et seq.

[392] [1972] Fam 173 at 182.

More recently, in *M v M (Divorce: Jurisdiction: Validity of Marriage)*,[393] a question arose, in the context of divorce proceedings:

> A couple married in 1980 in an Islamic ceremony in a flat in London. At the time of the ceremony, the husband was still married to an existing wife under the civil law of Egypt, which accorded with Islamic religious law and which permitted polygamy. The husband retained an Iraqi domicile throughout. The second wife had been domiciled in several Middle Eastern states before acquiring an English domicile of choice in 1992.

The court held that the ceremony was not a valid marriage under section 11 of the Matrimonial Causes Act 1973. HUGHES J stated that:

> When a marriage is characterised as monogamous or polygamous it is often, for convenience, referred to as a marriage in monogamous or polygamous form. That does not mean that a marriage derives its character from the contents of the ceremony. Some ceremonies plainly do refer either to the monogamous, or to the polygamous, rules under which they are conducted . . . But the marriage ceremony need not refer to the question at all . . . What characterises a valid marriage, at any rate at its inception, as monogamous or polygamous is the law of the country in which it is conducted . . . English law contemplates that a marriage will be monogamous.[394]

His Lordship continued:

> A valid English marriage may thus properly be described as monogamous. It may be entered into by persons whose personal laws would allow them to contract polygamous unions, but it remains, if a valid English marriage, a monogamous one.[395] . . . There is neither room for, nor occasion for, any category of potentially polygamous marriage contracted in England.[396]

Thus, the character of a marriage is determined not by the form of the ceremony, but by the law of the country in which it takes place.

One may conclude that, other than on the issue of capacity to marry,[397] all marriages in England are to be characterised as monogamous and that all marriages of English domiciliaries in a foreign country, according to polygamous forms or custom, will be regarded as polygamous. If there is a civil ceremony in England, followed by a religious one, it is the former which constitutes the legal monogamous marriage.[398]

(d) Can the nature of a marriage change?

One issue which has caused difficulty in the past is whether the nature of a marriage as monogamous or polygamous is to be determined as at the date of the marriage or of later legal proceedings. In other words, can the nature of a marriage change? This issue has usually arisen in the context of a claimed change in character from potentially polygamous to monogamous and has diminished in importance as the differences between the

---

[393] [2001] 2 FLR 6.
[394] Ibid, at [50].
[395] Ibid, at [51].
[396] Ibid, at [53].
[397] Infra, p 927 et seq.
[398] *Qureshi v Qureshi* [1972] Fam 173 at 186.

two kinds of marriage have narrowed.[399] Earlier cases rejected any possibility of change,[400] but it is now apparent from more recent decisions that English courts will recognise a change in the nature of a marriage after its inception. This is seen quite clearly from *Cheni v Cheni*,[401] where the facts were these:

> Two Sephardic Jews, uncle and niece domiciled in Egypt, were married in Cairo and a child was born to them two years later. By Jewish and Egyptian law the marriage was potentially polygamous in the sense that if no child was born within ten years the husband might take another wife subject to the approval both of his first wife and of the Rabbinical court. Five years after the parties had acquired an English domicile, the wife petitioned for a decree of nullity on the ground that she and her husband were within the prohibited degrees of consanguinity.

The court had no jurisdiction at the time[402] to entertain this suit if the marriage was potentially polygamous. Sir Jocelyn SIMON P was satisfied that at its inception it was undoubtedly of that nature, because of the remote possibility of an additional wife being taken, but he then held that the decisive date for considering its polygamous potential was the start of the instant proceedings. By that date the birth of the child had rendered the marriage monogamous, and the court assumed jurisdiction.

It is now accepted that there is a variety of ways in which the nature of a marriage may be changed from polygamous to monogamous. Furthermore, given that the nature of the marriage can change, then a corollary is that the relevant time for determining the nature of the marriage is that of the commencement of the proceedings in question.[403] Various examples of change from potentially polygamous to monogamous can be given, but it must always be remembered that the marriage must initially be regarded as valid. So a purported change in the nature of a *void* polygamous marriage will not turn it into a *valid* monogamous marriage. If the personal law of the parties refers the nature of their marriage to their religious law, then a change of religion may be held to alter the nature of the marriage.[404] If the law under which the marriage was celebrated later forbids polygamy, then such legislative action will render the marriage monogamous from henceforth,[405] and it has been seen that the birth of a child to the spouses can change the nature of their marriage under the relevant religious law.[406]

There is some authority that, where there is a marriage in polygamous form followed by a later marriage between the same parties in monogamous form, the parties are to be

---

[399] Infra, p 932.

[400] See *Hyde v Hyde* (1866) LR 1 P & D 130; *Mehta v Mehta* [1945] 2 All ER 690; *Sowa v Sowa* [1961] P 70.

[401] [1965] P 85.

[402] See now Matrimonial Causes Act 1973, s 47 as amended by the Private International Law (Miscellaneous Provisions) Act 1995, s 8(2), Sch, para 2.

[403] *Cheni v Cheni* [1965] P 85 at 92; *Parkasho v Singh* [1968] P 233 at 254–255.

[404] *Sinha Peerage Claim* (1939) 171 Lords Journals 350, [1946] 1 All ER 348 n. See also *Cheni v Cheni* [1965] P 85 at 90–91. An interesting, though undecided, issue is whether the change of religion of only one of the spouses has this effect: *A-G of Ceylon v Reid* [1965] AC 720 suggests that it might. See Webb (1965) 14 ICLQ 992, 996–997.

[405] *Parkasho v Singh* [1968] P 233, a decision on the effect of the Hindu Marriage Act 1955 prohibiting polygamy for Hindus in India, as to which the National Insurance Commissioners had much earlier reached the same conclusion: Decision No R (G) 2/56; and see *Poon v Tan* (1973) 4 Fam Law 161; *R v Sagoo* [1975] QB 885.

[406] *Cheni v Cheni*, supra.

regarded as monogamously married. In *Ohochuku v Ohochuku*[407] a potentially polygamous marriage in Nigeria was followed four years later by a ceremony of marriage in monogamous form, in England, between the same parties. Unable to grant a divorce dissolving the first marriage, the court dissolved the later marriage, thus apparently ignoring the polygamous nature of the union ascribed to the parties at the date of their first marriage. It is suggested that this decision is out of harmony with *Baindail v Baindail*[408] and *Thynne v Thynne*,[409] both decided by the Court of Appeal. As we shall see, it was held in the former case that a polygamous marriage valid according to the law of the parties' domicile is valid in the eyes of English law and therefore that it is an effective bar to a subsequent marriage with a third person in England.[410] *Thynne v Thynne* decided that what a decree of divorce dissolves is not any particular ceremony, but rather the existing status of the parties as husband and wife.[411] The parties in the *Ohochuku* case possessed a polygamous status according to the law of Nigeria where they were still domiciled and where the first marriage was celebrated. The parties could not be transformed from polygamists to monogamists simply by the nullifying of the English ceremony, because this would not affect their status under the still subsisting Nigerian marriage.[412] It is only if it can be said that the later English marriage altered the character of the first Nigerian marriage that the parties could claim to have acquired a monogamous status.[413]

Finally, *Ali v Ali*[414] provides authority for the proposition that, if a husband changes his domicile from a country which permits polygamy to one which does not, this change of domicile renders the marriage monogamous. The facts were these:

> The parties, both domiciled in India, entered into a valid potentially polygamous marriage there. Later they came to England and the wife left the husband. The husband acquired an English domicile in 1963 and petitioned for divorce on the ground of his wife's desertion. She cross-petitioned on the grounds of the husband's cruelty until she left him, and his adultery in 1964. The court's jurisdiction depended at that time on whether the marriage, at the time of the proceedings, was to be regarded as polygamous or monogamous.

CUMMING-BRUCE J concluded that the husband's acquisition of an English domicile and continued residence in England precluded him, apart from obtaining a divorce, from marrying a second wife in the lifetime of the first. This prohibition on remarriage was considered to have impressed a monogamous character on his previously polygamous

---

[407] [1960] 1 All ER 253; cf National Insurance Decision No R (G) 11/53; *Sowa v Sowa* [1961] P 70, supra, p 920.

[408] [1946] P 122.

[409] [1955] P 272.

[410] Infra, p 932.

[411] And see *Peters v Peters* (1968) 112 Sol Jo 311.

[412] The decision may perhaps be supported on the ground that the Nigerian law of the subsisting domicile would regard the decree as effective to dissolve the polygamous marriage, a question which the judge was not prepared to consider.

[413] *Cheni v Cheni* [1965] P 85 at 91; *Ali v Ali* [1968] P 564 at 578; *Parkasho v Singh* [1968] P 233 at 242; cf Carter (1965–1966) 41 BYBIL 443. Even so, if the Nigerian marriage was valid, how could they be married again in England? See *Ali v Ali*, supra.

[414] [1968] P 564; and see *R v Sagoo* [1975] QB 885; National Insurance Decision No R (G) 3/75; *Re Hassan v Hassan* (1976) 69 DLR (3d) 224; Social Security Decision No R (G) 1/95. A similar conclusion had been reached much earlier by the National Insurance Commissioners, see Decision No R (G) 12/56.

marriage, even though there was no conscious act on the part of the parties directed to this end. Furthermore, the court rejected the argument that the mutability of a marriage depends on whether the facts relied upon to effect the change are capable of taking place in the place of celebration, or probably, according to its law.[415] In other words, although the nature of the marriage is decided by the law of the place of celebration, the issue of mutability is not determined at the time of the marriage.

Now that the main raison d'être for the decision in *Ali v Ali*, namely the rule denying English matrimonial relief to the parties to an actually or potentially polygamous marriage, has disappeared,[416] both the decision and the difficulties posed by it[417] may, one hopes, be regarded as of little more than academic interest.

A marriage that is in fact polygamous cannot be changed to a monogamous one by, for example, a change of domicile by one[418] of the wives or by both;[419] but the problem might arise in the case of a marriage which, though once in fact polygamous, has ceased to be so, eg by divorce or by the death of a wife before the change. If, after the acquisition of an English domicile, the marriage ceased to be in fact polygamous, then that fact combined with the acquisition of an English domicile might well render the marriage monogamous.[420]

The discussion of mutability has centred so far on the change from a polygamous to a monogamous nature. Some consideration must be given to the possibility of change from monogamy to polygamy. If a marriage may be changed from polygamy to monogamy then it might seem logical to recognise a change the other way, based on similar circumstances, eg change of religion or change of law.[421] It has, however, been suggested that a marriage has the benefit of any doubt as to monogamy, ie that "it is sufficient that it is either monogamous in its inception or has become so by the time of the proceedings".[422] This would mean that even though it might be possible to change the nature of a marriage from monogamous to polygamous such change would not affect the attitude of English law towards it. Such an approach would afford a convenient way of dissipating the force of the argument that all monogamous marriages are potentially polygamous in that the spouses are free to change their religion or domicile and thus the nature of their marriage.[423]

There are very real difficulties with a view that, if parties marry in monogamous form, eg in England, one party (normally the husband) may change the whole nature of their marriage by changing his religion or domicile and thereby rendering the marriage

---

[415] [1968] P 564 at 575; cf Carter (1963) 39 BYBIL 474, 478. See the rejection of a similar argument in *Parkasho v Singh* [1968] P 233 at 244–245; cf Carter (1967) 42 BYBIL 300–301; and see the slight doubts of CUMMING-BRUCE J in *Radwan v Radwan* [1973] Fam 24 at 27.

[416] Infra, p 942.

[417] Carter (1965–1966) 41 BYBIL 442–444; Mendes da Costa (1966) 44 Can Bar Rev 293, 307–310; Tolstoy (1968) 17 ICLQ 721; cf Morris (1968) 17 ICLQ 1014.

[418] Eg *Onobrauche v Onobrauche* (1978) 8 Fam Law 107.

[419] Eg *Re Sehota* [1978] 1 WLR 1506.

[420] Law Com No 42 (1971), para 13.

[421] See *A-G of Ceylon v Reid* [1965] AC 720 for consideration of this problem under the law of Ceylon; but their Lordships, at 734, declined to express any opinion on "the situation in a purely Christian country"; and see Pearl [1972 A] CLJ 120, 139–142; cf *PP v White* (1940) 9 MLJ 214; and *M v M (Divorce: Jurisdiction: Validity of Marriage)* [2001] 2 FLR 6, per HUGHES J, at [53] and [54].

[422] *Cheni v Cheni* [1965] P 85 at 90. This is supported, further, by *Mehta v Mehta* [1945] 2 All ER 690 at 693; *Parkasho v Singh* [1968] P 233 at 243–244.

[423] See *Cheni v Cheni* [1965] P 85 at 90; *Parkasho v Singh* [1968] P 233 at 244.

potentially polygamous. To deny these difficulties would be to deny that polygamy is a different social and legal institution from monogamy.[424] The problem is seen most sharply where there is a possibility of a man being monogamously married to his first wife and polygamously married to his second, as where a husband domiciled in England marries his first wife, an English domiciliary, in England in a monogamous form and then, having acquired a domicile in Pakistan, marries a second wife, a Pakistan domiciliary, in Pakistan in polygamous form.[425] It would seem most unfair to the first wife that her marriage should, by the unilateral act of her husband, be changed in nature from monogamous to polygamous. This raises two issues—whether the second marriage is valid and, if so, what effect it has on the first marriage and on the rights of the first wife. Such authority as there is points in favour of the validity of the second marriage, which would satisfy general English choice of law rules.[426] It also appears that the fact that the husband has entered a second valid polygamous marriage does not change the nature of the first marriage as monogamous, leaving the first wife free, for example, to petition for divorce on the basis of adultery by the husband in taking a second wife.[427]

(e) Capacity to contract a polygamous marriage

(i) Common law choice of law rules

There has long been controversy in identifying the law that governs capacity in the case of a polygamous union, and the present law on this issue is a confusing mixture of common law and statute. There is support at common law for this issue to be referred to the ante-nuptial domicile of both parties,[428] the law of the intended matrimonial home[429] or the law of the place of celebration.[430] One argument in favour of the last view was that it is that law which determines whether a marriage is polygamous or monogamous[431] but this is not sufficient to outweigh the view that issues of marital status are to be referred to the law of the domicile and it was suggested that capacity to marry more than one spouse is an issue affecting status.[432] Indeed, there was a clear rejection of reference to the law of the place of celebration by CUMMING-BRUCE J in *Ali v Ali*.[433] He concluded that a husband domiciled in England and intending to reside there[434] did not have capacity to confer the status of "wife" on anyone else, no matter where he purported to "marry" a second wife.[435]

---

[424] See Carter (1982) 53 BYBIL 298, 299–300.

[425] The problem is the same if the husband was, at all times, domiciled in Pakistan.

[426] *Drammeh v Drammeh* (1970) 78 Ceylon Law Weekly 55, PC, infra, pp 943–944; *A-G of Ceylon v Reid* [1965] AC 720. In *Nabi v Heaton* [1981] 1 WLR 1052 at 1056–1057, VINELOTT J declined to decide the question; and see infra, pp 935–936.

[427] See infra, pp 943–944, and see Law Com No 146; Scot Law Com No 98 (1985), paras 4.10–4.24.

[428] Eg *Re Ullee* (1885) 53 LT 711 at 712; *Lendrum v Chakravarti* 1929 SLT 96 at 99 (overruled on another point by *Lendrum v Chakravarti* 1937 SC 390).

[429] *Kenward v Kenward* [1951] P 124 at 145; *Radwan v Radwan (No 2)* [1973] Fam 35, [1972] 3 All ER 1026.

[430] *Kaur v Ginder* (1958) 13 DLR (2d) 465. In *Sara v Sara* (1962) 31 DLR (2d) 566, varied on other grounds 36 DLR (2d) 499, it seems to have been assumed that capacity by the law of the place of celebration is all that is required.

[431] Supra, p 920 et seq.

[432] The reference in *Kaur v Ginder*, supra, to the law of the place of celebration was on the basis that power to enter a polygamous marriage was more an issue of form than capacity.

[433] [1968] P 564, supra, p 926.

[434] Thus avoiding a choice on the general question of capacity to marry between the ante-nuptial domiciliary laws of both parties and the law of the intended matrimonial home; see supra, p 896.

[435] [1968] P 564 at 576–577; but cf *A-G of Ceylon v Reid* [1965] AC 720.

If the law of the place of celebration is rejected, the choice used to lie between the law of the intended matrimonial home and the law of the domicile, and, as has been seen, there was authority in support of both. The fullest fairly recent discussion of the choice of law issue is to be found in *Radwan v Radwan (No 2)*[436] which supports the intended matrimonial home approach. Here, CUMMING-BRUCE J applied the law of Egypt to determine the issue of capacity to enter an actually polygamous marriage celebrated in the Egyptian Consulate General in Paris between a domiciled Egyptian and a domiciled Englishwoman, the parties intending to live in Egypt, which in fact they did. It was the judge's considered view that the law to determine capacity to enter a polygamous marriage, if no other question of capacity, should be that of the intended matrimonial home.

This decision was greeted with widespread,[437] though not unanimous,[438] criticism—primarily for its rejection of the dual domicile approach and for indicating that a special capacity rule in the case of polygamous marriages can be justified.[439] There is certainly a weight of authority supporting the view that capacity to contract a polygamous marriage is to be determined by the law of the ante-nuptial domicile,[440] whether the marriage is actually[441] or potentially[442] polygamous. Two further factors support this approach. In a number of cases since 1973 in which the validity of a polygamous marriage has arisen, the court or tribunal has simply applied the law of the domicile without any consideration of whether that country was the same as that of the intended matrimonial home.[443] The second factor is that Parliament seems also to have assumed that the dual domicile test was the law.[444] It is necessary now to look more closely at the current statutory provisions.

(ii) Statutory provisions

In the context of capacity to enter a polygamous marriage, it is necessary first to consider sections 11 and 14 of the Matrimonial Causes Act 1973, which in their original form provided as follows:

> 11 A marriage celebrated after 31 July 1971 shall be void on the following grounds only, that is to say . . .
> (b) that at the time of the marriage either party was already lawfully married . . .

---

[436] [1973] Fam 35.

[437] Karsten (1973) 36 MLR 291; Pearl [1973] CLJ 43; Wade (1973) 22 ICLQ 571.

[438] See Jaffey (1978) 41 MLR 38; Stone [1983] Fam Law 76; *Hassan v Hassan* [1978] 1 NZLR 385 at 389–390.

[439] This opposition was not unexpected; see [1973] Fam 35 at 54, and see supra, p 901.

[440] It may well be that the decision in *Re Bethell* (1988) 38 Ch D 220 can only be justified on the ground that the "husband" had no capacity by English law, the law of the domicile, to enter into a polygamous marriage. In *Risk v Risk* [1951] P 50, the court declined jurisdiction to consider this issue on the ground that the marriage, whether valid or not, was polygamous.

[441] *Crowe v Kader* [1968] WAR 122; *Ishiodu v Entry Clearance Officer, Lagos* [1975] Imm AR 56; *R v Immigration Appeal Tribunal, ex p Asfar Jan* [1995] Imm AR 440; Social Security Decisions Nos R (S) 2/92; R (G) 4/93.

[442] *Ali v Ali* [1968] P 564 at 576–577; *Afza Mussarat v Secretary of State for the Home Department* [1972] Imm AR 45; cf Hartley (1969) 32 MLR 155, 158–160.

[443] Eg *Hussain v Hussain* [1983] Fam 26; *Zahra v Visa Officer, Islamabad* [1979–80] Imm AR 48; *Rokeya Begum v Entry Clearance Officer, Dacca* [1983] Imm AR 163; National Insurance Decision No R (G) 3/75; and see Social Security Decision No R (G) 1/95.

[444] Matrimonial Causes Act 1973, s 11(d); Private International Law (Miscellaneous Provisions) Act 1995, s 5; and s 8(2), Sch, para 2 of the 1995 Act also amends the 1973 Act.

(d) in the case of a polygamous marriage entered into outside England and Wales, that either party was at the time of the marriage domiciled in England and Wales.

For the purposes of paragraph (d) of this subsection a marriage may be polygamous although at its inception neither party has any spouse additional to the other.

. . .

14 Where, apart from this Act, any matter affecting the validity of a marriage would fall to be determined (in accordance with the rules of private international law) by reference to the law of a country outside England and Wales, nothing in section 11 . . . above shall—

(a) preclude the determination of that matter as aforesaid; or
(b) require the application to the marriage of the grounds . . . there mentioned except so far as applicable in accordance with those rules.

Two rather different issues arise. The first is whether, in relation to marriages celebrated after 31 July 1971, these provisions embody a choice of law rule; and the second is to determine the effect of the provisions in cases to which they apply. As to the first issue, although as has been seen[445] some recent decisions have proceeded on the basis that section 11 of the 1973 Act applies whenever one party is domiciled in England, that approach was specifically rejected by CUMMING-BRUCE J in *Radwan v Radwan (No 2)*.[446] In considering the statutory predecessors of sections 11 and 14,[447] the judge concluded that the Law Commission,[448] the government and Parliament had laboured under a misapprehension as to the common law rules on capacity.[449] His conclusion that the choice of law rule is that the law of the intended matrimonial home should apply has the following effect. Section 11 would not apply in those cases where the parties did not intend to set up a matrimonial home in England, as was the position in *Radwan* itself. This was because section 14 of the 1973 Act expressly preserved the application of the substantive law of another country held to be applicable under our rules of private international law.[450] Put another way, section 11(d) could only apply to invalidate a marriage if one party was domiciled in England *and* the parties intended to live in England. Of course, if *Radwan* was not followed, section 11(d) would apply whenever one party was domiciled in England, irrespective of the intended matrimonial home.

We must now turn to examine the second issue, namely the effect of section 11 in those polygamous marriage cases where validity *is* governed by English law. From 1973 until 1983, anxiety had been expressed over the impact of section 11(d) in the following type of circumstance.

An immigrant to the United Kingdom from Pakistan becomes domiciled in England and then returns to Pakistan to marry, for the first time, in Moslem form bringing his new wife back to England with him. This marriage was regarded as

---

[445] Supra, p 928.
[446] [1973] Fam 35.
[447] Namely, s 4 of the Matrimonial Proceedings (Polygamous Marriages) Act 1972 and s 4 of the Nullity of Marriage Act 1971.
[448] The predecessor of s 11 is based on Law Com No 42 (1971).
[449] [1973] Fam 35 at 52.
[450] And see the Private International Law (Miscellaneous Provisions) Act 1995, s 5(2).

potentially polygamous with the result, so it was thought, that the marriage was void under section 11(d)—a conclusion which was much criticised.[451]

Had the Pakistani man been only resident, and not domiciled, in England, his marriage would have been valid[452] and, indeed, would become monogamous in character on his acquisition of an English domicile.[453] Furthermore, if the marriage had taken place in England, being monogamous in fact and in character, it would also have been valid.

Sustained criticism of the effect of section 11(d) in the case of a potentially polygamous marriage prompted the Law Commission to consider the case for reform. The day that its Working Paper was due to be sent for printing,[454] the Court of Appeal in *Hussain v Hussain*[455] cast a wholly new light on the effect of section 11 of the 1973 Act. The facts were as follows:

> The husband and wife married in Pakistan in 1979. They were Moslems and they married in a form appropriate for polygamous marriages. At all times the marriage was in fact monogamous. At the time of the marriage the husband was domiciled in England and the wife in Pakistan. When, on the subsequent breakdown of the marriage, the wife petitioned in England for judicial separation, the husband argued that the marriage was void by reason of section 11(d) in that it was polygamous in nature and that he was domiciled in England at the relevant time.

The Court of Appeal rejected the husband's argument and held the marriage to be valid. In so doing, it met many of the criticisms of section 11(d) and achieved a good deal, though not all, of the reform sought by the Law Commission; but the Court also created a range of further problems and turned on its head the law as it had been assumed to be for a decade by lawyers, immigrants and government officials alike.[456]

The reasoning of the Court of Appeal was as follows. Section 11(d) prevented an English domiciliary from entering a polygamous marriage, whether actually or potentially polygamous, but "a marriage can only be potentially polygamous if at least one of the spouses has the capacity to marry a second spouse".[457] However, in the case of a person domiciled in England, there was no capacity to enter an actually polygamous marriage because section 11(b) of the 1973 Act rendered a person who is actually married incapable of marrying a second spouse.[458] On this reasoning, the marriage in question was valid. It was not to be regarded as potentially polygamous, and thus falling within section 11(d), because the wife was incapable, under the Moslem law of Pakistan, of marrying a second husband, and the husband was incapable under English law, namely section 11(b) of the 1973 Act, of marrying a second wife.

---

[451] See Hartley (1971) 34 MLR 305, 306–307; Cretney (1972) 116 Sol Jo 654; Poulter (1976) 25 ICLQ 475, 503–508; James (1979) 42 MLR 533, 536.

[452] Eg *Ishiodu v Entry Clearance Officer, Lagos* [1975] Imm AR 56.

[453] Supra, p 923 et seq.

[454] Working Paper No 83 (1982), para 1.3.

[455] [1983] Fam 26.

[456] Law Commission Working Paper No 83 (1982), paras 4.3–4.39.

[457] [1983] Fam 26 at 32.

[458] The Court of Appeal assumed that s 11(d) of the 1973 Act applies to all English domiciliaries, without examining the claims of the intended matrimonial home rule laid down in *Radwan v Radwan (No 2)* [1973] Fam 35; and see *R v Junaid Khan* (1987) 84 Cr App Rep 44.

Whilst the actual decision of the Court of Appeal was welcomed, the process of reasoning by which it was reached and the implications to be drawn from it were widely criticised.[459] It only applied to marriages celebrated after 31 July 1971 because that was the limit of the scope of section 11. This meant that the validity of earlier polygamous marriages was governed by the common law under which a marriage in circumstances similar to *Hussain* would be void. Furthermore, even in the case of a marriage after 31 July 1971, it would be void if the position of the parties in *Hussain* had been reversed, ie the wife was domiciled in England and the husband in Pakistan. This was because the marriage would then be regarded as polygamous in nature, and thus within section 11(d), as the husband was capable under his personal law of marrying a second wife.[460]

This unsatisfactory state of the law on capacity to enter a polygamous marriage led the Law Commission to recommend[461] further reform in the wake of *Hussain*. These proposals were implemented by Part II of the Private International Law (Miscellaneous Provisions) Act 1995. The result is that section 11 of the Matrimonial Causes Act 1973 is amended so as to limit its operation to actually polygamous marriages.[462] Furthermore, section 5(1) of the 1995 Act provides that:

> A marriage entered into outside England and Wales between parties neither of whom is already married is not void under the law of England and Wales on the ground that it is entered into under a law which permits polygamy and that either party is domiciled in England and Wales.

The impact of these changes is that both men and women domiciled in England have capacity under English law to enter a marriage abroad which, though polygamous in form, is in fact monogamous. Two caveats must be expressed. The first is that these changes do not affect the determination of the validity of a marriage to which the law of another country is to be applied under English rules of private international law.[463] The second is that there is no change in the rule that there is no capacity under English law to enter an actually polygamous marriage.[464] The changes are also subject to a number of limitations. Although the changes have retrospective effect[465] and will, therefore, retrospectively validate some marriages thought to be invalid, there will be no such validation where a party to the marriage in question has entered a later marriage which was valid under the law as it was at the time it was celebrated,[466] or which is validated by the changes in the 1995 Act.[467] The retrospective effect of section 5 is also limited so as not to affect entitlement under the will or intestacy of a person dying before the provision came into effect, nor similarly to affect benefits, pensions, allowances, or tax, or succession to a dignity or title of honour.[468]

---

[459] Carter (1982) 53 BYBIL 298; Briggs (1983) 32 ICLQ 737; Pearl [1983] CLJ 26; Schuz (1983) 46 MLR 653; Poulter (1983) 13 Fam Law 72.

[460] Eg Social Security Decision No R (SB) 17/84.

[461] Law Com No 146; Scot Law Com No 96 (1985), Pt II.

[462] 1995 Act, Sch, para 2(2).

[463] Ibid, s 5(2); and see Law Com No 146; Scot Law Com No 96 (1985), paras 2.1–2.3.

[464] See Law Com No 146; Scot Law Com No 96 (1985), paras 4.2–4.8. Cf *Azad v Entry Clearance Officer, Dhaka* [2001] Imm AR 318, per JACOB J, at [4].

[465] 1995 Act, s 6(1).

[466] Ibid, s 6(2).

[467] Ibid, s 6(3)–(5).

[468] Ibid, s 6(6).

(f) Recognition of polygamous marriages in England

Although it is not possible to enter into a valid polygamous marriage in England, such a marriage abroad can be regarded as valid provided it has been validly created in the eyes of English private international law.[469] In short it must have been contracted between parties of full capacity and in accordance with the formal requirements of the law of the place of celebration.[470] The issue then arises as to the degree of recognition to be afforded by an English court to such a valid polygamous marriage.

Polygamous marriages are now recognised for a wide variety of purposes. In *Baindail v Baindail*,[471] Lord GREENE MR stressed that, since the status of a person depends on his personal law, the status of husband and wife conferred on the parties to a polygamous marriage by the law of their domicile must be accepted and acted on in other countries. Although he was careful to add that it must be accepted for certain purposes only, and not for all, the present state of the law is that a polygamous marriage is recognised for most purposes. The balance of definition has tipped from defining those instances where, exceptionally, such a marriage will be recognised to defining those few instances where it may not. A variety of situations needs to be considered.

The position used to be that neither party to a polygamous marriage could invoke "the remedies, the adjudication or the relief" given either by the High Court,[472] or by magistrates' courts,[473] in the exercise of their matrimonial jurisdiction. However, such matrimonial or declaratory relief may now be granted, under section 47 of the Matrimonial Causes Act 1973,[474] whether the marriage is actually or potentially polygamous.[475]

The English courts are prepared to recognise the validity of a polygamous marriage[476] as being a later marriage. This means that the second "spouse" is entitled to a nullity decree on the grounds of bigamy.[477] It might be thought that, in such a case, the spouse who "married" twice would also be guilty of the crime of bigamy. It has now been decided, however, in a lower court,[478] and approved by the Court of Appeal,[479] that a party to an existing polygamous marriage is not "married" for the purpose of founding a criminal

---

[469] See now the Private International Law (Miscellaneous Provisions) Act 1995, s 5(2).

[470] Proper investigation ought to be made by the court as to the validity of a particular marriage, and as to the status of an alleged second wife: *Ramsamy v Babar* [2003] EWCA Civ 1252, [2005] 1 FLR 113 (regarding the alleged second wife's occupation of property, as trespasser or spouse occupying the matrimonial home).

[471] [1946] P 122 at 127–128.

[472] *Hyde v Hyde* (1866) LR 1 P & D 130.

[473] *Sowa v Sowa* [1961] P 70.

[474] As amended by the Private International Law (Miscellaneous Provisions) Act 1995, s 8(2), Sch, para 2. See, eg, *El Fadl v El Fadl* [2000] 1 FLR 175; and *M v M (Divorce: Jurisdiction: Validity of Marriage)* [2001] 2 FLR 6.

[475] Infra, p 942.

[476] But the Irish courts have held that it cannot constitute a "common law" marriage: *Conlon v Mohamed* [1989] ILRM 523.

[477] [1946] P 122; and see *Srini Vasan v Srini Vasan* [1946] P 67; *Hashmi v Hashmi* [1972] Fam 36; *Alfonso-Brown v Milwood* [2006] EWHC 642, [2006] 2 FLR 265, per SINGER J, at [3]; Hartley (1967) 16 ICLQ 680, 691–694.

[478] *R v Sarwan Singh* [1962] 3 All ER 612; Polonsky [1971] Crim LR 401.

[479] *R v Sagoo* [1975] QB 885; Carter (1974–1975) 47 BYBIL 374; Morse (1976) 25 ICLQ 229. The Court of Appeal held that *R v Sarwan Singh*, supra, was wrongly decided, but only on the ground that no consideration had been given as to whether the marriage had become monogamous. The general principle was approved that "the marriage which is to be the foundation for a prosecution for bigamy must be a monogamous marriage": [1975] QB 885 at 889.

charge of bigamy against him. These decisions create an unfortunate distinction between the civil and the criminal law conceptions of bigamy.[480]

Turning to succession,[481] it seems fairly clear that the children of both a potentially and an actually polygamous marriage can succeed to property in England.[482] The only real doubt[483] on the issue of succession by children concerns whether a child of a polygamous marriage can succeed to a title of honour, or as an "heir" to real property or to an entailed interest.[484] This problem was discussed by Lord MAUGHAM in *The Sinha Peerage Claim*,[485] which concerned succession to a title of honour. In fact, the marriage of the claimant's father, celebrated in polygamous form, was held to have become monogamous by change of religion.[486] In holding that the claimant could succeed to the title, Lord MAUGHAM declined to express a view on succession as "heir" or to entails. It seems, however, that he was primarily concerned with problems which could arise in the case of an actually polygamous marriage: "If there were several wives, the son of a second or third wife might be the claimant to a dignity to the exclusion of a later born son of the first wife. Our law as to heirship has provided no means of settling such questions as these."[487] These problems relate only to actually polygamous marriages and it seems safe to assume, with the Law Commission,[488] that although a child of an actually polygamous marriage cannot succeed as "heir", no such disability attaches to the child of a potentially polygamous marriage.[489]

In the case of intestate succession by the widow of a potentially polygamous marriage, there is Privy Council authority in favour of her being able to succeed.[490] Such English authority as there is supports the view that such a widow would also be able to succeed

---

[480] Celebration of a "marriage" in England in polygamous form, in a private house, is not considered to be a celebration of a "marriage" within the meaning of s 75(2) of the Marriage Act 1949, under which it is an offence knowingly and willingly to solemnise a marriage in an unregistered building: *R v Bham* [1966] 1 QB 159; and see *R v Ali Mohamed* [1964] 2 QB 350 n. On the other hand, it might be noted that the parties to a valid polygamous marriage are married for the purposes of the crime of conspiracy so that the spouses are unable to conspire together: *Mawji v R* [1957] AC 126. If it is invalid it is of no effect in the law of evidence: *R v Junaid Khan* (1987) 84 Cr App Rep 44.

[481] Though the determination of legitimacy is now of very limited relevance (infra, Chapter 25), it might be noted that children of a valid potentially polygamous marriage are to be regarded as legitimate: *Sinha Peerage Claim* (1939) 171 Lords Journal 350, [1946] 1 All ER 348 n; *Baindail v Baindail* [1946] P 122 at 127–128. It would also appear that children of an actually polygamous marriage are to be regarded as legitimate: *Hashmi v Hashmi* [1972] Fam 36; and see *Yuen Tse v Minister of Employment and Immigration* (1983) 32 RFL (2d) 274. For criticism of *Hashmi*, see Goldberg and Lowe (1972) 35 MLR 430; Carter (1971) 45 BYBIL 413, 414.

[482] Cf *Bamgbose v Daniel* [1955] AC 107; and see National Insurance Decision No R (G) 11/53. In *Re Bethell* (1888) 38 Ch D 220, such a child was unable to succeed, but this is probably because the polygamous marriage there would not be regarded in England as a valid marriage, given the husband's incapacity by his domiciliary law, supra, p 922; cf Hartley (1969) 32 MLR 155, 171–172.

[483] See Law Commission Working Paper No 83 (1982), para 4.42.

[484] Cf Dicey, Morris and Collins, para 17-194.

[485] [1946] 1 All ER 348 n.

[486] Supra, p 923 et seq.

[487] [1946] 1 All ER 348 n at 349.

[488] Law Com No 146, Scot Law Com No 96 (1985), paras 3.5–3.6.

[489] It should be noted that, under s 6(6) of the Private International Law (Miscellaneous Provisions) Act 1995, the changes introduced by section 5, supra, p 931 do not, in the case of marriages entered into before that section came into force, affect succession rights, including succession to any dignity or title of honour.

[490] *Coleman v Shang* [1961] AC 481.

under the Administration of Estates Act 1925.[491] There appears to be no good reason for not applying a similar rule in the case of succession by the wives of an actually polygamous marriage,[492] and this approach is supported by *Re Sehota*.[493] Here the deceased husband was validly polygamously married to two wives. He left the whole of his estate to the second wife and the first wife applied successfully for reasonable provision as a "wife" out of the estate, under the Inheritance (Provision for Family and Dependants) Act 1975.[494]

Polygamous marriages are recognised for the purpose of determining other property rights. In *Shahnaz v Rizwan*[495] a Moslem woman, whose potentially polygamous marriage celebrated in India had been validly dissolved, was held entitled to recover deferred dower from her former husband. The agreement recorded in the marriage certificate placed the husband under a contractual obligation to pay a certain sum by way of dower in the event of a divorce. WINN J was careful to emphasise[496] that the wife's right arose not out of the relationship of husband and wife, but out of a contract made in contemplation and in consideration of a marriage that was lawful in the eyes of English law. There is statutory recognition of actually and potentially polygamous marriages for the purposes of the protection granted to a spouse by Part IV of the Family Law Act 1996;[497] and it has been held that the summary procedure, under section 17 of the Married Women's Property Act 1882, for determining property disputes between husband and wife extends to polygamous marriages.[498]

Statutory recognition of polygamy is also provided by social security legislation. Regulations made under or preserved by the Social Security Contributions and Benefits Act 1992[499] now govern the present position in relation to benefits falling within these Acts, eg widow's benefit, maternity benefit and child benefit. They allow a valid polygamous marriage to be treated as a monogamous marriage if it has either always been actually monogamous or for any day throughout which it was, in fact, monogamous.[500]

---

[491] In *Re Sehota* [1978] 1 WLR 1506, it was suggested (at 1511) that questions of succession had never fallen within the ambit of the rule in *Hyde v Hyde* (1866) LR 1 P & D 130; and see *Chaudhry v Chaudhry* [1976] Fam 148 at 152.

[492] See *Cheang Thye Phin v Tan Ah Loy* [1920] AC 369; cf *The Six Widows' Case* (1908) 12 Straits Settlements LR 120; though it must be admitted that there might be difficulty with distribution of the personal chattels.

[493] [1978] 1 WLR 1506.

[494] Contrast the result in *Gandhi v Patel* [2002] 1 FLR 603—a Hindu marriage ceremony in London amounted to a "non-marriage", and the parties thereto had not entered into it in good faith with regard to the need to satisfy English law, in particular s 25(4) of the Inheritance (Provision for Family and Dependants) Act 1975; see PARK J, at [28].

[495] [1965] 1 QB 390; and see *Qureshi v Qureshi* [1972] Fam 173.

[496] Because of the then existing inability of the court to grant matrimonial relief in the case of polygamous marriages.

[497] S 63(5).

[498] *Chaudhry v Chaudhry* [1976] Fam 148—a case of a potentially polygamous marriage.

[499] Ss 121 (1)(b), 147(5), as amended by the Private International Law (Miscellaneous Provisions) Act 1995, s 8(2), Sch, para 4, and the Civil Partnership Act 2004, Sch 24(3), para 40. The 1992 Act is a consolidation statute and regulations made under its forerunners, the Social Security Act 1975 and the Child Benefit Act 1976, continue in effect. See also State Pension Credit Act 2002, s 12; Tax Credits Act 2002, s 43; Age-Related Payments Act 2004, s 8(2); Welfare Reform Act 2007, Sch 1, para 6(7); SI 2006/213, reg 74(3); SI 2006/215, Pt 1, reg 2; SI 2007/688, Sch 2, para 1; and SI 2007/719, reg 2(7).

[500] SI 1975/561, regs 1(2), 2(2); and SI 2006/223, reg 35; and see National Insurance Decision Nos R (G) 2/75; R (G) 3/75; Social Security Decision Nos R (S) 2/92; R (G) 4/93; R (G) 1/95; *R v Department of Health*,

This means that when a marriage becomes monogamous through death or divorce or until it ceases to be monogamous by reason of a second valid marriage there is a right to qualification for these social security benefits. If the marriage is actually polygamous at the relevant times no widowed mother's allowance is payable.[501] In the case of income support, however, a crucial factor is the nature of the relationship between a man and a woman who are members of the same household, rather than whether they are validly married. The result is that the relevant legislation[502] extends to cases of actually polygamous marriages.[503]

An issue arose in *Azad v Entry Clearance Officer, Dhaka*[504] concerning the status of a child of an actually polygamous marriage in the context of an application for a right of abode under the British Nationality Act 1981.[505]

> The appellant asserted that he had acquired British citizenship as a result of the polygamous marriage in Bangladesh of his father, a British citizen and English domiciliary, and mother (the third wife of his father), resident in Bangladesh. The claim to British citizenship depended upon the applicant being the legitimate son of his father, which, in turn, rested upon the meaning and application of section 1(1) of the Legitimacy Act 1976.[506]

The Court of Appeal concluded that it was clear that the validity of the (third) marriage, for the purposes of the 1976 Act, was to be measured by English law alone (by which it was void, the father, as an English domiciliary, lacking capacity to contract such a marriage), and not by the Bangladeshi law of the place where the marriage was celebrated (according to which the marriage was valid).

The question of the application of tax legislation to polygamous marriages came before the courts in *Nabi v Heaton*[507] where the facts were these:

> The taxpayer claimed relief on the ground that his wife was wholly maintained by him[508] from 1970 to 1976. He had come to England from Pakistan in 1965 and married his first wife in England in 1968. They soon separated and in 1969, whilst still domiciled in Pakistan, he there married his second wife. She lived in Pakistan, maintained by him from England, until she came to join him here in 1975 when he divorced his first wife. The allowance was claimed in respect of the second wife.

---

ex p Misra [1996] 1 FLR 129. A similar approach is taken in the area of immigration control: *R v Immigration Appeal Tribunal, ex p Hasna Begum* [1995] Imm AR 249.

[501] *Bibi v Chief Adjudication Officer* [1998] 1 FLR 375. Cf *R (Shamsun Nahar) v The Social Security Commissioners* [2001] EWHC Admin 1049, [2002] 1 FLR 670

[502] Social Security Act 1986.

[503] See generally Wikeley, Ogus and Barendt, *The Law of Social Security* (2002) 5th edn; and see *Iman Din v National Assistance Board* [1967] 2 QB 213.

[504] [2001] Imm AR 318.

[505] Cf *R (Shamsun Nahar) v The Social Security Commissioners* [2001] EWHC Admin 1049, [2002] 1 FLR 670; and *SB (Bangladesh) v Secretary of State for the Home Department* [2007] EWCA Civ 28, [2007] Fam Law 494—concerning a polygamously married spouse's application for indefinite leave to remain in the United Kingdom as a dependent relative of a person present and settled in the United Kingdom.

[506] As amended by the Family Law Reform Act 1987, s 28.

[507] [1981] 1 WLR 1052, appeal allowed by consent [1983] 1 WLR 626; see Carter (1981) 52 BYBIL 322.

[508] Income and Corporation Taxes Act 1970, s 8(1); see now Income and Corporation Taxes Act 1988, s 257(1), as amended by the Income Tax Act 2007, Sch 1(1), para 29(6).

Although logically the first question to ask was whether the second marriage was to be regarded in England as valid.[509] VINELOTT J felt it unnecessary to answer it because he concluded that the taxpayer failed whether or not the second marriage was a valid actually polygamous marriage.[510] The reason for his conclusion was that he decided that reference to "his wife" in the Income and Corporation Taxes Act 1970 had to be construed in the singular.[511] Although it was the practice of the Revenue to grant the relief claimed in the case of potentially polygamous marriages,[512] VINELOTT J's decision would deny the relief in respect of any wife in the case of a valid actually polygamous marriage. When the taxpayer appealed, the Crown obviously had second thoughts, accepting that the appeal should be allowed by consent.[513] From this, one may conclude that, in practice, the relief will now be extended to all wives.

Other illustrations can be provided of the acceptance of polygamous marriages in English law. For example, it seems generally agreed[514] that a wife, or wives, of a polygamous marriage should be able to claim under the Fatal Accidents Act 1976 on the basis of dependence on the deceased husband. Finally, one of the most striking examples of recognition of the marital status conferred by a polygamous marriage is provided by *Mohamed v Knott*:[515]

> A Nigerian domiciled in Nigeria married a 13-year-old girl there according to Moslem law. This marriage was potentially polygamous and was valid under Nigerian law. Three months later they both came to England and a complaint was made against the husband that the girl was in need of care and protection within the meaning of section 2 of the Children and Young Persons Act 1963. The justices refused to recognise the marriage and concluded that a 13-year-old girl living with a man twice her age was in need of care and protection.

The Divisional Court differed and decided that this was a valid though potentially polygamous marriage, which should be recognised as conferring the status of a "wife" on the girl.[516]

A number of general conclusions may now be drawn as to the recognition afforded today by English law to polygamous marriages. The wheel has almost come full circle since 1866.[517] Instead of such marriages, whether actually or potentially polygamous, being denied recognition for all purposes, they are now widely recognised. The general pattern of legislative interpretation over the last few decades has been a liberal one, so that the term "wife" is generally taken to include the wives of an actually polygamous marriage. There is now a presumption in favour of the recognition of a polygamous marriage unless a good contrary reason can be shown. This has led to the suggestion that the rule in *Hyde v Hyde* has been entirely abolished.[518] If that is to be taken to mean that all *actually*

---

[509] Supra, p 927 et seq.

[510] [1981] 1 WLR 1052 at 1056–1057.

[511] Ibid at 1057–1059.

[512] Ibid at 1059.

[513] [1983] 1 WLR 626.

[514] Law Com No 42 (1971), para 124; Hartley (1969) 32 MLR 155, 169–170.

[515] [1969] 1 QB 1; Karsten (1969) 32 MLR 212.

[516] Whilst the court considered that an order under the 1963 Act could be made in respect of a married woman, it declined to make one in this case.

[517] *Hyde v Hyde* (1866) LR 1 P & D 130.

[518] *Re Sehota* [1978] 1 WLR 1506 at 1511.

polygamous marriages have the same effect and recognition as monogamous ones, it is too extravagant a statement. Obvious continuing areas of difference are capacity to marry[519] and the rules as to social security benefits.

The final issue is whether there are, or should be, any differences between monogamous and *potentially* polygamous marriages. The Law Commission identified[520] only two possible differences—the then rules on capacity to marry and on succession as an "heir" to real property, an entailed interest or a title of honour. The first difference has disappeared with the implementation of the Law Commission's recommendations in the Private International Law (Miscellaneous Provisions) Act 1995.[521] The second difference is more apparent than real because the restrictions on succession would seem to be limited to the children of actually polygamous marriages.[522] We can agree with the conclusion of the Law Commission that, provided a marriage remains actually monogamous, there should be no difference between a marriage celebrated in a monogamous form and a potentially polygamous one. The recent statutory changes now mean that this is, in fact, the law with the consequence that all references to potentially polygamous marriages can safely be removed from the statute book.[523] The concept is dead.[524]

6. CIVIL PARTNERSHIP AND DE FACTO COHABITATION[525]

(a) Introduction

Section 11(c) of the Matrimonial Causes Act 1973 provides that a marriage shall be void on the ground that the parties are not respectively male and female.[526] However, since 21 December 2005, by virtue of the Civil Partnership Act 2004, same sex partners have been able to register their relationship, in England and Wales, Scotland and Northern Ireland, as a civil partnership, a new form of regulated relationship bearing specified legal and personal consequences.[527] The 2004 Act is in eight Parts and has thirty Schedules. Part 1, section 1, describes a civil partnership as a relationship between two people of the same sex which is formed when they register as civil partners of each other in England and Wales under Part 2 of the Act; in Scotland under Part 3; in Northern Ireland under Part 4; outside the United Kingdom under an Order in Council made under Chapter 1 of Part 5 (registration at British consulates etc,[528] or by armed forces personnel[529]); or

---

[519] English domiciliaries continue to be incapable of contracting actually polygamous marriages, supra, p 931.

[520] Law Com No 146, Scot Law Com No 96 (1985), para 3.5.

[521] Ss 5, 6, supra, p 931.

[522] Supra, p 933.

[523] Law Com No 145, Scot Law Com No 96 (1985), paras 3.6–3.10.

[524] As it seems to be in the USA: *Royal v Cudahy Packing Co* (1922) 190 NW 427 at 428.

[525] See Swennen, "Atypical Families in EU (Private International) Family Law", Chapter 12 in Meeusen, Pertegas, Straetmans and Swennen (eds), *International Family Law for the European Union* (2007).

[526] See also *Bellinger v Bellinger* [2003] UKHL 21, [2003] 2 AC 467; *KB v NHS Pensions Agency* [2004] ECR I-541; *J v C (Void Marriage: Status of Children)* [2006] EWCA Civ 551, [2006] 2 FLR 1098; and *Wilkinson v Kitzinger* [2007] EWHC 2022 (Fam), [2007] 1 FLR 295.

[527] See also Civil Partnership Act 2004 (Overseas Relationships) Order, SI 2005/3135; and Civil Partnership (Jurisdiction and Recognition of Judgments) Regulations, SI 2005/3334.

[528] See supra, p 885, n 70.

[529] See supra, p 886, n 87.

which is registered as an equivalent overseas relationship in accordance with Chapter 2 of Part 5. Section 1(3) provides that a civil partnership ends only on death, dissolution or annulment. There follows, in this chapter, consideration of the private international law aspects of formation of civil partnerships, eligibility to register a partnership, and recognition of overseas relationships akin to civil partnership. Other relevant topics, including the dissolution and annulment of civil partnerships, will be addressed at relevant points throughout the book.

(b) Civil partnerships registered in England

A civil partnership registered in England must comply with the registration provisions (including provisions concerning formation, eligibility and parental, etc consent) set out in Chapter 1 of Part 2 of the Act.[530] Two people are to be regarded as having registered as civil partners of each other once each party has signed the civil partnership document at the invitation of, and in the presence of, a civil partnership registrar, and in the presence of each other and two witnesses.[531] No religious procedure is to be used during the officiation by the civil partnership registrar at the signing of the civil partnership document.[532] There are four procedures by which a civil partnership may be registered in England, each having its own particular rules.[533] Section 20 provides modified procedures for use in cases where a party who is resident in England intends to register a civil partnership in England with another party who is not so resident.[534]

As regards eligibility, two people are not eligible to register in England as civil partners of each other if (a) they are not of the same sex; (b) either of them is already a civil partner or lawfully married; (c) either of them is aged under 16; or (d) they are within the prohibited degrees of relationship.[535] The consent of appropriate persons[536] is required before a person under 18 years of age and another person may register in England as civil partners of each other.[537]

(c) Overseas relationships treated as civil partnerships

Chapter 2 of Part 5 of the Act concerns overseas relationships which are treated in the United Kingdom as equivalent to civil partnership. An overseas relationship is defined as one which (a) is either a specified relationship[538] or a relationship which meets the general conditions[539] laid down in the Act, and (b) is registered (whether before or after

---

[530] See also SI 2005/3176.

[531] S 2(1).

[532] S 2(5).

[533] S 5(1): the standard procedure (s 8); the procedure for house-bound persons (s 18); the procedure for detained persons (s 19); and the special procedure (for cases where a person is seriously ill and not expected to recover: s 21).

[534] S 20(2) where the other party resides in Scotland; (3) where s/he resides in Northern Ireland; and (4) where s/he is a member of HM forces serving abroad. See also ss 97, 150 and 239.

[535] S 3(1), and Sch 1. See *M v Secretary of State for Work and Pensions* [2006] 2 AC 91.

[536] See Sch 2, Pt 1.

[537] S 3(2), and Sch 2.

[538] S 213(1); and see Sch 20 and SI 2005/3135.

[539] S 214: that, under the relevant law, being the law of the country or territory in which the relationship is registered, including its rules of private international law, (a) the relationship may not be entered into if either of the parties is already a party to a relationship of that kind or lawfully married; (b) the relationship is of indeterminate

the passing of the Act) with a responsible authority in a country or territory outside the United Kingdom, by two people (i) who under the relevant law[540] are of the same sex at the time of registration of the relationship;[541] and (ii) neither of whom is already a civil partner or lawfully married.[542]

As a general rule, two people are to be treated as having formed a civil partnership as a result of having registered an overseas relationship if, under the law of the country or territory where the relationship is registered,[543] they (a) had capacity to enter into the relationship,[544] and (b) met all requirements necessary to ensure the formal validity of the relationship. If an overseas relationship has been registered by a person who was, at the relevant time,[545] domiciled in England and Wales, the two people concerned are not to be treated as having formed a civil partnership if, at that time, (a) either of them was under 16 years of age; or they would have been within the prohibited degrees of relationship under Part 1 of Schedule 1 to the Act had they been intending to register their relationship in England.[546] Accordingly, an English domiciliary cannot evade the provisions of his/her personal law as to eligibility by registering an overseas relationship. Moreover, two people are not to be treated as having formed a civil partnership as a result of entering into an overseas relationship if it would be manifestly contrary to public policy to recognise the capacity, under the law of the country or territory where the relationship is registered,[547] of one or both of them to enter into the relationship.[548]

(d) De facto cohabitation[549]

During the passage through Parliament of the Civil Partnership Act 2004, the House of Lords noted the lack of legal remedies under English law for couples who live together but do not marry or, in the case of same sex couples, register a civil partnership. This subject

---

duration; and (c) the effect of entering into it is that the parties are (i) treated as a couple either generally or for specified purposes, or (ii) treated as married.

[540] Meaning the law of the country or territory where the relationship is registered, including its rules of private international law: s 212(2). See, on renvoi, supra, Chapter 5.

[541] However, two people are not to be treated as having formed a civil partnership as a result of having registered an overseas relationship if, at the critical time, they were not of the same sex under United Kingdom law: s 216. See also Gender Recognition Act 2004.

[542] S 212.

[543] Including its rules of private international law: s 212(2). Cf *Taczanowska v Taczanowski* [1957] P 301. See supra, pp 890–891.

[544] See also ss 240 and 241 (certificates of no impediment to overseas relationships). The requirement of capacity according to the law of the country or territory where the relationship is registered is notably different from the current choice of law rule regarding capacity to marry, which, being characterised as a matter of essential validity, is governed by the dual domicile theory. See supra, p 898. See also Crawford and Carruthers, para 11-37.

[545] S 215(2): the time when the overseas relationship is registered under the relevant law as having been entered into; except where the overseas relationship is registered under the relevant law as having been entered into before 5 December 2005, in which case, the relevant time is 5 December 2005 (SI 2005/3175).

[546] S 217(2).

[547] Including its rules of private international law: s 212(2).

[548] S 218.

[549] Ie Cohabiting relationships (usually of a sexual rather than platonic nature, where the parties are living together "as if they were husband and wife", meaning that shared living arrangements between parent and adult child, or between siblings, or among friends, for economic or other reasons, are not generally to be included in this category), established otherwise than by means of formal registration and/or legal ceremony.

has been addressed recently by the Law Commission.[550] In the main, disputes arising in connection with *de facto* cohabitation concern matters of financial/proprietary relief rather than personal status.[551] It may be the case, however, that in order to qualify for financial/proprietary relief under a given system of law, an individual will require first to establish his/her status as "cohabitant".[552] Establishing qualifying status, it is submitted, is a matter to be determined by the law under which the relief and/or rights in question is/are claimed.

---

[550] Law Commission Consultation Paper No 179, "Cohabitation: The Financial Consequences of Relationship Breakdown—A Consultation Paper" (2006).

[551] See infra, p 1309; also Carruthers (2008) Edin LR 1.

[552] Eg in order to apply for financial/proprietary relief under the Family Law (Scotland) Act 2006, ss 25–30, an individual must establish that s/he is a "cohabitant", defined in s 25(1) of that Act as follows: "either member of a couple consisting of (a) a man and a woman who are (or were) living together as if they were husband and wife; or (b) two persons of the same sex who are (or were) living together as if they were civil partners".

Chapter 21

Matrimonial and Related Causes[1]

1. INTRODUCTION

Matrimonial causes are now generally taken to include petitions for divorce, nullity of marriage, judicial separation, and presumption of death and dissolution of marriage, as well as similar foreign proceedings which may fall for recognition in England.

---

[1] See North, *Private International Law of Matrimonial Causes*; (1990) I Hague Recueil 9, 97–126; Boele-Woelki (ed), *Perspectives for the Unification and Harmonisation of Family Law in Europe* (2003); Stark, *International Family Law* (2005), Chapters 3–6; and Meeusen, Pertegas, Straetmans and Swennen (eds), *International Family Law for the European Union* (2007).

The rules relating to the jurisdiction of the courts and to the recognition of foreign divorces, annulments and judicial separations are, in essence, the same for all three matrimonial causes, and will therefore be examined together, identifying where appropriate any rules which do not apply to all three. It will be seen that the one major area of difference remaining concerns the determination of the law to be applied by the English courts.[2] We shall then go on to examine, separately, proceedings for presumption of death and dissolution of marriage. Thereafter, consideration will be given to conflict rules concerning the dissolution, nullity and separation of civil partnerships.

Before these various matrimonial and related causes are considered, it is necessary to discuss a further preliminary issue, namely whether an English court will assume jurisdiction to grant matrimonial relief in the case of a polygamous marriage.

2. POLYGAMOUS MARRIAGES AND MATRIMONIAL RELIEF[3]

(a) At common law

Until 1972, the rule of English law was that the parties to a polygamous marriage were "not entitled to the remedies, the adjudication, or the relief of the matrimonial law of England".[4] It meant that, in the case of a polygamous marriage, the courts would decline to grant a divorce,[5] a decree of nullity even where the petitioner claimed lack of capacity to enter a polygamous marriage,[6] or a decree of judicial separation.[7] It came to be realised, however, that fundamental reform was called for in view of the number of immigrants from jurisdictions where they had contracted valid marriages in polygamous form. A substantial number of people, permanently resident though not domiciled in England, were denied all matrimonial relief.

(b) Matrimonial Causes Act 1973, section 47

All this has now changed. Section 47(1) of the Matrimonial Causes Act 1973[8] provides that: "A court in England and Wales shall not be precluded from granting matrimonial relief or making a declaration concerning the validity of a marriage by reason only that either party to the marriage is, or has during the subsistence of the marriage been, married to more than one person."

---

[2] Infra, p 966.

[3] See North, op cit, Chapter 7.

[4] *Hyde v Hyde* (1866) LR 1 P & D 130 at 138.

[5] *Hyde v Hyde*, supra; *Muhammad v Suna* 1956 SC 366.

[6] *Risk v Risk* [1951] P 50.

[7] Cf *Nachimson v Nachimson* [1930] P 217.

[8] As amended by the Private International Law (Miscellaneous Provisions) Act 1995, Sch, para 2(3). This amendment removes reference to potentially polygamous marriages which reference the Law Commission concluded was no longer necessary, given the absence of any difference between such marriages and monogamous ones: Law Com No 146 (1985), para 3.10; and see, supra, p 931.

This section makes available to the parties to an actually polygamous marriage[9] a wide range of matrimonial relief,[10] namely decrees of divorce, nullity, judicial separation, presumption of death and dissolution of marriage, orders for financial provision in the cases of neglect to maintain, variation of maintenance agreements, orders for financial relief or relating to children which are ancillary to any of the preceding decrees or orders,[11] orders made under Part I of the Domestic Proceedings and Magistrates' Courts Act 1978,[12] orders for financial relief after a foreign divorce, annulment or legal separation,[13] and any declaration under Part III of the Family Law Act 1986 involving a determination as to the validity of a marriage.[14] Indeed it has been said that the effect of section 47 of the 1973 Act is to abolish entirely the old rule, so that all forms of relief which can be classed as matrimonial are now available in the case of polygamous marriages.[15]

(c) Remaining problems

Whilst polygamous marriages will, for the purposes of such relief, normally be treated just as if they were monogamous marriages, they do pose certain peculiar problems in the, albeit rare, cases of actually polygamous marriages. Indeed, in such cases the 1973 Act makes specific provision for the making of rules of court to require notice of the proceedings to be served on any spouse other than one who is party to the proceedings and to confer on such a spouse a right to be heard.[16]

Where a party to an actually polygamous marriage brings proceedings for divorce alleging irretrievable breakdown of the marriage,[17] difficulties may arise over adultery, unreasonable behaviour or desertion as proof of breakdown.[18] If a wife alleges that her husband has committed adultery with another wife, such a claim will usually fail because "it is an essential element of adultery that intercourse has taken place outside the marriage relationship ie between persons not married to each other. This being so, intercourse with a wife could not be adultery".[19] In terms of policy, this conclusion seems right if both marriages were entered into in polygamous form. It has been said[20] that in such a case there has been no breach of the obligation of fidelity imposed by the law governing the marriage. Difficulties arise, however, in the case of a valid monogamous marriage,

---

[9] And see Matrimonial Causes Act 1973, s 47(4), as amended by the Private International Law (Miscellaneous Provisions) Act 1995, Sch, para 2(3); see eg *Onobrauche v Onobrauche* (1978) 8 Fam Law 107; *Quoraishi v Quoraishi* [1985] FLR 780, CA.

[10] Matrimonial Causes Act 1973, s 47(2).

[11] *Chaudhary v Chaudhary* [1976] Fam 148 at 151.

[12] See 1978 Act, Sch 2, para 39.

[13] Matrimonial and Family Proceedings Act 1984 Sch 1, para 15, infra, p 1063 et seq.

[14] Matrimonial Causes Act 1973, s 47(3), as substituted by the Family Law Act 1986, Sch 1, para 14.

[15] *Re Sehota* [1978] 1 WLR 1506 at 1511. Supra, pp 936–937.

[16] Matrimonial Causes Act 1973, s 47(4); see Family Proceedings Rules 1991, r 3.11.

[17] Ibid, s 1.

[18] Ibid, s 1(2)(a), (b) and (c). These "grounds" for divorce will no longer be relevant if and when Part II of the Family Law Act 1996 is brought into force.

[19] Law Com No 42 (1971), para 50; and see *Onobrauche v Onobrauche* (1978) 8 Fam Law 107.

[20] Clive, *The Law of Husband and Wife in Scotland* (1997) 4th edn, pp 109–110.

followed by a valid polygamous one,[21] as in the decision of the Privy Council in *Drammeh v Drammeh*:[22]

> H, domiciled in The Gambia, married W1 in England in monogamous form. Both professed the Christian faith. H then returned to The Gambia, reverted to his Moslem faith and married W2 in polygamous form. W1 petitioned for divorce, before the courts of The Gambia, alleging adultery by H and W2.

The Privy Council upheld the decision that W1 was entitled to a divorce, holding that even if the marriage to W2 was a valid polygamous marriage under the law of The Gambia, this should not affect the rights of W1 stemming from her valid English monogamous marriage. The nature of her marriage was not changed by H's unilateral change of faith. So far as W1's marriage was concerned, H had committed adultery with W2.[23] Had W1 chosen, as well she might, to have petitioned for divorce in England, it seems likely that an English court would have reached the same conclusion as the Privy Council.[24] When the Law Commission considered the effect of a later polygamous marriage on an earlier marriage, whether in monogamous or polygamous form, it concluded that legislative intervention was neither necessary nor desirable.[25]

If a wife's divorce petition is based on the husband's unreasonable behaviour,[26] the court will have to examine all the circumstances of the marriage.[27] It has been held that the taking by the husband of a second wife is unreasonable behaviour towards the first.[28] Similarly, if a husband's petition is based on desertion by the first wife,[29] the fact that he has validly married a second wife has been held to give the first wife reasonable grounds for leaving him.[30]

3. DIVORCE, NULLITY AND JUDICIAL SEPARATION

(a) Jurisdiction

(i) Bases of jurisdiction

The Domicile and Matrimonial Proceedings Act 1973, Part II,[31] lays down, in section 5, rules of jurisdiction for proceedings for divorce, judicial separation and nullity of marriage,[32] and for proceedings for death to be presumed and marriage dissolved pursuant to

---

[21] The question of the validity of the second marriage where the first was monogamous is discussed supra, p 923 et seq.

[22] (1970) 78 Ceylon Law Weekly 55.

[23] See also *A-G of Ceylon v Reid* [1965] AC 720 at 729; *Lendrum v Chakravarti* 1929 SLT 96 at 99.

[24] Law Com No 146 (1985), para 4.16.

[25] Ibid, para 4.23.

[26] Matrimonial Causes Act 1973, s 1(2)(b).

[27] *Gollins v Gollins* [1964] AC 644.

[28] *Poon v Tan* (1973) 4 Fam Law 161.

[29] Matrimonial Causes Act 1973, s 1(2)(b).

[30] *Quoraishi v Quoraishi* [1985] FLR 780, CA.

[31] As amended by the European Communities (Jurisdiction and Judgments in Matrimonial and Parental Responsibility Matters) Regulations, SI 2005/265.

[32] S 5(1)(a).

section 19 of the Act.[33] The rules contained in Part II of the 1973 Act were significantly changed, with effect from 1 March 2001, to take account of European harmonisation in the form of Council Regulation (EC) No 1347/2000 of 29 May 2000 on jurisdiction and the recognition and enforcement of judgments in matrimonial matters and in matters of parental responsibility for children of both spouses (known colloquially as "Brussels II").[34] Brussels II, in turn, was repealed, with effect from 1 March 2005, by Council Regulation (EC) No 2201/2003 of 27 November 2003 concerning jurisdiction and the recognition and enforcement of judgments in matrimonial matters and matters of parental responsibility ("Brussels II *bis*").[35] The rules of jurisdiction in matrimonial matters contained in Brussels II *bis* were taken substantially from Brussels II, which, in turn, were taken[36] from the Brussels II Convention of 28 May 1998 (never implemented) on the same subject.[37]

(a) Divorce or judicial separation

Section 5(2) of the Domicile and Matrimonial Proceedings Act 1973 provides that the High Court or a divorce county court shall have jurisdiction to entertain proceedings if, and only if: (a) the court has jurisdiction under Brussels II *bis*; or (b) no court of a Contracting State[38] has jurisdiction under Brussels II *bis*, and either of the parties to the marriage is domiciled in England on the date when the proceedings are begun. In other words, pre-eminent jurisdiction lies with the courts of a country which has jurisdiction in terms of Brussels II *bis*.

(i) Jurisdiction under Domicile and Matrimonial Proceedings Act 1973, section 5(2)(a)

Article 3[39] of Brussels II *bis* states the principles of general jurisdiction. Jurisdiction shall lie with the courts of the Member State:

    (a) in whose territory:
        —the spouses are habitually resident,[40] or
        —the spouses were last habitually resident, insofar as one[41] of them still resides[42] there, or

---

[33] S 5(1)(b).

[34] OJ 2000 L 160/19. See also the European Communities (Matrimonial Jurisdiction and Judgments) Regulations, SI 2001/310. For details of the rules of jurisdiction applying prior to 1 March 2001, see the 13th edition of this book (1999), p 764 et seq.

[35] OJ 2003 L 338/1. See generally Boele-Woelki and Beilfuss (eds), *Brussels II bis: Its Impact and Application in the Member States* (2007); McEleavy (2002) 51 ICLQ 883, and (2004) 53 ICLQ 503. The *Practice Guide for the Application of the New Brussels II Regulation* (2005) deals only with issues of parental responsibility.

[36] See Brussels II, Recital (6).

[37] See Borras, "Explanatory Report on the Convention on jurisdiction and the recognition and enforcement of judgments in matrimonial matters" OJ 1998 C 221/27.

[38] The expression "Contracting State" is defined in s 5(1A) as Belgium, Cyprus, Czech Republic, Germany, Greece, Spain, Estonia, France, Hungary, Ireland, Italy, Latvia, Lithuania, Luxembourg, Malta, Netherlands, Austria, Poland, Portugal, Slovakia, Slovenia, Finland, Sweden, the UK, and any party which subsequently has adopted Council Regulation (EC) No 2201/2003 of 27 November 2003. Denmark is not a Contracting State to this instrument (Brussels II *bis*, Recital (31)), and there has been no suggestion to date of the European Community entering into an agreement with Denmark pursuant to Brussels II *bis*, akin to the EC/Denmark Agreement which operates pursuant to the Brussels I Regulation (in respect of which, see supra, p 341).

[39] See generally Borras, *Explanatory Report*, paras 27–34.

[40] Eg *L-K v K (Brussels II Revised: Maintenance Pending Suit)* [2006] EWHC 153 (Fam), [2006] 2 FLR 1113.

[41] The claimant or the defendant.

[42] See infra, pp 947–949.

—the respondent is habitually resident,[43] or

—in the event of a joint application, either of the spouses is habitually resident, or

—the applicant is habitually resident if s/he resided[44] there for at least a year immediately before the application was made,[45] or

—the applicant is habitually resident if s/he resided[46] there for at least six months immediately before the application was made and is either a national of the Member State in question or, in the case of the United Kingdom and Ireland, has his/her domicile there;[47]

(b) of the nationality[48] of both[49] spouses or, in the case of the United Kingdom and Ireland, of the domicile[50] of both spouses.

The grounds of jurisdiction in Article 3 are set out as alternatives, and not in any order of precedence.[51] It is apparent that there is some overlap[52] in the provisions of Article 3; there is no need for a basis of jurisdiction on the ground of the spouses' common habitual residence (indent 1), if jurisdiction can be founded upon the respondent's habitual residence alone (indent 3). This overlap is a result of political compromise: "The grounds adopted are based on the principle of genuine connection between the person and a Member State. The decision to include particular grounds reflects their existence in various national legal systems and their acceptance by the other Member States or the effort to find points of agreement acceptable to all".[53]

---

[43] Eg *Armstrong v Armstrong* [2003] EWHC 777, [2003] 2 FLR 375; and *L-K v K (No 2)* [2006] EWHC 3280 (Fam).

[44] See infra, pp 947–949.

[45] Eg *Sulaiman v Juffali* [2002] 1 FLR 479—applicant's Saudi Arabian nationality considered irrelevant.

[46] See *Marinos v Marinos* [2007] EWHC 2047 (Fam), per MUNBY J, at [45] et seq, especially at [49]: "'Resided' means just that. It refers to residence; it does not connote habitual residence". Such a literal interpretation of Art 3(1)(a), indent 6, can be justified by reference to the precise language of the text. It would be illogical and inconsistent to take a different approach to the interpretation of "resided" where it appears in the similarly worded Art 3(1)(a), indent 5. What appears, therefore, to be required for the purpose of these two indents is: "(i) habitual residence on a particular day and (ii) residence, though not necessarily habitual residence, during the relevant immediately preceding period" (per MUNBY J, ibid, [46]). Contra Dicey, Morris and Collins, para 18-005. Dr Borras' *Explanatory Report* lends no assistance on this point of interpretation. MUNBY J's interpretation of "resided" would be more strained, however, if it were applied to Art 3(1)(a), indent 2, for that provision would appear to require, extending his Lordship's reasoning: (i) common habitual residence on the last day on which the parties cohabited and (ii) residence, though not necessarily habitual residence, on a subsequent day, namely, that on which proceedings are commenced. A requirement only of "residence" on the date on which proceedings are commenced would seem to be at odds with the importance otherwise attributed by Art 3(1)(a) to "habitual residence" as at the date of commencement of proceedings. However, as a matter of fact, it is unlikely, for the purposes of indent 2, that the "residence" of the "remaining" spouse, having regard to its continuing nature, would be other than "habitual".

[47] See *Marinos v Marinos*, ibid.

[48] Eg *L-K v K (Brussels II Revised: Maintenance Pending Suit)* [2006] EWHC 153 (Fam), [2006] 2 FLR 1113.

[49] Some states had wanted the condition to attach to one spouse only, but that was rejected on the ground that it would amount to pure "*forum actoris*": Borras, *Explanatory Report*, para 33.

[50] For the purposes of Brussels II *bis*, "domicile" has the same meaning it has under English law. See supra, p 153 et seq. See also *Re N (Jurisdiction)* [2007] EWHC 1274 (Fam Div), discussed by Douglas (2007) 37 Fam Law 901.

[51] See Borras, *Explanatory Report*, paras 28 and 44.

[52] And possibly gaps: see suggestions for reform in Proposal for a Council Regulation amending Regulation (EC) No 2201/2003 as regards jurisdiction and introducing rules concerning applicable law in matrimonial matters (COM (2006) 399 final, and Document 5274/07 LIMITE JUSTCIV 4 (12 January 2007)), discussed infra, p 952.

[53] Borras, *Explanatory Report*, para 30.

"Habitual residence"[54]   It can be seen that the principal connecting factor is habitual residence. This factor is nowhere defined in the instrument,[55] and it is not easy to define.[56] It has been held that the term "habitual residence" has an autonomous meaning for the purposes of the Brussels II *bis* Regulation.[57] Chapter 9, above, contains a full analysis of the concept of habitual residence, and so reference should be made to that treatment of the subject. In the context of jurisdiction in divorce, judicial separation and nullity of marriage, it suffices to make the following remarks.

With regard to the 1973 Act, the House of Lords held in *Mark v Mark*[58] that there was no reason for the word "lawfully" to be implied into section 5(2) of the Act: residence for the purpose of section 5(2) need not be lawful residence,[59] for the purpose of section 5(2) is to provide an answer to the question whether the parties and their marriage have a sufficiently close connection to the United Kingdom to make it desirable that English courts should have jurisdiction to dissolve the marriage.

Stipulation of a one-year period of residence for the purposes of habitual residence in Article 3, indent 5 of Brussels II *bis* should not be taken to be a definition of habitual residence for the purposes of the other indents in that provision. Indents 5 and 6 allow *forum actoris* in exceptional cases, on the basis of habitual residence coupled with another connection.[60]

It has been explained in Chapter 9[61] that a degree of continuity of residence is required: "a residence must be more than transient or casual; once established, however, it is not necessarily broken by a temporary absence".[62] Indeed, in the context of divorce jurisdiction, a respondent has been held[63] to be habitually resident in England even though she spent one-third of the relevant year either on holiday in Spain or visiting her children in the USA and Canada. The Court of Appeal in *Ikimi v Ikimi*[64] had to consider whether a Nigerian wife who filed a petition for dissolution of marriage in England on the basis of habitual residence had two such residences. The family had two matrimonial homes, of equal status, in Nigeria and in England, and the wife had spent 161 days of the year in England. The submission that it was not possible to be habitually resident in two places

---

[54] See, for detailed examination, supra, p 185 et seq. Also Bogdan, "The EC treaty and the Use of Nationality and Habitual Residence as Connecting Factors in International Family Law", and Pertegas, "Nationality and Habitual Residence: Other Connecting Factors in European Private International Law", both in Meeusen, Pertegas, Straetmans and Swennen (eds), *International Family Law for the European Union* (2007).

[55] See, for background, Borras, *Explanatory Report*, para 32.

[56] Though see suggested definition in Borras, *Explanatory Report*, para 32 ("the place where the person had established, on a fixed basis, his permanent or habitual centre of interests, with all the relevant facts being taken into account for the purpose of determining such residence"), cited with approval in *Marinos v Marinos* [2007] EWHC 2047 (Fam), per MUNBY J, at [33].

[57] *Marinos v Marinos* [2007] EWHC 2047 (Fam), per MUNBY J, at [17]–[18]; and *L-K v K (No 2)* [2006] EWHC 3280 (Fam), per SINGER J, at [35].

[58] [2005] UKHL 42, [2006] 1 AC 98. Cf *Witkowska v Kaminski* [2006] EWHC 1940 (Ch), [2007] 1 FLR 1547.

[59] For relevance of lawfulness of residence in relation to domicile, see supra, p 170.

[60] Borras, *Explanatory Report*, para 32. See also *Marinos v Marinos* [2007] EWHC 2047 (Fam); infra, p 948.

[61] Supra, p 153 et seq. See, in particular, *Armstrong v Armstrong* [2003] EWHC 777, [2003] 2 FLR 375, at [29].

[62] Law Com No 48 (1972), para 42. See also *Breuning v Breuning* [2002] EWHC 236, [2002] 1 FLR 888 (presence in England for medical treatment was not enough to establish habitual residence in England).

[63] *Oundjian v Oundjian* (1979) 1 FLR 198.

[64] [2001] EWCA Civ 873, [2001] 2 FLR 1288.

simultaneously was firmly rejected by the Court of Appeal,[65] but the Court took the view that the bodily presence required to form a basis for habitual residence had to be more than merely token in duration, probably amounting to residence for "an appreciable part of the relevant year".[66] Subsequently, in *Armstrong v Armstrong*,[67] Dame Elizabeth BUTLER-SLOSS concluded that the correct approach to the degree of continuity required to establish habitual residence in a country "cannot just be a counting of the days spent in the country. There has to be an element of quality of residence." [68]

In *Marinos v Marinos*[69] it fell to be decided whether, for the purposes of Brussels II *bis*, a person can be habitually resident in two different countries at the same time. MUNBY J considered that while it was clear that, for the purposes of English domestic law, one could be habitually resident contemporaneously in two different countries,[70] "the same is not necessarily true of the law laid down by the ECJ nor, specifically, for the purposes of the Regulation".[71] His Lordship suggested that the point of interpretation of Article 3 of the relevant Regulation (Brussels II) in *Armstrong* was inadequately argued and addressed, and that the decision of Dame Elizabeth BUTLER-SLOSS P, therefore, rests on a "frail foundation".[72] MUNBY J concluded in *Marinos*[73] that, "the language of Article 3(1)(a) of the Regulation [Brussels II *bis*[74]] is clear, as is the ECJ case-law. For the purposes of the Regulation, one cannot be habitually resident in more than one country at the same time." Of the two conflicting interpretations in *Armstrong* and *Marinos*, respectively, the latter commends itself as being technically more accurate,[75] whereas the former has the advantage of flexibility. Even adopting the strict interpretation of MUNBY J, however, to the effect that, for the purposes of the Brussels II *bis* Regulation, a party has only one habitual residence at any given time, there is room for disagreement[76] between the courts of different Member States on the question, where a party is habitually resident, particularly in cases such as these, where residence is divided. By reason of Article 19 (lis pendens),[77] however, such disagreement will emerge only consecutively, and not contemporaneously.

---

[65] Cf *Mark v Mark* [2005] UKHL 42, [2006] 1 AC 98.

[66] *Ikimi v Ikimi*, above, per THORPE LJ, at [35]. His Lordship favoured a liberal rather than restrictive approach to the determination of habitual residence, whilst noting that one consequence of liberality might be forum shopping.

[67] [2003] EWHC 777, [2003] 2 FLR 375.

[68] *Armstrong v Armstrong*, ibid, at [30]—pattern of respondent's visits to England, together with the number of days spent in the country—one-fifth of the year—did not demonstrate sufficient residence to meet the statutory requirement of habitual residence in the 1973 Act and Brussels II.

[69] [2007] EWHC 2047 (Fam).

[70] At [38].

[71] Ibid.

[72] At [42].

[73] At [43].

[74] Art 3 of which is in identical terms to Art 3 of Brussels II.

[75] *Marinos*, supra, [40].

[76] Pace MUNBY J in *Marinos v Marinos* [2007] EWHC 2047 (Fam), at [17]–[18], and SINGER J in *L-K v K (No 2)* [2006] EWHC 3280 at [35].

[77] Infra, pp 956–958.

The concept of alternating, or consecutive, habitual residences has been accepted in relation to a family that spends six continuous months in one home, followed by six continuous months in another.[78]

The time at which the personal law connecting factor (habitual residence or domicile, as the case may be) is to be determined is, as at common law and under the 1973 Act prior to 1 March 2001,[79] the time when proceedings are commenced, and not at the later time when the case is actually tried. If the rule were otherwise, a respondent habitually resident in England could frustrate a petition brought by the other spouse, domiciled and resident abroad, by changing his residence between the presentation of the petition and the hearing of the case. The rule is "once competent, always competent"[80] and this will be so even if the party habitually resident in England at the time of the English proceedings has since changed his residence and disassociated himself from the determination of his status by an English court.

Counterclaims In terms of Article 4 of Brussels II *bis*, a court which has jurisdiction on the basis of Article 3, and in which proceedings are pending, also has jurisdiction to examine a counterclaim, insofar as the counterclaim falls within the scope of the Regulation.[81]

Conversion of legal separation into divorce A Member State court which has given a judgment[82] on a legal separation has jurisdiction, by virtue of Article 5 of the Regulation, to convert that judgment into a divorce, if the law of that Member State so provides.[83] In some countries, legal separation is a necessary step prior to divorce, and so the conversion of legal separations into divorces is not infrequent in certain States.

Exclusive nature of jurisdiction under Articles 3, 4 and 5 and residual jurisdiction By virtue of Article 6 of Brussels II *bis*, a spouse who (a) is habitually resident in a Member State; or (b) is a national of a Member State,[84] or, in the case of the United Kingdom, has his/her "domicile" in that state, may be sued in another Member State only in accordance with Article 3, 4 or 5. In other words, national rules of residual jurisdiction, set out, for

---

[78] *Re V (Abduction: Habitual Residence)* [1995] 2 FLR 992. The concept breaks down, however, in the instance of a family moving between two jurisdictions on a weekly basis: *Ikimi v Ikimi* supra, per THORPE LJ at [32]. See also *In the Marriage of Hanbury Brown* (1996) FLC 92-671.

[79] *Leon v Leon* [1967] P 275; and see 13th edn of this book (1999), p 765.

[80] *Leon v Leon*, supra, at 284.

[81] Art 1(1) provides that Brussels II *bis* shall apply, whatever the nature of the court or tribunal, in civil matters relating to (a) divorce, legal separation or marriage annulment (but only to the dissolution of matrimonial ties, and not to issues such as the grounds for divorce, property consequences of marriage, or other ancillary measures: recital (8)); and (b) the attribution, exercise, delegation, restriction or termination of parental responsibility. The Regulation does not apply to: (a) the establishment or contesting of a parent-child relationship; (b) decisions on adoption, measures preparatory to adoption, or the annulment or revocation of adoption; (c) the name and forenames of a child; (d) emancipation; (e) maintenance obligations; (f) trusts or succession; (g) measures taken as a result of criminal offences committed by children.

[82] Defined in Brussels II *bis*, Art 2(4).

[83] Art 5.

[84] See discussion regarding non-Member State nationals in *Sulaiman v Juffali* [2002] 1 FLR 479, and conclusion of MUNBY J, at para 24, that Art 2 of Brussels II (Art 3 of Brussels II *bis*) is founded simply and solely on the habitual residence of one or other or both of the spouses, not on their nationality, rendering the Saudi Arabian nationality of both spouses, in the instant case, irrelevant. Cf *Singh v Singh* 2005 SLT 749, per Judge R F MACDONALD QC, at [12].

England, in section 5(2)(b) of the Domicile and Matrimonial Proceedings Act 1973, considered below, cannot be relied upon in respect of such a person.

Article 7(1) of Brussels II *bis* provides that, where no court of a Member State has jurisdiction pursuant to Article 3, 4 or 5 of the Regulation, jurisdiction shall be determined in each Member State by the laws of that state.[85] The European Court of Justice (ECJ) has stated that the application of Article 7(1) does not depend on the "position"[86] of the respondent, but solely on the question whether the court of a Member State has jurisdiction pursuant to Articles 3 to 5 of the Regulation.[87] By way of rationalisation of this statement, it should be noted that the rules for allocation of jurisdiction under Articles 3 to 5 envisage that jurisdiction can be established without reference to the "position" of the respondent as at the date of commencement of proceedings. This is true, however, only in respect of Article 3(1)(a), indents 5 and 6, based as they are upon principles of *forum actoris*, and potentially also in respect of indent 2.

By Article 7(2), as against a respondent who is not habitually resident and is not either a national of a Member State or, in the case of the United Kingdom and Ireland, does not have his domicile within the territory of one of the latter Member States, any national of a Member State who is habitually resident within the territory of another Member State may, like the nationals of that state, avail himself of the rules of jurisdiction applicable in that state.[88] For Article 7(2) to apply, the applicant must be a national of a Member State habitually resident in another Member State. Moreover, the respondent must satisfy two conditions: he must be habitually resident in a non-Member State country, and he must not be a citizen of a Member State (or, in the case of the United Kingdom and Ireland, must not be domiciled there).[89]

A question existed as to the extent to which the national rules of residual jurisdiction of one Member State could be used to trump the (putative) exercise by another Member State of jurisdiction under Article 3 of the Regulation. This very issue arose in Sweden, in the case of *Sundelind Lopez v Lopez Lizazo*.[90]

> The case concerned the commencement of divorce proceedings in the District Court of Stockholm by the female petitioner, a Swedish national, against her respondent husband, a Cuban national. The couple had lived together in France. At the date of commencement of proceedings, the petitioner continued to reside in France, whereas her husband, by then, was resident in Cuba.

The Swedish court dismissed the petition on the ground that, under Article 3(1)(a)[91] of Brussels II *bis*, only the French courts had jurisdiction and that, accordingly, Article 7 of the Regulation precluded Swedish rules on jurisdiction from applying. The Swedish Court of Appeal dismissed the appeal brought by the petitioner against that judgment. In a further appeal to the Swedish Supreme Court, the petitioner submitted that Article 6

---

[85] See McEleavy (2004) 53 ICLQ 605, at 614.
[86] *Sundelind Lopez v Lopez Lizazo* (Case C-68/07) [2008] IL Pr 4 at [25].
[87] Ibid, at [25].
[88] Art 7(2).
[89] See *Singh v Singh* 2005 SLT 749, per Judge R F MACDONALD QC, at [12].
[90] *Sundelind Lopez v Lopez Lizazo* (Case C-68/07) [2008] IL Pr 4.
[91] Indent 2 or indent 5; supra, pp 945–946.

of Brussels II *bis* implies that the courts of Member States do not have exclusive jurisdiction where the respondent neither has his habitual residence in, nor is a national of, a Member State. In February 2007, the Swedish Supreme Court referred the following question[92] to the ECJ for a preliminary ruling on the matter, namely:

> The respondent in a case concerning divorce is neither resident in a Member State nor a citizen of a Member State. May the case be heard by a court in a Member State which does not have jurisdiction under Article 3 [of Brussels II *bis*], even though a court in another Member State may have jurisdiction by application of one of the rules on jurisdiction set out in Article 3?

In November 2007, the ECJ delivered its judgment,[93] ruling as follows:

> Articles 6 and 7 of the Regulation are to be interpreted as meaning that where, in divorce proceedings, a respondent is not habitually resident in a Member State and is not a national of a Member State, the courts of a Member State cannot base their jurisdiction to hear the petition on their national law, if the courts of another Member State have jurisdiction under Article 3 of the Regulation.

The Court held that, according to Article 7(1), it is only where no court of a Member State has jurisdiction pursuant to Articles 3 to 5 of the Regulation that jurisdiction is to be governed, in each Member State, by the laws of that state. Moreover, according to Article 17 of the Regulation, where a court of one Member State is seised of a case over which it has no jurisdiction under the Regulation, and a court of another Member State has jurisdiction pursuant to the Regulation, the former is to declare of its own motion that it has no jurisdiction. Finally, the ECJ made clear that Article 6 does *not* lay down a general rule that the jurisdiction of the courts of a Member State to hear questions relating to a divorce in respect of a respondent who does *not* have his habitual residence in a Member State and is *not* a national of a Member State is to be determined, in all cases, under national law.[94]

The consequence, in *Sundelind Lopez v Lopez Lizazo*, was that since the French courts had jurisdiction to hear the divorce petition pursuant to Article 3(1)(a), the Swedish courts could not base their jurisdiction to hear that petition upon rules of their national law, pursuant to Article 7(1), but were required, in accordance with Article 17, to declare of their own motion that they had no jurisdiction, in favour of the French courts.[95]

(ii) Jurisdiction under Domicile and Matrimonial Proceedings Act 1973, section 5(2)(b)

For England,[96] the national rules of residual jurisdiction are to be found in section 5(2)(b) of the 1973 Act, ie: "the High Court or a divorce county court shall have jurisdiction to entertain proceedings if, and only if no court of a Contracting State[97] has jurisdiction under Brussels II *bis*, and either of the parties to the marriage is domiciled in England on the date when the proceedings are begun".

---

[92] *Kerstin Sundelind Lopez v Miquel Enrique Lopez Lizazo* (Case C-68/07).
[93] *Sundelind Lopez v Lopez Lizazo* (Case C-68/07) [2008] IL Pr 4.
[94] Ibid, at [24].
[95] Ibid, at [20].
[96] Cf residual rules of other Member States: Borras, *Explanatory Report*, para 47.
[97] See supra, p 945, n 38.

(iii) Proposed reform of rules of matrimonial jurisdiction in Brussels II bis

In July 2006, the European Commission published a Proposal for a Council Regulation amending Regulation (EC) No 2201/2003 as regards jurisdiction and introducing rules concerning applicable law in matrimonial matters (known colloquially as "Rome III").[98] One objective of the Proposal is to amend Brussels II *bis* as regards jurisdiction in matrimonial matters, to attain four objectives: (i) strengthening legal certainty and predictability; (ii) increasing flexibility by introducing limited party autonomy; (iii) ensuring access to court; and (iv) preventing a "rush to court" by one spouse.[99] In detail, it is proposed to insert a choice of court clause into Brussels II *bis*, to permit spouses in proceedings for divorce or legal separation (but not marriage annulment) to choose the jurisdiction of a "substantially connected"[100] Member State court.[101] This clearly could be advantageous to "international" couples. Additionally, it is proposed to introduce a new Article 7, providing a uniform and exhaustive rule on residual jurisdiction to replace national rules of residual jurisdiction. The concern is to ensure access to a Member State court for spouses who live in a non-Member State country but who retain strong links with a Member State of which they are nationals or in which they have resided for a certain period. On a point of Community competence, however, it is highly questionable what interest the Community has in residual cases such as these, which, by definition, fall outside the jurisdictional boundaries of Article 3 of Brussels II *bis*.[102] The United Kingdom government has decided not to opt into a resulting Community instrument.[103]

(b) Nullity of marriage

Section 5(3) of the 1973 Act provides that the High Court or a divorce county court shall have jurisdiction to entertain proceedings if, and only if: (a) the court has jurisdiction under Brussels II *bis*,[104] or (b) no court of a Contracting State[105] has jurisdiction under Brussels II *bis*, and either of the parties to the marriage (i) is domiciled in England on the date when the proceedings are begun,[106] or (ii) died before that date and either was

---

[98] COM (2006) 399 final, and Document 5274/07 LIMITE JUSTCIV 4, 12 January 2007. See also Green Paper on applicable law and jurisdiction in divorce matters (COM (2005) 82 final 14 March 2005); Commission Staff Working Paper, Annex to the Green Paper on applicable law and jurisdiction in divorce matters (SEC (2005) 331) 14 March 2005; and House of Lords EU Committee, 52nd Report, Session 2005/06, "Rome III—Choice of Law in Divorce" (2006).

[99] Proposal for a Council Regulation, Explanatory Memorandum, pp 2–3.

[100] See Proposal for a Council Regulation, Art 1(2).

[101] Party freedom of choice of court in relation to matrimonial matters presently is restricted in Brussels II *bis* to Art 3.1(a), indent 4 (joint application). See, however, Brussels II *bis*, Art 12, which permits parties, subject to certain conditions, to agree the competent court in matters of parental responsibility. See infra, p 1084.

[102] The label "extra-Community disputes", which, at one point, was considered as an alternative to the term "residual jurisdiction", perhaps better reveals the absence of Community interest in such cases. See Borras, *Explanatory Report*, para 47.

[103] See House of Lords, Written Statements, 18 April 2007: Column WS 7, per Baroness ASHTON of Upholland; and in Scotland, Report of the Justice I Committee of the Scottish Parliament, CJ1004/2005, 7 October 2005. Ireland also has decided not to opt into Rome III: Press Release 10 October 2006, at http://www.justice.ie/en/JELR/Pages/GovernmentrejectsEUdivorceproposals.

[104] As above.

[105] See supra, p 945, n 38.

[106] See, eg, *Singh v Singh* 2005 SLT 749—Scottish case under the equivalent rules of jurisdiction for Scotland, contained in Part III of the 1973 Act, s 7(3A) and (3B).

domiciled at death in England or had been habitually resident there for one year immediately prior to the date of death.

(i) Jurisdiction under Domicile and Matrimonial Proceedings Act 1973, section 5(3)(a)

Section 5(3)(a) refers to the rules of jurisdiction contained in Brussels II *bis* which, in
relation to petitions for nullity of marriage, are the same as those discussed above in relation to divorce and judicial separation.[107]

(ii) Jurisdiction under Domicile and Matrimonial Proceedings Act 1973, section 5(3)(b)

As with proceedings for divorce and judicial separation, Article 7 of Brussels II *bis* provides that where no court of a Member State has jurisdiction in annulment proceedings
pursuant to Article 3, 4 or 5 of Brussels II *bis*, jurisdiction shall be determined in each
Member State by the laws of that state. For England, the residual rules of jurisdiction for
proceedings for nullity of marriage are to be found in section 5(3)(b): either of the parties
to the marriage (i) is domiciled in England on the date when the proceedings are begun,
or (ii) died before that date and either was domiciled at death in England or had been
habitually resident there for one year immediately prior to the date of death.

The basis of jurisdiction in section 5(3)(b)(ii) is peculiar to nullity petitions, and is available only where either party to the marriage has died before the date when the proceedings for nullity were begun. The reason for this special jurisdictional rule is that, whilst
divorce and judicial separation petitions can be brought only if both spouses are alive, the
validity of a marriage may need to be tested in a nullity petition notwithstanding the death
of one spouse, or even after the death of both, as where succession issues are involved.

(c) Presumption of death and dissolution of marriage

Section 5(4) of the 1973 Act provides that the High Court or a divorce county court shall
have jurisdiction if, and only if the petitioner (a) is domiciled in England on the date when
the proceedings are begun; or (b) was habitually resident there for one year immediately
prior to the date of death. These bases of jurisdiction are unaffected by Brussels II *bis*.

(d) Jurisdiction to entertain other matrimonial proceedings in respect of the same marriage

By virtue of section 5(5) of the Domicile and Matrimonial Proceedings Act 1973, the
High Court or a divorce county court shall, at any time when proceedings are pending in
respect of which it has jurisdiction by virtue of section 5(2) or (3), discussed above, also
have jurisdiction to entertain other proceedings, in respect of the same marriage, for
divorce, judicial separation or nullity of marriage, notwithstanding that jurisdiction
would not be exercisable under section 5(2) or (3). The purpose of this somewhat cryptic
provision seems to be to deal with two jurisdictional problems. For example, let us assume
that a husband, habitually resident in France at the date the proceedings are begun, petitions for nullity in England on the basis of his wife's habitual residence in England, but,
before the petition is heard, she abandons her English residence. The wife, domiciled and
resident abroad, wishes to cross-petition for divorce in England. At that time, there is no
apparent jurisdictional basis for her petition; but section 5(5) confers jurisdiction because

---

[107] Supra, p 945 et seq.

proceedings for nullity are pending in respect of which the court does have jurisdiction. Secondly, the English court appears also to have jurisdiction where the petitioner changes his mind, as in the case where a spouse petitions for judicial separation, jurisdiction being based on the respondent's habitual residence, and then, before the petition is heard but after the respondent has lost her English habitual residence, the petitioner amends his petition to one for divorce. Finally, there is one further complication in that section 5(5) applies to cases where jurisdiction is conferred by reason of that sub-section itself. For example, proceedings are pending for divorce, jurisdiction being based on habitual residence; then a cross-petition is brought for divorce even though the original jurisdictional grounds no longer exist, jurisdiction being conferred by section 5(5); the original proceedings are abandoned; the cross-petitioner then wishes to amend the petition to one for nullity. The court has jurisdiction, again under section 5(5), to hear the final nullity petition so long as the cross-petition is still pending.

(ii) Impact of the statutory bases

If the statutory bases of jurisdiction are satisfied, the court does not have a general discretion to refuse to hear the petition. We shall see[108] that there is a discretion to stay the proceedings in cases where to proceed would lead to a clash with foreign proceedings in a non-European Community Member State or in Denmark, but there is no other discretion. For instance, leave is not required to serve a petition on a respondent overseas.[109] The position has been summed up by Bush J in a case where the respondent wife was resident in Ireland and could not afford to contest the English divorce proceedings: "If a court has jurisdiction . . . there is no way in which the court could decline jurisdiction on the ground of hardship, apparent unfairness or any other ground."[110]

(iii) Procedural issues

(a) Service of the petition

A copy of every petition for divorce, nullity or judicial separation must be served personally or by post on the respondent and every co-respondent,[111] and there is no need to obtain the leave of the court for service out of the jurisdiction.[112] An order for substituted service may be made in appropriate circumstances,[113] and service may even be dispensed with altogether in any case in which service is impracticable or dispensation otherwise appears necessary or expedient.[114] This discretion is unfettered, but it will be exercised in

---

[108] Infra, p 959 et seq.

[109] Family Proceedings Rules 1991, r 10.6.

[110] *Kapur v Kapur* [1984] FLR 920 at 922.

[111] Family Proceedings Rules 1991, r 2.9(1). See, however, in relation to the service of documents in proceedings instituted pursuant to Brussels II *bis*, Council Regulation (EC) No 1348/2000 of 29 May 2000 on the service in the Member States of judicial and extrajudicial documents in civil or commercial matters (Brussels II *bis*, Recital (15)); and Regulation (EC) No 1393/2007 of the European Parliament and of the Council of 13 November 2007 on the service in the Member States of judicial and extrajudicial documents in civil or commercial matters (service of documents), and repealing Council Regulation (EC) No 1348/2000.

[112] Ibid, r 10.6(1).

[113] Ibid, r 2.9(9). Eg *W v W (Preliminary Issue: Stay of Petition)* [2002] EWHC 3049, [2003] 1 FLR 1022.

[114] Ibid, r 2.9(11).

favour of the petitioner only in exceptional cases,[115] as, for instance, when the possible methods of substituted service are likely to be ineffective.[116]

(b) Staying proceedings[117]

The breadth of the English jurisdictional rules set out in the Domicile and Matrimonial Proceedings Act 1973 has the consequence that there is a greater risk of divorce and other matrimonial proceedings in respect of the same marriage being pursued in England and in some other country simultaneously. Indeed there could be several jurisdictions potentially in conflict, as where a wife habitually resident in England, but domiciled in Ireland, petitions for divorce from a husband habitually resident in Ontario, but domiciled in New York. There are related problems in that the concurrent matrimonial proceedings[118] may either be in some other part of the British Isles or in some politically foreign country. The provisions in Schedule 1 of the Domicile and Matrimonial Proceedings Act 1973 for the staying of the English proceedings vary according to the identity of the country in which the concurrent proceedings are taking place, ie: (i) a related jurisdiction in the British Isles; (ii) another European Community Member State, except Denmark; or (iii) a non-European Community Member State, or in Denmark. The rules are set out in section 5(6) and Schedule 1 to the 1973 Act, and are subject, by virtue of section 5(6A), to Article 19 of Brussels II *bis*. In every instance, however, there is an obligation on the petitioner, or a cross-petitioner, when proceedings are pending before the English court to furnish particulars of any proceedings[119] in respect of that marriage, or affecting its validity, which he knows are continuing in another jurisdiction.[120]

(i) Concurrent proceedings in a related jurisdiction—obligatory stays

Paragraph 8 of Schedule 1 to the 1973 Act provides for obligatory stays. Where it appears before the beginning of the trial[121] of proceedings for divorce, and only divorce,[122] that proceedings for divorce or nullity are continuing in a related jurisdiction elsewhere in the

---

[115] See *Akhtar v Rafiq* [2006] 1 FLR 27—no proper service on respondent wife; cogent evidence that the respondent was aware that divorce proceedings were under way might satisfy the judge prior to the issue of a special procedure certificate, but could not save the situation after the event, unless the circumstances were exceptional; *Ali Ebrahim v Ali Ebrahim* [1983] 1 WLR 1336 applied.

[116] *Luccioni v Luccioni* [1943] P 49 (no dispensation); *Weighman v Weighman* [1947] 2 All ER 852 (dispensation); *Paolantonio v Paolantonio* [1950] 2 All ER 404 (dispensation); *Spalenkova v Spalenkova* [1954] P 141 (no dispensation); and see *Whitehead v Whitehead* [1963] P 117 at 138. Different considerations are relevant in the case of a petition for presumption of death and dissolution of marriage: *N v N* [1957] P 385; infra, p 1029.

[117] Schuz (1987) 17 Fam Law 438; (1989) 38 ICLQ 946.

[118] Defined in the 1973 Act, Sch 1(2) as proceedings for divorce, judicial separation, nullity of marriage, a declaration as to the validity of a marriage of the petitioner, and a declaration as to the subsistence of such a marriage.

[119] Including non-judicial proceedings of a description prescribed by rules of court: Sch 1, paras 5 and 6; see Family Proceedings Rules 1991, rr 2.3, 2.27 (Stay under the Domicile and Matrimonial Proceedings Act 1973), 2.27A (Stay under the Council Regulation—inserted by SI 2001/821), and 4.27A (Stay under the Council Regulation—inserted by SI 2005/264). See *Trussler v Trussler* [2003] EWCA Civ 1830.

[120] Domicile and Matrimonial Proceedings Act 1973, s 5(6), Sch 1, para 7; see *Krenge v Krenge* [1999] 1 FLR 969 at 974–975.

[121] Trial of a preliminary issue of jurisdiction does not constitute trial of the proceedings for this purpose: Sch 1, para 4(1). Nor does trial of an issue as to custody or financial relief: *Thyssen-Bornemisza v Thyssen-Bornemisza* [1986] Fam 1.

[122] Where the proceedings are not only proceedings for divorce, then references to divorce apply only to the extent to which the proceedings are for divorce: Sch 1, para 8(2).

British Isles;[123] that the parties of the marriage have resided together after its celebration; that the place where they resided together when those proceedings began or where they last resided together before those proceedings began is that other related jurisdiction in the British Isles; and that either of the parties was habitually resident there throughout the year ending with the date on which they last resided there together, the English court must, on the application of one of the spouses,[124] order the English proceedings to be stayed.[125]

The salient features of this obligatory stay are that it only applies to English divorce proceedings and then only when the parties to the marriage are closely and clearly connected with the other jurisdiction in the British Isles. If the English proceedings are other than for divorce, or if the other British proceedings are other than for divorce or nullity, or if the residential connections with the other British jurisdiction are not all satisfied, this does not mean that the other proceedings cannot be stayed. It means, merely, that there will be no obligatory stay and that the question must be considered instead in the context of the court's *discretion* to stay the other proceedings. The object of the fairly elaborate criteria as to obligatory stays is to ensure that the proceedings are heard in the more appropriate forum; though it is possible to point to cases where the criteria produce the less appropriate forum.[126]

(ii) Concurrent proceedings in another European Community Member State, except Denmark—Brussels II bis, Article 19

Article 19 (Lis pendens and dependent actions) provides that:

1. Where proceedings relating to divorce, legal separation or marriage annulment between the same parties are brought before courts of different Member States, the court second seised shall of its own motion stay its proceedings until such time as the jurisdiction of the court first seised is established. . . .

3. Where the jurisdiction of the court first seised is established, the court second seised shall decline jurisdiction in favour of that court. In that case, the party who brought the relevant action before the court second seised may bring that action before the court first seised.

Article 3 of Brussels II *bis*, by its nature, often will confer jurisdiction on the courts of more than one Member State in respect of a single dispute, and so there is a clear need for a provision to deal with the problem of concurrent proceedings and conflicting judgments in the courts of different Member States.[127] Article 3 is limited to concurrent proceedings[128] in Member States, but it is not limited to proceedings under the bases of jurisdiction set out in the Regulation. Article 19 will apply equally where proceedings

---

[123] Defined by Sch 1, para 3(2), to mean Scotland, Northern Ireland, Jersey, Guernsey and the Isle of Man.

[124] But not by the court's acting of its own motion, see Law Com No 48 (1972), paras 90–93. See Family Proceedings Rules 1991, r 2.27(1).

[125] Sch 1, para 8(1); see *T v T (Custody: Jurisdiction)* [1992] 1 FLR 43. There are similar provisions requiring divorce proceedings in Scotland or Northern Ireland to be stayed when proceedings for divorce or nullity are continuing elsewhere in the British Isles: Sch 3, para 8.

[126] North, op cit, pp 37–38.

[127] Cf in relation to civil and commercial matters, the Brussels I Regulation, Art 27. See supra, p 303 et seq.

[128] Pending not concluded. See, in relation to civil and commercial matters, supra, p 309.

relating to divorce, legal separation or marriage annulment[129] between the same parties have been commenced in two Member States under their national rules of residual jurisdiction[130] (the bases of jurisdiction under Brussels II *bis* being inapplicable).[131]

Article 19, like Article 27 of the Brussels I Regulation, is a purely mechanical rule, which could lead to a race between the parties and which, arguably, is at odds with the prevailing culture of encouraging parties to attempt to engage in reconciliation and/or mediation processes rather than rushing to litigate.[132] Against that, however, the need for expensive litigation, generally conducted concurrently in two jurisdictions, as each party endeavours to establish that his/her favoured jurisdiction is the more appropriate, has been eliminated.[133] The court of the Member State first seised of the matter takes priority, and any court of another Member State must of its own motion decline jurisdiction,[134] once the jurisdiction of the court first seised is established in that state. The winner of the race to litigation is the spouse who can show that the court where s/he brought the action is first seised of jurisdiction.

The rule as to the time at which a court is seised is set out in Article 16 (Seising of a Court), which provides two alternatives,[135] namely:

1. A court shall be deemed to be seised:
   (a) at the time[136] when the document instituting the proceedings or an equivalent document is lodged with the court, provided that the applicant has not subsequently failed to take the steps he was required to take to have service effected on the respondent;[137] or
   (b) if the document has to be served before being lodged with the court, at the time when it is received by the authority responsible for service, provided that the applicant has not subsequently failed to take the steps he was required to take to have the document lodged with the court.

The steps which the petitioner is required to take to effect service will depend on the legal system in question. As with the seising of a court in civil and commercial matters, the fact

---

[129] Art 11 of Brussels II comprised two separate clauses dealing, respectively, with proceedings involving the same cause of action (Art 11.1), and proceedings not involving the same cause of action (Art 11.2) (see Borras, *Explanatory Report*, para 54), but the two clauses have been collapsed into a unitary clause in Art 19 of Brussels II *bis*.

[130] Sch 1(9)(1) of the 1973 Act supports this interpretation.

[131] See supra, p 951.

[132] See possible objections to the *lis pendens* doctrine in *Wermuth v Wermuth* [2003] EWCA Civ 50, [2003] 1 WLR 942, at [3].

[133] *Wermuth v Wermuth* [2003] EWCA Civ 50, [2003] 1 WLR 942, per THORPE LJ, at [3].

[134] Art 17 (Examination as to jurisdiction) provides that, "Where a court of a Member State is seised of a case over which it has no jurisdiction under this Regulation and over which a court of another Member State has jurisdiction by virtue of this Regulation, it shall declare of its own motion that it has no jurisdiction." See, eg *W v W (Preliminary Issue: Stay of Petition)* [2002] EWHC 3049, [2003] 1 FLR 1022; *Rogers-Headicar v Rogers-Headicar* [2004] EWCA Civ 1867, [2005] 2 FCR 1; *L-K v K (Brussels II Revised: Maintenance Pending Suit)* [2006] EWHC 153 (Fam), [2006] 2 FLR 1113; and *Moore v Moore* [2007] EWCA Civ 361, [2007] IL Pr 36.

[135] Cf in relation to civil and commercial matters, the Brussels I Regulation, Art 30. See supra, pp 308–309.

[136] The French language version of the instrument refers not to the "time", but to the date ("*la date à laquelle*") on which the court is seised; a verbal inconsistency noted, but not emphasised, by SINGER J in *L-K v K (Brussels II Revised: Maintenance Pending Suit)* [2006] EWHC 153 (Fam), [2006] 2 FLR 1113 at [15].

[137] Eg *W v W (Preliminary Issue: Stay of Petition)* [2002] EWHC 3049, [2003] 1 FLR 1022; and *L-K v K (Brussels II Revised: Maintenance Pending Suit)* [2006] EWHC 153 (Fam), [2006] 2 FLR 1113.

that Member States will not all be applying the same definition runs the risk that the race to become first seised will be run on unequal terms.[138] An English court may have to determine whether, and when, a foreign court has been seised; this should be a matter for the national law of that foreign Member State to determine.[139] An English court will determine whether and, if so, when it has been seised.[140] The court seised second cannot examine the jurisdiction of the court first seised. It was held in *Trussler v Trussler*[141] that "any litigant who asserts that there is a *lis alibi pendens* undertakes an obligation to prove the issue of the *lis* and the fact that it is still pending as at the date of issue of the proceedings in [England]".[142]

Once the jurisdiction of the court first seised has been established, the court second seised must then decline jurisdiction. This avoids the danger of the court second seised declining jurisdiction in favour of the court first seised, and that first court subsequently deciding that it has no jurisdiction.[143] There is no discretion given to the courts of either Member State as to whether they should take jurisdiction.

Article 19 is limited to concurrent proceedings in different Member States. It does not apply to concurrent actions in England and a non-Member State country, such as South Africa. In such cases, an English court will continue to employ traditional rules based upon the doctrine of *forum conveniens*, and given statutory expression in Schedule 1, paragraph 9 of the Domicile and Matrimonial Proceedings Act 1973, discussed later in this chapter.[144]

Brussels II *bis*, Article 20 (Provisional, including protective, measures) Article 20 provides that:

1. In urgent cases, the provisions of this Regulation shall not prevent the courts of a Member State from taking such provisional, including protective, measures in respect of persons or assets in that State as may be available under the law of that Member State, even if, under this Regulation, the court of another Member State has jurisdiction as to the substance of the matter.
2. The measures referred to in paragraph 1 shall cease to apply when the court of the Member State having jurisdiction under this Regulation as to the substance of the matter has taken the measures it considers appropriate.[145]

---

[138] Cf Brussels I Regulation, Art 30. See supra, pp 308–309.

[139] *W v W (Preliminary Issue: Stay of Petition)* [2002] EWHC 3049, [2003] 1 FLR 1022, citing *Overseas Union Ltd v New Hampshire Co* [1992] 1 QB 434; *C v C (Brussels II: French Conciliation and Divorce Proceedings)* [2005] EWCA Civ 68, [2005] 1 WLR 469; and *L-K v K (Brussels II Revised: Maintenance Pending Suit)* [2006] EWHC 153 (Fam), [2006] 2 FLR 1113.

[140] *Rogers-Headicar v Rogers-Headicar* [2004] EWCA Civ 1867, [2005] 2 FCR 1—the state of the pleadings cannot qualify the existence or otherwise of a court's jurisdiction to hear a suit; W's being given permission to amend her pleaded case was held to be only a case management decision which had no impact on the time at which the court was seised.

[141] [2003] EWCA Civ 1830.

[142] Ibid, per THORPE LJ, at [8].

[143] See *Wermuth v Wermuth* [2003] EWCA Civ 50, [2003] 1 WLR 942, per THORPE LJ, at [34]; and *L-K v K (Brussels II Revised: Maintenance Pending Suit)* [2006] EWHC 153 (Fam), [2006] 2 FLR 1113.

[144] Infra, p 959 et seq.

[145] See also Brussels II *bis*, Recital (16).

The rule on provisional and protective measures is not subject to the jurisdictional rules of Brussels II *bis*. It does not require provisional measures to be taken, but rather gives a discretion to a court which has no jurisdiction over the substance of the dispute if four conditions are satisfied:[146] (a) the measures are provisional within the meaning of the Regulation; (b) the court has power to grant the measures under national law; (c) the court considers that in the circumstances of the case it is appropriate to grant them; and (d) the case is urgent. In applying to "persons or assets", Article 20 affects matters outside the scope of the instrument, and is silent not only on the types of measures which may be taken, but also regarding the extent of their necessary connection with the matrimonial proceedings. The significance lies in the fact that the measures may be adopted by the court of one Member State even though the court of another Member State has jurisdiction over the main dispute. In invoking Article 20, the court of one Member State plays a supporting role to the court of another. The measures terminate, however, when a court in the Member State having jurisdiction over the main dispute delivers a judgment on the basis of Article 3 of the Regulation.

In *Wermuth v Wermuth*,[147] the Court of Appeal was required to consider whether an English order for maintenance pending suit in the sum of £12,500 per month, two-thirds of which was intended to provide the respondent wife with funds with which to litigate, was a protective measure in terms of Brussels II. It had been envisaged by the judge at first instance that the maintenance would run indefinitely. There was no realistic prospect of repayment by the wife, should that have been required by the substantive judgment of the German court in which the divorce proceedings were taking place. The Court of Appeal concluded that, in the light of the substance and duration of the maintenance order, it was neither a protective nor a provisional measure under Article 12 of Brussels II (Article 20 of Brussels II *bis*), for the maintenance order had not been urgent or protective in accordance with established principles, and it amounted to an unwarranted invasion of the proper function of the German court. Article 12 (Article 20, Brussels II *bis*) was to be narrowly construed since to do otherwise would be to usurp the power of the court first seised. Lawrence COLLINS J sounded a word of caution regarding the use of Article 12 (Article 20, Brussels II *bis*):

> Provisional measures vary from one context to another, and from one country to another, but what they have in common is that their object is to ensure that the rights of parties and the ultimate effectiveness of a judgment are not frustrated by the actions of one party pending resolution of their respective rights. In the international context it is vitally important to ensure that provisional measures are not used to frustrate internationally agreed principles of jurisdiction.[148]

(iii) Concurrent proceedings in a non-European Community Member State, or in Denmark—discretionary stays

As stated above, Article 19 of Brussels II *bis* is limited to concurrent proceedings in different Member States. It does not apply to concurrent actions in England and a

---

[146] Articulated in *Wermuth v Wermuth* [2003] EWCA Civ 50, [2003] 1 WLR 942, per Lawrence COLLINS J, at [40].

[147] ibid.

[148] At [38].

non-European Community Member State country, such as South Africa. In such cases, an English court will continue to employ traditional rules based upon the doctrine of *forum non conveniens*, and given statutory expression in paragraph 9 of Schedule 1 to the Domicile and Matrimonial Proceedings Act 1973. Where, before the beginning of the trial of any matrimonial proceedings[149] (other than proceedings governed by Brussels II *bis*[150]) which are continuing before the English courts, it appears that any proceedings[151] are pending in another jurisdiction[152] in respect of, or capable of affecting, the validity or subsistence of the marriage in question, then the English court has a discretion to stay its own proceedings. It has been held that proceedings in India for maintenance and for an injunction to allow the wife to reoccupy the matrimonial home do not affect the validity or subsistence of the marriage.[153] This discretion is wider than in the case of the obligatory staying provisions in that it applies to proceedings before other foreign[154] courts and it also applies to a much wider range of proceedings before the other courts.[155] In this case, the court may act not only on the application of a spouse but also of its own motion, and so it might exercise its discretion to stay proceedings in circumstances covered by the mandatory staying provisions where a spouse has not sought such a stay.

The basis on which the court's discretion is to be exercised is stated to be that the balance of fairness and convenience between the parties, having regard to all relevant factors, including the convenience of witnesses and delay or expense likely to result from a decision whether or not to stay the proceedings, is such that it is appropriate for the proceedings before the other court to be disposed of first.[156] It will depend on the facts of each case as to how the judge will draw this balance, but some guidance has emerged from the small number of reported cases directly concerned with the exercise of the discretion. What is clear is that, in determining the principles for the exercise of the discretion under the 1973 Act, the courts are to apply the general approach to the operation of the doctrine of *forum non conveniens* under the inherent jurisdiction which was developed in the context of commercial cases.[157] This means that the discretion under paragraph 9 of Schedule 1 to the 1973 Act ought to be exercised to grant a stay if the defendant can point to another forum which is the appropriate one for trial of the proceedings, provided that the petitioner does not show that justice cannot be done there.[158] However, it does not

---

[149] These are defined as proceedings for divorce, judicial separation, nullity, and declarations as to the validity or subsistence of the petitioner's marriage: Sch 1, para 2. Proceedings for presumption of death and dissolution of marriage, and for declarations of legitimacy or parentage are not included. Trial of an ancillary issue as to custody or financial relief is not trial of the matrimonial proceedings: *Thyssen-Bornemisza v Thyssen-Bornemisza* [1986] Fam 1.

[150] In respect of which, see supra, pp 956–959.

[151] The foreign proceedings may be of any kind, both as to the relief sought and the nature of the proceedings, including presumably administrative proceedings, so long as they are of a description prescribed by rules of court: Sch 1, paras 5 and 6; see Family Proceedings Rules 1991, rr 2.3, 2.27.

[152] Ie a non-EC Member State, or in Denmark.

[153] *Kapur v Kapur* [1984] FLR 920 at 922.

[154] Ie a non-EC Member State, or in Denmark.

[155] In so far as it applies also to cases covered by the mandatory staying provisions, the court shall not exercise its discretionary power whilst an application for a mandatory stay is pending: Sch 1, para 9(3).

[156] Sch 1, paras 9(1) and (2).

[157] *Spiliada Maritime Corpn v Cansulex Ltd* [1987] AC 460, supra, p 426 et seq.

[158] See *T v T (Jurisdiction: Forum Conveniens)* [1995] 2 FLR 660—English proceedings stayed in favour of those in Kenya, despite the absence of legal aid there.

seem that it has to be shown that the foreign forum is clearly or distinctly more appropriate than the English one.[159]

The drawing together of the statutory and common law approaches was achieved by the House of Lords in *De Dampierre v De Dampierre*:[160]

> The husband and wife were both French nationals who married in France in 1977. Two years later they moved to London. Then, in 1984, the wife established an antiques business in New York and in 1985 she took their child to live there with her. The wife refused to return and the husband started divorce proceedings in France, whereupon the wife then petitioned for divorce in England.[161] The husband sought to have the English proceedings stayed. This was resisted by the wife who claimed that, if she was found to be solely responsible for the breakdown of the marriage, she would receive less financial support from a French court than from an English one.

The House of Lords granted a stay, having little doubt that France was the more appropriate forum, given the wife's tenuous links with England and that "she voluntarily severed all connections with England before instituting her English divorce proceedings".[162] If France was the natural forum, then the issue had to be addressed as to whether substantial justice could be done there. In particular, what weight was to be given to the fact that the wife was likely to receive a lower level of financial support from a French than from an English court? In earlier decisions, this had proved to be a factor of considerable significance. For example, in *Gadd v Gadd*,[163] the fact that a wife would receive no financial support in divorce proceedings in Monaco tipped the scales in favour of refusing a stay. Courts should be less influenced by the issue of whether or not financial relief is available in a foreign court, given that the factor of advantage to the petitioner is of less significance since the *Spiliada* case,[164] and that the English courts now have power to grant such relief after a foreign divorce.[165] Certainly, in *De Dampierre*, the House of Lords did not find the difference between French and English matrimonial relief a convincing reason for refusing a stay of the English proceedings.[166] In other cases, as well as the availability of remedies,[167]

---

[159] *Butler v Butler* [1997] 2 All ER 822; cf *S v S* [1997] 2 FLR 100.

[160] [1988] AC 92, especially at pp 102, 108–109; and see *Gadd v Gadd* [1984] 1 WLR 1435; *K v K* [1986] 2 FLR 411; *Mitchell v Mitchell* 1993 SLT 123; see also *Kornberg v Kornberg* (1991) 76 DLR (4th) 379.

[161] Being pre-Brussels II, the English court had jurisdiction to entertain the wife's petition on the basis of the husband's habitual residence in England.

[162] [1988] AC 92 at 102. Cf *Breuning v Breuning* [2002] EWHC 236, [2002] 1 FLR 888; and *Armstrong v Armstrong* [2003] EWHC 777, [2003] 2 FLR 375. Another factor as to the appropriateness of the forum might be the language in which the proceedings are to be conducted and the availability of witnesses: *Shemshadfard v Shemshadfard* [1981] 1 All ER 726 at 734–735; *C v C (Divorce: Stay of English Proceedings)* [2001] 1 FLR 624; and *O v O (Appeal against Stay: Divorce Petition)* [2002] EWCA Civ 949, [2003] 1 FLR 192.

[163] [1984] 1 WLR 1435.

[164] [1987] AC 460 at 482–484, supra, p 426 et seq.

[165] Matrimonial and Family Proceedings Act 1984, Part III, infra, p 1063 et seq; referred to in *Gadd v Gadd* [1984] 1 WLR 1435 at 1442.

[166] [1988] AC 92 at 102, 110; cf *Armstrong v Armstrong* [2003] EWHC 777, [2003] 2 FLR 375. Contrast *R v R (Divorce: Stay of Proceedings)* [1994] 2 FLR 1036; *S v S* [1997] 2 FLR 100; and *O v O (Appeal against Stay: Divorce Petition)* [2002] EWCA Civ 949, [2003] 1 FLR 192.

[167] And see *Mytton v Mytton* (1977) 7 Fam Law 244; *Thyssen-Bornemisza v Thyssen-Bornemisza* [1985] FLR 670. The existence of a pre-nuptial agreement and mutual wills created by the spouses under French law was relevant in the decision to allow the application for stay of the English proceedings in *C v C (Divorce: Stay of English Proceedings)* [2001] 1 FLR 624.

other factors existing at the time of the application for a stay[168] which have been taken into account are whether any English decree or financial provision order will be recognised in the other country,[169] whether continuation of the English proceedings will lead to a speedier outcome of the issue,[170] the location of family property and the matrimonial home,[171] in the case of proceedings where the main issue relates to the children, their links with the jurisdiction in question,[172] and the costs of litigation.[173]

Finally, it should be mentioned that the English proceedings cannot be stayed once the trial of the main issues has begun, save that the court may stay the proceedings at a later time if the petitioner has failed to furnish particulars of concurrent proceedings in another jurisdiction.[174]

Implications of *Owusu v Jackson*[175]   A question arises in this connection regarding the potential implications for matrimonial proceedings of the ECJ ruling in *Owusu v Jackson*. Is it competent for an English court to accede to the plea of *forum non conveniens* (ie in this context, to grant a discretionary stay under the Domicile and Matrimonial Proceedings Act 1973[176]), in circumstances where a defendant, having been sued in a Member State court on the basis of jurisdiction under Article 3 of Brussels II *bis*, nevertheless argues that the balance of fairness, including convenience, is such that it is appropriate that the English proceedings be stayed in favour of another non-Member State court, which constitutes a competent forum in which the case might be tried more suitably for the interests of all the parties and the ends of justice? In other words, would it be consistent with the Brussels II *bis* Regulation, in a case where a claimant has commenced proceedings on the basis of Article 3, for a court of a Member State to exercise its discretionary power, available under its national law, to decline to hear proceedings brought against a person who is habitually resident in the territory of a Member State, or is a national of a Member State (or, in the case of the United Kingdom and of Ireland, has his domicile there), in favour of the courts of a non-Member State?

In light of the judgment in *Owusu v Jackson*, and by analogy with the Court's reasoning in that case, one might speculate that the ECJ would consider Article 3 of Brussels II *bis* to be mandatory[177] in nature, meaning that an English judge, being persuaded that another, non-Member State forum is appropriate, would *not* be permitted to stay proceedings against a defendant sued in England on the basis of Article 3. The likelihood is

---

[168] *Shemshadfard v Shemshadfard* [1981] 1 All ER 726 at 735.

[169] *Thyssen-Bornemisza v Thyssen-Bornemisza* [1985] FLR 670 at 687; and *Armstrong v Armstrong* [2003] EWHC 777, [2003] 2 FLR 375. See, however, *O v O (Appeal against Stay: Divorce Petition)* [2002] EWCA Civ 949, [2003] 1 FLR 192, per Thorpe LJ, at [60] et seq, criticising the reasoning of the judge at first instance, who attached significant weight to doubts about whether an English decree would be recognised in Nigeria.

[170] Ibid.

[171] *Armstrong v Armstrong* [2003] EWHC 777, [2003] 2 FLR 375.

[172] *A v A (Forum Conveniens)* [1999] 1 FLR 1; *Armstrong v Armstrong* [2003] EWHC 777, [2003] 2 FLR 375; and *O v O (Appeal against Stay: Divorce Petition)* [2002] EWCA Civ 949, [2003] 1 FLR 192 (the Nigerian cultural background of the family was a factor put on the scales in favour of a stay of the English proceedings).

[173] *O v O (Appeal against Stay: Divorce Petition)* [2002] EWCA Civ 949, [2003] 1 FLR 192; and *Armstrong v Armstrong* [2003] EWHC 777, [2003] 2 FLR 375.

[174] Sch 1, para 9(4). Trial of a preliminary issue of jurisdiction will, also, not terminate the power to order a stay: Sch 1, para 4(1).

[175] Case C-281-02, [2005] ECR I-1383, [2005] QB 801; supra, Chapter 11.

[176] Sch 1, paras 9(1) and (2); supra, pp 959–960.

[177] Cf reasoning of ECJ in *Owusu*, supra, at [32].

that the ECJ, if asked by means of a preliminary reference to give an interpretative ruling on the point, would deny the possibility of any derogation from the principles enshrined in Article 3, except such as is expressly provided for by Article 7 (residual jurisdiction). The Regulation provides no exception in relation to *forum non conveniens*, at least in relation to matrimonial proceedings.[178] It is highly probable that application, in a case such as has been conjectured, of the doctrine of *forum non conveniens* by means of the operation of a discretionary stay, would be deemed to undermine the desired objectives of certainty and predictability, which are inherent in the Regulation, as well as to jeopardise the legal protection of persons established in the European Community. Thus, by analogous reasoning, it is suggested that the decision in *Owusu* would be likely to preclude a court in a Member State from declining jurisdiction conferred upon it by Article 3 of Brussels II *bis*, on the ground that the court of another, non-Member State constitutes an appropriate forum for trial of the proceedings.

A related question which arises is whether the plea of *forum non conveniens* might be sustained (ie in this context, whether a discretionary stay might be granted in terms of the Domicile and Matrimonial Proceedings Act 1973[179]), in cases where jurisdiction is exercised by a Member State court on the basis of Article 7 (residual jurisdiction)[180] of Brussels II *bis*.[181] The situation envisaged here is where the proceedings in question are within the subject matter scope of Brussels II *bis*, but where none of the bases of jurisdiction set out in Article 3 comes into operation in a given case. According to Article 7 of the Regulation, jurisdiction in this situation is determined by the laws of each Member State.

Despite *Owusu*, it might be speculated that, where the jurisdiction of a court of a Member State is established pursuant to Article 7, the court in question would *not* be prevented from declining to exercise its jurisdiction, in accordance with the doctrine of *forum non conveniens* (ie in this context, on the basis of a discretionary stay under the 1973 Act), on the ground that the court of a *non-Member State* would be an appropriate forum for trial of the proceedings.[182] Where the alternative forum is a non-Member State, it may be assumed, with some confidence, that the exercise of a *forum non conveniens* discretion still would be available. Where, however, the alternative forum is another Member State, it seems most unlikely that the ECJ would interpret the provisions of the Regulation in such a manner as would sanction the continuing exercise of a *forum non conveniens* discretion.[183] A further consideration in support of this view, and a practical danger, corresponding to that mentioned previously in relation to civil and commercial matters,[184] is that even if an English court, the jurisdiction of which has been "established", should attempt to exercise its discretion and to stay English proceedings in favour of an alternative Member State forum, the court "second seised" would be bound to decline jurisdiction

---

[178] See, however, the transfer mechanism in Art 15, in relation to proceedings concerning matters of parental responsibility.

[179] Sch 1, paras 9(1) and (2); supra, pp 959–960.

[180] For England, under s 5(2)(b) of the Domicile and Matrimonial Proceedings Act 1973; supra, p 951.

[181] Cf, in civil and commercial matters, supra, pp 949–951.

[182] Cf reasoning in relation to matrimonial anti-suit injunctions, discussed, infra, pp 964–965.

[183] Irrespective, it is submitted, of the position which currently pertains with regard to civil and commercial matters, per *Sarrio SA v Kuwait Investment Authority* [1997] 1 Lloyd's Rep 113; supra, p 313 et seq.

[184] See supra, pp 309–310, regarding the operation of Art 27 of the Brussels I Regulation.

on the basis of Article 19 (lis pendens) of Brussels II *bis*.[185] The risk, therefore, would be that no court would exercise jurisdiction in the given case to hear the proceedings.

(iv) General matters

In the case of both obligatory and discretionary stays, the English court has a power, on application by one of the parties to the proceedings, to discharge the order staying any proceedings if the other proceedings are stayed or concluded, or if there has been unreasonable delay in prosecuting them.[186] Once an obligatory stay has been discharged the proceedings cannot again be obligatorily stayed;[187] though a discretion to stay remains but cannot normally be exercised once the trial of the English proceedings has begun. Special provision is made for the granting of ancillary relief in the case where English proceedings are stayed because proceedings are pending in another British jurisdiction.[188] It should be mentioned that the staying provisions contained in the Domicile and Matrimonial Proceedings Act 1973 are in addition to, and not in substitution for, any other power to stay proceedings.[189] The inherent power to stay was rarely used in matrimonial proceedings,[190] but, as we have seen, there is now little difference between the statutory power to stay and the developed common law doctrine of *forum non conveniens*.[191]

(c) Restraining foreign proceedings (anti-suit injunctions)

The English court has long had the inherent power, in matrimonial proceedings, to restrain by injunction a party who wished to pursue foreign matrimonial proceedings;[192] but it is a power which has been sparingly and carefully exercised. Lord GOFF in the Privy Council[193] and in the House of Lords[194] has laid down the principles on which this inherent power is to be exercised in the commercial context, and the Court of Appeal has made clear in *Hemain v Hemain*[195] that such principles are to be applied in matrimonial cases.[196]

---

[185] Supra, pp 356–358.

[186] Sch 1, para 10(1).

[187] Sch 1, para 10(2).

[188] Sch 1, para 11. These provisions are considered more fully in the context of jurisdiction to grant ancillary relief, infra, p 1050 et seq.

[189] S 5(6)(b). This seems to have been overlooked by DUNN LJ in *Gadd v Gadd* [1984] 1 WLR 1435 at 1438.

[190] *Sealey (otherwise Callan) v Callan* [1953] P 135—a divorce case where the court, in fact, declined to stay the English proceedings; and see *Baroness von Eckhardstein v Baron von Eckhardstein* (1907) 23 TLR 539 and 593 (judicial separation).

[191] But see *W v W (Financial Relief: Appropriate Forum)* [1997] 1 FLR 257; *Krenge v Krenge* [1999] 1 FLR 969.

[192] See *Orr-Lewis v Orr-Lewis* [1949] P 347, where, in the exercise of its discretion, the divorce court declined to issue an injunction; contrast *Bryant v Bryant* (1980) 11 Fam Law 85 where an injunction was issued restraining a husband from taking steps to have a Canadian divorce decree nisi made absolute in order to protect the wife's position in seeking relief from the English courts. In *Christian v Christian* (1897) 78 LT 86 the English courts hearing judicial separation proceedings did restrain the husband from pursuing divorce proceedings in Scotland.

[193] *Société National Industrielle Aérospatiale v Lee Kui Jak* [1987] AC 871 supra, p 460.

[194] *Airbus Industrie GIE v Patel* [1999] 1 AC 119, HL. See supra, p 457.

[195] [1988] 2 FLR 388.

[196] See also *Kornberg v Kornberg* (1991) 76 DLR (4th) 379; *Harris v Murray* (1995) 11 RFL (4th) 450; *B v B (Divorce: Stay of Foreign Proceedings)* [2002] EWHC 1711, [2003] 1 FLR 1 (injunction refused); and *R v R (Divorce: Hemain Injunction)* [2003] EWHC 2113, [2005] 1 FLR 386 (injunction granted).

In the commercial context, the decision in *Turner v Grovit*[197] made plain that the use by one European Community Member State forum of an anti-suit injunction to seek to restrain a party from litigating in the court of another Member State is not acceptable, as being tantamount to interference with the jurisdiction of the foreign court, and in breach of the obligation on the courts of Member States to refrain from acting in a manner that is incompatible with the Brussels I Regulation. Whether, in a family law context, the Brussels II *bis* Regulation would be construed in like manner, as precluding the grant by a court in one Member State of an injunction prohibiting a party to proceedings before it from commencing or continuing proceedings in the court of another Member State, is a matter of speculation. It is not clear whether it would be deemed inconsistent with the Brussels II *bis* Regulation for one Member State court to grant an injunction against a defendant who is threatening to commence or continue matrimonial proceedings in a "foreign" court.

In the light of the decision in *Turner v Grovit*, and by analogy with the Court's reasoning in that case, it might be thought likely that the ECJ, if asked by means of a preliminary reference to give an interpretative ruling on the point, would deny the availability of an injunction restraining foreign proceedings as a remedy in a matrimonial case, at least in the situation where it is sought to restrain proceedings in *another Member State*. This, it is suggested, would probably be the decision, regardless of whether the court exercising jurisdiction were doing so on the basis of Article 3 (general jurisdiction), or Article 7 (residual jurisdiction) of Brussels II *bis*. It is submitted that an injunction in these circumstances would be very likely to be judged incompatible with the regime put in place by Brussels II *bis*.

Where, however, the proceedings sought to be restrained are in a *non-Member State*, the position would be less clear. This would be the situation where an English court has jurisdiction under one of the bases set out in Article 3 of Brussels II *bis*, and the claimant in those proceedings seeks to restrain a party from commencing or continuing proceedings in a non-Member State. The injunction, if granted, would constitute, in effect, an interference with the jurisdiction of a non-Member State court only. In this situation, it could plausibly be argued that this would not be incompatible with the Brussels II *bis* regime. Indeed, as previously stated in relation to civil and commercial matters, in these circumstances the injunction, if anything, would be being utilised to uphold the jurisdiction allocated under Brussels II *bis*, and so its grant ought not to be viewed as being incompatible with the Regulation. Likewise, where the jurisdiction of a Member State court is established pursuant to Article 7 of the Regulation, this, it is submitted, should not prevent the court from granting an injunction prohibiting a party to proceedings before it from commencing or continuing proceedings in the court of a *non-Member State*.

---

[197] Case C-159/02, [2005] 1 AC 101; supra, p 458.

(b) Choice of law

(i) Divorce and judicial separation[198]

At common law, the sole basis of the jurisdiction of the English courts in divorce was domicile[199] and no choice of law problem arose. English law was applied and this could be justified either as the application of the law of the domicile[200] to issues affecting status or as the application of the law of the forum on the basis that dissolution of a marriage is a matter which "touches fundamental English conceptions of morality, religion and public policy",[201] and one which is governed exclusively by rules and conditions imposed by the English legislature.

The need for a choice of law rule arises when the court possesses jurisdiction on some basis other than domicile, as may be illustrated by *Zanelli v Zanelli*:[202]

> An Italian national, domiciled in England, married an Englishwoman in England in 1948. Later he was deported from England and thereupon reverted to his Italian domicile. The Matrimonial Causes Act 1937, which was then in force, had given the English court jurisdiction in divorce (and also judicial separation) in such a case,[203] but it did not impose a rule for the choice of law.

The court, applying English domestic law but without any consideration of the choice of law issue, granted the wife a decree of divorce, despite the rule of the Italian law of her domicile at that time that divorce was not permissible. A similar approach, namely the uniform application of English law, was seen in the case of judicial separation not only where, at common law, jurisdiction was taken on the basis of domicile,[204] but also on the basis of residence[205] or of a matrimonial home within the jurisdiction,[206] even though the parties were domiciled elsewhere.

The English common law rules were later extended to permit divorce and nullity (but not judicial separation) decrees to be granted on the basis of three years' residence in England by a wife,[207] and at that point a statutory choice of law rule was introduced both for this case and for that exemplified in *Zanelli v Zanelli*, ie the domicile of the wife in England immediately prior to the husband's desertion or deportation. This choice of law rule provided that the court should apply "the law which would be applicable thereto if both parties were domiciled in England at the time of the proceedings".[208]

---

[198] North, op cit, pp 146–151; North (1980) I Hague Recueil 9, 77–88; and see for separation Grodecki (1957) 42 Transactions of the Grotius Society 23, 41–43.

[199] *Le Mesurier v Le Mesurier* [1895] AC 517.

[200] *Lord Advocate v Jaffrey* [1921] 1 AC 146 at 152.

[201] Wolff, p 374; and see *Holland v Holland* 1973 (1) SA 897 (T) at 902.

[202] (1948) 64 TLR 556; see also *Niboyet v Niboyet* (1878) 4 PD 1 at 9.

[203] S13 (re-enacted in the Matrimonial Causes Act 1973, s 46(1)(a), itself repealed by the Domicile and Matrimonial Proceedings Act 1973). Jurisdiction could be assumed, in the case of a petition by a wife, on the basis of the husband's domicile in England prior to his desertion or deportation.

[204] *Eustace v Eustace* [1924] P 45.

[205] *Armytage v Armytage* [1898] P 178; *Ward v Ward* (1923) 39 TLR 440.

[206] *Wells v Wells* [1960] NI 122.

[207] Law Reform (Miscellaneous Provisions) Act 1949, s 1(1), re-enacted in the Matrimonial Causes Act 1973, s 46(1)(b), and repealed by the Domicile and Matrimonial Proceedings Act 1973.

[208] Ibid, s 1(4), re-enacted in the Matrimonial Causes Act 1973, s 46(2).

Strangely, this rule was cast in terms which pointed more to the law of the domicile than to the law of the forum. The latter approach could have been expressed far more simply by just saying that English law was applicable. Whilst the two statutory jurisdictional grounds available to the wife prevented considerable hardship in the case of divorce, they did not provide nearly so far-reaching an inroad into the basic jurisdictional rule dependent on domicile as was made by the Domicile and Matrimonial Proceedings Act 1973, and subsequently by the Brussels II and II *bis* Regulations.[209] Habitual residence is now, in practice, the main jurisdictional basis. The two statutory grounds available to a wife, and the attendant choice of law provision, have been abolished.[210] There is now no statutory choice of law rule. It was undoubtedly the intention of the Law Commission, in proposing the reforms which led to the 1973 Act, that English law should be applied,[211] but this does raise the issue whether such a rule is desirable.

Whilst some civil law jurisdictions are prepared to consider the relevance of the divorce law of countries other than the forum,[212] the general approach of the common law is to apply the law of the forum.[213] It is not self-evidently correct that this should be so. One argument in favour of the law of the forum is that divorce law may be regarded as part of the public law of the forum and so should be applied as part of that country's mandatory laws governing the continuance of a marital relationship within that particular society.[214] This argument is strongest in a jurisdiction, like many in the USA, with narrow rules for both jurisdiction and the recognition of foreign divorces. In England—where both sets of rules are broader—it may be much less obvious that parties have a close connection with the forum, especially if they can obtain a divorce abroad and readily have it recognised in England even though obtained on grounds unavailable under English law.[215] A further argument in favour of the law of the forum is that it would cause delay and create expense to apply foreign law to English petitions for divorce or judicial separation, most of which are undefended; and it has also been suggested that to "require English courts to dissolve marriages on exotic foreign grounds would be distasteful to the judges and unacceptable to public opinion".[216] These are dangerous arguments if carried too far. It is always easier and cheaper to apply the law of the forum, but nowhere else in English choice of law rules do we generally apply the law of the forum as such. If we are prepared to take jurisdiction over "exotic foreigners", under broad jurisdictional rules, it is arguably no more distasteful to apply their personal law to the dissolution than to apply it, as we do,[217] to the creation of their marriage.

There are certainly those who advocate the application of the party's personal law, ie the law of their domicile, to divorce and judicial separation—that being the law which should govern matters of status. The main argument in favour of applying the law of the domicile

---

[209] Supra, p 944 et seq.

[210] Domicile and Matrimonial Proceedings Act 1973, s 17(2).

[211] Law Com No 48, paras 103–108.

[212] Eg France, see Batiffol and Lagarde, *Droit International Privé* (1983) 7th edn, Vol II, pp 79–82; and see Palsson, *International Encyclopaedia of Comparative Law* Vol III, Chapter 16, p 129 et seq.

[213] Palsson, op cit, pp 126–129; though see *Alton v Alton* 207 F 2d 667 at 684–685 (1953).

[214] Wolff, *Private International Law* (1950) 2nd edn, 373–374; Cavers (1970) III Hague Recueil 75, 245–246.

[215] See infra, p 986 et seq.

[216] Morris, p 243.

[217] Supra, p 896 et seq.

is that dissolution of the marriage affects the status of the parties no less than does the creation of the marriage and is a substantive, not just a procedural, matter. Whilst the public policy of the forum may have a role to play, as elsewhere in choice of law matters,[218] this should not, it is said, be to the exclusion of other laws. There is, however, a practical difficulty with the application of the law of the domicile. Since a wife may acquire a separate domicile, and this is more likely to have occurred if the marriage has broken down and one spouse is petitioning for a divorce, it would have to be determined which spouse's domicile is to be regarded as the relevant one for choice of law purposes. The answer to such a question can be little more than arbitrary and militates against the application of the law of the domicile.

The arguments on choice of law in divorce and judicial separation have been summed up thus:

> The decision on choice of law rules in divorce must depend upon a balance between principle, which undoubtedly points to the application of the personal law, and pragmatism which favours the *lex fori*. It is no surprise that the civil law supports the former and the common law the latter. What is worrying about the common law approach is that a rule which was historically justified by its jurisdictional link has been maintained with little real consideration of the implications of breaking that jurisdictional link.[219]

The Matrimonial Causes Act 1973, unlike its predecessors, is silent on choice of law matters relating to divorce and judicial separation, though the fact that there is no express saving for the rules of private international law in the case of divorce and judicial separation, such as there is in the case of nullity,[220] provides some tacit support for the application of the law of the forum. There is no doubt, however, that in practice English law is applied to all petitions for divorce or judicial separation which come before the English courts.[221] The rules of English law existing at the time of the proceedings are applied and they will decide whether there is a good cause for divorce or judicial separation, and will determine the form of relief and the conditions on which the decree will be granted. Any other legal system, such as the law under which the parties married, the law(s) of their domiciles or nationalities, or the law of the place where the facts on which the petition is based took place, is completely irrelevant.[222] It should be mentioned that under English law it does not matter that the facts evidencing breakdown of the marriage did not constitute a basis for divorce in the country where they took place,[223] or in the country of the parties' domiciles.[224] Nor does it matter that the ground for divorce was not a ground under English law at the time that the cause arose.[225]

Rome III As stated above,[226] in July 2006, the European Commission published a Proposal for a Council Regulation amending Regulation (EC) No 2201/2003 as regards

---

[218] Supra, p 139 et seq.
[219] North (1980) I Hague Recueil 9, 87–88.
[220] Matrimonial Causes Act 1973, s 14, infra, pp 983–984.
[221] *Quoraishi v Quoraishi* [1985] FLR 780, especially at 783.
[222] *Czepek v Czepek* [1962] 3 All ER 990.
[223] Eg *Czepek v Czepek*, supra; and see *Holland v Holland* 1973 (1) SA 897 (T).
[224] See *Quoraishi v Quoraishi* [1985] FLR 780, [1985] Fam Law 308, CA; *Grummett v Grummett* (1965) 7 FLR 415.
[225] Eg *Pratt v Pratt* [1939] AC 417.
[226] Supra, p 952.

jurisdiction and introducing rules concerning applicable law in matrimonial matters ("Rome III").[227] The changes proposed in relation to jurisdiction have been considered already in this chapter. As regards choice of law, it is proposed to introduce a set of Community rules in respect of applicable law in matrimonial matters. The rule is based, in the first instance, on the possibility of choice of law by the spouses. The choice is confined to laws[228] with which the spouses are deemed to have a close connection (their last common habitual residence, in so far as one of them still resides there; the nationality/domicile of either spouse; their common habitual residence throughout a period of five years; the law of the forum[229]). In the absence of choice of the applicable law, a hierarchical rule has been suggested. It is proposed that the governing law should be the law of the state (a) where the spouses have their common habitual residence; failing that (b) where the spouses had their last common habitual residence, in so far as one of them still resides there; failing that (c) of which both spouses are nationals, or in the cases of the United Kingdom and of Ireland, domiciliaries; failing that (d) where the application is lodged.[230] It is proposed that renvoi should be excluded,[231] and that the applicable law would be subject to the public policy of the forum.[232]

The Proposal is flawed in many respects, eg it does not deal adequately with questions of mutability of the personal law connecting factor (ie it does not clearly identify the time at which the parties' habitual residence, nationality or domicile is to be determined), nor does it address the time at which parties are to be permitted to make agreements as to choice of court and/or choice of law. Whilst a harmonised choice of law rule in itself might be an attractive prospect,[233] and would help to offset any tactical advantage which a party intent on forum shopping (aided by the operation of the *lis pendens* doctrine) might enjoy,[234] the Proposal, as drafted, would override the certainty and ease of application afforded by the choice of law rule currently applied by the legal systems of the United Kingdom, in terms of which the applicable law is the domestic law of the forum.

---

[227] COM (2006) 399 final, and Document 5274/07 LIMITE JUSTCIV 4, 12 January 2007. See also Green Paper on applicable law and jurisdiction in divorce matters (COM (2005) 82 final) 14 March 2005; Commission Staff Working Paper, Annex to the Green Paper on applicable law and jurisdiction in divorce matters (SEC (2005) 331) 14 March 2005; and House of Lords EU Committee, 52nd Report, Session 2005/06, "Rome III—Choice of Law in Divorce" (2006).

[228] Although not explicitly stated in the Proposal, the draft instrument is intended to be of universal application, ie the parties' choice of law, and the applicable law in the absence of choice of law, would not be restricted to the law of an a European Community Member State. Although the principle of universal application is familiar in choice of law in contract (1980 Rome Convention, Art 2), and has been adopted in relation to choice of law concerning non-contractual obligations (Rome II, Art 3), its appropriateness in the context of family law is questionable; eg how desirable would it be for an English court to be required to apply the provisions of the Muslim Family Law Ordinance of Pakistan, were spouses to agree upon the application of the law of Pakistan?

[229] COM (2006) 399 final, Art 1(7)(1), Art 20(a). There is a lack of internal symmetry in the Proposal between Art 3(a) (choice of court by the parties) and Art 20(a) (choice of law by the parties).

[230] COM (2006) 399 final, Art 1(7)(1), Art 20(b).

[231] COM (2006) 399 final, Art 1(7)(1), Art 20(d).

[232] COM (2006) 399 final, Art 1(7)(1), Art 20(e). There is no reference, interestingly, to the concept of mandatory rules of potentially relevant/interested legal systems.

[233] Though, arguably, the Proposal is "an answer to a problem of the Commission's own making by its incursion into family law", and the provision, in Art 3 of Brussels II *bis*, of no fewer than seven possible divorce forums (Crawford and Carruthers, para 12-15).

[234] See Crawford and Carruthers, para 12-15.

As previously stated, the United Kingdom government has decided not to opt into a resulting Community instrument.[235]

(ii) Nullity[236]

(a) Introduction

Whilst divorce gives rise to few choice of law problems, the same cannot be said for nullity. The reasons for this are varied. A nullity decree is concerned with the validity of the creation of a marriage, unlike divorce which dissolves a marriage which is admittedly validly created. This means that the choice of law issues in nullity are essentially the same as those already examined in the context of marriage. The question to be asked is the same—is the marriage valid or invalid? General issues of formal and essential validity have already been examined[237] as matters relating to marriage. But others, such as lack of consent and physical defects, are considered here because they tend to arise in nullity petitions. Another reason why choice of law in nullity is a more difficult area than divorce is that the effects of annulment vary according to the particular ground in issue and they vary in relation to the same ground even within the United Kingdom. Some defects avoid a marriage *ab initio*, ie render it void, whilst others merely render it voidable. These distinctions can readily be exemplified. If one party is below the minimum age of marriage or is already married, English law regards the marriage as void.[238] If, however, a decree is granted in England on the ground of lack of consent, the marriage will be regarded as voidable.[239] In Scotland, on the other hand, lack of consent renders the marriage void *ab initio*.[240] Again, impotence or wilful refusal to consummate the marriage renders it voidable under English law;[241] whereas in Scotland, although impotence also renders the marriage voidable, wilful refusal has no effect on its validity.

The difference between void and voidable marriages is significant.[242] "A void marriage is no marriage. Considered literally the expression is self-destructive and contradictory. But without misleading anyone it serves to denote the situation where a ceremony of marriage does not bring about a marriage."[243] No proceedings are necessary to establish the fact of its nullity, though it may in practice be wise to take them, eg to obtain maintenance for the "wife" and any child of the "marriage" or to still doubts as to one's status where the position is disputed. Moreover, any member of the public may treat the marriage as void, notwithstanding the absence of a decree, as, for instance, by withholding

---

[235] See House of Lords, Written Statements, 18 Apr 2007: column WS7, per Baroness Ashton of Upholland; and in Scotland, Report of the Justice I Committee of the Scottish Parliament (CJ1004/2005, 7 October 2005). Ireland also has decided not to opt in to Rome III: Press Release 10 October 2006, at http://www.justice.ie/en/JELR/Pages/GovernmentrejectsEUdivorceproposals.

[236] North, op cit, chapter 8; Law Commission Working Paper No 89 (1985), Pt V.

[237] Supra, p 878 et seq.

[238] Matrimonial Causes Act 1973, s 11.

[239] Ibid, s 12.

[240] See, however, Family Law (Scotland) Act 2006, s 2, inserting s 20A into the Marriage (Scotland) Act 1977.

[241] Ibid.

[242] On the differences between void marriages and "non-marriages", see *Gereis v Yagoub* [1997] 1 FLR 854, at 857; and *Gandhi v Patel* [2002] 1 FLR 603 at [31] and [37]. Supra, p 879, n 28.

[243] *Ross Smith v Ross Smith* [1963] AC 280 at 314.

payment of money that is due to the woman conditionally on her being the wife of the man.

On the other hand: "A voidable marriage is one that will be regarded by every court as a valid subsisting marriage until a decree annulling it has been pronounced by a court of competent jurisdiction."[244] So the effect of a defect, like impotence, that renders a marriage voidable in England is such that the status of the parties as husband and wife, having sprung from a contract free from imperfection, cannot be affected until the existence of the defect has been proved, and therefore the rule is that the marriage is valid and must be treated as such by every court and every person until it has been judicially declared void. No one but the parties themselves can be heard to deny that they are married or can challenge, by nullity proceedings or otherwise, the validity of their marriage. Until either of them obtains a decree of nullity, all the normal consequences of the married status ensue, both *inter se* and as regards third parties.

There are also further differences in relation to the effects of an annulment. The annulment of a void marriage has retrospective effect; it declares the marriage never to have existed. However, the position is different in England in the case of a voidable marriage. Although the annulment of such a marriage had retrospective effect at common law, the position in the case of nullity decrees granted after 31 July 1971 is that the decree operates to annul the marriage prospectively only from the date of the decree absolute. Until that time the marriage must be treated as subsisting.[245]

A further difficulty in nullity cases is the all too common disregard of the elementary and primary distinction between jurisdiction and choice of law. The tendency of the judges, in cases involving lack of consent or physical incapacities, after surmounting the problem of jurisdiction, has been to apply the internal law of England as a matter of course.[246] Not only does this mean that the principles on which the choice of law depends are undeveloped, but it is particularly regrettable that the personal law should be deprived of its control over the married status.

(b) Classification of the nature of the defect

The ascertainment of the proper law in a nullity suit depends on analysing the various defects that may constitute cause for annulment, in order to determine their intrinsic nature. Once this is done, the legal system to which a particular defect is subject should become apparent. The consequence of this analysis is that, once the court has jurisdiction, then, in order to determine the law applicable to some alleged defect, it applies its own characterisation to decide whether the defect is as to form or essential validity. If, for example, it is the former, then it applies the rules of the law of the place of celebration to the issue in question. This may be illustrated by the British Columbia decision in *Solomon v Walters*,[247] where the facts were these:

---

[244] *De Reneville v De Reneville* [1948] P 100 at 111.
[245] Matrimonial Causes Act 1973, s 16.
[246] Eg *Easterbrook v Easterbrook* [1944] 1 All ER 90; *Hunter v Hunter* [1944] P 95; *Buckland v Buckland* [1968] P 296.
[247] (1956) 3 DLR (2d) 78; and see *Lepre v Lepre* [1965] P 52 at 60, where the law of the place of celebration considered the marriage to be valid rather than voidable or void.

> A marriage had been celebrated in Nevada between the husband, domiciled in British Columbia, and the wife, apparently domiciled in Alberta. The wife petitioned in British Columbia for a nullity decree on the ground of lack of parental consent as required by Nevada law, though by the domestic law of British Columbia the marriage was unaffected by the defect; by Nevada law it was rendered voidable.

The judge, having classified the defect as one of form, applied Nevada law and granted a decree of nullity. If the defect is as to capacity, then as has been seen,[248] the court should apply the ante-nuptial domiciliary law of the party alleged incapable.

It remains to consider other, more problematical, choice of law areas, namely lack of consent and personal physical defects.

(c) Lack of consent: is it formal or essential?

There is no settled authority as to whether defects affecting consent to marry are to be classified as akin to form, and thus to be governed by the law of the place of celebration, or as personal defects, thus raising questions of essential validity to be referred to the personal law of the parties.[249] There is a variety of different grounds on which an allegation of lack of consent can be based,[250] not all of which are sufficient in English domestic law. It may be argued that one party was mistaken as to the identity of the other party[251] or as to the marriage ceremony,[252] or that the marriage was entered into as the result of fraud[253]or fear caused by duress or coercion,[254] or during mental illness,[255] or there may have been a mistake as to the legal effects of the ceremony,[256] or as to the attributes of the other party,[257] or cases where one or both parties has/have made mental reservations as to the effect of the ceremony.[258] What is remarkable is that the English courts for many years failed to realise that a choice of law problem existed in such cases and invariably applied English law. It is a masterly understatement to say that, "there has been some difference of opinion as to what law applies".[259] Indeed, virtually the only cases in which there has been any discussion of the issue have been those where it was not necessary for the decision.

---

[248] Supra, p 896.

[249] Woodhouse (1954) 3 ICLQ 454.

[250] Neville Brown (1968) 42 Tul LR 837.

[251] Cf *C v C* [1942] NZLR 356.

[252] *Valier v Valier* (1925) 133 LT 830; *Parojcic v Parojcic* [1958] 1 WLR 1280; and see *Ford v Stier* [1896] P 1; and similarly *Mehta v Mehta* [1945] 2 All ER 690—belief that the marriage ceremony was merely one of conversion to Hinduism.

[253] *Johnson v Smith* (1968) 70 DLR (2d) 374.

[254] Either external pressure, such as political oppression, or for humanitarian reasons (*H v H* [1954] P 258; *Szechter v Szechter* [1971] P 286); or family/community pressure in respect of a forced marriage (*Hussein v Hussein* [1938] P 159; *Parojcic v Parojcic* [1958] 1 WLR 1280; *Buckland v Buckland* [1968] P 296; *Mahmood v Mahmood* 1993 SLT 589; *Mahmud v Mahmud* 1994 SLT 559; *Sohrab v Kahn* 2002 SLT 1255; *Hakeem v Hussain* 2003 SLT 515, and on appeal, *H v H* 2005 SLT 1025; *P v R (Forced Marriage: Annulment: Procedure)* [2003] 1 FLR 661; *Singh v Singh* 2005 SLT 749; and *NS v MI* [2006] EWHC 1646 (Fam)).

[255] Cf *Re Park's Estate* [1954] P 89; affd [1953] 2 All ER 1411.

[256] *Way v Way* [1950] P 71 at 79–80, approved [1951] P 124 at 133–134; *Kassim v Kassim* [1962] P 224.

[257] Cf *Mitford v Mitford* [1923] P 130.

[258] *Bell v Graham* (1859) 13 Moo PCC 242; *Silver v Silver* [1955] 1 WLR 728; cf *Johnson v Smith* (1968) 70 DLR (2d) 374. In Scotland, see *Akram v Akram* 1979 SLT (Notes) 87; *Hakeem v Hussain* 2003 SLT 515, and on appeal, *H v H* 2005 SLT 1025; and Family Law (Scotland) Act 2006, s 2, discussed infra, p 978.

[259] *Mahadervan v Mahadervan* [1962] 3 All ER 1108 at 111. This is omitted from the report in [1964] P 233.

(i) Application of the law of the forum

The only solution supported by all the direct authorities is reference to English law as the law of the forum in "consent" cases, but this is, in truth, an abdication from the problem. The decisions can be explained as having been reached *per incuriam*, and so reference to the law of the forum should only be accepted on such merits of principle as it may have. It has been suggested[260] that the law of the forum can be applied to cases of mistake as to the legal nature of the ceremony and to sham marriages, but not to cases of mistake as to the legal effects of the marriage which should be referred to the law of the mistaken party's ante-nuptial domicile.[261] The justification that the former concern issues of fact more appropriate for the forum than the issues raised in the latter case is not convincing, because the determination of a factual question, such as whether or not duress existed, does not of itself resolve the problem of the effect of such duress on the validity of the marriage.

The common judicial attitude of ignoring choice of law issues so far as the parties' consent is concerned may be illustrated by *Buckland v Buckland*.[262] Here a marriage celebrated in Malta between two Maltese domiciliaries was declared a nullity by an English court on the ground that the petitioner had gone through the ceremony because of fear of an unjust prosecution if he did not. Only English law was referred to, and yet the only connection with England was that, by the date of the proceedings, the petitioner had become domiciled in England. Determination of the applicable law could have been referred to other legal systems, whose varied claims we must now examine.

(ii) Application of the law of the place of celebration

In *Parojcic v Parojcic*,[263] DAVIES J referred the question of the effect of duress to English law as the law of the place of celebration. Despite this dictum, the view that that law should govern only "the method of giving consent as distinct from the fact of consent"[264] seems preferable. This is because, even in the sphere of commercial contracts, the issue of the parties' consent is not referred to the law of the place of contracting.[265] Indeed, it would seem that a marriage may comply with all the formal requirements of the law of the place of celebration and yet lack essential validity because of lack of consent.[266] Thus, even though reference to the law of the place of celebration is in accordance with many of the cases, there are certainly others which militate against it.[267]

(iii) Application of the law of the domicile

The same can also be said of the opinion that "no marriage is (*semble*) valid if by the law of either party's domicile he or she does not consent to marry the other".[268] There are at

---

[260] Webb (1959) 22 MLR 198, 202–204.

[261] Cf *Kassim v Kassim*, supra.

[262] [1968] P 296; see also *Kassim v Kassim*, supra; *Kelly v Ireland* [1996] 2 ILRM 364.

[263] [1958] 1 WLR 1280 at 1283.

[264] *Apt v Apt* [1948] P 83 at 88.

[265] Supra, pp 744–746.

[266] *Nane v Sykiotis* (1966) 57 DLR (2d) 118 at 122.

[267] *Bell v Graham*, supra; *Mehta v Mehta*, supra; *Apt v Apt* [1948] P 83 at 88; and see *H v H* [1954] P 258; *Silver v Silver*, supra; *Kassim v Kassim*, supra; *Buckland v Buckland*, supra.

[268] Dicey, Morris and Collins, para 17R-118.

least three English decisions[269] in which the validity of a marriage, so far as consent is concerned, has been considered without reference to the domiciliary law of one or both of the parties. The weight of opinion does, however, favour reference of the issue of consent to the law of the domicile. The view that lack of consent is a personal defect was accepted by HODSON J in *Way v Way*:[270]

> The petitioner, a British subject domiciled in England, went through a ceremony of marriage at Archangel with the respondent, domiciled in Russia, as the result of which he believed that he had been legally married. He later claimed annulment on the grounds (1) that certain formalities required by Russian law had been omitted and (2) that the marriage was void for want of consent, since he believed at the time of the ceremony that his wife would be allowed to accompany him to England (which was not permitted by the Soviet authorities) and also that it was the duty of both parties to live together. According to Russian law he was mistaken in both respects.

HODSON J began by finding that there had been no neglect of Russian formalities. He went on to propound the doctrine that "questions of consent are to be dealt with by reference to the personal law of the parties rather than by reference to the law of the place where the contract was made", with the result that "the matrimonial law of each of the parties" had to be applied.[271] He then held that, by English law, which was the personal law of the petitioner, consent is not nullified by a mistake of the kind pleaded, ie mistake as to attributes, a finding with which it is impossible to disagree.

The Court of Appeal[272] held the marriage to be void on the ground that the Russian formalities had not, in fact, been observed, and therefore anything that was said about the law to govern the question of consent was obiter. However, Sir Raymond EVERSHED MR was "prepared to assume" that HODSON J was correct in referring the question to the personal law of the parties.[273]

This decision to refer issues of consent to the law of the domicile was followed in *Szechter v Szechter*:[274]

> The husband, his first wife and his secretary, Nina, all were domiciled in Poland. The secretary was imprisoned for "anti-state activities" and her health deteriorated rapidly. In order to obtain her release from prison, the husband secretly divorced his first wife and in 1968 married Nina in prison. Shortly thereafter she was released from prison and all three came to England, where they acquired a domicile. Nina petitioned for the annulment of her marriage on the grounds of duress, so that the husband and first wife could resume their married life.

These facts undoubtedly raised an issue of choice of law. Polish law was the law of the place of celebration and the law of the domicile of both parties at the time of the marriage. English law was the law of the forum and the law of the domicile at the time of

---

[269] *Silver v Silver*, supra; *Kassim v Kassim*, supra; *Buckland v Buckland*, supra; and see *Cooper v Crane* [1891] P 369; *H v H*, supra; and see also *Parojcic v Parojcic* [1958] 1 WLR 1280 at 1283.

[270] [1950] P 71.

[271] Ibid, at 78.

[272] *Kenward v Kenward* [1951] P 124.

[273] Ibid, at 133.

[274] [1971] P 286; cf *Feiner v Demkowicz* (1973) 42 DLR (3d) 165; *Re Suria's Marriage* (1977) 29 FLR 308.

the proceedings. Both legal systems agreed that the marriage was void for duress. However, Sir Jocelyn SIMON P concluded that it was for Polish law, as the law of the domicile of the parties at the time of the marriage, to determine the validity of the marriage.[275] In so doing, he approved the proposition in Dicey and Morris[276] that "no marriage is valid if by the law of either party's domicile one party does not consent to marry the other".[277] The editors of that work have, however, accepted[278] the suggestion made in these pages[279] that the issue of a party's alleged lack of consent to marry should be determined by reference to that person's ante-nuptial domiciliary law, and not to the law of both parties' ante-nuptial domiciles.

It seems adequate to analyse the issue of consent as a personal issue to be referred to the law governing capacity, without requiring a wife to have consented not only according to her own law but also according to her husband's, or vice versa. This was the approach taken in Scotland in *Singh v Singh*.[280] The case concerned a United Kingdom citizen, domiciled in Scotland, who sought declaration of nullity of her marriage, celebrated in India, in 2001, to an Indian national, on the grounds of her lack of consent and that the marriage had been entered into under duress. The judge, RF MACDONALD QC, declining to follow the obiter dictum of Lord GUTHRIE in *Di Rollo v Di Rollo*[281] that the question of consent should be decided by the law of the place where the marriage was celebrated,[282] held that the law governing the issue of consent to marriage was the law of the domicile of the party claiming lack of consent.[283] In the instant case, by the law of the petitioner's Scottish domicile, the threats from her mother were deemed to be of a serious nature, amounting to threats of immediate danger to her liberty, which caused her will to be overborne, and vitiated her consent to marry. Declarator of nullity of marriage was granted.

Application of the law of the domicile to issues of consent was supported by the Court of Appeal in *Vervaeke v Smith*.[284] A major issue in this case was whether the English courts would recognise the validity of a Belgian nullity decree;[285] but the Court of Appeal also gave some consideration to the original validity of the marriage in question. The marriage had taken place in England between a woman domiciled in Belgium and a man domiciled in England. This was essentially a sham marriage whose purpose was to give the woman British nationality. Such a marriage, though valid under English law, was void under Belgian law. Nevertheless, its validity was upheld under the exception to the dual

---

[275] Nevertheless, he satisfied himself that the marriage was also invalid under English domestic law. Indeed so extensive was his examination of English law, that, had the marriage been valid by Polish law, the impression is given that he would, nevertheless, have held it to be void as contrary to English public policy; see Hartley (1972) 35 MLR 571, 580; cf Carter (1971) 45 BYBIL 406, 409.

[276] Dicey and Morris (1967) 8th edn, p 271. The proposition in the (2006) 14th edn, para 17R-118 is in substantially the same terms.

[277] [1971] P 286 at 294–295.

[278] See now Dicey, Morris and Collins (2006) 14th edn, para 17-122.

[279] 8th edn of this book, p 396.

[280] 2005 SLT 749.

[281] 1959 SLT 278.

[282] RF MACDONALD QC judged Lord GUTHRIE's approach to be "unsupported by reasoning and unvouched by authority" (at [22]).

[283] At [22].

[284] [1981] Fam 77 at 122.

[285] Infra, p 1014.

domicile rule provided by *Sottomayor v De Barros (No 2)*[286] in that the marriage was valid by English law, that of the domicile of one party and the place of celebration.[287]

(iv) Reform

In their examination of the choice of law rules relating to marriage, the Law Commission considered the issue of the law to be applied to matters of consent.[288] They suggested that, although some arguments can be advanced in favour of the application of the law of the forum, issues of consent are concerned with the essential or substantive validity of a marriage and that "it would be contrary to principle and inconvenient in practice to fragment the question of essential validity".[289] This led to the conclusion that the law of the domicile should govern issues of consent, as it probably does already; and the Law Commission favoured reference to the domiciliary law of the person whose consent is alleged to be defective, rather than the formulation approved in *Szechter v Szechter*.[290] Certain other piecemeal measures have been implemented concerning consent to marriage:

Forced Marriage (Civil Protection) Act 2007   Royal Assent was given on 26 July 2007 to the Forced Marriage (Civil Protection) Act 2007. The Act, which was introduced by Lord Lester of Herne Hill as a Private Member's Bill,[291] applies to England and Wales, and Northern Ireland. The aim of the Act, which inserts a new Part 4A into the Family Law Act 1996, is to provide civil protection against forced marriage[292] in England and Wales, and Northern Ireland. The Act does not create any specific new criminal offence of forced marriage.[293] It is hoped that the approach, using civil rather than criminal law measures, will encourage victims to seek protection. However, the Act does not affect any other protection or assistance which currently is available to victims of forced marriage, such as the inherent jurisdiction of the High Court, criminal liability, civil remedies under the Protection from Harassment Act 1997, or the law of marriage.[294] Forced marriage is defined in the Act as a situation in which one person, "A", is forced, by means of coercion by threats or other psychological means,[295] by another person, "B", into a marriage,[296]

---

[286] (1879) 5 PD 94, supra, pp 904–905.

[287] The House of Lords did not discuss the application of the *Sottomayor* rule; though Lord SIMON of Glaisdale was prepared to regard this issue of reality of consent as one of "quintessential validity" to be governed by the law of the country with which the marriage had the most real and substantial connection: [1983] 1 AC 145 at 166, supra, pp 911–912.

[288] Law Commission Working Paper No 89 (1985), paras 5.6–5.24. Their Report, Law Com No 165 (1987), adds little to this discussion, see paras 2.4, 2.8.

[289] Ibid, para 5.18.

[290] [1971] P 286, supra.

[291] It is the first House of Lords Private Member's Bill to become legislation since 2002 (House of Commons Library Research Paper 07/56, 28 June 2007, p 26).

[292] Distinguished from arranged marriages, where both parties fully and freely consent to the marriage.

[293] For details of the protection currently available under the criminal law of England, see House of Commons Library Research Paper 07/56, 28 June 2007, pp 8–10. The consultation paper, "Forced Marriage: A Wrong not a Right" issued in 2005 by the Foreign & Commonwealth Office and the Home Office, sought views on whether a specific offence of forced marriage ought to be introduced. The majority of respondents felt that the disadvantages of creating new criminal legislation would outweigh the advantages: see House of Commons Library Research Paper, supra, pp 17–19, and 36–38.

[294] Family Law Act 1996, s 63R. See also *NS v MI* [2006] EWHC 1646 (Fam), [2007] 1 FLR 444.

[295] Ibid, s 63A(6).

[296] Any religious or civil ceremony of marriage, whether or not legally binding: ibid, s 63S. "Although in the Western world, forced marriage is sometimes discussed as a religious practice, no major faith condones forced marriage." (House of Commons Library Research Paper 07/56, 28 June 2007, Summary).

with B or another person, without A's free and full consent.[297] It is irrelevant whether B's conduct is directed against A, B, or another person.[298] The Act empowers the High Court or a county court[299] to make a forced marriage protection order,[300] ie an order for the purposes of protecting (i) a person from being forced into a marriage or from any attempt to be forced into a marriage; or (ii) a person who has been forced into a marriage.[301] An application may be made for an order by the person who is to be protected by the order, or by certain third parties.[302] A forced marriage protection order may contain such prohibitions, restrictions, requirements, or other terms as the court considers appropriate for the purposes of the order.[303] In deciding whether to exercise its powers, the court must have regard to all the circumstances, including the need to secure the health, safety and well-being of the person to be protected.[304] In ascertaining that person's well-being, the court must have regard, in particular, to his/her wishes and feelings, so far as they are reasonably ascertainable, and as the court considers appropriate in the light of the person's age and understanding.[305]

Although the Act contains no conflict of laws provisions as such, it is intended to have extra-territorial import in so far as the terms of a forced marriage protection order may relate not only to conduct within England and Wales, but also (or instead of) to conduct outside England and Wales.[306] Thus, for example, a forced marriage protection order may be sought in England by a young girl living there who fears that she may be taken by her parents from the United Kingdom, against her will, for the purpose of forced marriage abroad.[307] An order may affect respondents who force, or attempt to force, a person to enter a marriage, as well as persons who aid, abet, counsel, procure, encourage or assist the forcing, or attempted forcing, of a marriage.[308]

Asylum and Immigration (Treatment of Claimants, etc) Act 2004 Sections 19 to 25 of the 2004 Act[309] establish a regime, for England and Wales, Scotland and Northern Ireland, the aim of which is to prevent the abuse of immigration rights by means of sham marriages entered into with the sole aim of procuring advantages under United Kingdom immigration rules. The regime requires that a marriage involving a person who is subject to immigration control[310] cannot take place without a Certificate of Approval first being granted by the Secretary of State. As regards England and Wales, the only marriages

---

[297] Family Law Act 1996, s 63A(4).

[298] S 63A(5).

[299] S 63M(1). It is possible that the power will be extended to magistrates' courts: s 63N.

[300] With or without power of arrest: s 63H.

[301] S 63A(1).

[302] Ss 63C and 63D.

[303] S 63B(1).

[304] S 63A(2).

[305] S 63A(3).

[306] S 63B(2)(a). Cf, for Northern Ireland, Forced Marriage (Civil Protection) Act 2007, Sch 1, para 2(2)(a).

[307] Cf *NS v MI* [2006] EWHC 1646 (Fam), [2007] 1 FLR 444.

[308] S 63B(2)(b) and (3).

[309] See also Immigration (Procedure for Marriage) Regulations, SI 2005/15, as amended by SI 2005/2917.

[310] Defined in s 19(4) as a person who is not a national of a state which is a party to the Agreement on the European Economic Area signed at Oporto on 2 May 1992, and who, under the Immigration Act 1971, requires leave to enter or remain in the United Kingdom.

which fall outside the regime are those conducted according to the rites of the Church of England.[311]

The position in Scots law   The subject of sham marriages and marriages of convenience has provoked considerable interest in recent years in Scots law.[312] The outcome has been a statutory response, in sections 2 and 38 of the Family Law (Scotland) Act 2006. Section 38, in the part of the Act headed "private international law", provides in sub-section (2) that the question whether a person who enters into a marriage (a) had capacity;[313] or (b) consented, to enter into it shall be determined[314] by the law of the place where, immediately before the marriage, that person was domiciled. This provision makes it clear, therefore, that consent to marry is a matter to be determined by a person's ante-nuptial domicile. Section 2 of the Act inserts a new section 20A (Grounds on which marriage void) into the Marriage (Scotland) Act 1977. Separate provision is made for marriages solemnised in Scotland where (a) at the time of the marriage ceremony a party to the marriage who was capable of consenting to the marriage purported to give consent, but did so by reason only of duress[315] or error;[316] and (b) at the time of the marriage ceremony a party to the marriage was incapable of (i) understanding the nature of the marriage; and (ii) consenting to the marriage. In each case, the marriage shall be void.[317] In contrast, if a party purported to give consent to the marriage other than by reason only of duress or error, the marriage shall not be void by reason only of that party's having tacitly withheld consent to the marriage at the time when it was solemnised.[318] The latter provision, which is aimed at tackling the problem of sham marriages, is a legislative answer to difficulties encountered by the Scottish courts, and "establishes a criterion of consent, objectively construed, to marriage".[319]

Rome III   As stated above,[320] in July 2006, the European Commission published a Proposal for a Council Regulation amending Regulation (EC) No 2201/2003 as regards jurisdiction and introducing rules concerning applicable law in matrimonial matters ("Rome III").[321] In its provisions concerning applicable law, the Proposal extends only to divorce and judicial separation. It does not apply to marriage annulment which, as is explained in Recital (6) of the Proposal, "is closely linked to the conditions for the validity of the marriage, and for which parties' autonomy is inappropriate". Although the Proposal

---

[311] See, eg, *R (on the Application of Baiai and Ors) v Secretary of State for the Home Department* [2006] EWHC 823 (Admin), [2007] 1 WLR 693; [2006] EWHC 1454 (Admin), [2007] 1 WLR 735; and [2006] EWHC 1035.

[312] See Crawford and Carruthers, para 12-38.

[313] See supra, p 895 et seq.

[314] Subject to s 38(3) and (4) of the Act, and s 50 of the Family Law Act 1986, supra, p 915.

[315] Eg *Mahmood v Mahmood* 1993 SLT 589; *Mahmud v Mahmud* 1994 SLT 559; *Sohrab v Kahn* 2002 SLT 1255; and *Singh v Singh* 2005 SLT 749.

[316] Error as to the nature of the ceremony, or error as to identity: s 20A(5).

[317] S 20A(1), (2) and (3).

[318] S 20A(4). Contrast *Akram v Akram* 1979 SLT (Notes) 87; and the Inner House decision in *H v H* 2005 SLT 1025.

[319] Crawford and Carruthers, para 12-38.

[320] Supra, p 952.

[321] COM (2006) 399 final, and Document 5274/07 LIMITE JUSTCIV 4, 12 January 2007. See also Green Paper on applicable law and jurisdiction in divorce matters (COM (2005) 82 final, 14 March 2005); Commission Staff Working Paper, Annex to the Green Paper on applicable law and jurisdiction in divorce matters (SEC (2005) 331, 14 March 2005), and House of Lords EU Committee, 52nd Report, Session 2005/06, "Rome III—Choice of Law in Divorce" (2006).

also contains provisions for determining the applicable law in the absence of party choice,[322] nevertheless, it is not proposed that these provisions should apply to marriage annulment.

(d) Physical defects[323]

It remains to identify the law which governs other personal physical defects. These can encompass a wide range of grounds of invalidity, as is illustrated by those which render a marriage voidable under section 12 of the Matrimonial Causes Act 1973: impotence, wilful refusal to consummate the marriage, mental disorder such as to render the person unfitted for marriage, venereal disease, that the woman was pregnant by another man, that, after the time of the marriage, an interim gender recognition certificate has been issued to either party to the marriage under the Gender Recognition Act 2004, or the respondent is a person whose gender at the time of the marriage had become the acquired gender under that Act. In the context of English law, a nullity petition on the ground of the respondent's pregnancy or suffering from venereal disease may only be brought if the petitioner is unaware of this fact and so such grounds could be regarded more properly as relating to the reality of the petitioner's consent and thus to be governed by the law appropriate to that issue.[324] However, other legal systems do not necessarily take the same approach and, in any event, the consent classification cannot so readily be applied to issues such as wilful refusal or impotence. Two issues are raised: what are the current choice of law rules to govern these personal physical defects, and are the rules appropriate and adequate?

(i) What is the present law?

It is not easy to resolve the first issue and state the current law with any confidence. The main defects to consider are impotence and wilful refusal, but the authorities are far from clear as to what law is to govern these defects. There is some authority to support the application of the law of the domicile, of the place of celebration or of the forum. The difficulty with the decisions is that in all but one of the cases[325] English law has been applied, often with little or no consideration of the choice of law issue. Even when that issue is considered, the varied dicta seem to be at odds with the facts of the reported decisions. For instance, in *Robert v Robert*[326] wilful refusal is characterised as an "error in the quality of the respondent"[327] to which the law of the place of celebration should be applied.[328] Against such classification may be cited *Way v Way*,[329] where English law was applied to a nullity petition based on wilful refusal arising from a marriage celebrated in

---

[322] Supra, p 952.

[323] Bishop (1978) 41 MLR 512; Law Commission Working Paper No 89 (1985), paras 5.25–5.43; Law Com No 165 (1987), para 2.9.

[324] Supra, p 972.

[325] *Robert v Robert* [1947] P 164.

[326] Ibid.

[327] Ibid, at 167–168. This is criticised by Morris, para 9-034.

[328] Though the court did consider that, if the defect was to be classified as a question affecting the capacity of one of the parties to contract a marriage, then the law of the domicile was applicable and this is supported by the citing of *Sottomayor v De Barros* (1877) 3 PD 1, and see *Addison v Addison* [1955] NI 1 at 30.

[329] [1950] P 71 at 80.

Russia; and *Ponticelli v Ponticelli*,[330] where English law was applied though the place of celebration was Italy.

The confused state of the cases can be further illustrated by the fact that application of the law of the husband's domicile at the time of the marriage is supported by some decisions[331] on impotence and wilful refusal but is inconsistent with others.[332] Again, application of English law as the law of the forum finds support in some cases,[333] but not in all.[334]

(ii) What ought the law to be?

If the cases provide no clear guide to the law to govern nullity petitions based on personal physical defects, are there obvious principles which might guide courts in the future? Application of the law of the place of celebration can be rejected. The defects in question cannot be classified as relating to formalities of marriage. Support can be found in principle for the application of both the law of the domicile and the law of the forum. If one regards defects such as impotence, pregnancy by another man, mental disorder, and the fact that the respondent was suffering from venereal disease, as matters of essential validity akin to capacity, then the relevant law to determine the effect of such alleged invalidity is that of the domicile.[335] It is, however, more difficult to adopt that approach in the case of wilful refusal to consummate the marriage. It is a post-nuptial defect and it might be thought inappropriate to apply the law of the domicile existing at the time of the marriage to a ground of annulment more akin to evidence of irretrievable breakdown of the marriage justifying divorce. Indeed, the divorce analogy would provide support for applying the law of the forum.[336]

It might seem that the easy answer would be to have different choice of law rules for defects which are ante-nuptial, eg impotence, as opposed to those which are post-nuptial, eg wilful refusal. This is, however, an impracticable solution because the two grounds are frequently pleaded in the alternative and, as the Law Commission has pointed out, "it would be undesirable and inconvenient if different choice of law rules were to apply, depending on whether non-consummation was due to inability to consummate or unwillingness to do so".[337] This means that either the law of the domicile or the law of the forum must apply to both impotence and wilful refusal.

Although arguments in favour of the law of the forum are good, they are not good enough. It is easier, and cheaper, to apply the law of the forum than any other law; but that argument can be used in relation to choice of law in any context, yet it is not generally accepted, save in the case of divorce. Wilful refusal may be like divorce in its post-nuptial character, but

---

[330] [1958] P 204.

[331] *Way v Way*, supra; *Ponticelli v Ponticelli*, supra.

[332] *Easterbrook v Easterbrook* [1944] P 10; *Hutter v Hutter* [1944] P 95, unless one can explain them on the ground that, when the foreign law is not pleaded, it is the same as English law. In so far as *Ramsay-Fairfax v Ramsay-Fairfax* [1956] P 115 at 125 can be considered an authority on choice of law, it militates against this view, unless Scots law, the law of the husband's domicile, is not only considered to be the same as English law (which is not the case), but it is accepted that this is a reason for applying English law as such.

[333] *Easterbrook v Easterbrook*, supra; *Hutter v Hutter*, supra; *Magnier v Magnier* (1968) 112 Sol Jo 233.

[334] *Robert v Robert* [1947] P 164; and see *Ponticelli v Ponticelli* [1958] P 204 at 214–216; *Sangha v Mander* (1985) 47 RFL (2d) 212 at 216.

[335] See *Robert v Robert* [1947] P 164 at 168; and see *Ramsay-Fairfax v Ramsay-Fairfax* [1956] P 115 at 125.

[336] Supra, p 966 et seq; for rejection of the analogy, see *Sangha v Mander* (1985) 47 RFL (2d) 212 at 216–217.

[337] Law Commission Working Paper No 89 (1985), para 5.30.

it is significant that English law has chosen to regard it as a ground of annulment. That being so, to apply the law of the domicile will ensure consistency with the treatment of all grounds of invalidity. It will also confirm the view that these personal defects go to the essential validity of a marriage and that all aspects of essential validity are to be governed by the law of the domicile.[338] Finally, it is hard to disagree with Lord Reid when he pointed out that application of the law of the forum is wrong in principle, saying: "Suppose a case where the law of the parties' domicile gives no relief on this ground [ie wilful refusal[339]], it seems to me quite contrary to principle that the wife should be able to come here and seek relief on that ground."[340]

Returning to the authorities, the most persuasive decision in favour of the application of the law of the domicile is *Ponticelli v Ponticelli*,[341] where the facts were these:

> The parties married by proxy in Italy. The wife was domiciled in Italy and the husband was domiciled in England. When the husband petitioned for a nullity decree on the ground of wilful refusal, the court had to face the choice of law issue, for wilful refusal was not in the circumstances a ground for annulment in Italian law.

SACHS J rejected a classification of wilful refusal as akin to an issue of form and so he rejected the law of the place of celebration, here Italian law, as the appropriate law.[342] He did not favour the analogy of wilful refusal with divorce, and so his arguments militated against the application of the law of the forum.[343] Although he applied English law, he did so rather because it was the law of the husband's domicile[344] at the time of the marriage and of the petition,[345] and it was also the law of the intended matrimonial home. Furthermore, he rejected any attempt to distinguish between the choice of law rules for wilful refusal and for impotence. He considered they should both be regarded as matters of personal capacity,[346] to be governed by the law of the domicile, for "it is surely a matter of some importance that the initial validity of a marriage should, in relation to all matters except form and ceremony . . . be consistently decided according to the law of one country alone . . . and that consistency cannot be attained if the test is *lex fori*".[347]

Agreeing that physical personal defects are to be governed by the law of the domicile does not, however, solve all problems in this area. It remains to decide which spouse's domiciliary law is to be applied and whether the domicile, and thus the applicable law, is to be determined at the date of the marriage or at the date of the nullity petition. Although in *Ponticelli* reference was made to the law of the husband's domicile, there seems little doubt that, since a married woman is now capable of acquiring a separate domicile, reference must be made to her domicile where appropriate. Various ways have been suggested to decide which domiciliary law should be applied. One approach is to look at the law of

---

[338] *De Reneville v De Reneville* [1948] P 100 at 114; *Szechter v Szechter* [1971] P 286 at 295; *Sangha v Mander* (1985) 47 RFL (2d) 212 at 217–218.

[339] As is the case in Scotland.

[340] *Ross Smith v Ross Smith* [1963] AC 280 at 306; and see *Ponticelli v Ponticelli* [1958] P 204 at 215.

[341] [1958] P 204; and see more recently *Sangha v Mander* (1985) 47 RFL (2d) 212.

[342] Thereby rejecting *Robert v Robert* [1947] P 164.

[343] He regarded *De Reneville v De Reneville*, supra, as supporting his view.

[344] The question of which spouse's domiciliary law should be applied is discussed infra.

[345] [1958] P 204 at 216; though reference to domicile at the time of the petition seems hard to justify.

[346] See *Ramsay-Fairfax v Ramsay-Fairfax* [1956] P 115 at 133.

[347] [1958] P 204 at 215–216.

each spouse's domicile and to annul the marriage if there are grounds for so doing under either law.[348] This tips the scales firmly in favour of annulling a marriage, with the result that the petitioner would succeed even though there were no grounds for annulment under the law of the domicile and even though he was the person alleged to lack capacity. The balance can be redressed by always applying the law of the petitioner's domicile.[349] Under this approach, however, a nullity decree will be denied in, say, a case of wilful refusal if that does not constitute a ground of annulment under the law of the petitioner's domicile even though it is a ground under that of the respondent, the respondent being the person who has refused. A third approach, which avoids this difficulty, is to apply the law of the domicile of the spouse who is alleged to be incapable, taking that in the case of non-consummation to be the spouse who is unable, or refuses, to consummate the marriage. In its turn, this approach would deny annulment in the case where wilful refusal was a ground for nullity under the law of the petitioner's, but not the respondent's domicile, assuming the refusal to be by the respondent.

No answer is perfect; but it is suggested that the third approach is the most appropriate in that it accords with the general choice of law rule relating to matters of essential validity, ie the application of the ground of invalidity under the domiciliary law of the person alleged to be incapable. This would still leave it open to a court to conclude that, in the special circumstances of non-consummation, it would be right to apply the law of the person who is rendered unable to consummate the marriage by reason of the conduct of the other party.

Finally, there is the question of the time at which the law of the domicile is to be determined. The general rule applicable to matters of essential validity is that the applicable law is that of the domicile immediately preceding the marriage—the ante-nuptial domicile.[350] There should be no doubt that this is the relevant time in all cases of alleged invalidity except wilful refusal.[351] The more doubtful case is that of wilful refusal. If it is also to be regarded as a straightforward issue of capacity, then the relevant time is again that of the marriage.[352] If, however, it is regarded more properly as an anomalous ground of nullity more like a basis for divorce, since it is post-nuptial, then the relevant date for determining domicile might be thought to be that of the proceedings.[353] However, the Law Commission would seem to be right in indicating that, if domicile is to be the test for determining the governing law in all issues of essential validity, consistency requires the domicile to be determined at the same time in all cases, ie immediately before the marriage, especially as wilful refusal and impotence are often pleaded in the alternative.[354]

---

[348] Palsson, *Marriage in Comparative Conflict of Laws* (1981), pp 314–315.

[349] Jaffey (1978) 41 MLR 38; Bishop (1978) 41 MLR 512.

[350] Supra, p 896.

[351] *De Reneville v De Reneville* [1948] P 100 at 114. This may have been lost sight of in *Savelieff v Glouchkoff* (1964) 45 DLR (2d) 520; Lysyk (1965) 43 Can Bar Rev 107, 121–121.

[352] Cf *Robert v Robert* [1947] P 164 at 167–168.

[353] Such a view might be supported by *Way v Way* [1950] P 71 at 80. In *Ponticelli v Ponticelli* [1958] P 204 it is expressly stated, at 216, that the husband was domiciled in England both at the date of the marriage and of the petition; cf *De Reneville v De Reneville* [1948] P 100 at 114 where Lord Greene's reference to the date of the marriage is made without qualification of the case of wilful refusal.

[354] Law Commission Working Paper No 89 (1985), para 5.41.

(e) Annulment on grounds unknown to English law

There is a further issue, closely connected with the question whether English law as the law of the forum should be applied to cases of impotence and wilful refusal. This is whether the English courts will annul a marriage on grounds unknown to English law. There is clear statutory provision for the application of foreign law to any question affecting the validity of a marriage. Section 14(1) of the Matrimonial Causes Act 1973 qualifies the grounds of annulment of void and voidable marriages laid down by that Act[355] by stating that, where any matter affecting the validity of a marriage would, in accordance with the rules of private international law, fall to be determined by a foreign law, nothing in the nullity provisions of the 1973 Act should preclude the application of the foreign law or require the application of the English law of nullity.[356]

There is no doubt that this provision contemplates that English courts will apply foreign law to nullity petitions in appropriate circumstances and, equally, there is no doubt that English courts will annul marriages on the basis of foreign rules as to invalidity. As has been seen when considering the validity of a marriage,[357] the English courts will annul a marriage celebrated in a foreign country if the formalities of the law of the place of celebration are not complied with, irrespective of the English law on such matters.[358] Similarly, the English courts will annul a marriage, even if celebrated in England, on a ground laid down by the parties' ante-nuptial domiciliary laws, whether or not that ground is co-extensive with a similar English ground. For instance, a marriage has been treated as void because the parties were within the prohibited degrees of relationship under their foreign domiciliary law, though not under English law.[359]

There appears to be no authority on whether an English court will annul a marriage on a ground which, under the law of the domicile, renders the marriage voidable but which falls quite outside the grounds on which a marriage might be declared voidable under English domestic law. Any determination of the question whether English courts would annul a marriage in such circumstances is speculative.[360] It is suggested, however, that an English court should be prepared fully to accept the general principle that questions as to the essential validity of the marriage are to be referred to the law of the domicile. In that event, it is submitted that it does not matter whether the English court applies foreign grounds verbally similar to English grounds, such as consanguinity or non-age, even though the substance of the rule is different. Similarly, it should make no difference if a foreign ground is applied which is a variant of the English ground, such as declaring a marriage voidable on the ground that at the time of the marriage another woman was pregnant by the husband,[361] or a foreign ground substantially different from any under

---

[355] Ss 11–13.

[356] S 14(2) also provides that the grounds on which a marriage is to be declared void, laid down in s 11, are without prejudice to other grounds under which a marriage celebrated under the Foreign Marriage Acts 1892–1947 or a common law marriage celebrated abroad might be declared void. See also the Marriage (Prohibited Degrees of Relationship) Act 1986, s 1(7).

[357] Supra, p 878.

[358] *Berthiaume v Dastous* [1930] AC 79—marriage with religious, but no civil, ceremony; *Kenward v Kenward* [1951] P 124—failure to comply with the Russian Marriage Code.

[359] *Sottomayor v De Barros* (1877) 3 PD 1.

[360] Morris, para 10-019.

[361] This used to be a ground in New Zealand. The English rule is limited to the case of a wife being pregnant by another man: Matrimonial Causes Act 1973, s 12(f).

English law, such as the incapacity of a person of one religion to marry a member of another[362] or annulment on the ground of a mistake as to the attributes of the other spouse.[363] It must not be forgotten that the English courts would always retain the power, as in the case of other issues of validity,[364] to refuse to apply a foreign provision laying down a rule of invalidity where the application of that rule would be contrary to English public policy.[365]

(f) What law determines whether a marriage is void or voidable?

It has been suggested[366] that, as the annulment of a voidable marriage and a divorce decree both only have prospective effect, the law of the forum should be applied to the former as to the latter. This would have the disadvantage of requiring the choice of law rule to depend on whether the marriage was void or voidable, and of deciding by what law that issue is to be determined—a difficult problem to which we must now turn.

It has been seen that different legal systems attribute different effects to invalidating factors. A clear example is provided by lack of consent, which renders a marriage void under Scots law[367] but voidable under English law.[368] This poses a problem. If an English court annuls the marriage of parties both domiciled in Scotland, applying the Scottish law on consent, is the marriage to be regarded in England as void or merely as voidable? At first sight it might seem that an English court ought to apply its own criteria for determining whether the problem is one of alleged voidness or of alleged voidability.[369] A moment's reflection, however, reveals the illogicality of this suggestion. Whether a marriage is void or voidable is merely a facet of the question whether it is valid or invalid. The law that determines its validity or invalidity must also determine what is meant by invalidity, ie whether it means voidness or voidability. The role of the proper law, whether it is the law of the place of celebration or the law of the parties' domiciles, is to determine whether the alleged defect is sufficient ground for annulment and if so what consequences ensue, assuming its existence to be proved. One of these consequences is the extent of the invalidity of the union, ie whether the marriage is merely voidable or void.

So far as authority is concerned, the weight of opinion supports the approach of characterisation by the law governing the substantive issue rather than by the law of the forum.[370] Nevertheless, it has been argued[371] that it is for English law as the law of the forum and

---

[362] Eg *Lendrum v Chakravarti* 1929 SLT 96; though see *MacDougall v Chitnavis* 1937 SC 390; cf *Corbett v Corbett* [1957] 1 WLR 486, a decision on recognition of a foreign decree.

[363] Cf *Mitford v Mitford* [1923] P 130, also a decision on recognition.

[364] Supra, p 908.

[365] *Vervaeke v Smith* [1983] 1 AC 145 provides some support for the view that English courts might not apply foreign rules invalidating sham marriages.

[366] Law Commission Working Paper No 89 (1985), para 5.47.

[367] But see, with regard to sham marriages, *Hakeem v Hussain* 2003 SLT 515, and on appeal, *H v H* 2005 SLT 1025 (especially per Lord PENROSE, at [28] and [35]); Clive, *Husband and Wife*, para 07-047; and Family Law (Scotland) Act 2006, ss 2 and 38, supra, p 978.

[368] Supra, p 970.

[369] This seems to have been what was done in *Corbett v Corbett* [1957] 1 WLR 486.

[370] See *De Reneville v De Reneville* [1948] P 100 at 114; *Casey v Casey* [1949] P 420 at 429–430; *Merker v Merker* [1963] P 283 at 297; *Szechter v Szechter* [1971] P 286 at 294; and see Law Commission Working Paper No 89 (1985), para 5.53.

[371] Morris (1970) 19 ICLQ 424.

not for some foreign governing law to determine whether a marriage is void or voidable,[372] and that any argument based upon or by analogy with *De Reneville v De Reneville*[373] "seems to have been overtaken by oblivion and no longer represents the law".[374] The main support for such a view would appear to be an unarticulated assumption of the House of Lords decision in *Ross Smith v Ross Smith*[375] where it was held that there was jurisdiction to annul a void but not a voidable marriage celebrated in England, even though the husband, who was alleged to be impotent or wilfully to have refused to consummate the marriage, was domiciled at all material times in Scotland. No reference was made to whether the marriage was void or voidable under Scots law. If their Lordships merely assumed[376] that Scots and English law was the same on the question whether impotence and wilful refusal rendered a marriage voidable,[377] this was a strange assumption.[378] Nevertheless, although a link in the chain of reasoning in the House of Lords is missing,[379] this is a feature all too common in nullity cases and the silence of the House of Lords on this issue provides scant authority against reference to the law of the domicile and in favour of the forum.

In conclusion, it is English law as the law of the forum which has to classify the type of defect as one of formalities (governed by the law of the place of celebration) or as a personal defect (governed by the law of the domicile). Once that classification is made, the effect of the defect on the validity of the marriage will be determined not by the law of the forum but by that law which, according to English choice of law rules, governs alleged defects of that kind. Any other approach would be highly unsatisfactory where the marriage was void under the governing law, but entirely valid under the law of the forum. To give the marriage full effect under the law of the forum notwithstanding its invalidity under the governing law would be to deprive the choice of law rule of any real impact.

(g) The law to govern the effect of a nullity decree[380]

Although it is right to determine whether a ground of invalidity renders a marriage void or voidable by the law applicable to that ground, the effect of any decree of nullity is a matter for the law of the forum which granted it.[381] So, if an English court grants a decree annulling a marriage, it is for English law, as the law of the forum governing procedure, to determine the effect of its own decree. That being so, the law of the domicile or of the place of celebration, depending on the type of defect in question, will decide whether the marriage is void or voidable, but English law will decide whether, in the light of that classification, the decree should have retrospective effect.

---

[372] Ibid.

[373] [1948] P 100.

[374] Morris (1970) 19 ICLQ 424, 427–428.

[375] [1963] AC 280.

[376] No evidence of Scots law would be necessary on this point as the House of Lords takes judicial knowledge of Scots law.

[377] Lysyk (1965) 43 Can Bar Rev 107, 119–120.

[378] Anton, p 440.

[379] Morris (1970) 19 ICLQ 424, 428.

[380] North, op cit, p 135; Law Commission Working Paper No 89 (1985), paras 5.54–5.55.

[381] For the effect of a foreign decree, see infra, pp 1026–1027.

(c) Recognition[382]

(i) Introduction

Until 1972, recognition of foreign divorces and legal separations was governed by common law rules. These rules were substantially, but not wholly, replaced by statutory grounds of recognition in the Recognition of Divorces and Legal Separations Act 1971, which was passed to implement the Convention on the Recognition of Divorces and Legal Separations adopted in 1970 by the Hague Conference on Private International Law. There had previously been criticism of the common law rules, and the implementation of the Convention in the 1971 Act provided an opportunity to introduce reforms rather broader in scope than the Convention required. However, the 1971 Act did not extend to the recognition of foreign annulments, which continued to be governed by common law recognition rules. The uncertainty of those rules and the fact that different regimes applied to divorce and nullity recognition was a source of criticism[383] which led the Law Commission, in 1984, to examine the varied rules for the recognition of divorces, annulments and legal separations and to propose that essentially the same statutory rules should apply in the case of all three matrimonial causes, and that those rules should be based on the Recognition of Divorces and Legal Separations Act 1971, subject to a number of amendments.[384] These recommendations were substantially carried into effect by Part II of the Family Law Act 1986.[385]

The general effect of the statutory rules in the 1986 Act is that, subject to a few minor exceptions mentioned later,[386] the same recognition rules apply to all three matrimonial causes. Furthermore, the common law rules of nullity recognition,[387] and those common law rules relating to the recognition of divorces and legal separations which survived the 1971 Act,[388] were replaced by the statutory regime of the 1986 Act, irrespective of where the divorce, annulment or legal separation was obtained and of whether it was obtained before or after the 1986 Act came into force.[389]

Different rules were provided in the 1986 Act for the recognition of divorces, annulments and judicial separations granted in other jurisdictions within the British Isles[390] and of divorces, annulments and legal separations[391] obtained in politically foreign countries. The 1986 Act governed the recognition of all overseas divorces, annulments and

---

[382] McClean, *Recognition of Family Judgments in the Commonwealth* (1983), Chapters 2 and 3; Gordon, *Foreign Divorces: English Law and Practice* (1988).

[383] Eg Carter (1979) 50 BYBIL 250, 252; Collier [1979] CLJ 289, 290.

[384] Law Com No 137 (1984).

[385] For discussion of Part II of the 1986 Act, see Pearl [1987] CLJ 35. The major difference between the Law Commission proposals and the 1986 Act is that the latter introduces separate, and more restrictive, recognition rules for foreign extra-judicial divorces obtained where there have been no judicial or other proceedings, discussed infra, p 999 et seq.

[386] Infra, p 992 et seq.

[387] See 10th edn of this book, pp 406–416; and see Law Com No 137 (1984), Pt II.

[388] Ibid, pp 366–369.

[389] This is subject to rules preserving the effect of common law recognition in very limited circumstances, infra, p 1024.

[390] This means the United Kingdom, the Channel Islands and the Isle of Man: see Interpretation Act 1978, Sch 1.

[391] The differing use of "judicial separation" and "legal separation" in the 1986 Act is discussed infra, p 998.

legal separations until 1 March 2001, when, as has been explained above,[392] the Brussels II Regulation took effect. With effect from 1 March 2005, account has had to be taken of the Brussels II *bis* Regulation.[393] Now, the rules for recognition of divorces, annulments and legal separations differ according to the identity of the state (the court of origin) in which the decree or judgment was issued: (i) a court elsewhere in the British Isles; (ii) a court or other authority in another European Community Member State, except Denmark; or (iii) a court or other authority in a non-European Community Member State, or in Denmark. These three situations must be considered separately.

(ii) Divorces, annulments and judicial separations granted elsewhere in the British Isles

Any decree of divorce, nullity, or judicial separation granted by a court of civil jurisdiction[394] in any part of the British Isles must be recognised in any part of the United Kingdom,[395] irrespective of when it was granted.[396] So, the English courts must[397] recognise any divorce, etc granted elsewhere in the British Isles and, similarly, such divorces, etc must be recognised in Scotland and Northern Ireland.[398]

Although such divorces, etc cannot be denied recognition on jurisdictional grounds,[399] two qualifications to recognition are provided. First, an English court can refuse recognition to a divorce or a judicial separation granted elsewhere in the British Isles at a time when there was no subsisting marriage between the parties, according to English law, including English rules of private international law.[400] This would cover such situations as where a marriage in England was invalid under English domestic law or a marriage abroad failed to satisfy English rules of private international law. In such circumstances, the English court has a discretion[401] to refuse recognition to, say, a Scottish divorce decree dissolving

---

[392] Supra, p 945.

[393] Supra, p 945; ibid.

[394] The significance of this is that extra-judicial divorces, etc are excluded: see Family Law Act 1986, s 44(1); Law Com No 137 (1984), para 4.14, and infra, p 999 et seq. There is one minor exception to the denial of recognition to extra-judicial divorces obtained in England, relating to those obtained before 1974, see infra, p 1024.

[395] s Family Law Act 1986, ss 44(2), 54(1). S 44 apparently has not been affected by the introduction of Brussels II *bis* (see SI 2005/265, reg 8), in spite of Art 66 (Member States with two or more legal systems) of that Regulation (see Crawford and Carruthers, para 12-16; Morris, para 11-009; and McEleavy (2004) 53 ICLQ 605, 615).

[396] Family Law Act 1986, s 52(1)(a), (3). This marks a change from the Recognition of Divorces and Legal Separations Act 1971 which only applied to the recognition of British divorces granted after the Act came into force. There are a number of transitional provisions which apply both to the recognition of other British and overseas divorces, etc, and which are discussed in the 13th edn of this book (1999), p 820.

[397] Subject to s 51 of the 1986 Act, infra, p 1012 et seq.

[398] The Isle of Man has enacted legislation similar to Part II of the 1986 Act: the Recognition of Divorces etc Act 1987; and there is also legislation, based on similar rules in the Recognition of Divorces and Legal Separations Act 1971, s 1, in the Channel Islands, see North, op cit, pp 309–310, 324–326, 343–346.

[399] Since 1974, the bases of divorce jurisdiction have been the same in England, Scotland and Northern Ireland: Domicile and Matrimonial Proceedings Act 1973, Parts II and III, as amended, and Matrimonial Causes (Northern Ireland) Order, SI 1978/1045, as amended. However, until 1974, there were significant differences between England and Scotland. The Scottish courts, but not the English, would grant a decree of divorce where a respondent was domiciled within the jurisdiction at the time of his adultery but not at the time of the proceedings: *Clark v Clark* 1967 SC 269; North, op cit, pp 26–27, 167–168. So a Scottish divorce granted in such circumstances before 1974 will be recognised in England.

[400] 1986 Act, s 51(2)(a).

[401] Under the 1971 Act, s 8(1)(a) refusal of recognition was mandatory. For the reasons for the change to a discretionary rule, see Law Com No 137 (1984) paras 4.6 and 6.66, and infra, p 1015.

that marriage. It may be noted that this provision does not apply to recognition of nullity decrees for which, given the invalidity of the marriage, it might be thought inappropriate. However, the second qualification does extend to other British nullity decrees, as well as to divorces and judicial separations.[402] It gives the English court a discretion to deny recognition on a *res judicata* basis, ie if the other British decree was granted at a time when it was irreconcilable with a decision on the validity of the marriage previously given either by an English court or given elsewhere and entitled to be recognised in England. So a Scottish decree annulling or dissolving an English marriage can be denied recognition if there is already an English decree, or a South African decree recognised in England, to similar effect. In the case of a divorce or judicial separation, if there is a previous decision ending the marriage, the court's discretion can be exercised under either of the two heads just mentioned.[403]

Because of the mandatory wording of section 44(2) of the Family Law Act 1986, which states that divorce, etc decrees granted by a court of civil jurisdiction elsewhere in the British Isles *shall be recognised* in England, such other British decisions cannot be denied recognition in England even though they may contravene the rules of natural justice or be manifestly contrary to English public policy.[404] The justification for this is that it was "thought that in such circumstances the complaining party should seek to have the decree set aside by the court which granted it,[405] or an appeal from that court, and that it would be objectionable to allow a court in another part of the British Isles[406] to refuse to recognise the decree".[407] However, an English court is not required under Part II of the 1986 Act to recognise any findings of fault or any maintenance, custody or other ancillary order made in the other British proceedings.[408]

(iii) Divorces, annulments and legal separations obtained in another European Community Member State, except Denmark

(a) Introduction

As has been stated previously in this book, the principle of mutual recognition of judgments has been fixed as the cornerstone for the creation of a European judicial area.[409] Alongside the objective of the free movement of judgments within the Member States in civil and commercial matters, the European Community has set the objective of creating an area of freedom, security and justice, in which the free movement of persons is ensured. "To this end, the Community is to adopt, among others, measures in the field of judicial co-operation in civil matters that are necessary for the proper functioning of the internal market."[410]

---

[402] S 51(1)(a).

[403] The two grounds for denying recognition are examined more fully in the context of the recognition of overseas divorces, etc, infra, p 1012 et seq.

[404] These are reasons for denying recognition to divorces, etc obtained in other, foreign countries: Brussels II *bis*, Art 22(a) (infra, pp 990–992), and 1986 Act, s 51(3), infra, p 1013 et seq.

[405] See *Gaffney v Gaffney* [1975] IR 133.

[406] This must mean "the United Kingdom".

[407] Law Com No 34 (1970), p 43; and see Law Com No 137 (1984), para 4.7.

[408] 1986 Act, s 51(5); for recognition of maintenance and custody orders generally, see infra, p 1069 et seq, p 1097 et seq.

[409] See generally supra, Chapter 16.

[410] Brussels II *bis*, Recital (1).

Article 1 (scope) of the Brussels II *bis* Regulation provides that, "1. This Regulation shall apply, whatever the nature of the court or tribunal, in civil matters relating to: (a) divorce, legal separation or marriage annulment".[411] It is interesting to compare this wording with that in Recital (9) of Brussels II, ie: "The scope of this Regulation should cover civil proceedings and non-judicial proceedings in matrimonial matters in certain States, and exclude purely religious procedures. It should therefore be provided that the reference to 'courts' includes all the authorities, judicial or otherwise, with jurisdiction in matrimonial matters."[412] According to the Explanatory Report on the Brussels II Convention, the term "civil" was to be understood not only as a means of including administrative (ie non-judicial) proceedings, but also as a means of excluding all merely religious proceedings.[413] The Report expressly states that: "The Convention excludes from its scope religious proceedings, which may become more frequent as a result of immigration (Muslim and Hindu marriages, for instance)."[414] Therefore, Brussels II *bis*, in covering civil matters, should be construed as applying to judicial or non-judicial (ie administrative) proceedings, but not to religious proceedings. All religious divorces, regardless of the country in which they are obtained, should be treated as falling under the scheme of recognition in Part II of the Family Law Act 1986.[415]

(b) General principle of recognition

It is stated in Brussels II *bis* that: "The recognition and enforcement of judgments given in a Member State should be based on the principle of mutual trust and the grounds for non-recognition should be kept to the minimum necessary."[416] Accordingly, Article 21 of the Regulation[417] states that;

1. A judgment[418] given in a Member State shall be recognised in the other Member States without any special procedure being required.
2. In particular, and without prejudice to paragraph 3, no special procedure shall be required for updating the civil-status records of a Member State on the basis of a judgment relating to divorce, legal separation or marriage annulment given in another

---

[411] Cf Recital (7): "The scope of this Regulation covers civil matters, whatever the nature of the court or tribunal."

[412] Cf Art 1, Brussels II: "This Regulation shall apply to: (a) civil proceedings relating to divorce, legal separation or marriage annulment; . . ."

[413] Borras, *Explanatory Report*, para 20.

[414] Ibid, para 20B.

[415] Infra, p 999. Cf Dicey, Morris and Collins, para 18-096; and Crawford and Carruthers, para 12-30.

[416] Recital (21).

[417] Applicable only to legal proceedings instituted, to documents formally drawn up or registered as authentic instruments and to agreements concluded between the parties after 1 March 2005: Arts 64 and 72. Transitional provisions are set out in Art 64.

[418] Meaning a divorce, legal separation or marriage annulment pronounced by a court of a Member State (including all the authorities in a Member State with jurisdiction in the matters falling within the scope of the Regulation pursuant to Art 1), whatever the judgment may be called, including a decree, order or decision: Art 2(1) and (4). Documents which have been formally drawn up or registered as authentic instruments and are enforceable in one Member State and also agreements between the parties that are enforceable in the Member State in which they were concluded shall be recognised and declared enforceable under the same conditions as judgments: Art 46. See Borras, *Explanatory Report*, paras 60 and 61.

Member State, and against which no further appeal lies under the law of that Member State.[419]

3. Without prejudice to Section 4[420] of this Chapter, any interested party[421] may, in accordance with the procedures provided for in Section 2[422] of this Chapter, apply for a decision that the judgment be or not be recognised . . .

4. When the recognition of a judgment is raised as an incidental question in a court of a Member State, that court may determine that issue.

(c) Grounds of non-recognition

Article 22[423] provides that a judgment relating to a divorce, legal separation or marriage annulment shall not be recognised:

(a) if such recognition is manifestly contrary to the public policy of the Member State in which recognition is sought;[424]

(b) where it was given in default of appearance, if the respondent was not served with the document which instituted the proceedings or with an equivalent document in sufficient time and in such a way as to enable the respondent to arrange for his or her defence[425] unless it is determined that the respondent has accepted the judgment unequivocally;[426]

(c) if it is irreconcilable with a judgment[427] given in proceedings between the same parties in the Member State in which recognition is sought;[428] or

(d) if it is irreconcilable with an earlier judgment given in another Member State[429] or in a non-Member State between the same parties, provided that the earlier judgment fulfils the conditions necessary for its recognition in the Member State in which recognition is sought.[430]

These grounds for non-recognition are very similar to those contained in Article 34 of the Brussels I Regulation.[431]

---

[419] Article 27 (Stay of proceedings) provides that: "1. A court of a Member State in which recognition is sought of a judgment given in another Member State may stay the proceedings if an ordinary appeal against the judgment has been lodged. 2. A court of a Member State in which recognition is sought of a judgment given in Ireland or the United Kingdom may stay the proceedings if enforcement is suspended in the Member State of origin by reason of an appeal." Cf Brussels I Regulation, Art 37.

[420] Enforceability of certain judgments concerning rights of access and of certain judgments which require the return of the child.

[421] See Borras, *Explanatory Report*, para 65: the concept of interested party is to be interpreted "in the broad sense under the national law applicable and may include the public prosecutor or other similar bodies where permitted in the State in which the judgment is to be recognised or contested".

[422] Application for a declaration of enforceability.

[423] By implication, Art 22 provides the only defences to recognition.

[424] See also Arts 24, 25 and 26, infra, pp 991–992. Cf Brussels I Regulation, Art 34(1), discussed supra, p 611 et seq.

[425] Cf Brussels I Regulation, Art 34(2), discussed supra, p 615 et seq.

[426] Eg by remarrying.

[427] Regardless of whether the judgment in the Member State in which recognition is sought pre- or post-dates the judgment given in the Member State of origin; *contra* Art 22(d).

[428] Cf Brussels I Regulation, Art 34(3), discussed supra, p 622 et seq. The situation envisaged here is, eg, where the Member State in which recognition is sought, having already issued a divorce decree in respect of a couple, subsequently is asked to recognise a legal separation in respect of the same couple granted by a court or other authority in another Member State (Borras, *Explanatory Report*, para 71).

[429] The *lis pendens* provision in Art 19 normally will prevent a judgment being given in the court second seised, but it will not do so if that court does not accept that the parties are the same.

[430] Cf Brussels I Regulation, Art 34(4), discussed supra, p 625.

[431] Supra, p 610 et seq.

Perhaps the most controversial of the Article 22 defences is that of public policy.[432] As with the Brussels I Regulation, the wording of Article 22(a) strongly suggests that the recognising court is to apply its own concept of public policy when considering this defence. National courts have a degree of latitude in determining the meaning of the concept, but it is to be expected that they will give it an interpretation which is appropriate in the context and spirit of the Regulation. The public policy defence should be used only sparingly, in exceptional cases, as is underscored by use of the word "manifestly".[433] It is recognition of the judgment, rather than the judgment itself, which must be contrary to public policy.

One possible challenge to recognition under Article 22(a) is in relation to the divorce, legal separation or annulment of a so-called same sex "marriage".[434] Neither "marriage" nor "divorce" is defined in Brussels II *bis*.[435] It is not clear whether the "divorce", etc of a same sex relationship falls within the scope of Brussels II *bis*; if so, it is unclear to what extent the courts of Member States have discretion to refuse recognition under Article 22 (bearing in mind the terms of Articles 24 and 25, discussed below); and where the demarcation should lie between the recognition rules contained in Brussels II *bis* and those in the Civil Partnership Act 2004.[436] There is potential for a reference to be made to the ECJ for a preliminary ruling on this point of interpretation.[437]

(d) Prohibition of review of jurisdiction of the court of origin

Article 24 of Brussels II *bis* narrates the important principle that: "The jurisdiction of the court of the Member State of origin may not be reviewed.[438] The test of public policy referred to in [Article 22(a)] may not be applied to the rules relating to jurisdiction set out in Articles [3 to 7]." It cannot be argued that the court of origin misapplied the jurisdictional rules in Brussels II *bis*, or its national rules of residual jurisdiction. In particular, this prohibition cannot be evaded by using the public policy defence.

(e) Differences in applicable law

By virtue of Article 25: "The recognition of a judgment may not be refused because the law[439] of the Member State in which recognition is sought would not allow divorce, legal separation or marriage annulment on the same facts." This provision is the counterbalance to Article 22(a), and is:

> designed to meet the concerns of States with more tolerant internal provisions on divorce who fear that the judgments given by their courts might not be recognised in another

---

[432] See Peruzzetto, "The Exception of Public Policy in Family Law within the European Legal System" in Meeusen, Pertegas, Straetmans and Swennen (eds), *International Family Law for the European Union* (2007).

[433] Unfortunately, the Borras *Explanatory Report* provides no examples of what might be a reasonable use of the public policy defence. It is stated, however, that, "the States are extremely sensitive on this issue on account of the major discrepancies between their laws on divorce. Those Member States in which dissolution of the marriage bond is easiest fear that their judgments may not be recognised in Member States with more stringent rules" (para 69).

[434] See supra, p 937 et seq.

[435] McEleavy (2004) 53 ICLQ 605, at 607, refers to the "gender neutral terminology" of the Regulation.

[436] See Crawford and Carruthers, para 12-25.

[437] As regards the recognition provisions of the Civil Partnership Act 2004, see infra, p 1035.

[438] Cf Brussels I Regulation, Art 35, discussed supra, p 625 et seq.

[439] Including its rules of private international law: Borras, *Explanatory Report*, para 76.

State because they are based on grounds unknown in the legislation of the State in which recognition is sought. The provision therefore limits indiscriminate use of public policy.[440]

(f) Non-review as to substance

Article 26 lays down the classic rule that under no circumstances may a judgment be reviewed as to its substance.[441] This buttresses the principle stated in Article 25, to the effect that recognition cannot be refused solely on the ground that there is a discrepancy between the legal rules applied, respectively, by the court of origin and by the recognising court. It cannot be alleged that the court of origin made a mistake of fact or of law. Procedural irregularities in the court of origin, however, can be examined in order to establish a defence under Article 22.

(iv) Divorces, annulments and legal separations obtained in a non-European Community Member State, or in Denmark

(a) Introduction

Part II of the Family Law Act 1986 deals with a range of matters relating to the recognition in England of divorces, annulments and legal separations which have been obtained in a country[442] outside the British Isles, other than those in respect of which provision as to recognition is made by Brussels II *bis*. Essentially, Part II applies to divorces, etc obtained in a state which is not an European Community Member State, or in Denmark; these are referred to in the 1986 Act as "overseas divorces", etc,[443] and references in this section of the chapter to "overseas divorces" or "foreign divorces" should be construed in like manner. No distinction is drawn in the 1986 Act, as there was in the 1971 Act,[444] between different kinds of foreign divorce, etc dependent on whether their recognition fell within or outside the Hague Convention of 1970. The consequence, as recommended by the Law Commission,[445] is a less complex set of recognition rules, especially in relation to issues of jurisdiction.[446] The areas to be examined here include the jurisdictional bases for recognition, the requirement of effectiveness of the divorce, etc in the country where it was obtained, the grounds on which recognition may be denied and the special problems and rules relating to different kinds of extra-judicial divorce.

---

[440] Borras, *Explanatory Report*, para 76.

[441] Cf Brussels I Regulation, Art 36, discussed supra, p 628.

[442] The meaning of "country" is discussed more fully, infra, pp 996–997.

[443] S 45, as amended by SI 2005/265, reg 17. Recognition by virtue of any other statute is preserved: s 45(1)(b), discussed infra, p 999.

[444] Contrast ss 2–5 with s 6 of the 1971 Act; and see North, op cit, pp 172–176.

[445] Law Com No 137 (1984), paras 6.3–6.6.

[446] Though the eradication of complexity has been somewhat offset by the decision, not recommended by the Law Commission, to have special rules for the recognition of some extra-judicial divorces, infra, p 999 et seq.

(b) General matters

The recognition rules laid down in Part II are exclusive.[447] It is not possible for the recognition of a foreign divorce, annulment or legal separation to be governed by common law recognition rules, whether or not it was obtained[448] before or after the 1986 Act came into effect.[449] As a result, the extension of the statutory regime for recognition to foreign annulments has the effect that it is now clear that an annulment of a void marriage will not be recognised on the basis that it was obtained in the country where the marriage was celebrated.[450] Furthermore, the general rule is that recognition is mandatory,[451] provided that the requirements of Part II (as to jurisdiction, etc) are satisfied and that one of the statutory grounds for denying recognition[452] is not relevant.

(c) Jurisdictional rules

Section 46(1) of the 1986 Act provides a number of jurisdictional grounds for the recognition of overseas divorces, annulments and legal separations which have been obtained by judicial or other proceedings.[453]

(i) Domicile

An overseas divorce, etc will be recognised if either party, whether petitioner or respondent, to the marriage was domiciled in the country where it was obtained[454] at the date of the commencement of the foreign proceedings.[455] In the case of the recognition of foreign divorces and legal separations, this involves a very slight limitation on the recognition rules available under the 1971 Act where it was possible for a divorce, etc to be recognised in England if its validity was recognised in the country of each spouse's domicile, though obtained in neither.[456] The Law Commission[457] concluded that there was no case for the retention of such an extended rule relating to domicile, given that there is no equivalent rule in relation to the other jurisdictional heads of habitual residence and nationality,[458] and that the old rule was inequitable if one of the spouses was domiciled in England and the other abroad. In such a case the divorce, etc would only be recognised if recognised in England, which was the very matter in issue; so recognition would have to be refused.[459]

---

[447] S 45.

[448] S 52, subject to certain saving provisions, discussed infra, p 1024.

[449] S 52(1).

[450] As in *Merker v Merker* [1963] P 283; Law Com No 137 (1984), paras 6.33–6.34.

[451] S 45.

[452] S 51, infra, p 1012 et seq.

[453] See the definition of "proceedings" in s 54. The jurisdictional rules relevant to extra-judicial divorces obtained without proceedings are discussed infra, p 999 et seq.

[454] S 46(1)(b)(ii).

[455] S 46(3)(a).

[456] Recognition of Divorces and Legal Separations Act 1971, s 6(3)(b); based on the common law decision in *Armitage v A-G* [1906] P 135.

[457] Law Com No 137 (1984), paras 6.27–6.30.

[458] Infra. Though the rules in the 1986 Act in relation to domicile are in other respects much wider than those in s 6 of the 1971 Act, where the domicile connection had to be satisfied in relation to both parties: see Law Com No 137 (1984), paras 6.21–6.26.

[459] See North, op cit, p 185.

There is, therefore, no counterpart of such an extended domiciliary rule in the 1986 Act[460] where there are foreign proceedings.[461]

It has been assumed so far, as is usual in private international law, that domicile means domicile in the English sense. However, section 46(1)(b) requires an overseas divorce, etc to be recognised if either party is domiciled in the foreign country in either the English or the foreign sense of domicile,[462] this latter being a ground of jurisdiction provided in the 1970 Hague Convention and in the 1971 Act. Hence an overseas divorce may have to be recognised on the basis of such foreign concept of domicile,[463] even though neither spouse was domiciled in the foreign country in the English sense of the term.[464]

It is possible that a country may have different concepts of domicile for different purposes;[465] and so section 46(5) of the 1986 Act makes clear that the concept of domicile relevant for recognition purposes is that used in the foreign country "in family matters".[466]

(ii) Habitual residence

An overseas divorce will be recognised if it was obtained in a country in which, at the time of the commencement of the proceedings,[467] either spouse was habitually resident as determined under English law.[468] No length of period of residence is specified or required;[469] and jurisdiction may be founded on the habitual residence of either spouse, whether petitioner or respondent.

(iii) Nationality

A similar rule applies in the case of nationality, so that divorces, etc obtained in a country of which, at the time of the proceedings,[470] either party was a national will be recognised in England.[471] No definition of nationality is provided,[472] but there seems little doubt

---

[460] Though there are saving provisions which preserve the validity of divorces and legal separations obtained before the 1986 Act came into effect and which would have been recognised under the now-abandoned rule: s 52(5)(b), (e), infra, p 1024.

[461] The common law rule is retained in cases where there are no proceedings: s 46(2), infra, p 1009 et seq.

[462] S 46(5). The same applies where there are no proceedings, infra, p 1009 et seq.

[463] See *Lawrence v Lawrence* [1985] Fam 106 at 121.

[464] Recognition does not depend, under the 1986 Act, on the foreign court having assumed jurisdiction on the basis of domicile.

[465] Indeed England has a special concept of domicile for the purposes of the Civil Jurisdiction and Judgments Acts 1982 and 1991, supra, p 222 et seq.

[466] This is consistent with Art 3 of the 1970 Hague Convention. It also involves dropping the requirement, to be found in s 3(2) of the 1971 Act, that the foreign country uses its concept of domicile as a ground of jurisdiction in divorce, etc. The Law Commission considered such a limitation to be ineffective, unnecessary and illogical, especially in the case of extra-judicial divorces: Law Com No 137 (1984), para 6.18.

[467] This head is inapplicable if there are no proceedings, infra, p 1009 et seq.

[468] S 46(1)(b)(i), (3)(a). See, eg, *Cruse v Chittum* [1974] 2 All ER 940; *Kendall v Kendall* [1977] Fam 208; *Joyce v Joyce* [1979] Fam 93 at 105; *Quazi v Quazi* [1980] AC 744 at 788, 821; Social Security Decision No R (P) 2/90.

[469] Cf the jurisdictional test in Pt II of the Domicile and Matrimonial Proceedings Act 1973, supra, pp 947–949, where the meaning of "habitual residence" is discussed.

[470] Again, this head is inapplicable if there are no proceedings, supra, pp 947–949.

[471] S 46(1)(b)(iii), 3(a); see, eg, *Broit v Broit* 1972 SLT (Notes) 32; *Quazi v Quazi* [1980] AC 744 at 805, 813, 821; *Lawrence v Lawrence* [1985] Fam 106 at 121.

[472] Though see s 54(2).

that, in the case of a person with dual nationality, recognition will be given to divorces, etc obtained in either country of the nationality.[473]

(d) The time at which the jurisdictional rules must be satisfied

As we have seen, the general rule is that the jurisdictional connection must be satisfied at the date of the commencement of the foreign proceedings by which the divorce, etc was obtained.[474] There are, however, two exceptions to this. The first is relevant only to the recognition of foreign annulments. It is possible both in England, and elsewhere, for an annulment of a void marriage to be obtained by a person other than a spouse and for that to be done after the death of either or both spouses. English jurisdictional rules make special provision for such a case,[475] as does section 46(4) of the 1986 Act in the case of recognition of an overseas annulment. If the annulment was obtained after the death of a party to the marriage, the jurisdictional requirements of domicile, habitual residence or nationality are satisfied if the appropriate connection existed at the date of the death.[476]

The second exception concerns cross-proceedings, where it is sufficient if the jurisdictional grounds of habitual residence, nationality and domicile in the English or the foreign sense existed either at the date of the original proceedings or of the cross-proceedings.[477] This applies irrespective of which proceedings led to the foreign divorce, etc. Of course, even if this special jurisdictional provision is satisfied, it is necessary to satisfy all the other requirements of Part II of the 1986 Act for the divorce, etc to be recognised.[478]

(e) Effectiveness

Not only must one of the various jurisdictional requirements be satisfied at the relevant time, but it is also necessary that the overseas divorce, etc be "effective under the law of the country in which it was obtained".[479] This requirement of effectiveness was also to be found in the 1971 Act[480] but did not there extend to recognition on the jurisdictional basis of domicile in the English sense. Following the recommendations of the Law Commission,[481] this requirement applies, under the 1986 Act, also to the domicile basis[482] and is extended, as is the whole of Part II of the 1986 Act, to the recognition of overseas annulments. This marks a change from the common law rules as to nullity recognition where, for example, a German decree was recognised in England even though it was regarded in Germany as invalid and of no effect there.[483]

---

[473] *Torok v Torok* [1973] 1 WLR 1066 at 1069.

[474] S 46(3)(a).

[475] Domicile and Matrimonial Proceedings Act 1973, s 5(3)(b), supra, p 953.

[476] See Law Com No 137 (1984), para 6.32; s 46(4).

[477] S 47(1)(a).

[478] S 47 (1)(b); and see Law Com No 137 (1984), para 6.39.

[479] S 46(1)(a). See *Kellman v Kellman* [2000] 1 FLR 785; and *Duhur-Johnson v Duhur-Johnson* [2005] 2 FLR 1042.

[480] S 2(b).

[481] Law Com No 137 (1984), paras 6.12–6.13.

[482] An example of a divorce recognised under common law domicile rules where the effectiveness requirement would not have been satisfied is provided by *Har-Shefi v Har-Shefi (No 2)* [1953] P 220; though see now the 1986 Act, ss 44(1), 52(5), infra, pp 1007–1008.

[483] *Merker v Merker* [1963] P 283. It might be argued that a foreign decree, though invalid in the country where granted, is effective there until actually set aside: *Kendall v Kendall* [1977] Fam 208 at 214.

Various examples of legal ineffectiveness might be provided, as, for instance, where a foreign divorce does not, in the foreign country, dissolve a marriage until a specified period has elapsed,[484] or whilst an appeal is pending,[485] or until a decree absolute is pronounced.[486] It is also possible[487] that, under the law of the foreign country, the divorce, etc might be regarded as ineffective there because that country's rules as to service on the parties or as to the jurisdiction of its courts had not been satisfied, even though the jurisdictional requirements of the 1986 Act[488] had been. This might be so even if the procedural defects did not fall within the heads listed in the 1986 Act[489] as grounds for denying recognition.[490]

(f) Meaning of "country"

So far, in examining the jurisdictional and other rules of Part II of the 1986 Act, it has been assumed that the requirement of a connection with the "country" in which the divorce, etc was obtained causes no difficulty.[491] There are, however, political countries which comprise different territories[492] and those territories may have different substantive or jurisdictional rules for obtaining divorces, etc. There were problems with the 1971 Act in deciding whether some or all of the references in that Act to "country" meant the political state or the individual territory.[493] In order to try to resolve these difficulties, section 49 of the 1986 Act[494] provides express modifications of the provisions of Part II of that Act in those cases where, in a country comprising different territories, there are different systems of law in force in relation to divorce, annulment or legal separation.[495] The general approach is to say that, in such cases, any requirement of domicile (in the English or foreign senses) or habitual residence in a country, and indeed effectiveness under the law of that country, means domicile or habitual residence in an individual territory.[496] This means that, as each American state has its own divorce, etc laws, New York or California is to be treated as a separate country for the purposes of determining domicile or habitual residence. On the other hand, Canada and Australia, both also federal

---

[484] Eg *Martin v Buret* 1938 SLT 479.

[485] Eg *Torok v Torok* [1973] 1 WLR 1066; cf Social Security Decision R (P) 2/90, p 6.

[486] Eg *De Thoren v Wall* (1876) 3 R (HL) 28. A further example in the case of an extra-judicial divorce by *talak* might be a delay whilst conciliation proceedings are continuing: National Insurance Decision Nos R(G) 5/74; R(G) 2/75.

[487] North, op cit, pp 175–176.

[488] S 46(1)(b), supra, p 993 et seq; see eg *Papadopoulos v Papadopoulos* [1930] P 55.

[489] S 51, infra, p 1012 et seq; see, eg, *Pemberton v Hughes* [1899] 1 Ch 781.

[490] Particular problems of effectiveness relating to extra-judicial divorces are discussed, infra, p 1008 et seq.

[491] Part II of the 1986 Act does not define "country" apart from saying that it includes a colony or other dependent territory of the United Kingdom, but that a person is to be treated as a national of such a territory only if it has a law of citizenship or nationality separate from that of the United Kingdom and he is a citizen or national of that territory under that law: s 54(2).

[492] Eg the USA, Canada, Australia, the United Kingdom.

[493] North, op cit, pp 173–175, 177, 179, 181; Law Com No 137 (1984), para 6.15.

[494] Following recommendations made in Law Com No 137 (1984), para 6.16.

[495] S 49(1). See *Kellman v Kellman* [2000] 1 FLR 785; and *Emin v Yeldag* [2002] 1 FLR 956.

[496] S 49(2), (4), (5), amending where appropriate the main jurisdictional rules in s 46(1)(b), and also the special jurisdictional rules where there are no proceedings, in s 46(2)(b); as well as the rules for the conversion of a legal separation into a divorce (s 47(2), infra, p 997) and relating to proof of finding of facts in the foreign proceedings (s 48, infra, p 998). Also amended are the provisions of s 52(3) and (4); but this appears to be a slip, as the appropriate provisions to be amended appear to be those in s 51(3) and (4). None of the provisions mentioned above are amended in relation to nationality, which is dealt with by s 49(3), infra.

states, have federal divorce laws;[497] so one must ask whether in divorce proceedings a spouse was habitually resident or domiciled in Canada or Australia, rather than in an individual province or state.

Nationality as a connecting factor poses rather different problems. Federal and other non-unitary states do not have different nationality rules, depending on a person's connection with a particular territory within the state. This would suggest that a connection with a territory is satisfied for jurisdictional purposes if either party is a national of the political state as a whole. This means that if a divorce, etc is obtained in New York, it will be recognised in England even though the only relevant connection for the purposes of the 1986 Act is that one spouse is a US citizen.[498] The provisions which state that connection by domicile or habitual residence with a territory will suffice[499] do not extend to connection by nationality.

It is necessary in the case of connection by nationality, as in other cases, not only that the divorce, etc was obtained in the country of the nationality but also that it was effective "under the law of the country in which it was obtained".[500] This raises the issue as to the meaning of "country" in this latter context. If, for instance, a divorce is obtained in California by an American citizen, and the only jurisdictional test which is satisfied is that of nationality, does the divorce have to be effective in California or throughout the USA? The 1971 Act was unclear on this question and academic views differed as to the answer; but section 49(3)(a) of the 1986 Act now makes it clear that, in such a case, effectiveness "throughout the country in which [the divorce] was obtained" is necessary.[501] So, in the example just given, the Californian divorce will only be recognised in England if it is recognised throughout the USA. Indeed, it has been thought to be "absurd" to recognise a divorce obtained in one American state which would not be recognised elsewhere in the USA.[502]

(g) Two procedural issues

(i) Conversion of legal separation into divorce

Some jurisdictions permit a legal separation automatically to be converted into a divorce at the end of a prescribed period. If the legal separation would be recognised on the jurisdictional grounds[503] of habitual residence, nationality, or domicile in the English or the foreign sense, then the later divorce will be recognised even though the jurisdictional criteria cannot be satisfied at that later date.[504] The conversion must, however, be in the country where the legal separation was obtained and the new divorce must be effective under the law of that country.

---

[497] The position would be different in Canada with regard to legal separation which, unlike divorce, is a provincial rather than a federal matter.

[498] S 46(1)(b)(iii).

[499] S 49(2), (4), (5).

[500] S 46(1)(a).

[501] There is a similar provision in s 49(3)(b) in relation to the effectiveness of the conversion into a divorce of a legal separation obtained in a country of which one party was a national.

[502] Morris (1975) 24 ICLQ 635, 641; and see Law Com No 137 (1984), para 6.16.

[503] Including the provisions as to cross-proceedings in s 47(1).

[504] S 47(2).

(ii) Findings of fact

If any finding of fact on the basis of which jurisdiction was assumed, such as to the domicile in the foreign sense,[505] habitual residence,[506] or nationality[507] of the parties,[508] is made in the foreign divorce, etc proceedings, it shall be conclusive evidence of the fact found if both spouses took part in the proceedings.[509] In any other case, eg an *ex parte* divorce, it shall be sufficient proof of that fact unless it is challenged and the contrary is shown.[510]

(h) Meaning of divorce, annulment or legal separation

As foreign matrimonial proceedings may differ markedly from English ones, it is necessary for the English court to decide whether the foreign proceedings come within one of the categories of divorce, annulment[511] or legal separation within the meaning of Part II of the 1986 Act. It has been held, for example, that the termination of a marriage by the husband's unilateral decision to change his religion and become a Moslem, which was evidenced by a declaration before witnesses in Malaysia, could not be regarded here as either a divorce or an annulment.[512] In the case of legal separations, it should be noted that, although the rules for the recognition of other British decrees refer to decrees of "judicial separation",[513] those for recognition of separations obtained outside the British Isles refer to "legal separations".[514] A legal separation is not defined in the 1986 Act, nor indeed in the 1970 Hague Convention on which the Act is based. It must be assumed that the Act extends to all foreign decrees or orders which are similar in character to an English decree of judicial separation and, indeed, to any order or decree made by a foreign court which has the effect that the parties are no longer obliged to live together, but not the effect of dissolving the marriage. The consequence of the use of different terminology is that, for example, a non-cohabitation order made in Northern Ireland will not be recognised in England because it is not a decree of judicial separation.[515] On the other hand, had it been made outside the British Isles, it is likely to be recognised as a legal separation.[516]

---

[505] It is not appropriate for a finding by a foreign court as to domicile in the English sense to be binding on an English court: see Law Com No 137 (1984), para 6.40.

[506] Eg *Cruse v Chittum* [1974] 2 All ER 940; cf Social Security Decision R (P) 2/90.

[507] Eg *Torok v Torok* [1973] 1 WLR 1066 at 1069.

[508] S 48(2).

[509] S 48(1)(a), as in *Lawrence v Lawrence* [1985] Fam 106 at 121; and appearance is to be treated as taking part in proceedings: s 48(3).

[510] S 48 (1)(b); eg *Mandani v Mandani* [1984] FLR 699 at 700. The court is not required under Part II of the 1986 Act to recognise any findings of fault made in any divorce, nullity or separation proceedings or any maintenance, custody or other ancillary order made in such proceedings: s 51(5); see *Sabbagh v Sabbagh* [1985] FLR 29. For recognition of maintenance and custody orders generally, see infra, p 1069 et seq and p 1097 et seq.

[511] A non-exclusive definition of annulment is provided in s 54(1) to include "any decree or declaration of nullity of marriage, however expressed".

[512] *Viswalingham v Viswalingham* (1979) 1 FLR 15. As the marriage was held to be ended under the law of Malaysia, the common domicile of the parties, prima facie this would be recognised in England; but recognition was in fact denied on public policy grounds.

[513] 1986 Act, s 44(2).

[514] Ibid, ss 46–52.

[515] North, op cit, pp 278–280.

[516] Ibid, pp 286–287.

(i) Irrelevance of the foreign jurisdictional rules or of the grounds for granting the divorce, etc

It should be pointed out that, as was the case at common law,[517] the grounds on which the foreign divorce, etc were obtained are irrelevant to the question of recognition.[518] It is immaterial that the divorce, etc was obtained on a ground unknown to English law. This is illustrated clearly by the fact that, at common law, a foreign nullity decree has been recognised as annulling a marriage, validly celebrated in England, on the ground of what English courts would class as formal invalidity.[519] A corollary of this is that a foreign divorce or annulment will be recognised though granted on grounds unknown to English law,[520] even where one spouse was domiciled in England.[521]

Furthermore, again as at common law, the jurisdictional basis assumed by a foreign court is similarly irrelevant. The English court is concerned only with the factual jurisdictional circumstances in the foreign country when the divorce, etc was obtained.

(j) Other statutory grounds of recognition

Section 45(1)(b) of the 1986 Act preserves the rules for the recognition of overseas divorces, annulments and legal separations which exist by virtue of any other enactment. However, at the same time, the 1986 Act repeals[522] as spent legislation most, if not all, of the other statutory provisions[523] under which overseas divorces, etc might be recognised, whilst also preserving the validity of past divorces, etc which would be recognised under that spent legislation, and might not be recognised under the 1986 Act.[524] Furthermore, it has been made clear[525] that an overseas divorce, etc not recognised under the 1986 Act cannot be recognised under the Foreign Judgments (Reciprocal Enforcement) Act 1933.[526]

(v) Extra-judicial divorces, annulments and legal separations[527]

(a) Introduction

Divorces may be obtained not only in judicial proceedings but also extra-judicially in a variety of ways. These include divorce by mutual consent,[528] by administrative process[529] or, more commonly, under religious laws.[530] For instance, a Jewish Rabbinical law allows

---

[517] *Indyka v Indyka* [1969] 1 AC 33 at 66.

[518] Subject to any public policy factor, infra, p 1018 et seq. Cf Brussels II *bis*, Art 25, discussed supra, pp 991–992.

[519] *De Massa v De Massa* (1931), reported in [1939] 2 All ER 150 n; *Galene v Galene (otherwise Galice)* [1939] P 237.

[520] *Corbett v Corbett* [1957] 1 WLR 486 at 490.

[521] *Mitford v Mitford* [1923] P 130.

[522] S 68(2) and Sch 2.

[523] The main ones are the Colonial and Other Territories (Divorce Jurisdiction) Acts 1926 and 1950 and the Matrimonial Causes (War Marriages) Act 1944, s 4; see Law Com No 137 (1984), paras 6.44–6.48.

[524] S 52(5)(c), (d); and see Law Com No 137 (1984), pp 115–116.

[525] *Maples v Maples* [1988] Fam 14.

[526] Supra, p 578.

[527] North, op cit, Chapter 11; (1975) 91 LQR 36; Young (1987) 7 Legal Studies 78; Edwards (1988) 18 Fam Law 419; Pilkington (1988) 37 ICLQ 131.

[528] National Insurance Decision No R(G) 1/72; and *H v H (Validity of Japanese Divorce)* [2006] EWHC 2989 (Fam), [2007] 1 FLR 1318 (divorce by *"kyogi rikon"*, ie by agreement, under Art 763 of the Japanese Civil Code).

[529] *Manning v Manning* [1958] P 112.

[530] Gordon, *Foreign Divorces: English Law and Practice* (1988), Chapters 1–3.

a husband to dissolve his marriage by delivering to his wife a letter of divorce, called a *gett* and, though this necessitates his appearance before a Rabbinical court, the proceeding is a formality and is not accompanied by a judicial finding and pronouncement.[531] Under Moslem law,[532] a husband is permitted to divorce his wife without any reference to a court. Such a divorce, by *talak*, merely requires him to state unequivocally three times his intention to repudiate the marriage. In some countries, no further formality is required than this—what is often called a "bare" *talak*.[533] In other jurisdictions where Moslem law is applied, it is necessary also either to register such a divorce with a court or administrative body[534] or, as under the Pakistan Muslim Family Laws Ordinance 1961,[535] to go through procedures giving the opportunity of conciliation proceedings.[536] Moslem law also provides other forms of divorce, such as by *khula*, a form of divorce by agreement on the suggestion of the wife.[537]

Examples of extra-judicial annulments are very much less easy to provide,[538] not least because few countries recognise religious or administrative annulment of marriage. However, examples can be provided of annulment by an ecclesiastical rather than civil tribunal.[539]

At common law, English courts were originally very reluctant to recognise the effectiveness and validity of extra-judicial divorces;[540] but attitudes have changed and it has come to be accepted that they should normally be recognised if the general jurisdictional criteria for recognition have been established.[541] Indeed, in 1970 recognition was given to a *talak* divorce pronounced in England, dissolving the marriage celebrated in England of spouses domiciled in Pakistan.[542]

---

[531] Eg *Har-Shefi v Har-Shefi (No 2)* [1953] P 220; *Broit v Broit* 1972 SLT (Notes) 32; *Maples v Maples* [1988] Fam 14; *Berkovits v Grinberg* [1995] Fam 142; and *O v O (Jurisdiction: Jewish Divorce)* [2000] 2 FLR 147; and see Berkovits (1988) 104 LQR 60, 81–93. See now Divorce (Religious Marriages) Act 2002 (and SI 2003/186), by which the English court may order that a decree of divorce is not to be made absolute until a declaration made by both parties that they have taken such steps as are required to dissolve the marriage in accordance with the usages of the Jews, or any other prescribed religious usages, is produced to the court. Cf in Scotland, Family Law (Scotland) Act 2006, s 15 (inserting s 3A into the Divorce (Scotland) Act 1976) and SSI 2006/253, discussed by Crawford and Carruthers, at para 12-18.

[532] See generally Rehman (2007) 21 International Journal of Law, Policy and the Family 108, 118 et seq; and *El Fadl v El Fadl* [2000] 1 FCR 685, per HUGHES J at 694 et seq.

[533] Eg *Sharif v Sharif* (1980) 10 Fam Law 216 (Iraq); *Zaal v Zaal* (1982) 4 FLR 284 (Dubai); *Chaudhary v Chaudhary* [1985] Fam 19 (Kashmir).

[534] Eg *Russ v Russ* [1964] P 315 (Egypt).

[535] See *Qureshi v Qureshi* [1972] Fam 173; *R v Registrar General of Births, Deaths and Marriages, ex p Minhas* [1977] QB 1; *Quazi v Quazi* [1980] AC 744; *R v Secretary of State for the Home Department, ex p Fatima* [1986] AC 527.

[536] See *Radwan v Radwan* [1973] Fam 24 (Egypt).

[537] *Quazi v Quazi* [1980] AC 744.

[538] Cases of extra-judicial separation have not come before the courts for many years: *Connelly v Connelly* (1851) 7 Moo PCC 438; North, op cit, p 280.

[539] *Di Rollo v Di Rollo* 1959 SC 75; *Butterley v Butterley* (1974) 48 DLR (3d) 351; see North, op cit, pp 264–266.

[540] Eg *R v Hammersmith Superintendent Registrar of Marriages, ex p Mir-Anwarrudin* [1917] 1 KB 634.

[541] Though the extra-judicial annulment in *Di Rollo v Di Rollo*, supra, was denied recognition on grounds of public policy.

[542] *Qureshi v Qureshi* [1972] Fam 173. Recognition was denied at common law if the spouses were domiciled in England, [1972] Fam 173 at 199; *Radwan v Radwan* [1973] Fam 24.

The rules for the recognition of foreign extra-judicial divorces and legal separations were placed by the Recognition of Divorces and Legal Separations Act 1971 on the same general statutory basis as the rules for the recognition of foreign divorces and legal separations obtained by court order; though the grounds for recognising extra-judicial divorces and legal separations obtained without there having been any proceedings (such as a bare *talak*) were narrower[543] than for those which involved some form of proceedings as in the case of a *gett*.[544] There were also special rules generally denying recognition to extra-judicial divorces and separations obtained in the British Isles but recognised as valid elsewhere.[545] This pattern has substantially been retained in Part II of the Family Law Act 1986, with the addition that the recognition rules now extend to the recognition of extra-judicial annulments.[546] The Law Commission[547] had proposed a more liberal approach[548] so that, for example, "bare" *talaks* would fall within the broader recognition rules applicable where there had been some proceedings. On the other hand, they also proposed that the requirement of some form of proceedings, albeit more liberally interpreted,[549] should apply to all divorces, etc irrespective of the jurisdictional basis of recognition. This would have had the effect that an entirely informal divorce could no longer be generally recognised[550] even though obtained in the country of the spouses' common domicile. This essentially more liberal approach was rejected[551] for three reasons, namely because of problems of proof in the case of informal divorces, because such divorces tend to discriminate against women (being usually obtained by men) and because they often provide little or no financial protection for the wife and family. These arguments are not wholly convincing. The last is met by the provisions in Part III of the Matrimonial and Family Proceedings Act 1984 allowing the courts to grant financial relief even though a foreign divorce is recognised in England.[552] If there is force in the first two arguments they militate against any recognition of such informal divorces, but in fact they continue to be recognised, provided they are obtained or recognised in the country of the domicile in the English sense.[553] It is not easy to see why a domicile connection provides any greater protection than one based, say, on habitual residence.[554]

The result is that, in relation to extra-judicial divorces, etc, Part II of the 1986 Act still follows very much the approach of the 1971 Act. We shall have to consider, therefore, the rules relating to extra-judicial divorces, etc obtained in the British Isles separately from those obtained overseas, and to determine where a divorce, etc is obtained, given that the

---

[543] Jurisdiction could only be based on domicile in the English sense under s 6 of the 1971 Act.

[544] Jurisdiction could also be based on habitual residence, nationality or domicile in the foreign sense under ss 2–5 of the 1971 Act.

[545] See the 1971 Act, ss 1, 6: Domicile and Matrimonial Proceedings Act 1973, s 16 (repealed by Family Law Act 1986, ss 68(2), 69, and Sch 2).

[546] Ss 44, 45; following the recommendations of the Law Commission: Law Com No 137 (1984), para 6.9.

[547] Law Com No 137 (1984), para 6.11.

[548] Similar to that in Australia (eg Family Law Act 1975, s 104).

[549] It was suggested that the statutory phrase "judicial or other proceedings" should include acts which constitute the means by which the divorce, etc may be obtained and which are done in compliance with the procedures required in the country where it was obtained.

[550] Under s 6 of the 1971 Act.

[551] 473 HL Official Report, cols 1082, 1103 (1986); see Young (1987) 7 Legal Studies 78, 81–83.

[552] Infra, p 1063 et seq.

[553] S 46(2).

[554] S 46(1).

recognition rules depend on this factor even though, because of the very informality of many of the divorces, etc under consideration, the parties may regard the place where it takes place as totally unimportant. In the context of overseas divorces, etc, it is also necessary to look separately at those obtained by some form of proceedings and, indeed, to consider what constitutes "proceedings".

Before turning to examine the detail of the 1986 Act, it should be borne in mind that the approach of English law and the attitude of English courts in this regard is one of tolerance, as is clear from the words of MUNBY J in *Sulaiman v Juffali*:[555]

> Although historically [England] is part of the Christian west, and although it has an established church which is Christian, I sit as a secular judge serving a multi-cultural community of many faiths in which all of us can now take some pride, sworn to do justice "to all manner of people". Religion—whatever the particular believer's faith—is no doubt something to be encouraged but it is not the business of government or of the secular courts. So the starting point of the law is an essentially agnostic view of religious beliefs and a tolerant indulgence to religious and cultural diversity. A secular judge must be wary of straying across the well-recognised divide between church and state. It is not for a judge to weigh one religion against another. All are entitled to equal respect, whether in times of peace or, as at present, amidst the clash of arms.

(b) General issues

Before examining the particular rules relating to the recognition of extra-judicial divorces, etc, it is necessary to examine, first, two of those inter-related general issues. As there are different rules for extra-judicial divorces, etc obtained in the British Isles and overseas, and for overseas divorces, etc depending on whether or not they were obtained by "proceedings", we shall consider here the two questions: where is an extra-judicial divorce, etc obtained and what constitutes proceedings?

(i) *Where is an extra-judicial divorce, etc obtained?*

This question may be asked in two main contexts. First, it is necessary that an overseas divorce, etc be effective in the country where it was obtained and that one of the relevant jurisdictional links with that country is satisfied.[556] The second context, which has proved in practice to be the more important, is to determine whether the divorce, etc was obtained in the British Isles or overseas. The significance of this is that the divorce, etc will normally be denied recognition if obtained in the British Isles.[557]

It might be thought that the proceedings or act[558] by which an extra-judicial divorce, etc is obtained could only occur in one country. Whilst this is usually true, particular difficulty has been caused by Moslem divorces by *talak*, especially where this religious requirement is also combined with a need for some further type of proceedings. This is illustrated

---

[555] [2002] 2 FCR 427, at 439.
[556] 1986 Act, s 46.
[557] Ibid, s 44, infra, p 1003.
[558] The need to decide where a divorce, etc was obtained arises whether or not it was obtained by judicial or other proceedings.

by a decision under the Recognition of Divorces and Legal Separations Act 1971, *R v Secretary of State for the Home Department, ex parte Fatima*:[559]

> The husband was a Pakistan national who married there in 1968, but had lived in England ever since. In 1978, he purported to divorce his wife by *talak* and in 1982 wished to marry Ghulam Fatima; but she was refused entry to England by an immigration officer at Heathrow Airport. This was because the officer concluded that the husband's *talak* divorce would not be recognised in England and so the husband was not free to marry again here.

The crucial issue with which the House of Lords was faced was to determine where the *talak* divorce in 1978 was obtained. If it was obtained in Pakistan, where it was effective, it would be recognised in England as a divorce obtained in the country of the nationality.[560] If it was obtained in England, it would be denied recognition.[561] The circumstances were that it was a "transnational" divorce:[562] some proceedings took place in England, others in Pakistan under the Muslim Family Laws Ordinance 1961 in force there. The husband had pronounced the *talak* in England and made a statutory declaration to that effect to an English solicitor. Copies of this were sent to Pakistan both to the wife and, as required by the Ordinance, to the chairman of the relevant local union council; and it would appear that all the necessary conciliation procedures in Pakistan were complied with. The effect of this was that the divorce became effective there ninety days after receipt of notice of the *talak* by the chairman. Lord ACKNER concluded that the divorce was not obtained by proceedings wholly in Pakistan because the pronouncement of the *talak* in England was an essential part of the proceedings.[563] This led him to the conclusion that the divorce was obtained by proceedings which took place in both countries and that recognition must be denied, because section 2 of the 1971 Act required an overseas divorce to be obtained by means of judicial or other proceedings in a country outside the British Isles and to be effective under the law of that country. Similarly, in *Sulaiman v Juffali*,[564] a bare *talak* pronounced by the husband in England, and registered with the Sharia Court in Saudi Arabia three days later was "obtained" in England for the purposes of the 1986 Act, since its effect was to dissolve the marriage as soon as it had been pronounced; the validity of this *talak* was in no way dependent upon the participation or authorisation of judicial authorities, and so, having been obtained in England other than through a court of civil jurisdiction, the divorce fell foul of section 44(1).

Such a result is wholly consistent with the policy of denying recognition to extra-judicial divorces, etc which have been obtained by proceedings in England,[565] but it does highlight the particular weight which the legislation places on where a divorce, etc is obtained. If the husband in this case had had the advice, or the funds, to go to Pakistan to pronounce the *talak*, it would have been recognised in England.[566]

---

[559] [1986] AC 527; affirming the CA, [1985] QB 190; Berkovits (1988) 104 LQR 60.
[560] Supra, pp 994–995.
[561] Infra, p 1004.
[562] [1985] QB 190 at 197, 207.
[563] [1986] AC 527 at 533–534; and see *Quazi v Quazi* [1980] AC 744 at 817, 826.
[564] [2002] 2 FCR 427.
[565] 1986 Act, s 44(1).
[566] See [1985] QB 190 at 199–200.

There is a difficult question as to whether the same result is compelled under the 1986 Act which is worded slightly differently. Section 46(1) requires an overseas divorce obtained by proceedings to be effective in the country where it was obtained but does not, in so many words, require the proceedings to be in that country. This led to the suggestion[567] that where the proceedings take place in more than one country, as in *Ex p Fatima*, the divorce may still be recognised if that element of the proceedings which renders the divorce effective takes place in the overseas country with which the necessary jurisdictional links may be established. So, it is argued,[568] a *talak* pronounced in England by a Pakistan national but perfected by proceedings in Pakistan is obtained (and effective) in Pakistan and should be recognised in England.

Whilst there is undoubted force in the argument both from the point of view of policy and on construction of the statutory provisions, it was rejected by WALL J in *Berkovits v Grinberg*.[569] In that case, a *gett* had been written in England but was delivered in Israel. Although it was effective under the law of Israel to dissolve the marriage, it was denied recognition in England. The judge accepted the argument that there was no evidence that the 1986 Act was intended to change the law and that it should be so construed.[570] Furthermore, other provisions of the 1986 Act, like their predecessors in the 1971 Act, are drafted on the basis that the divorce was obtained in the foreign proceedings.[571] This is particularly true of those provisions concerned with the giving of notice of the proceedings to the parties.[572] It is nonetheless undesirable to say, as was said by Lord ACKNER in *Ex p Fatima*, that there "must be a single set of proceedings which have to be instituted in the same country as that in which the relevant divorce was ultimately obtained".[573] This may be too sweeping a statement.[574] It is surely understandable to deny recognition to a divorce obtained by proceedings partly in England and partly abroad, given the prohibition on recognition of extra-judicial divorces, etc obtained in the British Isles.[575] It is less justifiable to deny recognition to, say, a *talak* pronounced in Dubai followed by conciliation proceedings in Pakistan, given that the divorce is effective in each of the countries where some of the proceedings took place.

If a divorce, etc is obtained in a consulate or embassy, it is to be taken to be obtained in the country where the consulate or embassy is situated, not in the country of the sending state. So it has been held that an extra-judicial divorce obtained in the Consulate-General

---

[567] Pilkington (1988) 37 ICLQ 130, 132–136; and see Young (1987) 7 Legal Studies 78, 87; Berkovits (1988) 104 LQR 60, 79–80; Gordon, op cit, pp 101–104.

[568] Pilkington (1988) 37 ICLQ 130, 135.

[569] [1995] Fam 142. McClean (1996) 112 LQR 230.

[570] Section 46(1) is essentially to the same effect as clause 3(1)(a) of the Law Commission's draft Bill on which the 1986 Act is based and the Commission expressed itself content with the decision in *Ex p Fatima*: see Law Com No 137 (1984), para 6.11 and p 94.

[571] Eg ss 47(1), 48(1).

[572] S 51(3), infra, p 1015 et seq. Had the 1986 Act changed the law, it would have been necessary also to amend Part III of the Matrimonial and Family Proceedings Act 1984, infra, p 1063; see *Berkovits v Grinberg* [1995] Fam 142 at 157–158.

[573] [1986] AC 527 at 534.

[574] Indeed it was made in answer to a question posed by Lord ACKNER which was restricted to proceedings which took place both in the British Isles and overseas: [1986] AC 527 at 533. See also Crawford and Carruthers, para 12-29.

[575] 1986 Act, s 44(1).

of the United Arab Republic in London was obtained in England and was not an overseas divorce.[576]

(ii) What constitutes proceedings?

The significance of this question is that, where the divorce, etc is obtained by judicial or other proceedings,[577] the jurisdictional bases of recognition are much wider than if there are no proceedings[578]—being limited in the latter case to domicile.[579] This is much the same as the position under the 1971 Act[580] in which context the courts had to consider the same question. Whilst there is no definition of "judicial or other proceedings" in the 1986 Act,[581] it has been suggested[582] that the phrase is limited to cases involving some act external to the parties themselves, such as registration, conciliation proceedings or some other form of approval.[583] The House of Lords has held in *Quazi v Quazi*[584] that a divorce obtained in Pakistan by *talak* and which then involved the procedures of the Pakistan Muslim Family Laws Ordinance 1961—namely the giving of notice to the wife and to the chairman of the local union council, with the prospect of conciliation proceedings—had been obtained by means of judicial or other proceedings. On the other hand, after a period of uncertainty, the Court of Appeal[585] has concluded that a "bare" *talak*, ie where there is no more than an oral pronouncement by the husband three times, whether or not before witnesses, that he divorces his wife, does not constitute proceedings.[586]

It has been suggested by OLIVER LJ that proceedings "must impart a degree of formality and at least the involvement of some agency, whether lay or religious, of or recognised by the state having a function that is more than simply probative",[587] and would exclude "a private act conducted entirely by parties *inter se* or by one party alone, as a proceeding, even though the party performing it may give it an additional solemnity or even an efficacy by performing it in the presence of other persons whose only involvement is that they witness the performance".[588] On this approach, it can be concluded that a divorce

---

[576] *Radwan v Radwan* [1973] Fam 24, supra, p 901; and see *Chaudhry v Chaudhry* [1976] Fam 148.

[577] To be distinguished from "procedure": *H v H (Validity of Japanese Divorce)* [2006] EWHC 2989 (Fam), [2007] 1 FLR 1318, per S WILDBLOOD QC, sitting as Deputy Judge of the High Court, at [101].

[578] 1986 Act, s 46(1).

[579] S 46(2). See *M v M (Divorce: Jurisdiction: Validity of Marriage)* [2001] 2 FLR 6 at [42].

[580] Contrast the broad recognition rules of ss 2–5 with the more limited domicile ground of s 6 which was the only ground of recognition if there were no proceedings.

[581] S 54(1), and nor was there in the 1971 Act; and see *Quazi v Quazi* [1980] AC 744 at 788–789. Contrast the proposed definition in Law Com No 137 (1984), pp 122–123.

[582] North, op cit, pp 225–230; Polonsky (1973) 22 ICLQ 343, 345.

[583] Including the delivery of a *gett* before a Rabbinical court, even though there is no judicial investigation: *Broit v Broit* 1972 SLT (Notes) 32; *Berkovits v Grinberg* [1995] Fam 142 and see Gordon, *Foreign Divorces: English Law and Practice* (1988) pp 96–97.

[584] [1980] AC 744; Karsten (1980) 43 MLR 202.

[585] This point had been left open by the House of Lords in *Quazi v Quazi* [1980] AC 744 at 817.

[586] *Chaudhary v Chaudhary* [1985] Fam 19; Canton (1985) 48 MLR 212. This confirms the view of WOOD J in *Sharif v Sharif* (1980) 10 Fam Law 216 in contrast to those of BUSH J in *Zaal v Zaal* (1982) 4 FLR 284 at 286–288 and TAYLOR J in *R v Secretary of State for the Home Department, ex p Ghulam Fatima* [1985] QB 190 at 195.

[587] [1985] Fam 19 at 41.

[588] Ibid. Cf *Baig v Entry Clearance Officer, Islamabad* [2002] INLR 117—*talak* divorce did not amount to "proceedings" as it was a personal act lacking formality other than ritual performance, and lacking the involvement or any contact with the state.

in Thailand by mutual consent based simply on an agreement signed by the spouses;[589] a divorce by consent under Chinese customary law, even if the agreement is presented to, and authenticated by, a local body;[590] or a divorce by "divorce letter" in The Gambia[591] will not be regarded as having been obtained by proceedings.[592] In taking this approach, the Court of Appeal does seem to have rejected the more liberal line of Lord SCARMAN in *Quazi v Quazi*.[593] He defined "proceedings" as "any act or acts officially recognised as leading to divorce in the country where the divorce was obtained and which itself is recognised by the law of the country as an effective divorce". On this basis, he was prepared to recognise, as obtained by proceedings, a divorce by *khula* in Thailand which involved no more than a written agreement witnessed by two persons.[594] The problem with Lord SCARMAN's approach is that it is so wide that it would include virtually every kind of effective divorce, etc and thus deprive of any content the special rules in Part II of the 1986 Act governing divorces, etc obtained where there are no proceedings.[595] Finally, there seems little doubt that, if the termination of a marriage by one spouse's unilateral declaration of his change of religion could be regarded as a divorce,[596] it is certainly not obtained by proceedings.[597]

In *El Fadl v El Fadl*,[598] HUGHES J recognised that the rules applicable to *talak* procedures differ to some extent from country to country, and that different varieties of *talak* may coexist within a single country, and so his Lordship viewed it as important to confine himself to the circumstances of the particular case, and to refrain from generalisation.[599] With regard to a *talak* divorce pronounced by a husband (a Lebanese national, habitually resident in the Lebanon), in front of two witnesses, and registered with the Sharia court in the Lebanon, as required by Lebanese law,[600] HUGHES J, in concluding that the divorce was a "proceedings divorce" was swayed by the requirement of registration:

> If . . . this had been a talaq which depended for its effectiveness solely upon the pronouncement in front of witnesses I should have held . . . that it was not a proceedings divorce[601] . . . Although the Sharia court has no judicial decision to make whether there is to be divorce or no, what occurred before it with the assembly of the court, judge and clerk, and the duty to record into the register, having taken formal declarations, is properly described as "proceedings" and the local law explicitly requires such proceedings as an integral part of the divorce process.[602]

In *H v H (Validity of Japanese Divorce)*,[603] the court held that a form of consensual divorce under Japanese law ("*kyogi rikon*"), which required the parties to sign a form

---

589 Eg *Ratanachai v Ratanachai* [1960] CLY 480; *Varanand v Varanand* (1964) 108 Sol Jo 693.
590 Eg *Lee v Lau* [1967] P 14.
591 *Wicken v Wicken* [1999] Fam 224.
592 *Chaudhary v Chaudhary* [1985] Fam 19 at 42, 47.
593 [1980] AC 744 at 824.
594 Ibid.
595 S 46(2).
596 Supra, p 999 et seq.
597 *Viswalingham v Viswalingham* (1979) 1 FLR 15 at 19.
598 [2000] 1 FCR 685.
599 Ibid, at 694. Cf *Sulaiman v Juffali* [2002] 2 FCR 427, per MUNBY J, at [37].
600 Without any requirement, however, that notice be given to the wife: ibid, at 696.
601 As required by *Chaudhary v Chaudhary* [1985] Fam 19 at 42.
602 [2000] 1 FCR 685, at 700.
603 [2006] EWHC 2989 (Fam), [2007] 1 FLR 1318.

called a *rikon todoke* and which became effective only upon registration of the form in the manner prescribed by Japanese law, was within the ambit of "other proceedings". The involvement of the state in the form of requiring registration of a divorce by consent was more than "simply probative" and certainly was not to be regarded as "mere surplusage"; the state did not simply prove the divorce that the parties had achieved by their prior act of consent, for the consent of itself created nothing. Although the state exercised no discretionary power of veto, the formalities of registration by the state were essential to the divorce; no registration, no divorce.[604] The fact that the state employee who effected the registration played no more than an administrative role did not make the procedure as a whole purely administrative.

(c) Extra-judicial divorces and annulments obtained in the British Isles

The type of situation with which we are concerned here is illustrated by the case of the pronouncement of a *talak* in England,[605] whether it is a "bare" *talak* or one followed by further procedures in, say, Pakistan.[606] The common law position was that, if such divorces were recognised as valid under the common law recognition rules, ie if recognised by the law of the domicile,[607] then they would be recognised in England, notwithstanding the fact that the *talak* was pronounced in England.[608] The Recognition of Divorces and Legal Separations Act 1971 left this position unaffected;[609] but two years later section 16(1) of the Domicile and Matrimonial Proceedings Act 1973 denied recognition to any such divorces obtained after 1973. It provided that "no proceedings" in the British Isles "shall be regarded as validly dissolving a marriage unless instituted in the courts of law" there. This general approach is maintained in section 44(1) of the Family Law Act 1986, but with rather different wording:[610] "No divorce or annulment obtained in any part of the British Isles shall be regarded as effective in any part of the United Kingdom unless granted by a court of civil jurisdiction." This means that extra-judicial divorces and annulments wholly obtained in any part of the British Isles will not be valid in England, including of course such divorces and annulments obtained in England.[611] Nor will they be valid where some part of the proceedings takes place in England and others abroad.[612]

The inclusion of annulments marks an extension from the 1971 Act; but in the absence of evidence of extra-judicial separations in the British Isles it was not felt necessary to provide for denial of their recognition.[613] What now seems clear is that any form of

---

[604] Ibid, para 85.

[605] Including a consulate or embassy in England.

[606] A trans-national divorce, supra, p 1003.

[607] Under the rule in *Armitage v A-G* [1906] P 135.

[608] *Har-Shefi v Har-Shefi (No 2)* [1953] P 220; *Qureshi v Qureshi* [1972] Fam 173; provided in fact the law of the domicile regarded it as effective; National Insurance Decisions No R(G) 5/74, No R(G) 2/75.

[609] Such divorces fell through the provisions of the Act: North, op cit, p 223.

[610] The Law Commission's draft Bill followed the wording of s 16(1) of the 1973 Act: Law Com No 137 (1984), p 90.

[611] Eg *Chaudhary v Chaudhary* [1985] Fam 19 at 28; *Maples v Maples* [1988] Fam 14; and see Young (1987) 7 Legal Studies 78, 84, 86. A difficult "incidental question" (supra, Chapter 4) will arise if the spouses are domiciled in a country where the extra-judicial divorce in England is recognised and one of them remarries either there or in England. Does that spouse have capacity to remarry? See North, op cit, pp 224–225.

[612] Supra, pp 1002–1003.

[613] Law Com No 137 (1984), p 91.

extra-judicial divorce or annulment obtained in the British Isles will be denied effect in England. Finally, the 1986 Act follows the pattern of the earlier legislation[614] and preserves the effect of an extra-judicial divorce obtained in the British Isles before 1974 and which would be recognised under the common law rules then applicable.[615] This saving provision is limited to divorces and does not apply to extra-judicial annulments.

(d) Recognition of extra-judicial divorces, etc obtained overseas

It is necessary to examine separately the recognition rules for extra-judicial divorces, etc obtained overseas depending on whether or not there are "judicial or other proceedings".[616]

(i) Where there are proceedings

The basic approach where there are proceedings is that recognition of the divorce, etc is governed by the general rules as to recognition already discussed in relation to judicial divorces, etc. So, the divorce, etc must have been obtained in a country where one party to the marriage was domiciled (in the English or the foreign sense) or habitually resident or of which one party was a national,[617] and it must have been effective under the law of that country.[618] All the other provisions of Part II of the 1986 Act applicable to judicial divorces, etc apply to divorces, etc obtained by other types of proceedings.[619] It might be noted that, as at common law,[620] an extra-judicial divorce, etc obtained by proceedings can be recognised in England despite the fact that both spouses are domiciled in England. So, a *talak* obtained in Pakistan by a husband who is a Pakistan national can be recognised in England, notwithstanding the English domicile of both spouses.[621]

The application of these general rules as to recognition in the context of divorces, etc obtained by extra-judicial proceedings does raise a number of special problems. The jurisdictional rules assume that the divorce, etc is *obtained* by the particular proceedings,[622] that the divorce, etc is effective under the law of *the country* where it was obtained[623] and that the connecting factors of habitual residence, domicile or nationality in the country where it was obtained are satisfied at the date of the commencement of the proceedings.[624] These requirements mean that it is necessary to determine whether a divorce, etc is obtained by going through all, or only part of, the proceedings and to identify the date of the commencement of the proceedings by which it was obtained. These issues have arisen in the context of "transnational" *talak* divorces[625] where it has been held that, though conciliation proceedings are required, and have taken place, in Pakistan, the

---

[614] Domicile and Matrimonial Proceedings Act 1973, s 16(3).
[615] Family Law Act 1986, s 52(4), (5)(a); see, eg, *Chaudhry v Chaudhry* [1976] Fam 148.
[616] 1986 Act, s 54(1). The meaning of this phrase has been discussed, supra, p 1005 et seq.
[617] S 46(1)(b).
[618] S 46(1)(a).
[619] Ss 46(4), 47(1)—supplementary rules on jurisdiction; s 48 on proof of facts; s 49—the meaning of "country"; s 51—the grounds for refusing recognition; and s 52—transitional provisions.
[620] Eg *Manning v Manning* [1958] P 112.
[621] See 1986 Act, s 46(1)(b)(iii). It might, however, be denied recognition on the ground of public policy, infra, p 1018 et seq.
[622] S 46(1).
[623] S 46(1)(a).
[624] S 46(1)(b), (3)(a).
[625] Supra, p 1002 et seq.

earlier pronouncement of the *talak* in England constituted the commencement of the proceedings by which the divorce was obtained.[626]

Particular concerns arise, in the context of the recognition of extra-judicial divorces, etc in relation to the requirement that the divorce be effective "under the law of" the country where it was obtained.[627] The effectiveness of a divorce, nullity or legal separation decree will be tested in terms of its validity in the courts which granted it, but it will often be necessary to determine in the case of an extra-judicial divorce, etc whether it satisfies the domestic law requirements of the country where it was obtained.[628] For example, the House of Lords in *Quazi v Quazi*,[629] whilst satisfied that the *talak* divorce obtained in Pakistan had satisfied the procedural requirements of that country's Muslim Family Laws Ordinance 1961 (and thus was effective there[630]), expressed much greater doubt as to the effectiveness under Thai law of the divorce by *khula* obtained in that country.[631] It may also be the case that the country where the extra-judicial divorce, etc was obtained requires the parties to go through civil judicial proceedings, and the courts in Ontario have denied recognition on this basis to an extra-judicial annulment.[632] However, the validity of an extra-judicial divorce can be tested not simply according to the domestic law of the country where it was obtained but also according to that country's rules of private international law. Take the following example:

> The husband and wife are Jews, both Israeli nationals domiciled in Israel, but habitually resident in British Columbia in Canada. They are divorced by *gett* before a Rabbinical court in British Columbia.

The requirements of the 1986 Act that there be judicial or other proceedings if recognition is to be based jurisdictionally on habitual residence are satisfied.[633] The extra-judicial divorce is not valid under the domestic law of British Columbia but it will be recognised there under that province's divorce recognition rules.[634] On that basis it should be considered to be "effective" under the law of British Columbia and thus be recognised in England.[635]

(ii) Where there are no proceedings

We are concerned here with the special recognition rules for extra-judicial divorces, etc obtained overseas without any proceedings.[636] This type of case can best be illustrated by

---

[626] *R v Secretary of State for the Home Department, ex p Fatima* [1986] AC 527 at 533; *Berkovits v Grinberg* [1995] Fam 142 at 147.

[627] North, op cit, pp 231–232.

[628] See *D v D* [1994] 1 FLR 38.

[629] [1980] AC 744.

[630] Ibid, at 805, 818, 824–826.

[631] Ibid at 824; and see Carroll (1985) 48 MLR 434, 437–438.

[632] *Butterley v Butterley* (1974) 48 DLR (3d) 351.

[633] S 46(1).

[634] Because it was recognised in Israel: see *Walker v Walker* [1950] 4 DLR 253; *Viccari v Viccari* (1972) 7 RFL 241, applying *Armitage v A-G* [1906] P 135.

[635] Indeed a divorce obtained in England in similar circumstances before 1974 was recognised here: *Qureshi v Qureshi* [1972] Fam 173; and see the 1986 Act, s 52(5)(a).

[636] As to what constitutes "proceedings", see supra, p 1005 et seq. *El Fadl v El Fadl* [2000] 1 FCR 685, per Hughes J, at 698: " . . . it is not every form of activity by which legal divorce is achieved which can qualify as proceedings".

such Moslem religious divorces as consensual divorce by *khula*[637] or divorce by "bare" *talak*.[638] Under the Recognition of Divorces and Legal Separations Act 1971, such a divorce could only be recognised if the spouses were domiciled (in the English sense) in the country where it was obtained, or if it was recognised in the country or countries of their domicile.[639] It was not enough that one spouse was habitually resident[640] in, or a national of,[641] the country where the divorce was obtained. It was not, however, a specific statutory requirement that the divorce should be effective in the country in which it was obtained.[642]

As has been indicated earlier,[643] the Law Commission's proposals[644] to have one set of recognition rules for all overseas divorces, etc, coupled with a broadening of the concept of proceedings, was not accepted. Part II of the Family Law Act 1986 follows the general approach of the 1971 Act and provides special, and limited, recognition rules for overseas divorces, etc obtained where there are no proceedings. The central provision is section 46(2):

> The validity of an overseas divorce, annulment or legal separation obtained otherwise than by means of proceedings shall be recognised if—
> (a) the divorce, annulment or legal separation is effective under the law of the country[645] in which it was obtained;
> (b) at the relevant date[646]—
>   (i) each party to the marriage was domiciled in that country; or
>   (ii) either party to the marriage was domiciled in that country and the other party was domiciled in a country under whose law the divorce, annulment or legal separation is recognised as valid; and
> (c) neither party to the marriage was habitually resident in the United Kingdom throughout the period of one year immediately preceding that date.

It will be seen that the divorce, etc must be obtained in one country and be effective there. This can raise the same type of problem as has been discussed in relation to divorces obtained by proceedings in the case of a transnational divorce.[647] It will be necessary to decide where, in the case of a divorce by mutual agreement, as in the Moslem *khula*, the divorce is obtained if the spouses are in different countries. It is also necessary that the

---

[637] See *Quazi v Quazi* [1980] AC 744 at 824; and see *Wicken v Wicken* [1999] Fam 224.

[638] *Chaudhary v Chaudhary* [1985] Fam 19.

[639] 1971 Act, s 6, as substituted by the Domicile and Matrimonial Proceedings Act 1973, s 2.

[640] Eg *Chaudhary v Chaudhary* [1985] Fam 19.

[641] Eg *Sharif v Sharif* (1980) 10 Fam Law 216; *Chaudhary v Chaudhary* [1985] Fam 19.

[642] This was because the requirement of effectiveness in s 2 of the 1971 Act did not apply to recognition on the domicile basis under s 6 of the Act.

[643] Supra, p 1001.

[644] Law Com No 137 (1984), para 6.11.

[645] "Country" in s 46(2) means territory within a political state if each territory has different laws on divorce, etc: s 49(1), (4), supra, pp 996–997.

[646] This means the date on which the divorce, etc was obtained: s 46(3)(b), with appropriate amendments in the rare case of an extra-judicial annulment without proceedings after the death of one spouse (s 46(4)). Although the special rules on cross-proceedings (s 47(1)) and proof of facts made in foreign proceedings (s 48) cannot apply where there are no proceedings, the special jurisdictional rule on conversion of a legal separation into a divorce (ss 47(2), 49(4)) does, in theory at least, apply to an extra-judicial divorce, etc obtained without proceedings.

[647] Supra, p 1002 et seq.

divorce, etc be "obtained" in the country of the domicile. Where there are no proceedings, a divorce is not obtained in the sense of being granted or approved by a third party; it is only obtained in the sense of being obtained by reason of legal provision made for it.

The rules laid down in section 46(2) of the 1986 Act reveal three particular changes from the rules applicable under the 1971 Act, in addition to their extension to extra-judicial annulments.

The first is that there is an express statutory requirement that the divorce, etc be effective in the country in which it was obtained[648] and, indeed, recognition may be refused if no official documents can be produced certifying that effectiveness.[649]

The second change concerns the jurisdictional test. Section 46(2) follows the pattern of the 1971 Act in limiting the jurisdictional basis to domicile. It also provides, as did the 1971 Act,[650] that such a divorce, etc will be recognised not only if it was obtained in the overseas country in which both spouses were domiciled, but also if it was obtained in the overseas country in which one spouse was domiciled and was recognised in the country of the domicile of the other spouse.[651] So, if a husband domiciled in Dubai obtains a "bare" *talak* there which is recognised in Pakistan, where the wife is domiciled, the essential requirements of section 46(2) are satisfied.[652] There is no express requirement that the country of one spouse's domicile in which the divorce, etc is recognised is an overseas country, to the exclusion of a part of the British Isles, including even England. Nevertheless, if one spouse was domiciled in England, recognition would be refused. There is here a circular problem, which also arose under the 1971 Act.[653] The divorce will be recognised only if recognised in England and that is the very matter at issue. That being so, recognition must be refused.[654] However, the domicile test under section 46(2) is more narrowly drawn than under the 1971 Act. Under that Act, recognition was allowed even though the overseas divorce, etc was obtained in a country in which neither spouse was domiciled, provided it was recognised either in their common domicile or in the countries of their separate domiciles.[655] The 1986 Act, however, contains no such jurisdictional basis of recognition.

The third change from the jurisdictional rules under the 1971 Act is that, under those provisions, the reference to domicile was to domicile in the English sense. However, domicile under section 46(2) of the 1986 Act includes, rather surprisingly, domicile in

---

[648] S 46(2)(a); see *Wicken v Wicken* [1999] Fam 224.

[649] S 51(3)(b)(i).

[650] S 6(3)(a).

[651] This is a statutory perpetuation of the common law recognition rule in *Armitage v A-G* [1906] P 135. Recognition may be refused if no official document certifying effectiveness in the country of the domicile of the second spouse can be produced: s 51(3)(b)(ii).

[652] The result would be the same if the situations were reversed, ie if the husband, domiciled in Pakistan, obtained the divorce in Dubai—provided it is valid in both countries. It does not matter with which of the spouses the two jurisdictional links are established.

[653] S 6; see North, op cit, p 185.

[654] As was probably the case in *R v Secretary of State for the Home Department, ex p Fatima* [1986] AC 527, especially at 535.

[655] S 6(3)(b). An overseas divorce or legal separation which would have been recognised under this provision and which was obtained before Part II of the 1986 Act came into force will continue to be recognised: Family Law Act 1986, s 52(5)(b), (e).

both the English sense and that of the country where the divorce was obtained or recognised.[656] So a "bare" *talak* obtained in, say, Dubai will be recognised in England if the spouses were domiciled in Dubai according to the law of Dubai on domicile in family matters, even though not so domiciled according to English law.

There is one major limitation on the recognition of overseas divorces, etc obtained where there are no proceedings, and that is the provision in section 46(2)(c) that recognition will be denied, despite the validity of the divorce, etc under the law of the domicile, if either party had been habitually resident in the United Kingdom for a year immediately preceding the date on which the divorce was obtained.[657] The major purpose of this provision, like its predecessor in the earlier legislation,[658] is to prevent circumvention of the rule that, in the case of British divorces, etc, recognition will only be given to those "granted by a court of civil jurisdiction".[659] It is not possible for the ban on extra-judicial divorces in the British Isles to be evaded by one spouse going to the country of his domicile to pronounce a "bare" *talak*, relying on the fact that it will be recognised in England if recognised in the country of the other spouse's domicile, if either spouse has been habitually resident for one year anywhere in the United Kingdom, not just in England. In fact this type of anti-evasion provision is actually less necessary under the 1986 Act than under the previous legislation, because, under the old law, without such a prohibition, a "bare" *talak* pronounced in, for example, France by a husband on a day trip there would have been recognised in England if recognised in the domicile of both spouses.[660] This cannot happen under the 1986 Act because the divorce, etc has to be obtained in the country of the domicile of one spouse and be effective under that law. It is, therefore, rather surprising to find that the anti-evasion provision in section 46 of the 1986 Act applies if *either* spouse had been habitually resident in the United Kingdom for one year, whereas the old law required them *both* to have been.[661] Finally, it should be emphasised that this limitation on recognition of divorces, etc obtained in, or recognised under the law of, the spouses' domiciles applies only to extra-judicial divorces, etc obtained "otherwise than by means of proceedings". There is no general prohibition on the recognition in England of a divorce obtained in, for example, Pakistan, under the Muslim Family Laws Ordinance 1961, even if the spouses have both been habitually resident in England for years and even if they are both domiciled here, provided one of them is a Pakistan national.[662]

(vi) Grounds for non-recognition of divorces, annulments and legal separations

(a) Introduction

Not only does Part II of the 1986 Act provide an exclusive list of the jurisdictional bases on which overseas divorces, etc may be recognised in England,[663] it also provides,

---

[656] S 46(5).

[657] See *R v Immigration Appeal Tribunal, ex p Asfar Jan* [1995] Imm AR 440.

[658] Domicile and Matrimonial Proceedings Act 1973, s 16; *Sharif v Sharif* (1980) 10 Fam Law 216.

[659] 1986 Act, s 44(1); see Law Com No 137 (1984), para 6.30.

[660] 1971 Act, s 6(3)(b).

[661] Domicile and Matrimonial Proceedings Act 1973, s 16(2).

[662] 1986 Act, s 46(1); see *R v Secretary of State for the Home Department, ex p Fatima* [1985] QB 190 at 199–200. If recognition is to be denied in such a case, it would have to be on one of the discretionary grounds in s 51, most probably the public policy ground, infra, p 1020 et seq.

[663] It being borne in mind that recognition of other British divorces, etc is automatic so far as jurisdiction is concerned.

in section 51, an exclusive list of the grounds on which recognition may be denied both to other British[664] and to overseas divorces, etc.[665] There are only two discretionary grounds on which another British divorce, etc may be denied recognition: *res judicata* and that there was no subsisting marriage between the parties at the time of the divorce, etc.[666] On the other hand, an overseas divorce, etc may be denied recognition, not only on these grounds but also, if there have been judicial or other proceedings, on the grounds of want of notice of, or opportunity to take part in, the proceedings. Where there were no proceedings, recognition may be denied to an overseas divorce, etc if there is no certificate as to its effectiveness where it was obtained or, when recognition depends on reference to the law of the domicile of one of the parties in another country, if there is no certificate as to its validity under the law of that country. Finally, recognition will be denied to all overseas divorces if it would be manifestly contrary to public policy. It was thought to be inappropriate to allow a court in the United Kingdom to deny recognition to another British decree, etc on any of these further grounds. If it is felt necessary to attack a British decree on one of those bases, that should be done in the court which granted it.[667] All the grounds of non-recognition mentioned so far are discretionary.[668] There are, however, two further circumstances in which an overseas divorce, etc *must* be denied recognition, both of which have already been fully considered, namely if the jurisdictional requirements for recognition under the 1986 Act are not satisfied,[669] or if the divorce, etc is not effective in the country where it was obtained.[670] There is nothing in Part II of the 1986 Act to indicate that the right to challenge the recognition of a divorce, etc is confined to a party to the marriage. Such a restriction does not seem to have existed at common law,[671] and Part III of the 1986 Act contemplates the making of declarations as to the validity or invalidity of a divorce, etc obtained outside England and Wales on the application by a person other than a party to the marriage.[672]

The various grounds for non-recognition laid down in section 51 of the 1986 Act must now be considered in more detail.

(b) Res judicata

In the 1971 Act there was no ground of non-recognition based specifically on *res judicata*. Instead, another British or a foreign divorce or legal separation would be denied recognition if it was obtained at a time when there was no subsisting marriage between the parties.[673]

---

[664] *Eroglü v Eroglü* [1994] 2 FLR 287.

[665] The limiting of the grounds for non-recognition to those provided by the 1986 Act is effected by s 45. For non-recognition of European divorces etc, see supra, pp 990–992.

[666] Supra, pp 987–988.

[667] Supra, p 988.

[668] See *Duhur-Johnson v Duhur-Johnson* [2005] 2 FLR 1042, per Jeremy RICHARDSON QC, at [44], "The provisions [of s 51(3)] need not be exercised if the interests of the respondent spouses (as opposed to the petitioning spouse) are met by other means . . . The important point to note is that the judicial discretion is wide and the applicability of the section will vary depending on the many and varied circumstances of each case."

[669] S 46(1), (2).

[670] Ibid, supra, pp 995–996.

[671] Eg *Pemberton v Hughes* [1899] 1 Ch 781; *Powell v Cockburn* (1976) 68 DLR (3d) 700.

[672] S 55, infra, pp 1041–1042.

[673] 1971 Act, s 8(1), and there is a similar ground of non-recognition in s 51(2) of the 1986 Act, infra, p 1015.

One purpose of this provision was, however, to deal with issues of *res judicata*,[674] as where the marriage has already been brought to an end by either an English divorce or nullity decree or a foreign one which was recognised in England. Whilst such an approach may be appropriate for the recognition of divorces and legal separations, it is not appropriate in the case of annulments where the whole issue in the foreign nullity proceedings for which recognition is now sought in England may be to declare that the marriage was void *ab initio*. On the other hand, there is common law authority that a foreign nullity decree may be denied recognition on the basis of *res judicata*, as in *Vervaeke v Smith*:[675] in 1970, the wife sought to have her English marriage in 1954 annulled on the ground that her husband was already married at the time, even though he had gone through divorce proceedings in Nevada in 1946, and that it was a "sham" marriage, being celebrated simply to enable her to acquire British nationality. The English court refused to grant her a nullity decree—because the Nevada divorce was recognised in England and the fact her marriage was a "sham" was no ground for annulling it.[676] Then, in 1972, the wife obtained a nullity decree from a Belgian court on the ground, considered but rejected in England, that the marriage was a "sham". It was held, in the lower courts,[677] that the Belgian decree satisfied the common law jurisdictional rules for the recognition of foreign annulments.[678] Nevertheless, recognition was denied, on the basis of the doctrine of *res judicata*.[679] The House of Lords had no doubt that the issue before the Belgian courts was the very point earlier decided in the English courts.[680]

It was thought that it would be desirable to retain the effect of this decision in any statutory regime for recognition of annulments, but that it would be inappropriate to extend the existing statutory rule from divorces to annulments. So, a new head of non-recognition based more specifically on *res judicata* had to be introduced.[681] To this end, section 51(1) of the 1986 Act[682] provides:

> Subject to section 52 of this Act, recognition of the validity of—
> (a) a divorce, annulment or judicial separation granted by a court of civil jurisdiction in any part of the British Islands, or
> (b) an overseas divorce, annulment or legal separation,
> may be refused in any part of the United Kingdom if the divorce, annulment or separation was granted or obtained at a time when it was irreconcilable with a decision determining the question of the subsistence or validity of the marriage of the parties previously given (whether before or after the commencement of this Part) by a court of

---

[674] Implementing Art 9 of the 1970 Hague Convention: see Law Com No 34 (1970), para 16 and App B (notes on clause 8); Law Com No 137 (1984), paras 4.66, 6.64.

[675] [1983] 1 AC 145; Carter (1982) 53 BYBIL 302; Jaffey (1983) 32 ICLQ 500, [1986] Civil Justice Quarterly 35.

[676] *Messina v Smith* [1971] P 322.

[677] [1981] Fam 77.

[678] The wife had a real and substantial connection with Belgium at the relevant time: *Indyka v Indyka* [1969] 1 AC 33; *Law v Gustin* [1976] Fam 155.

[679] And also on more general public policy grounds, infra, pp 1018–1020. Estoppel is discussed generally, supra, p 544 et seq.

[680] [1983] 1 AC 145 at 156, 160, 161–163.

[681] See Law Com No 137 (1984), paras 4.6, 6.65–6.66.

[682] See the critical discussion in Jaffey [1986] Civil Justice Quarterly 35, 44–45, 47–49.

civil jurisdiction in that part of the United Kingdom or by a court elsewhere and recognised or entitled to be recognised in that part of the United Kingdom.

It is important to emphasise a number of points. Like the common law rule and the other statutory heads under section 51, this ground for non-recognition is discretionary. It applies to the recognition in England of divorces, annulments and legal separations whether they were granted elsewhere in the British Isles or obtained in some other foreign country. Furthermore, the earlier irreconcilable decision which brings the provision into play may be either an earlier English decision, as was the case in *Vervaeke v Smith*, or it could be an earlier decision from a court elsewhere but which is recognised in England under Part II of the 1986 Act. This statutory head does, however, only apply to an earlier decision of a court, and so the fact that there had been an earlier extra-judicial divorce which was recognised in England would not bring the provision into play.[683] Since the earlier decision must relate to the "subsistence or validity" of the marriage, the provision would seem inapplicable where there has been an earlier decision refusing to grant a divorce or legal separation unless that was because there was held to be no marriage between the parties.[684]

(c) No subsisting marriage

The English court has a discretion to refuse recognition to a divorce or legal separation, whether granted elsewhere in the British Isles, or obtained overseas, if it was obtained at a time when, according to English law, there was no subsisting marriage between the parties.[685] Under the 1971 Act, denial of recognition on this ground was mandatory[686] but, because of the possible overlap with the *res judicata* ground, it was thought more appropriate that this head also should become discretionary.[687] This head is limited to the recognition of divorces and legal separations because it is inappropriate in the case of annulments whose purpose is to declare that the marriage is invalid. Whilst there is some overlap with section 51(1), as where there is a prior "decision" dissolving or annulling the marriage, there are other cases for which this further provision is required. It may be, for example, that the marriage in question is regarded by English law (and this includes English rules of private international law) as void *ab initio*, even though there has been no annulment of it. Furthermore, the *res judicata* provisions of section 51(1) would not apply where the marriage is terminated by an extra-judicial annulment which is recognised in England.

(d) Want of notice of the proceedings

Recognition may[688] be refused to an overseas[689] divorce, etc which has been obtained by judicial or other proceedings if it was obtained without such steps having been taken for giving notice[690] of the proceedings to a party to the marriage as, having regard to the

---

[683] Though it would be relevant under s 51(2).

[684] See Jaffey [1986] Civil Justice Quarterly 35, 47–48.

[685] S 51(2).

[686] 1971 Act, s 8(1).

[687] Law Com No 137 (1984), para 6.66.

[688] *El Fadl v El Fadl* [2000] 1 FCR 685, at 700—emphasis on discretion to refuse recognition; and *Duhur-Johnson v Duhur-Johnson* [2005] 2 FLR 1042.

[689] This does not apply to the recognition of other British divorces, etc, supra, pp 987–988.

[690] Ie advance notice: *El Fadl v El Fadl* [2000] 1 FCR 685, at 700.

nature of the proceedings and all the circumstances, should reasonably have been taken.[691] This provision would seem to embody the common law rules for denying recognition to a divorce or annulment on the ground of want of notice of the proceedings;[692] so lack of notice will not normally affect the recognition of a foreign divorce, etc if the foreign court's rules as to service or dispensation therefrom had been complied with.[693] This is subject to the qualification that such rules are themselves not unreasonable.[694] Indeed, "it cannot be sufficient merely to comply with local procedure, otherwise the provisions of the Act would be nugatory".[695] Recognition should still be denied where the lack of notice is consequent upon the petitioner's fraud.[696] In determining whether to deny recognition because of want of notice, the court will have to examine a wide range of factors, including whether one party has already decided not to take part in the foreign proceedings.[697] In *Duhur-Johnson v Duhur-Johnson*,[698] Jeremy RICHARDSON QC concluded that, in determining whether reasonable steps have been taken by the petitioning spouse to notify the respondent spouse of the divorce proceedings in advance of their taking place, a judge should look at all the circumstances of the case, and the nature of the proceedings in the overseas jurisdiction. Whether reasonable steps have been taken is a question of fact in each case, to be judged by English standards. Importantly, "whether the respondent spouse has notice of the proceedings is not the issue. It is whether the petitioner spouse has taken reasonable steps to notify the other party. The focus of inquiry is upon the actions of the petitioning spouse not simply a question of whether the respondent spouse knew about the proceedings."[699]

The application of this ground of non-recognition may not prove to be easy in the case of extra-judicial divorces, etc. It is only relevant to those cases of extra-judicial divorce, etc which have been obtained by means of judicial or other proceedings. So there must have been sufficient formality for these to be considered to be "proceedings",[700] but recognition may only be denied if the steps taken to give notice are inadequate with regard, inter alia, to the nature of the proceedings.[701] It may be, therefore, that it is thought unreasonable to have to give notice of exiguous proceedings. This would certainly be compatible with the approach to the recognition of extra-judicial divorces at common law where recognition was given to informal divorces in the absence of any notice to the other spouse.[702] Indeed, it has been suggested that the requirement, in what is now the 1986 Act, to have regard to the nature of the proceedings in deciding whether to deny recognition must "contemplate the possibility of proceedings which preclude the

---

[691] S 51(3)(a)(i). This marks a slight, but possibly significant, change in approach from its predecessor, s 8(2) of the 1971 Act.

[692] *Kendall v Kendall* [1977] Fam 208, infra, pp 1021–1022.

[693] *Igra v Igra* [1951] P 404; *Hornett v Hornett* [1971] P 255.

[694] *Macalpine v Macalpine* [1958] P 35 at 45; *Sabbagh v Sabbagh* [1985] FLR 29 at 33–34.

[695] *Sabbagh v Sabbagh* [1985] FLR 29 at 33; and see *Joyce v Joyce* [1979] Fam 93 at 111.

[696] *Macalpine v Macalpine* [1958] P 35. Cf *Duhur-Johnson v Duhur-Johnson* [2005] 2 FLR 1042, at [44]; and *Abbassi v Abbassi* [2006] EWCA Civ 355, [2006] 2 FLR 415, per THORPE LJ, at [18].

[697] Eg *Sabbagh v Sabbagh* [1985] FLR 29.

[698] [2005] 2 FLR 1042 at [44].

[699] Ibid.

[700] Supra, pp 1005–1007.

[701] *D v D* [1994] 1 FLR 38.

[702] Eg *Maher v Maher* [1951] P 342 at 344–345.

possibility of notice or participation".[703] In *El Fadl v El Fadl*,[704] HUGHES J declined to exercise his discretion to refuse recognition of a *talak* divorce on the ground of want of notice, for four reasons: first, advance notice could avail the wife nothing, the nature of the proceedings being such as to render notice of practically no value; secondly, the proceedings in question were the prescribed form of divorce in the Lebanon, where both parties were domiciled and in which they had been married, and both parties were taken to have known what the procedure was there and to which they were both subject by their personal law; thirdly, the divorce was accomplished in the forum (the Lebanon) which was the natural forum for both parties; and fourthly, the divorce was obtained in 1981, and it was not a proper exercise of discretion to refuse to recognise a divorce which is valid by the personal laws of both parties and of which they have both had knowledge for such a long period.[705] Tellingly, his Lordship remarked: "I am certainly satisfied that it is not in the public interest to disturb a status which has existed according to the personal law of both parties for 17 years and on the basis of which I am satisfied that both parties have conducted themselves for at any rate two thirds of that period."[706]

(e) Want of opportunity to take part in the proceedings

Recognition of an overseas[707] divorce, etc obtained by proceedings may be refused if it was obtained without a party to the marriage having been given (for any reason other than lack of notice) such opportunity to take part in the proceedings as, having regard to the nature of the proceedings and all the circumstances, he should have been given.[708] There may be cases where a party is prevented by external events from taking part in the proceedings, as in time of war; but even then an English court has recognised a German nullity decree obtained in wartime despite the fact that the English respondent was unable to go to Germany.[709] The courts have examined a range of matters as relevant to the issue of opportunity to take part in the proceedings. These include the failure of lawyers in the foreign country to comply with the respondent's instructions,[710] whether the respondent has the financial resources and time to attend or be represented in the foreign proceedings,[711] or even the fact that the husband has the wife's passport.[712] The "opportunity" is not to be limited to the mere taking part in the proceedings; it must be an effective opportunity to place views before the court.[713] However, the opportunity to take part in the

---

[703] *Chaudhary v Chaudhary* [1985] Fam 19 at 44; and see at 48.

[704] [2000] 1 FCR 685, at 701.

[705] His Lordship noted, ibid, that even if he were wrong in his classification of the divorce as a "proceedings" divorce, nonetheless, if it were a "non-proceedings" divorce, it would qualify for recognition since both parties were domiciled in the Lebanon (where the divorce was obtained) at the material time, and in that event, questions of notice and participation would not arise.

[706] Ibid, 703. Cf *H v H (Validity of Japanese Divorce)* [2006] EWHC 2989 (Fam), [2007] 1 FLR 1318, per S WILDBLOOD QC, sitting as Deputy Judge of the High Court, at [183] (Japanese divorce obtained 20 years earlier).

[707] But not a British divorce, etc, supra, pp 987–988.

[708] S 51(3)(a)(ii).

[709] *Mitford v Mitford* [1923] P 130.

[710] *Newmarch v Newmarch* [1978] Fam 79 at 90–94.

[711] *Joyce v Joyce* [1979] Fam 93; *Quazi v Quazi* [1980] AC 744 at 780; *Sabbagh v Sabbagh* [1985] FLR 29 at 34; *Mamdani v Mamdani* [1984] FLR 699.

[712] *Sharif v Sharif* (1980) 10 Fam Law 216 at 217.

[713] *Joyce v Joyce* [1979] Fam 93 at 111–112.

proceedings does not necessarily require the spouse to attend the proceedings,[714] and it has been held in one case that five days' notice of foreign nullity proceedings was sufficient.[715] In the case of an extra-judicial divorce, etc the exiguous nature of the proceedings will not, as in the case of lack of notice,[716] necessarily constitute grounds for denial of recognition. Finally, the discretionary nature of the power to refuse recognition must be stressed.[717] Even if the necessary opportunity is lacking, the court may still recognise the foreign divorce, etc.[718]

(f) Public policy[719]

As has been mentioned earlier,[720] recognition can only be refused on the grounds laid down in the 1986 Act. One of these is that recognition would be manifestly contrary to public policy.[721] There was a similar discretionary ground for denying recognition at common law on public policy grounds, the decisions on which will be considered first as they continue to provide guidance for the exercise of the statutory discretion.

(i) The common law rules

The residual discretion[722] at common law to refuse to recognise a foreign divorce, annulment or legal separation where such recognition would be contrary to English public policy led, for example, to a foreign divorce being denied recognition where there had been fraud as to the jurisdiction of the foreign court[723] or duress had been exercised on the petitioner.[724] Recognition would also be refused if it would be contrary to English public policy to accept the foreign legal rules being applied. Although it has been said in the context of the recognition of foreign divorces that the residual discretion to deny recognition was one to be exercised sparingly,[725] the courts became increasingly willing to deny recognition, especially to foreign nullity decrees, on the ground that either the foreign legal rule, or its application in the particular circumstances,[726] was offensive to the judicial sense of "substantial justice".[727] So recognition was denied to a Maltese nullity decree based on a provision of Maltese law that the marriage of a Maltese domiciled Roman Catholic was void if he had not married in a Roman Catholic church.[728] The Maltese husband had in fact married in a register office in England and recognition of the Maltese decree would have involved acceptance of the invalidity of this English marriage.

---

[714] *Sabbagh v Sabbagh* [1985] FLR 29 at 34; cf *Joyce v Joyce* [1979] Fam 93 at 113.

[715] *Law v Gustin* [1976] Fam 155.

[716] Supra, pp 1015–1017.

[717] *Chaudhary v Chaudhary* [1985] Fam 19 at 43–44, 48.

[718] As in *Newmarch v Newmarch* [1978] Fam 79, where the factors relevant to the exercise of the discretion are discussed; and see Dickson (1979) 28 ICLQ 132.

[719] Carter (1984) 55 BYBIL 111, 127–130; (1993) 42 ICLQ 1, 5–10.

[720] Supra, p 1012.

[721] S 51(3), infra, p 1020 et seq.

[722] *Qureshi v Qureshi* [1972] Fam 173 at 201.

[723] *Middleton v Middleton* [1967] P 62. There is some authority for denying recognition to a foreign nullity decree if there had been fraud as to the merits of the foreign petition: *Von Lorang v Administrator of Austrian Property* [1927] AC 641 at 663, 671–672; but disapproval of such an approach in the field of divorce recognition is seen in *Middleton v Middleton* [1967] P 62 at 69; *Kendall v Kendall* [1977] Fam 208 at 213.

[724] *Re Meyer* [1971] P 298.

[725] *Varanand v Varanand* (1964) 108 Sol Jo 693; *Qureshi v Qureshi* [1972] Fam 173 at 198–199, 201.

[726] Carter (1978) 49 BYBIL 295, 297.

[727] *Pemberton v Hughes* [1899] 1 Ch 781 at 790; *Middleton v Middleton* [1967] P 62 at 69–70.

[728] *Gray v Formosa* [1963] P 259.

Although the breadth of that approach was much criticised,[729] and the courts have remained uncertain whether a foreign divorce should be denied recognition on the sole basis that the decree was granted on racial or religious grounds,[730] the high-water mark for the denial of recognition at common law on the ground of want of "substantial justice" was reached in the House of Lords decision in *Vervaeke v Smith*.[731] It will be recalled[732] that the petitioner had entered into a "sham" marriage in England in 1954 in order to obtain British nationality. Having failed to have that marriage annulled in England,[733] she obtained a nullity decree in Belgium annulling it and sought to have that decree recognised in England. Recognition was refused, not only on the basis that the matter was already *res judicata*,[734] but also because recognition would offend English public policy. Sham marriages are void in Belgium, but valid in England;[735] yet even though courts elsewhere in the United Kingdom were prepared to regard such marriages as invalid,[736] the House of Lords regarded the English rule as embodying a principle of English public policy so strong that it had to be applied in the international context. Lord HAILSHAM LC stated that the English rule:

> is a doctrine of public policy and so at least in the present case takes the case outside the rules for the recognition of foreign, and in particular, Belgian, decrees, that is at least as regards a marriage celebrated in England between a British national and an alien for an extraneous purpose of the kind contemplated by the parties in the present case, viz, using the marriage as a vehicle for conferring British nationality on the alien partner so as to save her from deportation for a criminal offence.[737]

It must be stressed that these were arguments for *upholding* the validity of the marriage and denying effect to the Belgian decree.

Other arguments in favour of non-recognition of the Belgian decree for public policy reasons were advanced by Lord SIMON of Glaisdale.[738] The essence of his approach was that no case had been made out why English law "should surrender its own concept of the public policy involved and defer to that of Belgian law as expressed in the Belgian judgment".[739] This approach is both suspect and dangerous. It is suspect because there is a variety of instances where English courts have accepted the validity of foreign decrees without anxiety that the foreign law applied is different from the English rule, and have done so even where the effect has been to render void a marriage celebrated in England

---

[729] Carter (1962) 38 BYBIL 497; Lewis (1963) 12 ICLQ 298. The decision was followed only with misgivings in *Lepre v Lepre* [1965] P 52 and a different approach was taken by the courts in Australia and South Africa: *Vassallo v Vassallo* [1952] SASR 129; *De Bono v De Bono* 1948 (2) SA 802.

[730] Contrast *Igra v Igra* [1951] P 404 with *Re Meyer* [1971] P 298 at 310.

[731] [1983] 1 AC 145; Smart (1983) 99 LQR 24; Jaffey (1983) 32 ICLQ 500; and see *Westacre Investments Inc v Jugo Import-SPDR Holding Co Ltd* [1999] QB 740 at 764–765; *Soleimany v Soleimany* [1999] QB 785 at 795–796.

[732] Supra, p 150.

[733] *Messina v Smith* [1971] P 322.

[734] Supra.

[735] [1983] 1 AC 145 at 152–153.

[736] *Orlandi v Castelli* 1961 SC 113; *Akram v Akram* 1979 SLT (Notes) 87; *Hakeem v Hussain* 2003 SLT 515, and on appeal *H v H* 2005 SLT 1025. See now, however, Family Law (Scotland) Act 2006, ss 2 and 38.

[737] [1983] 1 AC 145 at 156–157.

[738] Ibid, at 163–167.

[739] Ibid, at 164.

and valid by English law.[740] The approach is dangerous because it would undermine the whole structure of English choice of law rules. English courts frequently apply foreign law different from English law, and it is only rarely that public policy is felt to justify not applying the foreign law.[741] Certainly the courts do not, and could not, weigh the policy of English law against that of the foreign law in every case.

The extraordinary conclusion in this case[742] can, perhaps, only really be explained by the fact that denying effect to the Belgian decree would render the petitioner's second marriage invalid and prevent her from succeeding as a widow to the second husband's estate, she having been a prostitute and he having managed her activities.[743] There is real danger in the adoption of so broad and vague an approach to the issue of public policy. It renders the law unpredictable on a matter vital to social stability and human happiness: "It is a common, natural and reasonable thing for people to adjust their lives according to the ostensible effect of a judgment disposing of their status pronounced by a competent court."[744] The more likely it is that a foreign divorce, etc will be denied recognition on unpredictable grounds of public policy, the harder is it for those reasonable expectations to be met.[745]

(ii) Under the 1986 Act

Denial of recognition to an overseas[746] divorce, etc on public policy grounds is specifically provided for in section 51(3) of the 1986 Act. The court has a discretion to refuse recognition if such recognition "would be manifestly contrary to public policy". It seems very likely that the courts will, in applying this provision, seek guidance from the common law decisions just discussed in deciding whether recognition would be contrary to public policy.[747] It should be emphasised that, again, the court has a discretion;[748] there is no requirement that recognition be refused on this basis and there is some authority for the unusual view that the discretion would be exercised in favour of recognition even if such recognition would be manifestly contrary to public policy.[749] Section 51(3) refers to recognition being "manifestly"[750] contrary to public policy. This does no more than confirm the stated attitude at common law that the discretion is one to be exercised sparingly.[751]

---

[740] Eg *Galene v Galene* [1939] P 237.

[741] Supra, p 139 et seq.

[742] Given that it was stated that the power to deny recognition should be exercised "with extreme reserve": [1983] 1 AC 145 at 164.

[743] Ibid, at 153; but Lord SIMON rejected these factors: ibid, at 166.

[744] *Merker v Merker* [1963] P 283 at 301.

[745] See Lewis (1963) 11 ICLQ 298, 301.

[746] But not a British divorce, etc, supra, pp 987–988.

[747] It is suggested that WOOD J was wrong, in *Chaudhary v Chaudhary* [1985] Fam 19 at 29, to indicate that there also coexisted a common law basis for denial of recognition on public policy grounds. Recognition is exclusively governed by what is now Part II of the 1986 Act, and the grounds for denying recognition are limited to those in the Act: s 45.

[748] See *H v H (Validity of Japanese Divorce)* [2006] EWHC 2989 (Fam), [2007] 1 FLR 1318 at [182].

[749] *Newmarch v Newmarch* [1978] Fam 79 at 97.

[750] The term is only in the statute in order to conform to Art 10 of the 1970 Hague Convention: Law Com No 34 (1970), p 43.

[751] *Eroglü v Eroglü* [1994] 2 FLR 287 at 289; *Tahir v Tahir* 1993 SLT 194; *El Fadl v El Fadl* [2000] 1 FCR 685, per HUGHES J, at 702; and *B v B (Divorce: Northern Cyprus)* [2001] 3 FCR 331 at 340. Cf the position under Brussels II *bis*, supra, p 991.

Indeed "manifestly" has been held to add nothing to the common law rule;[752] but the courts may prove to be willing to maintain the breadth which the common law rule had reached, and there is some evidence that the courts will deny recognition where the application of the foreign rule is, in the particular circumstances, felt to be contrary to public policy.[753]

The principles on which the statutory discretion should be exercised have been stated thus:

> In exercising its discretion . . . this court should have regard to all the surrounding circumstances which would include a full investigation of the facts relied upon to support a refusal of recognition; the likely consequences if the petitioning spouse had been given the opportunity to take part in the proceedings; an assessment of what the legitimate objectives of the petitioning spouse are, and to what extent those objectives can be achieved if the foreign decree remains valid, and what the likely consequences to the spouses and any children of the family would be if recognition were refused.[754]

Further, it has been stated[755] that the principle of comity is a relevant consideration;[756] the conduct of the parties leading up to the divorce may be a relevant factor; and motivation may be relevant.

In applying such principles, it has been held that the fact that a foreign decree has a different effect from an English one is not, as such, grounds of public policy for denying recognition to the former.[757] The operation of such principles might be illustrated by *Kendall v Kendall*:[758]

> H and W lived together in Bolivia. W decided to leave Bolivia, with their children, in 1974. Before leaving she signed documents, in Spanish (a language of which she had little understanding), which H told her were documents to permit her to take the children out of the country. In 1975 the Bolivian courts granted a decree of divorce, purporting to be a decree granted to W as petitioner. It was probably the case that the documents W signed constituted a power of attorney enabling a decree to be granted without W's presence before the court.

As H was habitually resident in Bolivia at the time of the decree it ought, prima facie, to be recognised in England.[759] It could not be denied recognition for want of notice under the relevant provisions of the Recognition of Divorces and Legal Separations Act 1971[760] because they only related to lack of notice of, or want of opportunity to take part in, the proceedings in the case of the respondent.[761] Here, the party disadvantaged was W, the

---

[752] *Sharif v Sharif* (1980) 10 Fam Law 216 at 217–218; *Chaudhary v Chaudhary* [1985] Fam 19 at 28–29.

[753] Eg *Newmarch v Newmarch* [1978] Fam 79; Carter (1978) 49 BYBIL 295, 297; *Joyce v Joyce* [1979] Fam 93 at 114; Dickson (1980) 43 MLR 81, 84–85; *Chaudhary v Chaudhary* [1985] Fam 19 at 39–40, 43–45.

[754] *Newmarch v Newmarch* [1978] Fam 79 at 95.

[755] *H v H (Validity of Japanese Divorce)* [2006] EWHC 2989 (Fam), [2007] 1 FLR 1318, per S WILDBLOOD QC, sitting as Deputy Judge of the High Court, at [182].

[756] *El Fadl v El Fadl* [2000] 1 FCR 685.

[757] Social Security Decision No R(G) 1/85.

[758] [1977] Fam 208.

[759] See now the 1986 Act, s 46(a)(i).

[760] S 8(2)(a).

[761] There is no such restriction in s 51(3)(a) of the 1986 Act, supra, pp 1015–1018.

apparent petitioner. However, HOLLINS J concluded that recognition of the decree would manifestly be contrary to public policy as the Bolivian court had been deceived, not just as to facts alleged in the petition, but as to the fundamental issue of whether W was petitioning at all.[762]

Finally, particular problems in relation to public policy may arise in the context of the recognition of extra-judicial divorces, etc. The recognition of extra-judicial divorces as such is not contrary to public policy.[763] However, when it was thought[764] that recognition of a "bare" *talak*, ie one delivered without any further proceedings, fell within the broad recognition rules of the Recognition of Divorces and Legal Separations Act 1971,[765] it was suggested that, though it would not be right to lay down a general rule for "bare" *talaks*, such a divorce could be denied recognition on the public policy grounds that it was done in secrecy and without the wife being in any way aware that it was about to happen.[766] It is now the case that specific provision is made in the 1986 Act for the recognition of "bare" *talaks* and other divorces, etc where there are no proceedings, but only on the limited jurisdictional basis of domicile.[767] "Bare" *talaks* cannot, therefore, be denied recognition, as such, on public policy grounds, because Parliament has provided clearly for their recognition. The courts will remain free, however, to take account of the particular circumstances of a case as justifying denial of recognition. In *El Fadl v El Fadl*,[768] HUGHES J remarked: "I am satisfied that however much a unilateral divorce without notice may offend English sensibilities comity between nations and belief systems requires at any rate this much, that one country should accept the conscientiously held but very different standards of another where they are applied to those who are domiciled in it."

It has also been suggested that recognition should be denied on public policy grounds to an extra-judicial divorce, etc if both parties were domiciled in England when it was obtained:

> It must plainly be contrary to the public policy of the law in a case where both parties to the marriage are domiciled in this country to permit one of them, whilst continuing his English domicile, to avoid the incidents of his domiciliary law and to deprive the other party to the marriage of her rights under that law[769] by the simple process of taking advantage of his financial ability to travel to a country whose laws appear temporarily to be more favourable to him.[770]

---

[762] Contrast *Eroglü v Eroglü* [1994] 2 FLR 287, where both spouses were party to the deception of a Turkish court whose divorce decree was recognised.

[763] *Quazi v Quazi* [1980] AC 744 at 781–782.

[764] That was shown to be incorrect in *Chaudhary v Chaudhary* [1985] Fam 19.

[765] Ie those based on nationality, habitual residence and domicile in the foreign sense, under ss 2–5 of the 1971 Act.

[766] *Zaal v Zaal* (1982) 4 FLR 284 at 288–289; and see *Quazi v Quazi* [1980] AC 744 at 783; *Chaudhary v Chaudhary* [1985] Fam 19 at 28–29, 39–41, 43–45.

[767] S 46(2)(b).

[768] [2000] 1 FCR 685 at 702–703.

[769] *Tahir v Tahir* 1993 SLT 194 makes clear that, in the light of the financial provisions for the benefit of a divorced spouse, contained in the Matrimonial and Family Proceedings Act 1984, Part III, infra, p 1063 et seq, recognition will not be denied on financial grounds alone.

[770] *Chaudhary v Chaudhary* [1985] Fam 19 at 45.

This suggestion was made in the context of the recognition of a "bare" *talak* and the problem cannot in fact now arise in that context because recognition is based on the domicile of the parties.[771] This approach has, however, been welcomed[772] as more widely appropriate to the case of extra-judicial divorces, etc where there are proceedings which could be recognised, even though both spouses are domiciled in England, because they have been obtained, for example, in the country of which one spouse was a national.[773] There are difficulties with so broad an approach. Why should such a rule be limited to extra-judicial divorces, etc as there may well be judicial divorces, etc where a spouse domiciled in England takes advantage of his financial resources to obtain a valid divorce abroad, to the disadvantage of the other spouse, also domiciled in England? If all divorces, etc obtained in such circumstances are to be denied recognition on public policy grounds, this seems to run counter to the policy of Parliament, for the legislation does not in terms preclude their recognition nor could it under the 1970 Hague Convention on which the 1986 Act is still based.[774]

(g) Special rules for extra-judicial divorces, etc where there are no proceedings

It will be recalled[775] that where a divorce, etc is obtained overseas but there are no judicial or other proceedings, eg a "bare" *talak*, the only jurisdictional basis for recognition is domicile in the English sense. However, even if the overseas divorce, etc satisfies that jurisdictional test and is effective in the relevant country of the domicile,[776] it may be denied recognition on any one of the following three bases for non-recognition already discussed: *res judicata*, no subsisting marriage or that recognition would manifestly be contrary to public policy.[777] However, the two bases concerned with notice of, or opportunity to take part in, the proceedings[778] are not applicable, for obvious reasons, where there are no proceedings. Instead, a foreign divorce, etc obtained without proceedings may be refused recognition if "there is no official document certifying that the divorce, annulment or legal separation is effective under the law of the country where it was obtained".[779] The purpose of this provision seems to be evidential, rather than going to issues of justice between the parties. An official document is defined as one "issued by a[780] person or body appointed or recognised for the purpose"[781] in the foreign country. So the operation of the provision will depend on whether court or other officials in the country where a bare *talak* or the like is obtained are prepared to provide such certification for the purposes of English proceedings, and certificates may not be easy to obtain.[782]

---

[771] 1986 Act, s 46(2).

[772] Carroll (1985) 101 LQR 175, 177; for a markedly different approach, see Gordon (1986) 16 Fam Law 169.

[773] 1986 Act, s 46(1).

[774] Art 1 of the Hague Convention envisages the recognition of at least some extra-judicial divorces and legal separations.

[775] Supra, p 1009 et seq.

[776] Supra, pp 993–994.

[777] S 51(1), (2), (3)(c).

[778] S 51(3)(a).

[779] S 51(3)(b)(i). See, eg, *Wicken v Wicken* [1999] 2 WLR 1166 (no justification for refusing recognition under s 51(3)(b)(i)).

[780] See *El Fadl v El Fadl* [2000] 1 FCR 685, per HUGHES J, at 702: "Many states will have more than one person or body capable of certifying officially and authoritatively."

[781] S 51(4).

[782] See Lord MESTON, 473 HL Official Report, col 1094 (1986).

Whilst proof of effectiveness of such divorces has been shown on occasions to be a problem,[783] one would hope that an English court is unlikely to deny recognition if it is satisfied as to the effectiveness of the divorce, etc even though no certificate is forthcoming. If that is so, it is hard to see what real purpose this provision serves.[784]

This provision on certification assumes that the divorce, etc is obtained in the country where both parties were domiciled at that time,[785] but there is a variant of it to deal with the case where the divorce, etc is obtained in the country where one spouse was domiciled and is recognised in the country of the domicile of the other spouse.[786] In such a case, recognition may be denied not only if there is no official certificate as to the effectiveness of the divorce where it was obtained, but also if there is no "official document" certifying that it is recognised as valid in the country of the domicile of the other spouse.[787] So, if a husband domiciled in Dubai obtains a "bare" *talak* there,[788] his wife being domiciled in Pakistan, the divorce may be denied recognition if there is no official certificate as to its effectiveness in Dubai or that it will be recognised in Pakistan.

(vii) Retrospectivity

The general rule in Part II of the 1986 Act is that its provisions govern the recognition of both British and overseas divorces, annulments and legal separations, whether they were obtained before or after the 1986 Act came into force.[789] There are two kinds of limitation on this general retrospective effect, both of which are fully explained in the previous edition of this book.[790]

(viii) Effect of a foreign divorce, annulment or legal separation[791]

One problem which is untouched by the 1986 Act and by Brussels II *bis* is as to the effect to be given in England to a divorce, annulment or legal separation obtained outside England (described in this section of the chapter as a "foreign" divorce, etc[792]) and whose recognition is governed by Part II of that Act, or by Brussels II *bis*. This is left to the common law and it is convenient to consider the three matrimonial causes separately.

(a) Divorce

The effect of a foreign divorce on the married status of the parties is obvious. If, in the eyes of English law, the divorce is valid, it effectively terminates that status;[793] if it is void for want of jurisdiction, the status remains unchanged. Nevertheless, the divorce may have an effect with regard to certain subsidiary purposes other than the assessment of status.

---

[783] *Quazi v Quazi* [1980] AC 744 at 824.

[784] No guidance can be found from Law Com No 137 (1984) because this basis of non-recognition is not one recommended by the Law Commission, who did not propose special rules for divorces, etc obtained where there were no proceedings; see *Wicken v Wicken* [1999] 2 WLR 1166 at 1180.

[785] S 46(2)(b)(i).

[786] S 46(2)(b)(ii).

[787] S 51(3)(b)(ii).

[788] Cf *Zaal v Zaal* (1982) 4 FLR 284.

[789] 1986 Act, s 51(1), (2), (3).

[790] See 13th edn of this book (1999), p 820.

[791] North, op cit, pp 135, 191–201, 266–268, 287–292.

[792] Including both those granted elsewhere in the British Isles and those obtained overseas.

[793] For discussion of its effect on capacity to remarry, see supra, p 915.

The question of the effect of a foreign divorce seldom arises in practice, but three situations merit some discussion.

First, although a valid divorce terminates the married status of the parties, it does not automatically terminate a maintenance order in favour of the wife made by an English court at a time when they were living permanently in England.[794] The court has discretion to retain, vary or discharge it, and in exercising this discretion it is relevant to consider whether the wife participated in the divorce proceedings, whether the question of maintenance was raised in the foreign court and whether the basis for the divorce was insufficient by English law.[795]

It is rare that a foreign divorce will be denied recognition in England for want of jurisdiction, given the breadth of English recognition rules under the 1986 Act, and the prohibition upon review of jurisdiction of the court of origin under Article 24 of Brussels II *bis*. If, however, lack of jurisdiction were to render the foreign divorce invalid in England, it would not be altogether devoid of effect even though it leaves the married status of the parties undisturbed.[796] It may at least require consideration in the context of desertion and estoppel. There is little authority on the question whether the effect of an invalid divorce is to exclude from consideration the period during which the respondent may have been in desertion prior to the divorce. This may be a critical factor if the petitioner later institutes divorce proceedings in England on the ground that the marriage has broken down in that the respondent has deserted the petitioner for a period of at least two years immediately preceding the presentation of the petition.[797] Although the answer no doubt depends on the conduct of the parties, it would appear from the two relevant decisions, both concerned with a Jewish divorce by delivery of a *gett*, that the desertion is not terminated unless the respondent initiated or instigated the foreign suit or at least freely consented to its institution.[798]

Another question is whether a foreign divorce, invalid for want of jurisdiction, is affected by the doctrine of estoppel. It is clear that there is no estoppel so far as the married status of the parties is concerned. Neither party is precluded from denying that in the eyes of English law the parties are still husband and wife.[799] It is, however, unclear whether the doctrine of estoppel can be invoked for other purposes. Can, for instance, a woman who has obtained an invalid divorce in a foreign country claim a widow's share of her deceased husband's estate? To succeed, she must show that she was the "wife" of her late husband at the time of his death, which involves relying on the invalidity of the divorce. But can it not be maintained that she is estopped from impugning the decision of the court whose jurisdiction she herself invoked? This question has met with conflicting answers in

---

[794] See infra, p 1061.

[795] *Wood v Wood* [1957] P 254; Carter (1957) 33 BYBIL 336; *Qureshi v Qureshi* [1972] Fam 173 at 200–201; *Newmarch v Newmarch* [1978] Fam 79.

[796] Subject to problems of the "incidental question", discussed, supra, Chapter 4, and see North, op cit, pp 199–200.

[797] Matrimonial Causes Act 1973, s 1(2)(c).

[798] *Joseph v Joseph* [1953] 1 WLR 1182 (desertion terminated); *Corbett v Corbett* [1957] 1 WLR 486.

[799] *Travers v Holley* [1953] P 246 at 254; and see *Bonaparte v Bonaparte* [1892] P 402; *Schwebel v Schwebel* (1970) 10 DLR (3d) 742; *Gaffney v Gaffney* [1975] IR 133. Indeed it has been said, in *Hornett v Hornett* [1971] P 255 at 261, that "there are great difficulties about applying a doctrine of estoppel to a legal decree affecting status"; and see Carter (1971) 45 BYBIL 410.

Canada, though the Supreme Court of Canada[800] has expressed itself in favour of there being no conclusive overriding principle of estoppel, and certainly there is no estoppel in the case of a person not a party to the foreign divorce.[801] So far as English courts are concerned, there is in principle no room for estoppel, since the paramount issue from which all else flows is the marital status of the parties at the time of the husband's death, and of that there can be no doubt.[802]

(b) Annulment[803]

In considering the effect in England of a foreign annulment which is recognised in England, it is necessary to investigate what effect the annulment has in the country where it was obtained and compare that effect with the effect of an English nullity decree. Where the foreign annulment has the same effect on the status of the parties as an equivalent English decree, there will be little difficulty in giving full effect to it.[804] Difficulty may arise where, for example, a decree annulling a voidable marriage is retrospective in effect, whilst an equivalent English decree is only prospective in effect.[805] This problem has arisen in a decision concerned with the recognition in Scotland of a Northern Ireland nullity decree. It concerned a claim to social security: Social Security Decision No R (G) 1/85 where the facts were these:

> The wife lived in Scotland. Her first husband died in 1966 and she had received a widow's pension ever since. In 1980, in Northern Ireland, she went through a ceremony of marriage with M with whom she lived for just seven weeks before returning to Scotland. As soon as she married, her widow's pension ceased to be paid. In 1982, she obtained a decree absolute from the Northern Ireland court declaring her second marriage void on the ground of non-consummation because of M's impotence. In the light of that, she sought, in Scotland, to have her widow's pension reinstated retrospectively. The effect in Northern Ireland of the nullity decree was that the marriage was voidable, and the decree had only prospective effect.[806] However, an equivalent decree in Scotland would render the marriage void and have retrospective effect.

The two issues for the Social Security Commissioner were whether the Northern Ireland nullity decree should be recognised in Scotland and, if so, whether it should be given prospective or retrospective effect. If the former, the wife would lose; if it had the Scottish retrospective effect, she would succeed. The Commissioner had no hesitation in holding that the Northern Ireland nullity decree should be recognised in Scotland.[807]

---

[800] *Downtown v Royal Trust Co* (1972) 34 DLR (3d) 403.

[801] *Fromovitz v Fromovitz* (1977) 79 DLR (3d) 148; cf *Knight v Knight* (1995) 16 RFL (4th) 48.

[802] And see *Gaffney v Gaffney* [1975] IR 133; *PK v TK* [2002] IR 186 (Sup Ct); and *CK v JK* [2004] IR 224, referred to by Dicey, Morris and Collins, para 18-144

[803] See Law Com No 137 (1984), paras 2.32–2.38. The Law Commission recommended (at para 6.60) that the effect in this country of a foreign annulment should not be the subject of legislation; and see Jaffey (1983) 32 ICLQ 500.

[804] *Von Lorang v Administrator of Austrian Property* [1927] AC 641 at 654–655. For its effect on capacity to marry, see supra, p 915.

[805] Matrimonial Causes Act 1973, s 16, supra, p 971.

[806] Matrimonial Causes (Northern Ireland) Order 1978, Art 18.

[807] Applying common law recognition rules, based on the fact that M, though not the wife, was domiciled in Northern Ireland.

Having rejected arguments that to recognise the Northern Ireland effect of the decree as prospective only would be contrary to Scottish public policy or that the effect was simply a matter of procedure to be ignored in Scotland,[808] he followed the approach recommended by the Law Commission[809] that the foreign effects of the annulment should normally be recognised and gave the Northern Ireland decree only prospective effect. To do otherwise would have given the decree greater effect in Scotland than it had in Northern Ireland as well as differing effects as between the two "spouses" who were domiciled in different countries.

Where the foreign annulment is not recognised, it should be treated in the same way as a foreign divorce that is not recognised.[810] There is Canadian authority[811] for the application of the doctrine of estoppel; but it is suggested that an English court should deny operation to the doctrine, whether the matter at issue is the direct one of marital status or a less central question, such as succession.

(c) Legal separation

An English decree of judicial separation entitles the petitioner to live apart from the respondent,[812] but does not dissolve the married status of the parties.[813] It is permanent in the sense that it remains in operation unless and until a discharge of the decree is ordered. The effect to be given to a foreign legal separation which is recognised in England was considered at common law in *Tursi v Tursi*:[814]

> Two Italian subjects, domiciled in Italy, married there in 1942. The husband deserted the wife and never returned to her. In 1947, the wife obtained in Rome a decree of judicial separation, substantially similar in effect to an English decree, on the ground of the husband's desertion. In 1955, the wife, who had been resident in England since 1949, petitioned for divorce on the ground of the husband's desertion for three years,[815] he being still domiciled and resident in Italy.

In deciding to recognise the foreign decree granted by the law of the domicile, SACHS J had to consider its effect under English law. He held that it should have the same effect with respect to desertion as an English decree of judicial separation, namely that a decree of judicial separation did not put an end to desertion, as at common law,[816] but that the wife could treat any period of desertion occurring before the decree as occurring immediately before the petition for divorce.[817] There seems no reason why the same conclusion should not be reached, under the Matrimonial Causes Act 1973, in respect of a petition for divorce on the ground of breakdown of marriage being evidenced by

---

[808] Social Security Decision No R(G) 1/85, 8–10.

[809] Law Com No 137 (1984), para 2.33; North, op cit, p 267; cf Smith (1980) 96 LQR 380, 390–393.

[810] Supra, p 1024 et seq.

[811] *Re Capon* (1965) 49 DLR (2d) 675; *Schwebel v Schwebel* (1970) 10 DLR (3d) 742.

[812] Matrimonial Causes Act 1973, s 18(1).

[813] Though if a spouse dies intestate whilst such a decree is in force, his property will devolve as if the other spouse was dead: Matrimonial Causes Act 1973, s 18(2).

[814] [1958] P 54.

[815] The equivalent ground of divorce under the Matrimonial Causes Act 1973, s 1(1) and (2)(c) is breakdown of marriage as evidenced by two years' desertion immediately preceding the petition.

[816] *Harriman v Harriman* [1909] P 123.

[817] Under the Matrimonial Causes Act 1950, s 7(3).

two years' desertion, so that a period of desertion preceding a foreign legal separation may be deemed to precede the English petition.[818] Similarly, it may be argued that the provision barring one spouse, judicially separated from the other, from succeeding to the latter's estate on intestacy[819] applies equally to foreign legal separations.[820]

More recent discussion of the effect to be given to a foreign legal separation which is recognised in England is found in *Sabbagh v Sabbagh*:[821]

> The spouses were married in Brazil in 1965, where they were domiciled. Shortly thereafter they came to England and acquired a domicile in England; but in 1980 the marriage broke up. The husband returned to Brazil and became domiciled and habitually resident there, whilst the wife remained in England. In 1983 the husband obtained a decree of judicial separation in Brazil, the effect of which was to freeze the proprietary rights of the parties, without dissolving the marriage. The wife then petitioned for divorce in England and two issues arose: should the Brazilian decree be recognised and, if so, what effect did recognition have on the rights of the English court to grant the wife financial and other relief on her divorce petition?

There was no doubt in the mind of BALCOMBE J that the Brazilian decree, being a decree of the country of the petitioner's domicile and habitual residence,[822] should be recognised.[823] The question remained, however, as to what effect was to be given to it. If its effect was the same as that of an English decree of judicial separation, it would prevent the English court from itself making a decree.[824] However, the effects of the Brazilian decree on the property rights of the parties were not to be recognised in England. This was not required by the statute[825] and "there is no basis here for the contention that the Brazilian decree of judicial separation will have the effect of excluding the English court's powers to deal with the wife's financial application once she has been granted a decree of divorce in England".[826]

4. PRESUMPTION OF DEATH AND DISSOLUTION OF MARRIAGE[827]

An English court may dissolve a marriage where a petition is brought for a decree of presumption of death of one of the parties and also for the dissolution of the marriage. Section 19 of the Matrimonial Causes Act 1973 allows any married person, who alleges

---

[818] Matrimonial Causes Act 1973, s 1(3), as amended by the Domestic Proceedings and Magistrates' Courts Act 1978, s 62.

[819] Ibid, s 18(2).

[820] Dicey, Morris and Collins, para 18-147.

[821] [1985] FLR 29.

[822] Applying s 3 of the Recognition of Divorces and Legal Separations Act 1971; see now s 46(1) of the 1986 Act.

[823] None of the grounds for non-recognition in s 8 of the 1971 Act (s 51 of the 1986 Act) were made out.

[824] [1985] FLR 29 at 35.

[825] S 8(3) of the 1971 Act; now s 51(5) of the 1986 Act.

[826] [1985] FLR 29 at 36. The availability of financial relief after foreign divorces, etc is discussed generally infra, p 1062 et seq.

[827] North, op cit, pp 68, 71, 151, 297–299; and see Kelly and Varsanyi (1971) 20 ICLQ 535.

reasonable grounds for supposing that the other party is dead, to petition the court not only to have it presumed that such party is dead, but also to have the marriage dissolved. Strictly speaking, once a person is dead in the eyes of the law, it is superfluous to dissolve his marriage. Nevertheless, its express dissolution is desirable to meet the contingency of the presumption being proved wrong. Such decrees are, therefore, *sui generis*, because in the case of divorce the court proceeds on the assumption that the respondent is alive, whilst here the opposite is assumed.[828]

(a) Jurisdiction

The jurisdiction of the English court is provided for in section 5(4) of the Domicile and Matrimonial Proceedings Act 1973.[829] The sole grounds are that the petitioner:

(a) is domiciled in England on the date when the proceedings are begun;[830] or
(b) was habitually resident in England throughout the period of one year ending with that date.[831]

This basis of jurisdiction is unaffected by Brussels II *bis*, the scope of which does not include presumption of death.

(b) Choice of law

So far as choice of law is concerned, the problem is similar to that in divorce.[832] The courts appear consistently to have applied English law, even though the petitioner was domiciled elsewhere,[833] but their statutory obligation to do so[834] has been repealed.[835]

(c) Recognition

The rules as to recognition of foreign decrees of presumption of death and dissolution of marriage are not wholly clear, for no statutory provision has expressly been made for them.[836] If such a foreign decree is granted in circumstances which, *mutatis mutandis*, would have conferred jurisdiction on an English court, then it will be recognised in England.[837] So, an English court will recognise decrees granted in the country where the petitioner was domiciled or had been habitually resident for one year.[838] It is quite possible that the common law rules for the recognition of divorces might be applied by analogy so as to permit recognition in England of a decree granted in a jurisdiction with

---

[828] *Wall v Wall* [1950] P 112 at 122–123, 125; *N v N* [1957] P 385 at 391.

[829] In relation to civil partnerships, see Civil Partnership Act 2004, ss 37(1)(c), 55 and 222, discussed infra, p 1030 et seq.

[830] S 5(4)(a).

[831] S 5(4)(b). It might be noted that there is here no statutory ground of jurisdiction based on the court having jurisdiction over other proceedings involving the same marriage. Nor is any statutory provision made for the staying of proceedings for presumption of death and dissolution of marriage; see the definition of "matrimonial proceedings" in Sch 1, para 2 of the Domicile and Matrimonial Proceedings Act 1973.

[832] Discussed, supra, p 966 et seq; see North, op cit, p 151.

[833] *Wall v Wall* [1950] P 112.

[834] Matrimonial Causes Act 1973, s 19(5).

[835] Domicile and Matrimonial Proceedings Act 1973, s 17(2).

[836] See North, op cit, pp 297–299.

[837] *Szemik v Gryla* (1965) 109 Sol Jo 175.

[838] Cf s 5(4) of the Domicile and Matrimonial Proceedings Act 1973.

which the petitioner had a "real and substantial connection".[839] If the foreign decree can, properly, be classed as a decree of divorce[840] then it may be recognised under the rules laid down in Part II of the Family Law Act 1986.[841] Neither that Act nor the Convention on which it is based defines what is meant by a "divorce". However, a foreign decree of presumption of death not coupled with one for dissolution of marriage might well not be recognised in England, on the ground that it was merely a matter of procedure and not of substantive law.[842] Matters relating to the presumption of death were not within the contemplation of the drafters of Brussels II *bis*. As mentioned previously, the term "divorce" is not defined in the Regulation, but the recognition rules contained in Chapter III of the instrument[843] should not be construed as applying to matters concerning the presumption of death, since such matters go beyond the "dissolution of matrimonial ties".[844]

5. DISSOLUTION, NULLITY AND SEPARATION OF CIVIL PARTNERSHIPS

(a) Jurisdiction

(i) Bases of jurisdiction

(a) Introduction

Chapter 2 (Dissolution, nullity and other proceedings)[845] of Part 2[846] of the Civil Partnership Act 2004 sets out the orders that an English court can make to bring a civil partnership to an end, or to provide for the separation of the parties. In particular, by virtue of section 37(1), the High Court or a county court[847] has power to make four orders: (a) a dissolution order, which dissolves a civil partnership on the ground that it has broken down irretrievably;[848] (b) a nullity order, which annuls a void or voidable civil partnership;[849] (c) a presumption of death order, which dissolves a civil partnership on the ground that one of the civil partners is presumed to be dead;[850] and (d) a separation order, providing for the separation of civil partners.[851] The power which is conferred on English courts by Chapter 2 of Part 2 of the Act, to grant orders of a type specified in

---

[839] Cf *Indyka v Indyka* [1969] 1 AC 33, [1967] 2 All ER 689; North (1968) 31 MLR 257, 281.

[840] On the question of classification, see North, op cit, p 203.

[841] Supra, p 992 et seq; and see Law Com No 48 (1972) para 74 n 21.

[842] *Re Wolf's Goods* [1948] P 66, [1947] 2 All ER 841; though see *In the Goods of Schlesinger* [1950] CLY 1549.

[843] Supra, p 988 et seq.

[844] Brussels II *bis*, Recital (8).

[845] Ss 37–64.

[846] Headed "Civil Partnership: England and Wales".

[847] S 37(4)(b).

[848] S 44 provides that an application may be made to the court by either civil partner on the ground that the civil partnership has broken down irretrievably.

[849] Ss 49 and 50, respectively, state the grounds on which, by English law, a civil partnership is void or voidable. See special provision for civil partnerships registered in Scotland, in Northern Ireland, at British consulates abroad, etc by members of armed forces serving abroad, or overseas: s 54.

[850] S 55 states the grounds on which, by English law, a presumption of death order may be granted.

[851] S 56 narrates the bases on which, by English law, an application for a separation order may be made.

section 37(1), is expressly subject[852] to sections 219 to 224 of the Act, discussed below. If, by virtue of sections 219 to 224 (jurisdiction of the court), an English court has jurisdiction in respect of a civil partnership, then the court is empowered to make an order under section 37.

(b) Civil Partnership (Jurisdiction and Recognition of Judgments) Regulations 2005 ("section 219 regulations")[853]

Chapter 3 (Dissolution etc: jurisdiction and recognition[854]) of Part 5[855] of the Civil Partnership Act 2004 makes provision concerning the exercise of jurisdiction by courts in England and Wales for the dissolution or annulment of a civil partnership, or for the legal separation of civil partners. Section 219 of the Act empowers the Lord Chancellor to make provision as to the jurisdiction of courts in England and Wales[856] in respect of civil partnerships, corresponding to the Brussels II *bis* Regulation,[857] for cases where one partner is, or has been, habitually resident in a Member State, or is a national of a Member State, or is domiciled in a part of the United Kingdom.

The regulations made by virtue of section 219 are the Civil Partnership (Jurisdiction and Recognition of Judgments) Regulations 2005[858] (known as the "section 219 regulations"), which apply to proceedings for the dissolution, annulment or legal separation of all civil partnerships, including overseas relationships entitled to be treated as civil partnerships by virtue of the 2004 Act.[859]

(c) Proceedings for dissolution or separation

Section 221(1) of the 2004 Act provides that the English court[860] has jurisdiction to entertain proceedings for a dissolution order or a separation order in three situations. First, under section 221(1)(a), if the court has jurisdiction under the section 219 regulations.[861] Regulation 4[862] of the section 219 regulations provides that the courts in England shall have jurisdiction in relation to proceedings for the dissolution or annulment of a civil partnership or for the legal separation of civil partners where:[863] (a) both civil partners are habitually resident in England; (b) both civil partners were last habitually resident in England and one of the civil partners continues to reside there; (c) the respondent is habitually resident in England; (d) the petitioner is habitually resident in England and has resided there for at least one year immediately preceding the presentation of the

---

852 S 37(5).
853 SI 2005/3334. See, for Scotland, SSI 2005/629.
854 Ss 219–238.
855 Headed "Civil partnership formed or dissolved abroad etc".
856 S 219(a).
857 S 219(3).
858 SI 2005/3334.
859 Rule 3.
860 High court or a county court: s 220.
861 SI 2005/3334.
862 Rule 5 makes corresponding provision for Northern Ireland.
863 Cf generally Art 3, Brussels II *bis*, discussed supra, pp 945–946. However, there is no ground of jurisdiction in the s 219 regulations equivalent to Brussels II *bis*, Art 3, indent 4 (joint applications).

petition;[864] or (e) the petitioner is domiciled and habitually resident in England and has resided there for at least six months preceding the presentation of the petition.[865]

Secondly, section 221(1)(b) of the 2004 Act provides that the English court has jurisdiction to entertain proceedings for a dissolution order or a separation order if no court has, or is recognised as having, jurisdiction under the section 219 regulations, and either civil partner is domiciled in England on the date when the proceedings are begun.

Thirdly, section 221(1)(c) of the 2004 Act provides that the English court has jurisdiction to entertain proceedings for a dissolution order or a separation order if the following conditions are met: (i) the parties registered as civil partners in England or Wales; (ii) no court has, or is recognised as having, jurisdiction under the section 219 regulations; and (iii) it appears to the court to be in the interests of justice to assume jurisdiction in the case.

(d) Proceedings for nullity

Section 221(2) of the 2004 Act provides that the English court[866] has jurisdiction to entertain proceedings for a nullity order in three situations. First, under s 221(2)(a), if the court has jurisdiction under the section 219 regulations.[867] Secondly, section 221(2)(b) of the Act provides that the English court has jurisdiction, if no court has, or is recognised as having, jurisdiction under the section 219 regulations and either civil partner (i) is domiciled in England on the date when the proceedings are begun, or (ii) died before proceedings were begun and was, at death or for one year immediately preceding death, habitually resident in England. Thirdly, section 221(2)(c) of the Act provides that the English court has jurisdiction, if the following conditions are met: (i) the parties registered as civil partners in England; (ii) no court has, or is recognised as having, jurisdiction under the section 219 regulations; and (iii) it appears to the court to be in the interests of justice to assume jurisdiction in the case.

(e) Other proceedings in relation to the same civil partnership

Section 221(3) of the 2004 Act provides that when proceedings are pending in respect of which the court has jurisdiction by virtue of section 221(1) or (2), it also has jurisdiction to entertain other proceedings for dissolution, separation or nullity in respect of the same civil partnership, notwithstanding that jurisdiction would not be exercisable in those proceedings under section 221(1) or (2).[868]

(f) Proceedings for presumption of death order

Section 222 of the 2004 Act provides that the English court[869] has jurisdiction to entertain proceedings for a presumption of death order only if: (a) the applicant is domiciled in England on the date when the proceedings are begun; (b) the applicant was habitually

---

[864] This wording is slightly different from that in Brussels II *bis*, Art 3, indent 5, on which the provision is based.

[865] This wording is slightly different from that in Brussels II *bis*, Art 3, indent 6, on which the provision is based.

[866] High court or a county court: s 220.

[867] Detailed supra.

[868] Cf Domicile and Matrimonial Proceedings Act 1973, s 5(5), supra, pp 953–954.

[869] High court or a county court: s 220.

resident in England throughout the period of one year ending with that date;[870] or (c) the parties registered as civil partners of each other in England and it appears to the court to be in the interests of justice to assume jurisdiction in the case.

(ii) Procedural issues

(a) Service of the petition

The rules on service of a petition for dissolution, etc are the same as those concerning petitions for divorce, etc.[871]

(b) Staying proceedings

The Family Proceedings (Civil Partnership: Staying of Proceedings) Rules 2005,[872] made under section 223 of the 2004 Act, make provision for civil partnerships corresponding to that which is made for marriages in Schedule 1 to the Domicile and Matrimonial Proceedings Act 1973.[873] The Rules make equivalent provision, *mutatis mutandis*, for obligatory[874] and discretionary[875] stays of civil partnership proceedings in England for cases where civil partnership proceedings[876] are continuing in another jurisdiction outside England. Given the close similarity between the regime set out in the 2005 Rules and that which applies to concurrent matrimonial proceedings, it is not proposed to examine the Rules in detail. In outline, however, rule 2 requires a party who is seeking an order in civil partnership proceedings to furnish the court with particulars of relevant civil partnership proceedings in another jurisdiction. Rule 3 provides for obligatory stays in relation to proceedings in a related jurisdiction.[877] Rule 4 concerns discretionary stays of civil partnership proceedings in a non-related jurisdiction.[878] Rule 5 relates to discharge of orders staying proceedings under rules 3 and 4. Rule 7 concerns the court's power to make ancillary relief orders where a stay is imposed, and rule 8 deals with the effect of orders already made in civil partnership proceedings which have been stayed.

(b) Choice of law

(i) Dissolution, separation orders and presumption of death orders

There is no direct reference in the Civil Partnership Act 2004 to choice of law. In the case of proceedings for dissolution of a civil partnership in England, a decree of dissolution will be granted only in accordance with sections 44 to 48 of the 2004 Act (ie English domestic law provisions on dissolution). Similarly, as regards proceedings for separation

---

[870] Cf Domicile and Matrimonial Proceedings Act 1973, s 5(4), supra, p 953. There is no equivalent in the Domicile and Matrimonial Proceedings Act 1973 to the discretionary basis of jurisdiction contained in s 222(c).

[871] Supra, pp 954–955.

[872] SI 2005/2921.

[873] Discussed supra, p 959 et seq.

[874] Rule 3.

[875] Rule 4.

[876] Defined in r 1(2) as proceedings for one or more of: a dissolution order; a separation order; a nullity order; a declaration as to the validity of a civil partnership of the petitioner; or a declaration as to the subsistence of such a civil partnership .

[877] Defined in r 1(2)(d) as Scotland, Northern Ireland, Jersey, Guernsey and the Isle of Man.

[878] Any state, European Community or non-European Community; Brussels II *bis* does not apply to civil partnerships, and so Art 19 (lis pendens) has no application here.

orders, such an order will be granted only in accordance with sections 56 and 57 of that Act (ie English domestic law provisions on separation). Finally, the court may make a presumption of death order only if the provisions of section 55 are satisfied (ie English domestic law provisions on presumption of death orders).

(ii) Nullity

The position is more complicated in relation to nullity. In the case of civil partnerships registered in England, a decree of nullity will be granted by an English court only in accordance with sections 49 to 53 of the 2004 Act.[879]

Section 54 of the Act lays down special rules as to the validity of civil partnerships registered *outside* England and Wales, to be used by the English court (having jurisdiction under section 221(2) of the Act[880]) when determining whether, under English law, a civil partnership is void or voidable where the parties did not register as civil partners in England and Wales.[881] Thus, a civil partnership registered: (a) in Scotland will be void if it would be void in Scotland under section 123 of the Act,[882] and will be voidable if the circumstances fall within section 50(1)(d)[883] of the Act;[884] (b) in Northern Ireland will be void if it would be void in Northern Ireland under section 173 of the Act,[885] and will be voidable if the circumstances fall within section 50(1)[886] of the Act;[887] (c) at a British consulate abroad etc,[888] will be void if it would be void under section 210[889] of the Act, and will be voidable if section 54(4)(b) of the Act is satisfied;[890] or (d) by members of armed forces serving abroad,[891] will be void if it would be void under section 211[892] of the Act, and will be voidable if section 54(4)(b) of the Act is satisfied.[893]

---

[879] Having, in the case of a voidable civil partnership, only prospective effect: s 37(3).

[880] Supra, p 1032.

[881] Explanatory Notes, para 104. For civil partnerships registered: in Scotland, see s 54(1); in Northern Ireland, s 54(2); at British consulates, etc or by armed forces personnel, s 54(3) and (4); overseas, s 54(7), (8) and (10).

[882] Scottish domestic law provisions on nullity as regards civil partnerships registered in Scotland.

[883] An interim gender recognition certificate under the Gender Recognition Act 2004 has, after the time of formation of the civil partnership, been issued to either civil partner. The Explanatory Notes (para 105) point out that if the case were being considered in Scotland, this would instead be grounds for dissolution of the civil partnership under s 117(2)(b).

[884] S 54(1).

[885] Northern Irish domestic law provisions on nullity as regards civil partnerships registered in Northern Ireland.

[886] Grounds on which a civil partnership registered in England is voidable. These are all circumstances which would render the civil partnership voidable in Northern Ireland under s 174 (Explanatory Notes, para 106).

[887] S 54(2).

[888] S 54(3) and (4).

[889] Discussed, supra, p 885.

[890] This ensures that questions of nullity are dealt with in exactly the same way as would apply under English law if the parties had registered as civil partners in England (Explanatory Notes, para 107).

[891] S 54(3) and (4).

[892] Discussed, supra, pp 886–887.

[893] This ensures that questions of nullity are dealt with in exactly the same way as would apply under English law if the parties had registered as civil partners in England (Explanatory Notes, para 107).

As far as an apparent or alleged overseas relationship[894] is concerned, it will be held to be void[895] if (a) the relationship is not an overseas relationship,[896] or (b) even though the relationship is an overseas relationship, the parties are not treated as having formed a civil partnership under Chapter 2 of Part 5 of the Act.[897] A civil partnership registered overseas is voidable[898] if: (a) it is voidable under the law of the country where the relationship was registered, including its rules of private international law;[899] (b) the circumstances fall within section 50(1)(d)[900] of the Act; or (c) where either party was domiciled in England or in Northern Ireland at the time of registration of the relationship, the circumstances fall within section 50(1)(a), (b), (c) or (e).[901] The Explanatory Notes to the Act make clear that where a civil partnership is voidable under section 54, the provisions of section 51 (bars to relief where civil partnership is voidable) are applicable. Where, however, a civil partnership is voidable by virtue of application of foreign law, the bars to relief will apply only to the extent that they are applicable under the foreign law.[902]

(c) Recognition of dissolution, annulment and separation

(i) Introduction

Chapter 3 (Dissolution etc: jurisdiction and recognition)[903] of Part 5[904] of the Civil Partnership Act 2004 makes provision in sections 233 to 238 concerning recognition of the dissolution or annulment of a civil partnership or the legal separation of civil partners.

(ii) Effect of dissolution, annulment or separation obtained in the United Kingdom

Section 233[905] of the 2004 Act states that no dissolution or annulment obtained in one part of the United Kingdom is effective in any part of the United Kingdom, unless obtained from a court of civil jurisdiction. The validity of a dissolution, etc which has been obtained from a court of civil jurisdiction elsewhere in the United Kingdom shall be recognised in England, subject only to limited defences, namely: (a) if the dissolution, etc was obtained at a time when it was irreconcilable with a decision determining the question of the subsistence or validity of the civil partnership previously given by a court in England, or entitled to be recognised in England;[906] or (b) if the dissolution,

---

[894] S 54(6).

[895] S 54(7).

[896] Defined in ss 212–214, discussed supra, pp 938–939.

[897] Eg if, under the law of the country in which the relationship was registered, the necessary formalities were not complied with, or there was no capacity to enter the relationship. See ss 215–218, discussed supra, pp 937–939.

[898] S 54(8).

[899] S 54(8) and (10).

[900] An interim gender recognition certificate under the Gender Recognition Act 2004 has, after the time of formation of the civil partnership, been issued to either civil partner.

[901] Grounds on which a civil partnership registered in England (and, by virtue of s 174, in Northern Ireland) is voidable.

[902] Explanatory Notes, para 111. See ss 51 and 54(9).

[903] Ss 219–238.

[904] Headed "Civil partnership formed or dissolved abroad etc".

[905] Cf Family Law Act 1986, s 44(1).

[906] S 233(3).

etc was obtained at a time when, according to English law, there was no subsisting civil partnership.[907]

(iii) Recognition in the United Kingdom of dissolution, annulment or separation granted in a Member State[908]

Section 234 of the 2004 Act provides that the validity of an overseas dissolution, etc is to be recognised in the United Kingdom only by virtue of the scheme of recognition imposed by sections 235 to 237 of the Act, which, in turn, are subject to the recognition rules set out in the section 219 regulations.[909] Section 219 of the Act empowers the Lord Chancellor to make provision as to the recognition in England and Wales of any judgment of a court of another Member State which orders the dissolution or annulment of a civil partnership, or the legal separation of civil partners.[910] Part 2[911] of the section 219 regulations lays down rules concerning the recognition and refusal of recognition of judgments[912] made by a court[913] in another Member State.[914] The scheme[915] of recognition of overseas judgments is a peculiar conglomerate of provisions, partly modelled upon the provisions of Chapter III, Section 1 of Brussels II *bis*, and partly upon Part II of the Family Law Act 1986.[916] Whilst it was no doubt convenient to draft the regulations in this manner, the wisdom of so doing is far from clear. The overall policy has been to provide, where possible, parity of treatment between civil partners and spouses.

As a matter of policy, it is not entirely clear, in relation to dissolutions, etc of same sex "marriages"[917] granted by a court of a European Community Member State, whether recognition thereof is to be effected under the rules of recognition in Brussels II *bis*, or under section 234 of the 2004 Act. "By which law is the relationship to be characterised as 'marriage' or 'partnership'? Upon that categorisation rests the decision as to which set of jurisdiction and recognition rules to apply."[918] What is to happen, for example, if an English court is called upon to recognise a Dutch dissolution of a Dutch same sex relationship, a relationship which, in the eyes of Dutch law, amounts to "marriage", and is therefore to be governed by Brussels II *bis*, but which, in the eyes of English law, amounts

---

[907] S 233(4).

[908] Defined in r 6(3) of the section 219 regulations: see infra, n 914.

[909] Civil Partnership (Jurisdiction and Recognition of Judgments) Regulations, SI 2005/3334; supra, p 1031. See, for Scotland, SSI 2005/629.

[910] S 219(1)(b).

[911] Rules 6–12.

[912] Defined in r 6(1) as an order for the dissolution or annulment of a civil partnership or the legal separation of civil partners, pronounced by a court of a Member State, however termed by that state.

[913] Defined in r 6(2) as meaning all authorities, whether judicial or administrative, having jurisdiction in matters falling within the scope of the s 219 regulations.

[914] Defined in r 6(3): Belgium, Cyprus, Czech Republic, Germany, Greece, Spain, Estonia, France, Hungary, Ireland, Italy, Latvia, Lithuania, Luxembourg, Malta, Netherlands, Austria, Poland, Portugal, Slovakia, Slovenia, Finland, Sweden, and, notably, Denmark.

[915] See also SI 2005/3104, which includes provisions to deal with countries which comprise territories having different systems of law (r 2); cross-proceedings (r 4); the recognition of dissolutions obtained following the conversion of legal separations (r 5); and the facilitation of the proof of certain facts relevant to recognition and established in proceedings abroad (r 6), analogous to the rules found in ss 47, 48 and 49 of the Family Law Act 1986, discussed, supra, pp 997–998.

[916] Supra, p 886 et seq.

[917] In respect of which see Norrie (2006) 2.1 J Priv Int L 137, 161.

[918] Crawford and Carruthers, para 12-48.

to "civil partnership" and is subject, therefore, to the recognition provisions of the 2004 Act?[919] It is submitted that an English forum is likely to prefer its own characterisation.[920]

Given the close similarity between the rules for recognition of judgments set out in the section 219 regulations and those which have been examined in the context of Brussels II *bis* and the Family Law Act 1986,[921] it is not proposed to examine the former in detail. In outline, regulation 7 states that an overseas judgment shall be recognised in England without any special formalities. Regulation 8 sets out criteria for refusal of recognition of a judgment, adopting,[922] peculiarly, the bifurcated scheme contained in Part II of the 1986 Act, according to whether or not the judgment has been obtained by means of proceedings. Regulations 9, 10 and 11, based on Brussels II *bis*,[923] prevent the court from reviewing the jurisdiction of the Member State of origin, and from reviewing the substance of that judgment, and ensure that a judgment is recognised notwithstanding that there might have been a different result if English law had been applied to the facts of the case. Regulation 12 allows the court to stay proceedings for recognition when there is an appeal outstanding against that judgment.[924]

(iv) Recognition in the United Kingdom of dissolution, annulment or separation granted other than in a Member State[925]

Section 234 states that the validity of an overseas (ie non-Member State[926]) dissolution, etc is to be recognised in the United Kingdom only by virtue of the scheme of recognition imposed by sections 235 to 237 of the 2004 Act. The grounds for recognition are set out in section 235(1) and (2), and for refusal of recognition in section 236, and essentially mirror the terms of sections 46(1) and (2) and 51 of the Family Law Act 1986. Given the close similarity of wording, it is not proposed to examine sections 235 and 236 in detail.[927] Two provisions which merit comment, however, are section 235 (1A) and (2A), which were inserted[928] to deal with situations where section 235 would be insufficient to ensure proper recognition of the validity of certain overseas dissolutions, etc because one or both of the civil partners is either habitually resident or domiciled in a country whose law does not recognise legal relationships between persons of the same sex. The need for this provision is said to rest on the fact that there are many countries where the legal status of civil partnership is not established, and where, therefore, foreign dissolution of that status may not be recognised.[929]

---

[919] Ibid: "A further dilemma of delimitation might arise in relation to conflicting proceedings concerning the same relationship, in order to decide which set of conflicting jurisdiction rules should apply . . . those in Regulation 2201, or those in the 2004 Act."

[920] Cf *Wilkinson v Kitzinger* [2006] EWHC 2022 (Fam), [2007] 1 FLR 295.

[921] See, in relation to Family Law Act 1986, s 46, supra, p 992 et seq.

[922] Reg 8(3).

[923] Arts 24, 26 and 25 (in that order), discussed supra, pp 991–992.

[924] Cf Brussels II *bis*, Art 27.

[925] For list of Member States, see supra, p 1036, n 914.

[926] Member State judgments are governed by the s 219 regulations: s 234(2). For Member States, see SI 2005/3334, r 6(3).

[927] See, in relation to ss 46 and 51 of the Family Law Act 1986, supra, p 992 et seq and p 1012 et seq.

[928] By SI 2005/3104, r 3.

[929] Explanatory Memorandum to SI 2005/3104, para 7.3.

The remaining provisions in Chapter 3 of Part 5 of the 2004 Act are based upon provisions in the Family Law Act 1986, including, in particular, those concerning the meaning of "domicile",[930] and the fact of non-recognition elsewhere of a decree of dissolution, etc being no bar to remarriage.[931]

[930] S 237 (1); cf 1986 Act, s 46(5), supra, pp 993–994.
[931] S 238; cf 1986 Act, s 50, supra, p 915.

Chapter 22

Declarations

1. INTRODUCTION

For many years, the courts had power, both under their inherent jurisdiction[1] and by statute,[2] to make declarations as to status. The purpose of such a declaratory judgment is not to determine the rights of the parties and to grant the appropriate relief but merely to affirm what their rights are without any reference to the enforcement of such rights. For many years, the courts had statutory power[3] to grant declarations of legitimacy,[4] of legitimation, of the validity of a marriage or that the petitioner is a British subject. They have exercised their inherent powers to declare that a foreign divorce or annulment should, or should not, be recognised in England.[5] There was no power, however, to declare

---

[1] Under RSC Ord 15, r 16.
[2] Matrimonial Causes Act 1974, s 45 (repealed by Family Law Act 1986, ss 68(2), 69 and Sch 2).
[3] Ibid.
[4] But not of illegitimacy: *Mansel v A-G* (1877) 2 PD 265; affd 4 PD 232; *B v A-G* [1967] 1 WLR 776.
[5] *Har-Shefi v Har-Shefi* [1953] P 161; *Law v Gustin* [1976] Fam 155; *Kendall v Kendall* [1977] Fam 208; *Lepre v Lepre* [1965] P 52 at 57; *Lawrence v Lawrence* [1985] Fam 106.

the invalidity of a marriage by declaration: that had to be done in nullity proceedings.[6] Whether a marriage could be declared valid under the inherent jurisdiction was a matter of doubt and uncertainty.[7] Certainly declarations were made as to the subsisting validity of a marriage;[8] but it has also been said[9] that declarations as to the initial validity of a marriage could only be made in the exercise of the statutory powers. The significance of this was that the jurisdictional grounds varied as between the two heads of jurisdiction and, furthermore, various procedural safeguards were available under the statutory jurisdiction but not in the exercise of the inherent powers.

In 1984, the Law Commission expressed concern as to the general state of the law on declarations in family matters, identifying a number of major defects.[10] They proposed a clean sweep and a fresh start, recommending "a new legislative code, based on consistent principles [to] replace the existing hotchpotch of statutory and discretionary relief".[11] That was achieved in Part III of the Family Law Act 1986. In that year, the Law Commission also recommended that there should be a power to grant declarations of parentage and that such declarations should be governed by essentially the same rules as those contained in the 1986 Act for other declarations, particularly those of legitimacy.[12] That particular recommendation was implemented by amendments to Part II of the 1986 Act, as introduced by the Family Law Reform Act 1987.[13]

2. FAMILY LAW ACT 1986, PART III

Part III of the 1986 Act states what kinds of declaration may be granted under the Act and what are the relevant jurisdictional rules for each class of declaration. The four classes of declaration, ie declarations as to marital status, of parentage, as to parentage, legitimacy or legitimation, and as to adoptions effected overseas will be considered separately. A number of matters which are common to all four classes will then be examined. It ought to be noted at the outset that the various types of declaration listed in Part III may only be granted by the court[14] on the basis of the rules there laid down; section 45 of the Matrimonial Causes Act 1973 has been repealed[15] and the inherent jurisdiction of the High Court is inapplicable to matters falling within Part III.[16]

---

[6] *Kassim v Kassim* [1962] P 224.

[7] See Law Com No 132 (1984), paras 2.7–2.8; North, op cit, Chapter 6.

[8] Eg *Garthwaite v Garthwaite* [1964] P 356; *Re Meyer* [1971] P 298.

[9] *Collett v Collett* [1968] P 482; *Aldrich v A-G* [1968] P 281; *Vervaeke v Smith* [1981] Fam 77; affd [1981] Fam 77, CA, [1983] 1 AC 145; *Williams v A-G* [1987] 1 FLR 501; though this was actually done in *Woyno v Woyno* [1960] 1 WLR 986.

[10] Law Com No 132 (1984), para 2.12.

[11] Ibid, para 2.13.

[12] Law Com No 156 (1986), para 3.14.

[13] S 22.

[14] The High Court or a county court.

[15] This means that there is no longer a statutory power to grant a declaration that the applicant is a British citizen. Any inherent power to make a declaration that a person is a British citizen is unaffected, as in *Bulmer v A-G* [1955] Ch 558; *A-G v Prince Ernest Augustus of Hanover* [1957] AC 436; *Motala v A-G* [1990] 2 FLR 261, revsd on another point [1992] 1 AC 281, infra, p 1148.

[16] S 58(4). It is unlikely that foreign declaratory judgments in personam would be recognised in England— and no rules have been devised for the recognition of foreign declarations in rem. This is probably because it

(a) Declarations as to marital status

There are five declarations which the court may make in this category,[17] all of which had been made under the old law, ie:

(i)   that the marriage[18] was valid at its inception;[19]

(ii) that it did subsist on a date specified in the application;

(iii) that it did not so subsist on a date so specified;

(iv) that the validity of a divorce, annulment or legal separation obtained outside England and Wales is entitled to recognition in England and Wales;[20] and

(v)   that the validity of such a divorce, etc so obtained is not entitled to recognition in England and Wales.

The jurisdictional rules for granting any of those five types of declaration are as follows:[21] that either party to the marriage is domiciled in England and Wales on the date of the application, or has been habitually resident in England and Wales throughout the period of one year ending with that date. If a party to the marriage is dead then the jurisdictional requirements of domicile or one year's habitual residence in England and Wales have to be satisfied at the date of death.[22] The jurisdictional connection is not with the applicant but rather with a party to the marriage and this accounts for the need for a rule, as in nullity, dealing with the case where a party to the marriage had died.[23] The reason for the connection being with the party to the marriage is because section 55 of the 1986 Act allows anyone to apply for one of the five listed declarations. If, however, the applicant is not a party to the marriage, the court has a discretion to refuse to hear the application if it considers that the applicant does not have a sufficient interest in the determination of the application.[24] As under the old law, a declaration may not be made that a marriage was void at its inception.[25] That is to be determined by means of a nullity petition, the powers to grant which are unaffected by Part III of the 1986 Act.[26] In this way, a party will be unable to avoid the ancillary relief powers of the court available on a nullity petition, by seeking instead a declaration where such powers are unavailable.[27]

---

would usually require an English declaration to recognise the foreign one: see North, *Private International Law of Matrimonial Causes*, p 300.

[17] S 55(1). See also the Family Proceedings Rules 1991, rr 3.12, 3.16.

[18] For equivalent rules pertaining to civil partnership, see infra, p 1047.

[19] Eg *Bellinger v Bellinger* [2003] 2 AC 467. See also *Westminster City Council v IC (A Protected Part by His Litigation Friend) and Ors* [2008] EWCA Civ 198, [2008] WCR (D) 92—the only route to a judicial conclusion that a marriage was void at its inception is a petition for nullity.

[20] Eg *Berkovits v Grinberg* [1995] Fam 142; *Abbassi v Abbassi* [2006] EWCA Civ 355; [2006] 2 FLR 648.

[21] S 55(2). The rules are modelled on those which applied to nullity decrees prior to the entry into force of Council Regulation (EC) No 1337/2000 of 29 May 2000 on jurisdiction and the recognition and enforcement of judgments in matrimonial matters and in matters of parental responsibility for children of both spouses. cf Domicile and Matrimonial Proceedings Act 1973, s 5(3). Supra, p 944 et seq.

[22] S 55(2)(c). The effect of these rules is to abolish the common law ground of jurisdiction that a declaration could be granted as to the validity of a foreign divorce if that was a necessary step in adjudicating on a matter within the jurisdiction of the court: *Lepre v Lepre* [1965] P 52; see Law Com No 132 (1984), para 3.45.

[23] This can be very useful, as in *Re Meyer* [1971] P 298.

[24] S 55(3); see *Berkovits v Grinberg* supra—application by Jewish ecclesiastical judge. See Law Com No 132 (1984), paras 3.29–3.33 for discussion of the issue of who should be able to apply for these declarations.

[25] S 58(5)(a).

[26] S 58(6).

[27] *Kassim v Kassim* [1962] P 224. It will, however, be possible for a petitioner to seek in the alternative a nullity decree or a declaration as to the validity of the marriage: Law Com No 132 (1984), paras 3.26–3.27.

The Domicile and Matrimonial Proceedings Act 1973 provides[28] that, in the case of any proceedings[29] for a declaration as to the validity of a marriage of the petitioner or as to the subsistence of such a marriage, the court has a discretion to stay the English proceedings before the beginning of the trial thereof. This would seem to cover all five declarations as to marital status falling within section 55 of the 1986 Act. The statutory discretion is the same as that in divorce proceedings and has been fully discussed in that context.[30]

(b) Declarations of parentage

Section 55A of the 1986 Act,[31] inserted by section 83(2) of the Child Support, Pensions and Social Security Act 2000, introduced a new, wider power whereby any person[32] may apply to a civil court[33] for a declaration as to whether or not a person named in the application is or was the parent of another person so named. Section 55A is intended to provide a single procedure for obtaining a declaration of parentage to replace the two discrete provisions contained in the 1986 Act and in section 27 of the Child Support Act 1991 (effective only for the purposes of child support and maintenance proceedings). The court can entertain an application only if either of the persons named therein is domiciled in England on the date of the application, or has been habitually resident in England throughout the period of one year ending with that date; or if either of the persons named in the application died before the date of application, and was at death domiciled in England, or had been habitually resident in England for one year preceding his/her death.[34]

If the applicant is not the child or one of the alleged parents concerned, then the court shall refuse to hear the application unless it considers that the applicant has a sufficient personal interest in the determination of the application.[35] Additionally, the court may refuse to hear the application if one of the persons named in it is a child, and it considers that the determination would not be in the best interests of that child.[36]

---

[28] Sch I, para 9.

[29] Other than proceedings governed by Council Regulation (EC) No 2201/2003 of 27 November 2003 concerning jurisdiction and the recognition and enforcement of judgments in matrimonial matters and matters of parental responsibility, repealing Regulation (EC) No 1347/2000. Supra, p 956 et seq.

[30] Supra, p 959 et seq.

[31] See also Family Proceedings Rules 1991, rr 3.13, 3.16, and 4.7–4.8 (in relation to which see *Re B (A Child) (Parentage: Knowledge of Proceedings)* [2003] EWCA Civ 1842; [2004] 1 FLR 473).

[32] The power is wider than that in s 56 (discussed, infra, p 1043). Subject to s 55A(3) and (4), *any* person may apply under s 55A(1) for a declaration of parentage of a person named in the application, whereas application may be made under s 56 only by an applicant in respect of his own parentage/status. See *Leeds Teaching Hospital NHS Trust v A and Ors* [2003] EWHC 259 (QB); [2003] All ER (D) 374; *Secretary of State for Work and Pensions v Jones* (2003) Times, 13 August; and *Re B (A Child) (Parentage: Knowledge of Proceedings)* [2003] EWCA Civ 1842; [2004] 1 FLR 473.

[33] The High Court or a county court or a magistrates' court: s 55A(1). By virtue of s 60(5), an appeal shall lie to the High Court against the making by a magistrates' court of, or refusal to make, a declaration under s 55A.

[34] S 55A(2).

[35] S 55A(3) and (4).

[36] S 55(A)(5); *Re R (A Child)* [2003] EWCA Civ 182; [2003] Fam 129 per HALE LJ at [32].

(c) Declarations of parentage, legitimacy or legitimation

Section 56 of the 1986 Act[37] retains and slightly extends the previous statutory power[38] to make declarations as to legitimacy and legitimation,[39] and introduces a new power to make declarations of parentage.[40] The court[41] may make four kinds of declaration in this category:

(i)   that a person is or was the applicant's parent;

(ii) that the applicant is the legitimate child of his parents; and

(iii) that the applicant has, or has not, become a legitimated person.[42]

Declarations as to legitimation[43] may relate to legitimation by statute, or to foreign legitimations which are recognised in England either under statutory provisions or at common law.[44] Declarations may be sought, for example, to acquire nationality, to establish rights of inheritance or to amend a birth certification. Only a person alleging that he is the child of someone may apply for a parentage declaration; and an application for a declaration as to legitimacy or legitimation may be made only by the person whose status is in issue.[45]

The jurisdictional rules for granting any of these declarations are the simple and familiar ones that the applicant is, at the time of the application, domiciled in England or has been habitually resident in England for one year immediately preceding that date.[46]

(d) Declarations as to adoptions effected overseas

Although recognition in England of adoption orders made elsewhere in the British Isles is automatic,[47] this is not true of foreign adoptions.[48] Although there is no reported case of an application for a declaration as to the validity of a foreign adoption,[49] the Law Commission concluded[50] that it would be desirable to take the opportunity to make clear

---

[37] As substituted by s 22 of the Family Law Reform Act 1987; and see Family Proceedings Rules 1991, rr 3.14, 3.16.

[38] See the Matrimonial Causes Act 1973, s 45; and see *Motala v A-G* [1990] 2 FLR 261; revsd on another point [1992] 1 AC 281, infra, p 1148.

[39] Such declarations are still needed notwithstanding the major reforms of the law relating to legitimacy contained in the Family Law Reform Act 1987, infra, p 1142, see Law Com No 118 (1982), para 10.2; Law Com No 157 (1986), para 3.14.

[40] See Norrie (1994) 43 ICLQ 757.

[41] The High Court or a county court.

[42] These may be sought in the alternative: s 56(2).

[43] S 58(5)(b) (prohibition of declaration of illegitimacy) has been excised from the Act by virtue of s 83(3) of the Child Support, Pensions and Social Security Act 2000. The reason for this is that the effect of a declaration of parentage under s 55A could be that a child is or was illegitimate, which is inconsistent with s 58(5)(b) as was.

[44] S 56(5). Recognition of foreign legitimations is discussed infra, p 1151 et seq.

[45] Contrast applications for declaration of parentage under s 55A, discussed, supra, p 1042.

[46] S 56(3); and see Law Com No 132 (1984), paras 3.34–3.36; *Motala v A-G* [1990] 2 FLR 261; revsd on another point [1992] 1 AC 281.

[47] Adoption Act 1976, s 38(1)(c); Adoption and Children Act 2002, ss 66(1) and 105–108.

[48] Infra, p 1170 et seq; and see Law Com No 132 (1984), para 3.15.

[49] The issue of the validity of a foreign adoption has always arisen in the course of other proceedings such as entitlement under a settlement (*Re Valentine's Settlement* [1965] Ch 831), a will (*Re Marshall* [1957] Ch 507), or an intestacy (*Re Wilson* [1954] Ch 733).

[50] Law Com No 132 (1984), paras 3.15–3.16.

provision for such declarations and to provide appropriate procedural safeguards.[51] Under section 57(2) of the Family Law Act 1986[52] the court[53] may grant a declaration that the applicant either is[54] or is not the adopted child of a particular person.[55] The only person who can apply for a declaration as to the validity of a foreign adoption is the child himself, and he can apply whether he has been adopted by a Convention adoption, or an overseas adoption, within the meaning of the Adoption and Children Act 2002, or an adoption recognised by English law and effected under the law of any country outside the British Islands.[56] Again the jurisdiction of the court is based on the domicile of the applicant in England on the date of the application or his habitual residence in England for one year immediately preceding that date.[57]

(e) Limits on the courts' powers

The basic approach of Part III of the 1986 Act is that the court may make the declarations listed there in family matters but may make no others.[58] Thus, as was mentioned earlier, there is express provision that no court may make a declaration as to the initial invalidity of a marriage,[59] and that the declarations available under Part III of the 1986 Act may only be made under that Part.[60] This latter provision excludes any possibility of the exercise of an overlapping jurisdiction under the inherent powers of the court.[61] It is also not possible for a court to make a "negative declaration", ie to declare the opposite of what is sought,[62] eg that a marriage was not subsisting on a particular date when a declaration is sought that it was.[63] There is nothing, however, to prevent a petitioner in that case from petitioning for the two declarations in the alternative, and indeed the Act expressly refers to this possibility in relation to declarations as to legitimation and adoption.[64]

(f) Safeguards and other procedural matters

All declarations made under Part III of the 1986 Act are binding in rem, ie they bind not only the parties but all other persons including the Crown.[65] It is important that in matters of personal status some finality is brought to the proceedings in order to still any doubts on the issue, and declarations as to the validity of a marriage, for example, are very

---

[51] Infra, p 1170 et seq.

[52] And see the Family Proceedings Rules 1991, rr 3.15, 3.16.

[53] The High Court or a county court.

[54] For the purposes of s 39 of the Adoption Act 1976, or s 67 of the Adoption and Children Act 2002, in respect of which, see infra, pp 1175–1176.

[55] These declarations may be sought in the alternative: s 57(1).

[56] S 57(1). See, for detailed consideration of adoption, infra, Chapter 25.

[57] S 57(3).

[58] It might also be noted that the power to grant declarations under the Greek Marriages Act 1884 has been abolished as has the right to petition for jactitation of marriage: ss 61, 62: and see Law Com No 132 (1984), paras 4.1–4.13.

[59] S 58(5).

[60] S 58(4).

[61] S 58(3); and see Law Com No 132 (1984), para 3.28.

[62] S 58(3); and see Law Com No 132 (1984), paras 3.24–3.27.

[63] Under s 55(1).

[64] Ss 56(2), 57(1). As has been mentioned, supra, p 1041, it is also possible to petition for a nullity decree and a declaration of initial validity in the alternative.

[65] S 58(2).

close in nature to decrees of divorce or nullity which do operate in rem. Although it is always possible for a declaration, like any other judgment, to be rescinded for fraud, the binding nature conferred on declarations under Part III does call for a number of procedural safeguards to protect the interests of third parties and of the public.

The first concern is that a declaration should only be granted on convincing evidence, and it is provided that the truth of the proposition to be declared has to be proved "to the satisfaction of the court".[66] A further safeguard is provided by involvement of the Attorney-General to enable him to protect the public interest.[67] The outcome of a petition for a declaration could be highly relevant, for example, on issues of nationality[68] or immigration. To meet these concerns, it is provided that the court may at any stage of the proceedings, either of its own motion or on the application of a party to the proceedings, direct that all papers be sent to the Attorney-General who may, whether or not he has been sent the papers, intervene in the proceedings in such manner as he thinks necessary or expedient.[69] It is also desirable that adequate provision be made for giving notice of the proceedings to all interested parties and to the Attorney-General, and power is given to make rules of court for that purpose.[70]

Finally, there is the issue of whether declarations under Part III should be available as of right, or only within the discretion of the court. The power of the court to grant a nullity decree is not discretionary,[71] and it has been said that "the right to obtain a declaration of status is a human right which should not be subject to the court's discretion".[72] Consequently, section 58(1) of the 1986 Act requires the court to make a declaration if the truth of the proposition to be declared is proved to the satisfaction of the court. There is, however, one exception to this in that the court may refuse to grant a declaration if to do so "would manifestly be contrary to public policy". This follows the approach of the earlier law, when courts were prepared to refuse a declaration as to the subsisting validity of a marriage, under section 45 of the Matrimonial Causes Act 1973, on grounds of public policy:

> It cannot be the intention of the statute that a decree must be pronounced (to the permanent prejudice of the Crown) when, although there has been no fraud at the hearing, the whole history is of fraud and perjury and the facts to found a decree have been brought about by criminal acts and offences and a fraudulent, deceitful course of conduct.[73]

---

[66] S 58(1).

[67] S 59.

[68] Eg *Puttick v A-G* [1980] Fam 1.

[69] S 59(2).

[70] S 60; and see Law Com No 132 (1984), paras 3.60–3.63. In the case of declarations of parentage under s 55A, and of parentage and of legitimacy under s 56, if a declaration is made the Registrar General must be notified: Family Law Act 1986, ss 55A(7) and 56(4), respectively.

[71] *Kassim v Kassim* [1962] P 224 at 234.

[72] Law Com No 132 (1984), para 3.39.

[73] *Puttick v A-G* [1980] Fam 1 at 22.

3. CHILD ABDUCTION AND CUSTODY ACT 1985

In terms of Article 15 of the 1980 Hague Convention on the Civil Aspects of International Child Abduction,[74] the judicial or administrative authorities of a Contracting State may, prior to the making of an order for the return of the child, request that the applicant obtain from the authorities of the state of the habitual residence of the child a decision or other determination that the removal or retention was wrongful within the meaning of Article 3 of the Convention, where such a decision or determination may be obtained in that state. The Central Authorities of the Contracting States shall, so far as practicable, assist applicants to obtain such a decision or determination.

Section 8 of the Child Abduction and Custody Act 1985, which gives effect to the Convention in the United Kingdom, provides that the High Court[75] may, on an application made for the purposes of Article 15 of the Convention[76] by any person[77] appearing to the court to have an interest in the matter, make a declaration that the removal of any child from, or his retention outside, the United Kingdom was wrongful within the meaning of Article 3 of the Convention.[78]

A declaration should not be sought in a case where it is likely unnecessarily to delay or hamper the application for a return order.[79] A declaration made for the purposes of Article 15 is not binding on the requesting authority or the Courts of that country, but is designed to be of assistance. Although, strictly, a declaration so obtained is no more than persuasive,[80] it has recently been held by the House of Lords that a determination under Article 15 should be treated as determinative unless clearly out of line with the international understanding of the Convention's terms.[81]

---

[74] See generally infra, Chapter 24. Also Family Proceedings Rules 1991, Part VI.

[75] In Scotland, the Court of Session.

[76] Though see *Re D (A Child) (Abduction: Rights of Custody)* [2007] 1 AC 619, per Lord BROWN of Eaton-under-Heywood, at [79]: the terms of s 8 of the 1985 Act "contemplate and empower [the English court] to make … a declaration even before there are any proceedings in, or any request from, a foreign contracting state".

[77] Not only persons having rights of custody or rights of access. *Re P (A Minor) (Child Abduction: Declaration)* [1995] 1 FLR 831; [1995] Fam Law 398.

[78] *Re D (A Child) (Abduction: Rights of Custody)* [2007] 1 AC 619; *Hunter v Murrow (Abduction: Rights of Custody)* [2005] EWCA Civ 976; [2005] 2 FLR 1119; *Re H (Child Abduction) (Unmarried Father: Rights of Custody)* [2003] EWHC 492; [2003] 2 FLR 153; *Re G (Abduction: Rights of Custody)* [2002] 2 FLR 703; [2002] Fam Law 732 (Fam Div); *Re L (Children) (Abduction: Declaration)* [2001] FCR 1; *Re J (Abduction: Rights of Custody)* [1999] 3 FCR 577; *Re P (Abduction: Declaration)* [1995] 1 FLR 831; and *Re J (A Minor) (Abduction: Ward of Court)* [1989] Fam 85; [1990] Fam Law 177. See also *Re A (Abduction: Declaration of Wrongful Removal)* [2002] NI 114.

[79] *Re P (Diplomatic Immunity: Jurisdiction)* [1998] 1 FLR 1026; *Hunter v Murrow (Abduction: Rights of Custody)* [2005] EWCA Civ 976; [2005] 2 FLR 1119, per THORPE LJ at [40]–[41] (eg where the question for determination in the requested state turns on a point of autonomous (ie Hague Convention) law); and DYSON LJ, at [50]–[51]; and *Re D (A Child) (Abduction: Rights of Custody)* [2007] 1 AC 619, per Lord HOPE of Craighead, at [6]. See also *Re A (Abduction: Declaration of Wrongful Removal)* [2002] NI 114, per GILLEN J at [120].

[80] *Hunter v Murrow (Abduction: Rights of Custody)* [2005] EWCA Civ 976; [2005] 2 FLR 1119, per THORPE LJ, at [27]; and *Re D (A Child) (Abduction: Rights of Custody)* [2007] 1 AC 619, per Lord CARSWELL at [71]; and Lord BROWN of Eaton-under-Heywood, at [82]–[83].

[81] *Re D (A Child) (Abduction: Rights of Custody)* [2007] 1 AC 619, per Baroness HALE of Richmond, at [43] and [44] (eg where the ruling was obtained by fraud or in breach of the rules of natural justice); Lord CARSWELL at [71]; and Lord BROWN of Eaton-under-Heywood, at [81] (eg where there was a manifest misdirection as to the autonomous meaning of the Convention term "rights of custody").

4. CIVIL PARTNERSHIP ACT 2004

Section 58 of the Civil Partnership Act 2004 provides that any person may apply to the High Court or a county court for one or more of the following five[82] declarations in relation to a specified civil partnership:

  (i) that the civil partnership was valid at its inception;
 (ii) that it subsisted on a date specified in the application;
(iii) that it did not so subsist on a date so specified;
 (iv) that the validity of a dissolution, annulment or legal separation obtained outside England and Wales is entitled to recognition in England and Wales; and
  (v) that the validity of such a dissolution, etc so obtained is not entitled to recognition in England and Wales.

Sections 59 (general provisions as to making and effect of declarations), 60 (the Attorney General and proceedings for declarations) and 61 (supplementary provisions as to declarations) of the 2004 Act reproduce the terms of sections 58, 59 and 60 of the Family Law Act 1986,[83] *mutatis mutandis*, with regard to declarations in relation to civil partnerships.

---

[82] Cf declarations as to marital status: s 55, Family Law Act 1986. Supra, p 1041.
[83] Supra, pp 1041–1042.

Chapter 23

Financial Relief

In many petitions for financial relief, the parties are not only, or indeed primarily, concerned with the determination of their personal status, but are also concerned with the powers of the court to make orders as to financial support, rights to the family home and property, and the like.[1] These forms of relief, often ancillary to that obtained in the

---

[1] Their other main concern is with orders concerning the welfare of the children, infra, p 1075 et seq.

main proceedings, give rise to three main questions of private international law—the jurisdiction of the English court; the power to order relief after a foreign divorce/dissolution, annulment or legal separation; and the recognition of foreign decrees or orders in relation to financial relief.[2]

1. JURISDICTION OF THE ENGLISH COURT

As the types of relief available to the parties to a marriage or civil partnership are varied, the jurisdictional issues raised thereby must be considered separately. The position is complicated by the fact that general jurisdiction over claims for maintenance is conferred by the Brussels/Lugano system (comprising four different sets of rules: those contained in the Brussels I Regulation; the EC/Denmark Agreement; the Brussels Convention; and the Lugano Convention), as well as under the Modified Regulation.[3] There are also special rules for married couples under Part III of the Matrimonial and Family Proceedings Act 1984, and corresponding rules for civil partners in terms of section 72(4) and Schedule 7 to the Civil Partnership Act 2004,[4] as to the powers and jurisdiction of the English courts to grant financial relief following the obtaining of a foreign divorce/dissolution, annulment or legal separation. It is necessary, therefore, to examine separately the jurisdictional rules governing the various heads of English financial relief, and those which are uniform within the European Community and the EFTA States under the Brussels/Lugano system, before considering the position under Part III of the 1984 Act.

(a) General jurisdictional rules

(i) Relief ancillary to an English decree of divorce, nullity or judicial separation

On granting a decree of divorce, nullity or judicial separation,[5] or at any time thereafter, the English court may make a variety of financial provision orders,[6] eg an order for the payment of periodical payments, which may be ordered to be secured, or that a lump sum shall be paid by one spouse to the other, or that similar payments may be made by one spouse to or for the benefit of a child of the family,[7] or that a spouse shall transfer to or settle property on the other spouse or a child or for the benefit of a child,[8] or the court may order the variation of any settlement made on the parties to the marriage or order the extinction or reduction of the interest of either party thereunder.[9] The court also

---

[2] See Martigny (1994) III Hague Recueil 131.

[3] See generally, supra, Chapter 10.

[4] The rules which apply to civil partners under the 2004 Act are based upon those which apply to married couples, and so all references in this chapter to "marriage" and "married persons" should be construed as including civil partnership and civil partners.

[5] Provision is also made for the payment of maintenance pending suit: Matrimonial Causes Act 1973, s 22. See *Harb v Aziz (No 1)* [2005] EWCA Civ 632, [2005] 2 FLR 1108.

[6] Matrimonial Causes Act 1973, s 23(1)(a)–(c).

[7] Ibid, s 23(1)(d)–(f). This relief may be ordered before a decree is granted, or if the proceedings are dismissed: ibid, s 23(2).

[8] Ibid, s 24(1)(a),(b).

[9] Ibid, s 24(1)(c) and (d). For consent orders, see the Matrimonial and Family Proceedings Act 1984, s 7.

has power[10] to restrain or set aside transactions intended to prevent or reduce relief and will, in appropriate circumstances, exercise this power in relation to immovables abroad.[11]

The court has jurisdiction to make such orders and grant such ancillary relief whenever it has jurisdiction in the main proceedings for divorce, nullity or judicial separation.[12] This means, primarily, when the court has jurisdiction under Article 3 of the Brussels II *bis* Regulation,[13] ie where:

(a) both parties are habitually resident in England and Wales;

(b) both parties were last habitually resident in England and Wales and one of them still resides there;

(c) the respondent is habitually resident in England and Wales;

(d) in the event of a joint application, either party is habitually resident in England and Wales;

(e) the applicant is habitually resident in England and Wales if s/he resided there for at least a year immediately before the application was made;

(f) the applicant is habitually resident in England and Wales if s/he resided there for at least six months immediately before the application was made and s/he has his/her domicile there; or

(g) both parties are domiciled in England and Wales.[14]

On the basis of jurisdiction in the main suit, an order for periodical payments has been made against a husband domiciled and resident in France and with no assets in England but where there was a real probability of his appearing before the English courts.[15] As the power to make orders for ancillary relief is discretionary,[16] the court will decline to make such an order where to do so would be quite ineffective.[17] The fact that there has been a legal separation abroad which is recognised in England does not prevent the English court from granting relief ancillary to a later English divorce petition.[18]

The power to make orders for ancillary relief may be exercised at any time after the granting of the main decree,[19] and there is authority for the opinion that, so long as there was

---

[10] Matrimonial Causes Act 1973, s 37.

[11] *Hamlin v Hamlin* [1986] Fam 11 (subject always to exclusive jurisdiction under the Brussels/Lugano system: see supra, p 276 et seq; and Carruthers (2005), paras 2.51–2.67).

[12] *Cammell v Cammell* [1965] P 467.

[13] Domicile and Matrimonial Proceedings Act 1973, s 5(2)(a) and (3)(a). Residual national rules of jurisdiction apply if no court of a Member State has jurisdiction under the Regulation (s 5(2)(b) and (3)(b)). See p 951, supra.

[14] Notably, the Brussels II *bis* Regulation (Recital (8)), like its predecessor, the Brussels II Regulation (Recital (10)), applies only to the dissolution of matrimonial ties; it does not deal with issues such as the property consequences of marriage or any other ancillary measures.

[15] *Cammell v Cammell*, supra (preceding the Brussels II *bis* Regulation); and see the power to vary a marriage settlement exercised over foreign settlements in *Nunneley v Nunneley* (1890) 15 PD 186; *Forsyth v Forsyth* [1891] P 363; and see *Hunter v Hunter and Waddington* [1962] P 1, infra, pp 1324–1326. See now Matrimonial Causes Act 1973, s 23.

[16] Eg, the Matrimonial Causes Act 1973, ss 23, 24.

[17] *Tallack v Tallack* [1927] P 211; *Goff v Goff* [1934] P 107; *Wyler v Lyons* [1963] P 274.

[18] *Sabbagh v Sabbagh* [1985] FLR 29. Relief after a foreign divorce, etc is discussed more fully, infra, p 1061 et seq.

[19] Matrimonial Causes Act 1973, ss 23(1), 24(1).

jurisdiction in the main suit, ancillary relief may still be granted notwithstanding that the jurisdictional ground in the main suit no longer exists.[20]

It will be recalled that the jurisdiction of the English courts to grant decrees of divorce, nullity and judicial separation is subject to a discretionary power in the court to stay the proceedings if similar proceedings are continuing in another, non-European Community jurisdiction.[21] If English proceedings are stayed because similar proceedings are continuing in another jurisdiction in the British Isles,[22] the English court does not have power to make, inter alia, orders for periodical payments or the payment of lump sums, except in circumstances of urgency.[23] Furthermore, any order, other than a lump sum order, already made in connection with the stayed proceedings ceases to have effect three months after the proceedings were stayed.[24] If an order for periodical payments or any provision relating to a child which could be made under section 8 of the Children Act 1989 has been made in the other British proceedings, then any English order made in connection with the stayed English proceedings in relation to the same matters shall cease to have effect and no such order may be made.[25]

(ii) Failure to provide reasonable maintenance

The court has power to order periodical payments, which may be ordered to be secured, or lump sum payments to be made to a spouse or to or for the benefit of a child if the other spouse has failed to provide reasonable maintenance.[26] This relief may be sought during the continuance of the marriage, during the joint lives of the spouses,[27] and is not ancillary to a petition for divorce, nullity or judicial separation. Indeed it assumes that the spouses are still married, though such relief may be granted after there has been a decree of judicial separation.[28] The court has jurisdiction to make such orders on three bases:[29]

(a) Domicile of the applicant or respondent in England on the date of the application;

(b) Habitual residence of the applicant in England for one year immediately preceding the application; or

(c) Residence of the respondent in England on the date of the application.[30]

(iii) Alteration of maintenance agreements

The court has power to order alterations, by variation or revocation, to a maintenance agreement on application by either of the parties thereto.[31] The court must be satisfied

---

[20] *Moss v Moss* [1937] QSR 1.

[21] Supra, p 959 et seq. The discretionary power does not exist in the case of competing proceedings in another European Community Member State: Brussels II *bis* Regulation, Art 19. See p 956 et seq, supra.

[22] A "related jurisdiction", per Domicile and Matrimonial Proceedings Act 1973, Sch 1, para 3.

[23] Domicile and Matrimonial Proceedings Act 1973, Sch 1, para 11(2)(c).

[24] Ibid, Sch 1, para 11(2)(b).

[25] Ibid, Sch 1 para 11(3), as amended by the Children Act 1989, Sch 13, para 33, Sch 15.

[26] Matrimonial Causes Act 1973, s 27. The differing obligations of maintenance on a husband and a wife are laid down in s 27(1), as substituted by s 63 of the Domestic Proceedings and Magistrates' Courts Act 1978; and see the Matrimonial and Family Proceedings Act 1984, s 4; Family Law Reform Act 1987, Sch 2, para 52.

[27] *Harb v Aziz (No 2)* [2005] EWCA Civ 1324, [2005] 1 FLR 825.

[28] *King v King* [1954] P 55.

[29] Matrimonial Causes Act 1973, s 27(2), as amended by the Domicile and Matrimonial Proceedings Act 1973, s 6(1). This is subject to the effects of the Brussels/Lugano system, supra, Chapter 11.

[30] For the meaning of "residence", see *Sinclair v Sinclair* [1968] P 189 and cases there cited. Also *Harb v Aziz (No 1)* [2005] EWCA Civ 632, [2005] 2 FLR 1108; and *Harb v Aziz (No 2)* [2005] EWCA Civ 1324, [2005] 1 FLR 825.

[31] Matrimonial Causes Act 1973, s 35.

that the financial circumstances of the parties have changed or that the agreement fails to make proper arrangements for a child of the family. Jurisdiction is based on the domicile or residence in England of each party to the agreement at the time of the application.[32] If an application is made to a magistrates' court, both parties must be resident in England and one must be resident in the local justice area for which the court is appointed.[33]

(iv) Financial provision in magistrates' courts[34]

(a) Under the Domestic Proceedings and Magistrates' Courts Act 1978

Magistrates' courts have power under Part I of the Domestic Proceedings and Magistrates' Courts Act 1978 to order either party to a marriage to make financial provision for the other spouse or for a child of the family. Jurisdiction to make such orders, and other orders covered by Part I of the 1978 Act, is based on either the applicant or respondent ordinarily residing, at the date of the making of the application, within the local justice area for which the particular magistrates' court is appointed.[35] This is a matter of internal jurisdiction only.[36] The one truly international jurisdictional provision in the 1978 Act is that the domicile of the parties is irrelevant to matters of jurisdiction.[37] All other issues remain to be determined, as they were with the forerunners of this Act, by the common law. The general principle is that, if the defendant is resident outside the United Kingdom, an English magistrates' court will lack jurisdiction.[38] However, it is arguable that a claim for financial provision is not a matter of status but is to be regarded simply as an action in personam,[39] in which event mere presence within the jurisdiction should suffice.[40] There is some authority[41] that any want of jurisdiction cannot be cured by submission because, in the case of an inferior court such as a magistrates' court, submission cannot extend "a limited and circumscribed jurisdiction"[42] conferred by statute. However, the only jurisdiction conferred by the 1978 Act relates to intra-United Kingdom jurisdiction and it is suggested that, if a claim for financial provision is characterised as an action in personam, submission by a respondent resident outside the United Kingdom should confer jurisdiction.

(b) Under the Maintenance Orders (Facilities for Enforcement) Act 1920 and the Maintenance Orders (Reciprocal Enforcement) Act 1972

If the defendant resides in a country outside the United Kingdom, the English courts may have jurisdiction to make a maintenance order against him if the circumstances are

---

[32] Ibid, s 35(1). If an agreement provides for the continuation of payment after the death of one party, and that party died domiciled in England, the court has jurisdiction over any application by the survivor or the personal representatives of the deceased: s 36.

[33] Ibid, s 35(3).

[34] For the impact on these rules of the Brussels/Lugano system, see infra, p 1055 et seq.

[35] S 30(1), as amended by the Courts Act 2003, Sch 8, para 194(b).

[36] The only international jurisdictional rules were contained in s 30(3), dealing with conflicts of jurisdiction within the United Kingdom, but they were repealed, without replacement, by the Courts and Legal Services Act 1990.

[37] S 30(5).

[38] *Forsyth v Forsyth* [1948] P 125.

[39] See *Berkley v Thompson* (1884) 10 App Cas 45 at 49.

[40] *Forsyth v Forsyth* [1948] P 125 at 136; *Collister v Collister* [1972] 1 WLR 54 at 59.

[41] *Forsyth v Forsyth*, supra, at 132.

[42] *Re Dulles' Settlement* [1951] Ch 265 at 274.

such that either the Maintenance Orders (Facilities for Enforcement) Act 1920[43] or the Maintenance Orders (Reciprocal Enforcement) Act 1972[44] is applicable.[45] Both these statutes deal with the problem of reciprocal enforcement of maintenance orders. As the basis of the operation of both statutes is reciprocity, they both deal with the recognition of foreign maintenance orders as well as the jurisdiction of the English court, but only the latter aspect is considered here.[46]

The 1920 Act applies only to those Commonwealth countries to which it has been extended by Order in Council. If a defendant is resident in such a country, then an English magistrates' court may make a provisional order against him in his absence,[47] even though the applicant's basis of complaint did not arise in England.[48] A copy of such an order is then sent by diplomatic channels to the Commonwealth country where the defendant resides with a view to its being confirmed by the courts of that country. In other words, there are proceedings in England for a provisional order, followed by proceedings in the foreign country for confirmation thereof.

Part I of the 1972 Act establishes a similar procedure but it is wider in scope. It applies to all countries with whom reciprocal agreements have been reached and not just Commonwealth countries,[49] and it contains a wider definition of the type of orders to which it applies than does the 1920 Act.[50] Furthermore, the "shuttlecock" procedure of provisional order in one country followed by confirmation in the other also applies to variation and revocation of maintenance orders.[51] Such variation or revocation may be made either by the court which made the original provisional order or the court which confirmed it.

Part II of the 1972 Act gives effect in the United Kingdom to the United Nations Convention on the Recovery Abroad of Maintenance (1956). If a person, usually the wife, in the United Kingdom claims maintenance from a person "subject to the jurisdiction" of a convention country,[52] she makes an application through the designated officer for the local justice area

---

[43] As amended by the Maintenance Orders (Reciprocal Enforcement) Act 1992, Sch 1, Part I; SI 1992/709, Art 4; Access to Justice Act 1999, Sch 15, Pt V; and the Courts Act 2003, Sch 8, para 68 and Sch 10. See Dicey, Morris and Collins, paras 18-182–18-186; McClean, *Recognition of Family Judgments in the Commonwealth* (1983), Chapter 5.

[44] As amended by the Domestic Proceedings and Magistrates' Courts Act 1978, ss 54–61, and by the Maintenance Orders (Reciprocal Enforcement) Act 1992, Sch 1, Part II. See McClean, op cit, Chapters 6 and 7.

[45] Dicey, Morris and Collins, paras 18-187–18-198.

[46] Recognition is discussed, infra, p 1069 et seq.

[47] S 3, as amended by Courts Act 2003, Sch 10, para 1.

[48] *Collister v Collister* [1972] 1 WLR 54.

[49] Indeed the 1920 Act is being replaced in the case of Commonwealth countries by new Orders made under the 1972 Act; see, eg, SIs 1983/1124, 1983/1125, 2002/788 and 2002/789.

[50] S 21, as amended by Courts Act 2003, Sch 10, para 1.

[51] 1972 Act, ss 5, 9, as amended by the Domestic Proceedings and Magistrates' Courts Act 1978, s 54; the Civil Jurisdiction and Judgments Act 1982, Sch 11, para 12; the Maintenance Enforcement Act 1991, Sch 1, para 14; the Maintenance Orders (Reciprocal Enforcement) Act 1992, Sch I, Part II; Access to Justice Act 1999, Sch 13, para 71; and the Courts Act 2003, Sch 8, para 153. For an example, see *Killen v Killen* 1981 SLT (Sh Ct) 77.

[52] By s 25(1) the Crown, by Order in Council, may declare that any country or territory specified in the Order, being a country or territory outside the United Kingdom to which the 1956 Maintenance Convention extends, is a Convention country for the purposes of Part II of the 1972 Act. See SIs 1975/423, 1978/279, 1982/1530, 1996/1925, and 2002/2839.

in which the applicant resides.[53] This application is forwarded through diplomatic channels to that foreign country and there are no judicial proceedings in England. In the converse case, where a foreign application is received in England by the designated officer for the magistrates' court which is acting in the local justice area in which the defendant resides,[54] the court proceeds just as if the complainant was before the English court.[55]

Under section 40 of the 1972 Act,[56] special recognition arrangements may be made with countries designated by Order in Council, applying modified versions of either Part I or Part II to such countries. Under this provision, there are, for example, reciprocal arrangements applying an amended version of Part I[57] to the Republic of Ireland,[58] to a majority of the states in the USA,[59] and to countries which are parties to the 1973 Hague Convention on the Recognition and Enforcement of Decisions Relating to Maintenance Obligations.[60] A modified version of Part II has also been applied to certain states in the USA.[61]

(b) Jurisdiction under the Brussels/Lugano system

As previously mentioned, the Brussels/Lugano system (comprising four different sets of rules, ie: those contained in the Brussels I Regulation; the EC/Denmark Agreement; the Brussels Convention; and the Lugano Convention), confers general jurisdiction over claims for maintenance, as does the Modified Regulation.[62] The scope of application of each instrument has been explained in Chapter 10 above, and so discussion in this chapter is restricted to the subject of maintenance claims.

The Brussels I Regulation is based on, and updates, the earlier Brussels Convention,[63] which it replaces in virtually all cases.[64] Under the EC/Denmark Agreement,[65] the provisions of the Brussels I Regulation, with minor modifications, are applied by international law to the relations between the Community and Denmark.[66] The Lugano Convention has

---

[53] S 26(3) and (6), as substituted by the Access to Justice Act 1999, Sch 13, paras 71, 76, and as amended by the Courts Act 2003, Sch 8, para 158. In Scotland, the application is submitted to the sheriff clerk for the sheriffdom in which the applicant resides.

[54] S 27B, as substituted and amended by the Courts Act 2003, Sch 8, para 159.

[55] Under s 28A of the 1972 Act (as substituted by the Maintenance Orders (Reciprocal Enforcement) Act 1992, Sch 1, Part II, para 13) an English magistrates' court can entertain an application for maintenance from a person who is residing in England, even though the spouses' marriage had been dissolved or annulled by an overseas decree which is recognised as valid in England.

[56] As amended by the Civil Jurisdiction and Judgments Act 1982, Sch 11, para 17.

[57] See SI 2001/410.

[58] SI 1993/594; see *Macaulay v Macaulay* [1991] 1 WLR 179; *R v West London Magistrates' Court, ex p Emmett* [1993] 2 FLR 663; and see *Sachs v Standard Chartered Bank (Ireland) Ltd* [1987] ILRM 297.

[59] SI 1995/ 2709, as amended by SI 2003/776.

[60] SI 1993/593, SI 1994/1902, SI 1999/1318, SI 2001/2567, SI 2002/2838; and see *Armitage v Nanchen* (1983) 4 FLR 293.

[61] SI 1993/591.

[62] See supra, Chapter 10.

[63] Although the Brussels Convention has been largely replaced by the Brussels I Regulation, the Convention still applies in relation to certain territories of Member States (see, generally, supra, Chapter 10). The Brussels Convention rule on special jurisdiction in matters relating to maintenance does not differ from that in the Brussels I Regulation.

[64] Art 68(1) of the Brussels I Regulation.

[65] In respect of which see, generally, supra, Chapter 10.

[66] For the purposes of the Agreement, application of the provisions of the Regulation is modified, but such modifications as concern maintenance do not relate to jurisdiction. For modifications in relation to enforcement, see supra, p 637 and infra, p 1071.

been aligned with the Brussels I Regulation, and the terms of the two are very similar.[67] Similarly, the maintenance provision of the Modified Regulation[68] mirrors, with only minor modification, that contained in the Brussels I Regulation.[69] Unless stated otherwise, references in this section to the Brussels I Regulation should be read as including reference to the Brussels Convention, the EC/Denmark Agreement, and the Lugano Convention.

(i) What are maintenance orders?

Article 1 of the Brussels I Regulation declares that: "This Regulation shall apply in civil and commercial matters whatever the nature of the court or tribunal." No definition is given of "civil and commercial matters", but there is a ground of special jurisdiction under Article 5(2) dealing with maintenance, from which it can be inferred that the term "civil matters" includes maintenance.[70] The concept of "matters relating to maintenance"[71] is not defined in the Regulation.[72] Whether an application is to be regarded as a "matter relating to maintenance" depends on an autonomous interpretation of the term, derived from the judgments of the European Court of Justice: "the label given to the claim by national law is not decisive".[73] "Whether a claim relates to maintenance will depend on its purpose, and in particular whether it is designed to enable one spouse to provide for himself or herself or if the needs and resources of each spouse are taken into consideration in the determination of its amount, or where the capital sum set is designed to ensure a predetermined level of income."[74] Some assistance may be derived from *De Cavel v De Cavel*[75] which illustrates that financial relief in its common form of periodical payments falls within the meaning of maintenance. There an order was made in the course of divorce proceedings for interim payments to be paid on a monthly basis. This was held to be within the Brussels Convention (and now, therefore, the Brussels I Regulation), but the court stressed that the payments were designed to support the spouse and were based on need. It has also been authoritatively stated that maintenance can include lump sum orders or transfers of property, if these are intended to ensure the support of a spouse.[76] The fact that a financial relief order is ancillary to a divorce order or

---

[67] See generally supra, Chapter 10. As far as rules of jurisdiction are concerned (Title 2, Arts 2–31), there are only two differences of substance between the Brussels I Regulation/Brussels Convention and the Lugano Convention, one of which concerns special jurisdiction in matters relating to maintenance. See supra, p 341.

[68] See generally supra, Chapter 10.

[69] See supra, p 345.

[70] But see *Gemeente Steenbergen v Baten* [2002] ECR I-10527, [2003] 1 WLR 1996 — claimant Dutch public authority not acting under the civil law rules governing maintenance obligations: where the action under a right of recourse is founded on provisions by which the legislature conferred on the public body a prerogative of its own, that action cannot be regarded as being brought in "civil matters" (at [36]).

[71] Art 5(2).

[72] See Schlosser Report, pp 101–105.

[73] *Moore v Moore* [2007] EWCA Civ 361, [2007] IL Pr 36, per THORPE LJ, at [80].

[74] Ibid, per THORPE LJ, at [80].

[75] Case 120/79 [1980] ECR 731, [1980] 3 CMLR 1. It does not matter whether the order is interim or final: *De Cavel v De Cavel* Case 143/78 [1979] ECR 1055, [1979] 2 CMLR 547.

[76] Schlosser Report, p 102. *Moore v Moore* [2007] EWCA Civ 361, [2007] IL Pr 36, per THORPE LJ, at [76] and [80].

decree or other judgment outside the Brussels/Lugano system[77] does not mean that the financial relief order is excluded. Indeed, specific mention is made of such a case in Article 5(2).

Applying these criteria to the various financial orders that can be made by English courts, it is clear that financial orders (periodical or lump sum) made during the subsistence of a marriage, both for a spouse and for children being designed for support, must rank as maintenance orders within the Brussels I Regulation. The position where there is a divorce, or annulment, is more difficult. Financial orders for periodical payments to be made to a child or spouse are designed to support that person and must, therefore, be within the Regulation. The position in respect of lump sum payments is more problematical. Sometimes these are undoubtedly concerned with the support of a spouse, and will constitute "maintenance";[78] whereas other lump sum payments may be more in the nature of compensation for non-material damage or a division of matrimonial property[79] and will fall outside the meaning of maintenance.[80] Consequently, the latter will fall outside the special jurisdictional rules for "maintenance".[81] Such non-maintenance lump sum payments are also likely to fall outside the scope of the Brussels I Regulation altogether because they will be caught by the exclusion relating to rights in property arising out of a matrimonial relationship.[82] It is not clear whether orders made by the English courts under Part III of the Matrimonial and Family Proceedings Act 1984 after the marriage has been ended by a foreign divorce or annulment[83] fall within the meaning of maintenance. It can be argued that, as the marriage is already at an end before the proceedings in England begin, such orders are not "maintenance" orders.[84]

(ii) Jurisdictional rules

(a) General rules

A person who is seeking an order for financial relief which falls within the Brussels I Regulation has a number of jurisdictional options open to him. First, he can sue under any of the generally applicable jurisdictional rules of the Regulation. This means that the English courts will have jurisdiction if the respondent is domiciled in England[85] within the special meaning of domicile for the purposes of the Regulation;[86] if the parties have

---

[77] Divorce, being a matter of status, is outside the scope of the Brussels I Regulation (Art 1(2)(a)), the EC/Denmark Agreement, the Brussels Convention, and the Lugano Convention.

[78] Case C-220/95 *Van den Boogard v Laumen* [1997] QB 759, discussed supra, p 245 et seq.

[79] *Moore v Moore* [2007] EWCA Civ 361, [2007] IL Pr 36, per THORPE LJ, at para [80]: "Where the provision is solely concerned with dividing property between the spouses, the decision will be concerned with rights in property arising out of a matrimonial relationship and will not therefore be enforceable under Brussels I."

[80] Eg *Moore v Moore* [2007] EWCA Civ 361, [2007] IL Pr 36, per THORPE LJ, at [76] and [80]. The essential object of H's application was to achieve sharing of the property on his terms (cf *Miller v Miller, McFarlane v McFarlane* [2006] UKHL 24, [2006] 2 AC 618, at [16] and [141]), rather than an order based on financial needs, and so there was no scope for application of Art 5(2) of the Brussels Convention.

[81] Art 5(2), infra.

[82] Art 1(2)(a), discussed in this context supra, pp 218–219.

[83] Infra, pp 1063–1064.

[84] The inter-relation of Part III of the 1984 Act with the Brussels/Lugano system is discussed, infra, p 1060 et seq.

[85] Art 2, supra, pp 222–224.

[86] S 41 of the 1982 Act, as amended by the 1991 Act, Sch 2, para 16, SI 2001/3929, and SI 2007/1655. See generally supra, p 223.

chosen the jurisdiction of the English courts;[87] or if the respondent submits to the jurisdiction of the English courts.[88]

(b) Special rules

In addition to the rules of general application just discussed, Article 5(2)[89] of the Brussels I Regulation provides special jurisdictional rules for maintenance cases. It states that claims may be brought against a respondent domiciled in another Member State, as follows:

> In matters relating to maintenance, in the courts for the place[90] where the maintenance creditor is domiciled or habitually resident or, if the matter is ancillary to proceedings concerning the status of a person, in the court which, according to its own law, has jurisdiction to entertain those proceedings, unless that jurisdiction is based solely on the nationality of one of the parties.[91]

The effect of this provision is to add two more bases of jurisdiction.[92] The jurisdictional link must be with the maintenance creditor, a concept which has been given an autonomous Community meaning. It covers any person applying for maintenance, including a person bringing a maintenance action for the first time.[93] A maintenance creditor does not need to have obtained a maintenance order recognising his/her entitlement to maintenance. An English court will be able to entertain maintenance proceedings against a defendant domiciled in another Member State if the petitioner is domiciled in England in the Regulation sense, or is habitually resident in England. Article 5(2) is a rare case where the Regulation uses the concept of habitual residence. The domicile of an individual is defined under the Civil Jurisdiction and Judgments Order 2001[94] in a way that is so close to the English concept of habitual residence that the use of habitual residence[95] as an alternative to domicile under Article 5(2) is unlikely to widen the scope of the provision. Nonetheless, Article 5(2) is more obviously pro-claimant in its terms than any other form of special jurisdiction, and is designed to protect the weaker party,[96] the maintenance creditor. The claimant's domicile is an appropriate forum for trial, since a court there is best able to gauge the claimant's needs. So, what happens if the maintenance debtor wants to sue, for example, for a reduction in his periodical payments? The English courts will have jurisdiction if one of the general jurisdictional bases is satisfied, the most

---

[87] Art 23, supra, p 283 et seq.

[88] Art 24, supra, p 296 et seq.

[89] Discussed more fully, supra, pp 245–246.

[90] Being another Member State.

[91] The proviso at the end of Art 5(2) is meaningless in the light of Art 3 of the Brussels II *bis* Regulation, which does not allow jurisdiction to be exercised in the courts of a Member State in matters relating to divorce, legal separation or marriage annulment on the basis of only one party's nationality. Art 3(b) provides that jurisdiction shall lie with the courts of the Member State of the nationality of both spouses (or, in the case of the United Kingdom and Ireland, of the "domicile" of both spouses).

[92] If a maintenance obligation arises from an agreement and not from a court order, Art 5(2) will be inapplicable; but the special contractual head of jurisdiction under Art 5(1) of the Brussels I Regulation may be applicable, supra, p 229 et seq. See the Schlosser Report, pp 101–102.

[93] Case C-295/95 *Farrell v Long* [1997] ECR I-1683: "maintenance creditor" is to be interpreted as covering any person claiming maintenance, as well as a person whose status as a maintenance creditor and entitlement to maintenance has been recognised by a previous judicial decision.

[94] SI 2001/3929; see also SI 2007/1655. Supra, p 223.

[95] Supra, p 185 et seq.

[96] Cf Sections 3, 4 and 5 of Chapter II of the Brussels I Regulation, discussed, supra, p 266 et seq.

obvious being if the maintenance creditor is domiciled in England.[97] What if he is only habitually resident in England? The maintenance creditor can undoubtedly bring proceedings in England, by reason of Article 5(2), but can the maintenance debtor sue in England on the basis of the creditor's habitual residence? Opinions are divided on this, for the wording of Article 5(2) does not contain any indication as to the party who may be the applicant, but if, in a case under the Brussels I Regulation, the European Court of Justice follows the authoritative Schlosser Report,[98] jurisdiction will be denied.[99] However, it has been held that a public body which seeks reimbursement from the maintenance debtor of sums paid by way of an education grant to a maintenance creditor, to whose rights it is subrogated, cannot rely on the special jurisdiction provision since the public body is not in a weaker position with regard to the maintenance debtor.[100] The derogation in Article 5(2) is intended to protect maintenance creditors, who are usually regarded as being the weaker party, by providing an alternative basis of jurisdiction.

Article 5(2) also confers jurisdiction on the English courts if the maintenance proceedings are ancillary to "proceedings concerning the status of a person", provided the court already has jurisdiction over those status proceedings under the relevant jurisdictional rules.[101] This is important because, as we have seen, many applications for financial relief are made in conjunction with divorce proceedings, and there is a recognised practice of combining maintenance claims (which on their own are within the scope of the Brussels I Regulation) with main proceedings for divorce (which on their own are outside the scope of that Regulation). Whilst no definition is provided in the Brussels I Regulation of proceedings concerning status, there seems little doubt that the term will cover proceedings for divorce, nullity or judicial separation. So, an English court will be able to make a maintenance order in such proceedings against a respondent habitually resident in another Member State if the court has jurisdiction over the main proceedings on the basis of, inter alia, both spouses being domiciled in England.[102]

Maintenance orders are often varied and sometimes revoked. A court which made the original order may only vary or revoke it, at a later date, if it still has jurisdiction under the Brussels I Regulation.[103] There should be no problem with maintenance orders made in England which are ancillary to divorce, etc proceedings, because the English court, under English rules, retains jurisdiction to vary or revoke the order, even though the original basis of jurisdiction has gone.[104] If, however, jurisdiction is based on the domicile or habitual residence of the maintenance creditor under Article 5(2), an English court will be unable to vary or revoke its own order if the maintenance creditor is neither domiciled nor habitually resident in England at the time of the later proceedings, assuming

---

[97] In such a case the maintenance creditor's domicile also satisfies Art 2.

[98] Para 107.

[99] Collins, *The Civil Jurisdiction and Judgments Act 1982*, p 58; Anton and Beaumont's, *Civil Jurisdiction in Scotland* (2nd edn), para 5.36; Kaye, *Civil Jurisdiction and Enforcement of Judgments*, p 545; cf Hartley, *Civil Jurisdiction and Judgments*, pp 49, 50.

[100] Case C-433/01 *Freistaat Bayern v Jan Blijdenstein* [2004] ECR1-981, [2004] IL Pr 8.

[101] Domicile and Matrimonial Proceedings Act 1973, s 5 (supra, p 944 et seq), referring, in the first instance, to the rules contained in the Brussels II *bis* Regulation, Chapter II, Section I, discussed, supra, pp 945–946.

[102] Brussels II *bis* Regulation, Art 3(b).

[103] Jenard Report, p 25; Schlosser Report, paras 107–108.

[104] Supra, p 949.

that the maintenance debtor is still domiciled in a Member State.[105] If he is not, the Brussels I Regulation will cease to apply and the English courts will have to decide the jurisdictional issue for themselves and, following the approach to variation of orders ancillary to divorce, etc proceedings, ought to take jurisdiction.

As far as jurisdiction under the Lugano Convention is concerned,[106] there are only two differences of substance between the Brussels I Regulation and the Lugano Convention, one of which concerns the special jurisdiction in matters relating to maintenance. Article 5(2) of the Lugano Convention sets out an additional alternative state (bound by the Convention) in which a person domiciled in a state bound by the Convention may be sued, namely, "(c) in the court which, according to its own law, has jurisdiction to entertain proceedings concerning parental responsibility, if the matter relating to maintenance is ancillary to those proceedings, unless that jurisdiction is based solely on the nationality of one of the parties". The aim of new sub-paragraph (c) is limited to ensuring equivalence between Community law and the Lugano Convention. In particular, Recital (11) of the Brussels II *bis* Regulation clarifies the jurisdiction rule for maintenance claims where these are ancillary to proceedings concerning parental responsibility, by providing that jurisdiction for such claims shall be determined on the basis of Article 5(2) of the Brussels I Regulation. In order to eliminate doubt on this matter in the Lugano Convention, the new Article 5(2)(c) has been included in the instrument.

The rule of special jurisdiction laid down in rule 3(b) of the Modified Regulation[107] states that a person domiciled in a part of the United Kingdom may, in another part of the United Kingdom be sued:

> in matters relating to maintenance, in the courts for the place where the maintenance creditor is domiciled or habitually resident or, if the matter is ancillary to proceedings concerning the status of a person, in the court which, according to its own law, has jurisdiction to entertain those proceedings, unless that jurisdiction is based solely on the nationality of one of the parties.

This wording, which is designed to give local jurisdiction, allocates jurisdiction to the courts in a part of the United Kingdom.

(c) Inter-relation of the Brussels/Lugano system with other bases of jurisdiction

Finally, there is the question of the inter-relation of jurisdiction under the Brussels/Lugano system with the other jurisdictional bases already discussed. Difficulty arises from the fact that, for example, the jurisdictional rules of the Brussels/Lugano system provide that only the courts given jurisdiction under the Brussels I Regulation/EC-Denmark Agreement/Brussels Convention/Lugano Convention, as appropriate, may exercise it. This means that, in the case of a respondent who is domiciled (in the Brussels I Regulation sense) in another part of the United Kingdom or in another Member State and the proceedings concern "maintenance" in the Regulation sense, there may be

---

[105] And will have to recognise a variation or revocation made by a court in another Member State.
[106] Title 2, Arts 2–31. See, eg, *Bentinck v Bentinck* [2007] EWCA Civ 175 (CA (Civ Div)).
[107] SI 2001/3929, as amended by SI 2007/1655. See generally supra, Chapter 10.

circumstances in which an English court is deprived of jurisdiction. There is no difficulty with the jurisdiction ancillary to divorce, etc proceedings because the Brussels I Regulation itself provides for that. Nor is there any difficulty[108] with jurisdiction under Part II of the Maintenance Orders (Reciprocal Enforcement) Act 1972, which applies to all European Community Member States except Ireland. There is probably no difficulty either in the case of Ireland, because the amended version of Part I of the 1972 Act applicable to Ireland under section 40 of the 1972 Act[109] would seem to constitute a convention containing jurisdictional rules within the meaning of Article 71 of the Brussels I Regulation. However, in the case of the amended version of Part I of the 1972 Act which, under section 40, gives effect to the 1973 Hague Maintenance Convention,[110] there is more difficulty. Although the 1973 Convention extends to a number of European Community Member States,[111] the jurisdictional provisions in the Order in Council,[112] which provides an amended version of Part I of the 1972 Act, are not derived from that Convention. Similar difficulties arise in relation to the Lugano Convention because the 1973 Hague Convention applies to two EFTA States also.[113] This suggests that Article 71 of the Brussels I Regulation[114] does not apply, with the apparent result that, if the case falls within the Brussels I Regulation, the parties cannot use the procedures provided under section 40 of the 1972 Act. Furthermore, the English courts will be unable to exercise any of their other heads of jurisdiction where the respondent is domiciled in a Member State and the claim is within the terms of the Brussels I Regulation. This will, for example, exclude jurisdiction to make orders for failure to provide maintenance on the basis of the respondent's residence in England,[115] or the jurisdiction of the magistrates' courts to make orders based on the residence of the respondent,[116] or orders under the Maintenance Orders (Facilities for Enforcement) Act 1920 or under Part I of the Maintenance Orders (Reciprocal Enforcement) Act 1972 (in the case of a person domiciled in a Member State to which Part I does not apply).

2. FINANCIAL RELIEF AFTER A FOREIGN DIVORCE/DISSOLUTION, ANNULMENT OR LEGAL SEPARATION

There are two issues to be examined in this context: the effect of a foreign divorce, annulment or legal separation on a pre-existing English order for financial relief, and the powers of the English court to grant such relief notwithstanding a prior foreign divorce, etc.

---

[108] This is because Art 71 of the Brussels I Regulation gives overriding effect to other conventions which govern jurisdiction or recognition and enforcement to which the Member States are parties. Cf Lugano Convention, Art 67.

[109] Supplemented by SI 2001/410.

[110] Infra, pp 1070–1071.

[111] Denmark, France, Germany, Italy, Luxembourg, the Netherlands, Portugal, Spain, Finland and Sweden.

[112] SI 1979/1317, SI 1993/593, SI 1994/1902, SI 1999/1318, SI 2001/2567, and SI 2002/2838.

[113] Norway and Switzerland.

[114] Cf Lugano Convention, Art 67.

[115] Matrimonial Causes Act 1973, s 27(2).

[116] Supra, p 1053.

(a) Effect of foreign divorce, etc on financial relief already granted in England

Under English domestic law, a maintenance order granted by a magistrates' court could be continued in the discretion of the magistrates even after the marriage had been dissolved in England.[117] The Court of Appeal has decided that the position is the same if the marriage is dissolved by a foreign divorce recognised in England;[118] and the same principle has been applied to an interim order for maintenance made by a divorce county court, notwithstanding a later foreign divorce recognised in England.[119] The English court retains its discretion to continue, vary or discharge the English maintenance order, but the changed marital circumstances of the parties may well affect their financial position and the view taken thereof by the court, as where dower became payable on the termination of a marriage by *talak*.[120]

(b) Powers of English court to grant financial relief, despite an earlier foreign divorce/dissolution, annulment or legal separation

(i) The common law position

Until Part III of the Matrimonial and Family Proceedings Act 1984 came into force, the general rule was that, once a marriage had been dissolved or annulled, the English court's power to grant financial relief came to an end.[121] No ancillary relief could be granted on the basis of a foreign divorce. The more liberal the English rules for the recognition of foreign divorces, etc, the greater the problem for spouses who wished to seek financial relief in England.[122] Various devices were utilised by the courts to minimise the difficulties of those who sought financial relief in England, such as expediting English proceedings if there were parallel foreign ones,[123] or granting relief in favour of a child though none could be granted to a parent.[124] Useful though these devices were, the law was undoubtedly unsatisfactory in that, if the foreign proceedings had included no, or inadequate, financial provision for an English spouse (usually the wife) she could find herself destitute in England with social security as her only source of financial support. This could be so even though her husband lived in England and had substantial assets in England. Furthermore, the inability of the English courts to grant relief if a foreign divorce was recognised in England led regularly to challenges to the validity of such divorces for recognition purposes. This problem[125] led to proposals for reform being made by the Law Commission[126] which were carried into effect by Part III of the Matrimonial and Family Proceedings Act 1984; and this applies whether the foreign divorce was obtained before or after Part III came into effect.[127]

---

[117] *Bragg v Bragg* [1925] P 20; and see Matrimonial Causes Act 1973, s 28; Domestic Proceedings and Magistrates' Courts Act 1978, s 4.

[118] *Wood v Wood* [1957] P 254.

[119] *Newmarch v Newmarch* [1978] Fam 79.

[120] *Qureshi v Qureshi* [1972] Fam 173 at 200–201.

[121] *Moore v Bull* [1891] P 279.

[122] Eg *Turczak v Turczak* [1970] P 198.

[123] Eg *Torok v Torok* [1973] 1 WLR 1066; *Bryant v Bryant* (1980) 11 Fam Law 85.

[124] See *P (LE) v P (JM)* [1971] P 318; *Hack v Hack* (1976) 6 Fam Law 177.

[125] Exemplified by *Quazi v Quazi* [1980] AC 744.

[126] Law Com No 117 (1982).

[127] *Chebaro v Chebaro* [1987] Fam 127.

(ii) Part III of the Matrimonial and Family Proceedings Act 1984[128]

In considering the powers of the English court[129] to grant matrimonial relief after a foreign divorce, etc, it is necessary to consider the orders which the court may make, the bases of jurisdiction available for the making of such orders and certain limitations or controls on the courts' powers.

Powers equivalent to those set out in Part III of the 1984 Act operate in respect of civil partners by virtue of section 72(4) of the Civil Partnership Act 2004. Schedule 7 to the 2004 Act makes provision for financial relief in England after a civil partnership has been dissolved or annulled, or civil partners have been legally separated, in a country outside the British Islands. The following commentary on Part III of the 1984 Act should be read as applying, *mutatis mutandis*, to the grant of financial relief in respect of civil partnerships, in terms of the 2004 Act.

(a) Orders which the court can make

The powers conferred by Part III of the 1984 Act apply to the High Court and to certain divorce county courts, but not to magistrates' courts.[130] The general approach is that the court can make any of the orders which it could make on granting an English decree of divorce, annulment or judicial separation,[131] including consent orders,[132] orders for the transfer of tenancies[133] and orders relating to children.[134] So, notwithstanding a foreign divorce, the English court will, for example, be able to make periodical payments orders lump sum orders, property adjustment orders, and pension sharing orders.[135] In deciding whether to make any of the orders which it could make on granting a decree, the court must have regard to a range of matters[136] which are essentially the same as if it were granting a decree itself.[137] In addition, section 18(6) provides as follows:

> Where an order has been made by a court outside England and Wales for the making of payments or the transfer of property by a party to the marriage, the court in considering in accordance with this section the financial resources of the other party to the marriage or a child of the family shall have regard to the extent to which that order has been complied with or is likely to be complied with.

The purpose of this provision is to enable the court to take account of any foreign order which has been made and of its likely effectiveness.[138] Furthermore, the English

---

[128] See the Family Proceedings Rules, 1991, rr 3.17–3.19; and see Gordon, *Foreign Divorces: English Law and Practice*, Chapter 11.

[129] Part IV of the 1984 Act confers similar, but more limited, powers on the Scottish courts, following the report of the Scottish Law Commission in Scot Law Com No 72 (1982). See Crawford and Carruthers, para 13-24.

[130] S 27.

[131] Supra, p 944 et seq.

[132] S 19.

[133] Ss 17, 19, 21–22. There are also provisions similar to those in the Matrimonial Causes Act 1973 for avoiding transactions designed to defeat applications for financial relief (s 23) and, for preventing transactions intended to defeat prospective applications (s 24). The court's powers are limited to orders relating to the matrimonial home (s 20) in cases when jurisdiction is taken solely on the basis of the presence of that home in England, infra, p 1064.

[134] Children Act 1989, s 8(4)(g).

[135] S 17, as amended by the Welfare Reform and Pensions Act 1999.

[136] S 18, as amended by the Welfare Reform and Pensions Act 1999.

[137] See Matrimonial Causes Act 1973, ss 25, 25A.

[138] Eg *M v M (Financial Provision After Foreign Divorce)* [1994] 1 FLR 399.

court may, if it thinks it appropriate, make an order in relation to matrimonial assets which are abroad, just as would seem to be the case in normal English matrimonial proceedings.[139]

(b) Jurisdiction of the English courts

There are three main bases of jurisdiction laid down by section 15(1) of the 1984 Act,[140] ie:

(a) the domicile in England and Wales of either party to the marriage—this can be at one of two dates: either the start of the English proceedings for relief[141] or the date when the foreign divorce, etc took effect in the foreign country;[142]

(b) the habitual residence in England and Wales of either party to the marriage for one year ending on either of the two dates relevant to domicile, ie the date of application for leave to bring the English proceedings or the date on which the foreign divorce, etc took effect in the country in which it was obtained;

(c) either or both of the parties to the marriage had at the date of application for leave to bring the English proceedings a beneficial interest in possession in a dwelling-house[143] in England and Wales which was at some time during the marriage a matrimonial home of the parties to the marriage.

In the Law Commission's view, the use of the same jurisdictional criteria of domicile and habitual residence as then[144] applied to divorce petitions struck the proper balance of formulating "jurisdictional rules strict enough to prevent persons, whose marriage is insufficiently connected with this country to make it appropriate for the English court to adjudicate on financial matters, from invoking the court's powers; but not so strict as to exclude meritorious cases".[145] The third head of jurisdiction, that there had been a matrimonial home in England, might be thought to cause more problems in terms of striking the correct balance and, indeed, was provisionally rejected by the Law Commission at one stage.[146] It was, however, felt necessary[147] to give the court power to deal with the quite common situation where the parties, though living abroad at the date of the divorce, had lived previously in England and where their only substantial asset was the former matrimonial home. The danger perceived by the Law Commission[148] that this head of jurisdiction could be too wide, in giving the court power to make orders in relation to all the property of persons who had left England long ago, has been met by limiting the

---

[139] *Razelos v Razelos (No 2)* [1970] 1 WLR 392 at 400, 401; and see *Hunter v Hunter* [1962] P 1; *Tallack v Tallack* [1927] P 211; *Hamlin v Hamlin* [1986] Fam 11.

[140] Cf, for civil partnerships, Civil Partnership Act 2004, Sch 7, para 7.

[141] Technically, the date of the application for leave, under s 13 of the 1984 Act, infra, p 1066.

[142] For detailed discussion of the reasons for selecting these alternative dates, see Law Commission Working Paper No 77 (1980), paras 33, 38.

[143] Defined in s 27.

[144] See now Domicile and Matrimonial Proceedings Act 1973, s 5, referring primarily to the rules of jurisdiction contained in the Brussels II *bis* Regulation (supra, p 945).

[145] Law Commission Working Paper No 77 (1980), para 31, and see Law Com No 117 (1982), paras 2.7–2.8.

[146] Ibid, para 44.

[147] Law Com No 117 (1982), paras 2.8–2.9.

[148] Ibid, para 2.10.

orders which the court may make, when exercising this head of jurisdiction alone, to orders relating to the former matrimonial home.[149]

Part III of the Matrimonial and Family Proceedings Act 1984 also provides for dovetailing these rules of jurisdiction into the structure of the Brussels/Lugano system.[150] It will be recalled[151] that the Brussels I Regulation extends the jurisdiction to grant maintenance orders, that no definition of maintenance orders is to be found in that instrument, and that it is possible that the Court of Justice in a case falling under the Brussels I Regulation might decide that an order made under Part III of the 1984 Act is not within that Regulation because it is first granted after the spouses' marriage has come to an end. Nevertheless, this possibility cannot be relied on because, even if the Regulation is applicable, it will not apply to those orders under the 1984 Act which concern "rights in property arising out of a matrimonial relationship".[152] In order to deal with the possibility of clashes between the jurisdictional rules of the Brussels I Regulation and of the 1984 Act, section 15(2) of the 1984 Act provides that where the jurisdiction of the court to entertain proceedings under Part III of the 1984 Act would fall to be determined by reference to the jurisdictional requirements imposed by virtue of Part I of the 1982 Act, or by virtue of the Brussels I Regulation,[153] then (a) satisfaction of the jurisdiction provisions laid down in section 15(1) of the 1984 Act shall not obviate the need to satisfy the requirements imposed by the Regulation or the 1982 Act; and (b) satisfaction of the requirements imposed by virtue of the Regulation or the 1982 Act shall obviate the need to satisfy the requirements of section 15(1) of the 1984 Act.[154] Assuming that some orders, at least, made under Part III of the 1984 Act fall within the Brussels I Regulation,[155] the Regulation[156] shall apply, in all cases where a defendant is domiciled in a country which is a European Union Member State,[157] and in such cases the court of the defendant's domicile will have jurisdiction, as will that of the country where the "maintenance creditor" is domiciled or habitually resident.[158] Where the maintenance order is ancillary to divorce or similar proceedings, the court which has jurisdiction over those proceedings may also make a maintenance order.[159]

(c) "Filter" mechanisms

In making proposals for giving the courts power to make financial relief orders after foreign divorces, etc the Law Commission was much concerned that the relief should be

---

[149] 1984 Act, s 20; and there is in such cases no power to make interim maintenance orders under s 14 (s 14(2)).

[150] Defined supra, Chapter 11. 1984 Act, s 15(2), as amended by Sch 1(1), para 13 of the Civil Jurisdiction and Judgments Regulations, SI 2007/1655.

[151] Supra, p 1055.

[152] Art 1(1). The meaning of this exclusion from the scope of the Brussels I Regulation is not clear; see supra, pp 218–219.

[153] As amended from time to time, and as applied by the EC/Denmark Agreement. 1984 Act, s 15(2), as amended by Sch 1(1), para 13 of the Civil Jurisdiction and Judgments Regulations, SI 2007/1655.

[154] S 15(2), as amended by Sch 1(1), para 13 of the Civil Jurisdiction and Judgments Regulations, SI 2007/1655.

[155] Or the EC/Denmark Agreement, or the Brussels Convention, or the Lugano Convention, respectively.

[156] Or the EC/Denmark Agreement, or the Brussels Convention, or the Lugano Convention, as appropriate.

[157] Or Denmark, by virtue of the EC/Denmark Agreement; or a Contracting State to the Brussels Convention; or a State bound by the Lugano Convention, as appropriate.

[158] Art 5(2). Or, in the case of the Lugano Convention, when Art 5(2)(c) applies; see supra, p 345.

[159] Ibid.

"confined to those cases in which it is appropriate for the English court to intervene".[160] In addition to rules as to jurisdiction, Part III of the 1984 Act contains two further means[161] for limiting relief to appropriate cases.[162] The first is a filter mechanism for applications to the court. Under section 13 of the 1984 Act no application for a financial relief order can be made unless the leave of the court has been obtained, and "the court shall not grant leave unless it considers that there is substantial ground for the making of an application".[163] The paradigm case creating the need for the legislation is one where the foreign court offered no rights to financial provision,[164] but the existence of a foreign financial provision order is no bar as such to the English application.[165] This is because the foreign order may be inadequate or inappropriate.[166] Furthermore, leave may be granted subject to such conditions as the court thinks fit,[167] such as an undertaking not to enforce a foreign order. If, however, the court concludes that it would not be appropriate (under the second filter mechanism) for an order to be made because, for example, the matter of financial relief is properly before or has been appropriately decided by a foreign court, it should refuse leave.[168] The English court will be cautious about making an order for financial relief in England when "a mature, foreign jurisdiction with its own statutory approach, properly seised of the matter, has already investigated and ruled on financial relief".[169] It is not necessary[170] in order to obtain the court's leave for the applicant to

---

[160] Law Com No 117 (1982), para 2.1.

[161] To be read in conjunction: *Holmes v Holmes* [1989] Fam 47, per Purchas LJ, at 53; *Jordan v Jordan* [2000] 1 WLR 210, per Thorpe LJ, at 218; and *Moore v Moore* [2007] EWCA Civ 361, [2007] IL Pr 36, per Thorpe LJ, at [107].

[162] To block unmeritorious applications under the Act and to avoid abuse of its underlying purpose: *M v L (Financial Relief after Overseas Divorce)* [2003] EWHC 328, [2003] 2 FLR 425.

[163] *Jordan v Jordan* [2000] 1 WLR 210, per Thorpe LJ, at 220; and *Ella v Ella* [2007] EWCA Civ 99, per Charles J, at [62]. It is necessary for the applicant to place all the material facts before the court: *W v W* [1989] 1 FLR 22; *M v M (Financial Provision After Foreign Divorce)* [1994] 1 FLR 399. Cf, for civil partnerships, Civil Partnership Act 2004, Sch 7, para 4.

[164] *Jordan v Jordan* [2000] 1 WLR 210, per Thorpe LJ, at 219.

[165] S 13(2). *Jordan v Jordan* [2000] 1 WLR 210, per Thorpe LJ, at 219: "after Parliament had provided the remedies for the paradigm case, attempts were repeatedly made to extend the statutory provisions to obtain for the applicant some specific outcome or target which she had failed to achieve in the jurisdiction where the marriage had been dissolved".

[166] Eg *A v S (Financial Relief after Overseas US Divorce)* [2002] EWHC 1157, [2003] 1 FLR 431, per Bodey J, at [66]: "When looking at the overall justice as between the parties ..., an important distinction may be as between when the foreign jurisdiction has fully determined all relevant issues of fact which might go to the justice of the case and when it has not."

[167] S 13(3).

[168] *Holmes v Holmes* [1989] Fam 47; *M v M (Financial Provision After Foreign Divorce)* [1994] 1 FLR 399; *Hewitson v Hewitson* [1995] Fam 100, CA; *N v N (Foreign Divorce: Financial Relief)* [1997] 1 FLR 900. *Jordan v Jordan* [2000] 1 WLR 210, per Thorpe LJ, at 219: "*Holmes v Holmes* and the subsequent cases are in the main restrictive and negative in conclusion, defining and policing the boundary between relieving hardship in the paradigm case and disqualifying the forum shopper for the applicant seeking a second bite of the cherry". Cf *A v S (Financial Relief after Overseas US Divorce)* [2002] EWHC 1157, [2003] 1 FLR 431, per Bodey J, at [76]; and *M v L (Financial Relief after Overseas Divorce)* [2003] EWHC 328, [2003] 2 FLR 425, per Coleridge J, at [37] and [54].

[169] *A v S (Financial Relief after Overseas US Divorce)* [2002] EWHC 1157, [2003] 1 FLR 431, per Bodey J, at [75].

[170] *Jordan v Jordan* [2000] 1 WLR 210, per Thorpe LJ, at 221: "Parliament might have so legislated, but it did not. The statutory criteria are fully expressed." Also *Moore v Moore* [2007] EWCA Civ 361, [2007] IL Pr 36, per Thorpe LJ, at [108]; and *A v S (Financial Relief after Overseas US Divorce)* [2002] EWHC 1157, [2003] 1 FLR 431, per Bodey J, at [75]: it is not necessary to look for financial hardship or injustice "although an applicant's case is stronger if such exist".

prove some hardship or injustice: "A case in which the applicant crosses the barriers contained in sections 13 and 16 without proving some specific hardship or injustice is perfectly conceivable."[171]

The second control or filter mechanism operates at the time of the actual hearing of the application, ie once leave to apply has been given[172] and even if the jurisdictional rules are satisfied. Under section 16 the court has to be satisfied that in all the circumstances of the case it is appropriate for a court in England and Wales to make the order and the court is directed to consider a wide range of matters in determining the appropriateness of the venue.[173] These include[174] the connection of the parties with England, with the country where the divorce, etc was obtained or with any other country, the relief ordered in a foreign country and the likely effectiveness of that order,[175] whether there is a right to apply for relief abroad, the existence of property in England in respect of which an order under Part III could be made, the likelihood of any order made under Part III of the 1984 Act being enforceable, and the length of time which has elapsed since the date of the foreign decree.[176] In determining the appropriateness of the English court granting relief, the court will have regard, where there are proceedings in a foreign country, to questions of comity[177] and to the general law relating to the doctrine of *forum non conveniens*.[178]

(d) Other matters

Part III of the 1984 Act gives the English court power to make orders for financial relief not only when a foreign divorce, but also when a foreign annulment or legal separation,[179] is recognised in England. The case for having the same powers in the case of divorce and annulment is strong. In both cases the marriage is at an end[180] and the rules for the recognition of foreign divorces and annulments are now the same.[181] They are also

---

[171] *Jordan v Jordan* [2000] 1 WLR 210, per THORPE LJ, at 221, criticising CAZALET J in *N v N (Foreign Divorce: Financial Relief)* [1997] 1 FLR 900. But see *M v L (Financial Relief after Overseas Divorce)* [2003] EWHC 328, [2003] 2 FLR 425, per COLERIDGE J, at [30].

[172] The court has power to make interim orders between the granting of leave to apply and the full hearing of the application: ss 14, 21.

[173] *Jordan v Jordan* [2000] 1 WLR 210, per THORPE LJ, at 221–228; and *A v S (Financial Relief after Overseas US Divorce)* [2002] EWHC 1157, [2003] 1 FLR 431, per BODEY J, at [74] – [75]. Cf, for civil partnerships, Civil Partnership Act 2004, Sch 7, para 8.

[174] S 16(2); see *Z v Z (Financial Provision: Overseas Divorce)* [1992] 2 FLR 291; *A v S (Financial Relief after Overseas US Divorce)* [2002] EWHC 1157, [2003] 1 FLR 431; and *M v L (Financial Relief after Overseas Divorce)* [2003] EWHC 328, [2003] 2 FLR 425, per COLERIDGE J, at [32].

[175] *Jordan v Jordan* [2000] 1 WLR 210, per THORPE LJ, at 220: "Prima facie, the primary jurisdiction offering comparable rights of equitable redistribution will also offer comparable powers of implementation and enforcement."

[176] *N v N (Foreign Divorce: Financial Relief)* [1997] 1 FLR 900; cf *Lamagni v Lamagni* [1995] 2 FLR 452, CA; and *M v L (Financial Relief after Overseas Divorce)* [2003] EWHC 328, [2003] 2 FLR 425.

[177] *Moore v Moore* [2007] EWCA Civ 361, [2007] IL Pr 36, per THORPE LJ, at [109].

[178] *Holmes v Holmes*, supra; *Ella v Ella* [2007] EWCA Civ 99, per CHARLES J, at [33] – [34]; and see supra, p 426 et seq.

[179] S 12(1).

[180] If a party remarries or forms a civil partnership, then he or she loses the right to apply for relief under the 1984 Act: s 12(2), (3).

[181] Brussels II *bis* Regulation, Ch III; and Family Law Act 1986, Part II, supra, p 986 et seq.

the same in the case of legal separations but in that case the marriage still subsists and there would be no bar to taking divorce proceedings in England and seeking the usual ancillary relief in England.[182] If, however, a divorce decree was not sought, proceedings could be brought on the ground of failure to provide maintenance.[183] The powers of the English court are less extensive in such a case than those provided in Part III of the 1984 Act, and so it was felt desirable[184] to make the latter powers available also in the case of legal separations.

The powers of the court under Part III of the 1984 Act depend not only on there having been a foreign divorce, annulment or legal separation but also on its being entitled to recognition in England.[185] However, the powers are limited to divorces, etc obtained in an "overseas country" which is defined as a country or territory outside the British Islands.[186] This means that the English court has no power to make an order under Part III following, for example, a Scottish divorce or Northern Ireland annulment. It was thought more appropriate, and not too inconvenient, in such a case for the party seeking relief to return to the court which granted the original decree.[187] Furthermore, the powers are limited to divorces obtained "by means of judicial or other proceedings",[188] thus excluding informal divorces despite the fact that they will be recognised in England by virtue of section 46(2) of the Family Law Act 1986.[189]

3. CHOICE OF LAW

There is little doubt that, when an English court is considering an application for maintenance or similar relief, it applies English domestic law,[190] irrespective of the domicile of the parties or any other factors connecting them with some other jurisdiction.[191] However, in cases to which the Maintenance Orders (Facilities for Enforcement) Act 1920 or the Maintenance Orders (Reciprocal Enforcement) Act 1972 apply, there may be a limited number of circumstances where foreign law is relevant by reason of the reciprocal provisions.[192]

---

[182] *Sabbagh v Sabbagh* [1985] FLR 29.

[183] Matrimonial Causes Act 1973, s 27.

[184] See Law Commission Working Paper No 77 (1980), para 64.

[185] S 12(1)(b); *B v B (Divorce: Northern Cyprus)* [2002] 2 FLR 707; and *Emin v Yeldag* [2002] 1 FLR 956 — application for leave granted on the basis of recognition of divorce granted by Turkish Republic of Northern Cyprus, notwithstanding non-recognition by the United Kingdom Government of Northern Cyprus as a country. See Law Commission Working Paper No 77 (1980), para 59. The rules for recognition are discussed supra, p 986 et seq.

[186] S 27.

[187] Law Commission Working Paper No 77 (1980), paras 65–66.

[188] S 12(1)(a).

[189] Supra, p 1010.

[190] 1984 Act, s 18. Eg *A v S (Financial Relief after Overseas US Divorce)* [2002] EWHC 1157, [2003] 1 FLR 431, per BODEY J, at paras 78–80; and *M v L (Financial Relief after Overseas Divorce)* [2003] EWHC 328, [2003] 2 FLR 425, per COLERIDGE J, at [39] et seq.

[191] Eg *Sealey v Callan* [1953] P 135; and see Law Commission Working Paper No 77 (1980), para 56.

[192] See Dicey, Morris and Collins, para 18-208.

4. RECOGNITION AND ENFORCEMENT OF FOREIGN ORDERS

All forms of financial relief, such as orders for periodical payments, the payment of lump sums or maintenance orders granted by a foreign court, may be regarded as foreign judgments in personam.[193] Usually, the foreign court has a power to vary the amounts of such payments, in which event the order will not be recognised in England as it is not "final or conclusive".[194] Where the power to vary is only prospective, any arrears of past payments may be recovered in England.[195] This is an atypical situation and the rules for the recognition and enforcement of foreign orders have not been left to the common law but are essentially statutory in formulation.

(a) Relief ancillary to a foreign divorce, annulment or legal separation

The main legislative provisions in this area are negative in effect. Article 1(3)(e) of the Brussels II *bis* Regulation states that it shall not apply to maintenance proceedings.[196] Similarly, the Family Law Act 1986 provides that nothing in that Act shall be construed as requiring the recognition in England of any maintenance, custody or other ancillary order made in any foreign proceedings for divorce, annulment or legal separation.[197] In such cases, recognition depends on the common law rules for the recognition of foreign judgments,[198] unless covered by any of the statutory provisions considered below. An English court will not recognise a foreign maintenance order ancillary to a foreign divorce, etc where it considers, under the English rules for the recognition of foreign divorces, etc, that the foreign court lacked jurisdiction.[199] For "if the main order goes, then any order which is merely ancillary to that order should go with it".[200]

(b) Maintenance orders made elsewhere in the United Kingdom

A maintenance order made elsewhere in the United Kingdom may, under Part II of the Maintenance Orders Act 1950,[201] be registered in an English court if the person liable to make the payments resides in England and it is regarded as convenient that the order should be enforceable in England.[202]

---

[193] Discussed supra, p 516 et seq, and see especially the critical discussion of *Phillips v Batho* [1913] 3 KB 25, supra, p 533. See McClean, *Recognition of Family Judgments in the Commonwealth* (1983), Chapter 4.

[194] Supra, p 536 et seq; contrast *McC v McC* [1994] 1 IR 293.

[195] *Beatty v Beatty* [1924] 1 KB 807; and see *G v G* [1984] IR 368; *Sachs v Standard Chartered Bank (Ireland) Ltd* [1987] ILRM 297.

[196] See also Recitals (8) and (11).

[197] S 51(5).

[198] Supra, p 516 et seq.

[199] *Simons v Simons* [1939] 1 KB 490, [1938] 4 All ER 436; and see *Papadopoulos v Papadopoulos* [1930] P 55.

[200] *Simons v Simons*, supra, at 499.

[201] By virtue of the Civil Jurisdiction and Judgments Act 1982, s 18(5)(a), the enforcement of a maintenance order made elsewhere in the United Kingdom continues to be governed by the Maintenance Orders Act 1950.

[202] S 18(1), as amended by the Courts Act 2003, Sch 8, para 88(2). Such orders are brought within the provisions of the Maintenance Orders Act 1958 as to registration and enforcement by reason of the amendments to that Act contained in the Administration of Justice Act 1977, s 3, Sch 3; Civil Jurisdiction and Judgments Act 1982, Sch 11, para 2; and the Matrimonial and Family Proceedings Act 1984, s 46(1), Sch 1, paras 4 and 5.

This procedure applies to a wide range of orders, including those for periodical payments ancillary to decrees of divorce, nullity or judicial separation, or for failure to provide reasonable maintenance, and orders for maintenance or other financial provision made by magistrates' courts.[203] Registration is in the discretion of the court making the original order and not the court which is asked to register it, as is also normally the case with variation or discharge of a registered order; but once registered, the order may be enforced as if an order of the registering court.[204]

(c) Recognition under the Maintenance Orders (Facilities for Enforcement) Act 1920

Under the Maintenance Orders (Facilities for Enforcement) Act 1920, provision is made for the reciprocal enforcement of maintenance orders between England, on the one hand, and, on the other, those Commonwealth countries to which the Act has been extended by Order in Council. The "shuttlecock" procedure applicable to English proceedings is equally applicable to foreign proceedings, so that if a provisional order is made in a Commonwealth country in the absence of the defendant, it may be confirmed by the English magistrates' court in the area where the defendant resides.[205] The defendant may raise any defence which he might have raised in the foreign proceedings and the English court has a discretion whether or not to confirm the foreign provisional order.

There are further reciprocal provisions in the 1920 Act whereby an English maintenance order may be registered in the Commonwealth country[206] or a Commonwealth order may be registered in England.[207] These provisions assume that the court making the original order had jurisdiction to make it but that there is difficulty in enforcing it in that jurisdiction, as where the defendant was resident in the Commonwealth country when the order was made, but is resident in England when enforcement is sought. Registration is mandatory if a certified copy of the maintenance order is sent from the Commonwealth court to the designated officers of the English court. The order also has the same effect as if it were an English order, though there is no power to rescind or vary such an order.[208]

(d) Recognition under the Maintenance Orders (Reciprocal Enforcement) Act 1972

There is reciprocal machinery in the 1972 Act, similar to that contained in the 1920 Act, for the recognition of maintenance orders made in any foreign reciprocating country.[209] A foreign provisional order made in the absence of the defendant may be sent

---

[203] Discussed, supra, p 1053.

[204] Recognition of liability orders, made elsewhere in the United Kingdom under the Child Support Act 1991, is governed by regulations made by the Secretary of State: Child Support Act 1991, s 39. The jurisdiction of a child support officer to make an original maintenance assessment is based on the relevant person's habitual residence in the United Kingdom: 1991 Act, s 44, as amended by the Child Support, Pensions and Social Security Act 2000, Sch 3, para 11(2).

[205] S 4 of the 1920 Act, amended by the Maintenance Enforcement Act 1991, Sch 1, para 1; the Maintenance Orders (Reciprocal Enforcement) Act 1992, Sch 1, Part I, para 2; and the Courts Act 2003, Sch 8, para 69(3)(b).

[206] S 2.

[207] S 1.

[208] *Pilcher v Pilcher* [1955] P 318; and see *Sethi v Sethi* 1995 SLT 104.

[209] S 1.

to the English court within whose jurisdiction the defendant resides and that court has a discretion as to whether or not to confirm the order.[210] The defendant may raise any defences open to him in the original proceedings; but, once confirmed, the order is registered and has effect as if made by the English court. Variation or revocation of such orders may normally be made by either the English or the foreign court.[211]

As with the 1920 Act, there is also provision for the registration of a foreign order in an English court[212] and vice versa.[213] Again, it is assumed that the original court had jurisdiction to make the order, but it is more convenient for it to be enforced in the other country. If a certified copy of a foreign order is sent to the designated officer of the magistrates' court where the defendant resides, registration is mandatory and the order has effect as if made by the English court.

We have seen[214] that section 40 of the 1972 Act allows Part I of the Act to be applied, by Order in Council, in amended form to specified countries. These amended versions extend to recognition as well as to jurisdiction.[215] The variations can be illustrated by the fact that, although registration (and thus recognition) of a certified foreign order is mandatory under the 1972 Act itself,[216] there are a number of grounds on which it can be refused under the version implementing the 1973 Hague Convention on the recognition of maintenance orders,[217] including that "registration is manifestly contrary to public policy".[218]

(e) Recognition under the Brussels/Lugano system

The general rules laid down in the Brussels I Regulation for the recognition and enforcement in England of judgments obtained in other Member States[219] extend to maintenance orders[220] provided they fall within the meaning of "maintenance" under the Regulation.[221] Thus a maintenance order made in another Member State[222] can be

---

[210] S 5(5), including a foreign provisional order varying an original English order: *Horn v Horn* [1985] FLR 984.

[211] Eg *Hinkley v Hinkley* (1984) 38 RFL (2d) 337.

[212] S 6.

[213] S 2.

[214] Supra, p 1055.

[215] Eg *R v West London Magistrates' Court, ex p Emmett* [1993] 2 FLR 663. The implementation of international Conventions under this power, as well as under Part II itself, is effective even if the other state is a European Community Member State or a state bound by the Lugano Convention: see the Brussels I Regulation, Art 71 and the Lugano Convention, Art 67, and supra, pp 1060–1061.

[216] S 6; though it has been suggested that it might be possible to challenge the validity of the order itself: *Sethi v Sethi* 1995 SLT 104.

[217] SI 1993/593, para 6(6).

[218] Ibid, para 6(6)(a); *Armitage v Nanchen* (1983) 4 FLR 293.

[219] Or in Denmark, by virtue of the EC/Denmark Agreement, or in an EFTA State, by virtue of the Lugano Convention. See generally supra, Chapter 10. But note the Civil Jurisdiction and Judgments Act 1982, s 18(5)(a), as regards enforcement of a maintenance order made elsewhere in the United Kingdom (supra, pp 1069–1070).

[220] Schlosser Report, pp 132, 134; and see 1982 Act, s 5 (as amended by the Courts Act 2003, Sch 8, para 268(3)). See also with regard to maintenance orders, SI 1993/604 and SI 2001/3928.

[221] Supra, pp 1056–1057.

[222] Or in Denmark, by virtue of the EC/Denmark Agreement, or in an EFTA State, by virtue of the Lugano Convention. See generally supra, Chapter 10.

enforced in England in accordance with the rules set out in Chapter 16, above, in relation to civil and commercial judgments generally.[223] The application for registration is sent to the magistrates' court in the place where the respondent is domiciled (in the sense used in the 1982 and 1991 Acts and the Civil Jurisdiction and Judgments Order 2001) and the decision on registration is taken by the designated officer of the court. Once it is registered, the order is treated for enforcement purposes as if it were an English order made by the court and the methods of enforcement are the same as for an English order.[224]

Although the main enforcement route is by way of the Brussels I Regulation, there is scope also for enforcing a claim for maintenance payment using the European Enforcement Order for Uncontested Claims.[225] The advantage of this procedure is that it permits the free circulation of judgments,[226] court settlements and authentic instruments[227] throughout the Member States without the need for intermediate proceedings being brought in the Member State of enforcement[228] prior to recognition and enforcement.[229]

There are three particular issues which arise in connection with the recognition and enforcement of maintenance orders under the Brussels/Lugano system. The first arises from Article 27(4) of the Brussels Convention[230] which provides, in effect, that, if the court which made the order has decided a preliminary question as to the status or legal capacity of the parties, or as to rights in property arising out of a matrimonial relationship, in a way which conflicts with an English rule of private international law, the order is not to be recognised in England unless an English court would have reached the same result applying English rules of private international law. So, if a French court awards maintenance to a woman who is regarded as a "wife" under French law, but whose marriage is invalid according to English choice of law rules, the French maintenance order is not to be recognised or enforced in England. This ground of non-recognition has not been included in the Brussels I Regulation, or the (revised) Lugano Convention.[231]

The second issue concerns a particular example of a problem discussed earlier,[232] namely that of conflicting judgments covered by Article 34(3) of the Brussels I Regulation. Maintenance orders fall within the Regulation, but foreign divorce decrees do not. If, for example, the parties have been divorced in a Member State where enforcement is sought of a maintenance order granted in another Member State, such enforcement may be refused under the Brussels I Regulation on the ground that the award of maintenance in

---

[223] For the detailed procedures for registration, see the 1982 Act, s 5 (as amended by the Courts Act 2003, Sch 8, para 268(3)); SI 1986/1962; SI 2002/194 and SI 2005/617.

[224] 1982 Act, s 5(4). Interest is payable on the order according to the law of the country making the order (s 7(1)) but, in the case of a maintenance order, only if the order is re-registered for enforcement in the High Court under s 2A of the Maintenance Orders Act 1958 (1982 Act, s 7(4)). Sums payable in England under the foreign order are to be paid in sterling, converted as at the date of registration: 1982 Act, s 8.

[225] Regulation (EC) No 805/2004 creating a European Enforcement Order for Uncontested Claims, which applies in all the Member States with the exception of Denmark. See generally supra, p 640 et seq.

[226] Defined in Art 4(1).

[227] Defined in Art 4(3).

[228] Defined in Art 4(5).

[229] Recital (9) and Art 1.

[230] Supra, p 637.

[231] See Art 34 of each instrument.

[232] Supra, pp 622–624.

the first state depends on the parties' still being married.[233] It is debatable, however, whether an English court could refuse enforcement in such a case, given the powers under Part III of the Matrimonial and Family Proceedings Act 1984 to award maintenance after a foreign divorce.[234] The problem, however, is unlikely to arise now as a result of the mutual recognition rules contained in the Brussels II *bis* Regulation.[235]

The third issue concerns the inter-relation of the recognition and enforcement provisions of the Brussels I Regulation with other legislation and conventions. It seems clear that, where there are conventions with states which are European Community Member States,[236] the procedures available thereunder are still available[237] and indeed, that the maintenance creditors can choose whether to follow those procedures or the procedures of the Regulation.[238]

5. INTERNATIONAL INITIATIVES

(a) Hague Conference on Private International Law

Work has been ongoing at the Hague Conference since 1999 on a new global instrument on the international recovery of child support and other forms of family maintenance,[239] with a view to modernising the rules in the existing Conventions. In November 2007, the new Hague Convention on the International Recovery of Child Support and other Forms of Family Maintenance, and a Protocol on the Law Applicable to Maintenance Obligations, were adopted by the twenty-first Diplomatic Session of the Hague Conference. The Convention will enter into force after the deposit of two instruments of ratification, acceptance or approval.[240] The United Kingdom is a party to the 1973 Hague Convention on the Recognition and Enforcement of Decisions relating to Maintenance Obligations, but not to the 1973 Hague Convention on the Law Applicable to Maintenance Obligations. By reason of work also having been commenced in this general area at a European level, it appears that a transfer of competence has been effected by European Community Member States[241] to the Community, in respect of matters covered by the 2007 Hague Convention.[242] It has been a point of controversy[243] and disagreement whether the European Community should direct its efforts towards harmonisation on a regional or a global level. The Hague project has continued in parallel with work ongoing in the Community, described below.[244]

---

[233] Case 145/86 *Hoffman v Krieg* [1988] ECR 645; *Macaulay v Macaulay* [1991] 1 WLR 179; *R v West London Magistrates' Court, ex p Emmett* [1993] 2 FLR 663.

[234] Supra, p 1063 et seq.

[235] Supra, p 988 et seq.

[236] As under the Maintenance Orders (Reciprocal Enforcement) Act 1972, supra, pp 1070–1071.

[237] Brussels I Regulation, Art 71. Cf Lugano Convention, Art 67.

[238] Cf *Macaulay v Macaulay* [1991] 1 WLR 179.

[239] See generally http://www.hcch.net.

[240] Art 60(1).

[241] Including the United Kingdom, even although the United Kingdom has declined to exercise its "opt-in" to a future European instrument in this area: see infra, p 1074.

[242] Art 59 of the Convention permits signature, acceptance, approval or accession to the Convention by a Regional Economic Integration Organisation. See further supra, Chapter 1.

[243] See, eg, COM (2004) 254 final, para 3.2 (Relationship between the Community Instruments and the Hague Conventions); and COM (2005) 649 final, para 1.1.2.

[244] COM (2005) 649 final, para 1.1.2: "The relationships between the negotiations undertaken in The Hague and Community work should be seen in terms of the search for possible synergies between them; these two exercises are not contradictory, but consistent and complementary."

(b) Proposal for a Council Regulation

In April 2004, the European Commission published a Green Paper on Maintenance Obligations,[245] followed, in December 2005, by a Proposal for a Council Regulation on jurisdiction, applicable law, recognition and enforcement of decisions and co-operation in matters relating to maintenance obligations.[246] The Proposal is within the political mandate given by the Tampere European Council in 1999 and the Hague Programme adopted by the European Council in November 2004.[247]

To date, the treatment of maintenance obligations in Community law has been a patch-work. As has been seen already in this chapter, maintenance obligations are an integral part of the Brussels I Regulation,[248] and fall also within the scope of the European Enforcement Order Regulation,[249] but they are excluded from the Brussels II *bis* Regulation.[250] Unlike the Brussels I Regulation and the European Enforcement Order Regulation, the Proposal deals exclusively with maintenance obligations. It seeks to pro-vide specific measures applicable to maintenance obligations, rather than treating such obligations as ancillary issues in the application of the rules pertaining to civil and com-mercial claims. The aim of the Proposal is to eliminate all obstacles which prevent the recovery of maintenance within the European Union.[251] It is said that the new European legal order cannot be limited to the fine-tuning of the current mechanisms: "ambitious measures have to be taken in all relevant areas of the civil judicial co-operation: jurisdic-tion, applicable law, recognition and enforcement, cooperation and elimination of obsta-cles for the good conduct of proceedings. The solutions to this multifaceted problem shall be contained in a single instrument."[252]

In April 2006, in accordance with the 1997 Protocol,[253] the United Kingdom government informed the Council of the European Union of its decision not to "opt in" to the Proposal. If the United Kingdom maintains that position, it will not be bound by a resulting instru-ment concerning maintenance obligations, and the existing instruments[254] will continue to apply.

---

[245] COM (2004) 254 final.

[246] COM (2005) 649 final. See also COM (2005) 648 final (Communication from the Commission to the Council calling on the Council to provide for measures relating to maintenance obligations taken under Article 65 of the Treaty establishing the European Community to be governed by the procedure laid down in Article 251 of that Treaty), transferring maintenance obligations from the unanimity to the co-decision procedure (the "*pas-sarelle*"), on the basis that maintenance though "familial by its roots ... [is] ... pecuniary in its implementation." (COM (2005) 649 final, para 3.1). See, further, European Parliament, Committee on Civil Liberties, Justice and Home Affairs Report on the Proposal (26 November 2007; Rapporteur, G Grabowska) (A6-0468/2007).

[247] The Hague Programme: Strengthening Freedom, Security and Justice in the European Union (OJ 2005 C 53/1) and the Council and Commission Action Plan Implementing the Hague Programme on Strengthening Freedom, Security and Justice in the European Union (OJ 2005 C 198/1). See generally supra, Chapter 1.

[248] Art 5(2); even though family law matters generally are excluded from the Regulation. See supra, pp 218–219.

[249] See supra, p 640 et seq.

[250] Art 1(3)(e) and Recital (11).

[251] COM (2005) 649 final, para 1.2.

[252] ibid.

[253] Protocol No 4 to the Treaty of Amsterdam on the Position of the United Kingdom and Ireland (OJ 1997 C 340/99).

[254] Brussels I Regulation, Art 5(2), and European Enforcement Order Regulation.

Chapter 24

Children[1]

1. INTRODUCTION

We are concerned in this chapter with the private international law rules regulating orders concerning children. The most important of these, so far as English law is concerned, are orders determining with whom a child shall live or with whom he may have contact.[2]

Until relatively recently, many of the private international law rules in this field were provided by an unclear and inconsistent mixture of statutory provision and common law decisions.[3] Indeed, the English jurisdictional rules to make orders concerning the welfare

---

[1] See North (1990) I Hague Recueil 9, 127 et seq.
[2] Under the Children Act 1989, s 8.
[3] See Law Com No 138 (1985), Part II.

of children were a mixture of very broad and very narrow rules, statutes and common law, detail and vagueness, clarity and confusion, and the rules were, above all, bewilderingly complex.[4] By contrast, the rules for the recognition or enforcement of orders made outside England, whether elsewhere in the British Isles or overseas, were simple. Whilst such orders would be given "grave consideration",[5] they had no direct effect in England and their relevance lay only in assisting an English court in deciding whether to exercise its own discretion to make an order and, if so, to what effect.

It came increasingly to be realised that, in an age of great mobility, a situation in which there are no rules for the recognition of other countries' parental responsibility and similar orders, at least on a reciprocal basis, was capable of engendering great anguish for parents and for children who might be shuttled from country to country. The legal position was in danger of verging on anarchy; indeed, the Law Commission described the position as a "state of legal disorder".[6] It was the source of potential and, sometimes, actual conflict between the courts in England and Scotland, with each claiming jurisdiction, making conflicting orders and not recognising orders made in the other country.[7] On the broader international scene, child abduction by, or on behalf of, one parent often unsuccessful in custody proceedings became so serious an international issue that action at last was taken.

This area of law has been characterised, since 1980, by a proliferation of legislative intervention on a national, regional and global scale.[8] Nationally, the Child Abduction Act 1984[9] introduced criminal offences governing the taking of a child under 16 out of the United Kingdom without consent. The statute covers abduction both by a parent and by others. Secondly, more effective powers have been given to the courts to order the disclosure of the whereabouts of a child, to order its recovery, to order the surrender of the child's passport and to prohibit the removal of the child from the United Kingdom.[10] The administrative procedures to prevent children being removed by stopping them at airports or ports have also been improved.[11] On the civil side, Part I of the Family Law Act 1986[12] was introduced to amend the law relating to the jurisdiction of courts in the United Kingdom to make orders with regard to the custody of children; to make provision as to the recognition and enforcement of such orders throughout the United Kingdom; and to make further provision as to the imposition, effect and enforcement of restrictions on the removal of children from the United Kingdom. The Law Commission

---

[4] Ibid, paras 2.5, 2.32, 2.48, 2.52.

[5] *McKee v McKee* [1951] AC 352 at 365.

[6] Law Com No 138 (1985), para 1.9.

[7] Eg *Johnstone v Beattie* (1843) 10 Cl & Fin 42; *Babington v Babington* 1955 SC 115; *Hoy v Hoy* 1968 SC 179; though courts tried more recently to avoid such conflicts: *Re H* [1966] 1 WLR 381; *Re L* [1974] 1 WLR 250; *Campbell v Campbell* 1977 SLT 125; *Thomson, Petitioner* 1980 SLT (Notes) 29; *Girven, Petitioner* 1985 SLT 92.

[8] See de Boer [2002] XLIX NILR 307.

[9] Amended by the Family Law Act 1986, s 65, the Children Act 1989, Sch 12, paras 37–40, Sch 15, and the Adoption and Children Act 2002, Sch 3, para 42. For evidence of its use, see [1991] Fam Law 202; and see *R v C (Kidnapping: Abduction)* [1991] 2 FLR 252.

[10] Family Law Act 1986, ss 33–37 (in respect of s 33, *Re G (Children) (Residence: Same Sex Partner)* [2006] EWCA Civ 372, [2006] 2 FLR 614); Children Act 1989, s 13; *Practice Direction (Disclosure of Addresses: 1989)* [1989] 1 WLR 219.

[11] *Practice Direction (Minor: Preventing Removal Abroad)* [1986] 1 WLR 475.

[12] References to the 1986 Act are to the Act as later amended, most significantly by the Children Act 1989, Schs 13, 15 and by SI 1991/1723.

and the Scottish Law Commission, on whose recommendations[13] Part I of the 1986 Act is based, concluded that, if there was to be a scheme for intra-United Kingdom recognition of such orders, the acceptability of such a scheme would be advanced by uniform jurisdictional rules throughout the United Kingdom for the making of the orders—a step which would also provide the opportunity of curing the varied defects in the then English rules. The statutory jurisdictional rules, however, are limited to the making of such orders as are defined by section 1 of the Act (ie Part I orders).

At a regional level, with effect from 1 March 2001, Council Regulation (EC) No 1347/2000 of 29 May 2000 on jurisdiction and the recognition and enforcement of judgments in matrimonial matters and in matters of parental responsibility for children of both spouses[14] (known colloquially as "Brussels II"[15]), came into operation. Brussels II, in turn, was repealed, with effect from 1 March 2005, by Council Regulation (EC) No 2201/2003 of 27 November 2003 concerning jurisdiction and the recognition and enforcement of judgments in matrimonial matters and matters of parental responsibility ("Brussels II *bis*").[16] This Europeanisation of rules relating to parental responsibility matters resulted in significant changes being made to the Family Law Act 1986, to ensure compliance with the Brussels regime.[17]

On a global platform, two organisations, the Hague Conference on Private International Law and the Council of Europe, have been responsible for the introduction of various instruments concerning children. Work at The Hague has resulted in, among other conventions,[18] the 1980 Hague Convention on the Civil Aspects of International Child Abduction,[19] and the 1996 Hague Convention on Jurisdiction, Applicable Law, Recognition, Enforcement and Co-operation in respect of Parental Responsibility and Measures for the Protection of Children.[20] The Council of Europe, meanwhile, has produced the 1980 European Convention on Recognition and Enforcement of Decisions concerning Custody of Children and on the Restoration of Custody of Children,[21] and the 2003 Convention on Contact concerning Children.[22]

The scope of application of each instrument, national and international, and the manner of their interlocking is not always as clear as might be hoped or expected.[23] We must now

---

[13] Law Com No 138 (1985).

[14] OJ 2000 L 160/19.

[15] Based upon the Brussels II Convention of 28 May 1998 (never implemented) on the same subject, in respect of which, see Borras, "Explanatory Report on the Convention on jurisdiction and the recognition and enforcement of judgments in matrimonial matters" (OJ 1998 C 221/27).

[16] OJ 2003 L 338/1.

[17] See The European Communities (Matrimonial Jurisdiction and Judgments) Regulations, SI 2001/310; and The European Communities (Jurisdiction and Judgments in Matrimonial and Parental Responsibility Matters) Regulations, SI 2005/265.

[18] Eg 1961 Hague Convention concerning the Powers of Authorities and the Law Applicable in respect of the Protection of Minors (to which the United Kingdom is not a party) and 1993 Hague Convention on Protection of Children and Co-operation in respect of Intercountry Adoption (to which the United Kingdom is a party: infra, p 1155).

[19] Given force of law in the United Kingdom by the Child Abduction and Custody Act 1985, Sch 1; infra, p 1103.

[20] The United Kingdom is not yet a party to this Convention; infra, p 1136.

[21] Otherwise known as the "Luxembourg Convention", and given force of law in the United Kingdom by the Child Abduction and Custody Act 1985, Sch 2; infra, p 1123 et seq.

[22] The United Kingdom is not yet a party to this Convention; infra, p 1139.

[23] The area has been described by THORPE LJ as a "treaty jungle": *Re G (Children) (Foreign Contact Order: Enforcement)* [2003] All ER (D) 144 at [32].

turn to consider the instruments in detail, examining, in turn, the rules governing the jurisdiction of the English courts as regards parental responsibility matters, the choice of law rules applied, and, finally, the varied provisions for the recognition and enforcement of parental responsibility and related orders made elsewhere.

2. JURISDICTION IN MATTERS OF PARENTAL RESPONSIBILITY

(a) Background

The Children Act 1989 introduced major changes in the law relating to children and, in particular, as to the orders which the English courts may make concerning them. Out went the old terminology of custody and custodianship orders; indeed the wardship jurisdiction is now described as the inherent jurisdiction. Instead the court may make orders under section 8 of the Children Act 1989 which are contact, prohibited steps, residence or specific issue orders—generally described as "section 8 orders". The powers of the court to make such orders[24] may be exercised in a range of "family proceedings"[25] which include both proceedings under the statutory jurisdiction[26] and under the inherent jurisdiction of the High Court in relation to children.[27] The court also has power to make orders for the appointment of a guardian of a child[28] which, again, are regarded as orders made in family proceedings.[29]

Part I of the Family Law Act 1986[30] establishes the jurisdictional rules of the English courts to make "Part I orders" in relation to children under the age of 18.[31] The principles on which the jurisdictional rules under Part I of the 1986 Act are founded are that they should be: clear, systematic and uniform throughout the United Kingdom; designed to reduce the likelihood of courts in more than one part of the United Kingdom having concurrent jurisdiction; and normally result in the case being heard in the country with which the child has the closest long-term connection.[32] These objectives are achieved in the following ways. First, Part I of the 1986 Act contains essentially identical jurisdictional rules for England and Wales, Scotland, and Northern Ireland.[33] Secondly these rules in places interlock, with the result that a court in one country usually will not have jurisdiction

---

[24] Under the Children Act 1989, ss 9–11.

[25] 1989 Act, s 8(3), (4).

[26] Ibid, s 8(3)(b), (4); namely the Children Act 1989, Parts I, II, IV; Matrimonial Causes Act 1973; Schs 5 and 6 to the Civil Partnership Act 2004; Adoption and Children Act 2002; Domestic Proceedings and Magistrates' Courts Act 1978; Matrimonial and Family Proceedings Act 1984, Part III; Family Law Act 1996; and ss 11 and 12 of the Crime and Disorder Act 1998.

[27] Ibid, s 8(3)(a).

[28] Ibid, ss 5, 6.

[29] Because made under Part I of the 1989 Act.

[30] As amended by the Children Act 1989, and by The European Communities (Jurisdiction and Judgments in Matrimonial and Parental Responsibility Matters) Regulations, SI 2005/265, regs 8–18.

[31] Family Law Act 1986, s 7(a); though under the Children Act 1989, s 9(7) such orders (other than one varying or discharging an existing order) will only be made in relation to children of 16 or over in exceptional cases.

[32] Law Com No 138 (1985), para 3.10.

[33] Chapters II, III and IV respectively of Part I. There is also power under s 43 of the 1986 Act to extend Part I by Order in Council to the rest of the British Isles and to any colony and, as has been seen, this has been done in the case of the Isle of Man: SI 1991/1723.

if jurisdiction lies with a court elsewhere. Thirdly, the rules are exclusive. Part I orders falling within the 1986 Act may be made only if the jurisdictional provisions of that Act are satisfied.[34]

The rules contained in Part I of the 1986 Act were significantly changed, with effect from 1 March 2001, to take account of European harmonisation in the form of the Brussels II Regulation.[35] Brussels II, in turn, was repealed, with effect from 1 March 2005, by the Brussels II *bis* Regulation.[36] Although the rules of jurisdiction in matrimonial matters contained in Brussels II *bis* were taken substantially from Brussels II, which, in turn, were taken[37] from the Brussels II Convention of 28 May 1998 (never implemented) on the same subject,[38] more significant changes were wrought by Brussels II *bis* in relation to matters of parental responsibility.[39]

In examining the jurisdictional rules for making parental responsibility orders, it is necessary to look separately at the harmonised rules of jurisdiction which apply throughout the European Community Member States (except Denmark) by virtue of Brussels II *bis*, and at the residual national rules of jurisdiction contained, for the United Kingdom, in the Family Law Act 1986.

(b) Bases of jurisdiction[40]

(i) Introduction

Section 2 of the Family Law Act 1986 deals with the jurisdiction of courts in England and Wales to make a "Part I order", ie, an order to which Part I of the 1986 Act applies,[41] namely: (a) an order made under section 8 of the Children Act 1989, other than an order varying or discharging such an order;[42] (b) a special guardianship order made under the

---

[34] Ss 2, 2A and 3.

[35] Council Regulation (EC) No 1347/2000 of 29 May 2000 on jurisdiction and the recognition and enforcement of judgments in matrimonial matters and in matters of parental responsibility for children of both spouses (OJ 2000 L 160/19). See The European Communities (Matrimonial Jurisdiction and Judgments) Regulations, SI 2001/310. For detail on the origins of Brussels II, see McEleavy (2002) 51 ICLQ 883 at 888, and Crawford and Carruthers (2006), paras 14-06–14-07. On the impact of Brussels II on the 1986 Act, see Lowe [2002] Fam Law 39.

[36] Council Regulation (EC) No 2201/2003 of 27 November 2003 concerning jurisdiction and the recognition and enforcement of judgments in matrimonial matters and matters of parental responsibility (OJ 2003 L 338/1). See The European Communities (Jurisdiction and Judgments in Matrimonial and Parental Responsibility Matters) Regulations, SI 2005/265. See also *Practice Guide for the Application of the New Brussels II Regulation* (2005) (the *Practice Guide* is not legally binding, and does not prejudge any opinion given by the ECJ, or decision issued by national courts, concerning interpretation of the Regulation); Boele-Woelki and Beilfuss (eds), *Brussels II bis: Its Impact and Application in the Member States* (2007); McEleavy (2002) 51 ICLQ 883, and (2004) 53 ICLQ 503. With regard to transitional provisions, see Art 64, *M v H (Custody: Residence Order)*, 27 July 2005 (unreported) (Fam Div), and *W v W (Foreign Custody Order: Enforcement)* [2005] EWHC 1811.

[37] See Brussels II, Recital (6).

[38] See Borras, "Explanatory Report on the Convention on jurisdiction and the recognition and enforcement of judgments in matrimonial matters" (OJ 1998 C 221/27).

[39] See *Practice Guide*, para 2.2.2.

[40] For details of the rules of jurisdiction applying prior to 1 March 2001, see the 13th edn of this book (1999) p 858 et seq.

[41] As regards courts in England and Wales. See s 1(1)(b) as regards orders made by a court in Scotland, and s 1(1)(c) and (e) as regards orders made in Northern Ireland.

[42] 1986 Act, s 1(1)(a).

Children Act 1989;[43] (c) an order made under section 26 of the Adoption and Children Act 2002, other than an order varying or discharging such an order;[44] or (d) an order in the exercise of the inherent jurisdiction of the High Court with respect to children.[45]

(ii) Jurisdiction to make "section 8 orders"

Section 2(1) of the 1986 Act provides that a court in England and Wales shall not make a "section 8 order"[46] with respect to a child unless (a) it has jurisdiction under Brussels II *bis*; or (b) Brussels II *bis* does not apply but (i) the question of making the order arises in, or in connection with, matrimonial proceedings or civil partnership proceedings and the condition in section 2A[47] of the 1986 Act is satisfied, or (ii) the condition in section 3[48] of the Act is satisfied. In other words, pre-eminent jurisdiction lies with the courts of the country which has jurisdiction in terms of Brussels II *bis*.

(a) Jurisdiction under the 1986 Act, s 2(1)(a)

Section 2(1)(a) of the 1986 Act provides that a court in England and Wales shall not make a "section 8 order"[49] with respect to a child unless it has jurisdiction under Brussels II *bis*.

(i) Scope of Brussels II bis

In order to ensure equality for all children, the ambit of Brussels II *bis* is more extensive than was that of Brussels II, which applied only to matters of parental responsibility for children of both spouses on issues that were closely linked to proceedings for divorce, legal separation or marriage annulment.[50] Brussels II *bis* covers all decisions on parental responsibility, including measures for the protection of children, independently of any link with matrimonial proceedings.[51] Parental responsibility is defined in the Regulation as meaning, "all rights and duties relating to the person or the property of a child which are given to a natural or legal person by judgment, by operation of law or by an agreement having legal effect".[52] In particular, Brussels II *bis* shall apply, whatever the nature of the court or tribunal, in civil matters[53] relating to the attribution, exercise, delegation, restriction or termination of parental responsibility.[54] Specifically included are: (a) rights of custody[55] and rights of access;[56] (b) guardianship, curatorship and similar institutions; (c) the designation and functions of any person or body having charge of the child's

---

[43] Ibid, s 1(1)(aa).
[44] Ibid, s 1(1)(ab).
[45] Ibid, s 1(1)(d).
[46] An order made by a court in England under the Children Act 1989, s 8, other than an order varying or discharging such an order: 1986 Act, s 1(1)(a).
[47] Infra, p 1086.
[48] Infra, p 1087.
[49] See supra, n 46.
[50] Brussels II, Recital (11).
[51] Brussels II *bis*, Recital (5).
[52] Ibid, Art 2(7).
[53] To be interpreted autonomously: *Re C* (Case C-435/06) 2008 IL Pr 1.
[54] Ibid, Art 1(1)(b).
[55] Defined in Art 2(9) as rights and duties relating to the care of the person of a child, and in particular the right to determine the child's place of residence.
[56] Defined in Art 2(10) as including in particular the right to take a child to a place other than his habitual residence for a limited period of time.

person or property, representing or assisting the child; (d) the placement of the child in a foster family or in institutional care;[57] (e) and measures for the protection of the child relating to the administration, conservation or disposal of the child's property.[58] It is important to note that, as regards the property of a child, the Regulation applies only to protective measures.[59] Brussels II *bis* does not apply to (a) the establishment or contesting of a parent-child relationship;[60] (b) decisions on adoption, measures preparatory to adoption, or the annulment or revocation of adoption;[61] (c) the name and forenames of the child; (d) emancipation; (e) maintenance obligations;[62] (f) trusts or succession;[63] or (g) measures taken as a result of criminal offences committed by children.[64] Not specifically mentioned in Article 1, but excluded from the scope of the Regulation by virtue of Recital (10), are other questions linked to the status of persons, matters relating to social security, public measures of a general nature in matters of education or health, and decisions on the right of asylum and on immigration.

Unlike most other instruments concerning children, Brussels II *bis* does not define "child", or set a maximum age regarding the children who are affected by its provisions. This question is left to be determined by national law.

(ii)   Rules of jurisdiction in Brussels II bis

The rules of jurisdiction in matters of parental responsibility are set out in Chapter II, section 2 of the Regulation. Unlike the grounds of jurisdiction set out in Article 3 in relation to divorce, legal separation and marriage annulment, which are set out as alternatives, and not in any order of precedence,[65] the rules of jurisdiction in relation to parental responsibility are set out in quasi-hierarchical form. The general rule is set out in Article 8, and the exceptions to that rule are to be found in Articles 9, 10, 12 and 13.

General jurisdiction—Article 8   Article 8(1) provides that, subject to Articles 9, 10 and 12,[66] examined below, the courts of a Member State shall have jurisdiction in matters

---

[57] The first reference for a preliminary ruling from the ECJ on interpretation of Brussels II *bis*, lodged by the Finnish *Korkein hallinto-oikeus* on 17 October 2006 (Case C-435/06, OJ 2006 C 326/33), concerned the question whether the Regulation applies to the enforcement of a public law decision in connection with child welfare, relating to the immediate taking into custody of a child and his placement in a foster family outside the home, taken as a single decision, in its entirety (or solely to that part of the decision relating to placement outside the home in a foster family). The ECJ held that Art 1(1) of the Regulation is to be interpreted to the effect that a single decision ordering a child to be taken into care and placed outside his original home in a foster family is covered by the term "civil matters" for the purposes of that provision, where that decision was adopted in the context of public law rules relating to child protection: *Re C* (Case C-435/06) 2008 IL Pr 1. See also third reference for a preliminary ruling from the ECJ on interpretation of Brussels II *bis*, lodged on 23 November 2007, also by the Finnish *Korkien hallinto-oikeus*, Case C-523/07.

[58] Ibid, Art 1(2).

[59] Ibid, Recital (9). Eg, the Regulation applies in all cases where a child's parents are in dispute as regards the administration of his property. Measures relating to the child's property which do not concern the protection of the child continue to be governed by the Brussels I Regulation, supra, Chapter 11.

[60] The establishment of parenthood is a different matter from the attribution of parental responsibility: Recital (10).

[61] See infra, Chapter 25.

[62] See supra, Chapter 23.

[63] See infra, Chapters 32 and 34.

[64] Brussels II *bis*, Art 1(3).

[65] Supra, pp 945–946.

[66] Art 9 (continuing jurisdiction of the child's former habitual residence); Art 10 (jurisdiction in cases of child abduction); and Art 12 (prorogation of jurisdiction).

of parental responsibility over a child who is habitually resident in that Member State at the time the court is seised. The grounds of jurisdiction established in the Regulation are said to have been:

> shaped in light of the best interests of the child, in particular on the criterion of proximity. This means that jurisdiction should lie in the first place with the Member State of the child's habitual residence, except for certain cases of a change in the child's residence or pursuant to an agreement between the holders of parental responsibility.[67]

The fundamental principle of the Regulation is that the court of the Member State in which the child is habitually resident is best placed to determine matters of parental responsibility.

"Habitual residence"[68] The meaning of habitual residence has been considered fully in relation to jurisdiction in divorce, legal separation and marriage annulment.[69] As has been seen, this connecting factor is nowhere defined in Brussels II *bis*,[70] and must be determined "by the judge in each case on the basis of factual elements".[71] Curiously, however, the *Practice Guide* states that:

> The meaning of the term should be interpreted in accordance with the objectives and purposes of the Regulation. It must be emphasised that this does not refer to any concept of habitual residence under national law, but an "autonomous" notion of Community law. If a child moved from one Member State to another, the acquisition of habitual residence in the new Member State should, in principle, coincide with the "loss" of habitual residence in the former Member State. Consideration by the judge on a case-by-case basis implies that whilst the adjective "habitual" tends to indicate a certain duration, it should not be excluded that a child might acquire habitual residence in a Member State on the very day of the arrival, depending on the factual circumstances of the concrete case.[72]

It has been thought that a child can have only one habitual residence at any one time,[73] though may have more than one during a year.[74] In the context of divorce proceedings, however, the submission that it is not possible to be habitually resident in two places simultaneously was firmly rejected by the Court of Appeal in *Ikimi v Ikimi*.[75] The Court took the view that the bodily presence required to form a basis for habitual residence had to be more than merely token in duration, probably amounting to residence for "an appreciable part of the relevant year".[76] If an adult is capable of being habitually resident

---

[67] Brussels II *bis*, Recital (12).

[68] See, for detailed examination, supra, p 185 et seq. Also Bogdan, "The EC Treaty and the Use of Nationality and Habitual Residence as Connecting Factors in International Family Law", and Pertegas, "Nationality and Habitual Residence: Other Connecting Factors in European Private International Law" in Meeusen, Pertegas, Straetmans and Swennen (eds), *International Family Law for the European Union* (2007).

[69] Supra, pp 947–949.

[70] See, for background, Borras, *Explanatory Report*, para 32.

[71] *Practice Guide*, para II.1.

[72] Ibid.

[73] *Re V (Abduction: Habitual Residence)* [1995] 2 FLR 992; *In the Marriage of R and S S Hanbury-Brown* (1996) 20 Fam LR 334; *Cameron v Cameron* 1996 SLT 306. Rarely will a child be without an habitual residence, though see the unusual circumstances of *W v H (Child Abduction: Surrogacy) (No 1)* [2002] 1 FLR 1008.

[74] *Re A (Abduction: Habitual Residence)* [1998] 1 FLR 497.

[75] [2001] EWCA Civ 873, [2001] 2 FLR 1288, considered supra, pp 947–948. But contra *Marinos v Marinos* [2007] EWHC 2047 (Fam), per MUNBY J, at [43].

[76] *Ikimi v Ikimi*, above, per THORPE LJ, at [35]. His Lordship favoured a liberal rather than restrictive approach to the determination of habitual residence, whilst noting that one consequence of liberality might be forum shopping.

in two places simultaneously, it is difficult to see why the same should not be true also of a child. Doubt has been cast, however, on whether, *for the purpose of the Brussels II bis Regulation*, an adult can be habitually resident in more than one country at the same time.[77] The wording of the *Practice Guide*,[78] coupled with the approach in *Marinos v Marinos*,[79] would appear to indicate that, at least for the purpose of Brussels II *bis*, a child may have only one habitual residence at any given time. It is apparent from the *Practice Guide* that if a competent court is seised, in principle it retains jurisdiction under Article 8, even if the child subsequently should acquire a new habitual residence in another Member State; this is the principle of *perpetuatio fori*.[80]

Continuing jurisdiction of the child's former habitual residence—Article 9 Where a child moves lawfully from one Member State to another and acquires a new habitual residence there,[81] the courts of the Member State of the child's former habitual residence shall, by way of exception to Article 8, retain jurisdiction during a three-month period following the move for the purpose of modifying a judgment on access rights issued in that Member State before the child moved, where the holder of access rights pursuant to the judgment continues to have his habitual residence in the Member State of the child's former habitual residence.[82] This does not apply, however, if the holder of access rights has accepted the jurisdiction of the courts of the Member State of the child's new habitual residence by participating in proceedings before those courts without contesting their jurisdiction.[83] It may be that the holder of the access rights wishes to seise the courts of the new Member State for the purpose of having those rights reviewed.

Article 9, which is limited to jurisdiction in respect of access rights:

> provides a guarantee that the person who can no longer exercise access rights as before does not have to seise the courts of the new Member State, but can apply for an appropriate adjustment of access rights before the court that granted them during a period of three months following the move. The courts of the new Member State do not have jurisdiction in matters of access rights during this period.[84]

It is important to recognise that Article 9 applies only in cases where a child has been moved lawfully from one Member State to another; the lawfulness of the removal is a matter to be determined by the law (including private international law) of the Member State of origin. Cases of wrongful removal or retention are dealt with according to Article 10.

---

[77] *Marinos v Marinos* [2007] EWHC 2047 (Fam), per MUNBY J, at [43]; supra, p 948.

[78] *Practice Guide*, para 11.1; supra, p 1079, n 36.

[79] [2007] EWHC 2047 (Fam).

[80] *Practice Guide*.

[81] Art 9 presupposes that the child in question has attained a new habitual residence within only three months of arriving in the new Member State. See criticism by McEleavy (2004) 53 ICLQ 503 at 508.

[82] See also Arts 40 and 41, infra, p 1100.

[83] Art 9(2).

[84] *Practice Guide*, para II.2(a). However, "Article 9 does not . . . prevent a holder of parental responsibility who has moved with the child to another Member State from seising the courts of that Member State on the question of custody rights during the three-month period following the move" (ibid).

Jurisdiction in cases of child abduction—Article 10 Special rules apply in cases of child abduction, and will be considered in that context, below.[85]

Prorogation of jurisdiction—Article 12 Article 12(1) provides that the courts of a Member State exercising jurisdiction by virtue of Article 3[86] of Brussels II *bis* on an application for divorce, legal separation or marriage annulment shall have jurisdiction in any matter relating to parental responsibility connected with that application where two conditions are satisfied: (a) at least one of the spouses has parental responsibility in relation to the child; and (b) the jurisdiction of the courts has been accepted expressly or otherwise in an unequivocal manner by the spouses and by the holders of parental responsibility, at the time the court is seised, and is in the superior[87] interests of the child.[88] Jurisdiction under Article 12(1) shall cease as soon as (a) the judgment allowing or refusing the application for divorce, legal separation or marriage annulment has become final;[89] (b) a final judgment is issued in parental responsibility proceedings which were still pending on the date when the divorce, etc proceedings became final; or (c) the divorce, etc proceedings referred to in (a) and the parental responsibility proceedings referred to in (b) have come to an end for another reason.[90]

The courts of a Member State shall also have jurisdiction[91] in relation to parental responsibility in proceedings other than matrimonial proceedings where: (a) the child has a substantial connection with that Member State,[92] in particular by virtue of the fact that one of the holders of parental responsibility is habitually resident in that Member State or that the child is a national of that Member State; and (b) the jurisdiction of the courts has been accepted expressly or otherwise in an unequivocal manner by all the parties to the proceedings at the time the court is seised and is in the best[93] interests of the child.

Where the child is habitually resident in a non-Member State which is not a contracting party to the 1996 Hague Convention on jurisdiction, applicable law, recognition, enforcement and co-operation in respect of parental responsibility and measures for the protection of children,[94] jurisdiction in a Member State under Article 12 shall be deemed to be in the child's interest, in particular if it is found impossible to hold proceedings in the non-Member State in question.[95]

Jurisdiction based on child's presence—Article 13 Where a child's habitual residence cannot be established, and jurisdiction cannot be determined on the basis of Article 12,

---

[85] Infra, p 1118.

[86] Supra, pp 945–946. See *C v FC (Brussels II: Freestanding Application for Parental Responsibility)* [2001] 1 FLR 317.

[87] The *Practice Guide* explains that: "No distinction was intended by the drafters between the term 'superior interests of the child' [Art 12(1)(b)] . . . and the term 'best interests of the child' [Art 12(3)(b)] . . . Versions of the Regulation in other languages employ an identical wording in both paragraphs" (para II(2)(c)).

[88] Eg *Re ML and AL (Children) (Contact Order: Brussels II Regulation) (No 1)* [2006] EWHC 2385 (Fam), [2007] 1 FCR 475.

[89] See, in relation to Brussels II, Art 3(3), *Re A (A Child) (Foreign Contact Order: Jurisdiction)* [2003] EWHC 2911, [2004] 1 FLR 641,

[90] Eg the application for divorce, etc has been withdrawn.

[91] Art 12(3). Eg, *S v D* 2007 SLT (Sh Ct) 37.

[92] See, in relation to operation of Art 66, infra, pp 1085–1086.

[93] See supra, n 87, regarding the difference in wording between Art 12(1)(b) and (3)(b).

[94] Discussed infra, p 1136.

[95] Art 12(4).

the courts of the Member State where the child is present shall have jurisdiction. This provision also applies to refugee children or children internationally displaced because of disturbances occurring in their country.[96]

Transfer to a court better placed to hear the case—Article 15[97]

(iii) Allocation of jurisdiction within the United Kingdom

Article 66 of Brussels II *bis* applies to Member States in which two or more systems of law apply. The precise meaning of Article 66 is not clear.[98] It mentions only references to (a) the "habitual residence" of a person in a Member State; (b) the "nationality" or "domicile" of a person in a Member State; (c) the "authority" of a Member State"; and (d) "the rules of the requested Member State". The references to a Member State are to be interpreted as references to the relevant territorial unit within that state. Article 66 does not mention the "courts of a Member State", referred to in Articles 12 and 15; "presence in a Member State", which is the connecting factor relied upon in Article 13; or the "courts of different Member States" referred to in Article 19.[99] The question arises whether the jurisdiction provisions of Brussels II *bis* operate so as to allocate jurisdiction among the territorial units of the United Kingdom. Chapter II of Part I of the Family Law Act 1986, dealing with the jurisdiction of courts in England and Wales, gives priority to the rules of jurisdiction contained in Brussels II *bis*, but does not expressly state whether those rules are intended to allocate jurisdiction as between the different territorial units of the United Kingdom. In contrast, Chapter III of Part I of the Act, dealing with the jurisdiction of courts in Scotland, in section 17A,[100] provides that the provisions of Chapter III are subject to sections 2 and 3 of Chapter II of Brussels II *bis*, ie Articles 8 to 20. By inference, it seems that the jurisdiction provisions in Articles 8, 9 and 10, all of which rely upon personal law connecting factors mentioned in Article 66, should operate to allocate jurisdiction within the United Kingdom. However, the extent of application of Article 12, as well as of Articles 13, 15 and 19, is more difficult, since those provisions refer to the "courts of a Member State", "substantial connection with a Member State", "presence in a Member State" or the "courts of different Member States", expressions to which no reference is made in Article 66. As regards Article 12(3), it was held in *S v D*[101] that a proper interpretation of Article 66 requires that the child in question has a "substantial connection" with the relevant territorial unit of the United Kingdom, and not generally with the United Kingdom as a Member State.[102] For reasons of clarity and simplicity, it is submitted that it is preferable to construe Articles 8, 9, 10 and 12 of the Regulation as applying to the allocation of jurisdiction intra-United Kingdom in parental responsibility disputes,[103] but strictly, and bearing in mind issues of European Community competence,

---

[96] Art 13(2).

[97] Discussed infra, pp 1092–1093.

[98] Eg *S v D* 2007 SLT (Sh Ct) 37.

[99] Infra, pp 1093–1094.

[100] Added by SSI 2005/42, reg 4(3).

[101] 2007 SLT (Sh Ct) 37, criticised by Maher 2007 SLT (News) 117.

[102] Since, in the instant case, the child no longer had a substantial connection with Scotland, the "robust conditions" of Art 12(3) were not satisfied.

[103] See, eg, Lowe [2004] IFLJ 205; Morris, p 279; and Crawford and Carruthers (2006), para 14-43. This is in line with the Scottish position, in terms of the Family Law Act 1986, s 17A, added by SSI 2005/42, in respect of Chapter III of the 1986 Act (Jurisdiction of Courts in Scotland).

this expansive interpretation of Articles 12 and 66 may be open to challenge.[104] At any rate, however: "To assume the operation of Regulation 2201 in intra-UK cases is the less complex interpretative option."[105]

(b) Jurisdiction under the 1986 Act, Section 2(1)(b)

By virtue of Article 14 of Brussels II *bis*, where no court of a Member State has jurisdiction pursuant to Articles 8 to 13 (either because of the factual circumstances of the case, ie the matter in dispute falls outside the subject matter scope of the Regulation;[106] or by reason of a lack of relevant geographical connecting factor[107]), jurisdiction shall be determined, in each Member State, by the laws of that state. The residual rules of jurisdiction are to be found, for England and Wales, in section 2(1)(b) of the 1986 Act.

Section 2(1)(b) provides that a court in England and Wales shall not make a "section 8 order"[108] with respect to a child unless Brussels II *bis* does not apply, but (i) the question of making the order arises in, or in connection with, matrimonial proceedings or civil partnership proceedings and the condition in section 2A[109] of the 1986 Act is satisfied, (ii) or the condition in section 3[110] of the 1986 Act is satisfied.

(i) *Jurisdiction in or in connection with matrimonial proceedings or civil partnership proceedings*

A court may make a "section 8 order" if the question of making the order arises in, or in connection with, matrimonial proceedings or civil partnership proceedings[111] in respect of the marriage or civil partnership of the parents of the child concerned, and (a) the proceedings, being ones for divorce or nullity of marriage,[112] or dissolution or annulment of civil partnership, are continuing;[113] or (b) the proceedings, being ones for judicial separation or legal separation, are continuing, and no proceedings for divorce or nullity proceedings, or dissolution or annulment proceedings, are continuing in Scotland or Northern Ireland.[114] The jurisdictional basis for so doing is that the court has jurisdiction over the matrimonial proceedings or civil partnership proceedings.[115]

The rules are dovetailed with those applicable in the other parts of the United Kingdom in two respects. First, if the English proceedings are merely for judicial separation or legal separation, the English court will lose its power to make a section 8 order therein if, after

---

[104] Maher 2007 SLT (News) 117.

[105] Crawford and Carruthers (2006), para 14-43.

[106] Supra, pp 1080–1081.

[107] Art 14(1) is in the same terms, mutatis mutandis, as Art 7(1) (residual jurisdiction in divorce, etc). Notably, however, there is no provision in Art 14 which corresponds to Art 7(2), discussed, supra, pp 950–951.

[108] A section 8 order made by a court in England under the Children Act 1989, other than an order varying or discharging such an order: 1986 Act, s 1(1)(a). See, eg, *Re H (Residence Order: Placement out of Jurisdiction)* [2004] EWHC 3243, [2006] 1 FLR 1140.

[109] Infra.

[110] Infra, p 1087.

[111] Defined in Family Law Act 1986, s 7(aa) as proceedings for the dissolution or annulment of a civil partnership or for legal separation of the civil partners.

[112] The English courts have power in proceedings under the Matrimonial Causes Act 1973 for divorce, nullity and judicial separation to make section 8 orders relating to children. See *T v T (Custody: Jurisdiction)* [1992] 1 FLR 43.

[113] See *V v V* [2006] EWHC 3374 (Fam), [2007] Fam Law 304.

[114] 1986 Act, ss 2A(1) and (2).

[115] Supra, pp 944 and 1030.

the granting of the decree of judicial separation and at the date of the application,[116] divorce or nullity, or dissolution or annulment proceedings are continuing in Scotland or Northern Ireland.[117] It seems right that the court dealing with the continued existence of the marriage should assume the position of primacy. Secondly, an English court in which the appropriate matrimonial proceedings or civil partnership proceedings are continuing may conclude that it is more appropriate for an application for a Part I order to be determined outside England. In that event it may direct that no section 8 order may be made by an English court in those matrimonial or civil partnership proceedings.[118] The need for this provision is caused by the fact that matrimonial/civil partnership proceedings once begun, and not dismissed, may continue indefinitely[119] even though, for instance, a divorce has been granted. This could have the result that the English divorce court retains its prime jurisdiction to make a section 8 order long after all the parties have ceased to have a close, or any, connection with England. Therefore, a power to decline jurisdiction where appropriate is desirable.[120]

(ii) Habitual residence or presence of the child

Alternatively, a court may make a "section 8 order" if, on the date of the application for an order,[121] the child concerned is (a) habitually resident in England and Wales, or (b) is present in England and Wales and is not habitually resident in any part of the United Kingdom, and, in either case, so long as matrimonial proceedings or civil partnership proceedings are not continuing in respect of the marriage or civil partnership of the child's parents in Scotland or Northern Ireland.[122] If matrimonial proceedings or civil partnership proceedings are continuing elsewhere in the United Kingdom,[123] then the English court must not exercise jurisdiction to make a section 8 order, despite the habitual residence or presence of the child in England. English jurisdiction must yield to the primacy of the courts of the country of the matrimonial/civil partnership proceedings.[124]

Habitual residence[125] No period of habitual residence is specified.[126] This is hardly surprising, given that Part I orders may be made in relation to very young children. There is, however, a danger that one parent, by taking the child to another jurisdiction, often wrongfully, could change his habitual residence and thus deprive the English court of its jurisdictional power to make a Part I order.[127] To combat this, section 41 of the 1986 Act[128] provides that, if a child under 16 who is habitually resident in a part of the United Kingdom is removed

---

[116] Or when the court is considering making the order if no application is made: 1986 Act, s 7(c).

[117] S 2A(1), (2).

[118] S 2A(4); see *R S (A Minor) (Jurisdiction to Stay Application)* [1995] 1 FLR 1093. It can always reinstate the basis of jurisdiction by revoking such direction.

[119] English proceedings may be treated by s 42(2) of the 1986 Act as continuing until the child is 18.

[120] Law Com No 138 (1985), para 4.97.

[121] 1986 Act, s 7(c). It is irrelevant that the jurisdictional link is later broken.

[122] 1986 Act, s 3.

[123] Eg *B v B (Scottish Contact Order: Jurisdiction to Vary)* [1996] 1 FLR 688.

[124] See *Dorward v Dorward* 1994 SCCR 928.

[125] See, for detailed examination, supra, p 185 and p 191 et seq.

[126] See *F v S (Wardship: Jurisdiction)* [1993] 2 FLR 686.

[127] Cf *Re A (A Minor) (Wardship: Jurisdiction)* [1995] 1 FLR 767.

[128] Cf *Scullion v Scullion* 1990 SCLR 577.

from or leaves that part[129] and becomes habitually resident outside that part,[130] either in contravention of an English court order[131] or without the consent of anyone having the right to determine where he resides,[132] then he is still treated as continuing to be habitually resident in England for a year from the date he left,[133] or until he becomes 16 or there is agreement to his living elsewhere.[134] In *Re S (A Child) (Abduction: Residence Order)*[135] the Court of Appeal held that section 41 of the 1986 Act is a deeming provision to resolve conflicts between the constituent parts of the United Kingdom, and not between the United Kingdom and any jurisdiction that is not a constituent part.

Presence   This basis of jurisdiction operates, irrespective of the child's nationality,[136] if the child is present in England at the date of the application for the Part I order. The retention of presence as a residual basis of jurisdiction is desirable in order to ensure that a range of appropriate cases may be entertained by the English courts. For example, if a child habitually resident abroad is brought to England against the wishes of the person entitled to exercise parental responsibilities in relation to the child[137] in the country of habitual residence, that person would be deprived of any effective remedy[138] unless the English court took jurisdiction on the basis of the presence of the child in England.[139]

(iii) Jurisdiction to make special guardianship orders, and orders under Children and Adoption Act 2002, section 26

Section 2(2A) of the 1986 Act provides that a court in England and Wales shall not have jurisdiction to make a special guardianship order under the Children Act 1989 unless the condition in section 3 of the 1986 Act is satisfied, ie the child concerned is (a) habitually resident in England and Wales, or (b) is present in England and Wales and is not habitually resident in any part of the United Kingdom, and, in either case, so long as matrimonial proceedings or civil partnership proceedings are not continuing in respect of the marriage or civil partnership of the child's parents in Scotland or Northern Ireland.

---

[129] S 41 also covers the case where the child was temporarily out of England, eg on holiday or at school, and is not returned when he should have been.

[130] *Re M (Minors) (Residence Order: Jurisdiction)* [1993] 1 FLR 495, the Court of Appeal concluded that a child who never in his life had left the United Kingdom, having always lived in England or Scotland, was not habitually resident in either country. The result was that s 41 could not apply and jurisdiction was based on presence in England. The criticism of this decision seems fully justified: Cretney (1993) 109 LQR 538. Contrast *Morris v Morris* 1993 SCLR 144.

[131] The English order must precede the removal: *Re E (Child: Abduction)* [1991] FCR 631 at 636; revsd on other grounds: [1992] 1 FCR 541.

[132] In relation to acquisition of parental responsibility by unmarried fathers and by step-parents, see Children Act 1989, ss 4 and 4A.

[133] Eg *D v D (Custody: Jurisdiction)* [1996] 1 FLR 574.

[134] Provided in this last case, there has been no contravention of a court order.

[135] [2002] EWCA Civ 1949, [2003] 1 FLR 1008.

[136] *Findlay v Matondo and Secretary of State for the Home Department* [1993] Imm AR 541.

[137] Cf Children Act 1989, ss 2, 3, 4 and 4A.

[138] Unless the child could be returned under the provisions of the Child Abduction and Custody Act 1985, infra, p 1103 et seq.

[139] For other examples, see Law Com No 138 (1985), para 4.25. See also *Re P (A Child) (Mirror Orders)* [2000] 1 FLR 435—as a matter of comity and common sense it is desirable to continue the practice of making mirror orders so that the court in one jurisdiction can be confident that there will be redress in another jurisdiction should the parent refuse to comply.

The same condition applies, by virtue of section 2(2B) of the 1986 Act, to jurisdiction in respect of orders for contact under section 26 of the Adoption and Children Act 2002.

(iv) Jurisdiction to make orders in the exercise of the inherent jurisdiction of the High Court

Section 2(3) of the 1986 Act provides that a court in England and Wales shall not have jurisdiction to make an order under section 1(1)(d) of the Family Law Act 1986 (ie, an order in the exercise of the inherent jurisdiction of the High Court so far as it gives care of a child to any person or provides for contact with, or the education of, a child[140])unless: (a) it has jurisdiction under Brussels II *bis*;[141] or (b) Brussels II *bis* does not apply but (i) the condition in section 3 of the Act is satisfied,[142] or (ii) the child concerned is present in England on the relevant date,[143] and the court considers that the immediate exercise of its powers is necessary for his protection.[144]

Whilst there is much to be said for a carefully constructed, interlocking set of jurisdictional rules, there is a danger that a hierarchy of jurisdictions may provide too cumbersome a set of rules to deal with those not infrequent, cases, where courts are called upon to act very quickly in matters concerning the welfare of children. To address this difficulty, section 2(3)(b)(ii) of the 1986 Act confers an emergency basis of jurisdiction on a court to make an order in exercise of the inherent jurisdiction of the High Court with regard to children. As the Law Commission noted: "Where a child is in immediate danger, his protection must take precedence over procedural considerations."[145] The effect of section 2(3)(b)(ii) is to allow the inherent jurisdiction of the High Court to be exercised to make such "emergency orders" even though, for example, the child is habitually resident elsewhere in the United Kingdom, or matrimonial proceedings between its parents are continuing in Scotland or Northern Ireland. The exercise of the inherent jurisdiction to make such orders is described as that of the High Court and would seem to be limited to that jurisdiction.[146] The English "emergency order" can be superseded at any time by an order of a court in the country with primacy of jurisdiction.

In relation to wardship proceedings,[147] it is necessary to distinguish between the jurisdictional rules for making orders under the inherent jurisdiction of the High Court giving

---

[140] Excluding an order varying or revoking such an order: 1986 Act, s 1(1)(d)(ii).

[141] Pre-eminent jurisdiction lies with the courts of the Member State which has jurisdiction in terms of Brussels II bis, Arts 8–14, examined supra, p 1081 et seq. See, in particular, Art 20 (provisional, including protective, measures), infra, pp 1094–1095.

[142] Ie the child concerned is (a) habitually resident in England and Wales, or (b) is present in England and Wales and is not habitually resident in any part of the United Kingdom, and, in either case, so long as matrimonial proceedings or civil partnership proceedings are not continuing in respect of the marriage or civil partnership of the child's parents in Scotland or Northern Ireland.

[143] The date of application for an order or variation thereof or, where no such application is made, the date on which the court is considering whether to make or, as the case may be, vary the order: 1986 Act, s 7(c). It is irrelevant that the jurisdictional link is later broken.

[144] *H v D* [2007] EWHC 802 (Fam). See also Brussels II *bis*, Art 20, infra, pp 1094–1095.

[145] Law Com No 138 (1985), para 4.19.

[146] 1989 Act, s 8(3)(a). The power to transfer family proceedings from the High Court to a county court, though it includes wardship proceedings, excludes applications for a child to be or cease to be a ward of court and "any proceedings which relate to the exercise of the inherent jurisdiction of the High Court with respect to minors": Matrimonial and Family Proceedings Act 1984, s 38(2)(b), as amended by the Children Act 1989, Sch 13, para 51.

[147] See Law Com No 138 (1985), para 1.25.

the care of a child to any person, or providing for contact with, or the education of, a child, which are governed by the Family Law Act 1986,[148] and the jurisdictional rules governing the exercise of the inherent jurisdiction making a child a ward of court. The difference is important because the High Court[149] may make orders under the inherent jurisdiction in wardship proceedings relating to matters other than the care of the child, such as orders as to his property;[150] and, indeed, the jurisdictional rules of the 1986 Act concerning orders as to the care of the child will apply only if the court had had jurisdiction to entertain the original wardship application.[151] Although a child becomes a ward of court on the making of the application,[152] the wardship lapses unless a wardship order is made within the prescribed period and no order as to the care of the child will be made if it is shown that the jurisdictional criteria, stated above, were not satisfied. "Wardship cannot be used to circumvent the application of the Brussels II Regulation and proceedings must be stayed pending a determination under it."[153] The inherent jurisdiction of the High Court to make a child a ward of court is founded on the prerogative power of the Crown acting in its capacity as *parens patriae* to do what is necessary for the welfare of children. It has long been held that this royal prerogative delegated to the courts should benefit those who owe allegiance to the Crown. It has been well established, therefore, that the High Court may exercise this jurisdiction in respect of any British subject[154] aged under 18, even though he possesses no property in England and even if he is out of the country at the time of the proceedings.[155] Jurisdiction has also been extended to an alien child who, at the time of the proceedings, is either (i) physically present though not domiciled in England,[156] or (ii) ordinarily resident, though not in fact present, in England.[157] That said, in fact there is no reported case of jurisdiction being assumed over a child who was neither resident nor present in England.[158] In *Al-H v F*,[159] Lord Justice THORPE opined that English courts should be extremely circumspect in assuming jurisdiction in relation to children physically present in some other jurisdiction founded only on the basis of nationality, explaining that:

> In order to achieve essential collaboration internationally it has been necessary to relax reliance upon concepts understood only in common law circles. Thus our historic emphasis

---

[148] 1986 Act, s 1(1)(d).

[149] Wardship jurisdiction is limited to the High Court.

[150] Lowe and Douglas, *Bromley's Family Law* (2007) 10th edn, p 885 et seq.

[151] Because s 1(1)(d) refers to orders made in the exercise of the inherent jurisdiction, which latter must be validly established.

[152] Law Reform (Miscellaneous Provisions) Act 1949, s 9(1); and he cannot then marry, or be taken out of the jurisdiction, subject to the Family Law Act 1986, s 38; and see Law Com No 138 (1985), para 1.26.

[153] Lowe and Douglas, op cit, p 890.

[154] Which would probably now mean a "British citizen" within the meaning of the British Nationality Act 1981.

[155] *Hope v Hope* (1854) 4 De G M & G 328; *Re Willoughby* (1885) 30 Ch D 324; *Harben v Harben* [1957] 1 WLR 261; *Re P (GE)* [1965] Ch 568 at 582, 587, 592; *McM v C (No 2)* [1980] 1 NSWLR 27; *Romeyko v Whackett (No 2)* (1980) 25 SASR 531; *Brown v Kalal* (1986) 7 NSWLR 423; cf *McM v C* [1980] 1 NSWLR 1.

[156] *Re D* [1943] Ch 305; *Re P (GE)* [1965] Ch 568 at 582, 588, 592; *J v C* [1970] AC 668 at 700–701, 720; *Re A* [1970] Ch 665.

[157] *Re P (GE)* [1965] Ch 568 at 584–586; and see *Scheffer v Scheffer* [1967] NZLR 466; *Holden v Holden* [1968] VR 334; *Nielsen v Nielsen* (1970) 16 DLR (3d) 33; *Glasson v Scott* [1973] 1 NSWLR 689; *Re Allison* (1979) 96 DLR (3d) 342; and *Re A (A Child) (Wardship: Habitual Residence)* [2006] EWHC 3338 (Fam), [2007] 1 FCR 390.

[158] See Law Com No 138 (1985), para 2.11.

[159] [2001] EWCA Civ 186, [2001] 1 FLR 951.

on the somewhat artificial concept of domicile has had to cede to an acknowledgement that the simpler fact based concept of habitual residence must be the currency of international exchange. The *parens patriae* concept must seem even more esoteric to other jurisdictions than the concept of domicile. If we are to look for reciprocal understanding and co-operation . . . we must refrain from exorbitant jurisdictional claims founded on nationality.[160]

In the past, orders made by the High Court under the inherent jurisdiction in wardship proceedings were quite often for the appointment of a guardian to a child.[161] The Children Act 1989[162] abolished this power and introduced, both in its place and in place of the previous statutory rules[163] relating to the making of guardianship orders, a statutory regime for the appointment of a guardian under that Act.[164] Guardianship falls now within the scope of Brussels II *bis*.[165]

(c) Variation and duration of Part I orders

One characteristic of orders relating to the welfare of children is that parents may well return to the courts to claim that their circumstances, or those of the child, have changed and to seek the variation of the order. Such applications inevitably pose jurisdictional problems, such as whether the court which made the original order should retain jurisdiction to vary it, even though in the meantime its jurisdictional link with the child has been broken.[166] The general approach of Part I of the 1986 Act is that the power to vary[167] continues, despite the loss of the jurisdictional link.[168] If, however, a Part I order (or a variation of such an order) made by a court in Scotland or Northern Ireland comes into force with respect to a child at a time when an English Part I order has effect, the original English order shall cease to have effect so far as it makes provision for any matter for which the same or different provision is made by the Scottish or Irish order.[169] Where the original English order ceases to have effect, an English court shall not have jurisdiction to vary that order.[170] Further, an English court shall not have jurisdiction to vary a Part I order if, on the date of application for variation of the order, matrimonial proceedings or civil partnership proceedings are continuing in Scotland or Northern Ireland in respect of the marriage or civil partnership of the parents of the child concerned, unless the original English order was made (a) in connection with divorce or nullity proceedings, or dissolution or annulment proceedings, in respect of the marriage or civil partnership of the parents of the child concerned, and those proceedings are continuing; or (b) in connection with proceedings for a judicial separation or legal separation in respect of the

---

[160] Ibid, at [42].
[161] Eg *Hope v Hope* (1854) 4 De G M & G 328; *Re Willoughby* (1885) 30 Ch D 324.
[162] S 5(13). The appointment of a guardian of the estate of a child may be made under the inherent jurisdiction, if so provided by rules of court: Children Act 1989, s 5(11), (12).
[163] Eg the Guardianship of Minors Act 1971.
[164] S 5.
[165] Art 1(2)(b).
[166] The answer in the past was unclear: see Law Com No 138 (1985), para 2.33.
[167] As to what constitutes a variation, see the 1986 Act, ss 6, 42 (5), (6).
[168] Eg *Re S (Residence Order: Forum Conveniens)* [1995] 1 FLR 314.
[169] 1986 Act, s 6(1).
[170] Ibid, s 6(2). See *Re K (A Minor: Wardship: Jurisdiction: Interim Order)* [1991] 2 FLR 104, [1991] Fam Law 226: *T v T (Custody: Jurisdiction)* [1992] 1 FLR 43; *S v S (Custody: Jurisdiction)* [1995] 1 FLR 155; and *A v A (Forum Conveniens)* [1999] 1 FLR 1.

marriage or civil partnership of the parents of the child concerned, and those proceedings are continuing and the decree has not yet been granted.[171] The English court will not lose its power, in proceedings under the inherent jurisdiction of the High Court, in an emergency to vary a Part I order relating to a child then present in England.[172]

(d) Refusal of application and stay of proceedings

The two main principles underlying the jurisdictional rules—a clear hierarchy of jurisdictional rules, coupled with a desire that an application for an order relating to the welfare of a child is to be heard by the court with the most appropriate links with the issue—are bound at times to come into conflict.

(i) Refusal of application

The power of the English court to refuse an application or to stay proceedings is set out in section 5 of the Family Law Act 1986. Section 5(1) provides that a court in England and Wales which has jurisdiction to make a Part I order may refuse an application for the order in any case where the matter in question has already been determined in proceedings outside England and Wales. This provision is concerned with the case where the issue in question had already been determined in proceedings elsewhere. This situation is separate from that of recognition of any other order. No matter where the other order has been made and irrespective of whether or not it may be recognised and enforced in England, the English court may decline jurisdiction, on any basis, to make a Part I order.[173] The English court is free to take the view that it does not wish to interfere with a decision as to the child's welfare which has already been made.[174]

(ii) Transfer to a court better placed to hear the case—Brussels II bis, Article 15

Where, at any stage of the proceedings on an application to a court in England and Wales for a Part I order, or for variation of such an order, it appears to the court that it should exercise its powers under Article 15 of Brussels II *bis*, the court may proceed accordingly. Uniquely in a European private international law Regulation, Brussels II *bis* incorporates what is, in effect, a *forum conveniens* rule. "It is a provision negotiated for the comfort of those jurisdictions who have reservations about the introduction of a strict *lis alibi pendens* rule into family litigation."[175] Article 15(1) provides, by way of exception,[176] and only if it is in the best interests of the child, that the courts of a Member State having jurisdiction as to the substance of the matter may, if they consider that a court of another Member State, with which the child has a particular connection, would be better placed to hear the case, or a specific part of it: (a) stay the case, or the part in question, and invite

---

[171] Ibid, s 6(3).

[172] Ibid, s 6(5).

[173] S 5(1). This may be very significant where the child has been "kidnapped" from another jurisdiction. The difficulties arising in such cases are discussed more fully, infra, p 1103 et seq.

[174] This general system of interlocking rules makes it very important for the court to be aware of other proceedings which relate to the child, whether in the United Kingdom or elsewhere, including administrative proceedings; see 1986 Act, ss 39, 42(7).

[175] *Re Clark (A Child)* [2006] EWCA Civ 1115, per THORPE LJ, at [18].

[176] As regards civil law jurisdictions, "truly exceptional" cases (THORPE LJ, ibid).

the parties to introduce a request before the court of that other Member State, in accordance with Article 15(4); or (b) request a court of another Member State to assume jurisdiction, in accordance with Article 15(5).

The operation of Article 15 may be triggered in one of three ways: by application from a party;[177] of the court's own motion; or upon application from a court of another Member State with which the child has a particular connection,[178] in accordance with Article 15(3). In the case of a transfer made of the court's own motion, or by application of a court of another Member State, the transfer must be accepted by at least one of the parties.[179] In order for a transfer to take place, the child must have a "particular connection" with the "receiving State". By Article 15(3), a child shall be considered to have such a connection if the receiving state: (a) has become the habitual residence of the child after the court of the state of origin was seised; (b) is the former habitual residence of the child; (c) is the place of the child's nationality; (d) is the habitual residence of a holder of parental responsibility; or (e) is the place where the child's property is located and the case concerns measures for the protection of the child relating to the administration, conservation or disposal of this property.

If the court of the state of origin stays the case, or part thereof, and invites the parties to introduce a request before the court of another Member State, Article 15(4) provides that the first court must set a time limit[180] by which the courts of the other Member State shall be seised. If the courts of another Member State have not been seised by that time, the first court shall continue to exercise jurisdiction in accordance with Articles 8 to 14. The courts of the "receiving State" may, where due to the specific circumstances of the case, this is in the best interests of the child, accept jurisdiction within six weeks of their seizure. In this event, the court first seised shall decline jurisdiction. Otherwise, the court first seised shall continue to exercise jurisdiction in accordance with Articles 8 to 14.

In order for the transfer mechanism to operate effectively, the courts shall co-operate either directly,[181] or through the Central Authorities designated pursuant to Article 53 of the Regulation.[182] In the event of a transfer under Article 15, the court in the "receiving State" is not allowed to make a further transfer of the case to a third court.[183]

(iii) Concurrent proceedings in another European Community Member State, except Denmark—Brussels II bis, Article 19

Article 15 of Brussels II *bis* concerns "consecutive" rather than "concurrent" proceedings. The rule in respect of concurrent, or parallel, proceedings in two or more European

---

[177] See Family Proceedings Rules 1991, r 7.53.
[178] Ibid, r 7.54.
[179] Brussels II *bis*, Art 15(2).
[180] The Regulation does not prescribe a specific limit.
[181] See, on the practicalities, *Practice Guide*, para II(3).
[182] Ibid, Art 15(6).
[183] Ibid, Recital (13).

Community Member States is contained in Article 19 (lis pendens and dependent actions), which provides that:

2. Where proceedings relating to parental responsibility relating to the same child[184] and involving the same cause of action are brought before courts of different Member States, the court second seised shall of its own motion stay its proceedings until such time as the jurisdiction of the court first seised is established. . . .

3. Where the jurisdiction of the court first seised is established, the court second seised shall decline jurisdiction in favour of that court. In that case, the party who brought the relevant action before the court second seised may bring that action before the court first seised.

Articles 8 to 14 of Brussels II *bis*, by nature, may confer jurisdiction on the courts of more than one Member State in respect of the same child and the same cause of action, and so there is a need for a provision dealing with the problem of concurrent proceedings and conflicting judgments in the courts of different Member States.[185] Article 19, like Article 27 of the Brussels I Regulation, but unlike Article 15 of Brussels II *bis*, is a purely mechanical rule. The court of the Member State first seised of the matter takes priority, and any court of another Member State must of its own motion decline jurisdiction,[186] once the jurisdiction of the court first seised is established in that state. The rule as to the time at which a court is seised is set out in Article 16 (Seising of a Court), examined earlier in relation to concurrent matrimonial proceedings.[187] Although the court second seised must decline jurisdiction, there is scope, nonetheless, in a suitable case,[188] for application to be made by that court to the court first seised for a transfer in terms of Article 15.[189]

Article 19 is limited to concurrent proceedings in different Member States. It does not apply to actions proceeding concurrently in England and in a non-Member State country, such as South Africa. In such cases, an English court will continue to employ traditional rules based upon the doctrine of *forum conveniens*, and given statutory expression in section 5 of the Family Law Act 1986.[190]

Brussels II *bis*, Article 20 (provisional, including protective, measures)

Article 20 of Brussels II *bis* provides that:

1. In urgent cases, the provisions of this Regulation shall not prevent the courts of a Member State from taking such provisional, including protective, measures in respect of persons or assets in that State as may be available under the law of that Member State, even if, under this Regulation, the court of another Member State has jurisdiction as to the substance of the matter.

---

[184] Perhaps surprisingly, there is no requirement in Art 19 that parental responsibility matters in respect of two or more children of the same family are to be determined in the same proceedings in the same Member State.

[185] Cf in relation to civil and commercial matters, Brussels I Regulation, Art 27. See supra, p 303 et seq.

[186] Article 17 (Examination as to jurisdiction) provides that: "Where a court of a Member State is seised of a case over which it has no jurisdiction under this Regulation and over which a court of another Member State has jurisdiction by virtue of this Regulation, it shall declare of its own motion that it has no jurisdiction." See *W v W (Preliminary Issue: Stay of Petition)* [2002] EWHC 3049, [2003] 1 FLR 1022; *Rogers-Headicar v Rogers-Headicar* [2004] EWCA Civ 1867, [2005] 2 FCR 1; *L-K v K (Brussels II Revised: Maintenance Pending Suit)* [2006] EWHC 153 (Fam), [2006] 2 FLR 1113; and *Moore v Moore* [2007] EWCA Civ 361, [2007] IL Pr 36.

[187] Supra, pp 957–958.

[188] Ie where the child in question has a "particular connection" with the Member State whose court was second seised: Art 15(2)(c) and (3).

[189] Supra, pp 1092–1093.

[190] Infra, p 1096.

2. The measures referred to in paragraph 1 shall cease to apply when the court of the Member State having jurisdiction under this Regulation as to the substance of the matter has taken the measures it considers appropriate.[191]

This rule, which is not subject to the jurisdictional rules of Brussels II *bis*, and does not require that provisional measures be taken (but rather gives a discretion to certain courts), has been examined already in the context of matrimonial proceedings.[192] The Article provides the courts of all European Community Member States with an emergency jurisdiction.[193] Article 20 should not be used illegitimately to seise jurisdiction validly vested in the first court.[194] The emergency jurisdiction can be compared to the making of orders by a court in England and Wales in the exercise of the inherent jurisdiction of the High Court.[195] It has already been noted that the inherent jurisdiction of the High Court can operate in cases where the court has jurisdiction under Brussels II *bis*.[196] In relation to the operation of protective emergency jurisdiction by a court in England, the demarcation between these two bases of jurisdiction is not entirely clear. Arguably, Article 20 of Brussels II *bis* confers wider powers than does section 1(1)(d) of the 1986 Act to protect not only the person, but also the assets, of a child.

(iv) Concurrent proceedings in a related United Kingdom jurisdiction

The question whether the jurisdiction provisions of Brussels II *bis* should be interpreted as operating so as to allocate jurisdiction among the territorial units of the United Kingdom has been considered previously in this chapter.[197] A similar interpretative difficulty arises in connection with the manner of treatment of concurrent proceedings in different territorial units of the United Kingdom. Article 19(2) (lis pendens) of Brussels II *bis* refers to the "courts of different Member States", an expression to which no reference is made in Article 66. If, as has been submitted is appropriate, the rules of allocation of jurisdiction contained in Brussels II *bis* are taken to apply so as to allocate jurisdiction to disputes within the United Kingdom, then it would be illogical to provide that concurrent proceedings in a related United Kingdom jurisdiction should be resolved by any means other than by the *lis pendens* rule set out in Article 19. If, however, an

---

[191] See also Brussels II *bis*, Recital (16).

[192] Supra, pp 958–959.

[193] See, for an example of the utility of Art 20, *Practice Guide*, para 2.3: "A family is travelling by car from Member State A to Member State B on their summer holiday. Once arrived in Member State B, they are victims of a traffic accident, where they are all injured. This child is only slightly injured, but both parents arrive at the hospital in a state of coma. The authorities of Member State B urgently need to take certain provisional measures to protect the child who has no relatives in Member State B. The fact that the courts of Member State A have jurisdiction under the Regulation as to the substance does not prevent the courts or competent authorities of Member State B from deciding, on a provisional basis, to take measures to protect the child. These measures cease to apply once the courts of Member State A have taken a decision." Another instance, suggested by Nicholas Mostyn QC in *Re ML and AL (Children) (Contact Order: Brussels II Regulation) (No 1)* [2006] EWHC 2385 (Fam), [2007] 1 FCR 475, at [35], is where there is evidence that children are about to be removed from the second state in order to frustrate the enforcement of a contact order there; the court of that state would be well justified in making an Art 20 order preventing the removal pending enforcement of the contact order. See also third reference for a preliminary ruling from the ECJ on interpretation of Brussels II *bis*, lodged on 23 November 2007 by the Finnish *Korkein hallinto-oikeus*, Case C-523/07.

[194] *Re ML and AL (Children) (Contact Order: Brussels II Regulation) (No 1)* [2006] EWHC 2385 (Fam), [2007] 1 FCR 475.

[195] 1986 Act, s 2(3).

[196] Ibid, s 2(3)(a).

[197] Supra, pp 1085–1086.

expansive interpretation of this sort is to be taken in respect of Article 19, then the same should be true also of Article 15, providing for the availability in such cases of the transfer mechanism,[198] by way of exception and in the best interests of the child.

(v) Concurrent proceedings in a non-European Community Member State, or in Denmark

Where, at any stage of the proceedings on an application to a court in England and Wales for a Part I order, or for variation of such an order, it appears to the court that proceedings with respect to the same matter are continuing in a non-European Community Member State, or in Denmark; or that it would be more appropriate for those matters to be determined elsewhere, the court may stay the proceedings.[199] This flexibility is particularly relevant where there are two sets of proceedings continuing simultaneously, but no Part I order has been made in either. This could happen, for example, where proceedings are started in England for a Part I order, in relation to a child who is habitually resident in England, followed by divorce proceedings in South Africa where the father is habitually resident. In such a case, the English court has a power to stay its proceedings if it thinks it appropriate to do so. It seems clear that "appropriateness" is not directly concerned with the welfare of the child, but rather with the suitability of the court to entertain the proceedings.[200] This was certainly the view of the Law Commission who gave,[201] as an example of appropriate circumstances for a waiver of jurisdiction, the case where a divorce had been granted in England five years earlier, with no application for an order relating to a child, but where, at the time of the later application for such an order, the parents and the child were habitually resident in another country. This view has been accepted,[202] despite earlier decisions to the contrary.[203]

3. CHOICE OF LAW

There seems little doubt that, when an English court takes jurisdiction to make orders with respect to children, it will apply English law as the law of the forum.[204] The application of English law is reinforced by the requirement imposed on the court to regard the welfare of the child as the paramount consideration.[205] There are no provisions in Brussels II *bis* concerning applicable law.[206]

---

[198] Supra, pp 1092–1093.

[199] S 5(2)(b); see, eg, *Hill v Hill* 1990 SCLR 238, OH. It can also lift the stay as appropriate: s 5(3).

[200] See *Spiliada Maritime Corpn v Cansulex Ltd* [1987] AC 460 at 474–475; and *A v A (Forum Conveniens)* [1999] 1 FLR 1.

[201] Law Com No 138 (1985), para 9.97.

[202] *Re S (Residence Order: Forum Conveniens)* [1995] 1 FLR 314; *M v B (Residence: Forum Conveniens)* [1994] 2 FLR 819; *Re F (Residence Order: Jurisdiction)* [1995] 2 FLR 518; *M v M (Stay of Proceedings: Return of Children)* [2005] EWHC 1159 (Fam), [2006] 1 FLR 138—in the application for a stay of English divorce proceedings, the welfare of the two children of the marriage was important, but not paramount; but in the application for the children's summary return to South Africa, their welfare was paramount; see remarks of WILSON J, at [9]; and *V v V* [2006] EWHC 3374 (Fam), [2007] Fam Law 304.

[203] Eg *Hallam v Hallam (Minors) (Forum Conveniens) (Nos 1 and 2)* [1993] 1 FLR 958; and see *Re S (A Minor) (Stay of Proceedings)* [1993] 2 FLR 912.

[204] Cf the Children (Scotland) Act 1995, s 14(3).

[205] Children Act 1989, s 1(1).

[206] See infra, pp 1137–1138, in relation to the choice of law provisions contained in the 1996 Hague Convention on Jurisdiction, Applicable Law, Recognition, Enforcement and Co-operation in respect of Parental Responsibility and Measures for the Protection of Children.

4. RECOGNITION AND ENFORCEMENT

(a) Introduction

The historic attitude of English courts to the recognition of orders relating to children, such as custody, guardianship and wardship orders, made in other countries was simple. Though they might be given careful consideration by an English court in deciding whether and, if so, what order to make, they were never recognised as such. The reasons for this attitude were primarily[207] because the English courts are instructed to regard the welfare of the child as the paramount consideration,[208] and this could conflict with recognition of a foreign order; and because such orders relating to children are never final, being always subject to review by the courts which made them.[209] This attitude contrasted strikingly with that, for example, in Canada, Australia and the USA, where there has for some time been legislation regulating the recognition of such foreign orders. Significant change in the English attitude was apparent with the introduction of legislation governing the recognition and enforcement of orders falling under Part I of the Family Law Act 1986 and made elsewhere in the United Kingdom, and with two international conventions, given the force of law in England by means of the Child Abduction and Custody Act 1985, which provide for the recognition of custody orders granted in, or custody rights under the law of, a number of foreign countries. Most important of all, however, has been the European objective of attaining the free movement of judgments in matrimonial matters and in matters of parental responsibility within the Community, leading ultimately to the implementation of Brussels II *bis*. The historic denial of recognition now is greatly reduced, affecting only orders granted in those countries not covered by Brussels II *bis*, the Family Law Act 1986, or the Child Abduction and Custody Act 1985. These varied rules must be considered in turn.

(b) Orders granted in another European Community Member State, except Denmark[210]

(i) Principle of recognition

As has been stated already in this book, the principle of mutual recognition of judgments has been fixed as the cornerstone of the European judicial area.[211] Alongside the objective of the free movement of judgments within the Member States in civil and commercial matters, the European Community has set the objective of creating an area of freedom, security and justice, in which the free movement of persons is ensured. "To this end, the Community is to adopt, among others, measures in the field of judicial co-operation in civil matters that are necessary for the proper functioning of the internal market."[212]

It is stated in Brussels II *bis* that: "The recognition and enforcement of judgments given in a Member State should be based on the principle of mutual trust and the grounds for

---

[207] See Law Com No 138 (1985), para 2.45.
[208] Children Act 1989, s 1(1).
[209] *McKee v McKee* [1951] AC 352 at 364–365.
[210] See the Family Proceedings Rules 1991, Pt VI.5.
[211] See generally supra, Chapter 16.
[212] Brussels II *bis*, Recital (1).

non-recognition should be kept to the minimum necessary."[213] Accordingly, Article 21 of the Regulation[214] states that:

1. A judgment[215] given in a Member State[216] shall be recognised in the other Member States without any special procedure being required.
2. In particular, and without prejudice to paragraph 3, no special procedure shall be required for updating the civil-status records of a Member State on the basis of a judgment relating to divorce, legal separation or marriage annulment given in another Member State, and against which no further appeal lies under the law of that Member State.[217]
3. Without prejudice to Section 4[218] of this Chapter, any interested party[219] may, in accordance with the procedures provided for in Section 2[220] of this Chapter, apply for a decision that the judgment be or not be recognised . . .
4. When the recognition of a judgment is raised as an incidental question in a court of a Member State, that court may determine that issue.

(ii) Grounds of non-recognition

Article 23[221] provides that a judgment relating to parental responsibility shall not be recognised: (a) if such recognition is manifestly contrary to the public policy of the Member State in which recognition is sought taking into account the best interests of the child;[222] (b) if it was given, except in cases of urgency, without the child having been given an opportunity to be heard, in violation of fundamental principles of procedure of

---

[213] Recital (21).

[214] Applicable only to legal proceedings instituted, to documents formally drawn up or registered as authentic instruments, and to agreements concluded between the parties after 1 March 2005: Arts 64 and 72. Transitional provisions are set out in Art 64.

[215] Meaning a divorce, legal separation or marriage annulment, as well as a judgment relating to parental responsibility, pronounced by a court of a Member State (including all the authorities in a Member State with jurisdiction in the matters falling within the scope of the Regulation pursuant to Art 1), whatever the judgment may be called, including a decree, order or decision: Art 2(1) and (4). Documents which have been formally drawn up or registered as authentic instruments and are enforceable in one Member State and also agreements between the parties that are enforceable in the Member State in which they were concluded shall be recognised and declared enforceable under the same conditions as judgments: Art 46. See Borras, *Explanatory Report*, paras 60 and 61. "The aim is to encourage parties to reach agreement on matters of parental responsibility outside court" (*Practice Guide*, para 2.2).

[216] Whether that Member State was seised of jurisdiction on the basis of Arts 8–13 of Brussels II *bis*, or founded its jurisdiction on the basis of its own residual rules, per Art 14. In the case of the latter: "Such decisions are to be recognised and declared enforceable in other Member States pursuant to the rules of the Regulation" (*Practice Guide*, para II(2)(e)).

[217] Article 27 (Stay of proceedings) provides that: "1. A court of a Member State in which recognition is sought of a judgment given in another Member State may stay the proceedings if an ordinary appeal against the judgment has been lodged. 2. A court of a Member State in which recognition is sought of a judgment given in Ireland or the United Kingdom may stay the proceedings if enforcement is suspended in the Member State of origin by reason of an appeal." Cf Brussels I Regulation, Art 37.

[218] Enforceability of certain judgments concerning rights of access and of certain judgments which require the return of the child.

[219] See Borras, *Explanatory Report*, para 65: the concept of interested party is to be interpreted "in the broad sense under the national law applicable and may include the public prosecutor or other similar bodies where permitted in the State in which the judgment is to be recognised or contested".

[220] Application for a declaration of enforceability.

[221] By implication, Art 23 provides the only defences to recognition.

[222] See also Arts 24 and 26, infra, p 1099, and under Brussels II, *Re S (Brussels II: Recognition: Best Interests of Child) (No 1)* [2003] EWHC 2115, [2004] 1 FLR 571. Cf Brussels I Regulation, Art 34(1), discussed supra, p 611 et seq.

the Member State in which recognition is sought; (c) where it was given in default of appearance if the person in default was not served with the document which instituted the proceedings or with an equivalent document in sufficient time and in such a way as to enable that person to arrange for his or her defence[223] unless it is determined that such person has accepted the judgment unequivocally; (d) on the request of any person claiming that the judgment infringes his or her parental responsibility, if it was given without such person having been given an opportunity to be heard; (e) if it is irreconcilable with a later judgment relating to parental responsibility given in the Member State in which recognition is sought;[224] (f) if it is irreconcilable with a later judgment relating to parental responsibility given in another Member State[225] or in the non-Member State of the habitual residence of the child provided that the later judgment fulfils the conditions necessary for its recognition in the Member State in which recognition is sought;[226] or (g) if the procedure laid down in Article 56[227] has not been complied with.

(iii) Prohibition of review of jurisdiction of the court of origin

Article 24 of Brussels II *bis* narrates the important principle that: "The jurisdiction of the court of the Member State of origin may not be reviewed.[228] The test of public policy referred to in [Article 23(a)] may not be applied to the rules relating to jurisdiction set out in Articles 3 to 14." It cannot be argued that the court of origin misapplied the jurisdictional rules in Brussels II *bis*, or its national rules of residual jurisdiction. In particular, this prohibition cannot be evaded by using the public policy defence.

(iv) Non-review as to substance

Article 26 lays down the classic rule that under no circumstances may a judgment be reviewed as to its substance.[229] It cannot be alleged that the court of origin made a mistake of fact or of law. Procedural irregularities in the court of origin, however, can be examined in order to establish a defence under Article 23. The nature of parental responsibility matters, however, is such that it may be in the best interests of the child for custody and access arrangements to be reviewed by a court having jurisdiction in terms of Articles 8 to 14.

(v) Application for a declaration of enforceability

Article 28(1) provides that a judgment on the exercise of parental responsibility in respect of a child given in a Member State which is enforceable in that Member State and has been served shall be enforced in another Member State when, on the application of any interested party, it has been declared enforceable there ("*exequatur* procedure"). Article 28(2) sets out a special rule in respect of the United Kingdom, providing that such a judgment shall be enforced in England and Wales, Scotland or Northern Ireland, only

---

223 Cf Brussels I Regulation, Art 34(2), discussed supra, p 615 et seq.

224 Cf Brussels I Regulation, Art 34(3), discussed supra, p 622 et seq.

225 The *lis pendens* provision in Art 19 normally will prevent a judgment being given in the court second seised, but it will not do so if that court does not accept that the parties are the same.

226 Cf Brussels I Regulation, Art 34(4), discussed supra, pp 624–625.

227 Concerning the placement of a child in institutional care or with a foster family in another Member State.

228 Cf Brussels I Regulation, Art 35, discussed supra, pp 625–626.

229 Cf Brussels I Regulation, Art 36, discussed supra, p 628.

when, on the application of any interested party, it has been registered for enforcement in that part of the United Kingdom.[230]

(vi) Enforceability of certain judgments concerning rights of access

Chapter III, Section 4 of Brussels II *bis* (Articles 40 to 45) concerns rights of access[231] and the return of a child entailed by a judgment given pursuant to Article 11(8).[232] Article 41 provides that the rights of access granted[233] in an enforceable judgment given in a Member State shall be recognised and enforceable in another Member State without the need for a declaration of enforceability and without any possibility of opposing its recognition if the judgment has been certified in the Member State of origin in accordance with Article 41(2),[234] thereby demonstrating that the necessary procedural safeguards have been complied with in that state.[235] The judgment shall be certified in the Member State of origin only if all parties concerned (including the child, if appropriate, having regard to his age and maturity) were given an opportunity to be heard; and where the judgment was given in default, the person defaulting was served with the document which instituted the proceedings or with an equivalent document in sufficient time and in such a way as to enable him to arrange for his defence,[236] unless it is determined that such person has accepted the judgment unequivocally. The *Practice Guide* makes plain that the consequence of this special rule for rights of access is two-fold: "(a) it is no longer necessary to apply for an '*exequatur*' and (b) it is no longer possible to oppose the recognition of the judgment".[237]

(vii) Enforcement procedure

Enforcement procedure is governed, not by the Regulation, but by the law of the Member State of enforcement.[238] However, "it is of the essence that national authorities apply rules which secure efficient and speedy enforcement of decisions issued under the Regulation so as not to undermine its objectives".[239] As regards practical arrangements for the exercise of rights of access, the courts of the Member State of enforcement may make the necessary arrangements if they have not already been made in the judgment delivered by the courts of the Member State having jurisdiction as to the substance of the matter and provided that the essential elements of the judgment are respected.[240]

---

[230] See Family Proceedings Rules 1991, rr 7.42–7.46. An application for registration under Art 28(2) shall be made without notice being served on any other party, but notice of the registration of a judgment must be served on the person against whom judgment was given.

[231] Art 2(10): "rights of access" shall include in particular the right to take a child to a place other than his or her habitual residence for a limited period of time.

[232] In respect of the latter, see infra, pp 1120–1121.

[233] Art 41 does not apply to judgments which refuse a request for rights of access.

[234] Using the standard form certificate in Annex III to the Regulation. See Family Proceedings Rules 1991, rr 7.51 and 7.52.

[235] See, however, Austrian court's failure to enforce an English contact order judged by the Deputy Judge of the High Court, relevant experts, and the children's guardian to be in the children's best interests, in *Re ML and AL (Children) (Contact Order: Brussels II Regulation) (No 2)* [2006] EWHC 3631 (Fam), [2007] 1 FCR 496.

[236] Cf Brussels I Regulation, Art 34(2), discussed supra, p 615 et seq.

[237] *Practice Guide*, para VI(1).

[238] Art 47(1). See Family Proceedings Rules 1991, r 7.47.

[239] *Practice Guide*, para VIII.

[240] Art 48.

(viii) Role of Central Authorities

In parental responsibility cases, it is especially important that the designated Central Authorities of Member States cooperate both in general matters and in specific cases,[241] to achieve the purpose of the Regulation. Each Central Authority is required to take all appropriate steps in accordance with the law of its Member State to collect and exchange information concerning the child, to provide information and assistance to holders of parental responsibility who are seeking the recognition and enforcement of decisions, to facilitate agreement between holders of parental responsibility through mediation or other means, and to facilitate communications between courts.[242]

(c) Orders granted in Scotland[243] and Northern Ireland

In 1985 the Law Commissions recommended not only that there should be uniform jurisdictional rules throughout the United Kingdom for the making of "custody orders", but also as a corollary that such orders should be recognised and enforceable elsewhere in the United Kingdom. In this way, protracted, expensive and disruptive proceedings might be avoided. The Commissions said: "In broad terms, our proposals are that the custody orders of the courts of each country [in the United Kingdom] should be recognised in the other countries but should only be enforceable if centrally registered in the courts of the receiving country and should only be enforced through the process of the receiving country."[244] These proposals were carried into effect in that form by Part I of the Family Law Act 1986.[245]

The extent of application of the jurisdiction provisions contained in Brussels II *bis* and of the *lis pendens* provision in Article 19 as regards intra-United Kingdom proceedings has been considered previously in this chapter.[246] The opaque wording of Article 66 of Brussels II *bis* generates a similar interpretative difficulty in relation to the recognition and enforcement of "Part I Orders" as between the territorial units of the United Kingdom. Article 66 of Brussels II *bis* does not refer to "judgments given in a Member State", which is the concern of the Article 21 recognition provisions of the Regulation. It does, however, provide, in Article 66(d), that, "any reference to the rules of the requested Member State shall refer to the rules of the territorial unit in which jurisdiction, recognition or enforcement is invoked". Except for the special Scottish rule of recognition contained in section 26 of the 1986 Act,[247] the recognition and enforcement provisions in Chapter V of the Family Law Act 1986 (sections 25 to 33) appear, from the fact of the Act, to be unaffected by Brussels II *bis*, and untouched by secondary legislation passed subsequent to Brussels II *bis*.[248] The assumption, therefore, is that the intra-United Kingdom

---

[241] Recital (25).

[242] Art 55.

[243] See Crawford and Carruthers (2006), paras 14-43 et seq.

[244] Law Com No 138 (1985), para 3.19.

[245] See the Family Proceedings Rules 1991, Part VII, C. 3. There is power under s 43 of the 1986 Act to extend Part I of the Act by Order in Council to the rest of the British Isles and to any colony, and this power has been exercised in relation to the Isle of Man (with effect from 14 October 1991) and Jersey (with effect from 10 July 2006): SI 1991/1723, as amended by SI 2006/1456.

[246] Supra, pp 1085–1086 and 1095–1096.

[247] Which now is subject to Brussels II *bis*.

[248] SI 2005/265 does not purport to amend Pt V (ss 25–33) of the 1986 Act.

scheme of recognition and enforcement contained in sections 27 to 29 of the 1986 Act still applies, notwithstanding Chapter III (recognition and enforcement) of Brussels II *bis*.[249] Whether this outcome was intended by Article 66 is not clear. It seems inconsistent and anomalous to apply, in intra-United Kingdom cases, the jurisdiction provisions of the Regulation (or at least some of them), but not to apply the recognition and enforcement provisions in Brussels II *bis*;[250] "picking and choosing" selective parts of the Regulation to operate intra-United Kingdom seems, in principle, surprising and undesirable.

The recognition and enforcement provisions of the 1986 Act apply to exactly the same range and type of orders, ie Part I orders, as do the jurisdictional provisions.[251] However, whilst the English jurisdictional provisions govern all Part I orders made in relation to children under the age of 18, the recognition and enforcement provisions are limited to orders applying to children under the age of 16, and they cease to have effect when the child reaches this age. There are various reasons for this difference:[252] Scottish orders can only be made up to the age of 16; the international conventions are limited to children under 16;[253] English orders in relation to 16 and 17-year-olds are rare and their enforcement would be difficult against the wishes of the child.

Part I orders made elsewhere in the United Kingdom and still in force in relation to a child under 16 must be recognised in England.[254] This will be of practical importance to third parties, such as social workers and school teachers, to know that rights conferred by, say, a Scottish order are to be recognised in England.[255] A Scottish or Northern Ireland order cannot, however, be enforced in England until it has been registered in England,[256] and proceedings have been taken in England for its enforcement.[257] Registration is effected by applying to the court which made the order which, provided the order is still in force, passes a certified copy of the order and other relevant documents to the High Court[258] for registration.[259] If the order ceases to have effect, other than by revocation,[260] as where it is superseded by a later order, its registration will be cancelled by the English court.[261]

---

[249] Cf Crawford and Carruthers (2006), para 14-43; and Dicey, Morris and Collins, para 19R-066. In relation to Scotland, although s 17A of the 1986 Act gives priority to the rules of jurisdiction contained in Brussels II *bis*, there is no equivalent provision in relation to the recognition and enforcement provisions of the Regulation.

[250] Particularly when the special United Kingdom provision contained in Art 28(2) and concerning registration for enforcement (supra, pp 1099–1100) echoes the registration provisions in s 27 of the 1986 Act.

[251] 1986 Act, s 1, supra, pp 1079–1080.

[252] Law Com No 138 (1985), para 1.22.

[253] Infra, pp 1104–1123.

[254] 1986 Act, s 25(1). No recognition is given to parts of the order which may relate to enforcement, such as a requirement to hand over the child at a particular time or place: s 25(2). This is so as to ensure that all matters of enforcement are in the hands of courts in the receiving country.

[255] There is also power, under the Children (Scotland) Act 1995, s 33, for effect to be given in England to prescribed Scottish orders, and vice versa.

[256] Ss 25(3), 27. See Lowe [2002] Fam Law 39, at 54. Also *Re T (A Child) (Application for Parental Responsibility)* [2001] EWCA Civ 1067.

[257] S 29. They will fail if, by then, the order has ceased to have effect where granted: *T v T (Custody: Jurisdiction)* [1992] 1 FLR 43.

[258] S 32(1).

[259] S 27.

[260] If the order is cancelled, this is notified by the court which made the order: s 28(1).

[261] S 28(2).

Once registered in England, the Scottish and Northern Ireland order can be enforced in exactly the same way as if it was an English Part I order,[262] provided it remains in force where made.[263] However, enforcement proceedings may be stayed on the application of any interested party on the ground that he has taken or intends to take other proceedings, whether in the United Kingdom or elsewhere, as a result of which the order may cease to have effect or have a different effect.[264] So although the merits of the order cannot be attacked in the country of registration,[265] a parent might convince the English court that he was going to attack them before the Scottish court which made the order, or there argue that that court lacked jurisdiction, or, indeed, that he proposes to apply to another court for a new order.[266] In all such cases, the English court has a discretion to stay the enforcement proceedings and, indeed, to lift any stay.[267] If the English court is satisfied that the original order, now registered in England, has ceased to have effect, it will dismiss the enforcement proceedings.[268]

Whilst it is to be hoped that the system for the recognition and enforcement throughout the United Kingdom of orders made in one part thereof will eradicate the conflicts which arose in the past, particularly between English and Scottish courts,[269] attention has to be drawn to the fact that the recognition and enforcement procedures apply only to orders falling under Part I of the 1986 Act.

(d) Child Abduction and Custody Act 1985 [270]

Special rules have been developed to govern cases where a child has been unlawfully removed from the state of his habitual residence and taken to another state. The Child Abduction and Custody Act 1985[271] gives effect to two international conventions relating to the recognition of foreign custody rights and orders, both of which are scheduled to the Act and provide very similar mechanisms for their operation.[272] The first is the Hague Convention on the Civil Aspects of International Child Abduction (1980), in respect of which there are eighty Contracting States,[273] and which is implemented by Part I of the 1985 Act. The second is the Council of Europe Convention on Recognition and Enforcement of Decisions concerning Custody of Children and on the Restoration of Custody of Children (1980). There are currently thirty-five parties[274] to the European

---

[262] S 29; and see *Woodcock v Woodcock* 1990 SLT 848.

[263] *S v S (Custody: Jurisdiction)* [1995] 1 FLR 155.

[264] S 30.

[265] It is suggested that the Court of Session was incorrect in *Woodcock v Woodcock* 1990 SLT 848 at 853 in indicating the contrary; see Edwards (1992) 41 ICLQ 444.

[266] Such an argument failed in *Re M (Minors) (Custody: Jurisdiction)* [1992] 2 FLR 382.

[267] S 30(3).

[268] S 31. It is relevant in the context of enforcement, as of jurisdiction, that the English court knows of similar proceedings elsewhere, including administrative proceedings, ss 39, 42(7).

[269] Contrast the balanced approach under the 1986 Act as evidenced by *Re K (A Minor: Wardship)* [1991] 2 FLR 104, [1991] Fam Law 226.

[270] See the Family Proceedings Rules 1991, Part VI.

[271] As amended by the Family Law Act 1986, ss 67, 68, Sch 1, para 28, and by the Children Act 1989, Sch 13, para 57, Sch 15.

[272] In relation to both there is power to order the disclosure of a child's whereabouts: 1985 Act, s 24A. See *Re D (A Minor) (Child Abduction)* [1988] FCR 585, [1989] 1 FLR 97; and *M, Petitioner* 2000 GWD 32-1242.

[273] See SI 2005/1260. See status table at www.hcch.net.

[274] Ibid, Sch 2. See http://conventions.coe.int.

Convention, which is implemented by Part II of the 1985 Act. These two Conventions now must be examined in the light of Brussels II *bis*, which contains special provisions pertaining to international child abduction, and which, by virtue of Article 60 of the Regulation, takes precedence over the Hague Convention and the Council of Europe Convention as regards relations between European Community Member States.

(i) Part I of the 1985 Act: the Hague Convention[275]

(a) Aim of the Convention

The prime concern of the Hague Convention is the restoration of children who have been wrongfully removed or wrongfully retained, whether or not this is in breach of a custody order in one of the Contracting States. Not only does the Convention provide for the recognition and enforcement of custody orders, but it also protects rights of custody even where there has been no order.[276] The Convention does not provide for the enforcement of access rights in the same way as it seeks to uphold custody rights, but an application to make arrangements for organising or securing the effective exercise of rights of access nevertheless may be presented to the Central Authorities[277] of Contracting States.[278]

(b) Wrongful removal and wrongful retention

Essential elements of the Convention are that it applies to a child under the age of 16 who was habitually resident in a Contracting State at the time when he was wrongfully removed or retained.[279] The House of Lords[280] has made clear that both removal and retention are single events, so that if a child is wrongfully removed before the Convention

---

[275] See Beaumont and McEleavy, *The Hague Convention on International Child Abduction* (1999); Anton (1981) 30 ICLQ 537; Eekelaar (1982) 32 U Tor LJ 281, 305–325; Shapira (1989) II Hague Recueil 127, 189–200; Crawford (1990) 35 JLSS 277; Davis (1990) 4 Aus J Fam L 31; Crawford (1992) 2 JR 192; Silberman (1994) 28 Family Law Quarterly 9; Bruch, ibid, 35; Schuz (1995) 44 ICLQ 771; McClean and Beevers (1995) 7 Ch FLQ 128; Balfour and Crawford (1996) SLPQ 411; Reddaway and Keating (1997) 5 Int J of Children's Rights 77; Lowe and Pery (1999) 48 ICLQ 127; Armstrong (2002) 51 ICLQ 427; McEleavy (2005) 1.1 J Priv Int L 5; and Beevers and Perez Milla (2007) 3.1 J Priv Int Law 201. Reports by the Hague Conference on the operation of the Convention are to be found in (1990) 29 International Legal Materials 220; (1994) 33 International Legal Materials 225. For a database of cases on the Convention, see http://www.incadat.com.

[276] See *B v B (Minors: Enforcement of Access Abroad)* [1988] 1 WLR 526; *C v C (Minors) (Child Abduction)* [1992] 1 FLR 163; *Re G (A Minor; Enforcement of Access Abroad)* [1993] Fam 216; *Re T (Minors) (Hague Convention: Access)* [1993] 2 FLR 617; and see [1993] 1 WLR 1461; cf *S v H (Abduction: Access Rights)* [1997] 1 FLR 970.

[277] S 3 of the Child Abduction and Custody Act 1985 establishes that the functions of the Central Authority in England and Wales and in Northern Ireland shall be discharged by the Lord Chancellor, and in Scotland, by the Secretary of State. No obligation is imposed, however, upon judicial authorities: *Donofrio v Burrell* 1999 GWD 12-528, aff d 2000 SLT 1051.

[278] Art 21. See *B v B (Minors: Enforcement of Access Abroad)* [1988] 1 WLR 526; *C v C (Minors) (Child Abduction)* [1992] 1 FLR 163; *Re G (A Minor: Enforcement of Access Abroad)* [1993] Fam 216; *Re T (Minors) (Hague Convention: Access)* [1993] 2 FLR 617; and see [1993] 1 WLR 1461; cf *S v H (Abduction: Access Rights)* [1997] 1 FLR 970. See, for Scottish cases, Crawford and Carruthers (2006), para 14-21. See access provisions of Brussels II *bis*, supra, p 1100, and Council of Europe Convention on Contact concerning Children, infra, p 1139.

[279] Art 4. The Convention ceases to apply when the child attains the age of 16 years: *Re H (Abduction: Child of 16)* [2000] 2 FLR 51.

[280] *Re H (Minors) (Abduction: Custody Rights)* [1991] 2 AC 476; and see *Kilgour v Kilgour* 1987 SLT 568; *B v B (Minors: Enforcement of Access Abroad)* [1988] 1 WLR 526; *Re S (Minors) (Abduction: Wrongful Retention)* [1994] Fam 70; *Re S (Child Abduction: Delay)* [1998] 1 FLR 651; *Findlay v Findlay* 1994 SLT 709; *Findlay v Findlay (No 2)* 1995 SLT 492; *Re Gollogly and Owen's Marriage* (1989) 13 Fam LR 622; *In the Marriage of Murray and Tam* (1993) 16 Fam LR 982.

came into force, but not returned after that date, such latter conduct does not constitute "retention" within the meaning of the Convention[281] and section 2 of the Act. This means that, for those purposes, removal and retention[282] are mutually exclusive concepts: "Removal occurs when a child, which has previously been in the state of its habitual residence, is taken across the frontier of that state;[283] whereas retention occurs where a child, which has previously been for a limited period outside the state of its habitual residence,[284] is not returned to that state on the expiry of such limited period."[285] Furthermore, the wrongful removal or retention under the Convention must be "international" in nature,[286] ie the child must have been taken from, or retained outside, the country of his habitual residence in which the custody or access rights existed.[287] In other words, what is involved is wrongful removal from, or retention out of, that country, rather than just from or out of the care of the parent having custody rights.

(i) Habitual residence

The habitual residence of the child is the crucial connecting factor[288] and it is not defined in the Convention. The concept of habitual residence has been examined in detail in Chapter 9. It is essentially a question of fact[289] for the English court,[290] although questions of habitual residence in relation to Article 3 of the Convention are to be determined by reference to the international jurisprudence recorded on the INCADAT database of the Hague Conference.[291] The child's habitual residence is usually determined by the parents.[292] A removal from one country with the consent of both parents will change the child's habitual residence even though one parent later changes his or her mind.[293] However, a child's habitual residence cannot be changed by one parent without the

---

[281] [1991] 2 AC 476 at 499; cf *Re J (A Minor) (Abduction: Custody Rights)* [1990] 2 AC 562 at 578–579.

[282] Retention may be evidenced by the institution of proceedings for a court order preventing the return of the child: *Re AZ (A Minor) (Abduction: Acquiescence)* [1993] 1 FLR 682; *Re B (Minors) (Abduction) (No 2)* [1993] 1 FLR 993; and *Re S (A Minor) (Abduction: European Convention)* [1998] AC 750.

[283] *Re L (Abduction: Pending Criminal Proceedings)* [1999] 1 FLR 433; *Re L (Children) (Abduction: Declaration)* [2001] 2 FCR 1.

[284] *Re D (Abduction: Discretionary Return)* [2000] 1 FLR 24; *Re H (A Child) (Abduction: Habitual Residence: Consent)* [2000] 2 FLR 294; *Re M (Abduction: Conflict of Jurisdiction)* [2000] 2 FLR 372; *H v H* [2004] EWHC 2111; and *Re C (A Child) (Abduction: Residence and Contact)* [2005] EWHC 2205, [2006] 2 FLR 277.

[285] [1991] 2 AC 476 at 500. Retention may be wrongful where a parent decides not to return a child, even though the period for which the child is lawfully with that parent has not yet expired: *Re S (Minors) (Abduction: Wrongful Retention)* [1994] Fam 70.

[286] *Re H (Minors) (Abduction: Custody Rights)* [1991] 2 AC 476; *In the Marriage of R and S S Hanbury-Brown* (1996) 20 Fam LR 334.

[287] *B v B (Minors: Enforcement of Access Abroad)* [1988] 1 WLR 526 at 532.

[288] Eg *V v B (A Minor) (Abduction)* [1991] FCR 451, [1991] 1 FLR 266.

[289] *Re J (A Minor) (Abduction: Custody Rights)* [1990] 2 AC 562 at 578–579; *Re N (Child Abduction: Habitual Residence)* [1993] 2 FLR 124; *In the Marriage of R and S S Hanbury-Brown* (1996) 20 Fam LR 334. Contrast *Re R (Wardship: Child Abduction) (No 2)* [1993] 1 FLR 249. See also *Al-H v F* [2001] EWCA Civ 186, [2001] 1 FLR 951; *Re R (Abduction: Habitual Residence)* [2003] EWHC 1968, [2004] 1 FLR 216; *Re D (Abduction: Habitual Residence)* [2005] EWHC 518, [2005] 2 FLR 403; *Re A (Abduction: Consent: Habitual Residence: Consent)* [2005] EWHC 2998, [2006] 2 FLR 1; *E v E* [2007] EWHC 276, [2007] Fam Law 480; and *W v F* [2007] EWHC 779 (Fam), (2007) 104(18) LSG 28.

[290] A foreign finding as to habitual residence is not binding on the English court: *Re B (Child Abduction: Habitual Residence)* [1994] 2 FLR 915.

[291] *Re S (A Child) (Abduction: Residence Order)* [2002] EWCA Civ 1949, [2003] 1 FLR 1008, per THORPE LJ, at [31].

[292] *Re G (Abduction: Rights of Custody)* [2002] 2 FLR 703; and *W, Petitioner* 2003 GWD 28-772.

[293] *Re J (A Minor) (Abduction: Custody Rights)* [1990] 2 AC 562 at 572, CA; *Dickson v Dickson* 1990 SCLR 692.

consent of the other;[294] and a wrongful removal of the child will not alter his habitual residence for the purposes of the Convention.[295]

(ii) Rights of custody

"The world would be a simpler place if the Convention had provided that all removal or retention of a child outside the country where he or she is habitually resident without the consent of the other parent or the authority of a court is wrongful. But it does not."[296] Removal or retention is wrongful if it is, at that time,[297] in breach of custody rights under the law of the child's habitual residence which were being exercised.[298] Therefore, when determining whether removal or retention is wrongful within the meaning of Article 3 of the Convention, the first task for the court to which the application is made[299] is to establish what rights, if any, the abductor had under the law of the state in which the child was habitually resident immediately prior to his removal,[300] and whether those rights amount to "rights of custody" for the purpose of Articles 3 and 5(b) of the Convention.

> This is a matter of international law and depends on the application of the autonomous meaning of the phrase "rights of custody".[301] Where . . . an application is made in the courts of England and Wales, the autonomous meaning is determined in accordance with English law as the law of the court whose jurisdiction has been invoked under the Convention.[302]

---

[294] Provided both have the right to determine the child's residence: *Re J (A Minor) (Abduction: Custody Rights)* [1990] 2 AC 562 at 572; *Re AF (A Minor) (Abduction)* [1992] 1 FCR 269; *Re S (Minors) (Abduction: Wrongful Retention)* [1994] Fam 70; *Re N (Child Abduction: Habitual Residence)* [2000] 2 FLR 899; *M, Petitioner* 2005 SLT 2.

[295] *Re Barraclough's Marriage* (1987) 11 Fam LR 773; *Re Gollogly and Owen's Marriage* (1989) 13 Fam LR 622; *Re Brandon's Marriage* (1990) 14 Fam LR 181. Family Law Act 1986, s 41 (habitual residence after removal without consent, etc) has no application to questions of habitual residence under Art 3 of the Hague Convention, being a deeming provision to resolve conflicts between the constituent parts of the United Kingdom, not between the United Kingdom and any jurisdiction that is not a constituent part: *Re S (A Child) (Abduction: Residence Order)* [2002] EWCA Civ 1949, [2003] 1 FLR 1008, per THORPE LJ, at [31]; and *Re B (A Child) (Court's Jurisdiction)* [2004] EWCA Civ 681, [2004] 2 FLR 741, and [2005] EWCA Civ 675.

[296] *Re D (A Child) (Abduction: Rights of Custody)* [2006] UKHL 51, [2007] 1 AC 619, per Baroness HALE of Richmond, at [24].

[297] *Re S (A Minor) (Abduction)* [1991] FCR 656, [1991] 2 FLR 1; *Re H (Minors) (Abduction: Custody Rights)* [1991] 2 AC 476 at 484–485, CA, affd, ibid, at 491, HL; *S v S (Child Abduction: Custody Rights: Acquiescence)* 2003 SLT 344 (father considered not to have abandoned the exercise of legal rights, or ceased exercising rights of custody while mentally ill and compulsorily detained in hospital); *Re A (A Child) (Abduction: Rights of Custody: Imprisonment)* [2004] 1 FLR 1; *Re L (A Child)* [2005] EWHC 1237, [2006] 1 FLR 843 (incarceration in a Spanish prison did not preclude child's father from exercising rights of custody).

[298] Art 3; *Re W (Abduction: Procedure)* [1995] 1 FLR 878.

[299] Not the authorities of the requesting State: *Re D (A Child) (Abduction: Rights of Custody)* [2006] UKHL 51, [2007] 1 AC 619, per Lord HOPE of Craighead, at [7].

[300] Arts 14, 15; and see 1985 Act, s 8; *C v C (Minors) (Child Abduction)* [1992] 1 FLR 163. An English court can, therefore, make a declaration as to wrongfulness for the benefit of a foreign court considering whether to order the return of a child: *Re J (Abduction: Ward of Court)* [1989] Fam 85. There is, however, no absolute guarantee that it will be followed abroad, just as there is no obligation on an English court to follow a foreign court's ruling; see *Re J (A Minor) (Abduction: Custody Rights)* [1990] 2 AC 562 at 577–578. Nor is there a requirement to seek a ruling from a foreign court: *Taylor v Ford* 1993 SLT 654; *Perrin v Perrin* 1994 SC 45. In relation to Art 15 declarations, see supra, p 1046.

[301] Cf *Re D (A Child) (Abduction: Rights of Custody)* [2006] UKHL 51, [2007] 1 AC 619, per Lord HOPE of Craighead, at [8].

[302] *Hunter v Morrow* [2005] EWCA Civ 976, [2005] 2 FLR 1119, per DYSON LJ, at [47].

That said, the Convention cannot be construed differently in different jurisdictions: it must have the same meaning and effect under the laws of all Contracting States.[303] Whilst it is for the law of the country of the habitual residence to determine the nature and extent of the rights,[304] it is for English law to determine whether they amount to "rights of custody" within the Convention;[305] a broad, purposive interpretation has been encouraged.[306]

Custody rights include those which can be attributed to one parent, or to both jointly,[307] and which can arise "by operation of law or by reason of a judicial[308] or administrative decision,[309] or by reason of an agreement having legal affect under the law" of the child's habitual residence.[310] Rights of custody are not defined exclusively but include rights relating to the care of the person of the child[311] and to determine his place of residence.[312] A person with "parental responsibility" has rights of custody[313] and may even have such rights when exercising parental functions short of full parental responsibility.[314] They also include, in England, custody rights attributed to a court when a child is made a ward of court,[315] where the court is exercising its powers to determine the child's place of residence,[316] where a guardianship application is pending,[317] or where a parent awarded an interim custody order is prohibited from removing the child from the jurisdiction;[318] but

---

[303] *Re H (Abduction: Acquiescence)* [1998] AC 72 at 87 per Lord BROWNE-WILKINSON. Though, as noted in *Re D (A Child) (Abduction: Rights of Custody)* [2006] UKHL 51, [2007] 1 AC 619, per Lord HOPE of Craighead, at [15], the Convention has not provided any formal mechanisms to ensure that the international legal norms that it has created are applied uniformly and consistently in the numerous Contracting States (cf Baroness HALE of Richmond, at [28]). See also Silberman (2005) 38 U C Davis Law Review 1049, 1057, criticising *Croll v Croll* (2000) 229 F 3 d 133, (2001) 534 US 949.

[304] *Hunter v Morrow* [2005] EWCA Civ 976, [2005] 2 FLR 1119.

[305] *Re B (A Minor) (Abduction)* [1994] 2 FLR 249; *Re F (A Minor) (Abduction: Custody Rights Abroad)* [1995] Fam 224; *S v H (Abduction: Access Rights)* [1997] 1 FLR 970.

[306] *Re B (A Minor) (Abduction)*, supra; *Re M and J (Children) (Abduction: International Judicial Collaboration)* [2000] 1 FLR 803; *Re H (A Minor) (Abduction: Rights of Custody)* [2000] 2 AC 291; *Re G (Abduction: Rights of Custody)* [2002] 2 FLR 703.

[307] Art 3.

[308] See *Re E (A Child) (Abduction: Rights of Custody)* [2005] EWHC 848, [2005] 2 FLR 759, per Sir Mark POTTER: in summary proceedings under the Convention it is not appropriate for an English court to go behind the decision of a competent court of another Contracting State dealing with the custody of the child, where the terms of the foreign court's order, relied on as establishing custody rights under the Convention, were clear, apt for the purpose, and had not been appealed.

[309] *Re JS (Private International Adoption)* [2000] 2 FLR 638.

[310] Art 3.

[311] Though see *Re J (Abduction: Acquiring Custody Rights by Caring for Child)* [2005] 2 FLR 791: despite having shared care of the child with the mother for a period and having lived with them, the applicant father was held never to have acquired rights of custody within the meaning of the Convention.

[312] Art 5(a). See *C v C (Abduction: Rights of Custody)* [1989] 1 WLR 654; *C v C (Minors) (Child Abduction)* [1992] 1 FLR 163.

[313] *Re M (Minors) (Residence Order: Jurisdiction)* [1993] 1 FLR 495.

[314] *Re B (A Minor) (Abduction)* [1994] 2 FLR 249 at 261; *Re O (Child Abduction: Custody Rights)* [1997] 2 FLR 702; cf *Re B (Abduction) (Rights of Custody)* [1997] 2 FLR 594. Also *T, Petitioner* 2007 SLT 543, and 2007 GWD 11-200

[315] *Re J (Abduction: Ward of Court)* [1989] Fam 85. A Canadian court has held that rights of custody may be attributed to a North American Indian Tribe: *S (S M) v A(J)* (1990) 65 DLR (4th) 222. It was left open, in *Re K (Abduction: Consent: Forum Conveniens)* [1995] 2 FLR 211, as to whether a parent may apply for the return of a child wrongfully removed when the rights were attributed to a court rather than to the applicant parent.

[316] *B v B (Abduction: Custody Rights)* [1993] Fam 32; cf *The Ontario Court v M and M (Abduction: Children's Objections)* [1997] 1 FLR 475. Also *Re W (Minors) (Abduction: Father's Rights)* [1998] 2 FLR 146.

[317] *Re H (A Minor) (Abduction: Rights of Custody)* [2000] 2 AC 291.

[318] *Thomson v Thomson* (1994) 119 DLR (4th) 253; *W (V) v S(D)* (1996) 134 DLR (4th) 481.

the rights of the court do not appear to continue once a final custody order has been made.[319] It has been held[320] that a right of veto (but not a potential right of veto[321]), giving one parent the right to insist that the other parent does not remove the child from the home country without either his consent or a court order, amounts to "rights of custody". It is possible for someone who is not related by blood to the child to fall within a quasi-parental role in relation to the child, and so to acquire inchoate rights of custody, namely, those which are capable of being effected by an application to the court which has a reasonable prospect of success.[322] If one parent had no rights of custody under the law of the child's habitual residence at the time of the removal or retention by the other parent, then such conduct is not wrongful and falls outside the Convention even if such rights are acquired later.[323]

(c) Restoration of status quo: return of the child to his habitual residence

The Convention requires administrative structures and procedures to be established, in particular the use of a designated Central Authority for each Contracting State,[324] to enable a child to be returned to the country from which it has been wrongfully removed or outside which it has been wrongfully retained. If we assume that a child has been wrongfully removed from Australia to England, the procedures to ensure its return to Australia are as follows.[325] The parent or other person claiming the child applies to the Central Authority in Australia, or in any other Contracting State, for assistance in securing the return of the child. The application, which has to contain essential particulars of the child, the grounds of the claim and available information as to the child's whereabouts,[326] is sent without delay by the Central Authority which receives it to the Central Authority in the country where the child is thought to be.[327] In the case of a child thought to be in England, the application is sent to the Lord Chancellor,[328] who must then cause all appropriate measures to be taken to discover the whereabouts of the child, to prevent

---

[319] *Seroka v Bellah* 1995 SLT 304; and see *Thomson v Thomson*, supra, at 281.

[320] *Re D (A Child) (Abduction: Rights of Custody)* [2006] UKHL 51, [2007] 1 AC 619 (see especially Baroness HALE of Richmond, at [37]); and *Re A (A Child) (Abduction: Rights of Custody: Imprisonment)* [2004] 1 FLR 1.

[321] *Re D (A Child) (Abduction: Rights of Custody)*, supra, at [38]. Where, for instance, a parent has the right to go to court to ask for an order regarding the child's upbringing, including relocation abroad. Cf *Re J (A Minor) (Abduction: Custody Rights)* [1990] 2 AC 562; and *Re V-B (Abduction: Rights of Custody)* [1999] 2 FLR 192—distinction must be drawn between rights of custody and rights of access.

[322] *Re F (Abduction: Unmarried Father: Sole Carer)* [2002] EWHC 2896, [2003] 1 FLR 839.

[323] *Re J (A Minor) (Abduction: Custody Rights)* [1990] 2 AC 562; *Re W (Minors) (Abduction: Father's Rights)* [1998] 2 FLR 146; *Re D (Abduction: Custody Rights)* [1999] 2 FLR 626; *B v United Kingdom* [2000] 1 FLR 1; *Re C (Child Abduction) (Unmarried Father: Rights of Custody)* [2002] EWHC 2219, [2003] 1 FLR 252; *Re H (Child Abduction) (Unmarried Father: Rights of Custody)* [2003] EWHC 492, [2003] 2 FLR 153; and *Re JB (Child Abduction: Rights of Custody: Spain)* [2003] EWHC 2130, [2004] 1 FLR 796 (in respect of which see Beevers and Perez Milla (2007) 3.1 J Priv Int L 201, 212 et seq).

[324] See Arts 7–11. S 3 of the Child Abduction and Custody Act 1985 establishes that the functions of the Central Authority in England and Wales and in Northern Ireland shall be discharged by the Lord Chancellor, and in Scotland, by the Secretary of State. On the matter of costs, see Arts 22 and 26 and 1985 Act, s 11; also *EC-L v DM (Child Abduction)* [2005] EWHC 588, [2005] 2 FLR 772.

[325] Similar procedures apply, *mutatis mutandis*, where a parent in England seeks the recovery of a child wrongfully taken or retained abroad; see eg *Re J (Abduction: Ward of Court)* [1989] Fam 85.

[326] Art 8.

[327] Art 9.

[328] 1985 Act, s 3. In fact, the Official Solicitor acts on his behalf: *Re T (Minors) (International Child Abduction: Access)* [1993] 1 WLR 1461.

further harm to him and to try to secure the voluntary return of the child.[329] He must also initiate, or facilitate, the institution of judicial or administrative proceedings to secure the return of the child[330] without considering the merits of any custody issue;[331] and any judicial proceedings in England are in the High Court.[332] If less than one year has elapsed between the date of the wrongful removal and the English proceedings, the child must[333] be ordered to be returned forthwith; if more than a year has elapsed, the return of the child must be ordered "unless it is demonstrated that the child is now[334] settled in its new environment".[335]

Settlement of the child in his new environment

Settlement in this context means more than mere adjustment to surroundings. It involves both the physical element of being established in a community and an environment, and an emotional and psychological[336] constituent of security and stability.[337] The concept of "new environment" has been held to encompass place, home, school, people, friends, activities and opportunities, but not, per se, the child's relationship with the abductor.[338] In *Cannon v Cannon*[339] THORPE LJ identified three different categories of case in which the issue of settlement may arise. First, there are cases which demonstrate a delayed reaction, short of acquiescence, on the part of the bereft parent: "In that category of case the court must weigh whether or not the child is settled and whether nevertheless to order return having regard to all the circumstances, including the extent of the plaintiff's delay and his explanation for the delay."[340] The second category is where concealment or other subterfuge on the part of the abductor has contributed to the period of delay: "In those cases I would not support a tolling rule that the period gained by concealment should be disregarded and therefore subtracted from the total period of delay in order to ascertain whether or not the 12-month mark has been exceeded."[341] However, an abducting

---

[329] Arts 7, 11.

[330] The return of the child is to the country of its habitual residence: *Re A (A Minor) (Abduction)* [1988] 1 FLR 365 at 373.

[331] Art 19.

[332] 1985 Act, s 3. Once an application has been made to the court, it may give interim directions to secure the welfare of the child or to prevent a change in circumstances: s 5; see *Re D (A Minor) (Child Abduction)* [1988] FCR 585, [1989] 1 FLR 97 n; *Re N (Child Abduction: Jurisdiction)* [1995] Fam 96.

[333] Subject to the discretionary grounds for refusal of return, infra, p 1110 et seq.

[334] This means the date of the commencement of the proceedings: *Re N (Minors) (Abduction)* [1991] 1 FLR 413 at 417.

[335] Art 12. There is also power to stay or dismiss the application if it is thought that the child has been taken to another state. The Convention powers are in addition to any other powers to order the return of the child: Art 18.

[336] Though see *Re C (A Child) (Child Abduction: Settlement)* [2006] EWHC 1229 (Fam), [2006] 2 FLR 797—the fact that a child or teenager is "unsettled" in her own emotional or psychological state does not demonstrate that she is not well settled for the purposes of the Convention in the place where she resides.

[337] *Re N (Minors) (Abduction)* [1991] 1 FLR 413, [1991] Fam Law 367; and see *Re S (A Minor) (Abduction)* [1991] 2 FLR 1 at 23–24; *Perrin v Perrin* 1994 SC 45; *Soucie v Soucie* 1995 SLT 414; *Graziano v Daniels* (1991) 14 Fam LR 697. It is possible that in certain situations it may be thought appropriate to put to the child, for his view, the hypothetical scenario of return ("what if?"), but this should never be deemed necessary: *Re H (Children) (Child Abduction: Objection to Return)* [2005] EWCA Civ 319, (2005) 149 SJLB 178, per SEDLEY LJ, at [25].

[338] *Re C (A Child) (Child Abduction: Settlement)* [2006] EWHC 1229 (Fam), [2006] 2 FLR 797 at [46]. Also *Re N (Minors) (Abduction)* [1991] 1 FLR 413.

[339] [2004] EWCA Civ 1330, [2005] 1 FLR 169 at [50] et seq. See also *Re C (Abduction: Settlement) (No 2)* [2005] 1 FLR 938; and *Re M (Children) (Abduction)* [2007] UKHL 55, [2007] 3 WLR 975.

[340] *Cannon v Cannon*, supra, at [50].

[341] Ibid, at [51].

parent who has engaged in such clandestine and deceitful behaviour will find it harder to prove settlement, and the burden of demonstrating the necessary elements of emotional and psychological settlement will be much increased.[342] It is possible, nevertheless, that the turpitude of the abductor's conduct will be outweighed by the quality of the new environment: "the longer the [abductor] persists in her deceit the more likely she is to hold her advantage".[343] Thirdly, there is the category of "manipulative delay", where, by deliberate conduct, the abductor is successful in delaying the issue of proceedings beyond the 12-month limit. It is not the case that judges should disregard the "settlement" defence altogether in such cases, but they will look critically at any alleged settlement built upon intentional concealment and deceit, especially if the defendant is a fugitive from criminal justice.[344]

Even if settlement is established on the facts, the court retains a residual discretion to order the return of the child.[345] The discretion is specifically conferred by Article 18 of the Convention. Furthermore, if notice of a wrongful removal has been received in England, whether expressly or by inference,[346] the merits of the custody issue cannot be determined in England until a decision has been taken on the return of the child or unless an application for its return is not made within a reasonable time.[347]

(d) Defences

Although the purpose of the Hague Convention and Part I of the 1985 Act is to ensure the summary return of a child without consideration of the merits of the custody issue,[348] there are three grounds in Article 13 of the Convention on which return may be refused.

---

[342] Ibid, at [54]–[58]. See also *Re L (Abduction: Pending Criminal Proceedings)* [1999] 1 FLR 433—hiding children in England for 10 months unlikely to constitute settlement; *Re B (Abduction: False Immigration Information)* [2000] 2 FLR 835—due administration of justice requires the courts to be intolerant of attempts to deceive other bodies operating legal functions, such as immigration authorities; and *Re C (A Child) (Child Abduction: Settlement)* [2006] EWHC 1229 (Fam), [2006] 2 FLR 797.

[343] *Cannon v Cannon*, at [58]. Eg *Re C (A Child) (Abduction: Residence and Contact)* [2005] EWHC 2205, [2006] 2 FLR 277.

[344] Ibid, at [61]. Cf *P v S (Child Abduction: Wrongful Removal)* [2002] Fam LR 2—Lord Ordinary entitled to find child not settled in new environment given circumstances of mother who had moved around Europe for several years, who only recently moved to current location with child and who, upon receiving warning of impending arrest, undoubtedly would have taken steps to evade the authorities further.

[345] See *Re S (A Minor) (Abduction)* [1991] FCR 656, [1991] 2 FLR 1; *Re L (Abduction: Pending Criminal Proceedings)* [1999] 1 FLR 433; *J v K (Child Abduction: Acquiescence)* 2002 SC 450; *Cannon v Cannon* [2004] EWCA Civ 1330, [2005] 1 FLR 169; *Re C (A Child) (Child Abduction: Settlement)* [2006] EWHC 1229 (Fam), [2006] 2 FLR 797; and *Re M (Children) (Abduction)* [2007] UKHL 55, [2007] 3 WLR 975.

[346] *R v R (Residence Order: Child Abduction)* [1995] Fam 209, where a parent abroad had not initiated proceedings under the Convention in the case of what the court concluded was wrongful removal. The court sought to have the parent informed of his rights.

[347] Art 16. It seems hard to understand why, in *H v H (Child Abduction: Stay of Domestic Proceedings)* [1994] 1 FLR 530, the court felt able to order the return of the child to France but then allowed English proceedings to go ahead. Issues which in England are held to go to the merits are listed in the 1985 Act, s 9, as amended by the Children Act 1989, Sch 15, and the Children (Scotland) Act 1995, Sch 4. Furthermore, if an order is made by the High Court for the return of the child, any similar English order ceases to have effect: ss 25, 27, Sch 3 (as amended by the Children Act 1989, Sch 13, para 57, Sch 15).

[348] See *Re E (A Minor) (Abduction)* [1989] 1 FLR 135 at 145; *P v P (Minors) (Child Abduction)* [1992] 1 FLR 155; *Re F (A Minor) (Child Abduction)* [1992] 1 FLR 548; *Re K (Abduction: Child's Objections)* [1995] 1 FLR 977; *Re S (Child Abduction: Delay)* [1998] 1 FLR 651. Speed is strikingly illustrated by *Re J (A Minor) (Abduction: Custody Rights)* [1990] 2 AC 562 where less than 3 months elapsed between a request being made by the Australian Central Authority for the return of a child in England and the House of Lords decision.

Such refusal is discretionary and, whilst the court must have regard to the welfare of the child, it must do so in the context of "the overall purpose and philosophy of the Convention".[349] Significantly, the House of Lords has held that:

> It is wrong to import any test of exceptionality into the exercise of discretion under the Hague Convention.[350] The circumstances in which return may be refused are themselves exceptions to the general rule. That in itself is sufficient exceptionality. It is neither necessary nor desirable to import an additional gloss into the Convention.[351]

(i) Child's objections

The first ground of refusal is if the child objects at the date of the court hearing[352] to being returned to the country of his habitual residence, rather than objecting simply to living with a particular parent,[353] "and has attained an age and degree of maturity at which it is appropriate to take account of its views".[354] The proper approach to dealing with the child's objections was set out in *Re M (A Child)*.[355] There are three considerations: (i) whether or not the objections to return are made out;[356] (ii) whether the age and maturity of the child are such that it is appropriate for the court to take account of the objections (for unless this is so, the defence cannot be established); and (iii) whether or not the court should exercise its discretion in favour of retention or return.

The first and second issues are questions of fact within the province of the trial judge.[357] It will usually be necessary for the trial judge to find out why the child objects to being returned. Very occasionally, the court might order that the child should be separately represented, but only in exceptional circumstances,[358] and subject to the child being

---

[349] *Re A (Minors) (Abduction: Custody Rights) (No 2)* [1993] Fam 1; *A v A (Child Abduction)* [1993] 2 FLR 225; *W v W (Child Abduction: Acquiescence)* [1993] 2 FLR 211; *Re R (Abduction: Consent)* [1999] 1 FLR 828.

[350] Meaning that a judge need *not* find something utterly exceptional in a case, over and above the basic ground of opposition which has been established, before he can refuse to order the return of the child under the Convention: *Re M (Children) (Abduction)* [2007] UKHL 55, [2007] 3 WLR 975, per Baroness Hale of Richmond, at [35].

[351] *Re M (Children) (Abduction)*, supra, per Baroness Hale of Richmond, at [40].

[352] *Cameron v Cameron (No 2)* 1997 SLT 206.

[353] *Re R (Minors: Child Abduction)* [1995] 1 FLR 716.

[354] Art 13; and see *Re G (A Minor) (Abduction)* [1990] FCR 189, [1989] 2 FLR 475; *Re S (A Minor) (Abduction)* [1991] FCR 656, [1991] 2 FLR 1.

[355] [2007] EWCA Civ 260, (2007) 151 SJLB 434. See also *Re S (A Minor) (Abduction: Custody Rights)* [1993] Fam 242; cited with approval in *Re T (Children) (Abduction: Child's Objections to Return)* [2000] 2 FLR 192; and *Re J (Children) (Abduction: Child's Objections to Return)* [2004] EWCA Civ 428, [2004] 2 FLR 64.

[356] *C v B (Abduction: Grave Risk)* [2005] EWHC 2988, [2006] 1 FLR 1095—child's views not strong enough to amount to "objection" for the purposes of Art 13. See also *K v K* [2006] EWHC 2685, [2007] 1 FCR 355, where a 9-year-old child expressed conflicting opinions, court held insufficient strength and clarity of objection to warrant exercise of Art 13 discretion.

[357] *Re S (A Minor) (Abduction: Custody Rights)* [1993] Fam 242; *The Ontario Court v M and M (Abduction: Children's Objections)* [1997] 1 FLR 475; *Urness v Minto* 1994 SC 249; *De L v Director-General, New South Wales Department of Community Services* (1996) 139 ALR 417; further proceedings (1997) 21 Fam LR 413.

[358] Eg *Re T (A Child) (Abduction: Appointment of Guardian ad Litem)* [1999] 2 FLR 796—European Convention case; and *Re F (A Child) (Application for Child Party Status)* [2007] EWCA Civ 393—child party status has been granted only in those cases in which there has been some element of state intervention within the affairs of the family. See also *Re H (A Child) (Child Abduction)* [2006] EWCA Civ 1247, [2007] 1 FLR 242, per Thorpe LJ, at [16]: the test for grant of party status, if it is to be revised in any direction in future, should be more, rather than less, stringently applied, especially in view of strict time limits imposed under Brussels II *bis*, Art 11(3), examined infra, p 1119.

capable of giving instructions.[359] In relation to the age and degree of maturity of the child, it should be asked whether the child is more mature or less mature or as mature as his chronological age.[360] The House of Lords has indicated that the older the child is, the greater the weight his objections are likely to carry.[361] There is no minimum age below which the child's views are to be discounted,[362] nor has maturity been defined for this purpose, but it is rare for the courts to take account of the views of a child of seven or younger.[363] However, it is accepted that a child "may be mature enough for it to be appropriate for her view to be taken into account even though she may not have gained that level of maturity that she is fully emancipated from parental dependence and can claim autonomy of decision-making".[364]

The nature of the child's "right" under Article 13 of the Convention is a right to be heard, not a right to self-determination.[365] Once the child is judged to be of an age and maturity at which it is appropriate for the court to take account of his views, the court moves to the separate exercise of discretion,[366] in order to ascertain the strength and validity of those views.[367] If account is to be taken of the child's views, then they must be considered in conjunction with the other factors in the case.[368] In that process the views of a child as old as 13 have been discounted.[369] It is a question of balancing the nature and strength of the child's objections against both Convention considerations and also general welfare considerations.[370] WARD LJ, in *Re T (Children) (Abduction: Child's Objections to Return)*,[371] listed some of the factors which the court should consider at this stage, including: (a) the child's own perspective of what is in his interests in the short, medium and long term; (b) the extent to which the reasons underpinning the objection are rooted in reality; (c) the extent to which the child's views have been shaped or coloured by undue

---

[359] *Re T (A Child) (Abduction: Appointment of Guardian ad Litem)* [1999] 2 FLR 796; *Re J (Children) (Abduction: Child's Objections to Return)* [2004] EWCA Civ 428, [2004] 2 FLR 64; and *Re F (A Child) (Application for Child Party Status)* [2007] EWCA Civ 393.

[360] *Re T (Children) (Abduction: Child's Objections to Return)* [2000] 2 FLR 192.

[361] *Re M (Children) (Abduction)* [2007] UKHL 55, [2007] 3 WLR 975, per Baroness HALE of Richmond, at [46].

[362] *Re S (A Minor) (Abduction: Custody Rights)* [1993] Fam 242; *Re R (Minors: Child Abduction)* [1995] 1 FLR 716.

[363] *Re R (Minors: Child Abduction)*, supra, at 730; *Re K (Abduction: Child's Objections)* [1995] 1 FLR 977; *Cameron v Cameron (No 2)* 1997 SLT 206; cf *Re B (Abduction: Children's Objections)* [1998] 1 FLR 667.

[364] *Re T (Children) (Abduction: Child's Objections to Return)* [2000] 2 FLR 192, per WARD LJ.

[365] *C v W* [2007] EWHC 1349 (Fam), per Sir Mark POTTER, at [48]; and *Re M (Children) (Abduction)* [2007] UKHL 55, [2007] 3 WLR 975.

[366] A discretion fortified by Art 18: *Z v Z (Abduction: Children's Views)* [2005] EWCA Civ 1012, [2006] 1 FLR 410, per THORPE LJ, at [19].

[367] See *M, Petitioner* 2005 SLT 2, per Lady SMITH, at 43; *Re H (Children) (Child Abduction: Objections to Return)* [2005] EWCA Civ 319, (2005) 149 SJLB 178; and *Z v Z (Abduction: Children's Views)* [2005] EWCA Civ 1012, [2006] 1 FLR 410.

[368] *Re S (A Minor) (Abduction: Custody Rights)* supra; *Urness v Minto*, supra, at 266; *Re K (Abduction: Child's Objections)* [1995] 1 FLR 977; *Re S (Child Abduction: Delay)* [1998] 1 FLR 651; *W v W* 2003 SCLR 478; *H v H* [2004] EWHC 2111; *Re C (A Child) (Abduction: Residence and Contact)* [2005] EWHC 2205, [2006] 2 FLR 277; and *T, Petitioner (No 2)* 2007 GWD 11-200.

[369] *Marshall v Marshall* 1996 SLT 429; *Re H B (Abduction: Children's Objections)* [1997] 1 FLR 392; cf *Re M (A Minor) (Abduction: Child's Objections)* [1994] 2 FLR 126; *Re R (A Minor: Abduction)* [1992] 1 FLR 105; and *Re J (Abduction: Objections of Child)* [2004] EWHC 1985, [2005] 1 FLR 273.

[370] *Z v Z (Abduction: Children's Views)* [2005] EWCA Civ 1012, [2006] 1 FLR 410; and *Re C (A Child) (Child Abduction: Settlement)* [2006] EWHC 1229 (Fam), [2006] 2 FLR 797.

[371] [2000] 2 FLR 192.

influence and pressure, directly or indirectly exercised by the abductor;[372] and (d) the extent to which the objections will be mollified upon return and, where relevant, removal from any pernicious influence from the abductor. In cases where more than one child is involved, the proper procedure is for the judge to consider separately whether each child has objected to return and has attained an age and degree of maturity at which it is appropriate to take account of his views, but the exercise of discretion cannot properly be made by treating each child in isolation: "The child's place within the family, and the consequences of the exercise of discretion on that child must be considered."[373]

(ii) Consent or acquiescence

The second ground on which return may be refused requires opponents[374] of the child's return to establish that the person, institution or other body in the other country having care of the child was not actually exercising custody rights at the time of removal, or consented to or subsequently acquiesced in the removal or retention. So far as consent is concerned, it does not fall to be considered in order to establish the wrongfulness of a removal or a breach of custody rights pursuant to Article 3, but rather it is to be taken into account for the purpose of invoking the court's discretion pursuant to Article 13.[375] Whilst consent does not have to be evidenced in writing[376], and can be inferred from conduct,[377] there must be firm and unequivocal evidence of it.[378] Furthermore, purported consent obtained by deception or non-disclosure will be disregarded.[379] There is a timing issue in relation to consent and acquiescence. The former must be given before or at the time of removal or retention,[380] whilst the latter can be passive and can be inferred simply from lapse of time after the removal or retention without objection to it,[381] as in the case of a fourteen-month,[382] but not a four-month,[383] delay. Acquiescence may be implied from other circumstances,[384] as well, of course, as being expressly conveyed,[385]

---

[372] If it appears that a child has been "coached" by the abducting parent, then it is probable that little or no weight will be attributed to his views.

[373] *Z v Z (Abduction: Children's Views)* [2005] EWCA Civ 1012, [2006] 1 FLR 410, per WALL LJ, at [34].

[374] *T v T* 2004 SC 323; and *K v K* [2006] EWHC 2685, [2007] 1 FCR 355.

[375] *Re P (A Child) (Abduction: Custody Rights)* [2004] EWCA Civ 971, [2004] 2 FLR 1057, per WARD LJ, at [22].

[376] *Re C (Abduction: Consent)* [1996] 1 FLR 414 at 418–419; *Re K (Abduction: Consent)* [1997] 2 FLR 212 at 216–218; *Re R (Minors) (Abduction: Consent)* [1999] 1 FCR 87 at 90; all disapproving *Re W (Abduction: Procedure)* [1995] 1 FLR 878 at 888; but see now *Re M (Abduction: Consent: Acquiescence)* [1999] 1 FLR 171 at 187.

[377] *Zenel v Haddow* 1993 SC 612; and *Re R (Abduction: Consent)* [1999] 1 FLR 828.

[378] *Re C (Abduction: Consent)*, supra, at 419; *Re R (Minors) (Abduction: Consent)*, supra, at 90; *Re M (Abduction: Consent: Acquiescence)* [1999] 1 FLR 171; *C v C* 2003 SLT 793; and *Re A (Abduction: Consent: Habitual Residence: Consent)* [2005] EWHC 2998, [2006] 2 FLR 1.

[379] *Re B (A Minor) (Abduction)* [1994] 2 FLR 249; *Re B (Abduction: Article 13 Defence)* [1997] 2 FLR 573 at 575; *Re M (Abduction) (Consent: Acquiescence)* [1999] 1 FLR 171 at 189; *T v T (Child Abduction: Consent)* [1999] 2 FLR 912; and *H v H* [2004] EWHC 2111.

[380] *Re A (Minors) (Abduction: Custody Rights)* [1992] Fam 106 at 115; *Re C (Abduction: Consent)* [1996] 1 FLR 414; and *Re M (Abduction) (Consent: Acquiescence)* [1999] 1 FLR 171.

[381] *Re A (Minors) (Abduction: Custody Rights)* [1992] Fam 106.

[382] *Re M (Abduction: Acquiescence)* [1996] 1 FLR 315; and see *W v W (Child Abduction: Acquiescence)* [1993] 2 FLR 211. Undue delay could also lead to the proceedings being struck out: *Re G (Abduction: Striking Out Application)* [1995] 2 FLR 410; cf *Medhurst v Markle* (1995) 17 RFL (4th) 428.

[383] *Re R (Minors) (Abduction)* [1994] 1 FLR 190; and see *Re K (Abduction: Child's Objections)* [1995] 1 FLR 977.

[384] *Re M (Abduction) (Consent: Acquiescence)* [1999] 1 FLR 171; and *Re D (Abduction: Acquiescence)* [1999] 1 FLR 36.

[385] *A v A (Child Abduction)* [1993] 2 FLR 225; *Re O (Abduction: Consent and Acquiescence)* [1997] 1 FLR 924; and *Re B (A Child) (Abduction: Acquiescence)* [1999] 2 FLR 818.

but, like consent, it must be unequivocal.[386] It had been thought that, in determining whether a parent had acquiesced, a court was only to consider his actual intentions in a case of passive acquiescence.[387] This approach was rejected by the House of Lords in *Re H (Abduction: Acquiescence)*[388] where Lord BROWNE-WILKINSON made clear that "acquiescence is a question of the actual subjective intention of the wronged parent, not of the outside world's perception of his intentions."[389] This question is one of fact,[390] not law, and subject to one exception applies to all types of acquiescence. The exception is: "Where the words or actions of the wronged parent clearly and unequivocally show and have led the other parent to believe that the wronged parent is not asserting or going to assert his right to the summary return of the child and are inconsistent with such return, justice requires the wronged parent be held to have acquiesced".[391]

One factor that may be relevant in determining whether in fact there has been acquiescence is the extent to which the wronged parent has received correct legal advice as to, or is broadly aware of, his position.[392] The court will also be cautious of statements which might appear to amount to acquiescence if they were made when "the parties are in a state of confusion and emotional turmoil",[393] or in the heat of argument.[394] It has been said that "acquiescence is not a continuing state of affairs",[395] which would tend to indicate that acquiescence for however short a period before it is retracted will fall within this second ground. More recently, however, the courts have taken a broader view and discounted a very short period of acquiescence, certainly where it had not been relied on by the other parent.[396]

Notwithstanding a finding of consent or acquiescence, the court has discretion to order the child's immediate return,[397] in order that outstanding custody issues might be resolved in the court of the state where the child is habitually resident. Exercise of discretion in this respect is equivalent, in effect, to the court sanctioning a change of mind by the consenting or acquiescing party after the other parent (the "abductor") has acted in reliance upon that consent or acquiescence.[398]

(iii) Grave risk of harm

The third ground on which return may be refused is "that there is a grave risk that his or her return would expose the child to physical or psychological harm or otherwise place

---

[386] *T v T (Child Abduction: Consent)* [1999] 2 FLR 912; *Re I (Abduction: Acquiescence)* [1999] 1 FLR 778; *Re H (A Child) (Abduction: Habitual Residence: Consent)* [2000] 2 FLR 294; *Re A (Abduction: Consent: Habitual Residence: Consent)* [2005] EWHC 2998, [2006] 2 FLR 1; and *M v M* [2007] EWHC 1820 (Fam).

[387] Eg *Re A (Minors) (Abduction: Custody Rights)* [1992] Fam 106; and see *Re AZ (A Minor) (Abduction: Acquiescence)* [1993] 1 FLR 682; though doubts were expressed in *Re S (Minors) (Abduction: Acquiescence)* [1994] 1 FLR 819.

[388] [1998] AC 72.

[389] Ibid, at 88. See also *Re H (Abduction: Child of 16)* [2000] 2 FLR 51.

[390] Eg, *Re D (Abduction: Acquiescence)* [1998] 2 FLR 335.

[391] [1998] AC 72 at 90; eg, *Re AZ (A Minor) (Abduction: Acquiescence)* [1993] 1 FLR 682.

[392] *Re AZ (A Minor) (Abduction: Acquiescence)*, supra; *Re S (Abduction: Acquiescence)* [1998] 2 FLR 115.

[393] *Department of Health and Community Services v Casse* (1995) 19 Fam LR 474 at 480; and see *Re A (Abduction: Custody Rights)* [1992] Fam 106 at 121.

[394] *C v W* [2007] EWHC 1349 (Fam).

[395] *Re A (Abduction: Custody Rights)* [1992] Fam 106 at 121.

[396] *Re R (Child Abduction: Acquiescence)* [1995] 1 FLR 716 at 727; and see *Re R (Minors) (Abduction)* [1994] 1 FLR 190 at 200.

[397] *Re D (Abduction: Discretionary Return)* [2000] 1 FLR 24; and *T v T* 2004 SC 323.

[398] *M v M* [2007] EWHC 1404 (Fam), per SUMNER J, at [48]–[49].

the child in an intolerable position".[399] In *Re S (A Child) (Abduction: Custody Rights)*,[400] WARD LJ stated that:

> To the extent that three risks are named, there are three discrete defences. They are, however, linked by the use of the word "otherwise" ... The use of the word "otherwise" points inescapably to the conclusion that the physical or psychological harm contemplated by the first clause of Article 13(b) is harm to a degree that also amounts to an intolerable situation.[401]

His Lordship concluded that:

> the proper approach for a court considering a defence alleging a grave risk of physical or psychological harm should be to consider the grave risk of that harm as a discrete question but then stand back and test the conclusion by looking at the Article in the round, reflecting whether the risk of harm is established to an extent which would lead one to say that the child will be placed in an intolerable situation if returned.

Whilst it may be clear that a child will suffer psychological harm if its return is ordered, the court has to determine whether that is outweighed by the harm that would ensue if no order was made. It is clear that the harm must be substantial[402] and the risk of it must be "grave", ie greater than would normally be expected if a child was taken from one parent and passed to another.[403] In assessing the degree of risk, the court may look at the practical consequences involved in the return of the child, such as financial provision, accommodation, or language.[404]

Even if the threshold of grave risk is crossed, there still remains a discretion in the court whether to return the child. It is striking that the courts take a good deal of convincing that return should be refused on this ground to which they have given a strict and narrow interpretation:[405] "the court must steel itself against too freely allowing this exceptional

---

[399] Art 13(b).

[400] [2002] EWCA Civ 908, [2002] 2 FLR 815.

[401] Ibid, [38]. Cf *Director-General of Family and Community Services v Davis* (1990) 14 Fam LR 381.

[402] *Re Gsponer's Marriage* (1988) 94 FLR 164 at 177; *Director-General of Family and Community Services v Davis*, ibid; and *Re L (A Child)* [2005] EWHC 1237, [2006] 1 FLR 843.

[403] *Thomson v Thomson* (1994) 119 DLR (4th) 253; *E v E (Child Abduction: Intolerable Situation)* [1998] 2 FLR 980; *C v B (Abduction: Grave Risk)* [2005] EWHC 2988, [2006] 1 FLR 1095; and *M v M* [2007] EWHC 1820 (Fam).

[404] *Re A (A Minor) (Abduction)* [1988] 1 FLR 365, [1988] Fam Law 54; *Re A (Minors) (Abduction: Custody Rights)* [1992] Fam 106; *B v B (Abduction: Custody Rights)* [1993] Fam 32; *MacMillan v MacMillan* 1989 SLT 350; *C v C* 2003 SLT 793; *Re J (Abduction: Acquiring Custody Rights by Caring for Child)* [2005] 2 FLR 791; and *S v B (Abduction: Human Rights)* [2005] EWHC 733, [2005] 2 FLR 878. See also *Re C (Abduction: Interim Directions: Accommodation by Local Authority)* [2003] EWHC 3065, [2004] 1 FLR 653.

[405] Eg *P v P (Minors) (Child Abduction)* [1992] 1 FLR 155; *Starr v Starr* 1999 SLT 335; and *Re C (Minors) (Abduction: Grave Risk of Psychological Harm)* [1999] 1 FLR 1145. But see *Re M (Children) (Abduction)* [2007] UKHL 55, [2007] 3 WLR 975. In exercising its discretion, the court may well be influenced by undertakings given by the parties: *C v C (Abduction: Rights of Custody)* [1989] 1 WLR 654; *Re G (A Minor) (Wrongful Removal of Child)* [1990] FCR 189, [1989] 2 FLR 475; McClean (1990) 106 LQR 375; *Re O (Child Abduction: Undertakings)* [1994] 2 FLR 349; *Re M (Minors) (Child Abduction: Undertakings)* [1995] 1 FLR 1021; *Police Comr of South Australia v Temple* (1993) 17 Fam LR 144; *P v B (Child Abduction: Undertakings)* [1994] 3 IR 507; *Re W (A Child) (Abductions: Conditions for Return)* [2004] EWCA Civ 1366, [2005] 1 FLR 727; *Re R (Abduction: Immigration Concerns)* [2004] EWHC 2042, [2005] 1 FLR 33; *C v W* [2007] EWHC 1349 (Fam); and *LL v PL*, 29 March 2007 (unreported) (Fam Div). There may be anxieties as to how far undertakings can be enforced in the country to which the child is returned: *In the Marriage of McOwan* (1993) 17 Fam LR 377; cf *Re K (Abduction: Psychological Harm)* [1995] 2 FLR 550; and *Walley v Walley* [2005] EWCA Civ 910, [2005] 3 FCR 35, where an order with stringent conditions attached has been breached, the proper course is to apply for the order to be set aside in light of the non-compliance, rather than to appeal.

defence and the defendant must be put to strict proof".[406] So English courts have ordered the return of a child to Australia even though the mother would have serious accommodation problems there,[407] or would face the prospect of arrest and imprisonment;[408] they have ordered return of a child to Israel, in spite of political instability and random, indiscriminate terrorist attacks;[409] and a Scottish court has concluded that a child is unlikely to be placed in an intolerable position by being returned to Canada even though a grandparent who was likely to look after the child spoke no English.[410] Indeed, an intolerable situation has to be "something extreme and compelling".[411] Put another way, "a very high degree of intolerability must be established".[412] The courts have regularly emphasised that they are concerned here not with the "paramount consideration" of the child's welfare, but rather with whether the child should be returned speedily to the jurisdiction most appropriate for the determination of that issue.[413] "No requested country can be expected to return children to a situation where they will be at serious risk, but this must not be turned into a substitute for the welfare test, usurping the function of the courts of the home country."[414] Usually, it is reasonable to expect the "home country" to be able to provide adequate protection.[415] The role of the "home country" cannot be thwarted by a parent refusing to return with the child and then arguing that the child will suffer grave psychological harm from being separated from that parent.[416] To accept such an argument would "drive a coach and four through the Convention, at least in respect of applications by young children".[417] However, the notion that a parent cannot be allowed to create a situation

---

[406] Re S (A Child) (Abduction: Custody Rights) [2002] EWCA Civ 908, [2002] 2 FLR 815, per WARD LJ, at [49]. Cf Re M (A Child) (Abduction: Brussels II Revised) [2006] EWCA Civ 630, [2006] 2 FLR 1180, per WALL LJ, at [75]: "For the child's Article 13 defence to prevail over the policy of the Convention, there must be something in the facts of the case which takes it out of the ordinary into the exceptional."

[407] Re A (A Minor) (Wrongful Removal of Child) [1988] Fam Law 383; and see C v C (Abduction: Rights of Custody) [1989] 1 WLR 654; Re E (A Minor) (Abduction) [1989] 1 FLR 135, [1989] Fam Law 105; Re G (A Minor) (Abduction) [1989] 2 FLR 475, [1989] Fam Law 473; V v B (A Minor) (Abduction) [1991] FCR 451, [1991] 1 FLR 266; Parsons v Styger (1989) 67 OR (2d) 1.

[408] Re L (Abduction: Pending Criminal Proceedings) [1999] 1 FLR 433.

[409] Re S (A Child) (Abduction: Custody Rights) [2002] EWCA Civ 908, [2002] 2 FLR 815. See also Re M (A Child) [2007] EWCA Civ 260, (2007) 151 SJLB 434, per Sir Mark POTTER, at [84].

[410] Viola v Viola 1988 SLT 7.

[411] Re N (Minors) (Abduction) [1991] 1 FLR 413 at 419; Re R (A Minor: Abduction) [1992] 1 FLR 105 at 107; Re C (Abduction: Grave Risk of Psychological Harm) [1999] 1 FLR 1145.

[412] B v B (Abduction: Custody Rights) [1993] Fam 32 at 42; C (A child) (Abduction: Grave Risk of Physical or Psychological Harm) (No 1) [1999] 2 FLR 478; and Re M (A Child) (Abduction: Intolerable Situation) [2000] 1 FLR 930.

[413] Eg C v C (Abduction: Rights of Custody) [1989] 1 WLR 654 at 661; V v B (A Minor) (Abduction) [1991] 1 FLR 266 at 273; Re Gsponer's Marriage (1988) 94 FLR 164 at 178–180; and I, Petitioner [1999] Fam LR 126.

[414] TB v JB (Abduction: Grave Risk of Harm) [2001] 2 FLR 515, per HALE LJ, at [38].

[415] TB v JB (Abduction: Grave Risk of Harm), ibid; Re M (A Child)(Abduction: Intolerable Situation) [2000] 1 FLR 930; Re H (Children) (Child Abduction: Grave Risk) [2003] EWCA Civ 355, [2003] 2 FLR 141; and Re W (A Child) (Abductions: Conditions for Return) [2004] EWCA Civ 1366, [2005] 1 FLR 727. But see Q, Petitioner 2001 SLT 243, and Re S (A Child) (Abduction: Custody Rights) [2002] EWCA Civ 908, [2002] 2 FLR 815, per WARD LJ, at [85].

[416] TB v JB (Abduction: Grave Risk of Harm) [2001] 2 FLR 515, per ARDEN LJ, at [96]. The situation may be different where it is impossible or impractical for the abductor to return with the child: C v C 2003 SLT 793; Re A (Abduction: Consent: Habitual Residence: Consent) [2005] EWHC 2998, [2006] 2 FLR 1. But see AL, Petitioner [2007] CSOH 55—respondent mother unable to accompany child on flight to Australia due to pregnancy, but other travel options identified by court, and so return ordered.

[417] C v C (Abduction: Rights of Custody) [1989] 1 WLR 654 at 661; V v B (A Minor) (Abduction) [1991] 1 FLR 266 at 274; N v N (Abduction: Article 13 Defence) [1995] 1 FLR 107; McCarthy v McCarthy 1994 SLT 743; Thorne v Dryden-Hall (1995) 18 RFL (4th) 15; and S v B (Abduction: Human Rights) [2005] EWHC 733, [2005] 2 FLR 878 at [49].

and then rely on it to his/her benefit "is not a principle articulated in the Convention or the [1985] Act and should not be applied to the effective exclusion of the very defence itself, which is in terms directed to the question of risk of harm to the child and not the wrongful conduct of the abducting parent".[418] The return of a child to Sweden has been ordered, despite allegations of sexual abuse by the mother's partner, given that the English court was satisfied that the Swedish authorities would both provide protection for the child and fully investigate the matter.[419] The burden of establishing grave risk is high, but not impossibly so. The kind of risk which would justify a refusal of the return order is return to a war zone, or to a child abuser, or to some other risk of that nature and gravity.[420] For example, a Scottish court has refused to return a child to Canada in the face of evidence of the Canadian father's depression and alcoholism;[421] and an English court has refused to return a child to the USA, given the violence shown by the father both to the child and to his mother.[422]

Sibling solidarity A difficult issue, and one which "requires no less stringent a test than the rest of Article 13(b)",[423] may arise where there appears to be a good case for declining to order the return of one child but not his sibling, as where the former child is older and objects to the return, or indeed vice versa. Courts have concluded that it would place one child in an intolerable situation to return one without the other and this has led them to return both[424] or neither.[425] A Canadian court, on the other hand, has ordered the return of a 3-year-old child, but not her 14-year-old sister, who objected to her return.[426]

(e) Impact of Brussels II *bis*[427]

Recital 17 of Brussels II *bis* narrates that, in cases of wrongful removal or retention[428] of a child, the return of the child should be obtained without delay. To this end, it is said that the 1980 Hague Convention should continue to apply, *as complemented by* the provisions

---

[418] *S v B (Abduction: Human Rights)* [2005] EWHC 733, [2005] 2 FLR 878, per Sir Mark POTTER, at [49].

[419] *Re S (Abduction: Return into Care)* [1999] 1 FLR 843.

[420] *M, Petitioner* 2007 SLT 433, per Lord MALCOLM, at 436; and *Re L (A Child) (Abduction: Jurisdiction)* [2002] EWHC 1864, [2002] 2 FLR 1042.

[421] *Macmillan v Macmillan* 1989 SLT 350. See also *Q, Petitioner* 2001 SLT 243. Contrast *McCarthy v McCarthy* 1994 SLT 743; *Medhurst v Markle* (1995) 17 RFL (4th) 428.

[422] *Re F (A Minor) (Abduction: Custody Rights Abroad)* [1995] Fam 224; cf *N v N (Abduction: Article 13 Defence)* [1995] 1 FLR 107; *Re M (A Minor) (Abduction: Leave to Appeal)* [1999] 2 FLR 550; and *Re D (Children) (Article 13(b): Non-Return)* [2006] EWCA Civ 146, [2006] 2 FLR 305.

[423] *Re T (Children) (Abduction: Child's Objections to Return)* [2000] 2 FLR 192.

[424] *Re HB (Abduction: Children's Objections)* [1997] 1 FLR 392.

[425] *B v K (Child Abduction)* [1993] 1 FCR 382; *Urness v Minto* 1994 SC 249; *The Ontario Court v M and M (Abduction: Children's Objections)* [1997] 1 FLR 475; *Re T (Children) (Abduction: Child's Objections to Return)* [2000] 2 FLR 192; *Q, Petitioner* 2001 SLT 243; and *W v W* 2003 SCLR 478.

[426] *Chalkley v Chalkley* (1995) 10 RFL (4th) 442.

[427] For background, see McEleavy (2004) 53 ICLQ 503, 509.

[428] Defined in Art 2(11). Cf definition in 1980 Hague Convention, Art 3. The Regulation expressly states that: "Custody shall be considered to be exercised jointly when, pursuant to a judgment or operation of law, one holder of parental responsibility cannot decide on the child's place of residence without the consent of another holder of parental responsibility." In consequence of this, removal of a child from one European Community Member State to another Member State without the consent of such a person amounts to wrongful removal under Brussels II *bis*. Where the removal is lawful according to the Member State of origin, Art 9 may apply. Supra, p 1083.

of the Regulation,[429] in particular Article 11. The 1980 Hague Convention has been ratified by all EC Member States, but the provisions of Brussels II *bis* will prevail in relation to "intra-Community" abductions, ie any case where a child is "abducted" from one European Community Member State (except Denmark) (the "Member State of origin") and taken to another European Community Member State (the "requested Member State").

(i) Jurisdiction in cases of child abduction

The 1980 Hague Convention does not lay down rules of jurisdiction, and so to this extent the special rule of jurisdiction contained in Article 10 of Brussels II *bis* complements the Convention. Where a child is abducted from the Member State of origin to the requested Member State, Article 10 ensures that the courts in the first state retain jurisdiction to determine questions of custody.[430] In a case of wrongful removal or retention of a child, the courts of the Member State where the child was habitually resident immediately before the wrongful removal or retention shall retain their jurisdiction until the child has acquired a habitual residence in another Member State and: (a) each person, institution or other body having rights of custody has acquiesced in the removal or retention; or (b) the child has resided in that other Member State for a period of at least one year after the person, institution or other body having rights of custody has had or should have had knowledge of the whereabouts of the child and the child is settled in his new environment and at least one of four conditions is met, namely: (i) within one year after the holder of rights of custody has had or should have had knowledge of the whereabouts of the child, no request for return has been lodged before the competent authorities of the Member State where the child has been removed or is being retained; (ii) a request for return lodged by the holder of rights of custody has been withdrawn and no new request has been lodged within the time limit set in (i); (iii) a case before the court in the Member State where the child was habitually resident immediately before the wrongful removal or retention has been closed pursuant to Article 11(7) because the parties have not made relevant submissions within three months of notification;[431] or (iv) a judgment[432] on custody that does not entail the return of the child has been issued by the courts of the Member State where the child was habitually resident immediately before the wrongful removal or retention.

(ii) Return of the child

Where the court of a Member State receives a request for return of a child pursuant to the 1980 Hague Convention, it must apply the rules in the Convention as complemented by Brussels II *bis*, in particular Article 11(2) to (8).[433]

---

[429] Art 60 of the Regulation states that Brussels II *bis* takes precedence over the 1980 Hague Convention as regards relations between European Community Member States. See also Child Abduction and Custody Act, s 1(3). As regards the relationship between Brussels II and the 1980 Hague Convention, see *Re L (A Child) (Abduction: Jurisdiction)* [2002] EWHC 1864, [2002] 2 FLR 1042.

[430] See, eg, *Re A, HA v MB (Brussels II Revised: Article 11(7) Application)* [2007] EWHC 2016 (Fam).

[431] Infra, p 1120.

[432] See remarks of Singer J in *Re A, HA v MB (Brussels II Revised: Article 11(7) Application)* [2007] EWHC 2016 (Fam) at [122] et seq.

[433] Art 11(1).

(iii) Expeditious procedure

Article 11(3) stipulates that a court to which an application for return of a child is made shall act expeditiously in proceedings on the application, using the most expeditious procedures available in national law. In particular, save where exceptional circumstances render it impossible, the court shall issue its judgment no later than six weeks after the application is lodged.[434] "Article 11(3) does not specify that such decisions . . . shall be enforceable within the same period. However, this is the only interpretation which would effectively guarantee the objective of ensuring the prompt return of the child within the strict time-limit."[435] Article 11(3) is designed to eliminate detailed examination of welfare considerations.[436] The Regulation allows the judge to weigh only the nature and strength of the child's objection to return against the policy of the Regulation, and the fact that the essential welfare investigations and decisions must be taken in the state of the child's habitual residence.[437]

(iv) Child's views

It is expressly stated that, "the hearing of the child plays an important role in the application of this Regulation".[438] This is true generally,[439] and in particular in relation to cases of wrongful removal or retention. Article 11(2) establishes that, when applying the provisions of Articles 12 and 13 of the 1980 Hague Convention, the competent authorities in a Member State shall ensure that the child is given the opportunity to be heard during the proceedings,[440] unless this appears inappropriate having regard to his age or degree of maturity.[441] The child's views may be ascertained for the purposes of the Regulation according to normal procedures.[442] The grant of party status is to be made only in exceptional cases. Although it is vital that the child's voice be heard, "the method by which the voice of the child is heard admits of a wide degree of appreciation in the individual member state",[443] and can be achieved without the child being joined as a party to the proceedings.[444]

(v) Applicant's views

Article 11(5) forbids a Member State court from refusing to return a child unless the person who requested the return of the child has been given an opportunity to be heard.

---

[434] It was indicated in *Re M (A Child) (Abduction: Brussels II Revised)* [2006] EWCA Civ 630, [2006] 2 FLR 1180, per THORPE LJ, at [44], that compliance with this time limit generally will require "queue-jumping" for cases proceeding under Brussels II *bis*. Priority will be given to Brussels II *bis* abduction cases over other cases on the Family Division list, which seems barely justifiable. It may well be necessary to reconsider the 6-week target. See also *Re H (A Child) (Child Abduction)* [2006] EWCA Civ 1247, [2007] 1 FLR 242, per THORPE LJ, at [16]–[18].

[435] *Practice Guide*, para VII.2.4.

[436] See, for criticism of the approach of the judge at first instance, *Re M (A Child) (Abduction: Brussels II Revised)* [2006] EWCA Civ 630, [2006] 2 FLR 1180, per THORPE LJ, at [32]–[34].

[437] Ibid, at [34].

[438] Recital (19).

[439] Hearing the child's views is a requirement of the abolition of *exequatur* procedure in relation to rights of access (Arts 40 and 41), and also may be a ground for refusing to recognise a judgment relating to parental responsibility (Art 23(b)).

[440] Recital 20 allows the hearing of a child in another Member State to take place under the arrangements laid down in Council Regulation (EC) No 1206/2001 (supra, p 84 et seq).

[441] This exception is to be interpreted restrictively: *Practice Guide*, para IX.

[442] Recital (19). Eg *C v W* [2007] EWHC 1349 (Fam); and *K v K* [2007] EWCA Civ 533.

[443] *Re H (A Child) (Child Abduction)* [2006] EWCA Civ 1247, [2007] 1 FLR 242, per THORPE LJ, at [16].

[444] *Re F (A Child) (Application for Child Party Status)* [2007] EWCA Civ 393.

(vi) Enquiry as to adequate arrangements to secure child's protection

Article 11(4) prevents a Member State court from refusing to return a child on the basis of Article 13(b) of the 1980 Hague Convention if it is established that adequate arrangements have been made to secure the protection of the child after his return. The fact that protective measures are available in the state of the child's habitual residence should nullify an Article 13(b) defence.[445] The Article 13(b) exception to the return of the child is to be kept to a "strict minimum".[446] The court is obliged to return the child where, despite it having been established that return could expose the child to physical or psychological harm or otherwise place him in an intolerable situation, the authorities in the Member State of origin have made adequate arrangements, ie "concrete measures",[447] to secure the protection of the child upon his return. The involvement of relevant Central Authorities is likely to be necessary in order to assist the judge in the receiving Member State to assess the factual circumstances in the Member State of origin.

(vii) Non-return orders

If a Member State court has issued a non-return order pursuant to Article 13(b) of the 1980 Hague Convention, the court must immediately,[448] either directly or through its Central Authority, transmit a copy of that order and relevant documents to the court with jurisdiction or Central Authority in the Member State where the child was habitually resident immediately before the wrongful removal or retention, as determined by national law. Unless the court in that state (the Member State of origin) has already been seised by one of the parties, it must notify the parties of the receipt of information and invite them to make submissions to the court within three months of the date of notification, so that it can examine the question of custody of the child.[449] If no submission is received by the court within the time limit specified, it shall close the case. If the court of the Member State of origin receives submissions, it is competent to deal with the substance of the case in its entirety, eg custody and access rights: "The judge should, in principle, be in the position that he or she would have been in if the abducting parent had not abducted the child but instead had seised the court of origin to modify a previous decision on custody or to ask for a [sic] authorisation to change the habitual residence of the child."[450]

The significance of Brussels II *bis* in this regard concerns Article 11(8), which provides that, notwithstanding a non-return order pursuant to Article 13(b) of the 1980 Hague Convention, any subsequent judgment which requires the return of the child issued by a court having jurisdiction in terms of Brussels II *bis* shall be enforceable in accordance with Articles 40 to 45 of the Regulation.[451] Article 11(8) is a surprising,

---

[445] *Re M (A Child) (Abduction: Brussels II Revised)* [2006] EWCA Civ 630, [2006] 2 FLR 1180, per Thorpe LJ, at [36] *Re A (A Child) (Custody Decision after Maltese Non-Return Order)* [2006] EWHC 3397 (Fam), [2007] 1 FCR 402, per Singer J, at [109] and *K v K* [2007] EWCA Civ 533.

[446] *Practice Guide*, para VII.2.2.

[447] Ibid, para VII.2.2.

[448] Within 1 month of the date of the non-return order: Art 11(6).

[449] Art 11(7); and Recital (17). See *Re A, HA v MB (Brussels II Revised: Article 11(7) Application)* [2007] EWHC 2016 (Fam).

[450] *Practice Guide*, para VII.4. See *Re A (A Child) (Custody Decision after Maltese Non-Return Order)* [2006] EWHC 3397 (Fam), [2007] 1 FCR 402.

[451] See eg *Re A (A Child) (Custody Decision after Maltese Non-Return Order)* [2006] EWHC 3397 (Fam), [2007] 1 FCR 402.

and arguably unnecessary, intervention, given the notable reluctance of Contracting State courts to invoke the Article 13(b) exception in the first place.[452] Recital (17) explains the rationale:

> The courts of the Member State to or in which the child has been wrongfully removed or retained should be able to oppose his or her return in specific, duly justified cases. However, such a decision could be replaced by a subsequent decision by the court of the Member State of habitual residence of the child prior to the wrongful removal or retention. Should that judgment entail the return of the child, the return should take place without any special procedure being required for recognition and enforcement of that judgment in the Member State to or in which the child has been removed or retained.

In other words, the Member State of origin has the final say in the matter.

Recital (17) envisages the situation where a *subsequent* decision by the court of the Member State of habitual residence requires return; it does not deal with the situation where a decision already has been made by that court sanctioning *ex post facto* the removal of a child.[453] In *Re T and J (Children) (Abduction: Recognition of Foreign Judgment)*,[454] Sir Mark POTTER stated:

> If . . . proceedings under the Hague Convention are commenced at a time when the issue sought to be resolved, namely where and with which parent the child should be residing, is already before the Court of the Member State where the child is habitually resident, and if, prior to the Hague Convention hearing, that issue is resolved in favour of the abducting parent, then the whole thrust and purpose of Brussels II b (as well as in spirit, if not the letter of the Hague Convention itself) operates in favour of an order for non-return.[455]

(viii) Enforceability of certain judgments requiring return of the child

If return of the child is entailed by a judgment given pursuant to Article 11(8) (ie a judgment by the Member State of origin), that shall be recognised and enforceable in another Member State[456] without the need for a declaration of enforceability (*exequatur*) and without any possibility of opposing its recognition,[457] if the judgment has been certified in the Member State of origin in accordance with Article 42(2),[458] demonstrating that necessary safeguards have been complied with in that state.[459] The judgment shall be certified in the Member State of origin only if: (a) the child, if appropriate having regard

---

[452] See *Re M (A Child) (Abduction: Brussels II Revised)* [2006] EWCA Civ 630, [2006] 2 FLR 1180, per WALL LJ, at [79].

[453] As in *Re T and J (Children) (Abduction: Recognition of Foreign Judgment)* [2006] EWHC 1472, [2006] 2 FLR 1290. See comments of Sir Mark Potter, at [42]: Art 11 of Brussels II *bis* "does not touch on the situation where the court of the State to which the child has been removed has available to it, before its decision is made, a court decision from the State of the child's habitual residence which sanctions the removal of the child". Recognition of judgments is addressed by Arts 21 and 23, examined, supra, p 1097 et seq.

[454] [2006] EWHC 1472, [2006] 2 FLR 1290.

[455] Ibid, at [52].

[456] Ie in all Member States, and not just the Member State in which the non-return order was made.

[457] Art 42(1).

[458] Using the standard form certificate in Annex IV to the Regulation. If the court takes measures to ensure the protection of the child after its return to the State of habitual residence, the certificate shall contain details of such measures (Art 42(2)). See Family Proceedings Rules 1991, rr 7.51 and 7.52. Eg *Re A (A Child) (Custody Decision after Maltese Non-Return Order)* [2006] EWHC 3397 (Fam), [2007] 1 FCR 402.

[459] Cf Arts 40 and 41 regarding rights of access. Supra, p 1100.

to his age and degree of maturity, was given an opportunity to be heard; (b) the parties were given an opportunity to be heard; and (c) the court has taken into account in issuing its judgment the reasons for and evidence underlying the order issued pursuant to Article 13 of the 1980 Hague Convention.[460] It is improbable that the abductor and child will return to the Member State of origin in order to give evidence, and so it is likely that evidence will be taken by means of video-conferencing or tele-conferencing.

(f) Implications of the Human Rights Act 1998

Article 20 of the 1980 Hague Convention provides that: "The return of the child under the provisions of Article 12 may be refused if this would not be permitted by the fundamental principles of the requested State relating to the protection of human rights and fundamental freedoms." Article 20 was not included in the provisions incorporated into the law of the United Kingdom by virtue of the Child Abduction and Custody Act 1985, for the reason that it would have been difficult to state with certainty at that time what were the fundamental principles of the law relating to the protection of human rights and fundamental freedoms.[461] In the light of the Human Rights Act 1998, however, the position now is clearer. Since 2000, there has been a growing trend in abduction cases for bereft parents to lodge complaints under the European Convention on Human Rights (ECHR). Claims typically are based upon alleged violation of the right to a fair trial (Article 6), and/or the right to respect for private and family life (Article 8).[462] Whilst the object of Article 8 is to protect the individual against arbitrary interference by public authorities, there may also be positive obligations[463] inherent in an effective "respect" for family life, which "may involve the adoption of measures designed to secure respect for family life even in the sphere of relations between individuals".[464] Such measures include enforcement mechanisms aimed at protecting individuals' rights, including the right of a parent to have measures taken with a view to his being reunited with the child, and an obligation upon the national authorities to take such measures. However, there is no absolute obligation upon national authorities to ensure contact between a child and his non-custodial parent following divorce.[465] Moreover, any obligation to apply coercion must be limited since the interests, as well as the rights and freedoms, of all concerned must be taken into account, especially those of the child.[466] The key question is whether those authorities have taken all necessary steps to facilitate contact as can reasonably be demanded in the special circumstances of each case.[467] Time is of particular significance

---

[460] The *Practice Guide* envisages that the judges in the Member State of origin and in the requesting Member State, respectively, will liaise closely in this regard, either directly or through their Central Authorities: para VII.5.

[461] *Re J (A Child (Custody Rights: Jurisdiction)* [2005] UKHL 40, [2006] 1 AC 80, at [44].

[462] Also, occasionally, on Art 14 (prohibition of discrimination), eg, *Re J (A Child (Custody Rights: Jurisdiction)* [2005] UKHL 40, [2006] 1 AC 80; and *EM (Lebanon) v Secretary of State for the Home Department* [2006] EWCA Civ 1531, [2007] 1 FLR 991.

[463] To be interpreted in the light of the 1980 Hague Convention: *Sylvester v Austria* [2003] 2 FLR 210, (2003) 37 EHRR 17; *Maire v Portugal* [2004] 2 FLR 653, (2006) 43 EHRR 13; and *Iglesias Gil v Spain* [2005] 1 FLR 190, (2005) 40 EHRR 3.

[464] *G v United Kingdom (Children: Rights of Contact)* [2001] 1 FLR 153, (2001) 33 EHRR 1.

[465] *Sylvester v Austria* [2003] 2 FLR 210, (2003) 37 EHRR 17.

[466] Ibid, at [H6]. But see *Maire v Portugal* [2004] 2 FLR 653, (2006) 43 EHRR 13, where use of coercive measures could not be ruled out in the event of manifestly unlawful behaviour by the abductor parent. See also *S v B (Abduction: Human Rights)* [2005] EWHC 733, [2005] 2 FLR 878; and *Re C (A Child) (Abduction: Residence and Contact)* [2005] EWHC 2205, [2006] 2 FLR 277.

[467] *G v United Kingdom (Children: Rights of Contact)* [2001] 1 FLR 153, (2001) 33 EHRR 1.

as there is always a risk that any procedural delay will result in the *de facto* determination of the issue before the court.[468] The European Court of Human Rights has consistently ruled that once the authorities of a Contracting State to the 1980 Hague Convention have determined that a child has been wrongfully removed or retained, there is a duty incumbent upon them to make "adequate and effective efforts"[469] to secure the return of the child to his/her habitual residence, with due expedition. Reasonableness in terms of length of proceedings will be assessed by reference to the circumstances of the particular case, including its complexity, the conduct of the applicant and the relevant authorities, and what is at stake for the applicant.[470] Failure to make due effort is likely to amount to violation of Articles 6 and/or 8. It was held in *Sylvester v Austria*[471] that a change in the relevant facts exceptionally might justify the non-enforcement of a foreign order, but the court must be satisfied that the change was not brought about by the state's failure to take all measures that reasonably could be expected to facilitate execution of the order.

(ii) Part II of the 1985 Act: the Council of Europe Convention[472]

(a) Operation of the Convention

This Convention governs the recognition and enforcement of decisions relating to custody, whether made by a judicial or administrative authority, in force in relation to children under 16.[473] The Council of Europe Convention has not been widely used in the United Kingdom, and so there is very little authority on its construction and ambit. It has been remarked that its utility lies more in the enforcement of access orders than custody orders, since the 1980 Hague Convention "has not been construed . . . to provide for the recognition and enforcement of an access decision which was made in another contracting state".[474] A decision relating to custody is one which "relates to the care of the person of the child, including the right to decide on the place of his residence or to the right of

---

[468] Ibid, per Costa J, at [66]. Cf *Sylvester v Austria* [2003] 2 FLR 210, (2003) 37 EHRR 17, per Rozakis J, at [60].

[469] Brussels II *bis, Practice Guide*, para VIII. See, eg, *Sylvester v Austria* [2003] 2 FLR 210, (2003) 37 EHRR 17—9 months' delay in enforcing a return order under the 1980 Hague Convention amounted to violation of Art 8; *Maire v Portugal* [2004] 2 FLR 653, (2006) 43 EHRR 13—failure by Portuguese authorities to take sanctions against abducting parent to enforce return of the child amounted to violation of Art 8; *Iglesias Gil v Spain* [2005] 1 FLR 190, (2005) 40 EHRR 3—refusal to issue an international search and arrest warrant breached applicant's rights under Art 8; *Monory v Romania* (2005) 41 EHRR 37—overall time taken by Hungarian authorities in divorce and child custody proceedings—4 years and 3 months—exceeded what was reasonable in the circumstances; the Romanian authorities failed to make adequate and effective efforts for child's return in breach of Art 8; *HN v Poland* [2005] 3 FCR 85—absence of satisfactory explanation for delay in obtaining expert opinion, or for dormant period during the 3 year proceedings, amounted to violation of Art 6; *Karadzic v Croatia* [2006] 1 FCR 36, (2007) 44 EHRR 45—periods of inactivity by the Croatian authorities violated Art 8; and *Iosub Caras v Romania* [2007] 1 FLR 661—18 months' delay between lodging of request for return of child under the 1980 Hague Convention and the final decision amounted to violation of Art 8. Contra *Mattenklott v Germany (Admissibility)* (2007) 44 EHRR SE 12—order to return applicant's daughter to USA, if necessary by force, not in violation of Art 8.

[470] *Monory v Romania* (2005) 41 EHRR 37.

[471] [2003] 2 FLR 210, (2003) 37 EHRR 17.

[472] See Jones (1981) 30 ICLQ 467; Shapira (1989) II Hague Recueil 127, 200–206. The Council of Europe has reviewed the operation of the Convention: DIR/JUR (89) 1.

[473] 1985 Act, Sch 2, Art 1. It does not apply to a child under 16 if he has the right to decide the place of his residence under the law of his habitual residence, nationality or of the Contracting State where recognition and enforcement is sought.

[474] *Re G (Children) (Foreign Contact Order: Enforcement)* [2004] 1 FLR 378, per Thorpe LJ, at [17]. Eg *Donofrio v Burrell* 1999 GWD 12-528, affd 2000 SLT 1051. Art 21, supra, p 1104. "Rights of access" is defined for English purposes by s 27(4) of the 1985 Act, added by the Children Act 1989, Sch 13, para 57.

access to him".[475] Let us assume that such a decision has been made in Turkey and the person who obtained it wishes to have it recognised and enforced in England. The procedure is much the same as under the Hague Convention.[476] An application, accompanied by the relevant documents and information as to the child's whereabouts,[477] is made to the Central Authority in any Contracting State and, if it is not sent in our example to the English Central Authority,[478] it must be sent directly and without delay to the Lord Chancellor by the Central Authority in the Contracting State to which the application was made.[479] Unless it is manifestly clear that the conditions of the Convention are not satisfied,[480] steps must be taken in England without delay to find the child, prevent any prejudice to his or the applicant's interests, and to secure the recognition and effective enforcement of the Turkish decision.[481] The foreign decision will be recognised in England, unless the High Court[482] has declared that such recognition shall be denied on any of the stated grounds.[483] It cannot, however, be enforced in England until it is registered in the High Court, and registration can be refused if the custody decision would not be recognised in England, if it is not enforceable where it was made, or if an application under the Hague Convention is pending.[484] Once registered, the foreign decision can be enforced as if it was an English one.[485] Registration, or an application for registration, of a foreign custody decision will limit the powers of the English courts in English proceedings relating to the welfare of the child started later than the foreign ones.[486]

Although the basic approach of the Convention is that all custody decisions given in one Contracting State should be recognised and enforced in all others[487] without any review of the substantive custody issue,[488] there are quite broad and elaborate grounds in Articles 9 and 10 on which recognition and enforcement may be refused:[489]

(i) where the decision was given in the absence of the defendant or his lawyers and the defendant was not duly served with the necessary documents, unless he concealed his whereabouts,[490] *or*

The application of the Convention to rights of access is illustrated by *Re A (Foreign Access Order: Enforcement)* [1996] 1 FLR 561; *RJ v MR* [1994] 1 IR 271; *SM v AJB* [1994] 3 IR 491.

[475] Art 1(c).

[476] It also works in a similar way where it is sought to enforce an English order in a foreign country.

[477] Listed in Art 13.

[478] 1985 Act, s 14: the functions of the Central Authority in England and Wales and in Northern Ireland shall be discharged by the Lord Chancellor, and in Scotland, by the Secretary of State.

[479] Art 4.

[480] Art 4(4).

[481] Art 5(1). If the child is thought to be in another Contracting State, the application must be passed on to the Central Authority there.

[482] 1985 Act, s 27(2).

[483] Ibid, ss 15(2), 27(1).

[484] Ss 15(2)(b), 16. If the original decision is varied or revoked, the registration can be varied or cancelled: s 17.

[485] S 18; and the court has interim powers once an application for registration has been made: s 19.

[486] S 20, as amended by the Children Act 1989, Sch 15. If there is an earlier English custody order, it will cease to have effect on registration of the foreign one: ss 25, 27, Sch 3, as amended by the Children Act 1989, Sch 13, para 57, Sch 15.

[487] Art 7.

[488] Art 9(3); though there is power to vary the detailed provisions relating to access: Art 11(2); *Re A (Foreign Access Order: Enforcement)* [1996] 1 FLR 561.

[489] 1985 Act, s 15(2)(a). These apply to permit refusal of enforcement, even though the foreign order has been registered in England: *Re H (A Minor) (Foreign Custody Order: Enforcement)* [1994] Fam 105.

[490] Eg *Re G (A Minor) (Child Abduction: Enforcement)* [1990] FCR 973, [1990] 2 FLR 325.

the jurisdiction of the authority making the decision was not based on the habitual residence of the defendant or of the child, or the last common habitual residence of both parents which is still the habitual residence of one of them;[491]

(ii) if the decision is incompatible with a custody decision which became enforceable in the state addressed before the child was improperly[492] removed unless the child had been habitually resident in the requesting state for one year before his removal;[493]

(iii) where the effects of the custody decision are "manifestly incompatible with the fundamental principles of the law relating to the family and children in the State addressed";[494]

(iv) if the effects of the original decision are manifestly no longer in accordance with the welfare of the child, by reason of change in circumstances, including lapse of time, but excluding the change in the residence of a child improperly removed;[495]

(v) if at the time of the original proceedings, the child was a national of, or habitually resident in, the state addressed and there was no such connection with the state of origin, or the child was a national of both states and habitually resident in the state addressed;[496]

(vi) if the original decision is incompatible with a decision of, or enforceable in, the State addressed, proceedings in which were begun before the submission of the request for recognition and enforcement, and if refusal of recognition and enforcement of the original decision is in accordance with the welfare of the child.[497]

It will be noted first, that this catalogue of grounds for refusal is lengthy and, secondly, that, in a number of instances, it may be necessary to consider the substantive merits of the original decision, despite the general requirement of recognition and enforcement.[498] The most significant of these instances is (iv), above, namely that the effects of the original decision are manifestly no longer in accordance with the welfare of the child. This has led an English court to refuse the return of young children who had lived in England for a year since the making of the foreign order, even though their original removal was wrongful.[499] It has also led a Scottish court to refuse to order the return of a teenager against his wishes when such return would have disrupted his schooling.[500] More recently, the English courts have adopted what seems to be a more robust view and have ordered

---

[491] Art 9(1)(a), (b).

[492] 1985 Act, s 15(3). Improper removal is defined in Art 1(d), and see Art 12; *Re S (Abduction: European Convention)* [1996] 1 FLR 660.

[493] Art 9(1)(c).

[494] Art 10(1)(a). The provision is to be construed and applied stringently: *Re G (Children) (Foreign Contact Order: Enforcement)* [2004] 1 FLR 378. This may, in England, include the welfare principle: see *Re G (A Minor) (Child Abduction: Enforcement)* [1990] FCR 973, [1990] 2 FLR 325, and *W v W (Foreign Custody Order: Enforcement)* [2005] EWHC 1811.

[495] Art 10(1)(b). The provision also is to be construed and applied stringently: *Re G (Children) (Foreign Contact Order: Enforcement)* [2004] 1 FLR 378. Where practicable, the views of the child are to be sought: Art 15; see, eg, *Re A (Foreign Access Order: Enforcement)* [1996] 1 FLR 561.

[496] Art 10(1)(c). See *Re T (Children) (Abduction: Child's Objections to Return)* [2000] 2 FLR 192.

[497] Art 10(1)(d); see *Campins-Coll, Petitioner* 1989 SLT 33; and *Re M (Child Abduction) (European Convention)* [1994] 1 FLR 551.

[498] Art 7, coupled with the prohibition on review of the substance of the foreign decision, in Art 9(3).

[499] *F v F (Minors) (Custody: Foreign Order)* [1989] Fam 1; Hall [1989] CLJ 189.

[500] *Campins-Coll, Petitioner* 1989 SLT 33.

the return of children who have been in England for a year or more.[501] Nevertheless, although the burden of proof of this ground for refusing enforcement is high, it has been discharged where the child was undoubtedly in fear of her foreign father.[502]

The Convention distinguishes between cases of improper removal[503] and others, with more limited bases for refusal of recognition in the former case;[504] but the United Kingdom in exercising a power of reservation under the Convention[505] has extended the full range of grounds for refusal of recognition and enforcement to all custody decisions, whether or not there was wrongful removal.

(b) Impact of Brussels II *bis*

Article 60 of Brussels II *bis* provides that in relations between Member States the Regulation shall take precedence over the 1980 Council of Europe Convention.[506] In *Re G (Children) (Foreign Contact Order: Enforcement)*[507] the Court of Appeal held that enforcement proceedings raised under the 1980 European Convention were a nullity because by virtue of Article 37 of Brussels II that Regulation had superseded the Convention with effect from 1 March 2001, and so the proceedings ought to have been brought under the provisions of the Regulation.

(iii) The Conventions compared [508]

All but one (Liechtenstein) of the countries who are party to the Council of Europe Convention are also parties to the Hague Convention. Where a person's claim could fall under both Conventions, there appears to be no restriction[509] on him choosing which procedure to follow or, indeed, to follow both. It should be noted, however, that an application under the Hague Convention will prevent registration of a foreign custody decision under the Council of Europe Convention.[510] Whilst there are considerable similarities between the two Conventions—they both apply to children under the age of 16, and their procedures follow the same pattern—there are also major differences. The Hague Convention protects custody rights, whether or not there has been a custody order; but this protection is only provided in cases of wrongful removal of children habitually resident in a Contracting State. The Council of Europe Convention is limited to the registration and enforcement of foreign custody decisions, but applies in all circumstances and not just in improper removal cases. One further significant difference is that the grounds, under the Hague Convention, for refusing to return the child are narrower than those under the Council of Europe Convention for refusing

---

[501] *Re K (A Minor) (Abduction)* [1990] FCR 524, [1990] 1 FLR 387; *Re G (A Minor) (Child Abduction: Enforcement)* [1990] FCR 973, [1990] 2 FLR 325; *Re A (Foreign Access Order: Enforcement)* [1996] 1 FLR 561; and see *Re L (Child Abduction: European Convention)* [1992] 2 FLR 178.

[502] *Re H (A Minor) (Foreign Custody Order: Enforcement)* [1994] Fam 105.

[503] Eg *Re S (A Minor) (Abduction: European Convention)* [1998] AC 750.

[504] Arts 8 and 9.

[505] Art 17, and see 1985 Act, s 12(2).

[506] Child Abduction and Custody Act 1985, s 12(3). Cf Brussels II, Art 37.

[507] [2004] 1 FLR 378.

[508] Eekelaar (1982) 32 U Tor LJ 281, 321–325.

[509] Subject to Brussels II *bis*, Art 60; and Child Abduction and Custody Act 1985, ss 1(3) and 12(3).

[510] 1985 Act, s 16(4)(c); *Re R (Abduction: Hague and European Conventions)* [1997] 1 FLR 663; contrast the position in Ireland: *RJ v MR* [1994] 1 IR 271.

recognition and enforcement of the foreign decision. This suggests that, given a choice, the Hague Convention is to be preferred,[511] not least because in the context of intra-Community abductions, Article 11 of Brussels II *bis* ensures utilisation of the most expeditious procedures available in national law for applications under the Hague Convention.

(iv) Permission to remove children from the jurisdiction

Difficult tensions emerge in cases where one parent wishes to relocate with his/her child, against the wishes of another person having parental responsibilities.[512] The proposed relocation might be internal to the United Kingdom, to another European Community Member State, or to a non-Member State country;[513] and it might be temporary or permanent, exposing the child to varying degrees of upheaval and loss of the familiar.[514] Relocation cases often bear common characteristics "(a) the applicant is invariably the mother and the primary carer; (b) generally the motivation for the move arises out of her remarriage[515] or her urge to return home;[516] and (c) the father's opposition is commonly founded on a resultant reduction in contact and influence".[517] Section 13 of the Children Act 1989 provides that where a residence order is in force with respect to a child, no person may remove[518] him from the United Kingdom without either the written consent of every person who has parental responsibility for the child, or the leave of the court. Additionally, under section 8 of the 1989 Act, the English court can make a prohibited steps order, or impose conditions on a residence order under section 11(7).

There is a clear link between relocation cases and abduction cases.[519] In *Payne v Payne*, a case concerning a mother's desire to return to her country of origin following the failure of her marriage, THORPE LJ opined that, "if individual jurisdictions adopt a chauvinistic approach to applications to relocate then there is a risk that the parent affected will resort

---

[511] North (1990) I Hague Recueil 9, 150–151.

[512] Defined in Children Act 1989, s 3.

[513] With "gradations of hurdles" according to the destination: *Re H (Children: Residence Order: Relocation)* [2001] EWCA Civ 1338, [2001] 2 FLR 1277, per THORPE LJ, at [20].

[514] The considerations relevant to an application for permission to relocate permanently are not automatically, if at all, applicable to an application for temporary relocation: *Re A (A Child) (Temporary Removal from Jurisdiction)* [2004] EWCA Civ 1587, [2005] 1 FLR 639.

[515] Eg *Re B (Children) (Removal from Jurisdiction), Re S (Children) (Removal from Jurisdiction)* [2003] EWCA Civ 1149, [2003] 2 FLR 1043.

[516] Usually following marital breakdown, as in *Payne v Payne*; *Re S (Children: Application for Removal from Jurisdiction)* [2004] EWCA Civ 1724, [2005] 1 FCR 471—leave to remove children from England to Spain, mother's country of origin, granted on appeal; and *C v S* [2006] EWHC 2891—leave to remove children from England to Australia, mother's country of origin, granted. *Contra Re Y (Leave to Remove from Jurisdiction)* [2004] 2 FLR 330—leave to remove child from Wales to USA, mother's country of origin, refused; *R v R (Leave to Remove)* [2004] EWHC 2572, [2005] 1 FLR 687—leave to remove children from England to Paris refused; *Re G (Removal from Jurisdiction)* [2005] EWCA Civ 170, [2005] 2 FLR 166—leave granted, on appeal, to remove children to Argentina, mother's country of origin; and *Re J (Children)* [2006] EWCA Civ 1897, [2007] 2 FCR 149—leave granted, on appeal, to remove children to Bulgaria, father's country of origin.

[517] *Payne v Payne* [2001] EWCA Civ 166, [2001] Fam 473, 483–484.

[518] For a period longer than 1 month: 1989 Act, s 13(2).

[519] *Re A (A Child) (Temporary Removal from Jurisdiction)* [2004] EWCA Civ 1587, [2005] 1 FLR 639. See also *Re K (A Minor) (Removal from Jurisdiction: Practice)* [1999] 2 FLR 1084—utmost vigilance is required where a parent seeks to take a child to a country that is not a signatory to the 1980 Hague Convention, infra, p 1129 et seq; and *F v R* [2007] EWHC 64 (Fam).

to flight".[520] Conversely, an order for return of the child to his habitual residence, following wrongful removal or retention, will not infrequently lead to an application to relocate being issued in that jurisdiction. THORPE LJ stated that the judge in the second application must be free to carry out a fully independent function unfettered by the conclusion of the judge in the earlier return proceedings, and without any fear of breaching the principle of comity, for the functions of the two judges are quite different and will require an assessment of the circumstances as they are, rather than as they were.[521]

Equally, there is a clear conflict between the desire and ambitions of the relocating parent (recognised in the right of mobility in Article 2 of Protocol 4 to the ECHR[522]), and the right of the other parent to respect for his/her private and family life (Article 8 of the ECHR).[523] As THORPE LJ remarked in *Payne v Payne*,[524] however: "Once a family unit disintegrates the separating members' separate rights can only be to a fragmented family life . . . the absent parent has the right to participation to the extent and in what manner the complex circumstances of the individual case dictate."

The Court of Appeal, in *Payne*, carried out a review of relocation jurisprudence over a thirty-year period,[525] and concluded that relocation cases have been consistently decided on the basis of two propositions: (a) although each member of the "fractured family" has rights to assert, the welfare of the child is the paramount consideration;[526] and (b) refusing the primary carer's reasonable proposals for the relocation of her family life is likely to impact detrimentally on the welfare of dependent children,[527] especially in cases where the applicant has forged a new family unit by marriage or other relationship. The court must evaluate factors such as the child's emotional and psychological dependency upon the primary carer; the relationship between the child and the non-respondent parent; the relationship between the child and extended family, including siblings, grandparents and step-parents; the reasonableness of the proposals and motivation of the parent who

---

[520] *Payne v Payne* [2001] EWCA Civ 166, [2001] Fam 473 at 484.

[521] Ibid, at 492.

[522] Yet to be ratified by the United Kingdom. But THORPE LJ, in *Payne*, ibid, at 487, stated that refusal to recognise such a right beyond the jurisdictional boundary "represents a stance of disproportionate parochialism".

[523] *Re A (Permission to Remove Child from Jurisdiction: Human Rights)* [2000] 2 FLR 225.

[524] [2001] EWCA Civ 166, [2001] Fam 473, at 486.

[525] *Poel v Poel* [1970] 1 WLR 1469; *Nash v Nash* [1973] 2 All ER 704; *Re A v A (Child: Removal from Jurisdiction)* [1979] 1 FLR 380; *Moodey v Field*, 13 February 1981 (unreported); *Chamberlain v de la Mare* [1982] 4 FLR 434; *Lonslow v Hennig* [1986] 2 FLR 378; *Belton v Belton* [1987] 2 FLR 343; *Tyler v Tyler* [1989] 2 FLR 158; *MH v GP (Child: Emigration)* [1995] 2 FLR 106; *Re H (Application to Remove from Jurisdiction)* [1998] 1 FLR 848; *Re C (Leave to Remove from Jurisdiction)* [2000] 2 FLR 457; and *Re L (A Child) (Contract: Domestic Violence)* [2001] Fam 260.

[526] Children Act 1989, s 1(1). See also *Re S (Violent Parent: Indirect Contact)* [2000] 1 FLR 481; *Re H (Children: Residence Order: Relocation)* [2001] EWCA Civ 1338, [2001] 2 FLR 1277; *R v R (Leave to Remove)* [2004] EWHC 2572, [2005] 1 FLR 687; and *Re A (Leave to Remove: Cultural and Religious Considerations)* [2006] EWHC 421, [2006] 2 FLR 572.

[527] Eg, *Re B (Children) (Removal from Jurisdiction), Re S (Children) (Removal from Jurisdiction)* [2003] EWCA Civ 1149, [2003] 2 FLR 1043—relocation to South Africa and Australia, respectively, in furtherance of each mother's new relationship; leave granted, on appeal, to remove children; *Re B (Children) (Leave to Remove: Impact of Refusal)* [2004] EWCA Civ 956, [2005] 2 FLR 239—leave granted, on appeal, to remove children to Australia, following mother's remarriage; *Re A (A Child) (Temporary Removal from Jurisdiction)* [2004] EWCA Civ 1587, [2005] 1 FLR 639—leave granted, on appeal, to remove 4-year-old child to South Africa for 2 years, in furtherance of mother's academic career; surprisingly, scant attention was paid to the fact that 2 years in the life of a 4-year-old child is a very substantial period of time; *Re G (Removal from Jurisdiction)* [2005] EWCA Civ 170, [2005] 2 FLR 166; and *C v S* [2006] EWHC 2891.

wishes to relocate; and, perhaps most importantly of all, the likely effect of the refusal of the application upon the psychological and emotional stability of the parent who wishes to relocate. In assessing the reasonableness of the relocation proposal, THORPE LJ has suggested the following discipline:[528] (a) Is the applicant's proposal genuine, ie not motivated by a selfish desire to reduce or terminate contact between the other parent and the child, and realistic, ie founded upon well conceived and well researched proposals?[529] (b) Is the respondent parent's opposition motivated by genuine concern for the future of the child's welfare or is it driven by an ulterior motive? (c) What would be the impact upon the applicant parent of a refusal of a genuine and realistic proposal? (d) What does an overriding review of the child's welfare as the paramount consideration indicate is best for the child? Whilst there is no presumption in favour of the applicant parent,[530] the reasonable proposals of such a person having a residence order in respect of the child typically will be granted unless the court concludes that this is incompatible with the child's welfare.[531]

The *Payne* principles were articulated with cases of permanent relocation in mind; the more temporary the proposed removal, the less regard should be had to the principles.[532] Moreover, in *Re B (Children)*,[533] a case in which both parents had strong connections with other jurisdictions, the mother with Holland, and the father with Dubai, the judge was required to determine, removal from England being inevitable, which of two jurisdictions would better advance the children's welfare,[534] and so *Payne*, being factually distinct (the respondent in that case having resisted the application for removal of the children to New Zealand in order that they might stay within the jurisdiction of England and Wales) was distinguished.

(e) Common law rules[535]

(i) Recognition of foreign orders

Despite the recent legislative developments, the common law rules as to the recognition of foreign orders continue to be important. This is because the Child Abduction and Custody Act 1985 and its Conventions apply to a relatively restricted (though continually growing) number of countries. Thus the common law rules apply in the case of all orders (whether custody, guardianship or wardship orders) made in other "non-Convention" countries[536] outside the United Kingdom; to any orders made in countries covered by the 1980 Hague Convention or by the European Convention but which do not fall within their

---

[528] *Payne v Payne*, [2001] EWCA Civ 166, [2001] Fam 473 at 488. Applied in *R v R (Leave to Remove)* [2004] EWHC 2572, [2005] 1 FLR 687.

[529] *H v F* [2005] EWHC 2705, [2006] 1 FLR 776—leave to remove child from England to Jamaica refused since proposal was ill-conceived, unrealistic and speculative in terms of income and probable benefit to family. *Contra McShane v Duryea* [2006] Fam LR 15; and *Re A (Leave to Remove: Cultural and Religious Considerations)* [2006] EWHC 421, [2006] 2 FLR 572.

[530] *Payne v Payne* [2001] EWCA Civ 166, [2001] Fam 473, at 483, per BUTLER-SLOSS P, at 500.

[531] Ibid.

[532] *Re A (A Child) (Temporary Removal from Jurisdiction)* [2004] EWCA Civ 1587, [2005] 1 FLR 639.

[533] [2005] EWCA Civ 643.

[534] The judge concluded that the children's best interests would be served by relocating with their father to Dubai.

[535] See McClean, *Recognition of Family Judgments in the Commonwealth* (1983), pp 252–262.

[536] See, eg, in respect of Singapore, Ong (2007) 21 International Journal of Law, Policy and the Family 220.

definitions of "rights of custody"[537] or "decisions relating to custody";[538] to orders made in a European Community Member State which are outside the scope of Brussels II *bis*;[539] and to any orders made elsewhere in the United Kingdom which are not "Part I orders" within the meaning of the 1986 Act. The common law position is simple. No automatic recognition or enforcement is given to a foreign custody order.[540] Arguments of comity or reciprocity, however potent they may be, are held to be outweighed by the principle that the welfare of the child is the paramount consideration of the English court in all proceedings concerned with the upbringing of the child or the administration of his property.[541] Even though a custody order has been made by a foreign court, the English judge can still make such order as he thinks is in the best interest of the child;[542] for "national status is merely one of the factors which the judge in exercising his discretion will take into consideration".[543]

The Court of Appeal made it clear in *Re F (A Minor) (Abduction: Custody Rights)*[544] that there are two contexts in which the court must consider the welfare of the child:

> The first is the context of which court shall decide what the child's best interests require. The second context, which only arises if it has first been decided that the welfare of the child requires that the English rather than a foreign court shall decide what are the requirements of the child, is what orders as to custody, care and control and so on should be made.[545]

Although, in deciding whether to order the immediate return of a child abducted from his habitual residence in a non-Convention country, the welfare of the child is the court's paramount consideration, the Court of Appeal in *Osman v Elasha*[546] made clear that the welfare principle is not an absolute standard: "What constitutes the welfare of the child must be subject to the cultural background and expectations of the jurisdiction striving to achieve it."[547] In particular, it is not for an English court to criticise the standards of, or paramount principles applied by, the family justice system in such a country, except in exceptional circumstances, such as persecution or ethnic, sex[548] or other discrimination.[549] With regard to three boys abducted by their mother from the Sudan to England, the welfare principle in *Osman* had to be looked at in the context of Sudanese custom and culture, which applied Islamic law and which was familiar and acceptable to a practising Muslim family. The point was made by Baroness HALE of Richmond in *Re J (A Child (Custody Rights: Jurisdiction)*[550] that: "In a world which values difference, one culture is

---

[537] Child Abduction and Custody Act 1985, Sch 1, Art 5(a).

[538] Ibid, Sch 2, Art 1(c).

[539] Art 1(3), supra, pp 1080–1081.

[540] For ease of exposition, we shall take recognition of custody orders as the prime example.

[541] See Children Act 1989, s 1; and *Re J (A Child) (Custody Rights: Jurisdiction)* [2005] UKHL 40, [2006] 1 AC 80, in which Baroness HALE of Richmond pointed out, at [20], that application of the welfare principle might be specifically excluded by statute as, for example, by the Child Abduction and Custody Act 1985.

[542] *Re G (JDM)* [1969] 1 WLR 1001 at 1004; *J v C* [1970] AC 668 at 700–701, 714, 720; and *AB v CD* [2000] Fam LR 91.

[543] [1970] AC 668 at 701; cf *Re B (Infants)* [1971] NZLR 143.

[544] [1991] Fam 25.

[545] Ibid, at 31.

[546] [2000] Fam 62.

[547] Ibid, at 69. Cf *B v El-B (Abduction: Sharia Law: Welfare of Child)* [2003] 1 FLR 811; and *Re J (A Child) (Custody Rights: Jurisdiction)* [2005] UKHL 40, [2006] 1 AC 80, per Baroness HALE of Richmond, at [37].

[548] See *EM (Lebanon) v Secretary of State for the Home Department* [2006] EWCA Civ 1531, [2007] 1 FLR 991.

[549] Cf, under 1980 Hague Convention, *Re S (Abduction: Intolerable Situation: Beth Din)* [2000] 1 FLR 454.

[550] [2005] UKHL 40, [2006] 1 AC 80, at [37], and [38].

not inevitably to be preferred to another. Indeed, we do not have any fixed concept of what will be in the best interests of the individual child." It is necessary that this realisation informs judicial policy with regard to the return of children abducted from "non-Convention" countries. If, however, as was the case in *Re J*, there is a genuine issue between the parents as to whether it is in the best interests of the child to live in England or in a non-Convention country, it must be relevant whether that issue is capable of being tried freely and fully in the courts of that country:

> If those courts have no choice but to do as the father wishes, so that the mother cannot ask them to decide, with an open mind, whether the child will be better off living [in England] or there, then our courts must ask themselves whether it will be in the interests of the child to enable that dispute to be heard. The absence of a relocation jurisdiction must do more than give the judge pause . . .; it may be a decisive factor.[551]

A leading common law authority is *McKee v McKee*:[552]

> A husband and wife, American citizens, separated and agreed in writing that neither of them, without the permission of the other, would remove their son out of the USA. A year later the husband obtained a decree of divorce from a Californian court and an order awarding him the custody of the child and confirming the written agreement. About four years later, the same court, on the applications of both parties, awarded custody to the wife, whereupon the husband took his son to Ontario without the leave or knowledge of his wife. The wife thereupon took *habeas corpus* proceedings in Ontario. The trial judge, after a careful review of the circumstances, awarded custody of the child to the husband, but his decision was reversed by the Supreme Court of Canada.

The Privy Council restored the Ontario decision. The two charges levelled against the husband, that he had broken the agreement with his wife and had flouted the order of the Californian court, had been adequately considered by the trial judge, who, in the opinion of the court, was justified in concluding that in the light of the other circumstances the interests of the child would best be served by leaving him in the custody of his father. The order of the Californian court was a factor of great importance, but it was not decisive:

> It is the law . . . that the welfare and happiness of the infant is the paramount consideration in questions of custody . . . To this paramount consideration all others yield. The order of a foreign court of competent jurisdiction is no exception. Such an order has not the force of a foreign judgment: comity demands not its enforcement, but its grave consideration. This distinction . . . rests on the peculiar character of the jurisdiction and on the fact that an order providing for the custody of an infant cannot in its nature be final.[553]

Giving a foreign order "grave consideration" certainly does not prevent the English court from making a contrary order if the judge thinks it is in the best interests of the child to do so;[554] but it must not be forgotten that the judge who made the first order will have

---

[551] Ibid, [39].
[552] [1951] AC 352.
[553] [1951] AC 352 at 365; and see *Re B's Settlement* [1940] Ch 54; *Re G (JDM)* [1969] 1 WLR 1001.
[554] *McKee v McKee* [1951] AC 352 at 364–365; *J v C* [1970] AC 668 at 700–701, 714, 720, 728; *Re L* [1974] 1 WLR 250 at 264; *Re C* [1978] Fam 105; *Re R* (1981) 2 FLR 416 at 425; *Sinclair v Sinclair* 1988 SLT 87.

had the advantage of seeing the parties and hearing cross-examination of witnesses.[555] The court will be influenced by a variety of factors in deciding whether to make an order in terms similar to, or different from, those of the foreign order. If the foreign order was made some years ago, and the family circumstances have changed, the English order may well be in different terms and a further significant time factor is that the children will be older and their views more important.[556]

Attitudes towards the basic common law rule have changed over time,[557] with the acceptance of statutory provisions within the United Kingdom and elsewhere of Conventions providing for the speedy return of children. For a time, there was a view that the principles of the Hague Convention should be applied, by analogy, where there has been wrongful removal of a child from a country not, at the relevant time, a party to that Convention.[558] This approach, however, has been declared wrong by the House of Lords in what now is the leading case on "non-Convention" child abduction, *Re J (A Child) (Custody Rights: Jurisdiction)*.[559] An issue of principle arose in *Re J* regarding the proper approach to be taken in applications for the summary return of children to "non-Convention" countries. Baroness HALE of Richmond directed that there is no warrant, either in statute or authority, for the principles of the Hague Convention to be extended or applied by analogy to countries which are not parties to it.[560] Rather, where a non-Convention country is involved, a trial judge must focus on the individual child in the particular circumstances of the case:

> Hence, in all non-Convention cases, the courts have consistently held that they must act in accordance with the welfare of the individual child. If they do decide to return the child, that is because it is in his best interests to do so, not because the welfare principle has been superseded by some other consideration . . . the child's welfare is paramount and the specialist rules and concepts of the Hague Convention are not to be applied by analogy in a non-Convention case.[561]

There are decisions under the common law rules, just as there are under the 1980 Hague and Council of European Conventions, involving cases where children have been brought within the jurisdiction of the English courts by one parent against the wishes of the other, often in flagrant contempt of the order of a foreign court;[562] though in other cases the

---

[555] *McKee v McKee*, supra, at 360; *Re Kernot* [1965] Ch 217; *Re S(M)* [1971] Ch 621.

[556] *Re T* [1969] 1 WLR 1608, at 1611; and see *E v F* [1974] 2 NZLR 435; and *Re Z (A Child)* [2006] EWCA Civ 1291.

[557] *McKee v McKee*, supra, has been described as "somewhat discredited": *Re Taylor's Marriage* (1988) 92 FLR 172 at 178.

[558] *Re F (A Minor) (Abduction: Custody Rights)* [1991] Fam 25; *G v G (Minors) (Abduction)* [1991] 2 FLR 506; *Re S (Minors) (Abduction)* [1994] 1 FLR 297; *D v D (Child Abduction: Non-Convention Country)* [1994] 1 FLR 137; *Re M (Abduction Non-Convention Country)* [1995] 1 FLR 89; *Re P (Abduction: Non-Convention Country)* [1997] 1 FLR 780; *Re Z (Abduction: Non-Convention Country)* [1999] 1 FLR 1270; *Re Lavitch* (1985) 24 DLR (4th) 248; *Re H's Marriage* (1985) FLC 80, 164; *Re Bannios and Sanchez's Marriage* (1989) 96 FLR 336; *ZP v PS* (1994) 122 CLR 639; *Re Z (Abduction: Non-Convention Country)* [1999] 1 FLR 1270; and *Re Z (A Child)* [2006] EWCA Civ 1219, per WALL LJ, at [14].

[559] [2005] UKHL 40, [2006] 1 AC 80.

[560] Ibid, at [22]. See also *Re H (Abduction: Dominica: Corporal Punishment)* [2006] EWHC 199 (Fam), [2006] 2 FLR 314—in determining whether the courts of Dominica could offer children the protection they needed, it had to be borne in mind that that jurisdiction condoned treating children with physical violence, and therefore the English court could not contemplate returning the children there.

[561] Ibid, per Baroness HALE of Richmond, at [25].

[562] Eg *McKee v McKee* [1951] AC 352; *Re H* [1966] 1 WLR 381; *Re E(D)* [1967] Ch 761, [1967] 2 WLR 1370; *Re T* [1968] Ch 704; *Re L* [1974] 1 WLR 250; *Re C* [1978] Fam 105; *Re R* (1981) 2 FLR 416; *Re G* (1983)

"kidnapping" has been done before there has been a foreign order,[563] sometimes to frustrate foreign proceedings.[564] These cases raise the issue of whether the English court should, despite any foreign custody order, examine the merits of the case concerning the child or make a summary order and send the child back to the jurisdiction from which he has come. *Re F (A Minor) (Abduction: Custody Rights)*[565] establishes[566] that the first task for the court in assessing the welfare of the child is to decide whether the return of the child to the country from which it has been wrongfully taken should be ordered. It was argued on behalf of the bereft father in *Re J (A Child) (Custody Rights: Jurisdiction)*[567] that there should be a "strong presumption" that it is "highly likely" to be in the best interests of a child, subject to unauthorised removal or retention, to be returned to his country of habitual residence so that any issues which remain can be decided in the courts there.[568] Such an approach, however, is open to the objection that, "it would come so close to applying the Hague Convention principles by analogy that it would be indistinguishable from it in practice".[569] Instead, Baroness HALE of Richmond stated that: "The most one can say . . . is that the judge may find it convenient to start from the proposition that it is likely to be better for a child to return to his home country for any disputes about his future to be decided there. But the weight to be given to that proposition will vary enormously from case to case."[570] Important variables are the degrees of connection of the child with each country (including his nationality, where he has lived for most of his life, his first language, his race or ethnicity, his religion, his culture, and his education), and the length of time he has spent in each country. The extent to which it is relevant that the legal system of the other country differs from that of England will depend on the facts of the particular case.[571] "Our law does not start from any a priori assumptions about what is best for any individual child. It looks at the child and weighs a number of factors in the balance."[572] The evaluation and balancing of these factors is a matter for the trial judge: "only if his decision is so plainly wrong that he must have given far too much weight to a particular factor is the appellate court entitled to interfere".[573] Only in the relatively rare case of immediate return not being ordered, will the English court decide what order, in the best interests of the child, to make under section 8 of the Children Act 1989.[574]

(ii) Effect of a foreign order in England

Foreign custody and guardianship orders may not be devoid of effect in England even though, as we have seen, there are no rules at common law regulating their recognition

---

5 FLR 268; and *Re S (Children) (Child Abduction: Asylum Appeal)* [2002] EWCA Civ 843; [2002] 2 FLR 465.

[563] Eg *Re T* [1968] Ch 704; *Re L* (1982) 4 FLR 368.

[564] Eg *Re B* (1982) 4 FLR 492.

[565] [1991] Fam 25.

[566] And see *Re P (Abduction: Non-Convention Country)* [1997] 1 FLR 780; cf *Re L* [1974] 1 WLR 250; *Re R* (1981) 2 FLR 416.

[567] [2005] UKHL 40, [2006] 1 AC 80.

[568] Ibid, at [30].

[569] Ibid, per Baroness HALE of Richmond, at [31].

[570] Ibid, at [32].

[571] Ibid, at [36].

[572] Ibid, at [38].

[573] Ibid, at [12].

[574] Taking account of the "check-list" in s 1(3) of the Children Act 1989.

and enforcement. Whilst there is no clear judicial authority in the case of custody orders, the Law Commission has suggested that "in practice a third person, such as an English headmaster, would be held to have acted properly if he acted on the assumption that a custody order made [elsewhere] was effective in England and Wales".[575]

There is some old authority in relation to foreign guardianship orders which supports the idea that effect will be given to such an order in England as it affects third parties, even though the English courts will remain free to make their own order.[576] A major question which arises is whether the foreign guardian is entitled to exercise, in England, those rights over the person and property of his ward that are recognised by English internal law. It is clear in the first place that, with or without an English order, his powers are limited to those recognised by English internal law.[577] This rule is in sharp contrast to the practice adopted in civil law countries, where it is admitted in general that a tutor appointed under the personal law of the child enjoys the same rights over his ward's movable property in other countries as he possesses in the country of his appointment. The problem, then, is whether a foreign guardian is justified if he acts in England within the limits of English internal law. The answer would appear to be that he occupies in effect the same position as a person appointed in England as the child's guardian. What he does within the limits of English internal law will be recognised as validly done provided that his authority has not been challenged;[578] but if his position or his authority is challenged, then, as in the case of an English guardian, it lies within the discretion of the court to decide whether he should be replaced by another person or whether his acts or proposed acts should be approved. Perhaps the major difference in this respect between a foreign and an English guardian is that the court would be more ready to displace the former than the latter.[579]

So, a foreign guardian whose authority was unchallenged in England would act properly if he took the child abroad, as he would be doing no more than an English guardian could do in exercising parental responsibility for the child.[580] Conversely, the English courts have recognised a foreign guardian and ordered that his ward, the young Prince Rainier of Monaco, at school in England, be delivered up to him.[581]

With regard to property rights, English practice has also shown a tendency to recognise the right of a foreign guardian to claim movable property in England.[582] Again, however, if his right is challenged it is at the discretion of the court whether, having regard to the interests of the child, the property shall be delivered to the guardian or to some

---

[575] Law Com No 138 (1985), para 5.6.

[576] See Dicey, Morris and Collins, paras 19R-058–19-064.

[577] *Johnstone v Beattie* (1843) 10 Cl & Fin 42 at 114.

[578] *Nugent v Vetzera* (1866) LR 2 Eq 704 at 712.

[579] Old cases in which foreign guardianship orders were recognised without regard to the paramount importance of the welfare of the child would not, in that respect, now be followed, ie *Nugent v Vetzera* (1866) LR 2 Eq 704; *Di Savini, Savini v Lousada* (1870) 18 WR 425; see *Re S (Hospital Patient: Foreign Curator)* [1996] Fam 23 at 30–31.

[580] Children Act 1989, s 5(6); and see *Nugent v Vetzera* (1866) LR 2 Eq 704 at 714; provided removal was done with the appropriate consent required under the Child Abduction Act 1984, s 1.

[581] *Monaco v Monaco* (1937) 157 LT 231.

[582] *Mackie v Darling* (1871) LR 12 Eq 319; *Re Crichton's Trust* (1855) 24 LTOS 267; *Re Brown's Trust* (1865) 12 LT 488.

other person.[583] The question generally arises where money is due to a foreign child under an English settlement, will or intestacy. Where the money has not been paid into court, it has been said that the trustees are legally discharged if they make payment to the foreign guardian and take his receipt.[584] Where the money is in court, then the court is entitled, but not compelled, to order payment to the guardian, and whether it does so or not depends on whether it is satisfied that the property will be properly administered for the child's benefit.[585]

(iii) UK-Pakistan Judicial Protocol on Child Contact and Abduction[586]

In *Osman v Elasha*,[587] THORPE LJ remarked that, although the 1980 Hague Convention has been extremely successful, there has been an obvious limitation to its success: "The member states by and large all derive their sense of law and justice from the Judaeo-Christian root. No state that settles civil and family disputes according to Islamic law has joined the club."[588] His Lordship recognised that: "The further development of international collaboration to combat child abduction may well depend upon the capacity of states to respect a variety of concepts of child welfare derived from differing cultures and traditions."[589] International collaboration of a different sort, specifically intended to address relations between the United Kingdom and Pakistan, can be seen in the consensus reached in January 2003, between the President of the Family Division in England and Wales, and the Hon Chief Justice of the Supreme Court of Pakistan, in consultation with senior members of the family judiciary of the United Kingdom and Pakistan, with regard to child contact and abduction. The Protocol was prompted by a desire to protect children of the United Kingdom and Pakistan from the harmful effects of wrongful removal or retention from one country to the other, and a concern to promote judicial co-operation, enhanced relations and the free flow of information between the judiciaries of the United Kingdom and Pakistan. Use of the Protocol will arise mainly in the context of abductions to or from Pakistan, but also in relation to an application for leave to take a child temporarily from the United Kingdom to Pakistan.

It has been agreed that, "1. In normal circumstances the welfare of a child is best determined by the courts of the country of the child's habitual/ordinary residence". In particular:

2. If a child is removed from the UK to Pakistan, or from Pakistan to the UK, without the consent of the parent with a custody/residence order or a restraint/interdict order from the court of the child's habitual/ordinary residence, the judge of the court of the

---

[583] *Ex p Watkins* (1752) 2 Ves Sen 470; *Re Hellmann's Will* (1866) LR 2 Eq 363; *Re Chatard's Settlement* [1899] 1 Ch 712. Cf *Dharamal v Lord Holm-Patrick* [1935] IR 760: A, domiciled in Indore in India, was not entitled as of right to the Irish Sweep winnings of his daughter, aged 7, though by the law of Indore he could give a good discharge.

[584] *Re Chatard's Settlement* [1899] 1 Ch 712 at 716.

[585] Children Act 1989, s 1.

[586] [2003] Fam Law 199; Guidance Note from the President of the Family Division at [2004] Fam Law 609; and [2006] Fam Law 5. See also *A v A*, 2 February 2004 (unreported); *A v A*, 25 February 2004 (unreported), discussed by Binns at [2004] Fam Law 359; *Re Z (A Child)* [2006] EWCA Civ 1219, per WILSON LJ, at [31]; and in Scotland, *A v N* 2007 GWD 01-2; and the high profile case of Molly Campbell/Misbah Rana (2006), settled out of court.

[587] [2000] Fam 62.

[588] Ibid, at 69. Cf *Re J (A Child) (Custody Rights: Jurisdiction)* [2005] UKHL 40, [2006] 1 AC 80, per Baroness HALE of Richmond, at [21].

[589] Ibid, at 70.

country to which the child has been removed shall not ordinarily exercise jurisdiction over the child, save in so far as it is necessary for the court to order the return of the child to the country of the child's habitual/ordinary residence.[590]

These principles are to apply without regard to the nationality, culture or religion of the parents and shall apply to "children of mixed marriages".[591] If the habitual/ordinary residence of the child is a matter of dispute, this should be determined as a preliminary issue by the court to which the application is made.

The Protocol differs from the 1980 Hague Convention in so far as there is no role to be played by Central Authorities. A liaison judge, however, has been appointed in each jurisdiction.[592]

5. OTHER DEVELOPMENTS

(a) 1996 Hague Convention

In 1996, the Hague Conference concluded a Convention on Jurisdiction, Applicable Law, Recognition, Enforcement and Co-operation in respect of Parental Responsibility and Measures for the Protection of Children.[593] The Convention was signed on 1 April 2003 by the then fourteen European Community Member States, including the United Kingdom, but it has not yet been ratified or acceded to by those states. Member States are no longer free to conclude the Convention on their own; since its provisions affect Community rules as contained in Brussels II *bis*, competence to conclude the Convention is shared between the Community and the Member States.[594]

The 1996 Convention is the broadest in scope of the Hague Conference's children conventions.[595] As its name indicates, not only does it contain rules on jurisdiction,

---

[590] In analogous cases which fall outside the strict terms of the Protocol, it is thought to be consistent with the predominant approach of the Court of Appeal to apply a presumption of return, provided that return is in the best interests of the child: Guidance Note from the President of the Family Division at [2004] Fam Law 609, para 7.

[591] Protocol, para 4.

[592] With a remit capable of extending, potentially, to other matters of family law arising between the two jurisdictions: see remarks of Thorpe LJ in *Abbassi v Abbassi* [2006] EWCA Civ 355, [2006] 2 FLR 451 at [20].

[593] See generally Lagarde, *Explanatory Report* (1996). Also Detrich [1996] Hague Yearbook of Int L 77; Lagarde (1997) 86 Rev Crit Dr Int Priv 217; Clive [1998] Jur Rev 169; Nygh (1998) 45 Neth Int L R 1; and Clive [2002] Fam Law 131. The Convention was designed to replace the 1961 Hague Convention concerning the Powers of Authorities and the Law Applicable in respect of the Protection of Minors, to which the United Kingdom was not a party, mainly because of the role given to the authorities of the state of the child's nationality. The 1996 Convention, which entered into force on 1 January 2002, currently has 15 Contracting States.

[594] See Council Decision of 19 December 2002 authorising the Member States in the interest of the Community to sign the Convention (OJ 2003 L 48/1); Commission Proposal for a Council Decision authorising the Member States to ratify, or accede, in the interest of the European Community, to the 1996 Convention (COM (2003) 348 final 17 June 2003) and Council (JHA) decision, Luxembourg, 6 June 2008. The stumbling block to ratification of the Convention (and other mixed competence conventions) by EC Member States concerns outstanding issues between the British and Spanish governments over operations in Gibraltar: see Parliamentary Debates, House of Commons (2006–07), Vol 459, 1174w (25 April 2007); and Communication from the European Commission to the Council and the European Parliament (Report on the implementation of the Hague programme for 2006), COM (2007) 373 final, para 91.

[595] Cf 1980 Convention on Civil Aspects of International Child Abduction, supra, p 1104 et seq; and 1993 Convention on Protection of Children and Co-operation in Respect of Intercountry Adoption, infra, p 1155.

applicable law, recognition and enforcement of measures on parental responsibility and protection of children,[596] it also establishes a framework for co-operation among Contracting States. The scope of application of the Convention[597] is very similar to that of Brussels II *bis*, although the latter, as has been seen, does not deal with choice of law. It is said that the Convention would make a "valuable contribution to the protection of children in situations that transcend the boundaries of the Community and thus usefully complement existing and future Community rules in this area".[598]

Chapter II (Articles 5 to 14) of the Convention contains rules of jurisdiction. Jurisdiction in respect of the person and property[599] of the child rests principally with the authorities of the Contracting State in which the child is habitually resident.[600] Article 10 permits the authorities of a Contracting State exercising jurisdiction in respect of the divorce, legal separation or annulment of marriage of a child's parents, also to take measures for the protection of the child.[601] A special rule for cases of wrong removal or retention of the child is laid down in Article 7,[602] and there exists also an emergency jurisdiction based upon presence of the child in the jurisdiction of a Contracting State.[603] A mechanism for the transfer of jurisdiction, akin to that contained in Article 15 of Brussels II *bis*,[604] is set out in Articles 8 and 9, and operates by way of exception and in the best interests of the child. Like Brussels II *bis*, the Convention adopts a principle of priority of process (*lis pendens*) to resolve problems of conflicting jurisdiction.[605]

Chapter III (Articles 15 to 22) of the Convention concerns applicable law. This chapter is particularly significant in so far as Brussels II *bis* makes no provision for choice of law, meaning that, if European Community Member States should ratify the instrument, the applicable law provisions contained in the 1996 Convention would apply.[606] In exercising jurisdiction under Chapter II of the Convention, the authorities of Contracting States shall apply their own law.[607] Since jurisdiction is conferred, as a general rule, on the

---

[596] Applying to children from the moment of their birth until they reach 18 years: Art 2.

[597] Art 3.

[598] Commission Proposal for a Council Decision authorising the Member States to ratify, or accede to, in the interest of the European Community, to the 1996 Convention (COM (2003) 348 final), para 4 17 June 2003.

[599] See Art 55 reservation in respect of immovable property: a Contracting State may reserve the right not to recognise any parental responsibility or measure in so far as it is incompatible with any measure taken by its authorities in relation to that property. See Carruthers (2005), para 2.71. The reservation, which was not included in the preliminary draft Convention, was proposed by the United Kingdom delegation.

[600] Art 5. Cf Brussels II *bis*, Art 8, supra, p 1081 et seq. "Article 5 is based on the supposition that the child has his or her habitual residence in a Contracting State. In the contrary case, Article 5 is not applicable and the authorities of the Contracting States have jurisdiction under the Convention only on the basis of provisions other than this one (Art 11 and 12). But nothing prevents these authorities from finding themselves to have jurisdiction, outside of the Convention, on the basis of the rules of private international law of the State to which they belong" (Lagarde, *Explanatory Report*, para 39).

[601] Cf Brussels II *bis*, Art 12, supra, p 1084.

[602] Cf Brussels II *bis*, Art 10, supra, p 1118.

[603] Art 11; see also Art 12 with regard to jurisdiction to take provisional protective measures. Cf Brussels II *bis*, Arts 13 and 20, supra, pp 1084–1085 and 1094–1095.

[604] Supra, pp 1092–1093.

[605] Art 13. Cf Brussels II *bis*, Art 19, supra, pp 1093–1094.

[606] Supra, p 1096.

[607] Art 15(1). "Law" means the law in force in a state other than its choice of law rules: Art 21 (subject to Art 21(2), which makes special provision for cases where the law applicable according to Art 16 is that of a non-Contracting State). The instrument adopts a principle of universal application, meaning that the law designated by the Convention shall apply, whether or not it is the law of a Contracting State: Art 20.

authorities of the Contracting State in which the child is habitually resident, the law of the forum, in most cases, will be the most appropriate law to apply. Exceptionally, the forum may apply or take into consideration the law of another state with which the situation has a substantial connection.[608] It is said that this provision is based "not on the principle of proximity (the closest connection), but on the best interests of the child".[609] If the child should become habitually resident in another Contracting State, the law of that state, from the time of the change, will govern the conditions of application of the measures taken in the state of former habitual residence.[610]

The attribution or extinction of parental responsibility by operation of law,[611] without the intervention of a judicial or administrative authority, is governed, by virtue of Article 16 by the law of the state in which the child is habitually resident.[612] Similarly, the attribution or extinction of parental responsibility by agreement or unilateral act (eg a will by which a parent nominates a guardian for the child) is governed by the law of the child's habitual residence at the time when the agreement or act takes effect.[613] Likewise, the exercise of parental responsibility is governed by the law of the state of the child's habitual residence from time to time.[614]

The Convention confers a certain degree of third party protection: the validity of a face-to-face[615] transaction entered into between a third party and another person who would be entitled to act as the child's legal representative under the law of the state where the transaction was concluded cannot be contested, and the third party cannot be held liable, on the sole ground that the other person was not entitled to act as the child's legal representative under the law designated by the Convention, unless the third party knew or ought to have known that the parental responsibility was governed by the latter law.[616]

Chapter IV (Articles 23 to 29) of the Convention, concerning recognition and enforcement, in essence is the same as Chapter III of Brussels II *bis*.[617] The same is true of Chapter V (Articles 29 to 39) of the Convention, on the topic of co-operation between the Central Authorities of Contracting States, which is akin to Chapter IV of Brussels II *bis*.[618]

Article 61 of Brussels II *bis* specifically deals with the relationship between the Regulation and the 1996 Convention. It provides that the Regulation would apply (a) where the child concerned has his habitual residence on the territory of a Member state; and (b) as concerns the recognition and enforcement of a judgment given in a court of one Member State in the territory of another Member State, even if the child is habitually resident in a third state which is a Contracting State to the 1996 Convention. By virtue of Article 61,

---

[608] Art 15(2). Eg, in relation to immovable property, where application of the law of the situs might be more appropriate (Lagarde, *Explanatory Report*, para 89).

[609] Lagarde, *Explanatory Report*, para 89.

[610] Art 15(3). See also Art 5(2).

[611] Recognising that most children are not subject to parental responsibility measures.

[612] Art 16(1).

[613] Art 16(2).

[614] Art 17. This provision, unlike Art 16 (attribution or extinction of parental responsibility), incorporates a mutability principle.

[615] Art 19(2).

[616] Art 19(1). Cf 1980 Rome Convention, Art 11, supra, pp 752–753.

[617] Supra, p 1097 et seq.

[618] Supra, p 1101.

however, the 1996 Hague Convention would have effect in relation to matters not governed by the Regulation; principally, and most significantly, applicable law. If a case were to arise concerning a matter covered by the Regulation (on a point of jurisdiction, or recognition and enforcement), and the child in question was habitually resident in a European Community Member State, Brussels II *bis* would take priority. If a case were to arise concerning the recognition and enforcement of a judgment issued by a court in another Community Member State, Brussels II *bis* would apply, even if the child in question lives in a third state which is a Contracting Party to the 1996 Hague Convention.[619]

If, by exercise of shared competence, the European Community and Member States should decide to ratify the 1996 Hague Convention, the outcome, in the United Kingdom, will be the introduction of yet another regime to govern parental responsibility and related issues. The result would be the operation of one regime for intra-United Kingdom cases; another for intra-European Community cases; still another for 1996 Hague Convention cases; and of residual common law rules for such cases as fall outside the scope of application of all the various instruments. Such a multiplicity of regimes is unnecessarily complicated and so, for the sake of clarity and simplicity, determined efforts should be made to streamline the rules.

(b) Council of Europe Convention on Contact concerning Children

On 15 May 2003, the Council of Europe Convention on Contact concerning Children[620] opened for signature. The Convention entered into force on 1 September 2005, and to date there have been five ratifications.[621] As with the 1996 Hague Convention, European Community Member States are no longer free to conclude the 2003 Convention on their own, since its provisions affect Community rules as contained in Brussels II *bis*, meaning that competence is shared between the Community and the Member States.[622]

The Convention aims at reinforcing the fundamental right of children and their parents and other persons having family ties with the child to maintain contact on a regular basis, and seeks to "improve the machinery for international co-operation especially as regards transfrontier access to children in order to establish safeguards for the return of children after a period of access".[623] The risk of unnecessary duplication and overlap with the provisions of Brussels II *bis*, the 1980 Hague Convention, the 1980 Council of Europe Convention and the 1996 Hague Convention, is obvious, but nevertheless the view has been advanced that the 2003 Convention will "contribute to the realisation of the aims underlying existing and future Community rules in the field of recognition and enforcement of judgments in the area of parental responsibility".[624] The preamble to the 2003

---

[619] See Brussels II *bis*, *Explanatory Report*, para XI.

[620] CETS No 192. See also *Explanatory Report*, adopted 3 May 2002.

[621] Albania, Czech Republic, Romania, San Marino, and Ukraine.

[622] Art 22(1) of the 2003 Convention allows for accession by the European Community. See Proposal for a Council Decision on the signing by the EC of the Council of Europe Convention on Contact concerning Children (COM 2002/0520 final), OJ 2003 C 20E/369. No decision as yet has been taken. In relation to England and Wales, see Department for Constitutional Affairs Consultation Paper 02/04, 28 May 2004.

[623] *Explanatory Report*, para I.

[624] Proposal for a Council Decision on the signing by the EC of the Council of Europe Convention on Contact concerning Children (COM 2002/0520 final), Recital (4).

Convention states that, "an additional instrument is necessary to provide solutions relating in particular to transfrontier contact concerning children".[625] Given the proliferation of instruments in this field of law, it is scarcely possible to justify this statement.

"Contact" is defined in the Convention as including direct and indirect contact with a child.[626] In particular, it includes "(i) the child staying for a limited period of time with or meeting a person[627] . . . with whom he or she is not usually living; (ii) any form of communication between the child and such person; (iii) the provision of information to such a person about the child or to the child about such a person".[628] "Contact", arguably, is broader than "rights of access" referred to in Brussels II *bis*,[629] and use of the expression is intended to demonstrate that children are the holders of certain rights.[630]

Article 20(1) of the Convention provides that it shall not prejudice the application of the 1980 Hague Convention, the 1980 Council of Europe Convention[631] or the 1996 Hague Convention.[632] Moreover, by virtue of Article 20(3), if the European Community and its Member States should accede to/ratify the 2003 Convention, in their mutual relations those Member States would give preference to the application of Brussels II *bis*, meaning that the 2003 Convention would apply only in so far as there is no Community rule to govern the particular issue arising.

The 2003 Convention is merely a "good practice guide". It does not lay down rules of jurisdiction, or a mechanism for the recognition and enforcement of contact orders. Rather, it is a "medium for promoting co-operation and consistency of practice".[633] Since the procedure for recognition and enforcement of orders has been laid down already in other instruments operating in the field, the advantages to be gained from ratification of yet another instrument are not obvious. Ratification of the Convention is more likely to confuse than to enhance regulation of contact concerning children.[634] It is to be hoped, therefore, that political pressure alone will not compel the United Kingdom to become a state party to this Convention.

---

[625] Recital (16).

[626] A person under 18 years of age in respect of whom a contact order may be made or enforced in a state party to the Convention: Art 2(c).

[627] A parent (Art 4) or a person other than the parent having family ties with the child (Art 5).

[628] Art 2(a).

[629] Art 2(10). Supra, p 1080.

[630] *Explanatory Report*, para 6.

[631] Though see special provision in Art 19 of the 2003 Convention.

[632] *Explanatory Report*, para 11.

[633] Department for Constitutional Affairs Consultation Paper 02/04 (28 May 2004), para 4.

[634] Cf remarks of THORPE LJ in *Re G (Children) (Foreign Contact Order: Enforcement)* [2003] All ER (D) 144 at [32].

Chapter 25

Legitimacy, Legitimation and Adoption

1. INTRODUCTION

The three matters that require consideration in this chapter are legitimacy, legitimation and adoption.[1] None of these topics falls within the scope of the Brussels II *bis* Regulation.[2] Legitimacy ordinarily means the status acquired by a person who is born to

---

[1] For a speculative discussion of private international law problems arising from issues of parentage, see Norrie (1994) 43 ICLQ 757.

[2] Recital (10) and Art 1(3)(a) and (b).

parents who are married to one another at the time of the birth. Legitimation means that a person who has not been born to married parents acquires the status of a legitimate person as the result of some act, such as the subsequent marriage of his parents, that occurs after the date of his birth. Adoption, in English law, involves the extinction of the parental links between the child and the biological parents and the creation of similar links between the child and the adoptive parents.

Whether a person is legitimate or has been legitimated or adopted has, in the past, been of considerable importance in the field of succession. If the will of a domiciled Englishman contained a gift to the "children" of a specified person it had to be asked whether this included not only legitimate children but also those who were illegitimate, legitimated or adopted. English domestic law has moved from a position in which it was rare that a will or intestacy applied to other than legitimate children to the situation where, as a consequence of a process culminating in the Family Law Reform Act 1987, there has been a very substantial assimilation of the rights of children, irrespective of the circumstances of their birth.[3] This legislation does not, however, abolish the distinction between legitimacy and illegitimacy, nor the concept of legitimation. Though they have become far less important,[4] it will still be necessary to determine whether or not the parents of a child are married, or whether the child is legitimate, for the purposes, for example, of domicile, as well as in determining the rights of the father.[5]

The general effect of these developments has been to diminish, though not to eradicate,[6] the need for rules of private international law to determine a person's legitimacy or the validity of his legitimation. It might, for example, also be necessary for a child domiciled in England to have his legitimacy determined for the purposes of succession under a foreign law. On the other hand, there has if anything been an increase in the need to determine the validity in England of foreign adoptions, resulting from the increase in the number of foreign children adopted, sometimes abroad, by English parents.

We have examined already[7] the powers and jurisdiction of the English courts to make declarations relating to legitimacy, legitimation and adoption. We have now to consider the choice of law rules relating to legitimacy, legitimation and adoption. It is also necessary, with regard to adoption, to discuss the further questions of the rules for the jurisdiction of the English courts to make adoption orders and for the recognition of foreign adoptions.

2. LEGITIMACY[8]

(a) Legitimacy to be governed by the law of the domicile

Before the passing of the Legitimacy Act 1959, the rule of domestic English law was that no child acquired the status of legitimacy unless he was born in lawful wedlock, ie, born

---

[3] 1987 Act,s 1, as amended by the Adoption and Children Act 2002, Sch 3, para 51.

[4] Eg, regarding citizenship, in respect of which see now the British Nationality Act 1981, ss 1 and 50(9), as substituted by the Nationality, Immigration and Asylum Act 2002, Pt 1, s 9(1); and SI 2006/1496, reg 2. In relation to the previous position, see, eg, *R (On the Application of Montana) v Secretary of State for the Home Department* [2001] 1 FLR 449; and *Azad v Entry Clearance Officer (Dhaka)* [2001] Imm A R 318.

[5] Children Act 1989, ss 2 (as amended by the Adoption and Children Act 2002, Pt 2, s 111(5)) and 4.

[6] See Law Com No 132 (1984), paras 3.9–3.14; Law Com No 158 (19860, para 3.14.

[7] Supra, p 1043 et seq.

[8] Welsh (1947) 63 LQR 65; Lipstein (1954) *Festschrift für Ernst Rabel*, Vol I, p 611.

of parents whose marriage was valid at the time of his birth. This exclusive test, however, was exceptional, for most countries, including Scotland,[9] had long recognised the doctrine of the putative marriage, according to which a child even of a void marriage is also legitimate. A common, though not a universal, qualification of this doctrine is that the spouses should have bona fide believed in the validity of their marriage. A question of choice of law might therefore arise if a child were born out of lawful wedlock in the country where X and Y, his parents, were domiciled and where the doctrine of the putative marriage was recognised.

Several writers have expressed the view that in such circumstances the English test of birth in lawful wedlock becomes applicable. This is open to the insuperable objection that it fails to appreciate the true function of English law in such a case. If an English will bequeaths a legacy to the "legitimate children" of parents who were domiciled abroad at the time of their son's birth and if his legitimacy is disputed, there are two separate questions to be resolved. The first is a question of construction—what did the testator intend by his use of the phrase "legitimate children"? This is a matter for English domestic law as the law governing succession. If the answer is that he referred to legitimate children, then the second question, whether the children are in fact legitimate, is a question not of construction, but of status determinable by the law of their domicile.[10] The subject of inquiry is not whether the marriage of the legatee's parents is valid, but whether he is legitimate in the eyes of the law of his domicile—the only law that is entitled to pass upon his status.[11] English law is, indeed, relevant so far as concerns the construction of the will, but as ROMER J said in one case: "The only relevant rule of construction is that a bequest in an English will to the children of A means to his legitimate children[12] and that does not carry the matter very far, for the question remains who are his legitimate children, and that is not a question of construction at all, it is a question of law."[13]

(b) Shaw v Gould

(i) The decision

This principle, that any person legitimate according to the law of his domicile, though not born in lawful wedlock, is legitimate for the purpose of succeeding to movables under an English will or intestacy has been repeatedly affirmed in a stream of cases from at least 1835 onwards;[14] but, with few exceptions,[15] these statements were made in cases concerned with legitimation. It is sometimes said, therefore, that they are of little value

---

[9] If by the law of the domicile of the innocent "spouse" he is legitimate: *Smijth v Smijth* (1918) 1 SLR 156. See Crawford (2005) 54 ICLQ 829, 851; and Crawford and Carruthers, para 14-02. See also Family Law (Scotland) Act 2006, ss 21 and 41.

[10] See, eg, *Wright's Trs v Callender* 1993 SC (HL) 13; discussed by Crawford 1994 SLT (News) 225, and Leslie 1995 SLT 264.

[11] See, eg, *Re Andros* (1883) 24 Ch D 637 at 639 where the position is stated with great clarity.

[12] Before the operation of what is now the Family Law Reform Act 1987, s 19, as amended by the Adoption and Children Act 2002, Sch 3, para 52.

[13] *Re Bischoffsheim* [1948] Ch 79 at 86.

[14] *Doe and Birtwhistle v Vardill* (1835) 2 Cl & Fin 571 at 573, 574; *Re Don's Estate* (1857) 4 Drew 194 at 197–198; *Re Goodmans' Trusts* (1881) 17 Ch D 266 at 291, 296–297; *Re Andros* (1883) 24 Ch D 637 at 639; and *Re Bischoffsheim* [1948] Ch 79 at 92.

[15] *Re Bischoffsheim*, supra; *Motala v A-G* [1990] 2 FLR 261; revsd on another point [1992] 2 AC 281; and see *Hashmi v Hashmi* [1972] Fam 36; *Re Karnenas* (1978) 3 RFL (2d) 213.

having regard to the decision of the House of Lords in *Shaw v Gould*,[16] which raised a question of legitimacy. The facts of this case were as follows:

> Funds were bequeathed by a testator domiciled in England in trust for Elizabeth Hickson for life and after her death in trust for her children. English land was also devised after her death to "her first and other sons *lawfully begotten*". Elizabeth, at the age of 16, was induced by fraud, without the knowledge of her family, to marry a domiciled Englishman, named Buxton, at Manchester. Her friends, however, succeeded in taking her away just after the ceremony, and she never lived with her husband. Sixteen years later, Elizabeth, having become engaged to a domiciled Englishman named Shaw, devised a scheme for obtaining a divorce in Scotland from Buxton. Shaw acquired a domicile in Scotland, and Buxton was paid £250 to go to that country for forty days. The marriage was dissolved by the Court of Session. Elizabeth then married Shaw in Edinburgh and had by him two daughters and one son, all of whom were born in the lifetime of Buxton. At the time of the present action Buxton, Elizabeth and Shaw were dead. The questions before the English court were whether the daughters and son were entitled under the will of the testator to the funds as being the "children" of Elizabeth, and also whether the son was entitled to the land as being her "son lawfully begotten". Evidence was given that by Scots law the divorce and second marriage were valid; also, that children born of a putative marriage, ie one regular in point of form but void owing to the prior existing marriage of one of the parties, were regarded as legitimate, provided that the parents were justifiably ignorant of the prior existing marriage.

It was the opinion of the Scottish advocates who gave evidence that justifiable ignorance existed if the parents believed in the validity of the divorce. The House of Lords unanimously held that the children were not entitled to take under the will.[17] Their Lordships appear to have been impressed by the supposedly logical reason that since Buxton, and therefore Elizabeth, remained domiciled in England, the Scottish divorce was not recognised in England; therefore the union between Elizabeth and Shaw was not a valid marriage according to English law; and that therefore the children were not born to lawfully married parents (being the test of legitimacy according to English domestic law). Lord COLONSAY, though impressed with the logic of the reasoning, was perplexed with doubts as to whether the status of legitimacy ought to be denied to the children. He felt that this denial was difficult to reconcile with general principles of jurisprudence or with the generally recognised rules of international law.[18]

(ii) Criticisms

It is difficult to resist the conclusion that the House of Lords lost its direction through its persistent concentration on one general principle to the exclusion of others. It certainly was a general principle that a divorce not recognised as valid by the law of the husband's domicile is invalid in England. But another principle, affirmed many times by the judiciary, is that legitimacy is determined by the law of the father's domicile at the time of the

---

[16] (1868) LR 3 HL 55.

[17] Though see now the Family Law Reform Act 1987, s 19, as amended by the Adoption and Children Act 2002, Sch 3, para 52.

[18] (1868) LR 3 HL 55 at 96–97.

child's birth. Both these principles demanded attention in *Shaw v Gould*. There is nothing inconsistent in them, and they are not mutually antagonistic. It was easy to argue in this manner:

> The father cannot be granted the status of a husband, since the woman whom he purported to marry is, owing to the continuance of her earlier marriage, the wife of another man. Therefore the children of the father by this woman cannot be regarded as legitimate.

Nevertheless, the conclusion is a non sequitur. The issue was the status of the children, not of their parents. The fact that Mrs Buxton could not claim to be Mrs Shaw was not necessarily a bar to the legitimate status of the children. The legitimacy of a child happened at the time of the case to depend according to English domestic law on the validity of the marriage of which he was born; but this is not and was not the case in all legal systems. If the two questions are separable by the law of the child's domicile of origin, they should be kept separate by an English court when dealing with a private international law case. The courts of other countries have found no difficulty in this. Thus in South Africa it was held that the children of a polygamous union, born when the father was domiciled in India, were to be regarded as legitimate in Natal, which was his domicile at death. For the purpose of fixing the rate of succession duty payable on the father's death, the status of the mother as a "wife" was tested by the internal law of Natal; but the status of the children was referred to their domicile of origin.[19] INNES CJ stated that:

> It is essential to bear in mind the distinction between the points to be decided in each instance. With regard to the wife, the issue is the validity of the marriage to which she was a party; with regard to the children, the issue is their right to the status of legitimacy. The wife's position cannot be considered apart from the marriage, but the position of the children may be.[20]

It is submitted that in any event *Shaw v Gould* ought to be regarded as an abnormal decision and one to be interpreted in the light of the exceptional circumstances involved. "My opinion in this case", said Lord CHELMSFORD, "is founded entirely upon the peculiar circumstances attending it."[21] It was, indeed, distinguished by a number of special features among which may be mentioned the following:

> The Scots divorce was granted in 1846, eleven years before judicial divorce was possible in England and at a time when the prevalent view, in accordance with the unanimous opinion of the judges in *Lolley's* case,[22] was that no foreign proceedings in the nature of a divorce could affect a marriage that had been contracted in England. In fact, in the court of first instance, KINDERSLEY V-C said: "By the English law of marriage, an English marriage is absolutely indissoluble by the sentence of any court (of course I am speaking of the law as it stood at the time of the

---

[19] *Seedat's Executors v The Master* 1917 AD 302.

[20] Ibid, at 311–312. In the New York case of *Re Hall* (1901) 61 App D 266, a woman obtained a divorce in Dakota that was not regarded as valid in New York. She then married a man domiciled in Dakota and a child was born of the marriage. It was held that the child was legitimate for the purposes of taking under the will of a testator who died domiciled in New York.

[21] *Shaw v Gould* (1868) LR 3 HL 55 at 79.

[22] (1812) Russ & Ry 237. The view was finally repudiated in *Harvey v Farnie* (1882) 8 App Cas 43.

transactions in question which was long before the Act establishing the Divorce Court). . . . Any decree or judgment or sentence of any foreign court, purporting to dissolve such marriage, is treated as a mere nullity".[23] It must be observed, however, that this view did not appeal to the House of Lords. The conduct of the Shaws was calculated to arouse the suspicion of any court. In the greatest secrecy and with every precaution against discovery, they contrived a scheme to obtain a divorce in a court which, to their knowledge, had no jurisdiction in the eyes of English law.[24]

The children were legitimate by Scots law if either of the Shaws was justifiably ignorant that there was an impediment to their marriage, ie in their case, a prior invalid divorce. After a careful examination of the facts, KINDERSLEY V-C found himself unable to agree that even Mrs Shaw was justifiably ignorant of the true position.

(c) Other authorities

It is significant that, in the much later case of Re Stirling,[25] Swinfen EADY J was far from repudiating the suggestion that a child might be legitimate although the previous divorce of one of his parents was invalid. It was not necessary, however, to decide the point, for it was held that the doctrine of putative marriage, on which the argument for the child turned, did not obtain in Scotland unless at least one of the parties was ignorant of the impediment that invalidated the second marriage. The party had to be mistaken as to some fact;[26] but here the ignorance alleged was that the mother of the child was unaware that her divorce from her first husband was invalid, and this was an error of law, not of fact.

Another authority that is sometimes said to support Shaw v Gould is Re Paine.[27] The question there was whether the children of W were legitimate for the purpose of the effect of a disposition to W contained in an English will:

> In 1875 W, when domiciled in England, was married in Germany to the widower of her deceased sister. At that date a marriage between such persons was prohibited. The husband was held to have been domiciled in Germany at the time of the ceremony. The parties cohabited in England until the husband's death in 1919.

BENNETT J adopted the dual domicile doctrine of capacity and held the three children of the union to be illegitimate, since they had sprung from a void marriage. But, as in Shaw v Gould, the possibility that the children might be legitimate according to the German law of their domicile of origin, despite the absence of lawful wedlock between their parents, was not canvassed.

However, despite all attempts to rationalise Shaw v Gould the fact remains that, until the decision of ROMER J in Re Bischoffsheim,[28] it seemed to provide an embarrassing obstacle

---

[23] Re Wilson's Trusts (1865) LR 1 Eq 247 at 257–258.
[24] For the details see ibid, at 260–262.
[25] [1908] 2 Ch 344.
[26] Crawford (2005) 54 ICLQ 829 at 851. See Smijth v Smijth (1918) 1 SLT 156.
[27] [1940] Ch 46; supra, p 902.
[28] [1948] Ch 79.

to the prevalent judicial view that the legitimacy of a child is a matter for the law of his domicile of origin. This view, however, was translated into action in *Bischoffsheim's* case where the facts were these:

In 1919 W was married in New York to H, the brother of her deceased husband. It may be taken that at that time both parties were domiciled in England. The marriage was void by English law, but valid by the law of New York. After they had acquired a domicile in New York a son was born to them. The question was whether the son was the legitimate child of his mother so as to entitle him to benefit under the will of a testator who had died domiciled in England.

ROMER J found in favour of the son on the following principle:

Where succession to personal property depends upon the legitimacy of the claimant, the status of legitimacy conferred on him by his domicile of origin (ie the domicile of his parents at birth) will be recognised by our courts; and that, if that legitimacy be established, the validity of his parents' marriage should not be entertained as a relevant subject for investigation.[29]

He distinguished *Shaw v Gould* by showing that, since in that case the House of Lords chose to concentrate their attention on the validity of the divorce, they were bound to find it invalid and consequently to fix the children's domicile of origin in England. This left no room for a claim based on the ground that their legitimacy stood apart from the validity of the divorce and that, if so, their domicile of origin was in Scotland.[30]

It has been argued that this decision should be dismissed as being inconsistent with higher authority, an opinion that has been expressed on several occasions.[31] To do so would have the startling result that in the same context legitimacy is subject to one rule, legitimation to another. Where a question has arisen of succession under an English testacy or intestacy, it has long been settled that, if a claimant has been legitimated by the law of the country where at the time of his birth (and of the subsequent marriage) his father was domiciled, English law "recognises and acts on the status thus declared by the law of the domicil".[32] There is no substantial difference between legitimacy and legitimation[33] and no reason of logic or convenience why the law should relegate them to mutually exclusive categories. If from the date of the act of legitimation the child assumes the status that he would have possessed had he been born legitimate, it is incomprehensible that these two causes of the same result should be subject to divergent rules for the choice of law.

---

[29] [1948] Ch 79 at 92. Approved by the Privy Council in *Bamgbose v Daniel* [1955] AC 107 at 120; and see *Re Jones* (1961) 25 DLR (2d) 595, and *Re Karnenas* (1978) 3 RFL (2d) 213.

[30] [1948] Ch 79 at 92.

[31] Morris (1948) 12 Conveyancer (NS) 223; F A Mann (1948) 64 LQR 199; Falconbridge, *Conflict of Laws* (2nd edn), p 747 et seq. On the other hand, it is approved by Wolff, p 388.

[32] *Re Goodman's Trusts* (1881) 17 Ch D 266 at 299; and see *Boyes v Bedale* (1863) 1 Hem & M 798; *Re Andros* (1883) 24 Ch D 637; *Re Grey's Trusts* [1892] 3 Ch 88.

[33] *Re Bischoffsheim* [1948] Ch 79 at 92.

Fortunately, Sir Stephen BROWN P in *Motala v A-G*[34] clearly rejected any such divergence of approach:

> H and W, domiciled at all material times in India, went to live in Northern Rhodesia (now Zambia) where in 1950 they went through a ceremony of marriage according to Sunni Moslem law. The marriage was invalid under the law of Northern Rhodesia and, in 1968, the parties went through another ceremony of marriage there, valid by that law. The first marriage, however, was regarded as valid by Indian law. The question arose of the legitimacy of some of the spouses' children in the context of their claims to British citizenship.

An immediate question to be considered was whether the children had been legitimated by their parents' subsequent marriage. This was referred to Indian law, being that of the domicile of the parents of the children at all material times, and Indian law did not recognise legitimation by subsequent marriage. That left the question of legitimacy which was answered by means of the same process. Legitimacy, being regarded as an issue of status, was referred to the law of the children's domicile of origin, India, which law regarded the children as legitimate because Indian law regarded the parents' first marriage as valid. *Shaw v Gould* was distinguished as being concerned with the validity of the Scottish decree, and the decision in *Re Bischoffsheim* was approved.

What is striking about this decision is that the children were regarded in England as legitimate, notwithstanding the fact that their parents' marriage was, in the eyes of English private international law, invalid. Had the parents petitioned for a declaration as to the validity of their first marriage, it would have been refused on the ground that the marriage was invalid as to form according to the law of the place of celebration.[35] This strengthens the view that a child's legitimacy depends on the law of his domicile of origin.

(d) Effect of doctrine of putative marriage

It is submitted, then, even if there had been no statutory alteration of English domestic law in 1959 the courts would have endorsed the approach to the subject made in *Bischoffsheim's* case and would have restricted the decision in *Shaw v Gould* to the exceptional circumstances of the case. This submission was considerably fortified once the doctrine of putative marriage was accepted in the Legitimacy Act 1959.[36] Birth in lawful wedlock no longer represents the sole test of legitimacy according to English domestic law.

Section 1(1) of the Legitimacy Act 1976 provides as follows:[37]

> The child of a void marriage, whenever born,[38] shall . . . be treated as the legitimate child of his parents if at the time of the insemination resulting in the birth or, where there was no

---

[34] [1990] 2 FLR 261; revsd on another point by the House of Lords [1992] 1 AC 281; and see *R v Secretary of State for the Home Department, ex p Brassey* [1989] 2 FLR 486 at 494; *A-G for Victoria v Commonwealth of Australia* (1961–1962) 107 CLR 529 at 596; *Re Sit Woo-tung* [1990] 2 HKLR 410.

[35] See *Berthiaume v Dastous* [1930] AC 79, supra, p 878, n 15.

[36] See now Legitimacy Act 1976, infra.

[37] First introduced by the Legitimacy Act 1959, s 2. Special provision is introduced in the Family Law Reform Act 1987, s 27 to deal with the status of a child born to a married couple by artificial insemination, with the semen of a man other than the husband. However, no choice of law rule is laid down, though the provisions are limited to the case of a child born in England. See *J v C (Void Marriage: Status of Children)* [2006] EWCA Civ 551, [2007] Fam 1.

[38] Provided the child was born after the marriage was entered into: *Re Spence* [1989] 2 All ER 679.

such insemination, the child's conception (or at the time of the celebration of the marriage if later) both or either of the parties reasonably believed that the marriage was valid[39],[40]

This provision does not apply unless the father of the child was domiciled in England at the time of the birth or, if he died before the birth, was so domiciled immediately before his death.[41] Where this condition is not satisfied, the legitimacy of a child born of a void marriage must be determined by the law of his domicile of origin. Where the father is domiciled in a foreign country where a similar doctrine is recognised, there would be even less justification than before for denying the legitimate status of a child born of a void marriage.[42]

In a provision that is susceptible of more than one interpretation,[43] a void marriage for the purposes of the Act is defined as "a marriage, not being voidable only, in respect of which the High Court has or had jurisdiction to grant a decree of nullity, or would have or would have had such jurisdiction if the parties were domiciled in England and Wales".[44] Although the meaning of this provision is far from clear, its probable object is to exclude any union which in the eyes of English law has no claim to be a marriage at all, as for example one springing from concubinage.[45]

(e) Meaning of "domicile of origin"

ROMER J's statement[46] that the domicile of origin means the country in which the parents are domiciled at the birth of the child is not supported by indisputable authority. Some of the judges have preferred to refer to the domicile of the father,[47] though others, probably having in mind the usual case where the father and mother possess a common domicile, with ROMER J, have preferred to speak of "the domicile of the parents", a view which, if adopted, would require the law of each domicile to be satisfied. It is, of course, true that to attribute to the child the domicile of his father where his parents have different domiciles is to beg the question of his legitimacy, for, since the domicile of a child is said to be that of his father if legitimate but of his mother if illegitimate,[48] it would appear to be impossible to fix his domicile until the question of his legitimacy has been settled.

This vicious circle would disappear if it could be said that the legitimacy of a child was to be referred to the domicile of one of his parents, but that his domicile of origin depended on the validity of his parents' marriage. Some nineteenth-century cases[49] on the domicile of origin

---

[39] According to English law: *Azad v Entry Clearance Officer (Dhaka)* [2001] Imm A R 318, per JACOB J, at p [15].

[40] S 1(1), amended by the Family Law Reform Act 1987, s 28(1). A presumption of reasonable belief is introduced by s 28(2) of the 1987 Act.

[41] S 1(2). See *Re Barony of Moynihan* [2000] 1 FLR 113.

[42] Jones (1959) 8 ICLQ 722, 725.

[43] For various views on its almost identical predecessor, s 2(5) of the Legitimacy Act 1959, see Jones (1959) 8 ICLQ 725, 726; Tucker (1960) 9 ICLQ 321, 322; and Kahn-Freund (1960) 23 MLR 58, 59.

[44] S 10(1).

[45] It is clear, at least, that the validity of a marriage for the purposes of s 1 of the 1976 Act is to be measured by reference only to English law, and not, eg, the law of the place of celebration: *Azad v Entry Clearance Officer (Dhaka)* [2001] Imm A R 318, per JACOB J, at p [13]–[15].

[46] *Re Bischoffsheim* [1948] Ch 79 at 92.

[47] Eg *Yuen Tse v Minister of Employment and Immigration* (1983) 32 RFL (2d) 274.

[48] Supra, p 174. See Crawford (2005) 54 ICLQ 829, at 852.

[49] Eg, in *Forbes v Forbes* (1854) Kay 341 at 343 it is said that "every person born in wedlock acquires by birth the domicil of its father".

of a child are compatible with such a view. The present difficulty stems from Lord WESTBURY's statement that "the law attributes to every individual as soon as he is born the domicil of his father, if the child be legitimate, and the domicil of his mother if illegitimate".[50] As in *Shaw v Gould*, the questions of the legitimacy of a child and of the validity of his parents' marriage seemed to nineteenth-century judges inextricably to be the same. The later acceptance that a child might be legitimate notwithstanding the invalidity of his parents' marriage[51] must inevitably cast doubt on the acceptability of Lord WESTBURY's views.[52]

If one must accept that Lord WESTBURY's statement has stood the test of time too well and cannot now be confounded, the vicious circle must be broken; for logic must not be allowed to impede the best solution of the problem. It is not easy to determine whether the domicile of the father or of the mother should predominate.[53] In an age of equality of treatment between the sexes, there is no particular reason or justification for preferring the application of the personal law of one parent over that of the other,[54] and so a cumulative test seems appropriate, ie a child not born of a marriage valid by English conflict rules is legitimate only if he is legitimate by the law of the domicile of *each* parent at the date of his birth. Of course, the disadvantage of a cumulative test is that it requires that two legal systems be satisfied, arguably making it more difficult for a child to attain the status of legitimacy, but this is a problem caused by current rules for the ascription of a domicile of origin. The decisive date for fixing the domicile of origin is the birth of the child. A child, no doubt, is for various purposes deemed at birth to have been in existence from the time of conception,[55] and if the parents change their domicile between the time of conception and of birth it is arguable that the law of the father's domicile at the former time deserves consideration.[56] However, despite the lack of authority in point, it is probable that the English courts would regard the domicile at the time of birth as decisive. A somewhat analogous question arises in the case of a posthumous child whose mother has changed her domicile since the death of the father. Is the law of the father's domicile at the time of his death or the law of the mother's domicile at the time of the child's birth to determine the question of legitimacy? The latter is probably the correct solution because the domicile of origin of a posthumous child is that of his mother.[57]

---

[50] *Udny v Udny* (1869) LR 1 Sc & Div 441 at 457.

[51] Eg putative marriage under the Legitimacy Act 1976, s 1.

[52] The vicious circle also disappears under the view in the Restatement 2d, § 287 that a child's legitimacy may be determined as to one parent only by reference, normally, to the domicile of that parent, so that a child may be legitimate with respect to one parent, but illegitimate with respect to the other.

[53] Some cases, arbitrarily, favour application of the law of the mother's domicile (eg *Smijth v Smijth* (1918) 1 SLT 156), whereas others favour application of the law of the father's domicile (eg *Re Grove* (1888) 40 Ch D 216; *Re Don's Estate* (1857) 4 Drew 194 at 198; *Re Andros* (1883) 24 Ch D 637 at 642; *R and McDonell v Leong Ba Chai* [1954] 1 DLR 401 at 403; *Perpetual Executors and Trustees Association of Australia Ltd v Roberts* [1970] VR 732 at 756, 575; and *Hashmi v Hashmi* [1972] Fam 36).

[54] Cf the position in Scots law where, by s 22 of the Family Law (Scotland) Act 2006, the domicile of a person under 16 years of age no longer is tied to the issue of the marital status of his parents. Where the child's parents are not domiciled in the same country as each other, the child shall be domiciled in the country with which he has for the time being the closest connection (s 22(3)). See also s 21 of the 2006 Act (abolition of status of illegitimacy). For criticism of the s 22 rule, see Crawford and Carruthers, paras 6-06 and 14-01.

[55] *Re Salaman* [1908] 1 Ch 4; *Re Callaghan* [1948] NZLR 846. But see *Elliot v Lord Joicey* [1935] AC 209.

[56] Taintor (1940) 18 Can Bar Rev 589, 596, 597.

[57] There seems to be no English authority on the domicile of a posthumous child, but academic opinion favours the view that it is the same as the mother's: Westlake (7th edn), s 250; Dicey, Morris and Collins, para 6-028.

(f) Relevance of the incidents of status

The question whether a child is legitimate or not by the law of the domicile is to be determined by examining the incidents of his status under that law rather than the title used to describe it. Take, for example, the situation where the law of the domicile is that of a country such as New Zealand,[58] where there is no distinction drawn between legitimate and illegitimate children. In such a case, the child would have all the incidents of the status of a legitimate child in England, though only described in New Zealand as a "child",[59] and should therefore be regarded in England as legitimate, even though not born to parents who are married. Indeed, the Supreme Court of Canada[60] has concluded that a child born in Mexico to parents who are not married, who was described by Mexican law as illegitimate, was to be considered to have the status of a legitimate child in Canada. Under Mexican law she had all the capacities and obligations of such a child, though certain social limitations attached to her position in Mexico causing her to be described there as "illegitimate".

(g) Where birth to parents who are married does not confer legitimacy

The rule suggested above[61] allocates a question of legitimacy to the law of the domicile of origin. Principle requires that this personal law should apply exclusively, since it is the only law competent to determine the status of the child. Nevertheless, if a case were to arise in which a child, though born to married parents, was for some reason not regarded as born legitimate, as for example because he was not conceived during the marriage, it is probably a safe assumption that an English court would be satisfied with the practically universal test of birth to parents married to one another.[62] This break with principle might be justified by the paramount importance of communicating to the child the beneficial status of legitimacy if some rational ground for doing so exists.

3. LEGITIMATION[63]

In the various legal systems of the world two main methods are found by which a person, not born with the status of legitimacy, may be later legitimated. These are: subsequent marriage of the parents and recognition of the child by the father. Each of these methods requires separate consideration. Here again, however, it should be emphasised that our concern is to examine the law which should determine the status. It is, for example, for

---

[58] Status of Children Act 1969 (New Zealand). Cf, in Scots law, Family Law (Scotland) Act 2006, ss 21 and 41.

[59] Ibid, s 3.

[60] *Re MacDonald* (1962) 34 DLR (2d) 14; affd 44 DLR (2d) 208; and see *Khoo Hooi Leong v Khoo Hean Kwee* [1926] AC 529 at 543; *Re Sit Woo-tung* [1990] 2 HKLR 410.

[61] Supra, p 174.

[62] See, for Scotland, the rule in s 41 of the Family Law (Scotland) Act 2006, which states that: "Any question arising as to the effect on a person's status of—(a) the person's parents being, or having been, married to each other; or (b) the person's parents not being, or not having been, married to each other, shall be determined by the law of the country in which the person is domiciled at the time at which the question arises."

[63] On the subject generally see Taintor (1940) 18 Can Bar Rev 589 and 691; F A Mann (1941) 57 LQR 112; Lipstein (1954) *Festschrift für Ernst Rabel*, Vol I, p 611. For problems connected with legitimation under a foreign statute, see Dicey, Morris and Collins, paras 20-065–20-069.

the law governing succession to decide whether a child who has been legitimated may or may not succeed by will or under an intestacy.

(a) Legitimation by subsequent marriage

(i) Introduction

It has been accepted that children born before marriage were made legitimate by the subsequent marriage of their parents. This rule became part of canon law around the twelfth century, and was later adopted by practically all the legal systems on the Continent and in South America. It has received statutory recognition in most of the common law world. Until the Legitimacy Act 1926, however, it formed no part of the law of England and Wales or of Ireland, though it obtained in Scotland, the Isle of Man and the Channel Islands.

(ii) Common law rule

The role of private international law is to choose the system of law which shall determine whether legitimation by this method is effective or not. The rule finally established at common law by *Re Grove*,[64] after some hesitation,[65] is that a foreign legitimation by subsequent marriage is not recognised in England unless the father is domiciled, *both at the time of the child's birth and also at the time of the subsequent marriage*, in a country whose law allows this method of legitimation.[66]

A simple illustration of the working of the rule is afforded by the case of *Re Goodman's Trusts*,[67] where a domiciled Englishwoman had died intestate in respect of a large sum of money, and it was necessary to decide which of her brother's children were entitled to share therein, as being her "next of kin" under the Statutes of Distribution. The relevant events in her brother's life were chronologically as follows.

(a) While domiciled in England he had three children by Charlotte Smith, to whom he was not married.

(b) He acquired a Dutch domicile, and had a fourth child, Hannah, by Charlotte Smith.

(c) He married Charlotte Smith in Amsterdam.

(d) While still domiciled in the Netherlands he had a fifth child, Anne, by Charlotte Smith.

Legitimation by subsequent marriage was part of Dutch law. It was, therefore, held on the above facts that Hannah and Anne alone were legitimate for the purposes of the English intestacy. It was only in their cases that, at the two critical moments, birth and marriage, the law of the father's domicile recognised this particular form of legitimation.

(iii) Under the Legitimacy Act 1976

The operation of the common law rules, though not abrogated, was immensely curtailed by the Legitimacy Act 1926[68] which made legitimation by subsequent marriage part of the law of England. The present law is to be found in section 2 of the Legitimacy Act

---

[64] (1888) 40 Ch D 216.

[65] See, eg, *Boyes v Bedale* (1863) 1 Hem & M 798, disapproved in *Re Goodman's Trusts*, infra.

[66] *Re Goodman's Trusts* (1881) 17 Ch D 266; *Re Andros* (1883) 24 Ch D 637; *Re Grove* (1888) 40 Ch D 216; and see *Motala v A-G* [1990] 2 FLR 261 at 267.

[67] (1881) 17 Ch D 266.

[68] S 1; the status of a person legitimated thereunder is preserved by the Legitimacy Act 1976, Sch 1, para 1.

1976 which provides that, where the parents of an illegitimate person marry, the marriage shall, if the father is *at the date of the marriage* domiciled in England and Wales, render that person, if living, legitimate from the date of the marriage.

With regard to persons who are not domiciled in England and Wales, section 3 of the Legitimacy Act 1976 provides as follows:

> Where the parents of an illegitimate person marry one another and the father of the illegitimate person is not at the time of the marriage domiciled in England and Wales but is domiciled in a country by the law of which the illegitimate person became legitimated by virtue of such subsequent marriage, that person, if living, shall in England and Wales be recognised as having been so legitimated from the date of the marriage[69] notwithstanding that, at the time of his birth, his father was domiciled in a country the law of which did not permit legitimation by subsequent marriage.

This section discards the old rule that the law of the father's domicile at the time of the child's birth must be taken into account. The law of the father's domicile at the time of the marriage is the sole decisive factor.[70] It is this law that decides, for instance, whether something more than mere marriage, such as a formal acknowledgment, is necessary to effect legitimation.

(b) Legitimation by recognition

It has been assumed so far that the foreign legitimation is by subsequent marriage. However, in several states in Europe and in North and South America a father is allowed to legitimate his child by formally recognising it as his own. The first question that this raises in private international law is—which legal system will the English courts look to in order to determine the validity of this particular form of legitimation? Is it sufficient that it is valid by the law of the father's domicile at the time of recognition, or, like legitimation by subsequent marriage before the Legitimacy Act 1926, must it also be valid by the law of the father's domicile at the time of the child's birth? The matter has been considered in only one case—*Re Luck's Settlement Trusts*[71]—where the facts were as follows:

> Under the will of George Luck, a British subject domiciled in England, funds were held in trust for all his children attaining twenty-one. Each child was to receive the income of his share for life, and after his death the capital was to be divided equally among his children at twenty-one. The marriage settlement of George limited further sums in the same manner, except that only those grandchildren born within twenty-one years of the death of the survivor of George and his wife were to take a share of the capital. The survivor died in 1896. Therefore, no grandchild was entitled under the settlement trusts unless he was alive and legitimate in 1917 at the latest. Charles was a son of George Luck. He married in 1893, but in 1906, while still married, he became the father of an illegitimate son, David, in California. At this time both he and David's mother were domiciled in England. After the dissolution of his first marriage he married a second wife. In 1925 he signed a formal

---

[69] This applies even though the father or mother was married to a third person at the time of the child's birth; cf Legitimacy Act 1926, s 1(2) since repealed.

[70] See *Heron v National Trustees Executors and Agency Co of Australasia Ltd* [1976] VR 733.

[71] [1940] Ch 864; and see *R and McDonnell v Leong Ba Chai* [1954] 1 DLR 401.

document with the assent of his second wife by which he acknowledged David to be his legitimate son and adopted him as such.[72] At this time Charles was domiciled in California. It was assumed by the Court of Appeal that David's mother was also domiciled there. By the law of California the acknowledgement in 1925 operated to legitimate David from his birth in 1906.

The question that arose on these facts was whether David was entitled to a share under the will and marriage settlement of his grandfather, George. At that time, to take under the latter he was required to be a legitimate grandchild alive as such in 1917.

The Court of Appeal held that David was entitled neither under the will nor under the settlement. The reasoning was that legitimation by subsequent marriage is disregarded at common law unless allowed by the law of the father's domicile at the time both of the birth and the marriage; that the relevant judgments regard this rule, not as confined to the single case of a subsequent marriage but as applicable to all forms of legitimation; and that in any case both convenience and principle demand the application of a uniform rule to all forms. Therefore David was disqualified, since at the time of his birth his father was subject to English law, by which legitimation by recognition is not allowed.

The common law rule based on capacity at birth was never in fact extended to cases other than legitimation by subsequent marriage. Even in this connection, it was curtailed substantially by the Legitimacy Act 1926.[73] Gratuitously to prolong its life and extend its operation is a retrograde step. In fact the decision has been most generally criticised on the ground that, though it is obviously convenient that one principle should govern all types of legitimation, it is a little eccentric to choose one whose operation has been greatly curtailed by statute.[74]

It is therefore to be hoped that, if the occasion arises, the House of Lords will prefer the dissenting judgment of SCOTT LJ, who argued in a convincing manner and at no little length that status, the outstanding characteristic of which is its "quality and universality", once determined by the law of the domicile, must be judicially recognised all the world over. At a time when David and his father and mother were domiciled in California, his father made a certain declaration according to Californian law. The effect of this by that law was to clothe David with the status of a legitimate person. Therefore, "that status, established by the law of that foreign country, was under English law one which it was the duty of the English court to recognise, and *prima facie* to enforce in accordance with its nature and attributes as determined by the law of that country".[75] It is the law of the domicile at the time when the legitimation is effected that should alone be considered.

It might also be added that the Legitimacy Act 1976 in referring to the recognition of legitimation at common law talks of a "legitimation (whether or not by virtue of the subsequent marriage of his parents)".[76]

---

[72] It is important to notice, as F A Mann has shown ((1941) 57 LQR 112, 119), that the Californian method was not adoption, but legitimation by recognition. The unwary might assume from the judgments in the Court of Appeal that it was equivalent to adoption in the English sense. See Adoption and Children Act 2002, s 55, by which an adoption order may be revoked, upon application, in circumstances where a child is legitimated by the marriage of his natural parents to each other, and s 67.

[73] S 8(1).

[74] Beckett (1944) 21 BYBIL 209; Taintor (1940) 18 Can Bar Rev 589, 652; F A Mann (1941) 57 LQR 112, 120.

[75] [1940] Ch 864 at 888.

[76] 1976 Act, s 10(1).

4. ADOPTION

Since 28 June 2007, intercountry adoption has been the responsibility of the United Kingdom Government Department for Children, Schools and Families. It is recognised that there are many children in the United Kingdom and abroad who are in need of a permanent home and an adoptive family, and for whom intercountry adoption offers the best prospects of stable domestic life.[77] Whilst the United Kingdom government does not actively promote intercountry adoption, it is willing to allow it where a child cannot be cared for in a suitable manner in his country of origin;[78] the adoption would be in his best interests, with respect to the child's fundamental rights as recognised by international law; and the prospective adopter has been assessed by a registered adoption agency as eligible[79] and suitable to adopt a child from abroad.[80]

A variety of issues arises from consideration of the private international law rules relating to adoption. There are wide differences among the laws of different countries on a number of matters, such as who can adopt, or be adopted, and the effects of adoption on, for instance, succession rights. For example, the requirements of English law that an adoption order may not be made in relation to a person who has attained the age of 19 years,[81] or who is or has been married,[82] are not found in all legal systems.

In examining the rules concerning adoption, it is important to consider the jurisdiction of the English courts to make adoption orders; the choice of law rules applied by English courts; and the rules for recognition of foreign adoptions. It is necessary also to distinguish the different types of intercountry adoption, according to the identity of the other country involved in the adoption process: (a) a Hague Convention country, being one which, like the United Kingdom, is a signatory to the 1993 Hague Convention on Protection of Children and Co-operation in respect of Intercountry Adoption;[83] (b) a country[84] on the United Kingdom's list of designated countries, as set out in the Adoption (Designation of Overseas Adoptions) Order 1973;[85] or a country which is neither a Hague Convention country, nor one which features on the United Kingdom's designated list.

(a) Adoption proceedings in England

(i) Introduction

Adoption, the process by which, under English law, a child is brought permanently into the family of the adopter and parental responsibility for the child is transferred to the

---

[77] For general information and statistics, see UK Government, Department for Children, Schools and Families website: http://dfes.gov.uk/intercountryadoption. Since 2000, approximately 2,240 applications have been made in the United Kingdom by persons wishing to adopt a child from overseas (average 319 per annum).

[78] "Intercountry adoption should never be considered as the first or only option for a child": Full Regulatory Impact Assessment for the Adoptions with a Foreign Element Regulations 2005 (SI 2005/392), p 2.

[79] There is no "right" to adopt a child.

[80] See House of Commons Library Research Paper 06/07, 7 February 2006, "Children and Adoption Bill"; and Full Regulatory Impact Assessment for the Adoptions with a Foreign Element Regulations 2005 (SI 2005/392), p 2.

[81] Adoption and Children Act 2002, s 47(9).

[82] Ibid, s 47(8).

[83] See Adoption (Intercountry Aspects) Act 1999, supplemented by the Intercountry Adoption (Hague Convention) Regulations, SI 2003/118; and Adoption and Children Act 2002, supplemented by the Adoptions with a Foreign Element Regulations, SI 2005/392.

[84] Which may, or may not, also be a Hague Convention Contracting State.

[85] SI 1973/19, as amended.

adopter,[86] was introduced into England by the Adoption of Children Act 1926, which was ultimately replaced by the consolidating legislation of the Adoption Act 1976.[87] Unlike the case in some other countries, adoption can be effected only by the order of a court,[88] after a judicial inquiry directed mainly to ensuring that such an order will be for the welfare of the child. The effect of an order is to take away from the child whatever legal benefits nature conferred upon him and to transfer all obligations towards him to the adoptive parents who, by nature, have no obligation towards him at all.[89] There is a complete and fundamental change in the status of the child. He becomes a child in law of his adoptive parent(s) to the exclusion of his natural parents.

(a) Adoption and Children Act 2002

The 2002 Act modernised the legal framework for domestic and intercountry adoption.[90] It largely replaces the Adoption Act 1976,[91] and incorporates most[92] of the provisions of the Adoption (Intercountry Aspects) Act 1999 (examined below), providing a statutory basis for the regulation of intercountry adoption, strengthening existing safeguards, introducing some new ones, and enabling the United Kingdom to ratify the 1993 Hague Convention on Protection of Children and Co-operation in respect of Intercountry Adoption. In introducing wide-ranging reform of the rules in England and Wales for domestic and intercountry adoption, it affects all adoptions in England, and all adoption applications from persons resident and settled in England who are seeking to adopt children living abroad. Part 1 of the Act sets out the framework of adoption law for England and Wales, including in Chapter 6 (sections 83 to 91) provision for intercountry adoption; Part 2 makes amendments to the Children Act 1989; and Part 3 makes miscellaneous provision on advertising and the Adoption and Children Act Register.

(b) Adoptions with a Foreign Element Regulations 2005[93]

The Adoptions with a Foreign Element (AFE) Regulations, which are one of a series of statutory instruments implementing the provisions of the Adoption and Children Act 2002,[94] set out safeguards and procedures for intercountry adoption. They apply to England and Wales with effect from 30 December 2005,[95] and are intended to replace

---

[86] 2002 Act, s 46(1).

[87] Only brought into force on 1 January 1988.

[88] This can be the High Court, county court, or magistrates' court: 2002 Act, ss 67(1) and 144(1); and the Family Procedure (Adoption) Rules, SI 2005/2795, r 5.

[89] 2002 Act, s 46.

[90] See also the Family Procedure (Adoption Rules), SI 2005/2795.

[91] Except provisions regarding the status of children already adopted. The 2002 Act includes some provisions amending the Adoption Act 1976, which enabled certain important elements of the new adoption framework to be implemented in advance of full implementation of the 2002 Act.

[92] Ss 1 and 2 (regulations to give effect to the 1993 Hague Convention), 7 (amendments to the British Nationality Act 1981), and Sch 1 (the text of the 1993 Hague Convention) continue in force. The remaining provisions of the 1999 Act have ceased to apply in England and Wales, and instead are incorporated in the 2002 Act.

[93] SI 2005/392 ("AFE Regulations"); made under powers conferred by ss 83(4)–(6), 84(3) and (6), 140 (7)–(8), 142(4)–(5) of the 2002 Act, and ss 1(1) and (3)–(5) of the 1999 Act.

[94] See generally Explanatory Memorandum to the AFE Regulations, paras 14 and 15. See also the Adoption Agencies Regulations, SI 2005/389 and the Adopted Children and Adoption Contact Register Regulations, SI 2005/924.

[95] Reg 1.

the Intercountry Adoption (Hague Convention) Regulations 2003[96] and the Adoption (Bringing Children into the United Kingdom) Regulations 2003,[97] both of which came into force only on 1 June 2003[98] and which were intended to be repealed when the Adoption and Children Act 2002 was fully implemented.

The AFE Regulations underpin a number of policy objectives, ie: to establish safeguards to ensure intercountry adoption takes place in the best interests of the child and with respect for his/her fundamental rights as recognised in international law; to ensure prospective intercountry adopters have been assessed and approved in accordance with the appropriate procedures; and to enable the United Kingdom to continue to meet its duties under international law.[99]

The AFE Regulations set out procedures in relation to incoming adoptions (adoption of children from abroad by British residents) and outgoing adoptions (adoption of children in England and Wales by persons resident abroad), and for Convention adoptions and non-Convention adoptions, respectively. The jurisdiction of the English court to make an adoption order and the law to be applied by the court depend on two different sets of legislative rules, namely general rules (for non-Convention adoptions) and Convention rules (for Hague Convention adoptions).

(ii) General rules

(a) Jurisdiction[100]

An application for an adoption order, other than a Convention adoption order, may be made, in terms of the Adoption and Children Act 2002, by a couple,[101] or by one person only, subject to satisfaction of one of two conditions.[102] In the case of adoption by a couple, an order may be made where both have attained 21 years,[103] or if one of the couple is the mother or father of the child and is at least 18 years of age, and the other has attained 21 years.[104] In the case of adoption by one person only, an order may be made if he has attained 21 years and is not married or a civil partner, or if he is the partner of a parent of the person to be adopted.[105] The two conditions, only one of which must be satisfied, are

---

[96] SI 2003/118; made under the Adoption (Intercountry Aspects) Act 1999, and applicable to Convention adoptions.

[97] SI 2003/1173; made under the transitional provisions in the 2002 Act (s 56A of the 1976 Act, as amended by the 2002 Act), and applicable to adoptions from non-Hague Convention countries, or from Contracting States that have acceded to the Convention, but in respect of which the United Kingdom has raised an objection.

[98] The 2003 Regulations put in place the necessary provisions to give effect in England and Wales to the 1993 Convention. See corresponding legislation in Scotland (SSI 2001/236, 2003/19 and 2003/67) and Northern Ireland (SR 2002/144 and 2006/336), which enabled the United Kingdom to ratify the 1993 Convention. Essentially, the 2003 Regulations required anyone habitually resident in England and wishing to adopt a child living in another country to be assessed and approved as suitable to adopt by a local authority or Voluntary Adoption Agency registered to work on intercountry adoption, regardless of the nature of that person's relationship to the child or the country from which they wished to adopt.

[99] Explanatory Memorandum to the AFE Regulations, para 7.

[100] See the 13th edn of this book (1999), p 903, for an examination of the rules operating prior to the entry into force of the Adoption and Children Act 2002.

[101] Ie a married couple, or two people (of different sexes or the same sex) living as partners in an enduring family relationship: 2002 Act, s 144(4), subject to s 144(5).

[102] Ibid, s 49(1).

[103] Ibid, s 50(1).

[104] Ibid, s 50(2).

[105] Ibid s 51(1) and (2); also (3), (3A) and (4).

that (i) at least one of the couple (in the case of a joint application), or the applicant (in the case of a sole applicant) is domiciled in a part of the British Islands;[106] or (ii) both applicants (in the case of a joint application), or the applicant (in the case of a sole applicant) have/has been habitually resident in a part of the British Islands for a period of not less than one year ending with the date of the application.[107] If only the domicile criterion is satisfied, the prospective adopters would not be eligible, in principle, to seek a Hague Convention adoption order,[108] habitual residence on the part of the applicant(s) being a requirement of such adoptions. If, on the other hand, only the habitual residence criterion is satisfied, the applicant(s) can consider adopting a child from any country. The domicile of the child to be considered for adoption is not relevant to the matter of allocation of jurisdiction. It should be borne in mind, however, that even if the applicant is domiciled or habitually resident in England, the court will be unable to make an adoption order if the other conditions set out in the 2002 Act are not satisfied.[109]

(b) Choice of law

The absence of any requirement in the 2002 Act that the child should be domiciled in England raises a question of choice of law. If an applicant, domiciled or habitually resident in England, applies for an adoption order in respect of a child domiciled abroad, will the court have regard to the substantive requirements of the foreign law of the child's domicile, which may differ widely from their English equivalents contained in the 2002 Act in such matters as the age of the respective parties and the required consents? The terms of the English legislation are such that an adoption order made by the court would not be vitiated by a failure to take account of the foreign law. In the absence of an express choice of law rule in the 2002 Act, the law of the forum must be assumed to apply. However, it is submitted that to refer exclusively to the law of the forum would be contrary to principle and often prejudicial to the well-being of the child. The admitted and basic feature of status as fixed by the law of the domicile is its universality.[110] The status attributed to a child in his domicile of origin is entitled to universal respect. It is, therefore, undesirable for the English court to make an adoption order which claims to destroy that status and to substitute another that is fundamentally different. Moreover, such an order would scarcely be recognised in the domicile of origin, with the result that the child would be the child of X in England, but of Y in all other countries, a situation which seems strangely at odds with the statutory requirement that, in making any decision relating to the adoption of a child, the paramount consideration of the court or adoption agency must be the child's welfare, throughout his life.[111] Certainly, the possibility of taking account of foreign law, whether or not the law of the child's domicile, is envisaged by the Family Procedure (Adoption) Rules 2005,[112] rule 139 of which sets out the procedure

---

[106] Ibid, s 49(2).

[107] Procedure for disputing the court's jurisdiction is set out in the Family Procedure (Adoption) Rules, SI 2005/2795, r 115.

[108] Infra, p 1160 et seq.

[109] Eg, s 47. See generally the 2002 Act, ss 18–65, especially ss 42–45 (preliminaries to adoption). Rules on service, including service out of the jurisdiction, are set out in SI 2005/2795, Pt 6.

[110] Re Luck's Settlement Trusts [1940] Ch 864 at 894.

[111] 2002 Act, s 1(2).

[112] SI 2005/2795.

which must be followed by a party who intends to put in evidence a finding on a question of foreign law by virtue of section 4(2) of the Civil Evidence Act 1972.

It might be extremely difficult to blend two opposing systems of adoption law, but nonetheless the fact remains that to impose a status on a child in conflict with that which he possesses in his domicile of origin, to create as it were a "limping child", would be a doubtful blessing to bestow upon him.

A resolution of the conflict between principle and the then applicable statutory wording[113] was found in *Re B (S) (An Infant)*:[114]

> An application was made by proposed adopters for the consent of the natural father to the adoption to be dispensed with. The natural father was domiciled in Spain and the child and the adoptive parents were resident in England where the adoptive parents were domiciled. It was assumed that the child was domiciled in Spain,[115] and this raised the issue of whether Spanish law should be considered relevant to the application.

GOFF J decided that the court had jurisdiction to make an adoption order "notwithstanding that by the law of the infant's domicil the court there could not make an order or could only make one having different consequences".[116] Nevertheless, he admitted that the law of the domicile is not to be ignored, for "the true impact of the domiciliary law is purely as a factor—albeit an important one—to be taken into account in considering whether the proposed order will be for the welfare of the infant, a matter upon which the Statute expressly provides[117] that the court must be satisfied before making an order".[118] Moreover, GOFF J took the view that "welfare", as used in the statute, "does not mean simple physical or moral well-being, but benefit in the widest sense which must include consideration of the effect the order, if made, will have on the infant's status".[119] If the adoption will not be recognised by such law, though here there was evidence that Spain would recognise the English order, then the court will have to weigh the serious disadvantages of being a "limping child" against the benefits which may accrue from adoption. This balancing process will inevitably result in cases, albeit rare ones, where an English adoption order will be made in circumstances where it will not be recognised by the law of the child's domicile.[120]

In none of the relevant English decisions has the court considered the effect of the adoption order on the status of the biological parents according to their own personal law(s). Although jurisdiction can be exercised without reference to the domicile of the biological parents, one might question[121] whether an order which deprives them in England of the status of parent should be made without consideration, not only of their interests in

---

[113] Adoption Act 1958, s 1(1).

[114] [1968] Ch 204; Blom-Cooper (1968) 31 MLR 219; Carter (1967) 42 BYBIL 309–310.

[115] The natural parents were divorced and the court would not decide whether in such a case a child took the domicile of the mother to whom custody had been awarded.

[116] [1968] Ch 204 at 210.

[117] Adoption Act 1958, s 7(1)(b); see now 2002 Act, s 1(2).

[118] [1968] Ch 204 at 211; approved in *Re G (An Infant)* [1968] 3 NSWR 483 at 485–486.

[119] Ibid.

[120] Eg *Re R (Adoption)* [1967] 1 WLR 34; cf *Re A (An Infant)* [1963] 1 WLR 231.

[121] See Blom-Cooper (1968) 31 MLR 219.

relation to matters such as consent, but also of the effect of the adoption order under the law governing their status.[122] Not only a child but also a parent can "limp". The Supreme Court of Canada, in 1981, decided[123] (though without detailed consideration of the choice of law issues) that the question whether a child was one who could be adopted should be referred not only to the domiciliary law of the applicants and of the child, but also, at least in contested cases, to that of the biological parents.

(iii) Convention rules

(a) Background

In 1964, the Hague Conference on Private International Law produced a Convention on Adoption, which was signed in 1965.[124] The Convention, which was ratified by the United Kingdom in 1978, related to jurisdiction, choice of law and recognition of foreign adoptions.[125] On 15 April 2003, however, the United Kingdom denounced the 1965 Convention,[126] with effect from 23 October 2003, in order that it could be replaced by the 1993 Hague Convention on Protection of Children and Co-operation in respect of Intercountry Adoption, signed by the United Kingdom on 12 January 1994.[127] With effect from 1 June 2003, in accordance with the Adoption (Intercountry Aspects) Act 1999, supplemented by the Intercountry Adoption (Hague Convention) Regulations 2003,[128] and the Adoption and Children Act 2002, supplemented by the Adoptions with a Foreign Element Regulations 2005,[129] the 1993 Convention came into force in the United Kingdom.

(b) 1993 Hague Convention on Protection of Children and Co-operation in respect of Intercountry Adoption[130]

Preparation of the 1993 Convention involved more than sixty-five countries, including the United Kingdom, as well as non-government organisations and voluntary bodies having an interest in intercountry adoption. The purpose of the Convention is to establish safeguards to ensure that intercountry adoptions take place in the best interests of the child and with respect for his fundamental rights as recognised in international law;

---

[122] In *J v C* [1970] AC 668, the House of Lords granted custody of a child to foster parents against the desire of the unimpeachable natural parents in Spain. Their Lordships were at pains to indicate they were not considering an application for an adoption order (see at 692, 714, 719), thus suggesting greater weight would be paid to the interests of the natural parents in the case of adoption because of its permanent effect.

[123] *Paquette v Galipean* [1981] 1 SCR 29; and see *Re L (HK)* [1989] 1 WWR 556; *Re S (H)* (1995) 13 RFL (4th) 301.

[124] Cmnd 2615. See Graveson (1965) 13 ICLQ 528; Lipstein [1965] CLJ 224; Unger (1965) 28 MLR 463.

[125] For examination of the 1965 Convention and the Adoption Act 1976, see the 13th edn of this book (1999), p 906 et seq.

[126] As also did Switzerland. Austria, the only other Contracting State to the 1965 Convention, denounced it on 20 April 2004.

[127] See van Loon [1993] VII Hague Recueil 191, [1994] Hague Yearbook of International Law 325–328; Pfund in Borras (ed), *E Pluribus Unum* (1996) 321–336; and Hinchliffe [2003] Fam Law 570.

[128] SI 2003/118.

[129] SI 2005/392.

[130] As at 1 April 2008, there are 75 Contracting States to the Convention. See Parra-Aranguren, *Explanatory Report on the Convention* (1994) (hereinafter "*Explanatory Report*"); and documents drawn up by the Permanent Bureau of the Hague Conference on Private International Law, regarding the Special Commissions of 2000 and 2005 on the practical operation of the 1993 Convention (http://www.hcch.net).

to establish a system of co-operation among Contracting States to ensure that those safe-guards are respected, and thereby prevent abduction, the sale of, or traffic in children;[131] and to secure the recognition in Contracting States of adoptions made in accordance with the Convention.[132]

The Convention applies where a child[133] who is habitually resident[134] in one Contracting State (the state of origin[135]) has been, is being, or is to be moved to another Contracting State (the receiving state), either after his adoption in the state of origin by a person or persons habitually resident in the receiving state, or for the purposes of such an adoption in the receiving state or in the state of origin.[136]

There is no express mention of choice of law in the 1993 Hague Convention. Instead, the Convention sets out the reciprocal obligations resting, respectively, upon the authorities in the state of origin and in the receiving state. The successful operation of the Convention depends to a large extent on effective collaboration between the two states.

Article 4 determines the duties of the state of origin.[137] It provides that a Convention adoption can proceed only if the competent authorities in the state of origin have (a) established that the child is adoptable; (b) determined, after possibilities for place-ment of the child within the state of origin have been given due consideration, that an intercountry adoption is in the child's best interests; (c) ensured that the persons,[138] insti-tutions and authorities[139] whose consent is necessary[140] for adoption have given their informed[141] consent, without coercion or financial incentive, and, in particular, that the consent of the child's biological mother, where required, has been given only after the birth of the child; and (d) ensured, having regard to the age and maturity of the child, that he has been duly counselled and informed of the effects of the adoption, that considera-tion has been given to his wishes and opinions, and that his consent, where required, was duly informed and freely given, not induced by payment or compensation of any kind.

---

[131] See, regarding breach of procedure, *Re C (A Minor) (Adoption: Illegality)* [1999] 1 FLR 370; and *Re M (Adoption: International Adoption Trade)* [2003] EWHC 219, [2003] 1 FLR 1111.

[132] Art 1.

[133] A person under the age of 18 on the date when the Central Authorities of the receiving state and the state of origin agree that the adoption may proceed: Art 3.

[134] The Convention does not define when a child or a prospective adopter shall be deemed to be habitually resident in a Contracting State.

[135] There was some early criticism of this expression, born of fear that it would cause misunderstandings, especially if interpreted as meaning the "State of the nationality". The drafters concluded, however, that the specific meaning for the purpose of the Convention was clear. Parra-Aranguren, *Explanatory Report*, para 73.

[136] Art 2. The Convention applies in every case where an application pursuant to Art 14, infra, has been received after the Convention has entered into force in the receiving state and the state of origin: Art 41.

[137] See Parra-Aranguren, *Explanatory Report*, paras 108–172; and *Pini v Romania* [2005] 2 FLR 596, (2005) 40 EHRR 13.

[138] Eg *Re A (A Child) (Adoption of a Russian Child)* [2000] 1 FLR 539; *Re C (A Child) (Foreign Adoption: Natural Mother's Consent: Service)* [2006] 1 FLR 318; *Re AMR (Adoption: Procedure)* [1999] 2 FLR 807—con-sent of Polish guardian— child's grandmother.

[139] Eg *Re N (A Child) (Adoption: Foreign Guardianship)* [2000] 2 FLR 431—consent of orphanage *qua* guardian; *Re J (A Child) (Adoption: Consent of Foreign Public Authority)* [2002] EWHC 766, [2002] 2 FLR 618; and *Re D (Adoption: Foreign Guardianship)* [1999] 2 FLR 865—consent of Romanian hospital not required as not guardian appointed in accordance with Children Act 1989.

[140] *Re K (A Minor) (Adoption: Foreign Child)* [1997] 2 FLR 221.

[141] *Re R (A Minor) (Inter-Country Adoptions: Practice) (No 1)* [1999] 1 FLR 1014; and *(No 2)* [1999] 1 FLR 1042.

Article 5 determines the duties of the receiving state,[142] providing that a Convention adoption can proceed only if the competent authorities in that state have determined that the prospective adoptive parents are eligible and suited to adopt, and have been counselled as may be necessary, and that the child is or will be authorised to enter and reside permanently in the receiving state.

The effective operation of the Convention is dependent upon co-operation and co-ordination among the designated Central Authorities of Contracting States.[143] The procedural requirements of intercountry adoption are detailed in Chapter IV (Articles 14 to 22). Article 14 states that persons habitually resident in a Contracting State, who wish to adopt a child habitually resident in another Contracting State, shall apply to the Central Authority in the state of their habitual residence.[144] The Parra-Aranguren Report makes clear that since Article 14 does not expressly regulate the formal requirements to be fulfilled by the application, these shall be determined by the law of the habitual residence of the prospective adoptive parents, it being understood, however, that they must identify themselves, and give all the necessary information to facilitate the preparation of the report prescribed by Article 15.[145] It follows from Article 14 that prospective adopters are not able to apply directly to the Central Authority or to any other public authority or accredited body of the state of origin of the child.

When the application is presented to the Central Authority of the receiving state (ie the state in which the prospective adopters are habitually resident), the Central Authority must ascertain whether the prospective adopters are eligible and suited to adopt, as is required by Article 5(a) of the Convention. Therefore, "it shall establish their compliance not only with all legal conditions prescribed by the applicable law, as determined by the receiving State, but also with the necessary socio-psychological requirements needed to guarantee the success of the adoption".[146] If the Central Authority of the receiving state is satisfied that the applicants are eligible and suited to adopt, it must prepare a report (an "Article 15 Report"), for transmission to the Central Authority of the state of origin,[147] including information about the applicants' identity, eligibility and suitability to adopt, background, family and medical history, social environment, reasons for adoption, ability to undertake an intercountry adoption, as well as the characteristics of the children for whom they would be qualified to care. The Parra-Aranguren Report explains that this is intended to be an additional safeguard to guarantee the success of the adoption. Preferences of the prospective adopters should be "expressed in general terms, *e.g.* age, religion and special needs (disability etc) of a child in accordance with their parenting

---

[142] Parra-Aranguren, *Explanatory Report*, paras 173–193.

[143] Cf the 1980 Hague Convention on the Civil Aspects of International Child Abduction, supra, p 1103 et seq. Ch III (Arts 6–13) of the 1993 Convention sets out the role and responsibilities of Central Authorities. The Central Authority for England and Wales is the Secretary of State. Chapter III should be read in conjunction with Art 22, which permits, within some limits and under certain conditions, delegation of the functions assigned to the Central Authority by Chapter IV to other public authorities or accredited bodies, or even non-accredited bodies or persons. See Parra-Aranguren, *Explanatory Report*, paras 194–279, especially para 196.

[144] Art 14.

[145] Parra-Aranguren, *Explanatory Report*, para 289.

[146] Ibid, para 294.

[147] Art 15(2).

skills and experiences, children professing a certain religion, and not make reference to a specific child in particular".[148]

If the Central Authority of the state of origin is satisfied that the child is adoptable, it shall prepare a report (an "Article 16 Report"), including information about the child's identity, adoptability, background, social environment, family history, medical history including that of his family, and any special needs.[149] The Central Authority of the state of origin must give due consideration to the child's upbringing and to his ethnic, religious and cultural background; ensure that relevant consents have been obtained,[150] and determine, on the basis of the Article 15 and 16 Reports, whether the envisaged placement is in the best interests of the child. Once it has been determined that the child should be entrusted to the prospective adopters,[151] the Central Authorities of both states shall take all necessary steps to obtain permission for the child to leave the state of origin and to enter and reside permanently in the receiving state.[152]

Article 28 makes clear that the Convention does not affect any law of the state of origin which requires that the adoption of a child habitually resident within that state take place in that state, or which prohibits the child's placement in, or transfer to, the receiving state prior to adoption. It is not the aim of the Convention to unify the substantive laws of Contracting States with regard to adoption.

In keeping with the objectives of the Convention, it is expressly stated that no-one shall derive improper financial or other gain from an activity related to an intercountry adoption; only proper costs and expenses, including reasonable professional fees, may be charged or paid.[153]

(c) Adoptions with a Foreign Element Regulations 2005[154]

(i) Convention adoptions where the United Kingdom is the receiving state

Chapter 1 of Part 3 of the Adoptions with a Foreign Element (AFE) Regulations deals with the requirements, procedure, recognition and effect of adoptions where the United Kingdom is the receiving state in relation to a Convention adoption, ie where a couple or a person habitually resident in the British Islands wish(es) to adopt a child who is habitually resident in a Convention country outside the British Islands in accordance with the Convention.

A prospective adopter in these circumstances must apply to an adoption agency for a determination of eligibility and an assessment of his suitability to adopt a child, and must give the agency such information as it may require for the purpose of the assessment.[155]

---

[148] Para 297.

[149] Art 30 imposes a duty on the competent authorities of a Contracting State to ensure that information held by them concerning the child's origin, in particular information concerning the identity of his parents, and medical history, is preserved. See Art 30(2) as regards the child's access to such information.

[150] See Art 4.

[151] Art 17.

[152] Art 18. The actual transfer of the child to the receiving state must be carried out in accordance with Art 19.

[153] Art 32. See, for an example of bad practice and exploitative intercountry adoption, *Re M (Adoption: International Adoption Trade)* [2003] EWHC 219, [2003] 1 FLR 1111.

[154] SI 2005/392.

[155] AFE Regulations, reg 13.

An application will not be considered unless, at the date thereof (a) in the case of an application by a couple, they have both attained 21 years and have been habitually resident in the British Islands for a period of not less than one year ending with the date of application; and (b) in the case of an application by one person, he has attained 21 years and has been habitually resident in the British Islands for a period of not less than one year ending with the date of application.

An assessment will be carried out by the adoption agency in accordance with regulations 14 to 34.[156] The assessment (or "home-study"), which involves detailed interviews with a social worker, as well as medical checks and police checks, will be considered by the agency's adoption panel. A prospective adopter's report must be prepared, including: the state of origin from which the prospective adopter wishes to adopt a child; confirmation that he is eligible to adopt a child under the law of that state; any additional information obtained as a consequence of the requirements of that state; and the agency's assessment of the prospective adopter's suitability to adopt a child who is habitually resident in that state.[157] If the applicant is deemed suitable to adopt, the application will be forwarded to the Department for Children, Schools and Families to be processed.[158] At that stage, a Certificate of Eligibility to adopt normally will be issued on behalf of the Secretary of State. Following notarisation and legalisation of documents, the papers will be forwarded to the Central Authority of the state of origin.[159]

Regulations 21 and 22 set out the requirements in respect of a prospective adopter proposing to enter the United Kingdom with a child, and the relevant adoption agency.[160] Regulations 24 to 27 lay down provisions following a child's entry into the United Kingdom where no Convention adoption was made or applied for in the state of origin. Regulation 31 provides that an adoption order shall not be made as a Convention adoption order unless (a) in the case of (i) an application by a couple, both have been habitually resident in the British Islands for a period of not less than one year ending with the date of application; or (ii) on application by one person, he has been habitually resident in the British Islands for a period of not less than one year ending with the date of application; (b) on the date when the Central Authorities of the state of origin and the receiving state agreed that the adoption may proceed,[161] the child was habitually resident in a Convention country outside the British Islands; and (c) in a case where one member of a couple (in the case of an application by a couple) or the applicant (in the case of an application by one person) is not a British citizen, the Home Office has confirmed that the child is authorised to enter and reside permanently in the United Kingdom.

(ii) Convention adoptions where the United Kingdom is the state of origin

Chapter 2 of Part 3 of the AFE Regulations deals with the requirements, procedure, recognition and effect of adoptions in England and Wales where the United Kingdom is the state of origin in respect of a Convention adoption, ie where a couple or a person

---

[156] See also Adoption Agencies Regulations, SI 2005/389.
[157] Reg 15(4).
[158] Reg 18. See reg 20 for procedure where the proposed adoption is not to proceed.
[159] Reg 19.
[160] Infra, p 1166 et seq.
[161] 1993 Hague Convention, Art 17(c).

habitually resident in a Convention country outside the British Islands wish(es) to adopt a child who is habitually resident in the British Islands.[162]

To a large extent, as is to be expected, the provisions of Chapter 2 of Part 3 are the mirror image of those in Chapter 1. Regulation 38 provides that the report which the relevant adoption agency is required to prepare in accordance with regulation 17 of the Adoption Agencies Regulations 2005[163] must include a summary of the possibilities for placement of the child within the United Kingdom, and an assessment of whether an adoption by a person in a particular receiving state is in the child's best interests. The relevant Central Authority in the receiving state, if satisfied that a prospective adopter who is habitually resident in that state is eligible and suited to adopt, will prepare an "Article 15 Report"[164] comprising information about the prospective adopter's identity, eligibility and suitability to adopt, background, family and medical history, social environment, reasons for adoption, ability to undertake an intercountry adoption, and the characteristics of the child for whom they would be qualified to care.[165] The United Kingdom adoption agency, when considering whether a proposed placement for adoption should proceed, must take into account the Article 15 Report[166] and any other information passed to it as a consequence of the AFE Regulations.[167]

Before a child will be placed for adoption with the prospective adopter, the Secretary of State may notify the Central Authority of the receiving state that it is prepared to agree that the adoption may proceed, subject to confirmation that, inter alia,[168] the prospective adopter is aware of the need to make an application under section 84 of the 2002 Act.[169]

Regulation 50 provides that an adoption order shall not be made as a Convention adoption order unless (a) in the case of (i) an application by a couple, both have been habitually resident in a Convention country outside the British Islands for a period of not less than one year ending with the date of application; or (ii) on application by one person, he has been habitually resident in a Convention country outside the British Islands for a period of not less than one year ending with the date of application; (b) on the date when the Central Authorities of the state of origin and the receiving state agreed that the adoption may proceed,[170] the child was habitually resident in any part of the British Islands; and (c) the competent authority has confirmed that the child is authorised to enter and remain permanently in the Convention country in which the applicant is habitually resident.

The meaning and application of regulation 50 was considered recently in *Greenwich LBC v S*:[171]

The case concerned the intercountry adoption of four siblings. The children had spent what was described as an "extended holiday" with the putative adopter, their

---

[162] Eg *Greenwich LBC v S* [2007] EWHC 820 (Fam).
[163] SI 2005/389.
[164] Supra, pp 1162–1163.
[165] Reg 42.
[166] Reg 43.
[167] Reg 44.
[168] Reg 47(1).
[169] Application for an order for transfer of parental responsibility prior to adoption abroad (infra, p 1167). See *Re G (A Child) (Adoption: Placement Outside Jurisdiction)* [2008] EWCA Civ 105, [2008] WLR (D) 56. See also reg 47(2).
[170] 1993 Hague Convention, Art 17(c).
[171] [2007] EWHC 820 (Fam).

maternal great-aunt, at her home in Canada. They had been in Canada, save for two breaks, for a period of one year, and a question arose as to whether they had lost their habitual residence in England. SUMNER J concluded[172] that whilst they had been in Canada for what might be described as an "appreciable time", there was no settled intention at that time by the local authority for the children to live in Canada. It was held that the placement of children overseas by a local authority, in the absence of a final plan for them, ought not to run the risk that they would lose their habitual residence after one year or two, unless there is compelling evidence leading to that conclusion. In the instant case, in the absence of such evidence, the children's habitual residence in England continued.

(iii) Power to charge

Section 13 of the Children and Adoption Act 2006[173] allows the Secretary of State to charge an administrative fee to adopters for services provided or to be provided by him in relation to intercountry adoptions.

(b) Procedures for taking children into and out of the United Kingdom

(i) Procedures under the AFE Regulations 2005[174]

Perceived deficiencies in the Adoption Act 1976 were intended to be remedied by the Adoption and Children Act 2002, and the Adoption (Bringing Children into the United Kingdom) Regulations 2003,[175] made in accordance with section 56A of the 1976 Act, as amended,[176] which enhanced the sanctions introduced in the Adoption (Intercountry Aspects) Act 1999 in respect of individuals who bring children into the United Kingdom in connection with adoption, without following proper procedures. This has now been replaced by the procedures set out in the AFE Regulations.

(a) Bringing children into the United Kingdom

Chapter 1 of Part 2 of the AFE Regulations deals with bringing children into the United Kingdom, for cases where the United Kingdom is the receiving state. This should be read in conjunction with section 83[177] of the 2002 Act, which imposes restrictions on British residents bringing or causing someone else to bring a child habitually resident outside the British Islands into the United Kingdom with the intention of adopting the child in the United Kingdom, unless the person complies with prescribed requirements and meets prescribed conditions.[178] It also makes it a criminal offence for a British resident to bring or cause someone else to bring a child habitually resident outside the British Islands whom he has adopted within the last twelve months into the United Kingdom, unless the

---

[172] [2007] EWHC 820 (Fam), at [27] et seq. Cf *Re JS (Private International Adoption)* [2000] 2 FLR 638.

[173] Inserting s 91A into the Adoption and Children Act 2002.

[174] SI 2005/392.

[175] SI 2003/1173, revoking (reg 7) the Adoption of Children from Overseas Regulations 2001.

[176] Substituted by the Adoption and Children Act 2002, Sch 4(12).

[177] Replacing and strengthening s 56A of the 1976 Act. Cf, for Scotland, s 133 of the 2002 Act, which amends ss 50 and 50A of the Adoption (Scotland) Act 1978. See also Children and Adoption Act 2006, s 9(2), infra, p 1169.

[178] 2002 Act, s 83(1) and (5). The conditions are set out in reg 4 of the AFE Regulations.

person complies with prescribed requirements and meets prescribed conditions.[179] The restrictions in section 83 do not apply if the child is intended to be adopted under a Convention adoption order, as the provisions in the 1993 Hague Convention will apply in such cases.[180]

By virtue of regulation 3 of the AFE Regulations, a prospective adopter falling within the circumstances described in section 83 of the 2002 Act must apply to an adoption agency for an assessment of his suitability to adopt a child, and must give the agency such information as it may require for the purpose of the assessment. The conditions applicable in respect of a child brought into the United Kingdom are set out in detail in regulation 4 of the AFE Regulations.

(b) Taking children out of the United Kingdom

Chapter 2 of Part 2 of the AFE Regulations applies in a situation where a person or couple wish(es) to remove a child from the United Kingdom for the purposes of adoption under the law of a non-Convention country, for cases where the United Kingdom is the state of origin of the child. This should be read in conjunction with sections 84 and 85 of the 2002 Act.

Section 84 provides that the High Court may make an order for the transfer of parental responsibility for a child to prospective adopters who are not domiciled or habitually resident in England and Wales, but who intend to adopt the child outside the British Islands.[181] Regulation 10 of the AFE Regulations, and regulation 48 in the case of a proposed Convention adoption, respectively set out the prescribed requirements which must be satisfied before an order will be made under section 84.[182] An application for an order may not be made unless at all times during the preceding ten weeks the child's home was with the applicant(s).[183]

Section 85 forbids the removal of a child who is a Commonwealth citizen or habitually resident in the United Kingdom to a place outside the British Islands for the purpose of adoption unless a section 84 order has been made conferring parental responsibility for the child on the prospective adopters. A person who removes a child in contravention of section 85 is guilty of an offence.[184]

(ii) Imposition of temporary suspensions

In June 2004, the then United Kingdom Minister for Children announced the Secretary of State's decision to impose a temporary[185] suspension of adoptions of Cambodian[186]

---

[179] Ibid, s 83(7).
[180] Ibid, s 83(2).
[181] Cf *Re A (Adoption: Placement Outside Jurisdiction)* [2004] EWCA Civ 515, [2004] 2 FLR 337.
[182] The 2002 Act, s 84(3). See *Re G (A Child) (Adoption: Placement Outside Jurisdiction)* [2008] EWCA Civ 105, [2008] WLR (D) 56.
[183] The 2002 Act, s 84(4).
[184] Ibid, s 85(4).
[185] To be reviewed in the event of new adoption legislation passed by the Cambodian government, or other significant development such as Cambodia's implementation of the 1993 Hague Convention.
[186] Cambodia is neither a Convention country nor a country designated in Sch 1 to the 1973 Order.

children by United Kingdom residents.[187] The suspension was introduced in response to concerns raised and investigated by United Kingdom officials regarding the Cambodian adoption system, including, in particular, lack of proper consents being given by birth parents,[188] and improper financial gain being made by individuals involved in the adoption process.[189] The Minister announced that: "Only in exceptional circumstances will I consider that the temporary suspension should not apply in a particular case. Any decision relating to a particular case will of course take account of what is in the best interests of the child and all the facts of the particular case."[190]

A question of the lawfulness of the Secretary of State's conduct with regard to intercountry adoptions generally, and the Cambodian suspension, in particular, arose in *R (On the Application of Thomson) v Minister of State for Children*:[191]

> The case concerned six couples (the third[192] to fourteenth claimants) who applied for judicial review of the Secretary of State's decision to impose the temporary suspension on intercountry adoptions from Cambodia, and her subsequent decisions in each of their cases not to allow them to proceed under the "exceptional circumstances" exception. The fifteenth claimant was the adopted daughter of one of the couples, whom they had adopted from Cambodia prior to imposition of the suspension.

MUNBY J noted that the regime prior to 1 June 2003 for adopting children from abroad had been problematic, and sometimes productive of serious concern.[193] His Lordship outlined two notable problems: the lack of effective regulation of intercountry adoptions,[194] and a growing sense that the best interests of children were not always served by such forms of adoption.[195] The claimants did not dispute the serious nature of these concerns, but they challenged the manner in which the problems had been addressed and the decisions taken by the Secretary of State.

The claimants' applications were refused. It was held that the Secretary of State's exercise of discretion in imposing the suspension, and in denying the claimants' adoption applications was consistent with the proper exercise of her powers in the context of the statutory scheme as a whole, and that her refusal to utilise the "exceptional circumstances" procedure met every common law requirement of "fairness" and was not incompatible with Article 6 of the European Convention on Human Rights (right to a fair trial),

---

[187] Hansard, 22 June 2004, cols WS61 and WS62. Concerns have been widely shared by the international community, leading a number of countries to impose suspensions: see *R (On the Application of Thomson) v Minister of State for Children* [2005] EWHC 1378, [2006] 1 FLR 175, per MUNBY J, at p [25].

[188] Including evidence of systematic falsification of Cambodian official documents relating to the adoption of children, and evidence relating to the procurement of children by facilitators' use of coercive tactics and financial incentives.

[189] See *R (On the Application of Thomson) v Minister of State for Children* [2005] EWHC 1378, [2006] 1 FLR 175, per MUNBY J, at p [23] et seq.

[190] Hansard, 22 June 2004, col WS62.

[191] [2005] EWHC 1378, [2006] 1 FLR 175. See Cordery [2006] (Mar) IFL 39.

[192] The first and second claimants having withdrawn their applications.

[193] [2005] EWHC 1378, [2006] 1 FLR 175, p at [4].

[194] Criminal prosecutions under ss 11 and 57 of the Adoption Act 1976 were seldom pursued: [2005] EWHC 1378, [2006] 1 FLR 175 p at [7].

[195] Cf Parliamentary Assembly, of the Council of Europe, Recommendation 1443 (2000), 26 January 2000; and UN General Assembly, Resolution 41/85, 3 December 1986.

assuming that Article 6 applied.[196] The judge considered there to be a pressing public interest that justified the introduction of the suspension without prior warning.

Given the nature and extent of the challenges to the exercise of powers by the Secretary of State in *R (On the Application of Thomson) v Minister of State for Children*, it is not surprising that the Children and Adoption Bill introduced in the House of Lords in June 2005[197] included provisions dealing with the suspension of intercountry adoptions.

(iii) The Children and Adoption Act 2006[198]

Part 2 of the 2006 Act[199] concerns adoptions with a foreign element. It makes express provision for the Secretary of State to suspend intercountry adoptions from a country if he has concerns about the practices there in connection with the adoption of children by British residents[200] in specified cases.[201] If the Secretary of State has reason to believe[202] that, because of practices[203] taking place in a foreign country (whether or not it is a Convention country[204]) in connection with the adoption of children, it would be contrary to public policy to further the bringing of children into the United Kingdom, he may declare, in relation to that country, that special restrictions are to apply.[205] The special restrictions are that the appropriate authority[206] is not to take any step which otherwise might have been taken in connection with furthering the bringing of a child into the United Kingdom.[207] The effect of the imposition of restrictions is that the Secretary of State no longer will process intercountry adoptions to or from a restricted country. There is scope, however, for the restrictions to be waived, exceptionally,[208] in an individual case, if the prospective adopters can satisfy the Secretary of State that the steps in question should be taken, ie that the adoption should proceed.[209] There is an obligation on the Secretary of State to keep the list of restricted countries under review.[210]

---

[196] [2005] EWHC 1378, [2006] 1 FLR 175 at [192].

[197] The Children (Contact) and Adoption Bill was published in draft on 2 February 2005 for pre-legislative scrutiny by an ad hoc joint committee of both Houses of Parliament.

[198] See [2006] (Sept) IFL 120; Cordery [2006] (Mar) IFL 139; and [2005] (Mar) IFL 51.

[199] Ss 9–14. Part 1 concerns the improved facilitation and enforcement of orders with respect to children in family proceedings.

[200] Ie persons habitually resident in the British Islands: 2006 Act, s 9(10)(a).

[201] 2006 Act, s 9(2): where a British resident (a) wishes to bring, or cause another to bring, a child who is not a British resident into the United Kingdom for the purpose of adoption by the British resident and, in connection with the proposed adoption, there have been, or would have to be, proceedings in the other country or dealings with authorities or agencies there, or (b) wishes to bring, or cause another to bring, into the United Kingdom a child adopted by the British resident under an adoption effected, within the period of 12 months ending with the date of bringing in, under the law of the other country. These cases mirror the cases to which s 83 of the Adoption and Children Act 2002 (restriction on bringing children in) applies, subject to the amendment of that section by s 14 of the 2006 Act.

[202] The Secretary of State must publish reasons for making the declaration in relation to each restricted country: 2006 Act, s 9(7).

[203] Eg child trafficking, or removal of children against their parents' wishes.

[204] 2006 Act, s 9(3).

[205] Ibid s 9(4).

[206] In a Convention case, the Central Authority (for England and Wales, the Secretary of State), and in any other case, the Secretary of State: ibid, s 11(4).

[207] Ibid, s 11(1).

[208] Eg where the child in question is a relative of the prospective adopter, or the sibling of a child already adopted by that person. See [2005] (Mar) IFL 51.

[209] 2006 Act, s 11(2).

[210] Ibid, s 10.

(c) Recognition of foreign adoptions

There may be a variety of circumstances in which a court in England is faced with the decision whether to recognise an adoption which has taken place abroad. The issue may arise incidentally in the course of other proceedings and the main examples in the reported cases concern property rights—eg whether a child adopted abroad can take under a will,[211] in an intestacy[212] or a settlement,[213] or whether a parent can succeed on his adopted child's intestacy.[214] The recognition of a foreign adoption may also affect the powers of the English court to make an adoption order itself,[215] social security issues,[216] or rights of entry to the United Kingdom as an immigrant.[217] Finally, it is possible that a child might simply wish to seek from the English courts a declaration as to his status, and thus ascertain whether his foreign adoption will be recognised in England.[218]

(i) Recognition of adoptions made elsewhere in the British Isles

Any adoption order made in Scotland,[219] Northern Ireland,[220] the Channel Islands, or the Isle of Man[221] will be recognised and given effect to in England.[222] Further, adoption records from Scotland, Northern Ireland, the Channel Islands or the Isle of Man, are receivable as evidence in England.[223]

(ii) Recognition of adoptions made in Hague Convention countries ("Convention adoptions")

As explained above, with effect from 1 June 2003, the 1993 Hague Convention on Protection of Children and Co-operation in respect of Intercountry Adoption came into force in the United Kingdom. Chapter V (Articles 23 to 27) of the Convention concerns the recognition and effects of the adoption. Recognition of an adoption includes recognition of (a) the legal parent-child relationship between the child and his adoptive parents; (b) the parental responsibility of the adoptive parents for the child; and (c) the termination of a pre-existing legal relationship between the child and his biological parents[224] (if the adoption has this effect in the Contracting State where it was made[225]). By Article 23, an adoption certified by the

---

[211] *Re Marshall* [1957] Ch 507; and see *Perpetual Trustee Co Ltd v Montuori* [1982] 1 NSWLR 710.

[212] *Re Wilson* [1954] Ch 733.

[213] *Re Valentine's Settlement* [1965] Ch 831; *Spencer's Trustees v Ruggles* 1982 SLT 165.

[214] *Re Wilby* [1956] P 174.

[215] *Re H (An Infant)* (1973) 4 Fam Law 77.

[216] Eg National Insurance Decisions Nos R(F) 1/65; R(F) 3/73.

[217] Eg *Mathieu v Entry Clearance Officer, Bridgetown* [1979–1980] Imm AR 157; *Secretary of State for the Home Department v Lofthouse* [1981] Imm AR 166. See infra, pp 1176–1177.

[218] The bases on which the court will grant a declaration in relation to a foreign adoption are considered, supra, p 1043.

[219] Adoption and Children Act 2002, s 105.

[220] Ibid, s 106.

[221] Ibid, s 108.

[222] See also Adoption Act 1976, s 38(1)(c).

[223] 2002 Act, s 107 (replacing s 60 of the 1976 Act, which did not extend to the Channel Islands or the Isle of Man).

[224] Art 26.

[225] Art 27 provides that where an adoption granted in the state of origin does not have the effect of terminating a pre-existing legal parent-child relationship, it may, in the receiving state be converted into an adoption

competent authority of the state of the adoption[226] as having been made in accordance with the Convention shall be recognised by operation of law[227] in the other Contracting States. This is one of the primary benefits of the instrument, thereby "superseding the existing practice that an adoption already granted in the State of origin is to be made anew in the receiving State only in order to produce such effects".[228] Recognition of a Convention adoption may be refused in a Contracting State only if the adoption is manifestly contrary to its public policy, taking into account the best interests of the child.[229]

The question as to the persons who could be prospective adoptive parents was discussed at length during negotiations, in particular whether the Convention should cover adoptions applied for by unmarried heterosexual couples, or by same sex persons, living as a couple or individually. The Parra-Aranguren Report states that:

> Notwithstanding the fact that these cases were thoroughly examined, the problems they raise may be qualified as false problems, since the State of origin and the receiving State shall collaborate from the very beginning and they may refuse the agreement for the adoption to continue, for instance, because of the personal conditions of the prospective adoptive parents. Moreover, in case they agree to those specific kinds of adoption, the other Contracting States are entitled to refuse its recognition on public policy grounds, as permitted by Article 24.[230]

Interestingly, the Parra-Aranguren Report notes that:

> The Convention does not specifically answer the question as to whether an adoption granted in a Contracting State and falling within its scope of application, but not in accordance with the Convention's rules, could be recognized by another Contracting State whose internal laws permit such recognition. Undoubtedly, in such a case, the Contracting State granting the adoption is violating the Convention, because its provisions are mandatory and such conduct may give rise to the complaint permitted by Article 33,[231] but the question of the recognition would be outside of the Convention and the answer should depend on the law applicable in the recognizing State, always taking into account the best interests of the child.[232]

Recognition in England of an adoption granted in a Contracting State which falls outside the scope of application of the Convention must be dealt with according to residual national rules.[233]

---

having such an effect if the law of the receiving state so permits and if relevant consents have been given. See, for England, infra, pp 1175–1176 (status conferred by adoption).

[226] The state of origin, or the receiving state, depending on the circumstances of the case.

[227] Ie automatically, without the need for a procedure for recognition, enforcement or registration: see Parra-Aranguren, *Explanatory Report*, para 409.

[228] Ibid, para 402.

[229] Art 24. See also *Singh (Pawandeep) v Entry Clearance Officer (New Delhi)* [2004] EWCA Civ 1075, [2005] QB 608.

[230] Parra-Aranguren, *Explanatory Report*, para 79.

[231] Concerning failure to respect the provisions of the Convention.

[232] Parra-Aranguren, *Explanatory Report*, para 411.

[233] For England, infra, pp 1173–1175.

(iii) Recognition of adoptions made in designated countries ("overseas adoptions")

The adoption of a child[234] effected in a country[235] or territory outside the British Islands which is included in the United Kingdom's list of designated countries, as set out in the Adoption (Designation of Overseas Adoptions) Order 1973,[236] and which is effected under the law in force in that place,[237] is known as an overseas adoption.[238] Overseas adoptions do not include Convention adoptions.[239] The 1973 Order applies in relation to any place which, at the time the adoption is effected, forms part of a country or territory which is then listed in Part I or Part II of the Schedule[240] to the Order. The list of countries in the Schedule to the 1973 Order, which was made pursuant to the Adoption Act 1976,[241] continues to have effect, by virtue of section 87(1)(a) of the Adoption and Children Act 2002.[242] The recognition of this wide range of foreign adoptions is not dependent, in any way, on reciprocity between England and the "overseas adoption" country.

Overseas adoption orders, being those of a description specified in the 1973 Order, are recognised automatically in England, and have the same incidents and effects as if they were made in England. Section 87 of the 2002 Act allows the Secretary of State to prescribe the requirements that must be met before a country will be included in the list of designated countries. Curiously, the only requirement for recognition appears to be that the adoption is effected under the law in force in the designated country; there is no scope for reviewing or challenging the jurisdiction of the country which effected the overseas adoption. There is no necessary link, such as is required in English law,[243] between the country where the adoption is effected and the adoptive parents.

Evidence that an overseas order has been effected may be given by the production of a document purporting to be a certified copy of any entry made, in accordance with the law of the country concerned, in a public register of adoptions, or of an adoption certificate signed, or purporting to be signed, by an authorised person.[244]

(iv) Annulment, etc of overseas or Hague Convention adoptions

Section 89 of the 2002 Act provides for the High Court to annul a Convention adoption or Convention adoption order on the ground that the adoption is contrary to public policy.[245] In particular, an intercountry adoption which has come about in circumstances in

---

[234] Any person who, at the time when the application for adoption is made, has not attained the age of 18 years and has not been married: SI 1973/19, rule 3(3).

[235] Which may, or may not, also be a Hague Convention Contracting State.

[236] SI 1973/19, as amended.

[237] The reference to "law" does not include customary or common law, meaning that the overseas adoption must be effected by means of legislative provision: SI 1979/13, rule 3(3).

[238] SI 1973/19, rule 3(1). Sometimes known also as a "designated country adoption".

[239] 2002 Act, s 87(1)(b).

[240] Part I comprises Commonwealth countries and United Kingdom dependent territories, and Part II comprises other countries and territories. By virtue of SI 1995/1614, art 2(b), as far as concerns Scotland, adoptions effected in the People's Republic of China also fall within the ambit of the Order: SI 1973/19, rule 3(2A) and (2B).

[241] S 72(2); repealed by the Adoption and Children Act 2002, Sch 5(1).

[242] Cf, in Scots law, 2002 Act, s 134 (amending s 65 of the Adoption (Scotland) Act 1978).

[243] Infra, p 1173 et seq.

[244] SI 1973/19, rule 4(1).

[245] See 1993 Convention, Art 24.

which little or no regard has been paid to the best interests of the child must be viewed with great caution.[246] Similarly, the High Court, on application, may provide for an overseas adoption or determination under section 91 of the 2002 Act to cease to be valid on the ground that it is contrary to public policy. An application for a section 89 order must be made within two years of the date on which the adoption (Convention or overseas) to which it relates was made.[247] Regulation 34 of the AFE Regulations provides that where a Convention adoption order or a Convention adoption is annulled under section 89, and the Secretary of State receives a copy of the order from the court, it must forward a copy to the Central Authority of the state of origin. The effect of any annulment is that the adoption will cease to have effect in the United Kingdom. Section 89(4) makes clear that except as provided for by section 89, the validity of a Convention adoption or overseas adoption order, or determination under section 91, cannot be called in question in proceedings in any court in England.

(v) Recognition of adoptions made in other foreign countries

The statutory recognition rules considered in relation to Convention adoptions and overseas adoptions are in addition to, and not in substitution for, the common law rules of recognition.[248] If an "overseas adoption" is denied recognition under the statutory rules because, for example, it was made under customary law, it may still be possible for the adoption to be recognised or given effect under the common law rules for recognition. Furthermore, although the list of countries whose adoptions have been included under the definition of overseas adoptions is extensive, it is not world-wide. In the case of such other countries[249] and "overseas adoptions" which, as has just been seen, fall outside the legislative rules, as well as those adoptions which have been effected in Convention countries but which fall outside the scope of application of the Convention, it is necessary to have resort to the common law recognition rules, to which we now turn.

The question of the extent to which, at common law, the English courts will recognise and give effect to an adoption order made abroad is of much less significance in the light of the statutory recognition provisions. It is still, however, of some importance and is an issue which the courts have not fully answered. The leading case on this subject is *Re Valentine's Settlement*.[250] The facts were these:

> A British subject, domiciled in what was then Southern Rhodesia, in 1946 made an English settlement of a fund on trust for her son, Alastair, for life and then to his children. Alastair had married only once and had one child, Simon, by the marriage. He and his wife had adopted two other children—Carol in 1939 and Timothy in 1944. These adoptions took place in South Africa where, at the date of their respective adoptions, Carol and Timothy were domiciled. Under the law of Southern Rhodesia an adoption order could not be made in respect of any child

---

[246] Though there may be cases where, although the order in question was made without regard to the best interests of the child, it could be seen, with hindsight, that adoption was in fact in the child's best interests, and that a family relationship sufficient to be recognised as family life had developed: *Singh (Pawandeep) v Entry Clearance Officer (New Delhi)* [2004] EWCA Civ 1075, [2005] QB 608.

[247] Family Procedure (Adoption) Rules, SI 2005/2795, r 109.

[248] Ibid, s 38(1)(e).

[249] Cf *Re H (An Infant)* (1973) 4 Fam Law 77.

[250] [1965] Ch 831; and see National Insurance Decisions Nos R(F) 1/65; R(F) 3/73.

who was not resident and domiciled there: so no Southern Rhodesian adoption order was made. Alastair and his wife were themselves domiciled and resident in Southern Rhodesia at all material times, and Alastair died domiciled there in 1962 without having exercised a power of appointment under the settlement. The trustees issued a summons to determine whether the trust fund devolved on Simon or equally among Simon, Carol and Timothy.

The fundamental question was as to whether the two adopted children were "children" of Alastair within the meaning of the settlement. The Court of Appeal by a majority answered this question in the negative. The whole Court was clearly prepared to countenance the recognition of foreign adoptions in some circumstances.[251] Lord DENNING MR stated that, "we should recognise an adoption order made by another country when the adopting parents are domiciled there and the child is resident there".[252] It was held, however, that the South African adoptions could not be recognised in the instant case because the adopting parents were not domiciled in South Africa.[253]

A number of further issues arise. The first is whether it is right to concentrate exclusively on the domicile of the adopters and ignore the domicile of the child or of the natural parents. The view was expressed obiter by Lord DENNING MR[254] that it would not have been necessary to show in addition that the children were domiciled in South Africa at the time of the adoptions. Residence would have sufficed.[255] At that time, an English court required the adoptive parents to be resident and domiciled in England and the child to be resident in England, so the basis of the reasoning was that English recognition rules should be based on an analogy with English jurisdictional rules. There is no agreement on the question among foreign legal systems. In some, the personal law of the child governs; in others, the personal law of the adopters is preferred; but in many, the doctrine of cumulation prevails by which the personal law of all three parties must be satisfied.[256] Whilst one may argue that the only law to pronounce on status is that of the domicile, the jurisdiction of the English court is based on the domicile or habitual residence of the prospective adopters—that of the child and the biological parents is ignored. It seems reasonable to recognise a foreign jurisdiction exercised in similar circumstances. There is no justification, by analogy with English jurisdictional rules, for looking especially to the domicile of the biological[257] rather than the adoptive parents.[258] If the domicile or habitual residence of the prospective adopters is accepted as the main jurisdictional criterion for recognition, then it is suggested that, on the analogy of the common law rule for divorce recognition in

---

[251] The earlier contrary decision in *Re Wilby* [1956] P 174 was said to have been wrongly decided.

[252] [1965] Ch 831 at 842; and see National Insurance Decision No R(F) 1/65; *Perpetual Trustee Co Ltd v Montuori* [1982] 1 NSWLR 710; *R v Secretary of State for the Home Department, ex p Brassey* [1989] FCR 423, [1989] 2 FLR 486; *Patel v Visa Officer, Bombay* [1990] Imm AR 297; *MF v An Bord Vehtala* [1991] ILRM 399.

[253] It was further held that, even if the South African adoptions were to be recognised, Carol and Timothy would be treated in English law (the law governing the settlement) as if they had been adopted in England. They would, therefore, be unable to take as the settlement was made before 1 January 1950, and English adopted children by virtue of s 5(2) of the Adoption of Children Act 1926 would have had no rights under it.

[254] [1965] Ch 831 at 842–843.

[255] This was approved in *Re B (S) (An Infant)* [1968] Ch 204 at 209–210.

[256] Mann (1941) 57 LQR 112, 123; Wolff, op cit, 398; Jones (1956) 5 ICLQ 205, 210–219. For a fuller discussion, see de Nova (1961) III Hague Recueil 75, 153; Lipstein (1963) 12 ICLQ 835.

[257] See *Re G (Foreign Adoption: Consent)* [1995] 2 FLR 534.

[258] Cf [1965] Ch 831 at 854.

Armitage v A-G,[259] an adoption should be recognised in England as conferring the status of child of the adopted person if recognised in the country (or countries) of the adopters' domicile or habitual residence, even though actually effected elsewhere.[260]

Another issue is whether it is still appropriate to demand that the child be resident in the country where the adoption is effected. That criterion was relied on in *Re Valentine's Settlement* because at that time there was a similar requirement for the jurisdiction of the English courts. There is no longer such a requirement and so jurisdictional reciprocity would support its abandonment when considering recognition of foreign adoptions.[261] Finally, it is not clear whether the English courts will be prepared to recognise foreign adoptions in wider circumstances such as those where, *mutatis mutandis*, an English court could not have jurisdiction, but where there was a "real and substantial connection" with the foreign court.[262]

We have seen that the statutory rules relating to the recognition of overseas adoptions and Convention adoptions provide that such adoptions may be denied recognition on grounds of public policy.[263] Public policy is similarly relevant to the recognition of foreign adoptions at common law.[264] Adoption law in other countries may be very different from English law, as, for example, with the adoption of adults and married persons.[265] Whilst great caution should be exercised in denying recognition on public policy grounds, the courts have power to do so both in relation to the incidents of the adoption, such as whether the child can succeed to the adoptive parents, and, in an extreme case, to the adoption's effect on the status of the parties, ie as to whether the parent and child relationship has been created at all.[266]

If a child is adopted from a country which is neither a Hague Convention country, nor on the United Kingdom list of designated countries in the 1973 Order, and the English court refuses to recognise the foreign adoption at common law, an adoption order will require to be made in England, under the Adoption and Children Act 2002, following the child's entry to the United Kingdom, ie there must be "re-adoption" in England, dependent upon the prospective adopter satisfying a registered adoption agency that he is eligible and suitable to adopt a child from abroad.

(d) Effect of foreign adoptions

(i) Status conferred by adoption

Section 67 of the Adoption and Children Act 2002 provides that, with effect from the date of adoption,[267] an adopted person is to be treated in law as if born as the child of the adopter. An adopted person is the legitimate child of the adopter and, if adopted by a

---

259 [1906] P 135, supra, p 993.
260 Some support for this may be drawn from *Re Valentine's Settlement* [1965] Ch 226 at 234, at first instance; and see ibid at 855.
261 On the analogy of the common law divorce recognition rule in *Travers v Holley* [1953] P 246.
262 Cf *Indyka v Indyka* [1969] 1 AC 33; North (1968) 31 MLR 257, 280–281.
263 Supra, p 1169 et seq.
264 See *Re C (A Child) (Foreign Adoption: Natural Mother's Consent: Service)* [2006] 1 FLR 318.
265 Eg *Ehrenclou v MacDonald* 12 Cal Rptr 3d 411 (Cal App 2004)—adult adoptees, discussed by Symeonides (2004) 52 AJCL 919, 986.
266 *Re Valentine's Settlement* [1965] Ch 831 at 842, 854; *Bouton v Labiche* (1994) 33 NSWLR 225.
267 2002 Act, s 67(5).

couple, or one of a couple under section 51(2), is to be treated as the child of the relationship of the couple in question.[268] The effect of the adoption is not determined by the law of the country of adoption.[269] If, for example, a child, adopted in New York, claims to succeed to the movable property of an adoptive parent dying domiciled in England, the adoption will be recognised and the child will, under English law as the law governing succession, have the same rights as an English adopted child.[270] This rule applies to succession, testate and intestate. It is important, however, to distinguish between the question of recognition and the determination of, for example, the succession rights of an adopted child once his status has been recognised. This latter issue should be determined by the appropriate law to govern matters of succession.[271] This means that the provisions of the 2002 Act, giving a child whose foreign adoption is recognised in England the same succession rights as an English adopted child, are relevant only if English law governs the succession. If the law governing the succession is foreign, it will be for that law to decide whether, and if so what, succession rights are given to an adopted child, even though the adoption is recognised in England.

Section 88 of the 2002 Act provides that the operation of section 67 may be modified in relation to Hague Convention adoptions. Where the High Court is satisfied that the conditions in section 88(2) have been met,[272] it may direct that section 67(3)[273] does not apply or does not apply to any extent specified in the direction, ie that the order does not have the effect of "full adoption".[274] The reason for this provision[275] stems from the fact that the United Kingdom recognises only "full adoption", in terms of which all legal ties between the child and his biological parents are severed, whereas some countries have other forms of adoption, known as "simple adoption" or "limited adoption", whereby not all ties between the child and his/her biological parents are severed. Article 26 of the 1993 Hague Convention provides for recognition of full and simple adoptions, and Article 27 allows a receiving state to convert a simple adoption into a full adoption if its law so permits, and provided the biological parents and relevant parties[276] give their consent to a full adoption.

(ii) British citizenship and immigration

(a) Adoption orders made in the United Kingdom

An adoption order made in a United Kingdom court (including, for this purpose, the Channel Islands and the Isle of Man) automatically confers British citizenship on the

---

[268] 2002 Act, s 67(2).

[269] *R v Secretary of State for the Home Department, ex p Brassey* [1989] FCR 423, [1989] 2 FLR 486.

[270] See the Family Law Reform Act 1987, ss 1 (as amended by the 2002 Act, Sch 3, para 51), 18 and 19 (as amended by the 2002 Act, Sch 3, para 52). See, in Scotland, *Salvesen's Trs* 1993 SC 14.

[271] See *Re Valentine's Settlement* [1965] Ch 831 at 843–845, rejecting suggestions to the contrary in *Re Marshall* [1957] Ch 507.

[272] Namely, under the law of the country in which the adoption was effected, the adoption is not a full adoption; the consents referred to in Art 4(c) and (d) of the 1993 Convention have not been given for a full adoption or the United Kingdom is not the receiving state; and it would be more favourable to the adopted child for a direction to be given under s 88(1).

[273] Whereby an adopted person is to be treated in law as not being the child of any person other than the adopter(s).

[274] Ie, one by virtue of which the child is to be treated in law as not being the child of any person other than the adopter: s 88(3).

[275] See Explanatory Notes to the 2002 Act, paras 229 and 230.

[276] 1993 Hague Convention, Art 4.

child if the adopter, or one of the adopters, is a British citizen on the date on which the adoption order is made.[277]

(b) Convention adoptions

A final adoption order under the Hague Convention, wherever made, will confer British citizenship on the child if the adopter (or one of them in the event of a joint adoption) is a British citizen and if the adopter was habitually resident in the United Kingdom on the date on which the Convention adoption is effected.[278] This ensures, in this respect at least, parity of treatment between Convention adoptions and adoption orders made in the United Kingdom. In *Re B (A Minor) (Adoption Order: Nationality)*[279] the House of Lords held that, in determining an adoption application, the judge was entitled to have regard to all the circumstances of the case, including the views of the Home Office on immigration policy, but that:

> In cases in which it appears to the judge that adoption would confer real benefits upon the child during its childhood, it is very unlikely that general considerations of "maintaining an effective and consistent immigration policy" could justify the refusal of an order. The two kinds of consideration are hardly commensurable so as to be capable of being weighed in the balance against each other.[280]

When a Convention order in consequence of which any person became a British citizen by virtue of section 1(5) of the British Nationality Act 1981 ceases to have effect, whether on annulment[281] or otherwise, the cesser shall not affect the status of that person as a British citizen.[282]

(c) Overseas adoptions

Overseas adoptions do not result in the automatic granting of British citizenship to the adopted child. An application for British citizenship must be submitted in respect of the child, and registration as such is at the discretion of the Secretary of State.[283]

(d) Immigration

British citizens are not subject to control under United Kingdom immigration legislation, but they must be able to prove their status when seeking admission to the United Kingdom. Except where a child is a British citizen, or is a national of another European Economic Area country, he will require entry clearance under United Kingdom immigration rules before travelling to the United Kingdom.[284] Where a prospective adopter is not a British citizen, he must have indefinite leave to remain in the United Kingdom to be able to sponsor an entry clearance application in respect of a child.

---

[277] Ibid, s 1(5)(a).

[278] British Nationality Act 1981, ss 1(5)(b) and (5A) ("acquisition by adoption").

[279] [1999] 2 AC 136.

[280] Ibid, per Lord HOFFMAN, at 141, distinguishing *Re K (A Minor) (Adoption Order: Nationality)* [1995] Fam 38. See also *SK (India) v Secretary of State for the Home Department* [2007] Imm A R 142.

[281] Supra, pp 1172–1173.

[282] British Nationality Act 1981, s 1(6).

[283] Ibid, s 3(1).

[284] For detailed information, see UK Government, Department for Children, Schools and Families website at http://dfes.gov.uk/intercountryadoption.

Chapter 26

Mental Incapacity

1. INTRODUCTION

Legal problems, both general and within the specific context of private international law, can arise in relation to persons suffering from mental incapacity. Some of these arise incidentally in other contexts. For example, special rules have had to be devised for determining the domicile of mentally disordered or incapacitated persons because they may be incapable of exercising a free choice as to where they are to live.[1] The inability of such people to grant full consent can affect issues relating to their marriage[2] or to contracts which they purport to have entered into. There is no direct authority on whether the issue of the capacity of a mentally disordered or incapacitated person should be governed by the law of his domicile or by the law governing the contract. Following the analogy of other contractual issues of capacity,[3] it is suggested that the law governing the contract should apply.

---

[1] Supra, pp 177–178.
[2] Supra, p 895 et seq.
[3] Supra, pp 750–753.

Mental incapacity may be, more directly, the source of private international law problems. It will be necessary, for example, to decide when an English court has jurisdiction to order the detention of a mentally disordered or incapacitated person or to place the management of his property and affairs in the hands of the court and what law is to be applied in such circumstances. The extent to which the English courts will recognise the powers conferred by a foreign court or under foreign law on someone (a curator) to manage the affairs of a mentally disordered or incapacitated person will also need to be determined.

In this chapter there will be considered the rules of private international law operating at common law and in terms of Parts VI and VII of the Mental Health Act 1983, as well as those rules put in place[4] by the Mental Capacity Act 2005.[5] The 2005 Act replaces Part VII[6] of the 1983 Act and the Enduring Powers of Attorney Act 1985.[7] For present purposes, the most significant provisions of the 2005 Act are section 63 (international protection of adults) and Schedule 3 to the Act, which give effect in England and Wales to the Convention on the International Protection of Adults signed at The Hague on 13 January 2000.[8] The Hague Convention and, in turn, Schedule 3 to the 2005 Act, concern adults[9] who, as a result of impairment or insufficiency of personal faculties, cannot protect their own interests.[10] The Convention lays down rules of jurisdiction, for determining the state(s) whose authorities can take measures directed to the protection of the person and/or property of such adults;[11] of applicable law;[12] of recognition and enforcement of measures for the protection of adults;[13] and of co-operation among Contracting States.[14] The Convention is not yet in force.[15] Section 63(b) of the 2005 Act makes related provision, in any event, regarding the private international law of England and Wales. When[16] the private international law provisions of the 2005 Act enter into force, nevertheless certain provisions of Schedule 3 to the Act[17] will not take effect until such time as the 2000 Hague Convention enters into force.

---

[4] See, to date, The Mental Capacity Act 2005 (Commencement No 1) Order, SI 2006/2814; The Mental Capacity Act 2005 (Commencement No 1) (Amendment) Order, SI 2006/3473; The Mental Capacity Act 2005 (Commencement No 1) (England and Wales) Order, SI 2007/563; Mental Capacity Act (Commencement No 2) Order, SI 2007/1897; and Mental Capacity Act 2005 (Transitional and Consequential Provisions) Order, SI 2007/1898.

[5] The 2005 Act extends only to England and Wales. For Scotland, see the Adults with Incapacity (Scotland) Act 2000, and the Mental Health (Care and Treatment) (Scotland) Act 2003.

[6] Ss 93–113.

[7] 2005 Act, ss 66 and 67; Sch 5, Parts 1 and 2; and Sch 6.

[8] See generally Lagarde, *Explanatory Report*.

[9] For the purposes of the 2005 Act being persons who have reached 16 years: Sch 3, para 4(b). Under Sch 3, para 23, however, a provision giving effect to, or deriving from, the Hague Convention in a country other than England, made in relation to a person under 16 years, shall be recognised and enforced in England as if it were a protective measure taken in relation to an adult: see infra, pp 1187–1189.

[10] Art 1; and 2005 Act, Sch 3, para 4.

[11] Art 2(a); also Arts 3 and 4. The Convention rules on jurisdiction are laid down in Chapter II (Arts 5–12).

[12] Chapter III (Arts 13–21).

[13] Chapter IV (Arts 22–27).

[14] Chapter V (Arts 28–37).

[15] It shall enter into force following deposit of the third instrument of ratification, acceptance or approval: Art 57. To date, it has been ratified only by the United Kingdom and Germany.

[16] 2005 Act, s 68: 1 October 2007 (Mental Capacity Act 2005 (Commencement No 2) Order, SI 2007/1987, art 2 (1) (b)).

[17] Sch 3, paras 8(2) and (3), 19(2) and (5), 23, 26, 27, 28 and 29.

2. JURISDICTION OF THE ENGLISH COURTS

(a) Prior to the Mental Capacity Act 2005

(i) Control of the person

Under Part II of the Mental Health Act 1983, a person may be compulsorily admitted to hospital and detained there, or may be placed under guardianship. As the steps taken under the 1983 Act are for the protection of the mentally disordered or incapacitated person and the public, it seems clear that the powers of the court can be exercised over anyone present in England, irrespective of their domicile or nationality.[18] It would seem that, conversely, if the person is not present in England, there is no jurisdiction over his person; though the court could order that he be returned within the jurisdiction of the court.[19]

(ii) Control of a patient's property

Under the Mental Health Act 1983, the management of the property and affairs of a person who is, by reason of mental incapacity, incapable of managing them himself is committed to the Lord Chancellor and certain judges of the Supreme Court nominated by him and to the Master and other officers of the Court of Protection.[20] The usual method of exercising this management is by the appointment of a receiver, who is invested with certain powers of dealing with the property of the patient and whose authority is restricted to the exercise of the particular powers so given.[21]

The jurisdiction of the Court of Protection[22] in terms of the 1983 Act extends to any person incapable by reason of mental disorder of managing his affairs who is actually present in England, whatever his nationality or domicile. This jurisdiction applies even though his property is, except for a few personal belongings, all situated abroad.[23] It also extends to any such person, whatever his nationality or domicile, who is outside the country provided that he has property in England.[24] British nationality or English domicile would not of itself appear to justify an exercise of the jurisdiction.

Where a foreign element arises, the exercise of the jurisdiction is, however, qualified in two ways. First, the Court of Protection cannot make an order directly affecting property situated in a country where the authority of the court is not recognised, but the Court achieves its object by directing the receiver to take such steps as may be necessary to effect the purposes of the court, eg by appointing an attorney to act in the name of the patient in selling property and accounting to the receiver for the proceeds. Secondly, the Court acts in accordance with the comity of nations and refrains from making orders that would be regarded as an infringement of a foreign jurisdiction.

---

[18] Eg *Re Sottomaior* (1874) 9 Ch App 677; *Re S (Hospital Patient: Foreign Curator)* [1996] Fam 23.

[19] See *Re Sykeham* (1823) Turn & R 537.

[20] Mental Health Act 1983, Pt VII.

[21] Ibid, s 99.

[22] In this context, the expression "Court of Protection" includes also the Lord Chancellor and the "nominated judges".

[23] *Re Houstoun* (1826) 1 Russ 312; *Re Princess Bariatinski* (1843) 1 Ph 375; *Re Burbidge* [1902] 1 Ch 426.

[24] *Ex p Southcote* (1751) 2 Ves Sen 401; *Re Scott* (1874) 22 WR 748.

Under section 110[25] of the Mental Health Act 1983, the powers of the English court over the property and affairs of a mentally disordered/incapacitated person also extend to his affairs and property (other than land) elsewhere in the United Kingdom, provided a receiver or person holding an equivalent office has not been appointed in the other part of the United Kingdom. There are reciprocal provisions relating to the powers of a receiver or equivalent appointed in Scotland or Northern Ireland over property or affairs in England.

(b) Under the Mental Capacity Act 2005

Under the 2005 Act,[26] a new Court of Protection, being a superior court of record, replaces the Court of Protection, being an office of the Supreme Court, which operates under the 1983 Act.[27] For England and Wales, Schedule 3 to the 2005 Act, in Part 2, establishes the rules of jurisdiction of the Court of Protection.[28] The Court of Protection may exercise jurisdiction under the Act[29] in relation to (a) an adult who is habitually resident in England and Wales;[30] (b) an adult's property situated in England and Wales; (c) an adult who is present in England and Wales or who has property there, if the matter is urgent; or (d) an adult who is present in England and Wales, if a protective measure[31] which is temporary and limited in its effect to England and Wales is proposed in relation to him. When the Hague Convention takes effect, the Court of Protection will be able to exercise jurisdiction in two further situations, in so far as it cannot otherwise do so under the provisions of paragraph 7(1) of Schedule 3. First,[32] the Court will have jurisdiction in relation to an adult of British nationality who has a closer connection with England and Wales than with Scotland or Northern Ireland, when the terms of Article 7[33] of the Hague Convention have been complied with. Secondly,[34] there will be jurisdiction if the Lord Chancellor, being the Central Authority for England and Wales,[35] agrees to a

---

[25] As amended by the Adults with Incapacity (Scotland) Act 2000.

[26] Pt 2.

[27] Ss 45 and 46.

[28] Under s 21 of the 2005 Act, the Lord Chancellor may order the transfer of proceedings relating to a person under 18 years from the Court of Protection to a court having jurisdiction under the Children Act 1989, or vice versa.

[29] Sch 3, para 7(1).

[30] For the meaning of habitual residence, see generally supra, Chapter 9. Specifically, however, in this context, by Sch 3, para 7(2), an adult present in England and Wales is to be treated for the purposes of jurisdiction as habitually resident there if (a) his habitual residence cannot be ascertained; (b) he is a refugee; or (c) he has been displaced as a result of disturbance in his country of habitual residence.

[31] Defined in Sch 3, para 5 as a measure directed to the protection of the person or property of the adult. Examples include the determination of incapacity and the institution of a protective regime (para 5(1)(1)); placing the adult in a place where protection can be provided (para 5(1)(e)); and administering, conserving or disposing of the adult's property (para 5(1)(f)). Infra, pp 1183–1185.

[32] Sch 3, para 8(1) and (2).

[33] Art 7 (concurrent subsidiary jurisdiction of the authorities of the State of nationality of the adult) establishes that, except for adults who are refugees or internationally displaced persons as a result of disturbances occurring in their state of nationality, the authorities of the Contracting State of which the adult is a national may take measures for the protection of the person or property of that adult if they consider that they are in a better position to assess his/her interests than are the authorities of the State having jurisdiction under Arts 5 or 6(2). See Lagarde, *Explanatory Report*, paras 56–64.

[34] Sch 3, para 8(1) and (3).

[35] Sch 3, para 6.

request under Article 8 of the Hague Convention (transfer of jurisdiction to an appropriate forum).[36]

It is clear, in terms of Article 12 of the Hague Convention, that any measure taken in reliance upon one of the Convention bases of jurisdiction shall remain in force, even if a change in circumstances[37] has eliminated the basis upon which jurisdiction was exercised. This principle applies equally to jurisdiction exercised under the 2005 Act.[38] Under Article 10(2) of the Convention, however, an urgent measure taken on the basis of mere presence in the jurisdiction in respect of an adult who is habitually resident in another Contracting State, shall lapse as soon as the authorities having jurisdiction on the basis of habitual residence or presence of property have taken the measures required by the situation. This will apply also to jurisdiction exercised in terms of paragraph 7(c) of Schedule 3 to the 2005 Act (presence of the adult or his property in England, if the matter is urgent).

3. CHOICE OF LAW

(a) Prior to the Mental Capacity Act 2005

There seems little doubt that, when exercising powers over the person, property or affairs of a mentally disordered or incapacitated person at common law or in terms of the Mental Health Act 1983, the English court will apply English law. The one specific statutory provision relating to choice of law is section 97(4) of the Mental Health Act 1983 which limits the effect of a will which a judge has authorised to be made on behalf of a patient.[39] The will is limited in its effect to matters governed by English law—and so has no effect in relation to foreign immovables or to the movable property of a person domiciled outside England unless the law of his domicile, by renvoi, refers the issue of his testamentary capacity to English law.

(b) Under the Mental Capacity Act 2005

In exercising jurisdiction under the 2005 Act, the Court of Protection will apply English law,[40] unless it thinks that the matter has a substantial connection with a country other than England and Wales, in which case it may apply the law of that other country.[41] In making a decision with regard to applicable law, the Court must act in the best interests

---

[36] In terms of Art 8 (transfer of jurisdiction to an appropriate forum), the authorities of a Contracting State having jurisdiction on the basis of Arts 5 (adult's habitual residence) or 6 (adults who are refugees, displaced or without habitual residence), if they consider that such is in the interests of the adult, may, on their own motion or on an application by the authority of another Contracting State, request one of a number of certain other states to take measures for the protection of the person or property of that adult. See Lagarde, *Explanatory Report*, paras 65–74.

[37] Eg change of the state in which the adult is habitually resident (Art 5) or physically present (Art 6): Lagarde, *Explanatory Report*, paras 86–89, and especially at 88.

[38] Sch 3, para 9(3).

[39] Mental Health Act 1983, s 96(1)(e).

[40] Cf Hague Convention, Art 13(1).

[41] Sch 3, para 11; cf Hague Convention, Art 13(2).

of the adult.[42] Renvoi is expressly excluded by virtue of Article 19 of the Convention and impliedly by paragraph 2(4) of Schedule 3 to the 2005 Act.

Where a protective measure is taken in one country, but implemented in another, the conditions of implementation are governed by the law of that other country.[43] Thus, the conditions of implementation of any protective measure taken abroad will be governed by English law, if implemented in England.

Sections 9 to 14 of the 2005 Act create a statutory form of power of attorney, the "lasting power of attorney", replacing the "enduring power of attorney" provided for by the Enduring Powers of Attorney Act 1985.[44] Paragraph 13(1)[45] of Schedule 3 provides that if the donor of a lasting power[46] is habitually resident in England and Wales at the time of granting the power, the law applicable to the existence, extent, modification or extinction of the power is (a) English law, or (b) if he specifies in writing the law of a connected country[47] for the purpose, that law. By paragraph 13(2), if the donor is habitually resident in another country at the time of granting the power, but England and Wales is a connected country,[48] the law applicable to the existence, extent, modification or extinction of the power is (a) the law of the other country, or (b) if he specifies in writing English law for the purpose, that law. As regards the manner of exercising a lasting power, the applicable law is the law of the country where it is exercised.[49] Where the law applicable to the power is other than English, the Court of Protection must, so far as possible, have regard to the law of the other country in that/those respect(s).[50]

Paragraph 16[51] of Schedule 3 operates to protect third parties who enter into transactions with a person (a "representative")[52] who purports to act in exercise of an authority to act on behalf of a mentally disordered/incapacitated adult. Where the representative and the third party are in England and Wales when entering into the transaction, the validity thereof may not be questioned in proceedings, nor may the third party be held liable, merely because by virtue of some foreign law applicable in terms of Schedule 3, the representative is not entitled to exercise the authority in that/those respect(s).[53]

---

[42] 2005 Act, s 1(5); cf Lagarde, *Explanatory Report*, para 92.

[43] Sch 3, para 12; cf Hague Convention, Art 14. See Lagarde, *Explanatory Report*, para 93.

[44] 2005 Act, ss 66 and 67; Sch 5, Parts 1 and 2; and Sch 6.

[45] Cf Hague Convention, Art 15. See Lagarde, *Explanatory Report*, paras 95–105.

[46] Defined in Sch 3, para 13(6) as a lasting power of attorney (in terms of s 9 of the 2005 Act); or an enduring power of attorney within the meaning of Sch 4 to the 2005 Act; or any other power of like effect (ie a foreign power akin to a lasting power of attorney).

[47] Defined in Sch 3, para 13(3) as a country of or in which the donor is (a) a national; (b) habitually resident; or (c) has property. In other words, the donor has restricted freedom of choice of law. Where the "connection" exists only by reason of the donor's property, para 13 applies in relation only to that property (para 13(4)).

[48] Ibid.

[49] Sch 3, para 13(5); cf Hague Convention, Art 15(3). See Lagarde, *Explanatory Report*, paras 106–107. For a power exercised in England and Wales, see the 2005 Act, Sch 1.

[50] Sch 3, para 14(2).

[51] Cf Hague Convention, Art 17. See Lagarde, *Explanatory Report*, paras 109–110.

[52] The provision does not apply where the third party deals with the adult personally, for such a situation is likely to be governed by the 1980 Rome Convention on the Law Applicable to Contractual Obligations, Art 11, in respect of which see pp 752–753, supra. Lagarde, *Explanatory Report*, para 110.

[53] Sch 3, para 16(2) and (3). If, however, the third party knew or ought to have known that the applicable law was the law of the other foreign country, the para 16 protection is not afforded to him: para 16(5)(a); cf Hague Convention, Art 17. See Lagarde, *Explanatory Report*, paras 109–110.

Conversely, where the representative and the third party are in a country other than England and Wales at the time of entering into the transaction, its validity may not be questioned in proceedings, nor may the third party be held liable, merely because by virtue of English law, the law applicable to the authority in terms of Schedule 3, the representative is not entitled to exercise the authority in that/those respect(s).[54]

Regardless of any system of law which otherwise would apply in relation to the matter, the mandatory provisions of English law will apply.[55] Similarly, a provision of the law of another country will not be applied by the English court if its application would be manifestly contrary to public policy.[56]

4. RECOGNITION AND ENFORCEMENT OF PROTECTIVE MEASURES TAKEN ABROAD

The question may arise whether someone appointed abroad to exercise powers in relation to the person, property or affairs of a mentally disordered or incapacitated person, whom we shall describe as a "foreign curator", can exercise any rights in England. It is necessary to consider, first, whether such a foreign curator will be recognised in England at all and then, if so, what rights he can exercise in England.

(a) Prior to the Mental Capacity Act 2005

Before a foreign curator can enforce in England any rights relating to the property or affairs of a mentally disordered or incapacitated person, the English courts must be satisfied, first, that the curator is entitled, according to the law under which he was appointed, to take proceedings in England (ie abroad) to recover the property or manage the affairs of that person.[57] Secondly, the English court must be prepared to recognise that the curator was appointed under the law of a country with which the patient was sufficiently closely connected. Whilst in many cases, the mentally disordered/incapacitated adult will be domiciled and present in, and a national of, the country where the curator was appointed,[58] presence alone will suffice at common law or under the Mental Health Act 1983.[59] The English courts have recognised a curator appointed in New York to manage the affairs of a widow domiciled in England;[60] though the rights of the curator in relation to proceedings in England concerning the patient's property are less extensive than if the patient had been domiciled in New York.[61] The English courts have also recognised a curator appointed in Norway to manage the affairs of a man domiciled in

---

[54] Sch 3, para 16(2) and (4); unless the third party knew or ought to have known that the applicable law was English law, in which case the para 16 protection is not afforded to him: para 16(5)(b).

[55] Sch 3, para 17; cf Hague Convention, Art 20. See Lagarde, *Explanatory Report*, para 113.

[56] Sch 3, para 18; cf Hague Convention, Art 21.

[57] *Re Barlow's Will* (1887) 36 Ch D 287, on which see *Didisheim v London and Westminster Bank* [1900] 2 Ch 15 at 49–50; and see *Re Piper* [1927] 4 DLR 924.

[58] Eg *Re De Linden* [1897] 1 Ch 453.

[59] *Re De Larragoiti* [1907] 2 Ch 14.

[60] *New York Security and Trust Co v Keyser* [1901] 1 Ch 666.

[61] Infra, p 1186.

Norway, but present in England.[62]A foreign curator can exercise, as of right, no control in England over the person of the patient;[63] but the English court can authorise the handing over of the mentally disordered or incapacitated person into the care of the foreign curator and the person's removal abroad.[64] Where a person who is neither a British nor Commonwealth citizen with a right of abode in the United Kingdom is detained in hospital as a patient receiving mental treatment, the Secretary of State, subject to the approval of a Mental Health Review Tribunal, can authorise the patient's removal to a country outside the British Isles[65] if he is satisfied as to the arrangements made for such removal, and that it is in the interests of the patient. Provision is also made relating to the removal of patients to and from Scotland, Northern Ireland, the Isle of Man and the Channel Islands on the authority of the Secretary of State or other appropriate authority.[66]With regard to the powers of a foreign curator over the property or affairs in England of a mentally disordered or incapacitated person, it must first be observed that the curator has no power to bring an action for the recovery of immovables.[67] He also has no power in the case of movables if a receiver has been appointed in England, because in that case all powers to deal with the person's property and affairs are vested in the Court of Protection.[68] Subject to this, the rule has been established that a foreign curator can sue in England as of right to claim money or property due to the mentally disordered/incapacitated person and to demand, and to give valid receipts for, property belonging to the patient which is held by persons in England.[69] This principle was finally laid down by the Court of Appeal in the leading case of *Didisheim v London and Westminster Bank*,[70] where the facts were as follows:

> A lady, domiciled and resident in Belgium, had securities of great value deposited with the defendant bank in London. She became insane in fact, though without being so found judicially, and Didisheim, having applied to the bank without success for the securities, brought an action for their recovery.

The Court of Appeal held that Didisheim was entitled to call for the securities and to give the bank a good discharge: "On general principles of private international law, the courts of this country are bound to recognise the authority conferred on him by the Belgian courts, unless lunacy proceedings in this country prevent them from doing so."[71] The court, however, ordered Didisheim to pay all the costs of the action, since the bank was justified in not complying with his demands until he had established his title by a successful action in the High Court. *Didisheim's* case has definitely established the right of a

---

[62] *Re S (Hospital Patient: Foreign Curator)* [1996] Fam 23.

[63] *Re Houston* (1826) 1 Russ 312.

[64] Eg *Re S (Hospital Patient: Foreign Curator)* [1996] Fam 23.

[65] Mental Health Act 1983, s 86.

[66] Ibid, ss 80–85; and Mental Health (Care and Treatment) (Scotland) Act 2003, ss 289, 290 and 309.

[67] *Grimwood v Bartels* (1877) 46 LJ Ch 788.

[68] *Re RSA* [1901] 2 KB 32.

[69] *Didisheim v London and Westminster Bank* [1900] 2 Ch 15; and see *Scott v Bentley* (1855) 1 K & J 281; *Re De Linden* [1897] 1 Ch 453; *Thiery v Chalmers Guthrie & Co* [1900] 1 Ch 80; *Kamouh v Associated Electrical Industries International Ltd* [1980] QB 199 at 205–206; *Re FN and the Mental Health Act 1958* [1984] 3 NSWLR 520.

[70] [1900] 2 Ch 15.

[71] Ibid, at 51.

foreign curator to demand property, and so if an English debtor insists on proceedings, he acts with an unreasonable excess of caution and will have to pay his own costs.[72]

Some limitations on the decision in *Didisheim's* case must be noticed. The foreign curator has no greater rights than his English counterpart. So, if there are funds in court, the payment out of which is in the discretion of the court, payment to a foreign creditor who claims the funds will be subject to such discretion.[73] Furthermore, in *Didisheim's* case, the owner of the property was an alien domiciled abroad over whom the court had no jurisdiction personally. If the patient is domiciled in England, then the foreign curator does not have a right to claim property in England, though the court has a discretion to order payment of appropriate sums.[74]

Although the principle established by *Didisheim's* case is of great benefit to foreign curators, its usefulness is limited not only by the fact that it has no application to immovable property but also because it does not enable the foreign curator to reduce into possession stock and shares registered in the name of the patient. This is because stock and shares can only be transferred by an instrument of transfer executed by the registered holder or by a person having authority to execute the document on his behalf, and a foreign curator is not recognised as having this power.

It is not, however, necessary in every case where stock and shares are concerned to appoint a receiver in England or to have independent medical evidence of mental incapacity. The reason for this is that the Court of Protection is empowered, if satisfied that the foreign curator has been appointed on the ground that the patient is incapable by reason of mental incapacity of managing his property, to direct any stock or shares standing in the name of the patient to be transferred to the curator or otherwise dealt with as he may direct.[75] The power is discretionary, and the court will not direct the capital to be transferred unless satisfied that it is required for the patient's maintenance or that there is other sufficient reason justifying a transfer.[76]

(b) Under the Mental Capacity Act 2005

Part 4 of Schedule 3 to the 2005 Act provides for the recognition and enforcement of protective measures[77] taken abroad. Protective measures may include: (a) the determination of incapacity and the institution of a protective regime; (b) placing an adult under the protection of an appropriate authority; (c) guardianship, curatorship or any corresponding system; (d) the designation and functions of a person having charge of the adult's person or property, or representing or otherwise helping him; (e) placing the adult in a place where protection can be provided; (f) administering, conserving or disposing of the adult's property; and (g) authorising a specific intervention for the protection of the person or property of the adult.[78]

---

72 *Pélégrin v Coutts & Co* [1915] 1 Ch 696.
73 *Re Garnier* (1872) LR 13 Eq 532; *Re De Linden* [1897] 1 Ch 453.
74 *New York Security and Trust Co v Keyser* [1901] 1 Ch 666.
75 Mental Health Act 1983, s 100.
76 *Re Knight* [1898] 1 Ch 257; *Re De Larragoiti* [1907] 2 Ch 14.
77 Defined in Sch 3, para 5.
78 Sch 3, para 5(1).

A protective measure taken under the law of the country in which an adult[79] is habitually resident will be recognised in England.[80] When the 2000 Hague Convention takes effect, a protective measure taken under the law of a Contracting State will be recognised if jurisdiction was exercised by that state on a ground equivalent to the bases of jurisdiction exercised by the Court of Protection, as detailed in paragraph 7 of Schedule 3.[81] An interested person may apply to the Court of Protection for a declaration as to whether a protective measure taken under the law of a foreign country is to be recognised in England.[82] Notably, any finding of fact relied on when the measure is taken is conclusive for the purpose of recognition.[83] The Court of Protection may not review the merits of a measure taken outside England except to establish, in so far as it may be necessary so to do, whether the measure complies with Schedule 3.[84]

Recognition of a protective measure taken abroad may be refused under paragraph 19(3) of Schedule 3, if the Court of Protection thinks that (a) the case in which the measure was taken was not urgent, (b) the adult was not given an opportunity to be heard, and (c) that omission amounted to a breach of natural justice.[85] Additionally, recognition may be refused, under paragraph 19(4) of Schedule 3, if (a) recognition of the measure would be manifestly contrary to public policy, (b) the measure would be inconsistent with a mandatory provision of English law, or (c) the measure is inconsistent with one subsequently taken or recognised in England in relation to the adult.[86] Further, when the Hague Convention takes effect, recognition of a protective measure taken by a Convention Contracting State may be refused, under paragraph 19(5) of Schedule 3, if Article 33 of the Convention (instituting a mandatory consultation procedure for cases of placement of an adult in another Contracting State[87]) has not been complied with in a suitable qualifying case.

An interested person may apply to the Court of Protection for a declaration as to whether a protective measure taken under the law of a foreign country, and enforceable there, is enforceable, or to be registered, in England, in accordance with the Court of Protection Rules.[88] A measure to which such a declaration relates is enforceable in England as if it were a measure of like effect taken by the Court of Protection.[89]

With regard to the powers of a foreign curator over the property or affairs in England of a mentally disordered/incapacitated adult, section 18(4) of the 2005 Act, incorporating Schedule 2(7) to the Act, provides for the vesting of stock[90] in a curator appointed outside England and Wales. If the Court of Protection is satisfied that under some foreign law a curator has been appointed to exercise powers in respect of the property and affairs

---

[79] See, with regard to persons under 16 years, Sch 3, para 23, and supra, p 1079 et seq.
[80] Sch 3, para 19(1).
[81] Supra, p 1182.
[82] Sch 3, para 20(1).
[83] Sch 3, para 21.
[84] Sch 3, para 24.
[85] Cf Hague Convention, Art 22(2)(b). See Lagarde, *Explanatory Report*, para 120.
[86] Cf Hague Convention, Art 22(2)(c) and (d). See Lagarde, *Explanatory Report*, paras 121–122.
[87] See Lagarde, *Explanatory Report*, paras 123 and 138–139.
[88] Sch 3, para 22(1); and ss 50 and 51.
[89] Sch 3, para 22(3).
[90] Defined in Sch 2, para 3.

of an adult on the ground that the latter lacks capacity to make decisions with respect to the management and administration of his property and affairs, the Court may, if it considers it expedient so to do, having regard to the nature of the appointment and the circumstances of the case, direct that any stocks standing in the incapable adult's name, or the right to receive dividends therefrom, be transferred into the curator's name, or otherwise be dealt with as required by the curator, and give such directions as it thinks fit for dealing with accrued dividends.[91]

5. CO-OPERATION AMONG HAGUE CONVENTION CONTRACTING STATES

Part 5 of Schedule 3 to the 2005 Act establishes a system of co-operation between public authorities[92] in England and authorities in other Convention countries to operate, when the Hague Convention takes effect, in two situations. First, as regards proposals for cross-border placements of mentally disordered/incapacitated adults,[93] where a public authority proposes to place an adult in an establishment in a foreign Convention country, it must consult an appropriate authority in that country, and provide it with a report on the adult and a statement of reasons for the proposed placement.[94] If the foreign authority opposes the proposed placement within a reasonable time, it cannot proceed.[95] Secondly, in respect of adults in "serious danger",[96] a public authority which is aware of such a person who is the subject of actual or proposed protective measures and who is, or has become, resident in another Convention country, must tell an appropriate authority in that foreign country of the danger and the measures in question.[97]

---

[91] Sch 2, para 7.

[92] Having the same meaning as "public authorities" under the Human Rights Act 1998: 2005 Act, s 64(1).

[93] Sch 3, para 26. cf Sch 3, para 19(5) and Hague Convention, Art 33. As regards the general powers of the Court of Protection concerning an adult's personal welfare, and property and affairs, see 2005 Act, ss 15–21.

[94] Subject to Sch 3, para 29, which provides that no information may be sought or communicated if to do so would be likely to endanger the adult or his property, or would amount to a serious threat to the liberty or life of a member of the adult's family.

[95] Sch 3, para 27.

[96] Eg illness requiring constant treatment, drugs, or influence of a sect: Lagarde, *Explanatory Report*, para 140.

[97] Sch 3, para 28; cf Hague Convention, Art 34. See Lagarde, *Explanatory Report*, para 140.

PART VI

The Law of Property

Chapters

The Law of Property

Chapter 27

The Distinction Between Movables and Immovables

1. INTRODUCTION[1]

In order to arrive at a common basis on which to determine questions involving a foreign element, English private international law classifies the subject matter of ownership into movables and immovables, and thus adopts a distinction that is accepted in other legal systems,[2] though even common law jurisdictions cannot agree whether some kinds of property are movable or immovable.[3] The first task of the court in a private international law case when required to decide some question of a proprietary or possessory nature is

---

[1] See Carruthers (2005), Chapter 1.

[2] *Re Hoyles* [1911] 1 Ch 179 at 185. For a critical examination of the relevant authorities, see Clarence Smith (1963) 26 MLR 16.

[3] Eg, the right of a mortgagee. England and Ontario consider it to be immovable: *Re Hoyles* [1911] 1 Ch 179; *Re Ritchie* [1942] 3 DLR 330; whereas New Zealand and Australia consider it to be movable: *Re O'Neill* [1922] NZLR 468; *Re Greenfield* [1985] 2 NZLR 662 at 664; Wills Amendment Act 1955, s 14(4); *Haque v Haque (No 2)* (1965) 114 CLR 98; see Sykes and Pryles, pp 648–651, 658–660. There are differing views in Canada as to whether mineral rights are movable or immovable property: *War Eagle Mining Co v Robo Management Co* [1996] 2 WWR 504.

to decide whether the item of property which is the subject of the dispute is movable or immovable. The legal system that will be applicable to the case depends on this preliminary decision. Rights over immovables are determined by the law of the situs; rights over movables are not necessarily governed by that law. In the sphere of private international law, then, the common law distinction between realty and personalty is abandoned, even though the case concerns a common law country where it is recognised in the sphere of domestic law. The importance of not confusing the domestic distinction between realty and personalty with the private international law distinction between movables and immovables can scarcely be exaggerated. They do not cover the same ground. The one cuts across the other in the sense that personalty includes both movables and immovables. Thus "realty" is not synonymous either with "land" or with "immovables", for though a life tenant, for instance, holds an interest in realty, a leaseholder holds an interest in personalty. For the purpose of private international law, however, a lease creates an interest in an immovable and is subject to the law of the situs.[4]

2. CLASSIFICATION BY THE LAW OF THE SITUS

The determination of whether the subject matter of ownership is movable or immovable generally presents no difficulty. English law and most other legal systems accept that interests in land, whether classified according to their nature, such as legal estates and equitable interests; or limited in duration, such as fees simple, entails and terms of years; or independent of the right to possession of the land, such as easements, profits and rent charges, are interests in immovable property. A more complex problem arises in those cases where a right over what is physically movable is regarded by a particular legal system as a right over immovable property. For instance, the owner of such obvious chattels as title-deeds, fixtures, fish in a pond and the key of a house is regarded by English internal law as having an interest in land.[5] Again, it seems obvious at first sight that a building erected for the purposes of an exhibition, and which cannot be removed without losing its identity, must be in the same category as normal buildings, yet in the USA[6] its owner has been deemed to hold an interest in movable property. If, therefore, the subject matter of ownership is regarded as immovable by one system of law but as movable by another, to which law is the decision left? The answer given by English law and by most foreign legal systems is: the law of the situs.[7] If the law of the situs attributes the quality of movability or of immovability to the property in question, the English court which is seised of the matter must proceed on that basis.[8]

---

[4] *Freke v Carbery* (1873) LR 16 Eq 461; *Duncan v Lawson* (1889) 41 Ch D 394; *Re Caithness* (1891) 7 TLR 354.

[5] Cf *The Islamic Republic of Iran v Berend* [2007] EWHC 132 (QB), [2007] 2 All ER (Comm) 132, where the parties agreed that a fragment of limestone relief dating from a building in 5th century BC Persepolis should be characterised as movable.

[6] Eg *Public Service Co of New Hampshire v Voudonas* 84 NH 387, 157 A 81 (1930). Cf Germany: BGB, s 95, and Cohn, *Manual of German Law* (2nd edn), Vol 1, p 72

[7] See Carruthers (2005), paras 1.20–1.46 for full discussion of the meaning of the "law of the situs", and infra, Chapter 29.

[8] *Johnstone v Baker* (1817) 4 Madd 474 n; Westlake, s 160, approved in *Re Hoyles* [1910] 2 Ch 333 at 341; affd [1911] 1 Ch 179; *Macdonald v Macdonald* 1932 SC (HL) 79; *Air Foyle Ltd and Anor v Center Capital Ltd* [2002] EWHC 2535; [2003] 2 Lloyd's Rep 753 at [41].

3. SOME EXAMPLES

(a) Mortgages

Mortgages provide an important illustration of this classification. It has been held that the right vested in a mortgagee of English land must be regarded by English law, being the law of the situs, as an interest in an immovable. This is notwithstanding that it is classified by English domestic law as personalty and that the debt, not the charge, is the principal characteristic of the transaction.[9]

(b) Trusts for sale

A further and important illustration is provided by *Re Berchtold*.[10] This case turned on the English doctrine of conversion,[11] namely, that: "Money directed to be employed in the purchase of land, and land directed to be sold and turned into money, are to be considered as that species of property into which they are directed to be converted."[12] What this equitable doctrine means in effect is that where there is such a direction the realty is treated as personalty for certain purposes, or in the reverse case, the personalty is treated as realty for certain purposes. If, for instance, land is conveyed to trustees on trust for sale and payment of the proceeds to A, and A dies before the actual sale, a bequest by him of all his personalty will include the money eventually arising from the sale. This, of course, does not alter the fact that until sold, the land is still immovable. This becomes material if the beneficiary under the trust dies domiciled in a foreign country before the conversion has actually been effected. *Re Berchtold* is just such a case:

> A party died intestate, domiciled in Hungary, and entitled to a freehold interest in English land which though subject to a trust for sale, had not been sold. The English choice of law rule is that intestate succession is governed by the law of the situs in the case of immovables, but by the law of the deceased's last domicile in the case of movables. It was, therefore, vital to decide whether the freehold interest, despite the doctrine of conversion, was still to be regarded as an interest in immovable property.

It was argued with some plausibility that by reason of the trust for sale the land was already money in the eyes of equity, that money is a movable, and that, therefore, the devolution was governed by Hungarian law. The fallacy of this argument, however, was demonstrated by RUSSELL J. The primary question before the court was whether the subject matter in which the deceased was interested was immovable. This had nothing to do with a subsequent question that might arise under the doctrine of conversion, namely, whether realty was to be treated as personalty, or vice versa. It was held that the unsold land was immovable, notwithstanding the binding direction for its conversion into money, and that therefore the appropriate law to govern its devolution on intestacy was the law of the situs.[13]

---

[9] *Re Hoyles* [1911] 1 Ch 179.

[10] [1923] 1 Ch 192; and see *Philipson-Stow v IRC* [1961] AC 727 at 762.

[11] On the uses to which this doctrine may be put in a conflict of laws situation, see Hancock (1965) 17 Stan LR 1095, and Carruthers (2005), paras 2.87–2.88.

[12] *Fletcher v Ashburner* (1779) 1 Bro CC 497 at 499; Pettit, *Equity and the Law of Trusts* (10th edn), Chapter 31.

[13] Cf *Murray v Champernowne* [1901] 2 IR 232.

The decision was distinguished by MORTON J in *Re Cutcliffe's Will Trusts*,[14] where the distinction between realty and personalty, and therefore the doctrine of conversion, were not strictly relevant.

> English land that was subject to an English settlement had been sold under the Settled Land Act 1882 and the proceeds had been invested in English debenture stock. The beneficiary under the settlement died intestate in 1897 domiciled in Ontario.

So far it seems obvious that the stock was in fact movable and that therefore under the relevant doctrine of private international law its devolution was governed by the law of the deceased's last domicile. The Settled Land Act 1882, however, provided that: "Capital money arising under this Act while remaining uninvested or unapplied and securities on which an investment of any such capital money is made shall, for all purposes of disposition, transmission and devolution, be considered as land."[15]

Deciding whether the stock was movable or immovable was the primary issue in trying to determine the governing law. It was held that it was immovable and subject as such to the English law of devolution. The decision has been attacked on the ground that the domestic doctrine of conversion was erroneously applied at the stage when the case was being considered internationally.[16] But this is to misinterpret the ratio of the case. How could the decision have been otherwise? The stock was physically situated in England. English law, therefore, had to determine whether it was to be treated as movable or immovable. An English statute peremptorily demanded that for all purposes, ie presumably including the choice of the applicable law, it should be regarded as land.

(c) Annuities

The character of annuities and other periodical payments depends on whether they issue out of, or are charged on, land. An annuity in the strict sense represents a right to movable property, but a rent charged on land is an interest in immovable property.[17]

4. RELEVANCE OF DISTINCTION BETWEEN REALTY AND PERSONALTY

Once the choice of law has been made, there may come a stage at which the distinction between realty and personalty then becomes relevant. This occurs where the choice falls on a law that recognises the distinction. The chosen law now has control of the case and it must be allowed to operate in its own way. In *Re Berchtold*,[18] for instance, the effect of deciding that the intestate died entitled to immovable property was to apply English law as the law of the situs, with the result that the immovable, being regarded as money under the domestic doctrine of conversion, devolved as personalty according to the rules of English internal law.

---

[14] [1940] Ch 565.
[15] S 22(5); see now Settled Land Act 1925, s 75(5).
[16] Falconbridge (1940) 18 Can Bar Rev 568.
[17] *Chatfield v Berchtoldt* (1872) 7 Ch App 192.
[18] Supra, p 1195.

5. DISTINCTION BETWEEN TANGIBLE AND INTANGIBLE MOVABLES[19]

By English domestic law, the subject matter of ownership, if not immovable, is property divisible into choses in possession, ie tangible physical objects, and choses in action, such as debts, patents, copyright, goodwill, shares and securities. Private international lawyers usually prefer, however, to classify movables as either tangible or intangible.[20] This is not only a linguistic solecism, since it is scarcely possible to move a thing that cannot be touched, but it provokes an unfortunate tendency to ascribe to a disembodied thing, such as a debt, the physical attributes of a corporeal object as, for instance, a definite situs. Although Lord HALSBURY once remarked that he was "wholly unable to see that goodwill itself is susceptible of having any local situation",[21] it is of course necessary for certain purposes, such as jurisdiction or probate, to assign a situs not only to goodwill, but to choses in action generally.[22] This is not without its dangers. Since the situs principle has furnished a simple and effective rule for questions relating to a physical thing, the natural inclination is to extend it to all questions and to regard it as the general determinant of rules for the choice of law concerning choses in action. This is a false analogy. Moreover, it frequently leads to forcing a rule, eminently adapted to one set of circumstances, to fit circumstances for which it is entirely inappropriate. It is reasonably clear that the appropriate law to govern goodwill or a debt depends on quite different considerations from those that are relevant to a physical thing. One must be aware of the danger of straining rules to fit categories.

---

[19] See Carruthers (2005), paras 1.13–1.14.
[20] For a criticism of the distinction, see Cook, pp 284 et seq.
[21] *IRC v Muller & Co's Margarines Ltd* [1901] AC 217 at 240.
[22] See Dicey, Morris and Collins, paras 22R-023–22-051; and Carruthers (2005), paras 1.31–1.42.

Chapter 28

Immovables

1. JURISDICTION

An English court, as we have seen earlier,[1] will not take jurisdiction to determine the issue of title, or right to possession of, foreign land. This rule stems from two sources. The first is the common law rule in *British South Africa Co v Companhia de Moçambique*.[2] The second, in the case of land within another European Community State or in an EFTA State, is derived from Article 22(1) of the Brussels I Regulation,[3] Article 16(1)(a) of the Brussels Convention, and Article 22(1) of the Lugano Convention, each of which gives exclusive jurisdiction in proceedings "which have as their object rights in rem in immovable property or tenancies of immovable property" to the courts of the country in which the property is situated.[4]

2. CHOICE OF LAW

(a) The law of the situs rule

In the USA[5] and in most European countries the general rule is that the law of the situs is the governing law for all questions that arise with regard to immovable property.[6]

---

[1] Supra, Chapter 14.

[2] [1893] AC 602.

[3] Under the EC/Denmark Agreement, the terms of the Brussels I Regulation, with minor modifications, are applied by international law to the relations between the Community and Denmark.

[4] Art 22(1), para 2 of the Brussels I Regulation, Art 16(1)(b) of the Brussels Convention and Art 22(1), para 2 of the Lugano Convention deal with jurisdiction over disputes concerning short-term tenancies, supra, pp 281–282.

[5] Scoles, Hay, Borchers and Symeonides, p 1056; and see Restatement 2d, §§ 222, 223.

[6] This proposition is so clear as scarcely to require authorities, but see *Birtwistle v Vardill* (1840) 7 Cl & Fin 895; *Coppin v Coppin* (1725) 2 P Wms 291; *Re Duke of Wellington* [1947] Ch 506; affd [1948] Ch 118;

The rule was authoritatively stated for English law in *Nelson v Bridport*,[7] where Lord Nelson, in his capacity as Duke of Bronte, had attempted to devise his Sicilian estate in a manner contrary to the law of Sicily. Lord LANGDALE MR said:[8]

> The incidents to real estate, the right of alienating or limiting it, and the course of succession to it, depend entirely on the law of the country where the estate is situated. Lord Nelson having accepted the Sicilian estate could deal with it only as the Sicilian law allowed; he had a right to appoint a successor, but no right to modify the estate, interest, or powers of disposition to which the successor was entitled by the law of Sicily. The successor became the holder of the estate subject to the incidents annexed to it by the grant and the law of Sicily and no others.

Whilst the situs rule may have been authoritatively stated, it has come under increasing criticism.[9] Indeed the rule has been condemned as a "taboo".[10] There is no doubt, however, that the law of the situs has a powerful interest in its rules being applied to a wide range of matters—essentially "with the manner in which land is used, occupied or developed".[11] This concern is seen at its strongest in the case of the transfer of title to land.[12] At the end of the day, only the law of the situs can control the way in which land, which constitutes part of the situs itself, is transferred. So, uniformity with the law of the situs is necessary in terms of effectiveness and justifies an English court applying that foreign law. Indeed this attitude is reinforced by the refusal of English courts to adjudicate on issues relating to title to foreign land[13] or to recognise foreign judgments to such effect.[14] In other cases, however, "where the parties are non residents and the policy of the situs does not concern the use, tenure or marketing of its land",[15] the case for the application of the law of the situs is much weaker. Although the courts have been prepared to apply a law other than that of the situs to govern a contract for the sale of land,[16] a foreign implied marriage settlement,[17] the division of property upon divorce,[18] or the formal validity of a will of immovables,[19] the generality of the situs rule remains in force, as is illustrated by the law on intestate succession to immovables[20] and on the essential validity of a will relating to immovables.[21] It seems unlikely that the entrenched position of the

---

Dicey, Morris and Collins, Rule 123, para 23R-061; Westlake, s 156; Story, Chapter X; and Carruthers (2005), Chapter 2.

[7] (1846) 8 Beav 547.

[8] Ibid, at 570.

[9] Cavers (1970) III Hague Recueil 75, 196 et seq.

[10] Hancock (1964) 15 Stan LR 561; (1965) 17 Stan LR 1095; (1966) 18 Stan LR 1299; (1967) 20 Stan LR 1; Weintraub (1966) 52 Cornell LQ 1; Morris (1969) 85 LQR 339; Alden (1987) 65 Texas LR 585; Anderson (1999) 48 ICLQ 167; and Carruthers (2005), paras 2.01–2.14.

[11] Scoles, Hay, Borchers and Symeonides, p 1056.

[12] Eg *Re Ross* [1930] 1 Ch 377; *Re Duke of Wellington* [1947] Ch 506.

[13] Supra, p 478 et seq. But consider the exercise of *in personam* jurisdiction by a non-situs court: eg *Ashurst v Pollard* [2001] Ch 595; and *Re Hayward (deceased)* [1997] Ch 45. Also *Gaillard v Chekili* (C/518/99) [2001] IL Pr 33. See Carruthers (2005), paras 2.30–2.50.

[14] Supra, p 532 et seq.

[15] Hancock (1966) 18 Stan LR 1299, 1321. See also Carruthers (2005), paras 2.51–2.86.

[16] See now supra, p 716.

[17] *Re De Nicols (No 2)* [1900] 2 Ch 410, infra, p 1302.

[18] *Hamlin v Hamlin* [1986] Fam 11; *Razelos v Razelos* [1970] 1 WLR 390. Cf *Holmes v Holmes* [1989] Fam 47.

[19] Infra, p 1279.

[20] Infra, pp 1277–1279.

[21] Infra, pp 1279–1280.

law of the situs as the choice of law rule for immovables is going to be altered other than by legislation.[22]

(i) Meaning of the "law of the situs"[23]

Before giving specific illustrations of the situs doctrine in operation it is essential that the true meaning of the expression "the law of the situs" should be understood. Most decisions and most writers have proceeded on the assumption that it means the relevant rule applicable at the situs to a purely domestic situation involving no foreign element at all. The assumption, however, is scarcely warranted. This, as we have seen in considering the renvoi doctrine, is one of those exceptional cases in which the court of the forum refers to the whole law of the foreign situs.[24] It may be that a court at the situs, if required to give a decision, would apply the relevant rule of its own law applicable to a purely domestic situation. This, however, is not necessarily so and the whole law of the foreign situs might either include its rules of private international law or might involve an examination of the rule applicable to a domestic situation to see whether it extends to a case with international elements. In order to determine this, the relevant rule should be examined in the light of its reason, the purpose that it is designed to effect and the policy on which it is based. It does not follow that a rule of land law designed to promote the welfare of persons domiciled in a country or to regulate local transactions should necessarily be extended to transactions completed abroad between domiciled foreigners. The truth of this is well brought out by Cook in his discussion of the New Hampshire case of *Proctor v Frost*:[25]

> This concerned a married woman, domiciled in Massachusetts, who, by the statute law of New Hampshire was incapable of becoming surety for her husband, but by the law of Massachusetts was free from this incapacity. By a transaction in Massachusetts she became surety for her husband, and by way of security she executed in that state a mortgage of her land in New Hampshire.

There was no dispute that her capacity to execute the mortgage as a surety fell to be determined by the law of the situs, but that did not inevitably mean that the New Hampshire statute applied to the instant case. A correct decision on that question could scarcely be reached without first considering the purpose of the statute. Was the purpose to regulate the conveyance of New Hampshire land, or to protect wives against the importunities of financially embarrassed husbands? If it was the latter, it would be unseemly and inexpedient to extend this paternal solicitude to wives domiciled in foreign jurisdictions. In the result, the Supreme Court of New Hampshire considered that the object of the statute was to protect married women within the jurisdiction, and they therefore held the mortgage to be valid.[26] This decision stands out as one of the few in which the matter has been approached in this manner.

---

[22] As in the case of the formal validity of wills, infra, p 1277.

[23] See Carruthers (2005), paras 1.20–1.21, and 1.43–1.45.

[24] Eg *Re Ross* [1930] 1 Ch 377; *Re Duke of Wellington* [1947] Ch 506, supra, p 69.

[25] 89 NH 304, 197 A 813 (1938); Cook, p 274; and see the articles by Hancock, supra, p 1200, n 10.

[26] Though their decision to apply the law of Massachusetts, essentially by way of renvoi, (see 197 A 813 at 815) as the place of execution of the mortgage, rather than as the place of the wife's domicile, is hard to justify: Cook, p 275. See the discussion of interest analysis, supra, pp 29–30.

It will be found, almost without exception, that the term "the law of the situs" is interpreted in its narrow literal sense as meaning that rule which applies to an analogous situation free from all trace of foreign elements. This narrow meaning must, of course, be adopted when the dispute concerns the legal effects of a conveyance, as, for example, when the question is whether there has been an infringement of the rule against perpetuities or whether the interest created is legally possible.[27] There is, however, no reason why it should be regarded as the only possible meaning.

(b) Specific issues

Problems relating to choice of the law applicable to immovables may arise in a variety of contexts. Some of these are considered separately in later chapters, such as the administration of estates of immovables and succession thereto, and the effect of marriage and other adult relationships on property, both movable and immovable. Nevertheless, some of the cases to be discussed in this chapter will be drawn from those fields, especially succession, where they illustrate principles generally applicable to immovables.

(i) Capacity to take and transfer immovables

Unless a person has capacity by the law of the situs to take immovables, he will be excluded from ownership. In *Duncan v Lawson*,[28] for instance, it was admitted that a bequest by a domiciled Scotsman of English leaseholds to trustees on trust for sale, and out of the proceeds to pay certain legacies to charities, was void as infringing the Mortmain and Charitable Uses Act 1888 (since repealed).[29] This was because the question whether a charity was competent to take English freeholds and leaseholds, even under a foreign will, must depend on English law. The same is true of capacity to transfer immovables, whether by sale, gift, mortgage or devise. If full age is attained in Country A at 18 and in Country B at 25, a person 22 years old, domiciled in A, cannot execute a valid conveyance of lands lying in B; whereas a person of the same age, even though domiciled in B, can effectually convey land in A.[30]

Bank of Africa Ltd v Cohen[31] unequivocally established that the situs rule is part of English law in relation to capacity to transfer land abroad. The facts were these:

> The defendant, a married woman domiciled in England, entered into a deed in England by which she agreed to make a mortgage of her land in Johannesburg in favour of the plaintiff. The mortgage was intended to secure money lent to her husband. The Roman-Dutch law prevailing in the Transvaal ordained that a married woman could not be bound as a surety unless she specifically renounced certain rights under that law. This renunciation had not been made in the formal manner required by the local law.

---

[27] Cook, p 270.

[28] (1889) 41 Ch D 394; and see *A-G v Parsons* [1956] AC 421.

[29] *Hewit's Trustees v Lawson* (1891) 18 R 793.

[30] Cf *Sell v Miller* 11 Ohio State 331 (1860); Scoles, Hay, Borchers and Symeonides, p 1058; Restatement 2d, § 223.

[31] [1909] 2 Ch 129.

In an action in England for specific performance of the English transaction, judgment was given both by the court of first instance and also by the Court of Appeal in favour of the defendant, based on her lack of capacity.

In the words of BUCKLEY LJ: "a person's capacity to make a contract with regard to an immovable is governed by the *lex situs*".[32] This decision is far from satisfactory. If the facts raised a true question of capacity, it did not follow that the object of the South African rule was to protect married women domiciled in other countries.[33] If a question of form was involved, it is difficult to distinguish the case from that of *Re Courtney*,[34] where a contrary decision was reached. Again, since the married woman had made a contract valid by English law, the governing law, was she not bound to do everything required by South African law to render it effective?

There is no English authority on the law governing capacity to transfer land in England where the transferor is domiciled abroad. However, there is clear Canadian authority in favour of applying the law of the situs in such a case. In *Landry v Lachapelle*:[35]

> A husband and wife were domiciled in Quebec, the wife owned land in Ontario which she conveyed to her husband, to be owned by them both as joint tenants. As a married woman, she had capacity to do this under the law of Ontario, but not of Quebec.

The Ontario Court of Appeal identified the issue as one relating to title, not to the validity of any contract. "The crucial question . . . may be stated as follows:—Is the law of Ontario inconsistent with the law of Quebec as regards the conveyance to the defendant of the lands in question? If so, the Ontario law must govern."[36]

It does not necessarily follow, however, that the substantive rules of law to be applied in the situs in the case of a foreign domiciliary are necessarily the same as would be applied to someone domiciled in the situs.[37]

(ii) Formalities of alienation

The formal validity of a transfer of immovables is determined by the law of the situs.[38] This is generally taken to mean that a transfer must comply with the formalities prescribed by the internal law of the situs for a purely domestic transaction containing no foreign element. For example, in *Adams v Clutterbuck*[39] it was held that a conveyance between two domiciled Englishmen of shooting rights in Scotland was valid, notwithstanding the fact that it was not under seal as required by English, but not Scots, law. Again it has been

---

[32] Ibid, at 143.

[33] See this aspect of the matter discussed supra, p 1202.

[34] (1840) Mont & Ch 239.

[35] [1937] 2 DLR 504.

[36] Ibid, at 508.

[37] Cf *Proctor v Frost*, supra, p 1201, where, although the New Hampshire court, by a process of renvoi, applied Massachusetts law, it could have achieved the same outcome by determining that the wife had capacity under New Hampshire law, given that the statutory restriction on capacity did not apply to her as a foreign domiciliary.

[38] Dicey, Morris and Collins, para 23-072. On the other hand, a contract to transfer an interest in land does not have to satisfy the formal requirements of the law of the situs: *Re Smith, Lawrence v Kitson* [1916] 2 Ch 206, infra, p 1205. But see Rome Convention, Art 9(6), and cf Rome I Regulation, Art 11(5), discussed supra, p 749.

[39] (1883) 10 QBD 403.

held in a case decided before the Wills Act 1837 that a devise which was valid by the law of the testator's domicile was ineffectual to pass English land, since it was not attested by three witnesses as then required by the Statute of Frauds.[40] Nevertheless, it does not inevitably follow that a local formality must in all circumstances be observed. Everything depends on how it is regarded by the law of the situs itself. This law may, indeed, regard it as essential for every conveyance, no matter where or by whom executed. On the other hand, it may regard the formality as necessary only for conveyances completed within the jurisdiction.[41]

(iii) Essential validity of transfers

The general rule laid down in *Nelson v Bridport*,[42] as we have already seen,[43] is that no disposition, though made in a country where it may be regular, can create an interest in immovables that is contrary to the law of the situs. The law of the situs obviously must decide whether an interest in land is permissible in nature or extent. That law exclusively governs the tenure, title and descent of immovables.[44] Although it is a general principle that a legal title duly acquired in one country is a good title all the world over,[45] yet, where the title concerns immovables, it must conform to the law of the situs. Thus a disposition of English land, whether by will or otherwise, which contains limitations that infringe the rules as to perpetuities and accumulations is void.[46]

A common application of the general principle occurs in the case of those restraints on alienation which are found in most systems of law. Prohibitions against alienation between certain persons, or for certain purposes or beyond a certain amount, are frequently met, and in fact most of the civil law systems forbid testators to dispose of more than a certain proportion of their property. When the subject matter of alienation is immovable property, the application of such restraints depends solely on the law of the situs.[47] Similarly, in determining whether a purported transfer infringes rules against perpetuities and accumulations, the law of the situs governs, and not the law of the testator's domicile.[48]

(iv) Contracts

Recognising the primacy of the law of the situs does not resolve all difficulties. The generality of the rule and the sweeping manner in which it is usually stated are apt to lead to error unless we notice the distinction between an actual transfer of land and a contract

---

[40] *Coppin v Coppin* (1725) 2 P Wms 291.

[41] In the USA many statutes have expressly provided that a transfer shall be valid if the formalities of the place of execution are observed; see the Uniform Acknowledgement Act 1957; Restatement 2d, § 223, comment e.

[42] (1846) 8 Beav 547.

[43] Supra, p 1200.

[44] *Fenton v Livingstone* (1859) 33 LTOS 335. Contrast the law governing the essential validity of contracts relating to land, infra, pp 1205–1206.

[45] *Simpson v Fogo* (1863) 1 Hem & M 195.

[46] *Re Grassi, Stubberfield v Grassi* [1905] 1 Ch 584 at 592; *Freke v Carbery* (1873) LR 16 Eq 461.

[47] *Re Hernando* (1884) 27 Ch D 284 (English land); *Re Ross* [1930] 1 Ch 377 (foreign land).

[48] *Curtis v Hutton* (1808) 14 Ves 537; *Duncan v Lawson* (1889) 41 Ch D 394; *Re Hoyles, Row v Jagg* [1911] 1 Ch 179. It seems no longer necessary to consider the unsatisfactory decision in *Canterbury (Mayor) v Wyburn* [1895] AC 89, PC; though see Hancock (1964) 16 Stan LR 561, 599–604. Though cf *Re Piercy* [1895] 1 Ch 83 (apparently approved in *Philipson-Stow v IRC* [1961] AC 727 at 744–745), where application of the Italian lex situs was somewhat limited. Cf *Brown v Gregson* [1920] AC 860 at 886.

to transfer.[49] So far as formalities are concerned, any transaction or instrument that purports to change, then and there, the ownership of immovables must satisfy the formal requirements of the law of the situs. But a different position arises where the inquiry relates not to the actual transfer of some interest, but to the rights and liabilities of the parties under a contract relating to immovables. A contract by A that he will transfer some interest in land to B brings into play the choice of law rules governing the validity of a contract, now to be found in the Rome Convention on the Law Applicable to Contractual Obligations, scheduled to the Contracts (Applicable Law) Act 1990.[50]

(a) Form

Under Article 9(1) of the Convention, a contract is binding, so far as relates to form, if it satisfies the requirements of the law of the place of contracting or of the law applicable to it under the other Convention rules.[51] So if A and B, two domiciled Englishmen, make a contract in London in such terms that its governing law is that of England, there is no doubt that it is exclusively subject to English law. The mere fact that it relates to foreign land does not affect the contractual rights and liabilities of the parties. Furthermore, a contract will be regarded as formally valid if so valid under its governing law or the law of the place of contracting, even if not formally valid under the law of the situs.[52]

There is, however, a special rule in Article 9(6) of the Convention which deals with the formal validity of a contract the subject matter of which is a right in immovable property or the right to use immovable property.[53] Such a contract shall:

> be subject to the mandatory requirements of form of the law of the country where the property is situated if by that law those requirements are imposed irrespective of the country where the contract is concluded and irrespective of the law governing the contract.

Such mandatory requirements, which must have overriding effect under the law of the situs, are "probably rather rare",[54] though there may be some such rules under Scots law.[55]

(b) Essential validity

Under Article 3(1) of the Convention, parties are free to choose the law to govern their contract relating to immovables;[56] but, in the absence of choice, the essential validity of the contract will, by reason of Article 4[57] and much as it was at common law,[58] be governed by the law of the country with which the contract is most closely connected.

---

[49] See Carruthers (2005), Chapter 4.

[50] See also Rome I Regulation. Supra, p 716 et seq.

[51] Supra, p 746 et seq. Cf Rome I Regulation, Art 11, discussed supra, pp 749–750.

[52] *Re Smith, Lawrence v Kitson* [1916] 2 Ch 206. See also *Hamilton v Wakefield* 1993 SLT (Sh Ct) 30.

[53] cf Rome I Regulation, Art 11(5), discussed supra, p 750.

[54] Report on the Convention by Giuliano and Lagarde, OJ 1980 c 282/32.

[55] Eg Requirements of Writing (Scotland) Act 1995, s 1(2)(a)(i).

[56] Reference is made to Arts 3 and 4 by Art 8 on material validity. Cf Rome I Regulation, Arts 3, 4 and 10. Supra, pp 744–746.

[57] Supra, p 707 et seq.

[58] See *British South Africa Co v De Beers Consolidated Mines Ltd* [1910] 2 Ch 502; revsd on other grounds [1912] AC 52; *Re Anchor Line (Henderson Bros) Ltd* [1937] Ch 483; cf *Carse v Coppen* 1951 SC 233 at 247–248.

In the nature of events, this is likely to be the law of the situs, and this is reinforced by a rebuttable presumption in Article 4(3) "that the contract is most closely connected with the country where the immovable property is situated".[59]

(c) Capacity

It would seem, on principle, that the distinction between an actual transfer and a contract to transfer must also be relevant in a question of capacity. Where a person contracts in one country to transfer land in another country, his capacity should be tested by the law[60] governing the essential validity of the contract. The difficulty, however, of maintaining this view is that, if the contracting party were subject to some incapacity in the true sense, eg nonage, by the law of the situs though not by the governing law, it would be futile to subject him to a decree of specific performance that the local law would forbid him to implement. The most that could be done would be to hold him liable in damages.

---

[59] Supra, p 716. See Carruthers (2005), paras 4.02–4.03. The Convention rules governing the validity of contracts relating to immovable property are, of course, subject to all the other general provisions of the Convention, discussed supra, Chapter 18. Cf Rome I Regulation, Art 4(1)(c); see also Art 4(1)(d), introducing an exceptional rule for short-term tenancies.

[60] See Carruthers (2005), para 4.04.

Chapter 29

The Transfer of Tangible Movables

1. INTRODUCTION

An assignment of movables can give rise to various problems. This chapter will focus on trying to determine the legal system according to which such matters should be resolved.[1] We are not concerned here with what are usually called general assignments, under which, on the occasion of marriage, death and bankruptcy, the entirety of a person's property may pass to another. Our inquiry is confined to particular assignments *inter vivos* of

---

[1] On this subject see especially Carruthers, *The Transfer of Property in the Conflict of Laws* (2005); Lalive, *The Transfer of Chattels in the Conflict of Laws* (1955); Zaphiriou, *The Transfer of Chattels in Private International Law* (1956); Falconbridge, *Conflict of Laws* (1954) 2nd edn, 442 et seq; Morris (1945) 22 BYBIL 232; Chesterman (1973) 22 ICLQ 213; North (1990) I Hague Recueil 9, 259 et seq; Prott (1989) V Hague Recueil 215, 262–281.

isolated or individual movables, of which the commonest examples are sales, gifts, mortgages and pledges. Further, the present discussion is limited to tangible movables.

This is one of the most intractable topics in English private international law, because many of the few relevant authorities are antiquated and they do not reveal with any certainty what principles govern the subject as a whole. A common but fallacious assumption is that all problems must be referred to one single law. In the course of time varied views on what this is have been advanced. The law of the situs of the property, the law of the place of the parties' domicile or of the transferor, the law of the place of acting, the proper law of the transfer—each of these has had its advocates. The assumption, however, is untenable. It represents an oversimplification of the position, because it is based on the fallacy that the possible questions arising out of a transfer of movables all fall into the same category and are all of the same juridical nature. This is not so. Suppose, for instance, the following facts:

> A, resident and domiciled in England, sells goods lying in a Barcelona warehouse to B, a Dutch businessman. He transmits the bill of exchange and the bill of lading to B to secure acceptance. B fails to accept the bill of exchange but takes the bill of lading to Antwerp and transfers it there to C, a Belgian businessman. Meanwhile, the goods have been shipped from Barcelona en route to Holland. The ship is wrecked off the coast of France, but the goods are salvaged and sold to D by the judicial authorities in Bordeaux.

A number of questions, some contractual others proprietary, differing fundamentally in character, may arise from these facts, and it does not require much acumen to appreciate that each one of these cannot satisfactorily be submitted to one system of law. Litigation may occur between A and B as to the formal or essential validity of the original transfer. A may claim as against B that he is entitled to stop the goods in transit. C may claim a derivative title from B which he alleges renders stoppage unlawful. D may claim that the effect of the judicial sale in France has been to divest all previous owners, original as well as derivative, of their former titles. If it is true to say that questions arising out of the transfer and acquisition of property in corporeal movables are determinable by one single law, what is that law in the instant case? Is Spanish law, which happened to be the law of the situs at the time of the original transfer, to determine, inter alia, the essential validity of the transaction between A and B, the effect of a failure by a Dutch buyer to accept a bill of exchange received by him from an English seller, and the title of a Frenchman who buys goods in France publicly sold by a French judicial authority? Furthermore, the law of the situs has not remained constant. Is it Spanish law for some questions, French law for others? If so, how are the questions to be classified for this purpose, and resolved? Consideration now will be given to the various theories that have been advanced with regard to the resolution of problems such as these.

2. THE VARIOUS THEORIES[2]

In choosing the proper law to govern the transfer of movable objects, arguments may be advanced in favour of the law of the domicile, the law of the situs, the law of the place of

---

[2] Carruthers (2005), paras 3.02–3.10.

acting, or the proper law of the transfer. It will be well to consider the relative merits of these legal systems before attempting a final statement of the law.

(a) The law of the domicile

Historically, the starting-point is the maxim *mobilia sequuntur personam*—goods follow the person. Some English writers have said that, "Personal property has no locality". Sweeping statements to the effect that rights over movables are to be governed by the law of the owner's domicile may be found in the earlier English authorities.[3] Now, however, it is generally agreed that to allow either party to invoke the law of his domicile in the case of a dispute arising out of a transfer of chattels would be commercially impracticable and contrary both to natural justice and to the normal expectations of the parties themselves. Indeed, it has been said by the Privy Council that the maxim *mobilia sequuntur personam* means, not that movables are deemed to be situated where their owner is domiciled, but merely that their devolution on his death is governed by his personal law.[4] Moreover, the application of the maxim might result in prejudice to innocent third parties, as can be seen from a hypothetical case:

> A, a domiciled Englishman, by a transaction which is valid by English law but void by the law of Illinois, executes a bill of sale in favour of X, another domiciled Englishman, over goods that are situated in Chicago, Illinois. Later, Y, also domiciled in England, causes a writ of attachment to be levied on the goods in Chicago in respect of a debt due to him from A. The attachment action proceeds to judgment and the goods are sold in satisfaction of Y's debt.

The result of holding in such a case that the original transaction conferred a valid and prior title to the goods on X, since it conformed to the law of the common domicile of A and X, would be to impose liability for conversion on the sheriff and the officer who conducted the sale in Chicago. Yet it is obvious that, though the sheriff must be presumed to know the law of the place where the goods are situate, he cannot be expected to investigate the law of their owner's domicile.

Again, whose domicile is decisive? Suppose, for instance, that the question is whether goods stored in Rotterdam belong to a domiciled Englishman or to a domiciled Frenchman. In such a case no decision is possible on the basis of the law of the domicile if the laws of France and of England differ, for there is no guide as to which of these laws shall be chosen. If the law of the claimant's domicile is chosen on the ground that the question of his title has been raised, this is a circular argument, since the sole issue is whether he possesses a title. The result is the same if the law of the defendant's domicile is chosen. Moreover, if the decisive factor is the domicile of one of the parties, the governing law would vary according to which of them began proceedings.

(b) The law of the situs[5]

An alternative to the law of the domicile is the law of the situs. This has obvious virtues. Where claimants have different domiciles or where they rely on transactions in different

---

[3] *Sill v Worswick* (1791) 1 Hy Bl 665 at 690; *Re Ewin* (1830) 1 Cr & J 151 at 156.
[4] *Alberta Provincial Treasurer v Kerr* [1933] AC 710 at 721.
[5] Carruthers (2005), paras 3.07–3.10, and Chapter 8.

countries, the law of the situs has the great advantage of being a single and exclusive system that can act as an independent arbiter of conflicting claims. Moreover, its right of control satisfies the expectations of the reasonable man, for a party to a transfer naturally concludes that the transaction will be subject to the law of the country in which the subject matter is at present situated.

> If a movable which is vested in A as the result of a transaction with B governed by English law is taken by B to France and there sold to C in circumstances which, by French law but not by English law, confer a valid title on C, it would be a travesty of justice to determine the mutual rights of A and C by English law, the relevancy of which would be entirely unknown to C.

Nevertheless, there may be cases where reference to the law of the situs appears arbitrary. If, for example, goods deposited temporarily in a Hamburg warehouse are sold by their owners, London importers, to another London dealer by a contract effected in England, there may seem to be no obvious reason why any question concerning the title to the goods should be governed by German law. However, there would seem to be good policy reasons to support reference to the law of the situs. "Two decisive considerations are, firstly, that the country of the situs has the effective power over the chattel, secondly that the exclusive application of the law of the situs alone can fulfil the need for security in international property transactions."[6]

As can be seen from the example suggested earlier,[7] difficulties may arise where the situs of the goods changes during the course of events leading to litigation. If this is so then the problem will be to identify the law of the particular situs that must govern.[8]

(c) The law of the place of acting

There is little to be said in favour of the law of the place of acting, ie the law of the country where the legal act of purported creation/acquisition etc, or the transfer/transaction took place. Here, as in other areas of law, the mere fact that a transaction is completed in a particular place is no adequate reason for admitting the control of the local law. If, for instance, an Englishman executes a document in Edinburgh granting a lien over his furniture in London to another Englishman it is unthinkable that this slight and perhaps incidental connection with Scotland should require the possessory rights of the parties to be determined by Scots law. Yet, curiously enough, there are decisions, dealing with negotiable instruments, which contain strong dicta in favour of the law of the place of acting. Thus in *Alcock v Smith*, ROMER J said:

> Generally, the rights of transferor and transferee, on a transfer in one country of a document of title to a debt or to an interest in personal property, are governed by the law of the country where the transfer takes place, although the debt may be due from persons living in, or the personal property may be situate in, a foreign country.[9]

---

[6] Lalive, op cit, p 115. But see, in contrast, Carruthers (2005), paras 8.16–8.71.
[7] Supra, p 1209.
[8] Morris (1945) 22 BYBIL 232, 233; and Carruthers (2005), paras 1.22–1.30.
[9] [1892] 1 Ch 238 at 255. See also *Embiricos v Anglo-Austrian Bank* [1905] 1 KB 677 at 683, 685.

On appeal, KAY LJ in terms said the same thing,[10] but it seems clear from the illustrations he gave that he had in mind a case where the law of the place of acting and the law of the situs coincided. Since the place of acting and the situs are necessarily the same in the transfer of a negotiable instrument, it is probable that in these cases the judges, despite their reference to the law of the place of acting, were in fact speaking in terms of the law of the situs.[11]

(d) The law governing the transfer

The last law that may be chosen to govern questions arising out of a transfer of movables is the law of the country with which the transfer has the most real connection, or more shortly, the law governing the transfer, analogous to the law governing a contract.[12] In most cases, its ascertainment will cause no difficulty, as for instance where the law of the place of acting and the law of the situs are identical or where two English businessmen meet in Paris and complete a transfer there of goods situated in England. But a more complex problem may arise, as where A, resident and domiciled in England, sells goods lying in a Naples warehouse to B, who is resident and domiciled in the Netherlands. Without more facts it is scarcely possible to say what the proper law would be in such a case. Before it could reach a decision, the court would require to know, inter alia: Where was the transfer effected? If reduced to writing, was it drafted in terms peculiar to English or Dutch law? Were the goods only temporarily in Italy? The danger to avoid, however, is the assumption that the law of the situs always constitutes the proper law.

It would seem that of the four laws proposed the choice lies between the law of the situs and the law governing the transfer.[13] Nevertheless, it cannot be said that either governs exclusively all the issues arising from a particular transfer. The choice between them depends, basically, on whether the issue under consideration is contractual or proprietary.[14]

3. THE MODERN LAW

(a) The general rule

The questions which arise in relation to a transfer of tangible movables may include a variety of matters, such as whether the transfer is void for incapacity, whether it is formally or essentially valid, whether it is voidable for misrepresentation or other cause, whether the transferor has a lien on the goods or a right to stop them in transit, and what is the nature of the interest created by the transfer. Some of these questions are of a contractual, others of a proprietary, character.

---

[10] Ibid, at 267.

[11] Lalive, op cit, p 79.

[12] Cf *Glencore International AG v Metro Trading International Inc* [2001] 1 Lloyd's Rep 284, discussed infra, p 1215.

[13] See further Carruthers (2005), paras 9.46 et seq, pp 249 et seq.

[14] Carruthers (2005), paras 4.05–4.09, 4.16–4.22. See also *Pattni v Ali and Dinky International SA* [2006] UKPC 51, per Lord MANCE, at [25].

It is clear that the contractual rights and obligations fall to be determined by the proper law of the transfer. This category includes such questions as whether there is an implied condition that the subject matter of the transfer is of satisfactory quality or is reasonably fit for a particular purpose, or whether the transfer itself is formally valid.

The solution is not so obvious, however, where the question relates not to the purely contractual rights but to claims to some possessory or proprietary right in the chattel itself. If, in such a case, the law of the situs and the proper law of the transfer do not coincide, which is to prevail? Although the authorities are few and whilst there is some support for reference to the proper law,[15] it is now established that the proprietary effect of a particular assignment of movables is governed exclusively by the law of the country where they are situated at the time of the assignment.[16] An owner will be divested of his title to movables if they are taken to a foreign country and there assigned in circumstances sufficient by the local law to pass a valid title to the assignee. The title recognised by the law of the foreign situs overrides earlier and inconsistent titles, no matter by what law they may have been created. As DIPLOCK LJ has said:[17]

> The proper law governing the transfer of corporeal movable property is the lex situs. A contract made in England and governed by English law for the sale of specific goods situated in Germany, although it would be effective to pass the property in the goods at the moment the contract was made if the goods were situate in England would not have that effect if under German law . . . delivery of the goods was required in order to transfer the property in them.

The application of the law of the situs rule must prevail on practical grounds of business convenience.[18]

The leading authority for the application of the law of the situs is *Cammell v Sewell*,[19] where the facts were these.

> A Russian seller shipped, in Russia, a cargo of timber on a Prussian vessel to English importers in Hull who insured the cargo with the plaintiffs as underwriters. The vessel having been wrecked off the coast of Norway, the timber was sold to X at a public auction held at the instance of the master in Norway. An action, brought by the underwriters in the Norwegian court to set aside the sale, failed. X shipped the timber to England and transferred it to the defendants. The underwriters sued the defendants for its value.

---

[15] Eg *Inglis v Usherwood* (1801) 1 East 515 where Russian law was the law of the situs, the law of the place of acting, and also, apparently, the proper law of the transfer.

[16] *Cammell v Sewell* (1858) 3 H & N 617; on appeal 5 H & N 728; *Winkworth v Christie, Manson and Woods Ltd* [1980] Ch 496; *Air Foyle Ltd & Anor v Center Capital Ltd* [2002] EWHC 2535; [2003] 2 Lloyd's Rep 753; *Government of the Islamic Republic of Iran v The Barakat Galleries Ltd* [2007] EWCA Civ 1374.

[17] *Hardwick Game Farm v Suffolk Agricultural Poultry Producers Association* [1966] 1 WLR 287 at 330; affd by the House of Lords [1969] 2 AC 31; and see *Bank voor Handel en Scheepvart NV v Slatford* [1953] 1 QB 248 at 257.

[18] *Re Anziani* [1930] 1 Ch 407; see obiter remarks of MAUGHAM J at 420, "I do not think that anybody can doubt that with regard to the transfer of goods the law applicable must be the law of the country where the movable is situate."

[19] (1858) 3 H & N 617; affd 5 H & N 728. In *Air Foyle Ltd and Anor v Center Capital Ltd* [2003] 2 Lloyd's Rep 753, GROSS J, at [42], described the *situs* rule, dating back to *Cammell v Sewell*, as "long established beyond challenge".

By English law, the auction sale had not affected the title vested in the English importers by the original contract and which was now vested in the claimants. The defendants, however, did not deny the effect of that contract. Their case was that, by virtue of what happened in Norway at the time when the timber was there, they had acquired a title which under Norwegian law overrode that of the earlier English purchaser. The Court of Exchequer gave judgment for the defendants on the ground that the decision of the Norwegian court was a judgment in rem which vested the property in X as against the whole world. On appeal, a majority of the Court of Exchequer Chamber, without giving a definite decision on the point, were of the opinion that the judgment was not a judgment in rem, but they decided that the title conferred on X by Norwegian law must prevail. CROMPTON J said: "We think the law on this subject was correctly stated by the Lord Chief Baron . . . when he says, 'If personal property is disposed of in a manner binding according to the law of the country where it is that disposition is binding everywhere'."[20]

Exclusive reference to the law of the situs will undoubtedly cause hardship to the previous owner if his movables are dealt with in a foreign country without his knowledge.[21] Thus, CROMPTON J acknowledged that the English law as to the distraint of a foreigner's goods for rent due from a tenant, or as to the title to stolen property acquired by a purchaser under a sale in market overt,[22] might appear harsh: "But we cannot think that the goods of foreigners would be protected against such laws, or that if the property once passed by virtue of them it would again be changed by being taken by the new owner into the foreigner's own country."[23]

This approach was applied by SLADE J in *Winkworth v Christie, Manson and Woods Ltd*[24] to the converse case of goods stolen in England, sold abroad and brought back to England.

> Works of art were stolen from the plaintiff's house in England. They were taken to Italy and there sold to the second defendant, an Italian, who then sent them back to England to be auctioned by the first defendants. It was agreed that, under Italian law, though probably not under English law,[25] the second defendant acquired a title to the goods, good against the world. It was crucial to decide whether title to the goods was governed by Italian law, as the law of the situs at the time of the transfer to the second defendant.

SLADE J upheld the law of the situs rule even though it seemed hard on the plaintiff to see goods which had been stolen from him in England being validly offered for sale in

---

[20] (1860) 5 H & N 728 at 744–745. See, more recently, *Pattni v Ali and Dinky International SA* [2006] UKPC 51.

[21] Eg *Winkworth v Christie, Manson and Woods Ltd* [1980] Ch 496.

[22] The market overt rule was abolished by the Sale of Goods (Amendment) Act 1994, s 1, but not with retrospective effect.

[23] (1860) 5 H & N 728 at 744; and see at 741, 743. In *Alcock v Smith* [1892] 1 Ch 238 at 267, KAY LJ said: "The goods of a foreigner sold in market overt by one who had no title to them could not be recovered from the purchaser." It seems likely that such a view would also be taken of transfers under such provisions as the Sale of Goods Act 1979, s 25, the Hire Purchase Act 1964, s 27 and the Factors Act 1889, ss 2, 8 and 9 (the 1889 and 1964 Acts as amended by the Consumer Credit Act 1974, s 192, Sch 4, Pt 1).

[24] [1980] Ch 496; Carruthers (2005), paras 3.24–3.30; Carter (1981) 52 BYBIL 329; Knott [1981] Conv 279; and see *Todd v Armour* (1882) 9 R 901.

[25] [1980] Ch 496 at 500.

England by the defendants. The judge would not accept that there should be any exception to the rule on the basis that the goods had been returned to England: "Security of title is as important to an innocent purchaser as it is to an innocent owner whose goods have been stolen from him. Commercial convenience may be said imperatively to demand that proprietary rights to movables shall generally be determined by the lex situs."[26] Furthermore, the fact that the goods were wrongfully removed from England to Italy was held not to affect the fact that their situs at the time of the transfer to the second defendant was Italian. SLADE J was not prepared to attribute a fictional English situs to them: "Intolerable uncertainty in the law would result if the court were to permit the introduction of a wholly fictional English situs when applying the principle to any particular case, merely because the case happened to have a number of other English connecting factors."[27]

The situs rule, though correct in general,[28] is not without its exceptions.[29] It was accepted in *Winkworth*[30] that there are a number of exceptions to the rule such as, for example, the rules applicable to goods in transit with a casual or unknown situs at the relevant time.[31] Again, succession is governed by separate choice of law rules.[32] Further, the law of the situs will not be applied if there is a mandatory statutory provision of English law which the courts are required to apply; though it should be pointed out that it is very rare for an English provision to be so interpreted. However, SLADE J was prepared to accept two further exceptions. The first is where the purchaser claiming title did not act bona fide. This is a dubious exception.[33] If good faith is required by the law of the situs, as it was in the present case, this is no exception. It can only be an exception if the English requirement of good faith is to be insisted upon, notwithstanding its absence under the law of the situs. It is suggested that this exception can only be justified, if at all, as an example of the broader public policy exception and that would mean that it would not apply in every case where the English concept of good faith had not been satisfied; but only in the rare case where the application of the law of the situs in the particular circumstances was quite unacceptable to English public policy. SLADE J himself described this second public policy exception as applicable to a case "where the content of the particular foreign law on which [the defendant] relied was so outrageous that this court regarded it as wholly contrary to justice and morality".[34] This is no more than the application of a general rule of private international law.[35]

---

[26] Ibid, at 512.

[27] Ibid, at 509.

[28] See *Bank voor Handel en Scheepvaart NV v Slatford* [1953] 1 QB 248, per DEVLIN J, at 257: "There is little doubt that it is the lex situs which as a general rule governs the transfer of movables when effected contractually"; *Kuwait Airways Corpn v Iraq Airways Co* [2002] 2 AC 883, per LORD NICHOLLS of BIRKENHEAD, at 1077; and *Government of the Islamic Republic of Iran v The Barakat Galleries Ltd* [2007] EWCA Civ 1374, per Lord PHILLIPS of Worth Matravers CJ at [132].

[29] Carruthers (2005), paras 3.23–3.78.

[30] [1980] Ch 496 at 501 and 514. See Carruthers (2005), paras 8.36 et seq.

[31] See infra, pp 1221–1222.

[32] See infra, p 1264 et seq.

[33] See Carruthers (2005), paras 8.38–8.46. Also *Glencore International AG v Metro Trading International Inc* [2001] 1 Lloyd's Rep 284, per MOORE-BICK, J at 295. Cf Knott (1981) 281.

[34] [1980] Ch 496 at 510.

[35] See supra, p 139 et seq. See also Carruthers (2005), paras 8.47–8.50.

An attempt by counsel for the claimants in *Glencore International AG v Metro Trading International Inc*[36]to have the court expand the categories of permitted exception to the situs rule was not successful. The litigation arose out of the collapse of an oil storage facility operated by the defendant ("MTI") in Fujairah, UAE.

> Each of the five claimants had entered into agreements with MTI, in terms of which they delivered oil products to MTI for storage. When MTI became insolvent the claimants asserted proprietary rights to the oil then held by MTI, and competing claims to the oil were made by several banks, and by the purchasers of various cargo parcels of fuel oil. The primary choice of law issue was this: what system of law governs title to oil delivered by the claimants to MTI, and by MTI to the purchasers, and what system of law governs any non-contractual liabilities which MTI and the purchasers may have incurred to the claimants? MTI and the purchasers alleged that the transfer of title to the oil in Fujairah was governed by the law of Fujairah (in terms of which the property had passed to MTI, and then to the purchasers). The claimants, on the other hand, sought to rely on the law which governed the contracts between themselves and MTI.

The issue was whether:

> as between the immediate parties to a contract under which goods are delivered by one party to the other, the passing of property is governed by the intention of the parties as expressed in the contract (the proper law) or by the law of the place where the property is situated (the lex situs) where these do not coincide in their effect.[37]

In the instant case, counsel for the claimant argued for the application of English law, being the proper law of the contract.[38]

Moore-Bick J, whilst recognising the attractiveness of the claimants' argument, preferred "consistency of principle . . . whether or not third party interests are involved",[39] and applied the law of Fujairah, as the situs of the oil, on the basis that, "it would be highly anomalous if questions of title to the goods were to be governed by English law as the proper law of the contract if the seller had not purported to re-sell the goods to a third party, but by . . . the lex situs if he had".[40] Arguably, however, such an approach would not be anomalous, but merely fact-sensitive, acknowledging that the dispute was between contracting parties and not merely between parties having no such contractual nexus.[41]

(b) Derivative claims

The principle of the situs rule is that title to movables acquired in one country by A under a transaction with B is good all over the world,[42] unless and until it is displaced by a new title vested in C as the result of an assignment effective by the law of the country to which the movables have been taken. As has been seen, the principle extends to a case where C

---

[36] [2001] 1 Lloyd's Rep 284. See Carruthers (2005), paras 3.60–3.77, pp 249, 257–272.

[37] Ibid, per Moore-Bick, J, at 290.

[38] Ibid, at 294.

[39] Ibid, at 295.

[40] Ibid.

[41] Carruthers (2005), para 3.75.

[42] *Simpson v Fogo* (1863) I Hem & M 195 at 222 where Page-Wood V-C said: "A good title acquired in one country shall be a good title all over the globe."

claims derivatively from one of the parties to the earlier transaction. This type of problem often arises from the conditional sale.[43]

> Suppose, for instance, that a car is delivered by A to B under a hire-purchase transaction concluded in England. By English law, which is both the law of the situs and the proper law of the transaction, the ownership of the car remains in A until all the instalments of the price have been paid. B takes the car to the Netherlands and sells it to C, a bona fide purchaser. Suppose also that Dutch internal law requires hire-purchase agreements to be recorded in a public register, and holds that whether a sale by the hirer binds the owner depends on whether the agreement has been recorded. Later C brings the car to England in the course of his holiday. A then brings an action against him claiming the return of the car or, alternatively, the payment of damages.

These facts raise the question whether the rights of the parties are determinable by Dutch or by English law. It would seem that on general principles English law should be preferred, for the alleged derivative title of C should depend on A's title from which its derivation is claimed. However, expediency demands that the bona fide assignee of movables should be protected if he acts according to the law of their situation, and there can be no doubt that a derivative title to them, recognised as valid by that law, will be recognised as valid by English law. In the present context, this means that, where there have been two transactions relating to the same subject matter, the first in one situs, the second in another situs to which the subject matter has been transferred, it is the law of the second situs that governs the conflicting claims of the parties.[44]

Two North American cases might be discussed as illustrations of the problem where goods are removed from one state to another, there having been a reservation of title in the first state. The first case is the Canadian decision in *Century Credit Corpn v Richard*:[45]

> X sold and delivered a car, in Quebec, to Y under a conditional sale agreement. This agreement reserved title in X, the unpaid seller, until full payment of the purchase price. Under Quebec law this agreement did not have to be, and was not, registered. Y took the car to Ontario and sold it to Z who was unaware of X's reservation of title. Under Ontario law such conditional sale agreements were required to be registered. Furthermore, under Ontario law, Y could pass a good title to Z despite any defects in his own title.

The Ontario court held that Z's title, good under the law of Ontario, prevailed against X. The reasoning was that, so far as the requirement of registration was concerned, X had made a valid reservation of title under Quebec law which was not affected by taking the car to Ontario. Ontario courts should recognise the validity of X's claim as against Y.[46] However, the sale of the car by Y in Ontario amounted, under Ontario law, to an overriding of X's reservation of title.

---

[43] See Schilling (1985) 34 ICLQ 86; Fawcett, Harris and Bridge, paras 18.112–18.118; and Carruthers (2005), para 3.59. For a discussion of the relevant authorities in Australia, Canada and the USA, see Davis (1964) 13 ICLQ 53; Ziegel (1967) 45 Can Bar Rev 284; Juenger (1978) 26 AJCL (Supp) 145.

[44] Davis (1964) 13 ICLQ 53, 56.

[45] (1962) 34 DLR (2d) 291; and see *Price Mobile Homes Centres Inc v National Trailer Convoy of Canada* (1974) 44 DLR (3d) 443; *Re Delisle* (1988) 52 DLR (4th) 106. For criminal law implications, see *R v Atakpu* [1993] 4 All ER (Ch D) 215, at 217–218.

[46] See, eg, *Taylor v Lovegrove* (1912) 18 ALR (CN) 22.

The second case is *Goetschius v Brightman*:[47]

> Y obtained possession of a car in California from X under a conditional sale contract by which the title remained in X until the whole price had been paid. The contract expressly provided that the car should not be removed from California. Y, however, took it to New York and there sold it to the defendant. The conditional sale was recorded neither in New York nor in California. By the domestic law of California applicable to a purely domestic case, the title of X would prevail over that of the defendant; by the equivalent law of New York the title of the defendant would be preferred. The plaintiff was the assignee of X.

Although the New York court applied its own law, as being the law of the situs, it found for the plaintiff. The judgment can be summarised as follows. The law that governs the interpretation and effect of the conditional sale is Californian law; by that law the title of the claimant is superior to that of the defendants; but, since the defendants bought the car while it was present in New York, it does not follow that New York law will recognise the superiority of the claimant's title. "No rule of comity requires this State to subordinate its public policy in regard to transfers made within the State of property situated here to the policy of the State where the owner of the property resides or where he acquired title."[48] The law of New York applies as being the law of the situs. But what is the New York rule applicable to the circumstances of this case? The law of a particular situs may prescribe that a person in the position of the present claimant may be divested of his title if the chattel has been removed out of his state with or without his consent. That, however, was not the rule in New York; by that law an owner shall not lose his title if the chattel is taken there without his consent. It is true that a conditional sale is void by New York statutory law against a purchaser unless it is filed, but this is confined to sales effected in New York, not in some other state or country.[49]

(c) Retention of title clauses[50]

There have been a number of Scottish and Irish decisions in which the effect of retention of title clauses in international contracts has had to be considered.[51] Foreign suppliers of goods have included terms in contracts of sale to Scottish or Irish buyers which purport to incorporate the provisions of the seller's law,[52] allowing him to reserve title to goods

---

[47] 245 NY 186 (1927).

[48] Ibid, at 191.

[49] In the converse case where title would not appear to have been effectively reserved in one jurisdiction and the chattel is taken to another jurisdiction where the reservation of title was effective, there is a tendency in the courts to protect the original owner's title, either by generous interpretation of the domestic law of the original jurisdiction (eg *A J Smeman Car Sales v Richardsons Pre-Run Cars* (1969) 63 QJPR 150; David (1970) 2 ACLR 50) or, apparently, of its territorial scope (eg *Marvin Safe Co v Norton* 48 NJL 410, 7 A 418 (1886); cf *Charles T Dougherty Co Inc v Krimke* 144 A 617 (1929)).

[50] North (1990) I Hague Recueil 9, 265–273; Fawcett, Harris and Bridge, paras 18.93–18.110; McCormack, *Reservation of Title* (1995) 2nd edn; and Morse [1993] JBL 168. For discussion of Directive (EC) No 2000/35 on Combating Late Payment in Commercial Transactions OJ 2000 L 200/35, see Fawcett, Harris and Bridge, paras 18.104–18.107, and Dicey, Morris and Collins, paras 33-131–33-384.

[51] *Hammer and Sohne v HWT Realisations Ltd* 1985 SLT (Sh Ct) 21; *Zahnrad Fabrik Passau GmbH v Terex Ltd* 1986 SLT 84; *Armour v Thyssen Edelstahlwerke AG* [1991] 2 AC 339; *Re Interview Ltd* [1975] IR 382; *Kruppstaal AG v Quitmann Products Ltd* [1982] ILRM 551.

[52] Often the foreign law is not pleaded, eg *Aluminium Industrie Vaassen BV v Romalpa Aluminium Ltd* [1976] 1 WLR 676; *Emerald Stainless Steel Ltd v South Side Distribution Ltd* 1983 SLT 162; *Deutz Engines Ltd v Terex*

which he has delivered until they have been fully paid for. Almost inevitably in this type of case, the situs of the goods will change with their delivery, raising issues as to what law is to govern the operation of the reservation of title clause. This may be illustrated by *Zahnrad Fabrik Passau GmbH v Terex Ltd*:[53]

> Plaintiffs in Germany agreed to supply vehicle components to a manufacturer in Scotland under a contact containing a reservation of title clause, the law governing the contract appearing to be German law. The components were used in the construction of earth-moving equipment and, when the Scottish buyer became insolvent,[54] the plaintiffs claimed title to the goods supplied by them.

Notwithstanding the fact that German law may have been the law governing the contract, the court concluded that, as the dispute was as to title to the goods, this issue fell to be decided by Scots law as that of the situs of the goods. The reason given for applying Scots law was that title was alleged by the defendants to have been acquired in Scotland by accession once the components were included in the equipment. A fuller analysis might have been to ask whether title was properly reserved in Germany when that was the situs of the goods and then to ask, when the goods were moved to Scotland, whether the reserved title was overridden by accession under the law of the new situs.[55]

(d) Meaning of "the law of the situs"

In determining the meaning and content of the law of the situs, there are two problems to consider. The first is whether, when English law refers to the law of the situs, the doctrine of renvoi[56] applies; ie will the English court apply the law, not of the situs itself, but of whichever country is selected as applicable by the choice of law rules of the law of the situs? Some tentative support for the application of renvoi in this context can be derived from *Winkworth v Christie, Manson and Woods Ltd* where SLADE J said: "It is theoretically possible that the evidence as to Italian law would show that the Italian court would itself apply English law. In this event I suppose it would be open to the plaintiff to argue that English law should, in the final result, be applied by the English court by virtue of the doctrine of renvoi."[57]

The question whether renvoi should be applied with regard to movable property arose in *The Islamic Republic of Iran v Berend*,[58] a case concerning the disputed ownership of a fragment of limestone relief believed to originate from fifth century BC Persepolis. The defendant claimed to have acquired title to the fragment when it was delivered to her in Paris in 1974, following purchase at auction in New York. EADY J was required to address the question whether, as a matter of English private international law, in determining the

---

Ltd 1984 SLT 273; *Armour v Thyssen Edelstahlwerke AG* [1991] 2 AC 339 at 350; or the parties may agree (rightly or wrongly) that the foreign law is the same as that of the forum, as in *E Pfeiffer Weinkellerei-Weineinkauf GmbH & Co v Arbuthnot Factors Ltd* [1988] 1 WLR 150.

[53] 1986 SLT 84.

[54] See now Council Regulation (EC) No 1346/2000 on Insolvency Proceedings, Art 7.

[55] If there is no further act in the second situs, the issue then will be whether the law of that situs accepts a reservation of title valid under the law of the first situs, see *Armour v Thyssen Edelstahlwerke AG* [1991] 2 AC 339.

[56] Supra, Chapter 5.

[57] [1980] Ch 496 at 514. See Carruthers (2005), paras 1.43–1.45.

[58] [2007] EWHC 132 (QB).

question of title to the fragment as movable property situated in France at the time of the event said to confer title, the English court should apply (as the defendant contended) only the relevant provisions of French domestic law, or (as the claimant contended) the relevant French conflict of laws rules as well as any relevant substantive provisions of French domestic law. His Lordship considered that, in the absence of binding authority to the effect that the renvoi doctrine should apply to such questions: "Whether or not it should apply in any given circumstances is largely a question of policy."[59] As a matter of policy, EADY J saw no room for the introduction of renvoi to problems concerning tangible movable property.[60] Accordingly, title to the fragment was to be determined in accordance with French domestic law, in terms of which the defendant was held to have acquired valid title in 1974.

The second problem is illustrated by the reasoning in *Goetschius v Brightman*.[61] It concerns the identification of the substantive rules which are to be applied once the appropriate legal system has been selected. The English judge must apply the law of the situs, but this will not necessarily be the same law as a court at the situs would apply to a domestic case containing no foreign element.[62] This simple truism, that the law of the situs means the law that a court at the situs would apply to the case in hand and not necessarily the domestic law applicable to a purely domestic case, illustrates the correct role of private international law so far as individual assignments of movables are concerned. Its role is to choose what law shall determine the conflicting claims of the parties. Its function in this regard is completed as soon as it has ruled that the law of the situs governs. Once this ruling has been given, ie once the choice of law has been made, we pass from the sphere of private international law; and it merely remains for the English court to ascertain as a fact what particular principle a court at the situs would follow in the actual circumstances.[63] Although this seems to be an obvious and elementary observation, it is sometimes overlooked. In dealing with the choice of law problem that arises where the subject matter of a hire-purchase agreement is removed to a foreign country and there sold, authors sometimes say that the governing law depends on whether the removal was with or without the consent of the owner. If the removal was without his consent, they say that the question arising between the owner and the purchaser is governed by the law to which the hire-purchase agreement is subject; otherwise it is governed by the domestic rule of the law of the situs. This distinction, however, forms no part of the English rule for the choice of law. The law of the situs of the goods at the time of their sale is chosen because, in the words of Wolff, "the place where a thing is situate is the natural centre of rights over it",[64] and it therefore follows that whether those rights depend on consent to removal or on any other factor is a matter solely for the law of that place to determine.

The authorities, so far as they go, appear to support the proposition that the English court, when required to apply English law as being the law of the situs in a case containing

---

[59] Ibid, at [20] and [31].
[60] Cf, with reference to intangible movable property, *Macmillan v Bishopsgate Investment Trust plc (No 3)* [1995] 1 WLR 978, per MILLETT J, at 1008. Also Carruthers (2005), para 1.44.
[61] 245 NY 186 (1927), discussed, supra, p 1217.
[62] Cook, pp 263 et seq.
[63] Eg *The Islamic Republic of Iran v Berend* [2007] EWHC 132 (QB), per EADY J, at [32]–[33], [57]–[58].
[64] *Private International Law* (1950) 2nd edn, p 512.

a foreign element, does not necessarily apply the ordinary domestic law of England. *Dulaney v Merry & Son*,[65] though it concerned a general assignment, may be given by way of analogy:

> Two domiciled Americans executed a deed in Maryland by which they assigned all their property wherever situate to another domiciled American for the benefit of their creditors. The deed was valid by the law of Maryland, but it was not registered under the English Deeds of Arrangement Act 1887.

The question was whether the assignee was entitled to goods situated in England. This was determinable by the English law of the situs. Had a similar assignment been effected in England between English traders concerning goods situated in England alone, there is no doubt that the deed would have been void. But this was a private international law case, and therefore a necessary inquiry was whether the English statute was designed to strike at all assignments, wherever made, affecting goods in England, or whether its operation was confined to assignments made in England. CHANNELL J said that the question before him reduced itself to the construction of the 1887 Act; he concluded that the policy of the Act was not to bring within its provisions an assignment by foreign debtors affecting goods abroad as well as goods in England. By internal English law, therefore, the Maryland assignment was valid with regard to the English goods.

(e) Attachment of movables by creditors

The attachment of movables by a creditor is also controlled by the law of the situs. The creditor enjoys the rights recognised by the law of the country where the movables are situated at the time of the attachment.[66] Those rights prevail against all persons claiming under some other law.[67]

The principle is illustrated by *Inglis v Robertson*,[68] where the facts were these:

> G, a domiciled Englishman, the owner of whisky stored in a warehouse at Glasgow, held delivery warrants issued by the warehouse-keeper stating that the whisky was held to G's order or "assigns by endorsement hereon". In return for a loan, G delivered in London to Inglis, an English merchant, a letter of hypothecation stating that the whisky was deposited with him as security for the loan, with power of sale. He indorsed the warrants and handed them to Inglis. Inglis gave no notice of his right to the warehouse-keeper. Robertson, claiming as personal creditor of G, arrested the whisky in the hands of the warehouse-keeper.

Presuming that by English law Inglis, claiming through G, had a better right to the whisky than Robertson, would that conclude the matter in his favour? It would not do so if Scots law were applicable, for the rule in Scotland was that a pledgee who wished to make his pledges effective in such circumstances had to give notice to the warehouse-keeper, otherwise his right was subordinated to the claims of the pledgor's creditor.

---

[65] [1901] 1 KB 536.

[66] But, for the distinction between the assignment of a movable and its attachment, see Lalive, op cit, p 156.

[67] *Liverpool Marine Credit Co v Hunter* (1867) LR 4 Eq 62; on appeal 3 Ch App 479; cf Lalive, op cit, p 69. See also Council Regulation (EC) No 1346/2000 on Insolvency Proceedings, Arts 5 (third parties' rights in rem) and 6 (set-off).

[68] [1898] AC 616.

The House of Lords gave judgment for Robertson. After stating that Robertson had done what was necessary by Scots law to acquire a real right against the whisky, Lord WATSON proceeded as follows:

> It would . . . be contrary to the elementary principles of international law, and . . . without authority, to hold that the right of a Scottish creditor when so perfected can be defeated by a transaction between his debtor and the citizen of a foreign country which would be according to the law of that country, but is not according to the law of Scotland, sufficient to create a real right in the goods.[69]

(f) Goods in transit

The transfer of movables while they are in course of transit raises a difficult question of choice of law.[70] Suppose, for instance, that goods have been dispatched overland from London to Vienna, and that before reaching their destination they have been the subject of a sale or some other commercial transaction. The problems that such circumstances raise become more complex if the parties have different domiciles, or if the transaction is effected in some third country, ie other than Austria or England.

So far, English courts have not had to address the issue of which law should be applied in such a case. The probable explanation is that goods in transit are generally represented by a bill of lading or other documentary symbol of ownership which is capable of an independent dealing.[71] Jurists have advocated several laws, such as the law of the situs, the law of the owner's domicile, the law of the place of ultimate destination, the law of the place of dispatch and the proper law of the particular transfer. Objections may be raised to each of these. The law of the situs, owing to its inconstancy, is an impracticable choice unless the movables have come to a definite resting-place at the time of the transfer.[72] The domicile of the owner, as well as begging the question potentially in issue (*who* is the owner?), is not a suitable criterion of the law to govern a mercantile transaction.[73] The law of the stipulated place of destination, though an appropriate choice in many circumstances, suffers from the disadvantage that it may be and frequently is altered during the course of the transit. The law of the place of dispatch is not well adapted to govern a transfer effected abroad when the transit is nearing completion. The proper law is, no doubt, suitable to govern questions dependent upon the effect of a particular transaction, but scarcely apposite to every question.

---

[69] Ibid, at 625.

[70] See *Winkworth v Christie, Manson and Woods Ltd* [1980] 1 Ch 496, per SLADE J, at 501. For a fuller discussion see Carruthers (2005), paras 1.27–1.30, and 3.31–3.35; Lalive, op cit, pp 186–193; and Wolff, pp 519–521.

[71] See, eg, the delivery warrants in *Inglis v Robertson*, supra. There is, however, no clear authority on what law governs the transfer of a bill of lading or other document of title to goods. The three possibilities seem to be the proper law of the bill of lading, the law of the situs of the bill at the time of its endorsement, and the law of the situs of the goods at that time. The point is important, since in some other countries the endorsement of a bill of lading does not pass the property in the goods. It is suggested that the correct choice is the law of the situs of the bill of lading at the time of its endorsement; see Zaphirou, op cit, pp 199–209; and Fawcett, Harris and Bridge, paras 18.78–18.92.

[72] Eg *Cammell v Sewell* (1858) 3 H & N 617; on appeal 5 H & N 728; and see *Hardwick Game Farm v Suffolk Agricultural Poultry Producers Association* [1966] 1 WLR 287 at 300; affd by the House of Lords [1969] 2 AC 31.

[73] Supra, p 1209.

The truth is that no single law can be made the exclusive arbiter of disputes arising out of a transfer of goods in transit. The problems must be broken down. A dispute between the parties to a particular transaction, as, for example, a mortgage of the goods granted by the assignee, will be governed by the proper law of the transaction.[74] If the movables come to rest sufficiently to admit of a dealing with them, as where they are seized by creditors in accordance with the local law or wrongfully sold by the carrier, the question of title must clearly be determined by the law of the situs.[75] Finally, if the transit is by sea in a single ship, there is much to be said for applying the law of the flag.[76]

(g) Gifts

Some special comment should be made on the transfer of movables by gift. The more common context for this issue to arise is that of *donatio mortis causa*—a gift in contemplation of death. Where such a gift has been characterised as a transfer of property,[77] then its validity and effect are governed by the law of the situs.[78] Even though FARWELL J in *Re Craven's Estate*[79] characterised such a gift as a testamentary disposition and applied the law of the testatrix's domicile, English law, by which law an effective parting with dominion was necessary to make the gift valid, he did not refer to the law of the situs to determine what was sufficient to pass the dominion.[80]

There is very little authority on transfer of movables by gift *inter vivos*, but it has been suggested that the validity of such transfers of property should be governed by the law of the situs.[81] In *Cochrane v Moore*[82] a donor, apparently domiciled and resident in England, purported, by words of gift spoken in England, to give to the defendant a quarter share in a horse at all relevant times stabled in Paris. Later, the plaintiff advanced money on the security of the horse and, when the horse was sold, he claimed that he was entitled to the whole proceeds of the sale. The issue whether any title had passed by the gift was decided solely by reference to English law, under which delivery was held to be necessary. However, as French law was not pleaded or referred to, the case is hardly strong authority against the application of the law of the situs.

The American decision in *Morson v Second National Bank of Boston*[83] is of interest in this context. The donor, whilst travelling in Italy with the donee, handed her an envelope containing shares in a Massachusetts company, thus purporting to transfer to her the title to the shares; later, the donor, whilst still in Italy, signed and delivered the stock certificate to the donee. This was adequate under Massachusetts law, but not under Italian law, to effect transfer of legal title to the shares. It was concluded by the Massachusetts court that the law of the situs should determine whether there had been a completed gift of a

---

[74] Cf *North Western Bank v Poynter* [1895] AC 56.
[75] *Cammell v Sewell* (1860) 5 H & N 728.
[76] Cf *Lloyd v Guibert* (1865) LR 1 QB 115.
[77] See Lalive, op cit, pp 26–29.
[78] *Re Korvine's Trust* [1921] 1 Ch 343.
[79] [1937] Ch 423 and see the fuller report in (1937) 53 TLR 694.
[80] Ibid, at 430; and see (1937) 53 TLR 694 at 698.
[81] Zaphiriou, op cit, pp 57–58. See, however, Carruthers (2005), para 3.12, for a situation where application of the situs rule may be inappropriate.
[82] (1890) 25 QBD 57.
[83] 306 Mass 589, 29 NE 2d 19 (1940).

tangible chattel and, had the shares been tangible chattels, Italian law, as the law of the situs, would have governed. This rule for the choice of law was, however, inapplicable since a transfer of shares fell to be governed by the law of the country in which the issuing company had been incorporated. On the other hand, the validity of the transfer of the actual certificate was subject to the law of the situs.[84]

(h) Cultural property[85]

Since 1970, there has been a developing landscape of regulation of what may be termed cultural property. The area is dominated by two international conventions, the 1970 UNESCO Convention on the Means of Prohibiting and Preventing the Illicit Import, Export and Transfer of Ownership of Cultural Property, and the 1995 UNIDROIT Convention on Stolen or Illegally Exported Cultural Objects.[86] To complement the United Kingdom's treaty obligations under the 1970 Convention, there has been created in England and Wales, by virtue of the Dealing in Cultural Objects (Offences) Act 2003, the criminal offence of trading in cultural objects in designated categories from desig-nated countries, which have been stolen, illegally excavated, or illegally exported from those countries. Moreover, at a European level, a 1993 Directive on the Return of Cultural Objects Unlawfully Removed from the Territory of a Member State[87] has been imple-mented in the United Kingdom by means of The Return of Cultural Objects Regulations 1994.[88]

The 1970 Convention and the 1994 Regulations impose duties only upon states, and not upon individuals. Consequently, recovery of cultural property is dependent upon state intervention, and property must be explicitly designated by a state if it is to warrant pro-tection under either instrument.

In practice, rules of private international law still govern legal questions arising in the United Kingdom concerning title to cultural property,[89] and to date no special choice of law rules have been introduced in the United Kingdom in respect of dealings with such property.[90] Anti-seizure legislation, however, was introduced in Part 6 of the Tribunals, Courts and Enforcement Act 2007 (Protection of Cultural Objects on Loan),[91] in terms of which protection from seizure and forfeiture is conferred on certain cultural objects

---

[84] The rules as to assignment of shares in English private international law are discussed infra, p 1244 et seq.

[85] See, generally, Carruthers (2005), Chapter 5.

[86] The 1970 Convention entered into force in the United Kingdom on 1 November 2002. The United Kingdom is not a party to the 1995 Convention. There are, in addition, various instruments concerning the import and export control of cultural objects.

[87] Council Directive (EEC) No 93/7, as amended.

[88] SI 1994/501, as amended by SI 1997/1719 and SI 2001/3972. See also Commission Proposal COM (2007) 873 final (11 January 2008).

[89] See eg *Government of the Islamic Republic of Iran v The Barakat Galleries Ltd* [2007] EWCA Civ 1374.

[90] See, in contrast, *The Islamic Republic of Iran v Berend* [2007] EWHC 132 (QB), in which evidence was led regarding a proposed exception (application of the law of the state of origin) to the French choice of law rule (application of the law of the situs). For an example of a special choice of law rule for cultural property, see the Belgian *Code de droit international privé* (16 July 2004), Art 90; cf Carruthers (2005), pp 265–272. Consider also the role and work of the United Kingdom's Spoliation Advisory Panel, created in 2000 to help to resolve claims in respect of cultural objects looted during the Nazi era and now held in national collections; to date the Panel has reported upon seven claims (see generally http://www.culture.gov.uk/what_we_do/Cultural_property/sap.htm).

[91] Ss 134–138.

("protected objects"[92]), which have been brought to the United Kingdom from overseas for public display in a temporary exhibition at a museum or gallery. Protected objects may not be seized or forfeited[93] unless by virtue of an order made by a court in the United Kingdom in circumstances where the court is required to make the order by reason of a Community obligation or any international treaty.[94]

(i) Human rights[95]

Article 1 of Protocol No 1 to the European Convention on Human Rights, implemented in the United Kingdom by means of the Human Rights Act 1998, provides that:

> Every natural or legal person is entitled to the peaceful enjoyment of his possessions. No one shall be deprived of his possessions except in the public interest and subject to the conditions provided for by law and by the general principles of international law.

> The preceding provisions shall not, however, in any way impair the right of a State to enforce such laws as it deems necessary to control the use of property in accordance with the general interest to secure the payment of taxes or other contributions or penalties.[96]

It is reasonable to inquire whether an English forum's strict application of the situs rule, where the effect of application is to deprive an "innocent" owner of his right to the peaceful enjoyment of his possessions, might be said to violate Article 1 of Protocol No 1. Where, by virtue of the situs rule, a deprived owner has no right of action or recourse in respect of his property, there would appear to be an *ex facie* violation of his proprietary rights. Legitimate interference with the exercise of the right to peaceful enjoyment of possessions must pursue an aim in the public interest. Arguably, however, the right to peaceful enjoyment does not attach to property which, by application of the situs rule, is deemed to belong to another.

---

92 Ie those which satisfy the conditions set out in the Tribunals, Courts and Enforcement Act 2007, s 134(2).

93 In respect of which, see s 135(3).

94 S 135(1). Eg "where . . . the court is asked to enforce an order for the seizure of an object made by the courts of another country to confiscate proceeds of crime" (Explanatory Notes to the Tribunals, Courts and Enforcement Act 2007, para 625).

95 See, generally, Carruthers (2005), paras 8.71–8.76.

96 See, eg, *Scotts of Greenock Ltd and Lithgows Ltd v United Kingdom* (1986) A 102; *Agosi v United Kingdom* (1986) A 108; *National and Provincial Building Society and Ors v United Kingdom* [1997] STC 1466.

Chapter 30

The Assignment of Intangible Movables

1. INTRODUCTION[1]

Intangible movables may be divided into rights which are mere rights of action, and rights which are represented by some document or writing that is not only capable of delivery but in the modern commercial world is negotiated as a separate physical entity. A debt, arising from a loan or from an ordinary commercial contract, is an example of the first class; while the second class is chiefly exemplified by negotiable instruments and shares. It is proposed here to keep the two classes separate, and to deal first with debts, secondly with negotiable instruments, and thirdly with shares and securities.[2]

---

[1] See, generally, Carruthers (2005), Chapter 6; Benjamin (2000), Chapter 1; and Ooi (2003), Chapters 1–5.
[2] On issues relating to intellectual property, see Fawcett and Torremans, *Intellectual Property and Private International Law* (1998).

2. DEBTS[3]

(a) The situs of a debt[4]

We have seen that the determination of the situs of immovable and tangible movable property may be necessary in order to determine the applicable law. It is possible also that a debt may be deemed by English law to have a definite locality of its own for several different purposes, such as the exercise of jurisdiction,[5] the payment of taxes, and the grant of probate or of letters of administration.[6] The test by which the locality is determined has been explained by ATKIN LJ in the following words:

> The test in respect of simple contracts was: Where was the debtor residing? . . . The reason why the residence of the debtor was adopted as that which determined where the debt was situate was because it was in that place where the debtor was that the creditor could, in fact, enforce payment of the debt.[7]

This rule, that an intangible movable, such as a right to recover a loan[8] or money due under an insurance policy,[9] is situated in the country where the debtor resides,[10] because that is where it can be enforced,[11] is a general but not a universal rule. It has been held that a debt which arises under an irrevocable letter of credit is situated in the place where it is in fact payable against the documents,[12] rather than the place of residence of the bank. The general rule of reference to the residence of the debtor encounters an apparent difficulty where, as will often occur in the case of a company, the residence extends to two or more countries. Although the place of residence is chosen because it is there that recovery by action is possible, eg being where the company can be found for service,[13] it is not clear what the situs of a debt is (if any) where a country in which the debt may be payable is not that of the residence of the debtor. One view is that the residence of the debtor is "an essential element in deciding the situs of the debt".[14] If, however, the debtor resides in two or more countries, then it is suggested that the debt is situated in the one in which "it is required to be paid by an express or implied provision of the contract or, if there is no such provision, where it would be paid according to the

---

[3] Moshinsky (1992) 109 LQR 591.

[4] Rogerson [1990] CLJ 441; and Carruthers (2005), paras 1.31–1.42.

[5] Kaye [1989] JBL 449.

[6] See, eg, *A-G v Bouvens* (1838) 4 M & W 171 at 191; *Stamps Comrs v Hope* [1891] AC 476 at 481–482; *A-G v Lord Sudeley* [1896] 1 QB 354 at 360–361; *Re Maudslay, Sons and Field* [1900] 1 Ch 602; Falconbridge (1935) 13 Can Bar Rev 265.

[7] *New York Life Insurance Co v Public Trustee* [1924] 2 Ch 101 at 119; *Kwok Chi Leung Karl v Comr of Estate Duty* [1988] 1 WLR 1035 at 1040. See, however, Carruthers (2005), paras 8.67–8.70.

[8] *Re Helbert Wagg & Co Ltd's Claim* [1956] Ch 323.

[9] *New York Life Insurance Co v Public Trustee* [1924] 2 Ch 101; *Jabbour v Custodian of Israeli Absentee Property* [1954] 1 WLR 139.

[10] *Swiss Bank Corpn v Boehmische Industrial Bank* [1923] 1 KB 673 at 678; *Sutherland v German Property Administrator* (1933) 50 TLR 107.

[11] *Alloway v Phillips* [1980] 1 WLR 888. In *Brooks Associates Inc v Basu* [1983] QB 220, it was held that a debt due from the National Savings Bank could be attached in England even though the head office of the Bank was in Scotland.

[12] *Power Curber International Ltd v National Bank of Kuwait SAK* [1981] 1 WLR 1233 at 1240.

[13] *Kwok Chi Leung Karl v Comr of Estate Duty* [1988] 1 WLR 1035 at 1041.

[14] *Deutsche Bank und Gesellschaft v Banque des Marchands de Moscou* (1930) (unreported), CA, cited in *Re Helbert Wagg & Co Ltd's Claim* [1956] Ch 323 at 343.

ordinary course of business".[15] If, however, the debtor resides only in one country, the debt is situated there alone, notwithstanding that it may be expressly or implicitly payable elsewhere.[16] This does not, however, deal adequately with the case where the debtor is not resident in any country where the debt is payable. An Australian court[17] has rejected the idea that such a debt has no situs and relied on the second part of the above quotation's reference to the place of payment in the ordinary course of business, notwithstanding the fact that the debtor is not resident there.

(b) The various theories

The conflict of opinion that impedes the search for the proper law to govern an assignment of tangible movables has been equally evident in the corresponding case of debts. Various theories have been propounded advocating the following legal systems: the law of the place where the creditor is domiciled; the law of the place where the debt may be said to have an artificial situation; the law of the place where the assignment is made; the proper law of the assignment; and the proper law of the transaction that created the debt.

There appears to be neither authority nor reason for choosing the law of the domicile as such, either of the creditor or the debtor, as the law to govern an assignment of a debt, and in fact cases may be put in which the choice would lead to absurdity.[18]

> If a domiciled Englishman, having acquired a right to receive a sum of money from a Belgian by reason of some commercial transaction governed by the law of France, were to assign that debt first to one man in Italy and then to another in Switzerland, it is difficult to adduce any principle that would justify the settlement of a dispute between the parties according to the law either of England or of Belgium. On the contrary, the assignee of a debt could not reasonably be expected to realise that he was subjecting his rights to the law of the domicile of either the creditor or the debtor, especially as the place of domicile might well be an unknown quantity.

As we have seen, a debt may possess a definite, though artificial, situation for certain purposes. This does not, however, necessarily imply that its assignment should be governed by the law of its situs, and there is authority rejecting reference to the law of the situs.[19]

English judges have more regularly said that an assignment is to be governed by the law of the place where it is executed.[20] Another theory is that the governing system is the

---

[15] *Jabbour v Custodian of Absentee's Property of State of Israel* [1954] 1 WLR 139 at 146; and see *Re Russo-Asiatic Bank* [1934] Ch 720; *Rossano v Manufacturers' Life Insurance Co Ltd* [1963] 2 QB 352 at 378–380. A debt due from a bank to a customer, for instance, is deemed by the general law to be situated at the branch where the account is kept: *Clare & Co v Dresdner Bank* [1915] 2 KB 576; *Joachimson v Swiss Bank Corpn* [1921] 3 KB 110 at 127; *Société Eram Shipping Co Ltd v Cie Internationale de Navigation and Ors* [2004] 1 AC 260, per Lord Hobhouse of Woodborough, at [73]; *Kuwait Oil Tanker Co SAK v Qabazard* [2004] 1 AC 300; and *Wight and Ors v Eckhardt Marine GmbH* [2004] AC 147.

[16] *Re Helbert Wagg & Co Ltd's Claim* [1956] Ch 323.

[17] *Cambridge Credit Corpn Ltd v Lissenden* (1987) 8 NSWLR 411.

[18] Carruthers (2005), paras 6.19–6.21.

[19] *Re Anziani* [1930] 1 Ch 407; *Macmillan Inc v Bishopsgate Investment Trust plc (No 3)* [1996] 1 WLR 387 at 401, and *Raiffeisen Zentralbank Österreich v Five Star General Trading LLC* [2001] EWCA Civ 68; [2001] QB 825, per Mance LJ, at [38]; Carruthers (2005), paras 6.24–6.30.

[20] *Lee v Abdy* (1886) 17 QBD 309; *Alcock v Smith* [1892] 1 Ch 238; *Embiricos v Anglo-Austrian Bank* [1905] 1 KB 677; *Republica de Guatemala v Nunez* [1927] 1 KB 669; *Re Anziani* [1930] 1 Ch 407. But see criticism in

lex actus, ie the law of the country with which the assignment is most closely connected.[21] This is preferable to the law of the place of acting, since it does not depend on the chance place of execution, but nevertheless it would seem to be less convenient than still another law which will now be discussed.

It is submitted that there is an obvious answer to the question—What is the most appropriate law to govern questions arising from the voluntary assignment of a debt as an intangible movable? The appropriate law is not the law governing the validity of the assignment, but the law governing the validity of the original transaction out of which the debt arose.[22] It is reasonable and logical to refer certain questions relating to a debt to the transaction in which it has its source and to the legal system which governs that transaction. If the transaction under which A lends money or sells goods to B is connected with no other country but England, A acquires a right that is admittedly governed by English law. The right thus created under the aegis of English law should, so far as its assignability is concerned, be governed throughout its existence by English law. Again, reference to such law is logical to determine most questions of priorities.[23] This is not to deny that certain questions might be determinable by the governing law of the assignment itself, as for example those concerned with the formal validity of a particular assignment and arising between the parties or their representatives.[24] But when the question travels beyond these boundaries—when, for example, it is denied that the right is capable of assignment—a solution must obviously be sought elsewhere. What is more reasonable than to refer to the law that admittedly continues to govern the subject matter of the assignment? One undeniable merit of this is that, where there have been assignments in different countries, no confusion can arise from a conflict of laws since all questions are referred to a single legal system. The same merit is not shared by the law of the situs, since this follows the residence of the debtor and is not therefore a constant.

An illustration may demonstrate the logic of the application of the law governing the validity of the original transaction out of which the debt arose:

> If an Englishman contracts a debt as a result of the purchase of goods from another Englishman in London, his obligation, if expanded in words, is to pay not only the seller but also an assignee of the seller, provided, however, that the assignment is regarded as good by English law. What governs his liability to the seller must also govern his liability to any person deriving title from the seller.

In such a case the attention of the debtor, when he assumes that role, is confined solely to the legal system under which he contracts the obligation, and the reasonable inference is that any transfer of the obligation made by the creditor shall be governed by the law of England as being the legal system to which the subject matter of the transfer owes its existence.

Macmillan Inc v Bishopsgate Investment Trust plc (No 3) [1996] 1 WLR 387, per STAUGHTON LJ, at 402. See also Carruthers (2005), paras 6.22–6.23.

[21] *Macmillan Inc v Bishopsgate Investment Trust plc (No 3)* [1996] 1 WLR 387, per STAUGHTON LJ, at 399; *Atlantic Telecom GmbH, Noter* 2004 SLT 1031, per Lord BRODIE, at 1043. See also Carruthers (2005), paras 6.31–6.32.

[22] *Macmillan Inc v Bishopsgate Investment Trust plc (No 3)* [1996] 1 WLR 387, per STAUGHTON LJ, at 401.

[23] Infra, pp 1234–1235.

[24] Carruthers (2005), paras 6.36–6.38, and 6.46–6.48.

Let us turn from the debtor and, taking the test of the reasonable man, contemplate the attitude of mind of an assignee.

> If B, the debtor under the original transaction from which the obligation sprang, takes up his residence in Italy, and A, the creditor, makes in France an assignment of the debt to X, it is reasonable to presume that X, as a prudent businessman, will concentrate his attention on the transaction which gave rise to B's obligation to pay, for it is the benefit of that obligation of which he is a purchaser.

It will naturally occur to him that an obligation having its origin in, and drawing its protection from, English law, will in all respects be subject to that law, just as much as if the subject matter of the assignment were goods situated in England or shares in an English company. Furthermore, we should naturally expect him to inquire what is necessary under English law for the completion of an effective assignment. What would not occur to him would be to consider the law of Italy merely because of the debtor's presence in that country. It would, perhaps, be convenient to allow the law of France, as the law governing the assignment, to govern the rights of A and X *inter se*, but, to take only one example, it cannot solve a question of priorities between X and an assignee claiming under an assignment made in some other country, except in the simplest case.[25]

In conclusion, it is suggested that the most appropriate law to govern the question at any rate of priorities is the law governing the transaction by which the subject matter of the various assignments was created.[26]

(c) The modern law

Leaving theory on one side, we must examine the present state of the law governing the assignment of a debt. An initial distinction has to be drawn, because there are two types of assignment, the voluntary (which may be contractual or non-contractual[27]) and the involuntary. The former occurs where the creditor of his own volition transfers his right to another party; the latter, where his right is transferred against his will by operation of law, as, for example, where in the course of execution the debt is attached as being part of his assets.

Furthermore, the questions in which the issue is the validity or effect of an assignment fall into two classes. The issue may depend solely on the validity and effect of the assignment itself, as, for example, where the dispute relates to capacity, form or essential validity; or it may depend on the validity and effect of the original transaction by which the debt was created, as, for example, where the question is whether the debt is capable of assignment, or to which of two or more competing assignees it is payable.[28]

---

[25] Cf *Bankhaus H Aufhauser v Scotboard Ltd* 1973 SLT (Notes) 87.

[26] Cf Carruthers (2005), paras 6.39–6.40. This principle seems to have been adopted by WARRINGTON J in *Kelly v Selwyn* [1905] 2 Ch 117, infra, p 1234; and see *Banque Paribas v Cargill International SA* [1992] 1 Lloyd's Rep 96 at 100; *Macmillan Inc v Bishopsgate Investment Trust plc (No 3)* [1996] 1 WLR 387 at 401. Contrast Goode, *Commercial Law* (1995) 3rd edn, pp 1128–1130 who would apply the law of the situs of the debt; and Moshinsky (1992) 108 LQR 591 at 613.

[27] Carruthers (2005), paras 6.12–6.17.

[28] On the distinction between an "original parties dispute" (where the problem arising stems from the original relationship between the debtor and his creditor) and a "remote parties dispute" (where the problem arising

(i) Voluntary assignments

The source of the modern law concerning the voluntary, contractual assignment of a right is the Contracts (Applicable Law) Act 1990 and Article 12 of the (1980) Rome Convention on the Law Applicable to Contractual Obligations, which is implemented by the Act.[29] This has made a major improvement to the relevant choice of law rules where the voluntary assignment is effected by a contract between assignor and assignee, having "the welcome effect of replacing a highly unsatisfactory and retrograde jurisprudence with rules which are at once both logical and practically defensible".[30]

(a) Contractual assignments—questions dependent solely on the validity and effect of the assignment[31]

Issues of form and essential validity are governed by Article 12(1) of the Rome Convention, which provides:

> The mutual obligations of assignor and assignee under a voluntary assignment of a right against another person ("the debtor") shall be governed by the law which under this Convention applies to the contract between the assignor and assignee.[32]

It will be seen that the effect of this provision is to require the application, to most questions which arise between assignor and assignee, of the law which governs the validity and effect of the contract between them.[33] So, in the case of essential validity, reference must be made to the law chosen by the parties where a choice is made or, in the absence of choice, to that determined by reference to the presumptions in Article 4 of the Convention.[34] This general approach confirms the view most recently adopted by the English courts.[35] Turning to formalities, the assignment will be formally valid, under Article 9 of the Convention,[36] if it satisfies the formal requirements of the governing law, or of the law of the place where it was concluded if both parties were in the same country, or, if they were in different countries, of the law of one of those countries.[37]

---

stems from the terms of the contract by which the debt is assigned), see Carruthers (2005), paras 6.41–6.62. The distinction between the two types of dispute is long-standing (*Dinwoodie's Executrix v Carruthers' Executrix* (1895) 23 R 234, at 239; *Scottish Provident Institution v Cohen* (1888) 16 R 112, at 113; *Scottish Provident Institution v Robinson* (1892) 29 SLR 733 at 734; and *Bankhaus H Aufhauser v Scotboard Ltd* 1973 SLT (Notes) 87, at 89), and is affirmed by Art 12 of the Rome Convention.

[29] Supra, p 667 et seq. Art 13 deals with the related matter of subrogation (which may result from both voluntary and involuntary assignment) but is limited to rights which are contractual in nature; see Fletcher, *Conflict of Laws and European Community Law* (1982), p 177. Cf Rome I Regulation, Art 14, which collapses into a single article, the provisions (modified and expanded) of Arts 12 and 13 of the Rome Convention.

[30] Fletcher, op cit, p 176.

[31] Carruthers (2005), paras 6.13–6.16.

[32] It might have been thought clearer to deal with the rights as between assignor and assignee after examining, for example, the question of assignability (Art 12(2)); but the reasons for this order are explained in the Report on the Rome Convention by Giuliano and Lagarde, OJ 1980 C 282/31, 34–35. No significant changes to the substance of the rule in Art 12(1) are proposed in the Rome I Regulation (Art 14(1); supra, p 669 et seq).

[33] Cf approach in Australia: *Pacific Brands Sport Leisure Pty Ltd v Underworks Pty Ltd* (2006) 149 FCR 395; [2006] FCAFC 40; and also (re non-contractual rights), *Salfinger v Niugini Mining (Australia) Pty Ltd (No 3)* [2007] FCA 1532.

[34] Supra, p 707 et seq. Cf Rome I Regulation, Art 4.

[35] *Trendtex Trading Corpn v Crédit Suisse* [1980] QB 629 at 658; affd on other grounds [1982] AC 679; and see *Lee v Abdy* (1886) 17 QBD 309 at 313; contrast *Re Anziani* [1930] 1 Ch 407.

[36] Supra, p 746 et seq. Cf Rome I Regulation, Art 11.

[37] This marks a distinct improvement on the confused state of the old law on formal validity stemming from *Republica de Guatemala v Nunez* [1927] 1 KB 669.

There remains the issue of capacity[38] which, save in one limited respect,[39] falls outside the ambit of the Rome Convention. So here, as in contract generally, reference must continue to be made to common law rules, and assuming that the contractual assignment of a debt stands in this respect on the same footing as a commercial contract, then the issue of capacity is to be governed by the proper law of the contract.[40] On this basis, the governing law will be the law of the country with which the assignment itself is more closely connected. This seems correct on principle, but unfortunately, in the few cases that have raised the question, the courts have shown a preference for the law of the place of acting. In *Lee v Abdy*:[41]

A policy of life insurance issued by an English company was assigned in Cape Colony by a husband to his wife. The assignment was valid by English law, but was invalid by the law of Cape Colony, where the parties were domiciled, because the assignee was the wife of the assignor. The insurance company, when sued by the wife for the recovery of the money, pleaded that the assignment was void.

It was held that the law of Cape Colony governed the assignment. There is much to be said for the view that the proper law of the assignment was the law of the Cape, for it was there that the parties were domiciled and the assignment was effected, but the judgments leave little doubt that the mechanical test of the place of the transaction was applied by the court.

In *Republica de Guatemala v Nunez*,[42] SCRUTTON LJ said that: "in cases of personal property, the capacity of the parties to a transaction has always been determined either by the *lex domicilii* or the law of the place of the transaction; and where, as here, the two laws are the same it is not necessary to decide between them".[43] It is a little surprising to meet the suggestion that the capacity of a person to enter into a commercial contract is determined by the law of his domicile; little less surprising is the suggestion that the determining law is the law of the place of acting, if that expression is to be taken literally. Is an assignment by an Englishman to his wife of a debt situated in London and governed by English law to be held void, merely because he executes the instrument of transfer in Cape Town while on a short visit to South Africa?

The only question is whether the judges in these two cases meant the idea of the application of the law of the place of acting to be taken literally and rigidly, or whether they intended to indicate the law governing the assignment.[44] The law of the place of contracting has so often in the past constituted the proper law of the contract that judges have tended to adopt the former expression when their intention seems to have been to refer to the proper law. This was especially true in the late nineteenth century when *Lee v Abdy* was decided. In fact, in that case, DAY J stated the rule for contracts in language that was scarcely felicitous, namely: "The general rule, . . . is that the validity and incidence of a contract *must be determined* by the law of the place where it is entered into."[45] Just as

---

[38] Carruthers (2005), paras 6.34–6.35.
[39] Article 11, supra, pp 752–753. Cf Rome I Regulation, Art 13.
[40] Supra, pp 750–751.
[41] (1886) 17 QBD 309.
[42] [1927] 1 KB 669.
[43] Ibid, at 689; and see LAWRENCE LJ at 701.
[44] Cf Morris, *Cases on Private International Law*, (1968) 4th edn, pp 362. See Carruthers (2005), para 6.35.
[45] Emphasis added.

there has been a development in the general common law rules of contract in favour of the proper law as the law to govern capacity,[46] so there should also be a similar development in the particular context of assignment.[47]

(b) Non-contractual assignments—questions dependent solely on the validity and effect of the assignment

It has been assumed, so far, that the assignments under consideration have been effected, as is usually the case,[48] by a contract between assignor and assignee. This does not necessarily have to be the case because a voluntary assignment may be effected, for example, by non-gratuitous, unilateral obligation or by outright gift.[49] The contractual or non-contractual character of the intangible right or claim which is the subject of the assignment should not be confused with the contractual or non-contractual character of the assignment; the latter of these is the focus of this discussion. The issue arises of whether *non-contractual assignments* fall within the scope of Article 12 of the Rome Convention.[50] It will be recalled[51] that Article 12(1)[52] makes provision for the law to be applicable to the mutual obligations[53] of assignor and assignee under a voluntary assignment, but without at that point restricting the provision to contractual assignments. However, the law to be applied is that which "applies to the contract between the assignor and assignee". If there is no such contract, then the rule cannot apply, leaving one with the conclusion that the Rome Convention, which is in terms to govern "contractual obligations",[54] does not in fact govern the voluntary, non-contractual assignment of rights, even of contractual rights.[55] The consequence of this is that reference must continue to be made to the common law rules,[56] which generally have been renowned for their unintelligibility.[57] Whilst there is some evidence of recent improvement,[58] it is to be hoped that the courts will now abandon the old rules and apply the provisions of Article 12 by analogy to cases of voluntary, non-contractual assignments.[59]

(c) Questions dependent on the nature of the right assigned

The assignment of a debt may raise questions that cannot be answered without considering the legal effect of the transaction to which the debt owes its origin. In such cases it is

---

[46] Supra, pp 750–751.

[47] Cf *Lowenstein v Allen* [1958] CLY 491; and Carruthers (2005), para 6.35.

[48] Eg *Lee v Abdy* (1886) 17 QBD 309; *Trendtex Trading Corpn v Crédit Suisse* [1980] QB 629.

[49] See *Re Westerton* [1919] 2 Ch 104; *Republica de Guatemala v Nunez* [1927] 1 KB 669; *Re Anziani* [1930] 1 Ch 407.

[50] Cf Rome I Regulation, Art 14.

[51] Supra, p 1230.

[52] Cf Rome I Regulation, Art 14(1).

[53] Cf Rome I Regulation, Art 14(1), which refers to "the relationship between assignor and assignee" rather than to the "mutual obligations" of the parties.

[54] Art 1(1). Cf Rome I Regulation, Art 1(1). For non-contractual obligations, see the Rome II Regulation, in particular Art 15(e).

[55] See Carruthers (2005), para 6.16.

[56] See 11th edn of this book (1987), pp 807–815; and Carruthers (2005), paras 6.17–6.33.

[57] Note (1906/07) 20 Harv LR 636, at 637; and Fletcher, *Conflict of Laws and European Community Law* (1982), p 176.

[58] See *Trendtex Trading Corpn v Crédit Suisse* [1980] QB 629; affd on other grounds [1982] AC 679.

[59] Dicey, Morris and Collins, Rule 126(2), and para 24R-050; and Carruthers (2005), para 6.32. For non-contractual obligations, see the Rome II Regulation, in particular Art 15(e).

imperative, if a satisfactory solution is desired, to be guided exclusively by the law governing that transaction. This was the view taken in a number of common law authorities,[60] and it is the view now adopted as English law by reason of Article 12(2) of the Rome Convention which provides:

> The law governing the right to which the assignment relates shall determine its assignability, the relationship between the assignee and the debtor, the conditions under which the assignment can be invoked against the debtor and any question whether the debtor's obligations have been discharged.[61]

It will be seen that a number of different types of problem may fall to be governed by the law governing the validity of the debt, the most important of which are whether the debt may be assigned, and the issue of priorities between successive assignments. These issues may be exemplified by common law decisions.

(i) Assignability[62]

The primary question of whether the right may be assigned at all may be illustrated by *Trendtex Trading Corpn v Crédit Suisse*:[63]

> A Swiss company sued a Nigerian bank in England for failing to honour a letter of credit. The Swiss company assigned this cause of action to one of its creditors, a Swiss bank, the assignment taking place in Geneva. The Swiss company then later took proceedings in England against the Swiss bank, alleging that the assignment was void, such a right of action being incapable of assignment as it offended against English rules relating to maintenance and champerty.

The Court of Appeal held that the Swiss company's right of action against the Nigerian bank was English, having been reduced into possession by the issue of the writ in England. In examining the nature and attributes of this right of action, it was necessary to refer to the legal system under which it arose, English law.[64] Neither its content nor its characteristics could be altered merely because it had been the subject of a later transaction that in certain respects was subject to a foreign system of law. Such questions as whether the assignment was voidable for fraud or unenforceable for lack of a written memorandum

---

[60] *Compañía Colombiana de Seguros v Pacific Steam Navigation Co* [1965] 1 QB 101 at 128, 129; and see *Pender v Commercial Bank of Scotland* 1940 SLT 306; *Bankhaus H Aufhauser v Scotboard Ltd* 1973 SLT (Notes) 87.

[61] Cf Rome I Regulation, Art 14(2), in terms of which the proposed applicable law is the law governing the assigned or subrogated claim.

[62] Carruthers (2005), paras 6.06–6.10.

[63] [1980] QB 629. In relation to the assignment of non-contractual obligations in civil and commercial matters falling within the scope of the Rome II Regulation (Art 1), the law applicable to the obligation under the Regulation shall govern the question whether a right to claim damages or a remedy may be transferred, including by inheritance (Art 15(e)). The applicable law under the Rome II Regulation will govern, therefore, the matter of assignability. See supra, p 847; and Rome II Explanatory Memorandum, p 24. In relation to the assignment of non-contractual obligations which fall outside the scope of the Rome II Regulation (Art 1), the matter of assignability will be determined by the proper law of the right transferred. Whether a copyright may be assigned has been held to be determined by the law governing the creation of the copyright: *Campbell Connelly & Co Ltd v Noble* [1963] 1 WLR 252; see Wadlow, *Enforcement of Intellectual Property in European and International Law* (1998), pp 441–451; Fawcett and Torremans, *Intellectual Property and Private International Law* (1998), pp 515–517.

[64] Cf approach in Australia: *Salfinger v Niugini Mining (Australia) Pty Ltd (No 3)* [2007] FCA 1532.

might be determinable by Swiss law, but the primary and fundamental question,[65] whether the subject matter was even capable of assignment, fell to be determined by English law.[66]

(ii) Priorities

The law governing the right to which the assignment relates is the most satisfactory legal system by which to determine the ranking of competing claimants where the creditor has made more than one contractual assignment. One exception to this principle is where there is a competition between two or more assignments which derive from the same creditor and which have the same governing law, in which case the assignees' rights *inter se* may be more appropriately governed by that common governing law, where that law differs from the law governing the right to which the assignment relates.[67] A true question of priorities arises where there have been two or more valid and competing assignments, the ranking of which is doubtful, as may be illustrated by *Kelly v Selwyn*:[68]

> By an assignment executed in 1891 in New York, X (domiciled in New York) assigned to his wife an interest in certain English trust funds. Notice was not given to the trustees until twelve years later, since none was required by the law of New York. In 1894, X assigned the same interest to the plaintiff by a deed executed in England. Immediate notice of this was given to the trustees.

It was held that the plaintiff ranked first, since the rights of the claimant fell to be regulated by English law. Warrington J said:

> The ground on which I decide it is that, the fund here being an English trust fund and this being the Court which the testator may have contemplated as the Court which would have administered that trust fund, the order in which the parties are to be held entitled to the trust fund must be regulated by the law of the Court which is administering that fund.[69]

The judge's language is somewhat ambiguous, leaving it a little doubtful whether he chose English law as that of the forum, the situs or the law governing the validity of the debt.[70] It is suggested, however, that the decisive factor in the mind of the judge, if his language is considered as a whole, was that the subject matter of the assignment consisted of a trust fund, the governing law of which was English law. Such an analysis is supported

---

[65] Ibid, at 652.

[66] In the House of Lords ([1982] AC 679) the choice of law issues were not addressed with any clarity. The House of Lords took the view that, under English law, the cause of action could not be assigned, but that nevertheless it was for Swiss law to determine the effect of the invalidity of the assignment on the agreement as a whole between the parties, there being issues involved other than just the validity of the assignment. See also *Grant's Trustees v Ritchie's Executor* (1886) 13 R 646; *Pender v Commercial Bank of Scotland* 1940 SLT 306; *Companhia Colombiana de Seguros v Pacific Steam Navigation Co* [1965] 1 QB 101, per Roskill J, at 128; and *Libertas-Kommerz GmbH v Johnson* 1977 SC 191.

[67] *Scottish Provident Institution v Robinson* (1892) 29 SLR 733. See Crawford and Carruthers (2006), para 17-28; and Carruthers (2005) para 6.39–6.40.

[68] [1905] 2 Ch 117; and see *Le Feuvre v Sullivan* (1855) 10 Moo PCC 1. In *Republica de Guatemala v Nunez* [1927] 1 KB 669, there were successive assignments but they were, for different reasons, held to be invalid.

[69] Ibid, at 122.

[70] Cf *Macmillan Inc v Bishopsgate Investment Trust plc (No 3)* [1996] 1 WLR 387; and *Raiffeisen Zentralbank Österreich v Five Star General Trading LLC* [2001] EWCA Civ 68; [2001] QB 825.

by *Le Feuvre v Sullivan*[71] where the law of the forum was the law of Jersey, but English law, which would appear to have been the law governing the debt,[72] was relied on to determine priorities. This is the approach now confirmed in the Contracts (Applicable Law) Act 1990 implementing the 1980 Rome Convention on the Law Applicable to Contractual Obligations; and Article 12(2) of that Convention[73] also applies the law governing the debt to such questions as whether notice of an assignment must be given to the debtor and whether an assignee takes subject to equities.

(iii) Substance or procedure?

The question whether an assignee must add the assignor as a party to his action raises the conflict between substance and procedure.

> Suppose, for instance, that a Frenchman assigns by way of charge to another Frenchman a sum of money due from a French debtor, the assignment being made in France and according to the law of that country.

According to the rules of private international law, the assignment has universal validity. According to English domestic law, the assignment is valid, but the assignee cannot recover the money unless he makes the assignor a party to the action against the debtor. If this rule as to the adding of parties is to be regarded as a procedural rule for the purposes of private international law,[74] it is governed by the law of the forum and it must be obeyed in an action brought in England notwithstanding that it is not recognised by French law. Such old authorities as there are would indicate, however, that the rule as to the adding of parties is substantive[75] and, thus, governed by the law governing the debt.[76]

(iv) Characterisation of the issue as contractual or proprietary

The operation of Article 12 of the Rome Convention was subjected to close judicial scrutiny in *Raiffeisen Zentralbank Österreich v Five Star General Trading LLC*,[77] a case which reveals that litigants seeking to rely on the prima facie clear direction offered by Article 12 may yet stumble on the preceding obstacle of characterisation. The facts of the case were as follows:

> The claimant Austrian bank lent money to the first defendants, Dubai shipowners, to assist them in the purchase of a vessel, the "Mount I". In turn, the owners mortgaged the vessel to the claimants, agreeing to assign to the bank the policy of marine insurance in respect of the vessel. Although the insurers were French, the insurance policy was governed by English law. By deed of assignment (also governed by English law), the owners purported to assign to the claimant "all their right, title and interest in and to the insurances". Two weeks after the assignment, the Mount I collided with a second vessel, causing the latter to sink. The owners of the sunken

---

[71] (1855) 10 Moo PCC 1.

[72] Ibid, at 13.

[73] Cf Rome I Regulation, Art 14(2).

[74] See supra, p 75 et seq.

[75] *Innes v Dunlop* (1800) 8 Term Rep 595; *O'Callaghan v Thomond* (1810) 3 Taunt 82; cf *Regas Ltd v Plotkins* (1961) 29 DLR (2d) 282.

[76] Rome Convention, Art 12(2).

[77] [2001] EWCA Civ 68, [2001] QB 825, [2001] 1 Lloyd's Rep 597.

vessel, together with the Taiwanese owners of its cargo, sought, in France, attachment orders in respect of the Mount I insurance proceeds. Accordingly, the claimant bank commenced proceedings, in England, against the Dubai owner, the French insurers, and the Taiwanese cargo owners, seeking various declarations, including one that, as from the date of the assignment, the owners had no right, title or interest in or to the insurances, or to moneys payable thereunder, and that, as from the same date, the bank was entitled to all such interests and money. The cargo owners, pleading French law, denied that the notice of assignment was valid or binding on them.

The principal issue for decision was whether the assignee of a marine insurance policy, made with French insurers, but governed by English law, was entitled to recover to the extent of his interest. According to French law, the assignment was invalid but, according to English law, it was valid. The choice of law issue was a complex one of characterisation, namely, whether the assignee's claim was to be determined by English law, as the proper law governing the underlying contract of insurance, or by French law, the law of the situs of the chose in action which had been assigned. Counsel for the claimant argued that the matter should be governed by Article 12(2) of the Rome Convention, whereas counsel for the defendant contended that, since the Convention was applicable only to contractual obligations, it did not apply to the dispute in hand. At first instance, LONGMORE J, having observed the difficulty inherent in the characterisation process,[78] concluded that certain of the issues arising in the case were contractual in nature, whereas certain others were proprietary.[79] His Lordship concluded that Article 12(2) was applicable, and, by virtue of that provision, the applicable law was deemed to be the law governing the right to which the assignment related, ie English law, the law of the underlying obligation.[80] The effect of the decision was that the claimants were entitled to the policy proceeds. The cargo owners appealed, but without success.

In the Court of Appeal, MANCE LJ appraised the conflicting contractual and proprietary analyses of the issues in dispute, which were advanced, respectively, on behalf of the respondent and the appellant. The respondent bank maintained that the issue in dispute was a contractual one, ie whether the insurance contract had been validly assigned by the owners to the bank. The appellant cargo owners, with whom the bank had no contractual nexus, maintained that the issue was essentially a proprietary one, concerning the validity against third parties of the assignment of an intangible claim against insurers. His Lordship pointed to the straitened nature of the litigants' respective approaches, stating that: "These opposing analyses both assume that the factual complex raises only one issue and, in their differing identification of that issue, emphasise different aspects of the facts. In my judgment a more nuanced analysis is required."[81] It is of note that MANCE LJ took the view that, "there is no hint in article 12(2) of any intention to distinguish between

---

[78] [2000] 2 Lloyd's Rep 684 at 687: "In the case of the sale of goods... one is entirely used to the different concepts of contract on the one hand and the transfer or conveyance of title on the other... It is much less easy to apply this analysis to intangible things... it is difficult, if not impossible, to divorce the concept of such title from the underlying contract which has created the chose in action in the first place."

[79] Ibid, at 687.

[80] Ibid, at 688.

[81] [2001] 1 Lloyd's Rep 597 at [20].

contractual and proprietary aspects of assignment. The wording appears to embrace all aspects of assignment."[82] Nevertheless, the Court of Appeal concluded that:

> Whatever might be the domestic legal position in any particular country . . . the Rome Convention now views the relevant issue—that is, what steps, by way of notice or otherwise, require to be taken in relation to the debtor for the assignment to take effect as between the assignee and debtor—not as involving any "property right", but as involving—simply—a contractual issue to be determined by the law governing the obligation assigned.[83]

Hence, the issue whether, following assignment to the bank of the benefits under the insurance policy, the French insurer had to pay the insurance proceeds to the bank as assignee, rather than to the vessel owner, was characterised as a contractual, not a proprietary, issue. In consequence, Article 12 was applicable and the tripartite dispute fell to be determined according to English law, the law governing the obligation assigned.

Although this approach is buttressed by the Giuliano and Lagarde Report,[84] characterisation of notice provisions as contractual, even vis-à-vis the debtor with whom the assignee has no contractual nexus, is a curious and anomalous conclusion. To characterise all the matters arising under Article 12(2) as contractual is rather strained. That said, to provide that the law governing the right to which the assignment relates is, by virtue of that law's relationship with the parties and their circumstances, the law which is appropriate to determine the issue in dispute, is a sensible rule of choice of law; the connecting factor and choice of law rule applied generally will be appropriate (as a matter of fact), even if characterisation of the issue as a purely contractual matter is not.

In transactions which concern intangible movable property, the borderland between contract and conveyance is more extensive than typically is the case regarding other types of property, and so a preferable approach to determination of the applicable law would be one which demands not strict characterisation of the issues arising as contractual or proprietary, but application, as the law of closest connection, of that law which governs the right to which the assignment relates.[85]

(ii) Subrogation

Article 13 of the Rome Convention concerns subrogation, and is to the effect that where a person (the "creditor") has a contractual claim upon another (the "debtor"), and a third person has a duty to satisfy the creditor, or has in fact satisfied the creditor in discharge of that duty, the law which governs the third person's duty to satisfy the creditor shall determine whether the third person is entitled to exercise against the debtor the rights which the creditor had against the debtor under the law governing their relationship and, if so, whether he may do so in full or only to a limited extent.[86] By virtue of Article 13(2), the same rule applies where several persons are subject to the same contractual claim and one of them has satisfied the creditor.

---

[82] Ibid, [45]. Contrast Giuliano & Lagarde Report (1980), comment 2 on Art 1, which reports that, "since the Convention is concerned only with the law applicable to contractual obligations, property rights... are not covered by these provisions".
[83] Ibid, at [48].
[84] At pp 34–35.
[85] Cf Plender and Wilderspin (2001), paras 11–25, and Rogerson [2000] All ER Annual Review 106.
[86] Art 13(1).

The Rome I Regulation[87] contains two provisions concerning subrogation: Article 14 (voluntary assignment and contractual subrogation) and Article 15 (legal subrogation). Article 15 reiterates, with modification, the wording of Article 13 of the Rome Convention, and is intended to apply, for example, where an insurer who has compensated a person who has suffered loss is subrogated to the victim's rights against the person who caused the loss.[88] Article 14, which is an expanded version of Article 12 of the Rome Convention, deals explicitly with contractual (ie voluntary) subrogation of claims. The Explanatory Memorandum accompanying the Commission Proposal for a Rome I Regulation justifies the expanded provision by stating that voluntary assignment and contractual subrogation "perform a similar economic function".[89]

It is worth noting in this regard the subrogation provision contained in the Rome II Regulation.[90] Article 19 of that instrument, which is in virtually identical terms to Article 15 of the Rome I Regulation, applies, *mutatis mutandis*, to the subrogation of non-contractual claims.

Multiple liability

Reference has been made to Article 13(2) of the Rome Convention, concerning multiple liability.[91] The corresponding provision in the Rome I Regulation is a freestanding Article (Article 16), which is to the effect that, if a creditor has a claim against several debtors who are liable for the same claim, and one of the debtors has already satisfied the claim in whole or in part, the law governing the debtor's obligation towards the creditor also governs the debtor's right to claim recourse from the other debtors. The other debtors may rely on the defences they had against the creditor to the extent allowed by the law governing their obligations towards the creditor. This is broadly equivalent, *mutatis mutandis*, to Article 20 of the Rome II Regulation, in respect of multiple liability for non-contractual claims.

(iii) Involuntary assignments[92]

The problem that affects private international law in the case of the involuntary assignment of a debt, as for instance where a customer's credit balance at a bank is vested by legislation in a custodian of enemy property,[93] is best illustrated by the process known formerly in England as garnishment and now by the making of a third party debt order, and in Scotland[94] and many other countries as arrestment. This is a process by which a judgment creditor attaches a sum of money that is due to the judgment debtor from a third party (formerly called the garnishee). If the necessary proceedings are taken, the court may order that the third party debtor shall pay the money direct to the judgment creditor.

In purely domestic proceedings, where the parties and the relevant transactions are connected solely with England,[95] the third party debtor is, of course, effectively discharged

---

[87] In respect of which, see generally supra, Chapter 18.
[88] Proposal for a Rome I Regulation (Commission version), Explanatory Memorandum, p 8.
[89] Ibid.
[90] In respect of which, see generally supra, Chapter 19.
[91] Supra, p 1237.
[92] See Carruthers (2005), paras 6.63–6.66.
[93] See eg *Arab Bank Ltd v Barclays Bank (Dominion, Colonial and Overseas)* [1954] AC 495. Also *Wight and Ors v Eckhardt Marine GmbH* [2004] 1 AC 147, per Lord HOFFMANN, at [12].
[94] Eg *Stewart v Royal Bank of Scotland* 1994 SLT (Sh Ct) 27. See Debt Arrangement and Attachment (Scotland) Act 2002.
[95] Cf *Brooks Associates Inc v Basu* [1983] QB 220, supra, p 1226, n 11.

from further liability once he has paid the judgment creditor. The position, however, is not so straightforward in a case containing a foreign element. The first problem arises where the third party debtor may be in one country and the debt situated in another. In debt attachment proceedings in England, it is necessary that the third party debtor be within the jurisdiction,[96] albeit temporarily, or have submitted to the jurisdiction.[97] It is not, however, necessary that the judgment debtor be within the jurisdiction nor, strictly speaking, that the debt be situated within the jurisdiction. If the debt is enforceable within the jurisdiction, even though payable elsewhere, the court has jurisdiction to make a third party debt order.[98] There is a risk in the case of a debt that is not situated within the jurisdiction that the third party debtor, having already complied with an order made in one country, will remain liable to pay his debt a second time if he is sued by the judgment debtor in a foreign court which refuses to recognise the validity of the order.[99] It had been thought that that risk was met by the court having a discretion whether or not to assume jurisdiction, being prepared to decline where the risk of the third party debtor being ordered to pay twice was real.[100] It was usually the case that the court would assume jurisdiction to make a third party debt order, confident that no such risk would materialise, as is illustrated by *Swiss Bank Corpn v Boemische Industrial Bank*.[101]

> In that case, the plaintiff had recovered judgment for a large sum of money against the defendant, a company carrying on business exclusively in Czechoslovakia. The defendant kept an account at a London bank where its balance was over £9,000. The plaintiff issued a garnishee summons against the bank. It was objected that to make a garnishee order in these circumstances would be inequitable, since the bank, if sued later in Czechoslovakia, would probably be ordered to pay the sum over again to the defendants.

The Court of Appeal nevertheless made the order in the confident belief that, having been made in the country where the debt was normally and properly recoverable, its validity and effect would not be repudiated in Czechoslovakia.

It must not be assumed, however, that where a debt is situated in England, there will never be a risk of double jeopardy and that jurisdiction always will be assumed, as is illustrated by the unusual decision in *Deutsche Schachtbau v Shell International Petroleum Co Ltd*.[102] The case concerned a garnishee order absolute (termed now a final third party debt order) made in respect of a debt situate in England. Lord GOFF, referring[103] to the court's "discretionary power" to make such an order, said[104] that it would be "inequitable" to

---

[96] CPR, r 72.1(1).

[97] *Société Eram Shipping Co Ltd v Cie Internationale de Navigation and Ors* [2004] 1 AC 260, per Lord BINGHAM of Cornhill, at [27]; *SCF Finance Co Ltd v Masri (No 3)* [1987] QB 1028; Kaye [1989] JBL 449, 455–459. See, for consideration of whether a third party debtor might be regarded as being "sued" within the meaning of the Brussels Regulation and the Brussels and Lugano Conventions, supra, Chapter 11, see Dicey, Morris and Collins, paras 24R-078–24-082.

[98] *Deutsche Schachtbau und Tiefbohrgesellschaft GmbH v Shell International Petroleum Co Ltd* [1990] 1 AC 295, CA, revsd in part, ibid, 323, HL; cf *Delaire v Delaire* [1996] 9 WWR 469.

[99] *Martin v Nadel* [1906] 2 KB 26.

[100] *SCF Finance Co Ltd v Masri (No 3)* [1987] QB 1028 at 1044; *Interpool Ltd v Galani* [1988] QB 738 at 741.

[101] [1923] 1 KB 673.

[102] [1990] 1 AC 295; see Briggs [1988] Lloyd's MCLQ 429; see also *Zoneheath Associates Ltd v China Tianjin International Economic and Technical Co-operative Corpn* [1994] CLC 348.

[103] [1990] 1 AC 295 at 350.

[104] Ibid, at 355.

make an order where there was a "real risk that [the third party] may be held liable in some foreign court to pay a second time." A majority in the House of Lords concluded that, even though the debt was situated in England, the exercise of jurisdiction in garnishment proceedings was discretionary and that it would be inequitable to exercise it in the instant case, bearing in mind that "the garnishee does not have to establish a certainty, or a very high degree of risk, of being compelled to pay the debt twice over; he has only to establish a real risk of being required to do so".[105] There is no doubt that the court's power to make an order in the case of an English debt is discretionary.[106]

Lord GOFF in *Deutsche Schachtbau* was not concerned with the court's power to refuse an order in the case of a foreign debt. That, however, was the issue which arose in *Société Eram Shipping Co Ltd v Cie Internationale de Navigation and Ors*,[107] in which the House of Lords was called to consider the power of an English court to make an order in relation to a foreign debt (in the instant case, a debt situated in Hong Kong and governed by the law of Hong Kong) and, if there were such a power, to determine the manner in which it ought to be exercised. Lord BINGHAM of Cornhill concluded:[108]

> It is not in my opinion open to the court to make an order in a case . . . where it is clear or appears that the making of the order will not discharge the debt of the third party or garnishee to the judgment debtor according to the law which governs that debt. In practical terms, it does not matter very much whether the House rules that the court has no jurisdiction to make an order in such a case or that the court has a discretion which should always be exercised against the making of an order in such a case. But the former seems to me the preferable analysis . . .[109]

The law of the situs of the debt is not only relevant in determining the question of jurisdiction, it is also relevant to the effect of the third party debt order as regards third parties.[110] If, for example, an involuntary assignment occurs after a voluntary assignment has already been made, the law of the situs determines whether the rights of the voluntary assignee have been postponed or defeated; if the involuntary assignment occurs first, the law of the situs determines what rights, if any, the voluntary assignee has acquired.

3. NEGOTIABLE INSTRUMENTS[111]

If a transfer of a negotiable instrument has been made abroad and its validity is disputed in an English action, the court is confronted with a problem of choice of law. What the choice should be depends on the manner in which the problem is analysed. It may be regarded as raising a question of form or interpretation to be governed by the Bills of

---

105 [1990] 1 AC 295, at 359.

106 *Société Eram Shipping Co Ltd v Cie Internationale de Navigation and Ors* [2004] 1 AC 260, per Lord MILLETT, at [105].

107 Ibid.

108 Ibid, at [26].

109 Cf Lord HOFFMANN, at [59]; Lord MILLETT, at [109]. See also *FG Hemisphere Associates LLC v Congo* [2005] EWHC 3103 (QBD); The Times, 27 February 2006; *Kuwait Oil Tanker Co SAK v Qabazard* [2004] 1 AC 300; and *Tasarruf Mevduati Sigorta Fonu (A Firm) v Demirel (Application to Set Aside)* [2006] EWHC 3354 (Ch); [2007] 1 Lloyd's Rep 223.

110 *Re Queensland Mercantile and Agency Co* [1891] 1 Ch 536; affd [1892] 1 Ch 219.

111 For a modern, specialised treatment, see Proctor, *International Payment Obligations* (1998), Chapter 27.

Exchange Act 1882; or as the transfer of a chattel, in which case the law of the situs will be applicable;[112] or as an assignment of a contractual right and therefore subject to the law governing the contract. *Koechlin et Cie v Kestenbaum*,[113] the leading decision on the matter, definitely treats the question as one of form or interpretation. Only the House of Lords can resolve the doubt as to whether the Court of Appeal reached this conclusion by reading too much into the earlier authorities.

The common law authorities[114] which preceded the Bills of Exchange Act 1882, with one exception,[115] showed a marked tendency to determine the validity of an indorsement by the law which governs the original contract of the acceptor or maker.

The relevant sub-sections of the Bills of Exchange Act 1882 are as follows:

72.—Where a bill drawn in one country is negotiated, accepted or payable in another, the rights, duties and liabilities of the parties thereto are determined as follows:
(1) The validity of a bill as regards requisites in form is determined by the law of the place of issue, and the validity as regards requisites in form of the supervening contracts, such as acceptance, or indorsement, or acceptance supra protest, is determined by the law of the place where such contract was made. Provided that—
(a) Where a bill is issued out of the United Kingdom it is not invalid by reason only that it is not stamped in accordance with the law of the place of issue.
(b) Where a bill, issued out of the United Kingdom, conforms as regards requisites in form, to the law of the United Kingdom, it may, for the purpose of enforcing payment thereof, be treated as valid as between all persons who negotiate, hold, or become parties to it in the United Kingdom.
(2) Subject to the provisions of this Act, the interpretation of the drawing, indorsement, acceptance, or acceptance supra protest of a bill, is determined by the law of the place where such contract is made.

The question now is whether these sections are concerned with the subject of transfer at all, and whether it is possible to ascertain from them the legal system that determines the validity and effect of an indorsement, or of a delivery, of a negotiable instrument.

There has been only a small number of relevant cases since the 1882 Act.[116] The first of these was *Alcock v Smith*:[117]

A bill of exchange, drawn by and on English firms, and payable in England to the order of X, was indorsed and delivered in Norway by X to Y. While in the hands of Y it was seized by a judgment creditor in Norway, and in the due course of Norwegian law was ultimately sold by public auction to Z. In fact, Z had no title to the bill by

---

[112] Such a classification was supported by STAUGHTON LJ in *Macmillan Inc v Bishopsgate Investment Trust plc (No 3)* [1996] 1 WLR 387 at 400.

[113] [1927] 1 KB 889.

[114] *Trimby v Vignier* (1834) 1 Bing NC 151; *Lebel v Tucker* (1867) LR 3 QB 77; *Re Marseilles Extension Rly and Land Co* (1885) 30 Ch D 598.

[115] *Bradlaugh v De Rin* (1868) LR 3 CP 538.

[116] *Alcock v Smith* [1892] 1 Ch 238; *Embiricos v Anglo-Austrian Bank* [1904] 2 KB 870; affd [1905] 1 KB 677; *Koechlin v Kestenbaum* [1927] 1 KB 616; revsd [1927] 1 KB 889. Brief reference was made to the 1882 Act in *Zebrarise Ltd and Anor v De Nieffe* [2004] EWCA 1842; [2005] 1 Lloyd's Rep 154—formal validity of a promissory note; and *Aspinall's Club Ltd v Fouad Al-Zayat* [2007] EWHC 362 (Comm)—English law applied qua law of place of issue.

[117] Ibid.

English law, but according to Norwegian law the property was duly passed to him as a result of the sale. In the action subsequently brought in England, it was held that the effect of the transactions in Norway must be governed by Norwegian law, and therefore that the title acquired thereunder by Z must prevail over one which by English law would have been stronger.

The judgments paid little heed to the statutory provisions, but in general applied Norwegian law as the law of the place of acting. ROMER J, indeed, held that the word "interpretation" in section 72(2) was wide enough to cover the "legal effect" of a contract and that therefore statutory effect had been given to the principle of the application of the law of the place of acting. In the Court of Appeal, however, no reliance was placed on the Act.

In the second case, *Embiricos v Anglo-Austrian Bank*:[118]

> A cheque on a London bank was drawn in Romania in favour of the plaintiffs, who specially indorsed it there to a firm in London and placed it in an envelope addressed to that firm. The cheque was stolen from the envelope in Romania by a clerk of the plaintiffs. Three days later the cheque, bearing an indorsement which purported to be that of the London firm but which was in fact a forgery, was presented for payment at a bank in Vienna. The Vienna bank cashed the cheque in good faith, indorsed it to the defendants, who were their London agents, and the latter collected the amount from the bank on which the cheque was drawn. The plaintiffs then sued the defendants in damages for conversion. Austrian law provided that, notwithstanding the theft and forgery, the Viennese bank acquired good title to the cheque, and judgment was given for the defendants.

In this case the title that was acquired under the law of the country where the instrument was situated at the time of the transaction was upheld by the English court.

Again Austrian law was chosen as being the law of the place of acting (though perhaps what was in the mind of the court was the law of the situs, since this necessarily coincided with the law of the place of acting),[119] and again the judgments attributed only trifling importance to the Bills of Exchange Act 1882. ROMER LJ thought that section 72(2) recognised the law of the place of acting as being applicable to the matter, an opinion which WALTON J was prepared to share if "interpretation" includes "legal effect". VAUGHAN WILLIAMS LJ was not clear that the sub-section covered the case, but according to STIRLING LJ its applicability was worthy of serious consideration.

Section 72, which, it will be observed, was only a secondary consideration in these two decisions, played, however, a decisive part in *Koechlin et Cie v Kestenbaum*:[120]

> In that case a bill of exchange was drawn in France by X on the defendants in London to the order of Y, who was X's father. It was accepted, payable in London, by the defendants. The bill was indorsed not by the payee, Y, but by X, and was then transferred for value to the plaintiffs in France. X's indorsement was affixed on behalf of, and with the authority of, Y. On presentment the defendants refused

---

[118] [1904] 2 KB 870; affd [1905] 1 KB 677.
[119] Supra, pp 1227–1228.
[120] [1927] 1 KB 889.

payment, on the ground that the bill did not bear the signature of Y by way of indorsement. English law requires that a bill payable to order shall be indorsed by the payee, or by an agent who expressly signs per pro the payee. French law, however, permits a valid indorsement to be made by an agent in his own name, provided that he so acts with the authority of the payee. Therefore, whether the plaintiffs were entitled to payment depended on whether the validity of the indorsement was to be determined by English or by French law.

BANKES LJ held that the proper law to govern the validity of a transfer had been definitely settled by section 72 of the Bills of Exchange Act in favour of the law of the place of acting, here French law. In his opinion this legal system was deliberately applied by the Court of Appeal in the *Embiricos* case long after the passing of the Act. The bill, he said, was drawn and indorsed in France in a form recognised by French law, and therefore it became valid in England by virtue of section 72(1).[121]

SARGENT LJ agreed, the essence of his judgment being contained in the following words:

> In my judgment the question whether this bill could properly be indorsed in the name of the payee . . . only or could rightly be indorsed by the son . . . in his own name if he had authority in fact to do so is purely a question of form, and is therefore covered in terms by s 72, sub-s (1); but if it is not covered by that subsection it is covered by sub-s (2), in view of the very wide effect of the decision in *Embiricos v Anglo-Austrian Bank* . . . If the indorsement in fact made is, according to the law of the place where it is made, sufficient to give a title to the indorsee, it appears to me that by the express terms of the Act the indorsee is entitled to sue. The effect is not to increase the liabilities of the acceptor, but merely to enlarge the methods by which the right to enforce those liabilities can be transferred by the person originally entitled to them to some subsequent indorsee.[122]

This case is a definite authority in favour of the law of the place of acting, though it is remarkable that it attributes to the judges who decided *Embiricos v Anglo-Austrian Bank* a confidence in the applicability of the Bills of Exchange Act 1882 that is not very apparent from their judgments.

It is necessary in stating the law with regard to the transfer of negotiable instruments to deal with both inland and foreign bills of exchange. An "inland bill" is one which is both drawn and payable within the British Isles, or one which is drawn within the British Isles upon some person resident there.[123] The Bills of Exchange Act 1882 expressly provides[124] that, when such a bill is indorsed in a foreign country, the indorsement shall, *as regards the payer*, be interpreted according to the law of the United Kingdom. This confirms the decision in *Lebel v Tucker*,[125] and means that the acceptor of an inland, as contrasted with a foreign, bill is liable only to holders who claim under an indorsement valid by English law. The enactment, however, is expressly confined to the liability of the payer.

---

[121] Cf *Aspinall's Club Ltd v Fouad Al-Zayat* [2007] EWHC 362 (Comm), per David STEEL J, at [16]; and *Zebrarise Ltd and Anor v De Nieffe* [2004] EWCA 1842; [2005] 1 Lloyd's Rep 154, per Judge HAVELOCK-ALLAN, QC, at[36].

[122] Ibid, at 899.

[123] Bills of Exchange Act 1882, s 4.

[124] S 72(2), proviso.

[125] (1867) LR 3 QB 77.

One must also consider the transfer of a foreign bill, ie one which does not satisfy the definition given in the preceding paragraph. The rule here is that whether a transfer is valid or not is determined by the law of the place where the transfer is effected, ie in the words of the Act, "where such contract is made".[126] This rule applies equally to a promissory note[127] and to a cheque.[128] The position was thus stated by Sargent LJ in *Koechlin v Kestenbaum*:[129]

> The result [of the 1882 Act] was that any one dealing with a foreign bill of exchange was in a less certain position than a person dealing with an inland bill, because in the case of an indorsement abroad on a foreign bill he might find substituted for the person to whom he was originally liable as acceptor not merely a person to whom the transfer would have been good if made in England, but a person to whom the transfer by indorsement would be good if made according to the law of the country in which it was made. That is rendered perfectly clear by s. 72, sub-ss 1 and 2, of the Act. The matter was carried probably further than was contemplated by the actual language of the sub-sections by the decision in *Embiricos v Anglo-Austrian Bank*.

The result of this distinction is scarcely satisfactory to the commercial world, but it certainly shows how important it is that as wide a unification as possible of the internal laws relating to negotiable instruments should be effected.

4. SHARES AND SECURITIES

(a) The traditional approach[130]

A share of stock is intimately connected with the place where the issuing company has its residence, since the general rule is that it can be effectively transferred only by a substitution of the name of the transferee for that of the transferor in the register of shareholders. This register is normally kept by the company at its principal place of business, though there may be branch registers in other countries for the purpose of recording transactions that are effected there.[131] Despite the fact that a share, traditionally, is generally represented by a certificate which may be pledged and otherwise dealt with as a document of value, it still remains true that by English law entry on the register alone constitutes legal ownership. In the context of private international law, it can be said that, as intangible property, questions relating to title to shares are to be governed by the law of the situs of the shares.[132] That leads to the conclusion that shares are deemed to be situated in the country where they can be effectively dealt with as between the shareholder and the company.[133]

---

[126] Bills of Exchange Act 1882, s 72(1), (2); *Embiricos v Anglo-Austrian Bank* [1904] 2 KB 870; affd [1905] 1 KB 677; *Alcock v Smith* [1892] 1 Ch 238; *Koechlin v Kestenbaum* [1927] 1 KB 889.

[127] *Zebrarise Ltd and Anor v De Nieffe* [2004] EWCA 1842; [2005] 1 Lloyd's Rep 154, per Judge Havelock-Allan, QC, at [36].

[128] *Embiricos v Anglo-Austrian Bank*, supra.

[129] [1927] 1 KB 889 at 898–899.

[130] See, generally, Carruthers (2005), paras 1.38–1.40, 7.01, 7.08–7.12; Ooi (2003), Chapters 1–5; and Benjamin (2001), Chapter 1.

[131] For instance, the Companies Act 2006, s 129 provides that an English company may keep a branch register (called an overseas branch register) in any of a given list of countries of members there resident. No transaction affecting shares so registered shall be registered in any other register (s 133(2)). An instrument of transfer of a share registered in an overseas branch register is regarded as a transfer of property situated outside the United Kingdom (s 133(3)).

[132] Carruthers (2005), paras 7.08–7.09; and *Shahar v Tsitsekkos* [2004] EWHC 2659 (Ch).

[133] On the situs of letters of allotment, see *Young v Phillips* [1984] STC 520.

In other words, shares that are transferable only by an entry in the register have been deemed to be situated, for tax purposes, in the country where the register or branch register is kept.[134] If a company keeps registers in two or more countries, in any of which transfers may be registered, the question where any particular shares are situated has been held to depend on the country in which according to the ordinary course of business the transfer would be registered.[135] On the other hand, there is Canadian authority in the context of expropriation of enemy property which refers to the place of incorporation.[136]

A question of choice of law may arise with regard to a transfer[137] of shares, as may be illustrated by *Macmillan Inc v Bishopsgate Investment Trust plc (No 3)*,[138] which concerned the issue of priorities:

> The plaintiff, a wholly-owned subsidiary of one of the Robert Maxwell group of companies, owned shares in a company which was incorporated in New York, where the share register was situated. The shares were transferred into the name of the first defendant as nominee and were deposited with the Depository Trust Co (DTC) in New York. Later, without the plaintiff's knowledge, some of the shares were used by Maxwell companies to secure loans from three banks who were further defendants in the proceedings. These loans were secured initially either by deposit of the share certificates in England or by transfer of the shares to the defendant banks through the DTC system in New York, but eventually all the shares were registered in New York in the names of the banks. The plaintiff company sought a declaration that it was beneficially entitled to the shares as being held by the defendants on trust for it.

The crucial issue was whether the plaintiff's claim was governed by New York law, under which it would fail as the defendants were bona fide purchasers without notice of the plaintiff's claim, or by English law under which the plaintiff could rely on constructive notice of its claim. The Court of Appeal rejected the argument that English law applied by reason of the claim being a restitutionary one and classified the particular issue as a proprietary one, namely whether the defendants had a good defence as bona fide purchasers for value without notice of the plaintiff's claim.[139] Given that conclusion, the central issue for the court was to determine the law to be applied to the issue of priority of title to the shares. The Court of Appeal concluded that the applicable law was that of

---

[134] *Brassard v Smith* [1925] AC 371; *Baelz v Public Trustee* [1926] Ch 863; *London and South American Investment Trust v British Tobacco Co (Australia)* [1927] 1 Ch 107; *Erie Beach Co v A-G for Ontario* [1930] AC 161; *R v Williams* [1942] AC 541.

[135] *R v Williams*, supra; *Treasurer of Ontario v Blonde* [1947] AC 24; *Standard Chartered Bank Ltd v IRC* [1978] 1 WLR 1160. See Ooi (2003), Chapter 2; and Goode, Kanda and Kreuzer, *Explanatory Report on the Hague Convention on the Law Applicable to Certain Rights in Respect of Securities Held with an Intermediary* (2005), Int 36, and para 4.3.

[136] *Braun v Custodian* [1944] 4 DLR 209.

[137] The term is used here for convenience, but see Ooi (2003), paras 4.01–4.15 for legal analysis of the correct terminology.

[138] [1996] 1 WLR 387; see Bird [1996] LMCLQ 57; J Stevens (1996) 59 MLR 541; R Stevens (1996) 112 LQR 198.

[139] On the classification issue, see Bird [1996] LMCLQ 57, 58–60; Briggs (1996) 67 BYBIL 604; J Stevens (1996) 59 MLR 741, 744–746; Forsyth (1998) 114 LQR 141. Also *Raiffeisen Zentralbank Österreich v Five Star General Trading LLC* [2001] EWCA Civ 68; [2001] QB 825, per MANCE LJ, at [27]–[28]; *Atlantic Telecom GmbH, Noter* 2004 SLT 1031, per Lord BRODIE, at 1043; and *Wight and Ors v Eckhardt Marine GmbH* [2004] AC 147, per Lord HOFFMANN, at [11]. For classification generally, see supra, p 41 et seq.

the situs of the shares, ie New York law.[140] Although the determination of the law to govern ownership of shares might be thought to be "a specific case",[141] the members of the Court of Appeal drew support for their conclusion[142] from the fact that the law of the situs also applies to immovable and tangible movable property, though not to debts.

There still remained the issue of determining what was the situs of the shares. On this issue, the Court of Appeal was agreed that the situs was New York, whose law was to be applied, but was less clear as to the basis for that conclusion. The situs of shares was variously described as the place where the company is incorporated, where the share register is kept or in the case of shares which are negotiable the place where the actual documents are at the time of transfer.[143] As to whether the place of incorporation or that where the share register is kept is to be preferred as the situs, there is undoubted support for the latter approach.[144] It has been pointed out,[145] however, that this may be a distinction without a real difference as the law of the place of incorporation may always override the law of another attributed situs.

It is necessary, however, to distinguish the situs of shares from the situs of the actual certificates, at least where the shares are non-negotiable. Indeed, the Court of Appeal in *Macmillan's* case was in agreement[146] that the situs of such share certificates is where the certificates physically are situated at the time of the transfer. This is well illustrated by *Colonial Bank v Cady*:[147]

> The executors of a deceased Englishman, owner of certain New York railroad shares, who wanted to be registered as owners in the books of the company. The executors sent the certificates to London brokers for transmission to New York. At the request of the brokers the executors signed the certificates in blank. The brokers deposited the certificates with the Colonial Bank as security for a debt, and later became bankrupt.

The question whether the deposit conferred a legal title on the bank depended on whether the transaction was to be governed by English or by New York law. By English law no title passed, but by New York law the delivery of the certificates operated to vest in the bank both the legal and the equitable ownership of the shares. Since the deposit was made in England, it was held that its effect must be determined by English law. Lord Herschell stated:

> I agree, that the question, what is necessary or effectual to transfer the shares in such a company, or to perfect the title to them, must be answered by a reference to the law of the State of New York. But I think that the rights arising out of a transaction entered into by parties in this country, whether, for example, it operated to effect a binding sale or pledge as against the owner of the shares, must be determined by the law prevailing here.[148]

---

[140] Rejecting the view of the trial judge, Millett J, ([1995] 1 WLR 978) that the applicable law was that of the country where the transaction had taken place—again new York.

[141] [1996] 1 WLR 387 at 402.

[142] Ibid, pp 399–402, 410–411, 424.

[143] Though Aldous LJ would also determine the situs in this way in the case of non-negotiable shares, at 411.

[144] Supra, p 1245; and see J Stevens (1996) 59 MLR 741, 744. For a preference for the law of the place of incorporation on the ground that there is always only one such place, see Bird [1996] LMCLQ 57, 62; R Stevens (1996) 112 LQR 198, 200.

[145] Dicey, Morris and Collins, para 22–045.

[146] [1996] 1 WLR 387 at 402–404, 412–413, 419–421.

[147] (1890) 15 App Cas 267; in the Court of Appeal, sub nom *Williams v Colonial Bank* (1888) 38 Ch D 388.

[148] (1890) 15 App Cas 267 at 283.

In the court below, BOWEN LJ simplified the problem with terse felicity:

> The key to this case is whether the defendants [the bank] have a right to hold these pieces of paper, these certificates. What the effect upon their ulterior rights in America would be, if we were to declare that they are entitled to these pieces of paper, is another question.[149]

It must be borne in mind that disputes in relation to the transfer of shares may give rise to choice of law issues in a related, but different,[150] context, namely as to the effect of the transfer as regards the parties to the transfer and persons claiming under them. If, for example, as in the *Macmillan* case, the certificates of a company incorporated in New York where the shares are registered have been transferred in England, New York law will decide whether the method by which the transfer has been effected entitles the transferee to be registered as a shareholder. However, the question whether the transferee is, for example, entitled by virtue of the transaction to retain the share certificates as against the transferor is determined by the proper law of the transaction, which will normally be the law of the place where the certificates were delivered—in the above example, English law. If English law decides in favour of the transferee, the question whether he can demand to be registered as a shareholder will, as seen above, be a matter for New York law.[151]

This type of issue might be illustrated by *Re Fry*,[152] where the facts were as follows:

> X was resident in New Jersey and domiciled in Florida. Whilst in New Jersey he executed transfers of shares, which he owned in an English company, by way of gift to a private company and to his son. The share certificates were sent to England to be registered but, under the Defence Regulations 1939, the English company could not register the shares without Treasury consent. The necessary forms were sent to X who signed and returned them but died before consent was actually obtained. As English law, the proper law of the transfers, had not been complied with, the transfers were incomplete and invalid.

(b) The modern holding system[153]

Market pressure, linked with technological and electronic advancement, has led to the development of a more efficient system for the holding and transfer of securities, namely, one which permits holding via an intermediary, and which allows for the transfer of interests by means of electronic book-entry to securities accounts. The traditional device of paper-based, materialised securities has been replaced by dematerialised securities, dealings with which are effected by virtue of electronic debit and/or credit book entries. Dematerialisation has been accompanied by immobilisation, which refers to the reduction in circulation of paper certificates as part of the transaction process, by means of their being deposited in a Central Securities Depositary, or International Central Securities Depositary, or other intermediary.

---

[149] (1888) 38 Ch D 388 at 408.

[150] This distinction was drawn by the Court of Appeal in *Macmillan Inc v Bishopsgate Investment Trust plc (No 3)* [1996] 1 WLR 387 at 404, 409–410, 419, 424.

[151] Falconbridge, op cit, pp 590–591.

[152] [1946] Ch 312.

[153] See, generally, Carruthers (2005), Chapter 7; Goode, Kanda and Kreuzer, *Explanatory Report on the Hague Convention on the Law Applicable to Certain Rights in Respect of Securities Held with an Intermediary* (2005); Benjamin (2000), Chapter 1; and Ooi (2003), Chapters 1–5.

Given the global nature of the financial market, it is increasingly likely that the players in, or the elements of, a securities transaction will be situated in different jurisdictions. Cross-border clearing and settlement processes, by definition, will necessitate the interaction of different legal systems, and a cross-border securities transaction frequently will trigger complex questions of choice of law, including, most importantly, the question, what law should govern all or part(s) of a transaction which is cleared and/or settled in more than one jurisdiction?

Efforts to apply the traditional situs rule to intermediated securities have involved the so-called "look-through" approach: "'looking through' the tiers of intermediaries to the laws of one or more of the following: the jurisdiction of incorporation of the issuer, the location of the issuer's register or the location of the actual underlying securities certificates"[154]. This amounts less to an application of the situs rule, than to a distortion of it, for it may be virtually impossible to ascertain the location of securities (materialised or dematerialised) held with an intermediary, particularly where securities are held in a multi-tier holding arrangement. The result is that it is not always clear to, or ascertainable by, market participants, which law is the governing law in relation to core issues such as enforceability, perfection of interests, and priority of interests.[155]

(i) European legislative measures

There have been piecemeal attempts within the European Community to deal with the issue of legal uncertainty in the securities market, namely, Directive (EC) No 98/26 of the European Parliament and of the Council of 19 May 1998 on settlement finality in payment and securities settlement systems (the "Settlement Finality Directive"),[156] and Directive 2002/47/EC of the European Parliament and of the Council of 6 June 2002 on financial collateral arrangements (the "Financial Collateral Directive").[157]

The Settlement Finality Directive[158] "aims at contributing to the efficient and cost effective operation of cross-border payment and securities settlement arrangements in the Community, which reinforces the freedom of movement of capital in the internal market ...".[159] It addresses the issue of choice of law in relation to the provision of collateral security in cases where the entitlement of the collateral taker is recorded on a register, account or a centralised deposit system (Central Securities Depositary) within a Member State. The choice of law rule favoured by the Directive embodies the place of the relevant intermediary approach (so-called "PRIMA"): the determination of the rights of the collateral holders shall be governed by the law of the Member State where the register, account or centralised deposit system is located.[160]

---

[154] Goode, Kanda and Kreuzer (2005), Int. 37.

[155] Ibid, Int. 5.

[156] OJ 1998 L166/45.

[157] OJ 2002 L168/43.

[158] Implemented in the United Kingdom by means of the Financial Markets and Insolvency (Settlement Finality) Regulations, SI 1999/2979. See also The Financial Markets and Insolvency (Settlement Finality) (Revocation) Regulations, SI 2001/1349. See Benjamin (2000), paras 7.46–7.51; and Ooi (2003), paras 12.03–12.80.

[159] Settlement Finality Directive, preamble (3).

[160] Art 9(2); and see SI 1999/2979, above, reg 23 (applicable law relating to securities held as collateral security).

The Financial Collateral Directive,[161] which is much wider in scope than the Settlement Finality Directive, sought to extend the PRIMA principle incorporated in that instrument, in order to create legal certainty regarding the use of book entry securities held in a cross-border context and used as financial collateral.[162]

From a choice of law perspective, the European instruments are notable, but from an economic perspective, the fragmented nature of the legislative framework means that the securities trading environment is less than ideal. Improvement in the system is not only desirable, but necessary.

(ii) The Hague Securities Convention

(a) Background

To address the demands of the global financial market for legal certainty and predictability as to the law applicable to securities, and conscious of the importance of "reducing legal risk, systemic risk and associated costs in relation to cross-border transactions involving securities held with an intermediary so as to facilitate the international flow of capital and access to capital markets",[163] the Hague Conference on Private International Law commenced work in May 2000 on a project concerning choice of law in relation to securities held with an intermediary. The Conference adopted a "fast-track" procedure which, together with industry involvement in, and transparency of, the negotiations, made it possible for the resulting Convention to be finalised in a remarkably short period of time: on 13 December 2002, the Convention on the Law Applicable to Certain Rights in respect of Securities Held with an Intermediary ("the Hague Securities Convention") was adopted,[164] and opened for signature and ratification by states.[165]

By reason of the adoption of a number of European Community Directives containing choice of law provisions relative to securities accounts, a transfer of competence has been effected by European Community Member States to the Community, in respect of matters covered by the Hague Securities Convention. The European Community qualifies as a Regional Economic Integration Organisation for the purposes of Article 18 of the Convention, but imminent signature and ratification appears unlikely,[166] principally because the regime adopted by the drafters of the Convention departs significantly from the choice of law rules currently applied in the Member States, as based on Community

---

[161] Implemented in the United Kingdom by means of The Financial Collateral Arrangements (No 2) Regulations, SI 2003/3226.

[162] Financial Collateral Directive, preamble (6) and (7), and Art 9(1); and see SI 2003/3226, above, reg 19 (standard test regarding the applicable law to book entry securities financial collateral arrangements). See Ooi (2003), paras 12.128–12.160.

[163] Convention on the Law Applicable to Certain Rights in respect of Securities Held with an Intermediary, preamble.

[164] The Convention is accompanied by an Explanatory Report prepared by Professor Roy Goode (United Kingdom), Professor Karl Kreuzer (Germany) and Professor Hideki Kanda (Japan), which, like the final text of the Convention, was reviewed and accepted by the Member States of the Conference. See also Goode (2005) 54 ICLQ 539; and Ooi [2005] LMCLQ 467.

[165] To date, the Convention has been signed by only two Contracting States (Switzerland and the USA), and has been ratified by none. Under Art 19, the Convention shall enter into force following deposit of the third instrument of ratification, acceptance, approval or accession.

[166] Serious reservations have been expressed by the European Banking Federation (Carruthers (2005), paras 7.46–7.49), and by the European Central Bank (OJ 2005 C 81/10) in response to a Proposal for a Council Decision concerning the signing of the Convention (COM (2003) 783 final).

legislation.[167] Further reflection and exploration is needed at a Community level before a decision is taken to replace the European regime with the Convention.[168]

(b) Detail

The purpose of the Convention is to harmonise rules of choice of law, not rules of substantive law, concerning certain rights in respect of securities held with an intermediary. The objective is to achieve certainty as to the applicable law, in order that market participants are capable of knowing in advance what law governs securities transactions,[169] thereby keeping legal risk and, in turn, economic risk, at a minimum.[170]

The Convention applies in all cases where securities are held with an intermediary, ie where the securities are credited to a securities account, "regardless of how the relevant substantive law classifies the nature of the right resulting from the credit of the securities to the securities account",[171] ie as proprietary or contractual.[172] The Convention does not apply to directly held securities.

The preamble to the Convention takes the line that the PRIMA ("place of the relevant intermediary") approach remains the basis of the choice of law rule contained in the Convention, but there is an important modification, in the form of party autonomy.

The primary choice of law rule is contained in Article 4 of the Convention, which recognises the relevance of party choice (albeit restricted choice). The rule settled upon gives effect to an express agreement on governing law[173] between an account holder and its immediate intermediary, subject only to the "qualifying office" requirement. The choice of law may be expressly agreed in the account agreement[174] between the parties as being the state whose law governs that account agreement,[175] or if the account agreement expressly provides that another law is applicable to the issues specified in Article 2(1) of

---

[167] Opinion of the European Central Bank OJ 2005 C 81/10, para 8.

[168] The European Central Bank has stressed the importance of assessing whether the Convention's approach would provide a greater degree of legal certainty and protection against systemic risk compared to the existing Community legislation (ibid, para 9).

[169] See Goode, Kanda and Kreuzer (2005) Int. 33.

[170] Ibid, Int. 34.

[171] Goode, Kanda and Kreuzer (2005) Int. 20, 24, and para 1-16. See Art 2(2).

[172] In terms of Art 2(3), however, the Convention does not determine the law applicable to (a) the rights and duties arising from the credit of securities to a securities account to the extent that such rights or duties are purely contractual or otherwise purely personal; (b) the contractual or other personal rights and duties of parties to a disposition of securities held with an intermediary; or (c) the rights and duties of an issuer of securities . . . whether in relation to the holder of the securities of any other person. See Goode, Kanda and Kreuzer (2005) para 4-2, Int. 25; and Int. 59, which cites the following examples of rights or duties which are considered purely contractual/personal: the content and frequency of account statements; the intermediary's standard of care in maintaining securities accounts; risk of loss; and deadlines in giving instructions.

[173] Art 9 adopts the principle of universality, according to which the Convention applies regardless of whether the applicable law is the law of a Contracting State. Art 10 excludes operation of the doctrine of renvoi, meaning that reference to the "law of a state" is to its internal law only; see, however, the limited appearance of renvoi in Art 12(2)(b) and (3) regarding multi-legal system states.

[174] Defined in Art 1(1)(e) as meaning, in relation to a securities account (ie an account maintained by an intermediary to which securities may be credited or debited: Art 1(1)(b)), the agreement with the relevant intermediary governing that securities account.

[175] See Goode, Kanda and Kreuzer (2005), Int. 60.

the Convention,[176] that other law shall govern those issues.[177] In any event, the law chosen will apply only if the relevant intermediary has, at the time of the agreement, a qualifying office[178] in that state.

Article 7 makes special provision for a case where an account agreement is amended so as to change the applicable law regarding Article 2(1) issues. One of the perceived benefits of allowing (limited) party autonomy in this sphere is that, as well as permitting greater legal certainty, it "reflects existing and foreseeable market practice".[179]

The secondary and subsequent choice of law rules (which are applicable either in the event of the parties failing to make an express agreement as to choice of law, or in the event of their choosing the law of a state in which, at the time of the agreement, the intermediary does not have a qualifying office) are narrated in Article 5 of the Convention. In terms of Article 5(1), if the applicable law is not determined under Article 4, but it is expressly and unambiguously stated in a written account agreement that the relevant intermediary entered into the account agreement through a particular office, then the law applicable to all the issues specified in Article 2(1) shall be the law of the state[180] in which that office then was located. However, as with Article 4, the law thus identified will apply only if the relevant intermediary has, at the time of the agreement, a qualifying office in that state.

If the applicable law is not determined under Article 5(1) (ie if there is no express and unambiguous statement in a written account agreement that the relevant intermediary entered into the account agreement through a particular office), then the applicable law, under Article 5(2), shall be the law in force in the state[181] under whose law the relevant intermediary is incorporated or otherwise organised at the time the written agreement is entered into or, if there is no such agreement, at the time the securities account was opened; and, failing which, under Article 5(3), the law in force in the state[182] in which the relevant intermediary has its (principal) place of business.

---

[176] Being the issues which are deemed to fall within the scope of the applicable law under the Convention, namely: (a) the legal nature and effects against the intermediary of the rights resulting from a credit of securities to a securities account; (b) the legal nature and effects against the intermediary and third parties of a disposition of securities held with an intermediary; (c) the requirements, if any, for perfection of a disposition of securities held with an intermediary; (d) whether a person's interests in securities held with an intermediary extinguishes or has priority over another person's interest; (e) the duties, if any, of an intermediary to a person other than the account holder who asserts in competition with the account holder or another person an interest in securities held with that intermediary; (f) the requirements, if any, for the realisation of an interest in securities held with an intermediary; and (g) whether a disposition of securities held with an intermediary extends to entitlements to dividends, income, or other distributions, or to redemption, sale or other proceeds. The list of issues in Art 2(1) is intended to be exhaustive: Goode, Kanda and Kreuzer (2005), Int. 54, and para 2-2.

[177] "The parties may expressly agree to have the law of one State govern all the Article 2(1) issues and that of a different State to govern the account agreement." (Goode, Kanda and Kreuzer (2005), Int. 60; also Int. 47).

[178] Defined in Art 4(1)(a) and (b), and meaning essentially that the intermediary must have in the state the law of which has been chosen by the parties, an office which is engaged in the activity of maintaining securities accounts (though not necessarily the account in question). See Goode, Kanda and Kreuzer (2005), Int. 62.

[179] Goode, Kanda and Kreuzer (2005), Int. 48; this is true, even though the rule is "counter-intuitive and . . . contrary to a well-established principle that two parties to a contract cannot by their agreement affect the rights of third parties, still less subject those rights to a given law." (Goode (2004) pp 1111–1112).

[180] Or relevant territorial unit of a multi-unit state.

[181] Or relevant territorial unit of a multi-unit state.

[182] Or relevant territorial unit of a multi-unit state.

Article 6 of the Convention lists certain factors of which no account may be taken in determining the applicable law under the Convention: (a) the place where the issuer of the securities is incorporated or otherwise organized; (b) the places where certificates representing or evidencing securities are located; (c) the place where a register of holders of securities maintained by or on behalf of the issuer of the securities is located; and/or (d) the place where any intermediary other than the relevant intermediary (ie an upper-tier intermediary) is located. What is significant is that Article 6, by its terms, deliberately severs any residual link with traditional situs thinking and methodology.

The customarily included public policy exception is to be found in Article 11(1) of the Convention, in terms of which application of the prima facie applicable law may be refused only if the effects of its application would be manifestly contrary to the public policy of the forum. So too, there is a saving provision in Article 11(2) regarding mandatory rules of the forum, according to which application is preserved of those provisions of the law of the forum which, irrespective of rules of conflict of laws, must be applied, even to international situations. Article 11(1) and (2), however, will be strictly construed, and in terms of Article 11(3), will not justify the application of those provisions of the law of the forum which impose requirements with respect to perfection, or relating to priorities between competing interests, *unless* the law of the forum is also the applicable law under the Convention.

Chapter 31

Administration of Estates

1. INTRODUCTION

The modern legal systems which have had their origin in English law differ fundamentally from the civil law jurisdictions with regard to the procedure by which property is administered after the death of its owner. In England the only person entitled to deal with the property is the person to whom a grant has been made by some public authority. This grant of the right of administration is made, according to the circumstances, to either an executor or an administrator. It is made to:

(a) an executor, when some person has been appointed as such by the will; or to

(b) an administrator *cum testamento annexo*, when a will has omitted to appoint an executor, or when the appointment fails, as, for instance, by the death or renunciation of the executor; or to

(c) an administrator, when the deceased has died intestate.

The executors and administrators or, to use a comprehensive expression, the personal representatives, become subject to two distinct duties. First, they must clear the estate of liabilities by the payment of funeral expenses and debts; secondly, they must distribute the residue of the estate among the beneficiaries according to the limitations of the will or the rules of intestacy. These two functions, debt-administration and beneficial distribution, are governed by different principles of private international law.

In the civil law countries, however, in the rare case where personal representatives are appointed, their duties and functions are generally of a supervisory nature widely different from those of their English counterparts.[1] The general civil law rule is that the entire property of a deceased person passes directly to his heirs, testate or intestate, or to his universal legatee, subject, of course, to their acceptance. These successors, broadly speaking, continue the existence of their predecessor.[2] For instance, unless they accept the inheritance with the benefit of an inventory, their liability for the debts of the deceased is not limited to the assets but is enforceable against their private property.

Thus, the striking difference between English and civil law practice is that in the latter case the property passes on death directly to the successor, but in England it cannot be dealt with by anyone without a public grant.[3] It is important, however, to observe at once that the automatic transfer recognised by civil law systems cannot operate on property of the deceased situated in England. Succession to movables is governed by the law of the deceased's domicile,[4] but, no matter what that domicile may be, nobody can rightfully and effectually obtain possession of movable property situated in England unless he gets an English grant of probate or of administration.[5] An English grant is always required in order to provide authority to administer English assets.

2. ENGLISH GRANTS

(a) Jurisdiction of English courts

One of the cardinal rules of private international law, as we shall see later,[6] is that the movable property of a deceased person, so far as concerns either testate or intestate succession, is regulated by the law of that country in which he died domiciled. It might be thought, therefore, that the courts of that domicile have jurisdiction to make a grant of administration, merely on the ground of domicile and regardless of whether there are assets actually within the jurisdiction.[7] Theoretically this principle is tenable, but two facts militate against its application. First, such a grant would be ineffective if there were no assets within the jurisdiction. Secondly, the jurisdiction of the old ecclesiastical courts, of which the High Court exercising jurisdiction in probate matters[8] is the successor, was

---

[1] See, eg, *Re Achillopoulos* [1928] Ch 433 at 435.

[2] Distinguish the English personal representative, who, strictly speaking, does not represent the deceased at all.

[3] But the Revenue Act 1889, s 19, provides that where a policy of life insurance has been effected by a person who dies domiciled elsewhere than in the United Kingdom, a grant of representation shall not be necessary to establish the right to receive the money payable; see *Haas v Atlas Assurance Co Ltd* [1913] 2 KB 209, where SCRUTTON J gives the genesis of the provision. For another case where no grant is necessary, see *Vanquelin v Bouard* (1863) 15 CBNS 341, infra, p 1260; and see the Administration of Estates (Small Payments) Act 1965.

[4] See infra, p 1264 et seq.

[5] *New York Breweries Co v A-G* [1899] AC 62. It should be noted, however, that an executor derives his title from the will, not from the grant of probate.

[6] Infra, p 1264 et seq.

[7] Cf *Hindocha and Ors v Gheewala and Ors* [2003] UKPC 77; [2004] 1 CLC 502.

[8] Supreme Court Act 1981, s 25. Under Sch 1, paras 1 and 3, non-contentious or common form probate business is assigned to the Family Division and all other probate business to the Chancery Division. As to what is included in non-contentious business, see *Re Clore* [1982] Fam 113 at 116; affd [1982] Ch 456.

universally founded on the presence within the jurisdiction of movables belonging to the deceased. In fact, for many years the rule has been that an English court can grant administration only if there is property in England.[9] However, the court now has statutory authority to make a grant notwithstanding that the deceased left no estate,[10] provided, probably, that the testator died domiciled in England.[11]

(b) Separate wills

Testators quite often have property both in England and abroad and, in such cases, they sometimes make separate wills, one disposing of their English property and the other of the foreign. This may be important if, for example, the law of the situs of foreign immovables has restrictive rules as to who may inherit them. In such cases, the normal practice is only to admit to probate the English will,[12] but it is also possible to admit to probate in England the foreign will, provided there is some appropriate reason for so doing.[13]

(c) Situs of assets

Except in the case of tangible movables, there may be some difficulty in establishing the situation of property, especially in the case of choses in action such as debts and shares.[14] It has long been established, however, that where there is a question as to the jurisdiction to make a grant of probate or administration with regard to choses in action and titles to property, then judgment debts are assets where the judgment is recorded; leases, where the land lies; specialty debts, where the instrument happens to be; and simple contract debts, where the debtor resides at the time of the testator's death.[15] Securities, such as bonds, promissory notes and bills of exchange which are transferable by delivery only, are assets if situated in England.[16] A share of stock, transferable only by registration, is not situated in the place where the certificates happen to be, but in the country where the shares may effectively be dealt with as between the shareholder and the company, ie in the country where registration must be effected.[17]

(d) Persons to whom grant will be made

Who are the persons in whose favour this jurisdiction ought to be exercised? Where the deceased dies domiciled in England, probate of his will is normally granted to the

---

[9] *Evans v Burrell* (1859) 28 LJP & M 82; *In the Goods of Tucker* (1864) 34 LJPM & A 29; Dicey, Morris and Collins, paras 26R-001–26-004.

[10] Supreme Court Act 1981, s 25(1); see *In the Estate of Wayland* [1951] 2 All ER 1041.

[11] *Aldrich v A-G* [1968] P 281 at 295.

[12] If the English will refers to and incorporates the foreign will, then the latter must be included in the probate; *Re Western's Goods* (1898) 78 LT 49; and see *Re Tinkler* [1990] 1 NZLR 621.

[13] *Re Wayland's Estate* [1951] 2 All ER 1041; see also *Re Baldry (Deceased)* [2004] WTLR 609 (Fam Div); and *Lamothe v Lamothe* [2006] EWHC 1387; [2006] WTLR 1431.

[14] Supra, Chapter 30.

[15] *A-G v Bouwens* (1838) 4 M & W 171 at 191.

[16] *Winans v A-G* [1910] AC 27.

[17] *A-G v Higgins* (1857) 2 H & N 339; *Brassard v Smith* [1925] AC 371; *Erie Beach Co v A-G for Ontario* [1930] AC 161; *R v Williams* [1942] AC 541, [1942] 2 All ER 95; *Standard Chartered Bank Ltd v IRC* [1978] 1 WLR 1160; supra, p 1244 et seq.

executors named in it.[18] On intestacy, letters of administration are usually granted to a person taking a beneficial interest in the estate.[19] What happens if the deceased died domiciled abroad? A case that commonly arises is where a person dies domiciled abroad, leaving the bulk of his property in the foreign country and a smaller amount in England. The ideal here is to have one administration in the domicile for the whole of the property, but such principle of unity is not found in practice and is attainable only by international agreement.[20] A separate grant of administration must be obtained from the English court with regard to the property in England. In such a situation, the administration in England is said to be "ancillary", whilst that in the country of the deceased's domicile is the "principal" administration.

The English court will normally make a grant to a person who has been entrusted with the administration of the deceased's estate by a court in the country of the deceased's last domicile.[21] However, in some countries, grants of representation, in the English sense, are not made by courts; or it could be that no application may in fact have been made in the country of the domicile. In such cases an English grant may then be made to the person beneficially entitled to the estate by the law of the place where the deceased died domiciled.[22] The making of such a grant is discretionary and the court may make a grant to such persons as it thinks fit, whether or not there is someone who fits into the above categories.[23] For example, in *Re Kaufman's Goods*[24] the deceased died domiciled in the Netherlands and the only person entitled to the estate under Dutch law died before the estate could be administered. The court made a grant, in the interests of convenience, to the deceased's brother who would have been entitled to a grant under English law if the deceased had died domiciled in England.

If the foreign domiciliary's will is in English or Welsh, then the court may grant probate to any executor named in the will.[25] It has also been held that a rule of the law of the foreign domicile restricting the authority of such an executor to a period of one year from the death of the testator must be disregarded in the English administration.[26] Furthermore, if the will, in whatever language, describes "the duties of a named person in terms sufficient to constitute him executor according to the tenor of the will"[27] probate may be granted to that person.

When the person who has been authorised to administer the estate in the country of the deceased's domicile seeks a grant of probate in England, the English court does not

---

[18] Tristram and Coote's *Probate Practice*, (2006) 30th edn, Chapter 4. Under the Supreme Court Act 1981, s 116, the court has a discretion to appoint someone else; see *IRC v Stype Investments (Jersey) Ltd* [1982] Ch 456.

[19] Tristram and Coote's *Probate Practice*, supra, Chapter 6.

[20] See, eg, the Hague Convention on the International Administration of the Estates of Deceased Persons (1972), which provides one international initiative, but one with a low success rate; see Law Com No 107 (1981), para 2.45; and also Nadelmann (1973) 21 AJCL 136, 139–149.

[21] Non-Contentious Probate Rules, SI 1987/2024, r 30(1)(a). Rule 31 is amended in minor respects by SI 1991/1876.

[22] Non-Contentious Probate Rules 1987, r 30(1)(b).

[23] Ibid, r 30(1)(c).

[24] [1952] P 325; and see *Bath v British and Malayan Trustees Ltd* [1969] 2 NSWLR 114.

[25] Non-Contentious Probate Rules 1987, r 30(3)(a)(i).

[26] *Re Goenaga's Estate* [1949] P 367. See Morris (1950) 3 ILQ 243 where it is shown that the decision, though correct in principle, is irreconcilable with *Laneuville v Anderson* (1860) 2 Sw & Tr 24.

[27] Non-Contentious Probate Rules 1987, r 30(3)(a)(ii).

examine the grounds of his appointment under the foreign law.[28] This does not mean, however, that the domiciliary executor or heir has an absolute right to administer the English assets. The court has a discretion, and although there are few cases where it refuses to follow the foreign grant, it will certainly do so if the foreign grantee is incompetent according to English law to act as administrator. Thus, for example, no grant will be made to a minor.[29] A further example is provided by the fact that where a minority or life interest arises in an estate, the grant of probate must normally be made to not fewer than two individuals or to a trust corporation.[30] Even if the law of the domicile allows one person to administer the estate, the court will not in such a case make a grant to just one individual.[31]

It might be thought that an English court is justified in following the grant made in the foreign country on the basis of consistency with the rule that succession to a deceased's movable estate is governed by his domicile on death.[32] The logic of such a justification breaks down, however, if the deceased's estate consists of immovables because succession to them is governed by the law of the situs.[33] Indeed the High Court of Australia has refused to follow the law of the domicile, England, and make a grant to the English personal representative in the case of a will of movables and immovables. The court required the title to administer the will, and its validity, to be determined by the law of the situs.[34] English law does not adopt so purist an approach, which is highly inconvenient where, as is often the case, the estate consists of both movables and immovables. The English court will make a grant following the one made in the domicile, even though the estate includes immovables.[35] Where, however, the whole or substantially the whole of the estate in England consists of immovables, the court may make a grant, in respect of the whole estate, in accordance with the law which would have been applicable if the deceased had died domiciled in England,[36] ie English law.

Under the Consular Conventions Act 1949 a grant of administration may be made to the consular officer of a foreign state where the executor or other such person is a national of that state and is not resident in England and where no other application is made by a person duly authorised by power of attorney.[37] A "foreign State" means one with which a Consular Convention has been concluded and so declared by Order in Council.[38]

(e) Title of administrator under an English grant

Although the theory may be that an English grant extends to property no matter where it is situated, it is obviously of no practical importance, because whether the administrator is entitled to the property of the deceased in a foreign country must necessarily depend

---

[28] *Re Hill's Goods* (1870) LR 2 P & D 89; *Re Humphries's Estate* [1934] P 78.

[29] *Re D'Orleans's (Duchess) Goods* (1859) 1 Sw & Tr 253; presumably *Re Da Cunha's Goods* (1828) 1 Hag Ecc 237 would not now be followed.

[30] Supreme Court Act 1981, s 114(2).

[31] Non-Contentious Probate Rules 1987, r 30(2).

[32] Infra, p 1264 et seq.

[33] Infra, p 1277 et seq.

[34] *Lewis v Balshaw* (1935) 54 CLR 188. See, more recently, *Weinstock v Sarnat* [2005] NSWSC 744.

[35] *Re Meatyard's Goods* [1903] P 125.

[36] Non-Contentious Probate Rules 1987, r 30(3)(b).

[37] S 1(1).

[38] For a list of current Orders in Council see Halsbury's *Statutes of England*, 4th edn, Vol 10 (2001 Reissue), p 579.

on the local law. The one certainty is that an administrator acting under an English grant, who does succeed in obtaining property in a foreign country, is accountable for it as administrator in England.[39]

His title extends not only to property situated in England at the death of the deceased,[40] but also to all property that comes to England thereafter.[41] Property, however, which comes to England after the death of the deceased does not pass to the administrator under an English grant if it has previously been appropriated abroad by an administrator acting under the law of the foreign situs.[42]

3. CHOICE OF LAW

Where an ancillary administrator has been authorised to deal with the movable English assets of a person dying domiciled abroad, the rule is that, though beneficial distribution is governed by the law of the domicile, the administration of the assets is governed exclusively by English law.[43] Thus the duty of an executor who receives a grant of administration from the English court is to pay all debts, whether domestic or foreign, according to the rules of English law. No distinction must be made between English and foreign creditors; no regard must be had to the corresponding rules of the law of the deceased's domicile. A foreign creditor seeking payment in England must take the law of England as he finds it. He can neither claim an advantage which his own or any other foreign law may allow him, nor can he be deprived of an advantage which belongs to him by English law though not by the law of the deceased's domicile. In particular, the priority of debts[44] and their extinction by lapse of time[45] are matters to be governed exclusively by English law. If, for instance, certain foreign debts owed by the deceased are statute-barred by English law but not so barred by the law of the domicile, the principal administrator in the country of the domicile is not entitled as of right to demand that the surplus English assets shall be handed over to him in order to satisfy the claims of the foreign creditors.[46] The only difficulty is to determine at what stage administration ends and beneficial distribution begins.[47] It has been held, for instance, that even though all debts have been paid and a net residue ascertained, yet, if the beneficiaries are minors, the administrator under the Administration of Estates Act 1925[48] can still exercise the right to postpone the realisation of the English assets. This is because postponement is a matter of administration.[49]

Once all debts have been paid by an ancillary administrator according to the law of England, the usual procedure is for him to remit any surplus assets to the principal administrator in the country of the deceased's last domicile. This is to allow them to be

---

[39] *Dowdale's Case* (1604) 6 Co Rep 46b; *Stirling-Maxwell v Cartwright* (1879) 11 Ch D 522.

[40] Administration of Estates Act 1925, s 1; *IRC v Stype Investments (Jersey) Ltd* [1982] Ch 456 at 473.

[41] See, eg, *Whyte v Rose* (1842) 3 QB 493 at 506; Dicey,Morris and Collins, para 26R-021, Rule 132(2).

[42] *Currie v Bircham* (1822) 1 Dowl & Ry KB 35; Dicey,Morris and Collins, para 26-023.

[43] *Re Kloebe* (1884) 28 Ch D 175; *Re Lorillard* [1922] 2 Ch 638; *Preston v Melville* (1841) 8 Cl & Fin 1 at 12, 13; *Enohin v Wylie* (1862) 10 HL Cas 1 at 13, 14.

[44] *Re Kloebe* (1884) 28 Ch D 175.

[45] *Re Lorillard* [1922] 2 Ch 638.

[46] Ibid.

[47] *Re Kehr* [1952] Ch 26.

[48] S 33, as amended by the Trustee Act 2000, Sch 2(II), para 27.

[49] *Re Wilks* [1935] Ch 645; cf *Re Northcote's Will Trusts* [1949] 1 All ER 442; *Re Kehr* [1952] Ch 26.

distributed among the beneficiaries according to the law of the domicile.[50] But this remission of assets is not a matter of course. It is within the discretion of the English court whether surplus assets shall be remitted to the domicile for purposes of beneficial distribution or whether that distribution shall be made from England. The sole function of the law of the domicile with regard to English assets is to regulate their beneficial distribution, not to allocate them in payment of debts. An immoderate use was made of this rational principle in *Re Lorillard*:[51]

> The testator, domiciled in New York, died leaving assets and creditors both in England and America. Administration proceedings were taken in both countries. The New York assets were exhausted, leaving unpaid certain creditors whose debts were statute-barred by English law but not so by the law of New York. There was a surplus of English assets after all creditors entitled under English law had been paid.

EVE J made an order that, if the American creditors did not within two months establish that their debts were payable by English law, the executor must not remit the assets in England to the New York executor, but must distribute them among the beneficiaries. The Court of Appeal refused to interfere with the exercise by EVE J of his discretion.

It does, however, seem strange to exercise judicial discretion to enrich beneficiaries at the expense of creditors who were entitled to payment in the place of the principal administration.[52] In any event, this attack on the creditors will not always succeed, and only succeeded in the instant case because the beneficiaries were resident in England. Had they resided in New York or, indeed, in any other country where statutes of limitation were not then classified as procedural,[53] they would have been liable at the suit of the creditors to disgorge what they had received.

4. FOREIGN ADMINISTRATORS

It is an absolute rule that the status of an administrator appointed by a foreign court is not recognised in England. His title relates only to property that lies within the jurisdiction of the country from which he derives his authority, and therefore he has no right to take or to recover by action property in England without a grant from the English court.[54] If, without the support of a grant, he succeeds in obtaining property in England, he is clearly liable as executor *de son tort* to account for the assets received.[55] Since a foreign administrator has no right to sustain actions or to receive property in England qua representative of

---

[50] *Re Achillopoulos* [1928] Ch 433; *Re Manifold* [1962] Ch 1; *In the Estate of Weiss* [1962] P 136; and see *Scottish National Orchestra Society Ltd v Thomson's Executor* 1969 SLT 325; *Re Lord Cable* [1977] 1 WLR 7 at 25–26.

[51] [1922] 2 Ch 638. The decision has been severely criticised by Nadelmann (1951) 49 Mich LR 1129, 1148–1149.

[52] But the decision was approved in *Government of India v Taylor* [1955] AC 491 at 509, per Lord SIMONDS; same case sub nom *Re Delhi Electric Supply and Traction Co Ltd* [1954] Ch 131 at 161, per EVERSHED MR, and at 165–166, per JENKINS LJ. On this aspect of the case see M Mann (1954) 3 ICLQ 502, 504–506. See also *Re Manifold* [1962] Ch 1; and *Permanent Trustee Co (Canberra) Ltd v Finlayson* (1968) 122 CLR 338.

[53] For the changes in English law introduced by the Foreign Limitation Periods Act 1984, see supra, pp 80–82.

[54] For discussion generally of the right to sue in a representative capacity, see supra, pp 90–91.

[55] *New York Breweries Co v A-G* [1899] AC 62; and see *Beavan v Lord Hastings* (1856) 2 K & J 724; and *IRC v Stype Investments (Jersey) Ltd* [1982] Ch 456 at 474.

the deceased,[56] it would appear clear on principle that a debtor from whom he receives payment is not discharged from liability to an English administrator.[57] As Story says,[58] however, there is much room for discussion and doubt on this matter. On the one hand, the domestic rule of English law is that "where an executor *de son tort* is really acting as executor, and the party with whom he deals has fair reason for supposing that he has authority to act as such, his acts shall bind the rightful executor, and shall alter the property".[59] On the other hand, there is the undoubted fact that a foreign administrator, as such, has no authority to receive or otherwise deal with English assets. There is no English case directly in point, but, if a debtor had reasonable grounds for believing that the foreign administrator was the bona fide representative of the deceased, it would seem justifiable to depart from strict principle and to regard the payment as a valid discharge. The majority of courts in the USA adopt this view.[60]

Although a foreign administrator is not permitted to sue in England as the representative of the deceased, it has long been established that he may enforce by action a right that is personal to himself and which he is entitled to assert in his own individual capacity, even though it is connected with the estate that he is administering.[61] If, for instance, in his official capacity he recovers judgment abroad against a debtor, he has effectually reduced the debt into his possession, and can sue on the judgment in England without taking out a separate administration.[62] In *Vanquelin v Bouard*:[63]

> A widow in France became donee of the universality of the succession of her deceased husband. By French law she was, as such donee, *personally* liable for her husband's debts and *personally* entitled to his property. She paid to an indorsee the amount of a bill of exchange that her husband had drawn, and later brought an action in England to recover this amount from the acceptor.

It was held that there were two grounds on which the widow must succeed. First, the right that she sought to enforce was one that she had acquired personally since it arose from a payment made by her after her husband's death. Secondly, her position as donee gave her, according to French law, a personal right to recover the sum from the acceptor.

The liabilities to which an administrator is subject are imposed on him in his capacity as the lawful representative of the deceased, and since the status of a representative appointed abroad is not recognised in England, it follows that a foreign administrator as such is not liable to be sued in England.[64] This is so even though he brings foreign assets to England. He cannot sue, neither can he be sued, in his capacity as administrator, but an action might lie, at the suit of a creditor or beneficiary, for the judicial administration of any unappropriated assets.[65]

---

[56] It even appears that a foreign personal representative cannot sue on behalf of the deceased's dependants under a Fatal Accidents Act claim: *Finnegan v Cementation Co* [1953] 1 QB 688, though see the criticisms at 699–700.

[57] Westlake, s 98; cf Dicey, Morris and Collins, para 26-039.

[58] Section 514.

[59] *Thomson v Harding* (1853) 2 E & B 630 at 640.

[60] Restatement 2d, § 322.

[61] *Vanquelin v Bouard* (1863) 15 CBNS 341.

[62] *Re Macnichol* (1874) LR 19 Eq 81; and see *Peterson v Bezold* (1970) 17 DLR (3d) 471.

[63] (1863) 15 CBNS 341.

[64] *Beavan v Lord Hastings* (1856) 2 K & J 724; *Degazon v Barclays Bank International Ltd* [1988] 1 FTLR 17; *Nova v Grove* (1982) 140 DLR (3d) 527; *Canadian Commercial Bank v Belkin* (1990) 73 DLR (4th) 678; Dicey, Morris and Collins, paras 26R-042–26-043.

[65] *Logan v Fairlie* (1825) 2 Sim & St 284; *Tyler v Bell* (1837) 2 My & Cr 89 at 110; Dicey, Morris and Collins, paras 26R-042(1) and 26-044.

But just as a foreign administrator can enforce in England a right that attaches to him personally, so he can be sued on a claim that is sustainable against him not in his representative, but in his personal, capacity, eg as trustee for legatees,[66] or as an executor *de son tort*.[67] An action will not lie against an administrator if it is based on a transaction entered into by the deceased, but it will lie on a transaction effected by the administrator after taking office. Thus, for instance, he will be liable on any contract connected with the winding up of the estate that he makes in England.[68] Indeed, the liability in England of a foreign executor would seem to go further than this, for if he has changed his character in any way from that of an executor to that of a trustee he would seem to incur liability within the principle of *Penn v Baltimore*.[69]

5. COMMONWEALTH AND OTHER UNITED KINGDOM GRANTS

A grant of administration made in any country to which the Colonial Probates Act 1892[70] has been extended by Order in Council may be sealed with the seal of the English probate registry, ie "resealed", and thus made effective with regard to English assets. An Order in Council, however, is not made until the country in question has made adequate provision for the recognition of English grants within its territory. The Act has been applied to most Commonwealth countries.[71] Resealing is discretionary and the court will not normally reseal a grant unless it was made to the person entitled to an English grant where the deceased died domiciled abroad,[72] eg the person entrusted with the administration of the estate by the court of the deceased's last domicile or the executor named in a will in English or Welsh.[73] Notice of the resealing is sent to the court which made the original grant.[74]

The position in the United Kingdom is that a grant of administration in Scotland or Northern Ireland is directly effective in England without the need for resealing.[75] Similarly, English grants may be directly recognised in Scotland[76] and Northern Ireland;[77] Scottish in Northern Ireland;[78] and vice versa.[79]

---

[66] Dicey, Morris and Collins, paras 26R-042(2) and 26-045.

[67] *New York Breweries v A-G* [1899] AC 62; cf *Charron v Montreal Trust* (1958) 15 DLR (2d) 240; *Re Pemberton* (1966) 59 DLR (2d) 44; *Canadian Commercial Bank v Belkin* (1990) 73 DLR (4th) 678 at 684–685.

[68] See the American case, *Johnson v Wallis* 112 NY 230 (1889); Restatement 2d, § 359.

[69] *Bond v Graham* (1842) 1 Hare 482 at 484; *Ewing v Orr-Ewing* (1885) 10 App Cas 453; *Penn v Baltimore* (1750) 1 Ves Sen 444 is fully discussed, supra, p 481.

[70] As amended by the Administration of Estates Act 1971, s 11, and the Supreme Court Act 1981, Sch 5.

[71] Colonial Probates Act 1892; extended to protected states and mandated territories by the Colonial Probates (Protected States and Mandated Territories) Act 1927, s 1. For the countries to which the legislation applies, see Halsbury's *Statutes of England*, 4th edn, Vol 17 (2002 Reissue), p 660.

[72] Supra, pp 1255–1257.

[73] Non-Contentious Probate Rules 1987, r 39(3).

[74] Ibid, r 39(6).

[75] Administration of Estates Act 1971, s 1 which is retrospective in effect; and see *Practice Direction* [1971] 1 WLR 1790.

[76] Administration of Estates Act 1971, s 3(1).

[77] Ibid, s 2(1).

[78] Ibid, s 2(2).

[79] Ibid, s 3(1).

Chapter 32

Succession[1]

1. INTRODUCTION

Presuming that the estate of the deceased has been cleared of debts and all taxes and duties paid, the duty of the administrator is to distribute the property among those to whom it beneficially belongs. These persons are to be identified by the choice of law rules relating to succession and these rules may vary according to whether the estate consists of movables or immovables and whether the deceased left a will or died intestate. It is also necessary to examine the rules relating to the exercise of powers of appointment by will.

Most foreign countries have adopted the principle of unity of succession by which questions relating to intestacy or wills are governed by one single law, the personal law of the

---

[1] See Miller [1988] Conv 30; (1990) 39 ICLQ 261; Scoles (1988) II Hague Recueil 9, 54–89; North (1990) I Hague Recueil 9, 273–282; Miller, *International Aspects of Succession* (2000); and Hayton, *European Succession Laws* (2002) 2nd edn.

deceased, irrespective of the nature of the subject matter. The common law of England has consistently adhered to what is called the principle of scission by which the issues are dealt with separately, with the result that the destination of movables on the death of the owner is governed by the law of his domicile, whilst the destination of immovables is governed by the law of the situs.[2] It is for that reason that we have to examine succession to movables separately from succession to immovables.

2. MOVABLES

(a) Intestate succession

The rule has been established for over two hundred and fifty years that movable property in the case of intestacy is to be distributed according to the law of the domicile of the intestate at the time of his death.[3] This law determines the class of persons to take, the relative proportions to which the distributees are entitled, the right of representation, the rights of a surviving spouse and all analogous questions.

The fate of movables situated in England and belonging to an intestate who has left no relatives recognised as his successors by the law of the domicile has already been fully discussed.[4] Summarily stated, the rule, which derives from the principle that the authority of the law of the domicile is rigorously confined to questions of succession, is this:

> If, by the law of the domicile, the movables pass to the state or some other body in the domicile by way of succession, English law gives effect to this ruling;[5] if, on the other hand, they are claimed by some body in the domicile as being no-one's property, they pass to the English Crown as *bona vacantia*. In this latter case, there is no question of succession to be referred to the law of the domicile.[6]

(b) Wills

The general rule, established both in England and in the USA, is that testamentary succession to movables is governed exclusively by the law of the domicile of the deceased as it existed at the time of his death.[7] When a testator dies domiciled abroad leaving assets

---

[2] For a fuller account of the opposing principles, see Wolff, p 567 et seq; Cohn (1956) 5 ICLQ 395. For criticism of the idea of scission, see *Re Collens* [1986] Ch 505 at 512–513. The Hague Conference on Private International Law concluded, in 1989, a Convention on the Law Applicable to Succession to the Estates of Deceased Persons. This Convention adopts the principle of unity of succession, applying the same rules to movables and immovables, and to testate and intestate succession. In most cases the law to be applied would be that of the deceased's habitual residence at the time of death. The Convention is not yet in force and has not been signed or ratified by the United Kingdom. For varied assessments of the Convention's merits, see von Overbeck (1989) 46 *Annuaire suisse de droit international* 138; Lagarde (1989) 78 Rev crit dr int privé 249; North (1990) I Hague Recueil 9, 278–282; Schoenblum (1991) 32 Va J Int L 83.

[3] *Pipon v Pipon* (1744) Amb 25. See, more recently, *Re Barton (Deceased), Tod v Barton* [2002] EWHC 264 (Ch); [2002] WTLR 469.

[4] Supra, pp 49–50.

[5] *In the Estate of Maldonado* [1954] P 223; Lipstein [1954] CLJ 22.

[6] *Re Barnett's Trusts* [1902] 1 Ch 847; *In the Estate of Musurus* [1936] 2 All ER 1666; cf *Re Mitchell, Hatton v Jones* [1954] Ch 525, on which see Ing, *Bona Vacantia*, pp 57–62.

[7] A subsequent change in the law of the domicile is in general of no effect: *Lynch v Provisional Government of Paraguay* (1871) LR 2 P & D 268; and see *Re Aganoor's Trusts* (1895) 64 LJ Ch 521; but see the Wills Act 1963,

in England, it is true that probate must be taken out in England, and it is also true that the assets must be administered in England according to English law, but nevertheless all questions concerning beneficial succession under a will must be decided in accordance with the law of the domicile. The duty of the executor is to ascertain who, by the law of the domicile, is entitled under the will and, once that is ascertained, to distribute the property accordingly.[8] It is necessary, however, to deal separately with the various questions that arise in the case of wills.

(i) Capacity

The capacity of a testator to make a will is determined by the law of his domicile;[9] and there is no distinction between "lack of capacity due to immaturity or status and incapacity arising from ill health".[10] The meaning of this statement is clear enough if the testator is domiciled in the same country at the time both of his making the will and of his death. If this is a foreign country, his capacity by English law is immaterial. Thus, in a case decided when a married woman possessed no testamentary capacity at common law,[11] the English court granted probate of the will of a married woman, a domiciled Spaniard, on proof that by Spanish law a wife was empowered to bequeath her movables.[12]

But what is the position where the testator has changed his domicile after making his will? Is the determinant of the governing law his domicile at death or at the time when he made the will? There is no decision on the matter. Some writers hold that it means the former.[13] This is curious, for by English internal law, and presumably by other legal systems, the decisive moment for testing capacity is the time when the will is made. A will made by a minor or by a person of unsound mind cannot be validated by subsequent events. No will can be valid unless it is valid when made. On principle it makes no difference that the subsequent event consists in a change of domicile to a new country where the law has a more favourable rule for capacity. For instance:

a domiciled Hungarian, 22 years of age, and therefore (it is assumed) lacking testamentary capacity by Hungarian law, makes a will, but ultimately dies domiciled in England.

It is submitted that the will is void. What is invalid for incapacity in its origin can scarcely be automatically validated by the change of domicile. If, on the other hand,

a domiciled German, 16 years of age, makes a will, as he is permitted to do by German law, but ultimately dies domiciled in England,[14]

---

s 6(3), infra, p 1266 et seq; cf succession to immovables where the relevant date is that of the proceedings: *Nelson v Lord Bridport* (1846) 8 Beav 547.

8 *Enohin v Wylie* (1862) 10 HL Cas 1 at 19.

9 *In the Estate of Fuld (No 3)* [1968] P 675 at 696; and see *Re Lewal's Settlement Trusts* [1918] 2 Ch 391.

10 *In the Estate of Fuld (No 3)*, supra, at 696.

11 Until the Married Women's Property Act 1882, a married woman could dispose by will of her separate estate or exercise a power of appointment, and she could bequeath personalty with the assent of her husband, but otherwise she had no testamentary capacity.

12 *In the Goods of Maraver* (1828) 1 Hag Ecc 498.

13 Westlake, s 86.

14 Cohn, *Manual of German Law* (2nd edn) Vol 1, § 614.

it is submitted that the will is valid. In fact it is difficult to disagree with the view that testamentary capacity, in the sphere of both internal law and private international law, is governed by the law of the testator's domicile at the time when the will is made.[15]

The capacity of a legatee to take a bequest is determined by either the law of his domicile,[16] or the law of the testator's domicile. These determine, for instance, whether he is of full age or whether an unincorporated association is capable of receiving a legacy. Thus, in the case of *Re Hellmann's Will*,[17] the court did not apply the law of the legatee's domicile exclusively, but adopted the principle that, where these two laws as to capacity conflict, the one which is most favourable to the *propositus* is selected.

(ii) Formal validity

According to the common law, domicile was the only connecting factor that determined the law to govern the formal validity of a will of movables. The formal requirements of the law of the country where the testator was domiciled at the time of his death had to be satisfied. His nationality, his domicile at the time of making the will and the place where he executed his will were inadmissible factors. The disadvantages of so rigid a principle were brought to light by the case of *Bremer v Freeman* in 1857,[18] where it was held that a will made in the English form by a British subject who died domiciled in France was invalid, since it neglected the formalities prescribed by French law. This decision led to the passing of the Wills Act 1861, often known as Lord Kingsdown's Act, which was designed to offer testators a wider choice of laws so far as formalities were concerned. Although that Act was a welcome step forward, it was disfigured by several serious blemishes.[19] It was badly drafted and was, for example, confined to the wills of British subjects, differentiating moreover between realty and personalty rather than between movables and immovables.

The 1861 Act was repealed and replaced by the Wills Act 1963[20] which applies to a will, whether of movables or immovables, made by any testator, irrespective of his domicile or nationality, provided that he died on or after 1 January 1964, even though it was executed before that time. A will made before 1964 that satisfies the Wills Act 1861, is, however, admissible to probate notwithstanding the repeal of that Act.[21]

The gist of the Act of 1963 is that it increased the relevant connecting factors by adding nationality and habitual residence to those which were already recognised by common law and the Wills Act 1861, namely domicile and the place of acting. It provides that

---

[15] See *Re Lewal's Settlement* [1918] 2 Ch 391; and see Dicey, Morris and Collins, paras 27R-021–27-023; Wolff, pp 581–582.

[16] *Re Hellmann's Will* (1866) LR 2 Eq 363; *Re Schnapper* [1928] Ch 420; and see *Re Pemberton* (1966) 59 DLR (2d) 44.

[17] Supra. By German law the boy's father was entitled as guardian to receive the legacy. Lord ROMILLY MR, however, refused to permit payment to him and ordered that during the minority the money should be treated as a minor's legacy.

[18] (1857) 10 Moo PCC 306.

[19] Morris (1946) 62 LQR 170, 173–176.

[20] This enabled the United Kingdom to ratify the 1961 Hague Convention on the Formal Validity of Wills, Cmnd 1729 (1961).

[21] Wills Act 1963, s 7(1), (2), (3), (4). For notes on the Act, see Morris (1964) 13 ICLQ 684; Kahn-Freund (1964) 27 MLR 55.

"a will shall be treated as properly executed" if its execution conforms to the internal law in force in any one of the following territories:[22]

(a) The territory where the will was executed, even if the testator was on a temporary visit.[23]

Where a will is made on board a vessel or aircraft, whether civil or not, the identity of the law of the place of execution receives special statutory treatment. If at the time of execution the aircraft grounded in a particular territory or the vessel is within territorial waters, the testator may comply with the internal law of that territory. Alternatively he may comply with the internal law of the territory with which, having regard to its registration and other relevant circumstances, the vessel or aircraft, whether in course of transit or not, has the closest connection.[24] Judged by this test, the law of the place of acting will normally be the law of the flag, which is represented by the law of the territory where the ship or aircraft is registered if the flag is common to a political unit containing a variety of legal systems.[25]

(b) The territory where the testator was domiciled either at the time of making the will or at death.

(c) The territory where the testator was habitually resident either at the time of making the will or at death.

(d) The state of which the testator, either at the time of making the will or at death, is a national.

This extension of the civil law principle of nationality, though it is a departure from the common law, does at least unify English and continental European rules so far as the formal validity of wills is concerned and will often save a will that under the old law would have failed. For instance, a will made at Zurich in Dutch form by a citizen of the Netherlands, domiciled and habitually resident at all material times in France, is properly executed even though it may be formally void in the eyes of French and Swiss law.

Where, however, reliance is placed on the national law of the testator, there are two situations in which it may be difficult to determine the relevant internal law. The first is where he is simultaneously a national of more than one country. The problem then is to decide whether it is necessary to select one particular nationality to denote the internal law or whether the will will be formally valid if it satisfies the internal law of any of the nationalities. If the former approach is to be adopted, it has been suggested that the court should select either the nationality of the country in which the testator is habitually and principally resident, or the nationality of the country with which in the circumstances he appears to be in fact most closely connected.[26] The other approach, namely of upholding the validity of the will if any of the relevant laws is satisfied, is said to conform more closely with the intentions of those who drafted the 1961 Hague Convention on which the Wills Act 1963 is based.[27]

---

[22] S 1.

[23] Eg *Re Wynn* [1984] 1 WLR 237; and see *Re Kanani* (1978) 122 Sol Jo 611.

[24] S 2(1)(a).

[25] Cf supra, p 859 et seq.

[26] This is the test laid down by the Hague Convention on Conflict of Nationality Laws (1930). If, however, the testator is a national of the forum, it is generally agreed that that nationality prevails; see Rabel, Vol 1, p 120.

[27] Mann (1986) 35 ICLQ 423.

The second situation that causes difficulty is where the state of which the testator is a national comprises various systems of internal law, as is the case for instance in the United Kingdom or the USA. The 1963 Act solves the problem by providing that the system to be applied shall be ascertained as follows. First, if there is in force throughout the state a rule indicating which of the various systems can properly be applied to the case in question, that rule shall be followed. Failing such a rule, the system shall be that with which the testator was most closely connected at the relevant time.[28] The first of these rules is likely to be of little practical benefit because there will be few composite states which have a unified conflict of laws rule but different domestic rules as to the formal validity of wills. It is reasonable to assume that under the second rule the court, in its search for the country with which the testator was most closely connected at the relevant time, will attribute most importance to his domicile and habitual residence. Where, however, he is domiciled and resident other than in the composite state of which he is a national, as is likely to be the case where he is relying on the law of his nationality as the basis of formal validity, the one remaining factor of significance seems to be the situation of his assets. The relevant time at which the connection must exist is specified in the 1963 Act as "the time of the testator's death where the matter is to be determined by reference to circumstances prevailing at his death, and the time of execution of the will in any other case".[29]

More generally, it will have been observed that the time at which the connecting factors of domicile, habitual residence or nationality may indicate an applicable law is either when the will is executed or when the testator dies. In effect, therefore, there are seven statutory rules for the choice of law.[30] It would seem that if in fact a will satisfies the requirement of any one of these possible laws it is valid as regards form even though the validating law was not deliberately chosen by the testator. This is the reasonable implication of the statutory provision that "a will shall be treated as properly executed if its execution conformed"[31] to one of the prescribed laws.

> A testator, for instance, domiciled in country X makes a will in country Y which is formally valid under the law of X but not under the law of Y. He believes that he has satisfied the requirements of the law of the place of execution.

It might be thought that the will is void, since the intention was to conform to the rules of the law of the place of execution, not of the law of the domicile. But the paramount intention of the testator in such a case is to make a valid will and if he achieves this purpose under one possible law his erroneous belief that he is achieving it under another is immaterial.[32]

The merit of the statutory provision that the legal system to govern formalities (whether it be based on nationality, domicile, habitual residence or place of execution) means the internal law of that system is that the doctrine of renvoi is excluded. This is fortified by the definition of "internal law" as the "law which would apply in a case where no question

---

[28] S 6(2).

[29] S 6(2)(b).

[30] In the case of immovables it is also sufficient to comply with the law of the situs: s 2(1)(b), infra, p 1279. The Law Reform Committee of British Columbia, in its Report on the Making and Revocation of Wills (1981), recommended (p 107) that a will should also be formally valid if it complies with the law of the situs of movables either at the time the will was made or at the date of death.

[31] S 1.

[32] Wolff, p 586.

of the law in force in any other territory or State arose".[33] Nevertheless, for three reasons, this does not mean that renvoi is wholly inapplicable in the case of the formal validity of wills. First, there is the transitional point that the Wills Act 1861 is still applicable to a will made before 1964 and the doctrine of renvoi has been applied under that Act.[34] Secondly, the Wills Act 1963 does not, despite the references to domicile, abolish the old common law rule whereby the formal validity of a will may be referred to the law of the testator's domicile on death,[35] including any further legal system referred to by that law.[36] Thirdly, the Wills Act 1963 does not take away the right to prove in England a will which has been accepted by a court of the deceased's last domicile,[37] even if that acceptance was based other than on that country's internal law.

In considering, under the Wills Act 1963, whether a will has been properly executed, regard must be had to the internal law as it existed at the time of execution. Any later alteration of the law, operating retrospectively to that time, may, however, be taken into account if it validates, but not if it invalidates, the will.[38]

Although it is clear that the capacity of a testator is governed by his personal law, and therefore not necessarily by the law that governs the formal validity of his will, it may sometimes be troublesome to determine whether or not a given rule affects capacity.

> Suppose, for instance, that the testator, Dutch by nationality and by domicile, makes a holograph will in France and leaves assets in England. Both English and French law recognise holograph wills, but the original Article 992 of the Netherlands Civil Code forbade a Dutch national to make such a will abroad.

If the proper execution of the will were to be questioned in England, the court would have to determine the scope of the rule contained in Article 992. If it imposed an incapacity upon the testator, it must be enforced; if it related to formalities, it must be ignored. Such a problem is dealt with by the following section of the Wills Act 1963.[39]

> Where (whether in pursuance of this Act or not) a law in force outside the United Kingdom falls to be applied in relation to a will, any requirement of that law whereby special formalities are to be observed by testators answering a particular description, or witnesses to the execution of a will are to possess certain qualifications, shall be treated, notwithstanding any rule of that law to the contrary, as a formal requirement.

In the hypothetical case suggested above, therefore, the will made in France would be formally valid in the eyes of English law.

International form of will

Increased mobility has meant an increase in the number of people who make wills in a country in which they are not domiciled or habitually resident or of which they are

---

[33] S 6(1).
[34] *In the Goods of Lacroix* (1877) 2 PD 94; *In the Estate of Fuld (No 3)* [1968] P 675.
[35] *In the Goods of Deshais* (1865) 4 Sw & Tr 13 at 17.
[36] *Collier v Rivaz* (1841) 2 Curt 855; cf *Bremer v Freeman* (1857) 10 Moo PCC 306; and see Morris, p 351.
[37] *Enohin v Wylie* (1862) 10 HL Cas 1; *Doglioni v Crispin* (1866) LR 1 HL 301.
[38] S 6(3). If this extends to alterations in the law made after the death of the testator, it reverses the effect of *Lynch v Provisional Government of Paraguay* (1871) LR 2 P & D 268, supra, p 1264, n 7.
[39] S 3.

not nationals. Undoubtedly the Convention which led to the Wills Act 1963 has done much to assist with this problem; but a further step has been taken with the United Kingdom's ratification of the Washington Convention on International Wills (1973).[40] The Annex to the Convention was brought into force by section 27 of the Administration of Justice Act 1982 and is scheduled to that Act. Its essential provision[41] is that a will will be formally valid in all the Contracting States if it complies with the formalities laid down in the Convention, irrespective of where the will was made, the location of the assets or the nationality, domicile or residence of the testator. The main formalities[42] are that the will be in writing (in any language) and signed or acknowledged by the testator in the presence of two witnesses and an "authorised person" (which in England is a solicitor or a notary public),[43] who have then to attest the will in the presence of the testator. The authorised person has to attach to the will a certificate in the form prescribed by the Convention,[44] authenticating the will and its proper execution.

In essence, the Convention provides a new, additional form for a will which a Contracting State must recognise as formally valid. It may also be recognised in a non-Contracting State under general choice of law rules, as where that state looks to the law of the domicile of the testator and the testator was domiciled in a state which is a party to the Convention and his will had complied with the Convention even though not with the formal require-ments of his domiciliary law.[45]

(iii) Essential validity

The essential, or material, validity of a will, and of any particular gift of movables therein is determined by the law of the country in which the testator was domiciled at death.[46] This rule is not affected by the Wills Act 1963. A will may be admitted to probate under that statute as having complied with the formalities of one of the legal systems that it makes available, but the actual effect of its dispositions must be measured by the law of the testator's domicile at death. The grant of probate is conclusive proof that the instru-ment proved is the will of the testator but it is not conclusive as to the validity of the dispositions.

> If, for instance, a British subject dies domiciled in France, having made a will in England according to English law, probate is necessarily granted. But if he has neglected to leave to his children that portion of the estate required by French law, the English court allows the will to take effect only as it would do in France. If French law regards the testamentary dispositions as ineffective, the court directs the

---

[40] Nadelmann (1974) 22 AJCL 365; Brandon (1983) 32 ICLQ 742; Kearney (1984) 18 Int Lawyer 613.

[41] Art 1.

[42] Arts 2–5.

[43] 1982 Act, s 28(1).

[44] Art 10.

[45] The Administration of Justice Act 1982, ss 23–26 also implements another international convention, namely the Council of Europe Convention on the Establishment of a Scheme of Registration of Wills (1972) which may also be of practical assistance to the person who makes a will away from home. It provides for the establishment of national registration schemes for wills and access to them from other Contracting States.

[46] *Thornton v Curling* (1824) 8 Sim 310; *Campbell v Beaufoy* (1859) John 320; *Macdonald v Macdonald* (1872) LR 14 Eq 60; *Re Groos, Groos v Groos* [1915] 1 Ch 572; *Philipson-Stow v IRC* [1961] AC 727 at 761; *Re Levick's Will Trusts* [1963] 1 WLR 311; *Re Barton (Deceased), Tod v Barton* [2002] EWHC 264 (Ch); [2002] WTLR 469; *Al-Bassam v Al-Bassam* [2004] EWCA Civ 857, [2004] WTLR 757.

property to be distributed according to the French law of intestacy;[47] if French law requires only part of the estate to go to the children, the will would be valid as to the rest with the bequests proportionately reduced.[48]

The principle that the law of the domicile at death is decisive is well illustrated by the reverse case to that just given. An example is afforded by *Re Groos, Groos v Groos*:[49]

A Dutch woman made her will in the Netherlands constituting her husband heir of her movable property except for the "legitimate portion to which her descendants were entitled". She died domiciled in England, leaving her husband and five children surviving. By Dutch law the "legitimate portion" of the children was three-fourths of the estate, but by English law it was nothing. It was held that, since the will operated under English law, the whole estate passed to the husband.

Whether a beneficiary is entitled to take under a will is determined by the law of the testator's domicile if the question turns on a rule of substantive law, not on procedure. In the case of *Re Cohn*:[50]

A testatrix and her daughter, both domiciled in Germany, were killed in an air raid in London in circumstances which left it uncertain which of them died first. The daughter's estate was entitled to movables under her mother's will, but only if she were the survivor. In such a case the English rule is that the younger person is presumed to have survived the elder,[51] but the presumption by German law was that they died simultaneously.

These presumptions were classified as falling within the sphere of substantive law, and it was held that the German view must be adopted. On the other hand, the English rule relating to the burden of proof of testamentary capacity has been classified as procedural and governed by the law of the forum.[52]

Other examples of questions of substance are whether a gift to an attesting witness, or to the relative of an attesting witness, is valid,[53] whether the testator acted under duress or undue influence,[54] and whether a beneficiary is put to his election.[55] Similarly, legislation empowering the court to make an order for such provision out of the estate as is adequate to support the dependants of the deceased would appear to be a matter of substance applicable only if the testator died domiciled within the jurisdiction.[56]

---

[47] *Thornton v Curling*, supra; *Campbell v Beaufoy*, supra.

[48] Eg *Re Annesley* [1926] Ch 692; *Re Adams* [1967] IR 424, especially at 452–458.

[49] [1915] 1 Ch 572.

[50] [1945] Ch 5; Morris (1945) 61 LQR 340.

[51] Law of Property Act 1925, s 184.

[52] *In the Estate of Fuld (No 3)* [1968] P 675 at 694–699.

[53] *Re Priest* [1944] Ch 58. This case has been much discussed; see RMW (1944) 60 LQR 114; Morris (1945) 61 LQR 124; (1946) 62 LQR 172, 173; Kahn-Freund (1946) 7 MLR 238; Wolff, p 586. See now the Wills Act 1968.

[54] *In the Estate of Fuld (No 3)* [1968] P 675 at 698–699.

[55] See *Re Ogilvie* [1918] 1 Ch 492, 500; *Re Mengel's Will Trust* [1962] Ch 791; Dicey, Morris and Collins, paras 27R-073–27-075. Election is discussed more fully in the context of succession to immovables, infra, p 1282 et seq.

[56] *Pain v Holt* (1919) 19 SRNSW 105; *Re Herron* [1941] 4 DLR 203; *Re Terry* [1951] NZLR 30; *Re Greenfield* [1985] 2 NZLR 662. The English legislation is limited in terms to testators dying domiciled in England and Wales: Inheritance (Provision for Family and Dependants) Act 1975, s 1(1), as amended by the Civil Partnership Act 2004, Sch 4(2), para 15(6); and see *Mastaka v Midland Bank Executor and Trustee Co Ltd* [1941] Ch 192;

It should not be assumed that because a testator dies domiciled in England his will is therefore inevitably subject to all the rules of English domestic law concerned with essential validity. This fact has not always been admitted. It has been said,[57] for instance, that whether a restraint on marriage or a gift to a charity is valid, or whether a limitation is void as infringing the rule against perpetuities,[58] must be determined by the law of the testator's domicile no matter what the domicile of the beneficiary may be. It is submitted that this view is neither consonant with principle nor warranted by the authorities. It entirely ignores the essential difference between the right to give and the right to receive. The two are not necessarily analogous. The right of a testator to give, for example as to whether he is free to bequeath the whole of his property as it pleases him or on the contrary whether he must reserve a legitimate portion for his children, is of necessity governed by the English law of succession from which his testamentary power of disposition is derived. But there is no reason why this law should restrict the right of a foreign legatee to enjoy a gift in accordance with the terms of the will, provided that the legacy is valid according to his personal law and provided that the limitations imposed on its enjoyment do not offend some rule of public policy so sacred in English eyes as to demand extra-territorial application.

> Suppose that a testator domiciled in England bequeaths a sum of money to a legatee domiciled in France, and that the legacy, though valid by French law, is void by English internal law as being obnoxious to the perpetuity rule.

If the English policy is to insist on the early vesting of interests regardless of where the property is to be enjoyed and administered then the legacy must be regarded as void. Such a suggestion is, however, untenable. The object of the perpetuity rule is to restrict the withdrawal of property from the channels of commerce, a purpose which is clearly local, and which, therefore, cannot justifiably be invoked to destroy a bequest of money that is to be enjoyed and administered in a foreign country. As Lord COTTENHAM said in an early case:

> The rules acted upon by the courts in this country with respect to testamentary dispositions tending to perpetuities relate to this country only . . . The fund [given by the English will] being to be administered in a foreign country is payable here though the purpose to which it is to be applied would have been illegal if the administration of the fund had been to take place in this country.[59]

This conclusion has been reached several times by the New York Court of Appeals[60] and on one occasion at least by an Australian court.[61] In the laconic words of one judge: "It is no part of the policy of the State of New York to interdict perpetuities or gifts in mortmain in Pennsylvania or California."[62]

Wilson v Jones (Preliminary Issue), 8 June 2000 (unreported), Ch D; *Cyganik v Agulian* [2006] EWCA Civ 129; [2006] 1 FCR 406.

[57] Westlake, p 154.

[58] Ibid; and Dicey, Morris and Collins, paras 27-046–27-048

[59] *Fordyce v Bridges* (1848) 2 Ph 497 at 515. An English testator gave the residue of his personal estate to trustees to convert it into money and lay it out in the purchase of land in England or Scotland according to the limitations of a Scottish entail. Such limitations infringed the English rule against perpetuities. The trustees were allowed to purchase land in Scotland in accordance with the terms of the will.

[60] Gray, *The Rule against Perpetuities* (1942) 4th edn, § 263.2; Morris and Leach, *The Rule against Perpetuities* (1962) 2nd edn, pp 22–23; and see *Re Chappell's Estate* 124 Wash 128, 213 P 684 (1923).

[61] *Re Mitchner* [1922] St R Qd 252.

[62] *Chamberlain v Chamberlain* 43 NY 424 at 434 (1870).

Again:

> Suppose that a testator, domiciled in England, leaves a sum of money in trust that the income thereof shall be used for purposes most conducive to the good of religion in a certain diocese in country X, and that persons domiciled in X are appointed to administer the trust.[63]

The trust is invalid by English law as not being charitable;[64] but, if it is valid by the law of X, must the court forbid payment of the money to the trustees? Again, such a ruling would be indefensible. English law confines the definition of a charity within comparatively narrow limits, presumably with the object of restricting the amount of money that may be withdrawn from circulation, but it cannot justifiably claim to impose this policy on foreign countries. The decisive factor is the law of the country where the trust is to be administered, ie its proper law, not the law that governs the instrument of gift.[65] Three conditions must be satisfied before transfer of the money to the foreign country will be authorised. First, the charitable bequest must be valid according to its proper law, the law of the country where it is to be administered. Secondly, there must be persons in that country willing and competent to undertake the task of administration.[66] Thirdly, the purposes for which the bequest is to be employed must not conflict with some rule of English public policy intended to operate extra-territorially. It can scarcely be maintained that a rule which confines within narrow limits the possible beneficiaries of a charitable gift is intended to be anything more than local in its operation.[67]

It would seem, then, that the principle which refers questions of substantial validity to the law of the testator's domicile is not unqualified.

(iv) Construction

The province of construction is to ascertain the expressed intentions of the testator, ie the meaning which the words of the will, when properly interpreted, convey. If the intention is expressed in a manner that leaves no room for doubt, the aid of private international law is unnecessary. This is because the duty of any court, no matter in which country it may sit, is to give effect to expressed intentions and, if these are clear, there can be no occasion to test the language of the will by reference to any particular legal system. If, however, the language of the will leaves the intention doubtful, or if it uses expressions which are ambiguous or equivocal or if the testator has failed to provide for certain events which have not been covered by his dispositions, a problem of choice of law arises, for it is essential that the doubtful intention of the testator should be ascertained by reference to rules of construction obtaining in one particular system of law. The consequences may be serious according to whether this law or that law is chosen, for when it is said that the intention of the testator is the sovereign guide in questions of construction, this does not mean that his language is necessarily to be construed in a manner that would commend

---

[63] The American position relating to charitable gifts is discussed by Hancock (1964) 16 Stan LR 561.

[64] *Dunne v Byrne* [1912] AC 407.

[65] The majority decision of the Supreme Court of Canada to the contrary: *Jewish National Fund Inc v Royal Trust Co* (1965) 53 DLR (2d) 577, has been strongly criticised: Picarda, *The Law and Practice Relating to Charities* (1995) 2nd edn, pp 783–785; Waters, *Law of Trusts in Canada* (2005) 3rd edn, Chapter 14.

[66] *New v Bonaker* (1867) LR 4 Eq 655.

[67] *Oliphant v Hendrie* (1784) 1 Bro CC 571; *Mackintosh v Townsend* (1809) 16 Ves 330; *A-G v Mill* (1827) 3 Russ 328 at 338; affd by the House of Lords 2 Dow and Clark 393; *Fordyce v Bridges* (1848) 2 Ph 497 at 515.

itself to an intelligent man, but that it must be read in the light of those technical rules of construction recognised by the governing legal system.

It will be seen, therefore, that in choosing a law to govern construction it is desirable to discover that system with which the testator was most intimately acquainted, and which it is just to presume that he had in mind when drafting his will.[68] Certain expressions, such as "next of kin", bear different meanings in different countries, and it is obvious that the intention of a testator may be defeated unless the legal system with reference to which he wrote his will is correctly ascertained.

The law with which the ordinary person is most familiar is the law of his existing domicile, and, despite the fact that certain authorities choose the domicile at death as the controlling factor,[69] it is more consonant with the desire of the court to implement the intention of the testator to say that the law of the domicile at the time when his will is made governs its construction, unless there is evidence indicating that his mind was directed to some other legal system. This approach is supported by section 4 of the Wills Act 1963 which provides that the "construction of a will shall not be altered by reason of any change in the testator's domicile after the execution of the will".[70]

In most cases, of course, the domicile does not change after the will has been made and examples can readily be provided of the application of the law of the domicile being unchanged between the making of the will and death. Where, for instance, a domiciled Englishman bequeathed a legacy to the "next of kin" of a foreigner, it was held that the legatees must be ascertained according to English law.[71] Whether a gift in the will of a domiciled Englishman was a satisfaction of a debt due under a Scottish settlement was tested by reference to English law.[72] Words of value or of quantity or of measurement, which vary in meaning in different countries, have been interpreted according to the law of the testator's domicile.[73]

There is, however, no absolute rule that the interpretation of a will depends on the law of the testator's domicile. It is merely a prima facie rule that is displaced if the testator has manifestly contemplated and intended that his will should be construed according to some other system of law.[74] Thus where a domiciled Frenchwoman left an unattested will valid by the law of France, in which she said that the will was to "be considered in England the same as in France", STIRLING J held, on the question whether the document operated as the execution of a power, that the testatrix wrote with reference to English law.[75]

---

[68] See *Re McMorran* [1958] Ch 624 at 634; *Durie's Trustees v Osborne* 1960 SC 444 at 450–451; *Re Adams* [1967] IR 424 at 458, 461.

[69] *Re Cunnington* [1924] 1 Ch 68; and see *Trotter v Trotter* (1828) 4 Bli NS 502; *Yates v Thompson* (1835) 3 Cl & Fin 544.

[70] And see *Philipson-Stow v IRC* [1961] AC 727 at 761. Cf *Re Levick's Will Trusts* [1963] 1 WLR 311.

[71] *Re Fergusson's Will* [1902] 1 Ch 483. But see *Re Goodman's Trusts* (1881) 17 Ch D 266, supra, p 1152; cf the Scottish view: *Mitchell's Trustee v Rule* 1908 SLT 189; *Smith's Trustees v Macpherson* 1926 SC 983; Anton, pp 692–694.

[72] *Campbell v Campbell* (1866) LR 1 Eq 383.

[73] *Saunders v Drake* (1742) 2 Atk 465.

[74] *Pierson v Garnet* (1786) 2 Bro CC 38; Westlake, s 123; cf *Re Cunnington* [1924] 1 Ch 68.

[75] *Re Price, Tomlin v Latter* [1900] 1 Ch 442. In *Re Wynn* [1984] 1 WLR 237, English law was applied to determine whether a will which revoked previous wills but made no fresh dispositions of the testatrix's property (apparently both movable and immovable) could have the effect of excluding her husband from taking on intestacy, even though it was not decided where the testatrix was domiciled at the material time.

(v) Revocation

Since the rules relating to revocation vary from country to country,[76] the problem is to ascertain the law that determines what suffices to revoke an existing will. According to English internal law, a will may be voluntarily revoked either by a fresh will or by its destruction, or obliteration, with the intention of revoking it, by the testator himself or by some authorised person in his presence. Further, its automatic revocation may result from the later marriage of the testator. These three methods will serve as the basis on which to discuss the problem of the choice of law.

(a) Revocation by later will

A will purporting to revoke an earlier will is formally valid and effective if it satisfies the requirements of any one of the laws by which, under the Wills Act 1963, its formal validity is determinable. Suppose, for instance, that a testator domiciled in England makes a will in the English form revoking an earlier will that he had made when domiciled in France. The revocation is effective even if ineffective according to French law.

The Wills Act 1963, however, goes further. It provides that the revoking will shall be effective if it complies with the requirements of any one of the laws qualified to govern the formal validity of the *earlier* will.[77] The mere fact that, at the time of his death, the testator has become subject to another testamentary law is not to upset what he lawfully and intentionally did according to a law that governed him in the past. Thus, to reverse the illustration suggested above, the revocation would be effective if contained in a will that was formally void by English law but valid according to the law of France.

It should be noted, however, that a testator may make a valid English will which does not revoke an earlier will in foreign form where the latter deals solely with property in a foreign country and the English will deals only with English property, even though it contains a revocation clause.[78]

(b) Revocation by destruction of the will

The Private International Law Committee recommended in 1958 that the effect of the destruction of a will should be determinable by any one of the laws capable of governing the formal validity of the testator's will, had he chosen to make one.[79] This proposal has not been accepted by the legislature. The Wills Act 1963 deals only with a testamentary revocation. Hence, the problem of choice of law in the case of acts such as destruction of the will, or obliteration of some of its provisions, must be solved on the basis of the common law principle of domicile.[80] But what is the decisive domicile in this context? The question is superfluous if the testator has lived in the same country throughout his life, since there is only one possible domiciliary law. It requires an answer, however, if he possessed one domicile at the time of the act of destruction, and another at the time of death,

---

[76] In relation to South Africa, see Neels (2007) 56 ICLQ 613.

[77] S 2(1)(c).

[78] *In the Estate of Wayland* [1951] 2 All ER 1041; *Guardian Trust and Executors Co of New Zealand Ltd v Darroch* [1973] 2 NZLR 143. Also *In the Estate of Vickers* (2001-02) 4 ITELR 584; *Re Baldry (Deceased)* [2004] WTLR 609 (Fam Div), in respect of which see Simm 2005 TEL & TJ (65) (Apr) 15; *Lamothe v Lamothe* [2006] EWHC 1387; [2006] WTLR 1431.

[79] (1958) Cmd 491, p 8.

[80] Cf *Velasco v Coney* [1934] P 143.

for what is an effective revocation by the earlier law of the domicile, may be ineffective by the later.

> Suppose, for instance, that a testator domiciled in Quebec sent written instructions to his solicitor to destroy his will. The will was accordingly burnt and was thereby revoked in the eyes of Quebec law. The testator died domiciled in England. English internal law would not regard the revocation as effective since the burning was not carried out in the presence of the testator.[81]

Since the testator died subject to English law, could it successfully be contended that his will, presuming its contents to be ascertainable, was still operative? It is submitted that such a contention would be ill-founded. The legal effect of the act of destruction fell to be determined at the time of its performance. The testator intended to revoke his will. He fulfilled his intention by an act that was regarded as final and effective by the law to which he was then subject. There was no other law available to him.[82] The mind recoils from the suggestion that the effect of such an act within the law might be nullified or changed merely because at some later period in his life he happened to be subjected to a different legal system. It requires something more than this to undo what has lawfully and intentionally been done in the past.

The same reasoning applies to the reverse case. If the act of destruction were sufficient by English law but insufficient by Quebec law, the will would remain unrevoked. A chance change of domicile could scarcely infuse life into an act that was legally stillborn.[83]

(c) Revocation by marriage

The rule of English law is that a will is revoked by marriage unless it is explicitly expressed to be made in contemplation of marriage.[84] Few other legal systems have adopted the rule and so choice of law problems may arise. When a person marries after making a will and then dies leaving movables in some other country, the question may arise as to whether the law of his domicile at the time of marriage or at the time of death determines the effect of the marriage on the will.[85] The answer to this question depends on whether the rule as to revocation by marriage is to be classified as a rule of matrimonial law or of testamentary law. If it is a rule concerning the former, then its effect must be tested by the law of the domicile at the time of marriage; if on the other hand, it has nothing to do with the matrimonial regime at all, its effect is to be measured by the law of the domicile at the date of death. It would seem scarcely open to doubt that it is essentially a doctrine connected with the relationship of marriage, and that this is so was affirmed in the case of *Re Martin, Loustalan v Loustalan*,[86] where a woman, after making a will, married a man domiciled in England and subsequently died domiciled in France. By English internal law a will is

---

[81] Wills Act 1837, s 20.

[82] See *Re Traversi's Estate* 189 Misc 251, 64 NYS 2d 453 (1946).

[83] Mann (1954) 31 BYBIL 217, 231.

[84] Wills Act 1837, s 18 (as substituted by the Administration of Justice Act 1982, s 18), and s 18A, as amended by the Law Reform (Succession) Act 1995, s 3 and the Family Law Act 1996, Sch 8). See also s 18B (will to be revoked by civil partnership) and s 18C (effect of dissolution or annulment of civil partnership on wills).

[85] There is also the fundamental question as to whether the relevant marriage was valid; see *Re Fleming* [1987] ILRM 638.

[86] [1900] P 211; and see *Re Micallef's Estate* [1977] 2 NSWLR 929.

revoked by marriage, but this is not so under French law. In order to decide whether the will was revoked it was necessary to decide whether this was a matrimonial question governed by English law or a testamentary question governed by French law. VAUGHAN-WILLIAMS LJ in the Court of Appeal held[87] that the question was one of matrimonial law, English law applied and the will was revoked.

As the relevant domicile is that at the time of the marriage, the effect of a change of domicile may be shown by the following two examples:

> A makes a will while domiciled in England; then he acquires a domicile in Scotland (where marriage does not revoke a will); he later marries in Scotland, and ultimately dies domiciled in England.[88]

In this case the will stands. English law applies only as being the governing testamentary law under which A dies, and therefore its doctrine as to the effect of marriage cannot affect a marriage that took place when the parties had a foreign domicile. The reverse case to that just put is as follows:

> A makes a will while domiciled in Scotland, then acquires an English domicile and later marries in England.

Here the question as to revocation is governed by English law as being the law applicable to all matters concerning the matrimonial regime.

It has been assumed so far that the spouses have a common domicile on marriage. However, this may not always be the case, given that a wife may have a domicile independent from that of her husband.[89] As domicile for the purposes of revocation of a will by marriage is to be determined as at the time of marriage, there may be some cases where a wife retains her separate domicile notwithstanding her marriage. If so, the law of that country will determine whether her will is revoked by marriage.

So far as English law is concerned, a marriage which is void under English rules of private international law will have no effect on the will;[90] but a voidable marriage will revoke it.[91]

3. IMMOVABLES

(a) Intestate succession

We have seen earlier[92] that, under the principle of scission, succession to immovables is governed, not by the law of the testator's domicile, but by the law of the situs.[93]

---

[87] Ibid, at 240.
[88] *In the Goods of Reid* (1866) LR 1 P & D 74; cf *In the Estate of Groos* [1904] P 269.
[89] Domicile and Matrimonial Proceedings Act 1973, s 1.
[90] *Mette v Mette* (1859) 1 Sw & Tr 416.
[91] *Re Roberts* [1978] 1 WLR 653.
[92] Supra, p 1264.
[93] This would seem to mean the law of the situs at the date of the proceedings, rather than at the time of death: *Nelson v Lord Bridport* (1846) 8 Beav 547.

Accordingly, where the owner of immovables dies intestate, the order of descent or distri-bution prescribed by the law of the situs is applied by the English court no matter what his domicile may have been.[94] This rule can be criticised on a number of grounds.[95] It is an historical anomaly from the time before 1926 when intestate succession to land was subject to rules different from intestate succession to personalty. Domestic legislation on intestate succession would seem to be based on the assumption, erroneous in fact, that succession to all the intestate's property will be governed by the same law. This is particu-larly striking with regard to the statutory legacies which go to a surviving spouse under the law of England[96] and of Northern Ireland.[97] Can a widow claim two such statutory legacies, one based on land in England and the other on personalty in Northern Ireland?[98] The operation of the rule may be illustrated by two decisions.

The first is an Irish case, *Re Rea*[99] in which:

> A domiciled Irishman died intestate without issue in Ireland, owning land in both Ireland and Victoria. In such circumstances a widow was entitled by a Victorian statute to a charge of £1,000 on land in the colony and by an Irish statute to a charge of £500 payable out of the real and personal estate in Ireland. The land in Victoria having been sold and the proceeds remitted to Ireland, it was held that the widow was entitled to the £1,000 under the Victorian statute, as well as the £500 under the Irish statute, since her rights were those conferred by the law of the situs.

The second, and more recent, decision is *Re Collens*:[100]

> The deceased died in 1966. He was intestate and died domiciled in Trinidad and Tobago, leaving property there, in Barbados and in England. The property in England included immovable property. There was a dispute over succession to the estate and it was agreed that the deceased's second wife should receive $1 million in settlement of any claim to the property in Trinidad and Tobago, but that succession to the estate in Barbados and England should be governed by their respective laws. It was not contested that English law as the law of the situs governed the intestate succession to the English immovables. The question for the court was whether the second wife could take, not only the $1 million agreed under the law of the deceased's domicile, but also the statutory legacy due to a widow under the English law of intestacy.

Sir Nicolas BROWNE-WILKINSON V-C was reluctant to see the widow succeed both under the law of the domicile and to the statutory legacy under English law, as the law of the situs. Nevertheless he was unable to interpret either the English statutory provisions or the choice of law rules so as to lead to any other result. Although he saw force in the

---

[94] *Balfour v Scott* (1793) 6 Bro Parl Cas 550; *Duncan v Lawson* (1889) 41 Ch D 394; cf *Re Ralston* [1906] VLR 689. When the immovables are situated in a country that adopts the principle of unity of succession this means that, subject to the acceptance of the renvoi doctrine by the law of the situs, the order of descent may be that of England; cf *Re Duke of Wellington* [1947] Ch 506; supra, pp 69–70.

[95] See Morris (1969) 85 LQR 339, 348–352.

[96] Administration of Estates Act 1925, s 46(1)(i), para (3), as amended.

[97] Administration of Estates Act (Northern Ireland) 1955, s 7, as amended.

[98] Morris and North, p 575. A clear negative answer has been given in Canada: *Re Thom* (1987) 40 DLR (4th) 184; *Vak Estate v Dukelow* (1994) 117 DLR (4th) 122; cf *Train v Train's Executor* (1899) 2 F 146.

[99] [1902] 1 IR 451.

[100] [1986] Ch 505.

criticisms of this state of the law, he felt obliged to conclude that "my job is to administer the law as it now is".[101]

(b) Wills

The general rule in the case of testamentary succession to immovables is, as with intestate succession, that it is the law of the situs of the immovables which governs. Though there are fewer authorities relating to wills of immovables, it may be helpful to consider the various issues that may arise in the same order as with wills of movables.

(i) Capacity

There seems little doubt that the law of the situs exclusively determines whether the testator has capacity to make a will of immovables,[102] and also probably capacity to take a bequest.

(ii) Formal validity

At common law, a will of immovables had to comply with the formal requirements of the law of the situs.[103] However, as with wills of movables,[104] the common law principles have been much enlarged by the Wills Act 1963. It is sufficient for the will to comply with any one of the seven laws specified in section 1 of the Act in relation to movables, name-ly the territory where the testator was domiciled or habitually resident or of which he was a national, either when the will was executed or when the testator died, or the territory where the will was executed. Furthermore, the common law rule, ie compliance with the formalities of the law of the situs, is also retained in the case of immovables.[105] However, reference in the Wills Act to the law of the situs is in terms of "the internal law in force in the territory where the property was situated"[106] and the reference to the "internal law" of the situs seems to exclude the doctrine of renvoi.[107]

(iii) Essential validity

There is no doubt[108] that the law of the situs, including its choice of law rules (which means that the doctrine of renvoi[109] is applicable), governs matters of essential validity. This rule has been applied to such issues as whether the bequest contravenes the rule against perpetuities or against accumulations,[110] whether gifts to charities are valid,[111] whether a proportion of the estate has to be left to the children or to a surviving spouse,[112]

---

[101] Ibid, at 513. See Carruthers (2005), paras 2.76–2.86

[102] See *Re Hernando, Hernando v Sawtell* (1884) 27 Ch D 284, where the proposition, so far as related to English land, was undisputed; and see Mental Health Act 1983, s 97 (4)(a).

[103] *Coppin v Coppin* (1725) 2 P Wms 291, supra, p 1204, *Pepin v Bruyère* [1900] 2 Ch 504.

[104] Supra, p 1266 et seq.

[105] Wills Act 1963, s 2(1)(b).

[106] Ibid.

[107] Cf wills of movables, supra, p 1267.

[108] Note, however, in the USA, the gradual erosion of the situs rule for testate succession to immovable property: *Saunders v Saunders* 796 So 2d 1253 (Fla App 2001), cited in Symeonides (2002) 50 AJCL 1, 94.

[109] Supra, Chapter 5.

[110] *Freke v Carbery* (1873) LR 16 Eq 461.

[111] *Duncan v Lawson* (1889) 41 Ch D 394; supra, pp 1222–1223.

[112] *Re Hernando* (1884) 27 Ch D 284; *Re Ross* [1930] 1 Ch 377; and see *Re Bailey* [1985] 2 NZLR 656.

whether a power to assign part of the estate is valid,[113] and, indeed, whether the land can be devised at all.[114]

A matter of considerable practical importance is whether a court can order payment to be made out of the estate for the support of dependants. In the case of movables, we have seen[115] that, under the Inheritance (Provision for Family and Dependants) Act 1975, an English court can make such an order only if the testator died domiciled in England. It might, therefore, have been expected that, in the case of an estate of immovable property, the 1975 Act would have been applicable if England was the law of the situs.[116] Unfortunately the 1975 Act is seriously defective[117] in that the court can only make an order in the case of immovables, as well as movables, if the testator died domiciled in England.[118] This means that, in the case of a testator who dies domiciled in a country which applies the law of the situs rule such as New South Wales[119] or New Zealand,[120] no provision for support can be made out of the English immovable property. The foreign court has no power because of the English situs and the English court has no power because of the foreign domicile.

(iv) Construction

A somewhat difficult question arises with regard to the construction of wills of immovables. It has been seen that a bequest of movables is construed according to the law intended by the testator, which is generally the law of his domicile at the time when he prepared his will.[121] The problem is whether the English authorities extend the same rule to wills of immovables, or whether they require that exclusive regard shall be paid to the law of the situs.

It is submitted that there is little difficulty if we resort to first principles, and determine what are the natural provinces of the law of the domicile and of the law of the situs respectively in this matter. The objective of all courts, when dealing with a will, is first to ascertain the intention of the testator and then to give effect to that intention so far as is consonant with the governing law. In the ascertainment of this intention in a case where the will has reference to more than one country, it may be a matter of great moment whether the testator's language is read in the light of this or that legal system. This is because it frequently happens that the same word or phrase, such as "heirs of the body", bears a different signification in different countries. It follows, therefore, in such a case that the result which the testator intended will not ensue unless we discover the system of law which he had in mind when he wrote the will. The presumption should be in favour of the law of the domicile at the time of the making of the will, for that is the system of law under which he lives and with which he is expected to be familiar.

---

[113] *Public Trustee v Vodjdani* (1988) 49 SASR 236.

[114] *Nelson v Bridport* (1846) 8 Beav 547.

[115] Supra, p 1271.

[116] See eg *Re Paulin* [1950] VLR 462 at 465.

[117] Morris (1946) 62 LQR 170, 178–179; cf Law Com No 61 (1974), paras 258–262.

[118] 1975 Act, s 1(1), as amended by the Civil Partnership Act 2004, Sch 4(2), para 15(6). See *Wilson v Jones (Preliminary Issue)*, 8 June 2000 (unreported), Ch D; *Cyganik v Agulian* [2006] EWCA Civ 129; [2006] 1 FCR 406.

[119] *Pain v Holt* (1919) 19 SRNSW 105.

[120] *Re Bailey* [1985] 2 NZLR 656.

[121] Supra, pp 1273–1274.

It may, of course, be some other system, such as the law of the situs, for the inquiry turns wholly on intention, and if there is anything clearly indicative of a desire to exclude the law of the domicile, the will must be construed accordingly.[122] Thus, if a domiciled Englishman, possessing land in Scotland, were to adopt in his will the terms "liferent" and "fee", it would be reasonable to conclude that he wished Scots law to govern his disposition; similarly, if he made one will for the land and a separate will for his English property.[123]

Where a testator is domiciled in one country and has land in another, the fact to be borne in mind, then, is that the law of the situs, as such, has no paramount claim to exclusive recognition.[124] Otherwise the result may be to defeat a testator's intention, for he may leave property, not to named persons, but to those persons who would be entitled were he to die intestate. It is obvious, in such a case, that his intention is to benefit the successors admitted by the law of his domicile, since it is that system with which he is familiar, and it can scarcely be denied that arbitrarily to make a new will for him by admitting a different line of succession imposed by the law of a foreign situs, merely because the will includes a certain amount of land situated abroad, would constitute a departure from principle.

The adoption of this principle does not infringe any local rule of the law of the situs; nor does it derogate from the sovereign power of the country in which the land is situated. All courts, in administering private international law, desire to give effect to expressed intentions, provided that this does not conflict with the public policy of the forum or of the situs, and it is a matter of indifference that A takes land under a will that has been construed according to the law of the testator's domicile, though B would have taken had the construction been that of the law of the situs. This, however, gives us the clue to the limits of the doctrine. If the rules of the law of the situs make it illegal or impossible to give effect to the will as construed by the system of law intended by the testator, the general principle must perforce give way, and the construction adopted must be that of the law of the situs.[125] Or, again, if the interest arising from a will that has been so construed possesses incidents different in the situs from those recognised by the law of the domicile, the law of the situs must prevail, for it is that law which determines the nature and extent of estates and interests in immovables.

The principle may, then, be stated as follows:

> A will of immovables must be construed according to the system of law intended by the testator. This is presumed to be the law of the domicile at the time when the will is made, but the presumption will be rebutted if evidence is adduced from the language of the will proving that he made his dispositions with reference to some other legal system. If, however, the interest that arises from such construction is not permitted or not recognised by the law of the situs, the latter law must prevail.

---

[122] *Public Trustee v Vodjdani* (1988) 49 SASR 236.
[123] As in *Re Duke of Wellington* [1947] Ch 506.
[124] Cf *Re Osoba, Osoba v Osoba* [1979] 1 WLR 247 at 250.
[125] *Philipson-Stow v IRC* [1961] AC 727 at 761.

It was decided in *Studd v Cook*,[126] an appeal to the House of Lords from the Court of Session in Scotland, that the size of estate which a devisee takes depends on the law of the testator's domicile. In that case:

A domiciled Englishman devised land in both England and Scotland to the use of X for his life, without impeachment of waste, remainder to the use of the first and every other son of X, "successively, according to their respective seniorities, in tail male". By English law X took a mere life interest, but by Scottish law he was entitled to the fee simple. It was held that the testator clearly intended the limitations of his will to be understood in their English sense, since he had used technical language familiar to English conveyancing, and that therefore his intention was effective so far as the law of Scotland permitted.

This case is distinguishable from *Re Miller, Bailie v Miller*,[127] in which:

By a trust disposition made in Scots form but sufficient to constitute a valid will by English law, A, a domiciled Scotsman, gave his lands in Scotland and England "for behoof of my eldest son, James ... and the heirs male of his body in fee", with remainders over. James died without issue and without having executed any disentailing assurance of the English land. He made, however, a trust disposition in Scots form, executed in the manner required by English law for the execution of wills, by which he disposed of the whole of his real and personal property. By English law, as it then stood, the will of James was ineffectual to pass the estate tail in the English land. By Scots law the will of A did not create a strict entail but gave James an interest that he could dispose of either *inter vivos* or by will. It was held that the question whether James had power to dispose of his London house by will must be decided according to English law.

It would seem that the decision in *Miller* is not inconsistent with *Studd v Cook*, where it was decided that a will should be construed according to the law of the domicile in order to ascertain the size and nature of the interest that the testator intended to give.

(v) Election

The idea that a will of immovables does not necessarily depend in all matters on the law of the situs may also be illustrated by decisions dealing with the doctrine of election.

Suppose, for instance, that a domiciled Englishman makes a will by which he devises his son's foreign land to X but gives £50,000 out of his own property to his son. The rule of domestic English law applicable to these circumstances is that, if the testator clearly intended to dispose of the land in favour of X, the son cannot claim the whole of the £50,000 unless he adopts the testamentary disposition of the land. He must elect, ie he must either keep the land and have the legacy correspondingly reduced, or must recognise the whole of the will by taking his legacy in full and abandoning the land to X. Election is based on the presumption that a testator intends his will to take effect in its entirety.

The rule of English private international law is now well settled that, where a testator disposes of property in more countries than one, the question whether a beneficiary is put

---

[126] (1883) 8 App Cas 577.
[127] [1914] 1 Ch 511. See also *Nelson v Bridport* (1846) 8 Beav 547; *Philipson-Stow v IRC* [1961] AC 727 at 761.

to his election is governed by the law of the testator's domicile.[128] This is so even though the subject matter of the election is land situated abroad, for, though the courts of the domicile cannot withhold the land from the person to whom it belongs according to the law of the situs, they can, in the administration of the movables which is their particular province, insist that if he retains the land contrary to the will he shall compensate the disappointed beneficiaries by relinquishing the whole or part of the legacy.[129] The English court in adopting this attitude does not interfere with the law of the situs. The foreign heir comes to the court, not as heir to the land, over which the court has no jurisdiction, but as legatee of movable property which is being administered in England. It can thus be said to him: "We have no power to dispense with the provisions of the foreign law relating to wills of land, but you come to us as legatee under the will of a testator domiciled in England; and if you claim the legacy you must also recognise the disposition which the will has purported to make of the land." It is always open to the heir to ignore the English administration and to claim the land under the territorial law.[130]

If a case involving the doctrine of election falls to be considered in England, the court turns to the law of the testator's domicile. That domicile may be English or foreign. If it is English, the court merely considers whether the domestic doctrine of election is applicable to the circumstances in question; if it is foreign, its sole guide is the law of the foreign domicile.[131] In *Balfour v Scott*:[132]

A person domiciled in England died intestate leaving immovables in Scotland. The heir to the Scottish land was also one of the next of kin, and as such he claimed a share of the English movables. It was objected to this claim that, by the law of Scotland, an heir could not share in movables unless he consented to the immovables being massed with the movables so as to form one common subject of division. This, however, was not the English rule, and it was therefore held that the heir could take his share as one of the next of kin without complying with the rule of the law of the situs.

As far as private international law is concerned, the question of election generally arises where the testator devises his own land away from the heir by a will that is void, either formally or essentially, according to the law of the situs, but bequeaths by a valid will a legacy to the rejected heir. An issue which arises here is whether the heir must elect, ie if he claims the land on the ground that the will is invalid, can he retain the legacy in full or must he make compensation out of it to the disappointed devisee?

---

[128] *Orrell v Orrell* (1871) 6 Ch App 302; *Dewar v Maitland* (1866) LR 2 Eq 834; *Re Ogilvie* [1918] 1 Ch 492. This rule was overlooked by COHEN J in *Re Allen's Estate* [1945] 2 All ER 264, as to which case see *Re Mengel's Will Trusts* [1962] Ch 791; Dicey, Morris and Collins, paras 27R-076–27-083; Morris (1945) 10 Conv (NS) 102; (1946) 24 Can Bar Rev 528.

[129] There is a conflict of authority in the USA in the case of immovables as to whether the law of the domicile or the law of the situs applies: Leflar, p 557. The Restatement 2d, § 242 supports the law of the situs. In the case of movables, whilst the predominant view is that expressed in the Restatement 2d, § 265 that the law of the domicile applies, this conclusion has been justified by reference to a balancing of the predominant interests of the jurisdictions involved: *Re Clark's Estate* 21 NY 2d 478, 236 NE 2d 152 (1968); *Re Mulhern's Estate* 297 NYS 2d 485 (1969).

[130] The present account of election is confined to a case where movables are bequeathed to the owner of the foreign land, and in such a case the law of the domicile governs. If English land is left to the foreign heir and foreign land left away from the heir, then English law as that of the situs governs, irrespective of domicile.

[131] *Dundas v Dundas* (1830) 2 Dow & Cl 349.

[132] (1793) 6 Bro Parl Cas 550.

This situation was possible in England prior to 1837 *in a purely domestic case*, for, until the law was altered by the Wills Act 1837, the formalities necessary for a valid will varied according to whether the subject matter of the disposition was realty or personalty. In this state of the law it was established as early as 1749 in *Hearle v Greenbank*[133] that, if a testator devised his English freeholds to a stranger and bequeathed legacies to the heir-at-law in a will that was valid as to personalty but void as to realty, the heir was not bound to elect, unless there was an express direction that anyone who disputed any part of the will should forfeit all benefits.[134] He was entitled both to the land and to the legacies. Although this situation can no longer arise in the case of an English will disposing of English property, it may well be so where the testator is domiciled abroad. Suppose that a testator domiciled in Italy makes a will by which he devises his English entailed interests to X and bequeaths a legacy to Y, who is his heir-at-law according to English law. The will is formally valid by Italian law but ineffective by English law. In such a case as this it has been held, following the principle of *Hearle v Greenbank*, that the English heir is not put to his election.[135] He can claim the land as heir against the invalid will of realty, and retain the legacy under the bequest which, since its validity falls to be determined by the law of the domicile, is invulnerable. This is an example of that "special tenderness" which the courts have always shown to the heir-at-law of English land,[136] though given that the heir has been abolished for fee simple estates in England it is doubtful whether a similar indulgence will be extended to those relatives who are entitled to the residuary estate of an intestate person. It is an inequitable privilege established by the courts at a time when they particularly favoured the heir-at-law and frowned on any attempt to defeat his rights.

This tenderness has never been shown to a foreign heir, ie to the heir entitled to take foreign land under the rules of intestate succession recognised by the law of the situs. The attitude of English law with regard to election in a case of this sort can be illustrated by *Re Ogilvie*,[137] where the facts; were as follows:

> A domiciled Englishwoman devised her land in Paraguay to a charity and gave legacies to the persons who were the obligatory heirs of the land according to Paraguayan law. The charitable devise was void by the law of the situs to the extent of four-fifths, which was the portion reserved for the obligatory heirs. Moreover, according to the law of the situs, the right of an heir to his legal portion was not affected by any other benefit that he might have received under the will.

In a case of this description, English law, as being the law of the testator's domicile, determines whether the foreign heir is to be put to his election. This raises the question of construction whether the testator has manifested an intention to pass the foreign land for, if he has, then despite the invalidity of the will by the law of the situs the doctrine of election becomes applicable.[138] The rule evolved by English courts on this matter is that the foreign property must be described either specifically or by necessary implication.[139]

---

[133] (1749) 1 Ves Sen 298.
[134] *Boughton v Boughton* (1750) 2 Ves Sen 12.
[135] *Re De Virte* [1915] 1 Ch 920.
[136] *Re Ogilvie* [1918] 1 Ch 492 at 496.
[137] [1918] 1 Ch 492.
[138] *Trotter v Trotter* (1828) 4 Bli NS 502.
[139] *Maxwell v Maxwell* (1852) 16 Beav 106; *Orrell v Orrell* (1871) 6 Ch App 302.

Thus, if a testator uses only general descriptive words, as for example where he says, "I devise all my estate, whatsoever or wheresoever, whether in possession or reversion", he is taken to intend that his disposition shall be restricted to such land as he is empowered to pass by a will executed in that particular form.[140] There was no difficulty of this sort in *Re Ogilvie*, since the testatrix had shown a plain intention to pass the Paraguayan property, and therefore it was held that the obligatory heirs must elect between what they took under the law of the situs owing to the invalidity of the charitable devise and what they were given in the shape of legacies by the will.[141]

(vi) Revocation

As with the case of a will of movables,[142] a will relating to immovables may be revoked by a later valid will and its validity will depend on the rules discussed earlier.[143] It should be mentioned that the provisions of the Wills Act 1963 relating to the testamentary revocation of an earlier will apply to a will of immovables as to a will of movables.[144] In the case of revocation by destruction or obliteration of the will, there is US authority for referring this issue to the law of the situs, as in *Re Barrie's Estate*[145] where the testatrix, who was domiciled in Illinois, wrote "void" across the will several times. The effect of such an act was determined not by the law of Illinois but by that of Iowa, the situs of her immovable property.

Finally, in the case of revocation by subsequent marriage, we have seen[146] that, in the case of movables, such revocation is generally to be regarded as an aspect of matrimonial law to be governed by the domiciliary law at the time of marriage rather than of death. Such an approach would indicate that, in the case of the revocation of a will of immovables by a subsequent marriage, reference should also be made to the law of the domicile at marriage and not to the law of the situs. Despite one English decision to the contrary,[147] it is suggested that the view just expressed is correct and support for it is to be found in the Australian decision in *Re Micallef's Estate*:[148]

> The testator, who was at all material times domiciled and resident in Malta, owned land in New South Wales. In 1970 he made a valid will disposing of all his property, including the land. He married in Malta in 1972 and died in 1973. Under Maltese law, the marriage did not revoke the will; under New South Wales law it did.

The court could find no policy justifying the imposition of New South Wales law on Maltese parties to a Maltese marriage. Furthermore, there was no justification for departing from the rule applicable to movable property.[149]

---

[140] *Maxwell v Maxwell*, supra.

[141] Cf the decision in *Brown v Gregson* [1920] AC 860, where it was held that a foreign heir will not be put to his election if it would be impossible by the law of the situs to give effect to the disposition of the foreign land intended by the testator.

[142] Supra, pp 1275–1277.

[143] Supra, p 1279 et seq; see also *In the Estate of Vickers* (2001-02) 4 ITELR 584; *Re Baldry (Deceased)* [2004] WTLR 609 (Fam Div), in respect of which see Simm 2005 TEL & TJ (65) (Apr) 15; *Lamothe v Lamothe* [2006] EWHC 1387; [2006] WTLR 1431.

[144] 1963 Act, s 2(1)(c), supra, p 1275.

[145] 240 Iowa 431, 35 NW 2d 658 (1949).

[146] Supra, pp 1276–1277.

[147] *Re Caithness* (1891) 7 TLR 354. See Dicey, Morris and Collins, para 27-089.

[148] [1977] 2 NSWLR 929; and see *Davies v Davies* (1915) 24 DLR 737 at 740.

[149] [1977] 2 NSWLR 929, at 933.

4. PROPOSED EUROPEAN HARMONISATION CONCERNING SUCCESSION AND WILLS

Previous harmonisation measures in the field of succession have been of mixed result. The successful harmonisation of choice of law rules in relation to the formal validity of wills[150] is to be contrasted with the disappointing outcome of work at the Hague Conference on Private International Law in producing the 1989 Hague Convention on the Law Applicable to Succession to the Estates of Deceased Persons.[151]

With regard to the European Community, the 1998 Vienna Action Plan[152] placed among its priorities the adoption of a European instrument concerning conflict rules of succession.[153] The Hague Programme[154] called upon the European Commission to present a Green Paper covering jurisdiction, applicable law, and recognition, together with administrative measures relating to wills. The Commission's Green Paper on Succession and Wills was issued in 2006,[155] commencing a broad-based consultation process concerning testate and intestate succession having an international dimension. The initiative is premised on the "growing mobility of people in an area without internal frontiers and the increasing frequency of unions between nationals of different Member States, often entailing the acquisition of property situated in the territory of several Union countries".[156] The issues raised in the Green Paper are wide-ranging, and the scope of any draft instrument is likely to be ambitious, seeking to deal not only with the administration of estates, but also with applicable law, and the removal of administrative and practical obstacles in the winding up of estates.

The general reaction to the initiative to date in the United Kingdom has been negative, in principle and in detail, and United Kingdom "opt-in" to any instrument, at this stage at least, is unlikely.[157] A legislative proposal drawn up by the Commission is currently awaited.

5. POWERS OF APPOINTMENT EXERCISED BY WILL[158]

Under English law, instead of disposing directly of his property, a person, either in a settlement or in his will, can nominate a person who, in his own will,[159] shall have the power

---

[150] 1961 Hague Convention on the Conflicts of Laws Relating to the Form of Testamentary Dispositions, leading in the United Kingdom to the Wills Act 1963.

[151] See supra, p 1264, n 2.

[152] OJ 1999 C 19.

[153] See generally supra, Chapter 1; Crawford and Carruthers [2005] Jur Rev 251.

[154] OJ 2005 C 53.

[155] COM (2005) 65 final. See also Commission Staff Working Paper, Annex to the Green Paper on Succession and Wills (SEC (2005) 270); Opinion of the European Economic and Social Committee on the Green Paper on Succession and Wills (OJ 2006 C 28); and European Parliament Report with Recommendations to the Commission (A6-0359/2006).

[156] COM (2005) 65 final, p 2. The United Kingdom government view is that there is not at present adequate evidence to justify European Union legislation. See House of Commons European Scrutiny Committee, 37th Report (2005–06), para 25.9.

[157] House of Commons European Scrutiny Committee, supra, paras 25.1–25.20. For Scotland, see Crawford and Carruthers, para 18-05.

[158] Fridman (1960) 9 ICLQ 1.

[159] It could also be a further settlement, *inter vivos*, but our concern here is with powers exercised by will.

to specify the ultimate recipient of the property which is the subject matter of the original settlement or will. For example:

> A in his will could leave the property to trustees to pay the income to B and then to transfer the capital to whoever B, in his will, appointed. In this case, A is described as the donor of the power of appointment and B is the donee of the power, or appointor. Whoever B selects as the beneficiary is described as the appointee.

There are two kinds of powers of appointment—general and special—and we shall see that this may be of significance in determining the appropriate choice of law rules. If the donee of the power, B in the above example, can appoint anyone he chooses, including himself, the power is general. If, however, the donor of the power, A, limits, in the instrument creating the power, the people or class of people among whom B can appoint, the power is special. One significance of the difference is that in the case of a special power B, the appointor, is clearly seen to be disposing of A's property, rather than his own, for A, the donee, has determined the class within which B must choose. In the case of a general power, though it may in strict theory still be true that B is disposing of A's property, this is more apparent than real, as B has the same freedom of choice as if the property was his own, including the power to appoint himself.

Choice of law problems may arise from powers of appointment exercised by will in a number of ways. It may be that the donor, the appointor and appointee all have different domiciles. Whilst it might seem logical to refer the essential validity of, for instance, the will of the donor which created the power (the instrument of creation) to the law of his domicile on death and the validity of the exercise of the power by will (the instrument of appointment) to the law of the donee's domicile on death, problems arise if the donee dies domiciled in a civil law country, such as France, where the concept of a power of appointment is unknown. The only practical answer would seem to be to refer to the law governing the instrument of creation. There is the further problem that, in the case of immovables, the law of the situs may be different from that of any of the relevant domiciles, though most of the cases are in fact concerned with movables.[160]

It can readily be argued that the law governing the instrument of creation should govern in the case of a special power, for the donee is manifestly no more than the agent for disposal of the appointor's property. As we have seen, this is less obviously true in the case of a general power which then poses a preliminary choice of law problem. If the main choice of law rule may depend on whether a power is special or general, by what law is that issue to be determined? After examining that question, we shall consider the other more general choice of law matters relating to powers of appointment exercised by will.

(a) Special and general powers

It is not always easy in a domestic system of law to decide whether a power is general or special. Also, more significantly, different legal systems which are familiar with powers of appointment may classify them differently.[161] As a matter of principle, it seems right that

---

[160] It should be assumed that the discussion relates to movables, unless immovables are referred to.
[161] See Dicey, Morris & Collins, paras 27R-097–27-099.

the nature of the power, ie as to whether it is special or general, should be determined by the law governing the instrument which created the power.

(b) Capacity

Considerations different from those relevant to testamentary capacity[162] apply to the question of capacity to exercise a testamentary power of appointment given by an English instrument to an appointor domiciled abroad. The obvious principle here is that, just as in the case where a testator disposes of his own property, capacity must be tested by the law of the appointor's domicile. There is indeed no doubt that, if the domiciliary law's rule on the matter is satisfied, the appointment is good. It is enough, whether the power is general or special, that the appointor is of full capacity by the law of his own domicile, even though he is incapable by the law that governs the instrument by which the power was created, ie the will. For example, in *Re Lewal's Settlement Trusts*,[163] the wife had a general power of appointment under an English marriage settlement. She had originally been domiciled in England but on her marriage had acquired the French domicile of her husband. In her will, made when she was aged 19, she appointed her husband her "legataire universel", and ten years later she died domiciled in France. Under English law, she had no capacity to exercise the power, being under 21; under French law, she was capable of disposing of half the property she could have disposed of had she been 21. The court applied French law[164] to the issue of her capacity, with the result that half the property subject to the power went to her husband, and the other half went as in default of appointment.

But this does not conclude the matter. What of the converse case, ie where the appointor has capacity by the law governing the instrument by which the power was created, but not under the law of his domicile? The view taken by English law is that it is the instrument which creates the power, and not the one by which the power is exercised, which is the governing instrument, and that the appointor is a mere agent to carry out the wishes of the donor. The appointee takes under the instrument of creation, not under the will of the appointor. It follows, therefore, that an appointment is valid if the appointor has capacity by the law that governs the instrument of creation, though he may be incapable by the law of his own domicile. It may well be objected that even if the appointor is regarded as merely the agent of the donor he should not be free to do what, according to the law to which he is subject, he is incapable of doing. Nevertheless, to treat him as an agent is not unreasonable in the case of a special power, for here, as has been seen, his function is to select the beneficiaries from the class already designated by the donor. He is in no sense disposing of his own property. But there is little to justify a reference to the law governing the instrument of creation in the case of a general power, for the appointor in such a case can scarcely be regarded as a mere agent to implement the wishes of the donor.

The correct rule probably is, therefore, that the testamentary exercise of a general power is invalid for want of capacity unless the appointor is capable by the law of his domicile;

---

162 Supra, pp 1265 and 1279.
163 [1918] 2 Ch 391.
164 The English marriage settlement also provided that the appointment should be made by will "executed in such manner as to be valid according to the law" of the appointor's domicile.

but that in the case of a special power the exercise is valid if he is capable either by the law of his domicile or by the law that governs the instrument of creation.[165]

(c) Formal validity

A power of appointment exercisable by will is frequently given by an English settlement or an English will to a person who ultimately dies domiciled in a foreign country or who makes his will in a foreign country. In such circumstances it is essential to ascertain the legal system that determines whether the formalities attending the testamentary exercise of the power are sufficient. The Wills Act 1963 has extended and amended the previous law. The position now is as follows.

First, a will so far as it exercises a power of appointment is to be treated as properly executed if it complies with the requirements of any one of the legal systems specified in the Act.[166] Thus the connecting factors now qualified to determine the governing law are the place of execution of the will or the nationality, domicile or habitual residence of the testator, or the law of the situs in the case of immovables.

Secondly, the will is to be treated as properly executed if its execution conforms to the law that governs the essential validity of the instrument creating the power.[167] If the power is created by an English instrument, it will be validly executed if it conforms with English law;[168] and if creation is by a foreign instrument, then there should be conformity with that foreign law.[169]

There is a further provision in the 1963 Act, resolving some tiresome problems in the law before 1964,[170] that the testamentary exercise of a power of appointment is not formally invalid by reason only of a failure to observe a formality required by the instrument of creation.[171]

(d) Essential validity

The determination of the law to govern the essential validity of a disposition resulting from the exercise of a power of appointment depends on whether the power is general or special. The effect of the appointment in the case of a special power is determined by the legal system to which the instrument that created the power is subject, for, since the appointor is merely the agent through whom the donor of the power designates the beneficiaries, the latter take under the instrument of creation.[172] Thus, in *Pouey v Hordern*[173] a domiciled Frenchwoman, who had a special power of appointment given by an English settlement, was held capable under English law of exercising it in a manner that was incompatible with the French doctrine of community.

---

[165] Cf Fridman (1960) 9 ICLQ, 1, 2–11. For a full discussion of the whole subject see Dicey, Morris and Collins, paras 27R-096–27-102.

[166] Supra, p 1267.

[167] Wills Act 1963, s 2(1)(d). Essential validity of wills is discussed, supra, pp 1270–1273 and 1279–1280.

[168] Eg *Murphy v Deichler* [1909] AC 446.

[169] See (1958) Cmnd 491, para 11(c).

[170] See, eg, *Barretto v Young* [1900] 2 Ch 339.

[171] Wills Act 1963, s 2(2).

[172] See *Pouey v Hordern* [1900] 1 Ch 492 at 494.

[173] Ibid.

In the case of general powers, the property given thereunder may be treated by the donee either as if it were his own, ie as a mass combined with his own, or quite separately therefrom. It is a question of construction as to how it is to be considered.[174] In the first case, where the donee treats the settled property as his own, the Court of Appeal in *Re Pryce*[175] held that the operation and effect of the donee's appointment must be determined by the law that governs the will by which he exercises the power, ie by the law of his last domicile. DANCKWERTS J in *Re Waite's Settlement*[176] preferred to apply the law governing the instrument creating the power, rather than the law of the donee's domicile, despite the fact that the case related to a general power where the funds were massed, but his decision was disapproved in *Re Khan's Settlement*.[177] In the latter case:

> The testator, the Nawab of Bhopal, domiciled in India, made a settlement in which he reserved to himself a general power of appointment by will. This settlement was to be governed by English law, apart from a clause referring to his heirs under Indian law. His English will gave legacies to three of his seven heirs, in excess of the free estate under the will, and then executed the power of appointment in favour of all his heirs. Under Indian law, the domiciliary law, the consent of all heirs was necessary before payment of legacies to any heirs could be made, and this consent was refused. Thus, if Indian law governed, the legacies could not be paid out of the free estate or the settlement funds, whilst there was no such restriction under English law, the law governing the instrument of creation.

RUSSELL LJ concluded that he was bound to follow *Re Pryce*[178] rather than *Re Waite's Settlement*.[179] He decided that the free estate and the settled fund formed one mass, the distribution of which was to be governed by Indian law, and the legacies could not be paid. He thought "it a logical consequence of the grounds of those decisions in cases of blending or massing . . . that the settled funds are subjected to the whole succession law of the domicile of the appointor, including any restriction on testation".[180]

If, in the case of a general power, the settled funds are not treated as having been taken out of the settlement and massed with the donee's own funds, then, as in *Re Mégret*,[181] the validity of the exercise of the power of appointment is governed, not by the law of the domicile of the donee, but by the law governing the instrument of creation, as in the case of special powers. This can be justified on the ground that in neither of these cases is the donee in reality disposing of his own funds.

All the cases discussed so far concern movable property. In the case of the essential validity of the exercise by will of a general power of appointment over immovables, there is clear authority that this should be governed by the law of the situs of the property.[182]

---

174 *Re Pryce* [1911] 2 Ch 286 at 295.
175 Ibid; and see *Re Lewal's Settlement Trusts* [1918] 2 Ch 391.
176 [1958] Ch 100; and see *Re McMorran* [1958] Ch 624 at 633–634; for criticisms, see Dicey, Morris and Collins, paras 27-120–27-122.
177 [1966] Ch 567; cf *Re Fenston's Settlement* [1971] 1 WLR 1640 at 1647.
178 [1911] 2 Ch 286.
179 Supra.
180 [1966] Ch 567 at 578.
181 [1901] 1 Ch 547; and see *Re Pryce* [1911] 2 Ch 286 at 296–297; cf Fridman (1960) 9 ICLQ 1, 9–10.
182 *Re Hernando* (1884) 27 Ch D 284; and see *Murray v Champernowne* [1901] 2 IR 232.

(e) Construction

In accordance with the principle applicable to wills generally, the construction of a power of appointment is governed by the law intended by the testator (or appointor) which, in the case of movables, is presumed to be that of his domicile when the will was made.[183] This appears to be true whether the power is special[184] or general.[185] If it appears that the testator intended a law other than that of his domicile at the time of making the will to apply, as in *Re Price*,[186] then that other law governs the construction.

But the question has arisen whether the intention of the testator is decisive if it indicates a foreign law that has no knowledge of powers.

> Suppose, for instance, that a testator, domiciled in France and having a general power of appointment by virtue of an English settlement, makes a valid will according to French law. The will does not refer in any way to the power but merely disposes of the property in general words. A power to dispose of property not belonging to the donor (which is the true nature of a power of appointment) is unknown in French law.[187] The will, therefore, if construed according to French law, can scarcely be said to constitute an execution of the power. Can English law be applied to the issue of construction?

After considerable judicial conflict this question has been answered in the affirmative.[188] The French court, being ignorant of the peculiar power of disposition thus given by an English instrument, would have to turn to English law (with reference to which the testator obviously wrote) in order to ascertain the nature of the right and the manner in which it might be exercised.

A consequence of this conclusion is that section 27 of the Wills Act 1837 may apply to wills of persons who are domiciled other than in England. Under section 27 a general devise or bequest is construed as exercising a general power of appointment unless a contrary intention appears in the will. In the above example, the testator's French will falls to be construed in accordance with section 27 as exercising a general power of appointment.[189] Were the power merely special, it would not be held to be exercised under section 27.

(f) Revocation

A power of appointment over movables exercisable by will may be revoked under the law of the donee's domicile.[190] A power over movables or immovables will be revoked if it is

---

[183] Supra, pp 1273–1274.

[184] *Re McMorran* [1958] Ch 624; and see *Re Walker* [1908] 1 Ch 560.

[185] *Durie's Trustees v Osborne* 1960 SC 444; Gareth Jones (1961) 10 ICLQ 624.

[186] [1900] 1 Ch 442; and see *Mitchell and Baxter v Davies* (1875) 3 R 208.

[187] Contrast the position in Scotland: *Re McMorran* [1958] Ch 624 at 634–635; *Durie's Trustees v Osborne*, supra.

[188] *Re Simpson* [1916] 1 Ch 502; *Re Wilkinson's Settlement* [1917] 1 Ch 620; *Re Lewal's Settlement* [1918] 2 Ch 391; *Re Waite's Settlement* [1958] Ch 100; *Re Fenston's Settlement* [1971] 3 All ER 1092. Decisions to the contrary are *Re D'Este's Settlement Trusts* [1903] 1 Ch 898; *Re Scholefield* [1905] 2 Ch 408.

[189] Eg *Re Lewal's Settlement*, supra; cf *Re Fenston's Settlement*, supra, where the will, as construed by the law of the domicile, contained no "bequest" to anyone.

[190] *Velasco v Coney* [1934] P 143. Presumably, compliance with the law of the situs is required in the case of immovables.

revoked by a later will properly executed under the Wills Act 1963.[191] Under section 2(1)(d) of the 1963 Act,[192] a will so far as it exercises a power of appointment is validly executed if it complies with the law governing the essential validity of the power. This does not apply, however, to a will which merely revokes a power of appointment without providing another power in its place. Finally a power exercisable by will may be revoked by the subsequent marriage of the testator according to the law of his domicile at the time of his marriage, rather than of his death.[193] Where, however, the testator is domiciled in England at the time of his marriage then, under section 18(2) of the Wills Act 1837,[194] an exercise of a power of appointment by will takes effect, "notwithstanding the subsequent marriage unless the property so appointed would in default of appointment pass to his personal representatives".

---

[191] Ss 1, 2(1)(b), (c), supra, p 1267.
[192] Supra, p 1266 et seq.
[193] Supra, pp 1276–1277.
[194] As substituted by the Administration of Justice Act 1982, s 18(1).

Chapter 33

Matrimonial Property[1]

1. INTRODUCTION

The problem that confronts us in this chapter is how to determine what system of law regulates the rights of a husband and wife in the movable and immovable property which either of them may possess at the time of marriage or may acquire afterwards. Important consequences may ensue depending on which law is chosen. For instance, the result of choosing one particular legal system may be that the property of the wife passes entirely to the

---

[1] Marsh, *Marital Property in the Conflict of Laws* (1952); Goldberg (1970) 19 ICLQ 357; McLachlan (1986) 12 NZUL Rev 66; Scoles (1988) II Hague Recueil 9, 17–53; Davie (1993) 42 ICLQ 855; and Hartley in Fawcett (ed), *Reform and Development of Private International Law* (2002), Chapter 9. There is a Hague Convention on the Law Applicable to Matrimonial Property (1978) but it has not been signed by the United Kingdom: see Philip (1976) 24 AJCL 307; Glenn (1977) 54 Can Bar Rev 586. For proposed European legislation, see infra, p 1309.

husband, as was substantially the case in England prior to 1883. Again, if an Englishwoman marries a Belgian and Belgian law is regarded as the governing system, it may be that the parties become subject to "community of goods" under which everything that belongs to either spouse at the time of marriage or that is acquired by either afterwards is owned by them jointly. They become joint co-owners of everything by the mere fact of marriage.[2]

In determining the choice of law rules for identifying the appropriate matrimonial property regime, it will be necessary to look separately at two types of case—first where the parties have not made an ante-nuptial contract and, secondly, where there is such a contract.

2. ASSIGNMENT WHERE THERE IS NO ANTE-NUPTIAL CONTRACT[3]

(a) Movables

(i) Application of matrimonial domicile

The primary rule,[4] long-prevailing, was that the effect of marriage on the proprietary rights of the parties in movables should be determined by the law of the husband's domicile[5] at the time of the marriage.[6] In the words of LINDLEY MR: "It is not necessary to cite authorities to shew that it is now settled that, according to international law as understood and administered in England, the effect of marriage on the movable property of spouses depends (in the absence of any contract) on the domicil of the husband in the English sense." [7]

Whilst acceptable against the legal background of the unity of domicile principle,[8] it is highly doubtful that the rule in favour of application of the law of the husband's domicile is reasonable in light of the prohibition upon discrimination on the grounds of sex contained in the Article 14 of the European Convention on Human Rights. Since 1974 a wife has been capable of acquiring a domicile independent of her husband.[9] One effect of this

---

[2] For a valuable exposition of the different systems found in the world see Rheinstein and Glendon, *International Encyclopedia of Comparative Law* (1980), Vol iv, Chapter 4, pp 47–118. There is a tendency in civil law countries now to allow the spouses the separate administration of their property during marriage, but to constitute the community of property on death or divorce: "deferred community". See Hartley, op cit, p 231; for France, see Amos and Walton, *Introduction to French Law*, (1966) 3rd edn, pp 379–392; for Germany, see Leyser (1958) 7 AJCL 276.

[3] Cf Goldberg (1970) 19 ICLQ 557 who maintains that there is always a contract which may be express, implied or presumed.

[4] Or presumption: *Re Egerton's Will Trusts* [1956] Ch 593, per ROXBURGH J, at 607.

[5] Subject to the application of a foreign law not being contrary to the public policy of the forum: *Vladi v Vladi* (1987) 39 DLR (4th) 563.

[6] Dicey, Morris and Collins, para 28-008; *Welch v Tennent* [1891] AC 639 at 644. For a case where a retrospective change in the law to a community regime was accepted, see *Topolski v R* (1978) 90 DLR (3d) 66.

[7] *Re Martin, Loustalan v Loustalan* [1900] P 211 at 233. For an example of the application of this rule, see *Re Bettinson's Question* [1956] Ch 67; and see *Razelos v Razelos (No 2)* [1970] 1 WLR 392. There are statutory choice of law rules in Canada, as in Ontario, where the law to be applied is usually that of the parties' last common habitual residence: Family Law Act 1986, s 15; and see *Pershadsingh v Pershadsingh* (1988) 40 DLR (4th) 681; *Mittler v Mittler* (1988) 17 RFL (3d) 113.

[8] Supra, p 178. As Hartley points out, the "leading cases almost all date from the nineteenth century. They are based on social attitudes so at odds with those of today that the legal rules laid down may no longer be acceptable" (op cit, p 215).

[9] Domicile and Matrimonial Proceedings Act 1973, s 1.

is that it is no longer the case that the law of the husband's domicile ought automatically to govern the spouses' rights to movable property.[10] Instead, as a general presumption, the law of the matrimonial domicile ought to apply. The law of the matrimonial domicile should be ascertained thus: in cases where the husband and wife are of the same domicile at the time of the marriage, the law of the common domicile should apply;[11] and in cases where the parties are not of the same domicile at the time of the marriage, the law of the matrimonial domicile should be that of "the country with which the parties and the marriage have the closest connection, equal weight being given to connections with each party".[12] Equal weight, however, should not necessarily be given to each and every connection;[13] the test is a qualitative one, to ascertain the "centre of gravity"[14] of the marriage.

In those cases where the husband and wife are of the same domicile at the time of the marriage, it must be asked whether account should be taken of their intention to set up home soon after marriage in another legal system.[15] Should the presumption in favour of application of the matrimonial domicile at the time of the marriage be rebutted if, in pursuance of their previous agreement, the parties in fact acquire a fresh domicile within a reasonable time after the marriage? The merit of this approach is that it meets the not unusual case where the parties intend to settle immediately after marriage in another country and in fact do so.

That a rigid application of the law of the domicile at the time of the marriage[16] has caused hardship can be illustrated by the facts of the South African case, *Frankel's Estate v The Master*.[17]

> H, whose domicile of origin was German, and W, domiciled in Czechoslovakia, were married in Czechoslovakia in 1933. At the time of the marriage the parties had definitely agreed that they would leave Europe for good and settle permanently in Johannesburg. They established their home in that city four months after the marriage. After working there for four years, they moved to Durban with the intention of remaining there permanently. Eleven years later, H died. According to the law of South Africa, the parties had married in community of property, but according to German law the doctrine of community was inapplicable. If South African law applied, as W claimed, death duties were not payable. The Appellate Division of the Supreme Court of South Africa held unanimously that German law applied.

---

[10] Cf Dicey, Morris and Collins, paras 28-008–29-010; Hartley, op cit, pp 226–227; and for Scotland, Crawford and Carruthers, para 13-10.

[11] Dicey, Morris and Collins, para 28-020. Cf, for Scotland, Family Law (Scotland) Act 2006, s 39(2).

[12] Dicey, Morris and Collins, para 28-011. This solution is preferable to that which has been articulated for Scots law in s 39(3) of the Family Law (Scotland) Act 2006, which ignores the very fact of marriage. "if spouses are domiciled in different countries then, for the purposes of any question in relation to the rights of the spouses to each other's moveable property arising by virtue of the marriage, the spouses shall be taken to have the same rights to such property as they had immediately before the marriage".

[13] Eg the situs of the matrimonial home is likely to be more significant than the nationality/ante-nuptial domicile of the parties.

[14] Hartley, op cit, p 226.

[15] *Corbet v Waddell* (1879) 7 R (Ct of Sess) 200 at 208; and see Anton, pp 585–586; Story, paras 191–199; Westlake, s 36; Crawford and Carruthers, para 13-10.

[16] In this case, the law of the husband's domicile, not the matrimonial domicile.

[17] 1950 (1) SA 220 (AD), analysed by Ellison Kahn (1950) 3 ILQ 439; and Hartley, op cit, pp 227–229.

Thus the proprietary rights of the parties were subjected to the law of Germany, a country which the parties had abandoned and which, it may be surmised, they would be little inclined to revisit. To this extent, the civil status of a German was indelibly impressed on the husband against his will and, in turn, on the wife, against her will. Indeed, South African courts have applied the law of the domicile at marriage including retrospective changes in that law effected after the spouses had become domiciled in South Africa.[18] On the other hand, reliance on the intended matrimonial domicile does suffer from the disadvantage, here as elsewhere,[19] that there is no certainty that it will ever be acquired.

Whether the test of the intended matrimonial domicile would be accepted by English law was not squarely raised until the case of *Re Egerton's Will Trusts*,[20] where ROXBURGH J stated the law to the effect that there is a presumption that the mutual property rights of spouses are determined by the law of the husband's domicile[21] at the time of the marriage. In his Lordship's view, that presumption was capable of being rebutted by an express contract that some other law should apply,[22] or by a tacit contract inferred from the conduct of the parties.[23] It was judicially admitted that application of the law of the husband's domicile at the time of the marriage would be ousted if the intention to adopt the law of another domicile could be deduced from the facts of the particular case. A tacit agreement would be sufficient to rebut the primary presumption. It has not been judicially tested whether the presumption in favour of applying the matrimonial domicile at the time of the marriage is open to rebuttal in like manner. It is submitted that rebuttal should be available in these circumstances, to be inferred from the conduct of the parties, if the circumstances justify the inference.

But what the judge in *Egerton's* case repudiated is the suggestion that an ante-nuptial agreement to establish the matrimonial home in another country, even though carried out with reasonable promptitude, would be sufficient per se to rebut the presumption and to let in the law of the new domicile. To have this effect, the circumstances must warrant the inference that the parties intended not merely to acquire a new domicile, but also to subject their proprietary rights to the law of that domicile. The judgment makes it clear that everything must turn on the precise facts of each case, including the reliability of the evidence by which the alleged agreement to change the domicile is supported, the length of time that may have elapsed before the fulfilment of that agreement and even the financial circumstances of the spouses.[24]

In *Egerton's* case itself the particular circumstances did not warrant any such inference. The facts were these:

> In 1932, the testator domiciled in England married a woman domiciled in France. The parties agreed, before the marriage, to settle in France, but the testator did not acquire a French domicile until some time after September 1934, which he retained

---

[18] *Sperling v Sperling* 1975 (3) SA 707 (AD).
[19] This is discussed generally, supra, p 896.
[20] [1956] Ch 593; Carter (1957) 33 BYBIL 345.
[21] And now, the matrimonial domicile: see supra, p 1294 et seq.
[22] *Re Martin, Loustalan v Loustalan* [1900] P 211 at 240.
[23] [1956] Ch 593, at 607.
[24] [1956] Ch 593 at 605.

until his death. The question to be decided was whether his estate should be administered on the footing that he and his wife were subject to the French regime of community of property at the time of the marriage.

RoxBURGH J held that the parties' agreement to settle in France did not render their proprietary rights subject to French law. The equivocal nature of the agreement which contemplated no immediate change of home, but only one that should be effected "as soon as possible"; the long period that in fact elapsed before the new domicile was acquired; the lack of any evidence that the parties even appreciated the difference between the property regimes of the two countries: all these precluded the inference that in the minds of the parties the law of England was to be supplanted by that of France. On the other hand, it is submitted that in *Frankel's* case the only reasonable intention to attribute to the parties was to sever all links with the German domicile of origin of the husband as quickly as possible.[25]

(ii) Effect of a change of domicile

A further question may arise—what is the effect of a subsequent change of the matrimonial domicile? Are the mutual proprietary rights of the spouses affected by the change? Many legal systems adopt what has been called the doctrine of immutability,[26] according to which the rights of property in movables as fixed by the law of the matrimonial domicile at the time of the marriage are unaffected by the acquisition of a fresh domicile. Thus the established rule in France is that the law of the matrimonial domicile governs the rights of the spouses in movables, whether existing at the time of the marriage or acquired later, and continues to govern them despite a change of domicile. This is so even with respect to movables acquired in the new domicile.[27] The prevailing rule in the USA is not so comprehensive. The law of the matrimonial domicile at the time of the marriage continues to govern movables owned at that time, but movables acquired later are subject to the law of the parties' domicile at the time of acquisition.[28]

It has been said that, according to English private international law, if the marriage domicile[29] is abandoned, the proprietary rights of the spouses are governed by the law of the new domicile. It is extremely doubtful, however, whether English law is committed to this doctrine of mutability.[30] The one case invariably cited in support of this doctrine is

---

[25] *Devos v Devos* (1970) 10 DLR (3d) 603 might similarly be criticised, for there the matrimonial domicile was held to be Belgian, where the husband was domiciled at the time of the marriage, even though the parties emigrated to Canada less than 3 months later. Contrast *Vien Estate v Vien Estate* (1988) 49 DLR (4th) 558.

[26] Wolff, pp 360–361.

[27] Batiffol and Lagarde, *Droit international privé* (1983) 7th edn, Vol II, pp 356–365; and see Juenger (1981) 81 Col LR 1061, 1062–1066.

[28] Scoles, Hay, Borchers and Symeonides, Chapter 14; Juenger, op cit; cf Restatement 2d, § 258 which adopts a "most significant relationship" test, though retaining emphasis on the law of the domicile at the time of acquisition; see *Re Crichton's Estate* 20 NY 2d 124, 228 NE 2d 799 (1967) (the Louisiana courts have been constrained by the US Constitution to uphold this decision despite their clear view that the New York decision was erroneous: *Crichton v Successor of Crichton* 232 So 2d 109 (1970); though see now La Civ Code 2334 (1980)); cf *Wyatt v Fulrath* 16 NY 2d 169, 211 NE 2d 673 (1965).

[29] Formerly the law of the husband's domicile, but now the matrimonial domicile.

[30] Marsh, op cit, pp 103–108.

the Scots decision in *Lashley v Hog*.[31] When analysed, however, this appears to be quite irrelevant to the controversy. The facts were these:

Hog, a native of Scotland, married an Englishwoman at a time when he was domiciled in England. There was no marriage settlement. After living in England for fifteen years the parties acquired a domicile in Scotland. Hog survived his wife and died in 1789. After his death, his daughter, Mrs Lashley, brought an action in the Scottish court claiming as the representative of her mother a share in her father's movables which, according to the then law of Scotland, were subject to the doctrine of community of goods. The basis of her claim was that, on the change of domicile from England to Scotland, her father's proprietary rights vis-à-vis his wife became restricted by the Scottish rule of community.

The House of Lords held that Scots law governed Mrs Lashley's claim, and that she was entitled in right of her mother to a share of the movables owned by her father at the time of her mother's death.[32]

What was the ratio decidendi? Was it that the rights of the wife with regard to the matrimonial property were enlarged as a result of the change of domicile? It would seem not. The House of Lords took the view that the matter "turned on testamentary and not on matrimonial law".[33] The so-called community of goods did not give the wife on marriage a proprietary interest similar to that recognised, for instance, by Belgian law, but only a hope of succeeding to the property.[34] The question therefore, was not: Were the rights of the wife enlarged by the change of domicile? but: What were the succession rights of the wife or her representative on the death of her husband? Thus Lord HALSBURY, speaking of the decision in a later case, said:

If the wife by the marriage in Scotland[35] acquired no proprietary rights whatever, but only what is called a hope of a certain distribution upon the husband's death, it is intelligible that that right of distribution, or by whatever name it is called, should be dependent upon the husband's domicil as following the ordinary rule that the law of a person's domicil regulates the succession of his movable property. But if by the marriage the wife acquires as part of that contract relation a real proprietary right, it would be quite unintelligible that the husband's act[36] should dispose of what was not his; and herein, I think, is to be found the key to Lord ELDON's judgment.[37]

The last sentence of this statement is a repudiation of the doctrine of mutability, for if the wife's acquired rights cannot be defeated by a change of domicile, neither can they be enlarged.

---

[31] (1804) 4 Pat 581; analysed by Goldberg (1970) 19 ICLQ 557, 580–584; Crawford and Carruthers, para 13-02; and Hartley, op cit, pp 219–220.

[32] Cf Married Women's Property (Scotland) Act 1920, s 7 of which was repealed by the Family Law (Scotland) Act 1985, Sch 2. See now Succession (Scotland) Act 1964.

[33] Westlake, p 74; cf Dicey, Morris and Collins, para 28-052; and Crawford and Carruthers, paras 13-02 and 13-10.

[34] Falconbridge (1937) 53 LQR 537, 539–540. For the purposes of private international law, it is treated in Scotland as a right of succession; Anton, pp 672–673.

[35] The marriage in fact took place in London.

[36] Ie the act of changing his domicile.

[37] *De Nicols v Curlier* [1900] AC 21 at 27.

The position in Scots law now is governed by the Family Law (Scotland) Act 2006, section 39(5) of which provides that: "A change of domicile by a spouse (or both spouses) shall not affect a right in moveable property which, immediately before the change, has vested in either spouse." It is not always clear, however, when or how a right vests. Nor is it clear whether, with regard to what may be termed "non-vested rights", the rights of the spouses will vary according to the content of the "matrimonial property law" of their common domicile from time to time; the inference seemingly is that this should be the case.

In England, a more decisive authority than *Lashley v Hog* must be found, before it can be categorically asserted that the proprietary relations between husband and wife change with a change of their domicile (the doctrine of mutability). It is a strong assertion to make, for, as Westlake says, "justice is shocked by allowing the husband to affect the wife's position by a change for which he does not require her assent",[38] and which, of course, now does not affect her domicile. What is shocking is suspect, and it is in fact doubtful whether English law has adopted the doctrine of mutability to its full extent.

English law, then, is far from certain, but nevertheless an attempt must be made to state the modern rule. The clue to it seems to be the distinction between inchoate and vested rights. Even if the doctrine of mutability is part of English law it can scarcely operate without restriction, for not only justice but principle demands that a spouse shall not, by reason of a change of domicile, be divested of a right of property actually acquired under the law of the matrimonial domicile, even though enjoyment of the right may be post-poned until the death of the other spouse. Under the Dutch system of community of goods, for instance, all movables belonging to husband and wife fall on marriage into the common ownership of both. Thus, on marriage, the wife becomes co-owner of movables then belonging to the husband. She also becomes co-owner of future movables when and as they are acquired.[39] If parties domiciled in the Netherlands at the time of marriage acquire a fresh domicile in England where the husband dies, the wife cannot on principle be deprived by her husband's will of what she owned when she reached England. No doubt the will of her husband, since he dies domiciled in England, is governed by English law, and English internal law does not recognise community of goods, but that cannot entitle him to dispose of what is not his. His power of testamentary disposition is limited by the extent of his title. If he dies intestate, his distributable assets are diminished by the rights of property therein owned by his wife.

But vested rights must be distinguished from those that are inchoate. When the Dutch couple change their domicile from the Netherlands to England, it cannot be said that either of them has a vested right of property in movables not yet acquired. At the most they have the hope of acquiring. It is a hope that is not recognised by the law to which they are now subject and which alone can make its voice effective. If, therefore, it should ultimately be decided that the proprietary rights of spouses change with a change in their domicile, this would presumably be subject to the exception that rights vested in either

---

[38] *Private International Law* (7th edn), p 73.

[39] Rheinstein and Glendon, *International Encyclopedia of Comparative Law* (1980), Vol iv, Chapter 4, pp 52–57.

party under the law of some previous domicile remain unaffected. Indeed, this is the approach in Scots law,[40] and this view has been accepted in Canadian courts:

> The law appears to be that the mutual rights of husband and wife as to personal property are governed by the law of the matrimonial domicile, and such rights are not affected by a subsequent change, but rights acquired after such change are, of course, governed by the law of the actual domicile.[41]

The solution that the rights of the spouses in movable property change with a change of domicile, though leaving acquired rights unaffected, is complicated by the possibility that only one spouse may change his/her domicile.[42] To continue the example of spouses domiciled at marriage in the Netherlands, if only one spouse later becomes domiciled in England, the other remaining domiciled in the Netherlands, the court will be faced with the difficult question whether after-acquired property is governed by English law or by the community rules of Dutch law. It seems wrong that the rights of the spouse domiciled in the Netherlands should be prejudiced by the other spouse's change of domicile. A change of domicile by only one spouse should not affect a right in movable property which, immediately before the change, has vested in either party.[43]

(b) Immovables

Discussion so far has been concerned with the effect of marriage on the spouses' movable property in the absence of a marriage contract. With regard to immovables, the leading decision is *Welch v Tennent*,[44] a Scottish appeal to the House of Lords. The facts were these:

> The husband and wife were domiciled in Scotland. The wife owned land in England which she sold with her husband's agreement and the proceeds of sale were paid to him. Later the parties separated and the wife claimed that the proceeds of sale be paid to her, arguing that under Scots law she was entitled to recall any donation made by her to her husband.

Lord HERSCHELL disposed very rapidly of the argument that Scots law might be applied, saying: "The rights of the spouses as regards movable property must, in the circumstances of this case be regulated by the law of Scotland, but it is equally clear that their rights in relation to heritable estate are governed by the law of the place where it was situate."[45] English law was applied and the husband was entitled to keep the proceeds of sale of the land.

---

[40] Family Law (Scotland) Act 2006, s 39(5); see Crawford and Carruthers, para 13-11.

[41] *Pink v Perlin & Co* (1898) 40 NSR 260 at 262; *Re Heung Won Lee* (1963) 36 DLR (2d) 177.

[42] Supra, pp 178–179.

[43] Cf Family Law (Scotland) Act 2006, s 39(5).

[44] [1891] AC 639; discussed by Hartley, op cit, p 224; and see *Callwood v Callwood* [1960] AC 659 at 683–684; *Tezcan v Tezcan* (1992) 87 DLR (4th) 503 at 518–519.

[45] Ibid, at 645.

It has been suggested that an English court should refuse to follow *Welch v Tennent*, applying instead, to immovables as well as to movables, the law of the domicile.[46] Whilst this might be acceptable, indeed appropriate, for disputes between husband and wife, on the basis that it would "reflect the values, attitudes and expectations of the parties",[47] it would not be satisfactory in the case of disputes involving third parties.[48]

The choice of law rule now in Scots law rests on a statutory footing. Section 39(1) of the Family Law (Scotland) Act 2006 provides that: "Any question in relation to the rights of spouses to each other's immoveable property arising by virtue of the marriage shall be determined by the law of the place in which the property is situated." Section 39(1), however, is subject to section 39(6)(b), which permits party autonomy to override the choice of law rule set out in section 39(1).[49]

3. ASSIGNMENT WHERE THERE IS AN ANTE-NUPTIAL CONTRACT

(a) The general rule

When we turn to the situation where the parties have entered an ante-nuptial contract, it must be borne in mind that the choice of law issues which may arise are governed by common law rules.[50] This is because the Rome Convention on the Law Applicable to Contractual Obligations[51] does not apply to contractual obligations relating to "rights in property arising out of a matrimonial relationship".[52] If the parties have made an ante-nuptial contract to regulate their future proprietary relationship, then the difficulties, just discussed, concerning the identification of the governing laws or the effect of a change of domicile do not arise. The contract continues to govern the proprietary rights of the parties not only in the matrimonial domicile, but also in any other domicile that may later be acquired.[53] It must be recognised no matter where it may be put in suit[54] (subject to any overriding provisions of the law of the forum),[55] and it applies whether

---

[46] Dicey, Morris and Collins, para 28-028; and Hartley, op cit, p 225. See also Clarkson and Hill, p 440, where a distinction is drawn between the treatment of foreign immovables (to be governed, it is suggested, by the law of the situs) and immovables situated in England (to be governed, it is suggested, by the law of the matrimonial domicile).

[47] Hartley, op cit, p 225.

[48] Cf Hartley, op cit, pp 232–234.

[49] See Crawford and Carruthers, paras 13-10–13-11.

[50] Though where the marriage contract purports to create a trust, the Recognition of Trusts Act 1987 will apply. Where an ante-nuptial agreement is embodied in a trust, as in *Re Fitzgerald* [1904] 1 Ch 573, the rules relating to the essential validity of trusts fall to be considered; see infra, Chapter 34.

[51] Brought into force by the Contracts (Applicable Law) Act 1990, supra, p 667.

[52] Art 1(2)(b), supra, pp 682–683. Cf Art 1(2)(b) and (c) of the Rome I Regulation: supra, Chapter 18.

[53] Though the original law governing the contract may allow it to be amended under the law of a new domicile: *Duyvewaardt v Barber* (1992) 43 RFL (3d) 139.

[54] *Anstruther v Adair* (1834) 2 My & K 513: *Montgomery v Zarifi* (1919) 88 LJPC 20; *De Nicols v Curlier* [1900] AC 21 at 46; *Re Hannema's Marriage* (1981) 54 FLR 79.

[55] Eg *Stark v Stark* (1988) 16 RFL (3d) 257.

the property in question is movable[56] or immovable.[57] It may either define precisely what the rights shall be or state the system of law by which they are to be regulated.[58]

No distinction in this respect is made between an express and a tacit contract, as is illustrated by *De Nicols v Curlier*:[59]

> H and W, French both by nationality and by domicile, were married in Paris without making an express contract as to their proprietary rights. Nine years after their marriage, they came to England, acquired an English domicile and prospered as the owners of the Cafe Royal, in Regent Street. The husband died in 1897 leaving a considerable fortune in movable and immovable property. In his will, he disposed of all of his property without taking account of the wife's entitlement to a half share in the property under the French system of community of property. The issue was whether the spouses' change of domicile from French to English affected their legal position in relation to the property.

The position of the movable property was considered first by the House of Lords, and separately from that of the immovables. The expert evidence accepted by the court was that according to French law parties who marry without an express marriage contract are bound by a tacit contract to abide by the system of community. Therefore, said Lord MACNAGHTEN: "if there is a valid compact between spouses as to their property, whether it be constituted by the law of the land or by convention between the parties, it is difficult to see how that compact can be nullified or blotted out merely by a change of domicile".[60]

The question then arose whether the French contract or English law as that of the situs determined the rights of the surviving wife to the English immovables of her deceased husband. KEKEWICH J held,[61] after further argument, that the French implied contract must operate according to the intention of the parties so as to bind the immovable property of the deceased, unless there was any overriding rule of English law that would render it unenforceable. The only possible rule was the provision of section 4 of the Statute of Frauds 1677, requiring a written memorandum in the case of a contract concerning land;[62] but the judge held that, since this particular contract constituted a partnership between the spouses in the eyes of French law, it fell within the rule of English law that a parol agreement for a partnership was not caught by the statute and was enforceable despite the lack of written evidence. The accuracy of the view expressed by KEKEWICH J that the contract implied by French law included foreign immovables is open to doubt.[63] His decision might have been based more surely on counsel's other argument, namely that the land represented the investment of money acquired by the husband during marriage, and that the wife could follow the money, to which she was admittedly entitled, into whatsoever form it had been converted.

---

[56] *De Nicols v Curlier* [1900] AC 21.
[57] *Re De Nicols* [1900] 2 Ch 410. Cf Family Law (Scotland) Act 2006, s 39(6)(b).
[58] *Este v Smyth* (1854) 18 Beav 112.
[59] [1900] AC 21; and see *Tezcan v Tezcan* (1992) 87 DLR (4th) 503. Hartley, op cit, pp 220 et seq.
[60] Ibid, at 33.
[61] *Re De Nicols* [1900] 2 Ch 410.
[62] See now Law of Property (Miscellaneous Provisions) Act 1989, s 2.
[63] Or indeed that French law would today consider there was a tacit contract in such a case; see Dicey, Morris and Collins, paras 28-024–28-025.

Support for the application to immovables of the law governing the ante-nuptial contract is provided by *Chiwell v Carlyon*,[64] a case which appeared before both the English and the South African courts, in which the facts were as follows:

> In 1887 H married W at Kimberley in South Africa. No express ante-nuptial contract was made. The parties were domiciled at the time in South Africa, and while still domiciled there they made a joint will disposing of their joint estate, ie of the movables and immovables that they held in community. In 1892, after the parties had settled in England, certain land in Cornwall was bought by H and conveyed to him. W died in 1893, H in 1895. The question that arose before the Chancery Division was whether the Cornish land passed under the will of the joint estate.

STIRLING J felt that the law of the previous domicile at the time of their marriage could not be disregarded and he submitted two questions to the Supreme Court in the Cape of Good Hope. The second[65] question was this:

> Assuming H and W to have been domiciled in South Africa at the time of their marriage, but subsequently to have acquired an English domicile before the purchase of the land, would this change have any effect by South African law on their respective rights in regard to the land?

The Supreme Court held that this question must be answered in the negative. The marriage created a universal partnership between husband and wife in all property, movable and immovable, belonging to either of them before marriage or coming to either during marriage. DE VILLIERS CJ took the view that: "It is competent for the intended spouses, before marriage, to regulate their respective rights by express contract, but in the absence of such an express contract, they are understood to enter into a tacit contract that community of property between them shall prevail."[66] This tacit contract of community extended to foreign land. It was unaffected by a change of domicile.

On receipt of this opinion from the South African court, STIRLING J decided that: "in any event the joint estate passing under the said will includes all property which according to the law of the Cape of Good Hope would fall within the community of property which would have been created by the marriage of the testator and testatrix, if they were domiciled at the Cape of Good Hope at the time of their marriage".[67] He thereupon made an order declaring that the Cornish land passed under the will apparently in accordance with the tacit contract, though the decision is perhaps also explicable on other grounds.[68]

---

[64] (1897) 14 SC 61 (South Africa); but see *Tezcan v Tezcan* (1992) 87 DLR (4th) 503 at 517–518.

[65] The first question was whether the South African community system applied to immovables acquired outside South Africa. The Supreme Court held that it did. Had it decided the opposite, that would have been the end of the claim, as in *Callwood v Callwood* [1960] AC 659.

[66] (1897) 14 SC 61 at 65.

[67] This case is not reported in England, but the Public Record Office reference to the Entry Books of Decrees and Orders (Supreme Court of Judicature) is 1897 A 2919.

[68] One possible ground is that the land represented money already owned by the parties in South Africa. Another, that it was merely a question of testamentary construction—what did the parties intend? Being subject to and conversant with South African law at the time of making the will, they would naturally contemplate that the common property would include everything regarded as such by that law.

It remains now to consider specifically what law governs the three questions of capacity, formal validity and essential validity in the case of marriage contracts.

(b) Capacity[69]

The combination of circumstances which most neatly raises the question of capacity occurs where a woman, being a minor according to the law of her English domicile, makes a marriage contract in England prior to her marriage with a foreigner, by the law of whose domicile the woman is not subject to any incapacity. A variation, which occurred in *Viditz v O'Hagan*,[70] arises if the contract is made in a country which is the domicile neither of the woman nor of the man.

In relation to immovables, it is arguable that capacity to enter into a marriage contract should be governed by the law of the situs.[71] Strictly, however, the law of the situs should govern only capacity to convey immovable property, and not capacity to make a contract with regard to such property.[72] As regards movables, if we reason by analogy to commercial contracts, the proper law of the contract governs,[73] but if by analogy to the contract to marry, then the law of the parties' domicile[74] is the governing system. It is submitted, however, that on principle the proper law of the agreement should govern, and that the proper law is prima facie deemed to be the law of the matrimonial domicile.[75] It is that law which is universally recognised as controlling the personal and proprietary relations of the parties during their marriage.

The relevant cases[76] in chronological order are: *Re Cooke's Trusts*,[77] *Cooper v Cooper*,[78] and *Viditz v O'Hagan*.[79]

The facts of *Re Cooke's Trusts* were as follows:

> A domiciled Englishwoman under 21 married a Frenchman in France. Prior to the marriage, she made a notarial contract in France, which excluded the French doctrine of community of goods, and gave her "the entire administration of her property and the free enjoyment of her income". There were three children of the marriage. After having lived in Jersey for eight years separately from her husband, she went through a ceremony of marriage with X in 1853 under the mistaken belief

---

[69] On this difficult subject see Dicey, Morris and Collins, paras 28-038–28-042; Crawford and Carruthers, para 13-05; Morris (1938) 54 LQR 78; cf Goldberg (1970) 19 ICLQ 557, 569–573. Capacity to contract is largely unaffected by the Contracts (Applicable Law) Act 1990, supra, pp 750–753.

[70] [1900] 2 Ch 87. See Dicey, Morris and Collins, para 28-041.

[71] *Black v Black's Trs* 1950 SLT (Notes) 32. See, however, criticism in relation to *Bank of Africa Ltd v Cohen* [1909] 2 Ch 129 (not, however, a matrimonial property case): Morris, *Cases on Private International Law*, (1968) 4th edn, p 350.

[72] Carruthers (2005), para 4.04.

[73] It should be the proper law objectively ascertained, rather than deemed to be chosen by the parties; see supra, p 751.

[74] As to the law of the parties' domicile, see supra, p 896 et seq.

[75] On the meaning of this, see supra, pp 1294–1295.

[76] The practical significance of all three cases is now much less, given that the age of majority has been reduced to 18: Family Law Reform Act 1969, s 1.

[77] (1887) 56 LJ Ch 637.

[78] (1888) 13 App Cas 88.

[79] [1899] 2 Ch 569; revsd [1900] 2 Ch 87.

that her husband was dead. She resided with X and with her three children in New South Wales until her death in 1879. Her French husband did not die until 1877. She made a will leaving all her property to X. It was argued that a notarial contract was valid, and that it precluded the testatrix from depriving her children of the vested interests in her property given to them by French law.

STIRLING J, after deciding that the woman died domiciled in New South Wales, held that her capacity to make the notarial contract was governed by English law, as being the law of her ante-nuptial domicile. The consequence was that in his opinion her minority rendered the contract "void".[80] The reasoning which led the judge to this conclusion was not impressive. All that he did was to follow *Sottomayor v De Barros*,[81] relying on statements that personal capacity to contract is governed by the law of the domicile.[82] The decision is of little value on the question of capacity, for the right of the Englishwoman to dispose of her property by will was in no way restricted by the French contract on which the children relied. As Morris has said: "If a woman makes an ante-nuptial contract which merely excludes *communauté des biens* [community of goods] and gives her full powers of disposition, it is difficult to see how the children of the marriage can complain if they take nothing under the will."[83] The decision, in other words, would have been the same had she been of full age when she made the contract.

The facts of *Cooper v Cooper*,[84] a Scottish appeal to the House of Lords, were as follows:

A domiciled Irishwoman of 18 made an ante-nuptial contract in Dublin with her intended husband, a domiciled Scotsman, by which she purported to relinquish the proprietary rights that she would be entitled to under Scottish law on the death of her husband. Both parties contemplated, in accordance with what proved to be the fact, that the matrimonial home would be established in Scotland. The husband died thirty-five years after his wife attained her majority. On his death she sued to set aside the contract on the ground that at the time of its execution she was a minor by Irish law.

It was held that the woman's capacity must be governed by the law of Ireland, since that country was not only her domicile but also the place where the contract was made. Lord MACNAGHTEN rejected the notion that Scots law, as being the law of the matrimonial domicile, applied, saying: "It is difficult to suppose that Mrs Cooper could confer capacity upon herself by contemplating a different country as the place where the contract was to be fulfilled, if that be the proper expression, or by contracting in view of an alteration of personal status which would bring with it a change of domicil."[85] In any event the decision is not readily explicable. By Irish law, as well as by English law, a marriage contract was voidable, in the sense that it was to be treated as valid unless repudiated by the minor within a reasonable time after the attainment of majority.[86] Since there had been

---

[80] Though see *Edwards v Carter* [1893] AC 360.
[81] (1877) 3 PD 1.
[82] Ibid, at 5. This is no longer regarded as being so, see supra, pp 750–753.
[83] (1938) 54 LQR 78, 81.
[84] (1888) 13 App Cas 88.
[85] (1888) 13 App Cas 88 at 108.
[86] *Edwards v Carter* [1893] AC 360.

no repudiation within thirty-five years after the event, why was the contract not valid even by the law of the minor's ante-nuptial domicile? The true explanation seems to be that the House of Lords considered Scots law as well as Irish law to be a governing factor. By Irish law she might repudiate the contract or leave it in operation. By Scots law, the law of her new domicile, she could do nothing but repudiate it, since to ratify it or to leave it unrepudiated would constitute a gift that was revocable as being a gift between husband and wife.[87] The decision is far from convincing as an authority in support of the view that capacity to make a marriage settlement depends on the law of the domicile at the time of the contract.

Viditz v O'Hagan[88] is a curious case, in which the facts were these:

> A domiciled Englishwoman, under 21, made a marriage contract at Berne in view of her approaching marriage with a domiciled Austrian. The contract was voidable by English law, ie it could be rescinded by her after she attained majority, though it would become irrevocable if not rescinded within a reasonable time after that event. The rule of Austrian law, the law of the matrimonial domicile, was that the husband and wife might revoke the settlement agreement at any time. Twenty-nine years after the settlement, ie long after it had become irrevocable by English law, the husband and wife executed an instrument in the Austrian form by which they exercised the right of revocation. They then brought the present action against the English trustees claiming a declaration that the agreement had been annulled.

It was held by the Court of Appeal that they were entitled to the declaration, since the power of revoking the settlement agreement was a matter for Austrian law. In other words, by English law the wife could repudiate the contract, provided that she did so within a reasonable time after attaining her majority; by Austrian law, to which she later became subject, she could always repudiate it. Therefore the joint operation of the two laws rendered effective what the parties had done.

Neither *Cooper v Cooper* nor *Viditz v O'Hagan*, then, justifies the view that the law of each party's domicile governs capacity, for if this were the law the contract in each case would have been valid as not having been repudiated within a reasonable time.

(c) Formal validity

What is the appropriate legal system to determine the formalities that must be observed in the case of a marriage contract? If, for instance, an Englishwoman marries a man domiciled in a country in which the couple wishes to settle and where such a contract is void unless made by notarial act, and she wishes to make a settlement agreement with ordinary English limitations, it is important to know whether the English or the foreign form must be followed. The proper course is to execute the settlement as an English deed and then to re-execute it as a notarial act, but if this is not done a difficult question arises. If the deed is executed in the foreign country it neglects the forms required by the law of the place of contracting; if in England, it requires the parties to act under a transaction that is devoid of effect by the law of the matrimonial domicile.

---

[87] Morris, p 375, citing Lord LINDLEY in *Viditz v O'Hagan* [1900] 2 Ch 87 at 96, 98.
[88] [1900] 2 Ch 87.

Formerly, the traditional view was that a contract must observe the forms required by the law of the place of contracting. However it has been accepted at common law, as well as under the Contracts (Applicable Law) Act 1990,[89] that formalities, like essential validity, may be governed by the proper law. At common law, the form required by the law of the place of contracting is sufficient[90] but not essential. The English cases clearly show that in the case of marriage contracts relating to property it is sufficient to adopt the formalities of the proper law as an alternative to those of the law of the place of contracting.[91]

The exact point arose in *Van Grutten v Digby*:[92]

> Prior to a marriage between an Englishwoman and a domiciled Frenchman, a deed of settlement in the English form and containing the usual English limitations was executed at Dunkirk. The settlement was wholly void by French law, since it had not been executed before a notary public. Five years later the husband claimed that, owing to the formal invalidity of the contract by French law, the settled property was subject to the doctrine of community of goods.

Lord ROMILLY held, however, that the contract was binding on both parties:

> I hold it to be the law of this country that if a foreigner and an Englishwoman make an express contract previous to marriage, and if on the faith of that contract the marriage afterwards takes place, and if the contract relates to the regulation of property within the jurisdiction and subject to the laws of this country, then, and in that case, this court will administer the law on the subject as if the whole matter were to be regulated by English law.[93]

(d) Essential validity

The essential validity of a marriage contract is governed by its proper law. In relation to immovable property, at least as regards matters in rem, the law of the situs must surely be the proper law.[94] Otherwise, it seems clear that there may be express selection of the governing law, at least if it is connected with the transaction.[95] In the absence of choice, the proper law will be the law of the country with which the contract is most closely connected. In effect, the principles on which the proper law is to be determined are much the same as those relevant at common law to determine the proper law of a commercial

---

[89] Supra, p 746 et seq.

[90] Eg *Guépratte v Young* (1851) 4 De G & Sm 217.

[91] As to what is the proper law see infra, under (D) ESSENTIAL VALIDITY; see also *Ex p Spinazzi* 1985 (3) SA 650.

[92] (1862) 31 Beav 561; see also *Watts v Shrimpton* (1855) 21 Beav 97; *Re Barnard, Barnard v White* (1887) 56 LT 9; *Re Bankes* [1902] 2 Ch 333.

[93] (1862) 31 Beav 561 at 567.

[94] Cf *Teczan v Teczan* (1992) 87 DLR 503 (BCCA). Though see Dicey, Morris and Collins, para 28R-030, which in advocating the law of the matrimonial domicile as the proper law of a marriage contract makes no exception, or special mention, of the position with regard to immovable property.

[95] *Re Fitzgerald, Surman v Fitzgerald* [1904] 1 Ch 573 at 587–588; *Montgomery v Zarifi* 1918 SC (HL) 128; Crawford and Carruthers, para 13.07; cf *Re Bowen's Estate* 351 NYS 2d 113 (1973).

contract.[96] However, the nature of the subject matter is such that certain factors may predominate in significance, not least being the matrimonial domicile.[97] Indeed there would appear to be a presumption in favour of the law of the matrimonial domicile, but this may well be rebutted by other circumstances.[98] Other factors to which consideration may be given include: the nature and situation of the property; whether the form and contents of the document are appropriate to one law, but not to another; the place where the accounts, the shares and other indicia of title are kept; the fact that the contract is invalid under the law of the matrimonial domicile.

The proper law, once it has been identified in accordance with these principles, continues to govern the marriage contract even though the interested parties may establish their house in a country where a different law prevails.[99]

Where there is a marriage settlement creating trusts of that settlement, the essential validity of such trusts falls to be governed by the law determined by reference to the Recognition of Trusts Act 1987.[100]

4. PROPERTY RIGHTS ARISING FROM OTHER ADULT RELATIONSHIPS

(a) Civil Partnership Act 2004

The Civil Partnership Act 2004 introduced the status of civil partnership for same sex couples.[101] In the case of civil partnerships registered in England, the property and financial consequences of such relationships are detailed in Chapter 3 of Part 2 of the Act.[102] Provision for recognition in England of civil partnerships formed abroad is set out in Chapter 2 of Part 5 of the Act.[103]

The 2004 Act does not lay down express choice of law rules regarding the property rights of civil partners resulting from civil partnership[104] akin to those rights which apply at common law in relation to the property of married persons resulting from marriage.[105] It is submitted, however, that the property rights of civil partners should be determined under English conflict rules in the same manner as those of married persons.[106] The rules and principles set out in this chapter, therefore, should be treated as applying, *mutatis mutandis*, to civil partners as well as to married persons.

---

[96] Including the possibility that, exceptionally, different proper laws may govern different parts of a contract, eg as regards movable, and immovable, property, respectively: Cheshire, *International Contracts* (1948), p 42.

[97] Supra, p 1294 et seq. See Dicey, Morris and Collins, para 28-032.

[98] *Re Fitzgerald* [1904] 1 Ch 573; and see *Re Hannema's Marriage* (1981) 54 FLR 79, 7 Fam LR 542. Crawford and Carruthers, para 13-08.

[99] *Re Hewitt's Settlement* [1915] 1 Ch 228.

[100] Infra, p 1312 et seq.

[101] See generally pp 937–939, supra.

[102] Ss 65–72.

[103] See pp 938–939, supra.

[104] See, however, Sch 4 in relation to wills, administration of estates, and family provision; and Sch 7 regarding financial relief in England following the overseas dissolution of a civil partnership.

[105] As described in this chapter.

[106] Cf Dicey, Morris and Collins, para 28-005.

(b) Cohabitation[107]

Included in the Law Commission's Ninth Programme of Law Reform[108] is a project to consider the financial hardship suffered by cohabitants[109] or their children on the termination of the cohabiting relationship by reason of breakdown or death.[110] It is recognised that, "when cohabitants separate, the courts use a patchwork of statutory and non-statutory rules to determine what should happen to the couple's property".[111] The Law Commission's Consultation Paper, in proposing a new scheme for cohabitants, recognised that account must be taken of the international dimension, and so there were proposed in Part 11 new rules of jurisdiction[112] and applicable law relevant to cohabitation, including rules pertaining to cohabitation contracts and "opt-out agreements".[113]

This project is at an early stage and it remains to be seen whether domestic law reform will be introduced. It is possible that the project will be eclipsed by legislative reform now proposed at the European level.

5. EUROPEAN PROPOSALS FOR REFORM

In July 2006, the European Commission published a Green Paper on Conflict of Laws in Matrimonial Property Regimes.[114] Accompanying the Green Paper is an Annex,[115] partially comprising the fruits of an European-commissioned study entitled, "Matrimonial Property Regimes and the Property of Unmarried Couples in Private International Law".[116] The purpose of the Green Paper is to launch a wide-ranging consultation exercise on the legal questions which arise in an international context as regards matrimonial property regimes and the property consequences of other forms of personal unions,

---

107 See generally Carruthers (2008) 12 Edin LR 51.

108 Law Com No 293 (2005), para 3.6.

109 "Opposite-sex and same-sex couples in clearly defined relationships." The project excludes relationships between blood relatives and "caring" relationships, as well as "commercial" relationships (eg landlord and tenant/lodger). Law Commission Consultation Paper No 179, "Cohabitation: The Financial Consequences of Relationship Breakdown—A Consultation Paper" (2006), para 1.19. See also Report on Cohabitation: "The Financial Consequences of Relationship Breakdown", Law Com No 307, (2007).

110 The project is limited in scope. It is not a comprehensive review of all the law that currently applies to cohabitants, but rather deals only with the issue of financial relief between cohabitants upon termination of their relationship. Cf the position in Scotland where statutory rules recently have been introduced pertaining to the financial and proprietary consequences of cohabitation: Family Law (Scotland) Act 2006, ss 25–30. The 2006 Act does not clearly specify, from a conflict of laws perspective, when or in what circumstances the rights established therein should apply: Crawford and Carruthers, paras 13-12–13-15.

111 Consultation Paper, para 3.3.

112 See Report on Cohabitation: "The Financial Consequences of Relationship Breakdown", Law Com No 307, (2007), para 7.15.

113 See Carruthers, (2008) 12 Edin LR 51, 61 et seq.

114 COM (2006) 400 final. See, for comment, Carruthers, op cit, at 72 et seq. Matrimonial property regimes hitherto have been excluded from Community instruments. The Green Paper is one of several initiatives deriving from the Hague Programme, adopted by the European Council in November 2004 (The Hague Programme: Strengthening Freedom, Security and Justice in the European Union, OJ 2005 C 53/1; and the Council and Commission Action Plan Implementing the Hague Programme on Strengthening Freedom, Security and Justice in the European Union, OJ 2005 C 198/1) (in respect of which, see generally, supra, Chapter 1).

115 SEC (2006) 952.

116 JAI/A3/2001/03. Full reports explaining the English and Scottish positions as at that date are available on the Commission website: http://ec.europa.eu/justice_home/doc_centre/civil/studies/doc_civil_studies_en.htm.

including registered partnerships and *de facto* unions. The Green Paper, which has been prompted by the increased mobility of persons within the European Union and the "significant increase in all forms of unions between nationals of different member States or the presence of such couples in a Member State of which they do not have the nationality, often accompanied by the acquisition of property located on the territory of several Union countries",[117] addresses issues of jurisdiction, choice of law, and recognition and enforcement of judgments. The document seeks to explore avenues in which conflict rules across the Member States might be improved, and suggests possible options for future legislative action at Community level. In what is an area of considerable technical complexity, however, it is seriously questionable whether a satisfactory Community-wide solution is attainable.[118]

---

[117] Green Paper, p 3.

[118] Cf House of Commons European Scrutiny Committee, 37th Report (2005–06), Document 3.

Chapter 34

Trusts

1. INTRODUCTION

The common law rules concerning the validity of trusts in the international context were described in 1951 as "simply specific rules, evolved to meet particular difficulties. They do not reflect, or form part of a fully-developed system, and it is a matter for remark that they deal with so few of the many possible situations which may possibly arise."[1] In the intervening years the case law remained thin, with patchy analysis of the issues and uncertainty as to the relevant rules in a number of areas. It is, therefore, not surprising that the

---

[1] Keeton (1951) 4 Current Legal Problems 111, 119.

Recognition of Trusts Act was passed in 1987 to enable the United Kingdom to give effect to the Convention, formally concluded in 1985 by the Hague Conference on Private International Law, on the Law Applicable to Trusts and on their Recognition.[2] This Convention is implemented by being scheduled, with some omissions,[3] to the 1987 Act.[4]

It has to be said that the main reason for the initiation of work on this Convention was not the unsatisfactory nature of the private international law of trusts in those countries familiar with the law of trusts, but rather the fact that issues involving the validity of trusts or the powers of trustees may arise in countries where the trust concept is unfamiliar.[5] This accounts for the fact that the Hague Convention and the 1987 Act not only lay down choice of law rules but also extend to the question of the recognition of trusts, which is a particular problem if they are unknown in the domestic law.[6]

In considering the private international law rules governing trusts which are laid down in the Recognition of Trusts Act 1987 and its scheduled Convention,[7] it is necessary to examine a range of preliminary issues before turning to the specific rules governing choice of law and the recognition of trusts.

2. PRELIMINARY ISSUES[8]

(a) Definition of a trust

A major objective of the Convention is "to establish common provisions on the law applicable to trusts and to deal with the most important issues concerning the recognition of trusts";[9] but these common provisions are to be applied in countries some of which are familiar with the trust concept and others of which are not. Furthermore, as the Convention is an "open" and not a "reciprocal" Convention, the law to be applied to the validity or recognition of a trust may not be that of a Contracting State.[10] This led to

---

[2] See *Actes et Documents de la Quinzième session*, Vol II, especially the official Explanatory Report, at p 370, by von Overbeck; Harris (2002); Hayton (1987) 36 ICLQ 260; Gaillard and Trautman (1987) 35 AJCL 307; Klein, in *Mélanges Paul Piotet* (1990), p 467; Hayton, in Borras (ed), *E Pluribus Unum* (1996), p 121.

[3] It would have been more helpful to have scheduled a fuller version. Indeed reference is made in this chapter to some provisions which have not been scheduled.

[4] 1987 Act, s 1(1).

[5] *Actes et Documents de la Quartorzième* session, Vol I, p 189; see Paton and Grosso (1994) 43 ICLQ 654.

[6] The Convention rules apply to trusts regardless of the date on which they were created: Art 22; though other states have a power (not exercised by the United Kingdom) to limit the rules to trusts created after the Convention came into force in those states. S 1(5) of the 1987 Act makes clear that Art 22 is not to be construed as affecting the law to be applied to anything done or omitted to be done before the Act came into force, though the combined meaning of these provisions is not without doubt: see *Re Carapiet's Trust, The Armenian Patriarch of Jerusalem v Sonsino* [2002] EWHC 1304 (Ch); [2002] WTLR 989, per JACOB J, at [3]; and Harris (2002), pp 406–408.

[7] The rules apply to conflicts between the laws of parts of the United Kingdom as they do more generally internationally; though there is a power in the Convention (Art 24) which would have allowed the exclusion of intra-United Kingdom conflicts.

[8] See generally Harris (2002), Part One.

[9] Convention, Preamble.

[10] Though there is a power for Contracting States to make a reservation limiting the application of the rules on recognition to a trust the validity of which is governed by the law of a Contracting State: Art 21.

the decision to include, in Article 2 of the Convention, a description, if not a definition, of a trust for the purposes of the Convention:

> For the purposes of this Convention, the term "trust" refers to the legal relationships created—*inter vivos* or on death—by a person, the settlor, when assets[11] have been placed under the control of a trustee for the benefit of a beneficiary or for a specified purpose.
>
> A trust has the following characteristics—
> (a) the assets constitute a separate fund and are not a part of the trustee's own estate;
> (b) title to the trust assets stands in the name of the trustee or in the name of another person on behalf of the trustee;
> (c) the trustee has the power and the duty, in respect of which he is accountable, to manage, employ or dispose of the assets in accordance with the terms of the trust and the special duties imposed upon him by law.
>
> The reservation by the settlor of certain rights and powers, and the fact that the trustee may himself have rights as a beneficiary, are not necessarily inconsistent with the existence of a trust.

The effect of this is to include within the Convention the classic concept of trust known to the common law world, whilst also making it possible to extend the Convention to trust-like institutions familiar to other jurisdictions.

(b) Types of trust falling within the 1987 Act[12]

The definition of a trust in Article 2 ensures that the rules of the Convention apply both to trusts created *inter vivos* and on death, and that they apply both to trusts for the benefit of specific beneficiaries and for "a specified purpose", thus including charitable trusts. Under Article 3, it is stated that: "The Convention only applies to trusts created voluntarily and evidenced in writing." Whilst this does not require the trust to be in writing, merely evidenced in writing, it would appear to exclude purely oral trusts, trusts which are created by judicial decision and trusts created by statute. All three such categories of trust are, however, covered by the 1987 Act, though in differing ways.

The Convention[13] gives Contracting States the power to extend the provisions of the Convention to trusts created by judicial decision and this has, in fact, been done in the 1987 Act.[14] It should be noted that the extension is unlimited in that it applies to trusts created by virtue of a judicial decision whether in the United Kingdom or elsewhere. This means that trusts created by judicial decision elsewhere in the European Community or in the EFTA States will fall to be recognised under the Civil Jurisdiction and Judgments Acts 1982 and 1991 respectively.[15] If the trust is created by judicial decision in some other country its recognition will depend on whether that foreign judgment falls to be recognised under the general rules for the recognition of foreign judgments.[16]

---

[11] No distinction is drawn between movable and immovable property.
[12] See Harris (2002), pp 123–138.
[13] Art 20.
[14] S 1(2).
[15] Supra, p 595 et seq.
[16] Supra, p 513 et seq.

Oral trusts and trusts created by statute fall outside the Convention and there is no express power to extend the Convention provisions to them. Nevertheless, in the interests of ensuring that as many kinds of trust as is appropriate are governed by the same rules, the 1987 Act applies the rules in the Convention on both choice of law and recognition to "any other trusts of property arising under the law of any part of the United Kingdom".[17] There is no doubt that this includes purely oral trusts arising under English law, as well as trusts created by the operation of a statute[18] or by specific action under a statute.[19]

Although the rules of the Convention are to be applied to a wide variety of trusts, not every type of trust is included. For example, the validity of an oral trust which arises under the law of some country outside the United Kingdom will have to be determined by an English court according to the common law rules of private international law, which, notwithstanding the 1987 Act, will remain applicable to such a trust.[20] The extension of the provisions of the Convention to trusts of property created by judicial decision will ensure that many instances of constructive trust are included, but not cases where constructive trusts are created as a form of personal remedy.[21]

(c) Validity of the instrument of creation of the trust

In the case of a voluntary testamentary or *inter vivos* trust, there is an important preliminary issue to be faced, namely whether the instrument which creates the trust, ie the will or the settlement, is valid according to the relevant governing law. Article 4 of the Convention makes it quite clear that this preliminary issue as to validity falls outside the scope of the Convention. The relevant choice of law rules will be those governing, for example, the formal or essential validity of wills[22] or, in the fairly rare cases where there is a settlement, those governing the validity of contracts[23] or deeds. In the case of a testamentary trust it will also be for the law governing the validity of the will to determine, for example, whether the testator is required to leave a fixed portion of his estate to his/her spouse or children rather than on trust for other beneficiaries.[24]

(d) Transfer of trust assets

Not only does a voluntary trust depend on there being a valid instrument of creation, it is also necessary that the transfer of the trust assets is valid. This further preliminary issue is also excluded from the Convention by reason of Article 4, as being an act "by virtue of

---

[17] S 1(2).

[18] Eg under the Law of Property Act 1925, ss 34–36; Administration of Estates Act 1925, s 33; Administration of Justice Act 1925, s 42; *Re Kehr* [1952] Ch 26.

[19] Eg under the Mental Health Act 1983, s 96(1)(d), repealed by the Mental Capacity Act 2005, s 67(2) and Sch 7 (see, for transitional provisions, s 66(4) and Sch 5, Pt 1).

[20] Though there are unlikely to be major differences between the two sets of rules, see infra, p 1315 et seq. For the common law rules, see the 11th edn of this book (1987), Chapter 35.

[21] See Chong (2005) 54 ICLQ 855; Hayton (1987) 36 ICLQ 260 at 264; and see Barnard [1992] CLJ 474, 479. See also *Minera Aquiline Argentina SA v IMA Exploration Inc and Inversiones Mineras Argentinas SA* 2006 BCSC 1102. Whether most forms of resulting trust are included is unclear, see Hayton, supra, 263–264. For discussion of the law applicable to other equitable obligations, see supra, p 769.

[22] Supra, p 1264 et seq, p 1279 et seq.

[23] Supra, p 689 et seq.

[24] Eg *Re Hernando* (1884) 27 Ch D 284; *Re Annesley* [1926] Ch 692; *Re Ross* [1930] 1 Ch 377; and see supra, pp 1270–1271.

which assets are transferred to the trustee". The choice of law issue as to whether a trustee has effective legal title to the assets to hold them for the beneficiaries will normally be governed by the general rules applicable to the transfer of property, eg the law of the situs in the case of tangible movables[25] and of immovables.[26] If the instrument of creation of the trust is valid under its governing law, the trust will, nevertheless, fail if the law of the situs does not permit the transferee to hold the property other than absolutely, as where the concept of the trust is unknown to that legal system. *Re Pearse's Settlement*[27] provides an illustration of this type of problem:

> In 1897, the settlor conveyed property to trustees to hold on the trusts of a marriage settlement. In all respects this was an English settlement. She agreed to settle after-acquired property on the same trusts. In 1901 she became entitled to land in Jersey and the question was whether that land was caught by the covenant to settle after-acquired property. There was no doubt as to the validity under English law of the instrument creating the trust. However, since under the law of Jersey, the settlor could not transfer land in Jersey to trustees, in the absence of adequate pecuniary consideration, the Jersey land was not subject to the covenant to settle after-acquired property.

3. CHOICE OF LAW

(a) Choice by the settlor[28]

Article 6 of the Convention embodies party autonomy by providing:

> A trust shall be governed by the law chosen by the settlor. The choice must be express or be implied in the terms of the instrument creating or the writing evidencing the trust, interpreted, if necessary, in the light of the circumstances of the case.

This makes clear that either an express[29] or an implied choice by the settlor of the governing law is permitted. Such a rule confirms what had generally been accepted to be the position at common law in relation both to testamentary[30] and *inter vivos*[31] trusts, and whether the case is one of choice of a foreign law by an English domiciled testator or settlor or of English law by a foreign domiciliary.[32] To be effective the choice must be of the substantive law of the jurisdiction chosen[33] and cannot include its private international law rules; ie the doctrine of renvoi is excluded here as elsewhere in the Convention.[34]

---

[25] Supra, p 1211 et seq.

[26] Supra, p 1199 et seq.

[27] [1909] 1 Ch 304.

[28] See Harris (2002), pp 166–213.

[29] See *Re Barton (Deceased), Tod v Barton* [2002] EWHC 264 (Ch); [2002] WTLR 469, per Lawrence COLLINS J, at [34] and [35].

[30] See, eg, *Re Lord Cable* [1977] 1 WLR 7 at 20; *Re Healy's Will* 125 NYS 2d 486 (1953).

[31] See, eg, *Este v Smith* (1854) 18 Beav 112 at 122; *Re Hernando* (1884) 27 Ch D 284 at 292–293; *Re Fitzgerald* [1904] 1 Ch 573 at 587; *Augustus v Permanent Trustee Co (Canberra) Ltd* (1971) 124 CLR 245; *Re Pratt* 8 NY 2d 855, 168 NE 2d 709 (1960).

[32] Cf *Canterbury Corpn v Wyburn and Melbourne Hospital* [1895] AC 89.

[33] This includes, here as elsewhere in the Convention, the law of a part of a multi-territory state which has its own law of trusts, eg of a part of the United Kingdom or of a state within the USA: 1987 Act, s 1(4), and Art 23 of the Convention (not scheduled to the Act).

[34] Art 17; though see Art 15, discussed infra, pp 1321–1322.

No guidance is provided by the Convention on what will constitute an implied choice of the applicable law; though there is certainly a suggestion at common law in the case of testamentary trusts that the testator was presumed to intend that the law of his domicile governed the validity of such trusts.[35] In *Re Barton (Deceased)*, Lawrence COLLINS J concluded that, even if there had been no express choice of English law, the terms of the Will by which the trust was created, particularly the reference to charitable trusts under English law, would have pointed to an implied choice of English law.[36] In the case of *inter vivos* trusts there is a degree of common law authority indicating circumstances from which the settlor's intention can be determined.[37] For example, reference has been made to such factors as the place of making the original contract or deed,[38] the situs of the property subject to the trust[39] and the place of registration of the trustee company[40] or the place of administration of the trust.[41]

The Convention allows "a severable aspect of the trust" to be governed by a different law from that otherwise applicable.[42] So, a testator or settlor could choose English law to govern the administration of a trust but New York law to govern all other matters relating to the trust—or he could choose the law to govern just one aspect, leaving the determination of the law to govern the others to be decided by the rules applicable in the absence of choice. Where there are trust assets in different jurisdictions the Convention will have to be construed to decide whether choosing different laws to govern the different assets is permitted as "a severable aspect" of the trust.

There are some limits on the freedom of the settlor to choose the governing law. First, if he chooses the law of a country which "does not provide for trusts or the category of trust involved",[43] then such a meaningless choice is ineffective and the trust is governed by the law applicable in the absence of choice.[44] Secondly, there are certain rules which take precedence over any chosen applicable law, ie mandatory rules of the forum, mandatory rules of other countries applicable by reason of the forum's private international law rules and the forum's rules on public policy.[45] Thirdly, a factor which may inhibit choice of the applicable law is that recognition of a trust may be refused if the significant elements of the trust are, but for the choice of the applicable law, the place of administration and the habitual residence of the trustee, more closely connected with a state or states which do not have the institution of the trust or the category of trust involved.[46] So life may not be breathed into a trust in such circumstances by the choice of the law of a common law country.

---

[35] Eg *Peillon v Brooking* (1858) 25 Beav 218; *Re Aganoor's Trusts* (1895) 64 LJ Ch 521; *Re Lord Cable* [1977] 1 WLR 7 at 20; though this was not an invariable rule, see *A-G v Campbell* (1872) LR 5 HL 524.

[36] *Re Barton (Deceased), Tod v Barton* [2002] EWHC 264 (Ch); [2002] WTLR 469, per Lawrence COLLINS J, at [36].

[37] See *Revenue Comrs v Pelly* [1940] IR 122.

[38] *Harris Investments Ltd v Smith* [1934] 1 DLR 748.

[39] Ibid; *Lindsay v Miller* [1949] VLR 13.

[40] *A-G v Jewish Colonization Association* [1901] 1 KB 123.

[41] *Chellaram v Chellaram* [1985] Ch 409 at 424–425.

[42] Art 9. *Re Barton (Deceased), Tod v Barton* [2002] EWHC 264 (Ch); [2002] WTLR 469 at [35].

[43] Art 6.

[44] Art 7, infra. If that law also does not provide for trusts, then the Convention rules cease to apply: Art 5.

[45] Arts 15, 16, 18, discussed infra, pp 1322–1323.

[46] Art 13, infra, pp 1321–1322.

(b) Absence of choice[47]

If the settlor has not chosen the law to govern the validity of the trust, or has made an ineffective choice by selecting the law of a country where the trust concept is unknown, then Article 7 provides for the determination of the applicable law as follows:

Where no applicable law has been chosen, a trust shall be governed by the law with which it is most closely connected. In ascertaining the law with which a trust is most closely connected reference shall be made in particular to—
(a) the place of administration of the trust designated by the settlor;
(b) the situs of the assets of the trust;
(c) the place of residence or business of the trustee;
(d) the objects of the trust and the places where they are to be fulfilled.

The basic rule that a trust should be governed by the law of the country with which it is most closely connected[48] is in substance the same rule as applied at common law, in the absence of choice, both in the case of testamentary[49] and *inter vivos*[50] trusts.

Although Article 7 provides a list of factors for the court to consider, it is not an exclusive list and a court would remain free to attach importance, for example, to domicile.[51] What is not clear is the relative weight to be given to all the factors, whether or not listed in Article 7. All that can really be said is that it will vary with the circumstances of each individual case,[52] though there may be a tendency to favour the application of the law of a country under which the trust is valid.[53] If the trust assets consist of immovable property, it is likely that greater significance will be afforded to the law of the situs of the property.[54] Direct evidence of the settlor's intention as to governing law is not admissible.[55]

What is not made clear expressly by Article 7 is the time at which the factors determining closeness of connection must be considered. It is suggested, however, that, as express provision is made later in relation to change of the applicable law,[56] the appropriate time to consider the factors should be that of the creation of the trust. This would follow the

---

[47] See Harris (2002), pp 215–232.

[48] In theory, at least, Art 9 would allow different laws to be applied to different aspects of the trust more closely connected with different jurisdictions. If the court decides, unusually, that the most closely connected law is that of a country which does not provide for trusts or for trusts of this kind, then the Convention is inapplicable: Art 5.

[49] See, in the case of movables, *A-G v Campbell* (1872) LR 5 HL 524; and *Re Carapiet's Trust, The Armenian Patriarch of Jerusalem v Sonsino* [2002] EWHC 1304 (Ch); [2002] WTLR 989, at [3]. The position in relation to immovables was less clear, see the 11th edn of this book (1987), pp 884–885.

[50] Eg *Iveagh v IRC* [1954] Ch 364; *Chellaram v Chellaram* [1985] Ch 409; *Chellaram v Chellaram (No 2)* [2002] EWHC 632 (Ch); [2002] 3 All ER 17, per Lawrence COLLINS J, at [142] and [166]; *Perpetual Executors and Trustees Association of Australia Ltd v Roberts* [1970] VR 732; *Branco v Veira* (1995) 9 ETR (2d) 49.

[51] Cf *Iveagh v IRC* [1954] Ch 364; *Re Hewitt's Settlement* [1915] 1 Ch 228; and *Re Lord Cable* [1977] 1 WLR 7 at 20. In contrast, see *Re Barton (Deceased), Tod v Barton* [2002] EWHC 264 (Ch); [2002] WTLR 469, per Lawrence COLLINS J, at [36].

[52] See Wallace (1987) 36 ICLQ 455, 468–469.

[53] Hayton (1987) 36 ICLQ 260, 272.

[54] Art 7, para (b); and see, eg, *Freke v Lord Carbery* (1873) LR 16 Eq 461; *Peabody v Kent* 153 App Div 286, 13 NYS 32 (1912); affd 213 NY 154, 107 NE 51 (1914).

[55] *Chellaram v Chellaram* [1985] 1 Ch 409 at 425; *Re Carapiet's Trust, The Armenian Patriarch of Jerusalem v Sonsino* [2002] EWHC 1304 (Ch); [2002] WTLR 989 at [5] and [12].

[56] Art 10, infra, p 1320.

common law position where changes in the identity, and thus the domicile or residence, of the trustees,[57] or in the place of investment,[58] which took place after the trust was created were to be ignored.

Just as with a choice of the applicable law, there are certain limits on the application of the most closely connected law. The forum's mandatory rules and rules of public policy remain applicable despite the close connection of the trust with another law;[59] the mandatory rules of other countries which are to be applied by reason of the forum's private international law rules are also applicable.[60]

(c) Scope of the applicable law[61]

Article 8 makes it clear that the applicable law determined by reference to Articles 6 or 7 is to govern "the validity of the trust, its construction, its effects and the administration of the trust". The basic starting point is, therefore, that the same law governs all these issues; though, as has been seen, it is possible for a severable aspect of a trust to be governed by a different law.[62] This generality of approach has the effect that the same law will normally apply to a testamentary or *inter vivos* trust even though the trust property consists of both movable and immovable property.

Article 8 goes on to list a non-exclusive range of matters which are to be governed by the applicable law, namely:

(a) the appointment, resignation and removal of trustees, the capacity to act as a trustee, and the devolution of the office of trustee;

(b) the rights and duties of trustees among themselves;

(c) the right of trustees to delegate in whole or in part the discharge of their duties or the exercise of their powers;

(d) the power of trustees to administer or dispose of trust assets, to create security interests in the trust assets, or to acquire new assets;

(e) the powers of investment of trustees;

(f) restrictions upon the duration of the trust, and upon the power to accumulate the income of the trust;

(g) the relationships between the trustees and the beneficiaries including the personal liability of the trustees to the beneficiaries;[63]

(h) the variation or termination of the trust;[64]

(i) the distribution of the trust assets;

(j) the duty of trustees to account for their administration.

---

[57] *Iveagh v IRC* [1954] Ch 364 at 370; and see *Re Hewitt's Settlement* [1915] 1 Ch 228 at 233–234; *Duke of Marlborough v A-G* [1945] Ch 78 at 85.

[58] *Iveagh v IRC*, supra: and see *Re Fitzgerald* [1904] 1 Ch 573 at 588; *Duke of Marlborough v A-G*, supra.

[59] Arts 16, 18, infra, pp 1322–1323.

[60] Art 15, infra, pp 1322–1323.

[61] See Harris (2002), pp 233–280.

[62] Art 9, supra, p 1316.

[63] See Barnard [1992] CLJ 472.

[64] Discussed more fully, infra, p 1323 et seq; see also *Re Barton (Deceased), Tod v Barton* [2002] EWHC 264 (Ch); [2002] WTLR 469.

The reference of these matters to the law determined by Articles 6 or 7 very much follows the common law approach in the case of *inter vivos* trusts. This may be illustrated by *Augustus v Permanent Trustee Co (Canberra) Ltd*:[65]

> The settlor executed a voluntary deed of settlement in the Australian Capital Territory. He was resident and domiciled in New South Wales. The trusts were in favour of the settlor's children and grandchildren; and those who were alive at the date of the settlement were also domiciled and resident in New South Wales. The trustee was a corporation registered in Canberra which was where the funds were paid over by the settlor. The trust was void for perpetuity under the law of the Australian Capital Territory, but valid under the law of New South Wales.

In the High Court of Australia, WALSH J held that the issue of validity was to be determined by the proper law of the trust and, there being a clause in the trust deed which was interpreted as a reference to the law of New South Wales, he upheld the validity of the trust, applying the law of that state.

Article 8 specifically states that the applicable law is to govern the construction of the trust. Where no view, express or implied, has been indicated by the testator or settlor, no problem arises and the most closely connected law will be applied.[66] It may be, however, that it is possible to determine the law which was intended to govern the construction or interpretation of the trust and it would seem to be the case that, under the Convention, as under the common law, the court's first task is to try to find whether there is any such intention on the part of the testator or settlor.[67] If so, then the intended law should be applied by reason of Article 6 even though it may only be applied to this severable aspect of the trust.[68]

The law to govern the administration of the trust is also specifically included within the terms of Article 8. This means that, where there is a choice, express or implied, of the law to govern the administration of the trust, effect will be given to that choice,[69] even though a different law is held to govern the validity of the trust.[70] Indeed it may also be the case that the closest connection test, in the absence of choice, leads to a different law being applied to administration from that applied to validity.[71] One or two words of caution are, however, necessary here. It may not always be easy to determine the place of administration, as where a testator leaves property in two countries creating separate administrations in each with the trustees' investment powers varying as between the applicable laws of the two separate places of administration.[72] Whilst here it could be argued that there are two separate administrations governed by separate laws, that escape is not available where there are issues which affect the administration of the trust as a whole, such as

---

[65] (1971) 124 CLR 245; and see *Lindsay v Miller* [1949] VLR 13.

[66] As at common law in *Re Levick's Will Trusts* [1963] 1 WLR 311 at 319; *Philipson-Stow v IRC* [1961] AC 727; *Perpetual Executors and Trustees Association of Australia Ltd v Roberts* [1970] VR 732.

[67] Eg *Re Pilkington's Will Trusts* [1937] Ch 574; *Trustees Executors and Agency Co Ltd v Margottini* [1960] VR 417; *Philipson-Stow v IRC*, supra, at 761.

[68] Eg *Spencer's Trustees v Ruggles* 1982 SLT 165.

[69] As at common law, see *Chelleram v Chelleram* [1985] Ch 409 at 431–432; *In the Estate of Webb* (1992) 57 SASR 193.

[70] Art 9, in allowing a different law to be applied to a severable aspect of a trust, makes specific reference to matters of administration; and see *In the Estate of Webb*, supra, at 204.

[71] Eg *Re Wilks* [1935] Ch 645; *Re Kehr* [1952] Ch 26.

[72] Eg *Re Tyndall* [1913] SASR 39.

the appointment of a new trustee. For such an issue the law of just one place of administration needs to be identified; and whilst there is some common law authority supporting
reference to the place where the bulk of the assets is held,[73] a better view is to identify the
place of administration by reference to the place of residence of all, or a majority, of the
trustees.[74] It has been assumed so far that it is easy to decide whether a matter refers to
validity or administration but this may not always be the case.[75] Indeed the categorisation
may vary between legal systems, thus requiring the choice of a legal system to resolve the
issue. Whilst the Convention is silent on this issue, it has been suggested that it is for the
law governing validity to determine the matter.[76]

(d) Variation of the applicable law[77]

There is no doubt that a trust must have a law or laws governing its validity, construction
and administration from the moment of its creation. If further assets are later transferred to the trustees, that will not, as such, affect the law applicable to the trust. Article
10 of the Convention envisages, however, that as with contracts[78] the law to govern
some or all aspects of a trust may be varied during the lifetime of the trust, eg by a later
express choice of the governing law, the trust up to that point having been governed by
the law determined under Article 7. Article 10 does not lay down a substantive rule that
such variation is permitted but rather provides a choice of law rule for resolving this
issue by stipulating that "the law applicable to the validity of the trust shall determine
whether that law or the law governing a severable aspect of the trust may be replaced by
another law".[79] So, if English law is the law already applicable to the trust, it will decide
whether or not, for example, a provision in the trust allowing the trustees to replace the
law governing all or part of the trust shall have effect.[80] It should be noted that Article
10 assumes that one law can be identified as that applicable to the validity of the trust
even though different aspects of the trust are expressly governed by different laws. So if
validity is expressly governed by English law and administration by New York law, it is
for English law to decide whether the law governing the administration of the trust may
later be varied.

4. RECOGNITION[81]

Chapter III of the Hague Convention is concerned with the recognition of trusts, and, as
such, is of more practical importance for the recognition of trusts in civil law countries
where the concept of the trust is unfamiliar—though it is no doubt important that

---

[73] *Permanent Trustee Co (Canberra) Ltd v Permanent Trustee Co of New South Wales Ltd* (1969) 14 FLR 246 at
252–253.
[74] *Re Smyth* [1898] 1 Ch 89 at 94.
[75] *Chelleram v Chelleram* [1985] Ch 409; and see Wallace (1987) 36 ICLQ 454, 474–475.
[76] Harris (2002), pp 234, and 283–289.
[77] See Harris (2002), pp 297–308.
[78] Supra, pp 692–694.
[79] *Chellaram v Chellaram (No 2)* [2002] EWHC 632 (Ch); [2002] 3 All ER 17, at [146] and [160].
[80] Change could also be effected by agreement of the beneficiaries, though this really amounts to the making
of a new settlement: *Duke of Marlborough v A-G* [1945] Ch 78 at 85; *Iveagh v IRC* [1954] Ch 364 at 370.
[81] Harris (2002), pp 311–335.

English trusts secure recognition in other Contracting States. The approach of the Convention is, in Article 11, almost to state the obvious by providing that a trust created in accordance with the choice of law rules laid down in the Convention shall be recognised as a trust. It goes on, however, to make provision (really for the benefit of countries where the trust is unfamiliar) for the implications and effects of recognition:

> Such recognition shall imply, as a minimum, that the trust property constitutes a separate fund,[82] that the trustee may sue and be sued in his capacity as trustee, and that he may appear or act in this capacity before a notary or any person acting in an official capacity.
>
> In so far as the law applicable to the trust requires or provides, such recognition shall imply, in particular—
> (a) that personal creditors of the trustee shall have no recourse against the trust assets;
> (b) that the trust assets shall not form part of the trustee's estate upon his insolvency or bankruptcy;
> (c) that the trust assets shall not form part of the matrimonial property of the trustee or his spouse nor part of the trustee's estate upon his death;
> (d) that the trust assets may be recovered when the trustee, in breach of trust, has mingled trust assets with his own property or has alienated trust assets. However, the rights and obligations of any third party holder of the assets shall remain subject to the law determined by the choice of law rules of the forum.[83]

It is noticeable that these provisions concentrate, at least on their face, on the position of the trustee though they do by inference provide safeguards for beneficiaries. Attention has been drawn to the fact that the last part of paragraph (d) will restrict the ability of a beneficiary to trace trust assets into the hands of a third party where the assets are situated in a country where the trust concept is unknown.[84]

There are, however, limitations on the recognition to be given to a foreign trust. There are, first, the generally applicable limitations which allow for the application of the public policy or mandatory rules of the forum or those designated by its choice of law rules.[85] If these last rules prevent the recognition of a trust, then Article 15 stipulates that "the court shall try to give effect to the objects of the trust by other means". This is a very vague exhortation and is likely to prove particularly difficult to operate in civil law countries.

A further limitation on recognition is provided by Article 13:

> No State shall be bound to recognise a trust the significant elements of which, except for the choice of the applicable law, the place of administration and the habitual residence of the trustee, are more closely connected with States which do not have the institution of the trust or the category of trust involved.

This is designed to protect the interests of states where the trust concept is unknown and has, therefore, been excluded from the provisions of the Convention scheduled to the

---

[82] The trustee is entitled, under Art 12, to register trust assets in his capacity as trustee provided such registration is not prohibited by or inconsistent with the law of the country where registration is sought.

[83] Art 14 permits, also, the application of rules of law more favourable to recognition.

[84] Hayton (1987) 36 ICLQ 260, 275–276.

[85] Arts 15, 16 and 18, infra, pp 1322–1323.

1987 Act.[86] Nevertheless, lawyers in England need to be aware that the provision may limit the recognition abroad of a trust expressed to be governed by English law but which is generally more closely connected with a "non-trust" state.[87]

5. MANDATORY RULES AND PUBLIC POLICY

The provisions of the Convention dealing with mandatory rules and public policy apply, normally, both to the question of the determination of the applicable law and to that of the recognition of a foreign trust.

(a) Mandatory rules[88]

Article 16 embodies the generally accepted private international law provision that, notwithstanding choice of law or recognition rules, the mandatory rules[89] of the forum may continue to be applied.[90] It does so by describing such rules as "provisions of the law of the forum which must be applied even to international situations".[91] Article 16 goes on to allow a court to apply the mandatory rules of another sufficiently closely connected state. Such a provision was no more acceptable to the United Kingdom in the context of trusts than of contract[92] and a power of reservation[93] was exercised to exclude it.

Rather more complex, and loosely drafted, provisions as to mandatory rules are to be found in Article 15 which states that the "Convention does not prevent the application of provisions of the law designated by the conflicts rules of the forum, in so far as those provisions cannot be derogated from by voluntary act". There is a somewhat broader description here than under Article 16 of the rules which the forum may apply, notwithstanding the provisions of the Convention. Although Article 15 merely gives the forum court power to continue to apply those rules, the 1987 Act requires an English court to do so.[94] What is striking is that the mandatory rules in question are not those of the forum but rather of another country (not that governing the trust) the application of whose law has been determined by "the conflicts rules of the forum". Such conflicts rules must be rules other than those contained in the Convention, ie rules applicable to an issue

---

[86] Harris (2002), pp 341–350.

[87] It is also the case that a Contracting State may reserve the right to apply the recognition provisions only to trusts whose validity is governed by the law of a Contracting State: Art 21 (not included in the provisions scheduled to the 1987 Act as the United Kingdom has not exercised this power of reservation).

[88] Harris (2002), pp 355–385.

[89] Examples that have been given of such rules include those designed to prevent the export of currency or of cultural heritage objects: Hayton (1987) 36 ICLQ 260, 278.

[90] S 1(3) of the 1987 Act makes clear that, if there are such mandatory rules, then an English court must apply them. See, however, Harris (2005) 121 LQR 16, 21; Harris (2002) pp 264–267.

[91] Contrast the rather different description in Art 7(2) of the 1980 Rome Convention on Contractual Obligations, scheduled to the Contracts (Applicable Law) Act 1990, supra, p 731 et seq.

[92] See Rome Convention, Art 7(1), supra, p 738.

[93] Art 16, third para.

[94] S 1(3). See *C v C (Ancillary Relief: Nuptial Settlement)* [2004] EWCA Civ 1030; [2005] Fam 250.

classified as other than one concerning the validity or recognition of a trust.[95] Article 15 then goes on to give a non-exclusive list of such issues:

(a) the protection of minors and incapable parties;

(b) the personal and proprietary effects of marriage;

(c) succession rights, testate and intestate, especially the indefeasible shares of spouses and relatives;

(d) the transfer of title to property and security interests in property;

(e) the protection of creditors in matters of insolvency;

(f) the protection, in other respects, of third parties acting in good faith.

(b) Public policy[96]

Article 18 contains the provision generally to be found in Hague Conventions allowing the forum to disregard the Convention provisions "when their application would be manifestly incompatible with public policy".[97] This would enable an English court to impose some limit on the freedom to choose the applicable law under Article 6 if, for example, there had been an attempt to evade the English rule against perpetuities by the choice of a foreign law to govern what was essentially an English trust.[98]

6. VARIATION OF TRUSTS AND SETTLEMENTS

(a) Variation of Trusts Act 1958[99]

Section 1 of the Variation of Trusts Act 1958 provides that where property, whether movable or immovable, is held on trusts arising under any will, settlement or other disposition, the court may, if it thinks fit, approve any arrangement varying or revoking all or any of the trusts. The courts have held that the power of the English courts to exercise their jurisdiction under this provision is not limited to trusts governed by English law,[100] because to take such a restrictive view would mean "that the court would be unable to vary a settlement made (say) in 1920 and governed by (say) Australian law, even though the beneficiaries, the trustees and the trust property had been for many years in this country. It would be unfortunate if the court had no jurisdiction in such a case".[101]

The power under the 1958 Act has to be set against the provision in Article 8 of the Trusts Convention which makes clear that "the variation or termination of the trust"[102] is a matter to be governed by the law applicable to the trust and not, for example, by the law of

---

[95] *Re Barton (Deceased), Tod v Barton* [2002] EWHC 264 (Ch); [2002] WTLR 469, per Lawrence COLLINS J, at [42].

[96] Harris (2002), pp 390–395.

[97] Art 19 preserves the powers of states in fiscal matters. It appears not to have been thought necessary to include this in the provisions scheduled to the 1987 Act.

[98] Dicey, Morris and Collins, paras 29-044–29-046.

[99] Harris (2002), pp 261–264.

[100] *Re Kerr's Settlement Trusts* [1963] Ch 553; *Re Paget's Settlement* [1965] 1 WLR 1046.

[101] *Re Paget's Settlement*, supra, at 1050.

[102] Art 8, para (h).

the forum. In *Re Barton (Deceased)*,[103] in proceedings brought by one of the executors and trustees of Professor Sir Derek Barton, for directions in relation to a Deed of Variation executed by the deceased's beneficiaries, the principal question of law was whether English law (the law expressly chosen in terms of Article 6) or Texas law (the deceased having died domiciled in Texas) should govern the validity and effect of the Deed. The court concluded that Article 8 assigned to English law the question of the ability of the beneficiaries to end or reconstitute the trust.[104]

How does Article 8 inter-relate with the 1958 Act? The 1958 Act, as its long title states, is concerned with the jurisdiction of the courts to vary trusts, whereas Article 8 of the Trusts Convention is concerned with choice of law matters. On that basis the court still retains the power under the 1958 Act to vary a trust governed by foreign law but there would seem to be two limitations on the exercise of that power. The first is that, where there are substantial foreign elements in the case, the court should proceed with caution in deciding whether to assume jurisdiction in such a case, following the advice of CROSS J in *Re Paget's Settlement*:

> If, for example, the court were asked to vary a settlement which was plainly a Scottish settlement, it might well hesitate to exercise its jurisdiction to vary the trusts, simply because some, or even all, the trustees and beneficiaries were in this country. It may well be that the judge would say that the Court of Session was the appropriate tribunal to deal with the case.[105]

The second limitation is that, in exercising the jurisdiction under the 1958 Act, the court, in making a variation, should apply the substantive law of the country governing the trust, identified by reference to Articles 6 or 7 of the Convention. If the law governing the trust does not permit variation, then the jurisdiction under the 1958 Act should not be exercised.[106]

(b) Variation of marriage settlements

There is power in the English court when granting a divorce, nullity or judicial separation decree, or at any time after the decree, to vary any settlement of movable and immovable property made on the parties to the marriage, whether by an ante-nuptial or a post-nuptial settlement.[107] The court can also extinguish or reduce the interest of either of the parties to the marriage under such a settlement.[108] Whenever the court has jurisdiction in the main proceedings for divorce, nullity or judicial separation, then it also has jurisdiction to order such variations.[109] This application of English law as the law of the forum has not been restricted to settlements governed by English law or of English property.

---

[103] *Re Barton (Deceased), Tod v Barton* [2002] EWHC 264 (Ch); [2002] WTLR 469.

[104] Ibid, at [38] and [43].

[105] [1965] 1 WLR 1046 at 1050. It has, however, to be noted that the judge was in fact prepared to vary a trust which may have been governed by New York law.

[106] See further Harris (2007) 11(2) Jersey and Guernsey Law Review 184.

[107] Matrimonial Causes Act 1973, s 24(1)(c). See also the orders which can be made after a foreign decree, under the Matrimonial and Family Proceedings Act 1984, s 17, supra, p 1063 et seq. See *C v C (Ancillary Relief: Nuptial Settlement)* [2004] EWCA Civ 1030; [2005] Fam 250.

[108] Ibid, s 24(1)(d).

[109] *Cammell v Cammell* [1965] P 467, supra, p 1051.

For example, in *Nunneley v Nunneley and Marrian*,[110] the English court varied a settlement made in Scotland and in Scottish form of movables and immovables in Scotland. Is this power now limited by the Recognition of Trusts Act 1987 to settlements governed by English law? It would seem undesirable that the power of the court in such family proceedings should be limited by the choice of law rules in the 1987 Act; and the exclusion of those rules might well be supported by reference to Article 15[111] which allows the English forum still to apply its conflict rules, here in fact leading to the application of the substantive law of the forum, to, inter alia, "the personal and proprietary effects of marriage".

The issue of whether an English court might vary a trust governed by a foreign law in ancillary relief proceedings, and which law it should apply in so doing,[112] was addressed in *C v C (Ancillary Relief: Nuptial Settlement)*.[113] Mr and Mrs Charalambous married in 1984. Before the birth of their second child, Mr Charalambous' mother created a settlement, expressly governed by Jersey law, known as the Hickory Trust. In 2001, by deed of appointment, Mr and Mrs Charalambous ceased to be beneficiaries under the Hickory Trust. Their marriage broke down in 2002. Mrs Charalambous commenced ancillary relief proceedings, including an application under section 24 of the Matrimonial Causes Act 1973 for the variation of the Hickory Trust as a post-nuptial settlement. It is clear from Article 8(2)(h) of the Trusts Convention that, if a foreign law governs the trust, it is that foreign law's substantive provisions on variation of trusts which should be applied. The difficulty arose, however, from the interface between Article 8(2)(h), which would have led to the application of Jersey law, and Article 15(b), which would have secured the operation of English law. The Court of Appeal concluded that the statutory provisions to vary settlements under section 24(1)(c) were provisions which could not be derogated from by voluntary act within the meaning of Article 15. Accordingly, Mrs Charalambous' claim was excepted from the Convention, and governed by English law rather than by the law of Jersey.

It has been pointed out that Article 15 does not expressly mention the effects of divorce as an area of law in which the governing law's mandatory rules are preserved, and further, that even if Article 15 is deemed broad enough to encompass ancillary relief upon divorce, it should not necessarily be invoked to override the general rule in Article 8(2)(h).[114] Harris has argued that it would be better to apply the law applicable to the trust to determine whether to vary the trust upon divorce, subject only to the Article 18 public policy saving.[115] Whilst a restrained approach to the application of Article 15 may be desirable, arguably that is not permitted by the wording of section 1(3) of the 1987 Act;[116] but restraint may be shown, nevertheless, in the exercise of classifying rules as mandatory.[117]

---

[110] (1890) 15 PD 186; and see *Forsyth v Forsyth* [1891] P 363.

[111] Supra, pp 1322–1323.

[112] Harris (2005) 121 LQR 16.

[113] [2004] EWCA Civ 1030; [2005] Fam 250.

[114] Though see Von Overbeck Report, paras 138 and 139; and *C v C (Ancillary Relief: Nuptial Settlement)* [2004] EWCA Civ 1030; [2005] Fam 250, per THORPE LJ, at [32].

[115] Harris (2005) 121 LQR 16, 19.

[116] *Pace* Harris (2002), p 266.

[117] Cf Dicey, Morris and Collins, para 29-040.

The fact that the English court would seem to continue to have power to apply English law to the variation of such marriage settlements does not mean that all foreign elements are to be ignored. The jurisdiction of the court is discretionary and it may well choose not to exercise its power if its order would be ineffective in the foreign country, as where the respondent had no connection with England, no property in England and where any English order would not be recognised in the foreign country.[118] Indeed, such ineffectiveness may justify setting aside service of the claim form on the foreign trustees.[119]

---

[118] *Tallack v Tallack and Broekema* [1927] P 211; cf *Hunter v Hunter and Waddington* [1962] P 1.
[119] *Goff v Goff* [1934] P 107; *Wyler v Lyons* [1963] P 274.

Index